2001

FROM THE WADSWORTH SERIES IN MASS COMMUNICATION AND JOURNALISM

SIXTH EDITION

MASS COMMUNICATION LAW
Cases and Comment

DONALD M. GILLMOR
Silha Professor of Media Ethics and Law
University of Minnesota

JEROME A. BARRON
Lyle T. Alverson Professor of Law
George Washington University Law School

TODD F. SIMON
Professor and Director
A. Q. Miller School of Journalism and Mass Communications
Kansas State University

WADSWORTH PUBLISHING COMPANY
I(T)P®   An International Thomson Publishing Company

Belmont, CA • Albany, NY • Bonn • Boston • Cincinnati • Detroit • Johannesburg • London • Madrid
Melbourne • Mexico City • New York • Paris • Singapore • Tokyo • Toronto • Washington

Communications Editor: Randall Adams
Assistant Editor: Ryan Vesley
Editorial Assistant: Megan Gilbert
Marketing Manager: Mike Dew
Project Editor: Vicki Friedberg
Print Buyer: Barbara Britton

Permissions Editor: Robert M. Kauser
Cover Design: Norman Baugher
Interior Design: John Edeen
Copy Editor: Pat Lewis
Compositor: Parkwood Composition
Printer: R. R. Donnelley, Crawfordsville

Printed in the United States of America
1 2 3 4 5 6 7 8 9 10

For more information, contact Wadsworth Publishing Company, 10 Davis Drive, Belmont,
CA 94002, or electronically at http://www.thomson.com/wadsworth.html

International Thomson Publishing Europe
Berkshire House 168-173
High Holborn
London, WC1V 7AA, England

International Thomson Editores
Campos Eliseos 385, Piso 7
Col. Polanco
11560 México D.F. México

Thomas Nelson Australia
102 Dodds Street
South Melbourne 3205
Victoria, Australia

International Thomson Publishing Asia
221 Henderson Road
#05-10 Henderson Building
Singapore 0315

Nelson Canada
Birchmount Road
Scarborough, Ontario
Canada M1K 5G4

International Thomson Publishing Japan 1120
Hirakawacho Kyowa Building, 3F
2-2-1 Hirakawacho
Chiyoda-ku, Tokyo 102, Japan

International Thomson Publishing GmbH
Königswinterer Strasse 418
53227 Bonn, Germany

International Thomson Publishing
Southern Africa
Building 18, Constantia Park
240 Old Pretoria Road
Halfway House, 1685 South Africa

Library of Congress Cataloging-in-Publication Data

Mass communication law : cases and comment / Donald M. Gillmor . . . [et
  al.]. — 6th ed.
    p. cm.
  Includes bibliographical references and index.
  ISBN 0-314-20221-8
    1. Press law—United States—Cases. 2. Telecommunication—Law and
legislation—United States—Cases.   I. Gillmor, Donald M.
KF2750.A7G5   1997   97-27920
343.7309'94—dc21

This book is printed on acid-free recycled paper.

BRIEF CONTENTS

CONTENTS

TABLE OF CASES

PREFACE

As new perplexities confront mass communication law, we believe that you will find the sixth edition of Gillmor, Barron, and Simon, *Mass Communication Law: Cases and Comment,* the most up-to-date, detailed, and readable text of its kind. As in earlier editions, we allow the courts and administrative agencies to speak for themselves. Cases and rulings are the original sources of law, its building blocks. Difficult as the language of the law may seem at times, momentous decisions as to how our society will conduct itself are expressed in that language. Hence, journalists are implored, lawyers required, to learn that language. This book is designed for students of both law and journalism, but particularly for those who combine the two fields.

The cases have been carefully edited. We have included the legal core of the opinions and at the same time have tried to capture the philosophical and literary flavor of the various justices and commissioners who write them. We have also expended every effort in making the material relevant to journalists, especially those who desire more than a superficial understanding of the law of mass communication.

Much time has been spent with galley and page proofs in an effort to achieve consistency in style and content. Note that in cases we retain the original footnote numbers whereas commentary footnotes are presented in sequence.

It is fortunate that the end of our writing coincided with the end of the October 1996 term of the U.S. Supreme Court. *Reno v. American Civil Liberties Union,* decided on June 26, 1997, may be remembered as the first shot over the bow of the Internet. It will not be the last. How precedents and statutes dealing with libel, privacy, copyright, obscenity, and access to information will be applied to new technologies remains for the future to work out, but we can be sure that the complexities of such applications will challenge the minds of the next generation of media law scholars. Still, the past remains prologue. We can predict that new law will build on precedent, however ill adapted it may seem to as yet undreamed of methods of interactive mass communication. While new communication tech-

nologies may be revolutionary, law, of necessity, remains evolutionary. As we have said before, individuals and groups depend on legal predictability. Stable legal systems tell us, and others, what is likely to happen if we choose one course over another. This does not mean that a dramatic break with the past cannot occur in our legal system. It does, but infrequently.

In all of this, one constant remains: the dedication to the U.S. Constitution of the courts that interpret that document's guarantee of free speech. That dedication has been called a signature of the American society, even though major segments of public opinion, from time to time, opt out on the First Amendment.

With freedom of expression as its engine, our information age is past, present, and future. We trust that this book will illuminate the past, serve the present, and, to some small degree, anticipate the future.

The first three chapters set down the rationales, the methodologies, and the categories the courts use in applying the constitution to the speech and press cases that come before them. These chapters provide a historical and philosophical primer for talking about freedom of speech and press and their limits. These materials are especially useful for advanced courses and seminars where students may wish to develop their own "theories" of freedom of expression. The next four chapters—Chapters 4, 5, 6, and 7—deal with major concerns of working journalists and the media bar: libel, privacy, sources, and access to information. Chapter 8 deals with another kind of access: access of the public to the major organs of public opinion. In a world of corporate media giants, a real democracy may be only a fantasy if ordinary people surrounded by sophisticated technologies cannot make themselves heard. Chapter 9 dwells on the business of mass communication—advertising, monopoly and antitrust, labor law, taxation, and copyright. Chapter 10 deals exclusively with two topics, the first of which generally does not concern professional journalists but greatly interests theoreticians, cultural historians, and bookstore owners—obscenity. The second topic, student journalism, represents that vast pool from which future journalists and media attorneys will emerge. The final four chapters deal with the regulated media—broadcast and cable. Administrative rulings and court decisions presage how computer technologies may be dealt with in the future. Some of the court decisions look at the electronic media from the perspective of audience rather than speaker, the public interest factor, and what the public may need to know.

Chapter 11 deals with the regulation of broadcasting and tracks the regulation of that medium from that distant time when radio defined the electronic media. The chapter also confronts our own world of digital television and the complexities of the Telecommunication Act of 1996. Some of the difficult problems raised by that Act are discussed. How will the new license renewal provisions work? How and *why* does the new Act relax the FCC's long-established diversification of ownership policy?

Chapter 12 grapples with the political and public issue dimensions of broadcasting. These are issues of critical contemporary significance. What is equal time? What is reasonable access for politicians on television? What is the appropriate use of the broadcast media by presidential candidates?

Chapter 13 deals with the day-to-day regulation of indecency and obscenity in broadcasting by the FCC and the lower federal courts. Chapter 13 complements Chapter 10, which considers similar issues from the more theoretical perspective of the Supreme Court.

Finally, Chapter 14 deals with the regulatory and First Amendment issues presented by the rise of cable television. Should cable television be obliged to carry local over-the-air broadcast signals in order to preserve an audience for over-the-air broadcasting? Congress thought so when it enacted the "must-carry" provisions of the 1992 Cable Act. The cable industry launched a bitter challenge to these provisions in the name of the First Amendment. In the two *Turner* cases, in 1994 and in 1997, the Supreme Court upheld the "must-carry" provisions. In the process, the Court took a first—but not a final—step toward developing a First Amendment standard for cable.

Chapter 14 also discusses content regulation of cable television. To what extent can indecency on cable television be regulated? In the 1996 *Denver Area* case, the Court considered this

issue in the context of leased and public access channels on cable. In the decisional process, the Court acknowledged the difficulty—and in its view, the prematurity—of charting a uniform First Amendment standard for the regulation of cable in particular and the electronic media in general. The significance of the Court's skepticism on this point is highlighted in this chapter.

As is always the case, this book could not have been written without help from others. Elizabeth Hannan, a former editor at West Publishing Company, got the project off the ground. We were fortunate to have a gifted copyeditor, Patricia Lewis, to edit this manuscript as she did for *Fundamentals of Mass Communication Law.* Our new publisher, Wadsworth, has blessed us with a vigorous communications editor, Randall Adams; a helpful project editor, Vicki Friedberg; and a delightful and efficient freelance production coordinator, Melanie Field of Strawberry Field Publishing, who put the project to bed.

Closer to home, Don Gillmor thanks Silha Fellowship holders Genelle Belmas and Jennifer Lambe for research and computer assistance when it was needed. And, as always, Karen Stohl and Kathleen Paul provided the day-to-day clerical assistance that keeps an author and a teacher from severe mental strain—or worse.

Jerry Barron thanks Ryan Wallach of the George Washington Law School Class of 1998 for his excellent research assistance, creativity, and skill in helping to ferret out meaning from the ambiguities of the Telecommunication Act of 1996. He also wishes to thank Dan Oginsky of the George Washington Law School Class of 1999 for his help with the galleys and page proofs of the electronic media chapters. To both Ryan Wallach and Stephen Rockwell of the Class of 1996, who labored with me on the First Amendment chapters, my thanks for their insights and scholarship.

In sum, the sixth edition of this book is a teaching and learning tool for students of journalism and of law. It recounts, among other things, the adventures of the First Amendment since the publication of the fifth edition in 1990. It tells the complex story of what has happened to the exceptions that have accumulated around the First Amendment—exceptions like hate speech and commercial speech. This book also describes the way in which the First Amendment is used as a sword by a threatened technology—

broadcasting—to thwart an emerging technology—cable. That story is told here as well. Writing this book has stimulated us as authors and editors. We hope that you who use this book—both teachers and students—will be stimulated by it as well.

Donald M. Gillmor
Jerome A. Barron
Todd F. Simon
July 1997

UNDERSTANDING THE LEGAL SYSTEM AND FINDING THE LAW

UNDERSTANDING THE AMERICAN LEGAL SYSTEM

A basic understanding of the law governing the press is essential for any journalist. No journalist is, or should be, expected to play the role of lawyer in deciding whether or not to publish. However, a basic understanding of the law and the legal system may enable a journalist to spot a potential problem, something that may skirt the line between hard-hitting journalism and libel, for instance. For example, a story may involve a charge of wrong-doing against a prominent public official. Although the story sounds plausible, it cannot be substantiated. Once a journalist spots such an issue, a lawyer should be consulted to see whether the story should run as it is or be modified. In some circumstances, it may be concluded that a story simply poses too great a litigation risk and should be pulled. A journalist who fails to seek legal assistance with such an issue risks a costly and destructive lawsuit for her employer as well as for herself.

WHO MAKES THE LAW?

Under the federal system established by the U.S. Constitution, both the U.S. Congress and the state legislatures have power to enact laws. Under the Constitution, the states and the federal government each have spheres of power that both overlap and maintain some exclusivity. The Supremacy Clause makes federal laws made "in Pursuance" of the Constitution supreme over conflicting state laws. The Supremacy Clause, which is found in Article VI, Section 2 of the U.S. Constitution, provides for the supremacy of federal law:

> This Constitution, and the Laws of the United States which shall be made in Pursuance thereof; and all Treaties made, or which shall be made, under the Authority of the United States, shall be the supreme Law of the Land; and the Judges in every State shall be bound thereby, any Thing in the Constitution or Laws of any State to the Contrary notwithstanding.

An example of federal legislative power that has often been cited in this book is the Federal Communications Act of 1934. Under its power to regulate interstate commerce, Congress may regulate broadcasting. The Commerce Clause, Article I, Section 8, U.S. Constitution, is the constitutional basis for the Federal Communications Act of 1934, which, as amended, governs broadcasting to this day. Pursuant to the Commerce Clause, Congress enacted the Federal Communications Act and established the Federal Communications Commission as the agency to administer that law.

States have authority to legislate concerning the police power within their jurisdictions. This means that they may legislate in matters concerning the health, welfare, and morals of their people. Thus, states may legislate to secure the public order and safety. Crimes such as murder and robbery are prosecuted under state law. In some contexts, however, Congress has enacted legislation that allows the federal authorities to prosecute murder and robbery if such actions cross state lines. The formation and operation of corporations is largely governed by state law.

In addition to the division of legislative authority between the state and the federal government, the constitutional scheme is predicated on the separation of powers within the federal government. Article I deals with the power of the legislature, Article II with the executive, and Article III with the judiciary. The federal legislature or Congress, consisting of the House of Representatives and the Senate, is charged with making the laws. The executive—the president and the federal bureaucracy—has the responsibility of executing these laws. Increasingly, through executive orders and other actions, the executive itself has come to have a lawmaking function. The federal judiciary, through the Supreme Court and the lower federal courts, has the responsibility of interpreting the law. Under the doctrine of judicial review, the federal courts—and the state courts as well—also determine whether the actions of government are consistent with the Constitution. If they are not, such actions may be set aside.

Although the courts have the formal responsibility of interpreting the law, in truth, the courts themselves make law. Judicial lawmaking occurs in numerous ways. For example, when interpreting statutes and administrative orders, it often becomes necessary for courts to fill in the gaps caused by statutory omissions and ambiguities. In the final analysis, it is often very difficult to separate the process of interpretation from the process of lawmaking.

The foregoing account does not exhaust the sources of lawmaking in the United States. Administrative agencies must also be mentioned. For example, the Federal Communications Commission, like other administrative agencies both federal and state, "makes law." By way of illustration, the Federal Communications Act says that broadcast licenses should be granted only if it is in the public interest. The FCC has on occasion issued regulations and decisions that set forth the criteria that should inform a determination of whether, by precedent, it should be decided the same way again. Common law maintains itself as a coherent body of law rather than simply a compendium of cases by relying upon precedent and the doctrine of *stare decisis*. Of course, in this century statutory law has become far more important than case law. Precedent will only be adhered to in situations where the statutory law does not otherwise command.

Sometimes a court will be presented with a novel issue that has not been addressed by either a statute or a prior case. In that instance, the court's decision on this issue becomes a new precedent that may stand for many years as the controlling law on the point. In this way the common law continues to grow and develop.

The obligation to follow *stare decisis* will depend upon the origin of the precedent that is pressed upon the court. If the precedent, or past case law, is from the same jurisdiction in which the court sits, then the prior case law will have great force. If, on the other hand, the only precedent that is urged upon the court is from other jurisdictions, the court will feel less obliged to follow the precedent. For example, a decision on an issue of law by a lower state court in Alaska might have some precedential effect upon the decision of a state court in Florida that is confronted with the same issue. However, the Alaska state court decision would not have the same authoritative force on the

Florida state court as a Florida state supreme court decision.

The common law has grown and developed incrementally. Common law courts have historically displayed a preference for the particular over the general. Common law courts usually prefer to resolve only the specific issues actually presented to them. Therefore, all aspects of a rule of law are not necessarily enunciated in a decision. Typically, a court will decide only those aspects that are raised by the actual controversy between the parties. A common law court does not decide more than it has to. Finally, it should be emphasized that the doctrine of *stare decisis* is a general principle to which, in the main, American courts attempt to adhere. But if changing social *mores* or new scientific or technical information suggests that a precedent is based on obsolete or erroneous assumptions, a court will depart from precedent. *Stare decisis* is a guide to decision. It is not an inexorable command.

FINDING THE LAW

One of the first, and most useful, skills that law students master is that of legal research. With this skill, law students can find the cases, statutes, treaties, and other sources of law that they will encounter in their study of the law. Since journalists must often report law-related matters, they should also have a basic understanding of legal materials and legal research.

Books or textbooks on legal topics are called *treatises* and a library's holdings are indexed in its card catalogue or on-line data base. A *Horn Book* is a single volume summary of a field of law. A *Nutshell* is an even more drastic summary. There are a number of legal bibliographies, among them *Law Books in Print*, edited by Nicholas Triffin.

The American Law Institute's *Restatements of the Law* are attempts to reorganize, simplify, and move case law toward comprehensible codes. Begin searching with the *General Index to the Restatement of the Law*.

For legal style and citation forms see *A Uniform System of Citation* published by the Harvard Law Review Association, and sometimes referred to as the Harvard Blue Book. There is also the University of Chicago *Manual of Legal Citation*, known as the Maroon Book. Any standard text on legal research and writing will provide similar information.

To find a case or statute, you have to know its *citation* as well as what the citation signifies. The citation is a set form that allows legal researchers to find the case or statute in whatever form it is collected. The citation for *Red Lion Broadcasting,* an important case in mass communication law, is as follows: *Red Lion Broadcasting Co. v. FCC,* 395 U.S. 367 (1969). The citation gives you first the name of the case and at least some of the parties involved, *Red Lion Broadcasting Co. v. FCC.* The order of the parties does not tell you who was the original plaintiff or defendant, however, because the order is often switched in the appellate process. Next, "395 U.S. 367" tells you that the case can be found in volume 395 of the *United States Reports,* and that it starts on page 367 of that volume. The *United States Reports* is the official publication for the U.S. Supreme Court.

Reports of Supreme Court cases are also published in West Publishing Company's *Supreme Court Reporter* and the Lawyers Cooperative's *Lawyer's Edition.* Although these sources are unofficial, they are published long before cases appear in the *United States Reports.* These unofficial reports are abbreviated as "S.Ct." and "L.Ed.," respectively. The number "1969" in parentheses is the year in which the case was decided by the Supreme Court.

Decisions of the U.S. courts of appeals are found in the *Federal Reporter,* which is also published by West Publishing Company. The *Federal Reporter* has now gone into a third edition. A sample citation would be *Poole v. Wood,* 45 F.3d 246 (8th Cir. 1995). The "8th Cir." in the parentheses refers to the circuit in which the court of appeals sits, here the Eighth Circuit. Federal district court decisions are reported in a publication called the *Federal Supplement.* A sample citation would be *Bellsouth Corp. v. U.S.,* 868 F.Supp. 1335 (N.D.Ala. 1994). The reference to "F.Supp." indicates that the case is a federal district court decision. The reference to "N.D.Ala." in the parentheses refers to the fact that the decision is from the federal district court for the northern district of Alabama.

State court decisions cite to an official state reporter. An example of a state supreme decision reported in the official state reporter is the following Vermont state supreme court decision:

Greenmoss Builders, Inc. v. Dun & Bradstreet, 143 Vt. 66 (1983). Besides the official state reporters, state decisions can also be found in West Publishing Company's regional reporters. The various regional reporters publish the decisions of the state courts in a particular region. The *Atlantic Reporter,* for example, publishes the state court decisions for Connecticut, Delaware, District of Columbia, Maine, Maryland, Massachusetts, New Hampshire, New Jersey, Pennsylvania, Rhode Island, and Vermont. An example of a regional reporter citation would be *Greenmoss Builders, Inc. v. Dun & Bradstreet,* 461 A.2d 414 (Vt. 1983). The "A.2d" refers to the second series of the *Atlantic Reporter* published by West. The reference to "Vt. 1983" indicates that this particular decision is a Vermont state court decision and that the case was decided in 1983.

U.S. statutes are officially cited to the *United States Code* (U.S.C.). An example of a citation to a federal statute would be 47 U.S.C. § 315. The number in front of the "U.S.C." citation refers to the title or volume in which the statute is found. Different federal laws are collected under separate titles of the United States Code. Thus, Title 47 U.S.C. contains the Federal Communications Act of 1934 and its amendments. The reference to Sec. 315 refers to a particular provision of the Federal Communications Act. Sec. 315, for example, is the "equal time" rule discussed above.

Laws of the United States are eventually codified in the United States Code. The *United States Code Annotated* (U.S.C.A.), West's unofficial version of the United States Code, includes explanatory notes and citations to cases. The most recent amendments to a title can be found in the pocket parts at the end of the volume or title. When one researches a federal statute, therefore, it is important not only to read the statute in the hardbound volume but to check the pocket parts to see if the statute has been repealed or amended. Regulations adopted by federal administrative agencies such as the Federal Communications Commission are published in the *Code of Federal Regulations* (C.F.R.).

State statutes are published for each state. Amendments and new laws can be found in the pocket parts of the volumes containing these laws. A sample citation of a state statute or law that is discussed in this book is the citation for the Florida right of reply law struck down in *Miami Herald Publishing Co. v. Tornillo*, 418 U.S. 241 (1974). The citation for the Florida right of reply law was as follows: West's F.S.A. § 104.38. The citation "F.S.A." stands for Florida Statutes Annotated. "Annotated" means that short summaries of the cases interpreting the various statutory provisions appear under each provision. The reference to Sec. 104.38 indicates the specific provision of the Florida Electoral Code that contained the Florida right of reply law.

Lexis and *Westlaw* are electronic services that have made conducting legal research considerably quicker and provided access to legal researchers in even the most remote locations. They are subscriber online services that have a vast store of state and federal cases and statutes along with numerous other legal and nonlegal resources. Law students and practitioners refer to these services often. Although these services can be expensive, they offer instant access to a wealth of current information. The availability of these online up-to-date legal databases has made electronic research indispensable to anyone undertaking substantial legal research. For example, WESTLAW includes much material useful to media law students such as law reviews, texts, bar journals, Practicing Law Institute materials, Bureau of National Affairs materials, Commerce Clearing House materials, Dow Jones, Dialog, VU/TEXT, PHINet, and Information America. Most of the foregoing material is reprinted from Gillmor, Barron, Simon and Terry, *Fundamentals of Mass Communication Law* (West Pub. Co. 1996).

THE FEDERAL COURT SYSTEM

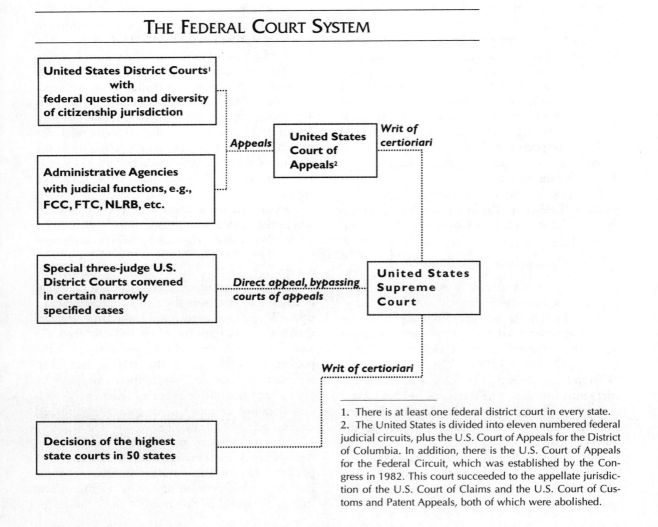

1. There is at least one federal district court in every state.
2. The United States is divided into eleven numbered federal judicial circuits, plus the U.S. Court of Appeals for the District of Columbia. In addition, there is the U.S. Court of Appeals for the Federal Circuit, which was established by the Congress in 1982. This court succeeded to the appellate jurisdiction of the U.S. Court of Claims and the U.S. Court of Customs and Patent Appeals, both of which were abolished.

A STATE COURT SYSTEM

The state court system outlined below is an example of one state court system. It is intended to provide a guide to the state judicial process for the student who is unfamiliar with the organization of state courts. There is substantial variation from state to state. The following figure illustrates the California court system.

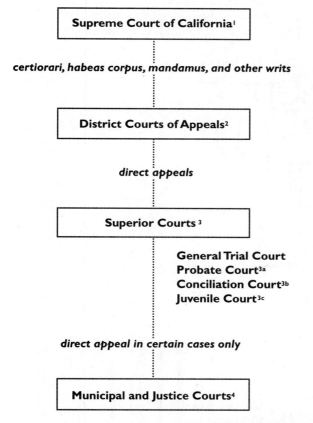

Supreme Court of California[1]

certiorari, habeas corpus, mandamus, and other writs

District Courts of Appeals[2]

direct appeals

Superior Courts [3]

General Trial Court
Probate Court[3a]
Conciliation Court[3b]
Juvenile Court[3c]

direct appeal in certain cases only

Municipal and Justice Courts[4]

Civil and Criminal Trials
Small Claims Court[4a]

1. Has no obligatory appellate jurisdiction; that is, it reviews cases by granting petitions for writs of certiorari and thus retains complete discretionary control of its jurisdiction.
2. Consequently the great bulk of cases reach final decision in these five District Courts of Appeals.
3. The Superior Court, the trial court of general jurisdiction, also has three special divisions: the General Trial Court, Probate Court, Conciliation Court, and Juvenile Court.
   3a. This court has jurisdiction over the administration of estates, wills, and related matters.
   3b. The Conciliation Court is a rather unique institution that takes jurisdiction over family disputes that could lead to the dissolution of a marriage to the detriment of a minor child.
   3c. The Juvenile Court considers certain types of cases involving persons under 18 years of age.
4. There is one Superior Court in each county. The Municipal and Justice Courts represent subdivisions of each county by population. These courts are trial courts with limited jurisdiction. They also have original and exclusive criminal jurisdiction for violations of local ordinances within their districts.
   4a. The Small Claims Court is the familiar forum used to settle small disputes using informal procedures and providing lawyers for the disputing parties.
   Note: Superior Court is usually the last state court to which a decision of these lowest courts can be appealed. It is possible that a case from one of these courts could be ineligible for further state review and could have further review only in the U.S. Supreme Court.

THE THIRTEEN FEDERAL JUDICIAL CIRCUITS

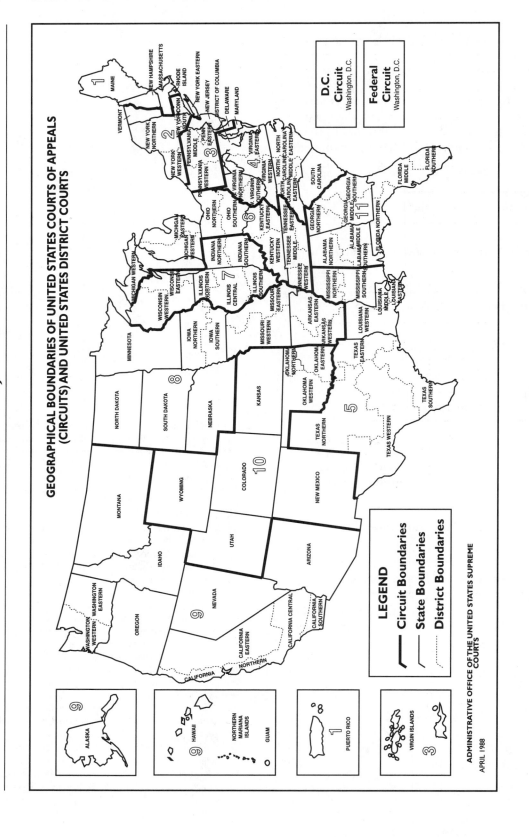

GEOGRAPHICAL BOUNDARIES OF UNITED STATES COURTS OF APPEALS (CIRCUITS) AND UNITED STATES DISTRICT COURTS

LEGEND
Circuit Boundaries
State Boundaries
District Boundaries

ADMINISTRATIVE OFFICE OF THE UNITED STATES SUPREME COURTS
APRIL 1988

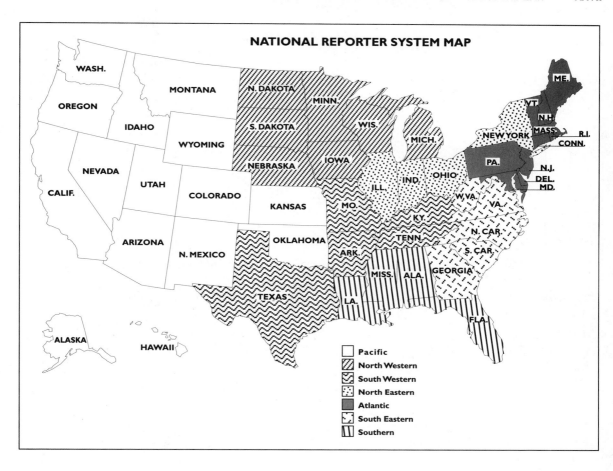

THE HISTORY AND RATIONALE OF THE FIRST AMENDMENT

CHAPTER OUTLINE

THE FIRST AMENDMENT AND THE EVOLUTION OF ITS MEANING

The language of the First Amendment to the U.S. Constitution is remarkably terse:

> Congress shall make no law respecting an establishment of religion, or prohibiting the free exercise thereof; or abridging the freedom of speech, or of the press; or the right of the people peaceably to assemble, and to petition the government for a redress of grievances.

The brevity of the First Amendment is in contrast to the volume of interpretation that has accumulated about it since its enactment in 1791. The freedom of expression portion of the First Amendment has two parts: a Free Speech Clause and a Free Press Clause. Significantly, the First Amendment is addressed to Congress and not to the states. The Framers of the First Amendment, and of the Bill of Rights of which it was a part, feared the new federal government they had created, not the states. They wished at the outset to prevent Congress from interfering with freedom of speech or press. Nothing in the original Constitution that was ratified by the states or in the Bill of Rights imposed any limitations on state legislatures with regard to freedom of speech or press.

Would the new state legislatures follow the darker pages in colonial history and hold newspaper editors guilty of legislative contempt if the editors offended them? If the new state governors were criticized in the press, would they follow the precedent set by the royal colonial governors and seek to have newspaper editors indicted for seditious libel? By its text, the First Amendment was not drafted to resolve such matters. They were to be governed by the freedom of expression provisions in the state constitutions.

The First Amendment, of course, has now been interpreted to apply to government in its entirety, state and federal. The vehicle for this development was the Fourteenth Amendment. The Fourteenth Amendment was enacted in 1868 to provide legal equality and constitutional protection for the recently emancipated slaves. One of the most famous provisions of that amendment states that no state shall "deprive any person of life, liberty, or property, without due process of law." The Due Process Clause of the Fourteenth Amendment has come to be the basis upon which the guarantees of the Bill of Rights such as freedom of speech and press have been made applicable to the states.

The watershed year in the evolution of this development was 1925. In *Gitlow v. New York*, 268 U.S. 652, 666 (1925), a case involving a now forgotten and ultimately repentant Communist, Benjamin Gitlow, Justice Edward Sanford made the following observation:

> For present purposes we may and do assume that freedom of speech and of the press—which are protected by the First Amendment from abridgment by Congress—are among the fundamental personal rights and "liberties" protected by the due process clause of the Fourteenth Amendment from impairment by the states.

The ruling that the Due Process Clause of the Fourteenth Amendment protects freedom of speech and of the press from infringement by the states was an important advance in the history of freedom of expression in the United States. The state constitutions have their own guarantees of freedom of expression, but sometimes these guarantees offer more comfort to state regulation than is the case with the more protective and encompassing interpretation that has been given to the First Amendment. For the view that state constitutions themselves gave early nurture to freedom of speech and press and greatly influenced the federal courts, see Blanchard, *Filling in the Void: Speech and Press in State Courts prior to Gitlow*, in Chamberlin and Brown, (eds.), *The First Amendment Reconsidered* (1982).

The use of the Fourteenth Amendment's Due Process Clause to extend the protection of the federal constitution to the states has been of enormous significance. Interpretation of federal constitutional provisions such as the First and Fourteenth Amendments is, ultimately, the responsibility of the U.S. Supreme Court. That Court's rulings bind the lower state and federal courts. Under Article III of the Constitution, justices of the Supreme Court essentially have life tenure. The president, it is true, has the power to nominate Supreme Court justices and the Senate has the power to advise and consent. Once appointed, however, the justice need answer only to her conscience. This fact gives Supreme Court justices great and necessary independence, greater independence certainly than state court judges in states where judges serve only for specific terms and must run for reelection. This independence enables Supreme Court justices to make unpopular decisions. In sum, the federal constitution's guarantee of freedom of speech and freedom of the press has placed the Supreme Court in a pivotal and dispositive role in enforcing and defining freedom of expression.

The English and Colonial Background of the First Amendment

The Framers' determination to assure protection for freedom of speech and press did not arise in a vacuum. English and American history prior to the American Revolution persuaded them of the need for such assurance. Essential to understanding both the origins and the development of the First Amendment is John Milton's great essay in defense of a free press, *Areopagitica*.

John Milton (1608–1674), was one of the greatest English poets. A republican in a monarchical age, the power of Milton's language and thought in his *Areopagitica* has made the essay a formidable obstacle to licensing and restraint of the press through the centuries. The *Areopagitica* was written as a protest against government licensing and censorship of the press.

On June 14, 1643, the English Parliament passed a law licensing the press. The statute forbad the publication of any book, pamphlet, or paper that was published or imported without registration by the Stationers' Company. The Stationers' Company, formed in 1557, has been described as follows:

> The exclusive privilege of printing and publishing in the English dominions was given to 97 London stationers and their successors by regular apprenticeship. All printing was thus centralised in London under the immediate inspection of the Government. No one could legally print, without special license, who did not belong to the Stationers' company. The Company had power to search for and to seize publications which infringed their privilege.[3]
>
> Jebb, ed., Introduction, Milton, *Areopagitica*, xxiii (Cambridge University, 1918).

Later the licensing authority was divided between various royal and ecclesiastical authorities. The 1643 law, against which Milton directed his pamphlet, authorized official searches for unlicensed presses and prohibited the publication of anything unlicensed. The statute was designed to prevent "the defamation of Religion and Government." In Milton's view, however, truth in both religion and government was more likely to emerge from free discussion than from repression.

The idea of liberty of expression is a challenge to the infirmity of the human condition. Even Milton was not an absolutist with regard to freedom of expression. He did not believe in religious freedom for Catholics and later served as a censor for Oliver Cromwell. Nevertheless, Milton's hostility to the licensing of the press by government and his evident passion for a higher plateau of freedom of expression have been a powerful influence in the development of freedom of the press in the United States. See Siebert, *Freedom of the Press in England, 1476–1766* (1952).

The licensing system ended in England in 1695, but licensing continued in the American colonies for several decades thereafter. Gradually, prosecution for criminal or seditious libel supplanted licensing as the instrument for governmental restraint of the press in America prior to the American Revolution. The common law crime of seditious libel made criticism of government a matter for criminal prosecution. Though such prosecutions were not frequent in colonial America, they did occur.

The most famous prosecution for seditious libel involved a New York printer, John Peter Zenger, editor of the *New York Weekly Journal*. Zenger's paper was used by politicians as a relentless forum for criticizing the colonial governor of New York, William Cosby. Zenger was arrested in 1734 on a charge of publishing seditious libels and was jailed for eight months before trial. In August 1735, a jury ignored the judge's instructions and found Zenger not guilty. The case became the most celebrated victory for freedom of the press in the prerevolutionary period.

It was no mean achievement for Zenger's attorney, Andrew Hamilton, to win the case because, under the common law of seditious libel, the truth of the utterance was irrelevant. In an account of the early history of freedom of the press in eighteenth-century America, Professor Norman Rosenberg points out that Hamilton sought help from the jury for his client. "Hamilton extolled the superior nature and wisdom of local juries." Hamilton "seldom mentioned the rights of a free press." Instead, he emphasized the right to resist an oppressive ruler and the right of "ordinary New Yorkers" to "complain about bad administration." In short, instead of talking about the right of a free press, Hamilton talked about the free speech rights of a free people. See Rosenberg, *Protecting the Best Men: An Interpretive History of the Law of Libel* 38-39 (1986).

In colonial seditious libel cases, the judge rather than the jury had the responsibility of deciding whether the publication in question constituted seditious libel. The role of the jury was simply to ascertain whether the defendant had published the offending publication. These features of the law of seditious libel did not give much breathing space to freedom of expression. In England it wasn't until 1792 that Fox's Libel Act finally altered the law of seditious libel and also gave the jury rather than the judge the power to determine whether the publication was seditious libel. See Emerson, *The System of Freedom of Expression* 99 (1970).

The Alien and Sedition Acts

Unfortunately, the law of seditious libel had proponents in the newly independent United States. In 1798, at the behest of the Federalist Party, Congress enacted four acts directed against the subversive activities of foreigners in the United States. The acts were inspired by the Federalists' fear of radical sympathizers with France and French agents and their hostility toward Republican journalist critics of the Federalist administration. Known collectively as the Alien and Sedition Acts, the acts included the Naturalization Act, the Act Concerning Aliens, the Act Respecting Enemies, and the Act for the Punishment of Crimes. The last, known as the Sedition Act, has been of great interest to First Amendment historians.

Unlike the common law crime of seditious libel, under the new law truth was permitted as a defense, proof of malice was required, and the jury was permitted to pass on both questions of law and fact. Punishment was set by the statute. Specifically, the Act provided that the publishing or printing of any false, scandalous, or malicious writings to bring the government, Congress, or the president into contempt or disrepute, excite popular hostility to them, incite resistance to the law of the United States, or encourage hostile designs against the United States was a misdemeanor. Republicans led by Thomas Jefferson and James Madison maintained that the law was a violation of the First Amendment, and among those convicted under the law were some of the leading Republican editors. The Republicans contended that the law was being interpreted to punish and silence Republican critics of the Federalist administration. The Federalists in turn defended the statute as necessary to the government's right of self-preservation.

Those who viewed the First Amendment as a rejection of the English law of seditious libel, contended that the Sedition Act was unconstitutional. Those who believed the First Amendment did not promise absolute protection of speech saw the enactment of the Sedition Act, so soon after the Revolution and the ratification of the Constitution, as proof that the First Amendment did not prohibit all governmental restraint of

expression. Did the Sedition Act violate the First Amendment? That question was never answered because the issue of the Act's validity did not come before the Supreme Court. Constitutional historians, however, contend that the Act would have been upheld by the justices who sat on the Court during John Adams's presidency. The Sedition Act expired on March 3, 1801.

Professor Leonard Levy, a noted American constitutional historian, initially argued that the First Amendment was designed to prohibit only prior restraint of the press (administrative prior censorship and licensing), not punishment for seditious libel. See Levy, *The Legacy of Suppression*, 247–48 (1960). Subsequently, however, Levy greatly moderated his views and now says that he erred when he said that "freedom of the press meant to the Framers merely the absence of prior restraints." Levy now considers that "freedom of the press merely began with its immunity from previous restraints." See Levy, *Emergence of a Free Press,* xi (1985). Levy has also altered his view that the eighteenth-century American understanding of freedom of the press did not include freedom from seditious libel:

> Some states gave written constitutional protection to freedom of the press after Independence; others did not. Whether they did or not, their presses operated as if the law of seditious libel did not exist.
> Id. at x.

The question of the constitutional status of the Alien and Sedition Acts was finally put to rest in the famous case of *New York Times v. Sullivan*, 376 U.S. 254 (1964), in which the Supreme Court narrowly contracted the scope of libel law. In *Sullivan,* Justice William Brennan, speaking for the Court, declared:

> "Although the Sedition Act was never tested in this Court, the attack upon its validity has carried the day in the court of history."
> Id. at 276.

For First Amendment scholar, Professor Harry Kalven, the *New York Times v. Sullivan* statement on seditious libel was a crucial step in the continuous reinterpretation the First Amendment receives from the Supreme Court. Seditious libel punished criticism of government. Criminalizing such criticism was incompatible with freedom of expression:

> The concept of seditious libel strikes at the very heart of democracy. Political freedom ends when

government can use its powers and its courts to silence the critics.

See Kalven, The New York Times Case: A Note on *"The Central Meaning of the First Amendment,"* 1964 Sup. Ct. Rev. 191, 205.

The repudiation of seditious libel furnished a new key to understanding the meaning of First Amendment protection:

The Court did not simply, in the face of an awkward history, definitively put to rest the status of the Sedition Act. More important, it found in the controversy over seditious libel the clue "to the central meaning of the First Amendment." The choice of language was unusually apt.

The central meaning of the [First] Amendment is that seditious libel cannot be made the subject of government sanction. It is now not only the citizen's privilege to criticize his government; it is his duty. At this point in its rhetoric and sweep, the opinion almost literally incorporated the citizen as ruler, Alexander Meiklejohn's thesis that in a democracy the citizen as ruler is our most important public official.

Kalven, 1964 Sup. CL. Rev. at 208–209.

FIRST AMENDMENT MODELS

Constitutional scholars have more or less agreed with Professor Zechariah Chafee's observation that the Framers of the Constitution did not have a very clear idea of what they intended the guarantee of freedom of speech and press to mean. Chafee, *Free Speech in the United States* (1954). Considerable judicial and scholarly effort has been devoted to developing a rationale for giving constitutional protection to freedom of speech and press. Not surprisingly, these rationales— sometimes called First Amendment models— offer quite different explanations to justify the guarantees of freedom of speech and freedom of the press.

The Marketplace of Ideas Model

Certainly, the most established First Amendment model or rationale is the marketplace of ideas theory. In a famous and widely quoted passage from the *Areopagitica,* John Milton eloquently stated the premise of the marketplace of ideas theory. Out of the unhindered combat of ideas, truth emerges:

And though all the winds of doctrine were let loose to play upon the earth, so Truth be in the field, we do injuriously by licensing and prohibiting to misdoubt her strength. Let her and Falsehood grapple; who ever knew truth put to the worse, in a free and open encounter?

Milton, *Areopagitica,* 58 (Jebb ed., Cambridge, University 1918).

John Stuart Mill (1806–1873), an English political philosopher and economist, was an influential nineteenth-century thinker who spoke against the silencing of ideas. It has been justly said that his essay, *On Liberty of Thought and Discussion* (1859), was his "most lasting contribution to political thought." For Mill, "freedom of thought and investigation, freedom of discussion, and the freedom of self-controlled moral judgment were goods in their own right." The unimpeded interaction of ideas was a social benefit:

But the peculiar evil of silencing the expression of an opinion is, that it is robbing the human race; posterity as well as the existing generation; those who dissent from the opinion, still more than those who hold it. If the opinion is right, they are deprived of the opportunity of exchanging error for truth; if wrong, they lose, what is almost as great a benefit, the clearer perception and livelier impression of truth, produced by its collision with error.

See Mill, *Utilitarianism, Liberty and Representative Government,* 104 (Lindsay, ed., 1957).

After World War I, the marketplace of ideas theory was given fresh life by Justice Oliver Wendell Holmes in a famous dissent in *Abrams v. United States,* 250 U.S. 616 (1919). Truth is best secured in the open marketplace of ideas, he said. Any government restraint that tends to distort or chill the free play of ideas, and thus the quest for truth, should not be permitted. In *Abrams* and other cases, Holmes used the marketplace of ideas metaphor to give theoretical underpinning to the First Amendment. The similarity between the Holmesian marketplace of ideas concept of freedom of expression and Mill's rationale for liberty of thought and discussion is striking.

Free speech issues did not get any extended or serious attention from the Supreme Court until cases involving a clash between government censorship and freedom of expression came about during and after World War I. It is not surprising that faced with these issues, the justices frequently cited Mill and Milton. Indeed, when justices serving after Holmes returned to the marketplace of ideas theory, the words they used to describe the theory are very close to the language of Mill. In dissent in *Dennis v. United States,* 341 U.S. 494, 584 (1951), a case upholding anti-Communist prosecutions against First Amendment challenge, Justice William O. Douglas wrote:

> When ideas compete in the market for acceptance, full and free discussion [exposes] the false and they gain few adherents. Full and free discussion even of ideas we hate encourages the testing of our own prejudices and preconceptions. Full and free discussion keeps a society from becoming stagnant and unprepared for the stresses and strains that work to tear all civilizations apart.

In *New York Times Co. v. Sullivan,* 376 U.S. 254 (1964), Justice Brennan cited Mill as well as Milton for the view that even a false statement, so long as it is not a calculated falsehood, merits First Amendment protection when the communication at issue involves criticism of elected government officials.

Is government intervention always inconsistent with marketplace of ideas theory? In the case of the electronic media, government has intervened in some respects in the marketplace of ideas. For example, the government mandated that broadcasters provide equal time to competing political candidates. In 1969 in *Red Lion Broadcasting Co. v. FCC,* 395 U.S. 367 (1969) the Supreme Court sustained the Federal Communication Commission's fairness doctrine and personal attack rules against First Amendment attack. In *Red Lion,* the Court quoted Mill in *support* of the governmental regulatory doctrines at issue:

> The expression of views opposing those which broadcasters permit to be aired in the first place need not be confined solely to the broadcasters themselves as proxies. "Nor is it enough that he should hear the arguments of his own adversaries from his own teachers, presented as they state them, and accompanied by what they offer as refutations. That is not the way to do justice to the arguments, or bring them into real contact with his own mind. He must be able to hear them from persons who actually believe them; who defend them in earnest, and do their very utmost for them." J.S. Mill, *On Liberty,* 32 (R.McCallum ed. 1947). 395 U.S. at 392 n.18.

For some, citing Mill to support any kind of governmental interference with the press seems heretical. Others see it as consistent with Mill's passion for liberty of discussion and hostility to censorship, whether public or private.

THE MARKETPLACE OF IDEAS THEORY AND ITS CRITICS   The marketplace of ideas rationale for freedom of expression has been subjected to severe criticism. Indeed, its fundamental premise that the full and free discussion of ideas is an ultimate good for society has been challenged. Herbert Marcuse, the political philosopher of the New Left in the 1960s, believed Mill's writings assumed that rational beings participate in free discussion. In Marcuse's view, though most contemporary human beings are not rational; instead, they are manipulated by the media for commercial purposes and by government for political ones. Thus, the glorious concept of tolerance for all ideas advocated by Milton and Mill is for Marcuse repressive tolerance. Not only was Marcuse hostile to the marketplace of ideas, but he wanted to substitute "precensorship" for "the more or less hidden censorship that permeates the free media." See Marcuse, *Repressive Tolerance in Wolff, Moore and Marcuse, A Critique of Pure Tolerance* (1965).

Marcuse submitted the traditional marketplace of ideas concept to the following Marxist critique:

> The tolerance which was the great achievement of the liberal era is still professed and (with strong qualifications) practiced, while the economic and political process is subjected to a ubiquitous and effective administration in accordance with predominant interests. The result is an objective contradiction between the economic and political structure on the one side, and the theory and practice of toleration on the other. *Id.* at 110.

Marcuse's evident wish to have an intellectual elite direct the media for predetermined social ends will not seem to many an improvement over the present situation. Yet there is concern as to whether a marketplace of ideas theory is meaningful when the marketplace is increasingly characterized by concentration of ownership and similarity of viewpoint.

Despite the assaults by its critics, the classic marketplace of ideas rationale still has great vitality. In *McIntyre v. Ohio Elections Commission,* 115 S. Ct. 1511 (1995), a state statute prohibiting the distribution of anonymous campaign literature was a violation of the First Amendment. In doing so, Justice John Paul Stevens relied squarely on the marketplace of ideas rationale of the First Amendment. See p. 36.

Another critic, Professor Jerome A. Barron, argues that a self-correcting marketplace of ideas is a romantic and unrealistic description of the opinion process: see Barron, *Access to the Press—A New First Amendment Right,* 80 Harv. L. Rev. 1641 (1967):

> There is inequality in the power to communicate ideas just as there is inequality in economic bargaining power; to recognize the latter and deny the former is quixotic. The "marketplace of ideas" has rested on the assumption that protecting the right of expression is equivalent to providing for it. But changes in the communications industry have destroyed the equilibrium in that marketplace. A realistic view of the first amendment requires recognition that a right of free expression is somewhat thin if it can be exercised only at the sufferance of the managers of mass communications.

In classic marketplace of ideas theory, the role of government is nonintervention. The marketplace of ideas functions in much the same way as the Darwinian theory of evolution: the assumption is that after combat, the best ideas will emerge triumphant. But the unstated assumption in the passage from Barron is that if the marketplace of ideas is to be something more than a metaphor, some government intervention is required. In this connection, Barron advocates recognition of public rights of reply and access to the media. This critique is a market failure critique; it seeks to correct the flaws in the marketplace of ideas theory and set them aright.

Some critics of the marketplace of ideas rationale have been skeptical of a solution that would involve government-mandated rights of access and reply: "For the government to determine what access is adequate involves the government implicitly judging what is the correct resolution of the marketplace debates." *See* Baker, *Scope of the First Amendment Freedom of Speech,* 25 U.C.L.A. L. Rev. 964, 986 (1978).

In *Turner Broadcasting v. FCC,* 512 U.S. 622 (1994), the "must-carry" case, involving federal legislation requiring cable operators to carry certain local over-the-air broadcasting signals, the Supreme Court declined to adopt a classic noninterventionist marketplace of ideas position and simply invalidate the legislation. Indeed, the Court expressed its willingness to entertain a corrective market failure approach. Professor C. Edwin Baker explains *Turner* in this regard as follows:

> Observing the "potential for abuse of [cable's] private power over a central avenue of communication," the Court relied on *Associated Press v. United States,* 326 U.S. 1, 20 (1945), for the proposition that the First Amendment does not disable the government from taking steps to ensure that private interests not restrict . . . the free flow of information and ideas. That is after rejecting the broadcasting analogy, the Court also rejected *Tornillo's* government-hands-off philosophy by relying on a different newspaper case, *Associated Press,* to assert the legitimacy of broad governmental power over cable. Interestingly, the four dissenters did not dispute any of this.
>
> C. Edwin Baker, *Turner Broadcasting: Content-Based Regulation of Persons And Presses,* 1994 S. Ct. Rev. 57, 58–59.

As *Turner* shows, the Court can still be persuaded to tolerate governmental intervention in defense of the free flow of information and ideas.

More avowed critics of the marketplace of ideas theory look to government to protect public discourse and its quality. Professor Owen Fiss argues that there is a legitimate role for government in First Amendment theory:

> The aim is not to free the various agencies of the state from the forces that dominate social structure (surely an impossible task), but only to make it more likely that they will exert a countervailing force. This goal might be achieved by creating within state agencies certain processes or mechanisms that would enhance the power of the weaker elements of society.
>
> Owen Fiss, *Why the State?* 100 Harv. L. Rev. 781, 792 (1987).

Fiss speaks of developing new mechanisms to counter market forces. What would these mechanisms be?

Professor Scott Powe distinguishes the views of Fiss and Barron: "For Barron, access was a way to add voices and ideas to the marketplace." Both marketplace and individual would thereby be promoted. "Fiss makes no such claim. His proposals are designed to abridge some speech so that what is thereafter allowed in the marketplace will be capable of proper evaluation by listeners." Individual autonomy is subordinated to a more important value: the quality of public discourse. See Powe, *Scholarship and Markets,* 56 Geo. Wash. L. Rev. 172, 181 (1987).

Powe challenges the idea that government intervention in defense of public discourse can be consistent with the First Amendment: "What Fiss leaves unexplained—because it is unexplainable—is how the First Amendment ceased being a bar to government action and instead became the vehicle to justify government regulation. Quite simply, Fiss is asking for an amendment to the Constitution rather than the interpretation of the Constitution." *Id.* at 184.

The Self-Governance Model: The Meiklejohn Theory of the First Amendment

In Professor Alexander Meiklejohn's judgment, the rationale for the absolute protection for freedom of speech was to ensure that the general citizenry would have the necessary information to make the informed judgments on which a self-governing society is dependent. Speech unrelated to that end was therefore not public speech and not within the scope of the First Amendment; hence, it was within the regulatory power of the legislatures. See generally A. Meiklejohn, *Free Speech And Its Relation to Self-Government* (1948).

Did Meiklejohn believe then that no manner of expression could be restricted by government—even "counselling to murder" or falsely shouting fire in a crowded theater? Meiklejohn did not go this far either. What he urged was that it is necessary to distinguish between two kinds of expression, one of which has absolute protection and one of which does not. Expression with regard to issues that concern political self-government was in Meiklejohn's view absolutely protected by the language of the First Amendment: "Congress shall make no law abridging . . . freedom of speech, or of the press." But private discussion that is nonpolitical in character, such as falsely shouting fire in a crowded theater, was not within the ambit of the First Amendment at all. Instead, it was within the ambit of the more flexible, and less restrictive, Due Process Clause of the Fifth Amendment: "nor shall any person . . . be deprived of life, liberty or property, without due process of law."

Meiklejohn thought it highly significant that the First Amendment prohibited the abridgment of "freedom of speech" rather than "speech itself." This for him was the clue that the Framers intended to give absolute protection to public or political speech. Levy, however, suggests that the historical background of the First Amendment by no means implies that the Framers contemplated the absolute freedom of expression championed by Meiklejohn. Levy, *Legacy of Suppression* (1960). For a revised opinion by Levy, see *Emergence of a Free Press* (1985). Did Meiklejohn underestimate the influence of nonpolitical forms of speech on the process of self-government?

MEIKLEJOHN AND THE BLASI CRITIQUE: THE CHECKING VALUE   The heart of Meiklejohn's thesis was that the First Amendment should be interpreted to safeguard and protect self-governance in a free and democratic society. This thesis has recently been exposed to a comprehensive critique by Professor Vincent Blasi, who believes that the view that the First Amendment is designed essentially to protect democratic decision making is outmoded:

> [T]he Meiklejohn thesis vision of active, continued involvement by citizens fails to describe not only the reality but also the shared ideal of American politics.
> See Blasi, *The Checking Value in First Amendment Theory,* 1977 Am. B. Found. Res. J. 523, 561.

Blasi suggests that the First Amendment should be viewed instead as a kind of counterpoise to government. The function of the press is to serve as the watchdog of government, and the purpose of the First Amendment is to provide the press with protection in its role of keeping government responsive and accountable. Professor Blasi describes this checking value of the First Amendment as follows:

> The central premise of the checking value is that abuse of government is an especially serious evil—more serious than abuse of private power, even by institutions such as large corporations which can affect the lives of millions of people.

The shift in emphasis between Meiklejohn and Blasi is very clear: protection of the media, rather than protection of the citizenry for purposes of self-expression, becomes the fundamental First Amendment objective. The press becomes the focal point of First Amendment theory because the press, and not the citizenry, is the essential "check" on government excess. Blasi's theory makes enduring constitutional interpretation out of the salutary role of the press in the Watergate case.

Under Blasi's "checking value," the function of citizens in a regime ordered by the First Amendment is very different than it would be in Meiklejohn's view:

> The checking value is premised upon a different vision—one in which the government is structured in such a way that built-in counterforces make it possible for citizens in most, but not all, periods to have the luxury to concern themselves almost exclusively with private pursuits.

In Meiklejohn's theory, the individual is at the heart of First Amendment theory. In Blasi's theory, the media occupy that role. But is this substitution necessary? First Amendment theory should be rich enough to give the media adequate protection and yet to continue to grant the citizens the pivotal role that Meiklejohn assigned them. The "checking value" theory quite properly recognizes the almost quasi-constitutional checking role the press plays vis-a-vis government. Yet the theory is perhaps somewhat defeatist because it posits the individual citizen as remote and helpless, at least when compared to the two major protagonists, government and the media.

CIVIC REPUBLICANISM: MEIKLEJOHN REVISED?

Does Blasi's theory of the checking value leave citizens as little more than spectators in society? A theory that has recently become influential is the idea that the Framers intended to create a society the hallmark of which would be "civic republicanism," a society characterized by civic virtue. Meiklejohn put great emphasis on the role of the individual citizen as participant in forging a democratic society. Professor Cass Sunstein argues that the structure of the Constitution itself provides that the institutions created by it will produce civic virtue, even though the individual citizens themselves are not the central actors in the society. Sunstein contends that the Framers of the Constitution wanted to "carry forward the republican belief in virtue." However, they wished to achieve "civic virtue" not by engaging in romantic assumptions but by assuring that the structure of the society they created would respond to "the real world of political life": "The commitment to these ideas explains many of the founding institutions. It helps explain why in the original system, the Senate and the President were to be chosen by deliberative representatives rather than directly elected by the people." Cass R. Sunstein, *The Partial Constitution*, 21 (1993).

Sunstein also notes that the Framers did not view the members of Congress as simply mouthpieces for their constituencies but rather as participants in a republic of reason. Questions remain, however: Does Sunstein's view submerge the role of the individual citizen as much as Blasi's view? Does the press have a role in achieving "civic virtue"? Should it?

DELIBERATIVE DEMOCRACY

Advocating what he calls "deliberative democracy," Sunstein criticizes the marketplace of ideas rationale: "Justice Holmes's metaphor of a 'marketplace of ideas' has produced considerable good, but is also misleading. Aggregate or marketplace notions disregard the extent to which political outcomes are supposed to depend on discussion and debate, on a commitment to political equality, and on the reasons offered for or against the alternatives." Cass R. Sunstein, *Democracy and The Problem of Free Speech*, 249 (1993).

Sunstein calls for a free speech New Deal and says that government regulation might usefully promote free speech. His proposal would include reforming campaign finance laws, requiring public interest programs on television, and providing for "rights of reply for dissenting views." Other suggestions include "controls on the power of advertisers to influence programming content, and limitations on advertising time during children's programming."

A critique of Meiklejohn's theory and the Sunstein theory is that presented by Professor Robert Post:

> Meiklejohn's work displays a structure of analysis that is common to all versions of the collectivist theory of the First Amendment. The theory postulates a specific "objective" for public discourse and it concludes that public debate should be regulated instrumentally to achieve this objective.
>
> Robert Post, *Meiklejohn's Mistake: Individual Autonomy and the Reform of Public Discourse*, 64 U. Colo. L. Rev. 1109, 1119 (1993).

Professor Robert Post contends that this "collectivist" theory "stands for the subordination of public discourse to a framework of managerial authority." *Id.* at 1120. Why does Professor Post call Meiklejohn's vision collectivist? Post says:

> Meiklejohn locates the essence of self-government, and therefore also "the final aim" of First Amendment freedom in democracy's effort to ensure "the voting of wise decisions." He sharply distinguishes this purpose from that of individual autonomy.
> *Id.* at 1111–12.

Incidentally, Post views Sunstein's theory as collectivist as well. Why?

The Liberty or Individual Autonomy Model

Yet another rationale that has been offered for the constitutional protection accorded to free expression is the liberty or individual autonomy model of the First Amendment. One of its principal proponents, Professor Edwin Baker, describes the liberty model this way:

> The liberty model holds that the free speech clause protects not a marketplace but rather an arena of individual liberty from certain types of governmental restrictions. Speech is protected not as a means to a collective good but because of the value of speech conduct to the individual.
> C. Edwin Baker, *Scope of the First Amendment Freedom of Speech*, 25 U.C.L.A. L. Rev. 964, 966 (1978).

Baker contends that the liberty model casts a broader net for First Amendment protection than its rivals: "[T]he broadened scope of protection required by the liberty model cures the major inadequacies of the marketplace of ideas as a model for finding or creating societal 'truth,' thereby providing protection for a progressive process of change."

Critics of the liberty model contend that its scope is too great and that, by attempting to protect so much, the model ends up protecting less than it should. Judge Robert Bork has argued that the liberty model makes it difficult to distinguish speech from other activities. In short, the liberty model by its inclusivity tends to depreciate freedom of speech. "[One] cannot on neutral grounds choose to protect speech [under the liberty model] more than [one] protects any other claimed freedom." Robert H. Bork, *Neutral Principles and Some First Amendment Problems*, 47 Ind. L. J. 1, 25 (1971).

Another proponent of the liberty or, as he calls it, self-realization model is Professor Martin Redish. He defends the reach of the self-realization model as follows:

> Just as individuals need an open flow of information and opinion to aid them in making their electoral and governmental decisions, they similarly need a free flow of information and opinion to guide them in making other life-affecting decisions. Thus there is no logical basis for distinguishing the role speech plays in the political process."
> Martin H. Redish, *The Value of Free Speech*, 130 U. Pa. L. Rev. 591, 604 (1982).

One might ask, however, whether this passage entirely responds to the concerns raised by Bork. How does the liberty model differ from the self-governance model? *Id.* at 619–25.

Alternative First Amendment Models and Values

The three First Amendment models discussed thus far—marketplace of ideas, self-governance, and liberty or autonomy—do not exhaust the approaches that have been offered to explain and ensure constitutional protection for freedom of expression. Several other ideas about the First Amendment have been influential, even though they lack the scope of the models. Dean Lee Bollinger has argued that the value of freedom of speech is in its capacity to stimulate tolerance in society. In this view, hateful as the Nazi symbol or the hooded sheet of the Klan member may be, freedom of speech is justified because it teaches self-restraint and tolerance to a heterogenous society that must espouse those values to endure. See Lee Bollinger, *The Tolerant Society: Freedom of Speech and Extremist Speech in America* (1986). This theory is a controversial one. In this view, racial and religious minorities must be not only the victims of the abuse of their tormentors but also martyrs to freedom of expression.

Another guideline to the First Amendment is suggested by Professor Steven Shiffrin who urges that First Amendment interpretation should have as its "organizing symbol" the "image of the dissenter." In case of doubt, the law should protect the dissenter and not the society that punishes him. See Steven Shiffrin, *The First Amendment, Democracy and Romance* (1990).

Still another approach to First Amendment interpretation finds its source in economics and public choice theory. Professor Daniel Farber contends that "the crucial insight of public choice theory is that because information is a public good, it is likely to be undervalued by both the market and the political system." Because information is undervalued by the market, the constitutional protection afforded information against governmental restriction is justified. See Farber, *Free Speech Without Romance: Public Choice and the First Amendment,* 105 Harv. L. Rev. 554, 555 (1991); *see generally,* Barron and Dienes, *First Amendment Law in a Nutshell,* 15–18 (1993).

Critics of a Special Protected Status for Freedom of Expression: An Assault on the First Amendment?

The proponents of the models discussed here usually assume that freedom of expression should have a special, protected status. Increasingly, however, these models and their assumptions are being severely criticized. For example, the marketplace of ideas rationale is being attacked not only as being structurally defective but for having harmful effects as well:

> Marketplace philosophy disables the government even from addressing serious distortions of the marketplace resulting from imbalances of private power. A philosophy shunning any government involvement in the "open and unregulated market for the trade in ideas" has significant disadvantages. Speech, after all, can do harm; marketplace theory leaves the government largely powerless to protect individuals from such harm.
>
> Jonathan Weinberg, *Broadcasting and Speech,* 81 Cal. L. Rev. 1101, 1144–45 (1993).

Opponents of sexism, pornography, and racism find in the marketplace of ideas theory a system that subordinates the oppressed. The feminist writer Catharine MacKinnon denies that women have an equal stake in the marketplace of ideas "supposedly" guaranteed by the First Amendment:

> First of all, the marketplace of ideas is literal; those with the most money can buy the most speech, and women are poor. Second, protecting pornographers as the First Amendment now does, does not promote the freedom of speech of women. It *has* not

done so. Pornography terrifies women into silence. Understanding free speech as an abstract system is a liberal position. Understanding how speech also exists within a substantive system of power relations is a feminist position.
>
> Catharine A. MacKinnon, *Feminism Unmodified: Discourses on Life and Law,* 140 (1987).

Professor Richard Delgado says that protectors of minorities seeking to punish racist speech see it "as not a mere isolated event, but as part of an interrelated series of acts, by which persons of color are subordinated." First Amendment advocates see protection of even racist speech as "part of the never-ending vigilance necessary to protect freedom of expression in a society that is too prone to balance it away." See Richard Delgado, *Campus Antiracism Rules: Constitutional Narratives in Collision,* 85 Nw. U. L. Rev. 343, 347–48 (1991). In Delgado's view, both positions have equal validity. First Amendment advocates, however, regard this as a *radical* claim because, in their view, the claims of free speech should trump the claims of those who suffer from its exercise even if the harms are undeniable. For more on the reconsideration of First Amendment theory that has been prompted by opponents of racist and other harmful speech, see Chapter 3.

PROBEMS OF FIRST AMENDMENT INTERPRETATION

The Supreme Court has generally treated free speech cases and freedom of the press cases as interchangeable. In 1975, however, Justice Potter Stewart declared that alone among constitutional guarantees "the Free Press Clause extends protection to an institution." Justice Stewart observed: "The publishing business is, in short, the only organized private business that is given explicit constitutional protection." *See* Stewart, *"Or of the Press,"* 26 Hastings L. J. 631, 633–34 (1975). In the Stewart thesis, the Free Press Clause is designed to protect the press *qua* press. In a sense, this idea is the antithesis of Justice Felix Frankfurter's conception of freedom of the press as reflected in his concurring opinion in *Pennekamp v. Florida,* 328 U.S. 331 (1946): "Freedom of the press, however, is not an end in itself but a means to the end of a free society." Justice Stewart interpreted the press clause "to create a fourth institution outside the government as an additional check on the three official branches."

Stewart's thesis that the press clause gives the press a special First Amendment status has not met with acceptance. In *First National Bank of Boston v. Bellotti,* 435 U.S. 765 (1978), Justice Lewis Powell observed for the Court that the inherent value of speech is not affected by the status of the speaker. Chief Justice Warren Burger, in a concurring opinion, also appeared to reject the idea that the press clause accords the press a uniquely privileged status: "In short, the First Amendment does not 'belong' to any definable category of persons or entities: it belongs to all who exercise its freedoms."

The constitutional protection given to freedom of speech and press covers the whole spectrum of the means of communication. The First Amendment has been extended to new communication media undreamed of in the eighteenth century, such as the sound truck, movies, radio, television, and cable television. The provisions of the Telecommunications Act of 1996 that limit indecent speech on the Internet are recent examples of a new technology raising First Amendment problems. Do such provisions raise the same First Amendment issues as those posed by indecency regulation on cable and broadcasting?

Should the Supreme Court try to deal with each new medium of communications in terms of its own technology and impact? Or should the Court apply broad First Amendment principles across the board? In *Joseph Burstyn, Inc. v. Wilson,* 343 U.S. 495, 502–03 (1952), Justice Tom Clark observed that "[t]o hold that liberty of expression by means of motion pictures is guaranteed by the First and Fourteenth Amendments is not the end of our problem. Each method [of expression] tends to present its own peculiar problems." In *Kovacs v. Cooper,* 336 U.S. 77 (1946), a case involving restrictions on the volume of sound trucks, Justice Robert Jackson urged that each medium be considered a law unto itself. Justice Hugo Black rejected this kind of "favoritism."

In October 1979, Justice William Brennan gave a provocative speech in which he suggested that there are two distinct First Amendment models—the "structural" model and the "speech" model—that they do not and need not receive the same degree of protection:

> Under one model—which I call the "speech" model—the press requires and is accorded the absolute protection of the First Amendment. In the other model—I call it the "structural" model—the press interests may conflict with other societal interests.
>
> The "speech" model is familiar. It is as comfortable as a pair of old shoes, and the press, in its present conflict with the Court, most often slips into the language and rhetorical stance with which this model is associated even when only the "structural" model is at issue. According to this traditional "speech" model, the primary purpose of the First Amendment is more or less absolutely to prohibit any interference with freedom of expression. The "speech" model thus readily lends itself to the heady rhetoric of absolutism.
>
> The "speech" model, however, has its limitations. It is a mistake to suppose that the First Amendment protects *only* self-expression, only the right to speak out. I believe that the First Amendment in addition fosters the values of democratic self-government.
>
> Another way of saying this is that the First Amendment protects the structure of communications necessary for the existence of our democracy. This insight suggests the second model to describe the role of the press in our society. This second model is structural in nature. It focuses on the relationship of the press to the communications functions required by our democratic beliefs. To the extent the press makes these functions possible, the model requires that it receive the protection of the First Amendment. A good example is the press' role in providing and circulating the information necessary for informed public discussion. To the extent the press or, for that matter, to the extent any institution uniquely performs this role, it should receive unique First Amendment protection.
>
> This "structural" model of the press has several important limitations. It significantly extends the umbrella of the press' constitutional protections. The press is not only shielded when it speaks out, but when it performs all the myriad tasks necessary for it to gather and disseminate the news. As you can easily see, the stretch of this protection is theoretically endless. Any imposition of any kind on the press will in some measure affect its ability to perform protected functions. Therefore this model requires a Court to weigh the effects of the imposition against the social interest which are served by the imposition. This inquiry is impersonal, almost sociological in nature. But it does not fit comfort-

ably with the absolutist rhetoric associated with the first model of the press I have discussed. For here, I repeat, the Court must weigh the effects of the imposition inhibiting press access against the social interest served by the imposition.

Justice William J. Brennan, Jr., *Address at the Dedication for the S.I. Newhouse Center for Law and Justice* (Oct. 17, 1979), in 32 Rutgers L. Rev. 173 (1979).

In First Amendment law, one confronts a continuous philosophical debate on the meaning and scope of freedom of expression. In this book, you will encounter numerous concepts such as freedom from prior restraint, clear and present danger, content-based versus content-neutral regulation, strict scrutiny, and compelled speech. Through these encounters, you will begin to learn and understand the vocabulary of First Amendment law. Sometimes these doctrines disguise the sources of a decision rather than illuminate them. Sometimes a Supreme Court decision owes more to the death, or retirement, of a justice and the appointment of a new one with a different worldview than it does to the demands of any particular doctrine. Nevertheless, the free speech and press doctrines discussed in this chapter, and elsewhere in this book, are of great importance. They represent attempts by judges and scholars to capture the variety and contradictions of First Amendment law. By understanding the scope and purpose of freedom of expression, we preserve and protect it.

FIRST AMENDMENT DOCTRINE IN THE SUPREME COURT: A RATIONALE FOR LIMITING THE REGULATION OF SPEECH CONTENT

The Rise of the Clear and Present Danger Doctrine

The American law of freedom of speech and press, as enunciated by the opinions of the U.S. Supreme Court, is mainly a post-World War I phenomenon. The use of conscription during World War I for the first time since the Civil War, the opposition of radical groups to participation in the war, and the antiradical "red scare" of the early 1920s combined to produce a collision between authority and libertarian values. Out of that collision came the first significant efforts to develop some guidelines for reconciling majoritarian impatience, as expressed in an assortment of repressive laws, with constitutional guarantees. The purpose of a constitution, of course, is in a sense to confound a legislative majority. What a constitution does is to remove certain matters from the reach of legislation.

The following case arose out of socialist hostility to the draft and to American participation in World War I. The clash of a federal antiespionage statute with socialist political protest provided a vehicle for an opinion by Justice Oliver Wendell Holmes.

Holmes became one of the early architects of American free speech and free press theory. In *Schenck*, Holmes launched a famous doctrine, the clear and present danger doctrine. Although this doctrine is less important today than it once was, the very structure of the doctrine shows that the absolutist approach to freedom of expression has not been favored by the Supreme Court. Further, the case illustrates the difficulties courts face in balancing the claims of national security against the claims of freedom of expression.

Schenck v. United States
249 U.S. 47, 39 S. CT. 247, 63 L. ED. 470 (1919).

[EDITORIAL NOTE: *Schenck, general secretary of the Socialist Party and others, mailed a document to draft-age men stating that the draft was in violation of the Thirteenth Amendment. The government contended the defendants thereby encouraged obstruction of the draft. Schenck and his associates were indicted and convicted for violation of the Espionage Act of 1917 for causing, and attempting to cause, insubordination in the military and obstruction of military recruiting when the United States was at war. On appeal to the Supreme Court, the defendants claimed that predicating a violation of the Espionage Act on their expression violated the First Amendment. Although the Supreme Court affirmed the conviction, Holmes set forth the embryo of the clear and present danger doctrine.*]

Justice HOLMES delivered the opinion of the Court:

The document in question [declared] that conscription was despotism in its purest form and a monstrous wrong against humanity in the interest of Wall Street's chosen few. It said, "Do not submit to intimidation," but in form at least confined itself to peaceful measures such as a petition for repeal of the act. The other and later printed side of the sheet was headed "Assert your Rights." [The document] denied the power to send our citizens away to foreign shores to shoot up the people of other lands, and added that words could not express the condemnation such cold-blooded ruthlessness deserves. Of course the document would not have been sent unless it had been intended to have some effect, and we do not see what effect it could be expected to have upon persons subject to the draft except to influence them to obstruct the carrying of it out. The defendants do not deny that the jury might find against them on this point.

But it is said, suppose that was the tendency of this circular, it is protected by the First Amendment. We admit that in many places and in ordinary times the defendants in saying all that was said in the circular would have been within their constitutional rights. But the character of every act depends upon the circumstances in which it is done. The most stringent protection of free speech would not protect a man in falsely shouting fire in a theatre and causing a panic. It does not even protect a man from an injunction against uttering words that may have all the effect of force. The question in every case is whether the words used are used in such circumstances and are of such a nature as to create a clear and present danger that they will bring about the substantive evils that Congress has a right to prevent. It is a question of proximity and degree.

When a nation is at war many things that might be said in time of peace are such a hindrance to its effort that their utterance will not be endured so long as men fight and that no Court could regard them as protected by any constitutional right. It seems to be admitted that if an actual obstruction of the recruiting service were proved, liability for words that produced that effect might be enforced. The statute of 1917 punishes conspiracies to obstruct as well as actual obstruction. If the act, (speaking, or circulating a paper,) its tendency and the intent to which it is done are the same we perceive no ground for saying that success alone warrants making the act a crime.

Judgments affirmed.

COMMENT

The *Schenck* case is an illustration of congressional power over political freedom. Abridgment of freedom of speech and press by Congress is not quite as unrestricted as a literal reading of the First Amendment might suggest. After all, Schenck was convicted for disseminating a pamphlet urging resistance to the draft, and the Supreme Court, in an opinion by one of its most libertarian judges, affirmed. In a companion case to *Schenck*, Justice Holmes remarked that "the First Amendment while prohibiting legislation against free speech as such cannot have been, and obviously was not, intended to give immunity for every possible use of language." *Frohwerk v. United States*, 249 U.S. 204, 206 (1919). Holmes made a similar observation in *Schenck* when he said that "free speech would not protect a man in falsely shouting fire in a theatre and causing a panic." In other words, there is no absolute freedom of expression; rather, the scope of protection for such freedom is a question of degree. Under the rubric of the clear and present danger doctrine, political expression can be punished if circumstances exist to "create a clear and present danger" that the communication in controversy would "bring about the substantive evils that Congress has a right to prevent." Does Holmes indicate in *Schenck* whether the determination of circumstances that would present a "clear and present" danger is a legislative or a judicial responsibility?

Since the pamphlet issued by a minor group of socialists was found sufficiently objectionable to place its distributors in jail, should we conclude that the clear and present danger doctrine operates to give relatively little protection to unpopular communications? Or does the fact that the expression punished in *Schenck* occurred in wartime limit its application?

Abrams v. United States
250 U.S. 616, 40 S. CT. 17, 63 L. ED. 1173 (1919).

[EDITORIAL NOTE: *Abrams and others were accused of publishing and disseminating pamphlets attacking the American expeditionary force sent to Russia to defeat the new Communist revolutionary government of Russia. The pamphlets also called for a general strike of munitions workers. The majority of the Supreme Court, per Justice Clarke, held that the publication and distribution of the pamphlets during the war were not protected by the First Amendment. Justice Clarke's opinion for the majority failed to make much impact on the law. The dissent of Justice Holmes, however, in which he was joined by Justice Louis Brandeis, became one of the significant documents in the literature of the law of freedom of expression.*]

Justice HOLMES, dissenting.

The indictment is founded wholly upon publication of two leaflets. The first of these leaflets says that the President's cowardly silence about the intervention in Russia reveals the hypocrisy of the plutocratic gang in Washington. [I]t seems too plain to be denied that the suggestion [in the second leaflet] to the [Russian emigrant] workers [in the United States] that they are producing bullets to murder their dearest, and the further advocacy of a general strike do urge curtailment of production of things necessary to the prosecution of the war within the meaning of the [1918 amendments to the Espionage Act.] But to make the conduct criminal that statute requires that it should be "with the intent by such curtailment to cripple or hinder the United States in the prosecution of the war." It seems to me that no such intent is proved.

I never have seen any reason to doubt that the questions of law that alone were before this Court in the cases of *Schenck, Frohwerk* and *Debs* were rightly decided. I do not doubt for a moment that by the same reasoning that would justify punishing persuasion to murder, the United States constitutionally may punish speech that produces or is intended to produce a clear and imminent danger that it will bring about forthwith certain substantive evils that the United States constitutionally may seek to prevent. The power undoubtedly is greater in time of war than in time of peace because war opens dangers that do not exist at other times.

But as against dangers peculiar to war, as against others, the principle of the right to free speech is always the same. It is only the present danger of immediate evil or an intent to bring it about that warrants Congress in setting a limit to the expression of opinion where private rights are not concerned. Now nobody can suppose that the surreptitious publishing of a silly leaflet by an unknown man, without more, would present any immediate danger that its opinions would hinder the success of the government arms or have any appreciable tendency to do so. Publishing those opinions for the very purpose of obstructing, however, might indicate a greater danger and at

any rate would have the quality of an attempt. [But] I do not see how anyone can find the intent required by the statute in any of the defendants' words.

In this case sentences of twenty years imprisonment have been imposed for the publishing of two leaflets that I believe the defendants had as much right to publish as the Government has to publish the Constitution of the United States now vainly invoked by them. Even if I am technically wrong and enough can be squeezed from these poor and puny anonymities to turn the color of legal litmus paper; I will add, even if what I think the necessary intent were shown; the most nominal punishment seems to me all that possibly could be inflicted, unless the defendants are to be made to suffer not for what the indictment alleges but for the creed that they avow—a creed that I believe to be the creed of ignorance and immaturity when honestly held, as I see no reason to doubt that it was held here but which, although made the subject of examination at the trial, no one has a right even to consider in dealing with the charges before the Court.

Persecution for the expression of opinions seems to me perfectly logical. If you have no doubt of your premises or your power and want a certain result with all your heart you naturally express your wishes in law and sweep away all opposition. To allow opposition by speech seems to indicate that you think the speech impotent, as when a man says that he has squared the circle, or that you do not care wholeheartedly for the result, or that you doubt either your power or your premises. But when men have realized that time has upset many fighting faiths, they may come to believe even more than they believe the very foundations of their own conduct that the ultimate good desired is better reached by free trade in ideas—that the best test of truth is the power of the thought to get itself accepted in the competition of the market, and that truth is the only ground upon which their wishes safely can be carried out. That at any rate is the theory of our Constitution. It is an experiment, as all life is an experiment. Every year if not every day we have to wager our salvation upon some prophecy based upon imperfect knowledge. While that experiment is part of our system I think that we should be eternally vigilant against attempts to check the expression of opinions that we loathe and believe to be fraught with death, unless they so imminently threaten immediate interference with the lawful and pressing purposes of the law that an immediate check is required to save the country. I wholly disagree with the argument of the Government that the First Amendment left the common law as to seditious libel in force. History seems to me against the notion. I had conceived that the United States through many years had shown its repentance for the Sedition Act of 1798, by repaying fines that it imposed. Only the emergency that makes it immediately dangerous to leave the correction of evil counsels to time warrants making any exception to the sweeping command, "Congress shall make no law abridging the freedom of speech." Of course I am speaking only of expressions of opinion and exhortations, which were all that were uttered here, but I regret that I cannot put into more impressive words my belief that in their conviction upon this indictment the defendants were deprived of their rights under the Constitution of the United States.

Justice BRANDEIS concurs with the foregoing opinion.]

COMMENT

Holmes's theory of freedom of expression is basically a laissez-faire idea. In this view, the clash of political ideas is a self-correcting and self-sustaining process. Under the marketplace of ideas theory, the responsibility of government is neither to suppress nor to influence the process. This approach is reconciled with the clear and present danger doctrine on the assumption that in a less than ideal world the doctrine permits only a minimum of governmental intervention into the opinion-making process. Holmes's *Abrams* dissent is a classic statement of the "marketplace of ideas" approach to First Amendment theory. In view of the rise of the electronic media, the information superhighway, and the increasing concentration of ownership in the media, what contemporary difficulties are encountered by ideas such as "the best test of truth is the power of the thought to get itself accepted in the competition of the market"? The "market" Holmes is talking about is basically what we today call the mass media and their mass audiences. Is "free trade in ideas" the distinguishing characteristic of these media? If it is not, what deficiencies do you see in

the "marketplace of ideas" theory? Do the advent of the Internet and the relative ease of individual access to it restore Holmes's vision of a working "marketplace of ideas"?

GITLOW v. NEW YORK
268 U.S. 652, 45 S. CT. 625, 69 L. ED. 1138 (1925).

[EDITORIAL NOTE: *Benjamin Gitlow, a member of the left wing section of the Socialist Party, was indicted and convicted under the criminal anarchy statute of New York for publishing a radical manifesto. Sixteen thousand copies of* The Revolutionary Age, *the house organ of the revolutionary section of the party that published the Manifesto, were printed. Some were sold; some were mailed. The New York Criminal Anarchy statute forbade the publication or distribution of material advocating, advising or "teaching the duty, necessity, or propriety of overthrowing or overturning organized government by force or violence." The Manifesto had urged mass strikes by the proletariat and repudiated the approach of the moderate socialists in seeking to obtain political power through democratic means. The state trial court convicted Gitlow under the state criminal anarchy statute, and the state appellate courts affirmed. The U.S. Supreme Court also affirmed. The Court utilized as the measure of constitutionality the question of whether there was a reasonable basis for the legislature to have enacted the statute.*]

Justice SANFORD delivered the opinion of the Court.

For present purposes we may and do assume that freedom of speech and of the press—which are protected by the First Amendment from abridgment by Congress—are among the fundamental personal rights and "liberties" protected by the due process clause of the Fourteenth Amendment from impairment by the States.

We cannot hold that the present statute is an arbitrary or unreasonable exercise of the police power of the State unwarrantably infringing the freedom of speech or press; and we must and do sustain its constitutionality.

This being so it may be applied to every utterance—not too trivial to be beneath the notice of the law—which is of such a character and used with such intent and purpose as to bring it within the prohibition of the statute. In other words, when the legislative body has determined generally, in the constitutional exercise of its discretion, that utterances of a certain kind involve such danger of substantive evil that they may be punished, the question whether any specific utterance coming within the prohibited class is likely, in and of itself, to bring about the substantive evil, is not open to consideration. It is sufficient that the statute itself be constitutional and that the use of the language comes within its prohibition.

It is clear that the question in such cases is entirely different from that involved in those cases where the statute merely prohibits certain acts involving the danger of substantive evil, without any reference to language itself, and it is sought to apply its provisions to language used by the defendant for the purpose of bringing about the prohibited results. There, if it be contended that the statute cannot be applied to the language used by the defendant because of its protection by the freedom of speech or press, it must necessarily be found, as an original question, without any previous determination by the legislative body, whether the specific language used involved such likelihood of bringing about the substantive evil as to deprive it of the constitutional protection. In such case it has been held that the general provisions of the statute may be constitutionally applied to the specific utterance of the defendant if its natural tendency and probable effect was to bring about the substantive evil which the legislative body might prevent. And the general statement in the *Schenck* case, that the "question in every case is whether the words used are used in such circumstances and are of such a nature as to create a clear and present danger that they will bring about the substantive evils,"—upon which great reliance is placed in the defendant's argument—was manifestly intended, as shown by the context, to apply only in cases of this class, and has no application to those like the present, where the legislative body itself has previously determined the danger of substantive evil arising from utterances of a specified character.

And finding, for the reasons stated, that the statute is not in itself unconstitutional, and that it has not been applied in the present case in derogation of any constitutional right, the judgment of the Court of Appeals is affirmed.

Justice HOLMES, disenting.

Justice BRANDEIS and I are of opinion that this judgment should be reversed. If what I think the correct test is applied it is manifest that there was no present danger of an attempt to overthrow the government by force on the part of the admittedly small minority who shared the defendant's views. It is said that this manifesto was

more than a theory, that it was an incitement. Every idea is an incitement. It offers itself for belief and if believed it is acted on unless some other belief outweighs it or some failure of energy stifles the movement at its birth. The only difference between the expression of an opinion and an incitement in the narrower sense is the speaker's enthusiasm for the result. Eloquence may set fire to reason. But whatever may be thought of the redundant discourse before us it had no chance of starting a present conflagration. If in the long run the beliefs expressed in proletarian dictatorship are destined to be accepted by the dominant forces of the community, the only meaning of free speech is that they should be given their chance and have their way.

If the publication of this document had been laid as an attempt to induce an uprising against government at once and not at some indefinite time in the future it would have presented a different question. The object would have been one with which the law might deal, subject to the doubt whether there was any danger that the publication could produce any result, or in other words, whether it was not futile and too remote from possible consequences. But the indictment alleges the publication and nothing more.

COMMENT

The *Gitlow* Court asserts that a test of "reasonableness" of the legislative judgment will be used when the legislature itself has determined that certain utterances create a danger of a substantive evil. The statements in the majority opinion in *Gitlow* concerning appropriate tests for legislation affecting freedom of expression are no longer authoritative. Instead, Brandeis's subsequent formulation of the clear and present danger doctrine in *Whitney v. California*, 274 U.S. 357 (1927), has prevailed. What proved durable in Justice Sanford's opinion in *Gitlow* were some *dicta*, or statements not actually necessary to the result reached by the Court, which offhandedly extended the First Amendment limitations on federal action curtailing freedom of expression to the states by reason of the Due Process Clause of the Fourteenth Amendment.

Previous *dicta* had indicated that the states were not bound by the federal constitutional guarantees of freedom of speech and press.

Justice Sanford's statement to the contrary in *Gitlow* was, therefore, of great importance. Were it not for his *Gitlow dictum,* Justice Sanford would be largely unremembered. Nevertheless, the substance of his *Gitlow* opinion did find a champion: Robert Bork argued at one point—although he has since changed his mind—that the opinion that should be praised in *Gitlow* is Sanford's rather than Holmes's:

> Speech advocating violent overthrow is not "political speech." It is not political speech because it violates constitutional truths about processes and because it is not aimed at a new definition of political truth by a legislative majority. Violent overthrow of government breaks the premises of our system concerning the ways in which truth is defined, and yet those premises are the only reason for protecting political speech. It follows that there is no constitutional reason to protect speech advocating forcible overthrow.
>
> See Bork, *Neutral Principles and Some First Amendment Problems,* 47 Ind. L. J. 1, 20 (1971).

Many will be concerned whenever political freedom is limited to those who believe in "constitutional truth." The fear is that those in control of government may define "constitutional truth" too narrowly. Compare the views of Herbert Marcuse with those of Robert Bork (both discussed earlier in this chapter). Are there any points of similarity? Any differences?

THE MEIKLEJOHN CRITIQUE OF THE CLEAR AND PRESENT DANGER DOCTRINE The political philosopher Alexander Meiklejohn was a severe critic of the views articulated by Justice Holmes. Holmes's clear and present danger doctrine sometimes permitted what, in Meiklejohn's judgment, the First Amendment prohibited: congressional legislation abridging freedom of expression. See A. Meiklejohn, *Free Speech and Its Relation to Self-Government,* 29 (1948). For Meiklejohn, the clear and present danger doctrine was merely a verbal dodge for permitting restriction of free speech and press whenever Congress was disposed to do so.

MEIKLEJOHN AND HOLMES: THE CHAFEE VIEW Meiklejohn's theory had the advantage of attempting to deal textually with the perplexing latitude of the First Amendment. The dilemma of First Amendment interpretation is that the more generously its language is interpreted, oddly enough, the less protection it renders. This is due to the fact that as a practical and political matter, legislative majorities are often unwilling to tolerate unlimited expression. Both Meiklejohn and Holmes, then, were attempting to provide a guide for indicating what is protected expression and what is not. Meiklejohn criticized Holmes because Holmes did not segregate the most important aspect of expression—political expression—for absolute protection.

Professor Zechariah Chafee subsequently criticized Meiklejohn on the ground that his attempt to immunize political speech—quite beyond the fact that separating what is public from what is private is no easy matter—was hopelessly unrealistic from a pragmatic point of view and historically invalid as well. Chafee's basic point was that the question is not, ideally, how much speech ought to be protected but rather, politically and practically, how much expression can be protected by a court that is asked to defy "legislators and prosecutors."

For Chafee, the merit of the clear and present danger doctrine was that it allowed Congress some room to legislate in the area of public discussion but in such a way that the scope for such legislation was very restricted. For Chafee, the alternative to the Holmesian interpretation of the First Amendment was not Meiklejohn's absolute immunity for public discussion but rather no "immunity at all in the face of legislation." See Chafee, *Book Review,* 62 Harv. L. Rev. 891, 898 (1949). It was obvious to Chafee that some concessions in the form of legislation must be made to popular intolerance in times of stress. Unless some concessions were made, the consequences for free expression in any time of turmoil and anxiety would, in his view, necessarily be worse than if some relaxation of the absolute language of the First Amendment were not permitted.

Whitney v. California
274 U.S. 357, 47 S. CT. 641, 71 L. ED. 1095 (1927).

[EDITORIAL NOTE: *Ms. Anita Whitney attended a Communist Labor Party Convention in California and was elected an alternate member of its state executive committee. Whitney was convicted under the California Criminal Syndicalism Act on the ground that the Communist Labor Party was formed to teach criminal syndicalism and, as a member of the party, she partic-*

ipated in the crime. The state Criminal Syndicalism Act defined criminal syndicalism "as any doctrine, advocating, teaching or aiding and abetting the commission of crime, sabotage [or] unlawful methods of terrorism as a means of accomplishing a change in industrial ownership or control, or effecting any political change."

On review to the U.S. Supreme Court, Whitney insisted that she had not intended to have the Communist Labor Party of California serve as an instrument of terrorism or violence. Whitney argued that, as the convention progressed, it developed that the majority of the delegates entertained opinions about violence that she did not share. She asserted she should not be required to have foreseen that development and that her mere presence at the convention should not be considered to constitute a crime under the statute. The Court, per Justice Sanford, said that what Whitney was really doing was asking the Supreme Court to review questions of fact that had already been determined against her in the courts below and that questions of fact were not open to review in the Supreme Court. The Supreme Court upheld Whitney's conviction on the ground that concerted action involved a greater threat to the public order than isolated utterances and acts of individuals.

But it was the concurrence of Justice Brandeis, joined by Justice Holmes, rather than Justice Sanford's opinion for the majority, that shaped the future development of the constitutional law of freedom of expression. Brandeis attempted to do two things in his concurrence in Whitney. *First, he sought to identify the responsibilities of the judiciary and the legislature under the clear and present danger doctrine so that the greatest possible protection was provided for freedom of expression. Second, Brandeis sought to explore the rationale of constitutional protection for freedom of expression.*

In reading the Brandeis opinion in Whitney, *the student should attempt to state and analyze the conclusions that Brandeis reached in trying to achieve these two goals.*]

Justice BRANDEIS concurring.

Miss Whitney was convicted of the felony of assisting in organizing, in the year 1919, the Communist Labor Party of California, of being a member of it, and of assembling with it. These acts are held to constitute a crime, because the party was formed to teach criminal syndicalism. The statute which made these acts a crime restricted the right of free speech and of assembly theretofore existing. The claim is that the statute, as applied, denied to Miss Whitney the liberty guaranteed by the Fourteenth Amendment.

The felony which the statute created is a crime very unlike the old felony of conspiracy or the old misdemeanor of unlawful assembly. The mere act of assisting in forming a society for teaching syndicalism, of becoming a member of it, or assembling with others for that purpose is given the dynamic quality of crime. There is guilt although the society may not contemplate imme-

diate promulgation of the doctrine. Thus the accused is to be punished, not for attempt, incitement or conspiracy, but for a step in preparation, which, if it threatens the public order at all, does so only remotely. The novelty in the prohibition introduced is that the statute aims, not at the practice of criminal syndicalism, nor even directly at the preaching of it, but at association with those who propose to preach it.

Despite arguments to the contrary which had seemed to me persuasive, it is settled that the due process clause of the Fourteenth Amendment applies to matters of substantive law as well as to matters of procedure. Thus all fundamental rights comprised within the term liberty are protected by the federal Constitution from invasion by the states. The right of free speech, the right to teach and the right of assembly are, of course, fundamental rights. These may not be denied or abridged. But, although the rights of free speech and assembly are fundamental, they are not in their nature absolute. Their exercise is subject to restriction, if the particular restriction proposed is required in order to protect the state from destruction or from serious injury, political, economic or moral. That the necessity which is essential to a valid restriction does not exist unless speech would produce, or is intended to produce, a clear and imminent danger of some substantive evil which the state constitutionally may seek to prevent has been settled.

It is said to be the function of the Legislature to determine whether at a particular time and under the particular circumstances the formation of, or assembly with, a society organized to advocate criminal syndicalism constitutes a clear and present danger of substantive evil; and that by enacting the law here in question the Legislature of California determined that question in the affirmative. Compare *Gitlow v. New York*. The Legislature must obviously decide, in the first instance, whether a danger exists which calls for a particular protective measure. But where a statute is valid only in case certain conditions exist, the enactment of the statute cannot alone establish the facts which are essential to its validity. Prohibitory legislation has repeatedly been held invalid, because unnecessary, where the denial of liberty involved was that of engaging in a particular business. The powers of the courts to strike down an offending law are no less when the interests involved are not property rights, but the fundamental personal rights of free speech and assembly.

This Court has not yet fixed the standard by which to determine when a danger shall be deemed clear; how remote the danger may be and yet be deemed present; and what degree of evil shall be deemed sufficiently substantial to justify resort to abridgment of free speech and assembly as the means of protection. To reach sound conclusions on these matters, we must bear in mind why a state is, ordinarily, denied the power to prohibit dissemination of social, economic and political doctrine which a vast majority of its citizens believes to be false and fraught with evil consequence.

Those who won our independence believed that the final end of the state was to make men free to develop their faculties, and that in its government the deliberative forces should prevail over the arbitrary. They valued liberty both as an end and as a means. They believed liberty to be the secret of happiness and courage to be the secret of liberty. They believed that freedom to think as you will and to speak as you think are means indispensable to the discovery and spread of political truth; that without free speech and assembly discussion would be futile; that with them, discussion affords ordinarily adequate protection against the dissemination of noxious doctrine; that the greatest menace to freedom is an inert people; that public discussion is a political duty; and that this should be a fundamental principle of the American government. They recognized the risks to which all human institutions are subject. But they knew that order cannot be secured merely through fear of punishment for its infraction; that it is hazardous to discourage thought, hope and imagination; that fear breeds repression; that repression breeds hate; that hate menaces stable government; that the path of safety lies in the opportunity to discuss freely supposed grievances and proposed remedies; and that the fitting remedy for evil counsels is good ones. Believing in the power of reason as applied through public discussion, they eschewed silence coerced by law—the argument of force in its worst form. Recognizing the occasional tyrannies of governing majorities, they amended the Constitution so that free speech and assembly should be guaranteed.

Fear of serious injury cannot alone justify suppression of free speech and assembly. Men feared witches and burnt women. It is the function of speech to free men from the bondage of irrational fears. To justify suppression of free speech there must be reasonable ground to fear that serious evil will result if free speech is practiced. There must be reasonable ground to believe that the danger apprehended is imminent. There must be reasonable ground to believe that the evil to be prevented is a serious one. Every denunciation of existing law tends in some measure to increase the probability that there will be violation of it. Condonation of a breach enhances the probability. Expressions of approval add to the probability. Propagation of the criminal state of mind by teaching syndicalism increases it. Advocacy of law-breaking heightens it still further. But even advocacy of violence, however reprehensible morally, is not a justification for denying free speech where the advocacy falls short of incitement and there is nothing to indicate that the advocacy would be immediately acted on. The wide difference between advocacy and incitement, between preparation and attempt, between assembling and conspiracy, must be borne in mind. In order to support a finding of clear and present danger it must be shown either that immediate serious violence was to be expected or was advocated, or that the past conduct furnished reason to believe that such advocacy was then contemplated.

Those who won our independence by revolution were not cowards. They did not fear political change. They did not exalt order at the cost of liberty. To courageous, self-reliant men, with confidence in the power of free and fearless reasoning applied through the processes of proper government, no danger flowing from speech can be deemed clear and present, unless the incidence of the evil apprehended is so imminent that it may befall before there is opportunity for full discussion. If there be time to expose through discussion the falsehood and fallacies, to avert the evil by the processes of education, the remedy to be applied is more speech, not enforced silence. Only an emergency can justify repression. Such must be the rule if authority is to be reconciled with freedom. Such, in my opinion, is the command of the Constitution. It is therefore always open to Americans to challenge a law abridging free speech and assembly by showing that there was no emergency justifying it.

Moreover, even imminent danger cannot justify resort to prohibition of these functions essential to effective democracy, unless the evil apprehended is relatively serious. The fact that speech is likely to result in some violence or in destruction of property is not enough to justify its suppression. There must be the probability of serious injury to the State. Among free men, the deterrents ordinarily to be applied to prevent crime are education and punishment for violations of the law, not abridgment of the rights of free speech and assembly.

Whenever the fundamental rights of free speech and assembly are alleged to have been invaded, it must remain open to a defendant to present the issue whether there actually did exist at the time a clear danger, whether the danger, if any, was imminent, and whether the evil apprehended was one so substantial as to justify the stringent restriction interposed by the Legislature. The legislative declaration, like the fact that the statute was passed and was sustained by the highest court of the State, creates merely a rebuttable presumption that these conditions have been satisfied.

Whether in 1919, when Miss Whitney did the things complained of, there was in California such clear and present danger of serious evil, might have been made the important issue in the case. She might have required that the issue be determined either by the court or the jury. She claimed below that the statute as applied to her violated the federal Constitution; but she did not claim that it was void because there was no clear and present danger of serious evil, nor did she request that the existence of these conditions of a valid measure thus restricting the rights of free speech and assembly be passed upon by the court or a jury. On the other hand, there was evidence on which the court or jury might have found that such danger existed. I am unable to assent to the suggestion in the opinion of the court that assembling with a political party, formed to advocate the desirability of a proletarian revolution by mass action at some date necessarily far in the future, is not a right within the protection of the Fourteenth Amendment. In the present case, however, there was other testimony which tended to establish the existence of a conspiracy, on the part of members of the International Workers of the World, to commit present serious crimes, and likewise to show that such a conspiracy would be furthered by the activity of the society

of which Miss Whitney was a member. Under these circumstances the judgment of the State court cannot be disturbed.

Justice HOLMES joins in this opinion.

COMMENT

It should be noted that Justice Brandeis only reluctantly agreed that the Due Process Clause of the Fourteenth Amendment applied to matters of substantive due process, that is, imposed a freedom of speech and press limitation on state power. Law and journalism students should observe how the modern American law of speech and press rests on judicial interpretation and creativity and how relatively small a role is played by the formal text, the actual language of the constitutional document.

In his discussion of the clear and present danger doctrine, Brandeis stressed that the crucial factor is the immediacy of the danger legislated against. As he puts it, "Only an emergency can justify repression." The corrective for communications objectionable to the state is expression to the contrary. It is only when the "evil apprehended is so imminent that it may befall before there is an opportunity for full discussion" that the legislature may act. Brandeis makes it very clear, however, that a legislative judgment that the danger is too immediate and too grave to justify reliance on corrective discussion is not conclusive. As he says, the "enactment of the state alone cannot establish the facts which are essential to its validity." There must be a reasonable basis for the legislative conclusion that a particular repressive statute should be applied because of the imminent danger of the occurrence of a prohibited substantive evil.

This insistence that the courts have the last word in analyzing whether the clear and present danger doctrine should be applied is of the utmost importance. Otherwise, all the legislature would have to do to comply formally with the clear and present danger doctrine would be to merely recite, as the California legislature did in its Criminal Syndicalism Act, that it is concerned with the "immediate preservation of the public peace and safety." By such formalism, the protection of a constitutional guarantee of freedom of speech and press would be effectively destroyed.

The Brandeis opinion in *Whitney*, as we have seen, was the charter for a revised clear and present danger doctrine. Yet, in the end, and despite the eloquence of Brandeis, the conviction of Anita Whitney was affirmed, a result that it should be noted, was joined by Justice Holmes.

Finally, a criminal syndicalism statute was struck down by the Supreme Court in *Brandenburg v. Ohio*, 395 U.S. 444 (1969). *Brandenburg* also reversed the decision of the Court in *Whitney:* "The contrary teaching of *Whitney v. California* cannot be supported and that decision is therefore overruled." See *Brandenburg v. Ohio* p. 27.

Dennis v. United States
341 U.S. 494, 71 S. CT. 857, 95 L. ED. 1137 (1951).

Chief Justice VINSON announced the judgment of the Court and an opinion in which Justice REED, Justice BURTON and Justice MINTON join.

Petitioners were indicted in July, 1948, for violation of the conspiracy provisions of the Smith Act during the period of April, 1945, to July, 1948. A verdict of guilty as to all the petitioners was returned by the jury on October 14, 1949. The Court of Appeals affirmed the convictions.

Sections 2 and 3 of the Smith Act provide as follows:

Sec. 2.
(a) It shall be unlawful for any person—
(1) to knowingly or willfully advocate, abet, advise, or teach the duty, necessity, desirability, or propriety of overthrowing or destroying any government in the United States by force or violence, or by the assassination of any officer of any such government;
(3) to organize or help to organize any society, group, or assembly of persons who teach, advocate, or encourage the overthrow or destruction of any government in the United States by force or violence; or to be or become a member of, or affiliate with, any such society, group, or assembly of persons, knowing the purposes thereof.
Sec. 3. It shall be unlawful for any person to attempt to commit, or to conspire to commit, any of the acts prohibited by the provisions of this title.

The indictment charged the petitioners with wilfully and knowingly conspiring (1) to organize as the Communist Party of the United States of America a society, group and assembly of persons who teach and advocate the overthrow and destruction of the Government of the United States by force and violence.

Our limited grant of the writ of certiorari has removed from our consideration any question as to the sufficiency of the evidence. Whether on this record petitioners did in fact advocate the overthrow of the Government by force and violence is not before us, and we must base any discussion of this point upon the conclusions stated in the opinion of the Court of Appeals, which treated the issue in great detail. That court held that the record amply supports the necessary finding of the jury that petitioners, the leaders of the Communist Party in this country, intended to initiate a violent revolution whenever the propitious occasion appeared.

The obvious purpose of the statute is to protect existing Government, not from change by peaceable, lawful and constitutional means, but from change by violence, revolution and terrorism. That it is within the *power* of the Congress to protect the Government of the United States from armed rebellion is a proposition which requires little discussion. Whatever theoretical merit there may be to the argument that there is a "right" to rebellion against dictatorial governments is without force where the existing structure of the government provides for peaceful and orderly change. We reject any principle of governmental helplessness in the face of preparation for revolution, which principle, carried to its logical conclusion, must lead to anarchy. No one could conceive that it is not within the power of Congress to prohibit acts intended to overthrow the Government by force and violence. The question with which we are concerned here is not whether Congress has such *power*, but whether the *means* which it has employed conflict with the First and Fifth Amendments to the Constitution.

One of the bases for the contention that the means which Congress has employed are invalid takes the form of an attack on the face of the statute on the grounds that by its terms it prohibits academic discussion of the merits of Marxism-Leninism, that it stifles ideas and is contrary to all concepts of a free speech and a free press.

The very language of the Smith Act negates the interpretation which petitioners would have us impose on that Act. It is directed at advocacy, not discussion. Thus, the trial judge properly charged the jury that they could not convict if they found that petitioners did "no more than pursue peaceful studies and discussions or teaching and advocacy in the realm of ideas." He further charged that it was not unlawful "to conduct in an American college and university a course explaining the philosophical theories set forth in the books which have been placed in evidence." Such a charge is in strict accord with the statutory language, and illustrates the meaning to be placed on those words. Congress did not intend to eradicate the free discussion of political theories, to destroy the traditional rights of Americans to discuss and evaluate ideas without fear of governmental sanction. Rather Congress was concerned with the very kind of activity in which the evidence showed these petitioners engaged.

But although the statute is not directed at the hypothetical cases which petitioners have conjured, its application in this case has resulted in convictions for the teaching and advocacy of the overthrow of the Government by force and violence, which, even though coupled with the intent to accomplish that overthrow, contains an element of speech. For this reason, we must pay special heed to the demands of the First Amendment marking out the boundaries of speech. The rule we deduce from [prior] cases is that where an offense is specified by a statute in nonspeech or nonpress terms, a conviction relying upon speech or press as evidence of violation may be sustained only when the speech or publication created a "clear and present danger" of attempting or accomplishing the prohibited crime, e.g., interference with enlistment. The dissents, we repeat, in emphasizing the value of speech, were addressed to the argument of the sufficiency of the evidence.

Although no case subsequent to *Whitney* and *Gitlow* has expressly overruled the majority opinions in those cases, there is little doubt that subsequent opinions have inclined toward the Holmes-Brandeis rationale. [But] neither Justice Holmes nor Justice Brandeis ever envisioned that a shorthand phrase should be crystallized into a rigid rule to be applied inflexibly without regard to the circumstances of each case. Speech is not an absolute, above and beyond control by the legislature when its judgment, subject to review here, is that certain kinds of speech are so undesirable as to warrant criminal sanction. Nothing

is more certain in modern society than the principle that there are no absolutes, that a name, a phrase, a standard has meaning only when associated with the considerations which gave birth to the nomenclature. To those who would paralyze our Government in the face of impending threat by encasing it in a semantic straitjacket we must reply that all concepts are relative.

In this case we are squarely presented with the application of the "clear and present danger" test, and must decide what that phrase imports. Overthrow of the Government by force and violence is certainly a substantial enough interest for the Government to limit speech. Indeed, this is the ultimate value of any society, for if a society cannot protect its very structure from armed internal attack, it must follow that no subordinate value can be protected. If, then, this interest may be protected, the literal problem which is presented is what has been meant by the use of the phrase "clear and present danger" of the utterances bringing about the evil within the power of Congress to punish.

Obviously, the words cannot mean that before the Government may act, it must wait until the *putsch* is about to be executed, the plans have been laid and the signal awaited. If Government is aware that a group aiming at its overthrow is attempting to indoctrinate its members and to commit them to a course whereby they will strike when the leaders feel the circumstances permit, action by the Government is required. Certainly an attempt to overthrow the Government by force, even though doomed from the outset because of inadequate numbers or power of the revolutionists, is a sufficient evil for Congress to prevent. The damage which such attempts create both physically and politically to a nation makes it impossible to measure the validity in terms of the probability of success, or the immediacy of a successful attempt. In the instant case the trial judge charged the jury that they could not convict unless they found that petitioners intended to overthrow the Government "as speedily as circumstances would permit." This does not mean, and could not properly mean, that they would not strike until there was certainty of success. What was meant was that the revolutionists would strike when they thought the time was ripe. We must therefore reject the contention that success or probability of success is the criterion.

Chief Judge Learned Hand, writing for the majority below, interpreted the phrase as follows: "In each case [courts] must ask whether the gravity of the 'evil,' discounted by its improbability, justifies such invasion of free speech as is necessary to avoid the danger." We adopt this statement of the rule. As articulated by Chief Judge Hand, it is as succinct and inclusive as any other we might devise at this time. It takes into consideration those factors which we deem relevant, and relates their significance. More we cannot expect from words.

Likewise, we are in accord with the court below, which affirmed the trial court's finding that the requisite danger existed. The mere fact that from the period 1945 to 1948 petitioners' activities did not result in an attempt to overthrow the Government by force and violence is of course no answer to the fact that there was a group that was ready to make the attempt. The formation by petitioners of such a highly organized conspiracy, with rigidly disciplined members subject to call when the leaders, these petitioners, felt that the time had come for action, coupled with the inflammable nature of world conditions, similar uprisings in other countries, and the touch-and-go nature of our relations with countries with whom petitioners were in the very least ideologically attuned, convince us that their convictions were justified on this score. And this analysis disposes of the contention that a conspiracy to advocate, as distinguished from the advocacy itself, cannot be constitutionally restrained, because it comprises only the preparation. It is the existence of the conspiracy which creates the danger. If the ingredients of the reaction are present, we cannot bind the Government to wait until the catalyst is added.

The judgments of conviction are affirmed.

Justice CLARK took no part in the consideration or decision of this case.

Justice FRANKFURTER, concurring.

Absolute rules would inevitably lead to absolute exceptions, and such exceptions would eventually corrode the rules. The demands of free speech in a democratic society as well as the interest in national security are better served by candid and informed weighing of the competing interests, within the confines of the judicial process, than by announcing dogmas too inflexible for the non-Euclidian problems to be solved.

But how are competing interests to be assessed? Since they are not subject to quantitative ascertainment, the issue necessarily resolves itself into asking, who is to make the adjustment?—who is to balance the relevant factors and ascertain which interest is in the circumstances to prevail? Full responsibility for the choice cannot be given to the courts. Courts are not representative bodies. They are not designed to be a good reflex of a democratic society. Their judgment is best informed, and therefore most dependable, within narrow limits. Their essential quality is detachment, founded on independence. History teaches that the independence of the judiciary is jeopardized when courts become embroiled in the passions of the day and assume primary responsibility in choosing between competing political, economic and social pressures.

Primary responsibility for adjusting the interests which compete in the situation before us of necessity belongs to the Congress. The nature of the power to be exercised by this Court has been delineated in decisions not charged with the emotional appeal of situations such as that now before us. We are to set aside the judgment of those whose duty it is to legislate only if there is no reasonable basis for it. We are to determine whether a statute is sufficiently definite to meet the constitutional requirements of due process, and whether it respects the safeguards against undue concentration of authority secured by separation of power.

Justice JACKSON, concurring.

The "clear and present danger" test was an innovation by Justice Holmes in the *Schenck* case, reiterated and refined by him and Mr. Justice Brandeis in later cases, all arising before the era of World War II revealed the subtlety and efficacy of modernized revolutionary techniques used by totalitarian parties.

I would save [the clear and present danger test], unmodified, for applications as a "rule of reason" in the kind of case for which it was devised. When the issue is criminality of a hot-headed speech on a street corner, or circulation of a few incendiary pamphlets, or parading by some zealots behind a red flag, or refusal of a handful of school children to salute our flag, it is not beyond the capacity of the judicial process to gather, comprehend, and weigh the necessary materials for decision whether it is a clear and present danger of substantive evil or a harmless letting off of steam. It is not a prophecy, for the danger in such cases has matured by the time of trial or it was never present. The test applies and has meaning where a conviction is sought to be based on a speech or writing which does not directly or explicitly advocate a crime but to which such tendency is sought to be attributed by construction or by implication from external circumstances. The formula in such cases favors freedoms that are vital to our society, and, even if sometimes applied too generously, the consequences cannot be grave. But its recent expansion has extended, in particular to Communists, unprecedented immunities. Unless we are to hold our Government captive in a judge-made verbal trap, we must approach the problem of a well-organized, nation-wide conspiracy, as our predecessors faced the trivialities that were being prosecuted until they were checked with a rule of reason.

Justice BLACK, dissenting.

[L]et us assume, contrary to all constitutional ideas of fair criminal procedure, that petitioners although not indicted for the crime of actual advocacy, may be punished for it. Even on this radical assumption, the other opinions in this case show that the only way to affirm these convictions is to repudiate directly or indirectly the established "clear and present danger" rule. This the Court does in a way which greatly restricts the protections afforded by the First Amendment. The opinions for affirmance indicate that the chief reason for jettisoning the rule is the expressed fear that advocacy of Communist doctrine endangers the safety of the Republic. Undoubtedly, a governmental policy of unfettered communication of ideas does entail dangers. To the Founders of this Nation, however, the benefits derived from free expression were worth the risk. They embodied this philosophy in the First Amendment's command that "Congress shall make no law abridging the freedom of speech, or of the press." I have always believed that the First Amendment is the keystone of our Government, that the freedoms it guarantees provide the best insurance against destruction of all freedom. At least as to speech in the realm of public matters, I believe that the "clear and present danger" test does not "mark the furthermost constitutional boundaries of protected expression" but does "no more than recognize a minimum compulsion of the Bill of Rights." *Bridges v. California*, 314 U.S. 252, 263.

Public opinion being what it now is, few will protest the conviction of these Communist petitioners. There is hope, however, that in calmer times, when present pressures, passions and fears subside, this or some later Court will restore the First Amendment liberties to the high preferred place where they belong in a free society.

Justice DOUGLAS, dissenting.

If this were a case where those who claimed protection under the First Amendment were teaching the techniques of sabotage, the assassination of the President, the filching of documents from public files, the planting of bombs, the art of street warfare, and the like, I would have no doubts. The freedom to speak is not absolute; the teaching of methods of terror and other seditious conduct should be beyond the pale along with obscenity and immorality. This case was argued as if those were the facts. But the fact is that no such evidence was introduced at the trial. So far as the present record is concerned, what petitioners did was to organize people to teach and themselves teach the Marxist-Leninist doctrine.

There comes a time when even speech loses its constitutional immunity. Speech innocuous one year may at another time fan such destructive flames that it must be halted in the interests of the safety of the Republic. That is the meaning of the clear and present danger test. When conditions are so critical that there will be no time to avoid the evil that the speech threatens, it is time to call a halt. Otherwise, free speech which is the strength of the Nation will be the cause of its destruction. Yet free speech is the rule, not the exception. The restraint to be constitutional must be based on more than fear, on more than passionate opposition against the speech, on more than a revolted dislike for its contents. There must be some immediate injury to society that is likely if speech is allowed.

COMMENT

Functionally speaking, Chief Justice Vinson really follows the old "reasonableness" test of Justice Sanford in *Gitlow*. Vinson's formulation of the clear and present danger doctrine is hardly the same as that articulated by Justice Brandeis in his concurrence in *Whitney*. Vinson said he endorsed the test employed by Judge Learned Hand, which was "whether the gravity of the 'evil,' discounted by its improbability, justifies such invasion of free speech as is necessary to avoid the danger."

Substituting a test of probability for a test of imminence greatly broadened the scope of governmental power over freedom of expression. Such an approach focuses on the gravity of the problem (the "evil") with which the legislature is concerned. The Court said the Smith Act, under which the Communist Party leaders were prosecuted, was concerned with the "ultimate value of our society." The nature of this ultimate value was the governmental interest in self-preservation.

Vinson said that the clear and present danger test could not mean that government action is prohibited "until the *putsch* is about to be executed." Reasoning that "success or probability of success is not the criterion," Vinson disregarded the factor of time in applying the clear and present danger test.

For Brandeis, time was the key factor in determining whether legislation was designed to protect the security of the state. In Brandeis's view, the integrity of the public order was strengthened by free discussion. As Brandeis put it in *Whitney:* "the path of safety lies in the opportunity to discuss freely supposed grievances and proposed remedies."

The crucial inquiry, according to Brandeis, was whether the "evil apprehended is so imminent that it may befall before there is opportunity for discussion." But inquiry into the imminence of the danger—the factor of time—is precisely what Vinson excluded from his reformulation of clear and present danger. In *Dennis,* Vinson professedly used the clear and present danger doctrine to assess the constitutionality of the Smith Act, but, in truth, he completely revised it so that it provided far less protection to freedom of expression than Brandeis's conception of clear and present danger.

Vinson rejected the "contention that success or probability of success is the criterion." The danger must be grave (serious), but apparently, under *Dennis,* it was no longer necessary that it be immediate (present). The function of time or imminence in the clear and present danger doctrine, however, was to justify legislation restricting freedom of expression where there is reason to believe that there was not enough time for normal debate to counteract the dangers feared by the legislature. By removing time from the clear and present danger equation, Vinson

removed the most significant protection the doctrine provided for freedom of expression.

If the imminence of danger is quite remote, then in the weighing process that constitutional adjudication involves, the value of freedom of expression should not be subordinated to the value of national security. Arguably, under such an approach the Smith Act should be held unconstitutional because the Act has been interpreted by the Justice Department to proscribe "advocacy."

Vinson changed the clear and present danger doctrine to the "clear danger" or the "clear and probable danger" doctrine. Vinson's "clear danger" doctrine rationale, however, merely asked whether a grave threat was posed to the state in the future, if not now. Under such a weighing process, the likelihood of a statute being held violative of the First Amendment was far less likely.

Frankfurter's long concurrence in *Dennis* argued for a balancing approach for cases where the values of freedom of expression and national security are in conflict. But Frankfurter intended the balancing to be done by Congress rather than by the Court. The difference is important because the law under attack was passed by Congress in the first place. If the congressional determination is to be upheld on the theory that the congressional balancing decision should be respected, there is no place for judicial review.

Did Frankfurter's opinion in *Dennis* ignore the point that majoritarianism and constitutionalism are not necessarily synonymous? The idea of constitutional limitation, after all, is to protect certain values from legislative repression, to limit the majority. Therefore, it is somewhat anomalous to make majoritarianism the dominant value in considering the meaning of a constitutional limitation.

Vinson's view as to the ultimate societal value contrasted sharply with that of Justice Black, who in his dissent argued that free speech and press are the preferred values, the ultimate values, in the American constitutional system. In his dissent, Black said the "First Amendment provides the only kind of security system which can preserve a free government." What is the nature of Justice Black's argument here?

As a result of the *Dennis* decision, the government brought many prosecutions under the

Smith Act against minor Communist Party leaders. The Supreme Court refused to review any of these cases until 1955 when it finally granted *certiorari* in *Yates v. United States*, 354 U.S. 298 (1957). *Yates* ostensibly clarified the *Dennis* holding. *Yates* contracted the scope of the *Dennis* case, revived the constitutional law of freedom of expression, and made it far more difficult for the government to obtain convictions under the Smith Act. Of the fourteen defendants whose convictions were before the Court in *Yates*, five convictions were reversed, and new trials were ordered for the rest.

The most authoritative part of the *Yates* case is certainly Justice Harlan's statement that the "essence of the *Dennis* holding" only sanctioned the restriction of "advocacy found to be directed to 'action for the accomplishment of forcible overthrow.'" 354 U.S. at 321. In his dissent, Justice Tom Clark said that as he read Chief Justice Vinson's opinion in *Dennis*, he saw no basis for the distinction between advocacy of unlawful action and advocacy of abstract doctrine, which Harlan said was the heart of the *Dennis* case. At least this much can be said for Justice Clark's point of view: the two lower federal courts in *Yates* also joined him in "misconceiving" the *Dennis* case. Justice Harlan's "reading" of *Dennis* in *Yates* may have been merely an indirect way of reversing *Dennis*. The question then becomes, how does the distinction between advocacy of abstract doctrine and advocacy of unlawful action expand the area of expression the government may not restrict?

The *Dennis* case was decided in 1951 at the beginning of the red-baiting years that have since been called the "McCarthy" era after Senator Jospeh R. McCarthy of Wisconsin. By 1957, the reaction against "McCarthyism" had set in. Is there a political explanation for *Dennis* and, later, *Yates*? What does such an explanation contribute to the discussion in *Dennis* about whether it is more appropriate for the judiciary or the legislature to make ultimate societal decisions?

What was the status of the clear and present danger doctrine after *Dennis* and *Yates*? No clear answer to this question was provided by the Supreme Court until 1969 when the Court quietly resurrected the clear and present danger doctrine in *Brandenburg v. Ohio*.

Brandenburg v. Ohio
395 U.S. 444, 89 S. CT. 1827, 23 L. ED. 2D 430 (1969).

PER CURIAM.

The appellant, a leader of a Ku Klux Klan group, was convicted under the Ohio Criminal Syndicalism statute for "advocat[ing] the duty, necessity, or propriety of crime, sabotage, violence, or unlawful methods of terrorism as a means of accomplishing industrial or political reform" and for "voluntarily assembl[ing] with any society, group, or assemblage of persons formed to teach or advocate the doctrines of criminal syndicalism." Ohio Rev. Code Ann. §2923.13.

The prosecution's case rested on [films and testimony] identifying the appellant as the person [who] spoke at [a Klan rally]. One film showed 12 hooded figures, some of whom carried firearms. They were gathered around a large wooden cross, which they burned. [S]cattered phrases could be understood that were derogatory of Negroes and, in one instance, of Jews. Another scene on the same film showed the appellant, in Klan regalia, making a speech. The speech [in part] was as follows:

"We're not a revengent organization, but if our President, our Congress, our Supreme Court, continues to suppress the white Caucasian race, it's possible there might have to be some revengeance taken. We are marching on Congress July the Fourth, four hundred thousand strong."

The Ohio Criminal Syndicalism Statute was enacted in 1919. From 1917 to 1920, identical or quite similar laws were adopted by 20 States and two territories. In 1927, this Court sustained the constitutionality of California's Criminal Syndicalism Act, the text of which is quite similar to that of the laws of Ohio. *Whitney v. California*. The Court upheld the statute on the ground that, without more, "advocating" violent means to effect political and economic change involves such danger to the security of the State that the State may outlaw it. But *Whitney* has been thoroughly discredited by later decisions. See *Dennis v. United States*. These later decisions have fashioned the principle that the constitutional guarantees of free speech and free press do not permit a State to forbid or proscribe advocacy of the use of force or of law violation except where such advocacy is directed to inciting or producing imminent lawless action and is likely to incite or produce such actions.[1]

A statute which fails to draw this distinction impermissibly intrudes upon the freedoms guaranteed by the First and Fourteenth Amendments. It sweeps within its condemnation speech which our Constitution has immunized from governmental control.

Measured by this test, Ohio's Criminal Syndicalism Act cannot be sustained. The Act punishes persons who "advocate or teach the duty, necessity, or propriety" of violence "as a means of accomplishing industrial or political reform"; or who publish or circulate or display any book or paper containing such advocacy; or who "justify" the commission of violent acts "with intent to exemplify, spread or advocate the propriety of the doctrines of criminal syndicalism"; or who "voluntarily assemble" with a group formed "to teach or advocate the doctrines of criminal syndicalism." Neither the indictment nor the trial judge's instructions to the jury in any way refined the statute's bald definition of the crime in terms of mere advocacy not distinguished from incitement to imminent lawless action.

Accordingly, we are here confronted with a statute which, by its own words and as applied, purports to punish mere advocacy and to forbid, on pain of criminal punishment, assembly with others merely to advocate the described type of action. Such a statute falls within the condemnation of the First and Fourteenth Amendments. The contrary teaching of *Whitney v. California* cannot be supported, and that decision is therefore overruled.

Justice BLACK, concurring.

I agree with the views expressed by Mr. Justice DOUGLAS in his concurring opinion in this case that the "clear and present danger" doctrine should have no place in the interpretation of the First Amendment. I join the Court's opinion, which, as I understand it, simply cites *Dennis v. United States,* but does not indicate any agreement on the Court's part with the "clear and present danger" doctrine on which *Dennis* purported to rely.

Justice DOUGLAS, concurring.

While I join the opinion of the Court, I desire to enter a *caveat.* Though I doubt if the "clear and present danger" test is congenial to the First Amendment in time of a declared war, I am certain it is not reconcilable with the First Amendment in days of peace. I see no place in the regime of the First Amendment for any "clear and present danger" test, whether strict and tight as some would make it, or free-wheeling as the Court in *Dennis* rephrased it.

***BRANDENBURG* AND THE REVIVAL OF THE DANGER DOCTRINE** In *Brandenburg,* the Supreme Court held the Ohio criminal syndicalism statute void on its face for failing to distinguish between mere advocacy of ideas and incitement of unlawful conduct. Nearly a half century earlier, a California criminal anarchy statute suffering an identical weakness had been upheld by the Court in the case of *Whitney v. California,* 274 U.S. 357 (1927). In *Brandenburg,* the Supreme Court turned a corner in its approach to the legislative suppression of politically unpopular speech. *Brandenburg* expressly overruled *Whitney.*

Yet the Supreme Court's approach to the *Brandenburg* decision was perfunctory. The Court issued its *Brandenburg* decision as an anonymous *per curiam* opinion. Further, though it purported to summarize and clarify fifty years of free speech doctrine, the *Brandenburg* opinion was relatively short.

Note that Brandenburg, a Ku Klux Klan organizer, was tried and convicted under a criminal syndicalism statute that was enacted in the early 1900s to guard against nihilists, anarchists, and wobblies. Ohio was one of many states that passed such laws to meet a particular threat perceived at the time but long since lost in oblivion. Yet the Ohio statute remained on the books, to be resurrected in *Brandenburg* to meet a situation far afield from the subject of its origins.

Oregon Supreme Court Justice Hans Linde perceived several new and disturbing elements in the

---

1. It was on the theory that the Smith Act embodied such a principle and that it had been applied only in conformity with it that this Court sustained the Act's constitutionality. That this was the basis for *Dennis* was emphasized in *Yates* in which the Court overturned convictions for advocacy of the forcible overthrow of the Government under the Smith Act, because the trial judge's instructions had allowed conviction for mere advocacy, unrelated to its tendency to produce forcible action.

Brandenburg test. Linde, *"Clear and Present Danger" Re-examined: Dissonance in the Brandenburg Concerto,* 22 Stan. L. Rev. 1163 (1970). If, as *Brandenburg* suggests, proscription of free speech is to be judged by the actual danger posed by the advocacy, doesn't this make an examination of the statute on its face useless? Under such an approach, Professor Linde is concerned that a criminal anarchy statute "might well be unconstitutional now but might be constitutional in the light of the diverse events in 1945, in 1951, in 1957, and in 1961, perhaps not in 1966, but again in 1968." But is such a result necessarily objectionable? If the American system of judicial review amounts to a continuous constitutional convention, isn't the situation Linde describes inevitable?

Does the *Brandenburg* decision even mention the clear and present danger doctrine by name? Is *Brandenburg* an attempt to abandon or revise the clear and present danger doctrine?

The *Brandenburg* test has received differing interpretations: "Some commentators interpret *Brandenburg* as adopting an 'incitement' test which focuses on the nature of the speech in question." In this view, freedom of speech is accorded absolute protection. However, speech that "incites to the violent overthrow of government" is deemed unprotected speech. Barron and Dienes, *Constitutional Law in a Nutshell,* 314 (1995).

Others, however, view *Brandenburg* as the merger of an incitement test and the Holmes-Brandeis danger test that examines the context in which the speech occurs. Under this interpretation, *Brandenburg* means this: "In order to punish speech, the speaker must use both the language of action and the context must be sufficient to establish imminence and the probability of the serious substantive evil which the government is seeking to prevent." *Id.*

Professor Vincent Blasi has advanced the thesis that courts should bring a pathological perspective to the resolution of First Amendment issues. The objective of First Amendment theory in this view "should be to equip the first amendment to do maximum service in those historical periods when intolerance of unorthodox ideas is most prevalent and when governments are most able and most likely to stifle dissent systematically. The first amendment, in other words, should be targeted for the worst of times." See Blasi, *The Pathological Perspective And the First Amendment,* 85 Colum. L Rev. 449, 449-50 (1985).

For Blasi, from the pathological perspective the particular vice of the clear and present danger doctrine, is that it "directs courts to focus on the quality or quantity of danger generated by dissenting speech." This focus tends to promote "the view that the nature of the danger generated by certain forms of speech constitutes the dominant, indeed sole, determinant of first amendment protection. Such a legitimation of risk aversion can only lend support to the forces of repression in times of widespread worry about internal or external threats to the society." *Id.* at 483. Is the *Brandenburg* test exclusively focused on the "quantity or quality of danger"?

Professor Martin Redish has challenged Blasi's pathological perspective: "An emphasis in first amendment analysis on the concrete danger of the advocacy sought to be suppressed is quite probably the best possible form of judicial self-defense against the excesses of pathology." See Redish, *The Role of Pathology in First Amendment Theory: A Skeptical Examination,* 38 Case W. Res. L. Rev. 618, 629 (1988).

THE CLEAR AND PRESENT DANGER DOCTRINE TODAY   Developed during World War I to deal with the antiwar radicals who objected to the war and the draft, the clear and present danger doctrine has been used in more recent times in cases involving fact patterns far removed from antigovernmental activities. For example, in *Nebraska Press Association v. Stuart,* 427 U.S. 539 (1976), the Supreme Court, per Chief Justice Burger, invalidated a "gag order" prohibiting reporting or commentary on judicial proceedings held in public (see text, p. 58).

The Court viewed "gag orders" as prior restraints. Interestingly, however, the Court said that the clear and present danger doctrine should be applied to determine whether gag orders are warranted in a particular situation. Barrett Prettyman, press counsel in the *Nebraska Press Association* case, objected to the use of the clear and present danger doctrine in the gag order context. Prettyman said that although the Court used the danger doctrine to enforce freedom of the press, lower courts might be tempted by the imprecise language of the doctrine to use it to validate gag orders.

At the Supreme Court level, on the relatively few occasions when the Court has used the danger doctrine since *Nebraska Press Association,* the result has been in favor of free expression. Thus, in *Landmark Communications, Inc. v. Virginia,* 435 U.S. 829 (1978), where sanctions were imposed on a newspaper that had reported matters concerning the confidential proceedings of a state judicial disciplinary proceeding, the sanctions were set aside. Even though such reporting was contrary to state law, the Court said the *Brandenburg* test had not been satisfied.

Similarly, in *NAACP v. Claiborne Hardware Co.,* 458 U.S. 886 (1982), a state court judgment awarding damages to white merchants against participants in a civil rights boycott was reversed by the Supreme Court. NAACP leader Charles Evers had warned African Americans who did not participate in the economic boycott of white merchants that they would be disciplined. The Supreme Court, per Justice Stevens, ruled that "mere *advocacy* of the use of force or violence does not remove speech from the protection of the First Amendment." Justice Stevens concluded: "The emotionally charged rhetoric of Charles Evers' speeches did not transcend the bounds of protected speech set forth in *Brandenburg.*"

In summary, the clear and present danger doctrine is not, currently, of major importance in Supreme Court First Amendment case law. Of course, the Court always has the option of resorting to it. A question remains. Are even the Court's infrequent uses of the doctrine justified? The more commonly used strict scrutiny test is simpler to apply, better understood, and probably would yield the same results (see the discussion of the strict scrutiny standard in Chapter 2).

Compelled Speech

The right to speak without fear of punishment is obviously an important right. But the right to refrain from speaking is also important. As the controls the state exercises over individuals increase, the scope of the law of free expression must be extended as well. The Court has, therefore, constructed a doctrine restricting compelled or involuntary speech. In *Abood v. Detroit Board of Education,* Justice Stewart, for the Court, cautioned that the state in a regime ordered by the First Amendment could not require an individual to express or support an ideology he did not share.

Abood v. Detroit Board of Education
431 U.S. 209, 97 S. CT. 1782, 52 L. ED. 2D 261 (1977).

[EDITORIAL NOTE: *The Court held that a law imposing compulsory service charges, equivalent to union dues, imposed on union members violated the First Amendment when those charges were to be used for political or ideological purposes not related to the union's role as a collective bargaining agent.*]

Justice STEWART delivered the opinion of the Court.

One of the principles underlying the Court's decision in *Buckley v. Valeo,* 424 U.S. 1 (1976), was that contributing to an organization for the purpose of spreading a political message is protected by the First Amendment. The fact that appellants are compelled to make, rather than prohibited from making, contributions for political purposes works no less an infringement on their constitutional rights. For at the heart of the First Amendment is the notion that an individual should be free to believe as he will, and that in a free society one's beliefs should be shaped by his mind and his conscience rather than coerced by the State.

These principles prohibit a State from compelling any individual to affirm his belief in God, or to associate with a political party, as a condition of retaining public employment. They are no less applicable to the case at bar, and they thus prohibit the appellees from requiring any of the appellants to contribute to the support of an ideological cause he may oppose as a condition of holding a job as a public school teacher.

We do not hold that a union cannot constitutionally spend funds for the expression of political views, on behalf of political candidates, or towards the advancement of other ideological causes not germane to its duties as a collective bargaining representative. Rather the Constitution requires only that such expenditures be financed from charges, dues, or assessments paid by employees who do not object to advancing those ideas and who are not coerced into doing so against their will by the threat of loss of governmental employment.

Wooley v. Maynard

430 U.S. 705, 97 S. CT. 1428, 51 L. ED. 2D (1977).

[EDITORIAL NOTE: *A married couple, Jehovah's Witnesses, had covered up the state motto "Live Free or Die" on their New Hampshire automobile license plate because it was contrary to their religious and moral beliefs. Could New Hampshire constitutionally enforce criminal sanctions against the couple for so doing? The Court held that New Hampshire could not.*]

Chief Justice BURGER delivered the opinion of the Court.

We are thus faced with the question of whether the state may constitutionally require an individual to participate in the dissemination of an ideological message by displaying it on his private property in a manner and for the express purpose that it be observed and read by the public. We hold that the state may not do so.

We begin with the proposition that the right of freedom of thought protected by the First Amendment against state action includes both the right to speak freely and the right to refrain from speaking at all. See *West Virginia Bd. of Educ. v. Barnette,* 319 U.S. 624 (1943). A system which secures the right to proselytize religious, political and ideological causes must also guarantee the concomitant right to decline to foster such concepts. The right to speak and the right to refrain from speaking are complementary components of the broader concept of "individual freedom of mind." This is illustrated by the recent case of *Miami Herald Publishing Co. v. Tornillo.*

Here, as in *Barnette,* we are faced with a state measure which forces an individual as part of his daily life—indeed constantly while his automobile is in public view—to be an instrument for fostering public adherence to an ideological point of view he finds unacceptable. In doing so, the state "invades the sphere of intellect and spirit which it is the purpose of the First Amendment to our Constitution to reserve from all official control."

New Hampshire's statute in effect requires that appellees use their private property as a "mobile billboard" for the state's ideological message—or suffer a penalty, as Maynard already has. As a condition to driving an automobile—a virtual necessity for most Americans—the Maynards must display "Live Free or Die" to hundreds of people each day. The fact that most individuals agree with the thrust of New Hampshire's motto is not the test; most Americans also find the flag salute acceptable. The First Amendment protects the right of individuals to hold a point of view different from the majority and to refuse to foster, in the way New Hampshire commands, an idea they find morally objectionable.

Identifying the Maynards' interests as implicating First Amendment protections does not end our inquiry however. We must also determine whether the state's countervailing interest is sufficiently compelling to justify requiring appellees to display the state motto on their license plates. The two interests advanced by the state are that display of the motto (1) facilitates the identification of passenger vehicles, and (2) promotes appreciation of history, individualism and state pride.

[EDITORIAL NOTE: *The Court found that these interests did not outweigh the interest in free expression. The first interest could be achieved by means less destructive of First Amendment interests if indeed it was not accomplished by the letters and numbers already on the license plate anyway. The second interest was not ideologically neutral.*]

[W]here the state's interest is to disseminate an ideology, no matter how acceptable to some, such interest cannot outweigh an individual's First Amendment right to avoid becoming the courier for such message.

We conclude that the State of New Hampshire may not require appellees to display the state motto upon their vehicle license plates, and accordingly, we affirm the judgment of the district court.

Affirmed.

COMMENT

Where ideology is concerned, must the state be neutral? Does the fact that government may not compel belief mean that government cannot add its views to those of others? The view expressed in *Wooley* suggests that the state must be ideologically neutral. In *Wooley,* the Court found in the First Amendment a source of protection for individuals compelled by the state to affirm something they did not believe. In *Abood,* the Court found in the First Amendment a source of protection for union members compelled unwillingly to make political contributions. The two cases may be seen as aspects of an important First Amendment right—the right to be free from state-compelled expression.

To what extent may the state provide that privately owned shopping centers be open to messages that the property owner might otherwise not permit? In *PruneYard Shopping Center v. Robins*, 447 U.S. 74 (1980), the Supreme Court held that where state law authorized the use of a privately owned shopping center for speech purposes, such state law did not violate the free expression and association rights of the property owner. The shopping center owner in *PruneYard* sought refuge in the principle of *Wooley*. The state could not require the Jehovah's Witnesses to use their private property to publicize the ideas of the state. In the *Wooley* case, New Hampshire had mandated that motorists carry the state motto on their license plates.

In *PruneYard*, the message in question was not being ordered by the state. Moreover, unlike the private automobile in *Wooley*, the shopping center in *PruneYard* was not used by the owners alone. By definition, the shopping center's very existence constituted an invitation to the public to come and do business. Messages that are publicized by a shopping center are not necessarily to be identified with the owners of the shopping center.

First Amendment law as interpreted by the Supreme Court does not require a shopping center owner to permit the dissemination of views to which he is opposed on his property. See *Hudgens v. NLRB*, 424 U.S. 507 (1976). The California courts, however, had interpreted the guarantee of freedom of expression in the state constitution to provide that the public's rights of free speech and petition, if responsibly exercised, extended to privately owned shopping centers. The California courts declined to grant absolute protection to the property owner's claim of self-expression as the Supreme Court had done in interpreting the First Amendment in similar circumstances. *PruneYard* holds, therefore, that although the First Amendment does not grant rights of free expression in a privately owned shopping center, it does not preclude a State constitution from granting those rights.

To what extent must private organizations using public facilities be hospitable to the messages of those with whom they disagree? Can there be—should there be?—*compelled* participation? How do we reconcile the competing claims of individuals and groups to autonomy, equality, and freedom of expression? The *Hurley* case presented the Supreme Court with that formidable task.

Hurley v. Irish-American Gay, Lesbian and Bisexual Group of Boston
115 S. CT. 2338 (1995).

[EDITORIAL NOTE: Hurley *held that the First Amendment prohibition against compelled speech extends to privately organized parades as well. Justice David Souter, for the Court, held that application of a state public accommodations law to require private citizens organizing a parade to include a group or parade to convey a message that the organizers of the parade did not wish to convey violated the First Amendment.*

The South Boston Allied War Veterans Council, a private association of individuals elected from various South Boston veterans groups, had been authorized by the City of Boston to organize and conduct the St. Patrick's Day–Evacuation Day Parade since 1947. The Irish-American Gay, Lesbian and Bisexual Group of Boston (GLIB) applied to march in the 1992 parade, and the Council rejected its application. A state court ordered the Council to allow GLIB to march, and it did so without incident. The issue arose again in 1993, and the Council's second rejection of GLIB's application was overruled again, this time finally by the Supreme Judicial Court of Massachusetts. The state courts ruled that the Council's exclusion of GLIB from the St. Patrick's Day Parade violated the Massachusetts public accommodation law, which prohibits discrimination on account of sexual orientation in places of public accommodation.

By the time the case reached the Supreme Court, it was agreed that the parade itself did not constitute state action. Could the state public accommodations law be applied consistent with the First Amendment to require the Veterans Council to permit GLIB to express a message with which the Council disagreed?]

Justice SOUTER delivered the opinion of the Court.

[We] use the word "parade" to indicate marchers who are making some sort of collective point, not just to each other but to bystanders along the way. Parades are thus a form of expression, not just motion, and the inherent expressiveness of marching to make a point explains our cases involving protest marches.

Not many marches, then, are beyond the realm of expressive parades, and the South Boston celebration is not one of them. Spectators line the streets; people march in costumes and uniforms, carrying flags and banners with all sorts of messages. To be sure, we agree with the state courts that in spite of excluding some applicants, the Council is rather lenient in admitting participants. But a private speaker does not forfeit constitutional protection simply by combining multifarious voices, or by failing to edit their themes to isolate an exact message as the exclusive subject matter of the speech.

Respondents' [GLIB's] participation as a unit in the parade was equally expressive. GLIB was formed for the very purpose of marching [in order] to celebrate its members' identity as openly gay, lesbian, and bisexual descendants of the Irish immigrants, to show that there are such individuals in the community, and to support the like men and women who sought to march in the New York parade.

In the case before us, however, the Massachusetts law has been applied in a peculiar way. Its enforcement does not address any dispute about the participation of openly gay, lesbian, and bisexual individuals in various units admitted to the parade. The petitioners disclaim any intent to exclude homosexuals as such, and no individual member of GLIB claims to have been excluded from parading as a member of any group that the Council has approved to march. Instead, the disagreement goes to the admission of GLIB as its own parade unit carrying its own banner. Since every participating unit affects the message conveyed by the private organizers, the state courts' application of the statute produced an order essentially requiring petitioners to alter the expressive content of their parade. Although the state courts spoke of the parade as a place of public accommodation, once the expressive character of both the parade and the marching GLIB contingent is understood, it becomes apparent that the state courts' application of the statute had the effect of declaring the sponsors' speech itself to be the public accommodation. Under this approach any contingent of protected individuals with a message would have the right to participate in petitioners' speech, so that the communication produced by the private organizers would be shaped by all those protected by the law who wish to join in with some expressive demonstration of their own. But this use of the State's power violates the fundamental rule of protection under the First Amendment, that a speaker has the autonomy to choose the content of his own message. [O]ne impor-

tant manifestation of the principle of free speech is that one who chooses to speak may also decide "what not to say."

Respondents argue that any tension between this rule and the Massachusetts law falls short of unconstitutionality, citing the most recent of our cases on the general subject of compelled access for expressive purposes, *Turner Broadcasting*. Respondents contend on this authority that admission of GLIB to the parade would not threaten the core principle of speaker's autonomy because the Council, like a cable operator, is merely "a conduit" for the speech of participants in the parade "rather than itself as a speaker." But this metaphor is not apt here, because GLIB's participation would likely be perceived as having resulted from the Council's customary determination about a unit admitted to the parade, that its message is worthy of presentation and quite possibly of support as well.

In *Turner Broadcasting*, we found this problem absent in the cable context, because "given cable's long history of serving as a conduit for broadcast signals, there appears little risk that cable viewers would assume that the broadcast stations carried on a cable system convey ideas or messages endorsed by the cable operator."

Parades and demonstrations, in contrast, are not understood to be so neutrally presented or selectively viewed. Unlike the programming offered on various channels by a cable network, the parade does not consist of individual, unrelated segments that happen to be transmitted together for individual selection by members of the audience. Although each parade unit generally identifies itself, each is understood to contribute something to a common theme, and accordingly there is no customary practice whereby private sponsors disavow "any identity of viewpoint" between themselves and the selected participants. Practice follows practicability here, for such disclaimers would be quite curious in a moving parade.

An additional distinction between *Turner Broadcasting* and this case points to the fundamental weakness of any attempt to justify the state court order's limitation on the Council's autonomy as a speaker. A cable is not only a conduit for speech produced by others and selected by cable operators for transmission, but a franchised channel giving monopolistic opportunity to shut out some speakers.

In this case, of course, there is no assertion comparable to the *Turner Broadcasting* claim that some speakers will be destroyed in the absence of the challenged law. True, the size and success of petitioner's parade makes it an enviable vehicle for the dissemination of GLIB's views, but that fact, without more, would fall far short of supporting a claim that petitioners enjoy an abiding monopoly of access to spectators. Considering that GLIB presumably would have had a fair shot (under neutral criteria developed by the city) at obtaining a parade permit of its own, respondents have not shown that petitioners enjoy the capacity to "silence the voice of competing speakers," as cable operators do with respect to program providers who wish to reach subscribers.

When the [public accommodations] law is applied to expressive activity in the way it was done here, its apparent object is simply to require speakers to modify the content of their expression to whatever extent beneficiaries of the law choose to alter it with messages of their own. But in the absence of some further, legitimate end, this object is merely to allow exactly what the general rule of speaker's autonomy forbids.

It might, of course, have been argued that a broader objective is apparent: that the ultimate point of forbidding acts of discrimination toward certain classes is to produce a society free of the corresponding biases. Requiring access to a speaker's message would thus not be an end in itself, but a means to produce speakers free of the biases, whose expressive conduct would be at least neutral toward the particular classes, obviating any future need for correction. But if this indeed is the point of applying the state law to expressive conduct, it is a decidedly fatal objective.

The very idea that a noncommercial speech restriction be used to produce thoughts and statements acceptable to some groups or, indeed, all people grates on the First Amendment, for it amounts to nothing less than a proposal to limit speech in the service of orthodox expression. The Speech Clause has no more certain antithesis.

[The Court denied that *PruneYard* supported GLIB's position:] *PruneYard* did not involve any concern that access "might affect the shopping center owner's exercise of his own right to speak: the owner did not even allege that he objected to the content of the pamphlets." The principle of

speaker's autonomy was simply not threatened in that case.

Our holding today rests not on any particular view about the Council's message but on the nation's commitment to protect freedom of speech. Disapproval of a private speaker's statement does not legitimize use of the Commonwealth's power to compel the speaker to alter the message by including one more acceptable to others. Accordingly, the judgment of the Supreme Judicial Court is reversed and the case remanded for proceedings not inconsistent with this opinion. It is so ordered.

COMMENT

Despite the difficulties of the issues presented in *Hurley*, the Court rendered a unanimous opinion—an unusual example of the Court's liberal and conservative factions joining together in a controversial case. How can this unusual unanimity be explained?

Dwight G. Duncan, *Parading the First Amendment Through the Streets of South Boston*, 30 New Eng. L. Rev. 663 (1995–96), observes that *Wooley* was cited only once in *Hurley*. But he explains: "*Wooley* was not necessary. Because the Supreme Court had accepted the Veterans' argument that parades were inherently expressive, there was no need for authority for the proposition that even if they were not, private parties would still be entitled to freedom from government-coerced expression of someone else's message." *Id.* at 692.

The freedom from compelled speech principle of *Wooley* was in fact reaffirmed in *Hurley*. Justice Souter proclaimed in *Hurley* that an important aspect of the free speech principle is this: "[O]ne who chooses to speak may also decide 'what not to say.'" *Hurley* is very clear in its intent to protect speaker autonomy. But *Hurley* also protects group autonomy. Can a pluralistic society thrive if the expressive activities of the Knights of Columbus have to include the views of Planned Parenthood? The thesis of the *Hurley* decision is that free expression and diversity of expression are strengthened if individual and group autonomy are protected. Furthermore, the Court's efforts to distinguish *Turner Broadcasting* (text, p. 861) and *PruneYard* illustrate that the problem of access for expression is very much a matter of context.

A contrary view to *Hurley* is found in Note, *Hurley v. Irish-American Gay, Lesbian and Bisexual Group of Boston*, 6 De Paul-LCA J. of Art and Ent. L. 125 (1995): "[T]he exclusion of subordinated groups is more problematic than the exclusion of dominant groups because the subordinated groups are already at a power disadvantage." In this view, GLIB's First Amendment rights merited greater protection than did the First Amendment rights of the veterans. Is the purpose of the First Amendment to equalize power relationships or to protect expression? Are these objectives distinct?

Anonymous Speech

Talley v. State of California
362 U.S. 60, 80 S. CT. 536, 4 L. ED. 2D 559 (1960).

[EDITORIAL NOTE: *In Talley, the Court struck down, on First Amendment grounds, a Los Angeles city ordinance restricting the distribution of handbills. The ordinance provided that no handbills may be distributed without providing on their face the name and address of both their maker and their distributor. Petitioner was arrested and convicted of distributing handbills urging a boycott that did not include his name and address.*]

Justice BLACK delivered the opinion of the Court:

[Anonymous] handbills urged readers to help [an] organization carry on a boycott against certain merchants and businessmen whose names were given, on the ground that they carried products of "manufacturers who will not offer equal employment opportunities to Negroes, Mexicans and Orientals."

The broad ordinance now before us, barring distribution of "any hand-bill in any place under any circumstances," falls precisely under the ban of our prior cases unless this ordinance is saved by the qualification that handbills can be distributed if they have printed on them the names and addresses of the persons who prepared, distributed or sponsored them. For, the ordinance here is not limited to handbills whose content is "obscene or offensive to public morals or that advocates unlawful conduct." This ordinance simply bars all handbills under all circumstances anywhere that do not have the names and addresses printed on them in the place the ordinance requires.

We have recently had occasion to hold in two cases that there are times and circumstances when States may not compel members of groups engaged in the dissemination of ideas to be publicly identified. *Bates v. City of Little Rock; N.A.A.C.P. v. Alabama.* The reason for those holdings was that identification and fear of reprisal might deter perfectly peaceful discussions of public matters of importance. This broad Los Angeles ordinance is subject to the same infirmity. We hold that it is void on its face.

Justice CLARK dissented, joined by Justices FRANKFURTER and WHITTAKER.

[B]efore passing upon the validity of the ordinance, I would weigh the interests of the public in its enforcement against the claimed right of Talley. The record is barren of any claim, much less proof, that he will suffer any injury whatever by identifying the handbill with his name. Talley makes no showing whatever to support his contention that a restraint upon his freedom of speech will result from the enforcement of the ordinance. The existence of such a restraint is necessary before we can strike the ordinance down.

But even if the State had this burden, which it does not, the substantiality of Los Angeles' interest in the enforcement of the ordinance sustains its validity. Its chief law enforcement officer says that the enforcement of the ordinance prevents "fraud, deceit, false advertising, negligent use of words, obscenity, and libel," and, as we have said, that such was its purpose. In the absence of any showing to the contrary by Talley, this appears to me entirely sufficient.

I stand second to none in supporting Talley's right of free speech—but not his freedom of anonymity. The Constitution says nothing about freedom of anonymous speech.

Is Talley's anonymous handbill, designed to destroy the business of a commercial establishment, passed out at its very front door, and attacking its then lawful commercial practices, more compatible with First Amendment freedoms? I think not.

COMMENT

The *Talley* case refers to *NAACP v. Alabama*, 357 U.S. 449 (1958), where the Court held that the NAACP could not be required to divulge its membership lists to the state of Alabama because such disclosure might cause economic reprisal and physical jeopardy for NAACP members. Justice Clark said that Talley made no showing that similar restraints would befall him. Did Justice Black respond to Justice Clark's argument that anonymity can claim constitutional protection only when it is indispensable to the exercise of political rights? What counterarguments might be made to Justice Clark's position?

McIntyre v. Ohio Elections Commission
115 S.CT. 1511 (1995).

[EDITORIAL NOTE: *An Ohio statute forbade the distribution of anonymous campaign literature. McIntyre distributed to persons attending a public school meeting a leaflet without her name on it expressing her opposition to a proposed school levy. She was subsequently fined $100 for distributing unsigned leaflets. The Ohio Supreme Court upheld the statute's constitutionality; the Supreme Court reversed and held that the statute abridged freedom of speech in violation of the First Amendment.*]

Justice STEVENS delivered the opinion of the Court.

Whatever the motivation may be, at least in the field of literary endeavor, the interest in having anonymous works enter the marketplace of ideas unquestionably outweighs any public interest in requiring the disclosure as a condition of entry. Accordingly, an author's decision to remain anonymous, like other decisions concerning omission or additions to the content of a publication, is an aspect of the freedom of speech protected by the First Amendment. The freedom to publish anonymously extends beyond the literary realm. The specific holding in *Talley* related to advocacy of an economic boycott but the Court's reasoning embraced a respected tradition of anonymity in the advocacy of political causes. This tradition is perhaps best exemplified by the secret ballot, the hard-won right to vote one's conscience without fear of retaliation.

Ohio's statute does, however, contain a different limitation than [was the case in *Talley*]: It applies only to unsigned documents designed to influence voters in an election. In contrast, the Los Angeles ordinance [in *Talley*] prohibited all anonymous handbilling "in any place under any circumstances." For that reason, Ohio correctly argues that *Talley* does not necessarily control

the disposition of this case. We must, therefore, decide whether and to what extent the First Amendment's protection of anonymity encompasses documents intended to influence the electoral process.

[T]he category of speech regulated by the Ohio statute occupies the core of the protection afforded by the First Amendment. Indeed, the speech in which Mrs. McIntyre engaged—handing out leaflets in the advocacy of a politically controversial viewpoint—is the essence of First Amendment expression. That this advocacy occurred in the heat of a controversial referendum vote only strengthens the protection afforded to Mrs. McIntyre's expression: urgent, important, and effective speech can be no less protected than impotent speech, lest the right to speak be relegated to those instances when it is least needed. No form of speech is entitled to greater constitutional protection than Mrs. McIntyre's.

When a law burdens core political speech, we apply "exacting scrutiny," and we uphold the restriction only if it is narrowly tailored to serve an overriding state interest. Our precedents thus make abundantly clear that the Ohio Supreme Court applied a significantly more lenient standard than is appropriate in a case of this kind.

Ohio argued that it had two such interests: Ohio judges its interest in preventing fraudulent and libelous statements and its interest in providing the electorate with relevant information to be sufficiently compelling to justify the anonymous speech ban.

The simple interest in providing voters with additional relevant information does not justify a state requirement that a writer make statements or disclosures she would otherwise omit. Moreover, in the case of a handbill written by a private citizen who is not known to the recipient, the name and address of the author adds little, if anything, to the reader's ability to evaluate the document's message. Thus, Ohio's informational interest is plainly insufficient to support the constitutionality of its disclosure requirement.

[EDITORIAL NOTE: *The Court then noted that Ohio already had a statute that dealt specifically with the making of false or fraudulent statements during political campaigns.*]

These regulations apply both to candidate elections and to issue-driven ballot measures. Thus, Ohio's prohibition of anonymous leaflets plainly is not its principal weapon against fraud. We recognize that a State's enforcement interest might justify a more limited identification requirement, but Ohio has shown scant cause for inhibiting the leafletting at issue here.

[**EDITORIAL NOTE:** *The Court dismissed Ohio's attempts to analogize its law to disclosure requirements the Court had previously upheld in the corporate and campaign expenditures context.*]

Under our Constitution, anonymous pamphleteering is not a pernicious, fraudulent practice, but an honorable tradition of advocacy and of dissent. Anonymity is a shield from the tyranny of the majority. See generally J. S. Mill, On Liberty, in On Liberty and Considerations on Representative Government 1, 3–4 (R. McCallum ed. 1947). It thus exemplifies the purpose behind the Bill of Rights, and of the First Amendment in particular: to protect unpopular individuals from retaliation—and their ideas from suppression—at the hand of an intolerant society. The right to remain anonymous may be abused when it shields fraudulent conduct. But political speech by its nature will sometimes have unpalatable consequences, and, in general, our society accords greater weight to the value of free speech than to the dangers of its misuse. Ohio has not shown that its interest in preventing the misuse of anonymous election-related speech justifies a prohibition of all uses of that speech. The state may, and does, punish fraud directly. But it cannot seek to punish fraud indirectly by indiscriminately outlawing a category of speech, based on its content, with no necessary relationship to the danger sought to be prevented. One would be hard pressed to think of a better example of the pitfalls of Ohio's blunderbuss approach than the facts of the case before us.

Justice GINSBURG concurred.

In for a calf is not always in for a cow. The Court's decision finds unnecessary, overintrusive, and inconsistent with American ideals the State's imposition of a fine on an individual leafleteer who, within her local community, spoke her mind, but sometimes not her name. We do not thereby hold that the State may not in other, larger circumstances, require the speaker to disclose its interest by disclosing its identity.

Justice THOMAS concurred in the judgment.

[**EDITORIAL NOTE:** *Justice Thomas did not join the Stevens rationale but used an original intent approach.*]

Instead of asking whether "an honorable tradition" of anonymous speech has existed throughout American history, or what the "value" of anonymous speech might be, we should determine whether the phrase "freedom of speech, or of the press," as originally understood, protected anonymous political leafletting. I believe that it did.

Justice SCALIA, joined by the Chief Justice dissented.

[T]he Court invalidates a species of protection for the election process that exists, in a variety of forms, in every State except California, and that has a pedigree dating back to the end of the 19th century. Preferring the views of the English utilitarian philosopher John Stuart Mill, to the considered judgment of the American people's elected representatives from coast to coast, the Court discovers a hitherto unknown right-to-be-unknown while engaging in electoral politics. I dissent from this imposition of free-speech imperatives that are demonstrably not those of the American people today, and that there is inadequate reason to believe were those of the society that begat the First Amendment or the Fourteenth.

The first question is whether protection of the election process justifies limitations upon speech that cannot constitutionally be imposed generally. Our cases plainly answer that question in the affirmative—indeed, they suggest that no justification for regulation is more compelling than protection of the electoral process.

[**EDITORIAL NOTE:** *Justice Scalia contended that the disclosure requirements here are effective in protecting and enhancing democratic elections, and that similar disclosure requirements had been upheld by the Court in the past.*]

COMMENT

How extensive is the protection accorded to anonymous speech? In *McIntyre*, Justice Stevens declares that an author's decision to remain anonymous is "an aspect of the freedom of speech protected by the First Amendment." How extensive is the protection accorded to anonymous speech? Is the protection stronger than that provided by *Talley?* The answer may depend on what kind of anonymous speech is being considered.

Anonymous core political speech is given the highest protection in the majority opinion in *McIntyre*. The Court says such speech merits the application of the strict, or "exacting," scrutiny standard. But *McIntyre* also says that the "State's enforcement interest 'may' justify a more limited identification requirement." Note that Justice Ginsburg in her concurrence emphasizes exactly this qualification in the majority opinion. Does Justice Ginsburg believe the Court gave too much protection to anonymous political speech? Under what circumstances would a "limited identification requirement" be warranted?

CHAPTER 2

FIRST AMENDMENT METHODOLOGY

The U.S. Supreme Court's experience with First Amendment problems has produced a complex body of law replete with tests, doctrines, and standards of review developed for the varying contexts in which freedom of expression problems arise. Collectively, these tests, doctrines, and standards comprise the methodology of First Amendment law. We have already encountered one example of First Amendment methodology—the clear and present danger doctrine. In this chapter we will examine other examples of First Amendment methodology. The most venerable of these is the prior restraint doctrine—the idea, rooted in the common law and embraced by First Amendment law, that governmental restraints that prevent publication from taking

place are disfavored. A discussion of the prior restraint doctrine leads off this chapter.

This is followed by a discussion of various civil and criminal sanctions against expressive activity such as restraints on the circulation and distribution of mail. Some of the cases that have arisen in the course of government regulation of pamphleteering, solicitation, parades, and demonstrations are also examined. Sections of particular interest to students of communication law are those on newsrack regulation and the potential for taxation to serve as a vehicle for media censorship.

One of the most important contemporary tools for evaluating governmental regulation affecting freedom of expression is the distinction between content-based and content-neutral regulation. This distinction has become critical in contemporary First Amendment methodology. The courts subject content-based regulation to a much more exacting standard of review than that accorded to content-neutral regulation. What is the justification for this difference? Is it because government should not be in the business of making judgments based on the content of expression? Should this be true in all circumstances? Other doctrinal tools covered in this chapter are the symbolic speech concept and—of critical importance—the *O'Brien* test that is now widely used to evaluate regulation that only incidentally affects free expression.

This chapter concludes with the public forum doctrine, which was developed to grapple with the difficult issue of the extent to which public facilities may be used as public forums for expressive activity. The discussion presents cases and examples that illustrate the various types of public forums—the limited public forum, the traditional public forum, and the nonpublic forum.

The public forum materials also grapple with the question: Is the public forum doctrine a static or dynamic concept? The town common or the village green served as what we today would call the traditional public forum. Should we expand the concept of the public forum to embrace, for example, the modern airport terminal? How capacious should the concept be? In short, as this question illustrates, in this chapter we try to explain the nature of First Amendment methodology and the extent to which the concepts it embraces are subject to adaptation and change.

THE DOCTRINE OF PRIOR RESTRAINT

Near v. Minnesota
283 U.S. 697, 51 S. CT. 625, 75 L. ED. 1357 (1931).

[EDITORIAL NOTE: *The clear and present danger cases we have examined in studying the constitutional development of freedom of expression as a concept have dealt with what might be called subsequent punishment, that is, punishing the speaker or the publisher after the act of communication because of state objection to the contents of the communication. This kind of legal sanction over communication obviously performs a certain censorship function. But press censorship, in the sense of being required by law to submit copy to a state official before publication is allowed, is another very significant and even more direct method by which freedom of expression can be restricted. At common law this kind of censorship was known as prior restraint. In* Near v. Minnesota, *the U.S. Supreme Court produced a very valuable precedent for the law of the press because the Court dealt with the constitutionality of press censorship and specifically with prior restraint.*

As you read the opinion of the Court in Near, *be careful to note that the Court did not say prior restraints were absolutely forbidden by the constitutional guarantee of freedom of the press, but rather that they were prohibited except in certain areas. According to Chief Justice Charles Evans Hughes, what are the areas of exception where prior restraints apparently are permitted?*

The factual setting of the Near *case was as follows. A Minnesota statute provided for the abating as a public nuisance of "malicious, scandalous, and defamatory" newspapers or periodicals. The statute provided that all persons guilty of such a nuisance could be enjoined. Mason's Minnesota Statutes, 1927, §§ 10123–1 to 10123–3.*

Floyd Olson, the county attorney of Hennepin County (Minneapolis) and later a populist governor, brought an action under the statute to enjoin the publication of a "malicious, scandalous, and defamatory newspaper, magazine, or other periodical" known as The Saturday Press. *The complaint filed by the county attorney asserted that The Saturday Press had accused the law enforcement agencies and officials of Minneapolis with failing to expose and punish gambling, bootlegging, and racketeering, which activities, The Saturday Press alleged, were in control of a "Jewish gangster."*

The state trial court found that the editors of The Saturday Press *had violated the statute, and the court "perpetually enjoined" the defendants from conducting "said nuisance under the title of* The Saturday Press *or any other name or title." The state supreme court affirmed, and the defendant Near appealed to the U.S. Supreme Court. For an interesting and lively account of the background of the case, See Friendly,* Minnesota Rag *(1981).]*

Chief Justice HUGHES delivered the opinion of the Court:

This statute, for the suppression as a public nuisance of a newspaper or periodical, is unusual, if not unique, and raises questions of grave importance transcending the local interests involved in the particular action. It is no longer open to doubt that the liberty of the press and of speech is within the liberty safeguarded by the due process clause of the Fourteenth Amendment from invasion by state action. It was found impossible to conclude that this essential personal liberty of the citizen was left unprotected by the general guaranty of fundamental rights of person and property. In maintaining this guaranty, the authority of the state to enact laws to promote the health, safety, morals, and general welfare of its people is necessarily admitted. The limits of this sovereign power must always be determined with appropriate regard to the particular subject of its exercise. Liberty of speech and of the press is also not an absolute right, and the state may punish its abuse. Liberty, in each of its phases, has its history and connotation, and, in the present instance, the inquiry is as to the historic conception of the liberty of the press and whether the statute under review violates the essential attributes of that liberty.

First. The statute is not aimed at the redress of individual or private wrongs. Remedies for libel remain available and unaffected. The statute, said the state court (174 Minn. 457, 219 N.W. 770, 772, 58 A.L.R. 607), "is not directed at threatened libel but at an existing business which, generally speaking, involves more than libel." It is aimed at the distribution of scandalous matter as "detrimental to public morals and to the general welfare," tending "to disturb the peace of the community" and "to provoke assaults and the commission of crime." In order to obtain an injunction to suppress the future publication of the newspaper or periodical, it is not necessary to prove the falsity of the charges that have been made in the publication condemned. In the present action there was no allegation that the matter published was not true. It is alleged, and the statute requires the allegation that the publication was "malicious." But, as in prosecutions for libel, there is no requirement of proof by the state of malice in fact as distinguished from malice inferred from the mere publication of the defamatory matter. The judgment in this case proceeded upon the mere proof of publication. The statute permits the defense, not of the truth alone, but only that the truth was published with good motives and for justifiable ends.

Second. The statute is directed not simply at the circulation of scandalous and defamatory statements with regard to private citizens, but at the continued publication by newspapers and periodicals of charges against public officers of corruption, malfeasance in office, or serious neglect of duty. Such charges by their very nature create a public scandal. They are scandalous and defamatory within the meaning of the statute, which has its normal operation in relation to publications dealing prominently and chiefly with the alleged derelictions of public officers.

Third. The object of the statute is not punishment, in the ordinary sense, but suppression of the offending newspaper or periodical. The reason for the enactment, as the state court has said, is that prosecutions to enforce penal statutes for libel do not result in "efficient repression or suppression of the evils of scandal." Describing the business of publication as a public nuisance does not obscure the substance of the proceeding which the statute authorizes. It is the continued publication of scandalous and defamatory matter that constitutes the business and the declared nuisance. In the case of public officers, it is the reiteration of charges of official misconduct, and the fact that the newspaper or periodical is principally devoted to that purpose, that exposes it to suppression.

This suppression is accomplished by enjoining publication, and that restraint is the object and effect of the statute.

Fourth. The statute not only operates to suppress the offending newspaper or periodical, but to put the publisher under an effective censorship. When a newspaper or periodical is found to be "malicious, scandalous and defamatory," and is suppressed as such, resumption of publication is punishable as a contempt of court by fine or imprisonment. Thus, where a newspaper or periodical has been suppressed because of the circulation of charges against public officers of official misconduct, it would seem to be clear that the renewal of the publication of such charges would constitute a contempt, and that the judgment would lay a permanent restraint upon the publisher, to escape which he must satisfy the court as to the character of a new publication. Whether he would be permitted again to publish matter deemed to be derogatory to the same or other public officers would depend upon the court's ruling. In the present instance the judgment restrained the defendants from "publishing, circulating, having in their possession, selling or giving away any publication whatsoever which is a malicious, scandalous or defamatory newspaper, as defined by law." The law gives no definition except that covered by the words "scandalous and defamatory," and publications charging official misconduct are of that class. While the court, answering the objection that the judgment was too broad, saw no reason for construing it as restraining the defendants "from operating a newspaper in harmony with the public welfare to which all must yield," and said that the defendants had not indicated "any desire to conduct their business in the usual and legitimate manner," the manifest inference is that, at least with respect to a new publication directed against official misconduct, the defendant would be held, under penalty of punishment for contempt as provided in the statute, to a manner of publication which the court considered to be "usual and legitimate" and consistent with the public welfare.

If we cut through mere details of procedure, the operation and effect of the statute in substance is that public authorities may bring the owner or publisher of a newspaper or periodical before a judge upon a charge of conducting a business of publishing scandalous and defamatory matter—in particular that the matter consists of charges against public officers of official dereliction—and, unless the owner or publisher is able and disposed to bring competent evidence to satisfy the judge that the charges are true and are published with good motives and for justifiable ends, his newspaper or periodical is suppressed and further publication is made punishable as a contempt. This is of the essence of censorship.

The question is whether a statute authorizing such proceedings in restraint of publication is consistent with the conception of the liberty of the press as historically conceived and guaranteed. In determining the extent of the constitutional protection, it has been generally, if not universally, considered that it is the chief purpose of the guaranty to prevent previous restraints upon publication. The struggle in England, directed against the legislative power of the licenser, resulted in renunciation of the censorship of the press. The liberty deemed to be established was thus described by Blackstone: "The liberty of the press is indeed essential to the nature of a free state; but this consists in laying no *previous* restraints upon publications, and not in freedom from censure for criminal matter when published. Every freeman has an undoubted right to lay what sentiments he pleases before the public; to forbid this, is to destroy the freedom of the press; but if he publishes what is improper, mischievous or illegal, he must take the consequence of his own temerity." 4 Bl. Com. 151, 152. See Story on the Constitution, §§ 1884, 1889. The distinction was early pointed out

between the extent of the freedom with respect to censorship under our constitutional system and that enjoyed in England. Here, as Madison said, "the great and essential rights of the people are secured against legislative as well as against executive ambition. They are secured, not by laws paramount to prerogative, but by constitutions paramount to laws. This security of the freedom of the press requires that it should be exempt not only from previous restraint by the Executive, as in Great Britain, but from legislative restraint also." Report on the Virginia Resolutions, Madison's Works, vol. IV, p. 543. This Court said, in *Patterson v. Colorado*, 205 U.S. 454, 462: "In the first place, the main purpose of such constitutional provisions is 'to prevent all such previous restraints upon publications as had been practiced by other governments,' and they do not prevent the subsequent punishment of such as may be deemed contrary to the public welfare. *Commonwealth v. Blanding*, 3 Pick. (Mass.) 304, 313, 314 (15 Am.Dec. 214); *Respublica v. Oswald*, 1 Dall. 319, 325. The preliminary freedom extends as well to the false as to the true; the subsequent punishment may extend as well to the true as to the false. This was the law of criminal libel apart from statute in most cases, if not in all. *Commonwealth v. Blanding, ubi supra;* 4 Bl. Com. 150."

The criticism upon Blackstone's statement has not been because immunity from previous restraint upon publication has not been regarded as deserving of special emphasis, but chiefly because that immunity cannot be deemed to exhaust the conception of the liberty guaranteed by state and federal Constitutions. The point of criticism has been "that the mere exemption from previous restraints cannot be all that is secured by the constitutional provisions," and that "the liberty of the press might be rendered a mockery and a delusion, and the phrase itself a byword, if, while every man was at liberty to publish what he pleased, the public authorities might nevertheless punish him for harmless publications." 2 Cooley, Const. Lim. (8th Ed.) p. 885. But it is recognized that punishment for the abuse of the liberty accorded to the press is essential to the protection of the public, and that the common-law rules that subject the libeler to responsibility for the public offense, as well as for the private injury, are not abolished by the protection extended in our Constitutions. Id. pp. 883, 884.

The law of criminal libel rests upon that secure foundation. There is also the conceded authority of courts to punish for contempt when publications directly tend to prevent the proper discharge of judicial functions. We have no occasion to inquire as to the permissible scope of subsequent punishment. For whatever wrong the appellant has committed or may commit, by his publications, the state appropriately affords both public and private redress by its libel laws. As has been noted, the statute in question does not deal with punishments; it provides for no punishment, except in case of contempt for violation of the court's order, but for suppression and injunction—that is, for restraint upon publication.

The objection has also been made that the principle as to immunity from previous restraint is stated too broadly, if every such restraint is deemed to be prohibited. That is undoubtedly true; the protection even as to previous restraint is not absolutely unlimited. But the limitation has been recognized only in exceptional cases. No one would question but that a government might prevent actual obstruction to its recruiting service or the *publication of the sailing dates of transports or the number and location of troops.* On similar grounds, the primary requirements of decency may be enforced against obscene publications. The security of the community life may be protected against incitements to acts of violence and the overthrow by force of orderly government. These limitations are not applicable here. Nor are we now concerned with questions as to the extent of authority to prevent publications in order to protect private rights according to the principles governing the exercise of the jurisdiction of courts of equity. [Emphasis added.]

The exceptional nature of its limitations places in a strong light the general conception that liberty of the press, historically considered and taken up by the federal Constitution, has meant, principally although not exclusively, immunity from previous restraints or censorship. The conception of the liberty of the press in this country had broadened with the exigencies of the colonial period and with the efforts to secure freedom from oppressive administration. That liberty was especially cherished for the immunity it afforded from previous restraint of the publication of censure of public officers and charges of official misconduct.

The fact that for approximately one hundred and fifty years there has been almost an entire absence of attempts to impose previous restraints upon publications relating to the malfeasance of public officers is significant of the deep-seated conviction that such restraints would violate constitutional right. Public officers, whose character and conduct remain open to debate and free discussion in the press, find their remedies for false accusations in actions under libel laws not in proceedings to restrain the publication of newspapers and periodicals. The general principle that the constitutional guaranty of the liberty of the press gives immunity from previous restraints has been approved in many decisions under state constitutions.

The importance of this immunity has not lessened. While reckless assaults upon public men, and efforts to bring obloquy upon those who are endeavoring faithfully to discharge official duties, exert a baleful influence and deserve the severest condemnation in public opinion, it cannot be said that this abuse is greater, and it is believed to be less, than that which characterized the period in which our institutions took shape. Meanwhile, the administration of government has become more complex, the opportunities for malfeasance and corruption have multiplied, crime has grown to most serious proportions, and the danger of its protection by unfaithful officials and of the impairment of the fundamental security of life and property by criminal alliances and official neglect, emphasizes the primary need of a vigilant and courageous press, especially in great cities. The fact that the liberty of the press may be abused by miscreant purveyors of scandal does not make any the less necessary the immunity of the press from previous restraint in dealing with official misconduct. Subsequent punishment for such abuses as may exist is the appropriate remedy, consistent with constitutional privilege.

In attempted justification of the statute, it is said that it deals not with publication per se, but with the "business" of publishing defamation. If, however, the publisher has a constitutional right to publish, without previous restraint, an edition of his newspaper charging official derelictions, it cannot be denied that he may publish subsequent editions for the same purpose. He does not lose his right by exercising it. If his right exists, it may be exercised in publishing nine editions, as in this case, as well as in one edition. If previous restraint is permissible, it may be imposed at once; indeed, the wrong may be as serious in one publication as in several. Characterizing the publication as a business, and the business as a nuisance, does not permit an invasion of the constitutional immunity against restraint. Similarly, it does not matter that the newspaper or periodical is found to be "largely" or "chiefly" devoted to the publication of such derelictions. If the publisher has a right, without previous restraint, to publish them, his right cannot be deemed to be dependent upon his publishing something else, more or less, with the matter to which objection is made.

Nor can it be said that the constitutional freedom from previous restraint is lost because charges are made of derelictions which constitute crimes. With the multiplying provisions of penal codes, and of municipal charters and ordinances carrying penal sanctions, the conduct of public officers is very largely within the purview of criminal statutes. The freedom of the press from previous restraint has never been regarded as limited to such animadversions as lay outside the range of penal enactments. Historically, there is no such limitation; it is inconsistent with the reason which underlies the privilege, as the privilege so limited would be of slight value for the purposes for which it came to be established.

The statute in question cannot be justified by reason of the fact that the publisher is permitted to show, before injunction issues, that the matter published is true and is published with good motives and for justifiable ends. If such a statute, authorizing suppression and injunction on such a basis, is constitutionally valid, it would be equally permissible for the Legislature to provide that at any time the publisher of any newspaper could be brought before a court, or even an administrative officer (as the constitutional protection may not be regarded as resting on mere procedural details), and required to produce proof of the truth of his publication, or of what he intended to publish and of his motives, or stand enjoined. If this can be done, the Legislature may provide machinery for determining in the complete exercise of its discretion what are justifiable ends and restrain publication accordingly. And it would be but a step to a complete system of censorship. The recognition of authority to impose previous restraint upon publication in order to protect the community against the circulation of charges of misconduct, and especially of official misconduct, necessarily would carry with it the admission of the authority of the censor against which the constitutional barrier was erected. The preliminary freedom, by virtue of the very reason for its existence, does not depend, as this court has said, on proof of truth.

Equally unavailing is the insistence that the statute is designed to prevent the circulation of scandal which tends to disturb the public peace and to provoke assaults and the commission of crime. Charges of reprehensible conduct, and in particular of official malfeasance, unquestionably create a public scandal, but the theory of the constitutional guaranty is that even a more serious public evil would be caused by authority to prevent publication. "To prohibit the intent to excite those unfavorable sentiments against those who administer the Government, is equivalent to a prohibition of the actual excitement of them; and to prohibit the actual excitement of them is equivalent to a prohibition of discussions having that tendency and effect; which again, is equivalent to a protection of those who administer the Government, if they should at any time deserve the contempt or hatred of the people, against being exposed to it by free animadversions on their characters and conduct." There is nothing new in the fact that charges of reprehensible conduct may create resentment and the disposition to resort to violent means of redress, but this well-understood tendency did not alter the determination to protect the press against censorship and restraint upon publication.

For these reasons we hold the statute, so far as it authorized the proceedings in this action, to be an infringement of the liberty of the press guaranteed by the Fourteenth Amendment. We should add that this decision rests upon the operation and effect of the statute, without regard to the question of the truth of the charges contained in the particular periodical. The fact that the public officers named in this case, and those associated with the charges of official dereliction, may be deemed to be impeccable, cannot affect the conclusion that the statute imposes an unconstitutional restraint upon publication.

Judgment reversed.

Justice BUTLER (dissenting).

The Minnesota statute does not operate as a *previous* restraint on publication within the proper meaning of that phrase. It does not authorize administrative control in advance such as was formerly exercised by the licensers and censors, but prescribes a remedy to be enforced by a suit in equity. In this case there was previous publication made in the course of the business of regularly producing malicious, scandalous, and defamatory periodicals. The business and publications unquestionably constitute an abuse of the right of free press. The statute denounces the things done as a nuisance on the ground, as stated by the State Supreme Court, that they threaten morals, peace, and good order. There is no question of the power of the state to denounce such transgressions. The restraint authorized is only in respect of continuing to do what has been duly adjudged to constitute a nuisance. There is nothing in the statute purporting to prohibit publications that have not been adjudged to constitute a nuisance. It is fanciful to suggest similarity between the granting or enforcement of the decree authorized by this statute to prevent *further* publication of malicious, scandalous, and defamatory articles and the *previous restraint* upon the press by licensers as referred to by Blackstone and described in the history of the times to which he alludes.

It is well known, as found by the state Supreme Court, that existing libel laws are inadequate effectively to suppress evils resulting from the kind of business and publications that are shown in this case. The doctrine that measures such as the one before us are invalid because they operate as previous restraints to infringe freedom of press exposes the peace and good order of every community and the business and private affairs of every individual to the constant and protracted false and malicious assaults of any insolvent publisher who may have purpose and sufficient capacity to contrive and put into effect a scheme or program for oppression, blackmail or extortion.

The judgment should be affirmed.

Justice VAN DEVANTER, Justice MC-REYNOLDS, and Justice SUTHERLAND concur in this opinion.

COMMENT

Chief Justice Hughes said in *Near* that freedom from prior restraint was the general principle. But he also made it clear that it was not an absolute principle. The areas of exception were apparently three: (1) cases where national security was involved in time of war; (2) cases where the "primary requirements of decency" were involved, that is, the problem of obscene publications; and (3) cases where the public order was endangered by the incitement to violence and overthrow by force of orderly government.

The *Near* case produced a sharp 5–4 division in the Court. The narrow majority supporting the opinion of Chief Justice Hughes was accused by Justice Pierce Butler, a Minnesotan, of reaching out to decide the constitutional status of prior restraints that were not involved in the case at bar. Technically, Justice Butler was right. The prior restraint known at common law empowered administrative officials rather than judges to review in the first instance the material to be published. In *Near*, *The Saturday Press* had been able to publish what it chose in the first instance. Moreover, no requirement of submitting future copy to a court as a prerequisite to publication was asked of the editors. Yet, more broadly viewed, the court order probably did create a prior restraint.

In the landmark case of *New York Times v. Sullivan*, 376 U.S. 254 (1964), the Supreme Court sharply limited the ability of public officials to successfully sue newspapers for libel. For an extended discussion of the impact of the *Times* case on the law of libel, see Chapter 4, p. 169. In the *Times* case, the Court cited the statements in *Near* and other cases that the "Constitution does not protect libelous utterances." But the Court pointed out that neither *Near* nor any other case cited for this proposition actually involved the use of libel laws to restrain expression "critical of the official conduct of public officials." 376 U.S. at 268. In a decision of far-reaching scope, the Court proclaimed the latter kind of expression to be protected by the First Amendment. Justice William Brennan said for the Court in *New York Times* that the case of a public official suing a newspaper for libel must be considered "against the background of a profound national commitment to the principle that debate on public issues should be uninhibited, robust and wide-open, and that it may well include vehement, caustic, and sometimes unpleasantly sharp attacks on government and public officials." *Id.* at 270.

If *The Saturday Press* were to publish in Minneapolis today an attack on the members of the municipal government of that city—an attack, that, let us assume, until the *New York Times* case would have been actionably libelous— would an injunction now be available to restrain further publications of the attack?

From the point of view of freedom of the press, the legal concept of prior restraint is of the greatest importance. If, as a constitutional matter, freedom of the press included nothing more than prior restraint, considerable protection would still have been afforded the printed word. This is because freedom from prior restraint allows the material to be disseminated in the first place. Ideas, no matter how disturbing to established authority, are thus given legal protection in their emergent state. This freedom from prior restraint against the printed word contrasts with the legal concept of subsequent punishment, which refers to the imposition of legal sanctions on those who authored the offending words. Punishing Gitlow *after* the publication of his revolutionary newspaper is an example of subsequent punishment. Under what set of facts would *Gitlow* have been a prior restraint case?

The contribution of Chief Justice Hughes's opinion in *Near v. Minnesota* is that it enriched, in a formative case, the constitutional interpretation of freedom of the press to include *both* freedom from prior restraint and freedom from subsequent punishment. Yet which of these two forms of repression of the press, prior restraint or subsequent punishment, is the more dangerous in damaging the values for which freedom of press exists as a constitutional guarantee? Why?

For an excellent discussion of prior restraint, see generally Emerson, *The Doctrine of Prior Restraint*, 20 Law & Contemp. Prob. 648 (1955); Symposium, *Near v. Minnesota, 50th Anniversary*, 66 Minn. L. Rev. 1–208 (1981). See generally, Redish, *The Proper Role of the Prior Restraint Doctrine in First Amendment Theory*, 70 Va. L. Rev. 53 (1984).

The *Pentagon Papers* Case

The Pentagon Papers or the *New York Times* case of the summer of 1971 brought forth suddenly and with no particular warning one of the great First Amendment and one of the most dramatic prior restraint cases in American constitutional history. For students of the law of mass communication, the case can be approached under at least three familiar categories: (1) prior restraint, (2) journalists' privilege to protect their sources, and (3) the public's right to know. All the judges who considered the case had to weigh claims of freedom from prior restraint and freedom of information against claims of government interest and security advanced by the Justice Department lawyers. Was Dr. Daniel Ellsberg, one of the thirty-six authors of the papers, justified, legally or ethically, in taking classified papers to which he had access and turning them over to the *New York Times?*

The sequence of events that created the Pentagon Papers case came about as follows: In June 1971, the *New York Times,* after much soul-searching, decided to publish a secret, classified Pentagon Report outlining the process by which America went to war in Vietnam. At the request of the U.S. government, a temporary restraining order was issued against the *New York Times* by a newly appointed federal judge, Murray Gurfein, of the Federal District Court for the Southern District of New York. A few days later Judge Gurfein in a stirring decision refused to grant the government a permanent injunction to restrain the *New York Times* from publishing the Pentagon Papers. "A cantankerous press, an obstinate press, a ubiquitous press," said the judge, "must be suffered by those in authority in order to preserve the even greater values of freedom of expression and the right of the people to know."

But the U.S. Court of Appeals for the Second Circuit reversed this decision, holding that the issue of whether the materials should be published should be decided in further hearings where the government could develop and support its position that the publication of the papers presented a threat to the security of the United States. In the interim, the Second Circuit Court of Appeals ruled that the restraints on publication should be continued. Meanwhile, the *Washington Post* entered the fray. The government requested an injunction against the *Post* in the U.S. District Court in the District of Columbia, but Judge Gerhard Gesell denied the government's attempt to restrain publication of the Pentagon Papers by the *Post.* The government appealed, and the U.S. Court of Appeals for the District of Columbia came down on the side of the press.

The *Washington Post* and *New York Times* were not the only newspapers to publish the Pentagon Papers. The *Boston Globe* and the *St. Louis Post Dispatch* had each published one article on the papers. The government sought and obtained a restraining order against the papers in Boston and St. Louis. The *Chicago Sun Times* and the *Los Angeles Times* published stories based on the Pentagon Papers, but these newspapers were never the subject of lawsuits by the government. Because of the inconsistent actions with regard to the Pentagon Papers in the federal courts of appeals in New York and Washington, the *Washington Post* was free to publish the papers, but the *New York Times* was not.

On June 30, 1971, the great case, a historic confrontation between government and the press, was decided by the Supreme Court. The result was clear—every newspaper in the land was free to publish the Pentagon Papers. In the excitement of victory, however, the press did not immediately appreciate that the Supreme Court had not clearly resolved the bitter struggle between freedom of information and national security. The Court's actual order merely held that the government had not met the heavy burden that must be met to justify any government prior restraint on the press. As for the myriad issues raised by the momentous case, nine separate opinions (it would have been impossible to have more) reflected the ambiguities, contradictions, and fundamental disagreements among the justices on basic issues concerning the role of the press in American society.

For a detailed account of the events leading to the Supreme Court's action, see Ungar, *The Papers & The Papers* (1973).

New York Times v. United States
403 U.S. 713, 91 S. CT. 2140, 29 L. ED. 2D 822 (1971).

Per Curiam.

We granted certiorari in these cases in which the United States seeks to enjoin the New York Times and the Washington Post from publishing the contents of a classified study entitled "History of U.S. Decision-Making Process on Viet Nam Policy."

"Any system of prior restraints of expression comes to this Court bearing a heavy presumption against its constitutional validity." *Bantam Books,*

Inc. v. Sullivan, 372 U.S. 58, 70 (1963); see also *Near v. Minnesota,* 283 U.S. 697 (1931). The government "thus carries a heavy burden of showing justification for the enforcement of such a restraint." *Organization for a Better Austin v. Keefe,* 402 U.S. 415 (1971). The District Court for the Southern District of New York in the *New York Times* case and the District Court for the District of Columbia and the Court of Appeals for the District of Columbia Circuit in the *Washington Post* case held that the government had not met that burden. We agree. [Emphasis added.]

The judgment of the Court of Appeals for the District of Columbia Circuit is therefore affirmed. The order of the Court of Appeals for the Second Circuit is reversed and the case is remanded with directions to enter a judgment affirming the judgment of the District Court for the Southern District of New York. The stays entered June 25, 1971, by the Court are vacated. The judgments shall issue forthwith.

So ordered.

Justice BLACK, with whom Justice DOUGLAS joins, concurring.

I believe that every moment's continuance of the injunctions against these newspapers amounts to a flagrant, indefensible, and continuing violation of the First Amendment. In my view it is unfortunate that some of my Brethren are apparently willing to hold that the publication of news may sometimes be enjoined. Such a holding would make a shambles of the First Amendment.

Now, for the first time in the 182 years since the founding of the Republic, the federal courts are asked to hold that the First Amendment does not mean what it says, but rather means that the government can halt the publication of current news of vital importance to the people of this country.

In seeking injunctions against these newspapers and in its presentation to the Court, the executive branch seems to have forgotten the essential purpose and history of the First Amendment. When the Constitution was adopted, many people strongly opposed it because the document contained no Bill of Rights to safeguard certain basic freedoms. They especially feared that the new powers granted to a central government might be interpreted to permit the government to curtail freedom of religion, press, assembly, and speech. In response to an overwhelming public clamor, James Madison offered a series of amendments to satisfy citizens that these great liberties would remain safe and beyond the power of government to abridge. Yet the Solicitor General argues and some members of the Court appear to agree that the general powers of the government adopted in the original Constitution should be interpreted to limit and restrict the specific and emphatic guarantees of the Bill of Rights adopted later. I can imagine no greater perversion of history. Madison and the other Framers of the First Amendment, able men that they were, wrote in language they earnestly believed could never be misunderstood: "Congress shall make no law abridging the freedom of the press." Both the history and language of the First Amendment support the view that the press must be left free to publish news, whatever the source, without censorship, injunctions, or prior restraints.

In the First Amendment the Founding Fathers gave the free press the protection it must have to fulfill its essential role in our democracy. The press was to serve the governed, not the governors. The government's power to censor the press was abolished so that the press would remain forever free to censure the government. The press was protected so that it could bare the secrets of government and inform the people. Only a free and unrestrained press can effectively expose deception in government. And paramount among the responsibilities of a free press is the duty to prevent any part of the government from deceiving the people and sending them off to distant lands to die of foreign fevers and foreign shot and shell. In my view, far from deserving condemnation for their courageous reporting, the New York Times, the Washington Post, and other newspapers should be commended for serving the purpose that the Founding Fathers saw so clearly. In revealing the workings of government that led to the Vietnam war, the newspapers nobly did precisely that which the Founders hoped and trusted they would do.

The government's case here is based on premises entirely different from those that guided the Framers of the First Amendment. The Solicitor General has carefully and emphatically stated:

"Now, Mr. Justice [Black], your construction of [the First Amendment] is well known, and I certainly respect it. You say that no law means no law, and that should be obvious. I can only say,

Mr. Justice that to me it is equally obvious that 'no law' does not mean 'no law', and I would seek to persuade the Court that that is true. [T]here are other parts of the Constitution that grant power and responsibilities to the Executive and the First Amendment was not intended to make it impossible for the Executive to function or to protect the security of the United States."

And the government argues in its brief that in spite of the First Amendment, "[t]he authority of the Executive Department to protect the nation against publication of information whose disclosure would endanger the national security stems from two interrelated sources: the constitutional power of the president over the conduct of foreign affairs and his authority as Commander-in-Chief."

In other words, we are asked to hold that despite the First Amendment's emphatic command, the executive branch, the Congress, and the Judiciary can make laws enjoining publication of current news and abridging freedom of the press in the name of "national security." The government does not even attempt to rely on any act of Congress. Instead it makes the bold and dangerously far-reaching contention that the courts should take it upon themselves to "make" a law abridging freedom of the press in the name of equity, presidential power and national security, even when the representatives of the people in Congress have adhered to the command of the First Amendment and refused to make such a law. See concurring opinion of Justice Douglas. To find that the president has "inherent power" to halt the publication of news by resort to the courts would wipe out the First Amendment and destroy the fundamental liberty and security of the very people the government hopes to make "secure." No one can read the history of the adoption of the First Amendment without being convinced beyond any doubt that it was injunctions like those sought here that Madison and his collaborators intended to outlaw in this Nation for all time.

The word "security" is a broad, vague generality whose contours should not be invoked to abrogate the fundamental law embodied in the First Amendment. The guarding of military and diplomatic secrets at the expense of informed representative government provides no real security for our Republic. The Framers of the First Amendment, fully aware of both the need to defend a new nation and the abuses of the English and Colonial governments, sought to give this new society strength and security by providing that freedom of speech, press, religion, and assembly should not be abridged.

Justice DOUGLAS, with whom Justice BLACK joins, concurring.

While I join the opinion of the Court I believe it necessary to express my views more fully.

It should be noted at the outset that the First Amendment provides that "Congress shall make no law abridging the freedom of speech or of the press." That leaves, in my view, no room for governmental restraint on the press.

There is, moreover, no statute barring the publication by the press of the material which the Times and Post seek to use.

So any power that the government possesses must come from its "inherent power."

The power to wage war is "the power to wage war successfully." See *Hirabayashi v. United States,* 320 U.S. 81, 93. But the war power stems from a declaration of war. The Constitution by Article I, § 8, gives Congress, not the President, power "to declare War." Nowhere are presidential wars authorized. We need not decide therefore what leveling effect the war power of Congress might have.

These disclosures may have a serious impact. But that is no basis for sanctioning a previous restraint on the press.

As we stated only the other day in *Organization for a Better Austin v. Keefe,* 402 U.S. 415, "any prior restraint on expression comes to this Court with a 'heavy presumption' against its constitutional validity."

The government says that it has inherent powers to go into court and obtain an injunction to protect that national interest, which in this case is alleged to be national security.

Near v. Minnesota, 283 U.S. 697, repudiated that expansive doctrine in no uncertain terms.

The dominant purpose of the First Amendment was to prohibit the widespread practice of governmental suppression of embarrassing information. It is common knowledge that the First Amendment was adopted against the widespread use of the common law of seditious libel to punish the dissemination of material that is embarrassing to the powers-that-be. See Emerson, *The System of Freedom of Expression,* c. V (1970); Chafee, *Free Speech in the United States,* c. XIII

(1941). The present cases will, I think, go down in history as the most dramatic illustration of that principle. A debate of large proportions goes on in the Nation over our posture in Vietnam. That debate antedated the disclosure of the contents of the present documents. The latter are highly relevant to the debate in progress.

Secrecy in government is fundamentally antidemocratic, perpetuating bureaucratic errors. Open debate and discussion of public issues are vital to our national health. On public questions there should be "open and robust debate." *New York Times, Inc. v. Sullivan,* 376 U.S. 254, 269–270.

I would affirm the judgment of the court of appeals in the *Post* case, vacate the stay of the court of appeals in the *Times* case and direct that it affirm the district court.

The stays in these cases that have been in effect for more than a week constitute a flouting of the principles of the First Amendment as interpreted in *Near v. Minnesota.*

Justice BRENNAN, concurring.

I write separately in these cases only to emphasize what should be apparent: that our judgment in the present cases may not be taken to indicate the propriety in the future, of issuing temporary stays and restraining orders to block the publication of material sought to be suppressed by the government. So far as I can determine, never before has the United States sought to enjoin a newspaper from publishing information in its possession. The relative novelty of the questions presented, the necessary haste with which decisions were reached, the magnitude of the interests asserted, and the fact that all the parties have concentrated their arguments upon the question whether permanent restraints were proper may have justified at least some of the restraints heretofore imposed in these cases. Certainly it is difficult to fault the several courts below for seeking to assure that the issues here involved were preserved for ultimate review by this Court. But even if it be assumed that some of the interim restraints were proper in the two cases before us, that assumption has no bearing upon the propriety of similar judicial action in the future. To begin with, there has now been ample time for reflection and judgment; whatever values there may be in the preservation of novel questions for appellate review may not support any restraints in the future. More important, the First Amendment stands as an absolute bar to the imposition of judicial restraints in circumstances of the kind presented by these cases.

The error which has pervaded these cases from the outset was the granting of any injunctive relief whatsoever, interim or otherwise. The entire thrust of the government's claim throughout these cases has been that publication of the material sought to be enjoined "could," or "might," or "may" prejudice the national interest in various ways. But the First Amendment tolerates absolutely no prior judicial restraints of the press predicated upon surmise or conjecture that untoward consequences may result. Our cases, it is true, have indicated that there is a single, extremely narrow class of cases in which the First Amendment's ban on prior judicial restraint may be overridden. Our cases have thus far indicated that such cases may arise only when the Nation "is at war," *Schenck v. United States,* 249 U.S. 47, 52 (1919), during which times "no one would question but that a government might prevent actual obstruction to its recruiting service or the publication of the sailing dates of transports or the number and location of troops." *Near v. Minnesota,* 283 U.S. 697, 716 (1931). Even if the present world situation were assumed to be tantamount to a time of war, or if the power of presently available armaments would justify even in peacetime the suppression of information that would set in motion a nuclear holocaust, in neither of these actions has the government presented or even alleged that publication of items from or based upon the material at issue would cause the happening of an event of that nature. "The chief purpose of [the First Amendment's] guarantee [is] to prevent previous restraints upon publication." *Near v. Minnesota, supra,* at 713. Thus, only governmental allegation and proof that publication must inevitably, directly and immediately cause the occurrence of an event kindred to imperiling the safety of a transport already at sea can support even the issuance of an interim restraining order. In no event may mere conclusions be sufficient: for if the Executive Branch seeks judicial aid in preventing publication, it must inevitably submit the basis upon which that aid is sought to scrutiny by the judiciary. And therefore, every restraint issued in this case, whatever its form, has violated the First Amendment—and not less so because that restraint was justified as necessary to afford the

courts an opportunity to examine the claim more thoroughly. Unless and until the government has clearly made out its case, the First Amendment commands that no injunction may issue.

Justice STEWART, with whom Justice WHITE joins, concurring.

In the absence of the governmental checks and balances present in other areas of our national life, the only effective restraint upon executive policy and power in the areas of national defense and international affairs may lie in an enlightened citizenry—in an informed and critical public opinion which alone can here protect the values of democratic government. For this reason, it is perhaps here that a press that is alert, aware, and free most vitally serves the basic purpose of the First Amendment. For without an informed and free press there cannot be an enlightened people.

Yet it is elementary that the successful conduct of international diplomacy and the maintenance of an effective national defense require both confidentiality and secrecy.

I think there can be but one answer to this dilemma, if dilemma it be. The responsibility must be where the power is. If the Constitution gives the executive a large degree of unshared power in the conduct of foreign affairs and the maintenance of our national defense, then under the Constitution the executive must have the largely unshared duty to determine and preserve the degree of internal security necessary to exercise that power successfully.

This is not to say that Congress and the courts have no role to play. Undoubtedly Congress has the power to enact specific and appropriate criminal laws to protect government property and preserve government secrets. Congress has passed such laws, and several of them are of very colorable relevance to the apparent circumstances of these cases. And if a criminal prosecution is instituted, it will be the responsibility of the courts to decide the applicability of the criminal law under which the charge is brought. Moreover, if Congress should pass a specific law authorizing civil proceedings in this field, the courts would likewise have the duty to decide the constitutionality of such a law as well as its applicability to the facts proved.

But in the cases before us we are asked neither to construe specific regulations nor to apply specific laws. We are asked, instead, to perform a function that the Constitution gave to the executive, not the judiciary. We are asked, quite simply, to prevent the publication by two newspapers of material that the executive branch insists should not, in the national interest, be published. I am convinced that the executive is correct with respect to some of the documents involved. But I cannot say that disclosure of any of them will surely result in direct, immediate, and irreparable damage to our Nation or its people. That being so, there can under the First Amendment be but one judicial resolution of the issues before us. I join the judgments of the Court.

Justice WHITE, with whom Justice STEWART joins, concurring.

I concur in today's judgments, but only because of the concededly extraordinary protection against prior restraints enjoyed by the press under our constitutional system. I do not say that in no circumstances would the First Amendment permit an injunction against publishing information about government plans or operations. Nor, after examining the materials the government characterizes as the most sensitive and destructive, can I deny that revelation of these documents will do substantial damage to public interests. Indeed, I am confident that their disclosure will have that result. But I nevertheless agree that the United States has not satisfied the very heavy burden which it must meet to warrant an injunction against publication in these cases, at least in the absence of express and appropriately limited congressional authorization for prior restraints in circumstances such as these.

It is not easy to reject the proposition urged by the United States and to deny relief on its good-faith claims in these cases that publication will work serious damage to the country. But that discomfiture is considerably dispelled by the infrequency of prior restraint cases. Normally, publication will occur and the damage be done before the government has either opportunity or grounds for suppression. So here, publication has already begun and a substantial part of the threatened damage has already occurred. The fact of a massive breakdown in security is known, access to the documents by many unauthorized people is undeniable and the efficacy of equitable relief against these or other newspapers to avert anticipated damage is doubtful at best.

What is more, terminating the ban on publication of the relatively few sensitive documents the government now seeks to suppress does not mean that the law either requires or invites newspapers or others to publish them or that they will be immune from criminal action if they do. Prior restraints require an unusually heavy justification under the First Amendment; but failure by the government to justify prior restraints does not measure its constitutional entitlement to a conviction for criminal publication. That the government mistakenly chose to proceed by injunction does not mean that it could not successfully proceed in another way.

The criminal code contains numerous provisions potentially relevant to these cases. Section 797 makes it a crime to publish certain photographs or drawings of military installations. Section 798, also in precise language, proscribes knowing and willful publications of any classified information concerning the cryptographic systems or communication intelligence activities of the United States as well as any information obtained from communication intelligence operations. If any of the material here at issue is of this nature, the newspapers are presumably now on full notice of the position of the United States and must face the consequences if they publish. I would have no difficulty in sustaining convictions under these sections on facts that would not justify the intervention of equity and the imposition of a prior restraint.

The same would be true under those sections of the criminal code casting a wider net to protect the national defense.

It is thus clear that Congress has addressed itself to the problems of protecting the security of the country and the national defense from unauthorized disclosure of potentially damaging information. Cf. *Youngstown Sheet & Tube Co. v. Sawyer,* 343 U.S. 579, 585–586 (1952); see also id., at 593–628 (Frankfurter, J., concurring). It has not, however, authorized the injunctive remedy against threatened publication. It has apparently been satisfied to rely on criminal sanctions and their deterrent effect on the responsible as well as the irresponsible press. I am not, of course, saying that either of these newspapers has yet committed a crime or that either would commit a crime if they published all the material now in their possession. That matter must await resolution in the context of a criminal proceeding if one is instituted by the United States. In that event, the issue of guilt or innocence would be determined by procedures and standards quite different from those that have purported to govern these injunctive proceedings.

Justice MARSHALL, concurring.

The government contends that the only issue in this case is whether in a suit by the United States, "the First Amendment bars a court from prohibiting a newspaper from publishing material whose disclosure would pose a grave and immediate danger to the security of the United States." Brief of the government, at 6. With all due respect, I believe the ultimate issue in this case is even more basic than the one posed by the solicitor general. The issue is whether this Court or the Congress has the power to make law.

In this case there is no problem concerning the President's power to classify information as "secret" or "top secret." Congress has specifically recognized presidential authority, which has been formally exercised in Executive Order 10501, to classify documents and information. See, eg., 18 U.S.C.A. § 798; 50 U.S.C.A. § 783. Nor is there any issue here regarding the President's power as chief executive and commander in chief to protect national security by disciplining employees who disclose information and by taking precautions to prevent leaks.

The problem here is whether in this particular case the Executive Branch has authority to invoke the equity jurisdiction of the courts to protect what it believes to be the national interest. See *In re Debs*, 158 U.S. 564, 584 (1895). The government argues that in addition to the inherent power of any government to protect itself, the president's power to conduct foreign affairs and his position as commander in chief give him authority to impose censorship on the press to protect his ability to deal effectively with foreign nations and to conduct the military affairs of the country. Of course, it is beyond cavil that the President has broad powers by virtue of his primary responsibility for the conduct of our foreign affairs and his position as commander in chief. And in some situations it may be that under whatever inherent powers the government may have, as well as the implicit authority derived from the president's mandate to conduct foreign affairs and to act as commander in chief, there is a basis for the invocation of the equity jurisdiction of this Court as an aid to prevent the publication of material damaging to "national security," however that term may be defined.

It would, however, be utterly inconsistent with the concept of separation of power for this Court to use its power of contempt to prevent behavior that Congress has specifically declined to prohibit. There would be a similar damage to the basic concept of these coequal branches of government if when the executive has adequate authority granted by Congress to protect "national security" it can choose instead to invoke the contempt power of a court to enjoin the threatened conduct. The Constitution provides that Congress shall make laws, the President execute laws, and courts interpret law. *Youngstown Sheet & Tube Co. v. Sawyer,* 343 U.S. 579 (1952). It did not provide for government by injunction in which the courts and the Executive can "make law" without regard to the action of Congress. It may be more convenient for the executive if it need only convince a judge to prohibit conduct rather than to ask the Congress to pass a law and it may be more convenient to enforce a contempt order than seek a criminal conviction in a jury trial. Moreover, it may be considered politically wise to get a court to share the responsibility for arresting those who the executive has probable cause to believe are violating the law. But convenience and political considerations of the moment do not justify a basic departure from the principles of our system of government.

Even if it is determined that the government could not in good faith bring criminal prosecutions against the New York Times and the Washington Post, it is clear that Congress has specifically rejected passing legislation that would have clearly given the president the power he seeks here and made the current activity of the newspapers unlawful. When Congress specifically declines to make conduct unlawful it is not for this Court to redecide those issues—to overrule Congress. See *Youngstown Sheet & Tube v. Sawyer,* 345 U.S. 579 (1952).

Either the government has the power under statutory grant to use traditional criminal law to protect the country or, if there is no basis for arguing that Congress has made the activity a crime, it is plain that Congress has specifically refused to grant the authority the government seeks from this Court. In either case this Court does not have authority to grant the requested relief. It is not for this Court to fling itself into every breach perceived by some government official nor is it for this Court to take on itself the burden of enacting law, especially law that Congress has refused to pass.

I believe that the judgment of the United States Court of Appeals for the District of Columbia should be affirmed and the judgment of the United States Court of Appeals for the Second Circuit should be reversed insofar as it remands the case for further hearings.

Chief Justice BURGER, dissenting.

So clear are the constitutional limitations on prior restraint against expression, that from the time of *Near v. Minnesota,* 283 U.S. 697 (1931), until recently in *Organization for a Better Austin v. Keefe,* 402 U.S. 415 (1971), we have had little occasion to be concerned with cases involving prior restraints against news reporting on matters of public interest. There is, therefore, little variation among the members of the Court in terms of resistance to prior restraints against publication. Adherence to this basic constitutional principle, however, does not make this case a simple one. In this case, the imperative of a free and unfettered press comes into collision with another imperative, the effective functioning of a complex modern government and specifically the effective exercise of certain constitutional powers of the executive. Only those who view the First Amendment as an absolute in all circumstances—a view I respect, but reject—can find such a case as this to be simple or easy.

The prompt setting of these cases reflects our universal abhorrence of prior restraint. But prompt judicial action does not mean unjudicial haste.

Here, moreover, the frenetic haste is due in large part to the manner in which the Times proceeded from the date it obtained the purloined documents. It seems reasonably clear now that the haste precluded reasonable and deliberate judicial treatment of these cases and was not warranted. The precipitous action of this Court aborting a trial not yet completed is not the kind of judicial conduct which ought to attend the disposition of a great issue.

The newspapers make a derivative claim under the First Amendment; they denominate this right as the public right-to-know; by implication, the Times asserts a sole trusteeship of that right by virtue of its journalist "scoop." The right is asserted as an absolute. Of course, the First Amendment right itself is not an absolute, as Justice Holmes so long ago pointed out in his aphorism concerning the right to shout of fire in a

crowded theater. There are other exceptions, some of which Chief Justice Hughes mentioned by way of example in *Near v. Minnesota.* There are no doubt other exceptions no one has had occasion to describe or discuss. Conceivably such exceptions may be lurking in these cases and would have been flushed had they been properly considered in the trial courts, free from unwarranted deadlines and frenetic pressures. A great issue of this kind should be tried in a judicial atmosphere conducive to thoughtful, reflective deliberation, especially when haste, in terms of hours, is unwarranted in light of the long period the Times, by its own choice, deferred publication.

It is not disputed that the Times has had unauthorized possession of the documents for three to four months, during which it has had its expert analysts studying them, presumably digesting them and preparing the material for publication. During all of this time, the Times, presumably in its capacity as trustee of the public's "right to know," has held up publication for purposes it considered proper and thus public knowledge was delayed. No doubt this was for a good reason; the analysis of 7,000 pages of complex material drawn from a vastly greater volume of material would inevitably take time and the writing of good news stories takes time. But why should the United States Government, from whom this information was illegally acquired by someone, along with all the counsel, trial judges, and appellate judges be placed under needless pressure? After these months of deferral, the alleged right-to-know has somehow and suddenly become a right that must be vindicated instanter.

Would it have been unreasonable, since the newspaper could anticipate the government's objections to release of secret material, to give the government an opportunity to review the entire collection and determine whether agreement could be reached on publication? Stolen or not, if security was not in fact jeopardized, much of the material could no doubt have been declassified, since it spans a period ending in 1968. With such an approach—one that great newspapers have in the past practiced and stated editorially to be the duty of an honorable press—the newspapers and government might well have narrowed the area of disagreement as to what was and was not publishable, leaving the remainder to be resolved in orderly litigation if necessary. To me it is hardly believable that a newspaper long regarded as a great institution in American life would fail to perform one of the basic and simple duties of every citizen with respect to the discovery or possession of stolen property or secret government documents. That duty, I had thought—perhaps naively—was to report forthwith, to responsible public officers. This duty rests on taxi drivers, Justices and the New York Times. The course followed by the Times whether so calculated or not, removed any possibility of orderly litigation of the issues. If the action of the judges up to now has been correct, that result is sheer happenstance.

Our grant of the writ before final judgment in the *Times* case aborted the trial in the District Court before it had made a complete record pursuant to the mandate of the Court of Appeals, Second Circuit.

The consequence of all this melancholy series of events is that we literally do not know what we are acting on. I agree with Justice Harlan and Justice Blackmun but I am not prepared to reach the merits.

I would affirm the Court of Appeals for the Second Circuit and allow the district court to complete the trial aborted by our grant of certiorari meanwhile preserving the *status quo* in the *Post* case. I would direct that the district court on remand give priority to the *Times* case to the exclusion of all other business of that court but I would not set arbitrary deadlines.

I should add that I am in general agreement with much of what Justice White has expressed with respect to penal sanctions concerning communication or retention of documents or information relating to the national defense.

We all crave speedier judicial processes but when judges are pressured as in these cases the result is a parody of the judicial process.

Justice HARLAN, with whom the Chief Justice and Justice BLACKMUN join, dissenting.

With all respect, I consider that the Court has been almost irresponsibly feverish in dealing with these cases.

In order to decide the merits of these cases properly, some or all of the following questions should have been faced:

1. Whether the attorney general is authorized to bring these suits in the name of the United States. This

question involves as well the construction and validity of a singularly opaque statute—the Espionage Act, 18 U.S.C.A. § 793(e).

2. Whether the First Amendment permits the federal courts to enjoin publication of stories which would present a serious threat to national security. See *Near v. Minnesota,* 283 U.S. 697, 716 (1931) (dictum).

3. Whether the threat to publish highly secret documents is of itself a sufficient implication of national security to justify an injunction on the theory that regardless of the contents of the documents harm enough results simply from the demonstration of such a breach of secrecy.

4. Whether the unauthorized disclosure of any of these particular documents would seriously impair the national security.

5. What weight should be given to the opinion of high officers in the executive branch of the government with respect to questions 3 and 4.

6. Whether the newspapers are entitled to retain and use the documents notwithstanding the seemingly uncontested facts that the documents, or the originals of which they are duplicates, were purloined from the government's possession and that the newspapers received them with knowledge that they had been feloniously acquired.

7. Whether the threatened harm to the national security or the government's possessory interest in the documents justifies the issuance of an injunction against publication in light of—
   a. The strong First Amendment policy against prior restraints on publication;
   b. The doctrine against enjoining conduct in violation of criminal statutes; and
   c. The extent to which the materials at issue have apparently already been otherwise disseminated.

These are difficult questions of fact, of law, and of judgment; the potential consequences of erroneous decision are enormous. The time which has been available to us, to the lower courts, and to the parties has been wholly inadequate for giving these cases the kind of consideration they deserve. It is a reflection on the stability of the judicial process that these great issues—as important as any that have arisen during my time on the Court—should have been decided under the pressures engendered by the torrent of publicity that has attended these litigations from their inception.

Forced as I am to reach the merits of these cases, I dissent from the opinion and judgments of the Court. Within the severe limitations imposed by the time constraints under which I have been required to operate, I can only state my reasons in telescoped form.

It is plain to me that the scope of the judicial function in passing upon the activities of the executive branch of the government in the field of foreign affairs is very narrowly restricted. This view is, I think, dictated by the concept of separation of powers upon which our constitutional system rests.

The power to evaluate the "pernicious influence" of premature disclosure is not, however, lodged in the executive alone. I agree that, in performance of its duty to protect the values of the First Amendment against political pressures, the judiciary must review the initial executive determination to the point of satisfying itself that the subject matter of the dispute does lie within the proper compass of the president's foreign relations power. Constitutional considerations forbid "a complete abandonment of judicial control." Cf. *United States v. Reynolds,* 345 U.S. 1, 8 (1953). Moreover, the judiciary may properly insist that the determination that disclosure of the subject matter would irreparably impair the national security be made by the head of the executive department concerned—here the secretary of state or the secretary of defense—after actual personal consideration by that officer.

But in my judgment the judiciary may not properly go beyond these two inquiries and redetermine for itself the probable impact of disclosure on the national security.

Even if there is some room for the judiciary to override the executive determination, it is plain that the scope of review must be exceedingly narrow. I can see no indication in the opinions of either the district court or the court of appeals in the *Post* litigation that the conclusions of the executive were given even the deference owing to an administrative agency, much less that owing to a coequal branch of the government operating within the field of its constitutional prerogative.

Accordingly, I would vacate the judgment of the Court of Appeals for the District of Columbia Circuit on this ground and remand the case for further proceedings in the district court. Before the commencement of such further proceedings, due opportunity should be afforded the government for procuring from the secretary of state or the secretary of defense or both an expression of their views on the issue of national security. The

ensuing review by the district court should be in accordance with the views expressed in this opinion. And for the reasons stated above I would affirm the judgment of the Court of Appeals for the Second Circuit.

Pending further hearings in each case conducted under the appropriate ground rules, I would continue the restraints on publication. I cannot believe that the doctrine prohibiting prior restraints reaches to the point of preventing courts from maintaining the *status quo* long enough to act responsibly in matters of such national importance as those involved here.

Justice BLACKMUN, dissenting.

I join Justice Harlan in his dissent. I also am in substantial accord with much that Justice White says, by way of admonition, in the latter part of his opinion.

At this point the focus is on *only* the comparatively few documents specified by the government as critical. So far as the other material—vast in amount—is concerned, let it be published and published forthwith if the newspapers, once the strain is gone and the sensationalism is eased, still feel the urge so to do.

But we are concerned here with the few documents specified from the 47 volumes.

The New York Times clandestinely devoted a period of three months examining the 47 volumes that came into its unauthorized possession. Yet that newspaper stood before us at oral argument and professed criticism of the government for not lodging its protest earlier than by a Monday telegram following the initial Sunday publication.

The District of Columbia case is much the same.

Two federal district courts, two United States courts of appeals, and this Court—within a period of less than three weeks from inception until today—have been pressed into hurried decision of profound constitutional issues on inadequately developed and largely assumed facts without the careful deliberation that hopefully, should characterize the American judicial process.

The First Amendment, after all, is only one part of an entire Constitution. Article II of the great document vests in the executive branch primary power over the conduct of foreign affairs and places in that branch the responsibility for the Nation's safety. Each provision of the Constitution is important, and I cannot subscribe to a doctrine of unlimited absolutism for the First Amendment at the cost of downgrading other provisions. First Amendment absolutism has never commanded a majority of this Court. See, for example, *Near v. Minnesota,* 283 U.S. 697, 708 (1931), and *Schenck v. United States,* 249 U.S. 47, 52 (1919). What is needed here is a weighing, upon properly developed standards, of the broad right of the press to print and of the very narrow right of the Government to prevent. Such standards are not yet developed. The parties here are in disagreement as to what those standards should be. But even the newspapers conceded that there are situations where restraint is in order and is constitutional.

It may well be that if these cases were allowed to develop as they should be developed, and to be tried as lawyers should try them and as courts should hear them, free of pressure and panic and sensationalism, other light would be shed on the situation and contrary considerations, for me, might prevail. But that is not the present posture of the litigation.

The Court, however, decides the cases today the other way. I therefore add one final comment.

I strongly urge, and sincerely hope, that these two newspapers will be fully aware of their ultimate responsibilities to the United States of America. I hope that damage already has not been done. If, however, damage has been done, and if, with the Court's action today, these newspapers proceed to publish the critical documents and there results therefrom "the death of soldiers, the destruction of alliances, the greatly increased difficulty of negotiation with our enemies, the inability of our diplomats to negotiate," to which list I might add the factors of prolongation of the war and of further delay in the freeing of United States prisoners, then the Nation's people will know where the responsibility for these sad consequences rests.

COMMENT

The doctrine urged by the government was that the president has the right to enjoin publication of a news story when the context of the story threatens "grave and irreparable" injury to the public interest. Justice Byron White denied both the existence and the validity of this doctrine at least in the absence of legislation authorizing the courts to grant injunctions in such circumstances.

Freedom of the press can be viewed as providing two modes of protection. One is freedom from prior restraint. The second is freedom from subsequent punishment. Criminal prosecution of Sulzberger or Graham, publishers of the *New York Times* and the *Washington Post,* respectively, *after* publication of the Pentagon Papers would be an example of subsequent punishment. Apparently, Justice White was of the opinion that the "extraordinary protection" granted the press by the First Amendment against prior restraints is to be distinguished from the protection afforded the press by the First Amendment in the case of subsequent punishments.

If the publishers of newspapers are free from prior restraint *prior* to publication but know that *after* publication they may go to jail, doesn't this effectively restrain publication in the first place? The lesser protection against subsequent punishment itself may act as a prior restraint. In effect, the lesser freedom from subsequent punishment forces publishers and journalists to become martyrs when they want to publish information the government desires to suppress.

For Justice White, as for Justice Potter Stewart, the case for criminal convictions against those publishing the Pentagon Papers was much stronger than the case for preventing by injunction the publication of the papers: Why? Apparently in White's view, Congress had authorized criminal prosecutions, but it had not authorized the "injunctive remedy against threatened publication."

Congress had not by statute authorized the injunctions against the press to prevent publication of material posing a danger to the security interests of the nation, even though it had been asked to do so in two world wars. This single fact was determinative for Justice Thurgood Marshall, as it had been for Justices White and Stewart. The issue, said Justice Marshall, was whether the Court or the Congress should make law. But the Supreme Court has not hesitated to make law before.

Perhaps more squarely than any of the other opinions, Chief Justice Warren Burger's dissent raises the issue of accountability: Who should make the ultimate decisions about how far the reach of a free press can extend and to what extent should the demands of government for confidentiality in its dealings be honored?

Describing the public right to know as a derivative First Amendment claim, Burger protested the *Times*'s apparent position that it was the absolute trustee of the public right to know. He argued that the First Amendment itself was not an absolute, much less any radiations the amendment might throw off such as the public's right to know.

The Chief Justice said that the government should have been given an opportunity to review the papers in the possession of the *Times* in the hope that agreement about publication could have been reached. On the other hand, the fact that the papers were stolen was in Burger's view no bar to declassification of some of them.

Burger thought it was anomalous that the *Times* would not allow the government to examine the Pentagon Papers in the newspaper's possession for fear this might jeopardize its sources. Yet, said Burger, the *Times* denied the government the right to keep the papers secret. But is the government really interested in protecting sources in the same way the *New York Times* was interested in protecting its sources? Certainly, a respectable body of opinion in the country believed that the government was anxious to protect the identities of participants in decisions on the Vietnam involvement as well as the nature of some of the decisions themselves. The *Times*, however, was anxious to protect the sources who made it possible to learn the identities of participants in vital national decisions. In other words, the interest of the *Times* in protecting its sources was procedural in nature. From whom the newspapers receive information is, informationally speaking, much less significant than the information obtained. Secrecy over such sources is designed to protect the *future* of the information flow. The government, on the other hand, was interested in protecting confidentiality to shield *prior* decisions of the highest substantive character. As a First Amendment matter, doesn't this distinction support the *Times* and not the government?

Chief Justice Burger was truly astonished that the *Times* did not report to the government that papers stolen from the government were in its possession. But the responsibilities to government in this regard were surely overshadowed in the *Times*'s judgment by its obligations to the information process, a duty that it believed had

First Amendment significance. In the last analysis, the question presented was a choice between a newspaper's determination of the legitimate demands of the public's right to know and the executive's conception of what must remain secret. Which determination should prevail?

A majority of the Court appeared to agree with Justice Brennan's observation that the basic error in the entire proceeding was Judge Gurfein's issuance of the temporary restraining order against the *New York Times*. Why then were there so many opinions in the case? In an interview, Chief Justice Burger answered this question by saying that it was decided that if each justice wrote his own opinion, it would be easier to get an expedited decision of the case.

Justice Hugo Black emphasized the unprecedented character of the judicial restraint on the press. The Pentagon Papers case was the first time an American newspaper had been restrained by a court order from publishing articles and documents the content of which could only be surmised by the government and whose damaging properties therefore could only be assumed. Viewed from that perspective, the 6–3 Supreme Court determination that the issuance of a restraining order in such circumstances was unconstitutional was a victory for freedom of information and freedom of the press. In this regard, the victory was more than an abstract vindication of constitutional theory. The decision unquestionably would deprive the whole government classification program of its legitimacy and its mystery, developments that are in the long-term interest of opening up the information process.

The Freedom of Information Act will be discussed later in Chapter 7, but one might consider how the Freedom of Information Act could have been used to declassify the Pentagon Papers.

The *Times* agonized for three months over whether to publish the Pentagon Papers. It chose to publish and thereby invited a bitter conflict with the government. Why? Perhaps the *Times* was still feeling the burn it got when it "cooperated" with the administration prior to the Bay of Pigs fiasco and was determined never to get caught in that situation again. Five years after the abortive invasion, it was disclosed that the *New York Times* had prior knowledge of the operation but had declined to publish it, at the request of President John F. Kennedy, because of national security considerations. Clifton Daniel, then managing editor of the paper, combined this disclosure with his conclusion that the Bay of Pigs operation "might well have been canceled, and the country would have been saved enormous embarrassment, if the *New York Times* and other newspapers had been more diligent in the performance of their duty."

Finally, there is a minor but important theme in the whole Pentagon Papers case—the issue of whether government ought to be able to imprison history.

In the bizarre *Progressive* case, the federal government sought to prevent *The Progressive* magazine from publishing an article on how to make a hydrogen bomb. The article was based on material that was publicly available. At first, the federal district court granted the government's request for a temporary injunction, restraining publication of the article by *The Progressive* on the ground that the article fell "within the narrow area recognized by the court in *Near v. Minnesota* in which a prior restraint on publication is appropriate." Which *Near* exception was the court relying on? The federal district court also cited Justice Stewart's opinion in the Pentagon Papers case as support for its view that a temporary injunction should be issued. The Atomic Energy Act contained a provision authorizing the issuance of injunctive relief to prevent disclosure of particular types of information. Assuming that that provision applied to *The Progressive* article, would the existence of such a statutory provision distinguish *The Progressive* case from the Pentagon Papers case? Arguably, it would, because the fact that there was no statutory basis for granting injunctive relief in the Pentagon Papers case was relied on by a number of justices as ground for not granting relief for the government.

Assuming that the statutory provision did apply to the article in *The Progressive* case, would the statutory provision be valid under the First Amendment? This is a matter of speculation because other newspapers began to publish material similar to that contained in *The Progressive* article, and the government decided not to go forward in its effort to secure permanent injunctive relief concerning *The Progressive* article. *See United States v. Progressive, Inc.,* 467 F. Supp. 990 (W.D. Wis.), *appeal dismissed* 610 F.2d 819 (7th Cir. 1979).

Progressive editor Erwin Knoll is on record as saying that the greatest moral error of his life was *not* to have published the original article. Disobey a court injunction, Columbia University law professor Vincent Blasi argued in rebuttal, and you escalate the totalitarian dynamic. The government, as has been noted, based its arguments primarily on provisions of the Atomic Energy Act prohibiting communication, transmission, and disclosure of certain categories of information that, the government contended, were either "classified at birth" or of a technical nature not protected by the First Amendment.

Judge Warren in his opinion for the federal district court saw the issue as one between freedom of speech and press and the freedom to live. If our right to live is extinguished, he said, the right to publish becomes moot. His test would have been that of Justices White and Stewart in their Pentagon Papers opinions—"immediate, direct, irreparable harm to the interests of the United States . . . to our nation and its people."

With the government's abandonment of the case, the appellate courts lost another opportunity to face the ultimate and still unresolved question of what is to be the constitutional relationship between prior restraint and national security. In answering that question, the courts will eventually have to define both prior restraint and national security, two complex concepts in precarious balance.

Nebraska Press and the Doctrine of Prior Restraint

A major case involving the issue of the constitutional validity of prior restraints against the press is the so-called gag order case, *Nebraska Press Ass'n v. Stuart,* p. 386. Although the case is discussed primarily in the free press–fair trial materials, it has authoritative significance on the present status of prior restraints against the press.

The decision of the Court in *Nebraska Press Ass'n* stretched the thesis advanced in earlier cases that there is a presumption against prior restraints and that the state must meet a heavy burden before such a restraint can issue. The *Nebraska Press* case reached the same conclusion as had its predecessors—*Near* and the Pentagon Papers case. In each case, the Supreme Court refused to issue a prior restraint against the press.

Yet, although the press was victorious on each occasion, the Court appeared determined to keep alive the possibility that in some undescribed circumstances a prior restraint against the press might be permissible. In short, although the Court has erected the strongest possible obstacles to the issuance of a prior restraint in the context of a "gag order" case, it still appeared resolved to reject "the proposition that a prior restraint can never be employed." Justice White, in a concurring opinion, suggested that if the consequence of the Court's *Nebraska Press* decision is to refuse to issue "gag orders" against the press in case after case on the ground that they are invalid prior restraints, then "we should at some point announce a more general rule and avoid the interminable litigation that our failure to do so would necessarily entail."

Justice Brennan's passionate distaste for prior restraints against the press is made vividly clear in his concurring opinion in *Nebraska Press*. He comments proudly on "the rarity of prior restraint cases of any type in this Court's jurisprudence." Analyzing the prior case law, he finds only one occasion where the exception to the presumption against prior restraints against the press might be deemed sufficient to authorize suppression before publication, that is, the so-called military security exception in *Near*. This would be the situation where a newspaper plans to publish the sailing date of a troop ship in war or its modern counterpart. The "overriding countervailing" interests that justify such suppression in wartime were, in his view, hardly comparable to the case for a prior restraint against the press in the interests of a fair trial.

Perhaps the difference between Chief Justice Burger and Justice Brennan is that the Burger opinion kept open the possibility, no matter how remote, that some "gag orders" against the press were yet conceivable while the Brennan view would remove that possibility. Brennan would adhere to the military security exception, despite the general freedom he would accord the press from prior restraint,

but would not grant a new exception in the interest of fair trial. Yet the latter is a constitutional value, enshrined in the Sixth Amendment, while secrecy in wartime, although it may be a societal value of great importance, is not mentioned in the Constitution.

Alexander v. United States
509 U.S. 544, 113 S. CT. 2766, 125 L. ED. 2D 441 (1993).

[EDITORIAL NOTE: Alexander *upheld a forfeiture order against a business dealing in sexually explicit materials despite the contention that such an order constituted an impermissible prior restraint. The owner of a number of stores and theaters dealing in sexually explicit materials was convicted of violating federal obscenity laws. These convictions were based on jury findings that four magazines and three videotapes sold at one of the defendant's stores were obscene. The obscenity convictions served as the basis for convictions under the federal Racketeer Influenced and Corrupt Organizations Act (RICO). The RICO statute provides for forfeiture of assets related to racketeering. Consequently, on top of a prison sentence and a fine, the defendant was ordered to forfeit his businesses as well as almost $9 million acquired through racketeering activity.*
The forfeiture order was challenged on the ground that it "operates as a prior restraint because it prohibits future presumptively protected expression in retaliation for prior unprotected speech." The RICO forfeiture order was challenged as not being any different than the injunction found to be an invalid prior restraint in Near v. Minnesota.] See Chapter 2, p. 40.

Chief Justice REHNQUIST delivered the opinion of the Court.

By lumping the forfeiture imposed in this case after a full criminal trial with an injunction enjoining future speech, [the defendant] stretches the term "prior restraint" well beyond the limits established by our cases. To accept [this] argument would virtually obliterate the distinction between prior restraints and subsequent punishments.

[Unlike *Near*] [T]he RICO forfeiture order in this case does not *forbid* [the defendant] from engaging in any expressive activities in the future, nor does it require him to obtain prior approval for any expressive activities. It only deprives him of specific assets that were found to be related to his previous racketeering violations.

Because we have interpreted the First Amendment as providing greater protection from prior restraint than from subsequent punishments, it is important for us to delineate with some precision the defining characteristics of a prior restraint. To hold that the forfeiture order in this case constituted a prior restraint would have the exact opposite effect: it would blur the line separating prior restraints from subsequent punishments to such a degree that it would be impossible to determine with any certainty whether a particular measure is a prior restraint or not.

Justice KENNEDY, joined by Justices BLACK-MUN and STEVENS, dissented from the Court's conclusion that the forfeiture did not constitute a prior restraint:

The government's stated purpose under RICO, to destroy or incapacitate the offending enterprise, bears a striking resemblance to the motivation for the state nuisance statute the Court struck down as an impermissible prior restraint in *Near*. The purpose of the state statute in *Near* was not "punishment, in the ordinary sense, but suppression of the offending newspaper or periodical."

What is happening here is simple: Books and films are condemned and destroyed not for their own content but for the content of their owner's prior speech. Our law does not permit the government to burden future speech for this sort of taint. Though perhaps not in the form of a classic prior restraint, the application of the forfeiture statute here bears its censorial cast.

COMMENT

Alexander demonstrates that not all government regulation that has the effect of preventing future expression will be deemed a prior restraint. Indeed, *Madsen v. Women's Health Center*, 114 S. Ct. 2516 (1994), refused to view a state court *civil* injunction as a prior restraint. What is the point of making a distinction between prior restraints and subsequent punishments? Chief Justice William Rehnquist says that the rationale for the distinction is that our First Amendment law gives more protection to freedom from prior restraint than to freedom from subsequent punishment. But why is this so? Isn't it because from a free speech point of view the most important objective is to get the speech into the public arena? Should the forfeiture in *Alexander* have been treated as a prior restraint?

In the section that follows, we deal with subsequent punishments. The expressive activity has taken place, but the question is whether sanctions can attach to such activity consistent with the First Amendment.

CIVIL AND CRIMINAL SANCTIONS AGAINST EXPRESSIVE ACTIVITY

Restraints on Circulation and Distribution of the Mail

In *United States, ex. rel., Milwaukee Social Democratic Publishing Co. v. Burleson*, reported below, the Supreme Court, per Justice Clarke, upheld the provision of the Espionage Act that conferred power upon the Postmaster General to exclude from the mail any items that under Title 12 of the Espionage Act were considered "nonmailable." The *Milwaukee Leader*'s second-class mail privilege was revoked under the Act. The paper launched an unsuccessful First Amendment challenge.

United States, ex rel., Milwaukee Social Democratic Publishing Co. v. Burleson
255 U.S. 407, 41 S. CT. 352, 65 L. ED. 704 (1921).

Justice CLARKE delivered the opinion of the Court.

Without further discussion of the articles, we cannot doubt that they conveyed to readers of them false reports and false statements, with intent to promote the success of the enemies of the United States, and that they constituted a willful attempt to cause disloyalty and refusal of duty in the military and naval forces, and to obstruct the recruiting and enlistment service of the United States, in violation of the Espionage Act [*Schenck v. United States*], and that therefore their publication brought the paper containing them within the express terms of title 12 of that law, declaring that such a publication shall be "nonmailable" and "shall not be conveyed in the mails or delivered from any post office or by any letter carrier."

The order of the Postmaster General not only finds reasonable support in this record, but is amply justified by it.

Government is a practical institution, adapted to the practical conduct of public affairs. It would not be possible for the United States to maintain a reader in every newspaper office of the country, to approve in advance each issue before it should be allowed to enter the mails, and when, for more than five months, a paper had contained, almost daily, articles which, under the express terms of the statute, rendered it "nonmailable," it was reasonable to conclude that it would continue its disloyal publications, and it was therefore clearly within the power given to the Postmaster General by R.S. § 396, "to execute all laws relating to the postal service," to enter, as was done in this case, an order suspending the privilege until a proper application and showing should be made for its renewal. It was open to the relator to mend its ways, to publish a paper conforming to the law, and then to apply anew for the second-class mailing privilege. This it did not do, but for reasons not difficult to imagine, it preferred this futile litigation, undertaken upon the theory that a government competent to wage war against its foreign enemies was powerless against its insidious foes at home. Whatever injury the relator suffered was the result of its own choice and the judgment of the Court of Appeals is affirmed.

Justice BRANDEIS dissenting.

This case arose during the World War; but it presents no legal question peculiar to war. It is important, because what we decide may determine in large measure whether in times of peace our press shall be free.

In discussing whether Congress conferred upon the Postmaster General the authority which he undertook to exercise in this case, I shall consider, first, whether he would have had the power to exclude the paper altogether from all future mail service on the ground alleged; and, second, whether he had power to deny the publisher the second-class rate.

Power to exclude from the mails has never been conferred in terms upon the Postmaster General. If such power were possessed by the Postmaster General he would, in view of the practical finality of his decisions, become the universal censor of publications. For a denial of the use of the mail would be for most of them, tantamount to a denial of the right of circulation.

The Postmaster General does not claim here the power to issue an order directly denying a newspaper all mail service for the future. Indeed, he asserts that the mail is still open to the *Milwaukee Leader* upon payment of first, third, or fourth class rates. He contends, however, that in regard to second-class rates special provisions of law apply under which he may deny that particular rate at his discretion. This contention will now be considered.

It is insisted that a citizen uses the mail at second-class rates, not as of right, but by virtue of a privilege or permission, the granting of which rests in the discretion of the Postmaster General. The certificate evidencing such freedom is spoken of as a permit. But, in fact, the right to the lawful postal rates is a right independent of the discretion of the Postmaster General. The right and conditions of its existence are defined and rest wholly upon mandatory legislation of Congress. It is the duty of the Postmaster General to determine whether the conditions for any rate exist. And it is not a function which either involves or permits the exercise of discretionary power.

It clearly appears that there was no express grant of power to the Postmaster General to deny second-class mail rates to future issues of a newspaper because in his opinion it had systematically violated the Espionage Act in the past, and it seems equally clear that there is no basis for the contention that such power is to be implied.

Hannegan v. Esquire, Inc.

327 U.S. 146, 66 S. CT. 456, 90 L. ED. 586 (1946).

[EDITORIAL NOTE: *In* Hannegan v. Esquire, Inc., *Justice William O. Douglas allied himself with the ideas expressed in Brandeis's dissent in* Burleson. *Congress could not have meant to grant the power to the Postmaster General to exclude publications from the mails on the basis of his judgment as to the quality of the publication. Under the statute, 35 Stat. 1129, 18 U.S.C.A. § 334, a publication, to be admitted to the second-class mail, must:*

> [B]e originated and published for the dissemination of information of a public character, or devoted to literature, the sciences, arts, or some special industry, and having a legitimate list of subscribers. Nothing herein contained shall be so construed as to admit to the second class rate regular publications designed primarily for advertising purposes, or for free circulation, or for circulation at nominal rates.

The Postmaster General cited Esquire Magazine with an order to show cause why its publication should not be excluded from the mail as not fulfilling the above-stated conditions. The Postmaster General also stated:

A publication to enjoy these unique mail privileges and special preferences is bound to do more than refrain from disseminating material which is obscene or bordering on the obscene. It is under a positive duty to contribute to the public good and the public welfare.]

Justice DOUGLAS delivered the opinion of the Court.

The issues of Esquire Magazine under attack are those for January to November inclusive of 1943. The material complained of embraces in bulk only a small percentage of those issues. But the objectionable items, though a small percentage of the total bulk, were regular recurrent features which gave the magazine its dominant tone or characteristic. These include jokes, cartoons, pictures, articles, and poems. They were said to reflect the smoking-room type of humor, featuring, in the main, sex.

An examination of the items makes plain, we think, that the controversy is not whether the magazine publishes "information of a public character" or is devoted to "literature" or to the "arts." It is whether the contents are "good" or "bad." To uphold the order of revocation would, therefore, grant the Postmaster General a power of censorship. Such a power is so abhorrent to our traditions that a purpose to grant it should not be easily inferred.

The second-class privilege is a form of subsidy. From the beginning, Congress has allowed special rates to certain classes of publications.

The policy of Congress has been clear. It has been to encourage the distribution of periodicals which disseminated "information of a public character" or which were devoted to "literature, the sciences, arts, or some special industry," because it was thought that those publications as a class contributed to the public good. [These standards] have been criticized, but not on the ground that they provide for censorship.

We may assume that Congress has a broad power of classification and need not open second-class mail to publications of all types. The categories of publications entitled to that classification have indeed varied through the years. And the Court held in *Ex parte Jackson,* 96 U.S. 727, that Congress could constitutionally make it a crime to send fraudulent or obscene material through the mails. But grave constitutional questions are immediately raised once it is said that the use of the mails is a privilege which may be extended or withheld on any grounds whatso-

ever. See the dissents of Justice Brandeis and Justice Holmes in *United States ex rel. Milwaukee Social Democratic Publishing Co. v. Burleson.* Under that view the second-class rate could be granted on condition that certain economic or political ideas not be disseminated. The [statute] would have to be far more explicit for us to assume that Congress made such a radical departure from our traditions and undertook to clothe the Postmaster General with the power to supervise the tastes of the reading public of the country.

Lamont v. Postmaster General
381 U.S. 301, 85 S. CT. 1493, 14 L. ED. 2D 398 (1965).

Justice DOUGLAS delivered the opinion of the Court.

Here the Congress—expressly restrained by the First Amendment from "abridging" freedom of speech and of press—is the actor. The act sets administrative officials astride the flow of mail to inspect it, appraise it, write the addressee about it, and await a response before dispatching the mail. We do not have here, any more than we had in *Hannegan v. Esquire, Inc.,* 327 U.S. 146, any question concerning the extent to which Congress may classify the mail and fix the charges for its carriage. We rest on the narrow ground that the addressee in order to receive his mail must request in writing that it be delivered. This amounts in our judgment to an unconstitutional abridgment of the addressee's First Amendment rights. The addressee carries an affirmative obligation which we do not think the Government may impose on him. This requirement is almost certain to have a deterrent effect, especially as respects those who have sensitive positions. Their livelihood may be dependent on a security clearance. Public officials, like schoolteachers who have no tenure, might think they would invite disaster if they read what the federal government says contains the seeds of treason. Apart from them, any addressee is likely to feel some inhibition in sending for literature which federal officials have condemned as "communist political propaganda." The regime of this act is at war with the "uninhibited, robust, and wide-open" debate and discussion that are contemplated by the First Amendment. *New York Times Co. v. Sullivan,* 376 U.S. 254, 270.

COMMENT

Burleson arose in a wartime context. During wartime, First Amendment liberties, like other constitutionally protected civil liberties, have sometimes been subordinated to other governmental interests. Compare *Schenck v. United States*, p. 13. *Hannegan* does not reverse *Burleson*. The Court was interpreting different statutes in both cases. Yet, the wartime context aside, the cases are still inconsistent. Why?

The *Lamont* case was a more recent example of an attempt to use the mails for censorship purposes. In *Lamont,* the Supreme Court unanimously invalidated a federal statute that permitted the mail delivery of "communist political propaganda" that originated in a foreign country only if the addressee specifically requested such delivery.

Regulation of Pamphleteering, Solicitation, Parades, and Demonstrations

Alma Lovell, a Jehovah's Witness, was arrested in the town of Griffin, Georgia, for violating a city ordinance that banned any pamphleteering or leafleting without prior written permission from the Griffin city manager. She never sought permission from the manager. Lovell appealed her conviction under this ordinance and urged that it violated the First Amendment.

In a unanimous decision in *Lovell v. Griffin,* 303 U.S. 444 (1938), delivered by Chief Justice Charles Evans Hughes, the U.S. Supreme Court found the Griffin ordinance invalid on its face as a violation of freedom of speech and freedom of the press.

The chief justice pointed out that the ordinance "prohibits the distribution of literature of any kind, at any time, at any place, and in any manner without a permit from the city manager." The ordinance made no distinctions but covered all "literature" in all circumstances. This First Amendment infirmity is called overbreadth.

If the town was concerned about a particular problem, such as litter or scurrilous libels, it ought to have drafted the ordinance to meet that problem rather than embracing all forms of pamphleteering. Secondly, the ordinance as drafted created a one-man censorship board in the person of the city manager with no guidelines to direct his decisions prohibiting or permitting circulation of a particular leaflet. The Griffin city

manager had total unquestioned discretion to regulate the flow of printed communication in the town. Under the doctrine of *Lovell v. Griffin,* the officials who administer a permit system must have their authority specified and articulated in the legislation creating the system.

In *dictum* in *Lovell v. Griffin,* Chief Justice Hughes noted that the First Amendment is not confined to protection of newspapers and magazines, but includes pamphlets and leaflets as well. "The press," he wrote, "in its historic connotation comprehends every sort of publication which affords a vehicle of information and opinion." Furthermore, freedom to distribute and circulate press materials is as protected under the First Amendment as freedom to publish in the first place.

In *Lovell,* the Court spoke in strong terms of the threat to a free press posed by a licensing scheme. If a statute or regulation is narrowly drawn and contains procedural safeguards (unlike the pamphleteering ordinance in *Lovell*), would it be upheld despite overtones of "licensing?" Would noncompliance with the statute then be justified if someone had doubts about the validity of the statute?

Because the ordinance in *Lovell* was found "void on its face," the Court held that it was not necessary for Alma Lovell "to seek a permit under it." The Court held that she was "entitled to contest its validity in answer to the charge against her."

Isn't it the usual view that a court, rather than an individual, should decide the constitutionality of legislation? Why then didn't the Court insist that Alma Lovell first apply for a permit and show that she had been denied it before determining that the ordinance was invalid?

Cantwell v. Connecticut, 310 U.S. 296 (1940), was yet another case involving the imposition of state criminal penalties on Jehovah's Witnesses. The Cantwells, a father and two sons, were arrested in New Haven, Connecticut, for conducting door-to-door religious solicitation in a predominantly Catholic neighborhood of the city. They were charged with violating a Connecticut statute that provided in part that: "No person shall solicit money . . . for any alleged religious . . . cause . . . unless . . . approved by the [county] secretary of . . . public welfare." Any person seeking to solicit for a religious cause was required under the statute to file an application with the welfare secretary, who was empowered to decide whether the cause was "a bona fide object of charity" and whether it conformed to "reasonable standards of efficiency and integrity." The penalty for violating the statute was a $100 fine or thirty days' imprisonment or both.

The Cantwells' convictions were affirmed by the state courts of Connecticut. But the U.S. Supreme Court unanimously, per Justice Owen Roberts, declared the statute unconstitutional as applied to the Cantwells and other Jehovah's Witnesses.

The Cantwells argued that the Connecticut state statute was not regulatory but prohibitory, because it allowed a state official to ban religious solicitation from the streets of Connecticut entirely. Once a certificate of approval was issued by the state welfare secretary, solicitation could proceed without any restriction at all under the Connecticut statute. And once a certificate was denied, solicitation was banned.

The Supreme Court ruled that the Connecticut statute in effect established a prior restraint on First Amendment freedoms that was not alleviated by the availability of judicial review after the fact.

The Supreme Court also pointed out that if the state wished to protect its citizens against door-to-door solicitation for fraudulent "religious" or "charity" causes, it had the constitutional power to enact a regulation aimed at that problem. The present law, however, was not such a statute. The Court also noted that it is within the police power of the state to set regulatory limits on religious solicitation (as on other sorts of solicitation), such as the time of day or the right of a householder to terminate the solicitation by demanding that the visitor remove himself from the premises. The state may not, however, force people to submit to licensing of religious speech.

On the breach of the peace conviction, the Supreme Court held that the broad sweep of the common law offense was an infringement of First Amendment rights.

The state had argued that because the Cantwells' solicitation technique had been provocative, it tended to produce violence on the part of their listeners and, therefore, was an appropriate matter for sanction under the common law offense of disturbing the peace.

In the Court's view in *Cantwell*, if the state had defined what is considered to be a clear and present danger to the state in a precisely drawn breach of the peace statute, this might have presented a sufficiently substantial interest to make it appropriate to convict the Cantwells under such a statute. But because the breach of the peace offense was an imprecise common law offense rather than an offense set forth in a tightly drawn statute, the Court set aside the breach of the peace conviction. Justice Roberts made the following observations in *Cantwell*:

> When clear and present danger of riot, disorder, interference with traffic upon the public streets, or other immediate threat to public safety, peace, or order, appears, the power of the state to prevent or punish is obvious. Equally obvious is it that a state may not unduly suppress free communication of views, religious or other, under the guise of conserving desirable conditions.

Newsrack Regulation

City of Lakewood v. Plain Dealer Publishing Co.

486 U.S. 750, 108 S. CT. 2138, 100 L. ED. 2D 771 (1988).

[EDITORIAL NOTE: *In* City of Lakewood, *the Supreme Court, per Justice Brennan, invalidated a city ordinance because it allowed the mayor too much discretion in granting or denying applications for annual permits for placement of coin-operated newspaper vending machines or newsracks on city sidewalks. The ordinance authorized the mayor to grant or deny applications for annual newsrack permits. If the application for a permit was denied, the mayor was required to state the reasons for the denial. Prior to the enactment of this ordinance, Lakewood absolutely prohibited the "private placement of any structure on public property." The Cleveland* Plain Dealer *accordingly had been denied permission to place its coin-operated newspaper vending machines on city sidewalks. The* Plain Dealer *challenged the constitutionality of the new ordinance.*

Although the district court upheld the ordinance, the Court of Appeals for the Sixth Circuit reversed and found the ordinance unconstitutional for three reasons: (1) The ordinance gave the mayor "unbounded discretion to grant or deny a permit application and to place unlimited additional terms and conditions on any permit that issues." (2) The ordinance conditioned approval of a newsrack permit on approval of the newsrack design by the city's Architectural Board of Review. Because no express standards governed newsrack design, the design approval requirement effectively gave the board unbridled discretion to deny applica-

tions. (3) Approval of a newsrack permit was also conditioned on an agreement by the newsrack owner to indemnify the city against any liability arising from the newsrack, "guaranteed by a $100,000 insurance policy to that effect." The court of appeals felt these indemnity and insurance requirements violated the First Amendment "because no similar burdens are placed on owners of the structures or public properties."

In a 4–3 decision, the Supreme Court affirmed the court of appeals decision in part and remanded. The Court held that the portions of the City of Lakewood ordinance giving the mayor discretion to deny a permit application and authorizing him to grant a permit on any terms he considered "necessary and reasonable" were unconstitutional.]

Justice BRENNAN delivered the opinion of the Court:

[W]e have previously identified two major First Amendment risks associated with unbridled licensing schemes: self-censorship by speakers in order to avoid being denied a license to speak; and the difficulty of effectively detecting, reviewing, and correcting content-based censorship "as applied" without standards by which to measure the licensor's action. It is when statutes threaten these risks to a significant degree that courts must entertain an immediate facial attack on the law. Therefore, a facial challenge lies whenever a licensing law gives a government official or agency substantial powers to discriminate based on the content or viewpoint of speech by suppressing disfavored speech or disliked speakers. This is not to say that the press or a speaker may challenge as censorship any law involving discretion to which it is subject. The law must have a close enough nexus to expression, or to conduct commonly associated with expression, to pose a real and substantial threat of the identified censorship risks.

The regulatory scheme in the present case contains two features which, at least in combination, justify the allowance of a facial challenge. First, Lakewood's ordinance requires that the Newspaper apply annually for newsrack licenses. Thus, it is the sort of system in which an individual must apply for multiple licenses over time, or periodically renew a license. When such a system is applied to speech, or to conduct commonly associated with speech, the licensor does not necessarily view the text of the words about to be spoken, but can measure their probable content or viewpoint by speech already uttered. A speaker in this position is under no illusion

regarding the effect of the "licensed" speech on the ability to continue speaking in the future.

A second feature of the licensing system at issue here is that it is directed narrowly and specifically at expression or conduct commonly associated with expression: the circulation of newspapers. Such a framework creates an agency or establishes an official charged particularly with reviewing speech, or conduct commonly associated with it, breeding an "expertise" tending to favor censorship over speech. Indeed, a law requiring the licensing of printers has historically been declared the archetypal censorship statute. Here again, without standards to bound the licensor, speakers denied a license will have no way of proving that the decision was unconstitutionally motivated, and, faced with that prospect, they will be pressured to conform their speech to the licensor's unreviewable preference.

Because of these features in the regulatory system at issue here, we think that a facial challenge is appropriate, and that standards controlling the Mayor's discretion must be required. Of course, the city may require periodic licensing, and may even have special licensing procedures for conduct commonly associated with expression; but the Constitution requires that the City establish neutral criteria to insure that the licensing decision is not based on the content or viewpoint of the speech being considered.

[**EDITORIAL NOTE:** *Justice Brennan took issue with the dissent's contention that since a city could ban newsracks altogether, it could therefore set forth conditions for the placement of newsracks.*]

The key to the dissent's analysis is its "greater-includes-the-lesser" syllogism. But that syllogism is blind to the radically different constitutional harms inherent in the "greater" and "lesser" restrictions. Presumably in the case of an ordinance that completely prohibits a particular manner of expression, the law on its face is both content and viewpoint neutral. [E]ven if the government may constitutionally impose content-neutral prohibitions on a particular manner of speech, it may not *condition* that speech on obtaining a license or permit from a government official in that official's boundless discretion.

It is apparent that the face of the ordinance itself contains no explicit limits on the mayor's discretion. Indeed, nothing in the law as written requires the mayor to do more than make the statement "it is not in the public interest" when denying a permit application. Similarly, the Mayor could grant the application, but require the newsrack to be placed in an inaccessible location without providing any explanation whatever. To allow these illusory "constraints" to constitute the standards necessary to bound a licensor's discretion renders the guarantee against censorship little more than a high-sounding ideal.

We hold these portions of the Lakewood ordinance giving the Mayor unfettered discretion to deny a permit application and unbounded authority to condition the permit on any additional terms he deems "necessary and reasonable," to be unconstitutional. Accordingly, we remand this cause to the Court of Appeals to decide whether the provisions of the ordinance we have declared unconstitutional are severable, and to take further action consistent with this opinion.

It is so ordered.

The Chief Justice and Justice Kennedy took no part in the consideration or decision of this case.

[EDITORIAL NOTE: *Justice White, joined by Justices Stevens and O'Connor, wrote a strong dissent in* City of Lakewood. *Justice White first noted that the Court did "not establish any constitutional right of newspaper publishers to place newsracks on municipal property." Nor had the Court passed on the question of the constitutionality of an outright municipal ban on newsracks.*

Justice White said that "our precedents suggest that an outright ban on newsracks on city sidewalks would be constitutional, particularly where (as is true here) ample alternate means of 24-hour distribution of newspapers exists." Justice White concluded that "cities remain free after today's decision to enact" bans on newsracks on public property. Justice White dissented from the doctrine, set forth by the majority in Lakewood, *that licensing laws that give municipal officials "substantial power to discriminate based on the content or viewpoint of speech" are unconstitutional on their face without any showing of actual censorship and without the need even to apply for a license.*]

COMMENT

For Justice White, cases such as *Lovell v. Griffin,* 303 U.S. 444 (1938) and *Cantwell v. Connecticut,* 310 U.S. 296 (1940) did not support the invalidation of the *City of Lakewood* ordinance: "Streets, sidewalks, and parks are traditional public fora; leafletting, pamphleting, and speaking in such places may be regulated, *Cox v. New Hampshire; Cantwell v. Connecticut;* but they

may not be entirely forbidden, *Lovell v. Griffin.*" The cited cases dealt with First Amendment activities that the locality could not prohibit altogether. The line of cases represented by *Lovell v. Griffin* would be applicable if a newspaper like the Cleveland *Plain Dealer* had a constitutional right to distribute its papers on newsracks on public property. But in Justice White's view—and in the Court's—there was no such right. Because the activity in question, placing newspaper vending machines on public sidewalks, could be prohibited altogether, lesser regulations such as local licensing conditioned on administrative discretion were *a fortiori* permissible.

City of Lakewood promulgated new doctrine. While facial invalidity of ordinances striking at First Amendment expression had been upheld in the past, this doctrine was now extended to reach situations where the law being challenged had a close enough nexus to expression or to conduct usually associated with expression, to pose a real and substantial risk of censorship. Because placing newsracks on publicly owned sidewalks, unlike parades and demonstrations on public property, had never been deemed First Amendment activity, Justice White and the other dissenters thought *Lovell* and its progeny should not apply.

Five years later the Court struck down yet another newsrack ordinance. In *Cincinnati v. Discovery Network, Inc.,* 507 U.S. 410 (1993), the Court, per Justice John Paul Stevens, struck down a Cincinnati ordinance banning commercial newsracks. These newsracks distributed free magazines and circulars consisting mainly of advertisements. The ban did not apply to newspaper newsracks. Cincinnati attempted to justify the discrimination on the basis of safety and aesthetics. However, the ban only affected 62 commercial newsracks, while between 1,500 and 2,000 newspaper newsracks were unaffected. Using the standard set forth in *Central Hudson* and *Fox,* the Court held that the ban violated the First Amendment by unjustifiably discriminating against commercial speech. See page 109.

Justice Stevens also held that the commercial newsrack ban could not be upheld as a valid time, place, or manner regulation because the "city's [commercial] newsrack policy was neither content-neutral nor 'narrowly tailored.'" Why does Justice Stevens say that the commercial newsrack ban was not content-neutral?

Justice Stevens also observed that the Cincinnati regulatory scheme depended on a determination by a government official. Because the distinction between a newspaper and a commercial handbill was hardly clear, "the responsibility for distinguishing between the two carries with it the potential for invidious discrimination of disfavored subjects." Consequently, the Cincinnati ordinance presented some of the same problems raised by the ordinance invalidated in *City of Lakewood.*

TAXATION OF THE PRESS AND CENSORSHIP

Grosjean v. American Press Co.
297 U.S. 233, 56 S. CT. 444, 80 L. ED. 660 (1936).

[EDITORIAL NOTE *On July 12, 1934, the Louisiana legislature enacted a law that provided in essence that any newspaper selling advertisements that had a circulation of more than 20,000 copies would be required to pay a license tax of 2 percent on its gross receipts. The law was passed at the behest of Governor Huey Long and was aimed at the New Orleans* Times-Picayune, *a New Orleans daily that had been critical of the Long regime. Nine newspaper publishers, publishing thirteen newspapers, brought suit to enjoin the enforcement of the statute.*]

Justice SUTHERLAND delivered the opinion of the Court.

The validity of the act is assailed as violating the freedom of the press in contravention of the due process clause contained in section 1 of the Fourteenth Amendment.

For more than a century prior to the adoption of the amendment—and, indeed, for many years thereafter—history discloses a persistent effort on the part of the British government to prevent or abridge the free expression of any opinion which seemed to criticize or exhibit in an unfavorable light, however truly, the agencies and operations of the government. The struggle between the proponents of measures to that end and those who asserted the right of free expression was continuous and unceasing. As early as 1644, John Milton, in an "Appeal for the Liberty of Unlicensed Printing," assailed an act of Parliament which had just been passed providing for censorship of the press previous to publication. He vigorously defended the right of every man to make public

his honest views "without previous censure"; and declared the impossibility of finding any man base enough to accept the office of censor and at the same time good enough to be allowed to perform its duties. Collett, *History of the Taxes on Knowledge,* vol. I, pp. 4–6. The act expired by its own terms in 1695. It was never renewed; and the liberty of the press thus became, as pointed out by Wickwar *(The Struggle for the Freedom of the Press,* p. 15), merely "a right or liberty to publish without a license what formerly could be published only with one." But mere exemption from previous censorship was soon recognized as too narrow a view of the liberty of the press.

In 1712, in response to a message from Queen Anne *(Hansard's Parliamentary History of England,* vol. 6, p. 1063), Parliament imposed a tax upon all newspapers and upon advertisements. Collett, vol. I, pp. 8–10. That the main purpose of these taxes was to suppress the publication of comments and criticisms objectionable to the Crown does not admit of doubt. Stewart, *Lennox and the Taxes on Knowledge,* 15 Scottish Historical Review, 322–327. There followed more than a century of resistance to, and evasion of, the taxes, and of agitation for their repeal.

Citations of similar import might be multiplied many times; but the foregoing is enough to demonstrate beyond peradventure that in the adoption of the English newspaper stamp tax and the tax on advertisements, revenue was of subordinate concern; and that the dominant and controlling aim was to prevent, or curtail the opportunity for, the acquisition of knowledge by the people in respect of their governmental affairs. It is idle to suppose that so many of the best men of England would for a century of time have waged, as they did, stubborn and often precarious warfare against these taxes if a mere matter of taxation had been involved. The aim of the struggle was not to relieve taxpayers from a burden, but to establish and preserve the right of the English people to full information in respect of the doings or misdoings of their government. Upon the correctness of this conclusion the very characterization of the exactions as "taxes on knowledge" sheds a flood of corroborative light. In the ultimate, an informed and enlightened public opinion was the thing at stake; for, as Erskine, in his great speech in defense of Paine, has said, "The liberty of opinion keeps governments themselves in due subjection to their duties." Erskine's

Speeches, High's Ed., vol. I, p. 525. See May's Constitutional History of England (7th Ed.) vol. 2, pp. 238–245.

In 1785, only four years before Congress had proposed the First Amendment, the Massachusetts Legislature, following the English example, imposed a stamp tax on all newspapers and magazines. The following year an advertisement tax was imposed. Both taxes met with such violent opposition that the former was repealed in 1786, and the latter in 1788. Duniway, *Freedom of the Press in Massachusetts,* pp. 136, 137.

The framers of the First Amendment were familiar with the English struggle, which then had continued for nearly eighty years and was destined to go on for another sixty-five years, at the end of which time it culminated in a lasting abandonment of the obnoxious taxes. The framers were likewise familiar with the then recent Massachusetts episode; and while that occurrence did much to bring about the adoption of the amendment (see *Pennsylvania and the Federal Constitution,* 1888, p. 181), the predominant influence must have come from the English experience. It is impossible to concede that by the words "freedom of the press" the framers of the amendment intended to adopt merely the narrow view then reflected by the law of England that such freedom consisted only in immunity from previous censorship; for this abuse had then permanently disappeared from English practice. It is equally impossible to believe that it was not intended to bring within the reach of these words such modes of restraint as were embodied in the two forms of taxation already described. Such belief must be rejected in the face of the then well-known purpose of the exactions and the general adverse sentiment of the colonies in respect of them. Undoubtedly, the range of a constitutional provision phrased in terms of the common law sometimes may be fixed by recourse to the applicable rules of that law.

In the light of all that has now been said, it is evident that the restricted rules of the English law in respect of the freedom of the press in force when the Constitution was adopted were never accepted by the American colonists, and that by the First Amendment it was meant to preclude the national government, and by the Fourteenth Amendment to preclude the states, from adopting any form of previous restraint upon printed publications, or their circulation, including that which had theretofore been effected by these two well-known and odious methods.

It is not intended by anything we have said to suggest that the owners of newspapers are immune from any of the ordinary forms of taxation for support of the government. But this is not an ordinary form of tax, but one single in kind, with a long history of hostile misuse against the freedom of the press.

The predominant purpose of the grant of immunity here invoked was to preserve an untrammeled press as a vital source of public information. The newspapers, magazines, and other journals of the country, it is safe to say, have shed and continue to shed, more light on the public and business affairs of the nation than any other instrumentality of publicity; and since informed public opinion is the most potent of all restraints upon misgovernment, the suppression or abridgment of the publicity afforded by a free press cannot be regarded otherwise than with grave concern. The tax here involved is bad not because it takes money from the pockets of the appellees. If that were all, a wholly different question would be presented. It is bad because, in the light of its history and of its present setting, it is seen to be a deliberate and calculated device in the guise of a tax to limit the circulation of information to which the public is entitled in virtue of the constitutional guaranties. A free press stands as one of the great interpreters between the government and the people. To allow it to be fettered is to fetter ourselves.

In view of the persistent search for new subjects of taxation, it is not without significance that, with the single exception of the Louisiana statute, so far as we can discover, no state during the one hundred fifty years of our national existence has undertaken to impose a tax like that now in question.

The form in which the tax is imposed is in itself suspicious. It is not measured or limited by the volume of advertisements. It is measured alone by the extent of the circulation of the publication in which the advertisements are carried, with the plain purpose of penalizing the publishers and curtailing the circulation of a selected group of newspapers. [Emphasis added.]

Having reached the conclusion that the act imposing the tax in question is unconstitutional under the due process of law clause because it abridges the freedom of the press, we deem it unnecessary to consider the further ground assigned, that it also constitutes a denial of the equal protection of the laws.

Decree affirmed.

COMMENT

Grosjean makes clear that stamp taxes on newspapers and taxes on advertisements were similar practices and as such abhorrent to the eighteenth-century American. *Grosjean* illustrates why a larger definition of freedom of the press than one limited merely to freedom from prior restraint was necessary if the objectives of freedom of the press, as outlined by Justice George Sutherland, were to be secured, that is, "In the ultimate, an informed and enlightened public opinion was the thing at stake." Discriminatory taxes, like licensing on the basis of content and prior restraints, were all forbidden by the constitutional guarantee of freedom of the press. *But see United States ex rel. Milwaukee Social Democratic Publishing Co. v. Burleson,* 255 U.S. 407 (1921).

Which is more destructive of the purposes of freedom of the press: a prior restraint on printed matter itself or a tax on circulation of daily newspapers? How does Sutherland deal with the state defense that newspapers are a business and, as a business, the press, like other businesses, has no constitutional immunity from taxation?

Minneapolis Star and Tribune Co. v. Minnesota Commissioner of Revenue

460 U.S. 575, 103 S. CT. 1365, 75 L. ED. 2D 295 (1983).

Justice O'CONNOR delivered the opinion of the Court.

This case presents the question of a state's power to impose a special tax on the press and, by enacting exemptions, to limit its effect to only a few newspapers.

Since 1967, Minnesota has imposed a sales tax on most sales of goods for a price in excess of a nominal sum. In general, the tax applies only to retail sales. This use tax applies to any nonexempt tangible personal property unless the sales tax was paid on the sales price. Like the classic use tax, this use tax protects the State's sales tax by eliminating the residents' incentive to travel to States with lower sales taxes to buy goods rather than buying them in Minnesota.

The appellant, Minneapolis Star and Tribune Company "Star Tribune", is the publisher of a morning newspaper and an evening newspaper in Minneapolis. From 1967 until 1971, it enjoyed an exemption from the sales and use tax provided by Minnesota for periodic publication. In 1971, however, while leaving the exemption from the sales tax in place, the legislature amended the scheme to impose a "use tax" on the cost of paper and ink products consumed in the production of a publication. Ink and paper used in publications became the only items subject to the use tax that were components of goods to be sold at retail. In 1974, the legislature again amended the statute, this time to exempt the first $100,000 worth of ink and paper consumed by a publication in any calendar year, in effect giving each publication an annual tax credit of $4,000. Publications remained exempt from the sales tax.

After the enactment of the $100,000 exemption, 11 publishers, producing 14 of the 388 paid circulation newspapers in the state, incurred a tax liability in 1974. Star Tribune was one of the 11, and, of the $893,355 collected, it paid $608,634, or roughly two-thirds of the total revenue raised by the tax. See 314 N.W.2d 201, 203 and n. 4 (1981). In 1974, 13 publishers, producing 16 out of 374 paid circulation papers, paid a tax. That year, Star Tribune again bore roughly two-thirds of the total receipts from the use tax on ink and paper.

Star Tribune instituted this action to seek a refund of the use taxes it paid from January 1, 1974 to May 31, 1975. It challenged the imposition of the use tax on ink and paper used in publications as a violation of the guarantees of freedom of the press and equal protection in the First and Fourteenth Amendments. The Minnesota Supreme Court upheld the tax against the federal constitutional challenge.

Star Tribune argues that we must strike this tax on the authority of *Grosjean v. American Press Co., Inc.* Although there are similarities between the two cases, we agree with the State that *Grosjean* is not controlling.

Commentators have generally viewed *Grosjean* as dependent on the improper censorial goals of the legislature. See T. Emerson, *The System of Freedom of Expression* 419 (1970); L. Tribe, *American Constitutional Law* 592 n. 8, 724 n. 10 (1978). We think that the result in *Grosjean* may have been attributable in part to the perception on the part of the Court that the state imposed the tax with an intent to penalize a selected group of newspapers. In the case currently before us, however, there is no legislative history and no indication, apart from the structure of the tax itself, of any impermissible or censorial motive on the part of the legislature. We cannot resolve the case by simple citation to *Grosjean*. Instead, we must analyze the problem anew under the general principles of the First Amendment.

Minnesota, however, has not chosen to apply its general sales and use tax to newspapers. Instead, it has created a special tax that applies only to certain publications protected by the First Amendment.

By creating this special use tax, which, to our knowledge, is without parallel in the State's tax scheme, *Minnesota has singled out the press for special treatment.* We then must determine whether the First Amendment permits such special taxation.

There is substantial evidence that differential taxation of the press would have troubled the Framers of the First Amendment.

[These fears] were well-founded. When the state singles out the press, the political constraints that prevent a legislature from passing crippling taxes of general applicability are weakened, and the threat of burdensome taxes becomes acute. That threat can operate as effectively as a censor to check critical comment by the press, undercutting the basic assumption of our political system that the press will often serve as an important restraint on government.

Further, differential treatment, unless justified by some special characteristic of the press, suggests that the goal of the regulation is not unrelated to suppression of expression, and such a goal is presumptively unconstitutional. Differential taxation of the press, then, places such a burden on the interests protected by the First Amendment that we cannot countenance such treatment unless the state asserts a counterbalancing interest of compelling importance that it cannot achieve without differential taxation.

Addressing the concern with differential treatment, Minnesota invites us to look beyond the form of the tax to its substance. The tax is, according to the State, merely a substitute for the sales tax, which, as a generally applicable tax, would be constitutional as applied to the press.

There are two fatal flaws in this reasoning. First, the State has offered no explanation of why it chose to use a substitute for the sales tax rather than the sales tax itself.

The state asserts that this scheme actually *favors* the press over other businesses, because the same rate of tax is applied, but, for the press, the rate applies to the cost of components rather than to the sales price. We would be hesitant to fashion a rule that automatically allowed the state to single out the press for a different method of taxation as long as the effective burden was not different from that on other taxpayers or the burden on the press was lighter than that on other businesses. One reason for this reluctance is that the very selection of the press for special treatment threatens the press not only with the current *differential* treatment, but with the possibility of subsequent differentially *more burdensome* treatment.

A second reason to avoid the proposed rule is that courts as institutions are poorly equipped to evaluate with precision the relative burdens of various methods of taxation. The complexities of factual economic proof always present a certain potential for error, and courts have little familiarity with the process of evaluating the relative economic burden of taxes. In sum, the possibility of error inherent in the proposed rule poses too great a threat to concerns at the heart of the First Amendment, and we cannot tolerate that possibility.[13] Minnesota, therefore, has offered no adequate justification for the special treatment of newspapers.

Minnesota's ink and paper tax violates the First Amendment not only because it singles out the press, but also because it targets a small group of newspapers. The effect of the $100,000 exemption enacted in 1974 is that only a handful of publishers pay any tax at all, and even

---

13. If a state employed the same *method* of taxation but applied a lower *rate* to the press, so that there could be no doubt that the legislature was not singling out the press to bear a more burdensome tax, we would, of course, be in a position to evaluate the relative burdens. And, given the clarity of the relative burdens, as well as the rule that differential methods of taxation are not automatically permissible if less burdensome, a lower tax rate for the press would not raise the threat that the legislature might later impose an extra burden that would escape detection by the courts. Thus, our decision does not, as the dissent suggests, require Minnesota to impose a greater tax burden on publications.

fewer pay any significant amount of tax.[15] The state explains this exemption as part of a policy favoring an "equitable" tax system, although there are no comparable exemptions for small enterprises outside the press. Whatever the motive of the legislature in this case, we think that recognizing a power in the state not only to single out the press but also to tailor the tax so that it singles out a few members of the press presents such a potential for abuse that no interest suggested by Minnesota can justify the scheme.

A tax that singles out the press, or that targets individual publications within the press, places a heavy burden on the State to justify its action. Since Minnesota has offered no satisfactory justification for its tax on the use of ink and paper, the tax violates the First Amendment, and the judgment below is Reversed.

Justice White, concurring in part and dissenting in part.

Justice REHNQUIST, dissenting:

The Court recognizes in several parts of its opinion that the State of Minnesota could avoid constitutional problems by imposing on newspapers the 4% sales tax that it imposes on other retailers. Rather than impose such a tax, however, the Minnesota legislature decided to provide newspapers with an exemption from the sales tax and impose a 4% use tax on ink and paper; thus, while both taxes are part of one "system of sales and use taxes," 314 N.W.2d 201, 203 (1981), newspapers are classified differently within that system. The problem the Court finds too difficult to deal with is whether this difference in treatment results in a significant burden on newspapers.

Today the Court [refuses] to look at the record and determine whether the classifications in the Minnesota use and sales tax statutes significantly burden the First Amendment rights of petitioner and its fellow newspapers.

Wisely not relying solely on inability to weigh the burdens of the Minnesota tax scheme, the Court also says that even if the resultant burden on the press is lighter than on others:

"[T]he very selection of the press for special treatment threatens the press not only with the current *differential* treatment, but with the possibility of subsequent differentially *more burdensome* treatment."

Surely the Court does not mean what it seems to say. The Court should be well aware from its discussion of *Grosjean v. American Press Co., Inc.,* that this Court is quite capable of dealing with changes in state taxing laws which are intended to penalize newspapers.

In summary, so long as the state can find another way to collect revenue from the newspapers, imposing a sales tax on newspapers would be to no one's advantage; not the newspaper and its distributors who would have to collect the tax, not the state who would have to enforce collection, and not the consumer who would have to pay for the paper in odd amounts. The reasonable alternative Minnesota chose was to impose the use tax on ink and paper.

The Court finds in very summary fashion that the exemption newspapers receive for the first $100,000 of ink and paper used also violates the First Amendment because the result is that only a few of the newspapers actually pay a use tax. I cannot agree. Absent any improper motive on the part of the Minnesota legislature in drawing the limits of this exemption, it cannot be construed as violating the First Amendment. There is no reason to conclude that the State, in drafting the $4,000 credit, acted other than reasonably and rationally to fit its sales and use tax scheme to its own local needs and usages.

For the reasons set forth above, I would affirm the judgment of the Minnesota Supreme Court.

COMMENT

Legislation is unconstitutional if the motive of the legislation is to penalize the press. The Court in *Minneapolis Star* professes not to follow *Grosjean* even though its result led to the invalidation of the challenged legislation, as was the case in *Grosjean*.

Does *Minneapolis Star* in fact follow *Grosjean* but expand its approach? Reading *Grosjean* and *Minneapolis Star* together, if the motive of legislation is either to hinder or to help the press, then the legislation is impermissible. With respect to the press, the motive of the legislature must be neutral or indifferent. In response to this

15. In 1974, 11 publishers paid the tax. Three paid less than $1,000, and another three paid less than $8,000. Star Tribune, one of only two publishers paying more than $100,000 paid $608,634. In 1975, 13 publishers paid the tax. Again, three paid less than $1,000, and four more paid less than $3,000. For that year, Star Tribune paid $636,113 and was again one of only two publishers incurring a liability greater than $100,000. See 314 N.W.2d at 203–204 and nn. 4, 5.

it may be argued that that was not what was held in *Minneapolis Star*. The test the Court referred to a number of times is that a legislative tax that treats the press differently cannot stand, unless the purpose of the legislation is designed to accomplish an overriding governmental interest. In other words, the strict scrutiny approach to legislation involving the press was used. In short, because Minnesota could not advance any overriding governmental reason for the tax in question, its differential aspect, as far as the press was concerned, required its invalidation under the strict scrutiny standard of judicial review now accorded to legislation challenged on First Amendment grounds.

Arkansas Writers' Project, Inc. v. Ragland

481 U.S. 221, 107 S. CT. 1722, 95 L. ED. 2D 209 (1987).

Justice MARSHALL delivered the opinion of the Court.

The question presented in this case is whether a state sales tax scheme that taxes general interest magazines, but exempts newspapers and religious, professional, trade, and sports journals violates the First Amendment's guarantee of freedom of the press.

Since 1935, Arkansas has imposed a tax on receipts from sales of tangible personal property. Numerous items are exempt from the state sales tax, however. These include "[g]ross receipts or gross proceeds derived from the sale of newspapers," (newspaper exemption), and "religious, professional, trade and sports journals and/or publications printed and published within this State when sold through regular subscriptions" (magazine exemption).

Appellant *Arkansas Writers' Project, Inc.* publishes Arkansas Times, a general interest monthly magazine with a circulation of approximately 228,000. The magazine includes articles on a variety of subjects, including religion and sports. It is printed and published in Arkansas, and is sold through mail subscriptions, coin-operated stands, and over-the-counter sales. *Minneapolis Star & Tribune Co. v. Minnesota Comm'r of Revenue,* held unconstitutional a Minnesota tax on paper and ink used in the production of newspapers. In January 1984, relying on this authority, appellant sought a refund of sales tax paid since

October 1982, asserting that the magazine exemption must be construed to include Arkansas Times. It maintained that subjecting Arkansas Times to the sales tax, while sales of newspapers and other magazines were exempt, violated the First and Fourteenth Amendments. The Commissioner denied appellant's claim for refund.

We now reverse. In contrast to *Minneapolis Star,* and *Grosjean,* the Arkansas Supreme Court concluded that the Arkansas sales tax was a permissible "ordinary form of taxation."

Our cases clearly establish that a discriminatory tax on the press burdens rights protected by the First Amendment. See *Minneapolis Star* [and] *Grosjean.*

In *Minneapolis Star,* the discrimination took two distinct forms. First, in contrast to generally applicable economic regulations to which the press can legitimately be subject, the Minnesota use tax treated the press differently from other enterprises. Second, the tax targeted a small group of newspapers. This was due to the fact that the first $100,000 of paper and ink were exempt from the tax; thus "only a handful of publishers pay any tax at all, and even fewer pay any significant amount of tax."

Both types of discrimination can be established even where, as here, there is no evidence of an improper censorial motive. This is because selective taxation of the press—either singling out the press as a whole or targeting individual members of the press—poses a particular danger of abuse by the State.

Addressing only the first type of discrimination, the Commissioner defends the Arkansas sales tax as a generally applicable economic regulation. He acknowledges the numerous statutory exemptions to the sales tax, including those exempting newspapers and religious, trade, professional, and sports magazines. Nonetheless, apparently because the tax is nominally imposed on receipts from sales of *all* tangible personal property, he insists that the tax should be upheld.

On the facts of this case, the fundamental question is not whether the tax singles out the press as a whole, but whether it targets a small group within the press. While we indicated in *Minneapolis Star* that a genuinely nondiscriminatory tax on the receipts of newspapers would be constitutionally permissible, the Arkansas sales tax cannot be characterized as nondiscriminatory, because it is not evenly applied to all magazines. To the contrary, the magazine exemption means that only a few Arkansas magazines pay any sales tax; in that respect, it operates in much the same way as did the $100,000 exemption to the Minnesota use tax. Because the Arkansas sales tax scheme treats some magazines less favorably than others, it suffers from the second type of discrimination identified in *Minneapolis Star.*

Indeed, this case involves a more disturbing use of selective taxation than *Minneapolis Star,* because the basis on which Arkansas differentiates between magazines is particularly repugnant to First Amendment principles: a magazine's tax status depends entirely on its *content.* "[A]bove all else, the First Amendment means that government has no power to restrict expression because of its message, its ideas, its subject matter, or its content." *Police Dept. of Chicago v. Mosley,* 408 U.S., at 95. "Regulations which permit the Government to discriminate on the basis of the content of the message cannot be tolerated under the First Amendment." *Regan v. Time, Inc.,* 468 U.S. 641, 648–649 (1984).

If articles in Arkansas Times were uniformly devoted to religion or sports, the magazine would be exempt from the sales tax. However, because the articles deal with a variety of subjects (sometimes including religion and sports), the Commissioner has determined that the magazine's sales may be taxed. In order to determine whether a magazine is subject to sales tax, Arkansas' "enforcement authorities must necessarily examine the content of the message that is conveyed." *FCC v. League of Women Voters of California,* 468 U.S. 364, 383 (1984). Such official scrutiny of the content of publications as the basis for imposing a tax is entirely incompatible with the First Amendment's guarantee of freedom of the press.

Arkansas' system of selective taxation does not evade the strictures of the First Amendment merely because it does not burden the expression of particular *views* by specific magazines. We rejected a similar distinction between content and viewpoint restrictions in *Consolidated Edison Co. v. Public Service Comm'n of New York,* 447 U.S. 530. As we stated in that case, "[t]he First Amendment's hostility to content-based regulation extends not only to restrictions on particular viewpoints, but also to prohibition of public discussion of an entire topic."

Nor are the requirements of the First Amendment avoided by the fact that Arkansas grants an exemption to other members of the media that might publish discussions of the various subjects contained in Arkansas Times. For example, exempting *newspapers* from the tax does not change the fact that the State discriminates in determining the tax status of *magazines* published in Arkansas.

Arkansas faces a heavy burden in attempting to defend its content-based approach to taxation of magazines. In order to justify such differential taxation, the State must show that its regulation is necessary to serve a compelling state interest and is narrowly drawn to achieve that end. See *Minneapolis Star.*

The Commissioner has advanced several state interests.

The Commissioner suggests that the exemption of religious, professional, trade and sports journals was intended to encourage "fledgling" publishers, who have only limited audiences and therefore do not have access to the same volume of advertising revenues as general interest magazines such as Arkansas Times. Even assuming that an interest in encouraging fledgling publications might be a compelling one, we do not find the exemption of religious, professional, trade and sports journals narrowly tailored to achieve that end. To the contrary, the exemption is both overinclusive and underinclusive. The types of magazines enumerated are exempt, regardless of whether they are "fledgling;" even the most lucrative and well-established religious, professional, trade and sports journals do not pay sales tax. By contrast, struggling general interest magazines and struggling specialty magazines on subjects other than those specified are ineligible for favorable tax treatment.

Finally, the Commissioner asserted for the first time at oral argument a need to "foster communication" in the State. While this state interest might support a blanket exemption of the press from the sales tax, it cannot justify selective taxation of certain publishers. The Arkansas tax scheme only fosters communication on religion, sports, and professional and trade matters. It therefore does not serve its alleged purpose in any significant way.

Appellant argues that the Arkansas tax scheme violates the First Amendment because it exempts all newspapers from the tax, but only some magazines. Appellant contends that, under applicable state regulations, the critical distinction between newspapers and magazines is not format, but rather content: newspapers are distinguished from magazines because they contain reports of current events and articles of general interest. Just as content-based distinctions between magazines are impermissible under prior decisions of this Court, appellant claims that content-based distinctions between different members of the media are also impermissible, absent a compelling justification.

Because we hold today that the State's selective application of its sales tax to magazines is unconstitutional and therefore invalid, our ruling eliminates the differential treatment of newspapers and magazines. Accordingly, we need not decide whether a distinction between different types of periodicals presents an additional basis for invalidating the sales tax, as applied to the press.

We stated in *Minneapolis Star* that "[a] tax that singles out the press, or that targets individual publications within the press, places a heavy burden on the State to justify its action." In this case, Arkansas has failed to meet this heavy burden. It has advanced no compelling justification for selective, content-based taxation of certain magazines, and the tax is therefore invalid under the First Amendment. Accordingly, we reverse the judgment of the Arkansas Supreme Court and remand for proceedings not inconsistent with this opinion.

It is so ordered.

Justice STEVENS, concurring in part and concurring in the judgment.

To the extent that the Court's opinion relies on the proposition " 'that government has no power to restrict expression because of its message, its ideas, its subject matter, or its content,' " I am unable to join it. I do, however, agree that the State has the burden of justifying its content-based discrimination and has plainly failed to do so.

Justice SCALIA, with whom the Chief Justice joins, dissenting.

I dissent from today's decision because it provides no rational basis for distinguishing the subsidy scheme here under challenge from many others that are common and unquestionably lawful.

Here, as in the Court's earlier decision in *Minneapolis Star,* application of the "strict scrutiny" test rests upon the premise that for First Amendment purposes denial of exemption from taxation is equivalent to regulation. That premise is demonstrably erroneous and cannot be consistently applied. Our opinions have long recognized—in First Amendment contexts as elsewhere—the reality that tax exemptions, credits, and deductions are "a form of subsidy that is administered through the tax system," and the general rule that "a legislature's decision not to subsidize the exercise of a fundamental right does not infringe the right, and thus is not subject to strict scrutiny." *Regan v. Taxation With Representation of Washington,* 461 U.S. 540.

The reason that denial of participation in a tax exemption or other subsidy scheme does not necessarily "infringe" a fundamental right is that—unlike direct restriction or prohibition—such a denial does not, as a general rule, have any significant coercive effect. It may, of course, be manipulated so as to do so, in which case the courts will be available to provide relief. But that is not remotely the case here. It is implausible that the 4% sales tax, generally applicable to all sales in the State with the few enumerated exceptions, was meant to inhibit, or had the effect of inhibiting, this appellant's publication.

COMMENT

The infirmity of the Arkansas sales tax scheme was that it treated "some magazines less favorably than others." Was the selective discrimination worse than in *Minneapolis Star?* Justice Marshall said it was. Why? Arkansas differentiated between the tax status of magazines on the basis of the *content* of the magazine.

In evaluating the First Amendment validity of the Arkansas sales tax as applied to newspapers and magazines, the Court applied the strictest standard of review, that is, the so-called strict scrutiny standard: "[T]he state must show that its regulation is necessary to serve a compelling state interest and is narrowly drawn to achieve that end."

Arkansas Writers' Project illustrates that the strict scrutiny standard is increasingly being used in First Amendment cases. Usually, the standard is strict in theory but fatal in fact. In other words, the announcement of the use of the strict scrutiny standard transmits a message that the legislation under review is going to be invalidated. Therefore, the choice of standard of review becomes critical.

Justice Scalia in dissent in *Arkansas Writers' Project* believed that the "strict scrutiny" test should not have been used because such a test is designed to evaluate government regulation. In Scalia's view, denial of exemption from taxation is not "equivalent to regulation." In *Grosjean*, however, small circulation newspapers were exempt from the challenged tax, which applied to large circulation newspapers that were also critics of Governor Huey Long. In *Grosjean*, this differentiation (which was, in a sense, a refusal to extend an exemption) was determined to have a coercive effect.

Scalia says that if the state decision to tax or not to tax is manipulated for coercive purposes, "the courts will be available to provide relief." Like Rehnquist in *Minneapolis Star*, Scalia believes the legislation under review does not raise First Amendment problems because there is no evidence of improper censorial motive behind the legislation. A difficulty with this analysis is that it puts a premium on being able to identify the legislative motive.

It was suspected by the press that the *Minneapolis Star* tax was intended to be punitive, although it didn't turn out to be because the newspapers actually paid less in paper and ink taxes than they would have in sales taxes. It would have been difficult to demonstrate this legislative motive were it true, and no effort was ever made to do so.

Justice Stevens disagrees that content-based regulation of expression is always impermissible. In taking this view, he is consistent with the views he expressed in *FCC v. Pacifica Foundation*, 438 U.S. 726 (1978), where he approved FCC regulation, in narrow circumstances, of a category of "indecent" speech. But is the decision of Arkansas to exempt general interest magazines really content-based?

Leathers v. Medlock

499 U.S. 439, 111 S. CT. 1438, 113 L. ED. 2D 494 (1991).

[EDITORIAL NOTE: *In* Leathers v. Medlock, *the Court upheld a general Arkansas sales tax that applied to cable television services but not to newspapers, magazines, or satellite broadcast services.*]

Justice O'CONNOR delivered the opinion of the Court:

Cable television provides to its subscribers news, information, and entertainment. It is engaged in "speech" under the First Amendment, and is, in much of its operation, part of the "press." That it is taxed differently from other media does not by itself, however, raise First Amendment concerns. Our cases have held that a tax that discriminates among speakers is constitutionally suspect only in certain circumstances.

Minneapolis Star & Tribune Co. resolved any doubts about whether direct evidence of improper censorial motive is required in order to invalidate a differential tax on First Amendment grounds: "Illicit legislative intent is not the *sine qua non* of a violation of the First Amendment." *Arkansas Writers' Project, Inc.* reaffirmed the rule that selective taxation of the press through the narrow targeting of individual members offends the First Amendment.

[D]ifferential taxation of First Amendment speakers is constitutionally suspect when it threatens to suppress the expression of particular ideas or viewpoints. Absent a compelling justification, the government may not exercise its taxing power to single out the press. See *Grosjean; Minneapolis Star*. The press plays a unique role as a check on government abuse, and a tax limited to the press raises concerns about censorship of critical information and opinion. A tax is also suspect if it targets a small group of speakers. Again, the fear is censorship of particular ideas or viewpoints. Finally, for reasons that are obvious, a tax will trigger heightened scrutiny under the First Amendment if it discriminates on the basis of the content of taxpayer speech.

The Arkansas tax at issue here presents none of these types of discrimination. The Arkansas sales tax is a tax of general applicability. It applies to receipts from the sale of all tangible personal property and a broad range of services, unless within a group of specific exemptions. The tax does not single out the press and does not therefore threaten to hinder the press as a watchdog of government activity. We have said repeatedly that a State may impose on the press a generally applicable tax.

Furthermore, there is no indication in these cases that Arkansas has targeted cable television in a purposeful attempt to interfere with its First Amendment activities. Nor is the tax one that is structured so as to raise suspicion that it was intended to do so. Unlike the taxes involved in *Grosjean* and *Minneapolis Star,* the Arkansas tax has not selected a narrow group to bear fully the burden of the tax.

The danger from a tax scheme that targets a small number of speakers is the danger of censorship; a tax on a small number of speakers runs the risk of affecting only a limited range of views. There is no comparable danger from a tax on the services provided by a large number of cable operators offering a wide variety of programming throughout the State.

Finally, Arkansas' sales tax is not content based. There is nothing in the language of the statute that refers to the content of mass media communications. Moreover, the record establishes that cable television offers subscribers a variety of programming that presents a mixture of news, information, and entertainment. It contains no evidence, nor is it contended, that this material differs systematically in its message from that communicated by satellite broadcast programming, newspapers, or magazines.

[D]ifferential taxation of speakers, even members of the press, does not implicate the First Amendment unless the tax is directed at, or presents the danger of suppressing, particular ideas. That was the case in *Grosjean, Minneapolis Star,* and *Arkansas Writers',* but it is not the case here. The Arkansas Legislature has chosen simply to exclude or exempt certain media from a generally applicable tax. Nothing about that choice has ever suggested an interest in censoring the expressive activities of cable television. Nor does anything in this record indicate that Arkansas' broad-based, content-neutral sales tax is likely to stifle the free exchange of ideas. We conclude that the State's extension of its generally applicable sales tax to cable television services alone, or to cable and satellite services, while exempting the print media, does not violate the First Amendment.

Justice MARSHALL, joined by Justice BLACKMUN, dissented:

Because cable competes with members of the print and electronic media in the larger information market, the power to discriminate between these media triggers the central concern underlying the nondiscrimination principle: the risk of covert censorship. The nondiscrimination principle protects the press from censorship prophylactically, condemning any selective-taxation scheme that presents the "potential for abuse" by the State, inde-

pendent of any actual "evidence of an improper censorial motive," *Arkansas Writers' Project.* The power to discriminate among like-situated media presents such a risk. By imposing tax burdens that disadvantage one information medium relative to another, the State can favor those media that it likes and punish those that it dislikes.

COMMENT

Does *Medlock* illustrate that the Court has returned to the principles laid down in *Grosjean?* There was no evidence in *Medlock*—as there was in *Grosjean*—of the state seeking to disfavor the cable industry on content grounds. The risk of abuse by the state was simply too hypothetical to justify invalidating the application of the general sales tax to cable. But what about the dissent's point that a state tax scheme could be used to discriminate among media and to punish those media that government disfavored? Does this possibility present enough risk of discrimination to invalidate the tax? After all, *Minneapolis Star* declared that proof of illicit motive was not required. Is this position too absolutist?

CONTENT-BASED VERSUS CONTENT-NEUTRAL REGULATION

A basic tool of contemporary First Amendment law is the distinction between content-based regulation and content-neutral regulation. Content-based regulation is scrutinized with greater severity than content-neutral regulation. The distinction has been defined as follows: "Content-based regulation involves government regulation of expression based on what is being said—the content of the message. Content-neutral regulation involves restrictions which may burden First Amendment expression but without regard to the message being communicated."

Simon & Schuster, Inc. v. Members of the New York State Crime Victims Board
502 U.S. 105, 112 S. CT. 501, 116 L. ED. 2D 476 (1991).

Justice O'CONNOR delivered the opinion of the Court.

New York's "Son of Sam" law requires that an accused or convicted criminal's income from works describing his crime be deposited in an escrow account. These funds are then made available to the victims of the crime and the criminal's other creditors. We consider whether this statute is consistent with the First Amendment.

In the summer of 1977, New York was terrorized by a serial killer popularly known as the Son of Sam. The hunt for the Son of Sam received considerable publicity, and by the time David Berkowitz was identified as the killer and apprehended, the rights to his story were worth a substantial amount. Berkowitz's chance to profit from his notoriety while his victims and their families remained uncompensated did not escape the notice of New York's Legislature. The State quickly enacted the statute at issue.

The Son of Sam law, as later amended, requires any entity contracting with an accused or convicted person for a depiction of the crime to submit a copy of the contract to respondent Crime Victims Board, and to turn over any income under that contract to the Board. The Board is then required to deposit the payment in an escrow account "for the benefit of and payable to any victim . . . provided that such victim, within five years of the date of the establishment of such escrow account, brings a civil action in a court of competent jurisdiction and recovers a money judgment for damages against such [accused or convicted] person or his representatives." After five years, if no actions are pending, "the board shall immediately pay over any moneys in the escrow account to such person or his legal representatives." This 5-year period in which to bring a civil action against the convicted person begins to run when the escrow account is established, and supersedes any limitations period that expires earlier.

[The Act] broadly defines "person convicted of a crime" to include "any person convicted of a crime in this state either by entry of a plea of guilty or by conviction after trial and any person who has voluntarily and intelligently admitted the commission of a crime for which such person is not prosecuted." Thus a person who has never been accused or convicted of a crime in the ordinary sense, but who admits in a book or other work to having committed a crime, is within the statute's coverage.

This case began in 1986, when the Board first became aware of the contract between petitioner Simon & Schuster and admitted organized crime figure Henry Hill. In August 1981, Hill entered into a contract with author Nicholas Pileggi for the production of a book about Hill's life.

The result of Hill and Pileggi's collaboration was Wiseguy, which was published in January 1986. The book depicts, in colorful detail, the day-to-day existence of organized crime, primarily in Hill's first-person narrative. Throughout Wiseguy, Hill frankly admits to having participated in an astonishing variety of crimes. He discusses, among other things, his conviction of extortion and the prison sentence he served. The book was a commercial success: Within 19 months of its publication, more than a million copies were in print. A few years later, the book was converted into a film called Goodfellas, which won a host of awards as the best film of 1990.

From Henry Hill's perspective, however, the publicity generated by the book's success proved less desirable. The Crime Victims Board learned of Wiseguy in January 1986, soon after it was published. The Board determined that Simon & Schuster had violated the law by failing to turn over its contract with Hill to the Board and by making payments to Hill, and that all money owed to Hill under the contract had to be turned over the Board to be held in escrow for the victims of Hill's crimes. The Board ordered Hill to turn over the payments he had already received, and ordered Simon & Schuster to turn over all money payable to Hill at the time or in the future.

Simon & Schuster brought suit under 42 U.S.C. § 1983, seeking a declaration that the Son of Sam law violates the First Amendment and an injunction barring the statute's enforcement. After the parties filed cross-motions for summary judgment, the District Court found the statute consistent with the First Amendment. A divided Court of Appeals affirmed.

Because the Federal Government and most of the States have enacted statutes with similar objectives, the issue is significant and likely to recur. We accordingly granted certiorari, and we now reverse.

A statute is presumptively inconsistent with the First Amendment if it imposes a financial burden on speakers because of the content of their speech. As we emphasized in invalidating a content-based magazine tax, "official scrutiny of the content of publications as the basis for imposing a tax is entirely incompatible with the First Amendment's guarantee of freedom of the press." *Arkansas Writers' Project, Inc. v. Ragland.*

This is a notion so engrained in our First Amendment jurisprudence that last Term we found it so "obvious" as to not require explanation. It is but one manifestation of a far broader principle: "Regulations which permit the Government to discriminate on the basis of the content of the message cannot be tolerated under the First Amendment." *Regan v. Time, Inc.* In the context of financial regulation, it bears repeating, that the Government's ability to impose content-based burdens on speech raises the specter that the Government may effectively drive certain ideas or viewpoints from the marketplace. The First Amendment presumptively places this sort of discrimination beyond the power of the Government.

The Son of Sam law is such a content-based statute. It singles out income derived from expressive activity for a burden the State places on no other income, and it is directed only at works with a specified content. Whether the First Amendment "speaker" is considered to be Henry Hill, whose income the statute places in escrow because of the story he has told, or Simon & Schuster, which can publish books about crime with the assistance of only those criminals willing to forgo remuneration for at least five years, the statute plainly imposes a financial disincentive only on speech of a particular content.

The Son of Sam law establishes a financial disincentive to create or publish works with a particular content. In order to justify such differential treatment, "the State must show that its regulation is necessary to serve a compelling state interest and is narrowly drawn to achieve that end." *Arkansas Writers' Project.*

The Board disclaims, as it must, any state interest in suppressing descriptions of crime out of solicitude for the sensibilities of readers. The Board thus does not assert any interest in limiting whatever anguish Henry Hill's victims may suffer from reliving their victimization.

There can be little doubt, on the other hand, that the State has a compelling interest in ensuring that victims of crime are compensated by those who harm them. Every State has a body of tort law serving exactly this interest.

The State likewise has an undisputed compelling interest in ensuring that criminals do not profit from their crimes. The force of this interest is evidenced by the State's statutory provisions for the forfeiture of the proceeds and instrumentalities of crime.

The Board attempts to define the State's interest more narrowly, as "ensuring that criminals do not profit from storytelling about their crimes before their victims have a meaningful opportunity to be compensated for their injuries." Here the Board is on far shakier ground. The Board cannot explain why the State should have any greater interest in compensating victims from the proceeds of such "storytelling" than from any of the criminal's other assets. Nor can the Board offer any justification for a distinction between this expressive activity and any other activity in connection with its interest in transferring the fruits of crime from criminals to their victims. Thus even if the State can be said to have an interest in classifying a criminal's assets in this manner, that interest is hardly compelling. Like the government entities in the above cases, the Board has taken the effect of the statute and posited that effect as the State's interest. If accepted, this sort of circular defense can sidestep judicial review of almost any statute, because it makes all statutes look narrowly tailored.

In short, the State has a compelling interest in compensating victims from the fruits of the crime, but little if any interest in limiting such compensation to the proceeds of the wrongdoer's speech about the crime. We must therefore determine whether the Son of Sam law is narrowly tailored to advance the former, not the latter, objective.

As a means of ensuring that victims are compensated from the proceeds of crime, the Son of Sam law is significantly overinclusive. As counsel for the Board conceded at oral argument, the statute applies to works on any subject, provided that they express the author's thoughts or recollections about his crime, however, tangentially or incidentally. In addition, the state's broad definition of "person convicted of a crime" enables the Board to escrow the income of any author who admits in his work to having committed a crime, whether or not the author was ever actually accused or convicted.

These two provisions combine to encompass a potentially very large number of works. Had the

Son of Sam law been in effect at the time and place of publication, it would have escrowed payment for such works as The Autobiography of Malcolm X, which describes crimes committed by the civil rights leader before he became a public figure; Civil Disobedience, in which Thoreau acknowledges his refusal to pay taxes and recalls his experience in jail; and even the Confessions of Saint Augustine, in which the author laments "my past foulness and the carnal corruptions of my soul," one instance of which involved the theft of pears from a neighboring vineyard. Amicus Association of American Publishers, Inc., has submitted a sobering bibliography listing hundreds of works by American prisoners and ex-prisoners, many of which contain descriptions of the crimes for which the authors were incarcerated, including works by such authors as Emma Goldman and Martin Luther King, Jr. A list of prominent figures whose autobiographies would be subject to the statute if written is not difficult to construct: The list could include Sir Walter Raleigh, who was convicted of treason after a dubiously conducted 1603 trial; Jesse Jackson, who was arrested in 1963 for trespass and resisting arrest after attempting to be served at a lunch counter in North Carolina; and Bertrand Russell, who was jailed for seven days at the age of 89 for participating in a sit-down protest against nuclear weapons. The argument that a statute like the Son of Sam law would prevent publication of all of these works is hyperbole—some would have been written without compensation—but the Son of Sam law clearly reaches a wide range of literature that does not enable a criminal to profit from his crime while a victim remains uncompensated.

Should a prominent figure write his autobiography at the end of his career, and include in an early chapter a brief recollection of having stolen (in New York) a nearly worthless item as a youthful prank, the Board would control his entire income from the book for five years, and would make that income available to all of the author's creditors, despite the fact that the statute of limitations for this minor incident had long since run. That the Son of Sam law can produce such an outcome indicates that the statute is, to say the least, not narrowly tailored to achieve the State's objective of compensating crime victims from the profits of crime.

The Federal Government and many of the States have enacted statutes designed to serve purposes similar to that served by the Son of Sam law. Some of these statutes may be quite different from New York's, and we have no occasion to determine the constitutionality of these other laws. We conclude simply that in the Son of Sam law, New York has singled out speech on a particular subject for a financial burden that it places on no other speech and no other income. The State's interest in compensating victims from the fruits of crime is a compelling one, but the Son of Sam law is not narrowly tailored to advance that objective. As a result, the statute is inconsistent with the First Amendment.

Justice THOMAS took no part in the consideration or decision of this case.

Justice KENNEDY, concurring in the judgment.

The New York statute we now consider imposes severe restrictions on authors and publishers, using as its sole criterion the content of what is written. The regulated content has the full protection of the First Amendment and this, I submit, is itself a full and sufficient reason for holding the statute unconstitutional. In my view it is both unnecessary and incorrect to ask whether the State can show that the statute " 'is necessary to serve a compelling state interest and is narrowly drawn to achieve that end.' " That test or formulation derives from our equal protection jurisprudence, and has no real or legitimate place when the Court considers the straightforward question whether the State may enact a burdensome restriction of speech based on content only, apart from any considerations of time, place, and manner or the use of public forums.

There are a few legal categories in which content-based regulation has been permitted or at least contemplated. These include obscenity, defamation, incitement, or situations presenting some grave and imminent danger the government has the power to prevent. These are, however, historic and traditional categories long familiar to the bar, although with respect to the last category it is more difficult for the government to prevail. See *New York Times Co. v. United States.* While it cannot be said with certainty that the foregoing types of expression are or will remain the only ones that are without First Amendment protection, the use of these traditional legal categories is preferable to the sort of ad hoc balancing that the Court henceforth must perform in every case if the analysis here used becomes our standard test.

As a practical matter, perhaps we will interpret the compelling interest test in cases involving content regulation so that the results become parallel to the historic categories I have discussed, although an enterprise such as today's tends not to remain pro forma but to take on a life of its own. When we leave open the possibility that various sorts of content regulations are appropriate, we discount the value of our precedents and invite experiments that in fact present clear violations for the First Amendment, as is true in the case before us.

The case before us presents the opportunity to adhere to a surer test for content-based cases and to avoid using an unnecessary formulation, one with the capacity to weaken central protections of the First Amendment. I would recognize this opportunity to confirm our past holdings and to rule that the New York statute amounts to raw censorship based on content, censorship forbidden by the text of the First Amendment and well-settled principles protecting speech and the press. That ought to end the matter.

With these observations, I concur in the judgment of the Court holding the statute invalid.

COMMENT

Simon & Schuster sets forth the standard of review used to evaluate the First Amendment validity of content-based regulation. How do we know that the Son of Sam law is a content-based regulation? Justice Sandra Day O'Connor said the New York legislature had targeted criminal assets with a "particular content." The statute targeted income-producing expressive activities about the crime committed by a criminal, but not other assets or income of the criminal.

When the state engages in content-based discrimination, the strict scrutiny standard of review is used. Quoting *Arkansas Writers' Project*, p. 72, the Court in *Simon & Schuster* said " 'the state must show that its regulation is necessary to serve a compelling state interest and is narrowly drawn to achieve that end.' "

Employment of the strict scrutiny standard—theoretically the most demanding standard of review—does not mean that the regulation invariably fails. The strict scrutiny test is a two-part test. The court must inquire (1) whether the state has a compelling interest in the regulation

and (2) whether the regulation is narrowly tailored to achieve the state's objective in enacting the regulation. The Court concluded that victim compensation is a compelling state interest but that the Son of Sam law was not narrowly tailored to achieve that goal. Why not?

Justice Anthony Kennedy's concurrence in *Simon & Schuster* raised a challenging question. If the speech that was regulated by New York's Son of Sam law is protected by the First Amendment, why isn't it protected absolutely? What justification, he asks, is there for evaluating a content-based regulation of speech under the strict scrutiny standard? Basically, Justice Kennedy is advocating an absolute standard.

What difference does it make whether an absolute standard or a strict scrutiny test is used? One difference is that it is possible for the state to justify a content-based regulation under the strict scrutiny test. However, if an absolute standard is used, all one needs to do is show that the regulation is content-based and it is therefore invalid. Does Justice Kennedy's approach present any difficulties?

SYMBOLIC SPEECH

Today, as we have seen, the distinction between content-based and content-neutral regulation is critical. A generation ago, the distinction between speech and action was important in understanding the scope of First Amendment protection. Under this approach, speech was absolutely protected while action could be regulated. Out of this speech-action dichotomy arose the so-called absolutist interpretation of the First Amendment.

Although his definitions of protected speech and press were sometimes narrow, Justice Black was the foremost judicial exponent of the absolutist test, and Professor Thomas I. Emerson has been its foremost academic exponent. Professor Emerson has described the test as follows:

The Test is not that all words, writing and other communications are, at all times and under all circumstances, protected from all forms of government restraint.

Actually, the absolutist test involves two components:

1. The command of the first amendment is "absolute" in the sense that "no law" which

"abridges" "the freedom of speech" is constitutionally valid. [T]he point being stressed is by no means inconsequential. For it insists on focusing the inquiry upon the definition of "abridge," "the freedom of speech," and if necessary "law," rather than on a general de novo balancing of interests in each case.

2. The absolute test includes another component. It is intended to bring a broader area of expression within the First Amendment than the other tests do.

See Emerson, *Toward A General Theory of the First Amendment*, 72 Yale L.J. 877, 914–15 (1963); see generally, Emerson, *The System of Freedom of Expression* (1970).

Some scholars have attacked the usefulness of the speech-action dichotomy. Professor Baker has written: "Unfortunately, neither identifying protected 'expression' by determining the conduct's contribution to the purposes of the system nor by using common sense to distinguish between expression and action works." *See* Baker, *Scope of the First Amendment Freedom of Speech*, 25 U.C.L.A. L. Rev. 964, 1010 (1978). Professor Emerson has responded in defense as follows:

The expression-action dichotomy is, of course, not that simple. It attempts to formulate a definition of the kind of conduct that merits special protection under the first amendment.

See Emerson, *First Amendment Doctrine and the Burger Court*, 68 Cal. L. Rev. 422, 478 (1980).

The speech-action test proceeds on the assumption that speech or communication is entitled to full First Amendment protection. But sometimes action has a communicative or expressive element. In such circumstances, should function or form control? If a particular kind of activity is essentially communicative in character, then perhaps it should be viewed for what it is—symbolic speech. As symbolic speech, the activity is entitled to full First Amendment protection just as if it were as communicative in substance as it is in form.

Embryonic recognition by the Supreme Court that some modes of activity should be treated as symbolic expression is found as early as *Stromberg v. California*, 283 U.S. 359 (1931), where the Supreme Court struck down on First Amendment grounds a state statute that prohibited "the display of a red flag as a symbol of opposition by peaceful and legal means to organized government." A fuller and more famous statement that contained the roots of the symbolic speech idea may be found in *West Virginia State Board of Education v. Barnette*, 319 U.S. 624 (1943), where Justice Robert Jackson said:

There is no doubt that the [compulsory] flag salute is a form of utterance. Symbolism is a primitive but effective way of communicating ideas. The use of an emblem or flag to symbolize some system, idea, institution, or personality is a short cut from mind to mind.

If action is "symbolic," shouldn't it really be treated as "speech" for First Amendment purposes?

Is a speech-action dichotomy too mechanical an approach, or is it a useful way of thinking about and resolving First Amendment problems?

The *O'Brien* Test

The *O'Brien* case arose out of the "draft card" burnings that occurred in different parts of the country in the late 1960s during the Vietnam War controversy. The Supreme Court declined to use the symbolic speech doctrine when its advocates tried to use the doctrine literally under fire. Instead, the Court fashioned a new test, known today as the *O'Brien* test. The *O'Brien* test has become the doctrinal vehicle for dealing with regulation of activity that has both expressive and nonexpressive components. The *O'Brien* test provides a guide for determining when regulation of such activity violates the First Amendment and when it does not. In the years since *O'Brien* was decided, the test has been increasingly used to determine when content-neutral regulation violates the First Amendment.

United States v. O'Brien
391 U.S. 367, 88 S. CT. 1673, 20 L. ED. 2D 672 (1968).

Chief Justice WARREN delivered the opinion of the Court.

On the morning of March 31, 1966, David Paul O'Brien and three companions burned their Selective Service registration certificates on the steps of the South Boston Courthouse.

For this act, O'Brien was indicted, tried, convicted, and sentenced in the United States District Court for the District of Massachusetts. He did not contest the fact that he had burned the certificate. He stated in argument to the jury that he burned the certificate publicly to influence others to adopt his antiwar beliefs, as he put it, "so that other people would reevaluate their positions with Selective Service, with the armed forces, and reevaluate their place in the culture of today, to hopefully consider my position."

The indictment upon which he was tried charged that he "wilfully and knowingly did mutilate, destroy, and change by burning [his] Registration Certificate (Selective Service System Form No. 2); in violation of Title 50, App., United States Code, Section 462(b)." Section 462(b) is part of the Universal Military Training and Service Act of 1948. Section 462(b)(3), one of six numbered subdivisions of § 462(b), was amended by Congress in 1965, 79 Stat. 586 (adding the words italicized below), so that at the time O'Brien burned his certificate an offense was committed by any person, "who forges, alters, *knowingly destroys, knowingly mutilates,* or in any manner changes any such certificate." [Emphasis added.]

By the 1965 Amendment, Congress added to the 1948 act the provision here at issue, subjecting to criminal liability not only one who "forges, alters, or in any manner changes" but also one who "knowingly destroys [or] knowingly mutilates" a certificate. We note at the outset that the 1965 Amendment plainly does not abridge free speech on its face, and we do not understand O'Brien to argue otherwise. [The Amendment] on its face deals with conduct having no connection with speech. It prohibits the knowing destruction of certificates issued by the Selective Service System, and there is nothing necessarily expressive about such conduct. The Amendment does not distinguish between public and private destruction, and it does not punish only destruction engaged in for the purpose of expressing views. A law prohibiting destruction of Selective Service certificates no more abridges free speech on its face than a motor vehicle law prohibiting the destruction of drivers' licenses, or a tax law prohibiting the destruction of books and records.

O'Brien nonetheless argues that the 1965 Amendment is unconstitutional in its application to him, and is unconstitutional as enacted because what he calls the "purpose" of Congress was "to suppress freedom of speech." We consider these arguments separately.

O'Brien first argues that the 1965 Amendment is unconstitutional as applied to him because his act of burning his registration certificate was pro-

tected "symbolic speech" within the First Amendment. His argument is that the freedom of expression which the First Amendment guarantees includes all modes of "communication of ideas by conduct," and that his conduct is within this definition because he did it in "demonstration against the war and against the draft."

We cannot accept the view that an apparently limitless variety of conduct can be labelled "speech" whenever the person engaging in the conduct intends thereby to express an idea. However, even on the assumption that the alleged communicative element in O'Brien's conduct is sufficient to bring into play the First Amendment, it does not necessarily follow that the destruction of a registration certificate is constitutionally protected activity. This Court has held that when "speech" and "nonspeech" elements are combined in the same course of conduct, a sufficiently important governmental interest in regulating the nonspeech element can justify incidental limitations on First Amendment freedoms. To characterize the quality of the governmental interest which must appear, the Court has employed a variety of descriptive terms: compelling; substantial; subordinating; paramount; cogent; strong. *Whatever imprecision inheres in these terms, we think it clear that a government regulation is sufficiently justified if it is within the constitutional power of the government; if it furthers an important or substantial governmental interest; if the governmental interest is unrelated to the suppression of free expression; and if the incidental restriction on alleged First Amendment freedom is no greater than is essential to the furtherance of that interest.* We find that the 1965 Amendment to § 462(b)(3) of the Universal Military Training and Service Act meets all of these requirements, and consequently that O'Brien can be constitutionally convicted for violating it. [Emphasis added.]

The many functions performed by Selective Service certificates establish beyond doubt that Congress has a legitimate and substantial interest in preventing their wanton and unrestrained destruction and assuring their continuing availability by punishing people who knowingly and wilfully destroy or mutilate them.

We think it apparent that the continuing availability to each registrant of his Selective Service certificates substantially furthers the smooth and proper functioning of the system that Congress has established to raise armies. We think it also apparent that the Nation has a vital interest in having a system for raising armies that functions with maximum efficiency and is capable of easily and quickly responding to continually changing circumstances. For these reasons, the Government has a substantial interest in assuring the continuing availability of issued Selective Service certificates.

It is equally clear that the 1965 Amendment specifically protects this substantial governmental interest. We perceive no alternative means that would more precisely and narrowly assure the continuing availability of issued Selective Service certificates than a law which prohibits their wilful mutilation or destruction. The 1965 Amendment prohibits such conduct and does nothing more. In other words, both the governmental interest and the operation of the 1965 Amendment are limited to the noncommunicative aspect of O'Brien's conduct. The governmental interest and the scope of the 1965 Amendment are limited to preventing a harm to the smooth and efficient functioning of the Selective Service System. When O'Brien deliberately rendered unavailable his registration certificate, he willfully frustrated this governmental interest. For this noncommunicative impact of his conduct, and for nothing else, he was convicted.

O'Brien finally argues that the 1965 Amendment is unconstitutional as enacted because what he calls the "purpose" of Congress was "to suppress freedom of speech." We reject this argument because under settled principles the purpose of Congress, as O'Brien uses that term, is not a basis for declaring this legislation unconstitutional.

Since the 1965 Amendment to the Universal Military Training and Service Act is constitutional as enacted and as applied, the Court of Appeals should have affirmed the judgment of conviction entered by the District Court. Accordingly, we vacate the judgment of the Court of Appeals, and reinstate the judgment and sentence of the District Court. This disposition makes unnecessary consideration of O'Brien's claim that the Court of Appeals erred in affirming his conviction on the basis of the nonpossession regulation.

It is so ordered.

Justice MARSHALL took no part in the consideration or decision of these cases.

Justice HARLAN, concurred.

[Justice DOUGLAS dissented on the ground that the basic but undecided constitutional issue in the case was whether conscription was unconstitutional in the absence of a declaration of war.]

Symbolic Speech after *O'Brien*

One should not think that symbolic speech received no protection after *O'Brien*. In *Tinker v. Des Moines Independent Community School District*, 393 U.S. 503 (1969), the Supreme Court reviewed the controversy that ensued when public school children wore black armbands to school to protest the Vietnam War. The Des Moines school system had prohibited the wearing of armbands in advance. The Court held that wearing an armband was a "symbolic act" that was "closely akin to 'pure speech'" and, therefore, protected under the free speech clause of the First Amendment. Because only seven of 18,000 students actually wore armbands to school, Justice Abe Fortas held that a more positive showing of interference with normal school operations would have to be made before the prohibition on armbands could be sustained.

The Court did not cite or discuss *O'Brien* in the *Tinker* case. Is this defensible? If the *O'Brien* test had been applied to the facts of *Tinker*, would the prohibition on armbands still have been struck down? See page 83.

Spence v. Washington, 418 U.S. 405 (1974), was another case in which the Court also protected symbolic expressive activity. Spence had affixed a peace symbol to the American flag and then displayed the flag upside down from his window to protest the American invasion of Cambodia. He was prosecuted under a state statute punishing misuse of the flag. In 1974 the Court overturned his conviction under the flag misuse statute. The Court made it clear that it understood Spence's use of the flag was an attempt to communicate "through the use of symbols." On the basis of the factual context of this protest, the Court concluded that Spence had "engaged in a form of protected expression." The Court evidenced a willingness to consider action in certain circumstances to be the equivalent of communication. *Spence* set forth a two-part test. First, it is necessary to show that the speaker intends to make a particular communication. Second, it is necessary that the audience to whom the protest at issue is addressed understand that it is used as a communication. Is the *Spence* test more protective of freedom of expression than *O'Brien?* Why?

The *O'Brien* Test Today

The *O'Brien* test has four parts. First, is the regulation at issue within the constitutional power of government? Second, does the regulation further an important or substantial governmental interest? Third, is the governmental interest unrelated to the suppression of free expression? Fourth, is the regulation's incidental restraint on free expression no greater than what is essential to further the governmental interest served by the regulation?

In applying the *O'Brien* test, the courts have been deferential to the government's assertion that its interest is substantial. Furthermore, as *O'Brien* illustrates, the courts have declined to look into legislative motives to determine whether the governmental interest is unrelated to the suppression of free expression. Finally, *O'Brien* did not ask that the legislature use the alternative least onerous to freedom of expression. Instead, it simply required that the incidental restraint on free expression not be greater than what was essential to achieve the governmental interest. In *O'Brien*, Chief Justice Earl Warren simply asserted that the prohibition against draft card destruction served the governmental interest. Is the *O'Brien* test, as described, stacked in favor of upholding the government regulation?

Consider the following summary of *O'Brien* and its significance for First Amendment law: Professor Tribe has argued that *[O'Brien]* has introduced a two-track system into First Amendment analysis. If government is regulating the conduct without regard to the message being communicated, it is content-neutral and the less demanding *O'Brien* standard applies. If government is regulating because of some harm associated with the speaker's message, the law is content-based and *O'Brien* is inapplicable. Presumably, the strict scrutiny standard would then be applied—assuming that the speech is otherwise entitled to full First Amendment protection. Barron & Dienes, *First Amendment Law in a Nutshell* 222–23 (1993).

Texas v. Johnson

491 U.S. 397, 109 S. CT. 2533, 105 L. ED. 2D 342 (1989).

Justice BRENNAN delivered the opinion of the Court.

After publicly burning an American flag as a means of political protest, Gregory Lee Johnson was convicted of desecrating a flag in violation of Texas law. This case presents the question whether his conviction is consistent with the First Amendment. We hold that it is not.

While the Republican National Convention was taking place in Dallas in 1984, respondent Johnson participated in a political demonstration dubbed the "Republican War Chest Tour." [T]he purpose of this event was to protest the policies of the Reagan administration and of certain Dallas-based corporations.

The demonstration ended in front of Dallas City Hall, where Johnson unfurled the American flag, doused it with kerosene, and set it on fire. While the flag burned, the protestors chanted, "America, the red, white, and blue, we spit on you." After the demonstrators dispersed, a witness to the flag-burning collected the flag's remains and buried them in his backyard.

Johnson was convicted of flag desecration for burning the flag rather than of uttering insulting words. This fact somewhat complicates our consideration of his conviction under the First Amendment. We must first determine whether Johnson's burning of the flag constituted expressive conduct, permitting him to invoke the First Amendment in challenging his conviction. See, e.g., *Spence v. Washington*. If his conduct was expressive, we next decide whether the State's regulation is related to the suppression of free expression. See, e.g., *United States v. O'Brien; Spence, supra*. If the State's regulation is not related to expression, then the less stringent standard we announced in *United States v. O'Brien* for regulations of noncommunicative conduct controls. If it is, then we are outside of *O'Brien's* test, and we must ask whether this interest justifies Johnson's conviction under a more demanding standard. A third possibility is that the State's asserted interest is simply not implicated on these facts, and in that event the interest drops out of the picture.

Texas conceded that Johnson's conduct was expressive conduct. Johnson burned an American flag as part—indeed, as the culmination—of a political demonstration that coincided with the convening of the Republican Party and its renomination of Ronald Reagan for President. The expressive, overtly political nature of this conduct was both intentional and overwhelmingly apparent.

The Government generally has a freer hand in restricting expressive conduct than it has in restricting the written or spoken word. It may not, however, proscribe particular conduct *because* it has expressive elements. It is, in short, not simply the verbal or nonverbal nature of the expression, but the governmental interest at stake, that helps to determine whether a restriction on that expression is valid.

[W]e have limited the applicability of *O'Brien's* relatively lenient standard to those cases in which "the governmental interest is unrelated to the suppression of free expression." See also *Spence*. In stating, moreover, that *O'Brien's* test "in the last analysis is little, if any, different from the standard applied to time, place, or manner restrictions," we have highlighted the requirement that the governmental interest in question be unconnected to expression in order to come under *O'Brien's* less demanding rule.

In order to decide whether *O'Brien's* test applies here, therefore, we must decide whether Texas has asserted an interest in support of Johnson's conviction that is unrelated to the suppression of expression. If we find that an interest asserted by the State is simply not implicated on the facts before us, we need not ask whether *O'Brien's* test applies. The State offers two separate interests to justify this conviction: preventing breaches of the peace, and preserving the flag as a symbol of nationhood and national unity. We hold that the first interest is not implicated on this record and that the second is related to the suppression of expression.

Texas claims that its interest in preventing breaches of the peace justifies Johnson's conviction for flag desecration. However, no disturbance of the peace actually occurred or threatened to occur because of Johnson's burning of the flag.

The State's position, therefore, amounts to a claim that an audience that takes serious offense at particular expression is necessarily likely to disturb the peace and that the expression may be prohibited on this basis. Our precedents do not countenance such a presumption. On the contrary, they recognize that a principal "function of free speech under our system of government is to invite dispute."

Thus, we have not permitted the Government to assume that every expression of a provocative idea will incite a riot. *Nor* does Johnson's expressive conduct fall within that small class of "fighting words" that are "likely to provoke the average person to retaliation, and thereby cause a breach of the peace." *Chaplinsky v. New Hampshire.* No reasonable onlooker would have regarded Johnson's generalized expression of dissatisfaction with the policies of the Federal Government as a direct personal insult or an invitation to exchange fisticuffs.

We thus conclude that the State's interest in maintaining order is not implicated on these facts. The State need not worry that our holding will disable it from preserving the peace. We do not suggest that the First Amendment forbids a State to prevent "imminent lawless action."

The State also asserts an interest in preserving the flag as a symbol of nationhood and national unity. These concerns blossom only when a person's treatment of the flag communicates some message, and thus are related "to the suppression of free expression" within the meaning of *O'Brien*. We are thus outside of *O'Brien's* test altogether.

It remains to consider whether the State's interest in preserving the flag as a symbol of nationhood and national unity justifies Johnson's conviction.

Johnson was not, we add, prosecuted for the expression of just any idea; he was prosecuted for his expression of dissatisfaction with the policies of this country, expression situated at the core of our First Amendment values.

Moreover, Johnson was prosecuted because he knows that his politically charged expression would cause "serious offense." If he had burned the flag as a means of disposing of it because it was dirty or torn, he would not have been convicted of flag desecration under this Texas law:

federal law designates burning as the preferred means of disposing of a flag "when it is in such condition that it is no longer a fitting emblem for display," 36 U.S.C. § 176(k), and Texas has no quarrel with this means of disposal. The Texas law is thus not aimed at protecting the physical integrity of the flag in all circumstances, but is designed instead to protect it only against impairments that would cause serious offense to others.

Whether Johnson's treatment of the flag violated Texas law thus depended on the likely communicative impact of his expressive conduct. This restriction on Johnson's expression is content-based.

We must therefore subject the State's asserted interest in preserving the special symbolic character of the flag to "the most exacting scrutiny."

Texas argues that its interest in preserving the flag as a symbol of nationhood and national unity survives this close analysis. According to Texas, if one physically treats the flag in a way that would tend to cast doubt on either the idea that nationhood and national unity are the flag's referents or that national unity actually exists, the message conveyed thereby is a harmful one and therefore may be prohibited.

If there is a bedrock principle underlying the First Amendment, it is that the Government may not prohibit the expression of an idea simply because society finds the idea itself offensive or disagreeable.

We have not recognized an exception to this principle even where our flag has been involved. In *Street v. New York,* 394 U.S. 576 (1969), we held that a State may not criminally punish a person for uttering words critical of the flag. Nor may the Government, we have held, compel conduct that would evince respect for the flag.

In short, nothing in our precedents suggests that a State may foster its own view of the flag by prohibiting expressive conduct relating to it. To bring its argument outside our precedents, Texas attempts to convince us that even if its interest in preserving the flag's symbolic role does not allow it to prohibit words or some expressive conduct critical of the flag, it does permit it to forbid the outright destruction of the flag. The State's argument cannot depend here on the distinction between written or spoken words and nonverbal conduct. That distinction, we have shown, is of no moment where the nonverbal conduct is expressive, as it is here, and where

the regulation of that conduct is related to expression, as it is here.

Texas' focus on the precise nature of Johnson's expression, moreover, misses the point of our prior decisions: their enduring lesson, that the Government may not prohibit expression simply because it disagrees with its message, is not dependent on the particular mode in which one chooses to express an idea. If we were to hold that a State may forbid flag-burning wherever it is likely to endanger the flag's symbolic role, but allow it wherever burning a flag promotes that role—as where, for example, a person ceremoniously burns a dirty flag—we would be saying that when it comes to impairing the flag's physical integrity, the flag itself may be used as a symbol—as a substitute for the written or spoken word or a "short cut from mind to mind"—only in one direction. We would be permitting a State to "prescribe what shall be orthodox" by saying that one may burn the flag to convey one's attitude toward it and its referents only if one does not endanger the flag's representation of nationhood and national unity.

To conclude that the Government may permit designated symbols to be used to communicate only a limited set of messages would be to enter territory having no discernible or defensible boundaries. Could the Government, on this theory, prohibit the burning of state flags? Of copies of the Presidential seal? Of the Constitution? In evaluating these choices under the First Amendment, how would we decide which symbols were sufficiently special to warrant this unique status? To do so, we would be forced to consult our own political preferences, and impose them on the citizenry, in the very way that the First Amendment forbids us to do.

There is, moreover, no indication—either in the text of the Constitution or in our cases interpreting it—that a separate juridical category exists for the American flag alone.

It is not the State's end, but its means, to which we object. It cannot be gainsaid that there is a special place reserved for the flag in this Nation. To say that the Government has an interest in encouraging proper treatment of the flag, however, is not to say that it may criminally punish a person for burning a flag as a means of political protest.

The way to preserve the flag's special role is not to punish those who feel differently about these matters. It is to persuade them that they are wrong. We do not consecrate the flag by punishing its desecration, for in doing so we dilute the freedom that this cherished emblem represents.

Johnson was convicted for engaging in expressive conduct. The State's interest in preventing breaches of the peace does not support his conviction because Johnson's conduct did not threaten to disturb the peace. Nor does the State's interest in preserving the flag as a symbol of nationhood and national unity justify his criminal conviction for engaging in political expression.

Chief Justice REHNQUIST, with whom Justice WHITE and Justice O'CONNOR join, dissenting.

The flag is not simply another "idea" or "point of view" competing for recognition in the marketplace of ideas. Millions and millions of Americans regard it with an almost mystical reverence regardless of what sort of social, political, or philosophical beliefs they may have.

Here it may equally well be said that the public burning of the American flag by Johnson was no essential part of any exposition of ideas, and at the same time it had a tendency to incite a breach of the peace. As with "fighting words," so with flag burning, for purposes of the First Amendment: It is "no essential part of any exposition of ideas, and [is] of such slight social value as a step to truth that any benefit that may be derived from [it] is clearly outweighed" by the public interest in avoiding a probable breach of the peace.

Surely one of the high purposes of a democratic society is to legislate against conduct that is regarded as evil and profoundly offensive to the majority of people—whether it be murder, embezzlement, pollution, or flag burning. The government may conscript men into the Armed Forces where they must fight and perhaps die for the flag, but the government may not prohibit the public burning of the banner under which they fight. I would uphold the Texas statute as applied in this case.

Justice STEVENS, dissenting.

Even if the flag burning could be considered just another species of symbolic speech under the logical application of the rules that the Court has developed in its interpretation of the First Amendment in other contexts, this case has an intangible dimension that makes those rules inapplicable.

COMMENT

In *Texas v. Johnson*, Justice Brennan concluded that the Texas law under which Johnson was prosecuted should not be evaluated under the *O'Brien* test. In *O'Brien* the government had reasons independent of any message communicated by draft card destruction for protecting the physical integrity of the draft card. But Texas had no interest in punishing flag burning independent of enforcing its view that flag burning was harmful and should be prohibited.

In short, the federal law in *O'Brien* was content-neutral, but the Texas law was content-based: the flag as a symbol of national unity should be protected and those who desecrate it punished. In such circumstances, Justice Brennan declared, the state's interest in protecting the "special symbolic character of the flag" must be subjected "to 'the most exacting scrutiny.'" The interests Texas sought to serve were to protect the flag as a symbol of national unity and to punish those who desecrate it. The state had asserted no state interest so compelling as to override "the bedrock principle" that "government may not prohibit the expression of an idea" simply because it finds that idea offensive or unpleasant.

Because the Texas flag desecration law was fairly clearly content-based, why was the statute struck down by only a narrow 5–4 margin? Does this result argue for an absolute First Amendment protection against content-based regulation as Justice Kennedy argued in *Simon & Schuster?* Note that Justice Rehnquist's dissent does not argue that the Texas law survives strict scrutiny, instead, the dissent seeks to create a new category of unprotected speech. *See generally,* Chapter 3.

Barnes v. Glen Theatre, Inc.
501 U.S. 560, 111 S. CT. 2456, 115 L. ED. 2D 504 (1991).

[EDITORIAL NOTE: *In* Barnes v. Glen Theatre, Inc., *a plurality of the Court, Chief Justice Rehnquist joined by Justices O'Connor and Kennedy, upheld the application of an Indiana statute banning pubic nudity to prevent totally nude dancing. Erotic dancers and the establishments that employed them wanted to provide their customers with totally nude dancing. They unsuccessfully challenged the state law requiring them to wear "pasties" and a "G-string." Although conceding that nude dancing is expressive conduct, the Court rejected the claim that the First Amendment precluded the state from enforcing its public indecency law to prevent totally nude dancing.]*

Chief Justice REHNQUIST delivered the opinion of the Court.

[N]ude dancing of the kind sought to be performed here is expressive conduct within the outer perimeters of the First Amendment, although we view it as only marginally so. This, of course, does not end our inquiry. We must determine the level of protection to be afforded to the expressive conduct at issue, and must determine whether the Indiana statute is an impermissible infringement of that protected activity.

Applying the four-part *O'Brien* test, [Indiana's public indecency statute] is justified despite its incidental limitations on some expressive activity. The public indecency statute is clearly within the State's constitutional power. And it furthers a substantial governmental [interest]. It is impossible to discern, other than from the text of the statute, exactly what governmental interest the Indiana legislators had in mind when [enacting] this statute, for Indiana does not record legislative history, and the State's highest court has not shed additional light on the statute's purpose. Nonetheless, the statute's purpose of protecting societal order and morality is clear from its text and history. Public indecency statutes of this sort are of ancient origin, and presently exist in at least 47 states.

This and other public indecency statutes were designed to protect morals and public order. The traditional police power of the States is defined as the authority to provide for the public health, safety, and morals, and we have upheld such a basis for legislation. Thus, the public indecency statute furthers a substantial government interest in protecting order and morality.

This interest is unrelated to the suppression of free expression. Some may view restricting nudity on moral grounds as necessarily related to expression. We disagree. It can be argued, of course, that almost limitless types of conduct—including appearing in the nude in public—are "expressive," and in one sense of the word this is true. People who go about in the nude in the public may be expressing something about themselves by so doing.

But, the court rejected this expansive notion of "expressive conduct" in *O'Brien,* saying:

"We cannot accept the view that an apparently limitless variety of conduct can be labelled 'speech' whenever the person engaging in the conduct intends thereby to express an idea."

Respondents contend that even though prohibiting nudity in public generally may not be related to suppressing expression, prohibiting the performance of nude dancing is related to expression because the state seeks to prevent its erotic message. Therefore, they reason that the application of the Indiana statute to the nude dancing in this case violates the First Amendment, because it fails the third part of the *O'Brien* test, viz: the governmental interest must be unrelated to the suppression of free expression.

But we do not think that when Indiana applies its statute to the nude dancing in these nightclubs it is proscribing nudity because of the erotic message conveyed by the dancers. Presumably numerous other erotic performances are presented at these establishments without any interference from the state, so long as the dancers wear a scant amount of clothing, otherwise, the requirement that the dancers don pasties and a G-string does not deprive the dance of whatever erotic message it conveys; it simply makes the message slightly less graphic. The perceived evil that Indiana seeks to address is not erotic dancing, but public nudity. The appearance of people of all shapes, sizes and ages in the nude at a beach, for example, would convey little if any erotic message, yet the state still seeks to prevent it. Public nudity is the evil the state seeks to prevent, whether or not it is combined with expressive activity.

This conclusion is buttressed by a reference to the facts of *O'Brien.* It was assumed that O'Brien's act in burning the certificate had a communicative element in it sufficient to bring into play the First Amendment, but it was for the noncommunicative elements that he was prosecuted. So here with the Indiana statute; while the dancing to which it was applied had a communicative element, it was not the dancing that was prohibited but simply its being done in the nude.

The fourth part of the *O'Brien* test requires that the incidental restriction on First Amendment freedom be no greater than is essential to the furtherance of the governmental interest. As indicated in the discussion above, the governmental interest served by the text of the prohibition is not a means to some greater end, but an end in itself. It is without fail that the public indecency statute is "narrowly tailored;" Indiana's requirement that the dancers wear at least pasties and a G-string is modest, and the bare minimum necessary to achieve the State's purpose.

Justice SCALIA, concurring in the judgment:

In my view, however, the challenged regulation must be upheld, not because it survives some lower level of First Amendment scrutiny, but because, as a general law regulating conduct and not specifically directed at expression, it is not subject to First Amendment scrutiny at all.

Were it the case that Indiana *in practice* targeted only expressive nudity, while turning a blind eye to nude beaches and unclothed purveyors of hot dogs and machine tools, it might be said that what posed as a regulation of conduct in general was in reality a regulation of only communicative conduct. Respondents have adduced no evidence of that. Indiana officials have brought many public indecency prosecutions for activities having no communicative element.

Since the Indiana regulation is a general law not specifically targeted at expressive conduct, its application to such conduct does not in my view implicate the First Amendment. The First Amendment explicitly protects "the freedom of speech [and] of the press"—oral and written speech—not "expressive conduct." When any law restricts speech even for a purpose that has nothing to do with the suppression of communication, we insist that it meet the high, First Amendment standards of justification. But virtually *every* law restricts conduct, and virtually *any* prohibited conduct can be prohibited for an expressive purpose. It cannot reasonably be demanded, therefore, that every restriction of expression incidentally produced by a general law regulating conduct pass normal First Amendment scrutiny, or even—as some of our cases have suggested, see, e.g., *United States v. O'Brien*—that it be justified by an "important or substantial" governmental interest. Nor do our holdings require such justification: we have never invalidated the application of a general law simply because the conduct it reached was being engaged in for expressive purposes and the government could not demonstrate a sufficiently important state interest.

This is not to say that the First Amendment affords no protection to expressive conduct. Where the government prohibits conduct *precisely because of its communicative attributes,* we hold the regulation unconstitutional. See, e.g., *United States v. Eichman; Texas v. Johnson.*

In each of the foregoing cases, we explicitly found that suppressing communication was the object of the regulation of conduct. Where that has not been the case, however—where suppression of communicative use of the conduct was merely the incidental effect of forbidding for other reasons—we have allowed the regulation to stand.

Justice SOUTER concurring in the judgment.

I agree with the plurality and the dissent that an interest in freely engaging in the nude dancing at issue here is subject to a degree of First Amendment protection. [Souter also agreed that *O'Brien* was the appropriate test.] I nonetheless write separately to rest my concurrence in the judgment, not on the possible sufficiency of society's moral views to justify the limitations at issue, but on the State's substantial interest in combating the secondary effects of adult entertainment establishments of the sort typified by respondents' establishments [that encourage prostitution, and increase sexual assaults and other criminal activity].

It is, of course, true that this justification has not been articulated by Indiana's legislature or by its courts. This asserted justification for the statute may not be ignored merely because it is unclear to what extent this purpose motivated the Indiana Legislature in enacting the statute. Our appropriate focus is not an empirical enquiry into the actual intent of the enacting legislature, but rather the existence or not of a current governmental interest in the service of which the challenged application of the statute may be constitutional.

Justice WHITE, joined by Justices MARSHALL, BLACKMUN, and STEVENS, dissented:

The Court's analysis is erroneous in several respects. Both the Court and Justice Scalia in his concurring opinion overlook a fundamental and critical aspect of our cases upholding the States' exercise of their police powers. None of the cases they rely upon, including *O'Brien,* involved anything less than truly *general* proscriptions on individual conduct. In *O'Brien,* for example, individuals were prohibited from destroying their draft cards at any time and in any place, even in completely private places such as the home. By contrast, in this case Indiana does not suggest that its statute applies to, or could be applied to , nudity wherever it occurs, including the home. We do not understand the Court or Justice Scalia to be suggesting that Indiana could constitutionally enact such an intrusive prohibition.

Thus, the Indiana statute is not a *general* prohibition of the type we have upheld in prior cases. As a result, the Court's and Justice Scalia's simple references to the State's general interest in promoting societal order and morality is not sufficient justification for a statute which concededly reaches a significant amount of protected expressive activity. Instead, in applying the *O'Brien* test, we are obligated to carefully examine the reasons the State has chosen to regulate this expressive conduct in a less than general statute. In other words, when the State enacts a law which draws a line between expressive conduct which is regulated and nonexpressive conduct of the same type which is not regulated, *O'Brien* places the burden on the State to justify the distinctions it has made. Closer inquiry as to the purpose of the statute is surely appropriate.

[EDITORIAL NOTE: Justice White then stressed that nudity was an essential part of the expressive nature of nude dancing, and:]

It is only because nude dancing performances may generate emotions and feelings of eroticism and sensuality among the spectators that the State seeks to regulate such expressive activity, apparently on the assumption that creating or emphasizing such thoughts and ideas in the minds of the spectators may lead to increased prostitution and the degradation of women. But generating thoughts, ideas, and emotions is the essence of communication. The nudity element of nude dancing performances cannot be neatly pigeonholed as mere "conduct" independent of any expressive component of the dance.

Content-based restrictions "will be upheld only if narrowly drawn to accomplish a compelling governmental interest." [E]ven if there were compelling governmental interests, the Indiana statute is not narrowly drawn. If the State is genuinely concerned with prostitution and associated evils, it can adopt restrictions that do not interfere with the expressiveness of nonobscene nude dancing performances. For instance, the State could perhaps require that, while performing, nude performers remain at all times a certain minimum distance from spectators, that nude entertainment be limited to certain hours, or even that establishments providing such entertainment be dispersed throughout the city. Banning an entire category of expressive activity, however, does not satisfy the narrow tailoring requirement of First Amendment strict scrutiny.

COMMENT

Rehnquist for the Court, Souter in a concurrence, and White in dissent all agree that *O'Brien* is the appropriate test. Why then don't they agree on the result? A principal reason for the Court's conclusion that the Indiana law prohibiting nudity was valid under *O'Brien* was that the law was unrelated to the suppression of freedom of expression. The law was applied to prohibit nude dancing not because of the expressive component of such dancing but because of the nudity. Justice White in dissent disputed this analysis. He thought that the expressive element in nude dancing was central to the state's reason for prohibiting it. Rehnquist and White then disagree, among other things, about whether the third prong of the *O'Brien* test is satisfied—is the regulation unrelated to the suppression of freedom of expression?

Justice David Souter, although agreeing with the Court that *O'Brien* is the right test, has yet a different take on how the test should be applied. Souter says that it is not morality that satisfies the substantial governmental interest aspect of the *O'Brien* test, but rather the secondary effects that flow from nude dancing such as prostitution and the encouragement of criminal activity.

The secondary effects doctrine was enunciated in *Renton v. Playtime Theatres, Inc.*, 475 U.S. 41 (1986). There a municipal zoning ordinance required adult movie theaters to be located in a designated area in the city. As a result, 95 percent of the city's physical space was off-limits to such establishments. The ordinance was justified not because of the desirability of prohibiting the content of the movies shown at adult theaters but because of the adverse secondary effects that flow from adult theaters such as neighborhood deterioration and crime.

The difficulty with the secondary effects doctrine is that content-based regulation may be validated by insisting that what is being prohibited is not the message but the secondary effects of the message. Why do you think Souter prefers secondary effects to morality as the government interest justifying the application of the Indiana law to nude dancing? Recall that in the flag burning cases the majority said that, under the First Amendment, government may not proclaim what is orthodox and what is not.

Unlike the other justices, Antonin Scalia questions the propriety of using the *O'Brien* test in *Barnes*. What about it troubles him? Scalia says that the Indiana law prohibiting nudity is a general law regulating conduct. Such legislation should not be subjected to the four-part *O'Brien* test simply because it has some incidental effect on expression. In short, Scalia doesn't think the demanding *O'Brien* test should be used to evaluate general legislation regulating conduct. For general legislation regulating conduct—even if it has an incidental effect on restricting free expression—the rational basis test is the appropriate message of the validity of the law.

In the flag burning cases, *Texas v. Johnson* and *United States v. Eichman,* Scalia joined the majority in determining that the prosecutions violated the First Amendment and could not go forward. Why weren't the flag burning statutes, which forbade the desecration or mutilation of the flag, general laws regulating conduct? Scalia said that in those cases the conduct prohibited was punished *because of* its communicative aspects. He denies that this is true on the ban on nude dancing in *Barnes*.

Since the *O'Brien* test yielded such conflicting results among the justices in *Barnes,* how useful is it?

PUBLIC FACILITIES AND THE PUBLIC FORUM

To what extent may a public facility be used as a public forum? The public forum concept received its classic expression from Professor Harry Kalven, who argued that "in an open and democratic society the streets, the parks, and other public places, are an important facility for public discussion and political process. They are in brief a public forum that the citizen can commandeer." The public forum concept became a vehicle for providing First Amendment–based legitimacy to the civil rights protests of the 1960s. In *Edwards v. South Carolina,* 372 U.S. 229 (1963), the Court based a right to use the Columbia, South Carolina state capitol grounds for a civil rights protest on the First Amendment. Similarly, *Brown v. Louisiana,* 383 U.S. 131

(1966), upheld the right to stage a protest at a library practicing racial segregation. In these cases the particular protests were deemed not to be inconsistent with the public facility's primary use.

Not every public facility, however, may be used as a public forum. In 1967, in *Adderley v. Florida,* 385 U.S. 39 (1966), the Supreme Court, by a 5–4 vote, denied public forum treatment to jailhouse grounds. Justice Black for the Court said that the "state, no less than the private owner of property has power to preserve the property under its control for the use to which it is lawfully dedicated." Justice Black rejected the idea that "people who want to propagandize protests or views have a constitutional right to do so whenever and however and wherever they please." But it is not always easy to identify which public facilities are appropriate sites for public forums and which are not. In *Adderley,* Justice Douglas dissented and reminded his colleagues that prisons such as the Tower of London and Bastille had been sites of protest: "[W]hen a prison houses political prisoners or those who many think are unjustly held, it is an obvious center for protest." *Adderley* indicated that there were public forums and nonpublic forums. Expressive activity at nonpublic forums could be regulated as long as the regulation had some rational basis.

If the public facility is to be used as a public forum, such use must be consistent with the primary purposes of the facility. This was emphasized once again in *Greer v. Spock,* 424 U.S. 828 (1976). In *Greer,* Justice Stewart rejected a First Amendment challenge to military post regulations that prohibited partisan political activity as well as the dissemination of pamphlets without the prior approval of military authorities. The Court denied that "whenever members of the public are permitted freely to visit a place owned or operated by the Government then that place becomes a forum for the purposes of the First Amendment." The purpose of military reservations was to "train soldiers, not to provide a public forum."

Justice Brennan, joined by Justice Marshall, dissented in *Greer* and expressed grave concern that a narrow approach to whether the "form of expression is compatible with the activities occurring at the locale" might lead to a "rigid characterization" that a "given locale is not a public forum." The result would be that "certain forms of public speech at the locale" would be suppressed even though the expression involved was entirely compatible with the principal purposes of the public facility in question.

What merit is there in generally viewing public facilities as broadly hospitable to public forum purposes? Professor Emerson offers this rationale: "It forces the relevant community to listen to the expression of grievances rather than allowing them to be swept under the rug." *See* Emerson, *The Affirmative Side of the First Amendment*, 15 Ga. L. Rev. 795, 809 (1981).

The Public Forum and Time-Place-Manner Regulation

Are protests next to school grounds permissible? The answer to this question may depend on whether classes are in session. In *Grayned v. Rockford*, 408 U.S. 104 (1972), the Court held that raucous demonstrations next to a school where classes were being conducted were not protected under the First Amendment. Protests at such sites would be governed by time, place, and manner regulation:

> The nature of the place, "the pattern of its normal activities, dictates the kinds of regulations of time, place and manner that are reasonable." Although a silent vigil may not unduly interfere with a public library, making a speech in the reading room almost certainly would. The same speech should be perfectly appropriate in a park. The crucial question is whether the manner of expression is basically compatible with the normal activity of a particular place at a particular time. Our cases make clear that in assessing the reasonableness of regulation, we must weigh heavily the fact that communication is involved; the regulation must be narrowly tailored to further the State's legitimate interest.

The Limited Public Forum

In *Heffron v. International Society for Krishna Consciousness*, 452 U.S. 640 (1981), the Court held that a state regulation that limited the sale or distribution of Hare Krishna materials to a fixed location was valid. The Krishnas contended the regulation violated the First Amendment by suppressing their religious practice of going to public places to walk around to distribute and solicit donations for their beliefs. But the Court held that the state fair grounds were a limited public forum. In other words, the state could designate only a part of the public facility—in this case the state fair grounds—for First Amendment purposes.

Heffron held that the restriction by a state entity of distribution, sales, and solicitation activities to a fixed site was a permissible time, place, and manner regulation. What are the characteristics of a valid time, place, and manner regulation?

Justice White in *Heffron* identifies four such characteristics: (1) The restriction cannot be based on either the content or subject matter of the speech. (2) A valid time, place, and manner regulation must serve a significant governmental interest. (What significant governmental interest was served by the regulation in *Heffron?*) (3) A time, place, and manner regulation is not valid if the state could accomplish its purpose by less drastic means. (Were less drastic means open to the Minnesota State Fair?) (4) A time, place, and manner regulation is valid if alternative forums exist for the purpose of communicating the expression that is limited by the regulation in controversy. (Were such alternative forums present in the *Heffron* context?)

Clark v. Community for Creative Non-Violence

468 U.S. 288, 104 S. CT. 3065, 82 L. ED. 2D 221 (1984).

[EDITORIAL NOTE: *The National Park Service sought to prohibit demonstrators from sleeping in Lafayette Park and the Mall in Washington, D.C. The demonstrators built a tent city and then, by sleeping in these places, sought to publicize the plight of the homeless. The National Park Service justified this decision by relying on its regulation prohibiting camping in certain parks. The regulation was upheld as a valid time-place-manner regulation.*]

Justice WHITE delivered the opinion of the Court.

Expression, whether oral or written or symbolized by conduct, is subject to reasonable time, place and manner restrictions. We have often noted that restrictions of this kind are valid provided that they are justified without reference to the content of the regulated speech, that they are narrowly tailored to serve a significant governmental interest, and that they leave open ample alternative channels for communication of information. *City Council v. Taxpayers for Vincent*, 104 S.Ct. 2132 (1984); *Heffron v. International Society for Krishna Consciousness*.

It is also true that a message may be delivered by conduct that is intended to be communicative and that, in context, would reasonably be understood by the viewer to be communicative. *Spence v. Washington,* 418 U.S. 405 (1974); *Tinker v. Des Moines School District* [see, p. 83]. Symbolic expression of this kind may be forbidden or regulated if the conduct itself may constitutionally be regulated, if the regulation is narrowly drawn to further a substantial governmental interest, and if the interest is unrelated to the suppression of free speech. *United States v. O'Brien* [see, p. 81].

The United States submits, as it did in the Court of Appeals, that the regulation forbidding sleeping is defensible either as a time, place, or manner restriction or as a regulation of symbolic conduct. We agree with that assessment.

That sleeping, like the symbolic tents themselves, may be expressive and part of the message delivered by the demonstration does not make the ban any less a limitation on the manner of demonstrating, for reasonable time, place, and manner regulations normally have the purpose and direct effect of limiting expression but are nevertheless valid. Neither does the fact that sleeping, *arguendo,* may be expressive conduct, rather than oral or written expression, render the sleeping prohibition any less a time, place, or manner regulation. Considered as such, we have very little trouble concluding that the Park Service may prohibit overnight sleeping in the parks involved here.

The requirement that the regulation be content neutral is clearly satisfied. The courts below accepted that view, and it is not disputed here that the prohibition on camping, and on sleeping specifically, is content neutral and is not being applied because of disagreement with the message presented. Neither was the regulation faulted, nor could it be, on the ground that without overnight sleeping the plight of the homeless could not be communicated in other ways. The regulation otherwise left the demonstration intact, with its symbolic city, signs, and the presence of those who were willing to take their turns in a day-and-night vigil. Respondents do not suggest that there was, or is, any barrier to delivering to the media, or to the public by other means, the intended message concerning the plight of the homeless.

It is also apparent to us that the regulation narrowly focuses on the Government's substantial interest in maintaining the parks in the heart of our capital in an attractive and intact condition, readily available to the millions of people who wish to see and enjoy them by their presence. It is urged by respondents that if the symbolic city of tents was to be permitted and if the demonstrators did not intend to cook, dig, or engage in aspects of camping other than sleeping, the incremental benefit to the parks could not justify the ban on sleeping, which was here an expressive activity said to enhance the message concerning the plight of the poor and homeless. We cannot agree. In the first place, we seriously doubt that the First Amendment requires the Park Service to permit a demonstration in Lafayette Park and the Mall involving a 24-hour vigil and the erection of tents to accommodate 150 people. Furthermore, although we have assumed for present purposes that the sleeping banned in this case would have an expressive element, it is evident that its major value to this demonstration would be facilitative. Without a permit to sleep, it would be difficult to get the poor and homeless to participate or to be present at all. The sleeping ban, if enforced, would thus effectively limit the nature, extent, and duration of the demonstration and to that extent ease the pressure on the Parks.

If the Government has a legitimate interest in ensuring that the National Parks are adequately protected, which we think it has, and if the parks would be more exposed to harm without the sleeping prohibition than with it, the ban is safe from invalidation under the First Amendment as a reasonable regulation on the manner in which a demonstration may be carried out. As in *City Council v. Taxpayers for Vincent,* the regulation "responds precisely to the substantive problems which legitimately concern the [Government]." 466 U.S., at 810, 104 S.Ct., at 2132.

We have difficulty, therefore, in understanding why the prohibition against camping, with its ban on sleeping overnight, is not a reasonable time, place, and manner regulation that withstands constitutional scrutiny. Surely the regulation is not unconstitutional on its face. None of its provisions appears unrelated to the ends that it was designed to serve. Nor is it any less valid when applied to prevent camping in Memorial-core parks by those who wish to demonstrate and deliver a message to the public and the central government. Damage to the parks as well as their partial inaccessibility to other members of the public can as easily result from camping by demonstrators as by non-demonstrators. In neither case must the Government tolerate it. This is no more than a reaffirmation that reasonable time, place, and manner restrictions on expression are constitutionally acceptable.

Contrary to the conclusion of the Court of Appeals, the foregoing analysis demonstrates that the Park Service regulation is sustainable under the four-factor standard of *United States v. O'Brien, supra,* for validating a regulation of expressive conduct, which, in the last analysis is little, if any, different from the standard applied to time, place, and manner restrictions. No one contends that aside from its impact on speech a rule against camping or overnight sleeping in public parks is beyond the constitutional power of the Government to enforce. And for the reasons we have discussed above, there is a substantial government interest in conserving park property, an interest that is plainly served by, and requires for its implementation, measures such as the proscription of sleeping that are designed to limit the wear and tear on park properties. That interest is unrelated to suppression of expression.

We are unmoved by the Court of Appeals' view that the challenged regulation is unnecessary, and hence invalid, because there are less speech-restrictive alternatives that could have satisfied the government interest in preserving park lands. We do not believe that either *United States v. O'Brien* or the time, place, and manner decisions assign to the judiciary the authority to replace the Park Service as the manager of the Nation's parks or endow the judiciary with the competence to judge how much protection of park lands is wise and how that level of conservation is to be attained.

Accordingly, the judgment of the Court of Appeals is *Reversed.*

COMMENT

The application of a National Park Service no-camping regulation to prohibit demonstrators from sleeping in Lafayette Park and the Mall was deemed valid. Justice White concluded in *Clark* that the prohibition was valid under either the *O'Brien* standards, see p. 81, or the standards appropriate for judging the reasonableness of time-place-manner regulation in the public

forum. Justice White concluded that the *O'Brien* standards and the time-place-manner standards, see p. 92, were the same. Is there any problem with his conclusion?

Professor Keith Werhan believes that both *O'Brien* and *Clark* are "disturbingly insensitive to the facilitation of robust public debate." *See* Werhan, *The O'Briening of Free Speech Methodology,* 19 Ariz. State L.J. 635, 649 (1987). Although he thinks the regulation upheld in both cases had "little impact on the degree of public debate," Professor Werhan sees dangers in the use of the *O'Brien* balancing test:

> [*O'Brien*] compromises the hard problems of free speech methodology by largely ignoring them. Using an operational focus on the ends and means of government regulation, the Court decides cases without assessing the speech side of the controversy. Thus, in [*O'Brien*] the Court ruled for the government without deciding whether symbolic conduct was protected by the first amendment; in [*Clark*], the Court ruled for the government without deciding whether sleep could constitute symbolic conduct. *Id.* at 673.

By implication, the *Heffron* standards appear more sensitive to First Amendment values. Is this because *O'Brien* is too easily satisfied "by a legitimate governmental interest of whatever weight"? *See Werhan* at 651.

Boos v. Barry: Regulation of the Traditional Public Forum

Boos v. Barry, 485 U.S. 312 (1988), illustrates the continuing attachment of the Court to a heightened scrutiny standard of review in the case of content-based regulation of a public forum when significantly less restrictive regulatory alternatives are available. The facts that gave rise to the case follow.

A District of Columbia law prohibited the display of signs bringing foreign governments into "public odium" or "public disrepute" within 500 feet of foreign embassies. The statute also prohibited persons from congregating within 500 feet of an embassy and not dispersing when ordered to do so. Some individuals wished to carry signs critical of the governments of the Soviet Union and Nicaragua and also wished to congregate within 500 feet of those embassies. They brought a facial First Amendment challenge to these provisions. In *Boos,* the Court, per Justice O'Connor, held that the provision forbidding display of signs criticizing foreign governments violated the First Amendment. Justice O'Connor said the speech involved was political speech; that it was exercised in a traditional public forum, that is, a public street; and, finally, that the display provision was content-based.

To the argument that the statute was not content-based because the government did not itself select between viewpoints, Justice O'Connor responded that she agreed that the provision was not viewpoint-based: "The display clause determines which viewpoint is acceptable in a neutral fashion by looking to the policies of foreign governments." This would prevent the display clause from being "directly viewpoint-based," but it did not render the statute content-neutral. The government was enforcing a prohibition based on content against "an entire category of speech—signs and displays critical of foreign governments."

Justice O'Connor concluded that the "display clause is content-based." She pointed out that the city did not point to the secondary effects of picket signs in front of embassies such as congestion, interference with ingress or egress, visual clutter, or embassy security. Instead, reliance was in protecting the dignity of foreign diplomatic personnel "by sheltering them from speech that is critical of their governments." Such a justification for the display provision was focused "only on the content of the speech and the direct impact that speech has on its listeners."

Justice O'Connor concluded that as a content-based restriction on political speech in a public forum, the display provision of the District of Columbia law "must be subjected to the most exacting scrutiny":

> Thus, we have requested the State to show that the "regulation is necessary to serve a compelling state interest and that it is normally drawn to achieve that end."

Even assuming that "international law recognized a dignity interest" to the point that it should be considered "sufficiently 'compelling' to support a content-based restriction on speech," the display provision was still not narrowly tailored to serve that interest. A federal statute prohibiting intimidating or harassing foreign officials or obstructing them in the course of

their duties illustrated the ready availability of a significantly less restrictive alternative. This demonstrated that the display clause was not sufficiently narrowly tailored to withstand the rigors of the strict scrutiny standard.

The Court, per Justice O'Connor, concluded that the congregation clause was not overbroad:

> So narrowed, the congregation clause withstands First Amendment overbreadth scrutiny. It does not reach a substantial amount of constitutionally protected conduct; it merely regulates the place and manner of certain demonstrations.

The Public Forum— A Static or Dynamic Concept?

International Society for Krishna Consciousness, Inc. v. Lee

505 U.S. 672, 112 S. CT. 2701, 120 L. ED. 2D 541 (1992).

[EDITORIAL NOTE: *Chief Justice Rehnquist, for the Court in* International Society for Krishna Consciousness, Inc. v. Lee, *upheld a regulation prohibiting soliciting in the interior of a publicly owned airport terminal. The Court held 5–4 that an airport terminal was not a public forum. The regulation was challenged by the Krishnas who perform a ritual called "sankirtan" that includes going to public places to solicit funds to support their religion.*]

Chief Justice REHNQUIST delivered the opinion of the Court.

In this case we consider whether an airport terminal operated by a public authority is a public forum and whether a regulation prohibiting solicitation in the interior of an airport terminal violates the First Amendment.

It is uncontested that the solicitation at issue in this case is a form of speech protected under the First Amendment. But it is also settled that the government need not permit all forms of speech on property that it owns and controls. Where the government is acting as a proprietor, managing its internal operations, rather than acting as lawmaker with the power to regulate or license, its actions will not be subjected to the heightened review to which its actions as a lawmaker may be subject.

[Our] cases reflect, either implicitly or explicitly, a "forum based" approach for assessing restrictions that the government seeks to place on the use of its property. Under this approach, regulation of speech on government property that has traditionally been available for public expression is subject to the highest scrutiny. Such regulations survive only if they are narrowly drawn to achieve a compelling state interest. The second category of public property is the designated public forum, whether of a limited or unlimited character—property that the state has opened for expressive activity by part or all of the public. Regulation of such property is subject to the same limitations as that governing a traditional public forum. Finally, there is all remaining public property. Limitations on expressive activity conducted on this last category of property must survive only a much more limited review. The challenged regulation need only be reasonable, as long as the regulation is not an effort to suppress the speaker's activity due to disagreement with the speaker's view.

The parties do not disagree that this is the proper framework. Rather, they disagree whether the airport terminals are public fora or nonpublic fora. They also disagree whether the regulation survives the "reasonableness" review governing nonpublic fora, should that provide the appropriate category. [W]e conclude that the terminals are nonpublic fora and that the regulation reasonably limits solicitation.

[T]he government does not create a public forum by inaction. The decision to create a public forum must *instead* be made "by intentionally opening a nontraditional forum for public discourse." Finally, we have recognized that the location of property also has bearing because separation from acknowledged public areas may serve to indicate that the separated property is a special enclave, subject to greater restriction.

[G]iven the lateness with which the modern air terminal has made its appearance, it hardly qualifies for the description of having "immemorially . . . time out of mind" been held in the public trust and used for purposes of expressive activity. [T]he tradition of airport activity does not demonstrate that airports have historically been made available for speech activity. Nor can we say that these particular terminals, or airport terminals generally, have been intentionally opened by their operators to such activity; the frequent and continuing litigation evidencing the operators' objectives belies any such claim.

Thus, we think that neither by tradition nor purpose can the terminals be described as satisfying the standards we have previously set out for identifying a public forum. The restrictions here challenged, therefore, need only satisfy a requirement of reasonableness. We have no doubt that under this standard the prohibition on solicitation passes muster.

We have on many prior occasions noted the disruptive effect that solicitation may have on business. In addition, face-to-face solicitation presents risks of duress that are an appropriate target of regulation. The skillful, and unprincipled, solicitor can target the most vulnerable, including those accompanying children or those suffering physical impairment and who cannot easily avoid the solicitation.

The Port Authority has concluded that its interest in monitoring the activities can best be accomplished by limiting solicitation and distribution to the sidewalk areas outside the terminals. This sidewalk area is frequented by an overwhelming percentage of airport users. Thus the resulting access of those who would solicit the general public is quite complete. In turn we think it would be odd to conclude that the Port Authority's terminal regulation is unreasonable despite the Port Authority having otherwise assured access to an area universally traveled. [W]e conclude that the solicitation ban is reasonable.

Lee v. International Society for Krishna Consciousness, Inc.

505 U.S. 830, 112 S. CT. 2709, 120 L. ED. 2D 669 (1992).

PER CURIAM.

For the reasons expressed in the opinions of Justices O'Connor, Justice Kennedy, and Justice Souter in *[International Society for Krishna Consciousness v. Lee]*, the judgment of the Court of Appeals holding that the ban on distribution of literature in the Port Authority airport terminals is invalid under the First Amendment is affirmed.

[EDITORIAL NOTE: *In summary, in the two airport terminal Krishna cases, the Court upheld the ban on solicitation of funds but struck down the ban on distribution of printed or written materials within the terminals.*

Chief Justice Rehnquist's dissent in Lee v. International Society for Krishna Consciousness, Inc., *joined by Justices White, Scalia and Thomas, focused upon the similarities between the risks posed by solicitation and distribution:*]

Leafletting presents risks of congestion similar to those posed by solicitation. It presents, in addition, some risks unique to leafletting. And of course, as with solicitation, these risks must be evaluated against a backdrop of the substantial congestion problem facing the Port Authority and with an eye to the cumulative impact that will result if all groups are permitted terminal access. Viewed in this light, I conclude that the distribution ban, no less than the solicitation ban, is reasonable. I therefore dissent from the Court's holding striking the distribution ban.

Justice O'CONNOR, concurred in the judgment upholding the ban on solicitation but she struck down the ban on leafletting as unreasonable:

[W]e have expressly noted that leafletting does not entail the same kinds of problems presented by face-to-face solicitation. With the possible exception of avoiding litter, it is difficult to point to any problems intrinsic to the act of leafletting that would make it naturally incompatible with a large multipurpose forum such as those at issue here.

Because I cannot see how peaceful pamphleteering is incompatible with the multipurpose environment of the Port Authority airports, I cannot accept that a total ban on that activity is reasonable without an explanation as to why such a restriction "preserv[es] the property for the several uses to which it has been put."

Of course, it is still open for the Port Authority to promulgate regulations of the time, place, and manner of leafletting which are "content-neutral, narrowly tailored to serve a significant government interest, and leave open ample alternative channels of communication."

[EDITORIAL NOTE: *Justice KENNEDY concurred in the judgment upholding the solicitation ban. Although he believed that airport terminals should be viewed as traditional public forums, he thought the solicitation ban was valid because it was content-neutral. Justice Kennedy believed that the public forum concept should be dynamic and reflect the impact technological change has on communication.*]

Justice KENNEY concurring:

In my view the airport corridors and shopping areas outside of the passenger security zones, areas operated by the Port Authority, are public forums, and speech in those places is entitled to protection against all government regulation inconsistent with public forum principles. The Port Authority's blanket prohibition on the distribution or sale of literature cannot meet those stringent standards, and I agree it is invalid under the First and Fourteenth Amendments. The Port

Authority's rule disallowing in-person solicitation of money for immediate payment, however, is in my view a narrow and valid regulation of time, place, and manner of protected speech in this forum, or else is a valid regulation of the non-speech element of expressive conduct. I would sustain the Port Authority's ban on solicitation and receipt of funds.

Under [the] categorical view the application of public-forum analysis to airport terminals seems easy. Airports are of course public spaces of recent vintage, and so there can be no time-honored tradition associated with airports of permitting free speech. And because governments have often attempted to restrict speech within airports, it follows a fortiori under the Court's analysis that they cannot be so-called "designated forums." So, the Court concludes, airports must be nonpublic forums, subject to minimal First Amendment protection.

This analysis is flawed at its very beginning. It leaves the government with almost unlimited authority to restrict speech on its property by doing nothing more than articulating a non-speech related purpose for the area, and it leaves almost no scope for the development of new public forums absent the rare approval of the government. The Court's error lies in its conclusion that the public-forum status of public property depends on the government's defined purpose for the property, or on an explicit decision by the government to dedicate the property to expressive activity. In my view, the inquiry must be an objective one, based on the actual, physical characteristics and uses of the property.

The Court's analysis rests on an inaccurate view of history. The notion that traditional public forums are property which have public discourse as their principal purpose is a most doubtful fiction. The types of property that we have recognized as the quintessential public forums are streets, parks, and sidewalks. It would seem apparent that the principal purpose of streets and sidewalks, like airports, is to facilitate transportation, not public discourse, and we have recognized as much. Similarly the purpose for the creation of public parks may be as much for the beauty and open space as for discourse. Thus under the Court's analysis, even the quintessential public forums would appear to lack the necessary elements of what the Court defines as a public forum.

In my view the policies underlying the [public forum] doctrine cannot be given effect unless we recognize that open, public spaces and thoroughfares which are suitable for public discourse may be public forums, whatever their historical pedigree and without concern for a precise classification of the property. Without this recognition our forum doctrine retains no relevance in times of fast-changing technology and increasingly insularity. In a country where most citizens travel by automobile, and parks all too often become locales for crime rather than social intercourse, our failure to recognize the possibility that new types of government property may be appropriate forums for speech will lead to a serious curtailment of our expressive activity.

One of the places left in our mobile society that is suitable for discourse is a metropolitan airport. It is of particular importance to recognize that such spaces are public forums because in these days an airport is one of the few government-owned spaces where many persons have extensive contact with other members of the public. In my view, our public forum doctrine must recognize this reality, and allow the creation of public forums which do not fit within the narrow tradition of streets, sidewalks, and parks. We have allowed flexibility in our doctrine to meet changing technologies in other areas of constitutional interpretation, and I believe we must do the same with the First Amendment.

Justice SOUTER, with whom Justice BLACK-MUN and Justice STEVENS joined, concurred in the judgment in *Lee v. International Society for Krishna Consciousness* that the ban on distribution of literature was invalid but dissented from the judgment in *International Society for Krishna Consciousness v. Lee* that the ban on solicitation was valid.

I agree with Justice Kennedy's view of the rule that should determine what is a public forum and with his conclusion that the airports at issue here qualify as such.

From the Court's conclusion, however, sustaining the total ban on solicitation of money for immediate payment, I respectfully dissent.

As Justice Kennedy's opinion indicates, the respondent comes closest to justifying the restriction as one furthering the government's interest in preventing coercion and fraud. The claim to be preventing coercion is weak to start with. While a solicitor can be insistent, a pedestrian on the street or airport concourse can simply walk away or walk on. Since there is no evidence of any type of coercive conduct, over and above the merely importunate character of the open and public solicitation, that might justify a ban, the regulation cannot be sustained to avoid coercion.

As for fraud, our cases do not provide government with plenary authority to ban solicitation just because it could be fraudulent. The evidence of fraudulent conduct here is virtually nonexistent.

Even assuming a governmental interest adequate to justify some regulation, the present ban would fall when subjected to the requirement of narrow tailoring.

Finally, I do not think the Port Authority's solicitation ban leaves open the "ample" channels of communication required of a valid content-neutral time, place and manner restriction. A distribution of preaddressed envelopes is unlikely to be much of an alternative. The practical reality of the regulation, which this Court can never ignore, is that it shuts off a uniquely powerful avenue of communication for organizations like the International Society for Krishna Consciousness, and may, in effect, completely prohibit unpopular and poorly funded groups from receiving funds in response to protected solicitation.

COMMENT

Chief Justice Rehnquist's opinion in *International Society for Krishna Consciousness v. Lee* is instructive for his summary of the standards of review for the three kinds of public forums—the traditional public forum, the limited or designated public forum, and the nonpublic forum. Content-based regulation of speech or expressive activity in the public forum and the limited public forum must survive the strict scrutiny standard of review. But regulation of expressive activity in the nonpublic forum will be valid as long as it is reasonable and not viewpoint-based.

In a sense, the proof of these tests is in their application. Rehnquist said that the airport terminal was not a traditional or limited public forum and, therefore, the ban on solicitation need only meet the nonpublic forum standard of review. The regulation need only be shown to be reasonable. Justice Kennedy said the airport terminal should be looked at as if it were a traditional public forum. Nevertheless, he said the solicitation ban was valid because it was a content-neutral time-place-manner regulation.

Chief Justice Rehnquist's view of the traditional public forum is controversial. In his view, unless public facilities have traditionally and historically been used for purposes of expressive activity, they may not be viewed as public forums. Justice Kennedy's conception of the public forum is much more fluid and dynamic. In Kennedy's view, public space where people come together can be characterized as a public forum even though that space may have been created to serve the needs of a technology unknown to the common law. Justice Souter agreed with Justice Kennedy's conception of the public forum as a dynamic concept:

> To treat the class of such forums as closed by their description as "traditional," taking that word merely as a charter for examining the history of the particular public property claimed as a forum, has no warrant in a Constitution whose values are not to be left behind in the city streets that are no longer the only focus of our community life. We need not say that all "transportation nodes" or all airports are public forums in order to find that certain metropolitan airports are. *Thus, the enquiry may and must relate to the particular property at issue and not necessarily to the "precise classification of the property."* [Emphasis added.]

What would be an example of an airport that would *not* be a public forum? A military airport might be a possibility, but a journalist—or a civil libertarian—might quarrel with this characterization. Why? In a sense, Souter's explanation may unintentionally give support to Rehnquist's historical approach to identifying a traditional public forum. The Rehnquist approach is at least clear—traditional public forums are streets, parks, and sidewalks.

The purpose of the First Amendment is to protect freedom of communication. But Rehnquist's view does not take into account that technology changes the nature of communication. If First Amendment tools like the public forum doctrine that are used to confer protection are limited only to the forums of communication known to the past, can the First Amendment do its job?

CHAPTER 3

CATEGORIES OF EXPRESSION AND THE SCOPE OF FIRST AMENDMENT PROTECTION

CHAPTER OUTLINE

CATEGORIZING EXPRESSION

In the preceding chapter, some of the major features of contemporary First Amendment methodology were examined. An important part of this methodology is the categorical approach to free expression problems. In view of the impor-

tance this approach has had in First Amendment law, we have treated it separately in this chapter.

Under the categorical approach to free expression problems, some categories of speech are accorded full protection, some receive lesser protection, and some are accorded no protection at all. Political speech or discourse has been considered to merit the highest protection on the ground that the protection and encouragement of speech dealing with self-governance by a democracy's citizens are essential to its preservation. Obscenity, on the other hand, has been held not to merit First Amendment protection because it has been deemed to concern interests the First Amendment was not designed to protect (see Chapter 10).

In *R.A.V. v. City of St. Paul*, 505 U.S. 377 (1992), Justice John Paul Stevens in a concurring opinion gave a crisp summary of the categorical approach: "Our First Amendment decisions have created a rough hierarchy in the constitutional protection of speech. Core political speech occupies the highest, most protected position; commercial speech and non-obscene, sexually explicit speech are regarded as a sort of second-class expression; obscenity and fighting words receive the least protection of all."

The use of the categorical approach by the U.S. Supreme Court has not been static. Commercial speech evolved from an unprotected status to one of greater protection. On the other hand, the *R.A.V.* case in 1992 held that fighting words—a category of speech previously thought unprotected—were not subject to unlimited regulation. Subject discrimination with fighting words was deemed not permissible. Child pornography has been held to be an unprotected category (see Chapter 10, pp. 636–637). Pornography degrading women, it is urged, should similarly be added to the unprotected categories of expression (see Chapter 10, p. 645). Clearly, the categorical approach is currently subject to considerable ferment. This is illustrated by the passionate debate—chronicled in this chapter— about whether racist speech should be treated as an unprotected category of expression.

Finally, it should be noted that the categorical approach to freedom of expression is under general attack. Justice Stevens's concurring opinion in *R.A.V.*, pp. 139–141, subjects the entire categorical approach to severe criticism: "Few dividing lines in First Amendment law are straight and unwavering, and efforts at categorization inevitably give rise only to fuzzy boundaries. The quest for doctrinal certainty through the definition of categories and subcategories is, in my opinion, destined to fail." This viewpoint should be compared with Justice Antonin Scalia's observation at the outset of his opinion for the Court in *R.A.V.*: "[A] limited categorical approach has remained an important part of our First Amendment jurisprudence."

COMMERCIAL SPEECH

Commercial speech is accorded varying levels of protection depending upon its content. For example, if a company solicits investors on the basis of assets that it claims to own but in fact does not own, it may be prosecuted under the securities laws even though it has engaged in speech or expression. In this example, the expression is clearly false. This is commercial speech, but it is unquestionably subject to regulation and punishment. What about expression that is not false but is simply engaged in for the commercial benefit of the disseminator? What is its First Amendment status?

In *Valentine v. Chrestensen*, 316 U.S. 52, 54 (1942), the Supreme Court held that the Constitution placed no restraint on government "as respects purely commercial advertising." An exhibitor of a navy surplus submarine prepared a handbill that advertised the submarine and solicited visitors to come and look at it for a fee. When the exhibitor attempted to distribute the handbill, he was advised by the police commissioner that such activities would violate a municipal anti-litter ordinance. The exhibitor then had a bright idea. He prepared a message for the back of the handbill. The message protested the action of the City Dock Department that had refused him wharfage facilities at a city pier for the exhibition of the boat. In short, the exhibitor tried to insulate his commercial advertising by adding some protected political speech.

Could a municipal anti-litter ordinance be constitutionally enforced against the exhibitor of a submarine who criticized city decisions on the back of his advertising handbill? The Supreme Court held that the city could enforce the ordinance. The Court believed that Chrestensen printed his noncommercial message solely to evade the ordinance. Chrestensen's subjective intent, in other words, belied his claim for First Amendment protection because it was merely a ploy to escape a lawful municipal regulation. If Chrestensen were permitted to distribute his flyers, so could every merchant, simply by affixing to the advertising copy some expression of opinion or protest. The streets of New York would be filled with litter, the sanitary code provision to the contrary notwithstanding.

There may be a Keystone Kops air about *Valentine v. Chrestensen*, but the case for a time sowed the seeds of a siginificant constitutional doctrine: the doctrine that the First Amendment does not embrace "purely" commercial speech.

The commercial speech doctrine that developed around *Chrestensen* came under vigorous attack from academic critics. Professor Martin Redish argued that commercial information contributed to individual self-fulfillment—an important justification for First Amendment protection. Accordingly, Professor Redish argued that commercial speech served First Amendment purposes: "[S]ome advertising today does convey rational information, and to the extent that the modern individual is apprised of this information, in many cases he is more likely, for the reasons discussed earlier, to give it, rather than equally rational political appeals, serious, thoughtful consideration." Martin Redish, *The First Amendment in the Marketplace: Commercial Speech and the Value of Free Expression*, 39 Geo. Wash. L. Rev. 429, 443–47 (1971).

The first in a series of cases that dealt a body blow to the idea that commercial speech is beyond the pale of First Amendment protection occurred in 1975. In *Bigelow v. Virginia*, 421 U.S. 809 (1975), the Court set aside the conviction of a weekly newspaper that violated a Virginia state law by accepting an abortion advertisement. The ad announced that placements in hospitals and clinics for low-cost abortions could be obtained in New York State. The Virginia state law that forbade the circulation of publications encouraging the procuring of abortions was held unconstitutional.

Bigelow set forth a ground-breaking doctrine. The Court repudiated the idea that a category of commercial speech such as commercial advertising was "stripped of First Amendment protection merely because it appear[ed] in that form." *Bigelow* was merely the first development in the waning of the commercial speech doctrine set forth in *Valentine v. Chrestensen*. The *coup de grâce* to the traditional doctrine was dealt by the following case.

Virginia State Board of Pharmacy v. Virginia Citizens Consumer Council, Inc.
425 U.S. 748, 96 S. CT. 1817, 48 L. ED. 2D 346 (1976).

Justice BLACKMUN delivered the opinion of the Court.

The plaintiff-appellees in this case attack, as violative of the First and Fourteenth Amendments, that portion of §54-524.35 of Va. Code Ann. (1974), which provides that a pharmacist licensed in Virginia is guilty of unprofessional conduct if he "(3) publishes, advertises or promotes, directly or indirectly, in any manner whatsoever, any amount, price, fee, premium, discount, rebate or credit terms for any drugs which may be dispensed only by prescription." The three-judge district court declared the quoted portion of the statute "void and of no effect," and enjoined the defendant-appellants, the Virginia State Board of Pharmacy and the individual members of that Board, from enforcing it.

The plaintiffs are an individual Virginia resident who suffers from diseases that require her to take prescription drugs on a daily basis, and two nonprofit organizations. Their claim is that the First Amendment entitles the user of prescription drugs to receive information, that pharmacists wish to communicate to them through advertising and other promotional means, concerning the prices of such drugs.

Certainly that information may be of value. Drug prices in Virginia, for both prescription and non-prescription items, strikingly vary from outlet to outlet even within the same locality. It is stipulated, for example, that in Richmond "the cost of 40 Achromycin tablets ranges from $2.59 to $6.00, a difference of 140% [sic]", and that in the Newport News-Hampton area the cost of tetracycline ranges from $1.20 to $9.00, a difference of 650%.

The question first arises whether even assuming that First Amendment protection attaches to the flow of drug price information, it is a protection enjoyed by the appellees as recipients of the information, and not solely, if at all, by the advertisers themselves who seek to disseminate that information.

Freedom of speech presupposes a willing speaker. But where a speaker exists, as is the case here, the protection afforded is to the communication, to its source and to its recipients both. This is clear from the decided cases. If there is a right to advertise, there is a reciprocal right to receive the advertising, and it may be asserted by these appellees.

The appellants contend that the advertisement of prescription drug prices is outside the protection of the First Amendment because it is "commercial speech." There can be no question that in past decisions the Court has given some indication that commercial speech is unprotected.

Our question is whether speech which does "no more than propose a commercial transaction," *Pittsburgh Press Co. v. Pittsburgh Comm'n on Human Relations,* 413 U.S. 376 (1973), is so removed from any "exposition of ideas," *Chaplinsky v. New Hampshire,* and from "'truth, science, morality, and arts in general, in its diffusion of liberal sentiments on the administration of Government,'" *Roth v. United States,* that it lacks all protection. Our answer is that it is not.

Focusing first on the individual parties to the transaction that is proposed in the commercial advertisement, we may assume that the advertiser's interest is a purely economic one. That hardly disqualifies him from protection under the First Amendment.

As to the particular consumer's interest in the free flow of commercial information, that interest may be as keen, if not keener by far, than his interest in the day's most urgent political debate. Appellees' case in this respect is a convincing one. Those whom the suppression of prescription drug price information hits the hardest are the poor, the sick, and particularly the aged. A disproportionate amount of their income tends to be spent on prescription drugs; yet they are the least able to learn, by shopping from pharmacist to pharmacist, where their scarce dollars are best spent.

Advertising, however tasteless and excessive it sometimes may seem, is nonetheless dissemination of information as to who is producing and selling what product, for what reason, and at what price. So long as we preserve a predominantly free enterprise economy, the allocation of our resources in large measure will be made through numerous private economic decisions. It is a matter of public interest that those decisions, in the aggregate, be intelligent and well informed. To this end, the free flow of commercial information is indispensable. And if it is indispensable to the proper allocation of resources in a free enterprise system, it is also indispensable to the formation of intelligent opinions as to how that system ought to be regulated or altered. Therefore, even if the First Amendment were thought to be primarily an instrument to enlighten public decision making in a democracy, we could not say that the free flow of information does not serve that goal.

Arrayed against these substantial individual and societal interests are a number of justifications for the advertising ban. These have to do principally with maintaining a high degree of professionalism on the part of licensed pharmacists. Indisputably, the state has a strong interest in maintaining that professionalism.

It appears to be feared that if the pharmacist who wishes to provide the low cost, and assertedly low quality services is permitted to advertise, he will be taken up on his offer by too many unwitting customers. They will choose the low-cost, low-quality service and drive the "professional" pharmacist out of business. They will respond only to costly and excessive advertising, and end up paying the price. They will go from one pharmacist to another, following the discount, and destroy the pharmacist-customer relationship. They will lose respect for the profession because it advertises. All this is not in their best interests, and all this can be avoided if they are not permitted to know who is charging what.

There is, of course, an alternative to this highly paternalistic approach. That alternative is to assume that this information is not in itself harmful, that people will perceive their own best interests if only they are well enough informed, and that the best means to that end is to open the channels of communication rather than to close them. If they are truly open, nothing prevents the "professional" pharmacist from marketing his own assertedly superior product, and contrasting it with that of the low-cost, high-volume prescription drug retailer. But the choice among these alternative approaches is not ours to make or the Virginia General Assembly's. It is precisely this kind of choice, between the dangers of suppressing information, and the dangers of its misuse if it is freely available, that the First Amendment makes for us. Virginia is free to require whatever professional standards it wishes of its pharmacists; it may subsidize them or protect them from competition in other ways. But it may not do so by keeping the public in ignorance of the entirely lawful terms that competing pharmacists are offering. In this sense, the justifications Virginia has offered for suppressing the flow of prescription drug price information, far from persuading us that the flow is not protected by the First Amendment, have reinforced our view that it is. We so hold.

In concluding that commercial speech, like other varieties, is protected, we of course do not hold that it can never be regulated in any way. Some forms of commercial speech regulation are surely permissible. We mention a few only to make clear that they are not before us and therefore are not foreclosed by this case.

There is no claim, for example, that the prohibition on prescription drug price advertising is a mere time, place, and manner restriction. We have often approved restrictions of that kind provided that they are justified without reference to the content of the regulated speech, that they serve a significant governmental interest, and that in so doing they leave open ample alternative channels for communication of the information. Whatever may be the proper bounds of time, place, and manner restrictions on commercial speech, they are plainly exceeded by this Virginia statute, which singles out speech of a particular content and seeks to prevent its dissemination completely.

Nor is there any claim that prescription drug price advertisements are forbidden because they are false or misleading in any way. Untruthful speech, commercial or otherwise, has never been protected for its own sake. *Gertz v. Robert Welch, Inc.* Obviously, much commercial speech is not provably false, or even wholly false, but only deceptive or misleading. We foresee no obstacle to a State's dealing effectively with this problem. The First Amendment, as we construe it today, does not prohibit the State from insuring that the stream of commercial information flows cleanly as well as freely.

Also, there is no claim that the transactions proposed in the forbidden advertisements are themselves illegal in any way. Cf. *Pittsburgh Press Co. v. Pittsburgh Comm'n on Human Relations.* Finally the special problems of the electronic broadcast media are likewise not in this case.

What is at issue is whether a State may completely suppress the dissemination of concededly truthful information about entirely lawful activity, fearful of that information's effect upon its disseminators and its recipients. Reserving other questions, we conclude that the answer to this one is in the negative.

The judgment of the district court is affirmed.

Justice STEVENS took no part in the consideration or decision of this case.

Justice STEWART, concurring.

Justice REHNQUIST, dissenting.

In this case the Court has unfortunately substituted for the wavering line previously thought to exist between commercial speech and protected speech a no more satisfactory line of its own— that between "truthful" commercial speech, on the one hand, and that which is "false and misleading" on the other. The difficulty with this line is not that it wavers, but on the contrary that it is simply too Procrustean to take into account the congeries of factors which I believe could, quite consistently with the First and Fourteenth Amendments, properly influence a legislative decision with respect to commercial advertising.

COMMENT

Virginia Pharmacy unquestionably gave new constitutional protection to commercial speech. The consumer interest in accurate price information was deemed to be related to speech that dealt with self-governance in a democracy. Such information involved the allocation of economic resources. This information related to informed and intelligent decision making by the citizenry. Government barriers to the free flow of such information were not permissible.

Not everyone greeted the new protection for commercial speech with enthusiasm. Thomas H. Jackson and John Calvin Jeffries, Jr., *Commercial Speech: Economic Due Process and the First Amendment*, 65 Va. L. Rev. 1 (1979) declared that commercial speech was "remarkable for its insignificance." Commercial speech "neither contributes to self-government nor nurtures the realization of the individual personality." Jackson and Jeffries concluded that the advertising considered in *Virginia Pharmacy* "should be subject to government regulation on the same terms as any other aspect of the marketplace." Economic decisions about the wisdom of prescription drug price advertising belonged to the legislature and should not be transferred to the courts on the basis of an unjustified claim to First Amendment protection.

In contrast, Justice Harry Blackmun, and earlier Professor Redish, asserted that advertising and commercial speech have a legitimate claim to First Amendment protection. This claim has been challenged. Critics Ronald K. L. Collins and David M. Skover, *Commerce & Communi-*

cation, 71 Tex. L. Rev. 697, 732 (1993) provide this rebuttal:

> By associating itself with the defenders of the old reason, modern mass advertising claims a high level of constitutional protection. But it does so talismanically. Merely by invoking the norm of informed and rational decisionmaking, imagistic advertising professes to promote it. Exploiting the weighty importance of reason for its own ends, such advertising does precisely what it does best: it appropriates the symbols of informational advertising, reconstructs them in its own image, and returns them to the legal community in the form of constitutional defenses.

Commercial Speech—Still Less Equal

Even after *Virginia Pharmacy,* commercial speech was still, to steal a phrase from George Orwell, a little less equal than other kinds of speech. In a much quoted footnote in *Virginia Pharmacy,* Justice Blackmun explained why commercial speech was still not given the same kind of protection accorded news reporting or political commentary:

> In concluding that commercial speech enjoys First Amendment protection, we have not held that it is wholly undifferentiable from other forms. There are commonsense differences between speech that does "no more than propose a commercial transaction," and other varieties. Even if the differences do not justify the conclusion that commercial speech is valueless, and thus subject to complete suppression by the state, they nonetheless suggest that a different degree of protection is necessary to insure that the flow of truthful and legitimate commercial information is unimpaired. The truth of commercial speech, for example, may be more easily verifiable by its disseminator than, let us say, news reporting or political commentary, in that ordinarily the advertiser seeks to disseminate information about a specific product or service that he himself provides and presumably knows more about than anyone else. Also, commercial speech may be more durable than other kinds. Since advertising is the *sine qua non* of commercial profits, there is little likelihood of its being chilled by proper regulation and forgone entirely.

Attributes such as these, the greater objectivity and hardiness of commercial speech, may make it less necessary to tolerate inaccurate statements for fear of silencing the speaker. They may also make it appropriate to require that a commercial message appear in such a form, or include such additional information, warnings and disclaimers, as are necessary to prevent it being deceptive.

Not everyone has accepted this justification for continuing to validate some regulation of commercial advertising. Justice Blackmun in *Virginia Pharmacy* justified a greater measure of regulation for commercial speech than for political speech on the ground that commercial claims are more easily verified than political ones. Professor Martin Redish disagrees and argues that the difference in regulation between commercial and political speech has quite another rationale:

> We presumably find such regulation in the political process so abhorrent not because we wish to condone misleading political claims, but rather because of the dangers inherent in allowing the government to regulate on the basis of the misleading nature of assertions made in the political process. The fear is that those in power will use such authority as a weapon with which to intimidate or defeat the political opposition, a result that has been all too common in our political history. In contrast, there is no reason to believe that much regulation of misleading advertising is similarly motivated.
> *See* Redish, *The Value of Free Speech,* 130 U. Pa. L. Rev. 591, 634–35 (1983).

Alex Kozinski and Stuart Banner contend that the distinction between commercial speech and noncommercial speech is of relatively recent vintage: "The commercial/non-commercial speech distinction seemed 'common-sense' to the *Virginia Pharmacy* Court because it had been around for over thirty years; there's nothing quite so common sense as the familiar." Alex Kozinski and Stuart Banner, *The Anti-History and Pre-History of Commercial Speech,* 71 Tex. L. Rev. 747, 755 (1993).

Kozinski and Banner argue that prior to *Chrestensen* Supreme Court case law did not make such a distinction. They point out—correctly—that *Chrestensen* itself didn't even use the phrase "commercial speech" but instead referred to "advertising." They also point out that *Virginia Pharmacy* actually continues the distinction: "[T]he fact that *Virginia Pharmacy* was broadening the protection afforded speech, rather than narrowing it, focused the controversy on whether commercial speech was entitled to any protection at all, rather than on whether commercial speech was more regulable than noncommercial speech. *Valentine v. Chrestensen*'s legacy lives on in the very case that supposedly buried it."

Does advertising itself—apart from its content—undermine a free and democratic press? Professor C. Edwin Baker contends that advertising revenues adversely influence media content. Baker says advertising has four effects that constitute "a profoundly troubling failure from a democratic perspective." First, advertising creates a disincentive on the part of the media to cover defects or problems with advertiser products. Second, in order to reach the largest audience and to avoid offending any potential buyer, the media are disinclined because of the force of advertising to take strong positions on controversial matters. Third, lighter or more trivial material is favored, and coverage of controversial matters is avoided because this may conflict with the creation of a "'buying mood'" in the audience. Fourth, advertising causes the media to shape content to attract the "'desired'" audience. Because of its buying power, the "'desired'" audience turns out to be an audience of the affluent. C. Edwin Baker, *Advertising and Free Expression* 69–70 (1994). Professor Baker contends advertising should be subject to regulation because this aids rather than detracts from editorial control over content. *Id.* at 135–37.

Central Hudson Gas & Electric Corp. v. Public Service Corp.

447 U.S. 557, 100 S. CT. 2343, 65 L. ED. 2D 341 (1980).

Justice POWELL delivered the opinion of the Court.

This case presents the question whether a regulation of the Public Service Commission of the State of New York violates the First and Fourteenth Amendments because it completely bans promotional advertising by an electrical utility.

In December 1973, the Commission, appellee here, ordered electric utilities in New York State to cease all advertising that "promot[es] the use of electricity." The order was based on the Commission's finding that "the interconnected utility system in New York State does not have sufficient fuel stocks or sources of supply to continue furnishing all customer demands for the 1973–1974 winter."

Three years later, when the fuel shortage had eased, the Commission requested comments from the public on its proposal to continue the ban on promotional advertising. Central Hudson Gas & Electric Corporation, the appellant in this case, opposed the ban on First Amendment grounds. After reviewing the public comments, the Commission extended the prohibition in a Policy Statement issued on February 25, 1977.

The Policy Statement divided advertising expenses "into two broad categories: promotional—advertising intended to stimulate the purchase of utility services—and institutional and informational, a broad category inclusive of all advertising not clearly intended to promote sales." The Commission declared all promotional advertising contrary to the national policy of conserving energy. It acknowledged that the ban is not a perfect vehicle for conserving energy. Still, the Commission adopted the restriction because it was deemed likely to "result in some dampening of unnecessary growth" in energy consumption.

The Commission's order explicitly permitted "informational" advertising designed to encourage *"shifts* of consumption" from peak demand times to periods of low electricity demand. [Emphasis in original.] Informational advertising would not seek to increase aggregate consumption, but would invite a leveling of demand throughout any given 24-hour period. The agency offered to review "specific proposals by the companies for specifically described [advertising] programs that meet these criteria." Appellant challenged the order in state court, arguing that the Commission had restrained commercial speech in violation of the First and Fourteenth Amendments. The Commission's order was upheld by the trial court and at the intermediate appellate level. The New York Court of Appeals affirmed.

The Commission's order restricts only commercial speech, that is, expression related solely to the economic interests of the speaker and its audience. In applying the First Amendment to this area, we have rejected the "highly paternalistic" view that government has complete power to suppress or regulate commercial speech. Even when advertising communicates only an incomplete version of the relevant facts, the First Amendment presumes that some accurate information is better than no information at all.

Nevertheless, our decisions have recognized "the 'common-sense' distinction between speech proposing a commercial transaction, which occurs in an area traditionally subject to government regulation, and other varieties of speech." The Constitution therefore accords a lesser protection to commercial speech than to other constitutionally guaranteed expression. The protection available for particular commercial expression turns on the nature both of the expression and of the governmental interests served by its regulation.

The First Amendment's concern for commercial speech is based on the informational function of advertising. Consequently, there can be no constitutional objection to the suppression of commercial messages that do not accurately inform the public about lawful activity. The government may ban forms of communications more likely to deceive the public than to inform it.

If the communication is neither misleading nor related to unlawful activity, the government's power is more circumscribed. The State must assert a substantial interest to be achieved by restrictions on commercial speech. Moreover, the regulatory technique must be in proportion to that interest. The limitation on expression must be designed carefully to achieve the State's goal. Compliance with this requirement may be measured by two criteria. First, the restriction must directly advance the state interest involved; the regulation may not be sustained if it provides only ineffective or remote support for the government's purpose. Second, if the governmental interest could be served as well by a more limited restriction on commercial speech, the excessive restrictions cannot survive.

Under the first criterion, the Court has declined to uphold regulations that only indirectly advance the state interest involved. The second criterion recognizes that the First Amendment mandates that speech restrictions be "narrowly drawn." The regulatory technique may extend only as far as the interest it serves. The State cannot regulate speech that poses no danger to the asserted state interest, nor can it completely suppress information when narrower restrictions on expression would serve its interest as well.

In commercial speech cases, then, a four-part analysis has developed. At the outset we must determine whether the expression is protected by the First Amendment. For commercial speech to come within that provision, it at least must concern lawful activity and not be misleading. Next, we ask whether the asserted governmental inter- *est is substantial. If both inquiries yield positive answers, we must determine whether the regulation directly advances the governmental interest asserted, and whether it is not more extensive than necessary to serve that interest.* [Emphasis added.]

We now apply this four-step analysis for commercial speech to the Commission's arguments in support of its ban on promotional advertising.

The Commission does not claim that the expression at issue either is inaccurate or relates to unlawful activity. Yet the New York Court of Appeals questioned whether Central Hudson's advertising is protected commercial speech. Because appellant holds a monopoly over the sale of electricity in its service area, the state court suggested that the Commission's order restricts no commercial speech of any worth. The court stated that advertising in a "noncompetitive market" could not improve the decision making of consumers. The court saw no constitutional problem with barring commercial speech that it viewed as conveying little useful information.

We come now finally to the critical inquiry in this case: whether the Commission's complete suppression of speech ordinarily protected by the First Amendment is no more extensive than necessary to further the State's interest in energy conservation. The Commission's order reaches all promotional advertising, regardless of the impact of the touted service on overall energy use. But the energy conservation rationale, as important as it is, cannot justify suppressing information about electric devices or services that would cause no net increase in total energy use. In addition, no showing has been made that a more limited restriction on the content of promotional advertising would not serve adequately the State's interests.

The Commission also has not demonstrated that its interest in conservation cannot be protected adequately by more limited regulation of appellant's commercial expression. To further its policy of conservation, the Commission could attempt to restrict the format and content of Central Hudson's advertising. It might, for example, require that the advertisements include information about the relative efficiency and expense of the offered service, both under current conditions and for the foreseeable future. In the absence of a showing that more limited speech regulations would be ineffective, we cannot approve the complete suppression of Central Hudson's advertising.

Mr. Justice REHNQUIST, dissenting.

The Court's analysis in my view is wrong in several respects. Initially, I disagree with the Court's conclusion that the speech of a state-created monopoly, which is the subject of a comprehensive regulatory scheme, is entitled to protection under the First Amendment. I also think that the Court errs here in failing to recognize that the state law is most accurately viewed as an economic regulation and that the speech involved (if it falls within the scope of the First Amendment at all) occupies a significantly more subordinate position in the hierarchy of First Amendment values than the Court gives it today. Finally, the Court in reaching its decision improperly substitutes its own judgment for that of the State in deciding how a proper ban on promotional advertising should be drafted. With regard to this latter point, the Court adopts as its final part of a four-part test a "no more extensive than necessary" analysis that will unduly impair a state legislature's ability to adopt legislation reasonably designed to promote interests that have always been rightly thought to be of great importance to the State.

This Court has previously recognized that although commercial speech may be entitled to First Amendment protection, that protection is not as extensive as that accorded to the advocacy of ideas. The test adopted by the Court elevates the protection accorded commercial speech that falls within the scope of the First Amendment to a level that is virtually indistinguishable from that of noncommercial speech. I think the Court in so doing has effectively accomplished the "devitalization" of the First Amendment. New York's order here is in my view more akin to an economic regulation to which virtually complete deference should be accorded by this Court.

[I]n a number of instances government may constitutionally decide that societal interests justify the imposition of restrictions on the free flow of information. When the question is whether a given commercial message is protected, I do not think this Court's determination that the information will "assist" consumers justifies judicial invalidation of a reasonably drafted state restriction on such speech when the restriction is designed to promote a concededly substantial state interest. I consequently disagree with the Court's conclusion that the societal interest in the dissemination of commercial information is sufficient to justify a restriction on the State's authority to regulate promotional advertising by utilities; indeed, in the case of a regulated monopoly, it is difficult for me to distinguish "society" from the state legislature and the Public Service Commission. Nor do I think there is any basis for concluding that individual citizens of the State will recognize the need for and act to promote energy conservation to the extent the government deems appropriate, if only the channels of communication are left open. Thus, even if I were to agree that commercial speech is entitled to some First Amendment protection, I would hold here that the State's decision to ban promotional advertising, in light of the substantial state interest at stake, is a constitutionally permissible exercise of its power to adopt regulations designed to promote the interests of its citizens.

The notion that more speech is the remedy to expose falsehood and fallacies is wholly out of place in the commercial bazaar, where if applied logically the remedy of one who was defrauded would be merely a statement, available upon request, reciting the Latin maxim *"caveat emptor."* But since "fraudulent speech" in this area is to be remediable under *Virginia Board,* the remedy of one defrauded is a lawsuit or an agency proceeding based on common law notions of fraud that are separated by a world of difference from the realm of politics and government. What time, legal decisions, and common sense have so widely severed, I declined to join in *Virginia Board,* and regret now to see the Court reaping the seeds that it there sowed. For in a democracy, the economic is subordinate to the political, a lesson that our ancestors learned long ago, and that our descendants will undoubtedly have to relearn many years hence.

It is [in] my view inappropriate for the Court to invalidate the State's ban on commercial advertising here based on its speculation that in some cases the advertising may result in a net savings in electrical energy use, and in the cases in which it is clear a net energy savings would result from utility advertising, the Public Service Commission would apply its ban so as to proscribe such advertising. Even assuming that the Court's speculation is correct, I do not think it follows that facial invalidation of the ban is the appropriate course.

COMMENT

Usually, when government regulates speech on the basis of content, a strict scrutiny standard of review is used. As the *Central Hudson* case illustrates, this standard is not used with commercial speech. It may not be regulated *carte blanche* as an unprotected category of expression might be, but on the other hand, it does not receive the same protection as political speech, which would be evaluated under the strict scrutiny standard of review—a standard that is very hard for government to meet. Instead, the four-part test set forth in *Central Hudson* employs an intermediate standard of review.

Professor Steven Shiffrin argues that a great gulf exists between *Virginia Pharmacy* and *Central Hudson*. In his view, *Virginia Pharmacy* extended the reach of the First Amendment to commercial speech because "paternalistic suppression of information" was not permissible under the First Amendment. The state could not decide for the consumers of Virginia that they would be better off if the prices of prescription drugs were not advertised. Is *Central Hudson* a retreat from this position? Shiffrin contends that *Central Hudson* permits "paternalistic suppression of true commercial information" as long as the government has a substantial interest in suppressing the information. Shiffrin, *The First Amendment and Economic Regulation: Away from a General Theory of the First Amendment,* 78 Nw. U. L. Rev. 1212, 1221 (1984).

Does Shiffrin's view pay too little attention to the fourth prong of *Central Hudson*—the requirement that the government regulation be no more extensive than necessary?

Board of Trustees of State University of New York v. Fox, 492 U.S. 469 (1989), however, substantially weakened the fourth prong of the *Central Hudson* test. *Fox* involved a state university regulation barring private commercial activity on campus except for specifically exempted activities. The plaintiff students sued alleging that their First Amendment rights were violated when the campus police broke up a "Tupperware" party because such an activity was not exempted under the regulation.

Justice Scalia, speaking for the Court, framed the issue as follows: Was government regulation of commercial speech invalid if it did not use the least restrictive means to achieve the governmental interests at stake? What were the substantial interests served by the regulation? The state university said its regulation promoted an educational instead of a commercial atmosphere on campus. Other interests served were safety and security as well as preventing the "commercial exploitation of students." Finally, the regulation was said to preserve the tranquility of the campus.

Fox held that regulations on commercial speech that served substantial governmental interests did not need to employ least restrictive means analysis. Justice Scalia conceded that this conclusion appeared to be a departure from *Central Hudson*.

> [O]ther formulations in our commercial speech cases support a more flexible meaning for the *Central Hudson* test. Whatever the conflicting tenor of our prior dicta may be, we now focus upon this specific issue for the first time, and conclude that the reason of the matter requires something short of a least-restrictive-means standard. What our decisions require is a " 'fit' between the legislature's ends and the means chosen to accomplish those ends,"—a fit that is not necessarily perfect, but reasonable.

Justice Scalia denied that his revision of the fourth prong of *Central Hudson* was "too permissive." He pointed out that this test was not like the rational basis test—a test that government can usually meet fairly easily. Instead, he said: "[W]e require the governmental goal to be substantial, and the cost to be carefully calculated."

As one follows the path of the case law, it is clear that the larger measure of protection for commercial speech that *Virginia Pharmacy* appeared to promise has not been fulfilled: "*Fox*, therefore, represents a further weakening of the full First Amendment status for protected commercial speech seemingly offered by *Virginia Pharmacy,* since it further weakens the *Central Hudson* test—a test which itself has been criticized by defenders of commercial speech as insufficiently protective." Jerome A. Barron and C. Thomas Dienes, *First Amendment Law in a Nutshell* 158 (1993).

In *Cincinnati v. Discovery Network, Inc.*, 507 U.S. 410 (1993), the Court, per Justice Stevens, demonstrated that the application of the *Fox* revision to *Central Hudson* does not necessarily mean that government regulation of commercial speech will be upheld. The city of Cincinnati imposed a ban on newsracks containing commercial publications but not on newspaper newsracks. The purported rationale for the ban on commercial newsracks was attributed to the city's concerns for safety and aesthetics on its sidewalks. *Fox* was applied *and* the ban was invalidated. Justice Stevens said the city had not established a "reasonable fit" between its interests in safety and aesthetics and the means chosen to safeguard those interests—"selective prohibition of newsracks." The "reasonable fit" between goals and means required by *Fox* had simply not been met.

The Court pointed out that the ban on commercial newsracks would remove exactly 62 commercial newsracks from the streets of Cincinnati. Yet 1,500–2,000 newspaper racks would still be on the streets. In the light of this, it was hard to see how the city's safety and aesthetic concerns would be served by the selective and insignificant ban on commercial newsracks.

Cincinnati had wrongly assumed that commercial speech was really not accorded much First Amendment protection and thus was more easily susceptible to regulation than noncommercial speech, i.e., newspapers:

> [Cincinnati] attaches more importance to the distinction between commercial and noncommercial speech than our cases warrant and seriously underestimates the value of commercial speech. Cincinnati has enacted a sweeping ban that bars from its sidewalks a whole class of constitutionally protected speech. [W]e conclude that Cincinnati has failed to justify that policy. The regulation is not a permissible regulation of commercial speech, for on this record it is clear that the interests that Cincinnati has asserted are unrelated to any distinction between "commercial handbills" and "newspapers." For these reasons, Cincinnati's categorical ban on the distribution, via newsrack, of "commercial publications" cannot be squared with the dictates of the First Amendment.

Justice Blackmun remarked that it was "little wonder" that Cincinnati targeted commercial newsracks although a ban on such newsracks had nothing to do with the interests the city wished to serve. *Central Hudson* had watered down the substantial First Amendment protection accorded commercial speech in *Virginia Pharmacy:* "In this case, *Central Hudson*'s chickens have come home to roost." *Discovery Network* rejected what would have been an "extreme extension" of the logic of *Central Hudson* and *Fox*. Justice Blackmun concluded: "I hope the Court ultimately will come to abandon *Central Hudson*'s analysis entirely in favor of one that affords full protection for truthful, noncoercive commercial speech about lawful activities."

Chief Justice William Rehnquist, joined by Justices Byron White and Clarence Thomas, attacked the Court's opinion for not applying *Fox* properly:

> That there may be other—less restrictive—means by which Cincinnati could have gone about addressing its safety and esthetic concerns, then, does not render its prohibitions against [commercial] newsracks unconstitutional. Today's decision, though, places the city in the position of having to decide between restricting more speech—fully protected speech—and allowing the proliferation of the newsracks on its street corners to continue unabated. It scarcely seems logical that the First Amendment compels such a result.

In Rehnquist's view, the city should be allowed to decide for itself how to resolve its newsrack problem. The ban the city imposed was a "reasonable fit" under *Fox* and should have been upheld.

What Is the Definition of Commercial Speech?

In *Virginia Pharmacy,* Justice Blackmun gave a simple but not particularly rich definition of commercial speech, when he described it as speech that does "'no more than propose a commercial transaction.'" It will be recalled that the commercial transaction involved was the advertising of prescription drugs.

In *Central Hudson,* Justice Lewis Powell broadened the definition of commercial speech so that it reached "expression related to the economic interest of the speaker and its audience." From a speech-protective view, which definition of commercial speech is more desirable? Note that in *New York Times v. Sullivan* the editorial advertisement "Heed Their Rising Voices" was held not to constitute commercial speech.

In *Bolger v. Youngs Drug Product Co.*, 463 U.S. 60 (1983), the Court considered a federal statute banning the mailing of unsolicited promotional and informational advertising about contraceptives. The materials at issue included a discussion of venereal disease and family planning. Did these materials constitute commercial speech? The Court held that just because the material was included in an advertisement did not necessarily make it commercial speech. Nor did the commercial motivation of the sender make it commercial speech either. When added to the offer to sell, however, these factors led to the conclusion that the mailing *was* commercial speech. Even so, the statute survived a *Central Hudson* analysis. *Bolger* illustrates the difficulty involved in defining commercial speech: "[T]he difficulties in defining commercial speech as a category greatly contributed to the demise of the rigid categorical approach taken in the *Chrestensen* case." Jerome A. Barron and C. Thomas Dienes, *First Amendment Law in a Nutshell* 143 (1993).

Government Regulation of Truthful Advertising of Harmful But Not Illegal Activity

Posadas de Puerto Rico Associates v. Tourism Co. of Puerto Rico

478 U.S. 328, 106 S. CT. 2968, 92 L. ED. 2D 266 (1986).

[EDITORIAL NOTE: *In order to encourage tourism, Puerto Rico legalized casino gambling. Advertising of these casinos and gambling parlors to the Puerto Rican public was prohibited under the Games of Chance Act, but "restricted advertising" outside Puerto Rico to the U.S. mainland was permitted.*]

Justice REHNQUIST delivered the opinion of the Court.

The particular kind of commercial speech at issue here, namely, advertising of casino gambling aimed at the residents of Puerto Rico, concerns a lawful activity and is not misleading or fraudulent, at least in the abstract. We must therefore proceed to the three remaining steps of the *Central Hudson* analysis in order to determine whether Puerto Rico's advertising restrictions run afoul of the First Amendment. The first of these three steps involves an assessment of the strength of the government's interest in restricting the speech. The interest at stake in this case, as determined by the Superior Court, is the reduction of demand for casino gambling by the residents of Puerto Rico. These are some of the very same concerns, of course, that have motivated the vast majority of the 50 States to prohibit casino gambling. We have no difficulty in concluding that the Puerto Rico Legislature's interest in the health, safety, and welfare of its citizens constitutes a "substantial" governmental interest.

The last two steps of the *Central Hudson* analysis basically involve a consideration of the "fit" between the legislature's ends and the means chosen to accomplish those ends. Step three asks the question whether the challenged restrictions on commercial speech "directly advance" the government's asserted interest. In the instant case, the answer to this question is clearly "yes." The Puerto Rico Legislature obviously believed, when it enacted the advertising restrictions at issue here, that advertising of casino gambling aimed at the residents of Puerto Rico would serve to increase the demand for the product advertised. We think the legislature's belief is a reasonable one, and the fact that appellant has chosen to litigate this case all the way to this Court indicates that appellant shares the legislature's view.

Appellant argues, however, that the challenged advertising restrictions are underinclusive because other kinds of gambling such as horse racing, cockfighting, and the lottery may be advertised to the residents of Puerto Rico. Appellant's argument is misplaced for two reasons. First, whether other kinds of gambling are advertised in Puerto Rico or not, the restrictions on advertising of casino gambling "directly advance" the legislature's interest in reducing demand for games of chance. Second, the legislature's interest, as previously identified, is not necessarily to reduce demand for all games of chance, but to reduce demand for casino gambling. According to the Superior Court, horse racing, cockfighting, "picas," or small games of chance at fiestas, and the lottery "have been traditionally part of the Puerto Rican's roots," so that "the legislator could have been more flexible than in authorizing more sophisticated games which are not so widely sponsored by the people." In other words, the legislature felt that for Puerto Ricans the risks associated with casino gambling were significantly greater than those associated with the more traditional kinds of gambling in Puerto Rico. In our view, the legislature's separate classification of casino gambling, for purposes of the advertising ban, satisfies the third step of the *Central Hudson* analysis.

We also think it clear beyond peradventure that the challenged statute and regulations satisfy the fourth and last step of the *Central Hudson* analysis, namely, whether the restrictions on commercial speech are no more extensive than necessary to serve the government's interest. The narrowing constructions of the advertising restrictions announced by the Superior Court ensure that the restrictions will not affect advertising of casino gambling aimed at tourists, but will apply only to such advertising when aimed at the residents of Puerto Rico. Appellant contends, however, that the First Amendment requires the Puerto Rico Legislature to reduce demand for casino gambling among the residents of Puerto Rico not by suppressing commercial speech that might *encourage* such gambling, but by promulgating additional speech designed to *discourage* it. We reject this contention. We think it is up to the legislature to decide whether or not such a "counterspeech" policy would be as effective in reducing the demand for casino gambling as a restriction on advertising. The legislature could conclude, as it apparently did here, that residents of Puerto Rico are already aware of the risks of casino gambling, yet would nevertheless be induced by widespread advertising to engage in such potentially harmful conduct.

In short, we conclude that the statute and regulations at issue in this case, as construed by the Superior Court, pass muster under each prong of the *Central Hudson* test. We therefore hold that the Supreme Court of Puerto Rico properly rejected appellant's First Amendment claim.

Appellant argues, however, that the challenged advertising restrictions are constitutionally defective under our decisions in *Carey v. Population Services Int'l,* and *Bigelow v. Virginia.* [But] [i]n *Carey* and *Bigelow,* the underlying conduct that was the subject of the advertising restrictions was constitutionally protected and could not have been prohibited by the State. Here, on the other hand, the Puerto Rico Legislature surely could have prohibited casino gambling by the residents of Puerto Rico altogether. In our view, the greater power to completely ban casino gambling necessarily includes the lesser power to ban advertising of casino gambling, and *Carey* and *Bigelow* are hence inapposite.

Appellant also makes the related argument that, having chosen to legalize casino gambling for residents of Puerto Rico, the First Amendment prohibits the legislature from using restrictions on advertising to accomplish its goal of reducing demand for such gambling. We disagree. In our view, appellant has the argument backwards. [I]t is precisely *because* the government could have enacted a wholesale prohibition of the underlying conduct that it is permissible for the government to take the less intrusive step of allowing the conduct, but reducing the demand through restrictions on advertising. It would surely be a Pyrrhic victory for casino owners such as appellant to gain recognition of a First Amendment right to advertise their casinos to the residents of Puerto Rico, only to thereby force the legislature into banning casino gambling by residents altogether. It would just as surely be a strange constitutional doctrine which would concede to the legislature the authority to totally ban a product or activity, but deny to the legislature the authority to forbid the stimulation of demand for the product or activity through advertising on behalf of those who would profit from such increased demand.

Justice BRENNAN, with whom Justice MARSHALL and Justice BLACKMUN join, dissenting.

[N]o differences between commercial and other kinds of speech justify protecting commercial speech less extensively where, as here, the government seeks to manipulate private behavior by depriving citizens of truthful information concerning lawful activities. Accordingly, I believe that where the government seeks to suppress the dissemination of nonmisleading commercial speech relating to legal activities, for fear that recipients will act on the information provided, such regulation should be subject to strict judicial scrutiny.

The Court asserts that the Commonwealth has a legitimate and substantial interest in discouraging its residents from engaging in casino gambling. Neither the statute on its face nor the legislative history indicates that the Puerto Rico Legislature thought that serious harm would result if residents were allowed to engage in casino gambling; indeed, the available evidence suggests exactly the opposite. Puerto Rico has legalized gambling casinos, and permits its residents to patronize them. Thus, the Puerto Rico legislature has determined that permitting residents to engage in casino gambling will not produce the "serious harmful effects" that have led a majority of States to ban such activity.

The Court nevertheless sustains Puerto Rico's advertising ban because the legislature *could* have determined that casino gambling would seriously harm the health, safety, and welfare of the Puerto Rican citizens.[4] [I]t is incumbent upon the government to *prove* that the interests it seeks to further are real and substantial. [A]ppellee has not shown that "serious harmful effects" will result if Puerto Rico residents gamble in casinos, and the legislature's decision to legalize such activity suggests that it believed the opposite to be true. In short, appellees have failed to show that a substantial government interest supports Puerto Rico's ban on protected expression.

[E]ven assuming that an advertising ban would effectively reduce residents' patronage of gambling casinos, it is not clear how it would directly advance Puerto Rico's interest in controlling the "serious harmful effects", the Court associates with casino gambling. In particular it is unclear whether banning casino advertising would affect local crime, prostitution, the development of corruption, or the infiltration of organized crime. Because Puerto Rico actively promotes its casino to tourists, these problems are likely to persist whether or not residents are also encouraged to gamble. Absent some showing that a ban on advertising aimed only at residents will directly advance Puerto Rico's interests in controlling the harmful effects associated with casino gambling, Puerto Rico may not constitutionally restrict protected expression in that way.

Rather than suppressing constitutionally protected expression, Puerto Rico could seek directly to address the specific harms thought to be associated with casino gambling. [T]here has

been no showing that alternative measures would inadequately safeguard the Commonwealth's interest in controlling the harmful effects allegedly associated with casino gambling. Under these circumstances, Puerto Rico's ban on advertising clearly violates the First Amendment. I would hold that Puerto Rico may not suppress the dissemination of truthful information about entirely lawful activity merely to keep its residents ignorant.

Justice STEVENS, with whom Justice MARSHALL and Justice BLACKMUN join, dissenting.

Puerto Rico does not simply "ban advertising of casino gambling." Rather, Puerto Rico blatantly discriminates in its punishment of speech depending on the publication, audience, and words employed. Moreover, the prohibitions, as now construed by the Puerto Rico courts, establish a regime of prior restraint and articulate a standard that is hopelessly vague and unpredictable.

The general proposition advanced by the majority today—that a State may prohibit the advertising of permitted conduct if it may prohibit the conduct altogether—bears little resemblance to the grotesquely flawed regulation of speech advanced by Puerto Rico in this case. The First Amendment surely does not permit Puerto Rico's frank discrimination among publications, audiences, and words. Nor should sanctions for speech be as unpredictable and haphazardous as the roll of dice in a casino.

COMMENT

A principle that may be extracted from *Posadas* is that government may prohibit truthful and accurate advertising about an activity that is legal but nevertheless is thought to be harmful. So stated, it would seem that the new protection forged for commercial speech by *Virginia Pharmacy* has been undone. The significance of *Posadas*, however, is more subtle and more complicated. *Virginia Pharmacy* held that a whole category of truthful commercial advertising—the price of prescription drugs—cannot be banned. Arguably, *Posadas* does not change this. *Posadas* is distinguishable because it involves a selective rather than a total ban.

The *Posadas* Court, it should be noted, used the four-part *Central Hudson* test. Posadas does

---

[4] I do not agree that a ban on casino advertising is "less intrusive" than an outright prohibition of such activity. A majority of States have chosen not to legalize casino gambling, and we have never suggested that this might be unconstitutional. However, having decided to legalize casino gambling, Puerto Rico's decision to ban truthful speech concerning entirely lawful activity raises serious First Amendment problems. Thus, the "constitutional doctrine" which bans Puerto Rico from banning advertisements concerning lawful casino gambling is not so strange a restraint—it is called the First Amendment.

underscore the unpredictable and inherently sub-jective quality of that test. Justice Rehnquist, for example, says that the prohibition on advertising casino gambling to Puerto Ricans satisfies a sub-stantial governmental interest. Justice Brennan, however, in dissent questions whether this is so.

Any analysis of *Posadas* has to highlight Jus-tice Rehnquist's argument that the "greater includes the lesser." In other words, since Puerto Rico could prohibit casino gambling altogether, it may take the lesser step of prohibiting a certain category of advertising of casino gambling. Jus-tice Brennan's short response to this argument is that restraints on truthful and accurate speech are prohibited by the First Amendment. There-fore, the First Amendment precludes application of "greater-includes-the-lesser" analysis.

What alternative to *Central Hudson* would Justice Brennan use? Since the speech at issue here is in his view protected speech, he would use the strict scrutiny standard of review. In short, the Puerto Rico regulation would fall unless some compelling governmental interest could justify it. Since Puerto Rico permits casino gam-bling, Justice Brennan did not see how prevent-ing a segment of advertising concerning it can possibly serve a compelling governmental inter-est. Does *Posadas* authorize a ban on cigarette advertising in the print media?

In summary, in *Posadas* the combination of *Central Hudson* and the "greater-includes-the-lesser" analysis served as a lethal weapon against a First Amendment case for the protection of truthful and accurate advertising. Yet, in the post-*Posadas* era, *Cincinnati v. Discovery Net-work, Inc., supra,* and *Rubin v. Coors Beer, below,* show that commercial speech enjoys a larger measure of First Amendment protection than *Posadas* might have suggested.

In *United States v. Edge Broadcasting Co.,* 509 U.S. 418 (1993), a case involving commer-cial speech in the electronic media, *Central Hud-son* proved not to be a very reliable tool in serv-ing First Amendment ends. In this case, the Court upheld federal legislation, 18 U.S.C. §§ 1304 and 1307, that prohibited broadcasting of lottery advertising by stations located in states that ban lotteries. Federal law, however, did per-mit the broadcasting of lottery advertising by broadcasters licensed to a state that operated lot-teries. Edge Broadcasting Co. has a radio station in Elizabeth City, North Carolina, on the Vir-

ginia–North Carolina border. The great major-ity of Edge's audience are Virginians. Lotteries are legal in Virginia but not in North Carolina. Because of the federal legislation, Edge is not permitted to broadcast Virginia lottery advertise-ments and has, therefore, been deprived of large amounts of Virginia lottery advertising sales.

Edge asserted that this federal legislation vio-lated the First Amendment. But the Court, per Justice White, using the *Central Hudson* test, upheld the legislation: "[The] congressional pol-icy of balancing the interests of lottery and non-lottery States is the substantial governmental interest that satisfies *Central Hudson.*" What about the "reasonable fit" requirement? It was reasonable that Virginia's lottery policy should not control what stations in a neighboring state may broadcast. The federal law directly advanced the interest in federalism and consti-tuted a reasonable fit between ends and means even though it might not be served in a particu-lar case.

Justice Stevens, joined by Justice Blackmun, dissented. The selective ban on lottery advertis-ing was just not a "reasonable fit." The means selected were out of all proportion to the gov-ernment's "asserted interest in protecting the antilottery policies of nonlottery States." The sea change in public attitudes about lotteries under-mined the claim that a state's interest in discour-aging lotteries outweighed the "First Amend-ment right to distribute, and the public's right to receive, truthful, nonmisleading information about a perfectly legal activity conducted in a neighboring State."

In the *Coors* case that follows, the Supreme Court protects a form of truthful advertising despite *Posadas.* Moreover, *Coors* shows a tough application by the Court of the third prong of the *Central Hudson* test: Does the challenged regulation directly advance the interest asserted by the government?

Rubin v. Coors Brewing Co.
514 U.S. 476, 115 S. CT. 1585, 131 L. Ed. 2d 532 (1995).

[EDITORIAL NOTE: *A federal statute, 27 U.S.C. § 205(e)(2), prohibited beer labels from indicating the percentage of alcoholic content in the beer. The statute was enacted shortly after the adoption of the Twenty-first Amendment which ended Prohibition and repealed the Volstead Amendment. The Twenty-first*

Amendment largely left the regulation of alcoholic beverages to the states. A unanimous Court, per Justice Thomas, applying the Central Hudson test, invalidated the statute.]

Justice THOMAS delivered the opinion of the Court.

[The Government] has a significant interest in protecting the health, safety, and welfare of its citizens by preventing brewers from competing on the basis of alcohol strength, which could lead to greater alcoholism and its attendant social costs. We have no reason to think that strength wars, if they were to occur, would not produce the type of social harm that the Government hopes to prevent.

The Government attempts to bolster its position by arguing that the labeling ban not only curbs strength wars, but also "facilitates" state efforts to regulate alcohol under the Twenty-first Amendment. In the Government's view, this saves States that might wish to ban such labels the trouble of enacting their own legislation, and it discourages beer drinkers from crossing state lines to buy beer they believe is stronger. We conclude that the Government's interest in preserving state authority is not sufficiently substantial to meet the requirements of *Central Hudson.* Even if the Federal Government possessed the broad authority to facilitate state powers, in this case the Government has offered nothing that suggests that states are in need of federal assistance.

We conclude that Sec. 205(e)(2) cannot directly and materially advance its asserted interest because of the overall irrationality of the Government's regulatory scheme. While the laws governing labeling prohibit the disclosure of alcohol content unless required by state law, federal regulations apply a contrary policy to beer advertising. Like Sec. 205(e)(2), these restrictions prohibit statements of alcohol in advertising, but, unlike Sec. 205(e)(2), they apply only in States that affirmatively prohibit such advertisements. As only 18 States at best prohibit disclosure of content in advertisements, brewers remain free to disclose alcohol content in advertisements, but not on labels, in much of the country. The failure to prohibit the disclosure of alcohol content in advertising, which would seem to constitute a more influential weapon in any strength war than labels, makes no rational sense if the Government's true aim is to suppress strength wars.

Other provisions of the [federal law] and its regulations similarly undermine Sec. 205(e)(2)'s efforts to prevent strength wars. While Sec. 205(e)(2) bans the disclosure of alcohol content on beer labels, it allows the exact opposite in the case of wines and spirits. If combatting strength wars were the goal, we would assume that Congress would regulate disclosure of alcohol content for the strongest beverages as well as for the weakest ones.

To be sure, the Government's interest in combatting strength wars remains a valid goal. But the irrationality of this unique and puzzling regulatory framework ensures that the labeling ban will fail to achieve that end. There is little chance that Sec. 205(e)(2) can directly and materially advance its aim, while other provisions of the same act directly undermine and counteract its effects.

In sum, although the Government may have a substantial interest in suppressing strength wars in the beer market, the [law's] countervailing provisions prevent Sec. 205(e)(2) from furthering that purpose in a direct and material fashion. The [law's] defects are further highlighted by the availability of alternatives that would prove less intrusive to the First Amendment's protection for commercial speech. Because we find that Sec. 205(e)(2) fails the *Central Hudson* test, we affirm the decision of the court below.

Justice STEVENS, concurring in the judgment.

The Court's continued reliance on the misguided approach in *Central Hudson* makes this case appear more difficult than it is. [T]he borders of the commercial speech category are not nearly as clear as the Court has assumed. Whatever standard is applied, I find no merit whatsoever in the Government's assertion that an interest in restraining competition among brewers to satisfy consumer demand for stronger beverages justifies a statutory abridgment of truthful speech. Any "interest" in restricting the flow of accurate information because of the perceived danger of knowledge is anathema to the First Amendment; more speech and a better informed citizenry are among the central goals of the Free Speech Clause.

If Congress is concerned about the potential for increases in the alcohol content of malt beverages, it may, of course, take other steps to combat the problem without running afoul of the First Amendment—for example, Congress may limit directly the alcoholic content of malt beverages. But Congress may not seek to accomplish the same purpose through a policy of consumer ignorance, at the expense of the free speech rights of the sellers and purchasers. See *Virginia Pharmacy*. Although some regulations of statements about alcohol content that increase consumer awareness would be entirely proper, this statutory provision is nothing more than an attempt to blindfold the public.

COMMENT

As the *Coors* case illustrates, *Central Hudson* still endures as the test used to review the First Amendment validity of regulations of commercial speech. *Coors* also shows that application of *Central Hudson* does not necessarily mean that government regulation will be upheld. Despite its critics, *Central Hudson* has teeth. Notice also that the Court stresses that there were alternatives available to the government that were less destructive of First Amendment rights than the means selected by Congress.

In the *Coors* case, the government strongly urged that *Central Hudson* was too strict a standard to use for reviewing the federal law. Instead, as Justice Thomas observed in a footnote, the government urged the Court to adopt the "far more deferential" standard used in *Edge* and *Posadas*:

> [T]he Government suggests that legislatures have broader latitude to regulate speech that promotes socially harmful activities, such as alcohol consumption, than they have to regulate other types of speech.

Justice Thomas rejected this argument. Neither *Edge* nor *Posadas* required the Court to "craft an exception to the *Central Hudson* standards" for regulation concerning speech about socially harmful activities. In fact, Justice Thomas seemed to minimize the significance of *Edge* and *Posadas*:

> Indeed, *Edge Broadcasting* specifically avoided reaching the argument the Government makes here because the Court found that the regulation in question passed muster under *Central Hudson*. To be sure, *Posadas* did state that the Puerto Rican government could ban promotional advertising of casino gambling because it could have prohibited

gambling altogether. But the Court reached this argument only *after* it already had found that the state regulation survived the *Central Hudson* test.

Apparently, the *Coors* majority would apply *Central Hudson* whether the commercial speech regulation involved applies to socially harmful activities or not.

Justice Stevens, however, is dissatisfied with the *Central Hudson* test altogether. For one thing, he doubts that the divide between commercial and noncommercial speech is as clear as the Court thinks. What is important for him is not how one categorizes the expression but rather whether the information is true and accurate. If it is, it would take a very strong governmental interest to overcome the First Amendment protection that should naturally be extended to truthful and accurate speech. Justice Stevens seems to prefer the approach to commercial speech set forth in *Virginia Pharmacy* to the *Central Hudson* test now in vogue. Why do you think this is?

---

44 Liquormart, Inc. v. Rhode Island
116 S. CT. 1495, 134 L. Ed. 2d 711 (1996).

[EDITORIAL NOTE: *The Court, per Justice Stevens, invalidated as violative of the First Amendment a Rhode Island statutory bar against advertisements of retail liquor prices except at the place of sale. Rhode Island defended its statute on the ground that the Twenty-first Amendment gives the states the authority to regulate the use of alcoholic beverages within their borders. Rejecting this contention the Court held that "the Twenty-first Amendment does not qualify the constitutional prohibition against laws abridging the freedom of speech embodied in the First Amendment."*

With regard to the First Amendment rationale for its holding, the 44 Liquormart Court was doctrinally fractionated. Justice Stevens, joined by Justices Kennedy and Ginsburg, noted the Court's past hostility to complete bans on classes of advertising.]

Justice STEVENS delivered the opinion.

As our review of the case law reveals Rhode Island errs in concluding that *all* commercial speech regulations are subject to a similar form of constitutional review simply because they target a similar category of expression. When a State regulates commercial messages to protect consumers from misleading, deceptive or aggressive sales practices, or requires the disclosure of beneficial consumer information, the purpose of its regulation is consistent with the reasons for according constitutional protection to commercial speech and therefore justifies less than strict review. However, when a State entirely prohibits the dissemination of truthful, nonmisleading commercial messages for reasons unrelated to the preservation of a fair bargaining process, there is far less reason to depart from the rigorous review that the First Amendment generally demands.]

Precisely because bans against truthful, nonmisleading commercial speech rarely seek to protect consumers from either deception or overreaching, they usually rest solely on the offensive assumption that the public will respond "irrationally" to the truth. The First Amendment directs us to be especially skeptical of regulations that seek to keep people in the dark for what the government perceives to be their own good. That teaching applies equally to state attempts to deprive consumers of accurate information about their chosen products.

[**EDITORIAL NOTE:** *Justice Stevens, joined by Justices Kennedy, Souter, and Ginsburg, observed that* Central Hudson *cautioned that blanket prohibitions against truthful nonmisleading advertising should be examined with "special care." The Rhode Island ban failed the* Central Hudson *test. The ban did not directly advance the State's admittedly substantial interest in promoting temperance. The State had the burden of showing not only that the ban will advance its interest but that it will do so in a material way.*

The State had shown "no evidence to suggest that its speech prohibition will significantly *reduce marketwide consumption." Furthermore, the State failed to satisfy the* Central Hudson *requirement that a restriction on speech should not be more extensive than was necessary. Clearly, alternative modes of regulation such as mandating higher prices for liquor or increased taxation of liquor were available to promote the State interest in promoting temperance.*

Justice Stevens, joined by Justices Kennedy, Thomas, and Ginsburg, rejected the State's contention that it had simply exercised an appropriate legislative judgment in deciding that banning price advertising of liquor would encourage temperance. Furthermore, the State relied on Posadas *and its doctrine that deference should be accorded to its legislative decision electing the "lesser" regulation of banning price advertising because it could have elected the "greater" regulation of banning the sale of alcoholic beverages altogether. Although conceding that* Posadas *supported the State's reasoning, Justice Stevens declared that* Posadas *was in error and should not be followed:*]

Although we do not dispute the proposition that greater powers include lesser ones, we fail to see how that syllogism requires the conclusion that the State's power to regulate commercial *activity* is "greater" than its power to ban truthful, nonmisleading commercial *speech*. Contrary to the assumption made in *Posadas*, we think it quite clear that banning speech may sometimes prove far more intrusive than banning conduct. In short, we reject the assumption that words are necessarily less vital to freedom than actions, or that logic somehow proves that the power to prohibit an activity is necessarily "greater" than the power to suppress speech about it.

As a matter of First Amendment doctrine, the *Posadas* syllogism is even less defensible. The text of the First Amendment makes clear that the Constitution presumes that attempts to regulate speech are more dangerous than attempts to regulate conduct. That presumption accords with the essential role that the free flow of information plays in a democratic society. As a result, the First Amendment directs that government may not suppress speech as easily as it may suppress conduct, and that speech restriction cannot be treated as simply another means that the government may use to achieve its ends.

These basic First Amendment principles clearly apply to commercial speech; indeed, the *Posadas* majority impliedly conceded as much by applying the *Central Hudson* test. Thus, it is no answer that commercial speech concerns products and services that the government may freely regulate. Our decisions from *Virginia Pharmacy Bd.* on have made plain that a State's regulation of the sale of goods differs in kind from a State's regulation of accurate information about those goods.

Thus, just as it is perfectly clear that Rhode Island could not ban all obscene liquor ads except those that advocated temperance, we think it equally clear that its power to ban the sale of liquor entirely does not include a power to censor all advertisements that contain accurate and nonmisleading information about the price of the product.

Finally, we find unpersuasive the State's contention that the price advertising ban should be upheld because it targets commercial speech that pertains to a "vice" activity. [T]he scope of any "vice" exception to the protection afforded by the First Amendment would be difficult, if not impossible to define. [A] vice label that is unaccompanied by a corresponding prohibition against the commercial behavior at issue fails to provide a principled justification for the regulation of commercial speech about that activity.

Justice O'CONNOR, with whom the Chief Justice, Justice SOUTER, and Justice BREYER join, concurring in the judgment.

I agree with the Court that Rhode Island's price-advertising ban is invalid. I would resolve this case more narrowly, however, by applying our established *Central Hudson* test to determine whether this commercial-speech regulation survives strict scrutiny. Rhode Island's regulation fails the final prong [of *Central Hudson*]; that is, its ban is more extensive than necessary to serve the State's interest.

[I]n order for a speech restriction to pass muster under the final prong, there must be a fit between the legislature's goal and method, "a fit that is not necessarily perfect, but reasonable; that represents not necessarily the best single disposition but one whose scope is in proportion to the interest served." *Board of Trustees of State Univ. of N.Y. v. Fox.*

[EDITORIAL NOTE: *Justice O'Connor said that Rhode Island offered only one justification for its price-advertising ban: it would keep alcohol consumption low. But the fit between this goal and the means Rhode Island used to accomplish it was not reasonable.*]

If the target is simply higher prices generally to discourage consumption, the regulation imposes too great, and unnecessary, a prohibition on speech in order to achieve it. The State has other methods at its disposal—methods that would more directly accomplish this stated goal without intruding on sellers' ability to provide truthful, nonmisleading information to customers. A tax [w]ould have a far more certain and direct effect on prices without any restriction on speech. The principal opinion suggests further alternatives.

It is true that *Posadas* accepted as reasonable, without further inquiry, Puerto Rico's assertions that the regulation furthered the government's interest and were no more extensive than necessary to serve that interest. Since *Posadas,* however, this Court has examined more searchingly the State's professed goal, and the speech restriction put into place to further it, before accepting a State's claim that the speech restriction satisfies First Amendment scrutiny. *Rubin v. Coors Brewing Co.; Cincinnati v. Discovery Network, Inc.* The closer look that we have required since *Posadas* comports better with the purpose of the analysis set out in *Central Hudson,* by requiring the State to show that the speech restriction directly advances its interest and is narrowly tailored. Under such a closer look, Rhode Island's price-advertising ban clearly fails to pass muster.

Because Rhode Island's regulation fails even the less stringent standard set out in *Central Hudson,* nothing here requires adoption of a new analysis of the evaluation of commercial regulation. The principal opinion acknowledges that "even under the less than strict standard that generally applies in commercial speech cases, the State has failed to establish a reasonable fit between the abridgment of speech and its temperance goal." Because we need go no further, I would not here undertake the question whether the test we have employed since *Central Hudson* should be displaced.

Rhode Island's prohibition on alcohol-price advertising, as a means of keeping alcohol prices high and consumption low cannot survive First Amendment scrutiny. The Twenty-first Amendment cannot save this otherwise invalid regulation. While I agree with the Court's finding that the regulation is invalid, I would decide that issue on narrower grounds. I therefore concur in the judgment.

Justice SCALIA, concurring in part and concurring in the judgment.

I share Justice Thomas's discomfort with the *Central Hudson* test, which seems to me to have nothing more than policy intuition to support it. I also share Justice Stevens' aversion towards paternalistic governmental policies that prevent men and women from hearing facts that might not be good for them. On the other hand, it would also be paternalism for us to prevent the people of the States from enacting laws that we consider paternalistic, unless we have good reason to believe that the Constitution itself forbids them. Since I do not believe we have before us the wherewithal to declare *Central Hudson* wrong—or at least the wherewithal to say what ought to replace it—I must resolve this case in accord with our existing jurisprudence. I am not disposed to develop new law, or reinforce old, on this issue, and accordingly, I must concur in the judgment of the Court. [Scalia, however, joined Stevens in his treatment of the Twenty-first Amendment issue.]

Justice THOMAS, concurring and concurring in the judgment.

In cases such as this, in which the government's asserted interest is to keep legal users of a product or service ignorant in order to manipulate their choices in the marketplace, the balancing test adopted in *Central Hudson* should not be applied. Rather, such an "interest" is *per se* illegitimate and can no more justify regulation of "commercial" speech than it can justify regulation of "noncommercial" speech. I do not see a philosophical or historical basis for asserting that "commercial" speech is of "lower value" than "noncommercial" speech.

Both Justice Stevens and Justice O'Connor appear to adopt a stricter, more categorical interpretation of the fourth prong of *Central Hudson* than that suggested in some of our other opinions, one that could, as a practical matter, go a long way toward the position I take. [Their] opinions would appear to commit the courts to striking down restrictions on speech whenever a direct regulation (i.e., a regulation involving no restriction on speech regarding lawful activity at all) would be an equally effective method of dampening demand by legal users. [B]ut rather than "applying" *Central Hudson* to reach the inevitable result that all or most such advertising restrictions must be struck down, I would adhere to the doctrine adopted in *Virginia Pharmacy Bd.*, that all attempts to dissuade legal choices by citizens by keeping them ignorant are impermissible.

In my view, the *Central Hudson* test asks the courts to weigh the incommensurable—the value of knowledge versus the value of ignorance—and to apply contradictory premises—that informed adults are the best judges of their own interests, and that they are not. Rather than continuing to apply a test that makes no sense to me when the asserted state interest is of the type involved here, I would return to the reasoning and holding of *Virginia Pharmacy Bd.* Under that decision, these restrictions fall.

COMMENTS

Justice O'Connor says she would approach the issue in *44 Liquormart* more narrowly and would not use the "established *Central Hudson* test." But didn't Justice Stevens use the "established *Central Hudson* test" in *44 Liquormart?* In her view, he did not—probably because of his statement that *Central Hudson* should be applied with special care where a blanket ban on truthful advertising was concerned. Certainly, Stevens's opinion does not seem to express much enthusi-

asm for *Central Hudson*. This is not surprising given his refusal to follow it in the *Coors* case.

The opinions in *44 Liquormart* clearly throw into doubt the future precedential value of *Posadas*. Justice Stevens and those who joined with him would throw out *Posadas*. Justice O'Connor and those who joined with her declined to follow *Posadas* but stopped short of saying that *Posadas* is no longer good law. Why? Do they want to keep *Posadas* alive to use to validate legislation banning tobacco advertising?

More subtly, the various opinions also throw into doubt the future of the *Central Hudson* test. Clearly, Justice Stevens is more sympathetic to the *Virginia Pharmacy* approach than to *Central Hudson* even though he applied the latter test.

Justice Thomas candidly avows his desire to scuttle *Central Hudson* and return to *Virginia Pharmacy*. Justice Scalia would like to scuttle *Central Hudson*, but he is less clear on with what he would replace it.

In *Glickman v. Wileman Brothers & Elliott, Inc.* (1997), the Court declined either to apply *Central Hudson* or to repudiate it. California fruit growers attacked on First Amendment grounds assessments imposed by the Secretary of Agriculture to cover the cost of generic product advertising of California fruit. *Central Hudson* was deemed not applicable because the orders imposed no restraint on any producer's freedom "to communicate any message to any audience." The Court, 5-4, per Justice Sevens sustained the compulsory advertising orders under the deferential standard generally used to evaluate economic regulation.

First Amendment Protection and Professional Advertising

A significant development in the line of cases according a higher degree of First Amendment protection to commercial speech is the lawyer advertising case, *Bates v. State Bar of Arizona*, 433 U.S. 350 (1977). The case arose out of the following facts. The state bar concluded that the two lawyers violated the disciplinary rule against lawyer advertising, and the Arizona Supreme Court upheld that determination. The U.S. Supreme Court affirmed in part and reversed in part.

In *Bates*, the Supreme Court, per Justice Blackmun, ruled that the state bar association's prohibition on all lawyer advertising was unconstitutional: "Like the Virginia statutes, [involved in *Virginia Pharmacy*] the disciplinary rule serves to inhibit the free flow of commercial information and to keep the public in ignorance." The issue presented was a narrow one. Problems associated with the regulation of advertising claims related to the quality of legal services were not addressed. Also left for later resolution were "the problems associated with in-person solicitation of clients—at the hospital room or the accident site, or in any other situation that breeds undue influence" by lawyers or their agents. Justice Blackmun described the issue before the Court as follows:

The heart of the dispute before us today is whether lawyers also may constitutionally advertise the prices at which routine services will be performed. Numerous justifications are proffered for the restriction of such price advertising.

The Court rejected the various justifications offered for restricting price advertising for routine services. Next the Court discussed the application of the overbreadth doctrine to the lawyer advertising ban. Under First Amendment law, attack on overly broad statutes had been permitted even though "the person making the attack" could not "demonstrate that in fact his specific conduct was protected." The reason for this was that otherwise protected expression would be discouraged.

Justice Blackmun ruled that the overbreadth doctrine was strong medicine in the context of commercial speech:

But the justification for the application of the overbreadth analysis applies weakly, if at all, in the ordinary commercial context. As was acknowledged in *Virginia Pharmacy*, there are "commonsense differences" between commercial speech and other varieties. Since advertising is linked to commercial well-being it seems unlikely that such speech is particularly susceptible to being crushed by overbroad regulation.

The Court held that the advertising at issue was not misleading and that advertising by attorneys could not be subjected to "blanket suppression." But the Court made it clear that it was not immunizing all professional advertising from government regulation. False, deceptive, or misleading information, for example, was subject to restraint: "Since the advertiser knows his product

and has a commercial interest in its dissemination, we have little worry that regulation to insure truthfulness will discourage protected speech." Advertising related to the quality of services also might, in some circumstances, be subject to regulation because quality claims were "not susceptible to measurement or verification."

Suppression of advertising concerning illegal transactions was still permissible. Possibilities left open by *Bates* included "reasonable restrictions on the time, place, and manner of advertising." Resolution of the "special problems of advertising on the electronic broadcast media" were left for another day. The holding of the *Bates* case was a simple one: the state could not, consistent with the First Amendment, prohibit the truthful advertisement of the terms of routine legal services in a newspaper.

Justice Rehnquist dissented in *Bates,* arguing that the First Amendment was a "sanctuary for expressions of public importance or intellectual interest." The First Amendment was "demeaned by invocation to protect advertisements of goods and services." Reflect on Professor Meiklejohn's view of the kind of expression the First Amendment was designed to protect (see p. 8). Do you think it would embrace professional advertising?

Bates reflected the view that the state could protect the public from deceptive advertising because it was not in the same protected category as truthful advertising of factual information such as the price of routine services. Thus, in *Ohralik v. Ohio State Bar Ass'n,* 436 U.S. 447 (1978), state regulation of lawyers' in-person solicitation of accident victims for financial gain was upheld. An ACLU lawyer's in-person solicitation of a client that furthered political expression, however, was protected expressive activity despite the possibility of potential deception.

On the whole, where in-person solicitation is not involved, regulation of lawyer advertising based on the possibility of *potential* deception has not fared too well when subjected to First Amendment challenge. *Zauderer v. Office of Disciplinary Counsel of Supreme Court of Ohio,* 471 U.S. 626 (1985), invalidated an Ohio Supreme Court disciplinary reprimand against a lawyer for advertising in a newspaper to solicit legal business from women who had suffered injuries as a result of using Dalkon Shields: "Print advertising may convey information and ideas more or less effectively, but in most cases, it will lack the coercive force of the personal presence of a trained advocate." *Zauderer* also invalidated a disciplinary restriction on the use of illustrations in lawyer advertising because "commercial illustrations are entitled to the First Amendment protections afforded verbal commercial speech."

The First Amendment and Bans on Targeted Direct-Mail Advertising

Should regulation of direct-mail advertising by professionals be treated differently than regulation of newspaper ads by professionals? *Zauderer* held that newspaper advertisements by lawyers containing truthful and nondeceptive information or advice regarding specific legal problems could not be categorically banned. *Shapero v. Kentucky Bar Association*, 486 U.S. 466 (1988), held, per Justice William Brennan, that a state could not prohibit targeted direct-mail advertising by a lawyer to potential clients. Was *Shapero* distinguishable? Was newspaper advertising by lawyers on specific legal problems different from targeted direct-mail advertising on specific legal problems? The Court declined to make such a distinction.

A case that both *Shapero* and *Zauderer* were at pains to distinguish was *Ohralik v. Ohio State Bar Association*, 436 U.S. 447 (1978), which invalidated an Ohio rule prohibiting in-person solicitation. Was the lawyer's letter targeted to a particular potential client just *Ohralik* in writing? Justice Brennan in *Shapero* said it was not:

> Like print advertising, petitioner's letter and targeted, direct-mail solicitation generally "poses much less risk of overreaching or undue influence" than does in-person solicitation. A letter, like a printed advertisement (but unlike a lawyer), can readily be put in a drawer to be considered later, ignored, or discarded.

Of course, some targeted, direct-mail solicitation did present opportunities for "isolated abuse," but this did not justify "a total ban on that mode of protected commercial speech." The state had far less restrictive means to deal with such problems. Justice Brennan repeated the statement from *Zauderer* that "the free flow of information is valuable enough to justify imposing on would-be regulators the costs of distinguishing the truthful from the false, the helpful from the misleading, and the harmless from the harmful."

Justice Sandra Day O'Connor, joined by Chief Justice Rehnquist and Justice Scalia, dissented. The fundamental problem was that *Bates* was ill-considered. *Central Hudson* and its doctrine should have been applied to the advertising section in *Shapero*.

Although the Court had struck down state regulation of truthful and nondeceptive direct-mail advertising by professionals, an important turnabout came in *Florida Bar v. Went For It, Inc.*, 115 S. Ct. 2371 (1995). The Supreme Court upheld a rule of the Florida Bar prohibiting "personal injury lawyers from sending targeted direct-mail solicitations to victims and their relatives for 30 days following an accident or disaster." Not surprisingly, Justice O'Connor who had dissented in *Shapero* wrote the opinion for the Court. Joining her in the majority were Chief Justice Rehnquist, Justices Scalia, Thomas, and Breyer. Although Justice O'Connor gave lip service to *Bates,* she made it clear that *Central Hudson* had supplanted it. Unlike rational basis review, the *Central Hudson* test did not permit the Court to substitute "'the precise interests put forward by the State with other suppositions.'" The Florida Bar had substantial interests in protecting the privacy of accident victims as well as the reputation of the legal profession: "In *Fox*, we made clear that 'the least restrictive means' test has no role in the commercial speech context."

Justice O'Connor said there was a reasonable "fit" between the goals of the rule and the means selected to implement it. The ban was reasonably "well-tailored" to the elimination of "targeted mailings whose type and timing are a source of distress to Floridians." Furthermore, the Bar's rule was limited in its duration. Finally, there were many alternative means through which Floridians could get information about legal representation.

Justice Anthony Kennedy, joined by Justices Stevens, Souter, and Ginsburg, dissented. The dissenters agreed that the case could be resolved by applying the *Central Hudson* test, but the rub was that, under their application of *Central Hudson,* the rule should be invalidated rather than upheld. Moreover even if it were necessary to apply the reasonable "fit" requirement of *Central Hudson* and *Fox,* it was clear that the relationship between ends and means was not satisfied. There was a "wild disproportion between the harm supposed and the speech ban enforced." Justice Kennedy remarked that for the first time since *Bates*, the Court had undertaken a "major retreat" from the First Amendment protection accorded commercial speech.

Whether the pro-regulation application of *Central Hudson* found in *Went For It, Inc.* will be extended to other areas of commercial speech besides lawyer advertising remains to be seen. What is clear is that the ideas Justice O'Connor expressed in dissent in *Shapero* achieved majority support in the *Went for It* case.

FIGHTING WORDS

Some categories of expression have not been accorded First Amendment protection because they do not serve the interests the First Amendment is designed to protect. In the history of First Amendment law, a class of speech called "fighting words" has been assigned this unprotected status. In its origins, the "fighting words" doctrine was really a commonsense response to one of the most fundamental of free speech problems: the situation where the exercise of free speech so endangers the public order as to transform the protected speech into illegal action.

Chaplinsky v. New Hampshire
315 U.S. 568, 62 S. CT. 766, 86 L. ED. 1031 (1942).

[EDITORIAL NOTE: *The "fighting words" doctrine was born in that frequent spawning ground of First Amendment litigation, the activities of the Jehovah's Witnesses.*]

Justice MURPHY delivered the opinion of the Court.

[The complaint charged that Chaplinsky made the following remarks to the Marshal outside City Hall]:"You are a Goddamned racketeer and a damned Fascist and the whole government of Rochester are Fascists or agents of Fascists."

There is no substantial dispute over the facts. Chaplinsky was distributing the literature of his sect on the streets of Rochester [New Hampshire] on a busy afternoon. Members of the local citizenry complained to the City Marshal, Bowering, that Chaplinsky was denouncing all religion as a "racket." Bowering told them that Chaplinsky was lawfully engaged, and then warned Chaplinsky

that the crowd was getting restless. Some time later, a disturbance occurred and the traffic officer on duty at the busy intersection started with Chaplinsky for the police station, but did not inform him that he was under arrest or that he was going to be arrested. On the way, they encountered Marshal Bowering, who had been advised that a riot was under way and was therefore hurrying to the scene. Bowering repeated his earlier warning to Chaplinsky who then addressed to Bowering the words set forth in the complaint.

[EDITORIAL NOTE: *Chaplinsky for his part said that he asked the marshal to arrest those responsible for the disturbance. But the marshal, according to Chaplinsky, instead cursed him and told Chaplinsky to come along with him. Chaplinsky was prosecuted under a New Hampshire statute, part of which forbade "addressing any offensive, derisive or annoying word to any other person who is lawfully in any street or other public place." The statute also forbade calling such a person "by any offensive or derisive name."*]

[T]he right of free speech is not absolute at all times and under all circumstances. There are certain well-defined and narrowly limited classes of speech, the prevention and punishment of which have never been thought to raise any Constitutional problem. These include the lewd and obscene, the profane, the libelous, and the insulting or "fighting" words—those which by their very utterance inflict injury or tend to incite an immediate breach of the peace. It has been well observed that such utterances are no essential part of any exposition of ideas, and are of such slight social value as a step to truth that any benefit that may be derived from them is clearly outweighed by the social interest in order and morality.

[EDITORIAL NOTE: *The state supreme court put a gloss on the statute saying no words were forbidden except such as had a "direct tendency to cause acts of violence by the persons to whom, individually, the remark is addressed." This gloss launched the "fighting words" concept as a First Amendment doctrine. The U.S. Supreme Court quoted the New Hampshire Supreme Court with approval:*]

"The word 'offensive' is not to be defined in terms of what a particular addressee thinks. The test is what men of common intelligence would understand to be words likely to cause an average addressee to fight. The English language has a number of words and expressions which by general consent are 'fighting words' when said without a disarming smile. Such words, as ordinary men know, are likely to cause a fight."

"The statute, as construed, does no more than prohibit the *face-to-face words* plainly likely to cause a breach of the peace by the speaker— including 'classical fighting words,' words in current use less 'classical' but equally likely to cause violence, and other disorderly words, including profanity, obscenity and threats." [Emphasis added.]

We are unable to say that the limited scope of the statute as thus construed contravenes the constitutional right of free expression. It is a statute narrowly drawn and limited to define and punish specific conduct lying within the domain of state power, the use in a public place of words likely to cause a breach of the peace.

Nor can we say that the application of the statute to the facts disclosed by the record substantially or unreasonably impinges upon the privilege of free speech. Argument is unnecessary to demonstrate that the appellations "damned racketeer" and "damned Fascist" are epithets likely to provoke the average person to retaliation, and thereby cause a breach of the peace.

COMMENT

The fundamental question that *Chaplinsky* raises is this: What separates some categories of expression from a claim for First Amendment protection? Notice that the Court refers to "certain classes of speech" such as obscene speech, defamation, and fighting words that may be subject to sanction (obscenity and defamation are discussed in other chapters in this book). The *Chaplinsky* Court answered this question for fighting words in a statement that has been much quoted: "[S]uch utterances are no essential part of any exposition of ideas, and are of such slight social value as a step to truth that any benefit that may be derived from them is clearly outweighed by the social interest in order and morality." As this passage indicates, fighting words do not receive First Amendment protection because they are not the *kind* of expression with which the First Amendment is concerned. They are of "slight social value;" they form no integral part of "any exposition of ideas."

The fighting words doctrine may be explained apart from the categorical approach. In this view, fighting words fall on the action or conduct rather than the speech side of the line. The First Amendment extends full protection to speech but not action. The admixture of action with expression renders reasonable state regulation permissible. Of course, the language Chaplinsky spoke to the marshal was "pure speech." But it was speech, in the Court's analysis, that was bound to provoke a physical reaction. In other words, fighting words are words that are on the verge of action.

The fighting words doctrine has played an important theoretical role in the development of the categorical approach to free expression problems. But the idea of fighting words as a separate category of unprotected speech like obscenity received radical revision in *R.A.V. v. City of St. Paul* reported below.

Houston v. Hill: Fighting Words and the Overbreadth Doctrine

Even prior to *R.A.V.*, the Supreme Court had severely limited the scope of the fighting words doctrine by use of the overbreadth doctrine. Overbreadth problems can easily arise in fighting words cases. Some prosecutions for fighting words have been struck down when the ordinance or statute is overbroad and punishes both fighting words and words that do not by their utterance inflict damage or tend to incite an immediate breach of the peace.

The vital role that the overbreadth doctrine plays in fighting words cases was highlighted in *Houston v. Hill,* 482 U.S. 451 (1987). Raymond Hill became involved in a shouting match with a police officer during a traffic fracas. Hill shouted to one of the officers who was talking to a friend of Hill's: "Why don't you pick on somebody your own size?" The police officer responded: "Are you interrupting me in my official capacity as a Houston police officer?" Hill then shouted: "Yes, why don't you pick on somebody my size?" Hill was arrested under a municipal ordinance prohibiting "willfully or intentionally interrupting a city policeman [b]y verbal challenge during an investigation."

The Supreme Court, per Justice Brennan, held that a municipal ordinance making it unlawful to interrupt a police officer in performance of his duties was unconstitutionally broad under the First Amendment. The Court ruled that the ordinance was "not susceptible to a limiting construction because its language is plain and its meaning unambiguous."

On the overbreadth point, Justice Brennan said:

> The Houston ordinance [is] not limited to fighting words nor even to obscene or opprobrious language, but prohibits speech that "in any manner" interrupts an officer. The Constitution does not allow such speech to be made a crime. The freedom of individuals verbally to oppose or challenge police action without thereby risking arrest is one of the principal characteristics by which we distinguish a free nation from a police state. Houston's ordinance criminalizes a substantial amount of constitutionally protected speech, and accords the police unconstitutional discretion in enforcement. We conclude that the ordinance is substantially overbroad.

In sum, rigorous use of the overbreadth doctrine has greatly diminished the practical significance of fighting words as a separate and unprotected category of expression at the Supreme Court level. *R.A.V. v. City of St. Paul,* reported later in this chapter, further serves to limit the doctrine. Legal scholars have pointed out, however, that the status of the fighting words doctrine on the Supreme Court level should be distinguished from the status it enjoys in the lower courts. Nadine Strossen has pointed out that the fighting words doctrine has more vitality than a look at just Supreme Court opinions would suggest:

> Notwithstanding the Supreme Court's limitation of the doctrine's scope, Professor Gard's survey reveals that the lower courts apply it much more broadly. [See Gard, *Fighting Words as Free Speech,* 58 Wash. U. L. Q. 531, 580 (1980).] Since the Supreme Court only reviews a fraction of such cases, the doctrine's actual impact on free speech must be assessed in terms of these speech-restrictive lower court rulings.
> Nadine Strossen, *Regulating Speech on Campus: A Modest Proposal?* 1990 Duke L.J. 484, 512.

The Swastika in Skokie: "Fighting Words"?

In the litigation spawned by a planned march of the American Nazi Party through Skokie, Illinois, a suburb of Chicago with a substantial Jewish population, opponents of the march attempted to rely on the fighting words doctrine. In *Village of Skokie v. National Socialist Party,* 373 N.E.2d 21 (Ill. 1978), the Illinois Supreme Court held that the planned display of the swastika in a community containing thousands of concentration camp survivors did not consti-

tute "fighting words." The court overturned a lower court injunction against the display of the swastika on the ground that the display was protected symbolic political speech. Enjoining such a display was deemed to be an unconstitutional prior restraint on the right to free speech of the American Nazi Party:

> Plaintiff urges, and the appellate court has held, that exhibition of the Nazi symbol, the swastika, addresses to ordinary citizens a message which is tantamount to fighting words. Plaintiff further [asks us to hold] that the fighting words doctrine permits a prior restraint on defendants' symbolic speech. In our judgment we are precluded from doing so.
> The display of the swastika, as offensive to the principles of a free nation as the memories it recalls may be, is symbolic political speech intended to convey to the public the beliefs of those who display it. It does not, in our opinion, fall within the definition of "fighting words," and that doctrine cannot be used here to overcome the heavy presumption against the constitutional validity of prior restraint.

The Illinois Supreme Court opinion does not specifically say *why* the swastika does not constitute fighting words. Was it because unlike the marshal in *Chaplinsky* those offended by the sight of the swastika in a parade could avoid affront by not going to the parade? The marshal in *Chaplinsky* was confronted by the Jehovah's Witness who berated him. He did not have the option of avoiding him.

Professor Robert Post has stressed the importance of civility to public discourse in a democracy. But there is, he says, a public discourse paradox: "[T]he First Amendment, in the name of democracy, suspends legal enforcement of the very civility that makes rational discourse possible." Robert C. Post, *Racist Speech, Democracy and the First Amendment,* 32 Wm. & Mary L. Rev. 267, 287 (1991). However, Professor Post contends that the use of legal regulation to enforce societal civility norms may be required as an "option of last resort": "A paradigmatic example of this use may be found in the 'fighting words) doctrine of *Chaplinsky v. Hampshire.*"

Fighting Words: An Opportunity for Tolerance

The whole fighting words approach has been attacked on the ground that a goal of First

Amendment theory should be the furtherance of tolerance within society. *See* Lee Bollinger, *The Tolerant Society: Freedom of Speech and Extremist Speech in America* (1986). Professor Bollinger argues that considering categories of speech such as fighting words as exceptions to First Amendment protection is misguided. The theory of cases like *Chaplinsky* is that because such "speech possesses small benefits for truth seeking," withholding First Amendment protection is justified. But Bollinger argues that it is not the "absence of social value that determines whether the principle of free speech is applicable; indeed, the perceived absence of value is, if anything, a major reason for protection, or more accurately for toleration."

Even speech society does not value should be protected, says Bollinger, because of "the insights and lessons we obtain about ourselves and for the increase in our capacity for toleration generally." In Bollinger's view, the development of our capacity for toleration is a social interest that must be furthered. But why should this be a First Amendment objective? Even if developing a capability for tolerance is used as a yardstick for First Amendment protection, isn't it too imprecise a yardstick to provide any real guidance to distinguishing speech that is protected from speech that is unprotected? Finally, the emphasis on tolerance has to be weighed against the assault on human dignity and individual autonomy in Skokie. Tormenting the concentration camp survivors in Skokie with the sight of hateful and unwanted Nazi demonstrators and swastika symbols surely presented such an assault. *See* Bollinger at 181–82.

The Hostile Audience Problem

Related to the fighting words doctrine is the hostile audience problem. Whom should the police protect? The speaker or the audience hostile to the speaker? The fighting words doctrine focuses on the circumstances in which a speaker's words may not merit protection. The hostile audience problem focuses on audience attempts to silence controversial but protected speech. Although the hostile audience problem does not directly involve the categorical approach to expression, it is included here because hostile audiences are so frequently aroused by fighting words.

Terminiello v. Chicago, 337 U.S. 1 (1949), involved a racist speaker who spoke to more than eight hundred people in an auditorium. Outside a thousand people gathered to protest the meeting. The police tried to keep order but several disturbances broke out nevertheless. The crowd milling outside the building was "angry and turbulent." The speaker was arrested and convicted under a law that the jury charge interpreted as prohibiting speech that "stirs the public to anger, invites dispute or brings about a condition of unrest." The Supreme Court overturned the conviction, 5–4, and declared that the statute was overbroad in that it punished expression that had not been shown to present a clear and present danger. In a famous passage, Justice William Douglas for the Court observed:

> [A] function of free speech under our system of government is to invite dispute. It may indeed best serve its high purpose when it induces a condition of unrest, creates dissatisfaction with conditions as they are, or even stirs people to anger. Speech is often provocative and challenging. It may strike at prejudices and preconceptions and have profound unsettling effects as it presses for acceptance of an idea.

Terminiello suggests that a hostile audience is no justification for taking away the agitator who arouses the audience—at least until the exacting standards of the clear and present danger test can be met. However, it would be incorrect to conclude that First Amendment law always protects the speaker against the hostility of the audience.

In *Feiner v. New York*, 340 U.S. 315 (1951), the speaker did not receive First Amendment protection against a hostile audience. Feiner, a controversial speaker, was arrested in midsentence by a policeman who demanded that he step down from his soapbox because the street corner audience appeared to be getting restless. Feiner's speech included the following:

> Mayor Costello [of Syracuse] is a champagne-sipping bum; he does not speak for the negro people. President Truman is a bum. The American Legion is a Nazi Gestapo. The negroes don't have equal rights; they should rise up in arms and fight for their rights.

When Feiner refused to step down, he was arrested for disturbing the peace. The Supreme Court, per Chief Justice Fred Vinson, upheld the conviction against Feiner's contention that his arrest violated his First Amendment rights of free speech.

If the audience menaces the speaker to the point where his physical safety is at stake or a general melee is threatened, are the police ever justified in arresting the speaker even though he is not intentionally inciting to violence? One way of resolving the issue would be to compare the size of the audience with the number of police. Presumably, if the latter were far outnumbered by potentially dangerous audience members and there was a possibility some of them were armed, simple logistics would dictate that it is easier to cart away the speaker than the audience.

Justice Felix Frankfurter, concurring in *Feiner,* took an approach not unlike this logistics approach. If speech threatens to precipitate disorder, then the police, acting on a nondiscriminatory basis, might be justified in stopping the speech. In dissent in *Feiner,* Justice Hugo Black concluded that the speaker should have been protected. The case for arresting the speaker in a situation where the speaker is using "fighting words," that is, words that can be expected to enrage the audience and lead it to physical violence, is stronger than in the situation where—as in *Feiner*—the speaker's words, on a reasonable analysis, ought not to engender hostility leading to physical violence. Even if Feiner's speech ran a risk of arousing potential violence among the listening crowd, the duty of the police was to protect Feiner's right to speak by arresting menacing hecklers if necessary. Silencing Feiner at the behest of the audience or because of the police prejudice against the speaker's views was not an appropriate alternative.

Yet *Feiner* illustrates that the speaker will not always be protected in a hostile audience situation. The dissenters viewed the facts in *Feiner* as presenting no imminent danger of violence. Chief Justice Vinson for the Court drew the opposite conclusion from the facts. In short, hostile audience cases are especially fact specific and fact dependent.

The Heckler's Veto

One dimension of the hostile audience problem is the vexing question of the *heckler's veto.* Heckling may indeed be a medium of desperation, but hecklers have First Amendment rights. But the speaker who is being heckled also has First Amendment rights: You have a right to speak. I have a right to heckle. At what point may the state constitutionally intervene to assure that all

of these First Amendment rights are served?

In *Gregory v. City of Chicago,* 394 U.S. 111 (1969), civil rights activist Dick Gregory led a march to the home of the mayor to protest against segregation in the Chicago schools. Onlookers gathered to heckle the protesters. To prevent disorder, the police demanded that the marchers disperse. When they refused to do so, they were arrested and convicted. The Supreme Court set aside the convictions. The Court held that a peaceful and orderly protest march—and there was no evidence to the contrary—was conduct protected by the First Amendment. Thus, *Gregory* struck down a heckler's veto to lawful expressive activity. But in a long concurrence, Justice Black argued that narrowly drawn legislation might permissibly restrict some otherwise lawful demonstrations:

> [F]acts disclosed by the record point unerringly to one conclusion, namely, that when groups with diametrically opposed, deep-seated views are permitted to air their emotional grievances, side-by-side, on city streets, tranquility and order cannot be maintained even by the joint efforts of the finest and best officers and of those who desire to be the most law-abiding protesters of their grievances. [But] the Constitution does not bar enactment of laws regulating conduct, even though connected with speech, press, assembly, and petition if such laws specifically bar only the conduct deemed obnoxious and are carefully aimed at that forbidden conduct.

Does Justice Black's analysis permit recognition of a heckler's veto? Should it?

In *Collin v. Chicago Park District,* 460 F.2d 746, 754 (7th Cir. 1972), the federal court of appeals in Chicago ruled that it was not permissible for the city to deny a permit to a Nazi speaker to speak in Marquette Park because of fear that the speaker would provoke a hostile audience. Relying on *Terminiello* and *Gregory,* the court said: "[I]t has become patent that a hostile audience is not a basis for restraining otherwise legal First Amendment activity." Why wasn't the speaker protected against a hostile audience in *Feiner?*

OFFENSIVE SPEECH

Some words or speech although they may not provoke people to fight are nevertheless offensive to many. Certain epithets, insults, and four-letter words are offensive to many people. Should we say of offensive speech that like fighting words in *Chaplinsky* it forms "no essential part of any exposition of ideas?" Is offensive speech "of such slight social value as a step to truth" that its benefits are outweighed by the pain and offense it gives to others? The issue is whether the harmful effects of offensive speech should deprive it of First Amendment protection. In the following case, Justice John Marshall Harlan considers—and rejects—what has come to be called the harmful effects rationale for restricting offensive speech.

Cohen v. California

403 U.S. 15, 91 S. CT. 1780, 29 L. ED. 2D 284 (1971).

Mr. Justice HARLAN delivered the opinion of the Court.

This case may seem at first blush too inconsequential to find its way into our books, but the issue it presents is of no small constitutional significance. [Cohen] was convicted of violating that part of California Penal Code §415 which prohibits "maliciously and willfully disturb[ing] the peace or quiet of any neighborhood or person by offensive conduct." He was given 30 days' imprisonment. The facts upon which his conviction rests are as follows:

> On April 26, 1968, the defendant was observed in the Los Angeles County Courthouse in the corridor outside of division 20 of the municipal court wearing a jacket bearing the words "Fuck the Draft" which were plainly visible. There were women and children present in the corridor. The defendant was arrested. The defendant testified that he wore the jacket knowing that the words were on the jacket as a means of informing the public of the depth of his feelings against the Vietnam War and the draft.
>
> The defendant did not engage in, nor threaten to engage in, nor did anyone as the result of his conduct in fact commit or threaten to commit any act of violence. The defendant did not make any loud or unusual noise, nor was there any evidence that he uttered any sound prior to his arrest.

In affirming the conviction the Court of Appeal held that "offensive conduct" means "behavior which has a tendency to provoke *others* to acts of violence or to in turn disturb the peace," and that the State had proved this element because, on the facts of this case, "[i]t was certainly reasonably foreseeable that such conduct might cause others to rise up to commit a violent act against the person of the defendant or attempt to forcibly remove his jacket." The California Supreme Court declined review by a divided vote. We now reverse.

In order to lay hands on the precise issue which this case involves, it is useful first to canvass various matters which this record does *not* present. The conviction quite clearly rests upon the asserted offensiveness of the words Cohen used to convey his message to the public. The only "conduct" which the State sought to punish is the fact of communication. Thus, we deal here with a conviction resting solely upon "speech," not upon any separately identifiable conduct which allegedly was intended by Cohen to be perceived by others as expressive of particular views but which, on its face, does not necessarily convey any message and hence arguably could be regulated without effectively repressing Cohen's ability to express himself. Cf. *United States v. O'Brien* [p. 81].

Further, the State certainly lacks power to punish Cohen for the underlying content of the message the inscription conveyed. At least so long as there is no showing of an intent to incite disobedience to or disruption of the draft, Cohen could not, consistently with the First and Fourteenth Amendments, be punished for asserting the evident position on the inutility or immorality of the draft his jacket reflected.

Appellant's conviction, then, rests squarely upon his exercise of the "freedom of speech" protected from arbitrary governmental interference by the Constitution and can be justified, if at all, only as a valid regulation of the manner in which he exercised that freedom, not as a permissible prohibition on the substantive message it conveys.

In this vein, too, however, we think it important to note that several issues typically associated with such problems are not presented here.

In the first place, Cohen was tried under a statute applicable throughout the entire State. Any attempt to support this conviction on the ground that the statute seeks to preserve an appropriately decorous atmosphere in the courthouse where Cohen was arrested must fail in the absence of any language in the statute that would have put appellant on notice that certain kinds of otherwise permissible speech or conduct would nevertheless, under California law, not be tolerated in certain places.

In the second place, as it comes to us, this case cannot be said to fall within those relatively few categories of instances where prior decisions have established the power of government to deal more comprehensively with certain forms of individual expression simply upon a showing that such a form was employed. This is not, for example, an obscenity case. Whatever else may be necessary to give rise to the States' broader power to prohibit obscene expression, such expression must be, in some significant way, erotic. It cannot plausibly be maintained that this vulgar allusion to the Selective Service System would conjure up such psychic stimulation in anyone likely to be confronted with Cohen's crudely defaced jacket.

This Court has also held that States are free to ban the simple use, without a demonstration of additional justifying circumstances, of so-called "fighting words," those personally abusive epithets which, when addressed to the ordinary citizen, are, as a matter of common knowledge, inherently likely to provoke violent reaction. *Chaplinsky v. New Hampshire.* While the four-letter word displayed by Cohen in relation to the draft is not uncommonly employed in a personally provocative fashion, in this instance it was clearly not "directed to the person of the hearer." No individual actually or likely to be present could reasonably have regarded the words on appellant's jacket as a direct personal insult. Nor do we have here an instance of the exercise of the State's police power to prevent a speaker from intentionally provoking a given group to hostile reaction. Cf. *Feiner v. New York; Terminiello v. Chicago.* There is, as noted above, no showing that anyone who saw Cohen was in fact violently aroused or that appellant intended such a result.

Finally, in arguments before this Court much has been made of the claim that Cohen's distasteful mode of expression was thrust upon unwilling or unsuspecting viewers, and that the State might therefore legitimately act as it did in order to protect the sensitive from otherwise unavoidable exposure to appellant's crude form of protest. Of course, the mere presumed presence of unwitting listeners or viewers does not serve automatically to justify curtailing all speech capable of giving offense. While this Court has recognized that government may properly act in many situations to prohibit intrusion into the privacy of the home of unwelcome views and ideas which cannot be totally banned from the public dialogue, we have at the same time consistently stressed that "we are often 'captives' outside the sanctuary of the home and subject to objectionable speech." The ability of government, consonant with the Constitution, to shut off discourse solely to protect others from hearing it is, in other words, dependent upon a showing that substantial privacy interests are being invaded in an essentially intolerable manner. Any broader view of this authority would effectively empower a majority to silence dissidents simply as a matter of personal predilections.

Those in the Los Angeles courthouse could effectively avoid further bombardment of their sensibilities simply by averting their eyes. Given the subtlety and complexity of the factors involved, if Cohen's "speech" was otherwise entitled to constitutional protection, we do not think the fact that some unwilling "listeners" in a public building may have been briefly exposed to it can serve to justify this breach of the peace conviction where, as here, there was no evidence that persons powerless to avoid appellant's conduct did in fact object to it, and where that portion of the statute upon which Cohen's conviction rests evinces no concern, either on its face or as construed by the California courts, with the special plight of the captive auditor, but, instead, indiscriminately sweeps within its prohibitions all "offensive conduct" that disturbs "any neighborhood or person."

Against this background, the issue flushed by this case stands out in bold relief. It is whether California can excise, as "offensive conduct," one particular scurrilous epithet from the public discourse, either upon the theory of the court below that its use is inherently likely to cause violent reaction or upon a more general assertion that the States, acting as guardians of public morality, may properly remove this offensive word from the public vocabulary.

The rationale of the California court is plainly untenable. At most it reflects an "undifferentiated fear or apprehension of disturbance [which] is not enough to overcome the right to freedom of expression." *Tinker v. Des Moines Indep. Community School Dist.* We have been shown no evidence that substantial numbers of citizens are standing ready to strike out physically at whoever may assault their sensibilities with execrations like that uttered by Cohen. There may be some persons about with such lawless and violent proclivities, but that is an insufficient base upon which to erect, consistently with constitutional values, a governmental power to force persons who wish to ventilate their dissident views into avoiding particular forms of expression. The argument amounts to little more than the self-defeating proposition that to avoid physical censorship of one who has not sought to provoke such a response by a hypothetical coterie of the violent and lawless, the States may more appropriately effectuate that censorship themselves.

Admittedly, it is not so obvious that the First and Fourteenth Amendments must be taken to disable the States from punishing public utterance of this unseemly expletive in order to maintain what they regard as a suitable level of discourse within the body politic. We think, however, that examination and reflection will reveal the shortcomings of a contrary viewpoint.

The constitutional right of free expression is powerful medicine in a society as diverse and populous as ours. It is designed and intended to remove governmental restraints from the arena of public discussion, putting the decision as to what views shall be voiced largely into the hands of each of us, in the hope that use of such freedom will ultimately produce a more capable citizenry and more perfect polity and in the belief that no other approach would comport with the premise of individual dignity and choice upon which our political system rests.

To many, the immediate consequence of this freedom may often appear to be only verbal tumult, discord, and even offensive utterance. These are, however, within established limits, in truth necessary side effects of the broader enduring values which the process of open debate permits us to achieve. That the air may at times seem filled with verbal cacophony is, in this sense not a sign of weakness but of strength. We cannot lose sight of the fact that, in what otherwise might seem a trifling and annoying instance of individual distasteful abuse of a privilege, these fundamental societal values are truly implicated.

Against this perception of the constitutional policies involved, we discern certain more particularized considerations that peculiarly call for reversal of this conviction. First, the principle contended for by the State seems inherently boundless. How is one to distinguish this from any other offensive word? Surely the State has no right to cleanse public debate to the point where it is grammatically palatable to the most squeamish among us. Yet no readily ascertainable general principle exists for stopping short of that result were we to affirm the judgment below. For, while the particular four-letter word being litigated here is perhaps more distasteful than most others of its genre, it is nevertheless often true that one man's vulgarity is another's lyric. Indeed, we think it is largely because governmental officials cannot make principled distinctions in this area that the Constitution leaves matters of taste and style so largely to the individual.

Additionally, we cannot overlook the fact, because it is well illustrated by the episode involved here, that much linguistic expression serves a dual communicative function: it conveys not only ideas capable of relatively precise, detached explication, but otherwise inexpressible emotions as well. In fact, words are often chosen as much for their emotive as their cognitive force. We cannot sanction the view that the Constitution, while solicitous of the cognitive content of individual speech, has little or no regard for that emotive function which, practically speaking, may often be the more important element of the overall message sought to be communicated.

Finally, and in the same vein, we cannot indulge the facile assumption that one can forbid particular words without also running a substantial risk of suppressing ideas in the process. Indeed, governments might soon seize upon the censorship of particular words as a convenient guise for banning the expression of unpopular views. We have been able, as noted above, to discern little social benefit that might result from running the risk of opening the door to such grave results.

It is, in sum, our judgment that, absent a more particularized and compelling reason for its actions, the State may not, consistently with the First and Fourteenth Amendments, make the simple public display here involved of this single four-letter expletive a criminal offense. Because that is the only arguably sustainable rationale for the conviction here at issue, the judgment below must be reversed.

Justice BLACKMUN, with whom the Chief Justice and Justice BLACK join [dissenting].

Cohen's absurd and immature antic, in my view, was mainly conduct and little speech. Further, the case appears to me to be well within the sphere of *Chaplinsky v. New Hampshire,* where Justice Murphy, a known champion of First Amendment freedoms, wrote for a unanimous bench. As a consequence, this Court's agonizing over First Amendment values seems misplaced and unnecessary.

COMMENT

We have considered commercial speech and fighting words as separate categories of expression that have been accorded, in some circumstances, less First Amendment protection than other speech. The Court in *Cohen* was not inclined to expand the categories of unprotected speech to include a new one—offensive speech. Why not? A principal reason was that there were no boundaries to the category of offensive speech. The subjective quality of what constituted offensive speech was self-evident. As Justice Harlan put it in a memorable sentence: "[O]ne man's vulgarity is another's lyric." Government officials would be particularly inappropriate arbiters to determine in any objective fashion what words were offensive and what were not. The end result of government cleansing of the public discourse would likely be that not only would the offensive words be suppressed but also the idea they expressed.

Several questions are raised by *Cohen.* First, obscenity and fighting words—both unprotected categories of expression—are concepts that are difficult both to define and to confine. Yet the Court declines to place offensive speech in an unprotected category for those very reasons. Would offensive speech be even *more* difficult than obscenity and fighting words to define and confine? Why?

Second, why don't those who are involuntarily confronted with Cohen's vulgar message merit protection from the state? If a person is required to go to court, why should she be required to be offended as well?

Finally, if offensive speech merits First Amendment protection because discourse about ideas is necessarily fraught with the possibility of giving offense, why doesn't offensive speech

merit absolute protection? Note, however, that Justice Harlan does not rule that regulation of offensive speech is *per se* invalid. Instead, he uses what today we would call a strict scrutiny standard. Regulation of offensive speech will fail unless the state can come up with a "particularized and compelling reason for its actions."

HATE SPEECH

Besides fighting words and obscenity, are there other categories of speech that do not merit First Amendment protection? Increasingly, it has been urged that racist speech, speech that denigrates or defames entire ethnic and racial groups, should not merit First Amendment protection. The issue of whether hate speech should receive First Amendment protection is not a novel one.

In *Beauharnais v. Illinois,* 343 U.S. 250 (1942), the Supreme Court, per Justice Frankfurter, upheld, 5–4, an Illinois criminal libel law. The Illinois law punished publications that portrayed the "depravity, criminality, unchastity, or lack of virtue of a class of citizens of any race, color, creed or religion" and exposed such citizens "to contempt, derision, or obloquy which is productive of breach of the peace or riots." Among the grounds that Frankfurter relied on to validate the statute were a group status theory and a human dignity theory: "[A] man's job and his educational opportunities and the dignity accorded him may depend as much on the reputation of the racial and religious group to which he willy-nilly belongs, as on his own merits." The Illinois criminal libel statute upheld in *Beauharnais* was subsequently repealed by the legislature.

Is *Beauharnais* Still Good Law?

In *Garrison v. Louisiana,* 379 U.S. 64 (1964), which invalidated a Louisiana criminal libel statute as interpreted by the Louisiana Supreme Court, Justice Douglas, concurring, declared: "*Beauharnais v. Illinois,* [a] case decided by the narrowest margins, should be overruled as a misfit in our constitutional system and as out of line with the dictates of the First Amendment."

Professor Cass Sunstein argues that *Beauharnais* is not, and should not, be treated as good law today. But, Professor Sunstein agrees that

Justice Frankfurter's argument in *Beauharnais* has force. Hate speech "contributes to the maintenance of a caste system, based on race." Nevertheless, Sunstein concludes that the conventional view that hate speech is protected speech is probably the correct one:

> The conventional view—which the Supreme Court has not directly addressed—is that racial hate speech contains highly political ideas, and that it may not be suppressed merely because it is offensive or otherwise harmful.
>
> Sunstein, *Words, Conduct, Caste,* 60 U. Chi. L. Rev. 795, 814 (1993).

Defining Hate Speech

An increase in racist incidents and heightened sensitivity to such incidents in a multiracial and multicultural society has aroused interest in regulating racist speech. In an influential article, Professor Mari J. Matsuda, *Public Response to Racist Speech: Considering the Victim's Story,* 87 Mich. L. Rev. 2320, 2321 (1989), called for "legal sanctions for racist speech." Matsuda advances a "narrow definition of actionable racist speech." Three criteria should be satisfied, she suggests, before racist speech can be sanctioned. First, the message must be one of racial inferiority. Second, the message must be directed against a group that has been historically oppressed. Third, the message must be "persecutorial, hateful, and degrading."

Rationale for Regulating Speech— Charles Lawrence and Mari Matsuda

Matsuda explains the significance of her criterion that the racist message must be directed at a historically persecuted group: "Racism is more than race hatred or prejudice. It is the structural subordination of a group based on the idea of racial inferiority. Racist speech is particularly harmful because it is a mechanism of subordination, reinforcing a historically vertical relationship." *Id.* at 2358.

Under Matsuda's theory, Malcolm X's "white devil statements" could not be criminalized. Is the distinction between racist speech directed at dominant groups and racist speech directed at subordinate historically oppressed groups a defensible one? Matsuda explains why she thinks it is: "The harm and hurt is there, but it is of a different degree. Because the attack is not tied to the perpetuation of racist vertical relationships, it is not the paradigm worst example of hate propaganda. The dominant-group member hurt by conflict with the angry nationalist is more likely to have access to a safe harbor of exclusive dominant-group interactions. Retreat and reaffirmation of personhood are more easily attained for historically nonsubjugated-group members." *Id.* at 2357.

In short, Professor Matsuda believes racist speech reinforces existing patterns of societal racism and minority group subordination: "Gutter racism, parlor racism, corporate racism, and government racism work in coordination, reinforcing existing conditions of domination." Id. at 2335.

Professor Charles Lawrence believes that racist speech operates like a preemptive strike. Racist speech does not merit First Amendment protection because the speaker's intention is not to begin a dialogue or discover truth but to hurt the victim: "When racial insults are hurled at minorities, the result may be silence or flight rather than a fight, but the preemptive effect on further speech is just as complete as with fighting words." Charles R. Lawrence III, *If He Hollers Let Him Go: Regulating Racist Speech on Campus,* 1990 Duke L. J. 431, 452.

In essence, Lawrence contends that racist speech silences dialogue: "The subordinated victim of fighting words also is silenced by her relatively powerless position in society. Because of the significance of power and position, the categorization of racial epithets as 'fighting words' provides an inadequate paradigm. The fighting words doctrine presupposes an encounter between two persons of relatively equal power who have been acculturated to respond to face-to-face insults with violence. The fighting words doctrine is a paradigm based on a white male point of view." *Id.* at 453–54. Because the purpose of racist speech is not to create dialogue but to terminate it, there is no First Amendment interest in protecting it.

The Case against Hate Speech Regulation

Opponents of hate speech regulation, like ACLU leader Nadine Strossen, acknowledge the harm racist speech can do: "Contrary to Professor

Lawrence's apparent assumption, the conclusion that free speech protections must remain indivisible, even for racist speech, has nothing to do with insensitivity to the feelings of minority group members who are vilified by hate speech and suffer acutely from it. Traditional civil libertarians recognize the power of words to inflict psychic and even physical wounds." Nadine Strossen, *Regulating Racist Speech on Campus: A Modest Proposal?* 1990 Duke L. J. 484, 539. Nevertheless, Professor Strossen insists on the indivisibility of the free speech principle: "The justification for not outlawing 'words that wound' is not based on a failure to recognize the injurious potential of words. The refusal to ban words is due precisely to our understanding of how very powerful they are and of the critical role they play in our democratic society." *Id.* at 441.

Racial equality may not necessarily follow the enactment of racist speech legislation: "[E]quality concerns weigh on the anti-regulation, as well as on the pro-regulation side." Racist speech regulation, Professor Strossen points out, is exercised at the discretion of government officials such as prosecutors and judges: "One ironic, even tragic, result of this discretion is that members of minority groups themselves—the very people whom the law is intended to protect—are likely targets of punishment. For example, among the first individuals prosecuted under the British Race Relations Act of 1967 were black power leaders." *Id.* at 557.

Professor Cass Sunstein argues that hate speech and much of our public debate are inextricably intertwined:

> A good deal of public debate involves racial or religious bigotry or even hatred, implicit or explicit. If we were to excise all such speech from political debate, we would severely limit our discussion of such important matters as civil rights, foreign policy, crime, conscription, abortion, and social welfare policy. Even if a form of hate speech is involved, it might well be thought a legitimate part of the deliberative process—it bears directly on politics.
>
> Sunstein, Words, *Conduct, Caste,* 60 U. Chi. L. Rev. 795, 815 (1993).

How might advocates of hate speech regulation rebut Sunstein? They might suggest that hate speech distorts public debate and sets its agenda in advance of debate.

R.A.V. v. City of St. Paul: Hate Speech and Fighting Words Revisited

R.A.V. v. City of St. Paul
505 U.S. 377, 112 S. CT. 2538, 120 L. ED. 2D 305 (1992).

SCALIA, J., delivered the opinion of the Court, in which REHNQUIST, C.J., and KENNEDY, SOUTER, and THOMAS, JJ., joined. WHITE, J., filed an opinion concurring in the judgment, in which BLACKMUN and O'CONNOR, JJ., joined, and in which STEVENS, J., joined except as to Part I-A. BLACKMUN, J., filed an opinion concurring in the judgment. STEVENS, J., filed an opinion concurring in the judgment, in Part I of which WHITE and BLACKMUN, JJ., joined.

Justice SCALIA delivered the opinion of the Court.

In the predawn hours of June 21, 1990, petitioner and several other teenagers allegedly assembled a crudely-made cross by taping together broken chair legs. They then allegedly burned the cross inside the fenced yard of a black family that lived across the street from the house where petitioner was staying. Although this conduct could have been punished under any of a number of laws, one of the two provisions under which respondent city of St. Paul chose to charge petitioner (then a juvenile) was the St. Paul Bias-Motivated Crime Ordinance, which provides: "Whoever places on public or private property a symbol, object, appellation, characterization or graffiti, including, but not limited to, a burning cross or Nazi swastika, which one knows or has reasonable grounds to know arouses anger, alarm or resentment in others on the basis of race, color, creed, religion or gender commits disorderly conduct and shall be guilty of a misdemeanor." Petitioner moved to dismiss this count on the ground that the St. Paul ordinance was substantially overbroad and impermissibly content-based and therefore facially invalid under the First Amendment. The trial court granted this motion, but the Minnesota Supreme Court reversed. That court rejected petitioner's overbreadth claim because, as construed in prior Minnesota cases, the modifying phrase "arouses anger, alarm or resentment in others" limited the reach of the ordinance to conduct that amounts to "fighting words," i.e., "conduct that itself inflicts injury or tends to incite immediate violence . . . ," (citing *Chaplinsky v. New Hampshire*), and therefore the ordinance reached only expression "that the First Amendment does not protect." The court also concluded that the ordinance was not impermissibly content-based because, in its view, "the ordinance is a narrowly tailored means toward accomplishing the compelling governmental interest in protecting the community against bias-motivated threats to public safety and order."

I

In construing the St. Paul ordinance, we are bound by the construction given to it by the Minnesota court. Accordingly, we accept the Minnesota Supreme Court's authoritative statement that the ordinance reaches only those expressions that constitute "fighting words" within the meaning of *Chaplinsky*. Petitioner and his amici urge us to modify the scope of the *Chaplinsky* formulation, thereby invalidating the ordinance as "substantially overbroad." We find it unnecessary to consider this issue. Assuming, *arguendo,* that all of the expression reached by the ordinance is proscribable under the "fighting words" doctrine, we nonetheless conclude that the ordinance is facially unconstitutional in that it prohibits otherwise permitted speech solely on the basis of the subjects the speech addresses.

The First Amendment generally prevents government from proscribing speech, or even expressive conduct, because of disapproval of the ideas expressed. Content-based regulations are presumptively invalid. *Simon & Schuster, Inc. v. Members of N. Y. State Crime Victims Bd.* From 1791 to the present, however, our society, like other free but civilized societies, has permitted restrictions upon the content of speech in a few limited areas, which are "of such slight social value as a step to truth that any benefit that may be derived from them is clearly outweighed by the social interest in order and morality." *Chaplinsky.* We have recognized that "the freedom of speech" referred to by the First Amendment does not include a freedom to disregard these traditional limitations. See, e.g., *Roth v. United States* (obscenity); *Beauharnais v. Illinois* (defamation); *Chaplinsky v. New Hampshire* ("fighting words"). Our decisions since the 1960's have narrowed

the scope of the traditional categorical exceptions for defamation and for obscenity, see *Miller v. California,* but a limited categorical approach has remained an important part of our First Amendment jurisprudence.

We have sometimes said that these categories of expression are "not within the area of constitutionally protected speech," or that the "protection of the First Amendment does not extend" to them. Such statements must be taken in context, however, and are no more literally true than is the occasionally repeated shorthand characterizing obscenity "as not being speech at all." What they mean is that these areas of speech can, consistently with the First Amendment, be regulated because of their constitutionally proscribable content (obscenity, defamation, etc.) — not that they are categories of speech entirely invisible to the Constitution, so that they may be made the vehicles for content discrimination unrelated to their distinctively proscribable content. Thus, the government may proscribe libel; but it may not make the further content discrimination of proscribing only libel critical of the government.

Our cases surely do not establish the proposition that the First Amendment imposes no obstacle whatsoever to regulation of particular instances of such proscribable expression, so that the government "may regulate [them] freely," (WHITE, J., concurring in judgment). That would mean that a city council could enact an ordinance prohibiting only those legally obscene works that contain criticism of the city government or, indeed, that do not include endorsement of the city government. Such a simplistic, all-or-nothing-at-all approach to First Amendment protection is at odds with common sense and with our jurisprudence as well. It is not true that "fighting words" have at most a "de minimis" expressive content, or that their content is in all respects "worthless and undeserving of constitutional protection;" sometimes they are quite expressive indeed. We have not said that they constitute "no part of the expression of ideas," but only that they constitute "no essential part of any exposition of ideas." *Chaplinsky.*

The proposition that a particular instance of speech can be proscribable on the basis of one feature (e.g., obscenity) but not on the basis of another (e.g., opposition to the city government) is commonplace, and has found application in many contexts. We have long held, for example, that nonverbal expressive activity can be banned because of the action it entails, but not because of the ideas it expresses — so that burning a flag in violation of an ordinance against outdoor fires could be punishable, whereas burning a flag in violation of an ordinance against dishonoring the flag is not. Similarly, we have upheld reasonable "time, place, or manner" restrictions, but only if they are "justified without reference to the content of the regulated speech." And just as the power to proscribe particular speech on the basis of a noncontent element (e.g., noise) does not entail the power to proscribe the same speech on the basis of a content element; so also, the power to proscribe it on the basis of one content element (e.g., obscenity) does not entail the power to proscribe it on the basis of other content elements.

In other words, the exclusion of "fighting words" from the scope of the First Amendment simply means that, for purposes of that Amendment, the unprotected features of the words are, despite their verbal character, essentially a "nonspeech" element of communication. Fighting words are thus analogous to a noisy sound truck: Each is, as Justice Frankfurter recognized, a "mode of speech,"; both can be used to convey an idea; but neither has, in and of itself, a claim upon the First Amendment. As with the sound truck, however, so also with fighting words: The government may not regulate use based on hostility—or favoritism—towards the underlying message expressed.

The concurrences describe us as setting forth a new First Amendment principle that prohibition of constitutionally proscribable speech cannot be "underinclusiv[e]," (WHITE, J., concurring in judgment) — a First Amendment "absolutism" whereby "within a particular 'proscribable' category of expression, . . . a government must either proscribe all speech or no speech at all," (Stevens, J., concurring in judgment). That easy target is of the concurrences' own invention. In our view, the First Amendment imposes not an "underinclusiveness" limitation but a "content discrimination" limitation upon a State's prohibition of proscribable speech. There is no problem whatever, for example, with a State's prohibiting obscenity (and other forms of proscribable expression) only in certain media or markets, for

although that prohibition would be "underinclusive," it would not discriminate on the basis of content.

Even the prohibition against content discrimination that we assert the First Amendment requires is not absolute. It applies differently in the context of proscribable speech than in the area of fully protected speech. The rationale of the general prohibition, after all, is that content discrimination "rais[es] the specter that the Government may effectively drive certain ideas or viewpoints from the marketplace," *Simon & Schuster.* But content discrimination among various instances of a class of proscribable speech often does not pose this threat.

When the basis for the content discrimination consists entirely of the very reason the entire class of speech at issue is proscribable, no significant danger of idea or viewpoint discrimination exists. Such a reason, having been adjudged neutral enough to support exclusion of the entire class of speech from First Amendment protection, is also neutral enough to form the basis of distinction within the class. To illustrate: A State might choose to prohibit only that obscenity which is the most patently offensive in its prurience—i.e., that which involves the most lascivious displays of sexual activity. But it may not prohibit, for example, only that obscenity which includes offensive political messages. And the Federal Government can criminalize only those threats of violence that are directed against the President, since the reasons why threats of violence are outside the First Amendment (protecting individuals from the fear of violence, from the disruption that fear engenders, and from the possibility that the threatened violence will occur) have special force when applied to the person of the President. But the Federal Government may not criminalize only those threats against the President that mention his policy on aid to inner cities. And to take a final example (one mentioned by Justice Stevens), a State may choose to regulate price advertising in one industry but not in others, because the risk of fraud is in its view greater there. But a State may not prohibit only that commercial advertising that depicts men in a demeaning fashion.

Another valid basis for according differential treatment to even a content-defined subclass of proscribable speech is that the subclass happens to be associated with particular "secondary effects" of the speech, so that the regulation is "justified without reference to the content of the . . . speech." A State could, for example, permit all obscene live performances except those involving minors. Moreover, since words can in some circumstances violate laws directed not against speech but against conduct (a law against treason, for example, is violated by telling the enemy the nation's defense secrets), a particular content-based subcategory of a proscribable class of speech can be swept up incidentally within the reach of a statute directed at conduct rather than speech. Thus, for example, sexually derogatory "fighting words," among other words, may produce a violation of Title VII's general prohibition against sexual discrimination in employment practices. Where the government does not target conduct on the basis of its expressive content, acts are not shielded from regulation merely because they express a discriminatory idea or philosophy.

These bases for distinction refute the proposition that the selectivity of the restriction is "even arguably conditioned upon the sovereign's agreement with what a speaker may intend to say." There may be other such bases as well. Indeed, to validate such selectivity (where totally proscribable speech is at issue) it may not even be necessary to identify any particular "neutral" basis, so long as the nature of the content discrimination is such that there is no realistic possibility that official suppression of ideas is afoot. (We cannot think of any First Amendment interest that would stand in the way of a State's prohibiting only those obscene motion pictures with blue-eyed actresses.) Save for that limitation, the regulation of "fighting words," like the regulation of noisy speech, may address some offensive instances and leave other, equally offensive, instances alone.

II

Applying these principles to the St. Paul ordinance, we conclude that, even as narrowly construed by the Minnesota Supreme Court, the ordinance is facially unconstitutional. Although the phrase in the ordinance, "arouses anger, alarm or resentment in others," has been limited by the Minnesota Supreme Court's construction to

reach only those symbols or displays that amount to "fighting words," the remaining, unmodified terms make clear that the ordinance applies only to "fighting words" that insult, or provoke violence, "on the basis of race, color, creed, religion or gender." Displays containing abusive invective, no matter how vicious or severe, are permissible unless they are addressed to one of the specified disfavored topics. Those who wish to use "fighting words" in connection with other ideas—to express hostility, for example, on the basis of political affiliation, union membership, or homosexuality—are not covered. The First Amendment does not permit St. Paul to impose special prohibitions on those speakers who express views on disfavored subjects.

In its practical operation, moreover, the ordinance goes even beyond mere content discrimination, to actual viewpoint discrimination. Displays containing some words—odious racial epithets, for example—would be prohibited to proponents of all views. But "fighting words" that do not themselves invoke race, color, creed, religion, or gender—aspersions upon a person's mother, for example—would seemingly be usable *ad libitum* in the placards of those arguing in favor of racial, color, etc. tolerance and equality, but could not be used by those speakers' opponents. One could hold up a sign saying, for example, that all "anti-Catholic bigots" are misbegotten; but not that all "papists" are, for that would insult and provoke violence "on the basis of religion." St. Paul has no such authority to license one side of a debate to fight freestyle, while requiring the other to follow Marquis of Queensbury Rules.

What we have here, it must be emphasized, is not a prohibition of fighting words that are directed at certain persons or groups (which would be facially valid if it met the requirements of the Equal Protection Clause); but rather, a prohibition of fighting words that contain messages of "bias-motivated" hatred and in particular, as applied to this case, messages "based on virulent notions of racial supremacy." One must wholeheartedly agree with the Minnesota Supreme Court that "[i]t is the responsibility, even the obligation, of diverse communities to confront such notions in whatever form they appear," but the manner of that confrontation cannot consist of selective limitations upon speech. St. Paul's brief asserts that a general "fighting words" law would not meet the city's needs because only a content-specific measure can communicate to minority groups that the "group hatred" aspect of such speech "is not condoned by the majority." The point of the First Amendment is that majority preferences must be expressed in some fashion other than silencing speech on the basis of its content.

St. Paul concedes in its brief that the ordinance applies only to "racial, religious, or gender-specific symbols" such as "a burning cross, Nazi swastika or other instrumentality of like import."

The content-based discrimination reflected in the St. Paul ordinance comes within neither any of the specific exceptions to the First Amendment prohibition we discussed earlier, nor within a more general exception for content discrimination that does not threaten censorship of ideas. It assuredly does not fall within the exception for content discrimination based on the very reasons why the particular class of speech at issue (here, fighting words) is proscribable. As explained earlier, the reason why fighting words are categorically excluded from the protection of the First Amendment is not that their content communicates any particular idea, but that their content embodies a particularly intolerable (and socially unnecessary) mode of expressing whatever idea the speaker wishes to convey. St. Paul has not singled out an especially offensive mode of expression—it has not, for example, selected for prohibition only those fighting words that communicate ideas in a threatening (as opposed to a merely obnoxious) manner. Rather, it has proscribed fighting words of whatever manner that communicate messages of racial, gender, or religious intolerance. Selectivity of this sort creates the possibility that the city is seeking to handicap the expression of particular ideas. That possibility would alone be enough to render the ordinance presumptively invalid, but St. Paul's comments and concessions in this case elevate the possibility to a certainty.

[I]t is clear that the St. Paul ordinance is not directed to secondary effects within the meaning of *Renton*. As we said in *Boos v. Barry*, "[l]isteners' reactions to speech are not the type of secondary effects we referred to in *Renton*." "The emotive impact of speech on its audience is not a 'secondary effect.'"[3]

Finally, St. Paul and its amici defend the conclusion of the Minnesota Supreme Court that, even if the ordinance regulates expression based on hostility towards its protected ideological content, this discrimination is nonetheless justified because it is narrowly tailored to serve compelling state interests. Specifically, they assert that the ordinance helps to ensure the basic human rights of members of groups that have historically been subjected to discrimination, including the right of such group members to live in peace where they wish. We do not doubt that these interests are compelling, and that the ordinance can be said to promote them. But the "danger of censorship" presented by a facially content-based statute requires that that weapon be employed only where it is "necessary to serve the asserted [compelling] interest." The existence of adequate content-neutral alternatives thus "undercut[s] significantly" any defense of such a statute, casting considerable doubt on the government's protestations that "the asserted justification is in fact an accurate description of the purpose and effect of the law," *Burson v. Freeman* (KENNEDY, J., concurring). The dispositive question in this case, therefore, is whether content discrimination is reasonably necessary to achieve St. Paul's compelling interests; it plainly is not. In fact the only interest distinctively served by the content limitation is that of displaying the city council's special hostility towards the particular biases thus singled out. That is precisely what the First Amendment forbids. The politicians of St. Paul are entitled to express that hostility—but not through the means of imposing unique limitations upon speakers who (however benightedly) disagree.

---

[3]St. Paul has not argued in this case that the ordinance merely regulates that subclass of fighting words which is most likely to provoke a violent response. But even if one assumes (as appears unlikely) that the categories selected may be so described, that would not justify selective regulation under a "secondary effects" theory. The only reason why such expressive conduct would be especially correlated with violence is that it conveys a particularly odious message; because the "chain of causation" thus necessarily "run(s) through the persuasive effect of the expressive component" of the conduct, *Barnes v. Glen Theatre*, (SOUTER, J., concurring in judgment), it is clear that the St. Paul ordinance regulates on the basis of the "primary" effect of the speech—i.e., its persuasive (or repellant) force.

Let there be no mistake about our belief that burning a cross in someone's front yard is reprehensible. But St. Paul has sufficient means at its disposal to prevent such behavior without adding the First Amendment to the fire. The judgment of the Minnesota Supreme Court is reversed, and the case is remanded for proceedings not inconsistent with this opinion.

Justice WHITE, with whom Justice BLACKMUN and Justice O'CONNOR join, and with whom Justice STEVENS joins except as to Part I(A), concurring in the judgment.

This case could easily be decided within the contours of established First Amendment law by holding, as petitioner argues, that the St. Paul ordinance is fatally overbroad because it criminalizes not only unprotected expression but expression protected by the First Amendment. Instead, the Court holds the ordinance facially unconstitutional on a ground that was never presented to the Minnesota Supreme Court, a ground that has not been briefed by the parties before this Court, a ground that requires serious departures from the teaching of prior cases.

This Court ordinarily is not so eager to abandon its precedents. But in the present case, the majority casts aside long-established First Amendment doctrine without the benefit of briefing and adopts an untried theory. This is hardly a judicious way of proceeding, and the Court's reasoning in reaching its result is transparently wrong.

I A

This Court's decisions have plainly stated that expression falling within certain limited categories so lacks the values the First Amendment was designed to protect that the Constitution affords no protection to that expression. *Chaplinsky v. New Hampshire.*

Thus, as the majority concedes, this Court has long held certain discrete categories of expression to be proscribable on the basis of their content. For instance, the Court has held that the individual who falsely shouts "fire" in a crowded theatre may not claim the protection of the First Amendment. The Court has concluded that neither child pornography, nor obscenity, is protected by the First Amendment.

All of these categories are content based. But the Court has held that the First Amendment does not apply to them because their expressive content is worthless or of *de minimis* value to society. We have not departed from this principle, emphasizing repeatedly that, "within the confines of [these] given classification[s], the evil to be restricted so overwhelmingly outweighs the expressive interests, if any, at stake, that no process of case-by-case adjudication is required." This categorical approach has provided a principled and narrowly focused means for distinguishing between expression that the government may regulate freely and that which it may regulate on the basis of content only upon a showing of compelling need.

Today, however, the Court announces that earlier Courts did not mean their repeated statements that certain categories of expression are "not within the area of constitutionally protected speech." To the contrary, those statements meant precisely what they said: The categorical approach is a firmly entrenched part of our First Amendment jurisprudence.

Nevertheless, the majority holds that the First Amendment protects those narrow categories of expression long held to be undeserving of First Amendment protection—at least to the extent that lawmakers may not regulate some fighting words more strictly than others because of their content. The Court announces that such content-based distinctions violate the First Amendment because "the government may not regulate use based on hostility—or favoritism—towards the underlying message expressed." Should the government want to criminalize certain fighting words, the Court now requires it to criminalize all fighting words.

To borrow a phrase, "Such a simplistic, all-or-nothing-at-all approach to First Amendment protection is at odds with common sense and with our jurisprudence as well." It is inconsistent to hold that the government may proscribe an entire category of speech because the content of that speech is evil, but that the government may not treat a subset of that category differently without violating the First Amendment; the content of the subset is by definition worthless and undeserving of constitutional protection.

The majority's observation that fighting words are "quite expressive indeed," is no answer. Fighting words are not a means of exchanging views, rallying supporters, or registering a protest; they are directed against individuals to provoke violence or to inflict injury. Therefore, a ban on all fighting words or on a subset of the fighting words category would restrict only the social evil of hate speech, without creating the danger of driving viewpoints from the marketplace.

Therefore, the Court's insistence on inventing its brand of First Amendment underinclusiveness puzzles me. The overbreadth doctrine has the redeeming virtue of attempting to avoid the chilling of protected expression, but the Court's new "underbreadth" creation serves no desirable function. Instead, it permits, indeed invites, the continuation of expressive conduct that in this case is evil and worthless in First Amendment terms, until the city of St. Paul cures the underbreadth by adding to its ordinance a catch-all phrase such as "and all other fighting words that may constitutionally be subject to this ordinance."

Any contribution of this holding to First Amendment jurisprudence is surely a negative one, since it necessarily signals that expressions of violence, such as the message of intimidation and racial hatred conveyed by burning a cross on someone's lawn, are of sufficient value to outweigh the social interest in order and morality that has traditionally placed such fighting words outside the First Amendment. Indeed, by characterizing fighting words as a form of "debate," the majority legitimates hate speech as a form of public discussion.

B

In a second break with precedent, the Court refuses to sustain the ordinance even though it would survive under the strict scrutiny applicable to other protected expression. Assuming, *arguendo*, that the St. Paul ordinance is a content-based regulation of protected expression, it nevertheless would pass First Amendment review under settled law upon a showing that the regulation "is necessary to serve a compelling state interest and is narrowly drawn to achieve that end." *Simon & Schuster, Inc. v. New York Crime Victims Board.* St. Paul has urged that its ordinance, in the words of the majority, "helps to ensure the basic human rights of members of groups that have historically been subjected to discrimination." The Court expressly concedes that this interest is compelling and is promoted

by the ordinance. Nevertheless, the Court treats strict scrutiny analysis as irrelevant to the constitutionality of the legislation. Under the majority's view, a narrowly drawn, content-based ordinance could never pass constitutional muster if the object of that legislation could be accomplished by banning a wider category of speech. This appears to be a general renunciation of strict scrutiny review, a fundamental tool of First Amendment analysis.

II

Although I disagree with the Court's analysis, I do agree with its conclusion: The St. Paul ordinance is unconstitutional. However, I would decide the case on overbreadth grounds.

The Minnesota Supreme Court erred in its application of the *Chaplinsky* fighting words test and consequently interpreted the St. Paul ordinance in a fashion that rendered the ordinance facially overbroad.

In construing the St. Paul ordinance, the Minnesota Supreme Court drew upon the definition of fighting words that appears in *Chaplinsky*— words "which by their very utterance inflict injury or tend to incite an immediate breach of the peace." However, the Minnesota court was far from clear in identifying the "injur[ies]" inflicted by the expression that St. Paul sought to regulate. Indeed, the Minnesota court emphasized (tracking the language of the ordinance) that "the ordinance censors only those displays that one knows or should know will create anger, alarm or resentment based on racial, ethnic, gender or religious bias." I therefore understand the court to have ruled that St. Paul may constitutionally prohibit expression that "by its very utterance" causes "anger, alarm or resentment."

Our fighting words cases have made clear, however, that such generalized reactions are not sufficient to strip expression of its constitutional protection. The mere fact that expressive activity causes hurt feelings, offense, or resentment does not render the expression unprotected.

In the First Amendment context, "[c]riminal statutes must be scrutinized with particular care; those that make unlawful a substantial amount of constitutionally protected conduct may be held facially invalid even if they also have legitimate application." *Houston v. Hill.* The St. Paul anti-bias ordinance is such a law. Although the ordinance reaches conduct that is unprotected, it also makes criminal expressive conduct that causes only hurt feelings, offense, or resentment, and is protected by the First Amendment. The ordinance is therefore fatally overbroad and invalid on its face.

III

Today, the Court has disregarded two established principles of First Amendment law without providing a coherent replacement theory. Its decision is an arid, doctrinaire interpretation, driven by the frequently irresistible impulse of judges to tinker with the First Amendment. The decision is mischievous at best and will surely confuse the lower courts. I join the judgment, but not the folly of the opinion.

Justice BLACKMUN, concurred in the judgment of the Court.

[I]f a State cannot regulate speech that causes great harm unless it also regulates speech that does not (setting law and logic on their heads), the Court seems to abandon the categorical approach, and inevitably to relax the level of scrutiny applicable to content-based laws. As Justice WHITE points out, this weakens the traditional protections of speech. If all expressive activity must be accorded the same protection, that protection will be scant. The simple reality is that the Court will never provide child pornography or cigarette advertising the level of protection customarily granted political speech. If we are forbidden from categorizing, as the Court has done here, we shall reduce protection across the board.

[Perhaps] this case will not significantly alter First Amendment jurisprudence, but, instead, will be regarded as an aberration—a case where the Court manipulated doctrine to strike down an ordinance whose premise it opposed, namely, that racial threats and verbal assaults are of greater harm than other fighting words. I fear that the Court has been distracted from its proper mission by the temptation to decide the issue over "politically correct speech" and "cultural diversity," neither of which is presented here. If this is the meaning of today's opinion, it is perhaps even more regrettable.

I see no First Amendment values that are compromised by a law that prohibits hoodlums from driving minorities out of their homes by burning crosses on their lawns, but I see great harm in preventing the people of Saint Paul from specifically punishing the race-based fighting words that so prejudice their community. I concur in the judgment, however, because I agree with Justice WHITE that this particular ordinance reaches beyond fighting words to speech protected by the First Amendment.

Justice STEVENS, with whom Justice WHITE and Justice BLACKMUN join as to Part I, concurring in the judgment.

I agree that the St. Paul ordinance is unconstitutionally overbroad for the reasons stated in Part II of Justice WHITE's opinion, [but] I write separately to suggest how the allure of absolute principles has skewed the analysis of both the majority and concurring opinions.

I

Drawing on broadly worded dicta, the Court establishes a near-absolute ban on content-based regulations of expression and holds that the First Amendment prohibits the regulation of fighting words by subject matter. Thus, while the Court rejects the "all-or-nothing-at-all" nature of the categorical approach, it promptly embraces an absolutism of its own: within a particular "proscribable" category of expression, the Court holds, a government must either proscribe all speech or no speech at all. This aspect of the Court's ruling fundamentally misunderstands the role and constitutional status of content-based regulations on speech, conflicts with the very nature of First Amendment jurisprudence, and disrupts well-settled principles of First Amendment law.

Although the Court has, on occasion, declared that content-based regulations of speech are "never permitted," *Police Dept. of Chicago v. Mosley,* such claims are overstated. Contrary to the broad dicta in *Mosley* and elsewhere, our decisions demonstrate that content-based distinctions, far from being presumptively invalid, are an inevitable and indispensable aspect of a coherent understanding of the First Amendment.

Even within categories of protected expression, the First Amendment status of speech is fixed by its content. *New York Times Co. v. Sullivan* and *Dun & Bradstreet, Inc. v. Greenmoss Builders, Inc.,* 472 U.S. 749 (1985), establish that the level of protection given to speech depends upon its subject matter: Speech about public officials or matters of public concern receives greater protection than speech about other topics. It can, therefore, scarcely be said that the regulation of expressive activity cannot be predicated on its content: Much of our First Amendment jurisprudence is premised on the assumption that content makes a difference.

Disregarding this vast body of case law, the Court today goes beyond even the overstatement in *Mosley* and applies the prohibition on content-based regulation to speech that the Court had until today considered wholly "unprotected" by the First Amendment—namely, fighting words. This new absolutism in the prohibition of content-based regulations severely contorts the fabric of settled First Amendment law.

Assuming that the Court is correct that [fighting words are] not wholly "unprotected," it certainly does not follow that fighting words and obscenity receive the same sort of protection afforded core political speech. Yet in ruling that proscribable speech cannot be regulated based on subject matter, the Court does just that. Perversely, this gives fighting words greater protection than is afforded commercial speech. [I]t is ironic to hold that a city cannot regulate fighting words based on "race, color, creed, religion or gender" while leaving unregulated fighting words based on "union membership or homosexuality." The Court today turns First Amendment law on its head: Communication that was once entirely unprotected (and that still can be wholly proscribed) is now entitled to greater protection than commercial speech—and possibly greater protection than core political speech.

II

Although I agree with much of Justice White's analysis, I do not join Part I-A of his opinion because I have reservations about the "categorical approach" to the First Amendment.

Admittedly, the categorical approach to the First Amendment has some appeal: either expression is protected or it is not — the categories create safe harbors for governments and speakers alike. But this approach sacrifices subtlety for clarity and is, I am convinced, ultimately unsound. As an initial matter, the concept of "categories" fits poorly with the complex reality

of expression. Few dividing lines in First Amendment law are straight and unwavering, and efforts at categorization inevitably give rise only to fuzzy boundaries. The quest for doctrinal certainty through the definition of categories and subcategories is, in my opinion, destined to fail.

Perhaps sensing the limits of such an all-or-nothing approach, the Court has applied its analysis less categorically than its doctrinal statements suggest. The Court has recognized intermediate categories of speech (for example, for indecent nonobscene speech and commercial speech) and geographic categories of speech (public fora, limited public fora, nonpublic fora) entitled to varying levels of protection. The Court has also stringently delimited the categories of unprotected speech. In short, the history of the categorical approach is largely the history of narrowing the categories of unprotected speech.

This evolution, I believe, indicates that the categorical approach is unworkable and the quest for absolute categories of "protected" and "unprotected" speech ultimately futile. My analysis of the faults and limits of this approach persuades me that the categorical approach presented in Part I-A of Justice WHITE's opinion is not an adequate response to the novel "underbreadth" analysis the Court sets forth today.

III

As the foregoing suggests, I disagree with both the Court's and part of Justice WHITE's analysis of the constitutionality of the St. Paul ordinance. Unlike the Court, I do not believe that all content-based regulations are equally infirm and presumptively invalid; unlike Justice WHITE, I do not believe that fighting words are wholly unprotected by the First Amendment.

Whatever the allure of absolute doctrines, it is just too simple to declare expression "protected" or "unprotected" or to proclaim a regulation "content-based" or "content-neutral."

In applying this analysis to the St. Paul ordinance, I assume *arguendo*—as the Court does—that the ordinance regulates only fighting words and therefore is not overbroad. Looking to the content and character of the regulated activity, two things are clear. First, by hypothesis the ordinance bars only low-value speech, namely, fighting words. By definition such expression constitutes "no essential part of any exposition of ideas, and [is] of such slight social value as a step to truth that any benefit that may be derived from [it] is clearly outweighed by the social interest in order and morality." *Chaplinsky.* Second, the ordinance regulates "expressive conduct [rather] than . . . the written or spoken word." *Texas v. Johnson.*

Looking to the context of the regulated activity, it is again significant that the statute (by hypothesis) regulates only fighting words. Whether words are fighting words is determined in part by their context. Fighting words are not words that merely cause offense; fighting words must be directed at individuals so as to "by their very utterance inflict injury." By hypothesis, then, the St. Paul ordinance restricts speech in confrontational and potentially violent situations. The case at hand is illustrative. The cross-burning in this case—directed as it was to a single African-American family trapped in their home—was nothing more than a crude form of physical intimidation. That this cross-burning sends a message of racial hostility does not automatically endow it with complete constitutional protection. Significantly, the St. Paul ordinance regulates speech not on the basis of its subject matter or the viewpoint expressed, but rather on the basis of the harm the speech causes.

In sum, the St. Paul ordinance (as construed by the Court) regulates expressive activity that is wholly proscribable and does so not on the basis of viewpoint, but rather in recognition of the different harms caused by such activity. Taken together, these several considerations persuade me that the St. Paul ordinance is not an unconstitutional content-based regulation of speech. Thus, were the ordinance not overbroad, I would vote to uphold it.

COMMENT

THE CATEGORICAL APPROACH: THE SCALIA REVISED VERSION The doctrine set forth in Scalia's opinion in *R.A.V.* radically transforms the traditional understanding not only of fighting words but of the categorical theory of expression. As a First Amendment matter, regulation of an unprotected category of speech had been thought of as permissible. But Justice Scalia held

that such categories of speech were not "entirely invisible to the Constitution, so that they be made the vehicle for content discrimination unrelated to their distinctively proscribable content." By way of illustration, Justice Scalia said the government could "proscribe libel" but it couldn't proscribe just libel critical of the government. The vice of the St. Paul ordinance was that it didn't proscribe *all* fighting words. It merely proscribed a subset of fighting words that reflected a viewpoint of which the government disapproved.

Justice White challenged Scalia's analysis of the categorical approach to free expression problems by arguing that if a category of speech did not merit First Amendment protection, then a subset of that category may be regulated: "[T]he content of the subject is by definition worthless and undeserving of constitutional protection." Justice White also said that the "categorical approach is a firmly entrenched part of our First Amendment jurisprudence." After *R.A.V.*, is this still true? Blackmun suggests Scalia aimed to strike a blow against political correctness. Blackmun is doubtful whether the analysis of the *R.A.V.* majority will endure. Why the doubts?

Justice Scalia conceded that the St. Paul ordinance serves the compelling governmental interest in protecting the basic human rights of historically discriminated against minorities. The St. Paul ordinance thus survived that part of the strict scrutiny test. However, Justice White says that according to the Court the ordinance is still not valid because a subset of fighting words cannot be proscribed: "Under the majority's view, a narrowly drawn content-based ordinance could never pass constitutional muster if the object of that legislation could be accomplished by banning a wider category of speech."

In Justice White's view, Scalia's analysis deprives *more* rather than *less* expression of First Amendment protection. To be valid, the St. Paul ordinance would have to proscribe *all* fighting words, not just fighting words falling into the subcategory of racist speech. What is the answer to this criticism? For example, such a total ban would even reach fighting words that come up in a labor dispute. Arguably, the St. Paul city council is not likely to wish to proscribe all fighting words—particularly those used in a labor dispute. Therefore, it will enact no fighting words ordinance at all. Thus, the actual result of Scalia's approach is to free a wider area of expression from state regulation.

JUSTICE STEVENS'S CRITIQUE OF THE CATEGORICAL APPROACH Although Justice Stevens warns against the "allure of absolute principles" such as the categorical approach, he concedes its surface appeal: "[E]ither expression is protected or it is not." But he argues that the quest for "doctrinal certainty" through the creation of categories and subcategories of expression is bound to fail. In practice, the categorical approach does not neatly divide expression between protected and unprotected categories. There are intermediate categories of speech, such as indecent speech, and commercial speech, that are neither completely protected nor completely unprotected: "[O]ur decisions establish a more complex and subtle analysis, one that considers the content of the regulated speech, and the nature and scope of the restriction on speech."

Applying his contextual approach, Stevens concludes that the ordinance "restricts speech in confrontational and potentially violent situations" and is directed to the harm the speech causes and not to its subject matter or viewpoint. Absent the overbreadth problem with the ordinance, he would have sustained it. Note that Stevens's approach to First Amendment problems is both nondoctrinal and fact-specific. Does Stevens's analysis provide enough guidance and predictability for speakers and regulators?

STRICT SCRUTINY, HATE SPEECH AND _R.A.V._ Because the St. Paul ordinance was a content-based regulation, _R.A.V._ applied the strict scrutiny standard of review. Why did the St. Paul ordinance fail to survive this stringent standard of review? Consider the following explanation:

> While acknowledging that the governmental interest in protecting the basic human rights of historically disadvantaged groups is a compelling interest, the St. Paul ordinance was not necessary to serve that interest. There existed content-neutral alternatives, _i.e._, a law proscribing all fighting words "not limited to the favored topics." Barron and Dienes, _First Amendment in a Nutshell_ 182 (1993).

Professor Steven H. Shiffrin asks why the St. Paul ordinance doesn't fall within one of the exceptions to this doctrine that Justice Scalia himself identified in _R.A.V._—-"[the] subclass of fighting words which is most likely to provoke a violent response." Steven H. Shiffrin, _Racist Speech, Outsider Jurisprudence and the Meaning of America_, 80 Cornell L. Rev. 43, 58 (1994). Does the ordinance fit this exception?

Shiffrin also asks a more fundamental question—why is it just assumed that the appropriate standard for evaluating racist speech is strict scrutiny?

> But idea discrimination is not always a constitutional sin, and strict scrutiny is not a given. In determining that obscenity or some forms of discrimination are unprotected, for example, the Court has forthrightly balanced or deferred to the interests proferred by the state. Why, then, is strict scrutiny appropriate for racist speech in the form of fighting words, but not for defamation or obscenity?
>
> Id. at 60–61.

CONTENT DISCRIMINATION AND _R.A.V._ Professor Shiffrin argues that content-based judgments are inescapable:

> [U]nder Justice Scalia's content-"neutral" ordinance, a judge or jury could make on an ad hoc basis the same type of distinction the St. Paul City Council was not permitted to encode as a rule, deciding, for example, that comments about race are fighting words, but comments about union membership or politics are not.
>
> _Id._ at 65.

Shiffrin tries to identify what there is about content discrimination that troubles Justice Scalia:

> Justice Scalia is attracted to a particular vision of America, as a nation that spurns paternalism and tolerates different points of view, however hateful. It is a nation that is formally neutral in race relations (affirmative action programs from his perspective are undesirable), ideally neutral in the economic market (although the Constitution does not guarantee this), and neutral in the "marketplace of ideas."
>
> _Id._ at 66.

But then Shiffrin exposes the anti-paternalistic model to some hard questions:

A model of anti-paternalism, tolerance, and neutrality has difficulty explaining why, for example, commercial speech and obscenity get less than full protection.

Id. at 66.

The Supreme Court of Canada and the Harmful Effects Rationale

In the United States the harmful effects of speech have generally not been viewed as a justification for regulating them. Cf. *Cohen v. California.* Richard Delgado and David H. Yun, advocates of hate speech regulation, have noted with approval two Supreme Court of Canada cases that have "upheld the power of the state to prohibit certain types of offensive expression when they cause societal harm." Delgado and Yun, *Pressure Valves and Bloodied Chickens: An Analysis of Paternalistic Objections to Hate Speech Regulation,* 82 Cal. L. Rev. 871, 875 (1994).

Regina v. Keegstra, 3 S.C.R. 697 (Can. 1990), involved hate speech that violated a provision of the Canadian criminal code. Despite the guarantee of freedom of expression in Section 2 of the Canadian Charter of Rights and Freedoms, the Supreme Court of Canada, relying on a harmful effect rationale—the harm that racist speech causes to its victims and to society—upheld the challenged criminal code provision. Similarly, in *Regina v. Butler,* 89 D.L.R. 4th 449 (Can. 1992), a pornography case, the Supreme Court of Canada again relied on a harmful effect rationale. This time the harmful effects that pornography inflicts on women were relied on to support the decision to reverse a dismissal of criminal pornography charges. Delgado and Yun suggest that a harmful effects rationale would support hate speech regulation:

[A] hate speech rule could be patterned after an existing tort, such as intentional infliction of emotional distress or group libel, with the race of the victim a "special factor" calling for increased protection, as current rules and the Restatement of Torts already provide. This suggestion is strengthened by the two Canadian cases, *Keegstra* and *Butler.* Harms based rationales for punishing hate speech should be valid if the social injury from the speech outweighs its benefits."

Id. at 887.

Professor Elena Kagan argues that although the harmful effect rationale has a surface appeal, it presents some problems:

[I]f pornography and hate-speech regulation is harm-based, then we can have both it and a rule against viewpoint discrimination. But if we assume (as a meaningful system of free speech must) that speech has effects—that the expression of a view will often cause people to act on it—then the two phrasings should be considered identical for First Amendment purposes.

Kagan, *Regulation of Hate Speech and Pornography After R.A.V.,* 60 U. Chi. L. Rev. 873, 879 (1993).

Professor Kagan believes that support for viewpoint neutrality is so strong on the present Court that other methods of dealing with hate speech should be undertaken. Does *Wisconsin v. Mitchell,* the case, discussed below, offer an effective alternative?

Wisconsin v. Mitchell

In *Wisconsin v. Mitchell,* 508 U.S. 476 (1993), a Wisconsin statute enhancing criminal penalties when the victim is selected because of race was upheld, per Chief Justice Rehnquist, by a unanimous Supreme Court. After a group of black men and boys attacked and beat a white boy severely, the two-year sentence of one of the attackers was enhanced to seven years because the attacker had selected the victim because of his race. The Wisconsin Supreme Court held the law violated the First Amendment because it was overbroad and punished what the legislature deemed to be "offensive thought."

The U.S. Supreme Court was not bound by the state supreme court's conclusion that the Wisconsin statute punished bigoted thought and not conduct. The Wisconsin Supreme Court was not defining the meaning of a particular statutory word or phrase, in which case the Supreme Court would indeed be bound by the state court's construction of the state statute. Instead, the Wisconsin Supreme Court was simply characterizing the "'practical effect' of the statute for First Amendment purposes." The U.S. Supreme Court was therefore free to make its own judgment as to the "operative effect" of the Wisconsin law.

Unlike the ordinance in *R.A.V.*, the Wisconsin statute went beyond punishing expression and punished the underlying conduct: "[A] physical assault is not by any stretch of the imagination expressive conduct protected by the First Amendment." The defendant unsuccessfully contended that because the rationale for enhancing the criminal penalty was his discriminatory motive in selecting the victim, the Wisconsin law punished thoughts and beliefs in violation of the First Amendment. While a person may not be punished because of his abstract beliefs, motive is frequently an important factor in determining penalties for criminal conduct.

Further, motive plays the same role under the Wisconsin penalty enhancement law as it does under antidiscrimination laws. These laws are aimed at unprotected conduct, not expressive activity protected by the First Amendment. Chief Justice Rehnquist used this reasoning to distinguish *R.A.V.*:

> [W]hereas the ordinance struck down in *R.A.V.* was explicitly directed at expression (*i.e.*, "speech" or "messages"), the statute in this case is aimed at conduct unprotected by the First Amendment.

Chief Justice Rehnquist stressed the rationale for the Wisconsin penalty enhancement law:

> [T]he Wisconsin statute singles out for enhancement bias-inspired conduct because this conduct is thought to inflict greater individual and societal harm. For example, according to the State, and its *amici*, bias-motivated crimes are more likely to provoke retaliatory crimes, inflict distinct emotional harms on their victims, and incite community unrest. The State's desire to redress these perceived harms provides an adequate explanation for its penalty-enhancement provision over and above mere disagreement with offenders' beliefs and biases.

The Court also rejected the defendant's contention that the Wisconsin law was impermissibly overbroad because evidence of his prior speech or associations could be used to prove that he deliberately selected his victim "on account of the victim's protected status." The argument that this would chill free expression for those concerned about enhanced sentences "if they should in the future commit a criminal offense covered by the statute" was far too attenuated:

> We are left, then, with the prospect of a citizen suppressing his bigoted beliefs for fear that evidence of such beliefs will be introduced against him at trial if he commits a more serious offense against person or property. This is simply too speculative a hypothesis to support Mitchell's overbreadth claim.

The First Amendment did not preclude the "evidentiary use of speech" to prove motive or intent or the elements of a crime.

In view of the First Amendment problems confronting regulation of racist speech, Professor Kagan has urged regulation of conduct—hate crimes—as an appropriate course of action: "The typical hate crimes law, as the Supreme Court unanimously ruled last Term, presents no First Amendment problem." Kagan, *Regulation of Hate Speech and Pornography after R.A.V.*, 60 U. Chi. L. Rev. 873, 884 (1993).

In *Wisconsin v. Mitchell*, Chief Justice Rehnquist said that enhanced penalties for bias-motivated conduct were valid because hate crimes were more likely to provoke socially harmful consequences, such as retaliation, emotional harm, and civil disorder, than hate speech. Would advocates of hate speech regulation agree? Does *Wisconsin v. Mitchell* present problems for classic civil libertarians as well?

CHAPTER 4
LIBEL AND THE MASS MEDIA

CHAPTER OUTLINE

WHAT IS LIBEL?

Few areas of media law are more complex or confusing than libel. Among its confounding elements are nuance and interpretation of language, time and place, and the unanticipated responses of jury and jurisdiction. Public opinion and the idiosyncrasies of state statutes and common law also play their roles. The root offense is *defamation*. When defamation is fixed in print or broadcast script, *published* or posted on an Internet bulletin board, a bumper sticker, or a gravestone, or written in the sky with smoke, it is called libel. When defamation is spoken, it is called slander. California treats defamation by radio and television as slander; most states do not. Since slander requires the plaintiff to prove special damages or monetary loss, that may be to a California defendant's benefit. Special damages need not be proven, however, if it is slander *per se,* that is, an allegation of crime or moral failure damaging trade, business, or profession. The differences between libel and slander are not clearly drawn and may be less important now than in the past. Media are mostly concerned with libel. What does it mean to defame a person?

Technically, defamation is a *false* attack on someone's reputation that supports a claim of *injury* to that person's good name and leads to public hatred, degradation, disgrace, ridicule, mental suffering, humiliation, shame, or embarrassment. That someone must be a readily *identifiable* person. Reputation is what others think of you in a particular time, place, and social and cultural context. Words should be given their contemporary meaning because, as Oliver Wendell Holmes put it, "A word is not a crystal, transparent and unchanged: it is the skin of a living thought and may vary greatly in color and content according to the circumstances and the time in which it is used."[1] Most libel cases stem from false imputations of crime, followed in order of descending severity by allegations of unchastity or other forms of moral imperfection, professional incompetence, financial unreliability, or unethical practices, resulting in injury to reputation and business standing.

A report that a police chief was accepting bribes to assign town towing work to a particular towing company was said by an Illinois appeals court to be defamatory on its face (libel *per se*), libelous as a matter of law because it imputed the commission of a criminal offense that is indictable and punishable by a prison term. It also suggested moral turpitude.[2]

Given the semantic jungle the law has provided, journalists are often very much alone— sometimes even lost—in deciding whether or not to publish. And deciding to publish can have grave consequences.

For example, the *Alton* (Illinois) *Telegraph* was reduced to bankruptcy by a jury award to a developer. Two reporters, having insufficient evidence of criminality for publication, thought they were doing their duty as citizens when they sent what information they had to the Justice Department.[3] Belo Broadcasting Corporation

settled out of court for an undisclosed amount after a jury awarded Dallas lawyer Victor Feazell $58 million in damages in 1991, although that figure was reduced significantly by the court prior to the settlement.[4] A federal jury awarded entertainer Wayne Newton $22.7 million, mercifully reduced by the court to $5.2 million, for a broadcast that allowed audience members to infer that Newton had received help from organized crime figures in buying a Las Vegas hotel. It took NBC almost ten years to convince the federal judiciary—ultimately, a three-judge panel of the Ninth Circuit—that there was insufficient evidence of actual or constitutional malice to support any award for damages in the case.[5] In that decade of litigation, NBC's insurance company estimated its costs at $9 million, most of it in attorney's fees.[6]

Twenty-two years after publication of articles critical of a former assistant district attorney for quashing a homicide investigation as a favor to a police officer whose son had been involved, the *Philadelphia Inquirer* in 1996 was still fighting a 1990 jury award to the plaintiff of $34 million (reduced by a state appeals court to $21.5 million).[7] The newpaper finally agreed to a settlement. Though a very high percentage of cases are settled out of court for undisclosed amounts of money, getting to that point can still be expensive in legal fees and court costs.

Money is not all that is lost. Pretrial issues of discovery and constitutional privilege rob a newsroom of time and self-confidence. There is evidence that some plaintiffs do not sue to win but rather to distract and intimidate, or to put the world on notice that their reputations are worth fighting for.[8] Former Gov. Edward King of Massachusetts, for example, sued the *Boston Globe* claiming defamation in three cartoons, one editorial, an op-ed piece, and two political columns criticizing his administration. A decade

1. *Towne v. Eisner,* 245 U.S. 418, 425 (1918).

2. *Moore v. Streit,* 17 Med.L.Rptr. 1144, 537 N.E.2d 408 (Ill. App. Ct. 1989).

3. *Green v. Alton Telegraph Printing Co.,* 8 Med.L.Rptr. 1345, 438 N.E.2d 203 (Ill. 1982). Thomas B. Littlewood, *Coals of Fire: The Alton Telegraph Libel Case* (Carbondale: Southern Illinois University Press, 1986).

4. *Feazell v. Belo Broadcasting Corp.,* No. 86-227-11 (McLennan County, Texas District Court, April 19, 1991).

5. *Newton v. National Broadcasting Co.,* 18 Med.L.Rptr. 1001, 913 F.2d 652 (9th Cir. 1990).

6. Donald M. Gillmor and Melanie C. Grant, "Sedition Redux: The Abuse of Libel Law in U.S. Courts," Working Paper, Freedom Forum Media Studies Center, New York, 1991, p. 6.

7. *New York Times,* May 4, 1990, p. A16.

8. Randall P. Bezanson, Gilbert Cranberg, and John Soloski, *Libel Law and the Press* (New York: Free Press, 1987).

passed before the judicial system decided that the governor had no case on any count.[9]

Although the courts cannot decide which plaintiffs to put in which categories, a third of all libel suits are brought by *public officials* of varying degrees of status and by celebrities or those whom some courts call "public personalities." Business and professional people, some of whom are designated *public figures* by the courts, account for at least another third of plaintiffs. *Private persons,* those who do not fall into either of the other categories, account for yet another 20 or 30 percent.

More than 70 percent of all libel suits are brought against the mass media. Newspapers bear the brunt of these, accounting for at least two-thirds of all media libel cases and far outstripping broadcasters, magazines, and other media as libel defendants—those who are sued. Plaintiffs win something like 70 percent of the cases that go to trial; jurors appear hostile toward the media and generally make awards to libel plaintiffs that outstrip the awards made to plaintiffs in medical malpractice and product liability suits. The win-lose figures are reversed when jury verdicts are appealed, indicating that the law favors the media while the public may not.[10]

Many libel suits result from carelessness, haste, or lack of knowledge of the facts of a story or of the law. To call a person dishonest, corrupt, cruel, perverted, or a drug abuser, whether seriously or in jest, is to tempt fate. When the *National Enquirer* falsely accused comedienne Carol Burnett of being drunk and disorderly in a posh Washington, D.C., restaurant, she successfully sued for libel.[11] When the 1964 presidential candidate Barry Goldwater was alleged to be mentally ill on the basis of a phony medical survey run by *Fact* magazine, the magazine's publisher, Ralph Ginzburg, lost a libel suit to Goldwater. While mental incompetency does not normally carry with it any sense of moral fault, the context of the charge made it so in the minds

of jurors and subsequent appeals courts, and the allegation was believed especially damaging to a candidate for the nation's highest office.[12] In the long run, though, such prominent people seldom win against the media that provoke them.

Defamation Defined

Libel is essentially a false and defamatory attack on a person's reputation in print or electronic form. Reputation is essentially what other people think of you. Lawyers define libel as a "communication . . . (that) tends . . . so to harm the reputation of another as to lower him in the estimation of the community or to deter third persons from associating or dealing with him."[13] Words can be insulting but still not defamatory. In a Vermont case, a plaintiff was characterized by a political opponent as a "horse's ass," a "jerk," an "idiot," and "paranoid." Words used in the heat of a political campaign, said the state supreme court, would not be read in their literal sense and were clearly not intended to destroy the plaintiff in his profession as an accountant. Such words may be insulting, abusive, and objectionable, but they are not defamatory in and of themselves, and they reflect more on the character of the user than on the person at whom they were directed.[14] Calling a university's attorney "the David Duke of Chester County," said a Pennsylvania court, "may suggest racism [and] constitutes an insulting, impetuous statement which is not, in the context of current political discourse, actionable."[15]

Satire, parody and humor are given latitude. After Carl Sagan, perhaps the country's best-known astronomer, refused to permit Apple Computer to name one of its personal computers after him, Apple called one of its machines "butt-head astronomer" and Sagan sued. A California court said the reference was not actionable because it was humorous and satirical and did not imply an objective fact. Nor did it give rise to an action for intentional infliction of emotional distress. For the same reasons, references to Mother Teresa as "Miss Nerdy Nun and a fashion no-no" and the labeling of a $50

9. *King v. Globe Newspaper Co.,* 512 N.E.2d 241 (Mass. 1987).

10. Marc Franklin, "Suing Media for Libel: A Litigational Study," 1981 *Am. Bar Foundation Res. J.* 797–831; Cranberg, Soloski, *Libel Law,* Chap. 6; Donald M. Gillmor, *Power, Publicity and the Abuse of Libel Law* (New York: Oxford University Press, 1992), Chap. 8.

11. *Burnett v. National Enquirer,* 7 Med.L.Rptr. 1321 (Cal.Sup.Ct. 1981); 193 Cal.Rptr. 206 (1983), appeal dismissed, 104 S.Ct. 1260 (1984).

12. *Goldwater v. Ginzburg,* 414 F.2d 324 (2d Cir. 1969).

13. *Restatement (Second) of Torts,* sec. 559 (1977).

14. *Blouin v. Anton,* 7 Med.L.Rptr. 1714, 431 A.2d 489 (Vt. 1981).

15. *MacElree v. Philadelphia Newspapers, Inc.,* 22 Med.L.Rptr. 1157, 650 A.2d 1068 (Pa. 1994).

hotel room in Manhattan as a place for contracting Lyme disease were protected as exaggerated humor.[16] There are limits, of course, notably where such references are susceptible of factual interpretation.

A UPI story from Baltimore reported that a superior court jury there had ordered Bernard Gladsky to pay his sister, Gloria Kovatch, $2,000 in damages for an inscription he had had carved on their father's tombstone: "Stanley Gladsky, 1895–1977, abused, robbed and starved by his beloved daughter." Just a joke, said Bernard. Some joke! It was a publication written in stone. As part of a settlement, the tombstone carver was assessed $3,000 since he had taken part in the publication.

The U.S. Supreme Court in 1970 held that the term "blackmail" when used to characterize the negotiating position of a real estate developer was not slander (spoken defamation) when uttered in the emotional atmosphere of a city council meeting. Nor was it libel when reported accurately in the local newspaper.[17]

So how does a reporter or an editor know when unpleasant words have crossed the line into actionable libel? He or she doesn't. There is no general guideline. Every state has compiled its own record in libel law in state statutes and their interpretation in actual cases by state courts. This is where the cautious communicator should begin.

State rulings, of course, must comply with the constitutional standard established by the U.S. Supreme Court in the landmark 1964 case of *New York Times v. Sullivan,*[18] which grew out of the civil rights movement. *New York Times* and its progeny partially took libel out of tort law (a wrong done to another person) and made it a matter of the Constitution's First Amendment protecting speech and press. Public people henceforth would have to prove *actual malice* on the part of a defendant to win a libel suit. And actual malice was given a federal definition: knowing falsehood or reckless disregard as to truth or falsity. It will become clear how this *constitutional-*

izing of libel law fashioned the rules that govern libel today. Chief Judge Richard Posner of the Seventh Circuit Court of Appeals caught the spirit of *New York Times* in a commentary on today's media:

> Today's "tabloid" style investigative television reportage, conducted by networks desperate for viewers in an increasingly competitive television market constitutes—although it is often shrill, one-sided, and offensive, and sometimes defamatory—an important part of that market. It is entitled to all the safeguards with which the Supreme Court has surrounded liability for defamation. . . . If the broadcast itself does not contain actionable defamation, and no established rights are invaded in the process of creating it . . . then the target has no legal remedy even if the investigatory tactics used by the networks are surreptitious, confrontational, unscrupulous, and ungentlemanly.[19]

At the same time the Rehnquist Supreme Court in the 1980s and 1990s seemed to be encouraging state courts to depend more upon their own precedents, laws, and constitutions in deciding libel cases.

It can be said with some assurance, however, that words imputing crime, gross immorality, criminal associations, or financial chicanery must be handled with great care in every jurisdiction. Who makes the charge? What are the circumstances? How is it likely to be interpreted? By whom? What will be the effects?

Several states, New York, Massachusetts, Colorado, Connecticut, Florida, and Georgia among them, subscribe to what is called the *single instance* rule. That is, you may charge a professional person with a mistake on a single occasion and be safe from a libel suit as long as you do not imply overall incompetence or give that person a reason to plead special damages (actual money loss).[20] This rule is not without problems. It lends itself to contradictory interpretations, and you could find yourself a defendant in a libel suit after an initial reference to a person prepared to sue, even in a jurisdiction where the rule is in effect.

A minority of states follow the *innocent construction* rule. This means simply that language will be construed in its ordinary, commonly

16. *Sagan v. Apple Computer Inc.,* 22 Med.L.Rptr. 2141, 874 F.Supp. 1072 (D.C.C.Cal. 1994); *Blackwell v. Carson,* 22 Med.L.Rptr. 1665 (Cal. Ct.Appl. 1994); *Milford Plaza Associates v. Hearst Corp.,* 22 Med.L.Rptr. 1128, 606 N.Y.S.2d 184 (N.Y. Sup.Ct.App.Div. 1994).

17. *Greenbelt Co-op Publishing Association v. Bresler,* 398 U.S. 6 (1970).

18. 376 U.S. 254 (1964).

19. *Desnick v. American Broadcasting Companies, Inc.,* 23 Med.L.Rptr. 1161, 1168 (7th Cir. 1995).

20. *Bowes v. Magna Concepts, Inc.,* 18 Med.L.Rptr. 1303 (N.Y. Sup.Ct. 1990).

accepted meanings. Unfamiliar or strained interpretations will be rejected. This also can be a tricky rule to live by. In one case in Illinois, which subscribes to the rule, a newspaper, editorializing on behalf of higher salaries for village trustees, declared that good government had to be paid for. A trustee chose to interpret that as meaning bribery, but failed in his libel suit. In another Illinois case, however, no innocent construction could be made of the statement that "I think 240 pieces of silver changed hands—30 for each alderman."[21] Nor did the Kentucky Supreme Court consider it "innocent" to use the words "fix, bribe, payoff" in a story that led readers to believe, erroneously, that an attorney had solicited a high legal fee from a drug defendant in order to bribe a judge and "fix" the case.[22] In most states judges decide whether a statement could be defamatory; juries decide in what sense it was read by its audience.

Another hazard in libel law is that some states recognize *libel by implication*, inference, or innuendo (libel *per quod*), a libel that is not obviously damaging on its face. The question often is, did the communicator anticipate a defamatory implication? The legal term *inducement* refers to a situation where a libel occurs due to extrinsic circumstances over which the reporter has neither control nor knowledge. Can defamation be inferred from what two writers call the "gestalt" of an article? And should being aware of an implied defamatory meaning be enough to impose liability?[23]

Courts are divided on whether to permit liability for inferences made by readers, listeners, or viewers from accurate reports. Two Minnesota appeals courts held that accurate newspaper reports and opinions on a county attorney's lackluster performance in prosecuting domestic abuse cases could not support a suit for defamation by implication (libel *per quod*). Nor could a second county attorney succeed in a suit for defamation by innuendo unless he could show that unreported facts would change the whole tenor of stories suggesting his lack of enthusiasm in investigating a murder case.[24] A Louisiana court speculated that libel *per quod*, that is, libel by implication, may not be possible in libel cases involving public people. The lesson of that specific case was not to imply wrongdoing in the way you ask a question.[25]

Some jurisdictions, but not all, have abandoned the distinction between *per se* and *per quod* altogether. Other jurisdictions allow suits for defamatory inferences drawn from factually accurate news reports.[26] In a case brought against the *Washington Post* and NBC for reports on irregularities in routine drug testing procedures required for a police lieutenant's promotion to captain and his later elevation to head of the Washington, D.C., police department's narcotics squad, a federal appeals court noted that if style or language suggests that a reporter intends or endorses a defamatory inference from even a true report, she may be liable.[27] Here the police captain failed in his suit because such a defamatory inference could not be made. The *Post* was also protected by having published a fair and accurate report of a governmental proceeding. NBC would have enjoyed the same privilege had it attributed its story to an official investigation or to documents the investigation had generated. It had failed to do so, but as with the newspaper, NBC's report made no defamatory inference and that protected it from the libel claim.

21. *Kaplan v. Greater Niles Township Publishing Corp.,* 278 N.E.2d 437 (Ill. 1971); *Catalano v. Pechous,* 387 N.E.2d 714 (Ill. 1978), affirmed, 419 N.E.2d 350 (Ill. 1980).

22. *McCall v. Courier-Journal and Louisville Times Co.,* 7 Med.L.Rptr. 2118, 623 S.W.2d 882 (Ky. 1981), *cert. denied,* 456 U.S. 975 (1982).

23. C. Thomas Dienes and Lee Levine, *Implied Libel: Defamatory Meanings, and State of Mind: The Promise of New York Times v. Sullivan,* 78 Iowa L.Rev. 237 (1993). The authors conclude that a cause of action for implied libel, as well as a finding of liability, ought to depend on clear and convincing evidence that (1) the publication is capable of a defamatory meaning, which the publisher wishes to communicate, and he disseminates the publication despite his knowledge of falsity and recklessly disregards the truth of the defamatory meaning, and (2) the publication is reasonably capable of both a defamatory and nonactionable construction and the publisher, aware of the defamatory construction and knowing it to be false, proceeds nevertheless to disseminate it. The reader's interpretation is not enough since myriad interpretations can generally be derived from any particular publication.

24. *Diesen v. Hessburg,* 17 Med.L.Rptr. 1849, 455 N.W.2d 446 (Minn. Sup.Ct. 1990); *Foley v. WCCO-TV Inc.,* 17 Med.L.Rptr. 1233, 449 N.W.2d 497 (Minn. Ct.App. 1989).

25. *Sassone v. Elder,* 22 Med.L.Rptr. 1049, 626 So.2d 345, 354 (La. 1993).

26. *Southern Air Transport, Inc. v. American Broadcasting Companies, Inc.,* 877 F.2d 1010, 1014 (D.C.Cir. 1989).

27. *White v. Fraternal Order of Police,* 17 Med.L.Rptr. 2137, 909 F.2d 512, (D.C.Cir. 1990).

Perhaps the classic case of implied libel was the suit brought by Israeli General Ariel Sharon against *Time* magazine. Correspondent David Halevy admitted that he had merely inferred from a government report that the general had discussed revenge with Lebanese Phalangists, who would later massacre 500 Palestinian women and children, and was therefore responsible. Whether Halevy intended to indict Sharon would never be known because the general claimed victory when the jury, at the second stage of the case as defined by the judge, said, yes, the story was false. The question of fault, in this case *actual malice,* defined in *New York Times v. Sullivan* as knowing falsehood or reckless disregard as to truth or falsity, was never reached because the Israeli general abandoned his case at this point and went home claiming victory.[28]

Defamatory innuendo may be drawn from headlines, illustrations, photographs, film, audio and videotape, and myriad other forms of communication. The important point is that those bringing libel suits must demonstrate that the offending language carries a defamatory meaning. A Boston newspaper printed a picture of a witness before a congressional committee on its front page. Although the witness had testified as to how he had refused to take part in an alleged fraud, his picture appeared under the banner headline, "Settlement Upped $2,000: $400 Kickback Told." Although no reference was made to the witness in an accompanying article, the court said the innuendo was capable of being defamatory and that the plaintiff was entitled to a jury trial to prove that he was defamed.[29]

Since reporters seldom write headlines for their stories, they don't feel responsible when headlines and story are mismatched. Courts, however, sensitive to the fact that often only the headline is read, have upheld libel judgments on the basis of the headline alone. For example, in *Sprouse v. Clay Communication, Inc.,*[30] a state supreme court upheld a $250,000 award in actual damages against a newspaper that had libeled an unsuccessful gubernatorial candidate

by what the court called "misleading words in oversized headlines . . . lead[ing] the average reader to an entirely different conclusion than the facts cited in the body of the story. . . ." Other courts have held that a headline must be read in context with an entire article before a judgment can be made about libel.[31]

The danger of *misquotes,* especially where they change the meaning of what someone said to a reporter, was dramatically brought home by a Supreme Court ruling in June 1991. Writer Janet Malcolm was accused by former psychoanalyst Jeffrey Masson of deliberately misrepresenting what he had said to her in an interview for a *New Yorker* article that would later become a book. A federal district court granted Malcolm a summary judgment. An appeals court affirmed, and the Supreme Court reversed and remanded. In reinstating Masson's $10 million libel case against Malcolm, the Court said a jury would have to decide whether discrepancies between the writer's notes and tape recordings and the published references to Masson describing himself as an "intellectual gigolo" and quoting him as promising to turn Anna Freud's home into a place of "sex, women and fun" constituted actual malice and damaged him. Was this a deliberate or reckless falsehood on Malcolm's part? Masson had objected to the quotations before they were published. Or was it simply the compression of part of what Masson had said to Malcolm in a long series of informal interviews and conversations? Actual malice, the linchpin of libel law, will be discussed below. In a trial noted for its theatrics as much as its legal lessons, a federal court jury found in favor of the psychoanalyst, but disagreed on what amount of money damages he should receive. Malcolm, said the jury, had shown reckless disregard for the truth in publishing two quotations attributed to Masson. Her attorney proclaimed that Masson had damaged his own reputation more than Malcolm ever could have by his own utterances, including his claim that he had slept with a thousand women by the time he was twenty-nine. At the same time, *The New Yorker* and Alfred A. Knopf were dropped from the suit as defendants since they had depended upon a usually reliable contributor, Malcolm, a freelance writer rather than an employee. While the outcome for the publish-

28. *Sharon v. Time, Inc.,* 11 Med.L.Rptr. 1591, 609 F.Supp. 1291 (S.D.N.Y. 1984).

29. *Mabardi v. Boston Herald-Traveler Corp.,* 198 N.E.2d 304 (Mass. 1964).

30. 1 Med.L.Rptr. 1695, 211 S.E.2d 674 (W.Va. 1975).

31. *Gambuzza v. Time, Inc.,* 239 N.Y.S.2d 466 (1963).

ers could have been worse, at the very least the case warns writers and their publishers against fabricating quotations or condoning the practice—especially those publishers of high-quality books and magazines upon which readers have come to rely. Nevertheless, the line between fabrication and a fair rendering of what was said in a long and complex dialogue between the parties to the lawsuit may often be indistinct.

Masson v. New Yorker Magazine, Inc.
18 MED.L.RPTR. 2241, 501 U.S. 496, 111 S.CT. 2419, (1991).

Justice KENNEDY delivered the opinion of the Court.

In this libel case, a public figure claims he was defamed by an author who, with full knowledge of the inaccuracy, used quotation marks to attribute to him comments he had not made. The First Amendment protects authors and journalists who write about public figures by requiring a plaintiff to prove that the defamatory statements were made with what we have called "actual malice," a term of art denoting deliberate or reckless falsification. We consider in this opinion whether the attributed quotations had the degree of falsity required to prove this state of mind, so that the public figure can defeat a motion for summary judgment and proceed to a trial on the merits of the defamation claim.

* * *

Malcolm's work received complimentary reviews. But this gave little joy to Masson, for the book portrays him in a most unflattering light. According to one reviewer,

"Masson the promising psychoanalytic scholar emerges gradually, as a grandiose egotist—mean-spirited, self-serving, full of braggadocio, impossibly arrogant and, in the end, a self-destructive fool. But it is not Janet Malcolm who calls him such: his own words reveal this psychological profile—a self-portrait offered to us through the efforts of an observer and listener who is, surely, as wise as any in the psychoanalytic profession." Coles, Freudianism Confronts Its Malcontents, *Boston Globe,* May 27, 1984, pp. 58, 60.

Petitioner wrote a letter to the New York Times Book Review calling the book "distorted." In response, Malcolm stated:

"Many of [the] things Mr. Masson told me (on tape) were discreditable to him, and I felt it best not to

include them. Everything I do quote Mr. Masson as saying was said by him, almost word for word. (The 'almost' refers to changes made for the sake of correct syntax.) I would be glad to play the tapes of my conversation with Mr. Masson to the editors of The Book Review whenever they have 40 or 50 short hours to spare."

Petitioner brought an action for libel under California law in the United States District Court for the Northern District of California. During extensive discovery and repeated amendments to the complaint, petitioner concentrated on various passages alleged to be defamatory, dropping some and adding others. The tape recordings of the interviews demonstrated that petitioner had, in fact, made statements substantially identical to a number of the passages, and those passages are no longer in the case. We discuss only the passages relied on by petitioner in his briefs to this Court.

Each passage before us purports to quote a statement made by petitioner during the interviews. Yet in each instance no identical statement appears in the more than 40 hours of taped interviews. Petitioner complains that Malcolm fabricated all but one passage; with respect to that passage, he claims Malcolm omitted a crucial portion, rendering the remainder misleading.

"Intellectual Gigolo." Malcolm quoted a description by petitioner of his relationship with Eissler [Dr. Kurt, project director of the Archives] and Anna Freud as follows:

" 'Then I met a rather attractive older graduate student and I had an affair with her. One day, she took me to some art event, and she was sorry afterward. She said, "Well, it is very nice sleeping with you in your room, but you're the kind of person who should never leave the room—you're just a social embarrassment anywhere else, though you do fine in your own room." And you know, in their way, if not in so many words, Eissler and Anna Freud told me the same thing. They like me well enough "in my own room." They loved to hear from me what creeps and dolts analysts are. I was like an intellectual gigolo—you get your pleasure from him, but you don't take him out in public. . . .' "

The tape recordings contain the substance of petitioner's reference to his graduate student friend, but no suggestion that Eissler or Anna Freud considered him, or that he considered himself, an " 'intellectual gigolo.' " Instead, petitioner said:

"They felt, in a sense, I was a private asset but a public liability. . . . They liked me when I was alone in their living room, and I could talk and chat and tell them the truth about things and they would tell me. But that I was, in a sense, much too junior within the hierarchy of analysis, for these important training analysts to be caught dead with me."

"Sex, Women, Fun." Malcolm quoted petitioner as describing his plans for Maresfield Gardens, which he had hoped to occupy after Anna Freud's death:

" 'It was a beautiful house, but it was dark and sombre and dead. Nothing ever went on there. I was the only person who ever came. I would have renovated it, opened it up, brought it to life. Maresfield Gardens would have been a center of scholarship, but it would also have been a place of sex, women, fun. It would have been like the change in The Wizard of Oz, from black-and-white into color.' "

The tape recordings contain a similar statement, but in place of the reference to "sex, women, fun," and *The Wizard of Oz,* petitioner commented:

"[I]t is an incredible storehouse. I mean, the library, Freud's library alone is priceless in terms of what it contains: all his books with his annotations in them; the Schreber case annotated, that kind of thing. It's fascinating."

Petitioner did talk, earlier in the interview, of his meeting with a London analyst:

"I like him. So, and we got on very well. That was the first time we ever met and you know, it was buddy-buddy, and we were to stay with each other and [laughs] we were going to pass women on to each other, and we were going to have a great time together when I lived in the Freud house. We'd have great parties there and we were [laughs]— . . . going to really, we were going to live it up."

* * *

"I Don't Know Why I Put It In." The article recounts part of a conversation between Malcolm and petitioner about the paper petitioner presented at his 1981 New Haven lecture:

"[I] asked him what had happened between the time of the lecture and the present to change him from a Freudian psychoanalyst with somewhat outré views into the bitter and belligerent anti-Freudian he had become.

"Masson sidestepped my question. 'You're right, there was nothing disrespectful of analysis in that

paper,' he said. 'That remark about the sterility of psychoanalysis was something I tacked on at the last minute, and it was totally gratuitous. I don't know why I put it in.' "

The tape recordings instead contain the following discussion of the New Haven lecture:

Masson: "So they really couldn't judge the material. And, in fact, until the last sentence I think they were quite fascinated. I think the last sentence was an in, [sic] possibly, gratuitously offensive way to end a paper to a group of analysts. Uh,—"

Malcolm: "What were the circumstances under which you put it [in]? . . ."

Masson: "That it was, was true."

* * *

". . . I really believe it. I didn't believe anybody would agree with me.

* * *

". . . But I felt I should say something because the paper's still well within the analytic tradition in a sense. . . .

* * *

". . . It's really not a deep criticism of Freud. It contains all the material that would allow one to criticize Freud but I didn't really do it. And then I thought, I really must say one thing that I really believe, that's not going to appeal to anybody and that was the very last sentence. Because I really do believe psychoanalysis is entirely sterile. . . ."

"Greatest Analyst Who Ever Lived." The article contains the following self-explanatory passage:

"A few days after my return to New York, Masson, in a state of elation, telephoned me to say that Farrar, Straus & Giroux has taken *The Assault on Truth* [Masson's book]. 'Wait till it reaches the best-seller list, and watch how the analysts will crawl,' he crowed. 'They move whichever way the wind blows. They will want me back, they will say that Masson is a great scholar, a major analyst—after Freud, he's the greatest analyst who ever lived. Suddenly they'll be calling, begging, cajoling: "Please take back what you've said about our profession; our patients are quitting." They'll try a short smear campaign, then they'll try to buy me, and ultimately they'll have to shut up. Judgment will be passed by history. There is no possible refutation of this book. It's going to cause a revolution in psychoanalysis. Analysis stands or falls with me now.' "

This material does not appear in the tape recordings. Petitioner did make the following statements on related topics in one of the taped interviews with Malcolm:

"... I assure you when that book comes out, which I honestly believe is an honest book, there is nothing, you know, mean-minded about it. It's the honest fruit of research and intellectual toil. And there is not an analyst in the country who will say a single word in favor of it."

"Talk to enough analysts and get them right down to these concrete issues and you watch how different it is from my position. It's utterly the opposite and that's finally what I realized, that I hold a position that no other analyst holds, including, alas, Freud. At first I thought: Okay, it's me and Freud against the rest of the analytic world, or me and Freud and Anna Freud and Kur[t] Eissler and Vic Calef and Brian Bird and Sam Lipton against the rest of the world. Not so, it's me. It's me alone."

The tape of this interview also contains the following exchange between petitioner and Malcolm:

Masson: "... analysis stands or falls with me now."

Malcolm: "Well that's a very grandiose thing to say."

Masson: "Yeah, but it's got nothing to do with me. It's got to do with the things I discovered."

* * *

Malcolm submitted to the District Court that not all of her discussions with petitioner were recorded on tape, in particular conversations that occurred while the two of them walked together or traveled by car, while petitioner stayed at Malcolm's home in New York, or while her tape recorder was inoperable. She claimed to have taken notes of these unrecorded sessions, which she later typed, then discarding the handwritten originals. Petitioner denied that any discussion relating to the substance of the article occurred during his stay at Malcolm's home in New York, that Malcolm took notes during any of their conversations, or that Malcolm gave any indication that her tape recorder was broken.

* * *

In general, quotation marks around a passage indicate to the reader that the passage reproduces the speaker's words verbatim. They inform the reader that he or she is reading the statement of the speaker, not a paraphrase or other indirect interpretation by an author. By providing this information, quotations add authority to the statement and credibility to the author's work.

Quotations allow the reader to form his or her own conclusions, and to assess the conclusions of the author, instead of relying entirely upon the author's characterization of her subject.

A fabricated quotation may injure reputation in at least two senses, either giving rise to a conceivable claim of defamation. First, the quotation might injure because it attributes an untrue factual assertion to the speaker. An example would be a fabricated quotation of a public official admitting he had been convicted of a serious crime when in fact he had not.

Second, regardless of the truth or falsity of the factual matters asserted within the quoted statement, the attribution may result in injury to reputation because the manner of expression or even the fact that the statement was made indicates a negative personal trait or an attitude the speaker does not hold. John Lennon once was quoted as saying of the Beatles, "We're more popular than Jesus Christ now." Time, Aug. 12, 1966, p. 38. Supposing the quotation had been a fabrication, it appears California law could permit recovery for defamation because, even without regard to the truth of the underlying assertion, false attribution of the statement could have injured his reputation. Here, in like manner, one need not determine whether petitioner is or is not the greatest analyst who ever lived in order to determine that it might have injured his reputation to be reported as having so proclaimed.

A self-condemnatory quotation may carry more force than criticism by another. It is against self-interest to admit one's own criminal liability, arrogance, or lack of integrity, and so all the more easy to credit when it happens. This principle underlies the elemental rule of evidence which permits the introduction of admissions, despite their hearsay character, because we assume "that persons do not make statements which are damaging to themselves unless satisfied for good reason that they are true."

Of course, quotations do not always convey that the speaker actually said or wrote the quoted material. "Punctuation marks, like words, have many uses. Writers often use quotation marks, yet no reasonable reader would assume that such punctuation automatically implies the truth of the quoted material." Baker v. Los Angeles Examiner, 42 Cal.3d, at 263, 228 Cal.Rptr., at 211, 721 P.2d, at 92. In Baker, a television reviewer printed a hypothetical conversation between a station vice president and writer/producer, and the court found that no reasonable reader would conclude the plaintiff in fact had made the statement attributed to him. Writers often use quotations as in *Baker,* and a reader will not reasonably understand the quotations to indicate reproduction of a conversation that took place. In other instances, an acknowledgment that the work is so-called docudrama or historical fiction, or that it recreates conversations from memory, not from recordings, might indicate that the quotations should not be interpreted as the actual statements of the speaker to whom they are attributed.

The work at issue here, however, as with much journalistic writing, provides the reader no clue that the quotations are being used as a rhetorical device or to paraphrase the speaker's actual statements. [Emphasis added.] To the contrary, the work purports to be nonfiction, the result of numerous interviews. At least a trier of fact could so conclude. The work contains lengthy quotations attributed to petitioner, and neither Malcolm nor her publishers indicate to the reader that the quotations are anything but the reproduction of actual conversations. Further, the work was published in The New Yorker, a magazine which at the relevant time seemed to enjoy a reputation for scrupulous factual accuracy. These factors would, or at least could, lead a reader to take the quotations at face value. A defendant may be able to argue to the jury that quotations should be viewed by the reader as nonliteral or reconstructions, but we conclude that a trier of fact in this case could find that the reasonable reader would understand the quotations to be nearly verbatim reports of statements made by the subject.

The constitutional question we must consider here is whether, in the framework of a summary judgment motion, the evidence suffices to show that respondents acted with the requisite knowledge of falsity or reckless disregard as to truth or falsity. This inquiry in turn requires us to consider the concept of falsity; for we cannot discuss the standards for knowledge or reckless disregard without some understanding of the acts required for liability. We must consider whether the requisite falsity inheres in the attribution of words to the petitioner which he did not speak.

In some sense, any alteration of a verbatim quotation is false. But writers and reporters by necessity alter what people say, at the very least to eliminate grammatical and syntactical infelicities. If every alteration constituted the falsity required to prove actual malice, the practice of journalism, which the First Amendment standard is designed to protect, would require a radical change, one inconsistent with our precedents and First Amendment principles. Petitioner concedes this absolute definition of falsity in the quotation context is too stringent, and acknowledges that "minor changes to correct for grammar or syntax" do not amount to falsity for purposes of proving actual malice. We agree, and must determine what, in addition to this technical falsity, proves falsity for purposes of the actual malice inquiry.

Petitioner argues that, excepting correction of grammar or syntax, publication of a quotation with knowledge that it does not contain the words the public figure used demonstrates actual malice. The author will have published the quotation with knowledge of falsity, and no more need be shown. Petitioner suggests that by invoking more forgiving standards the Court of Appeals would permit and encourage the publication of falsehoods. Petitioner believes that the intentional manufacture of quotations does not "represen[t] the sort of inaccuracy that is commonplace in the forum of robust debate to which the *New York Times* rule applies," and that protection of deliberate falsehoods would hinder the First Amendment values of robust and well-informed public debate by reducing the reliability of information available to the public.

We reject the idea that any alteration beyond correction of grammar or syntax by itself proves falsity in the sense relevant to determining actual malice under the First Amendment. An interviewer who writes from notes often will engage in the task of attempting a reconstruction of the speaker's statement. That author would, we may assume, act with knowledge that at times she has attributed to her subject words other than those actually used. Under petitioner's proposed standard, an author in this situation would lack First Amendment protection if she reported as quotations the substance of a subject's derogatory statements about himself.

Even if a journalist has tape recorded the spoken statement of a public figure, the full and exact statement will be reported in only rare circumstances. The existence of both a speaker and a reporter; the translation between two media, speech and the printed word; the addition of punctuation; and the practical necessity to edit and make intelligible a speaker's perhaps rambling comments, all make it misleading to suggest that a quotation will be reconstructed with complete accuracy. The use or absence of punctuation may distort a speaker's meaning, for example, where that meaning turns upon a speaker's emphasis of a particular word. In other cases, if a speaker makes an obvious misstatement, for example by unconscious substitution of one name for another, a journalist might alter the speaker's words but preserve his intended meaning. And conversely, an exact quotation out of context can distort meaning, although the speaker did use each reported word.

In all events, technical distinctions between correcting grammar and syntax and some greater level of alteration do not appear workable, for we can think of no method by which courts or juries would draw the line between cleaning up and other changes, except by reference to the meaning a statement conveys to a reasonable reader. To attempt narrow distinctions of this type would be an unnecessary departure from First Amendment principles of general applicability, and, just as important, a departure from the underlying purposes of the tort of libel as understood since the latter half of the 16th century. From then until now, the tort action for defamation has existed to redress injury to the plaintiff's reputation by a statement that is defamatory and false. * * * If an author alters a speaker's words but effects no material change in meaning, including any meaning conveyed by the manner or fact of expression, the speaker suffers no injury to reputation that is compensable as a defamation.

* * *

Deliberate or reckless falsification that comprises actual malice turns upon words and punctuation only because words and punctuation express meaning. Meaning is the life of language. And, for the reasons we have given, quotations may be a devastating instrument for conveying false meaning. In the case under consideration, readers of *In the Freud Archives* may have found Malcolm's portrait of petitioner especially damning because so much of it appeared to be a self-portrait, told by petitioner in his own words. And if the alterations of petitioner's words gave a dif-

ferent meaning to the statements, bearing upon their defamatory character, then the device of quotations might well be critical in finding the words actionable.

* * *

The protection for rational interpretation serves First Amendment principles by allowing an author the interpretive license that is necessary when relying upon ambiguous sources. Where, however, a writer uses a quotation, and where a reasonable reader would conclude that the quotation purports to be a verbatim repetition of a statement by the speaker, the quotation marks indicate that the author is not involved in an interpretation of the speaker's ambiguous statement, but attempting to convey what the speaker said. This orthodox use of a quotation is the quintessential "direct account of events that speak for themselves." *Time, Inc. v. Pape,* 401 U.S., at 285, 91 S.Ct., at 637. More accurately, the quotation allows the subject to speak for himself.

The significance of the quotations at issue, absent any qualification, is to inform us that we are reading the statement of petitioner, not Malcolm's rational interpretation of what petitioner has said or thought. Were we to assess quotations under a rational interpretation standard, we would give journalists the freedom to place statements in their subjects' mouths without fear of liability. By eliminating any method of distinguishing between the statements of the subject and the interpretation of the author, we would diminish to a great degree the trustworthiness of the printed word, and eliminate the real meaning of quotations. Not only public figures but the press doubtless would suffer under such a rule. Newsworthy figures might become more wary of journalists, knowing that any comment could be transmuted and attributed to the subject, so long as some bounds of rational interpretation were not exceeded. We would ill serve the values of the First Amendment if we were to grant near absolute, constitutional protection for such a practice. We doubt the suggestion that as a general rule readers will assume that direct quotations are but a rational interpretation of the speaker's words, and we decline to adopt any such presumption in determining the permissible interpretations of the quotations in question here.

We apply these principles to the case before us. On summary judgment, we must draw all justifiable inferences in favor of the nonmoving party, including questions of credibility and of the weight to be accorded particular evidence. *Anderson v. Liberty Lobby, Inc.,* 477 U.S., at 255, 106 S.Ct., at 2513. So we must assume, except where otherwise evidenced by the transcripts of the tape recordings, that petitioner is correct in denying that he made the statements attributed to him by Malcolm, and that Malcolm reported with knowledge or reckless disregard of the differences between what petitioner said and what was quoted.

Respondents argue that, in determining whether petitioner has shown sufficient falsification to survive summary judgment, we should consider not only the tape-recorded statements but also Malcolm's typewritten notes. We must decline that suggestion. To begin with, petitioner affirms in an affidavit that he did not make the complained of statements. The record contains substantial additional evidence, moreover, evidence which, in a light most favorable to petitioner, would support a jury determination under a clear and convincing standard that Malcolm deliberately or recklessly altered the quotations.

First, many of the challenged passages resemble quotations that appear on the tapes, except for the addition or alteration of certain phrases, giving rise to a reasonable inference that the statements have been altered. Second, Malcolm had the tapes in her possession and was not working under a tight deadline. Unlike a case involving hot news, Malcolm cannot complain that she lacked the practical ability to compare the tapes with her work in progress. Third, Malcolm represented to the editor-in-chief of The New Yorker that all the quotations were from the tape recordings. Fourth, Malcolm's explanations of the time and place of unrecorded conversations during which petitioner allegedly made some of the quoted statements have not been consistent in all respects. Fifth, petitioner suggests that the progression from typewritten notes, to manuscript, then to galleys provides further evidence of intentional alteration. Malcolm contests petitioner's allegations, and only a trial on the merits will resolve the factual dispute. But at this stage, the evidence creates a jury question whether Malcolm published the statements with knowledge or reckless disregard of the alterations.

We must determine whether the published passages differ materially in meaning from the tape recorded statements so as to create an issue of fact for a jury as to falsity.

* * *

Because of the Court of Appeals' disposition with respect to Malcolm, it did not have occasion to address petitioner's argument that the District Court erred in granting summary judgment to The New Yorker Magazine, Inc., and Alfred A. Knopf, Inc. on the basis of their respective relations with Malcolm or the lack of any independent actual malice. These questions are best addressed in the first instance on remand.

The judgment of the Court of Appeals is reversed, and the case is remanded for further proceedings consistent with this opinion. It is so ordered.

COMMENT

It was decided that the case would have to be retried so that damages could be assessed properly. In a second libel trial, a federal jury found in favor of Janet Malcolm: Masson had not proven actual malice. Masson appealed the jury verdict. In August 1995, while a third trial appeared possible, Malcolm's two-year-old granddaughter came upon a misplaced book of notes that Malcolm's lawyers said would help her case, should there be a third trial. Masson called the long lost notes a fabrication.[32]

Another form of libel is *disparagement* or *trade libel.* Special damages or actual money loss must be shown in such cases. A federal district case in *Bose Corporation v. Consumers Union*[33] defined trade libel:

> The tort of product disparagement, as distinguished from individual or corporate defamation, is a narrow cause of action. The interests protected are not those of the reputation of the corporation or the intangible concerns peculiar to individual reputation such as community standing, privacy and psychic well-being. . . . A cause of action for product disparagement is made out only when the plaintiff has satisfactorily proved that it suffered special damages flowing from a false statement concerning the nature or quality of plaintiff's product . . . . The tort exists to provide redress only for tangible and direct pecuniary loss, a purely economic injury to

---

32. *New York Times,* August 30, 1995, pp. B1, B4.
33. 7 Med.L.Rptr. 2481, 529 F.Supp. 357 (D.Mass. 1981).

which society accords a lesser value than reputational interests . . . . In a product disparagement case, the plaintiff must prove that special damages resulted from the publication and that the disparagement was a substantial factor in inducing others not to buy the plaintiff's product.

That case involved stereo speakers and would eventually reach the U.S. Supreme Court. An even more serious challenge to communicators involved apples. Eleven Washington State apple growers, claiming to represent 4,700, filed a disparagement suit against CBS's *60 Minutes*. The broadcast examined health risks that might be associated with the chemical Alar, a growth regulator used on apples. A U.S. district court granted the network's motion for summary judgment on the grounds that the broadcast dealt with an issue of public concern and that the growers would not be able to prove the falsity of the program's allegations.[34] In an amicus brief to the Ninth Circuit, forty-one publishers, broadcasters, and journalists reiterated that argument and urged the appeals court to affirm the lower court. They noted that plaintiffs did not demonstrate that the alleged defamation was "of and concerning them"; that is, there had been insufficient identification. Without that standard being met, said the communicators, media dealing with issues of public concern "would face the prospect of literally thousands of disparagement claims instituted by anyone with an economic stake in the generic product identified in a news report."[35]

In late 1995, a three-judge panel of the Ninth Circuit Court of Appeals dismissed the suit, upholding the district court's grant of summary judgment to the defendants on the grounds that the apple growers had not demonstrated disparagement of their product by CBS nor had they proven allegations in the broadcast false.[36] Nevertheless, at least eleven states have laws that permit trade libel suits against those who disparage agricultural produce.[37]

The federal Lanham Act (15 U.S.C. § 1125, et seq.) provides an independent basis for claiming trade libel, defined as false and misleading representations about the "nature, characteristics (or) qualities of any person's goods, services, or commercial activities." Not only is injunctive relief available in these cases, a remedy generally not available in libel cases, but attorney's fees and litigation costs may be added to an award of special damages.

Frequently, business plaintiffs are more clearly identifiable in small groups. This is called *corporate libel*. Corporations are collective persons—directors, managers, CEOs. Can the reputations of those persons be damaged when their companies or their products are disparaged? Courts are divided on the question. Most courts have held that corporations are not by definition public figures.[38] This means they do not have to demonstrate actual malice to win a libel suit. A more refined rule is that where corporations impinge upon the public interest, they are public figures for purposes of public comment and criticism. The greater the public interest, the higher the public figure status.[39] Oregon disagrees. "[M]erely opening one's doors to the public, offering stock for public sale, advertising, etc., even if considering thrusting one's self into matters of public interest, is not sufficient to establish that a corporation is a public figure."[40]

A typical case involved the manufacturer of an ozone-generating air purifier and a critical report in *Consumers Reports*. The company was designated a public figure by the court since the controversy it was involved in was a public matter that predated the alleged defamation. The plaintiff was actively engaged in the controversy and at all times had media access for purposes of rebuttal. More important, the plaintiff could prove neither falsity nor actual malice.[41] State and federal courts are divided on whether the *New York Times* doctrine applies to commercial advertising.

34. *Auvil v. CBS "60 Minutes,"* 21 Med.L.Rptr. 2059, 836 F.Supp. 740 (E.D.Wash. 1993).
35. News Notes, 22 Med.L.Rptr. No. 15 (April 12, 1994).
36. *Auvil v. CBS "60 Minutes,"* 23 Med.L.Rptr. 2454, 67 F.3d 816, (9th Cir. 1995).
37. Robert D. Sack, "1995 Developments in Defamation Law," in *Communications Law 1995,* vol. 1 (New York: Practicing Law Institute, 1995), pp. 727–28.

38. *Schiavone Construction Co. v. Time, Inc.,* 12 Med.L.Rptr. 1153, 619 F.Supp. 684 (D.N.J. 1985).
39. *Jadwin v. Minneapolis Star and Tribune Co.,* 11 Med.L.Rptr. 1905, 367 N.W.2d 476 (Minn. 1985).
40. *Bank of Oregon v. Independent News, Inc.,* 693 P.2d 35, 42 (Or. 1985), *cert. denied,* 474 U.S. 826 (1986).
41. *Quantum Electronic Corp. v. Consumers Union of U.S. Inc.,* 23 Med.L.Rptr. 1897 (U.S.D.C.R.I. 1995).

An earlier case suggested a test for determining the status of a corporate plaintiff: (1) Is it a public or merely a private controversy? (2) Did the controversy precede the defamatory statement? and (3) To what extent did the corporation participate in the controversy?[42]

Nonprofit organizations, foundations, special interest groups, and labor unions may attempt libel actions on behalf of their memberships, but successful suits in such cases are rare. Personal identification in such suits is impossible. Governments, political parties, and political interest groups are effectively barred from bringing libel suits because the citizen's right to criticize power brokers is fundamental to a democratic society. To view it otherwise would be to condone criminal or seditious libel, a jurisdiction that has all but disappeared in the evolution of American constitutional law and was very likely discredited altogether by the landmark 1964 case, *New York Times v. Sullivan.*

PUBLICATION

Publication in libel occurs when a defamation is published, communicated, circulated, or disseminated. This is when the most damage to reputation is likely to occur. Anyone taking part in the crafting of a libel or in its distribution is technically liable for damages.

Publication also assumes that someone has received the message. The recipient may be a single person or a substantial portion of the audience for which the publication was intended. Newspapers, broadcasting, books, magazines, and most other traditional forms of publication use editors as gatekeepers. Cyberspace tends not to. If an online service company exercises editorial control over the content of the messages posted on its computer bulletin boards, it is a publisher for libel law purposes. For example, an unidentified bulletin board user accused a securities investment firm of fraud and lying. Prodigy was treated as a newspaper. To enforce its guidelines, it had a prescreening system, an emergency delete function supervised by what the company called board leaders. Prodigy argued vainly before the trial court that it had abolished that

particular system long before the offensive statements were made.[43] The *New York Times* subsequently reported that the investment firm, in spite of the fact that it had been fined heavily by the Securities and Exchange Commission a year before the lawsuit for "fraudulent and deceptive sales practices," would drop its $200 million suit against Prodigy in exchange for an apology.[44]

CompuServe had no such supervisory system in place and so was not liable for statements published in its service by a third party.[45] The trick will be to distinguish a "publisher" from a "distributor." And perhaps "publishers" should be responsible only for what they produce. Since the CompuServe case may presage an important dimension of the future of libel in cyberspace, it is worth some attention:

Cubby Inc. v. CompuServe Inc.
19 MED. L. RPTR. 1525, 776 F.SUPP. 135 (S.D.N.Y. 1991).

LEISURE, J.:

* * *

CompuServe develops and provides computer-related products and services, including CompuServe Information Service ("CIS"), an online general information service or "electronic library" that subscribers may access from a personal computer or terminal. Subscribers to CIS pay a membership fee and online time usage fees, in return for which they have access to the thousands of information sources available on CIS. Subscribers may also obtain access to over 150 special interest "forums," which are comprised of electronic bulletin boards, interactive online conferences, and topical databases.

One forum available is the Journalism Forum, which focuses on the journalism industry. Cameron Communications, Inc. ("CCI"), which is independent of CompuServe, has contracted to "manage, review, create, delete, edit and otherwise control the contents" of the Journalism Forum "in accordance with editorial and technical standards and conventions of style as established by CompuServe."

---

42. *Bruno & Stillman, Inc. v. Globe Newspaper Co.,* 6 Med.L.Rptr. 2057, 633 F.2d 583, 589 (1st Cir. 1980).

43. *Stratton Oakmont, Inc. v. Prodigy Services Co.,* 23 Med.L.Rptr. 1794 (N.Y. Sup.Ct. 1995).

44. *New York Times,* October 25, 1995, pp. C1, C5.

45. *Cubby Inc. v. CompuServe Inc.,* 19 Med.L.Rptr. 1525, 776 F.Supp. 135 (S.D.N.Y. 1991).

One publication available as part of the Journalism Forum is Rumorville USA ("Rumorville"), a daily newsletter that provides reports about broadcast journalism and journalists. Rumorville is published by Don Fitzpatrick Associates of San Francisco ("DFA"), which is headed by defendant Don Fitzpatrick. CompuServe has no employment, contractual, or other direct relationship with either DFA or Fitzpatrick; DFA provides Rumorville to the Journalism Forum under a contract with CCI. The contract between CCI and DFA provides that DFA "accepts total responsibility for the contents" of Rumorville. The contract also requires CCI to limit access to Rumorville to those CIS subscribers who have previously made membership arrangements directly with DFA.

CompuServe has no opportunity to review Rumorville's contents before DFA uploads it into CompuServe's computer banks, from which it is immediately available to approved CIS subscribers. CompuServe receives no part of any fees that DFA charges for access to Rumorville, nor does CompuServe compensate DFA for providing Rumorville to the Journalism Forum; the compensation CompuServe receives for making Rumorville available to its subscribers is the standard online time usage and membership fees charged to all CIS subscribers, regardless of the information services they use. CompuServe maintains that, before this action was filed, it had no notice of any complaints about the contents of the Rumorville publication or about DFA.

In 1990, plaintiffs Cubby, Inc. ("Cubby") and Robert Blanchard ("Blanchard") (collectively, "plaintiffs") developed Skuttlebut, a computer database designed to publish and distribute electronically news and gossip in the television news and radio industries. Plaintiffs intended to compete with Rumorville; subscribers gained access to Skuttlebut through their personal computers after completing subscription agreements with plaintiffs.

Plaintiffs claim that, on separate occasions in April 1990, Rumorville published false and defamatory statements relating to Skuttlebut and Blanchard, and that CompuServe carried these statements as part of the Journalism Forum. The allegedly defamatory remarks included a suggestion that individuals at Skuttlebut gained access to information first published by Rumorville "through some back door"; a statement that Blanchard was "bounced" from his previous employer, WABC; and a description of Skuttlebut as a "new start-up scam."

Plaintiffs have asserted claims against CompuServe and Fitzpatrick under New York law for libel of Blanchard, business disparagement of Skuttlebut, and unfair competition as to Skuttlebut, based largely upon the allegedly defamatory statements contained in Rumorville. CompuServe has moved, pursuant to Fed.R.Civ.P. 56, for summary judgment on all claims against it. CompuServe does not dispute, solely for the purposes of this motion, that the statements relating to Skuttlebut and Blanchard were defamatory; rather, it argues that it acted as a distributor, and not a publisher, of the statements, and cannot be held liable for the statements because it did not know and had no reason to know of the statements. Plaintiffs oppose CompuServe's motion for summary judgment, claiming that genuine issues of material fact exist and that little in the way of discovery has been undertaken thus far.

* * *

A. The Applicable Standard of Liability

Plaintiffs base their libel claim on the allegedly defamatory statements contained in the Rumorville publication that CompuServe carried as part of the Journalism Forum. CompuServe argues that, based on the undisputed facts, it was a distributor of Rumorville, as opposed to a publisher of the Rumorville statements. CompuServe further contends that, as a distributor of Rumorville, it cannot be held liable on the libel claim because it neither knew nor had reason to know of the allegedly defamatory statements. Plaintiffs, on the other hand, argue that the Court should conclude that CompuServe is a publisher of the statements and hold it to a higher standard of liability.

Ordinarily, " 'one who repeats or otherwise republishes defamatory matter is subject to liability as if he had originally published it.' " *Cianci v. New Times Publishing Co.,* 639 F.2d 54, 61 [6 Med.L.Rptr. 1625] (2d Cir. 1980) (Friendly, J.) (quoting Restatement (Second) of Torts §578 (1977)). With respect to entities such as news vendors, book stores, and libraries, however, "New York courts have long held that vendors and distributors of defamatory publications are not liable if they neither know nor have reason to know of the defamation." *Lerman v. Chuckleberry Publishing, Inc.,* 521 F. Supp. 228, 235 [7

Med.L.Rptr. 2282] (S.D.N.Y. 1981); *accord Macaluso v. Mondadori Publishing Co.,* 527 F. Supp. 1017, 1019 [8 Med.L.Rptr. 1367] (E.D.N.Y. 1981).

The requirement that a distributor must have knowledge of the contents of a publication before liability can be imposed for distributing that publication is deeply rooted in the First Amendment, made applicable to the states through the Fourteenth Amendment. "[T]he constitutional guarantees of the freedom of speech and of the press stand in the way of imposing" strict liability on distributors for the contents of the reading materials they carry. *Smith v. California,* 361 U.S. 147, 152–53 (1959). In *Smith,* the Court struck down an ordinance that imposed liability on a bookseller for possession of an obscene book, regardless of whether the bookseller had knowledge of the book's contents. * * * Although *Smith* involved criminal liability, the First Amendment's guarantees are no less relevant to the instant action: "What a State may not constitutionally bring about by means of a criminal statute is likewise beyond the reach of its civil law of libel. The fear of damage awards. . . may be markedly more inhibiting than the fear of prosecution under a criminal statute." *New York Times Co. v. Sullivan,* 376 U.S. 254, 277 [1 Med.L.Rptr. 1527] (1964).

CompuServe's CIS product is in essence an electronic, for-profit library that carries a vast number of publications and collects usage and membership fees from its subscribers in return for access to the publications. CompuServe and companies like it are at the forefront of the information industry revolution. High technology has markedly increased the speed with which information is gathered and processed; it is now possible for an individual with a personal computer, modem, and telephone line to have instantaneous access to thousands of news publications from across the United States and around the world. While CompuServe may decline to carry a given publication altogether, in reality, once it does decide to carry a publication, it will have little or no editorial control over that publication's contents. This is especially so when CompuServe carries the publication as part of a forum that is managed by a company unrelated to CompuServe.

With respect to the Rumorville publication, the undisputed facts are that DFA uploads the text of Rumorville into CompuServe's data banks and makes it available to approved CIS subscribers instantaneously. CompuServe has no more editorial control over such a publication than does a public library, book store, or newsstand, and it would be no more feasible for CompuServe to examine every publication it carries for potentially defamatory statements than it would be for any other distributor to do so. "First Amendment guarantees have long been recognized as protecting distributors of publications. . . . Obviously, the national distributor of hundreds of periodicals has no duty to monitor each issue of every periodical it distributes. Such a rule would be an impermissible burden on the First Amendment." *Lerman v. Flynt Distributing Co.,* 745 F.2d 123, 139 [10 Med.L.Rptr. 2497] (2d Cir. 1984), *cert. denied,* 471 U.S. 1054 (1985); * * *

Technology is rapidly transforming the information industry. A computerized database is the functional equivalent of a more traditional news vendor, and the inconsistent application of a lower standard of liability to an electronic news distributor such as CompuServe than that which is applied to a public library, book store, or newsstand would impose an undue burden on the free flow of information. Given the relevant First Amendment considerations, the appropriate standard of liability to be applied to CompuServe is whether it knew or had reason to know of the allegedly defamatory Rumorville statements.

B. CompuServe's Liability as a Distributor

CompuServe contends that it is undisputed that it had neither knowledge nor reason to know of the allegedly defamatory Rumorville statements, especially given the large number of publications it carries and the speed with which DFA uploads Rumorville into its computer banks and makes the publication available to CIS subscribers. The burden is thus shifted to plaintiffs, who " 'must set forth specific facts showing that there is a genuine issue for trial.' " *Anderson v. Liberty Lobby, Inc.,* 477 U.S. 242, 250 (1986) (quoting Fed.R.Civ.P. 56(e)). Plaintiffs have not set forth anything other than conclusory allegations as to whether CompuServe knew or had reason to know of the Rumorville statements, and have failed to meet their burden on this issue. Plaintiffs do contend that CompuServe was informed that persons affiliated with Skuttlebut might be "hacking" in order to obtain unauthorized access to Rumorville, but that claim is wholly irrelevant to the issue of whether CompuServe was put on notice that the Rumorville publication contained statements accusing the Skuttlebut principals of engaging in "hacking."

Plaintiffs have not set forth any specific facts showing that there is a genuine issue as to whether CompuServe knew or had reason to know of Rumorville's contents. Because CompuServe, as a news distributor, may not be held liable if it neither knew nor had reason to know of the allegedly defamatory Rumorville statements, summary judgment in favor of CompuServe on the libel claim is granted.

Business Disparagement Claim

Plaintiffs base the claim for business disparagement of Skuttlebut on statements published in Rumorville in April 1990. Plaintiffs' contention is that "defendants made statements intentionally designed to discourage its [sic] own subscribers and others in the news business from associating with Skuttlebut, thus disparaging Skuttlebut's business." These statements include, *inter alia,* the allegedly defamatory remarks suggesting that plaintiffs inappropriately accessed information from Rumorville "through some back door" and describing Skuttlebut as a "new start-up scam."

New York courts rarely use the term "business disparagement" and have not articulated the elements of such a claim. New York's highest court, although not using the "business disparagement" label, has recognized a cause of action for tortious conduct similar to that alleged by plaintiffs. See *Ruder & Finn Inc. v. Seaboard Surety Co.,* 52 N.Y.2d 663, 670–71, 422 N.E.2d 518, 522, 439 N.Y.S.2d 858, 862 [7 Med.L.Rptr. 1833] (1981) ("[w]here a statement impugns the basic integrity or creditworthiness of a business, an action for defamation lies"). New York courts have applied other labels to similar conduct: "The tort of trade libel or injurious falsehood consists of the knowing publication of false matter derogatory to the plaintiff's business of a kind calculated to prevent others from dealing with the business or otherwise interfering with its relations with others, to its detriment." *Waste Distillation Technology, Inc. v. Blasland & Bouck Engineers, P.C.,* 136 A.D.2d 633, 633, 523 N.Y.S.2d 875, 876 (2d Dep't 1988).

Regardless of the label used, the substance of plaintiffs' "business disparagement" claim is similar to the action for defamation recognized in *Ruder & Finn,* as well as the action for trade libel or injurious falsehood recognized in *Waste Distillation Technology.* Under either formulation, plaintiffs would have to prove that CompuServe had knowledge or reason to know of Rumorville's publication of the allegedly disparaging statements in order to hold CompuServe liable for business disparagement. As discussed with respect to the libel claim, *supra,* plaintiffs have failed to meet their burden of setting forth specific facts showing that there is a genuine issue as to whether CompuServe had knowledge or reason to know of the April 1990 Rumorville statements. Summary judgment in favor of CompuServe on the business disparagement claim is therefore granted.

* * *

Conclusion

For the reasons stated above, CompuServe's motion for summary judgment pursuant to Fed.R.Civ.P. 56 is granted on all claims asserted against it.

COMMENT

Online services find themselves in the odd position of being held liable if they fail to delete what is offensive and being accused of censorship when they do. Should they be given common-carrier protection for the huge volume of material they can't control? If so, what First Amendment rights will they sacrifice? Or should a line be drawn somewhere before that point? Do those libeled in cyberspace have an opportunity for instant rebuttal? Should libelers in cyberspace have the same constitutional protections as the traditional media? Is every user in cyberspace a voluntary public figure in a particular news group? And where should a suit be brought? In the state where the bulletin board's computer is located? In the tortfeasor's state? The plaintiff's state? Since cyberspace is not the same as geographical space, should a federal law govern defamation in cyberspace?[46]

---

46. John D. Faucher, *Let the Chips Fall Where They May: Choice of Law in Computer Bulletin Board Defamation Cases,* 26 U of Calif.Davis L.Rev. 1045 (1993).

Choice of law questions[47] are not new to libel law, but they are complicated by nationally and internationally linked networks that pay little attention to state or national boundaries. Whose libel laws will govern? These and many additional questions remain unanswered. It is likely that online services will be held responsible for the content they generate and be treated as common carriers for what others generate. Online users have voluntarily entered a public arena and have ready access to cyberspace to dispute or correct defamatory comments made against them.

This raises the question of *republication*. The rule has been that a publisher is liable for what is consciously republished with consent and with foreseeable consequences. Mere distribution capability is not enough. The rule protects libraries, bookstores, and magazine vendors.

Some states, either by case law or by statute, subscribe to what is known as the *single publication* rule. Initial publication of a newspaper or magazine is one libel, one cause of action, regardless of how many people read it, when they read it, or how often they read it. A plaintiff may be able to plead and prove extent of circulation as evidence bearing on damages. Where the rule is in effect, the libel suit may have to be brought in the place where the libel was first published. Several courts have refused to let the single publication rule cross state lines and have allowed a separate cause of action in each state where publication occurred. The intention of the rule is to protect publishers from the perpetual harassment of multiple and never-ending libel suits. In spite of California's Uniform Single Publication Act, a new libel action based on the paperback edition of a book was permitted, even though identical passages in the original hardcover edition had already been litigated.[48]

A libel suit may be brought where the defendant resides or does business, in the place of largest circulation, or where the greatest harm was done, possibly the plaintiff's place of residence. What are called *long-arm statutes* can be applied to publishers of national newspapers without violating due process. For example, the

Los Angeles Times and other newspapers were sued in Wyoming for a story on organized crime that was researched in Wyoming by three *Times* reporters and had its major impact there.[49] Generally, however, a newspaper published in a distant place must have sufficient business and professional impact where the alleged libel has occurred to trigger a long-arm statute. In dismissing a libel suit for want of jurisdiction, a U.S. district court in Texas concluded that 28 daily copies of the *Detroit Free Press*, .0044 percent of the paper's total daily circulation, were insufficient to constitute the minimum contacts necessary to sustain jurisdiction under the Due Process Clause.[50]

Appellate courts are divided on who has jurisdiction when defendant media are engaged in interstate commerce, as they usually are. For example, a suit filed in South Dakota but based on a New York network program was removed to a federal court.[51] Again the test seems to be the degree to which the defendant is continuously and systematically involved in the forum where the plaintiff brings suit; that is, where was the information for the story researched, written, edited, and published? Another question: To what extent has the defendant been involved in the affairs of the plaintiff's state?[52] On the other hand, Maryland law applied in libel and privacy suits brought by Maryland residents against nationwide Fox television broadcasts.[53]

Most media and their messages do cross state lines, and therefore the plaintiff and defendant reside in different states. In such circumstances, federal courts assume jurisdiction in what is known as a *diversity suit*. The federal court may apply the law of the state in which the greatest injury to the plaintiff occurred. In *single publication rule* states, the libel suit may be brought where publication first took place, and that will usually be the place of greatest circulation. Where there is no *single publication* rule, some federal courts have allowed a sepa-

47. Arati Korwar and Ruth Walden, *Choice of Law in Multistate Media Law Cases: Have the 'Quaking Quagmires' Been Quelled?* Journalism & Mass Communication Monographs, No. 153 (October 1995).
48. *Kanarek v. Bugliosi*, 6 Med.L.Rptr. 1864, 166 Cal.Rptr. 526 (1980).
49. *Anselmi v. Denver Post, Inc.*, 2 Med.L.Rptr. 1530, 552 F.2d 316 (10th Cir. 1977).
50. *Kersh v. Angelosante*, 8 Med.L.Rptr. 1282 (N.D. Texas 1982).
51. *Federal Beef Processors Inc. v. CBS Inc.*, 22 Med.L.Rptr. 1833, 851 F.Supp. 1430 (D.C.S.C. 1994).
52. *Ticketmaster–New York, Inc. v. Alioto*, 22 Med.L.Rptr. 1682, 26 F.3d 201 (1st Cir. 1994).
53. *Crowley v. Fox Broadcasting Co.*, 22 Med.L.Rptr. 1904, 851 F.Supp. 700 (D.C.Med. 1994).

rate lawsuit in each state where the publication circulated.

A second step in publication occurs when the libel effectively reaches the readers, listeners, and viewers for whom it was intended. A number of courts have held that publication is effected when the libelous matter is delivered to common carriers for distribution, although retailers themselves are protected against libel suits in most states, as are carrier persons, broadcast engineers, and other innocent co-workers. Executives and managers are generally responsible for libel committed by permanent or contract employees.

The time of publication is also when the *statute of limitations* begins to run, setting a date of one, two, or three years from the date of publication after which a libel suit cannot be brought. If there is a conscious *republication* of a libel, the statute of limitations will begin running from the date of that second publication. An original author, as has been noted, will not be legally liable for a republication, however, unless she has given permission for it. The republisher, of course, will be liable.

In the *Alton* (Illinois) *Telegraph* case, the memo sent to the Justice Department constituted publication. No one at Justice seemed interested, and the memo found its way to the Home Loan Bank Board. The plaintiff, his credit sullied before the board, sued the *Telegraph* for $9.2 million, forcing it into bankruptcy. The plaintiff later tried to take over the newspaper in payment of a money judgment awarded him by a jury. Note that the newspaper had never published the story.

The case highlights another legal point. Clearly, in this case the corporate employer was responsible for libel committed by an employee, although the plaintiff could not prove that the editor knew the reporters had sent the memo to federal prosecutors. A majority of states hold the employer responsible for damages incurred by an employee committing a "malicious tort." Designed to encourage employers to know who their employees are and what they are doing, the rule is known as *respondeat superior*.

A minority of states, but a significant minority because it includes New York, California, and the District of Columbia, subscribes to what is called the *complicity rule*: employers are not liable, at least not for punitive damages, unless they authorize or participate in employee misconduct. An editor or publisher denying that he knew what his reporters were doing is hardly a

mark of responsible journalism. And yet it may be the mark of a professional that she operates with a full mandate from higher-ups.

Great care should be taken with delay devices used in radio talk shows. Stations have been held liable for what their callers say on the air.[54] The same is true of letters to the editor. All publishers, from the *Wall Street Journal* to the poorest leafleteer, are responsible for what they publish and distribute.

IDENTIFICATION

Identification must be precise. Whom does the libel damage? Is the person identifiable by name or nickname, initials, physical peculiarities, photograph, dress, address, or professional reputation? Patterns of behavior that by their sheer uniqueness identify a particular person in fiction or docudrama can establish identification. So can photographs, sketches, or cartoons—for example, a woman photographed on a street while a narrator discussed problems of neighborhood prostitution.[55] Names are not necessary for identification.[56]

Some jurisdictions hold plaintiffs to stringent standards of identification in order to protect works of the imagination. Superficial similarities are not enough.[57] Generally, a defamatory statement must be understood to identify a particular person. Someone other than the plaintiff must infer from a publication that the defamatory reference is to the plaintiff. The legal term for this requirement is *colloquium*.

Kimberly Pring, a former Miss Wyoming, claimed that she was identified in a salacious and phantasmagorical *Penthouse* magazine short story by the color of her costume and her baton-twirling ability. Her name was never mentioned.[58] No evidence was presented to support the allega-

54. *Snowden v. Pearl River Broadcasting Corp.,* 251 So.2d 405 (La. 1971); *Denman v. Star Broadcasting Co.,* 497 P.2d 1378 (Utah 1972).

55. *Clark v. American Broadcasting Cos. Inc.,* 8 Med.L.Rptr. 2049, 684 F.2d 1208 (6th Cir. 1982), *cert. denied, 460 U.S. 1040 (1983).*

56. *Desnick v. Capital Cities/ABC Inc.,* 22 Med.L.Rptr. 1937, 851 F.Supp. 303 (N.D. Ill. 1994).

57. *Springer v. Viking Press,* 8 Med.L.Rptr. 2613, 457 N.Y.S.2d 246 (1982).

58. *Pring v. Penthouse International,* 8 Med.L.Rptr. 2409, 695 F.2d 438 (10th Cir. 1982).

tion that the author had her in mind when he wrote his story. Her costume and talent alone were not enough to constitute identification.

Identification can be lost in a crowd. If a group is too large, individual identification is impossible and a libel suit cannot proceed. *Group libel,* as has been noted, has not found favor in Anglo-American law, partly because of its resemblance to criminal or seditious libel. Criminal libel is criticism of the government or words that disrupt public peace and good order. In a criminal libel case, the state is the plaintiff. Such laws, said Justice William O. Douglas, make someone a criminal because an audience can't hold its temper.[59] They turn a tort into a crime. He was referring to pamphlets critical of law enforcement and a newspaper publisher during a Kentucky miners' strike.

Nevertheless, much interest has been shown recently in protecting minority groups from the wrath of bigots and their sexist, racist, and homophobic speech. Some refer to these efforts, pejoratively, as "political correctness." An interesting and important question is to what extent, if at all, the "politically correct" speech movement would reinstate criminal libel, a crime, as we shall see, that the Supreme Court did away with in *New York Times v. Sullivan.*

The question remains: How big is too big for individual identification? As has been noted, under current law there is no way political parties and racial, religious, gender, occupational, or interest groups can successfully sue for libel. Many have tried and failed. Even a group of twenty-nine teachers, clearly identifiable in their own community, was said by a federal district court not to be "so small" that a newspaper article investigating possible sexual misconduct "may reasonably be understood to have personal reference to any member of the group."[60] But courts have waffled on the numbers, and a New York court suggested that numbers alone may not be determinant. The prominence of the group and individual roles within it would be, said the court. In that case, 53 of 71 police in Newburgh, New York, were allowed to sue for the defamatory implication that they had condoned what 18 indicted col-

leagues had done.[61] Generally, however, as a group gets smaller, the danger increases.

A Boston *Globe* editorial referred to the Manchester (N.H.) *Union Leader* as "probably the worst newspaper in America" and asserted that its publisher "runs a newspaper by paranoids for paranoids." For lack of identification, a federal district court disallowed a suit by 24 of the *Union Leader*'s 325 employees and three of its eight editors.[62] Care is definitely recommended when the number gets as small as eight. In that case the public nature of the controversy and the fact that the rhetoric reflected pure opinion influenced the court.

Until recently, the dead took their reputations with them. Now, however, in a number of states, the dead are rising to smite those who would defame them. Several states, including New York and Pennsylvania, recognize libel of the dead either by statute or by common law. The assumption, of course, is that a libel of a deceased reflects adversely on his survivors.

FALSITY

Falsehood has always been a central concept in libel. Before *New York Times v. Sullivan,* the falsity of a defamatory statement was presumed. Now it has to be proven by the plaintiff. Moreover, in *New York Times* the core of the Supreme Court's holding was that any public official from that day forward would have to prove falsity as well as actual malice to win a libel suit. Actual malice, as we shall see, would be given a constitutional definition—knowing falsehood or reckless disregard as to truth or falsity. Any doubts about who carried the burden of proof of falsity were dispelled by the U.S. Supreme Court in an important 1986 case, *Philadelphia Newspapers v. Hepps.*[63] At least where speech of public concern was involved, said the Court, all plaintiffs, whether private or public people, had the burden of proving falsity. This burden requires proving a negative, that is, proving that a libelous allegation is *not* true. Difficult though it may be to sep-

---

59. *Ashton v. Kentucky,* 384 U.S. 195 (1966).

60. *O'Brien v. Williamson Daily News,* 18 Med.L.Rptr. 1037 (E.D.Ky. 1990).

61. *Brady v. Ottaway Newspapers, Inc.,* 8 Med.L.Rptr. 1671, 445 N.Y.S.2d 786 (1981).

62. *Loeb v. Globe Newspaper Co.,* 6 Med.L.Rptr. 1235, 489 F.Supp. 481 (D.Mass. 1980).

63. 475 U.S. 767 (1986).

arate truth from falsehood in particular cases, the Constitution requires the scales to be tipped in favor of "true" speech. To ensure that true speech on matters of public concern is not deterred, the Court said that the common law presumption that defamatory speech is false could not stand. Hepps, a beer distributor, was alleged to have connections with organized crime:

Philadelphia Newspapers v. Hepps

12 MED.L.RPTR. 1977, 475 U.S. 767, 106 S.CT. 1558 (1986).

Justice O'CONNOR delivered the Opinion of the Court.

* * *

Our opinions to date have chiefly treated the necessary showings of fault rather than of falsity. Nonetheless, as one might expect, given the language of the Court in *New York Times,* a public-figure plaintiff must show the falsity of the statements at issue in order to prevail on a suit for defamation. See *Garrison v. Louisiana,* 379 U.S. 64, 74 (1 Med.L.Rptr. 1548) (1964) (reading *New York Times* for the proposition that "a public official [is] allowed the civil [defamation] remedy only if he establishes that the utterance was false"). See also *Herbert v. Lando,* 441 U.S. 153, 176 (1979) ("the plaintiff must focus on the editorial process and prove a false publication attended by some degree of culpability").

Here, as in *Gertz,* the plaintiff is a private figure and the newspaper articles are of public concern. In *Gertz,* as in *New York Times,* the common-law rule was superseded by a constitutional rule. We believe that the common law's rule on falsity— that the defendant must bear the burden of proving truth—must similarly fall here to a constitutional requirement that the plaintiff bear the burden of showing falsity, as well as fault, before recovering damages.

There will always be instances when the factfinding process will be unable to resolve conclusively whether the speech is true or false; it is in those cases that the burden of proof is dispositive. Under a rule forcing the plaintiff to bear the burden of showing falsity, there will be some cases in which plaintiffs cannot meet their burden despite the fact that the speech is in fact false. The plaintiff's suit will fail despite the fact that, in some abstract sense, the suit is meritorious. Similarly, under an alternative rule placing the burden of showing truth on defendants, there would be some cases in which defendants could not bear their burden despite the fact that the speech is in fact true. Those suits would succeed despite the fact that, in some abstract sense, those suits are unmeritorious. Under either rule, then, the outcome of the suit will sometimes be at variance with the outcome that we would desire if all speech were either demonstrably true or demonstrably false.

This dilemma stems from the fact that the allocation of the burden of proof will determine liability for some speech that is true and some that is false, but *all* of such speech is *unknowably* true or false. Because the burden of proof is the deciding factor only when the evidence is ambiguous, we cannot know how much of the speech affected by the allocation of the burden of proof is true and how much is false. In a case presenting a configuration of speech and plaintiff like the one we face here, and where the scales are in such an uncertain balance, we believe that the Constitution requires us to tip them in favor of protecting true speech. To ensure that true speech on matters of public concern is not deterred, we hold that the common-law presumption that defamatory speech is false cannot stand when a plaintiff seeks damages against a media defendant for speech of public concern.

In the context of governmental restriction of speech, it has long been established that the government cannot limit speech protected by the First Amendment without bearing the burden of showing that its restriction is justified. See *Consolidated Edison Co. v. Public Service Comm'n of N.Y.,* 447 U.S. 530, 540, 6 Med.L.Rptr. 1518 (1980) (content-based restriction); *First National Bank v. Bellotti,* 435 U.S. 765, 786, 3 Med.L.Rptr. 2105 (1978) (speaker-based restriction); *Renton v. Playtime Theaters, Inc.,* 475 U.S. 41, 12 Med.L.Rptr. 1721 (1986) (secondary-effects restriction). See also *Speiser v. Randall,* 357 U.S. 513 (1958) (striking down the precondition that a taxpayer sign a loyalty oath before receiving certain tax benefits). It is not immediately apparent from the text of the First Amendment, which by its terms applies only to governmental action, that a similar result should obtain here: a suit by a private party is obviously quite different from the government's direct enforcement of its own laws. Nonetheless, the need to encourage debate on public issues that concerned the Court in the governmental-restriction cases is of concern in a similar manner in this case involving a private suit for damages: placement by state law of the burden of proving truth upon media defendants who publish speech because of the fear that liability will unjustifiably result. See *New York Times*, 376 U.S. 279; *Garrison, supra*, at 74 ("Truth may not be the subject of either civil or criminal sanctions where discussion of public affairs is concerned"). Because such a "chilling" effect would be antithetical to the First Amendment's protection of true speech on matters of public concern, we believe that a private-figure plaintiff must bear the burden of showing that the speech at issue is false before recovering damages for defamation from a media defendant. To do otherwise could "only result in a deterrence of speech which the Constitution makes free."*Speiser, supra,* at 526.

We recognize that requiring the plaintiff to show falsity will insulate from liability some speech that is false, but unprovably so. Nonetheless, the Court's previous decisions on the restrictions that the First Amendment places upon the common law of defamation firmly support our conclusion here with respect to the allocation of the burden of proof. In attempting to resolve related issues in the defamation context, the Court has affirmed that "[t]he First Amendment requires we protect some falsehood in order to protect speech that matters." *Gertz,* 418 U.S. 341. Here the speech concerns the legitimacy of the political process, and therefore clearly "matters." See *Dun & Bradstreet,* 472 U.S., at __ (speech of public concern is at the core of the First Amendment's protections). To provide "breathing space," *New York Times, supra,* at 272 (quoting *NAACP v. Button,* 371 U.S. 415, 433 (1963)), for true speech on matters of public concern, the Court has been willing to insulate even *demonstrably* false speech from liability, and has imposed additional requirements of fault upon the plaintiff in a suit for defamation. See, *e.g., Garrison,* 379 U.S. 75; *Gertz, supra,* at 347. We therefore do not break new ground here in insulating speech that is not even demonstrably false.

We note that our decision adds only marginally to the burdens that the plaintiff must already bear as a result of our earlier decisions in the law of defamation. The plaintiff must show fault. A jury is obviously more likely to accept a plaintiff's contention that the defendant was at fault in publishing the statements at issue if convinced that the relevant statements were false. As a practical matter, then, evidence offered by plaintiffs on the publisher's fault in adequately investigating the truth of the published statements will generally encompass evidence of the falsity of the matters asserted. See Keeton, *Defamation and Freedom of the Press,* 54 Texas.L.Rev. 1221, 1236 (1976). See also Franklin & Bussel, *The Plaintiff's Burden in Defamation: Awareness and Falsity,* 25 Wm. & Mary L. Rev. 825, 856–857 (1984).

We recognize that the plaintiff's burden in this case is weightier because of Pennsylvania's "shield" law, which allows employees of the media to refuse to divulge their sources. But we do not have before us here the question of the permissible reach of such laws. Indeed, we do not even know the precise reach of Pennsylvania's statute. The trial judge refused to give any instructions to the jury as to whether it could, or should, draw an inference adverse to the defendant from the defendant's decision to use the shield law rather than to present affirmative evidence of the truthfulness of some of the sources. That decision of the trial judge was not addressed by Pennsylvania's highest court, nor was it appealed to this Court. In the situation before us, we are unconvinced that the State's shield law requires a different constitutional standard than would prevail in the absence of such a law.

For the reasons stated above, the judgment of the Pennsylvania Supreme Court is reversed, and the case is remanded for further proceedings not inconsistent with this opinion.

* * *

COMMENT

Justice Sandra Day O'Connor did not say what rule would apply to private plaintiffs who were not involved in matters of public concern, nor did she address the standing of nonmedia defendants. Some state laws and court opinions have extended the protections of *New York Times* to nonmedia defendants.

Hepps also holds that substantial falsity has to be established by *clear and convincing evidence,* at least where the plaintiff is a public person. This *standard of evidence or proof,* as shall be noted, is required in other areas of libel law as well, notably in proving actual malice. It is an intermediate position between the lesser standard of *fair preponderance* and the higher standard of *beyond a reasonable doubt* applied in criminal cases. Lower courts, however, have not always followed the Supreme Court on this matter. For example, in *Rattray v. City of National City,*[64] the Ninth Circuit court of Appeals held that a plaintiff need demonstrate falsity only by a preponderance of the evidence. Only actual malice, said the court, requires clear and convincing proof. Here the court correctly surmises that the "ultimate truth or falsity of a charge may be essentially unprovable."

Justice John Paul Stevens, recognizing the difficulty that having to prove a negative presents for the plaintiff, dissented in the 5–4 *Hepps* ruling. But he too assumed a clear-cut distinction between truth and falsity. While one might not be as sanguine as the courts in drawing a line between truth and falsehood, it is clearly incumbent upon editors to check the accuracy of every story they handle. Truth, when it can be measured and accurately assessed, is an absolute defense against libel suits.

ACTUAL INJURY

Although the U.S. Supreme Court has left to state courts the task of defining actual injury precisely, it did say in the important *Gertz* case[65] "that actual injury is not limited to out-of-pocket loss [so by inference it could mean monetary loss]. Indeed, the more customary types of actual harm inflicted by defamatory falsehood include impairment of reputation and standing in the community, personal humiliation, and mental anguish and suffering."

There is much debate in legal circles on what ought to be compensated. Some argue that loss of reputation alone deserves compensation.[66]

But aren't mental stress, anguish, and humiliation inevitable consequences of an attack on reputation? The Iowa Libel Research Project[67] found that most plaintiffs claim emotional suffering as a result of defamatory publication and seek restoration of their reputations rather than money damages. But what if humiliation and anguish occur without any damage to reputation? Could that be a libel suit? Thus, the question of damages is very much up in the air. Here an effort to define the various categories of damages will be made later in the chapter.

A mayor sued a Utah newspaper for asserting that he had attempted to "manipulate" the press. The suit failed because the mayor could not demonstrate that the publication had caused him any consequential injury.[68]

While we have attempted to define the *five prerequisites* to an actionable libel suit—defamation, publication, identification, falsity, and actual injury—we are not yet close to the heart of libel law. A new era of libel law began with *New York Times v. Sullivan* in 1964. How did we get there and where are we now?

FAULT: COMMON LAW LIBEL AND THE ORIGINS OF THE CONSTITUTIONAL DEFENSE

Strict Liability

Under the common law rule of *strict liability,* libel *per se* was defined as defamatory words published in reference to a plaintiff with obvious and substantial damage to reputation. Falsity as to fact, lack of justification as to opinion, malice on the part of the publisher, and injury to the plaintiff were all presumed. The plaintiff having met the then three threshold elements of actionable libel—defamation, identification, and publication—the burden of proof shifted to the defendant to present an affirmative defense of truth, privilege, or fair comment and criticism. Since these three common law defenses are still available to defendants, they will be discussed in more detail in later sections.

---

64. 23 Med.L.Rptr. 1779, 51 F.3d 793 (9th Cir. 1995).

65. *Gertz v. Robert Welch, Inc.,* 418 U.S. 323, 94 S.Ct. 2997 (1974).

66. David Anderson, "Reputation, Compensation, and Proof," 25 *William & Mary L.Rev.* 747 (1983–1984); William Van Alstyne, "First Amendment Limitations on Recovery from the Press—An Extended Comment on 'the Anderson Solution'," 25 *William & Mary L.Rev.* 793 (1983–1984).

---

67. Bezanson, Cranberg, Soloski, *Libel Law.*

68. *West v. Thomson Newspapers,* 23 Med.L.Rptr. 1097, 872 P.2d 999 (Utah 1994).

The problem with the rule of strict liability was that it took no account of a publisher's intent, degree of negligence, or level of professionalism, nor did it consider the extent of injury suffered by the plaintiff. Indeed, a publisher could be liable even where there was no apparent fault on his part. The rule begged timidity and self-censorship, although there is little evidence that such occurred.

Constitutionalizing the Law of Libel

Influenced by Alexander Meiklejohn's thesis that speech in the public realm is crucial to self-government and therefore warrants near absolute protection, Justice William Brennan in his 1964 opinion for the Court in *New York Times v. Sullivan* made libel of public officials a constitutional matter. But for the qualification of *actual malice,* Brennan would have reached the Meiklejohnian summit of protection for public speech.[69]

The *New York Times* case rose out of the turmoil of the Black Revolution. On March 29, 1960, a full-page editorial advertisement appeared in the *New York Times* under the headline, "Heed Their Rising Voices." The ad copy began by stating that the nonviolent civil rights movement in the South was being met by a wave of terror. The ad concluded with an appeal for funds in support of the student movement, voting rights, and the legal defense of Martin Luther King, Jr. In addition to the signatures of sixty-four prominent Americans, sixteen southern clergymen were purported to have signed the ad. Segments of two paragraphs of the text became the focal points of subsequent litigation:

> In Montgomery, Alabama, after students sang "My Country 'Tis of Thee" on the State Capitol steps, their leaders were expelled from school, and truckloads of police armed with shotguns and tear-gas ringed the Alabama State College Campus. When the entire student body protested to state authorities by refusing to re-register, their dining hall was padlocked in an attempt to starve them into submission. * * *
>
> Again and again the Southern violators have answered Dr. King's peaceful protests with intimidation and violence. They have bombed his home

almost killing his wife and child. They have assaulted his person. They have arrested him seven times—for "speeding," "loitering" and similar "offenses." And now they have charged him with "perjury"—a *felony* under which they could imprison him for *ten years.* * * *

L. B. Sullivan, one of three elected commissioners of Montgomery, brought a civil libel action against four black Alabama clergymen, whose names had appeared in the ad, and the *Times.* In accordance with Alabama law, Sullivan, before bringing action, demanded in writing a public retraction from the clergymen and the newspaper. The clergymen did not respond on the grounds that use of their names was unauthorized. The *Times* did not publish a retraction but wrote Sullivan asking how the statements in the ad reflected on him. The commissioner filed suit without answering the query.

Although not mentioned by name, Sullivan contended that he represented the "police" referred to in the ad; therefore he was being accused of ringing the campus with police and starving the students into submission. He also claimed that the term "Southern violators" was meant to apply to him; therefore he was being accused of "intimidation and violence," bombing Dr. King's home, assaulting his person, and charging the civil rights leader with perjury. Witnesses testified that they identified the commissioner in the ad.

With the elements of libel thus established, Sullivan proceeded to show that most of the charges could not in fact have applied to him because they referred to incidents that had occurred before his election. Moreover, there were serious inaccuracies in the ad, creating a presumption of general damages under Alabama law.

In its defense, the *Times* pointed out that the ad had come to it from a New York advertising agency representing the signatory committee. A letter from A. Philip Randolph accompanied the ad and certified that the persons whose names appeared in it had given their permission. It was not considered necessary to confirm the accuracy of the ad by the manager of the Advertising Acceptability Department or anyone else at the *Times.* Nor were there any doubts about the authorization of the ad by the individual southern clergymen (they were later absolved of any responsibility because they were unaware of the ad). The *Times* could not

---

69. Donald M. Gillmor, "Justice William Brennan and the Failed "Theory" of Actual Malice," 59 *Journalism Quarterly* 249 (Summer 1982).

see how any of the language of the ad referred to Sullivan.

The trial judge submitted the case to the jury under instructions that the statements in the ad were libelous *per se* and without privilege. He also left the door open for punitive damages by an imprecise definition of what was required to support them.

The Circuit Court awarded $500,000 to Sullivan. The Supreme Court of Alabama affirmed, and the *Times* appealed to the U.S. Supreme Court.

At the heart of the brief submitted to the Court on behalf of Sullivan was the argument that "the Constitution has never required that states afford newspapers the privilege of leveling false and defamatory 'facts' at persons simply because they hold public office. The great weight of American authority has rejected such a plea by newspapers." See *Brief for the Respondent*, 376 United States Supreme Court Records and Briefs 254–314 (Vol. 12), p. 23.

The argument for the *Times* was more provocative and, as it turned out, more persuasive. In part it stated:

> Under the doctrine of *libel per se* applied below a public official is entitled to recover "presumed" and punitive damages for a publication found to be critical of the official conduct of a governmental agency under his general supervision if a jury thinks the publication "tends" to "injure" him "in his reputation" to "bring" him "into public contempt" as an official. The publisher has no defense unless he can persuade the jury that the publication is entirely true in all its factual, material particulars. The doctrine not only dispenses with proof of injury by the complaining official, but presumes malice and falsity as well. Such a rule of liability works an abridgment of the freedom of the press. *Brief for the Petitioner*, 376 United States Supreme Court Records and Briefs 254–314 (Vol. 12), pp. 28–29.

Attorneys for the *Times* had deftly raised the specter of seditious libel, and the Court responded.

New York Times Co. v. Sullivan

376 U.S. 254, 84 S.CT. 710, 11 L.ED.2D 686 (1964).

Justice BRENNAN delivered the Opinion of the Court: * * *

Because of the importance of the constitutional issues involved, we granted the separate petitions for certiorari of the individual petitioners and of the *Times*. * * * We reverse the judgment. We hold that the rule of law applied by the Alabama courts is constitutionally deficient for failure to provide the safeguards for freedom of speech and of the press that are required by the First and Fourteenth Amendments in a libel action brought by a public official against critics of his official conduct. We further hold that under the proper safeguards the evidence presented in this case is constitutionally insufficient to support the judgment for respondent.

We may dispose at the outset of two grounds asserted to insulate the judgment of the Alabama courts from constitutional scrutiny. The first is the proposition relied on by the State Supreme Court—that "The Fourteenth Amendment is directed against State action and not private action." That proposition has no application to this case. Although this is a civil lawsuit between private parties, the Alabama courts have applied a state rule of law which petitioners claim to impose invalid restrictions on their constitutional freedoms of speech and press. * * *

The second contention is that the constitutional guarantees of freedom of speech and of the press are inapplicable here, at least so far as the *Times* is concerned, because the allegedly libelous statements were published as part of a paid, "commercial" advertisement. The argument relies on *Valentine v. Chrestensen*, 316 U.S. 52 (1942), where the Court held that a city ordinance forbidding street distribution of commercial and business advertising matter did not abridge the First Amendment freedoms, even as applied to a handbill having a commercial message on one side but a protest against certain official action on the other. The reliance is wholly misplaced. The Court in *Chrestensen* reaffirmed the constitutional protection for "the freedom of communicating information and disseminating opinion"; its holding was based upon the factual conclusions that the handbill was "purely commercial advertising" and that the protest against official action had been added only to evade the ordinance.

The publication here was not a "commercial" advertisement in the sense in which the word was used in *Chrestensen*. It communicated information, expressed opinion, recited grievances, protested claimed abuses, and sought financial support on behalf of a movement whose existence and objectives are matters of the highest public interest and concern. That the *Times* was paid for publishing the advertisement is as immaterial in this connection as is the fact that newspapers and books are sold. Any other conclusion would discourage newspapers from carrying "editorial advertisements" of this type, and so might shut off an important outlet for the promulgation of information and ideas by persons who do not themselves have access to publishing facilities—who wish to exercise their freedom of speech even though they are not members of the press. The effect would be to shackle the First Amendment in its attempt to secure "the widest possible dissemination of information from diverse and antagonistic sources." To avoid placing such a handicap upon the freedoms of expression, we hold that if the allegedly libelous statements would otherwise be constitutionally protected from the present judgment, they do not forfeit that protection because they were published in the form of a paid advertisement.

Under Alabama law as applied in this case, a publication is "libelous per se" if the words "tend to injure a person * * * in his reputation" or to "bring [him] into public contempt"; the trial court stated that the standard was met if the words are such as to "injure him in his public office, or impute misconduct to him in his office, or want of official integrity, or want of fidelity to a public trust * * *." The jury must find that the words were published "of and concerning" the plaintiff, but where the plaintiff is a public official his place in the governmental hierarchy is sufficient evidence to support a finding that his reputation has been affected by statements that reflect upon the agency of which he is in charge. Once "libel per se" has been established, the defendant has no defense as to stated facts unless he can persuade the jury that they were true in all their particulars. * * * His privilege of "fair comment" for expressions of opinion depends on the truth of the facts upon which the comment is based. * * * Unless he can discharge the burden of proving truth, general damages are presumed, and may be awarded without proof of pecuniary injury. A showing of actual malice is apparently a prerequisite to recovery of punitive damages, and the defendant may in any event forestall a punitive award by a retraction meeting the statutory requirements. Good motives and belief in truth do not negate an inference of mal-

ice, but are relevant only in mitigation of punitive damages if the jury chooses to accord them weight. * * *

The general proposition that freedom of expression upon public questions is secured by the First Amendment has long been settled by our decisions. The constitutional safeguard, we have said, "was fashioned to assure unfettered interchange of ideas for the bringing about of political and social changes desired by the people." "The maintenance of the opportunity for free political discussion to the end that government may be responsive to the will of the people and that changes may be obtained by lawful means, an opportunity essential to the security of the Republic, is a fundamental principle of our constitutional system." "[I]t is a prized American privilege to speak one's mind, although not always with perfect good taste, on all public institutions," and this opportunity is to be afforded for "vigorous advocacy" no less than "abstract discussion." * * * The First Amendment, said Judge Learned Hand, "presupposes that right conclusions are more likely to be gathered out of a multitude of tongues, than through any kind of authoritative selection. To many this is, and always will be, folly; but we have staked upon it our all." *United States v. Associated Press,* 52 F.Supp. 362, 372 (S.D.N.Y. 1943).

Thus we consider this case against the background of a profound national commitment to the principle that debate on public issues should be uninhibited, robust, and wide-open, and that it may well include vehement, caustic, and sometimes unpleasantly sharp attacks on government and public officials. [Emphasis added.] The present advertisement, as an expression of grievance and protest on one of the major public issues of our time, would seem clearly to qualify for the constitutional protection. The question is whether it forfeits that protection by the falsity of some of its factual statements and by its alleged defamation of respondent.

Authoritative interpretations of the First Amendment guarantees have consistently refused to recognize an exception for any test of truth—whether administered by judges, juries, or administrative officials—and especially one that puts the burden of proving truth on the speaker.

* * *

[E]rroneous statement is inevitable in free debate, and * * * it must be protected if the freedoms of expression are to have the "breathing space" that they "need * * * to survive." * * *

Just as factual error affords no warrant for repressing speech that would otherwise be free, the same is true of injury to official reputation. Where judicial officers are involved, this Court has held that concern for the dignity and reputation of the courts does not justify the punishment as criminal contempt of criticism of the judge of his decision. This is true even though the utterance contains "half-truths" and "misinformation." Such repression can be justified, if at all, only by a clear and present danger of the obstruction of justice. If judges are to be treated as "men of fortitude, able to thrive in a hardy climate," surely the same must be true of other government officials, such as elected city commissioners. Criticism of their official conduct does not lose its constitutional protection merely because it is effective criticism and hence diminishes their official reputations.

If neither factual error nor defamatory content suffices to remove the constitutional shield from criticism of official conduct, the combination of the two elements is no less inadequate. This is the lesson to be drawn from the great controversy over the Sedition Act of 1798, 1 Stat. 596, which first crystallized in national awareness of the central meaning of the First Amendment. See Levy, *Legacy of Suppression* (1960), at 258 et seq. * * * That statute made it a crime, punishable by a $5,000 fine and five years in prison, "if any person shall write, print, utter or publish * * * any false, scandalous and malicious writing or writings against the government of the United States, or either house of the Congress * * * or the President * * * with intent to defame * * * or to bring them * * * into contempt or disrepute; or to excite against them, or either or any of them, the hatred of the good people of the United States." The Act allowed the defendant the defense of truth, and provided that the jury were to be judges both of the law and the facts. Despite these qualifications, the Act was vigorously condemned as unconstitutional in an attack joined in by Jefferson and Madison. * * * Although the Sedition Act was never tested in this Court, the attack upon its validity has carried the day in the court of history. Fines levied in its prosecution were repaid by Act of Congress on the ground that it was unconstitutional. * * *

What a State may not constitutionally bring about by means of a criminal statute is likewise beyond the reach of its civil law of libel. The fear of damage awards under a rule such as that invoked by the Alabama courts here may be markedly more inhibiting than the fear of prosecution under a criminal statute. * * * Alabama, for example, has a criminal libel law which subjects to prosecution "any person who speaks, writes, or prints of and concerning another any accusation falsely and maliciously importing the commission by such person of a felony, or any other indictable offense involving moral turpitude," and which allows as punishment upon conviction a fine not exceeding $500 and a prison sentence of six months. * * * Presumably a person charged with violation of this statute enjoys ordinary criminal-law safeguards such as the requirements of an indictment and of proof beyond a reasonable doubt. These safeguards are not available to the defendant in a civil action. The judgment awarded in this case—without the need for any proof of actual pecuniary loss—was one thousand times greater than the maximum fine provided by the Alabama criminal statute, and one hundred times greater than that provided by the Sedition Act. And since there is no double-jeopardy limitation applicable to civil lawsuits, this is not the only judgment that may be awarded against petitioners for the same publication.[18] Whether or not a newspaper can survive a succession of such judgments, the pall of fear and timidity imposed upon those who would give voice to public criticism is an atmosphere in which the First Amendment freedoms cannot survive. * * *

The state rule of law is not saved by its allowance of the defense of truth. A defense for erroneous statements honestly made is no less essential here than was the requirement of proof of guilty knowledge which, in *Smith v. California,* we held indispensable to a valid conviction of a bookseller for possessing obscene writings for sale. * * * A rule compelling the critic of

---

18. The *Times* states that four other libel suits based on the advertisement have been filed against it by others who have served as Montgomery City Commissioners and by the Governor of Alabama; that another $500,000 verdict has been awarded in the only one of these cases that has yet gone to trial; and that the damages sought in the other three total $2,000,000.

official conduct to guarantee the truth of all his factual assertions—and to do so on pain of libel judgments virtually unlimited in amount—leads to a comparable "self-censorship." Allowance of the defense of truth, with the burden of proving it on the defendant, does not mean that only false speech will be deterred. Even courts accepting this defense as an adequate safeguard have recognized the difficulties of adducing legal proofs that the alleged libel was true in all its factual particulars. * * * Under such a rule, would-be critics of official conduct may be deterred from voicing their criticism, even though it is believed to be true and even though it is in fact true, because of doubt whether it can be proved in court or fear of the expense of having to do so. They tend to make only statements which "steer far wider of the unlawful zone." * * * The rule thus dampens the vigor and limits the variety of public debate. It is inconsistent with the First and Fourteenth Amendments.

The constitutional guarantees require, we think, a federal rule that prohibits a public official from recovering damages for a defamatory falsehood relating to his official conduct *unless he proves that the statement was made with "actual malice"—that is, with knowledge that it was false or with reckless disregard of whether it was false or not.* [Emphasis added.]

Such a privilege for criticism of official conduct is appropriately analogous to the protection accorded a public official when *he* is sued for libel by a private citizen. In *Barr v. Matteo,* 360 U.S. 564, 575 (1959), *this Court held the utterance of a federal official to be absolutely privileged if made "within the outer perimeter" of his duties.* [Emphasis added.] The States accord the same immunity to statements of their highest officers, although some differentiate their lesser officials and qualify the privilege they enjoy. But all hold that all officials are protected unless actual malice can be proved. The reason for the official privilege is said to be that the threat of damage suits would otherwise "inhibit the fearless, vigorous, and effective administration of policies of government" and "dampen the ardor of all but the most resolute, or the most irresponsible, in the unflinching discharge of their duties." *Barr v. Matteo.* Analogous considerations support the privilege for citizen-critic of government. It is as much his duty to criticize as it is the official's duty to administer. As Madison said, "the censo-

rial power is in the people over the Government, and not in the Government over the people." It would give public servants an unjustified preference over the public they serve, if critics of official conduct did not have a fair equivalent of the immunity granted to the officials themselves.

We conclude that such a privilege is required by the First and Fourteenth Amendments.

We hold today that the Constitution delimits a State's power to award damages for libel in actions brought by public officials against critics of their official conduct. Since this is such an action, the rule requiring proof of actual malice is applicable. While Alabama law apparently requires proof of actual malice for an award of punitive damages, where general damages are concerned malice is "presumed." Such a presumption is inconsistent with the federal rule. * * * Since the trial judge did not instruct the jury to differentiate between general and punitive damages, it may be that the verdict was wholly an award of one or the other. But it is impossible to know, in view of the general verdict returned. Because of this uncertainty, the judgment must be reversed and the case remanded. * * *

Since respondent may seek a new trial, we deem that considerations of effective judicial administration require us to review the evidence in the present record to determine whether it could constitutionally support a judgment for respondent. This Court's duty is not limited to the elaboration of constitutional principles; we must also in proper cases review the evidence to make certain that those principles have been constitutionally applied. This is such a case, particularly since the question is one of alleged trespass across "the line between speech unconditionally guaranteed and speech which may legitimately be regulated." In cases where that line must be drawn, the rule is that we "examine for ourselves the statements in issue and the circumstances under which they were made to see * * * whether they are of a character which the principles of the First Amendment, as adopted by the Due Process Clause of the Fourteenth Amendment, protect." * * * We must "make an independent examination of the whole record," * * * so as to assure ourselves that the judgment does not constitute a forbidden intrusion on the field of free expression.

Applying these standards, we consider that the proof presented to show actual malice lacks the *convincing clarity* which the constitutional standard demands, and hence that it would not constitutionally sustain the judgment for respondent under the proper rule of law. The case of the individual petitioners requires little discussion. Even assuming that they could constitutionally be found to have authorized the use of their names on the advertisement, there was no evidence whatever that they were aware of any erroneous statements or were in any way reckless in that regard. The judgment against them is thus without constitutional support. [Emphasis added.]

As to the *Times,* we similarly conclude that the facts do not support a finding of actual malice. The statement by the *Times'* Secretary that, apart from the padlocking allegation, he thought the advertisement was "substantially correct," affords no constitutional warrant for the Alabama Supreme Court's conclusion that it was a "cavalier ignoring of the falsity of the advertisement [from which], the jury could not have but been impressed with the bad faith of the *Times,* and its maliciousness inferable therefrom." The statement does not indicate malice at the time of the publication; even if the advertisement was not "substantially correct"—although respondent's own proofs tend to show that it was—that opinion was at least a reasonable one, and there was no evidence to impeach the witness' good faith in holding it. The *Times'* failure to retract upon respondent's demand, although it later retracted upon the demand of Governor Patterson, is likewise not adequate evidence of malice for constitutional purposes. Whether or not a failure to retract may ever constitute such evidence, there are two reasons why it does not here. *First,* the letter written by the *Times* reflected a reasonable doubt on its part as to whether the advertisement could reasonably be taken to refer to respondent at all. *Second,* it was not a final refusal, since it asked for an explanation on this point—a request that respondent chose to ignore. * * *

Finally, there is evidence that the *Times* published the advertisement without checking its accuracy against the news stories in the *Times'* own files. The mere presence of the stories in the files does not, of course, establish that the *Times* "knew" the advertisement was false, since the state of mind required for actual malice would have to be brought home to the persons in the *Times'* organization having responsibility for the publication of the advertisement. With respect to the failure of those persons to make the check, the record shows that they relied upon their knowledge of the good reputation of many of those whose names were listed as sponsors of the advertisement, and upon the letter from A. Philip Randolph, known to them as a responsible individual, certifying that the use of the names was authorized. There was testimony that the persons handling the advertisement saw nothing in it that would render it unacceptable under the *Times'* policy of rejecting advertisements containing "attacks of a personal character"; their failure to reject it on this ground was not unreasonable. We think the evidence against the *Times* supports at most a finding of negligence in failing to discover the misstatements, and is constitutionally insufficient to show the recklessness that is required for a finding of actual malice.

We also think the evidence was constitutionally defective in another respect: it was incapable of supporting the jury's finding that the allegedly libelous statements were made "of and concerning" respondent. Respondent relies on the words of the advertisement and the testimony of six witnesses to establish a connection between it and himself. * * * There was no reference to respondent in the advertisement, either by name or official position. A number of the allegedly libelous statements—the charges that the dining hall was padlocked and that Dr. King's home was bombed, his person assaulted, and a perjury prosecution instituted against him—did not even concern the police; despite the ingenuity of the arguments which would attach this significance to the word "They," it is plain that these statements could not reasonably be read as accusing respondent of personal involvement in the acts in question. The statements upon which respondent principally relies as referring to him are the two allegations that did concern the police or police functions: that "truckloads of police * * * ringed the Alabama State College Campus" after the demonstration on the State Capitol steps, and that Dr. King had been "arrested * * * seven times." These statements were false only in that the police had been "deployed near" the campus but had not actually "ringed" it and had not gone there in connection with the State Capitol demonstration, and in that Dr. King had been arrested only four times. The ruling that these discrepancies between what was true and what was asserted were sufficient to injure respondent's reputation may itself raise constitutional problems, but we need not consider them here. Although the statements may be taken as referring to the police, they did not on their face make even an oblique reference to respondent as an individual. Support for the asserted reference must, therefore, be sought in the testimony of respondent's witnesses. But none of them suggested any basis for the belief that respondent himself was attacked in the advertisement beyond the bare fact that he was in overall charge of the Police Department and thus bore official responsibility for police conduct; to the extent that some of the witnesses thought respondent to have been charged with ordering or approving the conduct or otherwise being personally involved in it, they based this notion not on any statements in the advertisement, and not on any evidence that he had in fact been so involved, but solely on the unsupported assumption that, because of his official position, he must have been. This reliance on the bare fact of respondent's official position was made explicit by the Supreme Court of Alabama. That court, in holding that the trial court "did not err in overruling the demurrer [of the *Times*] in the aspect that the libelous matter was not of and concerning the [plaintiff,]" based its ruling on the proposition that:

"We think it common knowledge that the average person knows that municipal agents, such as police and firemen, and others, are under the control and direction of the city governing body, and more particularly under the direction and control of a single commissioner. In measuring the performance or deficiencies of such groups, praise or criticism is usually attached to the official in complete control of the body."

This proposition has disquieting implications for criticism of governmental conduct. For good reason, "no court of last resort in this country has ever held, or even suggested, that prosecutions for libel on government have any place in the American system of jurisprudence." * * * The present proposition would sidestep this obstacle by transmuting criticism of government, however impersonal it may seem on its face, into personal criticism, and hence potential libel, of the officials of whom the government is composed. There is no legal alchemy by which a *State* may thus create the cause of action that would otherwise be denied for a publication which, as

respondent himself said of the advertisement, "reflects not only on me but on the other Commissioners and the community." Raising as it does the possibility that a good-faith critic of government will be penalized for his criticism, the proposition relied on by the Alabama courts strikes at the very center of the constitutionally protected area of free expression. We hold that such a proposition may not constitutionally be utilized to establish that an otherwise impersonal attack on governmental operations was a libel of an official responsible for those operations. Since it was relied on exclusively here, and there was no other evidence to connect the statements with respondent, the evidence was constitutionally insufficient to support a finding that the statements referred to respondent.

The judgment of the Supreme Court of Alabama is reversed and the case is remanded to that court for further proceedings not inconsistent with this opinion.

Reversed and remanded.

Justice BLACK, with whom Justice Douglas joins (concurring).

* * * In reversing, the Court holds that "the Constitution delimits a State's power to award damages for libel in actions brought by public officials against critics of their official conduct." I base my vote to reverse on the belief that the First and Fourteenth Amendments not merely "delimit" a State's power to award damages to "public officials against critics of their official conduct" but completely prohibit a State from exercising such a power. The Court goes on to hold that a State can subject such critics to damages if "actual malice" can be proved against them. "Malice," even as defined by the Court, is an elusive, abstract concept, hard to prove and hard to disprove. The requirement that malice be proved provides at best an evanescent protection for the right critically to discuss public affairs and certainly does not measure up to the sturdy safeguard embodied in the First Amendment. Unlike the Court, therefore, I vote to reverse exclusively on the ground that the *Times* and the individual defendants had an absolute, unconditional constitutional right to publish in the *Times* advertisement their criticisms of the Montgomery agencies and officials.

* * *

Expanding the *New York Times* Doctrine

Later the same year, the Court expanded the *New York Times* doctrine to reach *criminal libel* prosecutions. Historically, criminal libel laws were intended to protect the public peace and good order. Mob violence or other breaches of the peace, it was asserted, would be created by defamations against social groups (religious, racial, family, etc.) or government officials. The distinction between criminal and seditious libels was less than clear.

Accordingly, the state became plaintiff on behalf of the public. Truth, or truth published with good motives and for justifiable ends, was a defense. Privilege was a defense in some jurisdictions. As a result of *Garrison v. Louisiana,* 379 U.S. 64 (1964), actual malice had to be proven by the prosecution beyond a reasonable doubt in criminal libel cases.

Because of its closeness to sedition, criminal libel has not found favor in American courts. It reached its high-water mark in 1952 when the U.S. Supreme Court decided *Beauharnais v. Illinois,* 343 U.S. 250 (1952). See p. 130.

Beauharnais, a hatemonger who circulated pamphlets designed to pit white against black, was convicted under a 1949 Illinois criminal libel law, a law that would reappear in the *Skokie* cases twenty-five years later. The law made it a crime to exhibit in any public place any publication that "portrays depravity, criminality, unchastity, or lack of virtue of a class of citizens, or any race, color, creed or religion."

The law's constitutionality was upheld in a 5–4 decision in which Justice Felix Frankfurter for the Court answered no to the question, Is speech devoted to racial hatred so high on the scale of constitutional values that it cannot be abridged by lawmakers?

Frankfurter argued that the importance of protecting groups from harassment and vilification was so important that it justified some limitation on free speech. Furthermore, the Court had held in *Chaplinsky v. New Hampshire,* 315 U.S. 568 (1942) that "fighting words"—those which by their very utterance inspire violence or tend to incite an immediate breach of the peace—are not constitutionally protected; such expression forms no essential part of the exposition of ideas and has slight social value.

Black and Douglas in dissent contended that free speech is too important a part of the democratic commitment to be sacrificed to the comfort and protection of any single social group. They also advanced a shoe-on-the-other-foot argument: tomorrow, under a criminal libel law, advocacy of rejection of the Ku Klux Klan might be declared illegal.

This confrontation between free speech and social equality remains an interesting one. Which value do we risk? Do some of us need protection from the wrath of the bigot?[70]

Beauharnais has neither been followed nor reversed, but its minority opinions would seem to have carried the day. The fear that criminal libel laws would eventually suppress unpopular expression has prevailed.

For example, a labor organizer was sentenced to six months and fined $3,000 under Kentucky's common law of criminal libel for printing a pamphlet in support of striking miners and defamatory of law enforcement officials and a newspaper publisher. On appeal, Justice Douglas, writing for the Court, said "that to make an offense of conduct which is 'calculated to create disturbances of the peace' leaves wide open the standard of responsibility. It involves calculations as to the boiling point of a particular person or a particular group, not an appraisal of the nature of the comments *per se.* This kind of criminal libel 'makes a man a criminal simply because his neighbors have no self-control and cannot refrain from violence.' "[71]

It has been suggested that bad motives should never be assumed where public speech is concerned, and rather than limit discussion about minority groups, we should facilitate discussion *by* minority groups.[72]

The coup de grace for criminal libel in the United States may have come when the once notorious District Attorney Jim Garrison took it upon himself to criticize eight New Orleans judges.

---

70. David Riesman in "Democracy and Defamation: Control of Group Libel," 42 *Columbia L.Rev.* 727 (1942) relates how the Nazis used group defamation to purge their opposition, set up Jewish scapegoats, and prepare the way for the Holocaust.

71. *Ashton v. Kentucky,* 384 U.S. 195 (1966).

72. Beth, "Group Libel and Free Speech," 39 *Minn.L.Rev.* 167 (1955).

Garrison v. State of Louisiana
379 U.S. 64, 85 S.CT. 209, 3 L.ED.2D 125 (1964).

Justice BRENNAN delivered the opinion of the Court.

Appellant is the District Attorney of Orleans Parish, Louisiana. During a dispute with the eight judges of the Criminal District Court of the Parish, he held a press conference at which he issued a statement disparaging their judicial conduct. As a result, he was tried without a jury before a judge from another parish and convicted of criminal defamation under the Louisiana Criminal Defamation Statute. * * * The principal charges alleged to be defamatory were his attribution of a large backlog of pending criminal cases to the inefficiency, laziness, and excessive vacations of the judges, and his accusation that, by refusing to authorize disbursements to cover the expenses of undercover investigations of vice in New Orleans, the judges had hampered his efforts to enforce the vice laws. In impugning their motives, he said:

"The judges have now made it eloquently clear where their sympathies lie in regard to aggressive vice investigations by refusing to authorize use of the DA's funds to pay for the cost of closing down the Canal Street clip joints.

"* * * This raises interesting questions about the racketeer influences on our eight vacation-minded judges."

The Supreme Court of Louisiana affirmed the conviction. * * * The trial court and the State Supreme Court both rejected appellant's contention that the statute unconstitutionally abridged his freedom of expression. * * *

* * * At the outset, we must decide whether, in view of the differing history and purposes of criminal libel, the New York Times rule also limits state power to impose criminal sanctions for criticism of the official conduct of public officials. We hold that it does.

Where criticism of public officials is concerned, we see no merit in the argument that criminal libel statutes serve interests distinct from those secured by civil libel laws, and therefore, should not be subject to the same limitations. * * * At common law, truth was no defense to criminal libel. Although the victim of a true but defamatory publication might not have been unjustly damaged in reputation by the libel, the speaker was still punishable since the remedy was designed to avert the possibility that the utterance would provoke an enraged victim to a breach of peace. * * * [P]reference for the civil remedy, which enabled the frustrated victim to trade chivalrous satisfaction for damages, had substantially eroded the breach of the peace justification for criminal libel laws. In fact, in earlier, more violent, times, the civil remedy had virtually pre-empted the field of defamation; except as a weapon against seditious libel, the criminal prosecution fell into virtual desuetude. Changing mores and the virtual disappearance of criminal libel prosecutions lend support to the observation that "* * * under modern conditions, when the rule of law is generally accepted as a substitute for private physical measures, it can hardly be urged that the maintenance of peace requires a criminal prosecution for private defamation."

* * *

* * * In any event, where the criticism is of public officials and their conduct of public business, the interest in private reputation is overborne by the larger public interest, secured by the Constitution, in the dissemination of truth.

* * *

We held in New York Times that a public official might be allowed the civil remedy only if he establishes that the utterance was false and that it was made with knowledge of its falsity or in reckless disregard of whether it was false or true. The reasons which led us so to hold in New York Times apply with no less force merely because the remedy is criminal. The constitutional guarantees of freedom of expression compel application of the same standard to the criminal remedy. Truth may not be the subject of either civil or criminal sanctions where discussion of public affairs is concerned. And since "* * * erroneous statement is inevitable in free debate, and * * * it must be protected if the freedoms of expression are to have the 'breathing space' that they 'need * * * to survive' * * *," only those false statements made with the high degree of awareness of their probable falsity demanded by New York Times may be the subject of either civil or criminal sanctions. [Emphasis added.] For speech concerning public affairs is more than self-expression; it is the essence of self-government.

The use of calculated falsehood, however, would put a different cast on the constitutional question. Although honest utterance, even if inaccurate, may further the fruitful exercise of the right of free speech, it does not follow that the lie, knowingly and deliberately published about a public official, should enjoy a like immunity. At the time the First Amendment was adopted, as today, there were those unscrupulous enough and skillful enough to use the deliberate or reckless falsehood as an effective political tool to unseat the public servant or even topple an administration. * * * That speech is used as a tool for political ends does not automatically bring it under the protective mantle of the Constitution. For the use of the known lie as a tool is at once at odds with the premises of democratic government and with the orderly manner in which economic, social, or political change is to be effected. Calculated falsehood falls into that class of utterances which "are no essential part of any exposition of ideas, and are of such slight social value as a step to truth that any benefit that may be derived from them is clearly outweighed by the social interest in order and morality. * * *" Hence the knowingly false statement and the false statement made with reckless disregard of the truth, do not enjoy constitutional protection.

* * *

We do not think, however, that appellant's statement may be considered as one constituting only a purely private defamation. The accusation concerned the judges' conduct of the business of the Criminal District Court. Of course, any criticism of the manner in which a public official performs his duties will tend to affect his private, as well as his public, reputation. The New York Times rule is not rendered inapplicable merely because an official's private reputation, as well as his public reputation, is harmed. The public-official rule protects the paramount public interest in a free flow of information to the people concerning public officials, their servants. To this end, anything which might touch on an official's fitness for office is relevant. [Emphasis added.] Few personal attributes are more germane to fitness for office than dishonesty, malfeasance, or improper motivation, even though these characteristics may also affect the official's private character. * * *

Applying the principles of the New York Times case, we hold that the Louisiana statute, as authoritatively interpreted by the Supreme Court of Louisiana, incorporates constitutionally invalid standards in the context of criticism of the official conduct of public officials. For contrary to the New York Times rule, which absolutely prohibits punishment of truthful criticism, the statute directs punishment for true statements made with "actual malice." * * * The statute is also unconstitutional as interpreted to cover false statements against public officials. The New York Times standard forbids the punishment of false statements, unless made with knowledge of their falsity or in reckless disregard of whether they are true or false. But the Louisiana statute punishes false statements without regard to that test if made with ill-will; even if ill-will is not established, a false statement concerning public officials can be punished if not made in the reasonable belief of its truth. * * * The reasonable-belief standard applied by the trial judge is not the same as the reckless-disregard-of-truth standard. According to the trial court's opinion, a reasonable belief is one which "an ordinarily prudent man might be able to assign a just and fair reason for"; the suggestion is that under this test the immunity from criminal responsibility in the absence of ill-will disappears on proof that the exercise of ordinary care would have revealed that the statement was false. The test which we laid down in New York Times is not keyed to ordinary care; defeasance of the privilege is conditioned, not on mere negligence, but on reckless disregard for the truth.

Reversed.

COMMENT

Justice Douglas in a concurring opinion rejected "actual malice" as a constitutional standard, and of criminal libel he said:

Beauharnais v. Illinois, * * * a case decided by the narrowest of margins, should be overruled as a misfit in our constitutional system and as out of line with the dictates of the First Amendment. I think it is time to face the fact that the only line drawn by the Constitution is between "speech" on the one side and conduct or overt acts on the other. The two often do blend. I have expressed the idea before: "Freedom of expression can be suppressed if, and to the extent that, it is so closely brigaded with illegal action as to be an inseparable part of it * * *."

It should be noted that state constitutions may in some cases provide greater protection to free press than the U.S. Constitution, and the U.S. Supreme Court will be reluctant to review state court rulings based on those constitutions.

Having extended the *New York Times* rule to criminal libel, the next step in the onward march of the doctrine for the Supreme Court was to define, and by defining to expand, the term "public official."

In *Rosenblatt v. Baer,* 383 U.S. 75 (1966), Justice William Brennan, speaking for the Court, held "that the 'public official' designation applies at the very least to those among the hierarchy of government employees who have, or appear to the public to have, substantial responsibility for government operations * * * lest criticism of government itself be penalized." No matter that plaintiff in the case was a former supervisor of a county recreation area whose policy-making responsibilities were modest.

Within a few years, scores of unsuccessful libel plaintiffs in both state and federal courts learned that a public official could be anyone, past or present, who belonged, or had belonged, to a bureaucracy. Officials and quasi officials on the periphery of power were included.

There was a prophetic intimation in Justice Douglas's concurring opinion in *Rosenblatt* that the central question in such cases should not be who is a public official but rather whether a *public issue* is being discussed. The Court would come to that, but there was to be a prior step.

One of the fathers of the atomic bomb and a vocal pacifist, Dr. Linus Pauling, brought unsuccessful suits against the *New York Daily News* and William Buckley's *National Review.* Both had charged him with Communist and pro-Soviet sympathies. In the *Daily News* case, a federal court of appeals upheld a district court's characterization of Pauling as a *public figure,* open to the same comment and criticism as a public official.[73]

Two cases decided together, one involving a football coach and the other a retired army general, Edwin Walker, brought to its acme the *public figure* test and for a time provided a formula for measuring "reckless disregard for the truth."

The case of the coach began with an article entitled "The Story of a College Football Fix" in the March 23, 1963, issue of the *Saturday Evening Post.* The article reported a telephone conversation between Wally Butts, athletic director at the University of Georgia, and Paul Bryant, then head football coach at the University of Alabama, in which the two allegedly conspired to "fix" a football game between the two schools.

Notes had been taken on the conversation by an insurance salesman of questionable character, who, due to an electronic quirk, cut into the conversation when he picked up a telephone receiver at a pay station. Some of his notes appeared in the article, which compared this "fix" to the Chicago "Black Sox" scandal of 1919. The article went on to describe the game, the subsequent presentation of the salesman's notes to Georgia head coach, Johnny Griffith, and Butts's resignation. There was nothing subtle about the *Post's* charges against Butts.

Butts sued for $5 million compensatory and $5 million punitive damages. The *Post* tried to use truth as its defense, but the evidence contradicted its version of what had occurred. Expert witnesses supported Butts by analyzing the salesman's notes and films of the game. The jury returned a verdict of $60,000 in general damages and $3 million in punitive damages.

Soon after the trial, the *New York Times* decision was handed down, and the *Post* sought a new trial under its rules. The motion was rejected by the trial judge. He held *Times* inapplicable because Butts was not a "public official," and he ruled there was ample evidence of "reckless disregard" of the truth in the researching of the article. His judgment was affirmed by the U.S. Court of Appeals. From there the case went to the Supreme Court.

Justice John Marshall Harlan, who wrote the opinion for the Court, focused on the public interest in the circulation of the *Post* and in the activities of Butts. Did Butts, therefore, qualify as a "public figure"? The opinion was a study in the problems presented by the forward motion of *New York Times,* and it defined a separate test for public figures.

---

73. *Pauling v. News Syndicate Co., Inc.,* 335 F.2d 659 (2d Cir. 1964).

Curtis Publishing Co. v. Butts and Associated Press v. Walker

388 U.S. 130, 87 S.CT. 1975, 18 L.ED.2D 1094 (1967).

Justice HARLAN delivered the opinion of the Court: * * *

These similarities and differences between libel actions involving persons who are public officials and libel actions involving those circumstanced as were Butts and Walker, viewed in light of the principles of liability which are of general applicability in our society, lead us to the conclusion that libel actions of the present kind cannot be left entirely to state libel laws, unlimited by any overriding constitutional safeguard, but that the rigorous federal requirements of *New York Times* are not the only appropriate accommodation of the conflicting interests at stake. We consider and would hold that a "public figure" who is not a public official may also recover damages for a defamatory falsehood whose substance makes substantial danger to reputation apparent, *on a showing of highly unreasonable conduct constituting an extreme departure from the standards of investigation and reporting ordinarily adhered to by responsible publishers.* [Emphasis added.]

Nothing in this opinion is meant to affect the holdings in *New York Times* and its progeny.

* * *

Having set forth the standard by which we believe the constitutionality of the damage awards in these cases must be judged, we turn now, as the Court did in *New York Times,* to the question whether the evidence and findings below meet that standard. * * *

The *Butts* jury was instructed, in considering punitive damages, to assess "the reliability, the nature of the sources of the defendant's information, its acceptance or rejection of the sources, and its care in checking upon assertions." These considerations were said to be relevant to a determination whether defendant had proceeded with "wanton and reckless indifference." In this light we consider that the jury must have decided that the investigation undertaken by the *Saturday Evening Post,* upon which much evidence and argument was centered, was grossly inadequate in the circumstances. * * *

This jury finding was found to be supported by the evidence by the trial judge and the majority in the Fifth Circuit. * * *

The evidence showed that the Butts story was in no sense "hot news" and the editors of the magazine recognized the need for a thorough investigation of the serious charges. Elementary precautions were, nevertheless, ignored. The *Saturday Evening Post* knew that Burnett had been placed on probation in connection with bad check charges, but proceeded to publish the story on the basis of his affidavit without substantial independent support. Burnett's notes were not even viewed by any of the magazine's personnel prior to publication. John Carmichael, who was supposed to have been with Burnett when the phone call was overheard, was not interviewed. No attempt was made to screen the films of the game to see if Burnett's information was accurate, and no attempt was made to find out whether Alabama had adjusted its plans after the alleged divulgence of information.

The *Post* writer assigned to the story was not a football expert and no attempt was made to check the story with someone knowledgeable in the sport. At trial experts indicated that the information in the Burnett notes was either such that it would be evident to any opposing coach from game films regularly exchanged or valueless. Those assisting the *Post* writer in his investigation were already deeply involved in another libel action, based on a different article, brought against Curtis Publishing Co. by the Alabama coach and unlikely to be the source of a complete and objective investigation. The *Saturday Evening Post* was anxious to change its image by instituting a policy of "sophisticated muckraking," and the pressure to produce a successful exposé might have induced a stretching of standards. In short, the evidence is ample to support a finding of highly unreasonable conduct constituting an extreme departure from the standards of investigation and reporting ordinarily adhered to by responsible publishers.

Affirmed. * * *

COMMENT

Chief Justice Earl Warren concurred in the result but objected to the Court's making a distinction between "public official" and "public figure." Consistent with their absolutist rejection of libel actions against the press, Justices Black and Douglas dissented in *Butts* but concurred in the result in *Walker.*

But four members of the Court—Harlan, Tom Clark, Abe Fortas, and Potter Stewart—adopted a new standard, albeit a shaky one, for public figures. It would come to be known as the *prudent publisher* test, and it would reappear in *Gertz v. Robert Welch, Inc.* in modified form.

The *Walker* case did not divide the Court as did *Butts.* General Edwin Walker was clearly an actor in the tumultuous events surrounding the entry of James Meredith into the University of Mississippi. An Associated Press report stated that Walker, who was present on the campus, had taken command of the violent crowd and had personally led a charge against federal marshals. It also described Walker as encouraging rioters to use violence and providing them technical advice on combating the effects of tear gas.

Walker was a private citizen at the time of the riot but, since his resignation from the army, had become a political activist. There was little evidence relating to the preparation of the news dispatch. It was clear, however, that Van Savell, the reporter, was actually present during the events he described and had communicated them almost immediately to the Associated Press office in Atlanta.

Walker sought to collect millions in a *chain suit* against newspapers and broadcasting stations that had carried the AP reports. The present case began in Texas when a trial court awarded Walker $500,000 in general damages and $300,000 in exemplary or punitive damages. The trial judge, finding no actual malice to support the punitive damages, entered a final judgment of $500,000. The Texas Court of Civil Appeals, agreeing that the defense of fair comment did not apply because the press reports constituted "statements of fact," affirmed the judgment of the trial court. The Texas Supreme Court declined to review the case, and the case went up to the U.S. Supreme Court.[74]

Certainly, Walker was a public figure, said the Court, for he had cast his personality into the whirlpool of an important public controversy. Moreover, "in contrast to the *Butts* article, the dispatch which concerns us in *Walker* was news which required immediate dissemination. The Associated Press received the information from a correspondent who was present at the scene of the events and gave every indication of being trustworthy and competent. His dispatches in this instance, with one minor exception, were internally consistent and would not have seemed unreasonable to one familiar with General Walker's prior publicized statements on the underlying controversy. Considering the necessity for rapid dissemination, *nothing in this series of events gives the slightest hint of a severe*

departure from accepted publishing standards. We therefore conclude that General Walker should not be entitled to damages from the Associated Press." [Emphasis added.]

The *public figure* rule was subsequently applied to policemen and firemen seeking election to a public safety council,[75] to a head basketball coach,[76] to a well-known horse trainer,[77] to political party workers and precinct delegates,[78] to letter carriers who, upon refusing to join a union, were called "scabs, traitors, and men of low character and rotten principles,"[79] to a suspect in a $1.5 million mail robbery who chose to expose himself publicly by granting interviews and calling press conferences,[80] to a retired professional basketball player,[81] and to an escapee from a federal jail.[82]

A further attempt to define "reckless disregard" generated language that has persisted in court opinions. The case is *St. Amant v. Thompson*, 390 U.S. 727 (1968), and it involved defamatory charges made during the heat of a political campaign.

There Justice Byron White for the Court pointed out that "the defendant in a defamation action brought by a public official cannot * * * automatically insure a favorable verdict by testifying that he published with a belief that the statements were true. The finder of fact must determine whether the publication was indeed made in good faith. Professions of good faith will be unlikely to prove persuasive, for example, where a story is fabricated by the defendant, is the product of his imagination, or is based wholly on an unverified anonymous telephone call. Nor will they be likely to prevail when the publisher's allegations are so inherently improbable that only a reckless man would have put them in circulation. Likewise, recklessness may

---

74. *Associated Press v. Walker*, 388 U.S. 130 (1967).

75. *Tilton v. Cowles Publishing Co.*, 459 P.2d 8 (Wash. 1969).

76. *Grayson v. Curtis Publishing Co.*, 436 P.2d 756 (Wash. 1967).

77. *Lloyds v. United Press International, Inc.*, 311 N.Y.S.2d 373 (1970).

78. *Arber v. Stahlin*, 159 N.W.2d 154 (Mich. 1968).

79. *Old Dominion Branch No. 496, National Association of Letter Carriers, AFL–CIO v. Austin*, 418 U.S. 264 (1974).

80. *Tripoli v. Boston Herald-Traveler Corp.*, 268 N.E.2d 350 (Mass. 1971).

81. *Time, Inc. v. Johnston*, 448 F.2d 378 (4th Cir. 1971).

82. *McFarland v. Hearst Corp.*, 332 F.Supp. 746 (D.Md. 1971).

be found where there are obvious reasons to doubt the veracity of the informant or the accuracy of his reports." Justice White went on to say that "reckless conduct is not measured by whether a reasonably prudent man would have published, or would have investigated before publishing. There must be sufficient evidence to permit the conclusion that the *defendant in fact entertained serious doubts as to the truth of his publication.*" [Emphasis added.] "The occupation of public officeholder," said Justice Abe Fortas in an acerbic dissent, "does not forfeit one's membership in the human race."

Public official–public figure designations were to do yeoman service for the press in this period.

The Ocala (Fla.) *Star-Banner* may have come close to the outer limits of permissible comment when it confused a mayor who was a candidate for the office of county tax assessor with his brother and charged falsely that he had been indicted for perjury in a civil rights suit.

A new editor, who had never heard of the mayor's brother, changed the first name when a reporter phoned in the story. A jury awarded the mayor $22,000, but a precise application of the *New York Times* rule of knowing falsehood or reckless disregard of the truth had not been made, and the judgment was reversed.[83]

A deputy chief of detectives sued *Time* magazine when it implied in a story about a Civil Rights Commission report that the police officer was guilty of brutality. Although the news magazine had confused a complainant's testimony with the independent findings of the commission itself, the Supreme Court ruled that in the circumstances of the case the magazine had not engaged in a "falsification" sufficient in itself to sustain a jury finding of "actual malice."

"The author of the *Time* article," said Justice Potter Stewart for the Court, "testified in substance, that the context of the report of the * * * incident indicated to him that the Commission believed that the incident had occurred as described. He therefore denied that he had falsified the report when he omitted the word 'alleged.' The *Time* researcher, who had read the newspaper stories about the incident and two reports from a *Time* reporter in Chicago, as well as the accounts of [the deputy chief's] earlier

career, had even more reason to suppose that the Commission took the charges to be true. * * *

"These considerations apply with even greater force to the situation where the *alleged libel consists in the claimed misinterpretation of the gist of a lengthy government document. Where the document reported on is so ambiguous as this one was, it is hard to imagine a test of 'truth' that would not put the publisher virtually at the mercy of the unguided discretion of a jury.*" [Emphasis added.][84]

These examples are not meant to suggest that a plaintiff could not win a libel case in the period following *New York Times v. Sullivan.* As far back as 1964, a Kentucky court had disallowed application of the *New York Times* rule where it appeared that the published attack was not on the "official" conduct of a policeman.[85] And an Illinois appeals court would not accept the contention that a society columnist's remarks about the marital affairs of a prominent industrial family were privileged because the plaintiffs were "public" people.[86] The Supreme Court of Pennsylvania would not permit application of the rule when a defendant admitted that he knew his defamatory comments were false.[87]

Senator Barry Goldwater, the most notable plaintiff of the period, won a $75,000 judgment against Ralph Ginzburg, publisher of *Fact* magazine. Ginzburg had attempted to put together a "psychobiography" on Goldwater so as to alert the American people to what he perceived to be the potential danger of his presidency. Facts and comments on Goldwater were carefully selected to support Ginzburg's assumptions, including responses from more than 2,000 psychiatrists who had received a manifestly "loaded" questionnaire. The simplistic conclusion from all of this was that Goldwater was mentally ill—his "infantile fantasies of revenge and dreams of total annihilation of his adversaries," his "paralyzing, deep-seated, irrational fear," his "fantasy of a final conflagration," which Ginzburg compared with the "death-fantasy of another paranoiac woven in Berchtesgaden and realized in a Berlin bunker."

83. *Ocala Star-Banner v. Damron,* 401 U.S. 295 (1971).

84. *Time, Inc. v. Pape,* 401 U.S. 279 (1971).
85. *Tucker v. Kilgore,* 388 S.W.2d 112 (Ky. 1964).
86. *Lorillard v. Field Enterprises, Inc.,* 213 N.E.2d 1 (Ill. 1965).
87. *Fox v. Kahn,* 221 A.2d 181 (Pa. 1966).

At trial Ginzburg was unable to identify a single source for his statements. Nor could he document, in any medical sense, his reports that Goldwater had suffered two nervous breakdowns.

In upholding the judgment, a federal court of appeals relied on the "hot news" premise of the *Butts* and *Walker* cases and the less stringent actual malice definition of *St. Amant.*[88]

Nevertheless, some wondered how a candidate for the nation's highest office could argue that any part of his private life, particularly his psyche, should be immune from public comment, no matter how willfully distorted and inaccurate.

In dissenting vigorously to a denial of certiorari, Justice Black, joined by Justice Douglas, agreed:

This suit was brought by a man who was then the nominee of his party for the [p]residency of the United States. In our times, the person who holds that high office has an almost unbounded power for good or evil. The public has an unqualified right to have the character and fitness of anyone who aspires to the [p]residency held up for the closest scrutiny. Extravagant, reckless statements and even claims which may not be true seem to me an inevitable and perhaps essential part of the process by which the voting public informs itself of the qualities of a man who would be [p]resident. The decisions of the [d]istrict [c]ourt and the [c]ourt of [a]ppeals in this case can only have the effect of dampening political debate by making fearful and timid those who should under our Constitution feel totally free openly to criticize Presidential candidates. * * *

Another reason for the particular offensiveness of this case is that the damages awarded Senator Goldwater were, except for $1.00, wholly punitive. Goldwater neither pleaded nor proved any special damages and the jury's verdict of $1.00 nominal compensatory damages established that he suffered little if any actual harm. * * * It is bad enough when the First Amendment is violated to compensate a person who has actually suffered a provable injury as a result of libelous statements; it is incomprehensible that a person who has suffered no provable harm can recover libel damages imposed solely to punish a defendant who has exercised his First Amendment rights.

I would grant certiorari and reverse the [c]ourt of [a]ppeals summarily."[89]

A Doctrine Stretched to Its Limits: The Public Issue Test

Justice Douglas's notion that any matter of legitimate public interest, that is, any public issue, should be the standard for application of the *Times* doctrine was reminiscent of philosopher Alexander Meiklejohn's premise that the people of the United States are both the governors and the governed, and therefore "those activities of thought and communication by which we 'govern' must be free from interference."[90] Speech having social importance, whether of a political nature or not, must be free, said Meiklejohn, not because persons "desire to speak," but because people "need to hear." See p. 8.

There was still room for expansion. The Supreme Court held in 1970 that the term "blackmail," when used in characterizing the negotiating position of a real estate developer, was not slander when spoken in the heated public meetings of a city council and not actionable libel when subsequently reported accurately in newspaper articles.

The plaintiff in the case had entered into agreements with the city for zoning exemptions in the past and was again seeking such favors to expedite the construction of high-density housing units. At the same time, the city was trying to obtain land from the plaintiff for the purpose of building a school.

In addition, the trial judge's instructions to the jury, reflecting confusion in his mind as to what the Supreme Court had meant by "actual malice" in earlier cases, was considered by Justice Stewart to be an "error of constitutional magnitude." A trial court judgment against the newspaper was reversed.[91]

Final extension of the *New York Times* doctrine—and it would prove to be the breaking point—came in 1971 when a badly divided Court upheld a court of appeals reversal of a $275,000 trial court judgment in favor of a magazine distributor. Rosenbloom had been called a "smut distributor" and "girlie-book peddler" in a radio news report, although he was subsequently acquitted of criminal obscenity charges.

88. *Goldwater v. Ginzburg*, 414 F.2d 324 (2d Cir. 1969).
89. *Ginzburg v. Goldwater*, 396 U.S. 1049 (1970).

90. Meiklejohn, "The First Amendment Is an Absolute," 1961 *Sup.Ct.Rev.* 245 at 253–55. See also Meiklejohn, *Political Freedom* (1960).
91. *Greenbelt Co-op Publishing Association v. Bresler*, 398 U.S. 6 (1970).

Rosenbloom v. Metromedia

403 U.S. 29, 91 S.CT. 1811, 29 L.ED.2D 296 (1971).

Justice BRENNAN announced the judgment of the Court and an opinion in which The Chief Justice and Justice Blackmun join.

* * * The instant case presents the question whether the New York Times' knowing or reckless falsity standard applies in a state civil libel action brought not by a "public official" or a "public figure" but by a private individual for a defamatory falsehood uttered in a news broadcast by a radio station about the individual's involvement in an event of public or general interest. * * *

* * *

Petitioner concedes that the police campaign to enforce the obscenity laws was an issue of public interest, and, therefore, that the constitutional guarantees for freedom of speech and press imposed limits upon Pennsylvania's power to apply its libel laws to compel respondent to compensate him in damages for the alleged defamatory falsehoods broadcast about his involvement. As noted, the narrow question he raises is whether, because he is not a "public official" or a "public figure" but a private individual, those limits required that he prove that the falsehoods resulted from a failure of respondent to exercise reasonable care, or required that he prove that the falsehoods were broadcast with knowledge of their falsity or with reckless disregard of whether they were false or not. That question must be answered against the background of the functions of the constitutional guarantees for freedom of expression.

Self-governance in the United States presupposes far more than knowledge and debate about the strictly official activities of various levels of government. The commitment of the country to the institution of private property, protected by the Due Process and Just Compensation Clauses in the Constitution, places in private hands vast areas of economic and social power that vitally affect the nature and quality of life in the Nation. Our efforts to live and work together in a free society not completely dominated by governmental regulation necessarily encompass far more than politics in a narrow sense. * * *

Although the limitations upon civil libel actions, first held in New York Times to be required by the First Amendment, were applied in that case in the context of defamatory falsehoods about the official conduct of a public official, later decisions have disclosed the artificiality, in terms of the public's interest, of a simple distinction between "public" and "private" individuals or institutions. * * *

Moreover, the constitutional protection was not intended to be limited to matters bearing broadly on issues of responsible government. "[T]he Founders * * * felt that a free press would advance 'truth, science, morality, and arts in general' as well as responsible government."

* * *

If a matter is a subject of public or general interest, it cannot suddenly become less so merely because a private individual is involved, or because in some sense the individual did not "voluntarily" choose to become involved. The public's primary interest is in the event; the public focus is on the conduct of the participant and the content, effect, and significance of the conduct, not the participant's prior anonymity or notoriety. [Emphasis added.] The present case illustrates the point. The community has a vital interest in the proper enforcement of its criminal laws, particularly in an area such as obscenity where a number of highly important values are potentially in conflict: the public has an interest both in seeing that the criminal law is adequately enforced and in assuring that the law is not used unconstitutionally to suppress free expression. Whether the person involved is a famous large scale magazine distributor or a "private" businessman running a corner newsstand has no relevance in ascertaining whether the public has an interest in the issue. We honor the commitment to robust debate on public issues, which is embodied in the First Amendment, by extending constitutional protection to all discussion and communication involving matters of public or general concern, without regard to whether the persons involved are famous or anonymous.

* * * Drawing a distinction between "public" and "private" figures makes no sense in terms of the First Amendment guarantees. The New York Times standard was applied to libel of a public official or public figure to give effect to the Amendment's function to encourage ventilation of public issues, not because the public official

has any less interest in protecting his reputation than an individual in private life. While the argument that public figures need less protection because they can command media attention to counter criticism may be true for some very prominent people, even then it is the rare case where the denial overtakes the original charge. Denials, retractions, and corrections are not "hot" news, and rarely receive the prominence of the original story. When the public official or public figure is a minor functionary, or has left the position which put him in the public eye, see *Rosenblatt v. Baer,* the argument loses all of its force. In the vast majority of libels involving public officials or public figures, the ability to respond through the media will depend on the same complex factor on which the ability of a private individual depends: the unpredictable event of the media's continuing interest in the story. Thus the unproven, and highly improbable, generalization that an as yet undefined class of "public figures" involved in matters of public concern will be better able to respond through the media than private individuals also involved in such matters seems too insubstantial a reed on which to rest a constitutional distinction. Furthermore, in First Amendment terms, the cure seems far worse than the disease. If the States fear that private citizens will not be able to respond adequately to publicity involving them, the solution lies in the direction of ensuring their ability to respond, rather than in stifling public discussion of matters of public concern.

Further reflection over the years since *New York Times* was decided persuades us that the view of the "public official" or "public figure" as assuming the risk of defamation by voluntarily thrusting himself into the public eye bears little relationship either to the values protected by the First Amendment or to the nature of our society. We have recognized that "[e]xposure of the self to others in varying degrees is a concomitant of life in a civilized community." *Time, Inc. v. Hill,* 385 U.S. 374, 388 (1967). Voluntarily or not, we are all "public" men to some degree. Conversely, some aspects of the lives of even the most public men fall outside the area of matters of public or general concern. * * * Thus, the idea that certain "public" figures have voluntarily exposed their entire lives to public inspection, while private individuals have kept theirs carefully shrouded from public view is, at best, a legal fic-

tion. In any event, such a distinction could easily produce the paradoxical result of dampening discussion of issues of public or general concern because they happen to involve private citizens while extending constitutional encouragement to discussion of aspects of the lives of "public figures" which are not in the area of public or general concern.

* * *

We are aware that the press has, on occasion, grossly abused the freedom it is given by the Constitution. All must deplore such excesses. In an ideal world, the responsibility of the press would match the freedom and public trust given it. But from the earliest days of our history, this free society, dependent as it is for its survival upon a vigorous free press, has tolerated some abuse. * * * We thus hold that a libel action, as here, by a private individual against a licensed radio station for a defamatory falsehood in a newscast relating to his involvement in an event of public or general concern may be sustained only upon clear and convincing proof that the defamatory falsehood was published with knowledge that it was false or with reckless disregard of whether it was false or not. * * *

Petitioner argues finally that *WIP's* failure to communicate with him to learn his side of the case and to obtain a copy of the magazine for examination, sufficed to support a verdict under the *Times* standard. But our "cases are clear that reckless conduct is not measured by whether a reasonably prudent man would have published, or would have investigated before publishing. There must be sufficient evidence to permit the conclusion that the defendant in fact entertained serious doubts as to the truth of his publication." *St. Amant v. Thompson,* 390 U.S., at 731. Respondent here relied on information supplied by police officials. Following petitioner's complaint about the accuracy of the broadcasts, *WIP* checked its last report with the judge who presided in the case. While we may assume that the District Court correctly held to be defamatory respondent's characterizations of petitioner's business as "the smut literature racket," and of those engaged in it as "girlie-book peddlers," there is no evidence in the record to support a conclusion that respondent "in fact entertained serious doubts as to the truth" of its reports.

Affirmed.

———————————

COMMENT

In retrospect it was to be Justice Harlan's dissenting opinion in *Rosenbloom v. Metromedia* that would undo the *public issue* standard. "It is * * * my judgment," said Harlan, "that the reasonable care standard adequately serves those First Amendment values that must inform the definition of actionable libel and that those special considerations that made even this standard an insufficiently precise technique when applied to plaintiffs who are 'public officials' or 'public figures' do not obtain where the litigant is a purely private individual."

Justice Thurgood Marshall, joined by Justice Stewart in dissent, framed propositions that were also to reappear in *Gertz*. Agreeing with Harlan, he said that the plurality's doctrine would threaten society's interest in protecting private individuals from being thrust into the public eye by the distorting light of defamation. But beyond that he saw a formidable danger in punitive and presumed damages, and so made a proposal:

> The threats to society's interest in freedom of the press that are involved in punitive and presumed damages can largely be eliminated by restricting the award of damages to proven, actual injuries. The jury's wide ranging discretion will largely be eliminated since the award will be based on essentially objective, discernible factors. * * * [S]elf-censorship resulting from the fear of large judgments themselves would be reduced. At the same time society's interest in protecting individuals from defamation will still be fostered.

The Court seemed ready for *Gertz v. Robert Welch, Inc.*

The Present State of Libel: *Gertz* and Beyond

By removing libel from its ancestral home in tort law and putting it under the protection of the Constitution, *New York Times v. Sullivan* was truly a landmark case. Simply put, the Court had decided that in the interests of a vigorous social dialogue public officials would have to surrender their sensitivity to "vehement, caustic, and sometimes unpleasantly sharp" verbal assaults. But the Court left an opening to remedy injury to reputation. If the public official could with convincing clarity prove *actual malice,* that is, that the statement was published *with knowledge* that it was false or with reckless disregard of whether it was false or not, a libel suit could still be pursued and won. The major burden of proof, however, was now on the public-person plaintiff, and libel would be governed by a national, First Amendment–based standard of fault. Reviewing courts would make an independent examination of the record to assure that the plaintiff had satisfied the constitutional standard.

Much was made of *New York Times I,* as it would be called, to distinguish it from the *Pentagon Papers* case of 1971. Harry Kalven, Jr., saw it as laying to rest for all time sedition or libel of government—"an impossible notion for a democracy."[92] Kalven also reported that Meiklejohn had exclaimed that the ruling was "an occasion for dancing in the streets."

Justices Hugo Black, William O. Douglas, and Arthur Goldberg, however, had serious reservations. First Amendment theorist Thomas Emerson rejected the ruling for failing to take into account the value of even intentional falsehood in forcing people to defend, justify, and rethink their positions. Emerson referred to Brennan's actual malice test as a "relapse to the two level theory [the idea that certain forms of speech are exempt from First Amendment protection]," and he added:

> [S]uper-refined attempts to separate statements of fact from opinions, to winnow truth out of a mass of conflicting evidence * * * to probe into intents, motives and purposes—all these do not fit into the dynamics of a system of freedom of expression. * * * The health and vitality of the system depend more upon untrammeled freedom of discussion, in which all citizens contend vigorously, than in judicial attempts to establish the motives of participants.[93]

A perennial concern is that because of *New York Times* fewer people will choose to participate in public affairs as officeholders. This is based partly on the assumption that public persons have no superior access to publicity,[94] an assumption of doubtful validity.

92. Kalven, "The New York Times Case: A Note on the Central Meaning of the First Amendment," 1964 *Sup.Ct.Rev.* 205.
93. Emerson, *The System of Freedom of Expression,* 1970, pp. 530, 531, 538.
94. Schaefer, "Defamation and the First Amendment: The Coen Lecture," 52 *U. of Colorado L.R.* 1 (Fall 1980).

In the decade following *New York Times,* the Court stretched the application of its *actual malice* rule to public figures in *Butts* and *Walker* and finally, in the 1971 *Rosenbloom* case, to private persons caught up in matters of public interest, even though involuntarily. "We honor the commitment to robust debate on public issues," said Justice Brennan in his plurality opinion for the *Rosenbloom* Court, "* * * by extending constitutional protection to all discussion and communication involving matters of public or general concern, without regard to whether the persons involved are famous or anonymous."

But the Court was bitterly fragmented on the question of how far the First Amendment ought to go in protecting libel. Justice John Marshall Harlan, who dissented because he preferred a less severe proof than actual malice for private persons in pursuit of libel damages, was to have the last word. But for three years the press enjoyed a near immunity to libel laws. Whatever was published was, at least by an editor's definition, a matter of public interest and therefore subject to the actual malice test.

Gertz v. Robert Welch, Inc. swung the pendulum back, not all the way to the position of strict liability but to a point of recognizing the private person in libel law. The onward rush of *New York Times* had ended.

The family of a youth shot by a policeman had retained Elmer Gertz, a nationally known attorney and self-defined public person, to represent them in a civil suit for damages against the policeman. The policeman had already been convicted of second-degree murder. Meanwhile, the editor of the John Birch Society magazine, *American Opinion,* saw as his patriotic duty the publication of an article discrediting Gertz by identifying him with a "conspiracy" to undermine law enforcement in order to effect a Communist takeover of the United States.[95] In order to heap opprobrium upon Gertz, the article stated falsely that he had a criminal record, that he had planned the 1968 Chicago demonstrations, and that he was a Leninist and a front for Communists.

What he was, in fact, was one of Chicago's best-known lawyers, a legal expert on libel, censorship, civil rights, free speech, the death

penalty, and housing. He was also the author of books, pamphlets, magazine articles, book reviews, and radio plays; a professor of law; a civil rights leader; and a founder and member of countless organizations ranging from the Civil War Roundtable to the Henry Miller Literary Society.

Hardly a private person, Gertz was instrumental in writing a new Illinois constitution, having been elected to the post. He was a dedicated theater buff and literary dilettante. He founded the George Bernard Shaw Society. In 1931 he wrote his first book, a work on Frank Harris, the renegade literary libertine. He won a parole for Nathan Leopold and later a death sentence commutation for Jack Ruby.

Poet and historian Carl Sandburg once said that "Elmer Gertz fears no dragons." Probably true. More likely, though, he knew his libel law and had clearly discerned the divided nature of the Court in *Rosenbloom* and the significant changes in its membership since 1971.

Gertz sued *American Opinion,* and a sympathetic jury awarded him $50,000. A federal district court disallowed the award, agreeing with the magazine that the *public issue* rule of *Rosenbloom* protected it against that kind of judgment. The court of appeals affirmed, and Gertz sought review in the Supreme Court.

In an imprecise but significant opinion by Justice Lewis Powell, the Supreme Court reversed, declaring the very public Mr. Gertz to be a private person in the circumstances of the case. The Court pointed out that Gertz, unknown to the jury, was simply a lawyer serving a client. On the assumption that private persons don't have the same access to the media that public officials and public figures have—although it was doubtful that this was true of Elmer Gertz—the Court essentially rejected the public issue rule of *Rosenbloom* and held that henceforth purely private or nonpublic persons, to succeed as plaintiffs in a libel suit, need only show *negligence* on the part of the defendant, a much lighter burden than actual malice.

The Court said a lot more, however, and not all of it unfavorable to the press. No longer was it enough for a plaintiff to be falsely defamed (the traditional libel *per se* where falsity, malice, and damages are presumed). There now *must* be a showing of *negligence* for, said Powell, there can be *"no liability without fault."* And the sep-

---

arate states would be allowed "substantial latitude" in determining the standard of care required of publishers.

Moreover, to discourage damages, which may be destructive of unpopular ideas and of the press itself, private-person plaintiffs, said Powell, would have to come all the way up to the actual malice standard to claim punitive damages, which too often in the past had been out of all proportion to the harm inflicted by publication. Awards, then, in private-person suits would henceforth be restricted to actual damages for demonstrated injury, whether personal humiliation, mental anguish, or whatever. (Note how Powell's notion of actual damages appears to subsume what we will refer to later as compensatory or general damages.) A jury would assess injury on the basis of relevant testimony. In addition, there would be no punishment for opinions, no matter how pernicious. Under the First Amendment, said the Court, there is *no such thing as a false idea*. Facts and opinion would be distinguished whenever possible. *Gertz* governs the present law of libel. In April 1981, the plaintiff was awarded $100,000 in compensatory and $300,000 in punitive damages, and that result was affirmed by the Seventh Circuit Court of Appeals on June 16, 1982 (*Gertz v. Welch*, 8 Med.L.Rptr. 1769, 680 F.2d 527 [7th Cir. 1982].) Gertz had proven actual malice to the satisfaction of the district court jury, although there was some disagreement between the trial and appeals courts as to whether quotations from public documents of a time past required such proof. More than a decade of litigation finally ended in early 1983 when the Supreme Court declined to review the seventh circuit holding.

Gertz v. Robert Welch, Inc.
418 U.S. 323, 94 S.CT. 2997, 41 L.ED.2D 789 (1974).

Justice POWELL delivered the opinion of the Court:

* * *

The principal issue in this case is whether a newspaper or broadcaster that publishes defamatory falsehoods about an individual who is neither a public official nor a public figure may claim a constitutional privilege against liability for the injury inflicted by those statements. The Court considered this question on the rather different set of facts presented in *Rosenbloom v. Metromedia, Inc.,* 403 U.S. 29 * * * (1971). Rosenbloom, a distributor of nudist magazines, was arrested for selling allegedly obscene material while making a delivery to a retail dealer. The police obtained a warrant and seized his entire inventory of 3,000 books and magazines. He sought and obtained an injunction prohibiting further police interference with his business. He then sued a local radio station for failing to note in two of its newscasts that the 3,000 items seized were only "reportedly" or "allegedly" obscene and for broadcasting references to "the smut literature racket" and to "girlie-book peddlers" in its coverage of the court proceeding for injunctive relief. He obtained a judgment against the radio station, but the Court of Appeals for the Third Circuit held the *New York Times* privilege applicable to the broadcast and reversed. 415 F.2d 892 (1969).

This Court affirmed the decision below, but no majority could agree on a controlling rationale. The eight Justices who participated in *Rosenbloom* announced their views in five separate opinions, none of which commanded more than three votes. The several statements not only reveal disagreement about the appropriate result in that case, they also reflect divergent traditions of thought about the general problem of reconciling the law of defamation with the First Amendment. One approach has been to extend the *New York Times* test to an expanding variety of situations. Another has been to vary the level of constitutional privilege for defamatory falsehood with the status of the person defamed. And a third view would grant to the press and broadcast media absolute immunity from liability for defamation. To place our holding in the proper context, we preface our discussion of this case with a review of the several *Rosenbloom* opinions and their antecedents.

In affirming the trial court's judgment in the instant case, the Court of Appeals relied on Justice Brennan's conclusion for the *Rosenbloom* plurality that "all discussion and communication involving matters of public or general concern," warrant the protection from liability for defamation accorded by the rule originally enunciated in *New York Times Co. v. Sullivan,* 376 U.S. 254 * * * (1964). There this Court defined a constitutional privilege intended to free criticism of public officials from the restraints imposed by the common law of defamation. The *Times* ran a political advertisement endorsing civil rights demonstrations by black students in Alabama and impliedly condemning the performance of local law-enforcement officials. A police commissioner established in state court that certain misstatements in the advertisement referred to him and that they constituted libel *per se* under Alabama law. This showing left the *Times* with the single defense of truth, for under Alabama law neither good faith nor reasonable care would protect the newspaper from liability. This Court concluded that a "rule compelling the critic of official conduct to guarantee the truth of all his factual assertions" would deter protected speech, and announced the constitutional privilege designed to counter that effect:

> "The constitutional guarantees require, we think, a federal rule that prohibits a public official from recovering damages for a defamatory falsehood relating to his official conduct unless he proves that the statement was made with 'actual malice'—that is, with knowledge that it was false or with reckless disregard of whether it was false or not." [Fn. omitted.]

Three years after *New York Times,* a majority of the Court agreed to extend the constitutional privilege to defamatory criticism of "public figures." This extension was announced in *Curtis Publishing Co. v. Butts* and its companion, *Associated Press v. Walker,* 388 U.S. 130 * * * (1967). The first case involved the Saturday Evening Post's charge that Coach Wally Butts of the University of Georgia had conspired with Coach "Bear" Bryant of the University of Alabama to fix a football game between their respective schools. *Walker* involved an erroneous Associated Press account of former Major General Edwin Walker's participation in a University of Mississippi campus riot. Because Butts was paid by a private alumni association and Walker had resigned from the Army, neither could be classified as a "public official" under *New York Times.* Although Justice Harlan announced the result in both cases, a majority of the Court agreed with Mr. Chief Justice Warren's conclusion that the *New York Times* test should apply to criticism of "public figures" as well as "public officials." The Court extended the constitutional privilege announced in that case to protect defamatory criticism of nonpublic persons

who "are nevertheless intimately involved in the resolution of important public questions or, by reason of their fame, shape events in areas of concern to society at large."

In his opinion for the plurality in *Rosenbloom v. Metromedia, Inc.,* Justice Brennan took the *New York Times* privilege one step further. He concluded that its protection should extend to defamatory falsehoods relating to private persons if the statements concerned matters of general or public interest. He abjured the suggested distinction between public officials and public figures on the one hand and private individuals on the other. He focused instead on society's interest in learning about certain issues: "If a matter is a subject of public or general interest, it cannot suddenly become less so merely because a private individual is involved, or because in some sense the individual did not 'voluntarily' choose to become involved." Thus, under the plurality opinion, a private citizen involuntarily associated with a matter of general interest has no recourse for injury to his reputation unless he can satisfy the demanding requirements of the *New York Times* test.

Two Members of the Court concurred in the result in *Rosenbloom* but departed from the reasoning of the plurality. Justice Black restated his view, long shared by Justice Douglas, that the First Amendment cloaks the news media with an absolute and indefeasible immunity from liability for defamation. Justice White concurred on a narrower ground. He concluded that "the First Amendment gives the press and the broadcast media a privilege to report and comment upon the official actions of public servants in full detail, with no requirement that the reputation or the privacy of an individual involved in or affected by the official action be spared from public view." He therefore declined to reach the broader questions addressed by the other Justices.

Justice Harlan dissented. Although he had joined the opinion of the Court in *New York Times,* in *Curtis Publishing Co.* he had contested the extension of the privilege to public figures. There he had argued that a public figure who held no governmental office should be allowed to recover damages for defamation "on a showing of highly unreasonable conduct constituting an extreme departure from the standards of investigation and reporting ordinarily adhered to by responsible publishers." In his *Curtis Publishing Co.* opinion Justice Harlan had distinguished *New York Times* primarily on the ground that defamation actions by public officials "lay close to seditious libel. * * *" Recovery of damages by one who held no public office, however, could not "be viewed as a vindication of governmental policy." Additionally, he had intimated that, because most public officials enjoyed absolute immunity from liability for their own defamatory utterances under *Barr v. Matteo,* 360 U.S. 564 (1959), they lacked a strong claim to the protection of the courts.

In *Rosenbloom* Justice Harlan modified these views. He acquiesced in the application of the privilege to defamation of public figures but argued that a different rule should obtain where defamatory falsehood harmed a private individual. He noted that a private person has less likelihood "of securing access to channels of communication sufficient to rebut falsehoods concerning him" than do public officials and public figures, and has not voluntarily placed himself in the public spotlight. Justice Harlan concluded that the States could constitutionally allow private individuals to recover damages for defamation on the basis of any standard of care except liability without fault.

Justice Marshall dissented in *Rosenbloom* in an opinion joined by Justice Stewart. He thought that the plurality's "public or general interest" test for determining the applicability of the *New York Times* privilege would involve the courts in the dangerous business of deciding "what information is relevant to self-government." He also contended that the plurality's position inadequately served "society's interest in protecting private individuals from being thrust into the public eye by the distorting light of defamation." Justice Marshall therefore reached the conclusion, also reached by Justice Harlan, that the States should be "essentially free to continue the evolution of the common law of defamation and to articulate whatever fault standard best suits the State's need," so long as the States did not impose liability without fault. The principal point of disagreement among the three dissenters concerned punitive damages. Whereas Justice Harlan thought that the States could allow punitive damages in amounts bearing "a reasonable and purposeful relationship to the actual harm done * * *," Justice Marshall concluded that the size

and unpredictability of jury awards of exemplary damages unnecessarily exacerbated the problems of media self-censorship and that such damages should therefore be forbidden.

We begin with the common ground. *Under the First Amendment there is no such thing as a false idea.* However pernicious an opinion may seem, we depend for its correction not on the conscience of judges and juries but on the competition of other ideas. But there is no constitutional value in false statements of fact. Neither the intentional lie nor the careless error materially advances society's interest in "uninhibited, robust, and wide-open" debate on public issues. *New York Times Co. v. Sullivan,* 376 U.S., at 270. They belong to that category of utterances which "are no essential part of any exposition of ideas, and are of such slight social value as a step to truth that any benefit that may be derived from them is clearly outweighed by the social interest in order and morality." *Chaplinsky v. New Hampshire,* 315 U.S. 568, 572 (1942). [Emphasis added.]

Although the erroneous statement of fact is not worthy of constitutional protection, it is nevertheless inevitable in free debate. As James Madison pointed out in the Report on the Virginia Resolutions of 1798: "Some degree of abuse is inseparable from the proper use of every thing; and in no instance is this more true than in that of the press." 4 J. Elliot, *Debates on the Federal Constitution of 1787,* p. 571 (1876). And punishment of error runs the risk of inducing a cautious and restrictive exercise of the constitutionally guaranteed freedoms of speech and press. *Our decisions recognize that a rule of strict liability that compels a publisher or broadcaster to guarantee the accuracy of his factual assertions may lead to intolerable self-censorship.* Allowing the media to avoid liability only by proving the truth of all injurious statements does not accord adequate protection to First Amendment liberties. As the Court stated in *New York Times Co. v. Sullivan,* "Allowance of the defense of truth with the burden of proving it on the defendant, does not mean that only false speech will be deterred." The First Amendment requires that we protect some falsehood in order to protect speech that matters. [Emphasis added.]

The need to avoid self-censorship by the news media is, however, not the only societal value at issue. If it were, this Court would have embraced long ago the view that publishers and broadcasters enjoy an unconditional and indefeasible immunity from liability for defamation. Such a rule would, indeed, obviate the fear that the prospect of civil liability for injurious falsehood might dissuade a timorous press from the effective exercise of First Amendment freedoms. Yet absolute protection for the communications media requires a total sacrifice of the competing value served by the law of defamation.

The legitimate state interest underlying the law of libel is the compensation of individuals for the harm inflicted on them by defamatory falsehood. We would not lightly require the State to abandon this purpose, for, as Justice Stewart has reminded us, the individual's right to the protection of his own good name

> reflects no more than our basic concept of the essential dignity and worth of every human being— a concept at the root of any decent system of ordered liberty. The protection of private personality, like the protection of life itself, is left primarily to the individual States under the Ninth and Tenth Amendments. But this does not mean that the right is entitled to any less recognition by this Court as a basic of our constitutional system. *Rosenblatt v. Baer,* 383 U.S. 75, 92 (1966) (concurring opinion).

* * *

The *New York Times* standard defines the level of constitutional protection appropriate to the context of defamation of a public person. Those who, by reason of the notoriety of their achievements or the vigor and success with which they seek the public's attention, are properly classed as public figures and those who hold governmental office may recover for injury to reputation only on clear and convincing proof that the defamatory falsehood was made with knowledge of its falsity or with reckless disregard for the truth. This standard administers an extremely powerful antidote to the inducement to media self-censorship of the common-law rule of strict liability for libel and slander. And it exacts a correspondingly high price from the victims of defamatory falsehood. Plainly many deserving plaintiffs, including some intentionally subjected to injury, will be unable to surmount the barrier of the *New York Times* test. Despite this substantial abridgment of the state law right to compensation for wrongful hurt to one's reputation, the Court has concluded that the protec-

tion of the *New York Times* privilege should be available to publishers and broadcasters of defamatory falsehood concerning public officials and public figures. We think that these decisions are correct, but we do not find their holdings justified solely by reference to the interest of the press and broadcast media in immunity from liability. Rather, we believe that the *New York Times* rule states an accommodation between this concern and the limited state interest present in the context of libel actions brought by public persons. *For the reasons stated below, we conclude that the state interest in compensating injury to the reputation of private individuals requires that a different rule should obtain with respect to them.* [Emphasis added.]

* * *

The first remedy of any victim of defamation is self-help—using available opportunities to contradict the lie or correct the error and thereby to minimize its adverse impact on reputation. Public officials and public figures usually enjoy significantly greater access to the channels of effective communication and hence have a more realistic opportunity to counteract false statements than private individuals normally enjoy. Private individuals are therefore more vulnerable to injury, and the state interest in protecting them is correspondingly greater.

More important than the likelihood that private individuals will lack effective opportunities for rebuttal, there is a compelling normative consideration underlying the distinction between public and private defamation plaintiffs. An individual who decides to seek governmental office must accept certain necessary consequences of that involvement in public affairs. He runs the risk of closer public scrutiny than might otherwise be the case. And society's interest in the officers of government is not strictly limited to the formal discharge of official duties. As the Court pointed out in *Garrison v. Louisiana,* 379 U.S., at 77 * * *, the public's interest extends to "anything which might touch on an official's fitness for office. * * * Few personal attributes are more germane to fitness for office than dishonesty, malfeasance, or improper motivation, even though these characteristics may also affect the official's private character."

Those classed as public figures stand in a similar position. *Hypothetically, it may be possible for someone to become a public figure through no purposeful action of his own, but the instances of truly involuntary public figures must be exceedingly rare.* For the most part those who attain this status have assumed roles of especial prominence in the affairs of society. Some occupy positions of such persuasive power and influence that they are deemed public figures for all purposes. More commonly, those classed as public figures have thrust themselves to the forefront of particular public controversies in order to influence the resolution of the issues involved. In either event, they invite attention and comment. [Emphasis added.]

Even if the foregoing generalities do not obtain in every instance, the communications media are entitled to act on the assumption that public officials and public figures have voluntarily exposed themselves to increased risk of injury from defamatory falsehood concerning them. No such assumption is justified with respect to a private individual. He has not accepted public office or assumed an "influential role in ordering society." He has relinquished no part of his interest in the protection of his own good name, and consequently he has a more compelling call on the courts for redress of injury inflicted by defamatory falsehood. Thus, private individuals are not only more vulnerable to injury than public officials and public figures; they are also more deserving of recovery.

For these reasons we conclude that the States should retain substantial latitude in their efforts to enforce a legal remedy for defamatory falsehood injurious to the reputation of a private individual. The extension of the *New York Times* test proposed by the *Rosenbloom* plurality would abridge this legitimate state interest to a degree that we find unacceptable. And it would occasion the additional difficulty of forcing state and federal judges to decide on an *ad hoc* basis which publications address issues of "general or public interest" and which do not—to determine, in the words of Justice Marshall, "what information is relevant to self-government." *Rosenbloom v. Metromedia, Inc.,* 403 U.S., at 79. We doubt the wisdom of committing this task to the conscience of judges. Nor does the Constitution require us to draw so thin a line between the drastic alternatives of the *New York Times* privilege and the common law of strict liability for defamatory error. The "public or general interest"

test for determining the applicability of the *New York Times* standard to private defamation actions inadequately serves both of the competing values at stake. On the one hand, a private individual whose reputation is injured by defamatory falsehood that does concern an issue of public or general interest has no recourse unless he can meet the rigorous requirements of *New York Times.* This is true despite the factors that distinguish the state interest in compensating private individuals from the analogous interest involved in the context of public persons. On the other hand, a publisher or broadcaster of a defamatory error which a court deems unrelated to an issue of public or general interest may be held liable in damages even if it took every reasonable precaution to ensure the accuracy of its assertions. And liability may far exceed compensation for any actual injury to the plaintiff, for the jury may be permitted to presume damages without proof of loss and even to award punitive damages.

We hold that, so long as they do not impose liability without fault, the states may define for themselves the appropriate standard of liability for a publisher or broadcaster of defamatory falsehood injurious to a private individual. This approach provides a more equitable boundary between the competing concerns involved here. It recognizes the strength of the legitimate state interest in compensating private individuals for wrongful injury to reputation, yet shields the press and broadcast media from the rigors of strict liability for defamation. At least this conclusion obtains where, as here, the substance of the defamatory statement "makes substantial danger to reputation apparent." This phrase places in perspective the conclusion we announce today. Our inquiry would involve considerations somewhat different from those discussed above if a State purported to condition civil liability on a factual misstatement whose content did not warn a reasonably prudent editor or broadcaster of its defamatory potential. Such a case is not now before us, and we intimate no view as to its proper resolution. [Emphasis added.]

Our accommodation of the competing values at stake in defamation suits by private individuals allows the States to impose liability on the publisher or broadcaster of defamatory falsehood on a less demanding showing than that required by

New York Times. This conclusion is not based on a belief that the considerations which prompted the adoption of the New York Times privilege for defamation of public officials and its extension to public figures are wholly inapplicable to the context of private individuals. Rather, we endorse this approach in recognition of the strong and legitimate state interest in compensating private individuals for injury to reputation. But this countervailing state interest extends no further than compensation for actual injury. For the reasons stated below, we hold that the States may not permit recovery of presumed or punitive damages, at least when liability is not based on a showing of knowledge of falsity or reckless disregard for the truth. [Emphasis added.]

The common law of defamation is an oddity of tort law, for it allows recovery of purportedly compensatory damages without evidence of actual loss. Under the traditional rules pertaining to actions for libel, the existence of injury is presumed from the fact of publication. Juries may award substantial sums as compensation for supposed damage to reputation without any proof that such harm actually occurred. The largely uncontrolled discretion of juries to award damages where there is no loss unnecessarily compounds the potential of any system of liability for defamatory falsehood to inhibit the vigorous exercise of First Amendment freedoms. Additionally, the doctrine of presumed damages invites juries to punish unpopular opinion rather than to compensate individuals for injury sustained by the publication of a false fact. More to the point, the States have no substantial interest in securing for plaintiffs such as this petitioner gratuitous awards of money damages far in excess of any actual injury.

We would not, of course, invalidate state law simply because we doubt its wisdom, but here we are attempting to reconcile state law with a competing interest grounded in the constitutional command of the First Amendment. It is therefore appropriate to require that state remedies for defamatory falsehood reach no farther than is necessary to protect the legitimate interest involved. It is necessary to restrict defamation plaintiffs who do not prove knowledge of falsity or reckless disregard for the truth to compensation for actual injury. We need not define "actual injury," as trial courts have wide experience in framing appropriate jury instructions in tort actions. Suffice it to say that actual injury is not limited to out-of-pocket loss. Indeed, the more customary types of actual harm inflicted by defamatory falsehood include impairment of reputation and standing in the community, personal humiliation, and mental anguish and suffering. Of course, juries must be limited by appropriate instructions, and all awards must be supported by competent evidence concerning the injury, although there need be no evidence which assigns an actual dollar value to the injury. [Emphasis added.]

We also find no justification for allowing awards of punitive damages against publishers and broadcasters held liable under state-defined standards of liability for defamation. In most jurisdictions jury discretion over the amounts awarded is limited only by the gentle rule that they not be excessive. Consequently, juries assess punitive damages in wholly unpredictable amounts bearing no necessary relation to the actual harm caused. And they remain free to use their discretion selectively to punish expressions of unpopular views. Like the doctrine of presumed damages, jury discretion to award punitive damages unnecessarily exacerbates the danger of media self-censorship, but, unlike the former rule, punitive damages are wholly irrelevant to the state interest that justifies a negligence standard for private defamation actions. They are not compensation for injury. Instead, they are private fines levied by civil juries to punish reprehensible conduct and to deter its future occurrence. In short, the private defamation plaintiff who establishes liability under a less demanding standard than that stated by New York Times may recover only such damages as are sufficient to compensate him for actual injury. [Emphasis added.]

Notwithstanding our refusal to extend the New York Times privilege to defamation of private individuals, respondent contends that we should affirm the judgment below on the ground that petitioner is either a public official or a public figure. There is little basis for the former assertion. Several years prior to the present incident, petitioner had served briefly on housing committees appointed by the mayor of Chicago, but at the time of publication he had never held any remunerative governmental position. Respondent admits this but argues that petitioner's appearance at the coroner's inquest rendered him a "de facto public official." Our cases recognized no such concept. Respondent's suggestion would sweep all lawyers under the *New York Times* rule as officers of the court and distort the plain meaning of the "public official" category beyond all recognition. We decline to follow it.

Respondent's characterization of petitioner as a public figure raises a different question. That designation may rest on either of two alternative bases. *In some instances an individual may achieve such pervasive fame or notoriety that he becomes a public figure for all purposes and in all contexts. More commonly, an individual voluntarily injects himself or is drawn into a particular public controversy and thereby becomes a public figure for a limited range of issues.* In either case such persons assume special prominence in the resolution of public questions. [Emphasis added.]

Petitioner has long been active in community and professional affairs. He has served as an officer of local civic groups and of various professional organizations, and he has published several books and articles on legal subjects. Although petitioner was consequently well known in some circles, he had achieved no general fame or notoriety in the community. None of the prospective jurors called at the trial had ever heard of petitioner prior to this litigation, and respondent offered no proof that this response was atypical of the local population. We would not lightly assume that a citizen's participation in community and professional affairs rendered him a public figure for all purposes. *Absent clear evidence of general fame or notoriety in the community, and pervasive involvement in the affairs of society, an individual should not be deemed a public personality for all aspects of his life. It is preferable to reduce the public-figure question to a more meaningful context by looking to the nature and extent of an individual's participation in the particular controversy giving rise to the defamation.* [Emphasis added.]

In this context it is plain that petitioner was not a public figure. He played a minimal role at the coroner's inquest, and his participation related solely to his representation of a private client. He took no part in the criminal prosecution of Officer Nuccio. Moreover, he never discussed either the criminal or civil litigation with the press and was never quoted as having done so. He plainly

did not thrust himself into the vortex of this public issue, nor did he engage the public's attention in an attempt to influence its outcome. We are persuaded that the trial court did not err in refusing to characterize petitioner as a public figure for the purpose of this litigation.

We therefore conclude that the *New York Times* standard is inapplicable to this case and that the trial court erred in entering judgment for respondent. Because the jury was allowed to impose liability without fault and was permitted to presume damages without proof of injury, a new trial is necessary. We reverse and remand for further proceedings in accord with this opinion.

It is so ordered.

Reversed and remanded.

COMMENT

Gertz established definitively that (1) there could be *no liability without fault;* a plaintiff would have to demonstrate at least negligence on the part of the defendant to win a libel suit. (2) A plaintiff, whether a public or a private person, would have to prove actual malice to be awarded punitive damages. (The Court seemed to be discouraging punitive damages in libel suits. More about damages will follow.) (3) Jury awards in the future would be restricted to actual damages (although that term was given a flexible definition) for demonstrated injury, whatever form that injury might take, e.g., humiliation, shame, mental anguish, loss of standing in the community. (4) There could be no punishment for the expression of an opinion, or, as the Court put it, "there is no such thing as a false idea."

As in *Hepps,* the *Gertz* court did not deal with nonmedia defendants. Since *Hepps,* however, lower courts have tended to give them the benefit of the doubt; that is, the burden of proof of falsity is still on the person suing.[96]

Unlike the *Masson* case, in *Gertz* the publisher of *American Opinion*, Robert Welch, had hired an author who would present his ideological worldview without question, however much

---

96. For example, see *Burroughs v. FFP Operating Partners, L.P.,* 28 F.3d 543 (5th Cir. 1994); *Wheeler v. Nebraska State Bar Ass'n,* 508 N.W.2d 917, 921 (1993); *Underwager v. Salter,* 22 F.3d 730, 735 (7th Cir. 1994); and *Johnson v. Robbinsdale Ind. School Dist. 281,* 827 F.Supp. 1439, 1443 (D.Minn. 1993).

he might have to twist the facts to do so. No such purposeful distortion was planned in *Masson*.

Two years after *Gertz*, the Supreme Court decided *Time, Inc. v. Firestone*.[97] The case involved the scion of one of America's wealthiest industrial families and his socialite spouse. In dissolving their marriage, a Florida circuit court issued a judgment containing language such as "extramarital escapades . . . which would have made Dr. Freud's hair curl" and "bounding from one bedpartner to another with the erotic zest of a satyr." In an innocuous "Milestones" paragraph, *Time* erroneously reported that Mary Alice Firestone had been divorced for adultery. Technically, she hadn't. The marriage had been dissolved because, the court said, "neither of the parties has shown the least susceptibility to domestication." Mrs. Firestone sued for libel.

In spite of the fact that the plaintiff employed a clipping bureau to keep track of her social activities, called press conferences, and was a visible part of the Palm Beach, Florida, social whirl, then Justice William Rehnquist, writing for the Court, defined her as a private person who had "not thrust herself to the forefront of any particular public controversy . . . . She was compelled to go to court by the state in order to obtain legal release from the bonds of matrimony."

Privilege to report on judicial proceedings, Rehnquist added, did not include the false and inaccurate. Highly technical language had tripped up the *Time* stringer. In Florida, alimony did not have to be paid in divorce cases involving adultery. Mrs. Firestone was to be paid alimony because adultery had not been the grounds for divorce. The florid language of the judge had misled the reporter.

More important, Mrs. Firestone had withdrawn her claim for damages to reputation and had based her claim on "personal humiliation and mental anguish and suffering," what other courts have called the *intentional infliction of emotional distress*. That offense has been defined as conduct or behavior "so outrageous in character, and so extreme in degree as to go beyond all possible bounds of decency and to be regarded as atrocious and utterly intolerable in a civilized community."[98] Simple insults, indignities, and annoyances are not enough. Intent must be shown, and there must be proof of substantial emotional distress. (Mrs. Firestone's doctor had testified as to her suffering.) A majority of jurisdictions now recognize the tort. Emotional distress alone, however, will not support a libel claim in most states; there must also be a showing of damage to reputation.

The tort by itself was tested and greatly limited in a 1988 case brought by the Rev. Jerry Falwell against Larry Flynt's *Hustler* magazine.[99] Flynt, an albatross on the neck of the media bar, threatened metaphorically to assassinate Falwell. He attempted to do so by presenting a tasteless parody of a liqueur ad in which Falwell was quoted in the fine print as saying that his "first time" occurred in an outhouse with his mother when they were both drunk. A disclaimer was included at the bottom of the page. To assuage his deep emotional hurt, Falwell distributed copies of the ad far and wide and raised $800,000 for his ministry in the process.

Writing for the Court, Chief Justice Rehnquist explained:

> Generally speaking the law does not regard the intent to inflict emotional distress as one which should receive much solicitude, and it is quite understandable that most if not all jurisdictions have chosen to make it civilly culpable where the conduct in question is sufficiently "outrageous." But in the world of debate about public affairs, many things done with motives that are less than admirable are protected by the First Amendment. . . . Were we to hold otherwise, there can be little doubt that political cartoonists and satirists would be subjected to damages without any showing that their work falsely defamed its subject. . . . The art of the cartoonist is often not reasoned or even-handed, but slashing and one-sided. . . . "Outrageousness" in the area of political and social discourse has an inherent subjectiveness about it which would allow a jury to impose liability on the basis of the jurors' tastes or views, or perhaps on the basis of their dislike of a particular expression. An "outrageousness" standard thus runs afoul of our longstanding refusal to allow damages to be awarded because the speech in question may have an adverse emotional impact on the audience. . . . We conclude that public figures and public officials may not recover for the tort of intentional infliction

---

97. 424 U.S. 448, 96 S.Ct. 958 (1976).

98. *Restatement (Second) of Torts,* sec. 46 (1965); See Prosser, *Intentional Infliction of Mental Suffering: A New Tort,* 37 Michigan L.Rev. 874 (1939).

---

99. *Hustler Magazine v. Falwell,* 14 Med.L.Rptr. 2281, 485 U.S. 46, 108 S.Ct. 876 (1988).

of emotional distress by reason of publications such as the one here at issue without showing in addition that the publication contains a false statement of fact which was made with "actual malice," i.e., with knowledge that the statement was false or with reckless disregard as to whether or not it was true.

Did the Chief Justice intend in his opinion for the Court to discourage this kind of suit altogether? There is disagreement on that point.

A California appeals court ruled recently that triable issues of fact exist as to whether a television reporter exhibited extreme and outrageous conduct when he entered a private home, knowing no adults were present, and disclosed to three small children that neighborhood friends had been murdered by their mother, who had then committed suicide. The children were then videotaped as they reacted to the news and answered questions, although the interview was never broadcast.[100] The "new" tort is by no means dead.

Many fear that the spirit of *New York Times v. Sullivan* has not been sustained in the case law that has followed it. Writing in the *California Law Review,* Martin Shapiro concluded that libel no longer depends on outcome or a product of publication. Rather, *New York Times* constitutes a "process" standard that in time will generate judicial standards for news gathering and writing.[101] New York University law professor Diane Zimmerman notes that *Sullivan* has not reduced the number, cost, or uncertainty of libel suits. "The Court started out on a long road without an underlying shared agreement about exactly what it was doing and what the implications would be." Instead of protecting the press from harassment by public officials, the result has been greater confusion.[102] A sociologist described what lawyers do in evaluating stories for their tone, temper, imprecision, hyperbole, balance, fairness, and consistency as what experienced editors and copyreaders did in the past and ought to be doing still.[103] After a lengthy study of libel cases, a teacher of journalism con-

cluded that "libel litigation has become a devastatingly effective weapon for silencing those who dare to challenge the morality of power, privilege and prestige."[104]

There are then at least two major problems with the *New York Times* doctrine. First, it gives the judicial branch of government a creeping supervisory authority over the editorial process, traceable, perhaps, to Justice John Marshall Harlan's improvisation on *New York Times* in the *Butts* case in which he wrote:

> We consider and would hold that a "public figure" who is not a public official may also recover damages for a defamatory falsehood whose substance makes substantial danger to reputation apparent, *on a showing of highly unreasonable conduct constituting an extreme departure from the standards of investigation ordinarily adhered to by responsible publishers.*[105] [Emphasis added.]

This would become known as the *prudent publisher test,* and the courts would take the measure of journalistic prudence. But what are the standards of an industry as diverse and varied as mass communications? What are "normal" publishing practices? Will communicators who live by ethics codes be measured against them by the courts? Jurors may be even harsher judges: they seem to have trouble understanding that mistakes can be made without either actual malice or negligence being involved.

Secondly, the actual malice test could be implied to require the reading of a newsperson's mind and so to intrude into the editorial process in a most intimate way: What did newsroom personnel say to one another in informal conversation? What information did they have that wasn't published? Was a deadline imminent? And what efforts were made to investigate, verify, and document? The Court said as much in the 1979 case of *Herbert v. Lando.*[106] Justice Brennan, dissenting in part and concurring in part, defined the interior mental sets of newspeople as unprivileged matters of fact that, if regulated, would regulate expression itself. But, he added, and this makes the difference, if mental processes can't be regulated, they can be probed. Any other view, of course, would seriously have

100. *KOVR-TV Inc. v. Sacramento County Superior Court,* 23 Med.L.Rptr. 1371, 37 Cal.Rpts.2d 431 (1995).

101. *Libel Regulatory Analysis,* 74 *Calif.L.Rev.* 883, 886 (1986).

102. 22 Med.L.Rptr. No. 25, part of a report of a Practicing Law Institute libel litigation seminar, June 20, 1994.

103. Susan P. Shapiro, *Libel Lawyers as Risk Counselors: Prepublication and Pre-broadcast Review and the Social Construction of News,* 11 *Law & Policy* 281, 289–95 (July 1989).

104. Gillmor, *Power, Publicity, and the Abuse of Libel Law,* p. ix.

105. 388 U.S. 130, 87 S.Ct. 1975 (1967).

106. 441 U.S. 153, 99 S.Ct. 1635 (1979).

questioned the very actual malice test that Brennan himself had fashioned for the Court.

A federal district court in the case held that a Vietnam hero public figure who had brought a $45 million libel suit against a *60 Minutes* producer was entitled under the Federal Rules of Civil Procedure to undertake pretrial discovery of any and all documents in the network's files relevant to the broadcast in order to produce evidence of defendant's "slipshod and sketchy investigative techniques." The plaintiff, a maverick former army colonel critical of the army and with a nose for publicity, was permitted to appraise conclusions reached by CBS reporters during and after their investigations by having access to their informal conversations with one another, and with their sources, and by exploring their states of mind and intentions. Newspeople were distressed. Producer Lando's deposition required twenty-six sessions and stretched over a year. The nearly 3,000 pages of transcripts and 240 exhibits included reporters' notes, network memoranda, drafts and scripts, unused film, and videotapes of interviews, all intended to uncover the producer's "state of mind."

Justice White in his opinion for Court, and consistent with his dissent in *Gertz,* seemed to be pushing the Court back to the common law standards of strict liability, libel *per se,* and broader state definitions of malice. One study sees this trend toward common law concepts continuing in the absence of Justice White. *New York Times* is responsible for its own unintended consequences—the supervision of journalistic procedures by judges. "A check on the press may be necessary or inevitable, but the breadth of the current system's intrusion . . . is indefensible . . . . [L]awyers are transmitting judge-made norms to newsrooms, are counseling reporters on compliance, and in effect are legitimating the entire process."[107]

While the actual malice rule of *New York Times* doesn't keep libel cases out of court, it does make it extremely difficult for a plaintiff ultimately to win a victory.

ACTUAL MALICE

Having proved defamation, publication, identification, falsity, and actual injury, a plaintiff still has to prove *fault* on the part of the publisher to succeed in a libel suit. Fault, whether an actual malice standard for public plaintiffs or a negligence standard for private persons, may now be the central concept of libel law. The "knowing falsehood" part of the definition of actual malice suggests a defendant intentionally oblivious to evidence of falsity and motivated to use a false publication to hurt. *Gertz* called it "subjective awareness of probable falsity"; *Garrison* "a high degree of awareness of . . . probable falsity"; *Butts* an "awareness of probable falsity"; and *St. Amant* "serious doubts as to the truth of his publication."[108] All imply a subjective state of mind, an intention to hurt someone, whatever the truth of the allegation. "Reckless disregard," the second part of the definition and a seemingly lesser degree of fault and therefore the one usually employed by plaintiff's attorney, also suggests a lesser degree of premeditation, but a careless willingness to do harm nevertheless.

Actual malice must be distinguished from common law malice, traditionally defined as ill will, hostility, spite, or a capacity for revenge. The difference is important because common law malice must be demonstrated in trade libel and slander cases. It is not equivalent to or synonymous with actual malice.

While it is easier to find cases defining what actual malice is not, according to a particular set of facts, than to find cases that demonstrate what it is, at the very least actual malice would include elements of some or all of the following: (1) a fabricated story, a product of a reporter's imagination, with no warning to readers; (2) evidence that a reporter knew a story was false or had serious doubts about its truthfulness before it was published; (3) evidence that a reporter had no credible sources and made no independent investigation into the charges made in a story; and (4) dependence upon anonymous or unverified phone calls.

In *Harte-Hanks Communications, Inc. v. Connaughton,*[109] the Court condemned the

---

107. Brian C. Murchison, John Soloski, Randall Bezanson, Gilbert Cranberg, and Roselle Wissler, *Sullivan's Paradox: The Emergence of Judicial Standards of Journalism,* 73 North Carolina L.Rev. 99–100 (November 1994).

108. *St. Amant v. Thompson,* 390 U.S. 727 (1968).
109. 16 Med.L.Rptr. 1881, 491 U.S. 657 (1989).

newspaper's failure to interview the one witness that both plaintiff and source claimed would verify their conflicting accounts. In addition, the newspaper failed to listen to a tape that it had been told exonerated the plaintiff and that had been delivered to the newspaper by the plaintiff at the newspaper's request. Was this a purposeful avoidance of the truth? The plaintiff in the case was an unsuccessful challenger for a municipal judgeship. The newspaper supported the incumbent. Although the case is both complex and controversial, the newspaper was faulted for ignoring evidence it had before it and for failing to interview a key witness. "Although failure to investigate will not alone support a finding of actual malice," said the Court, "the purposeful avoidance of the truth is in a different category." While rejecting the prudent publisher test of *Butts,* the Court saw similarities between that case and the way the newspaper handled the information at its disposal in *Connaughton.* But the Court favored the original test for actual malice: plaintiff must prove by clear and convincing evidence that the defendant published the false and defamatory material with knowledge of falsity or with a reckless disregard for the truth. A desire to promote a political candidate or increase the newspaper's circulation had nothing to do with actual malice, said the Supreme Court. And, it added, the reviewing court must scrutinize the entire record of the case to make certain the precise constitutional standard has been met. That rule originated in *Bose Corp. v. Consumers Union of United States, Inc.*[110] Lower courts disagree as to whether this rule applies to falsity as well as to actual malice. Where it does, a high percentage of cases are either reversed or dismissed.[111] And there are objections in some quarters to judges assuming the fact-finding role of jurors[112] and substituting their own interpretations of actual malice for those of the jury, the trier of fact.[113]

---

110. 10 Med.L.Rptr. 1625, 466 U.S. 485, 104 S.Ct. 1949 (1984).

111. *Libel Defense Resource Council Bulletin,* April 30, 1994, pp. 1–6.

112. Marc E. Sorini, *Factual Malice: Rediscovering the Seventh Amendment in Public Person Libel Cases,* 82 *Georgetown L.Journ.* 563 (December 1993).

113. *McCoy v. Hearst Corp.,* 13 Med.L.Rptr. 2169, 42 Cal.3d 835, 727 P.2d 711 (Cal. 1986), *cert. denied,* 481 U.S. 1041 (1987).

A more clear-cut example of a court finding actual malice occurred when a tobacco company sued CBS for a news commentary accusing it of linking smoking to "pot, wine, beer, and sex" in order to "hook" young people. Chicago's WBBM-TV anchorman, Walter Jacobson, called the company "liars." In fact, the company had rejected an advertising agency's proposal that would have followed such a line in promoting its products. Jacobson's research assistant had uncovered information showing that what Jacobson was prepared to broadcast was false. His information was ignored.

Even more compelling evidence of actual malice was the research assistant's deliberate destruction of documents critical to the case while the case was pending, contrary to CBS's own policy. The result was a $3.05 million judgment against Jacobson and CBS, the largest libel award on record up to that time. The Supreme Court declined to review the case:

Brown & Williamson v. Jacobson
14 MED.L.RPTR. 1497, 827 F.2D 1119 (7TH CIR. 1987).

BAUER, C. J.

* * *

The attitude of most knowledgeable and disinterested persons toward the tobacco industry is certainly negative; at least it has been negative for the past decade. In such an atmosphere, it becomes difficult to imagine how the tobacco people can be libeled. The bashing of the industry by government and private groups has become a virtual cottage industry. This case, however, demonstrates that general bum raps against the whole tobacco industry are different from specific accusations of skulduggery by a specific company or person. And this case involves some very specific statements against a very specific company in the tobacco industry. The facts are as follows: Walter Jacobson, an employee of the CBS-owned Chicago television station WBBM-TV, has served for a number of years as the co-anchor for the 10 p.m. weekday newscasts. In addition to fulfilling his duties as an anchorman, Jacobson also delivers a nightly feature known as "Walter Jacobson's Perspective." When Jacobson delivers his Perspectives, he moves from his normal location at the anchor desk, which is located in the station's newsroom rather than in a separate studio, to a special "Perspective" section of the newsroom. During the feature, the word Perspective appears on the screen with Mr. Jacobson's signature below it. The Perspective segments are rebroadcast the following day during WBBM's early evening news broadcasts.

As part of its activities promoting the quality of its news personalities, CBS ran ads which stated that "[w]ith ten years of experience on our anchor desk, [Walter Jacobson] has established himself as the city's most savvy political reporter * * * with contacts as solid as his credentials." Jacobson was touted by CBS as someone who "pulls no punches" and "lays it on the line." According to the ads, he is a journalist who will "make you angry. Or make you cheer. Walter Jacobson is liable to evoke all kinds of reactions * * * and he'll always leave you informed." When he delivered his Perspective on November 11, 1981, he made the Brown & Williamson Tobacco Corporation very angry.

Jacobson's November 11 Perspective was the third in a series on the cigarette industry. The first in the series dealt with the political influence of tobacco manufacturers while the second in the series discussed the failure of cigarette manufacturers to incorporate fire prevention features into their products. The final segment in the series, which was promoted on the day of the broadcast as "[t]obacco industry hooks children * * * Tonight at 10:00," dealt with the marketing practices of the cigarette industry. After Jacobson had moved to the Perspective section of the newsroom, his co-anchor, Harry Porterfield, introduced Jacobson's Perspective by stating:

> For the past two nights in Perspective, Walter has been reporting on the companies that make cigarettes and the clout they carry in Washington.
>
> Tonight he has the last in his series of special reports, a look at how the cigarette business gets its customers.

Jacobson then delivered his Perspective:

> Ask the cigarette business how it gets its customers and you will be told over and over again, that it's hard these days to get customers; that the good old days are gone forever. The good old ads for cigarettes cannot be used anymore. Old St. Nick, for example, pushing Lucky Strikes because * * * "Luckies are easy on my throat." The cigarette business can't count on that kind of an ad anymore. Or

the doctors pushing Camels; more doctors smoke Camels than any other cigarette. The business can't count on an ad like [that] anymore, either.

> Nor can it count anymore on television. Pushing cigarettes on television is prohibited. Television is off limits to cigarettes. And so the business (the killer business) has gone to the ad business in New York for help; to the slicksters on Madison Avenue, with a billion dollars a year for bigger and better ways to sell cigarettes.

> Go for the youth of America. Go get 'em guys. Get some young women, give them some samples. Pass them out on the streets, for free, to the teenagers of America. Hook 'em while they're young. Make 'em start now. Just think how many cigarettes they'll be smoking when they grow up.

> Or, here's another cigarette-slickster idea. The Merit report wants your opinion; a survey, they say, on current events. A $270,000 Merit wagon. Walk in, children, and let us know what you think about President Reagan. Get involved, children. Thank you, on behalf of Merit cigarettes. Or another cigarette-slickster idea. Go for the children through sports. You'll never guess who's likely to be a winner at the Winter Olympics. How about Rudd Pyles, from Colorado? But better than that, how about Benson & Hedges? At-a-way. The best possible way to addict the children to poison. There are more subtle ways, as well. A scene, for example, in Superman II. A bus crashing into a truck. Could be any truck, couldn't it? But, in a movie that's being seen by millions of children who love Superman, the bus crashes into a Marlboro truck.

Jacobson then reached the portion of his Perspective that the jury and the district court found libeled Brown & Williamson:

> The cigarette business insists, in fact, it will swear up and down in public, it is not selling cigarettes to children; that if children are smoking (which they are, more than ever before), it's not the fault of the cigarette business. Who knows whose fault it is, says the cigarette business.

> That's what Viceroy is saying. Who knows whose fault it is that children are smoking? It's not ours. Well, there is a confidential report on cigarette advertising in the files of the federal government right now, a Viceroy advertising [sic]. The Viceroy strategy for attracting young people (starters, they are called) to smoking.

> "For the young smoker a cigarette falls into the same category with wine, beer, shaving, or wearing a bra," says the Viceroy strategy. "A declaration of independence and striving for self-identity. Therefore, an attempt should be made," says Viceroy, "to present the cigarette as an initiation into the adult world, to present the cigarette as an illicit pleasure,

a basic symbol of the growing-up maturity process. An attempt should be made," says the Viceroy slicksters, "to relate the cigarette to pot, wine, beer, and sex. Do not communicate health or health-related points."

That's the strategy of the cigarette-slicksters, the cigarette business which is insisting in public * * * we are not selling cigarettes to children.

They're not slicksters. They're liars.

While Jacobson was making his statements about Viceroy, superimposed on the screen was a current Viceroy ad featuring two packs of Viceroy Rich Lights, a golf ball, and a part of a golf club. The relation of that particular ad to "pot, wine, beer, and sex" advertisements is not clear. Jacobson testified that the golf club ad was used only as a means of identifying the brand name for the viewer.

The "confidential report in the files of the federal government" referred to by Jacobson was a report by members of the staff of the Federal Trade Commission (FTC). The report first came to the attention of Jacobson's researcher, Michael Radutzky, in the summer of 1981 when Radutzky saw an article in a Kentucky newspaper that referred to the FTC report. Radutzky, who went on to become the producer of the 5:00 p.m. and then the 10:00 p.m. news at WBBM-TV, received copies of the pertinent pages of the FTC report from the author of the newspaper article.

The FTC report stated that documents obtained from Brown & Williamson and one of its advertising agencies, Ted Bates & Company, "set forth the development of an advertising strategy for Viceroy cigarettes designed to suppress or minimize public concern about the health effects of smoking." The report stated that the documents showed that Bates, which had the Viceroy account in 1975, requested a marketing and research firm, Marketing and Research Counselors, Inc., (MARC) to assist Bates in developing a marketable image for Viceroy cigarettes. After conducting a number of focus group interviews on the subject of smoking, MARC delivered a report, which was authored by N. Kennan, to Bates. The MARC report made recommendations on what its author thought were the important elements of a successful cigarette advertising campaign. As summarized by the FTC report, "the basic premise of the [MARC] report's recommendations is that since there 'are not any real, absolute, positive qualities and attributes in

a cigarette,' the most effective advertising is designed to 'reduce objections' to the product by presenting a picture or situation ambiguous enough to provide smokers with a rationale for their behavior and a means of repressing their health concerns about smoking."

The MARC report discussed in a later chapter how "starters" could be introduced to the Viceroy brand. The FTC report quoted the MARC report's discussion of how the young smoker related to cigarettes. "For them," the MARC report opined, "a cigarette, and the whole smoking process, is part of the illicit pleasure category. * * * In a young smoker's mind a cigarette falls into the same category with wine, beer, shaving, wearing a bra (or *purposely* not wearing one), declaration of independence and striving for self-identity. For the young starter, a cigarette is associated with introduction to sex life, with courtship, with smoking 'pot' and keeping late studying hours." FTC report at 17 (quoting MARC report) (emphasis in MARC report). The MARC report went on to suggest a strategy for attracting "starters" to the Viceroy brand based "on the following major parameters":

> Present the cigarette as one of a few initiations into the adult world.
>
> Present the cigarette as part of the illicit pleasure category of products and activities.
>
> In your ads create a situation taken from the day-to-day life of the young smoker but in an elegant manner have this situation touch on the basic symbols of the growing-up, maturity process.
>
> To the best of your ability, (considering some legal constraints), relate the cigarette to "pot," wine, beer, sex etc.
>
> Don't communicate health or health-related points.

FTC report at 18 (quoting MARC report). The FTC report then stated that Brown & Williamson had adopted many of the ideas contained in the MARC report in the development of an advertising campaign for Viceroy. Specifically, the report noted that in a document it had received directly from Brown & Williamson, rather than from an advertising agency or a firm hired by the advertising agency, Brown & Williamson had indicated that it must provide consumers with a rationalization for smoking and a "means of repressing their health concerns about smoking a full flavor Viceroy." FTC report at 18 (quoting Viceroy strategy paper dated March 3, 1976).

The Viceroy strategy paper also indicated that other major full flavor brands had either consciously or unconsciously "coped" with the smoking and health issues in advertising by appealing to repression. The strategy paper suggested that Viceroy's advertising objective should be to "communicate effectively that Viceroy is a satisfying flavorful cigarette which young adult smokers enjoy, by providing them a rationalization for smoking, or, a repression of the health concern they appear to need." FTC report at 19 (citing Viceroy strategy paper).

The FTC report then cited three Viceroy advertising strategies that were used in a six-month media campaign conducted in three test cities in 1976. The first campaign was the "satisfaction" campaign which was intended to provide a "rationalization." Specifically, the intention was to convey the message that "Viceroy is so satisfying that smokers can smoke fewer cigarettes and still receive the satisfaction they want." The second campaign, the "tension release" campaign, was intended to convince the smoker that Viceroy's satisfying flavor would help the smoker in a tense situation. The third campaign, the "feels good" campaign, was intended to repress concerns that smokers might have about smoking by justifying it with the simple slogan "if it feels good, do it; if it feels good, smoke it." FTC report at 20 (citing internal memorandum dated July 14, 1976). None of these campaigns was cited in the FTC report as an example of Viceroy implementing the MARC report strategy to relate the cigarette to "pot," wine, beer, and sex. The FTC report stated, however, that Brown & Williamson documents did indicate that the company had "translated the advice on how to attract young 'starters' into an advertising campaign featuring young adults in situations that the vast majority of young people probably would experience and in situations demonstrating adherence to a 'free and easy, hedonistic lifestyle.' " FTC report at 20 (citing document titled Viceroy Marketing/Advertising Strategy dated January 26, 1976).

After reviewing the report, Radutzky contacted members of the FTC staff who had drafted the report to confirm that the partial copy of the report he had received from the Kentucky newspaper was accurate. The staff members told Radutzky that they could not send him the confidential documents cited in the report but did confirm that the report and its findings were accurate.

Radutzky also spoke on at least two occasions with Brown & Williamson public relations officer Thomas Humber. At trial, CBS introduced two internal Viceroy documents, which were written by Humber for his superiors, that relate the substance of the conversations that Humber had with Radutzky. In a conversation on November 4, 1981, Humber stated that the internal Viceroy memoranda could only be understood in context. The context included the fact that the Ted Bates agency was told prior to their submission of the memo that it was in trouble on the Viceroy account because Brown & Williamson was unhappy with its work. Humber told Radutzky that Brown & Williamson had not requested any ad campaign similar to the one suggested by Bates. Moreover, he stated that Brown & Williamson had rejected the strategy embodied in the documents submitted by Bates. Humber also noted that "thus far [we] have been unable to find copies of the proposed ads, to the best of our knowledge, no ads as described by the memo were ever actually published." Radutzky was also informed that partly as a result of Brown & Williamson's dissatisfaction with the specific proposal submitted by Bates, Brown & Williamson had terminated Bates' participation in Viceroy advertising. In a conversation with Radutzky on November 5, Humber told Radutzky that all Brown & Williamson ads must have the approval of the legal department and the highest levels of senior management. He also stated that the legal department did not get involved in the creative process and did not review the ads until they "are at the point of worked-up ads." Humber stated that the proposals referred to in the FTC report were similar to a proposed libelous story that a young inexperienced reporter might submit to his editors but that was corrected by a news organization's editors and attorneys. Humber stated that in such a case no legitimate criticism could be leveled at the news organization. He clearly implied that because Brown & Williamson had never run any of the controversial proposals as ads, it would be unfair to criticize Brown & Williamson simply because such proposals had been made by individuals who could not authorize an ad campaign.

In addition to contacting Brown & Williamson, Radutzky, on Jacobson's request, conducted a search for "pot," wine, beer and sex ads that were used by Viceroy. Unable to locate any such ads, Radutzky reported the result of his search to Jacobson. Radutzky also commented to Jacobson prior to the broadcast that Jacobson's script for the broadcast omitted Brown & Williamson's statement that it had never adopted a "pot," wine, beer or sex strategy. Jacobson did not alter his script.

During the course of his investigation, Radutzky made contemporaneous interview notes and extensive handwritten notes on his copy of the FTC report. In addition, he developed an eighteen-page sample script for the broadcast. The sample script, which was duplicated at least six times and distributed to various people in the newsroom including Walter Jacobson, reported "both sides of the issue." The jury never saw much of Radutzky's work product. Prior to trial, Radutzky destroyed all of his contemporaneous interview notes, five of the ten pages of the FTC report including those pages that contained the recommendations from the MARC report, and fifteen of the original eighteen pages of his sample script. CBS was unable to produce any of the copies of the sample script that Radutzky had distributed in the newsroom.

Radutzky testified that he destroyed his materials as part of a general housecleaning after the original complaint in this case had been dismissed by the district court but before he became aware that Brown & Williamson appealed that dismissal. His destruction of the documents contravened a CBS retention policy that provides that once litigation has commenced "any and all related materials should be retained until specifically released." The policy also provides that "[o]bviously if there is a * * * pending legal action, our policy is to retain all pertinent materials unless specifically released by the Law Department." Although Radutzky conceded that he did destroy the documents without the approval of the Law Department at CBS, he stated that he was unaware that the policy existed.

When Radutzky destroyed the documents, he was no longer assigned to the Perspective unit and therefore his desk was in a completely different section of the newsroom. Nonetheless, he apparently made a point of "cleaning house" in the Perspective section of the newsroom even though he had not worked there for several months.

Brown & Williamson attempted to prove that Jacobson's charges were false by introducing every Viceroy advertisement published between 1975 and 1982. They argued to the jury that none of these advertisements was a "pot," wine, beer, or sex ad. In addition, Robert Pittman, the Brown & Williamson Vice President whose approval was required before any Viceroy ad could be published, testified that he had never seen the MARC report prior to the litigation in this case. Pittman also stated that Brown & Williamson had never asked Bates to design any "pot," wine, beer, and sex ads. William Scholz, the Bates employee in charge of the Viceroy account, confirmed that Brown & Williamson had never asked Bates to utilize a "pot," wine, beer, and sex strategy in developing advertisements.

Brown & Williamson put forth evidence that it adhered vigorously to the Cigarette Advertising Code, which bars advertising to persons under 21. In addition to adhering to the Code, Brown & Williamson took the additional step of establishing a detailed procedure to ensure that its advertising agencies did not use models who either were or appeared to be younger than 25. When undertaking advertising campaigns that involved the distribution of samples, Brown & Williamson required the individuals distributing the samples to sign statements promising not to distribute cigarettes to people under 21.

Walter Jacobson also testified at trial. Jacobson indicated that he had read the FTC report prior to delivering his Perspective and was aware that the FTC report was quoting a document prepared by Market and Research Counselors. He agreed that the way in which the Perspective was delivered, with the Viceroy graphics on the screen at the time he was referring to the "pot," wine, beer, and sex strategy, would convey the impression that the "pot," wine, beer, and sex comment was made by Viceroy itself rather than MARC. After agreeing that such an impression would be created, Jacobson added that "I even said that 'Viceroy says.' "

Jacobson's testimony indicated that he had reviewed Radutzky's sample script prior to delivering the Perspective. Jacobson corroborated part of Radutzky's testimony by confirming that Radutzky had told him that he had been unable to find any ads showing that Brown & Williamson had implemented a "pot," wine, beer, and sex advertising strategy. Jacobson was also aware that Radutzky had spoken with Brown & Williamson and that the company denied adopting the strategy and therefore had no advertisements that they could supply that would reflect that strategy. According to Jacobson, he paraphrased Viceroy's denial in the broadcast when he stated "Viceroy insists * * * whose fault is it that children are smoking? It's not ours."

Jacobson also agreed, at least at one point, that it would be fair to say that when he wrote the Perspective script he wrote it in the present tense with respect to Viceroy and the purported "pot," wine, beer, and sex strategy. For example, he agreed that when he used a phrase such as "[t]hat's what Viceroy is saying," he realized that it would be interpreted by any reasonable listener as referring to the present tense. At other points during his testimony, however, Jacobson appeared to state that some language used during the broadcast was past tense. While recognizing that there was no indication in the Perspective that the strategy mentioned in the MARC report had been recommended in 1975, six years before the broadcast, Jacobson testified that because the FTC report described it as "the Viceroy strategy" he did not believe that he gave the viewer "an impression of time that varies from the facts." Under further questioning, Jacobson did agree that the phrase "[a]n attempt should be made, says the Viceroy slicksters' to relate the cigarette to 'pot,' wine, and beer" would be "more current" than the phrase "the Viceroy strategy."[2]

Jacobson also noted that there was a distinction between a report, an analysis, a commentary and an editorial. An example of a report, according to Jacobson, would be if a newsperson went on the air and said "[t]he FTC says that Viceroy did such and such, and Viceroy says it did not." He agreed that when delivering such a statement a reporter should try to be fair and accurate. Jacobson also stated that "[m]y life is research" and indicated that what he said in the Perspective was "absolutely true."

On direct examination, Jacobson's counsel brought out his client's state of mind at the time of the broadcast. Jacobson asserted that he "believed" at the time he delivered the Perspective that it was truthful and that it was a fair and accurate summary of what the Federal Trade Commission had said about Viceroy cigarettes. Jacobson also testified about what he "intend[ed]" to inform the viewers about Viceroy when he "sat down to write" the Perspective. When cross examined, Jacobson confirmed that he had testified on direct examination about what he was thinking when he wrote the script and attempted to refute the allegation that he "really [had] no recollection at all of what [he] thought about in" preparing the script by stating that such an assertion was "absolutely untrue." Brown & Williamson's counsel then read Jacobson's 1984 deposition in which the following exchange took place:

Question: I just want to know if you have a recollection whether in 1981, when you called the manufacturers of Viceroy cigarettes liars, you were attempting then to be objective?

Jacobson: I don't remember what I was thinking now when I wrote that three and a half years ago.

Question: Can you recall whether (when) you wrote the November 11, 1981 script, you were trying to fairly present both sides of the question?

Jacobson: I don't remember what I was thinking when I wrote that script. It's hard to remember three and a half years ago.

Question: You don't remember what was in your mind?

Jacobson: Right.

Question: You do remember you wrote the script though?

Jacobson: I don't remember writing it. I do see it.

Question: You don't remember writing it?

Jacobson: Yes, I mean—I don't remember sitting at my typewriter, what I was thinking and how my hands were working. I see the script. It has a date. I wrote it, obviously, and I remember being involved in a series of reports on that subject.

On redirect examination, Jacobson asserted that his recollection of his state of mind at the time of the broadcast had improved from the time of his deposition to the time of the trial because he had "gone over everything that ha[d] been given to [him] by a whole team of lawyers" including the script that he used during his Perspective and the videotape of the actual broadcast. Jacobson stated that as a consequence his memory was jarred and he was able to "just

---

2. Jacobson also agreed that when he said "Viceroy slicksters" he was talking about Brown & Williamson and the people who make Viceroy cigarettes as opposed to their advertising agency.

recall more specifically some things that I didn't recall from before."

* * *

Disregarding Jacobson's testimony (including his admission that he intended to attribute the MARC language to Viceroy), the evidence shows that Jacobson received and reviewed the FTC report. In addition, he was aware that Radutzky's search for "pot," wine, beer, and sex ads had been unsuccessful and that Brown & Williamson had denied publishing ads implementing the strategy. Defendants argue vigorously that each of these facts, standing alone, cannot provide clear and convincing proof of actual malice. Respondent Brief at 26–31 (citing *Time, Inc. v. Pape*, 401 U.S. 279, 289–92 (1971) (rational misinterpretation of government report that "bristled with ambiguities" does not create jury issue on actual malice); *Edwards v. National Audubon Society, Inc.*, 556 F.2d 113, 121 (2d Cir.), *cert. denied*, 434 U.S. 1002 (1977) (actual malice cannot be predicated solely on mere denials)); see also *Bose*, 466 U.S. at 511 (there is a significant difference between proof of actual malice and mere proof of falsity); *Woods v. Evansville Press*, 791 F.2d 480, 489 (7th Cir. 1986) (reporter's journalism skills are not on trial in a libel case). The cases defendants cite are unlike this one because none of them combines a distortion of a government report with a vehement denial of the "pot," wine, beer, and sex charge and an investigation by the journalist that tended to corroborate the denial. Moreover, none of those cases had evidence of document destruction. We conclude that when the intentional destruction of the sample script (which Jacobson did review prior to delivering the broadcast) is considered along with the distortion of the FTC report, Brown & Williamson's denial, and the corroboration of the denial, Brown & Williamson has met its burden of proving that Walter Jacobson and CBS acted with actual malice.[9]

Taking only the first two factors into account, we conclude that the district court's decision upholding the jury's punitive damage award was clearly correct. Brown & Williamson's attorney's fees were $1,360,000 prior to post-trial motions. Jacobson's net worth including his contract with CBS was over $5,000,000, while CBS's net worth was approximately one and one-half billion dollars. The punitive damage award of $50,000 against Jacobson is a modest one considering his net worth. It might provide some deterrent value without being destructive. In light of the attorney's fees that Brown & Williamson incurred and CBS's substantial net worth, the $2,000,000 award against CBS is reasonable. The award might provide some deterrence to future misconduct and yet will not burden CBS with a debt that it cannot easily discharge.[13] See also *Gertz v. Robert Welch, Inc.*, 680 F.2d 527, 540 (7th Cir. 1982), *cert. denied*, 459 U.S. 1226 (1983) (upholding $300,000 punitive damage award).

One of the most important functions of the court system in the United States is to protect the freedom of the press. See, *e.g., Bose v. Consumers Union*, 466 U.S. 485 (1984); *New York Times v. United States*, 403 U.S. 713 (1971); *New York Times v. Sullivan*, 376 U.S. 254 (1964). The federal courts of appeals including this one have played an important role in fulfilling this function. See, *e.g., Tavoulareas v. Piro*, 817 F.2d 762 (D.C. Cir. 1987) (en banc); *Sunward Corporation v. Dun & Bradstreet, Inc.*, 811 F.2d 511, 538 (10th Cir. 1987); *Woods v. Evansville Press*, 791 F.2d 480, 489 (7th Cir. 1986). In considering the merits of this case, this court has granted the defendants the fullest possible review; the standard of review that we have used, giving essentially no deference to the jury's findings, may be far broader than the review to which the defendants are entitled. See *Bose*, 466 U.S. at 499–500 (constitutionally based rule of independent review permits reviewing court to give "due regard" to the trial court's opportunity to observe the demeanor of the witnesses). After conducting such a review, it is unfortunate that we are forced to conclude that this case does not involve freedom of the press. Rather, it is one in which there is clear and convincing evidence

---

9. Brown & Williamson also argues that pressures to produce interesting stories brought on by the November "sweeps" is "strong proof of actual malice." Ratings during "sweeps" months such as November and May are especially important in determining the rates that advertisers will pay to stations to promote their products. * * *

13. Defendants also argue that the punitive damage award violates the Eighth Amendment which provides that "excessive bail shall not be required, nor excessive fines imposed, nor cruel and unusual punishments inflicted." Even if we were to accept the defendants' argument that the excessive fines clause applies to civil proceedings, we conclude that the punitive damage award in this case is not excessive.

that a local television journalist acted with actual malice when he made false statements about Brown & Williamson Tobacco Corporation. Because false statements of fact made with actual malice are not protected by the First Amendment, this court is required to affirm the district court's finding that Jacobson and CBS libeled Brown & Williamson.

Affirmed in Part, Reversed in Part.

COMMENT

In a case that gave her fans great satisfaction, comedienne Carol Burnett sustained a libel judgment in her favor against the *National Enquirer*.[114] A tipster reported to the magazine's gossip columnist that Burnett, near intoxication and rowdy in a Washington restaurant, had offered to share her dessert with none other than Henry Kissinger, had spilled wine on customers, and in turn had water spilled on her—a boisterous scene to say the least. Sources in Washington agreed with the gossip columnist that the tipster was untrustworthy (he would later himself become the magazine's gossip columnist). Burnett, it is true, had passed a fancy dessert to some other patrons, and she had had a brief and friendly conversation with Kissinger, but that was hardly newsworthy. The story needed embellishment and got it. It was published with all kinds of evidence of its falsity lying about.

A halfhearted and partial correction followed, but that was not enough. Burnett was especially sensitive to problems of alcoholism: both parents had died at forty-six from complications brought on by alcohol abuse. She was active in anti-alcohol causes and did not appreciate being portrayed as a hypocrite. Jury awards of $300,000 in compensatory damages and $1,300,000 in punitive damages were reduced to $50,000 and $750,000, respectively. The latter was further reduced to $150,000 by an appeals court.[115]

"Although failure to investigate fully," says a libel authority, "will not by itself be sufficient to prove actual malice, a failure to pursue the most obvious available sources for corrobora-

tion may be clear and convincing evidence of actual malice."[116]

Falsity is not to be confused with actual malice. Without a demonstration of falsity, the question of fault need not be reached. In a second and contemporaneous case involving a general, the court made the distinction between these two elements of libel equally as clear as had been done in the *Sharon* case. In a 1982 *60 Minutes* broadcast, "The Uncounted Enemy: A Vietnam Deception," General William Westmoreland was accused of conspiring to deflate the reported buildup of enemy troops facing his armies and of inflating the number of enemy dead. Westmoreland sued CBS for $120 million but abandoned his case in exchange for a rather cautious statement from the network saying that it had never intended to impugn the general's patriotism or loyalty. Again the jury had been pondering an answer to the first question—falsity. When two former aides to the general indicated that some of their testimony would contradict his, the general's chances of proving falsity diminished, at least in his own mind and in the minds of his legal supporters.

Though no damages were paid to Westmoreland, CBS paid dearly in terms of its credibility. CBS veteran Burton Benjamin, in an in-house investigation, found imbalance, coddling of sympathetic witnesses, misleading editing, and lack of supervision by editors.[117] Outside critics were even more vehement in their faulting of *Time* and CBS in the cases of the generals: the media giants were wrong, they refused to admit error, and they deployed huge financial and legal resources to obscure the truth. The question of actual malice, however, was moot in both cases. With stronger legal support, Westmoreland might have been able to prevail; most post-trial critics seemed to be on his side.

At the same time, the presiding judge in the *Westmoreland* case wrote: "Publishers and reporters do not commit a libel in a public figure case by publishing unfair one sided attacks. . . . A publisher who honestly believes in the truth of his accusations . . . is under no obligation under

---

114. *Burnett v. National Enquirer,* 7 Med.L.Rptr. 1321 (Cal.Sup.Ct. 1981).

115. *Burnett v. National Enquirer,* 9 Med.L.Rptr. 1921, 144 Cal.App.3d 991 (1983).

116. Rodney A. Smolla, *Law of Defamation,* Sec. 3.18(1) at 3–42 (1986).

117. Burton Benjamin, *Fair Play: CBS, General Westmoreland, and How a Television Documentary Went Wrong* (New York: Harper & Row, 1988).

the libel law to treat the subject of his accusations fairly or evenhandedly."[118]

When ABC used hidden cameras and planted employees to do a critical story of the way a food chain outlet handled meat, the company sued for fraud, negligent supervision, trespass, *respondeat superior* liability, unfair and deceptive trade practices, civil conspiracy, violations of the Racketeer Influenced and Corrupt Organizations Act (RICO), and federal wiretapping violations. The RICO and trespass allegations were dismissed on an initial motion by the defendant. To win a libel suit, though, said the court, the company would have to show falsity and actual malice, a difficult burden under the circumstances. Video techniques used in the story did spark a wide discussion about newsgathering ethics, however.[119]

An Alaska trial court did not err in granting the *Juneau Empire* summary judgment, said the Alaska Supreme Court, after the paper published criticism of a bankrupt company and its president and principal investor for the way hazardous wastes were handled at a project site. The plaintiff was a public figure, and the story dealt with a matter of public concern. The reporter's testimony that she published the story in good faith was not adequately countered by any evidence of actual malice on her part. And the newspaper's refusal to retract by itself did not demonstrate actual malice.[120]

Inadvertent transposition of the names of a rape defendant and a public defender was insufficient to establish actual malice.[121] A reporter's misunderstanding of the difference between charges leading to an arrest and formal charges brought by a state attorney did not constitute actual malice, although in this case a next-day retraction might have helped.[122] Nor was it actual malice to demonstrate confusion over the meaning of a court file. Inexperience, said the New Jersey Supreme Court, does not add up to

actual malice, but slipshod journalism does not help the credibility of the newspaper. And, as shall be noted, an inaccurate recounting or misrepresentation of a judicial process does not provide the media with a fair report privilege.[123] Even the use of multiple sources may negate a charge of actual malice.[124]

Regardless of the number of sources, courts will ask, how were they used? How discriminating was the editor in choosing sources? How probing and organized was the investigation into wrongdoing? What confirmation was sought? Was anything important learned from research omitted from the published story? Did the reporter have contradictory evidence before her? Was there deliberate distortion of the material? When the mayor of San Francisco sued *Look* magazine for alleging that he had strong personal ties to organized crime, it turned out that the reporter had relied on a single, uncorroborated underworld source and that apparent contradictory official sources were ignored.[125]

Reliance on a single, biased source, however, is not always indicative of actual malice. Craig Unger, relying on a former Israeli intelligence officer thought to be reliable by both FBI and congressional investigators, alleged in an *Esquire* magazine article that the Reagan-Bush campaign had engaged in an "arms for hostages" deal with Iran, leading to a delay in the release of American hostages until after the 1980 presidential elections. Robert McFarlane, former national security adviser, sued and lost. The court noted that the author had no information at hand either refuting his thesis or suggesting that he should investigate further.[126] Nor did an editor's failure to investigate an allegation concerning a public official in a letter to the editor constitute actual malice.[127]

118. *Westmoreland v. CBS, Inc.*, 11 Med.L.Rptr. 1703, 601 F.Supp. 66 (S.D.N.Y. 1984).

119. *Food Lion v. Capital Cities/ABC Inc.*, 23 Med.L.Rptr. 1673, 887 F.Supp. 81 (M.D.N.C. 1995).

120. *Mount Juneau Enterprises, Inc. v. Juneau Empire*, 23 Med.L.Rptr. 1685, 891 P.2d 829 (Alaska 1995).

121. *Parrish v. Gannett River States Publishing Corp.*, 22 Med.L.Rptr. 1413 (D.C.S.Miss. 1994).

122. *Clark v. Fernandina Beach News-Leader, Inc.*, 22 Med.L.Rptr. 2013 (Fla.Cir.Ct. 1994).

123. *Costello v. Ocean County Observer*, 22 Med.L.Rptr. 2129, 643 A.2d 1012 (N.J.S.Ct. 1994).

124. *Grutzmacher v. Chicago Sun Times, Inc.*, 22 Med.L.Rptr. 2397 (Ill.Cir.Ct. 1994).

125. *Alioto v. Cowles Communications, Inc.*, 2 Med.L.Rptr. 1801, 430 F.Supp. 1363 (N.D.Cal. 1977), *aff'd*, 6 Med.L.Rptr. 1573, 623 F.2d 616 (9th Cir. 1980), *cert. denied*, 449 U.S. 1102 (1981).

126. *McFarlane v. Esquire Magazine*, 22 Med.L.Rptr. 2033 (D.C.D.C. 1994).

127. *Pasculli v. Jersey Journal*, 7 Med.L.Rptr. 2574 (N.J. Super.Ct. 1981).

A rare example of a finding of actual malice occurred where an author before publication announced that he didn't like the plaintiff, then was advised that his information was false, and with time at his disposal made no further effort to confirm his facts.[128]

NEGLIGENCE

Mafia Kingfish, a book published by McGraw-Hill, was said by a Louisiana court to have embellished beyond all proportion a report of a House Select Committee on Assassinations and to have relied on unreliable sources. The book alleged that the plaintiff, a physician, was tied to the Mafia and had a role in hiring James Earl Ray to assassinate Dr. Martin Luther King, Jr. A book that would forever remain in the public domain, said the court, accused the plaintiff of a heinous crime. There was, the court added, clear and convincing evidence of actual malice, but as a private person, the doctor would only have to prove negligence by a preponderance of the evidence to support his claim.[129] Some states would have required proof of negligence by clear and convincing evidence.

Negligence is a lesser degree of fault. *Gertz* invited the states to define for themselves the appropriate standard of fault for defamation of private persons. Most states have accepted the invitation and follow the negligence rule of *Gertz.* Some have extended the standard to actual malice where private persons are involved in matters of public concern, suggesting the sturdiness of the *Rosenbloom* public issue test. Certainly, state laws and constitutions will continue to play a fluid and decisive role in guiding the evolution of libel in the states.

New York uses a test for private plaintiffs that falls somewhere between actual malice and negligence and tracks with the "prudent publisher" test of the *Butts-Walker* cases. A New York public school teacher sued a Utica newspaper for reporting erroneously that he was part of a trio arrested for a serious drug offense involving heroin. A trial court denied the newspaper's motion for summary judgment, but the appellate division reversed and was affirmed by the court of appeals, New York's highest court. The news report was said to fall within a sphere of legitimate public concern. In such circumstances, a New York plaintiff may recover only if it is established by a preponderance of evidence that the publisher acted in a *grossly irresponsible* manner and without due consideration for standards of information gathering and dissemination ordinarily followed by responsible journalists. The offending article was written after two authoritative sources had been consulted, and it was not published until it had been checked by at least two persons other than the writer.[130]

Negligence has been defined according to deadline pressure, the degree of public interest in a story, and the potential damage done to the subject of a report, given the intended audience. In applying the "standards of the profession," the door is opened to "expert" testimony, and this has become a particular temptation for professors of journalism.[131]

Whatever the standard of fault a plaintiff may have to meet, it is always safer for a reporter to have more than a single source and to have carried out his own investigation into serious allegations of wrongdoing. Assess the reliability of sources; some will have axes to grind. Check and recheck is still the best guide to accuracy. Contact the person about to be defamed when possible. Correct and apologize when wrong. Remember that it is difficult for jurors, drawn from the public at large, to believe that a false and defamatory story is written without negligence or actual malice.

Publications crossing state lines often have to defend themselves in federal courts. Although federal courts may defer to state libel laws, they can be expected to follow *Gertz* in defining actual malice and negligence.

To this point, numerous references have been made to "summary judgment" and "damages" without explaining what they entail. Those loose ends must now be gathered in.

128. *Stevens v. Sun Publishing Co.,* 240 S.E.2d 812 (S.C. 1978), *cert. denied,* 436 U.S. 945 (1978). See also *Widener v. Pacific Gas & Electric Corp.,* 75 Cal.App.3d 415 (1977), *cert. denied,* 436 U.S. 918 (1978).

129. *Deleo v. Davis,* 23 Med.L.Rptr. 1756 (E.D.La. 1995).

130. *Chapadeau v. Utica Observer-Dispatch,* 1 Med.L.Rptr. 1693, 379 N.Y.S.2d 61 (1975). In *Greenberg v. CBS,* 5 Med.L.Rptr. 1470, 419 N.Y.S.2d 988 (1978), the words "gross negligence" were substituted.

131. *Restatement (Second) of Torts,* sec. 5808, comment (h).

SUMMARY JUDGMENT

A motion for summary judgment in a libel case is made by the defendant communicator to prevent the case from going to trial. The motion is based on the assumption that there is no dispute as to the facts of the case and that the law is on the defendant's side. A next step, a motion to dismiss, has the same purpose. Parties to the suit make arguments in court, and the judge decides whether the case warrants dismissal or trial. The granting of a motion to dismiss frequently means that the plaintiff will be unable to show with convincing clarity that a defendant published with actual malice. Ninety percent of libel cases end in either a summary judgment or a dismissal. "Requiring media defendants to undergo full trial in nonmeritorious libel claims would stifle the constitutional guarantee of freedom of press," said a Louisiana court.[132] A federal court concluded: "Summary judgment is the preferred means of dealing with first amendment cases due to the chilling of first amendment rights inherent in expensive and time-consuming litigation.[133] Summary judgment was also warranted when a plaintiff was unable to cast any doubt on the truthfulness of *Prime Time Live* allegations that an "evangelist" had lied to his financial supporters about nonexistent orphanages, the geographic origin and use made of prayer paraphernalia, organized crime and drug smuggling ties, and a lavish lifestyle. In short, a religious scam was being conducted by a cynical and fraudulent individual and his money-raising organization.[134] One of the best expressions of the rationale for summary judgment in libel cases was made by Judge Skelly Wright in a 1966 case:

> In the First Amendment area, summary procedures are even more essential. For the stake here, if harassment succeeds, is free debate. One of the purposes of the *Times* principle, in addition to protecting persons from being cast in damages in libel suits filed by public officials, is to prevent persons from being discouraged in the full and free exercise of their First Amendment rights with respect to the conduct of their government. The threat of being put to the defense of a lawsuit brought by a popular public official may be as chilling to the exercise of First Amendment freedoms as fear of the outcome of the lawsuit itself, especially to advocates of unpopular causes. All persons who desire to exercise their right to criticize public officials are not as well equipped financially as the Post to defend against a trial on the merits. Unless persons, including newspapers, desiring to exercise their First Amendment rights are assured freedom from the harassment of lawsuits, they will tend to become self-censors. And to this extent debate on public issues and the conduct of public officials will become less uninhibited, less robust, and less wide-open, for self-censorship affecting the whole public is "hardly less virulent for being privately administered."[135]

Summary judgment was denied, however, where a newspaper inaccurately quoted a federal prosecutor as saying charges would be filed shortly against a Department of Public Works official, when in fact charges were never intended to be filed. Left unresolved, said the court, were genuine issues of fact on falsity and actual malice.[136] In a more serious case, an attorney had successfully represented a young girl in obtaining a multimillion dollar verdict for sexual abuse against her by her parents. A television talk show picked up the story and asked for photographs of the parents. The girl's attorney mistakenly sent pictures of her godparents who had nothing to do with the offense. The photographs were aired, and the godparents sued. Summary judgment for the broadcaster was reversed by a Minnesota appellate court because an accusation of child abuse is defamatory *per se* and does not lend itself to summary judgment. Paradoxically, the court went on to say that the godparents would still have to present evidence of harm to their reputations, a seeming contradiction in that libel *per se* statements are defamatory as a matter of law.[137] Other courts, notably the Second and Sixth Circuit Courts of

---

132. *Sassone v. Elder,* 22 Med.L.Rptr. 1049, 626 So.2d 345 (La.Sup.Ct. 1993).

133. *Hickey v. Capital Cities/ABC,* 792 F.Supp. 1195 (D.Or. 1992), *aff'd,* 999 F.2d 543 (9th Cir. 1993). The leading case on this side of the argument appears to be *Anderson v. Liberty Lobby,* 477 U.S. 242 (1986).

134. *Tilton v. Capital Cities/ABC Inc.,* 23 Med.L.Rptr. 2057, 905 F.Supp. 1514 (N.D.Okla. 1995).

135. *Washington Post Co. v. Keough,* 365 F.2d 965 (D.C.Cir. 1966).

136. *St. Surin v. Virgin Islands Daily News Inc.,* 22 Med.L.Rptr. 1545, 21 F.3d 1309 (3d Cir. 1994).

137. *Richie v. Paramount Pictures Corp.,* 532 N.W.2d 235 (Minn.App. 1995).

Appeal, have been neutral on the issue, preferring neither the granting nor the denial of motions for summary judgment.[138]

If motions for summary judgment or dismissal are denied, the judgment of the court can be appealed, although this is rare. The initial judgments can be affirmed, reversed, or reversed and remanded (sent back to the judge for reshaping). Before a case goes to a jury but after the evidence has been presented, it is possible for the judge to take the case out of the jury's hands and announce a directed verdict for the defense. Evidence for the defense must be compelling for a directed verdict, so it is also rare.

In a trial by jury, plaintiffs able to sustain the burden of proof usually receive a verdict in their favor and are awarded money damages. If not, the case is dismissed. Trial court judgments can be appealed and are affirmed, completely reversed, or reversed and remanded, and damages can be reduced in size (remittur) or enlarged (additur), although the latter seldom happens.

Actual malice is rarely found in libel cases, but the search for it, both in the discovery period when both sides gather and display their evidence, and in the courtroom, can be frightfully expensive in terms of time, energy, and money. Findings of negligence are also rare because private persons bring a relatively small proportion of libel suits. When they do bring suit and win, their chances of being reversed on appeal are only one-third that of public persons.

In a brief to a Minnesota district court on behalf of the Minneapolis *Star Tribune,* a Minneapolis lawyer[139] demonstrated how summary judgment should be approached. The dean of an unaccredited and, as it turned out, ephemeral law school had sued the newspaper for factual, dispassionate reporting on a faculty/student revolt within the school. The newspaper's attorney mustered all the relevant libel defenses in short, pithy paragraphs under the following headings: plaintiff must establish each element of his case by clear and convincing evidence; the statements of which plaintiff complains are true; certain statements of which plaintiff complains are nonactionable expressions of opinion; cer-

tain statements are not defamatory; the allegedly defamatory statements are privileged under the constitutions of the United States and Minnesota and at common law because plaintiff is a public figure and the statements concern matters of public interest and plaintiff can recover damages only upon clear and convincing evidence of actual malice; certain articles are conditionally privileged as fair and accurate reports of official actions and public proceedings; certain statements of which plaintiff complains are privileged as responses to his own accusations; others are privileged as neutral reportage of newsworthy statements and events; Minnesota law bars most of plaintiff's claims for general and punitive damages; and any award of punitive damages would be unconstitutional. Not only was the $14.7 million libel suit dismissed, but the plaintiff was ordered by the court to reimburse the newspaper for attorney's fees. An appeals court reversed the fees judgment.

DAMAGES

At least in the absence of a showing of actual malice, *presumed* damages have not survived *Gertz.* Perhaps *nominal* damages, token awards of a dollar, for example, symbolizing moral or technical victories rather than compensation for injury to reputation, also have disappeared with *Gertz,* since that case requires a showing of *actual injury* in all cases.

Compensatory damages in libel cases, which are meant to compensate for damage to one's reputation, take two forms: *actual* damages, which make amends for reputational injury and the mental distress that follows; and *special* damages, designed to pay back proven out-of-pocket money losses, say, medical expenses or documented loss of business income or employment. Confusion has resulted from the fact that in the past some authorities have used the terms *actual* and *special* interchangeably. Compensatory damages are sometimes called general damages or are considered a subset of general damages.

In many jurisdictions, special damages have to be proven for awards to be made in cases claiming *slander* (spoken defamation), in libel *per quod* (libel by implication or innuendo), and in *trade libel* (disparagement of someone's service or product). These forms of defamation fre-

138. *Yiamouyiannis v. Consumers Union,* 619 F.2d 932, 939–940 (2d Cir. 1980), *cert. denied,* 449 U.S. 839 (1980); *Schultz v. Newsweek,* 668 F.2d 911, 917 (6th Cir. 1982).
139. John P. Borger of Faegre & Benson.

quently require a showing of common law malice as well—ill will, hostility, a desire for revenge.

Punitive or *exemplary* damages, leading to what have come to be called "megaverdicts," often seem more useful in putting a publication out of business than in punishing it or making it an example for others. Punitive damages may also be a surviving form of presumed damages because there are no clear limits on the sums juries can award and on what grounds. Lawyers call them "smart money" because their gargantuan amounts "sting" defendants. The *Gertz* Court tied punitive damages to a showing of actual malice in what seemed to some to be an effort to discourage their use in all but the most egregious cases. At the same time, *Gertz* encouraged state courts to go their own way in fashioning their libel rules. And state courts have done just that.

Washington, Oregon, Massachusetts, and Michigan generally disallow punitive damages in libel cases under any circumstances. In other states, California and New York, for example, *common law malice* (ill will, spite, a desire for revenge) must be shown, as well as actual malice, to support a claim for punitive damages. In an unfortunate case of mistaken identity, discussed later in this chapter, New York's highest court, in granting a new trial to ABC-TV, largely on the issue of actual malice, had this to say about punitive damages:

Actual malice, as defined in *New York Times Co. v. Sullivan* (376 US 254), is insufficient by itself to justify an award of punitive damages, because that malice focuses on the defendant's state of mind in relation to the truth or falsity of the published information (*see, e.g., McCoy v. Hearst Corp.,* 727 P2d 711, 736 [Cal. 1986] [13 Med.L.Rptr. 2169], *cert denied* 481 US 1041; *compare Liberman v. Gelstein,* 80 NY2d 429, 437). This does not measure up to the level of outrage or malice underlying the public policy which would allow an award of punitive damages, i.e., "to punish a person for outrageous conduct which is malicious, wanton, reckless, or in willful disregard for another's rights" (*Vassiliades v. Garfinkle's, Brooks Bros.,* 492 A2d 580, 593 [D.C.] [11 Med.L.Rptr. 2057]; *see also, Liberman v. Gelstein,* 80 NY2d 429, *supra; Hartford Accident Indemnity Co. v. Village of Hempstead,* 48 NY2d 218, 227). This kind of common law malice focuses on the defendant's mental state in relation to the plaintiff and the motive in publishing the falsity—the pointed factors that punitive damages are intended to remedy.

While theoretically, and upon proof and instructions, punitive damages may be available in such cases, the evidence on this record did not support the conclusion that Prozeralik was reported as the victim of this violent crime out of hatred, ill will, spite, criminal mental state or that traditionally required variety of common law malice. Whether that could be shown on the new trial remains to be seen and demonstrated.[140]

Some states prohibit punitive damages when a request for a retraction is honored. Some consider a preponderance of evidence rather than clear and convincing evidence a sufficient level of evidence for punitive damages. Courts are divided on whether or not punitive damages depend upon a prior award of actual damages.

A development obviously distressing to defendants and their attorneys has been the propensity of some courts to assign damages according to a calculation of a defendant's net worth, the stated purpose being to punish and deter reprehensible conduct, not to destroy. Thus, in *Brown & Williamson v. Jacobson,*[141] a case that dramatically illustrates the concept of actual malice, the court measured damages against CBS's net worth of $1 billion and the commentator's assets of $5 million. Similarly, in Wayne Newton's suit against NBC, the network's net worth of $2 billion was computed by a federal district court in Nevada in constructing appropriate damages. The case against NBC was later reversed on the grounds that the network was not responsible for negative inferences concerning Newton that audience members may have drawn from its reports. A similar computation was made by California courts in the *Burnett* case.

Sometimes, in such judicial maneuvers, the purposes of the First Amendment become secondary. The result may be what Justice Powell in *Gertz* called "intolerable self-censorship."

Traditionally, courts have been instructed to make certain that punitive damages bear some relationship to the actual harm done or to the amount of actual damages awarded. Media lawyers argue that punitive damages thwart the central purpose of the First Amendment. Plaintiff attorneys argue that they discourage irresponsible

---

140. *Prozeralik v. Capital Cities Communications Inc.,* 21 Med.L.Rptr. 2257, 626 N.E.2d 34 (N.Y. 1993).
141. 827 F.2d 1119 (7th Cir. 1987).

journalism.[142] Congressional efforts to limit punitive damages in civil litigation generally have led to similar debates.

Excessive awards in punitive damages are often reduced by appeals courts, but not always. In 1993, the U.S. Supreme Court affirmed an award of $19,000 in compensatory damages and $10 million in punitive damages.[143] In a case that has kept the *Philadelphia Inquirer* in court for more than twenty-three years, a second jury award of $31.5 million in punitive damages, tacked on to $2.5 million in compensatory damages, was held to be excessive. It was reduced to $21.5 million, providing scant consolation to the newspaper. The plaintiff, a former assistant district attorney, claimed that the newspaper had engaged in a deliberate effort to destroy his reputation and public service career. A trial court agreed, finding actual malice in the lack of supervision given to what it called a mentally unstable reporter.[144] On April 2, 1996, a few days before the deadline for making a final appeal to the U.S. Supreme Court, the *Inquirer* agreed to a settlement for an undisclosed sum in the case that had begun in 1973.

In 1985, in the case of *Dun & Bradstreet v. Greenmoss Builders,*[145] the Supreme Court seemed to be endorsing a return to the discarded rule of presumed damages when it held that presumed and punitive damages, to use the Court's language, could be awarded "even absent a showing of actual malice" where *no* matters of public concern were involved. Perhaps contradicting its own holding in *Gertz,* the Court said that private plaintiffs in nonpublic situations might recover punitive damages *without* a showing of actual malice. Upheld was an award of $300,000 in punitive damages to a builder who had been mistakenly referred to as bankrupt in a credit reporting agency's newsletter that was sent to five subscribers.

Punitive damages in general have been under attack in the U.S. Congress. Under a House pro-

posal, for example, punitive damages would be limited to three times what was awarded in general damages. In the absence of state or federal legislation, however, libel defendants will have to depend on state constitutions or the First Amendment to protect them from excessive awards in punitive damages.

PUBLIC OR PRIVATE PLAINTIFF?

Courts have provided no sure way of distinguishing between public and private plaintiffs. Context is important. At first glance both Elmer Gertz and Mary Alice Firestone looked like public people. Firestone, a wealthy Palm Beach socialite, may have been a public figure in Palm Beach, even in Florida, and might have had to prove actual malice had she brought suit against the *Miami Herald.* In a national arena, however, she was closer to a nobody and entitled to private-plaintiff status in her libel suit against *Time,* a national news magazine. Justice William Rehnquist, writing for the Court in 1976, defined her as a private person who had "not thrust herself into the forefront of any particular public controversy" but who "was compelled to go to court by the state in order to obtain legal release from the bonds of matrimony."[146]

Context determined Firestone's status, making her a private person. The journalist, then, should pose these questions in trying to determine a plaintiff's legal status: (1) Is there a public controversy, and did it exist before the offending publication appeared? (2) Did the plaintiff voluntarily and prominently participate in the controversy so as to affect its outcome? (3) Did the plaintiff have access to communication media to dispute damaging publications?[147]

If the answer to all of these questions is yes, then the plaintiff may be what the courts call a *vortex* or *limited-purpose public figure:* people

142. For conflicting views on punitive damages, see, Jerome A. Barron, *Punitive Damages in Libel Cases: First Amendment Equalizer,* 47 Wash. & Lee L.Rev. 105 (1990), and P. Cameron DeVore and Marshall J. Nelson, *Punitive Damages in Libel Cases after Browning-Ferris,* 12 Comm-Ent 153 (1989).

143. *TXO Production Corp. v. Alliance Resources Corp.,* 113 S.Ct. 2711 (1993).

144. *Sprague v. Walter,* 656 A.2d 890 (Pa.Sup.Ct. 1995).

145. 472 U.S. 749 (1985).

146. *Time, Inc. v. Firestone,* 1 Med.L.Rptr. 1665, 424 U.S. 448, 96 S.Ct. 958 (1976).

147. For similar tests of vortex public-figure status, see, *Fitzgerald v. Penthouse International,* 525 F.Supp. 585, 592 (D.Md. 1981, *aff'd in part and rev'd in part,* 691 F.2d 666 (4th Cir. 1982), *cert. denied,* 460 U.S. 1024 (1983); *Greenberg, CBS,* 69 N.Y.A.D.2d 694, 704–705 (2d Dept. 1979); *Clark v. ABC,* 684 F.2d 1208, 1218 (6th Cir. 1982), *cert. denied,* 460 U.S. 1040 (1983).

who purposefully involve themselves in political, social, or literary controversies or causes, or loudly and prominently express their opinions, or play the role of promoters for products, services, political candidates, or causes of one kind or another. If the answer to these questions is no, then the plaintiff is probably a *private* person. The difference is important because public figures, like public officials, must prove *actual malice* to win libel suits. Private persons need only show *negligence* to achieve the same result. With few exceptions, final determination of plaintiff status is a matter of law for the courts.

"A private individual," wrote Justice Rehnquist for the Court in *Wolston v. Reader's Digest Association,* a 1979 case, "is not automatically transformed into a public figure by becoming involved in or associated with a matter that attracts public attention. To accept such reasoning would in effect re-establish the doctrine advanced by the plurality opinion in *Rosenbloom v. Metromedia.*"[148] In other words, media coverage alone does not create public figures, and where it tries to do so, courts have resisted by finding seemingly public figures to be private persons. In *Wolston,* a plaintiff who twenty years earlier had pleaded guilty to criminal contempt of court charges during grand jury investigations into spy charges involving the Rosenbergs, and others, was said not to be a public figure. The passage of time had dimmed the urgency of the matter, and Wolston had long since returned to private life.

Other courts, for example, the Sixth Circuit Court of Appeals, have held that "once a person becomes a public figure in connection with a particular controversy, that person remains a public figure thereafter for purposes of later commentary or treatment of that controversy."[149] Public people can and do fade back into anonymity, however. A federal district court said that a plaintiff who served as head of a U.S. Department of Justice Organized Crime Strike Force was not a *public official* in his libel suit against an Arizona newspaper for reporting on his activities after he left office.[150] Time and context had made him someone else. Surprisingly, an appointee to a city commission on human rights was also not a public official.[151]

The Fourth Circuit followed the Supreme Court's *Wolston* rule in preserving private-person status in a 1994 case. The case is also useful for its description of the "right of reply" defense against libel suits:

Foretich v. Capital Cities/ABC Inc.
22 MED.L.RPTR. 2353, 37 F.3D 1541 (4TH CIR. 1994).

MURNAGHAN, J.:

Vincent and Doris Foretich filed a defamation action against the producers and broadcasters of an ABC docudrama in which a character apparently referred to one or both of them as "abusers" of their granddaughter, Hilary A. Foretich, who had been the subject of a prolonged and highly publicized child-custody dispute. On the defendants' pretrial motion, the district court ruled that Vincent and Doris Foretich were "private individuals," not "limited-purpose public figures," and therefore would not have to prove at trial that the defendants acted with "actual malice." The issue of the Foretiches' proper status—"private individuals" or "limited-purpose public figures"—is now before us on interlocutory appeal. Although we conclude that the Hilary Foretich custody battle became a "public controversy," we hold that neither of her paternal grandparents was a "public figure" for the purpose of comment on that controversy because their public statements and actions were made predominantly in self-defense. We therefore affirm the district court's ruling and remand the case for further proceedings.

Hilary Foretich's parents, Dr. Elizabeth Morgan and Dr. Eric A. Foretich, were separated by the time she was born. By the time she learned to walk, the parents were divorced and embroiled in what would become one of the most notorious child-custody battles in American history.

In 1983, the Superior Court of the District of Columbia awarded temporary custody of Hilary

148. *Wolston v. Reader's Digest Association, Inc.,* 5 Med.L.Rptr. 1273, 443 U.S. 157 (1979).
149. *Street v. National Broadcasting Co.,* 645 F.2d 1227, 1235 (6th Cir. 1981), *cert. granted,* 454 U.S. 815, *cert. dismissed,* 454 U.S. 1095 (1981).
150. *Crane v. Arizona Republic,* 17 Med.L.Rptr. 1353, 729 F.Supp. 69, (D.C.C Cal. 1980).
151. *Mason v. Chattanooga News Weekly,* ___ S.W.2d ___ (Tenn.Ct.App. 1995).

to her mother, Dr. Morgan, subject to scheduled visitations by the child's father, Dr. Foretich. Over the next few years, Dr. Morgan allegedly came to believe that Hilary was being sexually abused during visitations with her father and the paternal grandparents, Vincent and Doris Foretich. Dr. Morgan sought a temporary suspension of the visitations, but the D.C. Superior Court denied her request.

Following one of Hilary's visitations with the Foretiches in February 1986, Dr. Morgan refused to permit any further visits. A flurry of motions and hearings ensued, and in July 1986 Dr. Morgan was held in contempt and briefly incarcerated. She still refused to turn the child over to her alleged abusers and, following another series of motions, hearings, contempt orders, and appeals, Dr. Morgan was again jailed for contempt in February 1987. Supervised weekend visitations then resumed for several months in compliance with the court's orders, while motions for emergency stays filed by Dr. Morgan, and by Hilary's guardian *ad litem*, (guardian for purposes of this lawsuit) were denied.

Also in 1986, Dr. Morgan and Hilary brought civil actions in the United States District Court for the Eastern District of Virginia, Alexandria Division, seeking damages and an end to Dr. Foretich's visitation rights. The plaintiffs claimed that Hilary had been physically and sexually abused by Eric, Vincent, and Doris Foretich, and that the Foretiches had threatened to kill or injure Hilary if she told anyone about the abuse. Specifically, the complaint accused the girl's grandfather, Vincent Foretich, of (1) manipulating Hilary's genitalia; (2) inserting various foreign objects into her vagina; (3) orally sodomizing her; (4) anally sodomizing her; and (5) masturbating himself and ejaculating into her face and hair. The complaint accused Doris Foretich of "various acts of sexual abuse and assault and battery upon her granddaughter, specifically including but not limited to acts in which she inserted objects into her vagina." The defendants filed counterclaims alleging defamation. In February 1987, following a four-day trial in which Hilary's parents and paternal grandparents testified, the jury returned a verdict against Dr. Morgan on the abuse claims and against the Foretiches on the defamation claims. Both sides appealed, and we reversed and remanded in part, but the case was never retried. None of the Foretiches was ever

indicted for, much less convicted of, any criminal act of child abuse.

In the meantime, Dr. Morgan hid Hilary. A District of Columbia Superior Court Judge ordered Dr. Morgan to disclose Hilary's whereabouts. She refused. Her third incarceration for civil contempt began in August 1987 and continued for twenty-five months, as Dr. Morgan steadfastly refused to reveal the location of Hilary's hideout.

While Dr. Morgan spent twenty-five months in a D.C. jail, the controversy generated a torrent of publicity. Dr. Morgan and Dr. Foretich (and their lawyers and surrogates) exchanged charges and countercharges. Each parent hired a public relations agent and commissioned a toll-free "800" number. Hundreds of newspaper and magazine articles where published about virtually every aspect of the controversy. The broadcast media devoted extensive coverage to the dispute and to the various public policy debates that it inspired. On Capitol Hill, the House Committee on the District of Columbia, having received "the largest outpouring of mail regarding a single issue" in its history, reported that the affair was "a local and national issue joining together various political, social, and religious organizations." Magazines termed it "a national cause, taken up by feminist groups, talk-show hosts, and columnists" and a "legal battle that made headlines around the world."

* * *

In 1990, a private investigator hired by Dr. Foretich found Hilary living with her maternal grandparents in Christchurch, New Zealand. Hilary's father and the paternal grandparents rushed to New Zealand, in whose courts the next chapter of the custody battle ensued. Ultimately, the New Zealand Family Court awarded Dr. Morgan full custody of Hilary, and Dr. Foretich agreed neither to contest custody nor to seek visitations. Today Dr. Morgan and her now-twelve-year-old daughter remain in New Zealand.

Central to the resolution of this interlocutory appeal is the nature and extent of Vincent Foretich's and Doris Foretich's participation in the controversy surrounding their granddaughter's custody. Therefore, we will recount the Foretich grandparents' media exposure in some considerable detail.

The record does not suggest that either grandparent ever actively sought out press interviews.

But, over a period of a few years, and most intensively during and immediately after Dr. Morgan's twenty-five months in jail, they did accede to requests for several newspaper and magazine interviews, attend at least three press conferences or rallies organized by or on behalf of their son, and appeared on at least two television shows. The grandparents did not simply confine their remarks to denying Dr. Morgan's allegations. They also described the positive environment that they had provided for Hilary, the negative influence that Dr. Morgan had on the girl, their belief that Dr. Morgan was mentally unstable, and the distress that they had suffered as a result of Dr. Morgan's allegations.

* * *

On November 29, 1992, American Broadcasting Companies, Inc. aired, as its "ABC Sunday Night Movie," a 91-minute docudrama entitled "A Mother's Right: The Elizabeth Morgan Story." Being a "docudrama," the made-for-TV movie presented a dramatized and perhaps somewhat fictionalized account, with actors and actresses playing the roles of Dr. Morgan, Dr. Foretich, Hilary, *et al.*

Among the docudrama's scenes was one in which Hilary, then four years old, visits with her father and paternal grandparents at the Washington, D.C. office of a court-appointed psychiatrist. In the scene, Hilary is initially agitated, gradually warms to her grandparents, and eventually climbs into her grandfather's lap after joining in the singing of "Row, Row, Row, Your Boat."

There immediately follows a conversation between Dr. Morgan and her friend, as they are leaving Washington by car. The friend had brought Hilary to the psychiatrist's office and had remained in an adjacent room during the visit. He describes to Dr. Morgan what he heard: "It was like a circus pony going through her tricks. You know, she even giggled on cue." Dr. Morgan responds, "It's just like the therapist said. . . . Classic response. *She's being kind to her abusers so she won't be hurt again.*" (emphasis added).

The above-quoted dialogue from ABC's docudrama gave rise to the case at bar. Vincent and Doris Foretich filed a diversity action for defamation, intentional infliction of emotional distress, and "insulting words" in the United States District Court for the Eastern District of Virginia, naming as defendants the producers and broadcasters of the ABC docudrama (collectively, "the defendants" or "ABC"). Plaintiffs' entire case is based on the utterance of a single sound—the "s" in the word "abuser*s*," which allegedly indicated that Hilary was being abused not only by her father but also by one or both of her paternal grandparents. At the present stage of the litigation, it is undisputed that the "s" that converted the singular "abuser" into the plural "abusers" was included unintentionally.

The defendants filed a motion to dismiss the complaint for failure to state a claim or, alternatively, for summary judgment, arguing that the statement at issue, as a matter of law, could not be construed to defame the plaintiffs. The district court denied the motion, finding the statement capable of defamatory meaning: "[T]he use of the term 'her abusers' [by the actress portraying Dr. Morgan] could be reasonably understood by a [viewer] . . . to refer to the plaintiffs as child abusers, and thus to be defamatory."

The defendants then filed a motion *in limine* (at the threshold) requesting a finding that the plaintiffs were "limited-purpose public figures" and therefore would have to prove at trial that the defendants acted with "actual malice" as defined in *New York Times Co. v. Sullivan,* 376 U.S. 254 [1 Med.L.Rptr. 1527] (1964). The district judge orally denied the motion and held that the plaintiffs were "private individuals" for purposes of their defamation action. Thus, the *New York Times* "actual malice" standard would not apply.

Specifically, the judge stated that the Morgan-Foretich custody fight "was a private controversy that got a lot of publicity [and] notoriety," not a "public controversy." Even if the controversy were "public," the court held that the nature and extent of the Foretich grandparents' participation in the controversy was insufficient to make them "public figures" for the limited purpose of comment on the controversy:

[I]f someone is accused as these grandparents were of fairly heinous behavior, ought they be required to sit silently on pain of being declared a public figure and be limited to doing no more than say, "I didn't do it"? Shouldn't they be allowed to attack their accuser without subjecting themselves to being a public figure?

* * *

[O]ught a person such as these plaintiffs be required to limit themselves to merely denials in order not to become a public figure?

When he announced the court's decision from the bench, the judge added,

> These plaintiffs did no more than defend themselves against fairly outrageous, even if true, accusations. And while they aggressively sought to defend themselves, I don't think they injected themselves into a point where they can be considered to have voluntarily assumed the role of prominence to the extent that this can be transformed into a public controversy in which they sought to influence the outcome.

The defendants requested an interlocutory appeal, pursuant to 28 U.S.C. § 1292(b). The district court issued a written order noting that "there is substantial ground for differences of opinion." Therefore, the district court stayed the proceeding and certified to this Court the question "whether the plaintiffs are limited-purpose public figures." The defendants filed a petition for interlocutory appeal, which we granted.

* * *

The first question we must address is whether there was a particular public controversy that gave rise to the alleged defamation.

* * *

In 1980, after carefully sifting through the Supreme Court cases, the United States Court of Appeals for the District of Columbia Circuit enunciated an express definition of a "public controversy":

> A public controversy is not simply a matter of interest to the public; it must be a real dispute, the outcome of which affects the general public or some segment of it in an appreciable way. . . . [E]ssentially private concerns or disagreements do not become public controversies simply because they attract attention. . . . Rather, a public controversy is a dispute that in fact has received public attention because its ramifications will be felt by persons who are not direct participants. *Waldman v. Fairchild Publications, Inc.,* 627 F.2d 1287, 1297 (D.C. Cir.), cert. denied, 449 U.S. 898 (1980) (defining a "public controversy" as "a specific public dispute that has foreseeable and substantial ramifications for persons beyond its immediate participants"). * * *

Next we must determine whether the above-quoted definition encompasses the Morgan-Foretich dispute.

* * *

There was ample evidence that the Morgan-Foretich dispute "received public attention because" it had "foreseeable and substantial ramifications for persons beyond its immediate participants." A search of Mead Data Central's NEXIS database reveals more than one thousand news reports on the Morgan-Foretich dispute. The custody battle heightened social awareness of child-abuse allegations and their role in custody disputes, and raised several substantial questions for public debate, including how best to determine which parent is more "fit," how courts can best protect a child's interests during a prolonged custody fight, and what should be the proper role of psychiatric and social-work experts.

* * *

Having concluded that there was indeed a public controversy that gave rise to the alleged defamation, we must next examine "the nature and extent of [Vincent Foretich's and Doris Foretich's] participation in [that] controversy." In conducting that examination, we are guided by the five-part test that we set forth in *Fitzgerald v. Penthouse Int'l, Ltd.,* 691 F.2d 666 (4th Cir. 1982), and reiterated in *Reuber v. Food Chemical News, Inc.,* 925 F.2d 703 (4th Cir.), *cert. denied,* 501 U.S. 1212 (1991): (1) whether Vincent and Doris Foretich had access to channels of effective communication; (2) whether Vincent and Doris Foretich voluntarily assumed roles of special prominence in the Morgan-Foretich public controversy; (3) whether Vincent and Doris Foretich sought to influence the outcome of the controversy; (4) whether the controversy existed prior to ABC's broadcast of the allegedly defamatory statement; and (5) whether Vincent and Doris Foretich retained public-figure status at the time of the broadcast. Because we find that neither Vincent nor Doris Foretich voluntarily assumed a role of special prominence in the Morgan-Foretich controversy in order to influence its outcome, we need not consider the other elements of the *Fitzgerald/Reuber* test.

* * *

[W]e now may proceed to examine the nature and extent of Vincent Foretich's and Doris Foretich's participation in the Morgan-Foretich controversy and to determine whether they voluntarily assumed roles of special prominence in that controversy in order to influence its outcome.

ABC has argued that Vincent and Doris Foretich voluntarily participated in the public controversy when they chose to support their son by publicly criticizing Dr. Morgan, by speaking with news reporters, and by appearing on television, at press conferences, and at public gatherings. The Foretiches' public comments and appearances, ABC has contended, were aimed at swaying public opinion in favor of their son and against his former wife. Furthermore, ABC has argued, the grandparents did not define their public comments and appearances to answering Dr. Morgan's charges against them; they also sought to improve their son's image and to convince the public of Dr. Morgan's instability, irrationality, and, ultimately, unfitness to retain custody of Hilary. Specifically, ABC has claimed that Dr. Foretich's parents wittingly allowed their son to use them as "props" in a strategy of "high theater"; Dr. Foretich would highlight the heinous charges that Dr. Morgan had leveled against his elderly and dignified-looking parents, and then ask his audiences rhetorically whether such grandparents could have possibly committed those vile acts, or whether, instead, the fact that Dr. Morgan had made such accusations demonstrated her "bizarre" and "unbalanced" personality. By ABC's account, the Foretiches—not Dr. Morgan—were responsible for the continued publicity surrounding the charges of grandparental abuse. Therefore, ABC has argued, both Vincent and Doris Foretich voluntarily assumed special roles of prominence in the Morgan-Foretich controversy in order to influence its outcome, and they may not now claim the protections of purely "private" persons.

We reject ABC's argument because it pays inadequate attention to the context in which the Foretiches made their public comments and appearances, and, as a result, undervalues their interest in defending their own reputations against the extraordinary attacks launched by Dr. Morgan. The complaint that Dr. Morgan filed in federal district court in 1986 accused the Foretich grandparents of performing very specific sex acts with Hilary, then a three-year-old girl. Those accusations were immediately publicized in *The Washington Post* and later were republished in dozens, if not hundreds, of news articles and broadcasts disseminated over the following months and years. The resultant publicity doubtless had the potential to destroy Vincent Fore-

tich's and Doris Foretich's reputations, and that potential may well have been realized.

The common law of defamation has long recognized that charges such as those leveled against the Foretich grandparents are so obviously and materially harmful to reputational interests that they must be deemed defamatory *per se*. We, too, recognize the devastation that public accusations of child sexual abuse can wreak, and we are extremely reluctant to attribute public-figure status to otherwise private persons merely because they have responded to such accusations in a reasonable attempt to vindicate their reputations.

Therefore, we hold that a person who has been publicly accused of committing an act of serious sexual misconduct that (if committed in the place of publication and proved beyond a reasonable doubt) would be punishable by imprisonment cannot be deemed a "limited purpose public figure" merely because he or she makes reasonable public replies to those accusations. Because Dr. Morgan publicly accused both Vincent and Doris Foretich of committing such acts, we next must consider whether the Foretiches' public comments and appearances predominantly were reasonable replies to Dr. Morgan's accusations of child sexual abuse. If they were, the Foretiches remain private individuals; if not, the Foretiches must be deemed public figures for purposes of the present litigation.

In determining the reasonableness of a reply, we need not plow entirely new ground: the common law on the conditional (or qualified) privilege of reply, also known as the privilege to speak in self-defense or to defend one's reputation, can help guide our discussion. Under the common law, the publication of a defamatory attack constitutes an "occasion" triggering the conditional privilege of reply, but the protection of that privilege is lost if it is "abused."

* * *

One may abuse, and thus lose, his conditional privilege of reply if, *inter alia*, (1) his reply includes substantial defamatory matter that is "irrelevant" or "nonresponsive" to the initial attack; (2) his reply includes substantial defamatory matter that is "disproportionate" to the initial attack; or (3) the publication of his reply is "excessive," *i.e.*, is addressed to too broad an audience. *See* Restatement (Second) of Torts §§

599, 603–605 (1977). * * * Our reading of the extensive case law on abuse of the privilege of reply demonstrates, however, that a public response to a public attack may be "uninhibited, robust, and wide-open," *New York Times,* 376 U.S. at 270, without stepping over the line into abuse.

Here, we will apply the same general principles to determine whether the Foretiches' public comments and appearances were (1) responsive to Dr. Morgan's attacks; (2) proportionate to those attacks; and (3) not excessively published. Together, those three inquiries will determine whether the Foretiches' public comments and appearances were predominantly, on the one hand, reasonable replies to Dr. Morgan's accusations of child sexual abuse, or, on the other hand, efforts to assume special roles of prominence in the Morgan-Foretich controversy in order to affect its outcome.[20] By borrowing well-established principles regarding the abuse of the privilege of reply, and applying them to the question of whether a defamation plaintiff is a public figure or a private individual, we hope to import decades of accumulated wisdom from the common law into a relatively recent constitutional doctrine.

As to the first requirement of reasonableness—that the reply be responsive to the initial attacks—we begin with Dean Prosser's admonition that a person attacked must not add "anything irrelevant and unconnected with the charges made against him, as where he attempts to refute an accusation of immorality by saying that [his accuser] has stolen a horse." *Prosser and Keeton on the Law of Torts,* § 115, at 825. A supposed "reply" is not truly a reply if it is "patently unrelated to the subject matter" of the antecedent attack.[21] One may not "publish any and all kinds of charges against

the offender, upon the theory that they tend to degrade him, and thereby discredit his [accusations]."[22] To be responsive, a reply's contents must clearly relate to its supposed objective—blunting the initial attack and restoring one's good name.[23] Statements that simply deny the accusations, or directly respond to them, or express one's impressions upon first hearing them are certainly responsive.[24] So, too, are statements impugning the motives of the accuser:[25] "One in self-defense is not confined to parrying the thrusts of his assailant."[26] If, however, one's reply exceeds the scope of the original attack,[27] and says more than reasonably appears to be necessary to protect his reputation,[28] it is not reasonably responsive.

The Foretiches' public comments and appearances were, in large part, relevant and responsive to Dr. Morgan's accusations against them. They made no public statements until *after* Dr. Morgan's federal complaint was filed and publicized in August 1986. At that time, their first reactions were to deny the allegations in a concise, forthright fashion. Later, they spoke to reporters in more detail about themselves, their son, and Dr. Morgan.

Most of the Foretiches' statements about themselves were relevant to the attacks against them. For example, it was clearly relevant for Doris Foretich to describe how she had taken Hilary to a doctor, who examined her and found

---

20. * * * On remand, the Foretiches will be able to recover damages only if they can prove that they never abused Hilary. *See Philadelphia Newspapers, Inc. v. Hepps,* 475 U.S. 767, 768–69, 775–76 (1986) (holding that, where a media defendant publishes speech of public concern, a private-figure plaintiff cannot recover damages without proving that the statement at issue were false); *see also Gazette, Inc. v. Harris,* 229 Va. at 15, 325 S.E.2d at 725 ("[T]he plaintiff must prove falsity . . . ."). Thus, our decision today provides no safe haven for actual sex abusers who deny true accusations against them.

21. *Reynolds v. Pegler,* 223 F.2d 429, 434 (2d Cir.), *cert. denied,* 350 U.S. 846 (1955).

22. *Brewer v. Chase,* 121 Mich. 526, 533, 80 N.W. 575, 577 (1899).

23. *See R. H. Bouligny, Inc. v. United Steelworkers of America,* 270 N.C. 160, 172, 154 S.E.2d 344, 355 (1967).

24. *See National Disabled Soldiers' League, Inc. v. Haan,* 4 F.2d 436, 442 (D.C. Cir. 1925); *Fram v. Yellow Cab Co.,* 380 F. Supp. 1314, 1328–30 (W.D. Pa. 1974).

25. *See Reynolds v. Pegler,* 223 F.2d at 433; *Shepherd v. Baer,* 53 A. at 791–92; *Conroy v. Fall River Herald News Publishing Co.,* 306 Mass. 488, 490, 28 N.E.2d 729, 730 (1940); *Shenkman v. O'Malley,* 2 A.D.2d 567, 574, 157 N.Y.S.2d 290, 297 (1956); *Collier v. Postum Cereal Co.,* 150 A.D. 169, 178, 134 N.Y.S. 847, 853 (1912); *Mencher v. Chesley,* 193 Misc. 829, 831, 85 N.Y.S.2d 431, 434 (1948).

26. *Collier v. Postum Cereal Co.,* 150 A.D. at 178, 134 N.Y.S. at 853; *accord Shenkman v. O'Malley,* 2 A.D.2d at 574, 157 N.Y.S.2d at 297; *Mencher v. Chesley* 193 Misc. at 831, 85 N.Y.S.2d at 434.

27. *See Reynolds v. Pegler,* 223 F.2d at 433; *Cartwright v. Herald Publishing Co.,* 220 S.C. 492, 68 S.E.2d 415, 417 (1951) (per curiam).

28. *See Afro-American Publishing Co. v. Jaffe,* 366 F.2d 649, 656 (D.C. Cir. 1966) (en banc).

absolutely no physical evidence of abuse. The Foretiches' more general self-descriptions—as "God-loving," "law-abiding," "honorable, clean-living people"—may or may not have sounded convincing, but they were certainly relevant to refuting Dr. Morgan's charges of child molestation. The same can be said for Doris Foretich's repeated attempts to explain that her loss of two children made it impossible for her to mistreat her granddaughters. Both Doris and Vincent Foretich described the sacrifices that they had made to assist their son in raising Hilary—moving from Gloucester to Great Falls; sewing quilts on which Hilary could play with her toys; supplying her with nice clothes and dolls and a pleasant room. Those selfless efforts to enhance the quality of their granddaughter's life tend to contradict the image that Dr. Morgan had painted of her former in-laws as depraved child molesters. Furthermore, the grandparents' descriptions of how they missed Hilary, and of their prayers for her, and of wanting to see her again all served to bolster their denials of Dr. Morgan's allegations. On the other hand, their lengthy descriptions of how the charges had damaged their own lives were not particularly relevant or responsive, but our examination of the record suggests that those descriptions were relatively innocuous.

The Foretiches' descriptions of their son Eric also were relevant to the accusations of child abuse. They described him as a "very honorable person" who stood up and fought for his parental rights and who loved and had attentively cared for his daughters. That description was bolstered by the Foretiches' willingness to stand beside him at press conferences and public gatherings. Doris Foretich's statement on the Donahue Show—that Eric had been "very much loved" as a child—was a clear, direct response to the showing of a videotape in which Dr. Morgan alleged that Eric had been abused as an adolescent (presumably either by his parents or with their acquiescence).

The grandparents' remarks about Dr. Morgan also were, in large part, relevant. Doris Foretich stated that Dr. Morgan "knows in her heart that it [the alleged sexual abuse of Hilary] never happened." Doris Foretich impugned Dr. Morgan's motives by describing the offers of book and movie contracts, the fame, and the high status in the women's movement that had accrued to Dr. Morgan, all as a result of her public campaign

against Hilary's father and paternal grandparents. Furthermore, Doris Foretich at least implied that Hilary had been mistreated, if not abused, at the hands of her mother. That allegation was highly relevant, for it suggested that Dr. Morgan may have accused the Foretiches in an attempt to camouflage her own misdeeds.

Neither Doris nor Vincent Foretich strayed far beyond those points. For example, neither attacked Dr. Morgan's qualifications or competence as a physician. Nor did they recount any general impressions of Dr. Morgan that they had formed during her brief marriage to their son. Moreover, they never commented directly on Dr. Morgan's contempt citation or imprisonment, on the legislation pending in Congress, or on how the D.C. courts should rule on the ultimate questions of custody and visitation rights. Rather, the Foretiches adhered quite closely to the topics most relevant to rebutting the allegations of child sexual abuse against them.

Next we must determine whether the Foretiches' public statements were "reasonably proportionate to the magnitude of the . . . first attack." In making that determination, we remain at all times aware that the allegation initially leveled here—concerning mistreatment of a little girl—was as destructive to reputation as virtually any charge imaginable. Thus, a reply would have to be truly outrageous before we would deem it "altogether disproportionate to the occasion." Nonetheless, we think it is important to sketch a few general guidelines for evaluating the proportionality of a reply to a public accusation of criminal sexual misconduct.

Turning again to the common law, we observe that a person under attack may properly allege, in Dean Prosser's words, "that his accuser is an unmitigated liar and the truth is not in him." *Prosser and Keeton on the Law of Torts*, § 115, at 825; Restatement (Second) of Torts § 594 cmt. k (1977).

* * *

We do not believe that the Foretiches' public comments came even close to being disproportionate to Dr. Morgan's attacks. They described their former daughter-in-law as "mentally ill," "sick," and "not in her right mind." They labeled her allegations as "heinous lie[s]," "downright filth," and "filthy dirt"—"like from the bottom of a cesspool." Those remarks may have been rather strong, but not when compared to Dr. Morgan's accusations. In explaining the common-law requirement of proportionality, a New York court once stated: "If a man, with equal physique, attacks another with his fists, it may not justify the use of a firearm in response." *Shenkman v. O'Malley*, 2 A.D.2d 567, 576, 157 N.Y.S.2d 290, 299 (1956). The present case more closely resembles the use of fists in response to firearms. Therefore, the Foretiches' public comments and appearances easily pass the "proportionality" test.

Finally, in considering the reasonableness of the Foretiches' public statements, we must ask to whom those statements were directed. "Excessive publication is conceptually parallel to the use of excessive force in self-defense [of one's person or property]." "The reply must reasonably focus on the audience which heard the attack." If an accusation of criminal sexual misconduct had been published only to a very limited audience, it obviously would be an abuse to respond in every newspaper and on every television and radio station in the country. But where the original attack was widespread, the response can be widely disseminated as well. In other words, the counterattack must be made primarily in the forums selected by the original attacker.[38]

The record evidence suggests that the Foretiches' public statements were made only to reporters from media outlets that had already aired, or were planning soon to air, Dr. Morgan's accusations against them and their son. The Foretich grandparents did not reach out to additional media outlets, and thereby to new audiences, in an effort to expand the circle of persons familiar with the controversy. Rather, they targeted their message toward those persons in whose eyes their reputations already had been (or soon would be) sullied. Thus, their replies were not excessive.

Because the Foretiches' public responses to Dr. Morgan's accusations were responsive, proportionate, and not excessively published, they were "reasonable." We acknowledge that some

of their public statements were probably intended (at least in part) to influence the outcome of the custody dispute or of the legislative debate in Congress. But we also recognize that, in the circumstances of this particular case, it is almost impossible to extricate statements made in self defense from statements intended to influence the outcome of the controversy. A favorable outcome of the ultimate dispute—*i.e.*, granting custody of Hilary, or at least unsupervised visitation rights, to Dr. Foretich—would have done more to vindicate Vincent and Doris Foretiches' reputations than any reply could have ever accomplished. Looking "through the eyes of a reasonable person at the facts taken as a whole," *Waldbaum*, 627 F.2d at 1292, we conclude that the Foretiches' primary motive was to defend their own good names against Dr. Morgan's accusations and that their public statements can most fairly be characterized as measured defensive replies to her attacks, rather than as efforts to thrust themselves to the forefront of a public controversy in order to influence its outcome. Therefore, we hold that Vincent and Doris Foretich were private individuals, not limited-purpose public figures.

Furthermore, we note that—were we to hold otherwise—our decision would necessarily have an unsettling breadth: the Foretiches would be required to demonstrate actual malice in order to recover damages for defamation not only from ABC, but also from any media *or nonmedia* defendant who repeated ABC's statement that they had abused Hilary. Such a result effectively "would create an 'open season' for all who sought to defame" Vincent and Doris Foretich. We see no reason to expose the Foretiches, or other similarly situated persons, to such a potential barrage.

In the three decades since the Supreme Court handed down its decision in *New York Times Co. v. Sullivan*, we have struggled to find the proper balance between the protection of reputational interests, on the one hand, and of free expression, on the other. * * * By allowing the Foretiches to defend their good names without succumbing to public-figure status, we protect not only their own interests in reputation, but also society's interest in free speech. Further extending the *New York Times* actual-malice standard here would serve only to muzzle persons who stand falsely accused of heinous acts and to

---

38. *See Barr v. Matteo*, 256 F.2d 890, 891 (D.C. Cir. 1958) (per curiam), *rev'd on other grounds*, 360 U.S. 564 (1959); *Mencher v. Chesley*, 193 Misc. at 831, 85 N.Y.S.2d at 434; *see also Richmond v. Southwire Co.*, 980 F.2d 518, 520 (8th Cir. 1992) (per curiam); *Dickins v. International Bhd. of Teamsters*, 171 F.2d at 25.

undermine the very freedom of speech in whose name the extension is demanded. By freely permitting the Foretiches to respond to Dr. Morgan's charges against them—charges that have never been proved in any court of law—we foster both the individual interest in self-expression and the social interest in the discovery and dissemination of truth—the very goals that animate our First Amendment jurisprudence.

Accordingly, we affirm the district court's ruling that both Vincent and Doris Foretich were private individuals, not public figures, and we remand the case for further proceedings consistent with this opinion.

Affirmed and Remanded.

COMMENT

A state court made the same point when it held that wide public concern about recruiting violations in college athletics did not in itself make an assistant basketball coach a public figure. Public interest alone does not create a public controversy, nor does it create a public figure. The same court ruled that arrest on a murder charge did not in itself raise a plaintiff to the status of public figure.[152] Media should be prepared to demonstrate why a plaintiff is a public person until the courts develop some guiding principles.

Whether from disdain for the peccadilloes of the press or concern for its power, courts seem reluctant to bestow public-figure status on even some of the most publicly engaged plaintiffs. Corporate officers, consultants, teachers, attorneys, physicians, drug dealers, appointees to governmental committees and commissions, and litigants are often classified as private persons. This makes the all-important distinction between private and public plaintiffs—all important because of the different standards of fault that apply—a crap shoot for reporters and editors. The distinctions drawn by the courts are often highly ambiguous and sometimes arbitrary. Again the context or the circumstances of the case may be the determining factor. Remember Elmer Gertz!

Those who voluntarily open themselves or their businesses to public scrutiny and create matters of legitimate public interest are public figures and will be held to the actual malice standard. Recent cases have expanded the category of public figure to include, for example, two psychologists who wrote about children's memories of sexual abuse.[153] The Supreme Court declined to use that case to clarify whether nonmedia defendants such as these also have to prove actual malice. The twin brother of a murder suspect who gave press interviews promoting a version of the case favorable to his brother was held to be a public figure,[154] as were the president of a nationwide charity fundraising organization,[155] a 1960s community activist,[156] and the owner of a lawnmower repair company.[157] But again, caution is in order. State courts apparently have the authority to expand the definition of "public figure" beyond what the U.S. Supreme Court has laid down.[158]

A well-known attorney who chose to represent the editor of *Hustler* magazine in a widely publicized suit was not—as the Supreme Court had held in *Gertz*—a vortex public figure.[159] "To hold otherwise," said the Third Circuit in a second case, "would place an undue burden on attorneys who represent famous or notorious clients."[160] But a little known public defender who represented a rape defendant over the period of a lengthy and highly publicized trial was a public figure.[161] A fine line? Or no line?

Involuntary public figures—criminals, political power brokers, financial manipulators, crime and accident victims, or those who find them-

---

152. *Warford v. Lexington Herald-Leader,* 17 Med.L.Rptr. 1785, 789 S.W.2d 758 (Ky.Sup.Ct. 1990); *Yancey v. Hamilton,* 17 Med.L.Rptr. 1012, 786 S.W.2d 854 (Ky.Sup.Ct. 1989).

153. *Underwager v. Salter,* 22 Med.L.Rptr. 1852, 22 F.3d 730 (7th Cir. 1994).

154. *Denney v. Lawrence,* 22 Med.L.Rptr. 1434, 27 Cal.Rptr. 2d 556 (Calif. Ct. App. 1994).

155. *Chapin v. Knight-Ridder, Inc.,* 21 Med.L.Rptr. 1449, 993 F.2d 1087 (4th Cir. 1993).

156. *Milsap v. Journal/Sentinel, Inc.,* 847 F.Supp. 406 (E.D.Wis. 1995).

157. *Turf Lawnmower Repair Inc. v. Bergen Record Corp.,* 22 Med.L.Rptr. 1461, 635 A.2d 575 (N.J. Super.Ct.App.Div. 1994).

158. *Harris v. Quadracci,* 23 Med.L.Rptr. 1296, 48 F.3d 247, 250, fn. 5 (7th Cir. 1995).

159. *Spence v. Flynt,* 19 Med.L.Rptr. 1129, 816 P.2d 771 (Wyo. 1991).

160. *Marcone v. Penthouse International,* 11 Med.L.Rptr. 1577, 754 F.2d 1072, 1085 (3d Cir. 1985), *cert. denied,* 474 U.S. 864 (1985).

161. *Parrish v. Gannett River States Publishing Corp.,* 22 Med.L.Rptr. 1430 (S.D.Miss. 1994).

selves, unexpectedly, embroiled in controversial topics about which substantial segments of society have different and strongly held views—are rare but also generally must meet the actual malice standard.[162] For obvious reasons, some of these people thrive in the shadows; publicity would spoil their game or expose their private lives. But here again state courts differ. In a 1976 case involving *Playboy* magazine and an alleged mobster, a federal district court in Georgia said that "Defining public figures is much like trying to nail a jellyfish to the wall." To rebut *Playboy's* evidence of extensive criminal contacts over the years, Louis Rosanova argued that he was not a public figure because he didn't have access to the media to contradict charges against him and because he had not thrust himself voluntarily into the vortex of a public controversy. *Playboy* won a summary judgment.[163]

One legal expert would label criminals in this category of plaintiff "notorious public figures," persons whose activities will sooner or later come to public attention. They should be libel-proof because they have reputations that cannot be further tarnished.[164] An example might be the convicted serial killer who sued an author and the publisher of a book on the grisly topic.[165] It can also be argued that criminals choose to commit crimes and therefore act voluntarily, even though they don't choose the publicity that follows.

In *Liberty Lobby, Inc. v. Anderson*,[166] the D.C. Circuit rejected the doctrine of the libel-proof plaintiff. In his column, Jack Anderson referred to Willis Carto, the Lobby's founder, as "racist, fascist, anti-semitic, and a neo-Nazi." Then D.C. Circuit Judge Antonin Scalia called the doctrine a "fundamentally bad idea." Other circuits have

adopted it, however.[167] It is partly dependent upon the *incremental harm doctrine*, the idea that a false but insignificant allegation may cause no appreciable harm beyond that already caused by an earlier and accurate but nonactionable statement. For example, a convicted rapist is falsely accused of a weapons violation. That doctrine is also recognized in some jurisdictions, though not in others, and may be traced to the appeals court ruling in *Herbert v. Lando*.[168]

For different reasons, it has been suggested that high-level public officials and dazzling celebrities also be made libel-proof.[169] More difficult to hold to the highest fault standard would be relatives of public people and accident victims or, for example, an air traffic controller who happened to be on duty when a plane crash occurred.[170] These people were in places where they would rather not have been.

A relatively stable category of public figure is the *pervasive or all-purpose public figure*, which may or may not include the celebrity, the cultural hero, and the person who may have become a *public personality*. The latter may be the all-purpose public figure most people would recognize at once. Nothing changes the status of public personalities; they include the stars of stage and screen, the greatest athletes of our time, the prizewinners, the creators of our fads and fashions, the great corporations that plead for our support, and the movers and shakers. People in

162. *Lerman v. Flynt Distributing Co.*, 10 Med.L.Rptr. 2497, 745 F.2d 123, 137–138 (2d Cir. 1984).

163. *Rosanova v. Playboy Enterprises, Inc.*, 411 F.Supp. 440 (D.Ga. 1976).

164. Bruce Sanford, *Libel and Privacy* (Englewood Cliffs, N.J.: Prentice-Hall, 1985), pp. 271–72. See, for example *Rogers v. Jackson Sun Newspapers*, 23 Med.L.Rptr. 1670 (Tenn.Cir.Ct. 1995).

165. *Schaefer v. Newton*, 22 Med.L.Rptr. 2239, 868 F.Supp. 246 (D.C.S.Ind. 1994).

166. 746 F.2d 1563 (D.C.Cir. 1984), vacated on other grounds, 477 U.S. 242 (1986).

167. *Herbert v. Lando*, 781 F.2d 298 (2d Cir. 1986), *cert. denied*, 476 U.S. 1182 (1986); *Masson v. New Yorker Magazine, Inc.*, 895 F.2d 1535 (9th Cir. 1989), *rev'd and remanded*, 111 S.Ct. 2419 (1991). The libel-proof doctrine may have originated in *Cardillo v. Doubleday & Co., Inc.*, 518 F.2d 638 (2d Cir. 1975). See, Note, *The Libel-Proof Plaintiff Doctrine*, 98 Harv.L.Rev. 1909 (1985). Opposition to the doctrine on grounds of equal protection and due process is found in Evelyn A. Peyton, Rogue's Rights: *The Constitutionality of the Libel-Proof Plaintiff Doctrine*, 34 Santa Clara L.Rev. 179 (1993).

168. 12 Med.L.Rptr. 1593, 781 F.2d 298 (2d Cir.), *cert. denied*, 476 U.S. 1182 (1986). Defined in *Desnick v. Capital Cities/ABC, Inc.*, 22 Med.L.Rptr. 1937, 851 F.Supp. 303 (N.D.Ill. 1994) as the harm "inflicted by the challenged statements beyond the harm imposed by the rest of the publication." Allegations of faked cataract surgery led to the suit in *Desnick*.

169. Gillmor, *Power, Publicity, and the Abuse of Libel Law*.

170. *Dameron v. Washington Magazine*, 12 Med.L.Rptr. 1508, 779 F.2d 736 (D.C.Cir. 1985).

this category might not exist without publicity. They include the famous singer and the football player, "whose success," said the Fifth Circuit Court of Appeals, "depends in large part on publicity,"[171] as well as the writer who strives for public acclaim and by his own purposeful activities had "thrust himself into the public eye. He had become a public personality."[172] But again caution is in order.

A Vermont insurance company, arguing that it did not thrust itself into a public controversy but had been forced into it, was nevertheless held to be a pervasive public figure.[173] So was a Florida television station.[174] At the same time, banks in Oregon and Virginia were held not to occupy this status because they lacked general fame and notoriety or widespread influence.[175]

Not all public employees are *public officials.* To qualify, an elected or appointed official should have control over the conduct of governmental affairs to the extent that the public has an interest in scrutinizing and discussing her qualifications and performance. To fit the category tightly, a public official should have some policy-making power and enjoy significantly greater access to the mass media than private persons for the purpose of contradicting false statements.[176] The farther down the ladder of public employment an individual is located, the more likely he is to qualify as a private person. More likely than not, law enforcement officers, political candidates, and financial administrators will be classified as public officials. Public school teachers and administrators, public defenders, and fire-fighters may or may not be.

In reviewing earlier Supreme Court rulings, the First Circuit in 1989 suggested that public-

official status depended on (1) the character of employment (its inherent attributes), (2) access to the media, and (3) assumed risk—those "who actively seek positions of influence in public life do so with the knowledge that, if successful in attaining their goals, diminished privacy will result."[177]

What about the private lives of public officials? Do they affect the body politic? Of course, they do: a political candidate's psychiatric profile or a U.S. senator's sexual behavior, for example, may be relevant. Here ethical guidelines may often serve the press better than legal guidelines.

THE COMMON LAW OR STATUTORY DEFENSES

Truth

In defending against libel actions, a news organization, as has been suggested, will use every available and relevant defense. Indeed, it will pile them up. At this point, libel attorneys need help from journalists. Where did you get the story? With whom did you check it out? Is there anything about it you should tell me that you haven't? Do you have documentation or other evidence that will help prove the truth of your report? The depth of a reporter's feeling about the truth of her story is not enough.

The traditional common law defenses were all journalists had before 1964. The major drawback of these defenses—and a drawback still if they are the only defenses presented—is that they put the burden of proof on those raising them, that is, on the defendant publication.

Truth or justification as a defense, however, has been largely absorbed by the *New York Times* doctrine. It has become part of the constitutional fabric of libel in that a plaintiff has to prove *falsity* at the threshold. The question of truth is dealt with early in the process. In the law, if something is not false, it is true. Under the *New York Times* doctrine, the initial burden of proof is on the plaintiff.

When truth is used as a separate or supplementary defense, however, the burden of proof

171. *Brewer v. Memphis Publishing Co.,* 6 Med.L.Rptr. 2025, 626 F.2d 1238, 1254–55 (5th Cir. 1980), *cert. denied,* 452 U.S. 962 (1981).

172. *Maule v. NYM Corporation,* 7 Med.L.Rptr. 2092, 54 N.Y.2d 880, 881–83 (1981).

173. *National Life Ins. Co. v. Phillips Publishing Inc.,* 20 Med.L.Rptr. 1393, 793 F.Supp. 627 (D.Md. 1992).

174. *WTSP-TV v. Vick,* 11 Med.L.Rptr. 1543 (Fla.Cir.Ct. 1985).

175. *Bank of Oregon v. Independent News,* 693 P.2d 35, *reh'g denied en banc,* 696 P.2d 1095, *cert. denied,* 474 U.S. 826 (1986): *Blue Ridge Bank v. Veribanc, Inc.,* 866 F.2d 681 (4th Cir. 1989).

176. *Mosesian v. McClatchy Newspapers,* 15 Med.L.Rptr. 2279, 252 Cal.Rptr. 586, *cert. denied,* 490 U.S. 1066 (1989).

177. *Kassel v. Gannett Co., Inc.,* 16 Med.L.Rptr. 1814, 875 F.2d 935, 939–40 (1st Cir. 1989).

would be on the defendant publisher. Where truth alone is pleaded as a defense, the proof must be at least as broad as the charge. "[I]t is generally agreed," said Dean Prosser, "that it is not necessary to prove the literal truth of the accusation in every detail, and it is sufficient to show that the imputation is substantially true, or as it is often put, to justify the 'gist,' the 'sting,' or the 'substantial truth' of the defamation."[178] Minor inaccuracies do not negate the defense of truth. A publication will be considered in its entirety and in relation to its structure, nuances, implications, and connotations. It is not enough to take sentences separately and demonstrate their individual accuracy, detached and wrenched out of context.

Luther Haynes claimed that he was libeled in a highly praised, best-selling book by Nicholas Lemann entitled *The Promised Land: The Great Black Migration and How It Changed America.* Part of the story involved the profligacy of Haynes as a husband and father in an earlier life that had since been reformed. In affirming a judgment for the defendant publisher, Chief Judge Posner of the Seventh Circuit Court of Appeals said this about the truth defense:

> The rule of substantial truth is based on a recognition that falsehoods which do no incremental damage to the plaintiff's reputation do not injure the only interest that the law of defamation protects . . . . Falsehoods that do not harm plaintiff's reputation more than full recital of the true facts about him would do are thus not actionable. The rule making substantial truth a complete defense and the constitutional limitations on defamation suits coincide.[179]

Posner's ruling on *Desnick v. American Broadcasting Companies, Inc.*[180] also finds that a target has no legal remedy, regardless of investigatory tactics, if the broadcast does not contain actionable defamation.

The Georgia Supreme Court, reversing a lower state court, held that a woman who sued the corporate parent and employees of a Cox newspaper that implied that she, a married

woman, had contracted chlamydia, a sexually transmitted disease, could not prove falsity in her libel action. The bacteria she was infected with had not been identified and remained unknown. Where there is doubt about truth, said the court, it will be resolved in favor of the newspaper.[181]

In using the truth defense, it is important to realize that it is not a defense to say that you accurately reported a false accusation made by someone else, unless, as we shall see, you are quoting from a trial transcript or some other governmental document or proceeding. It is the charge itself that you must be prepared to prove using a truth defense. Truth is a difficult defense because reporters seldom possess the kind of evidence that would "prove" truth in a court of law. Witnesses upon whom they have been counting often evaporate. Sources may disappear or change their stories. A reporter's sincerity or depth of feeling about the truth is not enough. Detailed documentation is usually a necessity for a truth defense. Truth alone can be a costly and hazardous defense. Under the *New York Times* doctrine, the focus is on falsity, not truth. But where truth can be demonstrated, it is a complete defense.

The Opinion Defense (Fair Comment and Criticism)

Also part of the constitutional fabric of libel, and much more important than in the past, is the opinion defense or what traditionally was referred to in the common law as *fair comment and criticism.* Recall that in *Gertz* Justice Powell said, "there is no such thing as a false idea." He went on to say: "However pernicious an opinion may seem, we depend for its correction not on the conscience of judges and juries but on the competition of other ideas."[182]

Under the common law defense of *fair comment,* one was permitted to go to the utmost lengths of denunciation, condemnation, and satirization when criticizing people and institutions seeking public attention and approval.[183] At the same time, common law malice (ill will, spite,

---

178. Prosser, *Handbook of the Law of Torts* (4th ed. 1971).
179. *Haynes v. Alfred A. Knopf Inc.,* 21 Med.L.Rptr. 2161, 8 F.3d 1222 (7th Cir. 1993); *Desnick v. American Broadcasting Companies, Inc.,* 23 Med.L.Rptr. 1161, 44 F.3d 1345 (7th Cir. 1995).
180. *Desnick v. American Broadcasting Companies, Inc.,* 23 Med.L.Rptr. 1161, 44 F.3d 1345 (7th Cir. 1995).

181. *Cox Enterprises Inc. v. Thrasher,* 22 Med.L.Rptr. 1799, 442 S.E.2d 704 (Ga. 1994).
182. *Gertz v. Robert Welch, Inc.,* 418 U.S. 323, 339 (1974).
183. That language is believed to have originated in the classic American case of fair comment, *Cherry Sisters v. Des Moines Leader,* 86 N.W. 323 (Iowa 1901), involving a somewhat grotesque but well-known vaudeville act of the time.

demonstrated hostility) could destroy the defense. So could an opinion based on false facts.

In 1984, a D.C. Circuit Court of Appeals ruling gave structure to the opinion defense.[184] Columnists Rowland Evans and Robert Novak criticized the appointment of professed Marxist Bertell Ollman to head the University of Maryland's Department of Politics and Government because, they said, he would use the classroom as an instrument for preparing for "revolution." They belittled his academic standing and challenged his pedagogic motives. Ollman asked for a retraction. It was refused, but a letter from Ollman was published in the *Washington Post*. Ollman sued, and a federal district court granted summary judgment to the columnists. Ollman appealed.

In a carefully crafted opinion, the federal appeals court affirmed a long tradition of judges' decisions on what was fact and what was opinion; the result was a four-part test to assist in making the distinction:

1. *Common usage.* Does the language have a precise meaning in ordinary usage, or is it indefinite and ambiguous?
2. *Verifiability.* Can the language be objectively characterized as true or false? The assumption is that facts can be so designated while opinions can only be called fair or unfair.
3. *Context and setting.* Where does the statement appear? In a column or an op-ed page, or in a news story? What kind of language surrounds it? How would the intended audience take the statement?
4. *Cautionary language.* Is the reader tipped off in any way that the statement is an opinion through the use of metaphor, hyperbole, or other figurative forms of speech?

The difficulty in distinguishing fact and opinion is still the central problem with the opinion defense, but this model is helpful.

Former Judge Robert Bork, concurring in the same case in a ringing defense of freedom of the press, added a fifth factor to *Ollman: political or public speech.* Those "who choose the pleasures and distractions of controversy," he wrote, "must be willing to bear criticism, disparagement, and even wounding assessments."

One of the first to feel the punch of *Ollman*'s fifth element was William Janklow, former governor of South Dakota. His libel claims were rejected first by a federal appeals court and later by the highest court of South Dakota on the grounds that assertions that he went "from raping an Indian teen-ager to raping Mother Earth" were "imprecise, unverifiable" and "presented in a forum where spirited writing is expected and involves criticism of the motives and intentions of a public official. . . ."[185]

As a result, with impunity in this period people began to call other people "unscrupulous charlatans," "cancer con artists," "Al Capone of the City," "neo-Nazis," "an unbelievably unscrupulous character," "a sleazebag" who "kind of slimed up from the bayou," and "an ignorant spineless politician."[186] All of these expressions led to libel suits, and all were held in 1987 to be protected expressions of opinion.

Judge Antonin Scalia's dissent in the *Ollman* case may have been a harbinger. Scalia reviled the press for descending from discussion of public issues to the intentional destruction of private reputations and called for solutions.

A partial solution, from Scalia's perspective, may have come with the Supreme Court's 1990 holding in *Milkovich v. Lorain Journal Co.*[187] A high school wrestling coach sued when the Willoughby (Ohio) *News-Herald* alleged that he had lied under oath about a fight at a wrestling match. There is no separate constitutional privilege, said the Court, this time in contradiction of *Gertz,* for anything called opinion, especially when it is based on false statements of fact, facts that cannot be supported, or facts that are simply implied. To write "in my opinion, Jones is a liar" is no defense. The charge implies a knowledge of facts. The Court seemed to be making *verifiability* the only consequential part of the now five-part opinion test for actionable libel set

184. *Ollman v. Evans,* 11 Med.L.Rptr. 1433, 750 F.2d 970 (D.C.Cir. 1984), *cert. denied,* 471 U.S. 1127 (1985).

185. *Janklow v. Newsweek,* 11 Med.L.Rptr. 1995, 12 Med.L.Rptr. 1961, 788 F.2d 1300 (8th Cir. 1986); *Janklow v. Viking Press,* 17 Med.L.Rptr. 2220, 459 N.W.2d 415 (S.D.Sup.Ct. 1990).
186. The cases are, in order, *Kirk v. CBS,* 14 Med.L.Rptr. 1263 (D.C.N.Ill. 1987); *Rowland v. Fayed,* 14 Med.L.Rptr. 1257 (D.C.Super.Ct. 1987); *Populist Party of Iowa v. American Black Hawk Broadcasting Co.,* 14 Med.L.Rptr. 1217 (Iowa Dist.Ct. 1987); *Chalpin v. Amordian Press,* 14 Med.L.Rptr. 1206, 515 N.Y.Supp.2d 434 (1987): *Henderson v. Times Mirror Co.,* 14 Med.L.Rptr. 1659 (D.C.Col. 1987): *Dow v. New Haven Independent,* 14 Med.L.Rptr. 1228, 41 Conn.Supp. 31 (Conn. Super.Ct. 1987).
187. 17 Med.L.Rptr. 2009, 497 U.S. 1, 110 S.Ct. 2695 (1990).

down by *Ollman.* If a statement could be proven, said the *Milkovich* Court, it was a fact, not opinion. The Court also reversed the long-held rule that separating fact from opinion was a task for the judge rather than the jury.

The media world was distressed. The 55,000 circulation newspaper paid Milkovich $116,000 in settlement of his suit and estimated that its legal costs over a sixteen-year period amounted to $500,000. Some state courts proceeded to use their own state constitutions to circumvent *Milkovich.*

For the media, the only redeeming feature of *Milkovich* was that the Court affirmed the rule laid down in *Hepps* that *falsity* had to be proved by the plaintiff. This constitutional requirement may be more protective of the media in the long run than a defendant having to convince a jury that what was written was opinion rather than fact. And, of course, pure opinion is still protected. The more fantastic, hyperbolic, unbelievable, implausible, and exaggerated a statement, the more likely it is to fall into the protected opinion category. Parody, satire, humor, and ridicule often fall into that category, but caution is advised.

In 1991, New York's highest court, in a case remanded by the U.S. Supreme Court, held that a letter to the editor of a scientific journal complaining about the handling of laboratory chimpanzees qualified as opinion under the state's constitution and common law. The content, tone, and apparent purpose of the letter when viewed in *context,* said the New York court, made it an expression of opinion on matters of public interest. In addition, the court said that New York's constitution often protected free speech and press more broadly than the federal constitution. While seeming to criticize the Supreme Court's narrow focus on the fact/opinion distinction in *Milkovich,* the New York court nevertheless recognized its responsibility to that body by noting that nothing in the letter had been proven false by the plaintiff, as the federal Constitution (presumably the First Amendment) and *Hepps* would require in a libel suit involving public matters.[188] In the post-*Milkovich* period,

other lower courts, Ohio's[189] as well as New York's and others, seemed persuaded by the logic of the *Ollman* test and were prepared to use their own constitutions and common law to apply it or something like it. For example, in *Cassidy v. Merin,*[190] a New Jersey court said, "[O]ur law (specifically the 'fair comment privilege') as applied in this case is at least as protective of free speech as federal law would be."

In a highly dramatic case, a three-judge panel of the influential D.C. Circuit Court of Appeals voted 2–1 to reverse a decision by a federal trial court granting a newspaper's motion for summary judgment.[191] Judge Harry Edwards, who wrote the opinion for the panel, would, within ten weeks, reverse himself and admit to making an error in judgment in his earlier holding.

The facts of the case were these. Dan Moldea, author of the book *Interference: How Organized Crime Influences Professional Football,* sued the *New York Times* for a review that accused him of "sloppy journalism" and thus, said the court, depicted him as an incompetent practitioner in his field. In its initial opinion, known as *Moldea I,* the appeals court majority said the newspaper would have to support its opinion with "true facts" to win a summary judgment. In response, the newspaper argued that the majority's reliance on *Milkovich's* verifiability requirement was misplaced because "sloppy journalism," a subjective evaluation of a writer's work, is not verifiable. Recall that in *Milkovich* the Supreme Court pulled back from the *Ollman* guidelines, where context was one of a number of additional requirements. Here again, the opinion defense appeared to be losing ground.

Then Judge Edwards changed his mind and in *Moldea II* adopted what had been the minority position in *Moldea I.* Context, he said, as *Ollman* held, is important. Here the criticism appeared in a book review, "a genre in which readers expect to find spirited critiques of literary works. . . ." Still, there would be no wholesale exemption from liability in defamation for statements of opinion "if they imply a provable false fact or

188. *Immuno A.G. v. Moor-Jankowski,* 18 Med.L.Rptr. 1625, 567 N.E.2d 1270, 77 N.Y.2d 235, 566 N.Y.S.2d 906 (1991), *cert. denied,* 111 S.Ct. 2261 (1991).

189. *Vail v. Plain Dealer Publishing Co.,* 23 Med.L.Rptr. 1881, 649 N.E.2d 182 (Ohio 1995).
190. 582 A.2d 1039 (N.J.Super. A.D. 1990).
191. *Moldea v. New York Times Co., Inc.,* 22 Med.L.Rptr. 1321, 15 F.3d 1137 (D.C.Cir. 1994).

rely upon stated facts that are provably false."[192] While not rejecting *Milkovich*'s holding that allegations of crime are not usually defensible as opinion (in that case, perjury), the appeals court seemed to be moving back toward *Ollman*. Weaving the threads of the opinion defense into a meaningful tapestry, the court's ruling in *Moldea II* is worth presenting in large part:

Moldea v. New York Times Co.
22 MED.L.RPTR. 1673, 22 F.3D 310 (D.C. CIR. 1994).

* * *

In the District Court and on appeal, Moldea alleged that six specific statements in the Times review had defamed him by accusing him of being an incompetent practitioner of his chosen profession, investigative journalism, and by supporting that accusation with false characterizations of his book. We held in *Moldea (I)* that one of these passages was a statement of opinion that implied defamatory facts because it accused Moldea of being an incompetent journalist. That statement read:

> But there is too much sloppy journalism to trust the bulk of this book's 512 pages including its whopping 64 pages of footnotes.

Moldea (I) went on to hold that the remaining statements Moldea challenged were offered by Eskenazi as factual examples of *Interference*'s alleged "sloppiness," and that "[i]n order for the review to be nonactionable as a matter of law, the Times must show that it offered true facts in support of its judgment that served to support its statement of opinion."

Our earlier decision in this cases held that three of the five remaining statements challenged by Moldea on appeal were not actionable in defamation. Of the three nonactionable passages, two were incontrovertibly true statements based upon facts revealed in the text of *Interference*, while the third was a supported statement of opinion. *Moldea (I)* held, however, that two of the challenged passages in the Times review were verifiable, and that a reasonable juror could conclude that they were false. First, the review stated:

Mr. Moldea tells as well of Mr. Namath's 'guaranteeing' a victory in Super Bowl III shortly after a sinister meeting in a bar with a member of the opposition, Lou Michaels, the Baltimore Colts' place-kicker. The truth is that the pair almost came to blows after they both had been drinking; and Mr. Namath's well-publicized 'guarantee' came about quite innocently at a Miami Touchdown Club dinner when a fan asked him if he thought the Jets had a chance. 'We'll win. I guarantee it,' Mr. Namath replied.

Second, the review opined that:

> [Moldea] revives the discredited notion that Carroll Rosenbloom, the ornery owner of the Rams, who had a penchant for gambling, met foul play when he drowned in Florida 10 years ago.

Our initial opinion in this case concluded that a reasonable juror could find that the Times review had mischaracterized *Interference*'s portrayal of each of the foregoing two events. Accordingly, we held that it was error for the trial court to grant summary judgment at so early a stage of this litigation.

Discussion

A. The Importance of Context

Moldea (I) noted that, "under the established case law, our analysis of this case is not altered by the fact that the challenged statements appeared in a 'book review' rather than in a hard news story." This statement is correct insofar as it suggests that there is no *per se* exemption from defamation for book reviews. Even the Times concedes this point in its Petition for Rehearing. ("No one doubts that a book review can be actionable.") A writer may not commit libel at will merely by labelling his work a "review." *Moldea (I)* is short-sighted, however, in failing to take account of the fact that the challenged statements were evaluations of a literary work which appeared in a forum in which readers expect to find such evaluations. As the Supreme Court has recognized, writers must be given some leeway to offer "rational interpretation" of ambiguous sources. *See Masson v. New Yorker Magazine, Inc.,* 111 S. Ct. 2419, 2434 [18 Med.L.Rptr. 2241] (1991). Thus, when a reviewer offers commentary that is tied to the work being reviewed, and that is a supportable interpretation of the author's work, that interpretation does not pre-

---

192. *Moldea v. New York Times Co., Inc.,* 22 Med.L.Rptr. 1673, 22 F.3d 310 (D.C.Cir. 1994).

sent a verifiable issue of fact that can be actionable in defamation.

The fundamental framework established in *Moldea (I)* for defamation actions is sound, and we do not modify it in this decision. As we stated in our initial opinion, the Supreme Court's decision in *Milkovich v. Lorain Journal Co.,* 497 U.S. 1 [17 Med.L.Rptr. 2009] (1990), and this court's decision in *White v. Fraternal Order of Police,* 909 F.2d 512 [17 Med.L.Rptr. 2137] (D.C. Cir. 1990), make clear that there is no wholesale exemption from liability in defamation for statements of "opinion." Instead, statements of opinion can be actionable if they imply a provably false fact, or rely upon stated facts that are provably false. *See generally Moldea (I),* 15 F.3d at 1143–45.

In *Milkovich,* the Supreme Court rejected the argument that an accusation of perjury was nonactionable merely because it was offered as the writer's "opinion." In that case, a high school wrestling coach argued that an Ohio newspaper libeled him by printing a column which alleged that he had perjured himself in his testimony to a state court concerning his role in an altercation between his team and an opposing squad at a wrestling match. The column stated that: "Anyone who attended the meet . . . knows in his heart that Milkovich . . . lied at the hearing." Although the statements at issue in *Milkovich* appeared in an "opinion column" in a newspaper sports section, the Court found no relevance in this fact in reaching its decision, apparently because an accusation of perjury is not the sort of discourse that even arguably is the usual province of such columns.[2] Sports columnists frequently offer intemperate denunciations of coaches' play-calling or strategy, and readers know this and presumably take such railings with a grain of salt; but an accusation of criminal conduct is a classic libel, and so *Milkovich* did not even pause to assess the effect that the column's context may have had on those who read it.

In *Moldea (I),* this court observed that *Milkovich* made no mention of the fact that the statements at issue in that case appeared in a sports column, and took that fact to mean that context was irrelevant in the instant case. We now recognize, however, as has the First Circuit, that *Milkovich* did not disavow the importance of context, but simply "discounted it in the circumstances of that case." *Phantom Touring, Inc. v. Affiliated Publications,* 953 F.2d 724, 729 n.9 [19 Med.L.Rptr. 1786] (1st Cir. 1992) (holding newspaper theater column nonactionable in part because "the context of each article rendered the language not reasonably interpreted as stating 'actual facts' about appellant's honesty."), *cert. denied,* 112 S. Ct. 2942 (1992). This conclusion is compelled by the logic of two Supreme Court cases expressly reaffirmed in *Milkovich,* and by the Court's decision in *Masson,* rendered the following term.

First, *Milkovich* reaffirmed the vitality of *Greenbelt Cooperative Publishing Association v. Bresler,* 398 U.S. 6 [1 Med.L.Rptr. 1589] (1970), and *Letter Carriers v. Austin,* 418 U.S. 264 (1974). In *Bresler,* a real estate developer had engaged in negotiations with a city council for a zoning variance, while simultaneously negotiating with the city over other land that the city wished to purchase from him. A local newspaper account stated that some people had characterized the developer's tactics as "blackmail," and the developer sued for libel. The court rejected the developer's argument that "blackmail" implied criminal activity, noting that "the word 'blackmail' *in these circumstances* was not slander when spoken . . . ." (emphasis added). In *Letter Carriers,* the Court held that the use of the word "traitor" to define a "scab" in the context of a labor dispute could not be the basis for a defamation action. Both *Bresler* and *Letter Carriers* rely in large part on the notion that the speech at issue in each case was intended as hyperbole; however, this fact reinforces the importance of context, because it is in part the *settings* of the speech in question that makes their hyperbolic nature apparent, and which helps determine the way in which the intended audience will receive them. Thus, the "lusty and imaginative expression of the contempt felt by union members" for a "scab" may lawfully find hyperbolic expression

---

2. *Milkovich* did briefly address whether the "general tenor" of the column negated the impression that the "writer was seriously maintaining that petitioner committed the crime of perjury," 497 U.S. at 21, but this assessment had to do with whether the statements at issue in that case were intended as hyperbole, not with the genre in which they appeared. The Court's decision in *Milkovich* provided that "loose, figurative, or hyperbolic" statements generally are not actionable in defamation, but this status derives from the constitutional protection afforded to parody, satire, and other imaginative commentary, not from a privilege for "opinion." *See Moldea (I),* 15 F.3d at 1143–44.

during a strike, because the context assures that no reader could understand the epithet "traitor" to be a charge that the "scab" has committed the criminal offense of treason.

Second, *Masson*, handed down in the term following *Milkovich*, is further evidence that the Supreme Court has not abandoned the consideration of context in defamation actions. In *Masson*, the Court addressed the question whether a writer's alteration of quotations attributed to the subject of an interview could establish the "actual malice" required for a defamation suit by a public figure. *Masson* observed that whether quotations will be interpreted by readers as the actual statements of a speaker depends on context for example, whether there is "an acknowledgment that the work is a so-called docudrama or historical fiction, or that it recreates conversations from memory, not from recordings. . . ." *Masson*, 111 S. Ct. at 2430–31.

In *Ollman v. Evans*, 750 F.2d 970, 983 [11 Med.L.Rptr. 1433] (D.C. Cir. 1984) *(en banc)*, *cert. denied*, 471 U.S. 1127 (1985), we recognized that courts have long "considered the influence that . . . well-established *genres* of writing will have on the average reader." (emphasis in original). Given that *Milkovich* was decided against the backdrop of this settled principle, and that it expressly reaffirmed two of the Court's key precedents in this area, we are, on reflection, convinced that *Moldea (I)* erred in assuming that *Milkovich* abandoned the principle of looking to the context in which speech appears. The Court's decision in *Masson* appears to confirm this interpretation of *Milkovich*. While *Milkovich* could be interpreted as we read it in our initial decision, we are unwilling to assume that the Court meant to sweep away so much settled law without a clearer indication that this was indeed its intent.

B. Relevance of the Book Review Context

In contrast to the situation in *Milkovich*, the instant case involves a context, a book review, in which the allegedly libelous statements were evaluations quintessentially of a type readers expect to find in that genre. The challenged statements in the Times review consist solely of the reviewer's comments on a literary work, and therefore must be judged with an eye toward readers' expectations and understandings of book reviews. This would not be the case if, for example, the review stated or implied that *Interference* was a badly written book because its author was a drug dealer. In that situation, this case would parallel *Milkovich*: the reviewer would simply be employing the medium of a book review as a vehicle for what would be a garden-variety libel, and the review would thus potentially be actionable.

There is a long and rich history in our cultural and legal traditions of affording reviewers latitude to comment on literary and other works. The statements at issue in the instant case are assessments of a book, rather than direct assaults on Moldea's character, reputation, or competence as a journalist. While a bad review necessarily has the effect of injuring an author's reputation to some extent—sometimes to a devastating extent, as Moldea alleges is true here—criticism's long and impressive pedigree persuades us that, while a critic's latitude is not unlimited, he or she must be given the constitutional "breathing space" appropriate to the genre. *New York Times Co. v. Sullivan*, 376 U.S. 254, 272 [1 Med.L.Rptr. 1527] (1964).

We believe that the Times has suggested the appropriate standard for evaluating critical reviews: "The proper analysis would make commentary actionable only when the interpretations are *unsupportable by reference to the written work*." Petition for Rehearing at 8 (emphasis added). This "supportable interpretation" standard provides that a critic's interpretation must be rationally supportable by reference to the actual text he or she is evaluating, and thus would not immunize situations analogous to that presented in *Milkovich*, in which a writer launches a personal attack, rather than interpreting a book. This standard also establishes boundaries even for textual interpretation. A critic's statement must be a rational assessment or account of something the reviewer can point to *in the text, or omitted from the text*, being critiqued. For instance, if the Times review stated that *Interference* was a terrible book because it asserted that African-Americans make poor football coaches, that reading would be "unsupportable by reference to the written work," because nothing in Moldea's book even hints at this notion. In such a case, the usual inquiries as to libel would apply: a jury could determine that the review falsely characterized *Interference*, thereby libeling its author by portraying him as a racist (assuming the other elements of the case could be proved).

Our decision to apply the "supportable interpretation" standard to book reviews finds strong support in analogous decisions of the Supreme Court, all decided or reaffirmed after *Milkovich*. These cases establish that when a writer is evaluating or giving an account of inherently ambiguous materials or subject matter, the First Amendment requires that the courts allow latitude for interpretation. For example, in *Bose Corp. v. Consumers Union of United States, Inc.*, 466 U.S. 485 [10 Med.L.Rptr. 1625] (1984), a decision the Court discussed and reaffirmed in *Masson*, a reviewer writing for *Consumer Reports* magazine described the experience of listening to music through a pair of stereo speakers: "[I]ndividual instruments heard through the Bose system seemed to grow to gigantic proportions and tended to wander about the room." Bose Corporation sued for defamation, alleging that the reviewer's unflattering portrayal was factually inaccurate. The Court held that the statements were not actionable, because they were not so obviously false as to sustain a finding of "actual malice." As the Court interpreted *Bose* in *Masson*:

> [T]he result was not an assessment of events that speak for themselves, but "one of a number of possible rational interpretations of an event that bristled with ambiguities and descriptive challenges for the writer." We refused to permit recovery for choice of language which, though perhaps reflecting a misconception, represented "the sort of inaccuracy that is commonplace in the forum of robust debate to which the New York Times rule applies."

Masson, 111 S. Ct. at 2434 (quoting *Bose*, 466 U.S. at 512, 513).

The Court's opinion in *Bose* relied heavily on its earlier decision in *Time, Inc. v. Pape*, 401 U.S. 279 [1 Med.L.Rptr. 1627] (1971). *Pape* reversed a libel judgment against a reporter who had summarized a report by the United States Commission on Civil Rights discussing civil rights abuses by police officers. The article quoted the Commission's summary of the facts of an alleged incident of police brutality, but failed to state that the Commission had qualified its remarks by noting that they were taken from a civil complaint. As in

Bose, the Court held that the claim was not actionable because the publication was not sufficiently false to sustain a finding of "actual malice." *Masson* explained that *Pape* "distinguished between a 'direct account of events that speak for themselves' and an article descriptive of what the Commission had reported. *Time, Inc. v. Pape* took into account the difficult choices that confront an author who departs from direct quotation and offers his own interpretation of an ambiguous source." *Masson*, 111 S. Ct. at 2434 (quoting *Pape*, 401 U.S. at 285).

Finally, *Masson* itself noted that: "The protection for rational interpretation serves First Amendment principles by allowing an author the interpretive license that is necessary when relying upon ambiguous sources." *Masson* concluded that in order to state a claim for defamation based upon the alteration of direct quotations, a plaintiff must show that the alterations resulted in "a material change in the meaning conveyed by the statement."[3] Although *Masson*, *Bose* and *Pape* all concerned the evidence necessary to establish "actual malice," those decisions are rooted in the question of a plaintiff's ability to prove *falsity* so as to show that a defendant presented information he or she knew to be false. Because of their focus on falsity, the reasoning of these decisions is fully applicable to the instant case. *Masson*, *Bose* and *Pape* recognized that some materials by their very nature require interpretation, and that the First Amendment affords latitude to those engaged in that task. Reasonable minds can and do differ as to how to interpret a literary work. Accordingly, as *Masson* counsels, we must allow a degree of "interpretive license."

---

3. *Masson* rejected a "rational interpretation" standard for quotations that are purportedly the actual words of a speaker, because such quotations signal readers that the quoted material is something more than just the writer's "interpretation." *See Masson*, 111 S. Ct. at 2433, 2434. In short, direct quotations are "the quintessential 'direct account of events that speak for themselves.' " *Id.* at 2434 (quoting *Pape*, 401 U.S. at 285). In the instant case, the Times review at no point purported to quote from *Interference*, but rather offered what was plainly the reviewer's interpretation of the book. Thus, in this regard, the instant case is much more like *Bose* and *Pape* than it is like *Masson*, and the "supportable interpretation" standard is appropriate.

C. Application of the "Supportable Interpretation" Standard to the Times Review

As we noted in our initial decision, this appeal presents a pure question of law, which we review *de novo*: whether Moldea can in fact state a claim for defamation. In this situation, we must determine as a threshold matter whether a challenged statement is capable of a defamatory meaning; and whether it is verifiable—that is, whether a plaintiff can prove that it is false. The Times review is, as we previously held, capable of a defamatory meaning insofar as it tends to injure Moldea's reputation as a practitioner of his chosen profession, investigative journalism. The key to this case is the question of verifiability.

Although *Moldea (I)* held that the Times review's statement that *Interference* contained "too much sloppy journalism" was a verifiable assessment of the book, we now recognize that, in the context of a book review, it is highly debatable whether this statement is sufficiently verifiable to be actionable in defamation. Arguably, our decision in *Moldea (I)* failed adequately to heed the counsel of both the Supreme Court and our own precedents that "[w]here the question of truth or falsity is a close one, a court should err on the side of nonactionability." *Liberty Lobby, Inc. v. Dow Jones & Co.,* 838 F.2d 1287, 1292 [14 Med.L.Rptr. 2249] (D.C. Cir.) (citing *Philadelphia Newspapers, Inc. v. Hepps,* 475 U.S. 767, 776 [12 Med.L.Rptr. 1977] (1986)), *cert. denied,* 486 U.S. 825 (1988). "The First Amendment requires that we protect some falsehood in order to protect speech that matters." *Gertz v. Robert Welch, Inc.,* 418 U.S. 323, 341 [1 Med.L.Rptr. 1633] (1974). The Court has cautioned in several cases that the First Amendment preserves a "breathing space" essential to the exercise of freedom of the press. "To that end [the Supreme] Court has extended a measure of strategic protection to defamatory falsehood." *Id.* at 342.

However, we need not determine whether "too much sloppy journalism" is verifiable, as the statements that the Times review offers in support of this assessment are supportable interpretations of *Interference.* Thus, even if the review's assertion that the book contains "too much sloppy journalism" is verifiable, that assessment is supported by revealed premises that we cannot hold to be false in the context of a book review. As we stated in *Moldea (I):* "Because the reader understands that such supported opinions represent the writer's interpretation of the facts presented, and because the reader is free to draw his or her own conclusions based upon those facts, this type of statement is not actionable in defamation."

As we noted above, *Moldea (I)* held that only two of the five challenged passages in the Times review could be proven to be false; the other three were held either to be true, or to be supported statements of opinion. In addition, Moldea did not challenge the review's assertion that *Interference* contains several spelling errors which the reviewer concluded "call into question [Moldea's] diligence at simple fact-checking." Thus, only two passages in the Times review are even potentially actionable: the statement that *Interference* "revives the discredited notion" that Carroll Rosenbloom was murdered, and the claim that Moldea described a meeting between opposing players just before the 1969 Super Bowl as "sinister."

Our initial decision in this case erred by basing its holding on a standard that failed to take into account the fact that the challenged statements appeared in the context of a book review, and were solely evaluations of a literary work. *Moldea (I)* considered whether a reasonable jury *could find* that the challenged statements were false because they mischaracterized *Interference.* Such a standard might be appropriate in the case of an ordinary libel such as that at issue in *Milkovich,* but it is an inappropriate measure of an interpretation of a book. Applying the "supportable interpretation" standard, the correct measure of the challenged statements' verifiability as a matter of law is whether *no reasonable person could find* that the review's characterizations were supportable interpretations of *Interference.* Applying this standard, we hold that the Times review is not actionable in defamation.

First, the Times review stated that:

> [Moldea] revives the discredited notion that Carroll Rosenbloom, the ornery owner of the Rams, who had a penchant for gambling, met foul play when he drowned in Florida 10 years ago.

Moldea discusses Rosenbloom's drowning in pages 319 through 326 of his book, closing his account with quoted observations from several of

Rosenbloom's friends, who speculate that he was murdered. *Interference* later reveals, on page 360, that Moldea has located previously unknown photographs, taken at Rosenbloom's autopsy, which make clear that he "died in a tragic accident and was not murdered." As we held in *Moldea (I)*, a reasonable jury could conclude that the Times review's characterization of *Interference*'s portrayal of Rosenbloom's death was false, and that the reviewer's account of the book creates the misleading impression that Moldea inadequately investigated this story. However, given that *Interference* does not reveal that Rosenbloom's death was accidental until 35 pages after giving undeniably titillating hints of homicide, we cannot hold that a reviewer could not reasonably suggest that Moldea sought to "revive" the notion that Rosenbloom was murdered in order to build suspense before disproving that theory.

The second potentially actionable review passage (involves Namath's meeting with opponent Michaels) . . . *Moldea (I)* concluded that a reasonable jury could find that Moldea did not describe the meeting as a "sinister" rendezvous, but rather made clear that the meeting was "quite accidental and even confrontational." Even applying the "supportable interpretation" standard, this review passage is close to the line. *Interference* not only states that the Namath-Michaels meeting was "accidental," but on the same page quotes Michaels as saying "What we talked about had no relationship to the game," and quotes another player present at the meeting as confirming that " 'nothing technical' about the game was discussed." The Times' petition for rehearing argues only that the review's characterization is supported by the fact that *Interference*'s description of the Namath-Michaels meeting appears in a chapter of the book largely devoted to probing allegations that there was something "suspicious" about Super Bowl III.

We are troubled by the "sinister meeting" passage, but are constrained to conclude that it does not give rise to an actionable claim. The review offered at least six observations to support the charge of "sloppy journalism": the five challenged passages, plus the unchallenged claim that Moldea made several spelling errors. At least five of these observations could not be proved false at trial, either because they are true, are

supported opinion, are reasonable interpretations, or are not challenged in this suit. Moldea is left with only the "sinister meeting" passage as a possible basis for his defamation claim, and this is a very weak basis indeed. For one thing, the "sinister meeting" passage is not defamatory on its face, but rather is simply one of the "interpretations" offered in support of the review's assessment of Moldea's book. Furthermore, even without the support of the "sinister meeting" passage, the review's assertion that *Interference* is marred by "too much sloppy journalism" is (as a legal matter) "substantially true," and so is not actionable in defamation.

As *Moldea (I)* noted, "substantial truth" is a defense to defamation. *Moldea (I)*, 15 F.3d at 1150. "Slight inaccuracies of expression are immaterial provided that the defamatory charge is true in substance." *Liberty Lobby v. Dow Jones*, 838 F.2d at 1296 (citing Restatement (Second) of Torts § 581A cmt. f (1977)); *accord Foretich v. CBS, Inc.*, 619 A.2d 48, 60 [21 Med.L.Rptr. 1001] (D.C. 1993) (citing *Liberty Lobby v. Dow Jones*). The Supreme Court explained this defense in *Masson* by noting that: "Minor inaccuracies do not amount to falsity so long as the substance, the gist, the sting, of the libelous charge be justified." 111 S.Ct. at 2433 (interpreting California law); *accord Liberty Lobby v. Dow Jones*, 838 F.2d at 1296 (a statement is nonactionable if "[t]he sting of the charge . . . is substantially true"). The difficulty here is that, as *Moldea (I)* pointed out, this circuit rejected the so-called "incremental harm rule" in *Liberty Lobby, Inc. v. Anderson*, 746 F.2d 1563, 1568 [11 Med.L.Rptr. 1001] (D.C. Cir. 1984), *vacated on other grounds*, 477 U.S. 242 [12 Med.L.Rptr. 2297] (1986). *See Moldea (I)*, 15 F.3d at 1149–50. Application on the "substantial truth" test when "incremental harm" is not tolerated can be conceptually confusing. However, on reconsidering the instant dispute, we believe *Moldea (I)* read this court's rejection of the incremental harm rule much too broadly, and that *Anderson*'s proscription is not applicable in this case.

Liberty Lobby v. Anderson rejected the defendants' claim that the plaintiffs in that case were "libel-proof" because "unchallenged portions of [defendants'] articles attribute[d] to the [plaintiffs] characteristics so much worse than those attributed in the challenged portions, that the latter could not conceivably do any incremental damage." 746 F.2d at 1568. Then-Judge Scalia observed that:

> The law, however, proceeds upon the optimistic premise that there is a little bit of good in all of us or perhaps upon the pessimistic assumption that no matter how bad someone is, he can always be worse. It is shameful that Benedict Arnold was a traitor; but he was not a shoplifter to boot, and one should not be able to make that charge while knowing its falsity with impunity."

However, the opinion goes on to note that:

> There may be validity to the proposition that at some point the erroneous attribution of incremental evidence of a character flaw of a particular type which is in any event amply established by the facts is not derogatory. If, for example, an individual is said to have been convicted of 35 burglaries, when the correct number is 34, it is not likely that the statement is actionable. That is so, however, not because the object of the remarks is "libel-proof," but because since the essentially derogatory implication of the statement ("he is an habitual burglar") is correct, he has not been libeled.

Id. at 1568–69 n.6. This latter point is dispositive of the instant case.

The disputed "sinister meeting" passage in the Times review is not inherently defamatory *i.e.*, it is not like calling Benedict Arnold a "traitor" *and* a "shoplifter," to cite the example used in *Anderson*. Rather, the discussion of the "sinister meeting" is but one of several interpretations of the book offered to support the claim of "sloppy journalism." As such, it does not come within the compass of "incremental harm." Because the review relies principally on statements that are true, supported opinions or supportable interpretations to justify the "sloppy journalism" assessment, we are constrained to find that it is substantially true and therefore not actionable.

Incidental Issues

Because we uphold the District Court's grant of summary judgment for the Times on Moldea's defamation claim, Moldea's related claim for false light invasion of privacy must also fail. As we noted in *Moldea (I)*, "a plaintiff may not avoid the strictures of the burdens of proof associated with defamation by resorting to a claim of false light invasion." *Moldea (I)*, 15 F.3d at 1151 (cit-

ing *Cohen v. Cowles Media Co.*, 111 S. Ct. 2513, 2519 [18 Med.L.Rptr. 2273] (1991); *Hustler Magazine, Inc. v. Falwell*, 485 U.S. 46, 56 [14 Med.L.Rptr. 2281] (1988)). Similarly, our resolution of Moldea's defamation claim requires that we uphold the District Court's denial of permission to amend the Complaint in the instant case. *See Moldea v. New York Times Co.*, 793 F. Supp. 338 [19 Med.L.Rptr. 1931] (D.D.C. 1992). Appellant sought to add four causes of action to his Complaint, based upon the Supreme Court's decision in *Cohen v. Cowles Media Co.* In light of our resolution of Moldea's libel claim, we agree with the trial court's assessment that the amended Complaint could not withstand a motion to dismiss, and so would be futile. As *Cohen* itself held, a plaintiff may not use related causes of action to avoid the constitutional requisites of a defamation claim. *See Cohen*, 111 S. Ct. at 2519.

Conclusion

Moldea has made a number of allegations in this suit that Gerald Eskenazi's negative review of *Interference* was prompted in part by Eskenazi's allegiance to the National Football League ("NFL"). Moldea alleged in his original brief to this court that Eskenazi has covered the NFL as a correspondent for over thirty years, and that he was therefore biased against *Interference* because he was dependent on the league's goodwill in order to gain access to information necessary to report on its activities. Indeed, Moldea's book predicts that the NFL's "loyal sportswriters" will try to discredit *Interference*. Even if true, however, these allegations do not make a case for appellant.

Any intelligent reviewer knows at some level that a bad review may injure the author of the book which is its subject. Indeed, some bad reviews may be written with an aim to damage a writer's reputation. There is nothing that we can do about this, at least not without unacceptably interfering with free speech. There simply is no viable way to distinguish between reviews written by those who honestly believe a book is bad, and those prompted solely by mischievous intent. To allow a plaintiff to base a lawsuit on claims of mischief, without some indication that the review's interpretations are unsupportable, would wreak havoc on the law of defamation.

See McBride v. Merrell Dow & Pharmaceuticals, Inc., 717 F.2d 1460, 1466 [9 Med.L.Rptr. 2225] (D.C. Cir. 1983) ("Libel suits, if not carefully handled, can threaten journalistic independence. Even if many actions fail, the risks and high costs of litigation may lead to undesirable forms of self-censorship.").

"As James Madison pointed out in the Report on the Virginia Resolutions of 1798: 'Some degree of abuse is inseparable from the proper use of everything; and in no instance is that more true than in that of the press.' " *Gertz,* 418 U.S. at 340. We are not insensitive to the fact that the "supportable interpretation" rule may permit some malicious reviews to go unchecked; however, "[b]ecause an *ad hoc* resolution of the competing interests at stake in each particular case is not feasible, we must lay down broad rules of general application." *Id.* at 343–44.

This is a difficult case, and we can easily understand the frustrations that have prompted Mr. Moldea's long legal battle. Upon reconsideration, however, we find that our first opinion in this case was misguided. Accordingly, we modify that opinion as indicated herein, and affirm the grant of summary judgment in favor of appellee New York Times Company.

So ordered.

COMMENT

As one might expect, the media bar rejoiced over *Moldea II.* Some thought it the most important case since *New York Times v. Sullivan.* Newspaper, book, and magazine publishers and Judge Kenneth Starr, then solicitor-general and author of the D.C. Circuit Court's opinion in *Ollman,* had joined the *Times* in asking the appeals court to reverse itself. *Moldea I* had made the media vulnerable to a potential deluge of libel suits.

In reversing its earlier decision, the court noted, "There is simply no way to distinguish between reviews written by those who honestly believe a book is bad, and those prompted solely by mischievous intent. To allow a plaintiff to base a lawsuit on claims of mischief, without some indication that the reviewer's interpretations are unsupportable, would wreak havoc on the law of defamation."[193] Now a defamatory

opinion tied to the work under review and a supportable interpretation of that work would be protected.

The plaintiff bar[194] thought *Moldea II* bad law. Both groups of lawyers speculated on how far beyond book reviews, and perhaps theater[195] and restaurant reviews, *Moldea II* might apply. At least for book reviews, the main question now would be whether offending statements are supportable interpretations of an author's work, and this would be decided up front by a judge as a matter of law, rather than as a question of fact to be determined through the long and expensive process of discovery and trial.[196]

But a problem remains. Like all dichotomies, including truth/falsehood and public/private, the fact/opinion dichotomy, if not false, is a gross simplification that promises more comfort than it gives. Legal commentators have called the fact/opinion dichotomy "enigmatic and intellectually opaque," "elusive" and "murky."[197] Robert Sack called the distinction "essentially a fiction" designed to maintain "liberality of expression."[198] However fictitious the distinction may appear to be in certain situations, it will nevertheless be made—one hopes in the context of all relevant circumstances and the perspectives of speaker, audience, and libel plaintiff.

What have been the consequences of the opinion defense as far as it has evolved? A few cases may partially answer that question. A school board member's allegation that a plaintiff engaging in discriminatory hiring practices was one of the "new night-riders of the KKK" was said by a New York court to be hyperbolic language that no reasonable reader would interpret as meaning that the plaintiff was actually a member of the

---

193. Id. at 1681.

194. For one vigorous and bitter voice of the plaintiff bar, see Martin London, *The "Muzzled Media": Constitutional Crisis or Product Liability Scam?* (New York: Twentieth Century Fund, Inc., 1993).

195. *Phantom Touring Inc. v. Affiliated Publications,* 19 Med.L.Rptr. 1786, 953 F.2d 724 (1st Cir. 1992), *cert. denied,* 112 S.Ct. 2942 (1992).

196. Lee Levine, *Diving Catch,* American Journ. Rev. 35 (July/August 1994).

197. Martin F. Hansen, "Fact, Opinion, and Consensus: The Verifiability of Allegedly Defamatory Speech," 62 *Geor. Wash. L.Rev.* 43 (November 1993).

198. Robert Sack, *Libel Slander, and Related Problems,* sec. 39 (1980), p. 156.

Ku Klux Klan.[199] A columnist's characterization of a political activist as a "neo-Nazi" was held by an Illinois court not to be defamatory *per se*, but rather to be protected opinion that might be applicable to a wide range of people and did not mean devotion to Adolf Hitler.[200] Name calling, said the Third Circuit Court of Appeals, is protected by the First Amendment.[201] "Cartoons," said the Eleventh Circuit, "are seldom vehicles by which facts are reported; quite the contrary, they are deliberate departures from reality designed forcefully, and sometimes viciously, to express opinion."[202]

A newspaper editorial calling on ousted basketball coach part of the "corruption of college athletics" was held not to be actionable because it was an opinion with no provably false assertions of fact. The writer had criticized the former coach specifically for the poor graduation record of his players and for using a scholarship fund for the benefit of his son.[203] Calling a political candidate's speech "gay-bashing" and a "right-wing, neo-numbskull tactic" is a statement of opinion rather than of fact and is protected by the state constitution, said the Ohio Supreme Court. Appearing in the commentary section of the paper, the statement was clearly an effort to sway public opinion with value-laden language and a subjective point of view.[204] Mischaracterizations and exaggerations in a satirical article

looking at a heated political controversy were also held to be protected opinion.[205]

The same could not be said for publication of a letter alleging that the plaintiff was involved in a "kickback" scheme. Here there was no loose, figurative or hyperbolic language, said a federal district court, but factual assertions that readers would interpret as such and that could be verified as to truth or falsity.[206] Nor did the opinion defense cover a letter to the editor in which the writer asked concerning a judge, "What do you think, was he paid off with drugs or money?"[207]

Nevertheless, there is still substantial latitude for criticism of public officials, incomplete or erroneous credit reports, letters of recommendation, and matters of public interest in general. But there is a difference between questioning someone's integrity or calling him a name and making that person a theft suspect, an extortionist,[208] or, as in *Milkovich*, a perjurer.

A 1994 case may have been the world's first libel suit over an Internet communication. A posting seeking to warn Internet users that a mail service might be a "scam" led to a libel suit that was settled out of court for $50,000. The defendant argued vainly, it would seem, that his research was sound, that his statements were, after all, only opinions, and that he had not published with actual malice. At the same time, the Internet as a new communication system lacked gatekeepers, was available to all, and provided opportunities for reply.[209]

Qualified Privilege (Fair Report)

Also known as the *fair report, public eye,* or *public record* privilege, this defense is rooted in the common law theory that in some situations

---

199. *Millus v. Newsday Inc.,* 22 Med.L.Rptr. 2122 (N.Y.Sup.Ct. 1994).

200. *Grutzmacher v. Chicago Sun-Times, Inc.,* 22 Med.L.Rptr. 2397 (Ill.Cir.Ct. 1994).

201. *Dunn v. Gannett New York Newspapers, Inc.,* 14 Med.L.Rptr. 1871, 833 F.2d 446 (3d Cir. 1987). See also *Partington v. Bugliosi,* 23 Med.L.Rptr. 1929, 56 F.3d 1147 (9th Cir. 1995), in which a lawyer in a memoir implies the incompetence of another lawyer, now a judge, who had lost a case similar to one that the first lawyer had won and that had been turned into a TV docudrama. The language, "if I defend you the way Partington is defending Walker, you'll spend the rest of your life in prison," led to suit but was said to be hyperbole designed to maintain the viewer's attention.

202. *Keller v. Miami Herald Publishing Co.,* 12 Med.L.Rptr. 1561, 778 F.2d 711, 718 (11th Cir. 1985). There are very few reported cases of American cartoonists losing libel cases.

203. *Maynard v. Daily Gazette Co.,* 22 Med.L.Rptr. 2337, 447 S.E.2d 293 (W.Va.Sup.Ct.App. 1994).

204. *Vail v. The Plain Dealer Publishing Co.,* 23 Med.L.Rptr. 1881, 649 N.E.2d 182 (1995).

205. *Gravelink v. Detroit News,* 22 Med.L.Rptr. 2503, 522 N.W.2d 883 (Mich.Ct.App. 1994), *appeal denied,* 448 Mich. 944 (1995).

206. *Coliniatis v. Dimas,* 22 Med.L.Rptr. 1916, 848 F.Sup. 462 (D.C.S.N.Y. 1994).

207. *Keohane v. Stewart,* 22 Med.L.Rptr. 2545, 882 P.2d 1293 (Col.Sup.Ct. 1994), *cert. denied,* 115 S.Ct. 936 (1995).

208. Compare *Hunt v. University of Minnesota,* 465 N.W.2d 88 (Minn.Ct.App. 1991) with *Weissman v. Sri Lanka Curry House, Inc.,* 469 N.W.2d 471 (Minn.Ct.App. 1991), and *Edwards v. Hall,* 19 Med.L.Rptr. 1969, 285 Cal.Rptr. 810 (Cal.Ct.App. 1991).

209. *Suarez Corp. Industries v. Meeks* (Ohio Ct. Common Pleas, 1994), unreported.

the public interest in full disclosure of official public business overrides any harm to individual reputation. The *Restatement* description of the privilege is more expansive: "The publication of defamatory matter concerning another in a report of an official action or proceeding or of a meeting open to the public that deals with a matter of public concern is privileged if the report is accurate and complete or a fair abridgment of the occurrence reported."[210]

Although historically the purpose of the privilege was to expose citizens to the process of self-government, nongovernmental or private meetings may be covered when their agendas are largely political. The question is always, how far does the privilege extend? New York law, for example, does not cover public meetings of nongovernmental bodies such as medical societies or publicly held corporations.

Here again state law may be determinative. Generally, a news organization may publish with impunity a fair and accurate report of any judicial, quasi-judicial, legislative, executive, or administrative proceeding at any level of government. Reports and documents relating to such proceedings are also protected. In some states, common law malice will destroy the defense. In most states, actual malice will have the same result, but in others it will not. Sometimes only the formal, official record of the proceedings is privileged. In a few states, cloakroom and corridor discussions may also be protected if they are related to the issues of the formal process. A New York court ruled that anything pertinent to a case, whether part of the record or not, would be privileged. "To be outside the privilege," the court held, "a statement made in open court must be so outrageously out of context as to permit one to conclude from the mere fact that the statement was uttered that it was motivated by no other desire than to defame."[211]

California's rule doesn't even require pertinence. Any publication that has a reasonable connection to a judicial proceeding, even reports of what was said outside the courtroom, including reports of closed grand jury hearings, may be privileged. There need only be some relationship

to what is going on in the courtroom.[212] Fair and accurate reports of information released by police are privileged under California law.[213] But be careful—few jurisdictions are as permissive as California.

When a Battle Creek, Michigan, newspaper reported oral statements made by police in connection with a plaintiff's arrest as a rape suspect, though he was never charged and was later exonerated, he sued. The newspaper's reliance on the state's privilege for a fair and accurate report of "any public and official proceeding" was rejected on the ground that an "arrest amounts to no more than an apprehension" and was not a "proceeding" under the law. The Michigan legislature intervened by changing the law to protect "a fair and true report of matters of public record, a public and official proceeding, or of a governmental notice, announcement, written or recorded report or record generally available to the public, or act or action of a public body."[214]

In covering an $80 million suit for civil rights and due process violations brought by a pharmacist who was mistakenly indicted for drug trafficking, an Ohio court said that the *Akron Beacon Journal* was not required to investigate beyond the record available to it. Its fair report privilege stood, even though it had failed to explain the misidentification or the reasons why the case against the pharmacist was dismissed.[215]

While reports of judicial proceedings are privileged, courts sometimes disagree as to when the judicial process has begun. The prevailing view is that a pleading, a deposition, or an affidavit filed in a case, but not yet acted upon, can be reported under the claim of privilege. In the minority of jurisdictions where such reporting is not privileged, the assumption is that false, defamatory, and uncontradicted charges in such documents

---

210. Restatement (Second) of Torts, sec. 611 comment (1977).

211. *Martirano v. Frost,* 307 N.Y.S.2d 425 (1969).

212. *Ascherman v. Natanson,* 100 Cal.Rptr. 656 (1972). See also *Dorsey a/k/a Engelbert Humperdinck v. National Enquirer, Inc.,* 20 Med.L.Rptr. 1745, 973 F.2d 1431 (9th Cir. 1992).

213. *Graziano v. Sun Co. of San Bernardino,* 23 Med.L.Rptr. 1028 (Cal.Super.Ct. 1994).

214. The case is *Rouch v. Enquirer and News of Battle Creek, Mich.,* 13 Med.L.Rptr. 2201, 398 N.W.2d 245 (Mich. 1986). The law is Mich. Comp. Laws, § 600.2911.

215. *Gamler v. Akron Beacon Journal,* 23 Med.L.Rptr. 1845 (D.C.N.D. Ohio 1995).

are for the courts and not for the public at large. To allow privilege at so early a point might encourage suits to be filed simply for their publicity value, only to be dropped when that was achieved.[216]

It is generally a good idea to indicate the source of privileged material in a news report.[217] And the news story need not be anything close to a verbatim report of what was said or documented, as long as it is a fair representation. Even errors of fact may be overlooked where highly technical and ambiguous language is involved.[218] Substantial, not perfect, accuracy appears to be the rule.

Unofficial police sources, police radios, and off-the-cuff remarks by police officers, witnesses, or attorneys have been held not privileged.[219] It can be safely reported that a crime has been committed and that a particular person is being held for questioning. Generally, an arrest should not be reported until a suspect is booked. A police blotter or log book is usually an official public record. Although some states have statutes extending privilege to reports of arresting officers, police chiefs, county prosecutors, and coroners, collateral details on investigations and speculation on evidence from such sources are generally not privileged.[220]

Separating the official from the unofficial can be a daunting task, although the constitutional or *New York Times* defense may now cover many doubtful situations. Some records and proceedings are sealed and closed by state statute—for example, juvenile, divorce, and sexual assault matters. Yet in *Cox Broadcasting Corp. v. Cohn,*[221] the Supreme Court held that where an accurate report from a judicial record broadcast the name of a rape-murder victim, contrary to Georgia law, the report was privileged. Recall that in *Firestone* the report of the judicial pro-

ceeding was inaccurate. Know the rules in the states where your reports are read or viewed.

The purposeful distortion of a record by a publication will negate the privilege. And not everything a public official publishes is part of his official duties and thereby privileged. Former U.S. Senator William Proxmire learned that lesson when making one of his often mindless Golden Fleece awards. This action was outside the perimeters of his official Senate duties and therefore not subject to absolute protection by the Constitution's Speech or Debate Clause, said the U.S. Supreme Court. A behavioral scientist, one of a number of such researchers ridiculed by the uninformed senator, settled his libel suit for $10,000, and the U.S. Senate paid $25,000 out of public funds for Proxmire's legal costs.[222]

State law may or may not extend this privilege to credit reports, job references, and family relationships.

SECONDARY AND TECHNICAL DEFENSES

Neutral Reportage

The defense of neutral reportage is similar to the fair report or qualified privilege defense and also bears a strong resemblance to *Rosenbloom*'s "public issue" test. In addition, judicial interpretations of the "reckless disregard" language of the *New York Times* defense have greatly limited the reporter's liability for communicating someone's libelous charges against public persons involved in matters of public concern and, in some jurisdictions, Ohio, for example, libelous charges against private persons as well.[223]

"While verification of the facts remains an important reporting standard," the Fifth Circuit Court of Appeals said in 1966, "a reporter, without a 'high degree of awareness of their probable falsity,' may rely on statements made by a single source even though they reflect only one side of the story without fear of libel prosecution. . . ."[224]

---

216. *Prosser & Keeton on Torts,* sec. 115 (5th ed. 1984).
217. *White v. Fraternal Order of Police,* 17 Med.L.Rptr. 2137, 909 F.2d 512 (D.C.Cir. 1990).
218. *Time, Inc. v. Pape,* 401 U.S. 279 (1971).
219. *Phillips v. Evening Star Newspaper Co.,* 6 Med.L.Rptr. 2191, 424 A.2d 78 (D.C. 1980), *cert. denied,* 451 U.S. 989 (1981).
220. See David A. Elder, *The Fair Report Privilege,* Stoneham, MA: Butterworth, 1988 for a detailed review of the status of press releases, news conferences, speeches, and private meetings at all levels of all branches of government.
221. 420 U.S. 469 (1975).

---

222. *Hutchinson v. Proxmire,* 5 Med.L.Rptr. 1279, 443 U.S. 111, 99 S.Ct. 2675 (1979).
223. *April v. Reflector Herald, Inc.,* 15 Med.L.Rptr. 2455, 546 N.E.2d 466 (Ohio App. 1988).
224. *New York Times v. Connor,* 365 F.2d 567, 576 (5th Cir. 1966).

Five years later, the constitutional rule of *Medina v. Time, Inc.*[225] was that news media reports of statements made by participants in a public controversy—the infamous My Lai massacre—are protected, where the leveling of charges by one participant against another is itself a newsworthy event.

It is even better when both sides or all sides of a controversial issue of public importance can be reported with a modicum of detachment. The defense of *neutral reportage* was first articulated by the Second Circuit Court of Appeals in a case involving a heated controversy between opponents and proponents of the use of the pesticide DDT. On one side was the National Audubon Society; on the other, a number of chemical companies and their scientific consultants, some of whom were prominent in the scientific community and Nobel laureates. In the middle was John Devlin, a science reporter for the *New York Times*.

The scientists were accused by their detractors of being "paid to lie." The reporter contacted as many of them as would talk to him and incorporated their angry responses into his stories. Nevertheless, his newspaper and the National Audubon Society were sued by three of the scientists, and a jury awarded them $20,000 in damages. The federal appeals court reversed, holding that "the First Amendment protects the accurate and disinterested reporting of those charges, regardless of the reporter's private views regarding their validity." The court went on to say:

Edwards v. National Audubon Society
556 F.2D 113 (2D CIR. 1977), CERT. DEN. 434 U.S. 1002.

Irving R. KAUFMAN, Chief Judge:

* * *

At stake in this case is a fundamental principle. Succinctly stated, when a responsible, prominent organization like the National Audubon Society makes serious charges against a public figure, the First Amendment protects the accurate and disinterested reporting of those charges, regardless of the reporter's private views regarding their validity. What is newsworthy

---

225. 439 F.2d 1129 (1st Cir. 1971).

about such accusations is that they were made. We do not believe that the press may be required under the First Amendment to suppress newsworthy statements merely because it has serious doubts regarding their truth. Nor must the press take up cudgels against dubious charges in order to publish them without fear of liability for defamation. The public interest in being fully informed about controversies that often rage around sensitive issues demands that the press be afforded the freedom to report such charges without assuming responsibility for them.

The contours of the press's right of *neutral reportage* are, of course, defined by the principle that gives life to it. Literal accuracy is not a prerequisite: if we are to enjoy the blessings of a robust and unintimidated press, we must provide immunity from defamation suits where the journalist believes, reasonably and in good faith, that his report accurately conveys the charges made. It is equally clear, however, that a publisher who in fact espouses or concurs in the charges made by others, or who deliberately distorts these statements to launch a personal attack of his own on a public figure, cannot rely on a privilege of *neutral reportage*. In such instances he assumes responsibility for the underlying accusations. See *Goldwater v. Ginzburg*, 414 F.2d 324 (2d Cir. 1969), cert. den., 396 U.S. 1049 (1970). [Emphasis added.]

* * * The *Times* article * * * was the exemplar of fair and dispassionate reporting of an unfortunate but newsworthy contretemps. Accordingly, we hold that it was privileged under the First Amendment.

COMMENT

To use this defense, a reporter should not have initiated an investigation leading to defamatory allegations. The controversy must have existed prior to the reporter's involvement. Nor should the reporter have taken sides at any point in the coverage. The reporter is no more than a pure channel, an honest broker, a conduit for the responsible representatives of the two sides of a public controversy involving public figures. Some reporters find this difficult; what should a reporter tell the public if she doesn't believe one side of a dispute? As a defense, neutral reportage does not fit the definition of investigative reporting. Where a reporter solicited charges in a public dispute stirred up by the reporter, neutral reportage did not apply.[226]

This defense has gained limited acceptance. A few federal district courts (the Eighth Circuit and the District of Columbia Circuit in part) and state courts in Ohio, Vermont, Florida, Wyoming, and Arizona, at last count, have recognized it. Many more reject it, including appellate courts in New York, Kentucky, Rhode Island, South Dakota, Texas, and Michigan and the Third Circuit Court of Appeals. There is uncertainty about the defense in the Ninth Circuit, and the courts are divided in some states, Illinois and New York, for example.

Justice Harry Blackmun gave the defense a modicum of respectability in a concurring opinion in a 1989 Supreme Court case.[227] In his concurrence, Blackmun said that the newspaper's decision to abandon neutral reportage "appears to have been unwise in light of the facts in this case . . . . Were this court to adopt the neutral reportage theory, the facts of this case arguably might fit within it."

The defense of neutral reportage ought to be approached cautiously. Because its requirements are high in those jurisdictions that recognize it,[228] it should never be substituted for a fair report defense. At the very least, it ought to involve accurate and dispassionate reporting on a preexisting controversy of public importance, where charges are made by responsible persons on two or more sides of the issue, preferably concerning public people. Using this defense may be difficult for broadcasters of talk radio shows, where partisans often take the opportunity to defame their opponents. The truth or falsity of a charge cannot be determined in the seven seconds afforded by an electronic delay mechanism. Is this kind of neutral reportage advancing the public dialogue on matters of public importance or is it an accommodation of verbal vitriol? Most courts have upheld the former interpretation.[229]

Consent

Another shaky defense is the implied consent a news source gives when publicly disputing charges someone else has made against him. A published denial requires republication of the original charge, of course, since a denial alone could be so out of context as to be meaningless. The very act of talking to a reporter indicates consent to publication. As the Fourth Circuit Court Appeals put it in a classic case: "In view of the fact that (the plaintiff) gave this statement to the press in an interview to be published, he is hardly in a position to complain of the publication with it of the charge to which it was an answer, even if the latter were otherwise objectionable."[230] Rev. Jerry Falwell's voluntary interview with *Penthouse* magazine made him vulnerable to the editorial predilections of that publication, in spite of conditions on the final product he thought he had imposed.[231]

Since consent can be a secondary defense, it is good practice for a reporter to contact all potential libel plaintiffs, get all sides of a controversy, and tell readers when relevant sources are unavailable for comment.

"Right" of Reply

There is a qualified privilege to make defamatory statements in defense of one's own reputation, that is, to answer back. Recall that in the *Foretich* case the grandparents had been charged by the mother with sexual abuse of their granddaughter. In upholding the right of the grandparents to respond, the court said:

> We, too, recognize the devastation that public accusations of child sexual abuse can wreak, and we are extremely reluctant to attribute public figure status

226. *McManus v. Doubleday & Co.*, 513 F.Supp. 1383, 1391 (S.D.N.Y. 1981).
227. *Harte-Hanks Communication Inc. v. Connaughton*, 16 Med.L.Rptr. 1881, 491 U.S. 657, 109 S.Ct. 2678 (1989).
228. *Crane v. Arizona Republic*, 17 Med.L.Rptr. 1353, 729 F.Supp. 698 (D.C.C.Cal. 1989).
229. For example, *Pacella v. Milford Radio Corp.*, 462 N.E.2d 355 (Mass. 1985), *aff'd*, 476 N.E.2d 595, *cert. denied*, 474 U.S. 844 (1985); *Adams v. Frontier Bdcst. Co.*, 555 P.2d 556 (Wyo. 1976); *Demman v. Star Bdcst. Co.*, 497 P.2d 1378 (Utah 1972).
230. *Pulverman v. A. S. Abell Co.*, 228 F.2d 797 (4th Cir. 1956).
231. *Falwell v. Penthouse International Limited*, 7 Med.L.Rptr. 1891, 521 F.Supp. 1204 (D.Va. 1981).

to otherwise private persons merely because they have responded to such accusations in a reasonable attempt to vindicate their reputations.[232]

The operative word is "reasonable." The conditional privilege is lost if abused by overstatement or disproportionate and irrelevant statements.

Another dimension of the defense occurs where a defamation has been circulated necessarily among those associated in a community of interests in pursuit of common goals—a family, a congregation, or a business or professional organization. One's social obligation to law enforcement may be another instance of the necessary circulation of a libel, although that defense did not work for the Alton (Illinois) *Telegraph*. Although the press is not often involved in these situations, the Kansas Supreme Court held that this defense did cover a meeting between editors of the *Kansas City Star* and power company officials who were concerned about a freelancer's investigative article on lack of recreational access to a nuclear power station's cooling lake. The freelancer unsuccessfully sued the power company for defamatory remarks that he said were made about him at the meeting.[233] Credit reports and letters of recommendation also invoke this defense.

The trick in using this defense is to stay within the boundaries of the areas of mutual interest and to make certain that a reply is measured and, as a counterattack, does not exceed in virulence the original verbal assault. In most jurisdictions, common law and/or actual malice will defeat the privilege.

Wire Service Defense

In one's own defense, one might argue that the offending story was an accurate republication of information from a usually reliable source. Major media, dependent upon wire services for a substantial portion of their nonlocal news, cannot be expected to verify every fact that comes across their desks, unless something in the story is highly improbable. Although one authority found only thirteen jurisdictions clearly adopting

this defense,[234] they do include New York, Massachusetts, Georgia, Wisconsin, North Carolina, and the D.C. Circuit. Massachusetts's highest court, for example, adopted the defense on its classic rationale after a convicted rapist-kidnapper sued a number of media outlets. In upholding motions for summary judgment made by thirty-three newspapers, the court wrote:

We think that the inference is inescapable that requiring verification of wire service stories prior to publication would impose a heavy burden on the media's ability to disseminate newsworthy material. "No newspaper could . . . assume in advance the burden of specially verifying every item of news reported to it by established news gathering agencies," [citing one of the earliest cases to discuss the wire service defense, *Layne v. Tribune Co.*, 108 Fla. 177, 188, 146 So.2d 234 (1933)] while at the same time publishing timely stories of worldwide or national interest. Because verification would be time-consuming and expensive, imposing such a burden would probably force smaller publishers to confine themselves to stories about purely local events . . . . We stress that this is not a case where the wire service stories are so inherently improbable or inconsistent that the defendants had, or should have had, some reason to doubt their accuracy."[235]

There is also, of course, the question of fault—actual malice or negligence, depending upon the court-designated status of the plaintiff. Accurate republication of a story provided by a reputable news agency, said a Wisconsin court, does not constitute "actual malice" or "negligence" as a matter of law.[236] The Eleventh Circuit Court of Appeals held that a newspaper that based its erroneous story on wire service reports marked "urgent" and "more" did not show actual malice, even though a subsequent wire service report that may have been available before the newspaper's deadline clarified the original report.[237]

Thus, the wire service defense is a repudiation of the common law's strict rule on republication.

---

232. *Foretich v. Capital Cities/ABC, Inc.*, 22 Med.L.Rptr. 2353, 37 F.3d 1541 (4th Cir. 1994).

233. *Knudsen v. Kansas Gas and Electric Co.*, 18 Med.L.Rptr. 1900, 807 P.2d 71 (Kan. 1991).

234. Kyu Ho Youm, "The 'Wire Service' Libel Defense," 70 *Journ. Q.*, 682, 684 (Autumn 1993).

235. *Appleby v. Daily Hampshire Gazette*, 11 Med.L.Rptr. 2373, 478 N.E.2d 71 (Mass. 1985).

236. *Van Straten v. Milwaukee Journal*, 16 Med.L.Rptr. 2408, 447 N.W.2d 105 (Wisc.Ct.Appl. 1989).

237. *Meisler v. Gannett Co. Inc.*, 22 Med.L.Rptr. 1214, 12 F.3d 1026 (11th Cir. 1994).

Retraction

While the secondary and technical defenses are seldom complete defenses, they are part of a defensive strategy and, at the very least, may serve to mitigate damages. Twenty-nine states by recent count[238] had retraction statutes of some kind. Even in states without retraction laws, prompt correction of a false and defamatory statement may influence the court to lessen damages when the plaintiff prevails. In some jurisdictions, a retraction will negate any claim of actual malice[239] and may suggest that a publisher does not believe that a plaintiff has been defamed[240] or that what was said about him was accurate. In other jurisdictions, a refusal to retract may be a factor in establishing actual malice; in still others, it will have no bearing whatsoever on the question of fault.

A libel plaintiff has no right to a retraction.[241] If she did, she would essentially enjoy the right of access and reply that the Court rejected in the *Tornillo* case. See p. 468. An editor's decision to run a retraction is voluntary, and he will decide the content of the retraction. In some states, California, for example, a libel plaintiff who seeks anything more than special damages must request a retraction.[242] In other states, for example, Minnesota, a retraction makes collection of punitive damages impossible and permits only a claim for special damages or out-of-pocket losses; the request must also be timely, that is, made within a stipulated time period. If the decision is made to retract, the retraction must be done in the format and form required by law (typeface, headline, location, and the like). In other states, Kentucky is one, failure to make a written request for a retraction rules out any possibility of punitive damages.[243]

Montana and Arizona are among the states that have declared retraction statutes to be unconstitutional denials of the libel remedy for compensating damaged reputations. Others consider retraction laws class legislation that favors wealthy publishers and thereby denies equal protection of the laws and the enjoyment of life, liberty, and property.

When retractions are printed, they should take the form of sincere apologies; they are more than mere corrections or clarifications, even though some statutes use these words interchangeably with the word *retraction*. Publication of a complainant's denial is not a retraction. A retraction implies that defamation has occurred and that the publisher is responsible; this may or may not be the case with corrections. Never use a retraction to take another shot at a newsmaker, even though the original libel will have to be referred to in the apology. Offended parties ought to be aware of that. When requests for retractions escalate to threats, have your lawyer take over.

No two retraction statutes are the same. Know what your state's law says. Aside from retracting, always correct mistakes willingly. Reader representatives or ombudsmen, preferably insulated from management, are a form of mediation that tells readers and viewers you care about accuracy and the feelings of those who become the focus of news coverage. Where there are honest disagreements about the accuracy of a report, the denial of a retraction ought to have no bearing on actual malice, if the intention of *New York Times v. Sullivan* is to be honored.

Libel-Proof Plaintiffs

Occasionally, an editor or a publisher may be successful in arguing that a plaintiff's reputation is already so bad that it could not be further impaired by a fresh accusation. Be careful, though. A plaintiff may be only partly libel-proof. Your defamatory publication may allude to a dimension of the person's life that did not contribute to loss of reputation or to a time and place having little to do with the story at hand. The totality of circumstances must be considered. In *Brooks v. American Broadcasting Companies, Inc.*,[244] however, a federal district court held that the plaintiff's reputation was so severely tarnished by his much publicized crimi-

---

238. Louise W. Hermanson, "Setting the Record Straight: A Proposal for Expanding the Role of Retraction in Libel Litigation," *Journ. Monographs*, No. 133 (June 1992), with an appendix summarizing the retraction statutes of 29 states in 1992.
239. *Hoffman v. Washington Post*, 3 Med.L.Rptr. 1143, 1146, 433 F.Supp. 600, 605 (D.D.C. 1977), aff'd, 578 F.2d 442 (D.C.Cir. 1978).
240. *Connelly v. Northwest Publications, Inc.*, 17 Med.L.Rptr. 1204, 448 N.W.2d 901 (Minn.Ct.App. 1989).
241. *Tackett v. KRIV-TV*, 22 Med.L.Rptr. 2092 (S.D.Tex. 1994).
242. *Denney v. Lawrence*, 22 Med.L.Rptr. 1434, 27 Cal.Rptr.2d 556 (Cal.Ct.App. 1994).
243. *White v. Manchester Enterprise, Inc.*, 23 Med.L.Rptr. 1309, 871 F.Supp. 934 (E.D.Ky. 1994).

nal history that he was libel-proof. That seems reasonable where reputation is the key question.

Statute of Limitations

The remaining defenses are indeed technical and, where they apply, absolute. Statutes of limitations define the time span within which legal actions can be brought. After the statutes have run, they are an *absolute* bar to libel actions. Their purpose is to protect defendants against stale claims that they might be totally unprepared to counter. Most statutes of limitations run for one, two, or three years, but occasionally they cover longer periods. A federal court in 1964 said that the statute begins running when a publication goes into general circulation. A few advance copies do not trigger the statute.[245] In some jurisdictions, however, the statute may not begin running until a plaintiff, by diligent effort, identifies the defendant. In *Bernson v. Browning-Ferris Industries of California Inc.,*[246] a divided California Supreme Court held that the state's one-year statute of limitations would not be available to the authors of a libel against a Los Angeles city councilman who had successfully concealed their identity for more than a year.

In 1977 Kathy Keeton, associate publisher of *Penthouse,* sued Larry Flynt and *Hustler* magazine for libel and invasion of privacy. Both claims were dismissed because Ohio's statute of limitations had run. Keeton then filed in New Hampshire where there was still time left because the state then had a six-year statute.

A federal district court dismissed the suit on the ground that the Due Process Clause of the Fourteenth Amendment forbade use of New Hampshire's *long-arm statute* (a state law that allows the courts of one state to claim jurisdiction over persons or property in another) to claim jurisdiction over *Hustler.* The court of appeals affirmed, largely because of Keeton's lack of contact with New Hampshire. Keeton appealed, and the Supreme Court reversed, much

to the distress of media attorneys. Justice Rehnquist, writing for a unanimous Court, found no problem in a plaintiff shopping for a jurisdiction with a stretched-out statute or more favorable rules. *Hustler* had chosen to enter the New Hampshire market and therefore had to cope with that state's laws.[247]

Equal Time

A second absolute bar to a libel suit occurs when a broadcaster who is required by the Federal Communications Act to give *equal time* or *equal opportunity* to federal candidates running for the same public office in either a primary or a general election is sued for something said in one of those broadcasts. Before 1959, broadcasters enjoyed no immunity from libel suits brought as a consequence of a candidate's defamatory speech, yet had no authority to edit those speeches to protect themselves. Surely, the broadcasting industry had argued for many years, if stations are required to carry libelous speeches and prevented from exerting any editing judgment, they should not be held responsible for damages.

The test case came in North Dakota. On October 29, 1956, A. C. Townley, a colorful remnant of the Progressive movement that had swept the Dakotas like a prairie fire four decades earlier, demanded equal time as an independent candidate for the U.S. Senate. Equal time was provided, and in a telecast over WDAY-TV, Fargo, a highly reputable station, Townley charged that the North Dakota Farmers Union was Communist controlled. WDAY had warned Townley that it believed his charge was libelous.

It was, and the Farmers Union brought a $100,000 damage suit against Townley and the station. A district court dismissed the complaint against WDAY on the ground that § 315 of the Radio Act of 1927 rendered the station immune from liability. The Farmers Union carried an appeal to the North Dakota Supreme Court, and that court became the first appellate court in the country to consider the question of whether a broadcasting station is liable for defamatory statements made by a political candidate using the station's facilities in accordance with federal law.

244. 17 Med.L.Rptr. 2041, 737 F.Supp. 431 (N.D. Ohio 1990). The concept may have originated in *Cardillo v. Doubleday & Co.,* 518 F.2d 638 (2d Cir. 1975). It has been recognized in a few appellate state courts and a number of federal appeals courts.
245. *Osmers v. Parade Publications,* 234 F.Supp. 924 (S.D.N.Y. 1964).
246. 22 Med.L.Rptr. 2065, 873 P.2d 613 (Cal. 1994).

247. *Keeton v. Hustler,* 10 Med.L.Rptr. 1405, 465 U.S. 770, 104 S.Ct. 1473 (1984).

Attorneys for the Farmers Union contended that § 315 did not apply in this case because a third party—the Farmers Union—was involved, making the case something more than a heated confrontation between opposing political candidates. They cited a Nebraska case, *Sorensen v. Wood*, 243 N.W. 82 (Neb. 1932), which they interpreted as holding that a station could not willingly join in publication of a libel and that the "no censorship" provision referred only to the political content of the speech.

In a 4–1 decision the North Dakota Supreme Court ruled that radio and television broadcasters are not liable for false or libelous statements made over their facilities by political candidates. Noting that WDAY had advised Townley that his remarks, if false, were libelous, the court said: "We cannot believe that it was the intent of Congress to compel a station to broadcast libelous statements and at the same time subject it to the risk of defending actions for damages." *Farmers Educational & Cooperative Union of America, North Dakota Division v. WDAY*, 89 N.W.2d 102, 109 (N.D. 1958).

The majority felt the attack on the Farmers Union was "in context" with a candidate's criticism of his opponent since "Communism" was a campaign issue. The majority added that the Farmers Union should have brought action against Townley alone. (The problem here was that Townley's income was a mere $98.50 a month—a promise of little satisfaction to an aggrieved party.)

The Farmers Union then appealed to the U.S. Supreme Court. The American Civil Liberties Union intervened on the side of WDAY and in support of the North Dakota Supreme Court decision. In its appeal, the Farmers Union posed two questions with First Amendment implications:

a. Does § 315 relieve radio and television stations from liability for broadcasting libelous statements by candidates when the statements defame a third party, not a competing candidate?
b. Did Congress, when it passed the 1934 act, intend to repeal or annul state laws covering liability?

In a surprisingly close 5–4 decision, the U.S. Supreme Court answered "yes" to the questions and affirmed the North Dakota decision upholding WDAY.

Farmers Educational and Cooperative Union of American v. WDAY Inc.

360 U.S. 525, 79 S.CT 1302, 3 L.ED.2D 1407 (1959).

Justice BLACK delivered the Opinion of the Court:

* * * Petitioner argues that § 315's prohibition against censorship leaves broadcasters free to delete libelous material from candidates' speeches, and that therefore no federal immunity is granted a broadcasting station by that section. The term censorship, however, as commonly understood, connotes *any* examination of thought or expression in order to prevent publication of "objectionable" material. We find no clear expression of legislative intent, nor any other convincing reason to indicate Congress meant to give "censorship" a narrower meaning in § 315. In arriving at this view, we note that petitioner's interpretation has not generally been favored in previous considerations of the section. Although the first, and for years the only judicial decision dealing with the censorship provision did hold that a station may remove defamatory statements from political broadcasts, subsequent judicial interpretations of § 315 have with considerable uniformity recognized that an individual licensee has no such power. And while for some years the Federal Communications Commission's views on this matter were not clearly articulated, since 1948 it has continuously held that licensees cannot remove allegedly libelous matter from speeches by candidates. Similarly, the legislative history of the measure both prior to its first enactment in 1927, and subsequently, shows a deep hostility to censorship either by the Commission or by a licensee. More important, it is obvious that permitting a broadcasting station to censor allegedly libelous remarks would undermine the basic purpose for which § 315 was passed—full and unrestricted discussion of political issues by legally qualified candidates. That section dates back to, and was adopted verbatim from, the Radio Act of 1927. In that Act, Congress provided for the first time a comprehensive federal plan for regulating the new and expanding art of radio broadcasting. Recognizing radio's potential importance as a medium of communication of political ideas, Congress sought to foster its broadest possible utilization

by encouraging broadcasting stations to make their facilities available to candidates for office without discrimination, and by insuring that these candidates when broadcasting were not to be hampered by censorship of the issues they could discuss. Thus, expressly applying this country's tradition of free expression to the field of radio broadcasting, Congress has from the first emphatically forbidden the Commission to exercise any power of censorship over radio communication. It is in line with this same tradition that the individual licensee has consistently been denied "power of censorship" in the vital area of political broadcasts.

The decision a broadcasting station would have to make in censoring libelous discussion by a candidate is far from easy. Whether a statement is defamatory is rarely clear. Whether such a statement is actionably libelous is an even more complex question, involving as it does, consideration of various legal defenses such as "truth" and the privilege of fair comment. Such issues have always troubled courts. Yet, under petitioner's view of the statute they would have to be resolved by an individual licensee during the stress of a political campaign, often, necessarily, without adequate consideration or basis for decision. Quite possibly, if a station were held responsible for the broadcast of libelous material, all remarks even faintly objectionable would be excluded out of an excess of caution. Moreover, if any censorship were permissible, a station so inclined would intentionally inhibit a candidate's legitimate presentation under the guise of lawful censorship of libelous matter. Because of the time limitation inherent in a political campaign, erroneous decisions by a station could not be corrected by the courts promptly enough to permit the candidate to bring improperly excluded matter before the public. It follows from all this that allowing censorship, even of the attenuated type advocated here, would almost inevitably force a candidate to avoid controversial issues during political debates over radio and television, and hence restrict the coverage of consideration relevant to intelligent political decision. We cannot believe, and we certainly are unwilling to assume, that Congress intended any such result.

Petitioner alternatively argues that § 315 does not grant a station immunity from liability for defamatory statements made during a political

broadcast even though the section prohibits the station from censoring allegedly libelous matter. Again, we cannot agree. For under this interpretation, unless a licensee refuses to permit any candidate to talk at all, the section would sanction the unconscionable result of permitting civil and perhaps criminal liability to be imposed for the very conduct the statute demands of the licensee. Accordingly, judicial interpretations reaching the issue have found an immunity implicit in the section. And in all those cases concluding that a licensee had no immunity, § 315 had been construed—improperly as we hold—to permit a station to censor potentially actionable material. In no case has a court even implied that the licensee would not be rendered immune were it denied the power to censor libelous material.

* * * Thus, whatever adverse inference may be drawn from the failure of Congress to legislate an express immunity is offset by its refusal to permit stations to avoid liability by censoring broadcasts. And more than balancing any adverse inferences drawn from congressional failure to legislate an express immunity is the fact that the Federal Communications Commission—the body entrusted with administering the provisions of the Act—has long interpreted § 315 as granting stations an immunity. Not only has this interpretation been adhered to despite many subsequent legislative proposals to modify § 315, but with full knowledge of the Commission's interpretation Congress has since made significant additions to that section without amending it to depart from the Commission's view. In light of this contradictory legislative background we do not feel compelled to reach a result which seems so in conflict with traditional concepts of fairness.

Petitioner nevertheless urges that broadcasters do not need a specific immunity to protect themselves from liability for defamation since they may either insure against any loss, or in the alternative, deny all political candidates use of station facilities. We have no means of knowing to what extent insurance is available to broadcasting stations, or what it would cost them. Moreover, since § 315 expressly prohibits stations from charging political candidates higher rates than they charge for comparable time used for other purposes, any cost of insurance would probably have to be absorbed by the stations themselves. Petitioner's reliance on the stations' freedom from obligation "to allow use of its station by any such candidate," seems equally misplaced. While denying all candidates use of stations would protect broadcasters from liability, it would also effectively withdraw political discussion from the air. Instead the thrust of § 315 is to facilitate political debate over radio and television. Recognizing this, the Communications Commission considers the carrying of political broadcasts a public service criterion to be considered both in license renewal proceedings, and in comparative contests for a radio or television construction permit. Certainly Congress knew the obvious—that if a licensee could protect himself from liability in no other way but by refusing to broadcast candidates' speeches, the necessary effect would be to hamper the congressional plan to develop broadcasting as a political outlet, rather than to foster it. We are aware that causes of action for libel are widely recognized throughout the States. But we have not hesitated to abrogate state law where satisfied that its enforcement would stand "as an obstacle to the accomplishment and execution of the full purposes and objectives of Congress." Here, petitioner is asking us to attribute to § 315 a meaning which would either frustrate the underlying purposes for which it was enacted, or alternatively impose unreasonable burdens on the parties governed by that legislation. In the absence of clear expression by Congress we will not assume that it desired such a result. Agreeing with the state courts of North Dakota that § 315 grants a licensee an immunity from liability for libelous material it broadcasts, we merely read § 315 in accordance with what we believe to be its underlying purpose.

Affirmed.

Settlement

A third way of resolving a libel suit once and for all is to take it out of the judicial process altogether. Here a lawyer should lead the way. A properly executed settlement will bar a suit for damages. While a settlement relieves a defendant of lawyer's fees, court costs, and damages, if not made cautiously, it may encourage suits by others more intent on monetary reward than vindication of reputation.

A dramatic example of a plaintiff gaining victory by avoiding the courtroom occurred in February 1993. General Motors held a news conference and methodically demonstrated how NBC had staged its depiction of incendiary gas tanks in pickup trucks to ensure that a fire would result. NBC settled and aired an apology, but still spent $2 million in investigating its own program and in legal fees.

A more ignominious and much criticized settlement took place when Capital Cities/ABC apologized in prime time for a prizewinning report charging that two large tobacco companies "spiked" their cigarettes with extra nicotine in order to hook their customers. In the settlement ABC also agreed to pay the legal expenses of Philip Morris and R. J. Reynolds, costs that approached $3 million. At the same time as it announced the settlement, ABC said that it stood by the "principal focus" of its original story, although it corrected the unsupported portion of its report. That qualification evoked strong allegations of "capitulation" on the part of the network from some lawyers and opponents of the tobacco industry. Others said that ABC was intimidated by Philip Morris's pursuit of $10 billion in damages, although internal Philip Morris documents, said to support ABC's charges, were not available to the network. It is also possible that ABC had a weak case and saw settlement as its only course; the report contained inaccuracies, notably in the promotional teasers preceding the program. In addition, ABC would not name its source (later dubbed Deep Cough), which made it more vulnerable to an actual malice claim. Philip Morris went to great lengths—unsuccessfully—to expose the source. An unanswered question is whether ABC's new owner, Walt Disney Company, will be more or less ready to settle in such cases. Will the financial demands of the marketplace do damage to journalistic values? The ABC correspondent and the producer of the report, both named as defendants, were said to have refused to sign the settlement.[248]

---

248. *New York Times,* August 22, 1995, pp. A1 and C6, and August 24, 1995, p. C2. See also Steve Weinberg, *Smoking Guns: ABC, Philip Morris and the Infamous Apology,* Columbia J.Rev. 29 (November/December 1995); Benjamin Weiser, "Bit Tobacco v. Big Media," *Washington Post,* January 15–21, 1996, R6; Lawrence R. Grossman, *CBS, 60 Minutes and the Unseen Interview,* Columbia J.Rev. 39 (January/February 1996).

Philip Morris took advantage of its temporary victory over its detractors and proclaimed its devotion to truth by running full-page ads in major newspapers around the world, reprinting ABC's acknowledgment of error with the heading "Apology accepted" in big, black letters. The threatened litigation did bring the smoking and addiction question to the attention of Congress and federal agencies.

A short time later, CBS lawyers advised management not to broadcast a planned *60 Minutes* interview with a tobacco company defector critical of the industry. Although the former tobacco executive had signed an agreement with Brown & Williamson not to discuss company matters upon his departure, some media lawyers doubted that their clients could be held liable for a violation of that agreement under the doctrine of tortious interference. If they were, newsgathering would be severely curtailed. As a substitute, ironically, CBS ran a program on how cigarette manufacturers block information to the public. CBS correspondent Mike Wallace said that ABC's settlement had influenced the CBS attorneys who, through management, were essentially in control of an editorial decision. James C. Goodale, in a *New York Times* editorial, complained that "CBS has now cultivated the impression that a company can bring and win an interference suit against the press."[249] Three months later, on February 4, 1996, the original program was broadcast on *60 Minutes*. The *Wall Street Journal* had cleared the way by essentially publishing the original interview a week earlier.

Insurance: A Practical Defense

The most practical way to mitigate or ease damages is to carry an *insurance policy* covering libel as well as other categories of media litigation. Though more than 80 percent of libel suits now end in settlements, and insurance companies press for settlement, it can cost $50,000 to reach that point. One insurance company estimates that 85 percent of its funds are spent defending libel actions and only 15 percent on settlements.

Gaining a summary judgment to end a case at its earliest stage can also cost $50,000. Suits that go through the judicial process can run up astronomical costs. Wayne Newton's unsuccessful suit against NBC cost the defendant's insurance company at least $9 million. Even without appeals, a case that goes to trial can cost hundreds of thousands of dollars.

At least four major insurance companies dominate the field, and premiums and deductibles have held fairly steady, although the trends for both are upward. Some insurance companies expect media clients to pay a percentage of expenses through the entire legal process, for example, 20 percent. Regardless of the expenses, no responsible publication or broadcast operation can afford to be without insurance. At the very least, lawyers' fees and court costs in the pretrial period as well as punitive damages should be covered. Acceptable policies will ensure that editors and publishers remain in control of the lawsuit so that appropriate journalistic and First Amendment values will be protected.

PROTECTING SOURCES

Approximately half of the states and many jurisdictions by their common law extend a qualified protection to the identity of a reporter's source and, in some cases, to the raw material and work product of reporting the news, such as notes, tapes, and outtakes. Most of these statutes and many courts in the absence of a statute have set down the qualifications in their statutes (shield laws) or common law. Thus, a person seeking the identity of a source would have to prove that there were no alternative sources, that there was a compelling public need for the information, and that the information sought was relevant. Some state laws, Minnesota's for example, make an additional exception: where a libel plaintiff can prove actual malice only by having access to the identity of a source or by showing that the reporter had no source at all and that the story was fabricated or dependent upon an unverified source, the reporter may have to identify that source.

In the early stages of Philip Morris's libel suit against ABC, a Richmond (Virginia) judge said the plaintiff had met all conditions for identification of ABC's sources. Six months later, the same

---

249. *New York Times*, November 9, 1995, pp. A1, A9; November 13, 1995, p. C8; November 17, 1995, p. A18. See also James C. Goodale, "CBS Must Clear the Air," *New York Times*, December 6, 1995, p. A23.

judge had second thoughts and withdrew his disclosure order until Philip Morris could provide more evidence of not being able to get the information it needed elsewhere and of having a compelling need for the information.[250]

Changes in the Federal Rules of Civil Procedure in 1993 will focus more attention on issues of confidentiality and editorial process. Defendants' counsel will have to protect sources, notes, and editorial techniques by making every effort to limit discovery on grounds of constitutional privilege. It will also be important for media lawyers to convince the judge at an early point that the offending story is fair and substantially true. In general, federal courts may be more hospitable to these appeals than state courts.

ALTERNATIVES TO LIBEL SUITS

Partly because of the damaging consequences libel suits can have on free expression, especially when those suits are brought, and most often lost, by highly visible public officials or public personalities, many recommendations have been made in recent years for modifications in the law or for alternatives to it.[251]

Far and away the most visible of these is the Uniform Correction or Clarification of Defamation Act, drafted by the National Conference of Commissioners on Uniform State Law in 1993 and approved by the American Bar Association six months later in 1994. The proposal focuses on correction or retraction in order to restore reputation and avoid the costs of a lengthy libel suit. It would work essentially like this:

1. An offended member of the public would have ninety days after becoming aware of what she considered a false and defamatory publication to request a correction. If the correction was made satisfactorily, only provable economic loss could be compensated.
2. A request for a correction would have to relate to the specifics of identity on both sides, publication,

defamation, and falsity. A publisher in turn could request evidence of falsity. If a response on the issue of falsity was not forthcoming, in a subsequent lawsuit the offended person would be limited to an award of provable economic loss. If information on falsity was provided, the publisher would then have twenty-five days to respond to the offended person's request for a correction.

3. Otherwise a publisher would have forty-five days from the receipt of a request for correction to publish the correction in a place sufficiently prominent for the audience of the original offending publication to see it. A correction could be written to overcome or correct a falsehood, claim the truth of the original allegation, clarify an implied meaning, deny an intent to defame, or endorse the truth of what a source had provided for publication.
4. If the time limitations are violated, a publisher may still offer to correct before trial. At this point, however, a publisher must also agree to pay reasonable litigation costs, including attorney's fees incurred prior to correction. If these conditions are met, the offended person is barred from bringing a libel suit. If the suit has already been brought, the court must dismiss the action after the publisher complies with the terms of the offer.

In 1996, the Uniform Law Commissioners were working with a legislative oversight group that includes newspaper organizations to persuade state legislatures to adopt the bill as written. In early 1996, only North Dakota's legislature had adopted the bill, though with modifications. A possible problem with this kind of legislation is that it assumes a distinct line between truth and falsehood that is not always discernible. Complex news stories do not always lend themselves to a clear truth or falsehood determination. If they did, the media would have nothing to lose by subscribing to this legislation. Another fear of both the authors of the bill and the media is that legislative committees will modify the proposal to the detriment of the media once it has been introduced into lawmaking bodies.

Proponents of the Uniform Correction Act use the *Prozeralik*[252] case to emphasize its advantages. In that case an inexperienced reporter misidentified a restaurateur as a beating victim

250. *Philip Morris Companies v. American Broadcasting Inc.,* 23 Med.L.Rptr. 1434 (Va.Cir.Ct. 1995); *New York Times,* July 12, 1995.
251. The most comprehensive examination of libel reform proposals is John Soloski and Randall P. Bezanson, eds., *Reforming Libel Law* (New York: Guilford Press, 1992).

252. *Prozeralik v. Capital Cities Communications, Inc.,* 21 Med.L.Rptr. 2257, 626 N.E.2d 34, 605 N.Y.S.2d 218 (1993). See Barbara W. Wall and Richard N. Winfield, "Uniform Correction Act Goes to States for Passage," *Editor & Publisher,* January 28, 1995, pp. 20–21.

with ties to organized crime, and the information was broadcast by a television station in Niagara Falls, New York. In 1994, after twelve years of litigation, a jury awarded the plaintiff $6 million for reputational harm, $3.5 million for emotional harm, $1.5 million for financial loss, and $500,000 in punitive damages. That verdict is still under appeal. The Uniform Correction Act, had it been available in New York, it is argued, would have saved the broadcaster a great deal of money.

A retired Philadelphia judge, Lois Forer, proposed a uniform federal libel statute in a 1987 book, *A Chilling Effect*.[253] In the same vein, journalism educator Louise Hermanson proposes a thirteen-point uniform federal Correction Act that would protect the media from mistakes and provide recourse to persons actually harmed by defamation. Retraction statutes, as they stand, are a hodge-podge of time limits and conditioned damages.[254]

Other proposals, which also depend upon a bright line between truth and falsehood, would follow an approach first suggested by Rep. Charles Schumer of New York in 1985 and end libel suits with a declaratory judgment: Was the publication true or false? The most notable of these was the *Annenberg* Washington Program Proposal for the Reform of Libel Law in which:

1. A complainant would seek specifically either a retraction or an opportunity to reply; failure to do so within thirty days of publication of the libel would bar any future legal action.
2. If either party elected to try the suit as an action for declaratory judgment, a suit would conclude with the court making a judgment as to truth or falsity.
3. Having chosen this process, the losing party would pay the winner's attorneys' fees in what is known as fee-shifting.

If this procedure was rejected, under the Annenberg proposal only actual or special damages would be considered in an ensuing libel action. Attorneys for both plaintiffs and defendants have criticized this no-money, no-fault proposal: the media side, because constitutional protections under *New York Times* would be lost; plaintiffs, because just compensation in dollar amounts would no longer be available to those

unjustly wronged by the media. Nowhere has this proposal been adopted. Pierre Leval, the federal judge who presided over the Westmoreland trial, has also recommended a no-money, no-fault libel suit. Only falsity would be measured; no money damages would be available to the plaintiff, but the losing communicator would have to promise to publicize a finding in the plaintiff's favor. No court rule or legislation would govern the process; it would simply be a mutual agreement. Plaintiffs would not have to overcome the unsurmountable obstacles of *New York Times v. Sullivan* in having to prove fault, and defendants would not suffer the grievous financial side effects of that case.[255]

A similar approach is the vindication remedy where a public acknowledgment of error is made and extensively circulated. Again an ascertainment of truth rather than a defendant's state of mind, plaintiff's status, or available privileges is the objective. A responsive retraction, summary judgment, or a settlement could precede vindication. But to make it compulsory would invite immediate constitutional challenge.[256]

Other proposals for reform include mandatory retractions or right of reply, or right of repair (correction), laws.[257] Fee-shifting, widely used in advanced legal systems around the world, is favored by the current Republican Congress but was overwhelmingly rejected by the American Bar Association in 1995 for limiting public access to the justice system. Alternative Dispute Resolution (ADR) mechanisms were first seriously pursued in 1987 by the Iowa Libel Dispute Resolution Program developed by the Iowa Libel Research Project in conjunction with the American Arbitration Association.[258] Generally, lawyers have resisted these approaches, although the Wisconsin Supreme Court adopted

---

253. New York: W. W. Norton & Company.
254. Hermanson, "Setting the Record Straight."

255. Pierre N. Leval, "Commentary: The No-Money, No-Fault Libel Suit—Keeping *Sullivan* in its Proper Place," 101 *Harv.L.Rev.* 1287 (1988).
256. James H. Hulme and Steven M. Sprenger, "Vindicating Reputation: An Alternative to Damages as a Remedy for Defamation," 30 *Am.U.L.Rev.* 375 (1981).
257. Rodney A. Smolla, *Suing the Press* (New York: Oxford University Press, 1986). See also Paul LeBel, Defamation and the First Amendment: The End of the Affair, 25 *Wm. & Mary L.Rev.* 779, 788–790 (1984).
258. Bezanson, Cranberg and Soloski, *Libel Law and the Press*.

an ADR plan in 1993, and Florida's dispute resolution program provides settlement procedures. From the media side, Oregon publisher Robert W. Chandler's Alternative Dispute Resolution system was being widely discussed in 1989. It included binding arbitration in which a plaintiff not only had an opportunity to persuade a news organization that it was wrong but would receive vindication when the news organization corrected or retracted. If the news medium stood by its story, it could allow rebuttal by letter or opinion piece. A few newspapers subsequently adopted the plan.

More aggressive news organizations go on the offensive and file countersuits to ward off and discourage prospective plaintiffs. This is where SLAPPs[259] come into the discussion. The acronym stands for Strategic Lawsuit Against Public Participation, the kind of libel suit that a powerful developer, for example, might bring against a community group to discourage them from opposing him before a city council. Condominium developers in Beverly Hills, California, sued the president of the League of Women Voters, the leader of an antidevelopment initiative, a local citizen, and 1,000 "John Does" for $63 million. California[260] and a number of other states have since passed anti-SLAPP laws, which, in the case of California, have been held to apply to lawsuits against the media.[261] Two journalism professors call countersuits "SLAPP-backs"; they are a way to get even when suits are filed out of spite and maliciousness in violation of Rule 11 of the Federal Rules of Civil Procedures or its state-level equivalents. In an examination of countersuits brought by media between 1980 and 1994, the authors found 70 percent were successful (35 of 51).[262]

Many argue for an end to or a limit on punitive damages, and a number of states have tried to do this through legislation. One of the authors of this text and others, however, see punitive damages as having the salutary effect of leveling the playing field for the relatively defenseless plaintiff.[263] Another writer recommends that policy-making public officials and celebrities, whatever their cultural, artistic, or athletic niche, should have no remedy in libel, but that media that attack them should provide voluntary opportunities for reply.[264]

The American Civil Liberties Union has opted for Justice Brennan's *Rosenbloom* test. Defamation suits, it believes, violate the First Amendment when brought by public officials on matters relating to their public position, by public figures on matters relating to their public status, and by private or public figures on matters of public concern.

Law professor David A. Anderson realistically concludes that only the U.S. Supreme Court can instigate libel reform. He would have the Court abandon the actual malice rule, then invite proposals for reform to begin a media/law dialogue. The Court would be final arbiter, although state courts might play a larger role than they do now, especially in moving toward greater uniformity across state lines.[265] In the meantime, courts enforce the libel laws as they stand.

PROBLEMS OF LIBEL LAW

Many problems of libel law have thus far been implied, if not squarely faced. Plaintiffs find fault so hard to prove that reputations are seldom

---

259. The term originated with Penelope Canan and George W. Pring, "Strategic Lawsuits Against Public Participation," 35 *Social Problems* 506 (December 1988).

260. A California superior court judge granted a motion to strike a libel complaint against the *San Francisco Chronicle* on the basis of a state statute providing that "a cause of action against a person arising from any act of that person in furtherance of the person's right of petition or free speech under the United States or California constitution in connection with a public issue shall be subject to a special motion to strike, unless the court determines that the plaintiff has established that there is a probability that the plaintiff will prevail on the claim." Much of the material in the *Chronicle* was based on public records having to do with More University, which described itself as a "sensuality school." See News Notes, 22 *Med.L.Rptr.* No. 38.

261. *Lafayette Morehouse, Inc. v. Chronicle Publishing Co.*, 23 Med.L.Rptr. 2389, 446 Cal.Rptr.2d 5462 (Cal.Ct.App. 1995), a case in which the newspaper commented on plaintiff More University's "Advanced Sensuality" course in terms that were neither obscene nor defamatory. The newspaper was awarded costs and attorneys' fees.

262. Kyu Ho Youm and Douglas A. Anderson, Media Countersuits in Libel Law: A Statutory and Judicial Framework, 17 *Hastings Comm/Ent L.J.* 383 (Winter 1995).

263. Barron, Punitive Damages in Libel Cases—First Amendment Equalizer? See fn. 142.

264. Gillmor, *Power, Publicity, and the Abuse of Libel Law.*

265. David A. Anderson, Is Libel Law Worth Reforming? 140 *U.Penn.L.Rev.* 487 (1991). Reprinted in Soloski and Bezanson, *Reforming Libel Law.*

restored. At the same time, powerful and affluent plaintiffs punish the news media for negative publicity by bringing frivolous suits, some of which vault them onto even higher levels of celebrity status.

Vindication by declaration of truth or falsity is laid on the foundation of a false dichotomy. Lawsuits abbreviated by declaratory judgment would save the media money at the cost of having to accept someone else's judgment as to truth.

Alternative Dispute Resolution proponents seldom mention that for twenty-three years Minnesota has had a mechanism for media accountability in place. It is called the Minnesota News Council, and it has already heard more than a hundred cases where a legal remedy was either doubtful or nonexistent.

Punitive damages continue to wreak havoc on a free press, and more and more courts are determining the financial assets of media companies before computing damages, as if to "beat" them within an inch of their lives. The public, suspicious of any concentration of power, including the media, is willing to go along. In the final analysis, the common law as finally applied by the Supreme Court, especially in light of new technologies, may be the best and most flexible way to change the law. In the meantime, American communicators will continue to be sued in foreign jurisdictions where plaintiffs have a better chance of winning. When possible, American courts will not enforce foreign libel judgments if judges believe they violate First and Fourteenth Amendment safeguards.[266]

RULES OF AVOIDANCE AND DAMAGE CONTROL

No responsible or professional publication can avoid libel altogether. It goes with the territory. But there are ways to lessen the expenditure of time, money, and energy so that journalists can do what news media must do. When plaintiffs win big, it is often because reporters and editors have misused or been overly dependent upon particular sources. They fail to consult other available sources, push sources toward desired responses, rely on sources with little credibility, and use sources with a grudge and then give their targets no opportunity to refute. Hidden tape recorders or other deceptive techniques are used to get the story. Reporters become emotionally involved to the point of changing quotations or using exaggerated language where it isn't called for. And potentially incriminating notes are lost or destroyed.[267]

Samuel Terilli, counsel for the *Miami Herald,* suggests other reasons for legal difficulties. Reporters may misinterpret what is in a document, misquote a source, or identify the wrong person or company in a story. Humor, sarcasm, eccentricity in style, and the careless use of synonyms can be trouble. Sometimes headlines or graphics misrepresent a fact. Past transgressions of newsmakers are presented in an accusatory manner, and morgue or library clippings are sometimes inaccurate.

In addition, these suggestions can help you avoid trouble:

1. Acknowledge mistakes generously and sympathetically. Always be prepared to check your facts and to clarify, correct, and retract where appropriate. None of these will keep you out of court, but they will help once you're there.
2. Confirm and verify to whatever extent deadlines and resources permit. Make certain photographs, headlines, and cutlines conform to the facts of stories.
3. What's true and what you can prove to be true are two different things. Having a source is not proof of truth.

---

266. See, for example, *Abdullah v. Sheridan Square Press, Inc.,* 23 Med.L.Rptr. 2210, 161 F.R.D. 25 (S.D.N.Y., May 4, 1994). The court dismissed a claim for libel under English law, holding that "establishment of a claim for libel under the British law of defamation would be antithetical to the First Amendment protection accorded the defendants." See also Kyu Ho Youm, *Suing American Media in Foreign courts: Doing an End-Run around U.S. Libel Law,* 16 *Comm/Ent* 235 (Winter 1994); and Derek Devgun, United States Enforcement of English Defamation Judgments: Exporting the First Amendment, 23 Anglo-American L.Rev. 195 (April/June 1994).

---

267. Thomas B. Kelley, *Summary and Analysis of Common Factors Present in Recent 'High' Plaintiff Verdicts in Libel Trials,* New York: Practicing Law Institute, 1994.

4. Make sure opinions do not infer or are not based upon false facts. Synonyms can be a problem: The words *inquiry*, *investigation*, and *probe* may suggest different levels of seriousness.

5. Always indicate the source of a story resulting from governmental proceedings or documents.

6. Avoid unofficial statements from law enforcement officers.

7. Get the other side of the story, especially that of the person you may defame.

8. Keep up to date on what is happening in media law in state and federal courts, especially those in your circulation or coverage area.

9. Finally, don't talk to a complainant's lawyer directly. Refer him to your lawyer.[268]

---

268. These suggestions are based partly on a list published by the Pennsylvania Newspaper Publishers Association and excerpted from a booklet, *Synopsis of the Law of Libel and the Right of Privacy*, distributed by the First Amendment Coalition's *Media Survival Kit.*

CHAPTER 5
PRIVACY AND THE PRESS

CHAPTER OUTLINE

WHAT IS PRIVACY?

There is much confusion about privacy and the law. As a philosophical matter, Americans have always prized their tradition of individualism and its corresponding emphasis on each person's integrity and autonomy.[1] Judge Thomas Cooley's often-invoked shorthand for privacy, "the

---

1. Copple, *Privacy and the Frontier Thesis: An American Intersection of Self and Society,* 24 American J. of Jurisprudence 87 (1989).

right to be let alone,"[2] describes the general concept of privacy most citizens support. But there is a great difference between encouraging respect for one another on the one hand and creating enforceable legal rights on the other. The rapid acceptance of privacy law by courts and legislatures in the twentieth century masks the fact that drawing lines to define what should be punishable behavior for publication is extremely difficult. Important differences exist between what is acceptable, what is tacky, and what is reprehensible. In a society operating under the First Amendment, any laws that punish publication of the truth should be, and have been, subject to rigorous review.[3]

Concern for breaches of social ethics in the late nineteenth century led law partners Samuel Warren and Louis Brandeis to propose formally that a right of privacy be recognized as a matter of common law in the state courts.[4] Their law review article, one of the most influential pieces of legal scholarship in history, drew upon a variety of contract, property, and tort law principles. Although the article's primary concern was to create a cause of action for damages when the press published personal or intimate information, it has led directly or indirectly to the establishment of at least five common law causes of action.

Unlike libel, privacy does not depend on how the opinions others have about you may have altered. Instead, privacy is based on how you are made to feel about yourself. It involves self-esteem. Warren and Brandeis were reacting to what they considered graceless newspaper gossip about the private social affairs of the Warren family. Their tone of injured gentility seems quaint today. But they were prophetic in anticipating that "mechanical devices" would eventually threaten almost all private information.

Their key argument was that law and society should make sacrosanct intimate information about individuals, though materials having public or general interest would be exempt. Unlike libel, though, truth would generally not be a defense. A privacy suit would be allowed where the "dignity and convenience" of the individual were intruded upon in an unwarranted fashion by either published text or photographs. Warren and Brandeis did not define what they meant by *unwarranted,* however. A plaintiff could claim mental suffering in addition to other damages.

Privacy gained momentum when New York passed a statute in 1903 making it both a tort and a misdemeanor to use someone's name or picture for trade purposes without consent (New York Civil Rights Law, §§ 50, 51). The legislature was reacting to the case of a woman who had no legal remedy after her portrait was used in an advertisement for flour that was pasted up in stores, warehouses, and saloons.[5] The right created by the statute remained one of property, comparable to copyright or trademark.

Soon the Georgia Supreme Court considered a similar case involving an insurance company's use of a person's photograph for advertising and became the first state to adopt privacy as a matter of common law.[6] Privacy spread rapidly. Soon courts and scholars were stretching the tort to accommodate other kinds of privacy interests. In 1960 the influential Dean William Prosser organized the developing body of common law privacy into four related causes of action that have provided a popular framework for analysis.[7] In reality, there was little case law to support Prosser's arguments for the intrusion on seclusion and portrayal in a false light actions, but his influence was so great that the state courts followed his lead.

When journalists or media professionals think of privacy, they have in mind the five tort actions of unreasonable disclosure of embarrassing private facts, intrusion upon seclusion, portrayal in a false light, appropriation for commercial purposes, and the right of publicity. Together the five actions are often referred to as "common law invasion of privacy," although the status of the action for right of publicity is disputed.[8] These causes of action are the primary focus of this chapter. In the 1980s and 1990s, however, plaintiffs have seldom won these cases. Consequently,

---

2. Cooley, *Torts* 29 (2d ed. 1888).
3. Schauer, *Free Speech: A Philosophical Enquiry* 173–1733 (1982).
4. Warren and Brandeis, *The Right to Privacy*, 4 Harv. L. Rev. 193 (1890).
5. *Roberson v. Rochester Folding Box Co.*, 171 N.Y. 538, 64 N.E.2d 442 (1902).
6. *Pavesich v. New England Life Insurance Co.*, 122 Ga. 190, 50 S.E. 68 (1905).
7. Prosser, *Privacy*, 48 Calif. L. Rev. 389 (1960).
8. *Crump v. Beckley Newspapers, Inc.*, 10 Med. L. Rptr. 2225, 320 S.E.2d 70, 84–85 (W. Va. 1983).

pressure has built to provide alternative liability actions against the press and the entertainment media. These efforts at imposing liability outside the privacy actions are the focus of the final section of the chapter.

Most states and the District of Columbia give common law or statutory recognition to the five causes of action.[9] Coverage varies widely, however. Of the fifteen states with statutes, only Rhode Island covers all of Prosser's four actions. Even when a statute does not provide a cause of action, state courts may create a right by common law, but the courts in many states have not had occasion to address all five causes of action. When federal courts hear privacy cases based on diversity of citizenship jurisdiction, they may be required to predict whether or not a state will recognize a cause of action, and in what form, risking that a state court will later conclude differently.[10] The press should be careful when relying upon a federal court decision on privacy grounds. In New York, the only privacy claims recognized are those adopted by statute, and as a result, there is no explicit common law or 'state constitutional law privacy action.[11]

Though common law invasion of privacy has always had critics, it remains the basis for many lawsuits against the mass media. Privacy is confusing, sometimes contradictory, and always in conflict with the First Amendment goal of a wide-open marketplace of ideas. Its demise has often been predicted or desired.[12] Because privacy cases often result in decisions for defendants, the vast majority of editorial decisions by the press are more a matter of ethics and good taste than of law.[13]

Common law invasion of privacy is a major worry for the mass media, but other branches of law also involve privacy. Citizens enjoy rights to data privacy, spatial privacy, and constitutional privacy that are protected by a variety of federal and state provisions—constitutional, statutory, and common law. While common law invasion of privacy is concerned with mass publication or distribution of private information, data, spatial, and constitutional privacy are aimed at preventing access to or interference with confidential information, private spaces, and intimate personal situations. The existence of multiple legal actions all bearing the label of privacy adds to the confusion surrounding privacy law.

Data privacy is primarily protected by statute or by private agreements such as contracts.[14] An individual's financial records, such as savings and checking account statements, are the classic example. Contract and custom have long kept this information secure; just in case, it is also covered by federal and state law. Other types of records—medical and educational, for example—have also been covered. The profusion of record keeping about individuals, especially in database form, has spurred efforts to increase protections that limit access to the information.[15] One of the most recent concerns has been the confidentiality of credit card data in Internet shopping transactions.

Whether these attempts to keep personal data private can succeed is widely doubted.[16] In any event, data privacy legislation has so far presented few problems for the news media,[17] mainly because the statutes have been aimed at those who compile and use private information in their normal trade or business activities. The press does not routinely create and retain files on matters such as student grades or checking

---

9. For a state-by-state listing, see *State-by-State Guide to Privacy Law,* News Media & the Law (Summer 1994), S5.

10. *State ex rel. Elvis Presley Int'l. Memorial Foundation v. Crowell,* 14 Med. L. Rptr. 1043, 733 S.W.2d 89 (Tenn.App. 1987).

11. *Arrington v. New York Times,* 6 Med. L. Rptr. 2354, 433 N.Y.S.2d 164 (Sup. Ct., App.Div. 1980).

12. Zimmerman, *False Light Invasion of Privacy: The Light That Failed,* 64 N.Y.U. L. Rev. 364 (1989); Zimmerman, *Requiem for a Heavyweight: A Farewell to Warren and Brandeis's Privacy Tort,* 68 Cornell L. Rev. 291 (1983).

13. See Special Issues, "Privacy I" and "Privacy II," 9 J. of Mass Media Ethics Nos. 3, 4 (1994).

14. Schwartz, *Privacy and Participation: Personal Information and Public Sector Regulation in the United States,* 80 Iowa L. Rev. 553 (1995).

15. *Golden Key Campaign Aims to Raise Public Awareness of Need for Privacy-Enhancing Technologies,* 1 Electronic Information Policy & L. Report 56 (BNA)(1996); Samoriski, Huffman, and Trauth, *Electronic Mail, Privacy, and the Electronic Communications Privacy Act of 1986: Technology in Search of Law,* 40 J. of Broadcasting & Electronic Media 60 (1996); Splichal, *The Evolution of Computer/Privacy Concerns: Access to Government Information Held in the Balance,* 1 Comm. L. & Policy 203 (1996).

16. Note, Petersen, *Your Life as an Open Book: Has Technology Rendered Personal Privacy Virtually Obsolete?* 48 Fed. Comm. L.J. 163 (1995).

17. Kirtley, *The EU Data Protection Directive and the First Amendment: Why a "Press Exemption" Won't Work,* 80 Iowa L. Rev. 639 (1995).

accounts. If a reporter "tapped" into the database of another without consent, however, it is unlikely that any defense would be availing against statutory charges based on the unauthorized entry.[18]

Spatial privacy is protected both by the Fourth Amendment's guarantee against unreasonable searches and seizures and by the common law of trespass. The Fourth Amendment explicitly protects against government interference, although it does not contain the word *privacy*. In a sense, the Fifth Amendment's guarantee against providing compelled self-incriminating information is also a privacy provision. Most of the cases have involved the application of the exclusionary rule, which was designed to prevent evidence obtained from an unreasonable search or seizure from being introduced into criminal trials.[19] When an individual is in a location where there is a "reasonable expectation of privacy," such as a home, office, or even telephone booth, the Fourth Amendment applies.[20]

When there is no expectation of privacy, however, as when someone leaves materials in "plain view" or allows material to be distributed to others, no violation of the constitutional guarantee occurs.[21] For example, police do not need a signed warrant from a judge—the usual requirement—to look through garbage left on a curbside. "It is common knowledge that plastic garbage bags left on or at the side of a public street are readily accessible to animals, children, scavengers, snoops and other members of the public," according to the Supreme Court.[22] The "plain view" concept has been influential as a defense in common law invasion of privacy actions.

The tort of trespass, like the Fourth Amendment, recognizes that a person's home or property is his castle and is not to be adversely affected either by private individuals or by government. Any tangible invasion of real property is regarded as a trespass, even if it actually causes no harm.[23] Common-sense exceptions to allow people to use sidewalks and knock on front doors are universally accepted. The common law invasion of privacy action of intrusion on seclusion is a close legal cousin to the tort of trespass.[24]

The U.S. Supreme Court has recognized constitutional privacy on a case-by-case and issue-by-issue basis. Although Court decisions protecting private activities date back to the latter part of the last century,[25] constitutional privacy has only been solidly established since the 1960s. In *Griswold v. Connecticut*, 381 U.S. 479 (1965), the Court struck down a state law that made contraceptives illegal, even when used by married couples. The law also forbade Planned Parenthood from giving advice about contraceptives. The Court was galled at the idea of government intruding into the bedroom. Justice William O. Douglas's opinion for the Court found a privacy interest scattered about the Bill of Rights:

> Specific guarantees in the Bill of Rights have penumbras, formed by emanations from those guarantees that give them life and substance. Various guarantees create zones of privacy. * * * We have had many controversies over these penumbral rights of "privacy and repose." * * * These cases bear witness that the right of privacy which presses for recognition here is a legitimate one.

The opinion found support for the right of privacy in the First, Third, Fourth, Fifth, and Ninth Amendments. Some Court watchers viewed the case as a shocking example of judicial improvisation and roundly criticized Douglas's opinion for being offhand. Others saw it as a necessary extension of civil liberties to invalidate a noxious law Connecticut's legislators were too timid to repeal.

Justice Harry Blackmun leaned on *Griswold* in his opinion for the Court in its historic 1973 abortion ruling, *Roe v. Wade*, 410 U.S. 113 (1973):

> In varying contexts the Court or individual justices have indeed found at least the roots of that right in the First Amendment; in the Fourth and Fifth

---

18. *America On-line, Inc. v. Cyber Promotions, Inc.*, 24 Med. L. Rptr. 2505 (E.D.Va. 1996).
19. Stewart, *The Road to Mapp v. Ohio and Beyond: The Origins, Development and Future of the Exclusionary Rule in Search-and-Seizure Cases*, 83 Columbia L. Rev. 1365, 1392 (1983).
20. *Coolidge v. New Hampshire*, 403 U.S. 443 (1971); *United States v. Calandra*, 414 U.S. 338 (1974).
21. *United States v. Weatherspoon*, 82 F.3d 1697 (6th Cir. 1996).
22. *California v. Greenwood*, 108 S. Ct. 1625 (1988).

---

23. *Prosser and Keeton on Torts*, § 13 (5th ed. 1984).
24. Id., § 117.
25. *Union Pacific Railway Co. v. Botsford*, 141 U.S. 250 (1891).

Amendments; in the penumbras of the Bill of Rights; in the Ninth Amendment; or in the concept of liberty guaranteed by the first section of the Fourteenth Amendment. These decisions make it clear that only personal rights that can be deemed "fundamental" or "implicit in the concept of ordered liberty" are included in this guarantee of personal privacy. They also make it clear that the right has some extension to activities relating to marriage, procreation, contraception, family relationships, and child rearing and education. [Case citations omitted.]

"This right of privacy," Blackman added, "* * * is broad enough to encompass a woman's decision whether or not to terminate her pregnancy. * * * We therefore conclude that the right of personal privacy includes the abortion decision, but that this right is not unqualified and must be considered against important state interests in regulation."

The constitutional right to privacy has been applied in many contexts, from cases invalidating state laws that prohibited interracial marriages to cases guaranteeing individuals the right to live in neighborhoods of their choice.[26] Nevertheless, the Court upheld a Georgia antisodomy law against homosexual activity in a private home, holding that the state's interest was stronger than the privacy interest.[27] The courts have generally limited application of constitutional privacy to issues where "fundamental" rights are at risk. In one case, the privacy interest in preventing disclosure of patient's HIV status was considered less than fundamental.[28]

As with other constitutional guarantees, privacy is protected only against government actions or those amounting to "state action."[29]

---

26. Barron, Dienes, McCormack, and Redish, *Constitutional Law Principles and Policy* 402–473 (4th ed. 1992).
27. *Bowers v. Hardwick,* 478 U.S. 186 (1986).
28. *Doe v. Wiggington,* 21 F.3d 733 (6th Cir. 1994).
29. *Movie Systems v. Heller,* 710 F.2d 492 (8th Cir. 1983). In *Heller,* the defendant was accused of stealing the signal for Home Box Office by using a device not authorized by the local microwave distributor, a violation of 42 U.S.C.A. § 605. Movie Systems used a van with electronic sensing equipment to patrol the streets of Minneapolis and St. Paul in search of unauthorized users. Since the surveillance was by a private party, the court concluded that Heller's Fourth Amendment rights had not been infringed. Heller also lost on state common law privacy grounds, since Minnesota is one of a handful of states that has refused to recognize the cause of action.

Violations by private parties must be addressed through common law or statute, if at all. State constitutions may offer protection that is broader than that available under the federal constitution. Some state constitutions include an explicit right to privacy,[30] while courts in some other states have interpreted the state constitution as granting greater privacy rights.[31]

The common law actions for invasion of privacy and their statutory counterparts, all banes for the press, remain the key concerns for mass media.

"PURE" PRIVACY: DISCLOSURE OF EMBARRASSING PRIVATE FACTS

Sidis, the Scope of "Outrage," the Defense of Newsworthiness, and the Elements of the Cause of Action

Unreasonable public disclosure of *embarrassing private facts* is the branch of invasion of privacy that Warren and Brandeis had most in mind, and it is the branch to which most current definitions of privacy apply. It is also the most difficult for a plaintiff to pursue. Yet, despite the odds against winning, plaintiffs file embarrassing private facts lawsuits frequently; only false light actions appear to outnumber them among all privacy cases.

Why do plaintiffs almost always fail? The major reason is that the defense of *newsworthiness,* adopted early in the development of the cause of action, has almost swallowed the tort. Newsworthiness, of course, means different things to different people, but the majority of cases applying an analysis of the newsworthiness defense have relied upon the tenets of the press itself in reaching conclusions. An editor or news director will likely consider any published story newsworthy—why else would it have been published? On occasion courts apply a narrower

---

30. *Ravin v. State,* 537 P.2d 494 (Alaska 1975) (use of marijuana in private home for noncommercial purposes protected).
31. *State v. Robertson,* 649 P.2d 569 (Ore. 1982); *Mark v. KING Broadcasting,* 618 P.2d 512 (Wash.App. 1980), affirmed, *Mark v. Seattle Times,* 635 P.2d 1081 (Wash. 1981); *People v. Brisendine,* 13 Cal.3d 528, 119 Cal.Rptr. 315, 531 P.2d 1099 (1975).

analysis, holding that issues that may directly affect audience members are newsworthy, but that information that is merely interesting is outside the scope of the defense.[32]

The problem with such interpretations is that they focus on the *value* of the story, especially its political or social value, rather than on the personal or intimate character of the information as Warren and Brandeis originally proposed. Narrow distinctions about newsworthiness also discount the significance of entertaining or novel information. Newsworthiness has been applied with a broad brush anyway, using a common-sense approach rather than one based on categories of speech. One of the ironies of the embarrassing private facts action is that not only do plaintiffs usually lose, but the lawsuit, a type of official government activity, brings additional publicity.

The leading case on embarrassing private facts arose from a story that asked the perennial reporter's question, "whatever happened to . . . ?" A writer for *The New Yorker* in 1937 decided to learn what had become of William James Sidis, a one-time child prodigy who had attracted extensive press attention in the early part of the century. Sidis had become an anonymous recluse. Although the magazine article was sympathetic, the privacy Sidis had carefully cultivated was shattered. In 1940, a federal appeals court rejected Sidis's privacy claim. Along the way, the court outlined most of the elements that define the unreasonable disclosure of embarrassing private facts to this day.

Sidis v. F-R Publishing Corp.
1 MED L. RPTR. 1775, 113 F.2D 806 (2D CIR. 1940).

CLARK, Circuit Judge

* * *

Warren and Brandeis realized that the interest of the individual in privacy must inevitably conflict with the interest of the public in news. Certain public figures, they conceded, such as holders of public office, must sacrifice their privacy and expose at least part of their lives to public scrutiny as the price of the powers they attain. But even public figures were not to be stripped bare.

* * *

Sidis today is neither politician, public administrator, nor statesman. Even if he were, some of the personal details revealed were of the sort that Warren and Brandeis believed "all men alike are entitled to keep from popular curiosity."

But despite eminent opinion to the contrary, we are not yet disposed to afford to all the intimate details of private life an absolute immunity from the prying of the press. Everyone will agree that at some point the public interest in obtaining information becomes dominant over the individual's desire for privacy. Warren and Brandeis were willing to lift the veil somewhat in the case of public officers. We would go further, though we are not yet prepared to say how far. At least we would permit limited scrutiny of the "private" life of any person who has achieved, or has had thrust upon him, the questionable and indefinable status of a "public figure."

William James Sidis was once a public figure. As a child prodigy, he excited both admiration and curiosity. Of him great deeds were expected. In 1910, he was a person about whom the newspapers might display a legitimate intellectual interest, in the sense meant by Warren and Brandeis, as distinguished from a trivial and unseemly curiosity. But the precise motives of the press we regard as unimportant. And even if Sidis had loathed public attention at that time, we think his uncommon achievements and personality would have made the attention permissible. Since then Sidis has cloaked himself in obscurity, but his subsequent history, containing as it did the answer to the question of whether or not he had fulfilled his early promise, was still a matter of public concern. The article in *The New Yorker* sketched the life of an unusual personality, and it possessed considerable popular news interest.

We express no comment on whether or not the newsworthiness of the matter printed will always constitute a complete defense. *Revelations may be so intimate and so unwarranted in view of the victim's position as to outrage the community's notions of decency.* [Emphasis added.] But when focused upon public characters, truthful comments upon dress, speech, habits, and the ordinary aspects of personality will usually not transgress this line. Regrettably or not, the misfortunes and frailties of neighbors and "public figures" are subjects of considerable interest and discussion to the rest of the population. And when such are the

32. *Buller v. Pulitzer Publishing Co.,* 684 S.W.2d 473 (Mo.App. 1984).

mores of the community, it would be unwise for a court to bar their expression in the newspapers, books, and magazines of the day.

COMMENT

The rule of *Sidis*—that revelations so intimate and so unwarranted in view of the victim's position as to outrage the community's notions of decency—has stood the test of time. Truth may be punished in some circumstances.

The Restatement (Second) of Torts, § 652 D (1977), drawing largely upon *Sidis,* appears to anticipate that a plaintiff must prove five points to establish a *prima facie* case for private facts. There must be publicity or publication. This is seldom an issue since most of the cases arise from mass distribution. The information must be "concerning the private life of another." As a defense, the defendant can offer evidence that the information is widely known or is not really private in nature. If, for example, one's sexual activities were provided to the press by lovers and ex-spouses, a plaintiff would be hard-pressed to claim that the information was really private any longer.[33] A plaintiff must then convince the fact- finder, jury or judge, of the third element: that the disclosure of the information would be highly offensive to a reasonable person. Most of the cases finding disclosures highly offensive have involved medical information or previously undisclosed physical characteristics.[34] The plaintiff must also show that the information is "not of legitimate public concern," a test that is somewhat different from the newsworthiness test. A plaintiff must apparently show in effect that the material published was in no way whatsoever of public concern. When a client at a substance abuse clinic was identified during news coverage of the clinic's anniversary celebration, her lawsuit failed in part because substance abuse treatment itself was a matter of legitimate public concern.[35] Finally, the courts have generally applied the "outrage to community decency" test from *Sidis* as a fifth element of the cause of action.

Judicial analysis in private facts cases is problematic. Courts often consider whether information is newsworthy or of public concern in deciding whether the same information is private in nature. Normally, the defense would apply only after a plaintiff establishes the elements of a cause of action. Here, however, the legitimate public concern element of the cause of action invites, and perhaps requires, that the status of the message be assessed at the outset.

Private facts is one area of communication law where the U.S. Supreme Court has not been very active. The media have tried to challenge the action for private facts as unconstitutional on the ground that publication of truth should always be protected by the First Amendment.[36] The Court, however, has always found narrower grounds for deciding the handful of private facts cases it has heard. As a result, just as in libel, the states retain ample latitude to develop their own standards of liability.

The Scope of the "Private Facts" Action and Its Constriction by the Defense of Newsworthiness

Just what is able to "outrage the community's notions of decency" has been addressed in many cases. Stories that resulted from routine reporting and publishing practices have seldom been subjected to liability. Only material that is truly intimate or media practices that are truly unreasonable have sufficed to impose liability.

A case in point involved a plastic surgeon who used "before and after" photographs of a patient for public demonstrations and television appearances. Mary Vassiliades, a retired secretary, underwent cosmetic surgery—apparently a facelift—in 1978. When photographs were taken during surgery and at postoperation visits, she was assured that taking photos was "part of the doctor's regular routine." In 1979, the doctor appeared on a Washington, D.C. talk show and gave a presentation at Garfinckel's department store. The doctor used four photos and identified Vassiliades by name. Acquaintances of Vassiliades

---

33. *Winstead v. Sweeney,* 23 Med. L. Rptr. 1563, 205 Mich.App. 664, 571 N.W.2d 874 (1994).

34. *Young v. Jackson,* 18 Med. L. Rptr. 2337, 572 So.2d 378 (Miss. 1990) (disclosure that plaintiff had had a hysterectomy would be offensive to a reasonable person).

35. *Friedrich v. Salinas Newspapers, Inc.,* 22 Med. L. Rptr. 1478 (Cal.Super. 1993).

36. *Cox Broadcasting v. Cohn,* 1 Med. L. Rptr. 1819, 420 U.S. 469 (1975).

saw the television show and began spreading the news of her surgery. Vassiliades herself testified that she was "devastated" and "went into a terrible depression" upon learning of the use of the photos. *Vassiliades v. Garfinckel's*, 11 Med. L. Rptr. 2057, 492 A.2d 580 (D.C.App. 1985).

Relying upon *Barber v. Time, Inc.*, 1 Med. L. Rptr. 1779, 159 S.W.2d 291 (Mo. 1942), an early case where a hospital patient with an eating disorder was photographed without consent while her attention was diverted, the court agreed that Vassiliades's privacy had been invaded. "Although the photographs may not have been uncomplimentary or unsavory, the issue is whether the publicity * * * was highly offensive to a reasonable person, * * *" the court said. The defense argued that plastic surgery is a matter of legitimate public interest. This newsworthiness argument was rejected. The court could find no "logical nexus" between the admittedly newsworthy subject and the use of Vassiliades's photo to explain the subject.

Similar arguments were used after the *Oakland Tribune* identified Toni Ann Diaz, the recently elected first female president of the student body at the College of Alameda, as having undergone sex change surgery some years before. Diaz had concealed the operation, telling only immediate family members and close friends. A reporter developed the story from a tip and confirmed it using confidential sources. The story also reported on an arrest record for Antonio Diaz from 1971. *Diaz v. Oakland Tribune*, 9 Med. L. Rptr. 1121, 139 Cal.App.3d 118, 188 Cal.Rptr. 762 (1983).

The court determined that sexual identity, Diaz's Puerto Rican birth certificate, and the arrest were all private matters. The *Tribune's* connection of Antonio Diaz to Toni Diaz, relying upon records that did not contain *both* names and on confidential sources, was seen as tenuous. Regarding the arrest record itself, the court noted, "[M]atter which was once of public record may be protected as private facts where disclosure of that information is not newsworthy." In addition, the court said that Diaz's status as student body president did not support a newsworthiness defense.

While *Diaz* and *Vassiliades* might seem to indicate that details of one's sex life or medical history are especially intimate details deserving

protection, such is not always the case. Oliver Sipple sued after he was identified in news stories as a member of San Francisco's gay community. The former Marine, who had kept his sexual preference from his family, suffered estrangement from his parents, brothers, and sisters. But Sipple had become a hero when he deflected Sara Jane Moore's gun hand as Moore tried to shoot President Gerald Ford in San Francisco in 1975. Since Sipple was a widely known and active member of the city's gay community, and that information was not capable of shocking his community, the court refused to consider his sexual preference a private fact. Even if it had, the court said, newsworthiness prevented any liability. While Sipple could perhaps not have foreseen the consequences, his voluntary actions made him subject to coverage, which "is not limited to the event that itself arouses the public interest. * * *" *Sipple v. Chronicle Pub. Co.*, 10 Med. L. Rptr. 1690, 154 Cal.App.3d 1040, 201 Cal.Rptr. 665 (1984). Is there any genuine difference between *Diaz* and *Sipple?*

Similarly, two minors who filed suit against *Hustler* magazine after its publication of nude photos taken years earlier and republished by the magazine as part of a review of two books containing the photos lost their case because the facts had ceased to be private. Their mother had originally consented to the taking of the photos and had signed a release. No matter how embarrassing the facts were today to the children and mother, that which had been allowed to become public could not later be made private by judicial fiat. *Faloona v. Hustler*, 13 Med. L. Rptr. 1353, 799 F.2d 1000 (5th Cir. 1980).

Note that, with the exception of *Sipple*, cases addressing issues of community standards seldom make explicit reference to the community in which the story appeared. The "community" that truly matters for private facts cases is the jury. Since what is private and what violates community standards is an issue of fact, it is initially for the jury to decide. And some appeals courts are reluctant to reverse juries.

In one case, a teenage mother told a newspaper reporter that Craig Hawkins was the father of her child. The reporter also talked to Hawkins himself. Despite what was apparently a fairly well-known fact, the court said a jury was entitled to find it a private fact. *Hawkins v. Multimedia*, 12 Med. L. Rptr. 1878, 344 S.E.2d 145

(S.C. 1986). The court also upheld a jury decision that the fact was not newsworthy. In addition, the court seemed to be influenced by the fact that Hawkins was a minor and that it was not clear that his telephone interview constituted consent. The court emphasized that, "the reporter never asked Craig if she could use his name in a newspaper article."

A case that addressed the community standards of decency test at length involved an eccentric bodysurfer and *Sports Illustrated*. Michael Virgil agreed to an interview but revoked consent when he learned that the picture story would include details of what can only be called eccentric behavior. The article was published anyway and included details of Virgil's unusual behaviors, including extinguishing cigarettes in his mouth, burning holes in his wrist, diving off billboards, and eating spiders and insects. A photo that accompanied the story read, "Mike Virgil, the wild man of the Wedge, thinks it possible his brain is slowly being destroyed."

The Ninth Circuit Court of Appeals rejected *Sports Illustrated*'s claim that truth should always be privileged. "The extent to which areas of privacy would continue to exist, then, would appear to be based not on rights bestowed by law but on the taste and discretion of the press. We cannot accept this result," the court said.

Nevertheless, the court added that news of legitimate concern to the public is protected by the First Amendment, and "in determining what is a matter of legitimate public interest, account must be taken of the customs and conventions of the community; and in the last analysis, what is proper becomes a matter of community mores. The line is to be drawn when the publicity ceases to be the giving of information to which the public is entitled, and becomes *a morbid and sensational prying into private lives for its own sake, with which a reasonable member of the public, with decent standards, would say that he had no concern.* * * * But if there is room for differing views as to the state of community mores or the manner in which it would operate upon the facts in question, there is room for the jury function." [Emphasis added.] *Virgil v. Time, Inc.,* 1 Med. L. Rptr. 1835, 527 F.2d 1122 (9th Cir. 1975). The case was returned to federal district court for trial.

The district court found that the Virgil story did not violate the "outrageousness" or "uncon-

scionability" standard adopted by the Ninth Circuit. While agreeing that the facts in the story were "generally unflattering and perhaps embarrassing," the court found the story just as positive about Virgil as negative (a concern more appropriate to libel cases). In any event, bodysurfing was a matter of legitimate public interest, and Virgil's prominence in the sport made him fair game. *Virgil v. Sports Illustrated,* 2 Med. L. Rptr. 1271, 424 F.Supp. 1286 (S.D.Cal. 1976).

Journalism practices were the focus of other cases. In *Pasadena Star-News v. Los Angeles Superior Court,* 15 Med. L. Rptr. 1867, 203 Cal.App.3d 131, 249 Cal.Rptr. 729 (1988), the mother of an abandoned baby girl filed a privacy suit after the *Star-News* published a story identifying by name the mother and her brother, who had deposited the baby in a cardboard box at a hospital. The plaintiff asserted that her name was not an integral part of the story, although she conceded the story's newsworthiness. The appeals court issued a writ of mandate ordering the superior court to grant the defendant's motion for summary judgment. The court focused on the consequences of plaintiff's argument in deciding against her. "Plaintiff's proposed rule—that a published report of embarrassing but newsworthy private facts is actionable unless the report omits the name of its subject—*would overhaul journalism as we know it,*" the court said. "The press could not without consent reveal the name of anyone other than a public official or a public figure. * * * This would change the tone of stories about matters of the greatest public concern, many of which are stories about individuals of no renown." [Emphasis added.]

Plaintiffs often file multiple claims, apparently hoping that one will survive. In *Van Straten v. Milwaukee Journal,* 16 Med. L. Rptr. 2408, 447 N.W.2d 105 (Wis.App. 1989), a prisoner in county jail who attempted suicide and later tested positive for the AIDS virus filed both libel and private facts claims over subsequent news coverage. On the libel claim, the court concluded that how prisoners with AIDS should be dealt with was a public controversy and that the plaintiff had become a limited-purpose public figure by slicing open his wrist and forearm. The same analysis inevitably found the story newsworthy, a matter of legitimate public interest, and thus squelched the private facts claim as well.

Iowa's Supreme Court held that a newspaper report of a patient subjected to sterilization was not an invasion of privacy because it was newsworthy and insufficiently intimate to outrage the community's notions of decency, and it was part of a public record. Of the story the court said:

> [I]t offered a personalized frame of reference to which the reader could relate, fostering perception and understanding * * * the editors also had a right to buttress the force of their evidence by naming names. We do not say it was necessary for them to do so, but we are certain they had a right to treat the identity of victims of involuntary sterilization as matters of legitimate public concern. * * * The specificity of the report would strengthen the accuracy of the public perception of the merits of the controversy. *Howard v. Des Moines Register and Tribune Co.*, 5 Med. L. Rptr. 1667, 283 N.W.2d 289 (Ia. 1979), *cert. denied* 445 U.S. 904 (1980).

A federal district court thought it had reached the outer boundaries of community decency when it denied a Minnesota television station's request to make copies of videotapes that had been shown to a jury in a kidnap-rape-murder trial. The defendant had made videotapes that recorded his multiple rapes of his former high school teacher. The victim and her daughter later escaped their captor. A boy who had been picked up during their abduction had been murdered.

Although not a privacy case as such, the judge relied on privacy notions in denying the motion to copy the videotapes. And the victim, who had agreed to the prosecution showing the tapes at trial, also opposed the motion. It is not clear if the denial was premised on private facts grounds or on bodily privacy grounds. The judge expressly declined to say, concluding that: "To now expose Mrs. Stauffer to public humiliation and degradation by releasing the tapes for public dissemination would, at best, be unseemly and shameless; it would constitute an unconscionable invasion of her privacy." *In re Application of KSTP-TV*, 65 Med. L. Rptr. 2249, 504 F.Supp. 360 (D.Minn. 1980).

The *KSTP* case seems to have more in common perhaps with nonmedia bodily privacy cases such as those involving police strip searches of women arrested for minor crimes and traffic offenses[37] or the surreptitious taking of photos of female patrons in the rest room of a bar.[38] A similar case involved a woman who, upon going to the police to report an assault, was asked to undress and was photographed nude; the photos were later circulated among the policemen for their amusement.[39]

The element of misbehavior was at work in a somewhat similar media privacy case involving what might be considered an "ambush" report. When police in Boise, Idaho, arrested a temporarily deranged man at his home for using a shotgun in a threatening manner, he was standing naked in his doorway. TV cameras filmed the arrest, and for a fraction of a second the man's buttocks and genitals appeared on the evening news. The news editor was fired. The arrested man, claiming embarrassment and humiliation, sued the television station for invasion of privacy, and a jury awarded him $15,000. On appeal to the Supreme Court of Idaho, the judgment was reversed, and the case remanded for retrial.[40] Does the fact that Taylor appeared naked in his front door, where anyone could have seen him, weaken his private facts claim? Does the fact that the reporter accompanied police make the (un)coverage newsworthy?

The behavior of journalists has also been challenged in cases alleging infliction of emotion distress and "tortious newsgathering." Those causes of action, however, are not based on the nature of information published but on unacceptable actions. They are often linked with a private facts or intrusion on seclusion claim.[41] Drawing a distinction between the story, which typically is newsworthy, and the manner in which it was reported can be difficult for both juries and judges.

A Florida case indicates that facts that might otherwise clearly be considered private will be newsworthy when official police involvement occurs or the magnitude of an event is sure to attract public attention. A Cocoa Beach jury

---

37. *Mary Beth G. v. City of Chicago*, 723 F.2d 1263 (7th Cir. 1983).

38. *Yoeckel v. Samonig*, 75 N.W.2d 925 (Wis. 1956). The facts also support an action for intrusion on seclusion since most people have a reasonable expectation of solitude in a rest room.

39. *York v. Story*, 324 F.2d 450 (9th Cir. 1963).

40. *Taylor v. KTVB, Inc.*, 525 P.2d 984 (Idaho 1974).

41. *KOVR-TV v. Sacramento County Superior Court*, 23 Med. L. Rptr. 1371, 31 Cal.App.4th 1023, 37 Cal. Rptr.2d 431 (1995); *Armstrong v. H&C Communications, Inc.*, 18 Med. L. Rptr. 1845, 575 So.2d 280 (Fla.App. 1991).

ordered a newspaper to pay $10,000 to a woman who was photographed fleeing from her home naked except for slight coverage from a hand towel after having been held captive by her estranged husband. An appeals court reversed. *Cape Publications v. Bridges,* 8 Med. L. Rptr. 2535, 423 So.2d 426 (Fla.App. 1982). The court explicitly noted that the Restatement of Torts regards police activities as newsworthy. The court also noted that the event itself provided a defense to the newspaper, because crimes—and by extension crime victims—are matters of public interest. The newspaper's photo, "which won industry awards, could be considered by some to be in bad taste," the court said. Matters of taste, however, should not be the basis for a court's substituting its judgment for that of editors. Notably, the photo run was one of the least revealing taken and "revealed little more than could be seen had appellee been wearing a bikini. * * *" Her claim for intentional infliction of mental distress was thrown out for failure to provide evidence of "outrageousness."

The newsworthiness tag appears to attach to any news coverage involving government or crime. When a television station ran stories, called "Your Kids on Board," about the criminal records of school bus drivers and identified the plaintiff, who had changed her name, as having served four years in jail for murder, she sued for both private facts and libel. She had changed her name since the incident, and the story was wrong—she had been convicted of attempted murder. A court concluded that the story involved a matter of public concern and, therefore, the private facts claim must fail even if the reporter did not rely on public records in reporting the name change. *Woodard v. Sunbeam Television Corp.,* 21 Med. L. Rptr. 1286, 616 So.2d 501 (Fla.App. 1993).

Even in cases of egregious bad taste and faulty editorial judgment, the public interest defense will protect a publisher. A newspaper printed photos of a murdered child's body, wrapped in chains, being pulled from a lake. Additional prints showing the gruesome effects of the crime were sold to the public. But a privacy claim brought by the parents was rejected because, said a Georgia court, the crime was a matter of urgent public interest, at least until its perpetrator was apprehended. *Waters v. Fleetwood,* 91 S.E.2d 344 (Ga. 1956).

Although the courts have not explicitly adopted the concept of plain view as a defense, it is closely related to the issues of newsworthiness and whether information is actually private. It stands to reason that any privacy interest has been waived when something occurs where anyone could have seen it. The cases that address the plain view concept typically involve plaintiffs who have been photographed and are embarrassed by the result. In *McNamara v. Freedom Newspapers,* 18 Med. L. Rptr. 1679, 802 S.W.2d 901 (Tex.App. 1991), the plaintiff had been photographed as a player in a high school soccer game. The newspaper ran a photo in which McNamara's genitals were exposed—apparently, the court said, because he'd failed to wear an athletic supporter. The court extended the concept of plain view in newsgathering to the level of constitutional privilege:

> We hold that because the published photograph accurately depicts a public, newsworthy event, the First Amendment provides the newspaper with immunity from liability for damages. . . .

Just to be safe, the court said that the Texas constitution requires the same result.

A similar analysis was applied in the case of a former Colombian judge who had fled her country following threats from a drug cartel and moved to Detroit. When *The Detroit News* ran a story reporting her presence in the city, and other news organizations followed, she sued, arguing private facts and several other claims. The court relied on evidence that she used her own name, had accepted appointment at the Columbian consulate in Detroit, and had been seen about as proof that she had effectively waived any privacy interest. *Sanchez Duran v. The Detroit News, Inc.,* 21 Med. L. Rptr. 1891, 200 Mich.App. 622, 504 N.W.2d 715 (1993).

Privileging Facts from Government Records and Proceedings

If journalists obtain information from public records or from attending open government proceedings, there is little basis for considering the information private in any normal sense. Government files often contain sensitive, intimate, and embarrassing information, it is true, but the courts have applied what amounts to a presumption that the fact that material comes from records or proceedings is almost *prima facie* evidence that the public interest is implicated. A decision that the material is newsworthy is almost inevitable. Use of information taken from court records is probably the safest, since judicial action is always considered to be a matter of public interest.

Although the federal Freedom of Information Act (FOIA) and the various state acts all contain privacy exceptions, the acts are directed at the custodians of the records, not at the press. Besides, the FOIA acts allow government officials to release records even if an exception applies. As a result, the courts have never held that these privacy exceptions in and of themselves create an enforceable privacy right plaintiffs may pursue.

More typical is direct government action designed to prevent publication of certain types of information. Statutes prohibiting the press from reporting the identities of rape victims are perhaps the best-known example. A court order prohibiting publication of certain information, normally in the form of an injunction or restraining order, is also direct.

The conflict between the state's interest in protecting rape victims and the right of the press to publish information obtained from public records has been addressed twice by the Supreme Court. Each time the press has prevailed, but for different reasons.

In the first case, a Georgia statute barred identification of rape victims. A father whose daughter had been raped and murdered brought a private facts suit after a television reporter used the daughter's name on the air. The name had been included in an official indictment that was open to the public.

The case raises two additional issues of more than passing interest. First, since the victim was dead, could the father, or another family member for that matter, maintain an action? Generally, in tort law, including privacy,[42] rights cease when an individual dies. A lawsuit could not have been maintained in the daughter's behalf, as it might have been in a contract or property law dispute. Second, the father was in effect arguing that his "relational privacy" rights had been violated. Although most state courts have concluded that a relational privacy action is not precluded, plain-

tiffs are almost always denied standing for the claim.[43] The Court did not address these issues because it decided the case on other grounds.

Cox Broadcasting Corp. v. Cohn
1 MED. L. RPTR. 1819, 420 U.S. 469, 95 S. CT. 1029, 43 L. ED. 2D 328 (1975).

Justice WHITE delivered the opinion of the Court.

* * *

Georgia stoutly defends both § 26-9901 and the State's common-law privacy action challenged here. Its claims are not without force, for powerful arguments can be made, and have been made, that however it may be ultimately defined, there *is* a zone of privacy surrounding every individual, a zone within which the State may protect him from intrusion by the press, with all its attendant publicity. * * *

More compellingly, the century has experienced a strong tide running in favor of the so-called right of privacy. * * * Nor is it irrelevant here that the right of privacy is no recent arrival in the jurisprudence of Georgia, which has embraced the right in some form since 1905 when the Georgia Supreme Court decided the leading case of *Pavesich v. New England Life Insurance Co.* * * * 50 S.E. 68 (Ga. 1905).

These are impressive credentials for a right of privacy, but we should recognize that we do not have at issue here an action for the invasion of privacy involving the appropriation of one's name or photograph, a physical or other tangible intrusion into a private area, or a publication of otherwise private information that is also false although perhaps not defamatory. The version of the privacy tort now before us—termed in Georgia "the tort of public disclosure,"—is that in which the plaintiff claims the right to be free from unwanted publicity about his private affairs, which, although wholly true, would be offensive to a person of ordinary sensibilities. * * * [I]t is here that claims of privacy most directly confront the constitutional freedoms of speech and press. The face-off is apparent, and the appellants urge

---

42. Restatement (Second) of Torts § 652 (1977).

43. *Barger v. Courier-Journal*, 20 Med. L. Rptr. 1189 (Ky. App., unpub., 1991); but see *Armstrong v. H&C Communications, Inc.*, 18 Med. L. Rptr. 1845, 575 So.2d 280 (Fla.App. 1991) (Sharp, J., concurring in part and dissenting in part).

upon us the broad holding that the press may not be made criminally or civilly liable for publishing information that is neither false nor misleading but absolutely accurate, however damaging it may be to reputation or individual sensibilities.

* * *

In this sphere of collision between claims of privacy and those of the free press, the interests on both sides are plainly rooted in the traditions and significant concerns of our society. Rather than address the broader question whether truthful publications may ever be subjected to civil or criminal liability consistently with the First and Fourteenth Amendments, or to put it another way, whether the State may ever define and protect an area of privacy free from unwanted publicity in the press, it is appropriate to focus on the narrower interface between press and privacy that this case presents, namely, whether the State may impose sanctions on the accurate publication of the name of a rape victim obtained from public records—more specifically, from judicial records which are maintained in connection with a public prosecution and which themselves are open to public inspection. We are convinced that the State may not do so.

In the first place, in a society in which each individual has but limited time and resources with which to observe at first hand the operations of his government, he relies necessarily upon the press to bring to him in convenient form the facts of those operations. Great responsibility is accordingly placed upon the news media to report fully and accurately the proceedings of government, and official records and documents open to the public are the basic data of governmental operations.

* * *

Appellee has claimed in this litigation that the efforts of the press have infringed his right to privacy by broadcasting to the world the fact that his daughter was a rape victim. The commission of crime, prosecutions resulting from it, and judicial proceedings arising from the prosecutions, however, are without question events of legitimate concern to the public and consequently fall within the responsibility of the press to report the operations of government.

* * *

The developing law surrounding the tort of invasion of privacy recognizes a privilege in the press to report the events of judicial proceedings.

* * *

Tentative Draft No. 13 of the *Second Restatement of Torts,* §§ 652A–652E, divides the privacy tort into four branches; and with respect to the wrong of giving unwanted publicity about private life, the commentary to § 652D states: "There is no liability when the defendant merely gives further publicity to information about the plaintiff which is already public. Thus there is no liability for giving publicity to facts about the plaintiff's life which are matters of public record. * * *" According to this draft, ascertaining and publishing the contents of public records are simply not within the reach of these kinds of privacy actions.

Thus even the prevailing law of invasion of privacy generally recognizes that the interests in privacy fade when the information involved already appears on the public record. The conclusion is compelling when viewed in terms of the First and Fourteenth Amendments and in light of the public interest in a vigorous press. The Georgia cause of action for invasion of privacy through public disclosure of the name of a rape victim imposes sanctions on pure expression— the content of a publication—and not conduct or a combination of speech and nonspeech elements that might otherwise be open to regulation or prohibition. * * *

By placing the information in the public domain on official court records, the State must be presumed to have concluded that the public interest was thereby being served.

* * *

We are reluctant to embark on a course that would make public records generally available to the media but forbid their publication if offensive to the sensibilities of the supposed reasonable man. Such a rule would make it very difficult for the media to inform citizens about the public business and yet stay within the law. The rule would invite timidity and self-censorship and very likely lead to the suppression of many items that would otherwise be published and that should be made available to the public. At the very least, the First and Fourteenth Amendments will not allow exposing the press to liability for truthfully publishing information released to the public in official court records. If there are privacy interests to be protected in judicial proceedings, the States must respond by means which avoid public documentation or other exposure of private information. Their political institutions must weigh the interests in privacy with the interests of the public to know and of the press to publish. Once true information is disclosed in public court documents open to public inspection, the press cannot be sanctioned for publishing it. In this instance as in others reliance must rest upon the judgment of those who decide what to publish or broadcast.

Appellant Wassell based his televised report upon notes taken during the court proceedings and obtained the name of the victim from the indictments handed to him at his request during a recess in the hearing. Appellee has not contended that the name was obtained in an improper fashion or that it was not on an official court document open to public inspection. Under these circumstances, the protection of freedom of the press provided by the First and Fourteenth Amendment bars the State of Georgia from making appellant's broadcast the basis of civil liability.

Reversed.

COMMENT

The Court's narrow opinion in *Cox* relied upon the common law privilege to report from records or proceedings, but went further by holding that the defense is required by the First Amendment. The Court also appears to constitutionalize the newsworthiness defense, almost in passing. But the Court refused to declare that truthful publications could never be the basis for liability.

The Court promoted further development of the private facts tort by encouraging states to balance privacy and press interests, emphasizing that it would not attempt to predict the constitutionality of measures designed to keep sensitive information from the press. In light of the Court's 1980s decisions recognizing a First Amendment right to obtain information about court activity and a recent string of decisions recognizing a right to gather news, see discussion in text, p. 397 ff, one might wonder if attempts by states to protect information normally obtainable from records or proceedings would be constitutional.

The Court's second case involved a Florida statute that made it unlawful to "print, publish, or broadcast" the name of a rape or sexual assault victim. The statute applied only to "mass communication." A reporter for *The Florida Star* was at the police station's press room preparing briefs for the paper's lengthy "Police Reports" section. Although the police department normally did not make records of sexual assaults available, a copy of an incident report identifying a rape and robbery victim by name had been left in the press room, where the reporter found it. The newspaper, which had a policy of not naming rape victims, nevertheless printed the story naming the victim.

B. J. F., the victim, filed a suit based on the statute, arguing that it created an enforceable privacy right for victims. The Florida courts declared that the statute barring publication created a presumption that identifying a rape victim was a *per se* invasion of privacy. When the case reached the Supreme Court, the newspaper argued that the case was governed by the *Cox* precedent. A majority of the Court disagreed, noting that, in *Cox*, the press's role in reporting on trials was at issue. Instead the majority used a test taken from a post-*Cox* case, *Smith v. Daily Mail Publishing Co.*, 5 Med. L. Rptr. 1305, 443 U.S. 97 (1979), which said it was unconstitutional for a state to punish a newspaper for violating a statute prohibiting publication of the names of juvenile offenders. Splitting fine hairs, the Court declared that the Florida statute violated the First Amendment, but argued that privacy interests might prevail in another context.

The Florida Star v. B.J.F.
16 MED L. RPTR. 1801, 491 U.S. 524, 109 S. CT. 2603, 105 L. ED. 2D 443 (1989).

Justice MARSHALL delivered the opinion of the Court.

* * *

We conclude that imposing damages on appellant for publishing B.J.F.'s name violates the First Amendment, although not for either of the reasons appellant urges. Despite the strong resemblance this case bears to *Cox Broadcasting,* that case cannot fairly be read as controlling here. The name of the rape victim in that case was obtained from courthouse records that were open to public inspection, a fact which Justice White's opinion for the Court repeatedly noted. Significantly, one of the reasons we gave in *Cox Broadcasting* for invalidating the challenged damages award was the important role the press plays in subjecting trials to public scrutiny and thereby helping guarantee their fairness. That role is not directly comprised where, as here, the information in question comes from a police report prepared and disseminated at a time at which not only had no adversarial criminal proceedings begun, but no suspect had been identified.

We continue to believe that the sensitivity and significance of the interests presented in clashes between First Amendment and privacy rights counsel relying on limited principles that sweep no more broadly than the appropriate context of the instant case.

In our view, this case is appropriately analyzed with reference to such a limited First Amendment principle. It is the one, in fact, which we articulated in *Daily Mail* in our synthesis of prior cases involving attempts to punish truthful publication: "[I]f a newspaper lawfully obtains truthful information about a matter of public significance then state officials may not constitutionally punish publication of the information, absent a need to further a state interest of the highest order." According the press the ample protection provided by that principle is supported by at least three separate considerations, in addition to, of course, the overreaching " 'public interest, secured by the Constitution, in the dissemination of truth.' " *Cox Broadcasting, supra,* at 491, quoting *Garrison, supra,* at 73 (footnote omitted). The cases on which the *Daily Mail* synthesis relied demonstrate these considerations.

First, because the *Daily Mail* formulation only protects the publication of information which a newspaper has "lawfully obtain[ed]," 443 U.S., at 103, the government retains ample means of safeguarding significant interests upon which publication may impinge, including protecting a rape victim's anonymity. To the extent sensitive information rests in private hands, the government may under some circumstances forbid its nonconsensual acquisition, thereby bringing outside of the *Daily Mail* principle the publication of any information so acquired. To the extent sensitive information is in the government's custody, it has even greater power to forestall or mitigate the injury caused by its release. The government may classify certain information, establish and enforce procedures ensuring its redacted release, and extend a damages remedy against the government or its officials where the government's mishandling of sensitive information leads to its dissemination. Where information is entrusted to the government, a less drastic means than pun-

ishing truthful publication almost always exists for guarding against the dissemination of private facts. * * *

A second consideration undergirding the *Daily Mail* principle is the fact that punishing the press for its dissemination of information which is already publicly available is relatively unlikely to advance the interests in the service of which the State seeks to act. It is not, of course, always the case that information lawfully acquired by the press is known, or accessible, to others. But where the government has made certain information publicly available, it is highly anomalous to sanction persons other than the source of its release. * * * The *Daily Mail* formulation reflects the fact that it is a limited set of cases indeed where, despite the accessibility of the public to certain information, a meaningful public interest is served by restricting its further release by other entities, like the press. As *Daily Mail* observed in its summary of *Oklahoma Publishing,* "once the truthful information was 'publicly revealed' or 'in the public domain' the court could not constitutionally restrain its dissemination." 443 U.S., at 103.

A third and final consideration is the "timidity and self-censorship" which may result from allowing the media to be punished for publishing certain truthful information. *Cox Broadcasting, supra,* at 496. *Cox Broadcasting* noted this concern with overdeterrence in the context of information made public through official court records, but the fear of excessive media self-suppression is applicable as well to other information released, without qualification, by the government. A contrary rule, depriving protection to those who rely on the government's implied representations of the lawfulness of dissemination, would force upon the media the onerous obligation of sifting through government press releases, reports, and pronouncements to prune out material arguably unlawful for publication.

* * *

The second inquiry is whether imposing liability on appellant pursuant to § 794.03 serves "a need to further a state interest of the highest order." *Daily Mail,* 443 U.S., at 103. Appellee argues that a rule punishing publication furthers three closely related interests: the privacy of victims of sexual offenses; the physical safety of such victims, who may be targeted for retaliation if their names become known to their assailants; and the goal of encouraging victims of such crimes to report these offenses without fear of exposure.

At a time in which we are daily reminded of the tragic reality of rape, it is undeniable that these are highly significant interests, a fact underscored by the Florida Legislature's explicit attempt to protect these interests by enacting a criminal statute prohibiting such dissemination of victim identities. We accordingly do not rule out the possibility that, in a proper case, imposing civil sanctions for publication of the name of a rape victim might be so overwhelmingly necessary to advance these interests as to satisfy the *Daily Mail* standard. For three independent reasons, however, imposing liability for publication under the circumstances of this case is too precipitous a means of advancing these interests to convince us that there is a "need" within the meaning of the *Daily Mail* formulation for Florida to take this extreme step. * * *

First is the manner in which appellant obtained the identifying information in question. As we have noted, where the government itself provides information to the media, it is most appropriate to assume that the government had, but failed to utilize, far more limited means of guarding against dissemination than the extreme step of punishing truthful speech. * * * Where, as here, the government has failed to police itself in disseminating information, it is clear under *Cox Broadcasting, Oklahoma Publishing,* and *Landmark Communications* that the imposition of damages against the press for its subsequent publication can hardly be said to be a narrowly tailored means of safeguarding anonymity. * * *

That appellant gained access to the information in question through a government news release makes it especially likely that, if liability were to be imposed, self-censorship would result. Reliance on a news release is a paradigmatically "routine newspaper reporting techniqu[e]." *Daily Mail,* 443 U.S., at 103. The government's issuance of such a release, without qualification, can only convey to recipients that the government considered dissemination lawful, and indeed expected the recipients to disseminate the information further.

* * *

A second problem with Florida's imposition of liability for publication is the broad sweep of the negligence *per se* standard applied under the civil cause of action implied from § 794.03. Unlike claims based on the common law tort of invasion of privacy, see Restatement (Second) of Torts § 652D (1977), civil actions based on § 794.03 require no case-by-case findings that the disclosure of a fact about a person's private life was one that a reasonable person would find highly offensive. On the contrary, under the *per se* theory of negligence adopted by the courts below, liability follows automatically from publication.

Third, and finally, the facial underinclusiveness of § 794.03 raises serious doubts about whether Florida is, in fact, serving, with this statute, the significant interests which appellee invokes in support of affirmance. Section 794.03 (the Florida statute) prohibits the publication of identifying information only if this information appears in an "instrument of mass communication," a term the statute does not define. Section 794.03 does not prohibit the spread by other means of the identities of victims of sexual offenses. An individual who maliciously spreads word of the identity of a rape victim is thus not covered, despite the fact that the communication of such information to persons who live near, or work with, the victim may have consequences equally devastating as the exposure of her name to large numbers of strangers.

Our holding today is limited. We do not hold that truthful publication is automatically constitutionally protected, or that there is no zone of personal privacy within which the State may protect the individual from intrusion by the press, or even that a State may never punish publication of the name of a victim of a sexual offense. We hold only that where a newspaper publishes truthful information which it has lawfully obtained, punishment may lawfully be imposed, if at all, only when narrowly tailored to a state interest of the highest order, and that no such interest is satisfactorily served by imposing liability under § 794.03 to appellant under the facts of this case. The decision below is therefore

Reversed.

COMMENT

The Court held out the possibility, "in a proper case," of imposing sanctions for publishing the name of a rape victim. Most observers thought otherwise, reasoning that the variation on the compelling interest test adopted by the Court effectively eviscerated the private facts tort, at least insofar as information relating to crime or government is concerned.[44] More than ever before, it appears that the decision on publishing the names of rape victims and similar sensitive information is an ethics issue for the press.[45] The case created quite a furor. A large majority of citizens believe the press ought not name rape victims, and the *Florida Star* case came at a time when the press had been using names in many high-profile stores. Most news organizations have traditionally had internal policies against publishing the names of rape victims,[46] although they may not always follow those policies.[47]

The Scope of the *Cox-Star* Defense

Following the *Star* case, the constitutionality of a number of state statutes was challenged. The Florida Supreme Court declared the *Star* statute unconstitutional on its face in a subsequent case arising from the William Kennedy Smith rape prosecution. The case attracted worldwide publicity. The state brought action against a Florida-based tabloid that had named the alleged victim. Notably, dozens of other news organizations also used her name and, on occasion, photo. Even though the U.S. Supreme Court had indicated that a statute might be upheld if it were narrowly tailored and not aimed at the press as in *Star,* the Florida court declined to offer an interpretation of the statute that would apply it to the public while also adding required constitutional defenses:

> The State is correct that whenever possible we will construe a statute so as not to conflict with the con-

stitution. We will resolve all doubts . . . in favor of its constitutionality, provided that we can give the statute a fair construction that is consistent with the Florida and federal constitutions and with legislative intent. * * * [E]xtensive rewriting and broadening of the statute's scope would be required to rehabilitate section 794.03. * * * [W]e do not rule out the possibility that the legislature could fashion a statute that would pass constitutional muster. *Florida v. Globe Communication Corp.,* 23 Med. L. Rptr. 1116, 648 So.2d 110 (Fla. 1994).

Other states have followed the hair-splitting approach of the *Star* majority. In *Macon Telegraph Publishing Co. v. Tatum,* 22 Med. L. Rptr. 1126, 436 S.E.2d 655 (Ga. 1993), a newspaper had published a story identifying by name Nancy Tatum, who had shot and killed an intruder who was apparently going to attempt rape. Two reporters had been given the name by police investigators. The newspaper also reported the name of the street where she lived. Tatum was later determined to have acted in self-defense. Relying upon a Georgia statute similar to Florida's, Tatum sued, but on common law grounds. In deciding for the newspaper, the Georgia Supreme Court relied on a newsworthiness analysis. The constitutionality of the statute itself was not addressed:

> [T]he commission of the crimes, police investigation, and departmental decision that Tatum acted in self-defense are matters of public interest. * * * Under the facts of this case, we hold that Tatum, who committed a homicide, however justified, *lost her right to keep her name private.* When she shot Hill, Tatum became the object of a legitimate public interest and the newspaper had the (constitutional) right . . . to accurately report the facts. . . ." [Emphasis added.]

The South Carolina Supreme Court found that state's statute banning naming of rape victims constitutional because it applied to all persons, not just to the news media. Nevertheless, the court held that the statute did not create a privacy cause of action for the plaintiff. As written, the statute allowed only criminal, not civil, enforcement. If the legislature intended a private cause of action, it would have to say so explicitly. *Dorman v. Aiken Communications, Inc.,* 18 Med. L. Rptr. 1394, 398 S.E.2d 687 (S.C. 1990).

Most courts have continued to find the *Cox* precedent applicable and more persuasive. For example, when a newspaper published names of

44. Arant, *Press Identification of Victims of Sexual Assault: Weighing Privacy and Constitutional Concerns,* 68 Journalism Q. 238 (1991); Comment, Stanton, Florida Star v. B.J.F.: *The Wrongful Obliteration of the Tort of Invasion of Privacy through the Publication of Private Facts,* 18 Hastings Const. L.Q. 391 (1991).

45. Black, *Commentary: Rethinking the naming of sex crime victims,* 16 Newspaper Res.J. 96 (1995).

46. Thomason, LaRocque, and Thomas, *Editors Still Reluctant to Name Rape Victims,* 16 Newspaper Res. J. 42 (1995); Wolf, Thomason, & LaRocque, *The Right to Know vs. the Right of Privacy: Newspaper Identification of Crime Victims,* 64 Journalism Q. 503 (1987).

47. Wexler, The *"Outing" of Kiri Jewell,* Quill, November/December 1995, at 31.

people who had been granted divorces that had been taken from court records, application of a constitutional public records privilege was almost automatic. The privilege analysis took only a paragraph, albeit a long one. *Doe v. Sherman Publishing Co.,* 19 Med. L. Rptr. 1028, 593 A.2d 457 (R.I. 1991). The state court decision in *Florida Star* seems to have been an isolated example. Apparently, no other case since 1975 has allowed recovery against a media defendant for information obtained from official records or proceedings. Thus, by common law, constitutional law, or statute, the right of privacy does not extend to matters of public record. *Doe v. New York City,* 21 Med. L. Rptr. 1734, 825 F.Supp. 36 (S.D.N.Y. 1993); *Lawton v. Georgia Television Co.,* 22 Med. L. Rptr. 2046 (Ga. Super. Ct. 1994). In recent years few cases involving information derived from official records or proceedings have been appealed, an indication that lawyers for plaintiffs are advising against appeal.

Another argument against media liability is that any invasion of privacy action based on records is the responsibility of the custodian of the record rather than of the press. Government officials enjoy qualified or absolute immunity in tort actions, so as a practical matter plaintiffs have no recourse if this argument is applied. *Woody v. West Publishing Co.,* 24 Med. L. Rptr. 1382, ___ F. Supp. ___ (N.D.Ill. 1995). In *Woody,* the defendant republished a court opinion that stated that the plaintiff had tested positive for HIV.

Generally, the burden of keeping information private falls upon either the individual or, in the case of a statutory provision, the government. When a rape victim relied on a promise that her name would not be disclosed and no photos would be taken of her if she testified at trial, she lost her subsequent privacy case against a local television station that ran a videotape with part of her testimony. *Doe v. Sarasota-Bradenton Television,* 9 Med. L. Rptr. 2074, 436 So.2d 328 (Fla.App. 1983). A similar result occurred when bar association ratings of nominees for judgeships were published, despite a state law stipulating that ratings be confidential. One nominee found "not qualified" sued both two newspapers and the bar association. Claims against the press were dismissed. "While the government may desire to keep some proceedings confidential and may impose the duty upon participants to maintain confidentiality, it may not impose criminal or civil liability upon the press for obtaining and publishing newsworthy information through routine reporting techniques." *Nicholson v. McClatchy Newspapers,* 12 Med. L. Rptr. 2009, 177 Cal.App.3d 509, 223 Cal.Rptr. 58 (1986).

Similar results have obtained when the press got information about a juvenile offense from a public parole report,[48] when a newspaper reported the name of a fourteen-year-old rape victim obtained in an open preliminary hearing,[49] and when a newspaper published medical details about a teenager's apparent hit-and-run death from a county sheriff's report.[50] In one case, a rationale similar to that in *Cox* was used to affirm dismissal of complaints by police officers whose names and addresses were reported in a newspaper story about a gun battle between police and gang members. The court reasoned that since a person's address appears in many public records, all open to public inspection, a home address is always a public fact. *McNutt v. New Mexico State Tribune,* 538 P.2d 804 (N.M.App. 1975).

Not all records have provided a defense. Government's interest in prosecuting criminals through changing witnesses' names was cited as a countervailing interest preventing summary judgment on newsworthiness grounds. A press release from a racing association had given the plaintiffs' former identities. Anthony Ciulla had been convicted of fixing horse races and was allowed to participate in the federal witness protection program in exchange for testimony. Relocated and renamed, his wife Helen applied for a license from the California Horse Racing Board. The defendant conducted an inquiry for the board, denied her application, and issued the press release. While noting that witness protection was a value that deserved weight, the court

---

48. *Montesano v. Las Vegas Review Journal,* 9 Med. L. Rptr. 2266, 668 P.2d 1081 (Nev. 1983).
49. *Poteet v. Roswell Daily Record,* 4 Med. L. Rptr. 1749, 584 P.2d 1310 (N.M.App. 1978).
50. *Moloney v. Tribune Pub.,* 6 Med. L. Rptr. 1426, 613 P.2d 1179 (Wash.App. 1980). The court relied upon the Restatement (Second) of Torts delineation of the official proceedings qualified privilege in libel rather than upon *Cox.* The action was also disallowed because the subject of the article was deceased, and privacy rights normally terminate at death under common law.

also urged the jury on remand to consider to what extent the plaintiffs had voluntarily exposed themselves to potential publicity. *Capra v. Thoroughbred Racing Ass'n.,* 12 Med. L. Rptr. 2006, 787 F.2d 463 (9th Cir. 1986). The press release was not on its own a public record, and the defendant was a private entity working on behalf of a government agency. Are those facts alone sufficient to distinguish *Capra* from *Cox?*

An individual's interest in personal safety and the state's interest in conducting criminal investigations were considered sufficient to allow trial on a privacy suit brought by a witness to a murder who was identified by name. *Times Mirror v. San Diego Superior Court,* 15 Med. L. Rptr. 1129, 198 Cal.App.3d 1420, 244 Cal.Rptr. 556 (1988). The plaintiff, identified in the opinion only as Doe, found her roommate's body. The roommate had been raped, beaten, and strangled. Looking up, she saw a man, then fled the apartment. She provided a description to the police, who withheld her identity. The *Los Angeles Times* published a story identifying Doe. The *Times* claimed it had obtained her name from an "unknown person" at the coroner's office. Doe sued for publication of private facts and for infliction of emotional distress. Newsworthiness would not support a summary judgment for the newspaper because the value to the public in being informed of a witness's name must be balanced against the effect publication might have on the witness. A dissenting opinion urged that the majority erred by failing to apply a "public event" analysis to the case. The majority seemed determined to find that no defense or privilege applied, at least at the pretrial stage.

The Passage of Time and Newsworthiness by Implication

Two additional lines of cases in private facts concern whether facts that occurred in the past and were of public interest or public record then will be considered public today if resurrected by the media, and whether a person who is closely associated with another who is newsworthy will also be considered newsworthy. Overall, the courts appear to take the position that a person who was newsworthy or an event that was newsworthy will remain so over time. One typical situation involved the *Iberville South*'s "Page From Our Past" column, which each week drew from

its files of stories on local events. Twice in four years, the paper published stories more than twenty years old about the plaintiffs'—three brothers—cattle theft trial and subsequent convictions. Asserting that the story was no longer of public concern, they filed a private acts suit. *Roshto v. Hebert,* 9 Med. L. Rptr. 2417, 439 So.2d 428 (La. 1983). The Court determined that controlling weight should be given to the fact that the stories were true and a matter of public record.

Mere allegations, when taken from public records, were sufficient to prevent liability when a newspaper published twenty-year-old charges based on FBI reports.[51] The existence of public records, of course, is not necessary to a finding of continued newsworthiness over time, as *Sidis* makes plain. For example, the Julius and Ethel Rosenberg espionage case has retained its public character. When Michael and Robert Meeropol, the natural children of Julius and Ethel Rosenberg, brought a multiclaim suit based on the book, *The Implosion Conspiracy,* they lost on privacy, defamation, and copyright grounds. An appeals court upheld a trial court determination that the events remained of public interest. *Meeropol v. Nizer,* 2 Med. L. Rptr. 2269, 560 F.2d 1061 (2d Cir. 1977). Ironically, the brothers were never referred to in the books by their adoptive name, and their identities were known to only a handful of individuals. By suing, they attracted the publicity they had shunned.

Newsworthiness by proximity to an event or to another person has been less of a concern. In *Campbell v. Seabury Press,* 5 Med. L. Rptr. 2612, 614 F.2d 395 (5th Cir. 1980), a federal appeals court seemed to answer that question when it decided that private facts based on references to a former sister-in-law in a civil rights leader's biography were nonactionable. Citing *Cox,* the court extended the public interest or newsworthiness privilege to entirely private persons because of a "logical nexus * * * between the complaining individual and the matter of legitimate public interest."

In *Gilbert v. Medical Economics,* 7 Med. L. Rptr. 2372, 665 F.2d 305 (10th Cir. 1981), the subject of an article entitled "Who Let This

---

51. *McCormack v. Oklahoma Pubg. Co.,* 6 Med. L. Rptr. 1618, 613 P.2d 737 (Okla. 1980).

Doctor in the O.R.?" found no remedy in privacy law because accurate personal facts about the doctor again were closely related to his malpractice suit.

Flora Schreiber, a criminal justice professor at New York University, wrote *The Shoemaker*, which detailed the psychological makeup of Joseph Kallinger, who had committed a series of rapes and murders during a string of robberies in New Jersey and Pennsylvania. The book recounted the ordeal of several people held hostage, including the murder of one, in 1975. When the book appeared in 1983, a number of the survivors sued for publication of private facts, false light privacy, libel, and unjust enrichment. The key to resolving all the claims lay in the incident's continued newsworthiness or lack thereof.

Romaine v. Kallinger
15 MED. L. RPTR. 1209, 537 A.2D 284 (N.J. 1988).

HANDLER, J.:

More than ten years ago Joseph Kallinger and his son went on a criminal rampage in Pennsylvania and New Jersey. The offenses were vicious, involving physical threats and sexual abuse of victims during the course of robberies of suburban homes. Kallinger murdered his victims on three occasions. In 1983, approximately eight years after Kallinger and his son had been apprehended, the defendant Simon & Schuster Publishing Inc. published a book entitled "The Shoemaker," written by the defendant Flora Rheta Schreiber, depicting the life and crimes of Joseph Kallinger. The book gave rise to this litigation.

The plaintiffs, Randi Romaine, Edwina Wiseman, Retta Romaine Welby, and Frank Welby, were victims of Kallinger, whose criminal acts against them resulted in the murder of a young woman, Maria Fasching. Plaintiffs sued the defendants Kallinger, Elizabeth Kallinger, his wife, Schreiber, Simon & Schuster, and Paul J. Giblin, claiming to have been legally injured by defamatory and offensively intrusive statements relating to those crimes contained in "The Shoemaker." Plaintiffs sought in separate counts the award of compensatory and punitive damages based respectively on libel and invasion of privacy by being cast in a false light; they also claimed that their privacy had been invaded

through the unreasonable publication of private facts.

* * *

The factual context of this litigation is important. Ms. Schreiber, the author of "The Shoemaker," is a professor at the City University of New York, John Jay College of Criminal Justice. Although she has no formal training as a psychologist, Ms. Schreiber has written extensively about psychological subjects, and has focused on the problem of child abuse in her work. She is the author of *Sybil,* a study of a woman who suffered from a multiple-personality disorder.

According to defendants, Professor Schreiber's work is an in-depth study of the psychological make-up of a killer. Specifically, the book explores the relationship between the abuse suffered by Kallinger as a child and the psychotic behavior that led to his criminal acts. "The Shoemaker" received a significant amount of critical praise and Schreiber was named "Author of the Year" by the American Society of Journalists and Authors in 1985 in recognition of her work.

The complaint focuses on a chapter of "The Shoemaker" called "The Hunting Knife." The chapter, which consists of twenty-one pages out of a total of 423, describes the murder of Maria Fasching on January 8, 1975, in Leonia, New Jersey. The chapter relates that Kallinger and his son broke into the home of Mr. and Mrs. DeWitt Romaine. Eight people, who were in the home, were held hostage by Kallinger and his son. Kallinger ordered several of them to remove their clothes, and tied them up. He committed acts of personal abuse and physical degradation on two of the women. While this was occurring, Maria Fasching, a friend of one of the victims, the plaintiff Randi Romaine, came into the house. She was also captured by Kallinger. He directed Ms. Fasching, a nurse, to perform an act of sexual mutilation on plaintiff Frank Welby, who was tied up and helpless. When she refused to do so, he killed her by slashing her throat several times. About one-half of the chapter is devoted to Kallinger's own recollections of the murder, obtained by Schreiber during interviews with him; those recollections are presented to indicate the extent that Kallinger's acts were the product of his mental illness. The balance of the chapter consists of the recreation of the murder, as derived from testimony offered at Kallinger's trial by the survivors of the incident.

* * *

Plaintiffs contend that the chapter "The Hunting Knife" publicizes matters pertaining to their private lives in a manner offensive to a reasonable person. They thus claim a cause of action based upon the invasion of privacy by the unreasonable publication of private facts. In making this claim, plaintiffs concede that the chapter is an accurate and truthful depiction of the events that occurred on January 8, 1975. However, they contend that their criminal victimization, personal degradation, and physical abuse at the hands of Kallinger occurred in private, and that disclosure of the details of these crimes eight years after their occurrence is highly offensive.

It is important to stress that this privacy tort permits recovery for *truthful* disclosures. For this reason the recognition of such a tort creates significant potential for conflict with the guarantees contained in the first amendment of the Constitution. * * *

The critical chapter describes the painful treatment, the humiliation, and abuse that the plaintiffs suffered at the hands of Kallinger. Such publicity is likely traumatic and profoundly disturbing for plaintiffs and would be highly offensive to a reasonable person because it exposes to the public eye the suffering and degradation that they were forced to endure. However, plaintiffs' appeal fails because the facts revealed are not private, and even if they were private, they are of legitimate concern to the public and so privileged under the "newsworthiness" exception to the "unreasonable publication of private facts" claim.

The determination as to whether published facts are actually private constitutes the first key element of this cause of action. If the facts are public information, even though they relate to matters of individual privacy, they cannot for these purposes be considered "private." The court must first determine then whether the published facts were in the public domain, and hence not private facts.

Public records that recount or disclose particular facts may serve to place such facts in the public arena and thus bar a claim for publication of private facts. While the term "public records" is not self-defining, we need not in this case determine the extent to which particular official governmental records place facts in the public domain. Here, the facts complained of were contained in nonconfidential official court records of the Kallinger trial. * * * The circumstances of this case fall squarely within the freedom to publish information contained in public court records sanctioned by *Cox Broadcasting*. The details and facts that plaintiffs claim invaded their privacy were made public by the testimony in court by plaintiffs and other witnesses. They were part of the court record in Kallinger's trial and were extensively reported on at the time of the trial.

Plaintiffs also contend that recovery should not be barred in this case because eight years passed between the crimes depicted in "The Shoemaker" and the publication of the book. This argument is unpersuasive. The *Cox Broadcasting* opinion does not suggest that the absolute privilege to publish matters contained in public records is limited if the events are not contemporaneous or recent. Moreover, courts after *Cox Broadcasting* have found a privilege to disseminate matters contained in public court records despite the passage of a significant period of time. * * *

The "newsworthiness" defense in privacy-invasion tort actions is available to bar recovery where the subject matter of the publication is one in which the public has a legitimate interest. * * * A publication is commonly understood to be "newsworthy" when it contains an "indefinable quality of information" that arouses the public's interest and attention." * * * In such cases it is for the court to determine whether a matter is of legitimate public interest. * * *

In addition, once a matter is found to be within the sphere of public interest, otherwise private facts that are related to the subject may also be considered "newsworthy," and therefore publishable. * * *

The events that occurred in the Romaine home on January 8, 1975, were newsworthy and matters of legitimate public concern. These events were the subject of widespread and intense publicity when they occurred. Extensive contemporaneous publicity of this sort is a strong indication that the subject is one that is clearly newsworthy. * * * Moreover, the facts surrounding the commission of a crime are subjects of legitimate public concern. * * * This concern extends to victims and other individuals who unwillingly become involved in the commission of a crime or its prosecution. * * *

The contention of plaintiffs that the publicized

matter is stale or remote may suggest that the publicized information was not "newsworthy" or a matter of legitimate public concern, and therefore recovery ought not be barred. The news value and public interest in criminal events are not abated by the passage of time.

* * *

For the reasons set forth in this opinion, we affirm the judgment below.

COMMENT

The plaintiffs sued not only the publisher but also the perpetrator, Kallinger, a somewhat unusual move apparently prompted by New Jersey's "Son of Sam" law, the Criminal Injuries Compensation Act, which was designed to prevent criminals from profiting by selling their stories; part of any profit would go to victims. Laws of this type have been declared unconstitutional because they discriminate on the basis of specific types of content. *Simon & Schuster v. New York State Crime Victims Board,* 19 Med. L. Rptr. 1609, 112 S. Ct. 501, 116 L. Ed. 2d 476 (1991). See p. 76.

The court noted in a separate section that the privacy claims were invalid in any event because the book relied upon interviews with Kallinger and transcripts from the trial. There was no evidence that any additional "prying" had occurred.

A similar analysis was applied in the case of the brother of a murderer who was written about extensively in the book *Life for Death.* Lee Dresbach sued after the story of his brother Wayne's murder of their parents appeared. The book contained details of the family's home life and of the dismal relationship between the brothers. The plaintiff argued that the murders were no longer of public interest and that he wasn't either. The courts disagreed. Further, the court said that the story of Wayne's rehabilitation contributed a more contemporary newsworthy angle. *Dresbach v. Doubleday,* 7 Med. L. Rptr. 2105, 518 F.Supp. 1285 (D.D.C. 1981). Can the retelling of a famous (or infamous) crime ever be the object of a private facts claim?

Have our sensitivities toward personal privacy diminished? We do know what has outraged some communities and their judicial systems in the past. For example, a woman's disfigured face photographed without her consent while she was semiconscious,[52] a published photograph of an employee's mangled thigh,[53] a photograph of a woman with her skirt blown over her head as she entered a county fair "fun house,"[54] and a newspaper piece that contained the words, "Wanna hear a sexy telephone voice? Call * * * and ask for Louise."[55] In the latter case, the court compared the objectionable language of the newspaper with that commonly found on the walls of public lavatories.

Any iota of voluntariness would seem to invoke a newsworthiness or consent defense. A man simply unfortunate enough to have been having a drink at a bar when police raided for drugs could not recover for television footage of the raid that included his likeness.[56] And a plaintiff, a heroin addict, who had consented to an interview, was said to have constructively consented to use of her photograph.[57] Older cases follow the same lines.

Even expunged—deleted—criminal records will support a defense, partly because accusations of crime retain their newsworthiness, and partly because underlying records such as police blotters and court documents were not expunged.[58]

Proof that a particular news story attracted tremendous publicity made it easier for a court to decide that an old, republished story was still newsworthy. The court also determined that, given the heavy news coverage, the information the plaintiff complained about was public, not private, anyway. *Heath v. Playboy Enterprises, Inc.,* 17 Med. L. Rptr. 1603, 732 F.Supp. 1145 (S.D.Fla. 1990).

A news report identifying a twelve-year-old mother, despite her objections, was protected. So were a news review ridiculing an inventor's invention and a photograph of corpulent women exercising in a gymnasium. A group of young

---

52. *Clayman v. Bernstein,* 38 D & C 543 (Pa. 1940).
53. *Lambert v. Dow Chemical Co.,* 215 So.2d 673 (La. 1968).
54. *Daily Times Democrat v. Graham,* 162 So.2d 474 (Ala. 1964).
55. *Harms v. Miami Daily News, Inc.,* 127 So.2d 715 (Fla. 1961).
56. *Penwell v. Taft Broadcasting,* 10 Med. L. Rptr. 1850, 469 N.E.2d 1025 (Ohio App. 1984).
57. *Little v. Washington Post,* 11 Med. L. Rptr. 1428 (D.D.C. 1985).
58. *Nilson v. Layton City,* 23 Med. L. Rptr. 1375, 45 F.3d 369 (10th Cir. 1995).

Americans who allowed themselves to be interviewed and photographed living in a communal cave in Crete had no privacy claim. Neither did a casino customer who got caught in a photograph that was later used to dress up an article on gambling and organized crime. The Boston "Strangler's" notoriety and the fact that he had consented to a film portrayal of his life, and had even offered technical advice to the filmmaker, left him without a privacy claim.[59]

As a general rule, information obtained in a public place will almost never be considered a private fact. When coverage of Ted Fry's death in a fire and of his rumored association with another women resulted in Mrs. Fry's suing, the court said that all the facts about the fire occurred in public.[60] Plaintiffs who have alleged invasions of privacy because they could be seen leaving or cleaning portable toilets have lost because anyone could have seen them.[61]

Does "Private Facts" Have a Future?

Where can a line be drawn between legitimate news and inappropriate prying? Considering the changes in what the public finds acceptable in its news and entertainment media, should a line be drawn at all? The answers await further analysis by the courts. In the meantime, it seems that fewer private facts cases are being filed, and that defendants are winning almost every time.

The rationale underlying the private facts cause of action was severely critiqued by the Oregon Supreme Court in a 1986 case. Justice Hans Linde's opinion for the court argued that the cause of action fails to serve the purposes it was created to protect, while doing considerable damage to the operations of the press. Richard Anderson filed suit after station KATU-TV used footage of him from an automobile accident in promotional advertising for its special report on emergency medical service. The material had never been used in a newscast. In the videotape Anderson was identifiable, shown injured and bleeding. He claimed violation of his right of privacy on private facts and appropriation grounds. A trial court gave the station summary judgment on the issue of newsworthiness. The court of appeals had reversed, holding that newsworthiness was a fact issue for the jury.

Anderson v. Fisher Broadcasting Cos.
12 MED. L. RPTR. 1604, 712 P.2D 803 (ORE. 1986).

LINDE, J.:

* * *

Plaintiff sued for general damages for mental anguish, alleging that defendant "violated plaintiff's right to privacy" by "appropriating to defendant's own use and advantage" the pictures its photographer had taken of plaintiff and by "publicizing" his picture in a condition "offensive to a reasonable person" and not of legitimate public concern. In defense, the broadcaster asserted that its use of plaintiff's picture occurred in advertising another news program, that this use was constitutionally privileged and that the undisputed facts gave rise to no common law claim. The trial court gave summary judgment for defendant. * * *

The Court of Appeals held that there was an issue of fact whether the film showing plaintiff's injured condition was newsworthy, because it was not used to report plaintiff's accident itself but only to draw viewers for a different program in which the accident was not mentioned.

* * *

In this court, defendant again stressed its constitutional claims along with its common law arguments, understandably so in defending against a tort claim for wrongful publicity to which media of mass communication are peculiarly vulnerable. The constitutional issues are significant. The right to "speak, write, or print freely on any subject whatever" guaranteed by Article I, section 8, of the Oregon Constitution accommodates laws providing civil responsibility and remedies (though not punitive damages) for an "injury done another in his person, property, or reputation," as guaranteed in Article I, section 10, if the interest said to be injured falls within section

---

59. *Meetze v. Associated Press,* 95 S.E.2d 606 (S.C. 1956); *Thompson v. Curtis Publishing Co.,* 193 F.2d 953 (3d Cir. 1952); *Sweenek v. Pathe News,* 16 F.Supp. 746 (D.N.Y. 1936); *Goldman v. Time, Inc.,* 336 F.Supp. 133 (D.Cal. 1971); *Holmes v. Curtis Publishing Co.,* 303 F.Supp. 522 (D.S.C. 1969); *DeSalvo v. Twentieth Century-Fox Film Corp.,* 300 F.Supp. 742 (D.Mass. 1969).

60. *Fry v. Ionia Sentinel-Standard,* 6 Med. L. Rptr. 2498, 300 N.W.2d 687 (Mich.App. 1980).

61. *Livingston v. Kentucky Post,* 14 Med. L. Rptr. 2076 (Ky.Cir.Ct. 1987); *Taggart v. Wadleigh-Maurice, Ltd.,* 489 F.2d 434 (3d Cir. 1973).

10 and if the defendant's expression meets the test of the word "abuse" in section 8.

* * *

We therefore included the constitutional issues among the questions that we submitted to counsel before argument. But we shall not decide this case on constitutional grounds when it is unnecessary to do so, and when a premature decision would foreclose legislative consideration. In the present case, we hold that the undisputed facts do not give rise to a claim for damages. We therefore reverse the Court of Appeals and reinstate the judgment of the circuit court.

* * *

The question whether truthfully publicizing a fact about a private individual that the individual reasonably prefers to keep private is, without more, a tort, has not yet been squarely decided by this court.

Generally, Oregon decisions have not allowed recovery for injury to a stranger's feelings as such, unless the infliction of psychic distress was the object of defendant's conduct or the conduct violated some legal duty apart from causing the distress. *See Norwest v. Presbyterian Intercommunity Hosp.,* 293 Or at 558–59, reviewing the cases. In the absence of some other duty or relationship of the defendant to plaintiff, it does not suffice for tort liability that defendant's offensive conduct is an intentional act. The conduct must be designed to cause severe mental or emotional distress, whether for its own sake or as a means to some other end, and it must qualify as extraordinary conduct that a reasonable jury could find to be beyond the farthest reach of socially tolerable behavior. Here the use of plaintiff's picture, of course, was intentional, but there is no claim or evidence that the broadcaster wished to distress plaintiff.

* * *

"Privacy" denotes a personal or cultural value placed on seclusion or personal control over access to places or things, thoughts or acts. "Privacy" also can be used to label one or more legally recognized interests, and this court has so used the term in several cases. * * * But like the older word "property," which it partially overlaps, "privacy" has been a difficult legal concept to delimit.

* * *

The common law tort claim based solely on publicizing private facts that are true but not newsworthy has met critical response. * * * Such a tort was not part of the "common law of England" adopted by Oregon in 1843, and after studying it was rejected in England, the home of the common law, in favor of alternative theories. Criticism has not implied a lack of sympathy with the feelings of persons whose past or present lives are brought to public attention against their own wishes; but the obstacles to defining when publicity as such is tortious, without more, are formidable.

What is "private" so as to make its publication offensive likely differs among communities, between generations, and among ethnic, religious, or other social groups, as well as among individuals. Likewise, one reader's or viewer's "news" is another's tedium or trivia. The editorial judgment of what is "newsworthy" is not so readily submitted to the *ad hoc* review of a jury as the Court of Appeals believed. It is not properly a community standard.

* * *

If the tort is defined to protect a plaintiff's interest in nondisclosure only against widespread publicity, as in the Restatement's § 652D, it singles out the print, film, and broadcast media for legal restraints that will not be applied to gossipmongers in neighborhood taverns or card parties, to letter writers or telephone tattlers. Finally, a successful tort action may serve to rectify a defamatory, appropriative, or "false light" publication, but in the pure "private facts" tort even success sacrifices rather than protect the plaintiff's interest in the privacy of the wrongfully publicized facts, for litigation only breeds renewed and often wider publicity, this time unquestionably privileged. Writing in 1979, Professor Dorsey D. Ellis, Jr., found that there had been no reported case in which a plaintiff successfully recovered damages for truthful disclosure by the press since the United States Supreme Court reversed a New York judgment in *Time, Inc. v. Hill,* 385 U.S. 374, 87 S. Ct. 534, 17 L. Ed. 2d 456 (1967), and he concluded that the tort's "very existence is in doubt, at least outside the law reviews." Ellis, *Damages and the Privacy Tort: Sketching a Legal Profile,* 64 Iowa L.Rev. 1111, 1133 (1979).

Doubtless in many instances a picture not only is worth a thousand words to a publisher but words would be worth nothing at all. * * * Some filmed or broadcast scenes compare to verbal reports in dramatic impact about as hearing music compares to reading a score, and the emotional reaction of the person who is depicted rather than described may likewise be greater. * * *

Nonetheless, the difference between undesired publicity by word or by picture seems to concern only the degree of the subject's psychic discomfort rather than the nature of the interest claimed to be invaded. Perhaps the present plaintiff would not have felt offended if KATU-TV had verbally described his bloodied and disheveled condition rather than showing it. But neither the courts nor the commentators have made a distinction in principle between one woman's objections to a book based on her experiences, *Cason v. Baskin,* 155 Fla. 198, 20 So.2d 243 (1944), and another's to a motion picture, *Melvin v. Reid,* 112 Cal. App. 285, 297 P. 91 (1931), and we perceive none.

* * *

Plaintiff in the present case concedes that KATU-TV would not be liable to him if it had included his picture in the ordinary news coverage of a traffic accident. He contends that the broadcaster became liable because instead it used the footage to draw audience attention to a later broadcast concerning emergency medical services, in which plaintiff's picture was not included. Does the distinction between "commercial" and "noncommercial" use of a person's name, likeness, or life history rest on a difference in the interest invaded by the publication or in the character of the publisher's motives and purposes? The reason should bear on the remedy.

* * *

This theory is not available, however, to a person whose image, with no established public familiarity, appears in a commercial context only incidentally, perhaps as one of several persons in a public scene, or otherwise under circumstances that plainly are not presented so as to convey any endorsement by that person.

* * *

In the present case, plaintiff does not claim that KATU-TV's promotional spots portrayed him as an accident victim in a manner implying that he endorsed its forthcoming program about emergency medical services, and the record on summary judgment suggests no such inference. His claim is not for the economic value of such an endorsement, nor for any gain unjustly realized by the broadcaster from appropriating a photograph belonging to plaintiff. The videotape was made at the accident scene by defendant's cameraman, and the identity of the accident victim was immaterial. Rather, plaintiff claims damages for mental distress from its publication. Without a showing that plaintiff's picture was either obtained or broadcast in a manner or for a purpose wrongful beyond the unconsented publication itself, that claim fails.

To summarize, we conclude that in Oregon, the truthful presentation of facts concerning a person, even facts that a reasonable person would wish to keep private and that are not "newsworthy," does not give rise to common-law tort liability for damages for mental or emotional distress, unless the manner or purpose of defendant's conduct is wrongful in some respect apart from causing the plaintiff's hurt feelings. * * * Because plaintiff has shown no such wrongful element in defendants' conduct, we have no occasion to anticipate constitutional questions in the event the legislature were to enter this field of tort law.

The decision of the Court of Appeals is reversed, and the judgment of the circuit court is reinstated.

COMMENT

Why did the court not adopt a state constitutional or First Amendment defense for the media against any private facts or appropriation lawsuit whenever the complained-of content was news? Such an analysis would have retained the common law actions for other, nonmedia or nonnews purposes. The court instead says that the content of media itself cannot become the basis for a suit, only a "wrongful element in defendants' conduct." In any event the publication of truthful information cannot, standing alone, support a privacy action in Oregon, no matter how private the facts may be. Oregon is nearly alone in its interpretation at present.[62] The logic

---

62. North Carolina rejected the private facts cause of action as unsound as a matter of common law and as constitutionally suspect. *Hall v. Post,* 15 Med. L. Rptr. 2329, 372 S.E.2d 711 (N.C. 1988). The court noted instead that a plaintiff could seek remedy through actions for intrusion or for infliction of emotional distress, both of which focus on a defendant's conduct rather than a defendant's content. North Carolina had previously rejected the false light cause of action as constitutionally suspect. *Renwick v. News & Observer,* 10 Med. L. Rptr. 1443, 312 S.E.2d 405 (N.C. 1984).

of not recognizing an action that, as the court notes, had resulted in "no reported case in which a plaintiff successfully recovered damages" seems sound. The factor of wrongful behavior is at the core of cases involving the other three branches of common law privacy, as we shall see. The courts have not always recognized that behavior, not content, is the central issue.

Looking to one's own state law is always important. The common law rules for unreasonable disclosure of embarrassing private facts vary greatly from jurisdiction to jurisdiction. Looking to state law is especially important in states where the courts do not recognize any common law privacy. In those states, only such protection as the legislature passes exists.[63]

"SPATIAL" PRIVACY: THE OFFENSE OF INTRUSION

Elements of the Cause of Action

The separate tort for intrusion upon seclusion focuses on newsgathering behaviors rather than on what information is published. The tort is designed to protect individual's right to be left alone in places where she would normally not expect to be subjected to observation by others. An act of intrusion occurs when one intentionally enters an area where another has a privacy interest. But to be actionable, the intrusion must be "highly offensive to a reasonable person." Consent or permission is a complete defense. By consenting, an individual has voluntarily waived her privacy interest, at least temporarily. Similarly, when news is gathered in a place where anyone could have gathered the same information, a plaintiff has no reasonable expectation of privacy; this analysis is much like the "plain view" defense in Fourth Amendment cases.

As a practical matter, intrusion suits have presented little serious danger to the mass media. Plaintiffs file few suits and win even fewer. Since the rules governing intrusion are fairly clear-cut, the press can easily avoid problems in most newsgathering. The clarity of intrusion analysis

seems to be due in part to its closeness to the common law of trespass. A case for trespass is made if it is shown that a defendant entered onto private property and to some extent interfered with the owner's rights of exclusive possession.[64] The property must be a place the plaintiff has a right to exclude others from. Just as with intrusion, consent or permission serves as a defense.

Another obvious similarity is found in the Fourth Amendment's guarantee against unreasonable searches and seizures by law enforcement personnel. The requirement of probable cause to support a search warrant recognizes that government bears the burden of proof in justifying an invasion of personal spaces.

Intrusion is also closely related to nuisance law, especially when surveillance reporting through electronic or photographic means is involved. The *conduct* of a journalist in obtaining information by extraordinary means may itself be considered offensive to a reasonable person. Extraordinary means may include unusually persistent and close tracking of a news subject in addition to electronic or mechanical means. In such cases, offensive reporting techniques are objectionable in the same way as extremely loud noises[65] or starting a pig farm near another's house.[66]

The element of control, whether it be of property or of information about oneself, is a common element in all of these actions. It is the interference with solitude or space, not the information published, that justifies an action. Although plaintiffs may be allowed to claim damages based on the effects of publication once the foundation for intrusion has been laid, if a plaintiff cannot prove the basic elements of intrusion, harm from publication is irrelevant.[67]

State courts that have adopted the action tend to follow the three elements of the cause of action developed in the Restatement (Second) of Torts § 652 B. Neither the Restatement nor the courts have focused much on developing defenses against intrusion actions. Defendants typically attempt to provide evidence that disproves one or more of the elements plaintiffs must satisfy.

When Bobby Berosini, an animal trainer and entertainer, was surreptitiously videotaped back-

---

63. *Fisher v. Richmond Newspapers, Inc.,* 22 Med. L. Rptr. 2372 (E.D.Va. 1994) (only appropriation branch of privacy recognized in Virginia); *Stubbs v. North Memorial Medical Center,* 17 Med. L. Rptr. 1090, 448 N.W.2d 78 (Minn.App. 1989) (no common law privacy recognized in Minnesota).

64. *Prosser and Keeton on Torts,* § 13 (5th ed. 1984).
65. *Fox v. Ewers,* 75 A.2d 357 (Md. 1950).
66. *Baldwin v. McClendon,* 288 So.2d 761 (Ala. 1974).
67. *Lovgren v. Citizens First National Bank,* 16 Med. L. Rptr. 1214, 534 N.E.2d 987 (Ill. 1989).

stage at the Stardust Hotel in Las Vegas, he sued, alleging multiple causes of action, one of which was intrusion. A dancer at the hotel, Ottavio Gesmundo, shot the tape, which showed Berosini "shaking, punching, and beating" his trained orangutans. The tape was then widely publicized by activist animal rights organizations. A trial court jury entered verdicts totaling $4.2 million on a variety of libel and privacy claims. On appeal, the Nevada Supreme Court reversed on every count. Its treatment of the intrusion claim provided a worthy overview of this cause of action.

People for the Ethical Treatment of Animals v. Berosini
23 MED. L. RPTR. 1961, 895 P.2D 1269 (NEV. 1995).

SPRINGER, J.:

Berosini claims that one of the Stardust dancers, Ottavio Gesmundo, has intruded upon his "seclusion" backstage, before his act commenced. We support the need for vigilance in preventing unwanted intrusions upon our privacy and the need to protect ourselves against the Orwellian nightmare that our "every movement [be] scrutinized."

* * *

To recover for the tort of intrusion, a plaintiff must prove the following elements: 1) an intentional intrusion (physical or otherwise); 2) on the solitude or seclusion of another; 3) that would be highly offensive to a reasonable person.

In order to have an interest in seclusion or solitude which the law will protect, a plaintiff must show that he or she had an actual expectation of seclusion or solitude and that the expectation was objectively reasonable. *M & R Investment Co.*, 103 Nev. at 719, 748 P.2d at 493. Thus, not every expectation of privacy and seclusion is protected by the law. "The extent to which seclusion can be protected is severely limited by the protection that must often be accorded to the freedom of action and expression of those who threaten that seclusion of others." 2 Fowler V. Harper, et al., *The Law of Torts*, § 9.6, at 636 (2d 3d 1986). For example, it is not invasion of privacy to photograph a person in a public place; *see, e.g.,* Gill v. Hearst Publication Co., 253 P.2d 441 (Cal. 1953); or for the police, acting within their powers, to photograph and fingerprint a sus-

pect. *See, e.g.,* Norman v. City of Las Vegas, 64 Nev. 38, 177 P.2d 442 (1947). Bearing this in mind, let us examine Berosini's claimed "right to be left alone" in this case and, particularly, the nature of Berosini's claim to seclusion backstage at the Stardust Hotel.

* * *

The focus, then, of Berosini's intrusion upon seclusion claim is Gesmundo's having "trespassed onto the Stardust Hotel with a video camera" and having "unlawfully filmed Plaintiff Berosini disciplining the orangutans without the Plaintiff's knowledge or consent." It is of no relevance to the intrusion tort that Gesmundo trespassed onto the Stardust Hotel, and it is of no moment that Gesmundo might have "unlawfully" filmed Berosini, unless at the same time he was violating a justifiable expectation of privacy on Berosini's part. The issue, then, is whether, when Gesmundo filmed Berosini "disciplining the orangutans without the Plaintiff's knowledge or consent," Gesmundo was intruding on "the solitude or seclusion" of Berosini.

The primary thrust of Berosini's expectation of privacy backstage at the Stardust was that he be left alone with his animals and trainers for a period of time immediately before going on stage. Berosini testified that "as part of his engagement with the Stardust," he demanded that "the animals be left alone prior to going on stage." Throughout his testimony, over and over again, he stresses his need to be alone with his animals before going on stage.

* * *

Persons who were backstage at the Stardust could hear what was going on when "Berosini [was] disciplining his animals," and, without interfering with Berosini's activities, could, if they wanted to, get a glimpse of what Berosini was doing with his animals as he was going on stage.

What is perhaps most important in defining the breadth of Berosini's expectation of privacy is that in his own mind there was nothing wrong or untoward in the manner in which he disciplined the animals, as portrayed on the videotape, and he expressed no concern about merely being seen or heard carrying out these disciplinary practices. To Berosini all of his disciplinary activities were completely "justified." He had nothing to hide—nothing to be private about.

As his testimony indicates, Berosini's "concern for privacy was based upon the animals," and not upon any desire for sight/sound secrecy or privacy or seclusion as such; and he "would have done the same thing if people were standing there." The supposed intruder, Gesmundo, was in a real sense just "standing there." By observing Berosini through the eye of his video camera, he was merely doing what other backstage personnel were also permissibly doing. The camera did not interfere in any way with Berosini's pre-act animal discipline or his claimed interest in being "secured from the other cast members and people before [he] went on stage." Having testified that he would have done the same thing if people were standing there, he can hardly complain about a camera "standing there."

If Berosini's expectation was, as he says it is, freedom from distracting intrusion and interference with his animals and his pre-act disciplinary procedures, then Gesmundo's video "filming" did not invade the scope of this expectation. Gesmundo did not intrude upon Berosini's *expected* seclusion. * * * For this reason the tort of intrusion cannot be maintained in this case.

On the question of whether Gesmundo's camera was *highly* offensive to a reasonable person, we first note that this is a question of first impression in this state. As might be expected, "[t]he question of what kinds of conduct will be regarded as a 'highly' offensive intrusion is largely a matter of social conventions and expectations."

A court considering whether a particular action is "highly offensive" should consider the following factors: "the degree of intrusion, the context, conduct and circumstances surrounding the intrusion as well as the intruder's motives and objectives, the setting into which he intrudes, and the expectations of those whose privacy is invaded."

Three of these factors are of particular significance here and, we conclude militate strongly against Berosini's claim that Gesmundo's conduct was highly offensive to a reasonable person. These factors are: the degree of the alleged intrusion, the context in which the actions occurred, and the motive of the supposed intruder. First, we note the nonintrusive nature of the taping process in the instant case. Berosini was concerned with anyone or anything interfering with his animals

prior to performance. The camera caused no such interference.

Secondly, as has been discussed fully above, the context in which this allegedly tortious conduct occurred was hardly a model of what we think of as "privacy." We must remember that the videotaping did not take place in a private bedroom (*see Miller*, 232 Cal. Rptr. at 668), or in a hospital room (*see* Estate of Berthiame v. Pratt, 365 A.2d 792, 796, (Me. 1976)), or in a restroom (*see* Harkey v. Abate, 346 N.W.2d 74 (Mich. Ct. App. 1983)), or in a young ladies' dressing room (*see* Doe by Doe v. B.P.S. Guard Services Inc., 945 F.2d 1422 (8th Cir. 1991)), or in any other place traditionally associated with a legitimate expectation of privacy. Rather, Gesmundo filmed activities taking place backstage at the Stardust Hotel, an area where Gesmundo had every right to be, and the filming was of a subject that could be seen and heard by any number of persons.

* * *

Finally, with regard to Gesmundo's motives, we note that Gesmundo's purpose was not to eavesdrop or to invade into a realm that Berosini claimed for personal seclusion. Gesmundo was merely memorializing on tape what he and others could readily perceive. Unlike the typical *intrusion* claim, Gesmundo was not trying to pry, he was not trying to uncover the covered-up. * * * Furthermore, even if Gesmundo was conspiring to put an end to the use of animals in entertainment, this is not the kind of motive that would be considered highly offensive to a reasonable person. Many courts, and Professor Prosser, have found the inquiry into motive or purpose to be dispositive of this particular element of the tort.

While we could reverse Berosini's intrusion upon seclusion judgment solely on the absence of any intrusion upon his actual privacy expectation, we go on to conclude that even if Berosini had expected complete seclusion from prying eyes and ears, Gesmundo's camera was not "highly offensive to a reasonable person" because of the nonintrusive nature of the taping process, the context in which the taping took place, and Gesmundo's well-intentioned (and in the eyes of some, at least, *laudable*) motive. If Berosini suffered as a result of the videotaping, it was not because of any tortious intrusion, it was because of subsequent events that, if remediable, relate to other kinds of tort actions than the *intrusion* upon seclusion tort.

COMMENT

The *PETA* case shows the difficulties plaintiffs face. To win an intrusion case almost requires showing that the defendant invaded the sanctity of one's home, office, locker, or automobile.[68] Plaintiffs have fared a bit better when they were able to prove active deception or abusive behavior, however.

A successful intrusion case arose when a *Life* magazine reporter and photographer gained access to a "healer's" home by pretending to be the friends of a friend, then surreptitiously took pictures and relayed tape recordings to law enforcement officials waiting outside while the subject of their investigation examined one of them for breast cancer.

Since the district attorney's office and the state department of health were in on the ruse, although they were not totally dependent upon *Life's* evidence, it did seem that the magazine was acting as an agent of law enforcement.

The "healer," who specialized in clay, minerals, herbs, and gadgetry, was subsequently arrested and charged with practicing medicine without a license. He pleaded *nolo contendere* and was cited for a number of misdemeanors. *Life's* illustrated article entitled "Crackdown on Quackery" became the basis of a subsequent privacy suit.

A federal district court awarded the plaintiff $1,000 for an invasion of his privacy, and *Life* appealed. The judgment was affirmed by a federal appeals court in an opinion that combined elements of both surveillance and trespass in its analysis.

Dietemann v. Time, Inc.
1 MED. L. RPTR. 2417, 449 F.2D 245 (9TH CIR. 1971).

HUFSTEDLER, Circuit Judge:

* * *

In jurisdictions other than California in which a common law tort for invasion of privacy is recognized, it has been consistently held that surreptitious electronic recording of a plaintiff's conversation causing him emotional distress is

actionable. Despite some variations in the description and the labels applied to the tort, there is agreement that publication is not a necessary element of the tort, that the existence of a technical trespass is immaterial, and that proof of special damages is not required.

Although the issue has not been squarely decided in California, we have little difficulty in concluding that clandestine photography of the plaintiff in his den and the recordation and transmission of his conversation without his consent resulting in his emotional distress warrants recovery for invasion of privacy in California. * * *

We are convinced that California will "approve the extension of the tort of invasion of privacy to instances of intrusion, whether by physical trespass or not, into spheres from which an ordinary man in plaintiff's position could reasonably expect that the particular defendant should be excluded." (*Pearson v. Dodd,* 410 F.2d at 704.)

Plaintiff's den was a sphere from which he could reasonably expect to exclude eavesdropping newsmen. He invited two of defendant's employees to the den. One who invites another to his home or office takes a risk that the visitor may not be what he seems, and that the visitor may repeat all he hears and observes when he leaves. But he does not and should not be required to take the risk that what is heard and seen will be transmitted by photograph or recording, or in our modern world, in full living color and hi-fi to the public at large or to any segment of it that the visitor may select. * * *

The defendant claims that the First Amendment immunizes it from liability for invading plaintiff's den with a hidden camera and its concealed electronic instruments because its employees were gathering news and its instrumentalities "are indispensable tools of investigative reporting." We agree that newsgathering is an integral part of news dissemination. We strongly disagree, however, that the hidden mechanical contrivances are "indispensable tools" of newsgathering. Investigative reporting is an ancient art; its successful practice long antecedes the invention of miniature cameras and electronic devices. *The First Amendment has never been construed to accord newsmen immunity from torts or crimes committed during the course of newsgathering.* [Emphasis added.] The First Amendment is not a license to trespass, to steal, or to intrude by electronic means into the precincts of another's home or office.

---

68. *Prosser and Keeton on Torts,* 854–855 (5th ed. 1984).

Privilege concepts developed in defamation cases and to some extent in privacy actions in which publication is an essential component are not relevant in determining liability for intrusive conduct antedating publication. Nothing in *New York Times* or its progeny suggests anything to the contrary. Indeed, the Court strongly indicates that there is no First Amendment interest in protecting news media from calculated misdeeds.

No interest protected by the First Amendment is adversely affected by permitting damages for intrusion to be enhanced by the fact of later publication of the information that the publisher improperly acquired. Assessing damages for the additional emotional distress suffered by a plaintiff when the wrongfully acquired data are purveyed to the multitude chills intrusive acts. It does not chill freedom of expression guaranteed by the First Amendment. A rule forbidding the use of publication as an ingredient of damages would deny to the injured plaintiff recovery for real harm done to him without any countervailing benefit to the legitimate interest of the public in being informed. The same rule would encourage conduct by news media that grossly offends ordinary men.

The judgment is affirmed.

COMMENT

The *Dietemann* opinion addressed several issues. It decided that clandestine newsgathering in a private place may be the basis for an intrusion case. It concluded that damages may be sought for harms caused by the intrusion itself and also for harms caused by subsequent publication. The Ninth Circuit's reasoning on these points has not been consistently persuasive with other courts, however. When reporters for ABC's *PrimeTime Live* newsmagazine program hired "undercover" patients to obtain both audio and video recordings of activities in the offices of opthamologists being investigated, the court found that the plaintiffs had in effect taken the risk of being reported upon by inviting the public onto the premises of the business.[69] *Dietemann* was not even cited. Even when another ABC reporter secretly recorded conversations while serving undercover as an employee at a chain grocery store, the court determined that an intrusion

claim must fail because conversations with co-workers are inherently not within the "private domain."[70] Regarding damages, the same court indicated that damages in intrusion cases should be limited to those arising from inappropriate behaviors only.

The major influence from *Dietemann* was the court's refusal to recognize a First Amendment–based privilege or defense akin to the one that had developed in libel. The court simply did not weigh the news value of the story. Why? In general, the news value of a story has been considered secondary to the offensiveness of intruding on someone's seclusion. For example, in *Anderson v. WROC-TV,* 7 Med. L. Rptr. 1987, 441 N.Y.S.2d 220 (1981), the fact that the reporter entered a private home at the invitation of a humane society officer executing a search warrant provided no defense to intrusion, although it would seem to support a newsworthiness defense if the suit was based on disclosure of private facts. Similarly, news value did not immunize reporters charged with trespass after they followed a group of protesters onto a nuclear power plant construction site after the protesters broke through a fence.[71]

Although not based on constitutional grounds, a defense based on motive and context is possible. Juries have been told to weigh a television news program's motives and the nature of the news story in deciding if an intrusion was highly offensive.[72] This in effect brings newsworthiness in by the back door.

Only one court has determined that a trespass onto private property was justified on First Amendment grounds, at least when there was no proof that the media knew they were trespassing. The judge in the case considered the distinction between newsgathering and news publication questionable in an era of live mini-cam television coverage, the type of coverage at issue in the case.[73] The decision, by a trial court, has no authority as precedent and has apparently not been adopted by any appeals courts.

---

69. *Desnick v. Capital Cities/ABC, Inc.,* 22 Med. L. Rptr. 1937, 851 F.Supp. 303 (N.D.Ill. 1994).

70. *Russell v. ABC, Inc.,* 23 Med. L. Rptr. 2428, ___ F.Supp. ___ (N.D.Ill. 1995).

71. *Stahl v. Oklahoma,* 9 Med. L. Rptr. 1945, 665 P.2d 839 (Okl.Crim.App. 1983).

72. *Magenis v. Fisher Broadcasting, Inc.,* 18 Med. L. Rptr. 1229, 798 P.2d 1106 (Ore.App. 1990).

73. *Allen v. Combined Communications,* 7 Med. L. Rptr. 2417 (Colo.Dist.Ct. 1981).

Another way of reading *Dietemann* is that the court was influenced by the fact that the defendant news reporters had exceeded the scope of the consent given. When people invite others onto their property, the court notes, they knowingly accept the risk that what is heard and seen will be reported.

In the celebrated case *Food Lion, Inc. v. Capital Cities/ABC, Inc.,* a jury imposed a punitive damages award of $5.5 million for a *PrimeTime Live* report on improper food-handling practices at one of the chain's stores. ABC reporters applied for jobs at the store, then reported using hidden cameras and microphones. Jurors said they were influenced by proof that the reporters lied in their employment applications. The substance of the story and the actual reporting appear not to have been the basis for the verdict. But journalists were put on notice that their newsgathering behaviors were being watched along with their news stories. Symposium, *Media Ethics,* vol. 8, no. 2, Spring 1997.

Is it reasonable to hold that inviting people also entails accepting the risk that they are wearing hidden recording devices, or may even be hooked up to a police radio receiver? Consent is a complete defense, and where the consent is ambiguous, newsgathering behaviors arguably within the scope of consent will be protected. In *Baugh v. CBS, Inc.,* 21 Med. L. Rptr. 2065, 828 F.Supp. 745 (N.D.Cal. 1993), the plaintiff complained that a reporter and camera crew had not sought consent when videotaping a crisis team response to a domestic violence call. Rather, she had the impression the taping was for internal use in the local district attorney's office. Her consent extended to the reporter and camera crew, who nevertheless had been on the property with consent. The plaintiff's allied claim that the deception supported an intentional infliction of mental distress action was allowed to proceed.

An action for a trespass form of invasion of privacy and for intentional infliction of emotional distress was brought against Florida news media by a mother whose daughter died in a fire in her home. So badly was she burned that, after her body was removed, its silhouette remained on a bedroom floor. The mother learned of the tragedy by reading a news story and seeing a picture of the silhouette in the *Florida Times-Union.*

Lower courts refused to grant summary judgment to the newspaper's publisher on the tresspass count. On appeal the Florida Supreme Court held that where there was an *implied consent by custom and usage* authorizing a news photographer to accompany police and fire marshals into a home, there was no trespass. In fact, a fire marshal had requested that the photographer take the "silhouette" picture for his official file.

Television networks, newspapers, wire services, and professional organizations had provided the court with affidavits attesting to the common practice of reporters accompanying officials into homes where there has been crime or tragedy. The court agreed that "as a matter of law an entry, that may otherwise be an actionable trespass, becomes lawful and nonactionable when it is done under common usage, custom and practice."

The court's opinion can be read to imply that had the plaintiff been present and objected to the photographer's entry, she would have had a stronger case. *Florida Publishing Co. v. Fletcher,* 340 So.2d 914 (Fla. 1976), *cert. denied* 431 U.S. 930 (1977).[74]

Reporters and photographers who entered "Son of Sam's" apartment after his arrest on suspicion of murder were not guilty of criminal trespass, said a New York city court. Although police had earlier entered the apartment with a warrant, they had no "possessory interest." Only the defendant himself, or the apartment owner, could have withheld consent from the newsmen. Police, however, could have excluded persons from the premises while a lawful criminal search was being conducted. *People v. Berliner,* 3 Med. L. Rptr. 1942 (Yonkers City Ct. 1978).

Some courts have rejected the custom and usage argument. These same courts also reason that, just because law enforcement officials have authority to enter property, the authority does not extend to journalists who are accompanying the search or raid. In *Ayeni v. CBS, Inc.,* 22 Med. L. Rptr. 1466, 848 F.Supp. 362 (E.D.N.Y. 1994), another videotaping case, the court emphasized that the point of conducting a search was to generate evidence, not news:

---

74. But see, *Prahl v. Brosamle,* 295 N.W.2d 768 (Wis. 1980). For a general discussion of "common usage, custom and practice," see Middleton, *Journalists, Trespass and Officials: Closing the Door on* Florida Publishing Co. v. Fletcher, 16 Pepperdine L. Rev. 259 (1989). The Supreme Court has never heard an intrusion case.

The images, though created by the camera, are part of the household; they cannot be removed without permission or official right. The television tape was a seizure of information for non-governmental purposes.

It did not help CBS that the Department of Treasury agent who had obtained the warrant had lost qualified immunity by behaving unreasonably and was also responsible for damages from the videotaping. *Ayeni v. Mottola*, 22 Med. L. Rptr. 2225, 35 F.3d 680 (2d Cir. 1994).

Ambush Journalism and Surveillance

Routine newsgathering in or from public places is almost always protected from an intrusion claim. When the newsgathering behaviors approach harassment, stalking, or nuisance levels, though, courts have occasionally been persuaded that intrusion or "tortious newsgathering," a term used to batch together intrusion, trespass, fraud, and related legal issues, has occurred.

In one striking case, a family was able to obtain a preliminary injunction prohibiting a reporter and crew from the syndicated tabloid news program *Inside Edition* from invading the privacy of a family. *Inside Edition* had been working on a story about salaries at U.S. Healthcare, one of the country's largest for-profit medical companies. Repeated attempts to get an interview with Leonard Abramson, chairman of the board and chief executive officer of U.S. Healthcare, had failed. Reporter Paul Wilson then focused instead on Abramson's daughter and her husband, Nancy and Richard Wolfson, both high-ranking officials within U.S. Healthcare. The couple's home in an affluent Philadelphia suburb was staked out. They were followed as they went to and from work. Their three-year-old daughter was followed to preschool. A one-year-old continued to be under surveillance at the family home. The crew used a variety of methods, including hidden cameras, sensitive boom microphones capable of picking up conversation from sixty yards, and a variety of powerful telephoto lenses. Both Wolfsons said they felt concerned about the family's safety. An ambush interview with either or both Wolfsons was planned. The family's reaction got stronger when Wilson phoned Nancy Wolfson and told her they meant no harm to the children. Abram-son and the family had previously received anonymous threats.

The company's security department tried to get *Inside Edition* to back off, but was told in response that the newsgathering was legally protected. A request for an interview with Abramson was again posed and declined. The Wolfsons decided hurriedly to take a trip to Abramson's beach home in Florida to get away from the journalists. *Inside Edition* followed. The crew rented a boat and set up business on the water about fifty yards from the house. They shot videotape and recorded conversations until sometime in the afternoon, when they moved to the highway and set up cameras. When the Wolfsons headed home a few days later, they had to sneak out escorted by security guards.

The Wolfsons raised a variety of claims, the most important being stalking, harassment, trespass, and intrusion. They also claimed that the sound recordings violated both Florida and Pennsylvania law assuring privacy in oral, wire, and electronic communications. Had a story already been run, a complaint based on disclosure of private facts might also have been added. The standard for obtaining a preliminary injunction is twofold: a plaintiff must show both a likelihood of success on the merits of the claim at trial and that the plaintiff will be irreparably harmed unless the injunction is issued. In the *Wolfson* case, the judge added a third factor—that issuing the injunction was in the public interest.

Wolfson v. Lewis
24 MED. L. RPTR. 1609, 924 F.SUPP. 1413 (E.D.PA. 1996).

BRODERICK, J.:

* * *

First Amendment freedoms can at times collide with another important cornerstone of democratic society—the right to privacy. The use of sophisticated video and recording equipment by T.V. journalists has increased the threat that a person's right to privacy may be violated. Furthermore, the television market for scandal and sensationalism has encouraged T.V. journalists to engage in forms of newsgathering that may bring about a clash between the right to privacy and freedom of the press. Recognizing this potential clash between privacy and the First Amendment, this Court must proceed with caution in making its determination as to whether the plaintiffs' privacy rights were invaded under the facts of this case.

* * *

Specifically at issue in this case is whether the defendants violated plaintiffs' right to privacy under Pennsylvania and Florida law.

* * *

An actionable intrusion upon seclusion consists of "an intentional interference with [a person's] interest in solitude or seclusion, either as to his person or his private affairs or concerns. . . ." Restatement (Second) of Torts § 6523, comment a. As stated in comment b of § 652B, the interference may be,

> by physical intrusion into a place in which the plaintiff has secluded himself, as when the defendant forces his way into the plaintiff's room in a hotel or insists over the plaintiff's objection in entering his home. It may also be by the use of the defendant's sense, with or without mechanical aids, to oversee or overhear the plaintiff's private affairs, as by looking into his upstairs windows with binoculars or taping his telephone wires.

* * *

Conduct that amounts to a persistent course of hounding, harassment and unreasonable surveillance, even if conducted in a public or semi-public place, may nevertheless rise to the level of invasion of privacy based on intrusion upon seclusion. The Restatement recognizes that conduct that is repeated with such persistence and frequency as to amount to a "course of hounding the plaintiff, [and] becomes a substantial burden to his existence" may constitute an invasion of privacy, § 652B, comment d. Pennsylvania courts, moreover, have specifically refused to recognize a separate tort of harassment on the ground that "an action for invasion of privacy will ordinarily be an adequate remedy for highly offensive conduct which unreasonably interferes with another's right to be left alone." *DeAngelo v. Fortney,* 515 A.2d 594, 596 (Pa. Super. 1986).

In ruling on a motion for a preliminary injunction, the district court must consider (1) the likelihood that the plaintiff will prevail on the merits at trial; (2) the extent to which the plaintiffs will suffer irreparable harm in the absence of an injunction; (3) the extent to which the defendant will suffer irreparable harm if the preliminary injunction is issued; and (4) the public interest.

The injunction should issue only if the plaintiff produces evidence sufficient to convince the district court that all four factors favor preliminary injunctive relief.

* * *

On February 12, 1996, when they were almost certain that Mr. Abramson would not provide an on-camera interview, Mr. Lewis and Mr. Wilson developed and began to implement a plan to engage in surreptitious surveillance of the Wolfsons. On February 12, 1996, Mr. Lewis called the *Inside Edition* crew coordinator in New York City to arrange for a cameraman and sound technician to begin work on February 13, 1996. In accordance with *Inside Edition* policy, a "One Interview Only Shoot" form was completed at the *Inside Edition* office in New York City documenting Mr. Lewis's request for a crew. This form clearly sets forth that Mr. Lewis needed a van with tinted windows and camera and sound crew for an "ambush."

As described by Mr. Wilson, Mr. Lewis and by their expert witness Robert Greene, a two-time Pulitzer prize winning journalist, an "ambush interview" refers to a confrontational, surprise interview with an unwilling subject, generally a person who has previously refused to be interviewed. The T.V. journalist approaches the subject surreptitiously with cameras and sound rolling and asks a question calculated to embarrass the subject. [Details of the surveillance are recounted.]

* * *

To escape what they perceived to be a danger to themselves and their children, Mr. and Mrs. Wolfson hurriedly made plans to go to Florida and spend a few days with Mr. and Mrs. Abramson at the "Abramson family home". Mr. Wolfson felt it imperative to the well-being of his family to "go to some other place where we believed we would not be followed or terrorized." Mr. and Mrs. Wolfson departed with their children from their home in Gwynedd Valley in the afternoon of the 14th, and arrived in Florida that evening.

* * *

Between 8:00 a.m. and 8:30 a.m. on February 18, 1996, a bright and sunny day, Mr. Wilson, Mr. Lewis, a cameraman and a sound technician anchored their rented motor boat a few feet from the rope which separates the public waterway from the Abramson family home. The boat was approximately 50 to 60 yards from the Abramson family home. The drapes to the Abramson family home were drawn when they arrived. Although it is common for recreational boats to take excursions on the Intracoastal Waterway, it is unusual for a boat to anchor so close to private property.

On board was a Sennheiser "shotgun mike", a television camera equipped with zoom lenses and a mounted microphone, a sound mixer, headsets, and binoculars. The "shotgun mike" was attached to a long stick called a "boom" and was covered by a "wind screen". As the name suggests, the wind screen protects the mike from wind blowing across its surface and interfering with its ability to pick up sound at a distance. Although the "shotgun mike" itself is approximately twelve inches long, the entire apparatus including the wind screen and boom is several feet in length.

* * *

As a result of the videotaping, and recording with the "shotgun mike", the Wolfsons were prisoners in the Abramson family home. As heretofore set forth, Mrs. Wolfson could not take her children out to play in the back yard because the boat was anchored there. As she testified, "I felt like a prisoner in my own house. I couldn't go outside. I couldn't leave the house, the kids couldn't go outside." When Mr. Wolfson returned from playing golf he found his family "huddled in the living room with all the windows to the back drawn." To make matters worse, soon after his return, the occupants of the Abramson family home learned that there was a T.V. crew stationed at the entrance to Admiral's Cove.

* * *

The Court finds that plaintiffs have presented sufficient evidence to support a reasonable likelihood of success on the merits of their claim for invasion of privacy based on intrusion upon seclusion under Florida and Pennsylvania law. A reasonable jury could well find that Mr. Wilson and Mr. Lewis intentionally intruded, in a manner that would be highly offensive to a reasonable person, upon the solitude and seclusion of the Wolfsons by engaging in a course of conduct apparently designed to hound, harass, intimidate and frighten them. The intrusions committed by Mr. Wilson and Mr. Lewis consisted of a pattern of conduct involving physical and sensory invasions into Mr. and Mrs. Wolfson's privacy. Mr.

Wilson's and Mr. Lewis's actions deprived the Wolfsons of the right to live their life quietly and peacefully.

* * *

The evidence is sufficient for the Court to find that there is a reasonable likelihood that plaintiffs will succeed in convincing a jury that the conduct of Mr. Wilson and Mr. Lewis in Pennsylvania and Florida was intentional and that it was undertaken to convince Mr. Abramson that his consent to be interviewed on T.V. would bring an end to the hounding and harassment of his daughters and grandchildren, who are the objects of his affection. During his conversations with Mr. Sebastianelli, Mr. Read made it abundantly clear that *Inside Edition* was interested in obtaining an on-camera interview with Mr. Abramson.

* * *

It is likely that a reasonable jury would conclude that the unreasonable surveilling, hounding and following of the Wolfsons in Pennsylvania literally drove them from their home in Pennsylvania. In Florida, Mr. Wilson's and Mr. Lewis's relentless surveillance, conducted with the aid of sophisticated sound and video equipment aimed directly at the home, virtually rendered Mr. and Mrs. Wolfson and their children captives in the Abramson family home. The evidence shows that in order to avoid being ambushed harassed, filmed or recorded by Mr. Wilson and Mr. Lewis, the Wolfsons drastically altered their normal routine and restricted their own and their children's activities. By engaging in such egregious actions, Mr. Wilson and Mr. Lewis trampled upon the Wolfsons' sense of emotional solitude and well-being. The evidence shows that Mr. Wilson's and Mr. Lewis's intrusive conduct caused the Wolfsons fear and anguish. Apprehension and wariness continues to plague the Wolfsons to such a degree that they have found it difficult to resume their normal lives.

* * *

The evidence shows that the Wolfsons' exceptionally well-trained security force was gravely concerned about Mr. Wilson's and Mr. Lewis's actions. The security guards reasonably interpreted their conduct as posing a threat to the safety and well-being of the Wolfson family. Although Mr. Gerken did not use his "semi automatic" weapon, all parties should be grateful that no greater violence ensued.

Unless enjoined, it is unlikely that Mr. Wilson's and Mr. Lewis's invasive conduct toward the Wolfsons will cease. Mr. Wilson and Mr. Lewis presented no evidence that they will discontinue their pursuit of the Wolfsons. They are convinced that their conduct is protected by the First Amendment.

Mr. Wilson and Mr. Lewis will not be irreparably harmed by an injunction narrowly tailored to preclude them from continuing their harassing conduct toward the Wolfsons. Such an injunction will not impair Mr. Wilson's and Mr. Lewis's legal newsgathering activities for their story on the salaries paid to executives at U.S. Healthcare.

COMMENT

The federal district court judge relied heavily upon the *Dietemann* case. Do the two cases seem comparable? The distinction between deception and openness was not addressed. In addition, intrusion claims normally require some type of "entry" onto property. For example, in *Dempsey v. National Enquirer*, 16 Med. L. Rptr. 1396, 702 F.Supp. 927 (D.Me. 1988), a reporter visited the plaintiff's house frequently, drove by repeatedly, and followed the plaintiff into a restaurant. "Although these contacts may well have been annoying, they cannot reasonably be seen as highly offensive," the court said. In the absence of an entry onto property, they were insufficient for an intrusion case. Is the use of sophisticated newsgathering and surveillance equipment enough to set the *Wolfson* case apart?

Another case the *Wolfson* judge relied on was *Galella v. Onassis*. In that case, the late Jacqueline Kennedy Onassis, widow of both President John Kennedy and Aristotle Onassis, one of the world's richest men, brought suit for damages and a permanent injunction against paparazzo Ron Galella, who had almost made a freelance career of photographing her and her family. The U.S. government joined the suit for an injunction against Galella's interference with Secret Service agents assigned to protect the former first lady and her children. Galella's strategy was aggressive pursuit, described by Onassis as constant stalking, with Galella popping up everywhere making a grunting sound that she said terrified her.

The two cases were joined, and a federal district court held that the photographer's antics were not protected by the First Amendment but constituted actionable assault, battery, and harassment, violation of the civil rights statute, and tortious infliction of emotional distress. Both Mrs. Onassis and the government were granted injunctive relief in a ruling in which the court expressed enormous distaste for Galella and rejected his claim along with what it called his perjured testimony. A portion of the ruling follows.

Galella v. Onassis
353 F.SUPP. 196 (S.D.N.Y. 1972).

COOPER, District Judge:

* * * [T]wenty further episodes are summarized in our supplemental findings of fact. These include instances where the children were caused to bang into glass doors, school parents were bumped, passage was blocked, flashbulbs affected vision, telephoto lenses were used to spy, the children were imperilled in the water, a funeral was disturbed, plaintiff pursued defendant into the lobby of a friend's apartment building, plaintiff trailed defendant through the City hour after hour, plaintiff chased defendant by automobile, plaintiff and his assistants surrounded defendant and orbited while shouting, plaintiff snooped into purchases of stockings and shoes, flashbulbs were suddenly fired on lonely black nights—all accompanied by Galella jumping, shouting and acting wildly. Many of these instances were repeated time after time; all preceded our restraining orders.

He was like a shadow: everywhere she went he followed her and engaged in offensive conduct; nothing was sacred to him whether defendant went to church, funeral services, theatre, school, restaurant, or board a yacht in a foreign land. While plaintiff denied so deporting himself, his admissions clearly spell out his harassment of her and her children.

* * *

The proposition that the First Amendment gives the press wide liberty to engage in any sort of conduct, no matter how offensive, in gathering news has been flatly rejected.

* * *

Invasion of Privacy. Plaintiff's endless snooping constitutes tortious invasion of privacy.

* * *

First let us reconsider plaintiff's close-shadowing of defendant. Continuously he has had her under surveillance to the point where he is notified of her every movement. He waits outside her residence at all hours. * * * His surveillance is so overwhelmingly pervasive that he has said he has not married because he has been unable to "get a girl who would be willing to go looking for Mrs. Onassis at odd hours."

* * * He has intruded into her children's schools, hidden in bushes and behind coat racks in restaurants, sneaked into beauty salons, bribed doormen, hatcheck girls, chauffeurs, fishermen in Greece, hairdressers and schoolboys, and romanced employees. In short, Galella has insinuated himself into the very fabric of Mrs. Onassis' life and the challenge to this Court is to fashion the tool to get him out.

* * *

The essence of the privacy interest includes a general "right to be left alone," and to define one's circle of intimacy; to shield intimate and personal characteristics and activities from public gaze; to have moments of freedom from the unremitted assault of the world and unfettered will of others in order to achieve some measure of tranquility for contemplation or other purposes, without which life loses its sweetness. The rationale extends to protect against unreasonably intrusive behavior which attempts or succeeds in gathering information.

* * *

COMMENT

Galella and his agents were enjoined by the district court from approaching within 300 feet of the Onassis and Kennedy homes and the schools attended by the children; they were also required to remain 225 feet from the children and 150 feet from Mrs. Onassis at all other locations. Galella was also prohibited from putting the family under surveillance or trying to communicate with them.

The Court of Appeals for the Second Circuit essentially upheld the lower court decision. The appeals court did something else. It sharply scaled down the distances Galella was to keep from Mrs. Onassis and her children. It reduced from 150 to 25 feet the distance the photographer had to put between himself and Mrs. Onassis; from 225 to 30 feet the distance he had to stay from Caroline and John; and it lifted the restriction on Mrs. Onassis's Fifth Avenue home. *Galella v. Onassis,* 487 F.2d 986 (2d Cir. 1973).

The court of appeals ruling essentially put Galella back in business. But it wasn't until 1982 that the original New York federal district court, more impatient with Galella than ever, held that the photographer's flagrant, deliberate, and persistent violations of federal court orders restricting coverage of Jacqueline Onassis and her children constituted a contempt of court. He had violated the court orders on distance-from-subject at least twelve times. *Galella v. Onassis,* 8 Med. L. Rptr. 1321, 533 F.Supp. 1076 (S.D.N.Y. 1982).

One irony of all the *Galella* litigation was that New York State had not and has never accepted intrusion or any other privacy right as a matter of common law. In the very first opinion in the case, the federal district court predicted, wrongly, that New York would accept intrusion once a proper case arose.

Clearly, Galella's behavior was more akin to a nuisance, even harassment, than to an intrusion. The positions of the various courts uphold the notion that we carry to some extent a zone of privacy wherever we go. While that "zone" may not be a legal construct, it is a practical one. Just try conducting an interview with a source at nose-to-nose closeness.

More typically, an intrusion involves places, not people. Just as in private facts cases, a plaintiff will not prevail when reporters or photographers only observed what anyone could have seen. For example, plaintiffs who objected to pictures of their home could not maintain an intrusion action.[75] Anybody could have taken the same pictures from the public street. Filming the interior of a pharmacy using telephoto lenses was not considered an intrusion when a television station was preparing a story on Medicaid fraud.[76]

---

75. *Wehling v. CBS,* 10 Med. L. Rptr. 1125, 721 F.2d 506 (5th Cir. 1983).
76. *Mark v. KING Broadcasting,* 6 Med. L. Rptr. 2224, 618 P.2d 512 (Wash.App. 1980).

Implicit in such cases is the notion that information readily seen is to some extent newsworthy, or at least eligible for news uses. A good general rule for those who would avoid publicity is not to conduct one's affairs where anybody can see. Search and seizure law's plain view doctrine applies—but by another name—in intrusion cases. Will photos taken from outer space be considered as defensible under a plain view rationale? See Lipschutz, *Mediasat and the Tort of Invasion of Privacy*, 65 Journalism Quarterly 507 (1988). Whether or not to report on or photograph what occurs in public places has been left primarily to the field of ethics, not law. Coleman, *Private Lives, Public Places: Street Photography Ethics*, 2 J. of Mass Media Ethics 60 (Spring/Summer 1987).

Newsworthiness can be a prodigious defense. Even though Wayne Williams's parents were practically prisoners in their own home and reporters themselves found the stakeout "gross" and "repellent," close coverage of the murder suspect was not enough to support a privacy claim.[77] Williams was convicted of the murders of two of twenty-eight young blacks slain in Atlanta.

On the other side of the law, a policeman had no privacy claim after being filmed by a television camera through a two-way mirror while investigating a massage parlor. Imagine the policeman's consternation when a door opened and someone suddenly cried, "Channel 7 News," and the camera crew exited filming the scene before them. After making suggestive remarks and physical advances to a "lingerie" model and after she had responded with "sufficient physical contact," the officer arrested her for solicitation.[78] His being a public official served to distinguish this case from *Dietemann*.

A Supreme Court case on another issue allowed a community to prevent intense but orderly and peaceful picketing in front of the house of a specific targeted individual.[79] Although the case was decided on time, place, and manner grounds, Justice O'Connor's opinion for the Court noted that, "[A] special benefit of the privacy all citizens enjoy within their own walls, which the State may legislate to protect, is an ability to avoid intrusions." The Court referred repeatedly to privacy interests, although the opinion appears to consider the picketing at issue more a form of nuisance or harassment than an invasion of privacy.

In one of the strangest cases alleging intrusion, the plaintiff claimed that repeated mailings from the Columbia Record Club constituted a privacy violation. The court agreed that a privacy interest extends to one's mailbox but could not explain how such a right would be effectuated. In any event, the court said, only unreasonable intrusions are triable and receiving junk mail simply cannot rise to the level of causing distress to a reasonable person.[80]

CBS News was less fortunate when one of its reporters and a camera crew "with cameras rolling" entered a posh French restaurant, Le Mistral, as a follow-up to a New York City Health Service Administration press release alleging health code violations at several city restaurants. Le Mistral sued for defamation and trespass following a WCBS-TV news report that included film clips of the restaurant's staff attempting to eject the CBS crew.

The trial court judge dismissed the defamation suit on "fair comment" grounds but granted a trial on the trespass count since, he said, "the right to publish does not include the right to break and enter upon and trespass upon the property of these plaintiffs." A year later a jury awarded Le Mistral $250,000 in punitive and $1,200 in compensatory damages for trespass. "Patronizing a restaurant," said the court, "does not carry with it an obligation to appear on television." *Le Mistral, Inc. v. CBS*, 3 Med. L. Rptr. 1913, 402 N.Y.S.2d 815 (N.Y.Sup.Ct., App.Div. 1978).

Receiving Stolen Information

A different type of intrusion or trespass issue arises when a journalist receives or obtains information that has been stolen. Clearly, journalists will be liable if they directly steal materials or pay another to steal materials. They are in effect perpetrators or accessories in such circumstances. But often information is passed along to

---

77. *Williams v. NBC*, 7 Med. L. Rptr. 1523 (D.Ga. 1981).
78. *Cassidy v. ABC*, 3 Med. L. Rptr. 2449, 377 N.E.2d 126 (Ill. 1978).
79. *Frisby v. Schultz*, 108 S.Ct. 2495 (1988).

80. *Bennett v. CBS*, 13 Med. L. Rptr. 1237, 798 F.2d 1413 (6th Cir. 1986).

journalists. Occasionally, that information will have been wrongfully obtained. What is the legal status of the journalist then? Is receiving information taken without authority the equivalent of receiving stolen property? Does it matter whether or not the journalist knew the material was stolen?

The leading case on the subject arose when syndicated columnist Drew Pearson and his associate Jack Anderson received photocopies of documents from the files of Connecticut Senator Thomas Dodd. Four of Dodd's former employees had removed the documents from the senator's office. The originals were returned. Pearson then ran columns using information from the files.

Dodd first sued for libel, but a trial court threw that out. He tried again, using a dual claim of invasion of privacy and of common law trover and conversion. The latter is "an unauthorized assumption and exercise of the right of ownership over goods or personal chattels belonging to another, to the alteration of their condition or the exclusion of an owner's rights."

The privacy claim was rejected, but a trial court granted partial summary judgment to Dodd on the conversion claim. *Dodd v. Pearson,* 279 F.Supp. 101 (D.D.C. 1968). He was entitled to attempt to convince a jury that Pearson knew the files were stolen and that Pearson had received and used another's property. The ruling was unique because it treated the information on the photocopies as if it were property. Obviously, Dodd technically had not been denied use of the files, as the originals had been returned. It was also unique because knowing use—scienter— is not part of the proof required under common law conversion.

Pearson appealed. The District of Columbia Circuit Court of Appeals reversed the conversion decision, emphasizing that Pearson could not be liable for intrusions committed by others. The court felt that Dodd was bringing the conversion claim only as a way of getting around the limitations of privacy or libel law:

> Appellee [Dodd] complains, not of the misappropriation of property bought or created by him, but of the exposure of information either (1) injurious to his reputation or (2) revelatory of matters which he believes he has a right to keep to himself. Injuries of this type are redressed at law by suit for libel and invasion of privacy respectively, where defendants'

> liability for those torts can be established under the limitations created by common law and by the Constitution.

> Because no conversion of the physical contents of appellee's files took place, and because the information copied from the documents in those files has not been shown to be property subject to protection by suit for conversion, the District Court's ruling that appellants are guilty of conversion must be reversed.

The court is on much stronger ground basing its arguments on the First Amendment and public interest. Since Pearson had not himself committed an intrusion and the information was of public interest, a First Amendment–based defense was sufficient. It would necessarily follow that active participation in intrusion or commissioning of others to commit an intrusion would prevent the application of a First Amendment defense. The public interest or newsworthiness defense only applies when considering the content *after* publication in any event. Wrongdoing in reporting is clearly separable from publication.

The court's distinction was based on the difference between the money value of the files themselves (negligible) and the money value of the information contained in the files (considerable). Does precluding liability based on whether or not the property is tangible remain persuasive today, or is it out of date in an information economy?

Dodd has generally been followed. And its rule that the journalist must be an active participant in or instigator of intrusion is easy to apply, both for judges and journalists.

There was no intrusion, said a Maryland appeals court, when newspaper reporters received the academic files of University of Maryland basketball players from an unnamed source. The press itself had not sought out, inspected, or solicited the files. *Bilney v. Evening Star Newspaper Co.,* 4 Med. L. Rptr. 1924, 406 A.2d 652 (Md. 1979).

Unconsented Recording

With the rapid spread of communication devices, including but not limited to cordless telephones, cellular telephones, telephonic computer software, and satellite linkages for private conversations, concern over the privacy of individuals communicating with one another over such system has grown. Statutes at the federal level and in many states are designed to safeguard the privacy of private communications.[81] Some courts have indicated that there is no privacy interest in messages distributed through unsecured means. *Edwards v. State Farm Insurance Co.*, 833 F.2d 535 (5th Cir. 1987). Federal law has been interpreted as creating an interest in the security of communication, not its confidentiality. *U.S. v. Cooper*, 365 F.2d 246 (6th Cir.), *cert. denied* 385 U.S. 1030 (1966).

Is a reporter liable to wiretap charges if telephone interviews with sources are recorded without consent? Ten states bar nonconsensual (one-party consent) recording either of telephone conversations or of individuals in person.[82]

In Florida such a law was upheld against a press challenge. There a reporter's tape recording of a caller who was unaware that the conversation was being recorded constituted an illegal wire intercept under Florida's Security of Communication Act, even though the reporter was using the recording only to help her write a news story.[83] The constitutionality of Florida's law requiring that all parties to an interception give prior consent was affirmed by the Florida Supreme Court in *Shevin v. Sunbeam Television*, 351 So.2d 723 (Fla. 1977). The United States Supreme Court declined review. A number of state courts, however, have construed their statutes so as to permit one-party participant recording of telephone conversations.[84]

Telephone interviews across state lines, then, may pose risks. One might expect that the applicable state law would be that of the state where the call originated. But one trial court has indicated otherwise, at least where tort claims are at issue. Applying the traditional tort law rule that the law of the state where the harm occurred applies, the judge in *Krauss v. Globe*

International, Inc., 24 Med. L. Rptr. 1509 (N.Y.Sup. 1995), decided that a plaintiff in a libel suit was bound by New York's statute, which does not require consent by both parties. The plaintiff had argued that Pennsylvania law should apply since the reporter had called from there. Federal law did not matter since, like New York's, it does not require mutual consent.

Journalists have not appreciated finding themselves at the other end of the tape recorder. In 1978 a D.C. Circuit Court panel held that the First Amendment was not violated by law enforcement officials' good faith inspection of the toll-call records of reporters released by the telephone company without prior notice. Any First Amendment newsgathering right, said the court, is subject to those general and incidental burdens that arise from good faith enforcement of valid civil and criminal laws. *Reporters Committee for Freedom of the Press v. AT & T*, 4 Med. L. Rptr. 1177, 593 F.2d 1030 (D.C. Cir. 1978), *cert. denied* 440 U.S. 949 (1979).

Federal court decisions have interpreted 18 U.S.C.A. § 2510 of Title III of the Omnibus Crime Control Act of 1968 (the Federal Wiretap Statute) to mean that if one party to a conversation records it, there is no illegal intercept. *United States v. Turk*, 526 F.2d 654 (5th Cir. 1976). See also *Boddie v. ABC*, 10 Med. L. Rptr. 1923, 731 F.2d 333 (6th Cir. 1984), and the Electronic Communications Privacy Act of 1986.

The FCC, in its supervisory capacity over broadcasting, prohibits the monitoring and divulging of nonpublic radio broadcasts such as police radios, a hallmark of most newsrooms, but it has not enforced the rule. It has admonished broadcasters to respect the rule and has pointed out the danger of attracting crowds to scenes of crime and disaster.[85]

The FCC also prohibits the private use of radio devices to monitor conversations without the consent of all parties,[86] and it requires broadcasters to give advance warning if a recorded telephone conversation is intended for broadcast.[87] Unannounced recording for broad-

---

81. See, Note, Lu, *Seeking Privacy in Wireless Communications: Balancing the Right of Individual Privacy with the Need for Effective Law Enforcement,* 17 Hastings Comm/Ent L.J. 529 (1995).
82. See Middleton, *Journalists and Tape Recorders: Does Participant Monitoring Invade Privacy?* 2 Comm/Ent L.J. 287 (1979–1980); Spellman, *Tort Liability of the News Media for Surreptitious Recording,* 62 Journalism Quarterly 289 (1985).
83. *News-Press v. Florida,* 2 Med. L. Rptr. 1240, 345 So. 2d 865 (Fla. 1977).
84. *State v. Birge,* 241 S.E.2d 213 (Ga. 1978); *Rogers v. Ulrich,* 52 Cal.App.3d 894, 125 Cal.Rptr. 306 (1975).

85. Monitoring of Police and Fire Radio Transmissions by Broadcast Stations, 1 Rad.Reg.2d (P & F) 291 (1963).
86. 47 C.F.R. §§ 2.701, 15.11 (1978).
87. *Use of Recording Devices in Connection with Telephone Service,* 38 FCC2d 579, 26 Rad.Reg.2d (P & F) 40 (1972). See also FCC 88–236 (Sept. 13, 1988).

cast purposes is not permitted, but the federal agency has made notable exceptions for reporters investigating crime.

Wiretapping and bugging by the media are illegal. Eavesdropping or recording conversations that are within hearing distance in public or quasi-public places is legal for both print and broadcast reporters. In 1980 a Kentucky court had an opportunity to address this question. An indicted drug dealer had given two reporters the impression that a lawyer had agreed to "fix" her case for $10,000. The reporters agreed to provide money to the suspect, if necessary, and asked her to meet with the lawyer in his office and record their conversation with a concealed recording device. The lawyer's privacy claims of intrusion by trespass and false light were rejected by the court, as were libel claims. The intrusion portions of the ruling follow.

McCall v. Courier-Journal
6 MED. L. RPTR. 1112 (KY.APP. 1980).

HOWERTON, Judge:

* * *

McCall is an attorney. He counseled with Kristie Frazier concerning two criminal charges. Frazier began spreading insinuations that she could buy her way out of her trouble. The appellees, Krantz and Van Howe, reporters for *The Louisville Times,* met with Frazier. In Frazier's words, McCall told her that "for $10,000.00 he would guarantee me that I'd walk in, but I would turn around and walk back out with him."

Krantz and Van Howe decided to investigate the possibility of bribery in the judiciary and met with Frazier again. They furnished her with a tape recorder and asked her to return to McCall's office. They also instructed her as to what questions to ask. They agreed to provide the $10,000.00 for her, if the dismissal of the criminal charges could be fixed.

On March 10, 1976, Frazier returned to McCall's office with the recorder. She asked the prearranged questions. The attorney told her there would be no "fix" and then inquired as to whether she had a recording device on her person. After Frazier's denial, McCall then stated that if he was able to keep Frazier out of jail, his fee would be $10,000.00, but if not, $9,000.00

would be returned to her. Although McCall's conduct was questionable in relation to the professional code, there was no evidence of bribery in the judicial system. Nevertheless, on March 17, 1976, *The Louisville Times* published and circulated a news article based on these events. On August 19, 1976, the newspaper carried an account of the lawsuit which resulted.

* * *

The first tort theory argued is labeled by McCall as invasion of privacy—intrusion/trespass. The appellees claim the nonexistence of this tort, stating that McCall created a hybrid cause of action. Prosser labels the tort "intrusion," which consists of "intrusion upon the plaintiff's physical solitude or seclusion, as by invading his home or other quarters * * *." Prosser extends the tort to include eavesdropping upon private conversations through wiretaps or microphones. Necessary elements of the tort include an intrusion in the nature of prying which is offensive or objectionable to a reasonable man. Also, the thing into which there is an intrusion must be private.

In this case, nothing was learned about McCall which was private or personal. The conversation dealt with Frazier and her legal problems and with how McCall proposed to resolve them. McCall spoke to her at his own risk, and Frazier was free to reveal the conversation to anyone. It is well settled that the attorney-client privilege "is not personal to the attorney but for the protection of the client." * * *

As to the allegation of trespass, we must conclude that neither the conduct of Frazier nor that of the newspaper or its reporters was sufficient under this theory. 75 Am.Jr.2d, *Trespass* § 14, states:

> The fact that a professional man, merchant, or other person opens an office to transact business with and for the public is a tacit invitation to all persons having business with him, and a permission for such persons to enter, unless forbidden. * * *

Thus, Frazier cannot be considered a trespasser. When McCall suspected a recorder on her person, he should have asked her to depart. By continuing the conversation, McCall consented to her presence and continued to discuss legal services for a fee. McCall argued that even if Frazier is considered an invitee, the newspaper and its reporters are trespassers. * * * However, since Frazier was not a trespasser, this argument must fail.

* * *

All concur.

COMMENT

It is important to note that the lower court in *McCall* distinguished *Dietemann* on grounds that no fraud or deception was involved in gaining access to the lawyer's office. As a client, the indicated drug dealer suspect was neither a trespasser nor an intruder. How about the reporters?

A year later the Kentucky Supreme Court reinstated the lawyer's libel and false light invasion of privacy suits while, at the same time, declining to discuss the intrusion claim. The court seemed to be saying that publication wrongs, i.e., libel and false light privacy violations, were more deserving of a jury's attention than the newsgathering wrong of intrusion. *McCall v. Courier-Journal*, 7 Med. L. Rptr. 2118, 623 S.W.2d 882 (Ky. 1981).

The two parties later reached a settlement, and McCall brought a libel suit against the newspaper for its report of the settlement. That suit was dismissed by a circuit court, and McCall appealed again seven years after the original publication.

A similar issue arose when ABC's *PrimeTime-Live* placed a reporter undercover as an employee at a national psychic advice company that relied on telemarketing. The reporter used hidden cameras. After material was broadcast, employees of the company argued that the reporter's behavior violated California's law barring eavesdropping on confidential conversations. They also argued an intrusion claim. Defendants moved for summary judgment, and the court said that both claims should go to trial. Under the statute, the employees must show a reasonable expectation of privacy in conversations at the workplace. Under intrusion, the employees must show that the behavior is offensive to reasonable people. State courts had previously determined that employees have a privacy interest against searches at work. *Kersis v. Capital Cities/ABC, Inc.*, 22 Med. L. Rptr. 2321 (Cal.Super.Ct. 1994). After trial, a jury assessed a total of more than $1 million in damages.

"IMPLICATIVE" PRIVACY: PORTRAYAL IN A FALSE LIGHT

Elements of and Defenses to the Cause of Action

Of the four common law invasion of privacy torts outlined in Prosser's famous 1960 law review article, invasion of privacy by portrayal in a false light has fared the worst. The action is a legal hybrid. Under common law, false light cases concern false assertions of fact or false implications of fact, just as in libel. The difference is that in false light the errors need not be defamatory, only embarrassing, to support the action. As a result, false light is a privacy tort rather than a part of libel law because the harm is usually considered to be to one's dignity rather than to one's reputation.

False light, then, walks a fine line. It is a line many of our most populous states do not adhere to. Massachusetts, New York, Ohio, and Texas all have refused to recognize the action at common law.[88]

In defining false light, the Restatement (Second) of Torts § 652 follows Prosser's example:

> One who gives publicity to a matter concerning another that places the other before the public in a false light is subject to liability to the other for the invasion of his privacy, if a) the false light in which the other was placed would be highly offensive to a reasonable person, and b) the actor had knowledge of or acted in reckless disregard as to the falsity of the publicized matter and the false light in which the other would be placed.

The latter portion reflects the "federalization" of both libel and false light under the First Amendment by the U.S. Supreme Court.

Prosser also emphasized that it is appropriate for plaintiffs to file dual claims for false light and libel in the same lawsuit. Partly as a result, false

---

88. *Brown v. Hearst Corp.*, 22 Med. L. Rptr. 2204, 862 F.Supp. 622 (D.Mass. 1994); *Torres v. CBS News*, 24 Med. L. Rptr. 1183 (N.Y.Sup., App. Div. 1995); *Celebrezze v. Dayton Newspapers, Inc.*, 15 Med. L. Rptr. 1589, 535 N.E.2d 755 (Ohio App. 1988); *Cain v. Hearst Corp.*, 22 Med. L. Rptr. 2161, 878 S.W.2d 577 (Tex. 1994). See also *Sullivan v. Pulitzer Broadcasting*, 12 Med. L. Rptr. 2187, 709 S.W.2d 475 (Mo.1986); *Renwick v. News & Observer Publishing Co.*, 10 Med. L. Rptr. 1443, 312 S.E.2d 405 (N.C. 1984).

light lawsuit filings remain numerous enough to constitute a significant concern for the press. Plaintiffs might prefer false light because the action as adopted in the Restatement does not require proof of a defamatory meaning, and a plaintiff might win if it can be shown that a defendant negligently overlooked an unfortunate meaning, resulting in embarrassment for the plaintiff. The uncertainty of the rules for false light has resulted in considerable criticism of the action.[89]

The similarity to libel has plagued attempts at consistent analysis in false light cases. Among the most typical instances of false light are coincidental uses of names, fictionalization, distortion, embellishment, and misuse of names or pictures through unfortunate juxtapositions in otherwise legitimate news stories. If there is a general clue to spotting what may constitute a false light privacy invasion, it appears to be that some interpretation or implication that is inaccurate must be drawn.

Because the two actions have become so similar, many jurisdictions have decided that the same rules apply to both.[90] One federal court hearing an appeal in a libel suit characterized the plaintiff's attempt to amend his complaint as an attempt to "avoid the strictures of the burden of proof associated with defamation. . . . ." *Moldea v. New York Times*, 22 Med. L. Rptr. 1321, 22 F.3d 310 (D.C. Cir. 1994). See p. 225.

A classic case illustrating false light is *Duncan v. WJLA-TV*, 10 Med. L. Rptr. 1395, 106 F.R.D. 4 (D.D.C. 1984). Linda Duncan was walking on a street in downtown Washington, D.C., at the same time a television crew was broadcasting a live 6 P.M. report on a new treatment for herpes. Duncan was clearly visible and recognizable to viewers. On the 11 P.M. newscast, the station

again used the video, but with a closer focus on Duncan. The anchor led into the story with the phrase "[f]or the twenty million Americans who have herpes, it's not a cure * * *." Duncan was looking directly at the camera during the voiceover.

Duncan sued for libel and false light. The court determined that the same analysis applied to both claims. The early story was not considered capable of a negative interpretation because it was in context: it showed other pedestrians nearby and did not zero in on Duncan. The 11 P.M. story was different:

> [P]laintiff was the only pedestrian who paused and unknowingly looked directly into the camera. As plaintiff turned and walked away from the camera, the film ended; viewers did not see Ms. Ashton [the reporter] as they did in the six o'clock report.
>
> The coalescing of the camera action, plaintiff's action, and the positions of the passersby caused plaintiff to be the focal point on the screen. The juxtaposition of this film and the commentary concerning twenty million Americans with herpes, is sufficient to support an inference that indeed plaintiff was a victim.

The court denied the station's motion for summary judgment. What distinguishes *Duncan* as more false light than libel is the absence of any assertion that the plaintiff had herpes. The audience had to reach, or not reach, that conclusion by considering the pictures and words together.

Analysis similar to that in *Duncan* was used to reverse a grant of summary judgment for a newspaper that used an old photo of a female coal miner. The picture had originally been used in a 1977 article on women miners, and was concededly nonobjectionable then. In 1979, another area newspaper obtained and used the photo to accompany an article concerning incidents of harassment of women miners. Plaintiff asserted that the use of the photo caused harm to her reputation and also caused embarrassment and humiliation. Since the court could not say as a matter of law that the photo failed to place plaintiff in a false light, as the paper claimed, it was considered best decided by a jury. *Crump v. Beckley Newspapers*, 10 Med. L. Rptr. 2225, 320 S.E.2d 70 (W.V. 1983).

Just as in deciding defamatory meaning in libel, however, whether or not the press has placed a plaintiff in a false light is initially a

---

89. See generally Zimmerman, *False Light Invasion of Privacy: The Light That Failed*, 65 N.Y.U.L.Rev. 364 (1989); Zuckman, *Invasion of Privacy—Some Communicative Torts Whose Time Has Gone*, 47 Wash. & Lee L.Rev. 253 (1990).

90. See, for example, *Brewer v. Rogers*, 22 Med. L. Rptr. 1180, 439 S.E.2d 343 (Ga.App. 1993) (high school football coach must prove actual malice in either false light or libel action); *Crowley v. Fox Broadcasting Co.*, 22 Med. L. Rptr. 1904, 851 F.Supp. 700 (D.Md. 1994) (under Maryland law, standards for false light and for libel are parallel); *Foreman v. Lesher Communications, Inc.*, 21 Med. L. Rptr. 1090, 16 Cal. Rptr. 2d 670 (Cal.App. 1993).

mixed question of fact and law that a trial judge may decide on a motion for summary judgment. In *Fox, Inc. v. Los Angeles Superior Court,* 22 Med. L. Rptr. 2347 (Cal.App., unpub. 1994), the plaintiff was shown being arrested for drunk driving on the program *America's Most Wanted.* He claimed that showing him in association with heinous criminals both libeled him and placed him a false light. "No reasonable person could possibly confuse [those] crimes with O'Connor's arrest for driving under the influence," the court noted.

Earlier false light cases followed a similar pattern. For example, in 1948 a federal district court granted relief to an honest taxi driver whose photograph had been used by the *Saturday Evening Post* to illustrate a story about crooked cabbies.[91] And an invasion of privacy was acknowledged by a New York court in 1955 when a law-abiding slum child's photo was used in a story about juvenile delinquents.[92] A more frequently cited case, and one that gave impetus to the false light category of suits, is *Leverton v. Curtis Publishing Co.,* 192 F.2d 974 (3d Cir. 1951). A newspaper photo of a child being helped to her feet after a car ran a stoplight and knocked her down was reprinted twenty months later in the *Saturday Evening Post* under the caption, "They Asked To Be Killed." Although the article was concerned with pedestrian carelessness, it erroneously implied that this particular child pedestrian had been at fault. A trial court judgment of $5,000 was sustained.

The original publication of the photo was not actionable because its legitimate news interest overbalanced any claim to privacy. But the magazine's use of the photo, said the court, exceeded the bounds of privilege and would be offensive to persons of ordinary sensibilities.

Since the *Post* had purchased the photograph from a commercial agency, was it aware of the misleading impression it would create? False light cases today turn on the answers to questions of this kind. How will a publisher know when an unaltered photograph has the capacity of placing someone in a false light or when something omitted from an article may embarrass?

The development of digital photography has caused concern in some circles. Today's hardware and software allow extensive modification, alteration, and even falsification of news photos.[93] *Time's* use of digital alteration on O. J. Simpson's Los Angeles Police Department mug shot at the time of his arrest set off a furor of media criticism. The ability to change news photos certainly increases the chances that individuals will be portrayed in a false light. To date, however, digital manipulation has not resulted in an increase in lawsuits.

The Constitutional Defense

The combination of libel rules with false light rules is somewhat at odds with the traditional common law formulation of false light. That formula, as given in the Restatement (Second) of Torts, allows recovery upon proof of offensiveness, that is, publicity "highly offensive to a reasonable person," but hedges on whether or not knowledge of falsity, reckless disregard, negligence, or the mere fact of having published materials placing someone in a false light constitutes a second requirement.

The overlap between false light and libel, always lurking in the tort, was brought to the forefront in 1967 when the Supreme Court, perhaps imbued with the spirit of *New York Times v. Sullivan,* invoked the First Amendment to defeat a privacy suit. In so doing, it tied together false light privacy, defamation, and the actual malice test.

The case began in 1952 when James Hill, his wife, and five children were held hostage in their suburban Philadelphia home by three escaped convicts. The Hills were not harmed; in fact, they were treated surprisingly well by the intruders. A year later, a novel, *Desperate Hours,* purported to describe the dramatic episode but with the fictionalized addition of captor violence against the father and a son and a verbal sexual assault on a daughter.

The novel led to a Broadway play and the play to a picture-and-story review in *Life* magazine. By then the Hills had moved to Connecticut, supposedly to avoid further public attention. Hill's

---

91. *Peay v. Curtis Publishing Co.,* 78 F.Supp. 305 (D.D.C. 1948).

92. *Metzger v. Dell Publishing Co.,* 136 N.Y.S.2d 888 (1955).

93. See generally Note, Potter, *Altered Realities: The Effect of Digital Imaging Technology on Libel and Right of Privacy,* 17 Hastings Comm/Ent L.J. 495 (1995).

privacy suit was brought under New York's privacy statute, which provides redress against appropriation and commercialization. Hill's suit, by contrast, contained all the elements of a common law false light action.

Hill found particularly offensive to his desire for anonymity *Life's* characterization of the play as "a heart-stopping account of how a family rose to heroism in a crisis." The play was set in the actual house the Hills had occupied in suburban Philadelphia; otherwise there was little resemblance between the docile captivity of the family and the sensationalized story line of the play. The incident inevitably became a Hollywood film starring a commando-like Frederick March as the father and Humphrey Bogart as the convict leader. So popular was the story that it was filmed again in 1990 with Anthony Hopkins as the father and Mickey Rourke as the top convict.

Hill won a $75,000 judgment from a jury. The Appellate Division of the New York Supreme Court upheld the verdict for Hill but ordered a new trial on the question of damages. A second jury awarded Hill $30,000 in compensatory damages. That judgment was affirmed by the Court of Appeals, New York's highest court. Time, Inc., appealed to the United States Supreme Court and argued that the rules pertaining to the standards of newsworthiness had not been measured against First Amendment guidelines as had been required since 1964 under *New York Times v. Sullivan.*

A majority of the Court agreed and applied the *New York Times* rule of actual malice to the *Life* article.

Time, Inc. v. Hill
1 MED. L. RPTR. 1791, 385 U.S. 374, 87 S.CT. 534, 17 L.ED.2D 456 (1967).

Justice BRENNAN delivered the opinion of the Court.

The question in this case is whether appellant, publisher of *Life* Magazine, was denied constitutional protections for speech and press by the application by the New York courts of §§ 50–51 of the New York Civil Rights Law, McKinney's Consol.Laws, c. 6 to award appellee damages on allegations that *Life* falsely reported that a new play portrayed an experience suffered by appellee and his family.

* * *

Although "Right to Privacy" is the caption of § 51, the term nowhere appears in the text of the statute itself. * * *

The New York courts have, however, construed the statute to operate much more broadly. * * * Specifically, it has been held in some circumstances to authorize a remedy against the press and other communications media which publish the names, pictures, or portraits of people without their consent.

* * *

The Court of Appeals sustained the holding that in these circumstances the publication was proscribed by § 51 of the Civil Rights Law and was not within the exceptions and restrictions for newsworthy events engrafted on the statute. * * *

The opinion goes on to say that the "establishment of minor errors in an otherwise accurate" report does not prove "fictionalization." Material and substantial falsification is the test. However, it is not clear whether proof of knowledge of the falsity or that the article was prepared with reckless disregard for the truth is also required. In *New York Times Co. v. Sullivan,* 376 U.S. 254, we held that the Constitution delimits a State's power to award damages for libel in actions brought by public officials against critics of their official conduct. Factual error, content defamatory of official reputation, or both, are insufficient to an award of damages for false statements unless actual malice—knowledge that the statements are false or in reckless disregard of the truth—is alleged and proved. * * * The Court of Appeals held that *New York Times* had no application.

* * *

If this is meant to imply that proof of knowing or reckless falsity is not essential to a constitutional application of the statute in these cases, we disagree with the Court of Appeals. We hold that the constitutional protections for speech and press preclude the application of the New York statute to redress false reports of matters of public interest in the absence of proof that the defendant published the report with knowledge of its falsity or in reckless disregard of the truth. [Emphasis added.]

The guarantees for speech and press are not the preserve of political expression or comment upon public affairs, essential as those are to healthy government. One need only pick up any newspaper or magazine to comprehend the vast range of published matter which exposes persons to public view, both private citizens and public officials. * * * Erroneous statement is no less inevitable in such case than in the case of comment upon public affairs, and in both, if innocent or merely negligent, "* * * it must be protected if the freedoms of expression are to have the 'breathing space' that they 'need * * * to survive' * * *." We create grave risk of serious impairment of the indispensable service of a free press in a free society if we saddle the press with the impossible burden of verifying to a certainty the facts associated in news articles with a person's name, picture or portrait, particularly as related to nondefamatory matter.

* * *

But the constitutional guarantees can tolerate sanctions against *calculated* falsehood without significant impairment of their essential function. We held in *New York Times* that calculated falsehood enjoyed no immunity in the case of alleged defamation of a public official's official conduct. Similarly calculated falsehood should enjoy no immunity in the situation here presented us. * * *

The judgment of the Court of Appeals is set aside and the case is remanded for further proceedings not inconsistent with this opinion.

COMMENT

By applying the actual malice test in *Hill*, the Court accepted the argument that false light and libel were in effect twin torts. Importing a test that apparently varies the rule to be applied depending upon the public interest in an event or person in effect brings the private facts newsworthiness defense into false light. A big difference is that, in private facts, the defense ends the case, while in false light it only changes the plaintiff's burden of proof.

Hill required proof of actual malice without regard to whether or not the plaintiff is a private figure or public figure, so long as the publicity concerned a matter of public interest. The rule strongly suggests that the interests served by libel and false light are parallel if not identical. But a number of scholars continued to urge that false light must be considered separately, as a privacy

tort addressing the individual's interest in personal well-being and peace of mind.[94]

The actual malice test of *Hill* has been applied in many cases. In *Machleder v. Diaz*, 13 Med. L. Rptr. 1369, 801 F.2d 46 (2d Cir. 1986), the court reversed a jury finding of actual malice stemming from an "ambush" interview of the plaintiff. Diaz, an investigative reporter for WCBS-TV, conducted an interview with plaintiff as part of a story on toxic waste dumping. Diaz spotted abandoned drums and approached the door of Flexcraft, the paint manufacturing plant Machleder managed. Diaz starting asking questions while the cameras rolled. Machleder got upset, told Diaz "I don't need any publicity," but then invited Diaz into the office for an interview. That evening, the station ran the story and included footage of the confrontation. Diaz opened the story by admitting he did not know who owned the barrels or had placed them there.

Machleder based his false light claim on two arguments—that viewers would assume he had put the barrels full of toxic waste where they were, and that he had been portrayed as "intemperate and evasive." Machleder was unable to prove that any false assertions or even implications had been made and lost on the first claim. A jury had awarded him $250,000 compensatory damages and $1 million punitive damages for having been portrayed as intemperate and evasive. There could be no falsity in the presentation, the court said, since "it was based on his own conduct, which was accurately captured by the cameras." The "true light" was that plaintiff had been intemperate and evasive.

A case in which actual malice was proved involved a surviving husband who was awarded $5,000 compensatory and $15,000 punitive damages when a *National Enquirer* story under the headline, "Happiest Mother Kills Her Three Children and Herself," was held sufficiently untruthful and offensive to constitute an invasion of privacy. The plaintiff said he suffered mental anguish, became unemployed, and was disdained by friends and acquaintances.

The "happiest" mother in reality had been extremely depressed and unstable, and only ficti-

---

94. Ashdown, *Media Reporting and Privacy Claims— Decline in Constitutional Protection for the Press,* 66 Kentucky L.J. 759 (1977–78); Nimmer, *The Right to Speak from Times to Time: First Amendment Theory Applied to Libel and Misapplied to Privacy,* 56 Calif.L.Rev. 935 (1968).

tious dialogue in the story could make her appear otherwise. The actual malice standard of knowing falsehood or reckless disregard of truth or falsity had been met. *Varnish v. Best Medium Publishing Co.*, 405 F.2d 608 (2d Cir. 1968).

The Supreme Court's plurality in *Rosenbloom*[95] would temporarily establish the same public interest or public issue standard for defamation. But that case was superseded by *Gertz*,[96] which substantially returned private persons to the protective cloak of libel law. *Time, Inc. v. Firestone*, 1 Med. L. Rptr. 1665, 424 U.S. 448 (1976), with its reluctance to consider a plaintiff who held press conferences a public figure and its recognition of the plaintiff's damage claim based on mental distress rather than harm to reputation, also appeared likely to affect privacy law. What was the effect of the two cases? Should a negligence test replace actual malice in false light as in libel for private figures? It is arguably illogical to use a newsworthiness test in privacy when it has been rejected in libel.[97]

A Post-*Gertz* case, *Cantrell v. Forest City Publishing Co.*, 1 Med. L. Rptr. 1815, 419 U.S. 245 (1974), provided the Court with an opportunity to either merge or distinguish false light and libel. In that case a story in the *Cleveland Plain Dealer* Sunday Magazine purported to describe an interview with Margaret Cantrell, whose husband had died in a bridge collapse, leaving her and her four children in proud but abject poverty. Mrs. Cantrell, however, had been absent when a reporter and photographer entered the home and talked with one of her children. Inaccuracy was inevitable since the article contained "quotes" from Margaret Cantrell although the reporter never spoke with her. The Court reinstated a trial court damages award that had been reversed by the Court of Appeals for the Sixth Circuit.

Since the actual malice test of *New York Times* had again been met, the Court found "no occasion to consider whether a state may constitutionally impose a more severe standard of liability for a publisher or broadcaster of false statements injurious to a *private individual* under a false light theory of invasion of privacy, or whether the constitutional standard announced in *Time, Inc. v. Hill* applies to all false light cases." [Emphasis added.]

"In essence," Justice Potter Stewart wrote, joined by seven of his colleagues, "the theory of the case was that by publishing the false feature story about the Cantrells and thereby making them the objects of pity and ridicule, the respondents damaged Mrs. Cantrell and her son William by causing them to suffer outrage, mental distress, shame and humiliation. * * * These were 'calculated falsehoods,' and the jury was plainly justified in finding that [the reporter] had portrayed the Cantrells in a false light through knowing or reckless untruth." The photographer was exonerated.

Cantrell, though clearly a private figure, had no occasion to charge negligence against the *Plain Dealer* because its falsehoods had already reached the level of actual malice. Since *Cantrell*, lower courts have disagreed on the amount to which *Hill* should be modified to coexist with *Gertz*.

In the *Crump v. Beckley Newspapers* case, discussed earlier, the West Virginia Supreme Court of Appeals explicitly held that that state's common law version of the false light tort served an interest different from defamation:

> [p]rivacy actions involve injuries to emotions and mental suffering, while defamation actions involve injury to reputation. * * * Second, the false light need not be defamatory, although it often is. * * * Finally, although widespread publication is not necessarily required for recovery under a defamation cause of action, it is an essential ingredient to any false light invasion of privacy claim.

On the conflict between *Hill* and *Gertz*, the court concluded that it would "eventually be resolved in favor of *Gertz*." The court engaged in an exhaustive review of other cases in deciding that a negligence standard was to be used in private person false light suits.[98]

A California appeals court opted to resurrect the public interest test of *Rosenbloom* in a 1981 libel and privacy suit.[99] In 1979 an Arkansas

---

95. *Rosenbloom v. Metromedia*, 1 Med. L. Rptr. 1597, 403 U.S. 29 (1971).

96. *Gertz v. Robert Welch, Inc.*, 1 Med. L. Rptr. 1633, 418 U.S. 323 (1974).

97. But see Walden and Netzhammer, *False Light Invasion of Privacy: Untangling the Web of Uncertainty*, 9 Comm/Ent L.J. 347, 359–364 (1987) (arguing for application of the *Hill* test).

98. See also *Deitz v. Wometco West Michigan TV*, 14 Med. L. Rptr. 1629, 407 N.W.2d 649 (Mich.App. 1987).

99. *Midwife v. Copley*, 7 Med. L. Rptr. 1393 (Cal.App. 1981).

court held that a private person must prove *actual malice* in a false light case if the publication is a matter of public concern.[100] An earlier case, *Rinsley v. Brandt,* 446 F.Supp. 850 (D.Kan. 1977), stood for the rule that *Gertz* limits the *actual malice* standard to false light claims brought by public persons and thus infers that private persons need only show *negligence.* Another federal district court crystallized that inference in *Dresbach v. Doubleday,* 7 Med. L. Rptr. 2105, 518 F.Supp. 1285 (D.D.C. 1981), by applying the District of Columbia's *negligence* standard for libel—to false light actions brought by private persons.[101]

Eventual adoption of the *Gertz* approach would aid the cause of legal symmetry, but the split in approaches remains. Some states have addressed narrower issues. For example, it is urged that if libel and false light are very similar, the measure and proof of damages should be as well.[102] In some states the statute of limitations for libel, which at one or two years is usually shorter than that for privacy, has been held to apply to both causes of action.[103] Most states, however, have retained a longer statute of limitations for false light—three years or more.[104]

Fictionalization and Embellishment

How can publishers anticipate fictional characters coming to life—and filing lawsuits? In recent years, a number of cases have charged that novels, and even biographies, contained characterizations that placed someone in a false light. In fiction, the claim typically is that a character is a too-thinly-disguised representation of a real person. In embellishment, the plaintiff usually admits the overall accuracy of a portrayal but claims that a small portion is exaggerated or misleading.

One area of special trouble has been the television docudrama, a dramatic form that blends fact, interpretation, and fiction.[105] Former aides to Senator Joseph McCarthy were portrayed without their consent in a television movie. Their real names were used in advertising and promoting the program. Their false light–type claim based on New York's privacy statute was dismissed on public interest grounds.[106] On the other hand, a false light claim was sustained when the real name of an attorney who had represented gangster Lucky Luciano was used in a wholly fictionalized, although not defamatory, episode in a novel.[107]

NBC found itself embroiled in litigation after it ran a docudrama entitled "Judge Horton and the Scottsboro Boys," which won several major awards. Dubbed "the most famous rape case of the twentieth century" by the Sixth Circuit, the case involved Victoria Price Street who, forty years before as Victoria Price, had charged nine black men with raping her on a train. Price was white. The evidence against the defendants consisted of little more than Price's accusations, but nevertheless, Price pressed charges that could have meant the death penalty. All nine were tried quickly in Scottsboro, Alabama, found guilty, and sentenced to death by all-white juries. Several convictions were reversed, some by the U.S. Supreme Court. Judge Horton presided over one of the retrials, setting the new guilty verdict aside as based on insufficient evidence—a decision that did not make Horton popular in the South at the time.

The drama was particularly harsh on Victoria Price, who throughout the many years of trials sought out the press to present her side of the story. NBC had good reason to be harsh. A book

100. *Dodrill v. Arkansas Democrat,* 5 Med. L. Rptr. 1385, 590 S.W.2d 840 (Ark. 1979), *cert. den.* 444 U.S. 1076 (1980).
101. The same rule was applied in *McCall v. Courier Journal,* 7 Med. L. Rptr. 2118, 623 S.W.2d 882 (Ky. 1981), a case that specifically rejects the public issue test of *Midwife v. Copley.* For the *Gertz* application, see also *Roberts v. Dover,* 7 Med. L. Rptr. 2296, 525 F.Supp. 987 (M.D.Tenn. 1981). *Fitzgerald v. Penthouse International, Limited,* 7 Med. L. Rptr. 2385, 525 F.Supp. 585 (D.Md. 1981), held that a limited purpose public figure must also show actual malice.
102. *Fellows v. National Enquirer,* 13 Med. L. Rptr. 1305, 42 Cal.3d 234, 228 Cal.Rptr. 215, 721 P.2d 97 (1986).
103. *Eastwood v. Cascade Broadcasting Co.* 13 Med. L. Rptr. 1136, 722 P.2d 1295 (Wash. 1986).
104. *Jensen v. Times Mirror,* 12 Med. L. Rptr. 2137, 634 F.Supp. 304 (D.Conn. 1986); *Wood v. Hustler Magazine,* 10 Med. L. Rptr. 2113, 736 F.2d 1084 (5th Cir. 1984).

105. Note, Lentzner, *My Life, My Story, Right? Fashioning Life Rights in the Motion Picture Industry,* 12 Hastings Comm/Ent L.J. 627 (1990).
106. *Cohn v. NBC,* 4 Med. L. Rptr. 2533, 414 N.Y.S.2d 906 (N.Y.Sup.Ct. , App.Div. 1979), *aff'd* 6 Med. L. Rptr. 1398, 430 N.Y.S.2d 265 (N.Y. 1980), *cert. den.* 449 U.S. 1022 (1981).
107. *Polakoff v. Harcourt Brace Jovanovich, Inc.,* 3 Med. L. Rptr. 2516 (N.Y.Sup.Ct. 1978), *aff'd* 413 N.Y.S.2d 537 (App.Div. 1979).

the network relied upon and Judge Horton's own comments supported the portrayal of Price as a perjurer and generally bad character. NBC also had been told that Price, who in the meantime had married and become an absolute nonentity in another state, was dead, and the dead, of course, cannot sue. Street filed, claiming both libel and false light. The court decided that Street, despite anonymity and a new name, remained a public figure so long as the case remained of public interest. A bristling dissent argued that Street's lifelong desire for anonymity deserved consideration; apparently, no one in her new hometown was aware of her past, and she had been completely rehabilitated. *Street v. NBC*, 6 Med. L. Rptr. 1001, 645 F.2d 1227 (6th Cir. 1981). Street appealed to the Supreme Court, and certiorari was granted. The parties reached a settlement, and the writ of certiorari was dismissed. How might the high court have approached the issues in the case?

Identification is obviously a key issue in fiction as opposed to "faction." Was Kimberly Pring, a former Miss Wyoming, identified by a salacious *Penthouse* short story about a baton-twirling former Miss Wyoming who wore a costume similar to Pring's? The Tenth Circuit did not reach the identification issue, privileging the story instead as satire.[108] Evidently, few of her neighbors in Cheyenne knew the story referred to her, or even knew of the story, until Pring announced it by filing suit.

In another identification case, an author was unwise enough to use the real name and physical description of a casual acquaintance for a fictional transsexual character.[109] Where there is no connection between author and plaintiff, the risk may not be as great.[110] In any case where identification is in doubt, it is initially a question for the jury.

Identification was no issue when A. J. Quinnell wrote and published *In the Name of the Father*, a novel about a plan concocted by three high Roman Catholic officials to assassinate the late Soviet leader Yuri Andropov. In a preface, readers were alerted that "some real people . . .

appear as characters in the book to give a sense of historical accuracy." One of those appearing was Paul Marcinkus, an archbishop who formerly headed the Vatican Bank. In the novel, Marcinkus is the central plotter. Ironically, the author himself had used a pseudonym. When Marcinkus filed suit, the court declared that the disclaimer was insufficient to protect against either false light assertions or a claim of appropriation. Adding insult to injury, the publisher had used Marcinkus's name in promoting and advertising the book.[111]

Traditional disclaimers, such as "all characters portrayed are wholly fictional and any resemblance to actual persons living or dead is purely coincidental," are useful, but they cannot cover every conceivable kind of character. Disclaimers should be explicit, although it is not clear that being explicit alone will provide more protection. Generally speaking, the better known a claimant, the strong a false light claim looks. Conversely, the rarer a work of imagination, the less vulnerable it should be. When the "real" T. J. Hooker filed a right of publicity suit against the network television show about a California policeman with the same name, the court had no difficulty finding that no reasonable person would have connected the two.[112] The real T. J. Hooker was a professional wood-carver from Woodstock, Illinois. Hooker would have fared no better under false light.

The most ominous example of a case of failed fictionalization and one that exercised the literary world was *Bindrim v. Mitchell*. Author Gwen Davis Mitchell not only lost a libel suit (the libel claim here being indistiguishable from a false light claim) to a "nude-encounter" therapist but was also sued by her publisher, which, under its contract with her, had a right to recover whatever costs might result from a libel suit. Doubleday had stuck with its author until she finally lost her case. Mitchell, who claimed that she had gone to great pains to change, disguise, and transmute—partly with vulgar dialogue—events at a nude therapy marathon into her novel *Touching*, maintained that there can be no libel in fiction.

108. *Pring v. Penthouse International,* 8 Med. L. Rptr. 2409, 695 F.2d 438 (10th Cir. 1982).
109. *Geisler v. Petrocelli,* 6 Med. L. Rptr. 1023, 616 F.2d 636 (2d Cir. 1980).
110. *Allen v. Gordon,* 6 Med. L. Rptr. 2010, 446 N.Y.S.2d 48 (N.Y.Sup.Ct. 1982).

111. *Marcinkus v. NAL Publishing,* 14 Med. L. Rptr. 2094 (N.Y.Sup.Ct. 1987).
112. *T. J. Hooker v. Columbia Pictures,* 551 F.Supp. 1060 (N.D.Ill. 1982).

The case was complicated by the fact that the plaintiff's appearance and academic credentials had changed to resemble those of the fictional character of "Dr. Herford" between publication and trial. Moreover, Mitchell had signed a contract with the plaintiff not to disclose in any manner what was to take place in the therapy sessions.

Essentially, Mitchell's disguise was inadequate, so again the question of identification arose. How many persons have to relate the fictional character to an actual person? In *Bindrim*, the California court said that one would suffice.

Bindrim v. Mitchell

5 MED. L. RPTR. 1113, 155 CAL. RPTR. 29 (CAL.APP. 1979), CERT. DENIED 444 U.S. 984, REHEARING DENIED 444 U.S. 1040 (1980).

KINGSLEY, J.:

* * *

There is clear and convincing evidence to support the jury's finding that defendant Mitchell entertained actual malice, and that defendant Doubleday had actual malice when it permitted the paperback printing of *Touching*, although there was no actual malice on the part of Doubleday in its original printing of the hardback edition.

Mitchell's reckless disregard for the truth was apparent from her knowledge of the truth of what transpired at the encounter, and the literary portrayals of that encounter. Since she attended sessions there can be no suggestion that she did not know the true facts. Since "actual malice" concentrates solely on defendants' attitude toward the truth or falsity of the material published * * * and not on malicious motives, certainly defendant Mitchell was in a position to know the truth or falsity of her own material, and the jury was entitled to find that her publication was in reckless disregard of that truth or with actual knowledge of falsity.

However, plaintiff failed to prove by clear and convincing evidence that the original hardback publication by Doubleday was made with knowledge of falsity or in reckless disregard of falsity. McCormick of Doubleday cautioned plaintiff that the characters must be totally fictitious and Mitchell assured McCormick that the characters in *Touching* were incapable of being identified as real persons. McCormick arranged to have the manuscript read by an editor knowledgeable in the field of libel. *.* * There must be sufficient evidence to permit the conclusion that defendant in fact entertained serious doubts as to the truth of his publication, and there is nothing to suggest that Doubleday entertained such doubts prior to the hardback publication.

Plaintiff suggests that, since the book did not involve "hot news," Doubleday had a duty to investigate the content for truth. * * * In the case at bar, Doubleday had been assured by Mitchell that no actual, identifiable person was involved and that all the characters were fictitious in the novel. Where the publication comes from a known reliable source and there is nothing in the circumstances to suggest inaccuracy, there is no duty to investigate. There was nothing in the record to suggest that, prior to the hardback printing defendant Doubleday in fact entertained serious doubts as to the truth or falsity of the publication, and investigatory failure alone is insufficient to find actual malice.

However, prior to the paperback printing there were surrounding circumstances to suggest inaccuracy, such that at that point Doubleday had a duty to investigate. Plaintiff did show that Doubleday sold the rights to the New American Library after receiving a letter from plaintiff's attorney explaining that plaintiff was Herford and the inscription in the paperback said, "This is an authorized edition published by Doubleday and Company." * * * The jury could have inferred that at that point Doubleday either had serious doubts, or should have had serious doubts, as to the possibility that plaintiff was defamed by "Touching" and that at that point Doubleday had some duty to investigate.

* * * Appellants claim that, even if there are untrue statements, there is no showing that plaintiff was identified as the character, Simon Herford, in the novel *Touching*.

Appellants allege that plaintiff failed to show he was identifiable as Simon Herford, relying on the fact that the character in *Touching* was described in the book as a "fat Santa Claus type with long white hair, white sideburns, a cherubic rosy face and rosy forearms" and that Bindrim was clean shaven and had short hair.

* * *

In the case at bar, the only differences between plaintiff and the Herford character in *Touching* were physical appearance and that Herford was a psychiatrist rather than psychologist. Otherwise, the character Simon Herford was very similar to the actual plaintiff. We cannot say, * * * that no one who knew plaintiff Bindrim could reasonably identify him with the fictional character. Plaintiff was identified as Herford by several witnesses and plaintiff's own tape recording of the marathon sessions show that the novel was based substantially on plaintiff's conduct in the nude marathon.

* * * In the case at bar, apart from some of those episodes allegedly constituting the libelous matter itself, and apart from the physical difference and the fact that plaintiff had a Ph.D., and not an M.D., the similarities between Herford and Bindrim are clear, and the transcripts of the actual encounter weekend show a close parallel between the narrative of plaintiff's novel and the actual real life events. * * * There is overwhelming evidence that plaintiff and "Herford" were one.

However, even though there was clear and convincing evidence to support the finding of "actual malice," and even though there was support for finding that plaintiff is identified as the character in Mitchell's novel, there still can be no recovery by plaintiff if the statements in *Touching* were not libelous. There can be no libel predicated on an opinion. The publication must contain a false statement of fact. (*Gregory v. McDonnell Douglas Corp.* (1976) 17 Cal.3d 596.)

* * *

Our inquiry then is directed to whether or not any of these incidents can be considered false statements of fact. It is clear from the transcript of the actual encounter weekend proceeding that some of the incidents portrayed by Mitchell are false: i.e., substantially inaccurate description of what actually happened. * * * [W]e regard the case at bench as involving a different issue. Defendants contend that the fact that the book was labeled as being a "novel" bars any claim that the writer or publisher could be found to have implied that the characters in the book were factual representations not of the fictional characters but of an actual nonfictional person. That contention, thus broadly stated, is unsupported by the cases. The test is whether a reasonable person, reading the book, would understand that the fictional character therein pictured was, in actual fact, the plaintiff acting as

described. * * * Whether a reader, identifying plaintiff with the "Dr. Herford" of the book, would regard the passages herein complained of as mere fictional embroidering or as reporting actual language and conduct, was for the jury. Its verdict adverse to the defendants cannot be overturned by this court.

* * *

COMMENT

Judge Files wrote a dissenting opinion expressing amazement and displeasure at the majority's reading of the facts and interpretation of libel law. The identification issue was resolved wrongly, the dissent argued, on the basis of three witnesses, all former therapy patients of Bindrim's rather than on the issue of whether a reader would have identified Bindrim as Dr. Herford. The dissent also urged that Bindrim had failed to prove adequately that a reasonable reader would consider Mitchell's account as containing assertions of fact. Most troubling, however, was the actual malice analysis:

> The majority opinion adopts the position that actual malice may be inferred from the fact that the book was "false." That inference is permissible against a defendant who has purported to state the truth. But when the publication purports to be fiction, it is absurd to infer malice because the fiction is false. * * * As the majority agrees, a public figure may not recover damages for libel unless "actual malice" is shown. * * * From an analytical standpoint, the chief vice of the majority opinion is that it brands a novel as libelous because it is "false," i.e., fiction; and infers "actual malice" from the fact that the author and publisher knew it was not a true representation of plaintiff. From a constitutional standpoint the vice is the chilling effect upon the publisher of any novel critical of any occupational practice, inviting litigation on the theory "when you criticize my occupation, you libel me."

* * *

The *Bindrim* case is the judiciary's strongest warning that authors should not get too close to describing real characters in their works.[113]

---

113. Note, Crook, *Welcome to the Nineties*, Bindrim v. Mitchell: *Now Drop Dead*, 12 Hastings Comm/Eng L.J. 517 (1990).

While the extent of Mitchell's actual malice can be debated forever, the fact that her portrayal of Herford is directly taken from her own experience should put all authors on notice to be careful when drawing characters based on people they know. Friends, families, business colleagues, and acquaintances after all are likely to be among the first to read one's work, and also the first to recoil at an unflattering portrait.

Embellishment presents similar problems of analysis to the courts. Embellishment typically occurs in feature stories. Commonly, a plaintiff admits the accuracy of a portrayal overall but focuses on a portion of the coverage that was exaggerated or was presented in a literary fashion with a bit of literary license.

When Shila Morganroth's singular method of styling hair caught the attention of *Detroit News* reporter Susan Whitall, the result was a feature article in the newspaper's Sunday magazine. Morganroth thought the personality profile cast her in a false, even foolish, light. Distressed, she sued claiming both libel and false light invasion of privacy.

Morganroth v. Whitall

14 MED. L. RPTR. 1411, 411 N.W.2D 859 (MICH.APP. 1987).

SAWYER, J.:

* * *

In this heated dispute, the trial court granted summary disposition in favor of defendants on plaintiff's claims of libel and invasion of privacy by false light. Plaintiff now appeals and we affirm.

Plaintiff alleges that she was libeled and cast in false light by an article written by defendant Whitall which appeared in the Sunday Supplement of the Detroit News on November 11, 1984. The article was entitled "Hot Locks: Let Shila burn you a new 'do.'" The article was accompanied by two photographs, one depicting plaintiff performing her craft on a customer identified as "Barbara X" and the second showing Barbara X and her dog, identified as "Harry X", following completion of the hairdressing. Central to the article was the fact that plaintiff used a blowtorch in her hairdressing endeavors. According to the article, plaintiff's blowtorch technique is dubbed "Shi-lit" and is copyrighted.

The article also describes two dogs, Harry and Snowball, the latter belonging to plaintiff, noting that the canines have had their respective coats colored at least in part. The article also indicates that the blowtorch technique had been applied to both dogs. Additionally, the article described plaintiff's somewhat unusual style of dress, including a silver holster for her blowtorch and a barrette in her hair fashioned out of a $100 bill.

* * *

Plaintiff's rather brief complaint alleges that the article, when read as a whole, is false, misleading and constitutes libel. More specifically, the complaint alleges that the article used the terms "blowtorch lady," "blowtorch technique" and the statement that plaintiff "is dressed for blowtorching duty in a slashed-to-there white jumpsuit" without any factual basis and as the result of defendants' intentional conduct to distort and sensationalize the facts obtained in the interview. The complaint further alleges that the article falsely portrays plaintiff as an animal hairdresser, again as part of a deliberate action by defendants to distort and sensationalize the facts.

* * *

In determining whether an article is libelous, it is necessary to read the article as a whole and fairly and reasonably construe it in determining whether a portion of the article is libelous in character. * * *

Reading the article as a whole, we believe that it is substantially true; therefore plaintiff's complaint lacks an essential element of her defamation claim, namely falsity. In looking at plaintiff's specific allegations of falsity, for the most part we find no falsehood. * * * In looking at the photographic exhibits filed by defendants, we believe that the instrument used by plaintiff in her profession can accurately be described as a blowtorch. Accordingly, while the use of the term "blowtorch" as an adjective in connection with references to plaintiff or her hairdressing technique may have been colorful, it was not necessarily inaccurate and certainly not libelous. As for the reference that plaintiff was "dressed for blowtorching duty in a slashed-to-there white jumpsuit", we have examined the photographic exhibits submitted by defendant at the motion hearing and we conclude that reasonable minds could not differ in reaching the conclusion that plaintiff did, in fact, wear a jumpsuit "slashed-to-there." * * *

In her brief, plaintiff claims that defendant inaccurately described her as being a hairdresser for dogs, giving dogs a Mohawk cut, and using a blowtorch on the dogs. While it appears that plaintiff did do hairdressing on dogs, it is not necessarily certain at this point that she did, in fact, use the blowtorch on the dogs. * * * Thus, there has been no showing by plaintiff that the statements relating to the dogs were false.

Moreover, inasmuch as it appears undisputed that plaintiff at least dyed the fur of the dogs, which would constitute hairdressing of dogs, we are not persuaded that the article, when read as a whole, becomes libelous because of an inaccurate reference to using the blowtorch on the dogs. This is particularly true since, by plaintiff's conduct, she asserts that blowtorching is a safe practice when performed on humans.

* * *

For the above-stated reasons, we conclude that, when reviewing the article and accompanying photographs as a whole, the article was not libelous.

On appeal, plaintiff also argues that the article invaded her privacy by casting her in a false light. * * * As indicated in the above discussion under the theory of defamation, with the exception of certain references to hairdressing dogs, none of the conduct attributed to plaintiff in the article was false. Therefore, it could not place plaintiff in a false light. With reference to the assertions concerning her hairdressing of dogs, we do not believe that a rational trier of fact could conclude that, even if inaccurate, those references are unreasonable or put plaintiff in a position of receiving highly objectionable publicity. The article did not indicate that plaintiff harmed, injured or inflicted pain upon the dogs. Rather, at most, the article inaccurately stated that plaintiff used techniques on the dogs, such as blowtorching, which she also used on humans. * * * Similarly, she cannot have been placed in a false light as being both the hairdresser of dogs and humans inasmuch as the tinting of the canines' fur would constitute hairdressing. Thus, it would not be placing plaintiff in a false light to indicate that she serves both dog and man. * * *

In summary, although the manner in which the present article was written may have singed plaintiff's desire for obtaining favorable coverage of her unique hairdressing methods, we cannot subscribe to the view that it was libelous. We believe that the trial court aptly summarized this case when it stated that "this Court is of the Opinion that the Plaintiff sought publicity and got it." Indeed, it would appear that the root of plaintiff's dissatisfaction with defendants' article is that the publicity plaintiff received was not exactly the publicity she had in mind. * * *

Affirmed. Costs to defendants.

COMMENT

The *Morganroth* case amply demonstrates the enduring difficulties in this area of the law. While the result ratifies the value of colorful, lively writing, reporters and authors should not rejoice. Consider that the plaintiff consented to the interview, then sued nevertheless. Excepting the disputed line about dog hairdressing, all else in the story appears to be an accurate description of what the reporter saw and heard.

When a Massachusetts reporter said that an interview subject was "passionate" and "bitter," the interview subject said the reporter was not entitled to make such an interpretation based on observation, and sued for false light. Characterizing the interpretation as opinion incapable of supporting a false light claim, a trial court judgment for the defendant was upheld.[114] In both this case and *Morganroth*, the major harm is that the claims ever made it to trial, much less to appeal.

Morganroth is like many other false light cases in the way it combines causes of actions and concepts. In addition to the explicit false light and libel claims, one can find familiar strains from intrusion on seclusion and from private facts cases. Shila Morganroth's case seems indistinguishable from Mike Virgil's a decade earlier but for the cause of action. There is even a hint of intellectual property law or appropriation to her complaint.

A major source of false light filing has been *Hustler* magazine's tendency to use photos of people who agreed to pose nude for other photographers—photos that later appeared in *Hustler* without the subjects' consent. The plaintiff's claim typically centers on objections to being

---

114. *Fox Tree v. Harte-Hanks Communications,* 14 Med. L. Rptr. 1090, 501 N.E.2d 519 (Mass. 1986).

allied with *Hustler* in the minds of readers. In general, cases involving the magazine have rejected the argument that one is portrayed in a false light simply by association. A false assertion must be proved, and a claim that appearance in the magazine asserts consent is unpersuasive.[115] Similarly, when footage of paraders at Mardi Gras found its way into a softcore sex film, the paraders could not complain about the company they were unwillingly keeping.[116] And plaintiffs who were photographed wearing negligible costumes at the Halloween Exotic Erotic Ball could not complain when they were later accurately portrayed in printed versions of the photo.[117]

From a journalistic perspective, having a level playing field is critical, and it may be best if false light and libel are eventually merged nationally through a Supreme Court opinion. Application of the *Gertz* public figure/private figure analysis would arguably be narrower than using the public interest test from *Hill*. Having judges and juries decide the news value of subject matter is risky, however.

Applying *Gertz* has advantages. For one, the plaintiff would clearly have the burden of proof on all elements. Presumed fault, damages, and, most likely, falsity would not be allowed. It would also clarify an unsettled issue on the malice standard. *Cantrell* appeared to approve of using common law malice rather than actual malice to allow punitive damages in false light cases, which seems plainly contradictory.

Obviously, false light invasions do not always harm reputation. The dramatizers of Hill's captivity made him a hero, for example. But the differences in the nature of the injury—to mental well-being rather than reputation—only suggest that the action is a bit different, not that it should be easier for plaintiffs to prevail in false light cases.

Until the tensions and ambiguities in false light privacy are resolved, the press can only hope that the actual malice bond that joins the two areas of mass communication law will remain sturdy and that, as a corollary, truth will remain a defense against both libel and false light privacy claims.

PERSONA AS PROPERTY: APPROPRIATION AND THE RIGHT OF PUBLICITY

Foundations of the Causes of Action

Appropriation of someone's name, picture, or distinctive personal characteristics was the first type of invasion of privacy tort to be widely accepted by states. It is committed more frequently by advertising, promotions, and merchandising personnel than by news reporters or photographers. Nevertheless, the tort is of concern for mass media.

At bottom, to prove appropriation, a person needs only to show that she was used in an identifiable fashion for a commercial purpose. The original tort was designed to protect the average person from having her "persona" used by the press. In the earliest common law appropriation case, an insurance company used the plaintiff's name and picture in an advertisement, which also contained a phony endorsement from the plaintiff.[118] The two elements—identification and commercial use—have remained to the present.

As originally put forth, appropriation like other privacy actions aimed to protect well-being and self-esteem. But starting in the 1950s and snowballing since, more and more cases have involved taking the name, likeness, or characteristics of the famous rather than the unknown. From this line of cases has sprung a separate tort, the right of publicity, which seeks to protect the monetary interests of those whose names, likenesses, and attributes are marketable.[119]

It should be obvious that the best defense against either an appropriation action *or* a right of publicity action will be a signed consent or release from the person whose identity is used.

---

115. *Ashby v. Hustler,* 13 Med. L. Rptr. 1416, 802 F.2d 856 (6th Cir. 1986); *Douglass v. Hustler Magazine, Inc.,* 11 Med. L. Rptr. 2264, 769 F.2d 1128 (7th Cir. 1985), *cert. denied* 106 S.Ct. 1489 (1986); *Braun v. Flynt,* 10 Med. L. Rptr. 1497, 726 F.2d 245 (5th Cir. 1984).

116. *Easter Seal Society v. Playboy Enterprises,* 15 Med. L. Rptr. 2384 (La.App. 1988).

117. *Martin v. Penthouse,* 12 Med. L. Rptr. 2059 (Cal.App. 1986).

118. *Pavesich v. New England Life Insurance Co.,* 50 S.E. 68 (Ga. 1905).

119. Halpern, *The Right of Publicity: Commercial Exploitation of the Associative Value of Personality,* 39 Vanderbilt L.Rev. 1199 (1986).

Actually, consent forms are applicable for defense in all of the privacy torts, although they are rarely sought in situations likely to provoke private facts, intrusion, or false light cases. Release forms are especially important where private figures are the subject of news or promotional activities. If minors or those incompetent to sign are involved, their parents or guardians should be asked to sign the release. If the signed release accurately reflects how a name or photo is going to be used, it should be a complete defense. The big difference with celebrities is that payment is normally required to get a release signed. Oral releases may be argued in court, but their validity or strength is dubious; generally they are worth the paper they're not printed on. *Miller v. Madison Square Garden Corp.*, 28 N.Y.S.2d 811 (1941).

Major alterations in a photograph or major changes in treatment will void consent and may open one to false light charges as well. Since passage of time and changed circumstances may nullify the reasons for consent, renewed releases should be sought if a picture or name is to be used for commercial or trade purposes again at a later time, or anytime if the use is for a different reason.

Hustler publisher Larry Flynt prevailed on false light grounds but lost the right of publicity claim filed against him by nascent actress Robyn Douglass. Flynt obtained nude photos of Douglass with another woman from a photographer who offered verbal assurances that Douglass consented. When the time came to offer proof, the consent forms introduced in evidence were not originals, and expert testimony for Douglass disputed the genuiness of her signature. Douglass had originally signed a valid release for the use of some photos of her alone to *Playboy*. The court, however, reduced her damages to the extent that they relied on distress from having appeared naked in *Hustler*, since she has appeared in the media frequently without clothes.[120]

Consent is apparently required of the heirs and assigns of deceased celebrities in many states that have adopted the right of publicity.[121]

There are only two other meaningful defenses against these two actions. The first is newsworthiness, usually claimed on either a common law, a statutory, or a First Amendment basis. If a person is caught up in a newsworthy event or voluntarily steps forward to debate on a public issue, and thereby becomes a public figure to any extent, appropriation or right of publicity claims are weak.[122] The second is similar to the fair use defense in copyright law. When the media make use of identifiable characteristics of the famous for purposes of commentary rather than purely for commercial profit, the use has been found defensible.[123]

Isolated references to television news reporters in the book *The Amityville Horror* did not support their invasion of privacy claims under New York's law since reports of psychic phenomena were matters of public interest.[124] Following allegations of fraud, they also became matters of public debate.

Joe Namath failed in a suit against *Sports Illustrated* when the magazine used a Super Bowl picture of the football hero it had published in 1969 to promote its subscriptions in other publications. The New York statute permits *incidental* use of once newsworthy photographs for trade purposes but not their direct or *collateral* use. The distinction is sometimes a fine one. But then newsworthiness is a broad and compassing defense. Since the photos had been taken during the 1969 Super Bowl while Namath was doing his job, it could also be argued that any interest

---

120. *Douglass v. Hustler,* 11 Med. L. Rptr. 2265, 769 F.2d 1128 (7th Cir. 1985); see also *Shields v. Gross,* 8 Med. L. Rptr. 1928, 451 N.Y.S.2d 419 (N.Y.Sup.Ct., App.Div. 1982) (consent signed by actress Brooke Shields's mother when Shields was ten may be disaffirmed at later age, and use of consented-to photographs made subject of action under New York privacy statute).

121. *Lugosi v. Universal Pictures,* 5 Med. L. Rptr. 2185, 25 Cal.3d 813, 160 Cal.Rptr. 323, 603 P.2d 425 (1979) (right of publicity remains valuable asset to heirs more than twenty years after celebrity's death).

122. *Anderson v. Fisher Broadcasting Cos.,* 11 Med. L. Rptr. 1839, 712 P.2d 803 (Ore. 1986) (appropriation); *Dora v. Frontline Video, Inc.,* 21 Med. L. Rptr. 1398, 18 Cal.Rptr. 790 (Cal.App. 1993).

123. *New Kids on the Block v. News America Publishing, Inc.,* 18 Med. L. Rptr. 1089, 745 F.Supp. 1540 (C.D.Cal. 1990). The lower court's "fair use" decision was based on the First Amendment. When an appellate court affirmed, it did so on the basis of trademark law. *New Kids on the Block v. News America Publishing, Inc.,* 20 Med. L. Rptr. 1468, 971 F.2d 302 (9th Cir. 1992).

124. *Bauman v. Anson,* 6 Med. L. Rptr. 1487 (N.Y.Sup.Ct. 1980).

in the publicity belonged to the New York Jets who, along with the leagues, had *invited* photographers to attend. *Namath v. Sports Illustrated,* 371 N.Y.S.2d 10 (N.Y.Sup.Ct., App.Div. 1975), aff'd 386 N.Y.S.2d 397 (N.Y. 1976).[125]

Note that the cases seldom focus on private figures. As a practical matter, appropriation of an unknown person to promote or sell something would be unusual. As a result, most of the true appropriation cases arise from news rather than from commercial contexts. For example, use of a murder suspect's picture by a gubernatorial candidate was held not to be for trade purposes under New York's statute. The First Amendment value of free political discussion outweighed individual injury.[126] When two infants were photographed at a public downtown festival in Baltimore and their pictures later used in an advertising campaign, the court held that the original news value extended to the later advertising use. In addition, the court said, no reader could see the use as an endorsement, a factor seldom addressed in appropriation cases.[127]

Apparently, not all subsequent uses will be considered news. In 1987, George Mendonsa filed a suit against *Life,* arguing that he was the sailor in Alfred Eisenstadt's famous cover photo from V-J day in 1945. The photo, which is one of the most famous of all time, showed a sailor kissing a nurse in Times Square. The sailor and nurse were never identified. In 1980, *Life* ran a copy of the picture and asked anyone who believed they were the two in the picture to contact the magazine. Mendonsa wrote to say he was the man in the photograph; *Life* never responded. In 1987, the magazine began selling copies of the photograph at $1,600. Although the court seemed dubious about Mendonsa's ability to prove that his image was being used for commercial purposes (the faces were largely unseen), it said he had a right to try convincing a jury. The newsworthiness issue was not addressed.[128] The bigger question is why Mendonsa did not step forward earlier. The photograph has been used for promotion many times.

Although unsettled by the film *Dog Day Afternoon,* the unidentified wife and children of the bank robber in that true story had not themselves been used in promoting the film, and plaintiffs had chosen subsequently to identify themselves.[129] A race car driver whose face and name were not used in a cigarette ad, but whose race car was, prevailed because the famous car was precisely identified with him.[130]

A shoe-on-the-other-foot situation occurred when a WCBS reporter, who had done a story on home insulation, found herself being used to promote a particular product. She brought a $4.5 million damage suit and asked for an injunction against the unauthorized use of the original news film.

"To be effective," said a New York appellate court in permitting the suit to continue, "a news reporter must maintain an image of absolute integrity and impartiality. The commercial exploitation of an impartial report by the use of a video tape or other reproduction of the name or picture of such reporter, for advertising or trade purposes, will not only tarnish the reporter's reputation for objectivity, but will have a chilling effect on reporters now involved in a field of expanding concern—consumer protection."[131]

Appropriation and the right of publicity began to separate in the early 1970s. The first action had always been seen as a personal action, one to redress mental anguish and distress. Appropriation also served to punish advertisers whose use of another's name or likeness falsely implied that that person endorsed a product or service. Justifications for the right of publicity, by contrast, were starting to be based on property law concepts, especially the intellectual property areas of copyright and trademark.

The switch to a property-based rationale for right of publicity cases received momentum

125. See also *Booth v. Curtis Publishing Co.,* 223 N.Y.S.2d 737 (N.Y.Sup.Ct., App.Div. 1962) (actress Shirley Booth's photo, taken on a public beach, used on cover of *Holiday* magazine); *Booth v. Colgate-Palmolive Co.,* 362 F.Supp. 343 (S.D.N.Y. 1973) (Booth's distinctive voice imitated in television commercial).
126. *Davis v. Duryea,* 5 Med. L. Rptr. 1937, 417 N.Y.S.2d 624 (N.Y.Sup.Ct. 1979).
127. *Lawrence v. A. S. Abell Co.,* 10 Med. L. Rptr. 2001, 475 A.2d 448 (Md.App. 1984).

128. *Mendonsa v. Time, Inc.,* 15 Med. L. Rptr. 1017, 678 F.Supp. 967 (D.R.I. 1988).
129. *Wojtowicz v. Delacorte Press,* 2 Med. L. Rptr. 2023, 395 N.Y.S.2d 205 (N.Y.Sup.Ct., App.Div. 1977), *aff'd* 3 Med. L. Rptr. 1992, 403 N.Y.S.2d 218 (N.Y. 1978).
130. *Motschenbacher v. R. J. Reynolds Tobacco Co.,* 498 F.2d 821 (9th Cir. 1974).
131. *Reilly v. Rapperswill Corp.,* 377 N.Y.S.2d 488 (1975).

when an entertainer explicitly claimed that a television station had taken his property by broadcasting film from his performance. The case also addressed connections between newsworthiness and consent. During the performance, Hugo Zacchini, reportedly one of the last human cannonballs in the nation, would shoot himself from a cannon into a net 200 feet away. It was a dramatic act, lasting about fifteen seconds.

Contending that the station had appropriated his professional property, Zacchini sued for $25,000. A trial court granted the station summary judgment. An appeals court reversed. The Ohio Supreme Court then reversed again. It first said that plaintiff's claim should be based on a right of publicity, not on appropriation, because the two serve different interests. Zacchini lost in any event because the Ohio court, apparently relying on *Time, Inc. v. Hill,* said a "legitimate public interest test" applied. On a third appeal, the U.S. Supreme Court again reversed. The Court held that the state might provide a newsworthiness defense on state law grounds but was not required to by the First Amendment. The Court also held that the right of publicity did not conflict with the First Amendment. Zacchini had won the battle.

Zacchini v. Scripps-Howard

2 MED. L. RPTR. 2089, 433 U.S. 562, 97 S.CT. 2849, 53 L.ED.2D 965 (1977).

Justice WHITE delivered the opinion of the Court.

* * *

The Ohio Supreme Court held that respondent is constitutionally privileged to include in its newscasts matters of public interest that would otherwise be protected by the right of publicity, absent an intent to injure or to appropriate for some nonprivileged purpose. If under this standard respondent had merely reported that petitioner was performing at the fair and described or commented on his act, with or without showing his picture on television, we would have a very different case. But petitioner is not contending that his appearance at the fair and his performance could not be reported by the press as newsworthy items. His complaint is that respondent filmed his entire act and displayed that film

on television for the public to see and enjoy. This, he claimed, was an appropriation of his professional property. The Ohio Supreme Court agreed that petitioner had a "right of publicity" that gave him "personal control over the commercial display and exploitation of his personality and the exercise of his talents." * * *

The Ohio Supreme Court nevertheless held that the challenged invasion was privileged, saying that the press "must be accorded broad latitude in its choice of how much it presents of each story or incident, and of the emphasis to be given to such presentation." * * * Under this view, respondent was thus constitutionally free to film and display petitioner's entire act.

The Ohio Supreme Court relied heavily on *Time, Inc. v. Hill,* but that case does not mandate a media privilege to televise a performer's entire act without his consent. * * *

Time, Inc. v. Hill, which was hotly contested and decided by a divided court, involved an entirely different tort than the "right of publicity" recognized by the Ohio Supreme Court. * * * It is also abundantly clear that *Time, Inc. v. Hill* did not involve a performer, a person with a name having commercial value, or any claim to a "right of publicity." * * *

The differences between these two torts are important. First, the State's interests in providing a cause of action in each instance are different. "The interest protected" in permitting recovery for placing the plaintiff in a false light "is clearly that of reputation, with the same overtones of mental distress as in defamation." Prosser, 48 Calif.L.Rev., at 400. By contrast, the State's interest in permitting a "right of publicity" is in protecting the proprietary interest of the individual in his act in part to encourage such entertainment. As we later note, the State's interest is closely analogous to the goals of patent and copyright law, focusing on the right of the individual to reap the reward of his endeavors and having little to do with protecting feelings or reputation. Second, the two torts differ in the degree to which they intrude on dissemination of information to the public. In "false light" cases the only way to protect the interests involved is to attempt to minimize publication of the damaging matter, while in "right of publicity" cases the only question is who gets to do the publishing. An entertainer such as petitioner usually has no objection to the widespread publication of his act as long as he gets the commercial benefit of such publication.

* * *

It is evident, and there is no claim here to the contrary, that petitioner's state-law right of publicity would not serve to prevent respondent from reporting the newsworthy facts about petitioner's act. Wherever the line in particular situations is to be drawn between media reports that are protected and those that are not, we are quite sure that the First and Fourteenth Amendments do not immunize the media when they broadcast a performer's entire act without his consent. The Constitution no more prevents a State from requiring respondent to compensate petitioner for broadcasting his act on television than it would privilege respondent to film and broadcast a copyrighted dramatic work without liability to the copyright owner. * * *

The broadcast of a film of petitioner's entire act poses a substantial threat to the economic value of that performance. As the Ohio court recognized, this act is the product of petitioner's own talents and energy, the end result of much time, effort and expense. Much of its economic value lies in the "right of exclusive control over the publicity given to his performance"; if the public can see the act for free on television, they will be less willing to pay to see it at the fair. The effect of a public broadcast of the performance is similar to preventing petitioner from charging an admission fee.

"The rationale for [protecting the right of publicity] is the straight-forward one of preventing unjust enrichment by the theft of good will. No social purpose is served by having the defendant get for free some aspect of the plaintiff that would have market value and for which he would normally pay." * * *

Of course, Ohio's decision to protect petitioner's right of publicity here rests on more than a desire to compensate the performer for the time and effort invested in his act; the protection provides an economic incentive for him to make the investment required to produce a performance of interest to the public. This same consideration underlies the patent and copyright laws long enforced by this Court.

* * *

These laws perhaps regard the "reward to the owner [as] a secondary consideration," *United*

States v. Paramount Pictures, 334 U.S. 131, 158 (1948), but they were "intended definitely to grant valuable, enforceable rights" in order to afford greater encouragement to the production of works of benefit to the public. * * *

Petitioner does not seek to enjoin the broadcast of his performance; he simply wants to be paid for it. Nor do we think that a state-law damages remedy against respondent would represent a species of liability without fault contrary to the letter or spirit of *Gertz.* Respondent knew exactly that petitioner objected to televising his act, but nevertheless displayed the entire film.

We conclude that although the State of Ohio may as a matter of its own law privilege the press in the circumstances of this case, the First and Fourteenth Amendments do not require it to do so.

Reversed.

Mr. Justice POWELL, with whom Mr. Justice BRENNAN and Mr. Justice MARSHALL join, dissenting.

Disclaiming any attempt to do more than decide the narrow case before us, the Court reverses the decision of the Supreme Court of Ohio based on repeated incantation of a single formula: "a performer's entire act." * * * I do not view respondent's action as comparable to unauthorized commercial broadcasts of sporting events, theatrical performances, and the like where the broadcaster keeps the profits. There is no suggestion here that respondent made any such use of the film. Instead, it simply reported on what petitioner concedes to be a newsworthy event, in a way hardly surprising for a television station—by means of film coverage. The report was part of an ordinary daily news program, consuming a total of 15 seconds. It is a routine example of the press fulfilling the informing function so vital to our system.

* * *

In my view the First Amendment commands a different analytical starting point from the one selected by the Court. Rather than begin with a quantitative analysis of the performer's behavior—is this or is this not his entire act?—we should direct initial attention to the actions of the news media: what use did the station make of the film footage? When a film is used, as here, for a routine portion of a regular news program, I would hold that the First Amendment protects the station from a "right of publicity" or "appropriation" suit, absent a strong showing by the plaintiff that the news broadcast was a subterfuge or cover for private or commercial exploitation.

* * *

COMMENT

The split between White and Powell is also the split that has pervaded right of publicity analysis generally. Powell focuses on the news or First Amendment value of the use to which the information is put, while White focuses on the economic value of the thing taken. Since there has been no other case in which a celebrity's entire act has been at issue, the viability of the "entire act" standard has not been tested.

One argument for a First Amendment "fair use" defense is based on the public's investment in celebrities. Since the value of their personae stems from the public, it is argued, the rights should be shared; placing all rights with the celebrity puts full control over information of general public interest in just a few hands. And it is argued that, after death, a celebrity's persona should fall into the public domain on the grounds that the celebrity has reaped the rewards of fame.[132] Most celebrities, after all, are able to protect heirs through contracts without relying on the right of publicity. In addition, copyright endures after death.

Note that the Court's opinions in *Zacchini* dealt with the right of publicity, not appropriation, in line with Ohio's view that the two torts serve different interests. The Court finds the right of publicity more akin to copyright, an intellectual property issue, than to privacy. Later right of publicity cases draw upon many related areas of law: copyright, trademark, service mark, unfair competition, and misappropriation.[133] As a result, publicity cases often become extremely complicated.

The Court never reached the issue of harm or damages, but it is difficult to conceive of how the news story actually cost Zacchini anything. Did the station gain extra viewers or advertisers? Such evidence would seem extremely relevant to proving that there was a commercial as opposed to news purpose. Might not the fifteen-second film be considered "free" advertising for Zacchini? The station in fact urged viewers that they should see the act in person. It is true that the public will be less willing to pay to see Zacchini after seeing the act for nothing? Certainly, general admission to the fair promised much more than just the human cannonball show.

In the years since *Zacchini*, many states have recognized a right of publicity, either on a common law basis or by statute. States with statutes include California, Florida, Kentucky, Massachusetts, Nebraska, New York, Oklahoma, Rhode Island, Tennessee, Utah, Virginia, and Wisconsin.[134]

Many actions that appear indistinguishable from right of publicity cases have been brought based upon New York's appropriation statute. Nevertheless, New York courts have repeatedly said the common law right of publicity is not recognized.[135] The New York statute has been influential in right of publicity analysis, however, due to New York's role as a media center.

On common law grounds, apparently every state that has had occasion to consider the right has recognized it. The general rule for establishing the existence of publicity rights in most states is twofold: the celebrity's name or likeness must have some value, and the celebrity must have exploited the right, although the ability to exploit the right may be sufficient.[136] Some states, such as California, treat the right as nearly identical to copyright. And like copyright it is descendible, even salable, after death.

In Tennessee, the right of publicity is viewed exclusively as a matter of property law, assignable and descendible in nature. And, much like a trademark, it retains its value so long as it is used and continues to have meaning to consumers. In *State ex rel. Presley v. Crowell*, 14 Med. L. Rptr.

---

132. See generally Goldman, *Elvis Is Alive, But He Shouldn't Be: The Right of Publicity Revisited,* 1992 B.Y.U. L.Rev. 597.

133. Simon, *Right of Publicity Reified: Fame as Business Asset,* 30 New York Law School L.Rev. 699 (1985).

134. Houdek, *Researching the Right of Publicity: A Revised and Comprehensive Bibliography of Law-Related Materials,* 16 Hastings Comm/Ent L.J. 385 (1994).

135. *Groden v. Random House, Inc.,* 23 Med. L. Rptr. 2203, 61 F.3d 1045 (2d Cir. 1995).

136. *Martin Luther King, Jr., Center for Social Change, Inc. v. American Heritage Products, Inc.,* 8 Med. L. Rptr. 2377, 296 S.E.2d 697 (Ga. 1982); *Grant v. Esquire, Inc.,* 367 F.Supp. 876 (S.D.N.Y. 1973) (actor Cary Grant objected to use of his likeness in sweater promotion largely because he never sold the highly marketable rights to his name or likeness).

1043, 733 S.W.2d 89 (Tenn.App. 1987), one of a large number of cases involving alleged misuses of the identity and characteristics of Elvis Presley, the state court gave the right of publicity a broad reading:

* * *

The concept of the right of property is multifaceted. It has been described as a bundle of rights or legally protected interests. These rights or interests include: (1) the right of possession, enjoyment and use; (2) the unrestricted right of disposition; and (3) the power of testimonial disposition. * * * Our courts have recognized that a person's "business," a corporate name, a trade name and the good will of a business are species of intangible personal property. * * * Tennessee's common law thus embodies an expansive view of property. Unquestionably, a celebrity's right of publicity has value. It can be possessed and used. It can be assigned, and it can be the subject of a contract. Thus, there is ample basis for this Court to conclude that it is a species of intangible personal property. * * * What remains to be decided by the courts in Tennessee is whether a celebrity's right of publicity is descendible at death under Tennessee law. * * * The only reported opinion holding that Tennessee law does not recognize a *postmortem* right of publicity is *Memphis Development Foundation v. Factors, Etc., Inc.* * * * We have carefully reviewed this opinion and have determined that it is based upon an incorrect construction of Tennessee law and is inconsistent with the better reasoned decisions in this field.

The United States Court of Appeals for the Sixth Circuit appears to believe that there is something inherently wrong with recognizing that the right of publicity is descendible. * * * We do not share this subjective policy bias. Like the Supreme Court of Georgia, we recognize that the "trend since the early common law has been to recognize survivability, notwithstanding the legal problems which may thereby arise." * * *

The court expressly noted that, as a music business center, the state had a strong policy interest in protecting celebrities. The court also listed six reasons to recognize descendability, all drawn from comparisons to real property, contract law, or intellectual property.

The court also traced the history of litigation involving the Presley estate, citing seven separate court opinions involving Elvis's right of publicity. It is an understatement to say that the estate zealously guards its right of publicity.

Once the property rights approach is accepted, descendability and transferability naturally follow. Unsettling to the media is that the courts give no weight or mention to public uses of the persona of Elvis Presley. One court found that an Elvis impersonator violated the "King's" right of publicity and service mark by presenting the "Big El Show." By all accounts the excellent Elvis impersonator, Rob Russen, may have been too good. Under the right of publicity, the court said, only Elvis's estate has the right to commission live imitations. But of course the estate could not provide the real thing. The argument that Russen was somehow in competition with the estate is hard to swallow since no reasonable audience member could be confused and think he *was* Elvis. In addition, the court shunted aside Russen's First Amendment arguments, saying that the show was not *informative*, only entertaining. While the "Big El Show" might have some value, this court concluded that some values are more protected than others.[137]

Much as in libel, right of publicity standards vary widely from state to state. But generally, all require a "taking" of a celebrity's persona for commercial gain. In some cases there is no commercial gain because the picture or attribute had already been used with consent. When a magazine published a photo from a movie of actress Ann-Margret partially clothed, she was unable to collect both because she is a public figure and because the rights belonged to the film owners. The court in addition seemed puzzled that she'd complained after millions had seen the movie.[138] Clint Eastwood established his right to sue for the *National Enquirer*'s nondefamatory use of his name and photo on the front page and in television advertising at common law, but to recover under the California statute, he would have to prove actual malice. The *Enquirer*'s claim of newsworthiness failed. The court said the statute had no news privilege but tracked libel law instead. The *Enquirer*'s argument that Eastwood was not portrayed as endorsing the publication was almost summarily dismissed.[139] Is this the

---

137. *Estate of Presley v. Russen,* 513 F.Supp. 1339 (D.N.J. 1981).
138. *Ann-Margret v. High Society Magazine,* 6 Med. L. Rptr. 1774, 498 F.Supp. 401 (S.D.N.Y. 1980).
139. *Eastwood v. Superior Court,* 10 Med. L. Rptr. 1073, 198 Cal.Rptr. 342 (Cal.App. 1983).

kind of fact pattern the right of publicity was meant to apply to? Is Eastwood trying to protect the commercial value of his name or his reputation? Can the two be separated?

Imitation and Satire

Elvis impersonators are not the only ones who have found themselves defendants in right of publicity cases. Recently, advertising agencies and their clients have been defending themselves, too. In 1988, the Circuit Court of Appeals for the Ninth Circuit, applying California law, determined that, "when a distinctive voice of a professional singer is widely known and is deliberately imitated in order to sell a product, the sellers have appropriated what is not theirs and have committed a tort in California." *Midler v. Ford Motor Co.*, 15 Med. L. Rptr. 1620, 849 F.2d 460 (9th Cir. 1988). The case arose as part of a television advertising campaign developed by the Young and Rubicam agency for Ford, Lincoln, and Mercury cars. To lure "yuppies" who had reached adulthood in the early 1970s, the campaign used familiar popular songs. Usually, the original artists were contracted but, when not, "sound alikes" were used.

An edited version of the song "Do You Want to Dance?" from Bette Midler's first album was suggested to her and her agent. The agent told Young and Rubicam no. Midler was presumptively disinclined toward endorsements. For a sound alike, the agency contracted Uta Hedwig, who had been a member of Midler's backup singers, the Harlettes, for ten years. The copy was very close; people who heard the commercial thought it was Midler's voice. Neither Midler's name nor her photo was used in the ad.

Although the court recognized that the right of publicity applied to voice imitation, it also endorsed a First Amendment defense when the purpose is "informative or cultural." If Hedwig had performed the imitation on stage or as part of a parody of Midler, the court apparently would have immunized the use. But the intent, purpose, and use were obviously solely commercial here.

The *Midler* case was followed by a second major imitation case a few years later. This case was different in several ways, but the basic facts were similar. Singer-actor Tom Waits sued snack food maker Frito-Lay and its advertising agency

after a sound alike was used in a radio commercial for SalsaRio Doritos. The most notable difference from the *Midler* case was Wait's well-known refusal to do commercial endorsements because he believes they detract from an artist's integrity. Knowing he would refuse, the advertising agency looked for a sound alike without even approaching Waits. Two other differences were also important. Waits asked for punitive damages, arguing that the interference was "willful" and "despicable." A final important difference was that Waits also claimed false endorsement under the federal Lanham Act's section 43, which provides a cause of action against unfair competition. Section 43 was amended shortly after the *Waits* case was filed to formally include a provision barring misrepresentation in advertising.[140]

A jury awarded Waits $375,000 in compensatory damages, $100,000 in Lanham Act damages, attorney fees under the Lanham Act, and $2 million in punitive damages. Frito-Lay appealed.

Waits v. Frito-Lay, Inc.
20 MED. L. RPTR. 1585, 978 F.2D 1093 (9TH CIR. 1992).

BOOCHEVER, J.:

* * *

The defendants argued at trial that although they had consciously copied Tom Waits' style in creating the Doritos commercial, they had not deliberately imitated his voice. They accordingly proposed a jury instruction which distinguished in detail between voice, which is protected under *Midler,* and style, which is not. The district court rejected this instruction. Instead, its instructions on voice misappropriation track closely the elements of the tort as they are formulated in *Midler.* The court's instruction directed the jury to decide whether Waits' voice is distinctive, whether his voice is widely known, and whether the defendants had deliberately imitated his voice.

The defendants argue that their proposed "style" instruction was crucial because of the deliberate stylistic similarities between the Doritos

---

140. 15 U.S.C. § 1125(a)(1982 and Supp. 1985); see generally Leatherbury, *Media Law: Explosion of Lanham Act Cases,* 14 Communications Lawyer 1, 16–18 (Spring 1996).

commercial and "Step Right Up" and because in instructing the jury on Waits' Lanham Act claim, the court told the jury that it could consider Waits' singing style, songwriting style, and manner of presentation. In failing to give their proposed instruction, the defendants contend, the court misled the jury into believing that it could also consider the defendants' admitted imitation of Waits' style in determining liability for voice misappropriation.

We disagree because, read as a whole, the instructions were not misleading. In charging the jury, the court repeatedly noted that two claims were presented for determination and gave separate instructions on each claim. The court's voice misappropriation instructions limited the jury's consideration to voice, and in no way implied that it could consider style. Indeed, in addressing the jury in closing argument, Waits' attorney agreed with the defendants that style was not protected. Moreover, the court included an additional instruction that effectively narrowed the jury's focus to Waits' voice and indicated that style imitation alone was insufficient for tort liability. For the defendants to be liable for voice misappropriation, the court stated, the imitation had to be so good that "people who were familiar with plaintiff's voice who heard the commercial *believed plaintiff performed it.* In this connection it is not enough that they were reminded of plaintiff or thought the singer sounded like plaintiff. . . ." (Emphasis added.)

* * *

The defendants next argue that the court's instruction concerning the meaning of "distinctive" was an unfair and inaccurate statement of the law because it confuses the "distinctiveness" of a voice with its identifiability or recognizability. The instruction given states in part: "A voice is distinctive if it is distinguishable from the voices of other singers . . . if it has particular qualities or characteristics that identify it with a particular singer." At trial the defendants' experts testified that identifiability depends, not on distinctiveness, but on the listener's expectations; that distinctiveness and recognizability are not the same thing; and that recognizability is enhanced by style similarity. The defendants argue that these theories were inadequately dealt with by the court's instruction and that because *anyone's* voice is identifiable by someone, it was

error for the court not to make clear the difference between distinctiveness and identifiability. We disagree.

The defendants' technical argument that distinctiveness is a separate concept from identifiability, while supported by their experts' testimony, has no basis in law. Identifiability is properly considered in evaluating distinctiveness, for it is a central element of a right of publicity claim. Our *Midler* holding is premised on the fact that a person is as identifiable by voice as by any other indicia of identity previously recognized as protectable. Although we did not define "distinctiveness" in *Midler,* we stated: "A voice is as *distinctive* and personal as a face. The human voice is one of the most palpable ways *identity is manifested.*"

* * *

The defendants next object to the district court's instruction concerning the element of "widely known" on the ground that it was too vague to guide the jury in making a factual determination of the issue. The court instructed the jury: "A professional singer's voice is widely known if it is known to a *large number* of people throughout a *relatively large* geographic area." (Emphasis added.) The court rejected an instruction proposed by the defendants, which reflected their contention at trial that Tom Waits is a singer known only to music insiders and to a small but loyal group of fans: "A singer is not widely known if he is only recognized by his own fans, or fans of a particular sort of music, or a small segment of the population."

The legal underpinnings of this proposed instruction are questionable. The defendants assert that because Waits has not achieved the level of celebrity Bette Midler has, he is not well known under the *Midler* standard. We reject this crabbed interpretation of *Midler.* The defendants' proposed instruction would have excluded from legal protection the voices of many popular singers who fall short of superstardom. "Well known" is a relative term, and differences in the extent of celebrity are adequately reflected in the amount of damages recoverable.

* * *

The defendants argue that in right of publicity actions, only damages to compensate for economic injury are available. We disagree. Although the injury stemming from violation of the right of publicity "may be largely, or even wholly, of an economic or material nature," we have recognized that "it is quite possible that the appropriation of the identity of a celebrity may induce humiliation, embarrassment, and mental distress." *Motschenbacher*, 498 F.2d at 824 & n.11. Contrary to the defendants' assertions, *Midler* neither discussed nor limited the damages recoverable in a voice misappropriation action. *Midler* makes reference to the market value of Midler's voice solely to support its conclusion that her voice has economic value and, therefore, is a protectable property right. *See* 849 F.2d at 463.

In assessing the propriety of mental distress damages, our focus is properly directed to the nature of the infringement and its embarrassing impact on the plaintiff.

* * *

The defendants argue, however, that merely taking offense is an insufficient basis for awarding mental distress damages, and that under California law the evidence was insufficient to support the award. In California, mental distress damages may be recovered for "shame, humiliation, embarrassment, [and] anger." Waits testified that when he heard the Doritos commercial, "this corn chip sermon," he was shocked and very angry. These feelings "grew and grew over a period of a couple of days" because of his strong public opposition to doing commercials. Waits testified, "[I]t embarrassed me. I had to call all my friends, that if they hear this thing, please be informed this is not me. I was on the phone for days. I also had people calling me saying, Gee, Tom, I heard the new Doritos ad." Added to this evidence of Waits' shock, anger, and embarrassment is the strong inference that, because of his outspoken public stance against doing commercial endorsements, the Doritos commercial humiliated Waits by making him an apparent hypocrite. This evidence was sufficient both to allow the jury to consider mental distress damages and to support their eventual award.

* * *

We have no doubt, in light of general tort liability principles, that where the misappropriation of identity causes injury to reputation, compensation for such injury is appropriate. See Cal. Civ. Code § 3333 (West 1970) (available damages are those "which will compensate for all of the detri-

ment" caused by defendant's tortious conduct). Reputational damages, moreover, have been awarded in the right of publicity cases. The central issue is not whether these damages were available, but whether the evidence was sufficient to establish injury to Waits' reputation. As we noted above, the jury could have inferred from the evidence that the commercial created a public impression that Waits was a hypocrite for endorsing Doritos. Moreover, it also could have inferred damage to his artistic reputation, for Waits had testified that "part of my character and personality and image that I have cultivated is that I do not endorse products." Finally, from the testimony of Waits' expert witness, the jury could have inferred that if Waits ever wanted to do a commercial in the future, the fee he could command would be lowered by $50,000 to $150,000 because of the Doritos commercial.

* * *

In California, exemplary or punitive damages are available "where it is proven by clear and convincing evidence that the defendant has been guilty of oppression, fraud, or malice." Cal. Civ. Code § 3294(a) (West Supp. 1992). The statute defines "malice" in pertinent part as "despicable conduct which is carried on by the defendant with a *willful and conscious disregard of the rights* or safety of others." *Id.* § 3294(c)(1) (emphasis added). The defendants contend that because *Midler* was so recently decided and so imprecise in the scope of its holding, they could not have been aware of the rights they were infringing upon in broadcasting the commercial. Thus, they reason, their conduct was not in "conscious disregard" of Waits' property right in his voice.

* * *

We believe that, viewed most favorably to Waits, this evidence was adequate to support a finding of high probability that Tracy-Locke and Frito-Lay acted with malice. Despicability reflects a moral judgment, "conscious disregard" a state of mind. A rational jury could have found the defendants' conduct despicable because they knowingly impugned Waits' integrity in the public eye. A rational jury also could have found that the defendants, in spite of their awareness of Waits' legal right to control the commercial use of his voice, acted in conscious disregard of that right by broadcasting the commercial. We therefore affirm the award of punitive damages.

* * *

At the time of the broadcast of the Doritos commercial, section 43(a) provided in pertinent part:

Any person who shall affix, apply, or annex, or use in connection with any goods or services . . . a false designation of origin, or any false designation or representation . . . shall be liable to a civil action . . . by any person who believes that he is or is likely to be damaged by the use of any such false designation or representation.

15 U.S.C. § 1125 note (Amendments) (1988). Courts in other jurisdictions have interpreted this language as authorizing claims for false endorsement.

* * *

The defendants next argue that Waits' false endorsement claim must fail on its merits because the Doritos commercial "did not represent that . . . Waits' sponsored or endorsed their product." We disagree. The court correctly instructed the jury that in considering Waits' Lanham Act claim, it must determine whether "ordinary consumers . . . would be confused as to whether Tom Waits sang on the commercial . . . and whether he sponsors or endorses SalsaRio Doritos." The jury was told that in making this determination, it should consider the totality of the evidence, including the distinctiveness of Waits' voice and style, the evidence of actual confusion as to whether Waits actually sang on the commercial, and the defendants' intent to imitate Waits' voice.

* * *

At trial, the jury listened to numerous Tom Waits recordings, and to a recording of the Doritos commercial in which the Tom Waits impersonator delivered this "hip" endorsement of SalsaRio Doritos: "It's buffo, boffo, bravo, gun-ho, tally-ho, but never mellow . . . try 'em, buy 'em, get 'em, got 'em." The jury also heard evidence, relevant to the likelihood of consumer confusion, that the Doritos commercial was targeted to an audience which overlapped with Waits' audience, males between the ages of 18 to 35 who listened to the radio. Finally, there was evidence of actual consumer confusion: the testimony of numerous witnesses that they actually believed it was Tom Waits singing the words of endorsement. This evidence was sufficient to support the jury's finding that consumers were likely to be misled by the commercial into believing that Waits endorsed SalsaRio Doritos.

* * *

AFFIRMED in part and VACATED in part.

COMMENT

The real gist of Waits's complaint was that the use of his voice in advertising diminished his long-standing and hard-earned reputation as an artist who made no compromises for purely commercial reasons. In that regard, the case is similar to a number of others where the celebrities based their right of publicity argument precisely on the fact that the value of their identity was even higher because it had never been sold or loaned.[141]

The *Waits* case should strike fear into the hearts of advertisers considering the use of a celebrity's attributes without consent. Some have argued that the court's opinion goes too far and overprotects celebrities who have plenty of alternative ways to protect themselves.[142]

The question of what constitutes a celebrity's attribute was at the heart of a suit game show co-host Vanna White brought against Samsung Electronics. After trying to persuade White to appear in a print advertising campaign with the durability of its products as the theme, Samsung and its ad agency instead used a robot dressed to closely resemble White, posed near a game board the same as the one used on the program *Wheel of Fortune*. The phrase "Longest-running game show, 2012 A.D." accompanied the picture. A typical ad in the humorous series featured a ludicrous long-term prediction and a depiction of an old Samsung product still working. White was not amused and sued. *White v. Samsung Electronics, Inc.*, 20 Med. L. Rptr. 1457, 971 F.2d 1395 (9th Cir.), *cert. denied* 113 S.Ct. 2443 (1992).

The Circuit Court of Appeals for the Ninth Circuit reversed a trial decision granting sum-

---

141. Bloom, *Preventing the Misappropriation of Identity: Beyond the "Right of Publicity,"* 13 Hastings Comm/Ent L.J. 489 (1991).

142. Note, Lurie, Waits v. Frito-Lay: *The Song Remains the Same,* 13 Cardozo Arts & Entertainment L.J. 187 (1994); Note, Weiler, *The Right of Publicity Gone Wrong: A Case for Privileged Appropriation of Identity,* 13 Cardozo Arts & Entertainment L.J. 223 (1994).

mary judgment for the defendants and sent the case back to trial on right of publicity grounds. Regarding celebrity attributes and consumer identification, the court said:

> Viewed separately, the individual aspects of the advertisement in the present case say little. Viewed together, they leave little doubt about the celebrity the ad is meant to depict. . . . Indeed, defendants themselves referred to their ad as the "Vanna White" ad. We are not surprised.

The defendants also posed a parody defense, arguing in effect that the ad poked fun at the automaton-like nature of White and her duties on *Wheel of Fortune*. The court rejected the parody defense, indicating that it would be available for traditional news, commentary, and entertainment, but not for spoofs that appear in commercial advertising. When Samsung sought an en banc rehearing, which was rejected, the humor issue galvanized Circuit Judge Alex Kozinski, who wrote an unusually sharp dissent:

> The panel's opinion is a classic case of overprotection. Concerned about what it sees as a wrong done to Vanna White, the panel majority erects a property right of remarkable and dangerous breadth: Under the majority's opinion, it's now a tort for advertisers to *remind* the public of a celebrity. . . . It raises serious First Amendment problems. It's bad law, and it deserves a long, hard second look. * * *
>
> Parody, humor, irreverence are all vital components of the marketplace of ideas. The last thing we need, the last thing the First Amendment will tolerate, is a law that lets public figures keep people from mocking them. . . .
>
> The majority dismisses the First Amendment issue out of hand because Samsung's ad was commercial speech. . . . Commercial speech is a significant, valuable part of our national discourse. *White v. Samsung Electronics America, Inc.*, 21 Med. L. Rptr. 1330, 989 F.2d 1512 (9th Cir. 1993).

The similarity between intellectual property law and the right of publicity is shown by the large number of cases in which plaintiffs raise a second claim that the defendant violated a trademark or service mark, or engaged in unfair competition prohibited by the Lanham Act. One such case arose when Johnny Carson's "trademark" introduction was used by a portable toilet company. The Sixth Circuit's opinion addressed both issues.

Carson v. Here's Johnny Portable Toilets, Inc.

9 MED. L. RPTR. 1153, 698 F.2D 831 (6TH CIR. 1983).

BROWN, J.:

This case involves claims of unfair competition and invasion of the right of privacy and the right of publicity arising from appellee's adoption of a phrase generally associated with a popular entertainer.

Appellant, John W. Carson (Carson), is the host and star of "The Tonight Show," a well-known television program broadcast five nights a week by the National Broadcasting Company. Carson also appears as an entertainer in night clubs and theaters around the country. From the time he began hosting "The Tonight Show" in 1962, he has been introduced on the show each night with the phrase "Here's Johnny." * * * The phrase "Here's Johnny" is generally associated with Carson by a substantial segment of the television viewing public. In 1967, Carson first authorized use of this phrase by a chain of restaurants called "Here's Johnny Restaurants." [The court recounts other Carson licensing ventures.]

Appellee, Here's Johnny Portable Toilets, Inc., is a Michigan corporation engaged in the business of renting and selling "Here's Johnny" portable toilets. Appellee's founder was aware at the time he formed the corporation that "Here's Johnny" was the introductory slogan for Carson on "The Tonight Show." He indicated that he coupled the phrase with a second one, "The World's Foremost Commodian," to make "a good play on a phrase."

Shortly after appellee went into business in 1976, appellants brought this action alleging unfair competition, trademark infringement under federal and state law, and invasion of privacy and publicity rights. They sought damages and an injunction prohibiting appellee's further use of the phrase "Here's Johnny" as a corporate name or in connection with the sale or rental of its portable toilets.

The [trial] court ordered the dismissal of the appellants' complaint. On the unfair competition claim, the court concluded that the appellants had failed to satisfy the "likelihood of confusion" test. On the right of privacy and right of publicity theories, the court held that these rights extend only to a "name or likeness," and "Here's Johnny" did not qualify.

* * *

Appellants' first claim alleges unfair competition from appellee's business activities in violation of § 43(a) of the Lanham Act, 15 U.S.C. § 1125(a) (1976), and of Michigan common law. The district court correctly noted that the test for equitable relief under both § 43(a) and Michigan common law is the "likelihood of confusion" standard.

* * *

In *Frisch's Restaurants* we approved the balancing of several factors in determining whether a likelihood of confusion exists among consumers of goods involved in a § 43(a) action. In that case we examined eight factors:

1. strength of the plaintiff's mark;
2. relatedness of the goods;
3. similarity of the marks;
4. evidence of actual confusion;
5. marketing channels used;
6. likely degree of purchaser care;
7. defendant's intent in selecting the mark;
8. likelihood of expansion of the product lines.

The district court first found that "Here's Johnny" was not such a strong mark that its use for other goods should be entirely foreclosed. 498 F.Supp. at 74. Although the appellee had intended to capitalize on the phrase popularized by Carson, the court concluded that appellee had not intended to deceive the public into believing Carson was connected with the product. *Id.* at 75. The court noted that there was little evidence of actual confusion and no evidence that appellee's use of the phrase had damaged appellants. For these reasons, the court determined that appellee's use of the phrase "Here's Johnny" did not present a likelihood of confusion, mistake, or deception. *Id.* at 75–77.

Our review of the record indicates that none of the district court's findings is clearly erroneous. Moreover, on the basis of these findings, we agree with the district court that the appellants have failed to establish a likelihood of confusion. The general concept underlying the likelihood of confusion is that the public believe that "the mark's owner *sponsored or otherwise approved* the use of the trademark."

* * *

The facts as found by the district court do not implicate such likelihood of confusion, and we affirm the district court on this issue.

The appellants also claim that the appellee's use of the phrase "Here's Johnny" violates the common law right of privacy and right of publicity. The confusion in this area of the law requires a brief analysis of the relationship between these two rights.

* * *

The district court dismissed appellants' claim based on the right of publicity because appellee does not use Carson's name or likeness. 498 F.Supp. at 77. It held that it "would not be prudent to allow recovery for a right of publicity claim which does not more specifically identify Johnny Carson." 498 F.Supp. at 78. We believe that, on the contrary, the district court's concept of the right of publicity is too narrow. The right of publicity, as we have stated, is that a celebrity has a protected pecuniary interest in the commercial exploitation of his identity. If the celebrity's identity is commercially exploited, there has been an invasion of his right whether or not his "name or likeness" is used. Carson's identity may be exploited even if his name, John W. Carson, or his picture is not used.

* * *

In *Ali v. Playgirl, Inc.,* 447 F.Supp. 723 (S.D.N.Y. 1978), Muhammad Ali, former heavyweight champion, sued Playgirl magazine under the New York "right of privacy" statute and also alleged a violation of his common law right of publicity. The magazine published a drawing of a nude, black male sitting on a stool in a corner of a boxing ring with hands taped and arms outstretched on the ropes. The district court concluded that Ali's right of publicity was invaded because the drawing was captioned "Mystery man." The district court found that the identification of Ali was made certain because of an accompanying verse that identified the figure as "The Greatest." The district court took judicial notice of the fact that "Ali has regularly claimed that appellation for himself." *Id.* at 727.

In *Hirsch v. S. C. Johnson & Son, Inc.,* 90 Wis.2d 379, 280 N.W.2d 129 (1979), the court held that the use by defendant of the name "Crazylegs" on a shaving gel for women violated plaintiff's right of publicity. Plaintiff, Elroy Hirsch, a famous football player, had been known by this nickname. * * *

In this case, Earl Braxton, president and owner of Here's Johnny Portable Toilets, Inc., admitted that he knew that the phrase "Here's Johnny" had been used for years to introduce Carson. Moreover, in the opening statement in the district court, appellee's counsel stated:

> Now, we've stipulated in this case that the public tends to associate the words "Johnny Carson," the words "Here's Johnny" with plaintiff, John Carson and, Mr. Braxton, in his deposition, admitted that he knew that and probably absent that identification, he would not have chosen it.

That the "Here's Johnny" name was selected by Braxton because of its identification with Carson was the clear inference from Braxton's testimony irrespective of such admission in the opening statement.

We therefore conclude that, applying the correct legal standards, appellants are entitled to judgment. The proof showed without question that appellee had appropriated Carson's identity in connection with its corporate name and its product.

* * *

The judgment of the district court is vacated and the case remanded for further proceedings consistent with this opinion.

COMMENT

The *Carson* and *White* cases give a sense of how enthusiastically the courts have supported right of publicity claims. The tort has indeed expanded from its origins in a 1954 law review article.[143] In both these cases, there was no proof that the plaintiffs had suffered financial harm or lost fees, as the cause of action originally anticipated. Furthermore, the evidence that the "use" of either Carson or White amounted to a fraud on the consuming public is scant. Might the concern celebrities have about their attributes really be more similar to the concerns of companies that fear their trademarks will become generic and available for anyone to use.[144]

One characteristic the right of publicity retains in common with common law invasion of privacy is the notion of wrongful use or wrongful behavior. Plaintiffs Carson, Eastwood, and Presley seem more concerned with exclusive control than with financial harm. Using anyone's name or likeness is wrongful in the sense that it falsely implies assent. But the cases are not consistent in requiring proof that the typical audience member interprets the use as assent, an apparently critical element to establishing that a defendant is profiting from a celebrity.

Judge Kennedy's dissent in *Carson* was based largely on the false implication of assent argument.

* * *

> There is nothing in the record to suggest that "Here's Johnny" has any nexus to Johnny Carson other than being the introduction to his personal appearances. * * * Appellee's use of the content "Here's Johnny," in light of its value as a double entendre, written on its product and corporate name, and therefore outside of the context in which it is associated with Johnny Carson, does little to rob Johnny Carson of something which is unique to him or a product of his own efforts. * * * The right of publicity, whether tied to name, likeness, achievements, identifying characteristics or actual performances, etc. conflicts with the economic and expressive interests of others.

* * *

In a similar case, Guy Lombardo's claim for appropriation of his "public personality" as "Mr. New Year's Eve" was allowed.[145]

One of the greatest risks for the media is that the right of publicity will spill over from advertising to other types of messages. What if a work is plainly newsworthy or creative, such as a biography or a stage play?

The greatest threat to the press and media generally comes from those cases that have allowed actions or recovery despite plainly creative or newsworthy ventures.[146] A Broadway musical's use in parody of the appearance and style of the Marx Brothers violated the deceased entertainers' right of publicity.[147] A First Amend-

---

143. Nimmer, *The Right of Publicity,* 19 Law & Contemporary Probs. 203 (1954).
144. See Heneghan and Wamsley, *The Service Mark Alternative to the Right of Publicity: Estate of Presley v. Russen,* 2 Loyola Entertainment L.J. 113 (1982).

145. *Lombardo v. Doyle, Dane & Bernbach, Inc.,* 2 Med. L. Rptr. 2321, 396 N.Y.S.2d 661 (N.Y.Sup.Ct., App.Div. 1977).
146. Weiler, Note, *The Right of Publicity Gone Wrong: A Case for Privileged Appropriation of Identity,* 13 Cardozo Art. & Ent. L. J. 223 (1994). *Cardtoons vs. Major League Baseball Players Ass'n.,* 95 F.3D 959 (10th Cir. 1996.)

ment defense was allowed when comedian Pat Paulsen, a perennial gag candidate for president, found his picture being sold on campaign posters.[148] A New York political activist's claim failed when he was satirized in print. The use of the public figure's identity was a fair one.[149]

The issues regarding the right of publicity, like so much else in the law of privacy and related areas of the law, are in flux. The best advice for those who would use another's likeness or name is to be sure to get a release or be confident that the use is newsworthy.[150] Some have suggested a federal right of publicity statute is needed.[151] Until such a statute is passed or the courts reach uniformity, it will be important to know local state law.

ALTERNATIVE MEDIA LIABILITY: EMOTIONAL DISTRESS, FORESEEABLE HARMS, AND OUTRAGEOUS BEHAVIOR

With the adoption of strenuous defenses, based on the constitution, common law, or statute, against invasion of privacy and libel actions, plaintiffs have attempted to substitute other causes of action when they believe media messages have caused them harm.[152] In addition, there is a widespread belief among the public that mass media messages have strong effects on audiences—effects perhaps strong enough to sway their behavior.[153] The 1980s and 1990s have seen an explosion of litigation against the media on alternative grounds. Among the actions that parallel both invasion of privacy and libel are infliction of mental distress (either negligent[154] or intentional[155]) and tortious newsgathering.[156] Among the libel substitutes are product disparagement[157] and interference with contractual relations.[158] And many of the cases feature novel arguments for media liability, including warranty,[159] incitement,[160] and products liability.[161] In addition, claims have been posed for breach of contract, fraud, harassment, deceptive business practices, and loss of consortium.[162] One surprisingly frequent claim has been that journalists have somehow conspired with government officials to deprive plaintiffs of their civil rights under U.S.C. § 1983. Since the statute requires state action—activity by government—claims against private individuals and companies have normally been dismissed.[163]

---

147. *Groucho Marx Productions v. Day and Night Co.,* 7 Med. L. Rptr. 2030, 523 F.Supp. 485 (S.D.N.Y. 1981).

148. *Paulsen v. Personality Posters,* 299 N.Y.S.2d 501 (N.Y.Sup.Ct. 1968).

149. *Velez v. VV Publishing,* 14 Med. L. Rptr. 2290, 524 N.Y.S.2d 186 (N.Y.Sup.Ct., App.Div. 1988).

150. *Midler v. Ford Motor Co.,* 15 Med.L.Rptr. 1620, 849 F.2d 460 (9th Cir. 1988).

151. Note, *The Right of Publicity Run Riot: The Case for a Federal Statute,* 69 Southern Calif. L. Rev. 1179 (1987).

152. See, e.g., *Howell v. Tribune Entertainment Co.,* 25 Med. L. Rptr. 1370, 106 F.3d 215 (7th Cir. 1997).

153. See generally Ballard, *See No Evil, Hear No Evil: Television, Violence and the First Amendment,* 81 Virginia L.Rev. 175 (1995); but see Chaudhuri and Buck, *Media Differences in Rational and Emotional Responses to Advertising,* 39 J. Broadcasting & Electronic Med. 109 (1995).

154. *Decker v. Princeton Packet,* 16 Med. L. Rptr. 2194, 561 A.2d 1122 (N.J. 1989).

155. *Raskin v. Swann,* 23 Med. L. Rptr. 2054, 454 S.E.2d 809 (Ga.App. 1995).

156. *Risenhoover v. England,* 24 Med. L. Rptr. 1705 (W.D.Tex. 1996).

157. *Auvil v. CBS "Sixty Minutes,"* 23 Med. L. Rptr. 2454, 67 F.3d 816 (9th Cir. 1995).

158. *Czuprysnki v. Bay City Times,* 23 Med. L. Rptr. 1634, No. 1449947 (Mich.App. 1994).

159. *Sinai v. Mitchell Books,* 21 Med. L. Rptr. 1691, 996 F.2d 1227 (9th Cir. 1993).

160. *Lewis v. Columbia Pictures,* 23 Med. L. Rptr. 1052, No. E011948 (Cal.App. 1994).

161. *Birmingham v. Fodor's Travel Publications, Inc.,* 20 Med. L. Rptr. 1521, 833 P.2D 70 (Haw. 1992).

162. See generally Brill, *The First Amendment and the Power of Suggestion: Protecting 'Negligent' Speakers in Cases of Imitative Harm,* 94 Columbia L. Rev. 984 (1994); Sims, *Tort Liability for Physical Injuries Allegedly Resulting from Media Speech: A Comprehensive First Amendment Approach,* 34 Arizona L. Rev. 231 (1992); Simon and Cronin, *Searching for Media Liability: The Law's Response to Perceived Changes in Harms Caused by Mass Media,* paper presented at the annual convention, Association for Education in Journalism and Mass Communication, Boston, Mass., August 1990.

163. *Starnes v. Capital Cities Media, Inc.,* 23 Med. L. Rptr. 1119, 39 F.3d 1394 (7th Cir. 1994).

Tortious newsgathering is clearly a potential substitute for an intrusion on seclusion claim or private facts claim. Two recent cases are demonstrative. In *KOVR-TV, Inc. v. Sacramento County Superior Court,* 23 Med. L. Rptr. 1371, 27 Cal.Rptr. 431 (Cal.App. 1995), a television reporter came to a house with cameras rolling to ask three children, ages 11, 7, and 5, about their neighbor's murder of her two children and subsequent suicide. The suit was filed by the children's parents. The appeals court considered the actions of the reporter "outrageous" and sent the multiple-issue case back to trial. "A free press is not threatened by requiring its agents to operate within the bounds of basic decency," the court noted. The case of *Armstrong v. H&C Communications, Inc.,* 18 Med. L. Rptr. 1845, 575 So.2d 280 (Fla.App. 1991) involved how news was presented. A television news reporter asked the local police chief to display the skull of a murdered child whose body was never found. The skull was shown on the evening news, which was being watched by the child's family. The suit was brought under the tort of outrage and of privacy. The court dropped the privacy claim, but let the case go back to trial on outrage. "[I]f the facts as alleged herein do not constitute the tort of outrage, then there is no such tort," the court said.

What these various causes of actions have in common is that they are pressed by plaintiffs who would surely lose under existing libel or privacy rules. Infliction of emotional distress has been brought most frequently. A key to this cause of action is that, much as with intrusion or private facts, liability hinges on the behavior of the press and sensitive content of the publication, not on truth, falsity, or privilege.

Like privacy, infliction of mental distress protects individual well-being, and has been adopted slowly as a common law tort against the media. Generally, negligent infliction requires that the defendant have published something where danger of harm is apparent.[164] For example, it would be reasonable to foresee that publication of names and pictures of undercover espionage agents places them at risk. The infliction of distress occurs when the risk was recognized and the information published anyway, or when the risk was not recognized but was of a nature that it should have been. The latter was the basis of a claim by a woman who had been assaulted. When the local newspaper obtained her address from the police and published it with the suspect still at large, she claimed they put her at risk, and sued both.

Hyde v. City of Columbia
637 S.W.2D 251 (MO.APP. 1982).

SHANGLER, Presiding J.:

The plaintiff Hyde sued the City of Columbia for the negligent disclosure of her name and address by the city police to reporter Brown of the *Columbia Daily Tribune* and to reporter Potter of the *Columbia Missourian* and for the negligent publication of that information subsequently by the newspapers. The petition alleges that on August 20, 1980, after midnight, the plaintiff was abducted and kidnapped by an unknown male assailant but escaped from his car; that she made a full report of that incident to the City of Columbia Police Department; that on that date, the police, without knowledge or authority of the plaintiff, released her name and address to the reporters for publication when the police knew the assailant was still at large; that on that very day the *Columbia Daily Tribune* published that information and on the next day, August 21, 1980, the *Columbia Missourian* published that information with the knowledge that the assailant was not in custody. The petition then alleges that the release and publication of her name and address identified the plaintiff to the unknown assailant who thereafter terrorized her on seven different occasions. The petition joined the reporters Brown and Potter, the newspapers *Columbia Daily Tribune* and *Columbia Missourian* and the City of Columbia as defendants. The prayer was for actual damages.

* * *

Actionable negligence encompasses essential proofs: a duty by the defendant to protect the plaintiff from harm, neglect of that duty, and injury to the plaintiff from that neglect. *Stevens v. Wetterau Foods, Inc.,* 501 S.W.2d 494, 498[7, 8]

---

164. Drechsel, *Mass Media and Negligent Infliction of Emotional Distress,* 62 Journalism Q. 523 (1985).

(Mo.App. 1973). To plead the ultimate fact of actionable negligence [and hence a substantive remedy well-stated], the petitioner must describe the duty owed by the defendant, the breach the petitioner charges, and the injury which results. *Einhaus v. O. Ames Co.*, 547 S.W.2d 821[4, 5] (Mo.App. 1977).

The pleadings enlarged by the interrogatory evidence, understood in legal effect, posit that the plaintiff reported the kidnapping and assault to the police as an official account of a crime and not for publication, and that the municipality owed the victim a duty not to disclose her identity and address to the reporter for publication without prior consent—and so protect her from the foreseeable risk of intentional harm by the assailant, when the police knew the assailant was still at large and the practice of disclosure was otherwise forbidden in the circumstances by internal policy, but that the municipality breached the duty and the plaintiff suffered emotional harm from the intentional threats of imminent death and injury proximately caused by the negligent conduct of the City of Columbia. The pleadings understood in legal effect posit also that the defendants reporter and newspaper owed a duty to the victim not to publish her identity and address and so protect her from the foreseeable risk of intentional harm by the assailant, when they knew the assailant was still at large and the practice of publication was otherwise forbidden by internal policy, but that reporter Brown and newspaper Columbia Daily Tribune breached the duty and the plaintiff suffered emotional harm from the intentional threats of imminent death and injury proximately caused by the negligent conduct of the reporter and newspaper.

The several defendants contend, nevertheless, that these averments amount to no duty the law fixes upon them, and so none they are bound to observe. The newspaper defendants contend moreover that such a duty were onerous to the free speech and free press the First Amendment protects, and so not a valid limitation to that exercise. The several defendants argue also that, in any event, a crime against persons report is a *public record* under the Sunshine law [§§ 610.010 to 610.120], thus, to give publicity to information already public can engender no liability.

In negligence jurisprudence, whether a duty exists presents a question of law. Restatement (Second) of Torts § 4 (1965). When the existence of a duty to use due care rests on a relationship between persons, the law has simply placed the actor under obligation for the benefit of another person—the plaintiff—in the given circumstances. Or, more simply, the law has determined that "the interest of the plaintiff which has suffered invasion [is] entitled to legal protection at the hands of the defendant." Thus, essential to liability for negligence is a relationship the law recognizes as the basis of a duty of care between the inflictor of injury and the person injured. * * * The judicial determination of the existence of a duty rests on sound public policy as derived from a calculus of factors: among them, the social consensus that the interest is worthy of protection; the foreseeability of harm and the degree of certainty that the protected person suffered injury; moral blame society attaches to the conduct; the prevention of future harm; considerations of cost and ability to spread the risk of loss; the economic burden upon the actor and the community—and others. * * * To these determinants we add that, when the actor is a public agency [or quasi-public institution, such as the press], the role the law assigns to that function.

* * *

Our law imposes the duty of an actor in some circumstances to foresee that the misconduct of a third person will result in injury to another [the plaintiff] and imposes liability for failure to protect against that risk of harm. * * * Thus, conduct may be negligent solely because the actor should have recognized that it would expose the person of another to an unreasonable risk of criminal aggression.

* * *

The allegations by the female plaintiff that she was abducted by an unknown assailant, made escape, then gave official report of the crime [and description of the assailant] to the municipal police, the release of the name and address of the victim by the police to the reporter without her consent and with knowledge that the assailant was still at large, and the publication of that information by the newspaper also with that knowledge, describe conditions which posed an especial temptation and opportunity to the third-party assailant for intentional and criminal aggression upon the victim to her injury, and so plead a prima facie breach of duty.

* * *

In the absence of an obligation imposed by the statute, the disclosure of the name and address of the victim-plaintiff by the municipal police department to the reporter was gratuitous. The disclosure served no essential criminal investigation role of the police, but rather was a foreseeable impediment to that function by the encouragement of an obstruction of justice by the assailant. The disclosure was also a threat to the very personal safety of the victim. The deliberate practice of the municipal police department to withhold information of that ilk from the general public attests to the fact that the risk of injury to the victim-plaintiff from disclosure was foreseeable.

* * *

The defendant reporter and newspaper contend that the report of the abduction by the victim to the police—facts pleaded in the petition—was her consent to the preparation of the formal crime report and its subsequent publication by the news medium. That argument disregards altogether the duty of citizenship to report criminal conduct—to raise a "hue and cry" of felony to the authorities. * * *

That the victim-name-and-address information kept by the municipal police department was by law confidential does not mean that once disclosed to a newspaper it retained its confidential character. Nor do allegations which suffice to plead a cause of action against the official keeper for the negligent release of that confidential record *ipso facto* suffice as a tort cause of action against a news medium for publication of that information. * * *

The defendants reporter and newspaper contend that the report of crime was a matter of legitimate public concern and interest so that the adjudication of tort liability for the publication of that information were an impermissible interference with the exercise of free speech and of a free press in violation of the First Amendment. The defendants develop argument in terms of *newsworthiness* of the publication and the status of the victim-plaintiff as a subject of public interest. They apply these considerations and commingle them with the invasion of privacy, outrageous conduct and defamation torts. The petition, however, pleads negligence—a tort which protects an interest distinctive from the other torts.

* * *

The petition of the victim-plaintiff taken at most favorable intendment states a cause of action in negligence against the news medium defendants free from the proof constraints of *New York Times v. Sullivan* as well as any constraints of common law privilege.

* * *

COMMENT

The court seemed to be influenced by evidence of the police practice of not ordinarily giving out addresses. The practice, the court said, "attests to the fact that the risk of injury to the victim-plaintiff from disclosure was foreseeable." While that may be true of the risk of injury, it does not explain how the newspaper could have or should have assessed the risk of mental distress.

The court refused to apply libel law's qualified privilege to report on matters in the public interest in this context. The privilege applies, the court said, "only as to information which affects a *sufficiently important public interest*." Why was not truth or newsworthiness a defense?

The *Hyde* case has understandably worried many. It is not easy to foresee the limits of its rationale. Can any information that carries the potential of causing harm now be the subject of a negligent infliction of mental distress action? For example, can the press harm people by printing truthful but defamatory stories? Is injured reputation the sort of harm the *Hyde* court has in mind?

While the newspaper's decision to publish the address and name certainly appears unwise, is the corollary of having judges and juries address these issues wiser? Such editorial judgments have traditionally been the province of ethics, not law. Under the *Sullivan* approach used in libel and much of privacy, the law will countenance much that is questionable, tacky, even undesirable. Does *Hyde* signal a judicial willingness to enforce social responsibility upon the press?[165]

---

165. See Drechsel, *The Legal Risks of Social Responsibility,* paper presented to Law Division, Association for Education in Journalism and Mass Communication convention, San Antonio, Texas, August 1987; Forer, *Autonomy and Responsibility: A Search for New Bases of Legal Rights and Obligations,* 1986 Utah L.Rev. 665 (1986); Barron, *The Search for Media Accountability,* 19 Suffolk U.L.Rev. 789 (1985); Weingarten, *Tort Liability for Nonlibelous Negligent Statements: First Amendment Considerations,* 93 Yale L.J. 744 (1983).

The courts have certainly been busy with mental and emotional distress claims. Few cases have succeeded. Some courts see the cause of action as duplicative of privacy or libel and tell plaintiffs to bring those suits instead.[166] Several cases have involved erroneous obituaries or telephone listings, with decisions for defendants.[167] One plaintiff failed after charging that an inadequate retraction constituted infliction.[168] But at the same time specific cases fail, many states have nevertheless recognized the cause of action as it applies to the media. The difficult part for plaintiffs has been foreseeability.

Intentional infliction requires proof of intent, normally by showing a pattern or course of behavior. In addition, the harmful material generally must be aimed directly at the person claiming distress. In common law cases not involving media, four factors were identified with proving intentional infliction. The defendant's conduct must be extreme and outrageous; the defendant must have acted with intent or recklessness; the defendant's conduct must have been the proximate cause of the distress; and, the distress must be severe.[169] Most of the elements were in place when Jerry Falwell sued Larry Flynt for libel, invasion of privacy, and intentional infliction of emotional distress over a parody that portrayed Falwell as a drunkard who was introduced to sex by his mother. There was no doubt about intent—Flynt stood on the steps of the Supreme Court to tell reporters he had aimed to cause Falwell distress. By the time the case reached the high court, only the infliction claim remained.

The Supreme Court's opinion in *Hustler Magazine, Inc. v. Falwell,* 14 Med. L. Rptr. 2281, 108 S.Ct. 876 (1988), see this text, p. 194, makes it plain that parody or satire of public figures is unlikely to result in liability. But the Court's holding implies that imposing liability will be easier for private figures:

> We conclude that public figures and public officials may not recover for the tort of intentional infliction of emotional distress by reason of publications such as the one here at issue without showing in addition that the publication contains a false statement of fact which was made with "actual malice," i.e., with knowledge that the statement was false or with reckless disregard as to whether or not it was true.

The Court applied a libel test to a case where truth or falsity is not the issue. It had already been decided that no reasonable reader would construe the parody as a statement of fact. So a test focusing on falsity seems misplaced. Why didn't the Court simply say that humor was absolutely protected? Perhaps it is willing to see how the tort develops in the lower courts. Based on *Falwell,* intentional infliction of emotional distress, like false light privacy before it, seems to be on its way to becoming a hybrid tort.

In 1986, the *Spartanburg Herald* ran a story, based on government sources, reporting that a young man who had collapsed and died was believed to have been using cocaine. The report was wrong; he had died of coronary artery disease. The family sued for intentional infliction of emotional distress. The newspaper argued that it had given a substantially true report as of the time of publication. The court disagreed, disallowing a truth defense, but would not allow the emotional distress claim on other grounds.

---

166. *Rutledge v. Phoenix Newspapers,* 12 Med. L. Rptr. 1969, 715 P.2d 1243 (Az.App. 1986); *Dworkin v. Hustler,* 14 Med. L. Rptr. 1673, 668 F.Supp. 1408 (C.D.Cal. 1987); *Smith v. Dameron,* 14 Med. L. Rptr. 1879 (Va.Cir.Ct. 1987).

167. *Decker v. Princeton Packet,* 15 Med. L. Rptr. 1775, 541 A.2d 292 (N.J.Super.Ct., App.Div. 1988) (obituary); *Rubinstein v. New York Post,* 11 Med. L. Rptr. 1329, 488 N.Y.S.2d 331 (N.Y.Sup.Ct. 1985) (obituary); *Tatta v. News Group Publications,* 12 Med. L. Rptr. 2318 (N.Y.Sup.Ct. 1986) (phone number listed in advertisement for a pay-per-call sex talk service).

168. *Beasley v. Hearst Corp.,* 11 Med. L. Rptr. 2067 (Cal.Super.Ct. 1985).

169. Restatement (Second) of Torts § 46(1) (1977).

Upchurch v. The New York Times Co.
21 MED. L. RPTR. 1568, 431 S.E.2D 558 (S.C. 1993).

HARWELL, C. J.:

* * *

On August 18, 1986, Bodie Upchurch, the son and brother of appellants, was lifting weights at the Gaffney YMCA. He began feeling unwell and decided to discontinue his workout. A short while later, while Bodie was driving home, he collapsed and died. He was twenty-three years old and in apparent good health.

The next morning, an autopsy to determine the cause of death commenced in the presence of two law enforcement officers from the Gaffney Police Department. A white, powdery substance was detected in Bodie's nostrils during the initial examination of his body. A swab of the substance was forwarded to State Law Enforcement Division (SLED) for analysis to determine whether the substance was cocaine. The law enforcement officers reported the discovery of the white, powdery substance to their chief of police, who cautioned them to divulge nothing about the discovery to anyone until the results of the SLED analysis revealed the identity of the substance.

Despite official secrecy regarding the discovery of the white, powdery substance, rumors quickly began circulating in the community that cocaine was implicated in Bodie's death. Soon respondents were seeking official confirmation that law enforcement suspected the white, powdery substance to be cocaine. Law enforcement refused to comment regarding the cause of Bodie's death. The request for a drug screen prepared by the coroner and forwarded to SLED was not in the possession of respondents, and there is no evidence that respondents were aware of the existence of the request. An alternative explanation was inferable that the white, powdery substance in Bodie's nostrils was chalk or talc used by Bodie when he was lifting weights. Nevertheless, respondents published a front page article and Bodie's picture under a banner headline exclaiming "Cocaine Suspected In Death." The same day the article was published, SLED toxicology reports came back negative as to the presence of cocaine.

* * *

Appellants brought this action for intentional infliction of emotional distress, alleging that the newspaper article contained false information that law enforcement suspected cocaine was involved in Bodie's death, that respondents knew or should have known that the statements contained in the article were false, and that their publishing the article constituted outrageous conduct entitled appellants to recover for the emotional harm they had suffered as a result of reading the article. At the conclusion of a jury trial, the trial judge directed a verdict in favor of respondents on the grounds that the statements contained in the article were substantially true at the time of publication.

* * *

As an initial matter, we find respondents' reliance on substantial truth as a defense to the tort of intentional infliction of emotional distress to be misplaced. This defense is applicable in defamation actions.

* * *

Moreover, we disagree with the trial judge that respondents' allegedly tortious acts are shielded simply by virtue of the protections guaranteed the press by the First Amendment. The publisher of a newspaper has no special immunity from the application of general laws, and he has no special privilege to invade the rights and liberties of others.

* * *

Thus, the fact that respondents' speech may be constitutionally privileged does not automatically protect them from private action. *See The Florida Star v. B.J.F.*, 491 U.S. 524 (1989). However, when a newspaper (1) lawfully obtains (2) truthful information about (3) a matter of public significance, liability may be imposed only if it serves a need to further a state interest of the highest order. If the test articulated in *Florida Star* is not met, torts committed by the press are actionable more readily, particularly when a private party is involved.

* * *

Accordingly, a correct analysis of respondents' liability to appellants would have addressed the threshold inquiry under *Florida Star*. We perceive that we need not review the facts under *Florida Star* in order to determine whether to uphold the directed verdict, however. We find that we must affirm the trial judge because appellants possess no basis upon which to assert a cause of action for intentional infliction of emotional distress.

The tort of intentional infliction of emotional distress arises when one by extreme and outrageous conduct intentionally or recklessly causes severe emotional distress to another. In order to recover for the intentional infliction of emotional distress, a plaintiff must establish that (1) the defendant intentionally or recklessly inflicted severe emotional distress, or was certain or substantially certain that such distress would result from his conduct; (2) the conduct was so extreme and outrageous as to exceed all possible bounds of decency and must be regarded as atrocious and utterly intolerable in a civilized community; (3) the actions of the defendant caused the plaintiff's emotional distress; and (4) the emotional distress suffered by the plaintiff was so severe that no reasonable person could be expected to endure it.

The law limits claims of intentional infliction of emotional distress to egregious conduct toward a plaintiff proximately caused by a defendant. It is not enough that the conduct is intentional and outrageous. It must be conduct directed at the plaintiff, or occur in the presence of a plaintiff of whom the defendant is aware.

* * *

The harm suffered by appellants arose only indirectly from respondents' publishing allegedly false information about Bodie. There are situations when plaintiffs may recover for intentional infliction of emotional distress for harm they suffer as the result of acts which have injured another. The Restatement (Second) of Torts § 46(2) (1965) provides:

§ 46. Outrageous Conduct Causing Severe Emotional Distress

* * *

(2) Where such conduct is directed at a third person, the actor is subject to liability if he intentionally or recklessly causes severe emotional distress
(a) to a member of such person's immediate family who is present at the time, whether or not such distress results in bodily harm, or
(b) to any other person who is present at the time, if such distress results in bodily harm.

As a matter of policy, courts have limited such recovery "to the most extreme cases of violent attack, where there is some especial likelihood of fright or shock."

* * *

There being no evidence that respondents physically attacked Bodie in the presence of appellants, we must hold that appellants do not possess a cause of action for intentional infliction of emotional distress arising under section 46(2). We agree with our sister state's disposition of a claim for intentional infliction of emotional distress which originated under strikingly similar facts. In *Briggs v. Rosenthal,* 73 N.C. App. 672, 327 S.E.2d 38, *cert. denied,* 314 N.C. 114, 332 S.E.2d 479 (1985), the plaintiffs brought an action for intentional infliction of emotional distress against an author and publisher as the result of a magazine article describing their son who had died in an automobile accident. The court noted that the magazine article had been published in a periodical intended for the public. The parents were not the subject of the article, but, like appellants herein, brought their action as third party family members distressed because they felt that their son had been disparaged in the magazine article. The *Briggs* court affirmed the trial court's dismissal of the parents' complaint because, among other reasons, the author and publisher of the magazine, like respondents herein, had not specifically directed their conduct toward the plaintiffs, and had not committed a violent act upon the son in the presence of the plaintiffs.

* * *

We may affirm the trial judge for any reason appearing in the record. We conclude that the trial judge did not err in directing a verdict in favor of respondents. Accordingly, the order of the trial judge is

AFFIRMED.

COMMENT

Closely related to negligent or intentional infliction are claims that media content led to physical injury. In the past, such cases have usually failed. When teens attempted suicide after listening to heavy metal rock music[170] and a child was injured trying to duplicate a trick from the Mickey Mouse Club,[171] they were barred from suit on First Amendment grounds. Although plaintiffs have not prevailed, again largely on the grounds that it was not reasonable to expect that defendants would have foreseen risks to specific plaintiffs, scholarly comment seems to favor recovery.[172]

When murder is the risk, attention gets focused. *Soldier of Fortune* magazine, a specialized publication for self-styled mercenary soldiers, lost twice in two separate cases in its attempts for summary judgment. In both cases, plaintiffs claimed that the magazine ran ads promoting murderers for hire. In the first case, the

---

170. *McCollum v. CBS,* 15 Med. L. Rptr. 2001, 202 Cal.App. 3d 989, 249 Cal.Rptr. 187, (1988); but see *Judas Priest v. Nevada District Court,* 15 Med. L. Rptr. 2010 (Nev. 1988).

171. *Walt Disney Productions, Inc. v. Shannon,* 276 S.E.2d 580 (Ga. 1981).

172. Dee, *Media Accountability for Real-Life Violence: A Case of Negligence or Free Speech?,* 37 J. of Communication 106 (1988).

murder was attempted but failed, in the second the victim was murdered.[173] The parties dispute whether the language of the advertisements clearly enough solicits contracts for murder to have placed the magazine on notice of the risk. Normally, publishers have no duty to investigate the contents of advertisements.

In an appeal of a third wrongful death case in which a mercenary responding to an ad had been hired by a man to kill his business partner, the Eleventh Circuit adopted an explicit duty test. In doing so, it attempted to balance First Amendment concerns so as to reach only "dangerous" content:

> We conclude that the First Amendment permits a state to impose upon a publisher liability for compensatory damages for negligently publishing a commercial advertisement where the ad on its face, and without the need for investigation, makes it apparent that there is a substantial danger of harm to the public. The absence of a duty to investigate . . . and the requirement that the substance of the ad itself must warn the publisher . . . guarantee that the burden placed on publishers will not impermissibly chill protected commercial speech. *Braun v. Soldier of Fortune Magazine, Inc.,* 20 Med. L. Rptr. 1777, 968 F.2d 1110 (11th Cir. 1992).

Does the argument that extreme risks justify imposing a standard of reasonable inspection seem persuasive?

The court in *Braun* was influenced by the "less protected" status of commercial speech under the First Amendment, see this text, p. 101. Are you persuaded that it should be easier to hold advertisements and media that carry them liable than it is to hold editorial content liable? Plaintiffs who claim that family members were murdered by contract killers who got information from the book *Hit Man: A Technical Manual for Independent Contractors* have sued the publisher for wrongful death, alleging that the publisher showed "intent" to cause harm.[174] The claim appears to be a variation of the argument used in incitement cases. The defense has argued that the plaintiffs must meet the incite-

ment test from *Brandenburg v. Ohio,* see this text, p. 27.

Foreseeability was central to the case of two plaintiffs who ate poisonous mushrooms after following erroneous instructions in the *Encyclopedia of Mushrooms.* The case was brought primarily under products liability principles, although several additional causes of action were also filed. The plaintiffs argued that how-to books should be more easily subject to liability precisely because authors and publishers create them with the expectation that the instructions in the books will be followed. A panel of the Ninth Circuit said that the book was "pure expression" and liability could not be imposed.

Winter v. G. P. Putnam's Sons
19 MED. L. RPTR. 1053, 938 F.2D 1033 (9TH CIR. 1991).

SNEED, J.:

* * *

FACTS AND PROCEEDINGS BELOW

The Encyclopedia of Mushrooms is a reference guide containing information on the habitat, collection, and cooking of mushrooms. It was written by two British authors and originally published by a British publishing company. Defendant Putnam, an American book publisher, purchased copies of the book from the British publisher and distributed the finished product in the United States. Putnam neither wrote nor edited the book.

Plaintiffs purchased the book to help them collect and eat wild mushrooms. In 1988, plaintiffs went mushroom hunting and relied on the descriptions in the book in determining which mushrooms were safe to eat. After cooking and eating their harvest, plaintiffs became critically ill. Both have required liver transplants.

Plaintiffs allege that the book contained erroneous and misleading information concerning the identification of the most deadly species of mushrooms. In their suit against the book publisher, plaintiffs allege liability based on products liability, breach of warranty, negligence, negligent misrepresentation, and false representations. Defendant moved for summary judgment asserting that plaintiffs' claims failed as a matter of law because 1) the information contained in a book is not a product for the purposes of strict

---

173. *Norwood v. Soldier of Fortune Magazine,* 13 Med. L. Rptr. 2025, 651 F. Supp. 1397 (W.D.Ark. 1987); *Eimann v. Soldier of Fortune,* 15 Med. L. Rptr. 1026, 680 F.Supp. 863 (S.D.Tex. 1988), *aff'd,* 16 Med. L. Rptr. 2148, 880 F.2d 830 (5th Cir. 1989), *cert. denied* 493 U.S. 1024 (1990).

174. *Rice v. Paladin Enterprises, Inc.,* No. AW-95-3811 (D.Md. filed December 13, 1995).

liability under products liability law; and 2) defendant is not liable under any remaining theories because a publisher does not have a duty to investigate the accuracy of the text it publishes. The district court granted summary judgment for the defendant. Plaintiffs appeal. We affirm.

* * *

DISCUSSION

A. Products Liability

The language of products liability law reflects its focus on tangible items. In describing the scope of products liability law, the Restatement (Second) of Torts lists examples of items that are covered. All of these are tangible items, such as tires, automobiles, and insecticides. The American Law Institute clearly was concerned with including all physical items but gave no indication that the doctrine should be expanded beyond that area.

The purposes served by products liability law also are focused on the tangible world and do not take into consideration the unique characteristics of ideas and expression. Under products liability law, strict liability is imposed on the theory that "[t]he costs of damaging events due to defectively dangerous products can best be borne by the enterprisers who make and sell these products." *Prosser & Keeton on The Law of Torts,* § 98, at 692–93 (W. Keeton ed. 5th ed. 1984). Strict liability principles have been adopted to further the "cause of accident prevention . . . [by] the elimination of the necessity of proving negligence." *Id.* at 693. Additionally, because of the difficulty of establishing fault or negligence in products liability cases, strict liability is the appropriate legal theory to hold manufacturers liable for defective products.

* * *

It is not a question of fault but simply a determination of how society wishes to assess certain costs that arise from the creation and distribution of products in a complex technological society in which the consumer thereof is unable to protect himself against certain product defects.

Although there is always some appeal to the involuntary spreading of costs of injuries in any area, the costs in any comprehensive cost/benefit analysis would be quite different were strict liability concepts applied to words and ideas. We place a high priority on the unfettered exchange of ideas. We accept the risk that words and ideas have wings we cannot clip and which carry them we know not where. The threat of liability without fault (financial responsibility for our words and ideas in the absence of fault or a special undertaking or responsibility) could seriously inhibit those who wish to share thoughts and theories.

* * *

Plaintiffs suggest, however, that our fears would be groundless were strict liability rules applied only to books that give instruction on how to accomplish a physical activity and that are intended to be used as part of an activity that is inherently dangerous. We find such a limitation illusory. Ideas are often intimately linked with proposed action, and it would be difficult to draw such a bright line. While "How To" books are a special genre, we decline to attempt to draw a line that puts "How To Live A Good Life" books beyond the reach of strict liability while leaving "How To Exercise Properly" books within its reach.

* * *

Plaintiffs' argument is stronger when they assert that *The Encyclopedia of Mushrooms* should be analogized to aeronautical charts. Several jurisdictions have held that charts which graphically depict geographic features or instrument approach information for airplanes are "products" for the purpose of products liability law.

* * *

Plaintiffs suggest that *The Encyclopedia of Mushrooms* can be compared to aeronautical charts because both items contain representations of natural features and both are intended to be used while engaging in hazardous activity. We are not persuaded.

Aeronautical charts are highly technical tools. They are graphic depictions of technical, mechanical data. The best analogy to an aeronautical chart is a compass. Both may be used to guide an individual who is engaged in an activity requiring certain knowledge of natural features. Computer software that fails to yield the result for which it was designed may be another. In contrast, *The Encyclopedia of Mushrooms* is like a book on how to *use* a compass or an aeronautical chart. The chart itself is like a physical "product" while the "How to Use" book is pure thought and expression.

Given these considerations, we decline to expand products liability law to embrace the ideas and expression in a book. We know of no court that has chosen the path to which the plaintiffs point.

B. The Remaining Theories

As discussed above, plaintiffs must look to the doctrines of copyright, libel, misrepresentation, negligent misrepresentation, negligence, and mistake to form the basis of a claim against the defendant publisher. Unless it is assumed that the publisher is a guarantor of the accuracy of an author's statements of fact, plaintiffs have made no case under any of these theories other than possibly negligence. Guided by the First Amendment and the values embodied therein, we decline to extend liability under this theory to the ideas and expression contained in a book.

In order for negligence to be actionable, there must be a legal duty to exercise due care. 6 B. Witkin. *Summary of California Law,* Torts § 732 (9th Ed. 1988). The plaintiffs urge this court that the publisher had a duty to investigate the accuracy of The Encyclopedia of Mushroom's contents. We conclude that the defendants have no duty to investigate the accuracy of the contents of the books it publishes. A publisher may of course assume such a burden, but there is nothing inherent in the role of publisher or the surrounding legal doctrines to suggest that such a duty should be imposed on publishers. Indeed the cases uniformly refuse to impose such a duty. Were we tempted to create this duty, the gentle tug of the First Amendment and the values embodied therein would remind us of the social costs.

Finally, plaintiffs ask us to find that a publisher should be required to give a warning 1) that the information in the book is not complete and that the consumer may not fully rely on it or 2) that this publisher has not investigated the text and cannot guarantee its accuracy. With respect to the first, a publisher would not know what warnings, if any, were required without engaging in a detailed analysis of the factual contents of the book. This would force the publisher to do exactly what we have said he has no duty to do—that is, independently investigate the accuracy of the text. We will not introduce a duty we have just rejected by renaming it a "mere" warning label. With respect to the second, such a warning is unnecessary given that *no* publisher has a duty as a guarantor.

For the reasons outlined above, the decision of the district court is affirmed.

COMMENT

Products liability normally applies to mechanical or physical aspects of manufactured goods. Under that approach, the plaintiffs in *Winter* might have been able to prevail if the book itself had caused harm, but not the words in it. In an information economy, is the distinction persuasive? The *Winter* court was following the lead of courts in numerous cases. The traditional view is that First Amendment principles preclude imposing liability. In addition, the courts have been reluctant to accept the notion that how-to books "invite" consumers to act, thereby creating a duty between authors, publishers, and readers. Indeed, most courts have decided that publishers of how-to books do not even have a duty to check accuracy,[175] even though such books are typically promoted based upon how reliable they are.

Most of the alternative actions have failed—for now. Modern tort law development has focused to a significant extent on preventing harms and on spreading the costs of injuries.[176] Perhaps recent developments in media liability for nondefamatory content are part of that trend.

---

175. Note, Arnold, *The Persistence of Caveat Emptor: Publisher Immunity from Liability for Inaccurate Factual Information,* 53 U. Pitt. L.Rev. 777 (1992).

176. Ingber, *Rethinking Intangible Injuries: A Focus on Remedy,* 73 Calif. L.Rev. 772 (1985).

CHAPTER 6

NEWSGATHERING RIGHTS

CHAPTER OUTLINE

PARALLEL RIGHTS— JOURNALIST'S PRIVILEGE AND ACCESS TO THE JUDICIAL SYSTEM

Two of the thorniest and most contentious areas of communication law during the 1970s and 1980s have become relatively calm in the 1990s. In the two previous decades, journalists and their lawyers fought to establish and clarify the constitutional, common law, and, in some cases, statutory standards for protecting newsgathering.

Investigative journalism increased in the late 1960s, and with it came an increased demand that reporters and editors appear later in lawsuits related to their investigations to name sources and provide background information. Many felt investigative journalism blossomed as a result of stronger media protections against libel suits stemming from *New York Times v. Sullivan*.[1] Whatever the reasons, journalists throughout the United States began looking to

---

1. 1 Med. L. Rptr. 1527, 376 U.S. 254, 84 S. Ct. 710, 11 L. Ed. 2d 686 (1964).

the courts to craft shields against intrusions into their newsgathering. The only Supreme Court case dealing with whether reporters have a First Amendment right not to identify confidential news sources, *Branzburg v. Hayes*,[2] appeared to crush the move to create a privilege. Instead the opinion became the basis for a constitutional privilege that has been accepted in almost every jurisdiction, federal and state, that has considered the issue. During the 1980s and 1990s, the courts have fine-tuned the privilege rules adopted in the 1970s. The privilege has been extended beyond sources to include notes, videotape, photographs, documents, and other materials acquired during newsgathering. Today the rules for claiming the journalist's privileges are well established as a result of judicial interpretation in hundreds of cases.

During the 1960s and 1970s, tensions between the news media and the judicial system were growing as saturation coverage of sensational trials, usually criminal trials, became more common. Prior to this century, few cases were publicized outside the immediate community. The spread of wire services, adoption of photography by newspapers, and the introduction of radio followed by television made it possible for trials to become spectacles. Judges feared that intense news coverage would distort the legal process, perhaps endangering defendants' Sixth Amendment right to a fair trial. Lawyers, too, feared that their clients' interests would be jeopardized. In *Sheppard v. Maxwell* in 1966,[3] the Supreme Court for the first time reversed a criminal conviction on the grounds that media coverage—and the behavior of journalists—had denied a defendant the right to a fair trial.

For two decades thereafter, the news media and the judicial system waltzed through a series of issues involving freedom of the press and the right to a fair trial. Judges imposed gag orders preventing journalists from reporting what they observed in court. Eventually, gag orders were declared presumptively unconstitutional First Amendment violations. Only a handful have been issued and upheld in twenty years. In another development, states began to experiment

with allowing television coverage of trials. The Supreme Court condoned cameras in the courts, and today video coverage is widely allowed. Judges, however, closed first pretrial proceedings and then trials. Eventually, the Supreme Court devised a right of access to courtrooms that applies to almost all proceedings. The right is currently being extended to evidentiary materials, court documents, and other materials submitted to the courts in litigation. The rules governing access to the judicial process are also well established today.

The legal tests set up by the courts for journalist's privilege and for access to the judicial system are remarkably similar. Each calls for application of a familiar judicially created constitutional law test, either the compelling interest test or the substantial interest test.[4] The major issues involving journalist's privilege and access to the judicial process today concern the scope of the rights rather than their existence.

Much of the protection for newsgathering is also procedural in nature. Under either journalist's privilege or judicial access, for example, news media are entitled to a hearing before newsgathering is invaded or restricted. An adverse decision on a motion to quash a subpoena or an opposition to closure of a court may qualify for accelerated appellate review as well.

That the courts have created tests to protect newsgathering rights does not mean that the issues have faded.[5] Attempts to force disclosure of sources and information apparently have not decreased,[6] and high-profile trials are producing ever more motions to restrict news coverage.[7] The developments of the last two decades assure, however, that in most cases a framework exists for resolving the issues.

JOURNALIST'S PRIVILEGE

Journalist's privilege is based on the argument that allowing forced disclosure of news sources

---

2. 1 Med. L. Rptr. 2617, 48 U.S. 665, 92 S. Ct. 2646, 33 L. Ed. 2d 626 (1972).
3. 1 Med. L. Rptr. 1220, 384 U.S. 333, 86 S. Ct. 1507, 16 L. Ed. 2d 600 (1966).

4. See Chapter 2, pp. 76–99.
5. See generally, Dyk, *Newsgathering, Press Access, and the First Amendment,* 44 Stanford L. Rev. 927 (1992).
6. "Report Finds Increased Reliance on Shield Laws to Quash Subpoenas," *The News Media and the Law,* Winter 1993, p. 49.
7. Mauor, "Simpson Trial Aftermath: Courts Closing Doors," *First Amendment News,* March 1996, p. 1.

or of materials gathered during reporting would have a "chilling effect" on the press. Subpoenas requesting identification of confidential sources were a primary focus in the earliest cases, with journalists arguing that protecting anonymous sources was essential if the free flow of information to the public was to continue. Pointing out that reporters often rely on anonymous sources for expert background,[8] the press argued that reluctant sources might not come forward at all without guaranteed anonymity. A chill might also occur if the press were to withhold publication due to fear of reprisals. Having a privilege, either by judicial decision or shield statute, thus appears to encourage more and better investigative reporting.[9]

Rapid increases in the number of subpoenas issued against journalists and news organizations in the late 1960s and early 1970s gave urgency to the call for privilege.[10] Most subpoenas sprang from criminal trials or grand jury investigations, where testimony from journalists could often be useful. Along with law enforcement officials and the parties to litigation, reporters are often the individuals most likely to have information on crimes or disputes that end up in court.

Privilege claims are not entirely new, having been made since the mid-1850s. Indeed, the practice of using anonymous sources, and even anonymous authors, dates to colonial times. Maryland passed the first shield law in 1896.[11] As a professional matter, almost all codes of ethics of journalism organizations now recognize an obligation on the part of reporters to protect their sources of information.

A journalist's privilege runs counter to the legal system's aversion to evidentiary privileges, however. Traditionally, "the public has a right to every man's evidence."[12] unless a privilege has been enacted by statute or court order. Even then, the courts interpret the privilege as narrowly as possible to assure that a maximum amount of evidence is obtained.[13] The courts argue that justice is best served by requiring all individuals who have relevant facts or information to testify in litigation.[14]

A number of privileges have long been accepted, but a privilege for reporters and journalists is not among them. Traditionally, the common law exempted compelled testimony concerning a lawyer-client relationship. Relationships between husbands and wives, priests and penitents, and doctors and patients were accorded a similar privilege. These privileges entered our legal system through the common law but are now usually covered by state and federal statutes.

Some jurisdictions have recognized a number of other privileges, including relationships between accountants, architects, and their clients. Even government informers have enjoyed anonymity unless their identities are needed to determine guilt or innocence.[15]

Similar recognition of privilege claims from journalists was slower to emerge. Courts and legislatures had to wrestle with competing values:

> [T]wo compelling interests are at stake: the interest in allowing the press unfettered access to sources of information and the interest in allowing courts and litigants unimpaired access to testimony and relevant information in civil litigation. *Senear v. Daily Journal American*, 6 Med. L. Rptr. 2070, 618 P.2d 536 (Wash.App. 1980), *reversed*, 8 Med. L. Rptr. 1151, 641 P.2d 1180 (Wash. 1982).

In *Senear*, the Washington Supreme Court acknowledged its difficulty with recognizing the privilege, but determined that

> Given both the complex and diffuse nature of modern society, the need for citizens in a representative democracy to make considered judgments, and the increasing importance of journalists to convey information to citizens, the confidential relationship is one we feel "in the opinion of the community ought to be sedulously fostered." [citation omitted]

---

8. Powers and Fico, *Influences on Use of Sources at Large U.S. Newspapers,* 15 Newsp. Res. J. 87 (1994).

9. Wirth, *Impact of State Shield Laws on Investigative Reporting,* 16 Newsp. Res. J. 64 (1995).

10. Osborn, *The Reporter's Confidentiality Privilege: Examining the Empirical Evidence After a Decade of Subpoenas,* 17 Columbia Human Rights L.Rev. 57, 59–60 (1985); Note, *The Case for a Federal Shield Law,* 24 U.C.L.A. L.Rev. 160, 162–164 (1976).

11. See Gordon, *The 1896 Maryland Shield Law: The American Roots of Evidentiary Privilege for Newsmen,* Journalism Monographs, No. 22 (February 1972).

12. Wigmore, *Evidence,* § 2192, at 70 (McNaughton rev. ed. 1961).

---

13. *United States v. Nixon,* 418 U.S. 683 (1974); E. Cleary, *McCormick on Evidence* §§ 72–77 (2d. ed. 1972).

14. *United States v. Bryan,* 339 U.S. 323, 331 (1950).

15. *Roviaro v. United States,* 353 U.S. 53 (1957).

Massachusetts has been one of the states most resistant to creating a privilege. Although a qualified First Amendment privilege has been accepted almost everywhere else, the Massachusetts Supreme Judicial Court has held that

> News reporters do not have a constitutionally based testimonial privilege that other citizens do not have. There is no such statutory privilege, nor is there any rule of court providing such a privilege. We have, however, recognized that common law principles may justify the denial of enforcement of a grand jury summons issued to a news reporter. [Citations omitted.] *In re John Doe Grand Jury Investigation*, 19 Med. L. Rptr. 1091, 574 N.E. 2d 373 (Mass. 1991).

Instead the court said that the competing free press and full testimony interests should be balanced as part of the general rules applicable to motions to quash, in which case "[A] judge would not have to reach any reporter's common law privilege issue."

Courts throughout the United States, not just in Washington and Massachusetts, have engaged in similar deliberations. Claims for absolute privilege on either constitutional or common law grounds have never been accepted. By its language, the federal constitution creates no privilege beyond the Fifth Amendment's provision against self-incrimination. As for common law, it is an awkward device for creating privileges when most are now statutory. Thus, in the early 1970s, hardly anyone would have predicted that most jurisdictions would eventually opt for a qualified privilege. In addition, the Supreme Court appeared to have rejected journalist's privilege altogether.

The Enigmatic *Branzburg* Case

In 1972, a divided Supreme Court appeared to strike the balance in favor of requiring reporters to testify when called. Recognizing a general duty to testify that compels even the president of the United States, the Court refused to fashion either an absolute or a qualified privilege from the First Amendment to protect reporters called to testify before a grand jury. *Branzburg v. Hayes*, 408 U.S. 665 (1972). Justice Byron White's prevailing opinion received four votes, while a minority of four justices, led by Justice Potter Stewart, vigorously pressed the case for privilege. Justice Lewis Powell saw merit in both sides of the argument.

In *Branzburg,* the Court considered three appeals. All three involved reporters who were called to testify before grand juries. Paul Branzburg, a reporter for the *Louisville Courier-Journal,* had written a story in 1969 describing his observations of marijuana being processed into hashish. He promised confidentiality as a condition of being allowed to observe. The published story noted the confidentiality promise. Branzburg was subpoenaed by the county grand jury, appeared, but refused to answer when asked to identify his sources. He based his refusal on Kentucky's reporters' privilege statute, the First Amendment, and the Kentucky Constitution. The state court said that the constitutional and statutory arguments did not permit a reporter to refuse to testify about events that had been personally observed. *Branzburg v. Pound,* 461 S.W.2d 345 (Ky.App. 1970).

A grand jury sought Branzburg's testimony a second time after a January 1971 story on drug use in Frankfort, Kentucky. Part of the report was based on information from sources also promised anonymity. Branzburg moved to quash the grand jury subpoena. He did obtain an order protecting him from revealing "confidential associations, sources, or information," but was told to testify concerning what he had witnessed. He refused to appear, and the court of appeals again rejected his privilege arguments.

Paul Pappas, a reporter for television station WTEV in New Bedford, Massachusetts, reported on civil disorders there. He planned to cover a Black Panther news conference, but the group was initially distrustful. The militant Black Panthers were believed by many officials to be planning guerrilla warfare against white society. Pappas was allowed to enter the group's headquarters on condition that he not disclose anything he saw or heard. He did not prepare a story based on the visit. Later he was called by the county grand jury. He appeared but refused to answer questions about what had taken place, claiming a privilege based on the First Amendment. A second summons was served, and Pappas this time refused even to appear. The Massachusetts Supreme Judicial Court denied Pappas's motion to quash, emphasizing the need for everyone's testimony. The claim that lack of privilege would chill newsgathering was deemed "indirect, theoretical, and uncertain." *In re Pappas,* 266 N.E.2d 297 (Mass. 1971).

Earl Caldwell, West Coast bureau chief for the *New York Times,* was in California also covering the Black Panthers. He received a subpoena *duces tecum* ordering him both to appear before a federal grand jury and to bring his notes, tape-recorded interviews, and other materials. Caldwell and his attorneys negotiated a continuance with federal government attorneys. A second subpoena ordered Caldwell to appear and testify. He moved to quash, arguing that appearing in secret before the grand jury would destroy his working relationship with sources among the Black Panthers. A federal district court issued a protective order preventing disclosure of sources and materials. *Application of Caldwell,* 311 F.Supp. 358 (N.D.Cal. 1970). The grand jury term expired.

A new grand jury was convened, and a third subpoena was issued to Caldwell. This time Caldwell's motion to quash was denied, and he was found in contempt. The Ninth Circuit reversed. Viewing the issue as whether Caldwell was required to appear before the grand jury at all, the court first agreed that the First Amendment provided a qualified testimonial privilege to journalists. The court accepted Caldwell's arguments that compelled testimony would deter informants and cause him to censor his writings. The court held that Caldwell was privileged to withhold his testimony unless there were compelling reasons for it. The Ninth Circuit began to fashion a three-part test to balance interests: (1) relevance, (2) lack of alternate sources, and (3) compelling public need. *Caldwell v. United States,* 434 F.2d 1081 (9th Cir. 1970). The three part test would reappear a year later in Alexander Bickel's oral arguments before the Supreme Court on the *New York Times*'s behalf in *Branzburg.*

The Ninth Circuit declared:

To convert news gatherers into Department of Justice investigators is to invade the autonomy of the press by imposing a governmental function upon them. To do so where the result is to diminish their future capacity as news gatherers is destructive of their public function. To accomplish this where it has not been shown to be essential to the Grand Jury inquiry simply cannot be justified in the public interest. Further it is not unreasonable to expect journalists everywhere to temper their reporting so as to reduce the probability that they will be required to submit to interrogation. The First

Amendment guards against governmental action that induces self-censorship.

The stage was set for a landmark decision.

Branzburg v. Hayes
1 MED. L. RPTR. 2617, 408 U.S. 665, 92 S. CT. 2646, 33 L. ED. 2D 626 (1972).

* * *

Opinion of the Court by Justice WHITE, announced by the Chief Justice.

* * *

Petitioners Branzburg and Pappas and respondent Caldwell press First Amendment Claims that may be simply put: that to gather news it is often necessary to agree either not to identify the source of information published or to publish only part of the facts revealed, or both; that if the reporter is nevertheless forced to reveal these confidences to a grand jury, the source so identified and other confidential sources of other reporters will be measurably deterred from furnishing publishable information, all to the detriment of the free flow of information protected by the First Amendment. Although petitioners do not claim an absolute privilege against official interrogation in all circumstances, they assert that the reporter should not be forced either to appear or to testify before a grand jury or at trial until and unless sufficient grounds are shown for believing that the reporter possesses information relevant to a crime the grand jury is investigating, that the information the reporter has is unavailable from other sources, and that the need for the information is sufficiently compelling to override the claimed invasion of First Amendment interests occasioned by the disclosure. * * *

We do not question the significance of free speech, press or assembly to the country's welfare. Nor is it suggested that news gathering does not qualify for First Amendment protection; without some protection for seeking out the news, freedom of the press could be eviscerated. But this case involves no intrusions upon speech or assembly, no prior restraint or restriction on what the press may publish, and no express or implied command that the press publish what it prefers to withhold. * * * The use of confidential sources by the press is not forbidden or restricted; reporters remain free to seek news from any source by means within the law. No attempt is made to require the press to publish its sources of information or indiscriminately to disclose them on request.

The sole issue before us is the obligation of reporters to respond to grand jury subpoenas as other citizens do and to answer questions relevant to an investigation into the commission of crime. [Emphasis added.] Citizens generally are not constitutionally immune from grand jury subpoenas; and neither the First Amendment nor other constitutional provision protects the average citizen from disclosing to a grand jury information that he has received in confidence. The claim is, however, that reporters are exempt from these obligations because if forced to respond to subpoenas and identify their sources or disclose other confidences, their informants will refuse or be reluctant to furnish newsworthy information in the future. * * *

It is clear that the First Amendment does not invalidate every incidental burdening of the press that may result from the enforcement of civil or criminal statutes of general applicability. * * *

The prevailing view is that the press is not free with impunity to publish everything and anything it desires to publish. Although it may deter or regulate what is said or published, the press may not circulate knowing or reckless falsehoods damaging to private reputation without subjecting itself to liability for damages, including punitive damages, or even criminal prosecution. See *New York Times Co. v. Sullivan.* * * *

It is thus not surprising that the great weight of authority is that newsmen are not exempt from the normal duty of appearing before a grand jury and answering questions relevant to a criminal investigation. At common law, courts consistently refused to recognize the existence of any privilege authorizing a newsman to refuse to reveal confidential information to a grand jury. * * *

The prevailing constitutional view of the newsman's privilege is very much rooted in the ancient role of the grand jury which has the dual function of determining if there is probable cause to believe that a crime has been committed and of protecting citizens against unfounded criminal prosecutions. Grand jury proceedings are constitutionally mandated for the institution of federal criminal prosecutions for capital or other serious crimes, and "its constitutional prerogatives are rooted in long centuries of Anglo-American history." The Fifth Amendment provides that "No

person shall be held to answer for a capital, or otherwise infamous crime, unless on a presentment or indictment of a Grand Jury." The adoption of the grand jury "in our Constitution as the sole method for preferring charges in serious criminal cases shows the high place it held as an instrument of justice." Although state systems of criminal procedure differ greatly among themselves, the grand jury is similarly guaranteed by many state constitutions and plays an important role in fair and effective law enforcement in the overwhelming majority of the States.

* * *

"It is a grand inquest, a body with powers of investigation and inquisition, the scope of whose inquiries is not to be limited narrowly by questions of propriety or forecasts of the probable result of the investigation, or by doubts whether any particular individual will be found properly subject to an accusation of crime." Hence the grand jury's authority to subpoena witnesses is not only historic, but essential to its task. * * * The long-standing principle that "the public has a right to every man's evidence," except for those persons protected by a constitutional, common law, or statutory privilege, 8 J. Wigmore, *Evidence* § 2192 (McNaughton rev. 1961), is particularly applicable to grand jury proceedings.

A number of States have provided newsmen a statutory privilege of varying breadth, but the majority have not done so, and none has been provided by federal statute. Until now the only testimonial privilege for unofficial witnesses that is rooted in the Federal Constitution is the Fifth Amendment privilege against compelled self-incrimination. We are asked to create another by interpreting the First Amendment to grant newsmen a testimonial privilege that other citizens do not enjoy. This we decline to do.

* * *

The argument that the flow of news will be diminished by compelling reporters to aid the grand jury in a criminal investigation is not irrational, nor are the records before us silent on the matter. But we remain unclear how often and to what extent informers are actually deterred from furnishing information when newsmen are forced to testify before a grand jury. The available data indicates that some newsmen rely a great deal on confidential sources and that some informants are particularly sensitive to the threat of exposure and may be silenced if it is held by this Court that, ordinarily, newsmen must testify pursuant to subpoenas, but the evidence fails to demonstrate that there would be a significant constriction of the flow of news to the public if this Court reaffirms the prior common law and constitutional rule regarding the testimonial obligations of newsmen. Estimates of the inhibiting effect of such subpoenas on the willingness of informants to make disclosures to newsmen are widely divergent and to a great extent speculative. * * * Reliance by the press on confidential informants does not mean that all such sources will in fact dry up because of the later possible appearance of the newsman before a grand jury. The reporter may never be called and if he objects to testifying, the prosecution may not insist. * * *

Accepting the fact, however, that an undetermined number of informants not themselves implicated in crime will nevertheless, for whatever reason, refuse to talk to newsmen if they fear identification by a reporter in an official investigation, we cannot accept the argument that the public interest in possible future news about crime from undisclosed, unverified sources must take precedence over the public interest in pursuing and prosecuting those crimes reported to the press by informants and in thus deterring the commission of such crimes in the future.

* * *

It is said that currently press subpoenas have multiplied, that mutual distrust and tension between press and officialdom have increased, that reporting styles have changed, and that there is now more need for confidential sources. * * * These developments, even if true, are treacherous grounds for a far-reaching interpretation of the First Amendment fastening a nationwide rule on courts, grand juries, and prosecuting officials everywhere.

* * *

The requirements of those cases, which hold that a State's interest must be "compelling" or "paramount" to justify even an indirect burden on First Amendment rights, are also met here. As we have indicated, the investigation of crime by the grand jury implements a fundamental governmental role of securing the safety of the person and property of the citizen, and it appears to us that calling reporters to give testimony in the manner and for the reasons that other citizens are called "bears a reasonable relationship to the achievement of the governmental purpose asserted as its justification." If the test is that the Government "convincingly show a substantial relation between the information sought and a subject of overriding and compelling state interest," it is quite apparent (1) that the State has the necessary interest in extirpating the traffic in illegal drugs, in forestalling assassination attempts on the President, and in preventing the community from being disrupted by violent disorders endangering both persons and property; and (2) that, based on the stories Branzburg and Caldwell wrote and Pappas' admitted conduct, the grand jury called these reporters as they would others—because it was likely that they could supply information to help the Government determine whether illegal conduct had occurred, and, if it had, whether there was sufficient evidence to return an indictment.

Similar considerations dispose of the reporters' claims that preliminary to requiring their grand jury appearance, the State must show that a crime has been committed and that they possess relevant information not available from other sources, for only the grand jury itself can make this determination.

* * *

We are unwilling to embark the judiciary on a long and difficult journey to such an uncertain destination. *The administration of a constitutional newsman's privilege would present practical and conceptual difficulties of a high order.* [Emphasis added.] Sooner or later, it would be necessary to define those categories of newsmen who qualified for the privilege, a questionable procedure in light of the traditional doctrine that liberty of the press is the right of the lonely pamphleteer who uses carbon paper or a mimeograph just as much as of the large metropolitan publisher who utilizes the latest photocomposition methods. Freedom of the press is a "fundamental personal right" which "is not confined to newspapers and periodicals. It necessarily embraces pamphlets and leaflets * * *." The informative function asserted by representatives of the organized press in the present cases is also performed by lecturers, political pollsters, novelists, academic researchers, and dramatists. Almost any author may quite accurately assert that he is contributing to the flow of information to the public, that he relies on confidential sources of information, and that these sources will be silenced if he is forced to make disclosures before a grand jury.

In each instance where a reporter is subpoenaed to testify, the courts would also be embroiled in preliminary factual and legal determinations with respect to whether the proper predicate had been laid for the reporters' appearance: Is there probable cause to believe a crime has been committed? Is it likely that the reporter has useful information gained in confidence? Could the grand jury obtain the information elsewhere? Is the official interest sufficient to outweigh the claimed privilege?

* * *

At the federal level, Congress has freedom to determine whether a statutory newsman's privilege is necessary and desirable and to fashion standards and rules as narrow or broad as deemed necessary to address the evil discerned and, equally important, to re-fashion those rules as experience from time to time may dictate. There is also merit in leaving state legislatures free, within First Amendment limits, to fashion their own standards in light of the conditions and problems with respect to the relations between law enforcement officials and press in their own areas. It goes without saying, of course, that we are powerless to erect any bar to state courts responding in their own way and construing their own constitutions so as to recognize a newsman's privilege, either qualified or absolute.

In addition, there is much force in the pragmatic view that the press has at its disposal powerful mechanisms of communication and is far from helpless to protect itself from harassment or substantial harm. Furthermore, if what the newsmen urged in these cases is true—that law enforcement cannot hope to gain and may suffer from subpoenaing newsmen before grand juries—prosecutors will be loath to risk so much for so little. Thus, at the federal level the Attorney General has already fashioned a set of rules for federal officials in connection with subpoenaing members of the press to testify before grand juries or at criminal trials. * * *

Finally, as we have earlier indicated, news gathering is not without its First Amendment protections, and grand jury investigations if instituted or conducted other than in good faith, would pose wholly different issues for resolution under the First Amendment. Official harassment of the press undertaken not for purposes of law enforcement but to disrupt a reporter's relationship with his news sources would have no justification. Grand juries are subject to judicial control and subpoenas to motions to quash. We do not expect courts will forget that grand juries must operate within the limits of the First Amendment as well as the Fifth.

From what we have said, it necessarily follows that the decision in *United States v. Caldwell* must be reversed. If there is no First Amendment privilege to refuse to answer the relevant and material questions asked during a good-faith grand jury investigation, then it is *a fortiori* true that there is no privilege to refuse to appear before such a grand jury until the Government demonstrates some "compelling need" for a newsman's testimony. * * *

The decisions in *Branzburg v. Hayes* and *Branzburg v. Meigs* must be affirmed. * * * In both cases, if what petitioner wrote was true, he had direct information to provide the grand jury concerning the commission of serious crimes.

The only question presented at the present time *In the Matter of Paul Pappas* is whether petitioner Pappas must appear before the grand jury to testify pursuant to subpoena. * * * We affirm the decision of the Massachusetts Supreme Judicial Court and hold that petitioner must appear before the grand jury to answer the questions put to him, subject, of course, to the supervision of the presiding judge as to "the propriety, purposes, and scope of the grand jury inquiry and the pertinence of the probable testimony."

So ordered.

Justice POWELL, concurring.

I add this brief statement to emphasize what seems to me to be the limited nature of the Court's holding. The Court does not hold that newsmen, subpoenaed to testify before a grand jury, are without constitutional rights with respect to the gathering of news or in safeguarding their sources. * * * The solicitude repeatedly shown by this Court for First Amendment freedoms should be sufficient assurance against any such effort, even if one seriously believed that the media—properly free and untrammeled in the fullest sense of these terms—were not able to protect themselves.

As indicated in the concluding portion of the opinion, the Court states that no harassment of newsmen will be tolerated. If a newsman believes that the grand jury investigation is not being conducted in good faith he is not without remedy. Indeed, if the newsman is called upon to give information bearing only a remote and tenuous relationship to the subject of the investigation, or if he has some other reason to believe that his testimony implicates confidential source relationships without a legitimate need of law enforcement, he will have access to the Court on a motion to quash and an appropriate protective order may be entered. The asserted claim to privilege should be judged on its facts by the striking of a proper balance between freedom of the press and the obligation of all citizens to give relevant testimony with respect to criminal conduct. The balance of these vital constitutional and societal interests on a case-by-case basis accords with the tried and traditional way of adjudicating such questions.

Justice STEWART, with whom Justice BRENNAN and Justice MARSHALL join, dissenting.

The Court's crabbed view of the First Amendment reflects a disturbing insensitivity to the critical role of an independent press in our society. The question whether a reporter has a constitutional right to a confidential relationship with his source is of first impression here, but the principles which should guide our decision are as basic as any to be found in the Constitution. While Justice Powell's enigmatic concurring opinion gives some hope of a more flexible view in the future, the court in these cases holds that a newsman has no First Amendment right to protect his sources when called before a grand jury. The Court thus invites state and federal authorities to undermine the historic independence of the press by attempting to annex the journalistic profession as an investigative arm of government. Not only will this decision impair performance of the press' constitutionally protected functions, but it will, I am convinced, in the long run, harm rather than help the administration of justice.

I respectfully dissent.

The reporter's constitutional right to a confidential relationship with his source stems from the broad societal interest in a full and free flow of information to the public. It is this basic concern that underlies the Constitution's protection of a free press because the guarantee is "not for the benefit of the press so much as for the benefit of all of us."

* * *

No less important to the news dissemination process is the gathering of information. News must not be unnecessarily cut off at its source, for without freedom to acquire information the right to publish would be impermissibly compromised. Accordingly, a right to gather news, of some dimensions, must exist. * * *

The right to gather news implies, in turn, a right to a confidential relationship between a reporter and his source. This proposition follows as a matter of simple logic once three factual predicates are recognized: (1) newsmen require informants to gather news; (2) confidentiality—the promise or understanding that names or certain aspects of communications will be kept off-the-record—is essential to the creation and maintenance of a news-gathering relationship with informants; and (3) the existence of an unbridled subpoena power—the absence of a constitutional right protecting, in *any* way, a confidential relationship from compulsory process—will either deter sources from divulging information or deter reporters from gathering and publishing information.

It is obvious that informants are necessary to the news-gathering process as we know it today. If it is to perform its constitutional mission, the press must do far more than merely print public statements or public prepared handouts.

* * *

It is equally obvious that the promise of confidentiality may be a necessary prerequisite to a productive relationship between a newsman and his informants. An officeholder may fear his superior; a member of the bureaucracy, his associates; a dissident, the scorn of majority opinion. All may have information valuable to the public discourse, yet each may be willing to relate that information only in confidence to a reporter whom he trusts.

* * *

Finally, and most important, when governmental officials possess an unchecked power to compel newsmen to disclose information received in confidence, sources will clearly be deterred from giving information, and reporters will clearly be deterred from publishing it, because uncertainty about exercise of the power will lead to "self-censorship."

After today's decision, the potential informant can never be sure that his identity or off-the-record communications will not subsequently be revealed through the compelled testimony of a newsman. A public spirited person inside government, who is not implicated in any crime, will now be fearful of revealing corruption or other governmental wrongdoing, because he will now know he can subsequently be identified by use of compulsory process.

* * *

Surveys have verified that an unbridled subpoena power will substantially impair the flow of news to the public, especially in sensitive areas involving governmental officials, financial affairs, political figures, dissidents, or minority groups that require in-depth, investigative reporting. And the Justice Department has recognized that "compulsory process in some circumstances may have a limiting effect on the exercise of First Amendment rights." *No* evidence contradicting the existence of such deterrent effects was offered at the trials or in the briefs here by the petitioners in *Caldwell* or by the respondents in *Branzburg* and *Pappas*.

The impairment of the flow of news cannot, of course, be proven with scientific precision, as the Court seems to demand. * * *

But we have never before demanded that First Amendment rights rest on elaborate empirical studies demonstrating beyond any conceivable doubt that deterrent effects exist; we have never before required proof of the exact number of people potentially affected by governmental action, who would actually be dissuaded from engaging in First Amendment activity.

* * *

Thus, we cannot escape the conclusion that when neither the reporter nor his source can rely on the shield of confidentiality against unrestrained use of the grand jury's subpoena power, valuable information will not be published and the public dialogue will inevitably be impoverished.

* * *

Accordingly, when a reporter is asked to appear before a grand jury and reveal confidences, I would hold that the government must (1) show that there is probable cause to believe that the newsman has information which is clearly relevant to a specific probable violation of law; (2) demonstrate that the information sought cannot be obtained by alternative means

less destructive of First Amendment rights; and (3) demonstrate a compelling and overriding interest in the information. [Emphasis added.]

This is not to say that a grand jury could not issue a subpoena until such a showing were made, and it is not to say that a newsman would be in any way privileged to ignore any subpoena that was issued. Obviously, before the government's burden to make such a showing were triggered, the reporter would have to move to quash the subpoena, asserting the basis on which he considered the particular relationship a confidential one.

The crux of the Court's rejection of any newsman's privilege is its observation that only "where news sources themselves are implicated in crime or possess information *relevant* to the grand jury's task need they or the reporter be concerned about grand jury subpoenas." But this is a most misleading construct. * * * As noted above, given the grand jury's extraordinarily broad investigative powers and the weak standards of relevance and materiality that apply during such inquiries, reporters, if they have no testimonial privilege, will be called to give information about informants who have neither committed crimes nor have information about crime. It is to avoid deterrence of such sources and thus to prevent needless injury to First Amendment values that I think the government must be required to show probable cause that the newsman has information which is clearly relevant to a specific probable violation of criminal law.

Similarly, a reporter may have information from a confidential source which is "related" to the commission of crime, but the government may be able to obtain an indictment or otherwise achieve its purposes by subpoenaing persons other than the reporter. It is an obvious but important truism that when government aims have been fully served, there can be no legitimate reason to disrupt a confidential relationship between a reporter and his source. To do so would not aid the administration of justice and would only impair the flow of information to the public. Thus, it is to avoid deterrence of such sources that I think the government must show that there are no alternative means for the grand jury to obtain the information sought.

Both the "probable cause" and "alternative means" requirements would thus serve the vital function of mediating between the public interest in the administration of justice and the constitutional protection of the full flow of information. These requirements would avoid a direct conflict between these competing concerns, and they would generally provide adequate protection for newsmen.

* * *

The sad paradox of the Court's position is that when a grand jury may exercise an unbridled subpoena power, and sources involved in sensitive matters become fearful of disclosing information, the newsman will not only cease to be a useful grand jury witness; he will cease to investigate and publish information about issues of public import. I cannot subscribe to such an anomalous result, for, in my view, the interests protected by the First Amendment are not antagonistic to the administration of justice. Rather, they can, in the long run, only be complementary, and for that reason must be given great "breathing space."

* * *

Accordingly, I would affirm the judgment of the Court of Appeals in United States v. Caldwell. In the other two cases before us, Branzburg v. Hayes and Branzburg v. Meigs, and In the Matter of Paul Pappas, I would vacate the judgments and remand the cases for further proceedings not inconsistent with the views I have expressed in this opinion.

COMMENT

Justice Douglas dissented separately, arguing that the First Amendment by its terms creates an absolute privilege against forced disclosure, be it of sources or information. He castigated the New York Times and the federal government for advocating "timid, watered-down, emasculated versions of the First Amendment." The Times had endorsed the qualified privilege in its brief.

The Branzburg case had been presaged by Justice Stewart while he was a Circuit Court of Appeals judge fourteen years earlier. In Garland v. Torre, 1 Med. L. Rptr. 2541, 259 F.2d 545 (2d Cir.), cert. denied 358 U.S. 910 (1958), he wrote for the court in a case where entertainer Judy Garland had sued newspaper columnist Marie Torre for libel. Garland wanted the identity of one of Torre's anonymous sources. Torre went to jail instead. The reliability of the source was essential to the libel case. As such, "The question asked of the appellant went to the heart of the plaintiff's claim." This reappeared in Stewart's Branzburg dissent as the "clearly relevant" first prong of the qualified privilege test.

Following Branzburg, Stewart became an advocate for the notion that the First Amendment creates a special status for the press.[16] Until his retirement in 1981, he consistently urged in his opinions that the news media needed rights broader than those applicable to the public.

The Branzburg case also represented the start of a consistent view by Justice White that laws of "general applicability" do not violate the First Amendment when applied to news organizations, even if those laws have some deterrent effect on the media.[17] Until his retirement in 1993, White resisted the growth of special status rights for the press, authoring several important majority opinions in cases on newsgathering issues.

Branzburg featured two elements that have come to play a large role in First Amendment litigation. The press presented itself as an "agent of the public," a notion White disputed, but which has become a key component in the development of newsgathering rights. The opinion also introduced a debate among the justices over how much proof is needed to establish a chilling effect on the media. Although the Court has never established any standards, and in fact continues to assess the chilling effects of actions against the media rather intuitively, it is common in newsgathering rights cases for courts to weigh the relative chilling effect of different types of interference. For example, in Idaho v. Salisbury, 24 Med. L. Rptr. 2454, 924 P.2d 208 (Id. 1996), the court determined that requiring a television reporter to testify about what occurred at the scene of a traffic accident was unlikely to have an effect on newsgathering.

> [R]equiring production of the nonconfidential and/or unbroadcast videotape will have little, if any, chilling effect on the ability of newspersons to gather news or on their editorial process. . . . Credibility balks at the idea that a TV station might stop covering fatal automobile accidents if a conse-

---

16. Stewart, Or of the Press, 26 Hastings L. Rev. 631 (1975).
17. Prendergast, Taming the Watchdog: Justice Byron White and the Repudiation of Press Privilege, 1 Comm. L. & Policy 177 (1996).

quence is that the station may be required to produce the videotape in a criminal prosecution.

The court held that the county prosecutor's request passed the qualified privilege test.

Most journalists, however, have seen protecting source confidentiality as an ethical and professional imperative. Few tenets of journalism are so sacred as that calling for reporters to abide by promises of confidentiality. Indeed, in some of the cases that have arisen, the potential harm to newsgathering seems so slight and the benefit to society from disclosure so great that only a stand based on principle can explain refusal to testify.

In Idaho in 1980, Ellen Marks of *The Idaho Statesman* wrote an article based on an interview with a father who had taken his daughter into hiding in violation of a court's custody order following divorce. The child's mother brought a habeas corpus proceeding to regain lawful custody, and Marks was called to testify while she covered the habeas corpus hearing. Marks refused to testify and moved to quash. The magistrate found her in contempt and levied a $500 per day fine. The Idaho Supreme Court ultimately affirmed the contempt order. *Marks v. Vehlow,* 9 Med. L. Rptr. 2361, 671 P.2d 473 (Id. 1983). Disclosure was ordered because both the writ of habeas corpus and the safety of the child constituted compelling interests, and Marks was the only person with any clue to the father's whereabouts.

Most cases where privilege is claimed present conflicts between newsgathering and law enforcement. William Farr of the *Los Angeles Herald-Examiner,* for example, refused to disclose to a county court judge the names of prosecution attorneys who had supplied him with a copy of a witness's deposition in the gruesome Charles Manson case, this after the judge had forbidden officers of the court to publicize the case. Farr spent two months in jail.[18]

Judges sometimes take umbrage when their direct orders are defied. In the *Rosato* case,[19] bribery-conspiracy indictments had been handed down by a Fresno County grand jury against three accused. A day before the grand jury transcripts would have become public documents, the judge sealed the record for the duration of the trial and issued a restrictive order prohibiting public communications by attorneys, parties, public officials, and witnesses. Stories replete with quotations from the sealed transcript nevertheless appeared in the *Fresno Bee,* and the judge demanded to know where they came from. When he asked reporters to name their sources, he was met with silence. Two reporters, the city editor, and the managing editor of the *Bee* were then cited for contempt.

The court's rationale was that in enforcing its power over its own officers, the concomitant interest of journalists in protecting their sources was irrelevant and the California "shield" law inapplicable. The journalists went to jail.

Punishment has most frequently resulted from refusals to cooperate with grand juries and in criminal trials. The Supreme Judicial Court of Maine affirmed a conviction of criminal contempt against Robert Hohler, a reporter for the *Concord Monitor* in New Hampshire. Hohler had refused to testify in a murder trial about an article based on an interview with the defendant that named the defendant as the source. The court reversed a Superior Court holding that Maine would recognize a qualified privilege against compelled testimony concerning nonconfidential, published information.[20]

In a celebrated case of yesteryear, Peter Bridge of the *Newark News* was jailed for three weeks because he would not reveal to a grand jury unpublished details of an interview with a state bureaucrat who alleged she had been offered a bribe. Bridge had forfeited protection under the New Jersey shield law, as it stood in 1972, by naming the source in the article. New Jersey's highest court declined to hear the case, and the U.S. Supreme Court denied a stay of his contempt sentence.[21]

At the opposite end are cases establishing broad protections for journalists. ABC was sued by the Food Lion grocery chain for fraud, trespass, and various other causes of action after the network aired reports alleging improper food handling by employees of the chain. In pretrial discovery, Food Lion sought testimony and

---

18. *Farr v. Superior Court of Los Angeles County,* 1 Med. L. Rptr. 2545, 99 Cal.Rptr. 342 (1971) *cert. denied* 409 U.S. 1011 (1972).
19. *Rosato v. Superior Court,* 1 Med. L. Rptr. 2560, 124 Cal.Rptr. 427 (1975), *cert. denied* 427 U.S. 912 (1976).

20. *Maine v. Hohler,* 15 Med. L. Rptr. 1611 (Maine 1988).
21. *In re Bridge,* 295 A.2d 3 (N.J. 1972), *cert. denied* 410 U.S. 991 (1973).

evidence from various nonparties, including hotels and delivery services. ABC sought to quash the subpoenas. The court quashed, noting that the attempted discovery would

> [C]learly infringe ABC's First Amendment rights with regard to its confidential sources. Although the discovery is not requested directly from ABC, the inquiries directed to third-parties nonetheless implicate ABC's privilege. . . . Food Lion has proposed that ABC can "screen out" confidential sources when subpoena productions are made, but the court would find this to be completely impracticable in view of the breadth of the subpoenas. *Food Lion, Inc. v. Capital Cities/ABC, Inc.,* 24 Med. L. Rptr. 2431 (M.D.N.C. 1996).

Journalists whose claims are denied and who face being jailed have recently had some success in getting their cases heard by a different judge or court based on filing for a writ of habeas corpus. In *Lenhart v. Texas,* 24 Med. L. Rptr. 2497 (S.D.Tex. 1996), a reporter persuaded a federal court to order her release after a state trial court had refused. A federal district court in Florida did the same after *Miami Herald* reporter David Kidwell had been jailed by a state trial court judge for refusing to testify about an interview with an accused murderer. *Kidwell v. McCutcheon,* No. 96-2888-CIV (S.D.Fla. 1996). Another case, *In re Willon,* 24 Med. L. Rptr. 2121, 55 Cal.Rptr. 245 (Cal.App. 1996), featured a direct habeas corpus appeal within the state court system.

It turned out that *Branzburg* was really the beginning rather than the end of the debate over journalist's privilege.

The Aftermath of *Branzburg*

The prevailing opinion in *Branzburg* attempted to limit the decision to the issue of whether or not journalists were required to appear and testify when called by a grand jury, but no Supreme Court case can be so limited in application and interpretation. Much as in libel law, the law of journalist's privilege varies from jurisdiction to jurisdiction and from context to context. Unlike libel law, however, the reporter who wants to understand the entire law of journalist's privilege must consider the standards of the federal circuit courts and of a number of federal district courts in addition to the laws of the fifty states.

The *Branzburg* decision has been given almost as many interpretations as there have been lower courts construing it. Some have declared that the opinion precludes creation of a journalist's privilege.[22] Others have declared that *Branzburg* itself creates a First Amendment privilege.[23] The dicta that state legislatures and courts are free to use statutes, common law, or state constitutional law to devise their own privileges have been widely followed.[24]

Some form of the privilege, most often a variation of the three-part test first offered by the Ninth Circuit in *Caldwell* and championed by Justice Stewart in *Branzburg,* has permeated the constitutional, statutory, and common law of both state and federal courts. The test was adopted quickly in several federal circuit courts of appeal.[25] Today only one circuit has declined to adopt a federal privilege when asked.[26] In states where the legislature did not adopt a shield law, the courts have commonly created a privilege.[27]

It is important to note, however, that none of the opinions in *Branzburg* discussed the constitutional status of notes, tapes, photographs, or other raw materials obtained or created during newsgathering. None of the justices addressed whether a privilege might apply if a reporter had not observed likely criminal activity. And none spoke to the status of journalist's privilege in civil actions or in nontrial proceedings.

One of the most typical narrow interpretations of *Branzburg* occurs when journalists are requested to provide testimony or evidence that does not implicate confidential sources or infor-

---

22. *In re Roche,* 6 Med. L. Rptr. 2121, 411 N.E.2d 466 (Mass. 1980); *Austin v. Memphis Publishing,* 9 Med. L. Rptr. 1986, 621 S.W.2d 397 (Tenn.App. 1981).
23. *Baker v. F&F Investment,* 470 F.2d 778 (2d Cir. 1972), cert. denied 411 U.S. 966 (1973); *Kansas v. Sandstrom,* 4 Med. L. Rptr. 1333, 581 P.2d 812 (Kan. 1978); *Winegard v. Oxberger,* 3 Med. L. Rptr. 1326, 258 N.W.2d 847 (Iowa 1977).
24. *Illinois v. Arya,* 19 Med. L. Rptr. 2079, 589 N.E.2d 832 (Ill.App. 1992) (extensive review of developments in other states and in federal courts).
25. Monk, *Evidentiary Privilege for Journalists' Sources: Theory and Statutory Protection,* 51 Missouri L.Rev. 1 (1986).
26. *Storer Communications v. Giovan,* 13 Med. L. Rptr. 2049, 810 F.2d 580 (6th Cir. 1987).
27. Simon, *Reporter Privilege: Can Nebraska Pass a Shield Law to Bind the Whole World?* 61 Nebraska L.Rev. 446, 469–475 (1982).

mation. Many courts reason that the position of journalists is no different from that of other citizens in such situations. Moreover, a journalist witnessing a crime clearly has no testimonial privilege under *Branzburg.*

Furthermore, the Court held narrowly in *Branzburg* that the First Amendment, because it is silent on the privilege, does not immunize a journalist from the usual duty of responding to a grand jury subpoena seeking evidence in a criminal case. Not even Justice Stewart believed that a subpoena could simply be ignored. Only Justice Douglas thought that. Both Stewart and Justice Powell in his concurring opinion stress the need for a judge to balance the interests of reporters and of justice by allowing a hearing before a reporter is compelled to testify.

The case is made even narrower by the majority's reliance upon the constitutionality guaranteed function of grand juries as an interest counterbalancing journalists' interests in First Amendment activities. Justice White consistently emphasizes that no privilege will be recognized due to the facts of the case. Perhaps the combined appeals in *Branzburg* did not represent the best occasion for the press to seek a constitutionally based privilege before the Supreme Court. It is clear from Powell's concurrence that he would have been more favorably disposed to a privilege claim under a different fact pattern.

CBS v. Jackson

18 MED. L. RPTR. 2110, 578 SO.2D 698 (FLA. 1991).

PER CURIAM:

During a law enforcement operation, police arrested Jackson on cocaine possession charges. A CBS news team videotaped portions of that operation and broadcast excerpts from the videotapes on television. In preparation for trial, Jackson deposed the arresting officer whose recounting of the arrest was inconclusive. Jackson then served a subpoena *duces tecum* on CBS, seeking the portions of the videotapes pertaining to him which were not televised (outtakes). In response, CBS moved to quash the subpoena, claiming that the outtakes were protected work product under the journalist's qualified privilege. The trial court denied the motion, finding the privilege inapplicable because the information was not from a confidential source. Moreover, the trial court

found that, if the qualified privilege indeed applied, the record showed that Jackson had met and overcome the burden of proof necessary to compel disclosure of the outtakes. The district court denied CBS's petition for certiorari and certified the aforementioned question to this Court as one of great public importance.

At the trial court and before the district court, CBS argued that journalists, because of the nature of their work and the implication of the first amendment guarantee of a free press, have a qualified privilege against the compelled disclosure of any information obtained while on a news-gathering mission. CBS contends that such information is privileged unless and until a judicial officer determines that the party seeking discovery has established that (1) the information sought to be obtained is relevant and material, (2) all alternative sources to obtain the information have been exhausted, and (3) there is a compelling need for the information. We disagree that such a qualified privilege exists under the circumstances of this case.

We accepted jurisdiction in this case before we published *Miami Herald Publishing Co. v. Morejon,* 561 So.2d 577 [17 Med. L. Rptr. 1920] (Fla. 1990). There, we observed that the journalist's qualified privilege originated from *Branzburg v. Hayes.* . . . In *Branzburg* the reporters claimed that, if forced to testify before a grand jury and reveal the identities of their confidential sources, those sources would refuse to furnish information in the future, thereby hampering the reporters' news-gathering ability. The plurality opinion rejected the reporters' claim, but, however, recognized that "without some protection for seeking out the news, freedom of the press could be eviscerated."

* * *

In *Morgan v. State,* 337 So.2d 951 [1 Med. L. Rptr. 2589] (Fla. 1976), and *Tribune Co. v. Huffstetler,* 489 So.2d 722 [12 Med. L. Rptr. 2288] (Fla. 1986), this Court held that journalists have a qualified privilege against the forced revelation of their confidential sources of information and applied the case-by-case balancing approach set forth by Justice Powell. In *Morejon,* however, we rejected the claim of a qualified privilege when the journalist was an eyewitness to a police search and subsequent arrest of the defendant. We held that "there is no privilege, qualified, limited, or otherwise, which protects journalists from testifying as to their eyewitness observations of a relevant event in a subsequent court proceeding. The fact that the reporter in this case witnessed the event while on a newsgathering mission does not alter our decision," *Morejon*, 561 So.2d at 580. We therefore found it unnecessary to balance the respective interests involved.

In the case under review, the sought-after discovery is the untelevised CBS videotapes of Jackson's arrest. From a first amendment privilege standpoint, we can perceive no significant difference in the examination of an electronic recording of an event and verbal testimony about the event. What Jackson seeks to discover is physical evidence of the events surrounding his arrest. His request does not implicate any sources of information. We see no realistic threat of restraint or impingement on the news-gathering process by subjecting the videotapes to discovery. Although the media may be somewhat inconvenienced by having to respond to such discovery requests, mere inconvenience neither eviscerates freedom of the press nor triggers the application of the journalists' qualified privilege. Because the qualified privilege does not apply under the circumstances of this case, we need not balance the respective interests involved.

* * *

While CBS seeks to implicate the first amendment, we think that its concern is more legitimately directed toward the trouble and expense of having to furnish the video outtakes. Neither CBS nor anyone else should be required to furnish photographs, videotapes, or similar tangible property acquired in the course of its business to a party with whom it is not in litigation without being reimbursed for the reasonable expenses incurred in making such property available. In the event the person who is subpoenaed to produce the property cannot obtain satisfactory reimbursement for its reasonable expenses, such person may seek a protective order under Florida Rule of Civil Procedure 1.280(c). These rules are broad enough to protect the media and similarly situated entities, as well as those seeking discovery.

In this case, the subpoena itself reflected the willingness to pay for the reasonable costs of preparation of the outtakes. Therefore, CBS has no basis to complain. We answer the certified question in the negative and approve the decision of the district court of appeal.

It is so ordered.

COMMENT

The reasoning of the courts in *CBS v. Jackson* and related cases is similar to that used in the plain view doctrine in criminal procedure law. Evidence of criminal activity that occurs in plain view—where any person might have been able to see it—is freely admissible in court. *Coolidge v. New Hampshire*, 403 U.S. 443 (1971). The courts often carefully distinguish between what anyone could have seen and what is exclusive to journalists. When an insurance company refused to pay a claim, basing its defense on a counterclaim of arson, a nonparty newspaper was subpoenaed to provide photographs taken by a staff member. The Michigan Court of Appeals refused to extend its qualified privilege to anything but confidential materials:

> After recognizing the *Branzburg* holding of no First Amendment privilege as to *confidential* sources, it would be anomalous for us to establish a First Amendment privilege for *nonconfidential* materials.
>
> [T]he argument journalists have made that their ability to gather news is dependent upon the right to protect confidentiality . . . simply has no applicability. . . .
>
> Although Booth [the newspaper company] would have us speculate that the administrative burden created by producing nonconfidential materials may someday grow to compete with, and ultimately consume, the journalist's time and resources essential to gathering and disseminating the news, we decline to engage in such speculation. In this regard, Booth relies upon a bald, self-serving conclusion which is totally unsupported. . . . *Marketos v. American Employers Insurance Co.*, 18 Med. L. Rptr. 1177, 460 N.W.2d 272 (Mich.App. 1990).

Use of anonymous sources was widespread in the early 1970s, with some reporters using them in half their stories. By 1984, however, reliance on anonymous sources had decreased significantly.[28] Since a majority of jurisdictions had accepted a privilege in some form, the declining reliance on anonymous sources cannot be attributed to a chilling effect alone. Journalists report that on-the-record sources are preferred to assure credibility. Many news organizations have also become more cautious in their use of confidential sources following nationwide embarrassment in 1981 when *Washington Post* reporter

---

28. St. Dizier, *Reporters' Use of Confidential Sources, 1974 and 1984: A Comparative Study*, 6 Newsp. Res. J. 44 (Summer 1985).

Janet Cooke admitted that statements attributed to a confidential source in an article that had won a Pulitzer Prize had been fabricated. Now reporters generally must seek editorial review and approval before using confidential sources,[29] and the casual use of anonymous sources is forbidden. Only extremely important stories that would go unreported in the absence of an anonymous source should use them, editors say. "It places an extra burden on the reporter to confirm the source's information from independent, disinterested records and, where possible, from on-the-record interviews with other participants in the story."[30]

Subsequent courts have agreed that the privilege, and with it the decision to disclose or not, lies with the journalist, not the source. *People v. LeGrand,* 4 Med. L. Rptr. 2524, 415 N.Y.S.2d 252 (N.Y.Sup.Ct., App.Div. 1979). The major reason for granting the journalist control over the privilege is that, unlike traditional evidentiary privileges journalists' privilege serves the public interest directly by enhancing the free flow of information. By contrast, in doctor-patient or lawyer-client privileges, the patient or client, not the professional, controls the privilege. The interest protected is primarily private, although these professional privileges assume that the public interest is indirectly enhanced by increased confidence in these professionals.

The greatest puzzle of the various opinions in *Branzburg* was the dispositive concurring opinion by Justice Powell. Although joining the result, Powell did not reject a qualified privilege based on the First Amendment. Powell instead emphasized that courts would be open to journalists' claims "under circumstances were legitimate First Amendment interests require protection."

Why didn't Powell join the dissenters? Apparently he thought journalists should obey the summons of a grand jury. Only after appearing could they press their privilege claims. This approach would have done Caldwell, who asserted that merely appearing would chill sources, no good.

Would Powell's approach be the same as Stewart's in contexts other than grand jury inquiries? No. For Powell, Stewart's three-part test placed too heavy a burden of proof on government. A balancing approach, on the other hand, placed the clashing interests in a more desirable state of rough equivalence. Do you agree with Powell that a journalist should at least appear before the grand jury and that rights to confidentiality should be determined after questions have been posed?

Enactment of a federal shield law, qualified or unqualified, seems unlikely. Bills to establish a federal privilege have been introduced repeatedly but have gone nowhere. One major reason is that the press itself is not sure it supports a federal shield law. Under the rationale that what Congress gives, Congress can take away, many members of the press oppose shield laws and prefer instead a privilege squarely based on the First Amendment. A careful count of the justices' votes in *Branzburg* makes clear that a majority supported some basis in the First Amendment for journalist's privilege. Under the Supremacy Clause of the U.S. Constitution, a First Amendment–based privilege would override any less protective statute.

Although the majority of federal circuits have recognized a First Amendment–based privilege, the state courts in those circuits have frequently ignored those precedents and applied a privilege on state law grounds alone. See, e.g., *Hopewell v. Midcontinent Broadcasting Corp.,* 24 Med. L. Rptr. 1091, 538 N.W.2d 780 (S.D. 1995). Sometimes the state privilege and the First Amendment privilege are said to be the same in nature and scope. See, e.g., *Kurzynski v. Spaeth,* 24 Med. L. Rptr. 1016, 538 N.W.2d 554 (Wis.App. 1995). Frequently, though, the lower courts have limited application of *Branzburg* to situations where journalists are called to appear before grand juries. See, e.g., *Vaughn v. Georgia,* 16 Med. L. Rptr. 2020, 381 S.E.2d 30 (Ga. 1989).

Apparently, only a decision by the Supreme Court will result in a uniform, nationwide rule or test, but the Court has never again heard a case requesting that it recognize the privilege. The issue arose indirectly in *Philadelphia Newspapers v. Hepps,* 12 Med. L. Rptr. 1977, 475 U.S. 767, 106 S. Ct. 1558 (1986), a libel case in which the Pennsylvania shield law was preventing a plaintiff from identifying sources used in a news story. The majority opinion's casual dismissal of the shield law issue indicated the Court is comfortable with how privilege law has developed. It does not constitute endorsement, however.

---

29. Day, *Ethics in Media Communications: Cases and Controversies* 134–139 (1991).
30. Williams, *Investigative Reporting and Editing* 64 (1978).

The great surprise of the *Branzburg* decision is that its most influential feature has not been Justice White's plurality decision but Justice Stewart's dissent advocating a qualified First Amendment–based journalist's privilege. The Stewart approach now governs much of the law of journalist's privilege in the context of civil *and* criminal proceedings. The three-part test of Stewart's *Branzburg* dissent has thus become enormously important.

Although the influence of Stewart's three-part test on the lower courts is clear, its application has not always been. Variations on the three-part test are sometimes semantic. At other times, they either expand or contract the test. Where "information going to the heart of the claim" subsumes "relevance" and "compelling public need," we have a two-part test. Where the information seeker's purpose must be more than "frivolous," we may have a four-part test.

Washington state's qualified privilege, which is part of its common law, requires all or part of a five-part test. The privilege can be defeated by showing that the request for information is necessary, there are no alternative sources, the purpose is nonfrivolous, the reporter got the information by unacceptable means, and the source had no reasonable expectation of confidentiality. *Senear v. Daily Journal-American,* 8 Med. L. Rptr. 1151, 641 P.2d 1180 (Wash. 1982). Why do some courts rely on a common law–based privilege rather than a constitutional privilege? In West Virginia, which also has a common law–based privilege, the burden may be placed on the reporter to show harm to the newsgathering process in support of a motion to quash. *Maurice v. NLRB,* 7 Med. L. Rptr. 2221, 691 F.2d 182 (4th Cir. 1982).

In addition to Washington and West Virginia, only a handful of courts, most notably the Third Circuit and Florida, have relied primarily on common law as the source of a journalist's privilege. Part of the reluctance to use common law is that common law traditionally opposes the creation of evidentiary privileges. Even courts that have used common law also use constitutional analysis, though, an indication perhaps that the First Amendment newsgathering arguments are viewed as stronger in any event. *In re Grand Jury Subpoena,* 20 Med. L. Rptr. 1232, 963 F.2d 567 (3d Cir. 1992); *Miami Herald Publishing Co. v. Morejon,* 561 So.2d 577 (Fla. 1991).

The use of federal common law by the Third Circuit is somewhat anomalous. Ordinarily, only state courts may create common law. *Erie Railroad Co. v. Tompkins,* 304 U.S. 64 (1938). But federal courts retain authority to create common law rules of evidence and procedure, which include journalist's privilege. *Riley v. City of Chester,* 5 Med. L. Rptr. 2161, 612 F.2d 708 (3d Cir. 1979). In *Riley,* the court said that the Federal Rules of Evidence justified its creation of a common law privilege. The test adopted mirrored Stewart's three-part test. In diversity of citizenship cases brought on state law grounds, federal courts are supposed to apply state substantive law, but may choose to use federal law for evidence or procedure.

Each part of the Stewart test has itself been interpreted in litigation. The requirement that there be "probable cause to believe that the newsman has information which is clearly relevant to a specific violation of law" has become a more generalized requirement, applicable to civil cases as well, that the journalist have information that can make a difference in the case. The party seeking disclosure must convince the court that the information sought addresses issues in the case directly. In *Campbell v. Klevenhagen,* 18 Med. L. Rptr. 2113, 760 F.Supp. 1206 (S.D.Tex. 1991), the trial judge denied a request by the defendant in a murder trial to force reporters to attend the trial on the chance that they would spot sources among the spectators. The request was speculative only; it failed the threshold requirement of relevance.

Similarly, the requirement that the requester "demonstrate that the information sought cannot be obtained by alternative means less destructive of First Amendment right" has generally been interpreted to have two meanings: one where confidential sources are at issue, another where they are not. Where a reporter's confidential sources are asked for, the vast majority of courts have held that testimony may be compelled only if all alternatives have been exhausted. In that event, forcing testimony from a journalist will be the least restrictive means for getting information. The courts are also careful to assure that no more disclosure is required than seems absolutely necessary. *Denk v. Iowa District Court,* 20 Med. L. Rptr. 1454 (Iowa 1992). When the information sought is not confidential, the requester need only show a reasonable attempt to identify alternative sources. *Shoen v. Shoen,* 23 Med. L. Rptr. 1522, 48 F.3d 412 (9th Cir. 1995).

The third part of the test, that a party must "demonstrate a compelling and overriding interest in the information," has also been subject to two major lines of interpretation. When information is confidential and the trial is criminal, only a showing of a compelling interest akin to a constitutional right has been accepted to force disclosure. *U.S. v. Burke,* 700 F.2d 70 (2d Cir. 1983). When the information is not confidential, some courts continue to apply the compelling interest analysis, *Grunseth v. Marriott Corp.,* 23 Med. L. Rptr. 1148, 868 F.Supp. 333 (D.D.C. 1994), but others reduce the burden on requesters to proof of a substantial interest or some like formula. *SEC v. Seahawk Deep Ocean Technology, Inc.,* 24 Med. L. Rptr. 1856, 166 F.R.D. 268 (D.Conn. 1996).

Justice White's opinion for the Court in *Branzburg* raises another problem with the privilege that has not been resolved. Who is a journalist or reporter? Who is covered by the constitutional or statutory shield? Can a workable definition be achieved? Was Daniel Ellsberg, who leaked the Pentagon Papers, covered? What about underground, minority, and student editors? Are pollsters, pamphleteers, book authors, freelancers, researchers covered? White believed that crafting a privilege would require courts to define categories of qualified, legitimate, or "respectable" journalists, a process that offends a First Amendment tradition hostile to any form of state certification or licensing.

Two reporters for the student newspaper at Hofstra University were ordered to testify at a pretrial hearing in a criminal case. Their argument that New York's shield law protected them was rejected because the law "* * * is limited to protecting the class of professional journalists, who, for gain or livelihood are engaged in preparing or editing of news for a newspaper." The shield law requires that a newspaper have paid circulation and a second class postal classification to qualify. Hofstra's paper had neither. *New York v. Hennessy,* 13 Med. L. Rptr. 1109 (N.Y.Dist.Ct. 1986).

The question of whether or not someone is qualified to claim the privilege arises only rarely, but when it does, the focus is typically on how well the person fits within the free flow of information principle announced by Stewart in *Branzburg. Matera v. Maricopa County Superior Court,* 19 Med. L. Rptr. 2053, 825 P.2d 971 (Ariz.App. 1992); *Silkwood v. Kerr-McGee,* 3 Med. L. Rptr. 1087, 563 F.2d 433 (10th Cir. 1977).

A student, Mario Brajuha, who was employed as a waiter at a restaurant while doing field research on "The Sociology of the American Restaurant" as part of his work for his Ph.D. degree, was subpoenaed to appear before a federal grand jury investigating a fire at the restaurant. Brajuha moved to quash on grounds that the material sought should be privileged. Academics doing scholarly research, he argued, would be chilled if material identifying parties to the research was routinely disclosable. The Second Circuit did not find a privilege under the facts of the case and remanded to a lower court for more fact-finding. The appeals court did say that a privilege should be available if a researcher can demonstrate the nature and seriousness of the research. *In re Grand Jury Subpoena,* 11 Med. L. Rptr. 1224, 750 F.2d 223 (2d Cir. 1984). How would a researcher demonstrate the nature and seriousness of a research project?

The Ninth Circuit expressly rejected the proffered scholar's privilege when a Ph.D. student at Washington State University was called before a grand jury to testify about his research on, and relationships with persons in, militant animal rights groups following a bombing on campus. *Scarce v. U.S.,* 21 Med. L. Rptr. 1972, 5 F.3d 397 (9th Cir. 1993).

State Law Privileges: Shield Laws, Constitutions, and Common Law

State courts and legislatures took the Supreme Court's recommendation to consider their own laws seriously. Prior to 1972, only a handful of states, estimated at ten to fourteen, had statutes or court rulings that created a privilege.[31] Since *Branzburg,* the number has increased to a total of forty-five states plus the District of Columbia. Twenty-nine states plus the District of Columbia have statutes, usually referred to as shield laws.

---

31. Comment, *Branzburg Revisited: The Continuing Search for a Testimonial Privilege for Newsmen,* 11 Tulsa L.J. 258 (1975).

The shield law jurisdictions include Alabama, Alaska, Arizona, Arkansas, California, Colorado, Delaware, District of Columbia, Georgia, Illinois, Indiana, Kentucky, Louisiana, Maryland, Michigan, Minnesota, Montana Nebraska, Nevada, New Jersey, New Mexico, New York, North Dakota, Ohio, Oklahoma, Oregon, Pennsylvania, Rhode Island, South Carolina, and Tennessee.[32] Sixteen states have recognized a privilege solely as a matter of state constitutional or common law. They are Connecticut, Florida, Idaho, Iowa, Kansas, Maine, Massachusetts, New Hampshire, North Carolina, South Dakota, Texas, Vermont, Virginia, Washington, West Virginia, and Wisconsin.[33] Ten jurisdic-

tions have adopted a common law or state constitutional privilege in addition to a shield law. They are Alaska, California, Delaware, District of Columbia, Illinois, Indiana, Louisiana, Michigan, Oklahoma, and Pennsylvania.[34] California has gone one step farther. Its residents incorporated a journalist's privilege into the text of the state constitution.[35] Thus, the only states that have not adopted a privilege are Hawaii, Mississippi, Missouri, Utah, and Wyoming.

The vast majority of the states have adopted some variation of Stewart's three-part test. As a result, the rules are fairly consistent. The major advantage to a reporter in relying upon state law rather than federal law is that a state court's interpretation cannot be overridden unless there is a direct conflict with federal law. That is also the biggest disadvantage, at least where federal law may offer stronger or broader protection.[36]

Although most states use the familiar three-part test, other aspects of state law vary greatly. One difference is in scope. In some states, the privilege applies to only a narrow range of judicial or other actions in the legal system, while in others it applies to all governmental proceedings of any type whatsoever.[37] Some states have specific exceptions making it easier to force disclosure of sources or information in certain types of cases, most notably libel suits or other cases where news media are likely to be parties.[38] The states also vary widely on who qualifies for the protection of the privilege, on whether a trial

32. Ala. Code § 12–21–142 (1986); Alaska Stat. §§ 09.25.150–.220 (1983); Ariz. Rev. Stat. Ann. §§ 12–2214, 12–2237 (1982); Ark. Code Ann. § 16–85–510 (1987); Calif. Evid. Code § 1070 (Supp. 1991); Colo. Rev. Code §§ 13–90–119, 24–72.5–101 (Supp. 1990); Del. Code Title 10 §§ 4320–4326 (1974); D.C. Code Ann. §§ 16–4701–4704 (1992); Ga. Code Ann. § 24–9–30 (1991 Supp.); Ill. Ann. Stat. Ch. 110, §§ 8–901–8–909 (1984 & 1991 Supp.); Ind. Code § 34–3–5–1 (1986); Ky. Rev. Stat. § 421.100 (1990); La. Rev. Stat. Ann. §§ 45:1451–1454 (1982); Md. Cts. & Jud. Proc. Code Ann. § 9–112 (1989); Mich. Comp. Laws § 767.5a (1982 & 1991 Supp.); Minn. Stat. Ann. §§ 595.012–.025 (West 1988); Mont. Code Ann. §§ 26–1–901–903 (1989); Neb. Rev. Stat. §§ 20–144–147 (1987); Nev. Rev. Stat. § 49.275 (1986); N.J. Stat. Ann. §§ 2A:84A–21 to 21.8, 29 (1976 & 1991 Supp.); N.M. Stat. Ann. § 38–6–7 (1978 and Supp. 1987); N.Y. Civil Rights Law § 79–h (McKinney 1981 & 1991 Supp.); N.D. Century Code § 31–01–06.2 (1978 & 1991 Supp.); Ohio Rev. Code Ann. §§ 2739.04, 2739.12 (1981 & 1990 Supp.); Okla. Stat. Ann. Title 12, § 2506 (1980 and 1991 Supp.); Ore. Rev. Stat. §§ 44.510–.540 (1989); Pa. C.S.A. § 5942 (1982); R.I. Gen. Laws §§ 9–19.1–1 to 1–3 (1985); S.C. Code Ann. § 19–11–100 (Supp. 1992); Tenn. Code Ann. § 24–1–208 (1980 & 1990 Supp.).
33. *Commercial Labor Relations Board v. Fagin,* 2 Med. L. Rptr. 1765, 370 A.2d 1095 (Conn.Super. 1976); *Morgan v. State,* 1 Med. L. Rptr. 2589, 337 So.2d 951 (Fla. 1976); *In re Wright,* 700 P.2d 40 (Id. 1985); *Winegard v. Oxberger,* 3 Med. L. Rptr. 1326, 258 N.W.2d 847 (Iowa 1977); *State v. Sandstrom,* 4 Med. L. Rptr. 1333, 581 P.2d 812 (Kan. 1978); *Maine v. Hohler,* 15 Med. L. Rptr. 1611, 543 A.2d 364 (Maine 1988); *In re Matter of John Doe Jury Investigation,* 19 Med. L. Rptr. 1091, 574 N.E.2d 373 (Mass. 1991); *Opinion of the Justices* 2 Med. L. Rptr. 2083, 373 A.2d 644 (N.H. 1977); *North Carolina v. Smith,* 13 Med. L. Rptr. 1940 (N.C.Super 1987); *Hopewell v. Midcontinent Broadcasting Corp.,* 24 Med. L. Rptr. 1091, 538 N.W.2d 780 (S.D. 1995); *Dallas Oil & Gas v. Mouer,* 533 S.W.2d 70 (Tex.Civ.App. 1976); *State v. St. Peter,* 1 Med. L. Rptr. 2671, 315 A.2d 254 (Vt. 1974); *Brown v. Commonwealth,* 204 S.E.2d 429 (Va. 1974); *Washington v. Rinaldo,* 10 Med. L. Rptr. 2448, 689 P.2d 392 (Wash. 1984); *Hudock v. Henry,* 389 S.E.2d 188 (W.Va. 1990); *Zelenka v. State,* 4 Med. L. Rptr. 1055, 266 N.W.2d 279 (Wis. 1978).

34. *Nebel v. Mapco Petroleum,* 10 Med. L. Rptr. 1871 (Alaska Super. 1984); *Mitchell v. Superior Court,* 11 Med. L. Rptr. 1076, 690 P.2d 625 (Cal. 1984); *Delaware v. McBride,* 7 Med. L. Rptr. 1371 (Del.Super. 1981); *Braden v. News World Communications,* 18 Med. L. Rptr. 2040 (D.C.Super. 1991); *Illinois v. Palacio,* 607 N.E.2d 1375 (Ill.App. 1993); *In re Stearns,* 12 Med. L. Rptr. 1837, 489 N.E.2d 146 (Ind.App. 1986); *In re Ridenhour,* 15 Med. L. Rptr. 1022, 520 So.2d 372 (La. 1988); *Marketos v. American Employers Insurance Co.,* 18 Med. L. Rptr. 1177, 460 N.W.2d 272 (Mich.App. 1990); *Taylor v. Miskorsky,* 7 Med. L. Rptr. 248, 640 P.2d 959 (Okla. 1981); *In re Taylor,* 193 A.2d 181 (Pa. 1963).
35. Calif. Const. Art. 1, § 2 (1983).
36. Alger, *Promises Not to Be Kept: The Illusory Newsgatherer's Privilege in California,* 25 Loyola L.A. L.Rev. 155 (1991); compare *Shoen v. Shoen,* 23 Med. L. Rptr. 1522, 48 F.3d 412 (9th Cir. 1995).
37. Simon, *Reporter Privilege: Can Nebraska Pass a Shield Law to Bind the Whole World?* 61 Nebraska L. Rev. 446 (1982).
38. See, e.g., Minn. Stat. Ann. § 595.025 (1988) (libel).

judge may order *in camera* review, and on what is required to defeat the qualified privilege.

The *Journal of the American Medical Association* (JAMA) and one of its editors found themselves defending a libel suit after asserting that a physician, Jean Cukier, who submitted a scientific manuscript had a financial interest in the proposed article. JAMA asked Cukier to submit a statement disclosing any financial interests, which he did. The article was eventually rejected, and Cukier sued for libel. To prove the case, he would need to find out the identity of the sources who brought his integrity into question. Cukier argued that JAMA and its staff were not covered by the Illinois shield law, and that the privilege had been overcome even if the shield applied. Cukier's petition for discovery gave the Illinois Appellate Court an opportunity to examine the operation of the shield.

Cukier v. The American Medical Association

22 MED. L. RPTR. 1696, 630 N.E.2D 1198 (ILL.APP. 1994).

MURRAY, J.:

The relevant facts are as follows. Cukier and his co-authors submitted a proposed scientific journal manuscript to JAMA in February 1991 for possible publication. Simultaneously, Cukier submitted a statement that he had no financial interest in the publication of the manuscript.

In September 1991 Cukier received a letter from Charles B. Clayman, contributing editor of the JAMA, indicating that it had come to their attention that Cukier might have "if not a direct, at least an indirect financial interest in the publication of [the] paper." The letter further stated that JAMA would require a statement of full disclosure of any and all financial interests relating to the publication. Clayman also sent to David A. Tentham, M.D., one of Cukier's co-authors, a letter indicating that allegations had been made concerning possible financial interests in the publication of the paper by Dr. Cukier.

In October 1991 petitioner again advised respondents that he had no financial interest in the publication of the submitted paper. In November 1991 petitioner was notified by JAMA that the submitted paper was declined for publication.

On September 29, 1992, Cukier filed his petition for pre-suit discovery in an attempt to ascertain what person, persons or entity made statements which called into question his professional honesty. . . .

On November 5, 1992, respondents filed a memorandum in opposition to the petition for discovery before suit, claiming: (1) the information sought was privileged under the Illinois Reporter's Privilege Act (735 ILCS 5/8–901 *et seq.* (West 1992)); (2) the petition violated the free press guarantees of the Illinois Constitution and the First Amendment to the United States Constitution; and (3) the information sought was privileged under the Medical Studies Act.

* * *

In ruling in favor of the respondents, the trial court applied section 8–907(2) of the Reporter's Privilege Act and found that the specified test had not been satisfied. The trial court stated that in order for petitioner to prevail, he would need to show that no other source for the information existed. In addition, the trial court found a public interest clearly existed in protecting the respondents' confidentiality. The court indicated that it would not rule on the applicability of the Medical Studies Act.

* * *

The respondents raise the following three points in support of their argument to affirm the trial court: (1) Compelling respondents to comply with Cukier's request would violate the Reporter's Privilege Act; (2) Compelling the AMA to disclose its source of the suggestion that Cukier had a financial interest would violate the protection conferred by the Medical Studies Act; and (3) The Illinois and United States Constitutions shield the respondents from discovery requests to the identity of their sources.

For the following reasons we affirm the decision of the trial court.

Both parties urge this court to rule on the applicability of both the reporter's privilege and the Medical Studies Act. * * * [T]he only issue properly before this court is the applicability and sufficiency of Cukier's complaint under the Reporter's Privilege Act.

The Reporter's Privilege Act provides that: "[n]o court may compel any person to disclose the source of any information obtained by a reporter except as provided in Part 9 of Article VII of this

Act." The Act defines "reporter" as "any person regularly engaged in the business of collecting writing or editing news for publication through a news medium on a full-time or part-time basis." The definition of "news medium" includes "any newspaper or other periodical issued at regular intervals and having a general circulation." Finally, "source" is defined as "the person or means from or through which the news or information was obtained." [Citations omitted.]

"The reporter's privilege has evolved from a common law recognition that the compelled disclosure of a reporter's sources could compromise the news media's first amendment right to freely gather and disseminate information." The objective of the privilege is "to preserve the autonomy of the press by allowing reporters to assure their sources of confidentiality, thereby permitting the public to receive complete, unfettered information."

* * *

JAMA is published in Chicago, Illinois, by the AMA and has approximately 371,000 subscribers in 148 countries. JAMA is also published in 16 international editions with a circulation of approximately 380,000 copies in 37 countries. During the previous year, although over 3,700 articles were submitted to JAMA, fewer than 700 submissions were published.

Dr. Lundberg's affidavit states that all manuscripts published in JAMA are subjected to peer review [Lundberg was the editor of JAMA]. In the peer review process, individuals with expertise in the subject matter of an article review the soundness of the article's methodology and conclusions. JAMA guarantees the confidentiality of its peer reviewers and other individuals who may provide information to JAMA in the course of the editorial process. * * *

JAMA requires all authors to submit a financial disclosure statement with their manuscripts. Financial disclosure information is not provided to peer reviewers and the fact that an author has a financial interest in the subject area of his article does not preclude publication of said article. The principal purpose of requiring financial disclosure is to determine whether the manuscript, if published, should be accompanied by a statement disclosing the author's financial interest to JAMA's readers.

We find that respondents meet the definitions of "reporter" and "news medium" as defined in the Reporter's Privilege Act. * * * Petitioner maintains that the present situation does not involve the news gathering activities of the respondents and that whether the petition did or did not have a financial interest in his article being published is not part of the news or information gathering activities. We disagree. Respondents allegedly learned of a possible financial interest on the part of the petitioner while evaluating his manuscript. Whether or not this information was relevant to the content of the manuscript does not preclude the possibility that the respondents learned the information during the news gathering process. Moreover, the language of the statute is very clear, that "[n]o court may compel any person to disclose the source of any information obtained by a reporter * * *."

However, once the reporter's privilege has been found to apply, a party may seek to divest the privilege. A party who seeks to divest a reporter or editor of this privilege must apply to the court for such an order. (See 735 ILCS 5/8—903 (West 1992).) The application provided in section 8–903 of the Act must allege:

"[t]he name of the reporter and of the news medium with which he or she was connected at the time the information sought was obtained; the specific information sought and its relevancy to the proceedings; and either, a specific public interest which would be adversely affected if the factual information were not disclosed, or in libel or slander cases, the necessity of disclosure of the information sought to the proof of plaintiff's case.

* * *

The court should only grant an order of divestiture when, the court has made findings that: (1) "the information sought does not concern matters, or details in any proceedings, required to be kept secret under the laws of this State or of the Federal government"; and (2) "that all other available sources of information have been exhausted and, either, disclosure of the information sought is essential to the protection of the public interest involved or, in libel or slander cases, the plaintiff's need for disclosure of the information used by a reporter as part of the news gathering process under the particular facts and circumstances of each particular case." [Citations omitted.]

An appellate court has held that "available sources" in section 8–907(2) means those sources that are identified or known or those sources that are likely to become known as a result of a thorough investigation. The Illinois Supreme Court has indicated that the provisions of the Act reflect a clear legislative intent to create a standard which balances the reporter's first amendment rights against the public interest in the information sought and the practical difficulties in obtaining the information elsewhere. Therefore, the extent to which an investigation must be carried prior to the time that the reporter's privilege should be divested cannot be reduced to any precise formula or definition, but rather must depend on the facts of each individual case.

In applying section 8–907(2) of the Reporter's Privilege Act, the trial court noted that Cukier failed to allege the lack of other available sources for the information requested as well as noting that a public interest exists in protecting confidentiality in the present case. * * * Since we have already determined that the trial court properly found the reporter's privilege applicable and petitioner did not plead allegations which would permit the court to grant divestiture of the privilege, we are compelled to affirm the decision of the trial court. * * *

JUDGMENT AFFIRMED.

COMMENT

Why did the court determine that JAMA was within the free flow of information principle of the shield law? Do you think that the legislature expected the shield to be applied to scholarly publications as well as to mass audience news media? If you were representing Cukier, how would you try to meet the court's command that alternative sources be exhausted? It would appear that the court is ordering the plaintiff to do the impossible. Compare *Minnesota v. Brenner*, 20 Med. L. Rptr. 1707, 488 N.W.2d 339 (Minn.Ap. 1992).

The *Cukier* opinion is a fairly typical, straightforward application of a state shield law. But it must be remembered that each state's privilege is structured and interpreted somewhat differently. In this area, it is essential to look up the actual statute or judicial opinions for each state.

While most states have relied on a combination of grounds for the privilege, others have taken the Court's invitation in *Branzburg* literally and narrowly. In an advisory opinion sought by state officials, the New Hampshire Supreme Court relied solely on that state's constitution in finding that a reporter has a privilege not to disclose sources in a civil proceeding.

In the absence of a statutory reporter's privilege we turn briefly to the question of whether such a privilege exists at common law. * * * No such general right existed at common law for civil proceedings.

However, in rejecting the proposed test in criminal proceedings before a grand jury the (U.S. Supreme) Court made clear that it was "powerless to bar state courts from responding in their own way." * * * The New Hampshire Constitution, part 1, article 22 provides that "liberty of the press" is "essential to the security of freedom in a state" and ought, therefore, "to be inviolably preserved."

Our constitution quite consciously ties a free press to a free state, for effective self-government cannot succeed unless the people have access to an unimpeded and uncensored flow of reporting. News gathering is an integral part of the process.

The court declined to offer an opinion on the scope of the privilege, what persons it applied to, or if the analysis would be different in a criminal proceeding. *Opinion of the Justices*, 2 Med. L. Rptr. 2083, 373 A.2d 644 (N.H. 1977). Advisory opinions are allowed in the states, but federal courts are prevented from rendering advisory opinions due to the federal constitution's requirement that there be a "case or controversy." Note how the New Hampshire court carefully used its specific state constitutional language in deciding in favor of a privilege. Are there advantages to this approach? Disadvantages?

The scope of material covered by the privilege has also been addressed on a common law or constitutional basis in a number of cases. The privilege has been held to include other material, such as unpublished notes and videotapes.[39] But the privilege has also been held inapplicable when a plaintiff in a libel suit was required to prove that a defendant entertained serious doubts about a news story.[40] When the reporter refused to disclose, the court said a jury would be entitled to consider that the reporter had no

---

39. *In re Pan Am Corp.*, 23 Med. L. Rptr. 2297 (S.D.Fla. 1995) (citing cases).

40. *Downing v. Monitor Publishing Co.*, 6 Med. L. Rptr. 1193, 415 A.2d 683 (N.H. 1980).

source—very close to directing a verdict.[41] The courts have generally not applied a privilege when a journalist is called to answer questions about published material and not about sources or background materials.[42]

The Scope of Shield Laws

State shield laws are perhaps a firmer form of protection because they are formalized in statutes and are therefore less susceptible to alteration or manipulation than is the case-by-case approach used under common law and constitutional tests. Shield laws are written in both absolute and conditional terms; most are conditional. Shield laws may cover only the identity of sources or may cover everything up to and including a reporter's thought processes; most protect sources, notes, and videotapes or negatives. Shield laws may be written so that they apply in only certain types of proceedings. They define who is protected and occasionally specify what newsgathering intent is required for a reporter to claim protection. However written, nearly all shield laws contain exceptions allowing compelled testimony or production of materials.

Shield laws range from stingy to generously absolute. Michigan's shield law is the stingiest, protecting journalists only before state grand juries and under no other circumstances. The statute was even narrower before Brad Stone, a reporter and producer for a Detroit television station, was subpoenaed to appear before a grand jury. He was also told to bring all written and filmed materials from his station's coverage of youth gangs in Detroit. The grand jury, investigating the death of an off-duty policeman, thought that Stone's materials and testimony might help identify suspects. Stone protested that many of his sources had been promised anonymity, and argued that the identities of youth gang members he interviewed were readily available to the police. Stone also relied on the state shield law. In a decision that is an example

of the tendency of state courts to construe privileges literally and narrowly, the Michigan Court of Appeals told Stone the shield law, written in 1949, did not apply to him:

> First, we note that the statute itself makes no mention of television or radio reporters. Rather, it refers to "reporters of newspapers or other publications." Appellant urges us to construe the statute broadly to read "publication" as including a television news show.
>
> Courts may not speculate as to the probable intent of the Legislature beyond the words employed in a statute. Ordinary words are given their plain and ordinary meaning. When the language of a statute is clear and unambiguous, judicial construction is neither required nor permitted. Such a statute * * * speaks for itself.
>
> As the trial court noted, reading the statute to include television news reporters would be an inappropriate exercise of the judicial function, and arguments concerning the fairness of the statute must be addressed to the Legislature.

The court also rejected Stone's claim that the statute as written violated the First Amendment by treating some members of the press preferentially. Only a broad interpretation, he argued, would render the statute constitutional. This argument too was rejected. *Michigan v. Storer Communications,* 13 Med. L. Rptr. 1901 (Mich.App. 1986). Stone's First Amendment equal protection argument was rejected later by the Sixth Circuit, which first read *Branzburg* as allowing no privilege under the circumstances, then said that, under a rational basis standard, "such action by a legislature is presumed to be valid." *Storer Communications v. Giovan,* 13 Med. L. Rptr. 2049, 810 F.2d 580 (6th Cir. 1987). Within months, the Michigan legislature amended the law to include broadcast reporters. At the same time, however, an exception allowing compelled disclosure when grand juries are investigating capital crimes was inserted into what had been an absolute shield law.[43]

Even the most absolutist privilege laws may fall before the Sixth Amendment rights of a criminal defendant.[44] In civil cases absolute shields

---

41. *Accord, Rancho La Costa, Inc. v. Superior Court,* 6 Med. L. Rptr. 1249, 165 Cal.Rptr. 347 (Cal.App. 1980).
42. *New Jersey v. Asbury Park Press,* 18 Med. L. Rptr. 2049, 589 A.2d 135 (N.J. 1991); *Ohio ex rel. NBC, Inc. v. Lake County Court of Common Pleas,* 17 Med. L. Rptr. 2209, 556 N.E.2d 1120 (Ohio 1990); *Maine v. Hohler,* 15 Med. L. Rptr. 1611, 543 A.2d 364 (Maine 1988).

---

43. Mich. Comp. Laws Annotated § 767. 5a (West 1982 and Supp. 1991).
44. *Hammarley v. Superior Court,* 4 Med. L. Rptr. 2055, 89 Cal. App. 3d 388, 153 Cal.Rptr. 608 (1979); *Oregon v. Knorr,* 8 Med. L. Rptr. 2067 (Ore. Cir.Ct. 1982).

are more likely to be applied absolutely,[45] but a demonstration that disclosure is needed for preservation of a constitutional or compelling interest may override the shield.[46]

The scope of shield laws shows complex variation from state to state. They may cover the source of information but not shield the information itself.[47] In others, shield laws discriminate between regular employees of the traditional news media and freelancers.[48] Still others differentiate, as Michigan does, among media, granting more protection to newspaper writers than magazine writers, for example.[49] In still others, the question of who is covered is determined solely by discerning an intent to disseminate to the public, regardless of the journalistic status of the individual claiming protection.[50]

Since sources may be inferred from a journalist's work product, the hazard of state laws that protect only sources should be recognized.[51] Some laws require that there be publication and an implied or express agreement of confidentiality between source and reporter for the privilege to be invoked.[52]

The argument for a nationwide, federal shield law is largely based on the uncertainty resulting from so much variation, an uncertainty that some consider unacceptable in a time when much journalism crosses state boundaries.[53] The potential for both uncertainty and overt conflict among and between state shields is more than theoretical. It has arisen frequently in cases where journalistic activities cross state borders. In a case where it is arguable that more than one state's law could apply, a court must choose which is the proper law to apply. Usually, that law will be the law of the state where the reporting occurred. But other courts may feel so strongly about local law that another state's law will not be applied, especially if the two conflict.

Former Senator Paul Laxalt of Nevada sued three California newspapers for libel over several articles implying he had relationships with organized crime figures. Nevada's federal district court applied that state's rules for deciding what law applies. Even though the newspapers had performed almost all reporting, writing, and editing in California and had only limited circulation in Nevada, the court decided that Nevada's shield law applied, not California's. Some of the sources apparently were from Nevada. Under Nevada's shield, the newspapers were protected from compelled source disclosure but were also told they could not rely on the sources in their libel defense. *Laxalt v. McClatchy,* 14 Med. L. Rptr. 1199, 116 F.R.D. 438, (D.Nev. 1987). Does the *Laxalt* case mean that reporters should consider the privilege law of another state when the subject of an article lives in that state? Could the reporters have anticipated that Nevada law applied to their reporter in California?

Other complications abound. In most—but not all—jurisdictions, a contempt order for failure to appear or disclose is considered a final, appealable judgment.[54] In some states the person seeking disclosure is expected to show that the material will be admissible at trial. There is uncertainty over the burden of proof applicable to those seeking disclosure. It may be preponderance of the evidence, clear and convincing evidence, or proof of a compelling interest.[55] And the burden of proof may vary depending upon the type of proceeding where disclosure is sought.

Nonetheless, a shield law works as the first line of defense for a journalist who is plainly covered by it. The "plain meaning" of the words of a statute can settle a dispute readily.

---

45. *Mazzella v. Philadelphia Newspapers,* 5 Med. L. Rptr. 1983, 479 F.Supp. 523 (E.D.N.Y. 1979).

46. *In re Farber,* 4 Med. L. Rptr. 1360, 394 A.2d 330 (N.J. 1978).

47. *Lightman v. State,* 295 A.2d 212 (Md. 1972); *New York v. Dupree,* 2 Med. L. Rptr. 2015, 388 N.Y.S.2d 1000 (N.Y.Sup.Ct. 1976); *Branzburg v. Pound,* 461 S.W.2d 345 (Ky. 1970).

48. *In re Haden-Guest,* 5 Med. L. Rptr. 2361 (N.Y.Sup.Ct. 1980); Mont. Code Ann. §§ 26–1–901–903 (1989); N.D. Century Code § 31–01–06.2 (1978 & 1991 Supp.); Ohio Revised Code Ann. §§ 2739.04, 2739.12 (1981 & 1991 Supp.)

49. *Application of Cepeda,* 233 F.Supp. 465 (S.D.N.Y. 1964).

50. Neb. Revised Stat. § 20–146 (1987); Minn. Stat. Ann. §§ 595.021 to 595.025 (West Supp. 1988).

51. *State v. Sheridan,* 236 A.2d 18 (Md. 1967); *Ohio v. Geis,* 7 Med. L. Rptr. 1675, 441 N.E.2d 803 (Ohio 1981).

52. *Lightman v. State,* 294 A.2d 149 (Md. 1972); *Andrews v. Andreoli,* 400 N.Y.S.2d 442 (1977).

53. Langley and Levine, *Broken Promises,* Columbia Journalism Rev., at 21 (July/August 1988); Note, *The Case for a Federal Shield Law,* 24 U.C.L.A. L.Rev. 160 (1976).

54. *Sinnott v. Boston Retirement Board,* 15 Med. L. Rptr. 1608, 524 N.E.2d 100 (Mass. 1988).

55. *State ex rel. Gerbitz v. Curriden,* 14 Med. L. Rptr. 1997, 738 S.W.2d 192 (Tenn. 1987).

Obviously, shield laws must be carefully drafted if they are to avoid judicial interpretations that puncture them. Minnesota's statute, stronger than most, provides an example of comprehensiveness, notably in its broad definition of newsgatherer and use of the three-part test. It also shows economy and clarity of language, which discourages strained constructions by the courts. But it proved to have one serious flaw. It did not protect work product—notes, tapes, negatives—unless their disclosure would identify a source.[56]

Journalist's Privilege in the Criminal Context

Consistent with *Branzburg,* a journalist who witnesses a crime remains highly vulnerable to subpoena. Traditional privilege analysis refuses to recognize a right to refuse to testify unless there is an understanding that a communication is privileged. When a reporter has simply seen what anyone else could have seen, no confidential relationship exists because no communication was understood as privileged. Typically, in *Pankratz v. Colorado District Court,* 6 Med. L. Rptr. 1269, 609 P.2d 1101 (Colo. 1980), the court held there was no state or federal constitutional privilege or common law privilege when a reporter witnesses a crime. The court noted that the reporter was not shielding the identity of a source, only testimony about a meeting attended by the reporter.

Even when a journalist witnesses a crime or has material amounting to a confession by a defendant under a confidentiality agreement, courts may look unfavorably on the claim. Following publication of a story in which a murder defendant made incriminating statements and prosecutors issued a subpoena, a New Jersey court determined that the state's shield law was waived so far as published information was concerned. *In re Schumann,* 15 Med. L. Rptr. 1113 (N.J. Super.Ct. 1988).

In other cases, courts have found that the compelling interest part of Stewart's three-part test is met by government's interest in public safety and in successful prosecution of criminals.

Reporters called to testify before grand juries may rely upon rules in addition to those of privilege. While federal and state constitutional privilege may apply, and so may state shield laws or state common law, grand jury subpoenas may also be attacked generally on grounds of overbreadth, prematurity, duplication, and harassment. The Fifth Amendment right against self-incrimination may be raised in appropriate cases, but a grant of immunity to the reporter witnesses will negate the right. A reporter who must "take the Fifth" probably has worries other than protecting sources or notes, however.[57]

In federal cases, the Department of Justice's *Guidelines on News Media Subpoenas*[58] and the *Federal Rules of Evidence* may be added. The *Guidelines* try to strike a balance between news flow and justice, between negotiation and demand. Reporters are not entitled under the First or Fourth Amendments to advance warning that a subpoena is coming. *Reporters Committee for Freedom of the Press v. American Telephone & Telegraph Co.,* 4 Med. L. Rptr. 1177, 593 F.2d 1030 (D.C. Cir. 1978), *cert. denied* 440 U.S. 949 (1979). In federal grand jury cases, express authorization by the U.S. Attorney General is required, and in all cases involving news media, alternative sources must be pursued. If the guidelines are not followed, a subpoena may be challenged and quashed. *United States v. Blanton,* 8 Med. L. Rptr. 1106, 534 F.Supp. 295 (S.D.Fla. 1982).

Federal Rules of Evidence § 403 allows a judge to exclude relevant evidence or quash subpoenas altogether if the testimony or subpoena is unlikely to produce significant new information. Any subpoena against a reporter that does not promise new information is premature. *United States v. Burke,* 9 Med. L. Rptr. 1211, 700 F.2d 70 (2d Cir. 1983). Section 501 provides that when state law supplies the rule for a defense, a federal court should apply state law when considering a privilege claim. If a federal circuit recognizes a privilege similar to Stewart's three-part test as a matter of federal constitutional law or federal common law, a federal court would nor-

---

56. Minn. Stat. Ann. §§ 559.021–0.25 (West Supp. 1988); *State v. Knutson v. Minnesota Daily.* 23 Med. L. Rptr. 1056, 523 N.W.2d 909; 24 Med. L. Rptr. 1530, 539 N.W.2d 254 (Minn. 1995).

57. *In re John Doe Grand Jury Investigation,* 19 Med. L. Rptr. 1091, 574 N.E.2d 373 (Mass. 1991).

58. *Guidelines on News Media Subpoenas,* 28 C.F.R. § 50.10, 1979, as amended Nov. 12, 1980, 6 Med. L. Rptr. 2153 (U.S. Dept. of Justice 1980).

mally apply federal privilege rules if there is no state law or if state privilege protection is less than the federal. Where the state's law provides greater protection, *Branzburg* itself may require that state law apply.

Under the *Federal Rules of Criminal procedure* § 17(c), only "evidentiary materials" may be subpoenaed—in other words, material that would be admissible at trial. State criminal procedure rules may be similar.

In the case that follows, lawyer Bruce Cutler was charged with criminal contempt. He was suspected of violating a rule of court prohibiting out of court statements that are likely to "interfere with a fair trial or otherwise prejudice the due administration of justice." Until he was replaced, Cutler was organized crime boss John Gotti's lawyer in Gotti's criminal trial. Apparently, Cutler was prone to trying his case in the press. He was quoted in numerous newspaper stories and appeared on several television shows. In defending himself against the contempt charge, Cutler sought both testimony and outtakes from journalists. The Second Circuit upheld denial of disclosure of testimony and unpublished notes, but ordered disclosure of outtakes and discovery of any testimony or evidence related to the outtakes.

U.S. v. Cutler

21 MED. L. RPTR. 2075, 6 F.3D 67 (2D CIR. 1993).

MAHONEY, J.:

The criminal contempt proceeding that gives rise to this appeal originated with the Gotti Case, in which Cutler served as Gotti's trial counsel until Cutler was disqualified in August 1991. Prior to Cutler's disqualification, Judge I. Leo Glasser, who was presiding over the Gotti trial, had warned counsel for both sides on December 21, 1990, January 9, 1991, and July 22, 1991 to comply with Rule 7 of the Criminal Rules of the United States District Courts for the Southern and Eastern Districts of New York ("Rule 7").

Rule 7 provides in part:

(a) It is the duty of the lawyer . . . not to release or authorize the release of information or opinion which a reasonable person would expect to be disseminated by means of public communication, in connection with pending . . . criminal litigation with which a lawyer . . . is associated, if there is a rea-

sonable likelihood that such dissemination will interfere with a fair trial or otherwise prejudice the due administration of justice.

Further, the rule specifies that lawyers shall not release extrajudicial statements that a reasonable person would expect to be publicly disseminated concerning, *inter alia,* "the character or reputation of the accused," "[t]he identity, testimony or credibility of prospective witnesses," or "[a]ny opinion as to the accused's guilt or innocence or as to the merits of the case or the evidence in the case." * * *

During the course of his representation of Gotti in the Gotti Case, and following his disqualification, Cutler was quoted in numerous newspaper articles making statements about Gotti and the Gotti Case, and appeared on several television programs during which he commented extensively on those subjects. In November 1991, in response to these public comments, Judge Glasser appointed a special prosecutor "'to prosecute, on behalf of the United States, Bruce Cutler for criminal contempt in that Bruce Cutler intentionally and willfully violated the orders of this court and Local Criminal Rule 7.'" In April 1992, Judge Glasser signed an order to show cause why Cutler should not be held in criminal contempt for violation of Judge Glasser's prior directions to comply with Rule 7. Judge Glasser then recused himself from the contempt proceeding, which was reassigned by random selection to Chief Judge Platt.

In preparation for a nonjury trial of this matter before Chief Judge Platt, the special prosecutor and defense counsel for Cutler served subpoenas upon the Reporters and the TV Stations. The special prosecutor's subpoenas to the Reporters called for the testimony of each of the Reporters "regarding the statements actually reported and attributed to Bruce Cutler" in the article(s) written by each reporter. His subpoenas to WNYW requested "[c]opies of televised news reports referring or relating to John Gotti that were actually broadcast on Fox's New York City local news program" on dates between December 12, 1990 and August 13, 1991. His subpoena to CBS requested a "copy of the television program '60 Minutes' that was actually broadcast on Channel 2 (New York)" on April 7 and August 11, 1991.

Defense counsel's subpoenas to the Reporters required the production of "[a]ny and all notes of any interviews of any person concerning the [article(s) written by that reporter]" and "[a]ll notes of any statements made by government officials, including but not limited to prosecutors, FBI agents, and any other employees of the United States Attorneys [sic] Office or the Justice Department concerning [the Gotti Case] and John Gotti." Defense counsel's subpoenas to WNYW requested a number of videotapes broadcast by WNYW from local and national news concerning the Gotti Case and related events, and "[a]ll videos, whether broadcast or not, of the Gotti trial or Bruce Cutler" for news programs on four specified dates. Defense counsel's subpoenas to CBS requested "[a]ll videos of segments that were broadcast concerning the John Gotti trial for the period of August 1, 1991 through and including August 12, 1991 from the local and national news," and "[a]ll videos filmed in the production of the '60 Minutes' story called 'Brucification,' broadcast on April 7, 1991 and rebroadcast on August 11, 1991, concerning Bruce Cutler and John Gotti whether or not those segments were actually broadcast."

The Reporters and the TV Stations moved to quash or, in the alternative, to modify the subpoenas on the ground that the scope of the subpoenas, particularly those of defense counsel, contravened the reporter's qualified privilege recognized by federal law. In the course of the oral argument before Chief Judge Platt on June 21, 1992 of the motions to quash, Cutler agreed to limit his subpoenas as follows: (1) the Reporters would not be required to produce unpublished notes of interviews of persons other than Cutler and the Government Officials; and (2) the TV Stations would be required to produce outtakes only respecting their interviews of Cutler.

At the conclusion of the oral argument, Chief Judge Platt denied the motions to quash and ordered the Reporters and the TV Stations to comply with the subpoenas, as modified. At an appearance before Chief Judge Platt the following day, the Reporters advised the court that they were willing to testify concerning "the substance and published aspects" of the Articles, but were unwilling to reveal confidential sources or to produce notes or other unpublished materials unless directed to do so by the Second Circuit Court of Appeals. The TV Stations advised the court that they would not disclose the Outtakes to Cutler's defense counsel, but were willing to offer the Outtakes for the court's *in camera* review on the

condition that if the district court found the Outtakes to be relevant, the TV Stations would have an opportunity to appeal the district court's ruling before the Outtakes were disclosed to Cutler.

Chief Judge Platt rejected the offer of the TV Stations, and ordered the Reporters and TV Stations to "be held in contempt and ordered to pay a fine of $1.00 per day until such time as they comply with the Court's instructions or are excused from doing so," but stayed imposition of the punishment pending an expedited appeal. The Reporters and TV Stations filed timely notices of appeal.

DISCUSSION

A.   The Governing Standard

The guiding precedent in this circuit for resolution of the issues presented by this appeal is *United States v. Burke*, 700 F.2d 70 (2d Cir.), *cert. denied*, 464 U.S. 816 (1983). In that case, we affirmed the quashing of a subpoena by which a defendant in a criminal case sought production of documents and tapes relating to a magazine article coauthored by a principal prosecution witness and a reporter for the magazine. The defendant sought to impeach the witness with these materials. The magazine moved to quash the subpoena, invoking "the First Amendment reporter's privilege." *Id.* at 76. We ruled that: "In light of [other] extensive impeachment evidence, the district court properly concluded that any information to be gleaned from the [magazine's] work papers would be merely cumulative and thus would not defeat the [reporter's] First Amendment privilege."

When a litigant seeks to subpoena documents that have been prepared by a reporter in connection with a news story, this Circuit's standard of review, at least in civil cases, is well settled:

> The law in this Circuit is clear that to protect the important interests of reporters and the public in preserving the confidentiality of journalists' sources, disclosure may be ordered only upon a clear and specific showing that the information is: highly material and relevant, necessary or critical to the maintenance of the claim, and not obtainable from other available sources. *Baker v. F&F Investment*, 470 F.2d 778, 783–85 (2d Cir. 1972), cert. denied, 411 U.S. 966, 93 S. Ct. 2147, 36 L.Ed.2d 686 (1973). *Accord, Zerilli v. Smith*, 656 F.2d 705, 713–15 (D.C. Cir. 1981); *Silkwood v. Kerr-McGee Corp.*, 563 F.2d 433, 438 (10th Cir. 1977).

Baker was this court's first assessment of the reporter's privilege in the aftermath of *Branzburg.* In *Baker,* we distinguished *Branzburg* as having only "tangential relevance" because *Baker* was a civil case. 470 F.2d at 784. Then, in *In re Petroleum Products Antitrust Litigation,* 680 F.2d 5, 7–8 [8 Med. L. Rptr. 1525] (2d Cir.) (per curiam), *cert. denied,* 459 U.S. 909 (1982), we adopted a rule, again in a civil context, that was explicitly based upon *Baker.* Finally, in *Burke,* perceiving "no legally-principled reason for drawing a distinction between civil and criminal cases" in defining the reporter's privilege, 700 F.2d at 77, we adopted the *Petroleum Products* rule for criminal cases.

B. Resolution of the Issues on Appeal

We consider first Cutler's demand for (1) the testimony, and production of the unpublished notes, of the Reporters regarding statements made by Cutler to the Reporters in connection with the Articles, and (2) the production of the Outtakes. For the reasons that follow, we conclude that Cutler is entitled to this testimony and the production of these materials.

Whatever the doctrinal considerations, we must certainly follow *Branzburg* when fact patterns parallel to *Branzburg* are presented for our decision. One of the reporters whose testimony was compelled in *Branzburg* had "refused to answer questions that directly related to criminal conduct that he had observed and written about," 408 U.S. at 708. The allegedly contemptuous conduct by Cutler in this case is precisely what the Reporters observed and wrote about, and what the TV Stations recorded on videotape.

The special prosecutor's subpoenas are no longer contested, so it is obvious that the Articles and "actually broadcast" videotapes whose production is required by the prosecutor's subpoenas can be admitted in evidence at Cutler's contempt trial. Cutler is clearly entitled to examine the Reporters regarding the context, background, and content of those statements, and to scrutinize their relevant unpublished notes that relate to these matters, as well as the Outtakes in the possession of the TV Stations, to defend against the charge that his statements were criminally contemptuous. *See United States v. Criden,* 633 F.2d 346, 359 (3d Cir. 1980) (most logical source of information about conversation is one of the participants), *cert. denied,* 449 U.S. 1113 (1981).

Other than Cutler's own testimony, which of course cannot be compelled, the evidence that Cutler seeks from the Reporters and the TV Stations is probably the *only* significant proof regarding his assertedly criminal behavior. Further, even if Cutler should choose to testify, we see no justification for consigning him to his unassisted memory when clearly relevant evidence is readily available from the Reporters and TV Stations. Finally, one of Cutler's major lines of defense is that the statements alleged to be contemptuous were in fact "repl[ies] to charges of misconduct" that are expressly precluded from the purview of Rule 7. That defense would be undercut if Cutler could not obtain relevant evidence regarding the context of his statements that is available only from the Reporters and the TV Stations.

The Reporters and TV Stations contend that they should not be required to produce the materials sought by Cutler, or testify on this subject, as to statements made by Cutler prior to any definitive order by Judge Glasser compelling Cutler's compliance with Rule 7.

* * *

The TV Stations also contend that the district court erred in denying the motion to quash the subpoenas rather than first reviewing the Outtakes *in camera.* In *Burke,* we encouraged *in camera* review as a precautionary measure before a definitive ruling to exclude access to assertedly privileged materials, especially when the materials are not voluminous. Given the clear relevance of the Outtakes to Cutler's defense, we perceive nothing in *Burke* that mandates an exercise of the district court's discretion to review them *in camera* before ordering their disclosure to Cutler. * * *

The remaining issue is posed by Cutler's demand for access to the Reporters' unpublished notes regarding statements by the Government Officials concerning Gotti and the Gotti Case, and for related cross-examination of the Reporters. * * *

We are unpersuaded. The comparative impact of Cutler's public statements and other publicity regarding the Gotti Case manifestly depends upon what was published on that subject, not upon what is in the Reporters' unpublished notes. * * *

In sum, whether judged by the *Branzburg* standard or *Burke's* special threshold standard,

Cutler's argument for production of the Reporters' testimony and unpublished notes regarding statements by Government Officials concerning Gotti and the Gotti Case does not prevail.

COMMENT

The journalists in *Cutler* were caught in a bind. The entire basis for the action was news coverage so, as a result, evidence about news coverage would necessarily make or break the case. Usually, courts have required significant proof that material from journalists goes to the heart of the claim before ordering that information be disclosed. *U.S. v. Hendron,* 21 Med. L. Rptr. 1506, 820 F.Supp. 715 (E.D.N.Y. 1993). The claim must virtually rise or fall with the information ordered disclosed. *In re Waldholz,* 24 Med. L. Rptr. 2395 (S.D.N.Y. 1996).

Another issue frequently encountered when demonstrative evidence such as videotapes or photos is sought is the availability of *in camera* review—a look at the material by the judge in chambers. Even this limited review has been found to violate the privilege. The party seeking disclosure through *in camera* review has a threshold burden of proving the material is relevant to the case and is likely not available from other sources. *U.S. v. Shay,* 21 Med. L. Rptr. 1415 (D.Mass. 1993).

An earlier somewhat similar case was *Brown v. Commonwealth,* 204 S.E.2d 429 (Va. 1974), where it was held that journalist's privilege could be pierced if the information was material to a defense or to reduction in the charge or penalty for the offense. While the opinion did not rely upon Stewart's three-part test, the court did require defendants to show that the information was (1) essential to the case and (2) not available from alternative sources. No mention was made of Stewart's third part—that there be a compelling interest for disclosure—but the court may have assumed that the Sixth Amendment fair trial right satisfies it. The court said that, once the defendant meets the test, "the defendant has a fair trial *right* to compel disclosure. * * * The newsman must, upon pain of contempt, yield to that right."

In *Brown,* the information sought concerned inconsistent statements of a prosecution witness. The Virginia Supreme Court appeared to rely upon both its state law and upon the First Amendment in recognizing a privilege. The material sought was held to be nonessential:

> [T]he record fails to show that either the statements made at trial or the prior statements were material to proof of the crime, to proof of Brown's defense, or to a reduction in the classification or penalty of the crime charged. Since the inconsistent statements were collateral and not material, the identity of the source was irrelevant.

In criminal cases, the greatest stumbling block for defendants or for prosecutors seeking disclosure of confidential sources or information has been the second prong of Stewart's three-part test, the requirement that there be no alternative method of obtaining the information sought. In *Hallissy v. Contra Costa Superior Court,* 15 Med. L. Rptr. 1325, 200 Cal.App.3d 1038 (Cal.App. 1988), a defendant in a murder trial argued that it was essential to his defense to call as a witness a reporter to whom the defendant had granted an interview. The interview resulted in an article in the *Contra Costa Times* entitled, "I kill many for pay," which included incriminating statements by the defendant. The prosecution relied on the article in pressing charges against the defendant. The trial judge considered a claim of First Amendment protection a "travesty" when the source was known, the information largely known, and the defendant was facing the death penalty.

The court of appeals reversed, noting that the defendant, who sought to attack his own credibility in the published interview, claimed to have confessed to others besides the reporter. This, the court held, indicated that alternative sources existed. In addition, under California's shield law, the defendant had failed to show that the material sought created a "reasonable possibility" that the evidence would exonerate him.

In *State ex rel., Gerbitz v. Curriden,* 14 Med. L. Rptr. 1797, 738 S.W.2d 192 (Tenn. 1987), the court applied the alternative means analysis to refuse to compel testimony before a grand jury by a reporter whose radio interview with a self-proclaimed killer had prompted a subpoena. The killer used a false name during the interview. The reporter said he did not know the identity of the killer and could provide only a general description. The court, applying the alternative means analysis, reasoned that the state had failed to investigate well enough:

There is no explanation of what information was sought from appellee or what other efforts, if any, the Attorney General or other law enforcement agencies had made to determine the identity of the criminal offense, the offender himself, or the site of the offense. It does not appear whether the alleged crime occurred in Hamilton County or was subject to the jurisdiction of the Hamilton County grand jury. No investigation or inquiry by Hamilton County officials with officials from surrounding counties appears to have been made, nor has any check of prison or parole records been shown.

In another case where a murder defendant had granted an exclusive interview to a reporter, however, the court ordered disclosure. *Waterman Broadcasting v. Reese*, 14 Med. L. Rptr. 2246, 523 So.2d 1161 (Fla.Ct.App. 1988). The court reasoned that (1) a confession is *always* relevant in a criminal case, (2) the exclusivity of the interview alone assured that no alternative sources existed, and (3) the state's interest in law enforcement constituted a compelling interest. Which approach is more persuasive—that of California and Tennessee refusing disclosure, or that of Florida requiring disclosure?

In jurisdictions with decisions less sympathetic to a journalist's privilege—California, Massachusetts, Michigan, and New York among them—neither state shield laws nor the First Amendment will protect journalists in all circumstances. In the *Rosato* case, a judge anxious to discover who defied his orders not to discuss a case recognized neither a privilege for unpublished material nor the requirement of exhausting alternative sources, despite the language of California's statute at the time.[59]

Similarly, in *CBS v. Superior Court*, 149 Cal.Rptr. 421, 4 Med. L. Rptr. 1568 (Cal.App. 1978), the California Court of Appeal required *in camera* disclosure of outtakes from the program "60 Minutes" showing negotiations for drug sales between undercover agents and the defendants in the case. The officers' identities had been revealed at a hearing on a motion to quash the subpoena. The court reasoned that all of the confidential material must be provided when part of it is revealed. This has sometimes been called the "exposure to view" theory.

Getting Too Close to Sources: *In re Farber* and *In re Decker*

One of the most famous controversies involving journalist's privilege was the 1978 *Farber* case. An investigative reporter for the *New York Times*, Myron Farber had dug into a series of old accusations that physician Mario Jascalevich was connected with mysterious deaths at a New Jersey hospital. Largely as a result of Farber's efforts, a grand jury was convened, and Jascalevich eventually faced trial for murder.

Farber and the *Times* received subpoenas requesting exhaustive production of notes and records for the judge to review. Farber demanded a hearing first but was refused. He appealed once and lost. He was sent to jail and the *Times* was fined $5,000 a day.

Farber and the *Times* appealed again. The New Jersey Supreme Court interpreted *Branzburg* as rejecting a First Amendment privilege. The court did agree that journalists deserved a hearing, but not necessarily before an order for *in camera* inspection. *In re Farber*, 4 Med. L. Rptr. 1360, 394 A.2d 330 (N.J. 1978). The court said that any interest Farber had in preventing disclosure of materials and confidential sources was overridden by Jascalevich's compelling Sixth Amendment interest in getting a fair trial and having an opportunity to confront witnesses. The court said that *in camera* review was valuable to determine the relevance of the requested materials and thus whether or not a privilege would be overcome.

Shortly afterward, the murder trial ended with Jascalevich being acquitted, and Farber was released from jail. The state shield law was soon amended to assure that reporters would have a hearing before being ordered to testify or face jail.[60] Then-governor Brendan Byrne pardoned both the *Times* and Farber in 1982 and returned $101,000 in criminal fines.

The case was unique in that Farber was essentially the sole expert on the case. His dealings with law enforcement officials were central to having charges brought. Almost two decades later, the case serves to warn journalists of possible dangers when they get very close to their sources or independently investigate crime.

---

59. *Rosato v. Superior Court,* 1 Med. L. Rptr. 2560, 51 Cal.App.3d 190, 124 Cal.Rptr. 427 (1975), *cert. denied* 427 U.S. 912 (1976).

60. *Maressa v. New Jersey Monthly,* 8 Med. L. Rptr. 1473, 445 A.2d 376 (N.J. 1982).

Reporter Twila Decker also spent time in jail as a result of getting close to official sources and promising them confidentiality. She was covering the pretrial proceedings in the case of Susan Smith, who was accused of murdering her two young sons by belting them into the family car and running it into a lake. The case attracted nationwide saturation coverage. After promising to keep her sources confidential, Decker obtained either a copy of or information from a secret mental competency report on Smith. The report had been distributed to prosecution and defense counsel by trial judge William Howard on the condition that the report be kept secret. When Decker wrote a story in *The State* of Columbia, South Carolina, using information from the report, it was obvious the judge's order had been violated. Determined to find out who had violated the order, Howard called Decker to testify. South Carolina had recently adopted a shield law for the first time, and Decker hoped it would keep her out of jail. It didn't.

In re Decker
23 MED. L. RPTR. 2542 (S.C. 1995).

PER CURIAM.

This case involves a newspaper article written by Decker about Susan Smith, who is charged with the murder of her two children. By order of the circuit court on March 23, 1995, Smith was ordered to submit to a psychiatric evaluation by the South Carolina Department of Mental Health (DMH). Due to extensive pre-trial publicity, the circuit court issued an order on May 16, 1995 requiring the report be disclosed only to defense counsel and the solicitor. They were not permitted to divulge the contents to any witness whose knowledge was not essential; disclosure "to any other party or individual prior to trial" was prohibited.

On May 25, 1995, *The State* published an article written by Decker which purported to summarize portions of DMH's psychiatric evaluation of Smith. The following day, the court conducted a hearing to determine the source of Decker's information. The court concluded that only four entities had had access to the report: The DMH, the 16th Circuit Solicitor, Smith's defense counsel, and the court itself. The court took the testimony of the DMH's Chief of Police

Safety, Freddie Lorick, who had conducted an investigation and testified that "there was not a breach of confidentiality on the part of the DMH or its employees in this case." The court then heard from Solicitor Pope who, as an officer of the court, advised that only three people in his office had viewed the report and none of them had breached confidentiality. Defense counsel submitted an affidavit indicating that the defense team was not the source of any breach.

Unable to ascertain the source of the breach of confidentiality, the trial judge called Decker as a witness. Decker acknowledged she had a contract with a confidential source who had provided her with information relative to the report, but she refused to reveal the source, citing the First Amendment to the United States Constitution, and the South Carolina "Reporter's Shield Law," S.C. Code Ann. § 19–11–100 (Supp. 1994). When Decker refused to reveal her source, the circuit court held her in contempt of court and ordered her incarcerated, provided that she could purge the contempt by revealing the identity of the confidential source. This Court stayed imposition of the contempt sanction pending disposition of the appeal.

ISSUES

1. Does the South Carolina Reporter's Shield Law provide Decker a qualified privilege to withhold her confidential source?
2. Does the First Amendment to the United States Constitution grant Decker a privilege to withhold her confidential source?

I. REPORTER'S SHIELD LAW

S.C. Code Ann. § 19–11–100 (Supp. 1994) provides, in pertinent part:

(A) A person . . . engaged in the gathering and dissemination of news for the public through a newspaper . . . has a qualified privilege against disclosure of any information . . . obtained . . . in the gathering or dissemination of news in any judicial . . . proceeding in which the compelled disclosure is sought and where the one asserting the privilege is not a party in interest to the proceeding.

(B) The person . . . may not be compelled to disclose any information . . . obtained . . . in the gathering or dissemination of news unless the party seeking to compel the production or testimony establishes by clear and convincing evidence that . . . the testimony or production sought:

(1) is material and relevant to the controversy for which the testimony or production is sought:

(2) cannot be reasonably obtained by alternative means:

(3) is necessary to the proper preparation or presentation of the case of a party seeking the information . . .

On its face, the reporter's shield law is inapplicable to the present case. A party is a person whose name is designated on the record as a plaintiff or defendant. Here, the disclosure of Decker's source is sought by the trial court, clearly not a party to the underlying proceedings. * * * Had the legislature intended the statute to apply in circumstances in which the trial court seeks disclosure, it would not have limited application of the statute to circumstances where a "party" seeks to compel production. Accordingly, we find the reporter's shield law inapplicable.

Moreover, the purpose of the reporter's shield law, as set forth in the preamble, is as follows:

> Whereas, the General Assembly finds that it is vital in a democratic society that the public have an unrestricted flow of information on *matters of concern to the public* and that the threat of compelled testimony or production of information . . . obtained . . . in gathering or disseminating news to the public interferes with the free flow of information to the public.

(Emphasis supplied). As noted previously, the mental health report is required by law to be kept confidential. * * * Contrary to Decker's contention, requiring her to disclose her source in no way contravenes the purpose of the reporter's shield law since the information is not public.

In any event, even were we to find the reporter's shield law applicable to the present case, we find the trial court complied with the three-prong inquiry set forth therein. Contrary to Decker's assertion, the record demonstrates, by clear and convincing evidence, that the information "cannot be reasonably obtained by alternative means."

The present record reveals that the trial judge made inquiry of every office known to him to have had access to the report. Uniformly, a representative of each office maintained the confidentiality of the report had not been breached by any of its employees. Contrary to Decker's asser-

tion, the only evidence on the present record is clear and convincing that no other person known to have had access to the report disclosed it. * * *

II. FIRST AMENDMENT

Decker contends she has a qualified privilege, pursuant to the First Amendment of the United States Constitution, to withhold her confidential source. Under these circumstances, we disagree.

* * * It has generally been held, however, that the First Amendment does not guarantee the press a constitutional right of special access to information not available to the public generally. The press may constitutionally be prohibited from publishing information about trials if necessary to assure a fair trial by an impartial tribunal. Consequently, the information Decker seeks to withhold is not protected by the First Amendment. Further, Decker's status as a news reporter affords her no privilege in the present case.

In *Branzburg v. Hayes,* the United States Supreme Court held that news reporters have no First Amendment privilege, either qualified or absolute, to refuse to divulge a confidential source in the context of a good faith grand jury investigation. * * *

A number of courts, citing *Branzburg,* have adopted a First Amendment qualified privilege requiring a balancing process prior to requiring disclosure of a news reporter's confidential source. These courts generally hold that a journalist's privilege protects confidential sources unless it is first demonstrated that the information is relevant, cannot be obtained by alternate means, and is necessary or critical to the claim.

However, notwithstanding the above decisions, a number of courts specifically reject the expansive reading given to *Branzburg* by other courts, and recognize that the balancing test implemented by those courts is precisely the type of approach the *Branzburg* court sought to avoid. *See Karem v. Priest,* 744 F.Supp. 136, 141 (W.D.Tex. 1990). . . .

Similarly, other courts acknowledge that *Branzburg* stands for the proposition that the press enjoys a qualified privilege only in certain *limited* situations, such as when the grand jury acts in bad faith or the press is being subjected to official harassment. Finally, a number of courts recognize that a criminal trial is at least as important as a grand jury proceeding, and a defendant's right to a fair trial outweighs any claimed qualified privilege, on its face.

We decline to adopt the view taken by those courts which utilize the three-prong balancing approach urged by the *Branzburg* dissent. Accordingly, we find no First Amendment privilege in this case.

Finally, even if we were to recognize a qualified First Amendment privilege, we find any such privilege is patently outweighed in the present case by the trial court's fundamental need to be able to enforce its own orders. As was recognized by the Ninth Circuit Court of Appeals in *Farr v. Pitchess,* 522 F.2d 464 [1 Med. L. Rptr. 2557], *cert. denied,* 427 U.S. 912, 96 S.Ct. 3200, 49 L.Ed.2d 1203 (1975):

> [T]he purpose of eliminating collaboration between counsel and the press is to protect the constitutionally guaranteed right of the defendants in criminal cases to due process by means of a fair trial. That constitutional right cannot be so protected if the authority of the court to enforce its orders is diluted. If the newsman's privilege against disclosure of news sources is to serve as a bar to disclosure of the names of those who disobey the court order, then the court is powerless to enforce this method of eliminating encroachment on the due-process right of defendants.

In *Farr,* the court concluded that the newsman's privilege must yield. . . .

As in *Farr,* we find the need for disclosure here far outweighs any asserted First Amendment privilege. Accordingly, Decker must divulge her source or suffer the consequences of the contempt of the circuit court's order. The judgment below is

AFFIRMED.

COMMENT

The South Carolina shield law was interpreted narrowly in *Decker.* It apparently will apply only when a journalist is called by a party to a lawsuit and disclosure is sought, a situation that rarely arises. Was that the intent of the South Carolina legislature? On the First Amendment side, the court found that no privilege applied except when a request is brought in bad faith or to harass the press. That too was a very narrow interpretation. Finally, the court determined that, even if a First Amendment privilege applied, it

was overcome by a court's "fundamental need to be able to enforce its own orders." Do you agree that this is equivalent to a compelling interest? The judge later rescinded his order after Decker, still refusing to name anyone, testified that her source was not someone subject to the judge's secrecy order.[61]

Notwithstanding the *Decker* opinion, if nothing else is certain when privilege is claimed in the context of a criminal investigation or trial, it is clear that "fishing expeditions" are disfavored and will typically result in a decision protecting the journalist's sources and materials. The *Journal of the American Medical Association* published an anonymous essay by a doctor who advocated euthanasia for some patients and who claimed to have actually killed a terminal patient. A Cook County, Illinois grand jury subpoenaed the magazine to name the source of its essay. Applying the Illinois shield law, the court refused to enforce the subpoena. Only if the state could provide more information would a subpoena be appropriate. Since there was no evidence that a crime had been committed, much less in Cook County, no basis for disclosure existed. The name of the source was not relevant. *In re Grand Jury Investigation,* 15 Med. L. Rptr. 1469 (Ill.Cir.Ct. 1988).

Journalist's Privilege in Libel Cases

Claims of privilege not to disclose identities of sources or not to provide materials create uneasy situations when the journalist or news organization—usually both—find themselves in the defendant's chair in a libel suit. The libel plaintiff frequently asserts that source identification or reporter work product materials are essential to proving the case. When the plaintiff is required to prove that a reporter acted negligently or with actual malice, that contention is often correct: the quality and credibility of sources, along with the scope and accuracy of reporting materials, may be the evidence needed to show the requisite evidence of fault.

Courts considering privilege claims in libel litigation have tended to be less solicitous of the privilege than in other contexts. A reporter-defendant has more than a principled desire to prevent a "chilling effect" on newsgathering as a

---

61. *The News Media and the Law,* Summer 1995, pp. 14–16.

result of government-ordered disclosures. In libel cases, a journalist also has self-interest in avoiding liability. The courts on occasion find it difficult to overlook the specter of media self-interest in addressing issues of principle.

For example, in *Downing v. Monitor Publishing Company,* 6 Med. L. Rptr. 1193, 415 A.2d 683 (N.H. 1980), the police chief of the town of Boscawen sued for libel after the *Concord Monitor* asserted in an article that the chief had failed a lie detector test. Downing sought disclosure of the names of undisclosed sources used in preparing the article. The newspaper refused, was ordered to disclose, and appealed to the New Hampshire Supreme Court. Holding that the plaintiff would be unable to prove that the defendant had "obvious reasons to doubt" the accuracy of its story without the identities of the sources, the court ordered disclosure. The police chief, a public official required to prove actual malice, would be "completely foreclosed" from recovery absent the informer's identity, the court said.

The newspaper argued that Downing should be required to make a facial showing of falsity prior to any disclosure order, reasoning both that falsity must be proved by any libel plaintiff and that a determination of truthfulness would eliminate any need for disclosure. The court instead held that disclosure may be ordered in libel cases if a plaintiff can show "that there is a genuine issue of fact regarding the falsity of the publication." The court's opinion implies a broad, general exception to the application of a journalist's privilege in libel litigation:

> Our earlier ruling in *Opinion of the Justices,* 117 N.H. 386, 373 A.2d 642 (1977), that there is a press privilege under the New Hampshire Constitution not to disclose the source of information when the press *is not a party* to an action is not applicable here. * * * In the case at hand we do not have * * * governmental involvement versus the press * * *. [Emphasis added.]

Concerned that the reporters involved might elect jail rather than reveal their sources, the court concluded that:

> Confining newsmen to jail in no way aids the plaintiff in proving his case. Therefore, we hold that when a defendant in a libel action, brought by a plaintiff who is required to prove actual malice under *New York Times,* refuses to declare his sources of information upon a valid order of the court, there shall arise a presumption *that the defendant had no source.* [Emphasis added.]

Such a presumption of course amounts to a direction by the court that a defendant acted recklessly, virtually assuring that the plaintiff will prove the necessary elements of constitutional libel.

The *Monitor* case highlights the collision of the principles of *New York Times v. Sullivan* with the First Amendment philosophy in Stewart's *Branzburg* dissent. In short, how can a libel plaintiff prove actual malice if the sources and information underlying the story cannot be obtained? If a public official or public figure plaintiff can show that identification of a news source will help prove actual malice, does the *New York Times* case in effect guarantee the plaintiff a right to disclosure?

Or, is the risk to the news media of an exception to privilege in libel suits greater because those suits may be filed primarily for the purpose of discovering the identities of confidential sources rather than to obtain money damages for harm to reputation? Regardless of a plaintiff's motivation, the media must bear the expense and inconvenience of litigation.

One of the earliest post-*Branzburg* cases to consider journalist's privilege in the libel context was *Cervantes v. Time, Inc.,* 1 Med. L. Rptr. 1751, 464 F.2d 986 (8th Cir. 1972), *cert. denied* 409 U.S. 1125 (1973). The mayor of St. Louis brought an action after a *Life* magazine story alleged he was involved with organized crime. Cervantes claimed he needed to know the magazine's confidential sources to prove actual malice. The court agreed that disclosure of sources might be needed in some libel suits, but not this one. At a minimum, the court said, a plaintiff will be required to show that the disclosure is likely to produce information relevant to actual malice. Since it was obvious that the sources were FBI and other government officials, obtaining their names from journalists was not essential to a showing of actual malice.

Since 1979, lower courts considering privilege claims in libel cases have addressed the issue in light of the Supreme Court's refusal to create a separate privilege to protect a media defendant's editorial process from inquiry by libel plaintiffs. *Herbert v. Lando,* 3 Med. L. Rptr. 1241, 568 F.2d 974 (2d Cir. 1977), *reversed,* 4 Med. L. Rptr.

2575, 441 U.S. 153 (1979). The Second Circuit, relying on *Branzburg*, had recognized such a privilege as a necessary corollary to newsgathering. But the Supreme Court, in an opinion by Justice White, declared that the privilege went too far by limiting a plaintiff's inquiry into a defendant's state of mind, necessary to show that a defendant had reason to doubt the accuracy of a story.

A number of courts, including the New Hampshire Supreme Court in *Downing*, read *Lando* as requiring an exception to privilege in libel cases. Other courts concluded instead that individual reputation was but one of many interests a state could choose to protect or not. *Mazzella v. Philadelphia Newspapers*, 5 Med. L. Rptr. 1983, 479 F.Supp. 523 (E.D.N.Y. 1979).

Pennsylvania's shield law, which had previously been held to protect against disclosure of source identities or of any material that might lead to identification of sources, was read narrowly when a libel plaintiff sought nonbroadcast material from a defendant television station. Relying in part on *Lando*, the court ordered that material be disclosed and placed the burden of deciding if a source might be identified from the material on the trial courts. In effect, the opinion called for *in camera* inspection. *Hatchard v. Westinghouse Broadcasting Company*, 14 Med. L. Rptr. 2000, 532 A.2d 346 (Pa. 1987). In passing, the court also added that reputation constitutes a "fundamental interest protected by the Pennsylvania Constitution. * * *" If reputation is considered a fundamental constitutional right, it would follow that reputation would constitute as compelling an interest as the Sixth Amendment's fair trial guarantee in criminal cases:

> [I]n interpreting the statute in question we must presume that the legislature did not intend to violate the Constitution of the United States or of this Commonwealth. Were we to interpret the Shield Law's protection as broadly as appellees urge, serious questions would arise as to the constitutionality of the statute in light of the protection of fundamental rights provided for in the Pennsylvania Constitution.

Contra, Maressa v. New Jersey Monthly, 8 Med. L. Rptr. 1473, 445 A.2d 376 (N.J. 1982) (New Jersey constitution does not create a fundamental right to reputation).

Some courts have held that just because the press is a party in a libel suit, the qualified privilege should not be abandoned. In 1984, Califor-

nia outlined how the interests of both libel plaintiffs and defendants could be respected. The case arose when the *Reader's Digest* ran a story about two journalists, David and Cathy Mitchell, who had written a series of articles on the Synanon Church. The magazine relied primarily upon previously published reports, most of them by the Mitchells. The church and its founder sued and subpoenaed seeking the names of sources used by the magazine. More importantly, the church sought the identification of sources used by the Mitchells and referred to in the magazine.

Mitchell v. Superior Court
11 MED. L. RPTR. 1076, 690 P.2D 625, 208 CAL.RPTR. 152 (CAL. 1984).

BROUSSARD, J.:

* * *

In brief summary, the Reader's Digest article, by staff writer David MacDonald, describes how the Mitchells won the Pulitzer Prize for a series of reports and editorials critical of Synanon which appeared in their weekly newspaper, the Point Reyes Light. The article contains the following statements: "Synanon was founded in 1958 by Charles Dederich, a reformed alcoholic, to rehabilitate drug addicts. Though his spectacular claims of success were never proved, Dederich and Synanon attracted publicity and enough cash donations to start a string of addiction centers. . . . Since 1968, minimal drug rehabilitation work had been attempted; funds, however, were still solicited on that basis." Plaintiffs charge that such language implies that plaintiffs were not successful at drug rehabilitation and that their claims of success were fraudulently made to enrich themselves.

* * *

The Reader's Digest revealed the sources for its article: the Mitchell's newspaper accounts, The Light on Synanon, Professor Ofshe's research papers, conversations with Ofshe and the Mitchells, and a few other, less significant, sources. Plaintiffs, however, want to discover the sources' sources. They sent the Mitchells two requests to produce documents, the first listing 27 broad categories of documents and the second specifying over 10 different documents. We do not set out the requests in full, as many are overlapping or duplicative. The breadth of the discovery sought is indicated by request number 8 from the first set of requests, which asks for "Each and every document, other than as described [and requested] above, referring to or relating to Synanon and/or Charles E. Dederich in the possession, custody or control of defendants prior to the publication of the Reader's Digest Article."

The Mitchells objected to request number 8 and many other requests on the ground "that it is vague and ambiguous and, to the extent it is intelligible, is overbroad, unduly burdensome, and calls for information protected from disclosure by, inter alia, The First Amendment to the Constitution of the United States, The First Amendment to the Constitution of the State of California and the common law." The superior court, however, ordered the Mitchells to identify every document responsive to the first and second requests, and to produce all documents described under specific items, including request number 8, of the first request to produce.

The Mitchells, uncertain whether the court had ruled on their claim of privilege, withheld documents tending to reveal confidential sources and asked the court to clarify its order. Ruling from the bench in response to the motion to clarify, the judge stated that he was ruling that the asserted privilege does "not exist in California." The Mitchells now seek a writ of prohibition to bar enforcement of the court's order requiring them to produce the withheld documents.

California by statute (Evid. Code, § 1070) and by constitutional amendment (art. I, § 2, subd. (b)) provides that "[a] publisher, editor, reporter, or other person connected with or employed upon a newspaper . . . shall not ["cannot" in Evid. Code] be adjudged in contempt . . . for refusing to disclose the source of any information procured while so connected or employed for publication in a newspaper . . . or for refusing to disclose any unpublished information." Since contempt is generally the only effective remedy against a nonparty witness, the California enactments grant such witnesses virtually absolute protection against compelled disclosure. A party to civil litigation who disobeys an order to disclose evidence, however, may be subject to a variety of other sanctions, including the entry of judgment against him.

We cannot ignore or subordinate the First Amendment values furthered by the protection of confidential sources and information; at the same time, we must recognize the parallel importance of the policy favoring full disclosure of relevant evidence. When called upon to weigh the fundamental values arguing both for and against compelled disclosure, the overwhelming majority of courts have concluded that the question of a reporter's privilege in civil cases must be decided on a case-by-case basis, with the trial court examining and balancing the asserted interests in light of the facts of the case before it. Thus, the courts conclude, there is neither an absolute duty to disclose nor an absolute privilege to withhold, but instead a qualified privilege against compelled disclosure which depends on the facts of each particular case.

We agree with those courts which have distinguished *Branzburg* and *Herbert* from the issue of discovery of sources in civil litigation. In criminal proceedings, both the interest of the state in law enforcement, recognized as a compelling interest in *Branzburg* (see 48 U.S. 665, 700) and the interest of the defendant in discovering exonerating evidence outweigh any interest asserted in ordinary civil litigation. * * * A confidential source, on the other hand, might well be deterred by the threat that his identity and information might be made public.

Synanon finally argues that the power of the superior court to issue discovery protective orders to protect against "annoyance, embarrassment, or oppression" (Code Civ. Proc., § 2019) is a sufficient safeguard against the abuse of discovery, and makes recognition of a qualified reporter's privilege unnecessary. But discovery which seeks disclosure of confidential sources, and information supplied by such sources, is not ordinary discovery. Judicial concern is not limited to cases of harassment, embarrassment, or abusive tactics; even a limited, narrowly drawn request may impinge upon First Amendment considerations. When a reporter's privilege has been defined by the courts, the limitations on that privilege described, and the relevant considerations set out, Code of Civil Procedure section 2019 provides the statutory basis for the issuance of protective orders safeguarding against harassment. The broad language of that section, however, cannot substitute for judicial explication of the basic privilege.

We conclude that in a civil action a reporter, editor, or publisher has a qualified privilege to withhold disclosure of the identity of confidential sources and of unpublished information supplied by such sources. The scope of that privilege in each particular case will depend upon the consideration and weighing of a number of interrelated factors.

First, the scope of the privilege depends on the nature of the litigation and whether the reporter is a party. In general, disclosure is appropriate in civil cases, especially when the reporter is a party to the litigation. * * * "[T]his will be particularly true in libel cases involving public officials or public figures. . . . Plaintiffs in those cases must prove both that the allegedly defamatory publication was false, and that it was made with 'actual malice.' Proof of actual malice will frequently depend on knowing the identity of the newspaper's informant, since a plaintiff will have to demonstrate that the informant was unreliable and that the journalist failed to take adequate steps to verify his story. Protecting the identity of the source would effectively prevent recovery in many *Times*-type libel cases. . . . We take care to point out, however, that disclosure should by no means be automatic in libel cases. Where other relevant factors suggest disclosure is inappropriate, the privilege should prevail." [Citation omitted.] Thus the present case, a libel suit in which discovery is sought from a party defendant, is of the type suitable for requiring disclosure, depending upon the balancing of other relevant considerations.

A second consideration is the relevance of the information sought to plaintiff's cause of action. The majority view, which we adopt, is that mere relevance is insufficient to compel discovery; disclosure should be denied unless the information goes "to the heart of the plaintiff's claim."

The parties before us dispute whether the disclosure plaintiffs seek goes to the "heart" of their suit against the Mitchells or is only peripheral to that matter. The dispute centers on the question of the liability of a reporter who furnishes defamatory material to the publisher, but does not control the content of the ultimate publication. Plaintiffs contend that through disclosure they will learn "[t]he extent to which the petitioners [Mitchells] were told, and then ignored, facts contrary to their defamations" and "[t]he extent to which petitioners sought only to find derogatory information. . . ." They suggest the possibility that they will discover that the Mitchells had no sources, or at least no reliable sources. * * *

If plaintiffs can show a sufficient causal link between the Mitchells and the Reader's Digest article, they can come within the rationale of the republication rule. The Mitchells would then be responsible for language in the article based on information furnished by them to the Reader's Digest.

The liability of the Mitchells, however, would depend upon proof that they acted with actual malice in the original publication of the defamatory matter. Discovery of the Mitchells' sources, and information derived from such sources, may be essential to proving actual malice, and thus goes to "the heart" of plaintiffs' claim against these defendants. The discovery sought by plaintiffs, however, is quite broad, and is not limited to sources whose information relates to the alleged libelous statements. The Reader's Digest article contains many other statements critical of Dederich and the Synanon operation. Knowledge of the source of such statements, while arguably relevant to the suit, is not sufficiently essential to justify overriding the reporter's privilege.

Third, virtually all cases agree that discovery should be denied unless the plaintiff has exhausted all alternative sources of obtaining the needed information.

In the present case plaintiffs made no showing that they have exhausted alternative sources of information. Many of the Mitchells' sources are known. . . . Such persons can be deposed to discover what information they furnished the Mitchells. Moreover, to the extent plaintiffs seek to prove that the Mitchells deliberately ignored information furnished them favorable to Synanon, it is likely that the sources of the information would readily come forward and cooperate with plaintiffs. There may well be an irreducible core of information which cannot be discovered except through the Mitchells, but plaintiffs have not yet reduced their discovery to that core.

Fourth, the court should consider the importance of protecting confidentiality in the case at hand. The investigation and revelation of hidden criminal or unethical conduct is one of the most important roles of the press in a free society—a role that may depend upon the ability of the press and the courts to protect sources who may justifiably fear exposure and possible retaliation. Thus when the information relates to matters of great public importance, and when the risk of harm to the source is a substantial one, the court may refuse to require disclosure even though the plaintiff has no other way of obtaining essential information.

Finally, the court may require the plaintiff to make a *prima facie* showing that the alleged defamatory statements are false before requiring disclosure. "The falsity of the . . . charges . . . should be drawn into question and established as a jury issue before discovery is compelled" because "to routinely grant motions seeking compulsory disclosure . . . without first inquiring into the substance of a libel allegation would utterly emasculate the fundamental principles [of *New York Times* and similar cases]." [Citations omitted.]

This requirement is closely related to the previous one. There is a great public interest in the truthful revelation of wrongdoing, and in protecting the "whistleblower" from retaliation; there is very little public interest in protecting the source of false accusations of wrongdoing. A showing of falsity is not a prerequisite to discovery, but it may be essential to tip the balance in favor of discovery.

The Reader's Digest article, and especially the earlier writings by the Mitchells, clearly relate to matters of public importance; they allege serious wrongdoing by a powerful private organization, and complicity by public officials. Defendants have hinted that sources might be subject to retaliation but have offered no proof on the point. Plaintiffs, on the other hand, have not attempted a *prima facie* showing of the falsity of the defamatory statements.

In conclusion, the superior court in this case ordered extensive disclosure of sources and information on the ground that there was no reporter's privilege in California. We have concluded that the basis for this ruling was erroneous; that the California courts should recognize a qualified reporter's privilege, depending upon a balancing of the relevant considerations in each case.

Let a peremptory writ of prohibition issue. . . .

COMMENT

Do you think the court succeeded in giving weight to the plaintiff's interest while also assur-

ing that the journalist's privilege, along with First Amendment libel protections, would not be set aside in libel cases? Since *Mitchell*, other courts have also taken pains to assure that requests for disclosure in libel cases are not used as "fishing expeditions." See, e.g., *Dallas Morning News Co. v. Garcia*, 19 Med. L. Rptr. 2033, 822 S.W.2d 675 (Tex.App. 1991).

A case that contrasts sharply with *Mitchell* is *Caldero v. Tribune Publishing* Co., 2 Med. L. Rptr. 1490, 562 P.2d 791 (Idaho 1977), *cert. denied* 434 U.S. 930 (1977). The Idaho Supreme Court apparently felt that *Branzburg* precluded recognition of a journalist's privilege, either qualified or absolute, in the libel case at hand or in other contexts. The *Lewiston Morning Tribune* ran a story about one of Caldero's experiences as an undercover agent for the Idaho Bureau of Narcotic Enforcement. During an arrest and scuffle, Caldero fired three shots through a car windshield, injuring a companion of the man being arrested. More than a year later the article appeared, questioning the "professional propriety of Caldero's conduct." The story quoted an off-the-record police expert who said Caldero's version of the story "didn't add up." The reporter refused to name his source when asked, was judged in contempt, and ordered to spend thirty days in jail. The order was stayed pending appeal.

The opinion in the *Caldero* case was remarkably insensitive to the journalist's interest in nondisclosure. It rejected all cases adopting a privilege as unpersuasive. Despite the breadth of the *Caldero* court's rejection or privilege even in civil litigation, the U.S. Supreme Court refused to review the case. The Idaho court did agree, however, that nondisclosure should be protected if the request was to harass the media or the information sought had an "unnecessary impact" on free expression rights. The court's position is summed up well in the last sentence of its opinion:

> We cannot accept the premise that the public's right to know the truth is somehow enhanced by prohibiting the disclosure of truth in the courts of the public.

Close to the trial date, the widow of the source consented to disclosure. The source was Caldero's boss. Idaho adopted a judicially created qualified privilege in a later case. *Marks v. Vehlow*, 9 Med. L. Rptr. 2361, 671 P.2d 473 (Id. 1983).

Can anything definitive be said, then, about the status of a journalist's privilege claim in libel litigation? Under most lower court interpretations of *Branzburg*, state statutes, state constitutions, or state common law, disclosure will be ordered if the libel suit is valid, especially in terms of its falsity, if other possible sources have been exhausted and if the information sought is relevant and critically important to the case. If the trial court is uncertain about those points, it can defer disclosure to conduct further discovery that may lead to summary judgment.

It may make a difference that a libel case is brought in federal court on the basis of diversity of citizenship. The federal courts have tended to apply federal rules of evidence—and hence a qualified First Amendment privilege—rather than a state privilege. Although Massachusetts recognized no privilege in any form, and all the reporting activities at issue in a libel suit occurred in that state, federal courts applied the First Amendment privilege. *Bruno & Stillman v. Globe Newspaper,* 6 Med. L. Rptr 2057, 633 F.2d 583 (1st Cir. 1980). In other words, a libel defendant in federal court may on occasion have protection unavailable to a defendant in state court. The reverse may be true in some instances, however.

On the other hand, many state shield statutes specifically provide an exception to the privilege in libel cases. Recall that Minnesota's shield law, while it may not be typical, has a section that makes the privilege inapplicable in any libel case where information sought would lead to "relevant evidence" about actual malice.

There may come a time when a reporter's string runs out. That person may then have to comply with a court order or face a contempt citation. Or, the reporter may be assumed to have had no source. Or, the reporter will be barred from using at trial any evidence based on anonymous sources or confidential information. As a consequence, the suit may be lost almost by default.

Journalist's Privilege in the Civil Context

Privilege claims in civil cases where journalists are third parties are much easier to sustain. The compelling need at stake in civil suits is less because the rights asserted by parties are unlikely to be of constitutional or equivalent magnitude. In addition, a greater array of alternative sources is typically available in civil cases.

One of the earliest and most influential post-*Branzburg* cases recognizing a qualified First Amendment privilege was *Baker v. F & F Investment,* 1 Med. L. Rptr. 2551, 470 F.2d 778 (2d Cir. 1972), *cert. denied* 411 U.S. 966 (1973). A number of potential African American home buyers brought a class action suit alleging racially discriminatory housing practices by the defendant. The plaintiffs sought the names of sources used in a 1962 *Saturday Evening Post* article, "Confessions of a Block-Buster," from the article's author, Alfred Balk, who by the time of trial was an editor of the *Columbia Journalism Review.* The federal district court refused to order disclosure, relying both upon First Amendment analysis and on the Illinois and New York shield laws.

The Second Circuit squarely adopted a First Amendment–based privilege. The court agreed that the plaintiffs had failed to prove that all sources had been exhausted or that disclosure was critical to protection of the public interest at issue in the case. Judge Kaufman emphasized that the nature of the claim was important in determining the scope of privilege. He distinguished *Branzburg,* noting, "No such criminal overtones color the facts in this civil case." Referring to *Branzburg,* he added:

> If, as Mr. Justice Powell noted in that case, instances will arise in which First Amendment values outweigh the duty of a journalist to testify even in the context of a criminal investigation, surely in civil cases, courts must recognize that the public interest in non-disclosure of journalists' confidential news sources will often be weightier than the *private interest* in compelled disclosure. [Emphasis added.]

Another case where a qualified First Amendment–based privilege was recognized was *Democratic National Committee v. McCord,* 356 F.Supp. 1394 (D.D.C. 1973). On motions to quash the subpoenas by news organizations, Federal District Judge Charles Richey granted their request and refused to enforce the subpoenas. Even though the issue was raised after the Supreme Court decision in *Branzburg* had declined to create a journalist's privilege in grand jury proceedings based on the First Amendment, Judge Richey held that in these circumstances the newspeople concerned were entitled to a qualified privilege under the First Amendment. The federal district court, reflecting Justice Stewart's dissent in *Branzburg,* stated that absent a showing that alternative sources of evidence had been exhausted and absent a showing of the materiality of the documents sought, an order quashing the subpoenas was warranted.

Federal courts have followed *Baker* and *McCord* almost religiously, and the analysis has been influential in state law cases as well. *Heaslip v. Freeman,* 22 Med. L. Rptr. 1347, 511 N.W.2d 21 (Minn.App. 1994). In *Grunseth v. Marriott Corp.,* 23 Med. L. Rptr. 1148, 868 F.Supp. 333 (D.D.C. 1994), where a former Minnesota gubernatorial candidate brought a suit against the Marriott hotel chain, the federal district court had its choice of a First Amendment privilege, the District of Columbia shield law, and the Minnesota shield law. Someone in the hotel had disclosed hotel registration records to a reporter; these were used along with other sources for a story about the candidate's long-standing affair. Grunseth claimed that the story forced him to drop out of the race and also cost him his job. The court said:

This is precisely the kind of newsgathering activity protected by the First Amendment, especially when the issue arises in a civil, rather than a criminal, context. . . .

While the information sought would be relevant, and therefore admissible if obtained in other ways . . . it certainly does not go to the heart of his claims and is not essential to establish liability. . . .

Nor has Plaintiff demonstrated, other than in conclusory language, that he has exhausted all other reasonable sources for obtaining the information.

Nor is this a case . . . where the reporter is a party and where, therefore, "the equities weigh somewhat more heavily in favor of disclosure." [Citation omitted.]

Finally, Plaintiff has demonstrated no overwhelming or compelling societal interest. . . .

Other seemingly lesser suits have been lost by the press. While a federal district court in Texas recognized a qualified privilege in a civil action brought by a suspended employee against the Dallas school district, it held a reporter in contempt for refusing to testify *in camera.* The plaintiff argued that the school district had released information to the reporter that led to his suspension after the resulting story was published. The court accepted the plaintiff's assertions that his case affected constitutional interests:

That claim includes assertion of a denial of constitutionally ordered due process in connection with Dr. Trautman's suspension from duty. * * * It bears repeating that we are here engaged in a sensitive and important balancing exercise of competing needs and interests rooted in constitutional values.

The plaintiff's claim was based on a denial of due process and liberty under the Fourteenth Amendment and also upon a federal civil rights provision, 42 U.S.C.A. § 1983. *Trautman v. Dallas School District,* 8 Med. L. Rptr. 1088 (N.D.Tex. 1982).

More typically, disclosure attempts in civil cases fail. Chilling effect "is a paramount consideration," said a federal district court in New York. A drug company had sought the identity of a source that had been consulted for evaluation of a drug in a medical newsletter article but had not met the three-part test. *Apicella v. McNeil Laboratories, Inc.,* 66 F.R.D. 78 (E.D.N.Y. 1975).

Are Confidentiality Promises Enforceable?

The traditional rule in journalist's privilege has been that the journalist, not the source, controls the privilege. Now, however, journalists must pay attention to the conditions attached to confidentiality.

During a three-party race for governor and lieutenant governor in Minnesota in 1982, Dan Cohen, a former city council member, provided information about a twelve-year-old shoplifting conviction against a candidate for lieutenant governor. Cohen, a Republican operative, secured a promise of anonymity from reporters employed by the *St. Paul Pioneer Press Dispatch* and the Minneapolis *Star Tribune.* Editors at both papers, thinking Cohen's disclosure a dirty trick, named him as the source. Cohen was fired from his public relations job the same day.

Cohen filed suit alleging that the promise of confidentiality was a contract that was breached by the two newspapers. After defenses based on both the First Amendment and contract law were rejected by the trial court, the case was tried before a six-person jury. The newspapers had argued that the promise of confidentiality was not substantial enough to constitute an enforceable contract and that the First Amendment in any event protected their editorial freedom to name Cohen in the stories. Cohen argued that the reporters, as agents of the newspapers, had legal authority to enter a binding contract on the newspapers' behalfs, and he argued fraud and misrepresentation. The jury agreed 5–1 and awarded $100,000 in actual damages and $250,000 in punitive damages against each newspaper, a total of $700,000.[62]

Part of the trial strategy in the Cohen case was to capitalize on public unease about news leaks to the mass media and about the media in general. Throughout the trial, Cohen's lawyer referred to notable issues such as revelations about Senator Joe Biden's plagiarism while a candidate for president in 1987, and Senator Thomas Eagleton's emotional disorders while the Democratic nominee for vice-president in 1972. The tactic drew criticism from trial judge Franklin Knoll.[63]

The newspapers appealed to the Minnesota Court of Appeals, which affirmed in part and reversed in part. *Cohen v. Cowles Media Co.*, 16 Med. L. Rptr. 2209, 445 N.W.2d 248 (Minn.App. 1989). The court upheld contract damages but set aside punitive damages and Cohen's claim for misrepresentation. Both sides appealed. The Minnesota Supreme Court determined that because nothing was written, Cohen would have to proceed under promissory estoppel rather than contract. It then held that application of estoppel against the newspapers would violate the First Amendment. *Cohen v. Cowles Media Co.*, 17 Med. L. Rptr. 2176, 457 N.W.2d 199 (Minn. 1990). Cohen appealed again.

Cohen v. Cowles Media Co.
18 MED. L. RPTR. 2273, 501 U.S. 663, 111 S.CT. 2513, 115 L.ED. 2D 586 (1991).

Justice WHITE delivered the opinion of the Court.

---

62. Oberdorfer, *"Is 'Burning a Source' A Breach of Contract?"* National L. J. (August 1, 1988), 8.
63. Cohen v. Cowles Media, 15 Med. L. Rptr. 2288 (Minn. Dist. Ct. 1988); Kauffman, "The Source Who Sued," paper presented to the Law Division, Association for Education to Journalism and Mass Communication, Washington, D.C., August 1989; Gillmor, "Broken Promises: Where Law and Ethics Met," in L. W. Hodges (ed.) Social Responsibility: Business, Journalism, Law, Medicine, Vol. XIX, 1993, p. 24; Barron, Cohen v. Cowles Media *and Its Significance for First Amendment Law and Journalism* 1994 William & Mary Bill of Rights J 419.

The question before us is whether the First Amendment prohibits a plaintiff from recovering damages, under state promissory estoppel law, for a newspaper's breach of a promise of confidentiality given to the plaintiff in exchange for information. We hold that it does not.

During the closing days of the 1982 Minnesota gubernatorial race, Dan Cohen, an active Republican associated with Wheelock Whitney's Independent-Republican gubernatorial campaign, approached reporters from the St. Paul Pioneer Press Dispatch (Pioneer Press) and the Minneapolis Star and Tribune (Star Tribune) and offered to provide documents relating to a candidate in the upcoming election. Cohen made clear to the reporters that he would provide the information only if he was given a promise of confidentiality. Reporters from both papers promised to keep Cohen's identity anonymous and Cohen turned over copies of two public court records concerning Marlene Johnson, the Democratic-Farmer-Labor candidate for Lieutenant Governor. * * *

After consultation and debate, the editorial staffs of the two newspapers independently decided to publish Cohen's name as part of their stories concerning Johnson. In their stories, both papers identified Cohen as the source of the court records, indicated his connection to the Whitney campaign, and included denials by Whitney campaign officials of any role in the matter. The same day the stories appeared, Cohen was fired by his employer.

Cohen sued respondents, the publishers of the Pioneer Press and Star Tribune, in Minnesota state court, alleging fraudulent misrepresentation and breach of contract. The trial court rejected respondents' argument that the First Amendment barred Cohen's lawsuit. A jury returned a verdict in Cohen's favor, awarding him $200,000 in compensatory damages and $500,000 in punitive damages. The Minnesota Court of Appeals, in a split decision, reversed the award of punitive damages after concluding that Cohen had failed to establish a fraud claim, the only claim which would support such an award. However, the court upheld the finding of liability for breach of contract and the $200,000 compensatory damage award. *Id.,* at 262.

A divided Minnesota Supreme Court reversed the compensatory damages award. After affirming the Court of Appeals' determination that

Cohen had not established a claim for fraudulent misrepresentation, the court considered his breach of contract claim and concluded that "a contract cause of action is inappropriate for these particular circumstances." The court then went on to address the question whether Cohen could establish a cause of action under Minnesota law on a promissory estoppel theory. * * *

In addressing the promissory estoppel question, * * * the court concluded that "in this case enforcement of the promise of confidentiality under a promissory estoppel theory would violate defendants' First Amendment rights." *Ibid.*

* * *

The initial question we face is whether a private cause of action for promissory estoppel involves "state action" within the meaning of the Fourteenth Amendment such that the protections of the First Amendment are triggered. For if it does not, then the First Amendment has no bearing on this case. The rationale of our decision in *New York Times Co. v. Sullivan,* 376 U.S. 254 (1964), and subsequent cases compels the conclusion that there is state action here. Our cases teach that the application of state rules of law in state courts in a manner alleged to restrict First Amendment freedoms constitutes "state action" under the Fourteenth Amendment. See, *e.g., id.,* at 265; *NAACP v. Claiborne Hardware Co.,* 458 U.S. 886, 916, n. 51 (1982); *Philadelphia Newspapers, Inc. v. Hepps,* 475 U.S. 767, 777 (1986). In this case, the Minnesota Supreme Court held that if Cohen could recover at all it would be on the theory of promissory estoppel, a state-law doctrine which, in the absence of a contract, creates obligations never explicitly assumed by the parties. These legal obligations would be enforced through the official power of the Minnesota courts. Under our cases, that is enough to constitute "state action" for purposes of the Fourteenth Amendment.

Respondents rely on the proposition that "if a newspaper lawfully obtains truthful information about a matter of public significance then state officials may not constitutionally punish publication of the information, absent a need to further a state interest of the highest order." *Smith v. Daily Mail Publishing Co.,* 443 U.S. 97, 103 (1979). That proposition is unexceptionable, and it has been applied in various cases that have found insufficient the asserted state interests in preventing publication of truthful, lawfully obtained information.

This case, however, is not controlled by this line of cases but rather by the equally well-established line of decisions holding that generally applicable laws do not offend the First Amendment simply because their enforcement against the press has incidental effects on its ability to gather and report the news. As the cases relied on by respondents recognize, the truthful information sought to be published must have been lawfully acquired. The press may not with impunity break and enter an office or dwelling to gather news. Neither does the First Amendment relieve a newspaper reporter of the obligation shared by all citizens to respond to a grand jury subpoena and answer questions relevant to a criminal investigation, even though the reporter might be required to reveal a confidential source. *Branzburg v. Hayes,* 408 U.S. 665 (1972). The press, like others interested in publishing, may not publish copyrighted material without obeying the copyright laws. See *Zacchini v. Scripps-Howard Broadcasting Co.,* 433 U.S. 562, 576–579 (1977). Similarly, the media must obey the National Labor Relations Act, *Associated Press v. NLRB,* 301 U.S. 103 (1937), and the Fair Labor Standards Act, *Oklahoma Press Publishing Co. v. Walling,* 327 U.S. 186, 192–193 (1946); may not restrain trade in violation of the antitrust laws, *Associated Press v. United States,* 326 U.S. 1 (1945); *Citizen Publishing Co. v. United States,* 394 U.S. 131, 139 (1969); and must pay nondiscriminatory taxes. *Murdock v. Pennsylvania,* 319 U.S. 105, 112 (1943); *Minneapolis Star and Tribune Co. v. Minnesota Commissioner of Revenue,* 460 U.S. 575, 581–583 (1983). It is therefore beyond dispute that "[t]he publisher of a newspaper has no special immunity from the application of general laws. He has no special privilege to invade the rights and liberties of others." *Associated Press v. NLRB, supra,* at 132–133. Accordingly, enforcement of such general laws against the press is not subject to stricter scrutiny than would be applied to enforcement against other persons or organizations.

There can be little doubt that the Minnesota doctrine of promissory estoppel is a law of general applicability. It does not target or single out the press. Rather, in so far as we are advised, the doctrine is generally applicable to the daily transactions of all the citizens of Minnesota. The First Amendment does not forbid its application to the press.

Justice Blackmun suggests that applying Minnesota promissory estoppel doctrine in this case will "punish" respondents for publishing truthful information that was lawfully obtained. This is not strictly accurate because compensatory damages are not a form of punishment, as were the criminal sanctions at issue in *Smith.* If the contract between the parties in this case had contained a liquidated damages provision, it would be perfectly clear that the payment to petitioner would represent a cost of acquiring newsworthy material to be published at a profit, rather than a punishment imposed by the State. * * * In any event, as indicated above, the characterization of the payment makes no difference for First Amendment purposes when the law being applied as a general law and does not single out the press. Moreover, Justice Blackmun's reliance on cases like *The Florida Star* and *Smith v. Daily Mail* is misplaced. In those cases, the State itself defined the content of publications that would trigger liability. Here, by contrast, Minnesota law simply requires those making promises to keep them.

* * *

The dissenting opinions suggest that the press should not be subject to any law, including copyright law for example, which in any fashion or to any degree limits or restricts the press' right to report truthful information. The First Amendment does not grant the press such limitless protection.

Nor is Cohen attempting to use a promissory estoppel cause of action to avoid the strict requirements for establishing a libel or defamation claim. As the Minnesota Supreme Court observed here, "Cohen could not sue for defamation because the information disclosed [his name] was true." Cohen is not seeking damages for injury to his reputation or his state of mind. He sought damages in excess of $50,000 for a breach of a promise that caused him to lose his job and lowered his earning capacity. * * *

Respondents and *amici* argue that permitting Cohen to maintain a cause of action for promissory estoppel will inhibit truthful reporting because news organizations will have legal incentives not to disclose a confidential source's identity even when that person's identity is itself newsworthy. But if this is the case, it is no more than the incidental, and constitutionally insignificant, consequence of applying to the press a generally applicable law that requires those who make certain kinds of promises to keep them. Although we conclude that the First Amendment does not confer on the press a constitutional right to disregard promises that would otherwise be enforced under state law, we reject Cohen's request that in reversing the Minnesota Supreme Court's judgment we reinstate the jury verdict awarding him $200,000 in compensatory damages. * * * These are matters for the Minnesota Supreme Court to address and resolve in the first instance on remand. Accordingly, the judgment of the Minnesota Supreme Court is reversed, and the case is remanded for further proceedings not inconsistent with this opinion.

So ordered.

Justice SOUTER, with whom Justice MARSHALL, Justice BLACKMUN and Justice O'CONNOR join, dissenting.

* * *

Because I do not believe the fact of general applicability to be dispositive, I find it necessary to articulate, measure, and compare the competing interests involved in any given case to determine the legitimacy of burdening constitutional interests, and such has been the Court's recent practice in publication cases.

Nor can I accept the majority's position that we may dispense with balancing because the burden on publication is in a sense "self-imposed" by the newspaper's voluntary promise of confidentiality. This suggests both the possibility of waiver, the requirements for which have not been met here, as well as a conception of First Amendment rights as those of the speaker alone, with a value that may be measured without reference to the importance of the information to public discourse. But freedom of the press is ultimately founded on the value of enhancing such discourse for the sake of a citizenry better informed and thus more prudently self-governed. "[T]he First Amendment goes beyond protection of the press and the self-expression of individuals to prohibit government from limiting the stock of information from which members of the public may draw." *First National Bank of Boston v. Bellotti,* 435 U.S. 765, 783 (1978). In this context, "'[i]t is the right of the [public], not the right of the [media], which is paramount,'" *CBS, Inc. v. FCC,* 453 U.S. 367, 395 (1981) (emphasis omitted) (quoting *Red Lion Broadcasting Co. v. FCC,* 395 U.S. 367, 390 (1969)), for "[w]ithout the information provided by the press most of us and many of our representatives would be unable to vote intelligently or to register opinions on the administration of government generally." *Cox Broadcasting Corp. v. Cohn*, 420 U.S. 469, 492 (1975); cf. *Richmond Newspapers, Inc. v. Virginia*, 448 U.S. 555, 573 (1980); *New York Times Co. v. Sullivan*, 376 U.S. 254, 278–279 (1964).

The importance of this public interest is integral to the balance that should be struck in this case. There can be no doubt that the fact of Cohen's identity expanded the universe of information relevant to the choice faced by Minnesota voters in that State's 1982 gubernatorial election, the publication of which was thus of the sort quintessentially subject to strict First Amendment protection. The propriety of his leak to respondents could be taken to reflect on his character, which in turn could be taken to reflect on the character of the candidate who had retained him as an adviser. An election could turn on just such a factor; if it should, I am ready to assume that it would be to the greater public good, at least over the long run.

Because I believe the State's interest in enforcing a newspaper's promise of confidentiality insufficient to outweigh the interest in unfettered publication of the information revealed in this case, I respectfully dissent.

COMMENT

The vote was close in *Cohen*, and the Court was sharply divided as to how the First Amendment should apply. Do you think the present Court would reach the same conclusion? On remand, the Minnesota Supreme Court held that the award of compensatory damages was allowable on promissory estoppel grounds. *Cohen v. Cowles Media Co.*, 19 Med. L. Rptr. 1858, 479 N.W.2d 387 (Minn. 1992).

Justice Souter's dissenting opinion was well received by members of the news media. Should it have been? He appears to be advocating a form of *ad hoc* balancing in which the Court's assessment of the importance of the information might be determinative. What if Cohen had given the reporters documents about a celebrity's cosmetic surgery rather than about a candidate for elected office? By contrast, White's majority opinion was greeted with dismay by the news media. The opinion is certainly no paean to journalism, but it *does* take chutzpah to argue that the First Amendment should protect a newspaper when its editors refuse to back up reporters' confidentiality guarantees. Avoiding the effects of *Cohen* should not be difficult for most news organizations.

Media lawyers see endless possibilities for plaintiffs using a contract approach. Would it be a breach of contract to quote someone inaccurately, to surprise a source by disparaging his views, or to disappoint a source by playing down statements she assumed would get front-page attention? And what if a confidential source lies to a reporter? Is the contract still binding? Will Cohen's victory mean that the privilege protects the source as much as it does the journalist? How much did the decision of Twin Cities's editors erode a fundamental proposition of American journalism—that journalistic privilege serves the flow of information to the public?

It is likely that the law of newsgathering will grow in the next decade, and courts may continue to give First Amendment arguments in this area less than their full attention.

Less than a month after the U.S. Supreme Court decision, a federal circuit court declared that a source interviewed for a magazine story about sexual abuse of patients by therapists could sue based on promissory estoppel. Jill Ruzicka agreed to the interview on the condition that she not be identified. She talked to a reporter from *Glamour* magazine about her anguish at being abused by her psychiatrist at a Minneapolis counseling center. Although the article as published did not identify Ruzicka by name, it referred to a Minneapolis attorney named Jill, to the source's lawsuit against the psychiatrist and state board of examiners, and her membership on a state task force to criminalize sexual abuse by therapists. In short, the description was specific enough that Ruzicka could be identified. *Ruzicka v. The Conde Nast Publications, Inc.*, 19 Med. L. Rptr. 1048, 939 F.2d 578 (8th Cir. 1991). When the case went back to the trial court, the judge ruled that the reporter's promise was too ambiguous to support a jury verdict based on promissory estoppel. The circuit court disagreed. Finding that the promise was that *Glamour* would neither name Ruzicka nor describe her in an identifiable fashion, the court stated: "These are terms of common usage and understanding. There is nothing vague or ambiguous about such a promise. . . ." The case was sent back again. *Ruzicka v. Conde Nast Publications, Inc.*, 21 Med. L. Rptr. 1821, 999 F.2d 1319 (8th Cir. 1993).

Numerous cases have featured arguments about media liability based on the *Cohen* decision. It appears that most courts considering arguments based on *Cohen* are interpreting the opinion narrowly to apply only to situations that are closely analogous.[64]

Newsroom Searches

One response to odds favoring journalists was a circumvention of the subpoena process altogether and the use of search warrants to permit the ransacking of an "innocent" third-party newspaper. Although fewer than thirty such searches occurred in ten states between the *Stanford Daily* case in 1978 and ameliorating intervention by federal legislation in 1981, they did represent one of the most serious ruptures ever in press-bench relationships.

Student reporters for *The Stanford Daily* at Stanford University had covered a student demonstration at a hospital that had resulted in violence and injuries to police officers. The newspaper published articles and photographs about the demonstration. At the request of the police, a municipal court judge issued a warrant authorizing a search of *The Stanford Daily*. He found probable cause to believe that photographs and negatives would be found on the newspaper premises that would help to identify the demonstrators who had assaulted the police officers. The warrant was issued even though the newspaper's personnel were not suspected of having committed a crime or of having participated in any unlawful acts.

The students brought an action in federal district court against the municipal judge and the law enforcement officers on the ground that their rights under the First and Fourth Amendments had been violated. The federal district court agreed with the students and rendered a declaratory judgment.

The lineup of the justices was similar to that in *Branzburg*. Justice White wrote the opinion for the Court in a 5–3 decision. Powell wrote an enigmatic concurring opinion. Stewart led three dissenters. White subjected the newsroom to the search warrant mandates of the Fourth Amendment with the same egalitarian approach used to apply the fair trial requirements of the Sixth Amendment in *Branzburg*. Powell steered a middle course, and Stewart urged that newsroom searches should be allowed only if something greater than probable cause was proved.

Zurcher v. The Stanford Daily
3 MED. L. RPTR. 2377, 463 U.S. 547, 948 S. CT. 1970, 56 L. ED. 2D 525 (1978).

Justice WHITE delivered the opinion of the Court.

* * *

But presumptively protected materials are not necessarily immune from seizure under warrant for use at a criminal trial. Not every such seizure, and not even most, will impose a prior restraint, and surely a warrant to search newspaper premises for criminal evidence such as the one issued here for news photographs taken in a public place carries no realistic threat of prior restraint or of any direct restraint whatsoever on the publication of the *Daily* or on its communication of ideas. The hazards of such warrants can be avoided by a neutral magistrate carrying out his responsibilities under the Fourth Amendment, for he has ample tools at his disposal to confine warrants to search within reasonable limits.

* * *

We accordingly reject the reasons given by the District Court and adopted by the Court of Appeals for holding the search for photographs at *The Stanford Daily* to have been unreasonable within the meaning of the Fourth Amendment and in violation of the First Amendment. Nor has anything else presented here persuaded us that the Amendments forbade this search. It follows that the judgment of the Court of Appeals is reversed.

So ordered.

Justice POWELL, concurring.

* * *

---

64. H. Martin, "*Cohen v. Cowles Media Co.* Revisited: An Assessment of the Case's Impact So Far," paper presented to the Law Division of the Association for Education in Journalism and Mass Communication, Anaheim, California, August 1996; Wall & Borger, *Broken Promises in the Aftermath of Cohen,* Communications Lawyer, Summer 1995, at 1, 16–19.

While there is no justification for the establishment of a separate Fourth Amendment procedure for the press, a magistrate asked to issue a warrant for the search of press offices can and should take cognizance of the independent values protected by the First Amendment—such as those highlighted by Justice Stewart—when he weighs such factors. If the reasonableness and particularity requirements are thus applied, the dangers are likely to be minimal.

In any event, considerations such as these are the province of the Fourth Amendment. There is no authority either in history or in the Constitution itself for exempting certain classes of persons or entities from its reach.

COMMENT

Press commentary on the case was bitter. How would the ruling have affected Watergate and the *Pentagon Papers* case had it been in place then? Suddenly, subpoenas didn't look so bad; at least you could see them coming.

Following *Stanford Daily*, a printer's office was searched in Flint, Michigan, a television newsroom in Boise, Idaho, the Associated Press in Butte, Montana, and the home of an editor in Albany, Georgia. On October 13, 1980, Congress passed the Privacy Protection Act (42 U.S.C. § 2000aa). While media organizations had lobbied Congress to prevent surprise invasions of the newsroom, they had asked for a ban on searches of the premises of all innocent third parties. What they got was legislation specific to them.

The law, which went into effect for federal searches on January 1, 1981, and for state searches on October 14, 1981, made it unlawful for law enforcement officers to search for or seize raw materials (photos, audio- and videotapes, interview notes) or work products (drafts of articles and notes) possessed by anyone engaged in the dissemination of news or information to the public through newspapers, books, or electronic broadcasts unless there was probable cause to believe that the person with the material was committing a crime.

Exceptions were threats to national defense, the theft of classified or restricted information, and seizures that would be necessary to prevent death or serious injury. Searches would also be permitted if there was reason to believe that a subpoena would lead to the destruction of material that would serve the needs of justice. Police are expected to request voluntary cooperation from news organizations and scholars or, if that fails, to seek a subpoena before going after a search warrant.[65]

State laws incorporating some or all of these provisions in ways having both more and less impact than the parent federal law have been passed in California, Connecticut, Illinois, Nebraska, New Jersey, Oregon, Texas, Washington, and Wisconsin.

The Privacy Protection Act does not by its terms prevent searches of newsrooms. Instead, it provides for an action for damages when its terms are violated. Obtaining an injunction is not an available remedy. When a television station argued that, to be valid under the act, a search warrant must specify what exception to the act applies, a federal circuit court refused to read the procedural requirement into the statute. *Citicasters v. McCaskill,* 24 Med. L. Rptr. 2196, 89 F.3d 1350 (8th Cir. 1996). The court said that the language of the act was plain and chastised the federal district judge who broadened the act's scope. It also said that law enforcement officials may be entitled to seek warrants based upon a "reasonable belief" that an exception applies without specifying the exception in advance. The act was amended in 1996 to provide an additional exception that allows searches when the materials sought either contain or are related to child pornography.[66]

ACCESS TO THE JUDICIAL SYSTEM

The Parameters of the Conflict

Although tensions between the judiciary and the news media are almost as old as the republic itself,[67] the number of reported cases of overt conflict between the two has exploded in recent years.

---

65. Atwater, *Newsroom Searches: Is "Probable Cause" Still in Effect despite New Law?* 60 Journalism Quarterly 4 (Spring 1983).

66. "Reasonable Belief Enough to Defeat Newsroom Act" *The News Media and the Law,* Summer 1996, p. 2.

67. Surette, *Media, Crime, and Criminal Justice: Images and Reality* 21–47 (1992).

One major reason is the media's increased capacity to cover legal proceedings. New technology, notably changes in cameras and in satellite, digital, and cable distribution, allow even small news organizations to cover major trials on an instantaneous, live basis. The number of media outlets offering news and information has also grown rapidly in the last decade. Hundreds of new television stations have been started. The Internet and World Wide Web have sprouted hundreds, probably thousands, of new sources of news.

Another major reason for increased conflict over journalists' rights to cover legal proceedings is the series of Supreme Court decisions that began in the 1980s and make it difficult for judges and magistrates to restrict news coverage. The First Amendment right to gather news about legal matters is now considered second nature to journalists and is part of their professional training and acculturation:

> The press vigorously opposes the closing of any court proceeding because it believes the public has a right to know what goes on in courtrooms as well as in other areas of government. Attorneys for newspapers and press associations stand ready to go into court and argue against closure.[68]

Almost all of the instances of conflict between the press and the legal system occur in the context of criminal trials and related proceedings. The Sixth Amendment by its terms does not assure criminal defendants a right to a "fair trial," but that is how its provisions are commonly summarized:

> In all criminal prosecutions, the accused shall enjoy the right to a speedy and public trial, by an impartial jury of the State and district wherein the crime shall have been committed. . . . U.S. Const., Amend. VI.

Fair trial concerns center on the jury. Generations of judges and lawyers have reasoned that extensive news coverage of a crime and pending trial will reach potential jurors and possibly sway them. Often judges and lawyers, whose first obligations are to protect the defendant's rights and to assure procedural fairness, have been persuaded to restrain news coverage.

The key question in free press–fair trial disputes is determining when and if publicity creates prejudgment in such a large number of potential jurors that impaneling an impartial jury becomes impossible. It is not essential that jurors be totally ignorant of news coverage about a case, though.[69] What is essential is that they have not drawn a conclusion from news coverage or other sources of information.[70] A juror capable of rendering a verdict based on the evidence presented and nothing else qualifies as impartial. The typical remedy for extensive news coverage is to ferret out any biased jurors during the *voir dire* stage of a trial. A potential juror will be challenged for cause when questioning shows bias. In addition, each side has a number of "peremptory" challenges that can be used to excuse jurors for any or no reason.[71]

An incongruity of the process is that the best potential jurors in terms of ability to judge are often those most likely to stay informed about the news. Those most likely to invest the most time and effort in staying informed tend to have more formal education.[72]

Crime and criminal trials make up the largest category of news coverage at the local level.[73] Since James Gordon Bennett and other penny press editors first emphasized crime news more than 160 years ago, crime news has aroused con-

---

68. Hough, *News Writing* 186–187 (5th ed. 1995); see also Brooks, Kennedy, Moen, and Ranly, *News Reporting & Writing* 485–487 (4th ed. 1992).

69. *United States v. Burr,* 25 Fed.Cas. 49 (No. 14692) (1807).

70. *Patton v. Yount,* 467 U.S. 1025 (1984).

71. *Chestnut v. Ford Motor Co.,* 445 F.2d 967 (4th Cir. 1971) (verdict overturned because juror who owned Ford stock allowed to sit); 28 U.S.C.A. § 1870 (federal courts allow three peremptory challenges).

In criminal cases, peremptory challenges may number fifteen to twenty. Federal court judges rather than attorneys control the examination of a prospective juror. Impaneling is faster, but the procedure is often less thorough than its counterpart in the state courts. Defense attorneys in criminal cases are especially critical of the federal procedure, believing lawyers are better equipped to elicit answers that accurately reflect a potential juror's opinion. See Garry and Riordan, *Gag Orders: Cui Bono?* 29 Stan.L.Rev. 575, at 583 (1977).

72. Stempel and Hargrove, *Mass Media Audiences In a Changing Environment,* 73 Journ. & Mass Comm. Q. 549 (1996).

73. Denniston, *The Reporter and the Law* 3–11 (1980). According to one recent study, in twenty-one major metropolitan daily newspapers stories about law enforcement and criminal legal proceedings were clearly the dominant type of local news coverage in terms of total stories published. These topics received almost a third more stories than the next largest category, local government. Simon, Fico, and Lacy, *Covering Conflict and Controversy: Measuring Balance, Fairness and Defamation in Local News Stories,* 66 Journalism Quarterly 427 (1989).

troversy. Famous crimes and trials are often as notorious for the news coverage that accompanied them as they are for the crimes themselves.

As early as 1807, John Marshall, the fourth chief justice of the United States, noted that the Alexandria (Virginia) *Expositor* had included extralegal comment in its coverage of Aaron Burr's treason trial. Crime reporting probably came into its own, however, when London's Bow Street police reporters discovered that crime news, when presented sensationally, had mass appeal.

Benjamin Day's *New York Sun,* the first successful penny press, specialized in news of crime and violence. Day hired George Wisner, a Bow Street veteran, to cover the courts, and within a year Wisner was co-owner of the paper. Charles Dickens was a Bow Street reporter *par excellence,* and in 1846 his own paper, the *Daily News,* carried a series of articles by Dickens on the brutalizing effects of the death penalty.

Crime news contributed to the success of Pulitzer's *World,* and James Gordon Bennett's *Herald* had no equal in sensational, aggressive, and even fictional crime coverage. William Randolph Hearst's *Journal* led America's "yellow" tabloids into the Jazz Age of journalism.

In 1907, Irwin S. Cobb wrote 600,000 words on the dramatic Harry K. Thaw murder trial for the *World.* Twelve years later the renowned stylist William Bolitho shocked the nation with his accounts in the *World* of the Paris trial of Henri Landru, better known as Bluebeard.

Ben Hecht and the *Daily News* were just right for Chicago in the roaring 20s. Bernarr Macfadden's *Graphic,* nicknamed the "pornographic," promoted the execution of Ruth Snyder in its inimitable style. The *New York Daily News* scored a coup, however, when one of its photographers strapped a tiny camera to his leg, smuggled it into Sing Sing's execution chamber, and took a picture of Snyder straining at the thongs of the electric chair moments after the current had been turned on. The picture was a front-page sensation. It sold 250,000 extra copies of the paper.

With the Lindbergh kidnapping trial, American crime reporting perhaps reached its zenith. As many as 800 newspersons and photographers joined by the great figures of stage and screen, U.S. senators, crooners, social celebrities, and 20,000 curious nobodies turned the little town of Flemington, New Jersey, into a midsummer Mardi Gras. The small courtroom became a twenty-four-hour propaganda bureau spewing out headlines such as "Bruno Guilty, But Has Aides, Verdict of Man in Street," and story references to Bruno Hauptmann as "a thing lacking human characteristics." According to one report, the jury was seriously considering an offer to go into vaudeville.

From Hauptmann's trial to the present, America has never for very long lacked a case *cause célèbre.* Other examples include the Scottsboro Boys case, the espionage trial of Julius and Ethel Rosenberg, the murder trial of Sam Sheppard, the Charles Manson case, and the criminal and civil trials of O. J. Simpson. Reacting to the coverage of both Simpson trials before the verdict in the civil suit, media critic Jon Katz argued that the relationship between journalism and justice needs to be reconsidered:

> Whatever the outcome, this trial won't begin to address the lingering issues the Simpson case has raised for the media, the size, ubiquity, and technologically driven imagery of which have poisoned the criminal justice system and threatened our ability to conduct high-profile inquiries—Simpson, Richard Jewell, and Anita Hill, Paula Jones—in anything like a rational or fair-minded way.
>
> Jury selection seems to depend, for example, on the myth that individuals in our society can be shielded from information, when the fact is that any sane process for choosing jurors should assume they can't, and react accordingly. . . . Jurors are locked up like prisoners for months in a vain effort to shield them from reporters and producers. . . . Katz, "O. J. Simpson and the Death of Justice," The Netizen, www.netizen.com/, January 27, 1997.

Crime coverage has long been criticized for having negative effects on individuals or society.[74] But having the press seek out the strangest, juiciest, and most prominent crime stories should be no surprise. Traditionally, journalists have used these factors to assess news value.[75] The classic response to extensive news coverage has been to either excuse potential jurors or admonish sitting jurors to disregard news coverage. *United States v. Leviton,* 193 F.2d 848 (2d Cir. 1951), *cert. denied* 343 U.S. 946 (1952).

---

74. Gordon and Heath, *The News Business, Crime, and Fears,* in Lewis (ed.), *Reactions to Crime* 227–250 (1981).
75. Romano, *The Grisly Truth about Bare Facts,* in Manoff and Schudson (eds.), *Reading the News* 38–78 (1986).

One judge has pointedly argued that the legal system's fears about publicity are exaggerated. In 1980, the FBI's investigation of bribe taking by government officials, nicknamed ABSCAM, attracted nationwide news coverage. One defendant, Philadelphia Congressman Michael Myers, opposed a motion by television networks to copy videotapes showing bribes being taken. He said the copying and airing of the tapes would prejudice his fair trial right. On appeal, Judge Newman's opinion noted:

Defendants, as well as the news media, frequently overestimate the extent of the public's awareness of news. In this very case, despite the extensive publicity about Abscam * * * about half of those summoned for jury selection had no knowledge of Abscam, and only a handful had more than cursory knowledge. *United States v. Myers*, 6 Med. L. Rptr. 1961, 635 F.2d 945 (2d Cir. 1980).

Most judges and lawyers in high-profile cases have probably agreed at some point with Justice Robert Jackson's statement, "The naïve assumption that prejudicial effects can be overcome by instructions to the jury, all practicing lawyers know to be unmitigated fiction." *Krulewitch v. United States*, 336 U.S. 440 (1949). Supreme Court cases addressing jury impartiality stretch back almost to the country's founding. In most, defendants have argued that their right to a fair trial was denied. The Court routinely has held that even proof of prior opinions about guilt or innocence will not overturn a conviction when a juror promised to decide only on the evidence. In such cases, the defendant bears the burden of proving unfairness.[76]

Researchers have given the issue of prejudicial publicity considerable attention over the last four decades. The goal was to measure the effects of news coverage either during pretrial or trial. The questions of how much prejudicial information appears in the media and whether or not it affects the public, and hence potential jurors,

have been studied frequently in both experimental and field settings. Two scholars recently reassessed dozens of earlier studies while also conducting a content analysis of their own to assess prejudicial publicity about criminal cases where the death penalty might be imposed. They concluded:

The effects of media coverage on criminal justice case processing, juror decision making and public opinion is [sic] difficult to document. The difficulty arises from the inability to dissect the effects of the news media from other potential influences on case outcomes. The media are but one influence on how the public constructs reality. This study cannot conclude that the media have a direct effect on capital jurors' or any criminal justice participants' behavior. Sandys and Chermak, *A Journey into the Unknown: Pretrial Publicity and Capital Cases*, 1 Comm. L. & Pol. 533, 575 (1996).

Interestingly, the authors also concluded "that media coverage of the criminal justice system is an important source of information for prosecutors [and] judges. . . ."

Social science findings may be beside the point in any event. They have seldom been referred to in court opinions, and with good reason. A court faced with a claim of prejudicial publicity violating a defendant's Sixth Amendment rights must base a decision on the specific facts of the case at hand. Proof of a prejudicial effect in one setting cannot prove the same effect in a different situation.

Action to restrain news coverage directly may arise from a variety of motions that are typically filed by the defendant's lawyer. The defendant might move to prevent publication of information—a gag order—to close a proceeding in whole or in part to the press and public, to limit access to materials introduced into evidence, or to prevent or limit electronic or broadcast coverage. Motions that indirectly affect the press may also be put forward, including motions to prohibit out-of-court statements by parties or court officers, to change venue, to obtain a continuance, or to sequester a jury.

The courts have decided hundreds of cases involving these issues since the landmark case of *Richmond Newspapers, Inc. v. Virginia*, 6 Med. L. Rptr. 1833, 448 U.S. 555, 100 S. Ct. 2814, 65 L. Ed. 2d 973 (1980). The general pattern of the case law, especially in the Supreme Court and the

---

76. *United States v. Reid*, 53 U.S. 361 (1851); *Reynolds v. United States*, 98 U.S. 145 (1878); *Hopt v. Utah*, 120 U.S. 430 (1886); *Ex parte Spies*, 123 U.S. 131 (1887); *Mattox v. United States*, 146 U.S. 140 (1892); *Holt v. United States*, 218 U.S. 245 (1910); *Shepherd v. Florida*, 341 U.S. 50 (1951); *Stroble v. California*, 343 U.S. 181 (1952); *U.S. ex rel. Darcy v. Handy*, 351 U.S. 454 (1956); and *Marshall v. United States*, 360 U.S. 310 (1959).

federal circuit courts of appeal, has been to allow limitations on the press only as a last measure, and then in as narrow a fashion as possible. The burden on those who would limit news coverage has been increased. Despite the trend, Professor Matthew Bunker suggests that the conflict is far from being resolved:

> Perhaps the greatest difficulty with the use of heightened scrutiny in most cases in which the press seeks to cover criminal proceedings is the notion that there are two fundamental rights in conflict. . . . Under the received view, these two rights are regarded as in some way incompatible. When judges perceive two rights in conflict, the most natural response is to balance the conflicting rights. . . . Bunker, *Justice and the Media: Reconciling Fair Trials and a Free Press* (1997).

Bunker notes that the tendency to balance will tilt toward protection of the rights of defendants for a variety of reasons. The issues are typically presented intuitively and under time pressure. Often a judge is presented with proof of extensive news coverage and urged that saturation coverage is jeopardizing a defendant's right to a fair trial. A "modest" limitation on newsgathering rights may seem the wiser course until more information is available to the judge. But, in general, "A trial court's apprehension that an open hearing would result in a 'barrage' of media coverage and damaging republication . . . is simply not a permissible reason to close the proceedings. . . . The trial court's findings must be specific enough to enable an appellate court to determine whether its decision was proper." *Ex Parte Birmingham News Co., Inc.*, 21 Med. L. Rptr. 1769, 624 So.2d 1117 (Ala.Crim.App. 1993).

The ultimate remedy is reversal of a conviction. Until 1961, the Supreme Court had not reversed a state conviction solely on the grounds that pretrial publicity had made an impartial jury impossible.

On April 8, 1955, Leslie Irvin, a parolee, was arrested by Indiana state police on suspicion of burglary and bad check writing. A few days later police in Evansville, Indiana, and the county prosecutor issued press releases proclaiming that their burglary suspect, "Mad Dog" Irvin, had confessed to six murders, including the killing of three members of a single family. Irvin went to trial in November, was found guilty, and sentenced to death.

The fact that 370 of 430 prospective jurors questioned by the court before trial said they thought Irvin guilty was bothersome. Defense counsel was never satisfied with the impartiality of the twelve jurors finally selected by the court. Between his conviction and the Supreme Court's reversal in 1961, Irvin's appeal, filed on *habeas corpus* grounds, was heard at least seven times. A unanimous Court concluded that he had not been accorded a fair trial before an impartial jury. Moreover he should have been granted a second change of venue, said the Justices, in spite of an Indiana law allowing only a single change in the place of the trial; and it was the duty of the court of appeals to evaluate independently the *voir dire* testimony of the jurors.

Justice Clark's opinion concluded that the evidence of bias was too strong to ignore:

> Here the "pattern of deep and bitter prejudice" shown to be present throughout the community, was clearly reflected in the sum total of the voir dire examination of a majority of the jurors finally placed in the jury box. Eight out of the 12 thought petitioner was guilty. With such an opinion permeating their minds, it would be difficult to say that each could exclude this preconception of guilt from his deliberations. *Irvin v. Dowd*, 1 Med. L. Rptr. 1178, 366 U.S. 717, 81 S. Ct. 1639, 6 L. Ed. 2d 751 (1961).

Irvin's case was remanded to the district court. He was retried in a less emotional atmosphere, found guilty, and sentenced to life imprisonment, a sentence for which, he confided to his attorney, he was grateful.

Irvin and the *Sheppard* case that follows are perhaps best seen as especially extreme departures from the normal role of journalism in the judicial process. The intensity and extent of coverage, along with the apparent *intent* of the press to affect the outcome, surely set these cases apart.

In the early 1960s, the judiciary retained memories of journalists' behavior from the 1920s and 1930s. Meanwhile the press still had a reputation for crime reporting that was sensational, not serious. The professional principle that reporting should be detached and neutral came relatively late to crime news. The colorful tradition of crime reporting began to change after 1966 when the Supreme Court reversed a second conviction because of the effects of news coverage.

The *Sheppard* Case and Its Aftermath

The trial of Dr. Samuel Sheppard illustrated the dangers of carnival-style news coverage. After a murder conviction and twelve years in prison, Sheppard's attorneys got his case heard by the Supreme Court. He was given a new trial and acquitted.

Sheppard was accused of the July 4, 1954 murder of his wife Marilyn at their home in Bay Village, a suburb of Cleveland. "From the outset officials focused suspicion on Sheppard," Justice Clark noted in his opinion for the Court. He recounted the press's role in subsequent events.

First the newspapers reported extensively on Sheppard's refusal to take a lie detector test. An editorial suggested that Sheppard should have been "subjected instantly to the * * * third degree." Another editorial demanded an inquest. When the coroner called an inquest, it was held in a school gymnasium, was attended by a "swarm" of reporters and photographers, and was broadcast live. The three-day inquest ended with a "public brawl." Sheppard's attorneys were allowed to attend but not to participate. The newspapers reported details of the investigation obtained from police that were never introduced at trial, all of which tended toward showing Sheppard's guilt. The newspapers reported extensively that Sheppard was a womanizer, implying motive, but that too was never introduced at trial. Later editorials asked "Why Don't Police Quiz Top Suspect?" and "Why Isn't Sam Sheppard in Jail?"

When Sheppard was arrested, a crowd of newscasters, reporters, and photographers was waiting for his arrival at city hall. Sensational coverage continued until the trial.

The trial itself began two weeks before elections in which the prosecutor was a candidate for municipal judge and the trial judge was a candidate for reelection. A list of seventy-five prospective jurors was drawn. The newspapers were given and printed each person's name and address. The courtroom was 26 by 48 feet. A temporary table was set up *inside* the bar for approximately twenty reporters who were given assigned seats. Four other rows of benches were assigned to media representatives for the duration of the trial. The press used all the other rooms on the same floor of the courthouse. Telegraph and telephone lines were installed. One radio station set up broadcasting facilities on the third floor, next to the jury room.

During trial, one television broadcast carried an interview with the judge as he entered the courthouse. Prospective jurors were photographed during *voir dire*. Witnesses, counsel, and jurors were all photographed and televised whenever they entered or left. Sheppard himself was brought into the courtroom about ten minutes before the start of each session to allow photographing, although picture taking was prohibited while court was in session. At *voir dire*, every juror testified of reading or hearing about the case in the media. During trial, pictures of the jury appeared in the Cleveland papers more than forty times. One feature story told of a juror's home life. On the second day of *voir dire*, a live debate was staged on radio. During the debate, reporters said Sheppard effectively admitted his guilt by hiring a prominent criminal defense attorney.

Sheppard's attorneys sought a continuance, a change of venue, and a mistrial, all denied. The jury was not sequestered, and no attempt was made to limit outside contacts and, thereby, exposure to news accounts.

Parties on both sides of the case had long agreed that responsibility for preventing "trial by newspaper" rests on judges, prosecutors, and police, not the press. For the second reversal of a state court conviction on due process grounds, the Supreme Court agreed.

Sheppard v. Maxwell
1 MED. L. RPTR. 1220, 384 U.S. 333, 86 S. CT. 1507, 16 L. ED. 2D 600 (1966).

Justice CLARK delivered the opinion of the Court:

* * *

A responsible press has always been regarded as the handmaiden of effective judicial administration, especially in the criminal field. Its function in this regard is documented by an impressive record of service over several centuries. The press does not simply publish information about trials but guards against the miscarriage of justice by subjecting the police, prosecutors, and judicial processes to extensive public scrutiny and criticism. This Court has, therefore, been unwilling to place any direct limitations on the freedom traditionally exercised by the news media for "[w]hat transpires in the court room is public property." *Craig v. Harney,* 331 U.S. 367 (1947).

* * * But the Court has also pointed out that "[l]egal trials are not like elections, to be won through the use of the meeting-hall, the radio, and the newspaper." *Bridges v. State of California,* 314 U.S. at 271 (1941). * * * And we cited with approval the language of Justice Black for the Court in *In re Murchison,* 349 U.S. 133, 136 (1955), that "our system of law has always endeavored to prevent even the probability of unfairness."

It is clear that the totality of circumstances in this case also warrant such an approach. * * * Sheppard was not granted a change of venue to a locale away from where the publicity originated; nor was his jury sequestered.

* * *

There can be no question about the nature of the publicity which surrounded Sheppard's trial. * * * Indeed, every court that has considered this case, save the court that tried it, has deplored the manner in which the news media inflamed and prejudiced the public.

* * *

Nor is there doubt that this deluge of publicity reached at least some of the jury. On the only occasion that the jury was queried, two jurors admitted in open court to hearing the highly inflammatory charge that a prison inmate claimed Sheppard as the father of her illegitimate child. Despite the extent and nature of the publicity to which the jury was exposed during trial, the judge refused defense counsel's other requests that the jury be asked whether they had read or heard specific prejudicial comment about the case, including the incidents we have previously summarized. In these circumstances, we can assume that some of this material reached members of the jury.

The court's fundamental error is compounded by the holding that it lacked power to control the publicity about the trial. From the very inception of the proceedings the judge announced that neither he nor anyone else could restrict prejudicial news accounts. And he reiterated this view on numerous occasions. Since he viewed the news media as his target, the judge never considered other means that are often utilized to reduce the appearance of prejudicial material and to protect the jury from outside influence. We conclude that these procedures would have been sufficient to guarantee Sheppard a fair trial and so do not consider what sanctions might be available

against a recalcitrant press nor the charges of bias now made against the state trial judge.

The carnival atmosphere at trial could easily have been avoided since the courtroom and courthouse premises are subject to the control of the court. * * * Bearing in mind the massive pre-trial publicity, the judge should have adopted stricter rules governing the use of the courtroom by newsmen, as Sheppard's counsel requested. The number of reporters in the courtroom itself could have been limited at the first sign that their presence would disrupt the trial. They certainly should not have been placed inside the bar. Furthermore, the judge should have more closely regulated the conduct of newsmen in the courtroom. * * *

Secondly, the court should have insulated the witnesses. All of the newspapers and radio stations apparently interviewed prospective witnesses at will, and in many instances disclosed their testimony. A typical example was the publication of numerous statements by Susan Hayes, before her appearance in court, regarding her love affair with Sheppard.

* * *

Thirdly, the court should have made some effort to control the release of leads, information, and gossip to the press by police officers, witnesses, and the counsel for both sides. Much of the information thus disclosed was inaccurate leading to groundless rumors and confusion.

* * *

Under such circumstances, the judge should have at least warned the newspapers to check the accuracy of their accounts. And it is obvious that the judge should have further sought to alleviate this problem by imposing control over the statements made to the news media by counsel, witnesses, and especially the Coroner and police officers. The prosecution repeatedly made evidence available to the news media which was never offered in the trial. Much of the "evidence" disseminated in this fashion was clearly inadmissible.

* * *

More specifically, the trial court might well have proscribed extra-judicial statements by any lawyer, party, witness, or court official which divulged prejudicial matters. * * * In addition, reporters who wrote or broadcast prejudicial stories, could have been warned as to the impropriety of publishing material not introduced in the proceedings. * * * In this manner, Sheppard's right to a trial free from outside interference would have been given added protection without corresponding curtailment of the news media.

* * *

From the cases coming here we note that unfair and prejudicial news comment on pending trials has become increasingly prevalent. Due process requires that the accused receive a trial by an impartial jury free from outside influences. Given the pervasiveness of modern communications and the difficulty of effacing prejudicial publicity from the minds of the jurors, the trial courts must take strong measures to ensure that the balance is never weighed against the accused, and appellate tribunals have the duty to make an independent evaluation of the circumstances. *Of course, there is nothing that proscribes the press from reporting events that transpire in the courtroom.* [Emphasis added.] But where there is a reasonable likelihood that prejudicial news prior to trial will prevent a fair trial, the judge should continue the case until the threat abates or transfer it to another county not so permeated with publicity. In addition, sequestration of the jury was something the judge should have raised *sua sponte* with counsel. If publicity during the proceedings threatens the fairness of the trial, a new trial should be ordered. But we must remember that reversals are but palliatives; the cure lies in those remedial measures that will prevent the prejudice at its inception. *The courts must take such steps by rule and regulation that will protect their processes from prejudicial outside interferences.* [Emphasis added.] Neither prosecutors, counsel for defense, the accused, witnesses, court staff nor enforcement officers coming under the jurisdiction of the court should be permitted to frustrate its function. Collaboration between counsel and the press as to information affecting the fairness of a criminal trial is not only subject to regulation, but is highly censurable and worthy of disciplinary measures.

* * *

The case is remanded to the District Court with instructions to issue the writ and order that Sheppard be released from custody unless the State puts him to its charges again within a reasonable time.

It is so ordered.

COMMENT

The clearest message from *Sheppard* is the Court's affirmation that it is primarily the judge's job to assure a fair trial. Only after considering a lengthy "laundry list" of alternative measures, apparently, would direct action affecting the press be justified. The *Sheppard* opinion is simultaneously a rebuke based on the effects of press coverage and a defense of the First Amendment. The requirement that alternative measures be tried first means that the defendant and not the press will be inconvenienced, at least initially.

Justice Clark specifically listed nine actions the trial judge ought to have considered to assure fairness:

> Control the courtroom behavior of the press via time, place, and manner restrictions.
>
> Insulate witnesses from the press.
>
> Control the release of information from the parties and the police.
>
> Caution reporters about potential issues of prejudice and accuracy in their coverage.
>
> Control, even prohibit, extra-judicial statements to the press by parties or their lawyers.
>
> Grant a continuance until the curiosity abates.
>
> Grant a change of venue to a location where press attention will be less.
>
> Sequester the jury to prevent them from getting access to news.
>
> Grant a new trial if all of the above fail.

In addition, there are traditional remedies that require no direct action against the press. One is admonishment of jurors. Conducting an intense *voir dire* to assure that any jurors actually seated have drawn no conclusions about guilt or innocence is also common. It is worth noting the practical effects of some of the alternatives Justice Clark said a trial judge should consider.

Change of venue is perhaps the most attractive of the alternatives. In most criminal cases, news coverage is local, not widespread. As a practical matter, that means that a shift to another county or another part of the state may remedy any potential publicity effects. Two problems are associated with change of venue, however. First, the Court's suggestion runs counter to the change of venue provisions of many state statutes. Second, it is of little help to the defendant who has attracted statewide or even nationwide news coverage.

Continuance means delaying the trial while waiting for the publicity to wane. It is useful only to allay the effects of pretrial publicity, since the trial itself will attract renewed press attention. Still, delay can make impaneling an impartial jury easier by allowing bias, if it exists, to erode with incomplete recollection. Unfortunately, the sort of recollection most likely to remain is an impression of guilt or innocence.

Sequestering the jury can help prevent publicity effects during the actual trial, but it presents tremendous practical problems. It is expensive; jurors may be fed and housed in hotels for weeks at court expense. Jurors would rather be home than effectively held prisoner to assure a fair trial. Court and police personnel must monitor jurors to assure that inappropriate contact or exposure does not occur.

Conducting an intense voir dire is perhaps the best of the remedies. It has been the primary method of guaranteeing an impartial jury almost as long as the jury system has been used. Ignorance itself is not necessarily a virtue, however. In *Murphy v. Florida*, 1 Med. L. Rptr. 1232, 421 U.S. 794 (1975), the defendant had been on trial for his part in a series of thefts, including theft of a famous sapphire, the Star of India. Although jurors admitted knowing of the highly publicized case, the Court could find no evidence of juror hostility toward the defendant in the *voir dire* record.

Admonishing the jury to disregard potentially irrelevant or prejudicial information is another traditional remedy, one in fact used by the trial judge in *Sheppard*. But how can a judge be confident that a warning to disregard will be heeded? Often jurors are admonished not to read a newspaper, watch television news, or listen to radio, but unless sequestered, a jury's adherence relies on an unspoken and hard-to-enforce honor system.

Insulating witnesses requires only that steps be taken to assure that the press does not have ready access. Having witnesses enter by back or side entrances have often been enough. Of course, whether or not a judge can prevent statements to the press by a willing witness is an entirely different issue.

Cautioning reporters has never been a common or popular practice. On occasion, a trial judge may meet with reporters in chambers to discuss some of the sensitive aspects of the case. In general, though, journalists feel uncomfortable taking advice from a government official. At the same time, judges are not likely to see educating the media as part of their responsibilities.

Controlling the release of information, typically in documents, has not proved as simple as Clark intimated in *Sheppard*. Reporters are usually able to find willing sources who voluntarily hand over documents. Judicial attempts to find out who leaked the information seldom meet with success. In *News-Journal Corp. v. Foxman*, 19 Med. L. Rptr. 1193, 939 F.2d 1499 (11th Cir. 1991), news organizations were apparently very successful at getting investigative and other records that became part of the extensive coverage of an unusual murder case. Although the trial judge decried the style of coverage, direct limitations were placed only on trial participants, not on the press.

Controlling statements made to the press is a thornier matter than the other remedies suggested. At the time *Sheppard* was decided in 1966, the Court appears to have simply assumed that prohibiting statements was within a court's power. But prohibiting statements amounts to a gag order, or a prior restraint. The major difference is that the First Amendment rights of parties, counsel, or others involved in the case are at stake, not the rights of the press. Many felt that Clark's casual endorsement of gag orders fueled court actions that resulted in the *Nebraska Press Association v. Stuart*, 427 U.S. 539 (1976) case ten years later. The propriety of gags against those who would speak to the press are now addressed in light of *Nebraska Press*.

The only direct action against the press approved in *Sheppard* is *time, place, and manner* **regulation** in the courtroom. A trial judge has an obligation to assure that the conduct of observers, including the press, does not have a detrimental effect on either the conduct or outcome of proceedings.

To be sure, these judicial remedies are useful, but they also present some obvious problems. The ubiquity of mass media, especially broadcasting, casts a shadow on the effectiveness of changes of venue and venire (importing jurors from distant jurisdictions). A continuance, or postponement, may lead to the disappearance of witnesses and evidence, and, if unable to raise bail, a defendant remains in jail. A mistrial subjects a defendant to the expense and trauma of a new trial. There is some debate over the usefulness of peremptory challenges to jurors and of challenges for cause, both part of *voir dire* pro-ceedings. Jurors as a rule don't like being sequestered, or locked up, and may react adversely to the party initiating such a motion; moreover, in most cases, they have already been exposed to pretrial publicity.

One survey reported that judges favored most of the above remedies appropriate to the pretrial period. Once the trial had begun, motion for a new trial on due process grounds was their choice. Most agreed that the reporting of crimi-nal records, confessions, and the results of pre-trial tests, such as the lie detector, were the most damaging forms of pretrial coverage. Bush, Wilcox, Siebert, & Hough, *Free Press and Fair Trial* (1971).

Clark did emphasize that "The courts must take such steps by rule and regulation that will protect their processes from prejudicial outside interferences," an admonition that could be interpreted as justifying if not advocating direct restraints on the press. The courts, the legal pro-fession, and journalists would all react differ-ently to the message of *Sheppard*.

Although Clark spoke sternly to trial judges, he also had strong words for the press. His pained account of press coverage showed disgust for the media's disregard for fairness. Clark's castigation of the press influenced lower court judges who, despite *Sheppard's* insistence that direct action against the press must be a last resort, issued hundreds of gag orders directly against the press in the next decade.

In the interim, and partly in response to criti-cism in the Warren Report on press coverage of Lee Harvey Oswald,[77] the American Bar Associ-ation set up an Advisory Committee on Fair Trial and Free Press under chairman Paul C. Reardon, then an associate justice on the Massachusetts Supreme Judicial Court.[78] While the Reardon Report, as it came to be called, primarily addressed officers of the courts, it recommended that judges use the long discredited power of *constructive contempt*.[79] Constructive contempt

allows judges to cite for contempt anyone who disseminates extrajudicial statements willfully designed to influence a trial's outcome, or any-one who violates a valid court order not to reveal information from a closed judicial hearing, despite the fact that the action took place outside the courtroom.[80]

The Reardon Report also favored closing pre-trial hearings to the press and public if the court believed that a fair trial was in jeopardy. Since 90 percent of criminal cases are disposed of in the pretrial stage, widespread closure of pretrial hearings would curtail newsgathering about criminal cases significantly.

The controversial report also established cate-gories of prohibited and publishable informa-tion. Prohibited comment included prior crimi-nal records; character references; confessions; test results; and out-of-court speculation on either guilt or innocence or the merits of evi-dence. Publishable information included facts and circumstances of arrests; identity of the per-son arrested; identity of the arresting officer or agency; descriptions of physical evidence; the charge; facts from public court records; and the next probable steps in the judicial process. The report was soon exerting nationwide influence on both press and bar.

The Reardon Report also had a positive side. The report gave momentum to the work of bar-press committees in the states. In most states, rep-resentatives of the legal and journalism communi-ties met to discuss what items of coverage were appropriate when the press covered criminal pro-ceedings. The press was motivated, at least in part, to seek better relations with the bar as a way of blunting the Reardon Report's effects after the report was formally adopted by the ABA.

The committees typically wrote bar-press guidelines, which the press hoped would assure limited judicial intervention in newsgathering and which the bar hoped would provide more balanced, less biased coverage. Voluntary guide-lines were adopted in about half the states during the 1960s and 1970s, and thereafter forgotten. Typically, they detailed information that was considered either appropriate or inappropriate

---

77. Report of the President's Commission on the Assassination of President John F. Kennedy (1964), 201–242 and *passim*.

78. American Bar Association Legal Advisory Committee on Fair Trial and Free Press, *The Rights of Fair Trial and Free Press*, 1969. See also Gillmor, *The Reardon Report: A Jour-nalist's Assessment*, 1967 Wisc.L.Rev. 215.

79. For a catalog of English contempt cases involving the press, see Gillmor, *Free Press and Fair Trial in English Law*, 22 Wash. & Lee L.Rev. 17–42 (1965).

---

80. *In re Stone*, 11 Med. L. Rptr. 2209 (Colo.Ct.App. 1985) (intent to interfere not required for civil contempt; sufficient if defendants knew that it was violation of the court order to contact murder trial jurors for interviews when jurors were under court order to not discuss case).

for publication. They also included guidelines for photography.[81]

The Contempt Power and Gag Orders

With *Sheppard*, the Reardon Report, and various states' guidelines in place, the stage was set for numerous confrontations between the judiciary and the press. The primary question anytime a judge orders the press not to report information is whether or not the order must be obeyed. The second question concerns the constitutional validity of the order.

While the news media were predictably negative toward broad prohibitions against publishing information in public records, such as criminal records, their strongest condemnation was reserved for the part of the Reardon Report that proposed punishing editors for what they printed. History was largely on the editors' side.

Traditionally, judges had extraordinary power. The general rule had been that judges had authority to punish out-of-court statements whenever the statements might obstruct the administration of justice. This so-called reasonable tendency test was rejected in *Nye v. United States*, 313 U.S. 33 (1941), which also required that the out-of-court statements be physically close to the judge's court.

The power of judges was even more severely limited in *Bridges v. California*, 314 U.S. 252 (1941). Labor leader Harry Bridges and the *Los Angeles Times* had both criticized a judge and the judicial process while a case was pending. The Court declared in this and subsequent cases that the contempt power could be used only against out-of-court comments creating a "clear and present danger" of impairing justice. "The assumption that respect for the judiciary can be won by shielding judges from published criticism wrongly appraises the character of American public opinion," Justice Hugo Black wrote for the Court. "[A]n enforced silence * * * would probably engender resentment, suspicion, and contempt much more than it would enhance respect." Dissenters in *Bridges* argued that applying a prior restraint analysis was inappropriate, because the punishment was for past conduct; they also thought the case upset the states'

traditional right to establish laws to protect the integrity of their courts.

Though perhaps of little moment to the journalist facing a contempt citation, it is important to note that American law provides for two types of contempt, civil contempt and criminal contempt. The difference refers to the actions of the person cited, however, and not to the nature of the action from which the contempt citation arose. Criminal contempt is more likely when the refusal to obey a court order is knowing and willful. The biggest difference is in penalties, with criminal contempt typically bringing harsher ones. The exact rules for contempt vary depending upon whether a court is federal or state and whether the action is civil or criminal; even then they vary tremendously among the states. Normally, persons cited for contempt are entitled to a hearing and counsel.

The traditional rule regarding court orders is that they must be obeyed, pending appeal, even when First Amendment interests are affected. The leading modern case on the duty of journalists to obey even an obviously invalid order constituting prior restraint developed from a 1971 Baton Rouge murder-conspiracy case.

At a preliminary hearing designed to determine whether the state had a legitimate motive in prosecuting a VISTA worker on a charge of conspiring to murder the city's mayor or whether its action was based on racial prejudice, a federal district judge prohibited the publication of testimony taken at a public hearing. Two *State-Times* reporters ignored the order, wrote their stories, and were adjudged guilty of criminal contempt of court. The reporters appealed to the Fifth Circuit, and that court upheld the principle that even an unconstitutional court order must be obeyed pending appeal. The court refused to make the First Amendment question of prior restraint the dispositive issue in the case.

Noting that no jury was yet involved in the case and that the press had not created a carnival atmosphere, the Fifth Circuit observed that the public's right to know the facts brought out in the hearing was particularly compelling because the issue being litigated was a charge that elected state officials had trumped up charges against an individual solely because of his race and civil rights activities. The federal district court's cure was worse than the disease, said the federal appeals court.

---

81. See, e.g., Bar/News Media Committee, *Journalists' Guide to Nebraska Courts* (1980), 43.

United States v. Dickinson
1 MED. L. RPTR. 1338, 465 F.2D 496 (5TH CIR. 1972).

John R. BROWN, Chief Judge:

* * *

The conclusion that the District Court's order was constitutionally invalid does not necessarily end the matter of the validity of the contempt convictions. There remains the very formidable question of whether a person may with impunity knowingly violate an order which turns out to be invalid. We hold that in the circumstances of this case he may not.

We begin with the well-established principle in proceedings for criminal contempt that an injunction duly issuing out of a court having subject matter and personal jurisdiction *must be obeyed,* irrespective of the ultimate validity of the order. Invalidity is no defense to criminal contempt. * * * "People simply cannot have the luxury of knowing that they have a right to contest the correctness of the judge's order in deciding whether to willfully disobey it. * * * Court orders have to be obeyed until they are reversed or set aside in an orderly fashion."

* * *

[T]he deliberate refusal to obey an order of the court without testing its validity through established processes requires further action by the judiciary, and therefore directly affects the judiciary's ability to discharge its duties and responsibilities. Therefore, "while it is sparingly to be used, yet the power of the courts to punish for contempts is a necessary and integral part of the independence of the judiciary, and is absolutely essential to the performance of the duties imposed on them by law. Without it they are mere boards of arbitration whose judgments and decrees would be only advisory."

* * *

Where the thing enjoined is publication and the communication is "news," this condition presents some thorny problems. Timeliness of publication is the hallmark of "news" and the difference between "news" and "history" is merely a matter of hours. Thus, where the publishing of news is sought to be restrained, the incontestable inviolability of the order may depend on the immediate accessibility of orderly review. But in the absence of strong indications that the appellate process was being deliberately stalled—certainly not so in this record—violation with impunity does not occur simply because immediate decision is not forthcoming, even though the communication enjoined is "news." * * * But newsmen are citizens, too. They too may sometimes have to wait. * * * [B]oth the District Court and the Court of Appeals were available and could have been contacted that very day, thereby affording speedy and effective but *orderly* review of the injunction in question swiftly enough to protect the right to publish the news while it was still "news."

* * *

Under the circumstances, reporters took a chance. As civil disobedients have done before they ran a risk, the risk being magnified in this case by the law's policy which forecloses their right to assert invalidity of the order as a complete defense to a charge of criminal contempt. Having disobeyed the Court's decree, they must, as civil disobeyers, suffer the consequences for having rebelled at what they deem injustice, but in a manner not authorized by law. * * *

Vacated and remanded.

COMMENT

The case was returned to the district court judge, and he again convicted the reporters and upheld their $300 fines. The appeals court also affirmed a second time. 476 F.2d 373 (5th Cir. 1972), *cert. denied* 414 U.S. 979 (1973).

The court of appeals urged *speedy* review of orders affecting the press, apparently echoing the Supreme Court's principle of accelerated review from the "Pentagon Papers" case. Ironically, the Fifth Circuit itself took nine months from initial appeal to opinion.

Speedy review of an order restraining broadcast of an NBC docudrama and ordering the network to produce the show for judicial scrutiny issued by a district court judge took less than a day in *Goldblum v. NBC,* 4 Med. L. Rptr. 1718, 584 F.2d 904 (9th Cir. 1978). The program was based on the plaintiff's business activities, which had landed him a prison sentence. Goldblum argued that the broadcast would prejudice his chances for parole and might bias juries should he be tried again in the future. The court of appeals concluded that Goldblum was not even close to meeting the requirements for a prior restraint.

Although the court in *Goldblum* did not directly chide the trial judge who issued the order, choosing rather to berate the plaintiff's case, the court did note that an action for a writ of mandamus on the network's part was appropriate to "correct an abuse of discretion" that affected First Amendment rights, and said in passing that there was "no authority which is even a remote justification for issuance of a prior restraint. * * *" To be reversed so summarily is surely embarrassing for a trial court judge and provides incentive for judges to "study up" on First Amendment issues before issuing restrictive orders affecting the press.

The principle of accelerated review is sufficiently well established today that when a North Carolina trial court issued an order prohibiting publication of the identity or photograph of a juvenile criminal defendant, the state supreme court reversed the trial judge just three days later. *In re Minor Charged,* 24 Med. L. Rptr. 1057 (N.C.Dist.Ct.), *reversed,* 24 Med. L. Rptr. 1064, 341 N.C. 415 (1995). Perhaps the most remarkable aspect of the case is that the North Carolina Supreme Court summarily reversed without any citation or discussion. In other cases, it has not been unusual to see an appellate decision the same day a restrictive order is issued by a trial judge. In *Sioux Falls Argus Leader v. Young,* 18 Med. L. Rptr. 1044, 455 N.W.2d 864 (S.D. 1990), the court was ready to take an appeal by fax the same day. Since the fax machine was turned off, however, the newspaper filed its appeal the next morning.

Not all courts will accelerate review this much. In *In re Charlotte Observer,* 18 Med. L. Rptr. 1365, 921 F.2d 47, (4th Cir. 1990) (designated as unpublished), the Fourth Circuit indicated that both sides should be given enough time to brief the issues. But the court found that about six days was enough time.

It may be important to distinguish restrictive orders issued by state courts and those issued by federal courts. Until it is overruled, *Dickinson* and federal cases upon which it rests hold that no disobedience to a court order will be permitted, even when the order violates the First Amendment. State law, however, may favor an attack on such orders, particularly where they violate state constitutional guarantees.[82]

Back in the 1970s, though, *Dickinson* gave impetus to the issuing of gag orders in criminal cases. The requirement that the press obey even an obviously invalid order virtually assured that the proceedings would have ended before the gag could be reviewed. Court proceedings and court records were closed. Names of jurors and witnesses, criminal records, and arrest records were sealed. Prior restraints were imposed by forbidding publication of information about exhibits, pleas, jury verdicts, and editorial comment on guilt or innocence.

Violation of an Order Redux—The *Providence Journal* Case

Although *Dickinson* has long been the prevailing opinion on whether or not court orders must be obeyed, the First Circuit challenged both the reasoning and result of that case in a dispute involving the *Providence Journal*'s ten-year attempt to report on the Patriarca crime family. In 1976, the *Journal* had requested logs and memoranda from FBI surveillance and wiretapping of Raymond L. S. Patriarca but was refused on the ground that disclosure would be an unwarranted invasion of personal privacy. After Patriarca's death, the *Journal* again sought the material and, along with other news organizations, received it.

Raymond J. Patriarca, son of Raymond L. S. Patriarca, brought an action for a temporary restraining order based on the federal Freedom of Information Act, the Omnibus Crime Control and Safe Streets Act of 1986, and the Fourth Amendment. Over the objections of both the newspaper and the federal government, the judge issued the order. Nevertheless, the next day the *Journal* published an article using the enjoined material. The district court, in a move that would prove crucial, appointed a special prosecutor, held a hearing, and found the newspaper in criminal contempt. Executive editor Charles M. Hauser received a suspended eighteen-month

---

82. See *S.N.E. v. R.L.B.,* 11 Med. L. Rptr. 2278, 699 P.2d 875 (Alaska 1985) (gag order preventing parties in child custody case from communicating with third parties, including the press, violates state constitution); *State ex rel. Superior Court of Snohomish County v. Sperry,* 483 P.2d 608 (Wash. 1971), *cert. denied* 404 U.S. 930 (1971).

jail term and an order to perform 200 hours of community service. The *Journal* itself was fined $100,000. The *Journal* appealed, and the First Circuit upheld its right to publish.

In re Providence Journal
13 MED. L. RPTR. 1945, 820 F.2D 1342 (1ST CIR. 1986).

WISDOM, J.:

This appeal propounds a question that admits of no easy answer. Each party stands on what each regards as an unassailable legal principle. The special prosecutor relies on the bedrock principle that court orders, even those that are later ruled unconstitutional, must be complied with until amended or vacated. This principle is often referred to as the "collateral bar" rule. The Journal relies on the bedrock principle that prior restraints against speech are prohibited by the First Amendment. In this opinion we endeavor to avoid deciding which principle should take precedence by reaching a result consistent with both principles.

* * *

[W]ell-established is the requirement of any civilized government that a party subject to a court order must abide by its terms or face criminal contempt. Even if the order is later declared improper or unconstitutional, it must be followed until vacated or modified. As a general rule, a party may not violate an order and raise the issue of its unconstitutionality collaterally as a defense in the criminal contempt proceeding.

* * *

Court orders are accorded a special status in American jurisprudence. While one may violate a statute and raise as a defense the statute's unconstitutionality, such is not generally the case with a court order. Nonetheless, court orders are not sacrosanct. An order entered by a court clearly without jurisdiction over the contemnors or the subject matter is not protected by the collateral bar rule. Were this not the case, a court could wield power over parties or matters obviously not within its authority—a concept inconsistent with the notion that the judiciary may exercise only those powers entrusted to it by law.

The same principle supports an exception to the collateral bar rule for transparently invalid court orders. Requiring a party subject to such an order to obey or face contempt would give the

courts powers far in excess of any authorized by the Constitution or Congress. Recognizing an exception to the collateral bar rule for transparently invalid orders does not violate the principle that "no man can be judge in his own case" anymore than does recognizing such an exception for jurisdictional defects. The key to both exceptions is the notion that although a court order—even an arguably incorrect court order—demands respect, so does the right of the citizen to be free of clearly improper exercises of judicial authority.

* * *

The line between a transparently invalid order and one that is merely invalid is, of course, not always distinct. As a general rule, if the court reviewing the order finds the order to have had any pretence to validity at the time it was issued, the reviewing court should enforce the collateral bar rule. Such a heavy presumption in favor of validity is necessary to protect the rightful power of the courts.

* * *

In its most recent decision on previous restraints on pure speech, *Nebraska Press Association v. Stuart,* the Court struck down a gag order issued to ensure the protection of a criminal defendant's Sixth Amendment right to a fair trial. Intending to keep "the barriers to prior restraint * * * high unless we are to abandon what the Court has said for nearly a quarter of our national existence and implied throughout all of it", the Court established a test so difficult to meet that Justice White was led to express his "grave doubt" that any prior restraint in the area would "ever be justifiable". The test requires proof to be established "with the degree of certainty our cases on prior restraint require", that (1) the nature and extent of pretrial publicity would impair the defendant's right to a fair trial; (2) there were no alternative measures which could mitigate the effects of the publicity; and (3) a prior restraint would effectively prevent the harm. It is patently clear that the order of November 13, 1985, fails to pass muster under the *Nebraska Press Association* test.

* * *

As the Supreme Court made clear in *Nebraska Press Association,* a party seeking a prior restraint against the press must show not only that publication will result in damage to a near sacred right, but also that the prior restraint will be effective and that no less extreme measures are available. The district court failed to make a finding as to either of these issues, an omission making the invalidity of the order even more transparent. Indeed, had the court considered the likely efficacy of the order it would have concluded that the order would not necessarily protect Patriarca's rights. Other media, including nonparties to the Patriarca litigation, had the same information that the government had disclosed to the Journal. Moreover, Patriarca's complaint specifically alleged that portions of the information disclosed by the FBI had already been "disseminated" by the media. It is therefore hard to imagine a finding that the prior restraint would accomplish its purpose.

An additional point to note is that the prior restraint was issued prior to a full and fair hearing with all the attendant procedural protections. A prior restraint issued in these circumstances faces an even heavier presumption of invalidity, and the transparent unconstitutionality of the order is made even more patent by the absence of such a hearing.

* * *

It must be said, it is misleading in the context of daily newspaper publishing to argue that a temporary restraining order merely preserves the status quo. The status quo of daily newspapers is to publish news promptly that editors decide to publish. A restraining order disturbs the status quo and impinges on the exercise of editorial discretion. * * * When, as here, the court order is a transparently invalid prior restraint on pure speech, the delay and expense of an appeal is unnecessary. * * * The absence of such a requirement will not, however, lead to a wide-spread disregard of court orders. Rarely will a party be subject to a transparently invalid court order. * * * And even when a party believes it is subject to a transparently invalid order, seeking review in an appellate court is a far safer means of testing the order. For if the party chooses to violate the order and the order turns out not to be transparently invalid, the party must suffer the consequences of a contempt citation.

* * *

The order of the district court finding the Providence Journal Company and its executive editor, Charles M. Hauser, in criminal contempt is therefore reversed.

COMMENT

The court dismissed Patriarca's claims for a prior restraint based upon the Freedom of Information Act, the Omnibus Crime Control and Safe Streets Act, and the Fourth Amendment almost out of hand. None of the three by their terms is designed to allow actions to restrain publication but might allow a postpublication action against either the government or the newspaper. A later action based on the Fourth Amendment would require proof that the *Journal* and the government "were somehow conspiring" to violate Patriarca's rights—hard to prove indeed. The court also dismissed Patriarca's claim that the restraining order was needed to protect privacy, arguing that he could always bring a privacy action later. Inasmuch as the material came from government records, it is unlikely that a privacy claim could succeed.

The court's conclusion that a transparently invalid restraining order affecting the press may be ignored without fear of punishment is based on First Amendment principles drawn from many Supreme Court opinions. The court especially relied on *Walker v. City of Birmingham,* 388 U.S. 307 (1967).

As important as the rule that transparently invalid orders can be disobeyed may appear to the press, the method for determining when an order is transparently invalid is just as important. The court in *Providence Journal* applied a three-part test drawn from the *Nebraska Press* case to determine that the district court's order was transparently invalid.

The *Nebraska Press* test, by its own terms, is intended to apply to issues involving pretrial publicity that may jeopardize a defendant's fair trial right. Here, Patriarca was neither a defendant nor involved in any legal action other than the one he himself brought. And, while *Nebraska Press* addressed the validity of a gag order, it did not explicitly address the matter of obeying an order.

Applying such a test places a significant burden on journalists, who may nevertheless feel somewhat chilled at attempting to determine if an order meets the prescribed three-part test. Even after receiving advice from counsel, an editor must recognize that there is no assurance that an order fails the test until a court agrees that it fails. And, while the press may have a First Amendment right to publish in the face of an order not to, the matter of punishment will still await determination in court, an expensive and inconvenient prospect.

The First Circuit, in a subsequent *en banc* opinion that the court itself saw as "technically dictum," affirmed but called for publishers facing a gag order "to make a good faith effort to seek emergency relief from the appellate court." If the appeals court does not act swiftly, then publication would be expected. "[S]uch a price does not seem disproportionate to the respect owing court processes; and there is no prolongation of any prior restraint." *In re Providence Journal,* 14 Med. L. Rptr. 1029, 820 F.2d 1354 (1st Cir. 1987).

The special prosecutor appointed by the district court judge appealed the decision. After having granted certiorari, apparently to review the First Amendment aspects of the First Circuit decision, the Supreme Court dismissed the writ of certiorari altogether on technical grounds and never reached the First Amendment issues. *United States v. Providence Journal,* 15 Med. L. Rptr. 1241, 108 S.Ct. 1502 (1988).

Since the Supreme Court did not address the First Amendment issues in *Providence,* the reasoning of the court of appeals decision apparently stands. But, if it does, journalists are caught in the middle of a conflict between the First Circuit's invitation to disregard invalid orders and the Fifth Circuit's warning that all orders must be obeyed. Technically, neither *Providence* nor *Dickinson* acts as precedent outside its circuit. Which can journalists rely upon when making a decision?

With *Sheppard,* the Reardon Report, and *Dickinson* as a base, restrictive orders were bolstered by *dicta* in the landmark journalist's privilege case, *Branzburg v. Hayes,* 1 Med. L. Rptr. 2617, 408 U.S. 665 (1972):

> Newsmen have no constitutional right of access to the scenes of crime or disaster when the general public is excluded, and they may be prohibited from attending or publishing information about trials if such restrictions are necessary to assure a defendant a fair trial before an impartial tribunal.

In 1976, under pressure from the Washington-based Reporters Committee for Freedom of the Press, the ABA agreed that no restraining order should be issued without the media's being afforded the basic elements of due process—

prior notice, the right to be heard, and an opportunity for speedy appellate review. Direct restraints on the press would generally be avoided, and any kind of restraint would be tailored to the specific circumstances of a criminal case.[83]

In 1978 the ABA's Committee on Fair Trial and Free Press proposed that there be no direct restraints on the news media, that press and public be excluded from hearings, and that records be sealed only on clear evidence of a clear and present danger to jury impartiality and a lack of alternative judicial remedies. The committee further recommended that reporters not be subject to the contempt power unless their potentially prejudicial information was acquired by means of bribery, theft, or fraud. Any judicial order affecting the press, said the committee, ought to be preceded by prior notice, a hearing, and, if the order is issued, an opportunity for prompt appellate review of the validity of the order. The committee, in effect, rejected the Fifth Circuit's holding in *United States v. Dickinson.*

In addition, the clear and present danger test was recommended for gagging lawyers and for closing pretrial hearings and court records.[84]

It was in this somewhat more conciliatory atmosphere that *Nebraska Press Association v. Stuart* came to the Supreme Court.

The *Nebraska Press* Case

On October 18, 1975, in the tiny prairie town of Sutherland, Nebraska, Erwin Simants walked across his yard to a neighbor's, raped and fatally

---

83. American Bar Association Legal Advisory Committee on Fair Trial and Free Press, *Preliminary Draft Proposed Court Procedure for Fair Trial–Free Press Judicial Restrictive Orders* (July 1975), revised *Recommended Court Procedure to Accommodate Rights of Fair Trial and Free Press* (Dec. 2, 1975), adopted by the ABA House of Delegates (August 1976). See also Landau, *Fair Trial and Free Press: A Due Process Proposal,* 62 ABA J. 55 (January 1976).

84. See Standing Committee on Association Communications of the American Bar Association, *The Rights of Fair Trial and Free Press: The American Bar Association Standards* (1981). Suggestions for making procedures for formulation and review of such guidelines or protective orders statutory came from the ABA's Legal Advisory Committee on Fair Trial–Free Press, The Twentieth Century Fund Task Force on Justice, Publicity and the First Amendment, *Rights in Conflict* (1976), and from *Fair Trial and Free Expression,* a report to the Subcommittee on Constitutional Rights of the Committee on the Judiciary of the United States Senate (1976).

shot ten-year-old Florence Kellie, then murdered all possible witnesses—her grandparents, her father, a brother, and a sister.

After spending the night in a cornfield, the thirty-year-old Simants turned himself in to authorities. A terrified community was relieved. At his arraignment on six counts of first-degree murder a few days later, County Judge Ronald Ruff, with an eye on the Nebraska Bar-Press Guidelines and without notice to the press, issued a broad order prohibiting publication of anything from public pretrial proceedings. In Nebraska, pretrial hearings must be open to the public. Because of an alleged confession and possibly incriminating medical tests relating to sexual assault, Judge Ruff feared that publicity might affect the fairness of the trial that Simants surely faced.

Within nine days a district court judge in Lincoln County, seeing a clear and present danger to a fair trial, set down essentially the same rules and said he would screen reporters to determine their "suitability" to be in the courtroom. Judge Hugh Stuart did something else. He incorporated the Nebraska Bar-Press Guidelines—or at least his interpretation of them—in his order and then forbade the press to talk about what he had done. "Voluntary" guidelines had become mandatory ones. A by-now infuriated press saw this as a "gag on a gag."

The Nebraska Press Association, firmly supported by broad elements of the national press, sped to the state supreme court and presented that body with a 120-hour ultimatum for extraordinary relief. But the Nebraska Supreme Court was in no hurry and told the press not to expect a ruling before February. The next step was an appeal to U.S. Supreme Court Justice Harry Blackmun, who was the overseeing Circuit Justice for the region that includes Nebraska. On November 13, in an almost unprecedented order, Blackmun told the Nebraska Supreme Court to consider the case "forthwith and without delay," because freedom of the press was being irreparably infringed by each passing day.

The state supreme court still did nothing. In the meantime, Justice Blackmun denied an application to stay Judge Stuart's order. *Nebraska Press Association v. Stuart*, 1 Med. L. Rptr. 1059, 423 U.S. 1319 (1975). Blackmun did, however, stay imposition of the bar-press guidelines, finding them "merely suggestive and,

accordingly . . . necessarily vague." Finding that Nebraska court delays had exceeded "tolerable limits," Justice Blackmun granted the press a partial stay of the original trial court order.

Blackmun told Judge Stuart that the language of his order was too vague for First Amendment purposes and that prohibitions on the reporting of details of the crime, the identities of the victims, and the testimony of a pathologist at a public preliminary hearing were unjustified. But the rest of Stuart's order stood.

Meanwhile the Nebraska Supreme Court had heard arguments in the case on November 25 as scheduled. Still reluctant to exercise concurrent jurisdiction with the high court, the Nebraska Supreme Court nevertheless upheld crucial parts of the original order in a 5–2 decision. Noting that "under some circumstances prior restraint may be appropriate," the state court concluded that a "clear and present danger" to a fair trial in North Platte, Lincoln, or even Denver overcame "the heavy presumption of unconstitutionality of the prior restraint." Missing in the court's analysis was evidence of how press coverage influences jury verdicts. *State v. Simants*, 236 N.W.2d 794 (Neb. 1975).

The state supreme court agreed with Justice Blackmun, however, that voluntary press-bar guidelines were not intended to be contractual or mandatory and could not be enforced as though they were. That part of Judge Stuart's order was overturned. But any information implying guilt or a confession was not to be published.

On December 12, 1975, the U.S. Supreme Court agreed to review the Nebraska court's order, but not with the speed Justices Marshall, Brennan, and Stewart thought necessary. The three would have lifted the Nebraska Supreme Court's order pending final resolution of the issue.

Simants was convicted on six counts of first-degree murder on January 17, 1976, and sentenced to death.

On June 30, 1976, in an otherwise unanimous decision striking down the Nebraska court's gag order in the Simants case, six justices held that in exceptional circumstances prior restraints might be constitutional in a criminal case. Surprisingly, Chief Justice Burger, speaking for the Court, used a test for prior restraint that had become symbolic of the repression of First Amendment rights: whether "the gravity of the 'evil,' discounted by its improbability, justifies such invasion of free speech as is necessary to avoid the danger." The language was Federal Circuit Court Judge Learned Hand's reformulation of the clear and present danger test that was applied by the Supreme Court in *Dennis v. United States*, 341 U.S. 494 (1951), the landmark, and since discredited, Communist conspiracy case.

Every justice writing an opinion in the case made an intuitive estimate of the effects of reporting on the fairness of a trial. No empirical literature was cited.

Nebraska Press Association v. Stuart
1 MED. L. RPTR. 1064, 427 U.S. 539, 96 S. CT. 2791, 49 L. ED. 2D 683 (1976).

Chief Justice BURGER delivered the opinion of the Court:

* * *

The thread running through all these cases is that prior restraints on speech and publication are the most serious and the least tolerable infringement on First Amendment rights. * * * If it can be said that a threat of criminal or civil sanctions after publication "chills" speech, prior restraint "freezes" it at least for the time.

The damage can be particularly great when the prior restraint falls upon the communication of news and commentary on current events. Truthful reports of public judicial proceedings have been afforded special protection against subsequent punishment. For the same reasons the protection against prior restraint should have particular force as applied to reporting of criminal proceedings, whether the crime in question is a single isolated act or a pattern of criminal conduct. * * *

Of course, the order at issue—like the order requested in *New York Times* [the *Pentagon Papers* case]—does not prohibit but only postpones publication. Some news can be delayed and most commentary can even more readily be delayed without serious injury, and there often is a self-imposed delay when responsible editors call for verification of information. But such delays are normally slight and they are self-imposed. Delays imposed by governmental authority are a different matter. * * * As a practical matter, moreover, the element of time is not unimportant if press coverage is to fulfill its traditional function of bringing news to the public promptly.

* * *

The Nebraska courts in this case enjoined the publication of certain kinds of information about the Simants case. There are, as we suggested earlier, marked differences in setting and purpose between the order entered here and the orders in *Near* * * * and *New York Times,* but as to the underlying issue—the right of the press to be free from *prior* restraints on publication—those cases form the backdrop against which we must decide this case.

We turn now to the record in this case to determine whether, as Learned Hand put it, *"the gravity of the 'evil,' discounted by its improbability, justifies such invasion of free speech as is necessary to avoid the danger."* [Emphasis added.] *United States v. Dennis*, 183 F.2d 201, 212 (1950), aff'd, 341 U.S. 494 (1951); see also L. Hand, *The Bill of Rights* 58–61 (1958). To do so, we must examine the evidence before the trial judge when the order was entered to determine (a) the nature and extent of pretrial news coverage; (b) whether other measures would be likely to mitigate the effects of unrestrained pretrial publicity; (c) how effectively a restraining order would operate to prevent the threatened danger.

* * *

Our review of the pretrial record persuades us that the trial judge was justified in concluding that there would be intense and pervasive pretrial publicity concerning this case. He could also reasonably conclude, based on common human experience, that publicity might impair the defendant's right to a fair trial. He did not purport to say more, for he found only "a clear and present danger that pretrial publicity *could* impinge upon the defendant's right to a fair trial." [Emphasis added.] His conclusion as to the impact of such publicity on prospective jurors was of necessity speculative, dealing as he was with *factors unknown and unknowable.* [Emphasis added.]

* * *

There is no finding that alternative measures would not have protected Simants' rights, and the Nebraska Supreme Court did no more than imply that such measures might not be adequate.

* * *

Finally, we note that the events disclosed by the record took place in a community of 850 people. It is reasonable to assume that, without any news accounts being printed or broadcast, rumors would travel swiftly by word of mouth. One can only speculate on the accuracy of such reports, given the generative propensities of rumors; they could well be more damaging than reasonably accurate news accounts. * * *

To the extent that this order prohibited the reporting of evidence adduced at the open preliminary hearing, it plainly violated settled principles: "there is nothing that proscribes the press from reporting events that transpire in the courtroom." The County Court could not know that closure of the preliminary hearing was an alternative open to it until the Nebraska Supreme Court so construed state law; but once a public hearing had been held, what transpired there could not be subject to prior restraint.

* * *

The record demonstrates, as the Nebraska courts held, that there was indeed a risk that pretrial news accounts, true or false, would have some adverse impact on the attitudes of those who might be called as jurors. But on the record now before us it is not clear that further publicity, unchecked, would so distort the views of potential jurors that 12 could not be found who would, under proper instructions, fulfill their sworn duty to render a just verdict exclusively on the evidence presented in open court. We cannot say on this record that alternatives to a prior restraint on petitioners would not have sufficiently mitigated the adverse effects of pretrial publicity so as to make prior restraint unnecessary. Nor can we conclude that the restraining order actually entered would serve its intended purpose. Reasonable minds can have few doubts about the gravity of the evil pretrial publicity can work, but the probability that it would do so here was not demonstrated with the degree of certainty our cases on prior restraint require.

* * *

It is significant that when this Court has reversed a state conviction, because of prejudicial publicity, it has carefully noted that some course of action short of prior restraint would have made a critical difference. However difficult it may be, we need not rule out the possibility of showing the kind of threat to fair trial rights that would possess the requisite degree of certainty to justify restraint. This Court has frequently denied that First Amendment rights are absolute and has consistently rejected the proposition that a prior restraint can never be employed.

Our analysis ends as it began, with a confrontation between prior restraint imposed to protect one vital constitutional guarantee and the explicit command of another that the freedom to speak and publish shall not be abridged. *We affirm that the guarantees of freedom of expression are not an absolute prohibition under all circumstances, but the barriers to prior restraint remain high and the presumption against its use continues intact.* [Emphasis added.] We hold that, with respect to the order entered in this case prohibiting reporting or commentary on judicial proceedings held in public, the barriers have not been overcome; to the extent that this order restrained publication of such material, it is clearly invalid. To the extent that it prohibited publication based on information gained from other sources, we conclude that the heavy burden imposed as a condition to securing a prior restraint was not met and the judgment of the Nebraska Supreme Court is therefore.

Reversed.

COMMENT

Prior restraints must be preceded by a clear demonstration of the harmful effects of publicity on a jury, the Court seemed to be saying, a relationship Burger at the same time considered "unknown and unknowable." In addition, the judge must show that a prior restraint would be effective and that no alternatives less destructive of First Amendment rights, such as the actions listed in *Sheppard*, are available. It is hard to imagine a judge ever hurdling these preliminary barriers. Trial judges were being asked to make judgments about juror prejudice before there were any jurors to examine.

The Court indicated that the effectiveness of the prior restraint must also be assured before such an order issues. This again is a tall order, given the difficulties of predicting media effects and human behavior. Furthermore, the court's jurisdiction would bind only those media organizations within the jurisdiction, limiting the order's effect in a case such as Simants's that drew broader coverage.

In *Nebraska Press*, Burger said a heavy First Amendment presumption against the validity of gag orders existed. Other justices would have gone further. Justice White wrote a short concurring opinion in which he doubted that a *Nebraska*-type order would ever be justified. He thought that a general rule banning gag orders would be preferable, so the Court could avoid "the interminable litigation that our failure to do so would necessarily entail."

Justice Brennan's exhaustive concurrence, joined by Stewart and Marshall, flatly declared that gag orders applied to the press are always unconstitutional. Brennan advocated a rule that gag orders are *per se* invalid under the First Amendment.

Simants's conviction was overturned on the grounds that a sheriff had lobbied a sequestered jury. On retrial he was found not guilty by reason of insanity, a result that did not sit well in some Nebraska circles.

The Court bolstered *Nebraska Press* in *Oklahoma Publishing Co. v. District Court*, 2 Med. L. Rptr. 1456, 430 U.S. 308 (1977), when it held that news media could not be prohibited from publishing the name or picture of a juvenile where the name had been reported in open court and the photograph taken without objection outside the courthouse. Both the open court proceeding and the courthouse exterior were considered public places; "what transpired there cannot be subject to prior restraint."

Two terms later, in *Smith v. Daily Mail Publishing Co.*, 5 Med. L. Rptr. 1305, 443 U.S. 97 (1979), the Court said that a West Virginia statute imposing criminal sanctions and barring publication of a juvenile offender's name lawfully obtained violated the First Amendment. The state's interest in protecting the anonymity of juveniles was insufficient to justify the encroachment on the press. The Court relied on *Landmark Communications, Inc. v. Virginia*, 3 Med. L. Rptr. 2153, 435 U.S. 829 (1978), which said a statute banning publication of information about confidential judicial review committee hearings against a judge violated the First Amendment.

Nebraska Press has reduced gag order litigation from a flood to a trickle, and gag orders are almost never upheld at the appeals level. Still, judges occasionally issue such restrictive orders, and the orders, if obeyed, suffice to stifle publicity until the appeal is decided—usually long after the trial.

Apparently, the only gag order against the media that has been successful on appeal in the federal courts occurred in *United States v. Noriega*, 18 Med. L. Rptr. 1348, 752 F.Supp. 1032 (S.D.Fla.), *aff'd*, *In re Cable News Network, Inc.*, 917 F.2d 1543 (11th Cir. 1990), *cert. denied* 498 U.S. 976 (1990). In that case, the court affirmed a federal district judge who had forbidden Cable News Network (CNN) from broadcasting sound tapes of conversations between Manuel Noriega and his defense lawyers. Noriega, a former president of Panama who was abducted by U.S. forces and taken to Florida for trial, was facing a variety of drug charges. At the time, the case attracted unusually heavy attention from the media. Although publication of the contents of privileged conversations with his lawyers might have affected Noriega's fair trial rights, the judge seemed as concerned with the breach of security and privilege. He ordered CNN to produce the tapes for *in camera* review, which might have helped identify how the tapes were made and leaked. When CNN refused, the judge issued a temporary injunction against airing the tapes. The appeals court opinion seemed more piqued at CNN's refusal to hand over the tapes than persuaded that Noriega's Sixth Amendment rights were in jeopardy. Supreme Court Justices Thurgood Marshall and Sandra Day O'Connor dissented from the denial of review. Marshall wrote that he felt the case was extremely important for freedom of the press. CNN was ultimately found in criminal contempt, fined a token $100, and ordered to air a statement saying it erred in disobeying the court's order. *United States v. Cable News Network, Inc.*, 23 Med. L. Rptr. 1033, 865 F.Supp. 1549 (S.D.Fla. 1994). The district court explicitly refused to endorse the "presumptively invalid" principle of the *Providence Journal* case. In the years since *Noriega* was decided, other courts have pointedly not cited the case, even where it might appear to have some relevance. *Ohio ex rel. New World Communications v. Character*, 23 Med. L. Rptr. 1478, 647 N.E.2d 1301 (Ohio App. 1995).

Another disconcerting case for the press arose when *Business Week* obtained documents from a $100 million civil lawsuit between Procter & Gamble and the Bankers Trust Co. The case had attracted much attention in the business press, but drew little general attention until the two parties agreed to a protective order that allowed them to designate discovery material as confidential. The magazine had obtained copies of some material that had been designated confidential. The federal district judge overseeing the civil case issued an order that *Business Week* not publish the materials unless the court approved. The order was issued without the magazine receiving either notice or a hearing. After failing to get either the Sixth Circuit or the Supreme Court to hear an expedited appeal, *Business Week* returned to federal district court to contest the order. In a decision made twenty days after the original order, the judge upheld the order, largely because the magazine had "knowingly violated" the protective order. *Procter & Gamble v. Bankers Trust Co.,* 23 Med. L. Rptr. 2505, 900 F.Supp. 186 (S.D. Ohio 1995).

On appeal, the Sixth Circuit found that the dispute was not moot even though the judge had subsequently modified the order and released the discovery documents to the public. To the appellate court, the order was obviously invalid:

> In short, at no time—even to the point of entering a permanent injunction after two temporary restraining orders—did the District Court appear to realize that it was engaging in a practice that, under all but the most exceptional circumstances, violates the Constitution: preventing a news organization from publishing information in its possession on a matter of public concern. . . .
>
> Not only did the District Court fail to conduct any First Amendment inquiry before granting the two TROs, but it compounded the harm by holding hearings on issues that bore no relation to the right of *Business Week* to disseminate the information in its possession. Weeks passed with the "gag order" in effect, while the court inquired painstakingly into how *Business Week* obtained the documents. . . . While these might be appropriate lines of inquiry for a contempt proceeding or a criminal prosecution, they are not appropriate bases for issuing a prior restraint. *Procter & Gamble v. Bankers Trust Co.,* 24 Med. L. Rptr. 1385, 78 F.3d 219 (6th Cir. 1996).

The appellate court also chided the trial court for its conclusion that a temporary restraining order was allowable to provide time so that the issues could be considered in a less-pressured fashion. No, said the Sixth Circuit. "In the case of a prior restraint, the hurdle is substantially higher [than likelihood of success on the merits]: publication

must threaten an interest more fundamental than the First Amendment itself."

One clear exception to the general rule invalidating prior restraints has been allowed. In *Seattle Times v. Rhinehart,* 10 Med. L. Rptr. 1705, 467 U.S. 20 (1984), the Court held that a trial court order barring the newspaper from publishing material it had obtained during pretrial discovery was valid. The *Times* was defending a libel suit brought by Keith Rhinehart, leader of a religious group, the Aquarian Foundation. Rhinehart had been the subject of numerous articles. Looking at the state's interest in the integrity of the legal process and at Rhinehart's claims of privacy and religious freedom that might be affected if material was published, the trial judge entered the order.

The Supreme Court unanimously upheld the order. Justice Powell, writing the majority opinion, noted that the state's interests were substantial. Substantial interest was sufficient to overcome press rights in the case, in part, because "an order prohibiting dissemination of discovered information before trial is not the kind of *classic* prior restraint that requires exacting First Amendment scrutiny." [Emphasis added.] Although the *Times'* status as a party was not technically a ground for decision, it appears to have weighed heavily, and it may be best to see the case as limited to its unique facts.

Although the Court's differentiation between classic prior restraints and other prior restraints suggests a risk that even the Supreme Court might apply a two-level public interest approach as was done in *KUTV,* Justice Brennan, concurring, saw a silver lining for the press. He stressed the importance of the Court's recognition "that pretrial protective orders, designed to limit the dissemination of information gained through the civil discovery process, are subject to scrutiny under the First Amendment." Brennan apparently had his eye on likely future cases in which the press was not a litigant but desired access to materials submitted in advance of trial.[85]

The bottom line for the media, then, is that, while *Nebraska Press* establishes the presump-

---

85. See, e.g., *Courier-Journal v. Peers,* 14 Med. L. Rptr. 1248 (Ky.Ct.App. 1987) (newspaper not a party to civil action lacks standing to unseal settlement records that ended action); *Rushford v. The New Yorker Magazine, Inc.,* 15 Med. L. Rptr. 1437, 846 F.2d 249 (4th Cir. 1988) (First Amendment right of access to documents filed in support of summary judgment motion in libel suit; protective order held invalid).

tive invalidity of judicial restraining orders, especially gag orders, a trial judge may nonetheless restrain publicity while an invalid order is contested, perhaps holding up news coverage for months. In some cases, state courts have upheld restraints and gag orders as either meeting *Nebraska Press* standards or by narrowly distinguishing cases.

As a standard practice, reporters should object promptly and strenuously, but diplomatically, to orders or for bidding publication or motions to close off parts of the judicial process. Notice and a hearing at which to oppose the orders or motions are required at the very least. Major news organizations have developed procedures and forms that are widely distributed to reporters to deal with these problems.

Although *Nebraska Press* and subsequent cases have simplified, if not completely resolved, issues about restraining orders directed at the press, it should be remembered that the opinions of the justices in that case mentioned without comment two alternatives: (1) gag orders against nonmedia personnel such as lawyers, accused, and officers of the court, and (2) exclusionary orders barring the public, including the media, from the courtroom. It is little wonder that such authoritative encouragement made these techniques the most commonly used devices to circumvent the *Nebraska Press* holding. As such, they have led to even more free press–fair trial litigation.

In retrospect, the Court's use of a modified clear and present danger test in *Nebraska Press* appears disingenuous. The *Simants* facts, objectively, seemed to meet the clear and present danger standard. The fact that the Court thought otherwise only supports the impropriety of the standard and the desirability of invalidating gag orders *per se*. While the test has not resulted in a torrent of gags, the danger of relying on it in such circumstances is that it will mislead courts into issuing gag orders, whether the orders can survive on appeal or not.

Gag Orders against Nonmedia Parties

While the *Nebraska Press* decision established a near-absolute prohibition against prior restraints against the news media in the form of gag orders in legal proceedings, it did not fully resolve the issue. A judge concerned that news coverage might have a prejudicial effect on the outcome of a trial could still consider placing limits on others involved in a case. Indeed, *Sheppard v. Maxwell* appeared to endorse gag orders on parties involved in cases, including lawyers, witnesses, jurors, plaintiffs, and defendants:

> [T]he trial court may well have proscribed extrajudicial statements by any lawyer, party, witness, or court official which divulged prejudicial matters.

It was inevitable that gagged parties would challenge these prohibitions. The news media challenged them as well, arguing that they were "indirect" prior restraints that violated the First Amendment newsgathering rights of the press.

The leading case to date on this issue arose when irate criminal defense attorney Dominic Gentile held a press conference during which he strongly criticized the conduct of the Las Vegas police investigation that had led to indictment of his client on drug possession and theft charges. Gentile was reprimanded for violating state bar rule 177, which provides, among other things, that:

> A lawyer shall not make an extrajudicial statement that a reasonable person would expect to be disseminated by means of public communication if the lawyer knows or reasonably should know that it will have a substantial likelihood of materially prejudicing an adjudicative proceeding.

The rule continues, listing six general categories of information to avoid, but also listing seven general categories of information that a lawyer remains free to comment on publicly. The Nevada rule is almost identical to the American Bar Association's Model Rule of Professional Conduct 3.6.

A state bar disciplinary board found that Gentile had violated the rule. Following reprimand, he appealed to the Nevada Supreme Court, which upheld the board. *Gentile v. State Bar of Nevada,* 787 P.2d 386 (Nev. 1990). Appeal to the U.S. Supreme Court followed. The high court decision featured two different five-justice majorities on two different First Amendment issues, rendered in separate opinions by Chief Justice William Rehnquist and Justice Anthony Kennedy. *Gentile v. State Bar of Nevada,* 501 U.S. 1030 (1991). The Rehnquist majority held that a state may proscribe lawyer comments on a "substantial likelihood" standard rather than the compelling interest standard that might otherwise apply, and upheld the constitutionality of the disciplinary rule in general. The Kennedy majority held that the provision listing allowable categories for extrajudicial comment was vague and therefore the rule violated Gentile's constitutional rights as applied. Justice Sandra Day O'Connor summed the positions up well in her concurring opinion:

> I agree with much of The Chief Justice's opinion. In particular, I agree that a State may regulate speech by lawyers representing clients in pending cases more readily than it may regulate the press. Lawyers are officers of the court and, as such, may legitimately be subject to ethical precepts that keep them from engaging in what otherwise might be constitutionally protected speech. See *In re Sawyer,* 360 U.S. 622, 646–647 (1959) (Stewart, J., concurring in the result). This does not mean, of course, that lawyers forfeit their First Amendment rights, only that a less demanding standard applies. I agree with The Chief Justice that the "substantial likelihood of material prejudice" standard articulated in Rule 177 passes constitutional muster. Accordingly, I join Parts I and II of The Chief Justice's opinion.
>
> For the reasons set out in Part III of Justice Kennedy's opinion, however, I believe that Nevada's rule is void for vagueness. Subsection (3) of Rule 177 is a "safe harbor" provision. It states that "notwithstanding" the prohibitory language located elsewhere in the rule, "a lawyer involved in the investigation or litigation may state without elaboration . . . [t]he general nature of the claim or defense." Gentile made a conscious effort to stay within the boundaries of this "safe harbor." In his brief press conference, Gentile gave only a rough sketch of the defense that he intended to present at trial. * * * When asked to provide more details, he declined, stating explicitly that the ethical rules compelled him to do so. Nevertheless, the disciplinary board sanctioned Gentile because, in its view, his remarks went beyond the scope of what was permitted by the rule. Both Gentile and the disciplinary board have valid arguments on their side, but this serves to support the view that the rule provides insufficient guidance. As Justice Kennedy correctly points out, a vague law offends the Constitution because it fails to give fair notice to those it is intended to deter and creates the possibility of discriminatory enforcement.

* * *

A key point from *Gentile* is that it is easier for judges to place limits on lawyers precisely because they are officers of the court—literally guardians of the proper operation of the legal system. Not all observers find this sort of argument persuasive.[86] The opinion also implies that the First Amendment rights of other trial participants should be stronger than the rights of lawyers. That was the conclusion of the U.S. Court of Appeals for the Fifth Circuit. Since the 1950s, the East Baton Rouge Parish School Board had been under federal district court supervision to end segregation. In 1996, when the board started to develop a new desegregation plan that might finally end the underlying legal action, the board asked the federal judge to issue an order prohibiting virtually all employees and school board members from discussing the plan with anyone, including the press. On February 6, 1996, the judge entered the order, which was challenged by a Baton Rouge newspaper and television station. Between February 14 and March 8, the district judge conducted a number of hearings and issued revised orders, most of which narrowed the scope of the original order. The challengers filed an emergency motion for expedited appeal. The Fifth Circuit stayed the order and declared it invalid on March 15.

Davis v. East Baton Rouge Parish School Board
24 MED. L. RPTR. 1513, 78 F.3D 920 (5TH CIR. 1996).

KING, J.:

Prior to 1954, the East Baton Rouge Parish school system was racially segregated as a matter of law. This school desegregation case was filed in 1956 following the decisions in *Brown v. Board of Educ.,* 347 U.S. 483 (1954) and *Brown v. Board of Educ.,* 349 U.S. 294 (1955). For the past forty years, the district court has maintained continuing jurisdiction over this case under *Swann v. Board of Educ.,* 402 U.S. 1 (1971), to ensure that the East Baton Rouge Parish School Board (the "Board") fulfills its duty to eliminate all vestiges of segregation from its school system. * * *

In late January or early February 1996, the newly elected Board, through its newly retained counsel, indicated to the district court that it was interested in formulating a proposed desegregation

---

86. Weisberg, *On a Constitutional Collision Course: Attorney No-Comment Rules and the Right of Access to Information,* 83 J. Crim.L. & Criminology 644 (1992); Swift, *Model Rule 3.6: An Unconstitutional Regulation of Defense Attorney Trial Publicity,* 64 B.U.L.Rev. 1003 (1984).

plan to finally end this litigation. The Board members indicated to the district court that they wished privately to discuss among themselves, their attorneys and some members of their staff, all aspects of a possible desegregation plan, as well as privately to plan the Board's strategy for negotiating the proposed plan with the adverse parties to the litigation.

At the Board's request, on February 6, 1996, the district court entered an order prohibiting the members of the Board, its attorneys, employees, and other agents from discussing "any aspects of any drafts of desegregation plans" with anyone other than the parties to the litigation (the "February 6th order"). The Board did not make a formal motion requesting this order, nor did the district court enter findings or written or oral reasons supporting the order. On February 14, 1996, the Capital City Press, Bill Pack, and the Louisiana Television Broadcasting Corporation d/b/a WBRZ-TV (collectively, the "news agencies") filed a motion to intervene to challenge the February 6th order as a violation of their First Amendment rights, and a motion to vacate the February 6th order. The Capital City Press publishes *The Advocate*, the Baton Rouge daily newspaper. Bill Pack is a reporter for *The Advocate* who has successfully investigated the Board's actions regarding desegregation in the past. The Louisiana Television Broadcasting Corporation d/b/a WBRZ-TV broadcasts one of the local news programs in Baton Rouge.

On February 22, 1996, the district court held a hearing on the news agencies' motions, and entered an order granting the motion to intervene and denying the motion to vacate (the "February 22nd order"). At the hearing, the district court orally explained its reasons for entering the February 6th order and for denying the news agencies' motion to vacate the February 6th order. The court, citing the oath of silence taken by the participants in the Constitutional Convention, reasoned that "there are some things, some public matters, that are better discussed and argued about in private than they are in public." * * * The court stated that it issued the February 6th order to give the Board an opportunity to hash out the relevant issues in private, without interference from the public or the news media, in order to facilitate and expedite the Board's formulation of a proposed desegregation plan.

* * * The district court stated that in entering its February 6th order, it "merely afforded the School Board an opportunity to negotiate in private—a chance for discussion unimpeded by outside sources." The court emphasized that its order expressly authorizes the Board to disseminate its proposal to the public once it has been created. Additionally, the court rejected the news agencies' arguments that the February 6th order was procedurally defective because it was entered without a written motion, without supporting findings, or without affording the press or public notice and an opportunity to be heard. * * * The court admitted that the order may have been "inartfully drawn," in that it applied to all of the more than 7,000 School Board employees, and accordingly, the court directed counsel for the Board to prepare and submit an amendment. The court concluded, however, that "[t]he necessity for the [February 6th] order clearly outweighs the 'amorphous "hope to hear"' rights of the news media." Finally, the court asserted that "there are no practical alternatives that would effectively safeguard the Board's progress in bringing this matter to a conclusion after forty years."

After filing a notice of appeal, on February 29, 1996, the news agencies filed an Emergency Motion for Expedited Appeal of District Court's Order Refusing to Vacate Confidentiality Order, and, Alternatively, Emergency Petition for Writ of Mandamus, as well as their original appellants' brief. On March 1, 1996, the district court entered an order amending the February 6th order by limiting the scope of the order to the members of the Board, the Superintendent, the Board's attorneys, and twenty-three specifically named staff members and employees (the "March 1st order" or the "confidentiality order").

On March 4, 1996, the news agencies filed an amended notice of appeal and an amended emergency motion for expedited appeal/petition for writ of mandamus, adding review of the March 1st order to their appeal. Also on March 4th, the Board filed a motion to dismiss the appeal, to which the news agencies responded. On March 7, 1996, the Board filed a memorandum in opposition to the motion to expedite the appeal. Later that day, we granted the news agencies' motion to expedite their appeal and we denied the Board's motion to dismiss.

On March 8, 1996, the district court entered a third order relating to the confidentiality of the Board's activities in formulating a desegregation plan (the "March 8th order"). The March 8th order directed the Board to conduct private meetings to compose a proposed desegregation plan and ordered the participants in the meetings to keep the meetings and any drafts of desegregation plans confidential. Having learned that the Board intended to meet secretly over the weekend of March 9 and 10, 1996, the news agencies immediately filed an emergency motion for a stay of the March 8th order pending this appeal. We granted the news agencies' motion and stayed the March 8th order.

* * *

DISCUSSION

In addressing this interlocutory appeal by a non-party, we must first examine two preliminary issues: whether appellate jurisdiction exists and whether the news agencies have standing to challenge the district court's March 1st and March 8th orders. We will then address the merits of the appeal—whether the March 1st and March 8th orders violate the First Amendment. [The court concluded that it had appellate jurisdiction and that the news media challengers had standing to pursue the case.]

1. The March 1st Order: The First Amendment

The Supreme Court has routinely held that prior restraints on protected speech are presumed to be constitutionally invalid. *See CBS, Inc.,* 522 F.2d at 238; *see, e.g., Nebraska Press Ass'n v. Stuart,* 427 U.S. 539, 556 (1976); *Bantam Books, Inc. v. Sullivan,* 372 U.S. 58, 70 (1963)). "An order that prohibits the utterance or publication of particular information or commentary imposes a 'prior restraint' on speech." *United States v. Salameh,* 992 F.2d 445, 446 (2d Cir. 1993). A prior restraint is constitutional only if the government demonstrates that the protected speech restrained poses a "clear and present danger, or a serious or imminent threat to a protected competing interest." *CBS, Inc.,* 522 F.2d at 238. Furthermore, "[t]he restraint must be narrowly drawn and cannot be upheld if reasonable alternatives are available having a lesser impact on First Amendment freedoms." *Id.*

The district court's March 1st order prohibits the Board, its attorneys, and certain of its employees from making "any written or oral comments to any other person or entity in connection with any aspect of any drafts of desegregation plans concerning the East Baton Rouge Parish School System." This order clearly constitutes a prior restraint on the speech of the Board members, attorneys, and employees to which it applies. Whether we should analyze the confidentiality order as a prior restraint in determining the First Amendment rights of the news agencies—the potential recipients of the restrained speech—is unclear. * * *

We need not decide whether the confidentiality order constitutes a prior restraint on the news agencies because, even assuming that the order is not a prior restraint, its effect on the news agencies' First Amendment rights must still be justified. *See Dow Jones & Co.,* 842 F.2d at 609 * * *

The Supreme Court has recognized "a First Amendment right to 'receive information and ideas'", and a right to receive speech protected by the First Amendment. *Virginia State Bd. of Pharmacy v. Virginia Citizens Consumer Council,* 425 U.S. 748, 757 (1976). Additionally, we have noted that "the Supreme Court recognized in *Branzburg v. Hayes,* 408 U.S. 665, 681 (1972), that newsgathering is entitled to [F]irst [A]mendment protection, for 'without some protection for seeking out the news, freedom of the press could be eviscerated.'" *In re Express-news Corp.,* 695 F.2d 807, 808 (5th Cir. 1982). However, neither the First Amendment right to receive speech nor the First Amendment right to gather news is absolute. *See id.* at 809. For example, the news media have no right to discover information that is not available to the public generally. *Id.*

Confidentiality orders, and denials of access to court proceedings as well, have been allowed when a strong governmental interest or a competing individual right outweighs the First Amendment rights asserted. *See Gurney,* 558 F.2d at 1209. For example, confidentiality orders have been held constitutional in criminal jury trials when necessary to protect a defendant's Sixth Amendment right to a fair trial by an impartial jury. * * *

In the context of a district court order preventing the press from conducting post-trial juror interviews, we have held that "an inhibition of press news-gathering rights must be necessitated 'by a compelling governmental interest, and . . . narrowly tailored to serve that interest.'" *In re Express-News,* 695 F.2d at 808–09 (quoting *Globe Newspaper v. Superior Court,* 457 U.S. 596, 607 (1982)). In *Dow Jones & Co.,* the Second Circuit stated that to justify a confidentiality order restraining participants in a criminal jury trial from speaking with the press, a "reasonable likelihood" that pretrial publicity would prejudice the criminal defendant's Sixth Amendment right to a fair trial by an impartial jury must be demonstrated. 842 F.2d at 610. Furthermore, the Second Circuit stated that the district court must consider whether alternative remedies less intrusive of First Amendment rights would serve to protect the criminal defendant's competing Sixth Amendment rights. *See id.* at 611. We need not decide whether to employ the strict scrutiny standard of *In re Express-News,* or some variant of the reasonable likelihood standard of *Dow Jones & Co.,* because the district court's March 1st order would not satisfy either standard.

The March 1st order is not justified, on this record, by any important governmental interest or countervailing individual right. First, we emphasize that this is not a criminal trial, nor even a civil jury trial. There is no possibility that publicity will prejudice potential jurors. The Board argues that the confidentiality order is necessary because the Fourteenth Amendment rights of the East Baton Rouge Parish school children to attend schools free of racial inequality outweighs any First Amendment rights of the news agencies. Indeed, the students' constitutional right to desegregated schools is compelling; however, the confidentiality order does not necessarily further their interests. The removal of the confidentiality order would in no way prevent the Board from desegregating the school system.

The purpose of the confidentiality order, as explained by the district court in relation to the February 6th order, is to allow the Board members privately—without interference from the public or the media—to discuss and formulate a proposed desegregation plan. Whatever the validity of this rationale for conducting private meetings may be, it does not, on this record, justify the sweep of the March 1st order prohibiting Board members and employees from making any written or oral comments to any other person or

entity in connection with any aspect of any drafts of any desegregation plan.

The Board argues that the damage to the news agencies' First Amendment rights is mitigated because the Board plans to disseminate the final draft of the proposed desegregation plan to the public and the press. The short answer to this argument is that the parties have stipulated that the process itself is newsworthy.

We hold that the district court's March 1st order is unconstitutional because, on this record, it intrudes severely upon the news agencies' First Amendment right to gather the news and receive speech and it is not justified by protection of any countervailing governmental interest or individual right. Accordingly, we vacate the March 1st order.

2. The March 8th Order

The March 8th order, in addition to requiring the Board to meet in private sessions, requires that "all of the above private sessions and all preliminary version(s) of the draft [of the desegregation plan] remain confidential and private." This confidentiality requirement suffers from the same constitutional infirmity as the March 1st order: the confidentiality, requirement violates the news agencies' First Amendment rights to gather news about the formulation of a desegregation plan. As no compelling governmental interest supports this confidentiality requirement, it must also be vacated.

The news agencies also contest the validity of the main portion of the March 8th order directing the Board to meet in private sessions to formulate a desegregation plan and negotiate the plan with the adverse parties to the litigation. The news agencies challenge the private sessions requirement under the First Amendment and also contend that this requirement of the March 8th order allows the Board to circumvent the requirements of the Louisiana Open Meetings Law, La. Rev. Stat. Ann. ("L.R.S.") § 42:4.1–11 (West 1990). Because we are able to dispose of the news agencies' challenge to the private sessions requirement of the March 8th order on nonconstitutional grounds, we do not reach their First Amendment argument.

Turning to the Louisiana Open Meetings Law, the Board defends the order by arguing that an exception to that law would allow it to conduct the private sessions contemplated by the March

8th order. The news agencies respond that, even if the private sessions would comply with the Louisiana Open Meetings Law, the court's order *requiring* such private sessions allows the Board to avoid taking the many procedural steps required by the Open Meetings Law before it meets in a closed session.

We express no opinion on whether the private sessions contemplated by the March 8th order would comply with the Louisiana Open Meetings Law. We note that, at least on the surface of it, the district court entered the March 8th order without even considering the Louisiana Open Meetings Law. In entering a confidentiality order protecting a public entity, or an order such as this requiring a public entity to meet in secrecy, the district court should consider the effect of the order on state freedom of information laws. * * *

The district court made no findings concerning whether the meetings contemplated by the March 8th order fit within any of the exceptions to the Louisiana Open Meetings Law. L.R.S. § 42:6.1(2); *see Pansy,* 23 F.3d at 786. The court made no effort to explain why the need for confidential Board meetings outweighed the news agencies' interest in attending Board meetings protected by the Louisiana Open Meetings Law. *See id.* Furthermore, the Board, although aware of its duty as a public entity to comply with the Louisiana Open Meetings Law, did not request that the district court determine whether the exceptions to the open meeting requirement covered the private sessions contemplated by the March 8th order.

The district court gave no notice to the news agencies of its intent to enter the March 8th order, although it must have known that the news agencies would oppose the order, as they had already intervened to contest the court's earlier confidentiality orders. The March 8th order requiring open sessions in effect immunizes the Board from enforcement of the Louisiana Open Meetings Law, as it removes the decision of whether to hold closed meetings from the Board. However, despite this effect, the district court also gave no notice of the March 8th order to the district attorney, who is required by law to enforce the provisions of the Open Meetings Law. L.R.S. § 42:10. We need not, and do not, hold that notice to the press or the district attorney is always required before entry of an order implicating state sunshine laws. At a minimum,

such notice, under the circumstances that obtained here, would have been prudential. In any event, the absence of such notice in this case had the effect of eliminating any opposition to the secret meetings aspect of the March 8th order. Because there was no opposition to the entry of the order, the district court took the wholly unacceptable step of entering the order without making any findings.

In short, the district court entered a sweeping order requiring a public entity to conduct confidential meetings which may or may not comply with state law. The court should not have entered this order without considering whether the meetings that it ordered complied with the Louisiana Open Meetings Law, or demonstrating compelling reasons for preempting Louisiana law.

* * *

For the foregoing reasons, we VACATE the district court's March 1st and March 8th orders.

COMMENT

Relying upon *Branzburg v. Hayes,* 408 U.S. 665 (1972), the opinion broadly and strongly interprets the press's right to gather news. Although no school board employees asserted that their First Amendment rights had been denied, the *Davis* case indicates that the First Amendment gives journalists the right to look for a willing speaker. The court accepted the argument that indirect gag orders stanch the free flow of information via the press just as direct gags do.[87] Interestingly, the *Gentile* opinion was not even cited; apparently, the court saw it as limited to cases involving comments by lawyers.

The trend in recent years has been to recognize the expression rights of both gagged trial participants and indirectly gagged journalists. There is widespread agreement on procedural requirements. A judge must consider less restrictive alternatives before filing an order and must provide written findings that support the order if one is filed. The order normally ceases the moment a proceeding has ended. *Butterworth v. Smith,* 494 U.S. 624, 110 S. Ct. 1376 (1990); *Ohio ex rel. Cincinnati Post v. Hamilton County Court of Common Pleas,* 59 Ohio St. 3d 103, 570 N.E.2d 1101 (1991).

---

87. See, e.g., Bjork, *Indirect Gag Orders and the Doctrine of Prior Restraint,* 44 U.Miami L. Rev. 165 (1989).

There is less agreement on whether the standard to be applied is the compelling interest or substantial interest test. Courts that view these restraints as indistinguishable from the type of gag orders in *Nebraska Press* make it almost impossible to enter a constitutional gag. *Breiner v. Takao,* 73 Hawaii 995, 835 P.2d 637 (1992). Other courts have concluded that the First Amendment interest is weaker and have used substantial interest. *In re the State-Record Co., Inc.,* 917 F.2d 124 (4th Cir. 1990).

Closed Courtrooms

Following the *Nebraska Press* decision, judges who wished to reduce the prospects that prejudicial publicity would affect a proceeding had very limited options. The major option, one that quite a number of judges must have felt was implied by the Court's pointed references to "judicial proceedings held in public" in *Nebraska Press,* was to make proceedings nonpublic by closing them.

The rules for closing courts to the public and press varied greatly from one state to another. Rules differed further depending upon what kind of proceeding was involved; evidentiary suppression hearings, competency hearings, bail hearings, deposition sessions, preliminary hearings, *voir dire,* juvenile hearings, post-trial motion hearings, and others could all have been assessed differently. In general, the right of access tended to depend on whether or not a state required openness.[88] Any right of access was significantly qualified, however, because the judge was always the final arbiter of what happened in court or, for that matter, who entered the courtroom.[89]

The argument for open courts is complicated because it can be argued that the Sixth Amendment's guarantee of a public trial is meant to protect the rights of the defendant, the rights of society through public oversight, and the rights of the press. Because no precedent prevented judges from closing trials, however, courtrooms were often routinely closed to the press and public to protect order and decorum, witnesses, public morality, trade secrets, police confidentiality,

national security, privacy rights, and the fragile psyches of juveniles. Judicial records were also often sealed if a judge was convinced doing so would protect a defendant from prejudice.

In 1979, a divided Court appeared to resolve doubts in favor of defendants. *Gannett v. DePasquale,* 5 Med. L. Rptr. 1337, 443 U.S. 368, 99 S. Ct. 2898 (1979). The Court narrowly held that the Sixth Amendment's public trial guarantee was waivable by the defendant, therefore raising no First Amendment issue. Pretrial suppression hearings could be closed by agreement of both the defense and the prosecution.

The majority opinion, written by Justice Stewart, noted that "a trial judge has an affirmative constitutional duty to minimize the effects of prejudicial pretrial publicity, and he may take protective measures even though they are not strictly and inescapably necessary."

The fragile majority did not support Stewart's position well. Although both Chief Justice Burger and Justice Powell joined Stewart's opinion, each concurred separately, apparently to narrow the opinion's scope. Burger openly doubted that the *Gannett* rationale could be applied to actual trials. Powell accepted a qualified First Amendment–based right of access to *all* criminal proceedings.

Justice Blackmun's vigorous dissenting opinion, which was joined by Justices Brennan, Marshall, and White, accepted the right of press and public access under the Sixth Amendment. Before allowing closure, he would require that a defendant show "substantial probability that irreparable damage" to a fair trial would result and that alternatives to closure were inadequate. But elsewhere, he referred to a "strict and inescapable necessity" formula.

Judges understood Stewart's admonition as a call to protect fair trial rights through closure whenever publicity seemed to pose a risk.

In the twelve-month period after the ruling, an estimated 270 efforts were made to close various phases of criminal proceedings: 131 closure motions were granted and upheld on appeal; 14 were reversed; and 111 were either denied by the trial court or withdrawn by counsel. Of the total number of motions, 171 sought to close pretrial hearings, and 49 to close trials. About half were granted in each category.

The Court changed direction one year later. *Gannett* had not addressed the issue of actual

88. *Detroit Free Press v. Macomb Circuit Judge,* 4 Med. L. Rptr. 2180, 275 N.W.2d 482 (Mich. 1979); *Philadelphia Newspapers v. Jerome,* 3 Med. L. Rptr. 2185, 387 A.2d 425 (Pa. 1978).

89. *Rapid City Journal v. Circuit Court,* 5 Med. L. Rptr. 1706, 283 N.W.2d 563 (S.D. 1979).

trial closures. It had also not decided whether the First Amendment independently provides the press or public a right to attend trials. Given the flood of closures and closure attempts in just one year's time, resolution of these issues was crucial to the press. In addition to resolving both issues in favor of access, the Court also appeared to recognize a general First Amendment–based right of access to information controlled by government.

Seven justices agreed on one point in *Gannett*: that the First Amendment, effective against the states through the Fourteenth Amendment, guarantees the press and public a right to attend criminal trials. The Court was split on the strength of that right and on what proof was needed to overcome it.

None of the justices has explained why a Sixth Amendment analysis was used in *Gannett* when a First Amendment approach would be used in *Richmond Newspapers, Inc. v. Virginia*. Only Blackmun seems to have had reservations about the locus of the access right.

Burger's opinion relied heavily upon history in establishing the value and tradition of openness in criminal trials. Much of the history had been presented by Blackmun in his comprehensive dissent in *Gannett*.

Richmond Newspapers, Inc. v. Virginia
6 MED. L. RPTR. 1833, 448 U.S. 555, 100 S. CT. 2814, 65 L. ED. 2D 973 (1980).

* * *

Chief Justice BURGER announced the judgment of the Court and delivered an opinion in which Justice WHITE and Justice STEVENS joined.

The narrow question presented in this case is whether the right of the public and press to attend criminal trials is guaranteed under the United States Constitution.

In March 1976, one Stevenson was indicted for the murder of a hotel manager who had been found stabbed to death on December 2, 1975. Tried promptly in July 1976, Stevenson was convicted of second-degree murder in the Circuit Court of Hanover County, Va. The Virginia Supreme Court reversed the conviction. * * *

Stevenson was retried in the same court. This second trial ended in a mistrial. * * *

A third trial, which began in the same court on June 6, 1978, also ended in a mistrial. It appears that the mistrial may have been declared because a prospective juror had read about Stevenson's previous trials in a newspaper and had told other prospective jurors about the case before the retrial began. * * *

Stevenson was tried in the same court for a fourth time beginning on September 11, 1978. Present in the courtroom when the case was called were appellants Wheeler and McCarthy, reporters for appellant Richmond Newspapers, Inc. Before the trial began, counsel for the defendant moved that it be closed to the public. * * *

The trial judge, who had presided over two of the three previous trials, asked if the prosecution had any objection to clearing the courtroom. The prosecutor stated he had no objection and would leave it to the discretion of the court. * * * Presumably referring to Virginia Code § 19.2–266, the trial judge then announced: "[T]he statute gives me that power specifically and the defendant has made the motion." He then ordered "that the Courtroom be kept clear of all parties except the witnesses when they testify." * * * The record does not show that any objections to the closure order were made by anyone present at the time, including appellants Wheeler and McCarthy.

Later that same day, however, appellants sought a hearing on a motion to vacate the closure order. The trial judge granted the request and scheduled a hearing to follow the close of the day's proceedings. When the hearing began, the court ruled that the hearing was to be treated as part of the trial; accordingly, he again ordered the reporters to leave the courtroom, and they complied.

At the closed hearing, counsel for appellants observed that no evidentiary findings had been made by the court prior to the entry of its closure order and pointed out that the court had failed to consider any other, less drastic measures within its power to ensure a fair trial. * * * Counsel for appellants argued that constitutional considerations mandated that before ordering closure, the court should first decide that the rights of the defendant could be protected in no other way.

* * *

The court denied the motion to vacate and ordered the trial to continue the following morning "with the press and public excluded." * * * Appellants then petitioned the Virginia Supreme Court for writs of mandamus and prohibition and filed an appeal from the trial court's closure order. On July 9, 1979, the Virginia Supreme Court dismissed the mandamus and prohibition petitions and, finding no reversible error, denied the petition for appeal. * * *

Appellants then sought review in this Court. * * * [W]e grant the petition.

We begin consideration of this case by noting that the precise issue presented here has not previously been before this Court for decision. In *Gannet Co., Inc. v. DePasquale,* 443 U.S. 386, (1979), the Court was not required to decide whether a right of access to *trials,* as distinguished from hearings on *pre* trial motions, was constitutionally guaranteed.

* * *

But here for the first time the Court is asked to decide whether a criminal trial itself may be closed to the public upon the unopposed request of a defendant, without any demonstration that closure is required to protect the defendant's superior right to a fair trial, or that some other overriding consideration requires closure.

The origins of the proceeding which has become the modern criminal trial in Anglo-American justice can be traced back beyond reliable historical records. We need not here review all details of its development, but a summary of that history is instructive. What is significant for present purposes is that throughout its evolution, the trial has been open to all who care to observe.

* * *

We have found nothing to suggest that the presumptive openness of the trial, which English courts were later to call "one of the essential qualities of a court of justice," *Daubney v. Cooper,* 10 B. & C. 237, 240, 109 Eng.Rep. 438, 440 (K.B. 1829), was not also an attribute of the judicial systems of colonial America. In Virginia, for example, such records as there are of early criminal trials indicate that they were open, and nothing to the contrary has been cited.

* * *

In some instances, the openness of trials was explicitly recognized as part of the fundamental law of the colony. The 1677 Concessions and Agreements of West New Jersey, for example, provided:

That in all public courts of justice for tryals of causes, civil or criminal, any person or persons,

inhabitants of the said Province may freely come into, and attend the said courts, and hear and be present, at all or any such tryals as shall be there had or passed, that justice may not be done in a corner nor in any covert manner. Reprinted in *Sources of Our Liberties* 188 (R. Perry ed. 1959). See also 1 B. Schwartz, *The Bill of Rights: A Documentary History* 129 (1971).

* * *

This is no quirk of history; rather, it has long been recognized as an indispensible attribute of an Anglo-American trial. Both Hale in the 17th century and Blackstone in the 18th saw the importance of openness to the proper functioning of a trial; it gave assurance that the proceedings were conducted fairly to all concerned, and it discouraged perjury, the misconduct of participants, and decisions based on secret bias or partiality.

* * *

This observation raises the important point that "[t]he publicity of a judicial proceeding is a requirement of much broader bearing than its mere effect on the quality of testimony." 6 J. Wigmore, *Evidence* § 1834, at p. 435 (Chadbourn rev. 1976). The early history of open trials in part reflects the widespread acknowledgment, long before there were behavioral scientists, that public trials had significant community therapeutic value. Even without such experts to frame the concept in words, people sensed from experience and observation that, especially in the administration of criminal justice, the means used to achieve justice must have the support derived from public acceptance of both the process and its results.

* * *

The crucial prophylactic aspects of the administration of justice cannot function in the dark; no community catharsis can occur if justice is "done in a corner [or] in any covert manner." * * *

To work effectively, it is important that society's criminal process "satisfy the appearance of justice," *Offutt v. United States,* 348 U.S. 11, 14 (1954), and the appearance of justice can best be provided by allowing people to observe it.

* * *

People in an open society do not demand infallibility from their institutions, but it is difficult for them to accept what they are prohibited from observing. When a criminal trial is conducted in the open, there is a least an opportunity both for understanding the system in general and its workings in a particular case:

> The educative effect of public attendance is a material advantage. Not only is respect for the law increased and intelligent acquaintance acquired with the methods of government, but a strong confidence in judicial remedies is secured which could never be inspired by a system of secrecy. 6 Wigmore, *supra*, at 438.

In earlier times, both in England and America, attendance at court was a common mode of "passing the time." See, *e.g.*, 6 Wigmore, *supra*, at 436. * * * With the press, cinema, and electronic media now supplying the representations or reality of the real life drama once available only in the courtroom, attendance at court is no longer a widespread pastime. * * * Instead of acquiring information about trials by firsthand observation or by word of mouth from those who attended, people now acquire it chiefly through the print and electronic media. In a sense, this validates the media claim of functioning as surrogates for the public. While media representatives enjoy the same right of access as the public, they often are provided special seating and priority of entry so that they may report what people in attendance have seen and heard. This "contribute[s] to public understanding of the rule of law and to comprehension of the functioning of the entire criminal justice system * * *."

From the unbroken, uncontradicted history, supported by reasons as valid today as in centuries past, we are bound to conclude that a presumption of openness inheres in the very nature of a criminal trial under our system of justice. * * *

Despite the history of criminal trials being presumptively open since long before the Constitution, the State presses its contention that neither the Constitution nor the Bill of Rights contains any provision which by its terms guarantees to the public the right to attend criminal trials. Standing alone, this is correct, but there remains the question whether, absent an explicit provision, the Constitution affords protection against exclusion of the public from criminal trials.

The First Amendment, in conjunction with the Fourteenth, prohibits governments from "abridging the freedom of speech, or of the press; or the right of the people peaceably to assemble, and to petition the Government for a redress of grievances." *These expressly guaranteed freedoms share a common core purpose of assuring freedom of communication on matters relating to the functioning of government.* Plainly it would be difficult to single out any aspect of government of higher concern and importance to the people than the manner in which criminal trials are conducted. [Emphasis added.]

* * *

It is not crucial whether we describe this right to attend criminal trials to hear, see, and communicate observations concerning them as a "right of access," * * * or a "right to gather information," for we have recognized that "without some protection for seeking out the news, freedom of the press could be eviscerated." *Branzburg v. Hayes,* 408 U.S. 665, 681 * * * (1972). The explicit, guaranteed rights to speak and to publish concerning what takes place at a trial would lose much meaning if access to observe the trial could, as it was here, be foreclosed arbitrarily.

The right of access to places traditionally open to the public, as criminal trials have long been, may be seen as assured by the amalgam of the First Amendment guarantees of speech and press.

* * *

Subject to the traditional time, place, and manner restrictions, * * * a trial courtroom also is a public place where the people generally—and representatives of the media—have a right to be present, and where their presence historically has been thought to enhance the integrity and quality of what takes place.

The State argues that the Constitution nowhere spells out a guarantee for the right of the public to attend trials, and that accordingly no such right is protected.

* * *

But arguments such as the State makes have not precluded recognition of important rights not enumerated. Notwithstanding the appropriate caution against reading into the Constitution rights not explicitly defined, the Court has acknowledged that certain unarticulated rights are implicit in enumerated guarantees. For example, the rights of association and privacy, the right to be presumed innocent and the right to be judged by a standard of proof beyond a reasonable doubt in a criminal trial, as well as the right to travel, appear nowhere in the Constitution or Bill of Rights.

* * *

[F]undamental rights, even though not expressly guaranteed, have been recognized by the Court as indispensable to the enjoyment of rights explicitly defined.

We hold that the right to attend criminal trials is implicit in the guarantees of the First Amendment; without the freedom to attend such trials, which people have exercised for centuries, important aspects of freedom of speech and "of the press could be eviscerated."

Having concluded there was a guaranteed right of the public under the First and Fourteenth Amendments to attend the trial of Stevenson's case, we return to the closure order challenged by appellants. * * * Despite the fact that this was the fourth trial of the accused, the trial judge made no findings to support closure; no inquiry was made as to whether alternative solutions would have met the need to ensure fairness; there was no recognition of any right under the Constitution for the public or press to attend the trial. * * * There was no suggestion that any problems with witnesses could not have been dealt with by their exclusion from the courtroom or their sequestration during the trial. * * * Nor is there anything to indicate that sequestration of the jurors would not have guarded against their being subjected to any improper information. All of the alternatives admittedly present difficulties for trial courts, but none of the factors relied on here was beyond the realm of the manageable. Absent an overriding interest articulated in findings, the trial of a criminal case must be open to the public.

Accordingly, the judgment under review is reversed.

Reversed.

COMMENT

In spite of the potential significance of the case and the near-unanimity of its result, the Court remained "badly splintered"[90] and imprecise on what anyone seeking closure must do to overcome the qualified right to attend criminal trials.[91] Of the eight justices participating, seven wrote separate opinions. Chief Justice Burger's plurality opinion was joined only by Stevens and White, both of whom also concurred separately

as well. Justices Blackmun, Brennan, and Stewart each wrote concurring opinions. Only Rehnquist dissented.

Burger's opinion addressed an issue not presented—whether the access right recognized also applies to civil trials. In an unusual example of anticipation, he added footnote 17, apparently to prevent a flood of closure attempts in civil suits:

Whether the public has a right to attend trials of civil cases is a question not raised by this case, but we note that historically both civil and criminal trials have been presumptively open.

The majority of courts that have had occasion to assess the issue have concluded that the First Amendment right of access does indeed apply to civil suits. Courts have also generally concluded that the right applies as strongly as in criminal trials. *NBC Subsidiary (KNBC-TV) Inc. v. Superior Court*, 25 Med. L. Rptr. 1065, 49 Cal.App. 487, 56 Cal.Rptr. 645 (1996).

In his concurrence, Justice Stevens accurately characterized the case as a watershed: "[F]or the first time, the Court unequivocally holds that an arbitrary interference with access to important information is an abridgment of the freedom of speech and of the press protected by the First Amendment." Stevens did not, however, specify what proof was needed to overcome the right of access to information, nor did he say what sort of information the right grants access to. In his decision, Chief Justice Burger was careful to distinguish the right of access to criminal trials from a more generalized right of access.

The press greeted *Richmond* with enthusiasm, interpreting it as creating a general right of access to news.[92] Lawyers and courts, however, tended to see the case as granting only a qualified newsgathering right. Media attorney Bruce Sanford, hoping that *Richmond* was the beginning of many successful access cases, cautioned journalists that, "A Court that can swing from [*Gannett*] to *Richmond Newspapers* within a year does not, after all, inspire a great feeling of confidence about what it may do in the future."[93]

The major unanswered question from *Richmond* was addressed two years later in *Globe*

---

90. Cox, *Freedom of Expression* (1982).

91. Powe, *The Fourth Estate and the Constitution* 192–197 (1991).

92. American Society of Newspaper Editors & American Newspaper Publishers Association, *Free Press & Fair Trial*, Washington, D.C. 1982.

93. Sanford, *Richmond Newspapers: End of a Zigzag Trail*, 19 Columbia Journalism Rev. 46 (1980).

Newspaper Co. v. Superior Court, 8 Med. L. Rptr. 1689, 457 U.S. 596 (1992). The facts in *Globe* looked unpromising from the point of view of the press. A Massachusetts trial court judge, relying on a state statute requiring that the public be excluded from testimony in sexual offense trials involving victims under age eighteen, ordered press and public from the courtroom during the trial of a defendant charged with raping three minors. The *Boston Globe* challenged, and the Massachusetts Supreme Judicial Court upheld the closure.

A six-member U.S. Supreme Court majority reversed. The First Amendment right of access to trials is violated by any mandatory closure. Justice William Brennan's opinion emphasized that blanket closure rules will never be narrowly tailored and so cannot comport with *Richmond.* Only a case-by-case determination will result in a narrowly tailored order.

Most importantly, Brennan's opinion applied the compelling interest test when closure of a trial is sought. The psychological and physical protection of minors, the primary interest underlying the closure statute, was considered compelling, but even that issue must be addressed on a case-by-case basis. Protecting the identities of minors seemed irrelevant to Brennan given the facts in *Globe:*

> Section 16A . . . requires closure even if the victim did not seek the exclusion of the press and the general public. In the case before us, for example, the names of the minor victims were already in the public record, and the record indicates that the victims may have been willing to testify despite the presence of the press.

A second interest, encouraging victims to come forward, help prosecutors, and testify, was also offered by the state. The Court rejected it as "speculative," in part because no evidence showed that closure resulted in more reporting of crime. It was "also open to serious question as a matter of logic and common sense" because the transcript and other sources of information were readily available.

Brennan relied upon prior restraint cases in his majority opinion, apparently reflecting the view that press exclusion was in effect a ban on publication of information.[94]

The Court's rejection of a blanket closure rule is apparently not meant to discourage enforcement of more narrowly drawn statutes. The recognition of compelling or overriding state interests—perhaps privacy in one of its myriad forms—would allow closure if the interest is better documented. The discretion to close, though, lies with the judge and not with the legislature.

Prior to and even after *Globe,* some state courts were quick to protect juvenile victims or witnesses,[95] to protect criminal defendants against revelation of past convictions,[96] and to protect defendants against embarrassment.[97] Others preferred to keep hearings and records open at all costs on state constitutional or common law grounds.[98]

Nevertheless, uncertainties remained. By their terms, both *Richmond* and *Globe* applied only to the main portion of the trial. That left room for maneuvering by lower courts. More clarification was needed.

The *Press-Enterprise* Cases

Two cases involving the Riverside (California) *Press-Enterprise* clarified the scope of *Richmond.* In the first case, the Supreme Court held that closure of *voir dire* violated the First Amendment. The newspaper was covering proceedings in a case where the defendant was accused of rape and murder. Apparently assuming that some potential jurors would be asked sensitive questions about their sexual experiences, the trial judge ordered closure on the basis of the jurors' privacy interests. Having been denied access to the *voir dire,* the newspaper requested a transcript and was refused. *Press-Enterprise v. Riverside County Superior Court,* 10 Med. L. Rptr. 1161, 464 U.S. 501 (1984) *(Press-Enterprise I).*

---

94. *Brown v. Hartlage,* 456 U.S. 45 (1982); *NAACP v. Button,* 371 U.S. 415 (1963).

95. *Connecticut v. McCloud,* 6 Med. L. Rptr. 1613, 422 A.2d 327 (Conn. 1980); *North Carolina v. Burney,* 7 Med. L. Rptr. 1411, 276 S.E.2d 693 (N.C. 1981).

96. *Capital Newspapers v. Clyne,* 7 Med. L. Rptr. 1536, 440 N.Y.S.2d 779 (1981).

97. *New York v. Jones,* 7 Med. L. Rptr. 2096, 418 N.Y.S.2d 359 (1979), *cert. denied* 444 U.S. 946 (1979).

98. *Oregonian Publishing Co. v. O'Leary,* 14 Med. L. Rptr. 1019, 736 P.2d 173 (Ore. 1987); *Capital Newspapers v. Moynihan,* 14 Med. L. Rptr. 2262, 525 N.Y.S.2d 24 (N.Y. 1988); *Seattle Times v. Ishikawa,* 8 Med. L. Rptr. 1041, 640 P.2d 716 (Wash. 1982); *Cowles Publishing v. Murphy,* 6 Med. L. Rptr. 2308, 637 P.2d 966 (Wash. 1981). See also *Lexington Herald Leader v. Tackett,* 6 Med. L. Rptr. 1436, 601 S.W.2d 905 (Ky. 1980), involving a sodomy prosecution.

All nine justices agreed that *voir dire* was part of the trial itself, and that therefore a First Amendment right of access applies. But Chief Justice Burger's majority opinion stated the applicable test in slightly different language than Brennan had in *Globe:*

> The presumption of openness may be overcome only by an overriding interest based on findings that closure is essential to preserve higher values and is narrowly tailored to serve that interest. The interest is to be articulated along with findings specific enough that a reviewing court can determine whether the closure order was properly entered.

Since Burger concluded that "The judge at this trial closed an incredible *six* weeks of *voir dire* without considering alternatives to closure," it was easy for the majority to hold that the test had not been met.

Burger found merit in the juror privacy argument, however, agreeing that it may "give rise to a compelling interest of a prospective juror when interrogation touches on deeply personal matters. . . ." He urged that "The privacy interests of such a prospective juror must be balanced against the historic values we have discussed and the need for openness of the process." Apparently, he would have required that an individual juror make an affirmative request to the trial judge before any privacy concern could be considered implicated. None had done so.

The privacy analysis has had some effect. One court required a trial judge to devise a procedure to decide if jurors should be questioned *in camera* about child abuse prior to being seated.[99] In another case, a court approved closing a civil case file containing material about a man later charged with rape. The court determined that privacy interests allowed closure. That the documents, some of which had been obtained in discovery, were not traditionally considered public information also influenced the decision.[100] On the whole, however, the exception does not appear to have led to many closures.

In *California v. Rollins,* 24 Med. L. Rptr. 2569 (Cal.Super. 1996), however, the trial judge imposed an array of restrictions on press access to a murder trial. A hearing on admissibility of evidence was closed to the press. *Voir dire* would

be open, but, "Should any juror request that his or her answers be given without media present, the court shall honor that request and conduct questioning in camera." All participants in the proceeding were ordered not to make any extrajudicial statements. The judge barred the broadcast of pictures of members of the jury panel, even when jurors were outside the courthouse. Journalists were also denied access to written questionnaires completed by members of the juror pool. The court said that a recently passed statute called for juror confidentiality. A local television station filed a petition for relief but was denied. *KGET-TV Channel 17 v. Superior Court,* No. FO26139 (Cal.App., June 7, 1996), No. 5th FO26139–SO54191 (Cal., June 25, 1996). A petition for a writ of certiorari filed with the U.S. Supreme Court was denied. No. 96–462 (U.S., Dec. 2, 1996).

The judge in *Rollins,* following California opinions that predated both the *Press-Enterprise* cases and also *Richmond,* applied the following test:

> [T]he judge need only be satisfied that there is a reasonable likelihood of prejudicial news which would make difficult the impaneling of an impartial jury and tend to prevent a fair trial. *Rosato v. Superior Court,* 1 Med. L. Rptr. 2560, 51 Cal.App.3d 190, 124 Cal.Rptr. 427 (1975), *cert. denied* 427 U.S. 912 (1976).

The Supreme Court's refusal to review a decision that appears to directly challenge the Court's access rules is puzzling. The station's petition explicitly raised the issue of inconsistent application of *Press-Enterprise I.*

The same year as *Press-Enterprise I,* the Court had occasion to revisit the Sixth Amendment's guarantee of a public trial. In *Waller v. Georgia,* 10 Med. L. Rptr. 1714, 467 U.S. 39 (1984), a trial judge had closed a pretrial evidentiary suppression hearing in a racketeering and gambling case against the objections of the defendant. Holding that "the explicit Sixth Amendment right of the accused is no less protective of a public trial than the implicit First Amendment right." Justice Powell's opinion for a unanimous Court ordered a new suppression hearing. The defendant had sought a new trial but was told he could get one only if *additional* material was suppressed in the second hearing. The trial judge had relied on a state wiretap law to close the hearing, but the Court, adhering to its analysis abjuring *per se* closures, said that the prosecu-

---

99. *Daily Herald v. Knight,* 13 Med. L. Rptr. 2199 (Wash. 1987).

100. *H. S. Gere and Sons, Inc. v. Frey,* 14 Med. L. Rptr. 1791, 509 N.E.2d 271 (Mass. 1987).

tion must meet the *Press-Enterprise* standards before closure may be had. Proving that the state's interest in secrecy is more compelling than a defendant's right to a public trial would be a difficult if not impossible task.

Although most lower courts had been or had begun applying *Richmond*-style tests to closures of even pretrial proceedings, some courts still interpreted the access right very narrowly. For example, *Midland Publishing v. District Court Judge*, 11 Med. L. Rptr. 1337, 362 N.W.2d 580 (Mich. 1984), involved both pretrial proceedings and a statute mandating closure. Three defendants were arrested on suspicion of criminal sexual conduct with children. Suppression orders pursuant to the statute were entered two days later. Comparing the closed documents and closed preliminary proceedings to pleadings in civil cases, the court opted for a statutory and common law approach upholding closure. *Globe* and *Press-Enterprise* were distinguished as limited to trials themselves, and the court then considered preliminary hearings as comparable to secret grand jury proceedings, because they had largely taken the place of grand juries under state law. The press and public were held to have neither constitutional nor common law access rights to the hearings or the records.

In California, where the preliminary hearing is also used to determine if probable cause exists to bring charges, the California Supreme Court had accepted a similar approach. The preliminary hearing of a nurse thought to have killed a dozen hospital patients using the heart drug lidocaine was closed for forty-one days. When the hearing was over and charges were brought, the magistrate in the case refused to release transcripts of the hearing. The deaths and hearing both occurred in Riverside, California, attracting the newsgathering attention of the *Press-Enterprise*. The result was another landmark case, *Press-Enterprise II*.

Press-Enterprise v. Riverside County Superior Court

13 MED. L. RPTR. 1001, 478 U.S. 1, 106 S. CT. 2735, 92 L. ED. 2D 1 (1986).

Chief Justice BURGER delivered the opinion of the Court.

We granted certiorari to decide whether petitioner has a First Amendment right of access to transcripts of a preliminary hearing growing out of a criminal prosecution.

On December 23, 1981, the State of California filed a complaint in the Riverside County Municipal Court, charging Robert Diaz with 12 counts of murder and seeking the death penalty. The complaint alleged that Diaz, a nurse, murdered 12 patients by administering massive doses of the heart drug lidocaine. The preliminary hearing on the complaint commenced on July 6, 1982. Diaz moved to exclude the public from the proceedings under California Penal Code Ann. § 868 (West 1985), which requires such proceedings to be open unless "exclusion of the public is necessary in order to protect the defendant's right to a fair and impartial trial." The Magistrate granted the unopposed motion, finding that closure was necessary because the case had attracted national publicity and "only one side may get reported in the media."

The preliminary hearing continued for 41 days. Most of the testimony and the evidence presented by the State was medical and scientific; the remainder consisted of testimony by personnel who worked with Diaz on the shifts when the 12 patients died. Diaz did not introduce any evidence, but his counsel subjected most of the witnesses to vigorous cross-examination. Diaz was held to answer on all charges. At the conclusion of the hearing, petitioner Press-Enterprise Company asked that the transcript of the proceedings be released. The Magistrate refused and sealed the record.

* * *

The California Supreme Court thereafter denied petitioner's peremptory writ of mandate, holding that there is no general First Amendment right of access to preliminary hearings. The court reasoned that the right of access to criminal proceedings recognized in *Press-Enterprise Co. v. Superior Court*, 464 U.S. 501, 10 Med. L. Rptr. 1161 (1984) (*Press-Enterprise I*), and *Globe Newspaper Co. v. Superior Court*, 457 U.S. 596, 8 Med. L. Rptr. 1689 (1982), extended only to actual criminal trials. 37 Cal.3d 772, 776, 691 P.2d 1026, 1028 (1984). Furthermore, the reasons that had been asserted for closing the proceedings in *Press Enterprise I* and *Globe*—the interests of witnesses and other third parties— were not the same as the right asserted in this case—the defendant's right to a fair and impartial trial by a jury uninfluenced by news accounts.

* * * Under the statute, the court reasoned, if the defendant establishes a "reasonable likelihood of substantial prejudice" the burden shifts to the prosecution or the media to show by a preponderance of the evidence that there is no such reasonable probability of prejudice.

* * *

It is important to identify precisely what the California Supreme Court decided:

"[W]e conclude that the magistrate shall close the preliminary hearing upon finding a reasonable likelihood of substantial prejudice which would impinge upon the right to a fair trial. Penal code section 868 makes clear that the primary right is the right to a fair trial and that the public's right of access must give way when there is conflict."

* * *

Plainly, the defendant has a right to a fair trial but, as we have repeatedly recognized, one of the important means of assuring a fair trial is that the process be open to neutral observers.

The right to an open public trial is a shared right of the accused and the public, the common concern being the assurance of fairness. * * *

The California Supreme Court concluded that the First Amendment was not implicated because the proceeding was not a criminal trial, but a preliminary hearing. However, the First Amendment question cannot be resolved solely on the label we give the event, *i.e.,* "trial" or otherwise, particularly where the preliminary hearing functions much like a full scale trial.

In cases dealing with the claim of a First Amendment right of access to criminal proceedings, our decisions have emphasized two complementary considerations. First, * * * we have considered whether the place and process has historically been open to the press and general public.

* * *

Second, in this setting the Court has traditionally considered whether public access plays a significant positive role in the functioning of the particular process in question. Although many governmental processes operate best under public scrutiny, it takes little imagination to recognize that there are some kinds of government operations that would be totally frustrated if conducted openly. A classic example is that "the proper functioning of our grand jury system depends upon the secrecy of grand jury proceed-

ings." * * * Other proceedings plainly require public access.

* * *

The considerations that led the Court to apply the First Amendment right of access to criminal trials in *Richmond Newspapers* and *Globe* and the selection of jurors in *Press Enterprise I* lead us to conclude that the right of access applies to preliminary hearings as conducted in California.

First, there has been a tradition of accessibility to preliminary hearings of the type conducted in California. Although grand jury proceedings have traditionally been closed to the public and the accused, preliminary hearings conducted before neutral and detached magistrates have been open to the public. * * * *United States v. Burr,* 25 F. Cas. 1 (CC Va. 1807) (No. 14,692). From *Burr* until the present day, the near uniform practice of state and federal courts has been to conduct preliminary hearings in open court. As we noted in *Gannett,* several states following the original New York Field Code of Criminal Procedure published in 1850 have allowed preliminary hearings to be closed on the motion of the accused. But even in these states the proceedings are presumptively open to the public and are closed only for cause shown. Open preliminary hearings, therefore, have been accorded "'the favorable judgment of experience.'"

* * *

The second question is whether public access to preliminary hearings as they are conducted in California plays a particularly significant positive role in the actual functioning of the process. * * * California preliminary hearings are sufficiently like a trial to justify the same conclusion.

* * *

It is true that unlike a criminal trial, the California preliminary hearing cannot result in the conviction of the accused and the adjudication is before a magistrate or other judicial officer without a jury. But these features, standing alone, do not make public access any less essential to the proper functioning of the proceedings in the overall criminal justice process. Because of its extensive scope, the preliminary hearing is often the final and most important step in the criminal proceeding. See *Waller v. Georgia,* 467 U.S., at 46–47. As the California Supreme Court stated in *San Jose Mercury-News v. Municipal Court,* * * * the preliminary hearing in many cases provides "the sole occasion for public observation of the criminal justice system."

* * *

Similarly, the absence of a jury, long recognized as "an inestimable safeguard against the corrupt or overzealous prosecutor and against the compliant, biased, or eccentric judge," *Duncan v. Louisiana* 391 U.S. 145, 156 (1968), makes the importance of public access to a preliminary hearing even more significant.

* * *

Denying the transcripts of a 41-day preliminary hearing would frustrate what we have characterized as the "community therapeutic value" of openness.

* * *

We therefore conclude that the qualified First Amendment right of access to criminal proceedings applies to preliminary hearings as they are conducted in California.

Since a qualified First Amendment right of access attaches to preliminary hearings in California under Cal. Penal Code Ann. §§ 858 *et seq.* (West 1985), the proceedings cannot be closed unless specific, on the record findings are made demonstrating that "closure is essential to preserve higher values and is narrowly tailored to serve that interest." * * * If the interest asserted is the right of the accused to a fair trial, the preliminary hearing shall be closed only if specific findings are made demonstrating that first, there is a substantial probability that the defendant's right to a fair trial will be prejudiced by publicity that closure would prevent and, second, reasonable alternatives to closure cannot adequately protect the defendant's fair trial rights.

* * *

The California Supreme Court, interpreting its access statute, concluded "that the magistrate shall close the preliminary hearing upon finding a reasonable likelihood of substantial prejudice." As the court itself acknowledged, the "reasonable likelihood" test places a lesser burden on the defendant than the "substantial probability" test which we hold is called for by the First Amendment. Moreover, that court failed to consider whether alternatives short of complete closure would have protected the interests of the accused.

In *Gannett* we observed that:

"Publicity concerning pretrial suppression hearings such as the one involved in the present case poses special risks of unfairness. The whole purpose of such hearings is to screen out unreliable or illegally obtained evidence and insure that this evidence does not become known to the jury."

* * *

But this risk of prejudice does not automatically justify refusing public access to hearings on every motion to suppress. Through *voir dire,* cumbersome as it is in some circumstances, a court can identify those jurors whose prior knowledge of the case would disable them from rendering an impartial verdict. And even if closure were justified for the hearings on a motion to suppress, closure of an entire 41-day proceeding would rarely be warranted. The First Amendment right of access cannot be overcome by the conclusory assertion that publicity might deprive the defendant of that right. And any limitation "'must be narrowly tailored to serve that interest.'"

The standard applied by the California Supreme Court failed to consider the First Amendment right of access to criminal proceedings. Accordingly, the judgment of the California Supreme Court is reversed.

COMMENT

The Court's voting lineup changed slightly, with Justices Stevens and Rehnquist dissenting from the majority opinion. Stevens's dissent seemed focused at least in part on what he saw as the Court's implicit rejection of *Gannett*, at least where the press is concerned.

Chief Justice Burger's majority opinion attracted six other votes, and no separate concurrences were filed, indicating numerically that the Court was now in accord. Nonetheless, Burger's opinion retains a potential for uncertainty. At one point he cites approvingly the "overriding interest" standard of *Press-Enterprise I*, but later applies a test consisting of "substantial probability" and lack of adequate alternatives. Is the result, then, a weaker right of press access for pretrial proceedings than for trials themselves?

The Court attempts to create a blueprint for future disputes over access to other parts of the judicial process by applying a two-part analysis to determine initially if a First Amendment right of access applies. First, history and tradition must be consulted. If a proceeding has traditionally been open, a presumption of openness should apply. Second, a reviewing court must consider if "public access plays a significant positive role in the functioning of the particular process in question." The second point stems from Justice Brennan's concurrence in *Richmond* and is an application of what he referred to as a "structural" model. Taking its cue from Brennan's argument that what occurs in courts is almost by definition a matter of public interest, this factor requires courts to consider the press's role in informing the public.

Preliminary hearings, at least as they are held in California, are often the beginning and end of the criminal justice process, as Burger noted. More than 85 percent of cases are resolved there.

Closures since the two *Press-Enterprise* cases have been the exception rather than the rule. The presumption against closure has been extended to a wide variety of proceedings, including sentencing hearings,[101] plea hearings,[102] mental competency hearings,[103] motion hearings,[104] bail hearings,[105] and judicial disqualification proceedings and records.[106] Access is most certain in criminal cases.

Truly sensational cases attracting saturation news coverage have often resulted in limitations, either in the form of partial closures or other types of restrictions. *U.S. v. McVeigh,* 24 Med. L. Rptr. 1737, 918 F.Supp. 1452 (W.D.Okla. 1996); *U.S. v. McVeigh,* 24 Med. L. Rptr. 1821, 918 F.Supp. 1467 (W.D.Okla. 1996); *U.S. v. McVeigh,* 24 Med. L. Rptr. 1908, 931 F.Supp. 756 (D.Colo. 1996); *Rufo v. Simpson,* 24 Med. L. Rptr. 2213, No. SC031947 (Cal.Super. August 23, 1996). But other cases just as notorious have not been subject to restrictions; for example, the prosecution of Dr. Jack Kevorkian, the trial of the Menendez brothers, *Menendez v. Fox Broad-*

casting Co., 22 Med. L. Rptr. 1702, No. 94 2339 R (C.D.Cal. April 19, 1994), and the trial of a male guest on the Jenny Jones show who later murdered another male guest who had revealed his amorous interest in the first guest, *Michigan v. Schmitz,* 24 Med. L. Rptr. 2535 (Mich.App. 1996).

The Supreme Court reinforced its insistence on pretrial proceedings being kept open in *El Vocero de Puerto Rico v. Puerto Rico,* 21 Med. L. Rptr. 1440, 113 S.Ct. 2004 (1993). Puerto Rico's rules called for all accused felons to have a hearing to determine if they would be held for trial. The rules also said the hearings would be "held privately" unless a defendant asked for an open hearing. The Supreme Court of Puerto Rico denied a challenge to the rule based on Puerto Rican history and traditions. In *per curiam* opinion, the U.S. Supreme Court reversed, noting that "At best, the distinctive features of Puerto Rico's preliminary hearing render it a subspecies of the provision this Court found to be infirm seven years ago."

Two Sixth Circuit cases have held that there is no First Amendment right of access to summary jury trials. In both cases, the court concluded that there was no history of access. Nor was openness seen as contributing to the proceeding. Only recently have summary jury trials gotten frequent use. In effect, they are "practice" trials designed to aid settlement—the parties are able to test the strength of their cases without the cost and time of a full-fledged trial. *In re The Cincinnati Enquirer,* 24 Med. L. Rptr. 2311, 94 F.3d 198 (6th Cir. 1996), *petition for cert. filed,* No. 96-1032 (1996). The earlier case had an identical result. *Cincinnati Gas & Electric Co. v. General Electric Co.,* 15 Med. L. Rptr. 2020, 854 F.2d 900 (6th Cir. 1988), *cert. denied,* 489 U.S. 1003 (1989). In *Cincinnati Gas,* the court relied heavily upon the fact that summary jury trials were nonbinding and did not preclude a later trial. But if they result in settlements, thereby substituting for formal proceedings, should they not be treated similarly?

Access to Evidence and Documents

The next step for news organizations was to attempt to extend the rationales of the *Richmond* and *Press-Enterprise* cases to establish a First Amendment right of access to documents

---

101. *In re Washington Post Co.,* 13 Med. L. Rptr. 1793, 807 F.2d 383 (4th Cir. 1986).

102. *United States v. Haller,* 14 Med. L. Rptr. 2166, 837 F.2d 84 (2d Cir. 1988).

103. *Society of Professional Journalists v. Bullock,* 14 Med. L. Rptr. 1737, 743 P.2d 1166 (Utah 1987).

104. *Mississippi Publishers Corp. v. Coleman,* 14 Med. L. Rptr. 2005, 515 So.2d 1163 (Miss. 1987) (closure upheld, however, as comporting with demands of *Press-Enterprise II*).

105. *In re Globe Newspaper Co.,* 10 Med. L. Rptr. 1433, 729 F.2d 47 (1st Cir. 1984) (but standard less than for trial itself).

106. *United States v. Presser,* 14 Med. L. Rptr 1417 (6th Cir. 1987).

and evidence filed with courts and with law enforcement agencies. The press in effect was trying to use the First Amendment as the equivalent of the Freedom of Information Act so far as courts and law enforcement were concerned.

The press and public have long had a common law right of access to records, documents, and various types of recorded material introduced into evidence at trial. The difficulty with a common law right, however, is its strength, or rather its lack thereof. The right may be overcome whenever a trial judge concludes that the interests on the side of denying access are greater than the interests on the side of access, essentially a type of balancing without explicit guidelines. *U.S. v. Edwards* 672 F.2d 1289 (7th Cir. 1982). In comparison, recognition of a First Amendment right would raise the burden on any party seeking to prevent access to materials. The burden would likely involve application of a substantial interest/probability test, similar to that in *Press-Enterprise II. In re Continental Illinois Securities Litigation,* 732 F.2d 1302 (7th Cir. 1984). Some courts have applied what amounts to strict scrutiny, compelling interest, to these types of materials. See, e.g., *Holland v. Eads,* 614 So.2d 1012 (Ala. 1993).

The extension of *Richmond* depends upon judicial acceptance of the argument that the public has as large a stake in the evidentiary materials in a public trial as in the trial itself. The argument has been fairly persuasive. A First Amendment right of access has been recognized in almost every jurisdiction that has considered the matter. *The Baltimore Sun v. Thanos,* 20 Med. L. Rptr. 1317, 92 Md.App. 227, 607 A.2d 565 (1992).

The extended right covers materials admitted for trial, but pretrial materials such as depositions and interrogatories generally have not been considered within the First Amendment access right. See e.g., *Doe v. Florida,* 587 So.2d 526 (Fla.App. 1991). One court decided that post-trial materials may be unsealed and made available to the press. The court indicated that both the common law right and a First Amendment right applied; it said the proper course was to assess an access claim under the common law first. Then, if access was denied under the common law analysis, a First Amendment test could be applied, although in the case at hand the court concluded that access was proper under both.

U.S. v. Gonzalez, 24 Med. L. Rptr. 2025, 927 F.Supp. 768 (D.Del. 1996).

Materials generated early in the criminal justice process, including videotapes of searches or of police lineups, have typically not been disclosed on the ground that they relate to an ongoing investigation.[107]

In the civil area, most courts have agreed that settlements and documents related to them are subject to an access right, although there is uncertainty over whether the First Amendment or the common law test should apply. *Brown v. Advantage Engineering, Inc.,* 960 F.2d 1013 (11th Cir. 1992).

Nondocumentary materials such as audiotapes, photographs, or videotapes have generally been available only as a matter of common law, making it easier for a party to prevent access. Requests to copy have been denied on privacy or dignity grounds, as well as on the right to a fair trial. The reasons for allowing ready access to texts but not to other material puzzle journalists, who see little legal difference between these types of material.

The public's right to inspect and copy official court records is well established at common law. Courts have been divided, however, on whether the common law right extends to records, including sound and videotapes, not admitted into evidence. Whether records were admitted or not, though, access could usually be easily denied on a "reasonable likelihood" of prejudice or harm standard.

In *Nixon v. Warner Communications, Inc.,* 3 Med. L. Rptr. 2074, 435 U.S. 589 (1978), the Supreme Court rejected claims of a Sixth or First Amendment right to make copies of Richard Nixon's tapes that had been introduced into evidence in the Watergate criminal trials of his presidential aides. The Court also determined that the normally applicable common law access right had been superseded by the Presidential Recordings and Materials Preservation Act. Under the act, reporters and the public were allowed only to hear the tapes in court, read their contents in a transcript, or listen to them where they were stored.

---

107. *U.S. v. Thomas,* 745 F.Supp. 499 (M.D.Tenn. 1990) (searches); *WBZ-TV4 v. District Attorney,* 408 Mass. 595, 562 N.E.2d 817 (1990) (lineups).

In the case of former Congressman Michael Myers, *United States v. Myers,* 6 Med. L. Rptr. 1961, 635 F.2d 945 (2d Cir. 1980), the Second Circuit said that the common law access right included a right to copy both visual and aural materials admitted into evidence in open court. Only the strongest showing of prejudice would justify denial. Copying, the court said, advances the interest in open trials identified in *Richmond.*

A similar result was reached by the Third Circuit in *In re Application of NBC (Criden)* 7 Med. L. Rptr. 1153, 648 F.2d 814 (3d Cir. 1981). The public has a right to see firsthand the impact of evidence, even if that impact extends beyond the courtroom, the court said. Since the media are surrogates for the public, media access serves that interest. Arguments that post-trial rebroadcasting of the tapes enhanced punishment or amounted to an invasion of privacy were rejected, as was the risk of prejudicing any retrial, which was seen as an issue based on speculation. Traditional judicial remedies would suffice to protect defendants, the court said.

A third common law case, involving former Congressman Thomas Jenrette, *In re Application of NBC,* 7 Med. L. Rptr. 1193, 653 F.2d 609 (D.C.Cir. 1981), produced mixed results. The Court reversed a trial court limit on access to tapes, noting that the lower court had failed to weigh adequately the strong tradition of public access. The appeals court told the trial judge to exercise discretion in excising portions of tapes that might harm innocent third parties, a practice that does not comport with common law traditions.

These cases and others, which were among the first to apply the principles of *Richmond,* if not its test, to access requests for court documents, presaged recent developments.

One case explored the weight to be given the First Amendment right of access to judicial documents, not the existence of the right. Relying on pre-*Richmond* federal court precedents, the court announced that denial of access to documents entered as evidence requires proof "that the denial serves an important governmental interest and that there is no less restrictive way to serve that governmental interest." In addition, the trial court should have held a hearing. The court recognized that a mere common law right of access "does not afford as much substantive protection * * * as does the First Amendment."

Rushford v. The New Yorker Magazine, Inc., 15 Med. L. Rptr. 1437, 846 F.2d 249 (4th Cir. 1988).

Similar results using a heightened standard have been based on common law,[108] on state constitutional law,[109] and on the status of documents as public records under the state statute.[110] Journalists should not assume that ready access may be had, though. Recall that the Supreme Court itself has only implied, not decided, that judicial records are subject to a First Amendment access right. In spring 1988, the Court denied certiorari in a case that recognized a right to transcripts of juror misconduct hearings but withheld the transcripts for fair trial reasons.[111]

Complications abound when access to records is sought. Getting access may depend on the nature of the records, for example. A number of courts hold to the distinction that records not introduced into evidence are not subject to any form of heightened review; usually, the denial of access is made on privacy grounds or on the ground that civil litigation is traditionally private.[112] The use to which materials, especially visual or audio records, might be put can also work against access. One court determined that allowing a television station access to a defendant's tape, even after trial, could prejudice the defendant's right to an appeal.[113] The records of a corporate dissolution were closed to protect

108. *Wilson v. American Motors Corp.,* 11 Med. L. Rptr. 2008, 759 F.2d 1568 (11th Cir. 1985) (applying a "compelling interest" test).
109. *Iowa Freedom of Information Council v. Wifvat,* 9 Med. L. Rptr. 1194, 328 N.W.2d 920 (Iowa 1983).
110. *Daily Gazette v. Withrow,* 14 Med. L. Rptr. 1447, 350 S.E.2d 738 (W.V. 1986).
111. *United States v. Edwards,* 14 Med. L. Rptr. 1399 (5th Cir. 1987). A similar rationale upheld denial of press access, despite a qualified First Amendment right, to materials used to support probable cause for search warrants in an ongoing criminal investigation. The public interest in effective law enforcement was given great weight. *In re Search Warrant,* 15 Med. L. Rptr. 1969, 855 F.2d 569 (8th Cir. 1988).
112. *In re Alexander Grant and Co. Litigation,* 14 Med. L. Rptr. 1370, 820 F.2d 352 (11th Cir. 1987).
113. *In re Pacific and Southern Co.,* 14 Med. L. Rptr. 1764, 361 S.E.2d 159 (Ga. 1987). One federal district court appeared to rely on a federal constitutional interest in physical or bodily privacy in refusing a television station's request to copy videotapes of an actual rape that had been entered into evidence at the defendant's trial. *In re Application of KSTP,* 6 Med. L. Rptr. 2249, 504 F.Supp. 360 (D.Minn. 1980).

trade secrets.[114] Access to juror names from venire lists has been denied based on privacy interests,[115] especially before trial. Litigants' privacy also was relied upon to uphold a restrictive order.[116]

The traditional reluctance to allow access to nondocumentary materials was recently upheld in an extraordinarily high profile case. President Bill Clinton was subpoenaed to testify in the savings and loan criminal fraud trial of defendants James McDougal, Susan McDougal, and Jim Guy Tucker. The court allowed Clinton to testify from the White House on videotape. The trial judge conducted the deposition personally by satellite link. The tape was ordered to be kept sealed. The Reporters Committee for Freedom of the Press requested physical access to the tape shortly after it was made. The judge refused. Instead, the judge ordered that a transcript of the tape would be made available after the videotape was played at trial. The Committee filed for expedited review with the Eighth Circuit, which affirmed the district court's order on August 12, 1996, two months after the tape had been played in court. On December 20, 1996, the Eighth Circuit issued its full opinion on the matter.

U.S. v. McDougal
25 MED. L. RPTR. 1097, NOS. 96–2606 AND 96–2671 (8TH CIR. 1996).

MCMILLIAN, J.:

A group of media organizations, including Reporters Committee for Freedom of the Press; Radio-Television New Directors Association; Capital Cities/American Broadcasting Companies, Inc.; Cable News Network, Inc.; National Broadcasting Company, Inc.; and CBS Inc. (hereinafter the Reporters), and a non-profit citizens' group, Citizens United (Citizens) (collectively appellants), each appeal from a final order entered in the United States District Court for the Eastern District of Arkansas denying their applications for access to a videotape recording of

---

114. *In re Crain Communications,* 14 Med. L. Rptr. 1951, 521 N.Y.S.2d 244 (N.Y.Sup.Ct., App.Div. 1987).
115. *Newsday v. Sise,* 14 Med. L. Rptr. 2140, 524 N.Y.S.2d 35 (N.Y. 1987); *contra, In re Baltimore Sun,* 14 Med. L. Rptr. 2379, 841 F.2d 74 (4th Cir. 1988).
116. *Courier-Journal v. Marshall,* 14 Med. L. Rptr. 1561, 828 F.2d 361 (6th Cir. 1987).

President William Jefferson Clinton's deposition testimony used at trial in the underlying criminal case. *United States v. McDougal,* No. LR–CR–95–173 (E.D. Ark. June 11, 1996). For reversal, appellants argue that the district court's denial of physical access to the videotape, so that they may make copies, violated their First Amendment and common law rights of access to judicial records. * * * Following oral argument on August 12, 1996, we entered an order which stated "[f]or reasons that will be stated in an opinion to follow, we affirm the district court's denial of access to the videotape." * * * We now set forth our reasons for affirming the district court's order.

BACKGROUND

* * *

In addition to the Reporters' request for access to the videotape, Citizens filed an application for access to the videotape and Dow Jones & Co. (Dow Jones) requested a copy of the unedited transcript and access to the unedited videotape of President Clinton's testimony. The President filed a motion for a protective order requesting that the original videotape and all copies thereof, whether edited or unedited, remain under seal.

Upon consideration of the outstanding motions and applications before it related to the videotapes and transcripts of President Clinton's deposition testimony, the district court granted Dow Jones's request for the unedited transcript but denied all requests for access to the videotape. * * * In the present case, the district court held that the press's First Amendment right of access to public information had been "fully satisfied in this instance by allowing the press to attend the playing of the videotaped deposition and in providing full access to the written transcript." As to the common law right of public access, the district court concluded that "[t]he Court need not decide at this time whether the common law right of access applies to videotaped testimony because even assuming it does, the Court finds, on balancing all the relevant factors, that the press's request to copy the videotape must be denied." The district court concluded that, on balance, the circumstances favored keeping the videotape under seal because: (1) substantial access to the information provided by the videotape had already been afforded; (2) release of the videotape would be inconsistent with the ban on cameras in the courtroom under Fed. R. Crim. P. 53; (3) in other cases involving videotaped testimony of a sitting president, the tapes were not released; and (4) there exists a potential for misuse of the tape, a consideration specifically recognized in *Nixon v. Warner Communications, Inc.,* 435 U.S. at 601 (noting President Nixon's argument that the audiotapes could be distorted through cutting, erasing, and splicing). * * * These appeals followed.

DISCUSSION

On appeal, appellants maintain that the district court's denial of access to the videotape violated their common law and First Amendment rights of access to judicial records. Thus, as a threshold matter, they argue that the videotape is a judicial record to which such rights attach, even though it is merely an electronic recording of a witness's testimony and was not itself admitted into evidence. Without citing any supporting authority, appellants argue that the videotape should be treated as a judicial record because "[t]he defendants should not be permitted to circumvent the common law and constitutional rights to access by marking only the transcript of the videotaped deposition." Brief for Appellants (Reporters) at 13. They also argue that, "[e]ffectively, the videotape was introduced into evidence by being played in open court." Appellants conclude that "[t]he videotape is like any other piece of evidence introduced or used in the courtroom. It becomes a judicial record subject to public review."

Assuming that the videotape is a judicial record, appellants contend that the denial of access violated their common law and constitutional rights under this court's holding in *In re Search Warrant for Secretarial Area Outside Office of Gunn,* 855 F.2d 569 (8th Cir. 1988) In *In re Search Warrant (Gunn),* a newspaper had unsuccessfully asked the district court to unseal documents that had been used to obtain a search warrant. This court considered the question of whether the documents in question were "judicial records" for purposes of the First Amendment analysis and opined that they were. *Id.* at 573. We nevertheless affirmed the district court's decision to keep the documents under

seal on grounds that they contained sensitive information concerning an ongoing nationwide criminal investigation, and line-by-line redaction was not practicable. * * * Appellants argue, in the present case, that their common law and First Amendment rights were violated because nondisclosure was not necessary to protect a compelling government interest. * * * On this point, appellants maintain that fear of misuse of the videotape in a political campaign does not constitute a compelling interest. They further assert, without citing authority, that "[t]he only government interest associated specifically with the Office of the President that might justify sealing a judicial record is national security." *Id.* at 23. The Reporters maintain that this court's holding in *In re Search Warrant (Gunn)* indicates that there is in this circuit "a strong presumption in favor of the common law right of access," Brief for Appellants (Reporters) at 4, notwithstanding our statement in *Webbe,* 791 F.2d at 106, that "[w]e decline to adopt *in toto* the reasoning of the Second, Third, Seventh, and District of Columbia Circuits in recognizing a 'strong presumption' in favor of the common law right of access." * * *

Appellants also challenge the district court's reliance on *Nixon v. Warner Communications, Inc.* and *Webbe.* They argue that *Nixon v. Warner Communications, Inc.* is not applicable to the present case because, in that case, the Presidential Recordings Act provided an alternative channel of access to the audiotapes in dispute. In *Webbe,* they note, the press was denied access to wiretap audiotapes, which had been admitted into evidence, in part because there was a chance that the tapes would be used again as evidence in future trials related to other pending criminal charges. Appellants argue that no similar considerations exist in the present case. * * *

Finally, as to the district court's reasoning that it was treating President Clinton's testimony in a manner equivalent to live testimony provided at trial (because cameras are not permitted in the courtroom under Fed. R. Crim. P. 53), appellants argue that the district court's decision to keep the videotape under seal actually gives the President special treatment because he was the one who requested permission to testify on videotape. Thus, they argue, the district court's disposition violates their common law and First Amendment rights. We disagree.

Common Law Right of Public Access to Judicial Records

Upon careful review, we hold that appellants' common law right of public access to judicial records was not violated as a consequence of the district court's denial of physical access to the videotape of President Clinton's testimony. To begin, we hold as a matter of law that the videotape itself is not a judicial record to which the common law right of public access attaches. Appellants are incorrect to assume that this issue turns on whether or not the videotape itself was admitted into evidence and that, therefore, the litigants at trial have control to decide whether or not the public's right may be exercised. Even if the defendants had moved for the admission of the videotape into evidence, the videotape itself would not necessarily have become a judicial record subject to public review. We conclude, for reasons unrelated to the fact that the videotape was never admitted into evidence, that the videotape itself is not a judicial record for purposes of this analysis.

The district court in the present case declined to decide whether the videotape itself was a judicial record to which the common law right attaches, but did note that courts are divided over whether a videotape of witness testimony, taken pursuant to Fed. R. Crim. P. 15, is a judicial record. * * *

In *Nixon v. Warner Communications, Inc.* and *Webbe,* the audiotapes in dispute were recordings of the primary conduct of witnesses or parties. Therefore, those recordings were similar to documentary evidence to which the common law right of public access ordinarily may apply. By contrast, the videotape at issue in the present case is merely an electronic recording of witness testimony. Although the public had a right to hear and observe the testimony at the time and in the manner it was delivered to the jury in the courtroom, we hold that there was, and is, no additional common law right to obtain, for purposes of copying, the electronic recording of that testimony. By comparison, Rule 53 of the Federal Rules of Criminal Procedure prohibits photography or other electronic recording of live witness testimony in the courtroom. Our holding today comports with Rule 53 because it mandates that Rule 15 deponents are treated equally to witnesses who testify in court, in person. In other words, contrary to appellants' argument, our holding does not give special treatment to Rule 15 deponents vis-a-vis witnesses who present live in-court testimony but rather puts them on equal footing. Accordingly, we conclude that appellants have failed to assert a cognizable common law claim in the present case because the videotape itself is not a judicial record to which the common law right of public access attaches.

Even if we were to assume that the videotape is a judicial record subject to the common law right of public access, we would hold that the district court did not abuse its discretion in denying access in the present case. The legal standards governing the common law right are well-established in this circuit. This court stated in *Webbe* "the consideration of competing values is one heavily reliant on the observations and insights of the presiding judge." * * *

Moreover, our deferential standard under the common law is in harmony with the Supreme Court's analysis in *Nixon v. Warner Communications, Inc.,* 435 U.S. at 598, in which the Court stated that "[e]very court has supervisory power over its own records and files, and access has been denied where the court files might become a vehicle for improper purposes." The Supreme Court concluded, with respect to the common law right of public access, "the decision as to access is best left to the sound discretion of the trial court, a discretion to be exercised in light of the relevant facts and circumstances of the particular case." *Id.* at 599.

We now turn to the district court's balancing of competing interests in the present case. As noted above, the district court concluded that, even assuming the videotape is a judicial record for purposes of the common law analysis, the circumstances favored keeping the videotape sealed because: (1) substantial access to the information provided by the videotape had already been afforded; (2) release of the videotape would be inconsistent with the ban on cameras in the courtroom under Fed. R. Crim. P. 53; (3) in other cases involving videotaped testimony of a sitting president, the tapes were not released; and (4) there exists a potential for misuse of the tape, a consideration specifically recognized in *Nixon v. Warner Communications,* 435 U.S. at 601 (noting President Nixon's argument that the audiotapes could be distorted through cutting, erasing, and splicing). In addition to these sound reasons stated by the district court, we note the following compelling considerations which further support the conclusion that the district court did not abuse its discretion.

In *Nixon v. Warner Communications, Inc.,* 435 U.S. at 602–03, the Supreme Court considered it a "crucial fact" that giving the press access to the audiotapes for purposes of making copies involved "a court's cooperation in furthering their commercial plans." The Supreme Court further explained that the courts have

> a responsibility to exercise an informed discretion as to release of the tapes, with a sensitive appreciation of the circumstances that led to their production. This responsibility does not permit copying upon demand. Otherwise, there would exist a danger that the court could become a partner in the use of the subpoenaed material "to gratify private spite or promote public scandal," with no corresponding assurance of public benefit.

Id. at 603 (quoting *In re Caswell,* 18 R.I. 835, 836 (1893)). We agree, as a matter of public policy, that courts should avoid becoming the instrumentalities of commercial or other private pursuits.

We also note that granting access to the videotape of President Clinton's testimony could harm the strong public interest in preserving the availability of material testimony in criminal trials. On the other hand, the public's interest in gaining access to the videotape recording is only marginal because the testimony has already been made visually and aurally accessible in the courtroom and the transcript has been widely distributed and publicized.

Finally, as a matter of historical interest and public policy, there has never been compelled incourt live testimony of a former or sitting president, nor has there ever been compelled dissemination of copies of a videotape recording of a sitting president's testimony. These facts, we think, suggest that there is a strong judicial tradition of proscribing public access to recordings of testimony given by a sitting president, which further supports our conclusion that the district court did not abuse its discretion in the present case.

First Amendment Right of Access to Public Information

Upon *de novo* review, we also agree, as a matter of law, with the district court's holding that the

First Amendment right of access to public information does not extend to the videotape of President Clinton's deposition testimony. As the district court noted, members of the public, including the press, were given access to the information contained in the videotape. Therefore, appellants received all the information to which they were entitled under the First Amendment.

In addressing the press's First Amendment right to public information as applied to the facts in *Nixon v. Warner Communications, Inc.,* the Supreme Court stated:

> The First Amendment generally grants the press no right to information superior to that of the general public. "Once beyond the confines of the courthouse, a news-gathering agency may publicize, within wide limits, what its representatives have heard and seen in the courtroom. But the line is drawn at the courthouse door; and within, a reporter's constitutional rights are no greater than those of any other member of the public."

In other words, in *Nixon v. Warner Communications, Inc.,* the Supreme Court held that, where access to audiotapes was sought by the press on grounds that they were public information, the press's First Amendment right was adequately protected because members of the public, including the press, were (1) permitted to listen to the audiotapes as they were played to the jury in the courtroom and (2) furnished with copies of the written transcript. Under these circumstances, the First Amendment right of public access did not extend to the audiotapes themselves. Similarly, in the present case, the First Amendment right does not extend to the videotape in dispute.

CONCLUSION

For the foregoing reasons, we affirm the district court's denial of access to the videotape. * * * The order of the district court is affirmed. Judgment shall be entered accordingly.

COMMENT

One plausible interpretation of the *McDougal* opinion is that the court was showing deference to the office of the president. The court relied almost solely upon the pre-*Richmond* case *Nixon v. Warner Communications, Inc.,* 3 Med.

L. Rptr. 2074, 435 U.S. 589 (1978), in deciding that the request to obtain and copy the tapes should be denied. There is a key difference between *Nixon* and *McDougal*, however: the Nixon tapes were not introduced into evidence at a trial. "What transpires in the court room is public property." *Craig v. Harney*, 1 Med. L. Rptr. 1310, 331 U.S. 367 (1947). Does it not follow that the tape itself, not just the playing of it in court, is public as well? "There is no special perquisite of the judiciary which enables it, as distinguished from other institutions of democratic government, to suppress, edit, or censor events which transpire in proceedings before it." *Id.*

The Status of Electronic Coverage: Cameras in the Courts

The majority of states today allow photographic, audio, and broadcast or cable coverage of judicial proceedings. Only Indiana, Mississippi, South Dakota, and the District of Columbia do not allow some type of access. Many states require the consent of the judge or of the parties in the case, but in just as many, access is automatic.

The federal courts currently bar electronic coverage. After allowing electronic coverage of civil actions in six federal district courts and two circuit courts of appeals as a test from 1991 to 1993, the Federal Judicial Center issued a report in 1994 that recommended continuing electronic coverage.[117] The U.S. Judicial Conference rejected the recommendation and also rejected a recommendation to open criminal cases to electronic coverage.[118] The conference later agreed to open circuit court of appeals proceedings to electronic coverage, but that meant little to journalists because oral arguments on appeal are seldom well suited to broadcast news. The Supreme Court has consistently declined to allow electronic coverage of its proceedings.

The 1994 report also included a summary and results of commissioned content analyses of broadcast coverage. The report concluded:

[T]he stories did not provide a high level of detail about the legal process in the cases covered. In addi-

tion, the analysis revealed that increasing the proportion of courtroom footage used in a story did not significantly increase the information given about the legal process.[119]

One of the main arguments of those advocating electronic coverage is that it will improve the quality of news coverage and will enable the public to better understand the legal system. Those claims have always been difficult to support.[120]

Whenever the question of whether to allow broadcast coverage has arisen, however, any potential benefits of electronic coverage have not been the issue. Instead, the major issue has been whether letting cameras and tape recorders in would somehow affect the process, either by affecting a criminal defendant's right to a fair trial or perhaps by skewing the proceedings generally. Bench and bar have tended to equate television's power to attract an audience with power to prejudice.

Prior to the 1960s, many states allowed audio and broadcast coverage of legal proceedings. Policemen posed suspects for the cameras and permitted them to announce their guilt to the world. In 1961 a jury reenacted its deliberations, theorized on the guilt or innocence of the defendant, and discussed the death penalty for a videotape rebroadcast the day before sentencing.[121] In the mid-1960s, two cases temporarily stopped such practices.

The Supreme Court first took note of these experiments in broadcasting in the case of Wilbur Rideau. After his arrest on suspicion of bank robbery and murder, Rideau was interviewed in jail by a film crew. A cooperative sheriff stood by posing his prisoner. He confessed, and his confession went out over the airwaves, not once but three times. A change of venue was denied; Rideau was tried, convicted, and sentenced to death.

When the case got to the U.S. Supreme Court, Justice Potter Stewart in his opinion for the Court reversed. "For anyone who has ever watched television," he said, "the conclusion

---

117. Federal Judicial Center, *Electronic Media Coverage of Federal Civil Proceedings: An Evaluation of the Pilot Program in Six District Courts and Two Courts of Appeal* 43–46 (1994).
118. "News Notes," Med. L. Rptr. Vol. 23, No. 1, January 3, 1995.

119. Federal Judicial Center, 36.
120. Harris, *The Appearance of Justice: Court TV, Conventional Television, and Public Understanding of the Criminal Justice System*, 35 Ariz. L. Rev. 785 (1993).
121. *United States v. Rees*, 193 F.Supp. 864 (D.Md. 1961).

cannot be avoided that this spectacle, to the tens of thousands of people who saw and heard it, in a very real sense was Rideau's trial—at which he pleaded guilty to murder. Any subsequent court proceedings in a community so pervasively exposed to such a spectacle could be but a hollow formality." *Rideau v. Louisiana,* 1 Med. L. Rptr. 1183, 373 U.S. 723 (1963).

There is a strong implication in the Court's opinion that no judicial remedies in either trial or pretrial period would have overcome the prejudicial effects of the broadcasts. Presumably, the power of the camera outstrips the power of the pen—an assumption that may no longer be safe.

The case of Billie Sol Estes came to the Court two years later. Estes, an erstwhile Texas financier and former confidant of Lyndon B. Johnson, went to trial in 1962 charged with theft, swindling, and embezzlement. Over Estes's objections, the trial judge permitted television coverage of the pretrial hearing and portions of the trial, as Texas law allowed. Upon conviction Estes appealed partly on the ground that the cameras deprived him of due process of law. By a narrow margin (5–4), the Supreme Court agreed, and courtroom doors closed to cameras throughout the land. *Estes v. State of Texas,* 1 Med. L. Rptr. 1187, 381 U.S. 532 (1965).

In *Estes,* the Court appeared to hold that television coverage constituted a *per se* violation of a defendant's Sixth Amendment right to a fair trial. In the majority opinion, Justice Clark noted four major reasons in support of a reversal. Television would have great impact on jurors. It would likely impair the quality of testimony. It adds a burden of oversight to a trial judge's work. In addition, television would amount to a form of mental harassment for the defendant. In sum:

> [T]he circumstances and extraneous influences intruding upon the solemn decorum of court procedure in the televised trial are far more serious than in cases involving only newspaper coverage.

Justice Clark granted to television a degree of influence and power that, if ever true, has certainly waned in the intervening decades.

Possible future changes in television technology and in public reactions to television prompted Justice Harlan to concur separately in *Estes.* Although "mischievous potentialities" had been at work in that case, *"the day may come,"* said Harlan, *"when television will have become*

so commonplace an affair in the daily life of the average person as to dissipate all reasonable likelihood that its use in courtrooms may disparage the judicial process." [Emphasis added.]

Add Justice Clark's own qualification— "When the advances in these arts permit reporting by printing press or by television without their present hazards to a fair trial we will have another case"—and you have almost an invitation for the camera to enter the courtroom.

Prior to the trial of Bruno Richard Hauptmann for the kidnapping of the Lindbergh baby, camera coverage depended on the presiding judge. Some welcomed it; some banned it. On balance, photographers acquitted themselves well in covering that notorious case, going so far as to pool their resources. Conventional history would have it otherwise. The transgressions of a newsreel crew are all that is remembered.[122]

After that confused and sensational case had concluded and the American Bar Association had time to think about it, the organization added Canon 35 to its statement of judicial ethics, recommending prohibition of all photographic and broadcast coverage of courtroom proceedings. In 1963 Canon 35 was amended to include television. In 1972 the Code of Judicial Conduct superseded the Canons of Judicial Ethics, and Canon 3A(7) reaffirmed and replaced Canon 35.

In 1978 the ABA Committee on Fair Trial– Free Press proposed revised standards that would permit camera coverage at a trial judge's discretion. Meanwhile, in 1978 the Conference of State Chief Justices, by a vote of 44 to 1, had approved a resolution recommending that the highest court of each state promulgate standards and guidelines regulating radio, television, and other electronic coverage of court proceedings.

By 1989, forty-four states were permitting video and/or audio coverage on either a permanent or an experimental basis, and federal courts had begun experimenting with video recording for record-keeping purposes.[123] Currently, only thirteen states require the consent of the defendant to allow coverage, down from about half in

---

122. Kielbowicz, *The Story behind the Adoption of the Ban on Courtroom Cameras,* 63 Judicature 14 (June/July 1979).
123. "Official Cameras in U.S. Courts," *The News Media and the Law* (Fall 1988), p. 53.

1983. Thirty-seven states allow coverage of any trials, civil or criminal. Most also allow coverage of appellate courts.

States with experimental programs usually later adopt permanent programs. No experimenting state has decided to return to banning coverage, although Ohio and Iowa have adopted less liberal permanent rules.

The rules themselves are diverse, Florida and a handful of states following Florida's lead place the burden of showing a necessity for closure on the party seeking closure. Most states leave closure to the discretion of the judge, who is usually admonished to close only if the fair administration of justice requires. The least broadcast access is available when a party's consent is needed.[124] When Michigan's experimental program, which required consent of *all* parties, resulted in no broadcast or photographic coverage in months, the Michigan Supreme Court amended its order to create a presumption of openness.[125]

Within the rules, specific limitations may be placed on which parties may be pictured. Many programs prohibit photographing juries, for example. Most plans require that the media pool resources to avoid intruding on the courtroom with large amounts of equipment. Judges generally have unappealable authority to regulate the time, place, and manner of coverage.

Still many states, including those with some provisions allowing coverage, keep trial proceedings closed to cameras. States often exempt, either by rule or statute, cases involving child custody, divorce, juvenile crimes, police informants, relocated witnesses, undercover agents, sex crimes, and evidentiary suppression hearings.

With Alabama, Georgia, New Hampshire, Texas, Washington, and Colorado, Florida was among the first states to experiment anew with the camera. Its test run began in July 1977. When the pilot program ended, the Florida Supreme Court received and reviewed briefs, reports, letters of comment, and studies. It conducted its own survey of attorneys, witnesses, jurors, and court personnel. A separate survey of judges was taken. The court studied the experience of other states allowing cameras and concluded that "on balance there [was] more to be gained than lost by permitting electronic media coverage of judicial proceedings subject to standards for such coverage."[126] The judge would be in control in the interests of the fair administration of justice, and limited quantities of equipment would be placed in fixed positions. Florida soon became the arena for testing the constitutionality of camera coverage.

The grand test of constitutionality came when two Miami Beach policemen challenged their convictions on burglary charges because portions of their trials had been televised over their objections.

In a unanimous decision grounded in federalism, the Supreme Court rejected their claim and found no constitutional problem with regulated access for cameras in states that so chose. But the ruling provided no right of camera access in states that forbade it or in the federal courts.

Calling for further experimentation to evaluate the camera's psychological and other effects, Chief Justice Burger's unanimous majority opinion seemed to be saying that *Chandler* would not be the last word on broadcast coverage. Justices Stewart and White suggested that *Estes* be formally overturned.

Chandler v. Florida
7 MED. L. RPTR. 1041, 449 U.S. 560, 101 S. CT. 802, 66 L. ED. 2D 740 (1981).

Chief Justice BURGER delivered the opinion of the Court:

* * *

At the outset, it is important to note that in promulgating the revised Canon 3A(7), the Florida Supreme Court pointedly rejected any state or federal constitutional right of access on the part of photographers or the broadcast media to televise or electronically record and thereafter disseminate court proceedings. It carefully framed its holding as follows:

> While we have concluded that the due process clause does not prohibit electronic media coverage

---

124. Dyer and Hauserman, *Electronic Coverage of the Courts: Exceptions to Exposure*, 75 Georgetown L.J. 1633 (1987).

125. *In re Film or Electronic Coverage*, Administrative Order No. 1988–1 (Mich. May 31, 1988).

126. *Petition of the Post-Newsweek Stations, Florida, Inc.*, 5 Med. L. Rptr. 1039, 370 So.2d 764 (Fla. 1979).

of judicial proceedings per se, by the same token we reject the argument of the [Post-Newsweek stations] that the first and sixth amendments to the United States Constitution mandate entry of the electronic media into judicial proceedings. Petition of the Post-Newsweek Stations, Florida, Inc., 370 So.2d at 774.

* * *

The Florida Supreme Court predicated the revised Canon 3A(7) upon its supervisory authority over the Florida courts, and not upon any constitutional imperative. Hence, we have before us only the limited question of the Florida Supreme Court's authority to promulgate the canon for the trial of cases in Florida courts.

This Court has no supervisory jurisdiction over state courts and, in reviewing a state court judgment, we are confined to evaluating it in relation to the Federal Constitution.

Appellants rely chiefly on *Estes v. Texas,* 381 U.S. 532 (1964), and Chief Justice Warren's separate concurring opinion in that case. They argue that the televising of criminal trials is inherently a denial of due process, and they read *Estes* as announcing a *per se* constitutional rule to that effect.

* * *

Parsing the six opinions in *Estes,* one is left with a sense of doubt as to precisely how much of Justice Clark's opinion was joined in, and supported by, Justice Harlan. * * * [W]e conclude that *Estes* is not to be read as announcing a constitutional rule barring still photographic, radio and television coverage in all cases and under all circumstances. It does not stand as an absolute ban on state experimentation with an evolving technology, which, in terms of modes of mass communication, was in its relative infancy in 1964, and is, even now, in a state of continuing change.

* * *

An absolute constitutional ban on broadcast coverage of trials cannot be justified simply because there is a danger that, in some cases, prejudicial broadcast accounts of pretrial and trial events may impair the ability of jurors to decide the issue of guilt or innocence uninfluenced by extraneous matter. The risk of juror prejudice in some cases does not justify an absolute ban on news coverage of trials by the printed media; so also the risk of such prejudice

does not warrant an absolute constitutional ban on all broadcast coverage. A case attracts a high level of public attention because of its intrinsic interest to the public and the manner of reporting the event. The risk of juror prejudice is present in any publication of a trial, but the appropriate safeguard against such prejudice is the defendant's right to demonstrate that the media's coverage of his case—be it printed or broadcast—compromised the ability of the particular jury that heard the case to adjudicate fairly. * * *

As we noted earlier, the concurring opinions in *Estes* expressed concern that the very presence of media cameras and recording devices at a trial inescapably give rise to an adverse psychological impact on the participants in the trial. This kind of general psychological prejudice, allegedly present whenever there is a broadcast coverage of a trial, is different from the more particularized problem of prejudicial impact discussed earlier. If it could be demonstrated that the mere presence of a photographic and recording equipment and the knowledge that the event would be broadcast invariably and uniformly affected the conduct of participants so as to impair fundamental fairness, our task would be simple; prohibition of broadcast coverage of trials would be required.

* * *

Not unimportant to the position asserted by Florida and other states is the change in television technology since 1962, when Estes was tried. It is urged, and some empirical data are presented, that many of the negative factors found in *Estes*—cumbersome equipment, cables, distracting lighting, numerous camera technicians—are less substantial factors today than they were at that time.

It is also significant that safeguards have been built into the experimental programs in state courts, and into the Florida program, to avoid some of the most egregious problems envisioned by the six opinions in the *Estes* case. Florida admonishes its courts to take special pains to protect certain witnesses. * * *

The Florida guidelines place on trial judges positive obligations to be on guard to protect the fundamental right of the accused to a fair trial. The Florida statute, being one of the few permitting broadcast coverage of criminal trials over the objection of the accused, raises problems not present in the statutes of other states. Inherent in electronic coverage of a trial is the risk that the very awareness by the accused of the coverage and the contemplated broadcast may adversely affect the conduct of the participants and the fairness of the trial, yet leave no evidence of how the conduct or the trial's fairness was affected. Given this danger, it is significant that Florida requires that objections of the accused to coverage be heard and considered on the record by the trial court. * * *

Whatever may be the "mischievous potentialities [of broadcast coverage] for intruding upon the detached atmosphere which should always surround the judicial process," *Estes v. Texas,* 381 U.S., at 587, at present no one has been able to present empirical data sufficient to establish that the mere presence of the broadcast media inherently has an adverse effect on that process. * * * The appellants have offered nothing to demonstrate that their trial was subtly tainted by broadcast coverage—let alone that all broadcast trials would be so tainted. * * *

The unanswered question is whether electronic coverage will bring public humiliation upon the accused with such randomness that it will evoke due process concerns by being "unusual in the same way that being struck by lightning" "is unusual." * * *

To say that the appellants have not demonstrated that broadcast coverage is inherently a denial of due process is not to say that the appellants were in fact accorded all of the protections of due process in their trial. As noted earlier, a defendant has the right on review to show that the media's coverage of his case—printed or broadcast—compromised the ability of the jury to judge him fairly. Alternatively, a defendant might show that broadcast coverage of his particular case had an adverse impact on the trial participants sufficient to constitute a denial of due process. Neither showing was made in this case.

To demonstrate prejudice in a specific case a defendant must show something more than juror awareness that the trial is such as to attract the attention of broadcasters. No doubt the very presence of a camera in the courtroom made the jurors aware that the trial was thought to be of sufficient interest to the public to warrant coverage. But the appellants have not attempted to show with any specificity that the presence of cameras impaired the ability of the jurors * * * to decide the case on only the evidence before

them or that their trial was affected adversely by the impact on any of the participants of the presence of cameras and the prospect of broadcast.

* * *

Absent a showing of prejudice of constitutional dimensions to these defendants, there is no reason for this Court either to endorse or to invalidate Florida's experiment.

* * *

We hold that the Constitution does not prohibit a state from experimenting with the program authorized by revised Canon 3A(7).

COMMENT

Although many difficult questions remain unanswered, they are not mainly legal questions. How does editing of proceedings affect the perceptions of the audience? Does broadcast coverage actually educate the public about the judicial system, as broadcasters have argued when seeking camera coverage? Does broadcast coverage affect the fairness of trials? Can photojournalists function with quiet dignity? Did televising of the O. J. Simpson criminal trial turn out to be a setback for cameras in the courtroom?

The biggest holdout from camera coverage is the federal court system. While he was Chief Justice, Warren Burger vowed that cameras would never be allowed in federal courts. He was as good as his word. Allowance of broadcast coverage has consistently been considered to be within the discretion of the various state and federal courts in their capacities as rulemakers.

The administration of electronic coverage rules is ultimately in the hands of the judges in proceedings the electronic media wish to cover. Almost all jurisdictions require at least some advance notice of media coverage, if only so that arrangements can be made for coverage. In general, a trial judge's discretionary decision to bar or closely limit electronic coverage is considered virtually unappealable. *Iowa v. Douglas,* 20 Med. L. Rptr. 1340, 485 N.W.2d 619 (Iowa 1992).

Judges in many states have been reluctant to grant access for electronic coverage despite state rules allowing it. In one case, a newspaper tired of its photographers being routinely refused access and asked a higher court to order a trial court judge to grant access.

Detroit Free Press v. Thirty-Sixth District Judge

24 MED. L. RPTR 1886, NO. 170071 (MICH. APP. 1996).

PER CURIAM:

Defendant appeals the circuit court's supplemental order of superintending control, entered following the circuit court's determination that defendant had violated an earlier order granting writ of superintending control, pertaining to defendant's handling of requests for media coverage of proceedings in his courtroom. We conclude that although the circuit court did not err in concluding it had authority to exercise superintending control and did not abuse its discretion in determining defendant had violated the initial writ, the supplemental order is overly broad. We thus affirm in part and vacate in part.

Plaintiff brought an action seeking a writ of superintending control in August 1992, alleging that defendant denied *Free Press* photographers access to court proceedings on five occasions over a six-month period, and had a standing policy never to allow cameras in his courtroom, which he had stated on the record. Plaintiff alleged defendant's blanket exclusion of cameras and failure to make findings and articulate them on the record violated Supreme Court Administrative Order No. 1989–1 (AO 1989–1), which states:

Film or Electronic Media Coverage of Court Proceedings

The following guidelines shall apply to film or electronic media coverage of proceedings in Michigan courts:

* * *

2. Limitations
   (a) Film or electronic media coverage shall be allowed upon request in all court proceedings. Requests by representatives of media agencies for such coverage must be made in writing to the clerk of the particular court not less than three business days before the proceeding is scheduled to begin. A judge has the discretion to honor a request that does not comply with the requirements of this subsection. The court shall provide that the parties be notified of a request for film or electronic media coverage.
   (b) A judge may terminate, suspend, limit or exclude film or electronic media coverage at any time upon a finding, made and artic-

ulated on the record in the exercise of discretion, that the fair administration of justice requires such action, or that rules established under this order or additional rules imposed by the judge have been violated. The judge has sole discretion to exclude coverage of certain witnesses, including but not limited to the victims of sex crimes and their families, police informants, undercover agents, and relocated witnesses.
   (c) Film or electronic media coverage of the jurors or the jury selection process shall not be permitted.
   (d) A trial judge's decision to terminate, suspend, limit, or exclude film or electronic media coverage is not appealable, by right or by leave.

* * *

Following a hearing, the circuit court entered an order granting writ of superintending control on October 13, 1992, which stated in pertinent part that defendant (the presiding judge):

. . . shall allow, upon proper request submitted not less than three business days in advance, pursuant to Supreme Court Administrative Order 1989–1, film or electronic media coverage of Court proceedings in his courtroom; . . . may deny a three-day advance request only for reasons specifically related to the court proceeding for which coverage is requested, and in which the fair administration of justice requires such action. These reasons must be articulated on the record at the time the request is denied. It is not sufficient reason to deny coverage on the basis that the parties or witnesses involved must receive notification under the Administrative Order or give their consent;

* * *

IT IS FURTHER ORDERED that the Court retains jurisdiction to enforce the terms of this Order.

* * *

Following entry of the writ granting superintending control, plaintiff made additional requests to photograph proceedings in defendant's courtroom and, after requests were allegedly denied or limited, moved to show cause why defendant should not be held in contempt for violation of the order granting writ of superintending control. At a show cause hearing in October 1993, there was testimony that defendant continued to deny plaintiff's requests for media coverage or imposed conditions more restrictive than AO 1989–1. One of plaintiff's requests was filed three days in advance but was denied as untimely. Another request was denied because it did not identify a particular proceeding, but rather indicated coverage was sought of proceedings on a particular day. There was also testimony that, although defendant approved several requests, the approvals were subject to conditions defendant imposed which were set forth in a document entitled "Special Court Rules for the Press," and attached to the approvals.

* * *

The circuit court determined defendant violated the initial order and issued a Supplemental Order of Superintending Control on October 22, 1993, which stated:

> . . . that Judge Bradfield committed three separate violations of this Court's October 13, 1992 Order Granting Writ of Superintending Control, the Court being of the opinion that a Supplemental Order should be issued further restricting Judge Bradfield's power to make decisions regarding media access to his courtroom in light of his violations of the Superintending Control Order . . .

> [1] IT IS ORDERED that Judge Bradfield must grant all requests for film or electronic media coverage of court proceedings, whether or not the request is made three business days before the proceeding;

> [2] IT IS FURTHER ORDERED that the request for film or electronic coverage of court proceedings need not specify a particular case;

> [3] . . . that the only proceedings for which Judge Bradfield has discretion to exclude film or electronic media coverage are those specifically enumerated in the last sentence of [paragraphs] 2(b), and in 2(c), of Supreme Court Administrative Order 1989–1;

> [4] . . . that Judge Bradfield can give reasonable directions to media regarding where any film or electronic cameras can be located in his courtroom when absolutely necessary to prevent disruption in the Court in a particular proceeding;

> [5] . . . that Judge Bradfield's authority to limit film or electronic media coverage is restricted to those situations set forth in this Supplemental Order, and shall be construed narrowly;

> [6] . . . that Judge Bradfield's "Special Court Rules for the Press," dated January 1, 1993 are VACATED, and Judge Bradfield shall not promulgate any such rules;

* * *

Defendant's initial argument, that the circuit court lacked authority to issue a writ of superintending control in the first instance, is not properly before us. Defendant concedes he was unsuccessful in his appeal from the original order. In any case, we believe the circuit court had both jurisdiction, MCR 3.302(D), and authority to issue the original order.

Generally, for superintending control to lie, a plaintiff must establish the absence of an adequate legal remedy and that the defendant failed to perform a clear legal duty. * * *

By its terms, all Michigan courts are subject to and bound by AO 1989–1. *See, e.g., Frederick v. Presque Isle Judge,* 439 Mich. 1, 9; 476 N.W.2d 142 (1991). Administrative orders are binding until changed or modified by the Supreme Court. *Detroit & Northern v. Woodworth,* 54 Mich.App. 517, 520; 221 N.W.2d 190 (1974). The circuit court properly determined defendant's general and non-particularized policy of excluding photographic coverage violated his clear legal duty under AO 1989–1.

The circuit court's initial order mandated compliance with AO 1989–1's requirement that denials of or limitations on timely requests for media coverage be articulated on the record, and precluded blanket exclusions of media coverage, in keeping with the AO's spirit that media coverage be allowed.

However, the supplemental order of superintending control, which defendant argues is overly broad, exceeded the dictates of AO 1989–1, and to the extent it did, we agree with defendant that the circuit court exceeded its superintending control power.

> The superintending court does not substitute its judgment or discretion for that of the magistrate; neither does it act directly in the premises. Rather it examines the record made before the magistrate to determine whether there was such an abuse of discretion as would amount to a failure to perform a clear legal duty; and in such case, the superintending court orders the magistrate to perform his duty.

Defendant was bound to obey AO 1989–1, and to obey the order of superintending control, as it was entered by a court with proper jurisdiction. *In the Matter of Hague,* 412 Mich. 523, 544–545; 315 N.W.2d 524 (1982). We conclude that the circuit court did not abuse its discretion in determining defendant's special rules for the press, which by their own terms "superseded" AO–1989–1, violated the original writ of super-intending control, as did his denials of certain press requests. Although the circuit court's issuance of a supplemental order under those circumstances was not an abuse of discretion, the supplemental order, in the paragraphs we have numbered [1], [3], and [5], goes beyond ordering defendant to perform his legal duties. We thus vacate those provisions.

Affirmed in part, and vacated in part.

COMMENT

The *Free Press* case was not much of a victory for the newspaper. The court of appeals approved only the circuit court's order that Judge Bradfield follow the rules regarding electronic coverage. The supplemental order that apparently required that Bradfield actually let electronic media in was seen as beyond its authority. In effect, the decision affirms that judges must consider access requests and must state reasons for refusing access on the record, but may not be required to have especially good reasons.

C H A P T E R   7

FREEDOM OF INFORMATION: ACCESS TO NEWS OF GOVERNMENT

CHAPTER OUTLINE

GOVERNMENT VERSUS PRESS AND PUBLIC?

Access to information and privacy/secrecy are interdependent: whatever is added to one must be taken from the other. Privacy and secrecy, however, are not synonymous. Privacy is personal: one's private space is intruded upon, or an intimate detail of one's persona is published without consent. Secrecy is institutional: an agency of government chooses to conduct its business in secret, to make its work product inaccessible to the public, or to conceal from the public what it is up to. The dichotomy is suggested in the very title of the Department of Justice's Office of Information and Privacy, which plays a role in balancing the two interests when defending a lawsuit brought against a federal agency for nondisclosure.

While the American press has its weaknesses and excesses, ultimately democracy is sustained by an informed public and by those institutions that seek out and distribute information about government, with some reasonable and adequately supported exceptions. James Madison may have put it best: "A popular government without popular information or the means of acquiring it is but a Prologue to a Farce or Tragedy; or perhaps both. Knowledge will forever govern ignorance: And people who mean to be their own Governors, must arm themselves with the power which knowledge gives."[1]

---

1. *Writings of James Madison* 103 (G. Hunt, ed. 1910).

Democratic societies have paid a high price for unnecessary governmental secrecy. The Gulf of Tonkin resolution[2] of August 10, 1964, for example, which was based on faulty and much disputed factual assertions by the White House, led Congress and the public closer to the abyss in the Vietnam War and, indeed, may have changed the course of American history.

The 1983 invasion of Grenada, another example of government business conducted in secret, seemed at the time like the apogee of a tug-of-war between press and government, between those accustomed to hiding information and those committed to uncovering it, however mixed the motives of both may have been. Outcries from the press against a government decision to exclude all eyewitness media coverage led to a postinvasion compromise: a pool of reporters would be allowed access to combat zones in the future.

This arrangement was applied with negative results to the Panama incursion on December 20, 1989. Rep. Charles Rangel (D-NY) had to file a formal Freedom of Information Act (FOIA) (5 U.S.C. § 552) request with Defense Secretary Dick Cheney to get Panama invasion footage. The FOIA, the federal open-records statute, and fifty state open meetings laws are not written exclusively for the press but for the public at large and will be discussed in more detail later.

Then came the Gulf War in January 1991 and the most draconian restrictions on press coverage of military actions in American history. Again pooling was imposed for coverage of specific military events. The mobility of journalists was strictly controlled; interviews could be conducted only in the presence of commanding or public affairs officers; and press copy, including photographs and videotapes, was subjected to prepublication review by military censors. The daily military briefings reminded some veteran reporters of what they had called the "Five O'Clock Follies" in Saigon—military information officers providing Vietnam War correspondents with carefully worded handouts and misleading or empty answers to questions about the conduct of the war.

To avoid charges that the Gulf War procedures constituted "prior restraint," an exhaus-

tive appeals process was written into the military's press guidelines: news organizations were permitted to make final judgments as to publication, but delays meant that many stories would no longer be news. "In the end," said a detailed Freedom Forum report on tension between media and military, "media coverage of the Gulf War was shaped far more by the military's concern for achieving a decisive victory than the media's paramount goals of comprehensive and accurate coverage."[3]

A legal challenge to these rules brought by *Nation* magazine, *Harper's,* the *Village Voice, Mother Jones,* and others was dismissed more than a year later by a federal district judge in New York as lacking specificity and as being moot because the war had ended.[4] A subsequent challenge to the military barring of press and public access to Dover (Delaware) Air Force Base, a receiving center for war fatalities, also failed.[5] One of the government's arguments was the "privacy" of grieving survivors, even though military family support groups joined the media as plaintiffs in that lawsuit.

One might have expected a major confrontation between press and government in Somalia, especially after television cameras met U.S. troops as they waded ashore. It didn't happen, but the Department of Defense still controls the development and composition of press pools in potential combat areas. Confrontation between press and media may reappear in Bosnia.

All governments deal in disinformation and secrecy for what they claim to be reasons of national security. Although some of the facts eventually emerged, the American public was for a time denied information about the bombing of a Pan Am airliner over Lockerbie, Scotland, American hostages in Lebanon, Soviet defense spending, the savings and loan scandals, the drug wars, and Gen. Manuel Noriega's overthrow by American forces, with its attendant Panamanian civilian casualties, to name only a few highly vis-

---

2. P.L. 88-408, House Joint Resolution 1145.

3. David Stebenne, Gannett Foundation Report, *The Media at War: The Press and the Persian Gulf Conflict* (New York: Gannett Foundation Media Center, 1991).
4. *The Nation Magazine v. Department of Defense,* 19 Med.L.Rptr. 1257, 762 F.Supp. 1558 (S.D.N.Y. 1991).
5. *JB Pictures Inc. v. Defense Dept.,* 21 Med.L.Rptr. 1564 (D.D.C. 1993).

ible examples. Another purpose of secrecy may be to control the direction of public debate. The government does this frequently, successfully, and sometimes necessarily with the forbearance of the mainstream American press.

For the sake of "national security," large segments of the federal budget are secret. As many as 20 million documents are classified annually. Foreign policy is often conducted undercover as, on occasion, it must be. Another argument for nondisclosure, as has been noted, is privacy. An example: the Farmers Home Administration refused to provide the names of thirty-one borrowers whose $1 million debts had been stricken from the records under new federal credit procedures. When the government argues "privacy," is it really making a case for secrecy—for removing itself from public scrutiny? In what appeared to be an affirmative answer to that question, President Bill Clinton on October 15, 1995, in Executive Order 12958, ordered the declassification of most government files more than twenty-five years old. They number in the hundreds of millions and will include CIA and nuclear test information.

On the front lines of this struggle, federal documents are still said by some record keepers to be packed away so thoroughly that it would cost tens of thousands of dollars to unpack them. Or they've been transferred to another agency. Or they've simply been misplaced. Or there's a terrible backlog in responding to requests. These kinds of excuses led one wag to call the FOIA the "Freedom to Delay" Act. The government certainly has the initial advantage when disclosure is requested. Many federal agencies, however, simply can't meet the FOIA time limits; there are too many requests and too few personnel to deal with them. The FBI and CIA can stretch a delay into years; other agencies give the impression that they wait until an appeal is made under FOIA procedures before taking a request seriously.[6]

Court cases claiming or denying access to federal and state records and meetings are probably more numerous than the cases in any other area of media law. An estimated 500,000 FOIA requests are filed annually by public and press. Some reporters file requests merely as a means of protesting government secrecy: the information they need never gets to them on time through the FOIA anyway.

Nevertheless, in passing the FOIA, Congress did for public and press what they could not have done for themselves. Although President Lyndon Johnson signed the FOIA reluctantly. Congress passed the act in 1966, and it went into effect, somewhat symbolically, on July 4, 1967. Although Congress in the past had tried to limit secret classifications of documents, the Reagan and Bush administrations did much to counter that pressure. In 1982, for example, President Ronald Reagan told officials through an executive order that they should favor the highest level of classification for national security materials and avoid automatic declassification.

In what was called an Openness In Government initiative, on October 4, 1993, President Clinton issued a White House memorandum to heads of departments and agencies, urging bureaucrats to handle FOIA requests in a "customer-friendly manner" and reduce unnecessary barriers, such as administrative backlogs. On the same day, Attorney General Janet Reno informed department and agency heads that the Justice Department—itself a chief offender in failing to respond to FOIA requests in a timely manner—would no longer defend an agency's withholding of information merely because there is a "substantial legal basis" for doing so. Instead, her department would operate on a "presumption of disclosure"; the "foreseeable harm" of disclosure to an agency or to the public would henceforth have to be demonstrated. Given the lack of sufficient personnel and funding to handle FOIA requests, however, these statements seem more rhetorical than real.

Not only are records often inaccessible, but in the past, the White House has attempted to muzzle for life all government employees with access to classified information and favored using espionage laws to punish unauthorized leakers, whistleblowers, and "deviant" reporters. One former CIA agent was forced to forgo all royalties from a book on America's shameful and panicky flight from Saigon as American involvement in the Vietnam War concluded. Frank Snepp had violated the requirements of an executive order

---

6. Allan R. Adler, ed., *Litigation under the Federal Open Government Laws*, 16th ed. (Washington, D.C.: ACLU Foundation, 1991), p. 22.

making those handling sensitive CIA material sign an enforceable order that they would write nothing without government clearance. The Supreme Court upheld the punishment.[7] The CIA has since reviewed hundreds of manuscripts, including an autobiography by its former head, Stansfield Turner, who complained about the procedure and now bemoans the reduced flow of unclassified material to the American public because of the CIA review process.

In 1982, Congress passed the Intelligence Identities Protection Act, making it a crime to engage in a "pattern of activities . . . intending to expose covert agents." A U.S. agent had been assassinated in Athens after exposure by an American writer. The writer's passport was revoked, and the Supreme Court let the decision stand.[8] In another case, Samuel Loring Morison was sentenced to two years in prison for theft and espionage after he sent spy satellite photographs of a partly built Soviet nuclear aircraft carrier to a British military magazine where he hoped to work. His prison conviction was affirmed on appeal.[9]

COMPUTER DATA

Technology, of course, has played an independent role in making records less accessible, more easily obscured or destroyed, and more expensive. New technologies, therefore, complicate as well as facilitate the request process, but time will transform FOIA procedures for getting information from cyberspace.[10] Computer tapes are records under the FOIA, but federal agencies are not required to create documents that do not

exist.[11] At least one federal district court has ruled that computer software used in manipulating file data is also a record under the FOIA,[12] unless a trade secret or a privacy exemption applies. Some states, however, claim copyright protection for their computer software and deny that software itself constitutes a public record. Other states reject this notion, but may permit extra charges for the use of government software. Charges vary; some are based on cost, others make a profit for an agency. Requesters may have to pay for search time, or it may be free. In some states, news media may be exempt from charges when operating in the public interest; in others, this makes no difference. While requesters may have no control over the form or format in which records are provided,[13] this situation may be changing. Copyright issues seldom arise when records are stored in traditional formats such as paper, disk, tape, or microfiche.

Some federal agencies continue to claim that the computer programming required to retrieve computer records constitutes record creation and point out that they are not required to "create" records under the FOIA. If no retrieval program is available, certain kinds of information may never be disclosed. Other agencies use private companies to computerize their records; the records are taken out of the agency, and the FOI officers offer the librarian's apology of "the book is in the bindery."

Federal court rulings also suggest that agencies may not have to go to the trouble of segregating nonexempt from exempt information held in computer files. For example, the Occupational Safety and Health Administration turned down a request for electronic data, claiming the request would require a significant computer reprogramming effort. Format continues to be a sticking point. Sometimes computer printouts are impossible to read, and agencies are under no compul-

---

7. *Snepp v. United States,* 5 Med.L.Rptr. 2409, 444 U.S. 280 (1981). See also *United States v. Marchetti,* 1 Med.L.Reptr. 1051, 466 F.2d 1309 (4th Cir. 1972), *cert. denied,* 409 U.S. 1063 (1972).
8. *Haig v. Agee,* 7 Med.L.Rptr. 1545, 453 U.S. 280 (1981).
9. *U.S. v. Morison,* 11 Med.L.Rptr. 1731, 604 F.Supp. 655 (D.Md. 1985); *U.S. v. Morison,* 15 Med.L.Rptr. 1369, 844 F.2d 1057 (4th Cir. 1988).
10. An excellent treatment of this subject in five Western democracies, including the United States, is David H. Flaherty, *Protecting Privacy in Surveillance Societies* (Chapel Hill: University of North Carolina Press, 1989). In the United States, the Justice Department's Office of Information and Privacy oversees FOIA compliance.

11. Computer Security Act of 1987, 40 U.S.C. §759 (1988). *Long v. IRS,* 5 Med.L.Rptr. 1165, 596 F.2d 362, 365 (9th Cir. 1979), *cert. denied,* 446 U.S. 917 (1980); *Yeager v. Drug Enforcement Administration,* 8 Med.L.Rptr. 1959, 678 F.2d 315, 321 (D.C.Cir. 1982).
12. *Cleary, Gottlieb, Steen & Hamilton v. Department of Health and Human Services,* 844 F.Supp. 770 (D.D.C. 1993).
13. *Dismukes v. Department of Interior,* 603 F.Supp. 760 (D.D.C. 1984).

sion to provide information in more readable form. Bills pending in Congress perennially seek to overcome these kinds of problems. The opponents often focus on the costs associated with computer searches and formats.

Some state and federal agencies provide the public with computer terminals to retrieve governmental information. Some states, notably California, Colorado, Hawaii, Minnesota, North Carolina, Utah and Wisconsin, and others, with or without a legislative mandate, are using the Internet to put official information on line, with access by telephone.

The Reporters Committee for Freedom of the Press, one of the vanguard freedom of information organizations, has prepared a readily available booklet, *Access to Electronic Records,* that explains how to approach and examine electronically stored information.[14] It includes a summary of state laws on electronic access as well as court cases and fee information. The booklet also describes the use of the Geographic Information System (GIS) where large databases can be superimposed on maps. At least twenty-five legislatures had connected with the system by 1994; some charged a fee to commercial users for the benefit of the state treasury. The Society of Professional Journalists and the Sigma Delta Chi Foundation (SPJ-SDX) publish annual freedom of information reports, and a number of other media and legal and public interest groups provide access assistance in special circumstances.

After eleven years of litigation, the Reporters Committee and a CBS news corespondent as plaintiffs, and the public by implication, suffered a setback in March 1989. The Supreme Court, while recognizing that computerization could make official data less accessible, ruled that the FBI did not have to disclose rap sheets, computerized compilations of individual criminal records, because they were compiled for law enforcement purposes and were therefore exempt during the lifetimes of their subjects under at least three of the FOIA's nine exceptions. The FOIA, said the Court, was meant to

monitor governmental, not private, affairs. The record sought in this case was that of an organized crime figure implicated in a scandal involving a Pennsylvania congressman who had pleaded guilty to soliciting campaign funds from government contractors. Personal privacy and agency discretion and convenience simply outweighed the public interest in the case.[15] The government saw "a great potential for mischief" in the reporter's request. The Reporters Committee saw a distinct public interest in the criminal record of a person selling missile and tank parts to the federal government. Once again the question arose: Was personal privacy a rationalization for secrecy? In a decision in which all members of the Court either joined or concurred, Justice John Paul Stevens, dealing largely with one subsection of one of nine FOIA exemptions, wrote in part:

Justice Department v. Reporters Committee

16 MED.L.RPTR. 1545, 489 U.S. 749, 109 S.CT. 1468 (1989).

STEVENS, J.

* * *

This case arises out of requests made by a CBS news correspondent and the Reporters Committee for Freedom of the Press (respondents) for information concerning the criminal records of four members of the Medico family. The Pennsylvania Crime Commission had identified the family's company, Medico Industries, as a legitimate business dominated by organized crime figures. Moreover, the company allegedly had obtained a number of defense contracts as a result of an improper arrangement with a corrupt Congressman.

The FOIA requests sought disclosure of any arrests, indictments, acquittals, convictions, and sentences of any of the four Medicos. Although the FBI originally denied the requests, it provided the requested data concerning three of the Medicos after their deaths. In their complaint in

---

14. Reporters Committee for Freedom of the Press, *Access to Electronic Records: A Guide to Reporting on State and Local Government in the Computer Age* (Washington, D.C.: 1994 [Suite 504, Eye St. NW 20006]).

---

15. See also *Department of Defense v. FLRA,* 23 Med.L.Rptr. 1417, 114 S.Ct. 1006 (1994).

the District Court, respondents sought the rap sheet for the fourth, Charles Medico (Medico), insofar as it contained "matters of public record."

The parties filed cross-motions for summary judgment. In their briefs, respondents urged that any information regarding "a record of bribery, embezzlement or other financial crime" would potentially be a matter of special public interest. In answer to that argument, the Department advised respondents and the District Court that it had no record of any financial crimes concerning Medico, but the Department continued to refuse to confirm or deny whether it had any information concerning nonfinancial crimes. Thus, the issue was narrowed to Medico's nonfinancial-crime history insofar as it is a matter of public record.

The District Court granted the Department's motion for summary judgment, relying on three separate grounds. First, it concluded that 28 U.S.C. §534, the statute that authorizes the exchange of rap-sheet information with other official agencies, also prohibits the release of such information to members of the public, and therefore that Exemption 3 was applicable. Second, it decided that files containing rap sheets were included within the category of "personnel and medical files and similar files the disclosure of which would constitute an unwarranted invasion of privacy," and therefore that Exemption 6 was applicable. The term "similar files" applied because rap-sheet information "is personal to the individual named therein." After balancing Medico's privacy interest against the public interest in disclosure, the District Court concluded that the invasion of privacy was "clearly unwarranted." Finally, the court held that the rap sheet was protected by Exemption 7(C) but it ordered the Department to file a statement containing the requested data *in camera,* to give it an opportunity to reconsider the issue if, after reviewing that statement, such action seemed appropriate. After the Department made that filing, the District Court advised the parties that it would not reconsider the matter but it did seal the *in camera* submission and make it part of the record on appeal.

The Court of Appeals reversed. 259 U.S. App. D.C. 426, 816 F.2d 730 (1987). It held that an individual's privacy interest in criminal-history information that is a matter of public record was minimal at best. Noting the absence of any statutory standards by which to judge the public interest in disclosure, the Court of Appeals concluded

that it should be bound by the state and local determinations that such information should be made available to the general public. Accordingly, it held that Exemptions 6 and 7(C) were inapplicable. It also agreed with respondent that Exemption 3 did not apply because 28 U.S.C. §534 did not qualify as a statute "specifically" exempting rap sheets from disclosure.

In response to rehearing petitions advising the court that, contrary to its original understanding, most States had adopted policies of refusing to provide members of the public with criminal-history summaries, the Court of Appeals modified its holding. 265 U.S. App. D.C. 365, 831 F.2d 1124 (1987). With regard to the public interest side of the balance, the court now recognized that it could not rely upon state policies of disclosure. However, it adhered to its view that federal judges are not in a position to make "idiosyncratic" evaluations of the public interest in particular disclosures; instead, it directed district courts to consider "the general disclosure policies of the statute." With regard to the privacy interest in nondisclosure of rap sheets, the court told the District Court "only to make a factual determination in these kinds of cases: Has a legitimate privacy interest of the subject in his rap sheets faded because they appear on the public record?" In accordance with its initial opinion, it remanded the case to the District Court to determine whether the withheld information is publicly available at its source, and if so, whether the Department might satisfy its statutory obligation by referring respondents to the enforcement agency or agencies that had provided the original information.

* * *

The Court of Appeals denied rehearing en banc, with four judges dissenting. Because of the potential effect of the Court of Appeals' opinion on values of personal privacy, we granted certiorari. 485 U.S. ___ (1988). We now reverse.

The preliminary question is whether Medico's interest in the nondisclosure of any rap sheet the FBI might have on him is the sort of "personal privacy" interest that Congress intended Exemption 7(C) to protect. As we have pointed out before "[t]he cases sometimes characterized as protecting 'privacy' have in fact involved at least two different kinds of interests. One is the individual interest in avoiding disclosure of personal matters, and another is the interest in independence in making certain kinds of important decisions." *Whalen v. Roe*, 429 U.S. 589, 598–600 (1977). Here, the former interest, "in avoiding disclosure of personal matters," is implicated. Because events summarized in a rap sheet have been previously disclosed to the public, respondents contend that Medico's privacy interest in avoiding disclosure of federal compilation of these events approaches zero. We reject respondent's cramped notion of personal privacy.

* * *

Exemption 7(C) requires us to balance the privacy interest in maintaining, as the Government puts it, the "practical obscurity" of the rap sheets, against the public interest in their release.

To begin with, both the common law and the literal understandings of privacy encompass the individual's control of information concerning his or her person. In an organized society, there are few facts that are not at one time or another divulged to another. Thus the extent of the protection accorded a privacy right at common law rested in part on the degree of dissemination of the allegedly private fact and the extent to which the passage of time rendered it private. According to Webster's initial definition, information may be classified as "private" if it is "intended for or restricted to the use of a particular person or group or class of persons: not freely available to the public." Recognition of this attribute of a privacy interest supports the distinction, in terms of personal privacy, between scattered disclosure of the bits of information contained in a rap sheet and revelation of the rap sheet as a whole. The very fact that federal funds have been spent to prepare, index, and maintain these criminal-history files demonstrates that the individual items of information in the summaries would not otherwise be "freely available" either to the officials who have access to the underlying files or to the general public. Indeed, if the summaries were "freely available," there would be no reason to invoke the FOIA to obtain access to the information they contain. Granted, in many contexts the fact that information is not freely available is no reason to exempt that information from a statute generally requiring its dissemination. But the issue here is whether the compilation of otherwise hard-to-obtain information alters the privacy interest implicated by disclosure of that

information. Plainly there is a vast difference between the public records that might be found after a diligent search of courthouse files, county archives, and local police stations throughout the country and a computerized summary located in a single clearing-house of information.

This conclusion is supported by the web of federal statutory and regulatory provisions that limit the disclosure of rap-sheet information. That is, Congress has authorized rap-sheet dissemination to banks, local licensing officials, the securities industry, the nuclear-power industry, and other law-enforcement agencies. * * * Further, the FBI has permitted such disclosure to the subject of the rap sheet and, more generally, to assist in the apprehension of wanted persons or fugitives * * *. Finally, the FBI's exchange of rap-sheet information "is subject to cancellation if dissemination is made outside the receiving departments or related agencies." This careful and limited pattern of authorized rap-sheet disclosure fits the dictionary definition of privacy as involving a restriction of information "to the use of a particular person or group or class of persons." Moreover, although perhaps not specific enough to constitute a statutory Exemption under the FOIA Exemption 3, * * * these statutes and regulations, taken as a whole, evidence a congressional intent to protect the privacy of rap-sheet subjects, and a concomitant recognition of the power of compilations to affect personal privacy that outstrips the combined power of the bits of information contained within.

Other portions of the FOIA itself bolster the conclusion that disclosure of records regarding private citizens, identifiable by name, is not what the framers of the FOIA had in mind. Specifically, the FOIA provides that "[t]o the extent required to prevent a clearly unwarranted invasion of personal privacy, an agency may delete identifying details when it makes available or publishes an opinion, statement of policy, interpretation, or staff manual or instruction." * * * Additionally, the FOIA assures that "[a]ny reasonably segregable portion of a record shall be provided to any person requesting such record after deletion of the portions which are exempt under [§(b)]." These provisions, for deletion of identifying references and disclosure of segregable portions of records with exempt information deleted, reflect a congressional understanding that disclosure of records containing personal details about private citizens can infringe significant privacy interests.

Also supporting our conclusion that a strong privacy interest inheres in the non-disclosure of compiled computerized information is the Privacy Act, codified at 5 U.S.C. §552a (1982 ed. and Supp. IV). The Privacy Act was passed in 1974 largely out of concern over "the impact of computer data banks on individual privacy." H. R. Rep. No. 93–1416, p. 7 (1974). The Privacy Act provides generally that "[n]o agency shall disclose any record which is contained in a system of records . . . except pursuant to a written consent of, the individual to whom the record pertains," * * *. Although the Privacy Act contains a variety of exceptions to this rule, including an Exemption for information required to be disclosed under the FOIA, see 5 U.S.C. §552a(b)(2), Congress' basic policy concern regarding the implications of computerized data banks for personal privacy is certainly relevant in our consideration of the privacy interest affected by dissemination of rap sheets from the FBI computer.

Given this level of federal concern over centralized databases, the fact that most States deny the general public access to their criminal-history summaries should not be surprising. As we have pointed out, * * * in 47 States *nonconviction* data from criminal-history summaries are not available at all, and even conviction data are "generally unavailable to the public." State-policies, of course, do not determine the meaning of a federal statute, but they provide evidence that the law-enforcement profession generally assumes— as has the Department of Justice—that individual subjects have a significant privacy interest in their criminal histories. It is reasonable to presume that Congress legislated with an understanding of this professional point of view.

In addition to the common-law and dictionary understanding, the basic difference between scattered bits of criminal history and a federal compilation, federal statutory provisions, and state policies, our cases have also recognized the privacy interest inherent in the nondisclosure of certain information even where the information may have been at one time public. Most apposite for present purposes is our decision in *Department of the Air Force v. Rose,* 425 U.S. 352 (1976). New York University law students sought Air Force Honor and Ethics Code case summaries for a Law Review project on military discipline. The Academy had already publicly posted these summaries on 40 squadron bulletin boards, usu-

ally with identifying names redacted (names were posted for cadets who were found guilty and who left the Academy), and with instructions that cadets should read the summaries only if necessary. Although the opinion dealt with Exemption 6's exception for "personnel and medical files and similar files the disclosure of which would constitute a clearly unwarranted invasion of personal privacy," and our opinion today deals with Exemption 7(C), much of our discussion in *Rose* is applicable here. We explained that the FOIA permits release of a segregable portion of a record with other portions deleted, and that *in camera* inspection was proper to determine whether parts of a record could be released while keeping other parts secret. * * * We emphasized the FOIA's segregability and *in camera* provisions in order to explain that the case summaries, *with identifying names redacted,* were generally disclosable. We then offered guidance to lower courts in determining whether disclosure of all or part of such case summaries would constitute a "clearly unwarranted invasion of personal privacy" under Exemption 6:

> Respondents sought only such disclosure as was consistent with [the Academy tradition of keeping identities confidential with the Academy]. Their request for access to summaries "with personal references or other identifying information deleted," respected the confidentiality interests embodied in Exemption 6. As the Court of Appeals recognized, however, what constitutes identifying information regarding a subject cadet must be weighed not only from the viewpoint of the public, but also from the vantage of those who would have been familiar, as fellow cadets or Academy staff, with other aspects of his career at the Academy. Despite the summaries' distribution within the Academy, many of this group with earlier access to summaries may never have identified a particular cadet, or may have wholly forgotten his encounter with Academy discipline. And the risk to the privacy interests of a former cadet, particularly one who has remained in the military, posed by his identification by otherwise unknowing former colleagues or instructors cannot be rejected as trivial. We nevertheless conclude that consideration of the policies underlying the Freedom of Information Act, to open public business to public view when no "clearly unwarranted" invasion of privacy will result, requires affirmance of the holding of the Court of Appeals . . . that although "no one can guarantee that all those who are 'in the know' will hold their tongues,

particularly years later when time may have eroded the fabric or cadet loyalty," it sufficed enjoining the District Court . . . that if in its opinion deletion of personal references and other identifying information "is not sufficient to safeguard privacy, then the summaries should not be disclosed to [respondents]." 425 U.S., at 380–381. * * *

In this passage we doubly stressed the importance of the privacy interest implicated by disclosure of the case summaries. First: We praised the Academy's tradition of protecting personal privacy through redaction of names from the case summaries. But even with names redacted, subjects of such summaries can often be identified through other, disclosed information. So, second: *Even though the summaries, with only names redacted, had once been public,* we recognized the potential invasion of privacy through later recognition of identifying details, and approved the Court of Appeals' rule permitting the District Court to delete "other identifying information" in order to safeguard this privacy interest. If a cadet has a privacy interest in past discipline that was once public but may have been "wholly forgotten," the ordinary citizen surely has a similar interest in the aspects of his or her criminal history that may have been wholly forgotten.

We have also recognized the privacy interest in keeping personal facts away from the public eye. In *Whalen v. Roe* we held that "the State of New York may record, in a centralized computer file, the names and addresses of all persons who have obtained, pursuant to a doctor's prescription, certain drugs for which there is both a lawful and an unlawful market." In holding only that the Federal constitution does not *prohibit* such a compilation, we recognized that such a centralized computer file posed a "threat to privacy":

> We are not unaware of the threat to privacy implicit in the accumulation of vast amounts of personal information in computerized data banks or other massive government files. The collection of taxes, the distribution of welfare and social security benefits, the supervision of public health, the direction of our Armed Forces, and the enforcement of the criminal laws all require the orderly preservation of great quantities of information, much of which is personal in character and potentially embarrassing or harmful if disclosed. The right to collect and use such data for public purposes is typically accompanied by a concomitant statutory or regulatory duty

to avoid unwarranted disclosures. Recognizing that in some circumstances that duty arguably has its roots in the Constitution, nevertheless New York's statutory scheme, and its implementing administrative procedures, evidence a proper concern with, and protection of the individual's interest in privacy." * * * ("The central storage and easy accessibility of computerized data vastly increase the potential for abuse of that information . . .").

In sum, the fact that "an event is not wholly 'private' does not mean that an individual has no interest in limiting disclosure or dissemination of the information." Rehnquist, Is an Expanded Right of Privacy Consistent with Fair and Effective Law Enforcement?, Nelson Timothy Stephens Lectures, University of Kansas Law School, pt. 1, p. 13 (Sept. 26–27, 1974). The privacy interest in a rap sheet is substantial. The substantial character of that interest is affected by the fact that in today's society the computer can accumulate and store information that would otherwise have surely been forgotten long before a person attains the age of 80, when the FBI's rap sheets are discarded.

Exemption 7(C), by its terms, permits an agency to withhold a document only when revelation "could reasonably be expected to constitute an *unwarranted* invasion of personal privacy." We must next address what factors might *warrant* an invasion of the interest described, *supra.*

Our previous decisions establish that whether an invasion of privacy is *warranted* cannot turn on the purposes for which the request for information is made. Except for cases in which the objection to disclosure is based on a claim of privilege and the person requesting disclosure is the party protected by the privilege, the identity of the requesting party has no bearing on the merits of his or her FOIA request. Thus, although the subject of a presentence report can waive a privilege that might defeat a third party's access to that report, *United States Department of Justice v. Julian*, 486 U.S. 1, (1988), and although the FBI's policy of granting the subject of a rap sheet access to his own criminal history is consistent with its policy of denying access to all other members of the general public, the rights of the two press respondents in this case are no different from those that might be asserted by any other third party, such as neighbor or prospective employer. As we have repeatedly stated, Congress "clearly intended" the FOIA "to give any member of the public as much right to disclosure as one with a special interest [in a particular document]." *NLRB v. Sears, Roebuck & Co.,* 421 U.S. 132, 149 (1975); *see NLRB v. Robbins Tire & Rubber Co.,* 437 U.S. 214, 221 (1978); *FBI v. Abramson,* 456 U.S. 615 (1982). * * *

Thus whether disclosure of a private document under Exemption 7(C) is warranted must turn on the nature of the requested document and its relationship to "the basic purpose of the Freedom of Information Act 'to open agency action to the light of public scrutiny,'" *Department of the Air Force v. Rose,* 425 U.S., at 372, rather than on the particular purpose for which the document is being requested. In our leading case on the FOIA, we declared that the Act was designed to create a broad right of access to "official information." *EPA v. Mink,* 410 U.S. 73, 80 (1973). * * * This basic policy of "full agency disclosure unless information is exempted under clearly delineated statutory language,'" indeed focuses on the citizens' right to be informed about "what their government is up to." Official information that sheds light on an agency's performance of its statutory duties falls squarely within that statutory purpose. That purpose, however, is not fostered by disclosure of information about private citizens that is accumulated in various governmental files but that reveals little or nothing about an agency's own conduct. In this case—and presumably in the typical case in which one private citizen is seeking information about another—the requester does not intend to discover anything about the conduct of the agency that has possession of the requested records. Indeed, response to this request would not shed any light on the conduct of any Government agency or official.

The point is illustrated by our decision in *Rose.* * * *

Respondents argue that there is a two-fold public interest in learning about Medico's past arrests or convictions: He allegedly had improper dealings with a corrupt Congressman and he is an officer of a corporation with defense contracts. But if Medico has, in fact, been arrested or convicted of certain crimes, that information would neither aggravate nor mitigate his allegedly improper relationship with the Congressman; more specifically, it would tell us nothing directly about the character of the *Con-gressman's* behavior. Nor would it tell us anything about the conduct of the *Department of Defense* (DOD) in awarding one or more contracts to the Medico Company. Arguably a FOIA request to the DOD for records relating to those contracts, or for documents describing the agency's procedures, if any, for determining whether officers of a prospective contractor have criminal records, would constitute an appropriate request for "official information." Conceivably Medico's rap sheet would provide details to include in a news story, but, in itself, this is not the kind of public interest for which Congress enacted the FOIA. In other words, although there is undoubtedly some public interest in anyone's criminal history, especially if the history is in some way related to the subject's dealing with a public official or agency, the FOIA's central purpose is to ensure that the *Government's* activities be opened to the sharp eye of public scrutiny, not that information about *private citizens* that happens to be in the warehouse of the Government be so disclosed. Thus, it should come as no surprise that in none of our cases construing the FOIA have we found it appropriate to order a Government agency to honor a FOIA request for information about a particular private citizen.

What we have said should make clear that the public interest in the release of any rap sheet on Medico that may exist is not the type of interest protected by the FOIA. Medico may or may not be one of the 24 million persons for whom the FBI has a rap sheet. If respondents are entitled to have the FBI tell them what it knows about Medico's criminal history, any other member of the public is entitled to the same disclosure— whether for writing a news story, for deciding whether or not to employ Medico, to rent a house to him, to extend credit to him, or simply to confirm or deny a suspicion. There is, unquestionably, *some* public interest in providing interested citizens with answers to their questions about Medico. But that interest falls outside the ambit of the public interest that the FOIA was enacted to serve.

Finally, we note that Congress has provided that the standard fees for production of documents under the FOIA shall be waived or reduced "if disclosure of the information is in the public interest because it is likely to contribute significantly to public understanding of the operations or activities of the government and is not primarily in the commercial interest of the requester. * * * Although such a provision obviously implies that there will be requests that do not meet such a "public interest" standard, we think it relevant to today's inquiry regarding the public interest in release of rap sheets on private citizens that Congress once again expressed the core purpose of the FOIA as "contribut[ing] significantly to public understanding *of the operations or activities of the government.*"

* * *

Finally: The privacy interest in maintaining the practical obscurity of rap-sheet information will always be high. When the subject of such a rap sheet is a private citizen and when the information is in the Government's control as a compilation, rather than as a record of "what the Government is up to," the privacy interest protected by Exemption 7(C) is in fact at its apex while the FOIA-based public interest in disclosure is at its nadir. Such a disparity on the scales of justice holds for a class of cases without regard to individual circumstances; the standard virtues of bright-line rules are thus present, and the difficulties attendant to ad hoc adjudication may be avoided. Accordingly, we hold as a categorical matter that a third party's request for law-enforcement records or information about a private citizen can reasonably be expected to invade that citizen's privacy, and that when the request seeks no "official information" about a Government agency, but merely records that the Government happens to be storing, the invasion of privacy is "unwarranted." The judgment of the Court of Appeals is reversed.

COMMENT

As a result of this ruling, privacy has been weighted more heavily than openness in subsequent cases. If privacy applies, the public interest is discounted. The privacy interest is categorical; the public interest is derived from the personal interest of the requester and therefore is less distinct. Lower courts are also condoning Justice Steven's endorsement of what the government called a "practical obscurity"—complete information buried in computer databases, if retrieved, would violate personal privacy more than scattered information that requires digging out. In addition, he wrote, a requester's purpose

in seeking the information should have no bearing on the agency's decision to disclose. In terms of the public interest and the reportorial function, that rule is a double burden.

State courts are divided on how far the privacy exemption should extend. In *Long v. IRS,*[16] the Ninth Circuit Court of Appeals recommended redaction or excision of personal information, a procedure that is more difficult with electronic data, but simpler than creating a new record.

One example from scores of lower federal court cases illustrates the change in favor of privacy. In *Gannett Satellite Information Network, Inc. v. U.S. Department of Education,*[17] the D.C. Circuit Court of Appeals in 1990 denied *USA Today*'s request for computerized data held by the department in its administration of the Guaranteed Student Loan Program. "The purpose of FOIA is not furthered," said the court, "by the disclosure of information about private citizens that is accumulated in various governmental files but that reveals little or nothing about an agency's own conduct." Some consider this such a narrow interpretation of the "public interest" that only Congress can remedy it. Justice Ruth Bader Ginsburg said as much in a subsequent case discussed below.

In *Department of Defense v. Federal Labor Relations Authority,*[18] the U.S. Supreme Court denied two labor unions access to federal civil service employees' home addresses, including those of nonmembers, in spite of a labor statute favoring disclosure of such information in the interests of collective bargaining.[19] Substantial precedent supported the statute. Such disclosure, said the Court, would be a violation of the FOIA's Exemption 6. Quoting liberally from *Reporters Committee,* Justice Clarence Thomas, speaking for a Court unanimous in its judgment, wrote:

> The relevant public interest supporting disclosure in this case is negligible, at best. Disclosure of the addresses might allow the unions to communicate more effectively with employees, but it would not appreciably further "the citizens' right to be informed about what their government is up to." . . . [and] would constitute "a clearly unwarranted invasion of personal privacy."

---

16. Op. cit. n. 11.
17. Unreported case.
18. 22 Med.L.Rptr. 1417, 114 S.Ct. 1006 (1994).
19. 5 U.S.C.A. §7103(a)(16) (1980).

The Court thus attaches the "agency conduct" rule of Exemption 7(c) to Exemption 6 as well. Responding in a concurring opinion, Justice Ginsburg wrote:

It is . . . doubtful that Congress intended a privacy interest, appraised by most courts as relatively modest, to trump the legislature's firmly-declared interest in promoting federal-sector collective bargaining. . . . The *Reporters Committee* "core purpose" limitation is not found in FOIA's language. A FOIA requester need not show in the first instance that disclosure would serve any public purpose, let alone a "core purpose" of "open[ing] agency action to the light of public scrutiny" or advancing "public understanding of the operations or activities of the government." . . . I am mindful, however, that the preservation of *Reporters Committee,* unmodified, is the position solidly approved by my colleagues . . . I therefore concur in the Court's judgment, recognizing that, although today's decision denies federal-sector unions information available to their private-sector counterparts, *"Congress may correct the disparity."* [Emphasis added.]

Voice recordings that may have revealed thoughts and feelings of the *Challenger* astronauts moments before their deaths in the tragic space shuttle explosion were denied the *New York Times* by a divided appeals court, also on the grounds that the recordings would constitute a clearly unwarranted invasion of personal privacy under Exemption 6.[20] This and other exemptions will be discussed in more detail in later sections.

FIRST AMENDMENT IMPLICATIONS: PAPERS AND PLACES

Until recently, the First Amendment has not helped communicators gain access to public documents or places. "There is no constitutional right to have access to particular government information, or to require openness from bureaucracy . . . ," said Justice Potter Stewart in a Yale University address. "The Constitution itself is neither a Freedom of Information Act nor an Official Secrets Act."[21] Yet in the *Pentagon Papers* case, he had written that "when everything is classified, then nothing is classified." His colleague Byron White had observed in his opinion for the Court in *Branzburg v. Hayes* that "without some protection for seeking out the news, freedom of the press would be eviscerated."[22] The problem, of course, is that the First Amendment mandates what government may *not* do; it does not provide a mandate for open government or for what the government can or must do. Courts traditionally have interpreted the First Amendment to mean primarily a right to publish without governmental restraint. And "publication" has not been equated with access to information or to places where news is being made. Some would change that.[23]

A series of cases concerning press access to prisons illustrates the point. In a case marking the first such effort by San Francisco television station KQED, Chief Justice Warren Burger said, "This Court has never intimated a First Amendment guarantee of a right to access to all sources of information within government control."[24] Earlier, the U.S. Supreme Court had applied this rule to requests by the press for interviews with prison inmates. The press, said the Court, has no rights beyond the rights of the public generally.[25]

In 1991, thirteen years after the first KQED case, the same station was again rebuffed when it sought camera access to prison execution chambers. The case set off a widespread debate on the ethics of photographing executions, with sometimes surprising arguments on both sides.[26] For example, those in favor thought photographing would make murderers think twice; others speculated that it would demonstrate to society the

---

20. *New York Times v. NASA,* 18 Med.L.Rptr. 1465, 920 F.2d 1002 (D.C.Cir. 1990).

21. Stewart, "Or of the Press," 26 *Hastings L.Rev.* 631, 636 (1976).

22. 408 U.S. 665 (1972).

23. Thomas I. Emerson, "The Affirmative Side of the First Amendment," 15 *Georgia L.Rev. 795* (Summer 1981); C. Edwin Baker, *Human Liberty and Freedom of Speech* New York: Oxford University Press, 1989.

24. *Houchins v. KQED,* 3 Med.L.Rptr. 2521, 438 U.S. 1 (1978).

25. *Pell v. Procunier,* 1 Med.L.Rptr. 2379, 417 U.S. 817 (1974); *Saxbe v. Washington Post Co.,* 1 Med.L.Rptr. 2314, 417 U.S. 843 (1974).

26. Walter Goodman, "Executions on Television: Defining the Issues," *New York Times,* May 30, 1991, p. B6.

horrors of capital punishment. Those opposed were largely concerned about security and the media "spectaculars" that would result. A federal district court said, however, that under California law, for reasons of security, the warden of San Quentin could impose clear limits on who could attend executions, although he could not bar all media representatives, who by tradition have been present with their pencils, paper, and sketch pads. "Prohibition of cameras, still or television, from the execution witness area," the court added, "is a reasonable and lawful regulation."[27]

Prison security was also the justification when another federal court allowed the Bureau of Prisons to reach far outside the prison and prohibit an inmate from writing for the *San Francisco Chronicle.* He had a First Amendment right to send what he wrote out of the prison with its content undisturbed, but he could not be a bylined reporter for the newspaper. When a prison regulation impinges upon an inmate's constitutional rights, said the court, "the regulation is valid if it is reasonably related to legitimate penological interests." The concern here was that the published articles could somehow lead to violence and threaten prison security.[28]

Restrictions on access have also been applied to disaster sites, both natural and human-made; military bases and operations, as noted earlier; and polling places. Distance limitations on exit polling have been held to restrict both access to information and the free speech of poll respondents. A Washington state law on exit polling was held unconstitutional because it did not protect a compelling governmental interest by the least restrictive means.[29]

Officials who prohibit press access to public places for compelling reasons must not discriminate among reporters, camerapersons, union members or nonmembers, or men and women for fear of raising both equal protection and First Amendment issues. A problem recognized by Justice White is his opinion for the Court in

Branzburg, however, is who defines the press? That problem is still unresolved.

First Amendment claims of access to places were strongly reinforced by the Supreme Court's 1980 decision in *Richmond Newspapers, Inc. v. Virginia,* which made access to a place traditionally open to press and public a matter of First Amendment protection. The place was the criminal trial courtroom. "[F]or the first time," said Justice Stevens in what he called a "watershed" case, "the Court unequivocally holds that an arbitrary interference with access to important information is an abridgment of the freedom of speech and of the press protected by the First Amendment."[30]

Two years later, a federal appeals court permitted the General Services Administration to segregate private from public material in the Nixon tapes to allow public access to papers labeled "presidential historical material."[31]

In their time, these victories were heartening for the press and public. Nevertheless, the fact remains that the right to gather information is by no means as sweeping as the right to publish information once in hand, although the Freedom of Information Act has sought to bridge that gap.

USING THE FOIA

Section 3 of the Administrative Procedure Act of 1946, amended in 1966 to incorporate the Freedom of Information Act, was based on a simple premise: unless specifically exempt under the act, public records are available for public inspection to anyone for whatever purpose. No longer could a government agency deny access on the grounds that the information seeker has no "personal" interest in the material sought or that its release would be contrary to a broad, undefined public interest.

Nine exemptions to disclosure make the release of information discretionary with either a federal agency or, in subsequent litigation, a federal court. In other words, under the FOIA and

---

27. *KQED v. Vasquez,* 18 Med.L.Rptr. 2323 (U.S.D.C. N. Cal. 1991). The Fifth Circuit reached the same conclusion in the 1977 case of *Garrett v. Estelle,* 2 Med.L.Rptr. 2265, 556 F.2d 1274 (5th Cir. 1977).

28. *Martin v. Rison,* 741 F.Supp. 1406 (N.D.Cal. 1990).

29. *Daily Herald v. Munro,* 14 Med.L.Rptr. 2332, 838 F.2d 380 (9th Cir. 1988).

30. 6 Med.L.Rptr. 1833, 448 U.S. 555 (1980). *Publicker Industries v. Cohen,* 10 Med.L.Rptr. 1777, 733 F.2d 1059 (3d Cir. 1984) extended the First Amendment right of attendance to civil trials.

31. *Nixon v. Freeman,* 8 Med.L.Rptr. 1001, 670 F.2d 346 (D.C.Cir. 1982).

its exemptions, protection of information in government files is not mandatory.[32] Often, however, agency discretion is exercised in favor of government.

A 1970 ruling by a federal district court summed up what many would like to think was the basic purpose of the FOIA: "Freedom of information is now the rule and secrecy the exception."[33] The Supreme Court would follow up by noting that the exemptions "do not obscure the basic policy that disclosure, not secrecy, is the dominant objective of the act."[34] The FOIA "seeks to permit access to official information long shielded unnecessarily from public view and attempts to create a judicially enforceable public right to secure such information from possibly unwilling hands."[35]

Nevertheless, bureaucrats still insist on substituting their definitions of the "public interest" and "news" for those of reporters and editors. Often they prefer interpretations of the law that lead to backlogs and lengthy delays in releasing information, especially when releasable and nonreleasable segments of documents have to be segregated and where requests are processed on a first in, first out basis. Sometimes fees for searches and duplication are so high and the prospects of litigation so forbidding that weaker publications and ordinary citizens are discouraged from appealing denials to their requests. An agency denying access still has the burden of proof in justifying its action.

The FOIA also requires that federal agencies publish their rules of procedure in the *Federal Register* and make available for inspection and copying their final opinions, statements of policy, interpretations, and staff manuals and instructions. Where someone has been adversely affected by noncompliance with these publication rules, agency actions or decisions of "general applicability" can be invalidated.[36]

In spite of the impediments, the act has succeeded in opening federal files to investigative reporters, scholars, public interest groups, and anyone else looking into government wrongdoing, unsafe working conditions and consumer products, nuclear power plants, toxic chemicals, drug trafficking, airport security, defense contract overruns, noncompliance with anti-discrimination laws, violations of the law by the CIA and FBI, and a host of other urgent public matters. For example, investigative reporters for the *Orange County Register* detected a pattern in military helicopter crashes. Information divulged through the FOIA revealed obsolete night vision goggles were involved in a third of the crashes. A congressional investigation led to new equipment and new regulations being issued. *Orlando Sentinel* reporters, using computerized prison records and publicly available criminal histories, were able to demonstrate the dire consequences of Florida's early release program. Freelancers without publishing contracts and anyone seeking information for personal profit or for purposes of litigation, however, may be viewed less favorably than identifiable reporters by record keepers and the courts.

Various amendments to the FOIA have sought either to improve or to restrict it. Examples of improvements were the 1974 amendments that led to more rigorous and specific deadlines for response; lower costs for actual search and duplication efforts or, in cases of substantial public interest, fee waivers; indexes of information held; and payment of court costs and lawyers' fees where appeals from agency decisions were found to be justified and where it would increase citizen access to government. Segregable portions of documents had to be provided, even though other parts could be kept secret. One circuit court of appeals, however, has since ruled that unclassified portions of a document need not be released if a compilation of individual unclassified items viewed together would require classification of the whole document.[37]

The 1974 amendments also included negative changes such as provisions giving Justice Department lawyers discretion to decide what was or was not in the public interest. The amendments also allowed extensions in time for agency response "under exceptional circumstances" such as huge backlogs—often the easiest justification for delay.

---

32. *Chrysler v. Brown,* 4 Med.L.Rptr. 2441, 441 U.S. 281, 293 (1979).

33. *Wellford v. Hardin,* 315 F.Supp. 768 (D.D.C. 1970).

34. *Department of the Air Force v. Rose,* 1 Med.L.Rptr. 2509, 425 U.S. 352, 96 S.Ct. 1592 (1976).

35. *John Doe Agency v. John Doe Corp.* 493 U.S. 146 (1989).

36. *Mada-Luna v. Fitzpatrick,* 813 F.2d 1006 (9th Cir. 1987), appeal after remand, 874 F.2d 816 (9th Cir. 1989).

37. *American Friends Service Committee v. Department of Defense,* 831 F.2d 441, 445 (3d Cir. 1987).

A federal district court in 1989 granted injunctive relief to an immigration attorney seeking to compel the Immigration and Naturalization Service to respond to the requests of aliens about to be deported. The court held that the "exceptional circumstances" rule would not apply where the requested material was easily retrievable and someone's life or liberty was at stake—in this case, a deportable alien.[38] The Ninth Circuit reversed on the question of summary judgment and remanded,[39] noting that both questions revolved around disputed facts: Did inadequate personnel create "exceptional circumstances," and did the INS act with "due diligence" given the urgency of the request? A later settlement in the case proposed, among other things, that requests be prioritized across agencies and that different processing tracks be used for simple and complex requests.[40]

The FOIA Reform Act of 1986, enacted as part of the Anti-Drug Abuse Act, was primarily intended to shield law enforcement officers and their confidential sources and records from disclosure. It also authorized the FBI to refuse to acknowledge the existence of records pertaining to foreign intelligence, counterintelligence, or international terrorism for "as long as the existence of records remains classified information." More sympathetically, the 1986 amendments also standardized fee schedules and made fee waivers easier to obtain, especially for those whose purpose was noncommercial news dissemination, scholarship, science, or otherwise in the public interest.[41] Journalism has not been considered a "commercial" activity. In an unreported 1988 case, a federal district court in Oregon would not accept the Department of Energy's argument that a fee waiver was not required when the documents sought were available in the agency's reading room—even though the reading room was 230 miles away.[42]

The 1986 amendments also empowered judges to review government documents at their discretion, *in camera,* in order to decide whether one or more of the nine exemptions had been properly applied. This partly overcame the effects of *Environmental Protection Agency v. Mink,* 1 Med.L.Rptr. 2448, 410 U.S. 73 (1973), in which the Supreme Court approved the use of Exemptions 1 and 5 (national security and inter- and intra-agency memos) to deny Rep. Patsy Mink and colleagues access to reports of a divided interdepartmental government committee considering the advisability of underground nuclear tests on Amchitka Island in the Aleutians.

Who Must Comply and What Are Records?

The FOIA applies to agencies, departments, commissions, and government-controlled corporations of the executive branch of the *federal* government. This includes cabinet-level departments such as State, Defense, Transportation, Interior, Justice, and Treasury. Independent regulatory agencies such as the Federal Communications Commission (FCC), the Federal Trade Commission (FTC), and the Securities and Exchange Commission (SEC) are also included, as are the U.S. Postal Service, the National Aeronautics and Space Administration (NASA), the Civil Service Commission, the United States Parole Board, the Smithsonian Institution, and executive offices such as the Office of Management and Budget (OMB). Their functions and rules are published in the *Federal Register.*

The FOIA does not apply to the president or his immediate staff or to consultants such as the president's Council of Economic Advisers,[43] the Defense Nuclear Facilities Safety Board,[44] and the United States Sentencing Commission.[45] A federal appeals court held in 1990 that neither the FOIA nor the Federal Advisory Committee Act (first passed in 1972 to open to public scrutiny the advising of government agencies by

38. *Mayock v. INS,* 714 F.Supp. 1558 (N.D.Calif. 1989).
39. *Mayock v. Nelson,* 938 F.2d 1006 (9th Cir. 1991).
40. See Eric J. Sinrod, Freedom of Information Act Response Deadlines: Bridging the Gap between Legislative Intent and Economic Reality, 43 *Am.U.L.Rev.* 325 (Winter 1994).
41. *National Security Archive v. Department of Defense,* 16 Med.L.Rptr. 2071, 880 F.2d 1381 (D.C.Cir. 1989), *cert. denied,* 494 U.S. 1029 (1990).
42. *Coalition for Safe Power, Inc. v. Department of Energy* (unreported).

43. *Rushforth v. Council of Economic Advisers,* 11 Med.L.Rptr. 2450, 762 F.2d 1038 (D.C.Cir. 1985).
44. *Energy Research Foundation v. Defense Nuclear Facilities Safety Board,* 18 Med.L.Rptr. 1294, 917 F.2d 581 (D.C.Cir. 1990).
45. *Andrade v. U.S. Sentencing Commission,* 989 F.2d 308 (9th Cir. 1993).

private persons) required the Office of Administration of the Executive Office of the President or the White House counsel to produce documents relating to the Tower Commission, which was investigating the Iran-Contra scandal. The Office of the President, said the court, is not an "agency" subject to the FOIA.[46]

Organizations that receive federal funds but are not under the direct control of the federal government, such as the Corporation for Public Broadcasting and the American Red Cross, are not subject to the act. Nor does the act apply to Congress, the federal courts, federally funded state agencies, or private corporations, unless their documents are filed with a federal agency. The FOIA is a federal law. It does not apply to state or municipal records. They are covered only by equivalent state laws.

The FOIA provides no definition of records. An agency must either "create or obtain" records and "must be in control of the material at the time the FOIA request is made." Furthermore, what is sought must be part of the "legitimate conduct of its [the agency's] official duties" for the act to apply. In *Forsham v. Harris,*[47] the Supreme Court held that records of a federally funded university research project were not subject to disclosure under the FOIA until a government agency had assumed exclusive control of the records for its own review or use. An agency is not responsible for documents that have escaped its control, and it has no obligation to retrieve them once they are gone.[48] Courts may enjoin an agency only when it *improperly withholds* agency *records.*[49] Courts may also discipline agency personnel who act arbitrarily or capriciously in withholding information. Failure to comply could eventually lead to a citation for contempt of court.

A "record" under the act appears to be almost anything in documentary form, including film, computer tapes, video and audio tapes, and photographs. Twenty years ago, the Ninth Circuit held that "computer-stored records, whether stored in the central processing unit, on magnetic tape or in some other form, are still 'records' for purposes of the FOIA," and this would also apply to computer tapes.[50] Generally speaking, as has been noted, the FOIA makes no distinction between manual and computer storage systems.[51] In another case, the D.C. Circuit denied that a document with some material deleted by computer manipulation to mask personal identities is a new document, but held that manipulation and restructuring of content are not part of an agency's obligation.[52] More recently, computer software programs were also held to be records under the FOIA,[53] although this issue and the question of how to define electronic mail records remain unsettled. The latter case involved efforts, so far unsuccessful, to gain access to the E-mail records of the Reagan White House.[54] In 1993, the D.C. federal district court, in ordering a periodic review of the electronic record-keeping practices of the National Security Council, held that E-mail constitutes records under the Federal Record Act.[55] To qualify for public inspection, any record should serve some official purpose, should have been prepared by the agency in question, and should be part of the agency's official function.[56] The act would not cover opinions about an agency expressed in a telephone interview.

Making a Request

A first step in using the act is to buy the Washington-based Reporters Committee for Freedom of the Press handbook, *How to Use the Federal FOI Act* (FOI Service Center, 800 18th Street, NW, Washington, D.C. 20006). It provides sample letters for formal requests, appeals, waivers of fee, and complaints to federal courts that may include a request for the making of indexes (called a *Vaughn* motion after a case requiring refusals to release records to be based

---

46. *National Security Archive v. U.S. Archivist,* 17 Med.L.Rptr. 2265, 909 F.2d 541 (D.C.Cir. 1990).
47. 5 Med.L.Rptr. 2473, 445 U.S. 169, 185–186 (1980).
48. *Kissinger v. Reporters Committee for Freedom of the Press,* 6 Med.L.Rptr. 1001, 445 U.S. 136, 100 S.Ct. 960 (1980).
49. Ibid.
50. Op. cit., n. 11.
51. Op. cit., n. 11.
52. Ibid.
53. Op. cit., n. 12.
54. *Armstrong v. Bush,* 721 F.Supp. 343 (D.D.C. 1989), aff'd in part, rev'd in part, 924 F.2d 282 (D.C.Cir. 1991); and *Armstrong v. Executive Office of the President,* 810 F.Supp. 335 (D.D.C. 1993).
55. *Armstrong v. Executive Office of the President,* 810 F.Supp. 335 (D.D.C. 1993).
56. *Illinois Institute for Continuing Legal Education v. U.S. Department of Labor,* 545 F.Supp. 1229 (N.D.Ill. 1982).

on a complete index of agency records requested and withheld and the reasons for withholding).[57] It also lists addresses of executive departments and agencies. In addition, the handbook explains how to use the federal Privacy Act of 1974,[58] which interconnects with the FOIA, as will be discussed later. The Reporters Committee handbook *Access to Electronic Records* suggests additional questions to ask: If there is a nonconfidential computer file, would it be available to an agency official? Is software needed, and will a tape or disk be compatible with the equipment used by the requester? Again, fees for retrieval should be discussed up front.

A more detailed and scholarly handbook, now in its eighteenth edition with a 1994 Supplement, is the American Civil Liberties Union Foundation publication, *Litigation under the Federal Open Government Laws*, edited by Allan Robert Adler (122 Maryland Avenue NE, Washington, D.C. 20002). The nuances, complexities, and cases of the FOIA, the Privacy Act, and the Government-in-Sunshine Act are all there.

Once you are familiar with the act, the first step is to make an informal request by telephone or, better, a written request to the agency's information officer. Be specific about who you are and what you want. Anyone can make a request. Ask about search and duplication costs early on. There is no need to say why you want the information, unless you think it will help you gain access. Each agency, bureau, or department of government will have an FOI officer to assist you. Some will be helpful; some will not. Indicate that you understand the appeals procedure and the obligation of an agency with respect to segregable materials. An agency claim of nonsegregability, that is, that confidential and nonconfidential material cannot be separated, must be made with the same degree of detail required for claims of exemption.[59] If a formal written request is asked for, send it by certified mail marked "FOIA request." Fax, of course, is a faster method of communication, and E-mail is sure to follow.

Technically, an agency has a legal duty to reply within ten working days—"technically"

because inadequate funding makes such a response virtually impossible. An extension of time may be needed for complex searches. The FBI and CIA and State and Justice Departments may argue "backlog" to avoid compliance, and the backlogs may be real. If your request involves health or safety, you may ask for an "expedited review." If a delay seems unreasonable, you may appeal in writing to the agency head or its FOI appeals officer who again—technically—is expected to respond within twenty working days. In your appeal, make as strong an argument as possible as to why your request should be granted. In spite of what may appear to be a built-in conflict of interests, the appeals officer can pressure a recalcitrant agency to comply. Attorney General Reno's 1993 memo conscripts the Justice Department's Office of Information and Privacy to assist both the public and agency appeals officers in making or responding to requests. Going directly to your federal representatives or senators might be a useful step, albeit a last resort.

Having followed these steps without success, you are entitled under the act to bring suit in the most convenient federal district court, that is, the one closest to home. If your case is strong enough, you should expect an expedited hearing, meaning that your case goes to the top of the docket and gets immediate attention. The burden of proof for nondisclosure is still on the government, which must justify its need for secrecy. If, in the final analysis, you have "substantially prevailed," you may be awarded attorneys' fees and court costs. The court decides.

Agencies are authorized to charge reasonable fees for searching and copying. Ask for estimates of cost before you order anything. Fee schedules for the various agencies are published in the *Federal Register*. If costs are prohibitive—computer searches can be very expensive—you may request a waiver on the ground you are serving a public benefit as a journalist, author, or scholar. But don't expect any uniformity of response across agencies to such an appeal. News media are not to be charged for the costs of searching for records. A trip to inspect documents, if within your financial resources, may better serve your research needs. Many agencies offer reading rooms and assistance once you get there. In response to a case holding that copies of documents need not be produced if agencies provide

---

57. *Vaughn v. Rosen,* 1 Med.L.Rptr. 2509, 484 F.2d 820 (D.C.Cir. 1973), *cert. denied,* 415 U.S. 977 (1974).

58. 5 U.S.C.A. §552a.

59. Op. cit., n 55.

some other form of access,[60] such as a reading room, the Justice Department advised as a matter of policy that the practice not be followed unless the requester agreed.

The *Vaughn* index referred to above and the case out of which it came also developed requirements for explaining decisions to withhold and for separating disclosable from nondisclosable information. The *Vaughn* court argued that, since the burden of proof for withholding was on the government, an agency would be required "to correlate statements made in its refusal justification with the actual portions of the document." This would allow adversaries to move quickly to the heart of the dispute as to protected and unprotected material and, hopefully, would result in greater disclosure. Unfortunately, *Vaughn* did not affect all agencies in the same way. A 1991 Ninth Circuit ruling attempted to clarify and regularize the *Vaughn* requirements and at the same time to celebrate the spirit of the FOIA.[61]

Wiener v. FBI

943 F.2D 972 (9TH CIR. 1991), *CERT. DENIED*, 112 S.Ct. 3013 (1992).

JAMES R. BROWNING, Circuit Judge:

Professor Jonathan M. Wiener, Professor of History at the University of California, Irvine, filed a request under the Freedom of Information Act ("FOIA") for disclosure of records of the Federal Bureau of Investigation concerning John Lennon, late member of the Beatles. Professor Wiener sought to further his research into John Lennon's life,[1] and to bolster his thesis that the investigation of Mr. Lennon by the FBI in the late 1960s and early 1970s reflected the use of executive agency power to suppress political dissent.

The FBI withheld some of the requested records as exempt from disclosure by the terms of

the Act. Wiener filed this action to compel complete disclosure and moved to require the FBI to explain why each document withheld was exempt. In response, the FBI filed affidavits of two FBI agents and one CIA agent justifying the withholdings in general terms. The district court ordered the FBI to submit in camera further justification for the withholdings. The FBI filed two additional affidavits and a copy of each withheld document. The court then granted the FBI's motion for summary judgment.

Wiener appealed contending: (1) the public affidavits were inadequate; (2) the district court's findings of fact and law were insufficient; and (3) there were triable issues of fact with respect to the propriety of the claims of exemption. We agree with Wiener's first two contentions and reverse. We do not find it necessary to reach Wiener's third claim.

Ordinarily, rules of discovery give each party access to the evidence upon which the court will rely in resolving the dispute between them. In a FOIA case, however, because the issue is whether one party will disclose documents to the other, only the party opposing disclosure will have access to all the facts. See *King v. Dep't of Justice*, 830 F.2d 210, 218 (D.C.Cir.1987); *Vaughn v. Rosen*, 484 F.2d 820, 823–25 (D.C.Cir.1973).

"This lack of knowledge by the party seeking disclosure seriously distorts the traditional adversary nature of our legal system[ ]." Vaughn, 484 F.2d at 824. The party requesting disclosure must rely upon his adversary's representations as to the material withheld, and the court is deprived of the benefit of informed advocacy to draw its attention to the weaknesses in the withholding agency's arguments. It is simply "unreasonable to expect a trial judge to do as thorough a job of illumination and characterization as would a party interested in the case." Id. at 825.

In recognition of this problem, government agencies seeking to withhold documents requested under the FOIA have been required to supply the opposing party and the court with a "Vaughn index," identifying each document withheld, the statutory exemption claimed, and a particularized explanation of how disclosure of the particular document would damage the interest protected by the claimed exemption. The purpose of the index is to "afford the FOIA requester a meaningful opportunity to contest, and the district court an adequate foundation to review, the

---

60. *Oglesby v. Department of the Army*, 920 F.2d 57, 65 (D.C.Cir. 1990).

61. An article demonstrating the importance of *Wiener's* standard for withholding to other federal circuit courts of appeal is Elizabeth A. Vitell, Toeing the Line in the Ninth Circuit: Proper Agency Justification of FOIA Exemptions Clarified in *Wiener v. FBI*, 42 DePaul L.Rev. 795 (Winter 1992). She notes that the D.C. Circuit still defers to government claims for secrecy.

1. Professor Wiener authored *Come Together: John Lennon In His Time* (Random House 1984), a study of Mr. Lennon.

soundness of the withholding." The index thus functions to restore the adversary process to some extent, and to permit more effective judicial review of the agency's decision.

The district court required a Vaughn index in this case. In response to the court's order, the FBI supplies the court and Wiener with the affidavits of three federal agents; the FBI later filed two additional public affidavits. Whether the government's public affidavits constituted an adequate Vaughn index is a question of law reviewed de novo. We conclude they did not.

The substance of the affidavits consisted of redacted copies of documents partially withheld and blacked out copies of documents withheld in their entirety, with one or more handwritten four digit codes written next to each exemption claimed by the FBI. For example, the notation "(b)(1)," is a reference to 5 U.S.C. §552(b)(1), and indicates that the exemption for properly classified documents ("Exemption 1") was claimed. The next two digits of each code refer to one of a number of categories of information listed in the affidavits into which the withheld information allegedly fell. For example "c3" refers to "detailed information pertaining to/or provided by an intelligence source." The affidavits list up to nine categories of information for each of the statutory exemptions claimed.

The affidavits then state in general terms why each category of information should be withheld.

* * *

These boilerplate" explanations were drawn from a "master" response filed by the FBI for many FOIA requests. No effort is made to tailor the explanation to the specific document withheld. Remarkably, in the original Vaughn index submitted by the FBI, John Lennon's name does not appear at all. The explanations offered are precisely the sort of "[c]ategorical description[s] of redacted material coupled with categorical indications of anticipated consequences of disclosure" the D.C. Circuit properly rejected in *King* as "clearly inadequate."

This categorical approach affords Wiener little or no opportunity to argue for release of particular documents. The most obvious obstacle to effective advocacy is the FBI's decision to state alternatively several possible reasons for withholding documents, without identifying the specific reason or reasons for withholding each particular document. Effective advocacy is possible

only if the requester knows the precise basis for nondisclosure. The agency may give alternative reasons for withholding a document only if each reason is applicable to the document at issue.

Moreover, the level of specificity in the index submitted in this case is insufficient. "Specificity is the defining requirement of the Vaughn index." Unless the agency discloses "as much information as possible without thwarting the [claimed] exemption's purpose," the adversarial process is unnecessarily compromised. The FBI did not disclose all it could. Indeed, the index provides no information about particular documents and portions of documents that might be useful in contesting nondisclosure—the two principal affidavits of Agents Chester and Peterson make no reference to any particular document at all.

In camera review of the withheld documents by the court is not an acceptable substitute for an adequate Vaughn index. *In camera* review does not permit effective advocacy. Therefore, resort to *in camera* review is appropriate only after "the government has submitted as detailed public affidavits and testimony as possible." *Doyle v. FBI*, 722 F.2d at 556; see also, *Ingle v. Dep't of Justice*, 698 F.2d 259, 266 (6th Cir.1983) ("no court should consider *in camera* review if a Vaughn Index can adequately resolve the issue"). *In camera* review may supplement an adequate Vaughn index, but may not replace it. Cf. *NLRB v. Robbins Tire & Rubber Co.*, 437 U.S. 214 (1978) ("*in camera* review . . . is designed to be invoked when the issue before the District Court could not be otherwise resolved").

In revising the Vaughn index on remand, the FBI must bear in mind that the purpose of the index is not merely to inform the requester of the agency's conclusion that a particular document is exempt from disclosure under one or more of the statutory exemptions, but to afford the requester an opportunity to intelligently advocate release of the withheld documents and to afford the court an opportunity to intelligently judge the contest.

We turn to a consideration of each of the four statutory exemptions claimed by the FBI in this case.

EXEMPTION 1: NATIONAL SECURITY

* * *

Though an executive agency's classification decisions are accorded substantial weight, the FOIA permits challenges to Exemption 1 withholdings, requires the district court to review the propriety of the classification, and places the burden on the withholding agency to sustain its Exemption 1 claims. * * * The government's affidavits did not provide Wiener a reasonable opportunity to contest the Exemption 1 withholdings.

(1) Confidential Source Information

Many of the Exemption 1 withholdings were based on the FBI's conclusion that release of the withheld documents would damage national security by leading to the disclosure of a confidential source. As discussed in more detail in connection with the FBI's withholdings under Exemption 7D (relating specifically to confidential sources), the withholding agency must provide the court and the FOIA requester with information sufficient to determine whether the source was truly a confidential one and why disclosure of the withheld information would lead to exposure of the source. Because the Vaughn index makes no effort to do so, it is inadequate.

Moreover, merely showing the source was confidential and would be revealed by production of the withheld document, is not sufficient to sustain an Exemption 1 claim. In addition, Exemption 1 is available only if disclosure of the source "could reasonably be expected to cause damage to the national security." To justify an Exemption 1 claim, the Vaughn index must provide (to the extent permitted by national security needs) sufficient information to enable the requester to contest the withholding agency's conclusion that disclosure will result in damage to the nation's security.

The index in this case does not meet this standard. The index lists eight categories of information the FBI asserts could expose a confidential source, and a single explanation of the harm to national security that may flow from disclosure of a source's identity:

Exposure of an intelligence source can result in termination of the source; discontinuance of the source's services; exposure of other ongoing intelligence gathering activities; modification or cancellation of future intelligence gathering activities; evaluation by hostile entities of the number and objectives of intelligence sources targeted against them, followed by appropriate countermeasures; and an overall chilling effect on the climate of cooperativeness with respect to the unwillingness of intelligence sources, both current and prospective, to risk the probability of exposure with its potential effect of possible loss of life, jobs, friends, status, etc., all of which can reasonably be expected to hamper intelligence collection ability and result in damage to the national security.

The index fails to tie the FBI's general concern about disclosure of confidential sources to the facts of this case. The index does not describe any particular withheld document, identify the kind of information found in that document that would expose the confidential sources, or describe the injury to national security that would follow from the disclosure of the confidential source of the particular document. The FBI must have made such an analysis in concluding that disclosure of some informants or classes of informants would damage national security and disclosure of others would not. Yet none of the information and analysis necessarily considered is made available to Wiener or the court. The index simply relies on general assertions that disclosure of certain categories of facts may result in disclosure of the source and disclosure of the source may lead to a variety of consequences detrimental to national security.

(2) Intelligence Activities and Methods

The discussion in the affidavits of withholdings based on the exemption from disclosure of information related to intelligence activities and method is particularly scanty.

We are once again given only a generalized, theoretical discussion of the possible harms which can result from the release of this category of information. The FBI has again failed to state the specific harms which may result from the release of a particular document. The explanations are simply too broad to be of any use to Wiener, the district court, or this court.

(3) Information about Foreign Relations and Governments

The same is true of the FBI's discussion of information concerning foreign relations and foreign governments. Again, we are given broad explanations of alternative harms that might result from the release of the withheld information. No explanation is given why seemingly farfetched harms, such as the FBI's claim that release of the withheld information will "[l]ead to . . . military retaliation against the United States," have any relevance to the particular documents withheld.

EXEMPTION 3: WITHHOLDING AUTHORIZED BY ANOTHER STATUTE

Exemption 3 authorizes the withholding of documents "specifically exempted from disclosure by statute" other than the FOIA itself. The FBI relied upon four separate statutes to support its Exemption 3 withholdings.

(1) Records Relating to Visa Applications

The FBI relied upon 8 U.S.C. §1202(f) (1988) in withholding three documents. * * * The Vaughn index does little more than recite the language of section 1202(f). This is not sufficient. The withholding agency's understanding of the scope of section 1202(f) may be incorrect. To enable the FOIA requester to challenge the FBI's conclusion that the documents withheld fell within section 1202(f), the Vaughn index must provide a description of the withheld documents, without breaching section 1202(f)'s mandate of confidentiality. Here, for example, without breaching confidentiality, the FBI could have disclosed that the withheld records concerned a foreign citizen's request for a temporary waiver of certain visa requirements, and included the investigating official's recommended disposition of the request.

(2) Records Relating to Tax Returns

The FBI relied upon 26 U.S.C. §6103 in withholding one document. Section 6103 states that "[tax] return information shall be confidential." The FBI's Vaughn index states only that tax return information was withheld.

Ordinarily, we would find such an explanation of a withholding of tax return information insufficient. Section 6103 contains a long and complex definition of tax return information. Reasonable people could differ as to its interpretation. * * * For this reason, the withholding agency must ordinarily provide the FOIA requester with a description of the withheld information sufficient to enable the FOIA

requester to challenge the agency's understanding of the scope of section 6103 reflected in the decision to withhold. The confidentiality guaranteed by section 6103 will not be compromised as long as the identity of the person about whom the tax return information relates is not revealed.

Here, however, the released portions of the document suggest the identity of the person whose privacy interests are protected by section 6103. Thus, if the withholding agency were to reveal the precise nature of the tax return information, the confidentiality guaranteed by section 6103 would be compromised. For this reason, the FBI could not disclose more than it did, and therefore was not required to do so.

(3) CIA Information

50 U.S.C. §403(d)(3) (1988) states "the Director of Central Intelligence shall be responsible for protecting intelligence sources and methods from unauthorized disclosure." 50 U.S.C. §403g (1988) states that "the [Central Intelligence] Agency shall be exempted from the provisions of . . . any other law which require[s] the publication or disclosure of the organization, functions, names, official titles, salaries, or numbers of personnel employed by the Agency." Both of these statutes specifically exempt information from FOIA disclosure.

The FBI relied upon §403(d)(3) and §403g in withholding parts of four documents. The FBI relied upon the affidavit of CIA Agent Dube to justify these withholdings. This affidavit, unlike those submitted by the FBI agents, discusses each document separately. It provides sufficient information with respect to all but one of the withholdings. Two of the withholdings consist only of codenames, identified as such in the Dube affidavit. Codenames plainly fall within section 403g's exemption of the names of CIA agents. No further disclosure would have enabled Wiener to argue for their release. One paragraph of a document labeled CIA-3 was withheld because it identified the location of a CIA installation outside the United States. The Dube affidavit describes how disclosure of this information would compromise "intelligence sources and methods," by leading to public pressure within the host nation to terminate its relationship with the CIA. This was sufficient to enable Wiener and the court to determine whether the government's conclusion that withholding was necessary to protect intelligence sources and methods was subject to challenge.[18]

The Dube affidavit is insufficient, however, with respect to the document labeled CIA-2. The Dube affidavit justifies the deletions of three paragraphs from this document with the statement that "disclosure of [the withheld] portions reasonably could be expected to lead to identification of the source of information." The affidavit fails to discuss the facts or reasoning upon which Agent Dube based his conclusion, and thus affords Wiener no opportunity to contest that conclusion.

EXEMPTION 7C: PRIVACY

Exemption 7C, 5 U.S.C. §552(b)(7)(C), permits the government to withhold documents and portions of documents "compiled for law enforcement purposes, but only to the extent that the production of such records would . . . (C)onstitute an unwarranted invasion of personal privacy." A disclosure is outweighed by the individual privacy interests that would suffer from disclosure. *Dep't of Justice v. Reporters Committee for Freedom of the Press*, 489 U.S. 749, 109 S.Ct. 1468, (1989). A Vaughn index must, to the extent possible without sacrificing the privacy interest in the process, provide the FOIA requester with the information necessary to contest the agency's conclusion that this balance tips in favor of withholding.

Wiener has not appealed Exemption 7C claims where only the name of an FBI agent or third person has been withheld. He challenges only the relatively few withholdings in which entire documents or paragraphs have been withheld to protect the privacy interests of persons whose names appear somewhere in the with-

held material. With respect to these withholdings, we conclude the FBI's affidavits are inadequate.

We focus upon the most substantial Exemption 7C withholdings—documents labeled HQ-8 and NY-88. Several pages of HQ-8 were withheld; NY-88 was withheld in its entirety.

Without violating the privacy interests of the informant or the third party, the FBI could have stated that HQ-8 recites information provided by a third party to an FBI informant detailing the third party's knowledge of several activists and protest activities planned at the 1972 Republican National Convention, discussing the possibility that John Lennon would organize a series of concerts to raise money to finance the activity, and describing rivalries and jealousies within activist organizations.

Had Wiener been provided with this information, he could have questioned whether the withholding of anything other than the names of the informant, the third party, and the individuals described, implicated privacy concerns. He could also have argued that the names of the activist leaders mentioned in the document should have been released because of the substantial public interest in exploring the scope and extent of the FBI's surveillance activities during a turbulent period of this nation's history. As this brief summary demonstrates, adequate specificity could have been achieved without compromising privacy interests. Instead, the FBI affidavits reveal only that the information in document HQ-8 relates to a third party who is mentioned in FBI files.

Without compromising privacy interests, the FBI could have stated that document NY-88 describes a series of meetings between a third person and various activists, discusses contests over the leadership of activist groups and complaints that activist leaders receive more publicity than the groups themselves, and reports tangential information about activist leaders, such as their habits of personal hygiene and even the peculiar behaviors of their pets. John Lennon's name appears only in the final paragraph in which it is stated that Lennon was willing to perform at a benefit concert if his appearance were not announced in advance. Without describing generally what the document contained, as we have, it was withheld in its entirety on the

---

18. Unlike withholdings under Exemption 1, a withholding agency relying upon section 403(d)(3) to protect an intelligence source need not demonstrate if disclosure of the source will damage national security. Nonetheless, the information provided in the Dube affidavit is sufficiently specific to constitute an adequate Vaughn index with respect to Exemption 1 as well. It states in detail the nature of the information (location of a CIA station) and the harm to national security likely to result form disclosure (the closing of that station).

ground that the information withheld relates to a third party.[23]

The FBI argues the decision in *Reporters Committee*, 489 U.S. 749 (1989), sanctions the categorical approach employed by the FBI in support of Exemption 7C claims. In holding that an individual's privacy interest in his "rap sheet" always outweighs the public interest in disclosure, the Court said "categorical decisions may be appropriate and individual circumstances disregarded when a case fits into a genus in which the balance characteristically tips in one direction." The FBI argues that the privacy interests of third persons whose names appear in withheld documents always outweigh the public interest in disclosure, and a Vaughn index therefore need only recite the fact that the document was withheld to protect the privacy interests of third persons. * * * We disagree.

The privacy interests of third persons whose names appear in FBI files, the public interest in disclosure, and a proper balancing of the two, will vary depending upon the content of the information and the nature of the attending circumstances.[24] Because it cannot be concluded that the privacy interests characteristically outweigh the public interest with respect to all the documents withheld under Exemption 7C, the FBI's categorical Vaughn index is inadequate.

The index also fails to explain with sufficient specificity the "law enforcement purposes" underlying its investigation of John Lennon. No withholding under any of the exemptions listed in section 552(b)(7) is valid unless the withholding agency establishes a "'rational nexus' between its law enforcement duties and the document for which Exemption 7 is claimed."[25]

The index states only that John Lennon was under investigation for possible violations of the Civil Obedience Act of 1968, 18 U.S.C. §231 (1988), and the Anti-Riot Act, 18 U.S.C. §2101 (1988), because of his association with a radical group known as the Election Year Strategy Information Center (EYSIC). The Civil Obedience Act and the Anti-Riot Act are very broad criminal statutes, prohibiting a wide variety of conduct. Citations to these statutes do little to inform Wiener of the claimed law enforcement purpose underlying the investigation of John Lennon. Without providing Wiener with further details of the kinds of criminal activity of which John Lennon was allegedly suspected, Wiener cannot effectively argue that the claimed law enforcement purpose was in fact a pretext.

EXEMPTION 7D: IDENTITY OF A CONFIDENTIAL SOURCE

Exemption 7D, 5 U.S.C. §552(b)(7)(D), permits the government to withhold documents and portions of documents "compiled for law enforcement

---

23. In contrast to the broad generalities offered to justify most of its Exemption 7C withholdings, the FBI provided model explanations with respect to two sets of documents. Wiener has not appealed these withholdings, and we mention them only to provide further examples of the level of specificity required in a Vaughn index.

The supplemental affidavit of Agent Flynn states that four documents were withheld because they document an "investigation . . . based on a citizen's inquiries to his Congressman about a nude photograph of Lennon and Yoko Ono on an album cover. The Congressman forwarded the inquiry to the FBI, which responded . . . that no violation [of obscenity laws] existed." This explanation makes clear what the documents contained and that they were withheld because their release might infringe upon the privacy interests of the citizen who made the inquiry. It afforded Wiener an opportunity to argue that this privacy interest was outweighed by other considerations. The FBI stated that Exhibit 00 pertained to the FBI's investigation of someone who threatened the Lennon family. The perpetrator was never identified. The FBI noted that details contained in the document were withheld because, if released, "media publicity would undoubtedly follow. It must be assumed that this unknown subject is alive and would be aware of such publicity. The resulting effect on him is obviously unknown but can be speculated upon. Perhaps this refreshing of his memory would cause him to resume this type of threatening activity against the Lennon family or possibly other well-known personalities. . . . In addition, its release could well be expected to cause John Lennon's widow and her family harassment and unwarranted public attention." This statement provided Wiener with sufficient information to argue in favor of the release of the withheld document had he chosen to do so.

24. In contrast, the Court in *Reporters Committee* noted that an individual's privacy interest in the confidentiality of his criminal record is always high, and the public interest in release of that information is always low, 109 S.Ct. at 1485.
25. Thus, our holding that the Vaughn index failed to adequately set forth the law enforcement purpose of the investigation of John Lennon applies equally to withholdings under Exemption 7D, protecting confidential sources. Both Exemption 7C and Exemption 7D exempt from disclosure only records "compiled for law enforcement purposes." 5 U.S.C. §552(b)(7).

purposes, but only to the extent that the production of such law enforcement records . . . could reasonably be expected to disclose the identity of a confidential source." The index does not provide Wiener with information necessary to challenge the FBI's conclusion that disclosure of documents withheld on this ground would in fact reveal the identity of a confidential source.

The most obvious flaw in the index in this respect is its failure to state whether the purported grant of confidentiality in each case was express or implied. An express grant of confidentiality is virtually unassailable. The FBI need only establish the informant was told his name would be held in confidence. An implied grant is a different matter. An informant's identity is protected by an implied grant of confidentiality only if he provides information under "circumstances from which . . . an assurance [of confidentiality] could be reasonably inferred." * * *

Without knowing whether the grant of confidentiality claimed was express or implied, the requester cannot challenge the claim intelligently.

Moreover, if the FBI is relying upon implied grants of confidentiality to justify its withholdings, the explanation given is inadequate. To serve its purpose, the index must state the circumstances surrounding the receipt of information which led the FBI to conclude the informant would not have given the information without an implicit assurance of confidentiality. Only if the requester has these facts can he intelligently argue no inference of confidentiality was justified; and only if the district court is apprised of these facts can its judgment on the merits be an informed one. * * *

Because the Vaughn index did not disclose the facts and circumstances surrounding the receipt of information from informants, the district court and opposing counsel were forced to look through a voluminous set of documents in an effort to find some evidence of the circumstances surrounding each purported grant of confidentiality. Moreover, the search necessarily accomplished little because the withheld documents, particularly in redacted form, did not provide much information of this kind.

An adequate Vaughn index would have guided the district court and opposing counsel to questionable claims of exemption. For example, without compromising confidentiality, the FBI

could have informed Wiener and the district court that during a hearing before the Immigration and Naturalization Service regarding the deportability of John Lennon, Mr. Lennon's attorney represented that Mr. Lennon had been offered a teaching post at New York University; that the FBI later investigated the truth of this claim; and that as part of its investigation, the FBI contacted an official at New York University who stated the University had in fact offered John Lennon a teaching position. The name of this University official, and all facts which could lead to his identity, are still being withheld by the FBI under Exemption 7D. Indeed, until 1984 this information was classified as "secret" by the FBI.

DISTRICT COURT FINDINGS

"Disclosure of the factual and legal basis for the trial court's decision is especially compelling in FOIA cases." *Van Bourg, Allen, Weinberg & Roger v. NLRB* (Van Bourg I), 656 F.2d 1356, 1357 (9th Cir.1981). The district court's findings of facts and conclusions of law must be "'sufficiently detailed to establish that the careful de novo review prescribed by Congress has in fact taken place.'" "The reviewing court should not be required to speculate on the precise relationship between each exemption claim and the contents of the specific document[s]." *Van Bourg I,* 656 F.2d at 1358 (quoting *Ray v. Turner,* 587 F.2d 1187, 1197 (D.C.Cir.1978)).

The district court's findings consist of a list of the affidavits submitted by government and the conclusory statement that "[t]he above-listed affidavits and declarations carry the government's burden of proof to show that the FOIA exemptions were properly applied in this case." Like the *Van Bourg I* court, "[w]e are unable to determine which exemption the court applied to each document withheld and what relevant undisputed facts provided the basis for non-disclosure." After receiving an adequate Vaughn index and conducting any additional proceedings the district court deems necessary on remand, the court must "state in reasonable detail the reasons for its decision as to each document in dispute."

The district court also erred by failing to make specific findings on the issue of segregability. 5 U.S.C. §552(b) provides that "[a]ny reasonably segregable portion of a record shall be provided to any person requesting such record after deletion of the portions which are exempt under this subsection." Here, many documents were withheld either in their entirety or in substantial part. It is reversible error for the district court "to simply approve the withholding of an entire document without entering a finding on segregability, or the lack thereof," with respect to that document. *Church of Scientology v. U.S. Postal Service*, 611 F.2d at 744. The court on remand must make a specific finding that no information contained in each document or substantial portion of a document withheld is segregable.

TRIABLE ISSUES OF FACT

Wiener argues summary judgment was inappropriate because triable issues of fact remain. In particular, he contends the FBI has failed to establish by uncontested facts that the documents withheld under Exemptions 7C and & 7D were "compiled for law enforcement purposes," 5 U.S.C. §552(b)(7), and that the documents withheld under Exemption 1 were not withheld merely "to conceal violations of law, inefficiency, or administrative error[, or] to prevent embarrassment to a person, organization, or agency." He points to a memorandum signed by FBI Director J. Edgar Hoover expressing concern that John Lennon might not be deported prior to the 1972 Republican National Convention; a memorandum from Acting FBI Director Gray stating the INS's belief that it had a weak case for deportation and that an arrest on narcotics charges would insure immediate deportation; and a memorandum to Senator Strom Thurmond, later forwarded to Attorney General John Mitchell, stating that termination of Lennon's visa would be a "strategic countermeasure" against the political strategies of anti-war and anti-Nixon groups.

It would be premature to address Wiener's claim. Without an adequate Vaughn index and sufficient findings of fact to guide us we cannot say whether these documents, in light of the rest of the record, raise a triable issue of fact.

REVERSED and REMANDED.

EXEMPTIONS

Nondisclosure under nine exemptions to the FOIA has led to hundreds of lawsuits. Though it is impossible to summarize all of this litigation in any meaningful way, each exemption will be discussed briefly, and a few representative cases will be mentioned.

1. NATIONAL SECURITY   Exemption 1 is the most difficult to dispute. Federal judges are authorized under the act to examine in chambers material that, if released, would cause, according to executive orders, "identifiable damage" to the national security or the foreign policy of the United States. "Expertise," initiative, and authority, however, remain with the government. All it has to show is that the material sought has been properly classified "top secret, secret, or confidential." If there is a "reasonable doubt" about the level of classification, the highest level pertains. Little if any balancing takes place where CIA records are involved. Exemptions 1 and 3 (federal laws covered by the latter)[62] put most CIA records beyond the reach of the public.[63] The question, then, is whether Congress's intent to enhance democratic self-rule by passing the FOIA is being honored.[64]

The difficulty of beating the national security exemption was dramatically demonstrated early on by the "Glomar Project," which was jointly financed by the CIA and the late Howard Hughes. The object was to raise an obsolete Russian submarine from the ocean floor. The public was told it was a deep-sea mining project. When more information was sought on the project, the D.C. Circuit Court of Appeals said, "It is well established that summary judgment is properly granted in Exemption 1 cases without an *in camera* inspection or discovery by the plaintiffs when the affidavits submitted by the agency are adequate to the task."[65]

---

62. CIA Information Act, 50 U.S.C. §431 (1988); National Security Act, 50 U.S.C. §403(g) (1988).

63. See *Hunt v. CIA*, 981 F.2d 1116 (9th Cir. 1992) in which the court acknowledged that ". . . we are now only a short step (from) exempting all CIA records from FOIA . . . contrary to what Congress intended." Similar results occurred in *Maynard v. CIA*, 986 F.2d 547 (1st Cir. 1993) in which the court, in complete deference to the agency, pled ignorance of intelligence operations, and in Sullivan v. CIA, 992 F.2d 1249 (1st Cir. 1993) in which the CIA Information Act was applied to uphold nondisclosure.

64. Amy E. Rees, Recent Developments Regarding the Freedom of Information Act: A Prologue to a Farce or a Tragedy; Or, Perhaps, Both, 44 *Duke L.J.* 1183 (April 1995).

65. *Military Audit Project v. Casey*, 7 Med.L.Rptr. 1708, 656 F.2d 724 (D.C.Cir. 1981).

Earlier, the same federal court had laid a foundation for that holding by ruling that in making a *de novo* (completely new) determination, the court must first "accord substantial weight to an agency's affidavit concerning the details of the classified status of the disputed record."[66] Two years later the court said it again: ". . . Congress intended reviewing courts to respect the expertise of an agency; for us to insist that the agency's rationale . . . is implausible would be to overstep the proper limits of the judicial role in FOIA review."[67] Although at least one circuit court has interpreted the FOIA to require agencies to justify their decisions to withhold with specific affidavits,[68] affidavits are given substantial weight by the courts. In other words, courts, seldom second-guess agency decisions in national security matters. While agency affidavits and judicial review may be acceptable compromises, they tend to leave the requester, the person seeking the information, out in the cold.

The *Glomar* case gave life to the much abused notion of "Glomarization," meaning that an agency is permitted to "neither confirm nor deny"[69] the existence of a document, although a federal court in 1985 said an agency might have to justify such a response.[70] This was followed by President Reagan's more constraining Executive Order 12356, which made classification of documents mandatory if their release "reasonably could be expected to cause damage to the national security." On the domestic front, the FBI can refuse to acknowledge the existence of records that are classified and relate to intelligence under the Anti-Drug Abuse Act of 1986.

Documents are sometimes reclassified after an FOIA request is made, the government being alerted and tempted by the request to engage in deeper classification. Congress has contributed to the *de facto* blanket exemption of CIA records through legislation such as the CIA Information Act, amending the National Security Act of 1947 to allow the CIA director to exempt certain "operational" files from the FOIA. At its discretion, the CIA may decline to search and review documents that by their very nature are likely to be classified. The judicial branch, as has been noted, is inclined to defer to the agency.

Under the Foreign Relations Authorization Act of 1991,[71] all State Department records are declassified after thirty years unless specifically reclassified. All records concerning the assassination of President Kennedy were to be released under a 1992 act of Congress.[72] Potential harm of any kind is to be balanced against the public's right to know.

Information that has leaked into the public domain may be less susceptible to classification.[73] Here again, though, "official acknowledgment" may have to precede declassification.[74]

2. INTERNAL RULES AND PRACTICES

Exemption 2 is a "housekeeping" claim. Matters "related solely to the *internal personnel rules and practices* of an agency" may be exempt. Basic rules were laid down in *Crooker v. Bureau of Alcohol, Tobacco and Firearms*[75] in 1981. Material is exempt if (1) "it is 'predominantly internal' in nature, meaning it is designed to establish rules and practices of interest to agency personnel, and is not applicable to matters where there is a substantial public interest in disclosure," and (2) disclosure "significantly risks circumvention of agency regulations or statutes." That part of the manual of the Bureau of Alcohol, Tobacco and Firearms, "Raids and Searches (Special Agent Basic Training—Criminal Enforcement)," dealing with the surveillance of premises and persons, was held not to be exempt under Exemption 2. "There can be little doubt," the court wrote, "that citizens have an interest in the manner in which they may

66. *Ray v. Turner*, 587 F.2d 1187 (D.C.Cir.1978).

67. *Hayden v. National Security Agency*, 5 Med.L.Rptr. 1897, 608 F.2d 1381 (D.C.Cir. 1979).

68. *Wiener v. FBI*, 943 F.2d 972 (9th Cir. 1991), *cert. denied*, 505 U.S. 1212 (1992).

69. The term was first suggested in *Phillippi v. CIA*, 2 Med.L.Rptr. 1208, 546 F.2d 1009, 1010 (D.C.Cir. 1976).

70. *Marrera v. U.S. Department of Justice*, 622 F.Supp. 51 (D.D.C. 1985).

71. P. L. 102–138, §198, 105 Stat. 685-691.

72. JFK Assassination Records Collection Act of 1992, P.L. 102-526, 106 Stat. 3443, codified at 44 U.S.C. §2107.

73. *Washington Post Company v. U.S. Department of Defense*, 766 F.Supp. 1, 9–14 (D.D.C. 1991).

74. *Afshar v. Department of State*, 702 F.2d 1125 (D.C.Cir. 1983); *Public Citizen v. Department of State*, 11 F.3d 198 (D.C.Cir. 1993); See also, David H. Morrissey, "Disclosure and Secrecy: Security Classification and Executive Orders," *Journalism and Mass Communication Monographs*, No. 161 (February 1997).

75. 7 Med.L.Rptr. 2411, 670 F.2d 1051, 1056–57, 1073–74 (D.C.Cir. 1981).

be observed by federal agents. . . . Neither exemption (b)(2) nor any other exemption prevents a citizen from satisfying his curiosity on these matters. The contents of this document . . . pertaining to surveillance of the public cannot possibly be assimilated to mere 'internal housekeeping' concerns."[76]

How are public interests to be separated from the particular interests of an agency? The Law Enforcement Manual of the IRS is not subject to disclosure because it contains "the kind of sensitive law enforcement information, disclosure of which will only serve to undermine law enforcement."[77] For similar reasons, FBI file numbers, classifying certain bank robbery investigation files for internal purposes, are exempt."[78] A complete draft manuscript of the Air Force's official history of the Vietnam War was held exempt from disclosure so as to protect the agency's deliberative process in editing and reviewing manuscripts.[79] Clearly, some rulings are meant to protect government secrecy. Yet an insurance company was able to get the names of personnel on an air base, even though the company's purpose was purely commercial.[80]

Since some agencies have gone so far as to claim exemptions for vacation schedules and parking lot assignments, courts must continue to search for that delicate balance between the genuine needs of government agencies and a legitimate public interest.

3. STATUTORY EXEMPTIONS Exemption 3 refers to federal statutes that already exempt certain classes of information. They are myriad: more than a hundred statutes have been cited to justify withholding information. Some qualify to override the FOIA, others don't. Statutes pertaining to the CIA generally qualify.[81] Statutes cited by less sensitive agencies often do not.[82] Some statutes fail to meet the standards for withholding because they are too broad to meet the requirement of identifying particular matters to be withheld.[83] Courts in such cases must weigh the purposes of the FOIA against the statute cited as an exemption, balancing one federal statute against another.

Exemption 3 requires the government to show (1) that the requested information falls within the scope of the statute cited and (2) that the statute either vests no discretion to disclose (that is, it mandates secrecy), or that the information fits criteria delineated to authorize withholding.

A 1984 amendment to the National Security Act removed from the ordinary search and review requirements of the FOIA all sensitive CIA "operational files" dealing mainly with foreign and counterintelligence operations. A year later, the Supreme Court certified broad authority for the CIA under the National Security Act to protect all of its sources of information.[84] Obviously, Exemptions 1 and 3 are frequently cited together as justification for nondisclosure. Exempt are files related to operations that Congress or other executive agencies might be investigating for possible CIA wrongdoing. That exception was relevant to the Walsh committee investigation of the Iran-Contra affair.

The Family Education Rights and Privacy Act of 1974,[85] sometimes referred to as the Buckley Amendment, gives students a right of access, within limits, to their own educational records maintained by institutions that receive federal funds, and it protects those files from public disclosure. Parents have access to these files until their postsecondary school children have reached the age of eighteen; at that point the consent of the student is required. School administrators, who also have access to such files under certain conditions, sometimes use the act for purposes not intended by Congress. For example, a Missouri federal judge ruled in 1991 that campus crime records were *not* exempt from disclosure by the act.[86] Remaining exempt are census records, tax returns, grand jury transcripts, and information pertaining to personnel of the National Security Agency.

76. Ibid.
77. *Roberts v. IRS,* 584 F.Supp. 1241 (E.D.Mich. 1984).
78. *McCoy v. Moschella,* unreported (D.D.C. 1991).
79. *Dudman Communications Corp. v. Department of Air Force,* 13 Med.L.Rptr. 245, 815 F.2d 1565 (D.C.Cir. 1987).
80. *Schwaner v. Department of the Air Force,* 898 F.2d 793 (D.C.Cir. 1990).
81. *CIA v. Sims,* 11 Med.L.Rptr. 2107, 471 U.S. 159 (1985).
82. *Church of Scientology v. U.S. Postal Service,* 6 Med.L.Rptr. 2434, 633 F.2d 1327 (9th Cir. 1980).
83. *Washington Post Company v. U.S. Department of State,* 8 Med.L.Rptr. 2206, 685 F.2d 698, (D.C.Cir. 1982), vacated, 464 U.S. 969 (1983).
84. *CIA v. Sims,* 471 U.S. 159 (1985).
85. 20 U.S.C. §1233g.
86. *Bauer v. Kincaid* (unreported).

4. TRADE SECRETS   Exemption 4 was designed to protect "trade secrets and commercial or financial information obtained from a person [that are] privileged or confidential." Like some of the other exemptions, Exemption 4 is frequently used by corporate rivals to gain competitive advantage or to circumvent civil discovery. Trade secrets may include profit and loss statements, market share information, secret formulas or product innovations bearing on the production process, and customer lists. All of this is commercially valuable secret information used in business and supplied to the government voluntarily by private firms; it is not information about private firms generated by the government itself, which could be made public. Nor does the information qualify for disclosure because it describes governmental procedures. Federal agencies are expected to prove that materials sought through the FOIA are indeed trade secrets; that is, that they are confidential and that their release would cause considerable business loss or competitive harm, or make it difficult for an agency to collect similar information in the future.[87]

The D.C. Circuit Court of Appeals drew a distinction between information that is submitted to the government involuntarily (by subpoena) and that submitted voluntarily; the latter is confidential "if it is the kind that the provider would not customarily make available to the public."[88] A divided court emphasized the government's interest in a continuing flow of uncompelled information, so crucial to an agency's concerns that the agency is prepared to limit public access to that information. The information at the center of this controversy involved nuclear power plant safety. A major drawback of the court's decision was that it could be inferred to encourage industry and government to conspire to keep information from the public by inviting voluntary submission of information that the government had the authority to compel. An agency would then have an excuse for secrecy. Perhaps the court had forgotten the original purpose of the FOIA, which is to disclose information to the

public when one of its agencies is playing an investigatory role.[89]

Before 1979, companies supplying information to the government would frequently sue to block disclosure to third parties. These were called reverse FOIA suits. In *Chrysler Corporation v. Brown,*[90] the U.S. Supreme Court held that the FOIA does not create a private right of action to prevent an agency from releasing documents covered by one or more of the nine exemptions. To release or not is within an agency's discretion, so long as it does not abuse that discretion and both requesters and submitters have been heard. Under Exemption 3, of course, it would be an abuse of discretion to release documents covered by the federal Trade Secrets Act,[91] especially if Exemption 4 also applied.

Justice Rehnquist's opinion for the Court in *Chrysler,* while acknowledging the difficulty of balancing secrecy against disclosure, seemed to opt for disclosure. Corporations do not like to disclose and have successfully exerted pressure on Congress to exempt documents relating to pricing policies, product safety, truth-in-advertising, and warranty data. A 1986 presidential executive order instructed agency heads to notify record submitters when confidential commercial information is requested by third parties.

5. EXECUTIVE PRIVILEGE: AGENCY MEMOS   Exemption 5 prevents disclosure of predecisional "inter-agency or intra-agency memoranda or letters which would not be available by law to a party other than an agency in litigation with the agency." Nothing that is part of or defined as "discovery" (two sides in a civil case looking at one another's evidence) is available under the FOIA. The act was not intended to be used to circumvent discovery proceedings, although Attorney General Reno's memo would ease Exemption 5 denials of access to predecisional information, even those involving litigation.

---

87. *National Parks & Conservation Ass'n v. Morton,* 498 F.2d 765, 770 D.C.Cir. 1974).

88. *Critical Mass Energy Project v. Nuclear Regulatory Commission,* 975 F.2d 871, 872 (D.C.Cir. 1992) (en banc).

89. Rees, "Recent Developments," p. 1207. For cases further complicating the analysis of Exemption 4, see, *A. Michael's Piano, Inc. v. FTC,* 18 F.3d 138 (2d Cir.), cert. denied, 115 S.Ct. 1579 (1994); and *GC Micro Corp. v. Defense Logistics Agency,* 33 F.3d 1109 (9th Cir. 1994).

90. 441 U.S. 281 (1979).

91. 18 U.S.C. §1905.

Exemption 5 has served as a major justification for withholding.

The exemption protects the lawyer-client privilege and other steps in the judicial process. For example, confidential, unsworn statements made to Air Force crash investigators did not have to be disclosed because they were part of pretrial discovery.[92]

To encourage frank discussion and protect the executive branch's deliberative process, predecisional documents (materials generated prior to a decision) are generally not disclosable, but postdecisional documents are. Final reports must be disclosed; working papers may be withheld. Memos, recommendations, opinions, policy statements, and staff comments that go into a final decision or report may be released, but only if they constitute the basis for the subsequent decision; the agency involved has final decisional authority.[93] More likely, such documents are supplemental to the decision and are therefore not releasable.

A Watergate Special Prosecution Force memorandum, for example, which was made as an integral part of that body's required report to Congress recommending that Richard Nixon not be indicted, was held disclosable. It was part of the final decision. Standing alone, it would have been exempt as a "pre-decisional intra-agency legal memorandum."[94]

If purely factual information, such as names and addresses of unsuccessful applicants for federal funds, can be segregated, it is not exempt from disclosure. Nor are factual portions of pre-decisional documents unless their disclosure would breach a promise of confidentiality and diminish an agency's ability to obtain similar information in the future. A compilation of facts, if complete enough, could also expose an agency's deliberative process.[95] A fact/opinion distinction was made in a case involving the attorney general's decision to make Kurt Waldheim, former president of Austria and secretary-general of the United Nations, an excludable alien because of his SS background. Factual material assembled through discretionary selection from a large number of primary documents was exempt under Exemption 5. A purely chronological account of Waldheim's military service was not exempt because it did not disclose the Justice Department's deliberative process.[96]

Government-generated commercial information may be withheld.[97] The reason is that disclosure would disadvantage the government in awarding contracts.

"Executive privilege" was first asserted early in American history by the Jefferson administration. Its purpose then and now is said to be to encourage frank discussion among agency or cabinet personnel prior to a decision. For example, a Justice Department staff attorney prepared legal analyses and conclusions to aid his superiors in responding to criticisms of legislation they had proposed to amend the FOIA. The documents were held to be exempt from disclosure under Exemption 5.[98]

Well-settled privileges such as those between lawyer and client (or agency) are covered by Exemption 5. National Public Radio reporter Barbara Newman found herself blocked by Exemption 5 when she tried to get information from the Justice Department on its investigation into the mysterious death of Karen Silkwood, an employee of a plutonium manufacturer. Silkwood, who was suspected of being contaminated by plutonium, died in a car accident while on her way to conduct business on behalf of her labor union and to talk with a *New York Times* reporter. There were suspicions that her car had been forced off the highway. A file of documents she was carrying was never recovered. Portions of a "death investigation" file held by the Justice Department contained working papers analyzing evidence and legal issues in the case. They fell under Exemption 5 as "memoranda prepared by an attorney in contemplation of litigation which set forth the attorney's theory of the case, his litigation strategy."[99]

---

92. *United States v. Weber Aircraft,* 10 Med.L.Rptr. 1477, 465 U.S. 792 (1984).

93. *Renegotiation Board v. Grumman Aircraft Engineering Corp.,* 1 Med.L.Rptr. 2487, 421 U.S. 168 (1975).

94. *Niemeier v. Watergate Special Prosecution Force,* 565 F.2d 967 (7th Cir.1977).

95. *Wolfe v. HHS,* 630 F.Supp. 546 (D.D.C. 1985).

96. *Mapother v. Department of Justice,* 3 F.3d 1533 (D.C.Cir. 1993).

97. *Federal Open Market Committee v. Merrill,* 5 Med.L.Rptr. 1221, 443 U.S. 340 (1979).

98. *Access Reports v. Justice Department,* 18 Med.L.Rptr. 1840, 926 F.2d 1192 (D.C.Cir. 1991).

99. *National Public Radio v. Bell,* 2 Med.L.Rptr. 1840, 431 F.Supp. 509 (D.D.C. 1977).

6. PERSONAL PRIVACY Next to national security, personal privacy, as protected in both Exemptions 6 and 7, may offer the most persuasive and pervasive argument for secrecy. Exempt under 6 are "personnel and medical files and similar files the disclosure of which would constitute *a clearly unwarranted invasion of personal privacy.*" Much litigation has focused on the meaning of the words "similar files," but courts have interpreted the term broadly to include many kinds of lists, records, files, summaries, letters, and the like. Major elements of the press are lobbying against a provision of the federal crime bill that would close public access to motor vehicle records (driver's licenses) after September 13, 1997.[100]

Because not all invasions of privacy fall under Exemption 6, courts ultimately will decide when the proper balance has been struck between individual privacy and the basic purpose of the FOIA to inform the public about governmental activities. It will be no easy task.

Courts have tried to balance these values by considering how the information being sought will be used. It may be important to explain to the record keeper why you are seeking the information and how it concerns the public interest. Courts also have considered the degrees of intimacy and personal detail in files. Names and other identifying data can be redacted (blacked out or otherwise deleted) before documents are released. Promises of confidentiality add weight to claims of exemption.

Even where the lives of two former Iranian officials might have been in jeopardy, the Supreme Court opted for disclosure, observing that the balance generally is heavily in favor of disclosure. The public had a right to know whether the Immigration and Naturalization Service had failed to enforce the law.[101]

This bias in favor of disclosure was reinforced when a federal appeals court observed, "The balance struck under FOIA Exemption Six overwhelmingly favors the disclosure of information relating to a violation of the public trust by a governmental official, which certainly includes the situation of misuse of public funds and facil-ities by a Major General of the United States Army."[102]

Nevertheless, it can be argued that the U.S. Supreme Court did shift the balance from "public" to "private" in *Reporters Committee,* discussed earlier in this chapter. Supporting the Court's tilt toward privacy is *U.S. Department of State v. Ray.*[103] This case involved an attempt by an immigration attorney and political asylum applicants to find out whether Haitians who had returned home had been persecuted. Their effort failed, partly on the basis of a *Reporters Committee* analysis.

"Mere speculations about hypothetical public benefits cannot outweigh a demonstrably significant invasion of privacy," wrote Justice John Paul Stevens for the Court. Interviews could lead to social embarrassment or retaliation for cooperating with the State Department. The advantages to the asylum applicants, and indirectly to the U.S. public, of having this information got short shrift. In *Ray* the Court made clear that the government's burden to disclose under Exemption 6 was heavier than its obligation under Exemption 7(C). The latter exempts files that *"could reasonably be expected to constitute an unwarranted invasion of personal privacy,"* a lesser standard for identifying a privacy interest and therefore a better protector of privacy, especially where the information sought is of a personal or intimate nature. In fact the Ninth Circuit has held that a "threat to privacy that may justify nondisclosure in an Exemption 7(C) case may warrant disclosure in an Exemption 6 case."[104]

Information having to do with medical conditions, job evaluations, welfare payments, and the legitimacy of children generally will be protected by Exemption 6. Personal privacy, of course, is waived when one applies for federal grants or contracts.

Because the "clearly unwarranted invasion of personal privacy" language of Exemption 6 is also found in the Federal Privacy Act of 1974 and, more generally, in the language of Exemption 7, we are not done with it yet.

---

100. Christopher Callahan, "License Revoked," *American J. Rev.* (November 1995), p. 40.

101. *Department of State v. Washington Post,* 8 Med.L.Rptr. 1521, 456 U.S. 595 (1982).

102. *Cochrane v. United States,* 770 F.2d 949 (11th Cir. 1985).

103. 502 U.S. 164 (1991).

104. *Dobronski v. FCC,* 22 Med.L.Rptr. 1309, 17 F.3d 275 (9th Cir.1994).

7. LAW ENFORCEMENT INVESTIGATIONS
Exemption 7 protects investigatory records or information compiled for law enforcement purposes, but only to the extent that the production of such records could reasonably be expected to (A) interfere with enforcement proceedings; (B) deprive a person of a right to a fair trial or an impartial adjudication; (C) constitute an unwarranted invasion of personal privacy; (D) disclose the identity of a confidential source, or the information itself in the case of a record compiled by a criminal law enforcement authority in the course of a criminal investigation, or by an agency conducting a lawful national security investigation; (E) disclose investigative techniques and procedures; or (F) endanger the life or physical safety of any individual.

Much public information is kept secret by interpretations of this exemption, even though it allows, but does not require, withholding of investigatory files compiled in response to suspicions of violations of federal law or national security. Technically, for information to qualify under Exemption 7, the government must first show that the record is both "investigatory" and contained in a file "compiled for law enforcement and prosecution" purposes. Then it must fall within one of the six exempt categories enumerated above under Exemption 7. But here, as with Exemptions 1 and 6, the government can present a *Glomar* defense: a denial of the existence of information about such matters as police informants, ongoing investigations, and classified FBI records. When the rationale for such a denial is not national security, it is often personal privacy.

Until recently, rap sheets, arrest and conviction records, department manuals, personnel rosters, and other routine compilations and records were not exempt. This is no longer the case. Balancing now seems to favor nondisclosure, as the discussion of *Reporters Committee* above suggested. In addition, documents no longer need to have been originally compiled for law enforcement purposes to be exempt from disclosure under the FOIA. In other words, documents not expressly gathered for law enforcement purposes may be withheld under Exemption 7 if they are subsequently combined with material gathered for that purpose. The word "originally" is key. Nonexempt records, as Justice Stevens noted in a dissenting opinion in a Supreme Court case, may now be transferred from a civilian agency to the FBI and constitute an "exempt compilation."[105]

For purposes of satisfying Exemption 7, all FBI investigatory records are compiled for law enforcement purposes. The legality of a particular investigation does not matter. In 1982, the Supreme Court upheld Exemption 7(C) claims against the request of an independent journalist that FBI documents on the Nixon administration "enemies list" be made public. On the list were such prominent citizens as Harvard economist John Kenneth Galbraith, political philosopher and theologian Reinhold Niebuhr, baby doctor Benjamin Spock, and farm worker organizer Cesar Chavez.

The crux of the Court's ruling was that material originally exempt under 7(C) does not lose that exemption simply because it is transmitted to a second agency in a slightly different form. The Court was assuming, of course, that the original list was compiled for law enforcement purposes. In justifying his opinion for the Court, Justice Byron White argued that the kind of people who had voiced suspicions about the loyalty of the celebrities on the list might be discouraged from informing in the future if disclosure were to occur. He rebuked Justice Sandra Day O'Connor for observing in her dissent that the Court had ignored the plain language of the FOIA and that the documents in question had been compiled for "political" not "law enforcement" purposes.[106]

More recently, the Supreme Court upheld the Department of Justice when it argued that it had a "categorical presumption" under 7(D) to protect all its sources in an FBI investigation into the death of a police officer by protecting all records that might disclose the identity of sources.[107] A confidential source was defined as anyone who has given information to law enforcement officials with the understanding (presumably either express or implied) that his or her identity would be protected. Even with no understanding of confidentiality, law enforcement officials could refuse to identify a source if they had a necessary law enforcement purpose in doing so. Noting,

105. Op. cit., n. 34.
106. *FBI v. Abramson*, 8 Med.L.Rptr. 1561, 456 U.S. 615 (1982).
107. *Department of Justice v. Landano*, 21 Med.L.Rptr. 1513, 508 U.S. 165 (1993).

however, that there was no blanket presumption of confidentiality for the great variety of FBI sources, the Court said that confidentiality would depend on the crime, the source's relation to it, and the source's expectation of confidentiality. The government agency still has the burden of proof for nondisclosure and must offer a case-specific rationale for its position. Thus, the decision was a partial win for press and public.

The Ninth Circuit also honored the spirit of the FOIA when it upheld a federal district court's rejection of an Exemption 7 rationale for FBI files concerning the Berkeley Free Speech Movement and reporter Marguerite Higgins.[108] The question of Berkeley President Clark Kerr's file was remanded since the file might have contained evidence as to whether subversive influences had been exerted on University of California students. This would have created a law enforcement purpose, as Exemption 7 requires. In general, however, the public interest in whether the FBI had been engaged in purely political activities outweighed privacy interests. Furthermore, the identity of confidential informants and investigative techniques were not revealed.

On occasion, the exemption does not work. When *Playboy* sued the Justice Department for release of a task force report on an FBI informer within the Ku Klux Klan, the department cited five FOIA exemptions. None applied, said a federal district court. When it came to Exemption 7, the department had failed to show that the report was an investigatory record compiled for law enforcement purposes.[109]

When an investigation or enforcement proceeding has concluded after trial, conviction, and sentencing, Exemption 7 no longer applies. Nondisclosure applies to ongoing investigations. But the word *ongoing* gets stretched. Two federal circuit court rulings involving the murder/disappearance of Jimmy Hoffa illustrate the rule. Despite the years that have passed since Hoffa disappeared, both courts held that investigations into the mystery of his whereabouts are still ongoing and that sources interviewed as part of

that investigation could still be considered confidential.[110] FBI informants in a 1931 murder investigation were still confidential sources in a 1990 case.[111]

Congress reinforced Exemption 7 in the Anti-Drug Abuse Act of 1986 by substituting the words "could reasonably be expected" to occur for "would" occur with reference to the enumerated harms that might follow from disclosure. It also included the language "state, local, and foreign agencies or authorities and private institutions" within the meaning of "confidential sources." As far as amended Exemption 7 is concerned, an agency need not acknowledge that records exist if they are part of an investigation, would identify informants, or have to do with intelligence or terrorists.[112]

Some records simply are not covered by the FOIA. This supports numerous refusals to provide access. The personnel file of an FBI agent containing a letter of reprimand was exempt.[113] U.S. Postal Service records containing the statements of identified persons interviewed during an investigation into the shooting of postal workers by a deranged fellow employee were records compiled for law enforcement purposes. Their disclosure, said a federal appeals court, would also constitute an invasion of privacy. Moreover, those interviewed had been given implied promises of confidentiality.[114]

8. AND 9. BANKS AND OIL WELLS   Exemption 8 protects reports and records "contained in or related to examination, operating, or condition reports prepared by, on behalf of, or for the use of an agency responsible for the regulation or supervision of financial institutions." Considering the number of bank, brokerage house, and savings and loan scandals that have rocked the nation in the past decades, this exemption has taken on new significance. If there was ever a

---

108. *Rosenfeld v. Justice Department*, 23 Med.L.Rptr. 2101, 57 F.3d 803 (9th Cir. 1995).

109. *Playboy v. U.S. Department of Justice*, 8 Med.L.Rptr. 1901, 516 F.Supp. 233 (D.D.C. 1981), *modified*, 677 F.2d 931 (D.C.Cir. 1982).

110. *Dickerson v. Department of Justice*, 992 F.2d 1426 (6th Cir. 1993), and *Crancer v. Department of Justice*, 999 F.2d 1302 (8th Cir. 1993).

111. *Schmerler v. FBI*, 17 Med.L.Rptr. 1709, 900 F.2d 333 (D.C.Cir. 1990).

112. *Freedom of Information Reform Act of 1986*, P.L. 99-570 §§1801–1804, 100 Stat. 3248 (1986).

113. *Dunkelberger v. Justice Department*, 17 Med.L.Rptr. 2298, 906 F.2d 779 (D.C.Cir. 1990).

114. *KTVY-TV v. U.S. Postal Service*, 18 Med.L.Rptr. 1479, 919 F.2d 1465 (10th Cir. 1990).

need for public accountability and an alert press, it was in the years immediately preceding the savings and loan disasters and the loss of millions of dollars of customer funds in collapsed savings institutions.

Federal courts have disagreed as to whether securities exchanges are "financial institutions" covered by Exemption 8.[115] The D.C. Circuit held in 1991 that the phrase "financial institutions" is not limited to depository institutions.[116]

To discourage speculation based on information about the location of private oil and gas wells and to protect competition, Exemption 9 covers geological and geophysical data and maps concerning wells. The Gulf War's implications for oil supplies may in time bring the light of more public scrutiny to this exemption also.

THE FEDERAL PRIVACY ACT

Surveillance by government in the name of the public, or surveillance by public and press for their own sakes, inevitably collides with personal privacy. How can the two social values be harmonized? A newspaper's request for arrest records may be motivated by a desire to assess the performance of a police department, but the consequence might be exposure of a third party's transgressions. It is important to know when denials of disclosure are based on a long tradition of official secrecy and suppression of information and when they are based on a genuine concern for a legal or constitutional right of personal privacy.

In 1974, Congress passed a comprehensive federal law to protect the privacy of government data on individuals created and stored by federal agencies. Under the law an individual has access to her files. After clearly identifying yourself, you can learn what information about you is on record, and you can correct it if it is inaccurate. The Reporters Committee includes a sample Privacy Act letter in its FOIA handbook.

Under this law you pay for duplication but not for search time. The Office of Management and Budget (OBM), which supervises the act, expects federal agencies to acknowledge receipt of a request within ten working days and to provide access, if it is granted, within thirty.

An important section of the act prohibits the government from creating any record having to do with the exercise of a First Amendment right—lawfully demonstrating, leafletting, placarding, street-corner speaking. This rule prevented the Internal Revenue Service from keeping records of its surveillance of speeches made by nuclear weapon and nuclear policy protesters.[117] Only a statute, a legitimate law enforcement activity, or your consent could change this rule.

Unless a record is open to public inspection under one of the Privacy Act's twelve exemptions or under the FOIA, a government agency must have the written consent of the subject of the record for disclosure. You can win damages, attorney's fees, and court costs if, in violating this rule, an agency "acted in a manner which was intentionally willful."

The Privacy Act might be thought of as an FOIA for the individual. Any disclosure of a record about a person to any member of the public, other than the individual to whom the record pertains, is forbidden under the Privacy Act, if the disclosure would constitute a "clearly unwarranted invasion of personal privacy." General exemptions to privacy protections apply to entire systems of records rather than to specific documents, as is the case with the FOIA. Again, CIA records, FBI rap sheets, and some other criminal records are examples. Specific exemptions deal with particular records that are part of a larger system of records, for example, "information compiled for the purpose of a criminal investigation" and "testing or examination material used solely to determine individual qualifications for appointment or promotion in the Federal service the disclosure of which would compromise the objectivity or fairness of the testing or examination process."

Exemption 2 of the Privacy Act provides that a record may be disclosed without written consent of the person to whom it pertains if disclosure

---

115. See *M. A. Schapiro & Co. v. SEC,* 339 F.Supp. 467 (D.D.C. 1972) and *Mermelstein v. SEC,* 629 F.Supp. 672 (D.D.C. 1986), arguing that the Government-in-Sunshine Act, passed after the FOIA, exempted brokerage firms.
116. *Public Citizen v. Farm Credit Administration,* 19 Med.L.Rptr. 1118, 938 F.2d 290 (D.C.Cir. 1991).

117. *Clarkson v. IRS,* 8 Med.L.Rptr. 1933, 678 F.2d 1368 (11th Cir. 1982), *cert. denied,* 481 U.S. 1031 (1987).

is required under the FOIA. In other words, *if a document is required to be made public by the FOIA it cannot be kept secret by the Privacy Act.* What is exempt from disclosure to an individual under the Privacy Act is not necessarily exempt from disclosure to the same person under the FOIA. Where a record is available under the Privacy Act, but exempt under the FOIA, the Privacy Act applies. Under the Privacy Act, an agency is *not* permitted to cite an FOIA exemption to prohibit a person from seeing her own file. Judicial review is available when such a file is withheld from amendment or correction. Requests for disclosures to third parties are made under the FOIA rather than the Privacy Act. In a sense openness trumps privacy.[118]

At the same time, the FOIA's Exemption 6 states that documents need not be disclosed if they are "personnel and medical files and similar files the disclosure of which would constitute *a clearly unwarranted invasion of personal privacy.*"

An understanding of the articulation of the two acts does not come without effort. Making privacy and openness work together is a challenge; they pull in opposite directions. Record keepers may try to exploit the confusion by arguing that they cannot risk penalties under the Privacy Act, even though the FOIA gives them clear discretion to decide whether or not to disclose.

THE FEDERAL OPEN MEETINGS LAW

A Government-In-Sunshine Act[119] was passed in March 1977 requiring fifty federal agencies, commissions, boards, and councils to hold their deliberative, policy-making meetings in public. The scope of application of the FOIA and of the Sunshine Act are essentially the same: If an agency is not subject to the FOIA, it is not subject to the Sunshine Act.[120] For a federal agency to be subject to the Sunshine Act, a majority of its board must have been chosen by the president, with the advice and consent of the Senate. If the board is not chosen by the president, the act does not apply.[121] Subdivisions of agencies are covered if they have agency authority to take final action.[122] Any meeting, whether formal, regular, or bare quorum, in which business is discussed or action is taken is presumed to be open. Minutes are to be kept, and set practices must be used for closing a meeting. Notice of the meeting including time, place, and person to contact must be given at least a week in advance. Though members of the public have a right to attend, they have no right to participate.[123] Nor does the Sunshine Act require agencies to hold meetings.

Communications to an agency from public interest groups or corporations must be made part of the public record. Public notice of a meeting is to be made at least a week in advance, preferably with an agenda included. Ways of getting around the federal open meetings law are almost as numerous as those for getting around the FOIA, however. Business is still conducted informally between meetings by telephone or at social gatherings.

Ten narrow exemptions, the first nine of which track with FOIA exemptions, allow closed meetings. Exemption 10 applies to agency litigation, arbitration, or adjudication. It is often invoked to save a case—or a reputation.

When the Nuclear Regulatory Commission sought to close its budget preparation meeting, Common Cause, a Washington-based public interest group, went to court. In deciding for Common Cause, a federal appeals court noted that, unlike the FOIA, the Sunshine Act was designed to open, not close, predecisional deliberations. The commission had cited Exemption 9, an exemption generally closing meetings where openness could lead to significant financial speculation, endanger the stability of a financial institution, or interfere with a proposed agency action.[124] The same commission's deliberations on the reopening of the Three Mile Island nuclear power plant were permitted to be closed, however, even though the accident evoked deep public concern.

118. *Greentree v. Customs Service,* 7 Med.L.Rptr. 1808, 674 F.2d 74 (D.C.Cir. 1982). See also *Department of Justice v. Provenzano,* 469 U.S. 14 (1984).
119. P.L. 94-409, 90 Stat. 1241 (March 12, 1977).
120. Op. cit., n. 42.
121. *Hunt v. NRC,* 611 F.2d 332 (10th Cir. 1979), *cert. denied,* 445 U.S. 906 (1980).
122. *FCC v. ITT World Communications,* 10 Med.L.Rptr. 1685, 466 U.S. 463, 465–66 (1984).
123. *We the People, Inc. v. Nuclear Regulatory Commission,* 746 F.Supp. 213 (D.D.C. 1990).
124. *Common Cause v. Nuclear Regulatory Commission,* 8 Med.L.Rptr. 1190, 674 F.2d 921 (D.C.Cir. 1982).

The law has not helped reporters cover international conferences attended by bureaucrats[125] or get into meetings of correctional institutions or public hospitals. Nor has it accommodated demonstrators—or reporters—on private property, even private property heavily regulated by government, such as a nuclear power plant.[126]

Rules granting press passes and establishing press access to scenes of crime and disaster should define "press" liberally. Otherwise, law enforcement officers are in the position of certifying "legitimate" news media, a role government should not play, although it does just that in granting postal and other subsidies or immunities.[127] When denied a press pass, a reporter should insist upon an explanation.

When the secretary of labor excluded press and public from meetings of the Mine Safety and Health Administration looking into the cause of a fatal mine fire, the Society of Professional Journalists brought suit and won. A federal district court ruled that the press and public had a constitutional right of access to such hearings, subject to reasonable rules of conduct set down by the secretary.[128] Attorney's fees may be awarded, at the court's discretion, when plaintiffs have "substantially prevailed" in Sunshine suits.

A federal district court's post-trial order prohibiting press interviews with jurors in a civil case was said to be impermissibly overbroad by an appeals court because the order included no time or scope of limitations and was not supported by compelling reasons.[129]

As noted earlier, laws prohibiting exit polling at voting places have been struck down in a number of states, including Florida, Minnesota, and Washington. Although voting places are not meetings in the usual sense of that term, they are places where news traditionally has been gathered and where people congregate and have a right to speak.

ACCESS TO LEGISLATURES

Access to legislative bodies and their committees should never be presumed. Legislators, after all, write the laws, and they are in a perfect position to exempt themselves from the irritations of press and public. Access to legislatures is governed by custom and practice, state and federal House and Senate rules, open meetings laws in some states, state constitutions, and well-formed First and Fourteenth Amendment arguments encased in the state's common law. For example, an Alaska court ruled in 1986 that the press and the public had an implied right under the Alaska Constitution to attend meetings of members of the state legislature so as to observe "every step" of the deliberative process.[130]

Periodically, the Reporters Committee publication *The News Media & the Law* summarizes the status of access to state legislatures. When covering a legislative body, protocols must be observed as to dress, positioning (coverage from the floor, galleries, or press boxes), cameras, and credentials.

Questions of due process and equal protection have arisen when particular reporters have been discriminated against in covering state lawmaking bodies and city councils.[131] State courts upheld both houses of the Maryland legislature in excluding tape recorders from their sessions. While recognizing some First Amendment protection for news gathering, a Maryland court held that the legislative rule did not interfere with the usual pencil-and-pad duties of reporters. There was no violation of due process in a rule intended to preserve order and decorum, even at the expense of news-gathering efficiency. As to equal protection, the court held that the tape recorder ban was against equipment, not a class of citizens.[132] This case and others illustrate the

---

125. *FCC v. ITT World Communications,* 10 Med.L.Rptr. 1685, 725 F.2d 732 (D.C.Cir. 1984).

126. *Stahl v. State,* 9 Med.L.Rptr. 1945, 665 P.2d 839 (1983), *cert. denied,* 464 U.S. 1069 (1984).

127. For example, the Newspaper Preservation Act.

128. *Society of Professional Journalists v. Secretary of Labor,* 11 Med.L.Rptr. 2474, 616 F.Supp. 569 (D.Utah 1985). On appeal, the Court of Appeals, McWilliams, C. J., held that the controversy had become moot by the time the district court entered judgment. The appeal was dismissed, and the cause remanded with directions, 14 Med.L.Rptr. 1827, 832 F.2d 1180 (10th Cir. 1987).

129. *Journal Publishing v. Mechem,* 13 Med.L.Rptr. 1391, 801 F.2d 1233 (10th Cir. 1981).

130. *League of Women Voters v. Adams,* 13 Med.L.Rptr. 1433 (Alaska Super.Ct. 1986).

131. *Kovach v. Maddux,* 238 F.Supp. 835 (D.Tenn. 1965); *Westinghouse Broadcasting Co. v. Dukakis,* 409 F.Supp. 895 (D.Mass. 1976); *Borreca v. Fasi,* 1 Med.L.Rptr. 2410, 369 F.Supp. 906 (D.Haw. 1974).

132. *Sigma Delta Chi v. Speaker, Maryland House of Delegates,* 310 A.2d 156 (Md. 1973).

sensitivity of one branch of government toward the prerogatives of another.

OPEN RECORDS AND MEETINGS IN THE STATES

Open Records

All states, the District of Columbia, and the territories have open records laws. They vary widely, change frequently, and do not lend themselves to generalization. Know the law of your state, how it has been applied, and its loopholes. No state has an ideal open records or open meetings law, but some are better than their federal counterparts. Most now deal with electronic records. Again the FOI Service Center of the Reporters Committee for Freedom of the Press and the Society of Professional Journalists' *Project Sunshine* can be helpful. Both publish booklets on model and actual open records meetings laws for each state and the District of Columbia.

From a press and public perspective, a *model* statute would define "records" broadly, by both physical format and origin or source, and make as few exceptions as possible. No particular reason or purpose for seeking access would be required, and access would include the right to inspect and copy. A state agency would be prepared to redact nonpublic or private information. Fees would be controlled so as not to discourage access. There would be penalties against state agencies for noncooperation and cynical delay, but no liabilities for disclosure. Denials of access would have to be justified in writing, and expedited judicial review would be available. Court costs and attorney's fees would be paid to requesters who prevailed in litigation.

As with the FOIA, state agencies are not required to create or acquire records in response to a request. They are responsible only for existing and identifiable records in their possession that are subject to the state open records law. Unfortunately, few state laws require indexes. A state-created agency that is federally funded and performs federal functions could be subject to *both* state and federal open records laws.

You will find quirks in many of these laws. In a few states, you must be a resident of the state to benefit from its open records laws. Others, taking their cue from the Federal Privacy Act,

have enacted huge data privacy or data practices acts, creating unanticipated complexities, loopholes, and interpretations. On the positive side, some states have set up FOI commissions or compliance committees, such as New York's Committee on Public Access to Records, and assigned deputy attorneys general to assist aggrieved record seekers and to assure rapid judicial review of denials.

Many of these open records laws have the same kind of exemptions that are found in the FOIA. Know what they are. And know how state courts have interpreted them. Exemptions should be discretionary rather than mandatory; that is, the agency itself should have the authority to make a decision to withhold or disclose.

Legal language can be troublesome. A number of state laws refer to "all official records *required by law* to be kept shall be open . . .," and these now include electronic or computer records. Records kept by tradition rather than by law, even if necessary for the functioning of a public body, may be claimed exempt from the law. As with the FOIA, there are statutory exemptions for records relating to welfare, medical information, child adoption or abuse, unemployment compensation, tax data, bank records, criminal histories, and other kinds of law enforcement information. Some records are closed for reasons no one can remember.

Delays can be egregious. Any survey of recent cases will show increasing evidence of bureaucrats, legislative bodies, including public school boards and university boards of regents, and law enforcement agencies circumventing state open records laws by erasing tapes,[133] making "computer" excuses,[134] and concocting strained interpretations of state law.[135] Many state laws do not require agencies to "manipulate" electronic

133. *Globe Newspaper Co. v. Pokaski,* 17 Med.L.Rptr. 1223 (D.C.Mass. 1989).

134. *Brownstone Publishers Inc. v. New York City Department of Buildings,* 17 Med.L.Rptr. 2237, 550 N.Y.S.2d 564 (N.Y.Sup.Ct. 1990).

135. *Buffalo News v. Commissioners of Buffalo Municipal Housing Authority,* 17 Med.L.Rptr. 2167, 558 N.Y.S.2d 364 (N.Y.Sup.Ct. App.Div. 1990); *Indianapolis Newspapers, Inc. v. Indianapolis Convention & Visitor Association, Inc.,* 17 Med.L.Rptr. 1215 (Ind.Cir.Ct. 1989); *Board of Regents of University System of Georgia v. Atlanta Journal,* 17 Med.L.Rptr. 1670, 378 S.E.2d 305 (Ga.Sup.Ct. 1989); *Brouillet v. Cowles Publishing Co.,* 17 Med.L.Rptr. 1982, 791 P.2d 526 (Wash.Sup.Ct. 1990).

data in order to present them in useful ways; some charge extra for manipulation. Others provide access to the data, but not to the software required for accessing the data. Some bureaucrats interpret state law as prohibiting publication even after information is in the hands of reporters and editors.[136] Getting information can become a never-ending game of cat and mouse. If arguments for privacy and imposition of excessive costs do not discourage records disclosure, then time will, and time is always on the side of the governmental institution.

Most state laws say little or nothing about time limits for responding to requests. And few provide penalties for violations of the law. Seemingly illegal denials of access to records should be challenged. As a reporter, ask a record keeper for written authority for a denial. Ask to speak to supervisors. Indicate that you know your rights under the law. Keep editors posted on what is happening.

Litigation continues over access to police blotters, investigative files, wiretap records, prison and hospital records, autopsy reports, and the documents developed by personnel search committees.

Recent examples of state records that have been opened by a liberal interpretation of open records laws are a California governor's appointment schedule, records having to do with the pensions of former legislators, a correctional department's videotapes of a prison uprising, police department records of the police shooting of a suspect, names and addresses of replacement teachers hired during a strike, legal memoranda prepared by a city's outside attorney for litigation purposes, a state university's response to National Collegiate Athletic Association charges, and department of health records concerning an investigation of nursing homes.

Examples of records closed to public inspection by interpretation of state open records laws include an assistant state's attorney's personnel file regarding matters of race, videotapes of the execution of a search warrant, names of state university students employed by the university's police department, mental health records of a person charged in a shooting, telephone billing

records of county board members, records of a corporate-administered local development program for small businesses, and reports evaluating the performance of a state's attorney. It is difficult to predict how such cases will be decided.

Open Meetings

All states, the District of Columbia, and the territories have open meetings laws or constitutional provisions guaranteeing some level of access to public meetings. These laws also differ substantially from state to state and are frequently amended. They are generally simpler to understand and apply than are open records laws, however.

From a press and public perspective, an ideal open meetings law would apply to both houses and the committees of the state legislature, state boards, commissions, county boards, city councils, and all executive branch agencies. Some laws use a public "funds" or "functions" test in deciding whether the law applies to a governmental body.

Executive sessions (special closed meetings of an organization's officers or committees) and other evasive devices for avoiding public scrutiny would not be permitted under an ideal law. A quorum would not be a condition of access. Advisory committees to public bodies would also be required to have open meetings. Minutes would be kept and all votes recorded. If exemptions must be written into the law, they would be limited and carefully defined. Open meetings and open records laws ought to be written so clearly and precisely that judicial discretion in applying them is at a minimum.

Any business transacted in a secret meeting would be null and void. Enforcement procedures should be practicable and available to ordinary citizens. There would be penalties for noncompliance, although penalties are not generally enforced in the state statutes that contain them. A recent exception was Minnesota. In 1994, a unanimous Minnesota Supreme Court ruled that the mayor of Hibbing, Minnesota, and two members of the city council should be removed from office for repeated violations of that state's open meeting law. Although this penalty for three violations of the law had been on the books for twenty-one years, it had never been enforced. The law was invoked, not by the press, but by

136. *Doe v. Florida Supreme Court,* 17 Med.L.Rptr. 1405, 734 F.Supp. 981 (D.S.Fla. 1990); *Providence Journal Co. v. Newton,* 17 Med.L.Rptr. 1033, 723 F.Supp. 846 (D.C.R.I. 1989).

four irate citizens.[137] The state legislature thereafter changed the law so that removal from office would no longer be an option. Instead, attorney's fees of up to $13,000 would be available to those alleging intentional violation of the open meetings law by public officials. Violations would more likely be considered "intentional" when a public official had been to open-meeting-law training sessions or had been in office for some length of time.

In a number of states, where intent to violate an open meeting law can be proven, criminal or civil penalties, usually in the form of fines, can be assessed and attorney's fees awarded to plaintiffs. In thirty-eight states, some business transacted in a secret meeting is null and void.[138]

Other remedies for so-called sunshine law violations are writs of mandamus (a judge orders something done to restore a right that has been illegally deprived) or injunctive relief (a judge prevents something from happening or permits it to happen).

Unannounced, irregular, or informal (telephone) meetings and social gatherings are still a major means of circumventing these laws. Parole and pardon boards are often closed by statute, although this can have disastrous consequences for society as when unrehabilitated prisoners are released or reformed prisoners are unjustly kept in prison. Law enforcement, state National Guard, and hospital board affairs are nearly always conducted in secret. Legislative bodies routinely go into executive session to discuss personnel matters, particularly where disciplinary action is anticipated. Attorney-client privilege applies where a council or an agency is planning its strategy for litigation or labor negotiations. Inquests are held in secret in some states, although state laws have been used to open them. State laws have also opened municipal library advisory boards. Public university and other governmental selection and search committees and in-house disciplinary hearings are closed in most states, although meetings of public university trustees or regents are generally open to the public. Reporters still have problems gaining access to law enforcement boards, jails, and accident scenes.

When wrongfully denied attendance at a meeting of a public body, ask for reasons and a vote of the membership. As a reporter, ask also that a record of your exclusion be kept in the minutes of the meeting. Do not leave a meeting until ordered to do so. If possible, photograph public officials escorting you out of a meeting. As with record keepers, of course, be respectful even when you are convinced that a public body is acting illegally. And keep in touch with the state press association; many have done an excellent job of monitoring open records and open meetings violations.

In cases of state and federal records and meetings, litigation opens more meetings and files than it closes. Nevertheless, in many states the long-range prospects for both openness and personal privacy are not good. The long-range prospects for government secrecy, on the other hand, are very good.

---

137. *Claude v. Collins,* 518 N.W.2d 836 (Minn. 1994).
138. Charles N. Davis and Milagros Rivera-Sanchez, University of Florida, *If You Do the Crime, Will You Do the Time? A Proposal for Reform of State Sunshine Law Enforcement Provisions,* (unpublished AEJMC paper, Atlanta, 1994).

CHAPTER 8
PUBLIC ACCESS TO THE MEDIA

CHAPTER OUTLINE

A RIGHT OF ACCESS TO THE PRESS?

Access to the Press—A New First Amendment Right
80 HARV. L. REV. 1641 (1967)

[EDITORIAL NOTE: *The press, long enshrined among
our most highly cherished institutions, was thought a
cornerstone of democracy when its name was boldly
inscribed in the Bill of Rights. Freed from governmental
restraint, initially by the first amendment and later by the
fourteenth, the press was to stand majestically as the
champion of new ideas and the watch dog against governmental abuse. Professor Barron finds this conception
of the first amendment, perhaps realistic in the eighteenth century heyday of political pamphleteering,
essentially romantic in an era marked by extraordinary
technological developments in the communications
industry. To make viable the time-honored "marketplace" theory, he argues for a twentieth century interpretation of the first amendment which will impose an affirmative responsibility on the monopoly newspaper to act
as sounding board for new ideas and old grievances.*]

There is an anomaly in our constitutional law.
While we protect expression once it has come to
the fore, our law is indifferent to creating opportunities for expression. Our constitutional theory
is in the grip of a romantic conception of free
expression, a belief that the "marketplace of
ideas" is freely accessible. But if ever there were
a self-operating marketplace of ideas, it has long
ceased to exist. The mass media's development of
an antipathy to ideas requires legal intervention
if novel and unpopular ideas are to be assured a
forum—unorthodox points of view which have
no claim on broadcast time and newspaper space
as a matter of right are in poor position to compete with those aired as a matter of grace.

The free expression questions which now come
before the courts involve individuals who have
managed to speak or write in a manner that captures public attention and provokes legal reprisal.
The conventional constitutional issue is whether
expression already uttered should be given first
amendment shelter or whether it may be subjected to sanction as speech beyond the constitutionally protected pale. To those who can obtain
access to the media of mass communications first

amendment case law furnishes considerable help. But what of those whose ideas are too unacceptable to secure access to the media? To them the mass communications industry replies: The first amendment guarantees our freedom to do as we choose with our media. Thus the constitutional imperative of free expression becomes a rationale for repressing competing ideas. First amendment theory must be reexamined, for only by responding to the present reality of the mass media's repression of ideas can the constitutional guarantee of free speech best serve its original purposes.

[A]n essentially romantic view of the first amendment has perpetuated the lack of legal interest in the availability to various interest groups of access to means of communication.

The possibility of governmental repression is present so long as government endures, and the first amendment has served as an effective device to protect the flow of ideas from governmental censorship: "Happily government censorship has put down few roots in this country. We have in the United States no counterpart of the Lord Chamberlain who is censor over England's stage." But this is to place laurels before a phantom—our constitutional law has been singularly indifferent to the reality and implications of nongovernmental obstructions to the spread of political truth. This indifference becomes critical when a comparatively few private hands are in a position to determine not only the content of information but its very availability, when the soap box yields to radio and the political pamphlet to the monopoly newspaper. Difficulties in securing access, unknown both to the draftsmen of the first amendment and to the early proponents of its "marketplace" interpretation, have been wrought by the changing technology of mass media.

Many American cities have become one newspaper towns. The failures of existing media are revealed by the development of new media to convey unorthodox, unpopular, and new ideas. Sit-ins and demonstrations testify to the inadequacy of old media as instruments to afford full and effective hearing for all points of view. Demonstrations, it has been well said, are "the free press of the movement to win justice for Negroes." But, like an inadequate underground press, it is a communication medium by default, a statement of the inability to secure access to the conventional means of reaching and changing public opinion. By the bizarre and unsettling nature of his technique the demonstrator hopes to arrest and divert attention long enough to compel the public to ponder his message. But attention-getting devices so abound in the modern world that new ones soon become tiresome. The dissenter must look for ever more unsettling assaults on the mass mind if he is to have continuing impact. Thus, as critics of protest are eager and in a sense correct to say, the prayer-singing student demonstration is the prelude to Watts. But the difficulty with this criticism is that it wishes to throttle protest rather than to recognize that protest has taken these forms because it has had nowhere else to go.

The Justices of the United States Supreme Court are not innocently unaware of these contemporary social realities, but they have nevertheless failed to give the "marketplace of ideas" theory of the first amendment the burial it merits. Perhaps the interment of this theory has been denied for the understandable reason that the Court is at a loss to know with what to supplant it. But to put off inquiry under today's circumstances will only aggravate the need for it under tomorrow's.

There is inequality in the power to communicate ideas just as there is inequality in economic bargaining power; to recognize the latter and deny the former is quixotic. The "marketplace of ideas" view has rested on the assumption that protecting the right of expression is equivalent to providing for it. But changes in the communications industry have destroyed the equilibrium in that marketplace. While it may have been still possible in 1925 to believe with Justice Holmes that every idea is "acted on unless some other belief outweighs it or some failure of energy stifles the movement at its birth," it is impossible to believe that now. Yet the Holmesian theory is not abandoned, even though the advent of radio and television has made even more evident that philosophy's unreality. A realistic view of the first amendment requires recognition that a right of expression is somewhat thin if it can be exercised only at the sufferance of the managers of mass communications.

A corollary of the romantic view of the first amendment is the Court's unquestioned assumption that the amendment affords "equal" protection to the various media. According to this view new media of communication are assimilated into first amendment analysis without regard to the enormous differences in impact these media have in comparison with the traditional printed word. Radio and television are to be as free as newspapers and magazines, sound trucks as free as radio and television.

This extension of a simplistic egalitarianism to media whose comparative impacts are gravely disproportionate is wholly unrealistic. It results from confusing freedom of media content with freedom of the media to restrict access. The assumption in romantic first amendment analysis that the same postulates apply to different classes of people, situations, and means of communication obscures the fact, noted explicitly by Justice Jackson in *Kovacs v. Cooper,* that problems of access and impact vary significantly from medium to medium.

An analysis of the first amendment must be tailored to the context in which ideas are or seek to be aired. This contextual approach requires an examination of the purposes served by and the impact of each particular medium. If a group seeking to present a particular side of a public issue is unable to get space in the only newspaper in town, is this inability compensated by the availability of the public park or the sound truck? Competitive media only constitute alternative means of access in a crude manner. If ideas are criticized in one forum the most adequate response is in the same forum since it is most likely to reach the same audience. Further, the various media serve different functions and create different reactions and expectations—criticism of an individual or a governmental policy over television may reach more people but criticism in print is more durable.

The test of a community's opportunities for free expression rests not so much in an abundance of alternative media but rather in an abundance of opportunities to secure expression in media with the largest impact.

The late Professor Meiklejohn, who has articulated a view of the first amendment which assumes its justification to be political self-government, has wisely pointed out that "what is essential is not that everyone shall speak, but that everything worth saying shall be said"—that the point of ultimate interest is not the words of the speakers but the minds of the hearers. Can everything worth saying be effectively said? Constitutional opinions that are particularly solicitous of the interests of mass media—radio, television, and mass circulation newspapers—devote little thought to the difficulties of securing access to those media. If those media are unavailable, can the minds of "hearers" be reached effectively? Creating opportunities for expression is as important as ensuring the right to express ideas without fear of governmental reprisal.

Today ideas reach the millions largely to the extent they are permitted entry into the great metropolitan dailies, news magazines, and broadcasting networks. The soap box is no longer an adequate forum for public discussion. Only the new media of communication can lay sentiments before the public, and it is they rather than government who can most effectively abridge expression by nullifying the opportunity for an idea to win acceptance. As a constitutional theory for the communication of ideas, laissez faire is manifestly irrelevant.

The constitutional admonition against abridgment of speech and press is at present not applied to the very interests which have real power to effect such abridgment. Indeed, nongoverning minorities in control of the means of communication should perhaps be inhibited from restraining free speech (by the denial of access to their media) even more than governing majorities are restrained by the first amendment—minorities do not have the mandate which a legislative majority enjoys in a polity operating under a theory of representative government. What is required is an interpretation of the first amendment which focuses on the idea that restraining the hand of government is quite useless in assuring free speech if a restraint on access is effectively secured by private groups. A constitutional prohibition against governmental restrictions on expression is effective only if the Constitution ensures an adequate opportunity for discussion. Since this opportunity exists only in the mass media, the interests of those who control the means of communication must be accommodated with the interests of those who seek a forum in which to express their point of view.

The potential of existing law to support recognition of a right of access has gone largely unnoticed by the Supreme Court. Judicial blindness to the problem of securing access to the press is dramatically illustrated by *New York Times Co. v. Sullivan,* one of the latest chapters in the romantic and rigid interpretation of the first amendment.

The constitutional armor which *Times* now offers newspapers is predicated on the "principle that debate on public issues should be uninhibited, robust, and wide-open, and that it may well include vehement, caustic, and sometimes unpleasantly sharp attacks on government and public officials." But it is paradoxical that although the libel laws have been emasculated for the benefit of defendant newspapers where the plaintiff is a "public official," the Court shows no corresponding concern as to whether debate will in fact be assured. The irony of *Times* and its progeny lies in the unexamined assumption that reducing newspaper exposure to libel litigation will remove restraints on expression and lead to an "informed society." But in fact the decision creates a new imbalance in the communications process. Purporting to deepen the constitutional guarantee of full expression, the actual effect of the decision is to perpetuate the freedom of a few in a manner adverse to the public interest in uninhibited debate. Unless the *Times* doctrine is deepened to require opportunities for the public figure to reply to a defamatory attack, the *Times* decision will merely serve to equip the press with some new and rather heavy artillery which can crush as well as stimulate debate.

The law of libel is not the only threat to first amendment values; problems of equal moment are raised by judicial inattention to the fact that the newspaper publisher is not the only addressee of first amendment protection. Supreme Court efforts to remove the press from judicial as well as legislative control do not necessarily stimulate and preserve that "multitude of tongues" on which "we have staked our all." What the Court has done is to magnify the power of one of the participants in the communications process with apparently no thought of imposing on newspapers concomitant responsibilities to assure that the new protection will actually enlarge and protect opportunities for expression.

If financial immunization by the Supreme Court is necessary to ensure a courageous press, the public officials who fall prey to such judicially reinforced lions should at least have the right to respond or to demand retraction in the pages of the newspapers which have published charges against them. The opportunity for counterattack ought to be at the very heart of a constitutional theory which supposedly is concerned with providing an outlet for individuals "who wish to exercise their freedom of speech even though they are not members of the press." If no such right is afforded or even considered, it seems meaningless to talk about vigorous public debate.

By severely undercutting a public official's ability to recover damages when he had been defamed, the *Times* decision would seem to reduce the likelihood of retractions since the normal mitigation incentive to retract will be absent.

Although the Court did not foreclose the possibility of allowing public officials to recover damages for a newspaper's refusal to retract, its failure to impose such a responsibility represents a lost opportunity to work out a more relevant theory of the first amendment. Similarly, the Court's failure to require newspapers to print a public official's reply ignored a device which could further first amendment objectives by making debate meaningful and responsive. Abandonment of the romantic view of the first amendment would highlight the importance of giving constitutional status to these responsibilities of the press.

However, even these devices are no substitute for the development of a general right of access to the press. A group that is not being attacked but merely ignored will find them of little use. Indifference rather than hostility is the bane of new ideas and for that malaise only some device of more general application will suffice. It is true that Justice Brennan, writing for the Court in *Times,* did suggest that a rigorous test for libel in the public criticism area is particularly necessary where the offending publication is an "editorial advertisement," since this is an "important outlet for the promulgation of information and ideas by *persons who do not themselves have access to publishing facilities*—who wish to exercise their freedom of speech *even though they are not members of the press.*" This statement leaves us at the threshold of the question of whether these individuals—the "non-press"—should have a right of access secured by the first amendment: should the newspaper have an obligation to take the editorial advertisement? As Justice Brennan appropriately noted, newspapers are an important outlet for ideas. But currently they are outlets entry to which is granted at the pleasure of their managers. The press having been given the *Times* immunity to promote public debate, there seems little justification for not enforcing coordinate responsibility to allocate space equitably among ideas competing for public attention. And, some quite recent shifts in constitutional doctrine may at last make feasible the articulation of a constitutionally based right of access to the media.

The *Times* decision operates on the assumption that newspapers are fortresses of vigorous public criticism, that assuring the press freedom over its content is the only prerequisite to open and robust debate. But if the *raison d'être* of the mass media is not to maximize discussion but to maximize profits, inquiry should be directed to the possible effect of such a fact on constitutional theory. The late Professor V. O. Key stressed the consequences which flow from the fact that communications is big business.[46]

> The networks are in an unenviable economic position. They are not completely free to sell their product—air time. If they make their facilities available to those who advocate causes slightly off color politically, they may antagonize their major customers.

The press suffers from the same pressures—"newspaper publishers are essentially people who sell white space on newsprint to advertisers"; in large part they are only processors of raw materials purchased from others.

Professor Key's conclusion—indifference to content follows from the structure of contemporary mass communications—compares well with Marshall McLuhan's view that the nature of the communications process compels a "strategy of neutrality." For McLuhan it is the technology or form of television itself, rather than the message, which attracts public attention. Hence the media owners are anxious that media content not get enmeshed with unpopular views which will undermine the attraction which the media enjoy by virtue of their form alone.

Whether the mass media suffer from an institutional distaste for controversy because of technological or of economic factors, this antipathy to novel ideas must be viewed against a background of industry insistence on constitutional immunity from legally imposed responsibilities. A quiet truth emerges from such a study: industry opposition to legally imposed responsibilities does not represent a flight from censorship but rather a flight from points of view. Points of view suggest disagreement and angry customers are not good customers.

The mass communications industry should be viewed in constitutional litigation with the same candor with which it has been analyzed by industry members and scholars in communication.

If the mass media are essentially business enterprises and their commercial nature makes it difficult to give a full and effective hearing to a wide spectrum of opinion, a theory of the first amendment is unrealistic if it prevents courts or legislatures from requiring the media to do that which, for commercial reasons, they would be otherwise unlikely to do. Such proposals only require that the opportunity for publication be broadened and do not involve restraint on publication or punishment after publication. When commercial considerations dominate, often leading the media to repress ideas, these media should not be allowed to resist controls designed to promote vigorous debate and expression by cynical reliance on the first amendment.

But can a valid distinction be drawn between newspapers and broadcasting stations, with only the latter subject to regulation? It is commonly said that because the number of possible radio and television licenses is limited, regulation is the natural regimen for broadcasting. Yet the number of daily newspapers is certainly not infinite and, in light of the fact that there are now three times as many radio stations as there are newspapers, the relevance of this distinction is dubious. Consolidation is the established pattern of the American press today, and the need to develop means of access to the press is not diminished because the limitation on the number of newspapers is caused by economic rather than technological factors. Nor is the argument that other newspapers can always spring into existence persuasive—the ability of individuals to publish pamphlets should not preclude regulation of mass circulation, monopoly newspapers

---

46. V. O. Key, *Public Opinion and American Democracy,* 378–79, 387 (1961).

any more than the availability of sound trucks precludes regulation of broadcasting stations.

The foregoing analysis has suggested the necessity of rethinking first amendment theory so that it will not only be effective in preventing governmental abridgment but will also produce meaningful expression despite the present or potential repressive effects of the mass media. If the first amendment can be so invoked, it is necessary to examine what machinery is available to enforce a right of access and what bounds limit that right.

One alternative is a judicial remedy affording individuals and groups desiring to voice views on public issues a right of nondiscriminatory access to the community newspaper. This right could be rooted most naturally in the letter-to-the-editor column and the advertising section. That pressure to establish such a right exists in our law is suggested by a number of cases in which plaintiffs have contended, albeit unsuccessfully, that in certain circumstances newspaper publishers have a common law duty to publish advertisements. In these cases the advertiser sought nondiscriminatory access, subject to even-handed limitations imposed by rates and space.

Although in none of these cases did the newspaper publisher assert lack of space, the right of access has simply been denied. The drift of the cases is that a newspaper is not a public utility and thus has freedom of action regardless of the objectives of the claimant seeking access.

The courts could provide for a right of access other than by reinterpreting the first amendment to provide for the emergence as well as the protection of expression. If monopoly newspapers are indeed quasi-public, their refusal of space to particular viewpoints is state action abridging expression in violation of even the romantic view of the first amendment.

Another, and perhaps more appropriate, approach would be to secure the right of access by legislation. A statute might impose the modest requirement, for example, that denial of access not be arbitrary but rather be based on rational grounds. Although some cases have involved a statutory duty to publish, a constitutional basis for a right of access has never been considered.

Constitutional power exists for both federal and state legislation in this area. Turning first to the constitutional basis for federal legislation, it

has long been held that freedom of expression is protected by the due process clause of the fourteenth amendment. The now celebrated section five of the fourteenth amendment authorizing Congress to "enforce, by appropriate legislation" the provisions of the fourteenth amendment, appears to be as resilient and serviceable a tool for effectuating the freedom of expression guarantee of the fourteenth amendment as for implementing the equal protection guarantee.

If public order and an informed citizenry are, as the Supreme Court has repeatedly said, the goals of the first amendment, these goals would appear to comport well with state attempts to implement a right of access under the rubric of its traditional police power. If a right of access is not constitutionally proscribed, it would seem well within the powers reserved to the states by the tenth amendment of the Constitution to enact such legislation. Of course, if there were conflict between federal and state legislation, the federal legislation would control. Yet, the whole concept of a right of access is so embryonic that it can scarcely be argued that congressional silence preempts the field.

The right of access might be an appropriate area for experimental, innovative legislation. The right to access problems of a small state dominated by a single city with a monopoly press will vary, for example, from those of a populous state with many cities nourished by many competing media. These differences may be more accurately reflected by state autonomy in this area, resulting in a cultural federalism such as that envisaged by Justice Harlan in the obscenity cases.

Utilization of a contextual approach highlights the importance of the degree to which an idea is suppressed in determining whether the right to access should be enforced in a particular case. If all media in a community are held by the same ownership, the access claim has greater attractiveness. This is true although the various media, even when they do reach the same audience, serve different functions and create different reactions and expectations. The existence of competition within the same medium, on the other hand, probably weakens the access claim though competition within a medium is no assurance that significant opinions will have no difficulty in securing access to newspaper space or broadcast time. It is significant that the right of access cases that have been litigated almost invariably involve a monopoly newspaper in a community.

The changing nature of the communications process has made it imperative that the law show concern for the public interest in effective utilization of media for the expression of diverse points of view. Confrontation of ideas, a topic of eloquent affection in contemporary decisions, demands some recognition of a right to be heard as a constitutional principle. It is the writer's position that it is open to the courts to fashion a remedy for a right of access, at least in the most arbitrary cases, independently of legislation. If such an innovation is judicially resisted, I suggest that our constitutional law authorizes a carefully framed right of access statute which would forbid an arbitrary denial of space, hence securing an effective forum for the expression of divergent opinions. With the development of private restraints on free expression, the idea of a free marketplace where ideas can compete on their merits has become just as unrealistic in the twentieth century as the economic theory of perfect competition. The world in which an essentially rationalist philosophy of the first amendment was born has vanished and what was rationalism is now romance.

Access and Its Critics

Professor Edwin Baker argued that access theory advocates really posit a "market failure" model of the First Amendment. Access theorists, in this view, basically support a marketplace of ideas rationale for the First Amendment and are really seeking to improve the functioning of that marketplace. As Professor Baker sees it, these marketplace of ideas dissidents are usually asking for government intervention to make the marketplace of ideas work better. Their heresy is not that a marketplace of ideas model for the First Amendment is mistaken, but rather that currently the marketplace of ideas does not work and should be improved. Professor Baker is critical of these melioristic efforts. See generally, Baker, *Scope of the First Amendment Freedom of Speech,* 25 U.C.L.A. L. Rev. 964, 986–87 (1978):

> The correction of market failures requires criteria to guide the state in its intervention. If provision of adequate access is the goal, the lack of criteria for

"adequacy" undermines the legitimacy of government regulation. For the government to determine what access is adequate involves the government implicitly judging what is the correct resolution of the marketplace debates—or, more bluntly, allows the government to define truth. If a purpose of the first amendment is to protect unpopular ideas that may eventually triumph over the majority's established dogma, then allowing the government to determine adequacy of access stands the first amendment on its head. (In other versions, where equality of input provides the criterion, the parallel problem will be defining equality.)

Is it possible (or desirable) to have access without having equal access?

A distinction has been made for First Amendment purposes between message composers and media owners. The former, in this view, enjoy a greater measure of protection. This distinction and a consequent novel response to the problem of encouraging access to the media is found in Nadel, *A Unified Theory of the First Amendment: Divorcing the Medium from the Message,* 2 Fordham Urb. L.J. 183 (1983):

> The theory of the first amendment discussed above distinguishes between the rights of the two groups comprising our system of communication: "hardware" medium owners and "software" message producers. First amendment rights belong solely to the latter—those who edit software messages which are normally entitled to copyrights. The amendment absolutely protects their thinking and editing (inclusion and exclusion of messages). If the expression of their message does not conflict with some other constitutional value then the government may not impose unreasonable restrictions on their access to media.
>
> The owners of the media are not entitled to any direct first amendment protection, although they may assert rights of inclusion on behalf of those who use their media. The owner's rights to include and exclude messages are solely economic property rights. These permit them to select which messages will gain access to their media. If, however, their economic power becomes great enough to enable them to censor messages and/or the advantages of permitting them to exercise discretion is minimal, then the government may regulate access and even impose common carrier obligations upon them.

Professor Nadel makes a case for greater protection for the editor of the copyrightable software message. If a newspaper were to publish an editorial reply, the reply would have been copyrightable. Why shouldn't this theory protect the access seeker as well as the editor? Why should there be special protection for editors as compared to other writers or speakers?

Other writers believe that the access concept is fundamentally at war with the First Amendment and believe that the defect in the existing law is precisely that it makes distinctions. In this view, *Red Lion* and *Tornillo* are inconsistent from a First Amendment point of view. Furthermore, in this view, the only way this inconsistency can be reconciled is to apply the rationale of the *Tornillo* case to broadcasting as well.

Turner Broadcasting System, Inc. v. FCC, 512 U.S. 622 (1994) introduced yet a new First Amendment model for application to new technologies. See p. 861. Professor Cass R. Sunstein says the *Turner* model stresses the "legitimacy and importance of ensuring general public (viewer) access to free programming." *Turner* suggests that "the government may provide access not only through subsidies, but also through regulation." See Cass R. Sunstein, *The First Amendment in Cyberspace*, 104 Yale L.J. 1757, 1774 (1995).

Access to the Print Press— The *Tornillo* Case

On June 7, 1971, the Supreme Court, in a further extension of the *New York Times* doctrine, in *Rosenbloom v. Metromedia, Inc.*, 403 U.S. 29 (1971), discussed in connection with the libel materials in this text, p. 182, justified further increasing the significant protection against libel newspapers already enjoyed by urging that the states establish a right of access to the press. Justice William Brennan, speaking for the Court, said in an opinion joined by Chief Justice Burger and Justice Blackmun:

> If the States fear that private citizens will not be able to respond adequately to publicity involving them, the solution lies in the direction of ensuring their ability to respond, rather than in a stifling public discussion of matters of public concern.

The Court, in footnote 15 of its opinion, accompanied this remark with a sympathetic discussion of the argument for the creation of a right of access to the press:

> Some States have adopted retraction statutes or right of reply statutes. See Donnelly, *The Right of Reply: An Alternative to an Action for Libel*, 34

Va.L.Rev. 867 (1984); Note, *Vindication of the Reputation of a Public Official*, 80 Harv. L. Rev. 1730 (1967). Cf. *Red Lion Broadcasting Co. v. FCC*, 395 U.S. 367 (1969).

> One writer, in arguing that the First Amendment itself should be read to guarantee a right of access to the media not limited to a right to respond to defamatory falsehoods, has suggested several ways the law might encourage public discussion. Barron, *Access to the Press—A New First Amendment Right*, 80 Harv. L. Rev. 1641, 1666–1678 (1967). It is important to recognize that the private individual often desires press exposure either for himself, his ideas, or his causes. Constitutional adjudication must take into account the individual's interest in access to the press as well as the individual's interest in preserving his reputation, even though libel actions by their nature encourage a narrow view of the individual's interest since they focus only on situations where the individual has been harmed by undesired press attention. A constitutional rule that deters the press from covering the ideas or activities of the private individual thus conceives the individual's interest too narrowly.

The Court's observations on access in *Rosenbloom* raised some intriguing questions. The Court said "constitutional adjudication" should take account of the individual's interest in access to the press. The Court's remarks in *Rosenbloom* appeared to *assume* the constitutionality of right to reply legislation that would have a much wider scope than merely to provide a response to defamation. Finally, the state action problem that had loomed so large in the lower courts was not mentioned at all.

In May 1973, in *CBS v. Democratic National Committee*, 412 U.S. 94 (1973), the Supreme Court dealt a blow to the view that the force of the First Amendment was sufficient in itself to require the broadcast networks to abandon their policy of refusing to sell time to political groups and parties for the dissemination of views about ideas. See p. 482. The Supreme Court took the position that so long as the Federal Communications Commission (FCC) neither forbade nor required the networks to take any particular position with regard to the sale of political time, what the networks did was private action and therefore removed from the realm of constitutional obligation.

In the much-publicized *Tornillo* case the tantalizing question was squarely presented for consideration: Was it consistent, under the First

Amendment, for a state to provide by statute for compelled publication by a general-circulation daily newspaper in certain specified circumstances?

A provision of the Florida Election Code, F.S. 104.38, enacted in 1913, provided that where the publisher of a newspaper assails the personal character of any political candidate or charges him with malfeasance or misfeasance in office, such newspaper shall upon request of the political candidate immediately publish free of cost any reply he may make thereto in as conspicuous a place and in the same kind of type as the matter that calls for the reply:

> F.S. § 104.38—Newspaper assailing candidate in an election; space for reply. If any newspaper in its columns assails the personal character of any candidate for nomination or for election in any election, or charges said candidate with malfeasance or misfeasance in office, or otherwise attacks his official record, or gives to another free space for such purpose, such newspaper shall upon request of such candidate immediately publish free of cost any reply he may make thereto in as conspicuous a place and in the same kind of type as the matter that calls for such reply, provided such reply does not take up more space than the matter replied to. Any person or firm failing to comply with the provisions of this section shall be guilty of a misdemeanor of the first degree, punishable as provided in § 775.082 or § 775.083.

The statute slumbered in the Florida sun for more than half a century. The rise of the idea that the First Amendment might suggest positive duties for the press as well as new immunities breathed new life into the statute in the late 1960s, and at least three lawsuits involving this little-known provision of the Florida Election Code were brought.

The most controversial came to involve a lawsuit by one Pat Tornillo, leader of the Dade County Classroom Teachers Association. In 1972, Tornillo ran as Democratic candidate for the Florida legislature.

In 1968, the Dade County Classroom Teachers Association went on strike. Under Florida law at the time, a strike by public school teachers was illegal. Tornillo led the strike in Miami.

On September 20, 1972, The *Miami Herald* published an editorial calling Tornillo a "czar" and a lawbreaker. The *Herald* said in an editorial that "it would be inexcusable of the voters if they sent Pat Tornillo to the legislature."

Tornillo demanded an opportunity to reply to both these attacks under the Florida right of reply statute. The *Herald* refused to print the reply, and Tornillo filed a suit against the *Herald* and sought, on the strength of the statute, a mandatory injunction requiring the printing of his replies.

The *Tornillo* case required a direct judicial consideration of the validity of affirmative implementation of First Amendment values.

The Florida lower court in the *Tornillo* case held that the right of reply statute was unconstitutional. But the Supreme Court of Florida in a 6–1 decision reversed that court and, in the first test of the validity of a newspaper right of reply statute, under the First Amendment held it to be constitutional. *Tornillo v. Miami Herald*, 287 So. 2d 78 (Fla. 1973).

The Supreme Court of Florida strongly relied on the endorsement of right of reply legislation contained in the opinion for the Court in *Rosenbloom*, p. 183. The idea expressed in *Rosenbloom* and the state supreme court decision in *Tornillo* may be outlined as follows: If damages are not to be a remedy for libel, perhaps a right of reply can perform that task. Damages won in a libel action are perhaps a burden on the information process. But a right of reply statute aids the information process in the sense that it provides for access for the person attacked.

Miami Herald Pub. Co. v. Tornillo
418 U.S. 241, 94 S. CT. 2831, 41 L. ED. 2D 730 (1974).

Chief Justice BURGER delivered the opinion of the Court.

The issue in this case is whether a state statute granting a political candidate a right to equal space to reply to criticism and attacks on his record by a newspaper, violates the guarantees of a free press.

In the fall of 1972, appellee, Executive Director of the Classroom Teachers Association, apparently a teachers' collective-bargaining agent, was a candidate for the Florida House of Representatives. On September 20, 1972, and again on September 29, 1972, appellant printed editorials critical of appellee's candidacy. In response to these editorials appellee demanded that appellant print verbatim his replies, defending the role of the Classroom Teachers Association and the organization's accomplishments for the citizens of Dade County. Appellant declined to print the appellee's replies, and appellee brought suit in Circuit Court, Dade County, seeking declaratory and injunctive relief and actual and punitive damages in excess of $5,000. The action was premised on Florida Statute § 104.38, a "right of reply" statute which provides that if a candidate for nomination or election is assailed regarding his personal character or official record by any newspaper, the candidate has the right to demand that the newspaper print, free of cost to the candidate, any reply the candidate may make to the newspaper's charges. The reply must appear in as conspicuous a place and in the same kind of type as the charges which prompted the reply, provided it does not take up more space than the charges. Failure to comply with the statute constitutes a first-degree misdemeanor.

Appellant sought a declaration that § 104.38 was unconstitutional. After an emergency hearing requested by the appellee, the Circuit Court denied injunctive relief because, absent special circumstances, no injunction could properly issue against the commission of a crime, and held that § 104.38 was unconstitutional as an infringement on the freedom of the press under the First and Fourteenth Amendments to the Constitution. *Tornillo v. Miami Herald Pub. Co.*, 38 Fla. Supp. 80 (1972). The Circuit Court concluded that dictating what a newspaper must print was no different from dictating what it must not print. The Circuit Judge viewed the statute's vagueness as serving "to restrict and stifle protected expression." 38 Fla. Supp. at 83. Appellee's cause was dismissed with prejudice.

On direct appeal, the Florida Supreme Court reversed holding that § 104.38 did not violate constitutional guarantees. *Tornillo v. Miami Herald Pub. Co.*, 287 So. 2d 78 (1973). It held that free speech was enhanced and not abridged by the Florida right of reply statute, which in that court's view, furthered the "broad societal interest in the free flow of information to the public." 287 So. 2d, at 82. It also held that the statute was not impermissibly vague; the statute informs "those who are subject to it as to what conduct on their part will render them liable to its penalties." 287 So. 2d, at 85. Civil remedies, including damages, were held to be available under this

statute; the case was remanded to the trial court for further proceedings not inconsistent with the Florida Supreme Court's opinion.

The challenged statute creates a right to reply to press criticism of a candidate for nomination or election. The statute was enacted in 1913 and this is only the second recorded case decided under its provisions.

Appellant contends the statute is void on its face because it purports to regulate the content of a newspaper in violation of the First Amendment. Alternatively it is urged that the statute is void for vagueness since no editor could know exactly what words would call the statute into operation. It is also contended that the statute fails to distinguish between critical comment which is and is not defamatory.

The appellee and supporting advocates of an enforceable right of access to the press vigorously argue that Government has an obligation to ensure that a wide variety of views reach the public.[8] The contentions of access proponents will be set out in some detail.[9] It is urged that at the time the First Amendment to the Constitution was enacted in 1791 as part of our Bill of Rights the press was broadly representative of the people it was serving. While many of the newspapers were intensely partisan and narrow in their views, the press collectively presented a broad range of opinions to readers. Entry into publishing was inexpensive; pamphlets and books provided meaningful alternatives to the organized press for the expression of unpopular ideas and often treated events and expressed views not covered by conventional newspapers. A true marketplace of ideas existed in which there was relatively easy access to the channels of communication.

Access advocates submit that although newspapers of the present are superficially similar to those of 1791 the press of today is in reality very different from that known in the early years of our national existence. In the past half century a communications revolution has seen the introduction of radio and television into our lives, the

---

8. See generally Barron, *Access to the Press—A New First Amendment Right,* 80 Harv. L. Rev. 1641 (1967).
9. For a good overview of the position of access advocates see Lange, *The Role of the Access Doctrine in the Regulation of the Mass Media: A Critical Review and Assessment,* 52 N.C. L. Rev. 1, 8-9 (1973).

promise of a global community through the use of communications satellites, and the spectre of a "wired" nation by means of an expanding cable television network with two-way capabilities. The printed press, it is said, has not escaped the effects of this revolution. Newspapers have become big business and there are far fewer of them to serve a larger literate population. Chains of newspapers, national newspapers, national wire and news services, and one-newspaper towns, are the dominant features of a press that has become noncompetitive and enormously powerful and influential in its capacity to manipulate popular opinion and change the course of events. Major metropolitan newspapers have collaborated to establish news services national in scope. Such national news organizations provide syndicated "interpretative reporting" as well as syndicated features and commentary, all of which can serve as part of the new school of "advocacy journalism."

The elimination of competing newspapers in most of our large cities, and the concentration of control of media that results from the only newspaper being owned by the same interests which own a television station and a radio station, are important components of this trend toward concentration of control of outlets to inform the public.

The result of these vast changes has been to place in a few hands the power to inform the American people and shape public opinion.[15] Much of the editorial opinion and commentary that is printed is that of syndicated columnists distributed nationwide and, as a result, we are told, on national and world issues there tends to be a homogeneity of editorial opinion, commentary, and interpretative analysis. The abuses of bias and manipulative reportage are, likewise, said to be the result of the vast accumulations of unreviewable power in the modern media empires. In effect, it is claimed, the public has lost any ability to respond or to contribute in a meaningful way to the debate on issues. The monopoly of the means of communication allows for little or no critical analysis of the media except in professional journals of very limited readership.

> This concentration of nationwide news organizations—like other large institutions—has grown increasingly remote from and unresponsive to the popular constituencies on which they depend and which depend on them. Report of the Task Force, *The Twentieth Century Fund Task Force Report for a National News Council, A Free and Responsive Press* 4 (1973).

Appellees cite the report of the Commission on Freedom of the Press, chaired by Robert M. Hutchins, in which it was stated, as long ago as 1947, that "The right of free public expression has lost its earlier reality." Commission on Freedom of the Press, *A Free and Responsible Press* 15.

The obvious solution, which was available to dissidents at an earlier time when entry into publishing was relatively inexpensive, today would be to have additional newspapers. But the same economic factors which have caused the disappearance of vast numbers of metropolitan newspapers,[16] have made entry into the marketplace of ideas served by the print media almost impossible. It is urged that the claim of newspapers to be "surrogates for the public" carries with it a concomitant fiduciary obligation to account for that stewardship.[17] From this premise it is reasoned that the only effective way to insure fairness and accuracy and to provide for some accountability is for government to take affirmative action. The First Amendment interest of the public in being informed is said to be in peril because the "marketplace of ideas" is today a monopoly controlled by the owners of the market.

Proponents of enforced access to the press take comfort from language in several of this Court's decisions which suggests that the First Amendment acts as a sword as well as a shield,

---

15. "Local monopoly in printed news raises serious questions of diversity of information and opinion. What a local newspaper does not print about local affairs does not see general print at all. And, having the power to take initiative in reporting and enunciation of opinions, it has extraordinary power to set the atmosphere and determine the terms of local consideration of public issues." B. Bagdikian, *The Information Machines* 127 (1971).

16. The newspapers have persuaded Congress to grant them immunity from the antitrust laws in the case of "failing" newspapers for joint operations. 15 U.S.C.A. § 1801 et seq.

17. "Freedom of the press is a right belonging, like all rights in a democracy, to all the people. As a practical matter, however, it can be exercised only by those who have effective access to the press. Where the financial, economic, and technological conditions limit such access to a small minority, the exercise of that right by that minority takes on fiduciary or quasi-fiduciary characteristics." A. MacLeish in W. Hocking, *Freedom of the Press,* 99 n.4 (1947).

that it imposes obligations on the owners of the press in addition to protecting the press from government regulation. In *Associated Press v. United States,* 326 U.S. 1, 20 (1945), the Court, in rejecting the argument that the press is immune from the antitrust laws by virtue of the First Amendment, stated:

> The First Amendment, far from providing an argument against application of the Sherman Act, here provides powerful reasons to the contrary. That amendment rests on the assumption that the widest possible dissemination of information from diverse and antagonistic sources is essential to the welfare of the public, that a free press is a condition of a free society. Surely a command that the government itself shall not impede the free flow of ideas does not afford non-governmental combinations a refuge if they impose restraints upon that constitutionally guaranteed freedom. Freedom to publish means freedom for all and not for some. Freedom to publish is guaranteed by the Constitution, but freedom to combine to keep others from publishing is not. Freedom of the press from governmental interference under the First Amendment does not sanction repression of that freedom by private interests. [Footnote omitted.]

In *New York Times Co. v. Sullivan,* 376 U.S. 254, 270 (1964), the Court spoke of "a profound national commitment to the principle that debate on public issues should be uninhibited, robust, and wide-open." It is argued that the "uninhibited, robust" debate is not "wide-open" but open only to a monopoly in control of the press. Appellee cites the plurality opinion in *Rosenbloom v. Metromedia, Inc.,* 403 U.S. 29, 47 & n. 15 (1971), which he suggests seemed to invite experimentation by the States in right to access regulation of the press.

Access advocates note that Justice Douglas a decade ago expressed his deep concern regarding the effects of newspaper monopolies:

> Where one paper has a monopoly in an area, it seldom presents two sides of an issue. It too often hammers away on one ideological or political line using its monopoly position not to educate people, not to promote debate, but to inculcate its readers with one philosophy, one attitude—and to make money. The newspapers that give a variety of views and news that is not slanted or contrived are few indeed. And the problem promises to get worse. *The Great Right* (Ed. by E. Cahn) 124–125, 127 (1963).

They also claim the qualified support of Professor Thomas I. Emerson, who has written that "[a] limited right of access to the press can be safely enforced," although he believes that "[g]overnment measures to encourage a multiplicity of outlets, rather than compelling a few outlets to represent everybody, seems a preferable course of action." T. Emerson, *The System of Freedom of Expression* 671 (1970).

However much validity may be found in these arguments, at each point the implementation of a remedy such as an enforceable right of access necessarily calls for some mechanism, either governmental or consensual. If it is governmental coercion, this at once brings about a confrontation with the express provisions of the First Amendment and the judicial gloss on that amendment developed over the years.[20]

The Court foresaw the problems relating to government enforced access as early as its decision in *Associated Press v. United States, supra.* There it carefully contrasted the private "compulsion to print" called for by the Association's Bylaws with the provisions of the District Court decree against appellants which "does not compel AP or its members to permit publication of anything which their 'reason' tells them should not be published." 326 U.S., at 20 n.18. In *Branzburg v. Hayes,* 408 U.S. 665, 681 (1972), we emphasized that the cases then before us "involve no intrusions upon speech and assembly, no prior restraint or restriction on what the press may publish, and no express or implied command that the press publish what it prefers to withhold." In *Columbia Broadcasting System, Inc. v. Democratic Nat. Comm.,* 412 U.S. 94, 117 (1973), the plurality opinion noted:

> The power of a privately owned newspaper to advance its own political, social, and economic views is bounded by only two factors: first, the acceptance of a sufficient number of readers—and hence advertisers—to assure financial success; and, second, the journalistic integrity of its editors and publishers.

An attitude strongly adverse to any attempt to extend a right of access to newspapers was

---

20. Because we hold that § 104.38 violates the First Amendment's guarantee of a free press we have no occasion to consider appellant's further argument that the statute is unconstitutionally vague.

echoed by several Members of this Court in their separate opinions in that case. 412 U.S. at 145 (Stewart, J., concurring); 412 U.S. at 182 n.12 (Brennan, J., dissenting). Recently, while approving a bar against employment advertising specifying "male" or "female" preference, the Court's opinion in *Pittsburgh Press Co. v. Pittsburgh Comm. on Human Relations,* 413 U.S. 376, 391 (1973), took pains to limit its holding within narrow bounds:

> Nor, *a fortiori,* does our decision authorize any restriction whatever, whether of content or layout, on stories or commentary originated by *Pittsburgh Press,* its columnists, or its contributors. On the contrary, we reaffirm unequivocally the protection afforded to editorial judgment and to the free expression of views on these and other issues, however controversial.

Dissenting in *Pittsburgh Press,* Justice Stewart joined by Justice Douglas expressed the view that no "government agency—local, state or federal—can tell a newspaper in advance what it can print and what it cannot." Id. at 400. See *Associates & Aldrich Co. v. Times Mirror Co.,* 440 F.2d 133, 135 (9th Cir. 1971).

We see the beginning with *Associated Press, supra,* the Court has expressed sensitivity as to whether a restriction or requirement constituted the compulsion exerted by government on a newspaper to print that which it would not otherwise print. The clear implication has been that any such a compulsion to publish that which " 'reason' tells them should not be published" is unconstitutional. A responsible press is an undoubtedly desirable goal, but press responsibility is not mandated by the Constitution and like many other virtues it cannot be legislated.

Appellee's argument that the Florida statute does not amount to a restriction of appellant's right to speak because "the statute in question here has not prevented the *Miami Herald* from saying anything it wished" begs the core question. Compelling editors or publishers to publish that which " 'reason' tells them should not be published" is what is at issue in this case. The Florida statute operates as a command in the same sense as a statute or regulation forbidding appellant from publishing specified matter. Governmental restraint on publishing need not fall into familiar or traditional patterns to be subject to constitutional limitations on governmental

powers. *Grosjean v. American Press Co.,* 297 U.S. 233, 244–245 (1936). The Florida statute exacts a penalty on the basis of the content of a newspaper. The first phase of the penalty resulting from the compelled printing of a reply is exacted in terms of the cost in printing and composing time and materials and in taking up space that could be devoted to other material the newspaper may have preferred to print. It is correct, as appellee contends, that a newspaper is not subject to the finite technological limitations of time that confront a broadcaster but it is not correct to say that, as an economic reality, a newspaper can proceed to infinite expansion of its column space to accommodate the replies that a government agency determines or a statute commands the readers should have available.

Faced with the penalties that would accrue to any newspaper that published news or commentary arguably within the reach of the right of access statute, editors might well conclude that the safe course is to avoid controversy and that, under the operation of the Florida statute, political and electoral coverage would be blunted or reduced. Government enforced right of access inescapably "dampens the vigor and limits the variety of public debate," *New York Times Co. v. Sullivan, supra,* 376 U.S., at 279. The Court, in *Mills v. Alabama,* 384 U.S. 214, 218 (1966), stated that

> there is practically universal agreement that a major purpose of [the First] Amendment was to protect the free discussion of governmental affairs. This of course includes discussion of candidates.

Even if a newspaper would face no additional costs to comply with a compulsory access law and would not be forced to forego publication of news or opinion by the inclusion of a reply, the Florida statute fails to clear the barriers of the First Amendment because of its intrusion into the function of editors. A newspaper is more than a passive receptacle or conduit for news, comment, and advertising. The choice of material to go into a newspaper, and the decisions made as to limitations on the size of the paper, and content, and treatment of public issues and public officials—whether fair or unfair—constitutes the exercise of editorial control and judgment. It has yet to be demonstrated how governmental regulation of this crucial process can be exercised consistent with First Amendment guarantees of a free press as they have evolved to this time. Accordingly, the judgment of the Supreme Court of Florida is reversed.

It is so ordered.

Justice WHITE, concurring.

The Court today holds that the First Amendment bars a State from requiring a newspaper to print the reply of a candidate for public office whose personal character has been criticized by that newspaper's editorials. According to our accepted jurisprudence, the First Amendment erects a virtually insurmountable barrier between government and the print media so far as government tampering, in advance of publication, with news and editorial content is concerned. *New York Times Co. v. United States*, 403 U.S. 713 (1971). A newspaper or magazine is not a public utility subject to "reasonable" governmental regulation in matters affecting the exercise of journalistic judgment as to what shall be printed. Cf. *Mills v. Alabama*, 384 U.S. 214, 220 (1966). We have learned, and continue to learn, from what we view as the unhappy experiences of other nations where government has been allowed to meddle in the internal editorial affairs of newspapers. Regardless of how beneficent-sounding the purposes of controlling the press might be, we prefer "the power of reason as applied through public discussion" and remain intensely skeptical about those measures that would allow government to insinuate itself into the editorial rooms of this Nation's press.

Of course, the press is not always accurate, or even responsible, and may not present full and fair debate on important public issues. But the balance struck by the First Amendment with respect to the press is that society must take the risk that occasionally debate on vital matters will not be comprehensive and that all viewpoints may not be expressed. The press would be unlicensed because, in Jefferson's words, "[w]here the press is free, and every man able to read, all is safe." Any other accommodation—any other system that would supplant private control of the press with the heavy hand of government intrusion—would make the government the censor of what the people may read and know.

To justify this statute, Florida advances a concededly important interest of ensuring free and fair elections by means of an electorate informed about the issues. But prior compulsion by government in matters going to the very nerve cen-

ter of a newspaper—the decision as to what copy will or will not be included in any given edition—collides with the First Amendment. Woven into the fabric of the First Amendment is the unexceptionable, but nonetheless timeless, sentiment that "liberty of the press is in peril as soon as the government tries to compel what is to go into a newspaper." 2 Z. Chafee, Jr., *Government and Mass Communications* 633 (1947).

The constitutionally obnoxious feature of § 104.38 is not that the Florida legislature may also have placed a high premium on the protection of individual reputational interests; for, government, certainly has "a pervasive and strong interest in preventing and redressing attacks upon reputation." *Rosenblatt v. Baer*, 383 U.S. 75, 86 (1966). Quite the contrary, this law runs afoul of the elementary First Amendment proposition that government may not force a newspaper to print copy which, in its journalistic discretion, it chooses to leave on the newsroom floor. Whatever power may reside in government to influence the publishing of certain narrowly circumscribed categories of material, see e.g., *Pittsburgh Press Co. v. Pittsburgh Comm. on Human Relations*, 413 U.S. 376 (1973); *New York Times Co. v. United States, supra*, at 730 (concurring opinion), we have never thought that the First Amendment permitted public officials to dictate to the press the contents of its news columns or the slant of its editorials.

But though a newspaper may publish without government censorship, it has never been entirely free from liability for what it chooses to print. Among other things the press has not been wholly at liberty to publish falsehoods damaging to individual reputation. At least until today, we have cherished the average citizen's reputation interest enough to afford him a fair chance to vindicate himself in an action for libel characteristically provided by state law. He has been unable to force the press to tell his side of the story or to print a retraction, but he has had at least the opportunity to win a judgment if he can prove the falsity of the damaging publication, as well as a fair chance to recover reasonable damages for his injury.

Reaffirming the rule that the press cannot be forced to print an answer to a personal attack made by it, however, throws into stark relief the consequences of the new balance forged by the Court in the companion case also announced today. *Gertz v. Robert Welch, Inc.* goes far towards eviscerating the effectiveness of the ordinary libel action, which has long been the only potent response available to the private citizen libeled by the press. Under *Gertz,* the burden of proving liability is immeasurably increased, proving damages is made exceedingly more difficult, and vindicating reputation by merely proving falsehood and winning a judgment to that effect are wholly foreclosed. Needlessly, in my view, the Court trivializes and denigrates the interest in reputation by removing virtually all the protection the law has always afforded.

Of course, these two decisions do not mean that because government may not dictate what the press is to print, neither can it afford a remedy for libel in any form. *Gertz* itself leaves a putative remedy for libel intact, albeit in severely emaciated form; and the press certainly remains liable for knowing or reckless falsehoods under *New York Times* and its progeny, however improper an injunction against publication might be.

One need not think less of the First Amendment to sustain reasonable methods for allowing the average citizen to redeem a falsely tarnished reputation. Nor does one have to doubt the genuine decency, integrity and good sense of the vast majority of professional journalists to support the right of any individual to have his day in court when he has been falsely maligned in the public press. The press is the servant, not the master, of the citizenry, and its freedom does not carry with it an unrestricted hunting license to prey on the ordinary citizen.

> In plain English, freedom carries with it responsibility even for the press; freedom of the press is not a freedom from responsibility for its exercise.
> Without a lively sense of responsibility a free press may readily become a powerful instrument of injustice. *Pennekamp v. Florida,* 328 U.S. 331, 356, 365 (1946) (Frankfurter, J., concurring).

To me it is a near absurdity to so deprecate individual dignity, as the Court does in *Gertz,* and to leave the people at the complete mercy of the press, at least in this stage of our history when the press, as the majority in this case so well documents, is steadily becoming more powerful and much less likely to be deterred by threats of libel suits.

Justice BRENNAN, with whom Justice Rehnquist joins, concurring.

I join the Court's opinion which, as I understand it, addresses only "right of reply" statutes and implies no view upon the constitutionality of "retraction" statutes affording plaintiffs able to prove defamatory falsehoods a statutory action to require publication of a retraction. See generally Note, *Vindication of the Reputation of a Public Official,* 80 Harv. L. Rev. 1730, 1739–1747 (1967).

COMMENT

In the context of the public law of libel in *Rosenbloom v. Metromedia,* p. 183, Justice Brennan expressed sympathy for the enactment of right to reply legislation. Yet he joined in the opinion for the Court in *Tornillo.* Furthermore, in *Gertz v. Welch,* p. 187, decided the same day as *Tornillo,* Brennan dissented from the Court's rejection of the *Rosenbloom* "public issue" approach to the public law of libel. If the *Gertz* Court was concerned that the "public issue" standard would make it too difficult for a libel plaintiff to vindicate his reputation by securing a judgment that the publication was false, Justice Brennan had just the remedy: "the possible enactment of statutes, not requiring proof of fault, which provide for an action for retraction or for publication of a court's determination of falsity if the plaintiff is able to demonstrate that false statements have been published concerning his activities."

But after the *Tornillo* decision, can a newspaper be compelled to publish a retraction against its will? Suppose a statute required a paper to publish the fact that a libel plaintiff was vindicated in a suit against the paper in that the offending publication was adjudicated as false? Wouldn't the newspaper challenge the statute and rely on the *Tornillo* case for the proposition that the "choice of material to go into the newspaper" is an editorial and not a legislative decision? Note that in *Tornillo,* Justice Brennan wrote a special concurrence to point out that the question of the constitutional validity of retraction statutes is not addressed by the decision of the Court in *Tornillo.* From a First Amendment point of view, how can the retraction statute be distinguished from the right of reply statute? Is it relevant that in the retraction situation the content of the retraction is composed by the newspaper, while in the reply situation the person who was attacked dictates the content of the reply?

In *Dun & Bradstreet, Inc. v. Greenmoss Builders, Inc.*, 472 U.S. 749 (1985), Justice White in a concurring opinion blasted the *New York Times v. Sullivan* rule and spoke sympathetically of the merits of a vindication statute as an alternative to libel damages:

> I can therefore discern nothing in the Constitution which forbids a plaintiff from obtaining a judicial decree that a statement is false—a decree he can then use in the community to clear his name and to prevent further damage from a defamation already published.

Can right of reply (or even a mandatory vindication statute) be used constitutionally as an alternative to libel damages? On the right of reply alternative, one commentator has suggested:

> One possible alternative is to provide a right of reply only for plaintiffs who prove they were defamed. Assuming a plaintiff meets this burden, the defendant would then have an option to respond in damages or to publish a reply authored by the successful libel plaintiff. In considering whether the "right" of reply, in such circumstances, coerces the defendant, it should be noted that the defendant must elect the reply course of action. The defendant's motive, reasonably enough, is to avoid damages.
> See Barron, *The Search for Media Accountability*, 19 Suffolk U. L. Rev. 789, 805 (1985).

Has the defendant who elects to use the right of reply remedy been coerced? Or is she, instead, freely exercising a choice to forgo damages in order to have a chance to correct misstatements?

The *Tornillo* decision has been criticized for setting forth the access arguments but not really answering them. One commentator, in an influential work on access, suggested what might prove to be a more reasoned and discriminating approach to the problem of access. See Schmidt, *Freedom of the Press v. Public Access* (1976).

Professor Schmidt said the access problem arises out of a conflict between a First Amendment historical tradition of editorial autonomy and an interpretation of the First Amendment that conceives as its function achievement of "the utilitarian goal of diversity of expression." Schmidt thought resolution of the access prob-lem should involve reconciliation of the "values of autonomy and diversity."

How would such a resolution proceed? Professor Schmidt outlines the following mode of analysis:

> The aim of analysis would be to determine which "publishers" should be protected from access so that the values of autonomy can be best preserved. And, conversely, analysis would have to determine which other "publishers" should be made accessible to serve the goals of diversity. Rights of access would have to be allocated to particular publishing units in such a way that the aim of diversity would be served to the maximum, but jeopardy to the values of autonomy would be kept to a minimum.
> See Schmidt, 36.

For a more appreciative response to the *Tornillo* case, see Abrams, *In Defense of Tornillo*, 86 Yale L.J. 361 (1976). For a more critical commentary, see *The Supreme Court, 1973 Term*, 88 Harv. L. Rev. 174, 177 (1974).

For some, the declaration in *Tornillo* that mandating the press to print something is the same thing as mandating that the press not print something remains unconvincing: "Viewed from the vantage of the public, a 'right of reply' gives John Citizen two sides of a question while suppression or prohibitions give him none." See Lewin, *What's Happening to Free Speech?*, The New Republic 13 (July 27, 1974).

From a legal point of view, the most remarkable aspect of the *Tornillo* decision is that it is innocent of any reference to the *Red Lion* decision. Is this a defensible omission? Perhaps the Court was reluctant to have to say that editorial decision making was less protected in the electronic media than in the print media, and yet, at the same time, it was unwilling to alter the *Red Lion* decision.

The aftermath of *Tornillo* has been an increase in voluntary opportunities for public access to newspapers. One study of the *Tornillo* case points to such developments as "op-ed pages, allocating more space to the letters to the editor column" and creation of press ombudsmen: "The solutions are not perfect, but with an intractable problem they could not be. Furthermore, as voluntary responses to a widely perceived problem, changes can be made as experience dictates. These attempts, even if imperfect, beat the potential errors of legislation, a possibility always lurking within *Tornillo.*" See Powe, *Tornillo,* 1987 Sup. Ct. Rev. 345, 394–95.

How important to the result in *Tornillo* was the concern that compulsory access might deter or chill speech? In *Pacific Gas & Electric v. Public Utilities Commission of California,* 475 U.S. 1 (1986), the Supreme Court concluded that it was central to *Tornillo. Pacific Gas & Electric* confronted the Supreme Court with the following question: Could the California Public Utilities Commission (CPUC) require Pacific, Gas & Electric (PG&E), a privately owned utility company, to include in the envelope with its monthly billing statement and newsletter, "Progress," the message of a third party, a ratepayers organization—Toward Utility Rate Normalization (TURN)—with which the utility disagreed? TURN's message was not required to be placed in PG&E's newsletter; instead, TURN'S message was required to be placed in PG&E's billing envelopes four months out of the year. The Court, per Justice Lewis Powell, relying on *Tornillo,* held that, the California Public Utilities Commission order violated the First Amendment on two grounds. First, the compulsory access order deterred the utility from saying things that might trigger an adverse response. Second, the order might cause the utility to respond to subjects about which it might otherwise prefer to remain silent.

The view of *Tornillo* taken in *Pacific Gas & Electric* sees concerns about deterrence of speech and compelling speech as central to that decision. *Pacific Gas & Electric* does concede, however, that editorial autonomy was an "independent ground for invalidating the statute." The Court in *Pacific Gas & Electric* used a strict scrutiny standard to judge the First Amendment impact of the Commission or CPUC compulsory access order.

In dissent, Justice William Rehnquist objected to applying the strictest standard of review to the Commission or CPUC access order on the basis of an unsubstantiated prophecy that the order would necessarily deter the utility's speech. Justice Rehnquist thought such a result unlikely: "TURN or any other group eventually given access will likely address the controversial subjects in spite of PG&E's silence. Accordingly, the right of access should not be held to trigger heightened scrutiny on the ground that it might somehow deter PG&E's right to speak."

ACCESS FOR ADVERTISING TO THE PRIVATELY OWNED DAILY PRESS

What is the status of a First Amendment–based right of access to the advertising columns of the privately owned press?

Has the *Tornillo* case, with its emphasis on unfettered editorial decision making, foreclosed all claims of access for advertising? Or is the advertising section of the paper more susceptible to access claims? See *Pittsburgh Press Co. v. Pittsburgh Comm. on Human Relations,* 413 U.S. 376 (1973). Moreover, *Tornillo* dealt with a statute compelling a newspaper to publish a reply to editorial attack, i.e., with the essential editorial product of the paper rather than with the traditionally open "advertising" section. The First Amendment–based access for advertising cases that follow illustrate the range of issues that occur in this area.

What is the significance of discrimination in deciding whether there is any legal duty to accept advertisements? In *Bloss v. Federated Publications,* 145 N.W.2d 800 (Mich. Ct. App. 1966), the plaintiff, a theater owner, wanted the Battle Creek *Enquirer and News,* the only daily newspaper in Battle Creek, Michigan, to publish certain advertisements concerning adult movies in the city. The paper informed the theater owner that it did not wish to "accept advertising for theaters concerning suggestive or prurient material." Although the Michigan Court of Appeals declared that a newspaper is "a business affected with a public interest," the court held that the plaintiff's case failed to survive a motion for summary judgment because the "essential element of discrimination is lacking."

On appeal to the Supreme Court of Michigan, that court affirmed. *Bloss v. Federated Publications,* 157 N.W.2d 241 (Mich. 1968).

The case of *Uhlman v. Sherman,* 22 Ohio N.P. (n.s.), 225, 31 Ohio Dec. 54 (1919), was discussed in the *Bloss* litigation. The theater owner relied heavily on it because it is the only American case that has recognized a right of access to the press. *Uhlman* concerned discrimination against a *commercial* advertiser.

Associates & Aldrich v. Times Mirror Co., 440 F.2d 133 (9th Cir. 1971), presented this question: "May a federal court compel the publisher of a daily newspaper to accept and print advertising in the exact form submitted?" The court answered: "No." A motion picture producer brought suit to prevent the *Los Angeles Times* from censoring its advertising copy. The court said it could find no legal basis to empower a court "to compel a private newspaper to publish advertisements without editorial control of their content merely because such advertisements are not legally obscene or unlawful."

Should the Ninth Circuit in *Associates & Aldrich* have distinguished between the exercise of editorial discretion in the news columns of newspapers and the exercise of editorial discretion in an "open" section of the paper such as the advertising columns? See generally Barron, *Freedom of the Press for Whom?,* 270–87 (1973).

Efforts to compel a First Amendment–based right of access to the advertising pages of the privately owned daily press persist but have yet to succeed. *Wisconsin Association of Nursing Homes, Inc. v. The Journal Co.,* 285 N.W.2d 891 (Wisc. 1979), is illustrative. When the *Milwaukee Journal* published a series of investigative reports dealing with the quality of care in Milwaukee area nursing homes, the Wisconsin Association of Nursing Homes prepared a full-page ad to respond to what it contended were "false and erroneous" allegations. The *Milwaukee Journal* refused to publish the ad, asserting that it contained possibly libelous material.

Plaintiffs sought an order compelling publication of the ads from the Wisconsin courts. Plaintiffs contended that the Journal Co. had a " 'monopoly' over all newspapers of general coverage in the Milwaukee metropolitan area, and that without access to defendant's newspapers, plaintiffs are deprived of any right to present their views to the public." The courts refused to issue an order compelling publication of the ad. The Wisconsin Supreme Court conceded that the "right of a publisher to refuse advertising in certain instances involving a claim of monopoly" is qualified in some circumstances. But the court said that there was no evidence of "any contracts, combinations, or conspiracies in restraint of trade" on the part of the defendant *Milwaukee Journal.*

Suppose a newspaper refuses to publish a union ad for fear of offending an advertiser? In *Chicago Joint Board, Amalgamated Clothing Workers, AFL-CIO, v. Chicago Tribune Co.,* 435 F.2d 470 (7th Cir. 1970), a union objected to the sale of imported clothing by Marshall Field and Company in Chicago on the ground that selling imports jeopardized the jobs of American clothing workers. When the union sought to place an ad explaining its position in each of the then four Chicago daily newspapers, none of the papers would publish the ad. The union sued the papers on an access theory to enjoin them from refusing to publish the ads and to pay compensatory and exemplary damages.

The union tried to show the interdependence between the Chicago daily newspapers and government in the hope that restraints on expression would be seen as quasi-public. Among the fascinating examples of state involvement with the Chicago daily press—unearthed by union lawyers—was a Chicago ordinance that restricted newsstands on public streets to selling daily newspapers printed and published in Chicago. Counsel for the union also argued that legal imposition of a duty to publish was not a foreign conception, as the newspaper lawyers claimed, because Illinois, like most states, required newspapers to publish certain legal notices. It was all to no avail.

The decision of the Court of Appeals for the Seventh Circuit, per Judge Castle, was a victory for the view that freedom of the press has as its primary focus the freedom of the publisher:

> The union's right to free speech does not give it the right to make use of the defendant's printing presses and distribution systems without defendant's consent.

In the *Chicago Joint Board* decision, Judge Castle rejected the union argument that "monopoly power in an area of vital public concern" is the equivalent of governmental action: the Chicago daily newspaper market was not a monopoly. This, of course, was true, but wasn't the union position really that in access terms the Chicago newspapers were functionally monopolistic? Because none of the papers would print the union's ad, for First Amendment purposes it was irrelevant that there was more than one daily newspaper in Chicago.

Despite the generally hostile reaction of the courts to lawsuits seeking access to the press, such suits continue to be brought. The West Virginia Supreme Court of Appeals, relying on *Tornillo,* reversed a trial court requiring a newspaper to accept and print a paid political advertisement that was submitted by a local political action committee. *Citizen Awareness Regarding Education v. Calhoun County Publishing, Inc.,* 19 Media L. Rep. 1061, 406 S.E.2d 65 (W. Va. 1991) The *Calhoun Chronicle* ran several ads from the committee, which was formed to oppose a school bond levy, but refused to print one particular committee ad because the paper had a policy of not publishing political ads in the last issue before an election. A previous West Virginia case requiring access for a union response to a paid employer ad was distinguished because it involved radio broadcasts produced by a state agency. *United Mine Workers of America v. Parsons,* 305 S.E.2d 343 (W. Va. 1983)

Indeed, whether the entity that refuses to publish an advertisement is a government instrumentality or a private entity can be crucial. This is illustrated by *Aids Action Committee v. Massachusetts Bay Transportation Authority,* 22 Media L. Rep. 2449, 42 F.3d 1 (1st Cir. 1994). Public entities, unlike private ones, must apply neutral standards and may not engage in content discrimination in accepting and refusing ads. The Massachusetts Bay Transportation Authority (MBTA) declined to run some public service ads composed by an Aids Action Committee. The ads promoted the use of condoms to help stop the spread of the AIDS virus. The MBTA refused to run some of the ads in its subway and trolley cars on the grounds that the ads were lewd, vulgar, and indecent, that the audience was a captive one, and that it contained children. Plaintiff pointed out that the MBTA had published sexually oriented and suggestive ads for the movie *Fatal Instinct.* The court of appeals determined that the MBTA's rejection of the ads was content-based:

> [W]e find, that in rejecting the 1993 ads while running the "Fatal Instinct" ads the MBTA engaged in a content discrimination which gave rise to an appearance of viewpoint discrimination and that it failed to explain that appearance away.

Ultimately, the MBTA might be able to validly exclude ads containing a certain quotient of "sexual innuendo and double entendre" from the interiors of its cars:

> To do so constitutionally, however, it will, at the least, need to act according to neutral standards, and it will need to apply these standards in such a way that there is no appearance that "the (government) is seeking to handicap the expression of particular ideas." *R.A.V. v. City of St. Paul,* 112 S. Ct. 2538, 2549 (1992).

In *United Food and Commercial Workers v. Ottaway Newspapers, Inc.,* 19 Media L. Rep. 1792, 1991 WL 328466 (D. Conn. 1991), a newspaper refused an ad by a union trying to organize employees at a retail store, which was one of the paper's advertisers. The paper refused to print the ad for fear that if it did the store would no longer advertise in the paper. The union argued unsuccessfully that the refusal to publish its ad violated the First Amendment and also constituted an unfair trade practice under the Connecticut Unfair Trade Practices Act. Relying on *Tornillo* and *Chicago Joint Board* the court rejected the union's claims: "[T]here is no place for a governmental check on a privately owned newspaper."

Outside the antitrust field, efforts to try to ground a right of access to the press on legislation not enacted for such purposes has not succeeded. In *Treanor v. Washington Post Co.,* 21 Media L. Rep. 1991, 826 F. Supp. 568 (D.D.C. 1993), a federal district court dismissed a claim that the Americans for Disabilities Act (ADA) obliged the *Washington Post* to publish a book review of a history of civil rights of disabled persons. The plaintiff, the author of the book, was a disabled individual. The plaintiff argued ingeniously that the newspaper was a place of "public accommodation" under the ADA. The court held that "newspaper columns are not 'public accommodations' within the meaning of the ADA."

Like the advertising columns, the letters to the editor column of a newspaper invites the readership to participate; the editorial and news columns do not. Is such space dedicated in some way to the public? Is there a First Amendment right to have a letter to the editor published? In *Georgescu v. Times Herald Paper,* 22 Media L. Rep. 2062, 1994 WL 525908 (Mich. Cir. Ct. 1994), it was held that there was no such right: "[U]nder the First Amendment, publishers have an absolute constitutional right to control the content of their publications. *Miami Herald v. Tornillo.* Plaintiff may not invoke the legal process to compel a change in editorial decision making—with respect to either the selection of letters for publication or the content of news coverage."

The *East West Journal of Natural Health and Living* refused to publish advertisements or a book review concerning a metabolic program for cancer treatment. The plaintiff, the developer of this treatment, stated that the *Journal* falsely asserted that he had retired and no longer provided the treatment, but that the metabolic treatment program could be obtained from another physician. The court dismissed the complaint, which had alleged fraud, deceit, constitutional tort, and antitrust violations: "[T]he printed press may publish or not publish advertising as it sees fit." *Kelley v. Gonzales,* 20 Media L. Rep. 1801, No. 92-1256 (D.W. Pa. 1992).

The Antitrust Laws and Access to the Press

Paradoxically, the antitrust laws rather than the First Amendment may turn out to be the breeding ground for a right of access to the press. Illustrative of this principle is *Home Placement Service v. Providence Journal,* 8 Media L. Rep. 1881, 682 F.2d 274 (1st Cir. 1982), Chapt. 9, which held that the refusal of a newspaper to accept classified advertising from a rental referral service that charges a fee violates the antitrust laws. Such conduct constituted "strangulation of a competitor."

Currently, a newspaper is free not to publish advertisements. But a newspaper was not free to decline publishing in circumstances where the rental referral business that seeks to place an ad is in competition with the newspaper. The newspaper's action was in violation of the Sherman Act. The newspaper was unlawfully using its control of the newspaper advertising market to preclude competition of the market seeking information about housing facts. The court of appeals in *Home Placement Service* remanded the case to the United States District Court for the District of Rhode Island for a determination of whether injunctive relief was appropriate and for an award of damages and attorney's fees.

Does the award suggest some reluctance by the court of appeals to order a newspaper to

accept an ad? Is the suggestion that the appropriate relief in lieu of an order to publish is monetary damages?

Home Placement Service should be contrasted with *Homefinders of America v. Providence Journal,* 6 Media L. Rep. 1018, 621 F.2d 441 (1st Cir. 1980), where the First Circuit held that the Sherman Act was not violated by a refusal to publish false and misleading advertisements that were submitted by a rental referral firm that charged fees to prospective renters. Judge Aldrich said for the First Circuit in *Homefinders*:

> Even when it might lack proof of actual fraud, we would hesitate long before holding that a newspaper, monopoly or not, armed with both the First Amendment and a reasonable business justification, can be ordered to publish advertising against its will. In the present case, we see no question. The antitrust laws are not a shield for deceptive advertising.

Homefinders was distinguished from *Home Placement Service* on the ground that in *Homefinders* the advertisements were deceptive and misleading and, therefore, the refusal to publish them was reasonable. The contention by the newspaper in *Home Placement Service* that the public should not have to pay to find rental housing was rejected by the court as an unacceptable "paternal judgment."

A RIGHT OF ACCESS TO THE PUBLIC PRESS—THE CASE OF THE STATE-SUPPORTED CAMPUS PRESS

In *Avins v. Rutgers, State University* 385 F.2d 151 (3d Cir. 1967), the plaintiff, Alfred Avins, alleged that he had submitted to the *Rutgers Law Review* an article that reviewed the legislative history of the Civil Rights Act of 1975 insofar as it was intended to affect school desegregation. The articles editor of the *Rutgers Law Review* rejected the article and stated that "approaching the problem from the point of view of legislative history alone is insufficient." Avins contended that a law review published by a state-supported university is a public instrumentality in whose columns all must be allowed to present their ideas: the editors do not have discretion to reject an article because in their judgment its nature or ideological approach is not suitable for publication.

The federal district court dismissed the suit, and the federal court of appeals affirmed. Judge Maris, for the court of appeals, rejected the plaintiff's contentions:

> [O]ne who claims that his constitutional right to freedom of speech has been abridged must show that he has a right to use the particular medium through which he seeks to speak. This the plaintiff has wholly failed to do. He says that he has published articles in other law reviews and will sooner or later be able to publish in a law review the article here involved. This is doubtless true. Also, no one doubts that he may freely at his own expense print his article and distribute it to all who wish to read it. However, he does not have the right, constitutional or otherwise, to commandeer the press and columns of the *Rutgers Law Review* for the publication of his article, at the expense of the subscribers to the *Review* and the New Jersey taxpayers, to the exclusion of other articles deemed by the editors to be more suitable for publication. On the contrary, the acceptance or rejection of articles submitted for publication in a law school law review necessarily involves the exercise of editorial judgment and this is in no wise lessened by the fact that the law review is supported, at least in part by the [s]tate.

The struggle for access to the press has had the most success in the high school and college press, and for a reason: the party denying access was acting pursuant to public authority, and therefore a public restraint on expression was involved. The *Wisconsin State University* case, which follows, is significant for access theory generally because it recognizes, almost without comment, what was formerly not recognized in American law at all: the First Amendment demands opportunity for expression. Therefore, prohibition against censorship does not exhaust the meaning of the First Amendment; the amendment has an affirmative dimension.

A ground-breaking case at the high school level was *Zucker v. Panitz*, 299 F. Supp. 102 (S.D.N.Y. 1969), that upheld the right of high school students to publish a paid ad opposing the war in Vietnam in their high school newspaper.

Lee v. Board of Regents of State Colleges, 441 F.2d 1257 (7th Cir. 1971), the *Wisconsin State University* case, affirmed a lower court determination that the Board of Regents of the Wisconsin State Colleges denied the freedom of the

plaintiffs who sought to publish editorial advertisements in the college paper, the *Royal Purple*. Because the state university authorities opened the campus newspaper to commercial and other types of advertising, they could not "constitutionally reject plaintiffs' advertisements because of their editorial character."

Lee, involved state-financed print media. Does *Lee* have much significance for the privately owned mass circulation newspaper? No, because the state is obliged not to censor but the private newspaper is not.

Note that a refusal by a public transit system to sell space for advertising by political candidates was upheld by the Supreme Court. See *Lehman v. City of Shaker Heights*, 418 U.S. 298 (1974). Should *Lehman* govern a case like *Lee*?

The *Mississippi Gay Alliance* Case— Access to the Public Press After *Tornillo*

Only in the tax-supported, state university campus press or some other form of public press has a right of access been recognized as set out in the foregoing cases. What is the status of cases like *Zucker* and *Lee v. Board of Regents* in light of the Supreme Court decision in *Miami Herald Publishing Co. v. Tornillo?* A case arising after *Tornillo* and raising this issue was *Mississippi Gay Alliance v. Goudelock*, 536 F.2d 1073 (5th Cir. 1976). The controversy occurred when the chairwoman of the Mississippi Gay Alliance (MGA) submitted an ad to *The Reflector*, the student newspaper at Mississippi State University (MSU). The contents of the ad were as follows:

> Gay Center—open 6:00 to 9:00 Monday, Wednesday and Friday nights.

> We offer—counselling, *legal aid* and a library of homosexual literature.

> Write to—The Mississippi Gay Alliance, P.O. Box 1328, Mississippi State University, Ms 39762.

The editor of *The Reflector* refused to publish the ad even though it was a paid advertisement. MGA, alleging a First Amendment violation, then brought suit to compel the editor to publish the ad. The federal district court refused to order publication. The federal court of appeals affirmed and distinguished cases like *Lee v. Board of Regents* and *Zucker* by contending that in the *MGA* case there was no state action because university officials did not control publishing decisions. A student editor rather than a state university official had declined to publish the ad.

The court of appeals speculated that if a state university official had ordered the newspaper not to publish such an ad, it would have been constitutionally impermissible. The reason for this conclusion, however, did not derive from the premise of *Lee v. Board of Regents* and *Zucker* that a state-sponsored press could not favor one idea and disfavor another. This conclusion derived instead from an idea set forth in *Miami Herald Publishing Co. v. Tornillo*—the inviolability of editorial autonomy. Courts could not review editorial decision making undertaken under either private or public auspices.

Protection of editorial autonomy, however, was only one component of the rationale of the decision in *MGA*. Because state law made sodomy a crime, the student editor was obliged not to publish an ad that had a connection, albeit peripheral, with such activity. Or as the court put it gingerly: "[S]pecial reasons were present for holding that there was no abuse of discretion by the editor of *The Reflector.*"

In a long and thoughtful dissent, Judge Goldberg denied that a state-sponsored newspaper could, for example, refuse to print a statement on the ground that "it expressed a political view contrary to that of the Governor."

Furthermore, Goldberg thought the principle of equal access to state student publications received implicit support from *CBS v. DNC*, reported below.

Judge Goldberg reasoned that because a "state" newspaper could not publish ads on one side of a public issue and reject ads taking the opposite point of view, it should also be assumed that it would be unconstitutional for a state newspaper to take advertisements dealing with public issues generally but to exclude, arbitrarily and selectively, advertisements on certain public issues.

For Goldberg, student editorial autonomy, a student right to edit even a state-sponsored press had to be recognized. At the same time the principle of nondiscriminatory access to state publications also had to be recognized. Judge Goldberg suggested accommodation between the two competing interests involved.

The "open" parts of the newspaper—the unedited advertising sections—were not involved in *Tornillo*. Others beside Judge Goldberg made the same distinction between the propriety of a claim for access to the advertising section but not to the news and editorial columns of a public press. See Canby, *The First Amendment and the State as Editor: Implications for Public Broadcasting,* 52 Tex. L. Rev. 1123, 1133–34 (1974). Where would a tendered reply to an "editorial advertisement" fit in Judge Goldberg's scheme if the paper involved didn't wish to publish the reply?

THE FIRST AMENDMENT AND ACCESS TO THE BROADCAST MEDIA

One immediate result of the decision in *Red Lion Broadcasting Co. v. FCC*, 395 U.S. 367 (1969), which validated the Fairness Doctrine, see p. 806, was the release of a pent-up demand for individual and group access to television. A manifestation of the dissatisfaction with complete broadcaster control over entry to broadcasting for political groups, indeed for political ideas, was the request made to the FCC by the Democratic National Committee in May 1970 that the FCC prohibit broadcasters from refusing to sell time to groups like the DNC for the solicitation of funds and for comment on public issues. The controversy that ensued from this request eventually found its way to the Supreme Court. One of the questions the case raised was whether there was a First Amendment right of access to the electronic media.

CBS v. Democratic National Committee
412 U.S. 94, 93 S. CT. 2080, 36 L. ED. 2D 772 (1973).

Chief Justice BURGER delivered the opinion of the Court:

In two orders announced the same day, the FCC ruled that a broadcaster who meets his public obligation to provide full and fair coverage of public issues is not required to accept editorial advertisements. A divided court of appeals reversed the commission, holding that a broadcaster's fixed policy of refusing editorial advertisements violates the First Amendment; the court remanded the cases to the commission to develop procedures and guidelines for administering a First Amendment right of access.

The complainants in these actions are the Democratic National Committee (DNC) and the Business Executives' Move for Vietnam Peace (BEM), a national organization of businessmen opposed to United States involvement in the Vietnam conflict. In January 1970, BEM filed a complaint with the commission charging that radio station WTOP in Washington, D.C., had refused to sell its time to broadcast a series of one-minute spot announcements expressing BEM views on Vietnam. WTOP, in common with many but not all broadcasters, followed a policy of refusing to sell time for spot announcements to individuals and groups who wished to expound their views on controversial issues. WTOP took the position that since it presented full and fair coverage of important public questions, including the Vietnam conflict, it was justified in refusing to accept editorial advertisements. WTOP also submitted evidence showing that the station had aired the views of critics of our Vietnam policy on numerous occasions. BEM challenged the fairness of WTOP's coverage of criticism of that policy, but it presented no evidence in support of that claim.

Four months later, in May 1970, the DNC filed with the commission a request for a declaratory ruling:

> That under the First Amendment to the Constitution and the Communications Act, a broadcaster may not, as a general policy, refuse to sell time to responsible entities, such as DNC, for the solicitation of funds and for comment on public issues.

DNC claimed that it intended to purchase time from radio and television stations and from the national networks in order to present the views of the Democratic Party and to solicit funds. Unlike BEM, DNC did not object to the policies of any particular broadcaster but claimed that its prior "experiences in this area make it clear that it will encounter considerable difficulty—if not total frustration of its efforts—in carrying out its plans in the event the commission should decline to issue a ruling as requested." DNC cited *Red Lion Broadcasting Co. v. FCC,* 395 U.S. 367 (1969) as establishing a limited constitutional right of access to the airwaves.

In two separate opinions, the FCC rejected respondents' claim that "responsible" individuals and groups have a right to purchase advertising

time to comment on public issues without regard to whether the broadcaster has complied with the Fairness Doctrine. The commission viewed the issue as one of major significance in administering the regulatory scheme relating to the electronic media, one going "to the heart of the system of broadcasting which has developed in this country." 25 FCC2d at 221. After reviewing the legislative history of the Communications Act, the provisions of the act itself, the commission's decisions under the act and the difficult problems inherent in administering a right of access, the commission rejected the demands of BEM and DNC. [The] FCC did, however, uphold DNC's position that the statute recognized a right of political parties to purchase broadcast time for the purpose of soliciting funds. The commission noted that Congress has accorded special consideration for access by political parties, see 47 U.S.C.A. § 315(a), and that solicitation of funds by political parties is both feasible and appropriate in the short space of time generally allotted to spot advertisements.[1]

A majority of the court of appeals reversed the commission, holding that "a flat ban on paid public issue announcements is in violation of the First Amendment, at least when other sorts of paid announcements are accepted." 450 F.2d at 646. Recognizing that the broadcast frequencies are a scarce resource inherently unavailable to all, the court nevertheless concluded that the First Amendment mandated an "abridgeable" right to present editorial advertisements. The court reasoned that a broadcaster's policy of airing commercial advertisements but not editorial advertisements constitutes unconstitutional discrimination. The court did not, however, order that either BEM's or DNC's proposed announcements must be accepted by the broadcasters; rather it remanded the cases to the FCC to develop "reasonable procedures and regulations determining which and how many 'editorial advertisements' will be put on the air." Ibid.

[W]e proceed to consider whether a broadcaster's refusal to accept editorial advertisements

---

1. The commission's rulings against BEM's Fairness Doctrine complaint and in favor of DNC's claim that political parties should be permitted to purchase airtime for solicitation of funds were not appealed to the court of appeals and are not before us here.

is governmental action violative of the First Amendment.

The Court has not previously considered whether the action of a broadcast licensee such as that challenged here is "governmental action" for purposes of the First Amendment. The holding under review thus presents a novel question, and one with far-reaching implications. See L. Jaffe, *The Editorial Responsibility of the Broadcaster,* 85 Harv. L. Rev. 768, 782–787 (1972).

The court of appeals held that broadcasters are instrumentalities of the government for First Amendment purposes, relying on the thesis, familiar in other contexts, that broadcast licensees are granted use of part of the public domain and are regulated as "proxies" or "fiduciaries of the people." 450 F.2d, at 652. These characterizations are not without validity for some purposes, but they do not resolve the sensitive constitutional issues inherent in deciding whether a particular licensee action is subject to First Amendment restraints.

The tensions inherent in such a regulatory structure emerge more clearly when we compare a private newspaper with a broadcast licensee. The power of a privately owned newspaper to advance its own political, social, and economic views is bounded by only two factors: first, the acceptance of a sufficient number of readers—and hence advertisers—to assure financial success; and, second, the journalistic integrity of its editors and publishers. A broadcast licensee has a large measure of journalistic freedom but not as large as that exercised by a newspaper. A licensee must balance what it might prefer to do as a private entrepreneur with what it is required to do as a "public trustee." To perform its statutory duties, the FCC must oversee without censoring. This suggests something of the difficulty and delicacy of administering the Communications Act—a function calling for flexibility and the capacity to adjust and readjust the regulatory mechanism to meet changing problems and needs.

The licensee policy challenged in this case is intimately related to the journalistic role of a licensee for which it has been given initial and primary responsibility by Congress. The licensee's policy against accepting editorial advertising cannot be examined as an abstract proposition, but must be viewed in the context of its journalistic role. It does not help to press on us the idea that editorial ads are "like" commercial ads for the licensee's policy against editorial spot ads is expressly based on a journalistic judgment that 10 to 60 second spot announcements are ill suited to intelligible and intelligent treatment of public issues; the broadcaster has chosen to provide a balanced treatment of controversial questions in a more comprehensive form. Obviously the licensee's evaluation is based on its own journalistic judgment of priorities and newsworthiness.

Moreover, the FCC has not fostered the licensee policy challenged here; it has simply declined to command particular action because it fell within the area of journalistic discretion. The commission explicitly emphasized that "there is of course no commission policy thwarting the sale of time to comment on public issues." 25 FCC 2d, at 226. The FCC's reasoning, consistent with nearly 40 years of precedent, is that so long as a licensee meets its "public trustee" obligation to provide balanced coverage of issues and events, it has broad discretion to decide how that obligation will be met. We do not reach the question whether the First Amendment or the Act can be read to preclude the FCC from determining that in some situations the public interest requires licensees to re-examine their policies with respect to editorial advertisements. The FCC has not yet made such a determination; it has, for the present at least, found the policy to be within the sphere of journalistic discretion which Congress has left with the licensee.

Thus, it cannot be said that the government is a "partner" to the action of broadcast licensee complained of here, nor is it engaged in a "symbiotic relationship" with the licensee, profiting from the invidious discrimination of its proxy. The First Amendment does not reach acts of private parties in every instance where the Congress or the commission has merely permitted or failed to prohibit such acts.

Our conclusion is not altered merely because the FCC rejected the claims of BEM and DNC and concluded that the challenged licensee policy is not inconsistent with the public interest.

Here, Congress has not established a regulatory scheme for broadcast licensees. More important, as we have noted, Congress has affirmatively indicated in the Communications Act that certain journalistic decisions are for the licensee, subject only to the restrictions imposed by evaluation of its overall performance under the public interest standard.

More profoundly, it would be anomalous for us to hold, in the name of promoting the constitutional guarantees of free expression, that the day-to-day editorial decisions of broadcast licensees are subject to the kind of restraints urged by respondents. To do so in the name of the First Amendment would be a contradiction. Journalistic discretion would in many ways be lost to the rigid limitations that the First Amendment imposes on government. Application of such standards to broadcast licensees would be antithetical to the very ideal of vigorous, challenging debate on issues of public interest. Every licensee is already held accountable for the totality of its performance of public interest obligations.

The concept of private, independent broadcast journalism, regulated by government to assure protection of the public interest, has evolved slowly and cautiously over more than 40 years and has been nurtured by processes of adjudication. That concept of journalistic independence could not co-exist with a reading of the challenged conduct of the licensee as governmental action. Nor could it exist without administrative flexibility to meet changing needs and the swift technological developments. We therefore conclude that the policies complained of do not constitute governmental action violative of the First Amendment.

By minimizing the difficult problems involved in implementing such a right of access, the court of appeals failed to come to grips with another problem of critical importance to broadcast regulation and the First Amendment—the risk of an enlargement of government control over the content of broadcast discussion of public issues. This risk is inherent in the court of appeals remand requiring regulations and procedures to sort out requests to be heard—a process involving the very editing that licensees now perform as to regular programming. Although the use of a public resource by the broadcast media permits a limited degree of government surveillance, as is not true with respect to private media, the government's power over licensees as we have noted, is by no means absolute and is carefully circumscribed by the act itself.

Under a constitutionally commanded and government supervised right-of-access system urged by respondents and mandated by the court of appeals, the FCC would be required to oversee far more of the day-to-day operations of broadcasters' conduct, deciding such questions as whether a particular individual or group has had sufficient opportunity to present its viewpoint and whether a particular viewpoint has already been sufficiently aired. Regimenting broadcasters is too radical a therapy for the ailment respondents complain of.

Under the Fairness Doctrine the FCC's responsibility is to judge whether a licensee's overall performance indicates a sustained good faith effort to meet the public interest in being fully and fairly informed. The commission's responsibilities under a right-of-access system would tend to draw it into a continuing case-by-case determination of who should be heard and when. Indeed, the likelihood of government involvement is so great that it has been suggested that the accepted constitutional principles against control of speech content would need to be relaxed with respect to editorial advertisements. To sacrifice First Amendment protections for so speculative a gain is not warranted, and it was well within the commission's discretion to construe the act so as to avoid such a result.

The FCC is also entitled to take into account the reality that in a very real sense listeners and viewers constitute a "captive audience." It is no answer to say that because we tolerate pervasive commercial advertisement we can also live with its political counterparts.

The judgment of the court of appeals is reversed.

Justice STEWART, concurring.

Justice BLACKMUN, with whom Justice POWELL joins, concurring.

Justice DOUGLAS.

While I join the Court in reversing the judgment below, I do so for quite different reasons.

My conclusion is that the TV and radio stand in the same protected position under the First Amendment as do newspapers and magazines.

If a broadcast licensee is not engaged in governmental action for purposes of the First Amendment, I fail to see how constitutionally we can treat TV and the radio differently than we treat newspapers. It would come as a surprise to the public as well as to publishers and editors of newspapers to be informed that a newly created federal bureau would hereafter provide "guidelines" for newspapers or promulgate rules that would give a federal agency power to ride herd on the publishing business to make sure that fair comment on all current issues was made.

The Fairness Doctrine has no place in our First Amendment regime. It puts the head of the camel inside the tent and enables administration after administration to toy with TV or radio in order to serve its sordid or its benevolent ends.

Justice BRENNAN, with whom Justice MARSHALL concurs, dissenting.

As the Court of Appeals recognized, "the general characteristics of the broadcast industry reveal an extraordinary relationship between the broadcasters and the federal government—a relationship which puts that industry in a class with few others." More specifically, the public nature of the airwaves, the governmentally created preferred status of broadcast licensees, the pervasive federal regulation of broadcast programming, and the FCC's specific approval of the challenged broadcaster policy combine in this case to bring the promulgation and enforcement of that policy within the orbit of constitutional imperatives.

Thus, given the confluence of these various indicia of "governmental action"—including the public nature of the airwaves, the governmentally created preferred status of broadcasters, the extensive Government regulation of broadcast programming, and the specific governmental approval of the challenged policy—I can only conclude that the Government "has so far insinuated itself into a position" of participation in this policy that the absolute refusal of broadcast licensees to sell air time to groups or individuals wishing to speak out on controversial issues of public importance must be subjected to the restraints of the First Amendment.

"[S]peech concerning public affairs is the essence of self-government," *Garrison v. Louisiana,* and the First Amendment must therefore safeguard not only the right of the public to *hear* debate, but also the right of individuals to *participate* in that debate and to attempt to persuade others to their points of view. And, in a time of apparently growing anonymity of the individual in our society, it is imperative that we take special care to preserve the vital First Amendment interest in assuring "self-fulfillment [of expression] for each individual." For our citizens may now find greater than ever the need to express their own views directly to the public, rather than through a governmentally appointed surrogate, if they are to feel that they can achieve at least some measure of control over their own destinies.

In light of these considerations, the Court would concede, I assume, that our citizens have at least an abstract right to express their views on controversial issues of public importance. But freedom of speech does not exist in the abstract. On the contrary, the right to speak can flourish only if it is allowed to operate in an effective forum—whether it be a public park, a schoolroom, a town meeting hall, a soapbox, or a radio and television frequency. For in the absence of an effective means of communication, the right to speak would ring hollow indeed. And, in recognition of these principles, we have consistently held that the First Amendment embodies, not only the abstract right to be free from censorship, but also the right of an individual to utilize an appropriate and effective medium for the expression of his views. Indeed, unlike the streets, parks, public libraries, and other "forums" that we have held to be appropriate for the exercise of First Amendment rights, the broadcast media are dedicated *specifically* to communication. And, since the expression of ideas—whether political, commercial, musical, or otherwise—is the exclusive purpose of the broadcast spectrum, it seems clear that the adoption of a limited scheme of editorial advertising would in no sense divert that spectrum from its intended use.

Moreover, it is equally clear that, with the assistance of the Federal Government, the broadcast industry has become what is potentially the most efficient and effective "marketplace of ideas" ever devised. Indeed, the electronic media are today "the public's prime source of information," and we have ourselves recognized that broadcast "technology supplants atomized, relatively informal communication with mass media as a prime source of national cohesion and news." *Red Lion Broadcasting Co. v. FCC.* Thus, although "full and free discussion" of ideas may have been a reality in the heyday of political pamphleteering, modern technological developments in the field of communications have made the soapbox orator and the leafleteer virtually obsolete. And, in light of the current dominance of the electronic media as the most effective means of reaching the public, any policy that *absolutely* denies citizens access to the airwaves necessarily renders even the concept of "full and free discussion" practically meaningless.

Regrettably, it is precisely such a policy that the Court upholds today. And, since effectuation of the individual's right to speak through a limited scheme of editorial advertising can serve only to further, rather than to inhibit, the public's interest in receiving suitable exposure to "uninhibited, robust, and wide-open" debate on controversial issues, the challenged ban can be upheld only if it is determined that such editorial advertising would unjustifiably impair the broadcaster's assertedly overriding interest in exercising *absolute* control over "his" frequency. Such an analysis, however, hardly reflects the delicate balancing of interests that this sensitive question demands. Indeed, this "absolutist" approach wholly disregards the competing First Amendment rights of all "non-broadcaster" citizens, ignores the teachings of our recent decision in *Red Lion Broadcasting Co. v. FCC,* and is not supported by the historical purposes underlying broadcast regulation in this Nation.

The First Amendment values of individual self-fulfillment through expression and individual participation in public debate are central to our concept of liberty. If these values are to survive in the age of technology, it is essential that individuals be permitted at least *some* opportunity to express their views on public issues over the electronic media. Balancing those interests against the limited interest of broadcasters in exercising "journalistic supervision" over the mere allocation of *advertising* time that is already made available to some members of the public, I simply cannot conclude that the interest of broadcasters must prevail.

COMMENT

A major portion of the Court's opinion in *CBS* is devoted to the question of whether private censorship is subject to constitutional sanction or obligation. The issue, said Chief Justice Warren Burger, is "whether the action of a broadcast licensee such as that challenged here is 'governmental action' for purposes of the First Amendment."

When constitutional lawyers say that state action must be present in order to invoke constitutional protection, they mean that constitutional limitations do not apply unless it is government that has restrained freedom. Because the First Amendment speaks to Congress and the Fourteenth Amendment speaks to the states, the argument is that if a nongovernmental source infringes freedom of expression, such an infringement does not rise to the dignity of a constitutional violation. In this respect, the fundamental issue of state action cuts across constitutional law generally. Should private power, specifically corporate power as reflected in the three corporations, CBS, NBC, and ABC, ever be constitutionalized, i.e., subject to constitutional obligation?

The Court, per Chief Justice Burger, answered this question, at least on the basis of the facts presented in the *CBS* case, in the negative.

Contrast the *CBS* case with *Miami Herald Publishing Co. v. Tornillo* where the Supreme Court invalidated the Florida right of reply to the press law.

Scholarly criticism of cases like *Red Lion* and *CBS v. DNC* has taken quite divergent directions depending on whether the critic takes an instrumental or classic libertarian approach to free speech theory. Professor Scott Powe takes the classic libertarian position: the First Amendment prevents any regulation of the media whether print or broadcast. In his view, the whole broadcast licensing scheme carries with it the danger of being used by government "to further impermissible agendas." See Powe, *American Broadcasting and the First Amendment*, 161 (1987). For him, the First Amendment exists to keep government out of the opinion process. Any government regulation that would be impermissible if applied to the printed press is impermissible if applied to broadcasting. Is this the theory of *CBS v. DNC?*

Professor Owen Fiss, on the other hand, has criticized this public-private distinction as a touchstone of First Amendment analysis:

> CBS is neither a state actor nor a private citizen but something of both. CBS's central property—the license—has been created and conferred by the government. It gives CBS the right to exclude others from its segment of the airwaves. CBS is thus a composite of the public and the private. The same is true of the print media, as it is of all corporations, unions, universities, and political organizations.

Because of the intermixed public and private character of basic institutions such as big media, Fiss thinks that the "classificatory game of deciding whether CBS" is really private or really public is pointless. Professor Fiss concludes: "Just as it is no longer possible to assume that the private sector is all freedom, we can no longer assume that the state is all censorship." See Fiss, *Free Speech and Social Structure*, 71 Iowa L. Rev. 1405, 1414–15 (1986).

Professor Jonathan Weinberg contends that in *CBS v. DNC*, the Supreme Court moved away from "the *Red Lion* philosophy to a more individualistic view of broadcast regulation." Jonathan Weinberg, *Broadcasting and Speech*, 81 Cal. L. Rev. 1103, 1188 (1993). This new philosophy emphasized the public-private distinction:

> Gone is the idea that broadcasters are mere "fidicuiaries" for the community, vessels of a larger will. Broadcasters were to be treated, to the extent possible, like ordinary First Amendment speakers, "journalistic 'free agent[s].' " Far from being mere altruistic voices of a larger community, broadcasters were individualistic autonomous speakers. Broadcasters were private entities, [the plurality] insisted; the government had no responsibility for their policies.
> *Id.* at 1189.

Chief Justice Burger observed in *CBS v. DNC* that if Congress were to impose access obligations on broadcasters, the result might be different. Does this observation serve to reconcile—at least—*Red Lion* with *CBS v. DNC?* In *Red Lion*, the Court was dealing with a federal statute. In *CBS v. DNC*, it was dealing with a claim based on an interpretation of the First Amendment. See *CBS v. FCC*, p. 490.

Forbes v. Arkansas Educational Television

22 MEDIA L. REP. 1616, 22 F.3D 1423 (8TH CIR. 1994).

[EDITORIAL NOTE: *The Arkansas Educational Television Network (AETN) sponsored a debate among the candidates for U.S. Representative for the Third Congressional District in Arkansas. AETN did not invite Ralph Forbes, an independent candidate for that office, to participate in the debate. Forbes sued AETN contending that his First Amendment rights were violated. Although the court of appeals denied Forbes's statutory Sec. 315 claim because it held that he should have first pursued that claim before the FCC, the court declared that candidates in his position had a qualified First Amendment right of access.]*

ARNOLD, C.J.:

Generally, speaking, it is true that a candidate does not have the right to demand air time. Under the circumstances of the present case, we hold that Forbes did have a qualified right of access created by AETN's sponsorship of a debate, and that AETN must have a legitimate reason to exclude him strong enough to survive First Amendment scrutiny. In *De Young v. Patten*, [898 F.2d 628 (8th Cir. 1990)], this Court concluded that a public television station such as AETN was a state actor. We adhere to this conclusion. AETN is not a private entity; it is a state-owned television network.

As a state actor, AETN is faced with constraints not shared by other television stations. When it comes to the First Amendment claim, we conclude that *De Young* was wrongly decided. *De Young* holds that no First Amendment right to appear in a televised debate exists, at least beyond that given by Sec. 315, and that the only remedy available to a candidate in Mr. Forbes' position is to seek remedial action through the FCC. This holding would allow a state-owned station to exclude all Republicans, or all Methodists, or all candidates with a certain point of view, except to the extent, if any, that the excluded candidates could obtain relief under the Communications Act. We believe the error of such a proposition is self-evident. The state may not, by statute or otherwise, take such a discriminatory action, absent a compelling state interest.

The AETN defendants suggest that the case should be governed by public-forum analysis. If it is, the same conclusion follows: a state agency does not have an absolute right to determine which of the legally qualified candidates for a public office it will put on the air. The reasons for such an exclusion must be ascertained and measured against First Amendment standards.

Since the key determination of whether a forum is a limited public one is the government's acquiescence in its use for expressive purposes, it is certainly possible that AETN created a limited public forum when it chose to sponsor a debate among the candidates for the Third Congressional seat. If it were determined that AETN had created a limited public forum, then Forbes would have a First Amendment right to participate in the debate and could be excluded only if AETN had a sufficient government interest.

Even in the context of the nonpublic forum certain minimum First Amendment requirements apply:

Control over access to a nonpublic forum can be based on subject matter and speaker identity so long as the distinctions drawn are reasonable in light of the purpose served by the forum and are viewpoint neutral.

Since Forbes was a member of the class of speakers for whose benefit the debate was held (candidates for the Third Congressional seat), and he wished to address the topic encompassed by the debate, [AETN] has violated his First Amendment rights.

AETN must provide a rational and viewpoint-neutral justification for its determination. On this record, AETN has not yet done so; therefore, Forbes has stated a claim upon which relief can be granted. So much of the judgement [below] as dismissed his claim under the First and Fourteenth Amendment for failure to state a claim is reversed, and the cause is remanded for further proceedings consistent with this opinion. That portion of *De Young v. Patten* which holds that the First Amendment places no restraint, beyond that imposed by the Communications Act, on the right of state agencies to sponsor candidates debates and pick and choose which candidates may take part, is overruled.

McMillian, J., joined by GIBSON, FAGG, MAGILL, and HANSEN, JJ., concurring in part and dissenting in part.

Although I agree with most of the majority opinion, for the reasons discussed below, I would affirm the order of the district court dismissing Forbes' complaint. I do not agree that Forbes, even though he was a legally qualified candidate, had a First Amendment right to be included in the candidate debate or that the candidate debate was a public forum for First Amendment purposes. In my view, the candidate debate was a nonpublic forum. Like private commercial television, public television is not a traditional public forum; it does not extend a general invitation to the public to appear on or participate in its programs. Nor did I think the candidate debate was a limited or quasi-public forum, the format of this candidate debate was not compatible with either unrestricted public access or with unrestricted access by all of the legally qualified candidates.

"Control over access to a nonpublic forum can be based on . . . speaker identity so long as the distinctions drawn are reasonable in light of the purposes served by the forum and are viewpoint neutral." *Cornelius v. NAACP Legal Defense & Educational Fund,* 473 U.S. 788, 806 (1985). Presumably, AETN decided to limit the number of candidates in order to maintain a traditional debate format, rather than to expand the format to a panel discussion. Because AETN has yet to file an answer, AETN's reasons for designing the format of the candidate debate as it did are not known. However, it would not have been unreasonable or veiwpoint-specific for AETN to have limited the candidate debate to only the two major party candidates, or, for that matter, to the two candidates who had the most support or who had the most likely chance of winning, for example, on the basis of poll results. It may not have been good programming, or even good politics, given voters' interest in and the occasional historical success of minor party and independent (and even fringe) candidates to limit the candidate debate to the two major party candidates. Nonetheless, I would hold that AETN had the editorial and programming discretion to structure the candidate debate along those lines and that excluding Forbes from the candidate debate for those reasons would be viewpoint neutral.

COMMENT

The *Forbes* case is significant because it departs from prior cases raising similar issues. For example, in *Chandler v. Georgia Public Telecommunications Commission (GPTC),* 917 F.2d 486 (11th Cir. 1990), the refusal by Georgia public television to allow the Libertarian candidates to participate in debates it was broadcasting between the Republican and Democratic candidates for lieutenant governor and governor was upheld. The *Chandler* court declared that "[m]embers of the public are not provided free access to GPTC air time." This seems to be another way of saying that GPTC was a nonpublic forum. Regulations governing such a forum need only be reasonable and not viewpoint restrictive:

[T]his content based decision is not veiwpoint restrictive and does not violate the First Amendment. GPTC makes content-based decisions on a regular basis in order to serve Georgians. A decision to air any show is necessarily content-based. GPTC chose to air a debate between only the Democratic and Republican candidates because it believed such a debate would be of the utmost interest and benefit to the citizens of Georgia. Such a decision promoted GPTC's function, was "reasonable" and was "not an effort to suppress expression merely because public officials oppose the speaker's views."

Why did *Forbes* conclude that the AETN-sponsored candidate debate was a limited public forum?

Note that *Forbes* observed, contrary to *Chandler,* that even if the AETN candidate debate was characterized as a nonpublic forum, the First Amendment might still require the participation of the independent candidate, Forbes, because his exclusion was unreasonable and possibly viewpoint-based. Forbes was a member of the class of speakers for whose benefit the debate was scheduled. His exclusion by AETN was, therefore, unreasonable. Furthermore, it was not shown that his exclusion was viewpoint-neutral.

The *Forbes* court combines the fact that the TV network was state operated with the public forum doctrine to reach the conclusion that the exclusion of a candidate from a debate might violate the First Amendment. In this respect, the decision is a rare example of a limited right of access based on the First Amendment itself.

Which position do you think is more sound—*Forbes* or *Chandler?*

On remand, Forbes' First Amendment claim was tried to a jury. The jury was instructed that the congressional debate was a non-public forum and judgment was entered for the defendant. In *Forbes v. Arkansas,* 93 F. 3d 497 (8th Cir. 1996), the court of appeals reversed and held that the debate was a limited public forum: "[B]y staging the debate [AETN had] opened its facilities to a particular group—candidates running for the Third Congressional District." Forbes was excluded from the debate, the court of appeals declared, because the television station concluded that he was not a "viable" candidate: "We hold that a governmentally owned and controlled television station may not exclude a candidate, legally qualified under state law, from a debate organized by it on such a subjective

ground. Whether [Forbes] was viable was ultimately a judgment to be made by the people of the Third Congressional District, not by officials of the government in charge of the channels of communication. Political viability is a tricky concept. We should leave it to the voters at the polls, and to the professional judgment of nongovernmental journalists. A journalist employed by the government is still a government employee." The court of appeals remanded the matter to the trial court to enter judgment for Forbes and to empanel a jury to determine the amount of actual damages owed by the station to Forbes. In March 1997, the Supreme Court agreed to review the *Forbes* case. *Arkansas Educational Television v. Forbes,* 117 S. Ct. 1243 (1997).

Same result if the television station had been owned by a private and not a public town entity?

Federal Statutory Access for Federal Political Candidates: Sec. 321(a)(7)

CBS, Inc. v. FCC
453 U.S. 367, 101 S. CT. 2813, 69 L. ED. 2D 706 (1981).

[EDITORIAL NOTE: *In CBS, Inc. v. FCC, the question of whether the "reasonable access for federal political candidates" provision of the Federal Communications Act, Sec. 312(a)(7), violated the First Amendment was considered by the Supreme Court. Jimmy Carter unsuccessfully sought time from the three major television networks for a thirty-minute program in early December 1979.*

Relying on Sec. 312(a)(7), the Carter-Mondale Presidential Committee filed a complaint with the FCC; the FCC ruled that the networks violated Sec. 312(a)(7), and the court of appeals affirmed. The Supreme Court in turn affirmed the court of appeals and held that Sec. 312(a)(7) required broadcasters "to respond to the individualized situation of a particular candidate" and was valid under the First Amendment. CBS contended that because the statute, Sec. 312(a)(7), afforded candidates a modified right of access, it violated the First Amendment in light of Tornillo and CBS v. DNC. The portion of the opinion dealing with these contentions follows.]

Chief Justice BURGER delivered the opinion of the Court.

Finally, petitioners assert that § 312(a)(7) as implemented by the FCC violates the First Amendment rights of broadcasters by unduly circumscribing their editorial discretion. Petitioners argue that the commission's interpretation of § 312(a)(7)'s access requirement disrupts the "delicate balanc[e]" that broadcast regulation must achieve. We disagree.

A licensed broadcaster is "granted the free and exclusive use of a limited and valuable part of the public domain; when he accepts that franchise it is burdened by enforceable public obligations." *Office of Communication of the United Church of Christ v. FCC.* This Court has noted the limits on a broadcast license:

A license permits broadcasting, but the licensee has no constitutional right to be the one who holds the license or to monopolize a frequency to the exclusion of his fellow citizens. There is nothing in the First Amendment which prevents the Government from requiring a licensee to share his frequency with others. *Red Lion Broadcasting Co. v. FCC.*

Although the broadcasting industry is entitled under the First Amendment to exercise "the widest journalistic freedom consistent with its public [duties]," *CBS, Inc. v. Democratic National Committee,* the Court has made clear that:

It is the right of the viewers and listeners, not the right of the broadcasters which is paramount. It is the purpose of the First Amendment to preserve an uninhibited marketplace of ideas in which truth will ultimately prevail, rather than to countenance monopolization of that market. It is the right of the public to receive suitable access to social, political, esthetic, moral, and other ideas and experience which is crucial here. *Red Lion Broadcasting Co. v. FCC.*

The First Amendment interests of candidates and voters, as well as broadcasters, are implicated by § 312(a)(7). We have recognized that "it is of particular importance that candidates have the opportunity to make their views known so that the electorate may intelligently evaluate the candidates' personal qualities and their positions on vital public issues before choosing among them on election day." *Buckley v. Valeo.* Section 312(a)(7) thus makes a significant contribution to freedom of expression by enhancing the ability of candidates to present, and the public to receive, information necessary for the effective operation of the democratic process.

Petitioners are correct that the Court has never approved a *general* right of access to the media. See, *e.g, FCC v. Midwest Video Corp.; Miami Herald Publishing Co. v. Tornillo; CBS, Inc. v. Democratic National Committee.* Nor do we do so today. Section 312(a)(7) creates a *limited* right to "reasonable" access that pertains only to legally qualified federal candidates and may be invoked by them only for the purpose of advancing their candidacies once a campaign has commenced. The FCC has stated that, in enforcing the statute, it will "provide leeway to broadcasters and not merely attempt *de novo* to determine the reasonableness of their judgments."

Section 312(a)(7) represents an effort by Congress to assure that an important resource—the airwaves—will be used in the public interest. We hold that the statutory right of access, as defined by the commission and applied in these cases, properly balances the First Amendment rights of federal candidates, the public, and broadcasters.

The judgment of the court of appeals is affirmed.

COMMENT

It has been argued that *Red Lion* and *Tornillo* "cannot be reconciled because the distinctions which have been drawn between them are constitutionally insignificant." But it is contended that "unlike *Red Lion, CBS v. FCC* can be reconciled with *Tornillo.*" See, Shelledy, *Note, Access to the Press: Teleological Analysis of a Constitutional Double Standard,* 50 Geo. Wash. L. Rev. 430 (1982). How?

The George Washington note distinguishes *Tornillo* from *CBS v. FCC* as follows:

Only one of the limiting characteristics of section 312(a)(7), the reasonableness standard, distinguishes it from the Florida right of reply on a level of constitutional significance: an editor's decision not to broadcast another's message is left undisturbed so long as the decision has been reached reasonably. The Florida statute the *Tornillo* Court invalidated constrained editorial discretion far more severely than Section 312(a)(7). Had the Florida statute been limited by the reasonableness standard, as is Section 312(a)(7), it would not have transgressed the Court's command in *Tornillo* that any "compulsion to publish that which 'reason' tells [editors] should not be published is unconstitutional."

Do you agree?

In *CBS v. Democratic National Committee,* 412 U.S. 94 (1973), the Supreme Court held that an "arbitrary" blanket network policy refusing to sell time to political groups for the discussion of social and political issues did not violate the First Amendment. Yet, in *CBS v. FCC,* the Court held that an "arbitrary" blanket ban by the networks on the use by a candidate of a particular length of time in a particular period could not be considered reasonable under § 312(a)(7). A blanket network ban on a certain category of programming was deemed permissible in one instance and impermissible in the other. Why? The difference is that in *CBS v. FCC* a *statute* conferred particular rights on individual political candidates. The FCC's construction of the statute made the candidate's "desires as to the method of conducting his or her campaign" a matter to be considered by the licensee in determining whether to grant reasonable access under the statute.

In short, the second *CBS* case involved a limited statutorily conferred right, whereas the first *CBS* case would have required a decision by the Supreme Court that the First Amendment itself was a barrier to the exercise of broadcast editorial judgment.

In an influential essay, Professor Owen Fiss argued that joining the general attack on the activist state "would expose us to an even greater danger: politics dominated by the market." See Fiss, *Why the State?*, 100 Harv. L. Rev. 781, 792 (1987). In the course of the essay, Professor Fiss makes these observations: "The powers of the FCC and CBS differ, one regulates while the other edits, but there is no reason for believing that one kind of power will be more inhibiting or limiting of public debate than the other."

Candidates for public office also gain access under § 315(a) of the Federal Communications Act. See p. 765.

ACCESS TO CABLE

In *Midwest Video Corp. v. FCC*, 571 F.2d 1025 (8th Cir. 1978), the court, per Chief Judge Markey, struck down as beyond the FCC's jurisdiction the 1976 Cable Report, 59 F.C.C.2d 399 (1976), which required cable operators to make available four channels for public access on a first-come, nondiscriminatory basis. The Eighth Circuit's decision in *Midwest Video* was affirmed by the Supreme Court in *FCC v. Midwest Video Corp.*, 4 Media L. Rep. 2345, 440 U.S. 689 (1979).

Justice Byron White invalidated the FCC's 1976 mandatory public access channel require-ments on the ground that the regulations imposed common-carrier obligations on cable operators without authorization by Congress. Under such circumstances, Justice White said it was not necessary to consider whether the public access requirements violated the "First Amendment rights of cable operators." But he did observe that the latter argument was not a frivolous one.

FCC v. Midwest Video Corp.
4 MEDIA L. REP. 2345, 440 U.S. 689, 99 S. CT. 1435, 59 L. Ed. 2d 692 (1979).

Justice WHITE delivered the opinion of the Court.

On petition for review, the Eighth Circuit set aside the FCC's access, channel capacity, and facilities rules as beyond the agency's jurisdiction. 571 F.2d 1025 (1978). The court was of the view that the regulations were not reasonably ancillary to the FCC's jurisdiction over broadcasting, a jurisdictional condition established by past decisions of this Court. The rules amounted to an attempt to impose common-carrier obligations on cable operators, the court said, and thus ran counter to the statutory command that broadcasters themselves may not be treated as common carriers. See Communications Act of 1934, § 3(h), 47 U.S.C. § 153(h). Furthermore, the court made plain its belief that the regulations presented grave First Amendment problems. We granted certiorari, and we now affirm.

The holding of the Court in [*CBS v. DNC*] was in accord with the view of the FCC that the act itself did not require a licensee to accept paid editorial advertisements. Accordingly, we did not decide the question whether the act, though not mandating the claimed access, would nevertheless permit the FCC to require broadcasters to extend a range of public access by regulations similar to those at issue here. The Court speculated that the FCC might have flexibility to regulate access and that "[c]onceivably at some future time Congress or the commission—or the broadcasters—may devise some kind of limited right of access that is both practicable and desirable." But this is insufficient support for the FCC's position in the present case. The language of § 3(h) is unequivocal; it stipulates that broadcasters shall not be treated as common carriers. As we see it, § 3(h), consistently with the policy of the act to preserve editorial control of programming in the licensee, forecloses any discretion in the commission to impose access requirements amounting to common-carrier obligations on broadcast systems. The provision's background manifests a congressional belief that the intrusion worked by such regulation on the journalistic integrity of broadcasters would overshadow any benefits associated with the resulting public access. It is difficult to deny, then, that forcing broadcasters to develop a "nondiscriminatory system for controlling access is precisely what Congress intended to avoid through § 3(h) of the Act."

In light of the hesitancy with which Congress approached the access issue in the broadcast area, and in view of its outright rejection of a broad right of public access on a common-carrier basis, we are constrained to hold that the commission exceeded those limits in promulgating its access rules. The commission may not regulate cable systems as common carriers, just as it may not impose such obligations on television broadcasters. We think authority to compel cable operators to provide common carriage of public-originated transmissions must come specifically from Congress.[19]

Affirmed.

COMMENT

Because its holding invalidating the public access rules was based on the lack of FCC jurisdiction to issue them, the court of appeals, per Judge Markey, declined to base its holding on constitutional grounds.

> Despite the Court's guidance in *Miami Herald*, the commission has attempted here to require cable operators, who have invested substantially to create a private electronic "publication"—a means of disseminating information—to open their "publications" to all for use as *they* wish. Though we are not deciding that issue here, we have seen and heard nothing in this case to indicate a constitutional distinction between cable systems and newspapers in the context of the government's power to compel public access.

Cable *can* be described as a technology of abundance, as compared with VHF television, a technology of scarcity. Should the First Amendment model applied to cable be the same as that applied to the newspaper press? *Tornillo*, rather than *Red Lion*, governs the public access obligations of the newspaper press, should *Tornillo*, rather than *Red Lion*, provide the appropriate First Amendment model for cable?

Are cable systems and newspapers equivalent? One commentator suggested there is a difference between newspapers and cable operators:

> There are some important differences, however, that tend to make the decision process in cable more like an economic activity and render the editorial aspects almost entirely theoretical. For the most part, cable personnel do not review any of the material provided by cable networks. Unlike expression originated by the cable operator, cable systems have no conscious control over program services provided by others. Conscious control does not operate uniformly in all other media either, but the tradition in newspaper editing is that the editor reviews all published material.

> See Brenner, *Cable Television and the Freedom of Expression*, 1988 Duke L. J. 329, 339.

This does not mean, however, that the cable operator should never be considered a communicator for First Amendment purposes. Brenner proposes this test: "The key to cable's first amendment regime lies in distinguishing as reasonably as possible, among the expressive and nonexpressive activities of operators. That regime should provide first amendment protection when content-related expressive activities are involved and pull back that protection when such activities are not." Id. at 331. In which of these categories do mandatory access rules fall?

Public Access and Municipal Franchise Agreements

The controversy about a right of access is still very much alive in the field of cable television. A common feature of cable franchise agreements

---

19. The court below suggested that the commission's rules might violate the First Amendment rights of cable operators. Because our decision rests on statutory grounds, we express no view on that question, save to acknowledge that it is not frivolous and to make clear that the asserted constitutional issue did not determine or sharply influence our construction of the statute. The court of appeals intimated, additionally, that the rules might effect an unconstitutional "taking" of property, or, by exposing a cable operator to possible criminal prosecution for offensive cablecasting by access users over which the operator has no control, might affront the Due Process Clause of the Fifth Amendment. We forgo comment on these issues as well.

between a cable operator and a municipality is a provision imposing some public access obligations on the cable operator. The question of the First Amendment validity of these provisions has divided the federal courts. Some courts have concluded that mandatory access rules for cable are governed by *Tornillo* and are invalid; others have felt that such rules are governed by *Red Lion* and are valid. Thus in *Erie Telecommunications, Inc. v. City of Erie,* 659 F. Supp. 580 (W.D. Pa. 1987), access requirements such as providing training and funding for public use of thirteen public channels were upheld as consistent with the First Amendment.

Contrasting sharply with *Erie* is *Group W Cable, Inc. v. Santa Cruz,* 14 Media. L. Rep. 1769, 669 F. Supp. 954, (N.D. Cal. 1987), where franchise provisions imposing a variety of access obligations on the cable operator were struck down on First Amendment grounds. The cable operator was required to operate separate access channels without fee to public, governmental, and institutional users. The court in the *Group W* case relied on *Tornillo to* invalidate the access obligations: The heart of the court's objections to the access requirements envisioned by Santa Cruz was that such obligations, if imposed on newspapers, would violate the First Amendment and cable operators were entitled to no less First Amendment protection than newspapers were.

In *Century Federal, Inc. v. City of Palo Alto, California,* 63 RR2d 1736 (1987), municipal requirements that cable franchises provide three public access educational channels and two governmental channels were held to violate the First Amendment rights of cable operators. Relying on *Tornillo* and *Pacific Gas,* the court, as in *Group W,* concluded that forcing access channels on a cable operator presented "the inherent risk that a franchise's speech will be chilled." This would have the "direct, undeniable impact of intruding into the franchise's editorial control and judgment of what to cablecast and what not to cablecast." Is the mere possibility of chilling the expression of a cable operator enough to invalidate a city's cable franchising scheme? *Century Federal* answered this question in the affirmative: "The Supreme Court has never required an actual showing of such an influence or chilling effect on the primary speaker's content. There was no such showing in either *Miami Herald* or *Pacific Gas;* it is the mere risk of such a chilling effect that is inconsistent with the First Amendment."

The First Amendment and Access to Cable Television Under the 1984 and 1992 Cable Acts

In the Cable Communications Policy Act of 1984, Congress permitted municipalities to require cable operators to reserve channels for public, educational, and governmental (PEG) use. See 47 U.S.C. § 531. The 1984 Act obliged cable operators to provide leased access channels. Cable systems with thirty-six or more channels were obliged to reserve 10 percent of their channel capacity for leased commercial use by persons not affiliated with the cable operator. 47 U.S.C. § 532(a). This meant that some channel capacity would be available on a for hire basis. The 1984 Cable Act prohibited cable operators from exercising any editorial control over either leased or PEG channels. Cable operators, however, were granted immunity from liability for programming transmitted on mandatory access channels.

In the following case, cable operators and programmers relying on the First Amendment unsuccessfully challenged provisions of the 1984 and 1992 Cable Acts authorizing local governments to require cable operators to dedicate part of their channel capacity for PEG and leased access purposes.

Daniels Cablevision v. U.S.
835 F. SUPP. 1 (D.D.C. 1993).

[EDITORIAL NOTE: *In the* Daniels *case, the mid-level O'Brien standard, rather than the more exacting strict scrutiny standard, was held to be the appropriate First Amendment standard for evaluating the validity for the PEG channels.*]

JACKSON, District Judge. [T]he crucial inquiry for determining the appropriate level of First Amendment scrutiny is not merely whether governmental regulation results in compelling certain speech, fetters the speaker's discretion in deciding what to say, or favors particular speakers at the expense of others, but is also whether the regulation is, overtly or covertly, content-based; that is, the government is telling the speaker what can or cannot be said. Constraints on speech, even if deriving from an exercise of government authority, need be strictly scrutinized only if the government has specified the speaker's message. Although the provisions here at issue may impose some limit on the autonomy of cable operators to speak only such speech as they would themselves pronounce, most do so only to serve regulatory goals unrelated to content. [These provisions] are constitutional if those goals serve significant governmental interests and do not burden substantially more speech than necessary to serve those interests. *Ward v. Rock Against Racism, United States v. O'Brien.*

[T]he plaintiffs reiterate that the PEG programming and leased access provisions force operators to engage in "speech" they might not otherwise undertake, and favor the speech of PEG programmers and non-affiliates over that of the operators themselves or other programmers the government deems less worthy.

The PEG and leased access provisions were enacted to serve a significant regulatory interest, *viz.,* affording speakers with lesser market appeal access to the nation's most pervasive video distribution technology. Enabling a broad range of speakers to reach a television audience that otherwise would never hear them is an appropriate goal and a legitimate exercise of federal legislative power.

The leased access provisions are likewise content-neutral, and they are designed to serve a similar market regulatory function. The provisions promote fair competition by overcoming the natural tendency of cable operators to enhance the profitability of their affiliated programmers.

Nor do the PEG and leased access provisions overreach. PEG use is negotiable, and leased access obligations are directly proportional to the number of channels a cable operator has available, never exceeding 15 percent of total capacity. Operators retain discretion over the remainder, and may, of course, utilize them as they wish, for their own programming or for that of affiliated programmers.

[EDITORIAL NOTE: *The 1992 Cable Act removed immunity for carriage of obscenity. Cable operators unsuccessfully contended that in the public access channel context this violated the First Amendment.*]

[C]able operators may not exercise any editorial control over the PEG or leased access channels they are required to carry. The 1984 Act conferred immunity from state law liability upon cable oper-

ators who transmitted obscene material included in the obligatory PEG and leased access programming. 47 U.S.C. § 558 (1988). Section 10(d) of the 1992 Act removes all immunity for carriage of obscenity.

The plaintiffs, and the ACLU as *amicus,* contend that potential liability for obscenity carried on PEG and leased access channels impermissibly burdens speech by creating an unacceptable incentive to operator self-censorship. Without immunity, they argue, operators will be forced to screen their PEG and leased access programming for material that might be deemed obscene, and the more timorous among them will become so apprehensive that they will voluntarily refuse to carry controversial programming that might nevertheless enjoy full constitutional protection.

The danger of self-censorship induced by the ambiguity inherent in the concept of obscenity itself has never been held to mandate a constitutional requirement for general immunity from obscenity laws for anyone. In other words, no speakers—cable operators included—have a constitutional *right* to immunity to relieve them of anxiety about crossing the threshold from the risque to the obscene. Congress' earlier decision to provide cable operators with immunity was a matter of grace that it has always been free to rescind.

COMMENT

In *Daniels,* Judge Jackson applied neither the *Red Lion* standard nor the *Tornillo* standard. Instead, he applied the *O'Brien* standard. Use of *Red Lion* would have analogized cable to broadcasting and made it easier to sustain federal legislation regulating cable. Use of *Tornillo* would have analogized cable to newspapers. *Tornillo* is a more stringent standard and would have made it more difficult to sustain federal regulation of cable. Note that Judge Jackson in *Daniels,* like Justice Anthony Kennedy later in *Turner Broadcasting System, Inc. v. FCC,* 512 U.S. 622 (1994), applied the *O'Brien* standard because the specific cable legislation being considered was deemed content-neutral.

The *Daniels* case was appealed to the United States Court of Appeals for the District of Columbia; *Time Warner Entertainment Co. v. FCC,* 93 F. 3d 957 (D.C. Cir. 1996), held that the leased access and public, educational and governmental (PEG) programming provisions of the 1984 Act do not violate the First Amendment. The court of appeals rejected Time Warner's contention that the leased access provisions were content-based and subjected to strict scrutiny: "There is nothing to this. The provisions are not content-based. They do not favor or disfavor speech on the basis of the ideas contained in the speech or the views expressed." On the question of the First Amendment validity of the PEG or public access channels, the court of appeals observed:

> We can of, course, imagine PEG franchise conditions that would raise serious constitutional issues. For example, were a local authority to require as a franchise condition that a cable operator designate three-quarters of its channels for "educational" programming, defined in detail by the city council, such a requirement would certainly implicate First Amendment concerns. At the same time, we can just as easily imagine a franchise authority exercising its power without violating the First Amendment. For example, a local franchise authority might seem to ensure public "access to a multiplicity of sources." *Turner*, by conditioning its grant of a franchise on the cable operator's willingness to provide access to a single channel for "public" use, defining "public" broadly enough to permit access to everyone on a nondiscriminatory, first-come, first-serve basis. Under *Turner*, such a scheme would be content-neutral, would serve an "important purpose unrelated to the suppression of free expression," and would be narrowly tailored to its goal. Time Warner's facial challenge therefore fails.

Finally, the court of appeals in *Time Warner* agreed with the district court in *Daniels* "that the 1992 Act's revocation of cable operators' immunity from liability" did not violate the First Amendment. Sec. 10(d) of the 1992 Cable Act simply imposed on cable operators the same liability for obscenity that all speakers face.

Should one conclude on the basis of *Time Warner* that the First Amendment validity of public access and leased access channels is now established?

Is the focus on whether requiring cable operators to provide public access channels is content-based or content-neutral misplaced? Consider the following:

> [A]lmost all regulation of the mass media will, at some level of generality, be justified with reference to the content of speech, because such regulation is generally concerned with *speech,* not other issues, and speech is about content. Thus, the interest in diversity is clearly about content, as are limitations on violence

or indecency, and the granting of access or reply rights. To attempt to distinguish between such regulations based on whether or not they are justified with reference to content therefore seems both impossible and of little value.

Ashutosh Bhagwat, *Of Markets and Media: The First Amendment, the New Mass Media, and the Political Components of Culture,* 74 N.C. L. Rev. 141, 193–94 (1995) (emphasis added).

Professor Cass Sunstein suggests that we have two First Amendment models and that *Turner* has not given us a third. One model is the marketplace model, that abhors content regulation. Another is the Madisonian model, that emphasizes "public deliberation." The *Turner* model has four parts:

> Under *Turner,* (a) government may regulate (not merely subsidize) new speech sources so as to ensure *access for viewers* who would otherwise be without free programming *and* (b) government may require owners of speech sources to provide access to *speakers,* at least if the owners are not conventional speakers too; *but* (c) government must do all this on a content-neutral basis (at least as a general rule); *but* (d) government may support its regulation not only by reference to the provision of "access to free television programming" but also by invoking such democratic goals as the need to ensure "an outlet for exchange on matters of local concern" and "access to a multiplicity of information sources."

See Cass R. Sunstein, *The First Amendment in Cyberspace,* 104 Yale L.J. 1757, 1774 (1995) (emphasis added).

The *Turner* model would provide the same result in *Daniels* as was obtained by using the *O'Brien* test. Is the *O'Brien* mid-level standard appropriate for cable? Isn't it too unpredictable in terms of outcome? *Turner* directly focuses on the communications issues that are actually presented.

The First Amendment and Regulation of Indecency on Public Access and Leased Access Channels

Access channels on cable pose a sensitive question—access for what? Can the cable operator exclude an entire category of speech, i.e., indecent speech? Does it matter that the material transmitted on these channels is by definition not selected by the cable operator?

The Cable Television Consumer Protection and Competition Act of 1992 made some changes in the regulation of public access and leased access channels on cable. Sec. 10(a) permitted a cable operator to refuse to carry leased access programming that "depicts sexual or excretory activities or organs in a patently offensive manner as measured by contemporary community standards." Sec. 10(b) sought to limit childrens' access to indecent programming. Accordingly, Sec. 10(b) instructs the FCC to issue rules obliging cable operators transmitting indecent material to carry such programming on a separate channel that is blocked unless the subscriber requests otherwise. Sec. 10(c) directs the FCC to issue regulations that permit cable operators to bar the use of PEG access channels for "programming which contains obscene materials, sexually explicit conduct, or material soliciting or promoting unlawful conduct." The FCC issued implementing regulations. Finally, Sec. 10(d), as was noted in *Daniels*, removed the immunity liability on access channels for obscene material that cable operators previously enjoyed.

First Amendment challenges to Secs. 10(a), (b), and (c) (47 U.S.C. § 532 (h) and (j), and note following § 531) were reviewed by the Supreme Court in *Denver Area Educational Telecommunications Consortium, Inc.*, reported below. On June 28, 1996, a badly fragmented Court upheld Sec. 10(a), allowing a cable operator to bar indecency on leased programming on public access channels, by a 7–2 vote. But Sec. 10(c), permitting operators to bar indecent programming on public access channels, was struck down, 5–4. Sec. 10(b), which required cable operators to segregate and block such programming, was struck down by a 6–3 vote. The following opinions deal with the First Amendment validity of the regulation of access channels on cable. The aspects of the *Denver* case dealing with indecency are set forth on pp. 881–884.

Denver Area Educational Telecommunications Consortium, Inc. v. FCC

116 S. CT. 2374 (1996).

[EDITORIAL NOTE: *Justice Breyer, joined by Justices Stevens, O'Connor, and Souter, found that Sec. 10(a) did not violate the First Amendment.*]

Justice BREYER:

[Petitioners] say, cable system operators have more power to "censor" program viewing than do broadcasters, for individual communities typically have only one cable system, linking broadcasters and other program providers with each community's many subscribers. Moreover, concern about system operators' exercise of this considerable power originally led government—local and federal—to insist that operators provide leased and public access channels free of operator editorial control. Under these circumstances, petitioners conclude, Congress' "permissive" law, in actuality, will "abridge" their free speech.

[T]he First Amendment embodies an overarching commitment to protect speech from Government regulation through close judicial scrutiny, thereby enforcing the Constitution's constraints, but without imposing judicial formulae so rigid that they become a straightjacket that disables Government from responding to serious problems.

Justices Kennedy and Thomas would have us further declare which [First Amendment approach] we are applying here. But no definitive choice among competing analogies (broadcast, common carrier, bookstore) allows us to declare a rigid single standard, good for now and for all future media and purposes. [A]ware as we are of the changes taking place in the law, the technology, and the industrial structure, related to communications, see Telecommunications Act of 1996, we believe it unwise and unnecessary definitively to pick one analogy or one specific set of words now.

We therefore think it premature to answer the broad questions that Justices Kennedy and Thomas raise in their efforts to find a definitive analogy, deciding for example the extent to which a private property can be designated a public forum; whether public access channels are a public forum; whether the government's viewpoint neutral decision to limit a public forum is subject to the same scrutiny as a selective exclusion from a pre-existing public forum; whether exclusion from common carriage must for all purposes be treated like exclusion from a public forum; and whether the interests of the owners of communications media always subordinate the interests of all other users of a medium.

Rather than decide these issues, we can decide this case more narrowly, by closely scrutinizing Sec. 10(a) to assure that it properly addresses an extremely important problem, without imposing, in light of the relevant interests, an unnecessarily great restriction on speech.

[Justice Breyer said that although Sec. 10(c), barring indecent material on public access channels, was similar to Sec. 10(a), barring indecent material on leased access channels, there were important differences. Cable operators dedicate channels for public access purposes "as part of the consideration they give municipalities that award them cable franchises." Thus, cable operators never had editorial control over public access channels: "Unlike Sec. 10(a), therefore, Sec. 10(c) does not restore to cable operators editorial rights that they once had, and the countervailing First Amendment interest is nonexistent, or at least much diminished." Second, public access cable systems are subject to locally accountable entities, which makes it "unlikely that many children will in fact be exposed to programming considered patently offensive in that community."

Justice Stevens in a concurrence explained why he believed Sec. 10(c) was unconstitutional.]

Justice STEVENS:

What is of critical importance to me, however, is that if left to their own devices, [local] authorities may choose to carry some programming that the Federal Government has decided to restrict. As I read Sec. 10(c), the federal statute would disable local governments from making that choice. It would inject federally authorized private censors into forums from which they might otherwise be excluded, and it would therefore limit local forums that might otherwise be open to all constitutionally protected speech.

[Justice SOUTER, concurring, shared the "Court's unwillingness to announce a definitive categorical analysis in this case"; he doubted the Court's capacity to develop a "definitive level-of-scrutiny" for cable.]

Justice SOUTER:[We] can hardly settle rules for review of regulation on the assumption that cable will remain a separable and useful category of First Amendment scrutiny. And as broadcast, cable, and the cyber-technology of the Internet and the World Wide Web approach the day of using a common receiver, we can hardly assume that standards for judging the regulation of one of them will not have immense, but now unknown and unknowable, effects on the others. Accordingly, in charting a course that will permit reasonable regulation in light of the values of competition, we have to accept the likelihood that the media of communication will become less categorical and more protean. [A] proper choice among existing doctrinal categories is not obvious.

I cannot guess how much time will go by until the technologies of communication before us today have matured and their relationships become known. Maybe the judicial obligation [can be captured] by a much older rule, familiar to every doctor of medicine: "First, do no harm."

Justice KENNEDY, joined by Justice GINSBURG, concurred in part and dissented in part.

The plurality opinion, insofar as it upholds Sec. 10(a) of the 1992 Cable Act, is adrift. The opinion treats concepts such as public forum, broadcaster, and common carrier as mere labels rather than as categories with settled legal significance; it applies no standard, and by this omission loses sight of existing First Amendment doctrine. When confronted with a threat to free speech in the context of an emerging technology, we ought to have the discipline to analyze the case by existing elaborations of constant First Amendment principles. Rather than undertake this task, however, the plurality just declares that, all things considered, Sec. 10(a) seems fine.

[Although Justice Kennedy agreed that Secs. 10(b) and (c) were invalid, he thought that past precedents required the Court to hold Sec. 10(a) invalid as well.]

Sections 10(a) and (c) are unusual. They do not require direct action against speech, but do authorize a cable operator to deny the use of its property to certain forms of speech. As a general matter, a private person may exclude certain speakers from his or her property without violating the First Amendment, and if Secs. 10(a) and (c) were no more than affirmations of this principle they might be remarkable. Access channels, however, are property of the cable operator dedicated or otherwise reserved for programming of other speakers or the government. A public access channel is a public forum, and laws requiring leased access channels create common carrier obligations. When the government identifies certain speech on the basis of its content as vulnerable to exclusion from a common carrier or public forum, strict scrutiny applies. However compelling Congress' interest in shielding children from indecent programming, the provisions in this case are not drawn with enough care to withstand scrutiny under our precedents.

While it protests against standards, the plurality does seem to favor one formulation of the question in this case: namely, whether the Act "properly addresses an extremely important problem, without imposing, in light of the relevant interests, an unnecessarily great restriction on speech." This description of the question accomplishes little, save to clutter our First Amendment case law by adding an untested rule with an uncertain relationship to the others we use to evaluate laws restricting speech. The novelty and complexity of this case is a reason to look for help from other areas of our First Amendment jurisprudence, not a license to wander into uncharted areas of the law with no compass other than our own opinions about good policy.

[Justice Kennedy discussed the emergence of access channels on cable.]

PEG access channels grew out of local initiatives in the late 1960's and early 1970's, before the Federal Government began regulating cable television. Local franchising was the first form of cable regulation, arising from the need of localities to control access to public rights of way and easements to minimize disruption to traffic and other public activity from the laying of cable lines. See D. Brenner, M. Price, & M. Meyerson, Cable Television and Other Nonbroadcast Video, Sec. 3.01 (3) (1996). From the early 1970's onward, franchising authorities began requiring operators to set aside access channels as a condition of the franchise.

Section 611 of the Communications Act of 1934, added by the Cable Communications Policy Act of 1984 (1984 Act), authorized local franchise authorities to set aside channel capacity for PEG access when seeking new franchises or renewal of old ones. 47 U.S.C. § 531(b). Prior to the passage of Sec. 10(c) of the 1992 Act, the cable operator, save for implementing provisions of its franchise agreement limiting obscene or otherwise constitutionally unprotected cable programming, § 544(b), was forbidden any editorial control over PEG access channels.

Congress has not, in the 1984 Act or since, defined what public, educational, or governmental access means or placed substantive limits on the types of programming on those channels. Those tasks are left to franchise agreements.

My principal concern is with public access channels (the P of PEG). These are the channels open to programming by members of the public. Petitioners here include public access programmers and viewers who watch their shows.

The public access channels established by franchise agreements tend to have certain traits. They are available at low or no cost to members of the public, often on a first-come, first-served basis. The programmer on one of these channels most often has complete control over, as well as liability for, the content of its show. The entity managing the technical aspects of public access, such as scheduling and transmission, is not always the cable operator; it may be the local government or a third party that runs the access centers, which are facilities made available for the public to produce programs and transmit them on the access channels.

Public access channels meet the definition of a public forum. Required by the franchise authority as a condition of the franchise and open to all comers, they are a designated public forum of unlimited character.

It is important to understand that public access channels are public forums created by local or state governments in the cable franchise. Section 10(c) does not, as the Court of Appeals thought, just return rightful First Amendment discretion to the cable operator. [T]he editorial discretion of a cable operator is a function of the cable franchise it receives from local government. The operator's right to exercise any editorial discretion over cable service disappears if its franchise is terminated. If the franchise is transferred to another, so is the right of editorial discretion. The cable operator may own the cables transmitting the signal, but it is the franchise—the agreement between the cable operator and the local government—that allocates some channels to the full discretion of the cable operator while reserving others for public access.

In providing access channels under their franchise agreements, cable operators are not exercising their own First Amendment rights. They serve as conduits for the speech of others. Section 10(c) thus restores no power of electrical discretion over public access channels that the cable operator once had; the discretion never existed.

Treating access channels as public forum [serves to define] the First Amendment rights of speakers seeking to use the channels. When property has been dedicated to public expressive activities, by tradition or government designation, access is protected by the First Amendment. Regulations of speech content in a designated public forum, whether of limited or unlimited character, are "subject to the highest scrutiny" and "survive only if they are narrowly drawn to achieve a compelling state interest." Unless there are reasons for applying a lesser standard, Sec. 10(c) must satisfy this stringent review.

Leased access channels, as distinct from public access channels, are those the cable operator must set aside for unaffiliated programmers who pay to transmit shows of their own without the cable operator's creative assistance or editorial approval. In my view, strict scrutiny also applies to Sec. 10(a)'s authorization to exclude indecent programming from these channels.

Two distinctions between public and leased access channels are important. First, whereas public access channels are required by state and local franchise authorities (subject to certain federal limitations), leased access channels are created by federal law. Second, whereas cable operators never have had editorial discretion over public access channels under their franchise agreements, the leased access provisions of the 1984 Act take away channels the operator once controlled. In this sense, Sec. 10(a) now gives back to the operator some of the discretion it had before Congress imposed leased access requirements in the first place.

The constitutionality under *Turner Broadcasting* of requiring a cable operator to set aside leased access channels is not before us. Laws requiring cable operators to provide leased access are the practical equivalent of making them common carriers, analogous in this respect to telephone companies: They are obliged to provide a conduit for the speech of others. The plurality resists any classification of leased access channels as a common carrier provision.

Laws removing common-carriage protection from a single form of speech based on its content should be reviewed under the same standard as content-based restrictions on speech in a public forum. A common-carriage mandate [fulfills] the same function as a public forum. It ensures open non-discriminatory access to the means of communication. [In the view of the House Committee reporting the 1984 cable bill], the leased access provisions were narrowly drawn structural regulations of private industry, cf. *Associated Press v. U.S.*, 326 U.S. 1 (1945), to enhance the free flow of diversity of information available to the public without government intrusion into decisions about program content. The functional equivalence of designating a public forum and mandating common carriage suggests the same scrutiny should be applied to attempts in either setting to impose content discrimination by law. Under our precedents, the scrutiny is strict.

The question remains whether a dispensation from strict scrutiny might be appropriate because Sec. 10(a) restores in part an editorial discretion once exercised by the cable operator over speech

occurring on its property. This is where public-forum doctrine gives guidance. Common-carrier requirements of leased access are little different in function from designated public forums, and no different standard of review should apply. It is not that the functional equivalence of leased access channels to designated public forum compels strict scrutiny; rather, it simply militates against recognizing an exception to the normal rule.

[This case is akin] to the Government's creation of a band shell in which all types of music might be performed except rap music. Giving government free rein to exclude speech it dislikes by delimiting public forum (or common carriage provisions) would have pernicious effects in the modern age. Minds are not changed in the streets and parks as they once were. To an increasing degree, the more significant interchanges of ideas and shaping of public consciousness occur in mass and electronic media. The extent of public entitlement to participate in those means of communication may be changed as technologies change; and in expanding those entitlements the Government has no greater right to discriminate on suspect ground than it does when it effects a ban on speech against the backdrop of the entitlement to which we have been more accustomed. It contravenes the First Amendment to give government a general license to single out some categories of speech for lesser protection so long as it stops short of viewpoint discrimination.

At a minimum the proper standard for reviewing Secs. 10(a) and (c) is strict scrutiny. I would hold these enactments unconstitutional because they are not narrowly tailored to serve a compelling interest. The Government has no compelling interest in restoring a cable operator's First Amendment rights of editorial discretion. As to Sec. 10(c), Congress has no interest at all, since under most franchises operators had no rights of editorial discretion over PEG access channels in the first place. As to Sec. 10(a), any governmental interest in restoring operator discretion over indecent programming on leased access channels is too minimal to justify the law. I dissent from the judgement of the Court insofar as it upholds the constitutionality of Sec. 10(a).

[Justice Kennedy conceded that Congress has a compelling interest in protecting children from indecent speech but said that Secs. 10(a) and (c) were not narrowly tailored to protect children from indecent programming on access channels. For a discussion of the indecency aspects of the Denver *case, see pp. 881–884.]*

Justice THOMAS, joined by Chief Justice REHN-QUIST and Justice SCALIA, concurred in the judgment in part and dissented in part.

I agree with the plurality's conclusion that Sec. 10(a) is constitutionally permissible, but I disagree with its conclusion that Secs. 10(b) and (c) violate the First Amendment. For many years, we have failed to articulate how and to what extent the First Amendment protects cable operators, programmers and viewers from state and federal regulation. I think is it time we did so, and I cannot go along with the plurality's assiduous attempts to avoid addressing that issue openly. The text of the First Amendment makes no distinction between print, broadcast, and cable media, but we have done so.

Our First Amendment distinctions between media, dubious from their infancy, placed cable in a doctrinal wasteland in which regulators and cable operators alike could not be sure whether cable was entitled to the substantial First Amendment protections afforded the print media or was subject to the more onerous obligations shouldered by the broadcast media. Over time, however, we have drawn closer to recognizing that cable operators should enjoy the same First Amendment rights as the nonbroadcast media.

Two terms ago, in *Turner Broadcasting, Inc., v. FCC,* we stated expressly what we had implied in *Leathers [v. Medlock,* pp. 75–76]: The *Red Lion* standard does not apply to cable television. While Members of the [*Turner*] Court disagreed about whether the must-carry rules imposed by Congress were content-based, and therefore subject to strict scrutiny, there was agreement that cable operators are generally entitled to much the same First Amendment protection as the print media. But see [*Turner*] (STEVENS, J., concurring in part and concurring in the judgment.) In *Turner,* by adopting much of the print paradigm, and by rejecting *Red Lion,* we adopted with it a considerable body of precedent that governs the respective First Amendment rights of competing speakers. In *Red Lion,* we had legitimized consideration of the public interest and emphasized the rights of viewers, at least in the abstract. After *Turner,* however, that view can no longer be given any credence in the cable context. It is the operator's right that is preeminent. If *Tornillo* and *Pacific Gas & Electric Co. v. P.U.C. of Cal.,* 475 U.S. 1 (1986), are applicable, and I think they are, then, when there is a conflict, a programmer's asserted right to transmit over an operator's cable system must give way to an operator's editorial discretion.

By recognizing the general primacy of the cable operator's editorial rights over the rights of programmers and viewers, *Turner* raises serious questions about the merits of petitioners' claims. None of the petitioners in these cases are cable operators; they are all cable viewers or access programmers or their representative organizations. It is not intuitively obvious that the First Amendment protects the interests petitioners assert, and neither petitioners nor the plurality have adequately explained the source or justification of those asserted rights.

In the process of deciding not to decide on a governing standard, Justice BREYER purports to discover in our cases an expansive, general principle permitting government to "directly regulate speech to address extraordinary problems, where its regulations are appropriately tailored to resolve those problems without imposing an unnecessarily great restriction on speech." This heretofore unknown standard is facially subjective and openly invites balancing of asserted speech interests to a degree not ordinarily permitted. It is true that the standard I endorse lacks the "flexibility" inherent in the plurality's balancing approach, but that relative rigidity is required by our precedents and is not of my own making.

[*Justice Thomas contended that "leased and public access were a type of forced speech." Accordingly,* Turner *required that the federal "access requirements" should have been subjected to "some form of heightened scrutiny." The access requirements restrict the free speech rights of cable operators and expand the speech opportunities of access programmers. But access programmers "have no underlying constitutional rights to speak through the cable medium." Consequently, the access programmers could not challenge the federal access scheme as an infringement on their freedom of speech.*]

Sections 10(a) and (c) do not burden a programmer's right to seek access for its indecent programming on an operator's system. Rather, they merely restore part of the editorial discretion an operator would have absent government regulation without burdening the programmer's underlying speech rights.

It makes no difference that the leased access restrictions may take the form of common carrier obligations. Nothing about common carrier status *per se* constitutionalizes the asserted interests of the petitioners in these cases, and Justice Kennedy provides no authority for his assertion that common carrier regulations "should be reviewed under the same standard as content-based restrictions on speech in a public forum."

[*In addition, Justice Thomas, unlike Justice Kennedy, was not persuaded that public access channels were public forums. Public access requirements were a "regulatory restriction on the exercise of cable operators' editorial discretion, not a transfer of a sufficient property interest in the channels to support a designation of that property as a public forum."*]

COMMENT

The *Denver* case takes us to a new stage in the elusive quest for an appropriate First Amendment standard for cable. Justice Stephen Breyer, for the plurality, declines, at least for the time being, to identify such a standard. New electronic media technologies are at too formative and embryonic a stage to warrant the imposition of a rigid First Amendment standard. Instead, Justice Breyer offers a reasonableness test: Section 10(a) should be scrutinized to make sure that "it properly addresses an extremely important problem, without imposing in light of the relevant interests, an unnecessarily great restriction on speech."

This "reasonableness" approach allows the Court to watch new communications technologies evolve before setting them into particular First Amendment molds. Justice David Souter, who joins Justice Breyer in his "go-slow" approach to choosing a First Amendment model for cable, says that at least the Breyer formula follows the age-old injunction given to medical students: "First, do no harm." But is that really true? Doesn't the "reasonableness" approach deprive First Amendment law of the precision and predictability it needs? Justice Kennedy accused the Breyer plurality opinion of substituting an "untested" standard for established First Amendment doctrine. Actually the Breyer standard is a throwback to the balancing test used by the Supreme Court in First Amendment case law in the 1950s and 1960s.

Justice Kennedy's account of the emergence of public access channels on cable is instructive. It also shapes his First Amendment views in the *Denver* case. For him, it is critical that cable operators never enjoyed editorial discretion with respect to public access channels as compared with leased access channels. Why then does Justice Kennedy conclude that the indecency restriction on leased access channels in Sec. 10(a) is invalid?

Justice Kennedy looks at leased access channels as equivalent to common-carrier requirements, which, he says, function the same as a designated public forum. Therefore, the strict scrutiny standard of review applies. Content restrictions on leased access channels are invalid unless some compelling interests can be identified to justify "giving government a general license to single out some categories of speech for lesser protection."

Although Justice Kennedy says that the First Amendment validity of requiring cable operators to set aside channels for leased access purposes was not before the Court, he implies that such requirements are valid. What distinguishes the leased access channels in *Denver* from the newspaper columns in *Tornillo*? Justice Kennedy views leased access channels as public forums whereas the columns of a newspaper are not. Why?

For Justice Clarence Thomas, joined by Chief Justice William Rehnquist and Justice Antonin Scalia, *Turner* should have marked the end of the quest for the appropriate First Amendment model for cable regulation. For example, Justice Thomas notes that the *Turner* Court refused to impose the governmentally deferential *Red Lion* standard on cable. But did it move closer, as he suggests, to the media-deferential *Tornillo* standard?

Turner said strict scrutiny should apply to content-based cable regulation. The difficulty is that in practice this standard proves less predictive than might have been thought. As *Turner* illustrated, the Court found it difficult to agree on whether the must-carry requirements were content-based or content-neutral. A majority concluded that they were the latter and applied the *O'Brien* standard—an intermediate standard occupying a place somewhere between the laxity of the *Red Lion* standard and the rigor of the *Tornillo* standard. In light of this, Justice Thomas's conclusion that by rejecting the *Red Lion* standard for cable, *Turner* stripped viewers of any First Amendment rights is a considerable overstatement.

The larger importance of the *Denver* case—and indeed of *Turner*—is that it demonstrates that the Court is extremely fragmented on the appropriate First Amendment treatment of cable. This has repercussions for other emerging communications technologies. For example, in the *Denver* case, Justice Thomas said *Turner* adopted "much of the print paradigm." In *ACLU v. Reno*, 929 F. Supp. 824 (E.D. Pa. 1996), a three-judge federal court granted, 2–1, a preliminary injunction against enforcement of the indecency restrictions in the Telecommunications Act of 1996 on communication over the Internet. Judge Dalzell, who wrote one of the two opinions declaring that these restrictions violated the First Amendment, read *Turner* differently than did Justice Thomas in the *Denver* case. Judge Dalzell reasoned that *Turner* did not apply *Red Lion* to cable because *Turner* involved a different technology than broadcasting, not because *Turner* wished to embrace the *Tornillo* standard.

Turner's refusal to apply the broadcast rules to cable television cannot be overstated. *Turner* thus confirms that the analysis of a particular medium of mass communication must focus on the underlying technology that brings the information to the user. The Internet has achieved, and continues to achieve, the most participatory marketplace of mass speech that this country—and indeed the world—has yet seen. If "the First Amendment erects a virtually insurmountable barrier between government and the print media," *Tornillo* (White J., concurring), a medium that *does* capture comprehensive debate and *does* allow for the expression of all viewpoints should receive at least the same protection from intrusion.

In *Reno v. ACLU,* 117 S. Ct. 2329 (1997), the Supreme Court struck down the restrictions imposed on the Internet and affirmed the lower federal court. Justice Stewart for the Court declared that "our cases provide no basis for qualifying the level of First Amendment scrutiny that should be applied to the medium."

CHAPTER 9

BUSINESS ISSUES

CHAPTER OUTLINE

ADVERTISING AND THE LAW

Advertising and the First Amendment

Protection of commercial speech under the First
Amendment has dominated discussions of advertising and the law in the last two decades. In a
series of cases that began in 1975[1] and continues

---

1. *Bigelow v. Virginia,* 1 Med. L. Rptr. 1919, 421 U.S. 809
(1975).

to the present,[2] the U.S. Supreme Court has crafted a measure of protection for promotional and advertising messages.

Prior to 1975, the Court had declared that speech promoting goods and services was not deserving of constitutional protection. *Valentine v. Chrestensen*, 1 Med. L. Rptr. 1907, 316 U.S. 52 (1942).[3] The Court's opinion devoted a mere sentence to explaining its apparently intuitive conclusion.

Valentine was influential. In later cases, a city ordinance barring sex-specific help wanted classified advertisements was upheld.[4] In another case, the Fifth Circuit flatly asserted that commercial reports lack the general public interest needed for First Amendment protection.[5]

Change came in 1976 when a citizens' group challenged a state ban on advertising of prices for prescription drugs. *Virginia State Board of Pharmacy v. Virginia Citizens Consumers Council, Inc.*, 1 Med. L. Rptr. 1930, 425 U.S. 748 (1976). As a focal case, it deserves review. The Court declared that advertising messages are entitled to some measure of protection, but did not indicate the exact degree. That it would be a lesser protection was apparent; the opinion's footnote 24 observed that commercial speech is hardier than other content and therefore is more amenable to government regulation. Nevertheless, *Virginia Pharmacy* is known best for what it says about the value of commercial speech.

In 1980, the Court created a four-part test that outlined the protection available to commercial speech. *Central Hudson Gas & Electric Corp. v. Public Service Commission*, 6 Med. L. Rptr. 1497, 447 U.S. 557 (1980). The Court invalidated a state regulation prohibiting advertising that promoted the use of electricity. The Court used a four-part test in assessing the constitutionality of regulation:

1. The commercial speech must concern a lawful activity;
2. it must not be false or misleading;
3. the state must prove the existence of a substantial interest to be served by regulation;

4. the regulation must in fact serve the government interest and be narrowly drawn.

In *Central Hudson*, the state's interest in conserving energy could have been accomplished in numerous ways less intrusive on First Amendment values than banning advertising. The substantial interest formula adopted by the Court provided a middle level of protection much akin to that accorded broadcasting, see *Red Lion Broadcasting Co. v. FCC*, but certainly less than that accorded print media or news content generally.

The potential for the first two parts of the test to result in an undervaluing of speech that appears to be misleading, but is not proved to be, was apparently rectified in *In re R.M.J.*, 7 Med. L. Rptr. 2545, 455 U.S. 191 (1982). An attorney's advertising prominently mentioned his specialization in an unusually large number of areas of legal practice. The state bar's attempts to regulate the message were declared invalid.

In 1986, the Court applied the *Central Hudson* test to uphold a Puerto Rico provision that prohibited advertisement of casino gambling directed at residents, within the commonwealth. The government, however, was eager that casinos be advertised to nonresidents. The Court, in an opinion by Chief Justice Rehnquist, said that the interest in protecting residents from the evils of gambling was substantial. Further, the Court said that the partial ban on advertising was valid, because Puerto Rico could have banned casino advertising altogether. *Posadas de Puerto Rico Associates v. Tourism Co.*, 13 Med. L. Rptr. 1033, 478 U.S. 328 (1986). Justice Brennan wrote a heated dissent. He thought the majority had turned the test on its head. The *Posadas* analysis was not well received among scholars.[6]

Two recent cases have limited what appeared to be a broad grant of regulatory authority in *Posadas*. In *44 Liquormart, Inc. v. Rhode Island*, 24 Med. L. Rptr. 1673, 116 S. Ct. 1495 (1996), a liquor store challenged a state law that prohibited advertising the prices of alcoholic beverages for sale. The Court declared the law unconstitutional, largely because the state had many other ways of achieving its goal of reducing harms

2. *44 Liquormart, Inc. v. Rhode Island,* 24 Med. L. Rptr. 1673, 116 S. Ct. 1495 (1996).
3. Fuller versions of *Valentine* and other commercial speech cases are found in Chapter 3.
4. *Pittsburgh Press v. Pittsburgh Commission on Human Relations,* 1 Med. L. Rptr. 1908, 413 U.S. 376 (1973).
5. *Hood v. Dun and Bradstreet,* 486 F.2d 25 (5th Cir. 1973).

6. See, e.g., Richards, *Clearing the Air about Cigarettes: Will Advertisers' Rights Go Up in Smoke?* 19 Pacific L. J. *1, 23–30 (1987)*; Nutt, *Trends in First Amendment Protection of Commercial Speech,* 41 Vanderbilt L. Rev. 173 (1988); Kurland, *Posadas de Puerto Rico v. Tourism Company: 'Twas Strange, 'Twas Passing Strange, 'Twas Pitiful. 'Twas Wondrous Pitiful,* 1986 Supreme Court Rev. 1.

caused by alcohol—ways that did not require restricting speech. In a number of separate opinions, all the justices, including Chief Justice Rehnquist, appeared to abandon *Posadas*. In 1993, in *Cincinnati v. Discovery Network, Inc.*, 21 Med. L. Rptr. 1161, 507 U.S. 410 (1993), the Court declared a city's limits on distribution of free-circulation shoppers invalid. Cincinnati placed no similar limits on regular newspapers. The Court in this case was skeptical of the city's claim that shopper limits were needed for aesthetic reasons and to reduce littering; the claim was just as valid for any publication distributed by vending machine. The Court majority said that the city should have generated solid, perhaps empirical, evidence to support its claims.

The limited protection afforded commercial speech has fueled debate over the First Amendment's role regarding advertising messages. On one side are those who think that the Court should go farther and provide the same level of protection as news messages receive. After all, if commercial information is as important to audiences as *Virginia Pharmacy* asserts, why should government decide, even on a limited basis, which messages should be allowed?[7] On the other side are those, far more numerous, who argue that commercial speech should have little or no First Amendment protection. Echoing the Court in *Virginia Pharmacy*, authors have argued that advertising is genuinely hardier than other speech because of the unavoidable need for businesses to advertise. In addition, some worry that protecting commercial messages, which are normally far removed from the "core" political speech that the Court protects most zealously, will have the effect of watering down protection for more important types of speech. In other words, it will trivialize free speech protection.[8] Another problem is how to distinguish commercial and corporate speech from noncommercial speech.

Free speech theory aside, the practical effect of the cases protecting commercial speech has been to make it difficult for states to regulate commercial messages.[9] The major area in which government regulations have been upheld is advertising by members of professions or trades that are licensed by the state.[10] In a relative handful of cases, the courts have upheld regulations involving the promotion of products that were illegal in whole or part[11] or the promotion of products or services that have traditionally been heavily regulated, including alcoholic beverages,[12] lotteries,[13] and the gambling in *Posadas*.

Whatever the future holds for the commercial speech doctrine, it seems clear that it poses no impediment to laws and regulations aimed at untruthful or deceptive advertising, the traditional target of regulation.

Direct Regulation of Advertising

The primary originator of advertising regulation nationwide is the Federal Trade Commission (FTC), although several other federal agencies engage in some advertising regulation, as do attorneys general or other officials in every state. Regulation varies from time to time and from one jurisdiction to another. Throughout the 1980s and into the 1990s, the FTC was relatively slow to bring action against advertisers.

One reason for the relative inactivity was the political climate. The Reagan and Bush administrations placed little emphasis on advertising regulation, apparently preferring to let market forces police advertising claims. The lack of activity at the federal level led to more

7. See, e.g., Neuborne, *A Rationale for Protecting and Regulating Commercial Speech*, 45 Brooklyn L. Rev. 437 (1980); Coase, *Advertising and Free Speech*, 6 J. Legal Stud. 1 (1977); DeVore, *The Two Faces of Commercial Speech under the First Amendment*, Comm. Law., Vol. 12, No. 1, 1, 23–28 (Spring 1994); Kozinski & Banner, *Who's Afraid of Commercial Speech?* 76 Va. L. Rev. 627 (1990).

8. See, e.g., Baker, *Press Rights and Government Power to Structure the Press*, 34 U. of Miami L. Rev. 785, 822 (1980); Shiffrin, *The First Amendment and Economic Regulation: Away from a General Theory of the First Amendment*, 78 Northwestern U. L. Rev. 1212 (1983); Farber, *Commercial Speech and First Amendment Theory*, 74 Northwestern U. L. Rev. 372 (1979).

9. See, e.g., *International Dairy Foods Association v. Amestory*, 24 Med. L. Rptr. 2089, 92 F.3d 67 (2d Cir. 1996).

10. See, e.g., *Anheuser-Busch v. Schmoke*, 24 Med. L. Rptr. 2491, 101 F.3d 325 (4th Cir. 1996); *Desnick v. Illinois Department of Professional Regulation*, 24 Med. L. Rptr. 2238, 665 N.E.2d 1346 (Ill. 1996).

11. See, e.g., *Princess Sea Industries v. State*, 635 P.2d 281 (Nev. 1981) (prostitution).

12. See, e.g., *Oklahoma Telecasters Ass'n. v. Crisp*, 699 F.2d 490 (10th Cir. 1983), *rev. on other grounds* 104 S. Ct. 2694 (1984); *S&S Liquor Mart v. Pastore*, 12 Med. L. Rptr. 1236, 497 A.2d 729 (R.I. 1985).

13. *U.S. v. Edge Broadcasting Co.*, 21 Med. L. Rptr. 1577, 113 S. Ct. 2696 (1993).

self-regulation by the advertising industry and increased activity at the state level.[14]

A second reason for the rather quiet regulatory front has been the First Amendment commercial speech doctrine. Some have argued that it casts doubt on the constitutionality of the FTC's long-accepted authority to regulate advertising.[15] See *Warner-Lambert Co. v. FTC*, text, p. 519. Indeed, in 1983 the FTC itself adopted a test for deception that makes its intervention less likely. Still, the FTC continued to bring enforcement actions during the 1980s and maintained a strong role in nonadversarial regulation, as it did in promulgating trade regulations and in pursuing informal agreement on rule violations.[16]

However subject to challenge a specific enforcement action of the FTC may be in potential litigation under the commercial speech doctrine, the agency's delegated legal authority under enabling legislation seems secure. Its authority to interpret its mandate freely has been the subject of a prolonged political battle with Congress, however.

In the early 1990s, the FTC began to step up its advertising regulatory activity.[17] In *Gerber Products Co.*, File No. 962 3173 (March 12, 1997) (proposed consent order), for example, the FTC investigated Gerber's claim that four out of five pediatricians recommended the company's baby foods. The FTC found that the study Gerber relied upon substantiated only that 16 percent of pediatricians who recommend specific brands recommended Gerber. The vast majority of pediatricians, 82 percent, did not make recommendations. The settlement prohibits Gerber from making similar claims in the future,

requires substantiation of future claims, and sets up multiyear record-keeping requirements. Gerber is, in effect, on advertising probation.

The regulation of advertising grew out of a general assault at the turn of the century on the excesses of *laissez-faire* capitalism and the cynical doctrine of *caveat emptor* (let the buyer beware). Stimulated by the writing of the muckrakers, notably Samuel Hopkins Adams's 1906 *Colliers* series on patent medicines, "The Great American Fraud," the regulatory movement took root in the passage of the Pure Food and Drug Act in 1906 and the creation of the FTC in 1914.

In 1914, Congress was primarily concerned with reinforcing the antitrust provisions of the Sherman and Clayton Acts. The FTC Act declared unfair methods of competition in commerce unlawful. Its purpose was to promote the "preservation of an environment which would foster the liberty to compete." In its early years, the courts used the Act to protect competitors against false and deceptive advertising; the protection of consumers was incidental.

In 1922, for example, Justice Louis Brandeis, in an opinion for the U.S. Supreme Court, upheld the FTC in a ruling against a manufacturer who had mislabeled underwear as wool when in fact it contained as little as 10 percent wool.

Although Brandies did recognize a public interest in prohibiting mislabeling, his main argument was that "the practice constitutes an unfair method of competition as against manufacturers of all wool knit underwear and as against those manufacturers of mixed wool and cotton underwear who brand their product truthfully. For when misbranded goods attract customers by means of the fraud which they perpetrate, trade is diverted from the producer of truthfully marked goods. * * *" *FTC v. Winsted Hosiery Co.*, 258 U.S. 483 (1922). See also *FTC v. Beech-Nut*, 257 U.S. 441 (1921).

That consumer rights in this period were peripheral to the welfare of competitors is best illustrated by the 1931 Supreme Court ruling in the *Raladam* case. Here the Court declared flatly, through Justice George Sutherland, that the FTC Act would not protect consumers against the phony advertising of an "obesity cure" unless competitive businesses were being hurt. *FTC v. Raladam Co.*, 283 U.S. 643 (1931).

Three years later, however, the Court repudiated *Raladam* in a case involving the deceptive

14. Rogers, *Advertising Self-Regulation in the 1980s: A Review*, 12 Current Issues and Research in Advertising 369 (1990); Sovern, *Private Actions under the Deceptive Trade Practices Acts: Reconsidering the FTC Act as Role Model*, 52 Ohio St. L.J. 437 (1991).

15. Reich, *Consumer Protection and the First Amendment: A Dilemma for the FTC?* 61 Minnesota L.Rev. 705 (1977); Note, *Commercial Speech and the FTC: A Point of Departure from Traditional First Amendment Analysis regarding Prior Restraint*, 16 New England L.Rev. 793 (1981); Thompson, *Antitrust, the First Amendment, and the Communication of Price Information*, 56 Temple L.Rev. 939 (1983).

16. Ford and Calfee, *Recent Developments in FTC Policy on Deception*, 50 J. of Marketing 82 (1986).

17. Petty & Kopp, *Advertising Challenges: A Strategic Framework and Current Review*, J. of Advertising Res. (March/April 1995) 41–55.

use of a lottery in marketing candy to children. *FTC v. R.F. Keppel & Brother, Inc.*, 291 U.S. 304, 1934). After *Keppel* unfair competitive practices were not limited to those violative of the antitrust laws. In 1937, Justice Hugo Black overruled a district court opinion by Judge Learned Hand that had struck down an FTC order against deceptive sales practices in selling encyclopedias. Black wrote for the Court:

> The fact that a false statement may be obviously false to those who are trained and experienced does not change its character nor take away its power to deceive others less experienced. There is no duty resting upon a citizen to suspect the honesty of those with whom he transacts business. Laws are made to protect the trusting as well as the suspicious. The best element of business has long since decided that honesty should govern competitive enterprises, and that the rule of *caveat emptor* should not be relied upon to reward fraud and deception. *FTC v. Standard Education Society,* 302 U.S. 112 (1937).

Congress legitimized this golden rule in 1938 by adding sec. 5(b) to the FTC Act: "Unfair methods of competition in commerce, and unfair or deceptive acts or practices in commerce, are declared unlawful." 15 U.S.C.A. § 45. And to sec. 12 was added language that declares false advertising of food, drugs, cosmetics, or devices to be an unfair or deceptive act and, as such, a violation of law.

Known as the Wheeler-Lea Amendments, these changes in the Act made "false" and "deceptive" advertising the keystones of the FTC's authority to protect consumers as well as competitors. The amendments provided the FTC with broad authority to prevent what it considered false, deceptive, or unfair. Only in the 1970s was that authority brought into question under the commercial speech doctrine.

In *Beneficial Corp. v. FTC,* 542 F.2d 611 (3d Cir. 1976), for example, the court, relying on *Virginia Pharmacy,* refused to enforce an FTC order on the ground that the First Amendment requires the commission to bear the burden of proof and to use the least restrictive remedy available. The court then recommended substitute language for an advertisement confusing an ordinary loan with a federal tax refund in lieu of litigation.

The goals of regulation remain fairness and efficiency in the marketplace and a lessening of competitor and consumer injury depending, in part, upon an increase in the flow of truthful information to the public. Under all the acts, the FTC is the primary interpreter of the meaning of "unfair" or "deceptive." The statutory terms are suggestive rather than definitive. It has been the commission's task to give them meaning.

FALSE, DECEPTIVE, AND UNFAIR ADVERTISING
False and deceptive advertising is regulated under secs. 5 and 12 of the FTC Act [18] and sec. 43(a) of the Lanham Act,[19] which is primarily concerned with trademark law. The FTC also enforces dozens of narrower, more specific consumer protection laws. Most of those laws permit consumers to sue for civil damages and to obtain attorney's fees.[20]

The definition of what is false, deceptive, or unfair has varied over time. From the Wheeler-Lea Amendments in 1938 until the mid-1980s, the FTC standard was whether or not an advertising assertion had a "tendency or capacity" to deceive consumers.[21] The courts generally upheld the standard, even when the FTC was basing its decision on whether gullible rather than ordinary consumers were likely to be deceived. See, e.g., *Charles of the Ritz Distributors Corp. v. FTC,* 143 F.2d 676 (2d Cir. 1944).

---

18. 15 U.S.C.A. § 45; 15 U.S.C.A. § 52. Under sec. 5(a)(1) it is unfair or deceptive to fail to disclose any safety risk in the use of a product for the purpose for which it is sold, which would not be immediately apparent to a casual purchaser or user. In particular, it is an unfair or deceptive act or practice to fail to disclose latent safety hazards relating to flammability. Where human safety is involved and the buyer must rely on a manufacturer's technical knowledge to assure the validity of its claims, it is an unfair and deceptive act or practice to make a specific advertising claim without supporting data from scientific tests. A scientific test is one in which persons with skill and expertise in the field conduct the test and evaluate its results in a disinterested manner using testing procedures that are generally accepted in the profession and that best ensure accurate results. See *Firestone Tire and Rubber Co.,* 81 FTC 398, 451, 463 (1972). *aff'd* 481 F.2d 246 (6th Cir. 1973), *cert. denied* 414 U.S. 1112 (1973). Disclosures are to be made in ways that arrest the eye or attract the attention of an average purchaser or user of the product.
19. 15 U.S.C.A. § 1125(a).
20. See, e.g., Truth in Lending Act, 15 U.S.C.A. §§ 1601–1667e; Fair Credit Reporting Act, 15 U.S.C.A. §§ 1681–1681t; Magnuson-Moss Warranty Act, 15 U.S.C.A. §§2301–2312; Energy Policy and Conservation Act, 42 U.S.C.A. §§ 6201–6422; Hobby Protection Act, 15 U.S.C.A. §§ 2101–2106.
21. Fueroghne, Law & Advertising 20–29 (1995).

The FTC has other responsibilities. It will issue formal opinions where there is a substantial question of law and no clear precedent, a proposed merger or acquisition is involved, or a matter of significant public interest is before it.

The commission may also issue Trade Regulation Rules. If the FTC finds evidence of unfair or deceptive practices across an entire industry, it can recommend a rulemaking proceeding. The public will have input, as will the commission staff, before a proposed rule is set down. Any rule may be challenged in any U.S. court of appeal. When issued, these rules have the force of law.

Unfair methods of competition, even when they do not violate antitrust laws directly and are not deceptive, were condemned in *FTC v. The Sperry & Hutchinson Co.*, 405 U.S. 233 (1972). "[L]egislative and judicial authorities alike convince us," said Justice Byron White for the Court, "that the Federal Trade Commission does not arrogate excessive power to itself if, in measuring a practice against the elusive but congressionally mandated standard of fairness, it, like a court of equity, considers public values beyond simply those enshrined in the letter or encompassed in the spirit of the antitrust laws."

The FTC, although independent as a matter of law, was buffeted during the 1980s by pressures from Congress. In 1980, Congress passed the FTC Improvements Act, which required the commission to submit all final rules to Congress. Under the Act, a rule would not take effect for ninety days, during which Congress could veto it. The Act also ordered the FTC to drop a long-term investigation of the effects of television advertising on children.[22] When the Act was declared an unconstitutional violation of separation of powers in *Immigration and Naturalization Service v. Chadha*, 462 U.S. 919 (1983), Congress responded by reducing the commission's budget.

Much of the pressure developed because members of Congress and businesses felt that the FTC's approach to what was unfair or deceptive was too amorphous. The FTC responded with a revised interpretation. Under the new approach,

an assertion will not be found deceptive unless it "is likely to mislead consumers" and the deception is material. In other words, an advertisement is deceptive if it can be predicted that the ad would trick the "reasonable consumer" into a purchase decision. *In re Cliffdale Associates, Inc.*, 103 F.T.C. 110 (1984). At the same time, the FTC indicated that it anticipated using extrinsic evidence, not intuition, to support charges. It has been suggested that prepublication prediction is possible and would save considerable time and money.[23]

Section 5 of the Federal Trade Commission Act was amended in 1994 to include language that is somewhat similar to that used in *Cliffdale*. Under the amendment, an act or practice will be unfair only if it "causes or is likely to cause substantial injury to consumers" and cannot be avoided by the consumers.[24]

The FTC's current definition of unfairness and deceptiveness, along with its interpretive authority, was examined in a case that attracted considerable national publicity.

Kraft, Inc. v. Federal Trade Commission
970 F.2D 311 (7TH CIR. 1992), *CERT. DENIED* **113 S. Ct. 1254 (1993).**

FLAUM, Circuit Judge:

Kraft, Inc. ("Kraft") asks us to review an order of the Federal Trade Commission ("FTC" or "Commission") finding that it violated §§ 5 and 12 of the Federal Trade Commission Act ("Act"), 15 U.S.C. §§ 45, 52. The FTC determined that Kraft, in an advertising campaign, had misrepresented information regarding the amount of calcium contained in Kraft Singles American Pasteurized Process Cheese Food ("Singles") relative to the calcium content in five ounces of milk and in imitation cheese slices. The FTC ordered Kraft to cease and desist from making these misrepresentations and Kraft filed this petition for review. We enforce the Commission's order.

Three categories of cheese compete in the individually wrapped process slice market:

---

22. Oppenheim, Weston, Maggs, & Schechter, Unfair Trade Practices and Consumer Protection 4th ed. 524–525 (1983); Petty, *FTC Advertising Regulation: Survivor or Casualty of the Reagan Revolution?* 30 Am.Bus. L.J. 1 (1982).

23. Richards & Preston, *Quantitative Research: A Dispute Resolution Process for FTC Advertising Regulation* 40 Okla. L. Rev. 593 (1987).

24. Preston, *Unfairness Developments in FTC Advertising Cases,* 14 J. Pub. Pol'y & Marketing 318 (1995).

process cheese food slices, imitation slices, and substitute slices. Process cheese food slices, also known as "dairy slices," must contain at least 51% natural cheese by federal regulation. 21 C.F.R. § 133.173(a)(5). Imitation cheese slices, by contrast, contain little or no natural cheese and consist primarily of water, vegetable oil, flavoring agents, and fortifying agents. While imitation slices are as healthy as process cheese food slices in some nutrient categories, they are as a whole considered "nutritionally inferior" and must carry the label "imitation." *Id.* at § 101.3(e)(4). Substitute slices fit somewhere in between; they fall short of the natural cheese content of process cheese food slices yet are nutritionally superior to imitation slices. *Id.* at § 101.3(e)(2). Consistent with FTC usage, we refer to both imitation and substitute slices as "imitation" slices.

Kraft Singles are process cheese food slices. In the early 1980s, Kraft began losing market share to an increasing number of imitation slices that were advertised as both less expensive and equally nutritious as dairy slices like Singles. Kraft responded with a series of advertisements, collectively known as the "Five Ounces of Milk" campaign, designed to inform consumers that Kraft Singles cost more than imitation slices because they are made from five ounces of milk rather than less expensive ingredients. The ads also focused on the calcium content of Kraft Singles in an effort to capitalize on growing consumer interest in adequate calcium consumption.

The FTC filed a complaint against Kraft charging that this advertising campaign materially misrepresented the calcium content and relative calcium benefit of Kraft Singles. The FTC Act makes it unlawful to engage in unfair or deceptive commercial practices, 15 U.S.C. § 45, or to induce consumers to purchase certain products through advertising that is misleading in a material respect. *Id.* at §§ 52, 55. Thus, an advertisement is deceptive under the Act if it is likely to mislead consumers, acting reasonably under the circumstances, in a material respect. * * * In implementing this standard, the Commission examines the overall net impression of an ad and engages in a three-part inquiry: (1) what claims are conveyed in the ad; (2) are those claims false or misleading: and (3) are those claims material to prospective consumers.

Two facts are critical to understanding the allegations against Kraft. First, although Kraft does use five ounces of milk in making each Kraft Single, roughly 30% of the calcium contained in the milk is lost during processing. Second, the vast majority of imitation slices sold in the United States contain 15% of the U.S. Recommended Daily Allowance (RDA) of calcium per ounce, roughly the same amount contained in Kraft Singles. Specifically then, the FTC complaint alleged that the challenged advertisements made two implied claims, neither of which was true: (1) that a slice of Kraft Singles contains the same amount of calcium as five ounces of milk (the "milk equivalency" claim); and (2) that Kraft Singles contain more calcium than do most imitation cheese slices (the "imitation superiority" claim).

The two sets of ads at issue in this case, referred to as the "Skimp" ads and the "Class Picture" ads, ran nationally in print and broadcast media between 1985 and 1987. The Skimp ads were designed to communicate the nutritional benefit of Kraft Singles by referring expressly to their milk and calcium content. The broadcast version of this ad on which the FTC focused contained the following audio copy:

> Lady (voice over): I admit it. I thought of skimping. Could you look into those big blue eyes and skimp on her? So I buy Kraft Singles. Imitation slices use hardly any milk. But Kraft has five ounces per slice. Five ounces. So her little bones get calcium they need to grow. * * *
>
> Singers: Kraft Singles. More milk makes 'em . . . more milk makes 'em good.

* * * The visual image corresponding to this copy shows, among other things, milk pouring into a glass until it reaches a mark on the glass denoted "five ounces." The commercial also shows milk pouring into a glass which bears the phrase "5 oz. milk slice" and which gradually becomes part of the label on a package of Singles. In January 1986, Kraft revised this ad, changing "Kraft *has* five ounces per slice" to "Kraft is *made from* five ounces per slice," (emphasis added), and in March 1987, Kraft added the disclosure, "one ¾ ounce slice has 70% of the calcium of five ounces of milk" as a subscript in the television commercial and as a footnote in the print ads.

The Class Picture ads also emphasized the milk and calcium content of Kraft Singles but, unlike the Skimp ads, did not make an express comparison to imitation slices. * * * The Class

Picture ads also included the subscript disclaimer mentioned above.

After a lengthy trial, the Administrative Law Judge (ALJ) concluded that both the Skimp and Class Picture ads made the milk equivalency claim. Specifically, the ALJ found that the juxtaposition of references to milk and calcium, along with the failure to mention that calcium is lost in processing, implied that each Kraft Single contains the same amount of calcium as five ounces of milk, and that the altered audio copy and subscript disclosure were confusing and inconspicuous and thus insufficient to dispel this impression. Further, the ALJ concluded that both sets of ads falsely conveyed the imitation superiority claim; he determined that reasonable consumers would take away the net impression that Kraft Singles contain more calcium than imitation slices because Kraft Singles contain five ounces and milk and imitation slices have little or no milk. According to the ALJ, both claims were material because they implicated important health concerns. He therefore ordered Kraft to cease and desist from making these claims about any of its individually wrapped slices of process cheese food, imitation cheese, or substitute cheese.

The FTC affirmed the ALJ's decision, with some modifications. *In re Kraft, Inc.,* FTC No. 9208 (Jan. 30, 1991). As to the Skimp ads, the Commission found that four elements conveyed the milk equivalency claim: (1) the use of the word "has" in the phrase "Kraft has five ounces per slice"; (2) repetition of the precise amount of milk in a Kraft Single (five ounces); (3) the use of the word "so" to link the reference to milk with the reference to calcium; and (4) the visual image of milk being poured into a glass up to a five-ounce mark, and the superimposition of that image onto a package of Singles. It also found two additional elements that conveyed the imitation superiority claim: (1) the express reference to imitation slices combined with the use of comparative language ("hardly any," "but"); and (2) the image of a glass containing very little milk during the reference to imitation slices, followed by the image of a glass being filled to the five-ounce mark during the reference to Kraft Singles. The Commission based all of these findings on its own impression of the advertisements and found it unnecessary to resort to extrinsic evidence; it did note, however, that the available extrinsic evidence was consistent with its determinations.

The Commission then examined the Class Picture ads—once again, without resorting to extrinsic evidence—and found that they contained copy substantially similar to the copy in the Skimp ads that conveyed the impression of milk equivalency. It rejected, however, the ALJ's finding that the Class Picture ads made an imitation superiority claim. * * *

The FTC next found that the claims were material to consumers. It concluded that the milk equivalency claim is a health-related claim that reasonable consumers would find important and that Kraft believed that the claim induced consumers to purchase Singles. The FTC presumed that the imitation superiority claim was material because it found that Kraft intended to make that claim. It also found that the materiality of that claim was demonstrated by evidence that the challenged ads led to increased sales despite a substantially higher price for Singles than for imitation slices.

Finally, the FTC modified the ALJ's cease and desist order by extending its coverage from "individually wrapped slices of cheese, imitation cheese, and substitute cheese" to "any product that is a cheese, related cheese product, imitation cheese, or substitute cheese." The Commission found that the serious, deliberate nature of the violation, combined with the transferability of the violations to other cheese products, justified a broader order. Kraft filed this petition to set-aside the Commission's order or, alternatively, to modify its scope.

Our standard for reviewing FTC findings has been traditionally limited to the highly deferential, substantial evidence test. *FTC v. Indiana Fed'n of Dentists,* 476 U.S. 447, 454 (1976). * * * However, Kraft argues as a threshold matter that two recent Supreme Court decisions, *Bose Corp. v. Consumers Union,* 466 U.S. 485, 510–11 (1984), and *Peel v. Attorney Registration and Disciplinary Comm'n,* 496 U.S. 91 (1990), compel us to review the FTC's factual findings *de novo* because they implicate Kraft's first amendment commercial speech rights.

A deferential standard in reviewing FTC findings long predates *Bose* and *Peel.* In *FTC v. Colgate–Palmolive Co.,* 380 U.S. 374, 385 (1965), the Supreme Court held that while the words "deceptive advertising" set forth a legal standard that derives its final meaning from judicial construction, an FTC finding is "to be given great weight by reviewing courts" because it "rests so heavily on inference and pragmatic judgment" and in light of the frequency with which the Commission handles these cases. However, *Colgate–Palmolive* preceded the extension of the first amendment protection to commercial speech. * * *

Bose was a libel case holding that appellate courts have a constitutional responsibility to review *de novo* a lower court finding of fact that a defamatory statement was made with actual malice. *Bose,* 466 U.S. at 510–11. The Court declared that judges, as expositors of the Constitution, must independently decide whether evidence in the record is sufficient to strip allegedly libelous speech of first amendment protection. The Court, however, explicitly left unresolved the question of whether this higher standard of review extended to commercial speech cases. *Peel* held that a state regulation prohibiting attorneys from advertising a specialty or certification violated the first amendment and, significantly, a plurality of four Justices reviewed this issue *de novo, Peel,* 496 U.S. at 108 (citing *Bose*) * * *. Thus, *Peel* arguably extended *de novo* review to another subcategory of constitutionally protected speech, commercial advertising.

Nonetheless, we decline to apply *de novo* review in this context. For one, the implications of *Bose* are not as clear as Kraft suggests, * * * and *Bose* itself suggests that commercial speech might not warrant the higher standard of review established for libel cases. * * * Although one might argue that *Bose* and *Peel* operating in tandem effectively overrule *Colgate–Palmolive,* we do not think that the Court intended that result. * * * The former involved review of court decisions, and courts generally lack the Commission's expertise in the field of deceptive advertising. While it could be posited that it is counter-intuitive to grant more deference to the Commission than to courts, Commission findings are well-suited to deferential review because they may require resolution of "exceedingly complex and technical factual issues." * * * In addition, the determination of whether an ad has a tendency to deceive is an impressionistic one more closely akin to a finding of fact than a conclusion of law. * * * *Beneficial Corp. v. FTC,* 542 F.2d 611, 617 (3d Cir.1976), *cert. denied,* 430 U.S. 983 (1977).

Most important, the restriction challenged in *Peel* is a completely different animal than the one challenged here. In *Peel,* the issue was whether a prophylactic regulation applicable to all lawyers, completely prohibiting an entire category of potentially misleading commercial speech, passed constitutional muster. * * * Here, by contrast, the issue is whether an individualized FTC cease and desist order, prohibiting a particular set of deceptive ads, passes constitutional muster. * * * We find the restriction at issue in *Peel* and the one here sufficiently distinct to justify differing levels of appellate review.

* * *

Kraft makes numerous arguments on appeal, but its principal claim is that the FTC erred as a matter of law in not requiring extrinsic evidence of consumer deception. Without such evidence, Kraft claims (1) that the FTC had no objective basis for determining if its ads actually contained the implied claims alleged, and (2) that the FTC's order chills constitutionally protected commercial speech. Alternatively, Kraft contends that substantial evidence does not support the FTC's finding that the Class Picture ads contain the milk equivalency claim. Finally, Kraft maintains that even if it did make the alleged milk equivalency and imitation superiority claims, substantial evidence does not support the FTC's finding that these claims were material to consumers.

* * *

In determining what claims are conveyed by a challenged advertisement, the Commission relies on two sources of information: its own viewing of the ad and extrinsic evidence. Its practice is to view the ad first and, if it is unable on its own to determine with confidence what claims are conveyed in a challenged ad, to turn to extrinsic evidence. *Thompson Medical,* 104 F.T.C. at 788–89; *Cliffdale Assocs.,* 103 F.T.C. 110, 164–66 (1984); *FTC Policy Statement,* 103 F.T.C. at 176. The most convincing extrinsic evidence is a survey "of what consumers thought upon reading the advertisement in question," *Thompson Medical,* 104 F.T.C. at 788–89 but the Commission also relies on other forms of extrinsic evidence including consumer testimony, expert opinion, and copy tests of ads. * * *

Kraft has no quarrel with this approach when it comes to determining whether an ad conveys *express* claims, but contends that the FTC should be required, as a matter of law, to rely on extrinsic evidence rather than its own subjective analysis in all cases involving allegedly *implied* claims. The basis for this argument is that implied claims, by definition, are not self-evident from the face of an ad. This, combined with the fact that consumer perceptions are shaped by a host of external variables—including their social and educational backgrounds, the environment in which they view the ad, and prior experiences with the product advertised * * *—makes review of implied claims by a five-member commission inherently unreliable. * * *

Kraft buttresses its argument by pointing to the use of extrinsic evidence in an analogous context: cases brought under § 43(a) of the Lanham Act. 15 U.S.C. § 1125(a). Courts hearing deceptive advertising claims under that Act, which provides a private right of action for deceptive advertising, generally require extrinsic proof that an advertisement conveys an implied claim. * * * Here, the Commission found implied claims based solely on its own intuitive reading of the ads (although it did reinforce that conclusion by examining the proffered extrinsic evidence). Had the Commission fully and properly relied on available extrinsic evidence, Kraft argues, it would have conclusively found that consumers do not perceive the milk equivalency and imitation superiority claims in the ads. While Kraft's arguments may have some force as a matter of policy, they are unavailing as a matter of law. Courts, including the Supreme Court, have uniformly rejected imposing such a requirement on the FTC, * * * and we decline to do so as well. We hold that the Commission may rely on its own reasoned analysis to determine what claims, including implied ones, are conveyed in a challenged advertisement, so long as those claims are reasonably clear from the face of the advertisement.

Kraft's case for a *per se* rule has two flaws. First, it rests on the faulty premise that implied claims are inescapably subjective and unpredictable. In fact, implied claims fall on a continuum, ranging from the obvious to the barely discernible. The Commission does not have license to go on a fishing expedition to pin liability on advertisers for barely imaginable claims falling at the end of this spectrum. However, when confronted with claims that are implied, yet conspicuous, extrinsic evidence is unnecessary because common sense and administrative experience provide the Commission with adequate tools to make its findings. * * * The implied claims Kraft made are reasonably clear from the face of the advertisements, and hence the Commission was not required to utilize consumer surveys in reaching its decision.

Second, Kraft's reliance on Lanham Act decisions is misplaced. For one, not all courts applying the Lanham Act rely on extrinsic evidence when confronted with implied claims, * * * but more importantly, when they do, it is because they are ill equipped—unlike the Commission—to detect deceptive advertising. * * *

The crux of Kraft's first amendment argument is that the FTC's current subjective approach chills some truthful commercial speech. Kraft acknowledges the novelty of its argument, but asserts that the issue warrants consideration in light of evolving commercial speech doctrine. * * *

Kraft contends that by relying on its own subjective judgment that an ad, while literally true, implies a false message, the FTC chills nonmisleading, protected speech because advertisers are unable to predict whether the FTC will find a particular ad misleading. Advertisers can run sophisticated pre-dissemination consumer surveys and find no implied claims present, only to have the Commission determine in its own subjective view that consumers would perceive an implied claim. Indeed, Kraft maintains that is precisely what happened here. * * *

Kraft's first amendment challenge is doomed by the Supreme Court's holding in *Zauderer,* which established that no first amendment concerns are raised when facially apparent implied claims are found without resort to extrinsic evidence. In *Zauderer,* a lawyer advertised that clients who retained him on a contingent-fee basis would not have to pay *legal fees* if their lawsuits were unsuccessful, without disclosing that these clients would be charged for *costs* * * *. In approving the state's action, the Supreme Court declared, "When the possibility of deception is as self-evident as it is in this case, we need not require the State to 'conduct a survey of the . . . public before it [may] determine that the [advertisement] had a tendency to mislead.'"

Zauderer 471 U.S. at 652–53 (quoting *Colgate-Palmolive*, 380 U.S. at 391–92).

Thus, *Zauderer* teaches that consumer surveys are not compelled by the first amendment when the alleged deception although implied, is conspicuous. In both *Zauderer* and here, an omitted piece of information—the definition of a key contractual term in *Zauderer*, the effect of processing on nutrient content here—led to potential consumer deception, and in both cases the ads were literally true, yet impliedly misleading. * * * Because we conclude that the Commission was not required to rely on extrinsic evidence, we need not examine the extrinsic evidence proffered by Kraft that it says contravenes the Commission's findings. We note, however, that the Commission did thoroughly examine this evidence, albeit after the fact, and found that it did not refute the implied claim findings and that some of the evidence was based on unsound consumer testing methodologies.

Our holding does not diminish the force of Kraft's argument as a policy matter, and, indeed, the extensive body of commentary on the subject makes a compelling argument that reliance on extrinsic evidence should be the rule rather than the exception. Along those lines, the Commission would be well-advised to adopt a consistent position on consumer survey methodology—advertisers and the FTC, it appears, go round and round on this issue—so that any uncertainty is reduced to an absolute minimum.

* * *

Kraft next asserts that the milk equivalency and imitation superiority claims, even if made, are not material to consumers. A claim is considered material if it "involves information that is important to consumers and, hence, likely to affect their choice of, or conduct regarding a product."

* * *

In determining that the milk equivalency claim was material to consumers, the FTC cited Kraft's surveys showing that 71% of respondents rated calcium content an extremely or very important factor in their decision to buy Kraft Singles, and that 52% of female, and 40% of all respondents, reported significant personal concerns about adequate calcium consumption. The FTC further noted that the ads were targeted to female homemakers with children and that the

60 milligram difference between the calcium contained in five ounces of milk and that contained in a Kraft Single would make up for most of the RDA calcium deficiency shown in girls aged 9–11. Finally, the FTC found evidence in the record that Kraft designed the ads with the intent to capitalize on consumer calcium deficiency concerns.

* * *

With regard to the imitation superiority claim, the Commission applied a presumption of materiality after finding evidence that Kraft intended the challenged ads to convey this message. (Recall that intent to convey a claim is one of three categories qualifying for a presumption of materiality. *See, e.g., Thompson Medical*, 104 F.T.C. at 816–17.) It found this presumption buttressed by the fact that the challenged ad copy led to increased sales of Singles, even though they cost 40 percent more than imitation slices.

* * *

To reiterate, the FTC's order does two things: it prohibits the Skimp ads and the Class Picture ads (as *currently* designed) and it requires Kraft to base future nutrient and calcium claims on reliable scientific evidence. Kraft mischaracterizes the decision as a categorical ban on commercial speech when in fact it identifies with particularity two nutrient claims that the Commission found actually misleading and prohibits only those claims. It further places on Kraft the (minor) burden of supporting future nutrient claims with reliable data. This leaves Kraft free to use any advertisement it chooses, including the Skimp and Class Picture ads, so long as it either eliminates the elements specifically identified by the FTC as contributing to consumer deception or corrects this inaccurate impression by adding prominent, unambiguous disclosures.

* * *

For the foregoing reasons, Kraft's petition to set-aside the order is DENIED and the Commission's order is ENFORCED.

COMMENT

The case was considered notable for two reasons. First, to many it represented a dramatic return to aggressive regulation by the FTC. Second, and probably more important for advertisers, the court approved the use of "its own reasoned analysis rather than extrinsic evidence" to assess claims. Broad agency discretion was upheld.[25]

In *Kraft,* the company raised a First Amendment argument that the cease-and-desist order was overbroad. The claim was rejected. Because Kraft's claims had been found to be misleading, they were outside the protection of the commercial speech doctrine. The order was narrowly tailored and satisfied the First Amendment in any event, the court added.

Another example of increased aggressiveness is *FTC v. Figgie International, Inc.,* 994 F.2d 595 (9th Cir. 1993). In *Figgie,* the commission brought claims against a distributor and seller of heat detectors. The FTC said that the company's advertising and marketing materials could not ignore the extrinsic scientific showing that smoke detectors provided earlier warnings than heat detectors. Figgie had claimed that heat detectors would provide adequate warning of fire. The commission interpreted this as an implied misrepresentation. The court found that the FTC had been a bit too aggressive, however. Its imposition of a remedy requiring that the company give funds to nonprofit fire safety groups was found to be a punitive damage award exceeding FTC authority under the act.

First Amendment issues are inherent in the regulatory process. The new interpretation tightens the inquiry. In the absence of evidence of intentional deception, the "reasonable person" standard comports with the common law and tends to discourage broad assaults on the First Amendment. It also legitimizes *puffery:* the exaggerated use of superlatives and hyperbole to describe goods and services, a form of expression defying objective measurement. Courts and commission have held words like "stupendous" to be romantic characterizations not to be read literally. So while a toothpaste may be said to "beautify the smile,"[26] a cigarette manufacturer may not safely say that his product is "less irritating." *Liggett & Myers Tobacco Co.,* 55 F.T.C. 354 (1958).

The trick seems to be to avoid factual or material claims or misrepresentation, but the distinction is vague and subjective. Puffery therefore has its articulate enemies who argue that the law has been systematically wrong in finding these falsities to be nondeceptive.[27]

In the past, higher truthfulness standards have been applied to advertising claims aimed at children,[28] especially nutrition and toy performance claims, and to other vulnerable groups.[29] It is not clear how the new FTC and congressional edicts will affect situations of this type.

Courts and commission have also been sensitive to misleading demonstrations, testimonials, and endorsements. The classic case began in 1959 when Colgate-Palmolive and its advertising agency Ted Bates presented TV ads suggesting by means of a mock-up that a shaving cream product could shave sandpaper. Seeing its case as having preventive as well as punitive purposes, the FTC stuck by its claim that viewers would be misled into thinking they were seeing an actual experiment all the way to the U.S. Supreme Court. The Court, in an opinion written by Chief Justice Warren, upheld the FTC:

> We agree with the [c]ommission that the undisclosed use of plexiglass in the present commercials, was a material deceptive practice, independent and separate from the other misrepresentation found. We find unpersuasive respondents' other objections to this conclusion. Respondents claim that it will be impractical to inform the viewing public that it is not seeing an actual test, experiment or demonstration, but we think it inconceivable that the ingenious advertising world will be unable, if it so desires, to conform to the [c]ommission's insistence that the public be not misinformed. *FTC v. Colgate-Palmolive Co.,* 380 U.S. 374 (1965).

---

25. Note, *The FTC's Reliance on Extrinsic Evidence in Cases of Deceptive Advertising: A Proposal for Interpretive Rulemaking,* 74 Neb. L. Rev. 352 (1995).

26. *Bristol-Myers Co.,* 46 F.T.C. 162 (1949), *aff'd* 185 F.2d 58 (4th Cir. 1950).

27. Preston, *The Tangled Web They Weave: Truth, Falsity, and Advertisers* (1994); Preston, *The Great American Blow-Up: Puffery in Advertising and Selling* (1975); Shimp, *Do Incomplete Comparisons Mislead?* 18 J. of Advertising 21 (1978).

28. *Topper,* FTC C–2073, and *Mattel,* FTC C–2071, 1973 CCH Transfer Binder ¶ 19,735 (1971); *Hudson Pharmaceutical Corp.,* 3 CCH Trade Reg.Rptr. ¶ 21,191 (1976), the "Spider Man" vitamins case.

29. *Doris Savitch,* 50 FTC 828 (1954), *Savitch v. FTC, aff'd per curiam* 218 F.2d 817 (2d Cir. 1955), women who fear they may be pregnant; *S.S.S. Co. v. FTC,* 416 F.2d 226 (6th Cir. 1969).

There have been few mock-up complaints since *Colgate-Palmolive,* and the commission has indicated that it will not go after smaller priced items unless public health or safety is involved. In *Bristol-Meyers Co.,* CCH 1973–76, Transfer Binder, ¶ 20,900, the 1975 "Dry Ban" case, the commission was perceived as being unwilling to pursue such supertechnical and inconsequential cases.

In *United States v. Reader's Digest,* 4 Med. L. Rptr. 2258, 464 F.Supp. 1037 (D.Del. 1978), the court proscribed "simulated checks" as a promotional device and found that the governmental interest in preventing deception outweighed *Reader's Digest's* free speech rights because regulation affected only the form of the message, not its content. The court imposed a civil penalty of $1,750,000 on *Reader's Digest.* The Third Circuit affirmed, 7 Med. L. Rptr. 1921, 662 F.2d 995 (3d Cir. 1981), and the Supreme Court let it stand, *cert. denied* 455 U.S. 908 (1982).

Claims of uniqueness have run afoul of the agency. When Wonder Bread implied in its advertising that it could cause dramatic growth in children, its makers were challenged. *In the Matter of I.T.T. Continental,* 90 F.T.C. 181 (1977).

The commission had *Sperry & Hutchinson* in mind when it decided its landmark *substantiation* case. Involved were advertisements for an ointment purporting to anesthetize nerves in sunburned skin on the basis of systematic scientific research, claims that were unsubstantiated. Affirming the decision of a hearing examiner that the commission's staff counsel had failed to establish with conclusive evidence that a cease-and-desist order should issue, FTC Chairman Miles Kirkpatrick nevertheless set the ground rules for future substantiation requirements.

> Given the imbalance of knowledge and resources between a business enterprise and each of its customers, economically it is more rational and imposes far less cost on society, to require a manufacturer to confirm his affirmative product claims rather than impose a burden upon each individual consumer to test, investigate, or experiment for himself. The manufacturer has the ability, the knowhow, the equipment, the time and the resources to undertake such information by testing or otherwise—the consumer usually does not. * * * Absent a reasonable basis for a vendor's affirmative product claims, a consumer's ability to make an economically rational product choice, and a competitor's ability to compete on the basis of price, quality, service or convenience are materially impaired and impeded. * * * The consumer is entitled, as a matter of marketplace fairness, to rely upon the manufacturer to have a "reasonable basis" for making performance claims. * * * A sale made as a result of unsupported advertising claims deprives competitors of the opportunity to have made that sale for themselves. *Pfizer, Inc.,* 81 F.T.C. 23 (1972).

"Substantial scientific test data," then, were required to support a claim that "involves a matter of human safety * * * which consumers themselves cannot verify since they have neither the equipment nor the knowledge to undertake the complicated * * * tests required [and therefore] must rely on the technical expertise of the manufacturers to assure the validity of its claims." *Firestone Tire & Rubber Co. v. FTC,* 81 F.T.C. 398, 451 (1972), *aff'd* 481 F.2d 246 (6th Cir. 1972), *cert. denied* 414 U.S. 1112 (1973).

THE REGULATORY PROCESS AND RULEMAKING

Federal Trade Commission consumer protection rules are promulgated under sec. 18 of the FTC Act (15 U.S.C. § 57a), as amended by the Magnuson-Moss Warranty—FTC Improvement Act of 1975, authorizing the commission to issue rules that "define with specificity" unfair or deceptive acts or practices proscribed by the Act.

Investigations may begin with letters from consumers or businesses, congressional inquiries, or media reports. In a pre-rulemaking investigative phase, the FTC staff gathers data to assess the seriousness of the problem. A proposal to move on to a formal investigation, which may lead to a rulemaking proceeding, must be approved by an evaluation committee of the Bureau of Consumer Protection and by that Bureau's director. The investigation then fans out to seek information from industry, state and local government officials, and knowledgeable persons generally. The FTC's Bureau of Economics is consulted. Subpoenas, with commission approval, and investigatory hearings are available in this stage, but voluntary information is preferred.

These efforts result in an initial staff report that includes findings and recommendations concerning the form of any proposed rule. This must be accompanied by a cost projection, an environmental impact assessment where needed, and a proposed initial notice of rulemaking—all approved by the Bureau of Economics—before forwarding to the commission.

An Initial Notice of proposed rulemaking includes (1) the terms or substance of the proposal or a description of the subjects and issues involved, (2) the legal authority under which the rule is proposed, (3) particular reasons for the rule, and (4) an invitation to all interested persons to propose issues within the framework of the proposal. A rulemaking proceeding begins with this invitation for comments and potential issues of disputed facts. These must be submitted within sixty days of the Initial Notice, and written comments are accepted until forty-five days before an informal hearing takes place.

A hearing officer then designates the disputed issues in a final notice, together with the hearing schedule, and deadlines for filing written comments and indications of interest to engage in examination, cross-examination, and rebuttal of witnesses. Ten days after publication of the final notice, interested persons may petition the commission for addition to, deletion from, or modification of a designated issue. An additional ten days are set aside for more submissions.

Hearings are held. A final staff report and a report by the presiding officer, who may be an administrative law judge and who has broad powers to make findings and conclusions, are forwarded to the commission. Both are open to public comment for a period of sixty days. After digesting these public comments, the commission may hold an open meeting at which interested parties are given a final limited opportunity to make oral presentations to the commission. Beyond this, the staff may add specialized memoranda, and counterproposals could come from the Bureau of Consumer Protection. The commission then deliberates and decides whether or not a rule shall issue. Once a rule is adopted, it is enforceable in the same way that a statute is.

RULE VIOLATIONS Federal Trade Commission actions against rule violations may begin with complaints from members of the public, but more frequently, they arise out of a commission investigation. The agency has broad investigatory powers and authority to enforce its own subpoenas. At an early point, the FTC may waive its right to bring a court action against a violator in return for consumer redress provisions in a *consent agreement,* provisions that could go beyond the statutory authority of the courts. The commission has noted that voluntary compliance through a consent agreement does not constitute an admission by respondents that they have violated the law. When issued by the commission on a final basis, a consent order carries the force of law with respect to future actions. It has the same effect as an FTC adjudication. Violation of such an order could result in a civil penalty of up to $10,000 per violation per day. Each broadcast of an advertisment may constitute a separate violation.

Adverse publicity and high litigation costs assure that more than 75 percent of cases will end this way. Since 1977, however, the FTC has had the power to ask an advertiser or its agency, during the sixty-day comment period, for documentary material related to the published consent order if releasable under the Freedom of Information Act. This could make consent agreements less attractive to advertisers.

CONSENT AGREEMENTS Consent agreements, incorporating refunds or other forms of equitable relief, are a major enforcement result of the Magnuson-Moss Act. Under the Act, consumer protection rules can be vigorously enforced. If the commission has reason to believe that the FTC Act or another federal consumer statute has been violated, an administrative complaint may initiate a *cease-and-desist* order.

A respondent then had the right to appear before an administrative law judge and show cause why such an order should not be made. An administrative law judge's order may be appealed to the full commission. If unsuccessful, that party would have sixty days to challenge a commission order in a federal court of appeals. The cease-and-desist order would not become effective until all stages in the process have been exhausted. This could take a long time. The commission took sixteen years to get the "Liver" out of Carter's Little Pills,[30] and in 1959, the year that case was concluded, the FTC began an investigation of Geritol. A complaint was issued in 1962, a cease-and-desist order in 1964; the Sixth Circuit Court of Appeals upheld the

---

30. *Carter Products, Inc. v. FTC,* 268 F.2d 461 (9th Cir. 1959), cert. denied 361 U.S. 884 (1959).

commission in 1967,[31] but two years later, finding the company in noncompliance, the commission turned the case over to the Department of Justice. Justice filed a $1 million suit against the company and in 1973 fined it and its advertising agency $812,000. In the intervening fourteen years, Geritol had spent an estimated $60 million on television advertising.

Under Magnuson-Moss, in lieu of cease-and-desist orders, rules are now directly enforceable in a U.S. district court with civil penalties of up to $10,000 per day per violation, plus consumer redress. Industry-wide Trade Regulation Rules may be enforced in the same manner.

Violations of cease-and-desist orders or other final orders of the commission empower district courts to grant temporary restraining orders or preliminary injunctions. In some cases the commission may seek and, after proof, a court may issue a permanent injunction. Injunctions are more common in antitrust cases than in consumer protection cases.

There has been some confusion over the legal standard that the FTC must meet to obtain an injunction. Prior to 1973, the apparent standard was whether there was "reason to believe" an advertisement was false or misleading. *FTC v. Rhodes Pharmacal Co.,* 191 F.2d 744 (7th Cir. 1951). A 1973 amendment to the FTC Act required a showing that the agency was likely to succeed on its claim, and also that the injunction was in the public interest. *National Commission on Egg Nutrition v. FTC,* 3 Med. L. Rptr. 2196, 570 F.2d 157 (7th Cir. 1977), *cert. denied* 439 U.S. 821 (1978). One court held that the FTC must show falsity to obtain an injunction, *FTC v. Simeon Management Corp.,* 532 F.2d 708 (9th Cir. 1976). The present FTC test would appear to meet the standard of the 1973 amendment.

Injunctions and other direct FTC actions are more likely to be triggered when consumer frauds involving foods, drugs, medical devices, and cosmetics are involved and where a violation is clear and immediately harmful. The Food and Drug Administration (FDA) has authority over the labeling of these kinds of products under the Food, Drug, and Cosmetic Act of 1938 (21 U.S.C.A. §§ 301–392). Recent regulatory issues

involving food labeling and limits on cigarette marketing and sales were in fact spearheaded by the Department of Agriculture and the FDA.[32]

In all, some twenty federal agencies regulate advertising in specifically defined areas. These agencies include the Securities and Exchange Commission, the Alcohol and Tobacco Tax Division of the Internal Revenue Service, the Civil Aeronautics Board, and the Federal Power Commission.

STATE REGULATION Most states except Alabama and the District of Columbia, Guam, Puerto Rico, and the U.S. Virgin Islands have "Little FTC" acts, paralleling to some degree the federal statute's sec. 5 proscription against unfair or deceptive trade practices. Some are as broad as sec. 5 itself. Others reach unfair or deceptive acts or practices but not unfair methods of competition. Still others reach only a specific list of prohibited practices. These "Little FTC" acts are drawn from a model statute, the Unfair Trade Practices and Consumer Protection Law, which was proposed by the FTC itself.[33] Many states also have provisions that largely track those of the Urban Deceptive Trade Practices Act (UDTPA).

Remedies vary. A number of states grant rule-making power to a state official, often the attorney general, who may bring suit to stop violations of the state law. By this route, consumers may gain restitution in most jurisdictions, while the state gains additional civil penalties in others.

The laws of nearly all of these jurisdictions authorize the use of subpoenas in civil investigations and the use of cease-and-desist orders or court injunctions to halt anticompetitive, unfair, unconscionable, or deceptive practices. Some jurisdictions permit class actions, and most jurisdictions allow *private actions by consumers.* Private actions are generally not allowed under the FTC Act's sec. 5.

Most state laws have been influenced by federal law and have been enacted relatively recently. The paucity of state court interpretations of these state statutes ensures that guidance

---

31. *J. B. Williams Co., Inc. v. FTC,* 381 F.2d 884 (6th Cir. 1967).

32. Choi, "The Constitutionality of the FDA's Tobacco Restrictions as a First Amendment Issue" (March 1997) (unpublished manuscript).

33. McManis, Unfair Trade Practices 3d ed. 353–354 (1992).

will be sought from administrative and judicial decisions under the federal act. Nearly half of state laws specifically encourage this.

The possibility of double or treble actual damages and punitive damages, and some attorney's fees and costs provides an incentive to litigate under state laws. Expectations are that state courts will eventually adopt the standards of the FTC Trade Practice Rules, the Trade Regulation Rules, and the concepts of other federal protection statutes enforced by the FTC. At least thirty-five states use federal standards in enforcing state food and drug laws.

The media are not liable for unlawful advertisements or injuries resulting from defective products,[34] and they have no duty to investigate each advertiser, even when placed on notice as to potential danger.[35] A problem can arise, however, if a publication plays an active role in a false and deceptive ad or specifically endorses a product. Indemnification clauses are now common in rate cards and advertising contracts, especially with regard to errors or omissions in ads, but they probably wouldn't protect a publication in the negligent preparation of an ad.

CORRECTIVE ADVERTISING

Corrective advertising, a powerful regulatory device, first came to the attention of the FTC in May 1970 when a group called SOUP (Students Opposing Unfair Practices) intervened in an action against the Campbell Soup Company in a situation reminiscent of the *Colgate-Palmolive* sandpaper case. Campbell had used marbles in its video advertising to make its soup appear thicker than it was. No order requiring corrective advertising was issued for lack of a significant public interest, but the commission made its point. *Campbell Soup,* 3 Trade Reg. Rptr. ¶ 19,261 (FTC May 25, 1970).

The FTC first sought corrective advertising in late 1970 in actions charging Coca-Cola with misrepresenting the nutritional value of Hi-C and Standard Oil of California with falsely claiming that its gasoline reduced air pollution.[36] Both complaints were later dropped.

The difference between a traditional order for affirmative disclosure and one for corrective advertising is that the corrective ad order refers to past rather than current advertising and is designed to dispel misconceptions the consumer may have gained from earlier ads. Although the commission may not impose criminal penalties or award compensatory damages for past acts, it does have a mandate to prevent illegal practices in the future.[37] A corrective order may remind consumers that a particular advertiser is a hard-core offender.

After a flurry of cases a hiatus occurred in corrective advertising partly because the somewhat ponderous process could not keep up with the fluid and ingenious advertising industry: ads were challenged long after they had served the purposes of advertisers. Then in 1975, in the first litigated corrective advertising case, an administrative law judge was upheld by the full commission in forbidding Warner-Lambert, the makers of Listerine, to advertise unless each ad included the following language: "Contrary to prior advertising, Listerine will not help prevent colds or sore throats or lessen their severity." *Warner-Lambert Co.,* 86 F.T.C. 1938 (1975). The corrective advertising was to continue until the company had spent $10 million on Listerine advertising, an amount roughly equal to the annual Listerine budget for 1962 to 1974. In the opinion that follows, the D.C. Circuit Court of Appeals affirmed the commission decision with the words "contrary to prior advertising" deleted.

Warner-Lambert Co. v. Federal Trade Commission

2 MED. L. RPTR. 2303, 562 F.2D 749 (D.C. CIR. 1977), CERT. DENIED, 435 U.S. 950 (1978).

WRIGHT, Circuit Judge:

* * *

The first issue on appeal is whether the Commission's conclusion that Listerine is not beneficial

---

34. *Goldstein v. Garlick* 318 N.Y.S. 2d 370 (1971); *Suarez v. Underwood,* 426 N.Y.S. 2d 208 (1980).
35. *Hernandez v. Underwood,* 7 Med. L. Rptr. 1535 (N.Y.Sup.Ct. 1981); *Pressler v. Dow Jones & Co., Inc.,* 8 Med. L. Rptr. 1680, 450 N.Y.S.2d 884 (N.Y.Sup.Ct., App.Div. 1982).
36. *Coca-Cola Co.,* 3 Trade Reg.Rptr. ¶ 19,351 (FTC 1970); *Standard Oil Co. of California,* 3 Trade Reg.Rptr. ¶ 19,352 (FTC 1970).
37. *FTC v. Ruberoid Co.,* 343 U.S. 470 (1952).

for colds or sore throats is supported by the evidence. The Commission's findings must be sustained if they are supported by substantial evidence on the record viewed as a whole. We conclude that they are.

Both the ALJ [Administrative Law Judge] and the Commission carefully analyzed the evidence. They gave full consideration to the studies submitted by petitioner. The ultimate conclusion that Listerine is not an effective cold remedy was based on six specific findings of fact.

* * *

Petitioner contends that even if its advertising claims in the past were false, the portion of the Commission's order requiring "corrective advertising" exceeds the Commission's statutory power. The argument is based upon a literal reading of Section 5 of the Federal Trade Commission Act, which authorizes the Commission to issue "cease and desist" orders against violators and does not expressly mention any other remedies. The Commission's position, on the other hand, is that the affirmative disclosure that Listerine will not prevent colds or lessen their severity is absolutely necessary to give effect to the prospective cease and desist order; a hundred years of false cold claims have built up a large reservoir of erroneous consumer belief which would persist, unless corrected, long after petitioner ceased making the claims.

The need for the corrective advertising remedy and its appropriateness in this case are important issues which we will explore. But the threshold question is whether the Commission has the authority to issue such an order. We hold that it does.

Petitioner's narrow reading of Section 5 was at one time shared by the Supreme Court. In *FTC v. Eastman Kodak Co.,* 274 U.S. 619, 623 (1927), the Court held that the Commission's authority did not exceed that expressly conferred by statute. The Commission has not, the Court said, "been delegated the authority of a court of equity."

But the modern view is very different. In 1963 the Court ruled that the Civil Aeronautics Board has authority to order divestiture in addition to ordering cessation of unfair methods of competition by air carriers. *Pan American World Airways, Inc. v. United States,* 371 U.S. 296 (1963). The CAB statute, like Section 5, spoke only of the authority to issue cease and desist orders. * * *

"Authority to mold administrative decrees is indeed like the authority of courts to frame injunctive decrees. * * * [The] power to order divestiture need not be explicitly included in the powers of an administrative agency to be part of its arsenal of authority. * * *"

Later, in *FTC v. Dean Foods Co.,* 384 U.S.. 597 (1966), the Court applied *Pan American* to the Federal Trade Commission. In upholding the Commission's power to seek a preliminary injunction against a proposed merger, the Court held that it was not necessary to find express statutory authority for the power. Rather, the Court concluded, "It would stultify congressional purpose to say that the Commission did not have the * * * power * * *. Such ancillary powers have always been treated as essential to the effective discharge of the Commission's responsibilities."

Thus it is clear that the Commission has the power to shape remedies which go beyond the simple cease and desist order. Our next inquiry must be whether a corrective advertising order is for any reason outside the range of permissible remedies. Petitioner and *amici curiae* argue that it is because (1) legislative history precludes it, (2) it impinges on the First Amendment, and (3) it has never been approved by any court.

* * *

We conclude that this legislative history cannot be said to remove corrective advertising from the class of permissible remedies.

Petitioner and *amici* further contend that corrective advertising is not a permissible remedy because it trenches on the First Amendment. *Petitioner is correct that this triggers a special responsibility on the Commission to order corrective advertising only if the restriction inherent in its order is no greater than necessary to serve the interest involved.* [Emphasis added.] But this goes to the appropriateness of the order in this case, an issue we reach [later in] this opinion. *Amici curiae* go further, arguing that, since the Supreme Court has recently extended First Amendment protection to commercial advertising, mandatory corrective advertising is unconstitutional.

A careful reading of *Virginia State Bd. of Pharmacy v. Virginia Citizens Consumer Council* compels rejection of this argument. For the Supreme Court expressly noted that the First Amendment presents "no obstacle" to government regulation of false or misleading advertising. The First Amendment, the Court said,

> as we construe it today, does not prohibit the State from insuring that the stream of commercial information flow[s] cleanly as well as freely.

The Supreme Court clearly foresaw the very question before us, and its statement is dispositive of *amici's* contention.

According to petitioner, "The first reference to corrective advertising in Commission decisions occurred in 1970, nearly fifty years and untold numbers of false advertising cases after passage of the Act." In petitioner's view, the late emergence of this "newly discovered" remedy is itself evidence that it is beyond the Commission's authority. This argument fails on two counts. First the fact that an agency has not asserted a power over a period of years is not proof that the agency lacks such power. Second, and more importantly, we are not convinced that the corrective advertising remedy is really such an innovation. The label may be newly coined, but the concept is well established. It is simply that under certain circumstances an advertiser may be required to make affirmative disclosure of unfavorable facts.

One such circumstance is when an advertisement that did not contain the disclosure would be misleading. For example, the Commission has ordered the sellers of treatments for baldness to disclose that the vast majority of cases of thinning hair and baldness are attributable to heredity, age, and endocrine balance (so-called "male pattern baldness") and that their treatment would have no effect whatever on this type of baldness. It has ordered the promoters of a device for stopping bedwetting to disclose that the device would not be of value in cases caused by organic defects or diseases. And it has ordered the makers of Geritol, an iron supplement, to disclose that Geritol will relieve symptoms of tiredness only in persons who suffer from iron deficiency anemia, and that the vast majority of people who experience such symptoms do not have such a deficiency.

Each of these orders was approved on appeal over objections that it exceeded the Commission's statutory authority. The decisions reflect a recognition that, as the Supreme Court has stated,

> If the Commission is to attain the objectives Congress envisioned, it cannot be required to confine

its road block to the narrow lane the transgressor has traveled; it must be allowed effectively to close all roads to the prohibited goal, so that its order may not be by-passed with impunity. FTC v. Ruberoid Co., 343 U.S. 470, 473 (1952).

* * *

Listerine has built up over a period of many years a widespread reputation. When it was ascertained that the reputation no longer applied to the product, it was necessary to take action to correct it. Here * * *it is the accumulated impact of *past* advertising that necessitates disclosure in *future* advertising. * * *

Having established that the Commission does have the power to order corrective advertising in appropriate cases, it remains to consider whether use of the remedy against Listerine is warranted and equitable. We have concluded that part 3 of the order should be modified to delete the phrase "Contrary to prior advertising." With that modification, we approve the order.

* * *

We turn next to the specific disclosure required: "Contrary to prior advertising, Listerine will not help prevent colds or sore throats or lessen their severity." Petitioner is ordered to include this statement in every future advertisement for Listerine for a defined period. In printed advertisements it must be displayed in type size at least as large as that in which the principal portion of the text of the advertisement appears and it must be separated from the text so that it can be readily noticed. In television commercials the disclosure must be presented simultaneously in both audio and visual portions. During the audio portion of the disclosure in television and radio advertisements, no other sounds, including music, may occur.

These specifications are well calculated to assure that the disclosure will reach the public. It will necessarily attract the notice of readers, viewers, and listeners, and be plainly conveyed. Given these safeguards, we believe the preamble "Contrary to prior advertising" is not necessary. It can serve only two purposes: either to attract attention that a correction follows or to humiliate the advertiser. * * *

The formula settled upon by the Commission is reasonably related to the violation it found.

Accordingly, the order, as modified, is Affirmed.

COMMENT

Judge Robb dissented because he believed the FTC had been conferred power only to prevent future deceptions or to impose a prospective remedy. Corrective advertising constituted a retrospective remedy, a remedy for past claims.

It has been urged that corrective orders not be confined to obvious cases such as *Warner-Lambert* where the proof presented to the commission of the success of a deceptive campaign is so striking. Noting the long history of a deceptive claim uniquely asserted for Listerine, the absence of consumer confusion as to which mouthwash was said to be effective against colds, and the persuasive evidence that consumers believed this claim after the false advertising had ceased, one commentator observed that "comparable proof of deception-perception-memory influence would be virtually impossible in most advertising cases. * * * If the commission is to do an effective job in regulating deceptive advertising, corrective advertising must apply to more than the one-in-a-million type of ad campaign present in *Warner-Lambert*." See Pitofsky, *Beyond Nader: Consumer Protection and the Regulation of Advertising,* 90 Harv.L.Rev. 661, 698 (1977).

What evidence established whether false claims about product characteristics create persistent misimpressions or other continuing effects and of what strength and duration? And what forms of corrective advertising would correct misimpressions? Answers to these kinds of factual questions should precede legal and policy considerations.

COMPARATIVE ADVERTISING If consumers deserve anything under either classical or contemporary theories of the First Amendment, it is fair and truthful comparative advertising.[38]

Courts have held it to be "in harmony with the fundamental objectives of free speech and free enterprise in a free society."[39] The FTC has endorsed it.[40]

Comparative advertising has exploded in the almost twenty years since the courts signaled that it is a good thing.[41] It appears that almost all parties agree that making direct comparisons between the products and services of competitors results in better information for consumers. Two problems arise, however. First, a comparative ad must use the brand names and trademarks of competitors, but businesses tend to get touchy when anyone else uses their exclusive markers. Second, the value to consumers of comparative advertising depends on the reliability of the comparison. If an advertisement misrepresents either the company advertised or a competitor named in the ad, consumers may be duped into making bad decisions.

The comparative advertising boom came during the 1980s when the FTC was rather inactive. Companies decided to attempt private actions rather than to press complaints with the FTC. Section 43(a) of the Lanham Act forbade a "false description or representation" in connection with the use of a trademark or service mark when a "person believes that he is or is likely to be damaged by the use of any such false description or representation."[42] One of the first cases to test whether comparative advertising claims could result in private damages shook the advertising world—and put the offending competitor out of business.

U-Haul International, Inc. v. Jartran, Inc.

793 F.2D 1034 (9TH CIR. 1986).

SNEED, Circuit Judge:

FACTS

The U-Haul System has dominated the self-move consumer rental industry for many years.

---

38. Defined by Leonard Orkin, Practising Law Institute, Legal and Business Problems of the Advertising Industry 1978, p. 304 as "Advertisements which direct the prospective customer's attention to similarities or differences between the advertised product and one or more competitors either explicitly or implicitly." Pompeo, *To Tell the Truth: Comparative Advertising and Lanham Act Secton 43(a),* 36 Cath. U. L. Rev. 565 (1987); Hasegawa, "Meeting the Public and Private Interest in Comparative Commercial Speech," paper presented to the Law Division, Association for Education in Journalism and Mass Communication, Montreal, Quebec, August 1992. See also Sterk, *The Law of Comparative Advertising: How Much Worse Is "Better" Than "Great."* 76 Columbia L.Rev. 80 (1976)

39. *Triangle Publications v. Knight-Ridder Newspapers,* 3 Med. L. Rptr. 2086, 445 F.Supp. 875 (S.D.Fla. 1978).
40. The FTC recommended comparative advertising on August 13, 1979 in 44 Fed.Reg. 4738.
41. Beller *The Law of Comparative Advertising in the United States and around the World: A Practical Guide for U.S. Lawyers and Their Clients,* 29 Int'l Law. 917 (1995).
42. 15 U.S.C.A. § 1125 (West 1982).

In mid-1979, Jartran entered that market on a national basis. It engaged in a nationwide newspaper advertising campaign comparing itself to U-Haul. The campaign lasted from the summer of 1979 to December of 1980 and included advertisements in forty-one states and the District of Columbia. While Jartran's revenues increased from $7 million in 1979 to $80 million in 1980, revenues of the U-Haul System declined for the first time in its history, from $395 to $378 million. The tremendous success of the advertisements is demonstrated not only by the financial growth of Jartran, but also by Jartran's receipt of the prestigious "Gold Effie" award, which the American Marketing Association awards annually in recognition of effective advertising campaigns.

The relations between U-Haul and the other entities that use the U-Haul trademark and make up what we designate as the U-Haul System are important to the understanding of the issues raised by this appeal. The plaintiff in this action, U-Haul International, Inc., owns the U-Haul trademark and operates both as a clearinghouse for distribution of U-Haul trucks and trailers and as a provider of accounting services to various entities. It does not, however, own the trucks and trailers. Most of these are rented to U-Haul by a variety of entities and individuals (the Fleet Owners). U-Haul's corporate parent is AMERCO, a holding company, which owns 100% of both U-Haul International, Inc. and the 97 U-Haul Rental Companies, each of the latter of which has an exclusive geographic region of service. The final members of the U-Haul system are the 6700 U-Haul Rental Dealers, local businessmen who have contracts with the geographically appropriate U-Haul Rental Company.

Each of these various parties receives a share of the revenue from any transaction in which it (or its equipment) is involved.

* * *

This litigation commenced on June 16, 1980, when U-Haul filed suit seeking damages and an injunction against further advertisement. * * * [I]n the spring of 1983, the district court tried the full case and found in favor of U-Haul under both the Lanham Act and the common law.

The district judge calculated damages with respect to each claim under two distinct methods. The first method relied on revenue projections for the U-Haul System as a whole. Those projections indicated that the U-Haul System experienced a substantial revenue shortfall because of the Jartran advertisements. Relying on this evidence, the district court awarded $20 million in actual damages. The second theory relied on the cost of the advertising campaign to Jartran, $6 million, and the cost of corrective advertising by the U-Haul System, $13.6 million. This also produced an award of $20 million. On the Lanham Act count, the district court doubled the $20 million under section 35 of the Lanham Act; on the common-law count, it awarded $20 million in punitive damages. Thus, the district court reached a $40 million verdict with respect to each claim. Only one recovery of full compensation is permissible, however.

* * *

LIABILITY

Jartran raises three challenges to the district judge's conclusion that Jartran is liable to U-Haul. First, it argues that the injury suffered by U-Haul was insufficiently direct to support a recovery under the Lanham Act. Second, it argues that the actual deception and reliance of consumers can be proved only by surveys of actual consumers. Finally, it argues that it is inappropriate to presume actual deception and reliance from proof of Jartran's intent to deceive. Because we reject the first and third challenges, we affirm the district court's findings of deception and reliance. Addressing the second challenge thus becomes unnecessary.

A. Directness of Injury

Jartran's basic complaint is that much of the injury in question was suffered by the other members of the U-Haul System, rather than by U-Haul itself. Relying on antitrust precedents, it argues that U-Haul cannot recover for these injuries. Our real-party-in-interest holdings may rob these precedents of force. If, on remand, the other members of the System are joined in or ratify U-Haul's action and their inclusion is related back, this contention would become moot.

B. Presumption of Consumer Deception and Reliance

In Conclusion of Law 10, the district court held that "[p]ublication of deliberately false comparative claims gives rise to a presumption of actual deception and reliance. Defendants have not rebutted this presumption." *U-Haul International, Inc. v. Jartran, Inc.,* 601 F.Supp. 1140, 1149 (D.Ariz.1984). Jartran argues that this conclusion is not supported by the law of this circuit.

To support the district court's conclusion, U-Haul cites a false advertising case granting injunctive relief, *McNeilab, Inc. v. American Home Products Corp.,* 501 F.Supp. 517 (S.D.N.Y.1980), and two of our "palming off" cases granting damages, *National Van Lines v. Dean,* 237 F.2d 688, 692 (9th Cir. 1956); *National Lead Co. v. Wolfe,* 223 F.2d 195, 202, 205 (9th Cir.), *cert. denied,* 350 U.S. 883 (1955). Jartran responds by pointing out that *McNeilab* was an injunction case, in which the burden of proof is substantially lower, and that the two "palming off" cases are not comparative advertising cases as is this one.

Jartran's distinctions do not undermine the force of U-Haul's argument. It is not easy to establish actual consumer deception through direct evidence. The expenditure by a competitor of substantial funds in an effort to deceive consumers and influence their purchasing decisions justifies the existence of a presumption that consumers are, in fact, being deceived. He who has attempted to deceive should not complain when required to bear the burden of rebutting a presumption that he succeeded.

The district judge's application of this presumption was fair and in keeping with our early "palming off" precedents. We hold that it was correct to apply it in this context.

CALCULATION OF THE AWARD

Jartran raises numerous challenges to the district court's calculation of the award. Because the court, quite helpfully, fixed the same amount of the award under two distinct theories, we must affirm the award if it is proper under either theory. We hold that the calculation of the award based on U-Haul's corrective-advertising-expenditures theory, as enhanced under section 35 of the Lanham Act, was correct.

A. Calculation of Damages

Jartran does not dispute the propriety of basing a damage award on corrective advertising expenditures. * * * Jartran does argue, however, that the

district court did not have discretion to award damages for corrective advertising expenditures more than twice the size of the original advertising expenditures. Jartran relies on *Big O Tire Dealers, Inc. v. Goodyear Tire & Rubber Co.,* 561 F.2d 1365, 1375 (10th Cir.1977), *cert. dismissed under Sup.Ct.R. 60,* 434 U.S. 1052 (1978). There the court reversed a jury verdict and held that the plaintiff's recovery for corrective advertising was limited to 25% of the defendant's wrongful expenditures. *Big O,* however, is plainly inapplicable. It explicitly distinguishes itself from the plentiful earlier precedent allowing recovery of *actual* corrective advertising expenditures. In *Big O* the plaintiff had not made any corrective advertising expenditures. * * * It provides no basis for overturning the district court's award in this case of actual corrective advertising expenditures.

Jartran's complaints as to the propriety of U-Haul's corrective advertising campaign should have been addressed to the district court. That court did consider arguments that the advertising was not necessary to correct harm to the U-Haul trademark; but it rejected them. We agree with the district court's conclusion.

B. Extraordinary Remedies under Lanham Act Section 35

Jartran attacks the district court's award, under section 35 of the Lanham Act, 15 U.S.C. § 1117, of Jartran's profits from false advertising, double damages, and attorney fees. Jartran's position is supported by the text of the section, which applies only to "a violation of any right of the registrant of a mark registered in the Patent and Trademark Office." U-Haul's trademark is not so registered.

Jartran, however, confronts the fact that these remedies have been held by this court to be available in actions under Lanham Act § 43(a). * * * In an earlier case we explained: "[W]e can see no reason to distinguish between registered and unregistered trademarks. . . . The type of conduct that these damages should deter is unrelated to the type of intellectual property protected." Jartran tries to distinguish this case on two grounds. First, that it is not a false advertising case. Second, that our decision in *Transgo,* 768 F.2d 1001 (9th Cir. 1985), expressly limited its holding to the attorneys' fee remedy, refusing to address the other remedies provided by section 35.

Neither argument is persuasive. Not only do we see no significant distinction between false advertising cases and other cases under Lanham Act § 43(a), *see id.,* but also the rationale for the *Transgo* decision, *viz.* the need for remedial consistency in the recovery of attorneys' fees, is no less pressing when a court considers awarding damages and unlawful profits. We hold that the district court was correct in applying section 35 to this case.

Finally, Jartran contends that the district court should not have included the $6 million cost of its advertising campaign as "profits" within the meaning of Lanham Act § 35 because Jartran did not make a profit during the relevant period. It is irrelevant that Jartran *as a whole* failed to turn a profit during the period of the advertising. The amount to be awarded is the financial benefit Jartran received because of the advertising. * * * The district court assumed that the financial benefit was at least equal to the advertising expenditures. Considering the detailed evidence that the court had of Jartran's swift revenue growth and the connection of that growth to Jartran's advertising, that finding is not clearly erroneous. We affirm the district court's award.

INJUNCTION

In Conclusion of Law 34, the district court held that U-Haul was entitled to a permanent injunction against Jartran's future publication of the "advertisements found to be false and deceptive in this proceeding." 601 F.Supp. at 1151. The district court was correct in granting this injunctive relief. Nothing is clearer in the emerging law of commercial free speech than that false or misleading commercial speech is clearly "subject to restraint." * * *

But the language of the injunction is much broader than the Conclusion of Law and, perhaps unintentionally, raises First Amendment concerns. As currently written, the injunction seems to prohibit future comparative advertising even if it is truthful. We are mindful of our obligation to prevent Jartran from misleading the public in the future with its deceptive ads. But we can fulfill that obligation while protecting Jartran's First Amendment rights—and simultaneously increase the "informed and reliable decisionmaking" that honest advertising can provide.

Affirmed in part; modified in part; reversed in part; and remanded for further proceedings.

COMMENT

Note that the plaintiff benefited from the statutory damage provisions of the Lanham Act. U-Haul received profits from Jartran, the $20 million damage award was doubled, and its attorneys' fees were paid. The message that comparative advertising had to use accurate, contextually relevant, and fair information about competitors was loud and clear.[43]

Section 43(a) of the Lanham Act was amended in 1988.[44] A new section, (a)(1)(B), bars the use of trade names and symbols that,

> in commercial advertising or promotion, misrepresents the nature, characteristics, qualities, or geographic origin of his or another person's goods, services, or commercial activities,

Besides creating a broad cause of action for competitors, the language appears to allow citizens to act as "private" attorneys general in bringing actions. The net result has been to encourage actions of this type. An unintended result is that the amendment has given trademark owners a potent weapon to use against the news and entertainment media when marks are used in news, editorials, or comedy.[45]

SELF-REGULATION   Advertising has developed the most impressive self-regulatory system in all of mass communication. The spearhead of self-regulation in advertising is the National Advertising Review Board, which acts on consumer and industry complaints about truth and accuracy in national advertising. National advertisers, delegates from advertising agencies, and representatives of the public comprise the Board's membership. It is sponsored by the American Advertising Federation, the American Association of Advertising Agencies, the Association of National Advertisers, and the Council of Better Business Bureaus. Complaints are handled initially by an investigating staff of

---

43. Best, *Monetary Damages for False Advertising,* 49 U. Pitt. L. Rev. 1 (1987).
44. 15 U.S.C.A. § 1125 (West Supp. 1993).
45. Leatherbury, *Media Law: Explosion of Lanham Act Cases,* Comm. Law., Vol. 14, No. 1, 1, 16–18 (Spring 1996).

the Council of Better Business Bureaus called the National Advertising Division (NAD). A query from the NAD can lead major national advertisers to modify or discontinue unsubstantiated advertising claims. The NAD monitors and advises and, in unresolved cases, carries appeals to the National Advertising Review Board (NARB). If an advertiser remains recalcitrant after an NARB panel reaches an adverse decision, the NARB will notify the appropriate government agency. This is seldom necessary. Of approximately 150 complaints made annually, half are found to have merit. Compliance with NAD recommendations is nearly perfect.

Individual newspapers and broadcast stations and the networks have their own advertising acceptability or broadcast standards departments. Network standards previously were considered higher than those of the legal regulators. In the late 1980s, however, standards and practices divisions of the three original networks experienced large staff cutbacks. Given network fare in the late 1990s, some would say standards themselves have been cut back.

Much of interest and importance is omitted from this brief account of some of advertising's legal problems. The Practising Law Institute's *Advertising Compliance Handbook* (2d ed. 1991) by Plevan and Siroky is an invaluable comprehensive reference. So too is Rosden and Rosden, *Law of Advertising* (1993).

Legal or Public Notice Advertising

The major premise of public notice advertising is that citizens should have an opportunity to know what the laws are, to be notified when their rights or property are to be affected, and to be apprised of how the administration of their government is being conducted. State laws define the classifications of information requiring promulgation. These may include statutes and ordinances, governmental proceedings, articles of incorporation, registration of titles, probate matters, notices of election, appropriation of public funds, tax notices, bids for public works, and judicial orders—this list is by no means exhaustive.

State laws also define the qualifications a newspaper must possess to carry public notices and how legally qualified and/or "official" newspapers are to be selected. See *New Jersey Subur-*

banite v. State, 384 A.2d 831 (N.J. 1978). Here the state supreme court denied review when a free distribution shopper challenged a state law restricting legal advertising to newspapers with a paid circulation, average news content of 35 percent, and a second-class mailing permit in effect for at least two years. The number of times a public notice is to be published and how publication is to be certified and paid for are generally statutory matters. Publications will make great efforts to qualify as the sort of newspaper allowed to carry public notice advertisements under state law. In one case, a paper that was inserted into another publication, then circulated, sought qualification and was refused.[46] Omission by a publication of legal notices it had agreed to run cannot result in liability, at least where the omission was inadvertent.[47]

"Official" and legally qualified newspapers are usually required to be stable publications of general and paid-for circulation, of general news coverage and general availability, printed in English, appearing frequently and regularly, and meeting specified minimum conditions of technical excellence. Close interpretation of state statutes has led to certain exceptions being made for specialized urban publications, known as commercial newspapers, which are designed to deal with the large volume of legal advertising that typical daily newspapers would find unprofitable. These interpretations have not gone unchallenged. See *King County v. Superior Court in and for King County,* 92 P.2d 694 (Wash. 1939); *In re Sterling Cleaners & Dyers, Inc.,* 81 F.2d 596 (7th Cir. 1936).

The Supreme Court has held that publication by newspaper will not constitute adequate notice to parties in litigation and will thus deny due process unless the notice is reasonably calculated actually to reach all the parties.[48] The rule of the case has been extended to many situations in which an individual might stand to lose something of value.[49]

---

46. *Gulf Coast Media v. Mobile Press Register,* 11 Med. L. Rptr. 2347, 470 So.2d 1211 (Alabama 1985).
47. *Indiana Construction Corp. v. Chicago Tribune,* 13 Med. L. Rptr. 1863, 648 F.Supp. 1419 (N.D.Ind. 1986).
48. *Mullane v. Central Hanover Bank & Trust Co.,* Trustee, 339 U.S. 306 (1950).
49. See *Walker v. City of Hutchinson,* 352 U.S. 112 (1956) (condemnation proceeding).

Finally, a newspaper does not have to accept public notice advertising; *Wooster v. Mahaska County*, 98 N.W. 103 (Iowa 1904); *Commonwealth v. Boston Transcript Co.*, 144 N.E. 400 (1924), but, if it does, it must comply with the statutory requirements of publication. *Belleville Advocate Printing Co. v. St. Clair County*, 168 N.E. 312 (Ill. 1929). Although issues surrounding legal or public notice advertising have been analyzed many times over the years, the importance of this source of revenue to publications still leads to quite a number of suits. See, e.g., *San Diego Daily Transcript v. San Diego Commerce*, 24 Med. L. Rptr. 1276, 40 Cal.App.4th 1229, 47 Cal.Rptr.2d 303 (1995).

Media Rights to Refuse and Control the Conditions of Advertising

In spite of First Amendment victories for commercial speech, the media have compromised none of their rights of control over access and display of advertising. They may refuse advertising and dictate the conditions of its sale.

In 1965 a Florida appeals court held that "in the absence of any statutory provisions to the contrary, the law seems to be uniformly settled by the great weight of authority throughout the United States that the newspaper publishing business is a private enterprise and is neither a public utility nor affected with the public interest. The decisions appear to hold that even though a particular newspaper may enjoy a virtual monopoly in the area of its publication, this fact is neither unusual nor of important significance. The courts have consistently held that in the absence of statutory regulation on the subject, a newspaper may publish or reject commercial advertising tendered to it as its judgment best dictates without incurring liability for advertisements rejected by it." *Approved Personnel, Inc. v. Tribune Co.*, 177 So.2d 704 (Fla. 1965).

An exception to the rule may be newspapers or periodicals that raise the issue of "state action," because they can be defined as publicly supported channels. See *Zucker v. Panitz*, 299 F.Supp. 102 (D.N.Y. 1969); *Lee v. Board of Regents of State Colleges*, 306 F.Supp. 1097 (E.D.Wis. 1969), *aff'd* 1 Med. L. Rptr. 1947, 441 F.2d 1257 (7th Cir. 1971). But see *Mississippi Gay Alliance v. Goudelock*, 536 F.2d 1073 (5th Cir. 1976), *cert. denied* 430 U.S. 982

(1977), and *AIDS Action Committee of Massachusetts, Inc. v. Massachusetts Bay Transportation Authority*, 22 Med. L. Rptr. 2449, 42 F.3d 1 (1st Cir. 1994).

A state university newspaper's refusal to run advertisements stating a person's sexual orientation was permissible because the paper was not a public forum. The refusal was protected as an editorial decision. *Sinn v. Daily Nebraskan*, 12 Med. L. Rptr. 2340, 638 F.Supp. 143 (D.Neb. 1986).

A court relied on *Tornillo*, text, p. 469, when denying an injunction to a plaintiff whose "tombstone advertisements" announcing an offer of shares in a pending lawsuit were rejected by a newspaper. The injunction would have required the newspaper either to publish the ad or to refrain from publishing all such ads in the future. Such a restraint, said the court, "runs squarely against the wall of freedom of the press. * * * That commercial advertising is involved makes no difference. * * * [A]ny such compulsion to publish that which 'reason' tells [a newspaper] should not be published" is unconstitutional. *Person v. New York Post*, 2 Med. L. Rptr. 1666, 427 F.Supp. 1297 (L.E.D.N.Y. 1977), *aff'd without opinion*, 3 Med. L. Rptr. 1784, 573 F.2d 1294 (2d Cir. 1977).

Newspapers may allocate their advertising space as they see fit,[50] and statutory requirements to the contrary will have difficulty passing constitutional muster. The Fifth Circuit affirmed a federal district court ruling in Florida that the First Amendment was violated by a provision of Florida's campaign financing law requiring newspapers to offer advertising to political candidates at the lowest available rate.[51]

If a refusal to accept advertising is in breach of contract or an attempt to monopolize interstate commerce, an injunction may issue. In *Lorain Journal Co. v. United States*, 342 U.S. 143 (1951), a publisher was prohibited from refusing to accept local advertisements from anyone who advertised on a competitive radio station.

In *Homefinders v. Providence Journal*, 6 Med. L. Rptr. 1018, 621 F.2d 441 (1st Cir. 1980), the

---

50. *National Tire Wholesale v. Washington Post*, 3 Med. L. Rptr. 1520, 441 F.Supp. 81 (D.D.C. 1977).
51. *Gore Newspapers v. Shevin*, 2 Med. L. Rptr. 1818, 397 F.Supp. 1253 (S.D.Fla. 1975), *aff'd* 2 Med. L. Rptr. 1818, 550 F.2d 1057 (5th Cir. 1977).

second circuit held that the Sherman Act was not violated by a newspaper's refusal to publish false and misleading advertisements submitted by a rental referral firm. Where the advertising was honest and above-board and the metropolitan daily, the only newspaper of its kind in town, was in direct competition with the advertiser, the result could be a Sherman Act violation. *Home Placement Service, Inc. v. Providence Journal Co.,* 8 Med. L. Rptr. 1881, 682 F.2d 274 (1st Cir. 1982).

Once a newspaper signs a contract to publish an ad, however, it has given up the right not to publish unless that right is specifically reserved in the contract or some other equitable defense is available to it. *Herald-Telephone v. Fatouros,* 8 Med. L. Rptr. 1230, 431 N.E.2d 171 (Ind. 1982).

In recent years, the media have been hit with numerous lawsuits filed by plaintiffs who claim that a refusal to accept advertising is a denial of civil rights under either 42 U.S.C. § 1983 or a state law provision. Such claims have been rather routinely denied. See, e.g., *Leeds v. Meltz,* 24 Med. L. Rptr. 1153, 898 F.Supp. 146 (E.D.N.Y.), *aff'd,* 24 Med. L. Rptr. 1924, 85 F.3d 51 (2d Cir. 1996); *World Peace Movement of America v. Newspaper Agency Corp., Inc.,* 22 Med. L. Rptr. 2193, 879 P.2d 253 (Utah 1994). Newspapers have also been charged with discrimination in real estate and housing advertising. Absent proof of intent to discriminate, however, winning such a case is almost impossible.[52]

On the other side, advertisers who conspire to withdraw advertising from a newspaper by waging an advertising boycott violate federal antitrust laws. A conglomerate corporation under single ownership, however, may withdraw all its advertising from a newspaper, as Howard Hughes did with the *Las Vegas Sun,* without violating federal law.[53]

Generally, courts have recognized that newspapers have a strong economic self-interest in limiting the kinds of advertising they will accept, because "in the minds of readers, a newspaper's advertising may be every bit as reflective of the policy of a newspaper as its editorial page." *Adult Film Association of America v. Times Mirror Co.,* 5 Med. L. Rptr. 1865, 97 Cal. App. 3d 77, 158 Cal. Rptr. 547 (1979).

Although the broadcast media are under more direct governmental supervision than other media, the U.S. Supreme Court in *CBS v. Democratic National Committee,* 1 Med. L. Rptr. 1855, 412 U.S. 94 (1973), was unwilling to grant a First Amendment right of access to editorial advertising on network television.

The Future

Typical of the kind of advertising case that may be expected in the future is *Cyber Promotions Inc. v. America Online Inc.,* 22 Med. L. Rptr. 1193, 948 F.Supp. 436 (E.D.Pa. 1996). There a U.S. district court held that a private online promotion company did not have a First Amendment right to send unsolicited electronic mail messages over the Internet to another private online company's subscribers. America Online (AOL) could block such messages without violating the First Amendment because it has not dedicated its private property to public use.

Cyber's main argument was that when AOL decided to provide subscribers with Internet e-mail, and access to the Internet as a whole, AOL became a mixed private and public system subject to the First Amendment because the Internet itself is a public system. Cyber also contended that it had no alternative avenues of communication for sending its e-mail to AOL subscribers.

The court rejected these arguments because no municipal power or public services traditionally exercised by the state were involved and Cyber did have alternative channels at its disposal, including the World Wide Web, the U.S. mail, telemarketing, cable, newspapers, magazines, and leaflets. And there were competing commercial online services such as CompuServe, the Microsoft Network, and Prodigy.

Moreover, the daily deluge of e-mail advertisements AOL receives over its servers, said the court, clogs them up and leads to a crush of complaints from subscribers and damage to AOL's reputation. Let Cyber develop its own Internet service, the court added. Also, AOL, using its Preferred Mail system, had given its subscribers the option of choosing to view Cyber's e-mail ads if they wished.

---

52. Williams, *Discriminatory Advertising: Do Large Dailies Comply with Fair Housing Act in Portrayal of Minorities in Housing Ads?* Newspaper Res. J., Vol. 15, No. 4, 77–86 (Fall 1994).

53. *Las Vegas Sun v. Summa Corp.,* 5 Med. L. Rptr. 2073, 610 F.2d 614 (9th Cir. 1979).

MONOPOLY, DIVERSITY, AND ANTITRUST LAW

Structural and Behavioral Elements of Antitrust

In the last decade of the nineteenth century, Congress decided that a market economy would not work well or fairly if monopolies were permitted to form, and so in 1890 it passed the Sherman Antitrust Act. The act prohibits contracts, combinations, trusts, and conspiracies that restrain trade or encourage monopoly, or attempt to do so. Its purpose is to influence and shape the *structure* of the entrepreneurial system.

In 1914 Congress supplemented the Sherman Act by passing the Clayton Act to discourage specific anticompetitive practices such as corporate mergers, interlocking directorates, discriminatory or predatory pricing (pricing so low that a competitor is destroyed), or tying (conditioning the sale of one product or service on the purchase of a second).

The Clayton Act's purpose is to discourage specific *behavioral* practices that would lessen competition now or in the future and, in doing so, tend to create a monopoly. The two acts together are designed to promote vigorous, fair business competition.

Clearly, then, antitrust violations can take both *structural* and *behavioral* form: a system can consolidate in such a way as to discourage diversity; or players within the system can achieve the same result by consciously breaking the law.

The Clayton Act has been amended many times since 1914 to sharpen its teeth against all forms of anticompetitive behavior. In addition, Congress has passed a number of complementary statutes. For example, in 1976 Congress passed the Hart-Scott-Rodino Antitrust Improvements Act (15 U.S.C. § 16A), which requires advance notice to the Justice Department and the FTC of impending mergers or acquisitions above a certain dollar size. Deals cannot be concluded until a government investigation is completed. The underlying assumption of all such congressional efforts is that fair competition among entrepreneurs ultimately benefits the consumer by providing both choice and quality, and so contributes to the general welfare.

Antitrust law affects media organizations in complex ways. Understanding it requires a knowledge of how the courts define such concepts as markets, products, services, and monopoly. For example, a "product market" is one in which purchasers might consider two or more services to be substitutable for one another: for example, advertising on radio station A or radio station B. A "geographic market" might be the metropolitan area in which a daily newspaper has the bulk of its circulation—a retail trading zone, an area of principal penetration, or an area of effective competition.

Courts, media managers, and media economists have generally declined to view communication markets as multimedia markets[54]—markets in which diverse media compete for advertisers and audiences. This curious position makes the single daily newspaper in Our Town seem more of a monopolist than it really is. Intermedia competition is now greater than it has ever been—a fact that the Justice Department does not always recognize. For example, local broadcasters compete with the local newspaper for a larger share of the advertising dollar, and the shopper competes with both; a national newspaper such as *USA Today* competes with CNN (Cable News Network) for national advertising, and *Time* magazine competes with both. Computer printing technologies encourage specialized advertising vehicles such as the various forms of direct mail that compete with all the old-line media. In a few major cities, direct broadcast satellite systems compete with cablecasters, and now telephone companies will compete with both. Electronic yellow pages compete with traditional newspaper classified ad sections. In such circumstances there is sometimes a temptation to resort to unlawful methods of competition. This is where the Antitrust Division of the Department of Justice, the Federal Trade Commission, and the Federal Communications Commission play their roles in enforcing the Sherman and Clayton Acts. Counterpart state agencies enforce parallel state antitrust laws.

Penalties for violation of either state or federal antitrust laws can be severe, and juries tend to be unsympathetic to large companies that seem to be preying on smaller competitors. Sections 1

---

54. *Valet Apt. Serv. v. Atlanta Journal & Constitution*, 865 F.Supp. 828 (N.D.Ga. 1994).

and 2 Sherman Act violations, for example, are felonies carrying penalties of imprisonment and fines of up to $10 million. Private plaintiffs injured by antitrust violations are sometimes entitled to treble damages and attorney's fees. It is recommended that media managers do nothing to reinforce the propensities of jurors to see big guys as bad guys. Antitrust compliance rules ought to be visible to all employees. In addition to facing fines, imprisonment, and huge legal fees, convicted antitrust violators may be prohibited from holding federal licenses or privileges, a substantial concern to broadcasters where licenses are required and profits are high.

An egregious example of lost licenses occurred in 1980 when RKO General was forced to give up three of its major television stations in Boston, New York, and Los Angeles. RKO's corporate parent, General Tire & Rubber, had engaged in reciprocal trade practices: RKO had said "advertise with us or no GT&R business." In addition, the company was alleged to have made illegal political contributions, to have defrauded business partners, bribed foreign officials, set up secret bank accounts, and falsified records, all to beat competitors. Worse, its reports to the FCC had been inaccurate. That alone can jeopardize a broadcast license.[55]

To avoid going to trial, many violators will accept consent agreements and discontinue certain illegal activities. If the problem is structural, they will sell off certain assets.

Monopolization of a product or a geographic market, of course, is not necessarily bad or illegal. It can happen naturally and unintentionally, as when competitor A leaves the market through no fault of competitor B but because A cannot match B's merchandising skill. Meanwhile a third competitor, C, may survive because it benefits from price increases imposed upon the market by the dominant player, competitor B.

Media markets being inherently concentrated, there has been, at least until recently, such a thing as a natural monopoly. For example, most communities cannot economically support more than a single daily newspaper or a single cable television company. What is illegal is the *abuse* of monopoly power, the exercise of market power to control prices or exclude viable competitors. A newspaper would run the risk of abusing its monopoly power if, for example, it priced its advertising space so low as to put a competing shopper or a suburban newspaper out of business, or if it required those who buy newspaper space to buy time on its radio station to the detriment of a competing radio station,[56] or if it refused to sell time or space to those who advertised on the independent station.[57] The former practice is "predation," the latter "forced combination rates and refusals to deal." Both are *behavioral* violations. "Tying" or "combination rates" are permitted if the cost savings involved are voluntary; that is, the buyer of advertising still has a choice. Volume discounts are also generally permissible. Newspapers and broadcasters must be sensitive and knowledgeable in setting advertising rates.[58] And there may be flexibility: in 1992, the Department of Justice gave the Newspaper Association of America permission to sell newspaper advertising space to a group of national advertisers at a single price.

There are other *behavioral* violations. A conspiracy across media to set advertising rates is known as "conscious parallelism" in the language of antitrust.[59] Zoned editions of a newspaper can be a problem if there is evidence of anticompetitive motives or collusion with advertisers.[60] Going too far in giving away free copies of a newspaper in order to hurt a competitor is called "blanketing."[61] "Vertical price fixing" occurs when a newspaper coerces an indepen-

---

55. *In re RKO General, Inc. v. FCC,* 78 FCC 2d 1 (1980), aff'd in part and rev'd in part sub nom., *RKO General, Inc. v. FCC,* 670 F.2d 215 (D.C.Cir. 1981), *cert. denied* 456 U.S. 927 (1982).

56. *Kansas City Star Co. v. United States,* 240 F.2d 643 (8th Cir. 1957), *cert. denied* 354 U.S. 923 (1957). At that time, the *Star* delivered to 96 percent of all homes in the metropolitan area and accounted for 94 percent of all available advertising revenues.

57. *Lorain Journal Co. v. United States,* 1 Med. L. Rptr. 2694, 342 U.S. 143 (1951).

58. For expert and detailed information on every aspect of antitrust law affecting the media, including the setting of advertising rates, see Conrad M. Shumadine, Walter D. Kelley, Jr., and Frank A. Edgar, Jr., "Antitrust and the Media," *Communication Law 1995,* Vol. 2 (New York: Practising Law Institute, 1995), pp. 801–1333.

59. *Ambook Enterprises v. Time, Inc.,* 5 Med. L. Rptr. 1989, 612 F.2d 604 (2d Cir. 1979), *cert. denied* 448 U.S. 914 (1980).

60. *Drinkwine v. Federated Publications, Inc.,* 12 Med. L. Rptr. 1676, 780 F.2d 735 (9th Cir. 1985), *cert. denied* 106 S.Ct. 1471 (1986).

61. *Morning Pioneer, Inc. v. Bismarck Tribune,* 342 F.Supp. 1138 (D.N.D. 1972), aff'd 493 F.2d 383 (8th Cir. 1974), *cert. denied* 419 U.S. 836 (1974).

dent distributor to keep prices at a certain level so as to maximize circulation for advertisers.[62] Advertising can be refused for legitimate business reasons. And, of course, a newspaper may refuse ads that violate its own clearly stated compliance standards, for example, ads that are false and misleading. "The antitrust laws," said a federal appeals court, "are not a shield for deceptive advertising."[63] But again caution is advised, for profit alone is not a compliance standard.

A Sherman Act violation was alleged when the San Jose *Mercury News* refused to accept advertising inserts from a company that competed with the newspaper's classified section for employee placement ads. Initially, the newspaper was granted summary judgment, but the Ninth Circuit Court of Appeals reversed, arguing that the dominant newspaper would have to prove that it was losing money because regular advertisers were switching to the insert just before the job fair, a time when advertising was heaviest. The court suspected that the newspaper might have intended to put its competitor out of business.[64] The newspaper's advertising director had written in a memo, "The only way we might recapture some of the advertising is if there were NO High Tech Careers Magazine" (the inserts company). Another difficulty with the newspaper's case was that it had accepted these same inserts in the past. Now it would have to show a valid business reason for refusing the ads. The case was remanded to the trial court where the newspaper was denied a motion for summary judgment because it could not satisfy the court's need for hard evidence as to lost revenue. A settlement was ordered.[65]

Another Sherman Act violation was alleged when AD/SAT, a company that beamed ads to newspapers via satellite, sued the Associated Press (AP), the Newspaper Association of America, the National Newspaper Network, and a number of individual newspapers for what it claimed was a conspiracy to put it out of business. AP, which is cooperatively owned by its membership, had begun a computer service called AD/SEND to provide essentially the same kind of service. One of the newspapers named in the suit, the Lexington (Kentucky) *Herald-Leader* was granted summary judgment against the Sherman Act claims. The court concluded:

> Plaintiff has not presented facts which tend to exclude the possibility that defendant was acting independently in the pursuit of its own self-interest. . . . In other words, based on the present record, AD/SAT, at best, can show that the *Herald-Leader* heard that AP was planning to introduce a new electronic delivery service, and decided, as a consequence, to terminate its affiliation with AD/SAT. In sum, AD/SAT has produced no evidence, either direct or circumstantial, that reasonably tends to prove that the *Herald-Leader* and others had a conscious commitment to a common scheme designed to achieve an unlawful objective.[66]

What the *Herald-Leader* was interested in was a lower price and better service. In 1996 the case was in the appeals courts.

While enforcing antitrust rules against predation has always been difficult, a federal court may have eased the problem in 1995 when it made it more difficult for a plaintiff to sustain a claim of predatory pricing. The result could be more price competition among sellers of advertising, or it could mean no competition at all, depending on the market and the facts of the situation. In *Advo, Inc. v. Philadelphia Newspapers Inc.,*[67] a federal appeals court in Pennsylvania ruled that a direct mail marketing company's suit against the *Philadelphia Inquirer* for predatory pricing was invalid because there was no direct evidence that the newspaper (1) had offered to distribute competing advertising circulars at below cost, (2) was attempting to create a monopoly for itself, or (3) if there was predation, had any hope of recouping the money it had spent. The court did not wish to do anything to chill competition in the absence of an intent and the power to harm. Nor did it consider the antitrust laws a way for a company to ensure higher profits, in this case Advo, the largest direct mail advertiser in the country. Even though it had already absorbed some of its own

---

62. *Albrecht v. The Herald Co.,* 390 U.S. 145 (1968); *Auburn News Co. v. Providence Journal Co.,* 7 Med. L. Rptr. 1969, 659 F.2d 273 (1st Cir. 1981).

63. *Homefinders of America v. Providence Journal,* 6 Med. L. Rptr. 1018, 621 F.2d 441 (1st Cir. 1980).

64. *High Technology Careers v. San Jose Mercury News,* 996 F.2d 987 (9th Cir. 1993). A seemingly contrary result was reached in *Alaska Airlines, Inc. v. United Airlines, Inc.,* 948 F.2d 536 (9th Cir. 1991), *cert. denied* 112 S.Ct. 1603 (1992).

65. 1994 WL 263841 (N.D.Cal.).

66. *AD/SAT a Division of Skylight, Inc. v. Associated Press,* 885 F.Supp. 511, 521–22 (S.D.N.Y. 1995).

67. 23 Med. L. Rptr. 1833, 51 F.3d 1191 (3d Cir. 1995).

direct mail competitors in the Philadelphia market, Advo brought suit under secs. 1 and 2 of the Sherman Act. A portion of the case follows, suggesting the complexity of this area of the law.

Advo Inc. v. Philadelphia Newspapers Inc.

23 MED. L. RPTR. 1833, 51 F.3D 1191 (3D CIR. 1995).

GREENBERG, J.:

Appellant Advo, Inc. sued appellee Philadelphia Newspapers, Inc. ("PNI") charging that PNI attempted to monopolize the market for delivering preprinted advertising circulars in the greater Philadelphia area, in violation of section 2 of the Sherman Antitrust Act, 15 U.S.C. § 2. Advo alleged that PNI has offered predatorily low prices to major purchasers of services for delivering circular advertising, and that, in light of specific features of the market, PNI's scheme to force Advo from the market has a dangerous probability of succeeding.

After extensive discovery, the district court entered summary judgment in favor of PNI. Because we concur that PNI could not have recouped the investment in predation it might have made, and because Advo failed to present evidence that could support a finding that PNI either priced below cost or had a specific intent to monopolize, we will affirm.

* * *

Advo is a national MC ["marketing communications"] services company and is the largest full-service direct mail marketing company in the country. It distributed at least three *billion* advertising packages in 1992, generating nearly a billion dollars in revenue. Advo began operating in the eight-county area that comprises the Philadelphia market in the mid-1960s, and appears to have grown rapidly since obtaining the Acme supermarket chain as a base advertiser for shared mailings in 1983.

Ironically, Advo faced a Sherman Act section 2 suit as a result of capturing the Acme account and expanding its business in Philadelphia. *Cassidy Distrib. Serv. v. Advo-Sys., Inc.,* No. 84-3464 (E.D. Pa. 1984). A small competitor that previously had serviced Acme sued Advo charging predatory conduct in furtherance of a plan to monopolize the market for distributing advertis-

ing circulars in the region. In the course of countering this charge, Advo argued that there are few, if any, barriers to entering the business of marketing communications, and thus there is little, if any, chance that a predator could recoup the costs of illegally obtaining a monopoly.

The market for circular advertising distribution appears to have become more competitive in recent years. When Advo changed its delivery schedule in 1989 to accommodate Acme, other major customers became dissatisfied and invited CBA, a MC services company from outside the area, to enter the Philadelphia market. Despite start-up costs of over $3,000,000, CBA turned a profit within 14 months. In a move admittedly taken to avert a "price war," Advo acquired CBA's Philadelphia preprint distribution operations in 1992. This acquisition apparently encountered no antitrust scrutiny.

THE EFFECT OF MARKETING COMMUNICATIONS SERVICES ON MAJOR PHILADELPHIA NEWSPAPERS, AND THEIR RESPONSE

Much of Advo's growth has come at the expense of PNI, publisher of the Philadelphia market's major daily newspapers, The Philadelphia Daily News and The Philadelphia Inquirer. PNI estimates that it has lost at least $4,000,000 per year in ROP ["run of press": advertising on editorial pages] and circular advertising to Advo and similar competitors.

To counter Advo's advantages in market penetration and the ability to target specific neighborhoods, PNI in 1991 began working on a "total market coverage" ("TMC") program to supplement ROP advertising with alternate delivery to non-subscriber households. PNI started implementing the program in small stages by 1992. Although it faced substantial start-up costs, PNI claims that it hoped to turn a profit on its TMC program by 1995.

Facing the same cost structure as Advo, PNI needed a base player to help cover the high fixed costs of delivering preprinted advertising packets door-to-door. In September 1992, and again in January of 1993, PNI offered to distribute circulars for the Super Fresh supermarket chain, a major Advo customer, for about $30 per thousand circulars. As part of its proposal, PNI offered discounts on ROP advertising tied to the total volume of advertising that Super Fresh purchased. Advo retained the account by cutting its rate by about 37%, from $58 to $36 per thousand circulars. Thus, Super Fresh retained Advo despite its base rate exceeding that in PNI's proposal by about 20%. Although the expert *opinion* testimony is conflicting, there appears to be no *factual* basis to Advo's claim that PNI's proposed prices were below its costs. There is also no support for Advo's claim that PNI tendered Super Fresh prices below those offered to comparable advertisers.

PNI made similar efforts to wrest the accounts of Acme and Fleming Foods supermarkets, Bradlees department stores, and Circuit City consumer electronics stores from Advo; in each case Advo retained the accounts after cutting its rates substantially. In fact no major account has switched from Advo. Thus, it is clear that to date PNI's activities have been pro-competitive, as they have resulted in lower prices.

PROCEDURAL HISTORY

Advo filed its complaint against PNI on June 17, 1993, alleging that PNI was engaged in a predatory pricing scheme designed to achieve a monopoly over the Philadelphia market for circular and ROP advertising in violation of section 2 of the Sherman Act, 15 U.S.C. § 2. Advo requested damages, 15 U.S.C. § 15, and injunctive relief, 15 U.S.C. § 26. The district court exercised subject matter jurisdiction over Advo's antitrust claims under 28 U.S.C. § 1331 (federal question jurisdiction) and 28 U.S.C. § 1337 (interstate commerce jurisdiction).

The parties undertook extensive discovery, including deposing at least 30 of each other's corporate officials as well as other industry experts. Each side presented expert economic analysis. In addition, the eight-volume appendix, running to over 2300 pages, includes relevant documents such as business plans, annual reports, and internal memoranda.

After reviewing this voluminous record, receiving extensive briefs, and hearing oral argument, the district court on June 13, 1994, granted PNI's motion for summary judgment on the antitrust claims. *Advo, Inc. v. Philadelphia Newspapers, Inc.*, 854 F. Supp. 367 (E.D. Pa. 1994). The court found that even if it accepted, *arguendo*, that PNI had engaged in predatory conduct with specific intent to monopolize, there was no dangerous probability that PNI could achieve a monopoly and maintain it long enough to recoup the costs of predation. The court reaffirmed its decision in response to Advo's motion under Fed. R. Civ. P. 59(e) for reconsideration on July 15, 1994.[2]

On August 11, 1994, Advo timely appealed from the district court's order of summary judgment and from the order denying the motion for reconsideration. We have jurisdiction under 18 U.S.C. § 1291.

* * *

In a nutshell, economic analyses stress that (1) predatory pricing, unlike collusion or merger, involves an expensive "investment in predation," since presumably the predator will have to price below costs; (2) this investment must be more than offset by *discounted* future monopoly profits; and (3) the ability to maintain a monopoly for long enough to recoup an investment in predation is uncertain, since supracompetitive prices will attract new entrants or returning competitors.

Empirical studies support these theoretical insights. While it once was believed widely that turn-of-the-century "robber barons" commonly practiced predatory pricing to eliminate competitors, research over the last few decades has exposed this belief as a myth. For instance, a seminal article demonstrated that John D. Rockefeller invariably used mergers, and not predatory pricing, to lessen competition in the oil industry.

Based on this combination of economic logic and empirical verification, the Court has concluded that "economic realities tend to make predatory pricing conspiracies self-deterring: unlike most other conduct that violates the antitrust laws, failed predatory pricing schemes are costly as to conspirators."* *Matsushita*, 475 U.S. at 595. "[I]f [the alleged predators] had no rational economic motive to conspire, and if their conduct is consistent with other equally

---

2. Because these rulings disposed of all federal questions in Advo's complaint, the court exercised its discretion and dismissed without prejudice a supplemental state law tort claim for tortious interference with prospective contractual relations.

* Japan's Matsushita company bought MCA's Universal Studios in 1990. After five years of heavy losses, it sold out to Seagram, the giant Canadian liquor company.

plausible explanations, the conduct does not give rise to an inference of conspiracy." *Id.* at 596–97.

Erroneous jury verdicts for plaintiffs in predatory pricing cases pose a unique threat. "[C]utting prices in order to increase business often is the very essence of competition. Thus, mistaken inferences in cases such as this one are especially costly, because they chill the very conduct the antitrust laws are designed to protect." *Matsushita,* 475 U.S. at 594. "[C]ourts should not permit factfinders to infer conspiracies when such inferences are implausible, because the effect of such practices is often to deter procompetitive conduct." *Id.* at 593. We cannot ignore the danger of chilling competition in this case, since PNI's acts clearly have benefited consumers, in the short run at least, with lower prices. There are antitrust problems only if PNI has the intent and the power to harm these consumers in the long run.

* * *

To summarize, then, in order to establish a "genuine issue" that entitles it to reach trial on its attempted monopolization claim premised on predatory pricing, Advo must present more than a scintilla of evidence that the alleged predatory conduct makes economic sense. In this appeal, the main hurdle for Advo is to show that PNI reasonably could expect to recoup an investment in the predatory pricing of distribution of circular advertising.

ELEMENTS OF PREDATION

"[I]t is generally required that to demonstrate attempted monopolization a plaintiff must prove (1) that the defendant has engaged in predatory or anticompetitive conduct with (2) a specific intent to monopolize and (3) a dangerous probability of achieving monopoly power." *Spectrum Sports, Inc. v. McQuillan,* 113 S.Ct. 884, 890–91 (1993). *See also Barr Labs. Inc. v. Abbott Lab.,* 978 F.2d 98, 112 (3d Cir. 1992). The district court assumed *arguendo* that Advo had demonstrated that there were genuine issues of material fact surrounding the first two elements of its attempted monopolization case: predatory conduct, in the form of predatory, below-cost pricing; and specific intent to monopolize. It nonetheless found no dangerous probability that PNI could achieve monopoly power.

While we concur with the district court's conclusion, we first examine Advo's evidence on predatory conduct and specific intent. We find that Advo failed to produce evidence sufficient to survive summary judgment on any of the three elements of its attempted monopolization claim against PNI.

1. Below-Cost Pricing

"[P]redatory pricing means pricing below some appropriate measure of cost." *Matsushita,* 475 U.S. at 584 n.8. Yet "[t]here is a good deal of debate, both in the cases and in the law reviews, about what 'cost' is relevant in such cases," *id,* and "[n]o consensus has yet been reached on the proper definition of predatory pricing in the antitrust context . . . ." *Cargill, Inc. v. Monfort of Colorado, Inc.,* 479 U.S. 104, 117 n.12. The Supreme Court, however, recently reaffirmed that "the reasoning in both [*Matsushita and Cargill*] suggests that only below-cost prices should suffice, and [that it has] rejected elsewhere the notion that above-cost prices that are below general market levels or the costs of a firm's competitors inflict injury to competition cognizable under the antitrust laws." *Brooke Group,* 113 S.Ct. at 2588. In *Brooke Group,* the Court accepted for the purposes of the case the parties' agreement to use average variable cost, but "again decline[d] to resolve the conflict among the lower courts over the appropriate measure of cost." *Id.* at 2587 n.1.

Under microeconomic theory, the most important measure is marginal cost—the cost of producing each incremental unit of output. As long as a firm's prices exceeds its marginal cost, each additional sale decreases losses or increases profits. Such pricing is presumably not predatory.

Like many economic abstractions, marginal cost is difficult to measure. The most widely cited approach to dealing with this problem, Phillip Areeda & Donald F. Turner, *Predatory Pricing and Related Practices Under Section 2 of the Sherman Act,* 88 Harv. L. Rev. 697, 716–18 (1975), divides costs into two categories: fixed costs that do not vary with the level of output (*e.g.,* interest on borrowings, insurance premiums), and variable costs that do vary with the level of output (*e.g.,* overtime wages, electricity bills, material costs). Because it is practically impossible to calculate the portion of variable costs attributable to each additional unit of output, Areeda and Turner argue that courts should use *average* variable cost as a proxy for marginal cost.

Regardless of the measure of a defendant's costs on which a plaintiff premises a predatory pricing claim, a plaintiff cannot anchor its case on theoretical speculation that a defendant is pricing below that measure. Indeed, "[a]s a practical matter, it may be that only *direct* evidence of below-cost pricing is sufficient to overcome the strong inference that rational businesses would not enter into conspiracies such as this one." *Matsushita,* 475 U.S. at 584 n.8 (emphasis added).

Despite extensive discovery, Advo apparently is unable to produce any direct evidence that PNI offered to distribute circulars at prices below any relevant measure of cost. As a key step of his analysis, Advo's economic expert states that "[a]verage variable costs for [PNI's TMC program] *were estimated.*" The basis for these estimates is weak. For instance, with no more foundation that a statement by PNI's publisher that inserting circulars involves "extensive costs," the expert concluded that PNI "potentially vastly understated" this variable cost. Other components of the expert's cost estimates similarly lack a factual basis.

As *Brooke Group* makes clear, expert testimony without such a factual foundation cannot defeat a motion for summary judgment. "When an expert opinion is not supported by sufficient facts to validate it in the eyes of the law, or when indisputable record facts contradict or otherwise render the opinion unreasonable, it cannot support a jury's verdict . . . . Expert testimony is useful as a guide to interpreting market facts, but it is not a substitute for them." *Brooke Group,* 113 S.Ct. at 2598. Advo failed to present *facts* establishing a genuine issue over whether PNI priced circular advertising distribution services below some measure of costs. This omission provided sufficient grounds for granting summary judgment.

2. Specific Intent to Monopolize by Predation

In addition to demonstrating predation, plaintiffs alleging monopolization under section 2 must produce intent evidence. Courts sometimes infer specific intent directly from proof of below-cost

pricing. Inasmuch as Advo failed to create a genuine issue over pricing, however, it needed to prove specific intent by other means. Its two attempts, based on (1) statements in internal PNI documents, and (2) PNI's alleged targeting of Advo's key customers, are not sufficient to withstand PNI's motion for summary judgment.

Antitrust plaintiffs often establish specific intent with "smoking gun" documents that articulate antitrust scienter in no uncertain terms. Advo found no such documents; instead, it attempted to cut and paste unrelated and innocent clauses together to produce guilty declarations. To take one example, Advo misrepresents that PNI's TMC Business Plan states that:

> [T]he 'ultimate benefit' of the TMC program was that PNI would be the 'one-stop buy,' i.e. the only competitor left, in the eight county Philadelphia market when rates would become 'upwardly adjustable.'

The phrases "ultimate benefit" and "one-stop buy" do occur in the same sentence in the plan and correctly portray PNI's overall objective. The phrase "upwardly adjustable," however, comes *eight paragraphs* later, as the discussion progresses from an overview of the plan to the nuts and bolts of various hypothetical business scenarios. PNI used the phrase "upwardly adjustable" in a scenario in which it assumed that prices "are deemed to be very competitively set . . ." This is a far cry from an admission that it was charging predatory prices to start with, or that it planned to charge monopolistic prices in the future.

Advo officials themselves have used aggressive-sounding language. Its CEO, Robert Kamerschen, once directed his managers "to seize the OPPORTUNITY inherent in the stumbling PROBLEMS of the newspaper industry," and quoted McDonald's founder Ray Kroc for the advice that "[w]hen [you] see the competition drowning, . . . stick a water hose down their throats."

The antitrust statutes do not condemn, without more, such colorful, vigorous hyperbole; there is nothing to gain by using the law to mandate "commercially correct" speech within corporate memoranda and business plans. Isolated and unrelated snippets of such language "provide no help in deciding whether a defendant has crossed the elusive line separating aggressive competition from unfair competition." *Morgan v.*

Ponder, 17 Med. L. Rptr. 1465, 892 F.2d 1355, 1359 (8th Cir. 1989). We thus conclude that nothing quoted from PNI's internal documents displays PNI's specific intent to monopolize the market for distribution of circular advertising.

Advo's claim that PNI's "targeting" of its key accounts demonstrates such specific intent is similarly unavailing. As we discussed, circular advertising distributors need "base players," that advertise frequently and on a large scale, to cover their high fixed costs. Inasmuch as there are relatively few base players in the Philadelphia market, any firm competing in the market for distribution of circular advertising necessarily would try, as a first step, to wrest one or more of these large accounts away from Advo. PNI's proposals to Advo's largest customers are exactly what we would expect from a legitimate competitor. That such behavior also might be consistent with predation does not mean that Advo can survive PNI's motion for summary judgment. "If [seemingly predatory] conduct is consistent with other, equally plausible explanations, the conduct does not give rise to an inference of conspiracy." *Matsushita,* 475 U.S. at 596–97.

3. Dangerous Probability of Recoupment

Finally, we concur with the district court's determination that Advo failed to establish a genuine issue of material fact about PNI's ability to recoup any investment made in predation. The Supreme Court instructs that "[i]f market circumstances or deficiencies in proof would bar a reasonable jury from finding that the scheme alleged would likely result in sustained supracompetitive pricing, the plaintiff's case has failed." *Brooke Group,* 113 S.Ct. at 2589. The district court found, in effect, that "[t]he evidence is inadequate to show that in pursuing this scheme, [PNI] had a reasonable prospect of recovering its losses from below-cost pricing," *id.* at 2592. We agree.

In addition, we reject Advo's theories that PNI can scare away potential entrants by "strategic deterrence" or can "leverage" its monopoly over ROP advertising to gain a monopoly over the distribution of circular advertising. Finally, we find no support for Advo's theories for how PNI could recoup an investment in predation via either price discrimination or long-term contracts.

* * *

CONCLUSION

We close with the following observation. There can be little doubt but that PNI's adoption of the TMC program has resulted in lower prices for distributing advertising circulars in the Philadelphia market. Yet Advo would have us condemn PNI because of what Advo contends, without basis, will be the long-range consequence of PNI's actions. We reject Advo's argument. This case is a text-book example of a situation in which a plaintiff is, in the words of *Matsushita,* using the antitrust laws in an attempt to chill the very conduct the laws were designed to protect.

Accordingly, because the district court correctly determined that PNI had no reasonable prospect of recouping any investment made to obtain predatorily a monopoly in the market for distributing circular advertising, we will affirm its order of June 13, 1994, granting summary judgment against Advo and its order denying reconsideration on July 15, 1994. As additional ground for affirming, we find that Advo failed to establish a genuine issue of material fact to support its case on the other two elements of its Sherman Act section 2 claims, predatory conduct and specific intent to monopolize. Finally, we note that the district court did not abuse its discretion in dismissing the state-law tortious interference with contractual relations claim once it had resolved all substantial federal questions in the case.

COMMENT

In 1970, a federal district court upheld a Justice Department claim that the *Boston Globe*'s exclusive feature syndicate contracts violated sec. 1 of the Sherman Act by assuring that the syndicates would not "license the features to any other newspaper published within an arbitrary and unreasonably broad territory surrounding the contracting newspaper's city of publication."[68] The case was subsequently settled by consent decree when the *Globe* agreed not to contest the challenge to its exclusivity where its penetration was less than 20 percent and its circulation less than 5,000.[69] Later, another federal

---

68. *United States v. Chicago Tribune–New York News Syndicate, Inc.,* 309 F.Supp. 1301 (S.D.N.Y. 1970).
69. *United States v. Chicago Tribune–New York News Syndicate, Inc.,* 1971–1 Trade Cas (CCH) Sec. 60,185 (S.D.N.Y. 1975).

district court held that circulation alone should not be conclusive. Local news and feature coverage should also be considered, presumably in the interests of diversity.[70]

In the media world, two simultaneous *structural* trends are observable. New and convergent technologies are providing new and diverse media of communication. Specialized cable channels have expanded, with some soon to be interactive (that is, you will be able to talk to your TV set). Within reach or here now are video dialtone, cellular telephony, VCR technology, digital compression, and the possibility of high-definition television (HDTV), direct broadcast satellite (DBS), a national fiber optics system with its elimination of spectrum space and greatly increased capacity for carrying messages, and, most important, new computer technologies and online service systems that will revolutionize the way information is gathered, transmitted, and stored. The Internet is the best example of how the computer has changed mass communication by turning passive audiences into active communicators. At the same time, fewer and fewer large concerns are coming to control more and more of the total system.

The Clayton Act's sec. 7 prohibits the acquisition of the assets of one company by another "where in any line of commerce in any section of the country, the effect of such acquisition may be substantially to lessen competition or tend to create a monopoly." Firm proof of such effects is not required.

Telecommunications developments in the twenty-first century may do away with "natural monopolies" altogether; there will be competition for information service customers in every market, but it may be competition among behemoths. One startling example: in 1994, TeleCommunications, Inc. (TCI) was the nation's largest multiple system operator (MSO) with approximately 10.5 million subscribers and annual revenues of more than $4.1 billion; in 1995, its revenues were topped only by Time Warner, Capital Cities/ABC/Disney, and CBS/Westinghouse, among media companies. TCI owned 49 percent of the Discovery Channel,

41 percent of Reiss Media, 27 percent of QVC Networks (fashion shopping channel), 15 percent of Heritage Media Interactive Network, and 22 percent of Turner Broadcasting, which owned HBO, WTBS, CNN, TNT, and the Cartoon Network and has since joined Time Warner. Through its sister corporation, Liberty Media Corporation, TCI owned 50 percent of American Movie Classics (AMC), 41 percent of Home Shopping Network (HSN), 21.6 percent of QVC, 17.5 percent of Black Entertainment Television (BET), 33 percent of Court TV, 90 percent of Encore, and 15.6 percent of the Family Channel.[71] In 1994, TCI added TeleCable Corporation to its holdings; TeleCable was the nation's eighteenth largest MSO. Turner Broadcasting and Liberty Media then ranked second and third behind TCI in programming revenues. TCI owns nearly 10 percent of Time Warner Turner.

Although an effort to merge TCI with Bell Atlantic was aborted when the FCC mandated lower cable television rates, other mergers or buy-ins between telephone companies and cable systems have been consummated. New York's telephone company (Nynex) has since bought Bell Atlantic. Cable companies provide program or content assets, telephone companies the infrastructure and capital assets. U.S. West's purchase of Continental Cablevision is an example. So far, mergers resulting in larger but fewer communication companies have not seemed to decrease whatever competition exists in local markets. As a result, antitrust laws have not been brought to bear. But there may be a consolidation level above which the Antitrust Division will take notice. Regulators did take notice when Time Warner agreed to acquire Turner Broadcasting System, an acquisition that nevertheless was concluded. The corporate interlockings are dazzling.

Given the opportunities for convergence of new information technologies, questions remain: Do we need more or less regulation by government? What is the ideal balance between First Amendment claims and regulatory policy?

HORIZONTAL MERGERS Chain or group ownership, a form of horizontal or market

---

70. *Woodbury Daily Times, Co., Inc. v. Los Angeles Times–Washington Post News Service,* 12 Med. L. Rptr. 1137, 616 F.Supp. 502 (D.N.J. 1985), *aff'd without opinion* 791 F.2d 924 (3d Cir. 1986).

71. Conrad M. Shumadine and Frank A. Edgar, Jr., "The Information Superhighway," *Communications Law 1994,* Vol. 3 (New York: Practising Law Institute, 1994), p. 845.

extension merger, now accounts for nearly 80 percent of daily newspapers. The 20 largest of 122 chains account for nearly 40 percent of all 1,538 U.S. dailies. Bigger chains buy smaller chains. In 1995, 75 percent of all newspapers sold passed from one group to another.[72] Even weekly newspapers attract chains. In 1994, there were 7,176 weekly newspapers, a thousand fewer than in 1960. This form of consolidation gets less attention than it deserves because, according to conventional wisdom, it can have a deadening effect on journalistic enterprise. Much of the evidence for the effects of corporate values on bold reporting is anecdotal, although dire expectations persist.[73] At the same time, higher newsprint costs, competition from innovative media, and weakening circulation compel organizational patterns that gain efficiencies from the economies of scale attendant upon chains. An example is American Publishing Company (Hollinger), a little known chain owned by Canadian businessman Conrad Black. Black owns more daily newspapers in the United States than anyone else—111.

Head-to-head newspaper competition is almost a thing of the past. Recent victims of the economic forces that lead to one-newspaper communities are New York's *Newsday,* the *Dallas Times-Herald,* the *Houston Post,* the Little Rock *Gazette,* the Anchorage *Times,* and the Los Angeles *Herald Examiner.* Newspaper groups have traditionally cushioned blows of this kind by investing in competing media. Gannett, Scripps-Howard, Pulitzer, and the New York Times Company, for example, have substantial broadcast holdings. When Gannett acquired Multimedia Entertainment, it added ten newspapers to its group, five television stations for a new total of fifteen, two radio stations for a new total of thirteen, and a cable company operating in five states. Knight-Ridder, Times Mirror, and Washington Post rank sixth, eighth, and tenth, respectively, in cable revenues. Reuters and the Associated Press both own advertising agencies.

VERTICAL MERGERS Another form of consolidation is the vertical merger where, for example, a newspaper company acquires a newsprint manufacturer; regulators call this a "backward vertical integration." If the same company were to buy an independent newspaper distribution system, regulators would call that a "forward vertical integration." In this way, the newspaper company could capture both suppliers and customers, making entry into the market by competitors extremely difficult. Other economic factors, however, may be even more fundamental than vertically organized competitors in constraining entry of a competitor. Capital Cities/ABC/Disney is another example. ABC will guarantee distribution of Disney programming.

CONGLOMERATE MERGERS A third form of merger is the conglomerate merger where the joined firms do not compete and may have very little in common. These mergers are particularly feared by purists in the media world because professional values may be overwhelmed or transformed by the acquiring firm. Conglomeration, the merging of unrelated businesses, has escalated rapidly in the 1990s. Magazines, record and film companies, movie theaters, book publishers, broadcast and cable companies, and even newspaper marketing and trade organizations were all affected. The danger of conglomeration is that the oil company or the electric company may not be sensitive to the public interest in a diverse and sometimes controversial and exasperating flow of information.

MERGERS AND THE ANTITRUST LAWS Horizontal mergers between companies that sell one or more competing products in the same geographic market get special scrutiny from the Justice Department. Seldom do newspapers qualify for this kind of attention. Where they do, the Justice Department and the federal courts have been hostile. A classic example occurred in 1964 when the Times-Mirror Company, publisher of the *Los Angeles Times,* acquired newspapers in nearby San Bernardino. The *Times,* a newspaper of national import, had the largest circulation in California, whereas the *San Bernardino Sun and Telegram,* the largest independent newspaper in southern California, dominated the market in San Bernardino

---

72. *New York Times,* February 19, p. C4.
73. A work vigorously disputing the conventional wisdom is David Pearce Demers, The Menace of the Corporate Newspaper: Fact or Fiction? (Ames: Iowa State University Press, 1996).

County, adjoining Los Angeles County. These newspapers, though occupying different categories, did engage in what the federal district court called "interlayer" competition. Both the Sherman and the Clayton Act had been violated. Competition within the relevant geographic and product market had been substantially lessened by the acquisition, and it is the purpose of the antitrust laws to protect competition, not individual competitors. A federal district judge had this to say in disallowing the merger:

United States v. Times Mirror Co.
274 F.SUPP. 606 (C.D.CAL. 1967), AFF'D PER CURIAM 390 U.S. 712 (1968).

FERGUSON, District Judge:

* * *

The Supreme Court, in *Brown Shoe Co. v. United States,* 370 U.S. 294, (1962), pointed out in setting forth the legislative history of the 1950 amendment to § 7 of the Clayton Act that:

"The dominant theme pervading congressional consideration of the 1950 amendments was a fear of what was considered to be a rising tide of economic concentration in the American economy. * * * Other considerations cited in support of the bill were the desirability of retaining 'local control' over industry and the protection of small businesses. Throughout the recorded discussion may be found examples of Congress' fear not only of accelerated concentration of economic power on economic grounds, but also of the threat to other values a trend toward concentration was thought to pose." 370 U.S. 295 at 315–16.

The Court declared:

Congress made it plain that § 7 applied not only to mergers between actual competitors, but also to vertical and conglomerate mergers whose effect may tend to lessen competition in any line of commerce in any section of the country. 370 U.S. at 317.

* * *

In actions under § 7 of the Clayton Act, a finding of the appropriate "product market" is a necessary predicate to a determination of whether a merger has the requisite anticompetitive effects. In *Brown Shoe Co. v. United States, supra,* it is set forth:

"Thus, as we have previously noted, '[d]etermination of the relevant market is a necessary predicate to a finding of a violation of the Clayton Act. * * *'"

In some of the services which they provide, daily newspapers compete with other media, such as radio and television, both for news and advertising. This does not mean, however, that all competitors of any service provided by a daily newspaper must be lumped into the same line of commerce with it. * * *

The defendant argues that each daily newspaper is so unique as to occupy a product market of its own. This argument stems more from pride of publication than from commercial reality. The contention is made that if a reader in Southern California wants depth in international, national and regional news, he buys the *Times* and if he wants depth in the local news of his own community, he buys his small local paper. In effect, it is claimed that the *Times* and the surrounding local daily newspapers are complementary toward each other. As set forth previously, the concept of two products being complementary toward each other is not a barrier to § 7 if the effect of the merger may have anticompetitive effects.

It is now firmly established that products need not be identical to be included in a § 7 analysis of the product market. Furthermore, in *Union Leader Corp. v. Newspapers of New England, Inc.,* the court of appeals recognized that numerous papers published all over New England could comprise a relevant daily newspaper market for both Clayton and Sherman Act purposes.

Finally, when a merger such as here results in a share of from 10.6% to 54.8% of total weekday circulation, from 23.9% to 99.5% of total morning circulation and from 20.3% to 64.3% of total Sunday circulation in the relevant geographic market, the acquisition constitutes a prima facie violation of the Clayton Act. As set forth in *United States v. Continental Can Co.:*

"Where a merger is of such a size as to be inherently suspect, elaborate proof of market structure, market behavior and probable anticompetitive effects may be dispensed with in view of § 7's design to prevent undue concentration." 378 U.S. at 458.

The *Times* competed with the *Sun* for advertising. The largest share of the revenue of a daily newspaper comes from its advertisements, and advertising is its lifeblood.

* * * After the acquisition, the advertising campaign that both papers waged against each other ceased.

It is necessary after defining the product market to determine the geographic market (the "section of the country") in order to determine the anticompetitive effect of the merger.

In 1964, the year of the acquisition, the *Times* had a weekday daily circulation of 16,650 and a Sunday circulation of 31,993 within San Bernardino County. This amounted to 10.6% of the total weekday circulation for both morning and evening newspapers, 23.9% of total morning circulation and 20.3% of the total Sunday circulation.

The *Sun* had its entire circulation, except for a very few copies, within the limits of San Bernardino County. The county therefore encompasses virtually the entire area of circulation and home delivery overlap between the *Times* and the *Sun*. * * *

The defendant contends that the County of San Bernardino is not commercially realistic because county boundaries do not define the boundaries of a newspaper market. It claims that counties are political and administrative boundaries, not necessarily market boundaries. This contention may be true as a generalized statement. * * * However, as stated previously, the newspaper industry has recognized San Bernardino County as a daily newspaper market. Most important of all, the *Times* itself, in evaluating the acquisition, used the daily newspaper business in the entire San Bernardino County as the relevant market.

* * *

At the time of the acquisition, there was already a heavy concentration of daily newspaper ownership in the ten counties of Southern California. * * *

There has been a steady decline of independent ownership of newspapers in Southern California. A newspaper is independently owned when its owners do not publish another newspaper at another locality. In San Bernardino County as of January 1, 1952, six of the seven daily newspapers were independently owned. On December 31, 1966, only three of the eight dailies published there remained independent.

* * *

In the ten-county area of Southern California in the same period of time, the number of daily newspapers increased from 66 to 82, but the number independently owned decreased from 39 to 20. In 1952, 59% of Southern California dailies were independent; in 1966 only 24% were independent.

The acquisition of the *Sun* by the *Times* was particularly anticompetitive because it eliminated one of the few independent papers that had been able to operate successfully in the morning and Sunday fields. * * *

The acquisition has raised a barrier to entry of newspapers in the San Bernardino County market that is almost impossible to overcome. The evidence discloses the market has now been closed tight and no publisher will risk the expense of unilaterally starting a new daily newspaper there.

An acquisition which enhances existing barriers to entry in the market or increases the difficulties of smaller firms already in the market is particularly anticompetitive.

* * *

The acquisition by The Times Mirror Company of The Sun Company on June 25, 1964, resulted in a violation of § 7 of the Clayton Act. It is an acquisition by one corporation (The Times Mirror Company) of all the stock of another corporation (The Sun Company), both corporations being engaged in interstate commerce, whereby in the daily newspaper business (the relevant product market) in San Bernardino County, California (the relevant geographic market), the effect is substantially to lessen competition.

The government seeks an order of divestiture and an injunction prohibiting the defendant from acquiring any other daily newspaper in the relevant geographic market.

Divestiture has become the normal form of relief when acquisitions have been found to violate § 7 of the Clayton Act. * * *

Complete divestiture here is the practical solution to correct the § 7 violation.

However, the request for a perpetual injunction must be denied. * * *

While it is recognized that injunctive relief has been granted in antitrust cases, the court is not able to predict the future of the daily newspaper business in San Bernardino County. * * * Based upon the evidence before it, the court cannot prejudge the newspaper business with sufficient certainty to grant the injunction. The dangers that could result from it outweigh any possible advantage that it may have.

* * *

COMMENT

Times Mirror is important for its support of the notion that competition among newspapers can be "interlayer" as well as "intralayer." That is, competition between newspapers of similar size and scope is less common than competition between different categories of newspapers— suburbans and metropolitans, for example. Had the merger been allowed, total morning circulation for the merged firm would have increased from 24 percent to 99 percent, and it would have eliminated one of the few independent papers that had been able to operate successfully in the morning and Sunday fields.

In 1982, when the *Orlando Sentinel* tried to buy several shoppers and weekly newspapers in a Florida county, the Department of Justice again took notice. A forced divestiture of the acquired publications followed.[74]

An even more directly monopolistic acquisition of a local daily newspaper by its competitor occurred in Arkansas in 1995. Government and private plaintiffs contended that purchase of the Northwest Arkansas *Times,* a Thomson newspaper, by a family group that owns most of the Donrey Media Group as well as the *Morning News of Northwest Arkansas,* would violate sec. 7 of the Clayton Act. The merged newspaper would lessen competition in the same geographic and product market by controlling more than 84 percent of circulation and 88 percent of advertising revenues. A federal district court held that monopolistic increases in prices would harm the public, advertisers, and a competing newspaper, the *Daily Record.* The latter, together with the *Arkansas Democrat-Gazette,* a statewide newspaper, had also tried to buy the *Times.*

Relying on vintage cases, the court accepted a definition of the market that included local daily newspapers only. Daily newspapers were viewed as a separate product in an integrated geographic region. But evidence showed that the three newspapers were competitive and that advertisers were the major beneficiaries of this competition. A merger of the *Morning News* and *Times* would leave the *Daily Record* out in the cold and would constitute what the courts call an "antitrust injury," not only to the independent newspaper but also to the public. Advertisers would have to buy space in the merged newspaper; it would become a "must-buy," even at higher advertising rates. Hence, little advertising would be left for the independent newspaper, and it would eventually go into a *"downward spiral"*. Subscriber and advertiser demands are interdependent. When circulation drops, advertising sales drop, and vice versa. The economies of scale dictate that fixed first-issue costs (paper, ink, labor, capital equipment, taxes, administration) diminish as circulation increases. When circulation decreases, fixed first-issue costs rise as a percentage of total costs. This leads to lower profitability, which can only be remedied by higher advertising and subscription rates or by cutting costs and thereby quality. Either course accelerates the "downward spiral." The weaker newspaper appears to be doomed.

Finding a Clayton Act sec. 7 violation, the court chose the remedy of "rescission"—meaning that the *Times* went back to its original owner, Thomson, restoring competition and giving the chain a chance to find its own buyer. The American Publishing Company (Hollinger) did buy the *Times.* Hopefully, daily newspaper competition will survive in Northwest Arkansas.[75] Private plaintiffs in the action were awarded $676,000 in attorney's fees.

A much maligned vertical merger was that of Warner Communication and Time, Inc., in 1989, creating the largest media firm in the United States in terms of revenues. Turner Broadcasting has since added a powerful player to the merged company. General Electric's acquisition of RCA and its NBC network three years earlier illustrates conglomeration. Ironically, more than sixty-five years ago, GE and RCA were separated for antitrust reasons. Now GE is one of the largest broadcast organizations in the United States in terms of revenues. In the 1990s, Walt

---

74. *United States v. Tribune Co.,* 4 Trade Reg. Reptr. Sec. 50,838.

75. *Community Publishers, Inc. v. Donrey Corp.,* 892 F.Supp. 1146 (W.D.Ark. 1995).

Disney Company acquired Capital Cities/ABC, and Westinghouse Electric took over the CBS network and its thirty-eight wholly owned television stations.

These developments toward even greater vertical integration have serious implications for the public interest in that they could lead to a lack of access for hard-hitting public affairs programming and a lessening of journalistic competition, the same concerns besetting the corporate newspaper. When a broadcaster with a strong news and public information tradition merges with a company dependent upon government defense contracts, is it logical to expect that critical reporting on government will be tempered? And will companies specializing in entertainment deemphasize information? Answers to such question have begun to emerge. Neil Hickey in an article entitled "So Big" (*Columbia Journalism Review,* January/February 1997) cites CBS's, NBC's and ABC's deference to China's feelings about reports on human rights, Taiwan, Chinese athletes' use of performance-enhancing drugs, and Martin Scorsese's movie about the Dalai Lama. Each network's parent company—Westinghouse, General Electric, Disney, respectively—has large engineering projects or business relations in and with China. Another question has been asked: Since when does a network have to apologize for telling the truth?

Rupert Murdoch, an Australian magnate who became a U.S. citizen, bought twelve UHF television stations in many of the nation's largest markets and with them Twentieth Century Fox studios to form a fourth network. He has since acquired New World Communications Group, making him the nation's leading television station owner with twenty-two outlets. In addition, he holds substantial shares in seventeen other television stations and has forged an alliance with MCI Communications. Murdoch also owns HarperCollins and *TV Guide.* Three of the original networks, NBC, ABC, and CBS, have traditionally been prohibited by the antitrust laws from this very kind of vertical integration of both production and distribution systems.

In the mid-1990s, with the financial help of Blockbuster Entertainment and Nynex, Viacomm Enterprises acquired another film studio, Paramount, to create a company with substantial assets in motion pictures, television networks, theaters, cable, and book publishing (Simon & Schuster)—clearly, a vertically integrated system.

THE TELECOMMUNICATIONS REFORM BILL

The Telecommunications Reform Bill, signed into law by President Clinton on February 8, 1996, and warmly greeted by industry, has had the effect of encouraging media mergers and joint ventures at a pace never before experienced. It reflects the beginning of a new era of mass communication, a new infostructure. In a decidedly deregulatory mode but with the industry still in its hold, the federal law substantially increases the number of individual units a broadcast organization may control nationally, the limit being accessibility to 35 percent of television homes. Without an exemption from the FCC, one TV station per market will still be the rule. Common ownership of TV and radio stations in a single market has been eased. In large radio markets (those with forty-five or more stations), a single broadcaster may own eight radio stations, but no more than five of them may be AM or FM. A decreasing scale applies to smaller markets. Broadcasters will now have eight-year license terms, with renewal pretty much assumed.

Television stations may now own cable systems in a single market, subject to existing FCC rules. Broadcast networks may also own cable systems, and they may start new networks. They cannot acquire already existing networks, however.

Cable rates for basic service will be deregulated in three years from passage of the bill in larger markets, immediately in smaller markets, defined as those with fewer than 50,000 subscribers, if unaffiliated with companies with assets of $250 million or more. Rates are also deregulated immediately for any cable system in competition with a telephone company, unless it is using direct broadcast satellite.

Telephone companies are barred from buying cable systems, and vice versa, unless the purchase takes place in a community with fewer than 35,000 people, and unless the share of the buy-in is less than 10 percent. But telephone companies can now provide video programming in their own service areas. They can choose to be regulated as a cable system, a common carrier, or what will be called an "open video system."

Cable systems operate under the rules of a local franchise; common carriers are heavily regulated, usually by public service commissions, in exchange for having a local monopoly; an "open video system" would require public access channels, but no local franchise.

Early in 1996, U.S. West's Media Group, a cable and wireless division separate from its telephone business (Communication Group), announced that it would buy Continental Cable, a company that serves approximately one-third of the U.S. cable audience with 4.2 million subscribers in twenty states. With its own 500,000 subscribers in the Atlanta area and a 25 percent share in Time Warner Entertainment (Warner Brothers and HBO), U.S. West would count 16.3 million households in its stable, making it the second largest cable operator in the country. Continental also has interests in a business telephone company, a satellite service, Turner Broadcasting's cable and film studios, home shopping, E! Entertainment, the Television Food Network, the Golf Channel, and New England Cable News. In addition it has cable holdings in Argentina, Australia, and Singapore.[76]

Industry generally didn't approve of the law's sex and violence V-chip provisions. Every new TV set will have a V-chip. Programs will be rated as to sex and violence and "other indecent material." Violations will lead to fines of up to $250,000 and up to six years in prison.[77] The American Civil Liberties Union (ACLU) didn't like these content restrictions any more than the application of unenforced and unenforceable "Comstock" laws to the Internet.

Long-distance carriers, cable television companies, software companies, and satellite operators all took such advantage of the newly competitive environment that charting the mergers, buy-outs, and buy-ins became as difficult as photographing a speeding jet. The Antitrust Division of the Department of Justice, the FTC, and the FCC will be busy. It is estimated that the FCC will engage in eighty rulemakings before the Telecommunications Reform Bill is on solid ground.

Constitutional Challenges

It should not be surprising that antitrust laws directed at the print and broadcast media have been challenged as unconstitutional. The first great challenge came in 1943 when the regulatory system governing broadcasting—the Federal Communications Act of 1934—was attacked by NBC and CBS as an unconstitutional infringement upon First Amendment rights. The U.S. Supreme Court upheld the constitutionality of the act in a 1943 decision that dealt in part with antitrust questions.

A 1938 study by the FCC had revealed that more than half the radio stations then in operation were affiliated with one of the two networks, and they were the more powerful stations. Of these stations, the most powerful were the eighteen owned by CBS and NBC. Stations affiliated with the national networks (including the Mutual Broadcasting System) utilized more than 97 percent of the total nighttime broadcasting power of all the stations in the country. NBC and CBS together controlled more than 85 percent of the total nighttime wattage, and the broadcast business of the three national network companies amounted to almost half of the total business of all stations in the United States. Network control over programming and advertising rates, the government argued, subverted the authority of local broadcasters and was anticompetitive. New networks were being kept from developing. This situation had led the FCC to adopt the "chain broadcasting regulations," limiting network power over local broadcasters. Now the constitutionality of those regulations and of the entire regulatory system as well was being challenged.

"If a licensee enters into a contract with a network organization which limits his ability to make the best use of the radio facility assigned him," said the Supreme Court in upholding the constitutionality of the FCC regulations, "he is not serving the public interest. . . . The net effect . . . has been that broadcasting service has been maintained at a level below that possible under a system of free competition."[78]

76. *New York Times,* February 28, 1996, pp. C1, C4.
77. "Much of this information was taken from Christopher Stern, "New Law of the Land," *Broadcasting & Cable,* February 5, 1996, pp. 8, 9, and 12.

78. *NBC v. United States,* 319 U.S. 190 (1943).

The next challenge to the constitutionality of antitrust laws came two years later from the Associated Press. Cooperatively owned by its newspaper members, the AP had denied membership to Marshall Field's *Chicago Sun,* a new paper founded to compete with the *Chicago Tribune.* The AP wire service, the *Sun* argued, was essential for its survival.

In a landmark opinion for the U.S. Supreme Court, Justice Hugo Black wrote that the AP bylaws used to exclude the *Sun* violated the Sherman act. To the argument that applying antitrust law in this way to an association of publishers constituted an abridgment of freedom of the press guaranteed by the First Amendment, Justice Black replied in language that is both puzzling and spirited:

> The First Amendment, far from providing an argument against application of the Sherman Act, here provides powerful reasons to the contrary. . . . Surely a command that the government itself shall not impede the free flow of ideas does not afford non-governmental combinations a refuge if they impose restraints upon that constitutionally guaranteed freedom. Freedom to publish means freedom for all and not for some. Freedom to publish is guaranteed by the Constitution, but freedom to combine to keep others from publishing is not. Freedom of the press from governmental interference under the First Amendment does not sanction repression of that freedom by private interests.[79]

Black's declaration is puzzling in that it suggests that private power as well as state action, i.e., governmental interference, may raise First Amendment barriers. Generally, the First Amendment has been interpreted as precluding only the federal government or Congress, or other branches or agencies of state and local government, from abridging First Amendment rights.

Together these two cases and others[80] left little doubt that antitrust laws, like all laws of general application, do apply to the media. Nor would the First Amendment protect a newspaper that refused classified ads in order to "strangle" a competitor.[81] Deceptive advertising, however,

would not warrant equal consideration, the same federal appeals court had said two years earlier: "[A] newspaper, monopoly or not, armed with both the First Amendment and a reasonable business justification, can[not] be ordered to publish advertising against its will."[82]

Newspaper Antitrust Immunity

When faced with a merger, the Antitrust Division defines the product and its geographical market. It then calculates the percentage of the market to be controlled by the new, merged firm and decides whether that figure is sufficient to create a "reasonable probability" of lessened competition through "the willful acquisition or maintenance of that power as distinguished from growth or development as a consequence of a superior product, business acumen, or historical accident," to use the language of the Sherman Act.

Economic pressures toward group ownership in the newspaper business have been enormous. Tax laws stimulate the investment of accumulated reserves. Undistributed earnings are not taxed as personal or corporate income if they are used to acquire additional newspaper properties. Those who already own newspapers generally know how to manage additional ones, and there are advantages to central management, pooled editorial services, and higher standing in the financial markets. At the same time, estate taxes are such that few aging publishers can resist the inflated purchase prices frequently offered by newspaper groups.

Powerful lobbying by the American Newspaper Publishers Association (ANPA)—now the Newspaper Association of America (NAA) as a result of mergers among a number of newspaper trade organizations—led to passage of the Newspaper Preservation Act in 1970.[83] Under certain conditions, the act *immunizes* newspapers from some structural constraints of the antitrust laws.

If there is no obvious intent to monopolize[84] and the geographic market is deemed unable to

---

79. *Associated Press v. United States,* 326 U.S. 1 (1945).
80. See, for example, *Citizen Publishing Co. v. United States,* 394 U.S. 131 (1969); *Lorain Journal Co. v. United States,* 342 U.S. 143 (1951).
81. *Home Placement Service v. Providence Journal,* 8 Med. L. Rptr. 1881, 682 F.2d 274 (1st Cir. 1982).

82. *Homefinders of America v. Providence Journal,* 6 Med. L. Rptr. 1018, 621 F.2d 441 (1st Cir. 1980).
83. Pub.L. 91–353, 84 Stat. 466 (codified at 15 U.S.C.A. §§ 1801–04).
84. *United States v. Harte-Hanks Newspapers, Inc.,* 170 F.Supp. 227 (N.D.Tex. 1959).

support competing daily newspapers,[85] the act permits the business, technical, and circulation departments of two papers, one of which is failing, to merge into a Joint Operating Agreement (JOA) for a fixed but renewable period of time. The editorial departments must remain separate, however, preserving two newspaper voices, and presumably editorial diversity, in the community. It is argued, therefore, that the act serves the First Amendment by saving editorial competition in a situation where it is in imminent danger of disappearing.

Since 1930, mergers in all businesses have been protected where there is clear evidence that a competing company is failing.[86] Thus, there must be a "failing newspaper" before the act permits a merger, and this is often a point of contention when these mergers are being considered. Is there sufficient evidence that the acquired newspaper's resources are depleted, that reorganization or financial rehabilitation of some kind would make no difference, and that no prospective buyers have appeared?

The act was an attempt in part to undo the work of the U.S. Supreme Court in *Citizen Publishing Co. v. United States,*[87] a case that began in Tucson, Arizona. In disallowing the merger, the Court stipulated that the acquired company, there a faltering evening newspaper, had to be so close to failing that nothing could save it. Otherwise price fixing, profit pooling, and market allocation schemes were *per se* illegal under the Sherman Act. That energized the ANPA to lobby the Congress for what was first called the Failing Newspaper Act and would become the Newspaper Preservation Act, a more congenial title. The latter act, however, does permit the U.S. attorney general to circumvent the criteria of "failing."

Before passage of the act, competing newspapers in twenty-three cities, beginning in Albuquerque, New Mexico, in 1933, had already merged into something like JOAs; they were "grandfathered" by the 1970 act, if they met the requirements of future JOAs.[88] In the past two decades, some JOAs have failed when the weaker newspaper in the agreement has ceased publication. This happened in Columbus, St. Louis, Miami, Tulsa, and Shreveport, Louisiana. In St. Louis, the Justice Department played an active role in selling the failing *Globe-Democrat,* but to the government's embarrassment, the purchaser itself failed in turn. In the last ten years, new JOAs have been made in Las Vegas, Detroit, and York, Pennsylvania. At about the same time, newspapers in Anchorage and Knoxville chose to regain their independence, and in Franklin–Oil City, Pennsylvania, the dominant newspaper ended the JOA by purchasing its partner. Buyouts, independent of JOAs, occurred in Little Rock when the *Arkansas Democrat* acquired the assets of the *Arkansas Gazette;* in Dallas when the A. H. Belo Corporation, publisher of the *Dallas Morning News,* bought out the *Dallas Times-Herald* (and the Providence *Journal-Bulletin*); and in Houston when the *Houston Chronicle* purchased the *Houston Post.* In the Houston case, the *Chronicle* had to demonstrate that the *Post* was unable to meet its financial obligations or to reorganize effectively under the Bankruptcy Act. It also had to show that good faith efforts had been made to find a buyer—essentially the "failing newspaper" test. Similar buy-outs have occurred in Anchorage; Atlanta; Laredo, Texas; Colorado Springs; Scranton, Pennsylvania; and Hudson County, New Jersey. The Justice Department made no objections to any of these transactions. In early 1996, seventeen JOAs were still in existence, and there was some concern about their future. The seventeen constitute nearly half of the thirty-six cities still claiming two or more dailies under separate ownership. Real daily newspaper competition prevails in no more than a dozen U.S. cities.

Again, under the "failing company" doctrine, newspapers have to show that the resources of one of the newspapers are about to be depleted; that is, the weaker newspaper must be in what has been referred to as a "downward spiral." A merger at any earlier point would be prohibited.

Two newspaper economists recommend that an exception to this prohibition be made for

---

85. *Union Leader v. Newspapers of New England, Inc.,* 180 F.Supp. 125 (D.Mass. 1959), *modified on other grounds,* 284 F.2d 582 (1st Cir. 1960), *cert. denied* 365 U.S. 833 (1961).
86. *International Shoe Company v. FTC,* 280 U.S. 291 (1930).
87. 1 Med. L. Rptr. 2704, 394 U.S. 131 (1969).

88. *Honolulu v. Hawaii Newspaper Agency,* 9 Med. L. Rptr. 1382, 559 F.Supp. 1021 (D.Hawaii 1983).

Sunday editions in what they would call a limited joint operation. They see benefits to both advertisers and subscribers from such an arrangement.[89]

Newspaper employees, advertisers, and the publishers of suburban newspapers generally oppose JOAs for obvious reasons—loss of jobs, higher advertising rates, and unfair or, at the very least, monolithic competition. They have also argued that JOAs represent a special privilege to powerful publishers who no longer wish to compete for advertisers and subscribers. Academicians often oppose JOAs because they suspect the motivations behind such mergers: Why would anyone want to take on a business that is truly failing? Is this the way a dominant newspaper eases into a monopoly? Will two independent voices remain when the same business values support them both? Will the press at some later date pay a price for what some will perceive as special statutory privilege for an elitist few—in other words, special legislation for the press? What the government gives the government can take away.

In recent years, JOAs in Seattle and Detroit experienced this kind of opposition. In Seattle, the U.S. attorney general, who must approve all such mergers, said the financial health of a newspaper could be considered apart from the financial condition of the chain to which it belonged. The "failing" *Post-Intelligencer* belonged to the financially sound Hearst organization. Nor was it necessary, said the attorney general, to prove the absence of a qualified buyer. A federal district judge disagreed with this interpretation of the act, but was reversed by the Ninth Circuit Court of Appeals. *The P-I, the appeals court held, was clearly in a "downward spiral."*[90] The critical question in determining whether a newspaper is "failing," said the court, is whether it is "suffering losses which more than likely cannot be reversed," despite reasonable management by either present or projected staff.

A battle of leviathans took place in Detroit where the two largest newspaper groups in the country, Gannett and Knight-Ridder, each had a newspaper. The latter claimed losses of $35 million over a five-year period for its *Free Press,* the second newspaper in Detroit and eighth largest in the country. Gannett claimed losses of $20 million for its *News,* the seventh largest U.S. daily.

Opponents charged that the two newspapers were engaging in what lawyers call self-predation: they were orchestrating their own failures by selling subscriptions and advertising space far below costs in order to be granted the privileges of a JOA. Knight-Ridder threatened to close the *Free Press* unless the merger was allowed. Jobs would be lost, and advertising and subscription rates would certainly go up if the JOA went through. It did, and advertising and subscription rates increased to a point where customers, it was said, were singing a tune dubbed the "JOA Blues."

In August 1988, the U.S. attorney general approved the merger, this time against the better judgment of one of his assistants and an administrative law judge. The *Free Press,* said the attorney general, had "satisfactorily demonstrated that the danger of its financial failure has moved well within the zone of 'probability,'" and that it could do nothing to reverse "the unbroken pattern of operating losses." Despite opposition from a committee of advertisers, readers, and employees, a federal district court approved the merger, defining the *Free Press* as a "failing newspaper."[91] In 1989, a divided panel of the District of Columbia Circuit Court of Appeals affirmed that decision, finding the attorney general's interpretation of both the law and the precarious position of the *Free Press* "reasonable." Portions of that decision follow:

Michigan Citizens for an Independent Press, et al., v. Richard Thornburgh, United States Attorney General, et al.
16 MED. L. RPTR. 1065, 868 F.2D 1285 (D.C. CIR. 1989).

SILBERMAN, Circuit Judge:

This case presents a challenge to a decision and order of the Attorney General, pursuant to

---

89. John C. Busterna and Robert G. Picard, *Joint Operating Agreements: The Newspaper Preservation Act and Its Application* (Norwood, N.J.: Ablex Publishing Corporation, 1993).
90. *Committee for an Independent P-I v. Hearst Corp.,* 9 Med. L. Rptr. 1489, 704 F.2d 467 (9th Cir. 1983), *cert. denied* 464 U.S. 892 (1983).

91. *Michigan Citizens for an Independent Press v. Attorney General of the United States,* 15 Med. L. Rptr. 1943, 695 F.Supp. 1216 (D.D.C. 1988).

the Newspaper Preservation Act ("NPA"), 15 U.S.C. § 1801–1804 (1982), approving a joint operating arrangement between the *Detroit Free Press* and *Detroit News* newspapers. Appellants, which include Michigan Citizens For An Independent Press,[1] seven individuals,[2] and the interest group Public Citizen, brought suit against the Attorney General and the two newspapers in the district court alleging that the Attorney General's decision violates the NPA and the Administrative Procedure Act, 5 U.S.C. § 706 (1982), because it is not based on substantial evidence, is arbitrary and capricious, and is otherwise in violation of law. The district court granted summary judgment in favor of defendants, and plaintiffs appealed to this court. We conclude that the Attorney General's decision was based on a permissible construction of the statute, and that his application of the legal standard to the facts of this case was not arbitrary, capricious, or an abuse of discretion. We therefore affirm the judgment of the district court.

* * *

Appellants allege that the Attorney General's determination is invalid both because it is based on an impermissible interpretation of the statute and is arbitrary or capricious. As is not unusual in appeals from agency actions, the claims are interrelated. At the core of appellants' case is the assertion that the Attorney General could not legally grant approval for a JOA because the *Detroit Free Press* was not in a tough enough spot to qualify as "in probable danger of financial failure." Whether the Attorney General legally decided that the *Free Press* did meet the statutory standard in turn depends to a large extent on whether his prediction of the newspaper's future course (if he did not approve the JOA) was reasonable. The Attorney General's interpretation of the probable danger of financial failure test draws content from the factual showing that he requires to meet that test. See *INS. v. Cardoza-Fonseca*, 107 S.Ct. 1207, 1221 (1987) (ambiguous statutory terms "can only be given concrete

meaning through a process of case-by-case adjudication"). And there is no question in our mind that if the Attorney General's statutory interpretation is reasonable, it is entitled to deference under *Chevron U.S.A. Inc. v. NRDC,* 467 U.S. 837, 842–43 (1984), because we are certainly unable to discern a specific congressional intent governing this case.

* * *

To be sure, the Attorney General had not previously faced a case such as this. Prior approvals of JOAs had always involved at least one newspaper that had actually entered the downward spiral, whereas the *Detroit Free Press* could be said to be poised on the brink of the spiral, its future dependent on the competitive behavior of the *News.* Still, the only prior case reviewing an Attorney General's approval of a JOA—the pre-*Chevron* decision of the Ninth Circuit in *Hearst*—phrased the question before the Attorney General in broader terms than whether one of the newspapers had entered a downward spiral. The court asked: "Is the newspaper suffering losses which more than likely cannot be reversed?" This interpretation of the statutory language, which the court called a "commonsense construction," *id.* at 478, was explicitly adopted by the Attorney General in this case, and thus made his own interpretation entitled to *Chevron* deference. Only for cogent reasons would we reject as unreasonable an interpretation of a statute that a sister circuit had considered a commonsense construction.

The Ninth Circuit thought implicit in its inquiry was an examination of alternative forms of relief for the putatively failing newspaper. Was there, for example, a group of interested buyers or a potential for improved management? Congress' reference to the *Third National Bank* case in the legislative history of the statute suggested to the Ninth Circuit that Congress intended the Attorney General to consider alternatives to a JOA before approving an application. We quite agree, but so apparently did the Attorney General. He concluded that if no form of relief was within the control of the sick newspaper—its survival depended only on improbable behavior by its competitor—the statutory test was satisfied. Appellants artificially construe the Attorney General's decision to permit a JOA without regard to consideration

---

1. At the time this suit was filed, Michigan Citizens For An Independent Press had twenty members who either read, purchased classified advertising in, or are employed by one of the newspapers.

2. The seven individual plaintiffs include persons who purchase advertising in the papers and allege that advertising prices will rise if the JOA is approved.

of the competitor's behavior, but that is not what the Attorney General said.

* * *

In this type of case * * * the Attorney General is called upon to balance two legislative policies in tension: The pro-consumer direction of the antitrust laws and a congressional desire embodied in the Newspaper Preservation Act that diverse editorial voices be preserved despite the unique economics of the newspaper industry. This is precisely the paradigm situation *Chevron* addressed. If the agency's choice "represents a reasonable accommodation of conflicting policies that were committed to the agency's care by the statute, we should not disturb it unless it appears from the statute or its legislative history that the accommodation is not one that Congress would have sanctioned." *Chevron*, 467 U.S. at 845 (quoting *United States v. Shimer*, 367 U.S. 374, 383 (1961)). To invoke the normal canon of construction is merely to say that the Attorney General put too much weight on the policy of preserving editorial diversity. We are not now after *Chevron*—if we ever were—permitted to accept such an argument.

Appellants argue that the Attorney General should receive less deference than *Chevron* requires, because "his interpretation of the statute was different from that of the Antitrust Division, where the Justice Department's expertise on the Newspaper Preservation Act resides." We have previously rejected the notion that *Chevron* deference is based solely on agency expertise. *Public Citizen v. Burke*, 843 F.2d 1473, 1477 (D.C.Cir. 1988); *Cablevision Systems Dev. Co. v. Motion Picture Ass'n of America*, 836 F.2d 599, 608–09 (D.C.Cir. 1988). The rationale of *Chevron* is also grounded in the principle that the political branches of government, rather than the judiciary, should make policy choices. *Chevron*, 467 U.S. at 865–66.

* * *

The only specific challenge, as far as we can determine, to the Attorney General's appraisal of the respective competitive strengths of the two newspapers is based on the different opinion of the ALJ (and the Antitrust Division's brief to the ALJ). It is true that the Attorney General's crucial conclusions that the *Free Press* "has no realistic prospect of outlasting the *News* given the latter's substantial advertising and persistent circulation

lead" and that the *News* "undoubtedly has the ability * * * to outlast the *Free Press* was predicated on the ALJ's findings recounting the *News'* lead in all major indices. It is also true that the ALJ went on to offer a somewhat different conclusion: that the *Free Press* was still within "striking distance" of the *News* and the latter's lead was "vulnerable." The Attorney General would not, however, be legally obliged to conform his judgment to that of a statutorily-required ALJ, much less this one, who was employed as a matter of discretion rather than law. * * * Both men relied on the very same facts to make different evaluations of the competitive strength of the *Free Press*. But, it is only the Attorney General's conclusions that have legal significance, and we cannot say that his determination is unreasonable. It is undisputed, after all, that the *News* has maintained the lead for a long time and that the *Free Press* had suffered extensive losses. Debatable, the Attorney General's appraisal may well be, but hardly unreasonable.

Similarly, appellants rely on the ALJ's contrary prediction to dispute the Attorney General's conclusion that the *News* would *not* release the pressure on the *Free Press* by raising prices if the JOA were disapproved. Gannett officials testified that they had no intention of raising prices regardless of the Attorney General's decision. The ALJ refused to credit this testimony, not on account of the witnesses' demeanor, but because he, the ALJ, thought that course would only cause more losses for the *News* and was therefore irrational. The Attorney General's judgment of the *News'* likely future behavior was premised on his determination, which we have already found reasonable, that the *News* had the competitive strength to outlast the *Free Press*. The ALJ never squarely found otherwise, and if the *News* had such strength, we do not see how the Attorney General's projection can be deemed unreasonable. Under those circumstances, Gannett's refusal to raise prices, as the Attorney General said, "hardly reflects unsound business judgment."

* * *

It may well be, as appellants argue and the ALJ found, that under ideal circumstances, Detroit could support two newspapers. The same could also be true of many cities that have lost competing newspapers and are now one newspaper monopoly towns. It is not at all clear whether the newspaper business in some cities is a natural monopoly, and, if so, in cities of what size. This sort of speculation, it seems to us, as it did to the Attorney General, is hardly conclusive. That an omniscient Detroit newspaper czar could set circulation and advertising prices that would permit both papers to return to profitable status is not a useful observation in this context. The Attorney General is required to determine what will actually happen in Detroit if his approval is withheld. It would, moreover, be anomalous for those responsible for enforcing the antitrust laws to try to guide and calibrate the competitive zeal of the two newspapers so as to reach that level of competition at which both newspapers could be profitable.

* * *

The real difficulty with this case—the factor that quite plainly underlies the ALJ's discomfort as well as appellants' quarrel with the Attorney General's decision—is the effect that the prospect of a JOA has on the behavior of competing newspapers. It is feared that the statute authorizing a JOA creates a self-fulfilling prophecy. Newspapers in two newspaper towns will compete recklessly because of a recognition that the loser will be assured a soft landing.

Appellants argue that the Attorney General inadequately considered whether or not "critical aspects of the newspapers' conduct were influenced by the prospect of obtaining a JOA." But his opinion addressed this "dual motive" concern at some length; he observed that this was not the classic case that had worried Congress, where a newspaper had "brought itself to the brink of financial failure through improper marketing practices or culpable management." Instead, the record of years of fierce competitive and consequent losses to both papers led the Attorney General reasonably to conclude that both papers were principally pursuing market domination and that their strategies had been followed before any mutual discussion of a JOA. Nevertheless, the Attorney General implicitly recognized that it would be impossible completely to preclude competing newspapers from factoring into their business strategy the prospect of a JOA. As he laconically put it, "newspapers cannot be faulted for considering and acting upon an alternative that Congress has created."

We can envision a perfectly rational different policy, one that would require a showing that the weaker paper was more bloodied before approving a JOA and therefore *might* discourage the sort of competition we saw in Detroit. Congress, however, delegated to the Attorney General, not to us, the delicate and troubling responsibility of putting content into the ambiguous phrase "probable danger of financial failure." We cannot therefore say that his interpretation of that phrase as applied to this case, with all of its obvious policy implications, was unreasonable. The judgment of the district court therefore is *affirmed.*

GINSBURG, RUTH B., Circuit Judge, dissenting:

* * *

Just as there is no dispute that the *Free Press* and the *News* have both incurred significant losses on an operating basis, so it is undisputed that neither paper has experienced any "downward spiral" effect. On the contrary, in the relevant time period, 1976 to 1986, the *Free Press* share of daily circulation was never less than 49%; its competitive position has remained essentially stable; the *News,* though retaining a "leading" edge, is not "dominant." Antitrust Division Brief at 7–11. In other words, the two papers, each now maintained by a "deep pocket," the *News* by Gannett, the *Free Press* by Knight-Ridder, have fought to a draw. Neither has achieved supremacy. The competition today "is as close, or closer, than it was a decade ago."

Gannett, it is also conceded, acquired the *News* only after obtaining expression of Knight-Ridder's willingness to consider a JOA. The nearly equal profit slit for the *Free Press* under the JOA indicates the "standoff" that existed; it reflects "a recognition on Gannett's part that the *Free Press* was not likely to exit the market in the near future." No "failing" paper in Newspaper Preservation Act history, it appears, has emerged so advantageously under an approved JOA. In these circumstances, I believe it incumbent on the Attorney General to recall—as our sister court observed—the legislature's "primary" concern "to prevent newspapers from allowing or encouraging financial difficulties in the hope of reaping long-term financial gains through a JOA." *Hearst,* 704 F.2d at 478.

* * *

The Newspaper Preservation Act's legislative history confirms that the "probable danger" standard was meant to have bite, to be "far more stringent" than the "not financially sound" test, 116 CONG.REC. 23,146 (statement of Rep. Kastenmeier), and thus "limited only to those situations where a joint newspaper operating arrangement is demonstrably essential to prevent a newspaper failure." *Id.* at 23,148 (statement of Rep. McCulloch). Given the congressional design, approval of a proposed JOA requires an affirmative answer to this question: "Is the [allegedly failing] newspaper suffering losses which more than likely cannot be reversed?" *Hearst,* 704 F.2d at 478.

The Attorney General's readiness to say "Yes" to a JOA for *Free Press-Detroit News* now, despite the view of the Antitrust Division and the ALJ that such a judgment remains premature, seems to me problematic on two counts. First, the Decision affords no assurance that the Attorney General has found a "middle ground" firmer than the pliant "not likely to * * * become financially sound" ground Congress thought inadequate for new agreements. The Decision never suggests any separate content for the "probable danger" standard to distinguish it from the more accommodating one. Second, the demonstration that satisfied the Attorney General allows parties situated as Gannett and Knight-Ridder are artificially to generate and maintain the conditions that will yield them a passing JOA. I remain unpersuaded that, with passage of the Newspaper Preservation Act, Congress opened the door to this sort of self-serving, competition-quieting arrangement. *Cf.* Attorney General's Decision at 12 (maintaining that "Congress opened the door to just this sort of response with passage of the Newspaper Preservation Act").

* * *

Detroit, as the Attorney General said, "is a highly prized $300 million dollar market." Attorney General's Decision at 4. That market could sustain two profitable newspapers. *Id.* at 9 n. 3. Market dominance is now beyond the grasp of the News as well as the Free Press. *Id.* at 13. The Attorney General has not cogently explained why, on the facts thus far found, the proposed JOA has become "an available option." Making the JOA an option now, in the situation artificially created and maintained by the *Free Press* and the *News,* moves boldly away from the "frame of reference [Congress] essentially embraced"—"the scenario of a strong newspaper

poised to drive from the market a weaker competitor," a newspaper experiencing, "due to external market forces," a decline in revenues and circulation "that in all probability cannot be reversed." *Id.* at 6, 13–14. I therefore dissent from the majority's disposition approving instanter [without delay] the giant stride the Attorney General has taken.

COMMENT

Judge Ruth Bader Ginsburg, now a Supreme Court justice, dissented. She did not see the *Free Press* in a downward spiral. Both papers were maintained by "deep-pocket" parent companies. Their competition was close. A JOA had been talked about when Gannett acquired the *News* some years before.

"No 'failing' paper in Newspaper Preservation Act history," she wrote, "has emerged so advantageously under an approved JOA." And she noted Congress's desire to prevent newspapers from engaging in destructive competition in the hope of gaining long-term financial rewards through a JOA—profit pooling, price fixing, and market allocation.

The U.S. Supreme Court affirmed the circuit court panel's decision in a tie vote[92] after the full appeals court had declined to hear the case. What would be a highly profitable merger went forward. The combined circulation of the two newspapers reached 1.2 million and then began to tumble, especially that of the *News.*

The success of the merger was by no means assured when a devastating 583-day strike hit the two newspapers in 1995. It is estimated that Gannett and Knight-Ridder lost between $100 and $200 million in strike-related costs and forgone profits. Labor took the hardest blows. Striking workers were replaced and most have not been rehired. In 1997, the National Labor Relations Board was considering their complaints of unfair labor practices, notably the hiring of "permanent replacements." As has happened in earlier newspaper walkouts, editorial staffs split on whether or not to strike. Management also lost. Though it won lower labor costs, the combined company lost half of its circula-

---

92. *Michigan Citizens for an Independent Press, et al. v. Thornburgh,* 490 U.S. 1045 (1989).

tion, half of its original editorial department, many of its advertisers, and, most seriously, the goodwill of a substantial segment of Detroit's population.

Then there were the possible long-range effects. Competition for readers and advertising could be stiffened as former newspaper subscribers and advertisers increasingly turned to cable, now in two-thirds of U.S. households, and to the more than two thousand consumer magazines, the growing number of news and talk radio stations, direct mail, and, of course, the Internet. Would subscribers come back?

After *Michigan Citizens,* an antitrust authority wrote:

> Under the Attorney General's interpretation of the Newspaper Preservation Act, two newspapers may enter into a price war, and create losses that provide the basis for seeking the protection of a JOA. That protection may be forthcoming even though neither newspaper has entered the downward spiral. Indeed, under the Attorney General's interpretation . . . a newspaper may be entitled to the protection of a JOA simply by demonstrating it is suffering losses that cannot be reversed. Since neither newspaper in a price war can afford to lose parity with its rival since the loss of parity typically results in a downward spiral, neither newspaper will be willing to withdraw from the price war that generates its losses. In short, a price war with its accompanying losses in and of itself arguably provides the basis for a JOA.[93]

In 1991, the Antitrust Division approved a proposed JOA between the weekly Manteca (Calif.) *News* and the daily Manteca *Bulletin,* the first merger of its kind, even though antitrust lawyers at first suspected that the weekly's financial difficulties were due primarily to bad management. The weekly died, however, before the marriage could be consummated.

Brief Antitrust Histories

BROADCASTING The FCC may consider antitrust behavior when measuring a licensee's performance against the "public interest, convenience, and necessity" standard applied in the licensing renewal process.

Although the FCC twice approved the proposed acquisition of ABC by International Tele-

phone and Telegraph (ITT) in the late 1960s, continuing Antitrust Division objections led to the canceling of the sale in 1968. In the 1980s, however, the same government agency raised no significant objections to the sale of the same network to Capital Cities Broadcasting, admittedly a more compatible takeover, and, ultimately, sale of the merged company to Disney. Nor were there objections to the acquisition of NBC by General Electric or CBS by Westinghouse.

In the 1970s, the Department of Justice limited network control over prime-time programming by severely restricting network control over production, syndication, and talent—controls that have been eliminated in light of the rapid growth of cable competition.

Also in the 1970s, the authority of the National Association of Broadcasters (NAB), a trade association, over programming was limited by antitrust forces. The Writers Guild of America argued that the NAB code exhorting broadcasters to implement socially responsible practices in both advertising and programming was *government* regulation in disguise. In particular, the guild saw "family viewing" rules, which set aside early evening hours for programming that would insulate children from sex and violence, as an infringement of writers' First Amendment freedoms.

A federal district court judge agreed, although his ruling was later vacated by an appeals court.[94] For the three years the rules were in effect, the NAB lived the public relations nightmare of being charged with violating the First Amendment rights of its own members. The prime-time access rules of the 1970s are now gone, but the debate over children viewing sex and violence is not.

At about the same time, the Department of Justice claimed that three provisions in the NAB television code limiting commercial time were a conspiracy to drive up the price of commercials and therefore violated the Sherman Act. A federal district court judge agreed in part.[95] A later settlement between the Department of Justice and the NAB closed the matter, but not before the NAB dropped its radio and television codes

---

93. Shumadine, Kelley, and Edgar, *op. cit.,* pp. 482–83.

94. *Writers Guild of America v. American Broadcasting Co.,* 609 F.2d 355 (1979).
95. *United States v. National Association of Broadcasters,* 536 F.Supp. 149 (D.D.C. 1982) and 553 F.Supp. 621 (1982).

altogether. However, the federal Children's Television Act of 1990 does limit commercial advertising time to 10.5 minutes per hour on weekends and 12 minutes per hour on weekdays for children under twelve.

One broadcast antitrust suit that did not end in a consent agreement or a settlement involved the question of whether the television contracts negotiated by the National Collegiate Athletic Association (NCAA) violated the Sherman Act. The Supreme Court ruled in 1984 that the association had monopolized the market for college football television in violation of the act.[96] The result of the ruling was a dramatic expansion in the amount of college football on both broadcast and cable television, as colleges signed contracts of their own or banded together in smaller regional or national associations.

Under the 1996 communications law, broadcasters may own an unlimited number of television stations if they account for less than 35 percent of the nationwide audience, a level that Westinghouse/CBS is already close to. With the purchase of Infinity Broadcasting, the corporation now owns seventy-seven radio stations. In what is termed "attribution," ownership will be defined at a certain level of stock ownership, to be decided by the FCC. Broadcasters may also own cable properties, and other forms of cross-media ownership are permitted in a single community. Under the new rules, the number of radio stations a company may own in a single community is limited, but no limit is placed on such ownership nationwide.

CABLE TELEVISION The Cable Communications Policy Act of 1984 and the Local Government Antitrust Act passed by Congress a year later relieved municipalities that license cable companies (usually one to a community) from having to worry about antitrust violations.

Cable may no longer be a natural monopoly. While local government franchisers have generally recognized this in choosing a single company to wire their communities, the 1996 communications act puts cable in direct competition with telephone and electric utility companies. Technological improvements, however, did lead to cable

competition in some larger cities. Under the law, most limits on cable rates will end by 1999. For small systems, rate regulation ended with the signing of the bill. Municipal cable regulators are immune to antitrust laws if what they do is based on "clearly articulated and affirmatively expressed state policy."[97]

An unsuccessful cable applicant was awarded $6 million after proving that Houston business leaders, the mayor, and the applicant who won the franchise had conspired to violate the Sherman Act in order to block him from the area. TCI, already described as one of the country's largest cable system operators, got into the same kind of trouble when it was proved that the company had conspired with the mayor and other city officials to retain its franchise in Jefferson City, Missouri. The penalty there was $35 million.

Cable has continued to consolidate both horizontally and vertically. Multiple system operators (MSOs) have bought more and more systems, and major MSOs have bought into many of their sources of programming. Cable's problems with antitrust laws are by no means over. In the early 1990s, Congress struggled with such questions as how to make cable more competitive, what power local authorities should have over cable rates and services where there was no local competition, and whether network television should be permitted to own cable systems, especially in large and competitive markets? Congress did pass a complex Cable Act in 1992.[98]

The ban on video programming by telephone companies continued, but a national debate immediately erupted over whether the Act's "must-carry" provisions (requiring cable companies to carry all local commercial and noncommercial broadcasts on top of their obligation to provide public access, educational, and governmental channels) violated cable's First Amendment rights. In 1994 and again in 1997, the U.S. Supreme Court declared that the "must-carry" rules are constitutional so long as they are content-neutral restrictions on speech that further a substantial governmental interest and are no more restrictive than necessary to serve that

---

96. *NCAA v. Board of Regents of the University of Oklahoma,* 468 U.S. 85 (1984).

97. *Community Communications Co. v. City of Boulder,* 455 U.S. 40 (1982).
98. Cable Television Consumer and Competition Act, 47 U.S.C. §§ 534 and 535.

interest. The 1994 case was remanded to a federal district court to consider the question.[99]

In late 1995, a divided three-judge panel of the U.S. District Court for the District of Columbia had upheld the "must-carry" rules because, it said, "the economic health of local broadcasters is in genuine jeopardy and in need of the protection afforded by must carry" as directed by the Supreme Court.[100] Cablecasters denied that there was "justification in any concern about free competition for giving the holders of government-granted broadcast licenses a mandated preference over independent cable programmers, equally seeking access to viewers in the same community." The issue was finally resolved by the Supreme Court in 1997 (see Chapter 14).

TELEPHONE On January 8, 1982, the Department of Justice and AT&T reached a settlement in a protracted antitrust suit against AT&T, Western Electric, and Bell Labs, Inc. Finally, AT&T agreed to give up control of local telephone service, but retain its long-distance operations in competition with new companies such as MCI and U.S. Sprint. It could also enter into new, unregulated businesses. A major consequence of this settlement was the spin-off of seven regional Bell companies or regional Bell operating companies (RBOCs). The breakup went into effect in 1984.[101]

In mid-1991, under intense lobbying pressure, Judge Harold Greene reluctantly removed the provision prohibiting the regional Bells from providing information services, but stayed his order until it could be reviewed by a higher court.[102] In the meantime, the Senate passed a bill allowing the seven Bell companies to participate in research, design, and manufacture of communication equipment.

Counterlegislation was immediately forthcoming. A bill introduced by Rep. Jim Cooper of Tennessee, supported by the newspaper lobby, would have barred the Bells from offering information services as long as they had a monopoly on local telephone services. The newspaper industry and twenty-three other media and consumer groups, joined by AT&T and other long-distance companies, urged reimposition of Judge Greene's stay delaying entry of the regional Bells into the information services business. The U.S. Supreme Court refused to allow this until the appellate court had considered the case.

"Fair competition cannot exist," the American Newspaper Publishers Association argued, "where you are forced to rely on a competitor for delivery of your product." Opponents retorted that restrictions on the Bell companies were unconstitutional because they denied them "the right to use their natural advantages to communicate with their intended audiences."

In 1992, the FCC modified the telco-cable cross-ownership rules to permit telcos (telephone companies) to originate video services on a common carrier basis (video dialtone).[103] In a series of 1994 cases, federal courts found the telco-cable ownership ban of sec. 533(b) of the 1984 Cable Communication and Policy Act an unconstitutional violation of the First Amendment. In one of those cases—*National Cable Television Assoc. Inc. v. Bell Atlantic Corp.*, 42 F.3d 181 (4th Cir. 1994)—a federal appeals court judge, in granting summary judgment to Bell Atlantic, refused to accept the proposition that potentially anticompetitive behavior was a sufficient reason for limiting the First Amendment rights of telephone companies. The Fourth Circuit said that sec. 533(b) was not narrowly tailored to serve the government's interest in promoting competition in the video programming market and in preserving diversity in ownership. That case and *United States v. Chesapeake and Potomac Telephone Co.*[104] were joined and granted certiorari by the U.S. Supreme Court. The Supreme Court sent the cases back to the Fourth Circuit to decide whether they were made moot by the 1996 Telecommunications Act.

99. *Turner Broadcasting System v. FCC*, 22 Med. L. Rptr. 1865, 114 S.Ct. 2245 (1994).
100. *Turner Broadcasting v. FCC*, 910 F.Supp. 734 (DDC 1995).
101. *United States v. AT&T*, 552 F.Supp. 131 (D.D.C. 1982), aff'd mem., sub nom., *Maryland v. United States*, 460 U.S. 1001 (1983).
102. *United States v. Western Elec. Co.*, 767 F.Supp. 308 (D.D.C. 1991), aff'd, *United States v. Western Elec. Co.*, 993 F.2d 1572 (D.C. Cir. 1992), cert. denied, 114 S.Ct. 487 (1993).

103. *In re Telephone Co.—Cable Television Cross-Ownership Rules, Sections 63.54–63.58, Second Report and Order, Recommendation to Congress and Further Notice of Proposed Rulemaking*, 7 F.C.C. 5781, 5783, sec. 1 (1992).
104. 24 Med. L. Rptr. 1352, 116 S.Ct. 1036 (1996).

MOTION PICTURES   The Sherman Act was first applied to the movies in 1923 in *Binderup v. Pathe Exchange, Inc.*[105] in order to free theater owners from having to show pictures foisted on them by a conspiracy of distributors. Seven years later, a take-it-or-get-nothing contract was declared anticompetitive in *Paramount Famous Lasky Corp. v. United States.*[106]

When Crescent Amusement Co., a monopoly chain in many towns, pressured distributors to give it monopoly rights in communities in which it had competition, the Supreme Court upheld an order to divest. The company was required to demonstrate that it would not restrain trade through any future acquisitions.[107] Theater chains and distributors were also prohibited from conspiring to concentrate the movie market in *Schine Chain Theatres, Inc. v. United States.*[108] In yet another case, independent distributors were unable to show certain producers' films until they had been shown in studio-owned theaters. The Supreme Court in *Bigelow v. RKO Radio Pictures, Inc.*[109] condemned such vertical producer-distributor-exhibitor combines.

The 1948 case of *United States v. Paramount Pictures, Inc.*[110] was particularly significant. Major film studios were required to divest their theaters in what was called at the time "the most significant change in the structure of a mass medium to be achieved to date under the antitrust laws."[111]

In *United States v. Loew's, Inc.*,[112] the Supreme Court considered the legality of block booking copyrighted motion pictures for television use. No conspiracy was alleged among defendants, but the lower courts had challenged the manner in which each defendant had marketed its product. Television stations were required to sign up for potboiler films in order to get the classics. Relying on *Paramount Pictures*, the Court held this form of *tying* to be a violation of the Sherman Act.

In 1986, a federal district court in California held that exclusive distribution agreements for first-run motion pictures between distributor and theater were *not* unreasonable restraints of trade.[113] The Ninth Circuit Court of Appeals affirmed, and the Supreme Court denied certiorari.[114]

THE MEDIA AND LABOR LAWS

A Free Press and the Journalist's Rights under Federal Labor Laws

Understanding the relationship of labor law and the press begins with a 1937 Supreme Court case, *Associated Press v. NLRB*, which established that labor laws may be applied to the press without violating the First Amendment.

Morris Watson, an editorial writer for AP, was fired for engaging in union activity. The American Newspaper Guild filed a charge with the National Labor Relations Board (NLRB) alleging that Watson's discharge violated sec. 7 of the National Labor Relations Act (NLRA)[115] and that AP had engaged in unfair labor practices as defined in the Act.[116] The Act forbids employers from interfering with employee attempts to "form, join, or assist labor organizations * * * for the purpose of collective bargaining. * * *"

AP first challenged the validity of the Act itself, alleging that Congress had overstepped its powers to regulate interstate commerce. It also argued that the specific dispute had no implications for interstate commerce. The Court dismissed the challenge, upholding what is now considered Congress's almost plenary authority over interstate commerce. The Court reasoned that "* * * it is obvious that strikes or labor disputes amongst this class of employees would have as direct an effect upon the activities of [AP] as similar disturbances amongst those who

105.   263 U.S. 291 (1923).
106.   282 U.S. 30 (1930).
107.   *United States v. Crescent Amusement Co.,* 323 U.S. 174 (1944).
108.   334 U.S. 110 (1948).
109.   327 U.S. 251 (1946).
110.   334 U.S. 131 (1948).
111.   Lee, *Antitrust Enforcement, Freedom of the Press, and the "Open Market:" The Supreme Court on the Structure and Conduct of Mass Media,* 32 Vanderbilt L.Rev. 1249 (1979).
112.   371 U.S. 38 (1962).

113.   *Three Movies of Tarzana v. Pacific Theatres, Inc.,* 1986-2 Trade Cas. (CCH), secs. 67,231, 61,172 (C.D.Cal. 1986).
114.   828 F.2d 1395 (9th Cir. 1987), *cert. denied* 484 U.S. 1066 (1988). See also Stanley I. Ornstein, *Motion Picture Distribution, Film Splitting, and Antitrust Policy,* 17 Hastings Comm/Ent L.J. 415 (1995).
115.   29 U.S.C.A. § 157.
116.   29 U.S.C.A. § 158(a).

operate the teletype machines or as a strike amongst the employees of the telegraph lines over which [AP's] messages travel."

The wire service's First Amendment argument was based on the assertion that " * * * it must have absolute and unrestricted freedom to employ and discharge those who, like Watson, edit the news, that there must not be the slightest opportunity for bias or prejudice personally entertained by an editorial employee to color or distort what he writes." The Act, AP said, was therefore a direct invasion of the freedom of the press. AP appeared to rely on the earlier decision in *Grosjean v. American Press Co.*[117] (text, p. 67), which had invalidated a state tax statute.

The Court in *AP* was not persuaded. There was no evidence that Watson's activities had resulted in any news bias, nor was there reason to expect bias from Watson in the future. The Court reasoned that the Act could only violate the First Amendment if it somehow interfered with the editorial judgment of management.

Associated Press v. National Labor Relations Board

1 MED. L. RPTR. 2689, 301 U.S. 103, 57 S. CT 650, 81 L. ED. 953 (1937).

Justice ROBERTS delivered the opinion of the Court.

* * * The act does not compel [AP] to employ any one; it does not require that [AP] retain in its employ an incompetent editor or one who fails faithfully to edit the news to reflect the facts without bias or prejudice. The act permits a discharge for any reason other than union activity or agitation for collective bargaining with employees. The restoration of Watson to his former position in no sense guarantees his continuance in petitioner's employ. The [AP] is at liberty, whenever occasion may arise, to exercise its undoubted right to sever his relationship for any cause that seems to it proper save only as a punishment for, or discouragement of, such activities as the act declares permissible.

The business of the Associated Press is not immune from regulation because it is an agency of the press. The publisher of a newspaper has no special immunity from the application of general

laws. He has no special privilege to invade the rights and liberties of others. He must answer for libel. He may be punished for contempt of court. He is subject to the antitrust laws. Like others he must pay equitable and nondiscriminatory taxes on his business. The regulation here in question has no relation whatever to the impartial distribution of news. The order of the Board in nowise circumscribes the full freedom and liberty of the [AP] to publish the news as it desires it published or to enforce policies of its own choosing with respect to the editing and rewriting of news for publication, and the [AP] is free at any time to discharge Watson or any editorial employee who fails to comply with the policies it might adopt.

Justice SUTHERLAND, dissenting.

Justice Van Devanter, Justice McReynolds, Justice Butler, and I think the judgment below should be reversed.

* * *

For many years there has been contention between labor and capital. * * * Such news is not only of great public interest; but an unbiased version of it is of the utmost public concern. To give a group of employers on the one hand, or a labor organization on the other, power of control over such a service is obviously to endanger the fairness and accuracy of the service. Strong sympathy for or strong prejudice against a given cause or the efforts made to advance it has too often led to suppression or coloration of unwelcome facts. It would seem to be an exercise of only reasonable prudence for an association engaged in part in supplying the public with fair and accurate factual information with respect to the contests between labor and capital, to see that those whose activities include that service are free from either extreme sympathy or extreme prejudice one way or the other.

* * *

COMMENT

The dissenting justices as a group had considered most of the New Deal legislation based on the commerce clause unconstitutional. Their dissents were consistently favorable to ownership and management. In the *Associated Press* case, however, the dissent argues in addition that a threat to unbiased reporting, presumably a tilt toward labor, exists with unionization. If there is a threat

---

117. 1 Med. L. Rptr. 2685, 297 U.S. 233 (1936).

of biased news coverage, does it not also exist if management is able to prevent coverage of labor issues? Apparently, it did not occur to the dissenters that ownership might be equally susceptible to the point of view of capital.

The case makes clear that the press is subject to the labor laws, just as it is subject to antitrust. The premise that the "publisher of a newspaper has no special immunity from the application of the general laws" has become the guideline by which subsequent issues involving business regulation of the press have been assessed. The continuing importance of *Associated Press* was stressed in the *Minneapolis Star* decision (text, p. 69), which invalidated a use tax on the costs of paper and ink products used in producing newspapers. In that case, Justice O'Connor said that *Associated Press* suggested the following:

> [A] regulation that singled out the press might place a heavier burden of justification on the [s]tate, and we now conclude that the special problems created by differential treatment do indeed impose such a burden.

Is Justice O'Connor's interpretation and application an extension of the *Associated Press* decision?

The holding that journalists have the same rights as other workers to collective bargaining has significant implications for the legal status of the press generally. Freedom of the press guaranteed under the First Amendment appears limited to matters of editorial judgment. Other interests and values may outweigh the usual freedom of publishers to act as they please.

A short time after the case was decided, Morris Watson was fired for "incompetency." Did the Court's decision effectively invite that result?

Key questions following *Associated Press* concerned the specific application of the NLR Act. Who is protected? What activities are so tied to the exercise of editorial judgment that they are solely the province of the publisher? When will management's actions be considered an unfair labor practice?

The Act does not apply to "professional" employees or to management employees. Similarly, the federal Fair Labor Standards Act (FLSA),[118] which sets standards for working conditions, exempts "professionals" from its coverage. A professional employee is defined as someone whose work is "predominantly intellectual and varied in character as opposed to routine mental, manual, mechanical, or physical work."[119] A natural conflict has developed, therefore, concerning who may claim the protection of the labor laws. Reporters and editors, it might be argued, are a far cry from the factory workers who were the primary targeted beneficiaries of the acts. That is precisely the argument the *Washington Post* used in opposing a claim for overtime pay filed by ninety-nine staff reporters, editors, and photographers.

Sherwood v. The Washington Post
15 MED. L. RPTR. 1692, 677 F.SUPP. 9 (D.D.C. 1988).

GESELL, J.:

Ninety-nine plaintiffs including reporters, editors or photographers presently employed by The Washington Post ("Post") have invoked Section 13(a)(1) of the Fair Labor Standards Act ("FLSA"), 29 U.S.C. § 213(a)(1) (1982), claiming they have been improperly denied time and a half pay for their overtime work.

* * *

Under longstanding practice, periodically reexamined in collective bargained agreements, The Washington Post since 1945 has paid time and a half wages for overtime work to all reporters/editors earning a salary of less than a stated amount per week. This complaint was filed after the last collectively bargained agreement failed to be renewed and negotiations for renewal had come to an apparent stalemate. There are 236 reporters and 160 editors who work full time out of the paper's Washington, D.C. newsroom. The approximately 60 reporters/editors who are plaintiffs earned an average of $50,000 per year with annual salaries ranging from $30,000 up to $60,000 at time of suit.

The FLSA provides an exemption from the Act's overtime pay requirements for employees working in a "bona fide executive, administrative or professional capacity." 29 U.S.C. § 213(a)(1). The individual plaintiffs each deny he or she is a professional within the meaning of this overtime exemption. Since they frequently gather information, write or edit outside the paper's 9:00 a.m. to

---

118. 29 U.S.C.A. §§ 213, 216.

119. 29 U.S.C.A. § 153(12).

6:00 p.m. hours, they seek to be paid time and a half wages for this work regardless of the amount of salary received or any arrangement included in a collectively bargained agreement.

The Washington Post contends that all of its reporters/editors, including the plaintiffs, are professionals within the meaning of the FLSA and therefore are exempt from the Act's time and a half overtime pay requirement. More specifically, it urges that the reporter/editor plaintiffs should be recognized as journalistic writers whose principal duty is to develop and write "original and creative" material and that, as such, they must be treated as members of an artistic profession within the meaning of the Department of Labor regulations found at 29 C.F.R. § 541.303 (1987) and other relevant interpretations of the FLSA.

* * *

The Washington Post is not an entry-level employer of reporters/editors. It employs only reporters and editors with proven experience who have acquired demonstrable newspaper writing skills that meet the particular, exacting needs of the Post. The paper does not rely heavily on other news services.

* * *

To this end, reporters are generally assigned a specific, broadly defined beat, general subject or institution. Thus, they are expected to become immersed in a particular field of activity and to be able to discern the significance of events as they occur and even to anticipate developments. Reporters write their own stories as semi-specialists, assisted by input from senior editors who aid in conceptualizing areas of interest to the newspaper as well as by other reporters in related fields.

* * *

Reporters/editors at the skill level of these 13 men and women are usually identified to the public by a by-line when their stories are printed. Their expertise becomes known and they are consulted by outsiders as well as colleagues. They may do a bit of teaching, free-lancing and/or talk show appearances on TV and radio on the side, always holding out their association with The Washington Post. By reason of their expertise they may also belong to professional societies or appear as speakers before such groups. * * *

Reporters have no set hours and their work may involve long hours; they are not generally required to be physically present at the Washington Post newsroom; they gather information at business or social encounters at any time of day and apparently are on call if the need arises.

* * * Their work is measured in terms of initiative, creativity, judgment, ability to handle multiple assignments, ability to complete daily assignments and projects, ability to help other reporters grow, use of language, ability to satisfy various exacting writing standards, ability to translate complicated situations into lucid prose, knowledge of subject covered, ability to expand their own knowledge, etc. * * *

The 13 reporters/editors under review here were hired at various times between 1967 and 1983 and they have had a wide variety of changing assignments. Most of them have college degrees, a long-term commitment to journalism, and all have well-tested newswriting skills gained through prior experience.

Following their employment by The Washington Post, most of them have won news awards and many have benefited from fellowships or full-time study at various universities, such as Duke for public policy, Harvard for law, etc.

* * *

When Congress enacted the FLSA in 1938, it was in response to President Roosevelt's call for legislation to establish minimum standards for free labor. The President sought a law to protect those receiving the bare necessities of life whose health was injured by long hours of toil. He spoke for those in the lowest income brackets, the underpaid and destitute receiving substandard pay. These are still the basic objectives of the statute.

No effort was made to list the precise jobs covered by the enactment. This was left to the Secretary of Labor to define and delineate; but bona fide professionals were exempted from the start. * * *

The professional exemption for artistic professions is stated, in relevant part, as follows:

Work of this type is original and creative in character in a recognized field of endeavor (as opposed to work which can be produced by a person endowed with general manual or intellectual ability and training), and the result of which depends primarily on the invention, imagination, or talent of the employee.

29 C.F.R. § 541.303(a). Writing is specifically defined as a field of artistic endeavor at § 541.303(b). The regulations then proceed at § 541.303(f) to consider newspaper writers and reporters and to emphasize that the exemption is available within this group for those doing written work which is "predominantly original and creative"; whether written work is "creative" is to be determined by its analytical, interpretive and individualized character. The work of columnists, cartoonists and editorial writers is apparently considered to be at the top of the scale measuring originality and creativity, the work of legmen at the bottom and a wide area of uncertainty left in between.

* * *

The Court is wholly satisfied that The Washington Post has met its burden and is entitled on the undisputed facts summarized above to treat each of the 13 reporters/editors as professionals exempted from the overtime pay requirements of the FLSA. They produce original and creative writing of high quality within the meaning of the regulations; they have far more than general intelligence; they are thoroughly trained before employment; their performance as writers is individual, interpretive and analytical both in the writing itself and in the process by which the writing must be prepared; and their performance is measured and paid accordingly. A special talent is necessary to succeed.

* * *

Plaintiffs' motion for summary judgment is denied; defendant's motion for summary judgment is granted; and the complaint of the 13 reporter/ editor plaintiffs is dismissed with prejudice.

* * *

COMMENT

The district court's grant of the newspaper's motion for summary judgment was the focus of the District of Columbia Circuit Court of Appeals when it overturned the decision. The appeals court noted that it was inappropriate for the trial judge to reach legal conclusions on the basis of facts that were still hotly contested. In other words, the appeals court thought the case

should go to trial and be decided by a jury rather than by a judge in pretrial.

Although decided under the FLSA, the interpretation of the district court in the *Sherwood* case would appear to apply as well to determinations under the NLRA. It is important to note that the decision is at odds with a long line of cases under the NLRA that determined that editorial employees are not considered professionals[120] or supervisors ordinarily part of management.[121] Newspaper management has long sought to have journalists considered professionals.

Back at the federal district court, Thomas Sherwood remained the lone plaintiff and lost again. *Sherwood v. The Washington Post*, 23 Med. L. Rptr. 1273, 871 F.Supp. 1471 (D.D.C. 1994). The court's opinion consisted largely of an exhaustive review of the types of work that Sherwood had done while a *Post* employee. Comparing newspaper journalism today with the 1940s, the court observed: "[T]he trade has changed so much in the intervening years that modern reporting jobs at the *Post* such as the one Sherwood held require invention, imagination, and talent."

Another federal district court expressly rejected the reasoning of *Sherwood* in a dispute between a television station and general assignment reporters, producers, directors, and assignment editors. In deciding for the employees, the court emphasized that the burden of proving an

---

120. See, e.g., *Express News*, 223 N.L.R.B. 223 (1976). In this case, the NLRB expressly refused to alter many prior decisions that journalists were not considered professionals. The board determined that recent developments in communication had not changed the essential nature of the jobs involved. A key to the decision was evidence that most news employees had not received advanced training in journalism. Advanced or specialized training is considered a major indicator of professional status under the NLRA. News organizations today report that up to 85 percent of new editorial hires have degrees from journalism and mass communication programs. American Newspaper Publishers Ass'n., *Facts about Newspapers* (1987).

121. See, e.g., *Passaic Daily News v. NLRB*, 736 F.2d 1543 (D.C. Cir. 1984) (bureau chief who lacked authority to hire, fire, or evaluate employees not a supervisor); *NLRB v. Medina County Publications*, 735 F.2d 199 (6th Cir. 1984) (sports editor who exercised authority in disciplining employee and in authorizing overtime pay considered a supervisor); *NLRB v. KDFW-TV, Inc.*, 790 F.2d 1273 (5th Cir. 1986) (directors, producers, and assignment editors who lacked authority over employees not supervisors).

FLSA exemption lies with the employer. It is otherwise assumed that the Act applies to employees. The station emphasized the specialized activities of the various jobs. The court described the duties of each position in detail, concluding that the work did not involve exempt "creative" activities, but rather "* * * depends primarily on intelligence, diligence, and accuracy * * * There is a well-established format and sameness * * *. Their work * * * is not predominantly original and creative because they do not produce analytical, interpretative, or highly individualized reporting." The station also claimed that the positions called for advanced or specialized education, which would exempt the employees from the FLSA as "learned" professionals. The district court concluded that preferring employees with journalism degrees was significantly different from requiring degrees. *Dalheim v. KDFW-TV*, 15 Med. L. Rptr. 2393, 706 F.Supp. 493 (N.D.Tex. 1988), *aff'd* 18 Med. L. Rptr. 1657, 918 F.2d 1220 (5th Cir. 1990).

Reporters at the Concord (New Hampshire) *Monitor* who earned less than $250 a week and who worked on general assignments rather than finding their own stories were found to be outside the professional and artistic professional exemptions in *Reich v. Newspapers of New England, Inc.*, 23 Med. L. Rptr. 1257, 444 F.3d 1060 (1st Cir. 1995). Both the trial and the appeals court relied on testimony from Ben Bagdikian, former dean of the Graduate School of Journalism at the University of California at Berkeley, who told the court that academic training in journalism was not especially important for entry-level reporters. The courts found that fairly close supervision was applied at the *Monitor*, an entry-level newspaper.

The cases suggest that to be considered a manager or a professional, the employee must have discretion *and* authority to act as an agent of the organization. Somewhat greater discretion and authority are required than would be involved in simply telling a news source that one is a reporter from a particular newspaper or television station.

Employees who participate in the formulation of editorial policy will likely be considered management without regard to their lack of authority over other employees. In one case, the court held that staffers who write editorials have the essential characteristics of managerial employees and are properly excluded from collective bargaining. "To hold that a person who was involved in the formulation of editorial content of a newspaper is not aligned with the newspaper's management would come perilously close to infringing upon the newspaper's First Amendment guarantee of freedom of the press." *Wichita Eagle & Beacon Publishing Co. v. NLRB*, 480 F.2d 52 (10th Cir. 1973), *cert. denied* 416 U.S. 982 (1974).

An employee who prepares the editorials that serve as the voice of the newspaper is indeed closely aligned with management, because an editorial writer is quite literally the "mouthpiece" of management.

In labor law generally, unfair labor practices specified in the NLRA prohibit employer interference with attempts to unionize; discrimination between employees based on union activity; attempts to dominate a recognized collective bargaining agent; discharge of employees after an employee files charges; and refusal to bargain.[122] When the *Passaic Daily News* pulled Mitchell Stoddard's weekly column after Stoddard participated in union-organizing activity, the court decided that the paper had canceled the column in an attempt to discourage membership in the union, an unfair labor practice. *Passaic Daily News v. NLRB*, 10 Med. L. Rptr. 1905, 736 F.2d 1543 (D.C. Cir. 1984). The court agreed with an administrative law judge that the action constituted an unfair labor practice. The court affirmed that the paper's action was retaliatory and discriminatory in nature and that Stoddard was effectively demoted following the union election. The newspaper argued that the First Amendment shields the decision from NLRB review. The court held that *Associated Press* indicates otherwise. If the newspaper had made a showing that its decision to cancel the column was based on editorial judgment rather than retaliation, the court said, its results might be different.

When the *Pottstown Mercury* management adopted and began enforcing a newsroom code of ethics without consulting with or bargaining with the Newspaper Guild chapter, the Guild

---

122. 29 U.S.C.A. § 158; Lacy & Simon, *The Economics and Regulation of United States Newspapers* 246–253 (1993).

asserted that the imposition of the code in such a fashion was a change in the terms and conditions of employment and an unfair labor practice. A federal district court disagreed, determining that "the editorial integrity of a newspaper lies at the very core of publishing control." Provisions of the code not related to the "core," however, might be appropriate for collective bargaining. *Newspaper Guild v. NLRB,* 6 Med. L. Rptr. 2089, 636 F.2d 550 (D.C. Cir. 1980). Other policy decisions less directly affecting editorial content, such as smoking policies or drug testing, would appear to require collective bargaining.[123] A newspaper's refusal to bargain over penalty provisions in a code of ethics, rather than the code itself, was considered an unfair labor practice, however. The decision to enhance editorial integrity with a code of ethics was not considered an economic decision that triggers mandatory bargaining. Penalties, though, directly affect job security. *The Capital Times Co. and Newspaper Guild of Madison, Local 64,* 223 NLRB No. 87 (1976).

The Fair Labor Standards Act, discussed earlier, was the subject of constitutional attack by newspapers shortly after its passage. In two cases in 1946, the Supreme Court upheld application of the FLSA to the press and upheld the authority of the Department of Labor to subpoena records for FLSA enforcement.

In the first case, *Mabee v. White Plains Publishing Co.,* the Court held that discrimination on the basis of circulation is a permissible method of classification to determine whether a newspaper will be regulated under the FLSA. A total of forty-five out-of-state subscribers was considered enough to place a newspaper in interstate commerce.

The FLSA established a minimum wage and maximum number of hours for employees engaged in interstate commerce unless specifically exempted. The act specifically provided that weekly or semiweekly newspapers with circulations of less than 3,000 were not covered. Daily newspapers, no matter how small their

out-of-state circulation, were apparently covered under the statute.

White Plains Publishing Co. contended that an out-of-state circulation of 45 out of 9,000 to 11,000 copies published was too weak a foundation on which to support a conclusion that the newspaper was in interstate commerce. Moreover, the company contended that the statutory exemption for small weekly newspapers was discriminatory. In *Grosjean v. American Press,* 297 U.S. 233 (1936), the Louisiana legislature had placed a tax on large-circulation papers but not on small-circulation newspapers. A duty to comply with the FLSA likewise was placed on some newspapers but not others. Therefore White Plains Publishing Co. argued that the statutory exemptions for small-circulation newspapers (weekly and semiweekly) represented discriminatory regulation.

Mabee v. White Plains Publishing Co.
327 U.S. 178, 66 S. CT. 511, 90 L. ED. 607 B(1946).

Justice DOUGLAS delivered the opinion of the Court.

* * *

* * * Volume of circulation, frequency of issue, and area of distribution are said to be an improper basis of classification. Moreover, it is said that the Act lays a direct burden on the press in violation of the First Amendment. The Grosjean case is not in point here. There the press was singled out for special taxation and the tax was graduated in accordance with volume of circulation. No such vice inheres in this legislation. As the press has business aspects it has no special immunity from laws applicable to business in general. *Associated Press v. NLRB,* 301 U.S. 103, 132–133. And the exemption of small weeklies and semi-weeklies is not a "deliberate and calculated device" to penalize a certain group of newspapers. *Grosjean v. American Press Co.* As we have seen, it was inserted to put those papers more on a parity with other small town enterprises. 83 Cong.Rec. 7445. The Fifth Amendment does not require full and uniform exercise of the commerce power. Congress may weigh relative needs and restrict the application of a legislative policy to less than the entire field. * * *

---

123. Rothstein, *Screening Workers for Drugs: A Legal and Ethical Framework,* 2 Employee Relations L.J. 422 (1985–1986); *Brotherhood of Locomotive Engineers v. Burlington Northern Railroad* (unpublished opinion) (D.Mont. 1985).

COMMENT

The FLSA had previously been challenged on the grounds that it might drive financially weak newspapers out of business entirely. *Sun Publishing Co. v. Walling*, 140 F.2d 445 (6th Cir. 1944). That court rejected the unusual proposition that the First Amendment grants publishers a guarantee of economic security.

The exemption of certain small newspapers was upheld, although discriminatory, because it was not designed to penalize other newspapers. Would the exemption survive under the *Minneapolis Star* test?

In the second case, the Court upheld that provisions of the FLSA requiring submission of pertinent records pursuant to a court order do not violate the First and Fourth Amendment rights of a newspaper publisher.

In this companion case to *Mabee*, a Department of Labor administrator sought judicial enforcement of *subpoenas duces tecum* issued in the course of investigations conducted pursuant to sec. 11(a) of the FLSA. The subpoenas sought records to determine whether Oklahoma Press Publishing Co. was violating the Act.

The Court quickly rejected the company's arguments that application of the FLSA to the publishing business and the classification method used to determine whether a newspaper may be regulated under the Act were in violation of its First Amendment rights.

Instead, the Court examined the contention that enforcement of the subpoenas would permit a general fishing expedition into the newspaper's records, without a prior charge, in violation of the Fourth Amendment's search and seizure provisions.

Oklahoma Press Publishing Co. v. Walling

327 U.S. 186, 66 S. CT. 494, 90 L. ED. 614 (1946).

Justice RUTLEDGE.

What petitioners seek is not to prevent an unlawful search and seizure. It is rather a total immunity to the act's provisions, applicable to all others similarly situated, requiring them to submit their pertinent records for the Administrator's inspection under every judicial safeguard, after and only after an order of court made pursuant to and in exact compliance with authority granted by Congress. This broad claim of immunity no doubt is induced by petitioners' First Amendment contentions. But beyond them it is rested also upon conceptions of the Fourth Amendment equally lacking in merit.

* * *

The matter of requiring the production of books and records to secure evidence is not as one-sided, in this kind of situation, as the most extreme expressions of either emphasis would indicate. With some obvious exceptions, there has always been a real problem of balancing the public interest against private security.

* * *

Whatever limits there may be to congressional power to provide for the production of corporate or other business records, therefore, they are not to be found, in view of the course of prior decisions, in any such absolute or universal immunity as petitioners seek.

* * *

The only records or documents sought were corporate ones. No possible element of self-incrimination was therefore presented or in fact claimed. All the records sought were relevant to the authorized inquiry, the purpose of which was to determine two issues, whether petitioners were subject to the act and, if so, whether they were violating it. * * * It is not to be doubted that Congress could authorize investigation of these matters. * * *

On the other hand, [*Oklahoma Press's*] view if accepted would stop much if not all investigation in the public interest at the threshold of inquiry and, in the case of the Administrator, is designed avowedly to do so. This would render substantially impossible his effective discharge of the duties of investigation and enforcement which Congress has placed upon him. And if his functions could be thus blocked, so might many others of equal importance. * * *"

COMMENT

The NLRA also stipulates that a labor organization may be found to engage in unfair labor practices in various circumstances. One such instance occurs when an employee prefers not to engage in collective bargaining activities.

In *Buckley v. American Federation of Television and Radio Artists* 496 F.2d 305 (2d Cir. 1974), the court of appeals held that a union shop agreement requiring television commentators to pay union dues as a condition of employment is not an infringement of their First Amendment right of free speech.

William F. Buckley, Jr., and M. Stanton Evans, television and radio commentators expressing a conservative point of view on public issues, brought suit in federal court for a declaratory judgment challenging the constitutionality of sec. 8(a)(3) of the National Labor Relations Act [29 U.S.C.A. § 158(a)(3)], as it applied to their relations with the American Federation of Television and Radio Artists (AFTRA). The main thrust of their complaint was that this provision of the act allowed AFTRA to require them to join in AFTRA strikes or work stoppages against the television and radio networks and to subject them to union discipline (fines or cancellation of membership) for continuing to broadcast their commentary in the face of AFTRA's orders to strike.

Both Buckley and Evans had joined AFTRA under protest and asserted that their continued membership under these conditions had a chilling effect on the exercise of their First Amendment rights of free press and free speech as commentators.

Against the constitutional rights asserted by plaintiffs, the Court balanced the legislative purpose underlying the "union shop" provision of the Act:

> Moreover, we find that the means adopted to achieve this proper purpose of reducing industrial strife are reasonable and do not "unwarrantedly abridge" free speech. The dues here are not flat fees imposed directly on the exercise of a federal right. To the contrary, assuming *arguendo* that government action is involved here, the dues more logically would constitute the employee's share of the expenses of operating a valid labor regulatory system which serves a substantial public purpose. If there is any burden on [plaintiffs'] free speech it would appear to be no more objectionable than a "nondiscriminatory [form] of general taxation" which can be constitutionally imposed on the communication media.

Buckley and Evans did not attack NLRA's general application to the broadcast industry on constitutional grounds.

Early cases relied for their rulings on the fact that local stations were in interstate commerce depending upon electricity purchased out of state, FCC licensing, and the fact that the station's signals could be picked up in other states. *Los Angeles Broadcasting, KMOX Broadcasting,* 10 NLRB 479 (1938). Later the NLRB relied upon such factors as network affiliation, subscription to the AP news service, advertising of nationally distributed products, and payment of copyright royalties to ASCAP or Broadcast Music, Inc. (BMI) in New York City or Chicago.

What is important to note about this history is that broadcasters fought the NLRB on jurisdictional grounds. Constitutional arguments, like those made in *AP v. NLRB,* were apparently rarely raised.

Isn't the rationale for union representation the need for equality of bargaining power? Do Dan Rather, Barbara Walters, or William F. Buckley, Jr., need a union to represent them? Perhaps the question misses the point. The rest of the AFTRA membership needed members like Buckley in order to have equality of bargaining power.

Are private labor agreements under the NLRA infused with sufficient "governmental action" to give rise to a cause of action under the First Amendment? Constitutional guarantees of free expression embrace only abridgments by the government. Whether union shop agreements like that in *Buckley* actually constitute governmental rather than individual action is a matter of conflicting interpretation. In *Buckley,* the Second Circuit avoided this issue, holding only that "if there were a burden on free speech it would appear to be no more objectionable than a 'nondiscriminatory [form] of general taxation' which can constitutionally be imposed on the communications media." See *Jensen v. Farrel Lines, Inc.,* 625 F.2d 379 (2d Cir. 1980).

Protection of Employee Rights in Contract Law

Many recent disputes between management and employees are a result of interpretation of specific contract provisions rather than of direct application of federal labor laws. Unless a condition or term of employment is specifically covered by federal or state statute or by collective bargaining, the contract of employment will be the basis for determining the relationship between employee and employer.

Traditionally, at common law, employment agreements were considered subject to the doctrine of employment at will. Under that rule, it was assumed that both parties freely entered into the employment relationship, and it was further assumed that either party could freely terminate the relationship for any or no reason. That rule still applies in the absence of evidence to the contrary. Contrary evidence may be found in a variety of places—employee handbooks, written statements of policy, even ethics codes. On occasion, even verbal agreements will be considered sufficient to overcome the presumption of employment at will.

Recent cases in many states have restricted the discretion of employers under the employment at will doctrine when an employee is able to show that explicit employment terms have been violated by the employer, or that the employer has somehow violated established public policy.[124] Claims that the First Amendment, as a statement of public policy, prevents management from interfering with the editorial discretion of journalists are almost certain to fail, however.

A public policy exception was rejected in a case flowing from the dismissal of Julianne Agnew from her job as lifestyle editor of the *Duluth Herald and News-Tribune.* When Agnew filed as a candidate for city council in 1978, she was discharged pursuant to the paper's conflict of interest policy. The state brought an action against the newspaper based on a Minnesota statute forbidding anyone from paying a person to induce him or her to become or refrain from becoming a political candidate. The court ordered that an indictment be dismissed because the prosecution was based on a "serious misunderstanding of both the First Amendment" and the corrupt practices statute. *Minnesota v. Knight-Ridder,* 5 Med. L.

Rptr. 1705 (Minn.Dist.Ct. 1979). The court implicitly upheld the ethics provisions as an integral part of Agnew's employment contract.

Patrick Sheehan's case against his former employer also shows that contract provisions freely bargained for by the employee are difficult to set aside. When Sheehan, a news anchor, began working for WFSB-TV in Hartford, Connecticut, he signed a noncompetition clause, a rather common clause in broadcast employment contracts. He was told in July 1979 that his contract would not be renewed, although it ran until November. He was no longer performing any work for the station when he began appearing for WTNH in New Haven. WFSB never invoked the noncompetition clause, and Sheehan signed a new contract in New Haven, again with a noncompetition clause. When he jumped stations once more, returning to Hartford, WTNH invoked its clause and sought an injunction. Sheehan eventually prevailed, but only because the clause had been written too broadly, limiting him from employment even in another state. A sharper definition of "market" would likely have made the clause enforceable. *Capital Cities Communications v. Sheehan,* 9 Med. L. Rptr. 2172 (Ct.Super.Ct. 1983).

When Ron Hunter was removed as anchor at a Louisiana television station, he sued for an injunction to reinstate him. Hunter argued that the removal was a violation of his "personal services contract." A lower court had granted a temporary restraining order reinstating Hunter. An appeals court reversed. *Hunter v. Gaylord Broadcasting Co.,* 12 Med. L. Rptr. 1591 (La.App. 1985). Being removed from the air was not the sort of immediate and irreparable injury needed for such an order, the court said. Hunter would receive his compensation for time remaining on the contract. Requiring that the station place him on air would interfere with its editorial judgment, the court added.

Many disputes of the last two decades have resulted from reductions in the number of production employees as a result of rapid technological change and of consolidation in the newspaper business. A case brought by dismissed production workers represented by the International Typographical Union following the closing of the *Cleveland Press* is illustrative.

124. Taylor, *Newspaper Ethics Code and the Employment-at-Will Doctrine,* paper presented to the Law Division, Association for Education in Journalism and Mass Communication, Portland, Oregon, July 1988.

The employees had negotiated a guarantee of employment in exchange for concessions on job duties. The contract, however, provided that the employment guarantee was terminated for a given paper's employees if either of the two Cleveland newspapers closed. The dismissed employees filed suit, claiming violations of federal labor law, antitrust law, and Ohio common law. *Province v. Cleveland Press Publishing Co.,* 787 F.2d 1047 (6th Cir. 1986).

The plaintiffs lost on all claims. No antitrust violation was proved because there was no evidence that the *Press* and the *Cleveland Plain Dealer* had conspired to terminate the agreement. The common law action was based on tortious interference with contract. Plaintiffs argued that the two newspapers' managements had worked together to destroy the employment guarantee. That claim also relied on proof of intent to cause harm, so it was dismissed. The express terms of the contract were held binding. The allegation that the *Press,* after years of losses delineated by the court, would conspire to cease publication primarily to avoid employment guarantees seems a bit strained.

For a case discussing a newspaper union's concern about the effect of new technology "on the bargaining unit, the extent of potential job displacement, and the result of new unit employees to operate the new equipment," see *Newspaper Printing Corp. v. NLRB,* 625 F.2d 956 at 959 (10th Cir. 1980). See Jaske, *Collective Bargaining Issues in Newspapers,* 4 Comm/Ent 595 at 596 (1982). See generally Ganzglass, *Impact of New Technology on Existing Bargaining Units in the Newspaper Industry,* 4 Comm/Ent 605 (1982).

The *Cincinnati Post* arranged to combine operations with the *Cincinnati Enquirer* on the ground that the *Post* was "a failing newspaper" under the provisions of the Newspaper Preservation Act, 15 U.S.C.A. § 1801 (1976). After the Joint Operating Agreement (JOA) was approved and the agreement between the Cincinnati newspapers was deemed to be exempt from the antitrust laws under the Act, the *Cincinnati Post* closed its composing room and fired all the printers. However, these printers earlier had been guaranteed that they would be continuously employed for the remainder of their working lives by the *Post.* After the approval of the JOA, however, the *Post* sought to abrogate the lifetime job guarantee. Is the agreement still enforceable? In *Heheman v. Scripps,* 6 Med. L. Rptr. 2089, 661 F.2d 1115 (6th Cir. 1981), Judge Merritt ruled as follows:

> In this case we are called upon to decide what effect should be given to an agreement in the newspaper industry guaranteeing lifetime job security for printers. The newspaper terminated the workers covered by the agreement following a partial reorganization and merger. We reverse the decision of the District Court which declined to give full effect to the job security agreement.

Union jurisdictional disputes resulting in labor strife such as strikes and picketing occur in the electronic as well as the print media. Illustrative is *American Broadcasting Companies, Inc. v. Writers Guild of America, West, Inc.,* 437 U.S. 411 (1978), involving three cases decided together by the Supreme Court. Among the antagonists were the Motion Picture and Television Producers, Inc., and the three television networks, NBC, CBS, and ABC, versus the Writers Guild.

Some employees perform various tasks that come within the jurisdiction of more than one union. The employee can be caught in a conflict between pressures from different unions and managements. When one union goes on strike, the other labor organizations may require that employees honor no-strike pledges in their contracts, and management may demand that employees perform duties that are not within the jurisdiction of the striking union. *American Broadcasting Companies* involved disciplinary proceedings brought by the Writers Guild against a union member, who was a supervisory employee with limited writing duties, for crossing the union's picket line during a strike and performing only his regular supervisory duties, which included acting as the employee's grievance representative.

The Supreme Court held that union action in issuing rules prohibiting producers, directors, and story editors from performing their supervisory duties during the course of the strike and imposing sanctions on those who did perform such duties was unlawful. The union violated the NLRA, which prohibits union attempts to coerce employers in the selection of their representatives for grievance adjustment purposes.

Four justices dissented contending that "The Court holds today that a labor union locked in a direct economic confrontation with an employer is powerless to impose sanctions on its own members who choose to pledge their loyalty to the adversary."

Other statutes may effectively modify an employment agreement as a matter of public policy. For example, federal and state civil rights provisions prohibiting discrimination based on race, sex, or age, as laws of general application, surely may be enforced against the media. Although dismissed news anchor Christine Craft lost her sex discrimination claim against her former employer, the court never doubted that the statutes may apply to the media.[125] African American reporters at the New York *Daily News* filed a race discrimination suit against the paper that attracted considerable adverse attention to the industry's record in minority hiring and promotion.[126] Much as in the case of an unfair labor practice charge, an employer who has based an employment decision on the conclusion that the plaintiff was less qualified will generally be upheld; it is the pretext that hides discrimination that may result in liability.

Another common statutory concern is with workers' compensation and disability provisions. In *Mulcahey v. New England Newspapers, Inc.*, the Rhode Island Supreme Court held that a widow was entitled to compensation benefits after her husband, the sports editor of the *Pawtucket Evening Times*, died of a cerebral hemorrhage spurred by the pressures and stress of his job.[127] In order to qualify for such benefits, an individual must qualify as an employee. Qualification has been an issue where part-time employees, stringers, and newspaper carriers are involved.[128]

TAXATION AND LICENSING OF THE PRESS

Constitutional Background

First Amendment analysis of restraints on the press today is dramatically different from what the framers envisioned. Threats against the press are seldom as direct as during the colonial period when the government formally licensed newspapers or used tax provisions to limit or hinder press activities.[129] Threats against the press are likely to be subtler, involving disputes over the placement of newsracks, application of state and federal tax laws, or enforcement of laws regulating public solicitation or distribution of materials.

The constitutional basics are fairly clear. Under *Grosjean v. American Press*,[130] tax statutes passed with the intent of hindering the press are invalid; it follows that other statutes aimed at punishing or hindering the press are also invalid. Under *Minneapolis Star & Tribune v. Minnesota Commissioner of Revenue*,[131] any statute that singles out the press from other businesses for differential treatment, even if beneficial, is suspect and likely invalid. Under *Associated Press v. NLRB*,[132] however, laws of general application that are applied evenly to all businesses will be valid when applied to the press. The general principle from these cases, taken together, is the traditional rule that government actions that affect media content will only be valid if justified by evidence of a compelling government interest. A similar analysis will apply when government treats some publishers or speakers differently from others.

The First Amendment's primary concern that government not be allowed to regulate content is implicated less directly, but implicated nonetheless, when regulation is addressed initially to business aspects of the media rather than editorial aspects.

Cases involving taxation or licensing-type issues take two main forms: disputes involving assertions that government is picking and

125. *Craft v. Metromedia, Inc.*, 766 F.2d 1205 (8th Cir. 1985) (court determined that reliance on audience surveys by employer avoided claim of sex discrimination); see Note, *Sex Discrimination in Newscasting*, 84 Michigan L. Rev. 443 (1985).

126. Cook, "In New York City, the 'News' Faces Reporters' Bias Charges," National L. J. (March 9, 1987), 6; see Stevens, *Discrimination in the Newsroom: Title VII and the Journalist,* Journalism Monographs, No. 94, September 1985.

127. Breton, "R.I. Newspaper Held Liable in Job-Related Stress Death," National L. J. (March 18, 1985), 10.

128. *Gittrich v. Dispatch Printing Co.*, 14 Med. L. Rptr. 1317 (Ohio App. 1987) (carriers independent contractors); Radolf, "Philadelphia NLRB says stringers are employees," *Editor & Publisher* (August 13, 1988), 28.

129. Smith, *Prior Restraint: Original Intentions and Modern Interpretations,* 28 William & Mary L. Rev. 439 (1987).

130. 1 Med. L. Rptr. 2685, 297 U.S. 233 (1936).

131. 9 Med. L. Rptr. 1369, 460 U.S. 575 (1983).

132. 1 Med. L. Rptr. 2689, 301 U.S. 103 (1937).

choosing from different media in allowing privileges or benefits, and claims that laws or rules applied to the press directly violate the First Amendment although the same laws might be valid if applied to other parties.

Regulation of Media Distribution

The 1980s and 1990s have seen a surge of cases where newspapers challenged the authority of cities, towns, airports, and other units of government to regulate the placement of newsracks.[133] The interests government has asserted include aesthetics, pedestrian traffic safety, and potential liability for injuries. In many cities, concern over congestion on sidewalks is merited. With racks featuring various national, regional, local, and specialized newspapers, there may not be a lot of room left. The sidewalk adjacent to one Washington, D.C. subway station recently sported sixteen newsracks.

In *Southern Connecticut Newspapers v. Greenwich,* 11 Med. L. Rptr. 1051 (D.Ct. 1984), the city passed an ordinance regulating newsracks. First, a newspaper must obtain a permit prior to placing a newsrack. To avoid liability for injuries, a certificate proving insurance for more than $1 million is required. The city's interest was apparently traffic safety, although no study was undertaken showing any danger to traffic. The ordinance placed discretion with the chief of police to prohibit newsracks whenever it appeared the rack could pose a danger to auto or pedestrian traffic. Under the traditional rules of analysis for time, place, and manner regulations, Greenwich's law was a virtual blueprint for invalidity.

The city of Keene, New Hampshire, went too far, a court said, when it used boltcutters to remove *Brattleboro Reformer* newsracks that had been chained to parking meters on Main Street. The city had no newsrack ordinance. The removal took place because the city attorney concluded that the racks were improperly situated. In court, the city argued public safety as its interest, but there was little to indicate that the newsracks on the sidewalks or streets of the small city presented a danger. The city failed the time, place, and manner test. *Miller Newspapers v. Keene,* 9 Med. L. Rptr. 1234, 546 F.Supp. 831 (D.N.H. 1982). The newspaper obtained an injunction preventing additional removals.

When Lakewood, Ohio, a suburb of Cleveland, attempted to enforce a newsrack ordinance against the *Cleveland Plain Dealer,* a newsrack case finally made its way to the Supreme Court. In a 4–3 case (Chief Justice Rehnquist and Justice Kennedy did not participate), Justice Brennan's opinion invoked the specter of prior restraint. (See text, page 64). The opinion concluded that the standards applicable to regulation of the distribution of leaflets and pamphlets should be applied to regulation of vending boxes. The city's attempt to distinguish the ordinance as a business regulation of general application failed. *Lakewood v. Plain Dealer Publishing Co.,* 15 Med. L. Rptr. 1481, 465 U.S. 750 (1988).

The opinion focused almost exclusively on the issue of official discretion. Since that issue was enough to declare the ordinance unconstitutional, the Court, as it typically does, left other issues alone. But would the result have been any different if the Court had more closely considered time, place, and manner factors or had assessed the city's asserted interest?

The *Lakewood* decision appears consistent with *Minneapolis Star* and *Associated Press.* A newsrack ordinance can never be of general application because it is aimed directly at the press, triggering greater scrutiny from the Court. Still, Brennan declined to cite *Minneapolis Star* in the case, perhaps indicating that the earlier case's compelling interest approach does not apply with full force in newsrack disputes.

The rule of *Lakewood* that an ordinance will be invalid if there is too much room for discretion by city officials was the basis for validating a Des Moines, Iowa ordinance less than a month after the Supreme Court decision. Limiting the opinion to the proposition that an ordinance will be valid if it assures that decisions are not based on the content of speech, the court denied a motion for a preliminary injunction. *Jacobsen v. Crivaro,* 15 Med. L. Rptr. 1958, 851 F.2d 1067 (8th Cir. 1988). The court also determined that a ten dollar annual license fee, which covered administrative costs, did not amount to an

133. See, e.g., *Chicago Observer, Inc. v. City of Chicago,* 929 F.2d 325 (7th Cir. 1991); *Providence Journal v. Newport,* 14 Med. L. Rptr. 1545, 665 F.Supp. 107 (D.R.I. 1987); *Gannett Satellite Information Network v. Metropolitan Transit Authority,* 10 Med. L. Rptr. 2424, 745 F.2d 767 (2d Cir. 1984); *Miami Herald v. City of Hallandale,* 10 Med. L. Rptr. 2049, 734 F.2d 666 (11th Cir. 1984).

unconstitutional attempt to license the press. The ordinance required the city director of traffic and transportation to issue a permit if the technical provisions were complied with.

In contrast, an ordinance that left significant discretion in the hands of a city manager was declared unconstitutional in *Chicago Newspaper Publishers Ass'n. v. Wheaton*, 15 Med. L. Rptr. 2297, 697 F.Supp. 1464 (N.D.Ill. 1988). Although the ordinance specified factors for the city manager to consider when reviewing a permit request, in the last analysis it vested final discretion to decide if there was a health or safety hazard or a sidewalk obstruction with the city manager.

Do the same principles apply when a different method of distribution is used? The Third Circuit said yes when Doylestown, Pennsylvania, enforced an ordinance banning door-to-door delivery of advertising materials. Plaintiff Ad World was the publisher of *Piggy Back,* a tabloid that was primarily advertising—a free "shopper"—but also carried a few pages of consumer and community information. The city claimed that the ordinance was backed by interests in preventing litter and vandalism and in protecting residents from receiving materials they had not asked for. The court determined that the shopper, however little news it carried, was entitled to full First Amendment protection like other newspapers. *Ad World v. Doylestown,* 8 Med. L. Rptr. 1073, 672 F.2d 1136 (3d Cir. 1982). Since the ordinance was not narrowly drawn and no reasonable alternatives were available to the *Piggy Back,* the ordinance was declared unconstitutional.

The question of whether newsracks filled with shoppers may be regulated more easily than traditional newspapers was addressed in *Cincinnati v. Discovery Network, Inc.,* 21 Med. L. Rptr. 1161, 113 S. Ct. 1505 (1993). The city argued that aesthetics and safety were its interests. The Court rebuked the city for having failed to show either that the regulation was related to improving aesthetics or that the newsracks posed a safety hazard. Just as importantly, the Court emphasized that shoppers could not be discriminated against simply because their contents were commercial speech.

The *Chicago Tribune* faced a similar problem when it ran into the Downers Grove solicitation ordinance. The law required commercial solicitors to obtain a permit and pay a fee. Then there was a minimum five-day waiting period. Finally, no more than fifteen commercial permits were allowed at any one time. *Tribune* solicitors without permits were stopped by Downers Grove police. No limit was placed on the number of permits for noncommercial solicitors, which included charitable, religious, and political groups. In addition, commercial permits were good only from 9 A.M. to 6 P.M., but noncommercial ones were good from 9 A.M. to 8 P.M. The court had little difficulty deciding that the ordinance was fatally overbroad. *Chicago Tribune v. Downers Grove,* 14 Med. L. Rptr. 1273, 508 N.E.2d 439 (Ill. App. 1987). Even if narrowly tailored, the court said, the ordinance was still objectionable because of its questionable discrimination between kinds of solicitation. There was no evidence that commercial solicitors posed more problems or greater dangers than noncommercial ones.

Cases involving municipal regulation of media distribution never involve situations where the city has undertaken licensing of the press in any formal sense. In invalidating regulations, however, the courts consistently refer to cases warning of the dangers of licensing. Much of the rationale applied seems related to the "slippery slope" argument—if any regulation or licensing is allowed, how much more will government seek?

Closely related to distribution is ownership. Newspapers have generally not been subject to as much regulation concerning ownership as have broadcast and cable. The authority of federal and even state government to place restrictions on broadcast and cable solely on the basis of ownership has been upheld repeatedly. For example, state requirements that cable franchisees provide access channels, a practice inapplicable to newspapers under *Tornillo,* have withstood challenge.[134]

The Media and Taxation

Following *Minneapolis Star,* in which the Court declared unconstitutional a sales and use tax plan that affected only the press, there has been a great deal of activity in the lower courts. On

---

134. *Berkshire Cablevision v. Burke,* 9 Med. L. Rptr. 2321, 571 F.Supp. 976 (D.R.I. 1983).

one side, the media have attempted to extend the *Minneapolis Star* rule against statutes that single out the press for differential treatment to other contexts. And governments, reminded that tax laws of general application are valid when enforced on the media, have considered broadening tax provisions to include the press where it had not been taxed before.

For example, most states exempt newspapers from sales tax. A major reason behind the exemptions is to encourage citizens to buy newspapers. It is also difficult to enforce a sales tax efficiently on such small transactions. Both points were raised in the Minnesota case. Following the *Minneapolis Star* case, it could be argued that the test used was equally able to invalidate laws favoring the press as those disfavoring it, and states might see the case as an occasion for changing their laws.[135] One of the first provisions reconsidered was the sales tax exemption. Other states began to consider taxing sales of services as well as goods.[136] A Florida advertising sales tax was controversial. Publishers and broadcasters argued that it violated the First Amendment, but it was upheld by the state supreme court. The media's argument appeared to be that a tax on advertising "singles out" the press in much the same way a newsrack ordinance does. The state's response was that selling advertising is just one of thousands of service transactions currently left untaxed. Most states do not impose a sales tax on services, although the temptation to do so grows as the service portion of the economy expands. In any event, the Florida statute was rescinded before the challenge could go far.[137]

Most states' sales tax statutes exempt from taxation purchases of materials that will themselves be incorporated into a product for sale. In this fashion, double taxation of the same material is avoided. Newspapers have traditionally benefited from such exemptions. For example, in *McClure Newspapers v. Vermont Department of Taxes*, 315 A.2d 452 (Vt. 1974), purchases of reporters' notebooks and even flashbulbs were held exempt as component parts of the final product.[138] Some states hold that virtually anything, including preprinted inserts, is a component part of the final product,[139] while others read the exemption narrowly as applying to materials such as newsprint and ink only.[140] A free-circulation publication, *Neighbor*, sought exemption from the sales tax provisions in Florida but was denied because it did not meet the administrative rule definition of a newspaper. One of the requirements is that the publication be sold and not given away. The court held that the provision was nonetheless not discriminatory because the sales tax "is widely applicable to businesses of all kinds. * * *" *North American Publications, Inc. v. Department of Revenue*, 436 So.2d 954 (Fla.App. 1983). The court said that *Minneapolis Star* was inapplicable because the Florida statute was not similar to a penalty. Did the court read *Minneapolis Star* correctly? A North Carolina court similarly upheld a sales and use tax that treated unpaid and paid circulation publications differently.[141]

Westinghouse Broadcasting v. Commissioner of Revenue, 7 Med. L. Rptr. 1066, 416 N.E.2d 191 (Mass. 1981), appeal dismissed 452 U.S. 933 (1981), involved a claim that the Massachusetts sales tax exemption for manufacturing should apply to the creation of television signals, and that to the extent the exemption favored newspapers, it violated the First Amendment. The court, in a pre–*Minneapolis Star* analysis, applied the traditional tax law rule that legislation may "make narrow distinctions without running into trouble on a constitutional level." Westinghouse sought review in the Supreme Court, advancing arguments remarkably similar

135. Simon, *All the News That's Fit to Tax: First Amendment Limitations on State and Local Taxation of the Press,* 21 Wake Forest L.Rev. 59 (1985).

136. For a complete listing of state sales and use taxes affecting newspapers, see *Six states now tax some form of advertising, but the number taxing newsprint and ink declines,* Presstime (February 1986), 42.

137. See Weber, *Florida's Fleeting Sales Tax on Services,* 15 Florida State University L.Rev. 613 (1987).

138. But see *Bodenstein v. Vermont,* 12 Med. L. Rptr. 2101, 510 A.2d 1314 (Vt. 1986) (materials used in producing newspaper advertisements not considered part of eventual product).

139. See, e.g., *In re Appeal of K-Mart,* 12 Med. L. Rptr. 1579 (Kan. 1985); *Allentown v. Call-Chronicle,* 13 Med. L. Rptr. 2329 (Pa.Ct.Common Pleas 1987).

140. *Sears, Roebuck & Co. v. Woods,* 12 Med. L. Rptr. 1897, 708 S.W.2d 374 (Tenn. 1986).

141. *Matter of Assessment of Additional North Carolina and Orange County Use Taxes,* 322 S.E.2d 115 (N.C. 1984).

to those used by the Court two years later in *Minneapolis Star.*

Media companies have attempted to extend *Minneapolis Star* with little success. The Supreme Court decision in *Arkansas Writers' Project v. Ragland*[142] was an exceptionally straightforward application of the test, because Arkansas's statute taxed some magazines but not others. *Texas Monthly v. Bullock,* 16 Med. L. Rptr. 1177, 489 U.S. (1989), involved a similar provision. Texas exempted from sales tax religious periodicals but not others. *Texas Monthly* sought to have the statute declared unconstitutional and to get a tax refund of about $150,000. The Texas Court of Appeals upheld the discriminatory provision on the ground that the state had a rational basis, and no more was needed. At oral argument before the Supreme Court, the state argued that the exemption serves the compelling interest of avoiding an entanglement with religion, also a First Amendment violation. How the exemption avoids entanglement when a state official must grant the exemption is problematic. In the lower court, the state said it granted the exemption to any group claiming it was a bona fide religious group. The Supreme Court, in an opinion by Justice Brennan, determined that the Texas law violated the First Amendment's establishment clause. The indirect tax subsidy for religious organizations had the effect of "endorsing" those organizations. Only Justice White, concurring, thought the press taxation cases dictated the result.

The limits of *Minneapolis Star* are suggested by *City of Alameda v. Premier Communications Network, Inc.,* 202 Cal.Rptr. 684 (Cal.App. 1984). In *Premier,* a cable television operator succeeded in having declared invalid a city business license fee that applied to cable, but not to newspapers. The provision, however, contained so many exceptions that Premier became one of only four categories of businesses actually taxed. The court noted that the city's only asserted interest was raising revenue, never enough under *Minneapolis Star.* On the other hand, by such analysis a cable operator might effectively escape taxation. Newspapers, as manufacturers, will likely be liable for use taxes if not sales taxes, but use or sales taxes are generally inapplicable as

applied to a cable system. The potential reach of *Premier* was limited in a subsequent case that upheld a city business tax that applied to all businesses in the community. *Times Mirror Co. v. Los Angeles,* 14 Med. L. Rptr. 1289, 237 Cal.Rptr. 346 (Cal.App. 1987). *Premier* was apparently limited to its specific facts. The court concluded that the business tax neither resembled a penalty nor operated like one. The court furthermore upheld different methods of computing taxes of media companies. "The inherent difference between these various forms of media is patent," the court said. As long as the effective tax burden was equal and nondiscriminatory, legislative classification would be allowed on a rational basis standard.

Is the result in *Times Mirror* a necessary limitation? Would *Minneapolis Star* otherwise provide the basis for challenges to any tax program applied to the media? The California court seemed to think so. Consider this case: In Chicago, the licensed cable franchise is exempt from the amusement tax. A provider of microwave-transmitted subscription movie services is not exempt. But the cable company pays a franchise fee. An Illinois appeals court said the difference was an unconstitutional one. The franchise fee was considered payment for the value of using public rights of way, etc. No attempt was made to assess the relative economic impact on the two payments.[143]

The confusion in the lower courts appears to be settling after *Leathers v. Medlock,* 18 Med. L. Rptr. 1953, 499 U.S. 439 (1991), in which the Supreme Court upheld an Arkansas sales tax imposed on cable subscribers. Recognizing that different types of media must necessarily be taxed differently, the Court indicated it would uphold tax provisions where there was discriminatory intent or effect. This apparently means that a statute is constitutional if it can be shown that the tax burden of different media companies is essentially the same. But the case has also been interpreted as allowing differential tax burdens.[144]

---

142. 13 Med. L. Rptr. 2313, 107 S.Ct. 1722 (1987).

143. *Statellink of Chicago, Inc. v. City of Chicago,* 523 N.E.2d 13 (Ill.App. 1988).

144. See, e.g., *Magazine Publishers of America v. Pennsylvania,* 23 Med. L. Rptr. 1337, 654 A.2d 519 (Pa. 1995); *Reuters America, Inc. v. Sharp,* 23 Med. L. Rptr. 1129, 889 S.W.2d 648 (Tex.App. 1994).

Regulation of Tax-Exempt Media

More than 600,000 groups or organizations qualify as exempt from taxation under the federal Internal Revenue Code. If a group also qualifies as educational or cultural, it may receive donations that are deductible from the donees' personal income taxes.[145] Tens of thousands of tax-exempt organizations produce publications, operate broadcast stations, or otherwise engage in creation of media content. University student newspapers, scholarly journals, and educational broadcasters are all typically considered tax-exempt, nonprofit educational organizations under the Code. Does the grant of tax-exempt status allow the government greater regulatory authority than it would have over other media?

The District of Columbia Circuit, in a pair of apparently contradictory decisions, answered both yes and no. Each case deals with the doctrine of unconstitutional conditions that stems from *Hannegan v. Esquire* (text, p. 61). Under that analysis, government may not condition receipt of a benefit or privilege upon the waiver of a constitutional right. But unless the IRS takes steps and passes regulations to assure that media produced by tax-exempt groups satisfy the purposes of providing educational or cultural benefits, how can the government avoid a severe drain on tax revenues? Tax exemption, after all, represents an indirect subsidy in the form of tax revenues forgone by government. The subsidy is therefore paid by elevated taxes for everyone else. When reading the excerpts from the two cases that follow, ask which party—government or the publisher—is better serving the public's interests.

Big Mama Rag, Inc. v. United States
631 F.2D 1030 (D.C. CIR. 1980).

MIKVA, Circuit Judge:

Plaintiff, Big Mama Rag, Inc. (BMR, Inc.), appeals from the order of the court below granting summary judgment to defendants and upholding the IRS's rejection of plaintiff's application for tax-exempt status. Specifically, BMR, Inc. questions the finding that it is not entitled to tax exemption as an educational or charitable

organization under section 501(c)(3) of the Internal Revenue Code, 26 U.S.C. § 501(c)(3) (1976), and Treas.Reg. § 1.501(c)(3) 1(d)(2) & (3) (1959). Appellant also challenges the constitutionality of the regulatory scheme, arguing that it violates the First Amendment and the equal protection component of the Fifth Amendment and that it unconstitutionally conditions tax exempt status on the waiver of constitutional rights.

Because we find that the definition of "educational" contained in Treas. Reg. § 1.501(c)(3) 1(d)(3) is unconstitutionally vague in violation of the First Amendment, we reverse the order of the court below.

BMR, Inc. is a nonprofit organization with a feminist orientation. Its purpose is "to create a channel of communication for women that would educate and inform them on general issues of concern to them." App. 76. To this end, it publishes a monthly newspaper, *Big Mama Rag (BMR)*, which prints articles, editorials, calendars of events, and other information of interest to women. BMR, Inc.'s primary activity is the production of that newspaper.

* * *

BMR, Inc. has a predominantly volunteer staff and distributes free approximately 2100 of 2700 copies of *Big Mama Rag's* monthly issues. Moreover, the organization has severely limited the quantity and type of paid advertising. As the district court found, BMR, Inc. neither makes nor intends to make a profit and is dependent on contributions, grants, and funds raised by benefits for over fifty percent of its income. 494 F.Supp. 473, 476 (D.D.C. 1979).

Because of its heavy reliance on charitable contributions, BMR, Inc. applied in 1974 for tax-exempt status as a charitable and educational institution. That request was first denied by the IRS District Director in Austin, Texas, on the ground that the organization's newspaper was indistinguishable from an "ordinary commercial publishing practice." After BMR, Inc. filed a protest and a hearing was held in the IRS National Office, the denial of tax-exempt status was affirmed on three separate grounds:

1. the commercial nature of the newspaper;
2. the political and legislative commentary found throughout; and
3. the articles, lectures, editorials, etc., promoting lesbianism.

---

145. Internal Revenue Code § 501(c)(3).

* * *

Appellant then brought a declaratory judgment action in the District Court for the District of Columbia. On cross-motions for summary judgment, the judge granted appellees' motion. Although the court rejected appellees' argument that BMR, Inc. was not entitled to tax-exempt status because it was a commercial organization, it agreed that appellant did not satisfy the definitions of "educational" and "charitable" in Treas.Reg. § 1.501(c)(3)–1(d)(2) & (3). The court found no constitutional basis for disturbing the IRS's decision.

* * *

The Treasury regulations also define some of the exempt purposes listed in section 501(c)(3) of the Code, including "charitable" and "educational." The definition of "educational" is the one at issue here:

The term "educational," as used in section 501(c)(3), relates to—

(a) The instruction or training of the individual for the purpose of improving or developing his capabilities; or

(b) The instruction of the public on subjects useful to the individual and beneficial to the community.

An organization may be educational even though it advocates a particular position or viewpoint so long as it presents a sufficiently full and fair exposition of the pertinent facts as to permit an individual or the public to form an independent opinion or conclusion. On the other hand, an organization is not educational if its principal function is the mere presentation of unsupported opinion. [Emphasis added.]

Treas.Reg. § 1.501(c)(3)–1(d)(3)(i) (1959).

The district court found that BMR, Inc. was not entitled to tax-exempt status because it had "adopted a stance so doctrinaire" that it could not meet the "full and fair exposition" standard articulated in the definition quoted above.

* * *

Even though tax exemptions are a matter of legislative grace, the denial of which is not usually considered to implicate constitutional values, tax law and constitutional law are not completely distinct entities. In fact, the First Amendment was partly aimed at the so-called "taxes on knowledge," which were intended to limit the circulation of newspapers and therefore the public's opportunity to acquire information about governmental affairs. * * *

Thus, although First Amendment activities need not be subsidized by the state, the discriminatory denial of tax exemptions can impermissibly infringe free speech. *Speiser v. Randall,* 357 U.S. 513 (1958). Similarly, regulations authorizing tax exemptions may not be so unclear as to afford latitude for subjective application by IRS officials. We find that the definition of "educational," and in particular its "full and fair exposition" requirement, is so vague as to violate the First Amendment and to defy our attempts to review its application in this case.

Vague laws are not tolerated for a number of reasons, and the Supreme Court has fashioned the constitutional standards of specificity with these policies in mind. First, the vagueness doctrine incorporates the idea of notice—informing those subject to the law of its meaning. * * * A law must therefore be struck down if "'men of common intelligence must necessarily guess at its meaning.'" *Hynes v. Mayor of Oradell,* 425 U.S. 610.

Second, the doctrine is concerned with providing officials with explicit guidelines in order to avoid arbitrary and discriminatory enforcement. * * * To that end, laws are invalidated if they are "wholly lacking in 'terms susceptible of objective measurement.'" *Keyishian v. Board of Regents,* 385 U.S. 589. * * *

These standards are especially stringent, and an even greater degree of specificity is required, where, as here, the exercise of First Amendment rights may be chilled by a law of uncertain meaning. * * * Vague laws touching on First Amendment rights, noted the Supreme Court * * *

require [those subject to them] to "steer far wider of the unlawful zone," than if the boundaries of the forbidden areas were clearly marked, . . . by restricting their conduct to that which is unquestionably safe. Free speech may not be so inhibited.

* * *

Measured by any standard, and especially by the strict standard that must be applied when First Amendment rights are involved, the definition of "educational" contained in Treas.Reg. § 1.501(c)(3)–1(d)(3) must fall because of its excessive vagueness.

We do not minimize the difficulty and deli-cacy of the task delegated to the Treasury by Congress under section 501(c)(3) of the Code. Words such as "religious," "charitable," "liter-ary," and "educational" easily lend themselves to subjective definitions at odds with the constitu-tional limitations we describe above. Treasury bravely made a pass at defining "educational," but the more parameters it tried to set, the more problems it encountered. * * *

We find similar problems inherent in the "full and fair exposition" test, on which the district court based affirmance of the IRS's denial of tax-exempt status to BMR, Inc. That test lacks the requisite clarity, both in explaining which appli-cant organizations are subject to the standard and in articulating its substantive requirements.

* * *

The uncertainty of the coverage of the "full and fair exposition" standard is evidenced by its application over the years by the IRS. The Trea-sury Department's Exempt Organizations Hand-book has defined "advocates a particular posi-tion" as synonymous with "controversial." Such a gloss clearly cannot withstand First Amend-ment scrutiny. It gives IRS officials no objective standard by which to judge which applicant organizations are advocacy groups—the evalua-tion is made solely on the basis of one's subjec-tive notion of what is "controversial." And, in fact, only a very few organizations, whose views are not in the mainstream of political thought, have been deemed advocates and held to the "full and fair exposition" standard.

The Treasury regulation defining "educa-tional" is, therefore, unconstitutionally vague in that it does not clearly indicate which organiza-tions are advocacy groups and thereby subject to the "full and fair exposition" standard. And the latitude for subjectivity afforded by the regulation has seemingly resulted in selective application of the "full and fair exposition" standard—one of the very evils that the vagueness doctrine is designed to prevent.

The Treasury definition of "educational" may also be challenged on the ground that it fails to articulate with sufficient specificity the require-ments of the "full and fair exposition" standard. The language of the regulation gives no aid in interpreting the meaning of the test.

* * *

An additional source of unclarity lies in the relationship between the two sentences compris-ing the "full and fair exposition" test. Appellant argues that the two should be read as counter-examples—an organization fails to satisfy the test only if "its principal function is the mere presen-tation of unsupported opinion." The Govern-ment, on the other hand, contends that tax-exempt status must be denied BMR, Inc. if a substantial portion of its newspaper consists of unsupported opinion. Again, the language of the regulation does not resolve this issue.

* * *

The futility of attempting to draw lines between fact and unsupported opinion is further illustrated by the district court's application of that test. The court did not analyze the contents of *BMR* under its proposed test but merely stated, without further explication, that the publication was not entitled to tax-exempt status because it had "adopted a stance so doctrinaire that it can-not satisfy this standard." 494 F.Supp. at 479. * * * We can conceive of no value-free mea-surement of the extent to which material is doc-trinaire, and the district court's reliance on that evaluative concept corroborates for us the impossibility of principled and objective applica-tion of the fact/opinion distinction.

Appellees suggest that the Treasury regulation at issue here embodies a related distinction—between appeals to the emotions and appeals to the mind. Material is educational, they argue, if it appeals to the mind, that is, if it reasons to a con-clusion from stated facts. Again, the required line-drawing is difficult, a problem which is com-pounded if the difference between the two relies on the aforementioned fact/opinion distinction.

Moreover, the Treasury regulation does not support such a narrow concept of "educational" and we cannot approve it. Nowhere does the regulation hint that the definition of "educa-tional" is to turn on the fervor of the organization or the strength of its language. As the Supreme Court has recognized in another context, the emotional content of a word is an important component of its message. See *Cohen v. Califor-nia,* 403 U.S. 15, 26 (1971).

* * *

The history of appellant's application for tax-exempt status attests to the vagueness of the "full and fair exposition" test and evidences the evils that the vagueness doctrine is designed to avoid. The district court's decision was based on the value-laden conclusion that *BMR* was too doctrinaire. Similarly, IRS officials earlier advised appellant's counsel that an exemption could be approved only if the organization "agree[d] to abstain from advocating that homosexuality is a mere preference, orientation, or propensity on par with heterosexuality and which should otherwise be regarded as normal." App. 1030. Whether or not this view represented official IRS policy is irrelevant. It simply highlights the inherent susceptibility to discriminatory enforcement of vague statutory language.

We are sympathetic with the IRS's attempt to safeguard the public * * * by closing revenue loopholes. And we by no means intend to suggest that tax-exempt status must be accorded to every organization claiming an educational mantle. Applications for tax exemption must be evaluated, however, on the basis of criteria capable of neutral application. * * *

This case is accordingly reversed and remanded for further proceedings consistent with this opinion.

National Alliance v. United States
710 F.2D 868 (D.C. CIR. 1983).

FAIRCHILD, Senior Circuit Judge:

On July 28, 1977, National Alliance applied to the IRS for a tax exemption as a charitable and educational institution under 26 U.S.C. § 501(c)(3). The IRS District Director in Arlington, Virginia denied the corporation's application on March 31, 1978, concluding that National Alliance was neither "charitable" nor "educational" as those terms are applied by Treas.Reg. § 1.501(c)(3)–(1)(d)(2) & (3).

National Alliance, a Virginia corporation, publishes a monthly newsletter and membership bulletin, organizes lectures and meetings, issues occasional leaflets, and distributes books; all for the stated purpose of arousing in white Americans of European ancestry "an understanding of and a pride in their racial and cultural heritage and an awareness of the present dangers to that heritage."

* * *

Having exhausted its available administrative remedies, National Alliance filed suit in federal district court for declaratory judgment pursuant to 26 U.S.C. § 7428.

The parties filed cross-motions for summary judgment.

This court had then recently decided *Big Mama Rag, Inc. v. United States,* 631 F.2d 1030 (D.C. Cir. 1980). This court there reversed a judgment upholding a denial of tax exemption, and held the IRS regulation defining the term "educational" unconstitutionally vague. The regulation in effect at the time of the IRS National Alliance decision was the same regulation held unconstitutional in *Big Mama.* In argument before the district court, the IRS presented four criteria which it designated the Methodology Test, contended the Methodology Test was an explanatory gloss to the "full and fair exposition" test held vague in *Big Mama,* and argued that National Alliance material was not "educational" under the Methodology Test.

The district court concluded that the Methodology Test was itself vague and would not cure the faults of the regulation found in *Big Mama.* * * *

Both parties appealed. The government argues that the district court should have declared National Alliance not tax-exempt. National Alliance contends the district court should have declared it exempt.

* * *

In large measure the parties, particularly the government, have argued the appeals as if the issue were whether reading the Methodology Test into the regulation would cure the vagueness found in *Big Mama.*

* * *

We think, however, that the appropriate first step is to examine the National Alliance materials to determine whether they could in any event qualify as "educational" within the exemption statute.

In response to an IRS request, National Alliance supplemented its application for exemption with back copies of its monthly newsletter, *Attack!,* and its membership bulletin, *Action.* It is these materials that IRS found noneducational.

The nature of these publications may be summarized as follows. *Attack!* is the organization's principal publication; it contains stories, pictures, feature articles and editorials in a form resembling a newspaper. The general theme of the newsletter is that "non-whites"—principally blacks—are inferior to white Americans of European ancestry ("WAEA"), and are aggressively brutal and dangerous; Jews control the media and through that means—as well as through political and financial positions and other means—cause the policy of the United States to be harmful to the interests of WAEA. A subsidiary proposition is that communists have persuaded "neo-liberals" of equality among human beings, the desirability of racial integration, and the evil of discrimination on racial grounds.

* * *

In sum, National Alliance repetitively appeals for action, including violence, to put to disadvantage or to injure persons who are members of named racial, religious, or ethnic groups. It both asserts and implies that members of these groups have common characteristics which make them sufficiently dangerous to others to justify violent expulsion and separation.

Even under the most minimal requirement of a rational development of a point of view, National Alliance's materials fall short. The publications before us purport to state demonstrable facts—such as the occurrence of violent acts, perpetrated by black persons, the presence of Jews in important positions, and other events consistent with National Alliance themes. The real gap is in reasoning from the purported facts to the views advocated; there is no more than suggestion that the few "facts" presented in each issue of *Attack!* justify its sweeping pronouncements about the common traits of non-whites and Jews or the need for their violent removal from society. It is the fact that there is no reasoned development of the conclusions which removes it from any definition of "educational" conceivably intended by Congress.

* * *

We recognize the inherently general nature of the term "educational" and the wide range of meanings Congress may have intended to convey. * * * We do not attempt a definition, but we are convinced that the National Alliance material is far outside the range Congress could have intended to subsidize in the public interest by granting tax exemption.

Aside from vagueness, it is clear that in formulating its regulation, IRS was attempting to include as educational some types of advocacy of views not generally accepted. But in order to be deemed "educational" and enjoy tax exemption some degree of intellectually appealing developing of or foundation for the views advocated would be required. * * * It is clear that the National Alliance material is not educational under that text.

One of the concerns in this area, because of First Amendment considerations, is that the government must shun being the arbiter of "truth." Material supporting a particular point of view may well be "educational" although a particular public officer may strongly disagree with the proposition advocated. Accordingly IRS has attempted to test the method by which the advocate proceeds from the premises he furnishes to the conclusion he advocates rather than the truth or accuracy or general acceptance of the conclusion.

Thus the Methodology Test presented in this proceeding contains the following four criteria:

1. Whether or not the presentation of viewpoints unsupported by a relevant factual basis constitutes a significant portion of the organization's communications.
2. To the extent viewpoints purport to be supported by a factual basis, are the facts distorted.
3. Whether or not the organization makes substantial use of particularly inflammatory and disparaging terms, expressing conclusions based more on strong emotional feelings than objective factual evaluations.
4. Whether or not the approach to a subject matter is aimed at developing an understanding on the part of the addressees, by reflecting consideration of the extent to which they have prior background or training.

Nothing in these criteria would suggest that the National Alliance material could be deemed educational.

* * *

We assume that the court in *Big Mama* viewed the activity of BMR, Inc. as falling within the range of reasonable interpretation of "educational" as used in the statute, or at least not clearly outside such range. Thus the vague test posed a real risk that BMR, Inc. might have been denied exemption under the test while others not distinguishable on any principled objective basis might be granted exemption.

* * *

We have no doubt that publication of the National Alliance material is protected by the First Amendment from abridgement by law. * * *

But it does not follow that the First Amendment requires a construction of the term "educational" which embraces every continuing dissemination of views.

* * *

We observe that, starting from the breadth of terms in the regulation, application by IRS of the Methodology Test would move in the direction of more specifically requiring, in advocacy material, an intellectually appealing development of the views advocated. The four criteria tend toward ensuring that the educational exemption be restricted to material which substantially helps a reader or listener in a learning process. The test reduces the vagueness found by the *Big Mama* decision.

The government does argue that the Methodology Test goes about as far as humanly possible in verbalizing a line separating education from noneducational expression.

* * *

We need not, however, and do not reach the question whether the application of the Methodology Test, either as a matter of practice or under an amendment to the regulation, would cure the vagueness found in the regulation by the court in *Big Mama*.

The judgment appealed from is reversed and the cause remanded with directions to enter judgment declaring National Alliance not tax-exempt.

COMMENT

In *National Alliance,* the court said that the vagueness that plagued the regulations had been addressed if not solved by applying the "Methodology Test." But doesn't that test necessarily require a government inquiry into the integrity of the publisher, the sort of inquiry the Supreme Court has often said is the exclusive province of publishers and editors? One must have some sympathy with the IRS in its quest to assure that exempt groups serve the intended statutory purpose. Among the dubious groups that have sought exemption as educational groups have been dog training schools, drag racing schools, and dance schools.[146] The IRS's

actions in *Big Mama Rag* and *National Alliance,* along with other tax disputes that never went to court, alarmed the press.[147]

First Amendment purists would argue that the IRS should never be in the business of deciding whether a publication's content is "educational." But the resolution under *Minneapolis Star,* to achieve constitutional equality, might be to eliminate tax exemption for such groups altogether. As government becomes more involved in encouraging free expression directly or indirectly, the sorts of issues addressed in these cases will be more critical.

COPYRIGHT, FAIR USE, AND UNFAIR COMPETITION

Copyright

Article 1, Section 8(8) of the United States Constitution stipulates that "The Congress shall have Power * * * To promote the Progress of Science and useful Arts, by securing for limited Times to Authors and Inventors the exclusive Right to their respective Writings and Discoveries. * * *"

The purpose is akin to that of the First Amendment: protect the property rights of authors in their creations, and in the end you will enhance the flow of information to the people.

The first copyright law was enacted in 1790. The most recent, which was enacted in 1976 and went into effect on January 1, 1978,[148] superseded the copyright law of 1909 and its patchwork amendments. The 1978 law has subsequently begun to acquire a patchwork of amendments of its own.[149] In general terms the law makes the author—the creative person—the focal point of protection.

For the mass media, protection of intellectual property interests, especially copyrights, is critically important. Infringements can cost copy-

146. Hopkins, The Law of Tax-Exempt Organizations 4th ed. 149–61 (1983).

147. MacKenzie, "When Auditors Turn Editors," *Columbia Journalism Review* (November/December 1981), 29; Caneff, "The Auditor as Editor," *Quill* (April 1985), 20; English, "Journalism: The Little Chill," *Mother Jones* (November 1984), 6.
148. 17 U.S.C.A. § 101 et seq.
149. See, e.g., Berne Convention Implementation Act of 1988, codified at 17 U.S.C. § 106A; Copyright Royalty Tribunal Act of 1993, 107 Stat. 2304 (1993).

right owners large sums in lost sales or license fees. For the student of mass communication law, the major concerns to be addressed are the basic elements of U.S. copyright law, the mechanics of registering for copyright, and the extent to which the fair use defense allows some copying without liability for damages. For fuller exploration, a comprehensive[150] text or a separate course in intellectual property is probably advisable.

Rapid changes in copyright laws are not far away. The spread of digital communications and the growing popularity of the Internet as a means of communication (and perfect copying) pose problems that the principles underlying U.S. copyright law are ill equipped to deal with.[151] All the copyright acts have been based on the premise that intangible intellectual property is identifiable and protectable because the intangible material is reproduced in a "tangible medium of expression."[152] This approach has emphasized the physical aspects of property and has resulted in a statutory system of protection that assumes works will be physically manufactured and distributed.

The agitation over digital distribution has led some observers to question the existence of copyright.[153] Given the constitutional admonition that Congress should spur creativity, the question is not whether there will be protection for intellectual property, but rather what form that protection may take. Lawmakers and judges have been slow to amend or reinterpret existing copyright law, however:

> As the pace of technological change quickens, Congress seems less able to adjust copyright laws to the changes. In the two centuries since it passed the first American copyright act, it has been playing catch-up with new technologies—first photographs, then phonograph records, motion pictures, radio, broadcast television, and cable television—usually about twenty years behind the new technologies. Goldstein, Copyright's Highway 32–33 (1994).

The student should be alert for news of changes in intellectual property protection.[154] For now, however, the basics of copyright remain as they have been since 1978—in some cases, since 1790. A quick summary of the basic features follows:

a. Duration of a copyright is now the author's life plus fifty years. If a copyright is in its first twenty-eight-year term under the old law, it may be renewed in the twenty-eighth year for an additional forty-seven years or a total copyright term of seventy-five years. Works in their second twenty-eight year term are automatically extended to seventy-five years from the date of original copyright. Joint or co-authored works are protected for fifty years after the last author dies. For works made for hire, the new term is seventy-five years from publication or one hundred years from creation, whichever is shorter. In such cases the employer becomes the "author."[155]

b. A work is now protected from the moment of its creation in a "fixed" or tangible form. The author is the first owner of all rights of copyright in every case.

c. An author need not sell all of his or her rights to a single publisher in order to obtain a copyright; under the 1978 law, any rights not specifically transferred in writing remain with the author. Copyright is now divisible. What may be copyrighted for newspaper or magazine purposes may be recopyrighted for book publishing or movie adaptation purposes.

d. A transfer of rights to a publisher may be terminated and renegotiated after thirty-five years, and the right to terminate may not be waived in

---

150. See, e.g., Nimmer & Nimmer, Nimmer on Copyright (1992); Foster & Shook, Patents, Copyrights, and Trademarks 2d ed. (1993).

151. See Samuelson & Glushko, *Intellectual Property Rights for Digital Library and Hypertext Publishing Systems*, 6 Harv. J. L. & Technology 237 (1993); Ballon, *Pinning the Blame in Cyberspace: Towards a Coherent Theory for Imposing Vicarious Copyright, Trademark and Tort Liability for Conduct Occurring over the Internet*, 18 Hastings Comm. & Entertainment L.J. 729 (1996); Meyer, *National and International Copyright Liability for Electronic System Operators*, 2 Global Legal Stud. J. <http://www.law.indiana.edu/g;sj/vol2/no2/> (1995); Litman, *Revising Copyright Law for the Information Age*, in Brock & Rosston, eds., The Internet and Telecommunications Policy 271–296 (1996).

152. 17 U.S.C. § 102(a).

153. Waldron, *From Authors to Copiers: Individual Rights and Social Values in Intellectual Property*, 64 Chicago-Kent L. Rev. 841 (1993); Reitenour, *Note, The Legal Protection of Ideas: Is It Really a Good Idea?* 18 Wm. Mitchell L. Rev. 131 (1992); Barlow, "The Economy of Ideas: A Framework for Rethinking Patents and Copyrights in the Digital Age," Wired, March 1994, 84.

154. General information and updates on proposed legislation can be obtained from the Copyright Office home page. <http://lcweb.loc.gov/copyright/>. A variety of links to sites devoted to intellectual property law developments are available. See, e.g., <http://www.kindone.com/html/ip.>

155. It has been proposed that the duration be extended to life plus seventy years. See Dixon, *Note, The Copyright Term Extension Act: Is Life Plus Seventy Too Much?* 18 Hastings Comm. & Entertainment L.J. 945 (1996).

advance. Any transfer of an author's rights must be validated by a signed contract. Without a written agreement, copyright remains with the creator.

e. Magazine publishers or other publishers of collected works acquire only first serial and limited reprint rights to articles or photographs. All other rights are retained by the author.

f. Sound recordings, including those played through jukeboxes, are protected, as are nondramatic literary works such as works of nonfiction, works of the performing arts such as musical compositions, television programs and motion pictures, and works of the visual arts such as photographs and advertisements. Public broadcasters must pay for noncommercial transmissions of published musical and graphic works. Cable systems must also pay for transmission of copyrighted works.

g. Originality is a key factor in obtaining a copyright. The test for originality is remarkably easy to meet, however. In general, the courts have found any work to be original to the author or creator if the work was the result of individual effort. The work need not be original in its ideas or even its expression so long as it is new to the author. The leading case on the originality requirement held that although the information in the residential listings of telephone books was not original enough to be copyrighted, the design and layout of presentation could still satisfy the requirement. *Feist Publications, Inc. v. Rural Telephone Service Co., Inc.,* 18 Med. L. Rptr. 1889, 499 U.S. 340 (1991). The case relied upon what is often called the fact-expression distinction. In copyright, an author's unique expression may be protected, but the ideas expressed cannot be. When a second author uses the underlying facts from another's work, the first author is without remedy. *Paul v. Haley,* 20 Med. L. Rptr. 2041, 588 N.Y.S.2d 897 (App.Div. 1992).

h. Exclusive rights of copyright owners are defined in 17 U.S.C. § 106. These include rights regarding (1) reproduction, (2) derivative works, (3) distribution for sale or rental, (4) performances, and (5) display. Any use by someone other than the author that conflicts with these exclusive rights is an infringement unless protected by the fair use defense.

i. Copyright owners have a variety of remedies available, including injunctions, impoundment and destruction of infringing copies, monetary damages, and statutory damages. Getting an injunction requires proof that the owner will suffer irreparable harm and is also likely to prevail at trial. Damages are usually based on either lost revenues on the part of the owner or on improper revenues gained by the infringer. Statutory damages are a special category. An owner whose copyright is registered with the U.S. Copyright Office may claim statutory damages. The amount varies, but the idea is to create a presumption of harm. A trial judge determines statutory damages on a discretionary basis from $250 to $10,000. If a plaintiff can prove willful infringement, statutory damages can be increased to $50,000. In addition, the owner may be granted attorney's fees. 17 U.S.C. §§ 501–505.

j. Infringement may also be subject to criminal penalties. These are applied primarily to large-scale copiers who are clearly competing with the owner of the copyrighted work. "Any person who infringes a copyright willfully and for purposes of commercial advantage shall be fined not more than $10,000, or imprisoned for not more than one year, or both." 17 U.S.C. § 506. Penalties are stiffer for infringements involving sound recordings.

COPYRIGHT REGISTRATION   As a technical matter, the 1978 Act does not require registration. Copyright may be claimed simply by placing the statutorily required notice on any publicly distributed copies of a work. The statute requires three pieces of information in the notice: an indication that copyright is claimed, the year of first publication, and the owner (usually the author or publisher). A typical notice would look like this:

© 1998 West Publishing Co.

The word "Copyright" or the abbreviation "Copr." may be used in lieu of the symbol. 17 U.S.C. § 401.

A notice, though, only tells the world that ownership is claimed. It is used most frequently for works prior to publication, as when, for example, an author sends an unpublished manuscript to various editors. Notice lets the editors know the author claims protection.

A work bearing notice may subsequently be formally registered. Works that have commercial value are typically registered formally at the earliest practical time. Registration conclusively establishes ownership rights and duration limits.

To register, the applicant fills out one of several forms, arranged by types of works, available from the U.S. Copyright Office, Library of Congress. The fee is nominal ($20 in 1997). The registrant in most cases must "deposit" two copies if the work has been published, one if unpublished, although the actual rules vary somewhat depending on the type of work. Downloadable forms and instructions are available at the Copyright Office home page. The applicant receives a certificate of registration once the office finds the paperwork and the deposit copies acceptable.

Mistakes made during registration and even an omission of notice can be corrected within time limits. Negligence by the author or publisher does not necessarily forfeit copyright, but publication without notice may provide a defense to an innocent infringer. Registration is no longer a condition of copyright protection, nor is placing a notice of copyright on published or unpublished works, but it is prerequisite to a copyright infringement suit seeking damages and attorney's fees and is therefore advantageous. Notice is particularly important for pre-1978 works, and any work without notice may be presumed to have found its way into the public domain.

All works now receive federal statutory protection from the moment of creation (the act of an author), without regard to whether or not they are published. All common law or state copyright protection is preempted by the uniform federal system,[156] unless the right in intellectual property at stake is not covered by the federal statute. The 1978 law is not retroactive, however. Works already in the public domain remain there, including anything published before September 19, 1906.

OWNERSHIP ISSUES   In practice, few copyrights are claimed or registered by the person or persons actually responsible for the creation of a work. In educational and professional publishing, for example, copyright is usually assigned by contract to the publishing company, not the writers. Under the terms of such an assignment, the publishing company will be deemed the "author" and hence the owner of the copyright. Authors of fiction and "trade" books, especially if they have reputations with market value, are more likely to file for copyright in their own names. In that case, the author gives the publishing company a license to use the work.

The biggest ownership issue involves the "works-made-for-hire" doctrine. This doctrine recognizes that most works are created on behalf of an employer. The Copyright Act specifies two work-made-for-hire situations:

1. Works "prepared by an employee within the scope of his or her employment."
2. Works "specially ordered or commissioned" and agreed to in writing to be works made for hire. In these circumstances the publisher may be considered the "author" and first copyright owner. These rights are nevertheless limited and divisible: an author may transfer part of a copyright to a publisher while retaining other parts.

Under the definition of works made for hire in sec. 101 of the 1978 Act, a newspaper publisher would be "author" of everything copyrightable in each issue of the newspaper; only by special agreement would a news reporter or a columnist retain rights in his or her copyrightable work. A columnist, for example, would have to make an agreement with a publisher in advance that future book publication rights remain with the column writer.

When such questions are litigated, courts consider the creative role played by the employer in guiding, supervising, or directing the work of an employee or an independent contractor—writers, filmmakers, translators, and text and test makers. A court ruled for example, that a university professor held copyright to his own lecture notes because the institution employing him played only an indirect role in their creation.[157] Likewise, Admiral Rickover, not the Navy, owned the copyright to his speeches on public education because the Admiral had not "mortgaged all the products of his brain to his employer."[158] And a local merchant, not the newspaper in which his ad appeared, owned the copyright to an advertisement because the merchant had directed what the ad should contain. On the other hand, a pamphlet written by a company chemist was clearly a project within the scope of his employment, so the copyright remained with the company.[159]

---

156. Ringer, *Finding Your Way Around in the New Copyright Law*, Practising Law Institute, Communications Law 1977, p. 114, reprinted from 22 New York Law School L.Rev. 477–495 (1976).

157. *Williams v. Weisser*, 273 Cal.App. 726, 78 Cal.Rptr. 542 (1969). The continuing strength of the case, based on preempted state common law copyright, is in doubt. See Simon, *Faculty Writings: Are They "Works Made for Hire" under the 1976 Copyright Act?* 9 J. College & University L. 485, 495–500 (1982–83).

158. *Public Affairs Associates v. Rickover*, 268 F.Supp. 444 (D.D.C. 1967).

159. *Brattleboro Publishing Co. v. Winmill Publishing Corp.*, 369 F.2d 565 (2d Cir. 1966) (advertisements); *U.S. Ozone Co. v. United States Ozone Co. of America*, 62 F.2d 881 (7th Cir. 1932) (pamphlet).

All the cases just referred to predate the 1978 Act. The Supreme Court held that the new law strengthens the interest of a work's creator. While the creations of employees will be presumed to be works made for hire unless there is written agreement to the contrary, creations of persons commissioned or contracted with are assumed to remain the property of the creator. Apparently, any intent by the parties that the party commissioning a work retain ownership must be stated unequivocally in writing. In a 1989 case, *Community for Creative Non-Violence v. Reid,* 16 Med. L. Rptr. 1769, 490 U.S. 730 (1989), the Court decided in favor of a sculptor who had created a statue at the urging of a community group. Both claimed ownership. In a unanimous opinion, the Court announced that the 1978 provisions superseded prior judicial interpretations. In all likelihood, the net effect is to improve the relative bargaining position of freelancers and other self-employed creators of works when negotiating a commissioned work. Especially for writers, future rights pale in comparison to getting desirable initial compensation. Reason may dictate exceptions. Work related to one's employment but done after business hours and for purposes outside the scope of that employment may be excepted.[160] For independent contractors, such as illustrators, songwriters, freelancers, and textbook authors, the fine print of the initial agreement or contract is important.

What some have called the "artistic-effort-invested" philosophy of copyright is reflected in cases decided both before and after passage of the 1978 Act. With a few exceptions, anything authored, created, performed, or produced and fixed or transcribed in a tangible or permanent way, rather than improvised, is copyrightable. Print, videotape, audiotape, film, television when taped at the time of transmission, computer programs, databases, art works, choreographies, musical compositions, maps, news programs, compilations like annotated bibliographies, and newsletters, either singly or in single-year groups, are included. Sedition, names, titles, slogans, standard symbols and emblems (although these may be protected as trademarks), and official works, both published and unpublished, of the United States and state governments cannot be copyrighted, although the government may protect its "physical" property.

For some time, there was an interesting debate as to whether the copyright law ought to have anything to say about content, for example, sedition or pornography. The prevailing view appears to be that it should not and does not.

By contrast, the Lanham Act prohibits registration of any trademark that "consists of or comprises immoral, deceptive or scandalous matter," 15 U.S.C.A. § 1052(a), and inventions must be shown to be "useful" before a patent is issued, 35 U.S.C.A. § 101. No such language appears in the 1909 or 1978 copyright laws.

"There is nothing in the Copyright Act," said the Ninth Circuit Court of Appeals in *Belcher v. Tarbox,* 486 F.2d 1087 (9th Cir. 1973), "to suggest that the courts are to pass upon the truth or falsity, the soundness or unsoundness, of the views embodied in a copyrighted work. The gravity and immensity of the problems, theological, philosophical, economic and scientific that would confront a court if this view were adopted are staggering to contemplate."

The Ninth Circuit relied on *Belcher* in 1982 when it held that the obscenity of a copyrighted film was not a valid defense against a claim of copyright infringement. Since *Miller v. California* made obscenity a matter of community definition, accepting an obscenity defense, said the court in *Clancy v. Jartech,* 8 Med. L. Rptr. 1404, 666 F.2d 403 (9th Cir. 1982), would fragment copyright enforcement, protecting registered material in one community and, in effect, authorizing pirating in another locale.

The *Clancy* court also cited an important Fifth Circuit ruling, involving the same plaintiffs, for the proposition that both the 1909 and 1978 copyright laws, using the inclusive language "all writings of an author" and "original works of authorship," respectively, were intended to be content-neutral. *Mitchell Brothers v. Cinema Adult Theater,* 5 Med. l. Rptr. 2133, 604 F.2d 852 (5th Cir. 1979), *cert. denied* 445 U.S. 917 (1980).

Mitchell Brothers arose when a number of adult theaters obtained unauthorized copies of the film *Beyond the Green Door* and showed them to audiences for profit. The film is unquestionably hard-core pornography within the meaning of the Supreme Court's obscenity

---

160. *Franklin Mint v. National Wildlife Art Exchange,* 3 Med. L. Rptr. 2169, 575 F.2d 62 (3d Cir. 1978).

holdings (see Chapter 10). *Beyond the Green Door* had been registered with the Copyright Office. The theaters defended on the ground that an obscene work should not be eligible for copyright protection. The court said that the 1909 Copyright Act was content-neutral. "The penalties for obscenity are defined by statute. Why should the courts add a new penalty out of their own heads by denying protection to a registered copyright which complies with every provision of the copyright act?"

The Fifth Circuit Court of Appeals also made it clear in *Miller v. Universal City Studios,* 7 Med. L. Rptr. 1785, 650 F.2d 1365 (5th Cir. 1981), that copyright protection extends only to the expression of facts or ideas and not to facts themselves or to the research involved in obtaining them. A *Miami Herald* reporter who covered the kidnapping of a wealthy businessman's daughter, who was buried alive and rescued after five days, collaborated with the victim to write a book about that terrifying experience. Titled *83 Hours Till Dawn,* the work was copyrighted, as was a condensed version of it in the *Reader's Digest* and a serialization in the *Ladies Home Journal.* Without the author's agreement, the book was turned into a television script, *The Longest Night,* and sold to ABC. A jury found infringement and awarded the reporter $200,000 in damages and profits.

"Obviously," said the appeals court in reversing and remanding, "a fact does not originate with the author of a book describing the fact. Neither does it originate with one who 'discovers' the fact. The discoverer merely finds and records. He may not claim that the facts are 'original' with him although there may be originality and hence authorship in the manner of reporting, i.e., the 'expression of the facts.' Nimmer, *Nimmer on Copyright* § 2.03(E), at 2–34 (1980). Thus, since facts do not owe their origin to any individual, they may not be copyrighted and are part of the public domain available to every person." The distinction between facts and copyrightable forms of expressing them is not always as clear as the foregoing statements suggest, however.

Nor is historical research copyrightable. In *Rosemont Enterprises, Inc. v. Random House, Inc.,* 366 F.2d 303 (2d Cir. 1966), *cert. denied* 385 U.S. 1009 (1967), the court said that it could not "subscribe to the view that an author is absolutely precluded from saving time and

effort by referring to and relying upon prior published material. * * * It is just such wasted effort that the proscription against the copyright of ideas and facts, and to a lesser extent the privilege of fair use, are designed to prevent." Defendant's biography was said to infringe the copyright on a series of *Look* magazine articles about Howard Hughes.

Similar litigation arose over books and films about the mysterious disaster involving the German dirigible *Hindenburg* with similar results. Interpretations of historical fact were not copyrightable. Nor were specific facts or the personal research behind them. *Hoehling v. Universal City Studios, Inc.,* 6 Med. L. Rptr. 1053, 618 F.2d 972 (2d Cir. 1980).

Works that become part of a federal agency's records, however, even though copyrighted by a third person, are public records under the Freedom of Information Act and cannot be withheld simply because they are copyrighted, said the D.C. Circuit in *Weisberg v. United States Department of Justice,* 6 Med. L. Rptr. 1401, 543 F.2d 308 (D.C.Cir. 1976). The case involved photographs in the government's possession that were taken at the scene of the assassination of Dr. Martin Luther King. Time, Inc., the copyright holder, would permit the photos to be viewed but not copied.

In 1988, the United States finally joined the Berne Convention, albeit under considerable pressure. Berne Convention Implementation Act of 1988, 102 Stat. 2853 (1988), 17 U.S.C. § 106A (West Supp. 1993). The Berne Convention is the major international copyright treaty and forms the basis for reciprocal recognition of intellectual property rights all over the world. One of the major concerns of U.S. trading partners was that American law did not recognize "moral rights" inhering to creators of works, be they owners or not. The issue of moral rights is examined later in this section. Joining the convention improves global protection of U.S. copyrights, but it also introduces complications in deciding what law applies where, and how it applies.[161]

In 1996, pending Senate ratification, the United States and 160 other countries signed

---

161. Fraser, *Berne, CFTA, NAFTA & GATT: The Implications of Copyright Droit Moral and Cultural Exemptions in International Trade Law,* 18 Hasting Comm. & Entertainment L.J. 287 (1996).

treaties extending copyright protection to creators of art, software, and music (a particularly abused creative product) distributed in cyberspace. How writers will be compensated when their works are distributed and so easily copied on the Internet has not been resolved, especially where newspapers have developed online editions. In 1997, the *Washington Post,* Time, Inc., Entertainment Weekly, Inc., CNN, the *Los Angeles Times,* Dow Jones, and Reuters brought suit complaining that a World Wide Web site was providing "framed" links to the plaintiffs' news service sites (contents of plaintiffs' Web sites, including trademarks and advertising, would be compressed into a frame occupying only a portion of the computer screen). Plaintiffs complained that this constituted copyright infringement, misappropriation, and trademark dilution and infringement—the equivalent of Internet pirating. *Washington Post Co. v. Total News Inc.,* DC SNY, 97 Civ. 1190 (PKL), complaint filed February 20, 1997.

Under the fair use doctrine, it would still be possible to make a limited number of copies of copyrighted material for noncommercial purposes, including news reports, criticism, and scholarship.

Fair Use

Fair use is a defense that allows limited reproduction of a copyrighted work for certain purposes. In effect, it excuses infringement. The doctrine of fair use is now enshrined in the Copyright Act, 17 U.S.C. § 107. Its source, though, is in more than one hundred years of common law decisions by the courts. Judges created the equitable defense of fair use as a "safety valve" against the otherwise absolute ownership rights of the copyright holder. Like copyright itself, fair use is designed to balance encouragement of creativity with the interest in assuring a free flow of information to the public.

Copying of another's work is allowed for purposes of "criticism, comment, news reporting, teaching (including multiple copies for classroom use), scholarship, or research." A defendant charged with infringement has the burden of proving that a use was one of the listed types. That only begins the inquiry, however.

Whether or not a use will be considered fair will be determined by looking at four factors taken from the judicial opinions that created the defense and specified in the 1978 Act: (1) the purpose and character of the use; (2) the nature of the work copied; (3) the amount used in relation to the size of the full work; and, (4) the effect of the use on the market for the work. See *Williams & Wilkins Co. v. United States,* 487 F.2d 1345 (Ct.Cl. 1973). *aff'd without opinion,* 420 U.S. 376 (1975). None of the factors alone is considered dispositive. As a general rule, copying is permitted when it does not substitute for purchase of a work and the use does not profit the copier financially.

Three major issues involving the fair use defense have developed since the new law took effect in 1978.

PHOTOCOPYING FOR TEACHING   At the urging of publishers and others interested in protecting the economic value of works, Congress appended a set of "Fair Use Guidelines" to the legislative history of the Act.[162] These guidelines are not a part of the law, but are used by some as a general indicator of what is allowed. The guidelines are detailed, and their purpose is plainly to ward off copiers.

Publishers have sued photocopy shops that produce coursepacks for university professors. The publishers' argument is that the coursepacks use large portions of copyrighted materials without permission and that the photocopy shop is infringing for profit. Along the way, the publishers have tried to persuade judges that the Fair Use Guidelines should be interpreted as somewhat binding.

The first, and probably best-known, case was *Basic Books, Inc. v. Kinko's Graphics Corp.,* 758 F.Supp. 1522 (S.D.N.Y. 1991). In the opinion, the district judge relied heavily on the guidelines in deciding that coursepacks prepared for New York University professors were not protected by the fair use defense. The commercial motivation of the defendant, its knowledge that copyrighted material was involved, and its use of copyright permissions in some instances also worked against a finding of fair use. Kinko's argued that it was merely acting as the agent of the professors or of the university, in whose hands the same copying would probably fit the defense. The court awarded $510,000 in damages.

Kinko's had immediate impact. Copy shops throughout the country began insisting on full

---

162. Johnston, Copyright Handbook 217 (1978).

copyright permissions. Universities set restrictive policies on copying in libraries and for classroom purposes. Kinko's itself eventually left the coursepack business. But *Kinko's* was merely a federal district court opinion, and although it was heeded as though it were precedent, it had no binding effect, except on the parties.

James M. Smith, owner of Michigan Document Service, Inc., a copying company serving Michigan State University, the University of Michigan, and Eastern Michigan University, thought the *Kinko's* decision was wrong. He publicly—and frequently—announced that he had no intention of abiding by it. Smith did not seek permissions in advance. When his shops paid use fees, the fees were based on estimates by Smith and his staff, not on fees set by the publishers. Smith pressed arguments similar to those raised by Kinko's: that the use was educational, that he was acting as an agent of the professors, and that his purpose, while commercial, was not to make money out of photocopying. After all, Smith earns the same amount for copying whether the materials are uncopyrighted or copyrighted.

The case Smith virtually invited, *Princeton University Press v. Michigan Document Services, Inc. (MDS)*, has been full of twists and turns. At the federal district court level, Smith lost. 855 F.Supp. 905 (E.D.Mich. 1994). The judge, essentially duplicating the *Kinko's* analysis, found fair use did not apply. A three-judge panel of the Sixth Circuit reversed. 74 F.3d 1512 (6th Cir. 1996). On a 2–1 vote, the panel accepted Smith's agency theory and also determined that the copying was not extensive enough to be substantial. It also said the publishers had failed to show evidence of economic harm. The publishers asked the court to rehear the case *en banc*. The thirteen judges split 8–5. Judge David Nelson, the dissenter in the earlier opinion, now authored the majority opinion.

Princeton University Press v. Michigan Document Services, Inc.

99 F.3D 1381 (6TH CIR. 1996).

DAVID A. NELSON, Circuit Judge:

The corporate defendant, Michigan Document Services, Inc., is a commercial copyshop that reproduced substantial segments of copy-righted works of scholarship, bound the copies into "coursepacks," and sold the coursepacks to students for use in fulfilling reading assignments given by professors at the University of Michigan. The copyshop acted without permission from the copyright holders, and the main question presented is whether the "fair use" doctrine obviated the need to obtain such permission.

* * *

Thanks to relatively recent advances in technology, the coursepack—an artifact largely unknown to college students when the author of this opinion was an undergraduate—has become almost as ubiquitous at American colleges and universities as the conventional textbook. From the standpoint of the professor responsible for developing and teaching a particular course, the availability of coursepacks has an obvious advantage; by selecting readings from a variety of sources, the professor can create what amounts to an anthology perfectly tailored to the course the professor wants to present.

The physical production of coursepacks is typically handled by a commercial copyshop. The professor gives the copyshop the materials of which the coursepack is to be made up, and the copyshop does the rest. Adding a cover page and a table of contents, perhaps, the copyshop runs off as many sets as are needed, does the necessary binding, and sells the finished product to the professor's students.

Ann Arbor, the home of the University of Michigan, is also home to several copyshops. Among them is defendant Michigan Document Services (MDS), a corporation owned by defendant James Smith. We are told that MDS differs from most, if not all, of its competitors in at least one important way: it does not request permission from, nor does it pay agreed royalties to, copyright owners.

Mr. Smith has been something of a crusader against the system under which his competitors have been paying agreed royalties, or "permission fees" as they are known in the trade. * * * After *Kinko's*, we are told, many copyshops that had not previously requested permission from copyright holders began to obtain such permission. Mr. Smith chose not to do so. He consulted an attorney, and the attorney apparently advised him that while it was "risky" not to obtain permission, there were flaws in the *Kinko's* decision. Mr.

Smith also undertook his own study of the fair use doctrine, reading what he could find on this subject in a law library. He ultimately concluded that the *Kinko's* case had been wrongly decided, and he publicized this conclusion through speeches, writings, and advertisements. * * *

Not surprisingly, Mr. Smith attracted the attention of the publishing industry. Three publishers—Princeton University Press, Macmillan, Inc., and St. Martin's Press, Inc.—eventually brought the present suit against Mr. Smith and his corporation.

Each of the plaintiff publishers maintains a department that processes requests for permission to reproduce portions of copyrighted works. * * * Macmillan and St. Martin's, both of which are for-profit companies, claim that they generally respond within two weeks to requests for permission to make copies for classroom use. Princeton, a non-profit organization, claims to respond within two to four weeks. Mr. Smith has not put these claims to the test, and he has not paid permission fees.

The plaintiffs allege infringement of the copyrights on six different works that were excerpted without permission.

* * *

The fair use doctrine, which creates an exception to the copyright monopoly, "permits [and requires] courts to avoid rigid application of the copyright statute when, on occasion, it would stifle the very creativity which that law is designed to foster." *Campbell v. Acuff-Rose Music, Inc.,* 114 S. Ct. 1164, 1170 (1994), quoting *Stewart v. Abend,* 495 U.S. 207, 236 (1990).

* * *

This language does not provide blanket immunity for "multiple copies for classroom use." Rather, "whether a use referred to * * * is a fair use in a particular case . . . depend[s] upon the application of the determinative factors."

When read in its entirety, as Judge Ryan's dissent correctly recognizes, the quoted sentence says that *fair use* of a copyrighted work for purposes such as teaching (including multiple copies for classroom use) is not an infringement. And the statutory factors set forth in the next sentence must be considered in determining whether the making of multiple copies for classroom use is a fair use in "any particular case," just as the statutory factors must be considered in determining whether any other use referred to in the first sentence is a fair use in a particular case. To hold otherwise would be to subvert the intent manifested in the words of the statute and confirmed in the pertinent legislative history.

The four statutory factors may not have been created equal. In determining whether a use is "fair," the Supreme Court has said that the most important factor is the fourth, * * *. We take it that this factor, "the effect of the use upon the potential market for or value of the copyrighted work," is at least *primus inter pares,* figuratively speaking, and we shall turn to it first.

The burden of proof as to market effect rests with the copyright holder if the challenged use is of a "noncommercial" nature. The alleged infringer has the burden, on the other hand, if the challenged use is "commercial" in nature. *Sony Corp. v. Universal City Studios, Inc.,* 464 U.S. 417,. 451 (1984). In the case at bar the defendants argue that the burden of proof rests with the publishers because the use being challenged is "noncommercial." We disagree.

It is true that the use to which the materials are put by the students who purchase the coursepacks is noncommercial in nature. But the use of the materials by the students is not the use that the publishers are challenging. What the publishers are challenging is the duplication of copyrighted materials for sale by a for-profit corporation that has decided to maximize its profits—and give itself a competitive edge over other copyshops—by declining to pay the royalties requested by the holders of the copyrights. * * *

The defendants' use of excerpts from the books at issue here was no less commercial in character than was *The Nation* magazine's use of copyrighted material in *Harper & Row,* where publication of a short article containing excerpts from the still unpublished manuscript of a book by President Ford was held to be an unfair use. Like the students who purchased unauthorized coursepacks, the purchasers of *The Nation* did not put the contents of the magazine to commercial use—but that did not stop the Supreme Court from characterizing the defendant's use of the excerpts as "a publication [that] was commercial as opposed to nonprofit. . . ."*Harper & Row,* 471 U.S. at 562.

* * *

One test for determining market harm—a test endorsed by the Supreme Court in *Sony, Harper & Row,* and *Campbell*—is evocative of Kant's categorical imperative. "[T]o negate fair use," the Supreme Court has said, "one need only show that *if the challenged use 'should become widespread, it would adversely affect the potential market* for the copyrighted work.'" * * * * Under this test, we believe, it is reasonably clear that the plaintiff publishers have succeeded in negating fair use.

As noted above, most of the copyshops that compete with MDS in the sale of coursepacks pay permission fees for the privilege of duplicating and selling excerpts from copyrighted works. The three plaintiffs together have been collecting permission fees at a rate approaching $500,000 a year. If copyshops across the nation were to start doing what the defendants have been doing here, this revenue stream would shrivel and the potential value of the copyrighted works of scholarship published by the plaintiffs would be diminished accordingly.

The defendants contend that it is circular to assume that a copyright holder is entitled to permission fees and then to measure market loss by reference to the lost fees. They argue that market harm can only be measured by lost sales of books, not permission fees. But the circularity argument proves too much. Imagine that the defendants set up a printing press and made exact reproductions—asserting that such reproductions constituted "fair use"—of a book to which they did not hold the copyright. Under the defendants' logic it would be circular for the copyright holder to argue market harm because of lost copyright revenues, since this would assume that the copyright holder had a right to such revenues.

* * *

Where, on the other hand, the copyright holder clearly does have an interest in exploiting a licensing market—and especially where the copyright holder has actually succeeded in doing so—"it is appropriate that potential licensing revenues for photocopying be considered in a fair use analysis." Only "traditional, reasonable, or likely to be developed markets" are to be considered in this connection, and even the availability of an existing system for collecting licensing fees will not be conclusive.

* * *

The potential uses of the copyrighted works at issue in the case before us clearly include the selling of permission to reproduce portions of the works for inclusion in coursepacks—and the likelihood that publishers actually will license such reproduction is a demonstrated fact. A licensing market already exists here, as it did not in a case on which the plaintiffs rely, *Williams & Wilkins Co. v. United States,* 487 F.2d 1345 (Ct. Cl. 1973), *aff'd by an equally divided Court,* 420 U.S. 376 (1975). Thus there is no circularity in saying, as we do say, that the potential for destruction of this market by widespread circumvention of the plaintiffs' permission fee system is enough, under the *Harper & Row* test, "to negate fair use."

* * *

In the context of nontransformative uses, at least, and except insofar as they touch on the fourth factor, the other statutory factors seem considerably less important. We shall deal with them relatively briefly.

A

As to "the purpose and character of the use, including whether such use is of a commercial nature or is for nonprofit educational purposes," we have already explained our reasons for concluding that the challenged use is of a commercial nature.

The defendants argue that the copying at issue here would be considered "nonprofit educational" if done by the students or professors themselves. The defendants also note that they can profitably produce multiple copies for less than it would cost the professors or the students to make the same number of copies. Most of the copyshops with which the defendants compete have been paying commission fees, however, and we assume that these shops too can perform the copying on a more cost-effective basis than the professors or students can. This strikes us as a more significant datum than the ability of a black market copyshop to beat the do-it-yourself cost.

As to the proposition that it would be fair use for the students or professors to make their own copies, the issue is by no means free from doubt. We need not decide this question, however, for the fact is that the copying complained of here was performed on a profit-making basis by a commercial enterprise. And "[t]he courts have . . . properly rejected attempts by for-profit users to stand in the shoes of their customers making nonprofit or noncommercial uses." As the House Judiciary Committee stated in its report on the 1976 legislation, "[I]t would not be possible for a non-profit institution, by means of contractual arrangements with a commercial copying enterprise, to authorize the enterprise to carry out copying and distribution functions that would be exempt if conducted by the non-profit institution itself." H.R. Rep. No. 1476, 94th Cong., 2d Sess. at 74 (1976).

* * *

B

The second statutory factor, "the nature of the copyrighted work," is not in dispute here. The defendants acknowledge that the excerpts copied for the coursepacks contained creative material, or "expression;" it was certainly not telephone book listings that the defendants were reproducing. This factor too cuts against a finding of fair use.

C

The third statutory factor requires us to assess "the amount and substantiality of the portion used in relation to the copyrighted work as a whole." Generally speaking, at least, "the larger the volume (or the greater the importance) of what is taken, the greater the affront to the interests of the copyright owner, and the less likely that a taking will qualify as a fair use." Pierre N. Leval, *Toward a Fair Use Standard,* 103 Harv. L. Rev. 1005, 1122 (1990).

The amounts used in the case at bar—8,000 words in the shortest excerpt—far exceed the 1,000-word safe harbor that we shall discuss in the next part of this opinion. * * * The defendants were using as much as 30 percent of one copyrighted work, and in no case did they use less than 5 percent of the copyrighted work as a whole. These percentages are not insubstantial. And to the extent that the third factor requires some type of assessment of the "value" of the excerpted material in relation to the entire work, the fact that the professors thought the excerpts sufficiently important to make them required reading strikes us as fairly convincing "evidence of the qualitative value of the copied material."

* * *

We turn now to the pertinent legislative history. The general revision of the copyright law enacted in 1976 was developed through a somewhat unusual process. Congress and the Register of Copyrights initiated and supervised negotiations among interested groups—groups that included authors, publishers, and educators—over specific legislative language. Most of the language that emerged was enacted into law or was made a part of the committee reports. See Jessica Litman, *Copyright, Compromise, and Legislative History,* 72 Cornell L. Rev. 857 (1987). The statutory fair use provisions are a direct result of this process. *Id.* at 876–77. So too is the "Agreement on Guidelines for Classroom Copying in Not-for-Profit Educational Institutions With Respect to Books and Periodicals"—commonly called the "Classroom Guidelines"—set out in H.R. Rep. No. 1476 at 68–71, 94th Cong., 2d Sess. (1976). The House and Senate conferees explicitly accepted the Classroom Guidelines "as part of their understanding of fair use," H.R. Conf. Rep. No. 1733, 94th Cong. 2d Sess. at 70 (1976), and the Second Circuit has characterized the guidelines as "persuasive authority . . . ."

Although the Classroom Guidelines purport to "state the minimum and not the maximum standards of educational fair use," they do evoke a general idea, at least, of the type of educational copying Congress had in mind. The guidelines allow multiple copies for classroom use provided that (1) the copying meets the test of brevity (1,000 words, in the present context); (2) the copying meets the test of spontaneity, under which "[t]he inspiration and decision to use the work and the moment of its use for maximum teaching effectiveness [must be] so close in time that it would be unreasonable to expect a timely reply to a request for permission;" (3) no more than nine instances of multiple copying take place during a term, and only a limited number of copies are made from the works of any one author or from any one collective work; (4) each copy contains a notice of copyright; (5) the copying does not substitute for the purchase of "books, publishers' reprints or periodicals;" and (6) the student is not charged any more than the actual cost of copying. The Classroom Guidelines also make clear that unauthorized copying to create "anthologies, compilations or collective works" is prohibited. H.R. Rep. No. 1476 at 69.

In its systematic and premeditated character, its magnitude, its anthological content, and its commercial motivation, the copying done by MDS goes well beyond anything envisioned by the Congress that chose to incorporate the guidelines in the legislative history. Although the guidelines do not purport to be a complete and definitive statement of fair use law for educational copying, and although they do not have the force of law, they do provide us general guidance.

* * *

The defendants attach considerable weight to the assertions of numerous academic authors that they do not write primarily for money and that they want their published writings to be freely copyable. The defendants suggest that unlicensed copying will "stimulate artistic creativity for the general public good."

This suggestion would be more persuasive if the record did not demonstrate that licensing income is significant to the publishers. It is the publishers who hold the copyrights, of course—and the publishers obviously need economic incentives to publish scholarly works, even if the scholars do not need direct economic incentives to write such works.

* * *

In the case at bar the district court was not persuaded that the creation of new works of scholarship would be stimulated by depriving publishers of the revenue stream derived from the sale of permissions. Neither are we. On the contrary, it seems to us, the destruction of this revenue stream can only have a deleterious effect upon the incentive to publish academic writings.

The district court's conclusion that the infringement was willful is somewhat more problematic, in our view. The Copyright Act allows the collection of statutory damages of between $500 and $20,000 for each work infringed. Where the copyright holder establishes that the infringement is willful, the court may increase the award to not more than $100,000. If the court finds that the infringement was innocent, on the other hand, the court may reduce the damages to not less than $200. Here the district court awarded $5,000 per work infringed, characterizing the amount of the award as "a strong admonition from this court." 855 F. Supp. at 913.

* * *

The plaintiffs do not contest the good faith of Mr. Smith's belief that his conduct constituted fair use; only the reasonableness of that belief is challenged. "Reasonableness," in the present context, is essentially a question of law. The facts of the instant case are not in dispute, and the issue is whether the copyright law supported the plaintiffs' position so clearly that the defendants must be deemed as a matter of law to have exhibited a reckless disregard of the plaintiffs' property rights. We review this issue *de novo*.

Fair use is one of the most unsettled areas of the law. The doctrine has been said to be "so flexible as virtually to defy definition." * * * The potential for reasonable disagreement here is illustrated by the forcefully argued dissents and the now-vacated panel opinion. In the circumstances of this case, we cannot say that the defendants' belief that their copying constituted fair use was so unreasonable as to bespeak willfulness.

* * *

The grant of summary judgment on the fair use issue is AFFIRMED. The award of damages is VACATED, and the case is REMANDED for reconsideration of damages and for entry of a separate judgment not inconsistent with this opinion.

* * *

MERRITT, Circuit Judge, dissenting.

The copying done in this case is permissible under the plain language of the copyright statute that allows "multiple copies for classroom use:" "[T]he fair use of a copyrighted work . . . for purposes such as . . . teaching (*including multiple copies for classroom use*), . . . is not an infringement of copyright." 17 U.S.C. § 107 (emphasis added). Also, the injunction the Court has upheld exceeds the protections provided by the Copyright Act of 1976 regardless of whether the use was a fair use and is so grossly overbroad that it violates the First Amendment.

This is a case of first impression with broad consequences. Neither the Supreme Court nor any other court of appeals has interpreted the exception allowing "multiple copies for classroom use" found in § 107 of the copyright statute. There is no legal precedent and no legal history that supports our Court's reading of this phrase in a way that outlaws the widespread practice of copying for classroom use by teachers and students.

For academic institutions, the practical consequences of the Court's decision in this case are highly unsatisfactory, to say the least. Anyone who makes multiple copies for classroom use for a fee is guilty of copyright infringement unless the portion copied is just a few paragraphs long. Chapters from a book or articles from a journal are verboten. No longer may Kinko's and other corner copyshops, or school bookstores, libraries and student-run booths and kiosks copy anything for a fee except a small passage. I do not see why we should so construe plain statutory language that on its face permits "multiple copies for classroom use." * * *

I disagree with the Court's method of analyzing and explaining the statutory language of § 107 providing a fair use exception. Except for "teaching," the statute is cast in general, abstract language that allows fair use for "criticism," "comment," "news reporting" and "research." The scope or extent of copying allowed for these uses is left undefined. Not so for "teaching." This purpose, and this purpose alone, is immediately followed by a definition. The definition allows "multiple copies for classroom use" of copyrighted material. The four factors to be considered, *e.g.,* market effect and the portion of the work used, are of limited assistance when the teaching use at issue fits squarely within the specific language of the statute, *i.e.,* "multiple copies for classroom use." In the present case that is all we have—"multiple copies for classroom use."

There is nothing in the statute that distinguishes between copies made for students by a third person who charges a fee for their labor and copies made by students themselves who pay a fee only for use of the copy machine. Our political economy generally encourages the division and specialization of labor. * * *

Neither the District Court nor our Court provides a rationale as to why the copyshops cannot "stand in the shoes" of their customers in making copies for noncommercial, educational purposes where the copying would be fair use if undertaken by the professor or the student personally.

Rights of copyright owners are tempered by the rights of the public. The copyright owner has never been accorded complete control over all possible uses of a work. * * *

Even if the plain language of the statute allowing "multiple copies for classroom use" were less clear, the Court's analysis of the fair use factors is off base. * * *

The copyshop makes its money based on the number of pages copied, not the content of those pages. The students paid the copyshop solely for the time, effort and materials that each student would otherwise have expended in copying the material himself or herself. The money paid is not money that would otherwise go to the publishers.

* * *

The statute also assess the "amount and substantiality of the portion used in relation to the copyrighted work as a whole." The excerpts here were a small percentage of the total work. The District Court recognized that the excerpts were "truly 'excerpts' and do not purport to be replacements for the original works." * * *

The Court also errs in analyzing the market effect of the classroom copying. The Court erroneously shifts the burden of proof as to market effect to the defendant by labeling the use "commercial" in nature. Generally the burden is on the plaintiff to demonstrate the alleged harm to the potential market value for the copyrighted work. If the challenge is to a noncommercial use of a copyrighted work, the plaintiff must prove by a preponderance of the evidence either that the particular use is harmful or that should it become widespread, it would adversely affect the potential market for the copyrighted work. The Court shifts the burden because it fails to acknowledge that the use in question—making "multiple copies for classroom use" for "teaching" purposes—precisely fits the plain language of the § 107 exception. The Court strains to relieve the plaintiffs of their normal burden of proof. * * *

Turning to the effect of the use upon the potential market for or value of the copyrighted work, plaintiffs here have failed to demonstrate that the photocopying done by defendant has caused even marginal economic harm to their publishing business. As the Court concedes, the publishers would prefer that students purchase the publications containing the excerpts instead of receiving photocopies of excerpts from the publications. What the publishers would "prefer" is not part of the analysis to determine the effect on the potential market. We are to examine what the facts tell us about the market effect. The facts demonstrate that it is only wishful thinking on the part of the publishers that the professors who assigned the works in question would have directed their students to purchase the entire work if the excerpted portions were unavailable for copying. * * *

The use complained of by plaintiffs here has been widespread for many years and the publishers have not been able to demonstrate any significant harm to the market for the original works during that time. The publishing industry tried to persuade Congress in 1976 to ban the type of copying done by defendant here. Congress declined to do so and the publishing industry has been trying ever since to work around the language of the statute to expand its rights.

It is also wrong to measure the amount of economic harm to the publishers by loss of a presumed license fee—a criterion that assumes that the publishers have the right to collect such fees in all cases where the user copies any portion of published works. The majority opinion approves of this approach by affirming the issuance of an injunction prohibiting defendant from copying any portion of plaintiffs' works. It does so without requiring a case-by-case determination of infringement as mandated by the Supreme Court.

The publishers have no right to such a license fee. Simply because the publishers have managed to make licensing fees a significant source of income from copyshops and other users of their works does not make the income from the licensing a factor on which we must rely in our analysis. * * *

The Court states that defendant has declined to pay "agreed royalties" to the holders of the copyrights. Agreed to by whom? Defendant has not "agreed" to pay the publishers anything. It is fair to label a royalty as "agreed to" only when the publisher has appropriately negotiated a fee with the copyshop for use of the copy in question.

The injunction upheld by the Court, as it stands now, extends the rights of the copyright owners far beyond the limits prescribed by Congress. * * * The injunction avoids the necessity of determining whether the copying is an infringement or a fair use—any copying and dissemination is forbidden.

COMMENT

Michigan Document Services now hopes to have the Supreme Court hear the case. No. 96-1219, pet. for cert. filed January 31, 1997. In its "Questions Presented" part of the petition, the appellant asks, "do teachers and students lose their rights of fair use when they ask a commercial copyshop to make classroom copies for them . . . ." It appears that the appeal is being based to a great extent on Judge Merritt's dissent.

The majority in *MDS* relied partly on *American Geophysical Union v. Texaco, Inc.*, 60 F.3d 913 (2d Cir. 1995) for its decision. In that case, publishers of technical and scientific journals sued because Texaco's 400–500 research scientists routinely copied articles, apparently to keep on file. The practice was found to be outside the fair use defense. In this case the court was persuaded that the reprint market for sale of individual copies of articles has been harmed. But the court limited its decision to "institutional, systematic, archival multiplication of copies . . . ." Do the two cases seem similar?

Sometimes the question is simply how much is too much use of a copyrighted work. When the Board of Cooperative Educational Services began making 10,000 videotapes a year of copyrighted motion pictures, a federal district court said that was too much. Applying *Williams & Wilkins* the court held that, while the purpose was educational and noncommercial, the effect on the copyright holder's market would be devastating. Entire films were reproduced, and the reproductions were interchangeable with the originals. Since this was not a fair use, an injunction against further copying was made permanent.[163]

Will the rules be interpreted differently for copying in other media? See Parsons, *Fair Use or Copyright Infringement: Off-Air Video in the Classroom*, 25 J.L. & Educ. 345 (1996).

The only authoritative case on noncommercial videotaping is *Sony Corp. of America v. Uni-*

---

163. *Encyclopedia Britannica v. Crooks,* 3 Med. L. Rptr. 1945, 447 F.Supp. 243 (W.D.N.Y. 1978).

versal City Studios, Inc., 464 U.S. 417 (1984). In this case, Universal and other companies that produced films and television shows accused Sony of contributory copyright infringement. Sony was the maker of the Betamax, the first home videocassette recorder to win consumer acceptance. Viewers used the units to copy and watch copyrighted shows and films at times other than the scheduled broadcast time. Perhaps more importantly, viewers were zipping past the commercials that formed the financial base for license fees to the studios. Sony defended by claiming that home videotaping was a fair use. The Supreme Court agreed, saying that the nature of the works—material broadcast for free reception—and the nominal effect on their market value made them fair use. That the works were copied whole was not deemed critical. The case may be as easily read as a concession to technology. Since there is no way to prevent videotaping of signals sent for free over the air, and since enforcement of the Copyright Act would make the everyday acts of a majority of ordinary citizens illegal, the safer course is to declare videotaping protected. At the time, the newspapers were full of editorial cartoons and columns anticipating the dawn of the "VCR police."

COPYING FOR NEWS USES The key modern fair use case involving news use arose when *Nation* magazine obtained proofs of former President Gerald Ford's memoirs. The magazine published only a few paragraphs, but they were the paragraphs that explained Ford's pardon of Richard Nixon, arguably the most intriguing sentences in the entire book. Ford's publisher, which had entered into a serialization agreement that was lost after the *Nation* story, claimed copyright infringement, arguing that the copying also cost book sales. The *Nation* claimed fair use; the copying had been done as part of reporting the news.

Harper & Row v. Nation Enterprises

11 MED. L. RPTR. 1969, 471 U.S. 539, 105 S. CT. 2218, 85 L. ED. 2D 588 (1985).

Justice O'CONNOR delivered the opinion of the Court.

* * *

In March 1979, an undisclosed source provided the *Nation* magazine with the unpublished manuscript of "A Time to Heal: The Autobiography of Gerald R. Ford." Working directly from the purloined manuscript, an editor of the *Nation* produced a short piece entitled "The Ford Memoirs—Behind the Nixon Pardon." The piece was timed to "scoop" an article scheduled shortly to appear in *Time* magazine. *Time* had agreed to purchase the exclusive right to print prepublication excerpts from the copyright holders, Harper & Row Publishers, Inc. (hereinafter Harper & Row) and Reader's Digest Association, Inc. (hereinafter Reader's Digest). As a result of the *Nation* article, *Time* canceled its agreement. Petitioners brought a successful copyright action against the *Nation*. On appeal, the Second Circuit reversed the lower court's finding of infringement, holding that the *Nation*'s act was sanctioned as a "fair use" of the copyrighted material.

* * *

In February 1977, shortly after leaving the White House, former President Gerald R. Ford contracted with petitioners Harper & Row and The Reader's Digest, to publish his as yet unwritten memoirs. The memoirs were to contain "significant hitherto unpublished materials" concerning the Watergate crisis, Mr. Ford's pardon of former President Nixon and "Mr. Ford's reflections on this period of history, and the morality and personalities involved." In addition to the right to publish the Ford memoirs in book form, the agreement gave petitioners the exclusive right to license prepublication excerpts, known in the trade as "first serial rights." Two years later, as the memoirs were nearing completion, petitioner negotiated a prepublication licensing agreement with *Time*, a weekly news magazine. *Time* agreed to pay $25,000, $12,500 in advance and an additional $12,500 at publication, in exchange for the right to excerpt 7,500 words from Mr. Ford's account of the Nixon pardon. The issue featuring the excerpts was timed to appear approximately one week before shipment of the full length book version to bookstores. Exclusivity was an important consideration; Harper & Row instituted procedures designed to maintain the confidentiality of the manuscript, and *Time* retained the right to renegotiate the second payment should the material appear in print prior to its release of the excerpts.

Two or three weeks before the *Time* article's scheduled release, an unidentified person secretly brought a copy of the Ford manuscript to Victor Navasky, editor of the *Nation,* a political commentary magazine. * * * He hastily put together what he believed was "a real hot news story" composed of quotes, paraphrases and facts drawn exclusively from the manuscript. Mr. Navasky attempted no independent commentary, research or criticism, in part because of the need for speed if he was to "make news" by "publish[ing] in advance of publication of the Ford book." * * * As a result of the *Nation*'s article, *Time* canceled its piece and refused to pay the remaining $12,500.

* * *

We agree with the Court of Appeals that copyright is intended to increase and not to impede the harvest of knowledge. But we believe the Second Circuit gave insufficient deference to the scheme established by the Copyright Act for fostering the original works that provide the seed and substance of this harvest. The rights conferred by copyright are designed to assure contributions to the store of knowledge a fair return for their labors. *Twentieth Century Music Corp. v. Aiken,* 422 U.S. 151, 156 (1975).

* * *

[T]he *Nation* has admitted to lifting verbatim quotes of the author's original language totaling between 300 and 400 words and constituting some 13% of the *Nation* article. In using generous verbatim excerpts of Mr. Ford's unpublished manuscript to lend authenticity to its account of the forthcoming memoirs, the *Nation* effectively arrogated to itself the right of first publication, an important marketable subsidiary right. For the reasons set forth below, we find that this use of the copyrighted manuscript, even stripped to the verbatim quotes conceded by the *Nation* to be copyrightable expression, was not a fair use within the meaning of the Copyright Act.

Fair use was traditionally defined as "a privilege in others than the owner of the copyright to use the copyrighted material in a reasonable manner without his consent." * * * The statutory formulation of the defense of fair use in the Copyright Act of 1976 reflects the intent of Congress to codify the common-law doctrine. 3 Nimmer § 13.05. Section 107 requires a case-by-case

determination whether a particular use is fair, and the statute notes four nonexclusive factors to be considered. This approach was "intended to restate the [pre-existing] judicial doctrine of fair use, not to change, narrow, or enlarge it in any way." H.R. Rep. No. 94-1476, p. 66 (1976) (hereinafter House Report).

"[T]he author's consent to a reasonable use of his copyrighted works ha[d] always been implied by the courts as a necessary incident of the constitutional policy of promoting the progress of science and the useful arts, since a prohibition of such use would inhibit subsequent writers from attempting to improve upon prior works and thus * * * frustrate the very ends sought to be attained." * * *

Perhaps because the fair use doctrine was predicated on the author's implied consent to "reasonable and customary" use when he released his work for public consumption, fair use traditionally was not recognized as a defense to charges of copying from an author's as yet unpublished works. Under common-law copyright, "the property of the author * * * in his intellectual creation [was] absolute until he voluntarily part[ed] with the same."

* * *

Though the right of first publication, like the other rights enumerated in § 106 is expressly made subject to the fair use provision of § 107, fair use analysis must always be tailored to the individual case. * * * The nature of the interest at stake is highly relevant to whether a given use is fair. * * *

The right of first publication implicates a threshold decision by the author whether and in what form to release his work. First publication is inherently different from other § 106 rights in that only one person can be the first publisher, as the contract with *Time* illustrates, * * * the commercial value of the right lies primarily in exclusivity.

* * *

We conclude that the unpublished nature of a work is "[a] key, though not necessarily determinative, factor" tending to negate a defense of fair use.

* * *

Respondents, however, contend that First Amendment values require a different rule under the circumstances of this case. The thrust of the decision below is that "[t]he scope of [fair use] is undoubtedly wider when the information conveyed relates to matters of high public concern." * * * Respondents advance the substantial public import of the subject matter of the Ford memoirs as grounds for excusing a use that would ordinarily not pass muster as a fair use—the piracy of verbatim quotations for the purpose of "scooping" the authorized first serialization. Respondents explain their copying of Mr. Ford's expression as essential to reporting the news story it claims the book itself represents. In respondents' view, not only the facts contained in Mr. Ford's memoirs, but "the precise manner in which [he] expressed himself was as newsworthy as what he had to say."

* * *

Respondents' theory, however, would expand fair use to effectively destroy any expectation of copyright protection in the work of a public figure. Absent such protection, there would be little incentive to create or profit in financing such memoirs and the public would be denied an important source of significant historical information. The promise of copyright would be an empty one if it could be avoided merely by dubbing the infringement a fair use "news report" of the book.

* * *

It is fundamentally at odds with the scheme of copyright to accord lesser rights in those works that are of greatest importance to the public. Such a notion ignores the major premise of copyright and injures author and public alike.

* * *

In view of the First Amendment protections already embodied in the Copyright Act's distinction between copyrightable expression and uncopyrightable facts and ideas, and the latitude for scholarship and comment traditionally afforded by fair use, we see no warrant for expanding the doctrine of fair use to create what amounts to a public figure exception to copyright. Whether verbatim copying from a public figure's manuscript in a given case is or is not fair must be judged according to the traditional equities of fair use.

Fair use is a mixed question of law and fact. * * * Thus whether the Nation article constitutes fair use under § 107 must be reviewed in light of

the principles discussed above. The factors enumerated in the section are not meant to be exclusive: "[S]ince the doctrine is an equitable rule of reason, no generally applicable definition is possible, and each case raising the question must be decided on its own facts." The four factors identified by Congress as especially relevant in determining whether the use was fair are: (1) the purpose and character of the use; (2) the nature of the copyrighted work; (3) the substantiality of the portion used in relation to the copyrighted work as a whole; (4) the effect on the potential market for or value of the copyrighted work.

* * *

In evaluating character and purpose we cannot ignore the Nation's stated purpose of scooping the forthcoming hardcover and Time abstracts. The Nation's use had not merely the incidental effect but the intended purpose of supplanting the copyright holder's commercially valuable right of first publication.

* * *

The fact that a work is unpublished is a critical element of its "nature." Our prior discussion establishes that the scope of fair use is narrower with respect to unpublished works. While even substantial quotations might qualify as fair use in a review of a published work or a news account of a speech that had been delivered to the public or disseminated to the press, the author's right to control the first public appearance of his expression weighs against such use of the work before its release. The right of first publication encompasses not only the choice whether to publish at all, but also the choices when, where and in what form first to publish a work.

* * *

Next, the Act directs us to examine the amount and substantiality of the portion used in relation to the copyrighted work as a whole. In absolute terms, the words actually quoted were an insubstantial portion of "A Time to Heal." The district court, however, found that "[t]he Nation took what was essentially the heart of the book." * * * A Time editor described the chapters on the pardon as "the most interesting and moving parts of the entire manuscript." The portions actually quoted were selected by Mr. Navasky as among the most powerful passages in those chapters. He testified that he used verbatim excerpts because simply reciting the information could not adequately convey the "absolute certainty with which [Ford] expressed himself," or show that "this comes from President Ford," or carry the "definitive quality" of the original. In short, he quoted these passages precisely because they qualitatively embodied Ford's distinctive expression.

* * *

In view of the expressive value of the excerpts and their key role in the infringing work, we cannot agree with the Second Circuit that the "magazine took a meager, indeed an infinitesimal amount of Ford's original language."

Finally, the Act focuses on "the effect of the use upon the potential market for or value of the copyrighted work." This last factor is undoubtedly the single most important element of fair use. "Fair use, when properly applied, is limited to copying by others which does not materially impair the marketability of the work which is copied." The trial court found not merely a potential but an actual effect on the market. *Time*'s cancellation of its projected serialization and its refusal to pay the $12,500 were the direct effect of the infringement. * * * Rarely will a case of copyright infringement present such clear cut evidence of actual damage.

* * *

The borrowing of these verbatim quotes from the unpublished manuscript lent the *Nation*'s piece a special air of authenticity—as Navasky expressed it, the reader would know it was Ford speaking and not the *Nation*. Thus it directly competed for a share of the market for prepublication excerpts. The Senate Report states:

> "With certain special exceptions * * * a use that supplants any part of the normal market for a copyrighted work would ordinarily be considered an infringement." Senate Report, at 65.

Placed in a broader perspective, a fair use doctrine that permits extensive prepublication quotations from an unreleased manuscript without the copyright owner's consent poses substantial potential for damage to the marketability of first serialization rights in general.

* * *

[T]he judgment of the Court of Appeals is reversed and remanded for further proceedings consistent with this opinion.

COMMENT

As Justice O'Connor emphasized, the determination of whether the fair use defense applies will always be a matter of context. In *Harper & Row* the last factor, harm to market, was determinative. That is undoubtedly because the case had undertones of unfair competition in addition to copyright law. The *Nation* was not merely copying a work to inform the public—it was "scooping" the work.[164] Had the memoirs been published already, there would never have been a case.

The opinion is a departure from traditional fair use analysis concerning materials copied for use in news stories. Although there are few such cases, generally the public interest in being informed has held up against infringement claims based on limited and, in some cases, unlimited copying.

In general, where it can be shown that material was copied either as part of news content or as part of news gathering and reporting, the use has been found to be fair. *Religious Technology Center v. Lerma,* 24 Med. L. Rptr. 1115, 908 F.Supp. 1362 (E.D.Va. 1995). In another case, the National Basketball Association (NBA) sued Motorola, a maker of handheld pagers, for providing basketball scores while the games were being played. The NBA claimed copyright infringement, commercial misappropriation under New York law, false advertising under the Lanham Act, and violation of the Communication Act. A federal appeals court disagreed in part holding that (1) professional basketball games were not "original works of authorship" protected by the Copyright Act, and (2) misstatements in advertising for the pagers did not violate the Lanham Act. Broadcasts of the game, however, would be protected by copyright. *National Basketball Association v. Motorola, Inc.,* 41 USPQ2d 1585 (2d Cir. 1997), 25 Med. L. Rptr. 1161 (1996).

Nevertheless, *Harper & Row* has had an effect. When videotapes of his speech to the 1988 Democratic Convention began appearing for sale, Jesse Jackson claimed copyright infringe-

---

164. See Baird, *Common Law Intellectual Property and the Legacy of International News Service v. Associated Press,* 50 University of Chicago L. Rev. 411 (1983); Abramson, *How Much Copying under Copyright? Contradictions, Paradoxes, Inconsistencies,* 61 Temple L.Rev. 133 (1988).

ment. The defendant claimed fair use and also argued that Jackson' speech, visible to all, contained no copyright notice and that any interest in the work was therefore abandoned. Jackson's original written copy of the speech was delivered to the Democratic National Committee without any copyright notice, and the speech was widely distributed by the party without apparent complaint from Jackson. Relying largely upon *Harper & Row*, a federal district court issued an injunction and temporary restraining order. The court said that defendant's marketing, which aimed to profit from Jackson's work, was unlikely to be found a fair use when the actual trial began. The court indicated that arguments based on lack of copyright notice and abandonment might succeed for defendant at trial. *Jackson v. MPI Home Video*, 15 Med. L. Rptr. 2065, 694 F.Supp. 483 (N.D.Ill. 1988). The court hinted that Jackson might have an additional claim that the sale of the tape implied endorsement.

Another *Harper's* magazine case, involving publication of copyrighted letters written by a creative writing teacher to his students, provides an excellent analysis and application of the four-part fair use test. The plaintiff prevailed against the magazine on three of the four fair use factors. See *Lish v. Harper's Magazine Foundation*, 20 Med. L. Rptr. 2073, 807 F.Supp. 1090 (S.D.N.Y. 1992).

When unpublished letters of reclusive author J. D. Salinger were obtained from public sources and used in an unauthorized biography, Salinger was able to get an injunction against the publisher. The unpublished nature of the letters, protected as a matter of common law copyright because they predated the 1978 Act, was the major factor. *Salinger v. Random House*, 13 Med. L. Rptr. 1954, 811 F.2d 90 (2d Cir. 1987). As noted earlier, cases were usually more kind to a news-based or hot-news fair use defense.

The *Miami Herald*, in promoting a new television supplement, used the cover of *TV Guide* in comparative advertising for its new service. Relying on Nimmer on Copyright § 14.4 at 62, a federal district court in Florida concluded that the cover of *TV Guide* "was encompassed within the protections afforded by the copyright registered for that magazine." Moreover there was no "fair use" justification in using the plaintiff's cover for promotional purposes. But a First Amendment purpose was being served in light of

judicial recognition of increased constitutional protection for commercial speech.

"Such comparative advertising, when undertaken in the serious manner that defendant did herein," said the court, "represents an important source of information for the education of consumers in a free enterprise system." Since *TV Guide* had not demonstrated irreparable injury and since the First Amendment outweighs any act of Congress, the magazine was denied an injunction against the *Herald*'s competitive promotional activities.[165]

Similarly, *Time* magazine failed in a copyright suit involving its copyrighted Zapruder film of the Kennedy assassination. *Time* had refused an author the use of certain frames of the film for a scholarly book on the assassination, and the author used sketches of the frames instead. The court said there was a *public interest* in the subject and the book would be purchased, not just for its pictures, but for the author's "theories."[166]

PARODY AND SATIRE   Parody has also been protected under fair use. In *Elsmere Music, Inc. v. NBC*,[167] "Saturday Night Live's" use of New York's public relations song "I Love New York" did not violate fair use because it was used as parody.

When *Screw* magazine portrayed the trade characters "Poppin Fresh" and "Poppie Fresh" in a compromising pose, the Pillsbury Company was understandably upset. A federal district court ruled, however, that the magazine's use of the copyrighted trade characters, while more pornographic than it needed to be, was intended as a social commentary and thereby protected. Since it did not cause significant economic harm to the company, the portrayal was fair use.[168]

There was no fair use, however, when a religious group presented what it called a "nonperverted" version of "Jesus Christ Superstar"

165. *Triangle Publications v. Knight-Ridder,* 3 Med. L. Rptr. 2086, 445 F.Supp. 875 (S.D.Fla. 1978), *aff'd* 6 Med. L. Rptr. 1734, 626 F.2d 1171 (5th Cir. 1980).
166. *Time, Inc. v. Bernard Geis Associates,* 293 F.Supp. 130 (S.D.N.Y. 1968).
167. 5 Med. L. Rptr. 2455, 482 F.Supp. 741 (S.D.N.Y. 1980), *aff'd* 6 Med. L. Rptr. 1457, 623 F.2d 252 (2d Cir. 1980).
168. *The Pillsbury Co. v. Milky Way Productions,* 3 Med. L. Rptr. 2328 (N.D.Ga. 1978); *The Pillsbury Co. v. Milky Way Productions,* 8 Med. L. Rptr. 1016 (N.D.Ga. 1981).

using, with sanctimonious modification, the plaintiff's original music and libretto.[169]

Humorous comment on an existing work through parody, satire, or lampoon has enjoyed considerable latitude from the courts. Intellectual property owners have become fairly thin-skinned in the last fifteen years, however, and have brought a flood of cases based not just on copyright, but also on trademark, right of publicity, and unfair competition.[170] The justification behind applying a fair use defense for humor may be based on the Copyright Act or on the First Amendment, but encouraging creativity is the common rationale. Another factor is that someone has created a work, symbol, or identity that has become so well known that it can be made fun of—public figures, via fair use, end up giving something up.[171]

Until recently, the protection of parody had not been formally reviewed at the U.S. Supreme Court. In *Hustler Magazine, Inc. v. Falwell,* 14 Med. L. Rptr. 2281, 485 U.S. 46 (1988), the Court had unanimously declared that Jerry Falwell could not recover for intentional infliction of emotional distress based on a salacious lampoon of Falwell in the context of a fake liquor ad. In deciding, the Court placed great weight on the history of political humor. Falwell, a public figure who had also been active in Republican politics, was fair game, the Court said. But *Falwell* did not involve copying.

The copyright parody case the Court eventually heard involved a spoof almost as raunchy as *Hustler*'s, although it was quite different in most other respects. Luther Campbell, the leader and main songwriter for the rap group 2 Live Crew, decided to spoof the song "Oh, Pretty Woman" on the group's new album. In so doing, the group used a background arrangement almost identical to the original; there was some evidence that the arrangement may have been digitally sampled from the original.

It probably did not help that 2 Live Crew sought approval from the copyright owner and then released the parody even though permission was not granted. And it probably did not help that the song being spoofed was the most-played song in the history of radio. And it probably did not help that Acuff-Rose, the copyright holder, is one of the biggest music publishers in the world. In the end, 2 Live Crew ended up representing all parodists and Acuff-Rose all copyright owners.

A federal district court had ruled that 2 Live Crew's parody was a fair use, but the Sixth Circuit reversed. *Acuff-Rose Music, Inc. v. Campbell,* 754 F.Supp. 1150 (M.D.Tenn. 1991), *rev'd,* 972 F.2d 1429 (6th Cir. 1992). The Supreme Court reversed the appeals court.

Campbell v. Acuff-Rose Music, Inc.
22 MED. L. RPTR. 1353, 114 S. CT. 1164 (1994).

Justice SOUTER delivered the opinion of the Court.

We are called upon to decide whether 2 Live Crew's commercial parody of Roy Orbison's song, "Oh, Pretty Woman," may be a fair use within the meaning of the Copyright Act of 1976. Although the District court granted summary judgment for 2 Live Crew, the Court of Appeals reversed, holding the defense of fair use barred by the song's commercial character and excessive borrowing. Because we hold that a parody's commercial character is only one element to be weighed in a fair use enquiry, and that insufficient consideration was given to the nature of parody in weighing the degree of copying, we reverse and remand.

In 1964, Roy Orbison and William Dees wrote a rock ballad called "Oh, Pretty Woman" and assigned their rights in it to respondent Acuff-Rose Music, Inc. Acuff-Rose registered the song for copyright protection.

Petitioners Luther R. Campbell, Christopher Wongwon, Mark Ross, and David Hobbs, are collectively known as 2 Live Crew, a popular rap music group. In 1989, Campbell wrote a song entitled "Pretty Woman," which he later described in an affidavit as intended, "through comical lyrics, to satirize the original work . . . ." 2 Live Crew's manager informed Acuff-Rose that 2 Live Crew had written a parody of "Oh, Pretty

169. *Robert Stigwood Group Ltd. v. O'Reilly,* 346 F.Supp. 376 (D.Conn. 1972).
170. Davidson Scott, *From Satirical to Satyrical: When Is a Joke Actionable?* 13 Hastings Comm. & Entertainment L.J. 141 (1991).
171. Denicola, *Trademarks as Speech: Constitutional Implications of the Emerging Rationales for the Protection of Trade Symbols,* 1982 Wis. L. Rev. 158; *L. L. Bean, Inc. v. Drake Publishers, Inc.,* 811 F.2d 26 (1st Cir. 1987).

Woman," that they would afford all credit for ownership and authorship of the original song to Acuff-Rose, Dees, and Orbison, and that they were willing to pay a fee for the use they wished to make of it. Enclosed with the letter were a copy of the lyrics and a recording of 2 Live Crew's song. Acuff-Rose's agent refused permission, stating that "I am aware of the success enjoyed by 'The 2 Live Crew', but I must inform you that we cannot permit the use of a parody of 'Oh, Pretty Woman.' " Nonetheless, in June or July 1989, 2 Live Crew released records, cassette tapes, and compact discs of "Pretty Woman" in a collection of songs entitled "As Clean As They Wanna Be." The albums and compact discs identify the authors of "Pretty Woman" as Orbison and Dees and its publisher as Acuff-Rose.

Almost a year later, after nearly a quarter of a million copies of the recording had been sold, Acuff-Rose sued 2 Live Crew and its record company, Luke Skyywalker Records, for copyright infringement. The District Court granted summary judgment for 2 Live Crew.

* * *

The Court of Appeals for the Sixth circuit reversed and remanded. 972 F.2d 1429, 1439 (1992).

* * *

We granted certiorari, 507 U.S. 1003 (1993), to determine whether 2 Live Crew's commercial parody could be a fair use.

It is uncontested here that 2 Live Crew's song would be an infringement of Acuff-Rose's rights in "Oh, Pretty Woman," under the Copyright Act of 1976, but for a finding of fair use through parody. * * * The fair use doctrine thus "permits [and requires] courts to avoid rigid application of the copyright statute when, on occasion, it would stifle the very creativity which that law is designed to foster."

The task is not to be simplified with bright-line rules, for the statute, like the doctrine it recognizes, calls for case-by-case analysis. The text employs the terms "including" and "such as" in the preamble paragraph to indicate the "illustrative and not limitative" function of the examples given. Nor may the four statutory factors be treated in isolation, one from another. All are to be explored, and the results weighed together, in light of the purposes of copyright.

A

The first factor in a fair use enquiry is "the purpose and character of the use, including whether such use is of a commercial nature or is for non-profit educational purposes." The enquiry here may be guided by the examples given in the preamble to § 107, looking to whether the use is for criticism, or comment, or news reporting, and the like. The central purpose of this investigation is to see, in Justice Story's words, whether the new work merely "supersede[s] the objects" of the original creation, or instead adds something new, with a further purpose or different character, altering the first with new expression, meaning, or message; it asks, in other words, whether and to what extent the new work is "transformative." Although such transformative use is not absolutely necessary for a finding of fair use, the goal of copyright, to promote science and the arts, is generally furthered by the creation of transformative works. Such works thus lie at the heart of the fair use doctrine's guarantee of breathing space within the confines of copyright, and the more transformative the new work, the less will be the significance of other factors, like commercialism, that may weigh against a finding of fair use.

* * * Suffice it to say now that parody has an obvious claim to transformative value, as Acuff-Rose itself does not deny. Like less ostensibly humorous forms of criticism, it can provide social benefit, by shedding light on an earlier work, and, in the process, creating a new one. We thus line up with the courts that have held that parody, like other comment or criticism, may claim fair use under § 107.

* * *

Modern dictionaries * * * describe a parody as a "literary or artistic work that imitates the characteristic style of an author or a work for comic effect or ridicule," or as a "composition in prose or verse in which the characteristic turns of thought and phrase in an author or class of authors are imitated in such a way as to make them appear ridiculous." For the purposes of copyright law, the nub of the definitions, and the heart of any parodist's claim to quote from existing material, is the use of some elements of a prior author's composition to create a new one that, at least in part, comments on that author's works. * * * Parody needs to mimic an original to make its point, and so has some claim to use the creation of its victim's (or collective victims') imagination, whereas satire can stand on its own two feet and so requires justification for the very act of borrowing.

The fact that parody can claim legitimacy for some appropriation does not, of course, tell either parodist or judge much about where to draw the line. Like a book review quoting the copyrighted material criticized, parody may or may not be fair use, and petitioner's suggestion that any parodic use is presumptively fair has no more justification in law or fact than the equally hopeful claim that any use for news reporting should be presumed fair. * * * Accordingly, parody, like any other use, has to work its way through the relevant factors, and be judged case by case, in light of the ends of the copyright law.

* * * As the District Court remarked, the words of 2 Live Crew's song copy the original's first line, but then "quickly degenerat[e] into a play on words, substituting predictable lyrics with shocking ones . . . [that] derisively demonstrat[e] how bland and banal the Orbison song seems to them." Judge Nelson, dissenting below, came to the same conclusion, that the 2 Live Crew song "was clearly intended to ridicule the white-bread original" and "reminds us that sexual congress with nameless streetwalkers is not necessarily the stuff of romance and is not necessarily without its consequences. The singers (there are several) have the same thing on their minds as did the lonely man with the nasal voice, but here there is no hint of wine and roses."

We have less difficulty in finding that critical element in 2 Live Crew's song than the Court of Appeals did, although having found it we will not take the further step of evaluating its quality. The threshold question when fair use is raised in defense of parody is whether a parodic character may reasonably be perceived. Whether, going beyond that, parody is in good taste or bad does not and should not matter to fair use.

* * *

The Court of Appeals, however, immediately cut short the enquiry into 2 Live Crew's fair use claim by confining its treatment of the first factor essentially to one relevant fact, the commercial nature of the use. The court then inflated the significance of this fact by applying a presumption ostensibly culled from *Sony*, that "every commercial use of copyrighted material is presumptively . . . unfair . . . ." *Sony*, 464 U.S., at 451. In giving virtually dispositive weight to the commercial nature of the parody, the Court of Appeals erred.

The language of the statute makes clear that the commercial or nonprofit educational purpose of a work is only one element of the first factor enquiry into its purpose and character. Section 107(1) uses the term "including" to begin the dependent clause referring to commercial use, and the main clause speaks of a broader investigation into "purpose and character." * * *

Sony itself called for no hard evidentiary presumption. There, we emphasized the need for a "sensitive balancing of interests," *Sony* noted that Congress had "eschewed a rigid, bright-line approach to fair use," and stated that the commercial or nonprofit educational character of a work is "not conclusive," but rather a fact to be "weighed along with other[s] in fair use decisions." The Court of Appeals's elevation of one sentence from *Sony* to a *per se* rule thus runs as much counter to *Sony* itself as to the long common-law tradition of fair use adjudication. Rather, as we explained in *Harper & Row, Sony* stands for the proposition that the "fact that a publication was commercial as opposed to nonprofit is a separate factor that tends to weigh against a finding of fair use." But that is all, and the fact that even the force of that tendency will vary with the context is a further reason against elevating commerciality to hard presumptive significance. * * *

B

The second statutory factor [is] "the nature of the copyrighted work." * * * This factor calls for recognition that some works are closer to the core of intended copyright protection than others, with the consequence that fair use is more difficult to establish when the former works are copied. * * * We agree with both the District Court and the Court of Appeals that the Orbison original's creative expression for public dissemination falls within the core of the copyright's protective purposes. This fact, however, is not much help in this case, or ever likely to help much in separating the fair use sheep from the infringing goats in a parody case, since parodies almost invariably copy publicly known, expressive works.

C

The third factor asks whether "the amount and substantiality of the portion used in relation to the copyrighted work as a whole," "the quantity and value of the materials used," are reasonable in relation to the purpose of the copying. Here, attention turns to the persuasivenes of a parodist's justification for the particular copying done, and the enquiry will harken back to the first of the statutory factors, for, as in prior cases, we recognize that the extent of permissible copying varies with the purpose and character of the use.

* * *

The Court of Appeals is of course correct that this factor calls for thought not only about the quantity of the materials used, but about their quality and importance, too. * * * We also agree with the Court of Appeals that whether "a substantial portion of the infringing work was copied verbatim" from the copyrighted work is a relevant question, for it may reveal a dearth of transformative character or purpose under the first factor, or a greater likelihood of market harm under the fourth; a work composed primarily of an original, particularly its heart, with little added or changed, is more likely to be a merely superseding use, fulfilling demand for the original.

Where we part company with the court below is in applying these guides to parody, and in particular to parody in the song before us. Parody presents a difficult case. Parody's humor, or in any event its comment, necessarily springs from recognizable allusion to its object through distorted imitation. Its art lies in the tension between a known original and its parodic twin. When parody takes aim at a particular original work, the parody must be able to "conjure up" at least enough of that original to make the object of its critical wit recognizable. What makes for this recognition is quotation of the original's most distinctive or memorable features, which the parodist can be sure the audience will know. * * *

We think the Court of Appeals was insufficiently appreciative of parody's need for the recognizable sight or sound when it ruled 2 Live Crew's use unreasonable as a matter of law. It is true, of course, that 2 Live Crew copied the char-

acteristic opening bass riff (or musical phrase) of the original, and true that the words of the first line copy the Orbison lyrics. But if quotation of the opening riff and the first line may be said to go to the "heart" of the original, the heart is also what most readily conjures up the song for parody, and it is the heart at which parody takes aim. Copying does not become excessive in relation to parodic purpose merely because the portion taken was the original's heart. If 2 Live Crew had copied a significantly less memorable part of the original, it is difficult to see how its parodic character would have come through.

This is not, of course, to say that anyone who calls himself a parodist can skim the cream and get away scot free. In parody, as in news reporting, context is everything, and the question of fairness asks what else the parodist did besides go to the heart of the original. It is significant that 2 Live Crew not only copied the first line of the original, but thereafter departed markedly from the Orbison lyrics for its own ends. 2 Live Crew not only copied the bass riff and repeated it, but also produced otherwise distinctive sounds, interposing "scraper" noise, overlaying the music with solos in different keys, and altering the drum beat. This is not a case, then, where "a substantial portion" of the parody itself is composed of a "verbatim" copying of the original. It is not, that is, a case where the parody is so insubstantial, as compared to the copying, that the third factor must be resolved as a matter of law against the parodists. * * * [W]e fail to see how the copying can be excessive in relation to its parodic purpose, even if the portion taken is the original's "heart." * * *

D

The fourth fair use factor is "the effect of the use upon the potential market for or value of the copyrighted work." It requires courts to consider not only the extent of market harm caused by the particular actions of the alleged infringer, but also "whether unrestricted and widespread conduct of the sort engaged in by the defendant . . . would result in a substantially adverse impact on the potential market" for the original.

* * *

In assessing the likelihood of significant market harm, the Court of Appeals quoted from language in *Sony* that " '[i]f the intended use is for commercial gain, that likelihood may be presumed. But if it is for a noncommercial purpose, the likelihood must be demonstrated.' " The court reasoned that because "the use of the copyrighted work is wholly commercial, . . . we presume a likelihood of future harm to Acuff-Rose exists." In so doing, the court resolved the fourth factor against 2 Live Crew, just as it had the first, by applying a presumption about the effect of commercial use, a presumption which as applied here we hold to be error.

* * *

But when * * * the second use is transformative, market substitution is at least less certain, and market harm may not be so readily inferred. Indeed, as to parody pure and simple, it is more likely that the new work will not affect the market for the original in a way cognizable under this factor, that is, by acting as a substitute for it. This is so because the parody and the original usually serve different market functions.

We do not, of course, suggest that a parody may not harm the market at all, but when a lethal parody, like a scathing theater review, kills demand for the original, it does not produce a harm cognizable under the Copyright Act. Because "parody may quite legitimately aim at garroting the original, destroying it commercially as well as artistically," the role of the courts is to distinguish between "[b]iting criticism [that merely] suppresses demand [and] copyright infringement[, which] usurps it." Fisher v. Dees, 794 F.2d, at 438.

* * *

2 Live Crew's song comprises not only parody but also rap music, and the derivative market for rap music is a proper focus of enquiry. * * * Of course, the only harm to derivatives that need concern us, as discussed above, is the harm of market substitution. The fact that a parody may impair the market for derivative uses by the very effectiveness of its critical commentary is no more relevant under copyright than the like threat to the original market.

Although 2 Live Crew submitted uncontroverted affidavits on the question of market harm to the original, neither they, nor Acuff-Rose, introduced evidence or affidavits addressing the likely effect of 2 Live Crew's parodic rap song on the market for a non-parody, rap version of "Oh, Pretty Woman." * * * [I]t is impossible to deal with the fourth factor except by recognizing that a silent record on an important factor bearing on fair use disentitled the proponent of the defense, 2 Live Crew, to summary judgment. The evidentiary hole will doubtless be plugged on remand.

* * *

We therefore reverse the judgment of the Court of Appeals and remand for further proceedings consistent with this opinion.

COMMENT

What was Acuff-Rose really after in the case? Sales of the original Roy Orbison song in various anthologies remain brisk almost a decade after the singer's death. One way of looking at this and similar cases[172] is that the intellectual property holder is trying to protect the integrity of the work, not to prevent copying or use as such. The real complaint appears to be that the work is besmirched as a result of the parodist's efforts. If Acuff-Rose had won, would celebrity impersonators and stand-up comedians have been at risk?

Will the owner of a well-known work ever be able to win an infringement case against a spoof after Acuff-Rose? The decision appears to provide a very broad defense. See Leval, Campbell v. Acuff-Rose: Justice Souter's Rescue of Fair Use, 13 Cardozo Arts & Entertainment L.J. 23 (1994).

The Acuff-Rose case bears some similarity to various "moral rights" cases brought over the years. Under moral rights doctrine, the integrity of a work is protected. An author or creator even retains rights to prevent revision or distortion when ownership of a work transfers.

A case that reflects a moral rights philosophy is Gilliam v. American Broadcasting Companies, Inc., 538 F.2d 14 (2d Cir. 1976), which is also of interest because it involved "Monty Python's Flying Circus." The case began when ABC bought from the BBC the right to show six Python episodes, then cut them in an apparently prudish manner to fit the commercial television format. The Pythons sued for copyright infringe-

---

172. See, e.g., Mutual of Omaha Insurance Co. v. Novak, 836 F.2d 397 (8th Cir. 1987) ("Mutant of Omaha" T-shirts); Carson v. Here's Johnny Portable Toilets, Inc., 698 F.2d 831 (6th Cir. 1983); MCA, Inc. v. Wilson, 677 F.2d 180 (2d Cir. 1981) (indecent lyrics in song parody).

ment and unfair competition, asking for a permanent injunction against ABC.

In what was by all accounts an entertaining trial, a federal district court, while recognizing a plaintiff's right to protect the artistic integrity of his creation (the film here had lost its "iconoclastic verve," said the judge), denied the injunction on grounds that it was not clear who owned the copyright. There was also a question as to whether the BBC and Time-Life—the latter had purchased the rights—should have been parties to the litigation. Further, ABC might suffer irreparable harm in its relationships with affiliates, public, and government if it were to withdraw the programs.

The trial judge suggested a disclaimer instead: "The members of Monty Python wish to disassociate themselves from this program, which is a compilation of their shows edited by ABC without their approval." ABC thought this distasteful, a dangerous precedent with respect to other artists and technicians, and a violation of its First Amendment rights. The best Monty Python could get was "Edited for Television by ABC."

A Second Circuit Court of Appeals panel subsequently reversed and remanded the lower court's denial of a preliminary injunction. Seeing Monty Python rather than ABC as the greater loser, the court held that "unauthorized editing of the underlying work, if proven, would constitute an infringement of copyright in that work similar to any other use of a work that exceeded the license granted by the proprietor of the copyright." Since the BCC itself had no right to make unilateral changes in the script, it could not grant such rights to Time-Life or ABC.

"Our resolution of these technical arguments," said the court somewhat in anticipation of the 1978 Copyright Act, "serves to reinforce our initial inclination that the copyright law should be used to recognize the important role of the artist in our society and the need to encourage production and dissemination of artistic works by providing adequate legal protection for one who submits his work to the public. * * * To deform his work is to present him to the public as the creator of a work not his own, and thus makes him subject to criticism for work he has not done."

The decision to join the Berne Convention will likely lead to increased debate about the moral rights of those who create materials. A congressional report prior to joining the convention indicated that, while the United States has no specific moral rights statute, moral rights are currently protected by the accumulated rights within other areas of intellectual property law. The assertion that rights under U.S. law are comparable to those in continental law is doubtful for a variety of reasons, but most obviously because U.S. law grants rights to owners rather than to creators of material.[173]

Unfair Competition

Unfair competition is prohibited under federal law by the Lanham Act[174] and by common law or statute in the states.[175] The cause of action is essentially a modern-day derivative from the common law actions of deceit and fraud. The essence of the action is the unauthorized taking from another of an intangible asset of value, then presenting it to the buying public as if it was one's own. The act is typically referred to as "passing off" another's material as your own. Disputes between competing businesses are the primary area for application of unfair competition principles. Typically, a competitor takes an attribute of another's product or business hoping to capitalize on it. For example, a manufacturer might put a product in a package that looks astonishingly like a competitor's.[176] A flood of imitative goods in recent years has sparked controversy.[177]

For the most part, the law of unfair competition, and its companion trademark and service mark law, seldom has a direct bearing on news media or, for that matter, mass media. It is primarily designed to assure that direct competitors compete reasonably. When a news organization uses a trademark like Kleenex, for example, in a news story, it may upset the trademark owner. But the use is not likely to be found an infringement because the news organization does not

---

173. See Ross, Comment, *The United States Joins the Berne Convention: New Obligations for the Authors' Moral Rights?* 68 N.C.L. Rev. 363 (1990).

174. 15 U.S.C.A. § 1125(a). The provision is commonly referred to as sec. 43(a), its designation in the original version of the act.

175. McManis, Unfair Trade Practices, 3d ed., 5–15 (1992).

176. *Johnson & Johnson v. Carter-Wallace, Inc.*, 631 F.2d 186 (2d Cir. 1980).

177. See Symposium, *Piracy and Gray Market Imports: Knocking out the Knock-offs,* 10 Comm/Ent L.J. 1045 (1988).

compete in the facial tissue market. Bonavita, *In the Beginning Was the Story*, Editor & Publisher, December 10, 1994. Most editors consider proper use of trademarks to be an issue of ethics, not law, and comply with owners' preferences for capitalization of marks. Doing so also prevents nasty letters.

Sometimes trademark owners bring an action for trademark dilution against media users, especially those who use a trademark in a parody. See *Anheuser-Busch, Inc. v. Balducci Publications*, 22 Med. L. Rptr. 2001, 28 F.3d 769 (8th Cir. 1994). The Eighth Circuit seems quite willing to find trademark dilution via media uses, but other circuits that have considered the issue disagree. Congress recently added an antidilution provision to the Lanham Act, the Federal Trademark Dilution Act. 15 U.S.C. § 1125(c). Previously, dilution had been a state law remedy only. The argument in essence is that the unauthorized user is conveying to the public the false implication that the trademark owner has consented to the use. Is this claim valid in light of the *Acuff-Rose* case?

For the media, unfair competition issues arise when one organization takes and uses the product of another, or when advertising or editorial materials incorporate an attribute of a person or organization.

The protection of news as "quasi property" against unfair competition was recognized in a broad and influential ruling by the U.S. Supreme Court in 1918. International News Service (INS) was alleged to have "pirated" news from the Associated Press for redistribution to its own customers. No direct question of fraud was raised, and the misappropriated material had not been copyrighted. In the absence of statutory protection, AP relied on the common law doctrine of unfair competition.

The court considered three major legal issues: (1) whether there is any property in news; (2) whether, if there be property in news collected for the purpose of being published, it survives the instant of its publication in the first newspaper to which it is communicated by the newsgatherer, and (3) whether INS's admitted course of conduct in appropriating for commercial use material taken from bulletins or earlier editions of AP newspapers constitutes unfair competition in trade. Each question was answered in favor of the AP. *International News*

Service v. Associated Press, 248 U.S. 215 (1918).[178]

News, being part of the public domain and like ideas "as free as the air,"[179] is excluded from specific copyright protection, but the doctrine of *INS v. AP* does apply to newsgathering and news presentation activities. Using one's competitor for news "tips" is an acceptable practice, but bodily appropriation of another's news copy is unfair competition subject to injunctive relief.

The *INS* case is more properly considered a common law action for misappropriation than one for unfair competition. INS did not attempt to pass off its product in a way that might lead buyers to think it was AP's. There is more theft and less deception in a misappropriation claim. In other respects the actions are alike, especially the factor of intending to benefit from another's efforts.

Since news itself is not copyrightable but only the style or pattern of words found in a story, copyright notices used by many newspapers when major news stories are broken cannot prevent others from using the facts within the story.

In *Associated Press v. KVOS*, 80 F.2d 575 (9th Cir. 1935), *reversed on other grounds* 299 U.S. 269 (1936), the appeals court ruled that appropriation for broadcast of an AP wire before neighboring AP newspapers could reach their subscribers—while the news was still "hot"—was enjoinable. An injunction was also granted to a Sitka (Alaska) newspaper whose AP stories were being read verbatim by a radio station even before the newspaper hit the streets. Instead of joining its member newspaper in the suit, AP sold the offending radio station an associate membership. Still preferring to read the newspaper's edited AP copy, the broadcaster found himself in a second suit. Nominal damages were awarded, and the radio station agreed to cease pirating news.[180]

In an unreported case, a Kentucky circuit court ruled that a defendant, who had without

---

178. For a discussion of this case and the whole question of news piracy, unfair competition, and misappropriation, see Sullivan, *News Piracy: Unfair Competition and the Misappropriation Doctrine*, 56 Journalism Monographs, May 1978.
179. *Desney v. Wilder*, 46 Cal.2d 715, 299 P.2d 257 (1956), a case dealing with the writing of a play from news stories and quoting Justice Brandeis.
180. *Veatch v. Wagner*, 109 F.Supp. 537 (Alaska 153) and 116 F.Supp. 904 (Alaska 1953).

permission used plaintiff's news stories sixteen to eighteen hours before the newspaper could be delivered to all its subscribers, would in future have to wait twenty hours after publication before engaging in his piracy.[181]

In 1963 the Supreme Court of Pennsylvania left no doubt that the broadcasting of news stories from a newspaper in a competitive situation was unfair competition and an invasion of a property right in uncopyrighted news. The court articulated a doctrine that had been expressed in earlier cases:

> Competition in business is jealously protected by the law and the law abhors that which tends to diminish or stifle competition. While a competitor may, subject to patent, copyright and trademark laws, imitate his rival's business practices, process and methods, yet the protection which the law affords to competition does not and should not countenance the usurpation of a competitor's investment and toil. *Pottstown Daily News Publishing Co. v. Pottstown Broadcasting Co.*, 192 A.2d 657, 663 (Pa. 1963).

Although consistently declared a type of unfair competition, the rip 'n' read practice of using local newspaper stories remains common at many radio stations.

In a 1966 case involving two business publications, defendant had appropriated information from the plaintiff's wire service in order to publish bond market news contemporaneously with his competitor and without expense or effort.

"It is no longer subject to question," said a New York appeals court, "that there is a property in the gathering of news which may not be pirated. Plaintiff's rights do not depend on copyright; they lie rather in the fact that the information has been acquired through an expenditure of labor, skill and money."[182]

After a period of some uncertainty, *INS v. AP* was reaffirmed by the 1973 ruling of the U.S. Supreme Court in *Goldstein v. California*, 412 U.S. 546 (1973). The case, involving record piracy, assures the validity of the misappropria-

tion doctrine and the use of state unfair competition laws.

A case with implications for source-reporter relations was *Sinatra v. Wilson*.[183] There a federal district court held that what a celebrity says to a columnist in an interview may be protected by common law copyright. Frank Sinatra said that he planned to publish an autobiography, but columnist Earl Wilson "scooped" him with a "boring" and unauthorized biography alleged to contain Sinatra's "private thoughts, statements, impressions and emotions." Action for a false-light invasion of privacy was also permitted on the basis of what plaintiff alleged to be false and fabricated statements. The issues could only be decided, said the court, after discovery and trial.

The *Sinatra* case illustrates the uncertain relationships between unfair competition and other areas of the law. Sinatra today would likely file a claim for invasion of his right of publicity. If the thing taken was his image or distinctive singing style, he might be able to claim instead violation of a service mark—essentially the same as a trademark. If Wilson had taken Sinatra's *written* comments and used them verbatim, there might be an action for plagiarism. The interest at stake in each is comparable to the notion of moral rights. The complicated strands of argument surrounding claims like these find courts struggling to separate claims. See *Carson v. Here's Johnny Portable Toilets*, 9 Med. L. Rep. 1153, 698 F.2d 831 (6th Cir. 1983), where the court initially said that plaintiff's unfair competition claim was inappropriate but decided for the plaintiff based on the right of publicity. See p. 313.

Trademarks, Patents, and Electronic Programming

Copyright protection should not be confused with trademark, or service mark, and patent protection. Trademark or service mark law protects a business's interest in a clearly identifiable sign, symbol, or slogan representing the company. Book titles, stage names, and even the call letters of broadcast stations can be registered with the Patent and Trademark Office. Unauthorized use of trademarks can lead to damages, forfeiture of profits, and payment of attorney's fees and court costs under the Federal Trademark Act. Trademark

181. *Madison Publishing Co., Inc. v. Sound Broadcasters, Inc.* (unreported 1966). In a 1956 case involving the *Toledo Blade* and radio station WOHO, the time period was set at twenty-four hours.

182. *Bond Buyer v. Dealers Digest Publishing Co.*, 267 N.Y.S.2d 944 (1966).

183. 2 Med. L. Rptr. 2008 (S.D.N.Y. 1977).

registration lasts for ten years, but infinite renewals are possible.

Whereas copyright protects the literary form or mode of the expression of an idea in a fixed, tangible form (a book, musical score, or video-tape), a patent protects the idea itself. Patent protection, which is good for seventeen years, is better protection than copyright for it seems to carry more weight in the courts. The distinction between copyright and patent in protecting some kinds of intellectual property, however, is not always clear. Software programs, for example, are patentable if described as a process. A company like IBM might apply for as many as two hundred software patents a year.

Various industries, notably advertising and public relations, routinely use computer scanning and modification to create illustrations derived from photographs, works of art, and other copyrightable images that may not even be recognized in the final product. What is fair use in such circumstances?

Congress has made various attempts to protect motion pictures, videocassettes, and digital audio tapes (DAT). DAT recorders are obviously a threat to digital recording copyrights. They can make perfect CDs.

Radio stations perform copyrighted music when they play records, tapes, and CDs over the air. Such performances require the permission of the copyright holders. Because it would be cumbersome to obtain these rights individually from all the composers who own them, composers typically assign some or all of their performance rights to performing rights societies. There are three of these in the United States: ASCAP (the American Society of Composers, Authors and Publishers); BMI (Broadcast Music, Inc.); and SESAC (the Society of European State Authors and Composers).

These societies simplify life for radio stations. Stations take out licenses from the societies to play music. In exchange for payment to the societies, the station gets the right to perform all recorded music that a society represents. Func-tioning as a clearinghouse, the society pays the rights-holders based on the amount their music is played. Under current U.S. law, performers of music, singers mainly, are not viewed as doing anything creative. The money goes to the authors—composers—of the songs or to the people to whom they have sold their rights. Performers resent this; they consider themselves to be creative artists, too. So far, however, they have been unable to persuade Congress to create a performer's right.

Cable TV has displayed some interesting variations on copyright law. Just as it would be cumbersome for radio stations to negotiate with all the rights-holders of copyrighted music, Congress has decided that cable systems should not have to negotiate with all the rights-holders involved in video programs carried on TV stations and retransmitted by cable systems. Congress gave the cable industry access to what is called a compulsory license. In exchange for an annual payment, a cable system obtains the automatic right to retransmit the copyrighted programming contained in over-the-air broadcast signals that the cable system can lawfully carry. The pooled money is redistributed to the rights-holders. Until December 1993, the collection and distribution was handled by a little-known agency called the Copyright Royalty Tribunal. Concluding that the Tribunal was both costly and useless, Congress abolished it. Now the Librarian of Congress selects arbitration panels to hammer out agreements over compulsory license rates and the distribution of money collected. Little money goes to broadcast or cable stations because they are not the authors of most of the programming they carry. Most of the money goes to the Hollywood studios that produce programming. A large amount also goes to the professional sports leagues such as the National Football League and the National Basketball Association. Sports leagues and the Hollywood studios believe cable pays too little for the content they produce.

CHAPTER 10

SELECTED PROBLEMS OF
MEDIA LAW

CHAPTER OUTLINE

OBSCENITY AND INDECENCY: AN OVERVIEW

Judicial Standards

OBSCENITY   *Obscenity* was defined for posterity by the U.S. Supreme Court in 1973. In *Miller v. State of California,* the Court said that the "average person" applying "contemporary community standards" could recognize obscenity as appealing to *prurient interest,* being *patently offensive,* and lacking in *serious literary, artistic, political, or scientific value.* A portion of that so far undisturbed ruling follows:

Miller v. State of California
412 U.S. 15, 93 S. CT. 2607, 37 L. E. 2D 419 (1973).

Chief Justice BURGER delivered the opinion of the Court.

* * *

This case involves the application of a state's criminal obscenity statute to a situation in which sexually explicit materials have been thrust by aggressive sales action upon unwilling recipients who had in no way indicated any desire to receive such materials. This Court has recognized that the states have a legitimate interest in prohibiting dissemination or exhibition of obscene material when the mode of dissemination carries with it a significant danger of offending the sensibilities of unwilling recipients or of exposure to juveniles. It is in this context that we are called on to define the standards which must be used to identify obscene material that a State may regulate without infringing the First Amendment as applicable to the States through the Fourteenth Amendment.

* * *

This much has been categorically settled by the Court, that obscene material is unprotected by the First Amendment. The First and Fourteenth Amendments have never been treated as absolutes. We acknowledge, however, the inherent dangers of undertaking to regulate any form of expression. State statutes designed to regulate obscene materials must be carefully limited. * * *

The basic guidelines for the trier of fact must be: (a) whether "the average person, applying contemporary community standards" would find that the work, taken as a whole, appeals to the prurient interest, (b) whether the work depicts or describes, in a patently offensive way, sexual conduct specifically defined by the applicable state law, and (c) whether the work, taken as a whole, lacks serious literary, artistic, political, or scientific value. [Emphasis added.] We do not adopt as a constitutional standard the *"utterly without redeeming social value"* test of *Memoirs v. Massachusetts;* that concept has never commanded the adherence of more than three Justices at one time. If a state law that regulates obscene material is thus limited, as written or construed, the First Amendment values applicable to the States through the Fourteenth Amendment are adequately protected by the ultimate power of appellate courts to conduct an independent review of constitutional claims when necessary.

We emphasize that it is not our function to propose regulatory schemes for the States. That must await their concrete legislative efforts. It is possible, however, to give a few plain examples of what a state statute could define for regulation under the second part (b) of the standard announced in this opinion, supra:

a. Patently offensive representations or descriptions of ultimate sexual acts, normal or perverted, actual or simulated.

b. Patently offensive representation or descriptions of masturbation, excretory functions, and lewd exhibition of the genitals.

Sex and nudity may not be exploited without limit by films or pictures exhibited or sold in places of public accommodation any more than live sex and nudity can be exhibited or sold without limit in such public places. At a minimum, prurient, patently offensive depiction or description of sexual conduct must have serious literary, artistic, political, or scientific value to merit First Amendment protection. For example, medical books for the education of physicians and related personnel necessarily use graphic illustrations and descriptions of human anatomy. In resolving the inevitably sensitive questions of fact and law, we must continue to rely on the jury system, accompanied by the safeguards that judges, rules of evidence, presumption of innocence and other protective features provide, as we do with rape, murder and a host of other offenses against society and its individual members.

* * *

Under the holdings announced today, no one will be subject to prosecution for the sale or exposure of obscene materials unless these materials depict or describe patently offensive "hard core" sexual conduct specifically defined by the regulating state law, as written or construed. We are satisfied that these specific prerequisites will provide fair notice to a dealer in such materials that his public and commercial activities may bring prosecution.

* * *

It is certainly true that the absence, since *Roth,* of a single majority view of this Court as to proper standards for testing obscenity has placed a strain on both state and federal courts. *But today, for the first time since Roth was decided in 1957, a majority of this Court has agreed on concrete guidelines to isolate "hard core" pornography from expression protected by the First Amendment.* Now we may abandon the casual practice of *Redrup v. New York,* and attempt to provide positive guidance to the federal and state courts alike. [Emphasis added.]

This may not be an easy road, free from difficulty. But no amount of "fatigue" should lead us to adopt a convenient "institutional" rationale— an absolutist, "anything goes" view of the First Amendment—because it will lighten our burdens. * * * Nor should we remedy "tension between state and federal courts" by arbitrarily depriving the States of a power reserved to them under the Constitution, a power which they have enjoyed and exercised continuously from before the adoption of the First Amendment to this day. * * *

Under a national Constitution, fundamental First Amendment limitations on the powers of the States do not vary from community to community, but this does not mean that there are, or should or can be, fixed, uniform national standards of precisely what appeals to the "prurient interest" or is "patently offensive." These are essentially questions of fact, and our nation is simply too big and too diverse for this Court to reasonably expect that such standards could be articulated for all 50 States in a single formulation, even assuming the prerequisite consensus exists. When triers of fact are asked to decide whether "the average person, applying contemporary community standards" would consider certain materials "prurient," it would be unrealistic to require that the answer be based on some abstract formulation. The adversary system, with lay jurors as the usual ultimate fact-finders in criminal prosecutions, has historically permitted triers-of-fact to draw on the standards of their community, guided always by limiting instructions on the law. To require a State to structure obscenity proceedings around evidence of a *national* "community standard" would be an exercise in futility.

* * *

We conclude that neither the State's alleged failure to offer evidence of "national standards," nor the trial court's charge that the jury consider state community standards, were constitutional errors. Nothing in the First Amendment requires that a jury must consider hypothetical and unascertainable "national standards" when attempting to determine whether certain materials are obscene as a matter of fact. * * *

It is neither realistic nor constitutionally sound to read the First Amendment as requiring that the people of Maine or Mississippi accept public depiction of conduct found tolerable in Las Vegas or New York City. People in different States vary in their tastes and attitudes, and this diversity is not to be strangled by the absolutism of imposed uniformity. * * * We hold the requirement that the jury evaluate the materials with reference to "contemporary standards of the State of California" serves this protective purpose and is constitutionally adequate.

* * *

In sum we (a) affirm the *Roth* holding that obscene material is not protected by the First Amendment, (b) hold that such material can be regulated by the States, subject to the specific safeguards enunciated above, without a showing that the material is "*utterly* without redeeming social value," and (c) hold that obscenity is to be determined by applying "contemporary community standards," * * * not "national standards."

Vacated and remanded for further proceedings.

INDECENCY Prohibition of "obscene, *indecent* or *profane* utterances" in broadcasting began with the Federal Radio Act of 1927 and was carried over to the Federal Communications Act of 1934 and to the criminal code in 1948. The Federal Communications Commission (FCC) is the initial enforcer.

Indecency may have become the key standard for broadcasting in 1970. WUHY-FM, a noncommercial radio station, interviewed the late Jerry Garcia ("Crazy Max" of *The Grateful Dead*) in a hotel room. Garcia used four-letter words with dazzling proficiency during the interview, and they were left in for broadcast. Saying that radio differed from other media, the FCC gave Garcia's language a reverberating rejection. Large numbers of children would be in the audience, and indecency, not obscenity, said the commission, should be the applicable standard. The station was fined $100.[1] (See pp. 830–833.)

Or, perhaps, indecency as a judicial standard originated in "topless radio" and was written into the law by the FCC in 1973.[2] (See pp. 827–830.) Certainly, it was legitimized by the Supreme Court five years later in *FCC v. Pacifica Foundation.* Creating a lower threshold for government intervention, the Court said that inde-

---

1. *In re WUHY-FM Eastern Education Radio*, 24 F.C.C.2d 48 (1970).

2. *Sonderling Broadcasting Corp., WGLD-FM*, 41 F.C.C.2d 777 (1973). The case involved what was then called "topless radio." ". . . (E)ven if it were not found to appeal to prurient interest," said the FCC ". . . it is within the statutory prohibition against the broadcast of *indecent* matter." The station was fined $2,000, and the FCC's action was upheld in *Illinois Citizens Committee for Broadcasting v. FCC*, 515 F.2d 397 (D.C.Cir. 1974), largely because of commercial exploitation and because children would be in the audience at the time of broadcast.

cency would apply to broadcast media, presumably because radio and television were more pervasive than print media and were thought to have a greater impact on their audiences, and because children who could not read could hear and see. Unfortunately, however, like obscenity, indecency is defined by synonym. Federal law prohibits "any obscene, indecent, or profane language by means of radio communication" and the mailing of anything "obscene, lewd, lascivious, indecent, filthy or vile." Whether these terms are conjunctive (substitutable) or disjunctive (distinctive in meaning) has never been determined in the courts. In a case involving the FCC's nonrenewal of a broadcast license, the D.C. Circuit added the words "coarse, vulgar, suggestive and susceptible of indecent, double meaning" to the lexicography of indecency.[3] What do these words really mean, to whom, and who should decide?

In *Pacifica*, the Court decided that George Carlin's "filthy words" fell somewhere within these definitional boundaries. In applying an indecency standard, the Court borrowed from its own earlier definition of obscenity. Carlin's monologue was "patently offensive" because it depicted sexual and excretory activities that way. And if it did not contain other elements of the obscene, then at least it was indecent. If one word did not fit, the other would. Obscenity and indecency continue to be used interchangeably, even though the Supreme Court did provide a comparatively definitive description of the former in *Miller.*

FCC v. Pacifica Foundation

3 MED. L. RPTR. 2553, 438 U.S. 726, 98 S. CT. 3026, 57 L. ED. 2D 1073 (1978).

Justice STEVENS delivered the opinion of the Court and an opinion in which the Chief Justice and Justice REHNQUIST joined in part.

This case requires that we decide whether the Federal Communications Commission has any power to regulate a radio broadcast that is indecent but not obscene.

A satiric humorist named George Carlin recorded a 12-minute monologue entitled "Filthy Words" before a live audience in a California theater. He began by referring to his thoughts about "the words you couldn't say on the public, ah, airwaves, um, the ones you definitely wouldn't say, ever." He proceeded to list those words and repeat them over and over again in a variety of colloquialisms. * * *

At about 2 o'clock in the afternoon on Tuesday, October 30, 1973, a New York radio station owned by respondent, Pacifica Foundation, broadcast the "Filthy Words" monologue. A few weeks later a man, who stated that he had heard the broadcast while driving with his young son, wrote a letter complaining to the commission. He stated that, although he could perhaps understand the "record's being sold for private use, I certainly cannot understand the broadcast of same over the air that, supposedly, you control."

The complaint was forwarded to the station for comment. In its response, Pacifica explained that the monologue had been played during a program about contemporary society's attitude toward language and that immediately before its broadcast listeners had been advised that it included "sensitive language which might be regarded as offensive to some."

* * *

On February 21, 1975, the commission issued a declaratory order granting the complaint and holding that Pacifica "could have been the subject of administrative sanctions." 56 FCC 2d 94, 99 (1975). The commission did not impose formal sanctions, but it did state that the order would be "associated with the station's license file, and in the event that subsequent complaints are received, the commission will then decide whether it should utilize any of the available sanctions it has been granted by Congress."

In its memorandum opinion the commission stated that it intended to "clarify the standards which will be utilized in considering" the growing number of complaints about indecent speech on the airwaves. Advancing several reasons for treating broadcast speech differently from other forms of expression, the commission found a power to regulate indecent broadcasting in two statutes: 18 U.S.C.A. § 1464, which forbids the use of "any obscene, indecent, or profane language by means of radio communications," and 47 U.S.C.A. § 303(g), which requires the commission to "encourage the larger and more effective use of radio in the public interest."

The commission characterized the language used in the Carlin monologue as "patently offen-

---

3. *Robinson v. FCC*, 334 F.2d 534 (D.C. Cir. 1964).

sive," though not necessarily obscene, and expressed the opinion that it should be regulated by principles analogous to those found in the law of nuisance where the "law generally speaks to *channeling* behavior more than actually prohibiting it. * * * [T]he concept of 'indecent' is intimately connected with the exposure of children to language that describes in terms patently offensive as measured by contemporary community standards for the broadcast medium, sexual or excretory activities and organs, at times of the day when there is a reasonable risk that children may be in the audience." 56 FCC 2d, at 98.

Applying these considerations to the language used in the monologue as broadcast by respondent, the commission concluded that certain words depicted sexual and excretory activities in a patently offensive manner, noted that they "were broadcast at a time when children were undoubtedly in the audience (i.e., in the early afternoon)," and that the prerecorded language, with these offensive words "repeated over and over," was "deliberately broadcast." In summary, the commission stated: "We therefore hold that the language as broadcast was indecent and prohibited by 18 U.S.C. 1464."

After the order issued, the commission was asked to clarify its opinion by ruling that the broadcast of indecent words as part of a live newscast would not be prohibited. The commission issued another opinion in which it pointed out that it "never intended to place an absolute prohibition on the broadcast of this type of language, but rather sought to channel it to times of day when children most likely would not be exposed to it." 59 FCC 2d 892 (1976). The commission noted that its "declaratory order was issued in a specific factual context," and declined to comment on various hypothetical situations presented by the petition. It relied on its "long standing policy of refusing to issue interpretive rulings or advisory opinions when the critical facts are not explicitly stated or there is a possibility that subsequent events will alter them."

The United States Court of Appeals for the District of Columbia reversed, with each of the three judges on the panel writing separately.

* * *

The relevant statutory questions are whether the commission's action is forbidden "censorship" within the meaning of 47 U.S.C.A. § 326 and whether speech that concededly is not obscene may be restricted as "indecent" under the authority of 18 U.S.C.A. § 1464. The questions are not unrelated, for the two statutory provisions have a common origin. Nevertheless, we analyze them separately.

Section 29 of the Radio Act of 1927 provided:

Nothing in this act shall be understood or construed to give the licensing authority the power of censorship over the radio communications or signals transmitted by any radio station, and no regulation or condition shall be promulgated or fixed by the licensing authority which shall interfere with the right of free speech by means of radio communications. No person within the jurisdiction of the United States shall utter any obscene, indecent or profane language by means of radio communication.

The prohibition against censorship unequivocally denies the commission any power to edit proposed broadcasts in advance and to excise material considered inappropriate for the airwaves. The prohibition, however, has never been construed to deny the commission the power to review the content of completed broadcasts in the performance of its regulatory duties.

There is nothing in the legislative history to contradict this conclusion. * * * In 1934, the anticensorship provision and the prohibition against indecent broadcasts were re-enacted in the same section, just as in the 1927 act. In 1948, when the Criminal Code was revised to include provisions that had previously been located in other titles of the United States Code, the prohibition against obscene, indecent, and profane broadcasts was removed from the Communications Act and re-enacted as § 1464 of Title 18. That rearrangement of the code cannot reasonably be interpreted as having been intended to change the meaning of the anticensorship provision.

We conclude, therefore, that § 326 does not limit the commission's authority to impose sanctions on licensees who engage in obscene, indecent, or profane broadcasting.

The only other statutory question presented by this case is whether the afternoon broadcast of the "Filthy Words" monologue was indecent within the meaning of § 1464. Even that question is narrowly confined by the arguments of the parties.

The commission identified several words that referred to excretory or sexual activities or organs, stated that the repetitive, deliberate use of those words in an afternoon broadcast when children are in the audience was patently offensive, and held that the broadcast was indecent. Pacifica takes issue with the commission's definition of indecency, but does not dispute the commission's preliminary determination that each of the components of its definition was present. Specifically, Pacifica does not quarrel with the conclusion that this afternoon broadcast was patently offensive. Pacifica's claim that the broadcast was not indecent within the meaning of the statute rests entirely on the absence of prurient appeal.

The plain language of the statute does not support Pacifica's argument. The words "obscene, indecent, or profane" are written in the disjunctive, implying that each has a separate meaning. Prurient appeal is an element of the obscene, but the normal definition of "indecent" merely refers to nonconformance with accepted standards of morality.

Pacifica argues, however, that this Court has construed the term "indecent" in related statutes to mean "obscene," as that term was defined in *Miller v. California.* Pacifica relies most heavily on the construction this Court gave to 18 U.S.C.A. § 1461 in *Hamling v. United States,* 418 U.S. 87. *Hamling* rejected a vagueness attack on § 1461, which forbids the mailing of "obscene, lewd, lascivious, indecent, filthy or vile" material.

* * *

In *Hamling* the Court agreed with Justice Harlan that § 1461 was meant only to regulate obscenity in the mails; by reading into it the limits set by *Miller v. California,* 413 U.S. 15, the Court adopted a construction which assured the statute's constitutionality.

The reasons supporting *Hamling's* construction of § 1461 do not apply to § 1464. * * * The former statute deals primarily with printed matter enclosed in sealed envelopes mailed from one individual to another; the latter deals with the content of public broadcasts. It is unrealistic to assume that Congress intended to impose precisely the same limitations on the dissemination of patently offensive matter by such different means.

Because neither our prior decisions nor the language or history of § 1464 supports the conclusion that prurient appeal is an essential component of indecent language, we reject Pacifica's construction of the statute. When that construction is put to one side there is no basis for disagreeing with the commission's conclusion that indecent language was used in this broadcast.

Pacifica makes two constitutional attacks on the commission's order. First, it argues that the commission's construction of the statutory language broadly encompasses so much constitutionally protected speech that reversal is required even if Pacifica's broadcast of the "Filthy Words" monologue is not itself protected by the First Amendment. Second, Pacifica argues that inasmuch as the recording is not obscene, the Constitution forbids any abridgment of the right to broadcast it on the radio.

The first argument fails because our review is limited to the question whether the commission has the authority to proscribe this particular broadcast. As the commission itself emphasized, its order was "issued in a specific factual context." 59 FCC 2d, at 893. That approach is appropriate for courts as well as the commission when regulation of indecency is at stake, for indecency is largely a function of context—it cannot be adequately judged in the abstract.

The approach is also consistent with *Red Lion Broadcasting Co. Inc. v. FCC,* 395 U.S. 367. In that case the Court rejected an argument that the commission's regulations defining the fairness doctrine were so vague that they would inevitably abridge the broadcasters' freedom of speech.

* * *

It is true that the commission's order may lead some broadcasters to censor themselves. At most, however, the commission's definition of indecency will deter only the broadcasting of patently offensive references to excretory and sexual organs and activities. While some of these references may be protected, they surely lie at the periphery of First Amendment concern.

* * *

When the issue is narrowed to the facts of this case, the question is whether the First Amendment denies government any power to restrict the public broadcast of indecent language in any circumstances. For if the government has any such power, this was an appropriate occasion for its exercise.

The words of the Carlin monologue are unquestionably "speech" within the meaning of the First Amendment. It is equally clear that the commission's objections to the broadcast were based in part on its content. The order must therefore fall if, as Pacifica argues, the First

Amendment prohibits all governmental regulation that depends on the content of speech. Our past cases demonstrate, however, that no such absolute rule is mandated by the Constitution.

* * *

The question in this case is whether a broadcast of patently offensive words dealing with sex and excretion may be regulated because of its content. Obscene materials have been denied the protection of the First Amendment because their content is so offensive to contemporary moral standards. *Roth v. United States.* But the fact that society may find speech offensive is not a sufficient reason for suppressing it. Indeed, if it is the speaker's opinion that gives offense, that consequence is a reason for according it constitutional protection. For it is a central tenet of the First Amendment that the government must remain neutral in the marketplace of ideas. If there were any reason to believe that the commission's characterization of the Carlin monologue as offensive could be traced to its political content—or even to the fact that it satirized contemporary attitudes about four letter words. First Amendment protection might be required. But that is simply not this case. These words offend for the same reasons that obscenity offends. * * *

Although these words ordinarily lack literary, political, or scientific value, they are not entirely outside the protection of the First Amendment. * * * Nonetheless, the constitutional protection accorded to a communication containing such patently offensive sexual and excretory language need not be the same in every context. It is a characteristic of speech such as this that both its capacity to offend and its "social value," to use Justice Murphy's term, vary with the circumstances. Words that are commonplace in one setting are shocking in another.

* * *

In this case it is undisputed that the content of Pacifica's broadcast was "vulgar," "offensive," and "shocking." Because content of that character is not entitled to absolute constitutional protection under all circumstances, we must consider its context in order to determine whether the commission's action was constitutionally permissible.

We have long recognized that each medium of expression presents special First Amendment problems. *Joseph Burstyn, Inc. v. Wilson,* 343 U.S. 495, 502–503. And of all forms of communication, it is broadcasting that has received the most limited First Amendment protection. Thus, although other speakers cannot be licensed except under laws that carefully define and narrow official discretion, a broadcaster may be deprived of his license and his forum if the Commission decides that such an action would serve "the public interest, convenience, and necessity." * * *

The reasons for these distinctions are complex, but two have relevance to the present case. *First, the broadcast media have established a uniquely pervasive presence in the lives of all Americans.* [Emphasis added.] Patently offensive, indecent material presented over the airwaves confronts the citizen, not only in public, but also in the privacy of the home, where the individual's right to be let alone plainly outweighs the First Amendment rights of an intruder. Because the broadcast audience is constantly turning in and out, prior warnings cannot completely protect the listener or viewer from unexpected program content. To say that one may avoid further offense by turning off the radio when he hears indecent language is like saying that the remedy for an assault is to run away after the first blow. One may hang up on an indecent phone call, but that option does not give the caller a constitutional immunity or avoid a harm that has already taken place.

Second, broadcasting is uniquely accessible to children, even those too young to read. [Emphasis added.] * * * Other forms of offensive expression may be withheld from the young without restricting the expression at its source. Bookstores and motion pictures theaters, for example, may be prohibited from making indecent material available to children. We held in *Ginsberg v. New York,* that the government's interest in the "well being of its youth" and in supporting "parents' claim to authority in their own household" justified the regulation of otherwise protected expression. The ease with which children may obtain access to broadcast material, coupled with the concerns recognized in *Ginsberg,* amply justify special treatment of indecent broadcasting.

It is appropriate, in conclusion, to emphasize the narrowness of our holding. This case does not involve a two-way radio conversation between a cab driver and a dispatcher, or a telecast of an Elizabethan comedy. We have not decided that an occasional expletive in either setting would justify any sanction or, indeed, that this broadcast would justify a criminal prosecution. The commission's decision rested entirely on a nuisance rationale under which context is all-important. The concept requires consideration of a host of variables. The time of day was emphasized by the commission. The content of the program in which the language is used will also affect the composition of the audience, and differences between radio, television, and perhaps closed-circuit transmissions, may also be relevant. As Justice Sutherland wrote, a "nuisance may be merely a right thing in the wrong place—like a pig in the parlor instead of the barnyard." We simply hold that when the commission finds that a pig has entered the parlor, the exercise of its regulatory power does not depend on proof that the pig is obscene.

The judgment of the court of appeals is reversed.

* * *

COMMENT

"[T]he concept of 'indecent'," said the Court, relying on the FCC, "is intimately connected with the exposure of children to language that describes in terms patently offensive as measured by contemporary community standards for the broadcast medium, sexual or excretory activities and organs at times of the day when there is a reasonable risk that children may be in the audience."

Obscene" and "indecent," the Court added, were meant to have different meanings, and indecent was defined as "nonconformance with accepted standards of morality." "Prurient appeal," a component of the Supreme Court's definition of obscenity, would not be necessary in defining what is indecent. But the Court did something else as well.

"The broadcast media have established a uniquely pervasive presence in the lives of all Americans," said the Court, and they are "uniquely accessible to children, even those too young to read." Because broadcasting has an impact on its audiences that other media do not have, the Court concluded, a more stringent level of regulatory and judicial supervision is warranted. The Court would also consider the manner in which the language was used and whether it was "concentrated," "repeated," "fleeting," or "isolated." The overall merit of the work would

be important, as would the question of whether the medium had some way of separating children and adults. Finally, contemporary community standards would refer to average broadcast listeners and viewers rather than to any specific local community.

Justices Stewart, Brennan, White, and Marshall, who dissented in *Pacifica*, anticipated the difficulties emerging electronic media would face in having the broader concept of *indecency* applied to their programming. "[L]anguage can be 'indecent' although it has social, political or artistic value and lacks prurient appeal," Justice Stewart noted. He also doubted that the FCC had the constitutional power to prohibit speech that would be constitutionally protected outside the context of electronic broadcasting.

Admitting to being unable to contain himself, Justice Brennan pointed to the voluntary nature of radio listening and argued for the right of listeners to hear broadcasts that some might find offensive: "I would place the responsibility and the right to weed worthless and offensive communications from the public airways where it belongs—in a public free to choose those communications worthy of its attention from a marketplace unsullied by the censor's hand . . . ." He added, "[T]he Court's decision may be seen for what, in the broader perspective, it really is: another effort to force those groups who do not share its mores to conform to its way of thinking, acting, and speaking."

Pacifica won immediate praise from those concerned about moral standards in broadcasting. At the same time, it aroused unease among broadcasters. Although indecency could not be banned altogether, it could be regulated as to time of broadcast. A plethora of complaints followed. For example, Morality in Media in Massachusetts asked the FCC to deny license renewal to WGBH-TV, an educational station in Boston, for consistently broadcasting "offensive, vulgar and material otherwise harmful to children without adequate supervision or parental warnings." Observing that the Court in Pacifica meant only to condemn the *repetition* of indecent words in that case, the FCC dismissed the petition and granted WGBH's application for renewal.[4] The FCC further discouraged complaints by

---

4. *In re Application of WGBH Educ. Found.* 69 F.C.C.2d 1250 (1978).

announcing that it would take action against broadcasters only after Justice Department prosecutions had concluded.

As for cable, a number of federal cases arose, but the courts said *Pacifica* did not apply to cable. No First Amendment theory for cable emerged from the cases, however. Similarly, state and local laws aimed at indecent cable programming usually did not survive constitutional challenge, even when they tried to incorporate the *Pacifica* standard. (See pp. 877–888.)

Meanwhile the FCC remained cautious. From the start of *Pacifica* in 1975 until 1987, it found no other broadcasters guilty of indecent utterances. In 1987, however, the FCC showed a renewed interest in indecent programming. Broadcasts that depicted or described sexual or excretory activities or organs in a patently offensive way when children might be in the audience faced renewed penalization.[5]

The American Civil Liberties Union (ACLU) and other groups challenged the new get-tough policy and eventually appealed to the D.C. Circuit Court of Appeals. In *Action for Children's Television v. FCC (ACT 1),*[6] the appeals court essentially upheld the stricter policy when "Shock Jock" Howard Stern, along with play and song titles such as "Jerker" and "Makin' Bacon," ran afoul of the commission. In 1995, Infinity Broadcasting, Stern's employer, paid the government $1.7 million in a settlement involving accusations of indecent radio broadcasts over a three-year span; Infinity called the payment a donation to the U.S. Treasury.

Pacifica had given the FCC authority to regulate broadcasts that were indecent but not obscene, clear of any challenge based on vagueness. Patent offensiveness, an element of the obscenity definition, would sufficiently define indecency; there need be no appeal to the prurient interest of children. Constrained by *Pacifica,* Judge Ruth Bader Ginsburg in her opinion for the D.C. Circuit Court in *ACT 1* nevertheless found the meaning of the generic term indecency

"clouded," if not constitutionally defective. Although indecent material qualifies for First Amendment protection, she said, it can be regulated to protect children. She found the FCC technically vague about what times of the day and night it meant to require channeling of programming and to what specific age groups. In other words, she asked, what was the "rational connection between the facts found and the choice made?"

"[I]n view of the constitutionally protected expression interest at stake," the court added, "the FCC must afford broadcasters clear notice of reasonably determined times at which indecent material safely may be aired." Two of the cases involved in *ACT 1* were therefore remanded to the FCC.

The FCC's somewhat cautious and reactive approach to this problem came to a dramatic end in 1989 when President Reagan signed an appropriations bill for the FCC and other federal agencies that ordered the FCC to enforce its indecency standards around the clock.[7] Broadcasters and public interest groups immediately challenged the policy on constitutional grounds. Early in 1989, the D.C. Circuit granted a motion to stay enforcement of the ban pending judicial review. At about the same time, a law was passed putting a similar ban on indecent commercial telephone messages, notably dial-a-porn. A lower court enjoined enforcement of that statute, and the Second Circuit agreed with the FCC that a scheme involving access codes, scrambling, and credit card payment was a feasible and effective way to serve the compelling governmental interest in protecting minors from obscene speech.[8] The U.S. Supreme Court agreed. In *Sable Communications of Calif., Inc. v. FCC,*[9] the Court concluded that "Because the statute's denial of adult access to telephone messages which are indecent but not obscene far exceeds that which is necessary to limit the access of minors to such messages, we hold the ban does not survive constitutional scrutiny." (See pp. 840–841.)

---

5. New Indecency Enforcement Standards to Be Applied to All Broadcast and Amateur Radio Licenses, 62 Rad.Reg. 2d (P&F) 1218 (1987). Cases leading to the new standards were *Pacifica Found.,* 2 F.C.C. Rcd 2698 (1987); *The Regents of the Univ. of California,* 2 F.C.C. Rcd 2703 (1987); and *Infinity Broadcasting Corp. of Pennsylvania,* 2 F.C.C. Rcd 2705 (1987).

6. 15 Med. L. Rptr. 1907, 825 F.2d 1332 (D.C. Cir. 1988).

7. *Enforcement of Prohibitions against Broadcast Obscenity and Indecency in 18 U.S.C. Sec. 1464,* 4 F.C.C. Rcd 457 (1988).

8. *Carlin Communications Inc. v. FCC,* 837 F.2d 546 (2d Cir. 1988).

9. 16 Med. L. Rptr. 1961, 492 U.S. 115 (1989).

The government had *not* used the "least intrusive means" for accomplishing its goal of protecting children. The FCC sought and obtained a remand from the D.C. Circuit so as to find data and obtain public comment supporting a total ban on indecent broadcasting. Upon analysis of this material, the FCC concluded that a twenty-four-hour ban would comport with the Supreme Court standards enunciated in *Sable.*[10]

A year later a panel of the D.C. Circuit Court of Appeals ruled that the FCC's twenty-four-hour ban on indecent programming intruded upon constitutionally protected speech. Sticking to its arguments in *ACT 1* that the FCC's definition of indecency was neither vague nor overbroad, but reassured by *Sable,* the appeals court criticized the "constitutional excesses" of Congress in eliminating the post–10 P.M. "safe harbor" for broadcasting constitutionally protected indecent, but not obscene, material when the audience would be predominantly adult. The circuit court ruling—*ACT 2*—sent the problem back to the commission.[11]

In 1995, federal courts were still wrangling over time periods. In *ACT 3*[12] the issue was the constitutionality of sec. 16(a) of the Public Telecommunication Act of 1992 that restricted indecent programs to the period midnight to 6 A.M. Public stations normally go off the air earlier, however, so the question was, could they broadcast indecency earlier? Again a remand asked the FCC to consider permitting indecent programming between 10 P.M. and 6 A.M. The case raised a number of questions—proof of harm to children, channeling versus banning, definitional vagueness, a narrowly tailored method of furthering a compelling governmental interest in protecting children—but all of them remained only partially answered in January 1996 when the Supreme Court declined to consider petitions asksing the Court to declare sec. 16(a) a violation of the First Amendment.[13]

The question of whether forefeiture for allegedly indecent broadcasting, as administered by the FCC, violated the First and Fourteenth Amendments, again came to the D.C. Circuit in 1995. In *ACT 4* the answer was, no, it did not, and the Supreme Court denied review.[14] (For more on the *ACT* cases, see pp. 833–846).

In an *en banc* hearing, a divided D.C. Circuit Court of Appeals also decided that under the Cable Television Consumer Protection and Competition Act, cable operators could, on the authority of an amendment to the act proposed by Sen. Jesse Helms, prohibit indecent programming on public, educational, and governmental (PEG) leased access channels. The amendment repealed an 1984 law that forbade cable-operator supervision of the content of leased channels. Judgments about the depiction of "sexual or excretory activities or organs in a patently offensive manner as measured by contemporary community standards" would now be the exercise of editorial discretion by cable operators; without state action there would be no First Amendment issue to debate.[15] Arguments in that case were heard before the U.S. Supreme Court in February 1996 and the ruling is reported on p. 627.

Neither the issues nor the players in this regulatory drama had changed in 1996. Obscenity and indecency were still interchangeable if not synonymous, especially where children were at risk. But the stage of debate and litigation was moving from print and broadcast media to cable and cyberspace.

While cable was in its "natural monopoly" phase, it was subject to regulation.[16] Though not a scarce resource like a broadcast frequency, cable could be regulated because it used the public byways (telephone poles and wires).[17] The extent of cable regulation remained unresolved, but it was understood that government could not

10. *Enforcement of Prohibitions Against Broadcast Indecency in U.S.C. Sec. 1464,* 5 F.C.C. Rcd 5297 (1990).
11. *Action for Children's Television v. FCC,* 18 Med. L. Rptr. 2153, 932 F.2d 1504 (D.C. Cir. 1991).
12. *Action for Children's Television v. FCC,* 58 F.3d 654 (D.C. Cir. 1995).
13. *Action for Children's Television v. FCC et al.,* 116 S.Ct. 701 (1996); *Pacifica Foundation v. FCC,* 116 S.Ct. 701 (1996).

14. *Action for Children's Television v. FCC,* 59 F.3d 1249 (D.C. Cir. 1995), *cert. denied* 116 S. Ct. 773 (1996).
15. *Alliance for Community Media v. FCC,* 56 F.3d 105 (D.C. Cir. 1995).
16. *Community Communications v. City of Boulder,* 660 F.2d 1370 (10th Cir. 1981), *cert. dismissed* 486 U.S. 1001 (1981).
17. *Preferred Communications, Inc. v. City of Los Angeles,* 754 F.2d 1396 (9th Cir. 1985), *aff'd on different grounds,* 476 U.S. 488 (1986).

restrain nonobscene, though indecent, programming. This gave cable greater First Amendment protection than broadcasting enjoyed in the same period.[18] At this point, Congress again entered the picture.

Congressional Standards: The Communications Decency Act of 1996

Prior to the signing of the Telecommunications Act by President Clinton on February 8, 1996, federal law forbade the use of telephone or cable for obscene, lewd, lascivious, filthy, or indecent comments, suggestions, or proposals.[19] Child pornography could not be sent or received by any technological means, including the computer. Obscene material could not be part of interstate or foreign commerce.

In a 1994 Tennessee federal district court trial, Robert and Carleen Thomas, a California couple using an electronic bulletin board called "Amateur Action," were found guilty of disseminating obscene material by computer and interstate telephone lines in violation of federal law. The Thomas's perverse material had failed to meet the community standards of Memphis, Tennessee, and they were sentenced to prison. The U.S. Court of Appeals for the Sixth Circuit upheld their convictions. The federal law punishing interstate distribution of obscene material included computer transmissions.[20]

For some, the case raised the question of whether there should be "cyberspace community standards," that is, standards defined by computer-connected people who avail themselves of sexually explicit material through on-line computer networks.[21] Similar indictments for distributing child pornography, some of it on Online America, have been issued in other states, among them Massachusetts, New Jersey, Texas, Florida, Arizona, and Mississippi. Some of this material depicted children aged two to thirteen, either nude or engaged in actual or simulated sexual acts.

Further discussion on this critical question was foreclosed when the much debated Exon Bill (named for Democratic Sen. James Exon of Nebraska) became the Communications Decency Act of 1995[22] and was passed and signed into law as part of the Telecommunications Act of 1996. The Act criminalizes any interstate or foreign telecommunication that is "obscene, lewd, lascivious, filthy, or indecent . . . [or] that depicts or describes, in terms patently offensive as measured by contemporary community standards, sexual or excretory activities or organs. . . ." Interactive computer services as well as cable television were subject to the law.

The first challenge to the constitutionality of the Act came when a federal district judge in Philadelphia, responding to an ACLU initiative, issued a temporary restraining order against enforcing regulations that prohibit *indecency* on the Internet on the grounds that "indecent" is too vague a term to survive constitutional scrutiny.[23] Scores of information providers, including associations of librarians, booksellers, publishers, editors, computer companies, on-line providers, and citizens' groups, followed the ACLU initiative and also brought suit. The main concern of the Citizens Internet Empowerment Coalition, as the alliance called itself, was that those who drafted the law appeared to know little about how the Internet worked. Here was a medium so abundant that it required no balance, no fairness, and certainly no government intervention. For Congress, cyberspace seemed an unexplored universe. In an effort to protect children, Congress was banning constitutionally protected adult speech.[24]

It may be useful to note here that in 1957 Justice Felix Frankfurter, writing for a unanimous Court, struck down a Michigan statute that prohibited distribution to the general reading public of material "containing obscene, immoral, lewd

18. *Cruz v. Ferre*, 571 F.Supp. 125 (S.D.Fla. 1983); *Community Television of Utah, Inc. v. Pay City*, 555 F.Supp. 1164 (D.Utah 1982).

19. 47 U.S.C.A. § 559 (1991); 47 U.S.C.A. § 532 (Supp. 1995).

20. *U.S. v. Thomas et al.*, 24 Med. L. Rptr. 1321, 74 F.3d 701 (6th Cir. 1996).

21. Steven Shapiro, *The Changing Landscape of First Amendment Jurisprudence in Light of the Technological Advances in Media*, Fordham Intellectual Property, Media & Entertainment L. J., 317–323 (1995).

22. 47 U.S.C. § 223 (1996).

23. *ACLU et al. v. Reno*, 24 Med. L. Rptr. 1379 (E.D.Pa. 929 F.Supp. 825 1996).

24. *American Library Association, Inc. et al. v. U.S. Department of Justice*, Complaint for declaratory and injunctive relief, U.S. District Court for the Eastern District of Pennsylvania, February 26, 1996.

or lascivious language . . . tending to incite minors to violent or depraved or immoral acts. . . ." "The incidence of this enactment," Frankfurter wrote in a frequently quoted line, "is to reduce the adult population of Michigan to reading only what is fit for children."[25]

Describing the Internet as a network of networks (linked groups of computers) and cyberspace as an unrestricted global medium of communication, plaintiffs wondered how the indecency law could be applied to 40 million World Wide Web users in 147 countries in the absence of any centralized system of supervision or control. By the turn of the century, 200 million persons may be connected. Although the Internet is subsidized by government, no one "owns" it. To those with personal computers, it functions like a combination printing press, telephone, post office, radio, and television system.

Unlike a radio or television audience, the cyberspace audience can become speakers at the push of a button. With another button the Internet user can screen out anything she finds indecent. With yet another button, the user can possess a forum for political discourse, cultural development, and intellectual activity. In passing the Decency Act, Congress seemed only vaguely aware of the promise of cyberspace. And government regulation of any such public dialogue has always been inappropriate.

Constitutionally protected Internet content in the areas of art and literature, popular culture, medicine, birth control, sexual behavior, gay rights, and what was once the anthropological allure of *National Geographic* may indeed be unsuitable for children. Although pornography can be found on the Internet (Usenet, for example, a collection of 16,000 bulletin boards) and in online sexual directories, software and hardware to aid in parental control are available, and warnings to parents are posted. But should adults also be denied access by threat of punishment? Vulgar words in a conversation with friends—legal on the telephone, in a letter or in face-to-face dialogue—would be illegal on the Internet. Something declared "indecent" in Typicalville would be indecent everywhere on the Internet and thereby everywhere in the world. Distinctions between what is private (e-mail) and

public (a popular Web site), as well as differences among cultures, would be lost.

An example of cultural misunderstanding occurred in a 1990 civil suit brought by a record store owner against a Florida sheriff who had confiscated all the store's copies of recordings by the rap music group 2 Live Crew. A judge found lyrics in the record "As Nasty As They Wanna Be" obscene. But confiscation of the recordings before a judicial determination of obscenity constituted a denial of due process and a prior restraint.[26]

A jury later acquitted the group of violating obscenity laws. The lyrics were nasty but not obscene. An award-winning Duke University professor of African American art and culture described the lyrics as "signifying," a rhythmic teasing and cajoling with roots in slavery; it features parody peppered with lewd remarks that can be meant as insult or compliment.

Opponents of rapping and what they saw as obscene about it, however, had learned how to get headlines, cancel concerts, and scare recordings off the shelves. The Decency Act would have done the same to the Internet by reducing its content to what is appropriate for children. Furthermore, much of the sexual content of the Internet enters the United States anonymously from foreign countries that are not subject to U.S. law. And domestic providers could always move their operations overseas if they had to.

The American Society of Newspaper Editors was particularly concerned that under the Decency Act online versions of a newspaper would be subject to censorship that the First Amendment would not permit with respect to hard-copy print editions. What is decent when published on newsprint would become indecent when published electronically.

Another problem with the Decency Act, and with all obscenity legislation, is the difficulty in reaching any consensus on the meaning of the terms used to describe the crime. To restate the *Miller* test for identifying obscenity: (a) Whether the average person applying *contemporary community standards* would find that the work taken as a whole appeals to *prurient interest,*

---

25. *Butler v. Michigan*, 352 U.S. 380 (1957).

26. *Skywalker Records, Inc. v. Navarro*, 17 Med. L. Rptr. 2073 (D.C.S. Fla. 1990); reversed by *Luke Records, Inc. v. Navarro*, 20 Med. L. Rptr. 1114, 960 F.2d 134 (11th Cir. 1992).

(b) whether the work depicts or describes in a *patently offensive* way sexual conduct specifically defined by the applicable state law, and (c) whether the work taken as a whole lacks *serious* literary, artistic, political, or scientific *value*. No effort was made in the 1996 Decency Act to define any elements of the test, particularly the central element, *indecency*. Aggressive prosecutors in intolerant communities would be free to fashion their own definitions.

Later in 1996, a three-judge federal district court panel, chaired by Chief Judge Dolores Sloviter of the Third Circuit Court of Appeals, did what Congress had failed to do. Consolidating three cases that had been brought challenging the constitutionality of the Act, the panel, in extensive findings of fact based on plaintiffs' briefs and its own study, explained the workings of cyberspace and its content in 123 numbered paragraphs. For example, at one point, the panel notes:

> The Internet is not exclusively, or even primarily, a means of commercial communication. Many commercial entities maintain Web sites to inform potential consumers about their goods and services, or to solicit purchases, but many other Web sites exist solely for the dissemination of non-commercial information. The other forms of Internet communication—e-mail, bulletin boards, newsgroups, and chat rooms—frequently have non-commercial goals. For the economic and technical reasons set forth in the following paragraphs, the Internet is an especially attractive means for not-for-profit entities or public interest groups to reach their desired audiences. . . . Plaintiff Human Rights Watch, Inc., offers information on its Internet site regarding human rights abuses around the world. Plaintiff National Writers Union provides a forum for writers on issues of concern for them. Plaintiff Stop Prisoner Rape, Inc., posts text, graphics, and statistics regarding the incidence and prevention of rape of prisoners. Plaintiff Critical Path AIDS Project, Inc., offers information on safer sex, the transmission of HIV, and the treatment of AIDS. . . .
>
> Because of the different forms of Internet communication, a user of the Internet may speak or listen interchangeably, blurring the distinction between "speakers" and "listeners" on the Internet. Chat rooms, e-mail, and newsgroups are interactive forms of communication providing the user with the opportunity both to speak and to listen.

Plaintiffs agreed that sexually explicit material, including text, pictures, and chat, ranging from the tamely titillating to the most hard-core, appeared on the Internet. They also agreed that they had no quarrel with the statute, or any future statute, to the extent that it covered child pornography or obscenity. But, they argued, children would not easily come upon the sexually explicit, and there are potential barriers such as credit card, password, and adult verification numbers and content tagging or labeling. None of these then seemed very promising, however, and, besides, 40 percent or more of Internet content originates outside the United States.

A portion of Chief Judge Sloviter's opinion follows:

American Civil Liberties Union v. Janet Reno

929 F.SUPP. 824 (E.D.Pa. 1996).

SLOVITER, Chief Judge, Court of Appeals for the Third Circuit:

* * *

Two aspects of these provisions stand out. First, we are dealing with criminal provisions, subjecting violators to substantial penalties. Second, the provisions on indecent and patently offensive communications are not parallel.

The government uses the term "indecent" interchangeably with "patently offensive" and advises that it so construes the statute in light of the legislative history and the Supreme Court's analysis of the word "indecent" in *FCC v. Pacifica Foundation*, 438 U.S. 726 (1978). However, the CDA does not define "indecent."

* * *

The failure to define "indecent" in § 223(a) is thus arguably a negative pregnant [a negative implying an affirmative, or a denial in form but an admission in fact] and subject to "the rule of construction that an express statutory requirement here, contrasted with statutory silence there, shows an intent to confine the requirement to the specified instance."

* * *

Subjecting speakers to criminal penalties for speech that is constitutionally protected in itself raises the spectre of irreparable harm. Even if a court were unwilling to draw that conclusion from the language of the statute itself, plaintiffs have introduced ample evidence that the challenged provisions, if not enjoined, will have a chilling effect on their free expression. Thus, this is not a case in which we are dealing with a mere incidental inhibition on speech, but with a regulation that directly penalizes speech.

Nor could there be any dispute about the public interest factor which must be taken into account before a court grants a preliminary injunction. No long string of citations is necessary to find that the public interest weighs in favor of having access to a free flow of constitutionally protected speech. See, e.g., *Turner Broadcasting System, Inc. v. FCC*, 114 S.Ct. 2445, 2458 (1994); *Virginia Bd. of Pharmacy v. Virginia Citizens Consumer Council*, 425 U.S. 748, 763–65 (1976).

Thus, if plaintiffs have shown a likelihood of success on the merits, they will have shown the irreparable injury needed to entitle them to a preliminary injunction.

The CDA [Communications Decency Act] is patently a government-imposed content-based restriction on speech, and the speech at issue, whether denominated "indecent" or "patently offensive," is entitled to constitutional protection. See *Sable Communications of California, Inc. v. FCC*, 492 U.S. 115, 126 (1989). As such, the regulation is subject to strict scrutiny, and will only be upheld if it is justified by a compelling government interest and if it is narrowly tailored to effectuate that interest. "[T]he benefit gained [by a content-based restriction] must outweigh the loss of constitutionally protected rights." *Elrod v. Burns,* 427 U.S. at 363.

The government's position on the applicable standard has been less than pellucid but, despite some references to a somewhat lesser burden employed in broadcasting cases, it now appears to have conceded that it has the burden of proof to show both a compelling interest and that the statute regulates least restrictively. In any event, the evidence and our Findings of Fact based thereon show that Internet communication, while unique, is more akin to telephone communication, at issue in *Sable,* than to broadcasting, at issue in *Pacifica,* because, as with the telephone, an Internet user must act affirmatively and deliberately to retrieve specific information online. Even if a broad search will, on occasion, retrieve unwanted materials, the user virtually always receives some warning of its content, significantly reducing the element of surprise or "assault" involved in broadcasting. Therefore, it

is highly unlikely that a very young child will be randomly "surfing" the Web and come across "indecent" or "patently offensive" material.

* * *

In part, our consideration of the government's showing of a "compelling interest" trenches upon the vagueness issue, discussed in detail in Judge Buckwalter's opinion but equally pertinent to First Amendment analysis. Material routinely acceptable according to the standards of New York City, such as the Broadway play *Angels in America* which concerns homosexuality and AIDS portrayed in graphic language, may be far less acceptable in smaller, less cosmopolitan communities of the United States. Yet the play garnered two Tony Awards and a Pulitzer prize for its author, and some uninhibited parents and teachers might deem it to be material to be read or assigned to eleventh and twelfth graders. If available on the Internet through some libraries, the text of the play would likely be accessed in that manner by at least some students, and it would also arguably fall within the scope of the CDA.

There has been recent public interest in the female genital mutilation routinely practiced and officially condoned in some countries. News articles have been descriptive, and it is not stretching to assume that this is a subject that occupies news groups and chat rooms on the Internet. We have no assurance that these discussions, of obvious interest and relevance to older teenage girls, will not be viewed as patently offensive—even in context—in some communities.

Other illustrations abound of non-obscene material likely to be available on the Internet but subject to the CDA's criminal provisions. Photographs appearing in *National Geographic* or a travel magazine of the sculptures in India of couples copulating in numerous positions, a written description of a brutal prison rape, or Francesco Clemente's painting "Labyrinth," all might be considered to "depict or describe, in terms patently offensive as measured by contemporary community standards, sexual or excretory activities or organs." But the government has made no showing that it has a compelling interest in preventing a seventeen-year-old minor from accessing such images.

By contrast, plaintiffs presented testimony that material that could be considered indecent, such as that offered by Stop Prisoner Rape or Critical

Path AIDS project, may be critically important for certain older minors. For example, there was testimony that one quarter of all new HIV infections in the United States is estimated to occur in young people between the ages of 13 and 20, an estimate the government made no effort to rebut. The witnesses believed that graphic material that their organizations post on the Internet could help save lives, but were concerned about the CDA's effect on their right to do so.

The government counters that this court should defer to legislative conclusions about this matter. However, where First Amendment rights are at stake, "[d]eference to a legislative finding cannot limit judicial inquiry." *Sable*, 492 U.S. at 129 (quoting *Landmark Communications, Inc. v. Virginia*, 435 U.S. 829, 843 (1978)). "[W]hatever deference is due legislative findings would not foreclose our independent judgment of the facts bearing on an issue of constitutional law." *Id.*

Moreover, it appears that the legislative "findings" the government cites concern primarily testimony and statements by legislators about the prevalence of obscenity, child pornography, and sexual solicitation of children on the Internet. Similarly, at the hearings before us the government introduced exhibits of sexually explicit material through the testimony of Agent Howard Schmidt, which consisted primarily of the same type of hard-core pornographic materials (even if not technically obscene) which concerned Congress and which fill the shelves of "adult" book and magazine stores. Plaintiffs emphasize that they do not challenge the Act's restrictions on speech not protected by the First Amendment, such as obscenity, child pornography or harassment of children. Their suit is based on their assertion, fully supported by their evidence and our findings, that the CDA reaches much farther.

I am far less confident than the government that its quotations from earlier cases in the Supreme Court signify that it has shown a compelling interest in regulating the vast range of online material covered or potentially covered by the CDA. Nonetheless, I acknowledge that there is certainly a compelling government interest to shield a substantial number of minors from some of the online material that motivated Congress to enact the CDA, and do not rest my decision on the inadequacy of the government's showing in this regard. Whatever the strength of the interest the government has demonstrated in preventing minors

from accessing "indecent" and "patently offensive" material online, if the means it has chosen sweeps more broadly than necessary and thereby chills the expression of adults, it has overstepped onto rights protected by the First Amendment.

The plaintiffs argue that the CDA violates the First Amendment because it effectively bans a substantial category of protected speech from most parts of the Internet. The government responds that the Act does not on its face or in effect ban indecent material that is constitutionally protected for adults. Thus one of the factual issues before us was the likely effect of the CDA on the free availability of constitutionally protected material. A wealth of persuasive evidence, referred to in detail in the Findings of Fact, proved that it is either technologically impossible or economically prohibitive for many of the plaintiffs to comply with the CDA without seriously impeding their posting of online material which adults have a constitutional right to access.

With the possible exception of an e-mail to a known recipient, most content providers cannot determine the identity and age of every user accessing their material. Considering separately content providers that fall roughly into two categories, we have found that no technology exists which allows those postings on the category of newsgroups, mail exploders or chat rooms to screen for age. Speakers using those forms of communication cannot control who receives the communication, and in most instances are not aware of the identity of the recipients. If it is not feasible for speakers who communicate via these forms of communication to conduct age screening, they would have to reduce the level of communication to that which is appropriate for children in order to be protected under the statute. This would effect a complete ban even for adults of some expression, albeit "indecent," to which they are constitutionally entitled, and thus would be unconstitutional under the holding in *Sable*, 492 U.S. at 131.

Even as to content providers in the other broad category, such as the World Wide Web, where efforts at age verification are technically feasible through the use of Common Gateway Interface (cgi) scripts (which enable creation of a document that can process information provided by a Web visitor), the Findings of Fact show that as a practical matter, non-commercial organizations and even many commercial organizations using the Web would find it prohibitively expensive and burdensome to engage in the methods of age verification proposed by the government, and that even if they could attempt to age verify, there is little assurance that they could successfully filter out minors.

The government attempts to circumvent this problem by seeking to limit the scope of the statute to those content providers who are commercial pornographers, and urges that we do likewise in our obligation to save a congressional enactment from facial unconstitutionality wherever possible. But in light of its plain language and its legislative history, the CDA cannot reasonably be read as limited to commercial pornographers.

* * *

It is clear from the face of the CDA and from its legislative history that Congress did not intend to limit its application to commercial purveyors of pornography. Congress unquestionably knew how to limit the statute to such entities if that was its intent, and in fact it did so in provisions relating to dial-a-porn services. It placed no similar limitation in the CDA. Moreover, the Conference Report makes clear that Congress did not intend to limit the application of the statute to content providers such as those which make available the commercial material contained in the government's exhibits, and confirms that Congress intended "content regulation of both commercial and non-commercial providers."

The scope of the CDA is not confined to material that has a prurient interest or appeal, one of the hallmarks of obscenity, because Congress sought to reach farther. Nor did Congress include language that would define "patently offensive" or "indecent" to exclude material of serious value. It follows that to narrow the statute in the manner the government urges would be an impermissible exercise of our limited judicial function, which is to review the statute as written for its compliance with constitutional mandates.

I conclude inexorably from the foregoing that the CDA reaches speech subject to the full protection of the First Amendment, at least for adults. In questions of the witnesses and in colloquy with the government attorneys, it became evident that even if "indecent" is read as parallel to "patently offensive," the terms would cover a broad range of material from contemporary films,

plays and books showing or describing sexual activities (e.g., *Leaving Las Vegas*) to controversial contemporary art and photographs showing sexual organs in positions that the government conceded would be patently offensive in some communities (e.g., a Robert Mapplethorpe photograph depicting a man with an erect penis).

We have also found that there is no effective way for many Internet content providers to limit the effective reach of the CDA to adults because there is no realistic way for many providers to ascertain the age of those accessing their materials. As a consequence, we have found that "[m]any speakers who display arguably indecent content on the Internet must choose between silence and the risk of prosecution." Such a choice, forced by sections 223(a) and (d) of the CDA, strikes at the heart of speech of adults as well as minors.

* * *

The government makes yet another argument that troubles me. It suggests that the concerns expressed by the plaintiffs and the questions posed by the court reflect an exaggerated supposition of how it would apply the law, and that we should, in effect, trust the Department of Justice to limit the CDA's application in a reasonable fashion that would avoid prosecution for placing on the Internet works of serious literary or artistic merit. That would require a broad trust indeed from a generation of judges not far removed from the attacks on James Joyce's *Ulysses* as obscene. See *United States v. One Book Entitled Ulysses*, 72 F.2d 705 (2d Cir. 1934); see also *Book Named "John Cleland's Memoirs of a Woman of Pleasure" v. Attorney General of Mass.*, 383 U.S. 413 (1966). Even if we were to place confidence in the reasonable judgment of the representatives of the Department of Justice who appeared before us, the Department is not a monolithic structure, and individual U.S. Attorneys in the various districts of the country have or appear to exercise some independence, as reflected by the Department's tolerance of duplicative challenges in this very case.

* * *

Finally, the viability of the defenses is intricately tied to the clarity of the CDA's scope. Because, like Judge Buckwalter, and for many of the reasons he gives, I believe that "indecent" and "patently offensive" are inherently vague, particularly in light of the government's inability to identify the relevant community by whose standards the material will be judged, I am not persuaded by the government that the statutory defenses in § 223(e) provide effective protection from the unconstitutional reach of the statute.

Minors would not be left without any protection from exposure to patently unsuitable material on the Internet should the challenged provisions of the CDA be preliminarily enjoined. Vigorous enforcement of current obscenity and child pornography laws should suffice to address the problem the government identified in court and which concerned Congress. When the CDA was under consideration by Congress, the Justice Department itself communicated its view that it was not necessary because it was prosecuting online obscenity, child pornography and child solicitation under existing laws, and would continue to do so. It follows that the CDA is not narrowly tailored, and the government's attempt to defend it on that ground must fail.

* * *

But the bottom line is that the First Amendment should not be interpreted to require us to entrust the protection it affords to the judgment of prosecutors. Prosecutors come and go. Even federal judges are limited to life tenure. The First Amendment remains to give protection to future generations as well. I have no hesitancy in concluding that it is likely that plaintiffs will prevail on the merits of their argument that the challenged provisions of the CDA are facially invalid under both the First and Fifth Amendments.

COMMENT

Federal District Judge Ronald Buckwalter, who had issued the original preliminary injunction, also focused on the unconstitutional vagueness of the terms "indecent" and "patently offensive." He noted that "Even Government counsel was unable to define 'indecency' with specificity." Judge Stewart Dalzell disagreed: "My analysis . . . leads ineluctably to the conclusion that the definition of indecency is not unconstitutionally vague." He then reviewed what the Supreme Court had done in the dial-a-porn case in providing adults access to indecent but nonobscene speech. Moreover, he said, the Internet, being closer to print and the telephone than to broadcasting, is a never-ending, worldwide con-

versation, the most participatory form of mass speech yet developed and a kind of chaos that is the strength of our liberty. As such, it "deserves the broadest possible protection." "We should also protect," he wrote, "the autonomy that such a medium confers to ordinary people as well as media magnates."

At the same time, Judge Dalzell, with his colleagues, believed that the government should continue to protect children from pornography on the Internet through vigorous enforcement of existing laws criminalizing obscenity and child pornography.

With a factual foundation firmly laid by detailed written briefs from plaintiff organizations such as the American Library Association and the American Civil Liberties Union and their use by the federal court in Philadelphia, the Supreme Court was well equipped to decide the landmark Internet case. On June 26, 1997, a near unanimous Court ruled the Communications Decency Act unconstitutional.

Reno v. American Civil Liberties Union
25 Med. L. Rptr. 1833, 1997 WL 348012 (U.S.).

Justice STEVENS delivered the opinion of the Court, in which SCALIA, KENNEDY, SOUTER, THOMAS, GINSBURG, and BREYER, JJ., joined. O'CONNOR, J., filed an opinion concurring in the judgment in part and dissenting in part, in which REHNQUIST, C. J., joined.

At issue is the constitutionality of two statutory provisions enacted to protect minors from "indecent" and "patently offensive" communications on the Internet. Notwithstanding the legitimacy and importance of the congressional goal of protecting children from harmful materials, we agree with the three-judge District Court that the statute abridges "the freedom of speech" protected by the First Amendment.

The District Court made extensive findings of fact, most of which were based on a detailed stipulation prepared by the parties. The findings describe the character and the dimensions of the Internet, the availability of sexually explicit material in that medium, and the problems confronting age verification for recipients of Internet communications.

* * *

The Internet is an international network of interconnected computers. It is * * * "a unique and wholly new medium of worldwide human communication." The Internet has experienced "extraordinary growth." * * * About 40 million people used the Internet at the time of trial, a number that is expected to mushroom to 200 million by 1999. * * * [T]hese tools constitute a unique medium—known to its users as "cyberspace"—located in no particular geographical location but available to anyone, anywhere in the world, with access to the Internet.

* * *

From the publishers' point of view, it constitutes a vast platform from which to address and hear from a world-wide audience of millions of readers, viewers, researchers, and buyers. Any person or organization with a computer connected to the Internet can "publish" information. Publishers include government agencies, educational institutions, commercial entities, advocacy groups, and individuals. Publishers may either make their material available to the entire pool of Internet users, or confine access to a selected group, such as those willing to pay for the privilege. "No single organization controls any membership in the Web, nor is there any centralized point from which individual Web sites or services can be blocked from the Web."

Sexually explicit material on the Internet includes text, pictures, and chat and "extends from the modestly titillating to the hardest-core." These files are created, named, and posted in the same manner as material that is not sexually explicit, and may be accessed either deliberately or unintentionally during the course of an imprecise search. "Once a provider posts its content on the Internet, it cannot prevent that content from entering any community." Thus, for example, "when the UCR/California Museum of Photography posts to its Web site nudes by Edward Weston and Robert Mapplethorpe to announce that its new exhibit will travel to Baltimore and New York City, those images are available not only in Los Angeles, Baltimore, and New York City, but also in Cincinnati, Mobile, or Beijing—wherever Internet users live. Similarly, the safer sex instructions that Critical Path posts to its Web site, written in street language so that the teenage receiver can understand them, are available not just in Philadelphia, but also in Provo and Prague."

Some of the communications over the Internet that originate in foreign countries are also sexually explicit.

Though such material is widely available, users seldom encounter such content accidentally. "A document's title or a description of the document will usually appear before the document itself . . . and in many cases the user will receive detailed information about a site's content before he or she need take the step to access the document. Almost all sexually explicit images are preceded by warnings as to the content." For that reason, the "odds are slim" that a user would enter a sexually explicit site by accident. Unlike communications received by radio or television, "the receipt of information on the Internet requires a series of affirmative steps more deliberate and directed than merely turning a dial. A child requires some sophistication and some ability to read to retrieve material and thereby to use the Internet unattended."

Systems have been developed to help parents control the material that may be available on a home computer with Internet access. A system may either limit a computer's access to an approved list of sources that have been identified as containing no adult material, it may block designated inappropriate sites, or it may attempt to block messages containing identifiable objectionable features. "Although parental control software currently can screen for certain suggestive words or for known sexually explicit sites, it cannot now screen for sexually explicit images." Nevertheless, the evidence indicates that "a reasonably effective method by which parents can prevent their children from accessing sexually explicit and other material which parents may believe is inappropriate for their children will soon be available."

The problem of age verification differs for different uses of the Internet. The District Court categorically determined that there "is no effective way to determine the identity or the age of a user who is accessing material through e-mail, mail exploders, newsgroups or chat rooms." The Government offered no evidence that there was a reliable way to screen recipients and participants in such fora for age. Moreover, even if it were technologically feasible to block minors' access to newsgroups and chat rooms containing discussions of art, politics or other subjects that potentially elicit "indecent" or "patently offensive" contributions, it would not be possible to block their access to that material and "still allow them access to the remaining content, even if the overwhelming majority of that content was not indecent."

Technology exists by which an operator of a Web site may condition access on the verification of requested information such as a credit card number or an adult password. Credit card verification is only feasible, however, either in connection with a commercial transaction in which the card is used, or by payment to a verification agency. Using credit card possession as a surrogate for proof of age would impose costs on non-commercial Web sites that would require many of them to shut down. For that reason, at the time of the trial, credit card verification was "effectively unavailable to a substantial number of Internet content providers." Moreover, the imposition of such a requirement "would completely bar adults who do not have a credit card and lack the resources to obtain one from accessing any blocked material."

Commercial pornographic sites that charge their users for access have assigned them passwords as a method of age verification. The record does not contain any evidence concerning the reliability of these technologies. Even if passwords are effective for commercial purveyors of indecent material, the District Court found that an adult password requirement would impose significant burdens on noncommercial sites, both because they would discourage users from accessing their sites and because the cost of creating and maintaining such screening systems would be "beyond their reach."

In sum, the District Court found:

"Even if credit card verification or adult password verification were implemented, the Government presented no testimony as to how such systems could ensure that the user of the password or credit card is in fact over 18. The burdens imposed by credit card verification and adult password verification systems make them effectively unavailable to a substantial number of Internet content providers." * * * The Telecommunications Act of 1996, Pub. L. 104-104, 110 Stat. 56, was an unusually important legislative enactment. * * * Title V—known as the "Communications Decency Act of 1996" (CDA)—contains provisions that were either added in executive committee after the hearings were concluded

or as amendments offered during floor debate on the legislation. An amendment offered in the Senate was the source of the two statutory provisions challenged in this case. They are informally described as the "indecent transmission" provision and the "patently offensive display" provision.

The first, 47 U.S.C.A. s 223(a) (Supp.1997), prohibits the knowing transmission of obscene or indecent messages to any recipient under 18 years of age. It provides in pertinent part:

"(a) Whoever—

"(1) in interstate or foreign communications—

. . .

"(B) by means of a telecommunications device knowingly—

"(i) makes, creates, or solicits, and

"(ii) initiates the transmission of, "any comment, request, suggestion, proposal, image, or other communication which is obscene or indecent, knowing that the recipient of the communication is under 18 years of age, regardless of whether the maker of such communication placed the call or initiated the communication;

. . .

"(2) knowingly permits any telecommunications facility under his control to be used for any activity prohibited by paragraph (1) with the intent that it be used for such activity, "shall be fined under Title 18, or imprisoned not more than two years, or both."

The second provision, s 223(d), prohibits the knowing sending or displaying of patently offensive messages in a manner that is available to a person under 18 years of age. It provides:

"(d) Whoever—

"(1) in interstate or foreign communications knowingly—

"(A) uses an interactive computer service to send to a specific person or persons under 18 years of age, or

"(B) uses any interactive computer service to display in a manner available to a person under 18 years of age, "any comment, request, suggestion, proposal, image, or other communication that, in context, depicts or describes, in terms patently offensive as measured by contemporary community standards, sexual or excretory activities or organs, regardless of whether the user of such service placed the call or initiated the communication; or

"(2) knowingly permits any telecommunications facility under such person's control to be used for an activity prohibited by paragraph (1) with the intent that it be used for such activity, "shall be fined under Title 18, or imprisoned not more than two years, or both."

The breadth of these prohibitions is qualified by two affirmative defenses. See s 223(e)(5). One covers those who take "good faith, reasonable, effective, and appropriate actions" to restrict access by minors to the prohibited communications. s 223(e)(5)(A). The other covers those who restrict access to covered material by requiring certain designated forms of age proof, such as a verified credit card or an adult identification number or code. s 223(e)(5)(B).

On February 8, 1996, immediately after the President signed the statute, 20 plaintiffs filed suit against the Attorney General of the United States and the Department of Justice challenging the constitutionality of ss 223(a)(1) and 223(d). A week later, based on his conclusion that the term "indecent" was too vague to provide the basis for a criminal prosecution, District Judge Buckwalter entered a temporary restraining order against enforcement of s 223(a)(1)(B)(ii) insofar as it applies to indecent communications. * * *

* * *

The judgment of the District Court enjoins the Government from enforcing the prohibitions in s 223(a)(1)(B) insofar as they relate to "indecent" communications, but expressly preserves the Government's right to investigate and prosecute the obscenity or child pornography activities prohibited therein. The injunction against enforcement of ss 223(d)(1) and (2) is unqualified because those provisions contain no separate reference to obscenity or child pornography.

The Government appealed under the Act's special review provisions, s 561, 110 Stat. 142–143, and we noted probable jurisdiction. In its appeal, the Government argues that the District Court erred in holding that the CDA violated both the First Amendment because it is overbroad and the Fifth Amendment because it is vague. While we discuss the vagueness of the CDA because of its relevance to the First Amendment overbreadth inquiry, we conclude that the judgment should be affirmed without reaching the Fifth Amendment issue.

* * *

The CDA's broad categorical prohibitions are not limited to particular times and are not dependent on any evaluation by an agency familiar with the unique characteristics of the Internet. * * * Moreover, the District Court found that the risk of encountering indecent material by accident is remote because a series of affirmative steps is required to access specific material. * * * [T]he CDA applies broadly to the entire universe of cyberspace. And the purpose of the CDA is to protect children from the primary effects of "indecent" and "patently offensive" speech, rather than any "secondary" effect of such speech. Thus, the CDA is a content-based blanket restriction on speech, and, as such, cannot be "properly analyzed as a form of time, place, and manner regulation." 475 U.S., at 46. See also *Boos v. Barry*, 485 U.S. 312, 321 (1988) * * * Neither before nor after the enactment of the CDA have the vast democratic fora of the Internet been subject to the type of government supervision and regulation that has attended the broadcast industry. Moreover, the Internet is not as "invasive" as radio or television. The District Court specifically found that "[c]ommunications over the Internet do not 'invade' an individual's home or appear on one's computer screen unbidden. Users seldom encounter content "by accident."' 929 F. Supp., at 844. It also found that "[a]lmost all sexually explicit images are preceded by warnings as to the content," and cited testimony that " 'odds are slim' that a user would come across a sexually explicit sight by accident." * * *

Regardless of whether the CDA is so vague that it violates the Fifth Amendment, the many ambiguities concerning the scope of its coverage render it problematic for purposes of the First Amendment. For instance, each of the two parts of the CDA uses a different linguistic form. The first uses the word "indecent," 47 U.S.C.A. s 223(a) (Supp.1997), while the second speaks of material that "in context, depicts or describes, in terms patently offensive as measured by contemporary community standards, sexual or excretory activities or organs," s 223(d). Given the absence of a definition of either term, this difference in language will provoke uncertainty among speakers about how the two standards relate to each other and just what they mean. Could a speaker confidently assume that a serious discussion about birth control practices, homosexuality, * * * or the consequences of prison rape would not violate the CDA? This uncertainty undermines the likelihood that the CDA has been carefully tailored to the congressional goal of protecting minors from potentially harmful materials.

The vagueness of the CDA is a matter of special concern for two reasons. First, the CDA is a content-based regulation of speech. The vagueness of such a regulation raises special First Amendment concerns because of its obvious chilling effect on free speech. See, e.g., *Gentile v. State Bar of Nev.*, 501 U.S. 1030, 1048–1051 (1991). Second, the CDA is a criminal statute. In addition to the opprobrium and stigma of a criminal conviction, the CDA threatens violators with penalties including up to two years in prison for each act of violation. The severity of criminal sanctions may well cause speakers to remain silent rather than communicate even arguably unlawful words, ideas, and images. See, e.g., *Dombrowski v. Pfister*, 380 U.S. 479, 494 (1965). As a practical matter, this increased deterrent effect, coupled with the "risk of discriminatory enforcement" of vague regulations, poses greater First Amendment concerns than those implicated by the civil regulation reviewed in *Denver Area Ed. Telecommunications Consortium, Inc. v. FCC*, 116 S.Ct. 2374 (1996).

The Government argues that the statute is no more vague than the obscenity standard this Court established in *Miller v. California*, 413 U.S. 15 (1973). But that is not so. In *Miller*, this Court reviewed a criminal conviction against a commercial vendor who mailed brochures containing pictures of sexually explicit activities to individuals who had not requested such materials. *Id.*, at 18. Having struggled for some time to establish a definition of obscenity, we set forth in *Miller* the test for obscenity that controls to this day:

"(a) whether the average person, applying contemporary community standards would find that the work, taken as a whole, appeals to the prurient interest; (b) whether the work depicts or describes, in a patently offensive way, sexual conduct specifically defined by the applicable state law; and (c) whether the work, taken as a whole, lacks serious literary, artistic, political, or scientific value." *Id.*, at 24.

Because the CDA's "patently offensive" standard (and, we assume arguendo, its synonymous "indecent" standard) is one part of the three-prong *Miller* test, the Government reasons, it cannot be unconstitutionally vague.

The Government's assertion is incorrect as a matter of fact. The second prong of the *Miller* test—the purportedly analogous standard—contains a critical requirement that is omitted from the CDA: that the proscribed material be "specifically defined by the applicable state law." This requirement reduces the vagueness inherent in the open-ended term "patently offensive" as used in the CDA. Moreover, the *Miller* definition is limited to "sexual conduct," whereas the CDA extends also to include (1) "excretory activities" as well as (2) "organs" of both a sexual and excretory nature.

The Government's reasoning is also flawed. Just because a definition including three limitations is not vague, it does not follow that one of those limitations, standing by itself, is not vague.[38] Each of *Miller's* additional two prongs—(1) that, taken as a whole, the material appeal to the "prurient" interest, and (2) that it "lac[k] serious literary, artistic, political, or scientific value"—critically limits the uncertain sweep of the obscenity definition. The second requirement is particularly important because, unlike the "patently offensive" and "prurient interest" criteria, it is not judged by contemporary community standards. See *Pope v. Illinois*, 481 U.S. 497, 500 (1987). This "societal value" requirement, absent in the CDA, allows appellate courts to impose some limitations and regularity on the definition by setting, as a matter of law, a national floor for socially redeeming value. The Government's contention that courts will be able to give such legal limitations to the CDA's standards is belied by *Miller's* own rationale for having juries determine whether material is "patently offensive" according to community standards: that such questions are essentially one of fact.[39]

---

38. Even though the word "trunk," standing alone, might refer to luggage, a swimming suit, the base of a tree, or the long nose of an animal, its meaning is clear when it is one prong of a three-part description of a species of gray animals.

39. 413 U.S., at 30 (Determinations of "what appeals to the 'prurient interest' or is 'patently offensive' . . . are essentially questions of fact, and our Nation is simply too big and too diverse for this Court to reasonably expect that such standards could be articulated for all 50 States in a single formulation, even assuming the prerequisite consensus exists.") The CDA, which implements the "contemporary community standards" language of *Miller*, thus conflicts with the Conferees' own assertion that the CDA was intended "to establish a uniform national standard of content regulation." S. Conf. Rep., at 191.

In contrast to *Miller* and our other previous cases, the CDA thus presents a greater threat of censoring speech that, in fact, falls outside the statute's scope. Given the vague contours of the coverage of the statute, it unquestionably silences some speakers whose messages would be entitled to constitutional protection. That danger provides further reason for insisting that the statute not be overly broad. The CDA's burden on protected speech cannot be justified if it could be avoided by a more carefully drafted statute.

We are persuaded that the CDA lacks the precision that the First Amendment requires when a statute regulates the content of speech. In order to deny minors access to potentially harmful speech, the CDA effectively suppresses a large amount of speech that adults have a constitutional right to receive and to address to one another. That burden on adult speech is unacceptable if less restrictive alternatives would be at least as effective in achieving the legitimate purpose that the statute was enacted to serve.

In evaluating the free speech rights of adults, we have made it perfectly clear that "[s]exual expression which is indecent but not obscene is protected by the First Amendment." *Sable*, 492 U.S., at 126. * * * As a practical matter, the Court also found that it would be prohibitively expensive for noncommercial—as well as some commercial—speakers who have Web sites to verify that their users are adults. *Id.*, at 845–848 These limitations must inevitably curtail a significant amount of adult communication on the Internet. By contrast, the District Court found that "[d]espite its limitations, currently available user-based software suggests that a reasonably effective method by which parents can prevent their children from accessing sexually explicit and other material which parents may believe is inappropriate for their children will soon be widely available."

The breadth of the CDA's coverage is wholly unprecedented. Unlike the regulations upheld in *Ginsberg* and *Pacifica*, the scope of the CDA is not limited to commercial speech or commercial entities. Its open-ended prohibitions embrace all nonprofit entities and individuals posting indecent messages or displaying them on their own computers in the presence of minors. The general, undefined terms "indecent" and "patently offensive" cover large amounts of nonporno-graphic material with serious educational or other value.[44] Moreover, the "community standards" criterion as applied to the Internet means that any communication available to a nation-wide audience will be judged by the standards of the community most likely to be offended by the message. The regulated subject matter includes any of the seven "dirty words" used in the *Pacifica* monologue, the use of which the Government's expert acknowledged could constitute a felony. It may also extend to discussions about prison rape or safe sexual practices, artistic images that include nude subjects, and arguably the card catalogue of the Carnegie Library.

For the purposes of our decision, we need neither accept nor reject the Government's submission that the First Amendment does not forbid a blanket prohibition on all "indecent" and "patently offensive" messages communicated to a 17-year-old—no matter how much value the message may contain and regardless of parental approval. It is at least clear that the strength of the Government's interest in protecting minors is not equally strong throughout the coverage of this broad statute. Under the CDA, a parent allowing her 17-year-old to use the family computer to obtain information on the Internet that she, in her parental judgment, deems appropriate could face a lengthy prison term. Similarly, a parent who sent his 17-year-old college freshman information on birth control via e-mail could be incarcerated even though neither he, his child, nor anyone in their home community, found the material "indecent" or "patently offensive," if the college town's community thought otherwise.

The breadth of this content-based restriction of speech imposes an especially heavy burden on the Government to explain why a less restrictive provision would not be as effective as the CDA. It has not done so. The arguments in this

---

44. Transmitting obscenity and child pornography, whether via the Internet or other means, is already illegal under federal law for both adults and juveniles. See 18 U.S.C. ss 1464–1465 (criminalizing obscenity); s 2251 (criminalizing child pornography). In fact, when Congress was considering the CDA, the Government expressed its view that the law was unnecessary because existing laws already authorized its ongoing efforts to prosecute obscenity, child pornography, and child solicitation. See 141 Cong. Rec. S8342 (June 14, 1995) (letter from Kent Markus, Acting Assistant Attorney General, U.S. Department of Justice, to Sen. Leahy).

Court have referred to possible alternatives such as requiring that indecent material be "tagged" in a way that facilitates parental control of material coming into their homes, making exceptions for messages with artistic or educational value, providing some tolerance for parental choice, and regulating some portions of the Internet—such as commercial web sites—differently than others, such as chat rooms. Particularly in the light of the absence of any detailed findings by the Congress, or even hearings addressing the special problems of the CDA, we are persuaded that the CDA is not narrowly tailored if that requirement has any meaning at all.

In an attempt to curtail the CDA's facial overbreadth, the Government advances three additional arguments for sustaining the Act's affirmative prohibitions: (1) that the CDA is constitutional because it leaves open ample "alternative channels" of communication; (2) that the plain meaning of the Act's "knowledge" and "specific person" requirement significantly restricts its permissible applications; and (3) that the Act's prohibitions are "almost always" limited to material lacking redeeming social value.

The Government first contends that, even though the CDA effectively censors discourse on many of the Internet's modalities—such as chat groups, newsgroups, and mail exploders—it is nonetheless constitutional because it provides a "reasonable opportunity" for speakers to engage in the restricted speech on the World Wide Web. This argument is unpersuasive because the CDA regulates speech on the basis of its content. A "time, place, and manner" analysis is therefore inapplicable. It is thus immaterial whether such speech would be feasible on the Web (which, as the Government's own expert acknowledged, would cost up to $10,000 if the speaker's interests were not accommodated by an existing Web site, not including costs for database management and age verification). The Government's position is equivalent to arguing that a statute could ban leaflets on certain subjects as long as individuals are free to publish books. In invalidating a number of laws that banned leafletting on the streets regardless of their content—we explained that "one is not to have the exercise of his liberty of expression in appropriate places abridged on the plea that it may be exercised in some other place." *Schneider v. State (Town of Irvington)*, 308 U.S. 147, 163 (1939).

The Government also asserts that the "knowledge" requirement of both ss 223(a) and (d), especially when coupled with the "specific child" element found in s 223(d), saves the CDA from overbreadth. Because both sections prohibit the dissemination of indecent messages only to persons known to be under 18, the Government argues, it does not require transmitters to "refrain from communicating indecent material to adults; they need only refrain from disseminating such materials to persons they know to be under 18."

This argument ignores the fact that most Internet fora—including chat rooms, newsgroups, mail exploders, and the Web—are open to all comers. The Government's assertion that the knowledge requirement somehow protects the communications of adults is therefore untenable. Even the strongest reading of the "specific person" requirement of s 223(d) cannot save the statute. It would confer broad powers of censorship, in the form of a "heckler's veto," upon any opponent of indecent speech who might simply log on and inform the would-be discoursers that his 17-year-old child—a "specific person . . . under 18 years of age," 47 U.S.C.A. s 223(d)(1)(A) (Supp. 1997)—would be present.

Finally, we find no textual support for the Government's submission that material having scientific, educational, or other redeeming social value will necessarily fall outside the CDA's "patently offensive" and "indecent" prohibitions.

The Government's three remaining arguments focus on the defenses provided in s 223(e)(5). First, relying on the "good faith, reasonable, effective, and appropriate actions" provision, the Government suggests that "tagging" provides a defense that saves the constitutionality of the Act. The suggestion assumes that transmitters may encode their indecent communications in a way that would indicate their contents, thus permitting recipients to block their reception with appropriate software. It is the requirement that the good faith action must be "effective" that makes this defense illusory. The Government recognizes that its proposed screening software does not currently exist. Even if it did, there is no way to know whether a potential recipient will actually block the encoded material. Without the impossible knowledge that every guardian in America is screening for the "tag," the transmitter could not reasonably rely on its action to be "effective."

For its second and third arguments concerning defenses—which we can consider together—the Government relies on the latter half of s 223(e)(5), which applies when the transmitter has restricted access by requiring use of a verified credit card or adult identification. Such verification is not only technologically available but actually is used by commercial providers of sexually explicit material. These providers, therefore, would be protected by the defense. Under the findings of the District Court, however, it is not economically feasible for most noncommercial speakers to employ such verification. Accordingly, this defense would not significantly narrow the statute's burden on noncommercial speech. Even with respect to the commercial pornographers that would be protected by the defense, the Government failed to adduce any evidence that these verification techniques actually preclude minors from posing as adults. Given that the risk of criminal sanctions "hovers over each content provider, like the proverbial sword of Damocles," the District Court correctly refused to rely on unproven future technology to save the statute. The Government thus failed to prove that the proffered defense would significantly reduce the heavy burden on adult speech produced by the prohibition on offensive displays.

We agree with the District Court's conclusion that the CDA places an unacceptably heavy burden on protected speech, and that the defenses do not constitute the worth of "narrow tailoring" that will save an otherwise patently invalid unconstitutional provision. In *Sable*, 492 U.S., at 127, we remarked that the speech restriction at issue there amounted to " 'burn[ing] the house to roast the pig.' " The CDA, casting a far darker shadow over free speech, threatens to torch a large segment of the Internet community.

* * *

In this Court, though not in the District Court, the Government asserts that—in addition to its interest in protecting children—its "[e]qually significant" interest in fostering the growth of the Internet provides an independent basis for upholding the constitutionality of the CDA. The Government apparently assumes that the unregulated availability of "indecent" and "patently offensive" material on the Internet is driving countless citizens away from the medium because of the risk of exposing themselves or their children to harmful material.

We find this argument singularly unpersuasive. The dramatic expansion of this new marketplace of ideas contradicts the factual basis of this contention. The record demonstrates that the growth of the Internet has been and continues to be phenomenal. As a matter of constitutional tradition, in the absence of evidence to the contrary, we presume that governmental regulation of the content of speech is more likely to interfere with the free exchange of ideas than to encourage it. The interest in encouraging freedom of expression in a democratic society outweighs any theoretical but unproven benefit of censorship.

For the foregoing reasons, the judgment of the district court is affirmed.

It is so ordered.

COMMENT

While agreeing with the Court that CDA was unconstitutionally overbroad as written, Justice O'Connor in dissent strove for a way to segregate indecent material from minors. Her message to those who drafted the Act was to go for a more precise rewrite of the bill in Congress. At least that's how the Act's proponents interpreted her. While Justice O'Connor thought parts of the Act constitutional, notably its "indecency transmission" and "specific person" provisions, she endorsed the idea of keeping children away from adult zones in cyberspace by the use of already existing screening software, even though she considered much of it to be so far inadequate. Not to be forgotten is that obscenity, once defined by an appropriate jury, is still outside the boundaries of First Amendment protection.

A much lower level of consensus greeted the Court when it was asked to consider the First Amendment status of patently offensive material on cable television. Three sections of the Cable Television Consumer Protection and Competition Act of 1992, collectively known as the Helms Amendment, were challenged by the Denver Area Educational Telecommunications Consortium, Inc., and the Alliance for Community Media. Section 10(a) permitted cable operators to prohibit leased access programming that "the cable operator reasonably believes describes or depicts sexual or excretory activities or organs in a patently offensive manner as measured by contemporary community standards." Section 10(b), deferring to an FCC definition of "indecent" similar to the foregoing, required cable operators to put "patently offensive" leased channel programming on a separate channel, to block it, and to unblock it within thirty days only if a subscriber made a written request for access, thus exposing his program predilections to the public. Section 10(c) would allow the FCC to create rules to enable cable operators to prohibit programming containing obscene material that solicits or promotes unlawful conduct on any public, educational, or governmental access channel. A 1984 law had denied cable operators any editorial discretion over leased channel programming. One consequence of that denial of judgment to cable managers was the hard-core sex show.

After riding out some heavy weather in the D.C. Circuit Court of Appeals, the case reached the Supreme Court. In a jumble of opinions, a splintered Court ruled that cable operators may ban indecent programming from leased commercial channels but not from leased public access channels—a holding reminiscent of 1960s decisions that permitted punishment of those who "commercially exploited" sexual content, even when that content failed to fit the Court's own definition of obscenity. At the same time, the Court struck down the requirement that subscribers request in writing, thirty days in advance, access to "patently offensive" programming on commercially leased channels when they were available. Justice Stephen Breyer's opinion for the Court on this point was the only opinion that commanded a majority, rather than a plurality, of the Court. That provision, said Breyer, ignored less intrusive alternatives and was not "narrowly or reasonably tailored to protect children." Viewers, he said, would be loath to identify themselves as part of an audience for indecent programming.

Justices John Paul Stevens and David Souter joined Justice Breyer in upholding and striking down secs. 10(a) and 10(b) of the Act, respectively, and concurred with the decision of the Court in striking down sec. 10(c). Justices Anthony Kennedy and Ruth Bader Ginsburg thought all three provisions of the Act were unconstitutional, while Chief Justice William Rehnquist and Justices Clarence Thomas and Antonin Scalia would have upheld all of them as constitutional. A number of justices admitted either explicitly or by implication that they were uncertain as to how the First Amendment would

apply to future communication technologies, but Justice Kennedy recommended that in the absence of any clear knowledge of future technological directions or consensus on indecency his colleagues "ought to begin by allowing speech, not suppressing it."

Justice Thomas saw a "doctrinal wasteland" in earlier decisions in which regulators and cable operators alike could not agree on whether cable was entitled to a print or broadcast level of First Amendment protection. Thomas would prefer the former. Access channel programmers, therefore, should not be able to force their programming on those who own cable channels. Nor, he said, are these channels public forums. He would restore full "editorial discretion" to cable operators.

The shifting majorities on the three provisions of the Act reflect deep differences and uncertainty among the justices about the level of First Amendment protection distinctive new communication systems deserve and how far the Court should be prepared to go in restricting content in order to protect the public from real or imagined evils. Accordingly, of the six separate opinions, only a portion of Justice Breyer's opinion will be presented. Breyer admitted equivocation, and even those justices who supported two-thirds of his opinion called it standardless and "adrift."

Denver Area Educational Telecommunications Consortium, Inc. v. FCC

116 S. CT. 2374, 135 L.Ed.2d 888 (1996).

BREYER, Justice:

* * *

We turn initially to the provision that permits cable system operators to prohibit "patently offensive" (or "indecent") programming transmitted over leased access channels. 1992 Act, Section(s) 10(a). The Court of Appeals held that this provision did not violate the First Amendment because the First Amendment prohibits only "Congress" (and, through the Fourteenth Amendment, a "State"), not private individuals, from "abridging the freedom of speech." Although the court said that it found no "state action," it could not have meant that phrase literally, for, of course, petitioners attack (as "abridg[ing] . . . speech") a congressional statute—which, by definition, is an Act of

"Congress." More likely, the court viewed this statute's "permissive" provisions as not themselves restricting speech, but, rather, as simply reaffirming the authority to pick and choose programming that a private entity, say, a private broadcaster, would have had in the absence of intervention by any federal, or local, governmental entity.

We recognize that the First Amendment, the terms of which apply to governmental action, ordinarily does not itself throw into constitutional doubt the decisions of private citizens to permit, or to restrict, speech—and this is so ordinarily even where those decisions take place within the framework of a regulatory regime such as broadcasting. Were that no so, courts might have to face the difficult, and potentially restrictive, practical task of deciding which, among any number of private parties involved in providing a program (for example, networks, station owners, program editors, and program producers), is the "speaker" whose rights may not be abridged, and who is the speech-restricting "censor." Furthermore, as this Court has held, the editorial function itself is an aspect of "speech," see *Turner,* 512 U.S., at ___, and a court's decision that a private party, say, the station owner, is a "censor," could itself interfere with that private "censor's" freedom to speak as an editor. Thus, not surprisingly, this Court's First Amendment broadcasting cases have dealt with governmental efforts to restrict, not governmental efforts to provide or to maintain, a broadcaster's freedom to pick and to choose programming. *(citations omitted)*

Nonetheless, petitioners, while conceding that this is ordinarily so, point to circumstances that, in their view, make the analogy with private broadcasters inapposite and make this case a special one, warranting a different constitutional result. As a practical matter, they say, cable system operators have considerably more power to "censor" program viewing than do broadcasters, for individual communities typically have only one cable system, linking broadcasters and other program providers with each community's many subscribers. See *Turner* (only one cable system in most communities; nationally more than 60% of homes subscribe to cable, which then becomes the primary or sole source of video programming in the overwhelming majority of these homes). Moreover, concern about system operators' exercise of this considerable power originally led

government—local and federal—to insist that operators provide leased and public access channels free of operator editorial control. To permit system operators to supervise programming on leased access channels will create the very private-censorship risk that this anticensorship effort sought to avoid. At the same time, petitioners add, cable systems have two relevant special characteristics. They are unusually involved with government, for they depend upon government permission and government facilities (streets, rights-of-way) to string the cable necessary for their services. And in respect to leased channels, their speech interests are relatively weak because they act less like editors, such as newspapers or television broadcasters, than like common carriers, such as telephone companies.

Under these circumstances, petitioners conclude, Congress' "permissive" law, in actuality, will "abridge" their free speech. And this Court should treat that law as a congressionally imposed, content-based, restriction unredeemed as a properly tailored effort to serve a "compelling interest." See *Sable Communications of Cal., Inc. v. FCC,* 492 U.S. 115, 126 (1989). They further analogize the provisions to constitutionally forbidden content-based restrictions upon speech taking place in "public forums" such as public streets, parks, or buildings dedicated to open speech and communication. See *Perry Ed. Assn. v. Perry Local Educators' Assn.,* 460 U.S. 37, 45 (1983). And, finally, petitioners say that the legal standard the law contains (the "patently offensive" standard) is unconstitutionally vague. See, e.g., *Interstate Circuit, Inc. v. Dallas,* 390 U.S. 676 (1968) (rejecting censorship ordinance as vague, even though it was intended to protect children).

Like the petitioners, Justices Kennedy and Thomas would have us decide this case simply by transferring and applying literally categorical standards this Court has developed in their contexts. For Justice Kennedy, leased access channels are like a common carrier, cablecast is a protected medium, strict scrutiny applies, Section(s) 10(a) fails this test, and, therefore, Section(s) 10(a) is invalid. For Justice Thomas, the case is simple because the cable operator who owns the system over which access channels are broadcast, like a bookstore owner with respect to what it displays on the shelves, has a predominant First Amendment interest. Both categorical approaches suffer from the same flaws: they import law developed in very different contexts into a new and changing environment, and they lack the flexibility necessary to allow government to respond to very serious practical problems without sacrificing the free exchange of ideas the First Amendment is designed to protect.

* * *

This Court, in different contexts, has consistently held that the Government may directly regulate speech to address extraordinary problems, where its regulations are appropriately tailored to resolve those problems without imposing an unnecessarily great restriction on speech. Justices Kennedy and Thomas would have us further declare which, among the many applications of the general approach that this Court has developed over the years, we are applying here. *But no definitive choice among competing analogies (broadcast, common carrier, bookstore) allows us to declare a rigid single standard, good for now and for all future media and purposes. That is not to say that we reject all the more specific formulations of the standard—they appropriately cover the vast majority of cases involving Government regulation of speech. Rather, aware as we are of the changes taking place in the law, the technology, and the industrial structure, related to telecommunications, see, e.g., Telecommunications Act of 1996, 110 Stat. 56, we believe it unwise and unnecessary definitively to pick one analogy or one specific set of words now. See Columbia Broadcasting, 412 U.S., at 102 ("The problems of regulation are rendered more difficult because the broadcast industry is dynamic in terms of technological change; solutions adequate a decade ago are not necessarily so now, and those acceptable today may well be outmoded 10 years hence"); Pacifica, supra, at 748 ("We have long recognized that each medium of expression presents special First Amendment problems.")* [Emphasis added.] We therefore think it premature to answer the broad questions that Justices Kennedy and Thomas raise in their efforts to find a definitive analogy, deciding, for example, the extent to which private property can be designated a public forum; whether public access channels are a public forum; whether the Government's viewpoint neutral decision to limit a public forum is subject to the same scrutiny as a selective exclusion from a preexisting public forum; whether exclusion from common carriage must for all purposes be treated like exclusion from a public forum; and whether the interests of the owners of communications media always subordinate the interests of all other users of a medium.

Rather than decide these issues, we can decide this case more narrowly, by closely scrutinizing Section(s) 10(a) to assure that it properly addresses an extremely important problem, without imposing, in light of the relevant interests, an unnecessarily great restriction on speech. The importance of the interest at stake here—protecting children from exposure to patently offensive depictions of sex; the accommodation of the interests of programmers in maintaining access channels and of cable operators in editing the contents of their channels; the similarity of the problem and its solution to those at issue in *Pacifica,* and the flexibility inherent in an approach that permits private cable operators to make editorial decisions, lead us to conclude that Section(s) 10(a) is a sufficiently tailored response to an extraordinarily important problem.

First, the provision before us comes accompanied with an extremely important justification, one that this Court has often found compelling—the need to protect children from exposure to patently offensive sex-related material.

Second, the provision arises in a very particular context—congressional permission for cable operators to regulate programming that, for but a previous Act of Congress, would have had no path of access to cable channels free of an operator's control. The First Amendment interests involved are therefore complex, and involve a balance between those interests served by the access requirements themselves (increasing the availability of avenues of expression to programmers who otherwise would not have them) and the disadvantage to the First Amendment interests of cable operators and other programmers (those to whom the cable operator would have assigned the channels devoted to access).

Third, the problem Congress addressed here is remarkably similar to the problem addressed by the FCC in *Pacifica* and the balance Congress struck is commensurate with the balance we approved there. In *Pacifica* this Court considered a governmental ban of a radio broadcast of "indecent" materials, defined in part, like the provisions before us, to include " 'language that describes, in terms patently offensive as measured by contemporary community standards for the broadcast medium, sexual or excretory activities and organs, at times of the day when there is a reasonable risk that children may be in the audience.' " 438 U.S., at 732 (quoting 56 F.C.C.2d 94, 98 (1975)).

The Court found this ban constitutionally permissible primarily because "broadcasting is uniquely accessible to children" and children were likely listeners to the program there at issue—an afternoon radio broadcast. In addition, the Court wrote, "the broadcast media have established a uniquely pervasive presence in the lives of all Americans," "[p]atently offensive, indecent material . . . confronts the citizen, not only in public, but also in the privacy of the home," generally without sufficient prior warning to allow the recipient to avert his or her eyes or ears, and "[a]dults who feel the need may purchase tapes and records or go to theaters and nightclubs" to hear similar performances.

* * *

Fourth, the permissive nature of Section(s) 10(a) means that it likely restricts speech less than, not more than, the ban at issue in *Pacifica*. The provision removes a restriction as to some speakers—namely, cable operators. Moreover, although the provision does create a risk that a program will not appear, that risk is not the same as the certainty that accompanies a governmental ban. In fact, a glance at the programming that cable operators allow on their own (nonaccess) channels suggests that this distinction is not theoretical, but real. Finally, the provision's permissive nature brings with it a flexibility that allows cable operators, for example, not to ban broadcasts, but, say, to rearrange broadcast times, better to fit the desires of adult audiences while lessening the risks of harm to children. * * * In all these respects, the permissive nature of the approach taken by Congress renders this measure appropriate as a means of achieving the underlying purpose of protecting children.

* * *

The existence of this complex balance of interests persuades us that the permissive nature of the provision, coupled with its viewpoint-neutral application, is a constitutionally permissible way to protect children from the type of sexual material that concerned Congress, while accommodat-

ing both the First Amendment interests served by the access requirements and those served in restoring to cable operators a degree of the editorial control that Congress removed in 1984.

Further, the statute protects against overly broad application of its standards insofar as it permits cable system operators to screen programs only pursuant to a "written and published policy." A cable system operator would find it difficult to show that a leased access program prohibition reflects a rational "policy" if the operator permits similarly "offensive" programming to run elsewhere on its system at comparable times or in comparable ways. We concede that the statute's protection against overly broad application is somewhat diminished by the fact that it permits a cable operator to ban programming that the operator "reasonably believes" is patently offensive. But the "reasonabl[e] belie[f]" qualifier here, as elsewhere in the law, seems designed not to expand the category at which the law aims, but, rather to provide a legal excuse, for (at least) one honest mistake, from liability that might otherwise attach. * * * And the contours of the shield—reasonableness—constrain the discretion of the cable operator as much as they protect it. If, for example, a court had already found substantially similar programming to be beyond the pale of "patently offensive" material, or if a local authority overseeing the local public, governmental, or educational channels had indicated that materials of the type that the cable operator decides to ban were not "patently offensive" in that community, then the cable operator would be hard pressed to claim that the exclusion of the material was "reasonable." We conclude that the statute is not impermissibly vague.

For the reasons discussed, we conclude that Section(s) 10(a) is consistent with the First Amendment.

The statute's second provision significantly differs from the first, for it does not simply permit, but rather requires, cable system operators to restrict speech—by segregating and blocking "patently offensive" sex-related material appearing on leased channels (but not on other channels). In particular, as previously mentioned, this provision and its implementing regulations require cable system operators to place "patently offensive" leased channel programming on a separate channel; to block that channel; to unblock the channel within 30 days of a subscriber's written request for access; and to reblock the channel within 30 days of a subscriber's request for reblocking. Also, leased channel programmers must notify cable operators of an intended "patently offensive" broadcast up to 30 days before its scheduled broadcast date.

These requirements have obvious restrictive effects. The several up-to-30-day delays, along with single channel segregation, mean that a subscriber cannot decide to watch a single program without considerable advance planning and without letting the "patently offensive" channel in its entirety invade his household for days, perhaps weeks, at a time. These restrictions will prevent programmers from broadcasting to viewers who select programs day by day (or, through "surfing," minute by minute); to viewers who would like occasionally to watch a few, but not many, of the programs on the "patently offensive" channel; and to viewers who simply tend to judge a program's value through channel reputation, i.e., by the company it keeps. Moreover, the "written notice" requirement will further restrict viewing by subscribers who fear for their reputations should the operator, advertently or inadvertently, disclose the list of those who wish to watch the "patently offensive" channel. Cf. *Lamont v. Postmaster General*, 381 U.S. 301, 307 (1965) (finding unconstitutional a requirement that recipients of Communist literature notify the Post Office that they wish to receive it). Further, the added costs and burdens that these requirements impose upon a cable system operator may encourage that operator to ban programming that the operator would otherwise permit to run, even if only late at night.

* * *

We agree with the Government that protection of children is a "compelling interest." But we do not agree that the "segregate and block" requirements properly accommodate the speech restrictions they impose and the legitimate objective they seek to attain. Nor need we here determine whether, or the extent to which, *Pacifica* does, or does not, impose some lesser standard of review where indecent speech is at issue. * * * That is because once one examines this governmental restriction, it becomes apparent that, not only is it not a "least restrictive alternative," and is not "narrowly tailored" to meet its legitimate

objective, it also seems considerably "more extensive than necessary." That is to say, it fails to satisfy this Court's formulations of the First Amendment's "strictest," as well as its somewhat less "strict," requirements. * * * The provision before us does not reveal the caution and care that the standards underlying these various verbal formulas impose upon laws that seek to reconcile the critically important interest in protecting free speech with very important, or even compelling, interests that sometimes warrant restrictions.

Several circumstances lead us to this conclusion. For one thing, the law, as recently amended, uses other means to protect children from similar "patently offensive" material broadcast on unleased cable channels, i.e., broadcast over any of a system's numerous ordinary, or public access, channels. The law, as recently amended, requires cable operators to "scramble or . . . block" such programming on any (unleased) channel "primarily dedicated to sexually-oriented programming." Telecommunications Act of 1996, Section(s) 505, 110 Stat. 136. In addition, cable operators must honor a subscriber's request to block any, or all, programs on any channel to which he or she does not wish to subscribe. Section(s) 504. And manufacturers, in the future, will have to make television sets with a so-called "V-chip"—a device that will be able automatically to identify and block sexually explicit or violent programs. Section(s) 551, id., at 139–142.

* * *

Consequently, we cannot find that the "segregate and block" restrictions on speech are a narrowly, or reasonably, tailored effort to protect children. Rather, they are overly restrictive, "sacrific[ing]" important First Amendment interests for too "speculative a gain." For that reason they are not consistent with the First Amendment.

The statute's third provision, as implemented by FCC regulation, is similar to its first provision, in that it too permits a cable operator to prevent transmission of "patently offensive" programming, in this case on public access channels. 1992 Act, Section(s) 10(c); 47 CFR Section(s) 76.702 (1995). But there are four important differences.

The first is the historical background. As Justice Kennedy points out, cable operators have traditionally agreed to reserve channel capacity for public, governmental, and educational channels as part of the consideration they give municipalities that award them cable franchises. In the terms preferred by Justice Thomas, the requirement to reserve capacity for public access channels is similar to the reservation of a public easement, or a dedication of land for streets and parks, as part of a municipality's approval of a subdivision of land. Significantly, these are channels over which cable operators have not historically exercised editorial control. Unlike Section(s) 10(a) therefore, Section(s) 10(c) does not restore to cable operators editorial rights that they once had, and the countervailing First Amendment interest is nonexistent, or at least much diminished.

The second difference is the institutional background that has developed as a result of the historical difference. When a "leased channel" is made available by the operator to a private lessee, the lessee has total control of programming during the leased time slot. Public access channels, on the other hand, are normally subject to complex supervisory systems of various sorts, often with both public and private elements. Municipalities generally provide in their cable franchising agreements for an access channel manager, who is most commonly a nonprofit organization, but may also be the municipality, or, in some instances, the cable system owner.

* * *

This system of public, private, and mixed nonprofit elements, through its supervising boards and nonprofit or governmental access managers, can set programming policy and approve or disapprove particular programming services. And this system can police that policy by, for example, requiring indemnification by programmers, certification of compliance with local standards, time segregation, adult content advisories, or even by prescreening individual programs. * * * Whether these locally accountable bodies prescreen programming, promulgate rules for the use of public access channels, or are merely available to respond when problems arise, the upshot is the same: there is a locally accountable body capable of addressing the problem, should it arise, of patently offensive programming broadcast to children, making it unlikely that many children will in fact be exposed to programming considered patently offensive in that community.

Third, the existence of a system aimed at encouraging and securing programming that the community considers valuable strongly suggests that a "cable operator's veto" is less likely necessary to achieve the statute's basic objective, protecting children, than a similar veto in the context of leased channels. Of course, the system of access managers and supervising boards can make mistakes, which the operator might in some cases correct with its veto power. Balanced against this potential benefit, however, is the risk that the veto itself may be mistaken; and its use, or threatened use, could prevent the presentation of programming, that, though borderline, is not "patently offensive" to its targeted audience. See Aufderheide, Public Access Cable Programming, Controversial Speech, and Free Expression (1992), App. 64–66 (describing the programs that were considered borderline by access managers, including sex education, health education, broadcasts of politically marginal groups, and various artistic experiments). And this latter threat must bulk large within a system that already has publicly accountable systems for maintaining responsible programs.

Finally, our examination of the legislative history and the record before us is consistent with what common sense suggests, namely that the public/nonprofit programming control systems now in place would normally avoid, minimize, or eliminate any child-related problems concerning "patently offensive" programming. * * * The upshot, in respect to the public access channels, is a law that could radically change present programming-related relationships among local community and nonprofit supervising boards and access managers, which relationships are established through municipal law, regulation, and contract. In doing so, it would not significantly restore editorial rights of cable operators, but would greatly increase the risk that certain categories of programming (say, borderline offensive programs) will not appear. At the same time, given present supervisory mechanisms, the need for this particular provision, aimed directly at public access channels, is not obvious. Having carefully reviewed the legislative history of the Act, the proceedings before the FCC, the record below, and the submissions of the parties and amici here, we conclude that the Government cannot sustain its burden of showing that Section(s) 10(c) is necessary to protect children or that it is appropriately tailored to secure that end. Consequently, we find that this third provision violates the First Amendment.

* * *

For these reasons, the judgment of the Court of Appeals is affirmed insofar as it upheld 10(a); the judgment of the Court of Appeals is reversed insofar as it upheld 10(b) and 10(c).

It is so ordered.

COMMENT

A week before the Supreme Court decided the Internet case, state courts in New York and Georgia ruled that state statutes similar to the Communications Decency Act were unconstitutional under both the First Amendment and the Commerce Clause. Also in 1997, a federal district court in New York enjoined application of the Military Honor and Decency Act of 1996 barring army PX's (post exchanges) from selling magazines like *Penthouse*. The government, said the court, has no authority to ban material just because it is offensive, vulgar, or indecent. A state interest in promoting core military values and improving the army's public relations was not a sufficiently compelling state interest. Equal protection and due process claims were also upheld by the court. *General Media Communications Inc., et. al. v. Perry et. al.* (S.D.N.Y. No. 96 Civ. 7525 [SAS], January 22, 1997).

Long before the Internet, the U.S. Supreme Court had had trouble applying the vague obscenity and indecency standards to the myriad cases it reviewed. In *Jenkins v. Georgia,*[27] the Court said the movie *Carnal Knowledge* was not "hard-core" because the camera did not focus on the genitals of actors Candice Bergen and Jack Nicholson during scenes of "ultimate sexual acts."

On the same day, the Court ruled in another case that expert testimony of any kind as to what was obscene to an average person could be barred from trial and that jurors, as average persons, could exercise their own judgments. The average person, however, said the Court, would be neither the most prudish nor the most tolerant in the community.[28] Some years later, the Court, in a vain effort to clarify, said that "community standards" did not mean a majority view and that an "average" or ordinary person had only to be "reasonable."[29]

In any case, said the Court, only "prurient interest" and "patent offensiveness" should be judged with reference to "community standards." "Serious value," the Court seemed to be saying, would be a fixed or intrinsic characteristic of any disputed work. It would not vary from community to community.[30] And, presumably, testimony on "value" would be available. Confusing? Yes.

It is safe to say that the words "obscenity," "pornography," and "indecency" are now used interchangeably. The dictionary defines "pornography" as obscene or licentious writing or painting, and "obscenity" as that which is offensive to chastity or to modesty and as the lewd, foul, and disgusting. The only difference is that "pornography," to some ears, may be a stronger word and may denote something worse than obscenity, especially when the adjective "hard-core" is attached. To add to this definitional imprecision, the Supreme Court itself has, in the past, referred to "soft-core" pornography. The law, however, has made no particular distinction between "obscenity" and "pornography."

"Indecency," however, does suggest a lesser problem for society, but still something profane and contrary to public morality. It also is generally regarded as a suitable standard for the protection of children where the more pervasive media are being used—networks of computers included.

A Brief History

From Venus figurines with exaggerated breasts and buttocks fired in clay 27,000 years ago to today's CD called "Cyborgasm," there is ample evidence of the durability of pornography.[31] But it was hateful attacks on the Roman Catholic church in English pamphlets that brought obscenity into the common law in *Curl's* case in 1727.[32] A century and a half later, in the *Hicklin* case, the lord chief justice of England laid down a test for obscenity that was designed to protect

---

27. 418 U.S. 153 (1974).
28. *Hamling v. United States,* 418 U.S. 87 (1974).
29. *Pinkus v. United States,* 436 U.S. 293 (1978).
30. *Pope v. Illinois,* 481 U.S. 497 (1987).
31. John Tierney, "Porn, the Low-Slung Engine of Progress," *New York Times,* January 9, 1994, pp. A1, 18.
32. 2 Strange 788, 93 Eng.Rep. 849 (K.B. 1727).

the feebleminded: "Whether the tendency of the matter charged as obscenity is to deprave and corrupt those whose minds are open to such immoral influence and into whose hands a publication of this sort should fall."[33]

Hicklin, reinforced by our own Comstock Act of 1876, was adapted to the United States and was the law until Judge John Woolsey in a 1933 federal district court case involving James Joyce's literary masterpiece, *Ulysses*, wrote an opinion for "normal" people. A better test, said the judge, would be the impact or the dominant effect of the whole book on the average person of normal sensual responses together with an evaluation of the writer's intent or purpose.[34] Judge Woolsey had read the book.

By 1945, postal censorship had also been declared unconstitutional in a case involving *Esquire* magazine in which Justice William O. Douglas wrote for a unanimous Court:

> Under our system of government there is an accommodation for the widest varieties of tastes and ideas. . . . The validity of the obscenity laws is recognition that the mails may not be used to satisfy all tastes, no matter how perverted. But Congress has left the Postmaster General with no power to prescribe standards for the literature or the art which a mailable periodical disseminates. . . .[35].

Later, the Court said that the Post Office would have to prove that nonmailable material was obscene.[36] But it upheld the constitutionality of the 1968 Pandering Advertisement Act[37] that permitted individual householders to define obscenity for themselves. If a person swears that he or she has been sexually aroused by unsolicited mail, the Post Office orders the sender to strike the name from its mailing list. Penalties for not doing so are substantial.[38] The only problem is that the Post Office has received as many as 300,000 complaints in a single year about the sexually stimulating effects of advertising for an astonishing array of goods and services.

Ulysses led directly to the 1957 Supreme Court ruling in *Roth v. United States* in which

Justice William Brennan for the Court defined the test of obscenity as "Whether to the average person, applying contemporary community standards, the dominant theme of the material taken as a whole appeals to prurient interest."[39] It was assumed in *Roth* that obscenity was *"utterly without redeeming social importance."* The "average" person remained a phantom. No one was certain how contemporary community standards would be measured. And who would willingly testify to being sexually aroused by something or other remained a mystery.

Cultural schizophrenia about sex will inexorably manifest itself in bizarre symptoms in the body politic. In 1977, for example, a Manhattan jury acquitted a wholesaler of selling films depicting bestiality because his wares were too disgusting to appeal to normal sexual urges. To be obscene, films would have to arouse healthy sexual responses in average, ordinary jurors.

Most attempts to distinguish good erotica from bad pornography have failed due in large part to the incredible diversity in human response to infinitely replaceable sexual stimuli. There is a neat contradiction in a market economy that depends in part upon sexual exploitation to sell its products at the same time as its government agencies pass and enforce laws to punish slightly more vulgar versions of identical themes. One is reminded of the proper Victorians who, while considering sex a topic unfit for polite conversation and forbidden to the poor, kept vast repositories of erotica in the libraries of their mansions.[40]

Between 1957 and the present, the concept of community standards has swung between local and national definitions.[41] Commercial exploitation has been punished.[42] Guilty knowledge was made a precondition of punishment for the crime of selling obscene books.[43] No assaults on personal privacy in attempts to suppress or punish

---

33. *R. v. Hicklin*, L. R. 3 Q.B. 360 (1868).

34. *United States v. One Book Called "Ulysses,"* 5 F. Supp. 182 (D.N.Y. 1933), aff'd, 72 F.2d 705 (2d Cir. 1934).

35. *Hannegan v. Esquire, Inc.*, 327 U.S. 146 (1946). See also *Walker v. Popenoe*, 149 F.2d 511 (D.C.Cir. 1945).

36. *Manual Enterprises, Inc. v. Day*, 370 U.S. 478 (1962).

37. 39 U.S.C.A. § 3008.

38. *Rowan v. United States Post Office Department*, 397 U.S. 728 (1970).

39. 1 Med. L. Rptr. 1375, 354 U.S. 476 (1957).

40. Stephen Marcus, *The Other Victorians* (1966).

41. *Jacobellis v. State of Ohio*, 378 U.S. 184 (1964).

42. *Ginzburg v. United States*, 1 Med. L. Rptr. 1409, 383 U.S. 463 (1966). Publisher Ralph Ginzburg was sentenced to three years in prison for distributing materials that were *not* obscene by the standards of the Supreme Court. But he promoted them as if they were, and the Court took him at his word. If a publisher guarantees that his material will stimulate certain glandular juices, then, the Court implied, that's what they do. The publishing world was shocked at the Court's holding, but indifferent to Ginzburg's plight.

43. *Smith v. California*, 351 U.S. 147 (1959).

obscenity would be allowed.[44] Children will be protected.[45] Prior restraint (censorship) was declared invalid.[46] And anyone accused of dealing in pornography must be accorded due process.[47] In obscenity cases due process meant that the government would demonstrate the offending material was unprotected, that a judicial hearing on the question would be held immediately, and that prior restraints would be of the shortest possible duration.

In the 1966 *Fanny Hill* case,[48] which involved the book *John Cleland's Memoirs of a Woman of Pleasure*, first published in England in 1748 and convicted of obscenity in Massachusetts in 1821, the U.S. Supreme Court revised its definition of obscenity. The Court was coached by a brilliant defense attorney,[49] who substituted *"redeeming social value"* in his arguments before the Court for the original language of *Roth*. Out of the case came a revision of the three-part definition for a finding of obscenity known as the *Roth-Memoirs* test: (1) the dominant theme of the material taken as a whole appeals to a prurient interest in sex; (2) the material is patently offensive because it affronts contemporary community standards relating to the description or representation of sex; and (3) the material is utterly without redeeming social value. *Value*, it was assumed, would be an easier test to satisfy than *importance*. All three elements would have to coalesce. Patent offensiveness and prurient appeal together could not outweigh social value, about which there would be some hope of getting testimony. Evidence on the first two parts of the test would remain a problem, however.

Despite this emancipating step, definitions of obscenity, pornography, and indecency remained elusive. *Roth-Memoirs* led to *Miller* and today's continuing search for meaning in the context of the Burger Court's definition of obscenity.

Justice Brennan, the principal architect of *Roth-Memoirs*, dissented in *Miller*.[50] He doubted the usefulness of everything he had fashioned in the law of obscenity since *Roth* in 1957. Now seeing nothing but confusion and the danger of infringing upon First Amendment rights, he concluded that "at least in the absence of distribution to juveniles or obtrusive exposure to unconsenting adults, the First and Fourteenth Amendments prohibit the state and federal governments from attempting wholly to suppress sexually oriented material on the basis of their allegedly 'obscene' contents"—essentially the position of the first Presidential Commission on Obscenity and Pornography (the 1970 Lockhart Commission).

Evidence of Harm

Fifty years of empirical study of the effects of erotic expression on attitudes and behavior have not satisfied large segments of society. The Lockhart Commission[51] found no evidence of a causal connection between obscenity and antisocial conduct. Its report recommended repeal of all federal, state, and local obscenity laws affecting adults, but it believed children and personal privacy deserved protection. In addition, it proposed sex education for everyone. Sixteen years later, the Attorney General's Commission on Pornography (Meese Commission)[52] came to opposite conclusions, blaming obscenity or pornography (the commission used the concepts interchangeably) for many of society's ills and calling for a legal crackdown.

Clearly, legislators do not have to wait for hard evidence before enacting laws to punish obscenity, nor, as has been noted, do jurors and judges have to give weight to so-called expert witnesses. Jurors can determine whether something is obscene simply by listening to it or

---

44. *Rowan v. United States Post Office Department,* 397 U.S. 728 (1970); *Stanley v. Georgia,* 394 U.S. 557 (1969).
45. *Ginsburg v. State of New York,* 1 Med. L. Rptr. 1424, 390 U.S. 629 (1968); *New York v. Ferber,* 8 Med. L. Rptr. 1809, 458 U.S. 747 (1982).
46. *Bantam Books v. Sullivan,* 1 Med. L. Rptr. 1116, 372 U.S. 58 (1963). It is important to note that in this case, which prohibited the Rhode Island Commission to Encourage Morality in Youth from book banning, the Supreme Court found its *Pentagon Papers* case rule: "Any system of prior restraints of expression comes to this Court bearing a heavy presumption against its constitutional validity." See also *Southeastern Promotions, Limited v. Conrad,* 1 Med. L. Rptr. 1140, 420 U.S. 546 (1975).
47. *Freedman v. State of Maryland,* 1 Med. L. Rptr. 1126, 380 U.S. 51 (1965).
48. *A Book, Etc. v. Attorney General of Commonwealth of Mass.,* 383 U.S. 413 (1966).
49. See Charles Rembar, *The End of Obscenity* (1968).

50. Brennan's dissent appears in a companion case, *Paris Adult Theatre I v. Slaton,* 413 U.S. 49 (1973).
51. *1970 Report of the Presidential Commission on Obscenity and Pornography* (New York: Bantam Books, 1970).
52. *Final Report* (Washington, D.C.: U.S. Department of Justice, 1986).

looking at it. And community standards are often whatever a judge or jury decides they are.

Courts are ambivalent about how to assess comparative evidence of obscenity's effects, expert testimony, and attitude surveys. At the federal level, comparative evidence has been discouraged because it may confuse the jurors more than they are already confused by their own subjective responses to obscenity. Chief Justice Warren Burger reflected this subjectivity when he wrote in a companion case to *Miller* that the films in the case "are the best evidence of what they represent." So did Justice Potter Stewart's famous line that while he couldn't define obscenity, "I know it when I see it."[53]

The highest court of Massachusetts held that a properly conducted public opinion survey would be admissible if it addressed itself to state obscenity standards.[54] An Illinois appellate court held that a trial court erred in not admitting into the record evidence from a public opinion poll. The survey results, it said, were strong evidence that community standards would not reject the portrayal of sexually explicit material in movies when access to the movies was limited to adult viewers.[55]

A Georgia court, however, held that survey evidence concerning Larry Flynt's *Hustler* and other magazines was admissible where "there was no attempt in the survey itself to determine whether respondents were of the opinion that the content of the . . . magazines would or would not exceed the limits of permissible candor in the depiction of 'nudity and sex.' "[56]

Even more confusion would result from efforts to test the limits of the public with respect to "prurient interest" and "patent offensiveness." As has been noted, evidence on these two elements of the definition of obscenity is hard to come by. A scientifically sound estimate of community standards for these two elusive concepts could expose scores of citizens to psychologically traumatizing words and pictures. How to avoid this without biasing the sample by using only "tolerant" members of the community would be a methodological

nightmare. Interviewer effects involving differences in age and gender would also pose problems, as would noncooperation rates.

For many, evidence of this kind is irrelevant anyway. As one writer puts it: "For Frederick Schauer and the Meese Commission, pornography is something more than speech. For [Catharine] MacKinnon, pornography is reality. Both views ascribe extraordinary powers to expression. Words and images take on fearsome attributes. They can literally drive history, by 'constructing' entire political, economic, and social structures."[57] Schauer and MacKinnon are both law professors. Schauer worked with the Meese Commission, named for then Attorney General Edwin Meese.

This is not to suggest that communities should reject the use of social surveys as a means of gaining a deeper and more complete understanding of community sentiment and response. Such studies may be the only way to reflect accurately the limits of community tolerance and the delicate balance between constitutional rights and governmental responsibilities.

Protection of Children

Courts as well as national commissions on obscenity have shown a keen interest in protecting children from viewing sexual materials and being involved in its manufacture. That interest was emphasized in a 1968 Supreme Court decision upholding the constitutionality of a New York statute prohibiting the sale of "girlie" magazines to anyone under seventeen. The law prohibited the sale to a minor of any depiction of nudity that included "the showing of . . . female buttocks with less than a full opaque covering, or the showing of the female breast with less than a fully opaque covering of any portion thereof below the top of the nipple. . . ."

Speaking for the Court, Justice Brennan held that the power of the state to control the conduct of children reached beyond the scope of its authority over adults. He also took note of the strong presumption made that parents supported the law.[58]

53. *Jacobellis v. State of Ohio,* 378 U.S. 184 (1964).
54. *Commonwealth v. Trainor,* 3 Med. L. Rptr. 2392, 374 N.E.2d 1216 (Mass. 1978).
55. *People v. Nelson,* 410 N.E.2d 476 (Ill. 1980).
56. *Flynt v. State,* 5 Med. L. Rptr. 2418, 264 S.E.2d 669 (Ga. 1980).

57. Steven G. Gey, *The Apologetics of Suppression: The Regulation of Pornography as Act and Idea,* 86 Mich.L.Rev. 1564, 1606 (June 1988).
58. *Ginsberg v. State of New York,* 390 U.S. 629 (1968).

The case illustrates the idea of variable obscenity: material that would not have been obscene if sold to adults was obscene when sold to juveniles or to the educationally underprivileged. The First Amendment rights of children are not equivalent to the First Amendment rights of adults. A 1982 New York case permitted the Court to go even farther.

In *New York v. Ferber*,[59] a case highly relevant to current computer-driven concerns, the Court supported an outright ban on the exhibition of films that visually depict sexual conduct by children under sixteen whether such presentations are obscene under the *Miller* guidelines or not. The Court seemed unwilling to take any chances where children were concerned. It noted that forty-seven states and the Congress had passed laws specifically directed at child pornography. Half of these did not require that the banned material be legally obscene.

While admitting its own struggle with "the intractable obscenity problem," notably the definition of obscenity, the Court remained firm in its position that "the states have a legitimate interest in prohibiting dissemination of obscene material when the mode of dissemination carries with it a significant danger of offending the sensibilities of unwilling recipients or of exposure to juveniles." A portion of the case follows:

New York v. Ferber
458 U.S. 747, 102 S. CT. 3348, 73 L. ED. 2D 1113 (1982).

* * *

Justice WHITE delivered the opinion of the Court.

* * *

First. It is evident beyond the need for elaboration that a state's interest in "safeguarding the physical and psychological well being of a minor" is "compelling." * * * "A democratic society rests, for its continuance, upon the healthy well-rounded growth of young people into full maturity as citizens." *Prince v. Massachusetts,* 321 U.S. 158, 168 (1944). Accordingly, we have sustained legislation aimed at protecting the

---

59. 458 U.S. 747 (1982).

physical and emotional well-being of youth even when the laws have operated in the sensitive area of constitutionally protected rights. In *Prince v. Massachusetts, supra,* the Court held that a statute prohibiting use of a child to distribute literature on the street was valid notwithstanding the statute's effect on a First Amendment activity. In *Ginsberg v. New York,* 390 U.S. 629 (1968), we sustained a New York law protecting children from exposure to nonobscene literature. Most recently, we held that the government's interest in the "well-being of its youth" justified special treatment of indecent broadcasting received by adults as well as children. *FCC v. Pacifica Foundation,* 438 U.S. 726 (1978).

The prevention of sexual exploitation and abuse of children constitutes a government objective of surpassing importance. The legislative findings accompanying passage of the New York laws reflect this concern:

> "There has been a proliferation of children as subjects in sexual performances. The care of children is a sacred trust and should not be abused by those who seek to profit through a commercial network based on the exploitation of children. The public policy of the state demands the protection of children from exploitation through sexual performances." *Laws of N.Y., 1977,* ch. 910, § 1.

We shall not second-guess this legislative judgment. Respondent has not intimated that we do so. Suffice it to say that virtually all of the States and the United States have passed legislation proscribing the production of or otherwise combatting "child pornography." The legislative judgment, as well as the judgment found in the relevant literature, is that the use of children as subjects of pornographic materials is harmful to the physiological, emotional, and mental health of the child. [There follows a substantial list of social science authority for the foregoing statement.] That judgment, we think easily passes muster under the First Amendment.

Second. The distribution of photographs and films depicting sexual activity by juveniles is intrinsically related to the sexual abuse of children in at least two ways. First, the materials produced are a permanent record of the children's participation and the harm to the child is exacerbated by their circulation. Second, the distribution network for child pornography must be closed if the production of material which requires the sexual exploitation of children is to be effectively controlled. Indeed, there is no serious contention that the legislature was unjustified in believing that it is difficult, if not impossible, to halt the exploitation of children by pursuing only those who produce the photographs and movies. While the production of pornographic materials is a low-profile, clandestine industry, the need to market the resulting products requires a visible apparatus of distribution. The most expeditious if not the only practical method of law enforcement may be to dry up the market for this material by imposing severe criminal penalties on persons selling, advertising, or otherwise promoting the product. Thirty-five States and Congress have concluded that restraints on the distribution of pornographic materials are required in order to effectively combat the problem, and there is a body of literature and testimony to support these legislative conclusions. * * *

Respondent does not contend that the State is unjustified in pursuing those who distribute child pornography. Rather, he argues that it is enough for the State to prohibit the distribution of materials that are legally obscene under the *Miller* test. While some States may find that this approach properly accommodates its interests, it does not follow that the First Amendment prohibits a State from going further. The *Miller* standard, like all general definitions of what may be banned as obscene, does not reflect the State's particular and more compelling interest in prosecuting those who promote the sexual exploitation of children. Thus, the question under the *Miller* test of whether a work, taken as a whole, appeals to the prurient interest of the average person bears no connection to the issue of whether a child has been physically or psychologically harmed in the production of the work. Similarly, a sexually explicit depiction need not be "patently offensive" in order to have required the sexual exploitation of a child for its production. In addition, a work which, taken on the whole, contains serious literary, artistic, political, or scientific value may nevertheless embody the hardest core of child pornography. "It is irrelevant to the child [who has been abused] whether or not the material * * * has a literary, artistic, political, or social value." * * * We therefore cannot conclude that the *Miller* standard is a satisfactory solution to the child pornography problem.

Third. The advertising and selling of child pornography provides an economic motive for and is thus an integral part of the production of such materials, an activity illegal throughout the nation. "It rarely has been suggested that the constitutional freedom for speech and press extends its immunity to speech or writing used as an integral part of conduct in violation of a valid criminal statute." *Giboney v. Empire Storage & Ice Co.,* 336 U.S. 490, 498 (1949). We note that were the statutes outlawing the employment of children in these films and photographs fully effective, and the constitutionality of these laws have not been questioned, the First Amendment implications would be no greater than that presented by laws against distribution: enforceable production laws would leave no child pornography to be marketed.

Fourth. The value of permitting live performances and photographic reproductions of children engaged in lewd sexual conduct is exceedingly modest, if not *de minimis.* We consider it unlikely that visual depictions of children performing sexual acts or lewdly exhibiting their genitals would often constitute an important and necessary part of a literary performance or scientific or educational work. As the trial court in this case observed, if it were necessary for literary or artistic value, a person over the statutory age who perhaps looked younger could be utilized. Simulation outside of the prohibition of the statute could provide another alternative. Nor is there any question here of censoring a particular literary theme or portrayal of sexual activity. The First Amendment interest is limited to that of rendering the portrayal somewhat more "realistic" by utilizing or photographing children.

Fifth. Recognizing and classifying child pornography as a category of material outside the protection of the First Amendment is not incompatible with our earlier decisions. "The question whether speech is, or is not protected by the First Amendment often depends on the content of the speech. * * * It is the content of an utterance that determines whether it is a protected epithet or an unprotected 'fighting comment.' " *Young v. American Mini Theatres,* [427 U.S. 50,] at 66.

* * * Leaving aside the special considerations when public officials are the target, *New York Times v. Sullivan,* 376 U.S. 254 (1964), a libelous publication is not protected by the Constitution. * * * Thus, it is not rare that a content-based classification of speech has been accepted because it may be appropriately generalized that within the confines of the given classification, the evil to be restricted so overwhelmingly outweighs the expressive interests, if any, at stake, that no process of case-by-case adjudication is required. When a definable class of material, such as that covered by § 263.15, bears so heavily and pervasively on the welfare of children engaged in its production, we think the balance of competing interests is clearly struck and that it is permissible to consider these materials as without the protection of the First Amendment.

* * *

Because § 263.15 is not substantially overbroad, it is unnecessary to consider its application to material that does not depict sexual conduct of a type that New York may restrict consistent with the First Amendment. As applied to Paul Ferber and to others who distribute similar material, the statute does not violate the First Amendment as applied to the States through the Fourteenth. The decision of the New York Court of Appeals is reversed and the case is remanded to that Court for further proceedings not inconsistent with this opinion.

So ordered.

COMMENT

Lower state and federal courts appear determined to protect the physical and psychological well-being of children.[60] Federal courts have since upheld the constitutionality of ordinances requiring stores to cover portions of some adult magazines with "blinder racks" or opaque covers. In 1986, however, the Fourth Circuit Court of Appeals overturned a Virginia statute prohibiting the display of sexually explicit materials to juveniles. The court feared that the law would lead vendors to restrict adult access to protected, nonobscene materials. Blinder racks, covers, adults-only sales areas, and similar devices, the court said, were either unconstitutional or ineffective.

The Supreme Court later sent two factual questions back to the Virginia Supreme Court, which subsequently ruled that the sixteen books in question were not harmful to juveniles and that the bookseller had made reasonable efforts to prevent juveniles from perusing potentially harmful material. The U.S. Supreme Court then vacated the Fourth Circuit's decision, and the constitutional questions originally raised by the case were left unanswered.[61]

Statutes regulating the display of materials deemed harmful to minors were neither constitutionally overbroad nor a prior restraint, said the Tennessee Supreme Court. Display ordinances did not suppress erotic materials and would have only an incidental effect on adults. Seizure of the material would depend upon its obscenity and require procedural safeguards. Material said to manifest "excessive violence" would be another matter, said the court, because that term is unconstitutionally vague.[62]

A federal district court in Missouri agreed in striking down a law that forbade sale or rental to persons under seventeen of videos that have "a tendency to cater or appeal to morbid interests in violence." The law was unconstitutionally vague and was not narrowly tailored to serve a compelling state interest. Violent expression, unlike obscenity, said the court, is protected by the First Amendment.[63] Violence is tolerable; sex is not.

A similar fate overtook Washington State's "erotic music statute." A King County court said that there was no way persons affected by the law could know what the law is. The vagueness of the word "erotic" offended the First Amendment and the Due Process Clause of the Fourteenth Amendment. The law required that "erotic" albums had to be sold with an "Adults Only" label affixed.[64]

---

60. *United States v. Evergreen Media Corp. of Chicago,* 21 Med. L. Rptr. 1942, 831 F.Supp. 1183 (N.D.Ill. 1993).

61. *American Booksellers Ass'n v. Virginia,* 12 Med. L. Rptr. 2271, 792 F.2d 1261 (4th Cir. 1986); *Commonwealth of Virginia v. American Booksellers Ass'n,* 15 Med. L. Rptr. 2078, 372 S.E.2d 618 (Va. 1988).

62. *David-Kidd Booksellers Inc. v. McWhorter,* 22 Med. L. Rptr. 1225, 866 S.W.2d 520 (Tenn. 1993).

63. *Video Software Dealers Ass'n v. Webster,* 19 Med. L. Rptr. 1649, 773 F.Supp. 1275 (W.D.Mo. 1991).

64. *Soundgarden v. Eikenberry,* 21 Med. L. Rptr. 1025 (Wash.Sup.Ct. 1992).

In 1990, the U.S. Supreme Court upheld prosecution of those who view child pornography in their homes. Reversing a decision it had made in 1969, the Court ruled that it was reasonable for a state to conclude that the production of child pornography would be reduced if there were penalties for those who possess and view it.[65]

Zoning Laws

Concern for protection of children is related to the permissiveness the courts have shown in letting a city's compelling interest in regulating the use of its commercial property override allegations of prior restraint.

A major issue for local authorities has been whether adult bookstores and theaters ought to be scattered through a community or clustered in what, in larger communities, sometimes comes to be called a "combat zone." While zoning ordinances must not be vague or overbroad, they do seem to win judicial approval when they are carefully drafted and allow for timely adjudication. But the absurd enters into this realm of control also.

In 1972, Detroit adopted ordinances requiring the dispersal of adult theaters, those that dealt with "specific sexual activities or anatomical areas." In addition, an adult theater could not be located within 1,000 feet of any *two* other "regulated uses." Regulated uses referred to other adult theaters or bookstores, cabarets, bars, pawnshops, hotels or motels, pool halls, public lodging houses, secondhand stores, shoeshine parlors, and taxi dance halls. Furthermore, an adult theater had to be at least 500 feet from any residential area. That would assure isolation?

The ordinances survived a constitutional challenge because, said the Supreme Court, the content affected was less important than ideas having social or political significance.[66] Ten years later, the Court relied on its opinion in the Detroit case to uphold a Renton (Washington) zoning ordinance as a time, place, and manner regulation designed to preserve the quality of urban life.[67] Unlike Detroit's "dispersal" ordinance, the Renton law "concentrated" adult theaters, but similar ordinances have been struck down.

An Ann Arbor (Michigan) law, for example, failed to survive. There a geographer testified that only 0.23 percent of the city's space could lawfully contain an adult bookstore under the law. Also flawed was the law's requirement that no more than 20 percent of a bookstore's total stock be adult in nature, the assumption being that everything "adult" is obscene. "It is clearly quite restrictive," said the Sixth Circuit Court of Appeals, "to permit a business to engage in . . . protected expression only 20 percent of the time."[68]

A New Jersey ordinance aimed at live nude dancing prohibited all live entertainment including plays, concerts, musicals, and dance. Such a law, said the Supreme Court, violated the First and Fourteenth Amendments.[69]

Lower courts are still perplexed about how to define "residential" areas and "community standards," and where to locate adult entertainment businesses. Meanwhile the definition of obscenity remains, in the words of Justice John Paul Stevens, "dim and uncertain."

The Politics of Pornography

Pornography readily lends itself to politicization. While the Meese Report may have engaged in the selective use of social evidence to support its moral assumptions, and in overkill in its prescriptions, its major recommendation was that state legislatures amend their obscenity statutes to incorporate provisions of the federal Racketeer Influenced and Corrupt Organizations (RICO) law, a subsection of the federal Organized Crime Control Act of 1970.[70] More than half the states have since complied.

Criminal penalties under the act include fines of up to $25,000 or imprisonment for up to twenty years, or both, and forfeiture of any and all assets acquired or maintained through a violation of the law—even though some of those assets may qualify as protected speech. The purpose of forfeiture is to confiscate material gains made through racketeering activities. Attached

65. *Osborne v. Ohio,* 495 U.S. 103 (1990), modifying *Stanley v. Georgia,* 394 U.S. 557 (1969).

66. *Young v. American Mini Theatres,* 1 Med. L. Rptr. 1151, 427 U.S. 50 (1976).

67. *City of Renton v. Playtime Theatres, Inc.,* 12 Med. L. Rptr. 1721, 475 U.S. 41 (1986).

68. *Christy v. Ann Arbor,* 14 Med. L. Rptr. 1483, 824 F.2d 489 (6th Cir. 1987).

69. *Schad v. Mont Ephraim,* 7 Med. L. Rptr. 1426, 452 U.S. 61 (1981).

70. 18 U.S.C. § 1467 (1988). Obscenity became a predicate offense in a 1984 amendment to the statute.

to criminal penalties are civil penalties, including divestment and treble damages. The federal statute has been applied with telling effect even in states without RICO laws.

An early application of the law by the Department of Justice's National Obscenity Enforcement Unit came in Virginia in 1987. Prosecutors closed down an adult bookstore by seizing the personal and business assets of four persons allegedly engaged in the distribution of obscene films and books. Convicted on three counts of racketeering and seven counts of interstate distribution of $105.30 worth of obscene materials, the defendants faced life imprisonment and the forfeiture of a warehouse, bank accounts, stock, the contents of their stores—both the obscene and the nonobscene—and eight videotape clubs valued at $1 million. All assets were considered part of a criminal enterprise.[71]

Not surprisingly, the constitutionality of laws as draconian as these has been challenged. In 1989, the U.S. Supreme Court, over the strong objections of Justice Stevens, upheld the constitutionality of Indiana's RICO statute when it was applied to obscene material; the law, said the Court, did not impose a prior restraint. The Court objected only to the seizure of the contents of a bookstore before an adversarial hearing had been held to determine whether the seized material was obscene—a denial of due process.[72]

The constitutionality of forfeiture was reinforced in a Minnesota case in which the defendant's entire adult entertainment business was confiscated, the constitutionally protected along with the obscene. Federal prosecutors in this case went so far as to attempt to indict the defendant's attorney. They failed. The U.S. Supreme Court, however, said that the penalties levied constituted subsequent punishment, not prior restraint, and that they had no chilling effect. Nor was RICO overbroad and its penalties cruel and unusual, or excessive, although on the latter point the case was remanded to the Eighth Circuit Court of Appeals. See p. 59.

Ferris Alexander forfeited his business and $9 million, said to have been acquired through rack-

eteering activities, and he was sent to a federal prison for six years. The Court's opinion follows:

Alexander v. United States
21 MED. L. RPTR. 1609, 113 S.CT. 2766 (1993).

REHNQUIST, C.J.:

After a full criminal trial, petitioner Ferris J. Alexander, owner of more than a dozen stores and theaters dealing in sexually explicit materials, was convicted on 17 obscenity counts and 3 counts of violating the Racketeer Influenced and Corrupt Organizations Act (RICO). The obscenity convictions, based on the jury's findings that four magazines and three videotapes sold at several of petitioner's stores were obscene, served as the predicates for his three RICO convictions. In addition to imposing a prison term and fine, the District Court ordered petitioner to forfeit, pursuant to 18 U.S.C. § 1963 (1988 ed. and Supp. III), certain assets that were directly related to his racketeering activity as punishment for his RICO violations. Petitioner argues that this forfeiture violated the First and Eighth Amendments to the Constitution. We reject petitioner's claims under the First Amendment but remand for reconsideration of his Eighth Amendment challenge.

Petitioner was in the so-called "adult entertainment" business for more than 30 years, selling pornographic magazines and sexual paraphernalia, showing sexually explicit movies, and eventually selling and renting videotapes of a similar nature. He received shipments of these materials at a warehouse in Minneapolis, Minnesota, where they were wrapped in plastic, priced, and boxed. He then sold his products through some 13 retail stores in several different Minnesota cities, generating millions of dollars in annual revenues. In 1989, federal authorities filed a 41-count indictment against petitioner and others, alleging operation of a racketeering enterprise in violation of RICO. The indictment charged 34 obscenity counts and 3 RICO counts, the racketeering counts being predicated on the obscenity charges. The indictment also charged numerous counts of tax evasion and related offenses that are not relevant to the questions before us.

Following a 4-month jury trial in the United States District Court for the District of Minnesota, petitioner was convicted of 17 substantive

---

71. *United States v. Pryba,* 674 F.Supp. 1518 (E.D.Va. 1987).
72. *Fort Wayne Books, Inc. v. Indiana,* 16 Med. L. Rptr. 1337, 109 S. Ct. 916 (1989), reversing *4447 Corp. v. Goldsmith,* 504 N.E.2d 559 (Ind. 1987).

obscenity offenses: 12 counts of transporting obscene material in interstate commerce for the purpose of sale or distribution, in violation of 18 U.S.C. § 1465; and 5 counts of engaging in the business of selling obscene material, in violation of 18 U.S.C. § 1466 (1988 ed. and Supp. III). He also was convicted of 3 RICO offenses which were predicated on the obscenity convictions: one count of receiving and using income derived from a pattern of racketeering activity, in violation of 18 U.S.C. § 1962(a); one count of conducting a RICO enterprise, in violation of § 1962(c); and one count of conspiring to conduct a RICO enterprise, in violation of § 1962(d). As a basis for the obscenity and RICO convictions, the jury determined that four magazines and three videotapes were obscene. Multiple copies of these magazines and videos, which graphically depicted a variety of "hard core" sexual acts, were distributed throughout petitioner's adult entertainment empire.

Petitioner was sentenced to a total of six years in prison, fined $100,000, and ordered to pay the cost of prosecution, incarceration, and supervised release. In addition to these punishments, the District Court reconvened the same jury and conducted a forfeiture proceeding pursuant to § 1963(a)(2). At this proceeding, the Government sought forfeiture of the businesses and real estate that represented petitioner's interest in the racketeering enterprise, § 1963(a)(2)(A), the property that afforded petitioner influence over that enterprise, § 1963(a)(2)(D), and the assets and proceeds petitioner had obtained from his racketeering offenses, §1963(a)(1), (3). The jury found that petitioner had an interest in 10 pieces of commercial real estate and 31 current or former businesses, all of which had been used to conduct his racketeering enterprise. Sitting without the jury, the District Court then found that petitioner had acquired a variety of assets as a result of his racketeering activities. The court ultimately ordered petitioner to forfeit his wholesale and retail businesses (including all the assets of those businesses) and almost $9 million in moneys acquired through racketeering activity.[1]

---

1. Not wishing to go into the business of selling pornographic materials—regardless of whether they were legally obscene—the Government decided that it would be better to destroy the forfeited expressive materials than sell them to members of the public. See Brief for United States 26–27, n. 11.

The Court of Appeals affirmed the District Court's forfeiture order. *Alexander v. Thornburgh*, 943 F. 2d 825 (CA8 1991). It rejected petitioner's argument that the application of RICO's forfeiture provisions constituted a prior restraint on speech and hence violated the First Amendment. Recognizing the well-established distinction between prior restraints and subsequent criminal punishments, the Court of Appeals found that the forfeiture here was "a criminal penalty imposed following a conviction for conducting an enterprise engaged in racketeering activities," and not a prior restraint on speech. The court also rejected petitioner's claim that RICO's forfeiture provisions are constitutionally overbroad, pointing out that the forfeiture order was properly limited to assets linked to petitioner's past racketeering offenses. Lastly, the Court of Appeals concluded that the forfeiture order does not violate the Eighth Amendment's prohibition again "cruel and unusual punishments" and "excessive fines." In so ruling, however, the court did not consider whether the forfeiture in this case was grossly disproportionate or excessive, believing that the Eighth Amendment " 'does not require a proportionality review of any sentence less than life imprisonment without the possibility of parole.' " We granted certiorari.

Petitioner first contends that the forfeiture in this case, which effectively shut down his adult entertainment business, constituted an unconstitutional prior restraint on speech, rather than a permissible criminal punishment. According to petitioner, forfeiture of expressive materials and the assets of businesses engaged in expressive activity, when predicated solely upon previous obscenity violations, operates as a prior restraint because it prohibits future presumptively protected expression in retaliation for prior unprotected speech. Practically speaking, petitioner argues, the effect of the RICO forfeiture order here was no different from the injunction prohibiting the publication of expressive material found to be a prior restraint in *Near v. Minnesota ex rel. Olson*, 283 U.S. 697 [1 Med. L. Rptr. 1001] (1931). As petitioner puts it, the forfeiture order imposed a complete *ban* on his future expression because of previous unprotected speech. We disagree. By lumping the forfeiture imposed in this case after a full criminal trial with an injunction enjoining future speech, petitioner stretches the term "prior restraint" well beyond the limits established by our cases. To accept petitioner's argument would virtually obliterate the distinction, solidly grounded in our cases, between prior restraints and subsequent punishments. The term prior restraint is used "to describe administrative and judicial orders *forbidding* certain communications when issued in advance of the time that such communications are to occur." M. Nimmer, Nimmer on Freedom of Speech § 4.03, p. 4–14 (1984) (emphasis added). Temporary restraining orders and permanent injunctions—*i.e.,* court orders that actually forbid speech activities—are classic examples of prior restraints. This understanding of what constitutes a prior restraint is borne out by our cases, even those on which petitioner relies. * * * And in *Vance,* we struck down a Texas statute that authorized courts, upon a showing that obscene films had been shown in the past, to issue an injunction of indefinite duration prohibiting the future exhibition of films that have not yet been found to be obscene. 445 U.S., at 311.

By contrast, the RICO forfeiture order in this case does not *forbid* petitioner from engaging in any expressive activities in the future, nor does it require him to obtain prior approval for any expressive activities. It only deprives him of specific assets that were found to be related to his previous racketeering violations. Assuming, of course, that he has sufficient untainted assets to open new stores, restock his inventory, and hire staff, petitioner can go back into the adult entertainment business tomorrow, and sell as many sexually explicit magazines and videotapes as he likes, without any risk of being held in contempt for violating a court order.

* * *

In this case * * * the assets in question were not ordered forfeited because they were believed to be obscene, but because they were directly related to petitioner's past racketeering violations. The RICO forfeiture statute calls for the forfeiture of assets because of the financial role they play in the operation of the racketeering enterprise. The statute is oblivious to the expressive or nonexpressive nature of the assets forfeited; books, sports cars, narcotics, and cash are all forfeitable alike under RICO. Indeed, a contrary scheme would be disastrous from a policy standpoint, enabling racketeers to evade forfeiture by investing the proceeds of their crimes in businesses

engaging in expressive activity. Nor were the assets in question ordered forfeited without according petitioner the requisite procedural safeguards, another recurring theme in our prior restraint cases. Contrasting this case with *Fort Wayne Books, Inc. v. Indiana,* 489 U.S. 46 [16 Med. L. Rptr. 1337] (1989), aptly illustrates this point. In *Fort Wayne Books,* we rejected on constitutional grounds the pretrial seizure of certain expressive material that was based upon a finding of "no more than *probable cause to believe* that a RICO violation had occurred." In so holding, we emphasized that there had been no prior judicial "determination that the seized items were 'obscene' or that a RICO violation *ha[d] occurred.*" "[M]ere probable cause to believe a legal violation ha[d] transpired," we said, "is not adequate to remove books or films from circulation." Here, by contrast, the seizure was not premature, because the Government established beyond a reasonable doubt the basis for the forfeiture. Petitioner had a full criminal trial on the merits of the obscenity and RICO charges during which the Government proved that four magazines and three videotapes were obscene and that the other forfeited assets were directly linked to petitioner's commission of racketeering offenses.

Petitioner's claim that the RICO forfeiture statute operated as an unconstitutional prior restraint in this case is also inconsistent with our decision in *Arcara v. Cloud Books, Inc.,* 478 U.S. 697 (1986). In that case, we sustained a court order, issued under a general nuisance statute, that closed down an adult bookstore that was being used as a place of prostitution and lewdness. In rejecting out-of-hand a claim that the closure order amounted to an improper prior restraint on speech, we stated:

> "The closure order sought in this case differs from a prior restraint in two significant respects. First, the order would impose no restraint at all on the dissemination of particular materials, since respondents are free to carry on their bookselling business at another location, even if such locations are difficult to find. Second, the closure order sought would not be imposed on the basis of an advance determination that the distribution of particular materials is prohibited—indeed, the imposition of the closure order has nothing to do with any expressive conduct at all."

This reasoning applies with equal force to this case, and thus confirms that the RICO forfeiture order was not a prior restraint on speech, but a punishment for past criminal conduct. Petitioner attempts to distinguish *Arcara* on the ground that obscenity, unlike prostitution or lewdness, has " 'a significant expressive element.' " But that distinction has no bearing on the question whether the forfeiture order in this case was an impermissible prior restraint.

Finally, petitioner's proposed definition of the term "prior restraint" would undermine the time-honored distinction between barring speech in the future and penalizing past speech. The doctrine of prior restraint originated in the common law of England, where prior restraints of the press were not permitted, but punishment after publication was. This very limited application of the principle of freedom of speech was held inconsistent with our First Amendment as long ago as *Grosjean v. American Press Co.,* 297 U.S. 233, 246 [1 Med. L. Rptr. 2685] (1936). While we may have given a broader definition to the term "prior restraint" than was given to it in English common law, our decisions have steadfastly preserved the distinction between prior restraints and subsequent punishments. Though petitioner tries to dismiss this distinction as "neither meaningful nor useful," we think it is critical to our First Amendment jurisprudence. Because we have interpreted the First Amendment as providing greater protection from prior restraints than from subsequent punishments, it is important for us to delineate with some precision the defining characteristics of a prior restraint. To hold that the forfeiture order in this case constituted a prior restraint would have the exact opposite effect: it would blur the line separating prior restraints from subsequent punishments to such a degree that it would be impossible to determine with any certainty whether a particular measure is a prior restraint or not.

In sum, we think that fidelity to our cases requires us to analyze the forfeiture here not as a prior restraint, but under normal First Amendment standards. * * *

Confronted with our decisions in *Fort Wayne Books* and *Arcara*—neither of which he challenges—petitioner's position boils down to this: stiff criminal penalties for obscenity offenses are consistent with the First Amendment; so is the forfeiture of expressive materials as punishment for criminal conduct; but the combination of the two somehow results in a violation of the First Amendment. We reject this counter-intuitive conclusion, which in effect would say that the whole is greater than the sum of the parts.

* * *

Petitioner contends that forfeiture of his entire business was an "excessive" penalty for the Government to exact "[o]n the basis of a few materials the jury ultimately decided were obscene." It is somewhat misleading, we think, to characterize the racketeering crimes for which petitioner was convicted as involving just a few materials ultimately found to be obscene. Petitioner was convicted of creating and managing what the District Court described as "an enormous racketeering enterprise." It is in light of the extensive criminal activities which petitioner apparently conducted through this racketeering enterprise over a substantial period of time that the question of whether or not the forfeiture was "excessive" must be considered. We think it preferable that this question be addressed by the Court of Appeals in the first instance.

For these reasons, we hold that RICO's forfeiture provisions, as applied in this case, did not violate the First Amendment, but that the Court of Appeals should have considered whether they resulted in an "excessive" penalty within the meaning of the Eighth Amendment's Excessive Fines Clause. Accordingly, we vacate the judgment of the Court of Appeals and remand the case for further proceedings consistent with this opinion.

It is so ordered.

COMMENT

Justices Kennedy, Blackmun, and Stevens, joined by Souter in part, dissented. Nonobscene material could not be constitutionally forfeited, they argued. Calling the Court's decision a grave repudiation of First Amendment principles, the minority argued that forfeiture, with its "unprecedented sweep," should not be equated with fines and imprisonment. Under the Act, a bookstore, is not temporarily closed—it is permanently destroyed.

"Under the principle the Court adopts," wrote Justice Kennedy, "any bookstore or press enterprise could be forfeited as punishment for even a single obscenity conviction." "Books and films," he added, "are condemned and destroyed not for their own content but for the content of their owner's prior speech. Our law does not permit the government to burden future speech for this sort of taint."

Under state and federal RICO laws, federal obscenity indictments have seen a huge increase. This trend has been accompanied by a nationwide crackdown, known as Project PostPorn, on firms that produce and mail obscene materials across state lines. The Department of Justice, as did the Meese Commission, has encouraged federal prosecutors to charge obscenity producers and distributors in several jurisdictions at the same time to increase the cost of defending the cases.

Reactions to the project have included charges of harassment, intimidation, violation of the First Amendment principle of no prior restraint, and denial of due process. Support for the laws has come from some conservatives playing the role of moral arbiters and radical feminists arguing with some force that pornography is an attack on the civil rights of women. The most prominent of the latter has been Professor Catharine MacKinnon of the University of Michigan Law School. She proposes what some have called "progressive censorship."

MacKinnon argues that pornography leads to the terrorization of women by men in such a way that the free speech accorded men silences the free speech of women. Pornography, she contends, is ultimately not speech but action leading to the submission of women.[73]

City councils in both Minneapolis and Indianapolis approved ordinances written by MacKinnon and feminist author Andrea Dworkin incorporating these ideas. Dworkin believes that most if not all gender relationships allow men to oppress women. After the Minneapolis city council approved the MacKinnon-Dworkin statute, the mayor vetoed it. The Indianapolis law, passed by the city council and signed into law by the mayor, did not survive its first federal appellate court test of constitutionality:

American Booksellers Association v. Hudnut

11 MED. L. RPTR. 2465, 771 F.2D 323 (7TH CIR. 1985).

EASTERBROOK, J.:

Indianapolis enacted an ordinance defining "pornography" as a practice that discriminates against women. "Pornography" is to be redressed through the administrative and judicial methods used for other discrimination. The City's definition of "pornography" is considerably different from "obscenity," which the Supreme Court has held is not protected by the First Amendment.

* * *

"Pornography" under the ordinance is "the graphic sexually explicit subordination of women, whether in pictures or in words, that also includes one or more of the following:

(1) Women are presented as sexual objects who enjoy pain or humiliation; or
(2) Women are presented as sexual objects who experience sexual pleasure in being raped; or
(3) Women are presented as sexual objects tied up or cut up or mutilated or bruised or physically hurt, or as dismembered or truncated or fragmented or severed into body parts; or
(4) Women are presented as being penetrated by objects or animals; or
(5) Women are presented in scenarios of degradation, injury, abasement, torture, shown as filthy or inferior, bleeding, bruised, or hurt in a context that makes these conditions sexual; or
(6) Women are presented as sexual objects for domination, conquest, violation, exploitation, possession, or use, or through postures or positions of servility or submission or display." Indianapolis Code § 16–3(q).

The statute provides that the "use of men, children, or transsexuals in the place of women in paragraphs (1) through (6) above shall also constitute pornography under this section." The ordinance as passed in April 1984 defined "sexually explicit" to mean actual or simulated intercourse or the uncovered exhibition of the genitals, buttocks or anus. An amendment in June 1984 deleted this provision, leaving the term undefined.

The Indianapolis ordinance does not refer to the prurient interest, to offensiveness, or to the standards of the community. It demands attention to particular depictions, not to the work judged as a whole. It is irrelevant under the ordinance whether the work has literary, artistic, political, or scientific value. The City and many amici point to these omissions as virtues. They maintain that pornography influences attitudes, and the statute is a way to alter the socialization of men and women rather than to vindicate community standards of offensiveness. And as one of the principal drafters of the ordinance has asserted, "if a woman is subjected, why should it matter that the work has other value?" Catharine

---

73. Catharine A. MacKinnon, *Feminism Unmodified* (Cambridge, Mass.: Harvard University Press, 1987).

A. MacKinnon, *Pornography, Civil Rights, and Speech,* 20 Harv. Civ. Rts.—Civ. Lib. L.Rev. 1, 21 (1985).

Civil rights groups and feminists have entered this case as amici on both sides. Those supporting the ordinance say that it will play an important role in reducing the tendency of men to view women as sexual objects, a tendency that leads to both unacceptable attitudes and discrimination in the workplace and violence away from it. Those opposing the ordinance point out that much radical feminist literature is explicit and depicts women in ways forbidden by the ordinance and that the ordinance would reopen old battles. It is unclear how Indianapolis would treat works from James Joyce's *Ulysses* to Homer's *Iliad;* both depict women as submissive objects for conquest and domination.

We do not try to balance the arguments for and against an ordinance such as this. The ordinance discriminates on the ground of the content of the speech. Speech treating women in the approved way—in sexual encounters "premised on equality" (MacKinnon, *supra,* at 22)—is lawful no matter how sexually explicit. Speech treating women in the disapproved way—as submissive in matters sexual or as enjoying humiliation—is unlawful no matter how significant the literary, artistic, or political qualities of the work taken as a whole. The state may not ordain preferred viewpoints in this way. The Constitution forbids the state to declare one perspective right and silence opponents.

The ordinance contains four prohibitions. People may not "traffic" in pornography, "coerce" others into performing in pornographic works, or "force" pornography on anyone. Anyone injured by someone who has seen or read pornography has a right of action against the maker or seller.

* * *

The district court held the ordinance unconstitutional. 598 F.Supp. 1316 (S.D. Ind. 1984). The court concluded that the ordinance regulates speech rather than the conduct involved in making pornography. The regulation of speech could be justified, the court thought, only by a compelling interest in reducing sex discrimination, an interest Indianapolis had not established. The ordinance is also vague and overbroad, the court believed, and establishes a prior restraint of speech.

* * *

Under the ordinance graphic sexually explicit speech is "pornography" or not depending on the perspective the author adopts. Speech that "subordinates" women and also, for example, presents women as enjoying pain, humiliation, or rape, or even simply presents women in "positions of servility or submission or display" is forbidden, no matter how great the literary or political value of the work taken as a whole. Speech that portrays women in positions of equality is lawful, no matter how graphic the sexual content. This is thought control. It establishes an "approved" view of women, of how they may react to sexual encounters, of how the sexes may relate to each other. Those who espouse the approved view may use sexual images; those who do not, may not.

Indianapolis justifies the ordinance on the ground that pornography affects thoughts. Men who see women depicted as subordinate are more likely to treat them so. Pornography is an aspect of dominance. It does not persuade people so much as change them. It works by socializing, by establishing the expected and the permissible. In this view pornography is not an idea; pornography is the injury.

There is much to this perspective. Beliefs are also facts. People often act in accordance with the images and patterns they find around them. People raised in a religion tend to accept the tenets of that religion, often without independent examination. People taught from birth that black people are fit only for slavery rarely rebelled against that creed; beliefs coupled with the self-interest of the masters established a social structure that inflicted great harm while enduring for centuries. Words and images act at the level of the subconscious before they persuade at the level of the conscious. Even the truth has little chance unless a statement fits within the framework of beliefs that may never have been subjected to rational study.

Therefore we accept the premises of this legislation. Depictions of subordination tend to perpetuate subordination. The subordinate status of women in turn leads to affront and lower pay at work, insult and injury at home, battery and rape on the streets. In the language of the legislature, "[p]ornography is central in creating and maintaining sex as a basis of discrimination." * * *

Yet this simply demonstrates the power of pornography as speech. All of these unhappy effects depend on mental intermediation. Pornography affects how people see the world, their fellows, and social relations. If pornography is what pornography does, so is other speech. Hitler's orations affected how some Germans saw Jews. Communism is a world view, not simply a *Manifesto* by Marx and Engels or a set of speeches. * * * The Alien and Sedition Acts passed during the administration of John Adams rested on a sincerely held belief that disrespect for the government leads to social collapse and revolution—a belief with support in the history of many nations. Most governments of the world act on this empirical regularity, suppressing critical speech. In the United States, however, the strength of the support for this belief is irrelevant. * * *

Racial bigotry, anti-semitism, violence on television, reporters' biases—these and many more influence the culture and shape our socialization. None is directly answerable by more speech, unless that speech too finds its place in the popular culture. Yet all is protected as speech, however insidious. Any other answer leaves the government in control of all of the institutions of culture, the great censor and director of which thoughts are good for us.

Sexual responses often are unthinking responses, and the association of sexual arousal with the subordination of women therefore may have a substantial effect. But almost all cultural stimuli provoke unconscious responses. * * * People may be conditioned in subtle ways. If the fact that speech plays a role in a process of conditioning were enough to permit governmental regulation, that would be the end of freedom of speech.

It is possible to interpret the claim that the pornography is the harm in a different way. Indianapolis emphasizes the injury that models in pornographic films and pictures may suffer. The record contains materials depicting sexual torture, penetration of women by redhot irons and the like. These concerns have nothing to do with written materials subject to the statute, and physical injury can occur with or without the "subordination" of women. As we discuss [below], a state may make injury in the course of producing a film unlawful independent of the viewpoint expressed in the film.

The more immediate point, however, is that the image of pain is not necessarily pain. In *Body Double,* a suspense film directed by Brian

DePalma, a woman who has disrobed and presented a sexually explicit display is murdered by an intruder with a drill. The drill runs through the woman's body. The film is sexually explicit and a murder occurs—yet no one believes that the actress suffered pain or died. * * * And this works both ways. The description of women's sexual domination of men in *Lysistrata* was not real dominance. Depictions may affect slavery, war, or sexual roles, but a book about slavery is not itself slavery, or a book about death by poison a murder.

Much of Indianapolis's argument rests on the belief that when speech is "unanswerable," and the metaphor that there is a "marketplace of ideas" does not apply, the First Amendment does not apply either. The metaphor is honored; Milton's *Aeropagitica* and John Stuart Mill's *On Liberty* defend freedom of speech on the ground that the truth will prevail, and many of the most important cases under the First Amendment recite this position. The Framers undoubtedly believed it. As a general matter it is true. But the Constitution does not make the dominance of truth a necessary condition of freedom of speech. To say that it does would be to confuse on outcome of free speech with a necessary condition for the application of the amendment.

A power to limit speech on the ground that truth has not yet prevailed and is not likely to prevail implies the power to declare truth. At some point the government must be able to say (as Indianapolis has said): "We know what the truth is, yet a free exchange of speech has not driven out falsity, so that we must now prohibit falsity." If the government may declare the truth, why wait for the failure of speech? Under the First Amendment, however, there is no such thing as a false idea, *Gertz v. Robert Welch, Inc.,* 418 U.S. 323, 339 (1974), so the government may not restrict speech on the ground that in a free exchange truth is not yet dominant.

* * *

At all events, "pornography" is not low value speech within the meaning of these cases. Indianapolis seeks to prohibit certain speech because it believes this speech influences social relations and politics on a grand scale, that it controls attitudes at home and in the legislature. This precludes a characterization of the speech as low value. True, pornography and obscenity have sex in common. But Indianapolis left out of its definition any reference to literary, artistic, political, or scientific value. The ordinance applies to graphic sexually explicit subordination in works great and small. The Court sometimes balances the value of speech against the costs of its restriction, but it does this by category of speech and not by the content of particular works. * * * Indianapolis has created an approved point of view and so loses the support of these cases.

Any rationale we could imagine in support of this ordinance could not be limited to sex discrimination. Free speech has been on balance an ally of those seeking change. Governments that want stasis start by restricting speech. Culture is a powerful force of continuity; Indianapolis paints pornography as part of the culture of power. Change in any complex system ultimately depends on the ability of outsiders to challenge accepted views and the reigning institutions. Without a strong guarantee of freedom of speech, there is no effective right to challenge what is.

The definition of "pornography" is unconstitutional. No construction or excision of particular terms could save it.

* * *

No amount of struggle with particular words and phrases in this ordinance can leave anything in effect. The district court came to the same conclusion. Its judgment is therefore affirmed.

COMMENT

A problem with this kind of moral maternalism, or paternalism, depending upon its origins, is that it depends upon arbiters outside the judicial structure where constitutional sensitivity is not always highly developed, and it poses the danger of spreading to all forms of "deviant" expression. It makes a crime out of what for many is a sin. It also is essentially reactionary because it would permit the state "to certify a realm of moral certainty in the face of a constitutional structure that denies the state that very power."[74]

Many feminists disagree with MacKinnon as to evidence of harm, questions of consent, and the consequences for feminism if feminism joins

forces with the radical Right to forbid forms of expression by the application of the police power.[75] Nevertheless, MacKinnon's work has altered the terms and the focus of the debate over what to do about obscenity, and it has had a direct effect upon Canadian law. Canada has adopted a federal law similar to what was proposed for the United States. Some of Dworkin's books are now denied entry into Canada.

Another radical approach is Oregon's. its courts have declared the punishment of obscenity unconstitutional under the state constitution, which says, in part: "No law shall be passed restraining the free expression of opinion, or restricting the right to speak, write or print freely *on any subject whatever . . .*" [emphasis added]. Of the *Miller* test, Oregon's Supreme Court has written:

> In a law censoring speech, writing or publication, such an indeterminate test is intolerable. It means that anyone who publishes or distributes arguably "obscene" words or pictures does so at the peril of punishment for making a wrong guess about a jury's estimate of "contemporary state standards" of prurience.[76]

Oregon found its constitutional protection of expression broader than that provided by the First Amendment and, by interpretation, admitting of no exceptions. Recognizing the futility of attempts to suppress the erotic, Oregon would nevertheless protect youth and unwilling viewers.

Uncertainties

The purely rhetorical distinction between obscenity and indecency remains a part of the law. Obscenity can be censored; indecency cannot, at least not where adults alone are concerned—unless it is transmitted electronically. Yet obscenity is used to define indecency. Two 1994 cases reflect these difficulties.

A Tennessee listener invoked the federal law imposing fines of up to $10,000 and up to two

---

74. Gey, *op. cit.,* p. 1613.

75. For example, see Joan Kennedy Taylor, *Does Sexual Speech Harm Women? The Split within Feminism,* 5 Stanford Law & Policy Rev. 49 (Spring 1994); Rosemarie Tong, "Women, Pornography, and the Law," *Academe,* September/October 1987; Wendy McElroy, *XXX: A Woman's Right to Pornography* (New York: St. Martin's Press, 1996).

76. *Oregon v. Henry,* 14 Med. L. Rptr. 1011, 732 P.2d 9 (Ore.S.Ct. 1987).

years in prison against National Public Radio (NPR). During its news program "All Things Considered," NPR had broadcast excerpts from wiretapped telephone conversations between convicted Mafia boss John Gotti and his underworld associates. Gotti's sentence structure depended upon an almost continuous stream of profanities that the listener found indecent. Much argumentation in the case revolved around the question of whether the irate listener had standing to sue. The FCC and the D.C. Circuit Court of Appeals decided that he did not. Furthermore, said the court, the listener's injury was an isolated instance.[77]

In amici briefs opposing the listener's request for review by the U.S. Supreme Court, it was further argued that the listener did not regularly tune in to "All Things Considered" and that he was making no effort through his litigation to protect a child from exposure to indecent material. To protect the rights of radio and television audiences in the future, however those who wrote the briefs would have granted the listener standing to sue in the first place. They were anticipating a positive outcome.

In the realm of obscenity and indecency, there is little agreement as to what is really being talked about. In cultural studies, pornography has been compared to a black mass, to science fiction, to a computer program, to the obliteration of privacy, to shamelessness and thereby inhumaneness in public life, and to various forms of political repression. This is testimony to the subjective responses the concept or concepts evoke.

At the same time, social science has had great difficulty demonstrating a connection between pornography and rape and other crimes. There is a connection between pornography and sexual fantasy, but sexual fantasy is a poor predictor of behavior, criminal or otherwise. Whether pornography harms adolescent boys or girls depends on prior sex education, sex roles, and the availability of alternative imagery.

Certainly, a society that always portrays women as sex objects contributes to the devaluation of women. And what about pornoviolence, that mixture of sex and violence so readily available to television audiences? A University of Wisconsin researcher in a comprehensive review of effects studies, including his own, concluded: "If you take out the sex and leave in the violence, you get increased violent behavior in the laboratory setting . . . if you take out the violence and leave the sex, nothing happens."[78] Violence ought to be a consideration of any repressive strategy.

Perhaps the proposed V-chip that has been mandated by Congress for all new television sets, or the lockbox, will ease the problems for parents—if expected First Amendment challenges to the V-chip fail. So might the complementary voluntary program content rating system accepted by network leaders at the White House on February 29, 1996. The program created a rating system similar to that used by film studios and went into effect in January 1997. CNN's Ted Turner, fearing the agreement would be detrimental to cutting-edge programming, said he was forced to do this "voluntarily." He also wondered how news magazines and cartoon shows would be rated.

A judge or a jury still has no precise constitutional guidelines to follow in deciding what is obscene or indecent. Community standards are pretty much what judges and juries say they are, as long as the judges and jurors act as "reasonable" people. But reasonable people often disagree. This places great pressure on the jury system.

Furthermore, no one knows what kind of evidence of prurient interest, patent offensiveness, and community standards will be admissible from one court to another. Expert witnesses can make a difference where "serious value" is the question, but in the final analysis, jurors, however unrepresentative of the public they may be, will decide what is obscene (and indecent) and not obscene under the standards of *Miller v. California.*

There is evidence that jurors, like the rest of us, often believe that deviant messages will have a more deleterious effect on others than on themselves and, therefore, that those others must be protected. In one study, women were more willing to censor than men, and age, religiosity and

---

77. *Branton v. FCC,* 21 Med. L. Rptr. 1532, 993 F.2d 906 (D.C. Cir. 1993).

78. Edward Donnerstein, Daniel, Linz and Steven Penrod, *The Question of Pornography: Research Findings and Policy Implications?* (New York: Free Press, 1987).

conservatism were positively associated with the desire to censor. But the sample in that study was purposive rather than random. Generalization was therefore discouraged.[79]

Another issue is whether particular bulletin boards operators (sysops) are to be considered publishers or distributors like bookstore owners. If they are publishers, is "guilty knowledge" the next question? The *CompuServe* and *Prodigy* libel cases suggest that publishers may be expected to control what is carried on their systems, whereas online distributors, who act more like common carriers, may not be. Is cyberspace the equivalent of a public street—and therefore a public forum—where increasingly large numbers of people can have verbal free-for-alls and where subscribers must take their chances? On the other hand, do Internet users have the capacity to protect their privacy by giving notice of what they do not wish to receive?[80] When the Decency Act was being enacted, a conservative coalition including former Attorney General Edwin Meese, Ralph Reed, formerly of the Christian Coalition, and Donald Wildmon of the American Family Association, appealed to Congress to criminalize access providers who knowingly distribute pornography.

What are the standards of the communities through which the information superhighway runs? Should they be assimilated into a national standard? A universal standard? How do small operators tailor their messages for selective transmission to meet the standards of uncountable communities? Can RICO statutes be applied to sysops? Should they be, especially if the operators are hobbyists only? If the statutes are applicable, in what jurisdiction should they be applied? Is the private accessing of a file and downloading of material an act of transporting and therefore a criminal act under court rul-

ings,[81] or is it considered to be for personal use only and therefore protected by privacy precedents?[82]

In the final analysis, however, the Internet may be legally unreachable. As one writer put it: "It would be like passing a law to block wind from Denmark."[83]

As society's norms evolve, perhaps its myriad publics and those elected to public office will ultimately decide what is to be outside the bounds of tolerance for erotic expression. "(I)t is better to leave a few . . . noxious branches to their luxuriant growth," wrote James Madison of free expression, "than, by pruning them away, to injure the vigour of those yielding the proper fruits."[84] Would anything on cable television or the Internet today have changed his mind?

STUDENT PRESS RIGHTS

Tinker, Bethel, and *Hazelwood*

In what was more a symbolic speech case than a student press case, the U.S. Supreme Court in 1969 held that certain First Amendment rights of students could *not* be abridged unless school authorities could convince the courts that the expression involved would "materially and substantially interfere with the requirements of appropriate discipline in the operation of the school." The case was *Tinker v. Des Moines Independent School District,*[85] and it involved the black armbands worn by seven schoolchildren to symbolize the opposition of their parents to the Vietnam War.

"It can hardly be argued," the Court declared, "that either students or teachers shed their constitutional rights to freedom of speech or expression at the schoolhouse gate." Citing a landmark case in which the Court had rejected compulsory flag salutes in the public schools of West Virginia during World War II, the Court added:

79. Hernando Rojas, Dhavan V. Shah, and Ronald J. Faber, "For the Good of Others: Censorship and the Third-Person Effect," *Int'l Jour. of Public Opinion Res.* 8 (Summer 1996), pp. 163–186.

80. Many of these questions are discussed in Colleen E. Boyle, "Community Standards in Cyberspace: Regulating Obscenity on Computer Information Services" (unpublished AEJMC convention paper, Washington, D.C., August 1995). See also, Note, *The Message in the Medium: The First Amendment on the Information Superhighway,* 107 Harv.L.Rev. 1062 (1994).

81. *United States v. Orito,* 413 U.S. 139 (1973); *United States v. 12 200 ft. Reels of Film,* 413 U.S. 123 (1973).

82. *Stanley v. Georgia,* 394 U.S. 557 (1969).

83. Charles Stough in the (Minneapolis) *Star Tribune,* February 19, 1996, p. A13.

84. 4 Writings of James Madison 544 (1865).

85. 393 U.S. 503 (1969).

That they are educating the young for citizenship is reason for scrupulous protection of Constitutional freedoms of the individual, if we are not to strangle the free mind at its source and teach youth to discount important principles of our government as mere platitudes.[86]

The rule of *Tinker*, that only a disruption of the educational process would permit interference with the First Amendment rights of students, was the rule before that case, and it is still the rule.

In a case closer to the core of student press rights, a more conservative Court nineteen years later held that a high school principal had the authority to remove two pages from the school newspaper without consulting the student staff or anyone else. The principal was concerned about the effects two stories on pregnancy and abortion and divorce would have on the privacy of students and the effects stories about divorce would have on the reputations of parents. A federal district court upheld the school district. The Eighth Circuit Court of Appeals reversed and was in turn reversed by the U.S. Supreme Court. Major portions of that ruling follow:

Hazelwood School District v. Kuhlmeier

14 MED. L. RPTR. 2081, 484 U.S. 160 (1988).

Justice WHITE delivered the opinion of the Court in which REHNQUIST, STEVENS, O'CONNOR, and SCALIA joined.

* * *

The District Court [607 F.Supp. 1450 (E.D.Mo. 1985)] concluded that school officials may impose restraints on students' speech in activities that are " 'an integral part of the school's educational function' "—including the publication of a school-sponsored newspaper by a journalism class—so long as their decision has " 'a substantial and reasonable basis.' " * * * The Court found that Principal Reynolds' concern that the pregnant students' anonymity would be lost and their privacy invaded was "legitimate and reasonable," given "the small number of pregnant students at Hazelwood East and several identifying characteristics that were disclosed in the arti-

cle." * * * The court held that Reynolds' action was also justified "to avoid the impression that [the school] endorses the sexual norms of the subjects" and to shield younger students from exposure to unsuitable material. The deletion of the article on divorce was seen by the court as a reasonable response to the invasion of privacy concerns raised by the named student's remarks. Because the article did not indicate that the student's parents had been offered an opportunity to respond to her allegations, said the court, there was cause for "serious doubt that the article complied with the rules of fairness which are standard in the field of journalism and which were covered in the textbook used in the Journalism II class." Furthermore, the court concluded that Reynolds was justified in deleting two full pages of the newspaper, instead of deleting only the pregnancy and divorce stories or requiring that those stories be modified to address his concerns, based on his "reasonable belief that he had to make an immediate decision and that there was no time to make modifications to the articles in question."

The Court of Appeals for the Eighth Circuit reversed. 795 F.2d 1368 (1986). The court held at outset that *Spectrum* was not only "a part of the school adopted curriculum," but also a public forum, because the newspaper was "intended to be and operated as a conduit for student viewpoint." The court then concluded that Spectrum's status as a public forum precluded school officials from censoring its contents except when " 'necessary to avoid material and substantial interference with school work or discipline . . . or the rights of others.' " [quoting *Tinker v. Des Moines Independent Community School Dist.*, 393 U.S. 503, 511 (1969)].

The Court of Appeals found "no evidence in the record that the principal could have reasonably forecast that the censored articles or any materials in the censored articles would have materially disrupted classwork or given rise to substantial disorder in the school." School officials were entitled to censor the articles on the ground that they invaded the rights of others, according to the court, only if publication of the articles could have resulted in tort liability to the school. The court concluded that no tort action for libel or invasion of privacy could have been maintained against the school by the subjects of the two articles or by their families. Accordingly,

---

86. *West Virginia State Board of Education v. Barnette,* 319 U.S. 624, 637 (1943).

the court held that school officials had violated respondents' First Amendment rights by deleting the two pages of the newspaper.

We granted certiorari, and we now reverse.

Students in the public schools do not "shed their constitutional rights to freedom of speech or expression at the schoolhouse gate." * * * They cannot be punished merely for expressing their personal views on the school premises—whether "in the cafeteria, or on the playing field, or on the campus during the authorized hours." * * * unless school authorities have reason to believe that such expression will "substantially interfere with the work of the school or impinge upon the rights of other students."

We have nonetheless recognized that the First Amendment rights of students in the public schools "are not automatically coextensive with the rights of adults in other settings," *Bethel School District No. 403 v. Fraser,* 478 U.S. 675 (1986), and must be "applied in light of the special characteristics of the school environment." * * * A school need not tolerate student speech that is inconsistent with its "basic educational mission," * * * even though the government could not censor similar speech outside the school. Accordingly, we held in *Fraser* that a student could be disciplined for having delivered a speech that was "sexually explicit" but not legally obscene at an official school assembly, because the school was entitled to "disassociate itself" from the speech in a manner that would demonstrate to others that such vulgarity is "wholly inconsistent with the 'fundamental values' of public school education." We thus recognized that "[t]he determination of what manner of speech in the classroom or in school assembly is inappropriate properly rests with the school board," rather than with the federal courts. It is in this context that respondents' First Amendment claims must be considered.

We deal first with the question whether *Spectrum* may appropriately be characterized as a forum for public expression. The public schools do not possess all of the attributes of streets, parks, and other traditional public forums that "time out of mind, have been used for purposes of assembly, communicating thoughts between citizens, and discussing public questions." * * * Hence, school facilities may be deemed to be public forums only if school authorities have "by policy or by practice" opened those facilities "for indiscriminate use by the general public," *Perry Education Assn. v. Perry Local Educators' Assn,* 460 U.S. 37, 47

(1983), or by some segment of the public, such as student organizations. *Id.,* at 46, n. 7. * * * If the facilities have instead been reserved for other intended purposes, "communicative or otherwise," then no public forum has been created, and school officials may impose reasonable restrictions on the speech of students, teachers, and other members of the school community. * * *

The policy of school officials toward *Spectrum* was reflected in Hazelwood School board Policy 348.51 and the Hazelwood East Curriculum guide. Board Policy 348.51 provided that "[s]chool sponsored publications are developed within the adopted curriculum and its educational implications in regular classroom activities." The Hazelwood East Curriculum Guide described the Journalism II course as a "laboratory situation in which the students publish the school newspaper applying skills they have learned in Journalism I." The lessons that were to be learned from the Journalism II course, according to the Curriculum Guide, included development of journalistic skills under deadline pressure, "the legal, moral, and ethical restrictions imposed upon journalists within the school community," and "responsibility and acceptance of criticism for articles of opinion." Journalism II was taught by a faculty member during regular class hours. Students received grades and academic credit for their performance in the course.

School officials did not deviate in practice from their policy that production of *Spectrum* was to be part of the educational curriculum and a "regular classroom activit[y]." The District Court found that Robert Stergos, the journalism teacher during most of the 1982–1983 school year, "both had the authority to exercise and in fact exercised a great deal of control over *Spectrum.*" * * * The District Court * * * found it "clear that Mr. Stergos was the final authority with respect to almost every aspect of the production and publication of *Spectrum,* including its content." Moreover, after each *Spectrum* issue had been finally approved by Stergos or his successor, the issue still had to be reviewed by Principal Reynolds prior to publication. Respondents' assertion that they had believed that they could publish "practically anything" in *Spectrum* was therefore dismissed by the District Court as simply "not credible."

* * *

The evidence relied upon by the Court of Appeals in finding *Spectrum* to be a public forum,

* * * is equivocal at best. For example, Board Policy 348.51, which stated in part that "[s]chool sponsored student publications will not restrict free expression or diverse viewpoints within the rules of responsible journalism," also stated that such publications were "developed within the adopted curriculum and its educational implications." One might reasonably infer from the full text of Policy 348.51 that school officials retained ultimate control over what constituted "responsible journalism" in a school-sponsored newspaper. Although the Statement of Policy published in the September 14, 1982, issue of *Spectrum* declared that "*Spectrum,* as a student-press publication, accepts all rights implied by the First Amendment," this statement, understood in the context of the paper's role in the school's curriculum, suggests at most that the administration will not interfere with the students' exercise of those First Amendment rights that attend the publication of a school-sponsored newspaper. It does not reflect an intent to expand those rights by converting a curricular newspaper into a public forum. Finally, that students were permitted to exercise some authority over the contents of *Spectrum* was fully consistent with the Curriculum Guide objective of teaching the Journalism II students "leadership responsibilities as issue and page editors." A decision to teach leadership skills in the context of a classroom activity hardly implies a decision to relinquish school control over that activity. In sum, the evidence relied upon by the Court of Appeals fails to demonstrate the "clear intent to create a public forum" * * * that existed in cases in which we found public forums to have been created. * * * School officials did not evince either "by policy or by practice" * * * any intent to open the pages of *Spectrum* to "indiscriminate use," by its student reporters and editors, or by the student body generally. Instead, they "reserve[d] the forum for its intended purpos[e]," as a supervised learning experience for journalism students. Accordingly, school officials were entitled to regulate the contents of *Spectrum* in any reasonable manner. It is this standard, rather than our decision in *Tinker,* that governs this case.

The question whether the First Amendment requires a school to tolerate particular student speech—the question that we addressed in *Tinker*—is different from the question whether the First Amendment requires a school affirmatively to promote particular student speech. The former question addresses educators' ability to silence a student's personal expression that happens to occur on the school premises. The latter question concerns educators' authority over school-sponsored publications, theatrical productions, and other expressive activities that students, parents, and members of the public might reasonably perceive to bear the imprimatur of the school. These activities may fairly be characterized as part of the school curriculum, whether or not they occur in a traditional classroom setting, so long as they are supervised by faculty members and designed to impart particular knowledge or skills to student participants and audiences.[3]

Educators are entitled to exercise greater control over this second form of student expression to assure that participants learn whatever lessons the activity is designed to teach, that readers or listeners are not exposed to material that may be inappropriate for their level of maturity, and that the views of the individual speaker are not erroneously attributed to the school. Hence, a school may in its capacity as publisher of a school newspaper or producer of a school play "disassociate itself," * * * not only from speech that would "substantially interfere with [its] work * * * or impinge upon the rights of other students," *Tinker,* 393 U.S., at 509, but also from speech that is, for example, ungrammatical, poorly written, inadequately researched, biased or prejudiced, vulgar or profane, or unsuitable for immature audiences.[4] A school must be able to set high standards for the student speech that is disseminated under its auspices—standards that may be

---

3. The distinction that we draw between speech that is sponsored by the school and speech that is not is fully consistent with *Papish v. Board of Curators,* 410 U.S. 667 (1973) *(per curiam),* which involved an off-campus "underground" newspaper that school officials merely had allowed to be sold on a state university campus.

4. The dissent perceives no difference between the First Amendment analysis applied in *Tinker* and that applied in *Fraser.* We disagree. The decision in *Fraser* rested on the "vulgar," "lewd," and "plainly offensive" character of a speech delivered at an official school assembly rather than on any propensity of the speech to "materially disrupt classwork or involve substantial disorder or invasion of the rights of others." 393 U.S., at 513. Indeed, the *Fraser* Court cited as "especially relevant" a portion of Justice Black's dissenting opinion in *Tinker* "disclaim[ing] any purpose * * * to hold that the Federal Constitution compels the teachers, parents and elected school officials to surrender control of the American public school system to public school students." 478 U.S., at ___ (citing 393 U.S., at 522). Of course, Justice Black's observations are equally relevant to the instant case.

higher than those demanded by some newspaper publishers or theatrical producers in the "real" world—and may refuse to disseminate student speech that does not meet those standards. In addition, a school must be able to take into account the emotional maturity of the intended audience in determining whether to disseminate student speech on potentially sensitive topics, which might range from the existence of Santa Claus in an elementary school setting to the particulars of teenage sexual activity in a high school setting. A school must also retain the authority to refuse to sponsor student speech that might reasonably be perceived to advocate drug or alcohol use, irresponsible sex, or conduct otherwise inconsistent with "the shared values of a civilized social order," * * * or to associate the school with any position other than neutrality on matters of political controversy. Otherwise, the schools would be unduly constrained from fulfilling their role as "a principal instrument in awakening the child to cultural values, in preparing him for later professional training, and in helping him to adjust normally to his environment." *Brown v. Board of Education,* 347 U.S. 483, 493 (1954).

Accordingly, we conclude that the standard articulated in *Tinker* for determining when a school may punish student expression need not also be the standard for determining when a school may refuse to lend its name and resources to the dissemination of student expression. Instead, we hold that educators do not offend the First Amendment by exercising editorial control over the style and content of student speech in school-sponsored expressive activities so long as their actions are reasonably related to legitimate pedagogical concerns.

We also conclude that Principal Reynolds acted reasonably in requiring the deletion from the May 13 issue of *Spectrum* of the pregnancy article, the divorce article, and the remaining articles that were to appear on the same pages of the newspaper.

The initial paragraph of the pregnancy article declared that "[a]ll names have been changed to keep the identity of these girls a secret." The principal concluded that the students' anonymity was not adequately protected, however, given the other identifying information in the article and the small number of pregnant students at the school. * * * Reynolds * * * could reasonably

have feared that the article violated whatever pledge of anonymity had been given to the pregnant students. In addition, he could reasonably have been concerned that the article was not sufficiently sensitive to the privacy interests of the students' boyfriends and parents, who were discussed in the article but who were given no opportunity to consent to its publication or to offer a response. The article did not contain graphic accounts of sexual activity. The girls did comment in the article, however, concerning their sexual histories and their use or nonuse of birth control. It was not unreasonable for the principal to have concluded that such frank talk was inappropriate in a school-sponsored publication distributed to 14-year-old freshmen and presumably taken home to be read by students' even younger brothers and sisters.

The student who was quoted by name in the version of the divorce article seen by Principal Reynolds made comments sharply critical of her father. The principal could reasonably have concluded that an individual publicly identified as an inattentive parent—indeed, as one who chose "playing cards with the guys" over home and family—was entitled to an opportunity to defend himself as a matter of journalistic fairness. * * *

Principal Reynolds testified credibly at trial that, at the time that he reviewed the proofs of the May 13 issue during an extended telephone conversation with [the printer], he believed that there was no time to make any changes in the articles, and that the newspaper had to be printed immediately or not at all. It is true that Reynolds did not verify whether the necessary modifications could still have been made in the articles, and that [the printer] did not volunteer the information that printing could be delayed until the changes were made. We nonetheless agree with the District Court that the decision to excise the two pages containing the problematic articles was reasonable given the particular circumstances of this case. * * *

In sum, we cannot reject as unreasonable Principal Reynolds' conclusion that neither the pregnancy article nor the divorce article was suitable for publication in *Spectrum.* Reynolds could reasonably have concluded that the students who had written and edited these articles had not sufficiently mastered those portions of the Journalism II curriculum that pertained to the treatment of controversial issues and personal attacks, the need to protect the privacy of individuals whose most intimate concerns are to be revealed in the newspaper, and "the legal, moral, and ethical restrictions imposed upon journalists within [a] school community" that includes adolescent subjects and readers. Finally, we conclude that the principal's decision to delete two pages of *Spectrum,* rather than to delete only the offending articles or to require that they be modified, was reasonable under the circumstances as he understood them. Accordingly, no violation of First Amendment rights occurred.

The judgment of the Court of Appeals for the Eighth Circuit is therefore

Reversed.

Justice BRENNAN, with whom Justice MARSHALL and Justice BLACKMUN join, dissenting.

When the young men and women of Hazelwood East High School registered for Journalism II, they expected a civics lesson. *Spectrum,* the newspaper they were to publish, "was not just a class exercise in which students learned to prepare papers and hone writing skills, it was a * * * forum established to give students an opportunity to express their views while gaining an appreciation of their rights and responsibilities under the First Amendment to the United States Constitution * * *." 795 F.2d 1368, 1373 (CA8 1986). "[A]t the beginning of each school year," the student journalists published a Statement of Policy—tacitly approved each year by school authorities—announcing their expectation that "*Spectrum,* as a student-press publication, accepts all rights implied by the First Amendment. * * * *Only speech that 'materially and substantially interferes with the requirements of appropriate discipline' can be found unacceptable and therefore prohibited*" [emphasis added]. The school board itself affirmatively guaranteed the students of Journalism II an atmosphere conducive to fostering such an appreciation and exercising the full panoply of rights associated with a free student press. "School sponsored student publications," it vowed, "will not restrict free expression or diverse viewpoints within the rules of responsible journalism." (Board Policy § 348.51). * * *

In my view the principal broke more than just a promise. He violated the First Amendment's prohibitions against censorship of any student expression that neither disrupts classwork nor invades the rights of others, and against any censorship that is not narrowly tailored to serve its purpose.

Public education serves vital national interests in preparing the Nation's youth for life and in our increasingly complex society and for the duties of citizenship in our democratic Republic. * * * The public school conveys to our young the information and tools required not merely to survive in, but to contribute to, civilized society. It also inculcates in tomorrow's leaders the "fundamental values necessary to the maintenance of a democratic political system. * * *" *Ambach v. Norwick,* 441 U.S. 68, 77 (1979). All the while, the public educator nurtures students' social and moral development by transmitting to them an official dogma of " 'community values.' " *Board of Education v. Pico,* 457 U.S. 853, 864 (1982).

* * *

Free student expression undoubtedly sometimes interferes with the effectiveness of the school's pedagogical functions. Some brands of student expression do so by directly preventing the school from pursuing its pedagogical mission: The young polemic who stands on a soapbox during calculus class to deliver an eloquent political diatribe interferes with the legitimate teaching of calculus. And the student who delivers a lewd endorsement of a student-government candidate might so extremely distract an impressionable high school audience as to interfere with the orderly operation of the school. See *Bethel School Dist. No. 403 v. Fraser,* 478 U.S. 675 (1986). Other student speech, however, frustrates the school's legitimate pedagogical purposes merely by expressing a message that conflicts with the school's, without directly interfering with the school's expression of its message: A student who responds to a political science teacher's question with the retort, "Socialism is good," subverts the school's inculcation of the message that capitalism is better. Even the maverick who sits in class passively sporting a symbol of protest against a government policy, * * * or the gossip who sits in the student commons swapping stories of sexual escapade could readily muddle a clear official message condoning the government policy or condemning teenage sex. Likewise, the student newspaper that, like *Spectrum,* conveys a moral position at odds with the school's official stance might subvert the administration's legitimate inculcation of its own perception of community values.

If mere incompatibility with the school's pedagogical message were a constitutionally sufficient justification for the suppression of student speech, school officials could censor each of the students or student organizations in the foregoing hypotheticals, converting our public schools into "enclaves of totalitarianism," that "strangle the free mind at its source" * * *. The First Amendment permits no such blanket censorship authority. While the "constitutional rights of students in public school are not automatically coextensive with the rights of adults in other settings," * * * students in the public schools do not "shed their constitutional rights to freedom of speech or expression at the schoolhouse gate."

* * *

The mere fact of school sponsorship does not, as the Court suggests, license such thought control in the high school, whether through school suppression of disfavored viewpoints or through official assessment of topic sensitivity. The former would constitute unabashed and unconstitutional viewpoint discrimination, see *Board of Education v. Pico,* * * * as well as an impermissible infringement of the students' " 'right to receive information and ideas.' " * * * Just as a school board may not purge its state-funded library of all books that " 'offen[d] [its] social, political and moral tastes,' " * * * school officials may not, out of like motivation, discriminatorily excise objectionable ideas from a student publication. The State's prerogative to dissolve the student newspaper entirely (or to limit its subject matter) no more entitles it to dictate which viewpoints students may express on its pages, than the State's prerogative to close down the schoolhouse entitles it to prohibit the nondisruptive expression of antiwar sentiment within its gates. * * *

The case before us aptly illustrates how readily school officials (and courts) can camouflage viewpoint discrimination as the "mere" protection of students from sensitive topics. Among the grounds that the Court advances to uphold the principal's censorship of one of the articles was the potential sensitivity of "teenage sexual activity." * * * Yet the District Court specifically found that the principal "did not, as a matter of principle, oppose discussion of said topi[c] in *Spectrum.*" 607 F.Supp., at 1467. That much is also clear from the same principal's approval of the "squeal law" article on the same page, dealing forthrightly with "teenage sexuality," "the use of contraceptives by teenagers," and "teenage pregnancy." If topic sensitivity were the true basis of the principal's decision, the two articles should have been equally objectionable. It is much more likely that the objectionable article was objectionable because of the viewpoint it expressed: it might have been read (as the majority apparently does) to advocate "irresponsible sex." * * *

The sole concomitant of school sponsorship that might conceivably justify the distinction that the Court draws between sponsored and nonsponsored student expression is the risk "that the views of the individual speaker [might be] erroneously attributed to the school." Of course, the risk of erroneous attribution inheres in any student expression, including "personal expression" that, like the Tinkers' armbands, "happens to occur on the school premises." Nevertheless, the majority is certainly correct that indicia of school sponsorship increase the likelihood of such attribution, and that state educators may therefore have a legitimate interest in dissociating themselves from student speech.

But " '[e]ven though the governmental purpose be legitimate and substantial, that purpose cannot be pursued by means that broadly stifle fundamental personal liberties when the end can be more narrowly achieved." * * * Dissociative means short of censorship are available to the school. It could, for example, require the student activity to publish a disclaimer, such as the "Statement of Policy" that *Spectrum* published each school year announcing that "[a]ll * * * editorials appearing in this newspaper reflect the opinions of the *Spectrum* staff, which are not necessarily shared by the administrators or faculty of Hazelwood East," or it could simply issue its own response clarifying the official position on the matter and explaining why the student position is wrong. Yet, without so much as acknowledging the less oppressive alternatives, the Court approves of brutal censorship.

* * *

Finally, even if the majority were correct that the principal could constitutionally have censored the objectionable material, I would emphatically object to the brutal manner in which he did so. Where "[t]he separation of legitimate from illegitimate speech calls for more sensitive tools" * * * the principal used a paper shredder. He objected to some material in two articles, but excised six entire articles. He did not so much as inquire into obvious alternatives, such as precise deletions or additions (one of which had already been made), rearranging the layout, or delaying publication. Such unthinking contempt for individual rights is intolerable from any state official. It is particularly insidious from one to whom the public entrusts the task of inculcating in its youth an appreciation for the cherished democratic liberties that our Constitution guarantees.

* * *

The young men and women of Hazelwood East expected a civics lesson, but not the one the Court teaches them today.

COMMENT

Between *Tinker* and *Hazelwood*, the court had dealt with *Bethel School District No. 403 v. Fraser*, a high school case more difficult than either of those. A student endorsing a candidate for a student office at a compulsory assembly, which included fourteen-year-olds, had used vulgar, lewd and plainly offensive sexual metaphors in his presentation. The speech was disruptive; students hooted, shouted, and made obscene gestures. Two of the student's teachers had warned the speechmaker of the possible consequences of his erotic rhetoric. After the speech, the student, who was otherwise in good standing, was suspended for three days and removed from the list of prospective commencement speakers.

The Supreme Court reversed lower federal courts on the grounds that schools have an interest in "teaching students the boundaries of socially appropriate behavior." "The pervasive sexual innuendo in Fraser's speech," the Court noted, "was plainly offensive to both teachers and students—indeed to any mature person. By glorifying male sexuality, and in its verbal content, the speech was acutely insulting to teenage girl students." (sic) Political speech or not, time, place, and manner were against this speaker and his captive audience.

Here Justice Brennan agreed. He reproduced some of the speech: "Jeff Kuhlman is a man who

takes his point and pounds it in. . . . He doesn't attack things in spurts—he drives hard, pushing and pushing until finally—he succeeds." Brennan decided that "in light of the discretion school officials have to teach high school students how to conduct civil and effective public discourse, and to prevent disruption of school educational activities, it was not unconstitutional for school officials to conclude, under the circumstances of this case, that respondent's remarks exceeded permissible limits." Justice Stevens dissented, partly on the grounds that the district and circuit court judges were in a better position to evaluate the speech than were Supreme Court justices.[87]

It could be argued that *Bethel* was the bridge between *Tinker* on one side and *Hazelwood* on the other. *Bethel* made *Hazelwood* possible. While not overturning *Tinker*, *Hazelwood* now seems to govern high school press law. In *Hazelwood* the Court chose not to direct its rule to college papers, but in a footnote suggested that such an application could be considered in the future. *Hazelwood* also may not apply to high school newspapers that are independent of the school curriculum, although that is a spongy distinction. The Hazelwood high school newspaper was part of a journalism class. So are some college and university newspapers; clearly, their independence is better assured when they are independent of the curriculum.

"A school," wrote Justice Byron White for the Court in *Hazelwood*, "need not tolerate speech that is inconsistent with its basic educational mission, even though the government could not censor similar speech outside the school." The Court was not prepared to equate student press rights with those of adults. So, when the contested school-sponsored expression takes place in a school setting, which is largely a nonpublic forum, and at the very most a limited public forum, a principal, a superintendent, or a school board, acting on behalf of the public, may suppress speech or press in the interests of education.

A more constitutionally sensitive approach would insist that school officials give adequate forewarning to students as to what forms and topics of expression may be subject to prior

----

87. *Bethel School District No. 403 v. Fraser*, 478 U.S. 675 (1986).

restraints; what constitutes disruption, defamation, obscenity, or an invasion of privacy; and what steps are available for a prompt hearing and appeal when an administrative interference with publication or distribution takes place. Few if any of these elements of due process were available to students in *Hazelwood.*

Responses to *Hazelwood*

JUDICIAL Some contend that *Hazelwood* wiped out twenty years of student press law, most of it forged in the federal appeals courts. They suggest that students may now have to look to state constitutions for protection.

Hazelwood is also authority for rejecting advertising in school-sponsored publications. Before *Hazelwood,* a journalism adviser at Portland College refused a Planned Parenthood ad because, he said, he did not want to lower the tone of the publicly funded college newspaper. Planned Parenthood sued. Had the state established a public forum? If it had, had it discriminated against a content category of speech that some might find offensive? A federal district court in Oregon answered yes to both questions.[88] After *Hazelwood,* similar questions were answered differently by a federal district court in Nevada. A high school publication was not a public forum, and the school district had not created a limited-purpose public forum for advertisers of lawful goods and services—here again, Planned Parenthood. The school's justifications for refusing to publish a family planning advertisement were reasonable: a desire to remain neutral on this controversial issue and to regulate its own sex education program.[89] A California school board that permitted placement of military service ads in the school paper but prohibited ads promoting alternatives to military service was said to have violated the First Amendment rights of the ad's antiwar sponsors.[90]

Hazelwood has also been used to justify removal of educational material from school curricula, in one case works by Aristophanes and Chaucer.[91] Before *Hazelwood,* the Supreme Court had held that books could not be removed from high school libraries simply because school authorities objected to their philosophical themes.[92] The First Amendment rights of students were violated, said a federal district court, when a school board removed all issues of *Ms.* magazine from a high school library without any showing of a countervailing governmental interest beyond the personal views of individual board members.[93]

In *Pratt v. Independent School District, No. 831,*[94] the Eighth Circuit Court of Appeals held that a "school board cannot constitutionally ban . . . films because a majority of its members object to the films' religious and ideological content and wish to prevent the ideas contained in the material from being expressed in the school."

For years, only serious disruptions of the educational process had justified restrictions on student expression. Fraudulent notices announcing the closing of a university met the test, as did leaflets calling for a boycott of registration, and the breaking up of campus meetings.[95] The majority of scholastic cases, however, had gone the other way.

In *Healy v. James,*[96] for instance, a unanimous Supreme Court held that fear of or a prediction of disruption was an inadequate reason for a college president to deny recognition to an SDS (Students for a Democratic Society) chapter on campus. Nor was the distinct possibility of public disapproval sufficient to keep a gay organization off a campus.[97]

The First Amendment would also prohibit school administrators from taking away a publication's funding or suspending its editor because of objections to editorial points of view. "We are

---

88. *Portland Women's Health Ctr. v. Portland Community College,* unreported, Oregon 1981.
89. *Planned Parenthood of Southern Nevada, Inc. v. Clark County School Dist.* 941 F.2d 817 (9th Cir. 1991).
90. *San Di Nego Committee v. Grossmont Union High School,* 790 F.2d 1471 (9th Cir. 1986).
91. *Virgil v. School Board,* 862 F.2d 1517 (11th Cir. 1989).
92. *Board of Education Island Trees Union Free School District No. 26 v. Pico,* 8 Med. L. Rptr. 1721, 457 U.S. 853 (1982).
93. *Salvail v. Nashua Board of Education,* 5 Med. L. Rptr. 1096, 469 F.Supp. 1269 (N.H. 1979).
94. 670 F.2d 771 (8th Cir. 1982).
95. *Speake v. Grantham,* 317 F.Supp. 1253 (S.D.Miss. 1970); *Jones v. State Board of Education,* 407 F.2d 834 (6th Cir. 1969).
96. 408 U.S. 169 (1972).
97. *Gay Students of University of New Hampshire v. Bonner,* 509 F.2d 652 (1st Cir. 1974).

well beyond the belief," said a federal district court in *Antonelli v. Hammond,*[98] "that any manner of state regulation is permissible simply because it involves an activity which is part of the university structure and is financed with funds controlled by the administration."

The Fourth Circuit Court of Appeals put it even more bluntly:

> It may well be that a college need not establish a campus newspaper, or, if a paper has been established, the college may permanently discontinue publication for reasons wholly unrelated to the First Amendment. But if a college has a student newspaper, its publication cannot be suppressed because college officials dislike its editorial comment. . . . Censorship of constitutionally protected expression cannot be imposed by . . . withdrawing financial support, or asserting any other form of censorial oversight based on the institution's power of the purse."[99]

Nor could a student fee system, a small portion of which supported a campus daily, be modified because of legal but distasteful editorial content.[100]

Shortly after *Hazelwood,* the Ninth Circuit Court of Appeals took the Supreme Court at its word by holding that a high school policy violated the First Amendment rights of students because it required that all student-written material not sponsored by the school be reviewed by school authorities before distribution. An off-campus newspaper had been brought to an on-campus barbecue. The appeals court seemed to be applying a *Tinker* standard. School sponsorship may be one key variable in school cases.[101] A federal court ruled in 1994 that a Lakeland, Florida elementary school policy that required students to submit non-school-sponsored written materials to school officials for approval prior to distribution on school grounds violated the First Amendment.[102]

The New Jersey Supreme Court in 1994 may also have softened the effects of *Hazelwood* somewhat by relying on the First Amendment—not the New Jersey Constitution—to decide whether school authorities had violated a student's free speech rights by disallowing publication in the junior high newspaper of reviews of R-rated movies he had written. *Rain Man* and *Mississippi Burning* were the movies at issue. No credits or grades were awarded for the assignment, but the publication was supervised by a designated faculty member and sponsored by the school.

Lower New Jersey courts had ruled against the school principal and his application of *Hazelwood.* The central question was whether valid pedagogical concerns justified the principal's action. The state supreme court agreed with the lower court decisions that justification here was absent.

The state appellate court had tried to distinguish *Hazelwood* by noting that the material there was censored because of its content and journalistic style. Content, the lower court added, is what is written. Here subject matter—or what was written about—was censored. The R-rating of the subject matter had led to the principal's action. The state supreme court, rejecting the lower court's effort to clarify the subtle distinction between an idea and the manner of expressing it, nevertheless agreed with the result.

Desilets v. Clearview Regional Board of Education
647 A.2D 150 (N.J. 1994).

* * *

PER CURIAM:

We need not, however, further address or resolve the significance of that alleged distinction between subject-matter and content or style in determining the scope and application of educational policy. We are satisfied that the evidence in this case concerning the school's educational policy was, at best, equivocal and inconsistent. The school board's position with respect to the policy that applied to student publications, specifically as related to matters such as movie reviews, was vague and highly conclusory. It conceded that it had no specific policy regarding movie reviews of R-rated films; nevertheless, it argued that the action taken by the principal and superintendent complied with that "policy." Further, how any "policy" was applied to the student's R-rated movie reviews remains unclear.

98. 308 F. Supp. 1329 (D.Mass. 1970).

99. *Joyner v. Whiting,* 477 F.2d 456 (4th Cir. 1973).

100. *Stanley v. Magrath,* 9 Med. L. Rptr. 2352, 719 F.2d 279 (8th Cir. 1976).

101. *Burch v. Barker,* 861 F.2d 1149 (9th Cir. 1988).

102. *Johnston-Loehner v. O'Brien,* 859 F.Supp. 575 (M.D.Fla. 1994).

The school authorities assert that the publication of Brien's R-rated movie reviews violated its official policy because those reviews constituted "material which advocated the use or advertised the availability of any substance believed to constitute a danger to student health." However, no one explained how such R-rated movie reviews posed a danger to student health. Moreover, if such R-rated movie reviews did violate that policy, the evidence strongly suggests that the policy was often ignored or applied inconsistently because R-rated movies were discussed in class, referred to and available in the school library, and, in fact, reviewed and published by the student newspaper.

The foregoing does not mean that the school had no legitimate pedagogical concerns over the publication of articles dealing with R-rated movies or, indeed, did not in fact have an educational policy dealing with that subject. Rather, the record suggests only that such a policy, if it exists, is vaguely defined and loosely applied and that its underlying educational concerns remained essentially undefined and speculative.

In sum, we agree with the Appellate Division that under *Hazelwood*, defendants failed to establish a legitimate educational policy that would govern the publication of the challenged materials and, as a consequence, the school authorities, under these circumstances, did violate the student's expressional rights under the First Amendment.

We thus agree, also, with the Appellate Division that because this case can be decided on federal constitutional grounds, we have no reason to consider the State constitutional claims.

* * *

The difficulty in resolving the basic question of whether defendants had an established and legitimate educational policy that would justify restrictions of expression by students is fully illustrated in this case, not only by the equivocal and vague evidence that was adduced to demonstrate the existence of such a policy, but also by the different explanations offered by the witnesses concerning the meaning and application of that policy. Those difficulties are further exemplified by the different conclusions with respect to the existence and meaning of such an educational policy reached by the several judges who participated at all levels of this litigation. The inherent complexity surrounding the nature and scope of educational policy affecting expressional activity demonstrates that the educational legitimacy of a school policy governing such activity should, if possible, first be considered and determined by the administrative agency charged with regulating public education.

* * *

In this case, the ultimate constitutional question—whether a student's constitutional expressional rights have been violated by restrictions imposed by school authorities—is answered in large measure by the determination of whether those restrictions are related to and effectuate "legitimate pedagogical goals." That determination clearly and unavoidably implicates "the highest level of professional expertise and judgment in the educational field," and, therefore, is one more appropriate reason for initial review and resolution by the Commissioner of Education.

For the reasons expressed in Judge Keefe's opinion, as well as those set forth here, the judgment of the Appellate Division is affirmed.

COMMENT

A federal district court in Kansas may also have put a slight dent in *Hazelwood*, by distinguishing it in a case involving the constitutionality of a district board of education and a superintendent removing from the school library a celebrated book, *Annie on My Mind*, that is sympathetic to a lesbian lifestyle. The superintendent thought the book was intended to inject homosexuality into the curriculum and create unnecessary controversy. The book's literary merits were never discussed. One board member, however, testified that homosexuality was a "mental disorder, immoral, and contrary to the teaching of the Bible and the Christian church . . . a lifestyle sinful in the eyes of God." Another stated that she "believes the library should contain only factual books, which would not include *Annie* or other works of fiction, but would include the Bible because . . . everything in the Bible is factual." Only two of six board members saw a First Amendment issue in the case.

Ironically, the board had accepted the American Library Association's School Library Bill of Rights recommending book choices that "reflect the ideas and beliefs of religious, social, political, historical, and ethnic groups and their contribution to the American and world heritage and culture, thereby enabling students to develop an intellectual integrity in forming judgment" and encourage "the development of literary, cultural and aesthetic appreciation and ethical standards."[103] After motions for summary judgment were decided, the court had this to say about the First Amendment questions:

Case v. Unified School District No. 233
24 MED. L. RPTR. 1161, 908 F.SUPP. 864 (D.KAN. 1995).

* * *

BEBBER, J.:

The District failed to follow its adopted procedures for the reconsideration of library materials. The District neither awaited a formal complaint, nor appointed a committee to consider the removal (as opposed to the donation) of *Annie on My Mind.* If the media specialists committee that was established to consider the donations also acted as a review committee for materials already on the shelves, its recommendation was ignored. The District's written guidelines forbid a reversal of the Review Committee's decision without an appeal to the superintendent by a complainant. No appeal was made. The District also ignored its own incorporation of the American Library Association's Library Bill of Rights, which affirms the importance of having a diversity of ideas available in the library "thereby enabling students to develop an intellectual integrity in forming judgment."

After the media specialists had concluded that the donation of *Annie on My Mind* should be accepted and that the books should be added to the existing copies on the shelves, Dr. Wimmer overrode that decision by promulgating new "book donation guidelines." Dr. Wimmer used the new book donation guidelines to rationalize the refusal of the donation and to remove existing copies of *Annie on My Mind* from the shelves, even though his newly-devised donation policy did not cover the removal action. In doing so, he disregarded the recommendation of the

media specialists as well as the District's established criteria for the reevaluation of library resources.

In voting to affirm Dr. Wimmer's decision and remove *Annie on My Mind,* the Board of Education did not follow the reconsideration policy, which requires that challenged materials be evaluated according to the District's established criteria for the selection of library materials. There was no discussion by the Board concerning the literary or educational merit of the book. The Board of Education ignored its own guidelines and criteria established for the reconsideration of library materials.

* * *

FIRST AMENDMENT CLAIM

Although local school boards have broad discretion in the management of school affairs, they must act within fundamental constitutional limits. See *Board of Educ. v. Pico,* 457 U.S. 853, 863–65, * * * and *Tinker v. Des Moines Independent Community Sch. Dist.,* 393 U.S. 503, 507 (1969). In *Pico,* the United States Supreme Court addressed the very issue that confronts the court in the present case: Does the First Amendment impose any limitations upon the discretion of school officials to remove library books from high school and junior high libraries? In a plurality opinion, the Court concluded there are limits. *Id.* at 871–72.

The *Pico* plaintiffs challenged the school board's removal of nine books from the school's libraries. A majority of the Court agreed that genuine issues of material fact precluded summary judgment in favor of the school board. *Id.* at 875–76, 883. Writing for the plurality, Justice Brennan opined that the motivations of school officials would be unconstitutional if the school officials "intended by their removal decision to deny respondents access to ideas with which [the officials] disagreed, and if this intent was the decisive factor in [the removal] decision." *Id.* at 871. The plurality went on to hold that "local school boards may not remove books from school library shelves simply because they dislike the ideas contained in those books and seek by their removal to 'prescribe what shall be orthodox in politics, nationalism, religion, or other matters of opinion.' " *Id.* at 872. The *Pico* plurality indicated that removal may be permissible if

---

103. *Case v. Unified School District No. 233,* 24 Med. L. Rptr. 1172, 895 F.Supp. 1463 (D.Kan. 1995).

the book contained "pervasive vulgarity" or if the book was "educationally unsuitable."

Writing separately, Justice Blackmun disagreed with the plurality's assertion that school children have a "right to receive information." *Id.* at 875–79 (concurring opinion). Instead, he focused on the school board's denial of access to ideas. Justice Blackmun would hold that "school officials may not remove books for the purpose of restricting access to the political ideas or social perspectives discussed in them, when the action is motivated simply by the officials' disapproval of the ideas involved." *Id.* at 879–80.

The plurality decision in *Pico* is not binding precedent. The court notes, however, that this is the only Supreme Court decision dealing specifically with the removal of books from a public school library. The court also notes that there are no Tenth Circuit Court of Appeals decisions directly on point. Thus, the court concludes that it should follow the *Pico* decision in analyzing the Olathe School District's removal of *Annie on My Mind* from the District's libraries.

In a recent Fifth Circuit decision, the court reversed the district court's grant of summary judgment in favor of plaintiffs who challenged the school board's removal of a book from the school library. *Campbell,* 64 F.3d at 191. The Fifth Circuit agreed that *Pico* should guide its book removal analysis. The court of appeals remanded the case for trial and directed the district court to determine the "actual motivation" behind the school board's removal of the book, *Voodoo & Hoodoo.* The court made the following observation in the path to its decision to remand:

[I]n light of the special role of the school library as a place where students may freely and voluntarily explore diverse topics, the School Board's non-curricular decision to remove a book well after it had been placed in the public school libraries evokes the question whether that action might not be an unconstitutional attempt to "strangle the free mind at its source."

The court also noted that the school board's failure to follow its own procedures raised suspicion that the motivation of the school board was unconstitutional. *Id.* at 190–91.

In the present case, the court must determine the "actual motivation" of the school board members in their removal decision. If the decisive factor behind the removal of *Annie on My Mind* was the school board members' personal disapproval

of the ideas contained in the book, then under *Pico* the removal was unconstitutional.

The Board of Education members who voted in favor of the removal of *Annie on My Mind* stated that they believed the book was "educationally unsuitable." The court is required to assess the "credibility of [school officials'] justifications for their decision." *Pico,* 457 U.S. at 875.

There is no basis in the record to believe that these Board members meant by "educational suitability" anything other than their own disagreement with the ideas expressed in the book. Here, the invocation of "educational suitability" does nothing to counterbalance the overwhelming evidence of viewpoint discrimination.

Accordingly, the court concludes that defendants removed *Annie on My Mind* because they disagreed with ideas expressed in the book and that this factor was the substantial motivation in their removal decision. Through their removal of the book, defendants intended to deny students in the Olathe School District access to those ideas. Defendants unconstitutionally sought to "prescribe what shall be orthodox in politics, nationalism, religion, or other matters of opinion." *Pico,* 457 U.S. at 872.

The highly irregular and erratic manner in which defendants removed *Annie on My Mind* from the District's libraries and their disregard of established policy and procedure are important evidence of their improper motivation. In addition, defendants did not consider or discuss less restrictive alternatives to complete removal of the book. This is also persuasive evidence of improper motivation.

Defendants have argued that they have broad discretion to transmit community values, and that they may remove library books based upon their personal social, political, and moral views. The Supreme Court in *Pico* expressly rejected this argument, noting that "petitioners' reliance upon that duty [to transmit community values through curriculum] is misplaced where, as here, they attempt to extend their claim of absolute discretion beyond the compulsory environment of the classroom, into the school library and the regime of voluntary inquiry that there hold sway." *Pico,* 457 U.S. at 869.

Defendants also have argued that plaintiffs' have not been denied access to the book because it is available from sources outside of the school library. The availability of *Annie on My*

Mind from other sources does not cure defendants' improper motivation for removing the book. "Restraint on expression may not generally be justified by the fact that there may be other times, places, or circumstances available for such expression." *Minarcini v. Strongsville City Sch. Dist.,* 541 F.2d 577, 582 (6th Cir. 1976) (removal of books because school board found them distasteful was unconstitutional).

In accordance with the analysis in *Pico* and *Campbell,* the court concludes that defendants' removal of *Annie on My Mind* from the Olathe School District libraries was a violation of plaintiffs' First Amendment rights. In addition, the Kansas Constitution, Bill of Rights § 11 entitles plaintiffs to prevail on their free speech claim to the same extent that they have prevailed on their First Amendment claim under the United States Constitution. . . .

LEGISLATIVE By 1996, six states—Arkansas, California, Colorado, Iowa, Kansas, and Massachusetts—had passed anticensorship laws to protect the scholastic press; other states, including Florida, Illinois, Michigan, Missouri, Nebraska, Oklahoma, and Oregon, had bills either awaiting introduction or somewhere in the legislative pipeline. California's legislation, the first of its kind, predates *Hazelwood;* other state laws appear to be efforts to overcome the effects of that Supreme Court ruling.

In the meantime it is worth speculating on why the scholastic press continues to face blatant censorship, funding threats, penalized faculty advisers, and theft of its product. On a microlevel these problems may have something to do with the training of school administrators. A national survey conducted shortly after *Hazelwood* was announced, indicated that principals were more concerned with discipline in the schools than with a free press. An overwhelming majority of principals and advisers thought all copy should be reviewed before publication, and two-thirds of principals and one-third of advisers thought "harmful" articles should be prohibited, even though they were not libelous, obscene, or disruptive. The surveyors concluded:

> Principals and advisers are human beings operating in a political society—more political than many would like to admit. Advisers may sense that they are caught between the administration and the stu-

dents. If the principal requests prior review of newspaper copy, the adviser will comply with the employer rather than advance student press freedom. Many are unqualified or marginally qualified in journalism, and many are alone in their schools. Smooth, relatively harmonious operation of the school may be higher on the priority list than freedom of the student press."[104]

Even experienced advisers tend to be caught in a crossfire of students, parents, administrators, school board members, the community at large, and constitutional commentators far removed from the situation. In a systematic and comprehensive study of high school journalism advisers, a University of Iowa researcher[105] found that control, hierarchy, and a sense of responsibility generally overcame notions of freedom of expression and freedom from censorship in high school settings. Level of journalism education, teaching assignment, length of service, and suburban location, as opposed to rural or inner city location, tempered this tendency. Stories about the competence of school personnel and articles on sex led to most disagreements among administrators, teachers, and students on whether or what to publish.

Looking at the question more broadly, it may be that majoritarianism (the majority rules) is gradually replacing constitutionalism (the First Amendment protects individual dissenters and rabble-rousers from the wrath of the majority) in our body politic.

More and more voices are calling for criminal or administrative sanctions to protect students from offensive or hateful speech. Even Congress has entertained legislation that would severely limit the distribution of student fees to political groups.[106] The campus is no longer a haven for conflicting views because speakers representing society's majority are believed to have an unfair advantage. Their voices are louder. Here the constitutional model is turned on its head: minorities

---

104. J. William Click and Lillian Lodge Kopenhaver, "Principals Favor Discipline More Than a Free Press," *Journalism Educator* 43 (Summer 1988), p. 48.

105. Mary Arnold, "Students' Freedom of Expression and High School Journalism Advisers: A Legal and Educational Dilemma," (unpublished convention paper, AEJMC): Washington, D.C., August 1995).

106. "Don't Gag Me with a Law," *Student Press Law Center Report* (Winter 1995–96), p. 21.

are being protected from majorities, as the Constitution prescribes, but minority persons are not speakers in these cases but audience—harassed individuals or members of a victimized group. It is hazardous to predict the future course of these cases or the public mood that may govern them.

Meanwhile classic forms of censorship are still abundant. Prior review boards are in place in schools all over the country. A superintendent in North Brunswick, New Jersey, had this to say about systems of prior restraint: school officials can censor if the articles are derogatory toward particular groups. "If it is harmful and poses a threat to safety . . . if it's prejudicial and alienates certain groups," he added, "I think the school has that right."[107] Generally, no journalism training is required for serving on these review boards.

Other Problems

DISTRIBUTION   When an entire edition of a newspaper is stolen or vandalized, distribution has come to an end. Disaffected groups regularly destroy offending newspapers. As justification they argue that you can't steal anything that's already "free" or that no one "owns" or that their student fees entitle them to take what's theirs. These arguments do not take into account the fact that only a minuscule part of what they are stealing is actually theirs and that advertisers under contract also have a stake in these assets. Moreover, such action is an affront to all other readers. Twenty-two such incidents were reported in the 1995–1996 school year, and only a few have been pursued as simple felonies.

School officials may restrict distribution of all forms of expression, political and commercial, if they can demonstrate that distribution will disrupt the educational process. A university campus is at the very least a limited public forum, depending upon what traditions, customs, and policies have evolved.[108] Content alone is not grounds for closing a limited public forum,[109] but reasonable time, place, and manner restric-

tions may be.[110] College plazas, malls, sidewalks, and indoor areas such as student unions or commons may be considered public forums or limited public forums. Faculty offices and classrooms are not. Policies and practices governing nonstudents may be determinative. One can expect that secondary schools generally will be less accommodating to free speech activities than college and university campuses.

ACCESS TO INFORMATION   Campus publication reporters and editors have always had trouble getting information from the various governing echelons of their own academic communities. Records, administrative hearings, and meetings are too often closed. The highest courts in New York, Michigan, and Georgia have reacted by agreeing that when student interest is shown, state open records and meeting laws apply against college administrations that prefer secrecy in such matters as presidential searches, faculty evaluations, disciplinary hearings, and law enforcement records.

Under some state open records laws, faculty evaluations of public school teachers are available. New York, North Dakota, Colorado, and Ohio are examples. In other states, the evaluations are closed; in still others, the question is clouded because the benefits of disclosure are to be balanced against the harm to privacy. This balancing is practiced in Iowa, Montana, West Virginia, Wisconsin, and a substantial number of other states.

Campus crime records have been particularly problematic. The Family Educational Rights and Privacy Act (FERPA), also known as the Buckley Amendment, was designed to protect the records and the procedures that generate records of college students from prying eyes of all kinds, including those of parents. In 1992, the Act was amended to exempt law enforcement records from the broader category of educational records. Two years later in 1994, the U.S. Department of Education issued regulations requiring all federally funded colleges and universities to issue annual campus crime reports. These developments were the culmination of efforts on campuses across the country, often led

107. "Nothing Left to Give," *Student Press Law Center Report* 16 (Spring 1995), pp. 5, 10.

108. *Widmar v. Vincent*, 454 U.S. 263, 267–68, n. 5 (1981).

109. *Police Department of Chicago v. Mosley*, 408 U.S. 92, 95–96 (1972).

110. *Ward v. Rock against Racism*, 491 U.S. 781, 791 (1989).

by women students, to disclose the level of safety of schools and surrounding environs. Student disciplinary records, still categorized as "education records," are still in the gray area.

SUBPOENAS   In early 1996, the editor of the *Minnesota Daily,* a national leader among major university student newspapers, was held in contempt of court and fined $250 per day pending the end of a criminal assault trial. A member of the Progressive Student Organization had been charged with hitting an alleged neo-Nazi. The court wanted to know if the neo-Nazi was wearing brass knuckles. A Minnesota district court judge, under pressure from county prosecutors and an appellate court, ordered negatives of photographs taken at the scene by the newspaper's photographer made available for *in camera* review. Due to ambiguity in the wording of Minnesota's shield law, photographs, notes, outtakes, and other miscellany of the reporter's trade could be construed to be protected only if they would divulge the identity of a source. The identity of a source was not an issue in this instance. Addressing the *Daily*'s First Amendment claim, the state appeals court decided that *in camera* review was an appropriate compromise between "a victim's right to confidentiality (in this case the reporter's qualified privilege) and the defendant's right to confront the accuser or procure all possible exculpating evidence." Quoting *Branzburg,* the court added that "The First Amendment does not invalidate every incidental burdening of the press that may result from the enforcement of civil or criminal statutes of general applicability."[111] The state supreme court declined without comment to hear the case, and representatives of the press asked the state legislature for an amendment to the shield law. Editors faced with having to provide evidence to prosecutors, especially in trivial cases, risk their credibility as honest brokers of news and public information. A jury acquitted the defendant in time to relieve the *Daily* editor of all but two days of punishment for contempt. See p. 350 and fn. 56, Chapt. 6.

High school newspaper photographers found themselves similarly vulnerable to police subpoenas when they took pictures of a parking lot fight between white and Asian students. The Mountlake Terrace High School *Hawkeye*'s editor refused to give her photos to the prosecutor despite a judicial order to do so. The "integrity" of the newspaper, the effect on sources, and a desire not to be seen as an "arm of the government" were the editor's reasons. Next step was the Washington Supreme Court.

SPEECH CODES   Highly restrictive speech codes at universities as prominent and as liberal in their traditions as Michigan and Wisconsin have been declared unconstitutional by federal courts.[112] In the Wisconsin case, a federal district judge wrote that "Content-based prohibitions such as in the UW Rule, however well intended, simply cannot survive the screening which our Constitution demands." Students were prohibited from directing discriminatory epithets at particular individuals with intent to demean them and create a hostile educational environment. The code, said the court, was overbroad and unduly vague and did not meet the requirements of the fighting words doctrine.

Similar codes have been prescribed by administrators for public college and high school student participation on the World Wide Web and the Internet. In these rules, "offensive" expression is often the threshold for state interference. Some regulations are less amorphous. Carnegie Mellon University, for example, announced in 1994 that in compliance with Pennsylvania law it would close out any bulletin board that distributed sexually explicit or obscene material.

Bans against the "sexually explicit" are also written into high school codes governing use of the Internet. When Bellevue, Washington high school student Paul Kim broke the rule, his principal withdrew the school's endorsement of Kim as a National Merit Finalist and sent faxes of his "crime" to every college and university to which he had applied. A year later, the Bellevue School District settled out of court with Kim after the

---

111. *Minnesota v. Knutson,* 24 Med. L. Rptr. 1530, 539 N.W.2d 254 (Min.Ct.App. 1995).

112. *Doe v. University of Michigan,* 721 F.Supp. 852 (E.D.Mich. 1989); *UW-M Post v. Bd. of Regents of U of W,* 774 F.Supp. 1163 (E.D.Wisc. 1991).

ACLU threatened a lawsuit based on free speech rights.

Normally, when high school students are given computer accounts, they are required to sign agreements that they will not enter areas containing pornography or other "inappropriate" language or materials. A Justice on Campus Web site, which attempts to document speech restraints of these kinds on high school and college campuses across the country, has itself felt the pressures of censorship. What is offensive, harassing, threatening, unwanted, disruptive, or neo-Nazi generally falls into the punishable category; the problem of vagueness remains.

Student Broadcasters

The FCC has had no trouble deciding "who's in charge" at campus broadcast stations. Though radio stations are rare on high school campuses, they are more common on college campuses, and so it is college students who are apt to find themselves in hot water on occasion. In 1978, the FCC voted to deny license renewal to a noncommercial, educational FM (WXPN) station at the University of Pennsylvania. There had been complaints about obscenity in a live call-in program, broadcast between 4 and 7 P.M. The FCC felt that the licensee, the trustees of the university, had lost control over the operation of the station.

Tracing control of the station through a bewildering campus bureaucracy, the commission concluded: "In sum, the daily operation of WXPN-FM was in the hands of student-run organizations and was considered by the licensee to be just one of many 'student' activities supervised by the Student Activities Council."

This was not good enough for the FCC. The station was licensed to the trustees, yet they exercised no control over what was broadcast. Under the law, the licensee is responsible for everything that goes out over the air.

The FCC said it did not wish to discourage student-run stations, but ultimate responsibility for content rested with the licensee, and total abdication of this role was unacceptable. The licensee was fined $2,000 and Penn lost its license. But a year later the FCC broke its own rule on how long one must wait to reapply and entertained a hasty reapplication from the trustees. A new license was granted but with the understanding that the station would be controlled by a professional manager and staff and that the president of the university and a Board of Governors would assume ultimate responsibility for programming.[113]

Conclusion

Cases such as *Hazelwood* and *Trustees of the University of Pennsylvania* may seem troublesome. If in any sense schools are breeding places for democratic citizenship, these cases could be said to breed only cynicism, although many would disagree. In any case, sooner or later scholastic journalists and broadcasters must learn to be responsible for their own mistakes and misjudgments. Although student groups may have difficulty getting broadcast licenses, their newspapers ought at least to consider the advantages of being free of credits, grades, and coursework. Although some excellent publications are woven into curricula, those independent of curricula seem to have many fewer problems with administrative censorship, and they are often better publications.

By serving on publication boards that include faculty and administrative representatives and play the role of publisher, students can learn how to judge their fellow students. This is how society functions. Libelous, obscene, or potentially disruptive content ought to be examined by faculty advisers and institutional or publication lawyers. This is how the commercial press does it. But responsible citizenship cannot be learned in an oligarchy.

Private school students will find the Constitution less available to them because censorship of their publications does not constitute state action. Nevertheless, they may still look to state constitutions, statutes, and legal precedents when they run afoul of the censor. Their institutions may also have traditions or written guarantees reflecting a respect for constitutional rights.

The Student Press Law Center (SPLC) in Washington, D.C.,[114] provides free assistance to students who have serious problems with censorship, access to information, libel, privacy, or any

---

113. *Trustees of the University of Pennsylvania,* 69 F.C.C.2d 1384 (1978). See also 45 R.R.2d 565 (1979).
114. Suite 504, 1735 Eye Street, N.W., Washington, D.C., 20006; (202) 466-5242.

part of the litigation process. Although few students litigants can generate the funds and the time necessary to take cases up the judicial appeals ladder, any issue of *Report,* the official publication of the SPLC, reflects the turmoil over free speech and press on high school and college campuses. The Center received 1,409 requests for legal assistance in 1995. In the past seven years, calls to the Center have increased almost 170 percent. Almost 40 percent of the calls are related to censorship by administrators. Another 23 percent have to do with libel, 17 percent with copyright, and 6 percent with access to information. Nearly half of the calls come from public colleges, while a quarter are from public high schools. The Center believes *Hazelwood* is in large part responsible for this increase.[115]

The Center also drafts model legislation, policy statements, and guidelines for advisers and administrators. The SPLC opposes prior review by anyone other than the designated publications

adviser, and then only for pedagogical purposes or to prevent disruption of the educational process. In a free press environment, or what is closer to a traditional public forum, students and their parents might be liable for damages resulting from expression or publication. Where teachers and advisers have taken it upon themselves to supervise and control what is said or published, they will be liable. To achieve shared responsibility, a publication board is a good idea. It would include students and publication staffs (hopefully in a majority), teachers, adviser, and administrators. Political correctness (PC), as interpreted by radicals of both left and right, is also taking its toll on traditional campus values of free expression. Although much of this conflict revolves around the appropriateness of library books, campus publications have not been immune. When "objectionable" material is printed in a school newspaper, a frequent response, as noted above, has been to steal and sometimes confiscate copies of the offending publication. Scholastic journalism is sometimes a perishable commodity.

---

115. Student Press Law Center *Report* (Spring 1994), pp. 3, 4.

CHAPTER 11

THE REGULATION OF BROAD-CASTING: SOME PROBLEMS OF LAW, TECHNOLOGY, AND POLICY

CHAPTER OUTLINE

INTRODUCTION: THE RATIONALE FOR BROADCAST REGULATION

One of the startling realities of the law of broadcasting is that its legal framework has long been altogether different from that of the print media. As Judge Warren Burger stated in *Office of Communication of the United Church of Christ v. FCC*, 359 F.2d 994, 1003 (D.C. Cir. 1966):

> A broadcaster seeks and is granted the free and exclusive use of a limited and valuable part of the public domain; when he accepts that franchise it is burdened by enforceable public obligations. A newspaper can be operated at the whim or caprice of its owners; a broadcast station cannot.

Under the Communications Act of 1934, broadcast regulation is extensive. The license period has been steadily extended. Until 1996, television licenses were issued for five years and radio licenses for seven years. As a result of the Telecommunications Act of 1996, the license period for both radio and television is now eight years. On January 23, 1997, the FCC implemented sec. 203 of the Telecommunications Act of 1996 by adopting rules that extend the license terms for television and radio stations to eight years, with the exception of experimental broadcast station license terms, which remain one year. The Act's language says that the license shall be granted and renewed "for a term of not to exceed 8 years." 47 U.S.C. § 307(c)(1). According to the Communications Act of 1934, the Federal Communications Commission (FCC) is to grant licenses, provided that "the public convenience, interest or necessity will be served thereby." 47 U.S.C. § 307(a).

In light of these and other provisions of the Act, the meaning of the "public interest" standard of sec. 307 has been a continuing issue in broadcast regulation. What criteria, for example, should govern the "public interest" standard? How extensive should regulation be? How directly can content be regulated without violating First Amendment standards?

In the 1940s, in the following case, NBC and CBS argued that the FCC's authority was limited solely to removing technical and engineering impediments that obstructed effective broadcasting. According to their argument, the FCC had no authority to make any particular qualitative demands of broadcast licensees.

When the FCC imposed restrictions on radio network/affiliate relationships, the networks (called chain broadcasters at the time) appealed ultimately to the U.S. Supreme Court. The Court addressed some very fundamental questions: Is broadcasting different than print? Should the FCC's function be limited to traffic control? Or should it be directed instead to determining the composition of the traffic, i.e., the character and quality of broadcast programming?

The Theory of Scarcity

NBC v. United States
319 U.S. 190, 63 S. CT. 997, 87 L. ED. 1344 (1943).

Justice FRANKFURTER delivered the opinion of the Court.

In view of our dependence upon regulated private enterprise in discharging the far-reaching role which radio plays in our society, a somewhat detailed exposition of the history of the present controversy and the issues which it raises is appropriate. On March 18, 1938, the FCC undertook a comprehensive investigation to determine whether special regulations applicable to radio stations engaged in chain broadcasting were required in the "public interest, convenience, or necessity."

The regulations, are addressed (directly) to station licensees and applicants for station licenses. They provide, in general, that no licenses shall be granted to stations or applicants having specified relationships with networks. Each regulation is directed at a particular practice found by the FCC to be detrimental to the "public interest," and we shall consider them seriatim.

The FCC found that at the end of 1938 there were 660 commercial stations in the United States, and that 341 of these were affiliated with national networks. It pointed out that the stations affiliated with the national networks utilized more than 97% of the total night-time broadcasting power of all the stations in the country. NBC and CBS together controlled more than 85% of the total night-time wattage, and the broadcast business of the three national network companies amounted to almost half of the total business of all stations in the United States.

The FCC recognized that network broadcasting had played and was continuing to play an important part in the development of radio. "The growth and development of chain broadcasting," it stated, "found its impetus in the desire to give widespread coverage to programs which otherwise would not be heard beyond the reception area of a single station. Chain broadcasting makes possible a wider reception for expensive entertainment and cultural programs and also for programs of national or regional significance which would otherwise have coverage only in the locality of origin. Furthermore, the access to

greatly enlarged audiences made possible by chain broadcasting has been a strong incentive to advertisers to finance the production of expensive programs. But the fact that the chain broadcasting method brings benefits and advantages to both the listening public and to broadcast station licensees does not mean that the prevailing practices and policies of the networks and their outlets are sound in all respects, or that they should not be altered. The FCC's duty under the Communications Act of 1934, 47 U.S.C. §151 *et seq.*, is not only to see that the public receives the advantages and benefits of chain broadcasting, but also, so far as its powers enable it, to see that practices which adversely affect the ability of licensees to operate in the public interest are eliminated." The FCC found [certain] network abuses were amendable to correction within the powers granted it by Congress.

> *Regulation 3.101—Exclusive affiliation of station.* The FCC found that the network affiliation agreements of NBC and CBS customarily contained a provision which prevented the station from broadcasting the programs of any other network. The effect of this provision was to hinder the growth of new networks.
>
> "Restraints having this effect," the FCC observed, "are to be condemned as contrary to the public interest irrespective of whether it be assumed that Mutual ['another network'] programs are of equal, superior, or inferior quality. The important consideration is that station licensees are denied freedom to choose the programs which they believe best suited to their needs; in this manner the duty of a station licensee to operate in the public interest is defeated."
>
> *Regulation 3.102—Territorial exclusivity.* The FCC found another type of "exclusivity" provision in network affiliation agreements whereby the network bound itself not to sell programs to any other station in the same area. The effect of this provision, designed to protect the affiliate from the competition of other stations serving the same territory, was to deprive the listening public of many programs that might otherwise be available.
>
> The FCC concluded that "[I]t is as much against the public interest for a network affiliate to enter into a contractual arrangement which prevents another station from carrying a network program as it would be for it to drown out that program by electrical interference."
>
> *Regulation 3.103—Term of affiliation.* The standard NBC and CBS affiliation contracts bound

the station for a period of five years, with the network having the exclusive rights to terminate the contracts upon one year's notice. The FCC, relying upon § 307(d) of the Communications Act of 1934, under which no license to operate a broadcast station can be granted for a longer term than three years, found the five-year affiliation term to be contrary to the policy of the Act.

The FCC concluded that under contracts binding the affiliates for five years, "stations become parties to arrangements which deprive the public of the improved service it might otherwise derive from competition in the network field; and that a station is not operating in the public interest when it so limits its freedom of action."

Regulation 3.104—Option time.   The FCC found that network affiliation contracts usually contained so-called network optional time clauses. Under these provisions the network could upon 28 days' notice call upon its affiliates to carry a commercial program during any of the hours specified in the agreement as "network optional time" [which] meant the entire broadcast day. In the FCC's judgment these optional time provisions, in addition to imposing serious obstacles in the path of new networks, hindered stations in developing a local program service.

Regulation 3.105—Right to reject programs.   The FCC found that most network affiliation contracts contained a clause defining the right of the station to reject network commercial programs. The NBC contracts provided simply that the station "may reject a network program the broadcasting of which would not be in the public interest, convenience, and necessity." While seeming in the abstract to be fair, these provisions, according to the FCC's finding, did not sufficiently protect the "public interest." As a practical matter, the licensee could not determine in advance whether the broadcasting of any particular network program would or would not be in the public interest. "In practice, if not in theory, stations affiliated with networks have delegated to the networks a large part of their programming functions. In many instances, moreover, the network further delegates the actual production of programs to advertising agencies. These agencies are far more than mere brokers or intermediaries between the network and the advertiser. To an ever increasing extent, these agencies actually exercise the function of program production. Thus it is frequently neither the station nor the network, but rather the advertising agency, which determines what broadcast programs shall contain. Under such circumstances, it is especially important that individual

stations, if they are to operate in the public interest, should have the practical opportunity as well as the contractual right to reject network programs. It is the station, not the network, which is licensed to serve the public interest." [FCC, Report on Chain Broadcasting, 1941, pp. 39, 66.]

Regulations 3.106—Network ownership of stations.   The FCC found that [the] 18 stations owned by NBC and CBS were among the most powerful and desirable in the country, and were permanently inaccessible to competing networks. The FCC concluded that "the licensing of two stations in the same area to a single network organization is basically unsound and contrary to the public interest," and that it was also against the "public interest" for network organizations to own stations in areas where the available facilities were so few or of such unequal coverage that competition would thereby be substantially restricted.

Regulation 3.108—Control by networks of station rates.   Under this provision the station could not sell time to a national advertiser for less than it would cost the advertiser if he bought the time from NBC. The FCC concluded that "it is against the public interest for a station licensee to enter into a contract with a network which has the effect of decreasing its ability to compete for national business. We believe that the public interest will best be served and listeners supplied with the best programs if stations bargain freely with national advertisers."

The appellants attack the validity of these regulations along many fronts. They contend that the FCC went beyond the regulatory powers conferred upon it by the Communications Act of 1934; and that, in any event, the regulations abridge the appellants' right of free speech in violation of the First Amendment. We are thus called upon to determine whether Congress has authorized the FCC to exercise the power asserted by the Chain Broadcasting Regulations, and if it has, whether the Constitution forbids the exercise of such authority.

The enforcement of the Radio Act of 1912 presented no serious problems prior to the World War. Questions of interference arose only rarely because there were more than enough frequencies for all the stations then in existence. The war accelerated the development of the art, however, and in 1921 the first standard broadcast stations were established. They grew rapidly in number, and by 1923 there were several hundred such stations throughout the country. The act of 1912 had not set aside any particular frequencies for the use of private broadcast stations; consequently, the Secretary of Commerce selected two frequencies, 750 and 833 kilocycles, and licensed all stations to operate upon one or the other of these channels. The number of stations increased so rapidly, however, and the situation became so chaotic, that the Secretary, upon the recommendation of the National Radio Conferences which met in Washington in 1923 and 1924, established a policy of assigning specified frequencies to particular stations. Since there were more stations than available frequencies, the Secretary attempted to find room for everybody by limiting the power and hours of operation of stations in order that several stations might use the same channel. [Courts declared that] the Secretary of Commerce [was] powerless to deal with the situation. From July, 1926, to February 23, 1927, when Congress enacted the Radio Act of 1927, 44 Stat. 1162, almost 200 new stations went on the air. These new stations used any frequencies they desired, regardless of the interference thereby caused to others. Existing stations changed to other frequencies and increased their power and hours of operation at will. The result was confusion and chaos. With everybody on the air, nobody could be heard. The situation became so intolerable that the President in his message of December 7, 1926, appealed to Congress to enact a comprehensive radio law.

The plight into which radio fell prior to 1927 was attributable to certain basic facts about radio as a means of communications—its facilities are limited, they are not available to all who may wish to use them; the radio spectrum simply is not large enough to accommodate everybody. In enacting the Radio Act of 1927, the first comprehensive scheme of control over radio communication, Congress acted upon the knowledge that if the potentialities of radio were not to be wasted, regulation was essential.

The Radio Act of 1927 created the Federal Radio Commission, composed of five members, and endowed the commission with wide licensing and regulatory powers. We do not pause here to enumerate the scope of the Radio Act of 1927 and of the authority entrusted to the Radio Commission, for the basic provisions of that Act are incorporated in the Communications Act of 1934, the legislation immediately before us. The

criterion governing the exercise of the commission's licensing power is the "public interest, convenience, or necessity." §§ 307(a)(d), 309(a), 310, 312.

The Act itself establishes that the FCC's powers are not limited to the engineering and technical aspects of regulation of radio communication. Yet we are asked to regard the FCC as a kind of traffic officer, policing the wave lengths to prevent stations from interfering with each other. But the Act does not restrict the commission merely to supervision of the traffic. It puts upon the FCC the burden of determining the composition of that traffic. The facilities of radio are not large enough to accommodate all who wish to use them. Methods must be devised for choosing from among the many who apply. And since Congress itself could not do this, it committed the task to the FCC.

The FCC was, however, not left at large in performing this duty. The touchstone provided by Congress was the "public interest, convenience, or necessity," a criterion which "is as concrete as the complicated factors for judgment in such a field of delegated authority permit." *FCC v. Pottsville Broad. Co.*, 309 U.S. 134, 138 (1940). The "public interest" to be served under the Communications Act is thus the interest of the listening public in "the larger and more effective use of radio." § 303(g). The facilities of radio are limited and therefore precious; they cannot be left to wasteful use without detriment to the public interest. The FCC's licensing function cannot be discharged, therefore, merely by finding that there are not technological objections to the granting of a license. If the criterion of "public interest" were limited to such matters, how could the commission choose between two applicants for the same facilities, each of whom is financially and technically qualified to operate a station? Since the very inception of federal regulation by radio, comparative considerations as to the services to be rendered have governed the application of the standard of "public interest, convenience, or necessity."

The avowed aim of the Communications Act of 1934 was to secure the maximum benefits of radio to all the people of the United States. To that end Congress endowed the FCC with comprehensive powers to promote and realize the vast potentialities of radio. Section 303(g) provides that the FCC shall "generally encourage the larger and more effective use of radio in the public interest"; subsection (i) gives the FCC specific "authority to make special regulations applicable to radio stations engaged in chain broadcasting," and subsection (r) empowers it to adopt "such rules and regulations and prescribe such restrictions and conditions, not inconsistent with law, as may be necessary to carry out the provisions of this act."

These provisions, individually and in the aggregate, preclude the notion that the FCC is empowered to deal only with technical and engineering impediments to the "larger and more effective use of radio in the public interest." We cannot find in the Act any such restriction of the FCC's authority. Suppose, for example, that a community can, because of physical limitations, be assigned only two stations. That community might be deprived of effective service in any one of several ways. More powerful stations in nearby cities might blanket out the signals of the local stations so that they could not be heard at all. The stations might interfere with each other so that neither could be clearly heard. One station might dominate the other with the power of its signal. But the community could be deprived of good radio service in ways less crude. One man, financially and technically qualified, might apply for and obtain the licenses of both stations and present a single service over the two stations, thus wasting a frequency otherwise available to the area. The language of the Act does not withdraw such a situation from the licensing and regulatory powers of the FCC, and there is no evidence that Congress did not mean its broad language to carry the authority it expresses.

In essence, the Chain Broadcasting Regulations represent a particularization of the FCC's conception of the "public interest" sought to be safeguarded by Congress in enacting the Communications Act of 1934. The basic consideration of policy underlying the Regulations is succinctly stated in its Report: "With the number of radio channels limited by natural factors, the public interest demands that those who are entrusted with the available channels shall make the fullest and most effective use of them. If a licensee enters into a contract with a network organization which limits his ability to make the best use of the radio facility assigned him, he is not serving the public interest. The net effect [of the practices disclosed by the investigation] has been that broadcasting service has been maintained at a level below that possible under a system of free competition. Having so found, we would be remiss in our statutory duty of encouraging 'the larger and more effective use of radio in the public interest' if we were to grant licenses to persons who persist in these practices."

We would be asserting our personal views regarding the effective utilization of radio were we to deny that the FCC was entitled to find that the large public aims of the Communications Act of 1934 comprehend the considerations which moved the commission in promulgating the Chain Broadcasting Regulations. True enough, the Act does not explicitly say that the FCC shall have power to deal with network practices found inimical to the public interest. But Congress was acting in a field of regulation which was both new and dynamic. "Congress moved under the spur of a widespread fear that in the absence of governmental control the public interest might be subordinated to monopolistic domination in the broadcasting field." *FCC v. Pottsville Broad. Co.* In the context of the developing problems to which it was directed, the Act gave the Commission not niggardly but expansive powers. It was given a comprehensive mandate to "encourage the larger and more effective use of radio in the public interest," if need be, by making "special regulations applicable to radio stations engaged in chain broadcasting." § 303(g)(i).

While Congress did not give the FCC unfettered discretion to regulate all phases of the radio industry, it did not frustrate the purposes for which the Communications Act of 1934 was brought into being by attempting an itemized catalogue of the specific manifestations of the general problems for the solution of which it was establishing a regulatory agency. That would have stereotyped the powers for the commission to specify details in regulating a field of enterprise the dominant characteristic of which was the rapid pace of its unfolding. And so Congress did what experience had taught it in similar attempts at regulation, even in fields where the subject-matter of regulation was far less fluid and dynamic than radio. The essence of that experience was to define broad areas for regulation and to establish standards for judgment adequately related in their application to the problems to be solved.

We conclude, therefore, that the Communications Act of 1934 authorized the FCC to promulgate regulations designed to correct the abuses disclosed by its investigation of chain broadcasting.

Since there is no basis for any claim that the FCC failed to observe procedural safeguards required by law, we reach the contention that the Regulations should be denied enforcement on constitutional grounds. Here, as in *New York Cent. Sec. Corp. v. United States,* 287 U.S. 12, 24, 25, the claim is made that the standard of "public interest" governing the exercise of the powers delegated to the FCC by Congress is so vague and indefinite that, if it be construed as comprehensively as words alone permit, the delegation of legislative authority is unconstitutional. But, as we held in that case, "It is a mistaken assumption that this is a mere general reference to public welfare without any standard to guide determinations. The purpose of the act, the requirements it imposes, and the context of the provision in question show the contrary." *Id.*

We come, finally, to an appeal to the First Amendment. The regulations, even if, valid in all other respects, must fall because they abridge, say the appellants, their right of free speech. If that be so, it would follow that every person whose application for a license to operate a station is denied by the FCC is thereby denied his constitutional right of free speech. Freedom of utterance is abridged to many who wish to use the limited facilities of radio. *Unlike other modes of expression, radio inherently is not available to all. That is its unique characteristic, and that is why, unlike other modes of expression, it is subject to governmental regulation. Because it cannot be used by all, some who wish to use it must be denied.* [Emphasis added.] But Congress did not authorize the FCC to choose among applicants upon the basis of their political, economic or social views, or upon any other capricious basis. If it did, or if the commission by these regulations proposed a choice among applicants upon some such basis, the issue before us would be wholly different. The question here is simply whether the FCC, by announcing that it will refuse licenses to persons who engage in specified network practices (a basis for choice which we hold is comprehended within the statutory criterion of "public interest"), is thereby denying such persons the constitutional right of free speech. The right of free speech does not include, however, the right to use the facilities of radio without a license. The licensing system

established by Congress in the Communications Act of 1934 was a proper exercise of its power over commerce. The standard it provided for the licensing of stations was the "public interest, convenience, or necessity." Denial of a station license on that ground, if valid under the Act, is not a denial of free speech.

Affirmed.

Justice MURPHY, dissenting.

Although radio broadcasting, like the press, is generally conducted on a commercial basis, it is not an ordinary business activity, like the selling of securities or the marketing of electrical power. In the dissemination of information and opinion radio has assumed a position of commanding importance, rivaling the press and the pulpit. Owing to its physical characteristics radio, unlike the other methods of conveying information, must be regulated and rationed by the government. Otherwise there would be chaos, and radio's usefulness would be largely destroyed. But because of its vast potentialities as a medium of communication, discussion and propaganda, the character and extent of control that should be exercised over it by the government is a matter of deep and vital concern. Events in Europe show that radio may readily be a weapon of authority and misrepresentation, instead of a means of entertainment and enlightenment. It may even be an instrument of oppression. In pointing out these possibilities I do not mean to intimate in the slightest that they are imminent or probable in this country but they do suggest that the construction of the instant statute should be approached with more than ordinary restraint and caution, to avoid an interpretation that is not clearly justified by the conditions that brought about its enactment, or that would give the FCC greater powers than the Congress intended to confer.

By means of these regulations and the enforcement program, the FCC would not only extend its authority over business activities which represent interests and investments of a very substantial character, which have not been put under its jurisdiction by the act, but would greatly enlarge its control over an institution that has now become a rival of the press and pulpit as a purveyor of news and entertainment and a medium of public discussion. To assume a function and responsibility of such wide reach and importance in the life of the nation, as a mere incident of its duty to pass on individual applications for permission to operate a radio station and use a specific wave length, is an assumption of authority to which I am not willing to lend my assent.

COMMENT

The FCC and the Supreme Court believed broadcasting to be "scarce" in the late 1930s and early 1940s. In 1940, there were 765 radio stations and a handful of TV stations on the air. Today the number of radio and TV stations is vastly greater. In addition, there has been an explosion in new electronic media including such widely used services as cable and DBS. Is the scarcity rationale obsolete? In *Turner Broadcasting System, Inc v. FCC*, 512 U.S. 622 (1994), Justice Kennedy observed: "Although courts and commentators have criticized the scarcity rationale, we have declined to question its continuing validity as support for our broadcast jurisprudence."

Is the limited-access-medium rationale the only plausible basis for broadcast regulation? Since Justice Murphy points out that radio "may be a weapon of authority and misrepresentation instead of a means of entertainment and enlightenment," why does he wish to overturn the Chain Broadcasting Regulations and thereby limit the concentration of communicating power?

Justice Murphy's dissent offers the basis for a new rationale for government regulation of broadcasting—the social impact rationale. Under this theory, the pervasiveness and the impact of broadcasting justify greater government regulation of broadcasting than of other media. For application of this theory, see *FCC v. Pacifica Foundation*, p. 606.

The Chain Broadcasting Regulations were an attempt by the FCC to do what Congress failed to do in the Communications Act of 1934, i.e., bring the networks under the regulatory authority of the FCC. The FCC was concerned that the station licensees, the parties regulated by the act, were becoming conduits for the largely unregulated networks. As with radio in 1943, at the present time television programming in the evening or "prime time" hours is largely dominated by the networks, although in the late 1980s network "share" of the audience dropped substantially due to increased competition from cable TV and independent television stations.

Currently, the networks, although not directly subject to regulation under the Communications Act of 1934, are actually responsive to FCC jurisdiction in at least two ways. First, FCC rules and regulations do, of course, bind broadcast licensees. To the extent these licensees are network affiliates, which in large part they are, the networks are affected by FCC policy. Second, although there are limits on how many broadcasting outlets a single entity may own, the networks own as many stations as the existing rules permit. See text, p. 751. Therefore, with respect to O and O's (stations owned and operated by the networks), the networks are directly regulated by the FCC. We have been considering the problem of the station owner who is a network affiliate, who does not know what programming his station will be emitting until he flicks the dial with the rest of the audience. The same problem, however, can arise with a station that is not a network affiliate.[1]

In June 1995, the FCC issued a Notice of Proposed RuleMaking to amend the rules governing the types of contracts that networks and local affiliates could agree to. *See In re the Commission's Regulations Governing Programming Practices of Broadcast Television Networks and Affiliates 47 C.F.R. § 73.658(a), (b), (d), (e) and (g), 10 F.C.C.R. 11951 (1995).* The Notice proposed amending the right-to-reject rule, the time option rule, the exclusive affiliation rule, the dual network rule, and the network territorial exclusivity rule.

First the FCC proposed to modify the right-to-reject rule—preventing networks from demanding that affiliates show all network programming—so that an affiliate could only reject programming for nonfinancial reasons. Second, the FCC proposed abandoning the time option rule, which prevents a network from reserving an option to use specified amounts of an affiliate's broadcast time. Under the FCC plan, however, if a network was not going to use a time slot, it would be required to notify the affiliate well in advance so that the affiliate could find alternative programming and advertisers.

---

1. See *Yale Broadcasting v. FCC*, 478 F.2d 594 (D.C. Cir. 1973), *cert. den.*, 414 U.S. 914 (1973).

Third, the FCC also proposed abandoning the exclusive affiliation rule, which prevents a network from restricting an affiliate's ability to show programming from other networks, because competing networks could gain access to a market in other ways. Fourth, rather than recommending a specific action on the dual network rule, which prevents anyone from owning more than one network, the FCC sought further comments on the benefits and drawbacks of the rule.

Finally, the FCC proposed partially abandoning the network territorial exclusivity rule, which prevents an affiliate from restricting a network's ability to market its programming to other stations inside and outside its community. The FCC proposed eliminating the restriction on preventing a network from offering programming to other stations within the same community. The FCC also stated, however, that affiliates should not be able to prevent a network from marketing its programming to stations in other communities. The FCC said that restricting network programming outside a market area would have no beneficial effects. The FCC has not yet acted on these proposals.

One study concludes that the *NBC* case has made three major contributions to communications law:

In *NBC,* the court addressed three points of continuing interest to the issue of the FCC's jurisdiction. First, the court confirmed that the FCC's licensing authority over broadcast stations permits it to promulgate regulations involving network practices addressed to broadcast station licensees that are network affiliates. Second, the Court suggested that courts should construe the 1934 act liberally in evaluating the commission's regulatory powers and responsibilities. Stated simply, courts should view the specific responsibilities assigned to the FCC as exemplary of its larger responsibilities. Third, the court implied by its silence that the FCC's overriding responsibility to regulate television broadcasting and its specific power to regulate stations engaged in chain broadcasting authorize it to regulate networks directly. See Krattenmaker and Metzger, *FCC Regulatory Authority over Commercial Television Networks: The Role of Ancillary Jurisdiction,* 77 Nw. U. L. Rev. 403, 431–32 (1982).

NBC v. United States determined that scarcity justified different treatment of broadcasting and print. A number of years passed, however, before the Supreme Court began to consider the manner in which broadcast and print First Amendment

theory vary. Does the "public interest" have a constitutional dimension? Does the public have First Amendment rights along with the broadcaster? In case of a conflict, whose rights should be subordinated?

Theories of Listeners' and Viewers' Rights

When a fundamentalist minister, Rev. Billy James Hargis, attacked a journalist, Fred Cook, who had been critical of presidential candidate Barry Goldwater, Hargis's strident attack implicated the "personal attack" rules that flowed from the FCC's fairness doctrine. In *Red Lion Broadcasting Co. v. FCC,* 395 U.S. 367 (1969), these doctrines and policies were challenged as violative of the First Amendment rights of broadcasters. At this point the student should read the *Red Lion* decision, text, p. 806.

The *Red Lion* decision indicated that the Supreme Court continued to believe that scarcity justified unique First Amendment treatment of broadcasters. Even more significantly, for the first time the Court parsed out and then rank ordered the interests of competing First Amendment claimants. To the surprise of broadcasters, the Court held that the fairness doctrine and personal attack rules not only did not abridge the First Amendment but actually enhanced First Amendment values.

Although the *Red Lion* decision professes allegiance to the scarcity rationale for broadcast regulation, does the case actually recognize a new justification for broadcast regulation? Does it add a new access-for-ideas justification for broadcast regulation that goes beyond the older rationalization of limited access to the spectrum?

The invalidation, in *Miami Herald Pub. Co. v. Tornillo,* 418 U.S. 241 (1974), of a state statutory right to reply to the print media in the case of an editorial attack presents a vivid contrast to the right of reply to personal attack in the broadcast media upheld in *Red Lion.* In *Tornillo,* the Supreme Court considered a Florida statute requiring a newspaper that editorially attacked a political candidate to grant the candidate equivalent space to reply; violated the First Amendment. The *Tornillo* decision does not so much as cite the *Red Lion* case decided only five years earlier. Henry Geller, former General Counsel of the FCC, has argued that "there is a direct conflict between *Tornillo* and *Red Lion.*" At the same time, he argues that the conflict is understandable. See Geller, *Does* Red Lion *Square with* Tornillo? 29 U. Miami L. Rev. 477 (1975).

Geller points out that even if the fairness doctrine were abolished, government regulation would still play a role in the broadcast media that it does not play in the print media:

> The point is that by eliminating the fairness doctrine, the problem of government control is not eliminated as long as regulation and licensing based on the public trust concept continues. But the public would be wholly unprotected from licensees based on presenting only one side of an issue. I, for one, would not accept that.

Judge Tamm spoke directly to the broadcasters argument that *Red Lion* and *Tornillo* were flatly inconsistent:

> I find the decisions "flatly consistent." Arguments advanced to the contrary are only reflective of broadcasters desires to become indistinguishable from the print media and to be freed of their obligations as public trustees. While the relevancy of *Red Lion* was fully briefed in *Tornillo,* that decision contained no reference to *Red Lion* or to implications for the broadcast media. I read the Court's striking down a reply rule for newspapers in *Tornillo* after upholding a similar rule for broadcasters in *Red Lion* as demonstrating the Court's continuing recognition of the distinction between the two media, which is primarily manifested in the unique responsibilities of broadcasters as public trustees. See *NBC v. FCC,* 516 F.2d 1101, 1193–94 (D.C. Cir. 1974).

Four years later, in *Columbia Broadcasting System, Inc. v. Democratic National Committee,* 412 U.S. 94 (1973), text, p. 796, the U.S. Supreme Court affirmed its belief in the First Amendment theory of *Red Lion.* While the Court refused to extend *Red Lion* into a First Amendment right of public access to broadcasting, it did so by arguing that the fairness doctrine was adequate to protect the public's First Amendment right of access to information.

Eight years after *CBS v. DNC,* the Court (a much more conservative Court by then) once again endorsed the notion that the public has First Amendment rights to be informed. The issue in *CBS, Inc. v. FCC* was the constitutionality of sec. 312(a)(7) of the Communications Act of 1934. That section requires broadcasters to provide "reasonable access" to candidates for federal elective office. The Court reasoned that sec. 312(a)(7), although impinging on the First Amendment rights of broadcasters, primarily advanced the paramount First Amendment rights of the public to receive political information.

Is the *Red Lion* case a viable First Amendment precedent today? In *Turner Broadcasting System, Inc. v. FCC,* 512 U.S. 622 (1994), Justice Kennedy spoke approvingly of the "more relaxed standard of scrutiny adopted in *Red Lion* and other broadcast cases" due to the "inherent physical limitation on the number of speakers who may use the broadcast medium." In *Denver Area Educational Telecommunications Consortium v. FCC,* 116 S. Ct. 2374 (1996), Justice Breyer spoke with similar approval of the *Red Lion* approach as the appropriate standard for broadcasting. See text, pp. 804–824.

Theories of Impact

Over the years scarcity theories and theories of listeners' and viewers' rights, which are at least partly derived from scarcity, have been the major reasons for treating broadcasting differently from print. In 1978, however, the U.S. Supreme Court announced a new justification for distinct treatment of broadcasting—the so-called impact or intrusiveness or accessibility theories. The context was the regulation of broadcast indecency. Congress had provided in 18 U.S.C. § 1464 that "obscene, indecent or profane" broadcasts were prohibited. Several times the FCC tried to distinguish indecent broadcasts from obscene broadcasts, but none of those cases reached the U.S. Supreme Court.

In 1975, however, the FCC chastised a noncommercial, educational radio station in New York City for airing a monologue by George Carlin. The case gradually worked its way up to the high court. The Court's eventual decision was not rooted in scarcity theory. Instead, the Court found other—new—reasons why broadcasters should be treated distinctly under the First Amendment. At this point, the student should read *FCC v. Pacifica Foundation,* 438 U.S. 726 (1978), text, p. 606. The law of broadcast indecency, as defined by Congress and the FCC, has changed substantially since 1978. The major continuing issues focus on how *Pacifica* will be applied in new contexts.

Does *Pacifica* stand the First Amendment on its head, saying that the more pervasive and influential a medium is, the more it is subject to government regulation? If so, is this not, perhaps, an argument for more extensive regulation of powerful media? Is the decision limited strictly to a concern for children? If so, then its impact may be narrow. If not, does it, as the dissenters argue, prohibit adults from receiving materials fit for them, but not considered fit for children?

Do the differences between obscenity and indecency that the FCC and the U.S. Supreme Court have attempted to create hold up? The FCC and the Court say that obscenity can be banned, but indecency may only be "channeled" to times of day when children are not likely to be in the audience. When are those times? See text, p. 833. Is *Pacifica* just a broadcasting case? It does not rely on "scarcity" to distinguish broadcasting from other media. Other media, however, are "pervasive" and, perhaps, intrusive. Should *Pacifica*'s arguments be extended to new, non-broadcast media?

In *Reno v. ACLU,* 117 S. Ct.—(1997), the Court held that the Internet unlike broadcasting was not an intrusive medium. But in *Denver Area Educational Telecommunications Consortium v. FCC,* 116 S. Ct. 2374 (1996), text, p. 627, the Supreme Court reacted differently. *Denver Area* involved First Amendment challenges to three provisions of the Cable Television Consumer Protection and Competition Act of 1992 regulating indecent expression. One of those provisions, sec. 10(a) of the Act, authorized cable operators to refuse to carry leased access programming depicting "sexual or excretory activities or organs in a patently offensive way as measured by contemporary community standards." The Supreme Court held, 7–2, that sec. 10(a) did not violate the First Amendment. Justice Breyer, joined by Justices Stevens, O'Connor, and Souter, commented approvingly on the applicability of *Pacifica:*

> [T]he problem Congress addressed here is remarkably similar to the problem addressed by the FCC in *Pacifica,* and the balance Congress struck is commensurate with the balance we approved there. All [the *Pacifica*] factors are present here. Cable television broadcasting, including access channel broadcasting, is as "accessible to children" as over-the-air broadcasting, if not more so. There is nothing to stop "adults who feel the need" from finding similar programming elsewhere, say, on tape or in theatres.

The *Denver Area* case reflects the staying power of the *Pacifica* decision but does not offer much guidance on whether indecent speech must meet some lesser standard of review than other "protected" speech. One of the other challenged

provisions of the 1992 Cable Act was sec. 10(b), which sought to limit the access of children to indecent programming on leased access channels. Section 10(b) required the FCC to issue rules obliging cable operators to segregate such programming on a separate channel and block it unless the subscriber requested otherwise. The Supreme Court held, 6–3, that sec. 10(b) was invalid but declined to pass on exactly what standard of review *Pacifica* had imposed:

> Nor need we here determine whether, or the extent to which, *Pacifica* does, or does not, impose some lesser standard of review where indecent speech is at issue. [T]his governmental restriction [is not] a "least restrictive alternative" and is not "narrowly tailored." [I]t fails to satisfy this Court's formulations of the First Amendment's "strictest" as well as its somewhat less "strict," requirements.

In short, the *Denver Area* case shows that the impact theory is very much alive. The Court showed no inclination to disavow *Pacifica* and, indeed, indicated a willingness to extend it to non-broadcast media such as cable television.

Marketplace-Based Theories

Major alternative theories of regulation—really theories for deregulation—began to be advanced in the late 1970s and throughout the 1980s. During that era, doubt was often raised about the wisdom of "New Deal" affirmative governmental regulation of many aspects of life. Transportation and banking came first, but communications was not far behind.

In the 1970s, the FCC was urged to intervene when radio stations changed their program format, but the commission, adopting a deregulatory philosophy, refused. The FCC reasoned that stations should be free to format in response to marketplace forces rather than in response to government mandates. The issue ultimately reached the Supreme Court. The Court upheld the FCC's decision to rely on marketplace forces.

FCC v. WNCN Listeners Guild
450 U.S. 582, 101 S. CT. 1266, 67 L. ED. 2D 521 (1981).

Justice WHITE delivered the opinion of the Court.

Sections 309(a) and 310(d) of the Communications Act of 1934, 47 U.S.C. § 151 *et seq.,* empower the FCC to grant an application for license transfer or renewal only if it determines that "the public interest, convenience and necessity" will be served thereby. The issue before us is whether there are circumstances in which the FCC must review past or anticipated changes in a station's entertainment programming when it rules on an application for renewal or transfer of a radio broadcast license. The FCC's present position is that it may rely on market forces to promote diversity in entertainment programming and thus serve the public interest. This issue arose when, pursuant to its informal rulemaking authority, the FCC issued a "policy statement" concluding that the public interest is best served by promoting diversity in entertainment formats through market forces and competition among broadcasters and that a change in entertainment programming is therefore not a material factor that should be considered by the FCC in ruling on an application for license renewal or transfer. Respondents, a number of citizen groups interested in fostering and preserving particular entertainment formats, petitioned for review in the Court of Appeals for the District of Columbia Circuit [hereinafter "D.C. Circuit"]. That court held that the FCC's policy statement violated the Act. We reverse the decision of the court of appeals.

Beginning in 1970, in a series of cases involving license transfers, the [D.C. Circuit] gradually developed a set of criteria for determining when the "public-interest" standard requires the FCC to hold a hearing to review proposed changes in entertainment formats. [T]he court of appeals ruled in 1974 that "preservation of a format [that] would otherwise disappear, although economically and technologically viable and preferred by a significant number of listeners, is generally in the public interest." *Citizens Comm. to Save WEFM v. FCC* [506 F.2d 246 (D.C. Cir. 1974)]. It concluded that a change in format would not present "substantial and material questions of fact" requiring a hearing if (1) notice of the change had not precipitated "significant public grumbling"; (2) the segment of the population preferring the format was too small to be accommodated by available frequencies; (3) there was an adequate substitute in the service area for the format being abandoned; or (4) the format would be economically unfeasible even if the station were managed efficiently. The court rejected the FCC's position that the choice of entertainment formats should be left to the judgment of the licensee, stating that the FCC's interpretation of

the public-interest standard was contrary to the Act.

In January 1976 the FCC responded to these decisions by undertaking an inquiry into its role in reviewing format changes. The FCC concluded in the policy statement that review of format changes was not compelled by the language or history of the act, would not advance the welfare of the radio-listening public, would pose substantial administrative problems, and would deter innovation in radio programming. The FCC also emphasized that a broadcaster is not a common carrier and therefore should not be subjected to a burden similar to the common carrier's obligation to continue to provide service if abandonment of that service would conflict with public convenience or necessity. The FCC also concluded that practical considerations as well as statutory interpretation supported its reluctance to regulate changes in formats. Such regulation would require the commission to categorize the formats of a station's prior and subsequent programming to determine whether a change in format had occurred; to determine whether the prior format was "unique"; and to weigh the public detriment resulting from the abandonment of a unique format against the public benefit resulting from that change. The FCC emphasized the difficulty of objectively evaluating the strength of listener preferences, of comparing the desire for diversity within a particular type of programming to the desire for a broader range of program formats and of assessing the financial feasibility of a unique format.

Finally, the FCC explained why it believed that market forces were the best available means of producing diversity in entertainment formats. First, in large markets, competition among broadcasters had already produced "an almost bewildering array of diversity" in entertainment formats. Second, format allocation by market forces accommodates listeners' desires for diversity within a given format and also produces a variety of formats. Third, the market is far more flexible than governmental regulation and responds more quickly to changing public tastes.

The court of appeals, sitting en banc, held that the FCC's policy was contrary to the Act as construed and applied in the court's prior format decisions. The court then responded to the commission's criticisms of the format doctrine. First, although conceding that market forces generally lead to diversification of formats, it concluded that the market only imperfectly reflects listener preferences and that the FCC is statutorily obligated to review format changes whenever there is "strong prima facie evidence that the market has in fact broken down." Second, the court stated that the administrative problems posed by the format doctrine were not insurmountable. Hearings would only be required in a small number of cases. Third, the FCC had not demonstrated that the format doctrine would deter innovative programming. Finally, the court explained that it had not directed the commission to engage in censorship or to impose common carrier obligations on licensees; it merely stated that the FCC had the power to consider a station's format in deciding whether license renewal or transfer would be consistent with the public interest.

Although conceding that it possessed neither the expertise nor the authority to make policy decisions in this area, the court of appeals asserted that the format doctrine was "law," not "policy," and was of the view that the FCC had not disproved the factual assumptions underlying the format doctrine. Accordingly, the court declared that the policy statement was "unavailing and of no force and effect."

Rejecting the FCC's reliance on market forces to develop diversity in programming as an unreasonable interpretation of the act's public-interest standard, the court of appeals held that in certain circumstances the commission is required to regard a change in entertainment format as a substantial and material fact in deciding whether a license renewal or transfer is in the public interest. With all due respect, however, we are unconvinced that the Court of Appeals' format doctrine is compelled by the Act and that the FCC's interpretation of the public interest standard must therefore be set aside.

The FCC has provided a rational explanation for its conclusion that reliance on the market is the best method of promoting diversity in entertainment formats. The court of appeals and the FCC agree that in the vast majority of cases market forces provide sufficient diversity. The court of appeals favors government intervention when there is evidence that market forces have deprived the public of a "unique" format, while the commission is content to rely on the market, pointing out that in many cases when a station changes its format, other stations will change their formats to attract listeners who preferred the

discontinued format. The Court of Appeals places great value on preserving diversity among formats, while the commission emphasizes the value of intra-format as well as inter-format diversity. Finally, the Court of Appeals is convinced that review of format changes would result in a broader range of formats, while the commission believes that government intervention is likely to deter innovative programming.

In making these judgments, the FCC has not forsaken its obligation to pursue the public interest. It did not assert that reliance on the marketplace would achieve a perfect correlation between listener preferences and available entertainment programming. Rather, it recognized that a perfect correlation would never be achieved, and it concluded that the marketplace alone could best accommodate the varied and changing tastes of the listening public. These predictions are within the institutional competence of the FCC.

Surely, it is argued, there will be some format changes that will be so detrimental to the public interest that inflexible application of the FCC's policy statement would be inconsistent with the FCC's duties. But radio broadcasters are not required to seek permission to make format changes. The issue of past or contemplated entertainment format changes arises in the courses of renewal and transfer proceedings; if such an application is approved, the FCC does not merely assume but affirmatively determines that the requested renewal or transfer will serve the public interest.

Under its present policy, the FCC determines whether a renewal or transfer will serve the public interest without reviewing past or proposed changes in entertainment format. This policy is based on the FCC's judgment that market forces, although they operate imperfectly, will not only more reliably respond to listener preference than would format oversight by the FCC, but will also serve the end of increasing diversity in entertainment programming. This court has approved of the commission's goal of promoting diversity in radio programming, *FCC v. Midwest Video*, 440 U.S. 689 (1979), but the FCC is nevertheless vested with broad discretion in determining how much weight should be given to that goal and what policies should be pursued in promoting it.

A major underpinning of its policy statement is the FCC's conviction, rooted in its experience, that renewal and transfer cases should not turn on the FCC presuming to grasp, measure and weigh the elusive and difficult factors involved in determining the acceptability of changes in entertainment format. To assess whether the elimination of a particular "unique" entertainment format would serve the public interest, the FCC would have to consider the benefit as well as the detriment that would result from the change. Necessarily, the FCC would take into consideration not only the number of listeners who favor the old and the new programming but also the intensity of their preferences. It would also consider the effect of the format change on diversity within formats as well as on diversity among formats. The FCC is convinced that its judgments in these respects would be subjective in large measure and would only approximately serve the public interest. It is also convinced that the market, although imperfect, would serve the public interest as well or better by responding quickly to changing preferences and by inviting experimentation with new types of programming. Those who would overturn the FCC's policy statement do not take adequate account of these considerations.

It is also contended that since the FCC has responded to listener complaints about nonentertainment programming, it should also review challenged changes in entertainment formats. But the difference between the FCC's treatment of nonentertainment programming and its treatment of entertainment programming is not as pronounced as it may seem. Even in the area of nonentertainment programming, the FCC has afforded licensees broad discretion in selecting programs.

We decline to overturn the FCC's policy statement, which prefers reliance on market forces to its own attempt to oversee format changes at the behest of disaffected listeners. The FCC seeks to further the interests of the listening public as a whole by relying on market forces to promote diversity in radio entertainment formats and to satisfy the entertainment preferences of radio listeners. This policy does not conflict with the First Amendment.

Contrary to the judgment of the court of appeals, the FCC's policy statement is not inconsistent with the act. It is also a constitutionally permissible means of implementing the public-interest standard of the Act. Accordingly, the judgment of the court of appeals is reversed and the case is remanded for further proceedings consistent with this opinion.

So ordered.

Justice MARSHALL, with whom Justice BRENNAN joins, dissenting.

COMMENT

The challenge to the scarcity of the spectrum rationale for radio regulation served as a justification for the Reagan-era FCC to repeal much of the prior regulatory structure applicable to radio, i.e., formal ascertainment procedures, guidelines regarding the amount of nonentertainment programming, and guidelines limiting commercial time. See *Report and Order, In re Deregulation of Radio*, 46 Fed. Reg. 1388 (1981), text, p. 719. How does radio deregulation affect the licensee's underlying public interest obligation to provide different types of programs and to know the needs of the audience? Justice White, in *WNCN*, appears to be sympathetic to allowing deregulation based on the FCC's perception of the public interest. Justice Marshall's dissent demonstrated his belief that nonentertainment programming issues remain relevant to the FCC's consideration of petitions to deny to grant or renew a license. Because the FCC will continue to examine the reasonableness of a broadcaster's nonentertainment programming decisions, licensees must still know what issues interest their communities. See *Office of Communication of the United Church of Christ v. FCC*, 707 F.2d 1413 (D.C. Cir. 1983).

Although doubts about intrusive government regulation of communications content first appeared in public policy under the Carter administration, the strongest drive to "unregulate"—to back away as far as possible from FCC regulation of broadcast content—emerged under President Reagan, specifically under Mark S. Fowler, the FCC chairman who served throughout most of the Reagan presidency.

Very early in the Fowler administration, a law review article outlined his philosophy of a marketplace approach to broadcast regulation. The philosophy expressed there not only had a profound effect during Fowler's seven-year term as FCC head, but continues to be influential. See Fowler and Brenner, *A Marketplace Approach to*

Broadcast Regulation, 60 Tex. L. Rev. 207 (1982):

Our thesis is that the perception of broadcasters as community trustees should be replaced by a view of broadcasters as marketplace participants. Communications policy should be directed toward maximizing the services the public desires. Instead of defining public demand and specifying categories of programming to serve this demand, the Commission should rely on the broadcasters' ability to determine the wants of their audiences through the normal mechanisms of the marketplace. The public's interest, then, defines the public interest. And in light of the first amendment's heavy presumption against content control, the Commission should refrain from insinuating itself into program decisions made by licensees.

In *FCC v. WNCN Listeners Guild,* 450 U.S. 582 (1981), decided in 1981, the Supreme Court expressly sanctioned the Commission's discretion to invoke market forces in its regulatory mission. In *WNCN* the Court found no inconsistency between the first amendment and the Commission's decision that the public interest in radio is best served by promoting diversity in entertainment formats through market forces and competition among broadcasters. The Court noted that the Commission had admitted that the marketplace would not necessarily achieve a perfect correlation between listener preferences and available entertainment programs. But given the choice of regulating format changes or leaving those decisions to the marketplace, the Court concluded that the Commission acted reasonably in adopting the latter. The Court recognized that the Commission was within its range of discretion in preferring a market approach to achieve the Communication Act's goal of providing "the maximum benefits of radio to all the people of the United States."

The market perspective diminishes the importance of the Commission's past efforts to define affirmatively the elements of operation "in the public interest." It recognizes as valid communications policy, well within Commission discretion, reliance on voluntary broadcaster efforts to attract audiences—whether by specialized formats, as in the case of major market radio, or with a mix of programs, as in the case of television—and to provide the best practicable programming service to the public. It concludes that governmental efforts to improve the broadcast market have led to distortions of programming that have merely yielded a different programming mix, not a better one, and that the costs of government intrusion into the marketplace outweigh the benefits. Important first amendment interests support this conclusion as well.

The marketplace approach to broadcast regulation has two distinct advantages from a first amendment perspective. First, it does not conflict with *Red Lion.* In basing editorial and program judgments on their perceptions of popular demand, broadcasters enforce the paramount interests of listeners and viewers. Even if licensees occasionally misperceive the wants of their audiences, the present regulatory system, which is based upon the Commission's judgment of the community's needs, does not ensure a better result. Second, the marketplace approach accords protection to the distinct constitutional status of broadcasters under the press clause. This first amendment interest is, or should be, coextensive with the first amendment rights of the print media, regardless of whether the public is best served by its uninhibited exercise. A broadcaster's first amendment rights may differ from its listeners' rights to receive and hear suitable expression, but once the call is close, deference to broadcaster judgment is preferable to having a government agency mediate conflicts between broadcasters and their listeners.

Fowler and Brenner proceeded to establish an agenda to implement their marketplace theories. Under Fowler, the FCC substantially deregulated radio and television. Other proposals include the suggestion that spectrum space could be sold or auctioned. Further, it has been proposed that the proceeds from sales or auctions of spectrum space—or perhaps from "taxes" imposed on commercial broadcasters—could be used to support public broadcasting.

Does the marketplace approach cover all the interests formerly embraced by the trusteeship concept? Will it protect the interests of children or the elderly who may participate in the marketplace in unique ways? Fowler and Brenner argue that the marketplace approach could be implemented under *Red Lion.* Do you agree with that, or are they just straining to find a way to implement their ideas without waiting for the Supreme Court to repudiate *Red Lion?*

Reconceptualization by the U.S. Supreme Court?

The "scarcity rationale," as recognized by *NBC v. United States,* and the "paramount rights of listeners and viewers," as articulated in *Red Lion,* have been the linchpins of First Amendment theory for broadcasting for decades—as even Fowler and Brenner recognize. In a 1984 decision involving the constitutionality of statutory restrictions on editorializing by some public broadcast licensees, the U.S. Supreme Court hinted that it might be willing to review these fundamental cases underlying so much broadcast First Amendment theory. In *dicta* in *FCC v. League of Women Voters*, 468 U.S. 364, (1984), see text, p. 738, Justice Brennan in two footnotes opened the door to fundamental reconsideration of broadcast First Amendment theory. Footnote 11 read, in part, as follows:

> The prevailing rationale for broadcast regulation based on spectrum scarcity has come under increasing criticism in recent years. Critics, including the incumbent Chairman of the FCC, charge that with the advent of cable and satellite television technology, communities now have access to such a wide variety of stations that the scarcity doctrine is obsolete. See, e.g., Fowler & Brenner, A Marketplace Approach to Broadcast Regulation, 60 Tex. L. Rev. 207, 221–226 (1982). We are not prepared, however, to reconsider our longstanding approach without some signal from Congress or the FCC that technological developments have advanced so far that some revision of the system of broadcast regulation may be required.

Footnote 12 made it clear, however, that there was no guarantee of eternal life for *Red Lion*:

> As we recognized in *Red Lion*, however, were it to be shown by the FCC that the fairness doctrine "has the effect of reducing rather than enhancing" speech, we would then be forced to reconsider the constitutional basis of our decision in that case.

Under Chairman Mark Fowler and his successor, Dennis Patrick, the FCC strove mightily to give a "signal" that scarcity was a thing of the past as far as broadcasting was concerned. Its efforts to do so will be discussed subsequently in sections dealing with broadcast deregulation. Congress, however, was reluctant to support the FCC in many of these areas. In the fairness doctrine area, discussed later, the FCC concluded that the doctrine had chilling effects and abandoned it. If scarcity is rejected as a basis for broadcast regulation, or if the listeners' and viewers' rights theories expressed in *Red Lion* are reconsidered, the rationale for treating broadcasting uniquely under the First Amendment would be profoundly altered.

TRAC v. FCC
801 F.2d 501 (D.C. CIR. 1986).

[EDITORIAL NOTE: *In* Telecommunications Research & Action Center (TRAC) v. FCC, *the court reviewed an FCC decision refusing to apply various political broadcasting policies to a new technology—teletext. In an influential decision, Judge Robert Bork for the court in* TRAC, *disagreed with the FCC that the political broadcasting policies at issue did not apply to teletext because the proper First Amendment model for teletext was* Tornillo *rather than* Red Lion. *He particularly took issue with a justification for broadcast regulation that rested on either scarcity or impact theories. His analysis poses a fundamental challenge to a bifurcated First Amendment—one First Amendment model for broadcasting and another for the print media.]*

BORK, J.:

With respect to the first argument, the deficiencies of the scarcity rationale as a basis for depriving broadcasting of full first amendment protection, have led some to think that it is the immediacy and the power of broadcasting that causes its differential treatment. Whether or not that is true, we are unwilling to endorse an argument that makes the very effectiveness of speech the justification for according it less first amendment protection. More important, the Supreme Court's articulation of the scarcity doctrine contains no hint of any immediacy rationale. The Court based its reasoning entirely on the physical scarcity of broadcasting frequencies, which, it thought, permitted attaching fiduciary duties to the receipt of a license to use a frequency. This "immediacy" distinction cannot, therefore, be employed to affect the ability of the FCC to regulate public affairs broadcasting on teletext to ensure "the right of the public to receive suitable access to social, political, esthetics, moral, and other ideas and experiences." *Red Lion*

The FCC's second distinction—that a textual medium is not scarce insofar as it competes with other "print media"—also fails to dislodge the hold of *Red Lion*. The dispositive fact is that teletext is transmitted over broadcast frequencies that the Supreme Court has ruled scarce and this makes teletext's content regulable. We can understand, however, why the Commission thought it could reason in this fashion. The basic difficulty in this entire area is that the line drawn between the print media and the broadcast media, resting as it does on the physical scarcity of the latter, is a distinction without a difference.

Employing the scarcity concept as an analytic tool, particularly with respect to new and unforeseen technologies, inevitably leads to strained reasoning and artificial results.

It is certainly true that broadcast frequencies are scarce but it is unclear why that fact justifies content regulation of broadcasting in a way that would be intolerable if applied to the editorial process of the print media. All economic goods are scarce, not least the newsprint, ink, delivery trucks, computers, and other resources that go into the production and dissemination of print journalism. Not everyone who wishes to publish a newspaper, or even a pamphlet, may do so. Since scarcity is a universal fact, it can hardly explain regulation in one context and not another. The attempt to use a universal fact as a distinguishing principle necessarily leads to analytical confusion.

Neither is content regulation explained by the fact that broadcasters face the problem of interference, so that the government must define usable frequencies and protect those frequencies from encroachment. This governmental definition of frequencies is another instance of a universal fact that does not offer an explanatory principle for differing treatment. A publisher can deliver his newspapers only because government provides streets and regulates traffic on the streets by allocating rights of way. Yet no one would contend that the necessity for these governmental functions, which are certainly analogous to the government's function in allocating broadcast frequencies, could justify regulation of the content of a newspaper to ensure that it serves the needs of the citizens. There may be ways to reconcile *Red Lion* and *Tornillo* but the "scarcity" of broadcast frequencies does not appear capable of doing so. Perhaps the Supreme Court will one day revisit this area of the law and either eliminate the distinction between print and broadcast media, surely by pronouncing *Tornillo* applicable to both, or announce a constitutional distinction that is more usable than the present one. In the meantime, neither we nor the FCC are free to seek new rationales to remedy the inadequacy of the doctrine in this area. The attempt to do that has led the FCC to find "implicit" considerations in the law that are not really there. The Supreme Court has drawn a first amendment distinction between broadcast and print media on a premise of the physical scarcity of broadcast frequencies. Teletext, whatever its similarities to print media, uses broadcast frequencies, and that, given *Red Lion,* would seem to be that.

The FCC, therefore, cannot on first amendment grounds refuse to apply to teletext such regulation as is constitutionally permissible when applied to other, more traditional, broadcast media.

COMMENT

Judge Bork says that "given *Red Lion*" he is not free to create a new rationale to remedy what he sees as the present inadequacy of First Amendment doctrine to explain the governance of the electronic media. What then is the point of his attack on the scarcity and impact rationales?

Is Judge Bork really writing a brief calling for the reversal of *Red Lion*? Should it be reversed? Should broadcasting be governed by market forces alone? If that happens, new problems may arise. Consider the following critique by Professor Owen Fiss of market theory as a system of governance for the electronic media:

> A fully competitive market might produce a diversity of programs, formats, and reportage, but to borrow an image of Renata Adler's, it will be the diversity of "a pack going essentially in one direction." [A] perfectly competitive market will produce shows or publications whose marginal cost equals marginal revenue. But there is no necessary, or even probabilistic, relationship between making a profit (or allocating resources efficiently) and supplying the electorate with the information they need to make free and intelligent choices about government policy, the structure of government, or the nature of society. This point was well understood when we freed our educational systems and our universities from the grasp of the market, and it applies with equal force to the media. Fiss, *Why the State?* 100 Harv. L. Rev. 781, 787–88 (1987).

In *Denver Area,* Justice Breyer argued against adopting a single First Amendment standard in an area of rapid technological change in the communications media:

> [N]o definitive choice among competing analogies (broadcast, common carrier, bookstore) allows us to declare a rigid single standard, good for now and for all future media and purposes. This is not to say that we reject all the more special applications of the standard. Rather, aware as we are of the changes taking place in the law, the technology, and

the industrial structure related to communications, see., *e.g.,* Telecommunications Act of 1996, we believe it unwise and unnecessary definitively to pick one analogy or one specific set of words now.

Instead, in *Denver Area* Justice Breyer urged a narrower approach: closely scrutinize the regulation "to assure that it properly addresses an extremely important problem, without imposing, in light of the relevant interests, an unncessarily great restriction on speech." Is this approach similar to the *Red Lion* standard? What are the merits and demerits of Justice Breyer's approach?

THE EMERGENCE OF "NEW" TECHNOLOGIES: REGULATING NONBROADCAST SERVICES

The last two decades have been filled with talk of "new communications technologies." Some of these technologies, however, were not very new; they just put old technologies to new uses. Others, such as direct broadcast satellites, were so "new" that they existed more in law and policy than in fact. What the "new technologies" have most in common is that they are not broadcasting. Discussion of them can be divided into two major categories: those that use the electromagnetic spectrum and those that do not.

Spectrum-Using Services

Four spectrum-using services created new legal problems in the 1970s and 1980s. The FCC expanded the range of uses broadcasters could make of carriers and subcarriers through "subsidiary communications authorizations" (SCAs). It converted what had been a rather limited low-power translator system to "retransmit" the signals of existing stations into a "Low Power Television Service" (LPTV) for which it had ambitious expectations. An old, but not extensively used, service called Multi-point Distribution Service was converted into something new known as "Multichannel, Multipoint Distribution Service" (MMDS). Finally, by authorizing "Direct Broadcast Satellites" (DBS), the FCC hoped to expand pay service alternatives, especially to sparsely populated areas. At least three of these four new services looked most promising if offered on a subscription, or pay, basis. This

eventually led the commission into a legal redefinition of what "broadcasting" itself was. Most broadcast stations do not use up all the spectrum space they are assigned just carrying programs for people to watch or listen to. In AM, FM, and TV, the technical capability exists to put some additional information on top of the broadcast signal in a piggyback fashion. People who just listen to radio or watch TV are not aware of the extra information. Their receivers are not affected by it; the radio sounds the same, and the TV looks the same even though additional information is being carried. People with special receivers, however, can pick up the piggyback signals and put them to special purposes.

LPTV   Low-power television has been around for years in the form of satellite and/or translator stations. The principle of these older services is simple. Full-power TV stations can have coverage problems. Their service is often blocked, for example, by mountains. Almost since the start of broadcasting, it was possible to add low-power TV stations that retransmitted the programming of a nearby full-power TV station, usually after shifting it to another channel, in ways that could serve the areas with reception difficulty. For many years, however, such translators or satellite stations operated with significant legal restrictions. While they could retransmit another station's signal, they could not originate programming of their own, except in the event of an emergency and to appeal for funds to support the service. Otherwise, they just retransmitted the signals of nearby full-power TV stations.

Under President Carter, the National Telecommunications and Information Administration (NTIA, a part of the Department of Commerce) decided that more could be done with this service. A spectrum management study convinced the NTIA that hundreds, perhaps even thousands of LPTV stations could be squeezed in among existing full-power stations to provide service to small areas without interfering with the full-power signals. The NTIA believed that these LPTV stations might serve very small communities, unable to support a full-power station, or serve urban neighborhoods or regions, including those heavily populated by minority group members, that tended to be ignored by the full-power stations. The barrier to achieving these goals was the FCC's rule that translators and satellite stations (the only low-power stations of their time) could only retransmit the programming of full-power TV broadcasters. The NTIA asked the FCC to change the rule and let low-power stations originate programming freely.

In 1982, the FCC went along. In line with its economic projections for the service (not optimistic) and with its general deregulatory philosophy of the time, the FCC imposed only minimal regulations. LPTV stations could originate whatever kind of programming they wished, whether that was over-the-air broadcasting, subscription (pay) scrambled services, or even hooking up to some satellite delivered service twenty-four hours per day and doing no locally originated programming. The FCC recognized that LPTV was using broadcast spectrum space but decided that broadcast rules (like the equal time provisions of sec. 315) would apply only to locally *originated* programming, which a LPTV station was free to completely ignore. The rationale for all this deregulation was that LPTV was new, experimental, and risky. The FCC chose not to burden it with the full panoply of broadcast regulations in hopes that some people would be able to make something out of the service if substantial freedom was granted. See *Low Power Television Service,* 51 R.R.2d 476 (FCC 1982). So far LPTV has not worked out as well as was hoped. The number of LPTV stations is not large, few serve small communities or minority groups (as the NTIA had hoped), and the service is still struggling. Nevertheless, many still hope for improvement in the future.

MMDS   MMDS introduces a new concept—that of a common carrier. In theory, a common carrier provides a transmission service but offers that service to anyone willing to pay established rates regardless of what they want to transmit. A common carrier normally does not discriminate among customers and does not control content. MMDS is, technically, still a common carrier service, as were its predecessors. The Multichannel Multipoint Distribution Services evolved out of three earlier services: the Multipoint Distribution Service (MDS), Instructional Television Fixed Services (ITFS), and Private Operational Television Fixed Services (OTFS). All are technically similar. Unlike broadcasting, they all used microwave transmitters (higher in frequency than broadcast stations) to transmit programming from a central point to scattered

sites. MDS operators often reached theaters to show events like prizefights; ITFS (and sometimes OTFS) operators sent programs to schools. Although the services had been around for years, they had not grown much. In the early 1980s, the FCC decided to change things. Whereas educators tended to underutilize the ITFS and OTFS channels reserved for them, MDS was limited to two channels per community—not enough, many argued. The FCC eventually set up a complex system under which some ITFS and OTFS spectrum space could be used for MDS services and a single MDS operator could get a package of several channels per community. The theory was that these newly defined MMDS providers could put together packages of about four channels per community and compete with cable television, at least where it was not yet offered. Indeed, the industry is coming to be known as wireless cable. An MMDS operator might sell, for example, a movie channel, a sports channel, a news channel, and a general entertainment channel—perhaps at a package price comparable to that of a cable system. Due to technological improvements and the MMDS operator's leasing of ITFS channels, MMDS systems can now carry twenty or more channels. As with LPTV, the FCC adopted a deregulatory attitude. Its position was that MMDS needed maximum freedom in order to prosper. See *Multichannel Multipoint Distribution Service,* 57 R.R.2d 943 (FCC 1985). Current rules are found at 47 CFR §§ 21.900-961 (1997).

DBS   In 1979, COMSAT, our nation's major international communications provider, threw a surprise at the FCC. COMSAT filed an application for a domestic Direct Broadcast Satellite Service, proposing to put a high-power satellite in a geosynchronous orbit and use small (one meter or less) earth stations to offer video service to people in the eastern United States. COMSAT hoped to offer a cablelike service (three or four channels of pay programming) primarily for people cable television had not yet reached. The major problem was that DBS, as a service, was not recognized by the FCC when COMSAT applied. Given that, it filled out a broadcast station application, specifying its transmitter location as "space" and proposed, initially, to serve the eastern time zone of the United States. The FCC eventually approved COMSAT's application and, at the same time, began to develop and adopt general DBS rules. As it had done with other new services at the time, the FCC adopted a deregulatory attitude. It decided that it would leave up to DBS providers many decisions as to what kinds of services they would provide. Most significantly, it said that it would not care, whether DBS applicants proposed to provide a broadcast service (as COMSAT had asked for), fully subject to the FCC's broadcast rules, or a common carrier service (where the satellite operator would simply put up the satellite and then let others buy time on it). The FCC tried to leave that choice to DBS service providers. See *Report and Order in Gen. Docket No. 80-603*, 90 F.C.C.2d 676, 51 R.R.2d 1341 (1982). This approach was challenged, first at the FCC and later in court, by the National Association of Broadcasters (NAB) and others. They argued that the Communications Act of 1934 created two regulatory systems—broadcasting and common carriage—and that the FCC had to choose which DBS fit into. They claimed that the FCC could not leave that choice up to DBS operators. The NAB took the FCC to court, and in 1984 the D.C. Circuit sided, in part, with the broadcasters. While generally supporting the FCC's authority to authorize DBS service, and agreeing with most of the rules it adopted, the court told the FCC that it had to decide whether DBS was broadcasting or common carriage. *NAB v. FCC*, 740 F.2d 1190, 56 R.R.2d 1005 (D.C. Cir. 1984). That led to an FCC redefinition of broadcasting, discussed below.

The D.C. Circuit's decision in *NAB v. FCC* threw many of the FCC's plans for new services for a loop. More than anything else, the FCC was trying to prevent broadcast law (e.g., the equal time provisions of sec. 315) from applying to these new services. The court, however, suggested that the FCC's ability to do this was limited, that the new services were either broadcasting, subject to most or all of those rules, or common carriage but not, as the FCC seemed to propose, some kind of a regulatory hybrid. To deal with this dilemma, the FCC began an inquiry into subscription (pay) video services. In 1987, it released a report and order that dealt with subscription services by redefining broadcasting. For years, the FCC explained, services that were designed to be of interest to a large number of listeners and could, in fact, be received by such a mass audience were "broad-

casting." The FCC had focused on the content of the service and its technological pervasiveness.

In its 1987 order, however, the FCC switched its focus to the intent of the transmitter of information. If the transmitter intended that the service be freely available to all, then the service was broadcasting and fully subject to broadcasting law. If, however, the service provider intended that the service be available only to a more limited, paying, audience—and took concrete steps such as scrambling to limit access—then the service was "point to multipoint nonbroadcast service" and not subject to broadcast rules. *Subscription Video*, 2 F.C.C.R. 1001 (1987). The new FCC policy was challenged in the D.C. Circuit. The court upheld the FCC's change, over the vigorous dissent of Judge Patricia Wald. See *National Ass'n for Better Broad. v. FCC*, 849 F.2d 665 (D.C. Cir. 1988).

HDTV One other "new technology" deserves brief mention—High Definition Television (HDTV). The television transmission system used in the United States is antiquated. The current analog television system is based on the NTSC standard, named for the National Television System Committee, an industry group that developed the monochrome television standard in 1940-1941 and the color television standard in 1950-1953. Though nearly state-of-the-art when adopted in 1941, the NTSC standard is now deficient in two major ways. First, its resolution is poor. Our TV "picture" consists of 525 lines running down the screen. European systems, adopted later than ours, use more lines and achieve slightly better picture resolution. The technology now exists to more than double the number of lines in a TV picture. The result would be an image that would have resolution comparable to 35 mm. slides or film, even when projected in a large-screen display.

The other problem with our TV system is that it uses a different aspect ratio (height-to-width ratio) than film does. Film uses an aspect ratio where the picture is wider, relative to its height, than the fairly boxy picture shown on TV. When films are transferred to television, they are either squeezed together optically or electronically (which makes the figures look like stick drawings), or part of the film image is cut out while the TV image concentrates on the most important part of the film frame. In any event, films broadcast on TV just do not look the way they do in theaters.

HDTV could fix this. Japanese electronics companies have developed equipment that has an aspect ratio much like film and uses 1,125 (instead of 525) lines. In other words, the picture would have more than twice the resolution of our current picture and would provide an image looking much more like film. The problem with HDTV is that all the extra lines and the expanded aspect ratio require more spectrum space to transmit. Using current technology, HDTV cannot be fit into the amount of spectrum space currently allocated for VHF and UHF television stations.

HDTV, ATV (ADVANCED TELEVISION SYSTEMS), AND DIGITAL BROADCAST TELEVISION In the late 1980s, discussion in communications circles centered on HDTV. Today the focus is on digital television. Digital television "created the possibility of broadcasting perhaps 10 signals where one had gone before. But in digital television, not analog." The terrestrial broadcaster could use digital to broadcast HDTV but, more significantly, "he could use it to compress more NTSC channels into the 6 mhz the FCC had been trying so hard to aggregate for HDTV." See Don West, *The Fateful Battle for the Second Channel*, Broadcasting & Cable, April 10, 1995 at 22. In the following report, the FCC chronicles the new developments in digital broadcast television that promise to transform the communications landscape. Part of this technological transformation involves the development of a so-called Second Channel for each existing channel. Who should get the additional channel? The incumbent, the present holder of the existing channel? Should the incumbent get it free? For how long? Should the Second Channel be auctioned off? Should it be available to all who apply for it?

In the Matter of Advanced Television Systems and Their Impact upon the Existing Television Broadcast Service

Further Notice of Proposed Rulemaking and Third Notice of Inquiry
10 F.C.C.R. 10540 (1995).

With this Fourth Further Notice of Proposed Rulemaking and Third Notice of Inquiry, we continue the process of moving toward the next era of *digital* broadcast television. In previous orders in this Advanced Television ("ATV") proceeding

[Advanced Television refers to any television technology that provides improved audio and video quality or enhances the current NTSC television system], our focus was on fostering the development of High Definition Television ("HDTV"). With that focus we made a series of decisions regarding, among other things, the nature of the ATV service, eligibility for ATV transition channels, and the transition period. Technological evolution now obliges us to revisit some of those decisions and consider new information which we do in this document. We tentatively conclude that many of our previous decisions—such as our decisions that initial eligibility for ATV transition channels should be limited to existing broadcasters—remain sound, even under the changed circumstances. We believe that a few decisions, however, required renewed consideration, such as our requirement that broadcasters must ultimately use the transition channel primarily for HDTV. In this document, we ask for comment on these and other issues. Our overarching goal is to ensure that the introduction of digital television fully serves the public interest.

The broadcast television service has seen a number of significant developments in the past half-century, including the allocation of UHF channels and the introduction of color broadcasting. When we began this proceeding in 1987, we believed that we were on the cusp of another similar development, the introduction of a major technical improvement in picture quality over the current NTSC television systems—High Definition Television. But the genius of the engineers who have labored to produce the technical advantages and system developments of the past few years has opened the door to an even more dramatic change in the nature of the broadcast television service: the introduction of a dynamic and flexible digital broadcast television technology.

Digital encoding and transmission technology has evolved and matured to the point where we are confident that it would not only permit the broadcast of a digital High Definition Television signal over a 6 MHz channel, but that it would also allow for an array of additional alternative uses. The current state of the art, which reflects advances in digital technology, and in particular, use of digital compression technology and a packetized transport scheme, allows for multiple streams, or "multicasting," of Standard Definition

Television ("SDTV") programming at a quality at least comparable to, and possibly better than the current analog system. [Standard Definition Television is a digital television system in which picture quality is approximately equivalent to the current NTSC television system.] For example, a broadcaster could transmit a news program consisting of four separate, simultaneous SDTV program streams for local news, national news, weather and sports; then transmit an HDTV commercial with embedded data about the product; then transmit a motion picture in an HDTV format simultaneously with unrelated data.

In deciding what rules should govern the transition to digital television, we recognize our obligation to manage the spectrum efficiently and in the public interest and to take account of the legitimate interests of all those with a stake in that transition. With the foregoing considerations in mind, we will pursue and balance the following goals in this proceeding: 1) preserving a free, universal broadcasting service; 2) fostering an expeditious and orderly transition to digital technology that will allow the public to receive the benefits of digital television while taking account of consumer investment in NTSC television sets; 3) managing the spectrum to permit the recovery of contiguous blocks of spectrum, so as to promote spectrum efficiency and to allow the public the full benefit of its spectrum; and 4) ensuring that the spectrum—both ATV channels and recovered channels—will be used in a manner that best serves the public interest.

[R]ecent developments do not change our view that the public interest is best served by affording incumbent broadcasters the means to provide digital ATV. Permitting broadcasters to transition to digital will ensure recovery of spectrum, to which we remain fully committed. Accordingly, temporary grant of an additional 6 MHz channel for digital broadcasting will be explicitly conditioned on, among other things, return of one of the channels at the end of the transition period. We invite comment on whether we should require that broadcasters also change their channels at the end of the transition period, so that the spectrum that will ultimately be recovered can be aggregated into *contiguous* blocks, thereby increasing its potential value for, as yet undefined, uses.

While recent developments do not change our view that existing broadcasters should be provided temporary use of an additional 6 MHz channel to permit a transition to digital technology without immediate loss of service to the NTSC-viewing public, they do change our view about, what if, any restrictions should apply to use of the second channel. Therefore, in this Notice, we ask what limits should be placed on use of the ATV channel.

Broadcasters are now subject to a number of public interest requirements, including the obligation to air issue-responsive programming, children's educational and informational programming, and to provide access to candidates for federal office. These public interest requirements were developed for the analog world in which each broadcast licensee could do no more than send one signal over its single channel. Digital technology allows each broadcast licensee to send several streams of video programming simultaneously, as well as a mix of video and nonvideo services. The technology also raises the possibility that a broadcaster can send a mix of subscription and non-subscription services. In this Notice, we ask for comments on how the conversion of digital broadcasting should affect broadcasters' public interest obligations. In sum, this Notice invites comment on a wide range of issues with respect to the conversion by television broadcasters to digital television, including some not addressed by the foregoing discussion.

Since we issued our last decision in this matter, significant developments have occurred. In May of 1992, 7 companies and institutions that had been proponents of the four tested digital ATV systems joined together in a "Grand Alliance" to develop a final digital ATV system for the standard. Rather than being limited to transmitting one HDTV service, a fully digital system such as that developed by the Grand Alliance can provide one HDTV service, several HDTV services, a host of nonbroadcast services alone or in combination with broadcast services. The system flexibility also permits switching among functions as needed.

In the *Second Report/Further Notice,* the FCC established that during the initial period, existing broadcasters would have the first opportunity to acquire ATV channels. We continue to believe that initial eligibility should be limited to existing broadcasters given the shortage of suitable spectrum and our decision not to allocate additional spectrum for this purpose. We are still asking existing broadcasters to inaugurate a television service that will deliver signals of superior quality.

While we reiterate our tentative conclusion to limit initial eligibility for ATV frequencies to existing broadcasters, we seek comment on the potential impact our proposal would have on the FCC's longstanding policy of fostering programming and ownership diversity. Specifically, we seek comment on what other measures, if any, the FCC may adopt to include new entrants into this emerging era of digital television.

Some parties have suggested that we should auction the spectrum intended to be used for ATV service. Section 309(j) of the Communications Act of 1934, as amended, limits the uses of spectrum that is subject to being auctioned. It specifically requires that "the principal use of such spectrum will involve or is reasonably likely to involve, the licensee receiving compensation from subscribers." Our experience and our judgment concerning market conditions lead us to believe that the broadcasters would use this spectrum for free over-the-air broadcast service; therefore, it cannot be auctioned under section 309(j). For this reason, as well as those set forth above, we reiterate our previous decision to limit eligibility to existing licensees. Commenters may address whether any changed circumstances should alter this conclusion.

We remain committed to enforcing our statutory mandate to ensure that broadcasters serve the public interest. Our current public interest rules, including those implementing specific statutory requirements, were developed for broadcasters essentially limited by technology to a single analog video programming service. The potential for more flexible and dynamic use of the advanced television channel than what broadcasters currently enjoy gives rise to important questions about the nature of public interest obligations in broadcasting. We request comment on how the conversion to digital broadcasting should affect broadcasters' obligation to serve the public interest.

Our future rules may allow broadcasters to use their advanced television channels to provide a high definition television service, multiple standard definition television services and perhaps other services, some of which may be on a subscription basis. Should a licensee's public interest obligations depend on the nature of the services it chooses to provide and if that is the case, how so? For example, if a broadcaster chooses to provide multiple standard definition

services, should public interest obligations attach to each one? What if one or more of the services are provided on a subscription basis? Alternatively, should public interest obligations be seen as attaching not to services but to licensees, each of whom would be required to operate the facilities associated with its 6MHz ATV channel in the public interest? We note that attaching a public interest requirement on one type of "service" could skew broadcaster investment away from providing that service—a situation that could potentially result in a net public interest loss. Commenters are requested to discuss whether, if Congress grants the FCC the requisite authority, we should consider imposing spectrum fees for that portion of the spectrum used by broadcasters to provide subscription services. We note that the use of spectrum fees may allow the FCC to establish a regulatory framework that does not discourage broadcasters from providing free over-the-air channels or other services to which public interest obligations might attach. We also invite comment on whether the conversion to digital broadcasting justifies other changes in our public interest framework.

As a related issue, we must revisit the question of whether licensees' NTSC and ATV station licenses should be considered a single license or two separate and distinct licenses. We previously decided to treat the licensee as having two paired licenses. That is each licensee's NTSC and ATV station would receive a separate license. We tentatively conclude that substantial benefits could be obtained if, instead of licensing the NTSC and ATV facilities separately, we authorized both under a single, unified license. It would ease administrative burdens on the FCC and broadcasters alike by reducing the number of applications that have to be filled out, filed and processed. Finally, treating the two facilities under a single license would retain the sound policy announced in the *Second Report/Further Notice* [7 F.C.C.R. 3340 (1992)] of treating both facilities the same from the revocation/non-renewal standpoint. We seek comment on this tentative conclusion.

[In conclusion], we request comments on the many issues pertinent to the conversion by television broadcasters to digital technology. The speedy conversion to digital technology will have profound public interest benefits, permitting efficient spectrum use, optimizing the development of new technologies and services to consumers, and fostering diversity and competition.

COMMENT

In the *Fourth Further Notice* on ATV, the FCC confronts the world of digital television and the multiple television services that ATV promises. Here the FCC wonders aloud about the nature of the public interest obligations that should attach to new services that licensees will be able to provide in the future. Should the public interest obligations of traditional broadcasters attach to each of a broadcaster's television channels? One might say that the answer should be in the affirmative on the ground that ATV still uses a limited spectrum. But the FCC points out that the downside to imposing the public interest obligations of traditional broadcasters on all ATV services is that it might deter broadcaster investment in new services. How do you think the FCC should handle this issue?

The *Fourth Further Notice* also asked for comment on other issues as well. The *Notice* proposes "to require the simulcast of all material being broadcast on the licensee's NTSC station (with the exception of commercials and promotions) on a program service of the ATV channel." Is it desirable for the FCC to impose a simulcast requirement on broadcast licensees?

In the *Fourth Further Notice,* the FCC observed that Congress in 1962 adopted the All Channel Receiver Act, which requires that all television sets "be capable of adequately receiving all frequencies allocated by the FCC to television broadcasting." 47 U.S.C. § 303(s). In light of this, the FCC asked for comment on "whether permitting the manufacture and sale of receivers that display only NTSC, SDTV, or HDTV signals, or a combination of two but not all three, would be consistent with the All Channel Receiver Act or otherwise would be in the public interest." In short, should the FCC set mandatory television receiver standards?

One should note that the *Fourth Further Notice* of July 1995 made it very clear that incumbent licensees should be allowed to provide the transition to digital television free of charge. Not everyone agrees. Some believe that broadcasters should pay for the digital spectrum. In December 1996 the computer and TV industries reached a general agreement on a digital TV standard. *Broadcasting & Cable* magazine reported that as part of the agreement the computer industry agreed not to join with those in Congress who want to auction off the spectrum "allocated for digital TV." One powerful voice in favor of auctioning off the spectrum was Senator John McCain (R-Ariz.), the new chair of the Senate Commerce Committee in 1997: "With McCain in the battle is a unique coalition of budget hawks and 'free-marketeers' who want an auction to help balance the federal budget. [Also joining them are public interest groups such as] Media Access Project which want to use spectrum revenue to fund 'public interest' projects including additional educational TV programming." See *Broadcasting & Cable,* Dec. 2, 1996, at 7.

Should licensees seeking to offer ATV services by means of digital TV have to pay for spectrum through an auction? If they do, should they be relieved of some—all?—of their public interest obligations? See *Sixth Report & Order In re Advanced Television Systems and Their Impact upon the Existing Television Broadcast Service,* 1997 WL 197153 (FCC, April 21, 1997).

In addition to auctioning off the new ATV digital licenses, Senator McCain also recommends auctioning off new analog licenses, i.e., traditional broadcast TV licenses. See Chris McConnell, *McCain Favors Auction of Analog TV Licenses,* Broadcasting & Cable, Jan. 13, 1997, at 3. Since *Bechtel v. FCC,* 10 F.3d 875 (D.C. Cir. 1993), the FCC has suspended comparative hearings and has accumulated over 710 applications for licenses in ninety-one markets. Senator McCain's proposal would allow the FCC to auction off these new licenses to raise additional revenues as well as speed up the licensing process.

Non-Spectrum-Using Services

Alternative, nonbroadcast, electronic communications services do not necessarily have to use the spectrum. One alternative, cable television, has been around since about 1949, although it grew explosively only in the 1970s and 1980s. Changes in the way our telephone system works have complicated the matter. The telephone system, once nothing more than a form of automated person-to-person (or company-to-company) communication, is used more and more as a means of one-to-many communication. That is the essence of mass communication. These new uses force policymakers to figure out how to reconcile mass communication law principles with the quite different traditions of telephone law and regulation.

CABLE TELEVISION   Cable television began in this country in the 1940s as a way of improving broadcast reception for people in mountainous or otherwise "shadowed" areas. By the 1980s, it had become something quite different—bringing broadcast programming plus a whole host of other cable-only services (e.g., HBO, ESPN, CNN) to more than half of all the people in the United States with televisions. These developments stressed the legal system for regulating cable television, which had never established a definite legal or regulatory identity. In the 1990s, the Supreme Court gave considerable attention to identifying an appropriate First Amendment standard for cable television. The details of this are discussed in the cable chapter.

CHANGES IN TELEPHONY   At about the same time, but accelerating after the break up of AT&T in 1984, the law of telephony assumed mass communications aspects. Traditionally, telephone systems were regarded as common carriers. They provided communications services but were neither responsible for nor much concerned about the nature of the content transmitted. In the 1980s, those attitudes changed. Using the telephone for one-to-many communications became more and more possible. For example, one could place a phone call and receive such diverse services as stock quotations, "Dial a Santa" or "Dial an Easter Bunny" during holiday seasons, "Gab Lines" (appealing primarily to teens), or "Dial-A-Porn" (sexually explicit recordings or "live" content). The result was the need, still much in progress, to rethink how mass communications law applied to telephony. The direction was toward a new synthesis of common carrier and mass communications law, although the precise outcome was hard to predict.

PROBLEMS OF BROADCAST LICENSING AND LICENSE RENEWAL

Under the Communications Act of 1934, broadcasting is subject to rather extensive regulation.

Until 1981, licenses for broadcasting stations were granted only for a period of three years under the Act. According to the Act, licenses are to be granted by the FCC provided that "the public convenience, interest, or necessity will be served thereby." 47 U.S.C. § 307(a). The Telecommunications Act of 1996 now provides that "[e]ach license granted for the operation of a broadcasting station shall be for a term of not to exceed 8 years." 47 U.S.C. § 307(c)(1) (1996). At the expiration of the licensing period, the licensee is required to apply for renewal, which may be granted "if the commission finds that public interest, convenience, and necessity would be served thereby."

The Sole Applicant Problem

One of the many problems the FCC encounters in licensing decisions occurs when only one applicant applies for a license. The rationale for FCC selection of licensees is that it must choose among competing licensees. But suppose there is only one applicant? The problem arose in *Henry v. FCC,* 302 F.2d 191 (D.C. Cir. 1962), where a new applicant sought a permit to construct the first commercial FM station in Elizabeth, New Jersey. In support of the application, the applicant submitted identical programming proposals to support its license applications for FM facilities in Berwyn, Illinois, and Alameda, California.

In *Henry,* the court upheld the FCC's authority to reject even the sole applicant for a new license:

> Appellants contend that the statutory licensing scheme requires a grant where, as here, it is established that the sole applicants for a frequency are legally, financially and technically qualified. This view reflects an arbitrarily narrow understanding of the statutory words "public convenience, interest, or necessity." It leaves no room for commission consideration of matters relating to programming.

The court concluded that the FCC could require that even a sole applicant for a license show an "earnest interest in serving a local community by evidencing familiarity with its particular needs and an effort to meet them." The FCC's action in denying the license application in *Henry* was held to involve "no greater interference with a broadcaster's alleged right to choose its programs free from commission control than the interference involved in *National Broadcasting Co.*"

Although the *Henry* case looks innocent enough, it actually represents a challenge to the entire rationale for broadcast regulation. The theory of the *NBC* case was that broadcasting was a limited access medium. Therefore, the commission was under obligation to play a role in determining the "composition of the traffic." But if only one applicant seeks a station license, why should the FCC play any role at all? At this point the limited access rationale presumably disappears. Does the *Henry* case result suggest an alternative theory of broadcast regulation? If so, what is it?

The Enforcement Powers of the FCC and the Licensing Process

In enforcing the Communications Act and the rules, policies, and regulations issued thereunder, the FCC has tremendous discretion in the range and severity of the sanctions available to it. Thus, in *FCC v. Pacifica Foundation* (see text, p. 606, the Supreme Court, per Justice Stevens, quoted with apparent approval the FCC's statement of its enforcement powers in *Pacifica, 56 F.C.C.2d 94, 96 n.3 (1972)*:

> The FCC noted "Congress has specifically empowered the FCC to (1) revoke a station's license, (2) issue a cease and desist order, or (3) impose a monetary forfeiture for a violation of Section 1464, 47 U.S.C. §§ 312(a), 312(b), 503(b)(1)(E). The FCC can also (4) deny license renewal or (5) grant a short term renewal. 47 U.S.C. §§ 307, 308."

ENFORCEMENT BY LETTER One regulatory procedure used by the FCC is enforcement by letter. This usually takes place when a third party protests some programming decision by a licensee. On rare occasions, the FCC dispatches a letter to the licensee stating its view of how the matter should be handled. This method has aroused some criticism because it is very difficult to get judicial review of the course of action outlined by the FCC in a letter. These letters of reprimand, which is what they often are, constitute the "raised eyebrow" technique. Do you see why such review would be difficult?

CEASE-AND-DESIST ORDERS From a reading of the Communications Act, one might expect that sec. 312(b) would play an important role in the enforcement of the commission's programming standards. That provision states:

> Where any person (1) has failed to operate substantially as set forth in a license, (2) has violated or failed to observe any of the provisions of this act, or (3) has violated or failed to observe any rule or regulation of the commission authorized by this act or by a treaty ratified by the United States, the commission may order such person to cease and desist from such action.

Although the FCC has seldom issued cease-and-desist orders, it nevertheless professes to be willing to use them.

DENIAL OF THE APPLICATION FOR LICENSE RENEWAL: THE DEATH PENALTY The most severe sanction in the FCC's enforcement arsenal is its power to deny any application for license renewal. The industry calls this sanction "the death penalty." It exists more as a specter than as a reality, however, because it is rarely used. The FCC, of course, may also revoke licenses under specified circumstances. See, for example, the discussion of 47 U.S.C. § 312(a)(7), permitting revocation of a license where there has been willful failure to provide "reasonable access" to broadcasting to a "legally qualified candidate for federal elective office." See generally, text, p. 790. Instead of denying the application for renewal outright, the FCC may grant an offending party a short-term renewal for one year rather than the eight-year renewal authorized under the Act. See 47 U.S.C. § 307(c)(1).

As should become clear from the materials in this chapter, denial of a license renewal application is an unusual event in broadcast regulation. Although the Communications Act does not provide for preferential treatment for incumbents, the "living law" certainly supports the view that a preference for incumbency exists. Why does the FCC exercise such solicitude toward applicants who have been licensed before?

An examination of the relatively few license renewal applications that have been denied reveals that misrepresentation by the licensee to the FCC is apparently deemed to constitute a sin of a fundamental kind. The leading case on misrepresentation as a ground for denial of license renewal is *FCC v. WOKO, Inc.*, 329 U.S. 223 (1946), where Justice Jackson stated:

> The fact of concealment may be more significant than the facts concealed. The willingness to deceive a regulatory body may be disclosed by immaterial and useless deceptions as well as by material and

persuasive ones. We do not think it is an answer to say that the deception was unnecessary and served no purpose.

In *Robinson v. FCC*, 334 F.2d 534 (D.C. Cir. 1964), the FCC took the unusual step of refusing to renew a license in a case where, among other issues, the licensee allocated a substantial amount of its programming to off-color jokes and remarks. One of the grounds for denial listed by the FCC was that Robinson had made misrepresentations in the license renewal proceeding. The court of appeals in a *per curiam* opinion affirmed the decision on that ground alone.

One of the FCC findings that the court of appeals refused to pass upon was that some of the disc jockey program material was "coarse, vulgar, suggestive, and susceptible of indecent, double meaning." Judge Miller, concurring, thought this and other FCC findings should have been upheld by the court of appeals. Judge Miller speculated on why the court's opinion in *Robinson v. FCC* nervously avoided the obscenity issue: "Perhaps, the majority refrained from discussing the other issues because of a desire to avoid approving any commission action which might be called program censorship."

See also *Brandywine–Main Line Radio, Inc. v. FCC*, 473 F.2d 16 (D.C. Cir. 1972), where radio station WXUR in Media, Pennsylvania, won the dubious honor of being the first licensee in the history of broadcast regulation to lose its license at renewal time because of failure to comply with the fairness doctrine. On the basis of the majority opinion in Brandywine, it is apparent that the group defamation practices of WXUR were a serious factor in the massive citizen group effort to persuade the FCC to deny WXUR's license renewal application. But the group defamation problem, however large it may have loomed in stimulating the movement against renewal of WXUR, does not loom very large in the formal rationalization for the result reached either by the FCC or by the court.

In fact, just a count of judicial votes at the court of appeals level shows that the real basis for decision in *Brandywine* was not the fairness doctrine but the misrepresentation issue. The only theory that any two judges of the three-judge appellate panel that reviewed the FCC decision in *Brandywine* agreed upon was that deception in obtaining a broadcast license is jus-

tification for denying renewal of that license as happened in *FCC v. WOKO, Inc.*

Why is misrepresentation preferred over violation of a programming standard as a ground for denial of a license renewal application?

Standing and License Renewal

Who is entitled to set the enforcement process in motion? If a licensee seeks renewal of a license, who can challenge that application? The law is clear that the other applicants for the license may certainly challenge a renewal application. Indeed, prior to the Telecommunications Act of 1996, in such a case a comparative hearing was required. All the applicants were joined in a single proceeding, and the merits and demerits of all the applicants were weighed against each other. See *Ashbacker Radio Corp. v. FCC*, 326 U.S. 327 (1945). 47 U.S.C. § 309(k)(4) now states that the FCC "shall not consider whether the public interest, convenience, and necessity might be served by the grant of a license to a person other than the renewal applicant."

But who beyond a licensee's competitors may institute and intervene in FCC proceedings? Until 1969, standing to challenge the programming activity of a licensee before the FCC was rather limited. The traditional view, established by *FCC v. Sanders*, 309 U.S. 470 (1940), was that a showing of economic injury was necessary for standing before the FCC. The theory behind this doctrine was that only someone who had an economically measurable interest in a proceeding could be considered to have a bona fide or nonmischievous stake in it. The theory proceeded on the belief that the public interest could best be defended by someone who was economically injured by the illegal behavior of a licensee since only she would have sufficient incentive to be steadily on the alert for noncompliance with the Communications Act. The difficulty with the doctrine was that it had an industry rather than a consumer orientation. The *Sanders* doctrine proceeded on the rather simplistic assumption that the competitive interests of other members of the broadcasting industry exhausted the range of values encompassed under the category of broadcasting in the "public interest." As a result, the stake of the listening audience in the social and informing function of broadcasting was largely unrepresented.

An approach to standing based on economic injury reflected a quantitative rather than a qualitative approach to the problems of broadcasting. In 1966, a heavy assault was finally made on the *Sanders* doctrine.

Office of Communication of the United Church of Christ v. FCC

359 F.2d 994 (D.C. CIR. 1966).

BURGER, Circuit Judge:

The petition claimed that WLBT failed to serve the general public because it provided a disproportionate amount of commercials and entertainment and did not give a fair and balanced presentation of controversial issues, especially those concerning Negroes, who comprise almost forty-five percent of the total population within its prime service area; it also claimed discrimination against local activities of the Catholic Church.

Appellants claim standing before the FCC on the grounds that:

1. They are individuals and organizations who were denied a reasonable opportunity to answer their critics, a violation of the Fairness Doctrine.
2. These individuals and organizations represent the nearly one half of WLBT's potential listening audience who were denied an opportunity to have their side of controversial issues presented, equally a violation of the Fairness Doctrine, and who were more generally ignored and discriminated against in WLBT's programs.
3. These individuals and organizations represent the total audience, not merely one part of it, and they assert the right of all listeners, regardless of race or religion, to hear and see balanced programming on significant public questions as required by the Fairness Doctrine and also their broad interest that the station be operated in the public interest in all respects.

Up to this time, the courts have granted standing to intervene only to those alleging electrical interference, *NBC v. FCC (KOA),* 132 F.2d 545 (1942), *aff'd,* 319 U.S. 239, or alleging some economic injury, e.g., *FCC v. Sanders,* 309 U.S. 470 (1940). We see no reason to believe that Congress through its committees had any thought that electrical interference and economic injury were to be the exclusive grounds for standing or that it intended to limit participation of the listening public to writing letters to the Complaints Division of the FCC. Instead, the Congressional reports seem to recognize that the issue of standing was to be left to the courts.

Since the concept of standing is a practical and functional one designed to insure that only those with a genuine and legitimate interest can participate in a proceeding, we can see no reason to exclude those with such an obvious and acute concern as the listening audience. There is nothing unusual or novel in granting the consuming public standing to challenge administrative actions.

After nearly five decades of operation the broadcast industry does not seem to have grasped the simple fact that a broadcast license is a public trust subject to termination for breach of duty. Such beneficial contribution as these Appellants, or some of them, can make must not be left to the grace of the FCC. Public participation is especially important in a renewal proceeding, since the public will have been exposed to the licensee's performance, as cannot be the case when the FCC considers an initial grant, unless the applicant has a prior record as a licensee. In a renewal proceeding, furthermore, public spokesmen, such as appellants here, may be the only objectors. In a community served by only one outlet, the public interest focus is perhaps sharper and the need for airing complaints often greater than where, for example, several channels exist. Even when there are multiple competing stations in a locality, various factors may operate to inhibit the other broadcasters from opposing a renewal application. An imperfect rival may be thought a desirable rival, or there may be a "gentleman's agreement" of deference to a fellow broadcaster in the hope he will reciprocate on a propitious occasion.

Thus, we are brought around by analogy to the Supreme Court's reasoning in *Sanders;* unless the listeners—the broadcast consumers—can be heard, there may be no one to bring programming deficiencies or offensive overcommercialization to the attention of the FCC in an effective manner. As to these appellants we limit ourselves to holding that the FCC must allow standing to one or more of them as responsible representatives to assert and prove the claims they have urged in their petition.

We hold further that in the circumstances shown by this record an evidentiary hearing was required in order to resolve the public interest issue. The FCC argues in this Court that it accepted all appellants' allegations of WLBT's misconduct and that for this reason no hearing was necessary.

The FCC in effect sought to justify its grant of the one-year license, in the face of accepted facts irreconcilable with a public interest finding, on the ground that as a matter of policy the immediate need warranted the risks involved, and that the "strict conditions" it imposed on the grant would improve *future* operations. However, the conditions which the commission made explicit in the one-year license are implicit in every grant.

We hold that the grant of a renewal of WLBT's license for one year was erroneous. The FCC is directed to conduct hearings on WLBT's renewal application, allowing public intervention pursuant to this holding. Since the commission has already decided that appellants are responsible representatives of the listening public of the Jackson area, we see no obstacle to a prompt determination granting standing to appellants or some of them. Whether WLBT should be able to benefit from a showing of good performance, if such is the case, since June 1965 we do not undertake to decide. The FCC has had no occasion to pass on this issue and we therefore refrain from doing so. The record is remanded to the FCC for further proceedings consistent with this opinion; jurisdiction is retained in this court.

Reversed and remanded.

The Petition to Deny and "Citizens" Groups

Suppose a citizens' group is dissatisfied with the job a broadcast licensee has been doing? What can the group do? If another applicant applies for a license, the group can enter the renewal proceeding as a result of the *United Church of Christ* decision. But suppose there is no hearing in which to participate. In that case, what can a citizens' group do? The group can file a petition to deny with the FCC, requesting that the incumbent's license renewal application be denied. But a license renewal application will hardly be denied without a hearing, and a petition to deny usually does not lead to the grant of a hearing.

Petitions to deny are sometimes used to pressure stations into making changes, particularly in personnel practices and minority programming

policies. In view of the difficulties in obtaining a hearing on a license renewal, citizens' groups sometimes file petitions to deny for their *in terrorem* effect and then bargain (often very successfully) privately and directly with the stations involved. If the group's requests are granted, the petition to deny is withdrawn. Sometimes the citizens' group bargains with the broadcaster first, usually just before renewal time, keeping the threat of filing a petition to deny in reserve for leverage. What criticisms would you make of these developments? Do you have suggestions for corrections? See Barron, *"The Citizen Group at Work," Freedom of the Press for Whom?* 233–248 (1973).

The FCC has set forth standards that, within limits, generally allow broadcasters to enter into agreements with citizen groups. See *In re Agreements between Broadcast Licensees and the Public,* 57 F.C.C.2d 42 (1975). The FCC made it clear that "a licensee is not obliged to undertake negotiations or agreements." If a licensee does enter into an agreement with citizens, the FCC stressed that "(t)he obligation to determine how to serve the public interest is personal to each licensee and may not be delegated, even if the licensee wishes to." The FCC warned that agreements should "not take responsibility for making public interest decisions out of the hands of a licensee."

On March 30, 1989, the FCC voted to limit broadcaster reimbursement of citizens' groups to "legitimate and prudent expenses." *FCC Revamps Rules to Stem Abuse of Process,* Broadcasting & Cable, April 3, 1989, at 27.

Minority and Gender Preferences in the Licensing Process

In 1973, the D.C. Circuit remanded a comparative proceeding where the FCC declined to give enhanced integration credit to a group including two local African American residents as owners/managers. The FCC's position was that it was "color-blind." The court, however, said that combined ownership interests and active managerial participation of the African Americans gave their group an advantage in providing "broader community representation and practicable service to the public by increasing diversity of content, especially of opinion and viewpoint." Twenty-five percent of the residents to be served by the proposed station were African American. *TV 9, Inc. v. FCC,* 495 F.2d 929 (D.C. Cir. 1973).

In subsequent years, the FCC, led largely by its Review Board, followed a policy of giving an enhancement to comparative advantages already held by applicants proposing integrated owners and managers when those persons were members of minority groups. See, for example, *Flint Family Radio, Inc.,* 41 R.R.2d 1155 (FCC 1977). For a summary of these developments, consult *West Michigan Broadcasting v. FCC,* 735 F.2d 601 (D.C. Cir. 1984). In plainer English, since the FCC already gave comparative advantages to groups where the owners promised to be active day-to-day managers, it simply decided to give even more comparative credit to applicants where the active owner/managers were minorities. These policies were not designed to promote minority ownership *per se.* Rather, they were intended to increase the number of minority owners involved in day-to-day management. The assumption was that ownership diversity would result in viewpoint diversity and better service in the public interest.

Subsequently, the FCC developed a number of other policies directly intended to promote minority ownership. It established a "distress sale" policy, under which licensees designated for renewal hearings could sell their stations to minority-controlled corporations despite their pending difficulties at the FCC. Although sales after designation for hearings normally are not permitted, these minority distress sales were allowed, but only if the sale was for no more than 75 percent of the fair market value of the station. *Minority Ownership of Broadcast Facilities,* 68 F.C.C.2d 979 (1978) and *Clarification of Distress Sale Policy,* 44 R.R.2d 479 (FCC 1978).

The FCC also awarded tax certificates to owners of broadcast stations and, eventually, cable television systems, who voluntarily sold their properties to minority-controlled corporations. Such certificates allow deferral (and sometimes complete avoidance) of capital gains taxes associated with sales. See *Minority Ownership of Broadcast Facilities,* 68 F.C.C.2d 979 (1978), *Minority Ownership in Broadcasting,* 52 R.R.2d 1301 (FCC 1982), and *Minority Ownership of Cable Television Facilities,* 52 R.R.2d 1469 (FCC 1983).

Women occasionally received preferences in traditional comparative proceedings. The FCC's Review Board, an intermediate appellate stop between the administrative law judges and the commissioners themselves, had developed a female preference policy modeled on the minority policy that grew from *TV 9.* The Review Board sometimes "enhanced" already existing credit for integration of ownership and management when the integrated owners/managers were female. In 1983, this policy led the board to award a radio station license to a group with integrated female ownership/management over other competitors. *Cannon's Point Broad. Co.,* 93 F.C.C.2d 643 (1983). The board refused to reconsider, 94 F.C.C.2d 72 (1983), and in 1984, without published opinion, the full FCC denied review. FCC 84-161 (April 13, 1984). The losers, including James Steele, appealed.

In *Steele v. FCC,* 770 F.2d 1192 (D.C. Cir. 1985), Steele, the disappointed applicant, brought an action challenging the FCC policy that extended preferential treatment to female applicants for FM radio stations in comparative proceedings. The court, per Judge Tamm, held that the FCC had exceeded its statutory authority in extending such preferential treatment absent a factual showing that such a preference promoted the public interest in fostering diversity of viewpoints in mass media. Unlike the minority preference, the court was unable to find any "(c)lear Congressional endorsement of the FCC's female preference policy."

Did the rationale underlying minority preference extend to women? The court answered this in the negative. It ran against the constitutional grain to assume that membership in a minority group would cause members to have distinct tastes and perspectives that would consciously or unconsciously be reflected in distinct programming. Such an assumption was a "(m)ere indulgence in the most simplistic kind of ethnic stereotyping." Instead, an individual's beliefs and tastes "should be assessed on their own merits."

Although conceding that these assumptions may be of merit with regard to cohesive ethnic cultures, the court declared that "women transcend ethnic, religious, and other cultural barriers." Thus, it was simply "(n)ot reasonable to expect that granting preferences to women will increase programming diversity." Consequently, the court invalidated the female preference policy and held that the FCC had exceeded its authority because "(t)he Commission had been unable to offer any evidence other than statistical under-representation to support its bald assertion that more women station owners would increase programming diversity." In a dissent, Judge Wald argued that it was not necessary for the FCC to demonstrate in advance that increasing female ownership in broadcasting would result in programming more responsive to the perspectives of women: "The Commission's reasonable expectation is sufficient." *Steele* was decided on August 23, 1985.

On October 31, 1985, the court, *en banc,* granted a rehearing and vacated the panel opinion. The court then issued an order asking the parties to file supplemental briefs addressing the FCC's statutory authority to grant gender-based preferences and the constitutionality of such grants. In response, the FCC, in an astonishing turnaround, expressed doubt that either its female or its minority preference policies satisfied statutory and constitutional requirements.

The FCC was especially concerned with several U.S. Supreme Court cases involving affirmative action programs that might have implicated the FCC's comparative preference, minority distress sale, and minority tax certificate programs. Collectively, these cases minimally established that classifications based on race or sex were subject to strict or heightened scrutiny. See *Wygant v. Jackson Bd. of Educ.,* 476 U.S. 267 (1986); *Mississippi Univ. for Women v. Hogan,* 458 U.S. 718 (1982); *Fullilove v. Klutznick,* 448 U.S. 448 (1980); *Regents of Cal. v. Bakke,* 438 U.S. 265 (1978).

To address these constitutional questions, the FCC initiated a notice of inquiry, *In re the Reexamination of the FCC's Comparative Licensing, Distress Sales and Tax Certificate Policies Premised on Racial, Ethnic or Gender Classifications,* 1 F.C.C.R. 1315 (1986). In this proceeding, the FCC invited commenters to focus on establishing a factual record that demonstrated an actual (i.e., not *assumed*) nexus between the preference scheme and enhanced program diversity, and also on whether such ownership was necessary to achieve such diversity (i.e., whether the policy was narrowly tailored).

Did ownership diversity result in program diversity? The *TV 9* court assumed that it would do so, if only the FCC would grant licenses to groups including minority owners/managers. The FCC had made the same assumption in adopting most of its minority and female preference policies. The *Steele* case could be interpreted as an invitation to the FCC to bring back evidence to support the assumption. The FCC's Notice of Inquiry could be interpreted as just an objective effort to gather the relevant information.

The Inquiry was also subject to other interpretations, however. Was the FCC's request for a remand an attempt to create a means to abandon, in one fell swoop, all the commission's minority and female preference policies? FCC officials, especially then FCC Chairman Mark Fowler, had given several speeches questioning gender- or race-based preferences. Parties, concerned that the FCC was going to use the proceeding to bring down minority and female preferences that the 1986 FCC had inherited from earlier commissions and did not like, appealed to the Congress for help. It took a while, but Congress intervened. In a bill providing appropriations for Fiscal Year 1988, Congress forced the FCC to terminate its inquiry and to reinstate its minority and female preference policies. Public Law 100-202, signed December 22, 1987, gave the FCC money to continue operating into 1988, but said that it could not use any of that money to:

> repeal, to retroactively apply changes in, or to continue a reexamination of, the policies of the FCC with respect to comparative licensing, distress sales and tax certificates granted under 26 U.S.C. § 1071, to expand minority and women ownership of broadcasting licenses, including those established in Statement of Policy on Minority Ownership of Broadcast Facilities, 68 FCC 2d 979 and 69 FCC 2d 1591, as amended 52 R.F.2d 1313 (1982) and Mid-Florida Television Corp., 60 FCC 2d Rev.Bd. 1978), which were effective prior to September 12, 1982, other than to close MM Docket No. 86-484 with a reinstatement of prior policy and a lifting of suspension of any sales, licenses, applications, or proceedings, which were suspended pending the conclusion of the inquiry. 101 Stat. 1329–32.

Put simply, Congress told the FCC to stop tinkering with the minority and female preference policies established and followed before *Steele.*

The FCC complied and reinstated delayed proceedings that turned on minority or female preference policies. See *Minority Preference Policy* [FCC Brief in *Winter Park Communications v. FCC*, 65 R.R.2d 424 (FCC 1988)]. The ban, of course, technically expired in fiscal year 1989—it only covered use of the 1988 continuing appropriations money—but Congress had told the FCC that it liked minority and female preferences. In the past, the FCC had taken the hint from such directions in appropriations bills and not reinstated policies killed by appropriations legislation.

Thus, the *Steele* case came to an end, pending, of course, any additional constitutional challenges to minority and female preferences. Several policies promoting minority and female ownership continue to be enforced by the FCC:

1. Minorities clearly receive "enhanced integration credit" when minority owners are also significantly involved in management.
2. Women, it appears, receive similar credit, although this policy is much more firmly recognized by the FCC's Review Board than by the commissioners themselves. It can also be argued that the preference extends only to FM broadcast applications—the only applications to which it has so far been applied.
3. Minority owners (but not females), even if not integrated as managers, are favored under the FCC's distress sale and tax certificate policies.
4. Minority (but again not female) owners are also given statistical advantages in lotteries for new licenses, at least under some circumstances.

In *City of Richmond v. J.A. Croson Co.*, 488 U.S. 469 (1989), the Supreme Court erected a heavier hurdle for state and local affirmative action plans to overcome. In *Croson*, a city ordinance required prime contractors awarded city construction contracts to subcontract at least 30 percent of the funds to minority contractors. The Court said that the standard of review for such state and local plans was strict scrutiny, the strictest standard of review; i.e., the plan must serve a compelling governmental interest and be narrowly tailored.

In an earlier case, *Fullilove v. Klutznick*, 448 U.S. 448 (1980), the Court upheld, 6–3, a 10 percent set-aside for minority contractors on federal public works. *Croson* said that the set-aside plan in *Fullilove* was enacted by Congress under sec. 5 of the Fourteenth Amendment. Congress has greater latitude to make findings that racial discrimination occurred in the past and requires remedial action now than do the states and localities. In *Fullilove*, there was no majority on

exactly what standard of review was appropriate for federal affirmative action programs. But a majority of the Court simply said that the federal set-aside plan satisfied either the strict scrutiny standard or the intermediate standard of review. The intermediate standard was an easier standard for affirmative action programs to meet. The government had to show only that the classification had an important purpose and that it was substantially related to the accomplishment of that purpose. *Fullilove* was understood to mean that a more deferential standard of review would be used to evaluate federal affirmative action programs. *Croson* spoke only to state and local plans and did not alter the *Fullilove* holding.

Meanwhile, the FCC's distress sale policy and the enhancement for minority-controlled ownership in comparative proceedings were challenged in the federal courts. The Supreme Court upheld the two FCC policies, 5–4, in the *Metro Broadcasting* case that follows. Would the Supreme Court apply the deferential intermediate standard of review to these two federal policies? Or would it apply the demanding strict scrutiny standard?

Metro Broadcasting, Inc. v. FCC
497 U.S. 547, 110 S. CT. 2997, 111 L. ED. 2D 445 (1990).

Justice BRENNAN delivered the opinion of the Court.

Although for the past two decades minorities have constituted at least one-fifth of the United States population, during this time relatively few members of minority groups have held broadcast licenses. [I]n 1986, [minorities] owned just 2.1 percent of the more than 11,000 radio and television stations in the United States. Moreover, these statistics fail to reflect the fact that, as late entrants who have often been able to obtain less valuable stations, many broadcasters serve geographically limited markets with relatively small audiences.

[In its *Statement of Policy on Minority Ownership of Broadcasting Facilities*, 68 F.C.C.2d 979 (1978)], the FCC outlined two elements of a minority ownership policy. First, the FCC pledged to consider minority ownership as one factor in comparative hearings for new licenses. In the *Policy Statement on Minority Ownership*, the FCC announced that minority ownership and participation in management would be considered in a comparative hearing as a "plus" to be weighed together with all other relevant factors. The "plus" is awarded only to the extent that minority owners actively participate in the day-to-day management of the station.

Second, the FCC outlined a plan to increase minority opportunities to receive reassigned and transferred licenses through the so-called "distress sale" policy. As a general rule, a licensee whose qualifications to hold a broadcast license come into question may not assign or transfer that license until the FCC has resolved its doubts in a noncomparative hearing. The distress sale policy is an exception to that practice, allowing a broadcaster whose license has been designated for a revocation hearing, or whose renewal application has been designated for hearing, to assign that license to an FCC-approved minority enterprise. The assignee must meet the FCC's basic qualifications, and the minority ownership must exceed 50 percent or be controlling. The buyer must purchase the license before the start of the revocation or renewal hearing, and the price must not exceed 75 percent of fair market value. These two FCC minority ownership policies are at issue today.

Our decision last term in *Croson*, concerning a minority set-aside program adopted by a municipality, does not prescribe the level of scrutiny to be applied to a benign racial classification employed by Congress. In fact, much of the language and reasoning in *Croson* reaffirmed the lesson of *Fullilove* [*v. Klutznick*, 448 U.S. 448 (1980)] that race-conscious classifications adopted by Congress to address racial and ethnic discrimination are subject to a different standard than such classifications prescribed by state and local governments.

We hold that the FCC ownership policies pass muster under the test we announce today. *First, we find that they serve the important governmental objective* of broadcast diversity. *Second, we conclude that they are substantially related to the achievement of that objective.* [Emphasis added.] Congress and the FCC did not justify the minority ownership policies strictly as remedies for victims of this discrimination, however. Rather, Congress and the FCC have selected the minority ownership policies primarily to promote programming diversity, and they urge that such diversity is an important governmental objective

that can serve as a constitutional basis for the preference policies. We agree.

[W]e conclude that the interest in enhancing broadcast diversity is, at the very least, an important governmental objective and is therefore a sufficient basis for the FCC's minority ownership policies. The benefits of such diversity are not limited to the members of minority groups who gain access to the broadcasting industry by virtue of the ownership policies; rather, the benefits redound to all members of the viewing and listening audience. As Congress found, "the American public will benefit by having access to a wider diversity of information sources."

We also find that minority ownership policies are substantially related to the achievement of the government's interest. One component of this inquiry concerns the relationship between expanded minority ownership and greater broadcast diversity; both the FCC and Congress have determined that such a relationship exists. The FCC has determined that increased minority participation in broadcasting promotes programming diversity. The FCC's conclusion that there is an empirical nexus between minority ownership and broadcast diversity is a product of its expertise, and we accord its judgment deference. Congress has made clear its view that the minority ownership policies advance the goal of diverse programming. We must give great weight to their joint determination.

Although all station owners are guided to some extent by market demand in their programming decisions, Congress and the FCC have determined that there may be important differences between the broadcast practices of minority owners and those of their nonminority counterparts. This judgment—and the conclusion that there is a nexus between minority ownership and broadcasting diversity—is corroborated by a host of empirical evidence. Evidence suggests that an owner's minority status influences the selection of topics for news coverage and the presentation of editorial viewpoint, especially on matters of particular concern to minorities. While we are under no illusion that members of a particular minority group share some cohesive, collective viewpoint, we believe it a legitimate inference for Congress and the FCC to draw that as more minorities gain ownership and policymaking roles in the media, varying perspectives will be more fairly represented on the airwaves.

Finally, we do not believe that the minority ownership policies at issue impose impermissible burdens on nonminorities. In the context of broadcasting licenses, the burden on nonminorities is slight. Applicants have no settled expectation that their applications will be granted without consideration of public interest factors such as minority ownership. Award of a preference in a comparative hearing or transfer of a station in a distress sale thus contravenes "no legitimate firmly rooted expectation[s]" of competing applicants.

Justice O'CONNOR, with whom the Chief Justice [REHNQUIST], Justice SCALIA and Justice KENNEDY join, dissenting.

Our traditional equal protection doctrine requires in addition to a compelling state interest, that the Government's chosen means be necessary to accomplish and narrowly tailored to further the asserted interest. The chosen means, resting as they do on stereotyping and so indirectly furthering the asserted end, could not plausibly be deemed narrowly tailored. The Court instead finds the racial classification to be "substantially related" to achieving the Government's interest, a far less rigorous fit requirement. The FCC's policies fail even this requirement.

Our equal protection doctrine governing intermediate review indicates that the Government may not use race and ethnicity as "a 'proxy for other, more germane bases of classification.'" The FCC has used race as a proxy for whatever views it believes to be underrepresented in the broadcast spectrum. This reflexive or unthinking use of a suspect classification is the hallmark of an unconstitutional policy. The ill fit of means to end is manifest. The policy is overinclusive; many members of a particular racial or ethnic group will have no interest in advancing the views the FCC believes to be underrepresented, or will find them utterly foreign. The policy is underinclusive: it awards no preference to disfavored individuals who may be particularly well versed in and committed to presenting those views. The FCC has failed to implement a case-by-case determination, and that failure is particularly unjustified when individualized hearings already occur, as in the comparative licensing process.

Moreover, the FCC's programs cannot survive even intermediate scrutiny because race-neutral and untried means of directly accomplishing the

governmental interest are readily available. The FCC could directly advance its interest by requiring licensees to provide programming that the FCC believes would add to diversity. Other race-neutral means also exist, and all are at least as direct as the FCC's racial classifications. The FCC could evaluate applicants upon their ability to provide and commitment to offer whatever programming the FCC believes would reflect underrepresented viewpoints. The FCC could develop an effective ascertainment policy, one guaranteeing programming that reflects underrepresented viewpoints.

Three difficulties suggest that the nexus between owners' race and programming is considerably less than substantial. First, the market shapes programming to a tremendous extent. Second, station owners have only limited control over the content of programming. Third, the FCC had absolutely no factual basis for the nexus when it adopted the policies and has since established none to support its existence.

Finally, the Government cannot employ race classifications that unduly burden individuals who are not members of the favored racial and ethnic groups. The challenged policies fail this independent requirement as well as the other constitutional requirements. The comparative licensing and distress sale programs provide the eventual licensee with an exceptionally valuable property and with a rare and unique opportunity to serve the local community. The distress sale imposes a particularly significant burden. The FCC has at base created a specialized market reserved exclusively for minority controlled applicants. There is no more rigid quota than a 100% set aside.

The comparative licensing program, too, imposes a significant burden. The Court's emphasis on the multifactor process should not be confused with the claim that the preference is in some sense a minor one. It is not. The basic nonrace criteria are not difficult to meet, and, given the sums at stake, applicants have every incentive to structure their ownership arrangement to prevail in the comparative process. Applicants cannot alter their race, of course, and race is clearly the dispositive factor in a substantial percentage of comparative proceedings.

In sum, the Government has not met its burden even under the Court's test that approves of racial classifications that are substantially related to an important governmental objective. Of course, the programs even more clearly fail the strict scrutiny that should be applied. The Court has determined that, in essence, Congress and all federal agencies are exempted, to some ill-defined but significant degree, from the Constitution's equal protection requirements. This break with our precedents greatly undermines equal protection guarantees, and permits distinctions among citizens based on race and ethnicity which the Constitution clearly forbids. I respectfully dissent.

COMMENT

The FCC's affirmative action policies were upheld in *Metro Broadcasting* by a narrow margin. Nevertheless, it was still a victory. The Court, per Justice Brennan, said race-conscious programs such as the enhancement for minority ownership in comparative hearings and the distress sale policy need only meet the deferential intermediate standard of review—the regulation must serve an important government objective and be substantially related to the achievement of that objective. The important government interest that was served was diversity in programming. Racial diversity in broadcast ownership could serve to some extent as a proxy for diversity in programming. Justice O'Connor wrote a powerful dissent that attracted the support of three other justices. She took particular aim at Justice Brennan's idea that race could be a proxy for program diversity.

Metro Broadcasting did not end the battle over affirmative action in the Supreme Court. The FCC policies upheld there were thrown into question again five years later in *Adarand Construction, Inc. v. Pena,* 115 S. Ct. 2097 (1995). Federal legislation provided for additional financial compensation to general contractors working on government projects if they hired "socially and economically disadvantaged individuals." Pursuant to this law, a contractor working on a U.S. Department of Transportation highway construction project hired a Hispanic American subcontractor even though a nonminority subcontractor had submitted a lower bid. The nonminority contractor brought suit alleging that he was denied equal protection of the laws. The court of appeals applied the intermediate standard of review and rejected his claim.

The Supreme Court in *Adarand,* per Justice O'Connor, 5–4, reversed and remanded. The upshot of *Adarand* was that it would be harder in the future for government affirmative action programs to survive a constitutional challenge. The Court said that *Metro Broadcasting* "[b]y adopting intermediate scrutiny as the standard of review for congressionally mandated 'benign' classifications" had erred:

> Accordingly, we hold today that all racial classifications imposed by whatever federal, state, or local governmental actor, must be analyzed by a reviewing court under strict scrutiny. In other words, such classifications are constitutional only if they are narrowly tailored measures that further compelling governmental interests. To the extent that *Metro Broadcasting* is inconsistent with that holding it is overruled.

The court of appeals was asked on remand to consider whether the subcontractor compensation clauses served a compelling state interest and whether the clauses were narrowly tailored. How could the court of appeals tell whether the program was narrowly tailored? The Supreme Court offered a couple of suggestions. First, the court of appeals should inquire whether race-neutral means to increase minority business participation had been considered. Second, the court of appeals should inquire whether the program was "'appropriately limited'" so that it would not last "longer than the discriminatory effects it was designed to eliminate."

Why did the Court take such a harsh view of affirmative action policies in *Adarand* in 1995 when in *Metro Broadcasting,* only five years earlier, it had been so sympathetic to the broadcast affirmative action policies at issue there? The short answer is that in the years between *Metro Broadcasting and Adarand,* a substantial personnel change occurred on the Supreme Court. The majority who joined in the opinion in *Metro Broadcasting* consisted of Justices Brennan, Marshall, White, Blackmun, and Stevens. At the time *Adarand* was decided, of that group only Justice Stevens remained on the Court. But all four dissenters in *Metro Broadcasting,* Justices O'Connor, Rehnquist, Kennedy, and Scalia, were still on the Court at the time of *Adarand.* Justice Thomas, who replaced Justice Marshall, joined the dissenters in *Metro Broadcasting* to form a new majority in *Adarand*—a majority that insisted on subjecting affirmative action plans to more intense scrutiny than in the past.

Does *Adarand* invalidate the FCC policies upheld in *Metro Broadcasting?*

On January 12, 1995, the FCC released a notice of proposed rulemaking on its diversity policies. *In re Policies and Rules Regarding Minority and Female Ownership of Mass Media Facilities,* 10 F.C.C.R. 2788 (1995). In the course of this notice, the FCC referred to *Lamprecht v. FCC,* 958 F.2d 381 (D.C. Cir. 1995) where the court held that the FCC preference for a woman owner in granting a permit to build a radio station was unconstitutional because it violated equal protection. The justification for such a preference was that it enhanced diversity in programming. But the court of appeals was not persuaded: "The FCC brief cites nothing that might support its predictive judgment that women owners will broadcast women's or minority or any other underrepresented type of programming at any different rate than will men." In addition, the court of appeals concluded that there was no "statistically meaningful link between [broadcast] ownership by women and programming of any particular kind."

In the 1995 notice, the FCC declared:

The FCC presently has no policies designed to promote women's ownership of mass media facilities. The FCC in the past awarded female owners a preference in comparative broadcast hearings, but that policy was invalidated in *Lamprecht.* [W]e are mindful of the court's decision in *Lamprecht.* Accordingly, we ask commenters to specifically address the extent to which female ownership contributes to diversity of programming distributed by the mass media and to provide evidence as appropriate.

As an alternative legal justification for providing incentives for greater ownership of mass media facilities by both minorities and women, apart from diversity of programming, we solicit comment on whether we should instead rely on an economic rationale. Specifically, we believe that women and minorities face economic disadvantages when they attempt to enter the mass media industry and that it may be appropriate to rectify such disadvantages, just as we have developed our EEO policies to encourage the hiring and promotion of women and minorities. We seek comment about whether in some cases, minorities and women lack access to capital when attempting to finance the purchase of a mass media outlet when others similarly situated have such access, and if so, an analysis of the reasons for this condition.

This Notice proposes specific mechanisms intended to increase minority and female ownership of mass media facilities, and solicits suggestions for other ways to further this goal. Our aim in proposing the mechanisms detailed here is to increase minority and female operators' access to capital which has consistently been identified as a crucial barrier to entry. First, we discuss ways to refine the FCC's previous proposal to create an "incubator" program whereby existing mass media entities would be encouraged, through ownership-based incentives, to assist new entrants to the communications industry. Next, we seek comment on whether and how to modify our ownership attribution rules to increase investment in minority and female-controlled properties and further to benefit minority and female owners. We then explore ways to expand our existing tax certificate policy to encourage entities to sell their mass media holdings to minorities and women, and to make it easier for minority and female operators to upgrade their facilities.

On June 30, 1995, the FCC authorized an extension of time for the filing of comments on its proposed rule making on minority and female ownership policies in light of the issues addressed in the *Adarand* case. 60 Fed. Reg. 34212. In this proposed rulemaking, the FCC suggests that an economic rationale for minority and female preference policies would be more likely to withstand a challenge in the courts than the diversity in programming rationale.

Problems of Incumbency and Media Diversification

In the *Policy Statement on Comparative Broadcast Hearings,* 5 R.R. 1901 (FCC 1965), the FCC emphasized maximum diffusion of control of the media of communications as a factor in selecting among competing applicants for the same facilities. The FCC also announced in the policy statement that it would be interested in full participation in station operation by the owner and in participation in civic affairs. The FCC insisted that broadcast experience be a factor, but that broadcast experience was not the same as a past broadcast record because, otherwise, newcomers would be unduly discouraged. The FCC also renewed its support for the programming criteria set out in the *Programming Inquiry,* 20 R.R. 1901 (FCC 1960) and declared that these criteria would still apply.

In *WHDH, Inc.,* 16 F.C.C.2d 1 (1969), the FCC held that where the applicant has substantial ownership interests in other media in the same community, his license renewal application may be denied if new applicants lacking such cross-media connections are competing for the same license. The broadcast industry did not react calmly to the *WHDH* decision and looked to Congress for an end to the insecurity the decision posed for renewal of existing licenses.

On January 15, 1970, the FCC announced the new but short-lived 1970 Policy Statement on Renewals. Under the policy statement, where there is a hearing in which an applicant seeks the license of an incumbent licensee, the incumbent shall be preferred if he can demonstrate substantial past performance not characterized by serious deficiencies. In such circumstances the incumbent "will be preferred over the newcomer and his application for renewal will be granted." Using "substantial service to the public," as the new criterion for renewal, rather than, say, choosing the applicant deemed most likely to render the best possible service, was justified by the FCC on the basis of "considerations of predictability and stability." The FCC feared that if there was no stability in the industry—if licenses were truly up for grabs at every renewal—it would not be possible for a station to render even substantial service. See *Policy Statements on Comparative Hearings Involving Regular Renewal Applicants,* 22 F.C.C.2d 424 (1970). If broadcasters' investments were not protected, the FCC warned, there would "be an inducement to the opportunist who might seek a license and then provide the barest minimum of service which would permit short run maximization of profit, on the theory that the license might be terminated whether he rendered a good service or not."

The FCC's decision in the *WHDH* case was affirmed. *Greater Boston Television Corp. v. FCC,* 444 F.2d 841 (D.C. Cir. 1970). The FCC's dramatic decision to take away a television station from an incumbent newspaper-affiliated licensee was upheld. The de facto automatic renewal process was dealt a body blow.[2]

Additionally, Judge Leventhal's opinion in *WHDH* fully approved the preference that the FCC gave to the diversification of control of mass communication media in the *WHDH* proceeding. In other words, the FCC had been authorized, in the Court's opinion, to choose a non-newspaper-affiliated applicant in a contest between it and a newspaper-affiliated incumbent. This endorsement of the diversification policy was an indication of rising judicial dissatisfaction with the FCC's automatic renewal policy.

THE *CITIZENS COMMUNICATION CENTER* CASE: THE RENEWAL CONTROVERSY RENEWED Two citizens' groups, the Citizens Communication Center and BEST, (Black Efforts for Soul in Television) challenged the legality of the 1970 policy statement. The citizens' groups prevailed, and on June 11, 1970, the D.C. Circuit directed the FCC to stop applying the policy statement. The FCC order refusing to institute rule-making proceedings was reversed. See *Citizens Communication Center v. FCC,* 447 F.2d 1201 (D.C. Cir. 1971).

The successful citizens' groups won on a three-pronged argument. First, the *Ashbacker* rule requiring a comparative hearing for mutually exclusive applicants was violated by depriving an applicant of such a hearing if the incumbent made a showing of substantial service. See *Ashbacker Radio Corp. v. FCC,* 326 U.S. 327 (1945). Further, the policy statement was unlawful because it deprived a competing applicant of a hearing in violation of sec. 309(c) of the Communications Act. Second, the policy statement was attacked on the ground that it violated the Administrative Procedure Act. Thirdly, the policy statement was successfully attacked on the ground that the decision unlawfully chilled the exercise of First Amendment rights.

The tremors *Citizens Communication Center (CCC)* sent through the broadcast industry rivaled the FCC's *WHDH* decision of January 1969. The unwritten rule of automatic renewal for a broadcast incumbent was once more under attack.

Communications lawyers in Washington read with particular care footnotes 35 and 36 of Judge Wright's decision in *CCC.* See *Broadcasting,* June 21, 1971. Footnote 35 said that the licenses of incumbents rendering "superior service" ought to be renewed, otherwise the public

---

2. As a result of the *WHDH* case, the *Boston Herald-Traveler,* which had been financially dependent upon WHDH, merged with the *Record-American.* Paradoxically, as a result of *WHDH,* Boston lost one daily newspaper voice. Was this cause for reconsideration of a policy aimed against cross-ownership? Indeed it had that effect, and *WHDH* would come to be considered an aberration.

will suffer. What is necessary, therefore, is to define "superior service." Wright suggested some criteria, i.e., avoidance of excessive advertising, quality programming, and reinvestment of profits "to the service of the viewing and listening public." Do you see any dangers in replacing a "superior service" standard with a "substantial service" standard? Isn't the key factor the FCC's attitude toward the renewal process?

In the exhaustive study of the comparative hearing procedure presented by the court in CCC, one of the most salient points made by Wright was his observation (footnote 28) that the FCC had in effect "abolished the comparative hearing mandated by §§ 309(a) and (e) and converted the comparative hearing into a petition to deny proceeding." Do you see why Judge Wright said this?

The issue of diversification of media ownership received considerable attention in CCC. This scrutiny was significant because it dealt a heavy blow to the efforts of broadcast owners with newspaper affiliations to escape the WHDH ruling on the cross-newspaper ownership point.

THE REACTION TO THE *CCC* CASE   Since the 1970 policy statement was invalidated in CCC, the FCC has moved warily in promulgating new guidelines for the renewal process. Deciding that it would rather "interpret" the CCC decision than appeal it and risk having the decision resoundly affirmed, the FCC did not appeal the decision to the Supreme Court.

In *Fidelity Television Inc. v. FCC*, 515 F.2d 684 (D.C. Cir.), *cert. denied*, 423 U.S. 926 (1975), an incumbent licensee whose past performance was judged to be "average" (rather than the "substantial" performance needed to earn a "plus of major significance") was renewed against a challenger. Although the challenger did not particularly impress the FCC, the challenger did have a comparative advantage over the incumbent in terms of diversification of ownership interests. Nevertheless, the FCC renewed the incumbent's license, and the appeals court affirmed.

In a 1977 report and order, the FCC terminated its inquiry into comparative renewal criteria to be used in determining whether a new applicant or the incumbent licensee should be chosen at renewal time. Although it said that it would prefer that Congress abolish the compar-

ative renewal process, the FCC decided that until Congress chose to act on this suggestion it would proceed on a case-by-case basis. The past performance of the incumbent licensee would continue to be examined. At the same time, the FCC emphasized that in making decisions at renewal time "there is no 'formula of general application' that can be applied to all cases." See *Formulation of Policies Relating to the Broadcast Renewal Applicant, Stemming from the Comparative Hearing Process*, 66 F.C.C.2d 419 (1977).

THE CENTRAL FLORIDA ENTERPRISES CASE: WEIGHING THE CLAIMS OF THE INCUMBENT AGAINST THE CHALLENGER?   Eventually, the FCC fashioned a comparative renewal approach satisfactory to the U.S. Court of Appeals. *Central Florida* sets forth some guidelines that, if applied, would mean that the incumbent will not necessarily prevail in renewal battles.

Central Florida Enterprises, Inc. v. FCC
683 F.2D 503 (D.C. CIR. 1982).

WILKEY, Circuit Judge:

This case involves a license renewal proceeding for a television station. The appeal before us is taken from a new decision by the FCC after our opinion in *Central Florida Enterprises v. FCC*, 598 F.2d 37 (D.C. Cir. 1978) (*Central Florida I*) vacated the FCC's earlier orders involving the present parties. The FCC had granted the renewal of incumbent's license, but we held that the FCC's fact-finding and analysis on certain issues before it were inadequate, and that its method of balancing the factors for and against renewal was faulty. On remand, while the FCC has again concluded that the license should be renewed, it has also assuaged our concerns that its analysis was too cursory and has adopted a new policy for comparative renewal proceedings which meets the criteria we set out in *Central Florida I*. Accordingly, and with certain caveats, we affirm the FCC's decision.

Central Florida Enterprises has challenged the FCC's decision to renew Cowles Broadcasting's license to operate on Channel 2 in Daytona Beach, Florida. In reaching a renewal/nonrenewal decision, the FCC must engage in a comparative weighing of pro-renewal considerations against anti-renewal considerations. In the case here, there were four considerations potentially cutting against Cowles: its illegal move of its main studio, the involvement of several related companies in mail fraud, its ownership of other communications media, and its relative (to Central Florida) lack of management ownership integration. On the other hand, Cowles' past performance record was "superior," i.e., "sound, favorable and substantially above a level of mediocre service which might just minimally warrant renewal."

In its decision appealed in *Central Florida I* the FCC concluded that the reasons undercutting Cowles' bid for renewal did "not outweigh the substantial service Cowles rendered to the public during the last license period." Accordingly, the license was renewed. Our reversal was rooted in a twofold finding. First, the FCC had inadequately investigated and analyzed the four factors weighing against Cowles' renewal. Second, the process by which the FCC weighed these four factors against Cowles' past record was never "even vaguely described" and, indeed, "the commission's handling of the facts of this case [made] embarrassingly clear that the FCC [had] practically erected a presumption of renewal that is inconsistent with the full hearing requirement" of the Communications Act. We remanded with instructions to the FCC to cure these deficiencies.

On remand the FCC has followed our directives and corrected, point by point, the inadequate investigation and analysis of the four factors cutting against Cowles' requested renewal. The FCC concluded that, indeed, three of the four merited an advantage for Central Florida, and on only one (the mail fraud issue) did it conclude that nothing needed to be added on the scale to Central's plan or removed from Cowles'. We cannot fault the FCC's actions here.

We are left, then, with evaluating the way in which the FCC weighed Cowles' main studio move violation and Central's superior diversification and integration, on the one hand, against Cowles' substantial record of performance on the other. This is the most difficult and important issue in this case, for the new weighing process which the FCC has adopted will presumably be employed in its renewal proceedings elsewhere. We therefore feel that it is necessary to scrutinize carefully the FCC's new approach, and discuss what we understand and expect it to entail.

For some time now the FCC has had to wrestle with the problem of how it can factor in some degree of "renewal expectancy" for a broadcaster's meritorious past record, while at the same time undertaking the required comparative evaluation of the incumbent's probable future performance versus the challenger's. As we stated in *Central Florida I*, "the incumbent's past performance is some evidence, and perhaps the best evidence, of what its future performance would be." And it has been intimated—by the Supreme Court in *FCC v. National Citizens Committee for Broadcasting (NCCB)* and by this court in *Citizens Communications Center v. FCC* and *Central Florida I*—that some degree of renewal expectancy is permissible. But *Citizens* and *Central Florida I* also indicated that the FCC has in the past impermissibly raised renewal expectancy to an irrebuttable presumption in favor of the incumbent.

We believe that the formulation by the FCC in its latest decision, however, is a permissible way to incorporate some renewal expectancy while still undertaking the required comparative hearing. *The new policy, as we understand it, is simply this: renewal expectancy is to be a factor weighed with all the other factors, and the better the past record, the greater the renewal expectancy "weight."* [Emphasis added.]

In our view (states the FCC), the strength of the expectancy depends on the merit of the past record. Where, as in this case, the incumbent rendered substantial but not superior service, the "expectancy" takes the form of a comparative preference weighed against [the] other factors. An incumbent performing in a superior manner would receive an even stronger preference. An incumbent rendering minimal service would receive no preference. This is to be contrasted with the FCC's 1965 Policy Statement on Comparative Broadcast Hearings, where "[o]nly unusually good or unusually poor records have relevance."

If a stricter standard is desired by Congress, it must enact it. We cannot: the new standard is within the statute.

The reasons given by the FCC for factoring in some degree of renewal expectancy are rooted in a concern that failure to do so would hurt broadcast consumers.

The justification for a renewal expectancy is threefold (l) There is no guarantee that a challenger's paper proposals will, in fact, match the incumbent's proven performance. (2) Licensees should be encouraged through the likelihood of renewal to make investments *to ensure quality service.* (3) Comparing incumbents and challengers as if they were both new applicants could lead to a haphazard restructuring of the broadcast industry especially considering the large number of group owners.

We are relying, then, on the FCC's commitment that renewal expectancy will be factored in for the benefit of the public, not for incumbent broadcasters. [Emphasis added.] As we concluded in *Central Florida I,* "[t]he only legitimate fear which should move [incumbent] licensees is the fear of their own substandard performance, and that would be all to the public good."

There is a danger, of course, that the FCC's new approach could still degenerate into precisely the sort of irrebuttable presumption in favor of renewal that we have warned against. But this did not happen in the case before us today, and our reading of the FCC's decision gives us hope that if the FCC applies the standard in the same way in future cases, it will not happen in them either. The standard is new, however, and much will depend on how the commission applies it and fleshes it out. Of particular importance will be the definition and level of service it assigns to "substantial"—and whether that definition is ever found to be "opaque to judicial review," "wholly unintelligible," or based purely on "administrative 'feel.'"[27]

In this case, however, the FCC was painstaking and explicit in its balancing. Having listed the relevant factors and assigned them weights, the FCC concluded that Cowles' license should be renewed. We note, however, that despite the finding that Cowles' performance was "'substantial,' *i.e.,* 'sound, favorable and substantially above a level of mediocre service,'" the combination of Cowles' main studio rule violation and Central's diversification and integration advantages made this a "close and difficult case." Again, we trust that this is more evidence that the commission's weighing did not, and will not, amount to automatic renewal for incumbents.

We are somewhat reassured by a recent FCC decision granting, for the first time since at least 1961, on *comparative* grounds the application of the challenger for a radio station license and denying the remedial application of the incumbent licensee.[38] In that decision the FCC found that the *incumbent deserved no renewal expectancy* for his past program record and that his application was inferior to the challenger's on comparative grounds. Indeed, it was the *incumbent's* preferences on the diversification and integration factors which were overcome (there, by the challenger's superior programming proposals and longer broadcast week). The commission found that the incumbent's "inadequate [past performance] reflects poorly on the *likelihood of future service in the public interest."* Further, it found that the incumbent had no "legitimate renewal expectancy" because his past performance was neither "meritorious" nor "substantial."

We have, however, an important caveat. In the FCC's weighing of factors the scale mid-mark must be neither the factors themselves, nor the interests of the broadcasting industry, nor some other secondary and artificial construct, but rather the intent of Congress, which is to say the interests of the listening public. All other doctrine is merely a means to this end, and it should not become more. If in a given case, for instance, the factual situation is such that the denial of a license renewal would not undermine renewal expectancy *in a way harmful to*

---

27. *Id.* at 50 [quoting earlier proceeding, 60 F.C.C.2d 372, 422 (1976)]. We think it would be helpful if at some point the commission defined and explained the distinctions, if any, among: substantial meritorious, average, above average, not above average, not far above average, above mediocre, more than minimal, solid, sound, favorable, not superior, not exceptional, and unexceptional—all terms used by the parties to describe what the FCC found Cowles' level of performance to have been. We are especially interested to know what the standard of comparison is in each case. "Average" compared to all applicants? "Mediocre" compared to all incumbents? "Favorable" with respect to the FCC's expectations? We realize that the FCC's task is a subjective one, but the use of imprecise terms needlessly compounds our difficulty in evaluating what the commission has done. We think we can discern enough to review intelligently the commission's actions today, but if the air is not cleared or, worse, becomes foggier, the FCC's decisionmaking may again be adjudged "opaque to judicial review."

---

38. *In re Applications of Simon Geller and Grandbanke Corp.,* [91 F.C.C.2d 1253 (1982)]. We intimate no view at this time, of course, on the soundness of the FCC's decision there; we cite it only as demonstrating that the FCC's new approach may prove to be more than a paper tiger.

the public interest, then renewal expectancy should not be invoked.[40]

Finally, we must note that we are still troubled by the fact that the record remains that an incumbent *television* licensee has *never* been denied renewal in a comparative challenge. American television viewers will be reassured, although a trifle baffled, to learn that even the worst television stations—those which are, presumably, the ones picked out as vulnerable to a challenge—are so good that they never need replacing. We suspect that somewhere, sometime, somehow, some television licensee *should* fail in a comparative renewal challenge, but the FCC has never discovered such a licensee yet. As a court we cannot say that it must be Cowles here.

We hope that the standard now embraced by the FCC will result in the protection of the public, not just incumbent licensees. And in today's case we believe the FCC's application of the new standard was not inconsistent with the commission's mandate. Accordingly the commission's decision is affirmed.

COMMENT

Under the FCC renewal policy described by Judge Wilkey in *Central Florida II,* will an incumbent television licensee that has other media affiliations be in a worse or better position in a renewal contest with a new applicant that has no media affiliations?

An interesting renewal case, that was mentioned in *Central Florida II* and involved the weight to be given the renewal expectancy factor was *Simon Geller,* 91 F.C.C.2d 1253, 52 R.R.2d 709 (1982). Simon Geller was the sole owner, operator, announcer, technician, salesman, and licensee of WVCA, the only broadcast station in Gloucester, Massachusetts, a town with a population of 28,000, twenty-five miles from Boston. He had held the license for more than twenty years. In 1968, Geller began to broadcast only symphonic music.

In his 1975 renewal application, Geller proposed an exclusively symphonic music format with only a small amount of nonentertainment programming. (In the license period immediately prior to the 1975 renewal application, Geller broadcast a total of less than 1 percent nonentertainment programming.) Grandbanke Corporation challenged Geller's license application and proposed a "musical medley" with approximately 28.7 percent of its broadcast week devoted to nonentertainment programming. A comparative hearing was held. The administrative law judge found that Geller was entitled to a renewal expectancy because of his favorable past record and granted him the license renewal.

The FCC, although agreeing with the ALJ's conclusion that both applicants were "basically qualified," denied Geller's renewal application and granted the license to Grandbanke. The FCC said that even though Grandbanke operated several other broadcast stations and Geller possessed no other media affiliations, Geller was entitled only to a moderate, rather than a strong, preference on the diversification of ownership criterion: "With no news, no editorializing and virtually no public affairs programming, Gloucester does not hear a separate information voice—indeed it hears no information at all. Therefore, while Geller's diversification showing is technically superior to Grandbanke's, he should receive no strong preference in this regard."

Geller appealed the FCC order denying his license renewal. The court of appeals remanded the case back to the FCC. See *Geller v. FCC,* 737 F.2d 74 (D.C. Cir. 1984). Judge Mikva began his opinion by relying on *Central Florida II:* "[W]e have too long hungered for just one instance in which the FCC properly denied an incumbent's renewal expectancy." But *Geller* was not that long-sought case. The FCC did not follow its own precedents with respect to the factors governing comparative renewals: "Therefore, while we affirm the Commission's denial of the incumbent's renewal expectancy, we remand the case so that the FCC can recalculate the comparative factors."

Judge Mikva's opinion for the D.C. Circuit in *Geller* is useful because it illustrates that the incumbent need not necessarily prevail under *Central Florida II.* The decision also illustrates that although deregulation has removed many

---

40. Thus, the three justifications given by the commission for renewal expectancy, should be remembered by the FCC in future renewal proceedings and, where these justifications are in a particular case attenuated, the commission ought not to chant "renewal expectancy" and grant the license.

obligations from licensees, some still remain. The court of appeals pointed out that although *Geller*'s formal ascertainment requirements had been eliminated, the licensee still must "determine the major issues in the community." The court also quoted from its decision approving the deregulation of radio: "For a radio licensee to provide programming responsive to issues facing the community, it must first ascertain just what those issues are." See *Office of Communication of the United Church of Christ v. FCC*, 707 F.2d 1413 (D.C. Cir. 1983).

The student will recall that in *Office of Communication of the United Church of Christ*, affirming the deregulation of radio, Judge Wright emphasized that licensees still had an obligation to provide issue-responsive programming. Judge Mikva picked up on this in the *Geller* case:

> Geller failed to comply with these substantive requirements. The (FCC) found that "Geller broadcast no news, no editorials, and none of his (nonentertainment) programming was locally produced. None of his programs, moreover, were presented in response to ascertained community needs and problems." 90 FCC 2d 265. Because Geller had not adequately ascertained community needs he could not, by definition, air responsive programs. Thus, it was reasonable for the (FCC) to conclude that Geller's previous service did not warrant a renewal expectancy.

Nevertheless, the court of appeals in *Geller* thought that the FCC had improperly changed its approach to the diversification of ownership criterion in a way that was inconsistent with its precedents. In the past "diversity of ownership" had been the "litmus test for diversity of viewpoints." For this and other reasons, the court of appeals remanded the *Geller* case back to the FCC. On remand, the FCC awarded Geller his license renewal. See *Simon Geller*, 102 F.C.C.2d 1443, 59 R.R.2d 579 (1985), *appeal dismissed, Grandbanke Corp. v. FCC*, No. 86-1230 (D.C. Cir. February 6, 1988).

Reforming the Renewal Process

On June 23, 1988, the FCC issued a *Second Further Notice of Inquiry and Notice of Proposed Rulemaking, In the Matter of Formulation of Policies and Rules Relating to Broadcast Renewal Applicants, Competing Applicants, and*

Other Participants to the Comparative Renewal Process and to the Prevention of Abuses of the Renewal Process, 3 F.C.C.R. 5179 (1988). A major proposal in this sixty-eight-page statement was that the comparative hearing process would not focus on programming but on compliance with the FCC's rules and policies. As Commissioner Dennis explained in a separate statement: "Under this alternative, we would still require licensees to maintain issues/programs lists and to broadcast issue-responsive programming to ensure that licensees meet public interest goals. But we would no longer force Administrative Law Judges to assume the role of TV critics, assessing the quality of each station's program service. The compliance-based approach could potentially allow us to apply a more consistent set of standards and to complete hearings more quickly, while still giving challengers their full legal rights under the Communications Act."

The FCC explained its new proposal as follows:

> [W]e believe that it would be helpful at this juncture to consider portions of two legislative proposals referred to earlier—S. 1277 and H.R. 3493.[17] Commenters should be aware that, procedurally, these legislative proposals would impose a two-step process, which generally eliminates comparative renewal hearings. In the first step, an incumbent's record is reviewed, on a noncomparative basis, to determine whether it has provided a meritorious level of service in response to community needs and whether there have been any serious violations of the Communications Act or Commission rules and policies. If these requirements have been met, then the incumbent's license is renewed. However, if the licensee has failed to satisfy these public interest tests, then, after an evidentiary hearing, its license renewal application may be denied. In the second step, competing applications would be accepted for the frequency in question, necessitating a comparative hearing to determine the best applicant if two or more mutually exclusive applications are filed.

---

17. See, *e.g.*, S. 1277, the Broadcasting Improvements Act of 1987 100th Cong., 1st Sess. (1987) introduced on May 27, 1987, by Senators Daniel Inouye and Ernest Hollings; H.R. 3493, the Broadcast License Reform Act of 1987, 100th Cong., 1st Sess. (1987), introduced on October 15, 1987, by Congressman Al Swift; and H.R. 1140 the Broadcast License Renewal Act of 1987, 100th Cong., 1st Sess., introduced on February 19, 1987, by Congressmen Tom Tauke and W. J. Tauzin.

Presumably, the incumbent could also file for the frequency.

In suggesting examination of portions of these bills, we are not proposing the use of a two-step procedural approach which obviates the need for comparative renewal hearings. Rather, we believe that consideration of the programming tests and other factors these bills use will help us in evaluating the various tests which we could use to determine whether a renewal expectancy is appropriately awarded in the context of our rules and procedures.

Under S. 1277, a broadcaster is renewed if, in the case of a radio licensee, its "programming as a whole has been meritorious and has responded to the interests and concerns of the residents in its service area, including through the coverage of issues of local importance." In the case of a television licensee, in addition to meeting this obligation, the licensees must also have provided meritorious service in "the nonentertainment programming and the programming directed towards children." In addition, the licensee must not have committed any willful or repeated failure to observe the Act or our Rules and must remain qualified under § 308(b) of the Act.

H.R. 3493 contains a similar test for determining whether a licensee is entitled to renewal. Specifically, it would grant renewal to a licensee which has provided "meritorious service responsive to issues, problems, and concerns of the residents of its service area" and which has committed "no serious violation" of the Act or our rules or policies and has committed no other violations which, taken together, constitute a pattern of abuse. In addition, H.R. 3493 adds features that are similar to our television and radio deregulation orders to the extent of permitting a licensee, in determining which issues to address and what responsive programming to air, to consider the composition of its audience, the number of other radio or television stations serving its service area, and the degree to which the programming of those stations has addressed these needs. H.R. 3493 also requires that, in determining whether a licensee's programming has been meritorious, the Commission shall accept the judgments of licensees concerning the issues addressed and the nature, duration, frequency, and scheduling of responsive programming, provided that such judgments are reasonable in the circumstances and made in good faith. It is also similar to the test set forth in the radio and television deregulation orders for reviewing licensee performance—that is, reasonableness in the selection of issues and in the broadcasting of responsive programming.

The student should recall that Judge Wilkey in *Central Florida II* observed caustically that "it would be helpful if at some point the commission defined and explained the distinctions, if any, among: substantial, meritorious, average" etc. Judge Wilkey also observed with similar asperity: "We are especially interested to know what the standard of comparison is in each case." Even standards oriented to issue responsiveness and compliance still have to provide a calculus upon which comparative estimates are based.

During the 1990s, comparative hearings and the broadcast renewal process underwent radical change. In *Bechtel v. FCC*, 10 F.3d 875 (D.C. Cir. 1993), the court, per Judge Stephen Williams, held that the FCC's use of the "integration criterion" as a renewal factor in comparative hearings was arbitrary and capricious. Judge Williams described the "integration criterion" as a preference the FCC awarded "applicants who promise that the station's owners will participate in its management."

Bechtel held that use of the "integration" factor in comparative hearings was arbitrary and capricious for three reasons. First, the FCC failed to substantiate its claims that integration served the public interest because owner-managers have greater incentives, take a more active interest in their stations, and are better positioned to gather relevant information about community needs. Second, because the FCC did not require licensees to maintain integration beyond one year, the alleged benefits of integration were often temporary. Third, the FCC placed too much weight on integration and did not sufficiently consider qualitative factors such as management experience.

The *Bechtel* court did not accept the FCC's assertion that integrated owners are more likely than absentee owners to take an active interest in the operation of their stations. Instead, the court pointed out that integration is not an adequate measure of an owner's interest in the operation of the station and said that broadcast experience may be a better measure. The FCC asserted that on-site owners have better sources of information than absentee owners because integrated owners, due to their presence at the station, are in a better position to learn "that the station is violating FCC rules or that people have asked the station to address particular community needs."

The court observed that "[t]he FCC cites no evidence that station visitors are a major source of information for broadcasters" and that "[f]amiliarity with a community seems much more likely than station visitors or correspondence to make one aware of community needs."

The court's most significant concern about integration seemed to be its lack of permanence: "Whatever the benefits of integration, they would last only if the FCC insisted on licensees maintaining the owner-manager relation or if successful licensees tended to adopt the integrated structure of their own free will. Neither appears to be the case." A licensee could sell its license after a year and as long as it did not misrepresent its intentions in its application, abandonment of integration proposals carried no consequences.

Bechtel remanded the case to the FCC with instructions not to consider integration as a factor. Although *Bechtel* did not hold comparative hearings to be arbitrary and capricious, it did hold that the integration factor that the FCC utilized in the comparative hearing process was arbitrary and capricious. The FCC responded to the *Bechtel* ruling by freezing all comparative hearings and issuing a Notice of Proposed Rulemaking to develop criteria to be used in the hearings. 9 F.C.C.R. 2821 (1994). But the blockbuster development since *Bechtel* is the Telecommunications Act of 1996, 47 U.S.C. § 309(k), which abolishes comparative hearings at least as far as incumbent applicants for renewal are concerned.

The Broadcast License Renewal Process and the Telecommunications Act of 1996

In the Telecommunications Act of 1996, signed into law by President Clinton on February 8, 1996, Congress conferred on broadcast licensees a greater security in their licenses than they had enjoyed in the past. Previously, incumbents' licenses had been overwhelmingly renewed as a matter of practice. Now under the 1996 Act, 47 U.S.C. § 309(k), the law reflects the practice. Section 309(k) provides for a two-step procedure. If a broadcast licensee applies for renewal of its license, the license will be renewed—and competing applications will not be entertained—if the FCC finds that the license renewal applicant has (1) served the public interest, (2) has committed no serious violations of the Communications Act or of FCC rules and regulations, and (3) has not committed other violations of the Act or FCC rules and regulations that "would constitute a pattern of abuse." 47 U.S.C. § 309(k)(1) [Standards for Renewal]. In short, the first step in the renewal procedure is an inquiry into whether the renewal applicant has served the public interest. If it has, the license will be renewed.

One commentator has observed that the FCC will now "be able to grant a licensee's renewal application without considering competing applications." As a consequence, "the incentive for parties to file challenges against a broadcaster's renewal application" will be diminished. See Mark D. Schneider, *Renewal Procedures and Expectancy before and after the Telecommunications Act of 1996,* 14 Comm. Law. 9 (1996).

Suppose that the FCC finds that a licensee does not meet the standards for renewal just described? What sanctions are available? The 1996 Act, 47 U.S.C. § 309(k)(2) [Consequence of Failure to Meet Standard] provides that the FCC can deny the application for renewal under sec. 309 (k)(3), or it can make a conditional grant of the renewal application "including renewal for a term less than the maximum otherwise permitted."

Section 309 (k)(3) provides that if after notice and hearing the FCC decides that a licensee has failed to meet the standards for renewal set forth in sec. 309(k)(1), the commission may deny the renewal application. After such denial, the FCC is then authorized to "accept and consider applications for a construction permit" for the channel or broadcasting facilities of the former licensee.

The new Act's hostility to comparative hearings is made clear by sec. 309(k)(4) [Competitor Consideration Prohibited] that provides: "In making the determinations specified in paragraph (1) [Standards for Renewal] or (2) [Consequences of Failure to Meet Standard], the FCC shall not consider whether the public interest, convenience, and necessity might be served by the grant of a license to a person other than the renewal applicant."

What does the new law mean? Here is the FCC's take on the new law.

In the Matter of Implementation of Sections 204(A) and 204(C) [47 U.S.C. § 309(k)] of the Telecommunications Act of 1996 [Broadcast License Renewal Procedures]

11 F.C.C.R. 6363 (1996).

New Two-Step Renewal Procedure. [T]he Telecom Act effects a major change in the way the FCC processes renewals. With respect to broadcast renewal applications filed after May 1, 1995, the statute eliminates comparative renewals and establishes, instead, a new two-step renewal procedure. It also codifies specific standards for the FCC to apply in considering broadcasters' renewal applications.

Additionally, the Telecom Act amends Sec. 309(d) to make the standard for filing petitions to deny conform to the statutory renewal standards. Thus, the statutory renewal standards are made applicable to the petitioner's required showing and the FCC's consequent findings in the case of a petition to deny a renewal application filed after the statutory effective date.

The Telecom Act does not define the terms contained in the renewal standards embodied in Sec. 309(k), and we likewise do not define those terms in this Order. It is our present intent to continue to apply existing policy statements and case law, refining these as appropriate on a case-by-case basis, in interpreting the statutory terms that govern the new renewal process. [Emphasis added.]

Termination of Comparative Renewal Rule Making. In light of the elimination of the comparative renewal procedure, we will terminate BC Docket No. 81-472, in which the FCC is considering reforming the comparative renewal process. Effective Dates. Pursuant to the Telecom Act, Sec. 309(k) will be applied to renewal applications filed after May 1, 1995. Pending comparative renewal proceedings and mutual exclusivities involving applications filed on or before May 1,1995, will be concluded pursuant to the current rules, and, accordingly, we will leave intact procedural provisions of the current rules that refer to comparative renewal proceedings until those pending proceedings and exclusivities are finally resolved.

COMMENT

Note that the italicized paragraph of the FCC's interpretation of the 1996 Act's new broadcast renewal procedures speaks of the "terms contained" in the renewal standards. These terms are found in sec. 309(k)(1) and include such terms as "public interest," "serious violations," and "other violations." A key aspect of the FCC's approach is that it says it will apply "existing policy statements and case law" to these terms. What would constitute a "serious violation"? Perhaps, failure to conform to FCC standards on children's programming would constitute such a violation. See text, pp. 723–729. Is *Bechtel* likely to have any future significance? What about *Central Florida II*, text, p. 705? Will any aspects of *Central Florida* still have continuing significance?

The 1996 Act, 47 U.S.C. § 308(d), provides that applicants for renewal of a television license, whether commercial or noncommercial, must attach as an exhibit to the renewal application a summary of comments and suggestions received from the public on the applicant's violent programming. Could this summary be used to support a finding by the FCC in the first stage of the new renewal procedure that the licensee has not performed in the public interest?

Consider the following assessment of the broadcast renewal procedures: "The new renewal procedures, however, will not insulate broadcasters from challenges and will maintain a premium on ensuring the compliance with significant FCC requirements placed on broadcasters." See Mark D. Schneider, *Renewal Procedures and Expectancy before and after the Telecommunications Act of 1996*, 14 Comm. Law. 9 (1996).

In *Ashbacker Radio Corp. v. FCC*, 326 U.S. 327 (1945), the Supreme Court directed the FCC to hold a comparative hearing when applicants file mutually exclusive applications. Do the new broadcast renewal procedures violate the *Ashbacker* doctrine?

PROGRAMMING, THE PUBLIC INTEREST, AND DEREGULATION

The Communications Act of 1934 and its predecessor, the Radio Act of 1927, were somewhat schizophrenic about the regulation of broadcast content. On the one hand, sec. 29 of the Radio Act (44 Stat 1162 [1927], now sec. 326 of the Communications Act, prohibited censorship by the Federal Radio Commission (FRC):

> Nothing in this chapter shall be understood or construed to give the Commission the power of censorship over the radio communications or signals transmitted by any radio station, and no regulation or condition shall be promulgated or fixed by the Commission which shall interfere with the right of free speech by means of radio communication.

At the same time, sec. 4(b) gave the FRC the power to "prescribe the nature of the service to be rendered by each class of licensed stations and each station within any class," sec. 18 required that broadcasters provide "equal opportunities" to candidates for public office to use broadcast stations, and several sections provided that the FRC was only to grant or renew licenses if doing so would serve the "public interest, convenience and necessity." The result, in the early days of broadcasting, was a substantial dispute over how far the government could go in its general supervision of broadcast content. Were the FRC and the FCC to be just traffic cops of the air—policing only technical aspects of spectrum use—or were they to have broad, general, regulatory powers over the content of American broadcasting?

Early in its short life, the FRC claimed the right to exercise general regulatory supervision over the content of American broadcasting. The FRC was faced with a problem—more stations were on the air than the technology of the time could accommodate without unacceptable interference. Under the circumstances, one alternative might have been to find purely technical reasons to reduce the number of stations. Another alternative, however, was to focus on the service being rendered and to order off the air those broadcasters that, in some overall sense, did not deserve licenses. The FRC chose the latter course—but not without warning.

As early as the "Great Lakes Statement," 3 FRC Ann. Rep. 32 (1929), the FRC warned broadcasters that it expected nondiscriminatory general service to the public, "in the public interest":

> [T]he service rendered by broadcasting stations must be without discrimination as between its listeners. Even were it technically possible so to design both transmitters and receiving sets that the signals emitted by a particular transmitter can be received

only by a particular kind of receiving set not available to the general public, the commission would not allow channels in the broadcast band to be used in such fashion. The entire listening public within the service area of a station, or of a group of stations in one community, is entitled to service from that station or stations. If, therefore, all the programs transmitted are intended for, and are interesting or valuable to, only a small portion of that public, the rest of the listeners are being discriminated against. This does not mean that every individual is entitled to his exact preference in program items. It does mean that the tastes, needs, and desires of all substantial groups among the listening public should be met, in some fair proportion, by a *well-rounded program, in which entertainment, consisting of music of both classical and lighter grades, religion, education and instruction, important public events, discussions of public questions, weather, market reports, and news, and matters of interest to all members of the family find a place.* [Emphasis added.] With so few channels in the spectrum and so few hours in the day, there are obvious limitations on the emphasis which can appropriately be placed on any portion of the program. There are differences between communities as to the need for one type as against another. The commission does not propose to erect a rigid schedule specifying the hours or minutes that may be devoted to one kind of program or another. What it wishes to emphasize is the general character which it believes must be conformed to by a station in order to best serve the public.

> In such a scheme there is no room for the operation of broadcasting stations exclusively by or in the private interests of individuals or groups so far as the nature of the programs is concerned. There is not room in the broadcast band for every school of thought, religious, political, social, and economic, each to have its separate broadcasting stations, its mouthpiece in the ether. If franchises are extended to some it gives them an unfair advantage over others, and results in a corresponding cutting down of general public-service stations. It favors the interests and desires of a portion of the listening public at the expense of the rest. Propaganda stations (a term which is here used for the sake of convenience and not in a derogatory sense) are not consistent with the most beneficial sort of discussion of public questions. As a general rule, postulated on the laws of nature as well as on the standard of public interest, convenience, or necessity, particular doctrines, creeds, and beliefs must find their way into the market of ideas by the existing public-service stations, and if they are of sufficient importance to

the listening public the microphone will undoubtedly be available. If it is not, a well-founded complaint will receive the careful consideration of the commission in its future action with reference to the station complained of.

Through policy guides like the "Great Lakes Statement," the FRC issued at least two warnings to the broadcasters of the day. First, service had to be well-rounded and nondiscriminatory—basically, something for everybody—in order to serve the "public interest, convenience and necessity" and justify granting licenses. Second, it was suggesting that opinions had to be handled carefully—that fairness was expected or the government might step in. Many broadcasters of the 1920s followed the FRC's warnings. A few did not. Some of the latter produced court cases that established fundamental, long-lasting principles about the federal government's general powers to regulate broadcast content.

The Government's Power to Regulate Broadcasting Content—The Early Public Interest

Two of the broadcasters who did not heed the warnings were the good "doctor" J. R. Brinkley, licensee of KFKB in Milford, Kansas, and the Reverend Doctor Shuler, pastor of Trinity Methodist Church in Los Angeles, California. Both essentially met the test of being propaganda broadcasters—they used their stations to promote their own interests. Brinkley was the more self-interested, using his station to promote the sale of patent medicines by members of the "Brinkley Pharmaceutical Association" throughout the United States. "Battling Bob" Shuler used his station as an electronic pulpit to present his strident views attacking Jews, the Roman Catholic church, law enforcement officials in Los Angeles, and many others. Shuler even raised funds for the station by vaguely threatening that (usually unnamed) folks would go to hell unless they contributed to its operation—an apparently successful fundraising technique.

Both broadcasters' license renewal applications were opposed. The FRC found itself having to decide whether or not to renew the licenses given that Brinkley was accused, by the AMA among others, of harming the public health and Shuler was accused of being hostile to opposing viewpoints. In 1930, the FRC decided not to renew Brinkley's license. Later the same year it

came to the same conclusion with regard to Shuler. Both unhappy broadcasters appealed these FRC decisions in court. In each case, the basic question was how far the FRC could go in regulating general programming. The decisions in both cases generally vindicated the right of the federal regulatory agency to be more than a technical traffic cop and, even, sustained overall content regulation of broadcasting against constitutional attack.

Brinkley's lawyers raised nothing but statutory objections to the FRC's nonrenewal of his license. They argued that the FRC should not consider broadcasting content in making licensing decisions, even in a general way. The court rejected that position:

> [T]he business of broadcasting, being a species of interstate commerce, is subject to reasonable regulation of Congress. It is apparent, we think, that the business is impressed with a public interest and that, because the number of available frequencies is limited, the commission is necessarily called upon to consider the character and quality of the service to be rendered. In considering an application for a renewal of the license, an important consideration is the past conduct of the applicant, for "by their fruits ye shall know them." Matt. VII:20. Especially is this true in a case like the present, where the evidence clearly justifies the conclusion that the future conduct of the station will not differ from the past. *KFKB Broad. Assn, Inc. v. FRC,* 47 F.2d 670 (D.C. Cir. 1931).

Shuler's lawyers raised additional arguments. They urged the Brinkley position (since their case was *argued* before Brinkley's was decided) that Congress had not intended for the FRC to be generally concerned with content. But they also argued that the FRC had breached Shuler's First Amendment rights to freedom of speech and press.[3] When the court decided Shuler's case in 1932, it had little difficulty disposing of both arguments. The statutory arguments were by then easy—the Brinkley case had decided them; Congress intended the FRC to be concerned, at least in an overall sense, with the "public interest" nature of service. The constitutional arguments were made more complex by the recently decided case of *Near v. Minnesota,* 283 U.S. 697 (1931), the first U.S. Supreme Court decision providing a mass media twist to the First Amend-

---

3. Interestingly, they did not argue that the FRC's actions violated Shuler's "freedom of religion" rights.

ment. *Near* said that "prior restraints" were nearly always unconstitutional, but that post-publication punishment (subsequent punishment) was permissible. The problem the Shuler court confronted was whether refusing to renew Shuler's license was a prior restraint under *Near* or just a postpublication punishment. The court came to the conclusion that refusal to renew broadcast licenses was, under the circumstances, more of a postpublication punishment than a prior restraint.

> We need not stop to review the cases construing the depth and breadth of the first amendment. It is enough to say that the universal trend of decisions has recognized the guaranty of the amendment to prevent previous restraints upon publication, as well as immunity of censorship, leaving to correction by subsequent punishment those utterances or publications contrary to the public welfare. In this aspect, it is generally regarded that freedom of speech and press cannot be infringed by legislative, executive, or judicial action, and that the constitutional guaranty should be given liberal and comprehensive construction. It may therefore be set down as a fundamental principle that under these constitutional guaranties the citizen has in the first instance the right to utter or publish his sentiments, though, of course, upon condition that he is responsible for any abuse of that right. *Near v. Minnesota.* But this does not mean that the government, through agencies established by Congress, may not refuse a renewal of license to one who has abused it to broadcast defamatory and untrue matter. In that case there is not a denial of the freedom of speech, but merely the application of the regulatory power of Congress in a field within the scope of its legislative authority.
>
> In the case under consideration, the evidence abundantly sustains the conclusion of the Commission that the continuance of the broadcasting programs of [Shuler] is not in the public interest. However inspired Dr. Shuler may have been by what he regarded as patriotic zeal, however sincere in denouncing conditions he did not approve, it is manifest, we think, that it is not narrowing the ordinary conception of "public interest" in declaring his broadcasts—without facts to sustain or to justify them—not within that term, and, since that is the test the Commission is required to apply, we think it was its duty in considering the application for renewal to take notice of appellant's conduct in his previous use of the permit, and, in the circumstances, the refusal, we think, was neither arbitrary nor capricious.
>
> If it be considered that one in possession of a permit to broadcast in interstate commerce may,

without let or hindrance from any source, use these facilities, reaching out, as they do, from one corner of the country to the other, to obstruct the administration, offend the religious susceptibilities of thousands, inspire political distrust and civic discord, or offend youth and innocence by the free use of words suggestive of sexual immorality, and be answerable for slander only at the instance of the one offended, then this great science [broadcasting], instead of a boon, will become a scourge, and the nation a theater for the display of individual passions and the collision of personal interests. This is neither censorship nor previous restraint, nor is it a whittling away of the rights guaranteed by the First Amendment, or an impairment of their free exercise. Appellant may continue to indulge his strictures upon the characters of men in public office. He may just as freely as ever criticize religious practice of which he does not approve. He may even indulge private malice or personal slander—subject, of course, to be required to answer for the abuse thereof—but he may not, as we think, demand, of right, the continued use of an instrumentality of commerce for such purposes, or any other, except in subordination to all reasonable rules and regulations Congress, acting through the Commission, may prescribe. *Trinity Methodist Church South v. FRC*, 62 F.2d 850 (D.C. Cir. 1932).

Taken together, these court decisions established two fundamental propositions. First, the FRC—and as things turned out, its successor, the FCC—was not intended by Congress to be just a technical traffic cop. In a general, overall way, at least, the licensing agency could take a broad look at the programming offered by licensees to decide whether or not it was in the "public interest, convenience and necessity." Second, such review did not automatically violate the First Amendment. Denial of a license at renewal time due to past overall programming deficiencies was not necessarily an unconstitutional prior restraint. Rather it was more a constitutional postpublication punishment for broadcasters who failed to meet their public interest obligations under the Radio Act of 1927 and, later, the Communications Act of 1934. On top of that, such regulation was justifiable because of the "scarcity" of broadcast spectrum space.

The FCC Speaks: The "Blue Book" and the *1960 Policy Statement*

This general vindication of its programming regulatory powers was used cautiously by the FCC in subsequent years. In the mid and late 1930s, the FCC forced most remaining "propaganda broadcasters" off the air, but it did not develop new, general programming policies until the mid-1940s. Then, largely because of changing economies of network radio, the FCC decided it was time for another general policy statement about radio. It directed its staff to consider the public interest implications of radio programming trends (at the time television was technologically possible, but not yet commercially viable) and essentially put the project in the hands of Dallas Smythe, an FCC economist with strong views on the "public interest" standard in the Communications Act. On March 7, 1946, the FCC released a staff report, *Public Service Responsibility of Broadcast Licensees,* that quickly became known as the "Blue Book" because of the hue of its cover.

The "Blue Book" was undeniably critical of American radio programming. According to its authors, radio stations were presenting (1) too little "sustaining" (unsponsored) programming (programming that the public might need even though nobody was willing to sponsor it); (2) too little programming that reflected local interests and activities or included local talent (in other words, too much network programming); (3) too few "discussions of public issues" (too little news and public affairs); and (4) too many commercials. Taking a dim view of all this, the report urged broadcasters to do better and subtly threatened that if they did not, some FCC remediation through regulation might be forthcoming.

Broadcasting industry reaction to the "Blue Book" was mixed. Many industry leaders did not respond at all. Some harshly criticized the FCC. Most argued that the FCC was going too far in regulating programming, maintained that the document was somehow a violation of either sec. 326 of the Communications Act or the First Amendment, and urged the commissioners to adopt a more "moderate" position. The FCC's response was to waffle. The FCC commissioners never adopted the staff report as their own official statement of policy, but from time to time, in subsequent cases, they admonished broadcasters for not living up to it. In other words, the FCC never adopted the "Blue Book," but neither did it repudiate it. Even though the "Blue Book" was never official FCC policy, until 1960 it, plus earlier FRC policy statements and FRC/FCC decisions, was the best guidance broadcasters had as

to how much the FCC would regulate programming in general.

On July 29, 1960, the FCC adopted a *Report and Statement of Policy re: Commission en banc Programming Inquiry,* 44 F.C.C. 2303—mercifully known as the "1960 Programming Policy Statement"—that, until the 1980s, was the primary policy guideline on general programming regulation. For the most part, the *1960 Policy Statement* reiterated well-established principles of broadcast regulation. The FCC regulation would be general, not specific. The FCC did not intend to second-guess specific program decisions, but it would exercise general oversight. Providing programming in the "public interest, convenience and necessity" was the licensee's responsibility. Failure to meet that test could not be blamed on network failure to provide appropriate programming or on advertiser failure to support it—that was the job of those lucky enough to hold FCC licenses. Programming designed only to serve the broadcaster's private interests rather than the "public interest" was inadequate. Broadcasters were expected to figure out what kind of programming the areas they were licensed to serve required—and that decision was not bound just by what advertisers would support. Years later, this 1960 standard evolved into a complex, highly formalized process of "community ascertainment"—to be discussed shortly—that the FCC abandoned in the 1980s. Finally, following earlier patterns, the FCC offered broadcasters a qualitative, nonquantitative list of kinds of programs that generally would adequately fulfill the "public interest" standards of the Communications Act. The FCC told broadcasters that programming in the public interest generally included:

(1) Opportunity for local self-expression, (2) the development and use of local talent, (3) programs for children, (4) religious programs, (5) educational programs, (6) public affairs programs (7) editorialization by licensees, (8) political broadcasts, (9) agricultural programs, (10) news programs, (11) weather and market reports, (12) sports programs, (13) service to minority groups and (14) entertainment programming.

Offering some reasonable mix of these kinds of programs was considered to be evidence that broadcasters were serving the public interest.

Enforcement of the *1960 Policy Statement* was not vigorous. How could it be, since the

FCC had been so vague? The statement—like the "Blue Book" that preceded it—was highly qualitative, but not very quantitative. The "Blue Book" urged broadcasters to present "more" sustaining, local, topical programs, but did not say how much was expected. The *1960 Policy Statement* set up fourteen categories of programming, but again did not say how much was expected in each category or when, in the broadcast day, it was expected to be offered. The result, quite predictably, was that broadcasters concentrated on the fourteenth category—"entertainment programming"—and looked to the FCC for more guidance as to what else they should do and how they should do it.

Over many years, the FCC provided that guidance. The general statement, in 1960, that broadcasters should know the problems, needs, and interests of their community—and design programming appropriate to meet those needs—evolved (largely at the request of attorneys representing broadcasters who wanted to know *exactly* what the FCC wanted) into a formal ritual of "ascertainment." At its height, a broadcaster had to talk continuously (throughout the license term) to community leaders to find out what they thought the "problems, needs and interests" of the community were, survey the general public (at least once during the then three-year license term) asking the same question, summarize the findings from the leaders and the public at license renewal time, and, finally, convert those findings into programming plans in order to convince the FCC that it should renew the broadcaster's license.

In addition, the FCC developed quantitative processing guidelines to be applied by the FCC staff when license renewals were sought by prospective broadcasters or, for that matter, when licenses were sought by new entrants into the industry. At their maximum state of development, these processing nonentertainment guidelines anticipated that FM broadcasters would propose to offer at least 6 percent noncommercial, nonentertainment programming. For AM broadcasters, the expectation was 8 percent; for television it was 10 percent. Failure to propose to offer these percentages when you sought a license from the FCC, either new or a renewal, did not necessarily mean that the license would not be granted. Rather, it meant that the FCC staff could not grant the license but would have

to refer the application to the full FCC (the seven commissioners). Because few broadcasters (or prospective broadcasters) wanted their applications held up by review by the full FCC, these quantitative standards were as effective as if they had been full-blown regulatory standards. Nearly all broadcasters provided the expected amounts of noncommercial, nonentertainment programming (or promised to do so if they were applying for new licenses) and also promised to limit the number of commercials, where other processing standards also existed. Everything was kept sort of honest by another FCC staff processing guideline system. Significant (not trivial—there were actually quantitative measures of this) failure to live up to previous promises about amounts of noncommercial, nonentertainment programming could prevent the FCC staff from granting renewal and force the application to be referred to the commissioners. Hence, most broadcasters made the appropriate promises and then were careful to keep them. Failure to do so held up license renewal. Except in extraordinary circumstances, it was not worth the delay.

Enforcement of all these guidelines required data. To provide the data, the FCC required continuous, detailed logging of programs and commercial matter by broadcasters. Broadcasters had to categorize and record their programming and commercials continuously. Daily program logs were available to the public, and at license renewal time, the FCC examined a sample week of those logs to see if the broadcasters had kept their programming promises. If not, the broadcasters were in trouble although, practically speaking, they almost never lost their licenses.

By the late 1970s and very early 1980s, then, general FCC regulation of programming consisted of the following:

1. To get new licenses, prospective broadcasters had to do formal ascertainments of community needs and make their proposals for licenses conform to the results of those ascertainments. They also were expected to promise minimal amounts of noncommercial, nonentertainment programming and observe limits on the amount of commercial time on their stations.
2. Incumbent broadcasters seeking license renewals had to do several things:
   a. They had to log all their programming so that the FCC and the public could check up on their performance at license renewal time.

b. They were required to conduct ascertainments of community needs throughout their license terms to prove that they knew, in a very formal sense, what the "problems, needs and interests" of the community were.

c. At license renewal time, they were expected to make certain maximal promises about how much time they would use for commercials (too much violated other FCC staff processing standards) and minimal promises about how much noncommercial, nonentertainment programming they would offer if granted renewal. The *1960 Policy Statement* provided the major guideline as to what kind of programming was expected. At renewal time, incumbent broadcasters were also held (somewhat loosely) to their prior promises. Too great a difference between what was promised to get a license and what was actually delivered during that term created at least some difficulty (usually resolved in the broadcaster's favor) in getting the license renewed.

At least on paper, the FCC's overall supervision of broadcast programming was more qualitative than quantitative. The commission expected some "public interest" programming, largely as defined by the *1960 Policy Statement*. It expected that programming would somehow respond to the "problems, needs and interests" of the communities broadcasters held licenses to serve. To make sure that was the case, the FCC expected such programming to be based on the results of a highly formal ascertainment process.

How much such programming was to be offered was, in theory, up to the broadcaster, but in practice, the processing guidelines told broadcasters what the FCC expected. More than anything else, broadcasters (and their attorneys), wanted to know what they had to do to secure their licenses. Over the years, broadcasters and broadcast attorneys asked the FCC for increasingly specific statements on licensing standards and generally got what they wanted. When the broadcasters wanted to know exactly how much programming of various kinds they had to provide to be assured license renewal, they got processing guidelines. When they wanted to know exactly how they had to log programming, they got precise marching orders from the commission. When they wanted to know exactly how the FCC expected them to ascertain community needs—so that they could do it "right" and not run into problems with the FCC—they got a series of ascertainment primers setting up a for-

mal system. By the late 1970s, all those ground rules were well understood. There were processing guidelines, ascertainment primers, and FCC "approved" forms for logging. It was a comfortable and predictable world that, according to the FCC of the 1980s, bore little relationship to real-world conditions.

Deregulation: The Reliance on Marketplace Forces

By the mid-1980s, most of the regulatory world we have just described was gone. Logging, formal ascertainment, expectations of minimal amounts of noncommercial, nonentertainment programming, and categorical lists of types of programs expected to be offered to gain licenses were eliminated. They were replaced by an expectation that "marketplace forces"—the forces of commercial (and noncommercial?) competition—would be just as effective as FCC rules. Nevertheless, the FCC did not officially abandon *all* general programming regulation. The result is a situation where licensees still face uncertainties—perhaps more uncertainties than they faced in the 1970s.

What happened is that deregulation caught up with the electronic media. The Roosevelt through Johnson presidencies typified a liberal attitude toward the relationship between government and society. Government, it was felt, could affirmatively take actions in many areas that would make society better. The Communications Act of 1934 is a characteristic piece of Roosevelt-era New Deal legislation. Although it largely recodified the earlier Radio Act of 1927, it clearly reflected the spirit of its time. Government could make broadcasting "good"—it could require broadcasters to serve its notions of what was in the "public interest, convenience and necessity." By the Carter administration, such faith in government's wisdom was failing. New Deal notions—if it is important, regulate it—were less widely and less automatically accepted. Alfred Kahn, as Carter's head of the Civil Aeronautics Board, argued that the board should be eliminated and that the marketplace, much distrusted in the 1930s after the Great Depression, could be trusted as an adequate regulator. Kahn became a generic guru of "deregulation."

In communications, Charles Ferris, the FCC chairman throughout most of the Carter administration, came forward as a "deregulator," even though many in the broadcasting industry distrusted his sincerity in this regard. Very late in the Carter administration, in fact, after Carter had been defeated for a second term as president, the Ferris-led FCC proved that it really wanted to import the general notions of "deregulation" into the electronic mass media field. The opportunity to do so came about through what came to be known as the "Radio Deregulation Proceeding." Although initiated under the Carter administration, the proceeding was obviously influenced by marketplace-based theories of regulation that came to have even greater force during the Reagan administration.

In *Deregulation of Radio,* 84 F.C.C.2d 968 (1981), the FCC scrapped (1) the nonentertainment guideline, (2) the ascertainment process (3) commercial guidelines, and (4) program logs. In a lengthy report, the FCC justified its decision to scrap a large part of its regulatory process. Among other things, the FCC said it was now convinced that even without the nonentertainment guidelines a significant quantity of nonentertainment programming would continue to be carried on commercial radio. The only nonentertainment obligation of radio broadcasters would be to provide "issue responsive programming." The only "nonstatutory programming obligation of a radio broadcaster should be to discuss issues of concern to its community license." How was this latter obligation to be met? The FCC explained:

> This includes programming [such as] public affairs, public service announcements, editorials, free speech messages, community bulletin boards, and religious programming. [W]e do not believe that it is advisable or necessary to specify precise quantities of programming that should be presented by all stations regardless of local needs and conditions. Therefore, we will eliminate our current guideline and will not specify any particular amount of total nonentertainment programming that should be presented.

Two separate but related developments occurred after the *Radio Deregulation* report was issued. The FCC began proceedings aimed at providing comparable deregulation to commercial TV broadcasters and noncommercial broadcasters, both radio and TV. Meanwhile opponents of broadcast deregulation challenged what the FCC had already done in court. On the first issue, the extension of deregulation, the FCC progressed relatively rapidly, especially under its

new deregulation-minded Republican chairman, Mark Fowler. In 1981, the FCC issued separate Notices of Proposed Rulemaking looking toward deregulation of commercial TV and noncommercial broadcasting. The notices relied heavily on the conclusions used to justify commercial radio deregulation. In 1984 the FCC released reports and orders generally granting to the rest of the broadcasting community the degree of deregulation accorded to radio in 1981. See *Revision of Programming and Commercialization Policies, Ascertainment Requirements, and Program Log Requirements for Commercial Television Stations,* 98 F.C.C.2d 1076 (1984) and *Revision of Program Policies and Reporting Requirements Related to Public Broadcasting Licensees,* 98 F.C.C.2d 746 (1984).

Essentially, the FCC argued, as it had in *Radio Deregulation,* that competitive marketplace forces would keep stations knowledgeable about and responsive to their communities and, in the case of commercial TV, prevent overcommercialization. The FCC, of course, had to admit that the TV and noncommercial "marketplaces" were different than the radio marketplace. In *Radio Deregulation,* the FCC had focused mostly on the level of competition among radio stations and found it sufficiently high to justify deregulation. In *Television Deregulation,* the FCC relied more heavily on competitors to TV stations beyond other TV broadcasters—cable television, videotapes, and the like. In fact, the FCC broadened the "marketplace" considerably and placed more emphasis on "competition" to TV from other information services such as books, magazines, and newspapers than it had done in deregulating radio.

Although there were significantly fewer TV stations than radio stations both nationally and in individual markets, the FCC concluded that competitive marketplace forces would be better than its own rules at keeping things in order. As to noncommercial broadcasting, the FCC noted the increasing reliance of public stations on corporate underwriting and their growing interest in attracting adequate audiences—a striving that put them, the commission reasoned, into a reasonably competitive marketplace as well. Thus, by 1984, the FCC had dropped many of its longstanding general programming regulations—programming guidelines, ascertainment standards, and logging requirements—for all broadcasters. Gone for commercial broadcasters were the guidelines concerning the amount of commercial matter offered. These changes were not quite final, however, because of the court challenges.

CHALLENGES TO DEREGULATION Because radio deregulation came first, it attracted the first court challenges. Since the logic and issues of the various deregulation proceedings were so similar, the outcome of the court challenges to radio deregulation had a substantial impact on the later deregulation proceedings. Many of the challenges to radio deregulation focused on the elimination of program logs. For citizens' groups seeking to challenge broadcaster license renewals, or at least to keep pressure on broadcasters to be responsive to the groups' perceptions of community needs, the detailed logs were useful tools. They provided a publicly available, comprehensive record of everything the broadcaster had aired. After radio deregulation, the groups feared, they would have much less data about broadcaster performance to use either in formal proceedings before the FCC or in much less formal negotiations with broadcasters. One of the leading broadcast citizens' groups, the Office of Communication of the United Church of Christ (UCC), took the lead in challenging radio deregulation.

The UCC looked for help from the D.C. Circuit. In 1983, however, that court generally upheld the FCC's 1981 radio deregulation order. See *Office of Communication of United Church of Christ v. FCC (UCC III)*, 707 F.2d 1413 (D.C. Cir. 1983). The court did, however, conclude that the FCC had not fully explained its decision to replace the logging requirements with an annual list of five to ten illustrative issues and programs. The court was particularly concerned about the FCC's admission that, under the new order, it would have to depend more than before on public complaints to identify broadcasters who were not performing adequately, yet without the logs the public might not have enough information to perform that task. Hence, the court remanded the logging issue to the FCC, essentially giving the commission a second chance to either justify that change or modify it.

The UCC went to the D.C. Circuit again, and in 1985, obviously somewhat tiring of the whole process, the court overturned the revised FCC standards and their justification. In *UCC IV*, 779 F.2d 702 (D.C. Cir. 1985), a frustrated panel of the court of appeals concluded that the FCC's

reliance on "illustrative" issues lists was irrational and argued that the FCC had unreasonably rejected alternatives proposed to it in the various related rule-making proceedings.

In *UCC IV*, the D.C. Circuit addressed a challenge to an FCC order that required radio broadcast licensees to maintain a list of at least five to ten community issues addressed by the station's programming during each quarter. This rule was enacted in response to *UCC III*, 707 F.2d 1413 (D.C. Cir. 1983), in which the court remanded a 1981 rule because of the FCC's failure to explain adequately why it had replaced its logging requirement with a requirement that licensees keep an illustrative issues/programs list.

Both *UCC III* and *UCC IV* arose out of the FCC's 1981 deregulation program that, among other things, eliminated the requirement that radio stations maintain program logs that recorded information about each program or commercial aired during the broadcast day. Instead the FCC required licensees to maintain an annual list of five to ten issues of concern to the community and provide examples of the programs presented in efforts to address those issues. The purpose of the new requirement was to reduce the paperwork burden borne by licensees. The *UCC III* court held that the issues/programs list would not provide the public with enough information to challenge a broadcaster's claims that it had served the public interest. The court then remanded the decision to the FCC.

In 1984, the FCC enacted a new rule that made some minor alterations to the public file requirements: (1) instead of an annual report the commission now required quarterly reports; and (2) instead of establishing a maximum of ten issues, the new rule left licensees free to determine the maximum number of issues on which they wished to report. In *UCC IV*, the court analyzed the 1984 rule and determined that it should be vacated for two reasons.

First, the court stated that an "agency's means [could] not undermine its purported goals." This meant that the FCC's rules governing the content of licensees' public files could not contradict its policy of relying on public participation in the license renewal process. "The agency relies, at least in part, on public participation in the form of petitions to deny to ensure that applicants for license renewal have met their public interest obligations."

In order to be granted a hearing on a petition to deny, the petitioner was required to make a *prima facie* case by filing affidavits making substantial and specific allegations of fact that would show that the "overall" programming efforts of the licensee failed to include adequate treatment of issues of public concern chosen by the licensee. The only way to maintain public participation in the renewal process was to allow the public access to information that could be used to determine whether the broadcaster had served the public interest. The FCC stated that "[i]nterested citizens need only visit [the public inspection file available at the station] to avail themselves of the information necessary to support a complaint or petition to deny."

The court rejected the issues/program list rule (1984 rule) because it was "impossible to determine whether the inadequate treatment of the issues on a merely illustrative list fairly reflect[ed] on the quality of a broadcaster's overall efforts." If the petitioner were to base its challenge solely on the FCC's revised issues list, any licensee would be free to respond by stating that "illustrative" lists did not provide an accurate picture of the applicant's overall programming efforts. "The licensee could argue that the petitioner lacks the complete picture[.] The petitioner would be unable to dispute that claim. Lacking a disputed material issue, the FCC would dismiss the petition."

Second, the court vacated the FCC rule because the commission had failed to explain adequately why it had rejected one of the alternatives suggested by a commenter. During the notice and comment period, it was suggested that the agency require licensees to list the programs that provided "significant treatment" of community issues. The petitioner could then rely on a list that the licensee certified to include programs in which it provided "significant treatment" of issues of community concern.

The court declared that the "significant treatment" alternative would allow the petitioner "to assert that by the broadcaster's own admission the programs on th[e] list represented the most significant treatment by that broadcaster of issues that the broadcaster itself thought to be of community concern." The court reasoned that if the licensee's best programs were insufficient to meet the public interest, then the rest of the licensee's programming was unlikely to be adequate.

The FCC argued that under the 1984 rule, licensees would voluntarily list their best programs. The court rejected this argument noting that some licensees "might decide to keep shoddy lists and take their chances" on being challenged at the renewal proceeding. In addition, the court noted that "in reviewing the Commission's public file regulations [it is] primarily concerned with the minimum requirements imposed by regulation, not with what the Commission hopes private parties will do if left free from such requirements."

The court vacated the 1984 rule because it believed that the "significant treatment" option was a reasonable alternative to the rule that was enacted and that "[t]he Commission's failure to provide a single word of explanation for its rejection of an option that appears to serve precisely the agency's purported goals suggests a lapse of rational decisionmaking."

Taking the court's command to heart, the FCC revised its programs/issues requirement along the lines the court had suggested. In *Deregulation of Radio*, 104 F.C.C.2d 505 (1986), the FCC decided to require licensees to maintain quarterly issues/program lists reflecting their "most significant programming treatment" of the issues as determined by the broadcaster's good faith judgment. This dropped the "illustrative" standard that the court found so objectionable and put the obligation on broadcasters to make sure that their lists included any number of issues that received "significant" treatment. Because this requirement was essentially what the court ordered, the FCC assumed (correctly as it turned out) that this new standard would survive judicial review.

The television situation was a little more complex. The 1984 television deregulation order was issued shortly after the FCC's first attempt to respond to the court's concerns about radio deregulation. Thus, TV broadcasters were, at first, required to prepare quarterly lists of at least five issues/programs. In its 1986 radio deregulation order that adopted the new "significant treatment" standard, the FCC decided to try to simplify things. It required commercial television broadcasters to also prepare quarterly issues/programs lists reflecting "significant programming treatment." Finally, in 1988, the FCC made everything consistent. In *Revision of Sec. 73.3527(A)(7) Relating to the Issues-Programs List for Public Broadcasting Licensees*, 3

F.C.C.R. 1032 (1988), the FCC established common standards for all broadcasters. The 1984 order deregulating noncommercial broadcasters had not been challenged, so they were still preparing quarterly lists of five to ten community issues/programs. Recognizing that it had argued that all broadcasters could be deregulated for essentially the same reasons, and placing a high value on regulatory consistency, the FCC decided that noncommercial broadcasters, too, should prepare quarterly lists of issues/programs receiving "significant programming treatment."

The dispute over how broadcasters should document their programming was essentially over. One more issue remained—growing, this time, from TV deregulation rather than radio deregulation. As will be discussed shortly, the FCC has often had special policies for children's television. Because the 1984 television deregulation order also affected those policies, it is not surprising that that order was challenged by children's advocates, notably Action for Children's Television (ACT). The forum was, again, the U.S. Court of Appeals for the D.C. Circuit, and, again, the FCC (mostly) won. In *ACT v. FCC*, 821 F.2d 741 (D.C. Cir. 1987), the court upheld most of the FCC's TV deregulation decision. The court remanded some portions of that decision directly dealing with children's television policy to the FCC for further review. Basically, the court was troubled that the FCC, after saying for so long that children were special (and did not participate in the "marketplace" as adults did), suddenly appeared to switch paths without justification. More on this issue can be found in the portions of this chapter dealing with children's television policy.

The Bedrock Obligation of Broadcasters to Offer "Issue-Responsive" Programming

By the late 1980s, then, much of the dust over changing general programming regulation appeared to have settled. Gone was the expectation that each broadcaster would try to meet the needs of everyone. Now specialization was legally permitted. Broadcasters could meet the needs of their audiences and argue that "other stations" were meeting the needs of others. Also gone was the expectation that most broadcasters would offer minimal amounts of noncommer-

cial, nonentertainment programming. Instead, broadcasters had a "bedrock obligation" to offer "issue-responsive" programming—with the amount, timing, and nature of that programming not specified in advance by the FCC.

In *Monroe Communications Corp. v. FCC*, 900 F.2d 351 (D.C. Cir. 1990), the court reversed the FCC's renewal of the license of Video 44, the licensee of a Chicago TV station. The rationale for reversal and remand to the FCC was significant. The court held that the FCC's renewal grant was arbitrary in light of the licensee's cutback on nonentertainment programming during the latter third of its license period:

> The [FCC] found that through the final year of its license term, Video 44 offered .08 percent news, 2.57 percent public affairs, and only 5.84 percent to other nonentertainment programming. These figures place Video 44 near the bottom of the pack, relative to other Chicago stations, in terms of news, public affairs, and other non-entertainment programming. Given that the license expectancy analysis focuses on the incumbent licensee's responsiveness to the ascertained problems and needs of its community, the FCC was arbitrary in awarding Video 44 a renewal expectancy in light of record evidence of a strong downward trend in Video 44's responsiveness to community needs in the form of news and non-entertainment programming.

The *Monroe* case put some teeth into the "issue-responsiveness" requirement. Would failure to meet the "issue-responsiveness" requirement constitute a "serious violation" under the broadcast renewal procedures of the Telecom Act of 1996? See text, p. 728.

The Impact of Deregulation

The consequences of deregulation were many. Gone were comprehensive, detailed program logs. Instead, broadcasters were to prepare quarterly lists of whatever number of community issues they believed received significant programming attention. Those lists never found their way to Washington, D.C., for FCC review unless somebody complained about a broadcaster's performance. Instead, they sat in the station's public files, used, if at all, only by the small number of knowledgeable members of the public who knew that the lists were there. Finally, commercial stations, both radio and TV, no longer faced any governmental pressure to hold down commercial loads. They were free to offer what the market-place would support.

The impact of radio and television deregulation on the public is very hard to assess. The consensus among communications scholars seems to be that many radio stations are offering fewer public service programming than they did before deregulation. Many stations have reduced the number of news and public affairs programming that they carry and have scheduled much of what they do offer in very early morning hours. At the same time, some of the specialization the FCC expected has occurred with some stations—especially AM stations—moving to more of a talk/information format.

The impact on broadcasters is also not very clear yet. Under the old rules, broadcasters knew what to do: stick to the programming and commercial guidelines and ascertain and log correctly. That world was a clear one. The revised world is murkier. Deregulation gives more discretion to broadcasters, which is almost certainly a good thing, but it has not completely eliminated general programming regulation. The broadcasting industry expected that a deregulatory-minded FCC such as that led by Mark Fowler, especially when constitutionally predisposed against content regulation, would pose few problems for broadcasters under the new standards. Whatever a broadcaster offered as "issue-responsive" programming would probably be adequate. When the FCC faces challenges to broadcast licenses that turn on "issue responsiveness," there is at least a chance that the FCC of the 1990s may find some broadcasters lacking. If so, case-by-case interpretation of the "issue-responsive" standard may, in the end, create new FCC standards as to what is expected. The result could well be the same process that played out in the 1960s and 1970s—case-by-case decisions summarized, eventually, in FCC policy statements and primers and, in effect, reregulation.

At the same time, significant features of the 1996 Telecom Act may work against reregulation. Under the Act, licenses for both radio and television may be granted for up to eight years. In addition, the new broadcast renewal procedures, text, p. 711, give broadcasters a new sense of security in their licenses. Of course, even under the new procedures, a license renewal application may still be denied. In short, renewal

pitfalls still exist, as is demonstrated by the increasing emphasis the FCC is giving to broadcaster obligations in the area of children's programming.

CHILDREN'S TELEVISION

For many years, the FCC treated children as special audience members. The *1960 Policy Statement,* for example, indicated that broadcasters were normally expected to provide programs for children. In 1974, largely in response to pressure from advocacy groups such as Action for Children's Television, the FCC adopted a comprehensive children's programming and advertising policy statement.

Although not as explicit as ACT wished, the 1974 Policy Statement prodded TV broadcasters to increase the amount of children's programming they offered, to schedule it throughout the week instead of clustering it in a Saturday morning children's TV ghetto, and to make a reasonable amount of it educational and informational and not just designed for entertainment. Relying on the NAB Television Code, which had not yet been discarded, the FCC urged broadcasters to sharply distinguish between program content and ads (notably by discouraging "host selling" in which, for example, a cartoon show host also pitches products) and appeared to rely on the NAB Code limits as to the maximum amount of commercial matter children's shows should contain. See *Children's Television Report and Policy Statement,* 50 F.C.C.2d 1, 31 R.R.2d 1228 (1974).

After five years of experience with the *1974 Policy Statement,* the FCC conducted a review of its effects. In 1979, the FCC concluded that the policy statement appeared to have little effect on the amount, type, or scheduling of children's programs, although it did seem to keep the commercial load of children's programs to the levels advocated. The FCC then opened a proposed rule-making in which it planned to explore five options, given its conclusion that the 1974 statement was having minimal effects. One option was to rescind the 1974 statement and rely on sources other than commercial broadcasters (such as cable television or VCRs) to fulfill children's needs. Other options were to strengthen the policy statement by regulating more pervasively, setting mandatory minimal children's TV standards for all broadcasters, developing firm renewal guidelines regarding children's programming, or working to increase the number of video outlets with hopes that some of the new outlets would better serve children. *Children's Television Programming and Advertising Practices,* 75 F.C.C.2d 138 (1979).

This proceeding, however, languished at the FCC for years. It was pending when Ronald Reagan became president, and the deregulation-oriented commissioners he named were not anxious to take it up. Finally, under prodding from the courts (see *Washington Ass'n for Television and Children v. FCC,* 712 F.2d 677 [D.C. Cir. 1983]), the FCC acted in late 1984.

As could easily be predicted, given the philosophy of the commissioners, the FCC chose the "deregulation" option first proposed in 1979. It concluded that sources other than commercial TV (public broadcasting, cable, VCRs, and the like) could also be considered in determining whether a licensee's programming would fulfill the needs of children and therefore abandoned most of its *1974 Policy Statement.* Specifically, the FCC indicated that it no longer had any minimal expectations about amounts of children's programming, no longer would try to mandate that at least some of it be educational or instructional, and no longer was concerned about forcing broadcasters to schedule at least some programming outside of the weekend. The FCC indicated that the marketplace would generally see to it that the needs of children were met or at least would do as good a job as FCC rules and regulations had done since 1974.

The FCC, however, did not totally deregulate children's TV. Under the public interest standard of the Communications Act of 1934, commercial TV broadcasters had to do at least something to meet the special needs of the child audience. The FCC refused, however, to be specific about what was required; this suggested a hands-off policy. But, plainly, it also invited those unhappy with a broadcaster's service to children to respond by filing petitions to deny when the broadcaster sought a license renewal. The FCC offered remarkably little guidance for either broadcasters or citizens' groups as to exactly what would be expected if a broadcaster's service to children was challenged. The FCC's new policies were generally upheld by the courts. *Children's Televi-*

sion Programming and Advertising Practices, 96 F.C.C.2d 634, 55 R.R.2d 199 (1984), *aff'd sub nom. ACT v. FCC,* 756 F.2d 899 (D.C. Cir. 1985).

One aspect of the FCC's regulation of children's programming was not immediately sustained by the court, however. In 1986, the FCC clarified its 1984 general television deregulation order by explaining that the order was intended to eliminate its prior children's television commercialization guidelines. *Memorandum Opinion and Order on Reconsideration,* 104 F.C.C.2d 358 (1986). Action for Children's Television appealed this decision to the D.C. Circuit. The court concluded that after years of saying that marketplace forces could not be relied upon to prevent overcommercialization toward children, the FCC had failed to adequately justify deregulation in the two paragraphs and two footnotes devoted to the subject in its 1986 decision. The court remanded the issue to the FCC, giving it an opportunity to develop a more complete justification for deregulation. *ACT v. FCC,* 821 F.2d 741 (D.C. Cir. 1987).

In response to the remand, the FCC expanded an existing notice inquiry and notice of proposed rulemaking to include new children's television issues. *Revision of Programming and Commercialization Policies, Ascertainment Requirements, and Program Log Requirements for Commercial Television Stations, Further Notice of Proposed Rulemaking/Notice of Inquiry,* 2 F.C.C.R. 6822 (1987). In addition to responding to the court's remand, the FCC also asked for comment on two previously filed petitions for rulemaking from ACT. One of the petitions dealt with so-called program-length children's commercials. To ACT, some children's shows (especially children's cartoon shows) had become so intertwined with the associated merchandising of toys that the entire program was, in effect, one long commercial. If so, its length would exceed almost any commercial guideline the FCC might adopt. ACT believed such programs were contrary to the public interest; the FCC asked for comment on the issue. Similarly, ACT complained to the FCC about "interactive" children's TV shows, which would contain signaling information that could activate toys, permitting a limited amount of interactive play with the television. ACT argued that these programs were contrary to the public interest because they could not be fully enjoyed without purchase of the home product. The FCC asked commenters to indicate whether they perceived any problem with such programs and, if so, why they might be contrary to the public interest.

The central issue in most of these matters was whether or not marketplace forces will meet the needs of children. The FCC generally took the position that the market *would* meet children's needs, especially if alternatives such as VCRs and cable television were included in the "marketplace." Meanwhile proponents of special policies for children argued that the children's marketplace is different and deserves special regulation.

The Children's Television Act of 1990

The Children's Television Act (CTA) of 1990 demonstrated that Congress was not content to rely solely on the market to meet the television needs of children. The Act provides in part:

Sec. 303(a). *Standards for Children's Television Programming.*

(a) The FCC shall . . . initiate a rulemaking proceeding to prescribe standards applicable to commercial television broadcast licensees with respect to the time devoted to commercial matter in conjunction with children's television programming.

(b) Except as provided in subsection (c), the standards prescribed under subsection (a) shall include the requirement that each commercial broadcast licensee shall limit the duration of advertising in children's television programming to not more than 10.5 minutes per hour on weekends and not more than 12 minutes per hour on weekdays.

(c) After January 1, 1993, the FCC—

(1) may review and evaluate the advertising duration limitations required by subsection (b); and (2) may after notice and public comment and a demonstration of the need for modification of such limitations, modify such limitations in accordance with the public interest.

(d) As used in this section, the term "commercial television broadcast licensee" includes a cable operator, as defined in section 602 of the Communications Act of 1934.

Sec. 303(b). *Consideration of Children's Television Service in Broadcast License Renewal.*

(a) After the standards required by section 102 [47 U.S.C. § 303] are in effect, the FCC shall, in its review of any application for renewal of a commercial or noncommercial broadcast license, consider the extent to which the licensee—

(1) has complied with such standards; and

(2) has served the educational and informational needs of children through the licensee's overall programming, including programming specifically designed to serve such needs.

(b) In addition to consideration of the licensee's programming as required under subsection (a), the FCC may consider—

(1) any special nonbroadcast efforts by the licensee which enhance the educational and informational value of such programming to children; and

(2) any special efforts by the licensee to produce or support programming broadcast by another station in the licensee's marketplace which is specifically designed to serve the educational and informational needs of children.

In 1991, the FCC adopted regulations to implement the CTA, but these regulations did not require that broadcasters provide any specific number of hours of educational and informational children's programming each week. See *Notice of Inquiry, In re Policies and Rules Concerning Children's Television,* 10 F.C.C.R. 6308 (1995). Although the FCC provided a definition of "educational and informational" programming in this document, broadcasters complained that they still lacked sufficient guidance on compliance with the CTA. A *Notice of Inquiry,* 8 F.C.C.R. 1841 (1993), was therefore initiated. During 1994, the FCC held hearings on the general subject of children's television programming. In the meantime, FCC Chairman Reed Hundt became convinced that some specific weekly quantity of children's programming should be required of broadcast licensees. Finally, the FCC issued a long-awaited *Report and Order.*

Report and Order in the Matter of Policies Concerning Children's Television Programming

11 F.C.C.R. 10660 (1996).
ADOPTED: AUGUST 8, 1996

By the Commission:

[O]ur initial regulations implementing the CTA have not been fully effective in prompting broadcasters "to increase the amount of educational and informational television programming available to children." Senate Report at 1. First, because of their imprecision, our rules have led to a variation on the level and nature of broadcasters' compliance efforts that is incompatible with the intent of the CTA. Indeed, some broadcasters are carrying very little regularly scheduled standard length programming specifically designed to educate and inform children. Second, some broadcasters are claiming to have satisfied their statutory obligations with shows that, by any reasonable benchmark, cannot be said to be "specifically designed" to educate and inform children within the meaning of the CTA. Third, parents and others frequently lack timely access to information about the availability of programming in their communities specifically designed to educate and inform children, exacerbating market disincentives. Therefore, as proposed in the *Notice of Proposed Rulemaking,* 10 F.C.C.R. 6308 (1995), we refine our policies and rules implementing the CTA to implement these policies.

First, we adopt a number of proposals designed to provide better information to the public about the shows broadcasters air to fulfill their obligation to air educational and informational programming under the CTA.

Second, we adopt a definition of programming "specifically designed" to educate and inform children (or "core" programming) that provides better guidance to broadcasters concerning programming that fulfills their statutory obligation to air such programming. *In order to qualify as core programming, a show must have serving the educational and informational needs of children as a significant purpose. The FCC will ordinarily rely on the good faith judgments of broadcasters as to whether programming satisfies this test and will evaluate compliance of individual programs with this definition only as a last resort. Our new definition of core programming includes other objective elements. A core program must be a regularly scheduled, weekly program of at least 30 minutes, and aired between 7:00 a.m. and 10:00 p.m. The program must also be identified as educational and informational for children when it is aired and must be listed in the children's programming report placed in the broadcaster's public inspection file.* [Emphasis added.]

Third, we adopt a processing guideline that will provide certainty for broadcasters about how

to comply with the CTA, and facilitate our processing efforts. [U]nder this guideline, broadcasters will receive staff-level approval of the CTA portion of the renewal applications if they air three hours per week of core programming or if, while providing somewhat less than three hours per week of core programming, they air a package of programming that demonstrates a level of commitment to educating and informing children that is at least equivalent to airing three hours per week of core programming. Broadcasters that do not meet this guideline will be referred to the full FCC for consideration, where they will have a full opportunity to demonstrate compliance with the CTA, including through efforts other than "core" programming and through nonbroadcast efforts.

By publishing our guideline for processing television renewal applications, and by identifying in advance those broadcasters who clearly are in compliance with the CTA and those who may be in compliance, a processing guideline will help ensure that broadcasters who wish to provide an ample amount of children's educational programming will not find themselves at an unfair disadvantage in the market relative to competing broadcasters who do not, and will not find themselves facing competitive pressure to forgo airing educational programs. A processing guideline will also facilitate speedy and consistent application processing by the FCC staff. In short, a processing guideline is a clear and fair and efficient way to implement the Children's Television Act.

A number of broadcasters submitted comments arguing that the FCC should assess not just the educational programming being provided over-the-air by broadcast stations, but rather the availability of educational programming in the marketplace. We believe, however, that the proper focus in this proceeding should be on the provision of children's educational programming by broadcast stations, not by cable systems and other subscription services such as direct broadcast satellite systems that, in contrast to broadcast service, require the payment of a subscription fee. The CTA itself expressly focuses on broadcast licensees. In enacting this statute, Congress found that, as part of their public interest obligations, *"television station operators and licensees should provide programming that serves the special needs of children"* [47 U.S.C. § 303 (emphasis added)], and the Act applies only to television broadcast stations. Thus the statute focuses on the provision of children's educational programming through broadcasting, a ubiquitous service, which may be the only source of video programming for some families that cannot afford, or do not have access to, cable or other subscription services. Although in 1991 we concluded that we should not quantify a broadcaster's CTA obligation, based on our experience over the past five years and the record in this proceeding, we believe a processing guideline approach is warranted at this time. We believe that three hours per week is a reasonable benchmark for all broadcast television stations to meet six years after enactment of the CTA. NAB states that commercial broadcasters were, on average, broadcasting two hours per week of regularly scheduled, standard length educational programming at the time the CTA passed in 1990.

While we do not know whether Congress was aware of this data in passing the CTA, the Act's legislative history makes clear that Congress was generally aware of the television programming being broadcast in 1990 when it found that "the marketplace had failed to provide an adequate supply of children's educational programming," and that it desired that the amount of such programming be increased. Thus, airing two hours per week of such programming six years after passage of the CTA clearly is not compatible with the long-term performance improvement Congress intended when it passed the CTA, and a processing guideline of three hours is clearly a reasonable means of implementing the statute at this time.

[A] safe harbor processing guideline will serve the public interest by providing a reasonable degree of certainty while also preserving a reasonable degree of flexibility for broadcasters. Renewal applications will be divided into two categories for purposes of staff-level CTA review. Applications falling into neither of these categories will be referred to the FCC for consideration. We will revise our license renewal form to reflect this processing guideline.

CATEGORY A

Broadcasters that air an average of three or more hours per week of programming that satisfies our new definition of programming "specifically designed" to serve children's educational and informational needs will have their applications

approved by the staff with respect to CTA compliance. A licensee seeking review under this category must simply check a box on our revised renewal form and provide supporting information, indicating that it has aired three hours per week of regularly scheduled, weekly shows that are 30 minutes or longer and that otherwise meet the definition of core programming.

To provide broadcasters scheduling flexibility, we will allow the three-hour core programming benchmark to be averaged over a six-month period. We will also allow repeats and reruns of core programming to be counted toward fulfillment of the three-hour guideline.

CATEGORY B

Broadcasters that air somewhat less than three hours per week of core programming will also receive staff-level approval if they show that they have aired a package of different types of educational and informational programming that demonstrates a level of commitment to educating and informing children that is at least equivalent to airing three hours per week of core programming. We do this to create a measure of flexibility as to how broadcasters may qualify for routine staff processing of their applications. Although core programming is our primary focus under the Children's Television Act, we believe that specials, regularly scheduled non-weekly programs, short-form programs, and PSA's with a significant purpose of educating and informing children ages 16 and under can help accomplish the objectives of the Act and can count toward the staff-level processing guideline.

FCC CONSIDERATION

Broadcasters that do not fall within Category A or B will have their renewal applications referred to the full FCC. Licensees referred to the FCC should be on notice by this order that they will not necessarily be found to have complied with the Children's Television Act. Given the modest nature of the guideline described in Categories A and B, we expect few broadcasters will fail to meet this benchmark. However, even if a licensee did not meet the guideline for staff approval, it will have an opportunity to make a showing before the FCC that it has satisfied its CTA obligations in other ways.

If we find that a broadcaster has not complied with the CTA, we will apply the same remedies that we use in enforcing other rules. These remedies will vary depending on the severity of the deficiency based on objective criteria. For less serious deficiencies, we will consider letters of admonition or reporting requirements. We may consider using a "promise versus performance" approach. This would be a prospective remedy under which a licensee would detail its plan for coming into full compliance with CTA programming obligations; if this plan meets with FCC approval, the station's license would be renewed on the condition that the licensee adheres to the plan absent special circumstances. For more serious violations, we will consider other sanctions, including forfeitures and short-term renewals. In extreme cases, we will consider whether the licensee's violations of the CTA and our implementing rules warrant nonrenewal under the standards set forth in Section 309(k) of the Communications Act.

Our new regulations, like the CTA itself, impose reasonable, viewpoint-neutral conditions on a broadcaster's free use of the public airwaves. They do not censor or foreclose speech of any kind. They do not tell licensees what topics they must address. They provide only that broadcasters report the educational objective of the program and the expected educational effects. Moreover, they expressly provide that broadcasters need *not* describe the viewpoint of the program or the opinions expressed on the program.

[T]he processing guideline that we adopt today does not limit [broadcaster] discretion. It provides a means by which a broadcaster can be certain that our staff will be in a position to process its renewal application without further review of the broadcaster's CTA efforts. As we explain above, any programming specifically designed to meet the educational and informational needs of children can "count" for purposes of meeting the processing guideline. In addition, a broadcaster can rely on other more general programming and related non-programming efforts to satisfy its CTA obligation—albeit after full FCC review.

[B]eginning September 1, 1997, we will begin to evaluate renewal applications to determine the extent to which licensees are providing educational programming that complies with the new definition of core programming using the new processing guideline. In this renewal cycle (i.e., for applications filed through April 1999)

such renewals will cover licensee performance that both pre-dates and post-dates these new rules. Licensee performance during the term that predates the relevant effective dates will be evaluated under existing standards and performance that post-dates these new rules will be judged under the new provisions.

CONCLUSION

For the reasons discussed above, we adopt this *Report and Order* designed to further the mandate of the Children's Television Act that broadcast television achieve its full potential in teaching the nation's children.

COMMENT

The *Report and Order* makes frequent reference to sec. 309(k) and the new broadcast renewal procedures. It seems clear that ignoring the FCC's new rules on children's programming could in egregious cases constitute a sufficiently "serious violation" to warrant denial of the license renewal application.

In the *Report and Order*, the FCC unanimously voted to require broadcasters to provide three hours of children's programming per week. FCC Chairman Reed Hundt contended that the new requirement does not place a new regulatory burden on broadcasters. Quantifying the industry's children's programming obligation, Hundt said, freed broadcasters from having to hire lawyers "to interpret unquantified [FCC] rules of the past." See *Communications Daily*, September 25, 1996.

Processing guidelines quantifying categories of programming to establish service in the public interest were scuttled in the deregulation of the 1980's. Does a processing guideline for children's programming run counter to the idea behind deregulation, that the market itself can be depended on to provide programming in the public interest? In a separate statement to the *Report and Order*, Chairman Hundt suggested that children's programming is an area where the market has failed the public interest: "[T]his vote affirms that market values are not the same as family values, and our concern ought to be with both. Even though the marketplace provides many television shows that interest the public, [i]t has been thought impossible that commercial television could provide a large amount of children's educational programming. With our vote today the impossible becomes inevitable."

Commissioner Quello joined in the unanimous vote. But in a separate statement he expressed concern that the FCC's action in the *Report and Order* might lead the FCC in the future "to apply similar quantitative programming requirements to other types of programming under the public trusteeship standard, even without Congressional direction." It might lead to "stipulated amounts of news or public affairs, or political broadcasting." Can this concern be answered by the argument that children's programming is unique?

BROADCAST LOTTERY REGULATION

Since 1934, broadcasters have been prohibited from promoting many kinds of lotteries. The original prohibition, still found in 18 U.S.C. § 1304, is sweeping. It prohibits the broadcast of "any advertisement of or information concerning any lottery." Until the 1970s, the prohibition was absolute. In the 1960s and 1970s, however, states began to run their own lotteries (e.g., the Illinois State Lottery), and in 1975 Congress was persuaded to amend the law slightly to permit limited advertising or promotion of state-run lotteries by broadcasters licensed to states with such lotteries. Under these amendments, a broadcaster in such a state could promote that state's official lottery and the state-run lotteries, if any, of adjacent states. Lotteries of more distant states, however, could not be promoted, nor could privately run lotteries—for example, bingo games run by local churches. In addition, a broadcaster licensed to a state without a state-run lottery was unable to promote any lotteries, even if a substantial portion of the station's audience was in a state that ran one.

In late 1988, however, Congress changed the law dramatically when it enacted the somewhat misnamed Charity Games Advertising Clarification Act of 1988, Pub. L. No. 100-625, 102 Stat. 3205. By May 1990, the Act had changed the ways broadcasters (and, for that matter, the print media) can advertise or promote lotteries—not just, as the name suggests, those run on behalf of charities but also those run for very commercial

purposes. Before discussing the law, however, one needs to know what a lottery is.

Lotteries Defined

A lottery consists of three elements. It is the distribution of (1) a prize, (2) by chance, (3) for consideration. If any of these three elements is lacking, there is no lottery. If any is missing, broadcasters are free to promote the activity without legal concern and without even considering the 1989 changes in the law.

The easiest element to define is prize. A prize is anything of value. Often it is money, as in a drawing where the prize is a cash award. It can, however, be other things. If a lucky person is given some other object of value, say, a car, that is clearly a prize. Even giving somebody a day off from work with his or her place being taken by a temporary worker is a prize. In most lottery law cases, the element of "prize" is not very debatable. To those who run lotteries, the prize is the most important aspect because it is what gets people to participate. Thus, the prize is usually quite obvious.

Chance is a bit harder to define. Fundamentally, something is decided by chance if it is not determined by knowledge or skill. In other words, chance is present if a person cannot do anything to determine the outcome. The selection of a winning ticket from a drum is obviously chance—there is no way that somebody can control whether a ticket is drawn or not. The situation becomes more complex when both chance and skill are involved. If "winners" are drawn from those who can give the name of the first president of the United States, chance prevails. If winners are chosen from a nontrivial test of knowledge administered to a randomly selected group of people, then the winner is determined by skill rather than by chance, and a lottery is not present. Obviously, most "games of chance" involve chance.

Finally, the third element is consideration. The idea here is simple. If somebody has to give up something of value in order to compete for a prize, then whatever is given up is the "consideration." In the classic raffle situation, for example, the consideration is whatever you paid for a ticket to enter the raffle. Sometimes consideration gets trickier. If you do something you would not routinely do—for example, take a test drive in an automobile—then the time you spend doing that can equal consideration. If, on the other hand, you are simply asked to do something most people do all the time—go to a grocery store and drop off an entry coupon or send in a postcard—then that is not consideration. Having to have a phone in order to respond to a station call-in contest is not consideration, but having to purchase a newspaper in order to get an entry form is. In this area, recent judgments of the FCC and similar authorities must sometimes be tracked carefully.

An important point to note is that consideration only "counts" under lottery law if it flows to the person providing the prize. Two examples will explain this principle. First, consider a classic raffle. Suppose a church has a bicycle to raffle off. The church sells tickets, keeps the money, and gives the bicycle to the winner. Consideration in a lottery law sense is present here. The consideration went to the party giving the prize. Now suppose that a bicycle store rents a booth at a state fair to promote its business. All persons who attend the fair are eligible to drop by the bicycle store's booth and receive a ticket that may win them a free bicycle at the end of the fair. Although people had to pay to enter the fairgrounds, tickets for the bicycle drawing are free. In this case, there is probably no consideration. The money paid did not go to the bicycle shop. Instead, it went to the fair authorities. Thousands of people go to the fair, and few probably do so just to enter the bicycle drawing. Advertising the fair and even advertising the bike shop would be allowed—even under pre-1988 lottery law.

The simplest way to avoid problems under lottery law is to take away any of these three elements. If there is no prize, no chance, or no consideration, there is no lottery. In that case, there is no need to be concerned about unlawfully promoting a lottery.

What Promotions of Lotteries Are Lawful?

Prior to 1975, the answer to this question for broadcasters was simple: none. Lotteries, even if run by churches for the noblest of causes, could not be promoted. They could be reported as news, but if the news account would tend to encourage others to gamble—especially by telling them exactly how to do so—even that was unlawful.

In 1975, Congress allowed broadcasters licensed to states that had state-run lotteries to promote those lotteries and the state-run lotteries, if any, of adjacent states. The law did not change with regard to private lotteries. Promotion of the church bingo game was still out.

The Charity Games Advertising Clarification Act of 1988 changed the situation substantially. The new law defers to federalism. Much more than in the past, what broadcasters can do will be determined by state law. Congress, in fact, delayed implementation of the Act for eighteen months after adoption so that states could change their laws dealing with lotteries and lottery advertising if they wanted to do so. The Act made the following basic changes in lottery promotion law.

STATE-RUN LOTTERIES   Congress removed the "adjacent state" provision of previous lottery law. Unless the state to which the broadcaster is licensed has or enacts a law to the contrary, broadcasters licensed to states with state-run lotteries may promote state-run lotteries anywhere in the United States. Broadcasters in states without state-run lotteries, however, will not be able to promote state-run lotteries at all. 18 U.S.C. §§ 1304, 1307.

Suppose a broadcaster is licensed to a community in a state that prohibits lotteries. The broadcaster derives the largest part of its advertising revenues from a neighboring state that has a state-run lottery. Can that broadcaster, consistent with the First Amendment, be precluded from carrying the neighboring state's lottery ads?

In *United States v. Edge Broad. Co.,* the Supreme Court answered that question in the affirmative and upheld the challenged federal broadcast lottery statutes. Edge Broadcasting, the operator of a radio station licensed to Elizabeth City, North Carolina, brought the case against the United States. Justice White observed for the Court in *Edge* that the station broadcast from Moyock, North Carolina, a scant three miles from the Virginia state line. Edge's station was much closer to the Virginia border than is Elizabeth City. Furthermore, 90 percent of Edge's audience were Virginians; the rest were North Carolinians.

United States v. Edge Broadcasting Co.

509 U.S. 418, 113 S. CT. 2696, 125 L. ED. 2D 345 (1993).

Justice WHITE delivered the opinion of the Court.

Because Edge is licensed to serve a North Carolina community the federal statute prohibits it from broadcasting advertisements for the Virginia lottery. Edge derives 95% of its advertising revenues from Virginia sources, and claims that it has lost large sums of money from its inability to carry Virginia lottery advertisements.

[EDITORIAL NOTE: *Edge's difficult situation notwithstanding, the Court upheld the federal law as a permissible regulation of commercial speech and concluded that the four-factor test for commercial speech set forth in* Central Hudson, *text, p. 106, was satisfied. Justice White ruled, contrary to the federal courts below, that the third factor set forth in* Central Hudson *was satisfied. The third factor inquires whether the statutes at issue directly advance the government interests at stake. On this point, Justice White declared:*]

Congress plainly made the commonsense judgment that each North Carolina station would have an audience in that State, even if its signal reached elsewhere and that enforcing the statutory restriction would insulate each station's listeners from lottery ads and hence advance the governmental purpose of supporting North Carolina's law against gambling. This congressional policy of balancing the interests of lottery and nonlottery states is the substantial governmental interest that satisfies *Central Hudson,* the interest which the courts below did not fully appreciate. It is also the interest that is directly served by applying the statutory restriction to all stations in North Carolina; and this would plainly be the case even if, as applied to Edge, there were only marginal advancement of that interest.

[EDITORIAL NOTE: *Another issue was* Central Hudson's *fourth factor: "whether the regulation is more extensive than is necessary to serve the governmental interest." Relying on Board of Trustees of State Univ. v.* Fox, *text, p. 109, Justice White said that while there had to be a fit between the regulation and the governmental interest, the fit did not have to be perfect:*]

[T]o prevent Virginia's lottery policy from dictating what stations in a neighboring State may air, it is reasonable to require Edge to comply with the restriction against carrying lottery advertising. In other words, applying the restriction to a broadcaster such as Edge directly advances the governmental interest in enforcing the restriction in nonlottery States, while not interfering with the policy of lottery States like Virginia.

Justice STEVENS, with whom Justice BLACKMUN joins, dissenting:

The Federal Government's selective ban on lottery advertising flunks [*Fox's* "reasonable fit"] test; for the means chosen by the Government, a ban on speech imposed for the purpose of manipulating public behavior, is in no way proportionate to the Federal Government's interest in protecting the antilottery policies of nonlottery States.

I would hold that suppressing truthful advertising regarding a neighboring State's lottery, activity which is, of course, perfectly legal, is a patently unconstitutional means of effectuating the Government's asserted interest in protecting the policies of nonlottery States.

[T]he United States has selected the most intrusive, and dangerous form of regulation possible—a ban on truthful information regarding a lawful activity imposed for the purpose of manipulating, through ignorance, the consumer policies of some of its citizens. Unless justified by a truly substantial governmental interest this extreme, and extremely paternalistic, measure cannot withstand scrutiny under the First Amendment.

In my view, the sea change in public attitudes toward state-run lotteries that this country has witnessed in recent years undermines any claim that a state's interest in discouraging citizens from participating in state-run lotteries is so substantial as to outweigh [Edge's] First Amendment right to distribute, and the public's right to receive, truthful, nonmisleading information about a perfectly legal activity conducted in a neighboring State.

The Federal Government and the States simply do not have an overriding or "substantial" interest in seeking to discourage what virtually the entire country is embracing, and certainly not an interest that can justify a restriction on constitutionally protected speech as sweeping as the one the Court today sustains.

COMMENT

The majority of the Court in *Edge* defer to an express congressional preference for federalism.

Some states wish to ban lotteries while others promote them. Congress has ordained that broadcasting should not frustrate these state preferences. For Justice Stevens, on the other hand, the critical factor is that Congress is seeking to regulate truthful information about a lawful activity.

In a footnote in *Edge,* Justice White criticized the federal court of appeals that had invalidated the statute: "We deem it remarkable and unusual that although the Court of Appeals affirmed a judgment that an Act of Congress was unconstitutional as applied, the court found it appropriate to announce its judgment in an unpublished *per curiam* opinion." How important was it to the result here that this was a federal statute regulating broadcasting? Is the Court predisposed to validate federal statutes regulating broadcasting even against First Amendment challenges? If so, why?

PRIVATELY RUN LOTTERIES

Assuming that the lottery is lawful under state law, and that the state in which the broadcaster is licensed has not adopted any contrary lottery advertising legislation, broadcasters may advertise or promote many private lotteries. All lawful lotteries run by "not-for-profit organizations or by a governmental organization" can be promoted. When it comes to lawful lotteries run by for-profit organizations, the test is whether or not the "advertisement, list of prizes, or other information concerning a lottery, gift enterprise, or similar scheme is conducted as a promotional activity by a commercial organization and is clearly occasional and ancillary to the primary business of that organization." Pub. L. No. 100-625, § 2(a). This seems to mean that businesses can run occasional lotteries, if allowed by state law, and that broadcasters can promote the business and its lottery, unless the state adopts laws restricting lottery advertising or promotion. Depending on state law, broadcasters may also run station promotions or contests that are lotteries. Promotion of unlawful lotteries, however, remains illegal.

LOTTERIES RUN BY NATIVE AMERICANS

Another law adopted in 1988, the Indian Gaming Statute, immediately permitted most broadcasters to advertise most forms of gambling conducted on Indian reservations. The law is very complex. Sometimes Indian games can be advertised only after approval of a compact between the Indian tribe and the Secretary of Interior or after approval by a newly established National Indian Gaming Commission. Sometimes games run by contractors rather than by Indians themselves also may not be readily promoted. Broadcasters view this as potentially a very lucrative market, because gambling on Indian reservations is now a multibillion dollar activity.

CASINO GAMBLING

The law, 18 U.S.C. § 1304, prohibits broadcasts of radio and television advertisements for casino gambling. Even where such gambling is lawful (for example, in Nevada or in Atlantic City), it is still contrary to federal law to promote it. Ads can be run for hotels where "casino" is part of the full name of the hotel, but the ads cannot promote the casino aspect of the operation. Instead they can stress accommodations, food, general entertainment, or the like—anything but gambling.

A group of broadcasters in the New Orleans area unsuccessfully challenged sec. 1304's ban on broadcasting ads for casino gambling. Applying *Central Hudson,* the U.S. Court of Appeals for the Fifth Circuit held that the statute directly advanced two substantial governmental interests: (1) discouraging public participation in gambling and (2) enforcing state antigambling policies. *Greater New Orleans Broad. Assn v. United States,* 24 Media L. Rep. 1146, 69 F.3d 1296 (5th Cir. 1995). One of the broadcasters' arguments was that *Edge* precluded "the assertion of any substantial federal interest other than protecting state choice in gambling decisions." The court rejected this contention:

> [Edge] did not determine the limit of a valid federal governmental interest. *Edge* in no way suggests that the general prohibition on casino gambling was rendered doubtful by the Court's approval of a "state choice" advertising policy for state lotteries. *Edge* supports rather than impairs the constitutionality of section 1304.

Did it matter that other media may advertise casino gambling while sec. 1304 singles out broadcasters alone? It did not. Again the court of appeals relied on *Edge.* "'Nor do we require that the Government make progress on every front before it can make progress on any front.'"

Furthermore, the court of appeals observed that the "*Edge* 'state choice' policy embodies a compromise that supports states' promotion of their own lotteries." Congress could have undertaken a similar compromise with respect to casino gambling, but it chose not to do so. Congress was not constitutionally required to do otherwise.

The Role of the States Under 18 U.S.C. § 1304

One of the most interesting aspects of the 1988 revision of sec. 1304 is how much control it gives the states over broadcast content. Generally, broadcast content regulation was preempted by the federal government, mostly by the FCC, and the states have been prohibited from dealing with it. Here, however, states have substantial control. Broadcasters will have to become very familiar with the specific provisions of state law, something quite new for most of them.

PUBLIC BROADCASTING

The Public Broadcasting Act of 1967

A significant development in American radio and television was the Public Broadcasting Act of 1967, 47 U.S.C. §§ 390–399b. One of the broad purposes of the Public Broadcasting Act is to assist through matching grants in the construction of noncommercial educational television or radio broadcasting facilities. 47 U.S.C. § 391. But the truly novel aspect of the act is the provision for the creation of the Corporation for Public Broadcasting. Great Britain has long experience with a public network run by an independent board—the much praised British Broadcasting Corp. or BBC. Similarly, the Canadian Broadcasting Corp., (CBC), which is sponsored by the federal parliament of Canada, is an integral part of Canadian life. But an American effort in the direction of government-sponsored broadcasting is a relatively recent development. Indeed, whether the federal government can finance an instrument that will influence the opinion-making process is itself a First Amendment question.

"Objectivity" and "Balance" in Public Broadcasting

The Corporation for Public Broadcasting(CPB) is supposed to facilitate the development of high-quality programming for educational broadcasting with "strict adherence to objectivity and balance in all programs or series of programs of a controversial nature." See 47 U.S.C. § 396(g)(1)(A). Is the requirement that public broadcasting must be "balanced" and "objective" enforceable? This issue was presented for decision in *Accuracy In Media, Inc. v. FCC*, 521 F.2d 288 (D.C. Cir. 1975).

Accuracy In Media (AIM), a feisty conservative citizens' organization and a professional thorn in many a media side, filed a complaint against the Public Broadcasting System (PBS) before the FCC, charging that two programs distributed by PBS to member stations did not provide a balanced or objective presentation of a subject. In its complaint, AIM contended that PBS had violated the law in two respects. First, AIM charged that the PBS programs violated the fairness doctrine. (The FCC rejected this contention.) AIM's other contention involved the little-known provision of the Public Broadcasting Act that required the CPB to adhere to a standard of objectivity or balance in programming of a controversial nature, 47 U.S.C. § 396(g)(1)(A) (1970). AIM contended that the two offending programs (one dealing with sex education and the other with the American criminal justice system) violated the balance and objectivity requirement of the Public Broadcasting Act.

The provision of the Public Broadcasting Act that required "balance" and "objectivity" authorizes the CPB to "facilitate the full development of educational television." The CPB's mandate is to obtain programs of "high quality from diverse sources" and to make them available to noncommercial broadcasters. This provision of the Act concludes that these responsibilities are to be accomplished "with strict adherence to objectivity and balance in all programs or series of programs of a controversial nature."

AIM argued that since the PBS programs it objected to were funded by the CPB, pursuant to this authorization, the programs were subject to the requirement of "strict adherence to objectivity and balance"—a requirement that AIM contended was "more stringent than the standard of balance and fairness in overall programming contained in the fairness doctrine."

If CPB programming must be balanced and objective, how does such a requirement differ from the fairness doctrine? AIM argued that there were two differences. With respect to the "balance" requirement, AIM argued that broadcasters must achieve a balanced presentation of the issues in each program. Balanced discussion in a broadcaster's overall programming, as suggested by the fairness doctrine, would not suffice. With respect to "objectivity" requirements, AIM contended that the FCC would have to conduct a "more searching inquiry into alleged factual inaccuracies than contemplated by the fairness doctrine."

The FCC refused to rule on the correctness of AIM's interpretation of the "balance and objectivity" standard in the Public Broadcasting Act because in its view it had no jurisdiction to enforce the Act. AIM then sought review in the D.C. Circuit. The federal court, per Judge Bazelon, a spokesman for the new liberal unease with the fairness doctrine, agreed with the FCC and not with AIM.

The D.C. Circuit's conclusion that the FCC had no jurisdiction to enforce the "balance and objectivity" standard was based on sec. 398 of the Public Broadcasting Act, which provides that no "agency . . . of the United States" should have authority to supervise or control the CPB. The court reasoned that because the FCC was an "agency of the United States," it could not "supervise" the CPB. Nevertheless, as Judge Bazelon conceded, the matter was hardly free from doubt. Another provision of the Public Broadcasting Act, sec. 399, mandates "supervision" of noncommercial licenses and contemplates FCC enforcement.

Judge Bazelon, however, made it clear that nothing in sec. 398 of the Communications Act served to limit FCC authority—"including the Fairness Doctrine"—over local noncommercial licensees. "While § 398 prohibits FCC jurisdiction over CPB and its program related activities, i.e., production, funding or distribution, the commission retains its authority concerning the broadcasting of programs, whether funded by CPB or not." Noncommercial licensees, therefore, were subject to FCC jurisdiction including

programming policies like the fairness doctrine. But the FCC could not enforce the objectivity and balance requirement imposed on the CPB by the Public Broadcasting Act.

The implication from the legislative history materials gathered by Judge Bazelon in his decision for the court of appeals is that permitting FCC supervision of the programming product of PBS would result in precisely that governmental supervision that Congress had desired to prevent.

If the FCC had no jurisdiction or authority to enforce the balance and objectivity requirement of the Public Broadcasting Act, who did? AIM argued that if the FCC was removed from enforcing the standard, then Congress's specific statutory directive was rendered meaningless. Judge Bazelon disagreed. The congressional appropriations process was the means designed to safeguard against "partisan abuse." As Bazelon put it: "Ultimately, Congress may show its disapproval of any activity of the Corporation [for Public Broadcasting] through the appropriations process."

Thus, AIM lost its effort to secure a judicial ruling that the FCC had a duty to enforce the objectivity and balance requirement of the Public Broadcasting Act. The court not only held that the FCC did not have jurisdiction to enforce the requirement, but went beyond the FCC's determination of no jurisdiction to in effect repeal the specific congressional directive that there be objectivity and balance in CPB programming. "The corporation is not required to provide programs with 'strict adherence to objectivity and balance' but rather to 'facilitate the full development of educational broadcasting in which programs will be made available.' We leave the interpretation of this hortatory language to the directors of the corporation and to Congress in its supervisory capacity."

The State in the Editor's Chair: Problems of Access in Public Broadcasting

Muir v. Alabama Educ. Television Comm'n, 688 F.2d 1033 (5th Cir. 1982), presented the access issue in the context of public broadcasting. The Alabama Educational Television Commission (AETC), a network of nine noncommercial educational television stations, is funded from state legislative appropriations, matching federal grants through the CPB, and private contributions.

On May 12, 1980, at 8:00 P.M., AETC was scheduled to broadcast "Death of a Princess," a dramatization of the public execution of a Saudi Arabian princess and her lover, who were executed for adultery in 1977. The announcement of the planned broadcast aroused protests for fear that its showing would jeopardize the physical security of Alabamians working in the Middle East. Two days prior to the planned broadcast, AETC announced that it would not air the film.

Residents of Alabama who had planned to watch the show filed suit in the federal district court under 42 U.S.C. § 1983 and the First and Fourteenth Amendments to compel AETC to broadcast the film and to enjoin it from making "political" program decisions. The district court refused to order AETC to broadcast the program and granted summary judgment for AETC. A panel of the U.S. Court of Appeals for the Fifth Circuit affirmed the decision of the district court.

In Texas, a federal district court reacted affirmatively to a viewer's request that KUHT-TV, a noncommercial broadcast station, owned and operated by the University of Houston, which had scheduled "Death of a Princess" but then canceled it, be compelled to show it. The federal district court held that KUHT-TV was a "public forum" and that the station could not deny access to speakers without meeting the strict scrutiny by which prior restraints are traditionally reversed. See *Barnstone v. University of Houston*, 487 F. Supp. 1347 (S.D. Tex. 1980). In the Houston case, the district judge said that the decision to cancel "Death of a Princess" was made by Patrick Nicholson, Vice President of University Relations for the University of Houston: "It was the government, the University of Houston, which decided not to program 'The Death of a Princess.' When the government gets involved in broadcasting, it has an obligation, at a minimum, to establish procedures that assure that programming decisions are not based on the political beliefs of its programmers and are not made arbitrarily and without due process of law."

In *Barnstone v. University of Houston*, 7 Media L. Rep. 2185, 660 F.2d 137 (5th Cir. 1981), *cert. denied*, 103 S. Ct. 1274 (1983), a Fifth Circuit panel reversed the federal district court on the basis of the earlier panel decision in *Muir v. Alabama Educational Television Commission*, 7 Media L. Rep. 1933, 656 F.2d 1012 (5th Cir. 1981). The Fifth Circuit directed that

the panel decisions in *Muir* and *Barnstone* be consolidated and reheard *en banc*. The Fifth Circuit in its *en banc* decision affirmed the judgment of the Alabama federal district court in *Muir* and reversed the decision of the Texas federal district court in *Barnstone*.

Do individual members of the public have a First Amendment right to compel public television stations "to broadcast a previously scheduled program which the licensees have decided to cancel"? In its *en banc* opinion in *Muir v. Alabama Educ. Television Comm'n*, 8 Media L. Rep. 2305, 688 F.2d 1033 (5th Cir. 1982), *cert. denied*, 103 S. Ct. 1274 (1983), the Fifth Circuit answered "No" to this question. The First Amendment protects private rather than government expression: "To find that the government is without First Amendment protection is not to find that the government is prohibited from speaking or that private individuals have the right to limit or control the expression of government."

The Fifth Circuit decision in *Muir* may serve as a kind of Magna Carta of the rights of public broadcasting:

> Under the existing statutes public licensees such as AETC and the University of Houston possess the same rights and obligations to make free programming decisions as their private counterparts; however, as state instrumentalities, these public licensees are without the protection of the First Amendment. This lack of constitutional protection implies only that government could possibly impose restrictions on these licensees which it could not impose on private licensees. The lack of First Amendment protection does not result in the lessening of any of the statutory rights and duties held by the public licensees. It also does not result in individual viewers gaining any greater right to influence the programming discretion of the public licensees.

An issue that continually arose in the "Death of a Princess" litigation was whether public television stations were "public forums." If public television stations were public forums, then, presumably, individual viewers could appropriately argue that they had a right of access to compel the broadcast of a program that was scheduled and then canceled.

The *en banc* decision of the court in *Muir* offered the following reasons for its conclusion that public television stations are *not* public forums:

In the cases in which a public facility has been deemed a public forum the speakers have been found to have a right of access because they were attempting to use the facility in a manner fully consistent with the "pattern of usual activity" and "the general invitation extended." The pattern of usual activity for public television stations is the statutorily mandated practice of the broadcast licensee exercising sole programming authority. The invitation extended to the public is not to schedule programs, but to watch or decline to watch what is offered. It is thus clear that the public television stations involved in the cases before us are not public forums. The plaintiffs have no right of access to compel the broadcast of any particular program.

The court of appeals in *Muir* also specifically rejected the public access argument of the plaintiffs. According to this argument, even if a public right of access were denied on the theory that public television stations are not public forums, the action of the public television stations in the "Death of a Princess" litigation was impermissible on the ground that public television stations could not "make programming decisions based on the communicative impact of a program."

Another issue that was resolved by the *en banc* decision of the court of appeals in *Muir* was whether the decision to cancel "Death of a Princess" by the public television stations should be deemed to constitute government censorship. The court found that it should not and drew distinction between state regulation of private expression and "the exercise of editorial discretion by state officials responsible for the operation of public television stations." Judge Hill, for the court in *Muir*, summarized the *en banc* court's reasons as follows:

Had the states of Alabama and Texas sought to prohibit the exhibition of the film by another party then indeed a question of censorship would have arisen. Such is not the case before us. The states have not sought to forbid or curtail the right of any person to show or view the film. In fact plaintiff Barnstone has already viewed the film at an exhibition at Rice University in Houston. The state officials in charge of AETC and KUHT TV have simply exercised their statutorily mandated discretion and decided not to show a particular program at a particular time. There is a clear distinction between a state's exercise of editorial discretion over its own expression, and a state's prohibition or suppression of the speech of another.

Judge Rubin concurred, joined by three other judges who participated in the *en banc* review of *Muir*, pointing out that the government was involved in the publication of a variety of informational media. Content neutrality was not necessarily required in the operation of these media.

The function of a state agency operating an informational medium is significant in determining first amendment restrictions on its actions. State agencies publish alumni bulletins, newsletters devoted to better farming practices, and law reviews; they operate or subsidize art museums and theater companies and student newspapers. The federal government operates the Voice of America and Radio Free Europe and Radio Liberty, publishes "journals, magazines, periodicals, and similar publications" that are "necessary in the transaction of the public business," including newspapers for branches of the Armed Forces, and pays the salaries of many federal officials who, like the President's press secretary, communicate with the public through the media. The first amendment does not dictate that what will be said or performed or published or broadcast in these activities will be entirely content neutral. In those activities that, like television broadcasting to the general public, depend in part on audience interest, appraisal of audience interest and suitability for publication or broadcast inevitably involves judgment of content.

Judge Frank Johnson, joined by four other judges, dissented from the *en banc* decision in *Muir*. The question as he saw it was this: Can executive officers of a state-operated public television station cancel a previously scheduled program because it presents a point of view disagreeable to the religious and political regime of a foreign country? Judge Johnson's answer was in the negative. He advocated a strict standard of review for programming decisions such as those involved in the cancellation of "Death of a Princess":

Once the plaintiff demonstrates that the government has silenced a message because of its substantive content, the government's decision becomes presumptively unconstitutional. The government should then be allowed to demonstrate that it would have taken the same action on the basis of legitimate reasons. Finally, the plaintiff should be given a full opportunity to refute the government's assertion.

COMMENT

Muir and *Barnstone* are not equivalent situations. In *Muir*, the editorial judgment of a broadcast journalist was the source of the decision to cancel. Broadcast journalists were the decision makers in *Muir*, and their exercise of editorial judgment was upheld. But the decision to cancel in *Barnstone* was a governmental and politically inspired judgment made by a university official, not a journalist.

The Fifth Circuit saw the "Death of a Princess" case as a conflict of First Amendment rights—freedom of the press versus freedom of speech and the derivative right to hear. The plaintiffs contended that the decision to cancel could not be viewed the same way as a decision to cancel a program by a private broadcaster. The presence of the state government as a sponsor and as a source of funds in part for AETC was said to have transformed AETC's programming decisions into "governmental action" and "governmental censorship." Judge Markey, author of the Fifth Circuit panel decision in *Muir*, disagreed. See *Muir v. AETC*, 656 F.2d 1012 (5th Cir. 1981). "The application of constitutional principles cannot, however, be controlled by the bare and barren fact that government plays some role."

Judge Markey was unimpressed with the argument that government funding of public broadcasting should provide the public with greater rights of participation in editorial decision making:

> Hence, if government ownership and partial funding alone be synonymous with government censorship of program content, government ownership and funding would doubtless have to cease. If initial rejection of some programs were considered a form of constitutionally forbidden censorship, every public television station would violate the Constitution with virtually every choice it made. It would demean the First Amendment to find that it required a public referendum on every programming decision made every day by every public television station solely because the station is "owned" and partially funded by a state government.

Judge Markey saw no difference between a decision canceling a scheduled broadcast and the initial scheduling decision as far as judicial oversight was concerned. Both suffered from the same infirmity. The use of court injunctions in either situation would destroy editorial freedom as well as involve excessive government entanglement in the editorial process.

What if there had been proof that the government sought to propagandize? The implication in the panel decision in *Muir* is that evidence of government intent to propagandize in editorial decision making would have made a difference and would be impermissible. Here then is a difference in the editorial freedom of a public broadcaster as compared to that of a private broadcaster. If private broadcasters cancel a television show out of a desire to propagandize, presumably the First Amendment is not violated although arguably some aspect of FCC law might be violated. But if a public broadcaster cancels a show out of a desire to propagandize, then presumably the First Amendment is violated. Government cannot mandate a point of view. This would be impermissible "compelled speech." See *Wooley v. Maynard*, 430 U.S. 705 (1977), text, p. 31.

Aldrich v. Knab, 858 F. Supp. 1480 (W.D. Wash.), *rev'd on other grounds*, 36 F.3d 1102 (9th Cir. 1994), addressed a challenge by volunteers of the University of Washington's radio station, KCMU, to the station's policy of banning all criticism of the university or the station. KCMU's policy prohibited criticism on the air or anytime an employee was acting in an official capacity. Several of the employees criticized the station in letters, e-mails, welcoming remarks at a concert, and in broadcasts. The employees were subsequently terminated and filed suit claiming that KCMU's policy was state action that suppressed their First Amendment rights to engage in free speech.

The *Aldrich* court used a "public forum" analysis to determine whether a state-owned broadcast station was entitled to ban certain speech. The court rejected the arguments that the station was a traditional public forum or a public area "which the state has opened for use by the public as a place for expressive activity." However, the court did note that KCMU had broad discretion to regulate speech but could not do so "based solely on the content of the speech:":

> Public property that is not a public forum may be reserved by the state "for its intended purposes, communicative or otherwise, as long as the

regulation on speech is reasonable and not an effort to suppress expression merely because public officials oppose the speaker's view." *Perry*, 460 U.S. at 46. "Although a speaker may be excluded from a nonpublic forum if he wishes to address a topic not encompassed within the purpose of the forum . . . or if he is not a member of the class of speakers for whose special benefit the forum was created . . . the government violates the First Amendment when it denies access to a speaker solely to suppress the point of view he espouses on an otherwise includible subject. *Lamb's Chapel v. Center Moriches Union Free Sch. Dist.*, 113 S. Ct. 2141, 2147 (1993).

The *Aldrich* court held that KCMU's policy was content-based suppression of speech and therefore was unconstitutional. The court stated that the station sought only to exclude speech that was critical of the university and KCMU. In addition, the station sought to limit not only on-air speech but off-air speech as well.

May Public Broadcasters Editorialize?

Commercial broadcasters may editorialize. See *Mayflower Broad. Corp.*, 8 F.C.C. 333 (1941); *Report on Editorializing by Broad. Licensees*, 13 F.C.C. 1246 (1949). The Public Broadcasting Act of 1967 did not give this opportunity to noncommercial broadcasters, however. Section 399 of the Public Broadcasting Act of 1967 was amended in 1981 to state the prohibition on editorializing as follows: "No noncommercial educational broadcasting station which receives a grant from the Corporation for Public Broadcasting under sub-part C of this part may engage in editorializing. No noncommercial educational broadcasting station may support or oppose any candidate for public office."

The constitutionality of an earlier version of this ban on editorializing was challenged by Pacifica Foundation, which owns and operates several noncommercial broadcasting stations in five metropolitan areas in the United States. The League of Women Voters of California and Congressman Henry Waxman, a regular listener and viewer of public broadcasting, joined in the Pacifica suit.

When the statute was amended as set forth above, Pacifica and the other challengers amended their complaint and continued their suit attacking the constitutionality of the ban. The federal district court held that sec. 399's ban

on editorializing was a violation of the First Amendment. The government appealed to the U.S. Supreme Court. The Court, per Justice Brennan, affirmed the district court and ruled that the no-editorializing ban of sec. 399 was unconstitutional. This marked the first time the Supreme Court had declared a federal statute dealing with broadcasting unconstitutional. The Court did not rule on the no-political-endorsement sentence in sec. 399 because that provision was not challenged.

FCC v. League of Women Voters
468 U.S. 364, 104 S. CT. 3106, 82 L. ED. 2d 278 (1984).

Justice BRENNAN delivered the opinion of the Court.

[A]lthough the broadcasting industry plainly operates under restraints not imposed upon other media, the thrust of these restrictions has generally been to secure the public's First Amendment interest in receiving a balanced presentation of views on diverse matters of public concern. As a result of these restrictions, of course, the absolute freedom to advocate one's own positions without also presenting opposing viewpoints—a freedom enjoyed, for example, by newspaper publishers and soapbox operators—is denied to broadcasters. But, as our cases attest, these restrictions have been upheld only when we were satisfied that the restriction is narrowly tailored to further a substantial governmental interest, such as ensuring adequate and balanced coverage of public issues, *e.g., Red Lion*. See also *Columbia Broadcasting System, Inc. v. FCC; Columbia Broadcasting System, Inc. v. Democratic National Committee, supra; Red Lion*. Making that judgment requires a critical examination of the interests of the public and broadcasters in light of the particular circumstances of each case.

We turn now to consider whether the restraint imposed by § 399 satisfies the requirements established by our prior cases for permissible broadcast regulation. Before assessing the government's proffered justifications for the statute, however, two central features of the ban against editorializing must be examined, since they help to illuminate the importance of the First Amendment interests at stake in this case.

First, the restriction imposed by § 399 is specifically directed at a form of speech—

namely, the expression of editorial opinion—that lies at the heart of the First Amendment protection. In construing the reach of the statute, the FCC has explained that "although the use of noncommercial educational broadcast facilities by licensees, their management or those speaking on their behalf for the propagation of the licensee's own views on public issues is not permitted, such prohibition should not be construed to inhibit any *other* presentations on controversial issues of public importance." *In re Complaint of Accuracy in Media, Inc.,* 45 F.C.C.2d 297, 302 (1973) (emphasis added). The Commission's interpretation of § 399 simply highlights the fact that what the statute forecloses is the expression of editorial opinion on "controversial issues of public importance." Indeed, the pivotal importance of editorializing as a means of satisfying the public's interest in receiving a wide variety of ideas and views through the medium of broadcasting has long been recognized by the FCC; the FCC has for the past 35 years actively encouraged commercial broadcast licensees to include editorials on public affairs in their programming. Because § 399 appears to restrict precisely that form of speech which the Framers of the Bill of Rights were most anxious to protect—speech that is "indispensable to the discovery and spread of political truth"—we must be especially careful in weighing the interests that are asserted in support of this restriction and in assessing the precision with which the ban is crafted. *Whitney v. California,* 274 U.S. 357, 375 (1927) (Brandeis, J., concurring).

Second, the scope of § 399's ban is defined solely on the basis of the content of the suppressed speech. A wide variety of non-editorial speech "by licensees, their management or those speaking on their behalf," *In re Complaint of Accuracy in Media , Inc., supra,* 45 F.C.C.2d, at 302, is plainly not prohibited by § 399. Examples of such permissible forms of speech include daily announcements of the station's program schedule or over-the-air appeals for contributions from listeners. Consequently, in order to determine whether a particular statement by station management constitutes an "editorial" proscribed by § 399, enforcement authorities must necessarily examine the content of the message that is conveyed to determine whether the views expressed concern "controversial issues of public importance."

As Justice Stevens observed in *Consolidated Edison Co. v. Public Service Commission,* 447 U.S. 530 (1980), however, "[a] regulation of speech that is motivated by nothing more than a desire to curtail expression of a particular point of view on controversial issues of general interest is the purest example of a 'law * * * abridging the freedom of speech, or of the press.' A regulation that denies one group of persons the right to address a selected audience on 'controversial issues of public policy' is plainly such a regulation." (concurring opinion). Section 399 is just such a regulation, for it singles out noncommercial broadcasters and denies them the right to address their chosen audience on matters of public importance. Thus, in enacting § 399 Congress appears to have sought, in much the same way that the New York Public Service Commission had attempted through the regulation of utility company bill inserts struck down in *Consolidated Edison,* to limit discussion of controversial topics and thus to shape the agenda for public debate. Since, as we observed in *Consolidated Edison,* "[t]he First Amendment's hostility to content-based regulation extends not only to restrictions on particular viewpoints, but also to prohibition of an entire topic," we must be particularly wary in assessing Sec. 399 to determine whether it reflects an impermissible attempt "to allow the government [to] control the search for political truth."

In seeking to defend the prohibition on editorializing imposed by § 399, the Government urges that the statute was aimed at preventing two principal threats to the overall success of the Public Broadcasting Act of 1967. According to this argument, the ban was necessary, first, to protect noncommercial educational broadcasting stations from being coerced, as a result of federal financing, into becoming vehicles for government propagandizing or the objects of governmental influence; and, second, to keep these stations from becoming convenient targets for capture by private interest groups wishing to express their own partisan viewpoints. By seeking to safeguard the public's right to a balanced presentation of public issues through the prevention of either governmental or private bias, these objectives are, of course, broadly consistent with the goals identified in our earlier broadcast regulation cases. But, in sharp contrast to the restrictions upheld in *Red Lion* or in *CBS, Inc. v. FCC,* which left room for editorial discretion and simply required broadcast editors to grant others access to the microphone, § 399 directly prohibits the broadcaster from speaking out on public issues even in a balanced and fair manner. The Government insists, however, that the hazards posed in the "special" circumstances of noncommercial educational broadcasting are so great that § 399 is an indispensable means of preserving the public's First Amendment interests. We disagree.

When Congress first decided to provide financial support for the expansion and development of noncommercial educational stations, all concerned agreed that this step posed some risk that these traditionally independent stations might be pressured into becoming forums devoted solely to programming and views that were acceptable to the Federal government. That Congress was alert to these dangers cannot be doubted. It sought through the Public Broadcasting Act to fashion a system that would provide local stations with sufficient funds to foster their growth and development while preserving their tradition of autonomy and community-orientation.

More importantly, an examination of both the overall legislative scheme established by the 1967 Act and the character of public broadcasting demonstrates that the interest asserted by the Government is not substantially advanced by § 399. First, to the extent that federal financial support creates a risk that stations will lose their independence through the bewitching power of governmental largesse, the elaborate structure established by the Public Broadcasting Act already operates to insulate local stations from governmental interference. Congress not only mandated that the new Corporation for Public Broadcasting would have a private, bipartisan structure, see §§ 396(c)–(f), but also imposed a variety of important limitations on its powers. The Corporation was prohibited from owning or operating any station, § 396(g)(3), it was required to adhere strictly to a standard of "objectivity and balance" in disbursing federal funds to local stations, § 396(g)(1)(A), and it was prohibited from contributing to or otherwise supporting any candidate for office, § 396(f)(3).

The Act also established a second layer of protections which serve to protect the stations from governmental coercion and interference. Thus, in addition to requiring the Corporation to operate

so as to "assure the maximum freedom [of local stations] from interference with or control of program content or other activities," § 396(g)(1)(D), the Act expressly forbids "any department, agency, officer, or employee of the United States [from] exercis[ing] any direction, supervision, or control over educational television or radio broadcasting, or over the Corporation or any of its grantees or contractors," § 398(a). The principal thrust therefore, has been to assure long-term appropriations for the Corporation and, more importantly, to insist that it pass specified portions of these funds directly through to local stations to give them greater autonomy in defining the uses to which those funds should be put. Thus, in sharp contrast to § 399, the unifying theme of these various statutory provisions is that they substantially reduce the risk of governmental interference with the editorial judgments of local stations without restricting those stations' ability to speak on matters of public concern.

Even if these statutory protections were thought insufficient to the task, however, suppressing the particular category of speech restricted by § 399 is simply not likely, given the character of the public broadcasting system, to reduce substantially the risk that the Federal Government will seek to influence or put pressure on local stations. An underlying supposition of the Government's argument in this regard is that individual noncommercial stations are likely to speak so forcefully on particular issues that Congress, the ultimate source of the stations' Federal funding, will be tempted to retaliate against these individual stations by restricting appropriations for all of public broadcasting. But, as the District Court recognized, the character of public broadcasting suggests that such a risk is speculative at best. There are literally hundreds of public radio and television stations in communities scattered throughout the United States and its territories. Given that central fact, it seems reasonable to infer that the editorial voices of these stations will prove to be as distinctive, varied, and idiosyncratic as the various communities they represent. More importantly, the editorial focus of any particular station can fairly be expected to focus largely on issues affecting only its community. Accordingly, absent some showing by the Government to the contrary, the risk that local editorializing will place all of public broadcasting in jeopardy is not sufficiently pressing to warrant § 399's broad suppression of speech.

Indeed, what is far more likely than local station editorials to pose the kinds of dangers hypothesized by the Government are the wide variety of programs addressing controversial issues produced, often with substantial CPB funding, for national distribution to local stations. Such programs truly have the potential to reach a large audience and, because of the critical commentary they contain, to have the kind of genuine national impact that might trigger a congressional response or kindle governmental resentment. The ban imposed by § 399, however, is plainly not directed at the potentially controversial content of such programs; it is, instead, leveled solely at the expression of editorial opinion by local station management, a form of expression that is far more likely to be aimed at a smaller local audience, to have less national impact, and to be confined to local issues. In contrast, the Act imposes no substantive restrictions, other than normal requirements of balance and fairness, on those who produce nationally distributed programs. Indeed, the Act is designed in part to encourage and sponsor the production of such programs and to allow each station to decide for itself whether to accept such programs for local broadcast.

Furthermore, the manifest imprecision of the ban imposed by § 399 reveals that its proscription is not sufficiently tailored to the harms it seeks to prevent to justify its substantial interference with broadcasters' speech. Section 399 includes within its grip a potentially infinite variety of speech, most of which would not be related in any way to governmental affairs, political candidacies or elections. Indeed, the breadth of editorial commentary is as wide as human imagination permits. But the Government never explains how, say, an editorial by local station management urging improvements in a town's parks or museums will so infuriate Congress or other Federal officials that the future of public broadcasting will be imperiled unless such editorials are suppressed. Nor is it explained how the suppression of editorials alone serves to reduce the risk of governmental retaliation and interference when it is clear that station management is fully able to broadcast controversial views so long as such views are not labeled as its own.

The Government appears to recognize these flaws in § 399, because it focuses instead on the suggestion that the source of governmental influence may well be state and local governments, many of which have established public broadcasting commissions that own and operate local noncommercial educational stations. The ban on editorializing is all the more necessary with respect to these stations, the argument runs, because the management of such stations will be especially likely to broadcast only editorials that are favorable to the state or local authorities that hold the purse strings. The Government's argument, however, proves too much. First, § 399's ban applies to the many private noncommercial community organizations that own and operate stations that are not controlled in any way by state or local government. Second, the legislative history of the Public Broadcasting Act clearly indicates that Congress was concerned with "assur[ing] complete freedom from any *Federal Government influence.*"

Finally, although the Government certainly has a substantial interest in ensuring that the audiences of noncommercial stations will not be led to think that the broadcaster's editorials reflect the official view of the government, this interest can be fully satisfied by less restrictive means that are readily available. To address this important concern, Congress could simply require public broadcasting stations to broadcast a disclaimer every time they editorialize which would state that the editorial represents only the view of the station's management and does not in any way represent the views of the Federal Government or any of the station's other sources of funding. Such a disclaimer—similar to those often used in commercial and noncommercial programming of a controversial nature—would effectively and directly communicate to the audience that the editorial reflected only the views of the station rather than those of the government.

In sum, § 399's broad ban on all editorializing by every station that receives CPB funds far exceeds what is necessary to protect against the risk of governmental interference or to prevent the public from assuming that editorials by public broadcasting stations represent the official view of government. The regulation impermissibly sweeps within its prohibition a wide range of speech by wholly private stations on topics that do not take a directly partisan stand or that have nothing whatever to do with federal, state or local government.

Assuming that the Government's second asserted interest in preventing noncommercial stations from becoming a "privileged outlet for the political and ideological opinions of station owners and management" is legitimate, the substantiality of this asserted interest is dubious. The patent over and underinclusiveness of § 399's ban "undermines the likelihood of a genuine [governmental] interest" in preventing private groups from propagating their own views via public broadcasting. *First National Bank of Boston v. Belloti.* If it is true, as the government contends, that noncommercial stations remain free, despite § 399, to broadcast a wide variety of controversial views through their power to control program selection, to select which persons will be interviewed, and to determine how news reports will be presented, then it seems doubtful that § 399 can fairly be said to advance any genuinely substantial governmental interest in keeping controversial or partisan opinions from being aired by noncommercial stations.

In short, § 399 does not prevent the use of noncommercial stations for the presentation of partisan views on controversial matters; instead, it merely bars a station from specifically communicating such views on its own behalf or on behalf of its management. If the vigorous expression of controversial opinions is, as the Government assures us, affirmatively encouraged by the Act, and if local licensees are permitted under the Act to exercise editorial control over the selection of programs, controversial or otherwise, that are aired on their stations, then § 399 accomplishes only one thing—the suppression of editorial speech by station management. It does virtually nothing, however, to reduce the risk that public stations will serve solely as outlets for expression of narrow partisan views. What we said in *CBS, Inc. v. Democratic National Committee,* applies, therefore, with equal force here: the "sacrifice [of] First Amendment protections for so speculative a gain is not warranted." 412 U.S. at 127.

Finally, the public's interest in preventing public broadcasting stations from becoming forums for lopsided presentations of narrow partisan positions is already secured by a variety of other regulatory means that intrude far less drastically upon the "journalistic freedom" of noncommer-

cial broadcasters. *CBS, Inc. v. Democratic National Committee, supra,* at 110. The requirements of the FCC's fairness doctrine, for instance, which apply to commercial and noncommercial stations alike, ensure that such editorializing would maintain a reasonably balanced and fair presentation of controversial issues. Thus, even if the management of a noncommercial educational station were inclined to seek to further only its own partisan views when editorializing, it simply could not do so. Since the breadth of § 399 extends so far beyond what is necessary to accomplish the goals identified by the Government, it fails to satisfy the First Amendment standards that we have applied in this area.

We therefore hold that even if some of the hazards at which § 399 was aimed are sufficiently substantial, the restriction is not crafted with sufficient precision to remedy those dangers that may exist to justify the significant abridgement of speech worked by the provision's broad ban on editorializing. The statute is not narrowly tailored to address any of the government's suggested goals. Moreover, the public's "paramount right" to be fully and broadly informed on matters of public importance through the medium of noncommercial educational broadcasting is not well served by the restriction, for its effect is plainly to diminish rather than augment "the volume and quality of coverage" of controversial issues. *Red Lion, supra,* at 393. Nor do we see any reason to deny noncommercial broadcasters the right to address matters of public concern on the basis of merely speculative fears of adverse public or governmental reactions to such speech.

In conclusion, we emphasize that our disposition of this case rests upon a narrow proposition. We do not hold that the Congress or the FCC are without power to regulate the content, timing, or character of speech by noncommercial educational broadcasting stations. Rather, we hold only that the specific interests sought to be advanced by § 399's ban on editorializing are either not sufficiently substantial or are not served in a sufficiently limited manner to justify the substantial abridgement of important journalistic freedoms which the First Amendment jealously protects. Accordingly, the judgment of the District Court is affirmed.

Justice REHNQUIST, with whom the Chief Justice and Justice White join, dissenting.

All but three paragraphs of the Court's lengthy opinion in this case are devoted to the development of a scenario in which the government appears as the "Big Bad Wolf," and appellee Pacifica as "Little Red Riding Hood." In the Court's scenario the Big Bad Wolf cruelly forbids Little Red Riding Hood from taking to her grandmother some of the food that she is carrying in her basket. Only three paragraphs are used to delineate a truer picture of the litigants, wherein it appears that some of the food in the basket was given to Little Red Riding Hood by the Big Bad Wolf himself, and that the Big Bad Wolf had told Little Red Riding Hood in advance that if she accepted his food she would have to abide by his conditions. Congress in enacting § 399 of the Public Broadcasting Act, 47 U.S.C. § 399 (Supp. V), has simply determined that public funds shall not be used to subsidize noncommercial, educational broadcasting stations which engage in "editorializing" or which support or oppose any political candidate. I do not believe that anything in the First Amendment to the United States Constitution prevents Congress from choosing to spend public monies in that manner. Perhaps a more appropriate analogy than that of Little Red Riding Hood and the Big Bad Wolf is that of Faust and Mephistopheles; Pacifica, well aware of § 399's condition on its receipt of public money, nonetheless accepted the public money and now seeks to avoid the conditions which Congress legitimately has attached to receipt of that funding.

The Court's three-paragraph discussion of why § 399, repeatedly reexamined and retained by Congress, violates the First Amendment is to me utterly unpersuasive. Congress has rationally determined that the bulk of the taxpayers whose monies provide the funds for grants by the CPB would prefer not to see the management of local educational stations promulgate its own private views on the air at taxpayer expense. Accordingly Congress simply has decided not to subsidize stations which engage in that activity.

The Court seems to believe that Congress actually subsidizes editorializing only if a station uses federal money specifically as editorializing expenses. But to me the Court's approach ignores economic reality. CPB's unrestricted grants are used for salaries, training, equipment, promotion, etc.—financial expenditures which benefit all aspects of a station's programming, including management's editorials. Given the impossibility of compartmentalizing programming expenses in any meaningful way, it seems clear to me that the only effective means for preventing the use of public monies to subsidize the airing of management's views is for Congress to ban a subsidized station from all on-the-air editorializing.

Here, in my view, Congress has rationally concluded that the bulk of taxpayers whose monies provide the funds for grants by the CPB would prefer not to see the management of public stations engage in editorializing or the endorsing or opposing of political candidates. Because Congress' decision to enact § 399 is a rational exercise of its spending powers and strictly neutral, I would hold that nothing in the First Amendment makes it unconstitutional. Accordingly, I would reverse the judgment of the District Court.

COMMENT

In dissent, Justice Stevens objected to considering the validity of the no-editorializing rule ban in sec. 399 without also considering the no-political-endorsement ban. Justice Stevens believed that sec. 399 was designed to keep the "Federal Government out of the propaganda arena." Congressional concern that the financial assistance it gave to public broadcasting might be used to fund government propaganda merited greater weight than it received:

> The court jester who mocks the King must choose his words with great care. An artist is likely to paint a flattering portrait of his patron. By enacting the statutory provision that the Court invalidates today, a sophisticated group of legislators expressed a concern about the potential impact of government funds on pervasive and powerful organs of mass communication. One need not have heard the raucous voice of Adolph Hitler over Radio Berlin to appreciate the importance of that concern.
>
> [T]he statutory prohibitions against editorializing and candidate endorsements rest on the same foundation. In my opinion that foundation is far stronger than merely "a rational basis" and it is not weakened by the fact that it is buttressed by other provisions that are also designed to avoid the insidious evils of propaganda favoring particular points of view. The quality of the interest in maintaining government neutrality in the free market of ideas—of avoiding subtle forms of censorship and propaganda—out-weigh the impact on expression that results from this statute.

One scholar, writing just before *League of Women Voters,* addressed the general problem of government-sponsored expression as well as the subject of public broadcasting. See Yudof, *When Government Speaks: Politics, Law and Government Expression in America* (1983). Professor Yudof believes that public broadcasting has escaped from government influence: "Ironically, the very localism advocated by the Nixon Administration [in public broadcasting] became the vehicle by which government attempts to influence programming were blunted."

Professor Yudof argues that the charge that "public broadcasting is a propaganda arm of the federal government is simply unfounded." Cultural elitism, however is a more serious charge. In this view, public broadcasting has been geared to the programming tastes of the cultured upper class rather than the programming needs of minorities or the poor. The solution? Professor Yudof suggests affirmative action by government:

> (W)hat of the obligation of government to expand the potential for choice by informing, teaching and leading? From this perspective, Congress could sensibly require that its funds be utilized to cover political conventions, to broadcast legislative hearings, to investigate and air controversial political matters, and to produce documentaries and other shows on the economy, on the adequacy of service delivery by government, and on world crises.

But would implementation of some of these proposals violate the strictures set forth in *League of Women Voters?* If so, how?

Comparative Standards for New Noncommercial Educational Applicants

On March 17, 1995, the FCC issued a Notice of Proposed Rulemaking (NPRM) seeking comments about criteria to be used in comparative hearings for evaluating applicants for *new,* mutually exclusive, noncommercial educational broadcast licenses. *Notice of Proposed Rulemaking, In re Reexamination of the Comparative Standards for New Noncommercial Educational Applicants,* 10 F.C.C.R. 2877 (1995) *(Reexamination NPRM).* The FCC declared that it was considering only criteria for new licenses and not the standards used in resolving applications filed against license renewals. The commission had also been considering new renewal standards.

See *Formulation of Rules and Policies Relating to Broadcast Renewal Applicants,* 4 F.C.C.R. 6363, 4 F.C.C.R. 4780 (1989), 3 F.C.C.R. 5179 (1988). Those proceedings have been mooted, however, because comparative hearings for all renewal applications, whether commercial or noncommercial, have been prohibited by sec. 309(k) of the Telecommunications Act of 1996, Pub. L. No. 104-104, 110 Stat. 56.

In a previous NPRM, the FCC stated that applicants for noncommercial stations were evaluated as to "the extent to which each of the proposed operations will be 'integrated into the overall operations and objectives' of the respective applicants." *NPRM in re Policy Statement on Comparative Broadcast Hearings (Policy Statement),* 7 F.C.C.R. 2664, 2669 (1992). The FCC declared that "such a vague standard may make rational choices among noncommercial applicants difficult, if not impossible." The FCC also tentatively concluded in the *Policy Statement* that the "vague standard" should be eliminated and that it should consider using a modified version of a "point system." The FCC invited comments on "(i) whether the criteria used to select commercial applicants were relevant in NCE [Noncommercial Educational] proceedings; (ii) whether different or additional criteria should be used; and (iii) whether a different comparative approach should be followed for state-owned public broadcasters as opposed to other NCE applicants."

The FCC received six comments in response to the 1992 *Policy Statement* and concluded in the 1995 *Reexamination NPRM* that the record was not sufficient to establish appropriate criteria for new applicants for noncommercial broadcast licenses. The FCC also noted that most of the commenters agreed that (1) commercial comparative criteria were inappropriate; (2) "time-sharing" and auxiliary power should be eliminated as a comparative criterion; and (3) a comparative coverage factor should be applied in some manner.

Two commenters in the 1992 proceeding, the Association of America's Public Broadcasters and National Public Radio, stated that the FCC should examine which applicant would best integrate the station operations with its educational and cultural objectives. Then the FCC should determine which applicant's proposed operations would "best meet community needs." Finally, the FCC should look to whether "any other factors demonstrate that one applicant will provide superior broadcast service."

Another commenter in the 1992 proceeding (National Federation of Community Broadcasters) urged the adoption of an all-or-nothing "point system" that relies on criteria such as "diversification (3 points); minority control (3 points); spectrum efficiency (a coverage comparison) (3 points); local program origination (2 points); local residence of principals (2 points); and finder's preference (only as a 'tiebreaker') (1 point)."

The FCC determined in the 1995 *Reexamination NPRM* that it did not have a sufficient record to institute a rule. Therefore the commission froze comparative hearings for new applicants. The FCC then noted that it would continue to accept NCE applications and to process any NCE applications that were not mutually exclusive. The FCC also declared in the 1995 *Reexamination NPRM* that it would continue to rule on and approve appropriate settlement agreements among mutually exclusive NCE applicants.

Since the 1995 *Reexamination NPRM* was issued, the FCC has not as yet determined the appropriate criteria to utilize. It has acknowledged, however, that comparative hearings will ultimately continue to be used for mutually exclusive new applications.

RELIGIOUS BROADCASTING

Regulating religious broadcasting has long been a minor problem for the FCC and its predecessor, the Federal Radio Commission. One of the earliest FRC enforcement actions came against the Reverend Doctor Shuler, whose Trinity United Methodist Church used its radio station to attack other religions, criticize the criminal justice system, and raise money through intimidation. The FRC refused to renew Shuler's license. On appeal, he argued that the First Amendment prohibited the FRC from considering past programming in making licensing decisions and that his First Amendment rights of freedom of speech and press had been violated. Shuler lost, but in the process helped the FRC establish the principle that it was not just a technical traffic cop of the

air—that it could consider content in making licensing decisions. *Trinity Methodist Church, South v. FRC*, 62 F.2d 850 (D.C. Cir. 1932). Interestingly, Shuler did not argue that the FRC had violated his freedom of religion rights, also guaranteed under the First Amendment. The future of First Amendment media law might have been quite different had he made that argument.

From time to time, the FCC has tried to encourage religious programming. The commission's *1960 Policy Statement*, for example, listed religious programming as one of the fourteen types of programming normally expected of licensees. The commission never took any sanctions against broadcasters for not offering religious programs, however, and with radio and TV deregulation in the early 1980s, it is unlikely that the FCC today expects broadcasters to offer religious programs.

When broadcasters have offered religious programming, however, the FCC has often been put in a tight spot when complaints about that programming have ensued. One of the major problems has been religious broadcaster compliance with the fairness doctrine. While that doctrine existed, the FCC maintained that it applied to religious and secular broadcasters alike. Religious broadcasters, in fact, stimulated some of the most important fairness doctrine cases. *Brandywine-Main Line Radio, Inc. v. FCC*, 473 F.2d 16 (D.C. Cir. 1972), *cert. denied*, 412 U.S. 922 (1973); text, p. 694. Broadcasts of an attack upon author Fred Cook on WGCB (W–God–Christ–Bible) in Red Lion, Pennsylvania, led to the U.S. Supreme Court's leading decision on the constitutionality of the doctrine, *Red Lion Broad. Co. v. FCC*. The FCC's position throughout has been consistent: it expects the same compliance with its rules from religious broadcasters as it expects from others.

Religious stations, like secular stations, have run afoul of lottery law. Many religious programs are aired for pay by stations that simply turn over large blocks of time to preachers, a practice known as time brokering. In theory, the FCC expects the licensee to know what is being aired and holds the licensee, not the paying preacher, responsible. A few unscrupulous "preachers" have used radio stations to run numbers games. Scripture references are marvelous devices for hiding numbers games and tips. When the FCC has discovered this, the broadcasters involved have encountered serious licensing difficulties. *United Broad. Co. v. FCC,* 565 F.2d 699 (D.C. Cir. 1977), *cert. denied,* 434 U.S. 1046 (1978).

The FCC long ago reserved frequencies in the FM and TV bands for "noncommercial, educational" radio and television. Religious stations can operate on commercial assignments, they can operate noncommercially on frequencies also available for commercial operation, or they can attempt to qualify for the reserved noncommercial channels. If they run noncommercially, they face certain limits on their operations: they cannot run routine ads for products or services. To qualify for the reserved educational channels, they have to show that the "primary thrust" of their operation will be "educational, albeit with a religious aspect to the religious activity. Recognizing that some overlap in purpose is, or can be, involved [the FCC] look[s] to the application as a whole to determine which is the essential purpose and which is incidental." *Bible Moravian Church, Inc.,* 28 F.C.C.2d 1, 21 R.R.2d 492 (1971). Reserved channel licenses are routinely granted to organizations, such as schools, that operate associated educational institutions. If a religious organization seeks a reserved noncommercial, educational license, it is usually required to prove that it operates a school in the community for which the license is sought. If that is not the case, the FCC sometimes finds itself in the delicate position of trying to decide whether the "primary thrust" of the application is religious or educational. The effort to make that distinction has sometimes led the FCC perilously close to making fine distinctions between religious content and nonreligious educational programming.

A good example of this complexity is *Moody Bible Institute,* 66 F.C.C.2d 162, 40 R.R.2d 1264 (1977). Moody Bible Institute applied for two reserved noncommercial, educational licenses in East Moline, Illinois, and Boynton Beach, Florida. The FCC, without opinion, found Moody qualified. Commissioner Margita White, however, was moved to release a lengthy concurring statement, questioning the FCC staff efforts to distinguish between religious and educational program proposals. The staff found it necessary to evaluate the application against 47 C.F.R. § 73.503, the basic standards for qualifying for the reserved channels. They evaluated Moody's proposed programs, trying to classify each as general educational or religious. Commissioner White took the extraordinary step of releasing copies of the staff analysis of Moody's application, showing penciled annotations. The staff had great trouble deciding whether programs such as the "Radio School of the Bible," described as "a daily instructional series offering courses in Bible subjects," or "Cleared for Take-Off," a "daily youth dramatic series, illustrating lives of missionary aviators in true-to-life situations," were religious or educational. White obviously believed that such an analysis had constitutional aspects, but because Moody got its licenses anyway, they were never further explored by the FCC or the courts.

The granting of noncommercial, educational licenses to religious organizations became particularly controversial when a pair of public interest (and community radio) advocates filed a petition with the FCC, asking it to look into two issues. First, were religious organizations, when granted noncommercial licenses, complying with the fairness doctrine? Second, was it sound public policy to grant reserved noncommercial licenses to religious organizations? The FCC quickly dismissed the petition, but rumors about it plagued the FCC for years.

Even though the matter was legally dead at the FCC, the rumor spread (often stimulated by conservative religious organizations) that the FCC was considering a petition from noted atheist Madalyn Murry O'Hair to ban religious broadcasting—a topic that was *never* the object of the original petition. Churches were encouraged to write to the FCC and complain; "Help Lines" in newspaper columns often published the FCC's address, and for years the FCC received hundreds of thousands of pieces of mail objecting to a petition that never existed. The FCC even found it necessary to set up a special phone number to answer queries about the petition. The monumental nature of this problem should not be underestimated. For several years, the FCC mailroom had to sort the large portion of its mail pertaining to the nonexistent petition (sometimes as much as 50 percent of all the mail received that day) from legitimate mail to the agency.

Once religious organizations get licenses, the FCC's expectation is the same as for secular broadcasters. Religious organizations must comply with the same rules and subject themselves to the same FCC supervision. On occasion, the FCC's investigation of alleged irregularities in the operation of religious stations has stirred controversy. In 1979, the FCC began an investigation into the operation of WJAN(TV) in Canton, Ohio. The objective was to find out whether the station had broadcast false information when it solicited funds. The station was closely affiliated with Heritage Village Church and Missionary Fellowship, Inc., of Charlotte, North Carolina. That religious organization did business as the PTL Television Network and was headed by the Reverend James O. Bakker. After several years of investigation, the FCC decided that there was smoke here but refused to look for the underlying fire. The commission terminated its investigation and referred its findings to the U.S. Department of Justice for possible prosecution, a referral the Justice Department did not pursue. Thus, the FCC missed a chance to blow open what was to become a major scandal for the religious broadcasting community in the late 1980s, the "affairs" of Jim Bakker. See *PTL of Heritage Village Church*, 71 F.C.C.2d 324 (1979).

In another case, however, the FCC pursued its investigation more doggedly. The minister here was the Reverend W. Eugene Scott, pastor of a religious organization called Faith Center Church, which was the licensee of radio and television stations. Upon receiving allegations similar to those in the Bakker case, that Scott was using the station for fraudulent solicitation of funds, the FCC launched an investigation. Scott argued that the investigation into his fundraising techniques, his contributors, and the "membership" of his electronic church violated both the Establishment and Free Exercise Clauses of the First Amendment. This, in effect, was the argument the Reverend Shuler had made more than fifty years earlier. The U.S. Court of Appeals for the Ninth Circuit eventually decided that the FCC's investigators had not transgressed upon Scott's freedom of religion rights. Although the FCC had inquired into religious activities, it had the right to do so under the facts of this case.

In *Scott v. Rosenberg*, 702 F.2d 1263 (9th Cir. 1983), Scott, the president and pastor of Faith Center Church, sued the FCC for an alleged violation of the First Amendment during an investigation of the church's television and radio stations. A former employee of one of the church's television stations sent a letter to the FCC in which he alleged that Scott solicited funds during broadcasts for projects that were never undertaken. In response, the FCC instituted an investigation of the church's California television and radio stations. Scott contended that the FCC's inquiry into his personal donations violated his free exercise rights under the First Amendment.

The *Scott* court noted that greater conflict with traditional First Amendment principles is tolerated with the broadcast media because of the limited number of available frequencies. The court rejected the argument that the FCC should be required to demonstrate a compelling governmental interest *prior* to investigating an allegation of fraud by one of its licensees that is owned by or affiliated with a religious organization. The court, however, did require the FCC to show a compelling governmental interest when a collision between portions of an FCC investigation and free exercise rights occurs. The court stated that not all burdens on religion are unconstitutional. "The government has a compelling interest in preventing the diversion of funds contributed for specific, identified purposes especially when such funds are obtained through the use of the public airwaves."

The court held that the government's investigation of Scott's pledge and donation records was necessary to further the compelling interest. "When Scott and the church decided to acquire television and radio stations, they availed themselves of facilities which, under congressional mandate, must be operated in the public interest." The court held that the FCC was justified in infringing on Scott's First Amendment rights in order to assure that the public interest was served. The court noted that the investigation was narrow and avoided any unnecessary interference with the free exercise of religion.

Scott v. Rosenberg
702 F. 2d 1263 (9TH CIR. 1983).

Before WALLACE, SCHROEDER, and CANBY, Circuit Judges.

WALLACE, Circuit Judge:

Scott, the president and pastor of Faith Center Church (the church), brought this action for injunctive relief and for actual and punitive damages against five present and former officers and employees (the government employees) of the

Federal Communications Commission (the FCC), alleging that they violated his first amendment rights during an investigation of the church's television and radio stations. The district court granted summary judgment for the government employees. We affirm.

Diederich, a former employee of one of the church's television stations, sent a letter to the FCC in which he alleged that Scott had solicited during broadcasts and subsequently received funds for projects which were never undertaken. He also stated his belief that Scott was using the stations for his personal gain. In response to that letter, the FCC instituted an investigation of the church's California television and radio stations. The FCC conducted a number of interviews during which further allegations were made: that the stations had failed to log paid religious programming as commercial broadcasting, that Scott had misstated the amount of his personal remuneration during broadcast solicitations, and that Scott had made personal pledges during the broadcasts which he had never fulfilled.

Subsequently, two FCC employees made an unannounced visit to the television station located in the main church building to interview employees and investigate records. There is some dispute with respect to how clearly they identified the purpose of their visit and with respect to the scope of their request for access to church and station records. In any event, the church subsequently made available some, but not all, of the materials requested, and thereafter the FCC issued an order designating for hearing the station's application for license renewal and a notice of apparent liability for forfeiture for violation of 18 U.S.C. § 1343, the statute governing fraud by use of radio and television. Scott brought this action not in any representative capacity, but to vindicate his individual rights. He apparently does not, in his personal capacity, contest the FCC's request for station logs and for his salary records. He does, however, allege that the FCC's inquiry into his personal donations violates his free exercise rights under the first amendment. Scott's claim that his religion requires donations to be made confidentially if they are to be received by God as sacrifices, is not disputed.

We must next decide whether Scott has a claim under the first amendment and, if so, what type of remedy is appropriate. We assume, with-

out deciding, that a private cause of action may be implied directly under the Constitution for violations of the first amendment. We must next examine the record to determine if there is any genuine factual dispute whether the government employees violated Scott's first amendment rights. Scott alleges that the government employees informed the press and public that they were investigating charges of fraud against Scott. He claims that those statements interfered with the free exercise of his religious obligation to convert others to his beliefs. He also argues that the FCC's demand, in conjunction with its investigation, that the church provide records of his personal pledges during 1976 and 1977, together with information showing the status of those pledges (paid, withdrawn, or outstanding) violates the free exercise clause of the first amendment.

In support of their motions for summary judgement, the government employees submitted affidavits in which they stated that they did not provide any information to the press or public with respect to the specific allegations made against the church. They further testified that they made no statements to the press or public accusing Scott of any criminal or dishonest activity. Scott introduced letters prepared by two of the government employees in response to public and congressional inquiries concerning the investigation. Those letters simply confirm that an investigation was in progress and that it was initiated in response to a complaint alleging irregular conduct. The letters further clarify the FCC's responsibility to investigate such complaints, including possible questions concerning the complainant's credibility. The letters do not, however, support Scott's allegations that the government employees dispatched charges of fraud to the press and public. Scott's allegations are unsupported by a factual presentation. Merely conclusory, they are insufficient to survive the government employees' motion for summary judgment.

Scott's second argument about the investigation of his pledges presents more difficult questions. It is complicated by the fact that the church owns the broadcast station. Our analysis must be on two levels: first, the result of the actions of the FCC in relation to the station and second, the result of its actions in relation to Scott.

The first question, therefore, is should the FCC be required to meet a different standard prior to investigation of broadcasters of religious programs than it is required to meet prior to investigation of broadcasters of secular programs? More specifically, should the FCC be required to demonstrate a compelling governmental interest prior to investigating an allegation of fraud by one of its licensees that is owned by or affiliated with a religious organization? We hold that such a requirement is not necessary.

The Federal Communications Act authorizes the FCC to regulate as required by the "public convenience, interest, or necessity," 47 U.S.C. § 303, and does not differentiate types of broadcast licensees. The FCC grants licenses and regulates the public airwaves without differentiating between religious and secular broadcasters.

Requiring the FCC to justify investigations undertaken in response to allegations of fraud by one of its licensees, religious or secular, is not supported by precedent, is impracticable, and might raise other first amendment obstacles. During the investigation, free expression conflicts may arise. This brings us to the second level of our analysis which pertains to the acts of the FCC in relation to Scott. When a collision between portions of an FCC investigation and free exercise rights occurs, free exercise rights can be protected by requiring the FCC to demonstrate a compelling governmental interest. A compelling governmental interest must be shown at that point because an action taken in the course of an investigation directly conflicts with a sincerely held religious belief.

Here, we conclude that it is necessary to employ compelling state interest analysis because of the unique factual setting. The FCC requested information, the release of which Scott alleges in and of itself violates his religious free exercise right. Thus, there is a direct conflict between a sincerely held religious belief and an action by government officials.

Therefore, we conclude that we can affirm the district court's order granting summary judgment only if the FCC's demand for the records of Scott's donations does not infringe on his first amendment freedoms or, if it does, a compelling governmental interest justifies the demand.

In support of his claim, Scott submitted personal affidavits in which he states that he believes that his church contributions are "sacrifices" and that disclosure of his sacrifices would violate their sacred nature. The government employees do not challenge the sincerity of

Scott's beliefs. Furthermore, Scott's claim is not "so bizarre, so clearly nonreligious in motivation, as not to be entitled to protection under the Free Exercise Clause." *Thomas v. Review Board of the Indiana Employment Security Division*, 450 U.S. 707, 715 (1981). We therefore conclude that the FCC's demand interferes with Scott's first amendment rights.

The conclusion that there is conflict between Scott's beliefs and the demand imposed by the FCC is "only the beginning, however, and not the end of the inquiry. Not all burdens on religion are unconstitutional." The state may justify its infringement on religious liberty if it is necessary to accomplish an overriding governmental interest. We must therefore determine whether the governmental interest in preventing the fraudulent practices alleged is sufficiently compelling to justify the burden upon Scott's right to the free exercise of his religion and, if so, whether the demand for church records of Scott's pledges and donations was necessary to further that interest.

The governmental interest in preventing some crimes is compelling, but that interest is not sufficient to permit interference with free exercise rights in every case. The Supreme Court has repeatedly stated that religious frauds can be penalized. Lower courts have applied this principle to religious organizations conducting fraudulent nonreligious activities and to individuals soliciting money for pretended religious purposes when religious beliefs were not sincerely held, and have concluded that the protections of the first amendment were not applicable.

Here, however, we face the question whether, when an allegedly fraudulent activity is connected with the exercise of sincerely held religious beliefs, the governmental interest in preventing fraud overrides the individual's right of religious freedom. We conclude that the answer depends, at least in part, on the nature of the fraud. Scott claims that in the framework of his religion, it is only important that the contributor give and, having made the gift, the contributor is spiritually blessed, no matter how his donation is used. Scott further states that he must follow "the leanings of the Lord" with respect to the utilization of donations. Scott does not claim, however, that contributors to identified projects know that their contributions may be used for any purpose which Scott determines to be in accordance with the will of the Lord. Scott does not claim that he clarified this aspect of his religious practice in his broadcast solicitations. At least under these limited circumstances, we conclude that the government has a compelling interest in preventing the diversion of funds from the specifically identified projects for which they have been solicited.

Our final inquiry is whether the government's investigation of Scott's pledge and donation records was necessary to further this compelling interest. We need not determine whether any other aspects of the FCC investigation were justifiable, for Scott contests only the FCC demand for those records. Although not every allegation of fraudulent solicitation would justify the government's interference with the religious practices of individuals and churches, we conclude that the allegations here justified the FCC's narrow and limited inquiry into Scott's donation records.

Several important considerations support this conclusion. First, we believe that the context in which the pledges were made is significant. When Scott and the church decided to acquire television and radio stations, they availed themselves of facilities which, under congressional mandate, must be operated in the public interest. 47 U.S.C. §§ 307(a), 309(a). With respect to the operation of broadcast facilities, the Supreme Court has held that the right of viewers and listeners, not that of broadcasters, is paramount. An allegation of fraud, even if not sufficiently specific or reliable generally to justify inquiry into solicitations made by a congregation in church, may nevertheless be sufficient to justify inquiry into broadcast solicitations.

Second, the FCC investigation in this case was premised on information sufficiently reliable to justify the limited intrusion on first amendment rights which it engendered. The FCC began its inquiry only after it received a complaint signed by Diederich, a former employee of the television station. In his former employment, Diederich was in a position in which he was likely to have received personal knowledge of the irregularities he alleged. His signed complaint, if knowingly false, could expose him to liability in tort for malicious prosecution and was therefore entitled to a greater inference of reliability than an unsigned statement would have been.

Third, the investigation in this case was narrow and avoided any unnecessary interference with the free exercise of religion. We can imagine circumstances in which the interference with religion could be substantial enough to overbalance a governmental interest that otherwise would be compelling, but that is not this situation. There was no request for wholesale investigation of the church's financial records, but rather specific requests for records of an FCC licensee concerning Scott's salary and donations, both of which he allegedly misrepresented during broadcast solicitations.

Finally, the FCC's demand for access to Scott's donation records was necessary to serve its compelling interest in investigating the alleged diversion of funds. If, as alleged, Scott solicited funds for projects which were never undertaken or if funds contributed to these projects were illegally diverted to other uses, Scott's misrepresentation of his personal pledges may have been intended to induce those contributions and therefore could constitute part of a scheme to defraud. Although other information might be only tangentially relevant to the objectives of a legitimate inquiry, the nexus between the investigations and the FCC's objective in this case was sufficiently close to comply with the principle that valid restrictions on first amendment rights must embody the least restrictive means of effectuating the government's compelling interest.

Scott also claims that the actions of the government employees violated the establishment clause of the first amendment. He apparently believes that inquiry into his donation record is only the first step in a contemplated program of pervasive regulation. The government employees have submitted affidavits in which they state that their inquiries were for the purpose of ascertaining the truth of Diederich's allegations and determining whether renewal of the church's license was in the public interest. Scott has alleged no facts from which we can infer that pervasive regulation is either planned or threatened.

AFFIRMED.

COMMENT

Scott eventually lost the license for KHOF-TV (and also sold WHOF-TV in Providence, Rhode Island, his other major TV station). He did not give up without a fight, however. The last few hours of broadcasting of KHOF-TV are unique in broadcast history. Scott spent most of his time berating the commission, presenting its members with a scroll describing them as "the antichrist," and displaying the antics of dozens of mechanical monkeys that he called the "FCC Monkey Band." As the plug on the station was pulled, Scott was shouting about the FCC and asking his listeners to contribute funds to keep up the fight.

The Bakker scandals and others (such as evangelist Jimmy Swaggart's alleged tryst with a prostitute and televangelist Oral Roberts's over-the-air claim that God would "call me home" unless he raised millions of dollars in a short period of time) stimulated increased self-regulation by many religious broadcasters. Under the guidance of the National Religious Broadcasters Association, a self-regulatory code was adopted in 1987. It requires religious broadcasters to submit to audits and open their books to broader scrutiny.

Religious programming also found a haven on cable television. Jim Bakker's "PTL" program was primarily distributed by cable, although many broadcast stations carried it too. The Christian Broadcasting Network of the Reverend Pat Robertson (a candidate for the Republican nomination for president in 1988) is primarily a cable programming service. Other religious broadcasters including the Reverend Jerry Falwell also found cable an effective (and less regulated) means of distributing their message. The "Eternal World" cable service provides programming for Catholics. There are other services for Jews and Muslims. Both the "ether" and the cable have become multidenominational.

PROBLEMS OF DIVERSIFICATION OF OWNERSHIP

The Demise of Multiple Ownership Rules and Broadcast Ownership under the Telecommunications Act of 1996

Until 1996, the FCC's so-called multiple ownership rules created a conclusive presumption that nationwide ownership by a single party of more than twelve AM radio stations, twelve FM radio stations, or twelve television stations was in itself contrary to the public interest. Although no specific provision in the Communications Act of

1934 dealt materially with the concentration of ownership in broadcasting, multiple ownership rules were held to lie within the administrative discretion of the FCC under the broad purposes of the Act. See *United States v. Storer Broad. Co.,* 351 U.S. 192 (1956).

In order "to promote minority participation in the broadcast industry," a minority-controlled entity was allowed to own fourteen stations of each type and was "allowed to reach a maximum of 30% of the national audience, provided that at least 5% of the aggregate reach of its stations is contributed by minority controlled stations." A minority station is a station with more than a 50 percent minority ownership. See, generally, *Report and Order on Amendment of FCC Rules Relating to Multiple Ownership,* 100 F.C.C.2d 74 (1985).

In addition to the ownership caps, television was subject to an audience-reach cap limitation. This limited "the aggregate ownership interests in TV stations to those which penetrate a maximum of 25 percent of the national audience." Due to the physical limitations of UHF stations, owners of those stations were attributed with only 50 percent of the television households in their service areas.

The Telecommunications Act of 1996 scuttled national ownership caps such as the rule of twelves. Telecommunications Act of 1996, Pub. L. No. 104-104, 110 Stat. 56, § 202(c)(1)(a). The audience-reach cap limitation was raised from 25 percent of the nation's television audience to 35 percent. 47 U.S.C. § 202(c)(1)(B).

For radio, the Telecommunications Act set forth ownership caps calibrated to the size of the market. In radio markets with 45 or more commercial radio stations, an entity could own up to 8 commercial radio stations. Not more than 5 of the 8 could be in the same service, AM or FM. In radio markets with 30-44 stations, one entity could own up to 7 commercial radio stations; only 4 of these could be in the same service, AM or FM. In radio markets with 15-29 stations, one entity could own up to 6 commercial radio stations; only 4 of the 6 could be in the same service, AM or FM. In radio markets with 14 or fewer commercial stations, one entity could own up to 5 commercial radio stations; not more than 3 of the 5 could be in the same service, AM or FM. Radio markets with 14 or fewer stations were subject to an additional limitation: no entity could own more than 50 percent of the stations in such a market. See generally, 47 U.S.C. § 202(b). See also, p. 542.

These developments were not exactly a surprise. As far back as the 1985 *Report and Order,* the FCC acknowledged that there was a strong case for the repeal of multiple ownership rules: "[T]he appropriate market for ideas is primarily local, and includes a broad variety of means of communication, especially cablecasting, newspapers and opinion magazines, in addition to radio and television." Insofar as "the idea market is a national one," it is sufficiently diverse, the FCC declared, to be unaffected by repeal of the multiple ownership rules.

The Duopoly Rule

In the past, the FCC prohibited the grant of a license to anyone already holding a license for the same type of facility in a given community. This was called the duopoly rule. For example, the holder of an AM radio station license in Middletown, Connecticut, could not acquire a license for another AM radio station in Middletown. See 47 C.F.R. §§ 73.35, 73.240, and 73.636. The duopoly in radio has been steadily relaxed, however. For example, on October 27, 1988, the FCC modified its radio duopoly rule to help commercial radio broadcasters in different but overlapping markets. This made it possible for commercial radio broadcasters "to take greater advantage of at least some of the economies of scale and related cost savings inherent in the joint ownership of stations in the same market." See *In re Amendment of Section 73.3555 of the Commission's Rules, the Broadcast Multiple Ownership Rules,* 4 F.C.C.R. 1723 (1988).

Section 202 of the 1996 Act has modified the duopoly rule even further for radio. Now, as we have seen, radio ownership in a single market, even ownership of stations offering the same type of service, is calibrated to the size of the market. As far as television is concerned, the 1996 Act specifically instructs the FCC to conduct a rule making on whether the duopoly rule ought to be retained, eliminated, or modified. See § 202(c)(2). In the past, the duopoly rule had prevented a broadcast entity from owning more

than one television station in a given market. The Telecommunications Act requires the FCC to reconsider this rule.

The One-to-a-Market Rule

In 1970, the FCC prohibited the "common ownership, operation, or control of more than one unlimited-time broadcast station in the same area, regardless of the type of broadcast service involved." *First Report and Order, Multiple Ownership of Standard, FM & TV Broadcast Stations,* 22 F.C.C.2d 306 (1970). Popularly known as the one-to-a-market rule, this rule has done little to alter concentration of ownership in the media because the FCC specifically exempted existing AM, FM, and TV combinations because of the disruptive effects a divestiture order would have. See *First Report and Order,* 22 F.C.C.2d at 323.

The history of the one-to-a-market rule is studded with exceptions. As early as 1971, the FCC amended the rule to permit AM and FM radio stations in the same market to be under common ownership. See *In re Amendment of Secs. 73.35, 73.240 and 73.636 of the FCC's Rules Relating to Multiple Ownership of Standard, FM, and Television Broadcast Stations,* 28 F.C.C.2d 662 (1971).

On December 12, 1988, the FCC modified its prohibition against the common ownership of radio and television stations in the same television market. Henceforth, the FCC looked favorably on case-by-case waiver applications "where those applications involve radio and television stations located in the top 25 markets where at least 30 separately owned or operated broadcast licensees or 'voices' would remain after the proposed combination." The FCC said such joint radio-television ownership "might lead to more news and public affairs programming, a greater diversity of program formats, and better technical facilities, and could enable struggling radio or television stations to remain on the air." See *FCC Report No. BC-1307.*

The 1996 Act further supports a policy of regarding radio-television joint ownership in a single market as encouraging rather than retarding diversity of ideas. The Act instructs the FCC to relax the one-to-a-market rule by extending "its waiver policy to any of the top 50 markets" where such waivers would be in the public interest. See § 202(d).

Newspaper-Broadcast Cross-Ownership

The one-to-a-market rule applies only to new common ownership situations it does not apply to existing licensees or to newspapers. In justification, the FCC pointed out in the AM-FM combination exception proceeding, 28 F.C.C.2d 662 (1971), that the whole point of the one-to-a-market rules was to produce more diversity of programming and viewpoints over the broadcast media. The rules did not "contemplate any action with regard to cross-ownership of newspapers and broadcast facilities." Still the FCC conceded that problems of divestiture and newspaper cross-ownership were reason for concern.

Simultaneous with the promulgation of the one-to-a-market rule, the FCC announced a rule making proceeding to consider whether it would be in the public interest to require divestiture by newspapers or multiple owners in a given market. See *Further Notice of Proposed Rulemaking, Multiple Ownership of Standard FM and TV Broadcast Stations*, 22 F.C.C.2d 339 (1970). This proceeding culminated in *FCC v. National Citizens Comm. for Broad.*, 436 U.S. 775 (1978). The Supreme Court decision in this case was the *denouement* of the long but inconsistent effort of the FCC to determine the role newspaper ownership should play in choosing from among applicants for a broadcast station license.

In 1975, the FCC set forth its new cross-ownership rules. The substance of the new rules was to prohibit the future licensing or transfer of broadcast stations to those who owned a newspaper in the same community. The rules were designed to prevent the operation of a broadcast station and a newspaper by a common owner in the same community. The rules were not as draconian as this summary might indicate, however. Existing cross-ownership situations were essentially "grandfathered" with the exception of sixteen communities where the only daily newspaper and the only television station in the community were under common ownership.

Broadcasters thought the new rules went too far, though, while citizens' groups thought they did not go far enough. On review to the federal court of appeals in Washington, D.C., Judge Bazelon, in a notable opinion, upheld the new FCC rules in part and reversed them in part. The court upheld the FCC's prospective ban on the future creation of cross-ownership situations in the same community. But the court held that the FCC had erred in "grandfathering" the existing cross-ownership situations. The FCC sought review in the Supreme Court. The Court agreed with the FCC and not with the court of appeals.

FCC v. National Citizens Committee for Broadcasting
436 U.S. 775, 98 S. CT. 2096, 56 L. Ed. 2d 697 (1978).

Justice MARSHALL delivered the opinion of the Court.

At issue in these cases are FCC regulations governing the permissibility of common ownership of a radio or television broadcast station and a daily newspaper located in the same community. Second Report and Order. 50 F.C.C.2d 1046 (1975) (hereinafter cited as Order), as amended upon reconsideration, 53 F.C.C.2d 589 (1975), codified in 47 C.F.R. 73.35, 73.240, 73.636 (1976). The regulations, adopted after a lengthy rulemaking proceeding, prospectively bar formation or transfer of co-located newspaper-broadcast combinations. Existing combinations are generally permitted to continue in operation. However, in communities in which there is common ownership of the only daily newspaper and the only broadcast station, or (where there is more than one broadcast station) of the only daily newspaper and the only television station, divestiture of either the newspaper or the broadcast station is required within five years, unless grounds for waiver are demonstrated.

The questions for decision are whether these regulations either exceed the commission's authority under the Communications Act of 1934, or violate the First or Fifth Amendment rights of newspaper owners; and whether the lines drawn by the commission between new and existing newspaper-broadcast combinations, and between existing combinations subject to divestiture and those allowed to continue in operation, are arbitrary or capricious within the meaning of § 10(e) of the Administration Procedure Act. For the reasons set forth below, we sustain the regulations in their entirety.

In setting its licensing policies, the FCC has long acted on the theory that diversification of mass media ownership serves the public interest by promoting diversity of program and service viewpoints, as well as by preventing undue concentration of economic power. See e.g., Multiple Ownership of Standard, FM and Television Broadcast Stations, 45 F.C.C. 1476, 1476–1477 (1964).

Thus, prior to adoption of the regulations at issue here, the fact that an applicant for an initial license published a newspaper in the community to be served by the broadcast station was taken into account on a case-by-case basis and resulted in some instances in awards of licenses to competing applicants.

Diversification of ownership has not been the sole consideration thought relevant to the public interest, however. The FCC's other, and sometimes conflicting goal has been to ensure "the best practicable service to the public." To achieve this goal, the FCC has weighed factors such as the anticipated contribution of the owner to station operations, the proposed program service, and the past broadcast record of the applicant—in addition to diversification of ownership—in making initial comparative licensing decisions. Moreover, the FCC has given considerable weight to a policy of avoiding undue disruption of existing service. As a result, newspaper owners in many instances have been able to acquire broadcast licenses for stations serving the same communities as their newspapers and the commission has repeatedly renewed such licenses on findings that continuation of the service offered by the common owner would serve the public interest.

Against this background, the FCC began the instant rulemaking proceeding in 1970 to consider the need for a more restrictive policy toward newspaper ownership of radio and television broadcast stations. Further Notice of Proposed Rulemaking, 22 F.C.C.2d 339 (1970). Citing studies showing the dominant role of television stations and daily newspapers as sources of local news and other information, the notice of rulemaking proposed adoption of regulations that would eliminate all newspaper-broadcast combinations serving the same market, by prospectively banning formation or transfer of such combinations and requiring dissolution of all existing combinations within five years. The Order explained that the prospective ban on creation of co-located newspaper-broadcast combinations was grounded primarily in First Amendment concerns while the divestiture regulations were based on both First Amendment and antitrust policies. In addition, the commission

rejected the suggestion that it lacked the power to order divestiture, reasoning that the statutory requirement of license renewal every three years necessarily implied authority to order divestiture over a five-year period.

The prospective rules, barring formation of new broadcast-newspaper combinations in the same market, as well as transfers of existing combinations to new owners, were adopted without change from the proposal set forth in the notice of rulemaking. While recognizing the pioneering contributions of newspaper owners to the broadcast industry, the FCC concluded that changed circumstances made it possible, and necessary, for all new licensing of broadcast stations to "be expected to add to local diversity." The prospective rules were justified, instead, by reference to the commission's policy of promoting diversification of ownership: increases in diversification of ownership would possibly result in enhanced diversity of viewpoints and, given the absence of persuasive countervailing considerations, "even a small gain in diversity" was "worth pursuing."

With respect to the proposed across-the-board divestiture requirement, however, the FCC concluded that "a mere hoped for gain in diversity" was not a sufficient justification. Characterizing the divestiture issues as "the most difficult" presented in the proceeding, the Order explained that the proposed rules, while correctly recognizing the central importance of diversity considerations, "may have given too little weight to the consequences which could be expected to attend a focus on the abstract goal alone." Forced dissolution would promote diversity, but it would also cause "disruption for the industry and hardship for individual owners, resulting in losses or diminution of service to the public."

The FCC concluded that in light of these countervailing considerations divestiture was warranted only in "the most egregious cases," which it identified as those in which a newspaper-broadcast combination has an "effective monopoly" in the local 'marketplace' of ideas as well as economically." The commission recognized that any standards for defining which combinations fell within that category would necessarily be arbitrary to some degree, but "[a] choice had to be made." It thus decided to require divestiture only where there was common ownership of the sole daily newspaper published in a community and either

1. the sole broadcast station providing that entire community with a clear signal, or
2. the sole television station encompassing the entire community with a clear signal.

The Order identified eight television-newspaper and 10 radio-newspaper combinations meeting the divestiture criteria. Waivers of the divestiture requirement were granted *sua sponte* to one television and one radio combination, leaving a total of 16 stations subject to divestiture. The FCC explained that waiver requests would be entertained in the latter cases, but, absent waiver, either the newspaper or the broadcast station would have to be divested by January 1, 1980. On petitions for reconsideration the FCC reaffirmed the rules in all material respects. *Memorandum Opinion and Order,* 53 F.C.C.2d 589 (1975).

Various parties petitioned for review of the regulations in the United States Court of Appeals for the District of Columbia Circuit.

Agreeing substantially with NCCB and the Justice Department, the court of appeals affirmed the prospective ban on new licensing of co-located newspaper-broadcast combinations, but vacated the limited divestiture rules, and ordered the FCC to adopt regulations requiring dissolution of all existing combinations that did not qualify for a waiver under the procedure outlined in the Order. 555 F.2d 938 (1977). The court held, first, that the prospective ban was a reasonable means of furthering "the highly valued goal of diversity" in the mass media, and was therefore not without a rational basis. The court concluded further that, since the FCC "explained why it considers diversity to be a factor of exceptional importance," and since the FCC's goal of promoting diversification of mass media ownership was strongly supported by First Amendment and antitrust policies, it was not arbitrary for the prospective rules to be "based on [the diversity] factor to the exclusion of others customarily relied on by the FCC."

The court also held that the prospective rules did not exceed the FCC's authority under the Communications Act. The court reasoned that the public interest standard of the Act permitted, and indeed required, the FCC to consider diversification of mass media ownership in making its licensing decisions, and that the FCC's general rule-making authority under 47 U.S.C. §§ 303(r) and 154(i) allowed the FCC to adopt reasonable license qualifications implementing the public interest standard. The court concluded, moreover, that since the prospective ban was designed to "increas[e] the number of media voices in the community," and not to restrict or control the content of free speech, the ban would not violate the First Amendment rights of newspaper owners.

After affirming the prospective rules, the court of appeals invalidated the limited divestiture requirement as arbitrary and capricious within the meaning of § 10(e) of the Administrative Procedure Act, 5 U.S.C. § 706(2)(A). The court's primary holding was that the FCC lacked a rational basis for "grandfathering" most existing combinations while banning all new combinations. The court reasoned that the FCC's own diversification policy, as reinforced by First Amendment policies and the FCC's statutory obligation to "encourage the larger and more effective use of radio in the public interest" 47 U.S.C. § 303(g), required the FCC to adopt a "presumption" that stations owned by co-located newspapers "do not serve the public interest." The court observed that, in the absence of countervailing policies, this "presumption" would have dictated adoption of an across-the-board divestiture requirement, subject only to waiver "in those cases where the evidence clearly discloses that cross-ownership is in the public interest." The countervailing policies relied on by the commission in its decision were, in the court's view, "lesser policies" which had not been given as much weight in the past as its diversification policy. And "the record [did] not disclose the extent to which divestiture would actually threaten these [other policies]." The court concluded, therefore, that it was irrational for the FCC not to give controlling weight to its diversification policy and thus to extend the divestiture requirement to all existing combinations.

The court of appeals held further that, even assuming a difference in treatment between new and existing combinations was justifiable, the FCC lacked a rational basis for requiring divestiture in the 16 "egregious" cases while allowing the remainder of the existing combinations to continue in operation. The court suggested that "limiting divestiture to small markets of 'absolute monopoly' squanders the opportunity where divestiture might do the most good," since "[d]ivestiture may be more useful in the larger markets." The court further observed that the record "[did] not support the conclusion that divestiture would be more harmful in the grandfathered markets than in the 16 affected markets," nor did it demonstrate that the need for divestiture was stronger in those 16 markets. On the latter point, the court noted that, "[a]lthough the affected markets contain fewer voices, the amount of diversity in communities with additional independent voices may in fact be no greater."

The FCC, NAB, ANPA, and several crossowners who had been intervenors below, and whose licenses had been grandfathered under the FCC's rules but were subject to divestiture under the court of appeals' decision, petitioned this court for review. We granted certiorari. And we now affirm the judgment of the court of appeals insofar as it upholds the prospective ban and reverse the judgment insofar as it vacates the limited divestiture requirement.

Petitioners NAB and ANPA contend that the regulations promulgated by the FCC exceed its statutory rulemaking authority and violate the constitutional rights of newspaper owners. We turn first to the statutory, and then to the constitutional, issues. NAB contends that, since the act confers jurisdiction on the FCC only to regulate "communication by wire or radio," 47 U.S.C. § 152(a), it is impermissible for the FCC to use its licensing authority with respect to broadcasting to promote diversity in an overall communications market which includes, but is not limited to, the broadcasting industry.

This argument undersells the FCC's power to regulate broadcasting in the "public interest." In making initial licensing decisions between competing applicants, the FCC has long given "primary significance" to "diversification of control of the media of mass communications."

Our past decisions have recognized, moreover, that the First Amendment and antitrust values underlying the FCC's diversification policy may properly be considered by the commission in determining where the public interest lies. "[T]he 'public interest' standard necessarily invites reference to First Amendment principles," *Columbia Broad. Sys., Inc. v. Democratic Nat'l. Comm.*, 412 U.S. 94, 122 (1973), and, in particular, to the First Amendment goal of achieving "the widest possible dissemination of information from diverse and antagonistic sources," *Associated Press v. United States.* And, while the

FCC does not have power to enforce the antitrust laws as such, it is permitted to take antitrust policies into account in making licensing decisions pursuant to the public interest standard.

It is thus clear that the regulations at issue are based on permissible public interest goals and, so long as the regulations are not an unreasonable means for seeking to achieve these goals, they fall within the general rulemaking authority recognized in the *Storer Broadcasting* and *National Broadcasting* cases.

Petitioner ANPA contends that the prospective rules are unreasonable in two respects: first, the rulemaking record did not conclusively establish that prohibiting common ownership of co-located newspapers and broadcast stations would in fact lead to increases in the diversity of viewpoints among local communications media; and second, the regulations were based on the diversification factor to the exclusion of other service factors considered in the past by the FCC in making initial licensing decisions regarding newspaper owners. With respect to the first point, we agree with the court of appeals that, notwithstanding the inconclusiveness of the rulemaking record, the FCC acted rationally in finding that diversification of ownership would enhance the possibility of achieving greater diversity of viewpoints. In these circumstances, the FCC was entitled to rely on its judgment, based on experience, that "it is unrealistic to expect true diversity from a commonly owned station-newspaper combination. The divergency of their viewpoints cannot be expected to be the same as if they were antagonistically run."

Petitioners NAB and ANPA also argue that the regulations, though designed to further the First Amendment goal of achieving "the widest possible dissemination of information from diverse and antagonistic sources," *Associated Press v. United States,* nevertheless violate the First Amendment rights of newspaper owners. We cannot agree, for this argument ignores the fundamental proposition that there is no "unbridgeable First Amendment right to broadcast comparable to the right of every individual to speak, write, or publish." *Red Lion Broad. Co. v. FCC.*

The physical limitations of the broadcast spectrum are well known. In light of this physical scarcity, government allocation and regulation of broadcast frequencies are essential, as we have often recognized. No one here questions the need for such allocation and regulation, and, given that need, we see nothing in the First Amendment to prevent the FCC from allocating licenses so as to promote the "public interest" in diversification of the mass communications media.

NAB and ANPA contend, however, that it is inconsistent with the First Amendment to promote diversification by barring a newspaper owner from owning certain broadcasting stations. In support, they point to our statement in *Buckley v. Valeo,* 424 U.S. 1 (1976), to the effect that "government may [not] restrict the speech of some elements of our society in order to enhance the relative voice of others." As *Buckley* also recognized, however, " 'the broadcast media pose unique and special problems not present in the traditional free speech case.' " quoting *CBS v. Democratic Nat. Committee.* Thus efforts to "'enhanc[e] the volume and quality of coverage' of public issues" through regulation of broadcasting may be permissible where similar efforts to regulate the print media would not be. Requiring those who wish to obtain a broadcast license to demonstrate that such would serve the "public interest" does not restrict the speech of those who are denied licenses; rather, it preserves the interests of the "people as a whole in free speech." *Red Lion Broad. Co.* As we stated in *Red Lion,* "to deny a station license because 'the public interest' requires it 'is not a denial of free speech.'" Quoting *NBC v. United States.*

Finally, petitioners argue that the FCC has unfairly "singled out" newspaper owners for more stringent treatment than other license applicants. But the regulations treat newspaper owners in essentially the same fashion as other owners of the major media of mass communications were already treated under the FCC's multiple ownership rules; owners of radio stations, television stations, and newspapers alike are now restricted in their ability to acquire licenses for co-located broadcast stations.

In the instant case, far from seeking to limit the flow of information, the FCC has acted, in the court of appeals' words, "to enhance the diversity of information heard by the public without on-going government surveillance of the content of speech." The regulations are a reasonable means of promoting the public interest in diversified mass communications; thus they do not violate the First Amendment rights of those who will be denied broadcast licenses pursuant to them. Being forced to "choose among applicants for the same facilities," the FCC has chosen on a "sensible basis," one designed to further, rather than contravene, "the system of freedom of expression." T. Emerson, *The System of Freedom of Expression* 663 (1970).

After upholding the prospective aspect of the FCC's regulations, the court of appeals concluded that the FCC's decision to limit divestiture to 16 "egregious cases" of "effective monopoly" was arbitrary and capricious within the meaning of the Administrative Procedure Act (APA), § 10(e), 5 U.S.C. § 706(2)(A).

In the view of the court of appeals, the FCC lacked a rational basis, first, for treating existing newspaper-broadcast combinations more leniently than combinations that might seek licenses in the future; and, second, even assuming a distinction between existing and new combinations had been justified, for requiring divestiture in the "egregious cases" while allowing all other existing combinations to continue in operation. We believe that the limited divestiture requirement reflects a rational weighing of competing policies, and we therefore reinstate the portion of the commission's order that was invalidated by the court of appeals.

The FCC was well aware that separating existing newspaper-broadcast combinations would promote diversification of ownership. It concluded, however, that ordering widespread divestiture would not result in the "the best practicable service to the American public", a goal that the commission has always taken into account and that has been specifically approved by this Court, *FCC v. Sanders Bros. Radio Station,* 309 U.S. 470 (1940). In particular, the FCC expressed concern that divestiture would cause "disruption for the industry" and "hardship to individual owners," both of which would result in harm to the public interest. Especially in light of the fact that the number of co-located newspaper-broadcast combinations was already on the decline as a result of natural market forces, and would decline further as a result of the prospective rules, the FCC decided that across-the-board divestiture was not warranted.

The Order identified several specific respects in which the public interest would or might be harmed if a sweeping divestiture requirement were imposed: the stability and continuity of meritorious service provided by the newspaper owners as a group would be lost; owners who had provided meritorious service would unfairly be denied the opportunity to continue in operation; "economic dislocations" might prevent new owners from obtaining sufficient working capital to maintain the quality of local programming; and local ownership of broadcast stations would probably decrease. We cannot say that the FCC acted irrationally in concluding that these public interest harms outweighed the potential gains that would follow from increasing diversification of ownership.

[W]hile diversification of ownership is a relevant factor in the context of license renewal as well as initial licensing, the FCC has long considered the past performance of the incumbent as the most important factor in deciding whether to grant license renewal and thereby to allow the existing owner to continue in operation. Even where an incumbent is challenged by a competing applicant who offers greater potential in terms of diversification, the FCC's general practice has been to go with the "proven product" and grant renewal if the incumbent has rendered meritorious service.

In the instant proceeding, the FCC specifically noted that the existing newspaper-broadcast cross-owners as a group had a "long record of service" in the public interest; many were pioneers in the broadcasting industry and had established and continued "[t]raditions of service" from the outset. Notwithstanding the FCC's diversification policy, all were granted initial licenses upon findings that the public interest would be served thereby, and those that had been in existence for more than three years had also had their licenses renewed on the ground that the public interest would be furthered. The FCC noted, moreover, that its own study of existing co-located newspaper-television combinations showed that in terms of percentage of time devoted to several categories of local programming, these stations had displayed "an undramatic but nonetheless statistically significant superiority" over other television stations. An across-the-board divestiture requirement would result in loss of the services of these superior licensees, and—whether divestiture caused actual losses to existing owners, or just denial of reasonably anticipated gains—the result would

be that future licensees would be discouraged from investing the resources necessary to produce quality service.

At the same time, there was no guarantee that the licensees who replaced the existing cross-owners would be able to provide the same level of service or demonstrate the same long-term commitment to broadcasting. And even if the new owners were able in the long run to provide similar or better service, the FCC found that divestiture would cause serious disruption in the transition period. Thus, the FCC observed that new owners "would lack the long knowledge of the community and would have to begin raw," and—because of high interest rates—might not be able to obtain sufficient working capital to maintain the quality of local programming.

The FCC's fear that local ownership would decline was grounded in a rational prediction, based on its knowledge of the broadcasting industry and supported by comments in the record, that many of the existing newspaper-broadcast combinations owned by local interests would respond to the divestiture requirement by trading stations with out-of-town owners. It is undisputed that roughly 75% of the existing co-located newspaper-television combinations are locally owned, and these owners' knowledge of their local communities and concern for local affairs, built over a period of years, would be lost if they were replaced with outside interests. Local ownership in and of itself has been recognized to be a factor of some—if relatively slight—significance even in the context of initial licensing decisions. It was not unreasonable, therefore, for the FCC to consider it as one of several factors militating against divestiture of combinations that have been in existence for many years.

In light of these countervailing considerations, we cannot agree with the court of appeals that it was arbitrary and capricious for the FCC to "grandfather" most existing combinations, and to leave opponents of these combinations to their remedies in individual renewal proceedings. In the latter connection we note that, while individual renewal proceedings are unlikely to accomplish any "overall restructuring" of the existing ownership patterns, the Order does make clear that existing combinations will be subject to challenge by competing applicants in renewal proceedings, to the same extent as they were prior to the instant rulemaking proceedings. That is, diversification of ownership will be a relevant but somewhat secondary factor. And, even in the absence of a competing applicant, license renewal may be denied if, *inter alia,* a challenger can show that a common owner has engaged in specific economic or programming abuses.

In concluding that the FCC acted unreasonably in not extending its divestiture requirement across-the-board, the court of appeals apparently placed heavy reliance on a "presumption" that existing newspaper-broadcast combinations "do not serve the public interest." The court derived this presumption primarily from the commission's own diversification policy, as "reaffirmed" by adoption of the prospective rules in this proceeding, and secondarily from "[t]he policies of the First Amendment," and the commission's statutory duty to "encourage the larger and more effective use of radio in the public interest" 47 U.S.C. § 303(g). As explained above, we agree that diversification of ownership furthers statutory and constitutional policies, and, as the FCC recognized, separating existing newspaper-broadcast combinations would promote diversification. But the weighing of policies under the "public interest" standard is a task that Congress has delegated to the FCC in the first instance, and we are unable to find anything in the Communications Act, the First Amendment, or the FCC's past or present practices that would require the FCC to "presume" that its diversification policy should be given controlling weight in all circumstances.

Such a "presumption" would seem to be inconsistent with the FCC's longstanding and judicially approved practice of giving controlling weight in some circumstances to its more general goal of achieving "the best practicable service to the public." Certainly, as discussed above, the FCC through its license renewal policy has made clear that it considers diversification of ownership to be a factor of less significance when deciding whether to allow an existing licensee to continue in operation than when evaluating applicants seeking initial licensing. Nothing in the language or the legislative history of § 303(g) indicates that Congress intended to foreclose all differences in treatment between new and existing licensees, and indeed, in amending § 307(d) of the Act in 1952, Congress appears to have lent its approval to the commission's policy of evaluating existing licensees on a somewhat different

basis than new applicants. Moreover, if enactment of the prospective rules in this proceeding itself were deemed to create a "presumption" in favor of divestiture, the commission's ability to experiment with new policies would be severely hampered.

We also must conclude that the court of appeals erred in holding that it was arbitrary to order divestiture in the 16 "egregious cases" while allowing other existing combinations to continue in operation. The FCC's decision was based not—as the court of appeals may have believed—on a conclusion that divestiture would be more harmful in the grandfathered markets than in the 16 affected markets, but rather on a judgment that the need for diversification was especially great in cases of local monopoly. This policy judgment was certainly not irrational, see *United States v. Radio Corp. of America,* 358 U.S., at 351–352, and indeed was founded on the very same assumption that underpinned the diversification policy itself and the prospective rules upheld by the court of appeals and now by this Court—that the greater the number of owners in a market, the greater the possibility of achieving diversity of program and service viewpoints.

As to the FCC's criteria for determining which existing newspaper-broadcast combinations have an "effective monopoly" in the "local market-place of ideas as well as economically," we think the standards settled upon by the commission reflect a rational legislative-type judgment. Some line had to be drawn, and it was hardly unreasonable for the commission to confine divestiture to communities in which there is common ownership of the only daily newspaper and either the only television station or the only broadcast station of any kind encompassing the entire community with a clear signal. It was not irrational, moreover, for the commission to disregard media sources other than newspapers and broadcast stations in setting its divestiture standards. The studies cited by the commission in its notice of rulemaking unanimously concluded that newspapers and television are the two most widely utilized media sources for local news and discussion of public affairs; and, as the FCC noted, "aside from the fact that [magazines and other periodicals] often had only a tiny fraction in the market, they were not given real weight since they often dealt exclusively with regional or national issues and ignored local issues." Moreover, the differences in treatment between radio and television stations were certainly justified in light of the far greater influence of television than radio as a source for local news. The judgment of the court of appeals is affirmed in part and reversed in part.

It is so ordered.

COMMENT

The Supreme Court decision in the cross-ownership case gave a new sense of security to incumbent or existing licensees by declaring that past performance by the incumbent licensee rather than diversification of ownership was the "most important factor in deciding whether to grant license renewals." See *Central Florida Enterprises v. FCC*, text, p. 705.

In its cross-ownership rules opinion, the FCC emphasized that the rules derived from First Amendment policy rather than antitrust policy. The FCC saw diversification of ownership as a First Amendment goal. The Supreme Court agreed with this perspective.

But is the whole philosophy of the diversification of ownership in broadcasting wrongheaded? The concept apparently assumes that the more diffuse the ownership of broadcast stations, the more diverse the content of broadcast programming will be. But is this assumption realistic? Apparently, Congress does not think so. The Telecommunications Act of 1996 allows a higher concentration of ownership in the broadcast industry than the FCC rules had previously allowed. Why?

Justice Marshall acknowledged that an FCC study of co-located newspaper-television combinations revealed that such combinations showed an "'undramatic but nonetheless statistically significant superiority'" in the percentage of programming time devoted to some local programming. If co-located newspaper-broadcast combinations display a measurably superior performance, how can a prospective ban on the formation of such combinations be justified?

Did the Court sustain the prospective ban based on the principle that the formation of broadcast regulatory policy is an FCC and not a judicial responsibility? Perhaps the FCC's decision to root the cross-ownership rules in First Amendment policy rather than antitrust policy indicates that the rules reflect a certain leap of First Amendment faith rather than any empirically or economically demonstrable policy.

If the Supreme Court had upheld the court of appeals's extension of the ban on cross-ownership to existing combinations, the result would not necessarily have been a substantial change in ownership patterns in the communications industry, at least not on a national basis. A ban on existing cross-ownership combinations would have encouraged trades. A newspaper in one city might sell its television station in that city to a newspaper in another and buy in its stead the television station in the other city.

Although the Supreme Court may have "grandfathered" existing cross-ownership combinations, such combinations are by no means impervious to future attack. The Court, per Justice Marshall, was careful to say: "And even in the absence of a competing applicant, license renewal may be denied if a challenger can show that a common owner has engaged in specific economic or programming abuses." What would constitute an economic abuse? What would a programming abuse be?

The Telecommunications Act of 1996 did not grapple with the newspaper-broadcast cross-ownership rule, but Chairman Reed Hundt of the FCC has indicated that he might reconsider the rule. Furthermore, the FCC has followed a liberal waiver policy with respect to the cross-ownership rule. See *Metropolitan Council of N.A.A.C.P. Branches v. FCC*, p. 763. Does the cross-ownership rule have a future? In a written question and answer interview with the editors of *Broadcasting and Cable*, President Clinton declared his opposition to relaxation of the cross-ownership rule. Earlier in the interview, President Clinton said: "I believe strongly that diverse ownership of the mass media is critical to the free flow of ideas and that we must work to insure that there are multiple voices available in each and every community." *Broadcasting and Cable*, September 23, 1996, at 24.

Congress, Cross-Ownership, and the Rupert Murdoch Caper

On March 19, 1988, the U.S. Court of Appeals for the District of Columbia, per Judge Williams, decided a much publicized case involving a clash between celebrated media magnate, Rupert Murdoch, and the cross-ownership rules. See *News America Pub. Inc. v. FCC,* 844 F.2d 800 (D.C. Cir. 1988). The case involved analysis of the meaning of the Supreme Court's decision in *FCC v. National Citizens Committee for Broadcasting (NCCB).* More important, the case considered a continuing resolution demonstrating congressional attachment to diversification of ownership policies such as the cross-ownership rules. The resolution also signaled congressional dissatisfaction with the relaxed enforcement of such policies by the FCC in its present deregulatory mode. The facts, as derived from Judge Williams's decision, are as follows. News America, Inc., controlled by K. Murdoch, is a corporation with huge broadcast and newspaper holdings around the world. Rupert Murdoch also owns Fox Television, Inc., which owns numerous television stations throughout the United States. In November 1985 and November 1986, Fox Television obtained permission from the FCC to acquire WNYW-TV in New York City and WXNE-TV in Boston. Because News America owned the New York *Post* and the Boston *Herald,* these acquisitions required waivers of the cross-ownership rules. (Do you see why, absent a waiver, these acquisitions would have violated the newspaper-broadcast cross-ownership rules?)

The FCC granted the temporary waivers—two years for the New York acquisition and eighteen months for the one in Boston. Murdoch was expected to sell the newspapers within these periods. The waiver extended to March 6, 1988, for the New York interests and to June 30, 1988, for those in Boston. News America sold the *Post* on March 7, but still retained the Boston paper.

On December 22, 1987, Congress passed and President Reagan signed a Continuing Resolution appropriating all of the funds for the federal government for the 1988 fiscal year. A provision in that resolution, an amendment introduced by Senator Hollings of South Carolina and Senator Kennedy of Massachusetts, would have deprived the FCC of any power to give Murdoch any additional waivers in these matters:

Provided further, that none of the funds appropriated in this Act or any other Act may be used to repeal, to retroactively apply changes in, or to begin or continue a re-examination of the rules of the Federal Communications Commission with respect to the common ownership of a daily newspaper and

a television station where the grade A contour of the television station encompasses the entire community in which the newspaper is published, *or to extend the time period of current grants of temporary waivers to achieve compliance with such rules.* [Emphasis added.] See Making Further Continuing Appropriations for the Fiscal Year Ending September 30, 1988, H.R. Rep. No. 100-498, at 34 (1987) (Conference Report).

Judge Williams analyzed the statute as follows: "As of December 22 the sole holder of any temporary waiver of the sort specified in the italicized phrase was News America Publishing Inc. [I]ts sole effect was to forbid extensions of those waivers." News America applied to the FCC for extensions of its waivers anyway on January 14, 1988. On the basis of the Hollings Amendment, the FCC issued an order denying these requests. Review was sought and obtained in the court of appeals, and the FCC's order was stayed.

The court of appeals ruled that the last eighteen italicized words of the Hollings Amendment were unconstitutional, but did not rule on the rest of the amendment. The court said that, under the First and Fifth Amendments, it had to "scrutinize" the legislation under a "test more stringent than the 'minimum rationality' criterion." The FCC argued that *FCC v. NCCB,* 436 U.S. 775 (1978), established "the minimum rationality standard for 'structural' regulations of the broadcast industry." Judge Williams, however, declared:

[T]he Hollings Amendment is far from purely structural. Indeed, it is structural only in form, as it applies to a closed class of one publisher/broadcaster. Thus, even if we were to accept the Commission's analysis of *NCCB,* we would not agree that the Amendment should be lumped with the cross-ownership rules and accorded the high deference that the Commission believes the latter received. We need not go so far as the Supreme Court in *League of Women Voters,* and require a showing that the Amendment's classification is narrowly drawn to serve a substantial governmental interest. What suffices for this case is that more is required than "minimum rationality.

Judge Williams concluded that the waiver request should be remanded back to the FCC:

Congress has denied a single publisher/broadcaster the opportunity to ask the FCC to exercise its discretion to extend its waivers. Whatever Congress' motives, the "potential for abuse" of First

Amendment interests is so great in such restrictions, *cf. Minneapolis Star,* 460 U.S. at 592, that bland invocation of Congress's conventional power to approach a problem one step at a time cannot sustain the Amendment.

Further, Judge Williams suggested that continuation of a waiver policy might be necessary if the cross-ownership rules were to avoid First Amendment challenge:

> [T]he Supreme Court in sustaining the cross-ownership rules against First Amendment attack found that their "reasonableness" was "underscored" by the availability of waivers where the station and newspaper "cannot survive without common ownership." NCCB 436 U.S. at 802 n.20. Thus, whether or not the waiver process is constitutionally compelled, First Amendment values are implicated in the process and require even-handed treatment of all applicants. We do not, of course, express any opinion as to whether News America is entitled to an extension of its remaining waiver.

As we saw earlier, the Hollings Amendment also forbade the FCC from changing its rules on cross-ownership of a daily newspaper and a television station in the community. Note that the *News America* decision did not invalidate that part of the resolution. Only the part concerning waiver extensions was invalidated.

In dissent, Judge Spottswood Robinson said that Congress feared that the FCC was about to repeal the cross-ownership rule; indeed, the FCC brief in the case conceded as much. Congress was also concerned, Judge Robinson said, by the FCC's use of waivers in connection with the cross-ownership rules: "Congress recognized the distinct possibility that through indefinite or successive extensions of a temporary waiver, the FCC could grant the equivalent of a permanent waiver without any showing that the heavy burden of justifying such a waiver had been met." Moreover Judge Robinson believed that the Hollings Amendment not only did not violate the First Amendment but in fact promoted First Amendment values as explained by Justice Marshall in *FCC v. NCCB.* How could this be?

Judge Robinson also did not believe that the standard of review employed in *League of Women Voters* should have been used:

> Congress has blocked News America's access to the Commission only for the purpose of requesting an extension of the waiver it presently enjoys. That is a far cry from the content focused restriction

involved in *League of Women Voters,* which outlawed a particular type of highly valued speech. The *League of Women Voters* standard of review is unsuitable here.

Are you persuaded by Judge Robinson's First Amendment defense of the provision against waiver extensions in the Hollings Amendment? Generally speaking, do you think cross-ownership rules frustrate or further First Amendment objectives?

The FCC's Cross-Ownership Rule Waiver Policy: The *Metropolitan Council* Case

Rupert Murdoch's continuing involvement with the New York *Post* led to more encounters with the FCC's cross-ownership rule. In 1988 Murdoch sold the *Post* to Peter Kalikow, a real estate developer. Kalikow declared bankruptcy in 1991, and the bankruptcy court granted real estate developer Abe Hirschfeld operational control on the basis of his pledge to invest $3 million in the *Post.* Hirschfeld soon fired the *Post*'s editor-in-chief and others, prompting a staff revolt. New York Governor Mario Cuomo then asked Murdoch to repurchase the *Post.* Murdoch agreed providing, among other conditions, that he could obtain a permanent waiver of the FCC cross-ownership ban.

Accordingly, Fox Television requested a permanent waiver from the cross-ownership rule. This request was sought because Fox's principal stockholder, Murdoch, had reacquired the New York *Post* and because Fox owned a television station in the New York market. Fox's basis for a waiver was as follows. No other viable purchaser had shown a willingness to undertake the financial burden of revitalizing the New York *Post.* Second, application of the cross-ownership rule in these circumstances would frustrate the underlying policy of diversity and instead would result in elimination of a competitive voice. The FCC considered Fox's waiver request in an expedited process and in a declaratory ruling granted the permanent waiver by a 2–1 vote. *Fox TV Stations,* 8 F.C.C.R. 5341 (1993).

Metropolitan Council of N.A.A.C.P. Branches, other civil rights organizations and various individuals appealed the FCC order granting Fox a permanent waiver. The following report of the federal appeals decision focuses only on the decision's discussion of cross-ownership issues.

Metropolitan Council of N.A.A.C.P. Branches v. FCC

46 F.3d 1154 (D.C. Cir. 1995).

SENTELLE, Circuit Judge:

The FCC observed that it devised waivers for the cross-ownership rule for four situations wherein application of the rule would be unduly harsh:

> (1) where there is an inability to dispose of an interest to conform to the rules; (2) where the only sale price possible is at an artificially depressed price; (3) where separate ownership and operation of the newspaper and station cannot be supported in the locality; and (4) where, for whatever reason, the purposes of the rule would be disserved by divestiture. [8 F.C.C.R.] at 5348.

The FCC therefore concluded that Fox's request fell under the fourth criterion for a waiver and that a waiver was warranted. The FCC reasoned that given the wide array of broadcast stations and newspapers in New York, Murdoch's potential for amassing an undue amount of control in the marketplace for ideas was unlikely and any cost to diversity from the waiver would be outweighed by the preservation of the *Post*.

[A]ppellants contend that not only does the grant of a permanent waiver to Fox, part of the world's largest media company, effectively eviscerate the long established cross-ownership rule, it violated Congress' direction that no federal funds be used to repeal or re-examine the rule. *See* Pub. L. No. 102-395, 106 Stat. 11846 (1992).

[The FCC] concluded that a permanent, rather than a temporary waiver was appropriate based on the persuasive business reasons Fox offered showing that a permanent waiver was necessary to its long-term strategy for revising the *Post*. For example, without a permanent waiver Fox would be unable to conclude meaningful negotiations with the *Post*'s labor unions, suppliers, distributors, creditors and advertisers. Also, Murdoch could not be expected to sustain the huge operating losses and undertake the enormous commitment necessary to revitalize the *Post* without knowing whether he would ultimately be forced to sell the newspaper or the TV station.

The FCC also concluded that a grant of the waiver was unlikely to have a significant impact on the diversity and competition concerns underlying the cross-ownership rule and that it has no authority to base its actions upon the anticipated content of the newspaper. It found that appellants' view of the New York market was not borne out since the record showed that not only was New York's media market uniquely competitive, the *Post* and Murdoch's TV station have a very small audience and advertising share of it. Furthermore, because waivers for extraordinary circumstances have been contemplated since the rule's adoption, the FCC determination that such circumstances obtain and warrant a waiver does not violate Congress' ban on repealing or reexamining the rule.

Because a forecast of the direction in which future public interest lies necessarily involves deductions based on the expert knowledge of the agency, in such circumstances complete factual support in the record for the FCC's judgment or prediction is neither possible nor required. *National Citizens Comm. for Broad.* Furthermore, the FCC properly disregarded arguments about the editorial content of the *Post* because the application of the cross-ownership rule cannot lawfully be based on a party's political, economic, or social views. Finally, the FCC did consider, but rejected, appellants' evidence of alleged anti-competitive conduct by the *Post* under Murdoch's control, and any future anti-competitive conduct can be raised and considered in the proceeding to renew the license for Fox's New York station.

The FCC's detailed decision granting Fox a permanent waiver was not arbitrary and capricious or unsupported by the record. Accordingly, the appeal is hereby denied.

COMMENT

If FCC policy is to be liberal in granting waivers to its cross-ownership rule, formal adherence to the rule by the FCC can become a trap for the unwary. Why? Where does the FCC get its authority to waive compliance to its cross-ownership rule?

CHAPTER 12

LEGAL CONTROLS ON POLITICAL AND PUBLIC ISSUE PROGRAMMING

CHAPTER OUTLINE

BROADCASTING AND POLITICAL DEBATE: SECTION 315 AND THE "EQUAL TIME" REQUIREMENT

Politicians believe that their fate is much influenced by how they are treated by broadcasters. In fact, they've been concerned about that since near the dawn of federal radio regulation. Section 18 of the Radio Act of 1927, the earliest general federal law governing broadcasting, imposed two requirements on broadcasters when dealing with political candidates. First, if a broadcaster let one legally qualified candidate for a public office use a station, then the broadcaster had to provide "equal opportunities" to that candidate's legally qualified opponents to use the same station. Second, whenever candidates used stations under this section, the broadcaster could not censor the candidate's use.

Seven years later, these provisions were incorporated into the Federal Communications Act of 1934, 47 U.S.C. §§ 151–614 (1990). They endure today as section 315 of that Act. The current version of the statute, 47 U.S.C. § 315(a) states:

Sec. 315 Facilities for Candidates for Public Office

a. [**Equal opportunities requirement;** censorship prohibition; allowance of station use; news appearances exemption; public interest; public issues discussion opportunities.]

If any licensee shall permit any person who is a legally qualified candidate for any public office to use a broadcasting station, he shall afford equal opportunities to all other such candidates for that office in the use of such broadcasting station: *Provided,* That such licensee shall have no power of censorship over the material broadcast under the provisions of this section. No obligation is hereby imposed under this subsection upon any licensee to allow the use of its station by any such candidate. Appearance by a legally qualified candidate on any—

1. bona fide newscast,
2. bona fide news interview,
3. bona fide news documentary (if the appearance of the candidate is incidental to the presentation of the subject or subjects covered by the news documentary), or
4. on-the-spot coverage of bona fide news events (including but not limited to political conventions and activities incidental thereto), shall not be deemed to be use of a broadcasting station within the meaning of this subsection. Nothing in the foregoing sentence shall be construed as relieving broadcasters, in connection with the presentation on newscasts, news interviews, news documentaries, and on-the-spot coverage of news events, from the obligation imposed upon them under this chapter to operate in the public interest and to afford reasonable opportunity for the discussion of conflicting views on issues of public importance.

b. [**Broadcast media rates**] The charges made for use of any broadcasting station by any person who is a legally qualified candidate for any public office in connection with his campaign for nomination for election, or election to such office shall not exceed—

1. during the forty-five days preceding the date of a primary or primary runoff election and during the sixty days preceding the date of a general or special election in which such person is a candidate, the lowest unit charge of the station for the same class and amount of time for the same period; and
2. at any other time, the charges made for comparable use of such station by other users thereof.

c. [**Definitions**] For purposes of this section—
1. the term "broadcasting station" includes a community antenna television system; and
2. the terms "licensee" and "station licensee" when used with respect to a community antenna television system mean the operator of such system.

d. [**Rules and regulations**] The Commission shall prescribe appropriate rules and regulations to carry out the provisions of this section.

The language of the Act reveals how interested Congress has been in political broadcasting over the years. The portions of the Act regulating rates [sec. 315(b)] were added in two stages. In 1952, Congress feared that some broadcasters were ripping off political candidates by setting artificially high candidate rates. Section 315(b) prohibits broadcasters from charging candidates more than they normally charge their other advertisers. In 1972, Congress decided that candidates should get the lowest rates available and hence added the lowest unit charge language to sec. 315(b). The four exceptions to the equal opportunities principle for news-related programming were added by Congress in 1959, after the Federal Communications Commission (FCC) ruled that equal opportunities—as the law was then written—applied to news appearances. Fearing that broadcasters would not cover the appearances of incumbent candidates, Congress hastily amended the law.

In 1972, Congress decided that sec. 315 needed a complement. As we'll see shortly, sec. 315 creates what could be called a contingent right of access. If a broadcaster provides access to one candidate, then that broadcaster must provide equal opportunity to use the station to that candidate's opponents. By itself, however, sec. 315 does not require that broadcasters provide any candidates with access to the station in the first instance. Recognizing that its "lowest unit charge" efforts to drive down candidate ad costs might lead broadcasters to turn away candidates altogether, in 1972 Congress amended sec. 312 of the Communications Act of 1934. Section 312 is where the most drastic remedies of the FCC are found—the conditions under which the FCC licenses broadcasters. Section 312(a)(7) states:

> (a) The Commission may revoke any station license or construction permit * * * (7) for willful or repeated failure to allow reasonable access to or to permit purchase of reasonable amounts of time for the use of a broadcasting station by a legally qualified candidate for Federal elective office on behalf of his candidacy.

Section 312 has been the subject of substantial litigation and interpretation (summarized below). Suffice it to say for now that it complements sec. 315 by opening up the airwaves to *federal* candidates—something sec. 315 by itself does not do.

Finally, by way of introduction to a complex subject, the FCC's "fairness doctrine" should be mentioned. This concept will be discussed later in this chapter, but a few initial points should be made here. First, the fairness doctrine has been scuttled. Firmly established by the FCC in 1949, it was abandoned by the FCC in 1987, and the federal courts have approved. Nevertheless, anyone interested in broadcasting law should have some understanding of the doctrine.

Unlike secs. 315 and 312, the fairness doctrine normally did not deal with how broadcasters treated persons; instead, it dealt with how broadcasters treated controversial issues of public importance. In its liveliest form, the doctrine said that broadcasters had to do two things; devote reasonable attention to controversial issues and provide reasonable opportunities for opposing viewpoints to be heard/seen on their stations.

Sections 312 and 315 remain solid law. The fate of the fairness doctrine, as already noted, is much more nebulous. Thus, those who want to understand how political content is regulated must try to (1) distinguish between secs. 312 and 315 of the Communications Act and (2) figure out the current status of the fairness doctrine. We begin with sec. 315.

Section 315: "Equal Opportunities"

Basically, sec. 315 says that if a broadcaster lets one "legally qualified candidate for public office" use his or her station, then, with some exceptions, "equal opportunities" must be given to "legally qualified opponents" to "use" the same station. In addition, it regulates what candidates can be charged for their uses. These statements set up a model for discussing what sec. 315 requires:

a. What's a "public office"? Who is a "legally qualified candidate" and who is a "legally qualified opponent"?
b. What's a "use" of a station?
c. When are "uses" exempt from creating equal opportunity rights/obligations?
d. What's an "equal opportunity"?
e. How are rates regulated?
f. What control can the broadcaster have over candidate uses?
g. Is this whole system constitutional?

WHAT IS A "PUBLIC OFFICE"? WHO IS A "LEGALLY QUALIFIED CANDIDATE" AND A "LEGALLY QUALIFIED OPPONENT"?   Although there are many public offices in this country, the FCC has interpreted sec. 315 as applying only to public offices where the electorate chooses the officeholder. The FCC has ruled that *all* elected offices come under sec. 315, regardless of their importance. Thus, for example, the president of the United States is covered, but so is the dogcatcher of Podunk—provided that the voters of Podunk elect their dogcatcher. Appointed offices, for example, a city manager in many communities, do not come under sec. 315 even if, by chance, somebody mounts a rather concerted campaign to be appointed. If the electorate does not vote for the office, it is not a "public office" under this portion of the Communications Act.

An inquiry into the meaning of the phrase "legally qualified" candidate is basic to understanding the statute. *Flory v. FCC,* 528 F.2d 124 (7th Cir. 1975), considered the problem. Ishmael Flory was nominated by the state committee of the Communist Party to run in the 1974 election for U.S. senator from Illinois. Because the Communist Party had not polled at least 5 percent of the vote in the preceding election, a nominating petition requiring 25,000 signatures was needed for its candidate to appear on the ballot.

Between the time of the nomination and the time when Flory eventually obtained the necessary signatures, he requested equal time in response to debates between the Republican and

Democratic candidates that were aired by broadcasters. The FCC refused to order the broadcasters to give equal time to Flory: because Flory had not yet secured a place on the ballot, he was not a legally qualified candidate at the time the debates were broadcast.

The court held that Flory was not precluded from seeking equal time where he indicated that he would run as a write-in candidate if he did not obtain a place on the ballot:

> We cannot agree with the argument of the Commission that the rule which provides qualification either by obtaining a place on the ballot or by becoming eligible by being a write-in candidate must be construed as setting up mutually exclusive routes.

Nevertheless, the court did not vacate the FCC order in the case on the ground that Flory should have sought review of the FCC rulings when they were made rather than attempting to obtain makeup time for past erroneous rulings.

As a result of the *Flory* case, the FCC amended its rules defining a "legally qualified" candidate. See *Amendment of the Commission's Rules Relating to Broadcasts by Legally Qualified Candidates,* 60 F.C.C.2d 615 (1976). Under the new rules, a candidate is legally qualified if he

1. has publicly announced his candidacy,
2. "meets the qualifications prescribed by the applicable laws to hold the office for which he is a candidate," and
3. either:
   a. has qualified for a place on the ballot, or
   b. "has publicly committed himself to seeking election by the write-in method, and is eligible under the applicable law" to be voted for by write-in or other method and "makes a substantial showing that he is a bona fide candidate for nomination or office."

With this definition, the FCC has attempted to clarify the questions left unanswered by *Flory.* The rules require that the candidate publicly commit himself to seeking election by the write-in method in the event that his attempts to get on the ballot fail. But the question remains: Is the candidate's word alone sufficient "public commitment"? The FCC's insistence on a "substantial showing" of bona fide candidacy suggests that more than a casual announcement by a candidate is necessary. Perhaps the pattern of continued assurance that the candidate will turn to a write-in candidacy, as found in *Flory,* will be sufficient. See also *Broadcasts and Cablecasts by Legally Qualified Candidates for Public Office,* 44 Fed. Reg. 32790 (1978).

The FCC recently summarized its understanding of who are "legally qualified" candidates as follows:

> Only "legally qualified candidates" are afforded equal opportunities rights under Section 15 of the Communications Act. Section 73.1940 of the Commission's rule defines a legally qualified candidate by reference to whether a candidate has qualified for a place on the ballot in accordance with the law of the election jurisdiction or has made a substantial showing of candidacy. A substantial showing involves the traditional indicia of an actual candidacy such as the establishment of campaign headquarters, speech making, fund raising, etc. In the Presidential context, a candidate who has so qualified in at least 10 states is deemed a candidate in all states. 47 C.F.R. § 73.1940. See *In re Requests of Fox Broad. Co., Pub. Broad. Serv., and Capital Cities/ABC, Inc.,* 11 F.C.C.R. 11101, 11106 n. 11 (1996).

Primary Elections and the "Equal Time" Rule Section 315, then, comes into play whenever there are declared, legally qualified candidates for elective office. The statute says that when that is the case, if broadcasters let one legally qualified candidate for an office "use" their station, then they have to give legally qualified opponents an equal opportunity to use the station. The question is, when do candidates oppose each other? As a result of FCC interpretation, it becomes important whether one is talking about a primary or a general election period.

During a primary, nobody—really—is running for a public office. Rather, various groups of candidates are running for the nomination of their respective party. The FCC treats each of these races as a campaign for "public office" under sec. 315 (even though, of course, they are really party, not public, offices, and even though, in the case of president, they are really campaigns to elect a group of electors rather than a candidate *per se*). A group of Democrats, for example, might run in a primary for the Democratic nomination for president. At the same time, a different group of Republicans might run for the Republican nomination for president. The FCC has ruled that during primary season, candidates from different parties are not "opponents" under sec. 315. Thus, use of a station by one of the Democratic candidates for an office during the primary would entitle the other legally qualified opponents for the Democratic nomination to claim "equal opportunity" rights. It would not enable any of the Republican candidates to claim equal opportunity rights, however. Once the primaries are over and parties have selected their candidates, then all of the candidates from different parties become opponents. During the general election season, "use" of a station by a Republican candidate for an office, for example, would entitle the Democratic opponent to claim equal opportunity rights. For that matter, independent or third-party candidates for that office would also be entitled to equal opportunities as well.

This interpretation can work to the disadvantage of minor candidates. Richard Kay, the unopposed candidate of the American Independent Party for the Ohio Senate, requested broadcast time equivalent to that afforded to major party candidates who were engaged in Ohio primary elections. Both the Democratic and Republican primaries were contested, and in each of these major party primaries the opponents matched against each other were well known: Governor Rhodes and Congressman Taft in the Republican primary and Howard Metzenbaum and John Glenn in the Democratic primary. The candidates for these races were offered broadcast time for appearances. The FCC refused to order the broadcasters to give Kay equal time. The federal court upheld the FCC. *Kay v. FCC,* 443 F.2d 638 (D.C. Cir. 1970).

While agreeing that primary elections were covered under sec. 315, the court ruled that primary elections held by one party are to be considered separately from primary elections of other parties. Equal opportunity need only be afforded candidates for nomination "for the same office in the same party's primary." Section 315 provides for equal opportunities only when candidates are competing against each other. Appearance on the broadcast media, prior to the primary, of candidates of one party does not entitle candidates of another party to equal time. Candidates in primary elections are running solely against other candidates from their own party and not against candidates from other parties.

The *Kay* case obviously presents some serious obstacles to the candidate of the minority party.

Where a candidate, as was the case in *Kay,* is unopposed in his party's primary, the equal time rule provides no assistance. In short, major-party candidates in contested primaries may gain great broadcast impact in terms of coverage and publicity before the equal time rule can be invoked. The *Kay* interpretation with respect to the application of the equal time rule to uncontested primaries is therefore particularly damaging to third-party candidates who are necessarily dependent on media exposure if they are to popularize and legitimize their parties and candidacies.

Does the *Kay* ruling open the door for potential abuse by broadcasters? Note that if Richard Kay had had an opponent in the American Independent Party primary, his opponent would have had rights to equal time if Kay was given the broadcast time he requested. The FCC recognized that primary elections were covered by sec. 315 when it stated that "both primary elections, nominating conventions and general elections are comprehended within the terms of Section 315."

Who Is "Qualified" Presidential or Vice-Presidential Candidate?   The FCC applies some special standards when it comes to candidates for president and vice-president. Sometimes these standards mean that broadcasters have to treat as "candidates" under sec. 315 persons whom their audience can't vote for. The problem is that the presidency and the vice-presidency are the only offices we elect nationally, and we do not even elect them directly. Instead, we use the electoral college system. This complicates sec. 315 as it applies to candidates for president and vice-president.

The FCC's rules work as follows. First, broadcasters must treat as candidates under sec. 315 *all* persons who have qualified for the presidential or vice-presidential ballot in their service area (or, if write-ins are allowed, are making a serious effort to get elected that way). This is so even if these persons have qualified in no other sections of the country and have no chance of being elected president or vice-president.

The voters the broadcaster serves have a choice—they can vote for such minor candidates—so the FCC applies sec. 315 to them. Second, all broadcasters must treat as candidates under sec. 315 persons who have qualified for the ballot in ten states anywhere in the United

States. Thus, sometimes, broadcasters have to consider sec. 315 implications for candidates their listeners or viewers cannot vote for and who are not on the local ballot. The theory here is that because a candidate could win the presidency or vice-presidency by taking the ten largest states—that would be enough electoral college votes to win—broadcasters should treat persons as "national candidates" once they have qualified in at least ten states. In other words, broadcasters have to treat as sec. 315 candidates for president and vice-president everybody who has qualified for a place on the local ballot (even if not nationally electible) plus any candidates who have qualified in ten states someplace in the nation even if they have not qualified in the broadcasters' local service area.

WHAT IS A "USE" OF A STATION?   The policies just described show that the FCC is not anxious to guess when somebody is a candidate. Nobody is a candidate until he or she says so. Similarly, the FCC has developed rather rigid notions of what a "use" of a station by a candidate is under sec. 315. Basically, a legally qualified candidate for public office "uses" a station whenever he or she appears on the station in an identifiable fashion. In television, it does not matter whether that appearance is audio or video. Candidates, for example, often produce commercials in which they do not appear—"person-on-the-street" spots in which ordinary folks say what a great person the candidate is. That is not a use of the station as far as the FCC is concerned, because the candidate has not appeared. If, however, the candidate appears in any way in the spot—in video, for example, in a brief still picture at the end of the spot or, in audio, reading the sponsorship ID lines explaining who has paid for the spot—then the same spot becomes a "use" under sec. 315 because it includes an identifiable candidate appearance.

Basically, the FCC does not want to get in the business of guessing which uses are political and which are not. Thus, the general rule is that *any* identifiable appearance by a legally qualified candidate for public office constitutes a use. This can lead to some interesting decisions.

In *In re Adrian Weiss*, 58 F.C.C.2d 342 (1976), the applicability of the equal time doctrine to nonpolitical broadcasts was tested dur-ing the 1976 presidential campaign when a broadcast station in California sought a ruling prior to airing old movies starring Ronald Reagan, a legally qualified candidate in the New Hampshire presidential primary. The FCC remarked that attempting to distinguish between political and nonpolitical use of broadcast facilities by candidates would require highly subjective judgments concerning content and would potentially enlarge government interference with broadcasting operations. Therefore the FCC declined to distinguish between political and nonpolitical appearances and ruled that "the broadcast of movies in which Ronald Reagan appears would be 'use' under Section 315 and would entitle opposing candidates to equal opportunities in the use of the broadcasting station."

At the time of the *Weiss* decision, Ronald Reagan was no longer engaged in an acting career. But what of an actor who is still performing on television and who is also campaigning for office? Should such an actor be successful in urging that his nonpolitical appearances should not impose "equal opportunities obligations upon broadcast licensees"? In *Paulsen v. FCC*, 491 F.2d 887 (9th Cir. 1974), the FCC responded in the negative to this question, and the federal court affirmed. The court explained:

> Paulsen's proposed distinction between political and non-political use would, the FCC contends, require it to make highly subjective judgments concerning the content, context, and potential political impact of a candidate's appearance. We agree.

Indeed, the FCC has ruled that, under certain circumstances, appearances of station news personnel performing their normal functions as broadcast journalists can amount to "uses" under sec. 315. See *Branch v. FCC*, 824 F.2d 37 (D.C. Cir. 1987), p. 785.

At one point, the FCC narrowed its definition of "use" under sec. 315 to reach only those nonexempt candidate appearances "that are controlled, approved, or sponsored by the candidate (or the candidate's authorized committee) after the candidate becomes legally qualified." *In re Codification of the FCC's Political Programming Policies*, 7 F.C.C.R. 678, 685 (1991). However, Tracy Westen and the National Association of Broadcasters contended that the broader *Paulsen*-type definition of "use" had been ratified in the 1959 amendment to sec. 315(a). Although disagreeing with this interpretation, the FCC has since returned to its "previous interpretation"—the broad *Paulsen* definition of "use." *In re Codification of the FCC's Political Programming Policies,* 9 F.C.C.R. 651, 652 (1994).

WHEN ARE "USES" EXEMPT FROM CREATING EQUAL OPPORTUNITY RIGHTS/OBLIGATIONS?

There are three exceptions to this notion that all "identifiable" uses count under sec. 315. The first exception occurs when a candidate "appears" in advertisements run by independent political groups. If such a group runs an ad supporting a candidate, but without that candidate's approval, appearance of the candidate in that spot will not entitle his or her opponents to equal opportunities. If a station allows a group to run a spot opposing a candidate, appearance by that candidate in the spot will not trigger equal opportunity rights for his or her opponents. It may, however, trigger the so-called Zapple Rule and obligate the station to stand willing to sell comparable time to the attacked candidate, if he or she can afford it and wishes to buy response time. The second exception recognized by the FCC is for so-called fleeting uses. The FCC will sometimes rule that a candidate's appearance is so brief or from such a wide angle that it should not count under sec. 315.

The most important exceptions to the idea that all appearances count as uses, however, were those created by Congress in 1959. The FCC had ruled that sec. 315, as then written, was absolute—any appearance, in any format (including news) meant that legally qualified opposing candidates were entitled to equal opportunities. Broadcasters had always, wrongly, assumed that news programs were somehow exempt from sec. 315, and they quickly urged Congress to change the law in response to the FCC's ruling. Congress, therefore, added four "exceptions" to sec. 315 within weeks of the FCC decision. The exceptions have been previously mentioned: (1) bona fide newscasts, (2) bona fide news interviews, (3) bona fide news documentaries (if the appearance of the candidate is incidental to the presentation of the subject or subjects covered by the news documentary), and (4) on-the-spot coverage of bona fide news events (including but not limited to political conventions and activities incidental thereto).

Note that Congress used the phrase "bona fide" in all these exemptions. Bona fide means true or genuine. Inclusion of the phrase gives the FCC the right to decide that some news-related appearances are not real or genuine but are, instead, just ways around the law. The FCC generally defers to what broadcasters, using reasonable, good faith judgment, believe to be exempt programs. The FCC, however, has issued some decisions that define what is a real or genuine use of the exemption and what is not.

The bona fide newscast exemption has presented few problems. Appearances by legally qualified candidates on the regularly scheduled newscasts of radio and TV stations do not create equal opportunity rights for their opponents. Thus, stations can take appearances that might not otherwise be exempt and include them in their newscasts, unless there is evidence showing that the reason for doing so was to deliberately favor one candidate over another. A newscast does not even have to be regularly scheduled to qualify for this exemption; special news bulletins have also been ruled to be bona fide newscasts.

When Congress exempted bona fide news interviews, it had in mind the news interview shows of 1959—venerable programs like *Meet the Press.* Such programs remain exempt today. If a news interview program is regularly scheduled, sticks to its normal format, is under the control of the broadcaster and not the candidate, and has chosen the people it interviews for their newsworthiness, the program will almost always be ruled exempt by the FCC. A couple of twists were added in recent years, however. For a long time, the FCC exempted only news interview shows that had been regularly scheduled in the past. This made it hard for a broadcaster to start a new interview show near election time. In 1984, the FCC ruled that some proposed news interview programs, if run according to guidelines submitted by the broadcasters to the FCC, would also be exempt. See *CBS Inc.,* 55 R.R.2d 864 (1984) and *NBC Inc.,* 56 R.R.2d 958 (1984). In subsequent years, the FCC has occasionally ruled that bona fide (newsworthy) interview segments of shows that are not wholly devoted to news interviews would also be exempt under this provision of sec. 315.

Bona Fide Newscasts and News Interviews:
Sections 315(a)(1) and (a)(2)

Telecommunications Research and Action Center v. FCC

26 F.3D 185 (D.C. CIR. 1994).

SENTELLE, Circuit Judge:

[A] typical *McLaughlin* program consists of several distinct "news reporting segments." [T]he moderator, John McLaughlin, reads a current news story that is accompanied by a videotaped clip of the events. These video clips are generally supplied by PBS, CNN, or one of the commercial broadcasting networks. After each news segment, a panel of four journalists discusses and debates the issues presented in the story. TRAC argues that [these] segments, cannot qualify as "newscasts" within the plain meaning of section 315 mainly because they do not present several uninterrupted stories in a row, as do typical network newscasts. The [FCC] responds that the statutory term "newscast" simply does not speak to issues of program formatting.

TRAC's petition for review rests upon its contention that the Commission [hereafter, FCC] misconstrued the "bona fide newscast" and "bona fide news interview" exemptions contained in section 315 of the Communications Act. We evaluate TRAC's arguments using the two-step framework set forth in *Chevron U.S.A. Inc. v. Natural Resources Defense Council, Inc.,* 467 U.S. 837 (1984).

[EDITORIAL NOTE: *Under the* Chevron *test, the court first asked whether Congress had spoken directly to the issue at hand in the Communications Act. If not, it will defer to the FCC's reasonable interpretation of its own statute.*]

In the first order under review in this case, the [FCC] denied TRAC's request for an expedited declaratory ruling vacating the [FCC]'s original decision in *Oliver [Productions, Inc.,* 3 F.C.C.R. 6642 (1988),] which held that the news reporting segments of McLaughlin are "bona fide newscasts" exempt from the equal opportunity requirements of Section 315. See *McLaughlin Group Decision,* 7 F.C.C.R. at 6039. TRAC argues that this ruling runs afoul of the plain language and legislative history of the Act.

TRAC first contends that the plain language of the phrase "bona fide newscast" forecloses the [FCC's] application of that term to *McLaughlin.*

The answer is: Congress's choice of the word "newscast" is not sufficiently precise to compel the multi-story program format TRAC suggests. The Communications Act does not define the term at all. And nothing else in the Act suggests that a news segment must present several stories in a row in order to qualify for the "bona fide newscast" exemption. Congress thus left the [FCC] to define the precise contours of the "bona fide newscast" exemption and decide what, if any, format characteristics are necessary to come within the exemption's coverage. Given the statute's silence regarding the required program format of exempt newscasts, we defer to the [FCC's] reasonable interpretation of the "newscast" exemption.

TRAC next contends that the statute's use of the adjective "bona fide" to modify "newscast" plainly excludes the news reporting segments of *McLaughlin.* TRAC argues that in order to qualify as "bona fide," a program's news segments must be selected for the journalistic purpose of informing viewers about current events. But the fact that the modifier "bona fide" may add a newsworthiness requirement to the "newscast" exemption does not mean that the news reporting segments of *McLaughlin* are non-exempt. [The FCC] specifically found that "[r]egarding the 'bona fide' requirement, there is no information before the [FCC] to indicate that the 'news reporting segments' are selected for reasons other than their genuine news value or are designed to advance or harm any particular candidacy." TRAC has come forward with nothing that would cause us to disturb this [FCC] finding.

TRAC finally charges that *McLaughlin* cannot qualify for an equal time exemption because Congress had considered, but refused to create, an exemption for "panel discussions." [T]his argument gets TRAC nowhere because the [FCC] did not exempt *McLaughlin's* panel discussion segments from the equal time requirement. The [FCC] exempted only the news reporting segments, and, there is "no suggestion in the legislative history that Congress also intended to render non-exempt news segments of hybrid programs that also include panel discussion segments."

[EDITORIAL NOTE: *TRAC next argued that the FCC decided incorrectly in a case brought by public broadcasters that "independently produced, bona fide news* interview programs" were exempt from the sec. 315 equal time requirement. Independent Producers Decision, 7 F.C.C.R. 4681 (1992). TRAC first contended that the "bona fide" exemption applies only to FCC licensees, and not to independent producers.]

One does not have to wrestle long with the statutory language to realize that TRAC cannot possibly win the argument that its interpretations of section 315 is compelled by the plain language of the statute. As the [FCC] rightly noted, the exemptions themselves "contain[] no reference to a requirement that only programs produced by particular entities can fall within the exemption[s]." Furthermore, although TRAC is correct to note that the Act subjects only FCC licensees to equal time obligations, it simply does not follow that only those shows produced by the licensees themselves can qualify as exempt programming. A broadcast licensee incurs equal time obligations *whenever* he permits a candidate to "use a broadcast station," regardless of who produced the show containing the candidate appearance. See 47 U.S.C. § 315(a). Similarly, then, a licensee will not incur equal time obligations whenever he airs a show that fits within one of the four categories of programming that are "not deemed to be use of a broadcasting station," regardless of who produced the program. In other words, the plain language of section 315 concerns itself only with the responsibilities of licensees who broadcast exempt or non-exempt programming. It simply does not speak to the identity of the program's producer.

[EDITORIAL NOTE: *TRAC next argued that the legislative history indicated that only news interviews produced by licensees and networks should be eligible for a sec. 315 exemption. The FCC itself previously held, as had a House Conference Report, that only licensees or networks could qualify for the "bona fide news interview" exemption. See H.R. Conf. Rep. No. 86–1069 at 4 (1959), reprinted in 1959 U.S.C.A.N. 2564, 2582.*]

However, in ruling on the public broadcasters' petition, the [FCC] reversed its course. The [FCC] explained that its re-reading of the Act's legislative history, its knowledge of the changed conditions of the broadcast and cable industries, and its duty to further the goals of the Communications Act led it to believe that news interviews produced by independent producers could indeed qualify for the news interview exemption.

[EDITORIAL NOTE: *The court emphasized the FCC's observation that the Conference Report referred to networks and licensees because when the Report was issued they "comprised almost the entire programming universe." The Report had referred to these two entities "to make clear that the candidates themselves could not produce or control exempt news programming." The court then noted that the FCC determined that the primary purpose of Congress in enacting the exemptions was "to ensure complete news coverage of political campaigns," and "that its past refusal to extend the news interview exemption to independent productions had frustrated this congressional intent in that it had deterred the production of news interviews with political candidates."*]

Furthermore, TRAC is simply wrong to assert that the FCC would be unable to enforce its equal time regulations if independent parties were allowed to produce exempt news programming. In the first place, a show that succumbs to candidate manipulation would lose its exempt status as a "bona fide" news interview or newscast, making it much more difficult for the independent producer to market the show to broadcasters. In addition, the broadcasters who actually air these programs are subject to the FCC's jurisdiction and remain responsible for either refusing to broadcast any candidate appearance that exceeds the boundaries of "bona fide" news programming or providing equal time to the candidate's opponents.

The [FCC's] order holding that the news reporting segments of the *McLaughlin Group* are "bona fide newscasts" exempt from the equal time provision of the Communications Act was based on a reasonable interpretation of the Act to which we defer. We likewise defer to the [FCC's] reasonable decision that the "bona fide news interview" and "bona fide newscast exemptions" to section 315 can extend to independently produced programming. We therefore deny the petitions for review.

COMMENT

By choosing a particular videotape clip, is the *McLaughlin* show engaging in a type of editorial selection that is at odds with the concept of bona fide newscast? Are any problems generated by allowing independent producers—and not just licensees—to benefit from the bona fide news exemption in the *TRAC* case?

Bona Fide News Documentaries: Section 315(a)(3) The bona fide news documentary provision of sec. 315 has not occasioned much interpretation, largely because the broadcasting industry's interest in documentaries has declined in recent years. The provision does, however, have an important twist. Documentaries about campaigns and candidates are not exempt. Documentaries are only exempt when the candidate's appearance is incidental to his or her status as a candidate. If, for example, a broadcaster were to run a documentary about "Campaign 1988" and include then presidential nominee George Bush in the documentary, that appearance would not be exempt because Bush is appearing because he was a candidate. If, on the other hand, the same broadcaster ran a documentary about the decline of the U.S. petroleum industry and that documentary included an appearance by former oilman George Bush, that appearance would presumably be exempt. In the latter example, Bush would be appearing not because he was a candidate but because of his affiliation with the subject of the documentary, and it would only be "incidental" that he was also a candidate for public office at the time.

On-the-Spot Coverage of Bona Fide News Events: Section 315(a)(4)   The final exemption, on-the-spot coverage of bona fide news events, has been the most controversial over the years. In 1959, Congress clearly exempted coverage of political conventions. The immediate question was what else, if anything, did Congress intend to include in this exemption? Early FCC rulings said, in effect, not much else. In the 1960s, the FCC ruled that this exemption did not apply to broadcaster-run candidate debates or coverage of press conferences called by candidates.

The famous John F. Kennedy–Richard M. Nixon television debates of 1960, which many think led to the election of John F. Kennedy, were made possible by an amendment to sec. 315 that suspended operation of the section during the presidential campaign of 1960. 74 Stat. 554 (1960). Why would the debate have been impossible otherwise? Suppose the presidential candidate of the Vegetarian or the Prohibition Party asked for "equal time" after the Kennedy-Nixon debate. If sec. 315 had been in effect, would the broadcasters have had to provide time?

Broadcasters apparently are willing to give time to major-party candidates but not to minority-party candidates. Is the way to deal with the problem a statute that simply repeals sec. 315 for

the purpose of those political contests where the minority-party candidates have no real popular support and no chance of victory? Does such a technique assure permanent minority status to minority parties?

In the 1976 presidential election, the equal time question, inevitable in presidential elections, arose once again: Could the television networks carry a live television debate between the candidates for the two major parties, Gerald Ford and Jimmy Carter, without incurring obligations to give equal time to third-party candidates?

On September 30, 1975, in response to petitions filed by CBS and the Aspen Institute, the FCC overruled past decisions (*The Goodwill Industries Station, Inc.*, 40 F.C.C. 362 [1962] and *National Broadcasting Co. (Wycoff)*, 40 F.C.C. 370 [1962] and held that the exemption in sec. 315(a)(4) for "on-the-spot coverage of bona fide news events" would free from "equal time" obligations broadcast coverage of debates between candidates sponsored by nonbroadcast entities, i.e., nonstudio debates. *In re Aspen Institute and CBS Inc.*, 55 F.C.C.2d 697 (1975). The FCC also held that press conferences by candidates for political office that are broadcast "live" and in their entirety would qualify for exemption under sec. 315(a)(4).

The FCC said that its decisions in the overruled cases were based on an incorrect reading of the legislative history of newscast exemptions. Language in a 1959 House Report suggested that for a candidate's appearance on the broadcast media to be exempt, it would have to be "incidental to" the main coverage of a news event. By definition, a debate could never qualify for exemption. The appearance of the candidates is the central focus of the event.

The FCC, however, said that "incidental to" language was removed by congressional conference before the amendment to the Communications Act was passed in 1959. Thus, the FCC's former conclusion that a candidate's appearance must be incidental to be exempt was held to be unsupported by legislative history. The FCC said that Congress did not intend the FCC "to take an unduly restrictive approach which would discourage news coverage of political activities of candidates." Accordingly, a program that is otherwise exempt does not lose that status because the appearance of a political candidate is central to the presentation. The FCC stressed that the broadcaster has reasonable latitude in making the initial determination of whether an event will be eligible for exemption under sec. 315. The FCC can overturn the licensee's determination if it was not reasonable or was not made in good faith.

Shortly after the *Aspen* decision, plans for a debate between Jimmy Carter and Gerald Ford, sponsored by the League of Women Voters, exclusive of any initiation or control by any broadcast media, were announced. The *Aspen* decision had done its work. A televised debate limited to the candidates of the two major parties had become a reality. Although there were numerous additional legally qualified candidates for president, none was invited by the League to take part in the debates. The League then invited the broadcast networks, ABC, CBS, and NBC, to air "live" each of the three scheduled debates before an invited audience. The panelists assigned to question the candidates were to be selected by the League and not by the broadcasters. Broadcasters would not be permitted to show the audience or its reaction.

When the networks agreed to air the debates on the basis of *Aspen*, the National Organization for Women (NOW) and Representative Shirley Chisholm, a legally qualified candidate for president, challenged the FCC ruling and the legality of the planned debates. In *Chisholm v. FCC*, 538 F.2d 349 (D.C. Cir. 1976), the court affirmed the FCC rulings in *Aspen*.

In *Chisholm*, the court upheld the FCC's new interpretation of the equal time rules. The court stressed the necessity for judicial deference to agency interpretation where Congress assigned the responsibility for dealing with specific situations to the agency. Moreover, an agency could change its mind about the meaning of a statute no matter how longstanding its prior interpretation. As a result of *Chisholm*, therefore, debates between qualified political candidates, which were initiated by nonbroadcast entities, would be exempt under sec. 315(a)(4) provided that they were covered "live" and that there was no evidence of broadcast favoritism. Once these requirements were met, the essential factor was that the decision to cover the debate was based on the good faith determination of the broadcast licensee that the debate was a "bona fide news event" worthy of broadcast coverage.

How does one explain the fact that Congress in 1960 had to change the law to permit what in 1976 was found to be permissible anyway, i.e., permitting broadcasters to televise a debate limited to the presidential candidates of the two major parties without incurring any equal time obligations? The court of appeals answered this argument in *Chisholm*: "[T]he 1960 suspension of Section 315 is more properly viewed as an isolated experiment in total repeal of the equal time requirements for presidential and vice presidential candidates, and not as a recognition or limitation of the scope of the news coverage exemption."

Fundamental changes, such as those created by *Aspen* and *Chisholm* were, of course, subject to further judicial and FCC interpretation. In 1980, the U.S. Court of Appeals for the D.C. Circuit sustained an FCC ruling that Senator Edward Kennedy, a challenger to Democratic President Jimmy Carter for the party's nomination in the 1980 elections, was not entitled to "equal opportunities" following a Carter press conference.

Section 315(a) and Presidential Elections after Aspen-Chisholm

---

Kennedy for President Committee v. FCC
6 MED. L. RPTR. 1705, 636 F.2D 432 (D.C. CIR. 1980).

ROBINSON, Circuit Judge:
This controversy arose when, on February 13, 1980, President Carter held a press conference carried live in prime time by the four major American television networks. On the day following, petitioner Kennedy for President Committee complained to the networks that the President had taken advantage of the occasion for purposes of his candidacy for the 1980 presidential nomination of the Democratic party. Petitioner asked for "an equal opportunity" for its candidate, Senator Edward M. Kennedy, "to respond to * * * calculated and damaging statements" allegedly made by the President "and to provide contrasting viewpoints." Each of the networks responded negatively, whereupon petitioner turned to the FCC for assistance. On March 7, that agency's Broadcast Bureau denied petitioner's request, and on May 6, by the order

now under review, the FCC sustained the Bureau's ruling.

Petitioner challenges the FCC's decision on several grounds. Foremost are contentions that the commission abdicated a duty to apply the equal opportunity mandate of Section 315(a) of the Communications Act of 1934, and ignored an independent responsibility to accord First Amendment considerations their just due. The FCC, on the other hand, insists that its action kept faith with principles of Section 315(a) interpretation formulated in its *Aspen* decision and approved by this court, and that its disposition furthered the common objective of Section 315(a) and the First Amendment by encouraging maximal coverage of events envisioned by the networks as newsworthy. We agree with the FCC and affirm.

The press conference precipitating this litigation transpired on the eve of the 1980 presidential primary in New Hampshire. Petitioner charges that the conference was staged as an integral part of President Carter's so-called "Rose Garden" campaign strategy. During the course of the telecast, the President was asked four questions regarding his candidacy for the Democratic presidential nomination and that of Senator Kennedy, his principal rival. In its protest to the networks, petitioner predicated its equal opportunity demand on allegedly "distorted and inaccurate statements" by the President in response to queries "about Senator Kennedy's views on a number of issues." In turning petitioner down, each network maintained that the telecast of the conference was free of Section 315(a)'s equal-opportunity obligation because it was an activity within that section's Exemption 4 for "[o]n-the-spot coverage of bona fide news events."

Petitioner then urged the FCC "to rule that President Carter's News Conference of February 13 constituted a 'use' of television facilities offered by the major networks and to direct the networks to afford equal time to Senator Kennedy." Petitioner claimed that the President had "devoted more than five minutes to a direct attack upon Senator Kennedy," with the consequence that "millions of viewers were misinformed about Senator Kennedy's views on national and international issues critical to voters in the campaign for the presidential nomination."

The FCC's Broadcast Bureau denied petitioner's request, primarily in reliance upon the commission's *Aspen* decision, affirmed by this court in *Chisholm v. FCC*. The bureau concluded that the telecast fell within *Aspen's* holding that press conferences featuring political candidates are exempt from Section 315(a)'s equal-opportunity requirement as "on-the-spot coverage of bona fide news events." The bureau felt that under *Aspen* the regulatory role in equal-opportunity proceedings is confined to determining "whether or not the broadcaster intends to promote the interest of a particular candidate in presenting coverage of a news event." Noting that petitioner had presented no evidence that the networks were not exercising good faith journalistic judgment in appraising the President's press conference as newsworthy, and detecting no indication of a purpose to favor the President's candidacy over the Senator's by televising the event, the Bureau rejected petitioner's plea for an order providing an opportunity to respond.

Four weeks later, on April 2, petitioner sought reexamination of the Bureau's ruling by the FCC. On May 6, the FCC denied petitioner's application for review. Since we later draw directly and heavily on the FCC's opinion, it suffices for now merely to say that essentially the FCC tracked the Bureau's reasoning, and ultimately adhered pivotally to its *Aspen* holding that "so long as a covered event is considered newsworthy in the good faith judgment of the broadcaster," it is encompassed by one or more of Section 315(a)'s exemptions from the duty to afford equal opportunity. It is the FCC's ensuing order that petitioner now brings before us. * * *

"Equal opportunities" is manifestly a comprehensive term, and the FCC has given it rather full sway. Four types of programming, however, are statutorily deemed nonuses of a broadcasting station, and thus are exempted from this requirement. One—embraced by Exemption 4—immunizes the "[a]ppearance by a legally qualified candidate on any on-the-spot coverage of bona fide news events (including but not limited to political conventions and activities incidental thereto)." This provision, in the FCC's view, relieved the networks of any equal-opportunity obligation consequent upon the telecasts of the president's February 13 press conference.

The question, then, is whether the FCC properly extended Exemption 4 to that conference, and in answering we do not write on a completely clean slate. *Aspen* marked the FCC's recognition that its original understanding—that candidate's press conferences were "uses" of station facilities enabling their opponents to demand broadcast privileges for their own purposes—was not congenial with the underlying purpose of the 1959 amendments. Accordingly, the FCC adopted the stance it deemed more in keeping with the legislative aims: that broadcasts of press conferences featuring candidates for political office qualified under Exemption 4 as "on-the-spot coverage of bona fide news events."

We upheld the FCC's new determination in *Chisholm*. Moreover, we found credible the FCC's declaration in *Aspen* that "any appearance by a candidate on the broadcast media is designed, to the best of the candidate's ability, to serve his own political ends." We thus held that the FCC acted reasonably in rejecting "the degree of control by the candidate, or the degree to which candidates tailor such events to serve their own political advantages," as a criterion for ascertaining whether the equal-opportunity provision of Section 315(a) had been triggered.

Having so concluded, we faced in *Chisholm* the further question whether the broadcaster's good faith judgment on newsworthiness—the element deemed crucial by the FCC—provided an acceptable measure of applicability of Section 315(a)'s exemptions. At the outset, we noted that this standard came directly from the legislative history of Section 315(a): the Chairman of the House Committee had explained during debate that "[i]t sets up a test which appropriately leaves reasonable latitude for the exercise of good faith news judgment on the part of broadcasters and networks."

Although we did not find sufficient authority either in the reports or the debates to substantiate the proposition that Congress intended this to be the sole factor the FCC could utilize in its calculus, we were satisfied that Congress wished to increase broadcaster discretion as a means of maximizing coverage of campaign activity. Accordingly, we upheld the FCC's revised approach.

Petitioner raises four principal objections to the FCC's handling of the statutory issues generated by this litigation. These include its use of *Aspen* and *Chisholm* as controlling precedents, the deference

accorded broadcaster discretion, the burden placed on petitioners to demonstrate the absence of good faith on the part of the networks, and the FCC's refusal to consider post hoc "corrective" action. These we now examine in turn.

The first contention advanced by petitioner is that the commission "woodenly applied" *Aspen* by improperly treating it as establishing a per se rule. Certainly we did not in *Chisholm* approve a per se exemption of press conferences from the equal opportunity requirement of Section 315(a), nor do we think the FCC attempted to apply *Aspen* in that manner here.

In *Chisholm*, we upheld the FCC's specification of three criteria to govern the decision on whether a candidate's press conference is exempt from the equal-opportunity provision. They are (1) whether the conference is broadcast live, (2) whether it is based upon the good faith determination of the broadcaster that it is a bona fide news event, and (3) whether there is evidence of broadcaster favoritism. It is clear enough that the FCC examined the President's February 13 press conference in each of these respects, and not in the least are we moved to impugn the conclusions the FCC reached.

Petitioner contends that the FCC effectively delegated to the networks its responsibility to determine whether a particular appearance of a candidate is a "use" entitling opponents to equal opportunities. This, petitioner says, the FCC did by attaching too great a weight to the broadcasters' good faith judgment of newsworthiness. The flaw in this argument is that, as we have noted, this criterion proceeds directly from the legislative history of Section 315(a). In *Chisholm*, we found congressional intent to expand the role of broadcasters under Section 315(a) and to place considerable reliance on the exercise of their journalistic discretion in order to insure attainment of goals viewed as even more important than equal responsive opportunities.

It would be pointless to restate the analysis carefully expounded in *Chisholm*. It is enough to say that in applying the challenged criterion the commission pursued the course approved by this court as consistent with the legislative history and objectives. Nor do we believe the commission acted improperly in requiring a candidate seeking an order affording equal opportunities to come forward with evidence that the broadcaster involved did not exercise a bona fide judgment on newsworthiness in covering an appearance by his opponent.

Petitioner has never even alleged that any of the networks failed to make or abide by a good faith estimate of newsworthiness Petitioner thus is hardly in position to complain that the evidentiary burden defined by the commission erects an impermissible barrier to complainants attempting to assert rights under Section 315(a). Requiring a complainant to substantiate his allegations at the outset effectuates this congressional purpose by promoting fearless exercise of the discretion Congress intended broadcasters to have.

Petitioner's apparent inability to satisfy the FCC's threshold burden—allegation and corroboration of either bad faith or nonexercise of judgment on newsworthiness by the networks—does not demonstrate that the standard on this score is improvident. On the contrary, it seems evident that one having a legitimate claim in this regard will ordinarily be able to point to something tending to support it. And we do not doubt that when a prima facie showing is made the FCC, as it has stated, will inquire into the honesty and reasonableness of a broadcaster's professed news judgment.

Finally, on statutory grounds, petitioner urges that the actual content of a candidate's press-conference broadcast should determine whether the equal-opportunity obligation of Section 315(a) is activated. This contention is linked with the further argument that the FCC erroneously failed to consider post hoc whether remedial action should be taken to mitigate damage allegedly wrought. It seems much too late to raise these objections, for petitioner never placed a transcript or other recording of the press conference before the FCC. In any event, we are convinced that one of the main purposes of Section 315(a) would be frustrated by requiring the FCC to make subjective judgments on the political content of a broadcast program.

As we have previously observed, a major goal of the 1959 amendments to Section 315(a) was preservation of broadcasters' journalistic judgment on news programming. Congress then decided that when broadcasters are allowed to exercise good faith discretion in evaluating the newsworthiness of candidates' appearances on the four exempted types of broadcast programs, the benefits to the public outweigh the detriments

to either the public or the candidates. We think the FCC steers the right course in declining to undertake assessments on the political or nonpolitical nature of a candidate's appearance, even assuming that there really is much of a difference. As the FCC aptly stated, "to draw such distinctions would require [it] to make subjective judgments concerning content, context and potential political impact of a candidate's appearance," and "neither Congress nor the commission desires to expand governmental oversight of broadcasters' professional journalistic functions."

We find eminently reasonable, too, the FCC's reading of Section 315(a) to require broadcasters to appraise newsworthiness prior to broadcast of the questioned event. Were the FCC to hinge operation of the equal-opportunity provision on after-the-fact reexamination of the event broadcast, the purposes for which Congress enacted the Section 315(a) exemptions would largely be set for naught. Broadcasters could never be sure that coverage of any given event would not later result in equal-opportunity obligations to all other candidates; resultantly, broadcaster discretion to carry or not to carry would be seriously if not fatally crippled.

We also deem irrelevant petitioner's assertion that the questioned press conference was "orchestrated as a partisan political event designed to gain maximum political advantage in the New Hampshire primary and subsequent elections—a fact recognized here and throughout the country if not at the FCC." When we decided *Chisholm,* we fully explained the insignificance of the candidate's motivation in appearing on the broadcast program. We perceive no good reason to reiterate the discussion here.

We thus are unpersuaded by petitioner's statutory arguments. Together they travel several routes, but they all lead to the same destination. In a word, petitioner's objections to the FCC's analysis of Section 315(a) do not warrant reversal of the order under review.

[EDITORIAL NOTE: *The court's discussion of Senator Kennedy's First Amendment claims is treated later in this chapter.]*

Significant Rulings in Applying Section 315(a) to Presidential Elections   Broadcasters liked the *Aspen-Chisholm* rulings but still viewed them as less than ideal. Under these rulings, debates had to be conducted by somebody else—usually the League of Women Voters—and had to be broadcast "live" and "in their entirety." Broadcasters would have preferred more flexibility but seemed fearful to ask for it themselves. In 1983 they got some help from former FCC General Counsel Henry Geller. Geller asked the FCC to broaden *Aspen* and to allow noncontemporaneous coverage of debates, including debates conducted by broadcasters themselves.

In *Petitions of Henry Geller et al.,* 95 F.C.C.2d 1236 (1983), the FCC concluded that broadcaster-run debates, as well as debates run by third parties, could be bona fide news events so long as there was no evidence of a broadcaster's intent to favor a candidate. Recognizing that third-party sponsors of debates might not always be available, the FCC noted that broadcasters may be "the ideal, and perhaps the only, entity interested in promoting a debate between candidates for a particular office, especially at the state or local level." It ruled that to be exempt, a debate—even if broadcaster run—had to be "of genuine news value and not be used to advance the candidacy of a particular individual."

The *Geller* decision also eliminated the idea that coverage within twenty-four hours to be "live," an interpretation that had grown up around the *Aspen* rule. Broadcasters could present delayed coverage of taped debates (and, presumably, press conferences) so long as they did not do so in a fashion intended to promote a single candidate. The U.S. Court of Appeals for the D.C. Circuit rejected appeals of the *Geller* decision. See *League of Women Voters v. FCC,* 731 F.2d 995 (D.C. Cir. 1984). Thus, by the late 1980s, broadcasters had substantial latitude to cover political debates. Provided they were not obviously attempting to promote one candidate, broadcasters could cover debates run by third parties (e.g., the League of Women Voters) without fear of having to provide equal opportunities to candidates the third party might choose not to include in the debate. They could even set up candidate debates themselves and leave out minor-party candidates if they did not intend to favor one of the candidates they included. They did not necessarily have to present their coverage "live." They could tape delay it if it retained its newsworthiness. It also appeared that they were not required to cover debates and press conferences "in their entirety," as *Aspen* had required, although no FCC decision squarely addressed this issue.

An example of the difficulties in interpreting sec. 315(a) in the context of presidential and vice-presidential elections is found in *Fulani v. FCC,* 49 F.3d. 904 (2d Cir. 1995). Ross Perot, an independent candidate for president of the United States in 1992, was interviewed on a special edition of the ABC news program *Nightline.* Subsequently, Lenora B. Fulani, another independent presidential candidate, asked ABC for equal time under sec. 315(a) of the Communications Act of 1934. ABC refused on the ground that the program was exempt from the equal time requirement as a "bona fide news interview" under sec. 315(a)(2). Fulani complained unsuccessfully to the FCC, which found that the program met the criteria for a "bona fide news interview." Fulani appealed this decision. The U.S. Court of Appeals for the Second Circuit, per Judge Cabranes, held that the FCC did not err in refusing to require ABC to provide presidential candidate Fulani airtime under sec. 315.

The court applied the highly deferential "arbitrary, capricious, or lacking in any rational basis" standard of review to the FCC's interpretation of its own statute. An examination of the FCC case law revealed that three criteria must be satisfied for the "bona fide news interview" exemption of sec. 315(a)(2) to apply. First, the program must be "regularly scheduled." Second, the broadcaster must have "control" over the program. Third, broadcaster decisions regarding "format, content and participants" had to be based on "reasonable, good faith journalistic judgment."

Fulani contended that the FCC acted "arbitrarily and capriciously" in applying these requirements. In particular, Fulani argued that the program was not "regularly scheduled" because it did not conform to the usual format of *Nightline* in several respects. The title "Nightline" did not appear in the broadcast, the usual host, Ted Koppel, did not conduct the interview, and the interview was both longer and in a different format, a town meeting, than the usual *Nightline* program. The court rejected these contentions. Since April 1988, *Nightline* had on thirteen occasions employed the same "town meeting" format used in "Who Is Ross Perot?" occasionally without using "Nightline" in the title. In addition, *Nightline* had run longer than its scheduled time period on many occasions. Further, Ted Koppel did not always act as host when the town meeting format was employed. Fulani responded that the occasions when the town meeting format was used and Koppel was absent represented only a small fraction of the shows in the *Nightline* series. Rejecting this argument, Judge Cabranes said: "But for a certain format to qualify as 'regularly scheduled,' there is no rigid requirement that it run on a daily or weekly basis; for example, the FCC has held that quarterly programs may qualify as 'regularly scheduled' news interviews."

Finally, although there was no precedent on *Nightline* for combining the town meeting format with a candidate's appearance, "it is undisputed that political issues and political candidates are a staple of the 'Nightline' series." The court concluded the FCC's finding that ABC's Perot telecast met the "regularly scheduled" requirement was "based on a permissible construction of the bona fide news interview exemption to § 315."

Observing that the "bona fide news interview" exemption requires that the broadcaster exercise control over the program, the court said:

> [W]e find that there was a reasonable basis for the FCC's finding that Jennings, and not Perot, was in control of the proceedings. First, Fulani claims that Jennings "turned the microphone over to Perot" at the outset of the live segment of the broadcast. From our reading of the transcript, however, we conclude that this episode was a limited opportunity for Perot to respond to the documentary on his career that ABC had just aired, not a transfer of control. Perot was not given carte blanche to give a campaign speech; characteristic of the typical news interview, Perot's remarks were frequently interrupted by Jennings' questions or elicitations of clarification.
>
> Second, although most audience members who asked questions were preselected by ABC and called upon by Jennings, Fulani points out that one audience member shouted out a question in an angry outburst, which Jennings permitted Perot to answer. To the extent that the impromptu question amounted to a fleeting surrender of control by ABC, the control did not shift to Perot, as the hostile tone and content of the question make clear."

The court next addressed the third requirement of the bona fide news exemption—that the broadcaster's programming decisions were based on "reasonable, good faith journalistic judg-

ment" rather than intent to advance any particular person's candidacy:

> We find that there was a "reasonable basis," for the FCC's finding that ABC's decisions were not motivated by an intention to advance Perot's candidacy. Our review of the transcript leads us to believe that the tenor of the proceedings was as critical as it was flattering, generally evidencing no undue favoritism by ABC toward Perot.

There was a final issue: Had the FCC erred in refusing to conduct an evidentiary hearing in connection with Fulani's complaint? Judge Cabranes answered this question in the negative. Section 315 did not require that the FCC conduct such hearings or indeed provide for any formal procedures. Fulani simply failed to establish that a substantial and material question of fact was in dispute.

King Broadcasting Co. v. FCC, 860 F.2d 465 (D.C. Cir. 1988), involved the application of the sec. 315(a)(4) exemption for on-the-spot coverage of bona fide news events. A broadcaster proposed to carry two program formats covering the major-party candidates in the 1988 presidential and vice-presidential races. Each format would be a pretaped studio event. The broadcaster described the two proposed formats as follows:

> The first [format] would be a one-hour program in which each of the two major party candidates would be allotted thirty minutes to "set forth their essential campaign message to the American people." [E]ach candidate would be recorded separately, but they would be broadcast back-to-back, with one candidate's presentation immediately followed by that of the other. There would be two such presentations, one at the start of the campaign season, and one just before the election. The order of presentation would be determined by a coin flip for the first show, and would be reversed in the second show.

The broadcaster who proposed these formats was worried that without a sec. 315(a) exemption, the proposed formats would not be feasible because he would then have to give thirty-minute presentations to all the minor-party candidates for president and vice-president. King Broadcasting contended that the sec. 315(a)(4) exemption should apply because there was no difference between an in-studio debate and in-studio joint or back-to-back candidate appearances in a program series. The FCC rejected this analysis of sec. 315(a)(4) on the ground that in presidential debates and press conferences the press was present to question the candidates and provide spontaneity. King's proposals, the FCC concluded, were "more like advertisements by the candidates than bona fide news programming."

The court of appeals did not agree with the FCC's sec. 315(a)(4) analysis." The FCC's "present construction of Sec. 315(a)(4) could not be squared with prior pronouncements on the issue." The court could "discern no reasonable explanation for the FCC's apparent departure from its own precedent." The court was particularly concerned that in *Aspen,* the FCC had required "two related inquiries when determining whether a program qualified for a 315(a)(4) exemption." Was the program genuinely "newsworthy"? Was the newsworthiness determination an exercise of good faith news judgment by the broadcaster? Failure to undertake either of these inquiries prompted the court to remand the case to the FCC for further consideration.

On remand, the FCC granted King Broadcasting's request that it rule that its format involving appearances by the candidates alone with no journalistic involvement constituted a bona fide news event under sec. 315(a)(4): "[T]he mere fact that the presentations allow the candidates to present their views in the most favorable light, without spontaneous interaction with the press or opposing candidates, does not preclude application of the news [event] exemption." *King Broadcasting Co.,* 6 F.C.C.R. 4998, 4999 (1991).

During the 1996 campaign, Fox Broadcasting Corp., Public Broadcasting Service, and Capital Cities/ABC, Inc. each submitted to the FCC proposed formats to offer the major candidates for the presidency free air time. Fox, PBS, and ABC all requested that their proposed formats be deemed bona fide news events and thus exempt from the obligations of sec. 315(a).

The FCC described the proposal as follows:

Fox: (1) A one-hour election eve program in which time would be split evenly among the candidates selected for inclusion in debates by the Commission on Presidential Debates; and (2) ten 60-second segments in which the candidates would address issue-oriented questions.

PBS: 2½ minutes of airtime scheduled at the same time each weeknight and rotated between/among the major presidential candidates without restriction as to content.

ABC: A one-hour prime-time special during the final week of the campaign. ABC states that this would be a "live unrestricted" event, with the candidates appearing without interruptions or questions from any third party.

The FCC granted the requests by Fox, PBS, and ABC that these proposals should be deemed bona fide news events and thus exempt from sec. 315(a). To put it more plainly, the FCC was really ruling that Fox, PBS, and ABC would not have to give free airtime to *all* candidates for the presidency if they gave free time under their respective proposals to the *major* presidential candidates. See *In re Requests of Fox Broad. Co., PBS, and Capital Cities/ABC,* 11 F.C.C.R 11101 (1996).

In justification of this conclusion, the FCC said that the legislative history behind the exemptions to sec. 315(a) "evidences Congress's recognition that the exemptions defied clear format characterizations." Furthermore, Congress intended the FCC to have broad discretion in interpreting the exemptions. The ruling on remand in *King Broadcasting Co.,* designed to encourage innovation, increased "broadcaster-initiated news event programming," and increased the amount of "election-related information available to the public."

The FCC noted that although its ruling on the Fox, PBS, and ABC requests relied on broadcaster discretion, it retained its obligation to see that "reasonable safeguards against broadcaster favoritism [of particular candidates]" existed with respect to the proposals being considered. For example, the FCC concluded that broadcaster favoritism would not be involved in the back-to-back statements of the candidates on election eve. The candidates would be selected by the Commission on Presidential Debates. The commission was described by the FCC as an organization set up "to plan and sponsor debates among the leading candidates for the Presidency and Vice-Presidency." A factor in the selection decisions of the Commission on Presidential Debates would be the newsworthiness of a candidacy.

Other proposals were held to be consistent with the law under sec. 315(a). With respect to the PBS proposal, the FCC said that "a licensee is not required to ask questions of candidates or to arrange for third parties to do so." Was the fact that the proposed PBS programming was not going to be aired "live" a problem? No. Under *Geller*, "the rebroadcast of any 'reasonably recent event'" would be deemed coverage of an "on the spot" news event. The presidential candidates spots proposed by Fox were all going to be aired at the same time of day; this was deemed an adequate safeguard against possible broadcaster favoritism.

The ABC proposal of a "one-hour prime-time 'live unrestricted event'" was deemed exempted under *King Broadcasting*. Unlike PBS, ABC was not going to delegate the selection of candidates. But that did not mean that its news judgment was not bona fide. The FCC observed that licensees were not obliged to delegate the selection of candidates to appear on their programming to a third party. The key point was that ABC was going to use objective criteria to make its selection, i.e., polling results, the "number of states in which a candidate has achieved ballot status, and the extent to which a candidate has engaged in a nationwide campaign."

Comments on the Free Time Proposal by Fox and Others Prior to issuing its declaratory ruling, the FCC issued a public notice asking interested parties to comment on the Fox request. Would a favorable ruling on the Fox request present greater risk of broadcaster favoritism at the local level? Professor Michael Meyerson contended that broadcaster favoritism is more likely to occur in "local races where multiple candidacies and parochial concerns abound." Why do local races present more opportunities for broadcaster favoritism in selecting political candidates for appearances? The FCC responded to this concern by saying that its declaratory ruling concerned presidential elections and did not "directly implicate other elections." But the FCC also declared that if problems arose in local races, they would be considered on a case-by-case basis and would be evaluated in keeping with the principles set forth in the *Fox* declaratory ruling.

The Media Access Project (MAP) suggested that the FCC change its definition of "legally qualified candidate." The theory behind this proposal was that if the category of legally qualified candidates were narrowed, the FCC "could at least at the national level reduce the number of candidates entitled to equal opportunities without having to assess the merits of particular news

programming." Factors in a redefinition of legally qualified candidate under the MAP proposal would include "support in independent opinion polls; signatures in nominating petitions; amount of campaign contributions; and votes in prior elections." For a summary of the present FCC definition of "legally qualified candidates," see p. 767. Do you favor the MAP proposal?

A number of commenters including the LaRouche Committee and the World Workers Party opposed the Fox proposal because they believed that granting it would result in the exclusion of the presidential candidates of minor political parties. This, of course, is what happened. Others like Frank J. Fahrenkopf, Jr., and Charles T. Manatt, former chairs, respectively, of the Republican and Democratic National Committees, supported the Fox proposal because it served the public interest by centering attention on the "major candidates through political broadcasts." Rupert Murdoch observed that it was simply not possible to offer time to political candidates who failed to win "significant public support." The Natural Law Party requested that the FCC rule that "all candidates achieving national party status, as evidenced by qualifying for matching funds with the Federal Election Commission, should be entitled to participate in Fox's programming."

As you analyze these comments, which ones do you agree with? Is there a tension between sec. 315(a)'s goal of providing political candidates equal opportunities and the FCC's interpretation of the exemptions, which emphasizes bona fide news judgment?

WHAT IS AN "EQUAL OPPORTUNITY"? When one candidate for a public office has made a nonexempt use of a broadcast station, broadcasters are obligated to provide upon request equal opportunities for all of that candidate's legally qualified opponents to "use" the station. Thus, the next sec. 315 issue is what "equal opportunity" to use a station means.

Section 315 is often erroneously called the "equal time" section of the Communications Act. It is that—but in three distinct ways. According to the FCC, equal opportunity to use a station includes three things. First of all, it means an equal amount of time. Thus, if Candidate A has appeared for five minutes, her opponent, Candidate B, gets five minutes of "use" as well. Here, the FCC divides between "spot" use and "program" use. If Candidate A appears in something of three minutes or less total time (say, a thirty-second ad), opposing Candidate B gets the same *total* amount of time as Candidate A had. Even if A's appearance was only for a few seconds, e.g., she read the tagline explaining who paid for the spot but did not otherwise appear in it, Candidate B still would get the total amount of time as the spot in which A's appearance occurred, in this example, thirty seconds. With longer formats (certainly, five minutes or longer), the FCC actually counts the time a candidate appears. Suppose, for example, that a movie featuring Fred Thompson is run at a time when Thompson is a candidate for a public office and has opponents. In this instance, the FCC would calculate how long Thompson appeared in the movie—either by visual image or just by voice—and the opposing candidates would be entitled to that total amount of time to use on the station that had aired the movie. Under most circumstances, then, sec. 315 does require an equal amount of time, but it also requires more.

Second, the FCC has ruled that opposing candidates are also allowed comparably desirable time. This policy prevents broadcasters from putting a favored candidate on during radio drive time, but providing equal amounts of time to opponents at 3:00 A.M. on Sunday mornings. The FCC recognizes that it is impossible for broadcasters to deliver exactly the same audience to opposing Candidate B that it allowed Candidate A to use, so it does not expect broadcasters to achieve that. Nor does it require that broadcasters put opposing candidates in exactly the same programs. Putting candidates in obviously discrepant time periods in terms of audience potential, however, will run afoul of sec. 315.

Finally, the FCC says that "equal opportunity" means that candidates must receive access to stations on the same commercial terms. Thus, if one candidate pays twenty-five dollars for a radio spot, his or her opponents must be given the opportunity to "use" the station at the same rate—twenty-five dollars. There is no obligation to give free time in response to paid time under sec. 315. If an impoverished candidate cannot afford what an opponent paid, the impoverished candidate is out of luck. All sec. 315 requires is that broadcasters treat opposing candidates

under the same rules. If Candidate A had to pay, opposing Candidate B must pay, too.

All of these claims for equal opportunity must be made with the FCC within seven days of what the FCC terms a "first prior use." These policies can get rather complex but can be exemplified simply. Suppose there is a three-candidate race for a public office. Candidate A makes some kind of use on the first of the month. Candidate B asks a broadcaster for an "equal opportunity" use on the sixth of the month. Candidate B is in time—within seven days of A's use. Assume that the third candidate, C, is not aware of A's use, but becomes aware of B's. Two days after B's use, C asks the station for an "equal opportunity." The station can deny the request. The "first prior use" was A's, on the first of the month. B's use flowed from that, and C has come in eight days after A's use. C is too late under the seven-days-after-first-prior-use rule. In the real world, working out these computations can be complex. The point, however, is that candidates cannot bank their rights to equal opportunity uses and claim them all at the last minute before an election.

HOW ARE RATES REGULATED?   What broadcasters can charge candidates to use their stations is regulated in three ways. First, since 1927, sec. 315 prevents broadcasters from charging one candidate more than they have charged an opposing candidate for a previous use. Thus, if candidate A paid twenty-five dollars for a radio spot, candidate B cannot be charged more than twenty-five dollars for a comparable spot under sec. 315.

Second, since 1952, broadcasters have been forbidden from having artificially high candidate rates. Broadcasters cannot charge candidates more for advertising time than they charge other advertisers. In the 1950s, broadcasters had two motivations for artificially high rates. Some broadcasters wanted to keep politicians off their stations altogether and sought to do so through exorbitant rates. Other broadcasters recognized that politicians needed broadcast advertising and sought to gouge them through high rates. The 1952 amendments to the Communications Act prohibited both kinds of broadcaster discrimination.

Finally, since 1972, Congress has required broadcasters to sell time to candidates at the "lowest unit charge" during periods just prior to elections—forty-five days before primaries and sixty days before general elections. This restriction arose from generalized congressional concerns about the high cost of campaigning, much of which was attributable to the cost of political broadcast ads. Accordingly, in 1971, Congress required broadcasters to sell time to candidates at their lowest unit rate.

The phrase is not as clear as it might seem, however. Prior to adoption of this law, broadcasters did not think in terms of unit rates, let alone "lowest" unit rates. Nevertheless, the concept is easy to express even though it is hard to work out in practice. Congress basically recognized that broadcast advertising time could be measured in two ways: amount of time (number of seconds/minutes) and desirability of time (prime time/drive time/class A time/etc.). What Congress basically said in 1972 was that if a broadcaster sold a particular length ad at a particular place in his or her schedule for a certain amount, and if that was the lowest price at which such a "class and amount of time" could be purchased, then the broadcaster had to be willing to cut the same deal with candidates during periods just before elections. Figuring out the lowest unit charge can be complicated in practice; for example, candidates get the benefit of volume purchase discounts even if they do not buy enough advertising to qualify for them. Still Congress's intent is clear—give candidates a break just before elections. Give them the benefit of the lowest price for which any other advertiser could buy the same ad at that time.

WHAT CONTROL CAN THE BROADCASTER HAVE OVER CANDIDATE USES?

Under sec. 315, broadcasters cannot censor candidate uses. Basically, this means that when a candidate gains a right to use a station under sec. 315, the broadcaster has no control over what the candidate does. Broadcasters must provide the same facilities to Candidate B as they provided voluntarily to his opponent, Candidate A. If Candidate B chooses to use those facilities in ways the broadcaster might not have expected and might not like, the broadcaster still must permit Candidate B to engage in those uses.

The no-censorship provision can create problems for broadcasters. In *Farmers Educational &* *Cooperative Union v. WDAY, Inc.*, 360 U.S. 525 (1959), the U.S. Supreme Court addressed some of these problems. A. C. Townley, a perennial candidate for public office in North Dakota, had run for the U.S. Senate and, in the eyes of the Farmers Educational and Cooperative Union, libeled the union. Townley had few resources, so the union sued the broadcast station that under sec. 315 had carried Townley's comments. A unanimous Supreme Court held that under sec. 315 of the Act, WDAY had no right to censor Townley's comments. The language of Congress was clear—broadcasters could not censor what candidates did under sec. 315. The Court split 5–4 on a different question: Should WDAY be financially responsible for Townley's remarks? Five members of the Court said no; Congress had given broadcasters no ability to prevent libelous candidate statements, so broadcasters should not be responsible for them when made. Four members of the Court took the position that if Congress intended through sec. 315 to make broadcasters immune to damages arising from defamatory remarks, then Congress should have said so. Thus, by the narrowest of margins, a fundamental principle was established. Broadcasters could not censor candidate uses under sec. 315, and they also were not legally responsible for comments they could not prevent. See p. 765.

Years later, when a candidate used the word "nigger" in a spot, the FCC ruled that broadcasters could not censor that use. *Letter to Lonnie King*, 36 F.C.C.2d 635 (1972). When Barry Commoner used the word "bullshit" in a spot in the 1976 campaign, broadcasters did not even bother to bring it to the FCC's attention; they ran the spot with a disclaimer that they were powerless to prevent it. *Hustler* magazine publisher Larry Flynt threw the broadcasting community into a panic when he threatened to run for president in 1980. Flynt claimed that one of his planks would be freedom for sexually explicit expression. Broadcasters feared that if Flynt became a candidate, they would have to run his ads. The chairman of the FCC at the time, Mark Fowler, made some public statements to the effect that he believed ways could be found for broadcasters to block Flynt's speech if it was obscene, despite the language of sec. 315. All this debate came to naught, however, when Flynt did not pursue his candidacy.

The Becker Case   A case that *did* raise the scope of the no-censorship clause of sec. 315(a) involved the request of Dan Becker, a legally qualified candidate for election to Congress from Georgia, that station WAGA-TV air a campaign advertisement that included photos of aborted fetuses. The ad was aired on July 19, 1992, at 7:58 P.M. and was the subject of many viewer complaints to the station.

In October 1992, Dan Becker sought to purchase time from WAGA-TV to broadcast a 30-minute political program, "Abortion in America: The Real Story" on November 1 between 4:00 P.M. and 5:00 P.M. following a pro football game. WAGA-TV said the ad was indecent but offered to carry it within the safe harbor hours of midnight to 6:00 A.M. Becker filed a complaint with the FCC. On November 22, 1994, the FCC issued a Declaratory Ruling that held in part that channeling the ad to a time when children would not be expected to be found in the audience would not violate the no-censorship provision of sec. 315(a). *In re Petition for Declaratory Ruling Concerning Section 312(a)(7),* 9 F.C.C.R. 7638 (1994).

A court of appeals panel, per Judge Buckley, joined by Judges Silberman and Rogers, vacated this Declaratory Ruling. *Becker v. FCC,* 95 F.3d 75 (D.C. Cir. 1996) The sec. 312(a)(7) issues raised in the *Becker* case are discussed at p. 803. Judge Buckley said the Declaratory Ruling violated sec. 315(a):

[P]etitioners assert that the [Declaratory] ruling compromises section 315(a)'s no censorship provision in two ways: First, by granting licensees the content-based discretion to refuse to broadcast particular advertisements during a particular period, it enables them not only to discriminate against a candidate on the basis of speech, but to inhibit the manner in which he is able to discuss public issues. Second, by enabling the licensee to determine when an advertisement that "may be harmful to children" will air, the ruling deprives the candidate of the ability to convey his message when and how he sees fit by presenting him with the choice of either changing its content or accepting a time slot that deprives him of his preferred audience.

In *WDAY, Inc.,* the Court held that section 315(a) prohibited a broadcaster from removing defamatory statements from the advertisements of a legally qualified candidate. From *[WDAY]*, we may discern two guiding principles: First, the basic purposes of section 315(a) is to permit the "full and unrestricted discussion of political issues by legally qualified candidates." Second, the section reflects Congress's "deep hostility to censorship either by the FCC or by a licensee."

Not only does the power to channel confer on a licensee the power to discriminate between candidates, it can force one of them to back away from what he considers to be the most effective way of presenting his position on a controversial issue lest he be deprived of the audience he is most anxious to reach. This self-censorship must surely frustrate the "full and unrestricted discussion of political issues envisioned by Congress."

The rationale behind *WDAY, Inc.,* requires us to agree with petitioners that "censorship" encompasses more than the refusal to run a candidate's advertisement or the deletion of material contained in it. We believe that a licensee's right to channel political advertisements will inevitably interfere with a candidate's freedom of expression by requiring him to choose between what he wishes to say and the audience he wishes to address.

Finally, section 315(a) not only prohibits censorship it also requires that candidates be given "equal opportunities" to use a broadcaster's facilities. [A] broadcaster must "make available periods of approximately equal audience potential to competing candidates to the extent that this is possible." *Political Primer 1984* 100 F.C.C.2d at 1505. [C]hanneling clearly implicates the equal opportunity provision of section 315(a).

This is so because if a station channels one candidate's message but allows his opponent to broadcast its message in prime time, the first candidate will have been denied the equal opportunity guaranteed by this section. On the other hand, if the station relegates the opponent's advertisements to the broadcasting Siberia to which the first Candidate was assigned, it would be violating the opponent's right of reasonable access under section 312(a)(7). We agree with petitioners that these provisions may not be read to create such a tension.

The [Declaratory Ruling] permits licensees to review political advertisements and to discriminate against candidates on the basis of their content, in violation of both the "no censorship" and "equal opportunities" provisions of section 315(a). Therefore, we grant the petitions for review and vacate the ruling.

IS THIS WHOLE SYSTEM CONSTITUTIONAL?

Obviously, broadcasting is subjected to regulation of political content that would not be acceptable in other media. Many constitutional challenges have been mounted to this scheme. Many turn on the oft-recognized position of the courts that broadcasting enjoys a unique

First Amendment status, as already discussed. By and large, the courts have sustained the constitutionality of sec. 315, although the U.S. Supreme Court has yet to speak on the matter.

One significant challenge came in 1980 when Senator Kennedy tested the FCC's interpretation of how sec. 315 applied to a press conference by President/Candidate Carter, already discussed in part. In *Kennedy for President Committee v. FCC*, 636 F.2d 432 (D.C. Cir. 1980). Judge Robinson rejected a First Amendment argument that private interests should not be permitted to restrict protected speech on the basis of a subjective assessment that it did not fit into the bona fide news exemption to sec. 315:

> Congress specifically exempted coverage of a number of arguably "political" news events in the belief that an overly-broad statutory right of access would diminish rather than augment the flow of information to the American public. The real question, then, is whether this legislative scheme transgresses the First Amendment interests of a candidate demanding an opportunity to respond to another candidate's statements on an excepted occasion. We think the answer is evident. As the commission states, "Congress has chosen to enforce the public's primary right in having 'the medium function consistently with the ends and purposes of the First Amendment' by relying on broadcasters as public trustees, periodically accountable for their stewardship, to use their discretion in insuring the public's access to conflicting ideas." More importantly, the Supreme Court has emphasized that no "individual member of the public [has a right] to broadcast his own particular views on any matter," rejecting the "view that every potential speaker is 'the best judge' of what the public ought to hear or indeed the best judge of the merits of his or her views."

In *Johnson v. FCC*, 829 F.2d 157 (D.C. Cir. 1987), the court of appeals rejected claims of Sonia Johnson and her running mate, Richard Walton—both nominees of the Citizens Party—that "by 1984 the televised Presidential and Vice-Presidential debates had become so institutionalized as to be a prerequisite for election." The court rejected First Amendment claims by Johnson and Walton that their exclusion from 1984 presidential and vice-presidential debates sponsored by the League of Women Voters restricted their access to the ballot and their opportunities to be elected.

Relying on *Kennedy for President Committee* and *CBS v. DNC*, the court declared:

> [P]etitioners present a far weaker constitutional thesis than the ones those cases rejected. They seek, not general access, as in *[CBS v. DNC]*, nor an opportunity to respond to a particular broadcast, as in *[Kennedy for President Committee]*, but rather the specific right to appear on a specific program—a program not organized by the broadcasters, but by a third party. Thus, viewed in light of the First Amendment balance struck in the statutory scheme, as delineated in the governing case law, petitioners have stated no legally cognizable claim to participate in the broadcast debates.

A final and significant First Amendment challenge to sec. 315 was mounted by a California TV journalist, William Branch. Branch became a candidate for public office and continued to appear regularly on his station's newscasts. The FCC had long taken the position that the bona fide newscast exemption to sec. 315 did not cover newscasts in which newscasters were also candidates. After the FCC changed its position, telling Branch's station that it would have to provide equal opportunity to his opponents if he appeared on newscasts, Branch appealed to the U.S. Court of Appeals for the D.C. Circuit. In 1987, that court upheld the FCC and, in the process, addressed generally the constitutionality of sec. 315.

Branch v. FCC

824 F.2D 37 (D.C. CIR. 1987); *CERT. DENIED*, 485 U.S. 959 (1988).

BORK, Judge:

A television news reporter who wishes to run for public office challenges the FCC's decision that the station which employs him would be required to provide "equal time" to his political opponents. This decision would require the station to offer his opponents opportunities to appear on the station that are equivalent to the newscaster's regular daily appearances. The FCC's determination rested on a federal statute. The reporter challenges both the interpretation of the statute and its constitutionality. We deny the petition for review.

Branch initially contends that the statute's "equal time" provisions do not apply to him because the statute exempts the television appearances of a newscaster candidate from their coverage. Branch reads the statutory language to mean: the "equal opportunities" requirement applies only when there is a "use" of a broadcasting station; a candidate's appearance on a bona fide newscast does not constitute such a "use"; thus Branch's appearances on KOVR's bona fide news broadcasts are not subject to the "equal opportunities" requirement. The apparent simplicity of this argument, however, is misleading.

The legislative history of the 1959 amendments conclusively establishes three critical and overlapping points. First, Congress' central concern in taking action was to overrule the FCC's *Lar Daly* decision. Second, the purpose of overruling *Lar Daly* was to restore the understanding of the law that had prevailed previously.

Third, Congress objected to the imposition of "equal opportunities" obligations on any station that carried news coverage of a candidate, because it deterred the broadcast media from providing the public with full coverage of political news events, and many other news events as well.

Thus Congress' intent in enacting the amended Section 315 is readily discernible. "Appearance by a legally qualified candidate," which is not "deemed to be use of a broadcasting station," is coverage of the candidate that is presented to the public as news. The "appearance" of the candidate is itself expected to be the newsworthy item that activates the exemption. "By modifying all four categories [not deemed to be 'use'] with the phrase 'bona fide,' Congress plainly emphasized its reliance on newsworthiness as the basis for an exemption."

The thrust of the language is brought out further in the third and fourth specific exemptions. The "news documentary" exemption applies only "if the appearance of the candidate is incidental to *the presentation of the subject or subjects covered by the news documentary.*" This passage relates the candidate's appearance to the subjects covered in the program. If the candidate's appearance has nothing to do with the subjects that are being covered as news— whether because the candidate is a regular employee on all such programs or, to take another example, because the candidate is being offered a gratuitous appearance that realistically is unrelated to the news content of the program—then the exemption does not apply. Similarly, the fourth exemption for "on-the-spot coverage" of news applies only to "coverage of bona fide news events." Here again the focus is on a

news *event* that is being covered, with the candidate's appearance expected to occur as part of the event *being covered.*

When a broadcaster's employees are sent out to cover a news story involving other persons, therefore, the "bona fide news event" is the activity engaged in by those other persons, not the work done by the employees covering the event. The work done by the broadcaster's employees is not a part of the event, for the event would occur without them and they serve only to communicate it to the public. For example, when a broadcaster's employees are sent out to cover a fire, the fire is the "bona fide news" event and the reporter does not become a part of that event merely by reporting it. There is nothing at all "newsworthy" about the work being done by the broadcaster's own employees, regardless of whether any of those employees happens also to be a candidate for public office.

Moreover, Congress' objection to *Lar Daly* was that it discouraged wide broadcast coverage of political news events by restricting a station's ability to determine which news *events* to present to the public. Congress solved this problem by exempting any on-air appearance by a candidate who is the *subject* of news coverage. It is irrelevant to that problem whether a station has broad discretion to determine which of its employees will actually present the news on the air.

In opposition to that consistent approach, Branch asks this court to read the phrase "[a]ppearance by a legally qualified candidate on any [news program]" as exempting from the "equal opportunities" rule all on-air work done by newscaster candidates. We cannot do so. As we have already noted, such a reading would be at odds with the law before *Lar Daly,* which Congress explicitly sought to restore through the 1959 amendments. In addition, this reading would raise a station's news employees to an elevated status not shared by any of its other employees: although the work done on the air by any other employee on any other program would not be exempt, the work done on the air by news employees would be. Yet this novel division was never endorsed, or even discussed, by Congress.

We have determined that Section 315 does not exempt newscaster candidates from the strictures of the "equal opportunities" rule. Branch challenges the statute, as so interpreted, on several constitutional grounds.

Branch's first objection is that the statute extinguishes his right to seek political office. That he has such a right is undeniable, though the Constitution and the Supreme Court's cases in the area do not pinpoint the precise grounds on which it rests. But whatever its source, the right is not implicated in this case. "In approaching candidate restrictions, it is essential to examine in a realistic light the extent and nature of their impact on voters." Here that impact is slight. The "equal opportunities" rule does not extinguish anyone's right to run for office. It simply provides that certain uses of a broadcast station by a candidate entitle other candidates for the same office to equal time. That the rule will affect some candidates favorably and others unfavorably is obvious. It may cause certain candidates to receive less time on the air than if the statute did not exist. But the Supreme Court has held that no individual has any right of access to the broadcast media. *Columbia B'casting System, Inc. v. Democratic Nat'l Comm.,* 412 U.S. 94 (1973).

The core of Branch's challenge on this point is that the statute imposes an undue burden on his ability to run for office because he cannot, during the time he is a candidate, do his normal work of reporting news on the air for Station KOVR. But nobody has ever thought that a candidate has a right to run for office and at the same time to avoid all personal sacrifice. Even if the practicalities of campaigning for office are put to one side, many people find it necessary to choose between their jobs and their candidacies.

Indeed, the burdens Branch complains of are borne by all other radio and television personalities under Section 315, though the exception he seeks would apply only to newscasters. In *Paulsen* the challenge was clothed in an equal protection guise, and perhaps at bottom Branch's challenge is also one of equal protection. However that may be, the argument is the same, and so is the result. Under established law, *Paulsen* was correct in finding the burdens imposed by Section 315 justifiable as "both reasonable and necessary to achieve the important and legitimate objectives of encouraging political discussion and preventing unfair and unequal use of the broadcast media."

Branch's second constitutional objection to Section 315 is that the "equal opportunities" rule violates the first amendment. He cites *Miami Herald Publishing Co. v. Tornillo* where the Supreme

Court broadly declared that a "[g]overnment-enforced right of access inescapably 'dampens the vigor and limits the variety of public debate.'" The "equal opportunities" rule, in Branch's view, is identical to a right-of-reply statute in its impact.

The Supreme Court has expressly held, however, that the first amendment's protections for the press do not apply as powerfully to the broadcast media. In *Red Lion B'casting Co. v. FCC,* the Court upheld the government's authority "to put restraints on licensees in favor of others whose views should be expressed on this unique medium." What makes the broadcast medium unique, in the Court's view, is the scarcity of broadcast frequencies.

While doubts have been expressed that the scarcity rationale is adequate to support differing degrees of first amendment protection for the print and electronic media, see, e.g., *Telecommunications Research & Action Center v. FCC, Meredith Corp. v. FCC,* it remains true, nonetheless that Branch's first amendment challenge is squarely foreclosed by *Red Lion.* In *Red Lion,* the Supreme Court upheld as constitutional the FCC's authority to enforce the fairness doctrine, which requires broadcast stations to give fair coverage to each side of a public issue, and in particular upheld "its specific manifestations in the personal attack and political editorial rules." In the course of its opinion, the Court held that the statutory "equal opportunities" rule in Section 315 and the FCC's own fairness doctrine rested on the same constitutional basis of the government's power to regulate "a scarce resource which the Government has denied others the right to use."

Nor can we adopt Branch's suggestion that this court would be justified in stepping away from *Red Lion.* The Supreme Court recently reaffirmed *Red Lion* and disavowed any intention "to reconsider our longstanding approach without some signal from Congress or the FCC that technological developments have advanced so far that some revision of the system of broadcast regulation may be required." *FCC v. League of Women Voters of California.* The FCC may now have sent just such a signal by issuing a report which concludes that Section 315 is unconstitutional and should be abandoned. But unless the Court itself were to overrule *Red Lion,* we remain bound by it.

Branch's final constitutional challenge to Section 315 is that it impermissibly limits the discretion of broadcast stations to select the particular people who will present news on the air to the public. Branch thus attempts to press the third-party rights of broadcasters who are not themselves parties to this case.

Nonetheless, the third-party challenge Branch advances is rebutted by *Red Lion*. A burden on the ability to present a particular broadcaster on the air, which applies to all broadcasters irrespective of the content of the news they present, is a much less significant burden than rules requiring the transmission of replies to personal attacks and political editorials, which were upheld in *Red Lion*. The latter provisions apply directly to political speech, and weigh more heavily on some messages than on others, depending on the precise content of the message conveyed. In contrast, the burdens on broadcasters that Branch asserts here do not "impair the discretion of broadcasters to present their views on any issue or to carry any particular type of programming." Moreover, we note again that there is no right of any particular individual to appear on television.

The petition for review is, therefore, denied.

COMMENT

As Judge Bork makes clear in *Branch*, when Congress in 1959 enacted exemptions from equal time obligation for bona fide newscasts, news interviews, news documentaries, and on-the-spot coverage of bona fide news events, its motivating force was the much criticized *Lar Daly* case. Lar Daly, a Chicago mayoral candidate, complained to the FCC that TV "newscasts had shown interviews of his opponents and a film clip of the incumbent mayor greeting the Argentine President at the airport." The FCC held that this was a "use" under sec. 315 and that, therefore, Lar Daly had a right to equal time. See *In re Telegram to CBS, Inc.*, 18 R.R. 238, *recon. denied*, 26 F.C.C. 715 (1959). This interpretation irritated Congress. Judge Bork quotes Senator Pastore of Rhode Island: " 'It was not until February of this year [1959], when the FCC issued its stupid, silly decision in the *Lar Daly* case, that we were confronted with any trouble.' "

In a concurring opinion in the *Branch* case, Judge Starr took a different view of sec. 315:

> When a newscaster reports the news, there is no "use" or "permitting" of a use in the ordinary sense of those words. Employers do not "permit" their employees to "use" broadcast facilities. Employees are *hired* to do their jobs. Once on the payroll, they have to carry on their duties; there is no "permission" being granted in the everyday sense of the word.

Judge Starr believed a "more natural statutory interpretation would exempt newscasters who are just doing their job from the 'equal opportunities' requirement of section 315(a)." The judge conceded, however, that the legislative history did indicate that Congress passed the 1959 amendments to restore the pre–*Lar Daly* law. That law "included the principle that a newscaster's appearance was indeed a 'use' within section 315(a)." Because the court was bound to accept the FCC's reasonable interpretation of its "governing statute," Judge Starr joined in the result. He noted, however, that the FCC was not bound by its interpretation of the *Branch* problem, which he believed to be "less natural" and "less sensible" than his.

In the *Branch* case, Judge Bork observed: "But unless the Court itself were to overrule *Red Lion*, we remain bound by it." Suppose that in a case involving the fairness doctrine, the Supreme Court overruled *Red Lion* only vis-à-vis the fairness doctrine? Would the "equal opportunities" rule still be valid?

Section 315 and Other Contingent Rights of Access

Like their print colleagues, broadcasters normally decide what content to air and, consequently, bear legal responsibility for it. Unlike the print media, however, broadcasters must by law provide access to their stations to others in certain instances. As just discussed, sec. 315 of the Communications Act is one such instance. It creates a contingent right of access. If a broadcaster permits one legally qualified candidate for a public office to use a station in a nonexempt format, then that broadcaster must be willing to provide equal opportunities to use the station to all of that candidate's legally qualified opponents.

Three related FCC policies create somewhat similar contingent rights of access: the so-called

Zapple Rule, the FCC's political editorializing rules, and its personal attack rules.

THE ZAPPLE RULE In 1970, Nicholas Zapple, at the time the leading staff member of the Senate Commerce Committee, sent a letter to the FCC. The committee's chairman, Senator John Pastore (D-RI) was concerned that broadcasters, especially the major networks, seemed willing to sell time to the Republican Party. He feared that they might not be similarly willing to sell time to the Democratic Party. The uses involved did not include candidate "appearances," hence sec. 315 did not apply. Pastore directed Zapple to ask the FCC how it would respond to unequal access to the airwaves among major political parties.

The FCC response has become known as the Zapple Rule. Conceptually, the FCC linked sec. 315 and the fairness doctrine. It said it would be contrary to the public interest (and, perhaps, a violation of the fairness doctrine) for a broadcaster to sell or provide time to one major political party without being willing to provide comparable access to the other major political party. This is sometimes also known as a "quasi-equal-opportunity" requirement. It basically says that if one major political party gets access, the other major party ought to be able to get comparable access on the same terms from the same broadcasters. As previously stressed, the rule creates a contingent right of access. Zapple does not require broadcasters to sell or provide time to political parties in the first place, but says that if they do, then they must provide quasi-equal opportunities to the other major party. *Letter to Nicholas Zapple*, 23 F.C.C.2d 707 (1970).

THE POLITICAL EDITORIALIZING RULES Broadcasters sometimes run editorials supporting or opposing candidates for public office. When a station takes such a formal position, as a licensee, on a candidate for public office, the FCC's political editorializing rules come into play. Within twenty-four hours of such a political editorial, the station must contact candidates. If a station opposes a candidate, that candidate must be given a reasonable opportunity to present a response. If the station supports a candidate in a race, then all the legally qualified opposing candidates must be notified and given a reasonable response opportunity. If it wishes, the station can tell candidates that they

must select a spokesperson to present their response, thus avoiding possible "equal opportunities" problems under sec. 315. If a station plans to run such editorials within seventy-two hours of the election or on election day itself, candidates must be notified "sufficiently far in advance of the broadcast" that a "reasonable opportunity to respond" is created. 47 C.F.R. § 73.1930 (1995). Again, contingent rights of access are created. If broadcasters run certain kinds of candidate-related editorials, they must provide access to candidates or, most commonly, to candidate spokespersons. Nothing, however, legally compels a broadcaster to take editorial positions on candidates for public office.

THE PERSONAL ATTACK RULES When it wrote the political editorializing rules, the FCC also adopted what have come to be known as the "personal attack rules." Derived from the fairness doctrine, these rules say that if a broadcaster attacks the "honesty, character or integrity" of an identified person or group while discussing a controversial issue of public importance, then that broadcaster must contact that person or group within a week, provide a script, tape, or accurate summary of the attack, and offer a reasonable opportunity to respond over the same station without charge. 47 C.F.R. § 73.1920 (1995). The FCC interprets the "personal" element of the rule strictly; attacks not going to personal character do not count.

Thus, broadcasters can vigorously criticize individuals and groups so long as they do not directly attack their "honesty, character or integrity." The FCC also adheres to its requirement that the only attacks that come under the rule are those occurring in the context of discussions of controversial issues of public importance. Generally, this phrase means the same thing in a personal attack case as it means in a fairness doctrine case, from which, of course, the phrase was derived.

Some kinds of personal attacks are exempt. To start with, attacks occurring in bona fide newscasts, news interviews, and on-the-spot coverage of bona fide news events do not bring on personal attack responsibilities. *These exemptions, derived from sec. 315, notably do not include the bona fide news documentary exemption also found there.* Attacks on foreign groups are also exempt. Most importantly, many attacks in a political context are also not covered. Attacks made by or on behalf of legally qualified candidates during a political campaign do not trigger the rules. If an attack is somehow made upon a legally qualified candidate, the broadcaster can offer the opportunity to respond to a candidate's spokesperson, again avoiding sec. 315 "equal opportunities" problems. 47 C.F.R. § 73.1920 (1995). As with the political editorializing rules, however, only a contingent right of access is created. Broadcasters do not have to attack in the first place—the rules simply say that if a personal attack occurs, some access must be given to the individual or, in a few instances, a spokesperson to respond.

It should be noted that the FCC has had proceedings going for years to repeal the personal attack and political editorializing rules. The FCC appears not to have acted on these proceedings out of concern for Congress's reaction. The fate of the rules is much linked to the fate of the fairness doctrine, discussed subsequently.

SECTION 312(a)(7) AND "REASONABLE ACCESS" FOR FEDERAL POLITICAL CANDIDATES

So far only one law requires broadcasters to provide noncontingent access to their facilities: sec. 312(a)(7) of the Communications Act of 1934. In 1972, Congress, concerned about the high cost of campaigning for federal office, adopted the Federal Election Campaign Act of 1971. In that Act Congress attempted to hold down the cost of campaigning by mandating that just before elections, broadcasters, if they sold time to candidates at all, had to sell that time at the "lowest unit charge"—basically, the lowest price available on the station on that date for that particular length and class of ad.

Having driven the price of political advertising time to its lowest levels, Congress logically became concerned that some broadcasters might decide not to sell any political advertising time at all. To prevent this, Congress amended sec. 312 of the Communications Act to add a provision saying that, at least in theory, the FCC could revoke the license of a broadcaster who refused to provide "reasonable access" to the station's

facilities for legally qualified candidates for federal office. No broadcaster has ever lost a license under sec. 312(a)(7), but the provision has occasioned substantial interpretation by the FCC and, eventually, a major decision by the U.S. Supreme Court. In *CBS, Inc. v. FCC*, 453 U.S. 367 (1981), the Court upheld the constitutionality of the "reasonable access" requirement. The context was the refusal of broadcast networks to sell time to the Carter-Mondale campaign in the early stages of their ultimately unsuccessful quest for reelection in 1979–1980. The Court concluded that sec. 312 was constitutional because it protected the public's right to receive political information.

CBS, Inc. v. FCC
7 MED. L. RPTR. 1563, 453 U.S. 367, 101 S. CT. 2813, 69 L. ED. 2D 706 (1981).

Chief Justice BURGER delivered the opinion of the Court.

We granted certiorari to consider whether the Federal Communications Commission properly construed 47 U.S.C. § 312(a)(7) and determined that petitioners failed to provide "reasonable access to [the] use of a broadcasting station" as required by the statute.

On October 11, 1979, Gerald M. Rafshoon, President of the Carter-Mondale Presidential Committee, requested each of the three major television networks to provide time for a 30-minute program between 8 P.M. and 10:30 P.M. on either the 4th, 5th, 6th, or 7th of December 1979. The committee intended to present, in conjunction with President Carter's formal announcement of his candidacy, a documentary outlining the record of his administration.

The networks declined to make the requested time available. Petitioner CBS emphasized the large number of candidates for the Republican and Democratic presidential nominations and the potential disruption of regular programming to accommodate requests for equal treatment, but it offered to sell two 5-minute segments to the committee, one at 10:55 P.M. on December 8 and one in the daytime. Petitioner ABC replied that it had not yet decided when it would begin selling political time for the 1980 Presidential campaign, but subsequently indicated that it would allow such sales in January 1980. Petitioner

NBC, noting the number of potential requests for time from presidential candidates, stated that it was not prepared to sell time for political programs as early as December 1979.

On October 29, 1979, the Carter-Mondale Presidential Committee filed a complaint with the FCC, charging that the networks had violated their obligation to provide "reasonable access" under Sec. 312(a)(7) of the Communications Act of 1934, as amended. Title 47 U.S.C. § 312(a)(7) states:

> The FCC may revoke any station license or construction permit * * * for willful or repeated failure to allow reasonable access to or to permit purchase of reasonable amounts of time for the use of a broadcasting station by a legally qualified candidate for federal elective office on behalf of his candidacy.

At an open meeting on November 20, 1979, the FCC, by a 4-to-3 vote, ruled that the networks had violated § 312(a)(7). In its Memorandum Opinion and Order, the FCC concluded that the networks' reasons for refusing to sell the time requested were "deficient" under its standards of reasonableness, and directed the networks to indicate by November 26, 1979, how they intended to fulfill their statutory obligations. 74 F.C.C.2d 631.

Petitioners sought reconsideration of the FCC's decision. The reconsideration petitions were denied by the same 4-to-3 vote, and, on November 28, 1979, the FCC issued a second Memorandum Opinion and Order clarifying its previous decision. It rejected petitioners' arguments that § 312(a)(7) was not intended to create a new right of access to the broadcast media and that the commission had improperly substituted its judgment for that of the networks in evaluating the Carter-Mondale Presidential Committee's request for time. November 29, 1979, was set as the date for the networks to file their plans for compliance with the statute. 74 F.C.C.2d 657.

The networks, pursuant to 47 U.S.C. § 402, then petitioned for review of the FCC's orders in the United States Court of Appeals for the District of Columbia Circuit. The court allowed the Committee and the National Association of Broadcasters to intervene, and granted a stay of the FCC's orders pending review.

Following the seizure of American Embassy personnel in Iran, the Carter-Mondale Presidential Committee decided to postpone to early January 1980 the 30-minute program it had planned to broadcast during the period of December 4–7,

1979. However, believing that some time was needed in conjunction with the president's announcement of his candidacy, the committee sought and subsequently obtained from CBS the purchase of five minutes of time on December 4. In addition, the committee sought and obtained from ABC and NBC offers of time for a 30-minute program in January, and the ABC offer eventually was accepted. Throughout these negotiations, the committee and the networks reserved all rights relating to the appeal.

The court of appeals affirmed the FCC's order, 629 F.2d 1 (1980), holding that the statute created a new, affirmative right of access to the broadcast media for individual candidates for federal elective office. As to the implementation of § 312(a)(7), the court concluded that the FCC has the authority to independently evaluate whether a campaign has begun for purposes of the statute, and approved the FCC's insistence that "broadcasters consider and address all non-frivolous matters in responding to a candidate's request for time." For example, a broadcaster must weigh such factors as: "(a) the individual needs of the candidate (as expressed by the candidate); (b) the amount of time previously provided to the candidate; (c) potential disruption of regular programming; (d) the number of other candidates likely to invoke equal opportunity rights if the broadcaster grants the request before him; and (e) the timing of the request." And in reviewing a broadcaster's decision, the FCC will confine itself to two questions: "(1) has the broadcaster adverted to the proper standards in deciding whether to grant a request for access, and (2) is the broadcaster's explanation for his decision reasonable in terms of those standards?"

Applying these principles, the court of appeals sustained the FCC's determination that the presidential campaign had begun by November 1979, and, accordingly, the obligations imposed by § 312(a)(7) had attached.

We consider first the scope of § 312(a)(7). Petitioners CBS and NBC contend that the statute did not impose any additional obligations on broadcasters, but merely codified prior policies developed by the FCC under the public interest standard. The FCC, however, argues that § 312(a)(7) created an affirmative, promptly enforceable right of reasonable access to the use of broadcast stations for individual candidates seeking federal elective office.

The Federal Election Campaign Act of 1971, which Congress enacted in 1972, included as one of its four titles the Campaign Communications Reform Act (Title I). Title I contained the provision that was codified as 47 U.S.C. § 312(a)(7).

We have often observed that the starting point in every case involving statutory construction is "the language employed by Congress." *Reiter v. Sonotone Corp.*, 442 U.S. 330, 337 (1979). In unambiguous language, § 312(a)(7) authorizes the FCC to revoke a broadcaster's license. It is clear on the face of the statute that Congress did not prescribe merely a general duty to afford some measure of political programming, which the public interest obligation of broadcasters already provided for. Rather, § 312(a)(7) focuses on the individual "legally qualified candidate" seeking air time to advocate "his candidacy," and guarantees him "reasonable access" enforceable by specific governmental sanction. Further, the sanction may be imposed for "willful or repeated" failure to afford reasonable access. This suggests that, if a legally qualified candidate for federal office is denied a reasonable amount of broadcast time, license revocation may follow even a single instance of such denial so long as it is willful; where the denial is recurring, the penalty may be imposed in the absence of a showing of willfulness.

The command of § 312(a)(7) differs from the limited duty of broadcasters under the public interest standard. The practice preceding the adoption of § 312(a)(7) has been described by the FCC as follows:

> Prior to the enactment of the [statute], we recognized political broadcasting as one of the fourteen basic elements necessary to meet the public interest, needs and desires of the community. No legally qualified candidate had at that time a specific right of access to a broadcasting station. However, stations were required to make reasonable, good faith judgments about the importance and interest of particular races. Based upon those judgments, licensees were to "determine how much time should be made available for candidates in each race on either a paid or unpaid basis. There was no requirement that such time be made available for specific "uses" of a broadcasting station to which Section 315 "equal opportunities would be applicable." [footnotes omitted.] Commission Policy in Enforcing Section 312(a)(7) of the Communications Act, 68 F.C.C.2d 1079, 1087–88 (1978) (1978 Report and Order).

Under the pre-1971 public interest requirement, compliance with which was necessary to assure license renewal, some time had to be given to political issues, but an individual candidate could claim no personal right of access unless his opponent used the station and no distinction was drawn between federal, state, and local elections. See *Farmers Educational & Cooperative Union v. WDAY, Inc.*, 360 U.S. 525, 534 (1959). By its terms, however, § 312(a)(7) singles out legally qualified candidates for *federal* elective office and grants them a special right of access on an individual basis, violation of which carries the serious consequence of license revocation. The conclusion is inescapable that the statute did more than simply codify the preexisting public interest standard.

The legislative history confirms that § 312(a)(7) created a right of access that enlarged the political broadcasting responsibilities of licensees. Perhaps the most telling evidence of congressional intent, however, is the contemporaneous amendment of § 315(a) of the Communications Act. That amendment was described by the Conference Committee as a "conforming statement" necessitated by the enactment of § 312(a)(7). Prior to the "conforming amendment," the second sentence of 47 U.S.C. § 315(a) read: "No obligation is imposed upon any licensee to allow the use of its station by any such candidate." This language made clear that broadcasters were not common carriers as to affirmative, rather than responsive, requests for access. As a result of the amendment, the second sentence now contains an important qualification: "No obligation is imposed *under this subsection* upon any licensee to allow the use of its station by any such candidate." 47 U.S.C. § 315(a) [emphasis added]. Congress retreated from its statement that "no obligation" exists to afford individual access presumably because § 312(a)(7) compels such access in the context of federal elections. If § 312(a)(7) simply reaffirmed the pre-existing public interest requirement with the added sanction of license revocation, no conforming amendment to § 315(a) would have been needed.

Thus, the legislative history supports the plain meaning of the statute that individual candidates for federal elective office have a right of reasonable access to the use of stations for paid political broadcasts on behalf of their candidacies without reference to whether an opponent has secured time.

Since the enactment of § 312(a)(7), the FCC has consistently construed the statute as extending beyond the prior public interest policy. In 1972, the commission made clear that § 312(a)(7) "now imposes on the overall obligation to operate in the public interest *the additional specific requirement* [emphasis added] that reasonable access and purchase of reasonable amounts of time be afforded candidates for Federal office." Use of Broadcast and Cablecast Facilities by Candidates for Public Office, 34 FCC 2d 510, 537–538 (1972) (1972 policy statement). In its 1978 Report and Order, the Commission stated: "When Congress enacted Section 312(a)(7), it imposed an additional obligation on the general mandate to operate in the public interest. Licensees were specifically required to afford reasonable access to or to permit the purchase of reasonable amounts of broadcast time for the "use" of Federal candidates. We see no merit to the contention that Section 312(a)(7) was meant merely as a codification of the FCC's already existing policy concerning political broadcasts. There was no reason to commit that policy to statute since it was already being enforced by the FCC." The FCC had adhered to this view of the statute in its rulings on individual inquiries and complaints.

Although Congress provided in § 312(a)(7) for greater use of broadcasting stations by federal candidates, it did not give guidance on how the FCC should implement the statute's access requirement. Essentially, Congress adopted a "rule of reason" and charged the commission with its enforcement. Pursuant to 47 U.S.C.A. § 303(r), which empowers the FCC to "[m]ake such rules and regulations and prescribe such restrictions and conditions, not inconsistent with law, as may be necessary to carry out the provisions of [the Communications Act]," the agency has developed standards to effectuate the guarantees of § 312(a)(7). See also 47 U.S.C. § 154(i). The FCC has issued some general interpretative statements, but its standards implementing § 312(a)(7) have evolved principally on a case-by-case basis and are not embodied in formalized rules. The relevant criteria broadcasters must employ in evaluating access requests under the statute can be summarized from the FCC's 1978 Report and Order and the Memorandum Opinions and Orders in these cases.

Broadcasters are free to deny the sale of air time prior to the commencement of a campaign, but once a campaign has begun, they must give reasonable and good faith attention to access requests from "legally qualified" candidates for federal elective office. Such requests must be considered on an individualized basis, and broadcasters are required to tailor their responses to accommodate, as much as reasonably possible, a candidate's stated purposes in seeking air time. In responding to access requests, however, broadcasters may also give weight to such factors as the amount of time previously sold to the candidate, the disruptive impact on regular programming, and the likelihood of requests for time by rival candidates under the equal opportunities provision of § 315(a). These considerations may not be invoked as pretexts for denying access; to justify a negative response, broadcasters must cite a realistic danger of substantial program disruption—perhaps caused by insufficient notice to allow adjustments in the schedule—or of an excessive number of equal time requests. Further, in order to facilitate review by the FCC, broadcasters must explain their reasons for refusing time or making a more limited counteroffer. If broadcasters take the appropriate factors into account and act reasonably and in good faith, their decisions will be entitled to deference even if the FCC's analysis would have differed in the first instance. But if broadcasters adopt "across-the-board policies" and do not attempt to respond to the individualized situation of a particular candidate, the FCC is not compelled to sustain their denial of access. 1978 Report and Order. Petitioners argue that certain of these standards are contrary to the statutory objectives of § 312(a)(7).

The FCC has concluded that, as a threshold matter, it will independently determine whether a campaign has begun and the obligations imposed by § 312(a)(7) have attached. Petitioners assert that, in undertaking such a task, the FCC becomes improperly involved in the electoral process and seriously impairs broadcaster discretion.

However, petitioners fail to recognize that the FCC does not set the starting date for a campaign. Rather, on review of a complaint alleging denial of "reasonable access," it examines objective evidence to find whether the campaign has already commenced, "taking into account the position of the candidate *and the networks* as well as other factors." [Emphasis added.] As the court of appeals noted, the "determination of when the statutory obligations attach does not control the electoral process, the determination is controlled by the process." 629 F.2d at 16. Such a decision is not, and cannot be, purely one of editorial judgment.

Moreover, the FCC's approach serves to narrow § 312(a)(7), which might be read as vesting access rights in an individual candidate as soon as he becomes "legally qualified" without regard to the status of the campaign. By confining the applicability of the statute to the period after a campaign commences, the FCC has limited its impact on broadcasters and given substance to its command of *reasonable access.*

Petitioners also challenge the FCC's requirement that broadcasters evaluate and respond to access requests on an individualized basis. In petitioners' view, the agency has attached inordinate significance to candidates' needs, thereby precluding fair assessment of broadcasters' concerns and prohibiting the adoption of uniform policies regarding requests for access.

While admonishing broadcasters not to " 'second guess' the 'political' wisdom or effectiveness" of the particular format sought by a candidate, the FCC has clearly acknowledged that "the candidate's request is by no means conclusive of the question of how much time, if any, is appropriate. Other factors, such as the disruption or displacement of regular programming (particularly as affected by a reasonable probability of requests by other candidates), must be considered in the balance." Thus, the FCC mandates careful consideration of, not blind assent to, candidates' desires for air time.

Petitioners are correct that the FCC's standards proscribe blanket rules concerning access; each request must be examined on its own merits. While the adoption of uniform policies might well prove more convenient for broadcasters, such an approach would allow personal campaign strategies and the exigencies of the political process to be ignored. A broadcaster's "even-handed" response of granting only time spots of a fixed duration to candidates may be "unreasonable" where a particular candidate desires less time for an advertisement or a longer format to discuss substantive issues. In essence, petitioners seek the unilateral right to determine in advance how much time to afford *all* candidates.

Yet § 312(a)(7) assures a right of reasonable access to *individual* candidates for federal elective office, and the FCC's requirement that their requests be considered on an *individualized* basis is consistent with that guarantee.

There can be no doubt that the FCC's standards have achieved greater clarity as a result of the orders in these cases. However laudable that may be, it raises the question whether § 312(a)(7) was properly applied to petitioners. Based upon the FCC's prior decisions and 1978 Report and Order, however, we must conclude that petitioners had adequate notice that their conduct in responding to the Carter-Mondale Presidential Committee's request for access would contravene the statute.

In the 1978 Report and Order, the FCC stated that it could not establish a precise point at which § 312(a)(7) obligations would attach for all campaigns because each is unique. An arbitrary "blanket" ban on the use by a candidate of a particular class or length of time in a particular period cannot be considered reasonable. A federal candidate's decisions as to the best method of pursuing his or her media campaign should be honored as much as possible under the "reasonable" limits imposed by the licensee.

Here, the Carter-Mondale Presidential Committee sought broadcast time approximately 11 months before the 1980 presidential election and 8 months before the Democratic national convention. In determining that a national campaign was underway at that point, the FCC stressed: (a) that 10 candidates formally had announced their intention to seek the Republican nomination, and two candidates had done so for the Democratic nomination; (b) that various states had started the delegate selection process; (c) that candidates were traveling across the country making speeches and attempting to raise funds; (d) that national campaign organizations were established and operating; (e) that the Iowa caucus would be held the following month; (f) that public officials and private groups were making endorsements; and (g) that the national print media had given campaign activities prominent coverage for almost 2 months. The FCC's conclusion about the status of the campaign accorded with its announced position on the vesting of § 312(a)(7) rights and was adequately supported by the objective factors on which it relied.

Nevertheless, petitioners ABC and NBC refused to sell the Carter-Mondale Presidential Committee any time in December 1979 on the ground that it was "too early in the political season." These petitioners made no counteroffers, but adopted "blanket" policies refusing access despite the admonition against such an approach in the 1978 Report and Order. Likewise, petitioner CBS, while not barring access completely, had an across-the-board policy of selling only 5-minute spots to all candidates, notwithstanding the FCC's directive in the 1978 Report and Order that broadcasters consider "a candidate's desire as to the method of conducting his or her media campaign." Petitioner CBS responded with its standard offer of separate 5-minute segments, even though the Carter-Mondale Presidential Committee sought 30 minutes of air time to present a comprehensive statement launching President Carter's reelection campaign. Moreover, the committee's request was made almost 2 months before the intended date of broadcast, was flexible in that it could be satisfied with any prime time slot during a 4-day period, was accompanied by an offer to pay the normal commercial rate, and was not preceded by other requests from President Carter for access. Although petitioners adverted to the disruption of regular programming and the potential equal time requests from rival candidates in their responses to the Carter-Mondale Presidential Committee's complaint, the FCC rejected these claims as "speculative and unsubstantiated at best." Under these circumstances, we cannot conclude that the FCC abused its discretion in finding that petitioners failed to grant the "reasonable access" required by Section 312(a)(7).[15]

Finally, petitioners assert that § 312(a)(7) as implemented by the FCC violates the First

Amendment rights of broadcasters by unduly circumscribing their editorial discretion. Petitioners argue that the FCC's interpretation of § 312(a)(7)'s access requirement disrupts the "delicate balanc[e]" that broadcast regulation must achieve. We disagree.

A licensed broadcaster is "granted the free and exclusive use of a limited and valuable part of the public domain; when he accepts that franchise it is burdened by enforceable public obligations." *Office of Communication of the United Church of Christ v. FCC.* The First Amendment interests of candidates and voters, as well as broadcasters, are implicated by Section 312(a)(7). We have recognized that "it is of particular importance that candidates have the opportunity to make their views known so that the electorate may intelligently evaluate the candidates' personal qualities and their positions on vital public issues before choosing among them on election day." *Buckley v. Valeo.* Section 312(a)(7) thus makes a significant contribution to freedom of expression by enhancing the ability of candidates to present, and the public to receive, information necessary for the effective operation of the democratic process.

Petitioners are correct that the Court has never approved a *general* right of access to the media. See, *e.g., FCC v. Midwest Video Corp.; Miami Herald Publishing Co. v. Tornillo; CBS, Inc. v. Democratic National Committee.* Nor do we do so today. Section 312(a)(7) creates a *limited* right to "reasonable" access that pertains only to legally qualified federal candidates and may be invoked by them only for the purpose of advancing their candidacies once a campaign has commenced. The FCC has stated that, in enforcing the statute, it will "provide leeway to broadcasters and not merely attempt de novo to determine the reasonableness of their judgments." If broadcasters have considered the relevant factors in good faith, the FCC will uphold their decisions. Further, § 312(a)(7) does not impair the discretion of broadcasters to present their views on any issue or to carry any particular type of programming.

Section 312(a)(7) represents an effort by Congress to assure that an important resource—the airwaves—will be used in the public interest. We hold that the statutory right of access, as defined by the FCC and applied in these cases, properly balances the First Amendment rights of federal candidates, the public, and broadcasters.

---

15. As it did here, the FCC with the approval of broadcasters, engages in case-by-case adjudication of § 312(a)(7) complaints rather than awaiting license renewal proceedings. Although the penalty provided by § 312(a)(7) is license revocation, petitioners simply were directed to inform the commission of how they intended to meet their statutory obligations. See 74 F.C.C.2d, at 651; 74 F.C.C.2d, at 676–677. In essence, the commission entered a declaratory order that petitioners' responses to the Carter-Mondale Presidential Committee constituted a denial of "reasonable access." Such a ruling favors broadcasters by allowing an opportunity for curative action before their conduct is found to be "willful or repeated" and subject to the imposition of sanctions.

The judgment of the court of appeals is Affirmed.

Justice WHITE, with whom Justice REHN-QUIST and Justice STEVENS join, dissenting.

While both the Court and the FCC describe other factors considered relevant such as the number of candidates and disruption in programming, the overarching focus is directed to the perceived needs of the individual candidate. This highly skewed approach is required because, as the Court sees it, the networks "seek the unilateral right to determine in advance how much time to afford *all* candidates." But such a right, reasonably applied, would seem to fall squarely within the traditionally recognized discretion of the broadcaster. Instead of adhering to this traditional approach, the Court has laid the foundation for the unilateral right of candidates to demand and receive any "reasonable" amount of time a candidate determines to be necessary to execute a particular campaign strategy. The concomitant FCC involvement is obvious. There is no basis in the statute for this very broad and unworkable scheme of access.

COMMENT

It has been argued that *Red Lion* and *Tornillo* "cannot be reconciled because the distinctions which have been drawn between them are constitutionally insignificant." But it is contended that "unlike *Red Lion*, *CBS v. FCC* can be reconciled with *Tornillo*." How? See Shelledy, *Note, Access to the Press: Teleological Analysis of a Constitutional Double Standard*, 50 Geo.Wash. L. Rev. 430 (1982). *CBS v. FCC* distinguished the right of access sought there from the Florida right of reply statute that was considered in *Tornillo*. The "identity of the medium" was not the critical factor. *Tornillo* is often distinguished from *Red Lion* on the ground that in a newspaper case the restraint that can be imposed under the First Amendment is far more severe in nature than that imposed upon the electronic media.

The *George Washington* note distinguishes *Tornillo* from *CBS v. FCC* as follows:

Only one of the limiting characteristics of section 312(a)(7), the reasonableness standard, distinguishes it from the Florida right of reply on a level of constitutional significance: an editor's decision not to broadcast another's message is left undisturbed so long as the decision has been reached reasonably. The Florida statute the *Tornillo* Court invalidated constrained editorial discretion far more severely than section 312(a)(7). Once a triggering editorial vested the Florida right of reply, the editor lost all control over the decision of whether to publish a response, what length to allot to the response, and placement and choice of typeset—notwithstanding reasonable alternatives the editor could have chosen. Had the Florida statute been limited by the reasonableness standard, as is section 312(a)(7), it would not have transgressed the Court's command in *Tornillo* that any "compulsion to publish that which 'reason' tells [editors] should not be published is unconstitutional."

Do you agree?

In *CBS v. Democratic National Committee*, 412 U.S. 94 (1973), the Supreme Court held that an "arbitrary" blanket network policy of refusing to sell time to political groups for the discussion of social and political issues did not violate the First Amendment. Yet, in *CBS v. FCC*, the Court held that an "arbitrary" blanket ban by the networks on the use by a candidate of a particular length of time in a particular period could not be considered reasonable under sec. 312(a)(7). A blanket network ban on a certain category of programming was deemed permissible in one instance and impermissible in the other. Why? The difference is that in *CBS v. FCC* a *statute* conferred particular rights on individual political candidates. The FCC's construction of the statute made the candidate's "desires as to the method of conducting his or her campaign" a matter to be considered by the licensee in determining whether to grant reasonable access under the statute.

In short, the second *CBS* case involved a limited, statutorily conferred right, whereas the first *CBS* case would have required a decision by the Supreme Court that the First Amendment itself was a barrier to the exercise of broadcast editorial judgment.

Did sec. 312(a)(7) of the Federal Election Campaign Act of 1971 create an affirmative, promptly enforceable right of access? Or did it merely codify prior FCC policies, i.e., the obligation to provide reasonable access to federal political candidates that was part of the public interest standard of the Federal Communications Act?

Chief Justice Burger's answer on this is very clear. Section 312(a)(7) of the Federal Election Campaign Act of 1971 created a *new,* affirmative, promptly enforceable right of access. Why? For one thing, the fact that the second sentence of sec. 315(a) was contemporaneously amended to make it clear that "no obligation is imposed *under this subsection* upon any licensee to allow the use of its station by any such candidate" is seen as quite significant. In *CBS v. FCC,* the Court interpreted this amendment as evidence of congressional awareness that sec. 312(a)(7) had imposed upon broadcast licensees an obligation to allow the use of their stations by federal political candidates in a manner that previously had not obtained under either the public interest standard of the act or the prior unamended text of the second sentence of sec. 315(a).

How does sec. 312(a)(7) differ anyway from the duty to provide access for political candidates that broadcasters had under the public interest standard? One answer to this question is that prior to the enactment of sec. 312(a)(7), no legislative candidate had a specific right of access to broadcasting. There was a general public interest obligation to give political candidates some time, but no particularized rights were lodged in the candidates. If one candidate was given time, then, of course, under sec. 315(a) rights to equal opportunities would be triggered for that office. If all candidates were denied time, however, then the candidates seeking time would have had to rely on the general public interest obligation of broadcasters to provide time for political campaigns. This obligation was difficult to enforce since no particular candidate had any specified rights under it.

For that matter, is there still a public interest–based duty to provide access to political candidates? The FCC and the U.S. Supreme Court concluded that such a duty existed prior to 1971 because the FCC "recognized political broadcasting as one of the fourteen basic elements necessary to meet the public interest, needs and desires of the community." The fourteen-point list was first announced in the FCC's "1960 Programming Policy Statement," *Report and Statement of Policy re: Commission en banc Programming Inquiry,* 44 F.C.C. 2303 (1960). It is generally believed that the FCC's 1981 *Radio Deregulation* and 1984 *Television Deregulation*

orders eliminated the 1960 Policy Statement's guidelines for broadcast programming. The deregulation orders said that the FCC's only expectation of programming in the public interest would be that broadcasters would provide some issue-responsive programming. Do these deregulation orders mean that the *only* obligations broadcasters have toward political speech are those found in secs. 312 and 315 of the Communications Act? Does this mean that broadcasters are under no legal obligation to provide any access to nonfederal candidates? Remember that broadcasters still have an obligation to provide issue-responsive programming. See, p. 722.

Do you agree with Justice White that the majority interpretation of sec. 312(a)(7) is an "open invitation to start campaigning early"? In sec. 312(a)(7), the FCC refuses to defer to the editorial judgment of the broadcasters about when a campaign may be deemed to have commenced and reserves that issue for itself. As a result, candidates may be encouraged to show a "need" to campaign early. If a candidate has a low recognition factor and a full treasury, the incentive to seek access for early campaigning is great. Does the majority opinion suggest any means by which such requests may be countered by the FCC? What are they?

CBS v. FCC requires that candidate requests under sec. 312(a)(7) be handled on a case-by-case basis and refused to accept an approach based on blanket network policies. The FCC has stated that blanket policies against selling candidates either program-length amounts of time or spot ads also violate sec. 312(a)(7). Broadcasters must be willing to consider expressed candidate needs for access to the electorate through long programs or short ads if that is what candidates desire.

"Reasonable Access" in Practice: What Lengths of Time Are Reasonable?

Michael H. Levinson, a legally qualified candidate for the Republican nomination for president of the United States on the Republican primary ballot, requested a three-hour block of prime-time programming from three noncommercial educational stations, WENH-TV (Durham, New Hampshire), WEKW-TV (Keene, New Hampshire), and WGBH-TV (Boston, Massachusetts).

In response, each of the licensees offered Levinson five minutes of prime-time programming. The licensees justified their denial on two grounds. First, they said that granting Levinson's request would significantly disrupt programming. Second, there were nineteen candidates for the Republican nomination for president on the New Hampshire ballot and thirty six candidates for the Democratic nomination.

The FCC Mass Media Bureau denied Levinson's complaints against the three licensees. The licensees had invoked the proper factors set forth in *CBS v. FCC*; the counteroffer of five minutes of prime time was appropriately geared to those factors. The FCC should not "second guess" a licensee's response to reasonable access requests. These were noncommercial stations obliged to "provide reasonable access without charge, except for reasonable production charges." Because these stations reasonably anticipated many "reasonable access" and equal opportunity requests, these factors were legitimate considerations in denying Levinson's request. *Letter to Michael S. Levinson*, 7 F.C.C.R. 1457 (1992).

On appeal to the FCC, the Mass Media Bureau was upheld. *In re Complaint of Michael S. Levinson v. N.H. Noncommercial TV Stations*, 9 F.C.C.R. 3018 (1994). The FCC rejected Levinson's contention that the stations had no reasonable basis for anticipating a large number of candidate requests for time because no others had been made at the time of his request. The controlling factor was that there was a reasonable probability that such requests would be made. The FCC also denied Levinson's complaints that NBC and PBS failed to respond to his request for a three-hour block of time. Levinson was not a national candidate because he had not qualified on the ballots of at least ten states: "Levinson was entitled to reasonable access only on those stations which serve New Hampshire. Neither of the networks is the licensee of a New Hampshire station, nor of any station whose normal service area includes New Hampshire."

The FCC rulings were summarily affirmed in *Levinson v. FCC*, 1995 WL224851, cert. denied, 116 S.Ct. 570 (1995) (D.C. Cir. 1995):

> [B]roadcasters must provide "careful consideration of, not blind assent to, candidates' desires for air time." [*CBS, Inc. v. FCC*] The FCC's determination

that the stations' counteroffer of air time did not violate 47 U.S.C. § 312(a)(7) is adequately supported by the record: the three-hour block of time requested would have significantly disrupted regular programming, and the stations would not have been able to provide comparable access to the large number of other qualified candidates for the presidency.

In *National Association of Broadcasters*, 9 F.C.C.R. 5778 (1994), the FCC considered a request by the National Association of Broadcasters (NAB) that "broadcast stations need not provide legally qualified candidates for federal candidates in increments other than those which the station ordinarily sells to commercial advertisers or which it ordinarily programs." Basically, the NAB was asking the FCC to rule that broadcasters did not have to sell odd blocks of time. The FCC went fairly far in meeting the NAB request, when it ruled:

> [B]roadcasters should be required to make available to federal candidates only the lengths of time offered to commercial advertisers during the year preceding a particular election period. We also believe that stations must make program time available to federal candidates in the same lengths they have programmed the station in the year preceding an election whether or not such lengths of programming time have been sold to commercial advertisers. A station's decision to *program* odd lengths of time should be treated in the same manner as its decision to *sell* odd lengths of time. In both cases, it is reasonable to require broadcasters to provide access to qualified federal candidates consistent with their own sales and programming decisions. (Emphasis supplied.)

Is the *NAB* ruling consistent with *CBS, Inc. v. FCC?*

Does Section 312(a)(7) Require Broadcasters to Make Free Time Available?

Kennedy for President Committee v. FCC
6 MED. L. RPTR. 1705, 636 F.2D 432 (D.C. CIR. 1980).

ROBINSON, Circuit Judge:

On March 14, 1980, the three major commercial television networks broadcast a half-hour speech by President Carter from 4:00 to 4:30 P.M. and a presidential press conference from 9:00 to

9:30 P.M. On each occasion, the principal topic of discussion was the state of the Nation's economy. Each event was presented in its entirety and, with but one exception, was televised live by each network. The president's statements were also reported in the course of the networks' regularly scheduled national and local newscasts.

The Kennedy for President Committee, the petitioner herein, charges that these programs saturated the American public with the president's views on the economy only four days before the 1980 Illinois presidential primary. That, petitioner asserts, diminished the chances of its candidate, Senator Edward M. Kennedy, of winning the Democratic Party's presidential nomination later in the year. Petitioner claims that Section 312(a)(7) of the Communications Act of 1934 and the well-known fairness doctrine separately entitle the senator to time for telecasts of his own ideas and proposals on economic conditions.

The networks denied petitioner's request for responsive time, and the FCC rejected petitioner's bid for an administrative directive therefor. Before us now is a petition for review of the FCC's order. We agree with the FCC that petitioner's reliance on Section 312(a)(7) is misplaced, and that petitioner failed to establish the elements of a prima facie case under the fairness doctrine. We accordingly affirm. Reacting to announcements of plans to televise President Carter's March 14 speech and press conference, petitioner implored the networks to provide Senator Kennedy with an opportunity to speak in prime time to the American people on the economy.

Independently, the networks refused. In each instance, they construed petitioner's request as an invocation of the equal-opportunity command of Section 315(a) of the Communications Act, and expressed the belief that the telecasts in question were exempt from that requirement as on-the-spot coverage of bona fide news events. Each network reminded petitioner that it had given extensive coverage to the senator's campaign, and to his position on economic issues. Two of the networks emphasized their earlier presentations of wide spectra of economic commentary and analysis encompassing numerous alternatives to the stratagems advanced by the president.

Petitioner then turned to the FCC for "redress [of] a pattern of conduct causing an unacceptably imbalanced presentation of important facts." Petitioner specifically identified Section 312(a)(7) of the Communications Act and the long-established fairness doctrine as bases for a commission order to the networks to make time available to the senator.

At the first level of FCC consideration, the Broadcast Bureau denied relief. It first declared that petitioner's dependence on Section 312(a)(7) was faulty; "[g]iven the availability of prime time for purchase," it said, "the networks' failure to furnish free time does not raise a Section 312(a)(7) question." With respect to the fairness doctrine, the bureau concluded that petitioner had not established a prima facie case of violation because it had neither alleged nor substantiated any instance of bad faith on the networks' part, or any failure to present contrasting views on economic issues in their overall programming.

In essence, then, the bureau held that Section 312(a)(7) does not entitle a candidate to free time when time is available for purchase, and that establishment of a prima facie case under the fairness doctrine demands more than a bare conclusory assertion that a broadcaster has not balanced his programming on an important and controversial issue. Without awaiting an application from petitioner, the FCC, in the interest of expedition, examined the bureau's decision and affirmed simply on the basis of the bureau's opinion. Then followed the instant petition for review by this court.

Petitioner's Section 312(a)(7) contention is that it required the networks to allot free time to Senator Kennedy, particularly in consequence of the so-called saturation coverage of President Carter's economic views shortly before the Illinois primary. Two theories are advanced in attempted support of this position. One is that Section 312(a)(7) provides a candidate for federal elective office with a contingent right of access to free time, triggered in this instance by the telecasts of the president's March 14 speech and press conference. The other is that independently of this contingent right, the section confers upon such a candidate direct and unqualified entitlement to use broadcast facilities without charge.

As we shall soon see, Sections 312(a)(7) and 315(a) of the Communications Act work in tandem to govern access to broadcast media by candidates for public office. With the interaction of these two sections at the heart of federal intervention in political broadcasting, we begin our assessment of petitioner's arguments with an analysis of their interrelationship. The first part of Section 315(a) is its equal-opportunity provision, frequently referred to as an equal-time grant.

The import of this language is clear: any broadcaster who permits a "use" of station facilities by a legally qualified candidate must provide equal opportunities to that candidate's opponents. As originally enacted, this was the full extent of Section 315(a), but in 1959 Congress amended it to exclude candidate appearances in bona fide newscasts and news interviews, bona fide documentaries in which the appearance is incidental, and on-the-spot coverage of bona fide news events—which no longer constitute a "use" of broadcast facilities, and therefore are unencumbered by the equal-opportunity obligation. Since Section 315(a), as its proviso specifically states, does not impose an unconditional obligation on broadcasters to allow use of their station facilities by any candidate, the equal-opportunity grant has aptly been characterized as a contingent right of access. It does not compel a broadcaster to afford access to any candidate in the first instance, but it does mandate parity for all candidates for a given office once access by one is permitted. The duty is thus no more or less than to accord equal treatment to all legally qualified candidates for the same public office, and "equal opportunity" encompasses such elements as hour of the day, duration and charges.

As we have noted, four categories of news-type programs are expressly exempted from this equal opportunity mandate. Those programs, like others, however, remain subject to the exigencies of the public interest and the demands of the fairness doctrine. The last sentence of Section 315(a) makes plain that broadcasters are not relieved, in connection with the presentation of newscasts, news interviews, news documentaries, and on-the-spot coverage of news events, from the obligation imposed upon them under [the Act] to operate in the public interest and to afford reasonable opportunity for the discussion of conflicting views on issues of public importance.

This language, placed in Section 315(a) in 1959 when Congress added the exemptions to the equal opportunity provision, codifies the fairness doctrine formulated by the FCC in 1949. So, while broadcast of an event exempted by Section 315(a) does not enliven the equal-opportunity

requirement, it does summon adherence to public-interest and "fairness" considerations. Since we address the ramifications as well as the confines of the fairness doctrine in detail at a later point, we need not dwell upon them now. It is sufficient merely to say that this is another means by which a candidate might gain entrée to broadcast facilities for use in his campaign.

The third leaf of the triad governing candidate access to broadcast media is Section 312(a)(7), which authorizes the FCC to

> revoke any station license or construction permit * * * for willful or repeated failure to allow reasonable access to or to permit purchase of reasonable amounts of time for the use of a broadcasting station by a legally qualified candidate for federal elective office on behalf of his candidacy.

This is not the first time that a controversy has arisen over interpretation of Section 312(a)(7). In our recent decision in *CBS v. FCC,* we addressed the question whether Section 312(a)(7) was enacted as a new and additional entitlement to broadcast media access for federal candidates, or whether it merely codified the pre-existing duty of broadcasters to provide time to such candidates pursuant to the general mandate to operate in the public interest. Reading Section 312(a)(7) in light of its legislative history, we concluded that it does indeed "create an affirmative right of access for individual candidates for federal elective office." We did not, however, attempt to define the monetary parameters of that right, for *CBS* involved refusal of requests to *purchase* time. To resolve the issues now before us—whether Section 312(a)(7) augments Section 315(a) as an additional but broader equal-opportunity exaction, and the extent to which it independently grants access on a free basis—we must return to the legislative history and undertake a somewhat broader analysis.

Section 312(a)(7) had its genesis in the Federal Election Campaign Act of 1971. Title I of that legislation, denominated the "Campaign Communications Reform Act," contained three distinct provisions: the reasonable-access requirement now embodied in Section 312(a)(7); the lowest-unit-cost specification which is now Section 315(b)(1); and a spending limitation on use of communications media by candidates for federal elective office, which has since been repealed. Each provision stemmed from serious congressional concern over the ever mounting expense of modern electioneering.

The most straightforward reading of the language of Section 312(a)(7) is that broadcasters may fulfill their obligation thereunder either by allotting free time to a candidate or by selling the candidate time at the rates prescribed by Section 315(b). Section 312(a)(7) in terms authorizes license or permit revocation "for willful or repeated failure to allow reasonable access to or to permit purchase of reasonable amounts of time for the use of a broadcasting station," and "or" normally connotes the disjunctive. While "or" permissibly may be accepted in the conjunctive sense when that adequately appears to have been the legislative intent, in this instance the disjunctive interpretation is clearly supported.

Each reference to Section 312(a)(7) in the legislative history of the Campaign Communications Reform Act speaks of the *sale* of time. This consistent characterization of the statutory text as a mandate for sale of a reasonable amount of time supplies firm support for a disjunctive reading. This conclusion is in harmony with Senator Pastore's declaration, a year after passage of that act, that "there was a great deal of pressure to mandate free time" but that Congress decided "to avoid that" and imposed something different.

Consequently, we discern no right to free time for candidates for federal elective office under Section 312(a)(7) either from a reading of the statutory text or from our analysis of its legislative history. Remaining to be answered, however, is the question whether the "reasonable access" language of Section 312(a)(7) sometimes accomplishes that and by affording a right of access to broadcast facilities auxiliary to the Section 315(a) right to equal opportunities.

An equal-opportunity quality for Section 312(a)(7) is mentioned only fleetingly in the legislative history. The very few references to the section as an equal-opportunity provision all concerned § 956 and the role that Section 312(a)(7) would play upon the anticipated—but ultimately aborted—revocation of the equal-opportunity mandate of Section 315(a) with respect to presidential and vice-presidential candidates. In this context, there was but one notable allusion to Section 312(a)(7) as a guaranty of fair treatment of such candidates by broadcasters. The idea, advanced by Senator Mathias, was that after excluding presidential

and vice-presidential candidates from the benefit of Section 315(a)'s equal-opportunity provision, Section 312(a)(7) could serve as a source of authority for requiring broadcasters selling time to one such candidate to do the same for his opponents. This suggestion seems to have contemplated no more, however, than that Section 312(a)(7) could operate as a means of assuring that broadcasters would make sufficient quantities of time for purchase available to candidates for presidential or vice-presidential office.

Even assuming that these references tended somewhat to depict Section 312(a)(7) as something of an equal-opportunity auxiliary, that justification eroded away when the proposed partial suspension of Section 315(a)'s equal-opportunity provision failed to pass. There was warm support for suspension, which we noted earlier, but many legislators were fearful of abolition of that provision. Consequently, the Conference Committee decided to eliminate the portion of the Senate bill proposing elimination of Section 315(a)'s equal-opportunity requirement in presidential and vice-presidential campaigns, and neither the final Conference Report nor the ensuing debate on the floor of either House again referred to Section 312(a)(7) as an equal-opportunity measure. Save for the instant proceeding, the FCC has not had occasion to consider whether Section 312(a)(7) grants an automatic right to respond to broadcast material additional to that defined in Section 315(a); and here the denial of petitioner's rather vague argument on that point was unelucidated. The Broadcast Bureau dismissed reliance on Section 312(a)(7) for that purpose as misplaced, stating merely that this "section of the law was intended to insure that broadcasters make available reasonable amounts of time for *use* by federal candidates," and the FCC affirmed without opinion of its own. To be sure, this deposition evinces an underlying construction of Section 312(a)(7) not at all inharmonious with its legislative reflections, but it adds nothing to an understanding of why. There is, however, a significant history of administrative interpretation with respect to whether Section 312(a)(7), when it does obtain, grants its right of access on a free or a paid basis.

The FCC has consistently read Section 312(a)(7) as giving broadcasters the option of fulfilling their obligation thereunder by offering to candidates either free time or the privilege of purchasing time. The Commission first took this position in 1972, shortly after passage of Section 312(a)(7), when it issued a public notice in the form of questions and answers:

5. Q. Does the "reasonable access" provision of Section 312(a)(7) require commercial stations to give free time to legally qualified candidates for Federal elective office?
    A. No, but the licensee cannot refuse to give free time and also [refuse] to permit the purchase of reasonable amounts of time. If the purchase of reasonable amounts of time is not permitted, then the station is required to give reasonable amounts of free time.
6. Q. If a commercial station gives reasonable amounts of free time to candidates for federal elective office, must it also permit purchase of reasonable amounts of time?
    A. No. A commercial station is required either to provide reasonable amounts of free time or permit purchase of reasonable amounts of time.

It is not required to do both.

The FCC brought this public notice to the attention of Congress in 1973, and neither then nor at any time thereafter has Congress expressed disagreement with the FCC's interpretation of Section 312(a)(7). To boot, the FCC has reiterated its original interpretation on subsequent occasions.

The Communications Act envisions integration of two of its sections in a relatively uncomplicated scheme of access to broadcast facilities by candidates for public office. Section 312(a)(7) supplies a right of access by requiring broadcasters, on pain of license revocation, to make reasonable amounts of time available for use by legally qualified persons seeking federal elective office. This right is unconditional in the sense that no prior use by any opponent of that candidate is necessary. Irrefutably, reasonable access is for the asking if the candidate is willing to pay, and the amount he can be charged is carefully limited by law. The measure of the right remains constant, however, at "reasonable access."

Section 315(a), in turn, ordains that whenever a broadcaster permits any candidate for any public office—federal, state or local—to "use" broadcast facilities, the broadcaster must afford an equal opportunity to any legally qualified rival of that candidate who seeks it. This right is contingent in nature; it does not come into fruition unless and until an opponent makes some "use" of station facilities, but once that occurs it ripens, and the candidate becomes unconditionally entitled to equal opportunities, though to no more. The Section 315(a) duty arises, however, only with respect to an opponent's "use" of broadcast facilities; and coverage of an event within the purview of the four exemptions to that section is statutorily deemed a nonuse, and therefore does not activate the equal-opportunity requirement.

The statutory language and historical precedents also make plain that this section does not, however, confer the privilege of using the broadcaster's facilities without charge. Rather, we have found that broadcasters may meet the demands of Section 312(a)(7) either by an allotment of free time or by making time available for purchase.

We are satisfied, too, that a candidate cannot secure broadcast time, free or otherwise, through the simple expedient of reading Section 315(a)(7) as just another equal-opportunity provision. Nothing in the history of the section's evolution or its administrative interpretation serves to validate the thesis that it confers a second responsive right to broadcast privileges that may be employed as a supplement to Section 312(a)'s equal-opportunity mandate. And without some clear indication that Congress so intended, we perceive no justification for such a reading. Settled principles of statutory construction militate strongly against that interpretation, for it would engender grave doubt as to the internal consistency of the statutory scheme.

If Section 312(a)(7) were to be viewed as an auxiliary source of entitlement to equal opportunities, the exemptions to Section 315(a) would easily be destroyed. The purpose of these exclusions, it will be recalled, was to free broadcasters who carried any of four types of newsworthy "political" events from the equal-opportunity burden, and thereby to encourage more complete coverage of these events. Should Section 312(a)(7) be construed as automatically entitling a candidate to responsive broadcast access whenever and for whatever reason his opponent has appeared on the air, Section 315(a)'s exemptions would soon become meaningless. Statutes are to be interpreted, if possible, to give operation to all of their parts, and to maintain them in harmonious working relationship. Congress has devised a comprehensive and cohesive plan in which Section 312(a)(7), Section 315(a) and the latter's exemptions all have well-defined missions. No provision may be misused to defeat the effective functioning of another.

Consequently, we do not find in Section 312(a)(7) a right of access that Section 315 denies. Petitioner has not advanced any claim under Section 315(a), nor has it quarreled with the networks' unanimous conclusion that the broadcasts of the President's March 14 speech and press conference were immune from the equal-opportunity command of that section. We hold that petitioner cannot use Section 312(a)(7) to circumvent the explicit exemptions of Section 315(a).

We further hold that petitioner is not in a position to utilize Section 312(a)(7) in the manner in which Congress designed it to function. Petitioner has never claimed that it was denied an opportunity to buy time; rather, it has insisted that the networks violated Section 312(a)(7) simply by refusing to provide free time to Senator Kennedy. We have seen that the section entitles a candidate to free time only if and when a broadcaster refuses to sell a reasonable quantity of time. No showing of that sort has been made, or indeed undertaken.

We thus find petitioner's Section 312(a)(7) arguments unpersuasive.

Affirmed.

Content Considerations and Licensee Discretion under Section 312(a)(7)

Gillett Communications, owner of WAGA-TV in Atlanta, Georgia, asked the FCC for a declaratory ruling on the following issue: May a licensee channel a use by a federal candidate to a safe harbor when children are not generally the audience if it determines an ad is indecent or unsuitable for children? The FCC found that Becker's ad was not indecent and that the channeling requested by Gillett was inconsistent with sec. 312(a)(7): "[C]hanneling material that is not indecent would deprive federal candidates of their rights to determine how best to conduct their campaigns." *Letter Ruling*, 7 F.C.C.R. 5599 (1992).

In October 1992, Dan Becker again sought to purchase time from WAGA-TV for a thirty-minute political program in the late afternoon on November 1 following a pro football game. Instead, WAGA-TV offered to carry it between midnight and 6:00 A.M. Becker complained to the FCC. On November 22, 1994, the FCC issued a Declaratory Ruling that held (1) that Becker's first ad was not indecent; (2) that the record showed "that graphic political advertisements at issue can be psychologically damaging to children"; (3) that sec. 312(a)(7) did not deprive broadcasters of discretion concerning placement of political ads to protect children; and (4) that channeling would not violate the non-censorship provision of sec. 315(a). *In re Petition for Declaratory Ruling Concerning Section 312(a)(7)*, 9 F.C.C.R. 7638 (1994).

A court of appeals panel, per Judge Buckley, joined by Judges Silberman and Rogers, vacated this Declaratory Ruling, holding that it violated both sec. 315(a) and sec. 312(a)(7). *Becker v. FCC*, 95 F.3d 75 (D.C. Cir. 1996). The sec. 315 issues in *Becker* were discussed earlier, p. 784. Judge Buckley's discussion of the sec. 312(a)(7) issues are set forth below:

> [T]he FCC [has] issued "formal guidelines for reasonable access for federal candidates' in which it states that commercial broadcasters "must make program time available during prime time and other time periods unless unusual circumstances exist that render it reasonable to deny access." *Codification of the Commission's Political Programming Policies*, 7 F.C.C.R. 678, 681 (1991) (1991 Policy Statement).

Judge Buckley noted that in the 1991 Policy Statement the FCC declared that denial of reasonable access could not be used as a means to censor political material. Nor could a licensee adopt a policy that flatly banned federal candidates "from access to the types, lengths, and classes of time which they sell to commercial advertisers." The Declaratory Ruling frustrated what the FCC itself has identified as Congress' primary purpose in enacting section 312(a)(7); namely, to ensure candidates access to the time periods with the greatest audience potential . . ." *Licensee Responsibility*, 47 F.C.C.2d at 517. Children are likely to be in the audience even during the so-called safe harbor.

Judge Buckley concluded that the Declaratory Ruling's approval of channeling violated sec. 312(a)(7):

> The Supreme Court has cautioned, however, that "endowing licensees with a 'blank check' to determine what constitutes 'reasonable access' would eviscerate Sec. 312(a)(7)." *CBS, Inc. [v. FCC]*. We believe that the standardless discretion that the FCC has granted broadcasters to channel political messages will do just that. [T]he [FCC] now allows licensees to

channel images based entirely on a subjective judgment that a particular advertisement might prove harmful to children. All that it asks is that that judgment be "reasonable" and made in good faith.

These are slippery standards, and it is of small solace to a losing candidate that an appellate court might eventually find that the FCC's approval of a licensee's channeling decision was an abuse of discretion or contrary to law. Moreover, the acceptance of a subjective standard renders it impossible to determine whether it was the advertisement's message rather than its images that the licensee found too shocking for tender minds. In many instances, of course, it will be impossible to separate the message from the image, when the point of the political advertisement is to call attention to the perceived horrors of a particular issue. And the political use of television for shock effect is not limited to abortion.

Finally, [the FCC] contends that "the public interest standard of the [Communications] Act clearly contemplates that appropriate measures may be taken to protect the well-being of children, as reflected in" other provisions of the Act. We have a couple of problems with this argument. First of all, the first of the cited provisions [The Children's Television Act of 1990, Sec. 102, 47 U.S.C. § 303] deals with the quantity and duration of advertisements during children's programs, not their content; and the second [Public Telecommunications Act of 1992, Sec. 16(a), 47 U.S.C. § 303 note ("instructing FCC to 'promulgate regulations to prohibit the broadcasting of indecent programming between 6 a.m. and 12 midnight'")] places no restraints on the broadcasting of materials that are not indecent. Secondly, the FCC offers no evidence that Congress intended to subordinate a candidate's right of reasonable access to a licensee's assessment of the public interest. To the contrary it seems to us that the right of access accorded candidates by sections 312(a)(7) and 315(a) overrides the programming discretion that is otherwise allowed licensees by the Act, except in those circumstances already specified in the FCC's policy guidelines.

The FCC's Declaratory Ruling violates the "reasonable access" requirement of section 312(a)(7) by permitting content-based channeling of non-indecent political advertisements, thus denying qualified candidates the access to the broadcast media envisioned by Congress.

So ordered.

COMMENT

In *Becker,* Judge Buckley says that "the right of access afforded candidates" under sec. 315(a) and sec. 312(a)(7) overrides the discretion that the Act might otherwise grant broadcasters. Arguably, the case for upholding broadcaster discretion in selecting the placement of political advertising is stronger under sec. 312(a)(7) because, unlike sec. 315(a), it contains no specific anti-censorship provision. Why then did the FCC treat the two provisions in the same way?

THE FAIRNESS DOCTRINE: ANACHRONISM OR PROTECTOR OF PUBLIC FIRST AMENDMENT RIGHTS?

A Preliminary Caution

For nearly forty years (1949–1987), the FCC enforced an administrative policy known as the fairness doctrine. Despite this long history, in August 1987 the FCC abandoned the policy. Many members of Congress advocate reimposition of the doctrine through amendments to the Communications Act of 1934. President Ronald Reagan vetoed one congressional effort to make the doctrine statutory and blocked another through a threatened veto.

One thing is certain. The constitutionality and public policy wisdom of the doctrine will continue to be debated for some time. Thus, we focus here on those matters, presenting the arguments on behalf of and in opposition to the doctrine. Our treatment of nitty-gritty application problems of the doctrine is limited and our focus is more on whether it should exist at all. If the doctrine is successfully reimposed by Congress, attention can turn, again, to the specific problems of its application.

A Fairness Doctrine Primer

To follow the debate over the fairness doctrine, it is essential to have a basic understanding of what it required. Under the doctrine, broadcasters had two affirmative responsibilities. First, they had to devote a "reasonable" amount of time to covering "controversial issues of public importance" in their service areas—the "first prong" of the doctrine. Second, once coverage of a controversial issue of public importance was opened, broadcasters had to provide a "reasonable opportunity" for significant opposing viewpoints on such issues to be heard—the "second prong" of the doctrine.

Although often confused with sec. 315 of the Communications Act—the "equal time" provision—the fairness doctrine actually worked quite differently. Section 315 provides little broadcaster discretion and works rather automatically. If a broadcaster allows one legally qualified candidate for a public office to use his or her station, then all legally qualified opponents of that candidate must be given precisely equal opportunities to use the same station—no ifs, ands, or buts. In contrast, a key concept in fairness doctrine enforcement was "reasonableness." Under the first prong of the doctrine, broadcasters did not have to cover *every* controversial issue of public importance—only those they chose to cover under a standard of "reasonableness and good faith." In practice, broadcasters got in trouble with the FCC under the first prong only if they failed to cover the most crucial of controversies in their communities; in fact, only once—ever—did the FCC find that a broadcaster had violated the first prong. *Rep. Patsy Mink*, 59 F.C.C.2d 987, 37 R.R.2d 744 (1976).

Under the second prong of the doctrine, broadcasters did not, as is true under sec. 315, have to provide "equal" opportunity for opposing views to be heard—only a "reasonable opportunity." In practice, the FCC was quite tolerant of unequal amounts of time being devoted to opposing views, stepping in only when the discrepancies became truly unreasonable. In addition, unlike sec. 315, the fairness doctrine never created a right for the proponents of views on controversial issues to demand access to stations. Under sec. 315, broadcasters must permit "opposing candidates" direct access to their stations, but under the fairness doctrine, all broadcasters had to do was see to it that the opposing views were presented somehow. While that might mean putting an advocate for those views on the air, the doctrine did not require that. Broadcasters could present opposing views in any way they chose; what was important was that the views got presented, somehow, in a reasonable fashion. Individual programs did not have to be "balanced," only the broadcaster's overall service.

Compared to fairness doctrine complaints, full-blown FCC fairness doctrine cases were relatively infrequent. Although the FCC received hundreds to thousands of complaints each year the doctrine was in effect, it deflected most of them from broadcasters. By placing many burdens of pleading and proof on complaining parties, the FCC usually managed procedurally to reject most fairness doctrine complaints rather than passing them along to broadcasters for response. Complaining parties had to prove that broadcasts concerned a "controversial issue of public importance." They had to assert that they were regular listeners or viewers of the station involved and, in a preliminary way, had to prove that the broadcaster had not "reasonably" treated opposing viewpoints on other programming. Complaints were referred to broadcasters only after these hurdles were cleared.

Broadcaster responses to submitted fairness complaints had to be accepted if they were reasonable. If, for example, a complaining party characterized an issue in a way that made it controversial and of public importance while the broadcaster characterized the issue in a different way that removed its controversial nature or public importance, courts told the FCC that they had to accept the broadcaster's reasonable characterization. *National Broad. Co. v. FCC*, 516 F.2d 1101 (D.C. Cir. 1974); see also *American Security Council Educ. Found. v. FCC*, 607 F.2d 438 (D.C. Cir. 1979). Even if a broadcaster was found to have violated the doctrine, the usual FCC response was simply to tell the broadcaster that somehow, someway he or she had to present additional programming dealing with the issue or, more commonly, the particular aspect presented "unreasonably." Only one broadcaster ever lost a license where fairness doctrine violations were a factor. In that case, it is unclear whether the license was lost for the fairness violations alone or, more likely, for a combination of the violations and the broadcaster's misrepresentation to the FCC about them. *Brandywine–Main Line Radio, Inc. v. FCC*, 473 F.2d 16 (D.C. Cir. 1972), *cert. denied* 412 U.S. 922 (1973).

At least once, the doctrine was subjected to fairly direct constitutional challenge. In the *Red Lion* case, the U.S. Supreme Court decided that the doctrine, as then applied and defended by the FCC, was constitutional.

The "Fairness" Doctrine and *Red Lion*

In November 1964, the Red Lion Broadcasting Co. of Red Lion, Pennsylvania, carried a program series entitled *The Christian Crusade*. One of the programs included an attack by Rev. Billy

James Hargis on a book entitled *Goldwater— Extremist of the Right* by journalist Fred Cook.

The *Red Lion* case concerns the "personal attack" rule, an aspect of the fairness doctrine that requires a station that carries a personal attack on an individual to give that individual an opportunity to reply. A question that had been unclear under the personal attack rule was whether the station had to furnish broadcast time free if the person attacked could not obtain a sponsor and was unable to pay for the time.

Cook asked the radio station for an opportunity to reply to Hargis. The radio station replied that the personal attack aspect of the fairness doctrine only required a licensee to make free time for reply available if no paid sponsorship could be secured. The station therefore insisted that Cook had to warrant that no such paid sponsorship could be found. Cook refused and instead complained to the FCC. The FCC took the position that the station had the duty to furnish reply time, paid or not. The FCC declared that it was not necessary for Cook to show that he could neither afford nor find sponsored time before the station's duty to make reply time available went into effect. The FCC ruled that the public interest required that the public be given an opportunity to learn the other side and that this duty remained even where the time had to be sustained by the station. The FCC entered a formal order to that effect, and the station appealed to the U.S. Court of Appeals for the District of Columbia, which held that the fairness doctrine and the personal attack rules were constitutional. *Red Lion Broad. Co. v. FCC,* 381 F.2d 908 (D.C. Cir. 1967).

With the *Red Lion* decision in the court of appeals, the fairness doctrine prevailed in the first court test of its validity under the First Amendment, as did its corollary, the personal attack rules. The broadcast industry was shocked by the court of appeals decision in the *Red Lion* case. The Radio Television News Directors Association decided to institute suit for judicial review of FCC orders upholding the personal attack rules and reply time for political editorials. Suit was filed in the U.S. Court of Appeals for the Seventh Circuit in Chicago, a forum that perhaps was selected because it was thought to be less sympathetic to government than the U.S. Court of Appeals for the District of Columbia in Washington. The Seventh Circuit ruled that the personal attack rules

and the political editorial rules would violate the First Amendment. *Radio Television News Directors Ass'n v. United States,* 400 F.2d 1002 (7th Cir. 1968).

The Seventh Circuit in the *RTNDA* case essentially adopted many of the prior restraint contentions that the D.C. Circuit rejected in *Red Lion.* Basically, the *RTNDA* decision took the position that broadcasters might forgo controversial commentary if they had to go to the expense of furnishing transcripts of personal attacks to those attacked, and if they had to furnish free time for responses to those who wished to avail themselves of the right of reply furnished by the personal attack rules. Under such circumstances, the *RTNDA* court reasoned, free speech would be unconstitutionally inhibited.

The Supreme Court had granted review in *Red Lion* but decided to defer decision until the Seventh Circuit decided the *RTNDA* case. When the FCC appealed the *RTNDA* ruling, the Supreme Court joined the two cases. The world of broadcast journalism eagerly watched to see how the Supreme Court would break the 1–1 score on the fairness doctrine and personal attack rules produced by the split between the two federal courts of appeals.

The Supreme Court affirmed the *Red Lion* decision and reversed the *RTNDA* decision. The fairness doctrine and the personal attack rules were upheld as consistent with the First Amendment by a unanimous Supreme Court consisting of all seven justices who participated in the case.

Red Lion Broadcasting Co., Inc. v. FCC
395 U.S. 367, 89 S. CT. 1794, 23 L. ED. 2D 371 (1969).

Justice WHITE delivered the opinion of the Court.

The FCC has for many years imposed on radio and television broadcasters the requirement that discussion of public issues be presented on broadcast stations, and that each side of those issues must be given fair coverage. This is known as the fairness doctrine, which originated very early in the history of broadcasting and has maintained its present outlines for some time. It is an obligation whose content has been defined in a long series of FCC rulings in particular cases, and which is distinct from the statutory requirement of § 315 of the Communications Act that equal time be allotted all qualified candidates for public office. Two aspects of the fairness doctrine, relating to personal attacks in the context of controversial public issues and to political editorializing, were codified more precisely in the form of FCC regulations in 1967. The two cases before us now, which were decided separately below, challenge the constitutional and statutory bases on the doctrine and component rules. *Red Lion* involves the application of the fairness doctrine to a particular broadcast, and *RTNDA* arises as an action to review the FCC's 1967 promulgation of the personal attack and political editorializing regulations, which were laid down after the *Red Lion* litigation had begun.

Not long after the *Red Lion* litigation was begun, the FCC issued a Notice of Proposed Rule Making, 31 Fed.Reg. 5710, with an eye to making the personal attack aspect of the fairness doctrine more precise and more readily enforceable, and also to specify its rules relating to political editorials. Believing that the specific application of the fairness doctrine in *Red Lion,* and the promulgation of the regulations in *RTNDA,* are both authorized by Congress and enhance rather than abridge the freedoms of speech and press protected by the First Amendment, we hold them valid and constitutional, reversing the judgment below in *RTNDA* and affirming the judgment below in *Red Lion.*

The history of the emergence of the fairness doctrine and of the related legislation shows that the commission's action in the *Red Lion* case did not exceed its authority, and that in adopting the new regulations the commission was implementing congressional policy rather than embarking on a frolic of its own. After an extended period during which the licensee was obliged not only to cover and to cover fairly the views of others, but also to refrain from expressing his own personal views, Mayflower Broadcasting Corp., 8 FCC 333 (1941), the latter limitation on the licensee was abandoned and the doctrine developed into its present form.

There is a twofold duty laid down by the FCC's decisions and described by the 1949 Report on Editorializing by Broadcast Licensees, 13 FCC 1246 (1949). The broadcaster must give adequate coverage to public issues, United Broadcasting Co., 10 FCC 515 (1945), and coverage must be fair in that it accurately reflects the opposing views. New Broadcasting Co., 6 P & F Radio Reg. 258 (1950). This must be done at the

broadcaster's own expense if sponsorship is unavailable. Cullman Broadcasting Co., 25 P & F Radio Reg. 895 (1963). Moreover, the duty must be met by programming obtained at the licensee's own initiative if available from no other source.

When a personal attack has been made on a figure involved in a public issue, both the doctrine of cases such as *Red Lion* and Times-Mirror Broadcasting Co., 24 P & F Radio Reg. 404 (1962), and also the 1967 regulations at issue in *RTNDA* require that the individual attacked himself be offered an opportunity to respond. Likewise, where one candidate is endorsed in a political editorial, the other candidates must themselves be offered reply time to use personally or through a spokesman. These obligations differ from the general fairness requirement that issues be presented, and presented with coverage of competing views, in that the broadcaster does not have the option of presenting the attacked party's side himself or choosing a third party to represent that side. But insofar as there is an obligation of the broadcaster to see that both sides are presented, and insofar as that is an affirmative obligation, the personal attack doctrine and regulations do not differ from preceding fairness doctrine. The simple fact that the attacked men or unendorsed candidates may respond themselves or through agents is not a critical distinction, and indeed, it is not unreasonable for the FCC to conclude that the objective of adequate presentation of all sides may best be served by allowing those most closely affected to make the response, rather than leaving the response in the hands of the station which has attacked their candidacies, endorsed their opponents, or carried a personal attack upon them.

The statutory authority of the FCC to promulgate these regulations derives from the mandate to the "commission from time to time, as public convenience, interest, or necessity requires" to promulgate "such rules and regulations and prescribe such restrictions and conditions as may be necessary to carry out the provisions of this chapter" 47 U.S.C. Sec. 303 and Sec. 303(r). The FCC is specifically directed to consider the demands of the public interest in the course of granting licenses, 47 U.S.C.A. §§ 307(a), 309(a); renewing them, 47 U.S.C. Sec. 307; and modifying them. Moreover, the FCC has included among the conditions of the Red Lion license itself the requirement that operation of the station be carried out in the public interest, 47 U.S.C. Sec. 309(h). This mandate to the FCC to assure that broadcasters operate in the public interest is a broad one, a power "not niggardly but expansive," *National Broadcasting Co. v. United States,* 319 U.S. 190, 219 (1943), whose validity we have long upheld. It is broad enough to encompass these regulations.

The fairness doctrine finds specific recognition in statutory form, is in part modeled on explicit statutory provisions relating to political candidates, and is approvingly reflected in legislative history. In 1959 the Congress amended the statutory requirement of § 315 that equal time be accorded each political candidate to except certain appearances on news programs, but added that this constituted no exception "from the *obligation imposed upon them under this act to operate in the public interest and to afford reasonable opportunity for the discussion of conflicting views on issues of public importance.*" Act of September 14, 1959, § 1, 73 Stat. 557, amending 47 U.S.C. § 315(a) [emphasis added]. This language makes it very plain that Congress, in 1959, announced that the phrase "public interest," which had been in the act since 1927, imposed a duty on broadcasters to discuss both sides of controversial public issues. In other words, the amendment vindicated the FCC's general view that the fairness doctrine inhered in the public interest standard. Subsequent legislation enacted into law and declaring the intent of an earlier statute is entitled to great weight in statutory construction. And here this principle is given special force by the equally venerable principle that the construction of a statute by those charged with its execution should be followed unless there are compelling indications that it is wrong, especially when Congress has refused to alter the administrative construction. Here, the Congress has not just kept its silence by refusing to overturn the administrative construction, but has ratified it with positive legislation. Thirty years of consistent administrative construction left undisturbed by Congress until 1959, when that construction was expressly accepted, reinforce the natural conclusion that the public interest language of the act authorized the FCC to require licensees to use their stations for discussion of public issues, and that the FCC is free to implement this requirement by reasonable rules

and regulations which fall short of abridgment of the freedom of speech and press, and of the censorship proscribed by § 326 of the act.

The objectives of § 315 themselves could readily be circumvented but for the complementary fairness doctrine ratified by § 315. The section applies only to campaign appearances by candidates, and not by family, friends, campaign managers, or other supporters. Without the fairness doctrine, then, a licensee could ban all campaign appearances by candidates themselves from the air and proceed to deliver over his station entirely to the supporters of one slate of candidates, to the exclusion of all others. In this way the broadcaster could have a far greater impact on the favored candidacy than he could by simply allowing a spot appearance by the candidate himself. It is the fairness doctrine as an aspect of the obligation to operate in the public interest, rather than § 315, which prohibits the broadcaster from taking such a step.

It is true that the personal attack aspect of the fairness doctrine was not actually adjudicated until after 1959, so that Congress then did not have those rules specifically before it. However, the obligation to offer time to reply to a personal attack was presaged by the FCC's 1949 Report on Editorializing, which the FCC views as the principal summary of its *ratio decidendi* in cases in this area.

When the Congress ratified the FCC's implication of a fairness doctrine in 1959 it did not, of course, approve every past decision or pronouncement by the FCC on this subject, or give it a completely free hand for the future. The statutory authority does not go so far. But we cannot say that when a station publishes a personal attack or endorses a political candidate, it is a misconstruction of the public interest standard to require the station to offer time for a response rather than to leave the response entirely within the control of the station which has attacked either the candidacies or the men who wish to reply in their own defense. When a broadcaster grants time to a political candidate, Congress itself requires that equal time be offered to his opponents. It would exceed our competence to hold that the FCC is unauthorized by the statute to employ a similar device where personal attacks or political editorials are broadcast by a radio or television station.

In light of the fact that the "public interest" in broadcasting clearly encompasses the presentation of vigorous debate of controversial issues of importance and concern to the public; the fact that the FCC has rested upon that language from its very inception a doctrine that these issues must be discussed, and fairly; and the fact that Congress has acknowledged that the analogous provisions of § 315 are not preclusive in this area, and knowingly preserved the FCC's complementary efforts, we think the fairness doctrine and its component personal attack and political editorializing regulations are a legitimate exercise of congressionally delegated authority. The Communications Act is not notable for the precision of its substantive standards and in this respect the explicit provisions of § 315, and the doctrine and rules at issue here which are closely modeled upon that section, are far more explicit than the generalized "public interest" standard in which the FCC ordinarily finds its sole guidance, and which we have held a broad but adequate standard before. We cannot say that the FCC's declaratory ruling in *Red Lion,* or the regulations at issue in *RTNDA,* are beyond the scope of the congressionally conferred power to assure that stations are operated by those whose possession of a license serves "the public interest."

The broadcasters challenge the fairness doctrine and its specific manifestations in the personal attack and political editorial rules on conventional First Amendment grounds, alleging that the rules abridge their freedom of speech and press. Their contention is that the First Amendment protects their desire to use their allotted frequencies continuously to broadcast whatever they choose, and to exclude whomever they choose, from ever using that frequency. No man may be prevented from saying or publishing what he thinks, or from refusing in his speech or other utterances to give equal weight to the views of his opponents. This right, they say, applies equally to broadcasters.

Although broadcasting is clearly a medium affected by a First Amendment interest, *United States v. Paramount Pictures, Inc.,* 334 U.S. 131, 166 (1948), differences in the characteristics of new media justify differences in the First Amendment standards applied to them. *Joseph Burstyn, Inc. v. Wilson,* 343 U.S. 495, 505 (1952). For example, the ability of new technology to pro-duce sounds more raucous than those of the human voice justifies restrictions on the sound level, and on the hours and places of use, of sound trucks so long as the restrictions are reasonable and applied without discrimination. *Kovacs v. Cooper,* 336 U.S. 77 (1949).

Just as the Government may limit the use of sound amplifying equipment potentially so noisy that it drowns out civilized private speech, so may the Government limit the use of broadcast equipment. The right of free speech of a broadcaster, the user of a sound truck, or any other individual does not embrace a right to snuff out the free speech of others. *Associated Press v. United States,* 326 U.S. 1, 20 (1945).

When two people converse face to face, both should not speak at once if either is to be clearly understood. But the range of the human voice is so limited that there could be meaningful communications if half the people in the United States were talking and the other half listening. Just as clearly, half the people might publish and the other half read. But the reach of radio signals is incomparably greater than the range of the human voice and the problem of interference is a massive reality. The lack of know how and equipment may keep many from the air, but only a tiny fraction of those with resources and intelligence can hope to communicate by radio at the same time if intelligible communication is to be had, even if the entire radio spectrum is utilized in the present state of commercially acceptable technology.

It was this fact, and the chaos which ensued from permitting anyone to use any frequency at whatever power level he wished, which made necessary the enactment of the Radio Act of 1927 and the Communications Act of 1934, as the Court has noted at length before. *National Broadcasting Co. v. U.S.* (1943). It was this reality which at the very least necessitated first the division of the radio spectrum into portions reserved respectively for public broadcasting and for other important radio uses such as amateur operation, aircraft, police, defense, and navigation; and then the subdivision of each portion, and assignment of specific frequencies to individual users or groups of users. Beyond this, however, because the frequencies reserved for public broadcasting were limited in number, it was essential for the Government to tell some applicants that they could not broadcast at all because there was room for only a few.

Where there are substantially more individuals who want to broadcast than there are frequencies to allocate, it is idle to posit an unabridgeable First Amendment right to broadcast comparable to the right of every individual to speak, write, or publish. If 100 persons want broadcast licenses but there are only 10 frequencies to allocate, all of them may have the same "right" to a license; but if there is to be any effective communication by radio, only a few can be licensed and the rest must be barred from the airways. It would be strange if the First Amendment, aimed at protecting and furthering communications, prevented the government from making radio communication possible by requiring licenses to broadcast and by limiting the number of licenses so as not to overcrowd the spectrum.

This had been the consistent view of the Court. Congress unquestionably has the power to grant and deny licenses and to delete existing stations. *Federal Radio Commission v. Nelson Bros. Bond & Mortgage Co.,* 289 U.S. 266 (1933). No one has a First Amendment right to a license or to monopolize a radio frequency; to deny a station license because "the public interest" requires it "is not a denial of free speech." *National Broadcasting Co. v. U.S.*

By the same token, as far as the First Amendment is concerned those who are licensed stand no better than those to whom licenses are refused. A license permits broadcasting, but the licensee has no constitutional right to be the one who holds the license or to monopolize a radio frequency to the exclusion of his fellow citizens. There is nothing in the First Amendment which prevents the government from requiring a licensee to share his frequency with others and to conduct himself as a proxy or fiduciary with obligations to present those views and voices which are representative of his community and which would otherwise, by necessity, be barred from the airwaves.

This is not to say that the First Amendment is irrelevant to public broadcasting. On the contrary, it has a major role to play as the Congress itself recognized in § 326, which forbids FCC interference with "the right of free speech by means of radio communications." Because of the scarcity of radio frequencies, the government is permitted to put restraints on licensees in favor of others whose views should be expressed on this unique medium. But the people as a whole retain their interest in free speech by radio and their collective right to have the medium function consistently with the ends and purposes of the First Amendment. *It is the right of the viewers and listeners, not the right of the broadcasters, which is paramount.* [Emphasis added.] Z. Chafee, Government and Mass Communications 546 (1947). It is the purpose of the First Amendment to preserve an uninhibited marketplace of ideas in which truth will ultimately prevail, rather than to countenance monopolization of that market, whether it be by the government itself or a private licensee. It is the right of the public to receive suitable access to social, political, esthetic, moral, and other ideas and experiences which is crucial here. That right may not constitutionally be abridged either by Congress or by the FCC.

Rather than confer frequency monopolies on a relatively small number of licensees, in a Nation of 200,000,000, the government could surely have decreed that each frequency should be shared among all or some of those who wish to use it, each being assigned a portion of the broadcast day or the broadcast week. The ruling and regulations at issue here do not go quite so far. They assert that under specified circumstances, a licensee must offer to make available a reasonable amount of broadcast time to those who have a view different from that which has already been expressed on his station. The expression of a political endorsement, or of a personal attack while dealing with a controversial public issue, simply triggers this timesharing. As we have said, the First Amendment confers no right on licensees to prevent others from broadcasting on "their" frequencies and no right to an unconditional monopoly of a scarce resource which the government has denied others the right to use.

In terms of constitutional principle, and as enforced sharing of a scarce resource, the personal attack and political editorial rules are indistinguishable from the equal-time provision of § 315, a specific enactment of Congress requiring stations to set aside reply time under specified circumstances and to which the fairness doctrine and these constituent regulations are important complements. That provision, which has been part of the law since 1927, Radio Act of 1927, c. 169, § 18, 44 Stat. 1162, 1170, has been held valid by this court as an obligation of the licensee relieving him of any power in any way to prevent or censor the broadcast, and thus insulating him from liability for defamation. The constitutionality of the statute under the First Amendment was unquestioned. *Farmers Educ. & Co-op. Union v. WDAY*, 360 U.S. 525 (1959).

Nor can we say that it is inconsistent with the First Amendment goal of producing an informed public capable of conducting its own affairs to require a broadcaster to permit answers to personal attacks occurring in the course of discussing controversial issues, or to require that the political opponents of those endorsed by the station be given a chance to communicate with the public.[18] Otherwise station owners and a few networks would have unfettered power to make time available only to the highest bidders, to communicate only their own views on public issues, people and candidates, and to permit on the air only those with whom they agreed. There is no sanctuary in the First Amendment for unlimited private censorship operating in a medium not open to all. "Freedom of the press from governmental interference under the First Amendment does not sanction repression of that freedom by private interests." *Associated Press v. U.S.*, 326 U.S. 1, 20 (1944).

It is strenuously argued, however, that, if political editorials or personal attacks will trigger an obligation in broadcasters to afford the opportunity for expression to speakers who need not pay for time and whose views are unpalatable to the licensees, then broadcasters will be irresistibly forced to self-censorship and their coverage of controversial public issues will be eliminated or at least rendered wholly ineffective. Such a result would indeed be a serious matter, for should licensees actually eliminate their coverage of

controversial issues, the purposes of the doctrine would be stifled.

At this point, however, as the FCC has indicated, that possibility is at best speculative. The communications industry, and in particular the networks have taken pains to present controversial issues in the past, and even now they do not assert that they intend to abandon their efforts in this regard. It would be better if the FCC's encouragement were never necessary to induce the broadcasters to meet their responsibility. And if experience with the administration of these doctrines indicates that they have the net effect of reducing rather than enhancing the volume and quality of coverage, there will be time enough to reconsider the constitutional implications. The fairness doctrine in the past has had no such overall effect.

That this will occur now seems unlikely, however, since if present licensees should suddenly prove timorous, the FCC is not powerless to insist that they give adequate and fair attention to public issues. It does not violate the First Amendment to treat licensees given the privilege of using scarce radio frequencies as proxies for the entire community, obligated to give suitable time and attention to matters of great public concern. To condition the granting or renewal of licenses on a willingness to present representative community views on controversial issues is consistent with the ends and purposes of those constitutional provisions forbidding the abridgment of freedom of speech and freedom of the press. Congress need not stand idly by and permit those with licenses to ignore the problems which beset the people or to exclude from the airways anything but their own views of fundamental questions. The statute, long administrative practice, and cases are to this effect.

The litigants embellish their first amendment arguments with the contention that the regulations are so vague that their duties are impossible to discern. Of this point it is enough to say that, judging the validity of the regulations on their face as they are presented here, we cannot conclude that the FCC has been left a free hand to vindicate its own idiosyncratic conception of the public interest or of the requirements of free speech. Past adjudications by the FCC give added precision to the regulations; there was nothing vague about the FCC's specific ruling in *Red Lion* that Fred Cook should be provided an

---

18. The expression of views opposing those which broadcasters permit to be aired in the first place need not be confined solely to the broadcasters themselves as proxies. "Nor is it enough that he should hear the arguments of adversaries from his own teachers, presented as they state them, and accompanied by what they offer as refutations. That is not the way to do justice to the arguments, or bring them into real contact with his own mind. He must be able to hear them from persons who actually believe them; who defend them in earnest, and do their very utmost for them." J. Mill, *On Liberty* 32 (R. McCallum ed. 1947).

opportunity to reply. The regulations at issue in *RTNDA* could be employed in precisely the same way as the fairness doctrine was in *Red Lion*. Moreover, the FCC itself has recognized that the applicability of its regulations to situations beyond the scope of past cases may be questionable, 32 Fed.Reg. 10303, 10304 and the scope of past cases may be questionable, 32 Fed.Reg. 10303, 10304 and n. 6, and will not impose sanctions in such cases without warning. We need not approve every aspect of the fairness doctrine to decide these cases, and we will not now pass upon the constitutionality of these regulations by envisioning the most extreme applications conceivable, *United States v. Sullivan*, 332 U.S. 689, 694 (1948), but will deal with those problems if and when they arise.

We need not and do not now ratify every past and future decision by the FCC with regard to programming. There is no question here of the commission's refusal to permit the broadcaster to carry a particular program or to publish his own views; of a discriminatory refusal to require the licensee to broadcast certain views which have been denied access to the airways; of government censorship of a particular program contrary to § 326; or of the official government view dominating public broadcasting. Such questions would raise more serious First Amendment issues. But we do hold that the Congress and the FCC do not violate the First Amendment when they require a radio or television station to give reply time to answer personal attacks and political editorials.

In view of the prevalence of scarcity of broadcast frequencies, the government's role in allocating those frequencies, and the legitimate claims of those unable without governmental assistance to gain access to those frequencies for expression of their views, we hold the regulations and ruling at issue here are both authorized by statute and constitutional. The judgment of the court of appeals in *Red Lion* is affirmed and that in *RTNDA* is reversed and the causes remanded for proceedings consistent with this opinion.

It is so ordered.

COMMENT

Why did the FCC in effect rule that if a person has a right of reply under the personal attack rules, the station must put him on free if he is not willing to pay? WGCB in Red Lion, Pennsylvania, was a small, independent station whose rates compared to network time were not high. Presumably, the FCC reasoned that if it followed a principle of permitting only paid reply time when the personal attack rules were involved, the high cost of network time, particularly television time, would make the rules a dead letter. Few could or would wish to pay for reply time under such circumstances.

Both the court of appeals and the Supreme Court in the *Red Lion* case cited *Cullman Broadcasting Co.*, 40 F.C.C. 516 (1963), for the proposition that once a fairness doctrine obligation arises, time must be provided by the licensee at his or her own expense if sponsorship is not available. In the *Democratic National Committee* case, the FCC described *Cullman* rights as follows:

> The paramount public interest, we stressed, is the right of the public to be informed. The licensee has adjudged that an issue is of importance to its area by presenting the first viewpoint; that being so, the public's right to hear the other side cannot turn on whether the licensee received money. This approach perfectly fits the public trustee concept. See *In re Democratic National Committee*, 25 F.C.C.2d 216 (1970).

The *Red Lion* case marks the extension of the *Cullman* principle of a right of free response from the fairness doctrine context to the context of the personal attack rules once a licensee obligation arises under the rules. When the FCC abandoned the fairness doctrine in 1987, it also abrogated the *Cullman* principle.

The decision in *Miami Herald Pub. Co. v. Tornillo*, 418 U.S. 241 (1974), in which the Supreme Court struck down a state statutory right to reply to the print media in the case of editorial attack presents a vivid contrast to the *Red Lion* decision upholding the right of reply to personal attack in the broadcast media. In *Miami Herald*, the Court held, in a unanimous opinion, that a Florida statute requiring a newspaper to grant a political candidate equivalent space to reply if the paper editorially attacked the candidate violated the First Amendment. (See p. 469.) The *Miami Herald* decision does not so much as cite the *Red Lion* case decided only five years earlier.

The Court noted in *Red Lion* that it did not intend the doctrine to endure for all time—a reservation of particular importance in the late

1980s when the FCC argued that the doctrine had become unconstitutional due to changed conditions. At least two subsequent U.S. Supreme Court decisions, *CBS v. DNC*, 412 U.S. 94 (1973) and *CBS v. FCC*, 453 U.S. 367 (1981), appeared to reinforce the *Red Lion* decision, but one more recent decision, *FCC v. League of Women Voters*, 468 U.S. 364 (1984), questioned it.

Speaking for the Court in *League of Women Voters*, Justice William Brennan discussed the question of the future of the fairness doctrine in footnote 12:

> We note that the FCC, observing that "[i]f any substantial possibility exists that the [fairness doctrine] rules have impeded, rather than furthered, First Amendment objectives, repeal may be warranted on that ground alone," has tentatively concluded that the rules, by effectively chilling speech, do not serve the public interest, and has therefore proposed to repeal them. Notice of Proposed Rulemaking In re Repeal or Modification of the Personal Attack and Political Editorial Rules, 48 Fed. Reg. 28295, 28298, 28301 (June 21, 1983). Of course, the Commission may, in the exercise of its discretion, decide to modify or abandon these rules, and we express no view on the legality of either course. As we recognized in *Red Lion*, however, were it to be shown by the Commission that the fairness doctrine "has the effect of reducing rather than enhancing" speech, we would then be forced to reconsider the constitutional basis of our decision in that case. 395 U.S. at 393.

FCC reexamination of the doctrine began in earnest on April 11, 1984, when the commission, then dominated by "unregulators" such as Chairman Mark Fowler, and much influenced by a First Amendment philosophy that electronic and print media should be treated alike, launched a major inquiry into the *General Fairness Doctrine Obligations of Broadcast Licensees*. Excerpts from that inquiry follow. They tell the story of the evolution of and justification for the doctrine. They also explain why, by 1984, the FCC had come to question it.

Inquiry Into the General Fairness Doctrine Obligations of Broadcast Licensees

49 FED. REG. 20317 (1984).

[A] new storm of controversy developed from an FCC decision in *WCBS-TV*, 8 F.C.C.2d 381, stay and recon. denied, 9 F.C.C.2d 921 (1967), aff'd

Banzhaf v. FCC, 405 F.2d 1082 (1968), cert. denied, 396 U.S. 842 (1969), to extend the doctrine to broadcast advertising. For the first time, the FCC applied the fairness doctrine to product advertising by ruling that the advertisement of cigarettes on broadcast stations raised a controversial issue of public importance. The FCC reasoned that cigarette smoking itself was a controversial health issue and, accordingly, required broadcasters to provide opportunities for contrasting viewpoints.

In subsequent cases, the FCC found itself unable to articulate any satisfactory standard by which to judge what types of programming would trigger fairness obligations. Thus, notwithstanding efforts to limit the scope of the cigarette advertising ruling, the FCC was unable to extricate itself from this area.

[I]n 1974, the FCC adopted the 1974 *Fairness Report,* which reaffirmed the earlier Report on Editorializing and upheld the application of a general fairness doctrine requirement for broadcast licensees on both statutory and constitutional grounds. The FCC's 1974 Report, including its decision to narrowly apply fairness doctrine obligations to broadcast advertising, was generally affirmed in *National Citizens Committee for Broadcasting v. FCC*, 567 F.2d 1095, (D.C. Cir. 1977), cert. denied, 436 U.S. 926 (1978).

Today, there appear to be many substitutes for the traditional broadcast media, radio and television, in their roles as sources of information and, similarly, substitutes for the traditional print media. This substitutability or interchangeability among media is witnessed to some extent by consumer acceptance of different media to satisfy individual information and entertainment needs.

Changes in communications technology are primarily responsible for dramatically increasing the means by which information reaches the public. As more fully described herein, distribution systems once thought to be quite different, such as broadcasting and print, are becoming interchangeable, merging into one mass media marketplace. We also see a dramatic increase in the number and different types of conventional television stations available throughout the United States, which is attributable in large measure to the FCC's establishment of the table of television station allocations in 1952. From 1950 to the present, the percentage increase in the total number of television stations alone is over 1100 percent.

In summary, the rapid growth of existing technologies, particularly throughout the 1970's, as well as the development of new ones that are or will soon be available throughout the remainder of the 1980's suggests that a proliferation of programming and information sources presently exists and will be even further augmented in the future. Although the above information is based on media outlets nationwide, nevertheless, even the less densely populated areas of the country appear to have access to a variety of information sources, particularly, the electronic media.

This overview of the electronic and print mass media marketplace indicates the existence of a plethora of print, video, and voice outlets and, through such outlets, the availability of large amounts of information to the public through these outlets. It also suggests that continued imposition of fairness doctrine obligations may be inappropriate when significant technological developments contributing to dynamic growth in the electronic media and to continued convergence between the print and electronic media appear to be undercutting what might have been at one time legitimate distinctions between the print and electronic media.

Just as there is editorial diversity as between newspapers, there is, and will continue to be, editorial diversity as between different broadcasters. But should the print media or the broadcast media be considered mutually exclusive information sources? Individuals typically do not receive information from a single medium. Rather, they can be expected to consult a variety of sources in a wide array of media. Accordingly, we query not only whether a scarcity of information outlets exists but also whether it can be said that broadcast stations are not diverse when considered alone or in conjunction with other available media. Anything even approaching the intrusiveness of the fairness doctrine would not pass constitutional muster if applied to the print media. See, *e.g., Miami Herald Publishing Co. v. Tornillo,* 418 U.S. 241 (1974). Thus, we must ask whether such a doctrine remains appropriate to the broadcast media which appear more numerous and very diverse.

We believe that the costs borne by broadcasters and the public as a whole under this doctrine include the need for some degree of governmental oversight over the content of broadcasts to assure balanced programming, and concomitantly, the possibility that the surveillance required may lead to excessive and unnecessary interference with important editorial and journalistic functions performed by broadcast licensees. In sum, we query whether they can have the unintended effect of inhibiting or "chilling" the exercise of speech by broadcasters. If governmental censorship (or even the possibility thereof) leads to licensee self-censorship, then the benefits of diversity sought to be achieved by government regulation might well be outweighed by the detrimental effect upon the public and, under such circumstances, to paraphrase the Court in *CBS v. DNC,* the interests of the public sought to be achieved by governmental regulatory power over broadcasters' speech would not appear to outweigh the private journalistic interests of broadcasters. Additionally, because "inhibition as well as prohibition against the exercise of First Amendment rights is a power denied to government," such regulation which has the undesirable effect of chilling the exercise of speech would also appear to be constitutionally suspect.

At the outset, we do not believe that any significant question exists that, prior to the 1959 amendments to Section 315, the fairness doctrine was not statutorily required by any express statutory provision or by the general public interest standard of the Communications Act. It has been generally conceded that, before those amendments, the fairness doctrine had evolved as an aspect of the Commission's discretionary authority to formulate policies consistent with the broad public interest.

For this reason, we believe that the appropriate focus for purposes of this inquiry turns on Congress' enactment of the Act of September 14, 1959, which resulted in statutory amendment of section 315 of the Communications Act and, more specifically, inclusion of the statutory language at the end of that section which appears to reference the fairness doctrine.

At the end of the exemption language, Congress added a sentence that apparently references the second prong of the Commission's fairness doctrine. That sentence, which appears in the present version of the Act, read as follows:

> Nothing in the foregoing sentence shall be construed as relieving broadcasters, in connection with the presentation of newscasts, news interviews, news documentaries, and on-the-spot coverage of news events, from the obligation imposed upon

them under this Act to operate in the public interest and to afford reasonable opportunity for the discussion of conflicting views on issues of public importance. 47 U.S.C. § 315(a).

This proviso contains the statutory language that raises the question whether Congress meant to impose statutorily on broadcasters the fairness doctrine in its entirety, meant to ensure by the statutory language that the Commission would apply the doctrine to issues concerning candidates in news programs exempted from the reach of the equal opportunities requirements, or merely meant to acknowledge but not disturb the Commission's existing regulatory efforts in this area.

The statutory interpretation that Congress intended to impose fairness doctrine obligations only in the political contexts that were the subject of the other section 315 amendments also appears to be in accord with the Supreme Court's decision in *Red Lion,* where the Court, in upholding the personal attack and political editorializing rules, recognized that "the objectives of section 315 could readily be circumvented" by broadcasters banning all campaign appearances by candidates themselves while, instead, featuring the supporters of the one candidate or slate of candidates to the exclusion of others. The Court observed that "the fairness doctrine as an aspect of the obligation to operate in the public interest rather than § 315" prohibits a broadcaster "from taking such a step" and, specifically stated that "[t]he legislative history reinforces this view of the effect of the 1959 amendment."

By the same token, we are fully aware that support can be mustered for the opposite view that Congress did in fact intend to impose by statute general fairness doctrine obligations on broadcasters. Indeed, we have assumed, but without giving the matter extensive consideration, that our discretion was removed by enactment of the 1959 amendments. In our previous notice of inquiry into the fairness doctrine commenced in 1971, we expressed a similar view stating that the "commission cannot abandon the fairness doctrine" because "[t]he Communications Act is explicit in th[is] respect."

In addition, the Supreme Court's affirmance of the personal attack and political editorial rules in the *Red Lion* case can be viewed as adding weight to the view that Congress, by adding the proviso appearing at the end of section 315, intended to impose a statutory obligation of fair-

ness on broadcasters. This view turns on the Court's references, in dicta, to the fairness doctrine as being "ratified," finding "specific recognition in statutory form." Similarly, the plurality opinion in *CBS v. DNC,* discussed more fully previously, states on two occasions that the 1959 amendments "give statutory approval" to the fairness doctrine, and Justice Stewart, in his concurring opinion in the case, notes that "[t]he basis for a fairness doctrine is statutory." For these reasons, we also invite comment on the interpretation that the 1959 amendment was intended to codify the second prong of the fairness doctrine as it applies to all controversial issues of public importance.

In particular, we seek comment on the possible interpretation that Congress did not intend to impose by statute any part of the fairness doctrine and its obligations. Accordingly, we also seek views on the possibility that Congress may not have intended any statutory codification of the fairness doctrine at all.

The FCC, the Courts, President Reagan, and the Fairness Doctrine

On October 26, 1984, a little over five months after starting its inquiry, the FCC concluded that WTVH-TV, a Syracuse, New York television station owned by Meredith Corporation, had violated the fairness doctrine—the only such finding reached while Mark Fowler headed the FCC. Responding to a complaint brought by a group called Syracuse Peace Council, the FCC concluded that WTVH-TV acted unreasonably under the second prong of the doctrine in its treatment of a controversy surrounding construction of a nuclear power plant.

Things became more complex on August 7, 1985, when the FCC concluded its fairness doctrine inquiry. *Report Concerning General Fairness Doctrine Obligations of Broadcast Licensees,* 102 F.C.C.2d 142 (1985). The FCC concluded (1) that the doctrine was contrary to the public interest—it "chilled" expression more than it promoted it—and (2) that the doctrine was probably unconstitutional. Despite these conclusions, the FCC retained the doctrine. The FCC doubted that it was within its power to pass on the constitutionality of the doctrine (especially given the *Red Lion* precedent), and it believed that Congress had probably incorporated the doctrine into the Communications Act of 1934 when sec. 315 of the Act was amended in 1959. Thus, an anomalous situation was created by the time Meredith's request for "reconsideration" of its case was reviewed by the FCC. The outcome of the inquiry certainly suggested that the FCC did not like the doctrine. In its petition for reconsideration, Meredith pressed hard for the FCC to consider its constitutional objections to the doctrine. The FCC refused to do so, however, and, on reconsideration, upheld its earlier decision that Meredith had violated the doctrine. *Syracuse Peace Council*, 59 R.R.2d 179 (1985).

Many observers believed the FCC was actually attempting to have the courts declare the doctrine void. Members of the FCC knew well that many members of Congress would be angry if the FCC abandoned the doctrine. By sticking to its guns in the *Syracuse* case, some suspected, the FCC could force the courts to overturn the doctrine, an action that would accomplish the FCC's objectives without substantial political costs.

Indeed, the next development in this scenario came from the courts and favored the FCC's perspective. On September 19, 1986, a panel of the U.S. Court of Appeals for the D.C. Circuit declared, in a most unlikely context, that the fairness doctrine—contrary to the general understanding of the FCC as reflected in its 1985 Report—had not been specifically mandated by Congress through the 1959 amendments to the Communications Act. In *Telecommunications Research and Action Center [TRAC] v. FCC*, 801 F.2d 501 (D.C. Cir. 1986), the court held that the fairness doctrine did not apply to teletext and that Congress had, at most, intended to affirm that the FCC could promulgate a fairness doctrine but had not mandated it. *TRAC* galvanized the fairness doctrine's supporters in Congress.

Less than a month later, on October 15, 1986, Congress—as part of the 1986 appropriations for the FCC—ordered it to study "alternative means of enforcement of the Fairness Doctrine and to report to the Congress by September 30, 1987." Making Continuing Appropriations for the Fiscal Year 1987, Pub. L. No. 99-591, Title V, 100 Stat. 3341, 3341-67 (1986). Congress's goal was plain—tell the FCC not to tinker with the doctrine, despite the *TRAC* decision.

All of these developments influenced Meredith Corporation's pursuit of an appeal of the decision that it had violated the fairness doctrine. On January 16, 1987, panel decisions for the D.C.

Circuit made decisions that much influenced future developments. In *Meredith Corp. v. FCC*, 809 F.2d 863 (D.C. Cir. 1987), the court suggested that the FCC should consider a rulemaking proceeding aimed at figuring out whether the fairness doctrine was or was not in the public interest.

Responding to the congressional mandate of October 1986, the FCC on February 13, 1987, opened an inquiry into alternatives to the fairness doctrine, *Notice of Inquiry into Sec. 73.1910 of the Commission's Rules and Regulations Concerning Alternatives to the General Fairness Doctrine Obligations of B'Cast Licensees* (MM Dock. 87-26), 2 F.C.C.R. 1532 (1987). Congress, however, was not willing to wait for the report. On April 21, 1987 the Senate adopted sec. 742, a bill intended to write the fairness doctrine squarely into the Communications Act of 1934. On June 3, 1987, the House adopted sec. 742, sending the measure to President Reagan. On June 19, 1987, however, Reagan vetoed the bill. His veto message raised constitutional objections to the doctrine:

Veto of the Fairness in Broadcasting Act of 1987

I am returning herewith without my approval § 742, the "Fairness in Broadcasting Act of 1987," which would codify the so-called "fairness doctrine." This type of content-based regulation is, in my judgment, antagonistic to the freedom of expression guaranteed by the First Amendment.

In any other medium besides broadcasting, such federal policing of the editorial judgment of journalists would be unthinkable. The Supreme Court indicated in *Red Lion* a willingness to reconsider the appropriateness of the fairness doctrine if it reduced rather than enhanced broadcast coverage. It may now be fairly concluded that the growth in the number of available media outlets does indeed outweigh whatever justifications may have seemed to exist at the period during which the doctrine was developed. [T]he FCC found that the doctrine in fact *inhibits* broadcasters from presenting controversial issues of public importance and thus defeated its own purpose. § 742 simply cannot be reconciled with the freedom of speech and the press secured by our Constitution. I am compelled to disapprove of this measure. [23 *Weekly Compilation of Presidential Documents* 715–16 (1987).]

Reagan's resolve was probably reinforced by a U.S. Supreme Court decision released just eleven days prior to his veto. On June 8, 1987, the

Court refused to review *TRAC,* the court of appeals decision holding that Congress had not mandated the fairness doctrine in 1959. *Telecommunications Research and Action Center v. FCC,* 482 U.S. 919 (1987). Thus, at the time Reagan vetoed sec. 742, courts had held that the fairness doctrine had not been made statutory in 1959; and Reagan successfully vetoed the 1987 effort to write it into the act. By late June 1987, it became apparent to Congress that, although a majority of both the Senate and House supported the doctrine, the two-thirds votes necessary to overturn the president's veto were not to be had.

The result of all these developments was to put the matter back in the hands of the FCC. Courts had told the FCC that it had to consider Meredith's constitutional arguments and suggested that it ought to look harder at whether or not the doctrine, even if constitutional, served the public interest. They had told the FCC that it did not have to uphold the doctrine out of a belief that Congress had mandated it in 1959. The FCC had not gotten everything from the courts that it might have wished—no lower court had been willing to find the doctrine unconstitutional—but the courts certainly had left the FCC a free hand to do as it wished. On August 4, 1987, the FCC reached a momentous decision. In *Syracuse Peace Council,* 2 F.C.C.R. 5043 (1987), the FCC bit the bullet. It eliminated the doctrine—at least most of it—as both contrary to the public interest and unconstitutional.

Syracuse Peace Council
2 F.C.C.R. 5043 (1987).

In *Meredith Corp. v. FCC,* the U.S. Court of Appeals remanded this case to the FCC for further consideration of our decision, in this adjudication, to enforce the Fairness Doctrine against Station WTVH. The court found that the Commission, on the basis of the evidence of record, had properly concluded that the station failed to satisfy the requirements of the Fairness Doctrine. It determined, however, that the Commission had acted arbitrarily and capriciously in not considering WTVH's contentions that the enforcement of the Doctrine deprived the station of its constitutional rights.

Pursuant to the court's Order, we reopened this proceeding in order to consider the constitu-

tional and public interest issues raised by WTVH. As explained more fully below, based upon this record, our experience in administering the Fairness Doctrine, fundamental constitutional principles, and the findings contained in our comprehensive 1985 Fairness Report, we conclude that the Fairness Doctrine, on its face, violates the First Amendment and contravenes the public interest. Accordingly, we shall grant reconsideration of our earlier determinations in this proceeding, and our previous orders in this proceeding are hereby vacated. Any formal determination that WTVH failed to comply with the requirements of the Fairness Doctrine can no longer be used against WTVH in any subsequent renewal proceedings or in any other context.

As the court noted in *Meredith Corp. v. FCC,* the FCC recently conducted "a comprehensive reexamination of the public policy and constitutional implications of the fairness doctrine."

Based upon compelling evidence of record, the FCC, in its 1985 Fairness Report, concluded that the Fairness Doctrine disserved the public interest. While disclaiming any intention to "definitively resolve whether or not the Fairness Doctrine is constitutional," the FCC questioned whether the Doctrine is consistent with the guarantees of the First Amendment. It stated that "were the balance ours alone to strike, the Fairness Doctrine would thus fall short of promoting those interests necessary to uphold its constitutionality." The FCC recognized that the Supreme Court in 1969 had upheld the Doctrine in *Red Lion B'casting Co. v. FCC,* but determined that the factual predicates underlying that decision had been eroded.

In the 1985 Fairness Report, the FCC did not reach a definitive conclusion as to whether the Doctrine was codified. In light of the "intense Congressional interest in the Fairness Doctrine, the pendency of legislative proposals," as well as the uncertainty as to whether the Doctrine was in fact codified, the FCC concluded that "it would be inappropriate at this time to either eliminate or significantly restrict the scope of the Doctrine." Expressing its intention to continue to enforce the Fairness Doctrine, the FCC forwarded its Report to Congress so that the legislature would have "an opportunity to review the Fairness Doctrine in light of the evidence [in that Report]." While the general inquiry on the Fairness Doctrine was still pending before the agency, the FCC in this adjudication held that television Station WTVH in Syracuse, N.Y., had violated the Doctrine. The FCC determined that WTVH, by broadcasting a series of editorial advertisements advocating the construction of the Nine Mile Point 11 nuclear plant as a sound investment for New York, presented a controversial issue of public importance. Finding at that time that the station had failed to air any contrasting viewpoints on the issue, the FCC concluded that WTVH had not met its obligations under the Fairness Doctrine.

Meredith sought judicial review of the FCC's order in the U.S. Court of Appeals for the District of Columbia Circuit. [That court declared that the FCC] had acted improperly in holding that Meredith violated the doctrine without responding to the broadcaster's constitutional arguments. [*Meredith Corp. v. FCC,* 809 F.2d at 873, n. 11.] [T]he court admonished the FCC that the failure to consider Meredith's constitutional arguments in its defense was not only the "very paradigm of arbitrary and capricious administrative action," but may also have constituted a breach of the oath that each Commissioner took to support and defend the Constitution. The case was therefore remanded for rectification, and we now consider it, in light of that admonition.

[T]he policy and constitutional considerations in this matter are inextricably intertwined and it would be difficult, if not impossible, to isolate the policy considerations from the constitutional aspects underlying the Doctrine. The fundamental issue embodied in this Fairness doctrine litigation is the same as that presented in all other Fairness Doctrine cases; whether it is constitutional and thereby sound public policy for a government agency to reverse editorial decisions of broadcast journalists concerning the broadcast of controversial issues of public importance.

[EDITORIAL NOTE: *The FCC indicated its intention to consider the validity of both parts of the fairness doctrine. The FCC went on to explain why it believed the fairness doctrine "chilled" speech.*]

The record in the fairness inquiry demonstrates that [s]elf-censorship is not limited to individual programs. In order to avoid Fairness Doctrine burdens, the FCC found that the stations have adopted company "policies" which have the direct effect of diminishing the amount of controversial material that is presented to the public on broadcast stations. For example, some

stations refuse to present editorials; other stations will not accept political advertisements; still others decline to air public issue (or editorial) advertising; and others have policies to decline acceptance of nationally produced programming that discusses controversial subjects or to have their news staffs avoid controversial issues as a matter of routine.

In sum, the Fairness Doctrine in operation disserves both the public's right to diverse sources of information and the broadcaster's interest in free expression. Its chilling effect thwarts its intended purpose, and it results in excessive and unnecessary government intervention into the editorial processes of broadcast journalists. We hold, therefore, that under the constitutional standard established by *Red Lion* and its progeny, the Fairness Doctrine contravenes the First Amendment and its enforcement is no longer in the public interest.

[W]e recognize that technological advancements and the transformation of the telecommunications market described above have not eliminated spectrum scarcity. All goods, however, are ultimately scarce, and there must be a system through which to allocate their use. Although a free enterprise system relies heavily on a system of property rights and voluntary exchange to allocate most of these goods, other methods of allocation, including first-come, first-served, administrative hearings, lotteries, and auctions, are or have been relied on for certain other goods. Whatever the method of allocation, there is not any logical connection between the method of allocation for a particular good and the level of constitutional protection afforded to the uses of that good.

Additionally, there is nothing inherent in the utilization of the licensing method of allocation that justifies the government acting in a manner that would be proscribed under a traditional First Amendment analysis. Indeed, the fact that government is involved in licensing is all the more reason why the First Amendment protects against government control of content.

On the other hand, the fact that the government may not impose unconstitutional conditions does not preclude the FCC's ability to license broadcasters in the public interest. Nothing in this decision, therefore, is intended to call into question the validity of the public interest standard under the Communications Act.

Rather, we simply believe that, in analyzing the appropriate First Amendment standard to be applied in the electronic press, the concept of scarcity—be it spectrum or numerical—is irrelevant. [A]n evaluation of First Amendment standards should not focus on the *physical differences* between the electronic press and the printed press, but on the *functional similarities* between these two media and upon the underlying values of goals of the First Amendment. We believe that the function of the electronic press in a free society is identical to that of the printed press and that, therefore, the constitutional analysis of government control of content should be no different.

A cardinal tenet of the First Amendment is that government intervention in the marketplace of ideas of the sort involved in the enforcement of the Fairness Doctrine is not acceptable and should not be tolerated. The Fairness Doctrine is at odds with this fundamental constitutional concept. While the objective underlying the Fairness Doctrine is that of the First Amendment itself— the promotion of debate on important controversial issues—the means employed to achieve this objective, government coercion, is the very one which the First Amendment is designed to prevent. In this sense, the underlying rationale of the Fairness Doctrine turns the First Amendment on its head.

Because the dissemination of a particular viewpoint by a broadcaster can trigger the burdens associated with broadcasting responsive programming, the Doctrine directly penalizes—through the prospect or reality of government intrusion—the speaker for expressing his or her opinion on a matter of public concern. For even if the broadcaster has, in fact, presented contrasting viewpoints, the government, at the request of a complainant, may nevertheless question the broadcaster's presentation, which in and of itself is a penalty for simply covering an issue of public importance.

[B]roadcasters who intend to, and who do in fact, present contrasting viewpoints on controversial issues of public importance are nevertheless exposed to potential entanglement with the government over the exercise of their editorial discretion. Consequently, these broadcasters may shy away from extensive coverage of their issues. We believe that, in the absence of the Doctrine, broadcasters will more readily cover controversial issues, which, when combined with sound

journalistic practice, will result in more coverage and more diversity of viewpoint in the electronic media; that is, the goals of the First Amendment will be enhanced by employing the very means of the First Amendment: government restraint.

Finally, we believe that under the First Amendment, the rights of viewers and listeners to receive diverse viewpoints is achieved by guaranteeing them the right to receive speech unencumbered by government intervention. The *Red Lion* decision, however, apparently views the notion that broadcasters should come within the free press and free speech protection of the First Amendment as antagonistic to the interest of the public in obtaining access to the marketplace of ideas. As a result, it is squarely at odds with the general philosophy underlying the First Amendment, i.e., that the individual's interests in free expression and the societal interests in access to viewpoint diversity are both furthered by proscribing government regulation of speech. The special broadcast standard applied by the Court in *Red Lion,* which sanctions restrictions on speakers in order to promote the interest of the viewers and listeners, contradicts this fundamental constitutional principle.

Under a traditional First Amendment analysis, the type of governmental intrusion inherent in the Fairness Doctrine would not be tolerated if it were applied to the print media. We believe that the role of the electronic press in our society is the same as that of the printed press. There is no doubt that the electronic media is powerful and that broadcasters can abuse their freedom of speech. But the framers of the Constitution believed that the potential for abuse of private freedoms posed far less a threat to democracy than the potential for abuse by a government given the power to control the press. We concur. We therefore believe that the First Amendment protections against content regulation should apply equally to the electronic and the printed press.

The court in *Meredith Corp. v. FCC* "remand[ed] the case to the FCC with instructions to consider [Meredith's] constitutional arguments." In response to the court's directive, we find that the Fairness Doctrine chills speech and is not narrowly tailored to achieve a substantial governmental interest. We therefore conclude, under existing Supreme Court precedent, as set forth in *Red Lion* and its progeny, that the Fairness Doctrine contravenes the First Amendment and thereby disserves the public interest. *As a consequence, we determine that the editorial decision of Station WTVH to broadcast the editorial advertisements at issue in this adjudication is an action protected by the First Amendment from government interference. Accordingly, we reconsider our prior determinations in this matter and conclude that the Constitution bars us from enforcing the Fairness Doctrine against Station WTVH.* [Emphasis added.]

We further believe, as the Supreme Court indicated in *FCC v. League of Women Voters,* that the dramatic transformation in the telecommunications marketplace provides a basis for the courts to reconsider its application of diminished First Amendment protection to the electronic media. Despite the physical differences between the electronic and print media, their roles in our society are identical, and we believe that the same First Amendment principles should be equally applicable to both. This is the method set forth in our Constitution for maximizing the public interest; and furthering the public interest is likewise our mandate under the Communications Act. It is therefore to advance the public interest that we advocate these rights for broadcasters.

COMMENT

Several alternatives to the fairness doctrine were before the FCC at the time it was considering *Syracuse Peace Council.* Many of these alternatives had been previously considered and rejected. Among them: enforcement of the doctrine only at license renewal time, rather than on a case-by-case basis; enforcement of only the second prong of the doctrine; permitting stations to opt for voluntary systems of public access in lieu of compliance with the doctrine; and use of an "actual malice" standard, derived from the law of libel, in determining fairness doctrine violations. The FCC rejected all of these alternatives. Instead in *Syracuse Peace Council,* the FCC repealed the fairness doctrine.

The last chapter in the *Syracuse Peace* litigation occurred on February 10, 1989, when a federal appeals panel, per Judge Williams, upheld the FCC's refusal to enforce the fairness doctrine against Meredith Broadcasting Co. See *Syracuse Peace Council v. FCC,* 867 F.2d 654 (D.C. Cir. 1989). Judge Williams declared:

Although the FCC somewhat entangled its public interest and constitutional findings, we find that the FCC's public interest determination was an independent basis for its decision and was supported by the record.

Judge Kenneth Starr, concurring, believed that the FCC *had* decided *Syracuse Peace Council* on First Amendment grounds. He thought the First Amendment issue should be confronted. Nevertheless, he concluded that the FCC's abolition of the fairness doctrine in *Syracuse Peace Council* should be upheld:

Vindication of the constitutional reasoning in the [FCC] order would *not* constitute a judicial determination that the fairness doctrine as [currently administered] is "unconstitutional." To reiterate: I would hold only that the FCC's decision to eliminate the fairness doctrine correctly interprets *Red Lion* and is based, as the court's opinion effectively demonstrates, on an adequate factual record. Such a decision would therefore not foreclose a future FCC (or Congress) from reestablishing the fairness doctrine in its present (or some modified) form.

Do you agree that the FCC did not rely on the First Amendment to invalidate the fairness doctrine? Look at the italicized language in *Syracuse Peace Council,* p. 817. Why were the FCC and the court of appeals so anxious *not* to base the abolition of the fairness doctrine on the First Amendment? Consider the following explanation:

Two factors [might explain] the casuistry behind avoiding the constitutional issue in the panel decision. One was a desire not to challenge the *Red Lion* precedent; the other could have been a desire not to preclude efforts to reinstate the Fairness Doctrine by statute. Congress would be undercut by a judicial holding that the Fairness Doctrine violated the First Amendment since this would run counter to congressional efforts to revive the Fairness Doctrine—efforts which had been undertaken in the aftermath of the FCC abolition order. Jerome A. Barron, *What Does the Fairness Doctrine Controversy Really Mean?,* 12 Comment Hastings Comm. and Ent. L. J. 205, 219 (1989).

The Status of the Fairness Doctrine Corollaries after the Abolition of the Fairness Doctrine

In a largely unsuccessful effort to placate an irate Congress after the FCC's abolition of the fairness doctrine, in September 1987 FCC Chairman

Dennis Patrick wrote a letter to Representative John Dingell (D-Mich.), chairman of the House Commerce Committee. Patrick assured Dingell that the FCC has not eliminated the personal attack rules, the political editorializing rules, the Zapple Rule (quasi-equal access to stations for major political parties), or the application of the doctrine to ballot issues or political campaigns. (On the present status of a broadcaster's obligations with regard to ballot issues, see *Arkansas AFL-CIO v. FCC*, 11 F.3d 1430 [8th Cir. 1993], p. 822.)

The personal attack rules, p. 789, have clearly survived the abolition of the fairness doctrine. See *Personal Attack Rule*, 47 C.F.R. § 73.1920. The political editorializing rules, p. 789, have also survived abolition. See *Political Editorializing Rules*, 47 C.F.R. § 73.1930.

Although the personal attack rules survive, there is a real question as to whether that survival is meaningful. In 1991, Professor David Berkman brought a complaint against radio station WISN. A WISN talk show host discussing the Gulf War said Berkman "won't be happy until we see Iraqi soldiers jumping for joy." WISN said this did not constitute a personal attack but instead was merely a contention that Berkman and Iraqi troops would be happy if U.S. troops withdrew from Iraq. The FCC agreed that no *personal* attack had taken place and, therefore, the personal attack rules could not be invoked. The FCC affirmed the Mass Media Bureau's ruling, but Commissioner Duggan observed that the controversy probably could have been defused if WISN had given Professor Berkman a chance to respond. See *Letter to Professor David P. Berkman*, 6 F.C.C.R. 6640 (1991); *aff'd*, 7 F.C.C.R. 6001 (1992).

Another case where the FCC refused to consider that the complaint constituted a personal attack involved Bree Walker Lampley, an anchor on a local Los Angeles television station. Lampley filed a complaint with the FCC against radio station, KFI(AM), for violating, among other things, the personal attack rules. The radio station broadcast a two-hour talk show that criticized the attempt by Lampley and her spouse to have a child because there was a 50 percent chance that the child would be born with a genetic birth defect. The FCC ruled that Lampley failed to make out a prima facie case that KFI had violated the personal attack rules. The com-

plainant had failed to show the "controversiality of the issue" by providing evidence that members of the community were vigorously debating the issue. The FCC noted that mere criticism of a personal decision "does not rise to a personal attack." *In re Personal Attack Complaint of Bree Walker Lampley*, 7 F.C.C.R. 1385 (1992).

The radio station comments about David Berkman and Bree Walker Lampley did not constitute personal attacks. What comments would constitute a personal attack?

A complaint was filed against radio station WOL(AM) in Washington, D.C., on the ground that during a discussion of alleged government conspiracies surrounding the death of Rev. Martin Luther King, Jr., Cathy Hughes of WOL characterized the complainant as a "stalker involved in a government conspiracy against her." The FCC found that the complainant did not provide sufficient evidence to establish that WOL's broadcast constituted a personal attack. Moreover, the FCC found that the complainant had "[a]pparently failed to contact the station to give it an opportunity to respond." *Letter to Ms. Loretta Smith*, 9 F.C.C.R. 7814 (1994) (denying request for reconsideration of personal attack complaint against WOL[AM]).

When a personal attack complaint is made, what is the role of the FCC? In *Letter to Ms. Loretta Smith*, the FCC answered this question as follows:

> The FCC neither investigates nor interferes in any way with a licensee's judgment in this sensitive First Amendment area absent a showing that the licensee has been clearly unreasonable in failing to contact a particular group or individual and allow a response. To initiate an investigation of whether a licensee violated the personal attack rule, therefore, a complaint must pass the threshold test; i.e., make a showing that the alleged attack took place during the discussion of a controversial issue of public importance. See *Fairness Doctrine and Public Interest Standards*, 48 F.C.C.2d 1 (1974), *recon. denied*, 58 F.C.C.2d 691 (1976).
>
> The FCC's role in reviewing personal attack complaints is not to substitute its judgment for that of the licensee or network but rather to determine whether the station has acted reasonably and in good faith in ascertaining whether a personal attack has occurred. In the absence of a clear and convincing showing that the licensee has been unreasonable or that there has been an abuse of journalistic discretion, FCC action is not justified.

The Fairness Doctrine:
Requiem or Resurrection?

As a result of *Syracuse Peace Council,* if the FCC were to decide to re-institute the fairness doctrine it could do so under the public interest standard. Another way to resurrect the fairness doctrine, of course, would be for Congress to enact a statute clearly establishing the fairness doctrine and mandating its enforcement on broadcasters. Still another means of re-instituting the fairness doctrine would be for another federal court of appeals to rule, contrary to the *TRAC* case, p. 771, that sec 315(a) did in fact codify the fairness doctrine. Just such a course of action was urged on the U.S. Court of Appeals for the Eighth Circuit.

In *Arkansas AFL-CIO v. F.C.C.,* the Court of Appeals, per Judge Beam, affirmed the FCC's refusal to apply the fairness doctrine to KARK-TV, holding that the fairness doctrine is not statutorily required and that the FCC was within its discretion when it ruled that the doctrine also was not in the public interest. The Arkansas AFL-CIO and the Committee Against Amendment 2 filed a complaint with the FCC that KARK-TV was violating the fairness doctrine in its coverage of a ballot issue. The FCC dismissed the complaint, stating that the fairness doctrine was not statutorily compelled and that the FCC had repealed it in *Syracuse Peace Council v. WTVH,* 2 F.C.C.R. 5043 (1987). A panel of the court of appeals affirmed this decision on different grounds, *Arkansas AFL-CIO v. FCC,* 980 F.2d 1190 (8th Cir. 1992); then a petition for rehearing *en banc* was brought by both the FCC and the Committee and granted, resulting in the following case.

Arkansas AFL-CIO v. FCC
11 F.3D 1430 (8TH CIR. 1993).

BEAM, Circuit Judge, with whom Floyd R. GIBSON, Senior Circuit Judge, BOWMAN, MAGILL and LOKEN, Circuit Judges, join.

The Committee raises two issues for en banc review. First it contends that the 1959 amendment clearly and unambiguously codified the fairness doctrine. In the alternative, the Committee [joined by the FCC] argues that *Chevron [U.S.A., Inc. v. Natural Resources Defense Council, Inc.,* 467 U.S. 837 (1984)] dictates that this case be remanded to the agency.

[T]he 1959 amendment [to Sec. 315(a) was enacted to insure that Congress] did not unintentionally dismantle the FCC's fairness doctrine. The introductory phrase of this proviso states: "Nothing in the foregoing sentence shall be construed as relieving broadcasters [f]rom the obligation imposed upon them under this chapter." This wording indicates to us that the proviso was intended to maintain the status quo, rather than to impose any new statutory obligations. The language merely ensures that any obligations existing before the amendment would continue unchanged.

Red Lion contains dicta that could be interpreted to support the view that the 1959 amendment codified the fairness doctrine. However, these statements are counter-balanced by others tending to support the contrary view that the 1959 amendment merely expressed congressional approval for the administrative system of fairness. These apparent contradictions are all dicta; the issue of the codification of the fairness doctrine was not squarely before the Court in *Red Lion.* Our analysis is borne out by later Supreme Court opinions.

For example, the Seventh Circuit described the 1959 amendment in dicta as explicitly including the fairness doctrine in the Communications Act, and ratifying the doctrine with positive legislation. *Maier v. FCC,* 735 F.2d 220, 223 n. 4, 5 (7th Cir. 1984). The Fourth Circuit described the 1959 amendment as "providing a statutory basis for [FCC's] pre-existing version of the fairness doctrine." *Larus & Bro. Co. v. FCC,* 447 F.2d 876, 882 (4th Cir. 1971). On the other hand, the First Circuit stated, again in dicta, that the 1959 amendment merely approved the general tenets of the fairness doctrine. *PIRG v. FCC,* 522 F.2d 1060, 1066 (1st Cir. 1975), *cert. denied,* 424 U.S. 965 (1976).

Reading all of the cases together, we think that they reflect some uncertainty about the status of the fairness doctrine, rather than an unalloyed conclusion that the 1959 amendment to section 315(a) codified the doctrine. Thus, our decision in this case does not conflict with either Supreme Court precedent or the decisions of the other circuits. Having concluded that the 1959 amendment to section 315(a) did not codify the fairness doctrine, we turn to the Committee's contention that a remand to the FCC is warranted.

Deference to an agency becomes an issue when the first part of a *Chevron* analysis does not yield a clear congressional intent. The Committee contends that an affirmance of the FCC's decision is incompatible with the Supreme Court's directives for the second strand of a *Chevron* inquiry. They argue that the FCC's interpretation of "operate in the public interest" [as set forth in the 1959 amendment to Sec. 315(a)] to permit the abolition of the fairness doctrine was neither reasonable nor permissible. We disagree with the Committee's contention that the FCC advanced no explanation for its decision, and therefore find remand to be unnecessary.

The FCC clearly articulated its reasons for abandoning the fairness doctrine in *Syracuse Peace Council,* and invoked those same reasons in this case. In *Syracuse Peace Council,* the D.C. Circuit credited the FCC's testimony that the dramatic increase in media outlets since 1959 eliminated the need for the fairness doctrine. In addition, the FCC presented testimony that the fairness doctrine actually chilled speech. We think this kind of judgment about the way the world of broadcasting works is precisely the type of determination that the FCC is better equipped to make than are the courts. The reasons advanced by the FCC in *Syracuse Peace Council* are undeniably reasonable explanations for the change in agency position. Therefore, while *Syracuse Peace Council* does not bind this court, we agree with that well-reasoned decision, and find the elimination of the fairness doctrine to be a permissible agency response to changed circumstances.

[O]ur decision in no way implicates the FCC's discretion to determine whether "operate in the public interest" requires some notion of fairness. The fairness doctrine developed from the "operate in the public interest" requirement and that language is still a part of the statute. The FCC is free to reasonably interpret this statutory mandate as it sees fit.

Richard S. ARNOLD, Chief Judge, with whom LOKEN and Morris Sheppard ARNOLD, Circuit Judges, join concurring in the judgment.

For me, the balance is tipped by the First Amendment. Whether the Supreme Court reexamines *Red Lion* is its business, not ours. But developments subsequent to *Red Lion* appear at least to raise a significant possibility that the First Amendment balance struck in *Red Lion* would look different today. In order to avoid having to reach this important constitutional question, I would construe the statute not to require the [FCC] to impose the fairness doctrine.

John R. GIBSON, Circuit Judge, with whom MCMILLIAN, FAGG, WOLLMAN, and HANSEN, Circuit Judges, join, dissenting.

I differ, however, with the lead opinion's analysis of the 1959 amendment to section 315, particularly when it discusses the house conference report. The language the conference committee substituted clearly states that broadcasters are not relieved "from the obligation imposed upon them under this Act to operate in the public interest and to afford reasonable opportunity for the discussion of conflicting views on issues of public importance." That this language mandates the fairness doctrine is confirmed by the conference report passage I have cited above and particularly its reference "to the 'standard of fairness' which is imposed on broadcasters under the Communications Act of 1934."

After carefully examining *Red Lion,* however, I see far more support for the proposition that the Court saw the bill as a congressional ratification of the fairness doctrine. The idea that the fairness doctrine rests squarely on an affirmative congressional mandate is not new. From 1959 until 1981, the FCC consistently interpreted the 1959 amendment as codifying the doctrine. Indeed, in 1981 the FCC sought to repeal the doctrine through legislative, not agency, action. Only after the FCC's attempts to obtain congressional action failed did the FCC first contend that Congress had never codified the doctrine.

If the court accepted even the limited proposition that the legislative history, like the plain language of the statute, is ambiguous, it should remand to the [FCC] for further proceedings. It is far more prudent and practical to remand the case to allow the FCC to determine whether the 1959 amendment codified the fairness doctrine.

COMMENT

Who has the better of the codification issue in *Arkansas AFL-CIO*—Judge Beam or Judge Gibson? Judge Beam made the following observation in a footnote in *Arkansas AFL-CIO:*

While nothing in our decision prevents the FCC from reinstituting the fairness doctrine should the agency determine that "operate in the public interest" so requires, such a course of action would inevitably raise constitutional questions.

The federal court of appeals in *Syracuse Peace Council* went to great lengths to avoid upholding FCC abolition of the fairness doctrine on constitutional grounds. Why then does Judge Beam suggest that its reinstatement would raise "constitutional questions"? Can you outline a legal and policy rationale for re-instituting the fairness doctrine? Should it be re-instituted?

The battle over whether the fairness doctrine was statutorily codified in sec. 315(a) still continues. In *Coalition for a Healthy California v. FCC*, 24 Med. L. Rptr. 2176, 87 F.3d 383 (9th Cir. 1996), the FCC was asked to issue a declaratory order that the fairness doctrine was statutorily mandated. The FCC failed to act on this request. In light of the failure of the FCC to issue such an order, the court could not rule on the merits of the request. Federal courts of appeals are only authorized to review final orders of the FCC; in this case, a final order was lacking.

In view of the abolition of the fairness doctrine by the FCC, what is the status of the *Red Lion* decision today? In the cable must-carry case, *Turner Broadcasting System, Inc. v. FCC*, 512 U.S. 622 (1994), p. 861, Justice Kennedy for the Court commented on *Red Lion* as follows:

It is true that our cases have permitted more intrusive regulation of broadcast speakers than of speakers in other media. Compare *Red Lion Broadcasting v. FCC* and *NBC v. U.S.* with *Miami Herald Publishing Co. v. Tornillo*. But the rationale for applying a less rigorous standard of First Amendment scrutiny to broadcast regulation, whatever its validity in the cases elaborating it, does not apply in the context of cable regulation. The justification for our distinct approach to broadcast regulation rests upon the unique physical limitations of the broadcast medium. See *FCC v. League of Women Voters; Red Lion; NBC*. Although courts and commenta-

tors have criticized the scarcity rationale, we have declined to question its continuing validity as support for our broadcast jurisprudence, see *FCC v. League of Women Voters*, and see no reason to do so here.

The foregoing passage reflects (1) no disposition to repudiate *Red Lion* or the scarcity rationale upon which it is based and (2) an unwillingness to extend *Red Lion* to new electronic technologies. At the same time, this passage reflects no real enthusiasm for *Red Lion*.

In the cable public access indecency case, *Denver Area Educ. Telecom. Consortium v. FCC*, 116 S. Ct. 2374 (1996), p. 881, Justice Stephen Breyer for the Court declined to extend the First Amendment standard used in *Red Lion* to cable regulation. Justice Breyer described *Red Lion* as "employing [a] highly flexible standard in response to the scarcity problem unique to over-the-air broadcast." Justice Clarence Thomas, joined by Chief Justice William Rehnquist and Justice Antonin Scalia, concurred in part and dissented in part. As for *Red Lion*, Justice Thomas observed: "In *Turner*, by adopting much of the print paradigm, and by rejecting *Red Lion*, we adopted a considerable body of precedent that governs the respective First Amendment rights of competing speakers. In *Red Lion*, we had legitimized consideration of the public interest and emphasized the rights of viewers, at least in the abstract. After *Turner*, however, that view can no longer be given any credence in the cable context. It is the operator's right that is preeminent."

Note that the foregoing excerpts from the Breyer and Thomas opinions in the *Denver Area* case do not challenge *Red Lion* as the governing First Amendment model in broadcasting. This is true also of the reference to *Red Lion* in *Turner*. In light of the view that the scarcity rationale is now obsolete, why does the Court continue to adhere to the *Red Lion* standard in broadcast regulation?

REGULATING OBSCENITY AND INDECENCY IN BROADCASTING BEFORE THE FCC AND THE FEDERAL COURTS

CHAPTER OUTLINE

THE BASIS FOR REGULATION

The regulation of broadcast obscenity and indecency is a murky area because the FCC and the courts must reconcile two apparently contradictory statutes: 47 U.S.C. § 326 of the Communications Act of 1934, which prohibits FCC censorship, and 18 U.S.C. § 1464 of the criminal code, which prohibits broadcasting "any obscene, indecent, or profane language."

Section 326 states:

Nothing in this Act shall be understood or construed to give the commission the power of censorship over the radio communications or signals transmitted by any radio station, and no regulation

or condition shall be promulgated or fixed by the commission which shall interfere with the right of free speech by means of radio communication.

The Federal Criminal Code, 18 U.S.C. § 1464, provides as follows:

Whoever utters any obscene, indecent, or profane language by means of radio communication shall be fined not more than $10,000 or imprisoned not more than two years, or both.

In 1978, the Supreme Court in *FCC v. Pacifica Foundation, Inc.,* reported, pp. 605–613, summarized the legislative history of these two provisions and observed that they had a common origin. The Court insisted that the two statutes did not conflict:

A single section of the 1927 [Radio] act is the source of both the anticensorship provision and the [c]ommission's authority to impose sanctions for the broadcast of indecent or obscene language. Quite plainly, Congress intended to give meaning to both provisions. Respect for that intent requires that the censorship language be read as inapplicable to the prohibition on broadcasting obscene, indecent, or profane language.

Broadcasters who violate sec. 1464 can be punished directly by the Department of Justice (DOJ). Such suits would be tried in federal courts. If pursued, they could be much more serious than complaints brought by the FCC because they carry the risk of imprisonment. In recent years, the DOJ has not vigorously prosecuted such cases, however, so broadcasters have much more concern about how the FCC applies these standards. Although the prohibition of obscene, indecent, or profane utterances originated in the Radio Act of 1927 and was carried forward to the Communication Act of 1934, it was removed from that act in 1948 when Congress created the U.S. Criminal Code. The ability of the FCC to continue to enforce the prohibition, however, persisted under another part of the Communications Act, 47 U.S.C. § 503(b)(2), which authorizes the FCC to punish infractions of 18 U.S.C. § 1464 by assessing forfeitures (fines). The FCC could also seek cease-and-desist orders from federal judges to halt such speech, but it never has.

Most severely, the FCC can consider violations of sec. 1464 when licenses are sought—either by renewal applicants or by initial applicants. License applications have rarely been disqualified. Instead, the FCC has preferred to warn or admonish licensees, although occasionally exceptions have occurred. For a while in the 1980s, the FCC indicated that it would not pursue alleged violations of this section of the criminal code but would, instead, refer complaints to the DOJ for prosecution. *Video 44,* 103 F.C.C.2d 1204 (1986). Through this process, the FCC apparently sought to resolve a long-standing problem: How could commissioners in Washington, D.C., understand local attitudes toward obscenity or indecency? How could local community standards be assessed? It also sought to conserve its resources by having others do things it has done in the past. In the face of accusations, with associated political pressure, that the commission was abdicating its responsibility to

enforce these sections of the law, however, the FCC eventually retreated from this position and stated (and shortly thereafter concretely demonstrated) that it would indeed apply the standards itself. *Video 44,* 3 F.C.C.R. 757 (1988).

Section 1464 prohibits three kinds of "utterances": (1) profane, (2) obscene, and (3) indecent. Interpretation of the statute has posed many problems. Are all these terms in the conjunctive—just synonyms for the constitutional definition of obscenity? Or are all these terms disjunctive? Is there a difference among profanity, obscenity, and indecency? Do the differences in these utterances justify different forms of regulation? How are the terms to be defined? If there is a difference, especially between obscenity and indecency, how is it determined? Who makes these decisions? Is there something special about this statute because it applies to broadcasting? Is there a difference between how obscenity (or indecency) is to be judged in broadcasting as contrasted with other media? FCC and court decisions throw light on all these points.

PROFANITY

Profanity generally refers to using religious or sacred names or terms in an irreverent fashion. Because it so closely implicates freedom of religion, courts have been reluctant to endorse use of government power to prevent profanity. If the courts were to protect the religious terms of one faith, that might amount to an establishment of that religion, violating the First Amendment to the Constitution. Consequently, courts and the FCC are rarely concerned about an occasional "hell" or "damn" on broadcasting. The closest the FCC has come in recent—and, in fact, not very recent—years was its decision to deny license renewal to Palmetto Broadcasting Company's WDKD, owned by the late Hollywood "bad man" Edward G. Robinson, Jr. *Palmetto Broadcasting Co.,* 33 F.C.C. 250 (1962).

The FCC denied renewal for WDKD in Kingstree, South Carolina, largely because Robinson lied to the commission during a renewal proceeding. The formal FCC term was that Robinson "misrepresented" himself. Misrepresentation is a sin of major proportion to the FCC, which, being a small agency without an extensive police force, depends heavily on the honesty and trustworthiness of the people it regulates. Robinson said he never heard complaints about the allegedly objectionable programming of disc jockey Charlie Walker, which featured what at the time were considered off-color jokes and remarks, but numerous witnesses testified to the contrary. The FCC never really zeroed in on whether the programming was profane, indecent, or obscene. The most important factor was that Robinson lied to the FCC when it asked him about it. The FCC's decision not to renew the license was upheld by the U.S. Court of Appeals for the D.C. Circuit. *Robinson v. FCC*, 334 F.2d 534 (D.C. Cir. 1964).

OBSCENITY

The law of obscenity is extensively described in Chapter 10 of this text. In theory, it applies no differently to broadcasting than to other media. In practice, the FCC has had little opportunity to develop a law of broadcast obscenity. For most of broadcasting's history, commercial forces restrained radio and TV stations from pushing sexual frankness to its limit and, perhaps, crossing the dividing line into obscenity.

As discussed in the obscenity section of this book, the U.S. Supreme Court has varied its definitions of obscenity over the last few decades. Whenever the FCC has faced an allegation of broadcast obscenity, it has claimed to apply the then current definition of obscenity supported by the U.S. Supreme Court. To accommodate the so-called special characteristics of broadcasting, however, the FCC has gone further and proscribed as "indecent" speech that would not have been "obscene."

A significant FCC broadcasting obscenity case arose in 1973 when several stations adopted what was called a "topless radio" format. Basically a talk or call-in format, topless radio featured hosts—usually male—who encouraged members of the audience—usually female—to call in and discuss a topic of the day, which was nearly always sexual in nature. The format was popular for a while but attracted complaints to the FCC. The FCC eventually concluded that a station owned by Sonderling Broadcasting Company violated sec. 1464 by broadcasting obscene utterances, and imposed a forfeiture or fine. Because the *Roth-Memoirs* definition of obscen-

ity was then endorsed by the Supreme Court, the FCC claimed that Sonderling's broadcasts were obscene under that standard.

Sonderling Broadcasting Corp., WGLD-FM
41 F.C.C.2D 777 (1973).

WGLD-FM [has] been using a format sometime called "topless radio," in which an announcer takes calls from the audience and discusses largely sexual topics. On February 23, 1973, the topic was "oral sex." The program consisted of very explicit exchanges in which the female callers spoke of their oral sex experiences.

If discussions in this titillating and pandering fashion of coating the penis to facilitate oral sex, swallowing the semen at climax, overcoming fears of the penis being bitten off, etc., do not constitute broadcast obscenity within the meaning of 18 U.S.C.A. § 1464, we do not perceive what does or could. We also believe that the dominant theme here is clearly an appeal to prurient interest. The announcer coaxed responses that were designed to titillate—to arouse sexual feelings.

Our conclusions here are based on the pervasive and intrusive nature of broadcast radio, even if children were left completely out of the picture. However, the presence of children in the broadcast audience makes this an *a fortiori* matter. There are significant numbers of children in the audience during these afternoon hours—and not all of a pre-school age. Thus, there is always a significant percentage of school age children out of school on any given day.

[T]here is an alternative ground for action in this case. In WUHY we set out at some length our construction that the term "indecent," as used in 18 U.S.C.A. § 1464, constituted a different standard from "obscene" in the broadcast field. We therefore find, as an alternative ground, that the material, even if it were not found to appeal to a prurient interest, warrants the assessment of a forfeiture because it is within the statutory prohibition against the broadcast of indecent matter.

[W]e recognize that we are not the final arbiters in this sensitive First Amendment field. Therefore, we welcome and urge judicial eration of our action. As to the amou.

forfeiture, we believe that $2,000 is appropriate for the willful or repeated violations here involved (covering both the February 21 and 23, 1972, programs). While it is true that there has been no judicial consideration of obscenity or indecency in this specific broadcast situation we are not fashioning any new theory here. In view of the foregoing, we determine that, pursuant to Sec. 503(b)(1)(E) of the Communications Act of 1934, as amended, Sonderling Broadcasting Corporation has incurred an apparent liability of two thousand dollars ($2000).

COMMENT

In *Sonderling* the FCC invoked both the indecency and the obscenity standards of 18 U.S.C. § 1464 and found that a forfeiture was warranted under both standards. *Sonderling* specifically applied the *Roth-Memoirs-Ginzburg* obscenity standard to broadcasting while stating that "the special quality of the medium must be taken into account." The FCC says that on the basis of its discussion of obscenity in *Sonderling*, it is clear that the matter broadcast is "indecent" as well. Do you agree?

Commissioner Johnson, in dissent, attacked the FCC policy of enforcing both an obscenity standard and an indecency standard. The charge of "indecency" was too imprecise, and the FCC majority did not define the community whose standards were supposedly violated. This duty to define the relevant community is now much more fundamental than ever in light of the new importance given to the local community standard by *Miller v. California*, 413 U.S. 15 (1973), text, p. 603, a case that had not been decided at the time of the announcement of the FCC's *Sonderling* opinion. In light of *Miller*, how should community be defined in a case like Sonderling?

Commissioner Johnson said further that the enforcement of sec. 1464 is better left to the DOJ. This approach would leave the problem of defining sec. 1464 to the federal courts, and it is certainly arguable that federal judges are better equipped to deal with the sensitive First Amendment issues involved than is the FCC. On the other hand, the FCC in *Sonderling* was acting pursuant to sec. 503(b)(1)(E) of the Communications Act of 1934. It is not appropriate for the

agency to fail to enforce a provision of its enabling statute.

The Sonderling Broadcast Co. simply paid the forfeiture to the FCC and did not appeal. But the Illinois Citizens Committee for Broadcasting and the Illinois Division of the American Civil Liberties Union (ACLU) took up the fight and sought both a petition for reconsideration of the notice of apparent liability and remission of the forfeiture from the FCC. These requests were denied by the FCC, and the ACLU and the committee petitioned the federal court of appeals for review.

In *Illinois Citizens Committee for Broadcasting v. FCC*, 515 F.2d 397 (D.C. Cir. 1974), the court, per Judge Leventhal, upheld the FCC determination in the *Sonderling* case: The FCC did not unconstitutionally infringe on the listening alternatives of the public when it determined that a radio call-in show carrying an explicit discussion of ultimate sexual acts in a titillating context was an obscene broadcast.

The court reasoned that the station's approach in the radio call-in show in question, "Femme Forum," triggered the principles of *Ginzburg v. United States*, 383 U.S. 463 (1966), where Justice Brennan held that commercial exploitation of erotica could be decisive in the determination of obscenity. In *Ginzburg*, the "leering innuendo" was found in the modes of sales promotion. Here the "commercial exploitation" of titillation was found in the "tone" that was "set by the continuity provided by the announcer."

Perhaps most significant was Sonderling's choice of broadcast hours. "Femme Forum" was broadcast from 10 A.M. to 3 P.M. when the radio audience might include children, home from school for lunch, illness, or staggered school hours. Judge Leventhal concluded: "Given this combination of factors, we do not think that the FCC's evaluation of this material infringes upon rights protected by the First Amendment."

A problem arose in determining the obscenity standard that should be applied. The FCC found Sonderling's broadcasts obscene under the standards of *Roth v. United States* and *Memoirs v. Massachusetts*. Between the FCC's resolution of the case and the present appeal, the Supreme Court decided *Miller v. California*, which sets out the following guidelines for the trier of fact:

(a) whether "the average person, applying contemporary community standards" would find that the work taken as a whole, appeals to the prurient interest in sex * * * (b) whether the work depicts or describes, in a patently offensive way, sexual conduct specifically defined by the applicable state law, and (c) whether the work, taken as a whole, lacks serious literary, artistic, political, or scientific value.

Judge Leventhal rejected the contention that *Miller* required reversal of the FCC ruling in *Sonderling*:

We conclude that, where a radio call-in show during daytime hours broadcasts explicit discussions of ultimate sexual acts in a titillating context, the commission does not unconstitutionally infringe upon the public's right to listening alternatives when it determines the broadcast is obscene.

The petitioners then sought a rehearing *en banc* by the full court. On March 13, 1975, that request was denied. Judge Bazelon, however, disagreed with his colleagues in refusing to grant a rehearing. He questioned the conclusion of obscenity in light of the fact that *Miller* requires "local fact-finders to apply 'local community standards' of decency." Bazelon argued that the court should have required the FCC "to take evidence on 'local community standards' before reaching a decision under Miller."

Judge Bazelon set forth further objections to the court's reasoning:

There is another difficulty with the court's opinion. *Miller* retains the established requirement that material allegedly obscene must be "taken as a whole" in the judgment of obscenity. Here the commission made its judgment of obscenity on a 22 minute tape which eliminated the bulk of the Sonderling (and other broadcasters') talk show programming not involving sexual discussion. By the admitted facts the FCC did not take the material as a whole but rather viewed the material piece meal. I think this is grounds for a remand.

In Bazelon's view the condemnation of sex-oriented radio shows by then FCC Chairman Burch and the commencement a day earlier, by the FCC of a closed notice of inquiry into the broadcast of obscene, indecent, or profane material made it clear that what was involved was not a "specific attack on *Sonderling* but rather a general attack on all sex-oriented talk shows." An entire class of speech had been chased off the air.

Finally, there was a basic statutory defect in the FCC's regulation of obscenity in broadcasting as manifested by the *Sonderling* decision:

Judge Bazelon questioned whether "any FCC enforcement of obscenity prohibitions prior to a judicial determination of obscenity is consistent with the broad principles of First Amendment 'due process.'" Judge Bazelon elaborated on this point in a footnote in the *Illinois Citizens* case:

47 U.S.C.A. § 503(b)(1)(E) (1970) speaks in terms of one who "violates" 18 U.S.C.A. § 1464 (1970) and thus may refer only to one adjudicated in violation by the FCC (who can only charge a violation and not conclusively adjudicate a violation). The legislative history is similarly unclear. Originally, the FCC was given enforcement powers over obscene broadcasts. See *Duncan v. United States,* 48 F.2d 128 (9th Cir. 1931), *cert. denied,* 283 U.S. 863. In 1948, the prohibition on obscene broadcasts was moved to Title 18 and nothing in Title 47 authorized the FCC to consider obscenity in a forfeiture proceeding. In 1960 Congress added § 503 to grant authority to the FCC to aid in the enforcement of anti-quiz-fraud provisions. Public Law 86-752, 74 Stat. 889. It was not stated whether the FCC was to have co-ordinate enforcement powers with the Department of Justice. The commission in *Sonderling Broadcasting Corp.,* 41 F.C.C.2d 777, 778, 781 (1973) argues that *FCC v. American Broadcasting Co.,* 347 U.S. 284, 289–90 n.7 (1954) establishes this concurrent enforcement authority. The commission misinterprets this case. The Supreme Court therein referred only to the power to enforce the general law upon licensees by revoking or failing to renew a license and expressly declined to hold in a comprehensive footnote that the FCC has forfeiture powers. The power to adjudicate violations of a criminal statute to impose a forfeiture prior to judicial review of the adjudication is a far cry from considering adjudicated illegal conduct or allegations of illegal conduct at license renewal time. See the perceptive discussion of this argument in Note, Broadcasting Obscene Language, 43 Ariz. St. L.J. 457, 466–70 (1974).

Judge Bazelon then discussed whether the "FCC as a national administrative agency" is equipped "to make a finding of whether speech appeals to a prurient interest under contemporary community standards (qua *Memoirs-Roth*) or under a local community standard (qua *Miller*)." The court rejected this objection on the ground that "the Supreme Court has found that jury trials are not required in obscenity decisions." But Bazelon's rejoinder to this was that it was "irrelevant to the larger question of whether a national administrative agency can be compared even to a local trial judge."

Although considered shocking at its time, the content of "Femme Forum" might be hard to distinguish today from radio programs such as those hosted by "Dr. Ruth" and similar sex therapists. Does this help demonstrate the value of relying on *contemporary* community standards? It may be that nothing is obscene forever—it is obscene, if at all, only at the time it is judged to be so. Standards can and do change.

The *WPXN* Case

On January 27, 1975, WPXN(FM) created a furor with two allegedly obscene broadcasts of a "live" call-in program called "The Vegetable Report," broadcast Monday evenings between 4:00 and 7:00 P.M. The station was licensed to the Trustees of the University of Pennsylvania but admittedly was managed solely by the students of the university. The FCC found at least four particular segments of the January 27 broadcast obscene under the test set forth in *Miller v. California*. One of the segments dealt with sexual relations between husband and wife. The other three dealt with using an on-the-air conversation with a three-year-old boy for purposes of sexual titillation. In one instance, the program announcer asked the child, who had been put on the phone by his mother, "Johnny, can you say 'fuck'?"

Despite some corrective actions taken by the university, the FCC found a violation of sec. 1464 for the broadcast of obscene and indecent matter. The FCC fined the licensee $2,000. It then turned the case into a renewal matter, on its own motion setting the trustees' renewal application for hearing. The FCC was primarily concerned that the licensee (the trustees) had lost control of the station to the students. See, generally, *In re Notice to the Trustees of the University of Pennsylvania*, 57 F.C.C.2d 782 (1975). Eventually, after the trustees cleaned house and reestablished control over the station, the FCC granted a new license. See p. 666.

INDECENCY

Congress did not define indecency in sec. 1464, and the concept does not exist outside the electronic media. Perceiving that obscenity and indecency are somewhat related, the FCC's approach has been to define broadcast indecency by using

at least part of whatever at the time is the approved U.S. Supreme Court definition of obscenity. The pattern began with the *WUHY* case reprinted below. At the time, the *Roth-Memoirs* definition of obscenity was in favor with the U.S. Supreme Court. Under that definition, described in more detail earlier in this text, something was obscene only if, to the average person, applying contemporary community standards, the dominant theme of the material taken as a whole appealed to a prurient interest in sex, and the work, as a whole, was utterly without any redeeming social value. The FCC decided that it took much less than that for a radio broadcast to be indecent.

In Re WUHY-FM Eastern Education Radio
24 F.C.C.2D 408 (1970).

WUHY-FM, a non-commercial educational radio station, broadcasts a weekly program, CYCLE II, from 10:00 to 11:00 P.M. On January 4, 1970, Jerry Garcia, of a musical group called *The Grateful Dead*, was interviewed by WUHY on tape in his hotel room. In the interview two of the most celebrated Anglo-Saxon four letter words were used with remarkable frequency by Garcia. [The words were not edited out when WUHY eventually broadcast the interview]. The FCC investigated WUHY.

[T]he narrow issue is whether the licensee may present previously taped interview or talk shows where the persons intersperse or begin their speech with expressions like, "Shit, man and shit like that," or "900 fuckin' times,""right fucking out of ya," etc. We believe that if we have the authority, we have a duty to act to prevent the widespread use on broadcast outlets of such expressions in the above circumstances. For the speech involved has no redeeming social value, and is patently offensive by contemporary community standards, with very serious consequences to the "public interest in the larger and more effective use of radio" (Section 303(g)).

This brings us to the second part of the analysis—the consequence to the public interest. *And here it is crucial to bear in mind the difference between radio and other media.* Unlike a book which requires the deliberate act of purchasing and reading (or a motion picture where admission to public exhibition must be actively sought), broadcasting is disseminated generally to the public under circumstances where reception requires no activity of this nature. Thus, it comes directly into the home and frequently without any advance warning of its content. Millions daily turn the dial from station to station. While particular stations or programs are oriented to specific audiences, the fact is that by its very nature, thousands of others not within the "intended" audience may also see or hear portions of the broadcast. Further, in that audience are very large numbers of children. Were this type of programming (e.g., the WUHY interview with the above described language) to become widespread, it would drastically affect the use of radio by millions of people. There are two aspects of this issue. First, there is the question of the applicability of 18 U.S.C.A. § 1464, which makes it a criminal offense to "utter any obscene, indecent, or profane language by means of radio communications." This standard, we note, is incorporated in the Communications Act. See Sections 312(a)(6) and 503(b)(1)(E), 47 U.S.C.A. § 312(a)(6); 503(b)(1)(E). The licensee urges that the broadcast was not obscene "because it did not have a dominant appeal to prurience or sexual matters." We agree, and thus find that the broadcast would not necessarily come within the standard laid down in *Memoirs v. Massachusetts.* 383 U.S. 413, 418 (1965); see also *Jacobellis v. Ohio,* 378 U.S. 184, 191 (1963); *Roth v. United States,* 354 U.S. 476 (1956). However, we believe that the statutory term, "indecent," should be applicable, and that, in the broadcast field, the standard for its *applicability* should be that the material broadcast is (a) patently offensive by contemporary community standards; and (b) is utterly without redeeming social value. The Court has made clear that different rules are appropriate for different media of expression in view of their varying natures. We have set forth [above], the reasons for applicability of the above standard in defining what is indecent in the broadcast field. We think that the factors set out [above] are cogent, powerful considerations for the different standard in this markedly different field.

The licensee argues that the program was not indecent, because its basic subject matters "are obviously decent"; "the challenged language though not essential to the meaning of the pro-

gram as a whole, reflected the personality and life style of Mr. Garcia"; and "the realistic portrayal of such an interview cannot be deemed 'indecent' because the subject incidentally used strong or salty language." We disagree with this approach in the broadcast field.

The licensee itself notes that the language in question "was not essential to the presentation of the subject matter" but rather was "essentially gratuitous." We think that is the precise point here—namely, that the language is "gratuitous"—i.e., "unwarranted or [having] no reason for its existence." There is no valid basis in these circumstances for permitting its widespread use in the broadcast field, with the detrimental consequences described [above].

The matter could also be approached under the public interest standard of the Communications Act. The standard for such action under the public interest criterion is the same as previously discussed—namely, that the material is patently offensive by contemporary community standards and utterly without redeeming social value.

In sum, we hold that we have the authority to act here under Section 1464 (i.e., 503(b)(1)(E)), or under the public interest standard (Section 503(b)(1)(A)(B))—for failure to operate in the public interest as set forth in the license or to observe the requirement of Section 315(a) to operate in the public interest.

However, whether under Section 1464 or the public interest standard, the criteria for commission action thus remains the same, in our view—namely, that the material be patently offensive and utterly without redeeming value. We believe that the presentation of the Garcia material quoted [above] falls clearly within the two above criteria, and hence may be the subject of a forfeiture under Section 503(b)(1)(A)(B) and (E). We further find that the presentation was "willful" (503(b)(1)(A)(B)). We note that the material was taped. Further the station employees could have cautioned Mr. Garcia either at the outset or after the first few expressions to avoid using the "gratuitous" expressions; they did not do so. That the material was presented without obtaining the station manager's approval—contrary to station policy—does not absolve the licensee of responsibility. Indeed, in light of the facts here, there would appear to have been gross negligence on the part of the licensee with respect to its supervisory duties.

[T]he issue in this case whether to impose a forfeiture (since one of the reasons for the forfeiture provision is that it can be imposed for the isolated occurrence, such as an isolated lottery, etc.). On this issue, we note that, in view of the fact that this is largely a case of first impression, particularly as to the Section 1464 aspect, we could appropriately forego the forfeiture and simply act prospectively in this field.

However, were we to do so, we would prevent any review of our action and in this sensitive field we have always sought to insure such reviewability. Thus, while we think that our action is fully consistent with the law, there should clearly be the avenue of court review in a case of this nature (see Section 504(a)).

In view of the foregoing, we determine that, pursuant to Section 503(b)(1)(A), (B), (E) of the Communications Act of 1934, as amended, Eastern Education Radio has incurred an apparent liability of one hundred dollars ($100).

COMMENT

Did the FCC choose "indecency" as the actionable term precisely because it had not received a detailed and limiting construction by the courts but "obscenity" had? Did the FCC think that making "indecency" the key term would give itself more room to deal with the different kinds of obscenity problems presented by the broadcast media as compared with the print media?

The FCC's definition of indecency omits any necessity to make a finding that the "dominant theme of the material taken as a whole appeals to a prurient interest in sex." Obviously, if a case of indecency is made out by pointing out that a broadcast used a "verboten" word, the "dominant theme" requirement must be dropped.

But the function of *Roth*'s "dominant theme" requirement was to give maximum protection to expression, to prevent one objectionable word or a few words from being used to ban an entire book, play, or movie. Is there any reason why the most susceptible member of the audience and the single offensive word should be the touchstone of indecency when for the print media the "average reader" and "dominant theme" requirements suffice?

The *WUHY* decision was immediately the object of substantial criticism. The criticism focused on several points. The FCC regarded broadcasting as "different" than other media. In *WUHY* it said that content could be judged by deciding whether it was "patently offensive according to contemporary community standards *for the broadcast media*." The U.S. Supreme Court had never judged these issues in such a media-specific fashion. Was it permissible for the FCC to do this in defining broadcast indecency?

The FCC took a nominalistic approach to defining indecency. What bothered the FCC most were Garcia's "gratuitous expletives," especially since they were on tape and could have been deleted before broadcast. This seemed to run counter to the U.S. Supreme Court's approach to obscenity where works (and their words) were considered "as a whole" and with regard to their "dominant theme."

Some were concerned that the FCC had deleted from the obscenity definition the notion of an appeal to a prurient interest in sex. While Garcia's words were sexual in nature, in context they were unlikely to excite prurient interests. To the FCC, that didn't matter. The words were "gratuitous" and ought not have been aired.

Finally, note that the FCC's approach reflects a particular concern for possible effects of the broadcast on children. According to the U.S. Supreme Court, obscenity was to be decided with reference to the standards of "the average person," by which the Court usually meant adults. The FCC, however, seemed particularly anxious to prevent harm to children. Would the courts allow that?

Resolution of these matters did not come immediately. Although the FCC plainly invited the licensee to take it to court, WUHY-FM elected, instead, to pay its nominal $100 fine. Sonderling Broadcasting later did the same with its $2,000 fine. Not until 1975 did the FCC find a broadcaster willing to pursue obscenity or indecency litigation in the courts. The result, in 1978, was a U.S. Supreme Court decision, *FCC v. Pacifica Foundation*, text, p. 606, that clarified somewhat many of the issues *WUHY* left dangling. Like *WUHY*, *Pacifica* was an indecency, not an obscenity, case. Because the U.S. Supreme Court had replaced the *Roth-Memoirs* obscenity definition with the so-called *Miller* test in 1973, the FCC, in dealing with a 1975 complaint about Pacifica Foundation's WBAI-FM (New York), had to fashion a new definition of broadcast indecency.

In *WUHY-FM* the FCC decided that the reference to "indecent" utterance in 18 U.S.C. § 1464 permitted the FCC to expand its regulatory authority to prohibit programming that was allegedly patently offensive but did not otherwise meet the constitutional test for obscenity. Such a policy clearly ran a risk of judicial reversal because escaping the rigors of the constitutional definition of obscenity appeared to be the whole point of including a separate and distinct meaning in the reference to "indecent" utterance in 18 U.S.C. § 1464.

In the 1978 Supreme Court decision in *Pacifica Foundation,* the FCC's gamble in trying to create a new category of prohibited programming on broadcasting—"indecent" programming—succeeded. In a decision that surprised broadcasters and disappointed civil libertarians, the Supreme Court agreed that the FCC's authority to regulate "indecent" programming was not limited by the constitutional requirements associated with its authority to regulate "obscene" programming. In the *Pacifica* case, the Supreme Court specifically cited *WUHY-FM* along with other FCC cases for the point that the FCC "has long interpreted § 1464 as encompassing more than the obscene."

The Supreme Court's *Pacifica* decision won immediate praise from those concerned about moral issues in broadcasting and brought immediate concerns to broadcasters. At first, the FCC sought to assure broadcasters that it did not intend to exercise the potentially broad supervisory power over content that *Pacifica* could be read to provide. When it was alleged that WGBH–TV in Boston had broadcast offensive and vulgar material harmful to children, the FCC dismissed the petition to deny the station's application for license renewal. The FCC granted WBGH's petition for license renewal:

> *Pacifica* affords [the FCC] no general prerogative to intervene in any case where words similar or identical to those in *Pacifica* are broadcast over a licensed radio or television station. We intend strictly to observe the narrowness of the *Pacifica* holding. In this regard, the FCC's opinion, as approved by the Court, relied in part on the repetitive occurrence of the "indecent" words in question.

On April 29, 1987, however, this state of affairs changed when the FCC issued four decisions that suddenly indicated a substantial renewed interest in indecency. The FCC stated that it would no longer focus on *just* the "seven dirty words" and that it was abandoning its policy of acting only when it found repetitious use of those words. Instead, the FCC returned to the generic definition of broadcast indecency and said that action was likely whenever broadcasts depicted or described sexual or excretory activities or organs in a patently offensive fashion for the broadcast media at a time of day when children were likely to be in the audience. It even expressed reservations about some earlier FCC cases suggesting that broadcasters could assume that children were not in the audience between 10:00 P.M. and 6:00 A.M.—that that period was a kind of "safe harbor." See, generally, *New Indecency Enforcement Standards to Be Applied to All Broadcast and Amateur Radio Licensees,* 62 R.R.2d 1218 (1987).

FCC Regulation of Indecent Programming: The Channeling Approach

In *Pacifica*, the Supreme Court gave approval to channeling. A program that might not be appropriate for listening or viewing at 1:00 P.M. might be entirely appropriate at 1:00 A.M. Notwithstanding sporadic efforts at total bans of indecency on broadcasting, the idea that indecent programming can be channeled consistently with the First Amendment has shaped the course of regulation of indecency programming by Congress and the FCC.

This new "get tough" policy of the FCC was appealed to the U.S. Court of Appeals for the D.C. Circuit. For the most part, the new policy was upheld. Judge Ruth Bader Ginsburg held for the court of appeals that the FCC could use its "generic" definition of broadcast indecency. Broadcasters would have to do their best to apply it. The FCC might need to do some fine-tuning to justify a particular "safe harbor," but the court of appeals seemed to welcome the channeling concept, if only the FCC could justify it better. *Action for Children's Television v. FCC,* 852 F.2d 1332 (D.C. Cir. 1988) [*ACT I*]. The FCC began to gather the information it needed to defend some specific time period.

But in 1988, Congress entered the broadcast indecency scene and directed the FCC to enforce its indecency standard around the clock—twenty-four hours a day. Public Law 100-549. Because the congressional mandate eliminated the need to define and justify a new safe harbor, the FCC abandoned that effort. On December 21, 1988, the FCC adopted an order implementing the new total ban. A coalition of broadcasting and public interest groups challenged the total ban. In *Action for Children's Television v. FCC*, 932 F.2d 1504 (D.C. Cir. 1991) [*ACT II*], the court of appeals held that the FCC total ban order, enacted pursuant to congressional directive, violated the First Amendment. The D.C. Circuit in *ACT II* remanded the case to the FCC with instructions on how to construct a new and valid safe harbor. But Congress once again intervened by enacting a statute setting forth its own idea of an appropriate safe harbor. The validity of that statute was considered by the D.C. Circuit in *ACT III*, the case reported below.

As *ACT III* demonstrates, notwithstanding sporadic efforts at total bans of indecency on broadcasting, the idea that indecency programming can be channeled consistently with the First Amendment has shaped the course of regulation of indecency programming by Congress and the FCC.

Action for Children's Television v. FCC
58 F.3D 654 (D.C. CIR. 1995).

Harry T. EDWARDS, Chief Judge, dissented and filed an opinion. WALD, Circuit Judge, dissented and filed an opinion in which ROGERS and TATEL, Circuit Judges, joined.

BUCKLEY, Circuit Judge:

We are asked to determine the constitutionality of section 16(a) of the Public Telecommunications Act of 1992, which seeks to shield minors from indecent radio and television programs by restricting the hours within which they may be broadcast. Section 16(a) provides that, with one exception, indecent materials may only be broadcast between the hours of midnight and 6:00 A.M. The exception permits public radio and television stations that go off the air at or before midnight to broadcast such materials after 10:00 P.M.

We find that the Government has a compelling interest in protecting children under the age of 18 from exposure to indecent broadcasts. We are also satisfied that, standing alone, the "channel-ing" of indecent broadcasts to the hours between midnight and 6:00 A.M. would not unduly burden the First Amendment. Because the distinction drawn by Congress between the two categories of broadcasters bears no apparent relationship to the compelling Government interests that section 16(a) is intended to serve, however, we find the more restrictive limitation unconstitutional. Accordingly, we grant the petitions for review and remand the cases to the Federal Communications Commission with instructions to revise its regulations to permit the broadcasting of indecent material between the hours of 10:00 P.M. and 6:00 A.M.

While obscene speech is not accorded constitutional protection, "[s]exual expression which is indecent but not obscene is protected by the First Amendment." *Sable Communications of California, Inc. v. FCC*, 492 U.S. 115 (1989). Noting that broadcasting has received the most limited First Amendment protection because of its unique pervasiveness and accessibility to children, the Supreme Court has held that the FCC may, in appropriate circumstances, place restrictions on the broadcast of indecent speech. *FCC v. Pacifica Foundation.*

We reviewed the 24-hour ban in *Action for Children's Television v. FCC*, 932 F.2d 1504 (D.C. Cir. 1991) ("*ACT II* "). We again rejected petitioners' vagueness and overbreadth arguments, but we struck down the total ban on indecent broadcasts because "[o]ur previous holding in *ACT I* that the Commission must identify some reasonable period of time during which indecent material may be broadcast necessarily means that the FCC may not ban such broadcasts entirely."

Shortly after the Supreme Court denied certiorari in *ACT II*, 503 U.S. 913, Congress again intervened, passing the Public Telecommunications Act of 1992, Pub. L. No. 102-356, 106 Stat. 949 (1992). Section 16(a) of the Act requires the FCC to promulgate regulations to prohibit the broadcasting of indecent programming—(1) between 6 A.M. and 10 P.M. on any day by any public radio station or public television station that goes off the air at or before 12 midnight; and (2) between 6 A.M. and 12 midnight on any day for any radio or television broadcasting station not described in paragraph (1). 47 U.S.C. § 303 note (Supp. IV 1992). Pursuant to this congressional mandate, the Commission published a notice of proposed rulemaking, and, in 1993, it issued regulations implementing section 16(a). These are challenged in the petition now before us.

Petitioners present three challenges to the constitutionality of section 16(a) and its implementing regulations: First, the statute and regulations violate the First Amendment because they impose restrictions on indecent broadcasts that are not narrowly tailored to further the Government's interest, which petitioners define as the promotion of parental authority by shielding unsupervised children from indecent speech in the broadcast media; second, section 16(a) unconstitutionally discriminates among categories of broadcasters by distinguishing the times during which certain public and commercial broadcasters may air indecent material; and third, the Commission's generic definition of indecency is unconstitutionally vague. Petitioners also assert that our decisions in *ACT I* and *ACT II* compel the rejection of the newly enacted restrictions both because there are insufficient data to justify the new statutory ban and because the Commission continues to include children ages 12 to 17 in the protected class.

The FCC argues that the Government's interests extend beyond facilitating parental supervision to include protecting children from exposure to indecent broadcasts and safeguarding the home from unwanted intrusion by such broadcasts. The FCC asserts that restricting indecent broadcasts to the hours between midnight and 6:00 A.M. is narrowly tailored to achieve these compelling governmental interests. It defends the exception allowing public stations that go off the air at or before midnight to broadcast such materials after 10:00 P.M. on the basis that these stations would otherwise have no opportunity to air indecent programs.

It is common ground that "[s]exual expression which is indecent but not obscene is protected by the First Amendment." *Sable.* The Government may, however, regulate the content of constitutionally protected speech in order to promote a compelling interest if it chooses the least restrictive means to further the articulated interest. Thus, a restriction on indecent speech will survive First Amendment scrutiny if the "Government's ends are compelling [and its] means [are] carefully tailored to achieve those ends."

Unlike cable subscribers, who are offered such options as "pay-per-view" channels, broadcast audiences have no choice but to "subscribe" to the entire output of traditional broadcasters. Thus they are confronted without warning with offensive material. See *Pacifica,* 438 U.S. at 748–49. This is "manifestly different from a situation" where a recipient "seeks and is willing to pay for the communication. . . ." *Sable;* see also *Cruz v. Ferre,* 755 F.2d 1415, 1420 (11th Cir. 1985) (distinguishing *Pacifica* from cases in which cable subscriber affirmatively elects to have specific cable service come into home).

In light of these differences, radio and television broadcasts may properly be subject to different—and often more restrictive—regulation than is permissible for other media under the First Amendment. While we apply strict scrutiny to regulations of this kind regardless of the medium affected by them, our assessment of whether section 16(a) survives that scrutiny must necessarily take into account the unique context of the broadcast medium. In examining the Government's interests in protecting children from broadcast indecency, it is important to understand that hard-core pornography may be deemed indecent rather than obscene if it is "not patently offensive" under the relevant contemporary community standards.

The FCC identifies three compelling Government interests as justifying the regulation of broadcast indecency: support for parental supervision of children, a concern for children's well-being, and the protection of the home against intrusion by offensive broadcasts. Because we find the first two sufficient to support such regulation, we will not address the third. Petitioners do not contest that the Government has a compelling interest in supporting parental supervision of what children see and hear on the public airwaves. This interest includes "supporting parents' claim to authority in their own household" through "regulation of otherwise protected expression." *Pacifica.*

Although petitioners disagree, Government's own interest in the well-being of minors provides an independent justification for the regulation of broadcast indecency. *New York v. Ferber,* 458 U.S. 747, 756-57 (1982). While conceding that the Government has an interest in the well-being of children, petitioners argue that because "no causal nexus has been established between broadcast indecency and any physical or psychological harm to minors," that interest is "too insubstantial to justify suppressing indecent material at times when parents are available to supervise their children." That statement begs two questions: The first is how effective parental supervision can actually be expected to be even when parent and child are under the same roof; the second, whether the Government's interest in the well-being of our youth is limited to protecting them from clinically measurable injury.

[A] recent poll conducted by Fairbank, Maslin, Maulin & Associates on behalf of Children Now [found] that 54% of the 750 children questioned had a television set in their own rooms and that 55% of them usually watched TV alone or with their friends, but not with their families. With respect to the second question begged by petitioners, the Supreme Court has never suggested that a scientific demonstration of psychological harm is required in order to establish the constitutionality of measures protecting minors from exposure to indecent speech.

We are not unaware that the vast majority of States impose restrictions on the access of minors to material that is not obscene by adult standards. In light of Supreme Court precedent and the social consensus reflected in state laws, we conclude that the Government has an independent and compelling interest in preventing minors from being exposed to indecent broadcasts. See *Sable*, 492 U.S. at 126 (Government's compelling interest in well-being of minors extends "to shielding [them] from the influence of literature that is not obscene by adult standards").

Today parents who wish to expose their children to the most graphic depictions of sexual acts will have no difficulty in doing so through the use of subscription and pay-per-view cable channels, delayed-access viewing using VCR equipment, and the rental or purchase of readily available audio and video cassettes. Thus the goal of supporting "parents' claim to authority in their own household to direct the rearing of their children," is fully consistent with the Government's own interest in shielding minors from being exposed to indecent speech by persons other than a parent. Society "may prevent the general dissemination of such speech to children, leaving to parents the decision as to what speech of this kind their children shall hear and repeat." *Pacifica* (Powell, J., concurring in part and concurring in the judgment).

The Government's dual interests in assisting parents and protecting minors necessarily extends beyond merely channeling broadcast indecency to those hours when parents can be at home to supervise what their children see and hear. It is fanciful to believe that the vast majority of parents who wish to shield their children from indecent material can effectively do so without meaningful restrictions on the airing of broadcast indecency.

Least Restrictive Means

The Government may regulate the content of constitutionally protected speech in order to promote a compelling interest if it chooses the least restrictive means to further the articulated interest. . . . [B]ut to withstand constitutional scrutiny, it must do so by narrowly drawn regulations designed to serve those interests without unnecessarily interfering with First Amendment freedoms. *Sable*. Petitioners argue that section 16(a) is not narrowly drawn to further the Government's interest in protecting children from broadcast indecency for two reasons: First, they assert that the class to be protected should be limited to children under the age of 12; and second, they contend that the "safe harbor" is not narrowly tailored because it fails to take proper account of the First Amendment rights of adults and because of the chilling effect of the 6:00 A.M. to midnight ban on the programs aired during the evening "prime time" hours. We address these arguments in turn.

Definition of "Children"

[I]n its 1990 Report, the FCC defined "children" to include "children ages 17 and under." 5 F.C.C.R. at 5301. The agency offered three reasons in support of its definition: Other federal statutes designed to protect children from indecent speech use the same standard (citing 47 U.S.C. § 223(b)(3) (Supp. II 1990) (forbidding indecent telephone communications to persons under 18); most States have laws penalizing persons who disseminate sexually explicit materials to children ages 17 and under; and several Supreme Court decisions have sustained the constitutionality of statutes protecting children ages 17 and under (citing *Sable*, *Ginsberg*, and *Bethel School District*). We find these reasons persuasive.

In light of Supreme Court precedent and the broad national consensus that children under the age of 18 need to be protected from exposure to sexually explicit materials, the FCC was fully justified in concluding that the Government interest extends to minors of all ages.

The Midnight to 6:00 A.M. "Safe Harbor"

Although we will require the FCC to allow the broadcast of indecent material between 10:00 P.M. and 6:00 A.M., we will address the propriety of section 16(a)'s midnight to 6:00 A.M. safe harbor. We do so for two reasons: First, in addressing the "narrowly tailored" issue, the parties have focused their arguments on the evidence offered by the FCC in support of the section's 6:00 A.M. to midnight ban on indecent programming. Second, the principles we bring to bear in our analysis of the midnight to 6:00 A.M. safe harbor apply with equal force to the more lenient one that the FCC must adopt as a result of today's opinion. Although fewer children will be protected by the expanded safe harbor, that fact will not affect its constitutionality. If the 6:00 A.M. to midnight ban on indecent programming is permissible to protect minors who listen to the radio or view television as late as midnight, the reduction of the ban by two hours will remain narrowly tailored to serve this more modest goal.

In *Pacifica*, the Supreme Court found that it was constitutionally permissible for the Government to place restrictions on the broadcast of indecent speech in order to protect the well-being of our youth. We have since acknowledged that such restrictions may take the form of channeling provided "that the FCC ... identify some reasonable period of time during which indecent material may be broadcast. . . ." *ACT II*. The question, then, is what period will serve the compelling governmental interests without unduly infringing on the adult population's right to see and hear indecent material. We now review the Government's attempt to strike that balance.

The data on broadcasting that the FCC has collected reveal that large numbers of children view television or listen to the radio from the early morning until late in the evening, that those numbers decline rapidly as midnight approaches, and that a substantial portion of the adult audience is tuned into television or radio broadcasts after midnight. We find this information sufficient

to support the safe harbor parameters that Congress has drawn.

It is apparent, then, that of the approximately 20.2 million teenagers and 36.3 million children under 12 in the United States, see *1989 NOI*, 4 F.C.C.R. at 8366, n.33; Nielsen Television Index National TV Ratings February 24–March 1, 1992 127, a significant percentage watch broadcast television or listen to radio from as early as 6:00 A.M. to as late as 11:30 P.M.; and in the case of teenagers, even later. We conclude that there is a reasonable risk that large numbers of children would be exposed to any indecent material broadcast between 6:00 A.M. and midnight.

The remaining question, then, is whether Congress, in enacting section 16(a), and the FCC, in promulgating the regulations, have taken into account the First Amendment rights of the very large numbers of adults who wish to view or listen to indecent broadcasts. We believe they have.

While the numbers of adults watching television and listening to radio after midnight are admittedly small, they are not insignificant. Furthermore, as we have noted above, adults have alternative means of satisfying their interest in indecent material at other hours in ways that pose no risk to minors. We therefore believe that a midnight to 6:00 A.M. safe harbor takes adequate account of adults' First Amendment rights.

Petitioners argue, nevertheless, that delaying the safe harbor until midnight will have a chilling effect on the airing of programs during the evening "prime time" hours that are of special interest to adults. They cite, as examples, news and documentary programs and dramas that deal with such sensitive contemporary problems as sexual harassment and the AIDS epidemic and assert that a broadcaster might choose to refrain from presenting relevant material rather than risk the consequences of being charged with airing broadcast indecency. Whatever chilling effects may be said to inhere in the regulation of indecent speech, these have existed ever since the Supreme Court first upheld the FCC's enforcement of section 1464 of the Radio Act. The enactment of section 16(a) does not add to such anxieties; to the contrary, the purpose of channeling, which we mandated in *ACT I* and reaffirmed in *ACT II*, 852 F.2d at 1343-44; 932 F.2d at 1509, and which Congress has now codified, is to provide a period in which radio and television stations may let down their hair without worrying whether they have stepped over any line other than that which separates protected speech from obscenity. Thus, section 16(a) has ameliorated rather than aggravated whatever chilling effect may be inherent in section 1464.

Petitioners also argue that section 16(a)'s midnight to 6:00 A.M. channeling provision is not narrowly tailored because, for example, Congress has failed to take into consideration the fact that it bans indecent broadcasts during school hours when children are presumably subject to strict adult supervision, thereby depriving adults from listening to such broadcasts during daytime hours when the risk of harm to minors is slight. [E]ven if such fine tuning were feasible, we do not believe that the First Amendment requires that degree of precision.

In this case, determining the parameters of a safe harbor involves a balancing of irreconcilable interests. It follows, then, that in a case of this kind, which involves restrictions in degree, there may be a range of safe harbors, each of which will satisfy the "narrowly tailored" requirement of the First Amendment. We are dealing with questions of judgment; and here, we defer to Congress's determination of where to draw the line.

Recognizing the Government's compelling interest in protecting children from indecent broadcasts, Congress channeled indecent broadcasts to the hours between midnight and 6:00 A.M. in the hope of minimizing children's exposure to such material. Given the substantially smaller number of children in the audience after midnight, we find that section 16(a) reduces children's exposure to broadcast indecency to a significant degree. We also find that this restriction does not unnecessarily interfere with the ability of adults to watch or listen to such materials both because substantial numbers of them are active after midnight and because adults have so many alternative ways of satisfying their tastes at other times. Although the restrictions burden the rights of many adults, it seems entirely appropriate that the marginal convenience of some adults be made to yield to the imperative needs of the young. We thus conclude that, standing alone, the midnight to 6:00 A.M. safe harbor is narrowly tailored to serve the Government's compelling interest in the well-being of our youth.

The Public Broadcaster Exception

Section 16(a) permits public stations that sign off the air at or before midnight to broadcast indecent material after 10:00 P.M. See 47 U.S.C. § 303 note. Petitioners argue that section 16(a) is unconstitutional because it allows the stations to present indecent material two hours earlier than all others.

Congress has provided no [satisfactory] explanation for the special treatment accorded these stations other than the following. Congress has made no suggestion that minors are less likely to be corrupted by sexually explicit material that is broadcast by a public as opposed to a commercial station. Whatever Congress's reasons for creating it, the preferential safe harbor [for public broadcasters] has the effect of undermining both the argument for prohibiting the broadcasting of indecent speech before that hour and the constitutional viability of the more restrictive safe harbor that appears to have been Congress's principal objective in enacting section 16(a).

Congress has failed to explain what, if any, relationship the disparate treatment accorded certain public stations bears to the compelling Government interest—or to any other legislative value—that Congress sought to advance when it enacted section 16(a). [T]he section is unconstitutional insofar as it bars the broadcasting of indecent speech between the hours of 10:00 p.m. and midnight.

The Constitution, however, permits restrictions on speech where necessary in order to serve a compelling public interest, provided that they are narrowly tailored. We hold that section 16(a) serves such an interest. But because Congress imposed different restrictions on each of two categories of broadcasters while failing to explain how this disparate treatment advanced its goal of protecting young minds from the corrupting influences of indecent speech, we must set aside the more restrictive one. Accordingly, we remand this case to the FCC with instructions to limit its ban on the broadcasting of indecent programs to the period from 6:00 a.m. to 10:00 p.m.

It is so ordered.

COMMENT

Section 16(a) was a direct response by Congress to earlier D.C. Circuit rulings that invalidated similar regulations initiated by the FCC without a congressional mandate, see *Action for Children's Television v. FCC,* 852 F.2d 1332 (D.C. Cir. 1988) [*ACT I*], and a subsequent ruling that invalidated a congressional ban on *all* indecent programming, *see Action for Children's Television v. FCC,* 932 F.2d 1504 (D.C. Cir. 1991) [*ACT II*]. Section 16(a) was Congress's attempt to test the borders of indecent speech regulation. By channeling indecent programming to certain hours of the day, Congress attempted to proscribe indecent speech without completely banning it. Despite the forceful dissents in *ACT III,* the Supreme Court declined to review the case. *Cert. denied, Pacifica Foundation v. FCC,* 116 S. Ct. 701 (1996). As a consequence, much broader channeling than that at issue in *Pacifica* was given a status that many broadcasters and communications lawyers thought unjustified under existing First Amendment law.

The *ACT III* court, professing to follow *Sable,* declared that the government may "regulate the content of constitutionally protected speech in order to promote a compelling interest if it chooses the least restrictive means to further the articulated interest." The court held that the government had a compelling interest in protecting children under the age of eighteen from exposure to indecent broadcasts. Against this interest the court had to balance the interests of adults who wanted to receive the indecent broadcasts, parents who might want their children to be able to view the broadcasts, and broadcasters that wanted to air the indecent programs. The court found that channeling indecent broadcasts to the hours between 10:00 P.M. and 6:00 A.M. would not unduly burden the First Amendment rights of broadcasters and adults.

The *ACT III* court did, however, invalidate the more restrictive ban on indecent programming between 6:00 A.M. and midnight, because the distinction drawn by Congress between public broadcasters and commercial broadcasters had no apparent relationship to the compelling interest of protecting children from indecent programming.

Judge Harry T. Edwards, dissenting, took particular aim at the *ACT III* majority's view that broadcasting received less First Amendment protection than other media:

> Because no reasonable basis can be found to distinguish broadcast from cable in terms of the First Amendment protection the two media should

receive, I would review section 16(a) and the Enforcement Order under the stricter level of scrutiny courts apply to content-based regulations of cable. This means "the most exacting scrutiny" should be applied "to regulations that suppress, disadvantage, or impose differential burdens upon speech because of its content." In *Sable,* the Court indicated that the "exacting scrutiny" test has two prongs: the Government's interests must be "compelling," and the method of regulation chosen must be "the least restrictive means" to achieve those compelling interests. That is the essence of the test, I think.

In this case, the majority views the broadcast media as disfavored in the application of First Amendment rights, relying principally on *Pacifica;* however, my colleagues nonetheless agree that section 16(a) reflects a content-based regulation that is subject to exacting scrutiny. Indeed, even the FCC viewed the case in this way. In my view, there is no way that section 16(a) can survive exacting scrutiny.

Because section 16(a) and the Enforcement Order ban indecent expression, they constitute content-based regulations, which have traditionally raised the red flag of exacting scrutiny. At issue in this case is whether the Government's interests are indeed compelling and whether it has chosen the least restrictive means to further its asserted compelling interests.

To withstand constitutional scrutiny, the Government's regulations must serve its interests "'without unnecessarily interfering with First Amendment freedoms.'" The First Amendment rights at stake here are those of broadcasters and the adult broadcasting audience. The Supreme Court finds laws insufficiently tailored when they deny adults their free speech rights by allowing them to read, watch, or hear only what was acceptable for children.

Judge Edwards found the government's compelling interest in "promoting the well-being of minors" to be in conflict with its compelling interest in "support[ing] parental supervision of children." Judge Edwards noted that "not every parent will decide, as the FCC has, that the best way to raise its child is to have the Government shield children under eighteen from indecent broadcasts." By taking away parents' ability to expose their children to "indecent" programs, the government infringes on their First Amendment rights. Judge Edwards noted that in the cable context, the D.C. Circuit stated that parents retained this control because they could elect to receive pay-per-view or subscribe to channels that aired indecent programs. In the broadcasting medium parents did not have alternatives to obtaining indecent programs.

In discussing the least restrictive means prong, Judge Edwards said the FCC presented no data that channeling was the least restrictive means. Indeed in oral argument, the FCC stated that blocking technology was emerging that would facilitate the government's interests.

Judge Wald also filed a dissent in which she advocated a review of the court's determination in *ACT I*, that the FCC's definition did not chill protected speech from being broadcast during the banned hours. Judge Wald noted that because the FCC insisted that indecency decisions be made on a case-by-case basis and "depend on a multi-faceted consideration of the context of allegedly indecent material," broadcasters refrain from airing programs that might be deemed indecent but actually are not. Judge Wald rejected the majority conclusion and said that there are less restrictive means of controlling indecency that would not have such a drastic effect on the First Amendment rights of broadcasters and adults:

> In constructing a safe harbor the government needs to give more careful consideration to those hours in the evening when parental control could reasonably be relied upon in lieu of censorship to protect children. It is only in this manner that the government can genuinely strike the delicate balance between adult freedoms of expression and society's interest in shielding children from indecency and a truly safe harbor can be crafted that "serve[s] the compelling governmental interests without unduly infringing on the adult population's right to see and hear indecent material."

Despite the majority's valiant effort to extract evidence for the government's position from the sparse record before us, the pickings are too slim for constitutional legitimacy. There is no evidence at all of psychological harm from exposure to indecent programs aired inside the current safe harbor. There is no evidence either that parents cannot supervise their children in those safe harbor hours or that "grazing" is leading to any significant viewing of indecency. Finally, the imminence of "V-chip" technology to enable parental control of all violence- and indecency-viewing suggests that a draconian ban from 6 A.M. to midnight is decidedly premature.

The *Sable* Case

Sable Communications, Inc. v. FCC, 492 U.S. 115 (1989), the so-called dial-a-porn case,

received a great deal of attention from the court of appeals in *ACT III*. In *Sable*, the Supreme Court, per Justice White, validated a federal law that placed an outright ban on obscene commercial telephone messages but invalidated a provision that totally banned indecent commercial telephone messages or dial-a-porn. The *Sable* Court pointed out that *Pacifica* did not authorize the total ban on indecency that the federal law imposed:

> *Pacifica* is readily distinguishable from this case most obviously because it did not involve a total ban on broadcasting indecent material. The FCC rule was not "intended to place an absolute prohibition on the broadcast of this type of language, but rather sought to channel it to times of day when children most likely would not be exposed to it."
>
> The private commercial telephone communications at issue here are substantially different from the public radio broadcast at issue in *Pacifica*. *Placing a telephone call is not the same as turning on a radio and being taken by surprise by an indecent message. Unlike an unexpected outburst on a radio broadcast, the message received by one who places a call to a dial-a-porn service is not so invasive or surprising that it prevents an unwilling listener from avoiding exposure to it.* [Emphasis added.]

Although they reach different conclusions on the validity of the federal law at issue in *ACT III* both Judge Buckley for the majority in *ACT III* and Judge Edwards in dissent cite *Sable* as authority for their positions. Why? Judge Buckley agrees that under *Sable* the indecency safe harbor for commercial broadcasters set forth in sec. 16(a) is a content control and should be evaluated by a strict scrutiny standard. However, Judge Buckley is much less rigorous in applying the strict scrutiny standard than Judge Edwards because the indecency control in *ACT III* occurs in the context of broadcasting. Judge Buckley says broadcasting receives "the most limited First Amendment protection." On this point, Judge Buckley declared:

> [R]adio and television broadcast may properly be subject to different—and often more restrictive— regulation than is permissible for other media under the First Amendment. While we apply strict scrutiny to regulations of this kind regardless of the medium affected by them, our assessment of whether section 16(a) survives that scrutiny must necessarily take into account the unique context of the broadcast medium.

But Judge Edwards, in dissent, says that a content-based control such as the channeling required by sec. 16(a) cannot meet *Sable*'s exacting strict scrutiny standard. Moreover, broadcasting should not be accorded a lesser First Amendment status than other media.

Reno v. ACLU: The Internet Case

In *Reno v. ACLU*, 25 Med. L. Rptr. 1833 (1997), two extremely broad provisions of the Communications Decency Act of 1996 designed to protect minors from indecent and patently offensive material on the Internet were struck down. The Court, per Justice Stevens, distinguished the Internet from broadcasting, held that the *Pacifica* case did not authorize the challenged provisions, and strongly relied on *Sable*:

> The Internet is not as "invasive" as radio or television. We distinguished *Pacifica* in *Sable* on just this basis. [U]nlike the conditions that prevailed when Congress first authorized regulation of the broadcast spectrum, the Internet can hardly be considered a "scarce" expressive commodity. [O]ur cases provide no basis for qualifying the level of First Amendment scrutiny that should be applied to this medium.

The Advent of the V-Chip

Judge Wald's comments in her dissent in *Act III* about the imminence of the V-chip were right on the mark. Section 551 of the Telecommunications Act of 1996, 47 U.S.C. §§ 303(w), 303(x), provides that starting in 1998 all new television sets with picture screens thirteen or more inches in width must "be equipped with a feature designed to enable viewers to block display of all programs with a common rating, except as otherwise permitted by regulations pursuant to section 330(c)(4)." An electronic signal would identify programs deemed objectionable under the ratings, and the viewer could then block such programming. Because the V-chip would give a parent control over the programming that would enter the home, V-chip technology could render channeling unnecessary.

Does the V-chip render the reasoning of *ACT III* obsolete? A consequence of the V-chip could be that so-called indecent programming could be presented at any hour because those averse to such programming could simply block it out. Is the latter a likely outcome if V-chip use becomes widespread?

The V-chip provisions of the Telecommunications Act did not require the video technology industry to develop ratings. In March 1996, however, broadcast and cable "voluntarily" agreed to develop an industry-wide rating system by the end of 1996. In December 1996, the industry announced such a rating system.

In December 1996, the press reported that the television industry was planning to introduce six rating categories that would ultimately be used in connection with V-chip technology. Children's programming would have two ratings: TV-K, suitable for all children, and TV-K7, suitable for children over age seven. Programming for general audiences would be classified under four headings: TV-G, for general audiences, programming suitable for all ages; TV-PG, "parental guidance suggested, infrequent coarse language, limited violence, some suggestive sexual dialogue"; TV-14, "parents strongly cautioned, strong language, more intense violence and sexual content"; TV-M, "mature audiences only, graphic violence, explicit sexual content." Paul Farhi, "TV Ratings to Have 6 Vague Levels," *Washington Post*, December 10, 1996, at A1, A3. Already, the proposed ratings have drawn fire. Ed Markey (D. Representative Mass.) charged that the categories were confusing and that most programming would be categorized as TV-PG, which he characterized as "Too Vague–Parents Give Up." *Id.*

The fact that the electronic media readily agreed to develop a rating system is hardly surprising. Under the 1996 Act, if the industry did not develop such a system, or if the FCC does not approve of the industry plan, the FCC is obliged to appoint an advisory committee to develop guidelines and recommendations for a rating system. The 1996 Act provides that the FCC must appoint the advisory committee if the voluntary plan "for rating video programming that contains sexual, violent, or other indecent material about which parents should be informed before it is displayed to children is not acceptable.

Interestingly enough, the Telecommunications Act does not mandate that the video programming industry adopt the FCC advisory committee's rating system. Although the 1996 Act does not indicate its specific electronic media addressees, it has been assumed that it applies "to all electronic video distribution technologies—including broadcasting, cable, DBS and telcos—although the legislative history discusses only broadcasters and traditional cable systems." See generally, Richard E. Wiley, *The Telecommunications Act of 1996*, ed. James. C. Goodale, Communication Law 55–57 (PLI 1996).

On July 11, 1997, Vice President Al Gore praised both the networks and family advocacy groups for reading an agreement on July 9, 1997, for a more detailed rating system to supplement the age-group categories discussed previously. These categories had been criticized as providing insuffient information to parents. Under the system agreed to in July, television shows will carry both an age group rating and a letter rating system as follows:

V   Violent Content
S   Sexual Content
L   Coarse Language
D   Suggestive Dialogue

Furthermore, children's shows that contain combat-style violence will have an FV rating. FV equals Fantasy Violence. *New York Times*, Friday, July 11, 1997, p. A15.

Is the FCC's Forfeiture System for Indecency Violations Valid under the First Amendment? The *ACT IV* Case

In *Action for Children's Television v. FCC*, 59 F.3d 1249 (D.C. Cir. 1995) [*ACT IV*], the D.C. Circuit addressed a First Amendment challenge to the entire process by which the FCC imposes forfeitures for the broadcast of indecent materials. The challenge in *ACT IV* was brought by broadcasters and public interest groups who claimed that the delays in securing decisions in FCC proceedings and the lack of timely judicial review of those decisions inhibited and infringed their free speech rights. ACT (Action for Children's Television) contended that because the FCC procedures took so long to complete, the effect was that broadcasters conformed to FCC indecency standards even though they believed those standards violated the First Amendment. Nevertheless, the court, per Judge Ruth Bader Ginsburg, held that the FCC's procedures did not violate the First Amendment.

ACT IV, reported below, contains a valuable summary of the forfeiture procedure the FCC issues to enforce its indecency standards.

Action for Children's Television v. FCC
59 F.3D 1249 (D.C. CIR. 1995), *CERT. DENIED*, 116 S. Ct. 773 (1996).

GINSBURG, Circuit Judge:

Section 1464 of 18 U.S.C. provides: "Whoever utters any obscene, indecent, or profane language by means of radio communication shall be fined not more than $10,000 or imprisoned not more than two years, or both." In addition, the FCC may impose a civil forfeiture for each violation of the same statute. 47 U.S.C. § 503(b)(1)(D); see id. § 503(b)(2)(A) (maximum forfeiture penalty of $25,000 for each violation but not in excess of $250,000 for any continuing violation). The FCC's imposition of a penalty for the broadcast of indecent material—defined by the Commission as "patently offensive descriptions of sexual or excretory activities or organs as measured by contemporary community standards for the broadcast medium"—is not inconsistent with the first amendment. See *FCC v. Pacifica Foundation,* 438 U.S. 726 (1978).

Section 503(b) of the Communications Act of 1934 authorizes the FCC to impose a forfeiture for the violation of a FCC order or regulation. While these provisions govern all types of forfeitures, the appellants challenge them only insofar as they are used to impose forfeitures arising from the broadcast of allegedly indecent material. The FCC may take either of two routes to impose a forfeiture. First, the FCC may proceed against a broadcaster under 47 U.S.C. § 503(b)(3), which authorizes the FCC to determine the penalty after a hearing, subject to review in the court of appeals. 47 U.S.C. §§ 402(a), 503(b)(3)(A). If, once the forfeiture determination becomes final, the penalty is not paid, then the FCC may refer the matter to the Attorney General for collection in the appropriate district court. 47 U.S.C. § 503(b)(3)(B). In such a collection action, "the validity and appropriateness of the final order imposing the forfeiture penalty shall not be subject to review." *Id.* While the FCC has stipulated that it generally does not use the procedures of § 503(b)(3) in imposing forfeitures for broadcast indecency, it reserves the authority to do so whenever that would "better serve the ends of justice." 47 C.F.R. § 1.80(g). Although the appellants claim that these procedures "ensure neither prompt administrative adjudication nor prompt completion of judicial review," they do not seriously challenge their constitutionality. In any event, because the FCC does not use § 503(b)(3), we express no view upon the subject.

The alternative, and in practice the exclusive, means of imposing a forfeiture for the broadcast of indecent material is for the FCC to issue a "notice of apparent liability" to the broadcaster, setting forth the relevant facts and granting the potentially liable party "an opportunity to show, in writing, . . . why no such forfeiture penalty should be imposed." 47 U.S.C. § 503(b)(4). The FCC initiates the forfeiture process only after receiving a complaint from a listener or viewer. The agency staff reviews each complaint to determine whether it suggests that there has been a violation of the ban on indecent broadcasting. In the course of this review, the staff may send the broadcaster a Letter of Inquiry seeking more information or inviting the broadcaster to respond to the complaint. After further consideration, the FCC decides whether to issue a Notice of Apparent Liability (NAL). The stipulated facts in this case concerning the indecency cases pending when the complaint was filed in district court show that the Commission issues a NAL anywhere from six months to three years after the broadcast to which it relates. During that time, the broadcaster may or may not be aware that the agency is considering whether the broadcast at issue contained indecent material.

The NAL is both sent to the broadcaster and published in the FCC Record. The NAL advises the broadcaster of its "apparent liability for a forfeiture" in a stated amount for an "apparent violation of 18 U.S.C. § 1464," and gives the broadcaster 30 days to pay or otherwise to respond. Once the broadcaster has responded or the 30 days have run, the FCC decides whether to order the forfeiture. As far as we can discern from the current record, the FCC has never failed to impose a forfeiture after issuing a NAL.

The FCC's internal guidelines exhort the responsible officials "to initiate forfeiture orders expeditiously, generally within 60 days after issuance of [the NAL]." In the seven instances in which the FCC imposed a forfeiture between January 1987 and March 1993, it took from two to 23 months—and an average of approximately nine months—for the FCC to make its decision.

Generally the forfeiture order recapitulates the history of the case, addresses any arguments raised by the broadcaster in response to the NAL, and orders payment of the forfeiture within 30 days. As with any FCC order, the broadcaster may petition for reconsideration. If the order becomes final and the broadcaster does not pay the forfeiture, the FCC issues progressively stiffer dunning letters, and threatens to refer and after 165 days does indeed refer the matter to the Department of Justice "for commencement of [a] civil action to recover the forfeiture," in accordance with 47 U.S.C. § 504(a). In defending that suit the broadcaster is entitled to a trial de novo on the question whether its broadcast was indecent.

At the time the complaint in this case was filed, there were only three cases in which a broadcaster had held out long enough for the FCC to refer the matter to Justice, and the Department had actually filed only one case in district court. That case was settled after the court denied defense motions for partial judgment on the pleadings and for summary judgment. See *United States v. Evergreen Media Corp.,* 832 F. Supp. 1179 and 1183 (N.D. Ill. 1993). Thus, as far as we can discern, no broadcaster has yet gone to trial on the merits of an FCC indecency determination, as envisioned by the statute; every one has either paid the forfeiture imposed or is awaiting action by the Commission or the Department of Justice.

By all indications, a long wait promises to be the rule rather than the exception. The single forfeiture suit pending in district court as of March 1993 was filed two days before the five-year statute of limitations would have run, and was apparently close to disposition a little more than a year later. *Evergreen Media,* 832 F. Supp. 1179 and 1183. Based upon the shortest times reflected in the record, the earliest a broadcaster could hope to be brought into court is some two years after the offending broadcast.

This delay is unfortunate enough, but a number of other factors serve to exacerbate the effects of uncertainty about the outcome. First, a broadcaster claiming that a forfeiture is unconstitutional runs the risk of incurring an increased forfeiture for any subsequent indecency violation, see, e.g., *Letter to Mr. Mel Karmazin, President, Sagittarius Broadcasting Corporation,* 8 F.C.C. Rcd 2688, 2689 & n. 3 (December 18, 1992) (giving notice of intent to impose $600,000 forfeiture in light of "apparent pattern of indecent broadcasting"), and the possibility that the FCC will invoke the ultimate sanction, revocation of the broadcaster's license. See 47 U.S.C. §§ 307–309. Second, individual Commissioners have taken an active public role in criticizing broadcasters for airing indecent material and have let it be known that sanctions for such activity are likely to increase. Furthermore, the FCC will not, as a matter of policy, issue a declaratory ruling on whether a proposed broadcast is indecent. Thus, the only official guidance about the FCC's standards of decency available to a broadcaster is what can be gleaned from published NALs and forfeiture orders.

The appellants do not argue that the delay they face in getting a final decision under the FCC's procedures is in itself unconstitutional. Rather they claim that the delay allows the FCC to take action against them without affording them the procedural safeguards necessary to avoid any abridgment of their first amendment rights.

The appellants challenge the forfeiture scheme on both constitutional and statutory grounds. As to the former, they claim that by forcing broadcasters to comply with the FCC's unreviewed determinations of indecency the scheme operates as a system of "informal censorship" similar to the one held unconstitutional in *Bantam Books, Inc. v. Sullivan,* 372 U.S. 58 (1963). As to the latter, they argue that the FCC also forces broadcasters to comply with its (perhaps invalid) standards by taking unpaid and unreviewed forfeiture orders into account in assessing subsequent forfeitures, in violation of the antibootstrapping provision of the Act, 47 U.S.C. § 504(c). That section provides: In any case where the FCC issues a [NAL] looking toward the imposition of a forfeiture under this chapter, that fact shall not be used, in any other proceeding before the FCC, to the prejudice of the person to whom such notice was issued, unless (i) the forfeiture has been paid, or (ii) a court of competent jurisdiction has ordered payment of such forfeiture, and such order has become final.

[EDITORIAL NOTE: *Because the FCC has not had occasion to pass on this claim, the court of appeals felt it inappropriate for it to do so.*]

(1) Are the statutes that prescribe the procedures by which the Commission may impose a

forfeiture for the broadcast of indecent material capable of constitutional application? and (2) If so, then does the record show that the Commission is applying the statutes in a constitutional manner?

The Supreme Court has repeatedly emphasized that: A facial challenge to a legislative Act is, of course, the most difficult challenge to mount successfully, since the challenger must establish that no set of circumstances exists under which the [Act] would be valid. The fact that [the regulations] might operate unconstitutionally under some conceivable set of circumstances is insufficient to render [them] wholly invalid. *Rust v. Sullivan,* 500 U.S. 173, 183 (1991). With this teaching in mind, we readily reject the appellants' claim insofar as they are arguing that the statutory enforcement scheme is incapable of constitutional application with regard to indecency violations. Prompt and efficient enforcement by the FCC could surely expedite the administrative process to an extent that leaves ample breathing space for first amendment rights.

Certainly nothing in the statutes or regulations prevents the FCC from issuing a NAL, imposing a forfeiture, and if need be referring a case to the Department of Justice all within a period of time short enough virtually to eliminate any concern with delay. The whole course could probably be run in most cases within, say, 90 days. No case of this type is very complex; each turns simply upon whether a certain broadcast was indecent. Indeed, under the Commission's own internal guidelines, after a broadcaster has had 30 days to respond to the NAL, the target for imposing a forfeiture is only 60 more days. If the FCC met this goal and then allowed the broadcaster to stipulate that it will not pay unless ordered by a district court to do so, then judicial review could begin almost immediately. In practice, no case has moved through the pipeline that quickly, but we are aware of no reason why the Commission could not, in principle, act with such dispatch. Reducing delay would also cabin the Commission's opportunity to rely upon its own unreviewed forfeiture decisions in setting standards of decency, thereby reducing the tendency for one unconstitutional decision to beget others.

In short, the FCC's indecency-enforcement scheme is clearly capable of constitutional application. Indeed, were the administration of this scheme merely expedited it would be indistinguishable, relative to the first amendment concern, from the undoubtedly constitutional process whereby the Government may bring a criminal action in district court for a violation of 18 U.S.C. § 1464.

The more difficult question is whether the statutes as applied pass muster under the teaching *Bantam Books v. Sullivan,* 372 U.S. 58 (1963). We agree with the appellants that some of the FCC's procedures are troubling but, on the basis of the record before us, we cannot agree that those procedures violate the first amendment. The centerpiece of the appellants' grievance is that: [B]ecause of the delays of securing administrative and judicial determinations in indecency forfeiture proceedings, and uncertainties as to the permissible scope of FCC indecency regulation they attempt to conform their conduct to the indecency standards articulated by the FCC and its Commissioners, whether or not they believe those standards are constitutional. That simply does not establish a violation of the Constitution.

In *Bantam Books,* Rhode Island had established a Commission to Encourage Morality in Youth and authorized it to determine whether publications were "objectionable for sale, distribution or display to youths." 372 U.S. at 61. Upon an affirmative finding, the Morality Commission would send a letter urging the distributor of the offending material not to carry the publication, and would refer the matter to the local police for investigation and possible prosecution under the state obscenity law. The Supreme Court struck down this scheme because it "amount[s] to . . . governmental censorship devoid of the constitutionally required safeguards for state regulation of obscenity, and thus abridge[s] First Amendment liberties."

The lesson of *Bantam Books* is that the state may not move to suppress speech by means of a scheme that, as a practical matter, forecloses the speaker from obtaining a judicial determination of whether the targeted speech is unprotected, lest the state be able effectively to suppress protected speech.

The appellants argue that the FCC has similarly implemented a system of "prior administrative restraint" that, for want of appropriate procedural safeguards, forces protected and unprotected material alike off the air. See, e.g.,

Freedman v. Maryland, 380 U.S. 51 (1965) (striking down motion-picture censorship scheme for lack of such safeguards). Unlike the state in *Freedman,* however, the FCC is not administering anything akin to a literal prior restraint. Broadcasters are free to air what they want; if and only if what they air turns out to transgress established guidelines do they face a penalty—but that is very much after the fact, not prior thereto. The FCC's ability to penalize a broadcaster in this manner was upheld by the Supreme Court in *Pacifica,* where the Court specifically rejected the argument that the agency's enforcement of the ban on indecency violates the statutory prohibition of censorship by the FCC.

We cannot help but conclude that the appellants have failed to establish any essential similarity between this case and *Bantam Books.* Unlike the Rhode Island Commission, which sought to regulate materials that could not be proscribed as obscene, so far as this record shows the FCC is not enforcing the statutory ban on indecency against material that is not indecent. [W]e have no indication that the FCC has done anything actively to discourage judicial review of any indecency forfeiture it imposed. That no case has yet progressed to judicial review may be the effect of any of several inoffensive causes: the FCC has only recently stepped up its enforcement efforts; the violators penalized thus far may very well have broadcast the indecency as charged and thus seen no point in contesting the forfeiture in court; and broadcasters may be self-censoring only indecent material, eliminating the need for many prosecutions. Indeed, some degree of self-censorship is inevitable and not necessarily undesirable so long as proper standards are available.

Finally, there is no indication that the FCC has failed or will fail to follow judicial guidelines for determining what is indecent and what is not, as they have developed and will develop in judicial decisions. While the prospect of a forfeiture trial may understandably cause some broadcasters to forego judicial review of an FCC determination that a program was indecent, we find no indication in this record that the FCC is taking the opportunity afforded thereby to impose unconstitutional restrictions upon broadcast speech.

The allegation that the FCC is chilling protected speech by means of the forfeiture scheme is not nearly as compelling as was the corresponding claim in *Bantam Books*. There is no indication in the case law that such a scheme is unconstitutional absent some showing that the agency is forcing off the air material that is not indecent.

The judgment of the district court is affirmed.

HARRY T. EDWARDS, Chief Judge, concurring with reservations.

COMMENT

Judge Tatel, dissenting, noted that if broadcasters did not comply with the FCC's unreviewed decisions, the FCC threatened to increase fines, revoke licenses, and prevent acquisition of additional stations. These FCC threats, he charged, were a greater danger to the First Amendment freedom of broadcasters than the regulations overruled in *Bantam Books, Inc. v. Sullivan*, 372 U.S. 58 (1963). Why were these First Amend-

ment considerations so unpersuasive to the majority? Was it because the parties who were subjected to forfeitures under the process described in this case could have obtained judicial review but declined to do so?

A fundamental problem is that the D.C. Circuit's opinion in *ACT IV* does not give enough weight to the fact that the administrative agency that issues forfeitures to broadcast licensees is also the agency that decides whether those licensees will be renewed. Once again, as it had done in *ACT III*, the Supreme Court declined to review an important aspect of broadcast indecency regulation. This time, in *ACT IV*, it was the decision of the court of appeals sustaining the FCC's forfeiture procedures. *Cert. denied, ACT v. FCC*, 116 S. Ct. 773 (1996). By default, regulation of indecency apparently was going to be left to the First Amendment sensitivities of the Congress and the FCC.

REGULATORY AND FIRST AMENDMENT ISSUES IN CABLE TELEVISION

CHAPTER OUTLINE

A BRIEF HISTORY OF CABLE TELEVISION

Cable television is not as recent a development as it sometimes seems. The industry began in 1948 when appliance store owners, anxious to demonstrate television but unable to do so because of weak signals, erected large antennas connected to an amplification and distribution system. Early cable systems grew in communities with weak broadcast reception, either because of natural conditions (such as shading by mountains) or because the communities were at the fringes of the service areas of early television broadcasters. Known as Community Antenna Television

Systems (CATVs), they consisted of large antenna systems that fed into a coaxial cable–based distribution system. The primary purpose was to improve a community's reception of over-the-air TV programs, that were available but hard to receive.

As long as that was all early CATV systems did, they attracted little legal or policy interest. The FCC, in fact, early on disclaimed any interest in regulating such systems. See *CATV and TV Repeater Services,* 26 F.C.C. 403 (1959). Broadcasters liked the new medium because it added to their audiences. Only later, when cable began to offer competing services, did the broadcasting industry become concerned. Once agitated, broadcasters manipulated the policymaking system into several years of regulatory suppression of cable television growth. The FCC changed its mind about its regulatory authority. See *Carter Mountain Transmission Corp.,* 32 F.C.C. 459 (1962), *aff'd, Carter Mountain Transmission Corp. v. FCC,* 321 F.2d 359 (D.C. Cir. 1963) and *First Report and Order in Docket Nos. 14895 and 15233,* 38 F.C.C. 683 (1965). Complex regulations adopted in 1966, in effect, "froze" the growth of the cable industry by making it practically impossible to import "distant" (out-of-market) TV stations into cabled communities. While effectively prohibiting distant-signal importation, the rules required cable systems to carry all local TV signals and protected local stations against duplication of their programming by non-local stations. See *Second Report on CATV Regulation,* 2 F.C.C. 2d 725 (1966).

The U.S. Supreme Court eventually upheld the FCC's claimed authority to regulate cable. In *United States v. Southwestern Cable Co.,* 392 U.S. 157 (1968), the Court accepted the arguments of the broadcasting industry and the FCC that cable's impact on broadcasting justified its regulation. The Court ruled that the FCC had authority to regulate cable to the extent "reasonably ancillary to the effective performance of the Commission's various responsibilities for the regulation of television broadcasting." See also *United States v. Midwest Video Corp.,* 406 U.S. 649 (1972).

Armed with this vindication of its regulatory authority, the FCC continued vigorous cable regulation. In 1970, it required cable systems with 3,500 subscribers or more to originate programming, a requirement subsequently dropped. It prohibited cable systems from being owned by local telephone companies, local broadcasters, or national TV networks. In 1972, it extensively revised its cable rules and began to provide the cable industry with some regulatory relief. The new rules were much less restrictive of distant-signal importation but still contained complex signal carriage rules that limited the programming options of cable system operators.

By the late 1970s, however, many of those oppressive regulations were gone either through FCC repeal or judicial action. By the late 1980s, cable television was to a very substantial degree deregulated. Some argued that the result was not a "level playing field" and that it was unfair for cable to be deregulated while broadcasters remained subject to many FCC regulations that did not apply to their cable competitors. Others began to suspect that the deregulation of cable television had gone too far, that cable was at least a local natural monopoly, and that it might be time to reimpose some regulation, especially of cable television rates. All of these debates were made more complex by the simple fact that by the late 1980s, the U.S. Supreme Court had yet to adopt a First Amendment model for cable television. Lower courts split badly when cable First Amendment issues arose. Thus, by the late 1980s, cable law was still very much an evolving field with the final framework unclear.

Congress Intervenes—The Cable Communications Policy Act of 1984

Congress attempted to set the regulatory framework for cable in 1984 when it adopted the Cable Communications Policy Act of 1984, Pub. L. No. 98-549, 98 Stat. 2779, codified as 47 U.S.C. §§ 521–559 (1984 Cable Act). To a substantial degree, the 1984 Cable Act, ratified many of the aspects of cable law that had emerged in an ad hoc fashion from the 1960s through the 1980s. It clarified that operators of systems that used public rights-of-way required franchises from local governments and set up the basic system for granting "1 or more" franchises, as the franchising authority might choose. The law, however, limited the ability of franchising bodies to regulate programming services: they could demand that broad categories of service be provided—say, a music channel—but could not specify which service had to be used (e.g., MTV).

They could not take programming into account in making franchise grants. Congress deregulated "basic cable" rates (rates for the cable tiers containing broadcast stations) for most cable systems and made it perfectly clear that rates for premium services (e.g., HBO) were to be completely determined by marketplace forces. These changes greatly pleased the cable television industry.

The cities, however, got something in exchange for their concessions on rate and programming deregulation. Congress clarified that cities could demand franchise fees of up to 5 percent of total cable system revenues (basic service, premium services, and local cable system advertising, for example, all counted). The cities had charged franchise fees for years, but Congress had never before specifically authorized it. In addition, franchising bodies were given the right to demand that applicants set aside channels for public, educational, and governmental (PEG) or public access. Systems of over thirty-six channels also had to be prepared to provide channels for leased access. The number of these varied with the number of activated channels on the system.

The 1984 Cable Act was the product of a carefully crafted compromise between the franchising bodies (mostly represented by the National League of Cities) and the cable television industry (primarily the National Cable Television Association). Congress did not so much adopt the Act as simply ratify the compromise. Powerful members of Congress told all parties that if they could settle their differences and present Congress with a compromise bill, Congress would do all it could to adopt the bill. The compromise was struck, and Congress fulfilled its end of the bargain. Only as the late 1980s rolled around did some in Congress question what they had done and at least consider whether or not it was time to "revisit" the Act and, perhaps, reimpose some form of regulation.

As noted previously, the bill was deregulatory on two points that mattered most to the cable industry: rates and program service. At the same time, it ratified the franchising process and gave the cities substantial authority to set non-program-related demands or conditions as a part of franchising. The result in subsequent years was to tend to divide the development of cable television law. On one side of the line are the now-infrequent efforts (mostly focused on cable

obscenity and indecency) to directly regulate the content of cable communications. Courts, as we will see, have been highly skeptical about many of these attempts to regulate cable's most clearly expressive functions. On the other side of the line are cases arising from the cable television franchising process. Many of these cases involve, at most, rather indirect effects on cable content. As courts have struggled with First Amendment cases related to cable regulation, they have become deeply entangled in the fact that cable television is, at the moment, without a clear First Amendment model.

In general, these cases have involved three areas of cable regulation. One question has centered on the so-called must-carry requirements—whether the FCC can require cable systems to carry local broadcast signals. A second question, related to must carry, is whether it is consistent with the First Amendment for franchisors to require public access channels, as the 1984 Cable Act permits. A third area of intense action has involved the issue of cable obscenity and/or cable indecency.

The Cable Television Consumer Protection and Competition Act of 1992

In 1992, Congress enacted the Cable Television Consumer Protection and Competition Act, Pub. L. 102-38, 106 Stat. 1460. The 1992 Cable Act, as it is popularly known in the cable industry, responded to a public outcry over steadily increasing cable subscriber fees. Accordingly, the 1992 Act authorized the FCC and municipal franchising authorities to subject the cable industry to rate regulation. Other important provisions of the Act were outlined by Justice Kennedy for the Supreme Court in *Turner Broadcasting Co. v. FCC,* 512 U.S. 622, 630–32 (1994). These included prohibiting local franchising authorities from awarding exclusive franchises to cable operators. In addition, the 1992 Act imposed certain restrictions on cable programmers who were affiliated with cable operators. Some of the foregoing provisions of the 1992 Cable Act are considered in the *Daniels Cablevision* case reported below.

The 1992 Cable Act also imposed certain "must-carry" obligations on cable operators. For a discussion of the must-carry provisions and the *Turner* case that upheld them, see this text,

p. 861. In addition, the 1992 Act set forth some restrictions—designed to protect children—on indecent programming by public access and leased access cable channels. For a discussion of the First Amendment challenge to these restrictions, see this text, p. 881.

Judge Jackson in *Daniels Cablevision, Inc. v. United States*, reported below, characterized the 1992 Cable Act as "essentially a regulatory measure of economic rather than ideologic import." In the following excerpts from the *Daniels* case, Judge Jackson described the purpose of Congress in enacting the 1992 Cable Act. He also explained the ways in which provisions of the 1992 Cable Act interact with the 1984 Cable Act.

Daniels Cablevision, Inc. v. United States

835 F. Supp. 1 (D.D.C. 1993).

JACKSON, District Judge:

Congress undertook [in the 1992 Cable Act, Pub. L. No. 102-385, 106 Stat. 1460] to expand and tighten government's control over that segment of the television market in which the plaintiffs traded, namely the business of delivering video signals to a major portion of the nation's homes. Congress was largely unconcerned with what was being said with those signals. It *was* concerned, however, that the plexuses of wires linking video "speakers" and most of the television receivers across the country remain open to transmit a diverse mix of "voices," not only the messages chosen for delivery by those who owned or controlled the cables.

Several of the provisions of the 1992 Cable Act avowedly inhibit the cable operators and programmers in making full use of the capabilities of their systems to deliver signals to their subscribers. The plaintiffs challenge these provisions largely on the same grounds on which they based their challenge to the must-carry provisions in sections 4 and 5 of the 1992 Act.

Section 7(b) of the 1992 Act, in conjunction with section 611 of the 1984 Act, the "PEG programming" provisions, allows local franchising authorities to require that franchise proposals submitted by aspiring cable operators contain assurances that a portion of their channel capacity will be designated for "public, educational, or governmental use." Once the franchise is awarded, the franchising authority may enforce these "PEG" commitments, 47 U.S.C. § 531(c) (1988), and the franchisee is not thereafter permitted to exercise any editorial control over the PEG programming it is obliged to carry. *Id.* § 531(e).

Section 612(b) of the 1984 Act, the "leased access" provisions, obligates cable operators to reserve channel capacity for use by commercial programmers that are unaffiliated with the operator. 47 U.S.C. § 532(b)(1) (1988). Again the cable operator is prohibited from exercising editorial control over its lessees' programming, except to the extent that it may consider content in establishing a reasonable price to charge the unaffiliated lessee, *id.* § 532(c), and it may also decline to carry programming that it reasonably believes to be obscene. 1992 Cable Act § 10(a).

Section 19 of the 1992 Act, the "vertical integration" provisions, regulates the conduct of programmers in which a cable system operator has an attributable (i.e., a property) interest ("vertically integrated programmers" or "VPs"). Section 19 directs the FCC to promulgate regulations to "prohibit discrimination [by vertically integrated programmers] . . . in the prices, terms, and conditions of sale or delivery of . . . cable programming . . . between cable systems. . . ." 1992 Cable Act § 19(c)(2)(B).

Section 3 of the 1992 Act, the "rate regulation" provisions, requires cable operators to provide all subscribers with a basic service tier containing all section 4 and 5 mandatory carriage broadcast stations; all public, educational or governmental stations which must be carried pursuant to the franchise; and all regular nonsatellite broadcast stations regularly transmitted by the operators. The FCC and local franchise authorities are empowered to ensure that the rates charged by cable systems subject to rate regulation for the basic tier are reasonable, and the FCC is directed to establish a regulatory regime to entertain challenges to the reasonableness of rates charged for all other non-premium channels. Section 3 also requires all operators to maintain a uniform rate structure throughout the geographic region in which the operator offers its services. Finally, section 3 prohibits operators from requiring subscribers to purchase any service, other than the basic tier, as a precondition to receiving any other pay-per-view or pay-per-channel service, and the price structure for such channels must be uniform regardless of the quantity of services ordered by a subscriber.

The Court holds that these provisions all are content-neutral, are thus subject to O'Brien/Ward balancing only, and that they withstand that level of scrutiny.

[EDITORIAL NOTE: *Judge Jackson found that the public access and leased access provisions were designed to allow a broad range of speakers to reach an audience. Similarly, the provisions constraining vertical integration and the rate regulation provisions were enacted to promote competition and diversity.]*

Three provisions in the 1992 Cable Act appear clearly unconstitutional, either because they overtly impose content-related burdens on speech, or because they do not serve any identifiable regulatory purpose of significance to justify even the incidental burdens they impose. These provisions are the direct broadcast satellite ("DBS") service obligations; the premium channel notice provisions; and the provisions placing quotas on the number of subscribers allowed per cable operator.

Direct Broadcast Satellite Service Provisions

Section 25 of the 1992 Cable Act directs the FCC to impose mandatory carriage requirements on providers of DBS services. DBS distributors transmit their signals via earth-orbiting satellites directly into subscribers' receivers through dish antennas, not over coaxial cable strung along public rights-of-way. As a condition to authorization or renewal of any DBS service license, the DBS provider must allocate four to seven percent of its transmission capacity to "noncommercial programming of an educational nature."

The plaintiffs contend that the DBS educational programming set-aside is content-based. The DBS service provisions accord a preference to speakers whose ostensible mission is to enlighten rather than entertain, and therefore, have implicitly been judged by Congress to be more worthy of an audience. Nevertheless, the Court finds that it need not decide whether a preference for "noncommercial programming of an educational nature" is more content-related than, for example, the "local" broadcasting at issue in Must-Carry, because, to the extent it subsumes a content component at all, even under O'Brien/Ward scrutiny, the DBS provisions must fail.

Premium Channel Notice Provisions

Section 15 of the 1992 Cable Act requires a cable operator to give notice to its subscribers, at least 30 days in advance, if it proposes to provide a free preview of a "premium channel"—one offering movies rated X, NC-17, or R by the Motion Picture Association of America—to entice those who do not ordinarily receive that channel to buy it. The plaintiff operators, and ENCORE, an intervenor-plaintiff offering pay-per-view movie programming services, contend that this provision is unconstitutional because it is indisputably content-related; because it burdens protected speech as well as suppressing obscenity; and because it does not survive the strict scrutiny to which such legislation must be subjected. The Court agrees.

Section 15 is content-based. The section passes judgment on material on the basis of the ratings the motion picture industry assigns to the movies, which, of course, are determined in turn by the movies' content. Content-based "indecency" restrictions are constitutional only if they are a "carefully tailored" means of accomplishing a "compelling" interest. *Sable Communications v. FCC,* 492 U.S. 115 (1989).

The federal defendants assert that section 15 is necessary to protect unwilling viewers, especially children, from indecent television messages which, although possibly being a compelling interest, section 15 is not, in any sense, "carefully tailored" to accomplish.

Congress has simply incorporated the Motion Picture Association's rating system as the measure of indecency. The government has not and could not demonstrate that all movies rated R are indecent. It is simultaneously under-inclusive in failing to address identical uninvited indecency originating from non-cable television sources; the law does not apply to broadcasters that carry uncut R or NC-17 movies.

Premium channels offered on cable are not "pervasive" in the *Pacifica* sense, i.e., in that questionable material ambient in the airwaves can be made to appear without warning on a television screen merely by turning on the set or throwing a channel selector switch. Like a subscription to a publication with "indecent" material or "900" telephone numbers, someone in the household must take affirmative steps to bring a premium channel into the home. *See Sable; Bolger v. Youngs Drug Products Corp.* (1983). The householder must subscribe to it, and thereafter retain it by paying the bill. *Cruz v. Ferre,* 755 F.2d 1415, 1420 (11th Cir. 1985). Parents also have the ability to block the reception of certain channels by use of "lock boxes" or similar devices which must be provided by cable operators on request. 47 U.S.C. § 544(d) (1988).

Numerical Limitations on Subscribers

A portion of section 11(c) of the 1992 Act directs the FCC to prescribe rules and regulations "establishing reasonable limits on the number of cable subscribers" a cable operator is authorized to reach through cable systems it owns or in which it has an attributable interest. The government contends that this provision is essential to promote competition in the cable industry; horizontal, no less than vertical, combination and expansion threaten to concentrate cable facilities in a few market-dominant entities. The plaintiffs challenge this provision on the ground that it directly interferes with the operators' ability to "speak" to as large an audience of their choice as possible. The Court holds that this provision is unconstitutional.

The federal defendants counter that the subscription limitation statute is subject only to *O'Brien/Ward* scrutiny, serving content-neutral purposes as it does, namely, to stem horizontal concentration in the cable industry, as well as to promote diversity of speakers. Even if content-neutral, however, and *O'Brien/Ward* thus supplying the appropriate standard by which the provision is to be judged, there would appear to be no circumstances under which the FCC could adopt constitutionally compatible regulations. Even content-neutral regulations may not burden substantially more speech than necessary, and must leave open ample alternative means of reaching an audience. See *Ward,* 491 U.S. at 802–03.

Three of the provisions challenged by the plaintiffs fail, so far as this Court can discern, to implicate the First Amendment to any significant extent at all. These are the provisions abrogating the statutory immunity that private cable operators formerly enjoyed for liability for the transmission of obscenity; the provisions immunizing municipally owned cable operators from civil

liability to private competitors for money damages; and the retransmission consent provisions. All of these provisions are compatible with the First Amendment.

Elimination of Immunity for Obscenity Carried on PEG and Leased Access Channels

As previously noted, cable operators may not exercise any editorial control over the PEG or leased access channels they are required to carry. The 1984 Act conferred immunity from state law liability upon cable operators who transmitted obscene material included in the obligatory PEG and leased access programming. 47 U.S.C. § 558 (1988). Section 10(d) of the 1992 Act removes all immunity for carriage of obscenity.

Without immunity, [the plaintiffs] argue, operators will be forced to screen their PEG and leased access programming for material that might be deemed obscene, and the more timorous among them will become so apprehensive that they will voluntarily refuse to carry controversial programming that might nevertheless enjoy full constitutional protection.

[N]o speakers—cable operators included— have a constitutional right to immunity to relieve them of anxiety about crossing the threshold from the risqué to the obscene. Congress' earlier decision to provide cable operators with immunity was a matter of grace that it has always been free to rescind.

Retransmission Consent

Section 6 of the 1992 Act directs the FCC to implement regulations prohibiting cable operators from carrying broadcast signals without the consent of the originating broadcaster. In conjunction with the must-carry provisions of section 4 of the 1992 Act, section 6 thus provides broadcasters with the enviable election between demanding mandatory carriage of the programming they cannot sell, and negotiating a price for that which is in demand. Daniels Cablevision, Inc. ("Daniels") perceives the effect of section 6 as a "prior restraint" on cable operators' speech because it places a condition on their carriage of material that the broadcaster itself has placed in the public domain.

Congress has independent constitutional authority, however, to provide creative artists—

and broadcasters are arguably such—with copyright protection for their work. U.S. Const. Art. I, § 8, cl. 8; *see United Video, Inc. v. FCC,* 890 F.2d 1173, 1191 (D.C. Cir. 1989). Daniels responds that while Congress might have extended copyright protection to broadcasters it has not done so, at least in so many words. Instead, Daniels argues, Congress has passed a separate law ostensibly having to do with telecommunications, never once adverting to its copyright powers.

Similar arguments were dismissed by the D.C. Circuit in *United Video.* Congress clearly could have amended the copyright law to provide infringement remedies for cable retransmission of broadcast material. But it is not constitutionally significant that Congress has done in the Cable Act what it otherwise could have done in the Copyright Act. Whatever title of the United States Code Congress chooses to place its law in, the law is still authorized by Congress' Article I power.

Time Warner Entertainment Co. v. FCC
93 F.3d 957 (D.C. Cir. 1996).

[EDITORIAL NOTE: *A panel of the U.S. Court of Appeals for the District of Columbia Circuit, consisting of Judges Buckley, Randolph, and Tatel, reviewed the Daniels decision.*]

PER CURIAM:

These are facial challenges to nine provisions of the Cable Act of 1992 and two provisions of its predecessor, the Cable Act of 1984. A group of cable television system owner/operators and programmers contend that the following provisions infringe upon their First Amendment right to freedom of speech: sections 611 (public, educational, and governmental programming) and 612 (leased access) of the 1984 Act, and sections 3 (rate regulation), 10(d) (obscenity liability), 11(c) (subscriber limitation, channel occupancy, and program creation restrictions), 15 (premium channel preview notice), 19 (vertically integrated programming), 24 (municipal immunity), and 25 (direct broadcast satellite set-aside) of the 1992 Act.

We sustain the constitutionality of these provisions, with the exception of section 11(c)'s "program creation provision." We hold that the challenge to this portion of section 11(c) is not ripe for judicial decision, and we consolidate the remaining challenges to section 11(c) with *Time*

Warner Entertainment Co. v. FCC, No. 94-1035, which addresses the same issues and is being held in abeyance pending reconsideration by the FCC of regulations contested in that action.

Broadcast and cable television are distinct in their operations. [I]n cable systems the transmitter is physically connected to the sets of individual subscribers by conventional or optical fiber cables that are similar in function to telephone lines. Because these cables must be laid in public rights-of-way and easements, cable operators must secure the necessary permits from local governments. Thus, their operations must be franchised.

The cable industry is comprised of cable operators, who own the physical assets and franchises and transmit the signals, and cable programmers, who produce programs for sale or license to the operators. Cable operators will often have ownership interests in programmers, and vice versa. These are known as "vertically integrated" entities. Cable operators create some of their own programming, but much of it comes from outside sources, including local and distant broadcast stations and such national and regional cable programming networks as CNN, ESPN, and C-Span. Cable subscribers select the stations they wish to receive by choosing among various plans ("tiers") of cable service. At an additional cost, a subscriber may receive "premium" channels (such as HBO and Showtime). Many systems also offer "pay-per-view" programs for which a subscriber pays a fee each time a specific movie or program is selected.

[F]ive lawsuits challenging various provisions of the Cable Acts were filed in the United States District Court for the District of Columbia. After these cases were consolidated, the challenges to two provisions were severed and assigned for hearing by a three-judge panel of the district court in accordance with section 23 of the 1992 Act, 47 U.S.C. § 555(c)(1). *See Turner Broadcasting Sys., Inc. v. FCC,* 810 F. Supp. 1308 (D.D.C. 1992). A single-judge district court proceeded to consider the remaining issues, which are those that now concern us, and concluded that three of the challenged provisions were unconstitutional (the DBS set-aside obligation, the premium channel preview notice requirement, and the subscriber limitation), *Daniels Cablevision, Inc. v. United States,* 835 F. Supp. 1, 8–10 (D.D.C. 1993), but upheld the validity of the rest.

In this proceeding, the government appeals the district court's holdings of unconstitutionality while Time Warner appeal[s] the remainder of its conclusions on the merits. We will deal first with the jurisdictional issue and then address the constitutionality of the challenged provisions of the Cable Acts. Any arguments that Time Warner could have raised with regard to subsections (a)–(c) of section 10 have essentially been foreclosed by the Supreme Court's recent decision in *Denver Area.*

The Rate Regulation Provisions

Studies conducted by Congress subsequent to the passage of the 1984 Act concluded that cable operators possessed excessive market power at the expense of consumers because of a lack of competition. See 1992 Act, § 2(a)(2), 106 Stat. at 1460. As a consequence, Congress incorporated into section 3 of the 1992 Act a new definition of "effective competition," which empowers the FCC and local authorities to regulate the prices charged subscribers by the great majority of cable operators. See 47 U.S.C. § 543(a)(2) & (l)(1). The statute requires the FCC to adopt regulations that will ensure that the rates charged by the operators for their "basic service tier[s]" are reasonable, *id.* § 543(b)(1); it directs the FCC to establish criteria for determining when the rates charged for other cable services are unreasonable, *id.* § 543(c)(1); and it details the factors that the FCC must consider in carrying out these mandates, *id.* § 543(b)(2)(C) & (c)(2). Section 3 also requires cable operators to provide certain specified programming in their basic service tiers, *id.* § 543(b)(7)(A), and to maintain a uniform rate structure throughout their service areas. *Id.* § 543(d). Time Warner asserts that these provisions violate its First Amendment rights.

Subsequent to oral argument, Congress enacted the Telecommunications Act of 1996, Pub. L. No. 104-104, 110 Stat. 56 ("1996 Act"). Section 301 of that statute amends section 3 of the 1992 Act by, inter alia, phasing out the regulation of cable rates after March 31, 1999. 1996 Act, § 301(b)(1)(C), 110 Stat. at 115 (codified at 47 U.S.C. § 543(c)(3)). Because the 1992 provisions remain in effect until then, at least as to larger cable operators, Time Warner's challenge has not been rendered moot.

In this case, the district court upheld section 3 as a legitimate, content-neutral regulation. *Daniels Cablevision.* Time Warner disagrees. It contends that section 3 is subject to strict scrutiny because, among other reasons, regulating cable rates inevitably affects both the content and quantity of speech by limiting the amount of money that a cable operator can spend on programming. This question, however, is no longer open. In *Time Warner Entertainment Co. v. FCC,* 56 F.3d 151 (D.C. Cir. 1995) ("Time Warner I"), *cert. denied,* 116 S. Ct. 911 (1996), in which Time Warner made nearly identical arguments in its challenge to the constitutionality of rules promulgated by the FCC pursuant to section 3, we determined that intermediate scrutiny applied. We specifically rejected the contention that the rate regulations affected the content of cable operators' speech and observed that, as promulgated, they "adequately insulated cable operators" from the "potential for causing incidental effects on content."

We rejected strict scrutiny for another reason as well: "Strict scrutiny of laws directed only at one element of the media is unwarranted if the difference in treatment is 'justified by some special characteristic' of the medium"; we concluded "[t]hat cable rate regulation [was] so justified . . . [because] most cable television subscribers have no opportunity to select between competing cable systems." *Id.* at 183 (quoting *Turner*). Accordingly, we found that "the rate regulations must be analyzed by the same 'intermediate' standard . . . applied in *Turner Broadcasting.*" On applying that standard, we concluded that the cable rate regulations "[we]re not unconstitutional [because] [t]he government has demonstrated a substantial interest in reducing cable rates and the Commission's regulations issued pursuant to section 3 of the 1992 Act are narrowly tailored to meet that interest."

Time Warner I thus controls the level of review to be applied to section 3 in this case. Time Warner's assertion that the basic service tier requirements constitute a content-based restriction does not compel a contrary conclusion. If the government may require a cable system to carry certain stations without triggering strict scrutiny, it may require them to carry those stations in their basic service tiers without inviting a finding of content-based regulation.

Leased Access Provisions

"Leased access" was originally aimed at bringing about "the widest possible diversity of information sources" for cable subscribers. *Id.* § 532(a). Congress thought cable operators might deny access to programmers if the operators disapproved the programmer's social or political viewpoint, or if the programmers' offerings competed with those the operators were providing. "Diversity" referred not to the substantive content of the program on a leased access channel, but to the entities—the "sources"—responsible for making it available.

The 1984 Act gave cable operators the authority to establish the price, terms, and conditions of the service on their leased access channels. 1984 Act, § 2, 98 Stat. at 2783 (original version of 47 U.S.C. § 532(c)(1)). The 1984 legislation did not accomplish much. Unaffiliated programming on leased access channels rarely appeared. Exactly why is uncertain. Cable operators said the reasons were high production costs and low demand in the face of the already wide array of programming operators were already providing. Others laid the blame at the feet of the operators, claiming they had set unreasonable terms for leased access. The FCC, in a 1990 report, recommended amending the 1984 Act to provide a national framework of leased access rules and to streamline the section's enforcement mechanism. *Competition, Rate Deregulation, and the Comm'ns Policies Relating to the Provision of Cable Television Serv.,* 5 F.C.C.R. 4962, 5048–50 Paras. 177–83 (1990) (report).

Amendments enacted in 1992 authorized the FCC to establish a maximum price for leased access, to regulate terms and conditions, and to establish procedures for the expedited resolution of disputes. 47 U.S.C. § 532(c)(4)(A). At the same time, Congress added a second rationale for leased access: "to promote competition in the delivery of diverse sources of video programming."

Time Warner's initial point regarding the leased access provisions is that they should be subject to the most stringent of the standards used to evaluate restrictions on speech. As the company sees it, the provisions are content-based; the government therefore must demonstrate a compelling interest to overcome their presumptive invalidity. There is nothing to this.

The provisions are not content-based. They do not favor or disfavor speech on the basis of the ideas contained in the speech or the views expressed. *Turner.* The statutory objective, as well as the provisions carrying it forth, are framed in terms of the sources of information rather than the substance of the information. This is consistent with the First Amendment's "assumption that the widest possible dissemination of information from diverse and antagonistic sources" promotes a free society. *Associated Press v. United States,* 326 U.S. 1 (1945). The Supreme Court has determined that regulations along these lines are content-neutral. *Turner.*

Hence the standard must be intermediate scrutiny: it is enough if the government's interest is important or substantial and the means chosen to promote that interest do not burden substantially more speech than necessary to achieve the aim. *Time Warner I,* 56 F.3d at 184. Time Warner thinks the leased access provisions fail even this test.

Time Warner thinks it sufficient to allege in its brief that there is not now, nor will there be under new FCC regulations, any appreciable demand by unaffiliated programmers for access to cable systems because cable systems are already carrying a wide variety of programs from diverse sources and because leased access does not make economic sense in light of the costs of production. Would that render the leased access provisions unconstitutional? We think not. Under section 532(b)(4), a "cable operator may use any unused channel capacity" set aside for leased access "until the use of such channel capacity is obtained, pursuant to a written agreement, by a person unaffiliated with the operator." That is, if unaffiliated programmers have not and, as Time Warner predicts, will not exploit the leased access provisions, then the provisions will have no effect on the speech of the cable operators. *See Turner.* None of their programming would have to be dropped. The operators' editorial control will remain unimpaired and so will their First Amendment right to determine what will appear on their cable systems.

PEG Provision

Section 611 of the 1984 Cable Act provides that local franchising authorities "may . . . require as part of a [cable] franchise . . . [or] franchise renewal . . . that channel capacity be designated for public, educational, or governmental use." 47 U.S.C. § 531(b).

To prevail in its facial challenge, Time Warner must "establish that no set of circumstances exists under which the Act would be valid." Consideration of this standard is somewhat tricky here since rather than requiring PEG channel capacity, the statute merely permits local franchise authorities to require PEG programming as a franchise condition. In passing the PEG provision, Congress thus merely recognized and endorsed the preexisting practice of local franchise authorities conditioning their cable franchises on the granting of PEG channel access.

Time Warner must therefore show that no franchise authority could ever exercise the statute's grant of authority in a constitutional manner. We can, of course, imagine PEG franchise conditions that would raise serious constitutional issues. For example, were a local authority to require as a franchise condition that a cable operator designate three-quarters of its channels for "educational" programming, defined in detail by the city council, such a requirement would certainly implicate First Amendment concerns. At the same time, we can just as easily imagine a franchise authority exercising its power without violating the First Amendment. For example, a local franchise authority might seek to ensure public "access to a multiplicity of information sources," *Turner,* by conditioning its grant of a franchise on the cable operator's willingness to provide access to a single channel for "public" use, defining "public" broadly enough to permit access to everyone on a nondiscriminatory, first-come, first-serve basis. Under *Turner,* such a scheme would be content-neutral, would serve an "important purpose unrelated to the suppression of free expression," *id.,* and would be narrowly tailored to its goal. Time Warner's facial challenge therefore fails.

The DBS Provisions

A direct broadcast satellite ("DBS") service utilizes satellites to retransmit signals from the Earth to small, inexpensive terminals. It operates on a specified band of the radio frequency spectrum. The FCC prescribes the manner in which parts of that spectrum are made available for DBS systems. *See* 47 C.F.R. pt. 100. With the emergence

of DBS technology, nations of the Western Hemisphere entered into an agreement to assign orbital satellite positions and channels. *See Processing Procedures Regarding the Direct Broadcast Satellite Serv.,* 95 F.C.C.2d 250, 251 (1983). The United States was assigned 32 channels at each of eight orbital positions. Through the use of compression technology, one satellite channel can deliver up to four channels of video service. DBS providers are allotted a number of channels of a specified spectrum width.

Section 25 of the 1992 Act provides:

> The Commission shall require, as a condition of any provision, initial authorization, or authorization renewal for a provider of direct broadcast satellite service providing video programming, that the provider of such service reserve a portion of its channel capacity, equal to not less than 4 percent nor more than 7 percent, exclusively for noncommercial programming of an educational or informational nature.

47 U.S.C. § 335(b)(1). DBS providers have no editorial control over the educational or informational programming they are required to carry under this provision. *Id.* § 335(b)(3). The district court held that section 25 is invalid because the government provided no evidence that regulation of DBS providers is necessary to serve any significant interest. *Daniels Cablevision.*

Time Warner insists, for a variety of reasons, that the DBS set-aside provisions must be subjected to strict scrutiny; it also maintains that we may not consider the government's argument that DBS systems are analogous to broadcast television and therefore subject to no more than heightened scrutiny, because that argument had not been raised before the district court. Our resolution of the legal issue presented here does not require the consideration of facts not already in the record, and for us to ignore the obvious similarity between DBS and broadcasting would do nothing to preserve the integrity of the judicial process.

The Supreme Court recognized, in 1969, that because of the limited availability of the radio spectrum for broadcast purposes, "only a tiny fraction of those with resources and intelligence can hope to communicate by radio at the same time. . . ." *Red Lion.* The same is true for DBS today. Because the United States has only a finite number of satellite positions available for DBS use, the opportunity to provide such services will necessarily be limited. Even before the first DBS communications satellite was launched in 1994, the FCC found that "the demand for channel/orbit allocations far exceeds the available supply." *Continental Satellite Corp.,* 4 F.C.C.R. 6292, 6293 (1989). Recently, the last DBS license was auctioned off for $682.5 million, the largest sum ever received by the FCC for any single license to use the airwaves. As the Supreme Court observed,

> [w]here there are substantially more individuals who want to broadcast than there are frequencies to allocate, it is idle to posit an unabridgeable First Amendment right to broadcast comparable to the right of every individual to speak, write, or publish.

Red Lion, 395 U.S. at 388.

In such cases, the Court applies a "less rigorous standard of First Amendment scrutiny," based on a recognition that "the inherent physical limitation on the number of speakers who may use the . . . medium has been thought to require some adjustment in traditional First Amendment analysis to permit the Government to place limited content restraints, and impose certain affirmative obligations, on broadcast licensees." *Turner.* Because the new DBS technology is subject to similar limitations, we conclude that section 25 should be analyzed under the same relaxed standard of scrutiny that the court has applied to the traditional broadcast media.

The government asserts an interest in assuring public access to diverse sources of information by requiring DBS operators to reserve four to seven percent of their channel capacity for noncommercial educational and informational programming. This interest lies at the core of the First Amendment: "Assuring that the public has access to a multiplicity of informational sources is a governmental purpose of the highest order, for it promotes values central to the First Amendment." *Turner.*

Time Warner [contends] that the government made no findings regarding the need for channel set-asides on DBS.

In this instance, Congress could not have made DBS-specific findings for the simple reason that no DBS system was in operation at the time the 1992 Act was enacted. Congress had to base its decision to require set-asides on its long experience with the broadcast media.

Section 25, then, represents nothing more than a new application of a well-settled govern-ment policy of ensuring public access to non-commercial programming. The set-aside requirement of from four to seven percent of a provider's channel capacity is hardly onerous. We note, further, that the government does not dictate the specific content of the programming that DBS operators are required to carry. Because section 25 is "a reasonable means of promoting the public interest in diversified mass communications," it does not violate the First Amendment rights of DBS providers.

Vertically Integrated Cable Company Provisions

Time Warner challenges section 19's "program access" provision, which requires the Commission to prohibit vertically integrated video programmers from "discriminat[ing] . . . in the prices, terms, and conditions of sale or delivery of satellite programming among or between multichannel video programming distributors, or their agents or buying groups." Exempted from this provision are reasonable requirements for creditworthiness, as well as price distinctions resulting from either differences in cost or economies of scale. Time Warner also challenges section 19's restrictions on exclusive contracts between cable operators and vertically integrated programmers, and between operators and vertically integrated satellite broadcast vendors. For geographical areas served by cable on the statute's effective date, the Act bars exclusive contracts unless the Commission determines, according to enumerated criteria, that the contract is in the "public interest," *id.* § 548(c)(2)(D), (c)(4); for areas not served by cable on that date, the Act prohibits exclusive contracts altogether. *Id.* § 548(c)(2)(C). The district court upheld the vertically integrated programming provisions, finding that they are content-neutral and satisfy intermediate scrutiny. *Daniels Cablevision,* 835 F. Supp. at 7.

We first address the appropriate level of scrutiny. As the district court properly recognized, these provisions are content-neutral on their face, regulating cable programmers and operators on the basis of the "economics of ownership," a characteristic unrelated to the content of speech.

We thus apply intermediate scrutiny. Like one of its interests in the must-carry provision at issue in *Turner,* the government's interest in regulating vertically integrated programmers and operators is the promotion of fair competition in the video marketplace. According to *Turner,* this goal both furthers an important government interest and is unrelated to the suppression of free expression. *Turner.*

Time Warner contends that these provisions are not "narrowly tailored" since they prohibit vertically integrated programmers from favoring, or entering into exclusive contracts with, even non-affiliates. The Supreme Court has made clear, however, that to satisfy *O'Brien's* narrow-tailoring requirement, a statute need not be the "least speech-restrictive means of advancing the government's interests." *Turner.* Rather, "[n]arrow tailoring in this context requires . . . that the means chosen . . . not 'burden substantially more speech than is necessary to further the government's legitimate interest.'" *Id.* (quoting *Ward v. Rock Against Racism,* 491 U.S. 781, 799 (1989)). Both the "program access" provision and the prohibition against exclusive contracts satisfy this standard. That these provisions reach beyond Congress's goal does not mean that they burden substantially more speech than necessary, the crucial factor in whether a regulation satisfies "narrow tailoring," since they merely restrict Time Warner's ability to contract freely with non-affiliates.

Limitations on Ownership, Control, and Utilization

Time Warner challenges three subsections of section 11(c) of the 1992 Act: the "subscriber limitation," the "channel occupancy," and the "program creation" provisions. Rather than imposing any direct requirements on cable, these provisions either require the FCC to promulgate regulations or authorize it to consider the necessity of doing so. The "subscriber limitation" provision requires the FCC to limit the number of cable subscribers any one cable operator may reach. 47 U.S.C. § 533(f)(1)(A). The "channel occupancy" provision requires the FCC to limit the number of channels that vertically integrated programmers may occupy on affiliated cable systems. *Id.* § 533(f)(1)(B). The "program creation" provision directs the FCC to "consider the necessity" of imposing limitations on the degree to which cable distributors may "engage in the cre-

ation and production of video programming." *Id.* § 533(f)(1)(C).

The FCC has promulgated regulations pursuant to the "subscriber limitation" and "channel occupancy" provisions. *See Implementation of Sections 11 and 13 of the Cable Television Consumer Protection and Competition Act of 1992: Horizontal and Vertical Ownership Limits,* 8 F.C.C.R. 8565, 8567 (1993) (second report and order) (limiting each cable company to 30% of national cable market and precluding vertically integrated operators from having more than 40% of channels occupied by affiliated programmers). Time Warner has challenged these regulations in a direct appeal to this court in *Time Warner Entertainment Co. v. FCC,* No. 94-1035, a case currently held in abeyance pending FCC reconsideration. At this point, we express no opinion as to the constitutionality of either the statute or the regulations.

Although the Commission "considered the necessity" of "program creation" limits, it decided no such limits to be necessary at present. 8 F.C.C.R. at 8567–68. Accordingly, Time Warner's challenge to the "program creation" provision, which neither regulates nor requires the Commission to regulate video programming, is not ripe.

[EDITORIAL NOTE: *The D.C, Circuit agreed with the district court and upheld limiting the remedies available to cable operators, in suits against muncipal franchising authorities, to injunctive and declaratory relief.*]

Obscenity Liablility

We agree with the district court that the 1992 Act's revocation of cable operators' immunity from liability for obscene programming carried on PEG or leased access channels does not violate the First Amendment. Sec. 10(d). Time Warner complains that section 10(d) makes cable operators liable for programming the Cable Acts force them to carry. But section 506 of the 1996 Act amended 47 U.S.C. § 531(e) and 532(c)(2) to provide explicitly that cable operators may refuse to transmit obscene material on leased access and PEG channels. 1996 Act, § 506, 110 Stat. at 136-37 (to be codified at 47 U.S.C. §§ 531(e), 532(c)(2)). The constitutionality of section 506 is not before us, nor could it be. Constitutional challenges to the 1996 Act must be heard by three-judge district courts in accordance with 28

U.S.C. § 2284. See 1996 Act, § 561, 110 Stat. at 142–43. We therefore shall assume the validity of section 506. Because cable operators may, under that provision, refuse to transmit obscenity on PEG and leased access channels, section 10(d)'s revocation of cable operators' obscenity immunity does not make them liable for programming they are forced to carry.[7]

Premium Channel Notice Provision

Premium channels are offered only to those who sign up and agree to pay the extra fee. All other subscribers receive a scrambled signal on the premium channel. As a marketing technique, some cable systems provide free access to a premium channel for a limited time. During the free preview period, all cable subscribers receive the premium channel. Section 15 of the 1992 Act requires operators to give their subscribers thirty days notice before offering free previews of premium channels—defined as "any pay service offered on a per channel or per program basis, which offers movies rated by the Motion Picture Association of America as X, NC-17 or R"—and requires operators to block any preview if the subscriber so requests. 47 U.S.C. § 544(d)(3)(A). The district court struck down section 15 on the ground that it constituted a content-based restriction of speech. *Daniels Cablevision.*

Parents have a right to control what comes into their homes and what thus becomes available to their children. *Rowan v. Post Office Dep't,* 397 U.S. 728 (1970). And the government has a substantial interest in facilitating their ability to do so. *Sable Communications,* 492 U.S. at 126. Advance notice of free previews allows parents to decide if they will allow this type of programming to appear on their television screens.

See FCC v. Pacifica Foundation, 438 U.S. 726, 748-49 (1978). In fact, the premium channel notice provision imposes less of a burden than the safe-harbor restriction upheld in *Pacifica,* 438 U.S. at 732. The district court thought that section 15's thirty day notice requirement would make previews "less practicable and more costly." *Daniels Cablevision.* But operators already communicate with their subscribers on a monthly basis through billing, and the increased costs associated with the advance notice cannot be significant.

We are dealing with a disclosure statute, not a direct restriction on speech. Time Warner suggests, as did the district court, that "lockboxes" constitute a less intrusive and equally effective method of protecting children. But this would be so only if parents who had lockboxes—not all do—knew in advance what sort of programs may be carried on a premium channel to which they do not subscribe. Otherwise, why would anyone bother to place a lockbox in operation? For parents to make an informed judgment about which course to follow, and when, they must have information in advance, which is what section 15 gives them. Denver, 116 S.Ct. at 2393 (reasoning that informational requirements are a more appropriate complement to lockboxes than segregation and blocking requirements).

Time Warner also believes that annual notice would be sufficient to enable parents to make appropriate choices on behalf of their children. We cannot see how. It must be the rare family indeed that plans its television viewing one year in advance.

In summary, we sustain the constitutionality of sections 611 and 612 of the 1984 Act and sections 3, 10(d), 15, 19, 24, and 25 of the 1992 Act. We hold unripe the challenge to section 11(c)'s program creation provision and consolidate the remaining challenges to section 11(c) with *Time Warner Entertainment Co. v. FCC,* No. 94–1035.

So ordered.

TATEL, Circuit Judge, dissenting in part:

I concur in all of the court's opinion except [that part] which upholds section 15 of the 1992 Cable Act, the Premium Channel Notice Provision. I agree that the government has a compelling interest in protecting children. *See also Denver Area.* But because I do not believe we can sustain the statute's constitutionality on this record, I respectfully dissent.

---

7. By upholding section 10(a) of the 1992 Act, the Supreme Court's judgment in *Denver* permitted cable operators to prohibit the transmission of obscene (as well as indecent) programming on leased access channels. *See* 116 S.Ct. at 2382–90 (plurality opinion); *id.* at 2422–25 (opinion of Thomas, J., joined by Rehnquist, C.J., and Scalia, J.). The Court's judgment struck down section 10(c), which authorized operators to exert similar control over PEG channels. But the judgment appeared to rest on the principle that indecent material, unlike obscenity, is entitled to some measure of constitutional protection. Section 10(d), of course, deals only with obscene programming. *See id.* at 2428 n. 14 (opinion of Thomas, J., joined by Rehnquist, C.J., & Scalia, J.).

Section 15 plainly discriminates among programmers based solely on the content of their speech. While operators must provide thirty days advance notice to all subscribers when offering free previews of "pay service" channels carrying movies rated R, NC-17, or X—a rating system based solely on the movies' content—they need not provide such notice when offering free previews of pay channels not carrying such movies. The court does not dispute this.

- Section 15 is overbroad because it requires notice to even those customers already subscribing to the "premium channel," as well as notice every time a premium channel seeks to show a free preview, even a preview with no movies rated R, NC-17, or X. Section 15 would thus require a cable operator offering a free preview of Snow White and the Seven Dwarfs on a "premium channel" to give thirty days advance notice.
- Section 15 is underinclusive because it covers only "pay service" channels, not other stations seeking to show the same movies, see *Daniels Cablevision,* and it does not apply to indecent programming not rated by the MPAA.
- Because section 15 does not require operators to inform subscribers that the term "premium channel" is defined as a channel that shows movies rated R, NC-17, or X, the statute only marginally furthers the government's stated interest of warning parents about indecent programming. Subscribers unaware that "premium channels" show such movies would thus not have the very information the government believes to be so valuable: that the free preview may include materials inappropriate for their children. Section 15 thus "does not reveal the caution and care" First Amendment jurisprudence requires. *Denver,* 116 S.Ct. at 2392. Were the court to engage in ordinary First Amendment analysis, I have little doubt it would be hard-pressed to uphold section 15 under either strict scrutiny, *Sable Communications Inc. v. FCC,* 492 U.S. 115, 126 (1989) (requiring that content-based statute be "least restrictive means to further the articulated interest"), or even the "close judicial scrutiny" standard endorsed by four Justices in *Denver,* 116 S.Ct. at 2378 (plurality opinion) (invalidating statute if it imposes "unnecessarily great restriction on speech").

[T]he record contains abundant uncontroverted evidence that the costs of notice are not only significant, but also so prohibitive as to make free previews financially impractical. "A statute is presumptively inconsistent with the First Amendment if it imposes a financial burden on speakers because of the content of their speech." *Simon & Schuster, Inc. v. Members of the N.Y. State Crime Victims Bd. (quoting Leathers v. Medlock).*

Although I dissent from the court's conclusion that the notice requirement does not burden speech, I do not believe the district court should have granted Time Warner summary judgment without affording the Government an opportunity for further discovery. I would therefore remand for further development of the record on the factual question of whether section 15 imposes financial burdens on Time Warner's speech.

COMMENT

The D.C. Circuit denied a petition for rehearing *en banc* in the *Time Warner* case reported above. *Time Warner Entertainment Co. v. FCC,* 105 F.3d 723 (D.C. Cir., 1997). Judge Williams, joined by four others, dissented from the denial of rehearing *en banc.* Judge Williams said there were "fatal defects in the panel's legal *theory* for upholding the 1992 Cable Act's requirement that direct broadcast satellite ("DBS") providers set aside several channels for noncommercial programming of an educational or informational nature." The panel erred in concluding that DBS was analogous to broadcasting and that, therefore, the "relaxed First Amendment regime" set forth in *Red Lion* should be applied: "[T]he *Red Lion* doctrine relies on an idea of extreme physical scarcity. The new DBS technology already offers more channel capacity than the cable industry, and far more than traditional broadcasters." Although conceding that the Supreme Court had not abandoned *Red Lion,* Judge Williams made the following observation: "While *Red Lion* is not in such poor shape that an intermediate court of appeals could properly announce its death, we can think twice before extending it to another medium."

Judge Williams also contended that the DBS requirements could not be analogized to the must-carry rules upheld in *Turner* because the latter simply required cable systems to carry certain stations regardless of content whereas the DBS requirements are specific as to their content.

But is this distinction really significant? Isn't the rationale of the must-carry requirements that the local service programming provided by local over-the-air broadcasters will be protected by requiring carriage on cable?

THE "MUST-CARRY" RULES

Another contentious area has been that of "must carry." Few areas of cable law have been of more concern to the broadcasting industry. In most instances when customers connect to cable television, they disconnect (and often remove altogether) their over-the-air antenna. They become totally dependent on the cable system for the delivery of video services, including over-the-air broadcasting. The FCC's 1966 cable television rules required cable systems to carry all "significantly viewed" local TV channels, and for years "must carry" was a well-established cable regulatory policy.

In 1980, however, Turner Broadcasting System asked the FCC to delete the must carry rules. Turner's motives were obvious; the company was developing cable services (such as CNN II, later "Headline News"), but finding it hard to place the services on cable systems filled with must carry signals. At about the same time, a small twelve-channel cable system in Quincy, Washington, decided to challenge the FCC by not carrying all the required must carry signals. After the FCC fined the cable system $5,000 for violating the rules, Quincy appealed to the D.C. Circuit. The case was combined with Turner's petition to review the FCC's refusal to repeal the rules; in 1985, the court issued a decision, holding that the must carry rules as then drafted and justified by the FCC violated the First Amendment rights of cable operators. *Quincy Cable TV, Inc. v. FCC*, 768 F.2d 1434 (D.C. Cir. 1985), *cert den. sub nom. National Ass'n of Broadcasters v. Quincy Cable TV, Inc.*, 476 U.S. 1169 (1986). Pressured strongly by broadcasters, the FCC in 1986 issued revised must-carry rules that it thought would pass constitutional muster. After all, the court of appeals had not said that all "must-carry" rules were inherently unconstitutional. The new rules were, immediately challenged, however, and, relatively promptly in 1987, were also declared unconstitutional by the D.C. Circuit.

Turner Broadcasting System, Inc. v. FCC
512 U.S. 622, 1145 S.Ct. 2445,129 L.Ed.2d 497 (1994).

Justice KENNEDY announced the judgment of the Court and delivered the opinion of the Court, except as to Part III-B.

Sections 4 and 5 of the 1992 Cable Act require cable television systems to devote a portion of their channels to the transmission of local broadcast television stations. This case presents the question whether these provisions abridge the freedom of speech or of the press, in violation of the First Amendment.

The United States District Court for the District of Columbia granted summary judgment for the United States, holding that the challenged provisions are consistent with the First Amendment. Because issues of material fact remain unresolved in the record as developed thus far, we vacate the District Court's judgment and remand the case for further proceedings.

I

On October 5, 1992, Congress overrode a Presidential veto to enact the [1992 Cable Act]. At issue in this case is the constitutionality of the so-called must-carry provisions, which require cable operators to carry the signals of a specified number of local broadcast television stations.

Congress found that the physical characteristics of cable transmission, compounded by the increasing concentration of economic power in the cable industry, are endangering the ability of over-the-air broadcast television stations to compete for a viewing audience and thus for necessary operating revenues. Congress determined that regulation of the market for video programming was necessary to correct this competitive imbalance.

II

Through "original programming or by exercising editorial discretion over which stations or programs to include in its repertoire," cable programmers and operators "seek to communicate messages on a wide variety of topics and in a wide variety of formats." *Los Angeles v. Preferred Communications, Inc.* By requiring cable systems to set aside a portion of their channels for local broadcasters, the must-carry rules regulate cable speech in two respects: The rules reduce the number of channels over which cable operators exercise unfettered control, and they render it more difficult for cable programmers to compete for carriage on the limited channels remaining. Nevertheless, because not every interference with speech triggers the same degree of scrutiny under the First Amendment, we must decide at the outset the level of scrutiny applicable to the must-carry provisions.

A

We address first the Government's contention that regulation of cable television should be analyzed under the same First Amendment standard that applies to regulation of broadcast television. It is true that our cases have permitted more intrusive regulation of broadcast speakers than of speakers in other media. But the rationale for applying a less rigorous standard of First Amendment scrutiny to broadcast regulation, whatever its validity in the cases elaborating it, does not apply in the context of cable regulation.

The scarcity of broadcast frequencies required the establishment of some regulatory mechanism to divide the electromagnetic spectrum and assign specific frequencies to particular broadcasters. In addition, the inherent physical limitation on the number of speakers who may use the broadcast medium has been thought to require some adjustment in traditional First Amendment analysis to permit the Government to place limited content restraints, and impose certain affirmative obligations, on broadcast licensees. *Red Lion.*

The broadcast cases are inapposite in the present context because cable television does not suffer from the inherent limitations that characterize the broadcast medium. Indeed, given the rapid advances in fiber optics and digital compression technology, soon there may be no practical limitation on the number of speakers who may use the cable medium. Nor is there any danger of physical interference between two cable speakers attempting to share the same channel. In light of these fundamental technological differences between broadcast and cable transmission, application of the more relaxed standard of scrutiny adopted in *Red Lion* and the other broadcast cases is inapt when determining the First Amendment validity of cable regulation.

By a related course of reasoning, the Government and some appellees maintain that the must-carry provisions are nothing more than industry-specific antitrust legislation, and thus warrant rational basis scrutiny under this Court's "precedents governing legislative efforts to correct market failure in a market whose commodity is speech." But while the enforcement of a generally applicable law may or may not be subject to heightened scrutiny under the First Amendment, laws that single out the press, or certain elements thereof, for special treatment "pose a particular danger of abuse by the State," *Arkansas Writers' Project, Inc. v. Ragland,* and so are always subject to at least some degree of heightened First Amendment scrutiny. Because the must-carry provisions impose special obligations upon cable operators and special burdens upon cable programmers, some measure of heightened First Amendment scrutiny is demanded.

B

At the heart of the First Amendment lies the principle that each person should decide for him or herself the ideas and beliefs deserving of expression, consideration, and adherence. Our political system and cultural life rest upon this ideal. Our precedents thus apply the most exacting scrutiny to regulations that suppress, disadvantage, or impose differential burdens upon speech because of its content. Laws that compel speakers to utter or distribute speech bearing a particular message are subject to the same rigorous scrutiny. In contrast, regulations that are unrelated to the content of speech are subject to an intermediate level of scrutiny, because in most cases they pose a less substantial risk of excising certain ideas or viewpoints from the public dialogue.

C

Insofar as they pertain to the carriage of full power broadcasters, the must-carry rules, on their face, impose burdens and confer benefits without reference to the content of speech. Although the provisions interfere with cable operators' editorial discretion by compelling them to offer carriage to a certain minimum number of broadcast stations, the extent of the interference does not depend upon the content of the cable operators' programming. The rules impose obligations upon all operators, save those with fewer than 300 subscribers, regardless of the programs or stations they now offer or have offered in the past. Nothing in the Act imposes a restriction, penalty, or burden by reason of the views, programs, or stations the cable operator has selected or will select. The number of channels a cable operator must set aside depends only on the operator's channel capacity, hence, an operator cannot avoid or mitigate its obligations under the Act by altering the programming it offers to subscribers. Cf. *Miami Herald Publishing Co. v. Tornillo* (newspaper may avoid access obligations by refraining from speech critical of political candidates).

The must-carry provisions also burden cable programmers by reducing the number of channels for which they can compete. But, again, this burden is unrelated to content, for it extends to all cable programmers irrespective of the programming they choose to offer viewers. Cf. *Boos* (individuals may picket in front of a foreign embassy so long as their picket signs are not critical of the foreign government). And finally, the privileges conferred by the must-carry provisions are also unrelated to content. The rules benefit all full power broadcasters who request carriage—be they commercial or noncommercial, independent or network-affiliated, English or Spanish language, religious or secular. The aggregate effect of the rules is thus to make every full power commercial and noncommercial broadcaster eligible for must-carry, provided only that the broadcaster operates within the same television market as a cable system.

It is true that the must-carry provisions distinguish between speakers in the television programming market. But they do so based only upon the manner in which speakers transmit their messages to viewers, and not upon the messages they carry: Broadcasters, which transmit over the airwaves, are favored, while cable programmers, which do not, are disfavored. Cable operators, too, are burdened by the carriage obligations, but only because they control access to the cable conduit. So long as they are not a subtle means of exercising a content preference, speaker distinctions of this nature are not presumed invalid under the First Amendment.

That the must-carry provisions, on their face, do not burden or benefit speech of a particular content does not end the inquiry. Our cases have recognized that even a regulation neutral on its face may be content-based if its manifest purpose is to regulate speech because of the message it conveys.

Appellants contend, in this regard, that the must-carry regulations are content-based because Congress' purpose in enacting them was to promote speech of a favored content. We do not agree. Our review of the Act and its various findings persuades us that Congress' overriding objective in enacting must-carry was not to favor programming of a particular subject matter, viewpoint, or format, but rather to preserve access to free television programming for the 40 percent of Americans without cable.

By preventing cable operators from refusing carriage to broadcast television stations, the must-carry rules ensure that broadcast television stations will retain a large enough potential audience to earn necessary advertising revenue—or, in the case of noncommercial broadcasters, sufficient viewer contributions, to maintain their continued operation. In so doing, the provisions are designed to guarantee the survival of a medium that has become a vital part of the Nation's communication system, and to ensure that every individual with a television set can obtain access to free television programming.

The scope and operation of the challenged provisions make clear, in our view, that Congress designed the must-carry provisions not to promote speech of a particular content, but to prevent cable operators from exploiting their economic power to the detriment of broadcasters, and thereby to ensure that all Americans, especially those unable to subscribe to cable, have access to free television programming—whatever its content.

D

Appellants maintain that the must-carry provisions trigger strict scrutiny because they compel cable operators to transmit speech not of their choosing. Relying principally on *Miami Herald Publishing Co. v. Tornillo,* appellants say this intrusion on the editorial control of cable operators amounts to forced speech which, if not per se invalid, can be justified only if narrowly tailored to a compelling government interest.

Tornillo and *Pacific Gas & Electric* do not control this case for the following reasons. First, unlike the access rules struck down in those cases, the must-carry rules are content-neutral in application. They are not activated by any particular message spoken by cable operators and thus exact no content-based penalty.

Second, appellants do not suggest, nor do we think it the case, that must-carry will force cable operators to alter their own messages to respond to the broadcast programming they are required to carry. Given cable's long history of serving as a conduit for broadcast signals, there appears little risk that cable viewers would assume that the broadcast stations carried on a cable system convey ideas or messages endorsed by the cable operator.

Finally, the asserted analogy to *Tornillo* ignores an important technological difference between newspapers and cable television. Although a daily newspaper and a cable operator both may enjoy monopoly status in a given locale, the cable operator exercises far greater control over access to the relevant medium. A daily newspaper, no matter how secure its local monopoly, does not possess the power to obstruct readers' access to other competing publications—whether they be weekly local newspapers, or daily newspapers published in other cities. Thus, when a newspaper asserts exclusive control over its own news copy, it does not thereby prevent other newspapers from being distributed to willing recipients in the same locale.

The same is not true of cable. When an individual subscribes to cable, the physical connection between the television set and the cable network gives the cable operator bottleneck, or gatekeeper, control over most (if not all) of the television programming that is channeled into the subscriber's home. Hence, simply by virtue of its ownership of the essential pathway for cable speech, a cable operator can prevent its subscribers from obtaining access to programming it chooses to exclude. A cable operator, unlike speakers in other media, can thus silence the voice of competing speakers with a mere flick of the switch.

Second, appellants urge us to apply strict scrutiny because the must-carry provisions favor one set of speakers (broadcast programmers) over another (cable programmers). Appellants maintain that as a consequence of this speaker preference, some cable programmers who would have

secured carriage in the absence of must-carry may now be dropped. Relying on language in *Buckley v. Valeo,* appellants contend that such a regulation is presumed invalid under the First Amendment because the government may not "restrict the speech of some elements of our society in order to enhance the relative voice of others."

Our holding in *Buckley* does not support appellants' broad assertion. Rather, it stands for the proposition that speaker-based laws demand strict scrutiny when they reflect the Government's preference for the substance of what the favored speakers have to say (or aversion to what the disfavored speakers have to say). *Buckley* stands for the proposition that laws favoring some speakers over others demand strict scrutiny when the legislature's speaker preference reflects a content preference.

Finally, appellants maintain that strict scrutiny applies because the must-carry provisions single out certain members of the press—here, cable operators—for disfavored treatment. In support, appellants point out that Congress has required cable operators to provide carriage to broadcast stations, but has not imposed like burdens on analogous video delivery systems, such as multichannel multipoint distribution (MMDS) systems and satellite master antenna television (SMATV) systems. Relying upon our precedents invalidating discriminatory taxation of the press, appellants contend that this sort of differential treatment poses a particular danger of abuse by the government and should be presumed invalid.

Regulations that discriminate among media, or among different speakers within a single medium, often present serious First Amendment concerns. It would be error to conclude, however, that the First Amendment mandates strict scrutiny for any speech regulation that applies to one medium (or a subset thereof) but not others. The must-carry provisions, as we have explained above, are justified by special characteristics of the cable medium: the bottleneck monopoly power exercised by cable operators and the dangers this power poses to the viability of broadcast television.

In addition, the must-carry provisions are not structured in a manner that carries the inherent risk of undermining First Amendment interests. The regulations are broad-based, applying to almost all cable systems in the country, rather than just a select few.

For these reasons, the must-carry rules do not call for strict scrutiny.

III

A

We agree with the District Court that the appropriate standard by which to evaluate the constitutionality of must-carry is the intermediate level of scrutiny applicable to content-neutral restrictions that impose an incidental burden on speech. See *Ward; O'Brien.*

To satisfy this standard, a regulation need not be the least speech-restrictive means of advancing the Government's interests. Narrow tailoring in this context requires, that the means chosen do not "burden substantially more speech than is necessary to further the government's legitimate interests."

Congress declared that the must-carry provisions serve three interrelated interests: (1) preserving the benefits of free, over-the-air local broadcast television, (2) promoting the widespread dissemination of information from a multiplicity of sources, and (3) promoting fair competition in the market for television programming. None of these interests is related to the "suppression of free expression," *O'Brien*, or to the content of any speakers' messages. And viewed in the abstract, we have no difficulty concluding that each of them is an important governmental interest.

B

That the Government's asserted interests are important in the abstract does not mean, however, that the must-carry rules will in fact advance those interests. [I]n applying *O'Brien* scrutiny we must ask first whether the Government has adequately shown that the economic health of local broadcasting is in genuine jeopardy and in need of the protections afforded by must-carry. Assuming an affirmative answer to the foregoing question, the Government still bears the burden of showing that the remedy it has adopted does not "burden substantially more speech than is necessary to further the government's legitimate interests." On the state of the record developed thus far, and in the absence of findings of fact from the District Court, we are unable to conclude that the Government has satisfied either inquiry.

We agree that courts must accord substantial deference to the predictive judgments of Congress. That Congress' predictive judgments are entitled to substantial deference does not mean, however, that they are insulated from meaningful judicial review altogether. On the contrary, we have stressed in First Amendment cases that the deference afforded to legislative findings does "not foreclose our independent judgment of the facts bearing on an issue of constitutional law."

The paucity of evidence indicating that broadcast television is in jeopardy is not the only deficiency in this record. Also lacking are any findings concerning the actual effects of must-carry on the speech of cable operators and cable programmers—i.e., the extent to which cable operators will, in fact, be forced to make changes in their current or anticipated programming selections; the degree to which cable programmers will be dropped from cable systems to make room for local broadcasters; and the extent to which cable operators can satisfy their must-carry obligations by devoting previously unused channel capacity to the carriage of local broadcasters. The answers to these and perhaps other questions are critical to the narrow tailoring step of the *O'Brien* analysis, for unless we know the extent to which the must-carry provisions in fact interfere with protected speech, we cannot say whether they suppress "substantially more speech than necessary" to ensure the viability of broadcast television. Finally, the record fails to provide any judicial findings concerning the availability and efficacy of "constitutionally acceptable less restrictive means" of achieving the Government's asserted interests.

In sum, because there are genuine issues of material fact still to be resolved on this record, we hold that the District Court erred in granting summary judgment in favor of the Government. Because of the unresolved factual questions, the importance of the issues to the broadcast and cable industries, and the conflicting conclusions that the parties contend are to be drawn from the statistics and other evidence presented, we think it necessary to permit the parties to develop a more thorough factual record, and to allow the District Court to resolve any factual disputes remaining, before passing upon the constitutional validity of the challenged provisions.

Justice BLACKMUN, concurring.

I join Justice Kennedy's opinion, which aptly identifies and analyzes the First Amendment concerns and principles that should guide consideration of free speech issues in the expanding cable industry. I write to emphasize the paramount importance of according substantial deference to the predictive judgments of Congress, particularly where, as here, that legislative body has compiled an extensive record in the course of reaching its judgment. Nonetheless, the standard for summary judgment is high, and no less so when First Amendment values are at stake and the issue is of far-reaching importance. Because in this case there remain a few unresolved issues of material fact, a remand is appropriate.

Justice STEVENS, concurring in part and concurring in the judgment.

The must-carry provisions are amply "justified by special characteristics of the cable medium," namely, "the bottleneck monopoly power exercised by cable operators and the dangers this power poses to the viability of broadcast television." Cable operators' control of essential facilities provides a basis for intrusive regulation that would be inappropriate and perhaps impermissible for other communicative media.

While I agree with most of Justice Kennedy's reasoning, and join Parts I, II(C), II(D), and III(A) of his opinion, I part ways with him on the appropriate disposition of this case. In my view the District Court's judgment sustaining the must-carry provisions should be affirmed.

Economic measures are always subject to second-guessing. But the question for us is merely whether Congress could fairly conclude that cable operators' monopoly position threatens the continued viability of broadcast television and that must-carry is an appropriate means of minimizing that risk.

As Justice Kennedy recognizes, findings by the Congress, particularly those emerging from such sustained deliberations, merit special respect from this Court. Accorded proper deference, the findings in § 2 are sufficient to sustain the must-carry provisions against facial attack. Congress's conclusion, for example, that broadcasters who are denied carriage on cable systems will suffer serious and potentially terminal economic harm, requires no "further demonstration." [E]ven if Congress had had before it no historical evidence that terminations or refusals of carriage had already occurred, it could reasonably infer that

cable operators' bottleneck control, together with the already high degree of vertical integration in the industry, would motivate such conduct in the near future.

It is thus my view that we should affirm the judgment of the District Court. Were I to vote to affirm, however, no disposition of this appeal would command the support of a majority of the Court. Accordingly, because I am in substantial agreement with Justice Kennedy's analysis of the case, I concur in the judgment vacating and remanding for further proceedings.

Justice O'CONNOR, with whom Justice SCALIA and Justice GINSBURG join, and with whom Justice THOMAS joins as to Parts I and III, concurring in part and dissenting in part.

There are only so many channels that any cable system can carry. If there are fewer channels than programmers who want to use the system, some programmers will have to be dropped. In the must-carry provisions of the 1992 Cable Act, Congress made a choice: By reserving a little over one-third of the channels on a cable system for broadcasters, it ensured that in most cases it will be a cable programmer who is dropped and a broadcaster who is retained. The question presented in this case is whether this choice comports with the commands of the First Amendment.

The 1992 Cable Act implicates the First Amendment rights of two classes of speakers. First, it tells cable operators which programmers they must carry, and keeps cable operators from carrying others that they might prefer. Though cable operators do not actually originate most of the programming they show, the Court correctly holds that they are, for First Amendment purposes, speakers. Selecting which speech to retransmit is, as we know from the example of publishing houses, movie theaters, bookstores, and Reader's Digest, no less communication than is creating the speech in the first place.

Second, the Act deprives a certain class of video programmers—those who operate cable channels rather than broadcast stations—of access to over one-third of an entire medium. Cable programmers may compete only for those channels that are not set aside by the must-carry provisions. A cable programmer that might otherwise have been carried may well be denied access in favor of a broadcaster that is less appealing to the viewers but is favored by the must-carry rules.

Under the First Amendment, it is normally not within the government's power to decide who may speak and who may not, at least on private property or in traditional public fora. Laws that treat all speakers equally are relatively poor tools for controlling public debate, and their very generality creates a substantial political check that prevents them from being unduly burdensome. Laws that single out particular speakers are substantially more dangerous, even when they do not draw explicit content distinctions.

Preferences for diversity of viewpoints, for localism, for educational programming, and for news and public affairs all make reference to content. They may not reflect hostility to particular points of view, or a desire to suppress certain subjects because they are controversial or offensive. They may be quite benignly motivated. But benign motivation, we have consistently held, is not enough to avoid the need for strict scrutiny of content-based justifications. The First Amendment does more than just bar government from intentionally suppressing speech of which it disapproves. It also generally prohibits the government from excepting certain kinds of speech from regulation because it thinks the speech is especially valuable.

This is why the Court is mistaken in concluding that the interest in diversity—in "access to a multiplicity" of "diverse and antagonistic sources"—is content neutral. The interest in ensuring access to a multiplicity of diverse and antagonistic sources of information, no matter how praiseworthy, is directly tied to the content of what the speakers will likely say.

* * *

[T]he Court suggests, the findings show "nothing more than the recognition that the services provided by broadcast television have some intrinsic value and, thus, are worth preserving against the threats posed by cable." I cannot agree. The controversial judgment at the heart of the statute is not that broadcast television has some value— obviously it does—but that broadcasters should be preferred over cable programmers. The best explanation for the findings, it seems to me, is that they represent Congress' reasons for adopting this preference; and, according to the findings, these reasons rest in part on the content of broadcasters' speech.

Having said all this, it is important to acknowledge one basic fact: The question is not whether there will be control over who gets to speak over cable—the question is who will have this control. Under the FCC's view, the answer is Congress, acting within relatively broad limits. Under my view, the answer is the cable operator. Most of the time, the cable operator's decision will be largely dictated by the preferences of the viewers; but because many cable operators are indeed monopolists, the viewers' preferences will not always prevail. Our recognition that cable operators are speakers is bottomed in large part on the very fact that the cable operator has editorial discretion.

I have no doubt that there is danger in having a single cable operator decide what millions of subscribers can or cannot watch. And I have no doubt that Congress can act to relieve this danger. In other provisions of the Act, Congress has already taken steps to foster competition among cable systems. Congress can encourage the creation of new media, such as inexpensive satellite broadcasting, or fiber-optic networks with virtually unlimited channels, or even simple devices that would let people easily switch from cable to over-the-air broadcasting. And of course Congress can subsidize broadcasters that it thinks provide especially valuable programming.

But the First Amendment as we understand it today rests on the premise that it is government power, rather than private power, that is the main threat to free expression; and as a consequence, the Amendment imposes substantial limitations on the Government even when it is trying to serve concededly praiseworthy goals. Perhaps Congress can to some extent restrict, even in a content-based manner, the speech of cable operators and cable programmers. But it must do so in compliance with the constitutional requirements, requirements that were not complied with here. Accordingly, I would reverse the judgment below.

Justice GINSBURG, concurring in part and dissenting in part.

I conclude that Congress' "must-carry" regime, which requires cable operators to set aside just over one-third of their channels for local broadcast stations, reflects an unwarranted content-based preference and hypothesizes a risk to local stations that remains imaginary.

The "must-carry" rules Congress has ordered do not differentiate on the basis of "viewpoint," and therefore do not fall in the category of speech regulation that Government must avoid most assiduously. The rules, however, do reflect a content preference, and on that account demand close scrutiny.

COMMENT

In *Turner*, cable operators argued that the must-carry rules should be held unconstitutional because they were similar to the right-of-reply statute overturned in *Tornillo*. Does the cable operators' analogy of cable to newspapers make more sense than their rejection of the broadcasting analogy? Was the *Turner* court wise in dismissing both analogies and relying on the *O'Brien* test?

A significant question raised by the *Turner* decision, and later by the decision in *Denver Area Educational Telecommunications Consortium, Inc. v. FCC*, 116 S.Ct. 2374 (1996). text, pp. 627, 824, is whose First Amendment interests should the law be concerned with—the public's right to view certain programs, the cable operators' right to maintain editorial control over their medium, or the cable programmers' right to create the programs they want and to have those programs aired.

On remand, a three-judge federal court held, 2–1, that the must-carry legislation satisfied the *O'Brien* test and was, therefore, consistent with the First Amendment.

Turner Broadcasting System, Inc. v. FCC

910 F. Supp. 734 (D.D.C. 1995).

SPORKIN, District Judge:

This matter comes before this three-judge District Court on remand from the Supreme Court of the United States. The central question before the Court is whether the "must-carry" provisions of the 1992 Cable Act violate the First Amendment.

Although this case pits expert against expert, there is no dispute about several fundamental facts. Cable systems and over-the air broadcast-

ers are in "direct competition" as an "independent source of television programming." *Turner*. And cable systems are winning the competition, with over 60% of the "television households" currently subscribing to cable systems. The market power of cable systems is expected to increase. Once a television household has subscribed to cable, then the cable operator has "monopoly power"—the "physical connection between the television set and the cable network gives the cable operator . . . gatekeeper control over most (if not all) of the television programming that is channeled into the subscriber's home." *Turner*. This gatekeeper control which has been conferred upon the cable medium by local and federal regulation, allows the cable operator to "silence the voices of competing speakers." *Turner*.

There is also no dispute that these monopolists face virtually no competition from other monopolists because the vast majority of television communities are served by only one cable system. Accordingly, local broadcasters cannot look to other cable systems for recourse when they are denied carriage on the one cable system in their area.

Finally, the cable industry has become increasingly horizontally concentrated and vertically integrated. Power has been concentrated in the hands of fewer and fewer operators (horizontal concentration) which has led to increased vertical integration as the largest operators have begun to demand ownership interests in cable programming networks.

Having determined that the burden to the cable industry is quite small and is expected to diminish, the question becomes whether the burden on protected speech is "substantially more . . . than is necessary to achieve the government's legitimate interests." *Turner*.

Plaintiffs assert that the must-carry rules fail the narrow tailoring test because there are less-restrictive means for achieving the government's purpose. Specifically, the Plaintiffs contend that there were some five less restrictive alternatives. These are: 1) adoption of the *Century* Rules [The *Century* rules were a more modest version of the 1992 law. These rules were found to be unconstitutional by the D.C. Circuit in *Century Communications Corp. v. FCC*, 835 F.2d 292 (D.C.

Cir. 1987), *cert. denied,* 486 U.S. 1032 (1988)]; 2) use of A/B switches which allow viewers to switch from receiving cable reception to receiving over-the-air broadcast reception; 3) direct governmental subsidies to local disadvantaged, over-the-air broadcasters; 4) imposition of charges for carriage; and 5) policing of cable operators' alleged abuses of power through antitrust and FCC enforcement. But even assuming that they would be less burdensome, it is clear they are not in any respect as effective in achieving the government's objectives—1) promoting fair competition in the market for television programming; 2) preserving the benefits of free, over-the-air broadcast television; and 3) promoting the widespread dissemination of information from a multiplicity of sources.

Based on the foregoing analysis, the Court finds that sections 4 and 5 of the Cable Act of 1992 survive the "intermediate level of scrutiny applicable to content-neutral restrictions that impose only an incidental burden on speech" as set forth in *O'Brien. Turner.* Accordingly, the Court grants the Defendants' motion for summary judgment and denies the Plaintiffs' motions for summary judgment.

COMMENT

The Supreme Court affirmed Judge Sporkin's decision that there was substantial justification for the must-carry legislation and that the evidence was sufficient to satisfy the *O'Brien* intermediate standard of review. See *Turner Broadcasting System, Inc. v. FCC,* 117 S. Ct. 1174 (1997). Among the First Amendment issues presented to the Supreme Court in *Turner II* was whether the *O'Brien* test was properly applied. In a long dissent, Judge Stephen Williams had said it was not. Note that Justice Kennedy for the Supreme Court in *Turner II* found must-carry to be consistent with the *O'Brien* test.

Recall that Justice O'Connor expressed doubts in *Turner* I about whether Congress could, consistent with the First Amendment, favor local over-the-air broadcast programming. In her opinion this constituted impermissible content discrimination. How did *Turner II* deal with this issue? On this point particular attention

should be given to Justice Breyer's concurrence in *Turner II.*

Turner Broadcasting System, Inc. v. FCC
117 S. Ct. 1174, 137 L.Ed. 2d 369 (1997).

Justice KENNEDY delivered the opinion of the Court, except as to a portion of Part II-A-1.

Sections 4 and 5 of the Cable Television Consumer Protection and Competition Act of 1992 require cable television systems to dedicate some of their channels to local broadcast television stations. Earlier in this case, we held the so-called "must-carry" provisions to be content-neutral restrictions on speech, subject to intermediate First Amendment scrutiny under *United States v. O'Brien,* 391 U.S. 367 (1968).

On appeal from the District Court's grant of summary judgment for appellees, the case now presents the two questions left open during the first appeal: First, whether the record as it now stands supports Congress' predictive judgment that the must-carry provisions further important governmental interests; and second, whether the provisions do not burden substantially more speech than necessary to further those interests. We answer both questions in the affirmative, and conclude the must-carry provisions are consistent with the First Amendment.

II

We begin where the plurality ended in *Turner [Broadcasting System, Inc. v. FCC,* 512 U.S. 622 (1994) ("*Turner*")], applying the standards for intermediate scrutiny enunciated in *O'Brien.* A content-neutral regulation will be sustained under the First Amendment if it advances important governmental interests unrelated to the suppression of free speech and does not burden substantially more speech than necessary to further those interests. *O'Brien,* 391 U.S., at 377. We have been most explicit in holding that "'protecting noncable households from loss of regular television broadcasting service due to competition from cable systems' is an important federal interest." *Id.,* at 663. We have identified a corresponding "governmental purpose of the highest order" in ensuring public access to "a multiplicity of information sources," 512 U.S., at 663. And it is undisputed the Government has an interest in "eliminating restraints on fair competition . . ., even when the individuals or entities subject to particular regulations are engaged in expressive activity protected by the First Amendment." *Ibid.*

On remand, and again before this Court, both sides have advanced new interpretations of these interests in an attempt to recast them in forms "more readily proven." These alternative formulations are inconsistent with Congress' stated interests in enacting must-carry. In explicit factual findings, Congress expressed clear concern that the "marked shift in market share from broadcast television to cable television services," Cable Act § 2(a)(13), note following 47 U.S.C. § 521, resulting from increasing market penetration by cable services, as well as the expanding horizontal concentration and vertical integration of cable operators, combined to give cable systems the incentive and ability to delete, reposition, or decline carriage to local broadcasters in an attempt to favor affiliated cable programmers. § 2a(2)–(5), (15). Congress predicted that "absent the reimposition of [must-carry], additional local broadcast signals will be deleted, repositioned, or not carried" with the end result that "the economic viability of free local broadcast television and its ability to originate quality local programming will be seriously jeopardized." § 2(a)(16).

Congress was concerned that without must-carry "significant numbers of broadcast stations will be refused carriage on cable systems," and those "broadcast stations denied carriage will either deteriorate to a substantial degree or fail altogether." 512 U.S., at 666.

Nor do the congressional findings support appellants' suggestion that legitimate legislative goals would be satisfied by the preservation of a rump broadcasting industry providing a minimum of broadcast service to Americans without cable. We have noted that "'it has long been a basic tenet of national communications policy that the widest possible dissemination of information from diverse and antagonistic sources is essential to the welfare of the public.'" *Turner,* 512 U.S., at 663–664. "'[I]ncreasing the number of outlets for community self-expression'" represents a "'long-established regulatory goa[l] in the field of television broadcasting.'" *United States v. Midwest Video Corp.,* [406 U.S. 649, 667–68

(1972) (plurality opinion)]. Consistent with this objective, the Cable Act's findings reflect a concern that congressional action was necessary to prevent "a reduction in the number of media voices available to consumers." § 2(a)(4).

It is for Congress to decide how much local broadcast television should be preserved for non-cable households, and the validity of its determination "'does not turn on a judge's agreement with the responsible decisionmaker concerning' . . . the degree to which [the Government's] interests should be promoted." *Ward* [*v. Rock Against Racism,* 491 U.S. 781, 800 (1989)]. Congress has an independent interest in preserving a multiplicity of broadcasters to ensure that all households have access to information and entertainment on an equal footing with those who subscribe to cable.

A

The expanded record now permits us to consider whether the must-carry provisions were designed to address a real harm, and whether those provisions will alleviate it in a material way. We turn first to the harm or risk which prompted Congress to act. The Government's assertion that "the economic health of local broadcasting is in genuine jeopardy and in need of the protections afforded by must-carry" rests on two component propositions: First, "significant numbers of broadcast stations will be refused carriage on cable systems" absent must-carry. Second, "the broadcast stations denied carriage will either deteriorate to a substantial degree or fail altogether."

1

We have no difficulty in finding a substantial basis to support Congress' conclusion that a real threat justified enactment of the must-carry provisions.

[T]here was specific support for [Congress's] conclusion that cable operators had considerable and growing market power over local video programming markets. Cable operators exercise "control over most (if not all) of the television programming that is channeled into the subscriber's home . . . . [and] can thus silence the voice of competing speakers with a mere flick of the switch." *Turner.*

Evidence indicated the structure of the cable industry would give cable operators increasing ability and incentive to drop local broadcast stations from their systems, or reposition them to a less-viewed channel. Horizontal concentration was increasing as a small number of multiple system operators (MSO's) acquired large numbers of cable systems nationwide. The trend was accelerating, giving the MSO's increasing market power. Vertical integration in the industry also was increasing. As Congress was aware, many MSO's owned or had affiliation agreements with cable programmers.

Though the dissent criticizes our reliance on evidence provided to Congress by parties that are private appellees here, that argument displays a lack of regard for Congress' factfinding function.

The reasonableness of Congress' conclusion was borne out by the evidence on remand, which also reflected cable industry favoritism for integrated programmers.

In addition, evidence before Congress indicated that cable systems would have incentives to drop local broadcasters in favor of other programmers less likely to compete with them for audience and advertisers. Independent local broadcasters tend to be the closest substitutes for cable programs, because their programming tends to be similar, and because both primarily target the same type of advertiser: those interested in cheaper (and more frequent) ad spots than are typically available on network affiliates.

[C]able has little interest in assisting, through carriage, a competing medium of communication. As one cable-industry executive put it, "'our job is to promote cable television, not broadcast television.'" Congress could reasonably conclude that cable systems would drop broadcasters in favor of programmers—even unaffiliated ones—less likely to compete with them for audience and advertisers.

The dissent contends Congress could not reasonably conclude cable systems would engage in such predation because cable operators, whose primary source of revenue is subscriptions, would not risk dropping a widely viewed broadcast station in order to capture advertising revenues. However, if viewers are faced with the choice of sacrificing a handful of broadcast stations to gain access to dozens of cable channels (plus network affiliates), it is likely they would still subscribe to cable even if they would prefer the dropped television stations to the cable programming that replaced them. Substantial evidence demon-

strated that absent must-carry the already "serious" problem of noncarriage would grow worse because "additional local broadcast signals will be deleted, repositioned, or not carried."

The dissent cites evidence indicating that many dropped broadcasters were stations few viewers watch, and it suggests that must-carry thwarts noncable viewers' preferences. If cable systems refused to carry certain local broadcast stations because of their subscribers' preferences for the cable services carried in their place, one would expect that all cable programming services would have ratings exceeding those of broadcasters not carried. That is simply not the case.

This is not a case in which we are called upon to give our best judgment as to the likely economic consequences of certain financial arrange- ments or business structures, or to assess competing economic theories and predictive judgments, as we would in a case arising, say, under the antitrust laws. The issue before us is whether, given conflicting views of the probable development of the television industry, Congress had substantial evidence for making the judgment that it did. We need not put our imprimatur on Congress' economic theory in order to validate the reasonableness of its judgment.

2

The harm Congress feared was that stations dropped or denied carriage would *be at a* "serious risk of financial difficulty," 512 U.S., at 667, and would "deteriorate to a substantial degree or fail altogether." *Id.*, at 666. Congress had before it substantial evidence to support its conclusion. Congress was advised the viability of a broadcast station depends to a material extent on its ability to secure cable carriage.

We hold Congress could conclude from the substantial body of evidence before it that "absent legislative action, the free local off-air broadcast system is endangered."

The evidence assembled on remand confirms the reasonableness of the congressional judgment. Documents produced on remand reflect that internal cable industry studies "clearly establis[h] the importance of cable television to broadcast television stations.

The question is not whether Congress, as an objective matter, was correct to determine must-carry is necessary to prevent a substantial number of broadcast stations from losing cable carriage and suffering significant financial hardship. Rather, the question is whether the legislative conclusion was reasonable and supported by substantial evidence in the record before Congress. *Turner*, 512 U.S., at 665–666. We are not at liberty to substitute our judgment for the reasonable conclusion of a legislative body. See *Turner*, *supra*, at 665–666. A fundamental principle of legislation is that Congress is under no obligation to wait until the entire harm occurs but may act to prevent it. We think it apparent must-carry serves the Government's interests "in a direct and effective way." *Ward*, 491 U.S., at 800. Must-carry ensures that a number of local broadcasters retain cable carriage, with the concomitant audience access and advertising revenues needed to support a multiplicity of stations.

B

The second portion of the *O'Brien* inquiry concerns the fit between the asserted interests and the means chosen to advance them. Content–neutral regulations do not pose the same "inherent dangers to free expression," *Turner*, *supra*, at 661, that content-based regulations do, and thus are subject to a less rigorous analysis, which affords the Government latitude in designing a regulatory solution. Under intermediate scrutiny, the Government may employ the means of its choosing "'so long as the . . . regulation promotes a substantial governmental interest that would be achieved less effectively absent the regulation,'" and does not "'burden substantially more speech than is necessary to further'" that interest. *Turner*.

Appellants say the burden of must-carry is great, but the evidence adduced on remand indicates the actual effects are modest. Significant evidence indicates the vast majority of cable operators have not been affected in a significant manner by must-carry.

Appellants argue that the rate of growth in cable programming outstrips cable operators' creation of new channel space, that the rate of cable growth is lower than claimed, and that must-carry infringes First Amendment rights now irrespective of future growth. Finally, they say that regardless of the percentage of channels occupied, must-carry still represents "thousands of real and individual infringements of speech."

While the parties' evidence is susceptible of varying interpretations, a few definite conclusions can be drawn about the burdens of must-carry. It is undisputed that broadcast stations gained carriage on 5,880 channels as a result of must-carry. While broadcast stations occupy another 30,006 cable channels nationwide, this carriage does not represent a significant First Amendment harm to either system operators or cable programmers because those stations were carried voluntarily before 1992, and even appellants represent that the vast majority of those channels would continue to be carried in the absence of any legal obligation to do so. The 5,880 channels occupied by added broadcasters represent the actual burden of the regulatory scheme. Appellants concede most of those stations would be dropped in the absence of must-carry so the figure approximates the benefits of must-carry as well.

Because the burden imposed by must-carry is congruent to the benefits it affords, we conclude must-carry is narrowly tailored to preserve a multiplicity of broadcast stations for the 40 percent of American households without cable.

Appellants posit a number of alternatives in an effort to demonstrate a less-restrictive means to achieve the Government's aims. They ask us, in effect, to "sif[t] through all the available or imagined alternative means of regulating [cable television] in order to determine whether the [Government's] solution was 'the least intrusive means' of achieving the desired end," an approach we rejected in *Ward*, 491 U.S., at 797. This "'less-restrictive-alternative analysis . . . has never been a part of the inquiry into the validity'" of content-neutral regulations on speech. Our precedents establish that when evaluating a content-neutral regulation which incidentally burdens speech, we will not invalidate the preferred remedial scheme because some alternative solution is marginally less intrusive on a speaker's First Amendment interests.

In any event, after careful examination of each of the alternatives suggested by appellants, we cannot conclude that any of them is an adequate alternative to must-carry for promoting the Government's legitimate interests.

[EDITORIAL NOTE: *The Court addressed appellants' proposed alternatives to must-carry but determined that the record included sufficient evidence to support Congress's rejection of those alternatives.*]

III

Judgments about how competing economic interests are to be reconciled in the complex and fast-changing field of television are for Congress to make. Those judgments "cannot be ignored or undervalued simply because [appellants] cas[t] [their] claims under the umbrella of the First Amendment." *Columbia Broad. v. DNC*, 412 U.S., at 103. Appellants' challenges to must-carry reflect little more than disagreement over the level of protection broadcast stations are to be afforded and how protection is to be attained. We cannot displace Congress' judgment respecting content-neutral regulations with our own, so long as its policy is grounded on reasonable factual findings supported by evidence that is substantial for a legislative determination. Those requirements were met in this case, and in these circumstances the First Amendment requires nothing more. The judgment of the District Court is affirmed.

It is so ordered.

Justice STEVENS, concurring.

As Justice KENNEDY clearly explains, the policy judgments made by Congress in the enactment of legislation that is intended to forestall the abuse of monopoly power are entitled to substantial deference. That is true even when the attempt to protect an economic market imposes burdens on communication. If this statute regulated the content of speech rather than the structure of the market, our task would be quite different. Though I write to emphasize this important point, I fully concur in the Court's thorough opinion.

Justice BREYER, concurring in part.

I join the opinion of the Court except insofar as Part II-A-1 relies on an anticompetitive rationale. I agree with the majority that the statute must be "sustained under the First Amendment if it advances important governmental interests unrelated to the suppression of free speech and does not burden substantially more speech than necessary to further those interests." *United States v. O'Brien.* I also agree that the statute satisfies this standard. My conclusion rests, however, not upon the principal opinion's analysis of the statute's efforts to "promot[e] fair competition," but rather upon its discussion of the statute's other objectives, namely "'(1) preserving the benefits of free, over-the-air local broadcast television,'" and "'(2) promoting the widespread

dissemination of information from a multiplicity of sources.'" *Turner I.* Whether or not the statute does or does not sensibly compensate for some significant market defect, it undoubtedly seeks to provide over-the-air viewers who lack cable with a rich mix of over-the-air programming. I believe that this purpose—to assure the over-the-air public "access to a multiplicity of information sources" provides sufficient basis for rejecting appellants' First Amendment claim.

I do not deny that the compulsory carriage that creates the "guarantee" extracts a serious First Amendment price. This "price" amounts to a "suppression of speech."

But there are important First Amendment interests on the other side as well. The statute's basic noneconomic purpose is to prevent too precipitous a decline in the quality and quantity of programming choice for an evershrinking non-cable-subscribing segment of the public. This purpose reflects what "has long been a basic tenet of national communications policy," namely that "the widest possible dissemination of information from diverse and antagonistic sources is essential to the welfare of the public."

With important First Amendment interests on both sides of the equation, the key question becomes one of proper fit. The majority's opinion analyzes and evaluates those consequences, and I agree with its conclusions in respect to both of these matters.

I believe that Congress could reasonably conclude that the statute will help the typical over-the-air viewer (by maintaining an expanded range of choice) more than it will hurt the typical cable subscriber (by restricting cable slots otherwise available for preferred programming). The former's over-the-air choice is restricted; and, as cable becomes more popular, it may well become still more restricted insofar as the over-the-air market shrinks and thereby, by itself, becomes less profitable. In these circumstances, I do not believe the First Amendment dictates a result that favors the cable viewers' interests.

These and other similar factors discussed by the majority, lead me to agree that the statute survives "intermediate scrutiny," whether or not the statute is properly tailored to Congress' purely economic objectives.

Justice O'CONNOR, with whom Justice SCALIA, Justice THOMAS, and Justice GINSBURG join, dissenting.

In sustaining the must-carry provisions of the [1992 Cable Act], against a First Amendment challenge by cable system operators and cable programmers, the Court errs in two crucial respects. First, the Court disregards one of the principal defenses of the statute urged by appellees on remand: that it serves a substantial interest in preserving "diverse," "quality" programming that is "responsive" to the needs of the local community. Second, the Court misapplies the "intermediate scrutiny" framework it adopts. Although we owe deference to Congress' predictive judgments and its evaluation of complex economic questions, we have an independent duty to identify with care the Government interests supporting the scheme, to inquire into the reasonableness of congressional findings regarding its necessity, and to examine the fit between its goals and its consequences. The Court fails to discharge its duty here.

I

Much of the principal opinion treats the must-carry provisions as a species of antitrust regulation enacted by Congress in response to a perceived threat that cable system operators would otherwise engage in various forms of anticompetitive conduct resulting in harm to broadcasters.

I fully agree that promoting fair competition is a legitimate and substantial Government goal. But the Court nowhere examines whether the breadth of the must-carry provisions comports with a goal of preventing anticompetitive harms. Instead, in the course of its inquiry into whether the must-carry provisions are "narrowly tailored," the principal opinion simply assumes that most adverse carriage decisions are anticompetitively motivated, and that must-carry is therefore a measured response to a problem of anticompetitive behavior.

Perhaps because of the difficulty of defending the must-carry provisions as a measured response to anticompetitive behavior, the Court asserts an "independent" interest in preserving a "multiplicity" of broadcast programming sources. In doing so, the Court posits existence of "conduct that threatens" the availability of broadcast television outlets, quite apart from anticompetitive conduct. We are left to wonder what precisely that conduct might be. The proper analysis, in my view, necessarily turns on the present

distribution of broadcast stations among the local broadcast markets that make up the national broadcast "system." Whether cable poses a "significant" threat to a local broadcast market depends first on how many broadcast stations in that market will, in the absence of must-carry, remain available to viewers in noncable households. It also depends on whether viewers actually watch the stations that are dropped or denied carriage.

Neither the principal opinion nor the partial concurrence ever explains what kind of conduct, apart from anticompetitive conduct, threatens the "multiplicity" of broadcast programming sources. Pressed to explain the importance of preserving noncable viewers' access to "vulnerable" broadcast stations, appellees emphasize that the must-carry rules are necessary to ensure that broadcast stations maintain "diverse," "quality" programming that is "responsive" to the needs of the local community. Must-carry is thus justified as a way of preserving viewers' access to a Spanish or Chinese language station or of preventing an independent station from adopting a home-shopping format. Undoubtedly, such goals are reasonable and important, and the stations in question may well be worthwhile targets of Government subsidies. But appellees' characterization of must-carry as a means of protecting these stations, like the Court's explicit concern for promoting "'community self-expression'" and the "'local origination of broadcast programming'" reveals a content-based preference for broadcast programming. This justification of the regulatory scheme is, in my view, wholly at odds with the *Turner* Court's premise that must-carry is a means of preserving "access to free television programming—whatever its content," 512 U.S., at 649.

I do not read Justice BREYER'S opinion—which analyzes the must-carry rules in part as a "speech-enhancing" measure designed to ensure a "rich mix" of over-the-air programming—to treat the content of over-the-air programming as irrelevant to whether the Government's interest in promoting it is an important one. The net result appears to be that five Justices of this Court do not view must-carry as a narrowly tailored means of serving a substantial governmental interest in preventing anticompetitive behavior; and that five Justices of this Court do see the significance of the content of over-the-air programming to the Government's and appellees' efforts to defend the law. Under these circumstances, the must-carry provisions should be subject to strict scrutiny, which they surely fail.

II

The principal opinion goes to great lengths to avoid acknowledging that preferences for "quality," "diverse," and "responsive" local programming underlie the must-carry scheme, although the partial concurrence's reliance on such preferences is explicit. I take the principal opinion at its word and evaluate the claim that the threat of anticompetitive behavior by cable operators supplies a content-neutral basis for sustaining the statute. It does not.

Because I remain convinced that the statute is not a measured response to congressional concerns about monopoly power, in my view the principal opinion's discussion on this point is irrelevant. But even if it were relevant, it is incorrect.

1

[T]he principal opinion states that "[e]xtensive testimony" before Congress showed that in fact operators do have incentives to favor vertically integrated programmers. This testimony, noteworthy as it may be, is primarily that of persons appearing before Congress on behalf of the private appellees in this case. It is appropriate to regard the testimony of interested persons with a degree of skepticism when our task is to engage in "'independent judgment of the facts bearing on an issue of constitutional law.'" *Turner, supra*, at 666.

[A]ppellees claim that since cable operators compete directly with broadcasters for some advertising revenue, operators will profit if they can drive broadcasters out of the market and capture their advertising revenue. There is no dispute that a cable system depends primarily upon its subscriber base for revenue. A cable operator is therefore unlikely to drop a widely viewed station in order to capture advertising revenues— which, according to the figures of appellees' expert, account for between one and five percent of the total revenues of most large cable systems.

2

The Court accepts Congress' stated concern about preserving the availability of a "multiplicity" of broadcast stations, but apparently thinks it suffi-

cient to evaluate that concern in the abstract, without considering how much local service is already available in a given broadcast market.

Nor can we evaluate whether must-carry is necessary to serve an interest in preserving broadcast stations without examining the value of the stations protected by the must-carry scheme to viewers in noncable households. The issue is whether the Government can demonstrate a substantial interest in forced carriage of certain broadcast stations, for the benefit of viewers who lack access to cable. That inquiry is not advanced by an analysis of relative cable household viewership of broadcast and cable programming.

3

The record on remand does not permit the conclusion, at the summary judgment stage, that Congress could reasonably have predicted serious harm to a significant number of stations in the absence of must-carry.

The Court concludes that the evidence on remand meets the threshold of harm established in *Turner*. The analysis, however, does not focus on features of the market in which these stations were located or on the size of the audience they commanded.

Most of the anecdotal accounts of harm on which the Court relies are sharply disputed. Congress' reasonable conclusions are entitled to deference, and for that reason the fact that the evidence is in conflict will not necessarily preclude summary judgment in appellees' favor. Nevertheless, in the course of our independent review, we cannot ignore sharp conflicts in the record that call into question the reasonableness of Congress' findings.

A highly dubious economic theory has been advanced as the "substantial interest" supporting a First Amendment burden on cable operators and cable programmers. In finding that must-carry serves a substantial interest, the principal opinion necessarily accepts that theory. The partial concurrence does not, but neither does it articulate what threat to the availability of a "multiplicity" of broadcast stations would exist in a perfectly competitive market.

* * *

I turn now to the second portion of the *O'Brien* inquiry, which concerns the fit between the

Government's asserted interests and the means chosen to advance them.

The Court's logic is circular. Surmising that most of the 5,880 channels added by the regulatory scheme would be dropped in its absence, the Court concludes that the figure also approximates the "benefit" of must-carry. Finding the scheme's burden "congruent" to the benefit it affords, the Court declares the statute narrowly tailored. Without a sense whether most adverse carriage decisions are anticompetitively motivated, it is improper to conclude that the statute is narrowly tailored simply because it prevents some adverse carriage decisions.

In my view, the statute is not narrowly tailored to serve a substantial interest in preventing anticompetitive conduct. I do not understand Justice BREYER to disagree with this conclusion. Congress has commandeered up to one third of each cable system's channel capacity for the benefit of local broadcasters, without any regard for whether doing so advances the statute's alleged goals.

Finally, I note my disagreement with the Court's suggestion that the availability of less-speech-restrictive alternatives is never relevant to *O'Brien's* narrow tailoring inquiry. The Court's present position on this issue is puzzling.

Our cases suggest only that we have not interpreted the narrow tailoring inquiry to "require elimination of all less restrictive alternatives." Put another way, we have refrained from imposing a least-restrictive-means requirement in cases involving intermediate First Amendment scrutiny. *Ward.* [T]he availability of less intrusive approaches to a problem serves as a benchmark for assessing the reasonableness of the fit between Congress' articulated goals and the means chosen to pursue them. *Rubin v. Coors Brewing Co.,* 514 U.S. 476, 490–491.

If Congress truly sought to address anticompetitive behavior by cable system operators, it passed the wrong law. See *Turner, supra,* at 682 (O'CONNOR, J., concurring in part and dissenting in part) ("That some speech within a broad category causes harm . . . does not justify restricting the whole category"). Nevertheless, the availability of less restrictive alternatives—a leased-access regime and subsidies—reinforces my conclusion that the must-carry provisions are overbroad.

* * *

IV

In sustaining the must-carry provisions of the Cable Act, the Court ignores the main justification of the statute urged by appellees and subjects restrictions on expressive activity to an inappropriately lenient level of scrutiny. The principal opinion then misapplies the analytic framework it chooses, exhibiting an extraordinary and unwarranted deference for congressional judgments, a profound fear of delving into complex economic matters, and a willingness to substitute untested assumptions for evidence. In light of gaps in logic and evidence, it is improper to conclude, at the summary judgment stage, that the must-carry scheme serves a significant governmental interest "in a direct and effective way." *Ward,* 491 U.S., at 800.

Justice BREYER disavows the principal opinion's position on anticompetitive behavior, and instead treats the must-carry rules as a "speech-enhancing" measure designed to ensure access to "quality" programming for noncable households. Neither the principal opinion nor the partial concurrence explains the nature of the alleged threat to the availability of a "multiplicity of broadcast programming sources," if that threat does not arise from cable operators' anticompetitive conduct. Such an approach makes it impossible to discern whether Congress was addressing a problem that is "real, not merely conjectural," and whether must-carry addresses the problem in a "direct and material way." *Turner.*

I therefore respectfully dissent, and would reverse the judgment below.

COMMENT

In *Turner I,* the Court declined to apply the deferential *Red Lion* model to cable television regulation. The Court said that content-based regulation of cable should be reviewed under the demanding strict scrutiny standard of review. But the majority of the Court then ruled that the must-carry rules constituted *content-neutral* regulation.

In *Turner II,* Justice Kennedy's opinion for the Court once again concluded that the statutory must carry requirement was content neutral and that, therefore, the appropriate standard of review was intermediate scrutiny, i.e., the *O'Brien* test. This standard is more deferential to

Congress than the strict scrutiny standard. In Congress's judgment, the must-carry rules protected the economic health of local broadcasters. Absent must carry, the economic viability of local broadcasters might be at risk because cable operators would not be obliged to carry local broadcasters. The *Turner II* Court deferred to that congressional judgment.

The concurring opinion of Justice Breyer, who was not on the Court in *Turner I*, has attracted considerable attention. Justice Breyer upholds must carry because it preserves "the benefits of free, over-the-air broadcasting" *and* promotes "the widespread dissemination of information from a multiplicity of sources." Breyer is very much aware that both sides in the must carry controversy make strong First Amendment arguments. Cable operators have a point when they contend they should be allowed to make their own programming decisions. But cable's penetration of video programming makes those who are not cable subscribers particularly dependent on the survival of local over-the-air broadcasters for information. Breyer balances the interests and comes out in favor of the local over-the-air broadcasters. Recall that he used a balancing test in *Denver Area* as well (see text, pp. 627–633, 883–884). One First Amendment commentator, Prof. Cass Sunstein contends that Justice Breyer's opinion is the most significant of the opinions in *Turner II*: "Breyer says the First Amendment is basically about democracy. *Even content-based regulation can make democracy work better.* Breyer doesn't allow himself to be trapped by the categories of 'content-based' and 'content-neutral.'" See *Broadcasting*, April 7, 1997, at 30. Justice Breyer saw must-carry as enhancing rather than restricting expression. Why do you think he saw must-carry in this light?

Justice O'Connor in dissent contended that Justice Breyer's justification for maintaining local over-the-air broadcasting is "heavily content-based" because these broadcasters give voice to local community issues and community self-expression. As a technical matter, she is right on this. On a more fundamental level, can this analysis be seen as a criticism of the content-based versus content-neutral distinction? In addition, Justice O'Connor criticized Justice Kennedy's opinion for not really analyzing whether the must carry actually serves the goal of "preventing anti-competitive harms." In short, she suggests that by deferring to Congress the Court disserves the First Amendment.

Does the logic of *Turner II* require that the must carry obligation be imposed on DBS and DTV as well? See *Broadcasting*, April 7, 1997, at 32.

THE REGULATION OF CABLE TELEVISION CONTENT

Several portions of the 1984 Cable Act dealt with cable obscenity and, in some instances, indecency. Under the Act, operators of cable systems with more than thirty-six channels have to be willing to lease some channels to outsiders. Section 532(h) of 47 U.S.C., however, says that such leased access need not be provided if the franchising authority judges the access service to be "obscene, or in conflict with community standards in that it is lewd, lascivious, filthy, or indecent or is otherwise unprotected by the Constitution of the United States." Section 544(d) authorizes the franchising authority and cable operator to specify that certain cable services "shall not be provided, or shall be provided subject to conditions, if such cable services are obscene or are otherwise unprotected by the Constitution of the United States." Section 544(d)(2)(A) says that cable system operators have to provide "lockboxes" for sale or lease that cable subscribers can use to "prohibit viewing of a particular cable service during periods selected by that subscriber." In other words, a subscriber can use the lockbox to block out, for example, the Playboy Channel when the children are home alone. Finally, sec. 559 extends the previously existing criminal sanctions against broadcast obscenity to cable obscenity by providing that "whoever transmits over any cable system any matter which is obscene or otherwise unprotected by the Constitution of the United States shall be fined not more than $10,000 or imprisoned not more than 2 years, or both." In 1988, Congress amended this portion of the law to make it clear that both state and federal obscenity prosecutions were possible.

Oddly, these provisions of federal law have not yet been the object of much litigation. Instead, lawsuits have arisen when states and local governments have adopted statutes or ordinances aimed at restricting obscene or, more often, indecent cable programming. Challenges to these laws have forced courts to confront the basic lack of a First Amendment theory for cable television.

The major cases arose in Utah and Miami, Florida. In each instance, laws were adopted prohibiting cable "indecency." The effort, in each, was to transplant the principles of the regulation of broadcast indecency, largely as reflected in the U.S. Supreme Court's *Pacifica* decision, into the area of cable television. Although the courts that eventually struck down these laws did not establish a general First Amendment theory for cable, they did decide that the broadcast model derived from *Pacifica* did not apply. The Utah statute was initially struck down in *Community Television of Utah, Inc. v. Roy City,* 555 F.Supp. 1164 (D.C. Utah 1982). It was disapproved again in *Community Television v. Wilkinson,* 611 F. Supp. 1099 (D.C. Utah 1985), a decision upheld in *Jones v. Wilkinson,* 800 F.2d 989 (10th Cir. 1986). The U.S. Supreme Court affirmed without opinion, 107 S. Ct. 1559 (1987). Miami's rather similar ordinance was invalidated in *Cruz v. Ferre,* 571 F. Supp. 125 (S.D.Fla. 1983), a decision upheld in *Cruz v. Ferre,* 755 F.2d 1415 (11th Cir. 1985). This Eleventh Circuit Court of Appeals decision considers the propriety of applying broadcast indecency theories to cable television.

Cruz v. Ferre
755 F.2D 1415 (11TH CIR. 1985).

STAFFORD, District Judge:

This case involves a challenge to the constitutionality of a Miami ordinance regulating the distribution of obscene and indecent material through cable television. The district court found the provisions of the ordinance regulating the distribution of "indecent material" constitutionally overbroad. Additionally, the district judge held that the ordinance "violate[s] the notion of fairness implicit in one's right to due process of law." *Cruz v. Ferre,* 571 F.Supp. 125, 126 (S.D.Fla. 1983). We affirm on both first amendment and due process grounds.

On January 13, 1983, the city [of Miami] enacted a third cable ordinance, Ordinance No. 9538. This ordinance, which is the subject of this

lawsuit, is intended to regulate "indecent" and "obscene" material on cable television. The relevant portions of this ordinance provide:

> Section 1. No person shall by means of a cable television system knowingly distribute by wire or cable any obscene or indecent material.
> *Section 2.* The following words have the following meanings:
> (f) The test of whether or not material is "obscene" is:
> (1) whether the average person, applying contemporary community standards, would find that the work, taken as a whole, appeals to the prurient interest;
> (2) whether the work depicts or describes, in a patently offensive way, sexual conduct specifically defined by the applicable state law; and (3) whether the work, taken as a whole, lacks serious literary, artistic, political or scientific value.
> (g) "Indecent material" means material which is a representation or description of a human sexual or excretory organ or function which the average person, applying contemporary community standards, would find to be patently offensive.

Additionally, section 3 of the ordinance provides procedures for complaints alleging violations of the ordinance to be brought. Furthermore, the city manager is empowered to initiate such claims himself. All complaints, whether received or initiated by the city manager, are to be reviewed by him to determine whether there is probable cause to believe that a violation has been committed. If the city manager determines that such probable cause exists, [a hearing is held.] The city manager presides over the hearing and governs the admissibility of evidence. The burden of proof (a preponderance of the evidence) is on the city. Within ten days after the conclusion of the hearing, the city manager is to make his written findings and decision, including the nature and extent of any sanctions imposed and the reasons therefore. The only sanctions provided in the ordinance are suspension of the license for a period of time not to exceed nine days, or termination of the license.

This action for declaratory and injunctive relief was filed in February 1983 against appellants, the City of Miami, its mayor, and its city manager. Plaintiff-appellee Ruben Cruz is a Cablevision subscriber. The complaint sought a judgment declaring the ordinance void on its face and an injunction restraining the enforcement of the ordinance.

Appellants challenge the district court's resolution of the first amendment and due process issues. The United States Supreme Court has long recognized that the first amendment's prohibition against any "law abridging the freedom of speech" applies to the states and their subdivisions through the fourteenth amendment. *Gitlow v. New York* (1925). In *Miller v. California,* (1973), the Court reaffirmed that obscene material is unprotected by the first amendment and set forth the current permissible limits of regulation. However, the *Miller* court "acknowledge[d] the inherent dangers of undertaking to regulate any form of expression. State statutes designed to regulate obscene materials must be carefully limited."

Appellees did not challenge the Miami ordinance's definition of "obscene" material or the city's constitutional authority to regulate obscenity on cable television. (The ordinance's definition of obscenity is in fact closely derived from the test set forth in *Miller.*) Rather, appellees challenged the provisions of the ordinance which attempt to regulate "indecent" materials. The ordinance's definition of indecent materials goes beyond the *Miller* definition of obscenity in two significant respects. First, the ordinance does not require that the challenged materials, "taken as a whole, appeal to the prurient interest in sex." *Miller.* Second, the ordinance does not inquire whether the materials, "taken as a whole, do not have serious literary, artistic, political, or scientific value." Therefore, if materials falling within the ordinance's definition of "indecent" are to be regulated, the city's authority to do so must be found somewhere other than in the Supreme Court's obscenity cases.

Appellants' primary argument on appeal is that authority for the city's regulation is found in the Supreme Court decision *FCC v. Pacifica Foundation* (1978). In *Pacifica,* [f]ive members of the Court concluded that broadcasting of indecency could be regulated by the FCC under certain circumstances. The Court noted that "of all forms of communication, it is broadcasting that has received the most limited First Amendment protection." Moreover, the Court wrote that "differences between radio, television, and perhaps closed-circuit transmissions, may also be relevant."

The district court, after "a careful consideration of *Pacifica*," found *Pacifica* to be "inapplic-

able to the facts herein." *Cruz v. Ferre*, 571 F. Supp. at 131. After describing the cable television medium, the district court contrasted the cable medium with broadcast television. A Cablevision subscriber may avoid the unpleasant surprises that sometimes occur in broadcast programming. Additionally, the district court noted, the ability to protect children is provided through use of a free "lockbox" or "parental key" available from Cablevision.

In reaching his conclusions, the district judge relied in great part upon two cases from Utah, *Community Television, Inc. v. Roy City,* 555 F. Supp. 1164 (D. Utah 1982), and *Home Box Office, Inc.* v. *Wilkinson,* 531 F. Supp. 987 (d.Utah 1982). *Roy City* and *Wilkinson* are the only other federal cases to have adjudicated the applicability of *Pacifica* to cable television. The district court in *Roy City* summarized the "key concepts" in *Pacifica* as "the broadcasting of patently offensive material, its presence on public airwaves at a time when it could be available to children, audience surprise, and the power of the F.C.C. to control airwaves in the `public interest.'" After listing the differences between cable and broadcast television, the *Roy City* court examined these differences in greater detail and concluded, based upon these differences, that *Pacifica* is inapplicable to cable television. The Court gave particular emphasis to *Pacifica's* "pervasiveness" component and found that cable television, unlike broadcast television, is not pervasive.

[W]e are persuaded that *Pacifica* cannot be extended to cover the particular facts of this case. *Pacifica,* it must be remembered, focused upon broadcasting's "pervasive presence," and the fact that broadcasting "is uniquely accessible to children, even those too young to read." The Court's concern with the pervasiveness of the broadcast media can best be seen in its description of broadcasted material as an "intruder" into the privacy of the home. Cablevision, however, does not "intrude" into the home. The Cablevision subscriber must affirmatively elect to have cable service come into his home. Additionally, the subscriber must make the additional affirmative decision whether to purchase any "extra" programming services, such as HBO. The Supreme Court's reference to "a nuisance rationale," is not applicable to the Cablevision system, where there is no possibility that a non-cable subscriber will be confronted with materials carried only on cable. One of the keys to the very existence of cable television is the fact that cable programming is available only to those who have the cable attached to their television sets.[6]

Probably the more important justification recognized in *Pacifica* for the FCC's authority to regulate the broadcasting of indecent materials was the accessibility of broadcasting to children. This interest, however, is significantly weaker in the context of cable television because parental manageability of cable television greatly exceeds the ability to manage the broadcast media. Again, parents must decide whether to allow Cablevision into the home. [P]arents may obtain a "lockbox" or "parental key" device enabling parents to prevent children from gaining access to "objectionable" channels of programming. Cablevision provides these without charge to subscribers.

Pacifica represents a careful balancing of the first amendment rights of broadcasters and willing adult listeners against the FCC's interests in protecting children and unwilling adults. The Court held that under the particular facts of Pacifica, the balance weighed in favor of the FCC. Because we determine that under the facts of the instant case the interests of the City of Miami are substantially less strong than those of the FCC in *Pacifica*, we believe that we must hold *Pacifica* to be inapplicable to this case.[9]

─────────────

6. Appellants seem to want to extend Justice Stevens's "pig in the parlor" analogy. *See* Brief of Appellants at 16 ("it makes no difference whether the pig enters the parlor through the door of broadcast, cable, or amplified speech: government is entitled to keep the pig out of the parlor"). It seems to us, however, that if an individual voluntarily opens his door and allows a pig into his parlor, he is in less of a position to squeal.

9. Appellants and the State of Utah apparently argue that the limited number of stations on cable television somehow gives the city an interest in regulating indecency on cable television. This argument, however, misconstrues the rationale in *Pacifica* and in other Supreme Court cases such as *Red Lion Broadcasting Co. v. FCC*, 395 U.S. 367, 396 (1969). As Justice Brennan noted in *Pacifica*:

The opinions of my Brothers Powell and Stevens rightly refrain from relying on the notion of "spectrum scarcity" to support their result. As Chief Judge Bazelon noted below, "although scarcity has justified increasing the diversity of speakers and speech, it has never been held to justify censorship." *Pacifica*, 438 U.S. at 770 n. 4, (Brennan, J., dissenting) (quoting *Pacifica Foundation v. FCC*, 556 F.2d 9, 29 (D.C. Cir. 1977)).

Even if we were to find the rationale of *Pacifica* applicable to this case, we would still be compelled to strike the ordinance as facially overbroad. As the district judge noted, the ordinance "prohibits far too broadly the transmission of indecent materials through cable television. The ordinance's prohibition is wholesale, without regard to the time of day or other variables indispensable to the decision in *Pacifica*." The ordinance totally fails to account for the variables identified in *Pacifica*: the time of day; the context of the program in which the material appears; the composition of the viewing audience. In ignoring these variables, the ordinance goes far beyond the realm of permissible regulation envisioned by the *Pacifica* Court.

However noble may have been the city's intentions, we are constrained to recognize the limitations imposed by the Constitution and the opinions of the Supreme Court. The city's attempt through the challenged ordinance to regulate indecency on its cable television system exceeds these limitations.

For the reasons stated herein, we hold that the findings of the district court were correct as a matter of law. Accordingly, we AFFIRM.

──────────────

COMMENT

The focus of the *Cruz* case is very clearly on the distinctions between cable television and broadcasting. The significance of emphasizing these distinctions is very clearly to try to free cable television from the regulatory embrace of the Supreme Court's decision in *FCC v. Pacifica Foundation*, text, pp. 606–613. According to *Cruz*, cable is less pervasive than broadcasting in the sense that getting access to cable requires more effort than getting access to over-the-air broadcasting. To obtain cable, one has to subscribe. In *Pacifica*, Justice Stevens, although conceding that indecent speech was protected, also insisted that it could be channeled to times when children were less likely to be in the audience. Or, as Justice Stevens put it, government is "entitled to keep the pig out of the parlor." But Judge Stafford for the Eleventh Circuit in *Cruz* said it was different in the cable context: "[I]f an individual voluntarily opens his door and allows a pig into his parlor, he is in less of a position to squeal."

In 1996, in the *Denver Area* case below, the Supreme Court had to consider the application of *Pacifica* to cable. Once again the issue arose as to whether cable, like broadcasting, was pervasive and uniquely accessible to children. But the Court in *Denver Area* took a very different stance from the position espoused by Judge Stafford in *Cruz*.

Indecency and Cable Access Channels

In *Denver Area Educational Telecommunications Consortium, Inc. v. FCC*, 116 S. Ct. 2374 (1996), the Supreme Court considered First Amendment challenges to three provisions of the 1992 Cable Act as implemented by FCC regulations. Section 10(a) permits a cable operator to refuse to carry leased access programming that "depicts sexual or excretory activities or organs in a patently offensive way as measured by contemporary community standards." Section 10(b) requires the FCC to promulgate rules requiring cable operators transmitting indecent material on leased access channels to segregate such programming on a separate channel that is blocked unless the subscriber requests otherwise.

Section 10(c) mandates that the FCC issue regulations that authorize cable operators to deny the use of public, educational, and governmental channels (public access channels) for programming "which contains obscene material, sexually explicit conduct, or material soliciting or promoting unlawful conduct."

A sharply divided Court upheld sec. 10(a) by a 7–2 vote, struck down sec. 10(c) by a 5–4 vote, and struck down sec. 10 (b) by a 6–3 vote. As a result of the decision, indecency on public access channels receives more favored treatment than indecency on leased access channels. The requirement that indecent material be segregated on a separate channel was struck down, however. The *Denver Area*'s consideration of First Amendment issues relating to access channels is in the text, pp. 627–633, while its discussion of indecency regulation of cable access channels is set forth in the next paragraphs

Justice Breyer joined by Justices Stevens, O'Connor and Souter concluded that Sec. 10(a) was valid. First, *Sable Communications v. FCC*, 492 U.S. 115 (1991), *Ginsberg v. New York*, 390 U.S. 629 (1968), and *New York v. Ferber*, 458 U.S. 747 (1982) all support the compelling governmental interest in protecting "children from exposure to patently offensive sex-related

material." Second, sec. 10(a) is a very specialized provision. "[B]ut for a previous act of Congress" there would have been "no path of access of an operator's control." Third, the problem Congress addressed in *Pacifica* is remarkably similar to the problem addressed by Congress in the cable context:

> All [the *Pacifica* factors] are present here. Cable television broadcasting, including access channel broadcasting, is as "accessible to children" as over-the-air broadcasting, if not more so. See Heeter, Greenberg, Baldwin, Paugh, Srigley, & Atkin, Parental Influences on Viewing Style, in Cableviewing 140 (C. Heeter & B. Greenberg eds. 1988) (children spend more time watching television and view more channels than do their parents, whether their household subscribes to cable or receives television over the air.) Cable television systems, including access channels, "have established a uniquely pervasive presence in the lives of all Americans." *Pacifica*. [Studies showed that] cable subscribers tended to sample more channels before settling on a program, thereby making them more, not less, susceptible to random exposure to unwanted materials. There is nothing to stop "adults who feel the need" from finding similar programming elsewhere, say, on tape or in theaters.

Fourth, Justice Breyer pointed out that sec. 10(a) is permissive, i.e., it did not *require* the cable operator to ban indecent material on leased access channels but simply permitted the operator to do so: "[A]lthough [sec. 10(a)] does create a risk that a program will not appear, that risk is not the same as the certainty that accompanies a governmental ban." Justice Breyer rejected the contention that the material as defined in the provisions and as amplified by the FCC was too vague. FCC regulations had added as a guideline language similar to the definition of obscenity set forth in *Miller v. California*:

> The language, while vague, attempts to identify the category of materials that Justice Stewart thought could be described only in terms of "I know it when I see it." *Jacobellis v. Ohio*. Section 10(a) and the FCC regulations, with *Miller*'s qualifiers, [appear] to refer to material that would be offensive enough to fall within that category but for the fact that the material also has "serious literary, artistic, political or scientific value" or nonprurient purposes. This history suggests that the statute's language aims at the kind of programming to which its sponsors referred—pictures of oral sex, bestiality and rape. [W]e conclude that the statute is not impermissibly vague.

With respect to sec. 10(b), Justice Breyer delivered the opinion of the Court:

> [Section 10(b)] and its implementing regulations require cable operators to place "patently offensive" leased channel programming on a separate channel; to block that channel; to unblock that channel within 30 days of a subscriber's written request for access, and to reblock that channel within 30 days of a subscriber's request for reblocking. Also, leased access channel programmers must notify cable operators of an intended "patently offensive" broadcast up to 30 days before its scheduled broadcast date. These requirements have obvious restrictive effects. The several up-to-30-day delays, along with a single channel segregation, mean that a subscriber cannot decide to watch a single program without considerable advance planning. Moreover, the "written notice" requirement will further restrict viewing by subscribers who fear for their reputations. Further, the added costs and burdens that these requirements impose upon a cable system operator may encourage that operator to ban programming that the operator would otherwise permit to run, even if only late at night.

In response, the government contended that these "segregate and block" requirements were the least restrictive means of achieving the compelling governmental interest in protecting children. The government argued *Pacifica* did not require that regulation of indecency on television should be subject to the strictest First Amendment standard of review. Justice Breyer responded that it was not necessary to decide whether *Pacifica* "does, or does not, impose some lesser standard of review where indecent speech is at issue." This was because this restriction was not "'narrowly tailored' to meet its legitimate objective." Section 10(b) failed to satisfy both the strictest and less strict First Amendment standards. Congress has shown how to use less restrictive means in dealing with similar problems in the Telecommunication Act of 1996. For example, sec. 551 of the 1996 Act provides that in the future television sets will have to be manufactured "with a so-called 'V-chip'—a device that will be able automatically to identify and block sexually explicit or violent programs." Justice Breyer said of these measures:

> [T]hey are significantly less restrictive than the provision here at issue. They do not force the viewer to receive all "patently offensive" programming or none; they will not lead the viewer automatically to judge the few by the reputation of the many; and

they will not automatically place the occasional viewer's name on a special list.

Justice Breyer, joined by Justices Stevens and Souter, concluded that sec. 10(c) authorizing cable operators to ban obscene and indecent material on public access channels was unconstitutional. The government had failed to show that there was a sufficient problem regarding "patently offensive" broadcasts to children to warrant the restriction:

> [Section 10(c)] would not significantly restore editorial rights of cable operators, but would greatly increase the risk that certain categories of programming (say, borderline offensive programs) will not appear. [Further,] we conclude that the Government cannot show Sec. 10(c) is necessary to protect children or that it is appropriately tailored to secure that end.

Justice Souter, concurring, agreed with the plurality that cable indecency, should be governed by *Pacifica* for the present:

> [T]oday's plurality opinion observes rightly that the characteristics of broadcast radio that rendered indecency particularly threatening in *Pacifica*, that is, its intrusion into the house and accessibility to children are also present in the case of cable television. It would seem, then, that the appropriate category for cable indecency should be as contextually detailed as the *Pacifica* example.
>
> Rather than definitively settling the issue now, Justice Breyer wisely reasons by analogy rather than by rule, concluding that the speech and the restriction at issue in this case may usefully be measured against the ones at issue in *Pacifica*. [U]ntil a category of indecency can be defined both with reference to the new technology and with a prospect of durability, the job of courts will be just what Justice Breyer does today: recognizing established First Amendment interests through a close analysis that constrains the Congress, without wholly incapacitating it in all matters of significance apparent here.

Justice Kennedy, joined by Justice Ginsberg, dissenting in part and concurring in part, would hold sec. 10(a) as well as secs. 10(b) and (c) unconstitutional:

> [The government] argues the nature of the speech in question—indecent broadcast (or cablecast)—is subject to the lower standard of review it contends was applied in *Pacifica*. *Pacifica* did not purport, however, to apply a special standard for indecent broadcasting. Emphasizing the narrowness of its holding,

Pacifica conducted a context-specific analysis of the FCC's restriction on indecent programming during daytime hours. It relied on the general rule that "broadcasting has received the most limited First Amendment protection." We already have rejected the application of this standard of review to infringements on the liberties of cable operators, even though they control an important communications medium. *Turner Broadcasting*. There is even less cause for a lower standard here.

Justice Kennedy said that the appropriate standard for both secs. 10(a) and 10(c) was strict scrutiny. Under that standard, these provisions failed because they were not "narrowly tailored to serve a compelling interest":

First, to the extent some operators may allow indecent programming, children in localities those operators serve will be left unprotected. Second, to the extent cable operators prohibit indecent programming on access channels, not only children but adults will be deprived of it. Secs. 10(a) and (c) present a classic case of discrimination based on its content.

Justice Thomas, joined by Chief Justice Rehnquist and Justice Scalia, concurring in the judgment in part and dissenting in part, agreed that Sec. 10(a) did not violate the First Amendment but thought that Secs. 10(b) and (c) did not violate the First Amendment either:

Sec. 10(b) does nothing more than adjust the nature of government-imposed leased access requirements in order to emulate the market forces that keep indecent programming primarily on premium channels (without permitting the operator to charge subscribers for that programming.)

Unlike Secs. 10(a) and (c), Sec. 10(b) clearly implicates petitioners' free speech rights. Though Sec. 10(b) by no means bans indecent speech, it clearly places content-based restrictions on the transmission of private speech by requiring cable operators to block and segregate indecent programming that the operator has agreed to carry. Consequently, Sec. 10(b) must be subjected to strict scrutiny and can be upheld only if it furthers a compelling governmental interest by the least restrictive means available. The parties agree that Congress has a "compelling interest in protecting the physical and psychological well-being of minors" and that its interest "extends to shielding minors from the influence of [indecent speech] that is not obscene by adult standards." See *Ginsberg v. New York*. Because Sec. 10(b) is narrowly tailored to achieve that well-established compelling interest, I would

uphold it. I therefore dissent from the Court's decision to the contrary.

COMMENT

Notice that Justice Breyer is unequivocal on the point that cable, no less than broadcasting, is pervasive in the lives of Americans and that, like broadcasting, cable is uniquely accessible to children. Why does the Breyer plurality differ so sharply from the Eleventh Circuit in *Cruz* on this point? Is part of the answer that *Cruz* was decided in 1985 and *Denver Area* in 1996 and that cable'a penetration of American households was far greater in 1996 than it was in 1985?

Isn't there still a strong argument to the contrary? After all, it takes a good deal more effort to subscribe to cable than to turn on an over-the-air television set. The subscriber has to call the cable company to connect to the cable system and has to pay a fee for that service. Why don't these realities undermine the applicability of the *Pacifica* rationale to cable? Yet one must also acknowledge that Justice Breyer's endorsement of *Pacifica* was somewhat tentative. Why?

In *Reno v. ACLU*, text, p. 619, the Court declined to apply *Pacifica* to regulation of the Internet. Moreover, Justice Stevens viewed the Internet differently than Justice Breyer viewed cable: "[T]he Internet is not as 'invasive' as radio or television."

Justice Souter said *Pacifica* should be used for cable indecency problems until a better standard can be developed. What would that better standard be? Are you persuaded by Justice Kennedy's point that *Turner*, pp. 627, 861, should preclude the application of *Pacifica* to cable? Why does Justice Thomas say that sec. 10(b), unlike the other provisions at issue in *DenverArea*, clearly implicates the free speech rights of viewers and access programmers?

Professor Kathleen Sullivan of Stanford Law School noted that Justice Breyer's plurality opinion in *Denver Area* raised First Amendment issues that will be of continuing significance. The *Denver Area* case was significant, she said, because it offered a "sociological" alternative to First Amendment interpretation. This alternative inquires into the institutional characteristics of the speaker: "Breyer said that free speech cases may require a very content-specific review of who the speaker is—a conduit? a bookstore? a speaker?"

Such an approach, she said, "could undermine" the "content-based/content-neutral test for speech regulations." Further, the Breyer approach marked the triumph of a standards approach over bright line rules: "Breyer joined Stevens as favoring flexible standards and content- specific, fact-intensive balancing tests." *Constitutional Law Scholars Attempt to Distill Recent Supreme Court Term*, 65 U.S.L.W. 2285 (October 29, 1996) (Comments of Prof. Kathleen Sullivan).

Justice Breyer, writing for a plurality in *Denver Area*, noted that the application of a specific test to the regulation of cable programming was "unwise and unnecessary" because of "the changes taking place in the law, the technology, and the industrial structure, related to telecommunications." Should the guarantee of free speech vary for the different media? Does *Denver Area* foreshadow a cautious approach to developing a First Amendment standard for the Internet?

With the Internet in mind, Professor Cass Sunstein advocates that the Court take a cautious approach to developing First Amendment tests for new communications technology. See Cass R. Sunstein, *Constitutional Caution*, 1996 U. Chi. Legal F. 361. Professor Sunstein cites *Denver Area* to support his assertion that "[i]t is important [for the Court] to get a sense of the nature of the underlying problem before reaching confident conclusions." Professor Sunstein states further that "[a] narrow, and in my view correct, decision is *Denver Area*."

Reno v. ACLU, text, p. 615, distinguished broadcasting from the Internet. Unlike broadcasting, cyberspace was not characterized either by scarcity or invasiveness. The Court in *Reno* applied the strict scrutiny standard of review and held the Communications Decency Act violative of the First Amendment.

In *Turner* the Court refused to apply the scarcity rationale of broadcasting to justify the regulation of cable and went on to analyze the must-carry provisions under an intermediate scrutiny standard. In *Denver Area*, "Justice Breyer employed a general balancing test to evaluate [the challenged provisions], weighing 'the government's interest in protecting children, the permissive aspect of the statute and the nature of the medium' against leased programmers' and viewers' interests in viewing sexually explicit material." *Leading Cases*, 110 Harv. L. Rev. 135, 249 (1996).

Do you agree with *Leading Cases* that Justice Breyer's balancing test in *Denver Area* "likely will have little or no precedential value"?

Playboy Entertainment Group, Inc. v. United States
945 F. Supp. 772 (D. Del. 1996).

[EDITORIAL NOTE: *The lack of a well defined First Amendment standard of review for cable continues to impede judicial review of indecency regulation.*
The Playboy *court noted that after* Denver Area *"it is clear only that we should apply either strict scrutiny or something very close to strict scrutiny when a content-based law, applicable in the cable context, is challenged."*]

ROSH, Circuit Judge:

The plaintiffs in this action, Playboy Entertainment Group, Inc. ("Playboy") and Graff Pay-Per-View ("Graff"), challenge the constitutionality of section 505 of the Communications Decency Act of 1996, which is Title V of the Telecommunications Act of 1996, Pub. L. No. 104–104, 110 Stat. 56. Congress enacted section 505 in an effort to eliminate signal bleed, i.e., the partial reception of sexually explicit adult cable television programming in the homes of non-subscribers to that programming.

Cable system operators attempt to block non-subscribers from receiving [premium] programming by various scrambling techniques. Signal bleed occurs when the scrambling process is not fully successful.

The stated purpose of section 505 is to protect children from signal bleed. Section 505(a) requires a cable television operator to completely scramble or block the video and audio portions of any cable channel that is primarily dedicated to sexually explicit programming. If a cable operator is unable to comply in full with section 505(a), then section 505(b) requires "time channeling", i.e., that sexually explicit adult programming be transmitted only during those hours when children are not likely to view it. The FCC has determined these "safe harbor" hours to be from 10:00 P.M. to 6:00 A.M.

The principal issue facing us is whether government regulation of signal bleed from sexually explicit programming offends the free speech and equal protection rights of adult-programming networks and of their subscriber audience. Our analysis is narrowed by the fact that plaintiffs do not contend that signal bleed itself is protected speech.

[EDITORIAL NOTE: *Read as multi- channel video programming distributors.*]

Playboy and Graff provide MSOs with adult, sexually oriented video programming. The MSOs then transmit the plaintiffs' programming to premium subscribers and pay-per-view purchasers who request access to such programming.

Because the cost of premium and pay-per-view programming is in addition to the cost of basic programming, MSOs seek to secure premium network signals for subscribers only. To prevent a signal from reaching the home of a non-subscriber, MSOs "scramble" the signal by blocking a portion of it. Currently, most MSOs scramble premium channel signals using either "RF" or "baseband" technology. Generally, this scrambling affects only the video portion of the transmission.

The problem which § 505 was enacted to remedy is known as "signal bleed." Audio or video "bleed" occurs when a signal is not effectively scrambled by the MSO's RF or baseband equipment. Bleeding does not occur in TV sets with converter boxes that have a feature known as channel mapping. Cable-ready television sets, however, do not include this mapping feature. When a consumer with a cable-ready TV tunes to a scrambled premium channel to which the consumer does not subscribe, the consumer receives the jammed signal which under some circumstances includes a video picture or portions of a picture because of a phenomenon called random lockup. The non-subscribing consumer will also receive a clear audio signal unless the MSO's scrambling system is one which scrambles the audio. The severity of this signal bleeding problem varies from time to time and from place to place. This permits the child of a cable subscriber to tune the cable-ready TV to a premium or pay-per-view channel offered on the cable system and to receive discernible images even though the parent is a non-subscriber to that channel.

[A] non-subscriber may see and hear portions of a channel or program to which he or she does not subscribe. This result is of particular concern when the programming is sexually explicit, intended for an adult-only audience. Families, who do not subscribe to adult entertainment

channels, have found that sounds and images from these channels are at least partially discernible.

There are MSOs that already meet the requirements of § 505. For the MSOs that are not in compliance, several technologies may become available in the future that would allow an MSO to meet the requirements of § 505. Television manufacturers may soon be required by law to insert the so-called "V-chip," in all new televisions. Pub. L. No. 104-104, § 551, 110 Stat. at 139–41. The V-chip will allow parents to block types of programming which they find inappropriate for their children. The V-chip is currently being tested in Canadian markets. It is not clear, however, how long it will be before televisions with V-chips become widely available in the United States.

Because the currently used "RF" and "baseband" technologies are not capable of fully scrambling both the audio and video signal at all times, many MSOs would be required, if § 505(a) was enforced today, to resort to other and/or additional scrambling techniques. If an MSO was not able or willing to initiate additional scrambling techniques, it would be required to time channel adult programming.

In order to fully block access to sexually oriented programming at all times, each cable-connected TV set in the home would have to be connected to a lockbox. If MSOs that offer adult programming were to distribute one converter/lockbox to every nonsubscribing household currently without one, the total cost would be prohibitive, probably in excess of one billion dollars.

Finally, an MSO has the option of complying with § 505 by "time channeling" as provided in subsection (b). If an MSO cannot or chooses not to completely scramble audio and/or video signals as required by § 505(a), it must restrict adult programs to certain "safe harbor" hours. In preparation for implementing § 505, the FCC established a regulation that defines the safe harbor hours as the eight hour period between 10:00 P.M. and 6:00 A.M. If time channeling were adopted by an MSO, adult cable programming would not be available in the MSO's service area except during the safe harbor hours. Plaintiffs estimate that their revenues would fall approximately thirty per cent if time channeling were adopted.

Plaintiffs challenge § 505 on grounds that it (1) infringes the free speech protections provided by the First Amendment of the U.S. Constitution. [W]e conclude that Playboy and Graff have failed to meet the preliminary injunction test. They have not persuaded us that they are likely to prevail on the merits. Moreover, they have not demonstrated that the public interest is served by permitting signal bleed to invade nonsubscribers' homes.

Playboy and Graff claim that § 505 burdens their rights guaranteed under the First Amendment by inhibiting their freedom of speech. The Supreme Court has been exacting in its protection of this First Amendment right. [A]s circumstances and technologies have changed, the Court has adapted free speech protection to meet these changes.

We postponed our decision here until the Supreme Court reached its decision in a case dealing with a similar field of developing technology—that of leased and public access cable channels. See *Denver Area* [hereinafter *Denver Consortium*]. In *Denver Consortium*, [a] majority of the Supreme Court agreed that § 10(b) of the 1992 Cable Act was unconstitutional, but the Court was unable to form a majority regarding the constitutionality of the remainder of the Act.

One of the seemingly unresolved aspects of *Denver Consortium* is the standard of scrutiny we should apply in our analysis here. The plurality suggested that it was "unwise and unnecessary" to decide whether a lower standard of scrutiny, such as that applied in *F.C.C. v. Pacifica Foundation,* should apply in the cable context. It was unnecessary to specify a specific standard because § 10(b) could not pass constitutional muster either under strict scrutiny or under a less rigorous standard. And, it was unwise to declare a "rigid single standard" for fear of dampening the rapid rate of development in the field of communications technologies.

The other five members of the Court suggested that strict scrutiny remained the applicable standard where a law restricted speech on the basis of its content. Thus, these members of the Court would have required that the law be "narrowly tailored" to achieve a "compelling" government interest in order to survive constitutional review. In the aftermath of the *Denver Consortium* decision, it is clear only that we should apply either strict scrutiny or something

very close to strict scrutiny when a content-based law, applicable in the cable television context, is challenged on grounds that it violates the First Amendment.

However, whatever the standard of scrutiny, as Justice Breyer stated for the Court in *Denver Consortium*: "The essence of that protection is that Congress may not regulate speech except in cases of extraordinary need and with the exercise of a degree of care that we have not elsewhere required."

Section 505 differs, however, from the statute at issue in *Denver Consortium* and from most statutes that are directed at speech or at the regulation of speech in that the target of § 505 is not the speech itself, i.e., sexually explicit adult programming. The target is signal bleed, a secondary effect of the transmission of that speech. Moreover, § 505 is directed at this secondary effect because signal bleed is intruding into the homes of television viewers who have chosen not to receive the underlying sexually explicit programming.

This focus of § 505 on a secondary effect of speech leads us to our next inquiry, whether § 505 is "content-based" or "content-neutral." See *City of Renton v. Playtime Theaters, Inc.,* (1986). As we have noted, in *Denver Consortium* five justices agreed that a content-based strict scrutiny standard should apply. We conclude here, but not without considerable deliberation, that § 505 should be treated as a content-based restriction on speech. Even though § 505 is aimed at the content-neutral objective of preventing signal bleed, the section applies only when signal bleed occurs during the transmission of "sexually explicit adult programming or other programming that is indecent." It does not apply when signal bleed occurs on other premium channel networks, like HBO or the Disney Channel. Thus, Congress targeted signal bleed based on its sexually explicit content, rendering § 505 a "content-based" restriction. We will therefore apply content-based analysis.

We must, however, also consider content in context. We cannot ignore the fact that the households that receive signal bleed have not subscribed to the adult channel which transmits the unwanted images and sounds. Nor can we ignore the fact that cable television is a means of communication which is pervasive and to which children are easily exposed. The Supreme Court has recognized that cable television is as accessible to children as over-the-air broadcasting, if not more so. See *Denver Consortium.*

Moreover, the Supreme Court in its consideration of freedom of speech under the First Amendment has recognized the need to protect children from sexually explicit material, particularly in the context of a pervasive medium. See *Denver Consortium.*

As a result, we conclude that § 505 clearly addresses a recognized "compelling interest," and it remains only for us to determine whether the provision is carefully tailored to serve that end. For the reasons that we now develop, and particularly on the basis of the Supreme Court's ruling in *F.C.C. v. Pacifica Foundation,* we hold that Congress has adopted, at least in respect to § 505(b), a carefully tailored, and constitutional, solution. It was largely the pervasive nature of broadcast media that motivated the Court in *Pacifica Foundation* to uphold governmental restrictions placed on radio broadcasts of indecent material.

We wholeheartedly agree with the plurality's finding in *Denver Consortium* that cable television is now "uniquely pervasive." The plurality also noted that "[c]able television broadcasting . . . is as 'accessible to children' as over-the-air broadcasting if not more so."

[W]hen cable signal bleed occurs, children may be exposed to the sights and sounds of sexually explicit films and other adult programming. Such programming has the potential to affect not only a child's vocabulary, but also his or her capacity for inappropriate conduct that is sexual in nature. We believe that the danger of prematurely exposing children to video and audio transmissions of graphic adult sexual behavior is even more troublesome than the exposure to offensive language that was at issue in *Pacifica Foundation.*

Indeed, the parties do not dispute that the government has a well-established compelling interest in protecting children from unsupervised exposure to sexually explicit material.

We then turn to the solution which Congress crafted in § 505. Congress provided MSOs with two alternative methods of compliance with the section: (1) complete scrambling, or (2) time-channeling the programming into safe-harbor hours. Plaintiffs fear that MSOs will drop adult programming entirely, rather than

invest in technologies which will be made obsolete by the V-chip or that MSOs will transmit plaintiffs' networks for an unprofitably short eight-hour period. Not only do the plaintiffs foresee lost profits, they present the possibility of bankruptcy caused by implementation of § 505.

There is undoubtedly a substantial expense involved in complying with subsection (a). However, while an economic burden may warrant consideration when weighing the relative harms imposed by a law, economics alone cannot dictate the result where constitutional rights are at issue.

By including the time-channeling compliance option in § 505, Congress provided MSOs with decision-making flexibility and an economically less restrictive alternative. We thus find that the economic burden placed on MSOs by subsection (a) is not determinative of the result in light of the substantially less expensive option provided by time-channeling in subsection (b). It follows therefore that if the time-channeling alternative provides a constitutional means of compliance with § 505, then § 505 is constitutional.

Because the Supreme Court endorsed a time-channeling solution in very similar circumstances in *Pacifica Foundation,* we believe that time-channeling also survives constitutional scrutiny here. It is important to our reasoning that § 505 does not seek to ban sexually explicit programming, nor does it prohibit consenting adults from viewing erotic material on premium cable networks if they so desire. It is clearly established that a complete ban on indecent speech will rarely (if ever) be tolerated. See *Denver Consortium.*

[T]he cost to MSOs of creating an adequate shield from a widespread intrusion of signal bleed by supplying converter/lockboxes to households that don't subscribe to adult channels, would be close to the expense of providing converter/lockboxes to non-subscribing households under § 505(a). The main difference is that under § 504 the household has to request the box, while under § 505 the MSO must provide the box. We have no evidence in the present record that local cable operators or producers of sexually explicit programming are advertising the free availability of the § 504 lockbox or other blocking devices upon demand. Likewise, there is no evidence that parents are otherwise aware of the § 504 means of achieving complete blocking of undesired channels. Upon this record, the government has demonstrated an expectation that § 504 will not be a viable alternative.

Given the content of adult programming and the pervasive nature of cable television, we find that § 505 is an acceptable governmental response intended to prevent exposure of minors to sexually explicit signal bleed. We therefore conclude that plaintiffs have failed to show that they are likely to succeed in their claim that the provision violates their First Amendment rights to freedom of speech.

Plaintiffs have not satisfied the elements of the preliminary injunction test. We will therefore remove the temporary restraining order, which was previously granted by this court, and we will deny plaintiffs request for preliminary injunctive relief.

COMMENT

In *Denver Area*, the Supreme Court held that Congress's mandate requiring cable operators to segregate and block (scramble) indecent programming on leased or public access channels violated the First Amendment. In the *Playboy* case, however, a three-judge panel held that it was constitutional for Congress to mandate that if cable programmers choose to scramble an indecent signal, they must scramble it completely or time-channel the programming. Thus, on the one hand, Congress cannot require a cable operator to segregate and block indecent programming, Yet, on the other hand, Congress can require a cable operator to completely scramble a program that the cable operator has chosen to scramble for commercial purposes. Are these decisions consistent with each other?

The *Playboy* court attempted to distinguish *Denver Area* stating, "Section 505 differs, however, from the statute at issue in *Denver [Area]* in that the target of § 505 is not the speech itself , i.e., sexually explicit adult programming. The target is signal bleed, a secondary effect of the transmission of that speech." If Playboy decided to transmit its programming without any scrambling, would it receive greater protection? The *Playboy* court noted that *Playboy* did not claim that the partially scrambled programming was speech. Why did Playboy neglect to make that argument? Can a partially scrambled picture be considered speech?

Shortly after the decision of the three-judge court in *Playboy*, Playboy & Graff obtained a stay pending appeal to the Supreme Court. On March 24, 1997, the Supreme Court affirmed the lower court's decision without opinion. See *Playboy Entertainment Group, Inc. v. U.S.*, 117 S.Ct. 1309 (1997).

Government and Franchisee Controls on Nonindecent Content

Time Warner Cable v. City of New York
943 F. Supp. 1357 (S.D.N.Y. 1996).

COTE, District Judge:

This case concerns the power of a city to influence, control, and even coerce the programming decisions of an operator of a cable television system. It therefore goes to the heart of First Amendment concerns. [O]n October 1, 1996, the City of New York ("City") proposed to Time Warner a plan that called for the City to abandon one of its cable channels designated for public, educational and governmental use ("PEG") if Time Warner would place the new Fox News program on one of Time Warner's commercial cable channels. Time Warner refused to "swap" channels with the City in order to accommodate Fox News. Unwilling to accept Time Warner's decision, a decision protected by the First Amendment and a federal statute, the City raised the ante over the ensuing days in an effort to convince Time Warner to change its mind. This campaign culminated on October 10, 1996, when the City placed Bloomberg Information Television ("BIT") on one of its PEG channels—specifically, a channel set aside for educational or governmental use—and prepared to place Fox News on another PEG channel. This action, intended to compel Time Warner to capitulate, instead has brought the parties before this Court.

[I find that] the City's actions are far beyond acceptable PEG use, the City acted in contravention of the legislative purposes of the Cable Act, and, specifically, violated the provisions relating to PEG use and the editorial autonomy of a cable operator. [Cable Communications Policy Act of 1984, 47 U.S.C. § 521 et seq.] Most importantly, I find that by engaging in an effort to compel Time Warner to alter its constitutionally–protected editorial decision not to carry Fox

News, the City has violated Time Warner's First Amendment rights.

I find that the evidence establishes the following, when taken as a whole. In response to learning that it had not won the bidding battle with MSNBC, Fox used its direct access to the Mayor to seek the City's assistance. The City, in a strategy developed and executed by the Mayor's senior staff, then undertook to convince and, if necessary, force Time Warner to place Fox News on one of Time Warner's commercial channels. Fox and the City understood and agreed that Fox News could not run on television for any significant length of time without commercials, and, therefore, it was essential that Time Warner be convinced to place Fox News on a commercial channel.

After the rejection of the City's proposal, the City increased the pressure on Time Warner by linking Time Warner's satisfying Fox to the City's renewal of the franchises, which are due to expire in 1998.

Finally, the City took steps to put Fox News on Crosswalks [a public access channel], although stripped of its advertisements. Even in this format, however, the City was choosing programming for a PEG channel that had no precedent in the City or beyond and that was not contemplated by the Cable Act.

I find that Time Warner has established through compelling evidence that the City abused its power over the FCRC process and its control of the PEG programming on Crosswalks and has acted both to coerce Time Warner and to retaliate against it for its decision not to enter a contract with Fox News. The more difficult issue is whether such conduct provides a basis for continuation of the injunction. It is to that issue that I now turn.

The PEG provisions reflect an understanding of the industry standard and prior government regulation under the 1972 FCC regulations. Congress intended to codify this understanding by ensuring franchising authorities could continue to require cable operators to provide public channels for individual and community access, educational channels for educational institutions, and governmental channels to show local government at work.

The Cable Act does not require PEG access nor establish the exact meaning of PEG, but it does set an outer limit to PEG. Section 531(a)'s phrase "public, educational or governmental use" is not without meaning. It establishes a limit on both the identity of the user and the content of the program. A franchise agreement gives life to this provision, but neither a franchise agreement, nor a party's actions, may violate the substantive meaning of Section 531(a). While it is unnecessary to determine the exact limits of governmental use—nor do I want to, given the importance of governmental flexibility in the face of changing technology and public needs—as explained below, it is clear that no matter what the contours of that line, the City may not use its channels as it intends here.

The parties dispute the meaning of the term "governmental use" in the Cable Act. The City argues that the PEG provision sanctions any use by the government—if the actor is the government, the content of the program is irrelevant. The City argues that under Section 531(a) the requirement that a channel be reserved "'for public, educational or governmental use' is automatically satisfied if the user is the City of New York, because the City is a government." Thus, it contends that it could, if it desired, run any commercial programming it wanted. Time Warner argues that "governmental use" refers to the purpose of the channel: to provide programming related to governmental purposes.

I find the City's reasoning unpersuasive.

Moreover, if I were to follow the City's interpretation of the PEG provision, the entire statutory provision would be nonsensical. Channels for "public, educational, and governmental use" would have no meaning. Indeed, the government could become a competitor with a cable operator for the provision of commercial programming instead of providing access for those voices who generally will not have commercial access: the public at-large, educational institutions, and government programs.

To be clear, I am not determining whether a government can ever run "commercial" programming on a PEG station. I do not find that the Cable Act bans advertising on PEG stations. If a municipality determines advertising is useful to fund programming on local government at work or other appropriate PEG programming, I find nothing in the Cable Act that would prevent a municipality from doing so.

Finally, and most significantly, I simply do not agree with the City's interpretation of Section

531(a). The City argues that Section 531(a) only prescribes the identity of the user and not the type of use because such a reading of the statute is content-neutral.

I find the City's reasoning unpersuasive. While the statute refers only to "governmental use," the statute codified the idea that a governmental channel was to show "local government at work." H.R.Rep. 98-934. Therefore, an interpretation which states that the Cable Act sanctions any use by the government belies the intent and purpose of Section 531(a).

Applying Section 531(a) to the City's conduct here, I find that the City's decision to air a 24-hour news program, substantially identical in feed to that aired on commercial channels across the country, with the relatively minor exception of the inclusion of some minutes of local New York news, constitutes in the circumstances of this case a use of a PEG channel in a way clearly unintended by Congress. There are several underlying purposes to the PEG channels. These purposes include a desire to respond to local needs, create space for voices that would not otherwise be heard, air programs needed by a community that may not otherwise be commercially viable, and, for governmental channels, show local government at work. While a failure to serve any one of these purposes may not itself be dispositive, in the instant case, the City's use of Crosswalks is at odds with all four purposes.

First, neither Fox News nor BIT responds to local needs.

Second, neither Fox News nor BIT will contribute a voice that is not already heard.

Third, neither Fox News nor BIT needs a government subsidy in order to reach large audiences.

Finally, neither Fox News nor BIT will allow the citizenry to see local government at work, except in the most incidental fashion.

Our precedents apply the most exacting scrutiny to regulations that suppress, disadvantage, or impose differential burdens upon speech because of its content. Laws that compel speakers to utter or distribute speech bearing a particular message are subject to the same rigorous scrutiny.

As *Turner* itself reaffirmed, speakers have a First Amendment right not to be compelled to speak by the government. A second guiding principle, also discussed in *Turner*, is that the government regulation of speech based on its content is subject to strict scrutiny. A final principle of importance to this case is that viewpoint-based discrimination—as opposed merely to content-based discrimination—is particularly unacceptable under the First Amendment.

Time Warner contends that its First Amendment rights have been violated in two ways. First, Time Warner claims that it has First Amendment rights in the City's PEG channels. Time Warner argues that when the City placed programming on Crosswalks which was inappropriate for a PEG channel, the City lost the right to use that PEG channel, and the right "reverted" to Time Warner. Therefore, Time Warner argues, when the City placed on that channel programming which Time Warner did not wish to carry, the City forced Time Warner to speak in violation of the First Amendment. Second, Time Warner argues that the City's actions in this case are intended to compel Time Warner to reverse its initial decision and accept Fox News on its regular commercial channels.

The central issue in determining whether Time Warner has First Amendment rights in the City's PEG channels is essentially a "chicken and the egg" problem. On the one hand, Time Warner argues that it has an underlying right to all of the channels. Time Warner contends that because the City's right to use certain channels comes only from either Section 531(a) of the statute or the franchise agreements, once the City is violating that right, the channels revert to Time Warner. In contrast, the City argues that no one owned the channels first, and that Time Warner's only right to any channels arises from the franchise agreements. If this is true, then Time Warner has no reversionary rights

A statutory provision supporting Time Warner's contention is Section 531(a), which states that the City "may establish requirements in a franchise with respect to the designation or use of channel capacity for public, educational, or governmental use only to the extent provided in this section." 47 U.S.C. § 531(a). By only allowing the City to set aside PEG channels "to the extent provided in this section," Time Warner argues that unless the City is in compliance with the requirements of Section 531, it may not use the channels.

The best reading of the statutory framework is that the answer to who owned the channels first is neither party—the rights to the channels were created simultaneously at the time the franchise agreements were signed. Without the franchise agreements, neither the City nor the cable operator would have a right to use any channel. As explained by Justice Kennedy in his *Denver Area* concurrence/dissent, the editorial discretion of a cable operator is a function of the cable franchise it receives from local government.

Accordingly, I find that even though the City is misusing the PEG channels, Time Warner has no First Amendment right to editorial discretion over channels that it never had a right to use. See *Denver Area.*

Time Warner contends that by [attempting to force it] to carry Fox News on its commercial channels, the City has violated Time Warner's First Amendment right as a cable operator to exercise editorial discretion. I find that the City's justifications for its actions in this case are entirely unconvincing. With respect to the City's purported desire to increase the diversity of news programs available to New Yorkers, it must be observed as an initial matter that it is not self evident that this is in fact a constitutionally permissible purpose when the City has favored specific speakers in pursuit of this goal. [T]he City's intonation of the rubric "diversity" is a thinly disguised reference to its preference for the editorial content of Fox News. As such, this rationale for the City's actions cannot constitute a permissible purpose for its actions.

The City's second justification fares no better. While the economic health of a city and the preservation and creation of jobs is an appropriate and essential concern of city government, the record here does not indicate that this concern was other than pretextual in the context of this dispute.

Second, I find that Fox News and BIT also expect that placement on Crosswalks will significantly increase their ability to win places on Time Warner's commercial channels.

In addition, the City's actions create a chilling effect under which Time Warner will feel pressure to capitulate to City requests that it accommodate a New York City commercial programmer who has direct access to the City Hall. In such cases, if Time Warner refuses the City's request, then the City can simply turn Crosswalks into a competing commercial system of channels.

In sum, Time Warner has a right under the First Amendment to be free from government interference with its programming decisions. I find that the City has acted to compel Time Warner to add Fox News to its system of commercial channels and that these actions have had a direct, immediate, and chilling effect on Time Warner's exercise of its constitutionally-protected editorial discretion. Consequently, Time Warner has carried its burden of establishing irreparable harm.

The regulations at issue in *Turner* were content-neutral structural regulations designed to save the broadcast networks. The City's actions in this case are very different, and thus warrant strict scrutiny. First, the City's actions are viewpoint based, which *Turner* makes clear require strict scrutiny. Second, the City's actions are not the type of broad-based "structural" regulations faced by the *Turner* Court, but rather are specifically targeted to benefit two individual speakers. Finally, the City has not engaged in any fact finding, as did Congress in justifying the "must-carry" rules.

Accordingly, given the evidence here of content-based decisionmaking by the City, I find that strict scrutiny applies. As noted above, the City argues that it was acting to further two interests: to ensure a wide diversity of programming, and to promote city employment. I have found that these reasons have been used here as pretexts and were not the actual motivation for the City's actions. Even if the City had been motivated by these reasons, however, and even if they are compelling, I find that the City has not narrowly tailored its actions to accomplish these goals.

The City has simply failed to show that placing Fox News and BIT on the Crosswalks channels is necessary in order to further the goals of increasing the diversity of news programs or promoting City employment.

I must address one last issue. The City argues that its First Amendment right to speak would be infringed by the issuance of a preliminary injunction in this matter. In addition, as noted above, under Section 531(e) Time Warner may not interfere with the City's programming decisions for the PEG channels. Fox and Bloomberg also assert that they have First Amendment interests which would be injured if this Court issues an injunction. According to the City, Fox, and Bloomberg, an injunction would act as a prior restraint on their speech.

In sum, the City's actions fail strict scrutiny. Accordingly, I find that Time Warner has shown a likelihood of success on the merits of its claim that the City has violated its First Amendment right to exercise editorial discretion.

The City has engaged in a pattern of conduct with the purpose of compelling Time Warner to alter its constitutionally-protected editorial decision not to carry Fox News. The City's actions violate longstanding First Amendment principles that are the foundation of our democracy. In many instances the First Amendment has been invoked to protect the interests of those whose ideas are unpopular or even repugnant. Here the First Amendment is invoked by a powerful commercial enterprise with substantial resources to respond to the government's actions. Even though the government's power is nearly matched by that of its commercial adversary, in order to protect the values embodied in the First Amendment, we nevertheless must be vigilant against the abuse of governmental power present here.

Having found that Time Warner has carried the burden that applies at this preliminary proceeding and that it has sufficiently established that the City of New York violated Time Warner's rights under Section 544(f)(1) of the Cable Act and under the First Amendment of the United States Constitution, I preliminarily enjoin the City from placing Fox News and BIT on its Crosswalks channels in a manner inconsistent with this Opinion.

[EDITORIAL NOTE: *Sec. 544(f)(1) provides that no government agency may "impose requirements regarding the provision or content of cable services" unless expressly provided in the statute.*]

So ordered.

COMMENT

Time Warner Cable v. City of New York was a battle of titans: Gerald Levin of Time Warner versus Rupert Murdoch of Fox News. Levin tried to shut Murdoch's new cable news service, Fox News, out of New York City. Murdoch tried an end run around Levin by seeking help from Mayor Giuliani's administration. The City then tried to put Fox News on one of its PEG channels and succeeded. According to this case, the whole scheme was an effort to pressure Time Warner to assign a channel to Fox News. Can New York City use its PEG channels for these purposes? Here Judge Cote ruled very emphatically that it cannot.

Clearly, under *Turner*, New York City's decision to allocate one of its PEG channels to Fox News was a content-based decision. The City's efforts to favor particular programming are documented vividly in this opinion. Suppose, however, that there was no hint of favoritism in New York City's decision to assign one of its PEG channels to Fox News. Suppose the City simply wanted to enhance the informational mix of its PEG offerings by assigning one of its PEG channels to Fox News? Would that still be a content-based decision?

Is the court here holding that PEG channels created by a franchise agreement belong neither to the city nor to the cable operator? To whom then do they belong?

Judge Cote says that Time Warner's resources are nearly matched by those of New York City. In the end, a content control imposed by government was held to violate the First Amendment. But is there any remedy against the content control imposed on Murdoch by Time Warner?

First Amendment lawyer Floyd Abrams represented three New York City Democratic officials in the Fox–New York City–Time Warner litigation. In an essay on the case, he observed that Time Warner "may not limit the selection of commercial programmers to their own affiliates." As for the city, "[it] may not stray into the commercial area in determining what to show on the channels specially set aside for governmental and educational purposes." Mr. Abrams concluded:

> When the city tells Time Warner that it must carry Fox News (with commercials) or else the city will carry Fox on its government-access channels (without commercials), it is in forbidden First Amendment terrain. Floyd Abrams, *Tuning Out Free Speech,* New York Times, October 30, 1996, at A21.

For a discussion of public access channels generally, see the public access chapter, pp. 492–503.

REGULATION OF CABLE TELEVISION OWNERSHIP

The FCC began regulating cable television in the 1970s. By the late 1980s, regulation consisted of a combination of FCC rules, elements of the antitrust settlement in the *AT&T* case, and

Congressional intervention through the Cable Communications Policy Act of 1984. Several of the provisions in the 1984 Cable Act restricted a cable operator's ability to own other types of media, and vice versa. In addition, the FCC under its own initiative developed rules that placed limits on who could own a cable system and who could be owned by a cable operator.

Nationwide cable ownership is limited in several ways, including a limitation on television network ownership of cable systems, local broadcast station ownership of cable systems within the same market, and telephone company ownership of a cable system in the same market. Until 1993, there were no national ownership caps on cable, and some cable multiple system operators (MSOs) owned thousands of systems. Only antitrust law functioned as a theoretical limit. In 1993, the FCC adopted an Order limiting cable operators : "[N]o person or entity shall be permitted to reach more than 30 percent of all homes passed nationwide through cable systems owned by such person or entity or in which [it] holds an attributable interest." See 47 C.F.R. § 76.503. This Order was stayed by the court in *Daniels Cablevision, Inc. v. United States*, 835 F. Supp. 1 (D.D.C. 1993), text, pp. 850–853. The portion staying limits on subscribers is still on appeal with the D.C. Circuit. See *Time Warner Entertainment Co. v. FCC*, No.94–1035. The case is being held in abeyance pending FCC reconsideration.

Television Network/Cable Cross-Ownership

Prior to 1996, the FCC restricted the three major national broadcast TV networks from owning a cable system. See 47 C.F.R. § 76.501(a)(1) (1995). The FCC rule stated that a cable operator could only have an interest in a network if the operator's cable systems did not "pass" more than "10 percent of homes passed on a nationwide basis" and "50 percent of homes passed" within one television station's broadcast area. This meant that a cable operator could not own an interest in a TV network if its systems *were capable* of providing service to more than 10 percent of the U.S. population that *could* order cable service; or if its systems *could* provide service to 50 percent of the homes in a TV broadcast station's market. This rule, in effect, prohib-

ited any network or cable operator from owning interests in one another. Faced with this prohibition, the networks explored ownership of video programming services, such as ESPN and CNBC.

In order to allow broadcasters, telecommunications providers, and cable companies to compete against each other, in the Telecommunications Act of 1996 (1996 Act), Congress amended several provisions of the Communications Act of 1934 to permit cross-ownership between media. In sec. 202(f)(1) of the 1996 Act, Pub. L. No. 104-104, § 202, 110 Stat. 56, Congress instructed the FCC to revise its rules "to permit a person or entity to own or control a network of broadcast stations and a cable system." The FCC, however, was advised to adopt rules, if necessary to "ensure carriage, channel positioning and nondiscriminatory treatment of non-affiliated broadcast stations" by any network-owned cable system. See 1996 Act, Pub. L. No. 104-104, § 202(f)(2). On March 18, 1996, the FCC issued an Order amending its rules to reflect Congress's mandate. See *Implementation of Sections 202(F), 202(I) and 301(I) of the Telecommunications Act of 1996*, 11 F.C.C.R. 15115 (1996).

Broadcast Station/Cable Cross-Ownership

Cable operator ownership of local broadcast stations, and vice versa, was previously limited by FCC rules and later by congressional statute. Local full-power TV broadcasters could not own cable systems serving the same areas as their television stations. See 47 C.F.R. § 76.501(a). The FCC rule declared that a cable system could not "carry the signal of any television broadcast station if such system" had an interest in a TV broadcast station whose service area overlapped *any portion* of the cable system's franchise area. This rule was later codified as a congressional prohibition in the 1984 Cable Act, 47 U.S.C. § 533(a) (1984).

The 1996 Act repealed the statutory restriction on the ability of a local broadcaster to own a cable system in its market, or for a cable operator to own a broadcasting station in its franchise area. See 1996 Act, Pub. L. No. 104-104, § 202(i), 110 Stat. 112. The FCC's rule that prohibited this type of cross-ownership was not based on the statutory restriction. In the Conference Report that accompanied the 1996 Act,

Congress qualified the repeal of the statutory restriction by declaring that it "did not intend that this repeal of the statutory prohibition should prejudge the outcome of any review by the [FCC] of its rules." This qualification means that the prohibition on cross-ownership of local broadcast stations and cable systems in the same market will be maintained until the FCC amends its rules.

Telephone/Cable Cross-Ownership

Historically, local telephone companies (telcos) were similarly prohibited from acquiring cable systems in their service areas—originally under an FCC rule and subsequently under the 1984 Cable Act. The prohibition originated after cable TV began to experience substantial expansion in the late 1960s. Cable TV was provided by installing coaxial cable from the cable company's facility (the headend) to subscribers' homes. To reach the subscribers, cable operators attached the coaxial cable to telephone utility poles. The FCC was concerned that a telephone company that owned the utility poles could prevent a cable company from providing service by denying it access. The FCC feared that telephone companies would dominate the cable industry because of their ability to control the use of the telephone poles (pole-access discrimination) and because the telephone companies could subsidize their cable affiliates with revenue obtained from telephone services. See *Applications of Tel. Cos. for Section 214 Certificates for Channel Facilities Furnished to Affiliated Community Antenna Television Sys.*, Final Report & Order, 21 F.C.C.2d 307 (1970), *aff'd sub nom. General Tel. Co. v. U.S.*, 449 F.2d 846 (5th Cir. 1971). To ensure that telephone companies could not engage in anticompetitive activities, in 1970 the FCC adopted the telephone/cable cross-ownership rule.

The cross-ownership rule was codified by Congress as 47 U.S.C. § 533(b) in the 1984 Cable Act, Pub. L. No. 98–594, 98 Stat. 2785. Section 533(b) was enacted in conjunction with the other restrictions on cable system ownership, such as the network and broadcast station restrictions. Congress stated that the purpose of sec. 533 was to "prevent the development of local media monopolies, and to encourage a diversity of ownership of communications outlets." H.R. Rep. No. 98-934, at 55 (1984). Section 533(b) generally precluded telephone com-

panies from providing video programming directly to subscribers in their telephone service areas, except in rural areas. Besides the rural exception, the statute allowed the FCC to waive the rule and permit a telco to operate a cable system in the telco's service area if the FCC was convinced that nobody else could provide the cable service.

In 1988, the FCC granted a waiver to General Telephone Company (GTE) to build and partly operate a cable system in Cerritos, California; another company would operate most of the cable system, but it was argued that construction and ownership could not be done without GTE. In no other way, it was argued, could a system be built that would meet Cerrito's specifications. The FCC concluded that GTE was entitled to a waiver to ensure cable service to Cerritos. See *In re Application of General Tel. Co.*, 64 R.R.2d 1156 (1988). In granting the waiver, the FCC set a course for increased telco involvement in the video programming market—a course that Congress would follow in the 1996 Act.

THE *AT&T* CASE: JUDGE HAROLD GREENE AND THE MFJ Section 533(b) only limited a telco's ability to provide service in its own service area, but the large telcos were also prevented from providing service outside their service area. This restriction was not imposed by Congress or the FCC but was a result of the AT&T antitrust consent decree, later to become the Modification of Final Judgment (MFJ). See *United States v. AT&T*, 552 F. Supp. 131 (D.D.C. 1982), *aff'd sub nom., Maryland v. United States*, 460 U.S. 1001 (1983). The antitrust consent decree divided AT&T into seven regional Bell operating companies (RBOCs) and AT&T. The MFJ applied to AT&T, the major interstate telecommunications provider, and the RBOCs (U.S. WEST, NYNEX, Ameritech, etc.). The MFJ precluded the RBOCs from entering the cable industry. The MFJ was supervised by U.S. District Judge Harold Greene, who believed that barring the RBOCs from entering cable would enable a diverse, competitive, multimembered electronic information industry to develop. The fear was that the mighty RBOCs and AT&T would have an unfair competitive advantage in accessing subscribers. In addition, the notion of competing with a multibillion dollar corporation would intimidate most potential competitors.

GTE was not subject to the MFJ, even though it would eventually become the nation's largest corporation that provides local phone service. See Mike Mills, *Holding the Line on Phone Rivalry; GTE Keeps Potential Competitors, Regulators' Price Guidelines at Bay,* Washington Post, October 23, 1996, at C12.

THE *CHESAPEAKE & POTOMAC TEL. CO.* CASE AND THE REPEAL OF SECTION 533(b). In addition to waiver requests, the telephone companies gained access to the cable TV market by challenging sec. 533(b) in the federal courts. See *Chesapeake & Potomac Tel. Co. v. United States,* 42 F.3d 181 (4th Cir. 1994), *cert. granted* 115 S. Ct. 2608 (1995), *vacated and remanded* 116 S. Ct. 1036 (1996). In *Chesapeake* the Fourth Circuit held that sec. 533(b) was unconstitutional because it violated the telephone companies' First Amendment rights. The Fourth Circuit analyzed sec. 533(b) under an intermediate level of scrutiny because it was a regulation unrelated to the content of the telephone companies' speech. The intermediate level of scrutiny required the statute to be "narrowly tailored to serve a significant governmental interest, and . . . leave open ample alternative channels for communication of the information." The Fourth Circuit concluded that "Section 533(b) is not narrowly tailored because the [FCC] failed to demonstrate why Section 533(b) does not, by removing the 'irresistible' incentive which domination of that market provides, 'burden substantially more speech than is necessary.'" The FCC challenged the Fourth Circuit's decision and was granted certiorari in 1995. The 1996 Act mooted the case, however, by repealing sec. 533(b).

TELCO PROVISION OF VIDEO SERVICES UNDER THE 1996 ACT The 1996 Act has drastically changed the scope of telco participation in providing video programming services. In addition to eliminating the restrictions on telco/cable cross-ownership by repealing 47 U.S.C. § 533(b), the 1996 Act preempts the AT&T consent decree by stating: "Any conduct or activity that was . . . subject to any restriction or obligation imposed by the AT&T Consent Decree shall . . . be subject to the restrictions and obligations imposed by the Communications Act of 1934 . . . and shall not be subject to the

restrictions and obligations imposed by such Consent Decree." See Telecommunications Act of 1996, Pub. L. No. 104-104, § 601, 110 Stat. 143. Telephone companies and cable operators are now permitted to provide each other's services in the same market. Telephone companies can choose to provide video programming over a satellite master antenna TV or wireless cable system, to provide cable service directly as cable operators, or to develop an "open video system"—a system that uses the existing phone lines. Cable operators are permitted to provide telecommunications services over their own systems.

REMAINING TELCO/CABLE CROSS-OWNERSHIP RESTRICTIONS UNDER THE 1996 ACT Although Congress removed the cross-ownership restrictions, it was concerned about allowing telephone and cable companies to buy out one another in the same market. Therefore, Congress adopted 47 U.S.C. § 572 to prohibit telephone companies from buying out existing cable operators in the same market. This restriction also prevents cable companies from buying out telephone companies. Section 572 does not prevent a telco from building a new cable system or acquiring a small video provider, however; it only restricts the purchase of a cable system in a noncompetitive market.

Section 572(a) states that "[n]o local exchange carrier or any affiliate . . . may purchase or otherwise acquire directly or indirectly more than a 10 percent financial interest, or any management interest, in any cable operator providing cable service within . . . [the same] service area." Section 572(b) imposes the same restriction on cable operators, and sec. 572(c) restricts both types of providers from entering into joint ventures. Section 572, however, does provide for a number of exceptions to these buyout restrictions.

Rural Exemption—The restrictions on buyouts do not apply in a market where the cable system serves areas with fewer than 35,000 inhabitants outside an urbanized area, as long as all acquired systems do not total more than 10 percent of the households in the telco's telephone service area.
Smaller Telcos—If a cable system serves no more than 20,000 subscribers, of whom fewer than 12,000 are in an urban area, then the buyout restrictions do not apply.

Smaller Systems—Telcos may purchase a cable system, if the system serves fewer than 17,000 subscribers, of whom 8,000 are in an urban area and over 6,000 are in a nonurban area; if the system is not one of the top one hundred television markets as of June 1, 1995; and if the system is not owned by one of the top fifty (MSOs).

Small Market Overbuilds—An overbuild is a cable system that is built separate from an existing monopoly cable provider. The 1996 Act allows telcos to purchase an overbuild outside of the top twenty-five television markets if the cable system purchased is not the largest system in the market, the system's franchise area is the same as the larger cable competitor, the system is not owned by one of the top fifty MSOs, and the largest system is owned by one of the top ten MSOs.

Limited Joint Ventures—The 1996 Act allows telcos and cable operators to enter into joint ventures for constructing facilities. This is not expressly stated in sec. 572, but the conference report accompanying the Act states that "[s]uch carriers or cable operators may enter into a joint venture or partnership for other purposes, including the construction of facilities for the provision of such programming or services."

Telephone entry into the video programming market is in full swing. In 1996, U.S. West was permitted to purchase Continental Cable, one of the largest cable companies in the United States. Similarly, TCI Cable and Jones Cable are both in the process of entering the telecommunications markets. Most of these endeavors are being pursued by building new systems, but the future is likely to create new mergers and acquisitions.

A TELCO/CABLE HYBRID—OPEN VIDEO SYSTEMS

By eliminating the statutory barrier to entry imposed by the cross-ownership restriction, the 1996 Act has opened the video programming market to competition. Prior to the 1996 Act, the telcos were able to provide video on a common carrier basis via a system known as video dialtone. Video dialtone required the telcos to obtain authorization from the FCC prior to building their facilities. The 1996 Act directed the FCC to eliminate all of its video dialtone rules as well as the requirement that a common carrier obtain authorization pursuant to sec. 214 of the Communications Act for the provision of video programming. See 47 U.S.C. § 571(c).

VIDEO DIALTONE   The 1996 Act repealed the FCC's video dialtone rules and policies, which were established to permit telephone companies to participate in the video marketplace in a manner that was consistent with the statutory telephone/cable cross-ownership ban. See 1996 Act, § 302(b)(3), Pub. L. No. 104; *Further Notice of Proposed Rulemaking, First Report and Order and Second Further Notice of Inquiry in CC Docket No. 87-266,* 7 F.C.C.R. 300 (1991); *Memorandum Opinion and Order on Reconsideration,* 7 F.C.C.R. 5069, aff'd, *National Cable Television Ass'n v. FCC,* 33 F.3d 66 (D.C. Cir. 1994). Under video dialtone, telcos could provide common carrier video *transmission* service for programming provided by others, but, consistent with the statutory ban, they were generally prohibited from providing any programming themselves. See *Second Report and Order, Recommendation to Congress, and Second Further Notice of Proposed Rulemaking,* 7 F.C.C.R. 5781, 5820 (1992).

The 1996 Act adopted a different regulatory approach. The Act offers telcos several options for entering and competing in the video marketplace. The Conference Report issued at the time the 1996 Act was enacted stated:

> Recognizing that there can be different strategies, services and technologies for entering video markets, the conferees agree to multiple entry options to promote competition, to encourage investment in new technologies and to maximize consumer choice of services that best meet their information and entertainment needs. S. Conf. Rep. No. 104-230, at 172 (1996).

The Conference Report further noted that "the conferees recognize that telephone companies need to be able to choose from among multiple video entry options to encourage entry," and therefore systems under this section should be "allowed to tailor services to meet the unique competitive and consumer needs of individual markets." *Id.* at 177. Thus, the 1996 Act gives significant flexibility to telcos to determine how to enter the video marketplace.

ENTRY OPTIONS   Section 302 of the 1996 Act established a new Part V (Sections 651-653) of Title VI of the Communications Act, which established the regulatory systems that govern a telco's entry into video. Section 651 governs the entry options for telcos to provide video service.

See 47 U.S.C. § 571. Section 651 provides that common carriers may "(1) provide video programming to subscribers through radio communication under Title III of the Communications Act [47 U.S.C. § 571(a)(1)]; (2) provide transmission of video programming on a common carrier basis under Title II of the Communications Act [47 U.S.C. § 571(a)(2)]; (3) provide video programming as a cable system under Title VI of the Communications Act [47 U.S.C. § 571(a)(3)]; or (4) provide video programming by means of an 'open video system' under new Section 653 of the Communications Act, [47 U.S.C. § 571(a)(3)–(4)]." *In re Implementation of Section 302 of the Telecommunications Act of 1996*, Report and Order and Notice of Proposed Rulemaking, 11 F.C.C.R. 14639 (1996). The 1996 Act also allows the FCC to permit a cable operator or any other person to provide video programming through an open video system. 47 U.S.C. § 573(a)(1).

OPEN VIDEO SYSTEMS Section 653's open video system (OVS) option establishes a new method for telco entry into the video marketplace. Generally, sec. 653 provides that if a telco certifies that it complies with certain nondiscrimination and other requirements established by the FCC, its OVS will not be subject to regulation under Title II and will be entitled to reduced regulation under Title VI. See 47 U.S.C. § 573(a)(1), (c). The FCC must approve or disapprove any open video system certification request within ten days of receipt. *Id.* § 573(a)(1). This type of certification process is considerably shorter than the previous sec. 214 certification that was required for video dialtone.

An OVS operator's certification request must state that it complies with the requirements in subsection 653(b), which (1) prohibit the operator from discriminating among video programmers regarding carriage on its system; (2) require the operator to establish rates, terms, and conditions of carriage that are just, reasonable, and not unjustly or unreasonably discriminatory; (3) prohibit the operator or its affiliate, if carriage demand exceeds capacity, from selecting the video programming on more than one-third of its activated channels; (4) permit the operator to use channel sharing arrangements; (5) extend the FCC's sports exclusivity, network nonduplication and syndicated exclusivity regulations to

open video systems; and (6) prohibit the operator from discriminating with regard to information provided to subscribers for the purpose of selecting programming.

REDUCED REGULATORY BURDENS FOR OVS Subsection 653(c)(2)(A) requires the FCC to prescribe regulations applying Title VI must-carry and public, educational, and governmental (PEG) obligations, and Title III retransmission consent obligations, to OVS operators. Although an OVS operator will still be subject to some regulations under Title VI, sec. 653 provides a number of exemptions from Title VI regulation. Some of the Title VI provisions that would not apply to OVS include (1) sec. 612—"leased access" obligations; (2) sec. 621 and 622—franchise requirements and fees (although an OVS operator will be subject to a gross revenue fee at a rate not to exceed the franchise fee paid by the local cable operator, 47 U.S.C. § 573(c)(2)(B)); (3) sec. 623—rate regulation; and (4) sec. 632—consumer protection and customer service.

Congress envisioned telco entry into the video marketplace as the answer to rising cable rates. To promote entry, Congress concluded it was necessary to provide incentives, i.e., reduced regulatory burdens:

> There are several reasons for streamlining the regulatory obligations of [OVS]. First, the conferees hope that this approach will encourage common carriers to deploy [OVS] and introduce vigorous competition in entertainment and information markets. Second, the conferees recognize that common carriers that deploy open systems will be "new" entrants in established video programming markets and deserve lighter regulatory burdens to level the playing field. Third, the development of competition and the operation of market forces mean that government oversight and regulation can and should be reduced. S. Conf. Rep. No. 104-230, at 178.

The FCC has promulgated rules pursuant to sec. 653. See *Implementation of Section 302 of the Telecommunications Act of 1996 (Open Video Systems)*, Report and Order and Notice of Proposed Rulemaking, 11 F.C.C.R. 14639 (1996); *Implementation of Section 302 of the Telecommunications Act of 1996 (Open Video Systems)*, Second Report and Order, 11 F.C.C.R. 18223, FCC 96-249 (1996), *summarized at* 61 Fed. Reg. 28698 (June 5, 1996); *Implementation of Section 302 of the Telecommunications Act of 1996 (Open Video Systems),* Third Report & Order and Second Order on Reconsideration, 11 F.C.C.R. 20227, FCC 96-334 (August 8, 1996) *summarized at* 61 Fed. Reg. 43160 (August 21, 1996).

As of the end of 1996, the FCC had certified three OVS operators. On October 17, 1996, Bell Atlantic received approval for its certification to convert its Dover, New Jersey, video dialtone system to OVS. See *Bell Atlantic OVS Certification,* 11 F.C.C.R. 13249. MFS was granted certifications on December 9, 1996, for the operation of OVS systems in Boston and New York, both of which are being used to provide programming. See *Metropolitan Fiber Systems/New York, Inc. (Certification to Operate an Open Video System),* Consolidated Order, DA 96-2075 (CSB December 9, 1996). On October 10, 1996, Digital Broadcasting Open Video Systems received approval to offer OVS service in southern California. Telco entry into OVS has been slow, but the landscape is set for adoption of new rules that will stimulate entry into the video programming market.

THE CONSTITUTION OF
THE UNITED STATES

PREAMBLE

We the People of the United States, in Order to form a more perfect Union, establish Justice, insure domestic Tranquility, provide for the common defence, promote the general Welfare, and secure the Blessings of Liberty to ourselves and our Posterity, do ordain and establish this Constitution for the United States of America.

ARTICLE I

Section 1.   All legislative Powers herein granted shall be vested in a Congress of the United States, which shall consist of a Senate and House of Representatives.

Section 2.   The House of Representatives shall be composed of Members chosen every second Year by the People of the several States, and the Electors in each State shall have the Qualifications requisite for Electors of the most numerous Branch of the State Legislature.

No Person shall be a Representative who shall not have attained to the Age of twenty five Years, and been seven Years a Citizen of the United States, and who shall not, when elected, be an Inhabitant of that State in which he shall be chosen.

Representatives and direct Taxes shall be apportioned among the several States which may be included within this Union, according to their respective Numbers, which shall be determined by adding to the whole Number of free Persons, including those bound to Service for a Term of Years, and excluding Indians not taxed, three fifths of all other Persons. The actual Enumeration shall be made within three Years after the first Meeting of the Congress of the United States, and within every subsequent Term of ten Years, in such Manner as they shall by Law direct. The Number of Representatives shall not exceed one for every thirty Thousand, but each State shall have at Least one Representative; and until such enumeration shall be made, the State of New Hampshire shall be entitled to chuse three, Massachusetts eight, Rhode Island and Providence Plantations one, Connecticut five, New York six, New Jersey four, Pennsylvania eight, Delaware one, Maryland six, Virginia ten, North Carolina five, South Carolina five, and Georgia three.

When vacancies happen in the Representation from any State, the Executive Authority thereof shall issue Writs of Election to fill such Vacancies.

The House of Representatives shall chuse their Speaker and other Officers; and shall have the sole Power of Impeachment.

Section 3.   The Senate of the United States shall be composed of two Senators from each State, chosen by the Legislature thereof, for six Years; and each Senator shall have one Vote.

Immediately after they shall be assembled in Consequence of the first Election, they shall be divided as equally as may be into three Classes. The Seats of the Senators of the first Class shall be vacated at the Expiration of the second Year, of the second Class at the Expiration of the fourth Year, and of the third Class at the Expiration of the sixth Year, so that one third may be chosen every second Year; and if Vacancies happen by Resignation, or otherwise, during the Recess of the Legislature of any State, the Executive thereof may make temporary Appointments until the next Meeting of the Legislature, which shall then fill such Vacancies.

No Person shall be a Senator who shall not have attained to the Age of thirty Years, and been nine Years a Citizen of the United States, and who shall not, when elected, be an Inhabitant of that State for which he shall be chosen.

The Vice President of the United States shall be President of the Senate, but shall have no Vote, unless they be equally divided.

The Senate shall chuse their other Officers, and also a President pro tempore, in the Absence of the Vice President, or when he shall exercise the Office of President of the United States.

The Senate shall have the sole Power to try all Impeachments. When sitting for that Purpose, they shall be on Oath or Affirmation. When the President of the United States is tried, the Chief Justice shall preside: And no Person shall be convicted without the Concurrence of two thirds of the Members present.

Judgment in Cases of Impeachment shall not extend further than to removal from Office, and disqualification to hold and enjoy any Office of honor, Trust, or Profit under the United States: but the Party convicted shall nevertheless be liable and subject to Indictment, Trial, Judgment, and Punishment, according to Law.

Section 4.   The Times, Places and Manner of holding Elections for Senators and Representatives, shall be prescribed in each State by the Legislature thereof; but the Congress may at any time by Law make or alter such Regulations, except as to the Places of chusing Senators.

The Congress shall assemble at least once in every Year, and such Meeting shall be on the first Monday in December, unless they shall by Law appoint a different Day.

Section 5.   Each House shall be the Judge of the Elections, Returns, and Qualifications of its own Members, and a Majority of each shall constitute a Quorum to do Business; but a smaller Number may adjourn from day to day, and may be authorized to compel the Attendance of absent Members, in such Manner, and under such Penalties as each House may provide.

Each House may determine the Rules of its Proceedings, punish its Members for disorderly Behavior, and, with the Concurrence of two thirds, expel a Member.

Each House shall keep a Journal of its Proceedings, and from time to time publish the same, excepting such Parts as may in their Judgment require Secrecy; and the Yeas and Nays of the Members of either House on any question shall, at the Desire of one fifth of those Present, be entered on the Journal.

Neither House, during the Session of Congress, shall, without the Consent of the other, adjourn for more than three days, nor to any other Place than that in which the two Houses shall be sitting.

Section 6.   The Senators and Representatives shall receive a Compensation for their Services, to be ascertained by Law, and paid out of the Treasury of the United States. They shall in all Cases, except Treason, Felony and Breach of the Peace, be privileged from Arrest during their Attendance at the Session of their respective Houses, and in going to and returning from the same; and for any Speech or Debate in either House, they shall not be questioned in any other Place.

No Senator or Representative shall, during the Time for which he was elected, be appointed to any civil Office under the Authority of the United States, which shall have been created, or the Emoluments whereof shall have been increased during such time; and no Person holding any Office under the United States, shall be a Member of either House during his Continuance in Office.

Section 7.   All Bills for raising Revenue shall originate in the House of Representatives; but the Senate may propose or concur with Amendments as on other Bills.

Every Bill which shall have passed the House of Representatives and the Senate, shall, before it becomes a Law, be presented to the President of the United States; If he approve he shall sign it, but if not he shall return it, with his Objections to the House in which it shall have originated, who shall enter the Objections at large on their Journal, and proceed to reconsider it. If after such Reconsideration two thirds of that House shall agree to pass the Bill, it shall be sent together with the Objections, to the other House, by which it shall likewise be reconsidered, and if approved by two thirds of that House, it shall become a Law. But in all such Cases the Votes of both Houses shall be determined by Yeas and Nays, and the Names of the Persons voting for and against the Bill shall be entered on the Journal of each House respectively. If any Bill shall not be returned by the President within ten Days (Sundays excepted) after it shall have been presented to him, the Same shall be a Law, in like Manner as if he had signed it, unless the Congress by their Adjournment prevent its Return in which Case it shall not be a Law.

Every Order, Resolution, or Vote, to which the Concurrence of the Senate and House of Representatives may be necessary (except on a question of Adjournment) shall be presented to the President of the United States; and before the Same shall take Effect, shall be approved by him, or being disapproved by him, shall be repassed by two thirds of the Senate and House of Representatives, according to the Rules and Limitations prescribed in the Case of a Bill.

Section 8.   The Congress shall have Power.

To lay and collect Taxes, Duties, Imposts and Excises, to pay the Debts and provide for the common Defence and general Welfare of the United States; but all Duties, Imposts and Excises shall be uniform throughout the United States;

To borrow Money on the credit of the United States;

To regulate Commerce with foreign Nations, and among the several States, and with the Indian Tribes;

To establish an uniform Rule of Naturalization, and uniform Laws on the subject of Bankruptcies throughout the United States;

To coin Money, regulate the Value thereof, and of foreign Coin, and fix the Standard of Weights and Measures;

To provide for the Punishment of counterfeiting the Securities and current Coin of the United States;

To establish Post Offices and post Roads;

To promote the Progress of Science and useful Arts, by securing for limited Times to Authors and Inventors the exclusive Right to their respective Writings and Discoveries;

To constitute Tribunals inferior to the supreme Court;

To define and punish Piracies and Felonies committed on the high Seas, and Offenses against the Law of Nations;

To declare War, grant Letters of Marque and Reprisal, and make Rules concerning Captures on Land and Water;

To raise and support Armies, but no Appropriation of Money to that Use shall be for a longer Term than two Years;

To provide and maintain a Navy;

To make Rules for the Government and Regulation of the land and naval Forces;

To provide for calling forth the Militia to execute the Laws of the Union, suppress Insurrections and repel Invasions;

To provide for organizing, arming, and disciplining, the Militia, and for governing such Part of them as may be employed in the Service of the United States, reserving to the States respectively, the Appointment of the Officers, and the Authority of training the Militia according to the discipline prescribed by Congress;

To exercise exclusive Legislation in all Cases whatsoever, over such District (not exceeding ten Miles square) as may, by Cession of particular States, and the Acceptance of Congress, become the Seat of the Government of the United States, and to exercise like Authority over all Places purchased by the Consent of the Legislature of the State in which the Same shall be, for the Erection of Forts, Magazines, Arsenals, dock-Yards, and other needful Buildings;—And

To make all Laws which shall be necessary and proper for carrying into Execution the foregoing Powers, and all other Powers vested by this Constitution in the Government of the United States, or in any Department or Officer thereof.

Section 9.   The Migration or Importation of such Persons as any of the States now existing shall think proper to admit, shall not be prohibited by the Congress prior to the Year one thousand eight hundred and eight, but a Tax or duty may be imposed on such Importation, not exceeding ten dollars for each Person.

The privilege of the Writ of Habeas Corpus shall not be suspended, unless when in Cases of Rebellion or Invasion the public Safety may require it.

No Bill of Attainder or ex post facto Law shall be passed.

No Capitation, or other direct, Tax shall be laid, unless in Proportion to the Census or Enumeration herein before directed to be taken.

No Tax or Duty shall be laid on Articles exported from any State.

No Preference shall be given by any Regulation of Commerce or Revenue to the Ports of one State over those of another: nor shall Vessels bound to, or from, one State be obliged to enter, clear, or pay Duties in another.

No Money shall be drawn from the Treasury, but in Consequence of Appropriations made by Law; and a regular Statement and Account of the Receipts and Expenditures of all public Money shall be published from time to time.

No Title of Nobility shall be granted by the United States: And no Person holding any Office of Profit or Trust under them, shall, without the Consent of the Congress, accept of any present, Emolument, Office, or Title, of any kind whatever, from any King, Prince, or foreign State.

Section 10.   No State shall enter into any Treaty, Alliance, or Confederation; grant Letters of Marque and Reprisal; coin Money; emit Bills of Credit; make any Thing but gold and silver Coin a Tender in Payment of Debts; pass any Bill of Attainder, ex post facto Law, or Law impairing the Obligation of Contracts, or grant any Title of Nobility.

No State shall, without the Consent of the Congress, lay any Imposts or Duties on Imports or Exports, except what may be absolutely necessary for executing it's inspection Laws: and the net Produce of all Duties and Imposts, laid by any State on Imports or Exports, shall be for the Use of the Treasury of the United States; and all such Laws shall be subject to the Revision and Controul of the Congress.

No State shall, without the Consent of Congress, lay any Duty of Tonnage, keep Troops, or Ships of War in time of Peace, enter into any Agreement or Compact with another State, or with a foreign Power, or engage in War, unless actually invaded, or in such imminent Danger as will not admit of delay.

ARTICLE II

Section 1.   The executive Power shall be vested in a President of the United States of America. He shall hold his Office during the Term of four Years, and, together with the Vice President, chosen for the same Term, be elected, as follows:

Each State shall appoint, in such Manner as the Legislature thereof may direct, a Number of Electors, equal to the whole Number of Senators and Representatives to which the State may be entitled in the Congress; but no Senator or Representative, or Person holding an Office of Trust or Profit under the United States, shall be appointed an Elector.

The Electors shall meet in their respective States, and vote by Ballot for two Persons, of whom one at least shall not be an Inhabitant of the same State with themselves. And they shall make a List of all the Persons voted for, and of the Number of Votes for each; which List they shall sign and certify, and transmit sealed to the Seat of the Government of the United States, directed to the President of the Senate. The President of the Senate shall, in the Presence of the Senate and House of Representatives, open all the Certificates, and the Votes shall then be counted. The

Person having the greatest Number of Votes shall be the President, if such Number be a Majority of the whole Number of Electors appointed; and if there be more than one who have such Majority, and have an equal Number of Votes, then the House of Representatives shall immediately chuse by Ballot one of them for President; and if no Person have a Majority, then from the five highest on the List the said House shall in like Manner chuse the President. But in chusing the President, the Votes shall be taken by States, the Representation from each State having one Vote; A quorum for this Purpose shall consist of a Member or Members from two thirds of the States, and a Majority of all the States shall be necessary to a Choice. In every Case, after the Choice of the President, the Person having the greater Number of Votes of the Electors shall be the Vice President. But if there should remain two or more who have equal Votes, the Senate shall chuse from them by Ballot the Vice President.

The Congress may determine the Time of chusing the Electors, and the Day on which they shall give their Votes; which Day shall be the same throughout the United States.

No person except a natural born Citizen, or a Citizen of the United States, at the time of the Adoption of this Constitution, shall be eligible to the Office of President; neither shall any Person be eligible to that Office who shall not have attained to the Age of thirty five Years, and been fourteen Years a Resident within the United States.

In Case of the Removal of the President from Office, or of his Death, Resignation or Inability to discharge the Powers and Duties of the said Office, the same shall devolve on the Vice President, and the Congress may by Law provide for the Case of Removal, Death, Resignation or Inability, both of the President and Vice President, declaring what Officer shall then act as President, and such Officer shall act accordingly, until the Disability be removed, or a President shall be elected.

The President shall, at stated Times, receive for his Services, a Compensation, which shall neither be increased nor diminished during the Period for which he shall have been elected, and he shall not receive within that Period any other Emolument from the United States, or any of them.

Before he enter on the Execution of his Office, he shall take the following Oath or Affirmation: "I do solemnly swear (or affirm) that I will faithfully execute the Office of President of the United States, and will to the best of my Ability, preserve, protect and defend the Constitution of the United States."

Section 2.   The President shall be Commander in Chief of the Army and Navy of the United States, and of the Militia of the several States, when called into the actual Service of the United States; he may require the Opinion, in writing, of the principal Officer in each of the executive Departments, upon any Subject relating to the Duties of their respective Offices, and he shall have Power to grant Reprieves and Pardons for Offenses against the United States, except in Cases of Impeachment.

He shall have Power, by and with the Advice and Consent of the Senate to make Treaties, provided two thirds of the Senators present concur; and he shall nominate, and by and with the Advice and Consent of the Senate, shall appoint Ambassadors, other public Ministers and Consuls, Judges of the supreme Court, and all other Officers of the United States, whose Appointments are not herein otherwise provided for, and which shall be established by Law; but the Congress may by Law vest the Appointment of such inferior Officers, as they think proper, in the President alone, in the Courts of Law, or in the Heads of Departments.

The President shall have Power to fill up all Vacancies that may happen during the Recess of the Senate, by granting Commissions which shall expire at the End of their next Session.

Section 3.   He shall from time to time give to the Congress Information of the State of the Union, and recommend to their Consideration such Measures as he shall judge necessary and expedient; he may, on extraordinary Occasions, convene both Houses, or either of them, and in Case of Disagreement between them, with Respect to the Time of Adjournment, he may adjourn them to such Time as he shall think proper; he shall receive Ambassadors and other public Ministers; he shall take Care that the Laws be faithfully executed, and shall Commission all the Officers of the United States.

Section 4.   The President, Vice President and all civil Officers of the United States, shall be removed from Office on Impeachment for, and Conviction of, Treason, Bribery, or other high Crimes and Misdemeanors.

ARTICLE III

Section 1.   The judicial Power of the United States, shall be vested in one supreme Court, and in such inferior Courts as the Congress may from time to time ordain and establish. The Judges, both of the supreme and inferior Courts, shall hold their Offices during good Behaviour, and shall, at stated Times, receive for their Services a Compensation, which shall not be diminished during their Continuance in Office.

Section 2.   The judicial Power shall extend to all Cases, in Law and Equity, arising under this Constitution, the Laws of the United States, and Treaties made, or which shall be made, under their Authority;—to all Cases affecting Ambassadors, other public Ministers and Consuls;—to all Cases of admiralty and maritime

Jurisdiction;—to Controversies to which the United States shall be a Party;—to Controversies between two or more States;—between a State and Citizens of another State;—between Citizens of different States;—between Citizens of the same State claiming Lands under Grants of different States, and between a State, or the Citizens thereof, and foreign States, Citizens or Subjects.

In all Cases affecting Ambassadors, other public Ministers and Consuls, and those in which a State shall be a Party, the supreme Court shall have original Jurisdiction. In all the other Cases before mentioned, the supreme Court shall have appellate Jurisdiction, both as to Law and Fact, with such Exceptions, and under such Regulations as the Congress shall make.

The Trial of all Crimes, except in Cases of Impeachment, shall be by Jury; and such Trial shall be held in the State where the said Crimes shall have been committed; but when not committed within any State, the Trial shall be at such Place or Places as the Congress may by Law have directed.

Section 3.   Treason against the United States, shall consist only in levying War against them, or, in adhering to their Enemies, giving them Aid and Comfort. No Person shall be convicted of Treason unless on the Testimony of two Witnesses to the same overt Act, or on Confession in open Court.

The Congress shall have Power to declare the Punishment of Treason, but no Attainder of Treason shall work Corruption of Blood, or Forfeiture except during the Life of the Person attainted.

ARTICLE IV

Section 1.   Full Faith and Credit shall be given in each State to the public Acts, Records, and judicial Proceedings of every other State. And the Congress may by general Laws prescribe the Manner in which such Acts, Records and Proceedings shall be proved, and the Effect thereof.

Section 2.   The Citizens of each State shall be entitled to all Privileges and Immunities of Citizens in the several States.

A Person charged in any State with Treason, Felony, or other Crime, who shall flee from Justice, and be found in another State, shall on Demand of the executive Authority of the State from which he fled, be delivered up, to be removed to the State having Jurisdiction of the Crime.

No Person held to Service or Labour in one State, under the Laws thereof, escaping into another, shall, in Consequence of any Law or Regulation therein, be discharged from such Service or Labour, but shall be delivered up on Claim of the Party to whom such Service or Labour may be due.

Section 3.   New States may be admitted by the Congress into this Union; but no new State shall be formed or erected within the Jurisdiction of any other State; nor any State be formed by the Junction of two or more States, or Parts of States, without the Consent of the Legislatures of the States concerned as well as of the Congress.

The Congress shall have Power to dispose of and make all needful Rules and Regulations respecting the Territory or other Property belonging to the United States; and nothing in this Constitution shall be so construed as to Prejudice any Claims of the United States, or of any particular State.

Section 4.   The United States shall guarantee to every State in this Union a Republican Form of Government, and shall protect each of them against Invasion; and on Application of the Legislature, or of the Executive (when the Legislature cannot be convened) against domestic Violence.

ARTICLE V

The Congress, whenever two thirds of both Houses shall deem it necessary, shall propose Amendments to this Constitution, or, on the Application of the Legislatures of two thirds of the several States, shall call a Convention for proposing Amendments, which, in either Case, shall be valid to all Intents and Purposes, as part of this Constitution, when ratified by the Legislatures of three fourths of the several States, or by Conventions in three fourths thereof, as the one or the other Mode of Ratification may be proposed by the Congress; Provided that no Amendment which may be made prior to the Year One thousand eight hundred and eight shall in any Manner affect the first and fourth Clauses in the Ninth Section of the first Article; and that no State, without its Consent, shall be deprived of its equal Suffrage in the Senate.

ARTICLE VI

All Debts contracted and Engagements entered into, before the Adoption of this Constitution shall be as valid against the United States under this Constitution, as under the Confederation.

This Constitution, and the Laws of the United States which shall be made in Pursuance thereof; and all Treaties made, or which shall be made, under the Authority of the United States, shall be the supreme Law of the Land; and the Judges in every State shall be bound thereby, any Thing in the Constitution or Laws of any State to the Contrary notwithstanding.

The Senators and Representatives before mentioned, and the Members of the several State Legislatures, and all executive and judicial Officers, both of the United States and of the several States, shall be bound by Oath or Affirmation, to support this Constitution; but no religious Test shall ever be required as a Qualification to any Office or public Trust under the United States.

ARTICLE VII

The Ratification of the Conventions of nine States shall be sufficient for the Establishment of this Constitution between the States so ratifying the Same.

Amendment I [1791]

Congress shall make no law respecting an establishment of religion, or prohibiting the free exercise thereof; or abridging the freedom of speech, or of the press; or the right of the people peaceably to assemble, and to petition the Government for a redress of grievances.

Amendment II [1791]

A well regulated Militia, being necessary to the security of a free State, the right of the people to keep and bear Arms, shall not be infringed.

Amendment III [1791]

No Soldier shall, in time of peace be quartered in any house, without the consent of the Owner, nor in time of war, but in a manner to be prescribed by law.

Amendment IV [1791]

The right of the people to be secure in their persons, houses, papers, and effects, against unreasonable searches and seizures, shall not be violated, and no Warrants shall issue, but upon probable cause, supported by Oath or affirmation, and particularly describing the place to be searched, and the persons or things to be seized.

Amendment V [1791]

No person shall be held to answer for a capital, or otherwise infamous crime, unless on a presentment or indictment of a Grand Jury, except in cases arising in the land or naval forces, or in the Militia, when in actual service in time of War or public danger; nor shall any person be subject for the same offence to be twice put in jeopardy of life or limb; nor shall be compelled in any criminal case to be a witness against himself, nor be deprived of life, liberty, or property, without due process of law; nor shall private property be taken for public use, without just compensation.

Amendment VI [1791]

In all criminal prosecutions, the accused shall enjoy the right to a speedy and public trial, by an impartial jury of the State and district wherein the crime shall have been committed, which district shall have been previously ascertained by law, and to be informed of the nature and cause of the accusation; to be confronted with the witnesses against him; to have compulsory process for obtaining witnesses in his favor, and to have the Assistance of Counsel for his defence.

Amendment VII [1791]

In Suits at common law, where the value in controversy shall exceed twenty dollars, the right of trial by jury shall be preserved, and no fact tried by jury, shall be otherwise re-examined in any Court of the United States, than according to the rules of the common law.

Amendment VIII [1791]

Excessive bail shall not be required, nor excessive fines imposed, nor cruel and unusual punishments inflicted.

Amendment IX [1791]

The enumeration in the Constitution, of certain rights, shall not be construed to deny or disparage others retained by the people.

Amendment X [1791]

The powers not delegated to the United States by the Constitution, nor prohibited by it to the States, are reserved to the States respectively, or to the people.

Amendment XI [1798]

The Judicial power of the United States shall not be construed to extend to any suit in law or equity, commenced or prosecuted against one of the United States by Citizens of another State, or by Citizens or Subjects of any Foreign State.

Amendment XII [1804]

The Electors shall meet in their respective states, and vote by ballot for President and Vice-President, one of whom, at least, shall not be an inhabitant of the same state with themselves; they shall name in their ballots the person voted for as President, and in distinct ballots the person voted for as Vice-President, and they shall make distinct lists of all persons voted for as President, and of all persons voted for as Vice-President, and of the number of votes for each, which lists they shall sign and certify, and transmit sealed to the seat of the government of the United States, directed to the President of the Senate;—The President of the Senate shall, in the presence of the Senate and House of Representatives, open all the certificates and the votes shall then be counted;—The person having the greatest number of votes for President, shall be the President, if such number be a majority of the whole number of Electors appointed; and if no person have such majority, then from the persons having the highest numbers not exceeding three on the list of those voted for as President, the House of Representatives shall choose immediately, by ballot, the President. But in choosing the President, the votes shall be taken by states, the representation from each state having one vote; a quorum for this purpose shall consist of a member or members from two-thirds of the states, and a majority of all states shall be necessary to a choice. And if the House of Representatives shall not choose a President whenever the right of choice shall devolve upon them, before the fourth day of March next following, then the Vice-President shall act as President, as in the case of the death or other constitutional disability of the President.—The person having the greatest number of votes as Vice-President, shall be the Vice-President, if such number be a majority of the whole number of Electors appointed, and if no person have a majority, then from the two highest numbers on the list, the Senate shall choose the Vice-President; a quorum for the purpose shall consist of two-thirds of the whole number of Senators, and a majority of the whole number shall be necessary to a choice. But no person constitutionally ineligible to the office of President shall be eligible to that of Vice-President of the United States.

Amendment XIII [1865]

Section 1.   Neither slavery nor involuntary servitude, except as a punishment for crime whereof the party shall have been duly convicted, shall exist within the United States, or any place subject to their jurisdiction.

Section 2.   Congress shall have power to enforce this article by appropriate legislation.

Amendment XIV [1868]

Section 1.   All persons born or naturalized in the United States, and subject to the jurisdiction thereof, are citizens of the United States and of the State wherein they reside. No State shall make or enforce any law which shall abridge the privileges or immunities of citizens of the United States; nor shall any State deprive any person of life, liberty, or property, without due process of law; nor deny to any person within its jurisdiction the equal protection of the laws.

Section 2.   Representatives shall be apportioned among the several States according to their respective numbers, counting the whole number of persons in each State, excluding Indians not taxed. But when the right to vote at any election for the choice of electors for President and Vice President of the United States, Representatives in Congress, the Executive and Judicial officers of a State, or the members of the Legislature thereof, is denied to any of the male inhabitants of such State, being twenty-one years of age, and citizens of the United States, or in any way abridged, except for participation in rebellion, or other crime, the basis of representation therein shall be reduced in the proportion which the number of such male citizens shall bear to the whole number of male citizens twenty-one years of age in such State.

Section 3.   No person shall be a Senator or Representative in Congress, or elector of President and Vice President, or hold any office, civil or military, under the United States, or under any State, who having previously taken an oath, as a member of Congress, or as an officer of the United States, or as a member of any State legislature, or as an executive or judicial officer of any State, to support the Constitution of the United States, shall have engaged in insurrection or rebellion against the same, or given aid or comfort to the enemies thereof. But Congress may by a vote of two-thirds of each House, remove such disability.

Section 4.   The validity of the public debt of the United States, authorized by law, including debts incurred for payment of pensions and bounties for services in suppressing insurrection or rebellion, shall not be questioned. But neither the United States nor any State shall assume or pay any debt or obligation incurred in aid of insurrection or rebellion against the United States, or any claim for the loss or emancipation of any slave; but all such debts, obligations and claims shall be held illegal and void.

Section 5.   The Congress shall have power to enforce, by appropriate legislation, the provisions of this article.

Amendment XV [1870]

Section 1.   The right of citizens of the United States to vote shall not be denied or abridged by the United States or by any State on account of race, color, or previous condition of servitude.

Section 2.   The Congress shall have power to enforce this article by appropriate legislation.

Amendment VI [1913]

The Congress shall have power to lay and collect taxes on incomes, from whatever source derived, without apportionment among the several States, and without regard to any census or enumeration.

Amendment XVII [1913]

The Senate of the United States shall be composed of two Senators from each State, elected by the people thereof, for six years; and each Senator shall have one vote. The electors in each State shall have the qualifications requisite for electors of the most numerous branch of the State legislatures.

When vacancies happen in the representation of any State in the Senate, the executive authority of such State shall issue writs of election to fill such vacancies: *Provided,* That the legislature of any State may empower the executive thereof to make temporary appointments until the people fill the vacancies by election as the legislature may direct.

This amendment shall not be so construed as to affect the election or term of any Senator chosen before it be comes valid as part of the Constitution.

Amendment XVIII [1919]

Section 1.   After one year from the ratification of this article the manufacture, sale, or transportation of intoxicating liquors within, the importation thereof into, or the exportation thereof from the United States and all territory subject to the jurisdiction thereof for beverage purposes is hereby prohibited.

Section 2.   The Congress and the several States shall have concurrent power to enforce this article by appropriate legislation.

Section 3.   This article shall be inoperative unless it shall have been ratified as an amendment to the Constitution by the legislatures of the several States, as provided in the Constitution, within seven years from the date of the submission hereof to the States by the Congress.

Amendment XIX [1920]

The right of citizens of the United States to vote shall not be denied or abridged by the United States or by any State on account of sex.

Congress shall have power to enforce this article by appropriate legislation.

Amendment XX [1933]

Section 1.   The terms of the President and Vice President shall end at noon on the 20th day of January, and the terms of Senators and Representatives at noon on the 3d day of January, of the years in which such terms would have ended if this article had not been ratified; and the terms of their successors shall then begin.

Section 2.   The Congress shall assemble at least once in every year, and such meeting shall begin at noon on the 3d day of January, unless they shall by law appoint a different day.

Section 3.   If, at the time fixed for the beginning of the term of the President, the President elect shall have died, the Vice President elect shall become President. If the President shall not have been chosen before the time fixed for the beginning of his term, or if the President elect shall have failed to qualify, then the Vice President elect shall act as President until a President shall have qualified; and the Congress may by law provide for the case wherein neither a President elect nor a Vice President elect shall have qualified, declaring who shall then act as President, or the manner in which one who is to act shall be selected, and such person shall act accordingly until a President or Vice President shall have qualified.

Section 4.   The Congress may by law provide for the case of the death of any of the persons from whom the House of Representatives may choose a President whenever the right of choice shall have devolved upon them, and for the case of the death of any of the persons from whom the Senate may choose a Vice President whenever the right of choice shall have devolved upon them.

Section 5.   Sections 1 and 2 shall take effect on the 15th day of October following the ratification of this article.

Section 6.   This article shall be inoperative unless it shall have been ratified as an amendment to the Constitution by the legislatures of three-fourths of the several States within seven years from the date of its submission.

Amendment XXI [1933]

Section 1.   The eighteenth article of amendment to the Constitution of the United States is hereby repealed.

Section 2.   The transportation or importation into any State, Territory, or possession of the United States for delivery or use therein of intoxicating liquors, in violation of the laws thereof, is hereby prohibited.

Section 3.   This article shall be inoperative unless it shall have been ratified as an amendment to the Constitution by conventions in the several States, as provided in the Constitution, within seven years from the date of the submission hereof to the States by the Congress.

Amendment XXII [1951]

Section 1.   No person shall be elected to the office of the President more than twice, and no person who has held the office of President, or acted as President, for more than two years of a term to which some other person was elected President shall be elected to the office of President more than once. But this Article shall not apply to any person holding the office of President when this Article was proposed by the Congress, and shall not prevent any person who may be holding the office of President, or acting as President, during the term within which this Article becomes operative from holding the office of President or acting as President during the remainder of such term.

Section 2.   This article shall be inoperative unless it shall have been ratified as an amendment to the Constitution by the legislatures of three-fourths of the several States within seven years from the date of its submission to the States by the Congress.

Amendment XXIII [1961]

Section 1.   The District constituting the seat of Government of the United States shall appoint in such manner as the Congress may direct:

A number of electors of President and Vice President equal to the whole number of Senators and Representatives in Congress to which the District would be entitled if it were a State, but in no event more than the least populous state; they shall be in addition to those appointed by the states, but they shall be considered, for the purposes of the election of President and Vice President, to be electors appointed by a state; and they shall meet in the District and perform such duties as provided by the twelfth article of amendment.

Section 2.   The Congress shall have power to enforce this article by appropriate legislation.

Amendment XXIV [1964]

Section 1.   The right of citizens of the United States to vote in any primary or other election for President or Vice President, for electors for President or Vice President, or for Senator or Representative in Congress, shall not be denied or abridged by the United States, or any State by reason of failure to pay any poll tax or other tax.

Section 2.   The Congress shall have power to enforce this article by appropriate legislation.

Amendment XXV [1967]

Section 1.   In case of the removal of the President from office or of his death or resignation, the Vice President shall become President.

Section 2.   Whenever there is a vacancy in the office of the Vice President, the President shall nominate a Vice President who shall take office upon confirmation by a majority vote of both Houses of Congress.

Section 3.   Whenever the President transmits to the President pro tempore of the Senate and the Speaker of the House of Representatives his written declaration that he is unable to discharge the powers and duties of his office, and until he transmits to them a written declaration to the contrary, such powers and duties shall be discharged by the Vice President as Acting President.

Section 4.   Whenever the Vice President and a majority of either the principal officers of the executive departments or of such other body as Congress may by law provide, transmit to the President pro tempore of the Senate and the Speaker of the House of Representatives their written declaration that the President is unable to discharge the powers and duties of his office, the Vice President shall immediately assume the powers and duties of the office as Acting President. Thereafter, when the President transmits to the President pro tempore of the Senate and the Speaker of the House of Representatives his written declaration that no inability exists, he shall resume the powers and duties of his office unless the Vice President and a majority of either the principal officers of the executive department or of such other body as Congress may by law provide, transmit within four days to the President pro tempore of the Senate and the Speaker of the House of Representatives their written declaration and the President is unable to discharge the powers and duties of his office. Thereupon Congress shall decide the issue, assembling within forty-eight hours for that purpose if not in session. If the Congress, within twenty-one days after receipt of the latter written declaration, or, if Congress is not in session, within twenty-one days after Congress is required to assemble, determines by two-thirds vote of both Houses that the President is unable to discharge the powers and duties of his office, the Vice President shall continue to discharge the same as Acting President; otherwise, the President shall resume the powers and duties of his office.

Amendment XXVI [1971]

Section 1.   The right of citizens of the United States, who are eighteen years of age or older, to vote shall not be denied or abridged by the United States or by any State on account of age.

Section 2.   The Congress shall have power to enforce this article by appropriate legislation.

Amendment XXVII [1992]

No Law, varying the compensation for the services of the Senators and Representatives, shall take effect, until an election of Representatives shall have intervened.

GLOSSARY

A

Actionable. Providing legal reasons for a lawsuit.

Actual damages. Compensation for demonstrated injury, whatever form that injury might take. Sometimes referred to as general damages.

Ad libitum. Literally "at pleasure." At one's leisure.

Ad litem. Literally "For the suit"; for purposes of this lawsuit. An appointed temporary representative of a party to a lawsuit.

Affidavit. The sworn written statement of a party or a witness in a suit. The person who makes the statement is called an *affiant*.

Affirmed. Signifies that the appellate court agreed with the lower court's decision and has decided to let it stand after review, thus "affirming" it.

Amicus curiae. A friend of the court. Usually refers to legal briefs submitted to a court by persons or groups, not parties of record to an action. Briefs *amici curiae* are submitted to bring to the attention of the court factors and problems raised by a case that the parties to the action may not bring to the court's attention.

Appellant. The party who appeals a lower court decision rendered against him to a higher court is the appellant.

Appellee. The party who opposes an appeal and who is usually content with the lower court decision is the appellee. Courts sometimes use terms like "plaintiff-appellee" or "defendant-appellant" to indicate that the defendant lost at trial and now appeals and that the plaintiff won below and now opposes the appeal.

A priori. From cause to effect. Inferring specific facts from general principles.

Arguendo. Assume something true for the sake of argument.

B

Barratry. Provoking a lawsuit intentionally, e.g., a lawyer for profit.

Bill of attainder. A legislative act pronouncing a person guilty of a crime without a trial. Such acts are prohibited in the U.S. Constitution.

Bill of Rights. The first ten amendments to the U.S. Constitution.

Black letter law. Legal principles accepted by the judiciary in most jurisdictions.

Brandenburg **approach to the clear and present danger doctrine.** The approach currently in force was set forth in *Brandenburg v. Ohio* (1969): Advocacy of illegal action can only be prohibited "where such advocacy is directed to inciting or producing imminent lawless action and is likely to incite or produce such action."

Brief. The written legal arguments that are presented to the court by a party to a lawsuit. A brief is generally partisan. The brief states the facts and the relevant legal authorities on which a party relies for the result it seeks.

C

Categorical approach. Expression is divided among various categories. Some like political speech receive full First Amendment protection. Others like commercial speech receive different levels of protection. False and misleading commercial speech, for example, receives no protection. Other kinds of commercial speech are evaluated under the *Central Hudson* test.

Certiorari. A writ by which review of a case is sought in the U.S. Supreme Court. Technically, when the writ is granted, the Court orders the lower court to send the record of the case, a transcript of the proceedings below, up for review. The Supreme Court has discretion over which petitions for *certiorari* (*cert.*) it will grant and thus retains control over which cases it will review.

Civil action. A lawsuit brought to enforce a private, civil right or to redress a wrong, as distinguished from a criminal prosecution.

Civil law. Law based on codes originating with the Romans; the legal system that operates in France and Germany.

Clear and convincing proof (or evidence). A standard of proof in civil litigation more stringent than the normal requirement that the successful party be favored by a preponderance of the evidence. The standard is still less stringent than the standard of proof used in criminal litigation, which is that the evidence must show guilt beyond a reasonable doubt.

Collateral bar rule. A judicial order, e.g., an injunction, must be obeyed pending appeal on threat of contempt.

Common carrier standard. The legal approach used

Some of the definitions in this glossary are reprinted from Gillmor, Barron, Simon, and Terry, *Fundamentals of Mass Communication Law* (St. Paul: West, 1996).

to describe the obligation of public utilities such as phone companies to their subscribers. As a common carrier, the phone company must transmit the messages of all subscribers without regard to the message.

Common law. The legal system of the United States and Great Britain and other countries whose formative legal institutions derive in some measure from England. A common law system, which is based upon general rules and principles found in judicial decisions, is distinguished from the *civil law* systems of continental Europe, where rules and principles are codified in statutory law. Common law is judge-made law as opposed to law made by legislatures, or statutory law.

Complainant. The person who brings a lawsuit. It can also refer to the "complaining witness" or the person who has asked the state to bring criminal charges against the defendant. Often used as a synonym for plaintiff.

Compulsory license. Statutory permission to use a copyrighted work without consent of the owner. License fees are set by formula.

Concurring opinion. When a court, consisting of more than one judge, reaches its decision, one or more of the judges on the court comprising the majority may agree with the decision reached, but for different reasons than those found in the court's opinion. Such judges may decide to write a concurring opinion, stating their separate reasons for joining in the result reached by the majority of the court.

Constitutional law. Law based on the basic principles of the Constitution as to structure, rights, and functions of government.

Contempt of court. Any act that is deemed by a court to embarrass, hinder, or obstruct the court in the administration of justice or calculated to lessen its authority or its dignity. *Direct* contempt is committed in the presence of the court, or very near it, and can be punished summarily without a jury trial. *Constructive* or indirect contempt refers to actions outside of court that hinder the administration of justice, as when a court order is not obeyed.

Counterclaim. A claim brought by the defendant *against* the plaintiff. A counterclaim may be similar to the plaintiff's claim against the defendant, or it may be totally unrelated to the plaintiff's claim.

D

Damages. Money that a person receives as compensation, as the result of a court order, for injury to her person, property or rights because of the act, omission, or negligence of another.

Declaratory judgment. A judicial decision that sets out the rights and obligations of the parties to a dispute and expresses an opinion on a question of law, but does not necessarily order any coercive relief such as an injunction or damages.

Defendant. The party against whom a suit is brought. The defendant must answer the plaintiff's complaint and defend against his allegations. In criminal cases, the defendant is the party accused of crime by the state.

De jure. A matter of law whether or not consistent with fact.

De minimis. Something, or some act, that does not rise to a level of sufficient importance to be dealt with judicially.

De novo. Means anew or fresh. A new trial of a case is a "trial *de novo.*" A new trial can be granted by the trial judge or ordered by an appellate court.

Deposition. A sworn, recorded, oral statement made by a party or a witness out of court, either in the form of a narrative or as answers to questions posed by an attorney. The party whose deposition is taken is called the deponent. A deposition is often used to obtain testimony in advance of a trial or to secure the testimony of a person unable to come into court. The deposition can be used at trial to contradict a deponent's testimony at trial, or it can be used in the event of the deponent's unavailability.

Dicta. See *Obiter dictum.*

Directed verdict. Occurs when the trial judge decides that as a matter of law reasonable people cannot differ concerning the proper verdict in a case and directs the jurors to reach that verdict. The judge, in effect, makes the jury's decision for them; she takes it out of their hands.

Discovery. A period of information exchange between the parties in a lawsuit accomplished by interrogatories and deposition.

Disparagement. An untrue or misleading statement about a competitor's goods that is intended to influence or tends to influence the public not to buy the goods. Trade disparagement is distinguished from libel in that it is directed toward the goods rather than the personal integrity of the merchant.

Doctrine of judicial restraint. A doctrine associated in twentieth-century U.S. constitutional law with Supreme Court Justices Frankfurter, Harlan, and Scalia as well as jurists such as Judge Robert Bork. Under this view, courts should only rarely exercise their power to invalidate legislation on constitutional grounds. This doctrine holds that as long as the legislation in controversy is reasonable and has some constitutional authorization, it should be given a presumption of validity. The doctrine holds that in a democratic society nonelected judges should be reluctant to invalidate legislation enacted by the elected representatives of the people.

Duces tecum. A subpoena commanding a person to

appear in court with documentary evidence; a sub-poena *ad testificandum* commands a person to appear in court to give testimony.

Due process. A complex of rights guaranteed by the Fifth and Fourteenth Amendments to the U.S. Constitution, as interpreted by the Supreme Court. There are two kinds of due process. Procedural due process is offended when the fair procedures of the judicial process have not been complied with such as right to notice of the charges against one and a fair hearing concerning those charges. Substantive due process is offended by legislative action abridging substantive rights guaranteed by the Due Process Clause of the Fourteenth Amendment such as freedom of speech, freedom of religion, freedom of assembly, the right to privacy, etc.

Duopolies. Common ownership of two electronic media of the same type in the same community; for example, owning two TV stations in the same town. Or when two firms account for all businesses in the field.

E

Effect of the use. A factor to be considered in fair use claims; refers to the economic effects of copying. If the economic impact is great, a use is less likely to be considered fair.

Electronic yellow pages. The video services offered by telephone companies (telcos) such as sports results, news services, financial market quotations, and entertainment advertising.

En banc. A decision by all the judges of a court.

Equity. As distinguished from common law, equity means to be flexible where the common law is rigid. Equity fashions remedies to do substantial justice where the law is inadequate. Also, refers to the separate equity court system developed in England and to the remedies fashioned by those courts. Many of these remedies have now been adopted by U.S. courts. Thus courts have the broad power to order the equitable remedy of an injunction when money damages (the legal remedy) are inadequate.

Ex parte. Something done by, for, or on the application of *one party only*. An example of an *ex parte* proceeding is a hearing on a temporary restraining order. Such an order can be granted to a party in the absence of the party sought to be restrained.

Ex rel. Legal proceedings that are instituted by the attorney general in the name of and on behalf of the state, but on the information and at the instigation of an individual who has a private interest in the matter.

F

Fair comment. A traditional or common law defense in libel suits, now more generally referred to as the "opinion" defense. It is qualified by the requirement that opinions not be based on demonstrably false facts. It is meant to protect those who criticize persons, such as actors and authors, who seek public approval for their work. The more disconnected to fact, or the more outrageous, incredible, or unverifiable, the less the chance of a successful suit.

Fair use. A doctrine in copyright law that provides a limited legal right for others to use copyrighted materials without the owner's consent, especially where news, criticism or scholarship is involved. The fair use defense has had influence in right of publicity and trademark infringement cases.

Fairness doctrine. The fairness doctrine was abolished by the FCC in 1987 as part of President Reagan's deregulation program and out of First Amendment concerns. It required broadcasters to (1) present some programming about controversial issues of public importance and (2) reasonably present opposing viewpoints on those issues.

Federalism. The complex interaction between federal and state governments. This term is also sometimes used to emphasize the primacy of the role of the states in the U.S. federal system.

Felony. A serious crime, in contrast to a misdemeanor.

First-sale doctrine. Guarantees that the person who buys a copy of a copyrighted work is entitled to exercise complete ownership over that copy, including the right to resell or rent the copy.

G

Gloss. An annotation, explanation, or comment on any passage in the text of a work for purposes of elucidation or amplification.

Grand jury. A jury whose responsibility it is to decide whether probable cause exists to warrant the trial of an accused for a serious crime. A finding of probable cause is not equivalent to a finding of guilt. If the grand jury believes sufficient evidence exists to establish probable cause, it issues an indictment. The grand jury is termed a "grand jury" because it has more members than the trial or "petit" jury.

H

Habeas corpus. "You have the body." Often called the "Great Writ" because it has been considered basic to liberty in U.S. law. Typically, a writ of habeas corpus issues to order a warden or jailer to bring a prisoner before the court so that the court can determine whether the prisoner is lawfully confined. The writ can be used to secure review of a criminal conviction in the hope that the court will release the prisoner if it decides the prisoner is unlawfully confined.

Haec verba. In these exact words.

Hate speech. Expression that denigrates a racial, ethnic, or religious group. Some have contended that it should be treated as unprotected low-value speech, but so far, the Court has not made it a new, unprotected category of expression.

Holding. The authoritative core of a judge's holding or a court's decision.

I

In camera. In a judge's chambers, or in a courtroom with the public excluded.

Indictment. A written accusation made by a grand jury charging that the person named therein is accused of committing a crime. An indictment should be distinguished from an information (see below). Most jurisdictions require a grand jury indictment as the basis for charges of the most serious crimes.

Information. The *information* is an alternate method by which a criminal prosecution can be commenced. In states that allow a prosecutor to proceed by information as an alternative to a grand jury indictment, a preliminary hearing is first held before a magistrate to determine if there is "probable cause" to believe that a crime has been committed.

Infra. Refers to something printed later in the text. Used in the sense of "see below."

Injunction. A court-issued writ ordering a party either to refrain from doing something or to perform a specific act. When a court issues an injunction against a party, it *enjoins* that party. This equitable remedy is issued at the request of a litigant. An injunction may be granted temporarily to preserve the *status quo* while the issue in controversy is still pending before a court. This is called a preliminary injunction. A permanent injunction is granted only after a hearing on the merits.

In limine. On or at the threshold; at the very beginning; preliminarily.

Instanter. Immediately.

Inter alia. Literally "among other things"; reference to only a part of something.

Interlocutory appeal. An appeal of a judicial order in a case rendered by a court prior to final decision of that case. An order that is not final, or is not dispositive of the entire suit, is interlocutory in nature. Interlocutory appeals, except for a few statutory exceptions, are not permissible in federal practice. But this rule is sometimes circumvented by application to appellate courts for prerogative writs, such as writs of mandamus, that in effect do subject interlocutory orders to appeal.

Intermediate standard of review. This standard is used for gender and some other classifications; it is not as severe as the strict scrutiny standard that is used in racial discrimination cases. Under the intermediate standard of review, the state must show that the challenged classification is substantially related to achieving an important government objective.

Interrogatories. Written questions submitted by one party to the opposing party before the trial. The opposing party is then required under oath to provide specific written answers to the interrogatories of the other party. Interrogatories are part of the discovery process used by counsel prior to the actual trial to inform each other of the basic facts and issues in the case. The interrogatories are usually written and answered by counsel after consultation with the client.

Ipse dixit. To rely on one's own *ipse dixit* is to say something that rests not on independent evidence but solely on the say-so of the speaker.

J

Judgment. The final decision of the court defining the rights and duties of the parties to a lawsuit. A judgment should be distinguished from a verdict (see below), which is the name given to the decision of a jury rather than of a court.

Judgment n.o.v. (non obstante veredicto). A judgment notwithstanding the verdict occurs when the court renders a judgment in favor of one party after the jury has returned a verdict in favor of the other party. When a motion for a judgment *n.o.v.* is granted, the judge in effect overrules the jury's verdict. The motion is usually granted on the grounds that the jury's verdict was clearly unreasonable and not supported by the evidence. This decision by the judge can be the basis for an appeal.

Judicial activist. A judicial activist is the opposite of an exponent of a doctrine of judicial restraint (see this glossary). A judicial activist believes the judiciary may, in some circumstances, serve as a fulcrum for social change.

Judicial review. The invalidation or validation by courts of governmental action on the ground that that action is inconsistent or consistent with the Constitution.

Jurisprudence. The philosophy of law. Sometimes used as a synonym for law itself.

L

Lanham Act. The federal statute protecting trademarks used in interstate commerce. The act also prohibits types of unfair competition.

Lanham Trademark Law Revision Act. A 1989 federal law that provides remedies for those hurt by false advertising, as well as protecting competitors from one another.

Leased access channels. The Cable Communications Policy Act of 1984 required that cable systems with a specified channel capacity reserve some channels for leased commercial use by entities not affiliated with the cable system. This requirement was designed to prevent a cable operator from dominating programming.

Libel *per quod*. Indirect libel. A libel by innuendo, implication, or inference.

Libel *per se*. Libel on its face. An obvious libel.

Libel-proof. A reputation so tarnished that it cannot be further impaired by a fresh accusation.

Likelihood of confusion. Exists when a competitor uses a close copy of another's trademark and consumers are either misled or will likely be misled into mistaking the copy for the original.

M

Malfeasance. Usually refers to wrongdoing by a public official.

Mandamus. A writ ordering a lower court judge or other public official to perform a legal duty as to which he has no discretion.

Mandatory PEG channels. The Cable Communications Policy Act of 1984 authorized municipalities to require the dedication of some cable channels for public, educational, and governmental (PEG) programming.

Market failure theory. Argues that the marketplace of ideas does not work because even if entry to the marketplace is not restricted by government, entry is still restricted because the marketplace is dominated by large business interests.

Marketplace of ideas theory. Ideas should be allowed to compete freely without government censorship or intervention. Proponents contend that out of this competition the best or truest ideas will emerge.

Memorandum decision. A court ruling without written opinion or reasons given.

Mistrial. A trial interrupted and concluded for a major procedural defect.

Model acts. Laws proposed by law reform groups such as the National Conference of Commissioners on Uniform State Laws.

Moot. A case no longer needing judicial determination.

Movant (movent). One who makes a motion before a court; the applicant for a rule or order.

Moving papers. Papers that are made the basis of some motion in court proceedings.

N

Neutral reportage. A secondary libel defense based on the argument that the reporter, without malice or bias, is simply reporting both sides of a controversial issue of public importance. Courts are divided on its acceptability.

Nonpublic forum. Public areas such as airports that are not intended to be used as sites for expressive activity. Government may subject expressive activity in such forums to reasonable regulation. A place traditionally not thought to be suitable for speech activities, unless by invitation, e.g., a private home.

Nolle prosequi (nol. pros.). When the prosecuting attorney in a criminal suit decides that he will "prosecute the case no further," a *nol. pros.* is entered into the court records. The use of a *nol. pros.* usually terminates the lawsuit. Unless a *nol. pros.* is obtained with leave of court, the case will not be reopened at a later date; a *nol. pros.* usually signifies that the matter has been dropped altogether.

Nolo contendere. A defendant's plea of "no contest" in a criminal case, but implying or admitting of no guilt. Defendant submits to sentencing.

N.O.V. (*non obstante veredicto*). Notwithstanding the verdict of a jury, the judge gives judgment to the other side.

Nonfeasance. Usually failure of a public official to perform an assigned public duty.

Nunc pro tunc. Retroactive.

O

Obiter dictum, or dicta. Statements in a judge's opinion that strictly speaking are not necessary to the decision of the court. These "statements by the way" are often responsive to some suggestion that is made by the case's facts or its legal issue, but are not themselves part of the court's holding. To characterize a statement in a judicial decision as "dicta" means that the statement does not have the precedential value of a statement that recites the holding of the decision.

Original jurisdiction. Refers to a court's jurisdiction to permit a case to be commenced there in the first place.

Overbreadth. A law that proscribes both protected and unprotected expressive activity is overbroad and, therefore, invalid. The problem is that an individual may forgo protected expression for fear of being sanctioned for engaging in unprotected expression.

P

PEG access. Channels on cable television systems reserved for use by public, educational, or governmental (PEG) cablecasters.

Per curiam. When the opinion of a court or more than one judge is styled *per curiam*, the opinion is issued by and for the entire court, rather than by one judge writing for the court.

Peremptory. Conclusive, even if arbitrary, and requiring no explanation, e.g., peremptory challenges of prospective jurors.

Petitioner. One who seeks review of a lower court decision in the U.S. Supreme Court by petitioning for a writ of certiorari. The person who files the petition seeking review is called the petitioner. A person who petitions for any judicial relief such as a party who seeks other writs, such as mandamus, is also called a petitioner.

Plaintiff. The party who brings the lawsuit. The party who complains.

Pleading. The written statements of the parties containing their respective allegations, denials, and defenses. The plaintiff's complaint and the defendant's answer are examples of pleadings.

Police blotter. At the police station, the book in which a record is first made of the arrest of an accused person and the charges filed against her. Often used as a source for a journalist's report on the facts of the arrest.

Precedent. A judicial decision that is said to be authority for or to furnish a rule of law binding on the disposition of a current case. A precedent will involve similar facts or raise similar questions of law to the case at bar.

Preliminary hearing. A hearing before a judge to determine if enough evidence exists to show that there is probable cause to justify bringing a person accused of crime to trial. In some jurisdictions, if probable cause is shown to exist at the preliminary hearing, the accused will be bound over to the grand jury.

Preponderance of evidence. The standard of proof in civil as distinguished from criminal litigation. The greater weight of evidence, i.e., evidence that is more credible and convincing to the mind and therefore entitled to be given probative value (to be believed as proven true) in a civil law suit.

Prima facie. On the face of it, e.g., a *prima facie* or presumptively winning case.

Promissory estoppel. The doctrine that requires a promise to be enforced when someone has relied upon and acted, or refrained from acting, upon it and an injustice can be avoided only by enforcing the promise. Often established by statute.

Public law. The law defining the relationship between government and persons, and the operations of government, e.g., constitutional, administrative, and criminal law.

Punitive damages. Payment of money to an aggrieved party designed to punish or make an example of so as to discourage similar behavior in the future. Sometimes called exemplary damages.

R

Ratio decidendi. The essential rationale of a judicial decision.

Rational basis standard of review. This standard of review, used for legislation dealing with economic matters, gives great deference to the legislative judgment. Under this standard of review, a statutory classification, challenged under the Equal Protection Clause of the Fourteenth Amendment, will be deemed valid if it is rationally related to a permissible government interest.

Recusation. The process of disqualifying a judge for prejudice or a special interest in a lawsuit.

Remand. A remand is an order of a higher court directing the lower court to conform its decision to the mandates of the higher court.

Remittitur. When the jury awards the plaintiff excessive damages, the court may, in lieu of awarding the defendant a new trial, remit what it considers to be the excess and award the remaining damages to the plaintiff. The judge gives the plaintiff the option of accepting the damages the court believes authorized by the evidence in the form of reduction of damages by a *remittitur* or else facing a new trial.

Res judicata. Literally, the "thing judicially acted upon." This doctrine states the rule that a party cannot bring the same suit on the same facts against the same parties after these matters have already been decided once by a court. A party has only one "day in court," and once a case has been finally decided, he cannot bring the same suit again.

Respondeat superior. The legal doctrine whereby the employer can be held liable for the torts of an employee committed in the scope of his employment. Thus, in a media setting, the publisher may be required to respond in damages for defamation perpetrated in her newspaper by a journalist in her employ.

Respondent. The term used to identify the party opposed to granting a petition. The party petitioning for judicial relief is the petitioner; her opponent is the respondent.

Restatement of Torts. A publication of the American Law Institute that attempts to state in a comprehensive way the modern common law of torts on the basis of both a study of the judicial decisions and what it believes to be sound policy. The ALI also publishes restatements on other areas of the common law, such as contracts and conflicts of law.

Reversible error. An error in law or procedures by the trial court substantial enough to warrant reversal on appeal.

S

Scienter. Guilty knowledge. In some criminal prosecution, an allegation of scienter, or guilty knowledge, concerning the act or omission complained of is a prerequisite to prosecution. Proof of *scienter* has often been an issue in obscenity prosecutions.

Sealed records. The records of certain cases may be sealed and closed from public view by order of the court. Cases involving trade secrets or juveniles are examples of what a court might order sealed.

Sequester. To put aside, e.g., to lock up a jury.

Slip opinion. A copy of a court opinion printed and distributed immediately after it is delivered.

Standards of review. Tests employed by courts to determine the constitutional validity of legislation. Depending on the strength of the constitutional claim at issue, the state in defending its action will be held to one of the following standards of review: rational basis, intermediate, or strict scrutiny.

Stare decisis. Literally, to hold the decision. A doctrine intended to provide continuity in the common law system. The doctrine requires that when a court has developed a principle of law and has applied it to a certain set of facts, it will apply the same principle in future cases where the facts are substantially the same. The doctrine does not operate inexorably, and in contemporary U.S. law, particularly constitutional law, it has not been a barrier to legal, and thus to social, change as may have been the case in the past.

State action. The requirement that there be governmental involvement in a matter in order for the standards of the Fourteenth Amendment to be applicable.

Strict scrutiny standard of review. The standard of review that is used when a fundamental right is said to be significantly burdened by governmental action or when a government classification is deemed "suspect" because it classifies on the basis of race. Unlike the rational basis standard, this standard is not deferential to state legislation. Government action challenged under this standard will be valid only if the government can show that it serves a compelling state interest. Courts sometimes describe this standard as strict in theory but fatal in fact. Increasingly, this standard is used in free expression cases.

Sua sponte. To do something on one's own initiative. A term used when a court makes a ruling on its own even though the ruling has not been requested by counsel for either side.

Sub nom. When used in case citations, this abbreviation means that the same case as the previous case is being noted, but that it was decided on appeal under a *different name*.

Substantive law. The basic law of rights and duties.

Sui generis. One of a kind.

Summary judgment. A motion for summary judgment is a pretrial motion that will be granted when the pleadings, affidavits, and discovery materials disclose that there is no issue of material fact in controversy between the parties. In that event, the only issues left to resolve are questions of law, which can be decided by the court. Summary judgment, therefore, is a pretrial device that, if appropriate for rendition, will result in judgment to the successful party without the necessity of going through a trial.

Summons. A notice delivered by a sheriff or other official (or sometimes a private individual) to a person to inform him that he has been named as a defendant in a civil suit and must come to court on a certain day and answer the complaint against him.

Supra. Refers to something printed earlier in the text in the sense of "see above."

T

Tort. A civil wrong not based on contract. A tort may be accomplished with or without force against the person or property of another. Typical torts include trespass, assault, libel, slander, invasion of privacy, and negligence. The same word used to identify a tort may also be used to identify a crime, but the two meanings will often be quite different. Relief is usually sought through a suit seeking money damages.

Tortfeasor. One who commits a tort. A wrongdoer.

Trademark. A symbol, name, logo, or other device that is used to identify the source of a product for consumers. The most effective trademarks are immediately recognizable.

Traditional public forum. Public areas such as parks and streets that have long been opened or dedicated by government for expressive activity. Discussion and protest are available in such areas as a matter of right, subject to reasonable regulation.

TRO. Temporary restraining order. An injunction.

U

Ultra vires. Acts beyond the scope of the powers of a corporation, as defined by its charter or act of incorporation

Unconstitutional conditions. A doctrine used to void rules that require that the recipient of a government benefit or subsidy give up a constitutional right to get the benefit.

V

Vel non. (Latin for "or not"), i.e., the issue is the validity *vel non* of this statute. (The issue is the validity or invalidity of the statute.)

Venireman. A member of a panel of jurors.

Verdict. The decision of the trial or "petit" jury. The jury reaches its verdict on the basis of the instructions given by the trial judge. The verdict may be a general verdict of "guilty" in a criminal case or a general verdict for either the defendant or the plaintiff in a civil case.

A special verdict consists of answers in the affirmative or negative to specific questions posed by the judge.

Viva voce. Orally rather than in writing.

Void. Without legal effect.

Vortex or limited-purpose public figure. A person who momentarily or for a limited period becomes visible, controversial, or newsworthy.

W

Writ. A judge's order requiring or authorizing something to be done outside the courtroom.

Writ of prohibition. An extraordinary judicial writ from a court of superior jurisdiction directed to an inferior court or tribunal to prevent the latter from usurping a jurisdiction with which it is not lawfully vested, or from assuming or exercising jurisdiction over matters beyond its cognizance or in excess of its jurisdiction.

INDEX